Travel With Someone You Trust® visit us at aaa.com

Britain & Ireland Bed & Breakfast 2003

In association with AA Lifestyle Guides - the experts on Britain & Ireland

Assessments of the establishments in this guide are based on the experience(s) of the AA's professional hotel and restaurant inspectors on the occasion(s) of their visit(s) and therefore the descriptions given in this guide may contain an element of subjective opinion which may not dictate a reader's experience on another occasion.

Produced by AA Publishing

Directory generated by the AA Establishment Database, Information Research, AA Hotel Services

www.theAA.com/getaway

To contact us
Advertising Sales: advertisingsales@theAA.com
Editorial: lifestyleguides@theAA.com

Maps prepared by the Cartography Department of the Automobile Association Developments Limited.

Design by Kingswood Graphics, Theale Road, Burghfield, Reading, Berkshire

Typeset/Repro by Avonset, 11 Kelso Place, Bath

Printed by Printer Barcelona

Cover photograph: Thatches on the Green, Corby, Northamptonshire.

A CIP catalogue record for this book is available from the British Library.

Published by AA Publishing, which is a trading name of Automobile Association Developments Limited whose registered office is Millstream, Maidenhead Road, Windsor, Berkshire, SL4 5GD
Registered number 1878835

ISBN 0 7495 34338
A01264
Published in the USA by AAA

Contents

Welcome to the Guide 6

How to Use the Guide 8

AA Diamond Classification 10

Hints for Booking Your Stay
and useful information 11

AA Rosette Awards 14

Best Breakfast Award 15

Landlady of the Year Awards
Top Twenty Finalists 2002-2003 16

Feature – The Interest is Building 19

Guest Accommodation of the Year Awards
The 2002-2003 award winners 22

AA Hotel Booking Service 24

Premier Collection
A quick-reference list of AA five
diamond establishments 25

DIRECTORY OF ESTABLISHMENTS

ENGLAND 33
Channel Islands 489
Isle of Man 491

SCOTLAND 493
Scottish Islands 553

WALES 555

IRELAND
Northern Ireland 594
Republic of Ireland 599

County Map of UK and Ireland 652

Location Atlas 654

Index 674

Photo Credits 706

Readers' Report Forms 707

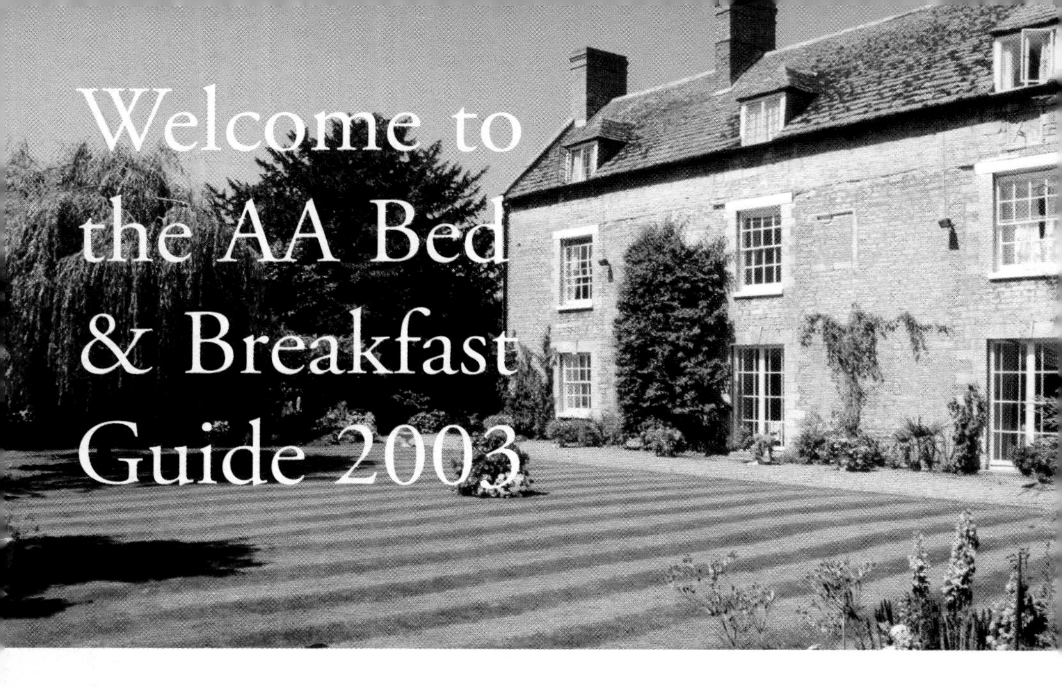

Welcome to the AA Bed & Breakfast Guide 2003

Fully updated for the new edition, the AA B&B Guide brings you a wide choice of accommodation across Britain and Ireland. All the establishments with diamond awards have been assessed under the quality standards agreed between the AA, English Tourist Council and the RAC, enabling you to make your choice with confidence. You can find out more about the AA's inspection process on page 7.

New for 2003

There are some changes to this year's guide. Most importantly, we have introduced the **AA Red Diamond Awards.** These recognise the very best ten percent of guest accommodation within the three, four and five Diamond rating levels. While the Diamond rating itself (see page 11) takes into account an assessment of **all** aspects of the establishment and how it is run, Red Diamond establishments are selected **only** on the basis of the quality of their bedrooms, bathrooms and public areas.

For the first time, we are also showing **AA Associate Entries.** These are places that have been inspected by one of the other organisations; the RAC, ETC, Welsh, Northern Ireland or Scottish Tourist Boards, rather than by the AA. They have paid to take a limited entry in our guide, with contact details, room, facilities and price information, as well as any restrictions. Descriptions for these establishments appear on the AA website, www.theAA.com.

This year for the first time we are indicating if an establishment has conference facilities, and also if any of the bedrooms are on the ground floor. N.B. ground floor rooms may be mentioned in the text but not in the FACILITIES information, depending on whether a questionnaire was received from the establishment for this edition. Always check that the place you have chosen can offer the facilities you require.

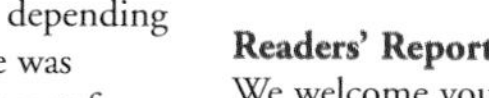

AA Awards 2002-2003

We present a range of awards in the B&B Guide, from AA Landlady of the Year, which showcases the very finest hospitality in the country, to the Best Breakfast Award, and the Guest Accommodation of the Year Awards, presented to those establishments in Scotland, Ireland, Wales and England that our Inspectors feel best demonstrate all that a B&B should be.

AA Accessible Awards

Presented to the establishment which has made the greatest effort in their accommodation for the independent disabled traveller. See page 23.

Readers' Reports

We welcome your feedback about the establishments we feature in the guide and about the guide itself. Readers' report forms appear at the back of the book, or you can e mail us at lifestyleguides@theAA.com

♦ AA INSPECTED FULL ENTRIES

The AA inspects and classifies more than 4000 small private hotels, guest houses, farmhouses and inns for its Guest Accommodation scheme, under quality standards agreed between the AA, English Tourism Council and RAC. AA recognised establishments pay an annual fee, this varies according to the classification level and the number of bedrooms. The establishment receives an unannounced inspection visit from a qualified AA inspector who recommends the appropriate classification. Return visits are made to check that standards are maintained and the classification is not transferable if an establishment changes hands.

ASSOCIATE ENTRIES

A These are establishments which have been inspected and rated by the RAC, English Tourist Council, Welsh Tourist Board, Northern Ireland Tourist Board or Scottish Tourist Board. In Northern Ireland the Tourist Board does not give ratings. They are rated with Diamonds by the RAC and ETC, or with stars ★ by the WTB or STB. They have paid to take a limited entry in our Guide. Descriptions for these establishments appear on our website www.theAA.com

U entries are establishments which joined the AA Guest Accommodation Scheme too close to Guide deadlines for a full inspection to take place.

STAYING AT A GUEST HOUSE

Many guest houses include the word 'hotel' in their name. Small and private hotels may choose to be rated with Diamonds, as guest houses, when they cannot offer all the services required for the AA hotel star rating (for example evening meals). The term does not imply that guest houses are inferior to hotels, just that they are different. Many offer a very high standard of accommodation, and a more personal level of service.

Please note that there may be restricted access to the guest house, particularly in the late morning and during the afternoon, so do ask about this when booking.

London

The majority of establishments in the London section of the book are small hotels. London prices tend to be higher than outside the capital, and normally only bed and breakfast is provided, although some do provide a full meal service.

STAYING AT A FARMHOUSE

Farmhouse accommodation generally represents good value for money and excellent home-cooking. Many listed are working farms, and some farmers are happy to allow visitors to look around, or even to help feed the animals, while others may discourage visitors from exploring the working land. Please note that modern farms are potentially dangerous places, especially where machinery and chemicals are concerned. Visitors should exercise care, in particular when accompanying children, and should never leave children unsupervised around the farm. Sometimes the land has been sold off and only the house remains. Although the directory entry states the acreage and the type of farming carried out, do check when booking to make sure that it matches your expectations.

All of the farmhouses are listed under town or village names, but many are fairly remote, so do ask for directions when booking.

STAYING AT AN INN

Traditional inns provide a cosy bar, convivial atmosphere, good beer and pub food. Inns with entries in the guide will provide breakfast in a suitable room, and should also serve light meals during licensing hours. Some small, fully licensed hotels are classified as inns, and the character of the properties will vary according to whether they are traditional country inns or large town establishments. Check details before you book, including arrival times as these may be restricted to opening hours.

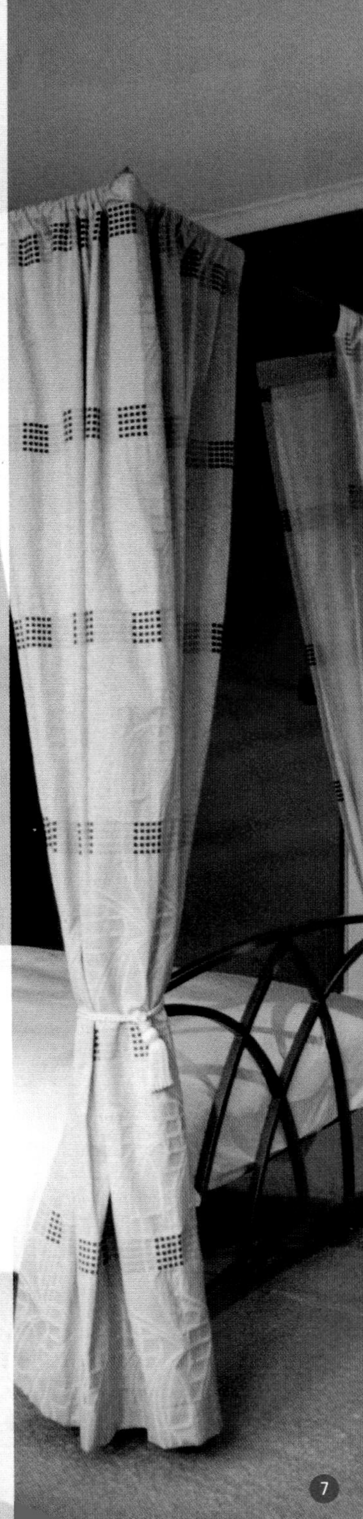

Symbols and Abbreviations

Red Diamonds (see page 6)	♦
Black Diamonds (see page 11)	♦
Associate Member (see page 9)	A
Unconfirmed rating - late entries into the guide	U
Rating from the Welsh Tourist Board/Scottish Tourist Board	★
Inn	
Farmhouse	
Telephone number	☎
Fax number	
Breakfast which exceeds quality requirements at this Diamond level	
Dinner which exceeds quality requirements at this Diamond level	
Best Breakfast Award (see page 15)	
Member of the Blue Book Consortium (Republic of Ireland – see page 13)	
Single room including breakfast per person per night	**s**
Double room (2 people sharing a room) including breakfast per night	**d**
Family bedroom	**fmly**
Ground floor bedroom	**GF**
Bed and breakfast for up to £19 per person per night	**BB**
Short breaks available	**LB**
2002 prices	✳
Full central heating	**Cen ht**
Special facilities for children (see page 10)	**ch fac**
Lounge with TV	TVL
TV in bedrooms	TVB
Satellite TV	STV
Credit cards (see page 10)	
Tea and coffee making facilities	**tea/coffee**
Conference facilities available and number of delegates	**CONF:** 60

Time last dinner can be ordered	**Last d**
Letting bedrooms in main building	**rms**
Easter	**Etr**
From	**fr**
Restricted service	**rs**

Sample Entry

ANY TOWN Map 00 NS00 1
♦♦♦ Any Place 2
Any Walk XX37 6XX 3
☎ 09689 24444144 4
e-mail: address@test.co.uk 5
Dir: on A422 900 yds NW of town centre 6
7
A charming 17th century thatched cottage, within walking distance of the town centre, offers a mixture of modern and traditional styles of bedroom. The attractive lounge/dining room is furnished in period style in keeping with the house, and sustaining cooked breakfasts make a cheerful start to the day. 8
FACILITIES: 10 en suite (5 fmly 3 GF) No smoking in lounge TVB STV tea/coffee No dogs 9
PRICES: s £40-£47.50; d £57.50-£111.00 LB BB 10
PARKING: 14 NOTES: Closed Dec; Civ Wed 25 11 12
CARDS: 13

How to use the Guide

1 The guide is divided into countries: England, Scotland, Wales, Northern Ireland and the Republic of Ireland. The Channel Islands and Isle of Man follow the England section. Scottish Islands follow the rest of Scotland. Each country is listed in county order, and then in alphabetical town/village order within each county.

The map reference refers to the town/village. The map page number refers to the atlas at the back of the Guide and is followed by the National Grid Reference. To find the location, read the first figure across and the second figure vertically within the lettered square.

Farmhouse entries only - as they are often in remote areas, we provide a six-figure map reference which can be used with Ordnance Survey maps. This Ordnance Survey map reference is shown in italics in brackets after the establishment name, e.g. *(SN191184)*. We also show the name of the proprietors, as often farms are known locally by this name, rather than their proper name.

Within a town or village, establishments are listed alphabetically in descending order of Diamonds.

2 **Diamond Classification**. Details of the Diamond Classification can be found on page 11 and Red Diamonds are explained on page 6. Those places that have gained five Diamonds have their entries highlighted in the directory. There is a quick reference list of five Diamond establishments on page 25.

Establishments in Britain with no identifying symbol are either guest houses or small hotels. In the Republic of Ireland, GH refers to Guest Houses, and T&C to the Town and Country Homes Association, an umbrella organisation for B&Bs which are officially recognised by Bord Failte and have six rooms or less.

Rosette Awards The AA's food award. Further explanation can be found on page 14.

Egg cups and pies These symbols denote the very best breakfasts and evening meals. Both indicate that, in the experience of our Inspector, either breakfast or dinner exceeded the required level for the Diamond rating achieved by the establishment.

Approximately 200 establishments in the Guide have an eggcup, and approximately 180 have a pie.

Many other establishments offer dinner, this is indicated in the FACILITIES section by the word Dinner.

3 **Establishment address and post code.** If the establishment's name is shown in italics, then details have not been confirmed by the proprietor for this edition.

4 **Telephone and fax** numbers may change during the currency of this book in some areas. In case of difficulty, check with the operator.

5 **E-mail** address where applicable.

6 **Directions** are given wherever they have been supplied by the proprietor.
Some establishments have a group or consortium name in brackets after their directions, e.g. (*The Independents*). This indicates that they belong to this group.

7 Establishments may choose to include a photograph in their entry.

8 **Description of the property.** Note - if there are rooms adapted for or suitable for disabled people reference may be made in the description. Ground floor rooms are listed under the FACILITIES heading. Guests with any form of disability should notify proprietors, so that arrangements can be made to minimise difficulties.

9 **FACILITIES** (For key to symbols and abbreviations, see page 8) The first figure shows the number of letting bedrooms (rms). The number of rooms with en suite bath or shower is also indicated. Bedrooms that have a private bathroom adjacent may be included as en suite.

Annexe - The number of bedrooms available in an annexe of equivalent standard are shown. Facilities may not be the same as in the main building, and it is a good idea to check the nature of the accommodation and prices before making a reservation.

fmly - indicates family bedrooms
GF – indicates ground floor bedrooms

Dinner - dinner is available. Guests may have to order dinner in advance - please check when booking

No smoking - 'No smoking' when used by itself indicates a total ban on smoking throughout the premises. If the establishment is only partly no-smoking, the

areas where smoking is not permitted are shown

TVB - television in bedrooms (TV12B - television in 12 bedrooms)

TVL - television in lounge

STV - satellite television

tea/coffee - tea and coffee making facilities in bedrooms

No dogs - Establishments which do not normally accept dogs may accept guide dogs. Some places that accept dogs may restrict the size and breed of dogs permitted and the rooms into which they may be taken. Generally, dogs are not allowed in the dining room, but this is at the discretion of the owners. Check when booking the conditions under which pets are accepted.

No children - indicates that children cannot be accommodated. A minimum age may be specified (e.g. No children 4 yrs = no children under four years old). Although establishments may accept children of all ages they may not necessarily be able to provide special facilities. If you have very young children, check before booking about provisions like cots and high chairs, and any reductions made.

ch fac - indicates establishments with special facilities for children, which will include babysitting service or baby intercom system, playroom or playground, laundry facilities, drying and ironing facilities, cots, high chairs and special meals.

cen ht - central heating available

last d 8.30pm - last orders for dinner

No coaches - this information is published in good faith from details supplied by the establishments concerned. Inns have well-defined legal obligations towards travellers, in the event of a query the customer should contact the proprietor or the local licensing authority.

Additional facilities such as lifts or any leisure activities available are also listed.

10 **PRICES** - these are prices per night.
s - bed and breakfast per person;
d - bed and breakfast for two people sharing a room.

BB - this indicates that the establishment expects to provide bed and breakfast for £19 and under per person, per night, but remember that circumstances and prices can change during the currency of the Guide.

LB - this indicates that Short or Leisure Breaks are available.

Prices given have been provided by the owner in good faith, and are indications rather than firm quotations. Some places offer free accommodation to children provided they share their parents' room. Check current prices before booking.

11 **PARKING** - number of private parking spaces available

12 **MEALS** - meal prices are shown for inns.

13 **NOTES** - Open/Closed details - unless otherwise stated, establishments are open all year, but where dates are shown they are inclusive: e.g. 'Dec-Feb' indicates that the establishment is closed from the beginning of December to the end of February.

Some places are open all year, but offer a restricted service off season. The abbreviation 'rs' indicates this. It may mean either that evening meals are not served or that other facilities listed are not available. If the text does not say what the restricted services are, you should check before booking.

Civ Wed 50 - the establishment is licensed for civil weddings and can accommodate 50 guests for the ceremony.

14 **CARDS** - the following credit/debit cards may be accepted, but check current details when booking

Mastercard
American Express
Connect
Delta
Visa
Switch
Diners

PLEASE NOTE - The Euro

The Euro is now the currency of the Republic of Ireland. See page 13 for further details.

Diamond Classification

The Diamond Awards classify guest accommodation at five levels of quality, from one Diamond at the simplest, to five Diamonds at the luxury end of the spectrum. The emphasis for the assessment for a Diamond rating is on guest care and quality rather than the provision of extra facilities.

This includes the style and quality of the furnishings and decor. To be recognised under the Quality Standards, establishments must provide sufficient quality in all areas of operation covered under the following headings to merit a minimum score of 1 out of 5.

- Cleanliness and Housekeeping
- Service and Hospitality
- Bedroom Facilities
- Bathroom Facilities
- Food Quality and Service
- Public Rooms
- Safety, Security and Maintenance

Establishments applying for AA quality assessment are visited on a 'mystery guest' basis by one of the AA's team of qualified accommodation inspectors. Inspectors stay overnight to make a thorough test of the accommodation, food, and hospitality offered. After paying the bill the following morning they identify themselves and ask to be shown round the premises. The inspector completes a full report, resulting in a recommendation for the appropriate quality level.

After this first visit, the establishment will receive an annual visit to check that standards are maintained. If it changes hands, the new owners must re-apply for classification, as AA recognition is not transferable.

Guests can expect to find the following minimum standards in Guest Accommodation at all Diamond levels:

- a pleasant, professional check in and check out, with a properly prepared bill
- comfortable accommodation equipped to modern standards
- furniture, soft furnishings and fittings in good condition. Bedding and towels changed for each new guest, and at least weekly if the room is taken for a long stay. Extra pillows and blankets available on request.
- adequate storage, heating, lighting and comfortable seating
- a sufficient hot water supply at reasonable times.
- well prepared, wholesome meals served at reasonable times, and presented in an appetising manner.
- A full, cooked breakfast to be available, but if this is not provided, the fact must be advertised and a substantial continental breakfast must be provided. This must include a reasonable selection from the following items: cold meats, cheeses, fresh fruit, fruit compotes, preserves, cereals, juices, yoghurts, bakery items and hot beverages (choice of tea and coffee).

Hints for Booking Your Stay and Useful Information

FOOD AND DRINK
Some guest houses offer bed & breakfast only, so you have to go out for the evening meal. Many guest houses do provide evening meals, ranging from a set meal to a full menu; some have their own restaurants. You may have to arrange dinner in advance, at breakfast, or on the previous day, so do ask about this when booking. If you book on bed, breakfast and evening meal terms, you may find that the tariff includes only the set menu. If there is a carte you may be able to order from this and pay a supplement. On Sundays, many establishments serve the main meal at midday, and provide only a cold supper in the evening. In some parts of Britain, particularly in Scotland, high tea (i.e. a savoury dish followed by bread and butter, scones, cakes, etc.) is sometimes served instead of dinner. Dinner may be available as an alternative. The last time at which high tea or dinner may be ordered on weekdays is shown, but this may vary at weekends.

BOOKING
Book as early as possible, particularly for the peak holiday period (beginning of June to the end of September) and bear in mind that Easter and other public holidays may be busy, too. In some parts of Scotland the skiing season is a peak holiday period.

Some establishments only accept weekly bookings from Saturday. Some will require a deposit on booking.

We have tried to provide as much information as possible about the establishments in our Guide, but if you require further information, contact the establishment itself. Do please mention the Guide in any enquiry. Although we try to publish accurate and up to date information, please remember that any details, particularly prices, are subject to change without notice and this may happen during the currency of the guide. Confirm details with the establishment at the time of booking.

PAYMENT
Always ask about payment methods when booking. If a guest house accepts credit or charge cards, this is shown by the appropriate symbol in its directory entry. Please note that credit card payment may incur extra charges.

Great Value BB
Establishments that have told us they are offering bed and breakfast for £19 or under per person per night or up to £38 per double room are indicated by this symbol against their entry.

PRICES

Daily terms quoted throughout this guide show minimum and maximum prices for both one (s) and two people (d) and include a full breakfast. If dinner is also included this will be indicated in brackets (incl. dinner).

VAT is payable in the United Kingdom and in the Isle of Man, on both basic prices and any service. VAT does not apply in the Channel Islands. With this exception, prices quoted in the Guide are inclusive of VAT (and service where applicable).

You should always confirm the current prices before making a booking. Those given in this book have been provided by proprietors in good faith, and must be accepted as indications rather than firm quotations.

Unconfirmed prices
In some cases, proprietors have been unable to provide us with their 2003 charges, but to give you a rough guide we publish the 2002 price, followed by an asterisk (*). It is also a good idea to check exactly what is included in the price. We cannot indicate whether or not you are able to arrive mid-week, so if this is your intention, do check when making your reservation. Where information about 2003 prices is not given, please make enquiries direct.

CANCELLATION

If you have to cancel a booking, let the proprietor know at once if the room you booked cannot be re-let, you may be held legally responsible for partial payment. This may mean losing your deposit, or being liable for compensation. You should consider taking out cancellation insurance.

SMOKING REGULATIONS

We have tried to get accurate information on this question from establishments, however the situation may change during the currency of this edition. If the freedom to smoke or to be in a smoke-free atmosphere is important to you, please ask about the rules when you book.

FIRE PRECAUTIONS

Many of the establishments listed in the Guide are subject to the requirements of the Fire Precautions Act of 1971. As far as we can discover, every establishment in this book has applied for, and not been refused, a fire certificate.

The Fire Precautions Act does not apply to Ireland, the Channel Islands or the Isle of Man, which exercise their own rules regarding fire precautions for hotels.

LICENSED PREMISES

The Guide entry will show whether or not the establishment is licensed to serve alcohol. Many places in the guest house category hold a residential or restaurant licence only, but all inns hold a full licence. Licensed premises are not obliged to remain open throughout the permitted hours, and they may do so only when they expect reasonable trade.

Note that in establishments which have registered clubs, club membership does not come into effect, nor can a drink be bought, until 48 hours after joining.

COMPLAINTS

Readers who have any cause to complain are urged to do so at the time. This should provide an opportunity for the proprietor to correct matters. If a personal approach fails, readers may write to: The Editor, B&B Guide, AA Hotel Services, Fanum House, Basingstoke, Hants, RG21 4EA. We cannot guarantee to enter into any correspondence.

CODES OF PRACTICE

The Hotel Industry Voluntary Code of Booking Practice was revised in 1986, and the AA encourages its use in appropriate establishments. Its prime object is to ensure that the customer is clear about the precise services and facilities s/he is buying and what price will have to be paid, before entering into a contractually binding agreement. If the price has not been previously confirmed in writing, the guest should be handed a card at the time of registration, stipulating the total obligatory charge.

The Tourism (Sleeping Accommodation Price Display) Order 1977 compels hotels, motels, guest houses, farmhouses, inns and self-catering accommodation with four or more letting bedrooms to display in entrance halls the minimum and maximum prices charged for each category of room. This order complements the Voluntary Code of Booking Practice. The tariffs quoted in the directory of this book may be affected in the coming year by inflation, variations in the rate of VAT and many other factors.

USEFUL INFORMATION – IRELAND

Map References

In the Irish Directory, the six-figure map references shown against establishments have been taken from the Irish National Grid.

Prices - The Euro

Irish notes and coins are no longer legal tender. Prices are quoted in Euros, indicated by the symbol €. Please consult your bank or the daily paper for the current exchange rate. Please check prices on booking.

Hotels must display tariffs, either in the bedrooms or at reception. Application of VAT and service charges varies, but all prices quoted must be inclusive of VAT.

Ireland's Blue Book is an association of privately owned country houses and restaurants.

Telephone Numbers

Area codes shown against the numbers in the Republic of Ireland only work within the Republic. If dialling from outside, you will need to check with the telephone directory. The area codes shown for Britain and Northern Ireland cannot be used directly from the Republic.

Fire Precautions

Northern Ireland: The Fire Services (NI) Order 1984 covers establishments accommodating more than 6 persons, and they must have a fire certificate issued by the Northern Ireland Fire Authority. Places accommodating fewer than 6 people must have adequate exits.

Republic of Ireland: safety regulations are a matter for local authority regulations.

For your own and others' safety, you must read the emergency notices displayed and be sure you understand them.

Licensing Regulations

Northern Ireland: public houses open from 11.30 - 23.00, and on Sun 12.30 - 14.30 and 19.00 - 22.00. Hotels can serve residents without restriction. Non-residents can be served from 12.30 - 22.00 on Christmas Day. Children under 18 are not allowed in the bar area and may neither buy nor consume liquor in hotels.

Republic of Ireland: Mon–Wed 10.30 – 23.30, Thurs-Sat 10.30-00.30,

Sun 12.30-23.00, St Patrick's Day 12.30-00.30.

Hotels can serve residents without restriction. There is no service on Good Friday or St Patrick's Day.

For the latest travel information in Ireland, check the AA Ireland website on www.aaireland.ie

AA Rosette Awards

How the AA assesses restaurants for Rosette Awards

The AA's rosette award scheme was the first nationwide scheme for assessing the quality of food served by restaurants and hotels. The rosette scheme is an award scheme, not a classification scheme and although there is necessarily an element of subjectivity when it comes to assessing taste, we aim for a consistent approach to our awards throughout the UK. It is important, however, to remember that many places serve enjoyable food but do not qualify for an AA award.

Our awards are made solely on the basis of a meal visit or visits by one or more of our hotel and restaurant inspectors who have an unrivalled breadth and depth of experience in assessing quality. They award rosettes annually on a rising scale of one to five.

So what makes a restaurant worthy of a Rosette Award?

For our inspectors the top and bottom line is the food. The taste of the food is what counts for them, and whether the dish successfully delivers to the diner what the menu promises. A restaurant is only as good as its worst meal. Although presentation and competent service should be appropriate to the style of the restaurant and the quality of the food, they cannot affect the rosette assessment as such, either up or down.

The following summaries attempt to explain what our inspectors look for, but are intended only as guidelines. The AA is constantly reviewing its award criteria and competition usually results in an all-round improvement in standards, so it becomes increasingly difficult for restaurants to reach award level.

Excellent local restaurants serving food prepared with care, understanding and skill, using good quality ingredients. These restaurants stand out in their local area. The same expectations apply to hotel restaurants where guests should be able to eat in with confidence and a sense of anticipation. Around 50% of restaurants with rosettes.

The best local restaurants, which aim for and achieve higher standards, better consistency and where a greater precision is apparent in the cooking. There will be obvious attention to the selection of quality ingredients. Around 40% of restaurants with rosettes.

Outstanding restaurants that achieve standards that demand recognition well beyond their local area. The cooking will be underpinned by the selection and sympathetic treatment of the highest quality ingredients. Timing, seasoning and the judgement of flavour combinations will be consistently excellent, supported by other elements such as intelligent service and a well-chosen wine list. Around 150 restaurants (less than 10% of those with rosettes).

Amongst the very best restaurants in the British Isles where the cooking demands national recognition. These restaurants will exhibit intense ambition, a passion for excellence, superb technical skills and remarkable consistency. They will combine appreciation of culinary traditions with a passionate desire for further exploration and improvement. Around a dozen restaurants with rosettes.

The finest restaurants in the British Isles, where the cooking stands comparison with the best in the world. These restaurants will have highly individual voices, exhibit breathtaking culinary skills and set the standards to which others aspire. Around half a dozen restaurants with rosettes.

AA Best Breakfast Awards 2002-2003

Winners

England and Overall Winner
Nonsuch House, Dartmouth, Devon

Scotland and Northern Ireland
Grange Lodge, Dungannon, County Tyrone

Wales
Tyddynmawr Farmhouse, Dolgellau, Gwynedd

Although this Guide features every kind of place, they do all have at least one thing in common, whether grand country houses, cosy bungalows, or the smartest of townhouses – breakfast. From the continental buffet to the full monty (English/Scottish/Welsh or Irish) and beyond, and from a tray in your room to a polished mahogany dining table seating fifteen, our establishments offer breakfast every which way. We give an Eggcup to those places that provide an outstanding breakfast, one that exceeds the expectation of our Inspector for the diamond rating of the establishment, and this gives us the basis for our Best Breakfast Award, now in its fifth year. We send out a questionnaire, asking about the nation's breakfast habits, the importance of the setting, unusual requests, special recipes and, most importantly, the proprietors' Breakfast Philosophy…

Olwen Evans of **Tyddynmawr Farmhouse** tells us that 'as we are situated in an idyllic location, it's important that the richness, quality and freshness of life is reflected in the food served to our guests.' Quality local produce is essential, and it always helps to 'make as much as possible yourself.' Her mother told her 'Your quality of life depends on the quality of the food you eat' and she agrees absolutely. Her speciality is home-made muesli, and a typical breakfast menu might feature fresh fruits, smoked mackerel, local Welsh yogurt and home-made jams and marmalades.

At **Grange Lodge**, Norah and Ralph Brown agree that to many people breakfast 'can be the most important meal of the day.' Like Olwen, they feel it is important to source as many ingredients as possible locally, including '… free range eggs, Moyallen dry cured bacon, Hulls sausages and all sorts of mushrooms grown nearby', as well as 'a lovely locally produced apple juice'. They make their own rhubarb compote, as well as wheaten and soda breads. Tea and coffee should be served 'when the guests want it… not when you think of it!' Their speciality is 'Bushmills Porridge', made with local organic oatflakes and Bushmills whiskey, prepared the night before and cooked in the plate-warming oven of their four oven Aga. One mouthful of that and 'many of our guests think they have died and gone to heaven!'

In the winter there's a roaring fire in the dining room at **Nonsuch House**, while in the warmer months you can eat on the terrace or in the conservatory, where the views over Dartmouth Harbour are so glorious that 'sometimes we watch people and find they have difficulty in finding their mouths because they are so entranced with the 'to-ings and fro-ings' on the river below!' Kit Noble tells us that 'we try to make each morning's breakfast a memorable one – a sort of benchmark for the rest of the day's meals.' As well as the usual fruit compotes, yogurt, cereal and full English, there are specials every day, which might include salmon fishcakes, kedgeree, pancakes with lemon and sugar, home-made waffles, or eggy bread with maple syrup. They source all their food locally where possible, 'and love shopping for good things to eat.' What else is important when it comes to breakfast? 'No sign of rush or bustle or horrid stares when a guest comes down later or earlier than expected. We would never ever refuse a visitor breakfast if they had slept in.' Everything on the menu is enjoyable to make, so they don't have a 'speciality' as such, but Kit's description of an omelette deserves to be repeated here… 'made the traditional way, fresh beaten eggs, thrown in a really hot sizzling buttered fry pan – swirled around quickly, a filling popped in (mushrooms, bacon, cheese or smoked fish) and then rolled over onto a hot hot plate – scrummy.' We can only agree and dream of delicious Devonshire breakfasts and that marvellous view.

Conservatory and terrace at Nonsuch House

AA Landlady of the Year Awards 2002-2003

from left, Sheila Runham-Williams, Mary McFadden (winner) and Geraldine Bailie

Now in its ninth year, this award is presented in recognition of the vital role played by Bed and Breakfasts, Guest Houses, Inns and Farmhouses in the tourist industries of the UK and Ireland; and as a celebration of the hard work, endless patience and good humour of those dedicated souls who strive to make your stay both pleasant and memorable.

A rather damp day in early May saw the cream of Britain's landladies and gentlemen gathered at the Savoy Hotel, London, for the presentation of this coveted award.

Mary McFadden, of Drumkeerin, Cushendun, County Antrim, was our first winner from Northern Ireland, and clearly thrilled to receive her impressive Caithness Glass trophy, presented by Nick Walter of Caithness Glass, and a large bouquet. She also won a weekend for two at Chewton Glen, a five star country house hotel in Hampshire.

Professional artist Mary has taught art at all levels, and in her spare time walks in the Glen of Antrim with her sketch book. She joined the AA Guest Accommodation Scheme in 1999, having opened Drumkeerin as a B&B in 1995. She has consistently impressed our inspectors, who have found her 'endearing hospitality and great food a real treat.'

Albert Hampson, Business Manager of AA Hotel Services, said 'Attention to detail carried Mary through tough tests. She gives every guest a warm welcome and makes you feel at home as soon as you walk through the door.'

The runners-up were Geraldine Bailie of Ballynester House, Newtonards, and Sheila Runham Williams of Gate House, Moretonhampstead, who also received trophies.

The process leading to the presentation began some months earlier, when nominations were collected from our team of Inspectors. Approximately 100 landladies and gentlemen were sent a questionnaire, asking them about their previous jobs, what drew them to the hospitality industry, and also about amusing or significant things which have happened to them in the job. This enabled us to reduce the list to about 35, who received a testing telephone enquiry. From this we produced a Top Five, and these were the establishments visited by an undercover journalist.

Our journalist was very impressed indeed with the standards of all five, saying she felt it was almost impossible to choose between them and that this reflected incredibly well on the B&B industry as a whole. Although a close run thing, her scores enabled us to choose the winner and runners up.

Former teachers Sheila Williams and husband John, of Gate House, Moretonhampstead, have belonged to the AA Scheme since 1993. Gate House is a charming medieval hall house, matched by the hospitality of the hosts.

Ballynester House nestles in the hills above Strangford Lough, in Newtownards, County Down. Geraldine Bailie has belonged to the AA Scheme since 2001, and our inspector enthused about her 'mothering approach to hospitality', which ensures that 'guests are cosseted at every turn.'

The Top Twenty with Nick Walter, Regional Sales Manager, Caithness Glass and John Howard, Special Advisor AA Publishing (second left and centre back)

AA Landlady Of The Year 2002-2003

Top Twenty

Geraldine Bailie – Runner Up
Ballynester House, Newtownards, Co Down

Jane Bennett
Victoria Lodge, Lynton

Anne Clarke-Kehoe
Alexander Lodge, Hotel, Bournemouth

Diana Cleaver
Newnham Farm, Ryde, Isle-of-Wight

Martin Eades
Coombe Farm Hotel, Looe

Elizabeth Goodbourn
Neuadd-Wen Guest House, Cwmduad, Carmarthen

Pat Hicks
Shamwari, Axminster

Calmyn Lamb
Priory Lodge, South Queensferry, Edinburgh

Kath Leadbeater
Hart Manor, Langholm

Sue Lindsay
Midway Cottage, Bradford-Upon-Avon

Mary McFadden – Winner
Drumkeerin, Cushendun, Co Antrim

Kit Noble
Nonsuch House, Kingswear ,Dartmouth

Jean Player
Crailing Old School, Crailing, Nr Jedburgh

Caroline Robins
Hotel Petit Champ, Sark, Channel Islands

Sheila Runham-Williams – Runner Up
Gate House, Moretonhampstead

Judith Sharpe
Amble House, Keswick

Elaine Sheldrake
Swan House Country Guest House, Newnham on Severn

Margaret Smith
Hurdon Farm, Launceston

Tricia Thorburn-Muirhead
Thamesmead House Hotel, Henley-on-Thames

Amanda Willats
Harrabeer Country House Hotel, Yelverton

The Interest is Building

Lavenham Priory

Off the beaten track or off the wall, you'll find B&Bs in some bizarre locations, including former railway stations, schools, a chapel, windmill, milking barn, morgue and maternity hospital. Buildings of great historic and architectural interest abound, so take your pick from our beautiful B&Bs.

The Bed & Breakfast Guide 2003 offers an intriguing choice of places to stay, ranging in scale from a one-up one-down former tallet barn to a Cumbrian Castle.

For the uninitiated, a tallet barn is a simple agricultural building with a loft. **The Tallett Barn B&B** at Long Compton, Warwickshire, once housed animals on the ground floor with a feed store above, accessed by external steps and a loft door, which are still there today.

Augill Castle, Brough, is a splendid specimen of Victorian Gothic with six turrets and a main central tower, gilded ceilings in the main public rooms, a vaulted stairwell below the tower, and a rare stained-glass window based on a design from Melrose Abbey. The castle was bought in a semi-derelict state in 1997, and has been completely refurbished using authentic period colours throughout.

A-list properties

Listed buildings figure prominently, with stunning examples like **Lavenham Priory** in Suffolk (Grade I listed), carefully restored to its 13th-century appearance, with a Great Hall, Merchants Room and courtyard herb garden. **Wallington Hall**, King's Lynn, is an Elizabethan Manor House dating from 1527. The front entrance porch is of particular significance with its grotesque heads and fascinating stonework. Another Grade I property is **Beeties**, a former warehouse now incorporating a shop with accommodation above. It is part of a model industrial village built by Titus Salt – Saltaire, near Shipley in West Yorkshire. The whole village has just been designated a World Heritage Site.

In an urban context are the likes of **Harrington Hall**, Dublin, and **Mayville Guest House**, Edinburgh, Georgian town houses, both notable for their fine moulding, plasterwork and other original features, including a large stained glass window at Mayville. The owners from Edinburgh write that 'no alterations of any kind can be made to the house without permission from Historic Scotland'.

While the listing process preserves the nation's precious buildings from destruction or passing fancy, it does mean that the owners have to work within the scheme's constraints. Most say they have no problem with painting, decorating and making alterations in consultation with their supervising authority, as they are equally committed to the integrity of their historic buildings, and enjoy decorating in period style. However it can be a problem when you aim to provide the highest standards of guest accommodation, and some owners have experienced difficulties in attempting to add bathrooms, or removing partition walls to enlarge a room.

The Coach House, in Melbourne, Derbyshire, is located in a conservation area, and the Conservation Officer from the local council, who dictated the colours for the building's exterior décor, also recommended refusal of planning permission for the internally illuminated AA lantern sign – unsuccessfully as it happens! Owners, June and Terry Lee won two local awards for their restoration work on the property.

English Heritage says that listing is not meant to 'fossilise a building', and that 'a building's long-term interests are often best served by putting it to good use …'.

Listed Buildings

In England and Wales listed buildings are graded as follows:

- **Grade I** buildings are those of exceptional interest (only about 2 per cent of listed buildings so far are in this grade).
- **Grade II*** are particularly important buildings of more than special interest (some 4 per cent of listed buildings).
- **Grade II** buildings are of special interest, warranting every effort to preserve them.

The main criteria for selecting listed buildings are architectural interest, historic interest, close historical association with nationally important buildings or events, and group value, such as an interesting square, terrace or model village.

The older and more rare a building is, the more likely it is to be listed. All buildings dating from before 1700, which survive in anything like their original condition, are listed, as are most built between 1700 and 1840. After that date, the criteria become tighter with time, so that post-1945 buildings have to be exceptionally important to be listed.

In Scotland listed buildings are graded as follows:

- **Category A:** Buildings of national or international importance, either architectural or historic, or fine little-altered examples of some particular period, style or building type.
- **Category B:** Buildings of regional or more than local importance, or major examples of some particular period, style or building type which may have been altered.
- **Category C(S):** Buildings of local importance, lesser examples of any period, style or building type, as originally constructed or altered; and simple, traditional buildings which group well together with others in categories A and B or are part of a planned group such as an estate or an industrial complex.

Ireland, both North and South, have similar schemes.

De-listed & deconstructed

'Yesterdays' an establishment in Newtown, Powys, is a former temperance hotel and boarding school dating from 1690. It was a listed building, but in 1990 when the house was being refurbished from its derelict condition, an earthquake caused considerable damage. As they had already re-roofed, and wanted to keep the original beams and staircase, the owners persuaded the builder to scaffold up the internal beams and roof and remove the walls (see picture on page 21). They then dug foundations and built the walls up to the roof – an incredible feat. The house is now de-listed.

In another act of reconstruction, **Glenaveron**, built in Brora during 1904, was taken down stone by stone in 1911, moved 200 yards to its present location and rebuilt.

The Big Sleep Hotel

Lavenham Priory

All change

Buildings don't have to be very old or even very beautiful to be appealing, as Cosmo Fry and Lulu Anderson have shown with their conversion of the former British Gas HQ in Cardiff. The 10-storey, green-glazed 1960s office block now provides the coolest accommodation – high on design values and low on price – in **The Big Sleep Hotel**. Extensive use of Formica furniture and fleece fabrics is a strong style statement.

Dramatic changes of use make for interesting accommodation. Both **Scuffits** and **Langley Oast**, near Maidstone, are former oast houses with roundels (tower-like kilns built for the drying of hops), converted to provide bedrooms, dining rooms and kitchens. **Bradford Old Windmill**, a 200-year-old windmill at Bradford-on-Avon has a round tower and conical roof spanning four storeys, a new tower and conical roof of two storeys and Gothic-style windows. A particular feature, set against the round rooms and conical ceiling, is a round bed.

Steep stairs, overhead gear, shafting and original millstones have all been retained at **Bolebroke Water Mill**, Hartfield, a building old enough to have been recorded in the Domesday Book.

Transports of delight

Both **Ye Olde Station Guest House** at Coleshill, Warwickshire, and **Eyarth Station** at Ruthin are old railway stations dating from the age of steam, Eyarth retaining its original platform and ticket office. The country's maritime heritage has also left a legacy of useful buildings like **Y Glennydd Hotel**, a former coast guard station at St David's, and the **Old Passage Inn** at Arlingham – once the ferry terminal.

Stores, cop shops & old schools

First a chemist shop and then a bank, **Redbank House**, Skerries, keeps its wine stocks safe in the old bank vault. You should also feel secure at **Henllys**, Betws-y-Coed, a former police station and magistrates' court with an original cell door on reception, a single room in an old cell, and a collection of police helmets. **Jeake's House** in Rye, dating from 1534, has seen duty as a chapel, wool store and Baptist school, while other educational establishments include **The Old School**, Stafford; **Crailing Old School**, Crailing, and the **Cholmondeley Arms**, Cholmondeley. The 400-year-old **Apothecary Guest House** at Kimbolton was a chemist's for 200 years and before that the village bath house.

In its earlier days, the **New Central Hotel** at Blackpool was a maternity hospital, and at the other end of life's journey, the thatched barn at **May Cottage**, Thruxton, was the village mortuary, as was the **Village House Hotel**, Findon. While on the subject of hatching and despatching, the **Library House** at Ironbridge has been a clinic, dentist's, village library and registrar's office – maybe a little matching there?

We started with a barn, and so we finish at the common end with **Common End Farm**, Ashbourne – delightful accommodation converted from cow barns with hayloft storage. Also on the rustic theme is the **Old Forge** at Compton Abbas near Shaftesbury. Tim and Lucy Kerridge bought the thatched, stone-built cottage and outbuildings in 1986. Attached was a slate-roofed workshop – former wheelwright's premises – and across the yard the old blacksmith's with the forge and tools still in place, apparently untouched since 1930. These outbuildings have been lovingly converted over the years, retaining many original features and all those wonderful artefacts, to provide the most attractive B&B accommodation.

Thanks to English Heritage for information on listed buildings www.heritage.co.uk

Thanks to Historic Scotland for information on listed buildings www.historic-scotland.gov.uk

Yesterdays

AA Guest Accommodation of the Year Awards 2002-2003

Every year we ask our Inspectors to nominate those establishments they feel come closest to the ideal of what a B&B should be. They consider location, food standards and quality of fittings, as well as those less tangible elements – charm, warmth and hospitality. From a shortlist of around twenty, one is selected to represent each country in the Guide.

A picture of the winner opens each country section.

England

Lakeshore House, Windermere

Enjoying a magnificent setting in manicured grounds, this luxurious house offers suites and bedrooms furnished to the very highest standards and featuring every conceivable extra. Public areas include a conservatory with swimming pool, and there is a real sense that nothing is too much trouble for the charming proprietors.

Scotland

Nether Underwood, Symington

A lovely country house set in a walled garden. Bedrooms are charming and elegant. Hospitality is unsurpassed, and great home-cooked food is served. The owners join their guests for dinner around the large polished table, creating a warm and friendly house party atmosphere. 'A really special place to stay' was the opinion of our Inspector.

Ireland

Ballywarren House, Cong

Attention to detail is evident throughout this delightful house, from the extremely comfortable bedrooms and public areas to the home-baking. Rustic country cooking from France and Holland features in the newly built conservatory dining room, and guests are asked on reservation for any dietary preferences or food allergies. The owners are an English couple with plenty of experience in running a guest house, previously having run the five Diamond Cockle Warren Cottage Hotel at Hayling Island.

Wales

The Talkhouse, Caersws

The Talkhouse may not be that imposing from the outside but it is outstanding inside. A 19th century country inn, it has been completely refurbished over recent years. The three bedrooms and the restaurant are just lovely. Rooms are not large, but are so well designed and comfortable that size does not matter. The chef/owner is passionate about food, and makes fine use of quality local produce.

AA Accessible Hotel of the Year Awards 2002-2003

These awards highlight establishments which are making particular progress in their welcome to disabled guests in the lead-up to the introduction of part 3 of the Disability Discrimination Act from 2004. From nearly 8000 establishments in the AA accommodation schemes, twenty finalists have been chosen. These include three Highly Commended and an outright winner. The selection process involves assessment of accessible facilities against an 80 point checklist, mystery telephone enquiry and overnight visit. The Top Twenty includes sixteen hotels and four establishments from the B&B Guide; Rosendale Lodge, Ely, Double-Gate Farm, Wells, Websters, Salisbury and Llety Ceiro Country House, Aberystwyth; of which Rosendale Lodge has been awarded Highly Commended.

Rosendale Lodge, Ely

The caring hosts at this superb detached property are very welcoming, and the spacious bedrooms, tastefully furnished with period pieces, have many thoughtful touches. The ground floor room has been very carefully designed, and proprietor Val Pickford is very aware of the details which can make or break the stay for the less mobile – such as raising the breakfast table on castors to allow wheelchair access. When compiling her list of accessible places to eat nearby, she checks their claims in person.

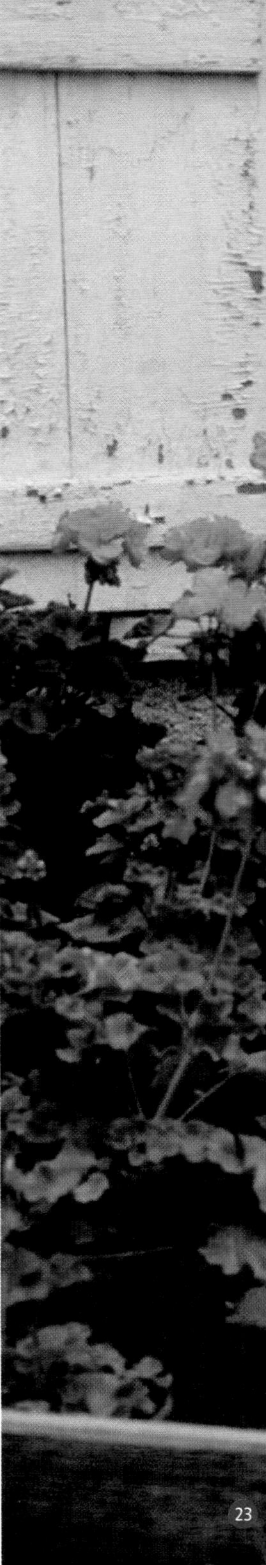

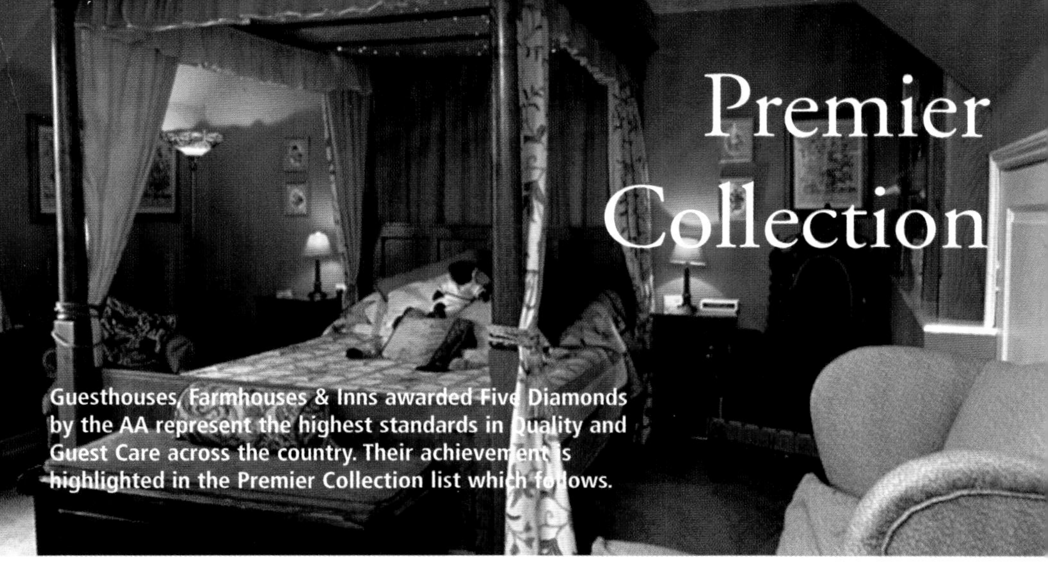
Premier Collection
Guesthouses, Farmhouses & Inns awarded Five Diamonds by the AA represent the highest standards in Quality and Guest Care across the country. Their achievement is highlighted in the Premier Collection list which follows.

CHANNEL ISLANDS

JERSEY

ST SAVIOUR
Champ Colin
☎ 01534 851877

ENGLAND

BEDFORDSHIRE

SANDY
Highfield Farm
☎ 01767 682332

BERKSHIRE

SULHAMSTEAD
The Old Manor
☎ 01189 832423

BUCKINGHAMSHIRE

BEACONSFIELD
The George Hotel
☎ 01494 673086

NEWPORT PAGNELL
The Limes
☎ 01908 617041

CAMBRIDGESHIRE

CHIPPENHAM
The Old Bakery
☎ 01638 721185

ELY
Rosendale Lodge
☎ 01353 667700

Springfields
☎ 01353 663637

HUNTINGDON
Holmefields Barn
☎ 01487 841435

CHESHIRE

CHESTER
Grove House
☎ 01829 740893

Redland Private Hotel
☎ 01244 671024

MALPAS
Tilston Lodge
☎ 01829 250223

NANTWICH
Oakland House
☎ 01270 567134

The Limes
01270 624081

WILMSLOW
Pear Tree Cottage
Country Guest House
☎ 0161 439 5755

CO DURHAM

DARLINGTON
Clow Beck House
☎ 01325 721075

CORNWALL & ISLES OF SCILLY

FALMOUTH
Dolvean Hotel
☎ 01326 313658

LAUNCESTON
Stenhill Farm
☎ 01566 785686

LOOE
St Aubyn's Guest House
☎ 01503 264351

PADSTOW
Cross House Hotel
☎ 01841 532391

Seafood Restaurant
☎ 01841 532700

St Petroc's Hotel and Bistro
☎ 01841 532700

The Old Cabbage Patch
☎ 01841 520956

PENZANCE
Chy-an-Mor
☎ 01736 363441

Ennys
☎ 01736 740262

The Summerhouse
☎ 01736 363744

PERRANUTHNOE
Ednovean Farm
☎ 01736 711883

POLPERRO
Trenderway Farm
☎ 01503 272214

ST AUSTELL
Anchorage House Guest Lodge
☎ 01726 814071

ST BLAZEY
Nanscawen Manor House
☎ 01726 814488

TINTAGEL
The Old Borough House
☎ 01840 770475

TRURO
Bissick Old Mill
☎ 01726 882557

CUMBRIA

AMBLESIDE
Grey Friar Lodge
Country House Hotel
☎ 015394 33158

Rowanfield Country House
☎ 015394 33686

BORROWDALE
Hazel Bank Country House
☎ 017687 77248

BRAMPTON
Cracrop Farm
☎ 016977 48245

BROUGH
Augill Castle
☎ 017683 41937

CARTMEL
Hill Farm
☎ 01539 536477

Uplands Hotel
☎ 015395 36248

CONISTON
Coniston Lodge Hotel
☎ 015394 41201

Wheelgate Country Guest House
☎ 015394 41418

KENDAL
Blaven Homestay
☎ 01539 734894

KESWICK
Derwent Cottage
☎ 017687 74838

The Grange Country House
☎ 017687 72500

LONGTOWN
Bessiestown Farm
Country Guest House
☎ 01228 577219

LORTON
New House Farm
☎ 01900 85404

Winder Hall Country House
☎ 01900 85107

NEAR SAWREY
Ees Wyke Country House
☎ 015394 36393

Sawrey House Country
Hotel & Restaurant
☎ 015394 36387

WINDERMERE
Howbeck
☎ 015394 44739

Lakeshore House
☎ 015394 33202

Newstead
☎ 015394 44485

The Beaumont
☎ 015394 47075

DERBYSHIRE

ASHBOURNE
Omnia Somnia
☎ 01335 300145

Turlow Bank
☎ 01335 370299

BELPER
Dannah Farm Country House
☎ 01773 550273

BUXTON
Grendon Guest House
☎ 01298 78831

HOPE
Underleigh House
☎ 01433 621372

ILKESTON
The Redhouse
☎ 0115 932 2965

NEWHAVEN
The Smithy
☎ 01298 84548

WESTON UNDERWOOD
Park View Farm
☎ 01335 360352

WIRKSWORTH
The Old Lock-Up
☎ 01629 826272

DEVON

ATHERINGTON
Springfield Garden
☎ 01769 560034

AXMINSTER
Kerrington House
☎ 01297 35333

Lea Hill
☎ 01404 881881

BAMPTON
The Bark House
☎ 01398 351236

BANTHAM
Widcombe House
☎ 01548 561084

BOVEY TRACEY
Brookfield House
☎ 01626 836181

Front House Lodge
☎ 01626 832202

CHAGFORD
Parford Well
☎ 01647 433353

CHILLATON
Tor Cottage
☎ 01822 860248

DARTMOUTH
Broome Court
☎ 01803 834275

Nonsuch House
☎ 01803 752829

Slide House
☎ 01803 770378

HAYTOR
Bel Alp House
☎ 01364 661217

HONITON
West Colwell Farm
☎ 01404 831130

HORN'S CROSS
Lower Waytown
☎ 01237 451787

LUSTLEIGH
Woodley House
☎ 01647 277214

LYDFORD
Moor View House
☎ 01822 820220

LYNMOUTH
Bonnicott House
☎ 01598 753346

LYNTON
Highcliffe House
☎ 01598 752235

Victoria Lodge
☎ 01598 753203

MORETONHAMPSTEAD
Blackaller Hotel & Restaurant
☎ 01647 440322

Gate House
☎ 01647 440479

POSTBRIDGE
Lydgate House
☎ 01822 880209

SIDMOUTH
The Old Farmhouse
☎ 01395 512284

The Salty Monk
☎ 01395 513174

SOUTH BRENT
Coombe House
☎ 01548 821277

SOUTH MOLTON
Kerscott Farm
☎ 01769 550262

TEIGNMOUTH
Thomas Luny House
☎ 01626 772976

TIVERTON
Hornhill Farmhouse
☎ 01884 253352

TORQUAY
Colindale Hotel
☎ 01803 293947

Mulberry House
☎ 01803 213639

WHIMPLE
Woodhayes Country House
and Cottage
☎ 01404 822237

DORSET

CHRISTCHURCH
Druid House
☎ 01202 485615

The Lord Bute Hotel & Restaurant
☎ 01425 278884

DORCHESTER
The Casterbridge Hotel
☎ 01305 264043

Yalbury Cottage Hotel & Restaurant
☎ 01305 262382

FARNHAM
The Museum Inn
☎ 01725 516261

SHERBORNE
Munden House
☎ 01963 23150

The Grange Hotel & Restaurant
☎ 01935 813463

The Old Vicarage
☎ 01963 251117

ESSEX

CHIPPING ONGAR
Diggins Farm
☎ 01277 899303

SAFFRON WALDEN
The Bonnet
☎ 01799 584955

THORPE-LE-SOKEN
The Olive Branch Brasserie, Bar & Rooms
☎ 01255 861199

WIX
Dairy House Farm
☎ 01255 870322

GLOUCESTERSHIRE

BLOCKLEY
The Old Bakery
☎ 01386 700408

CHELTENHAM
Cleeve Hill Hotel
☎ 01242 672052

Georgian House
☎ 01242 515577

FRAMPTON ON SEVERN
The Old School House
☎ 01452 740457

GUITING POWER
Guiting Guest House
☎ 01451 850470

NEWENT
Three Choirs Vineyards Restaurant & Rooms
☎ 01531 890223

STONEHOUSE
The Grey Cottage
☎ 01453 822515

STOW-ON-THE-WOLD
Rectory Farmhouse
☎ 01451 832351

STROUD
Hunters Lodge
☎ 01453 883588

The Priory
☎ 01453 834282

WINCHCOMBE
Isbourne Manor House
☎ 01242 602281

GREATER MANCHESTER

ALTRINCHAM
Ash Farm Country Guest House
☎ 0161 929 9290

HAMPSHIRE

BARTON-ON-SEA
Tower House
☎ 01425 629508

BROCKENHURST
Thatched Cottage Hotel & Restaurant
☎ 01590 623090

FORDINGBRIDGE
Cottage Crest
☎ 01725 512009

The Three Lions
☎ 01425 652489

LYMINGTON
Efford Cottage
☎ 01590 642315

The Olde Barn
☎ 01590 644939

RINGWOOD
Little Forest Lodge
☎ 01425 478848

SWAY
The Nurse's Cottage
☎ 01590 683402

HEREFORDSHIRE

LEOMINSTER
Hills Farm
☎ 01568 750205

ROSS-ON-WYE
Trecilla Farm
☎ 01989 770647

HERTFORDSHIRE

BISHOP'S STORTFORD
Harewood
☎ 01279 813907

ISLE OF WIGHT

RYDE
Little Upton Farm
☎ 01983 563236

Newnham Farm
☎ 01983 882423

KENT

CANTERBURY
Magnolia House
☎ 01227 765121

Thanington Hotel
☎ 01227 453227

DEAL
Sutherland House Hotel
☎ 01304 362853

DOVER
The Old Vicarage
☎ 01304 210668

FARNINGHAM
Beesfield Farm
☎ 01322 863900

FOLKESTONE
Harbourside Hotel
☎ 01303 246824

HAWKHURST
Southgate-Little Fowlers
☎ 01580 752526

The Wren's Nest
☎ 01580 754919

MAIDSTONE
Ringlestone Inn & Farmhouse Hotel
☎ 01622 859900

MARDEN
Merzie Meadows
☎ 01622 820500

ROYAL TUNBRIDGE WELLS
Danehurst House
☎ 01892 527739

The Old Parsonage
☎ 01892 750773

SITTINGBOURNE
Hempstead House Country Hotel
☎ 01795 428020

LANCASHIRE

BLACKPOOL
The Old Coach House
☎ 01253 349195

CARNFORTH
New Capernwray Farm
☎ 01524 734284

PRESTON
Whitestake Farm
☎ 01772 613005

YEALAND CONYERS
The Bower
☎ 01524 734585

LEICESTERSHIRE

KEGWORTH
Kegworth House
☎ 01509 672575

LINCOLNSHIRE

LINCOLN
Minster Lodge Hotel
☎ 01522 513220

STAMFORD
Rock Lodge
☎ 01780 481758

LONDON

N4
Mount View
☎ 020 8340 9222

MERSEYSIDE

SOUTHPORT
Cambridge Town House Hotel
☎ 01704 538372

NORFOLK

CLEY NEXT THE SEA
Old Town Hall House
☎ 01263 740284

HINDRINGHAM
Field House
☎ 01328 878726

KING'S LYNN
Wallington Hall
☎ 01553 811567

NORTH WALSHAM
White House Farm
☎ 01263 721344

NORWICH
Catton Old Hall
☎ 01603 419379

THURSFORD GREEN
Holly Lodge
☎ 01328 878465

WALCOTT
Holly Tree Cottage
☎ 01692 650721

NORTHUMBERLAND

CORNHILL-ON-TWEED
Ivy Cottage
☎ 01890 820667

HEXHAM
Montcoffer Bed & Breakfast
☎ 01434 344138

WOOLER
The Old Manse
☎ 01668 215343

NOTTINGHAMSHIRE

HOLBECK
Browns
☎ 01909 720659

OXFORDSHIRE

BURFORD
Burford House
☎ 01993 823151

Jonathan's at the Angel
☎ 01993 822714

HENLEY-ON-THAMES
Lenwade
☎ 01491 573468

Thamesmead House Hotel
☎ 01491 574745

OXFORD
Burlington House
☎ 01865 513513

Chestnuts Guest House
☎ 01865 553375

Cotswold House
☎ 01865 310558

THAME
The Dairy
☎ 01844 214075

SHROPSHIRE

CHURCH STRETTON
Jinlye Guest House
☎ 01694 723243

Willowfield Guest House
☎ 01694 751471

CLEOBURY NORTH
Cleobury Court
☎ 01746 787005

IRONBRIDGE
The Library House
☎ 01952 432299

LLANFAIR WATERDINE
The Waterdine
☎ 01547 528214

LUDLOW
Line Farm
☎ 01568 780400

Number Twenty Eight
☎ 01584 876996

WHITCHURCH
Dearnford Hall
☎ 01948 662319

SOMERSET

BATH
Apsley House Hotel
☎ 01225 336966

Athole Guest House
☎ 01225 334307
Cheriton House
☎ 01225 429862

Dorian House
☎ 01225 426336

Haydon House
☎ 01225 444919

Holly Lodge
☎ 01225 424042

Kennard Hotel
☎ 01225 310472

Leighton House
☎ 01225 314769

Monkshill Guest House
☎ 01225 833028

Paradise House Hotel
☎ 01225 317723

The Ayrlington
☎ 01225 425495

The County Hotel
☎ 01225 425003

BEERCROCOMBE
Whittles Farm
☎ 01823 480301

BURROWBRIDGE
Saltmoor House
☎ 01823 698092

CHARD
Bellplot House Hotel
☎ 01460 62600

Higher Beetham Farm
☎ 01460 234460

DULVERTON
Highercombe
☎ 01398 323451

ILMINSTER
The Old Rectory
☎ 01460 54364

MINEHEAD
Glendower Hotel
☎ 01643 707144

NORTON ST PHILIP
Bath Lodge
☎ 01225 723040

Monmouth Lodge
☎ 01373 834367

PORLOCK
Dunster Steep House
☎ 01643 863008

SOMERTON
Lydford House
☎ 01963 240217

TAUNTON
Heathfield Lodge
☎ 01823 432286

WELLS
Beaconsfield Farm
☎ 01749 870308

Riverside Grange
☎ 01749 890761

The Old Farmhouse
☎ 01749 675058

WEST BAGBOROUGH
Bashfords Farmhouse
☎ 01823 432015

Tilbury Farm
☎ 01823 432391

WESTON-SUPER-MARE
Church House
☎ 01934 633185

YEOVIL
Holywell House
☎ 01935 862612

STAFFORDSHIRE

CHEDDLETON
Choir Cottage and Choir House
☎ 01538 360561

OAKAMOOR
Bank House
☎ 01538 702810

TAMWORTH
Oak Tree Farm
☎ 01827 56807

SUFFOLK

BEYTON
Manorhouse
☎ 01359 270960

FRESSINGFIELD
Chippenhall Hall
☎ 01379 588180

HARTEST
The Hatch
☎ 01284 830226

KEDINGTON
The White House
☎ 01440 707731

LAVENHAM
Lavenham Priory
☎ 01787 247404

LOWESTOFT
Abbe House Hotel
☎ 01502 581083

SUSSEX, EAST

ARLINGTON
Bates Green
☎ 01323 482039

EASTBOURNE
Pinnacle Point
☎ 01323 726666

HARTFIELD
Bolebroke Watermill
☎ 01892 770425

HASTINGS & ST LEONARDS
Parkside House
☎ 01424 433096

HEATHFIELD
Old Corner Cottage
☎ 01435 863787

HERSTMONCEUX
Wartling Place
☎ 01323 832590

LEWES
Nightingales
☎ 01273 475673

PETT
Pendragon Lodge
☎ 01424 814051

RYE
Durrant House Hotel
☎ 01797 223182

Jeake's House
☎ 01797 222828

King Charles II Guest House
☎ 01797 224954

Little Orchard House
☎ 01797 223831

Manor Farm Oast
☎ 01424 813787

Playden Cottage Guesthouse
☎ 01797 222234

The Benson
☎ 01797 225131

The Old Vicarage Guest House
☎ 01797 222119

White Vine House
☎ 01797 224748

UCKFIELD
Hooke Hall
☎ 01825 761578

WILMINGTON
Crossways Hotel
☎ 01323 482455

SUSSEX, WEST

ARDINGLY
The Avins Bridge Restaurant & Rooms
☎ 01444 892393

ARUNDEL
Bonham's Country House
☎ 01243 551301

BOSHAM
Kenwood
☎ 01243 572727

CHILGROVE
Forge Hotel
☎ 01243 535333

HORSHAM
Random Hall
☎ 01403 790558

LINDFIELD
The Pilstyes
☎ 01444 484101

ROGATE
Mizzards Farm
☎ 01730 821656

WARWICKSHIRE

NUNEATON
Leathermill Grange
☎ 01827 714637

SHIPSTON ON STOUR
Chavignol at the Old Mill
☎ 01608 663888

STRATFORD-UPON-AVON
Glebe Farm House
☎ 01789 842501

WEST MIDLANDS

BIRMINGHAM
Westbourne Lodge
☎ 0121 429 1003

WILTSHIRE

BOX
Spinney Cross
☎ 01225 742019

White Smocks
☎ 01225 742154

BRADFORD-ON-AVON
Bradford Old Windmill
☎ 01225 866842

Widbrook Grange
☎ 01225 864750

BROAD CHALKE
Ebblesway Courtyard
☎ 01722 780182

CALNE
Chilvester Hill House
☎ 01249 813981

DEVIZES
Blounts Court Farm
☎ 01380 727180

LACOCK
At the Sign of the Angel
☎ 01249 730230

MALMESBURY
Horse & Groom Inn
☎ 01666 823904

MIDDLE WINTERSLOW
The Beadles
☎ 01980 862922

WARMINSTER
The Angel Inn
☎ 01985 213225

WHITEPARISH
Newton Farmhouse
☎ 01794 884416

WORCESTERSHIRE

BROADWAY
Mill Hay House
☎ 01386 852498

BROMSGROVE
Rosa Lodge
☎ 0121 445 5440

YORKSHIRE, EAST RIDING OF

BEVERLEY
Burton Mount Country House
☎ 01964 550541

WOLD NEWTON
The Wold Cottage
☎ 01262 470696

YORKSHIRE, NORTH

AMPLEFORTH
Shallowdale House
☎ 01439 788325

BEDALE
Elmfield Country House
☎ 01677 450558

GRASSINGTON
Ashfield House Hotel
☎ 01756 752584

Grassington Lodge
☎ 01756 752518

HARROGATE
Ruskin Hotel
☎ 01423 502045

PICKERING
The Moorlands Country House Hotel
☎ 01751 460229

THORNTON LE DALE
Allerston Manor House
☎ 01723 850112

YORK
Alexander House
☎ 01904 625016

YORKSHIRE, SOUTH

SHEFFIELD
Westbourne House Hotel
☎ 0114 266 0109

ISLE OF MAN

DOUGLAS
Engelwood Lodge
☎ 01624 616050

PORT ERIN
Rowany Cottier
☎ 01624 832287

PORT ST MARY
Aaron House
☎ 01624 835702

RAMSEY
The River House
☎ 01624 816412

SCOTLAND

ARGYLL & BUTE

CARDROSS
Kirkton House
☎ 01389 841951

DUNOON
The Anchorage Hotel
☎ 01369 705108

SALEN
Gruline Home Farm
☎ 01680 300581

CITY OF EDINBURGH

EDINBURGH
Bonnington Guest House
☎ 0131 554 7610

Dunstane House Hotel
☎ 0131 337 6169

Elmview
☎ 0131 228 1973

Kildonan Lodge Hotel
☎ 0131 667 2793

Newington Cottage
☎ 0131 668 1935

The Lodge Hotel
☎ 0131 337 3682

The Stuarts
☎ 0131 229 9559

The Witchery by the Castle
☎ 0131 225 5613

DUMFRIES & GALLOWAY

CASTLE DOUGLAS
Craigadam
☎ 01556 650233

Longacre Manor
☎ 01556 503576

DALBEATTIE
Auchenskeoch Lodge
☎ 01387 780277

EAST LOTHIAN

EAST LINTON
Kippielaw Farmhouse
☎ 01620 860368

FIFE

ANSTRUTHER
Beaumont Lodge Guest House
☎ 01333 310315

The Grange
☎ 01333 310842

CUPAR
Todhall House
☎ 01334 656344

Westfield House
☎ 01334 655699

ST ANDREWS
Fossil House Bed & Breakfast
☎ 01334 850639

HIGHLAND

AVIEMORE
The Old Minister's House
☎ 01479 812181

BALLACHULISH
Ballachulish House
☎ 01855 811266

BRORA
Glenaveron
☎ 01408 621601

FORT WILLIAM
Ashburn House
☎ 01397 706000

The Grange
☎ 01397 705516

GRANTOWN-ON-SPEY
Ardconnel House
☎ 01479 872104

The Pines
☎ 01479 872092

INVERNESS
Ballifeary House Hotel
☎ 01463 235572

Moyness House
☎ 01463 233836

Trafford Bank
☎ 01463 241414

KENTALLEN
Ardsheal House
☎ 01631 740227

KINGUSSIE
Osprey Hotel
☎ 01540 661510

MELVICH
The Sheiling Guest House
☎ 01641 531256

STRATHPEFFER
Craigvar
☎ 01997 421622

MORAY

ELGIN
The Croft
☎ 01343 546004

PERTH & KINROSS

PERTH
Over Kinfauns
☎ 01738 860538

PITLOCHRY
Dunfallandy House
☎ 01796 472648

RENFREWSHIRE

JOHNSTONE
Nether Johnstone House
☎ 01505 322210

LOCHWINNOCH

East Lochhead
☎ 01505 842610

PAISLEY
Myfarrclan Guest House
☎ 0141 884 8285

SCOTTISH BORDERS

JEDBURGH
The Spinney
☎ 01835 863525

MELROSE
Fauhope House
☎ 01896 823184

SOUTH AYRSHIRE

BALLANTRAE
Cosses Country House
☎ 01465 831363

DUNURE
Dunduff Farm
☎ 01292 500225

SYMINGTON
Nether Underwood
Country House
☎ 01563 830666

STIRLING

CALLANDER
Leny House
☎ 01877 331078

DUNBLANE
Rokeby House
☎ 01786 824447

WEST LOTHIAN

EAST CALDER
Ashcroft Farmhouse
☎ 01506 881810

WALES

CONWY

COLWYN BAY
Plas Rhos Hotel
☎ 01492 543698

CONWY
Sychnant Pass House
☎ 01492 596868

LLANDUDNO
Abbey Lodge
☎ 01492 878042

Bryn Derwen Hotel
☎ 01492 876804

GWYNEDD

DOLGELLAU
Tyddynmawr Farmhouse
☎ 01341 422331

ISLE OF ANGLESEY

PENTRAETH
Parc-yr-Odyn
☎ 01248 450566

MONMOUTHSHIRE

ABERGAVENNY
Oak Meadows
☎ 01873 850927

NEATH PORT TALBOT

NEATH
Green Lanterns Guest House
☎ 01639 631884

NEWPORT

NEWPORT
The Inn at the Elm Tree
☎ 01633 680225

PEMBROKESHIRE

SOLVA
Lochmeyler Farmhouse
☎ 01348 837724

POWYS

CAERSWS
The Talkhouse
☎ 01686 688919

CRICKHOWELL
Glangrwyney Court
☎ 01873 811288

NORTHERN IRELAND

DOWN

DOWNPATRICK
Pheasants' Hill Country House
☎ 028 44838707

HOLYWOOD
Beech Hill Country House
☎ 028 9042 5892

NEWTOWNARDS
Ballynester House
☎ 028 4278 8386

Edenvale House
☎ 028 9181 4881

LONDONDERRY

COLERAINE
Greenhill House
☎ 028 7086 8241

TYRONE

DUNGANNON
Grange Lodge
☎ 028 8778 4212

REPUBLIC OF IRELAND

CARLOW

CARLOW
Barrowville Town House
☎ 0503 43324

CLARE

BALLYVAUGHAN
Drumcreehy Guesthouse
☎ 065 7077377

LAHINCH
Moy House
☎ 065 708 2800

CORK

BLARNEY
Ashlee Lodge
☎ 021 4385346

FERMOY
Ballyvolane House
☎ 025 36349

KANTURK
Assolas Country House
☎ 029 50015

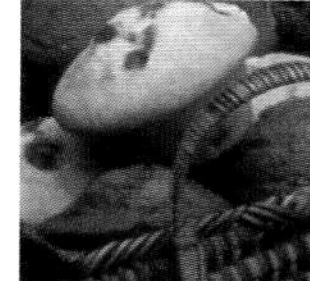

KINSALE
The Old Bank House
☎ 021 4774075

SHANAGARRY
Ballymaloe House
☎ 021 4652531

YOUGHAL
Ahernes
☎ 024 92424

DONEGAL

FAHAN
St John's Country House
& Restaurant
☎ 077 60289

DUBLIN

DUBLIN
Aberdeen Lodge
☎ 01 2838155

Ariel House
☎ 01 6685512

Blakes Townhouse
☎ 01 6688324

Brownes Townhouse & Brasserie
☎ 01 6383939

Butlers Town House
☎ 01 6674022

Cedar Lodge
☎ 01 6684410

Eglinton Manor
☎ 01 2693273

Glenogra Guest House
☎ 01 6683661

Merrion Hall
☎ 01 6681426

Pembroke Town House
☎ 01 6600277

Waterloo House
☎ 01 6601888

GALWAY

CLIFDEN
Byrne's Mal Dua House
☎ 095 21171

O'Grady's Sunnybank House
☎ 095 21437

CRAUGHWELL
St Clerans
☎ 091 846555

GALWAY
Killeen House
☎ 091 524179

OUGHTERARD
River Run Lodge
☎ 091 552697

Waterfall Lodge
☎ 091 552168

KERRY

CASTLEGREGORY
The Shores Country House
☎ 066 7139196

DINGLE
Emlagh House
☎ 066 9152345

Gormans Clifftop House
& Restaurant
☎ 066 9155162

Greenmount House
☎ 066 9151414

Milltown House
066 9151372

Pax House
☎ 066 9151518

KENMARE
Sallyport House
☎ 064 42066

KILLARNEY
Earls Court House
☎ 064 34009

Foleys Town House
☎ 064 31217

Kathleen's Country House
☎ 064 32810

Old Weir Lodge
☎ 064 35593

KILLORGLIN
Carrig House Country
House & Restaurant
☎ 066 9769100

KILDARE

ATHY
Coursetown Country House
☎ 0507 31101

LAOIS

PORTLAOISE
Ivyleigh House
☎ 0502 22081

LIMERICK

KILMALLOCK
Flemingstown House
☎ 063 98093

LOUTH

CARLINGFORD
Beaufort House
☎ 042 9373878/9

DROGHEDA
Boynehaven House
☎ 041 9836700

Tullyesker Country House
☎ 041 9830430

MAYO

CONG
Ballywarren House
☎ 092 46989

WESTPORT
Knockranny Lodge
☎ 098 28595

MEATH

BETTYSTOWN
Lis-Maura
☎ 041 9828387

TIPPERARY

THURLES
Inch House Country
House & Restaurant
☎ 0504 51348

The Castle B & B
☎ 0504 44324

WATERFORD

ANNESTOWN
Annestown House
☎ 051 396160

BALLYMACARBRY
Glasha Farmhouse
☎ 052 36108

Hanoras Cottage
☎ 052 36134

CAPPOQUIN
Richmond House
☎ 058 54278

DUNGARVAN
Powersfield House
☎ 058 45594

The Castle Country House
☎ 058 68049

WATERFORD
Foxmount Country House
☎ 051 874308

Sion Hill House & Gardens
☎ 051 851558

WESTMEATH

MOATE
Temple Country House & Spa
☎ 0506 35118

MULLINGAR
Crookedwood House
☎ 044 72165

WEXFORD

CAMPILE
Kilmokea Country Manor
& Gradens
☎ 051 388109

ENNISCORTHY
Ballinkeele House
☎ 053 38105

GOREY
Woodlands Country House
☎ 0402 37125

ROSSLARE HARBOUR
Churchtown House
☎ 053 32555

England

Lakeshore House, Windermere

ENGLAND

BEDFORDSHIRE

ASTWICK Map 04 TL23

♦♦♦ Tudor Oaks Lodge
Taylor's Rd SG5 4AZ ☎ 01462 834133 01462 834133
e-mail: tudoroakslodge@aol.com
Dir: *on A1, 1m past junct 10 northbound*
This 16th-century house has been renovated to provide open-plan public areas where a selection of real ales and imaginative food is served. Bedrooms are well-equipped, smartly presented and situated around an attractive courtyard.
FACILITIES: 13 en suite (13 GF) No smoking in 4 bedrooms No smoking in area of dining room No smoking in 1 lounge TVB tea/coffee Direct dial from bedrooms No dogs (ex guide dogs) Licensed Cen ht Jacuzzi in rooms 6 & 7, Sauna in 14 Dinner Last d 10pm **PRICES:** s £49.50-£59.50; d £62-£72✻ **CONF:** Thtr 30 Class 20 Board 12 **PARKING:** 200 **CARDS:**

See advert under HITCHIN

BEDFORD Map 04 TL04

♦♦♦♦ Knife & Cleaver
The Grove, Houghton Conquest MK45 3LA ☎ 01234 740387 01234 740900
e-mail: info@knifeandcleaver.com
Dir: *turn off A6 signed Houghton Conquest, 5m S of Bedford. Inn opposite church in village*
In a pleasant village setting, this relaxing restaurant-with-rooms consists of a cosy bar and an elegant conservatory restaurant. Interesting dishes are offered, complemented by a good wine list. Bedrooms come in a variety of styles, located in a separate garden wing, all comfortably appointed and well equipped; deluxe rooms are particularly good. Service is caring, friendly and helpful.
FACILITIES: 9 annexe en suite (1 fmly) (9 GF) No smoking in 2 bedrooms No smoking in dining room STV TVB tea/coffee Direct dial from bedrooms No dogs (ex guide dogs) Cen ht No coaches Dinner Last d 9.30pm **PRICES:** s £49-£59; d £49-£74✻ **MEALS:** Lunch fr £14.95&alc Dinner fr £20&alc✻ **CONF:** Thtr 16 Class 8 Board 12 Del from £69 ✻ **PARKING:** 35 **NOTES:** Closed 27-30 Dec rs Res & Bar closed Sun evening **CARDS:**

♦♦♦ Birch House
22 Clapham Rd MK41 7PP ☎ 01234 266972 01234 266972
e-mail: wkem1@aol.com
Dir: *On A6 N of town centre, approx. 1km. From W & S follow A6 Kettering signs, from N follow Bedford signs*
Within easy walking distance of central attractions, this impressive late-Victorian house has been sympathetically renovated. It provides a range of practically equipped bedrooms complemented by smart modern shower rooms. Breakfast is taken in an attractive conservatory overlooking the pretty garden.
FACILITIES: 4 en suite No smoking TVB tea/coffee No dogs (ex guide dogs) Cen ht TVL No children No coaches **PRICES:** s £30-£35; d £45✻ **PARKING:** 6 **CARDS:**

♦♦♦ Hertford House Hotel
57 De Parys Av MK40 2TR ☎ 01234 350007 & 354470 01234 353468
e-mail: carlo@noto.powernet.co.uk
Dir: *top end of high street near Robinson Swimming Pool*
This small, family-run hotel is within easy walking distance of Bedford town centre. The bedrooms are generally spacious, soundly appointed and well maintained. The public rooms include a ground-floor reception/lounge with an open fire place and comfortable seating, and a first-floor breakfast room, overlooking playing fields.
FACILITIES: 16 rms (14 en suite) (4 fmly) No smoking in 4 bedrooms No smoking in dining room No smoking in lounges STV TVB tea/coffee No dogs (ex guide dogs) Cen ht TVL **PARKING:** 14 **NOTES:** Closed 24 Dec-2 Jan **CARDS:**

BIGGLESWADE Map 04 TL14

♦♦♦ Crown Hotel
23 High St SG18 0JE ☎ 01767 312228 01767 312567
e-mail: terry@crownhotel.fsnet.co.uk
Dir: *Exit A1 into Biggleswade Town Centre. The hotel is between Lloyds Bank and National Westminster Bank. Opp Halifax Building Society*
The Crown is situated in the heart of this bustling market town; there has been an inn on this site since the 16th century. The bedrooms are well equipped and the bars have a good range of real ales. Food served in the cosy dining room is imaginative and tasty.
FACILITIES: 15 en suite (2 fmly) No smoking in dining room TVB tea/coffee Direct dial from bedrooms Cen ht Dinner Last d 9pm **PRICES:** s £40-£45; d £60; (room only) ✻ **CONF:** Thtr 30 Class 30 Board 30 **PARKING:** 20 **CARDS:**

LUTON Map 04 TL02

♦♦♦ Leaside Hotel
72 New Bedford Rd LU3 1BT ☎ 01582 417643 01582 734961
Dir: *Access to car park via Old Bedford Road & Villa rd*
Located a few minutes' walk from the town centre, this impressive Victorian villa retains many original features. The bar and games lounges have a traditional feel to them and there is an elegant restaurant where imaginative dishes are served. Bedrooms are well-equipped for both the business and leisure guest.
FACILITIES: 12 en suite 2 annexe en suite (1 fmly) STV TVB tea/coffee Direct dial from bedrooms No dogs (ex guide dogs) Licensed Cen ht TVL No coaches Three quarter size snooker table Dinner Last d 9.30pm/10pm Fri/Sat **PRICES:** s £40-£57.50; d £55-£67.50✻ **PARKING:** 30 **NOTES:** Closed 24-27 Dec **CARDS:**

♦♦♦ Arlington Hotel
137 New Bedford Rd LU3 1LF ☎ 01582 419614 01582 459047
e-mail: arlingtonhotel@btconnect.com
Dir: *on A6 opposite Wardown Park 0.75m from Luton town centre towards Bedford*
Set in the northern suburbs, this commercial hotel has a relaxed and informal atmosphere. The practical modern bedrooms come in a variety of sizes and include three outside chalet rooms. There is a small residents' bar and parking is a bonus.
FACILITIES: 23 rms (22 en suite) (3 fmly) No smoking in 4 bedrooms No smoking in dining room No smoking in 1 lounge STV TVB tea/coffee Direct dial from bedrooms No dogs (ex guide dogs) Licensed Cen ht TVL Dinner Last d 9.45pm **PRICES:** s £45-£48; d £50-£56✻ **LB PARKING:** 30 **CARDS:**

England

SANDY Map 04 TL14

Premier Collection

♦♦♦♦♦ Highfield (*TL166515*)

Great North Rd SG19 2AQ ☎ 01767 682332 01767 692503 Mrs M Codd
e-mail: margaret@highfield-farm.co.uk
Dir: *situated up long private drive directly off A1, 2.5m S of A1/A421 rdbt*

This charming farmhouse, with its white painted exterior is set in a peaceful location with superb views of the surrounding countryside. Bedrooms are comfortable, well-equipped and all feature modern facilities. Comprehensive, organic breakfasts are taken in the elegant dining room and there is a comfortable lounge for guests.
FACILITIES: 3 en suite 3 annexe en suite (2 fmly) (5 GF) No smoking TV10B tea/coffee Cen ht TVL 300 acres arable **PRICES:** s £40-£50; d £55-£60✻ **PARKING:** 10 **CARDS:**

SILSOE Map 04 TL03

♦♦ The Old George Hotel

High St MK45 4EP ☎ 01525 860218 01525 860218
Dir: *Slip Rd off A6 halfway between Bedford and Luton*
Situated in the heart of the village, this period inn retains many of its original features. Bedrooms are simply appointed and the four poster rooms offer particular charm. A wide range of restaurant and bar meals specialising in seafood and fish dishes are available. Gardens include a pet centre.
FACILITIES: 7 rms (2 en suite) (2 fmly) No smoking in bedrooms No smoking in dining room No smoking in 1 lounge TVB tea/coffee Cen ht Snooker Dinner Last d 9pm **PRICES:** s £35-£40; d £50-£75✻ **MEALS:** Lunch £13-£17&alc Dinner £20-£40alc✻ **PARKING:** 50 **CARDS:**

BERKSHIRE

ASCOT Map 04 SU96

♦♦♦♦ Ascot Corner

Wells Ln SL5 7DY ☎ 01344 627722 01344 873965
e-mail: susan.powell@easynet.co.uk
Dir: *A329 towards Virginia Water pass hospital, through Ascot pass BMW showroom. Proceed 0.75m and turn right into Wells Lane, then right into Ascot Corner*
FACILITIES: 3 en suite No smoking TVB tea/coffee No dogs (ex guide dogs) Cen ht TVL No children 10yrs No coaches Outdoor swimming pool (heated) **PRICES:** d £85-£90✻ **PARKING:** 8 **NOTES:** Closed 25-26 Dec **CARDS:**

HUNGERFORD Map 04 SU36

♦♦♦♦ The Swan Inn

Craven Rd, Inkpen RG17 9DX ☎ 01488 668326 01488 668306
e-mail: enquiries@theswaninn-organics.co.uk
Dir: *from M4 exit 14 S to Hungerford, S along High St under railway bridge, left to Hungerford common, right on common signed Inkpen, 3m*
Peacefully situated in the village, this delightful inn dates back to the 17th century in parts. The open fires and beams, together with a few local characters, are features of the bar, whilst the smart restaurant is an added bonus. Bedrooms are generally spacious and furnished in keeping with the style of the inn.
FACILITIES: 10 en suite (2 fmly) No smoking in bedrooms No smoking in dining room No smoking in 1 lounge TVB tea/coffee Direct dial from bedrooms No dogs Cen ht Organic farm shop Dinner Last d 9.30pm **PRICES:** s £40-£65; d £75-£90✻ **MEALS:** Lunch £18.95&alc Dinner £18.95&alc✻ **CONF:** Class 40 Board 12 **PARKING:** 50 **NOTES:** Closed 25-26 Dec **CARDS:**

♦♦♦♦ Crown & Garter

Great Common, Inkpen RG17 9QR ☎ 01488 668325 01488 669072
e-mail: mail@crownandgarter.com
Dir: *turn off A4 into Kintbury, turn opposite corner stores marked Inkpen Road, straight ahead for 2m, do not turn off this road.*

Located in the pretty rural village of Inkpen, this 17th century inn has been carefully extended to provide facilities for the modern traveller whilst retaining charm and character. A range of real ales and imaginative food is offered in the cosy dining room. The homely and comfortable bedrooms are located in quality chalets surrounding the pretty garden.
FACILITIES: 8 en suite No smoking in bedrooms TVB tea/coffee Cen ht Dinner Last d 9.30pm **PRICES:** s £45; d £65✻ **LB MEALS:** Lunch fr £10&alc Dinner £15-£25alc✻ **PARKING:** 40 **CARDS:**

England

HUNGERFORD continued

♦♦♦♦ *Marshgate Cottage Hotel*

Marsh Ln RG17 0QN ☎ 01488 682307 📠 01488 685475
e-mail: reservations@marshgate.co.uk
Dir: *from A338 turn right beside railway bridge into Church St, 0.5m pass used car garage & immediate right into Marsh Ln. At end on right*

This charming little cottage hotel backs onto the Kennet and Avon Canal. Hungerford town is just a short walk along the tow-path and the M4 is only three miles away making this an ideal base from which to explore. Bedrooms are attractively furnished and, together with the public rooms, create a cosy atmosphere here.
FACILITIES: 10 en suite (4 fmly) No smoking in bedrooms No smoking in dining room No smoking in 1 lounge TVB tea/coffee Direct dial from bedrooms No dogs (ex guide dogs) Licensed Cen ht TVL No coaches **PARKING:** 10 **CARDS:**

See advertisement on opposite page

♦♦♦ Beacon House

Bell Ln, Upper Green, Inkpen RG17 9QJ ☎ 01488 668640
e-mail: l.g.cave@classicfm.net
Dir: *A4 Newbury-Hungerford, S turn to Kintbury/Inkpen. At Kintbury, L (Inkpen Rd), 1m to x-rds, straight ahead, bear right to common, 3rd left after Crown & Garter pub*

Guests can be assured of a warm welcome at this peaceful house. Bedrooms are comfortably furnished and look south on to unspoilt fields. Guests can relax in a spacious sitting room complete with a log fire in the winter. Home-cooked evening meals are available and there is ample parking.
FACILITIES: 3 rms No smoking TVB Cen ht TVL No coaches Art Studio Dinner Last d 4pm **PRICES:** s £25; d £48✻ **LB PARKING:** 6

U Queen's Arms Hotel

Lambourn Rd, East Garston RG17 7ET ☎ 01488 648757
At the time of going to press the Diamond classification for this establishment had not been confirmed. Please check the AA website www.theAA.com for up-to-date information.
FACILITIES: 8 en suite 5 annexe rms (4 en suite)

MAIDENHEAD Map 04 SU88

♦♦♦♦ Beehive Manor

Cox Green Ln SL6 3ET ☎ 01628 620980 📠 01628 621840
e-mail: beehivemanor@aol.com
Dir: *M4 junct 8/9,take A404M to 1st exit signed Cox Green/ White Watham follow Cox Green signs and at second rdbt turn into Cox Green Rd, then left at Forresters Pub*

This delightful and quite unique 15th-century house is set in a peaceful location with good motorway access. Bedrooms are individually decorated and feature many thoughtful extras; two rooms have en suite facilities and the third has a private bathroom. Additional features include a large stone fireplace, wooden beams, a cosy lounge and fine period furniture in the breakfast room, where all guests share one table.
FACILITIES: 3 rms (2 en suite) No smoking TVB tea/coffee No dogs (ex guide dogs) Cen ht TVL No children 12yrs No coaches **PRICES:** s £50-£60; d £65-£75✻ **PARKING:** 6 **NOTES:** Closed Xmas/New Year **CARDS:**

♦♦♦♦ A Moor Farm

Ascot Rd, Holyport SL6 2HY ☎ 01628 633761 📠 01628 636167
e-mail: moorfm@aol.com
Dir: *M4 junct 8 or 9 onto A308m signed Maidenhead Central. At rdbt take final exit onto A330 to Holyport. After 0.5m right into Moor Farm*
FACILITIES: 2 en suite No smoking No dogs (ex guide dogs) Cen ht TVL No coaches **PRICES:** s £45-£50; d £50-£60✻ **PARKING:** 5

NEWBURY Map 04 SU46

♦♦♦♦ Rookwood Farm House

Stockcross RG20 8JX ☎ 01488 608676 📠 01488 657961
Dir: *from B4000/A34 junct, follow B4000 into Stockcross. 1st right signed Woodspean, bear left and establishment is 1st on right*

This delightful farmhouse with wonderful rural views, is located just outside the quiet village of Stockcross. The bedrooms are attractively presented with many fine pieces of furniture. Tasty English breakfasts are served in the dining room and parking is an added bonus.

continued

England

FACILITIES: 3 en suite (1 fmly) No smoking TVB tea/coffee Direct dial from bedrooms No dogs Cen ht TVL No coaches Outdoor swimming pool (heated) Croquet lawn **PRICES:** s £45; d £60✻ **CONF:** Board 12 Del £90 ✻ **PARKING:** 3 **CARDS:**

READING

See advert below

SLOUGH

Map 04 SU97

♦♦ *Colnbrook Lodge*

Bath Rd, Colnbrook SL3 0NZ ☎ 01753 685958
🖹 01753 685164

Dir: *airport side of Colnbrook between Punchbowl pub & level crossing*

This Edwardian house is conveniently located for the M4 and within easy reach of Heathrow Airport. No smoking bedrooms, which vary in size, are furnished in a modern style and well equipped. Breakfast is served in the spacious breakfast room and drinks can be obtained from the bar.

FACILITIES: 8 rms (6 en suite) No smoking in 6 bedrooms No smoking in dining room STV TVB tea/coffee No dogs (ex guide dogs) Licensed Cen ht TVL **PARKING:** 26 **NOTES:** Closed 23 Dec-2 Jan **CARDS:**

SULHAMSTEAD

Map 04 SU66

Premier Collection

♦♦♦♦♦ The Old Manor

Whitehouse Green, Sulhamstead RG7 4EA
☎ 01189 832423 🖹 01189 836262
e-mail: rags-r@theoldmanor.fsbusiness.co.uk

Dir: *M4 junct 12, A4 W, left for Theale Station, over railway, over river, right after 0.4km. Continue for 1km and turn left at x-roads & Old Manor entrance on left*

This fine period manor house, set in 10 acres of well kept gardens, is situated a couple of miles away from the M4. Bedrooms are elegantly furnished, one has a four-poster bed and a spa bath. Afternoon tea can be taken in the drawing room, and good food and a complimentary glass of wine are on offer at dinner in the dining room.

FACILITIES: 2 en suite No smoking No dogs Cen ht TVL No children 8yrs No coaches Croquet lawn Bowls Volley ball Dinner Last d previous day **PRICES:** s £50; d £70✻ **PARKING:** 8 **NOTES:** Closed 23 Dec-2 Jan

THEALE

See Sulhamstead

England

WINDSOR Map 04 SU97

♦♦♦ *Netherton Hotel*

96 St Leonards Rd SL4 3DA ☎ 01753 855508 🖹 01753 621267
e-mail: netherton@btconnect.com
This attractive Edwardian guest house is located in a quiet residential area, a few minutes' walk from the town centre. The bedrooms feature co-ordinated fabrics and a good range of facilities. Guests have the use of a small lounge to relax in. Ample off-street parking is provided to the rear of the hotel.
FACILITIES: 11 en suite (5 fmly) No smoking in dining room No smoking in lounges TVB tea/coffee Direct dial from bedrooms No dogs Cen ht TVL
PARKING: 9 **CARDS:**

♦♦♦ Oscar Hotel

65 Vansittart Rd SL4 5DB ☎ 01753 830613 🖹 01753 833744
e-mail: info@oscarhotel.com
Dir: *M4 junct 6 follow signs for Windsor 1st slip road on L which goes to rdbt, 1st L from rdbt and 1st R into Vansittart Road*

Ideally located for road systems and a few minutes' walk from the historic centre, this popular owner-managed commercial hotel provides modern, practically equipped bedrooms. Breakfast is taken in the cosy dining room, which also contains a bar.
FACILITIES: 13 en suite (4 fmly) TVB tea/coffee Direct dial from bedrooms No dogs Licensed Cen ht TVL No coaches **PRICES:** s £40-£60*
PARKING: 7 **CARDS:**

♦♦ Clarence Hotel

9 Clarence Rd SL4 5AE ☎ 01753 864436 🖹 01753 857060
Dir: *M4 J6 follow dual carriageway to Windsor, turn L at 1st rdbt into Clarence Rd*

This Grade II listed Victorian townhouse is situated in the heart of Windsor. Space in some rooms is limited, but all are well maintained and offer excellent value for money. Added facilities include a lounge with well stocked bar and steam room. Breakfast is served in the dining room overlooking attractive gardens.
FACILITIES: 20 en suite (6 fmly) No smoking in dining room TVB tea/coffee Licensed Cen ht TVL Sauna Steam room **PRICES:** s £40-£55; d £50-£67* **PARKING:** 4 **CARDS:**

BRISTOL

BRISTOL Map 03 ST57

♦♦♦♦ Downlands House

33 Henleaze Gardens, Henleaze BS9 4HH ☎ 0117 962 1639
🖹 0117 962 1639
e-mail: mjdownlands@compuserve.com
Dir: *M5 J17 (Westbury on Trym/City Centre), past private girls' schools, Henleaze Gdns on left*

An elegant Victorian property, conveniently located for the Downs, Clifton village and Bristol Zoo. It offers comfortable accommodation and a warm and friendly atmosphere. Bedrooms are well decorated, with extras such as reading material and quality toiletries. Breakfast can be served in the delightful conservatory.
FACILITIES: 10 rms (7 en suite) (1 fmly) No smoking TVB tea/coffee Cen ht TVL No coaches **PRICES:** s £34-£47; d £48-£60* **LB CARDS:**

♦♦♦♦ Downs Edge

Saville Rd, Stoke Bishop BS9 1JA
☎ 0117 968 3264 & 07885 866463 🖹 0117 968 3264
e-mail: welcome@downsedge.com
Dir: *M5 take J17 onto A4018. At 4th rdbt right into Parrys Lane B4054. 1st left Saville Rd, 3rd right Hollybush Ln, after 2nd speed ramp, left into drive*

Located on the edge of Bristol's famous Durdham Downs, this establishment benefits from a quiet yet convenient setting. The well-equipped bedrooms are all nicely decorated and furnished. At breakfast, an interesting variety of hot and cold dishes is on offer, and served family-style round one large table. Guests are also welcome to use the comfortable lounge.
FACILITIES: 4 en suite No smoking in bedrooms No smoking in dining room TVB tea/coffee No dogs (ex guide dogs) Cen ht No children 7 No coaches **PRICES:** s £45-£50; d £62-£68* **PARKING:** 8 **NOTES:** Closed Xmas/New Year **CARDS:**

England

♦♦♦♦ Greenlands
BS39 4ES ☎ 01275 333487 Fax 01275 331211
e-mail: greenlands.bandb@virgin.net
(For full entry see Stanton Drew (Somerset))

♦♦♦♦ Valley Farm *(ST595631)*
Sandy Ln BS39 4EL ☎ 01275 332723 & 07799 768161
Fax 01275 332723 Doreen & John Keel
e-mail: highmead.gardens@virgin.net
(For full entry see Stanton Drew)

♦♦♦♦ Westbury Park Hotel
37 Westbury Rd, Westbury-on-Trym BS9 3AU ☎ 0117 962 0465
Fax 0117 962 8607
e-mail: reception@westburypark-hotel.co.uk
Dir: *M5 junct 17, follow A4018 for 4.5m, hotel is on the left, opposite gates of Badmington School*

Situated by the famous Durdham Downs, this attractive Victorian property offers pleasantly decorated accommodation with all modern comforts. Drinks are served from a small bar in the lounge and at breakfast there is a choice of cooked dishes, served in a stylishly furnished dining room.
FACILITIES: 8 en suite (2 fmly) No smoking in bedrooms No smoking in dining room TVB tea/coffee Direct dial from bedrooms Licensed Cen ht No coaches **PRICES:** s £40-£50; d £55-£60✳ **PARKING:** 4 **CARDS:**

♦♦♦ Mayfair Lodge
5 Henleaze Rd, Westbury on Trym BS9 4EX ☎ 0117 962 2008
Fax 0117 962 2008
e-mail: avril@akitching.fsnet.co.uk
Dir: *exit M5 J17 (A4018) before 4th rdbt turn into Henleaze Rd. Hotel 50 yds on left*
This charming Victorian house is located in a residential area close to the Durdham Downs and Bristol Zoo. Mayfair Lodge offers comfortable, well-equipped bedrooms and a friendly, relaxed atmosphere. Breakfast is served at separate tables in the bright dining room. Off-street parking is also available.
FACILITIES: 9 rms (3 en suite) (1 fmly) No smoking in dining room No smoking in lounges TVB tea/coffee No dogs Cen ht No children 5yrs No coaches **PRICES:** s £28-£45; d £48-£52✳ **PARKING:** 6 **NOTES:** Closed Xmas & New Year **CARDS:**

♦♦♦ *Oakfield Hotel*
52-54 Oakfield Rd, Clifton BS8 2BG ☎ 0117 973 5556
Fax 0117 974 4141
Dir: *1.25m from city centre, nr BBC Whiteladies Rd, 1st L after passing BBC, 100 yds up Oakfield Rd on L*
Traditional standards of comfort and hospitality have been provided by the Hurley family for over 50 years. Rooms are well equipped; and dinner is available by arrangement and served in the spacious dining room. Guests may also choose a drink from the short selection of beers and wine. *continued*

FACILITIES: 27 rms (4 fmly) No smoking in dining room No smoking in 1 lounge TVB tea/coffee Licensed Cen ht TVL Dinner Last d 4pm
PARKING: 9 **NOTES:** Closed 24 Dec-1 Jan

♦♦♦ Rowan Lodge
41 Gloucester Rd North, Filton Park BS7 0SN ☎ 0117 931 2170
Fax 975 3601
Dir: *From M5 J16 to A38 follow Filton for approx 3.25m. Rowan Lodge on junct of A38 and Bronksea Rd*
This small private hotel, conveniently located for the nearby industrial and business areas and with easy access to the M4 and M5, offers a relaxed and friendly atmosphere. Bedrooms are all well equipped, some being suitable for families. A comfortable lounge/breakfast room is provided.
FACILITIES: 6 rms (3 en suite) (2 fmly) No smoking in dining room No smoking in lounges TVB tea/coffee Cen ht No coaches **PRICES:** s £27-£35✳ **LB PARKING:** 8 **NOTES:** Closed Xmas & New Year
CARDS:

♦♦♦ Shirehampton Lodge Hotel
62-64 High St, Shirehampton BS11 0DJ ☎ 0117 907 3480
Fax 0117 907 3481
Dir: *M5 J18, take B4054 to Shirehampton for 1m. Hotel on left above Alldays shop, entrance up ramp*
Situated above shops, this imaginatively converted warehouse offers easy access to the motorway network and the city centre. Bedrooms are equipped with many modern comforts and there is a well furnished lounge-dining room where guests are welcome to use the recently opened bar facilities.
FACILITIES: 12 en suite (3 fmly) STV TVB tea/coffee Licensed Cen ht TVL **PRICES:** s £30; d £50✳ **PARKING:** 10 **CARDS:**

England

BRISTOL continued

♦♦♦ Washington Hotel

11-15 St Pauls Rd, Clifton BS8 1LX ☎ 0117 973 3980
0117 9734740
e-mail: washington@cliftonhotels.com
Dir: *follow A4018 into city, turn right at lights opposite BBC buildings, hotel is 200yds on left*

A large guest house ideally located within walking distance of both the city centre and Clifton Village. This terraced property offers secure parking and a small rear patio garden. There is a smart new reception area and breakfast room, and many of the bedrooms have also been recently refurbished.

FACILITIES: 46 rms (40 en suite) (4 fmly) No smoking in 13 bedrooms No smoking in dining room STV TVB tea/coffee Direct dial from bedrooms Licensed Cen ht Hon. membership of nearby fitness centre Last d 11pm **PRICES:** s £35-£53; d £52-£67* **PARKING:** 20 **NOTES:** Closed 23 Dec-3 Jan **CARDS:**

♦♦♦ Arches Hotel

132 Cotham Brow, Cotham BS6 6AE ☎ 0117 924 7398
0117 924 7398
e-mail: ml@arches-hotel.co.uk
Dir: *A38 N out of city centre. At mini rdbt left into Cotham Brow and hotel 100mtrs on left*

FACILITIES: 9 rms (4 en suite) (3 fmly) (2 GF) No smoking TVB tea/coffee Cen ht No children 6yrs No coaches **PRICES:** s £25.50-£38.50; d £44.50-£53.50* **NOTES:** Closed Xmas & New year **CARDS:**

♦♦♦ Basca House

19 Broadway Rd, Bishopston BS7 8ES ☎ 0117 942 2182
Dir: *from A38 (Gloucester Road) turn into Berkeley Road then take 1st left into Broadway Road*

FACILITIES: 4 rms No smoking TVB tea/coffee No dogs Cen ht TVL No coaches **PRICES:** s £25-£35; d £45-£48* **NOTES:** Closed 23 Dec-3 Jan

EASTON-IN-GORDANO — Map 03 ST57

The Tynings B & B

Martcombe Rd BS20 0QE ☎ 01275 372608

At the time of going to press the Diamond classification for this establishment had not been confirmed. Please check the AA website www.theAA.com for up-to-date information.

FACILITIES: 6 rms (2 en suite)

BUCKINGHAMSHIRE

AYLESBURY — Map 04 SP81

♦♦♦ The Hamlet

3 Home Close, Weston Turville HP22 5SP ☎ 01296 612660
01296 612660
e-mail: gburg27705@aol.com
Dir: *Aylesbury to Wendover A413, turn left onto B4544 to Weston Turville. In village take 2nd right into Bates Lane & 1st left into Home Close*

This privately owned, semi-detached bungalow is located in the quite village of Weston Turville. Bedrooms are tastefully furnished and offer a thoughtful range of facilities. Guests have the use of the large, comfortable lounge and meals are taken at a family table in the conservatory dining room.

FACILITIES: 3 rms (1 en suite) No smoking in bedrooms No smoking in area of dining room No smoking in lounges TVB tea/coffee No dogs Cen ht TVL No children 6 mths No coaches **PRICES:** s £25; d £50* **LB** **PARKING:** 6 **CARDS:**

continued

The Hamlet

BEACONSFIELD — Map 04 SP99

Premier Collection

♦♦♦♦♦ George Hotel

Wycombe End, Old Town HP9 1LX ☎ 01494 673086
01494 674034
e-mail: info@thegeorgehotel.com
Dir: *Exit M40 J2, 0.5m into Beaconsfield. Hotel over main rdbt on right*

Located a few minutes drive from the M40 in the historic part of the town, this Grade II listed Tudor inn retains many original features, enhanced by the quality furnishing and decor schemes throughout. Bedrooms are spacious, homely, very well equipped, and three self-catering cottage suites are also available.

FACILITIES: 10 en suite (5 fmly) STV TVB tea/coffee Direct dial from bedrooms Licensed Cen ht No coaches **PRICES:** s fr £115.15; d fr £148.05* **CARDS:**

BLEDLOW — Map 04 SP70

♦♦♦♦ Cross Lanes

Cross Lanes Cottage HP27 9PF ☎ 01844 345339
01844 274165
e-mail: ronaldcoul@aol.com
Dir: *Exit M40 J6 (B4009). Continue & after passing Beldlow village sign, Cross Lanes 1st property on right, behind gates*

A warm welcome is assured at this beautifully maintained house located on pretty gardens and convenient for major road links. Parts of the property date from the 16th century and original features have been retained. Bedrooms are equipped with lots of thoughtful extras and a comfortable beamed lounge is also available.

FACILITIES: 3 en suite (1 GF) No smoking TVB tea/coffee No dogs Cen ht TVL No children 14yrs No coaches **PRICES:** s £45-£50; d £55-£60* **PARKING:** 6 **CARDS:**

England

BRILL — Map 04 SP61

♦♦♦ Poletrees Farm *(SP660160)*
Ludgershall Rd HP18 9TZ ☎ 01844 238276 🖷 01844 238276 Mrs A Cooper
e-mail: poletrees.farm@virgin.net
Dir: *from M40 take A41 towards Aylesbury 5m, from Bicester turn right signed Ludgershall/Brill after rail bridge 0.5m on left entrance to farm*

Located between the villages of Brill and Ludgershall, this 15th century farmhouse retains many original features including a wealth of exposed beams. Bedrooms are filled with homely extras and a guest lounge with welcoming wood burning stove is available in addition to a cosy dining room, the setting for wholesome breakfasts.

FACILITIES: 2 rms 1 annexe en suite No smoking TV1B tea/coffee No dogs Cen ht TVL 100 acres beef sheep Dinner Last d 24hrs prior **PRICES:** s £30-£60; d £50-£60✱ **PARKING:** 6 **NOTES:** Closed 23-31 Dec

DINTON — Map 04 SP71

♦♦♦ Wallace *(SP770110)*
HP17 8UZ ☎ 01296 748660 🖷 01296 748851 Mrs J M W Cook
e-mail: jackiecook@wallacefarm.freeserve.co.uk
Dir: *from A418 take turning marked Dinton/Ford, then 1st left signed Upton, farm on right*

Located between Aylesbury and Thame, this farm supports the Rare Breeds Survival Trust and many unusual species of animal and fowl are found in abundance. The 16th-century house retains many original features and has a great deal of charm. Bedrooms are equipped with thoughtful extras and a comfortable guest sitting room is also available.

FACILITIES: 3 en suite (1 fmly) No smoking in bedrooms No smoking in dining room tea/coffee No dogs (ex guide dogs) Cen ht TVL Fishing 24 acres beef cattle sheep **PRICES:** s fr £32; d £48 **PARKING:** 6
CARDS:

GAYHURST — Map 04 SP84

♦♦♦ Mill *(SP852454)*
MK16 8LT ☎ 01908 611489 🖷 01908 611489 Mrs K Adams
e-mail: adamsmillfarm@aol.com
Dir: *take B526 from Newport Pagnell, after 2.5m turn left into Haversham Rd, Mill Farm is 1m on left*

Located in peaceful surroundings north of Newport Pagnell, this well proportioned period house has been sympathetically renovated to provide high standards of comfort and facilities. The homely bedrooms are furnished with quality fabrics and an open plan living area includes an elegant dining section in addition to sumptuous lounge seating, enhanced by fine antiques and art.

FACILITIES: 3 rms (2 en suite) 1 annexe en suite (1 fmly) No smoking in 2 bedrooms No smoking in dining room No smoking in 1 lounge TVB tea/coffee Cen ht TVL Tennis (hard) Fishing Riding Croquet lawn Rough shooting Trout & Coarse fishing 550 acres mixed **PRICES:** s £20-£25; d £40-£50✱ **PARKING:** 13

HIGH WYCOMBE — Map 04 SU89

♦♦♦ Clifton Lodge Hotel
210 West Wycombe Rd HP12 3AR ☎ 01494 440095 & 529062 🖷 01494 536322
e-mail: sales@cliftonlodge.com
Dir: *West Wycombe road (A40 towards Aylesbury from town centre). Hotel on right, just beyond BP garage & opposite phone box*

Located to the west of the town centre, convenient for the M40, this well maintained owner-managed hotel provides a good range of business related facilities and also benefits from a private car park.

continued

FACILITIES: 32 rms (20 en suite) (1 fmly) (7 GF) No smoking in dining room TVB tea/coffee Direct dial from bedrooms No dogs Licensed Cen ht TVL Jacuzzi Dinner Last d 8.45pm **PRICES:** s £40-£80; d £65-£85✱ **LB CONF:** Thtr 30 Class 20 Board 15 **PARKING:** 28 **CARDS:**

MARLOW — Map 04 SU88

♦♦♦♦ Holly Tree House
Burford Close, Marlow Bottom SL7 3NE ☎ 01628 891110 🖷 01628 481278
Dir: *from M40 junct 4 take exit for Marlow Bottom, turn right into Marlow Bottom & follow road past shops. 1st left into Burford Close*

An impressive range of in-room facilities, combined with a variety of personal treasures, contributes to the homely atmosphere that is part of the charm of this family run guest house. Set in an acre of mature woodland, yet with easy access to the motorways. There is a heated outdoor swimming pool.

FACILITIES: 9 en suite No smoking STV TVB tea/coffee Direct dial from bedrooms No dogs (ex guide dogs) Cen ht TVL No coaches Outdoor swimming pool (heated) **PRICES:** s £69.50; d £84.50✱ **PARKING:** 13
CARDS:

♦♦♦♦ The Country House
Bisham Rd SL7 1RP ☎ 01628 890606 🖷 01628 890983
e-mail: countryhousemarlow@btinternet.com
Dir: *M4 junct 8/9, A404 to 1st rdbt. Left onto A308, through Bisham village. 1m from Bisham rdbt on right*

FACILITIES: 11 en suite (2 fmly) No smoking in 4 bedrooms No smoking in dining room No smoking in 1 lounge TVB tea/coffee Direct dial from bedrooms Cen ht TVL **PRICES:** s £80; d £109✱ **LB PARKING:** 12
CARDS:

MILTON KEYNES — Map 04 SP83

See also Gayhurst

♦♦♦♦ Apple Tree House
16 Verley Close, Woughton-On-The-Green MK6 3ER
☎ 01908 669681 🖷 01908 669681
e-mail: apples@mrobinson5.fsnet.co.uk
Dir: *From M1 junct 14 follow signs for Milton Keynes centre. At 2nd rdbt L, at next rdbt R into Chaffron Way. Straight over next rdbt, L at sign for Woughton-on-the-Green. 2nd R, then 3rd R, then 1st R, 2nd house on L.*

This impressive detached house is peacefully located in a quiet residential suburb close to the central amenities. The comfortable and homely bedrooms are filled with many thoughtful extras. Breakfast is taken at one family table in the elegant dining room and guests can enjoy full use of the comfortable lounge and immaculate mature gardens.

FACILITIES: 4 rms (2 en suite) No smoking STV TVB tea/coffee No dogs Cen ht No coaches Dinner Last d Noon **PRICES:** s fr £35; d fr £70✱ **LB PARKING:** 4

NEWPORT PAGNELL Map 04 SP84

Premier Collection

♦♦♦♦♦ The Limes

North Square MK16 8EP ☎ 01908 617041 Fax 01908 217292
e-mail: royandruth@8thelimes.freeserve.co.uk
Dir: *M1 junct 14, Newport Pagnell pass Aston Martin factory & at T-junct right into High St, 1st left onto North Sq 3rd house on right*

Set in pretty, immaculate gardens complete with river frontage and fine rural views, this well-proportioned early Victorian house (once the home of the Taylor's Mustard family) retains many original features, highlighted by the décor and period furniture in the public areas. The spacious bedrooms have a wealth of thoughtful extras, and wholesome breakfasts and imaginative dinners are taken in an elegant dining room with its large mahogany table and Queen Anne chairs which once graced London's American Embassy.
FACILITIES: 4 en suite (1 fmly) No smoking STV TVB tea/coffee No dogs (ex guide dogs) Cen ht No children 8yrs No coaches Fishing Croquet lawn Dinner Last d 10am **PRICES:** s £49.50; d £70 **CONF:** Board 8 Del from £95 ✳ **PARKING:** 7 **CARDS:**

OLNEY Map 04 SP85

♦♦♦ Queen Hotel

40 Dartmouth Rd MK46 4BH ☎ 01234 711924 Fax 01234 711924
Dir: *on A509, in Olney town centre*
Located in the heart of the historic town, this 18th-century hotel has been sympathetically renovated to provide thoughtfully equipped bedrooms with modern efficient bathrooms. Comprehensive breakfasts are taken in an elegant dining room and a small comfortable lounge with honesty bar is also available.
FACILITIES: 11 rms (9 en suite) (1 fmly) No smoking TV9B tea/coffee No dogs Licensed Cen ht **PRICES:** s fr £47.50; d fr £60✳ **LB PARKING:** 7 **CARDS:**

CAMBRIDGESHIRE

ALCONBURY Map 04 TL17

♦♦♦ Apple Tree House

4 Vinegar Hill, Alconbury Weston PE28 4JA ☎ 01480 890285
e-mail: book@appletree-house.co.uk
Dir: *A14 N from Huntingdon, exit at Alconbury. Follow B1043 signposted Alconbury Hill to flyover, turn right and right again over flyover, house on left*
Enthusiastic owners offer a warm welcome to this pleasant guest house, which sits in a quiet village with access to the A1 and A14. The attractive bedrooms come in a variety of sizes; some are particularly spacious. On the ground floor guests have the use of a lounge and a separate dining room.
FACILITIES: 5 rms (2 en suite) (1 fmly) No smoking TVB tea/coffee No dogs Cen ht No coaches **PRICES:** s £23-£30; d £50-£55✳ **PARKING:** 4 **NOTES:** Closed 25-26 Dec rs Xmas **CARDS:**

CAMBRIDGE Map 05 TL45

Premier Collection

♦♦♦♦♦ Holmefields Barn

16 High St, Bluntisham PE28 3LD ☎ 01487 841435
e-mail: roy.carlyle@btinternet.com
(For full entry see Huntingdon)

♦♦♦♦ *Acorn*

154 Chesterton Rd CB4 1DA ☎ 01223 353888 Fax 01223 350527
e-mail: info@acornguesthouse.co.uk
Dir: *From M1 J13. Right for city centre until mini rdbt. Turn left, straight for about 1m, house on right*
Ideally located close to the ring road system and city centre, this attractive yellow brick house has been carefully extended and renovated by Andrew and Helen Constantinides to provide homely and comfortable accommodation. Tasty English breakfasts are taken in the cosy dining room, and services are friendly and attentive.
FACILITIES: 10 en suite (1 fmly) No smoking TVB tea/coffee Direct dial from bedrooms No dogs (ex guide dogs) Cen ht TVL **PARKING:** 7 **CARDS:**
See advertisement on opposite page

♦♦♦♦ Aylesbray Lodge

5 Mowbray Rd CB1 7SR ☎ 01223 240089 Fax 01223 528678
e-mail: stay@aylesbray.com
Dir: *M11 junct 11 towards Cambridge, turn right into Long Rd, through lights & left at rdbt. Aylesbray Lodge 50yds on right*

A genuinely warm welcome is assured from Anna Pippas at this family run guest house. Bedrooms are tastefully furnished and very well equipped, each with a modern en suite shower room, and two rooms have attractive four-poster beds. Tasty English breakfasts are served in the elegant dining room and a guest lounge is also available.
FACILITIES: 6 en suite (1 fmly) No smoking STV TVB tea/coffee Direct dial from bedrooms No dogs Cen ht TVL **PRICES:** s £35-£45; d £45-£75✳ **PARKING:** 6 **CARDS:**

♦♦♦♦ *De Freville House*

166 Chesterton Rd CB4 1DA ☎ 01223 354993
Dir: *on ring road at junct of Chesterton Rd and Elizabeth Way*
Convenient for the town centre, this large Victorian house has been tastefully restored and is furnished throughout with some lovely pieces. There is an attractive, comfortable lounge and the lower

continued

ground floor dining room is appealing and cheerful for breakfast. Bedrooms are equipped with many thoughtful extras.
FACILITIES: 8 rms (6 en suite) No smoking TVB tea/coffee No dogs Cen ht TVL No children 10yrs No coaches **PARKING:** 2

♦♦♦♦ Hamden

89 High St, Cherry Hinton CB1 9LU ☎ 01223 413263
📠 01223 245960
Dir: *M11 junct 11 for Cambridge Road-A1309, at 2nd traffic lights right into Long Road - A1134 to Cherry Hinton, High St. From A14 at junct A1303 to Cambridge. Left at next rdbt to Cherry Hinton, pass next rdbt, traffic lights & railway crossing, establishment on right*
Guests can expect a warm welcome from Mr and Mrs Casciano at this small family run guest house. Bedrooms are generally spacious, pleasantly decorated and equipped with many thoughtful extras. Public areas are limited to a bright and airy open plan kitchen/breakfast room.
FACILITIES: 5 en suite (1 fmly) (2 GF) No smoking TVB tea/coffee Direct dial from bedrooms No dogs Cen ht No children 10yrs No coaches **PRICES:** s £35-£50; d £50-£60✱ **LB PARKING:** 6 **CARDS:**

♦♦♦♦ Helen Hotel

167 Hills Rd CB2 2RJ ☎ 01223 246465 📠 01223 214406
Dir: *1m E, follow signs to A604 Colchester*
This impressive detached house has been totally renovated during recent years and now offers very well equipped and comfortable bedrooms; the most recently refurbished bedrooms and bathrooms are particularly smart. Tasty English breakfasts are taken in the attractive dining room, which overlooks the pretty rear garden.
FACILITIES: 22 en suite (2 fmly) No smoking in bedrooms No smoking in dining room No smoking in 1 lounge STV TVB tea/coffee Direct dial from bedrooms No dogs (ex guide dogs) Licensed Cen ht TVL Dinner Last d 7.45pm **PRICES:** s £48-£58; d £69-£75✱ **PARKING:** 12 **NOTES:** Closed X-mas **CARDS:**

♦♦♦♦ Lensfield Hotel

53 Lensfield Rd CB2 1EN ☎ 01223 355017 📠 01223 312022
e-mail: reservations@lensfieldhotel.co.uk
Dir: *M11 J11, 12, or 13. Follow signs to city centre and join the city ring road. Approach hotel via Silver St or Trumpington St (turning left into Lensfield Rd*
Located close to colleges and the city centre, this Victorian house has been sympathetically extended and renovated to provide comfortable quality accommodation. Professional and friendly services are provided by the Paschalis family, and their Greek origins are reflected in the authentic specialities featured in the elegant restaurant.
FACILITIES: 30 rms (28 en suite) (4 fmly) No smoking in 27 bedrooms No smoking in area of dining room No smoking in lounges STV TVB tea/coffee Direct dial from bedrooms No dogs Licensed Cen ht TVL Dinner Last d 8pm **PRICES:** s £55-£80; d £90-£95✱ **LB PARKING:** 7 **NOTES:** Closed 2wks Xmas **CARDS:**

♦♦♦ Alpha Milton

61-63 Milton Rd CB4 1XA ☎ 01223 311625 📠 01223 565100
A warm welcome is assured at this constantly improving establishment, located on a mainly residential avenue within easy walking distance of city centre. Bedrooms are homely and other areas include an attractive open plan dining room with lounge area, overlooking the pretty garden.
FACILITIES: 6 en suite (2 fmly) No smoking in 2 bedrooms No smoking in dining room No smoking in lounges TVB tea/coffee No dogs Cen ht TVL **PRICES:** s £30-£45; d £50-£90✱ **LB PARKING:** 6 **CARDS:**

England

CAMBRIDGE continued

♦♦♦ *Arbury Lodge*

82 Arbury Rd CB4 2JE ☎ 01223 364319 & 01233 566988
🖷 01223 566988
e-mail: arburylodge@ntlworld.com
Dir: *turn off A14 onto A1309 (Milton Road) at 4th set of main traffic lights, turn right into Arbury Road*

Ideally located for the Science Park and A14, this house offers attractively decorated and very well-equipped bedrooms, most with quality modern en suite facilities. The resident proprietor provides friendly and attentive services.

FACILITIES: 5 rms (4 en suite) (1 fmly) No smoking TVB tea/coffee No dogs (ex guide dogs) Cen ht **PARKING:** 8 **NOTES:** Closed 24-26 Dec
CARDS:

♦♦♦ Assisi

193 Cherry Hinton Rd CB1 4AU ☎ 01223 211466 & 246648
🖷 01223 412900
Dir: *from W, continue past Addenbrook Hospital, take 1st right - Cherry Hinton Rd. From E continue up Hill Rd past rail station on left - Cherry Hinton Rd next left.*

This Victorian house is located within easy walking distance of the city centre. The well equipped modern bedrooms all have en suite or private facilities. There is a comfortable lounge in addition to an attractive breakfast room.

FACILITIES: 17 en suite (1 fmly) (4 GF) No smoking in 7 bedrooms No smoking in dining room No smoking in lounges TVB tea/coffee Direct dial from bedrooms No dogs Cen ht TVL **PRICES:** s £35; d £50✱
PARKING: 15 **NOTES:** Closed 18 Dec-6 Jan **CARDS:**

See advertisement on opposite page

♦♦♦ Benson House

24 Huntingdon Rd CB3 0HH ☎ 01223 311594 🖷 01223 311594
Dir: *on A604 near New Hall & Fitzwilliam College*

Popular guest house ideally placed for the city centre and visitors to New Hall and Fitzwilliam colleges. Although bedrooms vary in size and style they are all pleasantly decorated and well equipped.

FACILITIES: 5 en suite (1 GF) No smoking TVB tea/coffee No dogs Cen ht No children 12yrs No coaches **PRICES:** d £45-£60✱ **PARKING:** 5
CARDS:

♦♦♦ *Brooklands*

95 Cherry Hinton Rd CB1 7BS ☎ 01223 242035
🖷 01223 242035
e-mail: michelle@brooklandsguesthouse.co.uk

Located within a small shopping centre close to the ring road system, this Edwardian terraced house offers well equipped homely bedrooms. Home-cooked breakfasts are taken in the cosy dining room and a sauna is now provided.

FACILITIES: 5 en suite (1 fmly) No smoking STV TVB tea/coffee Direct dial from bedrooms Cen ht No coaches Snooker Sauna **PARKING:** 5
CARDS:

♦♦♦ Cristina's

47 St Andrews Rd CB4 1DH ☎ 01223 365855 & 327700
🖷 01223 365855
e-mail: cristinas.guesthouse@ntlworld.com

Located in a quiet residential road off the internal ring road system, this guest house house offers very well maintained accommodation. Comprehensive breakfasts are taken in the cosy dining room, and there is a comfortable lounge.

FACILITIES: 9 rms (7 en suite) (1 fmly) No smoking TVB tea/coffee No dogs Cen ht TVL **PRICES:** s £38-£49; d £47-£57✱ **LB**
PARKING: 8 **NOTES:** Closed 25-27 Dec

♦♦♦ Dykelands

157 Mowbray Rd CB1 7SP ☎ 01223 244300 🖷 01223 566746
e-mail: dykelands@fsbdial.co.uk
Dir: *A10/M11 junct 11, follow A1309, at 7th traffic lights turn right, continue to 1st rdbt, 1st exit, Mowbray Rd, last house on right*

This large detached house is located in a mainly residential area close to Addenbrooke's Hospital. Dykelands Guest House offers well-equipped and comfortable accommodation. Breakfasts are taken in the cosy dining room and there is also a small lounge available for guest use.

FACILITIES: 9 rms (7 en suite) (3 fmly) (2 GF) No smoking TVB tea/coffee Cen ht No coaches **PRICES:** s £30-£50; d £40-£50✱ **PARKING:** 7
CARDS:

♦♦♦ Fairways

141-143 Cherry Hinton Rd CB1 7BX ☎ 01223 246063
🖷 01223 212093
e-mail: mike.slatter@btinternet.com
Dir: *from city centre towards Addenbrooke's Hospital turn off A1307 (after bridge) then left into Cherry Hinton Rd*

Ideally located for the city and ring road system, this large Victorian house is being constantly improved and provides well-equipped bedrooms. Many of the bedrooms have attractive hand-crafted pine furniture and modern en suite shower rooms. Breakfast is taken in the ground floor dining room.

FACILITIES: 15 rms (8 en suite) (3 fmly) No smoking in dining room No smoking in lounges TVB tea/coffee No dogs (ex guide dogs) Cen ht
PRICES: s £25-£30; d £42-£48✱ **PARKING:** 20 **NOTES:** Closed 22 Dec-2 Jan **CARDS:**

See advertisement on opposite page

♦♦♦ Hamilton Hotel

156 Chesterton Rd CB4 1DA ☎ 01223 365664 🖷 01223 314866
e-mail: hamiltonhotel@talk21.com
Dir: *1m NE of city centre, off ring road A1134*

Close to the city centre, this hotel offers comfortable and well-equipped accommodation; all rooms have a range of extra facilities. The relaxing public areas include a restaurant with a small dispensing bar, where a selection of evening meals and snacks are served; service is both courteous and efficient. *continued*

Hamilton Hotel

FACILITIES: 25 rms (19 en suite) (4 fmly) No smoking in dining room TVB tea/coffee Direct dial from bedrooms No dogs (ex guide dogs) Licensed Cen ht No coaches Dinner Last d 8pm **PRICES:** s £25-£50; d £50-£70✱ **PARKING:** 20 **NOTES:** Closed 25 & 26 Dec **CARDS:**

♦♦♦ Southampton

7 Elizabeth Way CB4 1DE ☎ 01223 357780 📠 01223 314297
e-mail: southamptonhouse@telco4u.net

A friendly service is provided by the proprietors of this guest house, which is located on the inner ring road system, just a few minutes walk from the Grafton Centre. This period terraced house offers comfortable and well equipped bedrooms, which all have en suite facilities.

FACILITIES: 5 en suite (3 fmly) No smoking TVB tea/coffee Direct dial from bedrooms No dogs Cen ht **PRICES:** s £30-£45; d £45-£55✱ **PARKING:** 8

CHATTERIS — Map 05 TL38

♦♦♦ North Bank House

84 High St PE16 6NN ☎ 01354 695782 📠 01354 695782
Dir: *on A142 from Ely, house on left when reaching High St*

Situated at the quieter end of the main street, this Regency town house retains many original features, which are enhanced by the furniture and decor styles within. Bedrooms are well equipped and homely and friendly services are provided by the resident hosts Mr & Mrs Horsman. Private car park and garden for guests' use.

FACILITIES: 3 rms (2 en suite) No smoking TVB tea/coffee Cen ht No coaches **PRICES:** s £25; d £30-£35✱ LB BB **PARKING:** 4 **NOTES:** Closed 24 Dec-2 Jan

A indicates an Associate entry, which has been inspected and rated by the ETC or the RAC in England

England

CHIPPENHAM Map 05 TL66

Premier Collection

♦♦♦♦♦ The Old Bakery

22 High St CB7 5PP ☎ 01638 721185 01638 721185
e-mail: joycemgrimes@aol.com
Dir: *from A14 eastbound, join A11 towards Thetford/Norwich. Take 1st left signed Chippenham. After 1m turn left at T-junction and after 2 sharp bends pass church on right. Old Bakery is large cream house on left.*

Set in its own beautiful gardens, this delightful Grade II listed Tudor house has been carefully restored whilst retaining much of its original character. Bedrooms are well appointed and benefit from a host of thoughtful extras. Spacious, comfortable public rooms include an inviting lounge, conservatory and snooker room. Carefully prepared meals are served in the heavily beamed dining room around an enormous oak table.

FACILITIES: 3 en suite No smoking in bedrooms No smoking in dining room No smoking in lounges TVB tea/coffee No dogs (ex guide dogs) Licensed Cen ht TVL No children No coaches Pool Table Half size snooker table Dinner Last d by prior arrangement **PRICES:** s £35; d £65-£85 **PARKING:** 5 **NOTES:** Closed Xmas **CARDS:**

ELY Map 05 TL58

Premier Collection

♦♦♦♦♦ Rosendale Lodge

223 Main St, Witchford CB6 2HT ☎ 01353 667700
01353 667799
e-mail: valpickford@rosendalelodge.co.uk
Dir: *at rdbt on A10, turn onto A142 towards March, after 0.25m left turn into Witchford village, Lodge 1.25m on left just beyond restaurant*

Expect a warm welcome from the caring hosts at this superb detached property. The spacious bedrooms are tastefully furnished with period pieces and have many thoughtful touches; the ground floor room is suitably equipped for less mobile guests. Breakfast and dinner are served in the galleried dining room and guests also have the use of a comfortable lounge area. Rosendale Lodge was Highly Commended in the AA Accessible Hotel of the Year Awards 2002-2003.

FACILITIES: 4 en suite (1 fmly) (1 GF) No smoking TVB tea/coffee Cen ht No coaches Croquet lawn boule Dinner Last d 48 hrs notice **PRICES:** s £39-£45; d £50-£65✱ **LB PARKING:** 8 **CARDS:**

Premier Collection

♦♦♦♦♦ Springfields

Ely Rd, Little Thetford CB6 3HJ ☎ 01353 663637
01353 663130
e-mail: springfields@talk21.com
Dir: *on A10, 10m N of Cambridge*

Tea and homemade cake are offered on arrival at this attractive ranch-style bungalow, which is situated amidst landscaped grounds just a short drive from Ely. The individually decorated bedrooms are tastefully furnished and equipped with many thoughtful touches. Breakfast is served at a large communal table in the elegant dining room.

FACILITIES: 3 rms (3 GF) No smoking TVB tea/coffee No dogs Cen ht No children 12yrs No coaches **PRICES:** s £40; d £50✱
PARKING: 6 **NOTES:** Closed Dec

♦♦♦♦ Hill House *(TL589817)*

9 Main St, Coveney CB6 2DJ ☎ 01353 778369 01353 778369
Mrs H Nix
e-mail: Hill_house@madasafish.com
Dir: *off A142 3m W of Ely*

A Victorian farmhouse, in the unspoilt village of Coveney, just west of Ely offering tasteful bedrooms with quality soft furnishings. Those in the main house have their own entrance and great views of the surrounding countryside. There are new deluxe bedrooms and a lounge in the adjacent barn conversion. Breakfast is served at a highly polished communal table in the dining room, and there is also a comfortable sitting room in the main house.

FACILITIES: 3 en suite No smoking TVB tea/coffee No dogs Cen ht No children 12yrs 240 acres arable **PRICES:** s £30-£41; d £46-£50✱
PARKING: 6 **NOTES:** Closed Xmas **CARDS:**

♦♦♦♦ Anchor

Sutton Gault CB6 2BD ☎ 01353 778537 01353 776180
e-mail: AnchorInnSG@aol.com
Dir: *Sutton Gault signposted off B1381 at southern end of Sutton village (6m W of Ely)*

Superbly located beside the New Bedford River with stunning views over the surrounding countryside, this 17th-century inn retains many original features which are highlighted by the period furniture. Bedrooms are spacious, comfortable and equipped with lots of thoughtful extras.

FACILITIES: 2 en suite (1 fmly) No smoking TVB tea/coffee Direct dial from bedrooms No dogs (ex guide dogs) Cen ht No coaches Fishing Dinner Last d 9pm **PRICES:** d £66.50-£95✱ **LB MEALS:** Lunch £7.95&alc Dinner £20-£25alc✱ **PARKING:** 16 **NOTES:** Closed 26 Dec **CARDS:** 

♦♦♦ Castle Lodge Hotel

50 New Barns Rd CB7 4PW ☎ 01353 662276 Fax 01353 666606

Dir: *turn off A10 at 1st rdbt on Ely bypass, at lights turn left, over next lights and take next right. At top of rd turn left. Hotel on right*

Located within easy walking distance of the cathedral, this extended Victorian house offers well equipped bedrooms and public areas which include a traditional furnished dining room and comfortable bar lounge.

FACILITIES: 11 rms (6 en suite) (2 fmly) No smoking in dining room TVB tea/coffee Direct dial from bedrooms No dogs (ex guide dogs) Licensed Cen ht TVL No coaches Dinner Last d 9pm **PRICES:** s £25-£39.50; d £59.50✱ **PARKING:** 6 **NOTES:** Closed 23-27 Dec **CARDS:**

♦♦♦ The Nyton Hotel

7 Barton Rd CB7 4HZ ☎ 01353 662459 Fax 01353 666217

e-mail: nytonhotel@yahoo.co.uk

Dir: *from S A10 into Ely, pass golf course on right, then 1st right pass garage, Hotel 200yds on right*

Set in two-acre gardens, this family-run hotel offers comfortable bedrooms in a variety of sizes and styles. Informal meals are served in the bar with more serious dining in the wood-panelled restaurant; there is also a conservatory lounge.

FACILITIES: 10 en suite (3 fmly) TVB tea/coffee Direct dial from bedrooms No dogs (ex guide dogs) Licensed Cen ht TVL ch fac Dinner Last d 2pm **PRICES:** s £45; d £70✱ **LB** **PARKING:** 25 **CARDS:**

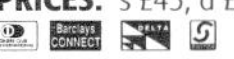

♦♦♦ Red Lion

47 High St, Stretham CB6 3JQ ☎ 01353 648132 Fax 01353 648327

e-mail: frank.hayes@ukgateway.net

Dir: *Turn right off A10 from Cambridge & 1st left into High St*

This 17th-century coaching inn has been fully renovated. Downstairs are two bustling bars, a cosy public bar with satellite television, and the larger lounge bar with a family conservatory restaurant to the rear. There are some bedrooms in the main house and some in the modern annexe.

FACILITIES: 6 en suite 6 annexe en suite (3 fmly) No smoking in 6 bedrooms No smoking in dining room TVB tea/coffee Cen ht TVL No children 4yrs Dinner Last d 9pm **PRICES:** s £34.75; d £45.75✱ **PARKING:** 19 **CARDS:**

Egg cups for excellence!
This symbol shows that breakfast exceeded our Inspector's expectations.

HILTON — Map 04 TL26

♦♦♦♦ Prince of Wales

Potton Rd PE28 9NG ☎ 01480 830257 Fax 01480 830257

Dir: *from A14 follow B1040 towards Biggleswade, follow road for approx. 2m into village Prince of Wales on the left*

Located in the heart of the village and very popular with locals, this cosy traditional inn offers a choice of bars serving good food and real ales. Bedrooms vary in size, although each room is well equipped and has modern en suite facilities.

FACILITIES: 4 en suite TVB tea/coffee Direct dial from bedrooms No dogs (ex guide dogs) Cen ht No children 5yrs Pool table Darts Dinner Last d 8.45pm **PRICES:** s £45-£50; d £65✱ **MEALS:** Lunch £12 Dinner £13✱ **PARKING:** 9 **NOTES:** Closed 1 Jan **CARDS:**

HUNTINGDON — Map 04 TL27

Premier Collection

♦♦♦♦♦ Holmefields Barn

16 High St, Bluntisham PE28 3LD ☎ 01487 841435

e-mail: roy.carlyle@btinternet.com

Dir: *take A1123 through Bluntisham to the High St. Holmefields is 300 yds on left, just before Baptist Church.*

Mrs Carlyle is a caring and friendly host who warmly welcomes guests to her home, a charming Grade II listed thatched cottage dating back to the 17th century, in its own mature grounds. The accommodation is in a converted barn with a private entrance and includes a double bedroom, lounge, kitchen and bathroom. Breakfast is served in the elegant dining room and features home-made bread and preserves.

FACILITIES: 1 en suite No smoking tea/coffee No dogs (ex guide dogs) Cen ht TVL No children None No coaches **PRICES:** d £60✱ **PARKING:** 2

KIMBOLTON — Map 04 TL16

♦♦♦♦ Apothecary

1 St Andrews Ln PE28 0HN ☎ 01480 860352

Dir: *A14 onto B660, from A1 S onto B645, establishment on High St in front of church.*

Located adjacent to the village church of St Andrews with its renowned Tiffany window, this 16th-century former pharmacy is now a comfortable home offering well-equipped bedrooms. Breakfast is taken at one family table in the dining hall, which retains many original features including polished stone floors and exposed beams.

FACILITIES: 3 rms (2 en suite) (3 fmly) No smoking TVB tea/coffee No dogs (ex guide dogs) Cen ht No coaches **PRICES:** d £45-£50✱

England

KIRTLING Map 05 TL65

♦♦♦ Hill *(TL685585)*
CB8 9HQ ☎ 01638 730253 01638 731957 Mrs C A Bailey

Located on arable land, south of Newmarket and in the heart of bloodstock country, this 400-year old property retains many original features, public areas are furnished in keeping with the period of the building. Hearty breakfasts are taken at one family table in the elegant dining room and friendly service is provided.
FACILITIES: 3 rms (2 en suite) TVB tea/coffee Direct dial from bedrooms No dogs (ex guide dogs) Cen ht TVL Games room 500 acres arable
PRICES: s £30; d £55* **LB PARKING:** 15

MAXEY Map 04 TF10

♦♦♦♦ Abbey House
West End Rd PE6 9EJ ☎ 01778 344642 01778 342706
e-mail: info@abbeyhouse.co.uk
Dir: *from rdbt on A15, 1m S of Market Deeping, turn left into Maxey. 1st right (Castle End Rd), 1st left (West End Rd), Abbey House 400yds on left*
Located in the quiet village of Maxey, this mellow stone building dates in part from the 12th century. Over the years it has been sympathetically renovated to provide facilities for the modern traveller yet still retain many original features. Bedrooms are well equipped and comfortable and an elegant dining room and comfortable lounge are provided.
FACILITIES: 4 en suite 6 annexe en suite (1 fmly) No smoking TVB tea/coffee Direct dial from bedrooms No dogs (ex guide dogs) Cen ht TVL No coaches Fishing **PARKING:** 10

PETERBOROUGH Map 04 TL19

See also Maxey

♦♦♦♦ Hawthorn House Hotel
89 Thorpe Rd PE3 6JQ ☎ 01733 340608 & 313470
01733 763800
e-mail: peggy.warren@tesco.net
Dir: *from south take A1, A1139, A1260, A1179, straight over next rdbt, hotel 0.25m on right*
A friendly welcome is assured at this lovely Victorian house, which sits within easy walking distance of the cathedral and city centre. Bedrooms are mostly well proportioned, equipped to a good standard and are comfortably appointed. Breakfast is served in an attractive dining room, which has a corner bar, and guests are welcome to use the small conservatory that overlooks the rear gardens.
FACILITIES: 7 en suite (2 fmly) (2 GF) No smoking in 3 bedrooms No smoking in dining room No smoking in lounges TVB tea/coffee Direct dial from bedrooms No dogs (ex guide dogs) Licensed Cen ht TVL No coaches
PRICES: s £32.50-£42.50; d £52-£60* **PARKING:** 5 **NOTES:** Closed Xmas & New Year **CARDS:**

♦♦♦♦ Lodge Hotel
130 Lincoln Rd PE1 2NR ☎ 01733 341489 01733 753437
Dir: *N of city at junct with Lincoln Road and Limetree Avenue*
Conveniently located for access to the town centre, this small, friendly hotel is just ten minutes walk from the cathedral. Bedrooms are pleasantly furnished and well-equipped. Guests have the use of a small lounge bar and a range of imaginative dishes are served in the no-smoking restaurant.
FACILITIES: 9 en suite No smoking in dining room TVB tea/coffee Cen ht No children 10yrs No coaches **PRICES:** s £37-£40; d £50-£55*
PARKING: 6 **CARDS:**

♦♦♦ Aaron Park Hotel
109 Park Rd PE1 2TR ☎ 01733 564849 & 751238
01733 564855
e-mail: aaronparkhotel@yahoo.co.uk
Dir: *off A1 onto A1139, Fletton Parkway to junct 5 city centre Boongate Rd turn left. Over next rdbt 3rd exit along Crawthorne Rd over traffic lights, next left onto Park Rd, near Cathedral*
This Victorian house is situated in a tree lined avenue just a short walk from the city centre and cathedral. Bedrooms come in a variety of styles and sizes; each room is nicely presented and has a good range of modern facilities. Breakfasts are carefully cooked, a good start to the day.
FACILITIES: 10 en suite (3 fmly) (2 GF) No smoking STV TVB tea/coffee No dogs (ex guide dogs) Licensed Cen ht No coaches Dinner Last d noon
PRICES: s £44; d £54* **PARKING:** 5 **NOTES:** Closed Xmas **CARDS:**

♦♦♦ Charlotte House
78 London Rd PE2 9BP ☎ 01733 315870 01733 313705
e-mail: charlottehouse@hotels.activebooking.com
Dir: *follow signs to city centre then follow A605 Whittsley/A1 London. Pass football club and at traffic lights fork right into London Rd*
Stella and Ernie Dunton offer a warm welcome to Charlotte House, a detached Victorian house, which is conveniently located just ten minutes' walk from the city centre. The house has been sympathetically refurbished to a good standard; bedrooms come in a variety of styles and sizes, each soundly appointed with modern facilities.
FACILITIES: 9 en suite (2 GF) No smoking in bedrooms No smoking in dining room No smoking in lounges STV TVB tea/coffee No dogs (ex guide dogs) Cen ht No coaches Dinner Last d 7pm **PRICES:** s £41-£44; d £52-£58* **PARKING:** 9 **NOTES:** Closed 19-31 Dec **CARDS:**

WATERBEACH Map 05 TL46

♦♦♦ Inspiration
92 Bannold Rd, Waterbeach CB5 9LQ
☎ 01223 863661 07761 140571
e-mail: b&b@richardguy.screaming.net
Dir: *From Ely on A10, left at sign Waterbeach, into Denny End Rd. 3rd left into Bannold Rd. From Cambridge on A10, pass Slap Up pub. right into Waterbeach, approx 0.5m then as above.*
Located on the outskirts of the town, this detached chalet bungalow offers self-contained accommodation that includes a first floor suite accessed via a spiral staircase. It has a homely comfortable bedroom and a combined lounge and dining area. A comprehensive continental breakfast is provided.
FACILITIES: 1 en suite No smoking No dogs Cen ht TVL No children 14yrs No coaches **PRICES:** s £20-£30; d £40-£50* **LB PARKING:** 1

Places with this symbol are farmhouses.

CHESHIRE

ALSAGER Map 07 SJ75

♦♦♦♦ Sappho Cottage

118 Crewe Rd ST7 2JA ☎ 01270 882033 📠 01270 883556
e-mail: reception@sappho-cottage.demon.co.uk

Dir: *5 mins from M6 J16, follow signs for Alsager, right at 1st lights, Sappho Cottage is 1m on right*

This attractive house, dating from the mid-19th century, is just a short drive from the Potteries and M6. It has pretty rear gardens and a cosy lounge. The bedrooms have individual decor to reflect the seasons they are named after. One room is on ground floor level. Warm hospitality and good home cooking is offered.

FACILITIES: 3 en suite No smoking TVB tea/coffee No dogs Cen ht ch fac No coaches **PRICES:** s £30-£40; d £45-£55✱ **PARKING:** 3

ASHLEY Map 07 SJ78

♦♦♦♦ Birtles Farm B&B

Ashley Rd WA14 3QH ☎ 0161 928 0458 📠 0161 928 0458
e-mail: birtles1@supanet.com

Dir: *left of A556 at the Swan Hotel, turn left until the T-junct, right to 2nd T-junct, then left, next right before narrow bridge up drive.*

FACILITIES: 3 rms (2 en suite) (1 fmly) TVB tea/coffee Cen ht TVL Riding Dinner Last d 5.30pm **PRICES:** s £25-£30; d £40-£44✱ **LB PARKING:** 10

AUDLEM Map 07 SJ64

♦♦♦ Little Heath Farm *(SJ663455)*

CW3 0HE ☎ 01270 811324 📠 01270 811324 Mrs H M Bennion
e-mail: littleheathfarm@btopenworld.com

Dir: *6m from Nantwich on A529. At 30mph sign in Audlem, farm on right*

This 200-year-old brick-built farmhouse retains much of its original character with low beamed ceilings and traditionally furnished public areas. These include a cosy sitting room and a separate dining room where guests dine family style. The friendly owners create a relaxing atmosphere for their guests.

FACILITIES: 3 rms (1 en suite) (1 fmly) No smoking TVB tea/coffee No dogs (ex guide dogs) Cen ht TVL 50 acres dairy / mixed. Dinner Last d 10am **PRICES:** s £20-£30; d £36-£50✱ **LB BB PARKING:** 3 **NOTES:** Closed Xmas & New Year

CHESTER Map 07 SJ46

See also Malpas

Premier Collection

♦♦♦♦♦ Grove House

Holme St, Tarvin CH3 8EQ ☎ 01829 740893
📠 01829 741769
e-mail: helen_s@btinternet.com

Dir: *take A51 from Chester then A54 at rdbt up slight hill and house on brow on left behind stone wall and stone gateposts.*

This impressive red brick late-Victorian house is set in its own pretty gardens, complete with croquet lawn. Bedrooms are spacious, comfortable and furnished with period pieces. The elegant dining room has a large polished table, and the drawing room is inviting.

FACILITIES: 3 en suite No smoking in bedrooms No smoking in dining room TVB tea/coffee No dogs Cen ht TVL No children 12yrs No coaches Croquet lawn **PRICES:** s £30-£40; d £60-£70✱ **PARKING:** 6 **NOTES:** Closed 20 Dec-5 Jan

continued

Grove House

Premier Collection

♦♦♦♦♦ Redland Private Hotel

64 Hough Green CH4 8JY ☎ 01244 671024
📠 01244 681309

Dir: *from Chester on A483 Wrexham rd, 1m & take A5104 Saltney rd for 200yds, opp Westminster Park*

This delightful hotel has been carefully and tastefully restored to its former Victorian splendour. Rooms are individually styled, many with antique four-poster and half-tester beds and bathrooms are spacious and appointed to a high standard. Public areas include an honesty bar and a spacious drawing room, as well as a sauna, solarium and laundry room.

FACILITIES: 13 en suite (3 fmly) No smoking in 6 bedrooms No smoking in dining room STV TVB tea/coffee Direct dial from bedrooms Licensed Cen ht No coaches Sauna Solarium **PRICES:** s £45; d £65-£85✱ **PARKING:** 12 **CARDS:**

♦♦♦♦ Alton Lodge Hotel

78 Hoole Rd CH2 3NT ☎ 01244 310213 📠 01244 319206
e-mail: enquiries@altonlodge.co.uk

Dir: *exit M53 junct 12 and take A56 into Chester, house 0.5m on right opposite playing field*

Located between the ring road and city centre, this Edwardian house has been sympathetically renovated and extended to provide quality pine furnished bedrooms with smart modern bathrooms. Comprehensive breakfasts are taken in an attractive dining room, which also contains a comfortable lounge area and dinner is available on weekdays.

FACILITIES: 4 en suite 13 annexe en suite (2 fmly) No smoking in bedrooms No smoking in dining room TVB tea/coffee Direct dial from bedrooms No dogs Licensed Cen ht TVL No coaches Dinner Last d 9pm **PRICES:** s £45-£50; d £60-£70✱ **LB PARKING:** 22 **NOTES:** Closed Xmas/New Year rs Fri-Sun (bar & restaurant closed) **CARDS:**

England

CHESTER continued

♦♦♦♦ *Cheltenham Lodge*

58 Hoole Rd, Hoole CH2 3NL ☎ 01244 346767

Dir: *M53 junct 12, at rdbt 3rd exit following signs for city centre, at next rdbt 2nd exit join A56 hotel 0.5m on right opposite All Saints Church*

This small and friendly personally run guest house is conveniently located near the city centre and M53. The modern bedrooms, which include rooms on ground floor level and a family room, are attractively appointed and well-equipped.

FACILITIES: 5 en suite (2 fmly) No smoking in 3 bedrooms No smoking in dining room No smoking in lounges TVB tea/coffee No dogs (ex guide dogs) Cen ht **PARKING:** 5 **NOTES:** Closed 23 Dec-7 Jan

♦♦♦♦ Craigleith Lodge

56 Hoole Rd CH2 3NL ☎ 01244 327186

Dir: *M53 junct 12 toward Chester on A56 for 0.5m*

Situated within walking distance of the city, this constantly improving late Victorian house provides comfortable bedrooms, equipped with both practical and homely extras. A cosy traditionally furnished dining room is the setting for comprehensive breakfasts and the private car park is a real benefit.

FACILITIES: 6 en suite (2 GF) No smoking in dining room TVB tea/coffee No dogs Cen ht No coaches **PRICES:** d £45-£55✻ **PARKING:** 9

♦♦♦♦ Golborne Manor

Platts Ln, Hatton Heath CH3 9AN

☎ 01829 770310 & 07774 695268 🖷 01829 770370

e-mail: ann.ikin@golbornemanor.co.uk

Dir: *5m S of A41 Whitchurch rd. Turn right after DP Motors & Demon Tyres into Platts Lane, then 400yds on left*

This elegant mid-Victorian manor house stands amidst beautiful gardens enjoying spectacular views across open countryside. Accommodation is in spacious, comfortable bedrooms, with either brass bedsteads or a richly carved antique Arabian bed. Breakfast is served around the one large table in the dining room, and residents have use of a very comfortable lounge.

FACILITIES: 3 en suite (1 fmly) No smoking TVB tea/coffee No dogs Cen ht Croquet lawn Threequarter snooker table,table tennis Dinner Last d 1 day advanced **PRICES:** s £28-£38; d £58-£68✻ **LB** **PARKING:** 6

♦♦♦♦ Green Gables

11 Eversley Park CH2 2AJ ☎ 01244 372243 🖷 01244 376352

Dir: *off A5116 signed 'Countess of Chester Hospital'*

This attractive Victorian house, set in its own pretty gardens and private car park, is located in a quiet residential area, yet is conveniently close to the city centre. Comfortable, well-equipped, bedrooms include a family room. A sitting room is provided and the breakfast room is light and strikingly decorated.

FACILITIES: 2 en suite (1 fmly) No smoking TV4B tea/coffee Direct dial from bedrooms No dogs (ex guide dogs) Cen ht TVL **PRICES:** s fr £28; d fr £42✻ **PARKING:** 11

♦♦♦♦ Lavender Lodge

46 Hoole Rd CH2 3NL ☎ 01244 323204 🖷 01244 329821

e-mail: bookings@lavenderlodge.co.uk

Dir: *turn off M53 junct 12 onto A56 towards Chester city centre, Stillington House 0.75m on right opposite All Saints Church*

Ideally located within easy walking distance of central attractions, this late Victorian house provides comfortable bedrooms filled with thoughtful extras, with modern efficient bathrooms. Comprehensive breakfasts are taken in an attractive dining room and a warm welcome is assured.

FACILITIES: 5 rms (4 en suite) (2 fmly) No smoking TVB tea/coffee Cen ht No coaches **PRICES:** s £25-£35; d £40-£60✻ **PARKING:** 7

♦♦♦♦ The Mount

Lesters Ln, Higher Kinnerton CH4 9BQ ☎ 01244 660275

🖷 01244 660275

e-mail: major@mountkinnerton.freeserve.co.uk

Dir: *turn off A55 onto A5104, left at 2nd rbt, through Broughton then 1st left signed Kinnerton. Follow lane for 0.75m, house on right*

This fine Victorian house is surrounded by extensive grounds and gardens. Bedrooms, and public areas are furnished with fine period pieces and equipped with modern facilities. Warm hospitality is provided by the friendly Major family and a relaxing atmosphere is created for guests. The house is a convenient base for Chester and for the North Wales tourist areas.

FACILITIES: 3 en suite No smoking TVB tea/coffee No dogs (ex guide dogs) Cen ht No children 12yrs No coaches Tennis (hard) Croquet lawn **PRICES:** s £30-£40; d £50✻ **PARKING:** 10 **NOTES:** Closed 22 Dec-6 Jan

♦♦♦♦ Rowton Poplars Hotel

Whitchurch Rd, Rowton CH3 6AF ☎ 01244 333010

🖷 01244 333020

e-mail: valwalley@rowtonpoplars.fsnet.co.uk

Dir: *M53 onto A55 at junct 2 follow signs for Whitchurch A41, hotel just before petrol station.*

A charming Victorian house that has been tastefully converted into a friendly family run hotel and is conveniently located for visiting Chester and the surrounding attractions. Bedrooms are freshly decorated and well-equipped. Downstairs there is a comfortable guests' lounge and residents' bar. Dinner is available by arrangement and meals are served in the attractive dining room.

FACILITIES: 8 en suite (4 fmly) No smoking in 6 bedrooms No smoking in area of dining room No smoking in lounges TVB tea/coffee Direct dial from bedrooms Licensed Cen ht TVL Dinner Last d 8.15pm **PRICES:** d £55-£70✻ **LB** **PARKING:** 15 **CARDS:**

If an establishment name appears in *italics*, details have not been confirmed for 2003.

♦♦♦ Derry Raghan
54 Hoole Rd CH2 3NL ☎ 01244 318740

Dir: *M53 junct 12 on to A56 towards Chester for 0.5m, establishment on right*

A friendly, Victorian guest house situated within easy reach of Chester town centre and the railway station. The tastefully decorated rooms are comfortable and some are on the ground floor.

FACILITIES: 6 en suite (4 fmly) No smoking in dining room TVB tea/coffee No dogs (ex guide dogs) Cen ht No coaches **PRICES:** s £25-£35; d £45-£55✻ **PARKING:** 12

♦♦♦ Gloster Lodge Hotel
44 Hoole Rd, Hoole CH2 3NL ☎ 01244 348410 & 320231 📠 01244 401468

Dir: *on A56. On main 'hotel' rd into Chester straight from M56 & joining A56. Hotel 0.5m on A56 on right opp All Saints Church*

This small family run hotel is located on the eastern approach to this historic city. Bedrooms are smart and well equipped with stained glass windows featuring in some. There is a pretty breakfast room and staff and owners are friendly and welcoming.

FACILITIES: 5 en suite 3 annexe en suite (2 fmly) (3 GF) No smoking in 1 bedrooms No smoking in dining room No smoking in lounges TVB tea/coffee Direct dial from bedrooms No dogs (ex guide dogs) Cen ht No coaches **PRICES:** s fr £22; d fr £45✻ **LB PARKING:** 9 **NOTES:** Closed 24-31 Dec **CARDS:**

♦♦♦ The Glann Hotel
2 Stone Place CH2 3NR ☎ 01244 344800

e-mail: glannhot@supanet.com

Dir: *approach city centre on A56, 0.75m from Hoole Rd rdbt, 4th turning on left after Church*

FACILITIES: 10 rms (9 en suite) (1 fmly) No smoking in 4 bedrooms No smoking in dining room TVB tea/coffee No dogs (ex guide dogs) Licensed Cen ht No coaches **PRICES:** s £26-£35; d £47-£55✻ **LB PARKING:** 10 **NOTES:** Closed 22 Dec-3 Jan **CARDS:** 

♦♦♦ Strathearn
38 Hoole Rd CH2 3NL ☎ 01244 321522 📠 01244 321522

e-mail: strathearn@breathemail.net

Dir: *at end of M53, follow signs for A56 to Chester. Proceed for 0.75m. Guest house is on right opposite All Saints Church).*

FACILITIES: 6 rms (3 en suite) (1 fmly) No smoking in dining room TVB tea/coffee No dogs Cen ht No coaches **PRICES:** s £20-£25; d £40-£50✻ **PARKING:** 4 **NOTES:** Closed 24 Dec-1 Jan

CHOLMONDELEY — Map 07 SJ55

♦♦♦ Cholmondeley Arms
SY14 8HN ☎ 01829 720300 📠 01829 720123

e-mail: cholmondeleyarms@cwcom.net

Dir: *on A49, 6m N of Whitchurch*

continued

Until 1982 this characterful inn was the village school. The conversion in 1988 was sympathetic and the inn is enhanced by period furniture and a welcoming real fire. Across the former playground, now the car park, what was once the headmaster's residence has been converted into six well equipped bedrooms.

FACILITIES: 6 en suite (1 fmly) No smoking in bedrooms TVB tea/coffee Direct dial from bedrooms Cen ht No coaches Dinner Last d 10pm **PRICES:** s £45; d £60✻ **LB MEALS:** Lunch fr £5&alc✻ **PARKING:** 60 **CARDS:**

CONGLETON — Map 07 SJ86

♦♦♦♦ Waggon and Horses
Manchester Rd, Eaton CW12 2JD ☎ 01260 224229 📠 01260 224248

Dir: *on A34 1.5m N of Congleton heading towards Manchester*

Situated north of Congleton on the A34, The Waggon and Horses provides good quality, well equipped and tastefully appointed modern bedrooms, all of which are located on the ground and first floors of a separate cottage. Facilities include a lounge bar and a spacious restaurant where a wide range of dishes is available.

FACILITIES: 6 annexe en suite No smoking in bedrooms No smoking in dining room TVB tea/coffee Direct dial from bedrooms No dogs (ex guide dogs) Cen ht Pool Table Dinner Last d 9pm **PRICES:** s fr £44; d fr £54✻ **LB MEALS:** Lunch £8.95-£13.50alc Dinner £8.95-£13.50alc✻ **PARKING:** 50 **CARDS:**

♦♦♦♦ Sandhole Farm
Hulme Walfield CW12 2JH ☎ 01260 224419 📠 01260 224766

e-mail: veronica@sandholefarm.co.uk

Dir: *2m N of Congleton on A34 Manchester road. Left down drive*

FACILITIES: 2 en suite 15 annexe en suite (3 fmly) (7 GF) No smoking TVB tea/coffee Direct dial from bedrooms Cen ht TVL **PRICES:** s fr £44; d fr £54✻ **CONF:** Thtr 30 Board 15 **PARKING:** 50 **CARDS:**

♦♦♦ Egerton Arms Hotel
Astbury Village CW12 4RQ ☎ 01260 273946 📠 01260 277273

e-mail: egertonastbury@totalise.co.uk

Dir: *1.5m S of Congleton just off A34 in Astbury Village next to St Marys Church*

This 15th-century country inn lies opposite the church in the pretty village of Astbury. A wide range of food is available in its bars and restaurant and this attracts a popular local following. Some bedrooms have recently been refurbished and these are well equipped and attractively decorated.

FACILITIES: 6 rms (2 en suite) No smoking in 2 bedrooms No smoking in dining room No smoking in 1 lounge TVB tea/coffee No dogs (ex guide dogs) Cen ht No coaches Golf & fishing can be arranged Dinner Last d 9pm **PRICES:** s £25-£40; d £35-£50✻ **BB PARKING:** 100 **CARDS:**

KINGSLEY — Map 07 SJ57

♦♦♦♦ Charnwood
Hollow Ln WA6 8EF ☎ 01928 787097 📠 01928 788566

e-mail: susan.klin@talk21.com

Dir: *from Frodsham take B5152 for approx 3m, then onto B5153 for Kingsley Hollow Lane. House just past church on right*

Set on the edge of a peaceful village, offering two well-furnished bedrooms that share a spacious bathroom and comfortable lounge. A separate entrance is provided, which is ideal for families or individuals. Breakfast is served in the dining room, which looks out onto the patio and pretty gardens.

FACILITIES: 2 rms (1 en suite) (1 fmly) No smoking TVB tea/coffee Direct dial from bedrooms No dogs Cen ht TVL No coaches **PRICES:** s £25-£35; d £36-£50✻ **BB PARKING:** 5

KNUTSFORD Map 07 SJ77

♦♦♦♦ Old Vicarage

Moss Ln, Over Tabley WA16 0PL ☎ 01565 652221
🖷 01565 755918

Dir: *exit M6 junct 19 onto A556 signposted Manchester Airport. Turn right after Little Chef into Moss Lane*

The Old Vicarage is a charming, delightfully restored 19th-century house set in two acres of landscaped, wooded grounds and gardens, convenient for access to the M6. Bedrooms are attractively furnished and thoughtfully equipped.

FACILITIES: 4 en suite (1 fmly) No smoking TVB tea/coffee No dogs (ex guide dogs) Licensed Cen ht TVL No children 10yrs Arrangements with 2 golf courses Last d 9pm **PRICES:** s £49.50; d £65✱ **PARKING:** 50 **NOTES:** Closed 2 -18 Jan **CARDS:**

♦♦♦♦ The Dog Inn

Well Bank Ln, Over Peover WA16 8UP ☎ 01625 861421
🖷 01625 864800
e-mail: dog-inn@paddockinns.fsnet.co.uk

Dir: *from A50 turn left at Whipping Stocks continue straight on for approx 2m*

Nestling in the heart of the Cheshire countryside, hanging baskets and tubs adorn the front of this 18th-century inn. Bedrooms are comfortable, attractively furnished, and equipped with many extras. The lounge bar and restaurant offer an all-day menu utilising local produce and a wide selection of ales making it a popular place with locals.

FACILITIES: 6 en suite No smoking in dining room TVB tea/coffee Direct dial from bedrooms No dogs (ex guide dogs) Cen ht Pool Table Dinner Last d 9.30pm **PRICES:** s £55-£60; d £75-£100✱ **MEALS:** Lunch £8.95-£13.95alc Dinner £8.95-£13.95alc✱ **PARKING:** 80 **CARDS:**

♦♦♦♦ The Hinton

Town Ln, Mobberley WA16 7HH ☎ 01565 873484
🖷 01565 873484

Dir: *on B5085. From Knutsford, Hinton on right just past shops. From Wilmslow, Hinton on left just past fieldside close*

Conveniently located for Manchester Airport, with good parking in a rural village setting, this delightful guest house is attractively decorated. Bedrooms are equipped with numerous modern facilities, and there is a two-bedroom suite especially suitable for families. There is a guest lounge, and a spacious dining room, which leads to the conservatory and patio.

FACILITIES: 5 en suite (1 fmly) No smoking TVB tea/coffee No dogs (ex guide dogs) Licensed Cen ht No coaches Dinner Last d 4.30pm **PRICES:** s £38-£44; d £50-£58✱ **PARKING:** 10 **CARDS:**

An asterisk ✱ indicates that prices given are for 2002.

♦♦♦♦ Laburnum Cottage

Knutsford Rd, Mobberley WA16 7PU ☎ 01565 872464
🖷 01565 872464

Dir: *on B5085 1.5m from Knutsford town centre, 250yds beyond Parish of Mobberley sign on left*

Set in an attractive garden, this guest house is within easy reach of the motorway network and Manchester Airport. Bedrooms are attractively furnished and well equipped. Guests have access to a comfortable lounge, and carefully prepared evening meals are available by prior arrangement.

FACILITIES: 5 en suite No smoking TVB tea/coffee No dogs (ex guide dogs) Cen ht TVL No coaches Dinner Last d 8pm **PRICES:** s £44; d £57✱ **PARKING:** 6 **CARDS:**

MALPAS Map 07 SJ44

Premier Collection

♦♦♦♦♦ Tilston Lodge

Tilston SY14 7DR ☎ 01829 250223 🖷 01829 250223

Dir: *A41 Chester towards Whitchurch (S) After 10m cross over Broxton rdbt. After 1.5m turn right for Tilston. In village turn left at T-junction. Tilston Lodge 200mtrs on R at 40mph sign*

Once a hunting lodge, this impressive Victorian house lies in 16 acres of pasture which is home to rare breeds of sheep and poultry. The pretty gardens have won awards. The individually decorated bedrooms are furnished with fine period pieces and public rooms are equally comfortable. Breakfast includes free-range eggs from the Lodge's own hens, and home-made preserves.

FACILITIES: 3 en suite (1 fmly) No smoking TVB tea/coffee No dogs (ex guide dogs) Cen ht TVL No coaches **PRICES:** s £45-£55; d £70-£76✱ **LB** **PARKING:** 10

♦♦♦♦ Millmoor Farm *(SJ518475)*

Nomansheath SY14 8DY ☎ 01948 820304 Mrs S Chesters
e-mail: dave-sal@millmoor-farm.fsnet.co.uk

Dir: *A41 S towards Whitchurch, R towards Nomansheath, 1m after Hampton Heath rdbt. L at mini rdbt in village, establishment signposted after 0.5m*

Parts of this tastefully modernised farmhouse date back to the late 17th century. Set in an attractive garden, it is quietly located on a beef and dairy farm near Nomansheath. The traditionally furnished accommodation includes a room with a four-poster bed, and there is a pleasant combined lounge and dining room, where welcoming real fires burn when the weather is cold.

FACILITIES: 3 en suite No smoking TVB tea/coffee Cen ht Fishing 240 acres dairy & beef Dinner Last d am day meal required **PRICES:** s £20-£22; d £36-£44✱ **LB** **BB** **PARKING:** 11

MIDDLEWICH Map 07 SJ76

♦♦♦ Forge Mill *(SJ704624)*

Forge Mill Ln, Warmingham CW10 0HQ ☎ 01270 526204
🖷 01270 526204 Mrs S Moss

Dir: *M6 junct 18. In Middlewich, left onto A533, after 40mph sign turn right, then 1st left, after 1.5m, at T-junct, right into Forge Mill Lane. After river bridge, on right with white railings*

The house, built of Cheshire red brick, is situated in large gardens on a working farm. The bedrooms, both commanding fine country views, are spacious. The lounge is comfortably furnished and has a cheery log fire in cooler months. Hearty breakfasts are served in the large breakfast room.

FACILITIES: 2 rms (1 fmly) No smoking in bedrooms No smoking in dining room No dogs (ex guide dogs) Cen ht TVL 150 acres mixed **PRICES:** s fr £26; d fr £38✱ **LB** **BB** **PARKING:** 10

NANTWICH Map 07 SJ65

See also Wybunbury

Premier Collection

◆◆◆◆◆ *The Limes*
5 Park Rd CW5 7AQ ☎ 01270 624081 📠 01270 624081
Dir: *M6 junct 16 follow signs for Nantwich & Stapeley Water Gdns, continue into Nantwich, then follow signs for A530 Whitchurch*
Lying in a quiet residential area, not far from the town centre, this impressive Victorian house is impeccably maintained and is surrounded by pleasant gardens. The spacious bedrooms are well equipped and one has a four-poster bed. The lounge is elegantly furnished and breakfast is taken in a delightful dining room.
FACILITIES: 3 en suite No smoking TVB tea/coffee No dogs (ex guide dogs) Cen ht TVL No children 10yrs No coaches
PARKING: 3 **NOTES:** Closed Nov-Jan

Premier Collection

◆◆◆◆◆ Oakland House
252 Newcastle Rd, Blakelow, Shavington CW5 7ET
☎ 01270 567134
Dir: *on A500 5m from M6 junct 16, and 2m from Nantwich, following the Norwich and Chester signs*

Conveniently located for the motorway, Oakland House offers a friendly and relaxed atmosphere. The bedrooms are attractively furnished and well equipped. There is a spacious sitting room and a modern conservatory which overlooks the garden toward the Cheshire countryside. A substantial breakfast is served around one family table.
FACILITIES: 3 en suite 6 annexe en suite (1 fmly) (6 GF) No smoking TVB tea/coffee Cen ht TVL No coaches **PRICES:** s £34; d £49✻ **LB**
PARKING: 14 **CARDS:**

SANDBACH Map 07 SJ76

◆◆◆ Poplar Mount
2 Station Rd, Elworth CW11 3JG ☎ 01270 761268 📠 01270 761268
e-mail: popmntgh@aol.com
Dir: *off A533 Sandbach-middlewich rd onto B5079, 50yds on L*
Conveniently located near the railway station this friendly guest house offers a cosy lounge for residents and home cooked meals. These are served in the attractively decorated dining room next to the comfortable lounge. Bedrooms are thoughtfully equipped and furnished.
FACILITIES: 7 rms (4 en suite) (1 fmly) No smoking in dining room TVB tea/coffee No dogs (ex guide dogs) Cen ht TVL No coaches Dinner Last d 6.30pm **PRICES:** s £21-£30; d £42✻ **PARKING:** 7 **CARDS:**

TARPORLEY Map 07 SJ56

◆◆◆◆ Alvanley Arms Hotel
Forest Rd, Cotebrook CW6 9DS ☎ 01829 760200
📠 01829 760696
Dir: *from Tarporley follow A49 N for 1.5m. Hotel on right at bottom of hill, as you enter Cotebrook*

The Alvanley Arms is located close to Delamere Forest and Oulton Park racecourse. Records show that a public house has been on this site since at least the 18th century and renovations have uncovered original beams in some of the bedrooms. Bedrooms are brightly furnished and an extensive range of dishes is offered in the various dining areas.
FACILITIES: 6 en suite No smoking in bedrooms No smoking in dining room TVB tea/coffee Cen ht No coaches Fishing Dinner Last d 9pm
PRICES: s £35-£40; d £60-£70✻ **MEALS:** Lunch £12.95-£24.95alc Dinner £14.95-£24.95alc✻ **PARKING:** 70 **CARDS:**

Hill House Farm
Rushton CW6 9AU ☎ 01829 732238
At the time of going to press the Diamond classification for this establishment had not been confirmed. Please check the AA website www.theAA.com for up-to-date information.
FACILITIES: 3 en suite (1 fmly)

TATTENHALL Map 07 SJ45

◆◆◆◆ Ivy Farm *(SJ452555)*
Ivy Farm, Coddington CH3 9EN ☎ 01829 782295
📠 01829 782583 Mrs B R Arden
Dir: *from A41/A534 towards Wrexham. Through village of Clutton to bottom of small hill and right to Coddington. Farm on left opposite fenced pond*
This impressive creeper-clad 18th century farmhouse is located in the beautiful Cheshire countryside and makes a convenient base for visitors to North Wales and Chester. It has well-equipped bedrooms and comfortably furnished public areas. Warm hospitality is offered and good hearty breakfasts are served.
FACILITIES: 3 rms (2 en suite) (1 fmly) No smoking TVB tea/coffee No dogs (ex guide dogs) Cen ht 75 acres beef **PRICES:** s £23; d £40✻
PARKING: 5 **NOTES:** Closed Xmas & New Year

A indicates an Associate entry, which has been inspected and rated by the ETC or the RAC in England

England

WILMSLOW Map 07 SJ88

See also Manchester Airport (Greater Manchester)

Premier Collection

♦♦♦♦♦ Pear Tree Cottage Country

Church Ln SK7 1PQ ☎ 0161 439 5755 📠 0161 439 5755
e-mail: P-T-cottage@fsbdial.co.uk
Dir: *A34/B5094, opposite Bramhall Cricket Club*

A warm welcome is assured at this beautifully maintained, extended cottage, parts of which date from the 16th century. Bedrooms are tastefully decorated and furnished, and are have modern efficient shower rooms. The dining room features period furniture and is the setting for comprehensive breakfasts, and imaginative dinners (by arrangement).

FACILITIES: 3 en suite No smoking TVB tea/coffee No dogs Cen ht TVL No children 12yrs No coaches leisure facilities nearby Dinner Last d 5pm **PRICES:** s £35-£45; d £55-£80* **LB PARKING:** 6 **CARDS:**

WYBUNBURY Map 07 SJ64

♦♦♦ Lea *(SJ717489)*

Wrinehill Rd CW5 7NS ☎ 01270 841429 📠 01270 841429
Mrs J E Callwood
e-mail: contactus@leafarm.co.uk
1st Jan - 20th Dec
Dir: *A500 (Nantwich) over 2 rdbts, over split railway bridge take 1st left to T-junct, turn left, 2nd farm on right*

This working dairy farm is surrounded by well presented gardens and the beautiful Cheshire countryside. Spacious bedrooms are equipped with modern facilities and the cosy lounge features a small snooker table. Hearty breakfasts are served in the attractive dining room and this looks out over the garden.

FACILITIES: 3 rms (2 en suite) (1 fmly) No smoking TVB tea/coffee Cen ht TVL Fishing Pool Table 150 acres dairy Dinner Last d 5pm **PRICES:** s £23-£28; d £40-£45* **PARKING:** 24 **NOTES:** Closed Xmas

CORNWALL & ISLES OF SCILLY

BODMIN Map 02 SX06

♦♦♦♦ Mount Pleasant

Mount PL30 4EX ☎ 01208 821342
e-mail: colette@capper61.fsnet.co.uk
Dir: *from Bodmin follow A30 signed Launceston for 4m, then turn right signed Millpool, continue for 3m*

Set in 10 acres, this 17th-century farmhouse has extensive facilities including games room, gymnasium and heated swimming pool. The cosy bedrooms are comfortable and well furnished. Guests also have use of a lounge with e-mail facilities, a bar, and sun lounge with an indoor garden. Breakfast and dinner (by arrangement) use excellent local produce.

FACILITIES: 6 en suite No smoking TVB tea/coffee No dogs Licensed Cen ht No children 5yrs No coaches Indoor swimming pool (heated) Pool Table Dinner **PRICES:** s £30-£45; d £60-£80* **LB PARKING:** 10 **NOTES:** Closed Oct-Etr **CARDS:**

♦♦♦ Tremeere Manor

Lanivet PL30 5BG ☎ 01208 831513 📠 01208 832417
e-mail: oliver.tremeere.manor@fwi.co.uk
Dir: *turn off A30 at end of Bodmin bypass, take 3rd exit signed Wadebridge/Lanivet, in Lanlivet turn right between SPAR village shop and Garage. 1st left before church, in 0.5m Tremeere is on right*

FACILITIES: 3 en suite No smoking tea/coffee No dogs (ex guide dogs) Cen ht No coaches **PRICES:** s £22-£26; d £36-£48* **LB BB PARKING:** 6 **NOTES:** Closed Xmas & New Year

BOSCASTLE Map 02 SX09

♦♦♦♦ Old Coach House

Tintagel Rd PL35 0AS ☎ 01840 250398 📠 01840 250346
e-mail: parsons@old-coach.demon.co.uk
Dir: *at junct of B3266 and B3263*

Over 300 years old, The Old Coach House enjoys splendid views over the village and the surrounding countryside. The pleasantly decorated bedrooms are well equipped and two rooms on the ground floor have been very well equipped for the less mobile. A hearty breakfast is served in the conservatory, which overlooks the well-kept garden.

FACILITIES: 8 en suite (3 fmly) No smoking in bedrooms No smoking in dining room No smoking in lounges TVB tea/coffee Cen ht TVL No coaches **PRICES:** s £25-£38; d £36-£44* **LB BB PARKING:** 9 **NOTES:** Closed Xmas **CARDS:**

♦♦♦♦ Tolcarne House Hotel & Restaurant

Tintagel Rd PL35 0AS ☎ 01840 250654 📠 01840 250654
e-mail: crowntolhouse@eclipse.co.uk
Dir: *at junct of B3266/B3263 in Boscastle*

Guests are assured of a warm welcome at this substantial Victorian residence set in its own delightful grounds and gardens. The well-equipped bedrooms are stylishly decorated and equipped with many extras. There is a lounge with an open fire and a separate cosy bar. Evening meals are available.

FACILITIES: 8 en suite (1 fmly) No smoking in 4 bedrooms No smoking in dining room No smoking in 1 lounge TVB tea/coffee Licensed Cen ht No children 10yrs No coaches Croquet lawn Dinner Last d 8.45pm **PRICES:** s £30-£32; d £50-£68* **LB PARKING:** 15 **NOTES:** Closed Nov-Feb **CARDS:**

BUDE Map 02 SS20

♦♦♦♦ Bude Haven Hotel & Annabel's Restaurant

Flexbury Av EX23 8NS ☎ 01288 352305 📠 01288 352662
e-mail: enquiries@budehavenhotel.com
Dir: *leave A39 at Bude, through shopping area, past golf course. Flexbury church on right, 1st left, 1st right*

continued

continued

Standing in a quiet area, within easy walking distance of the town centre and Crooklets Beach, this charming Edwardian hotel has recently been totally refurbished. Bedrooms are comfortable, bright and airy. Annabel's Restaurant serves an interesting choice of dishes at dinner. There is also a lounge and bar where guests can relax.
FACILITIES: 11 en suite (1 fmly) No smoking in 4 bedrooms No smoking in dining room No smoking in lounges TVB tea/coffee Direct dial from bedrooms Licensed Cen ht TVL Dinner Last d 9pm **PRICES:** s £25-£35; d £50-£65✳ **LB** **CONF:** Thtr 30 Class 24 Board 24 Del from £60 ✳ **PARKING:** 7 **CARDS:**

♦♦♦♦ Cliff Hotel

Maer Down, Crooklets Beach EX23 8NG
☎ 01288 353110 & 356833 Fax 01288 353110
Dir: *A39 through Bude. Left at top of High street and past Somerfields. 1st right between golf course, straight over X-rd, hotel at end of road*

Located on the clifftop overlooking the sea, this is a friendly and efficiently run hotel with attractive, well-equipped bedrooms. Public areas are numerous and include a bar and lounge in addition to various leisure facilities. An excellent choice of food is offered in the dining room both at dinner and at breakfast.
FACILITIES: 15 en suite (15 fmly) No smoking in dining room TVB tea/coffee Direct dial from bedrooms Licensed Cen ht TVL No coaches Indoor swimming pool (heated) Golf 18 Tennis (hard) Gymnasium Pool Table Putting green Bowling Green,Canal Fishing. Dinner Last d 6pm **PRICES:** s £35.40-£40.20; d £59-£67✳ **LB** **PARKING:** 18 **NOTES:** Closed Nov-March **CARDS:**

♦♦♦♦ Fairway House

8 Downs View EX23 8RF ☎ 01288 355059
e-mail: enquiries@fairwayguesthouse.co.uk
Dir: *Through town, past post office at top of main street. Follow brown tourist signs to Downs View from golf course.*
Genuine hospitality and attentive service await at this delightful Victorian terraced property, which overlooks the golf course and is close to the beach and town centre. Bedrooms are of a high standard, comfortable and with many thoughtful extra facilities. Dinners using quality, fresh ingredients are available by prior arrangement only.
FACILITIES: 7 rms (5 en suite) (1 fmly) No smoking TVB tea/coffee Cen ht TVL Dinner Last d noon **PRICES:** s £20-£30; d £34-£50✳ **LB** **BB**

♦♦♦♦ Seagulls

11 Downs View EX23 8RF ☎ 01288 352059 Fax 01288 359259
e-mail: contactus@seagullsguesthouse.co.uk
Dir: *off A39, at mini rdbt right to Bude town centre. Up hill, and pass golf course. 1st left at bottom of hill, then left again into Downs View, Seagulls on right*
FACILITIES: 6 rms (5 en suite) (1 fmly) No smoking TVB tea/coffee No dogs (ex guide dogs) Licensed Cen ht TVL No coaches **PRICES:** s £16-£25; d £36-£50✳ **LB** **BB** **NOTES:** Closed 24-26 Dec **CARDS:**

♦♦♦ Pencarrol

21 Downs View EX23 8RF ☎ 01288 352478
Dir: *turn off A39 to town centre follow signs to Crooklets Beach, Downs View Road is ahead at beach car park exit*
This cosy guest house is only a short walk from both the town centre and the beach, and benefits from glorious views over the golf course. Bedrooms are comfortable, attractively furnished and decorated. Breakfast is served at separate tables in the dining room and an attractive lounge is provided on the first floor.
FACILITIES: 7 rms (4 en suite) (2 fmly) (2 GF) No smoking TVB tea/coffee No dogs Cen ht TVL No coaches **PRICES:** s £16-£20; d £36-£44✳ **LB** **BB** **NOTES:** Closed Xmas

CALLINGTON — Map 02 SX36

♦♦♦ Dozmary

Tors View Close, Tavistock Rd PL17 7DY ☎ 01579 383677
e-mail: dozmarybb@aol.com
Dir: *from Callington town centre traffic lights, take A390 Tavistock Rd, left turning after 300yds into Tors View Close by 40mph sign*
A warm welcome is offered to guests at this deceptively spacious, dormer bungalow, located on the outskirts of town. In the well-equipped bedrooms, the best possible use has been made of the available space. Two rooms are located on the ground floor. A comfortable lounge/dining room overlooking the garden is provided for guests.
FACILITIES: 3 en suite (1 fmly) (2 GF) No smoking TVB tea/coffee No dogs (ex guide dogs) Cen ht No coaches **PRICES:** s £20-£21; d £34-£36✳ **LB** **BB** **PARKING:** 4 **NOTES:** Closed 22 Dec-2 Jan

♦♦♦ Green Pastures Bed & Breakfast

Longhill PL17 8AU ☎ 01579 382566
e-mail: greenpast@aol.com
Dir: *0.5m E of Callington on A390 to Tavistock*
Located on the southern side of Kit Hill, the property enjoys panoramic views across the Tamar Valley with distant views of Dartmoor. This modern bungalow is situated in five acres of land where Shetland ponies graze. Bedrooms are comfortably furnished and there is a large lounge in which guests may relax.
FACILITIES: 3 en suite (3 GF) No smoking TVB tea/coffee No dogs (ex guide dogs) Cen ht No children No coaches **PRICES:** s £20-£22; d £37-£44✳ **LB** **BB** **PARKING:** 8

♦♦♦ Penpill Farmhouse

near Stoke Climsland PL17 8QE ☎ 01579 370540
Fax 01579 371142
e-mail: penpill@btinternet.com
Dir: *on A388 6m S of Launceston, 2m on left past village of Treburley*
Set in a delightful rural location mid-way between Plymouth and Launceston and between Dartmoor and Bodmin Moor this charming stone farmhouse, with its wealth of beams, flagstone floors and an inglenook fireplace is also well placed for the Duchy Agricultural College. Country-style home cooked dinners, using fresh ingredients, are available by prior arrangement.
FACILITIES: 4 en suite (1 fmly) No smoking in bedrooms No smoking in dining room TVB tea/coffee No dogs (ex guide dogs) Licensed No coaches Dinner Last d 6pm **PRICES:** s £30; d £40✳ **LB** **PARKING:** 8

Smoking restrictions appear under the **FACILITIES** heading, please check when booking.

England

CAMELFORD Map 02 SX18

♦♦♦♦ Pendragon House

Davidstow PL32 9XR ☎ 01840 261131 📠 01840 261131
e-mail: john1pendragonho@aol.com
Dir: *Turn off A30 onto A395 Pendragon House is 9.5m on right*

Set in one and a half acres of well-tended gardens and grounds, and with glorious views across both Bodmin Moor and Dartmoor, this former Victorian rectory was originally built for the Bishop of Truro. Guests are welcomed as friends; and comfortable bedrooms are stylishly furnished and well-equipped.

FACILITIES: 4 en suite No smoking TVB tea/coffee No dogs (ex guide dogs) Cen ht TVL No children 10yrs No coaches Croquet lawn **PRICES:** s £23; d £46-£50* **PARKING:** 11 **NOTES:** Closed Dec-Jan **CARDS:**

♦♦♦ Silvermoon

Ln End PL32 9LE ☎ 01840 213736 📠 01840 213736
e-mail: silvermoonbandb-jennymetters@hotmail.com
Dir: *from A30 at Launceston take A395 then A39 towards Camelford turn right at 1st X-rds into Lane End, 2nd property on right*

Located at the edge of the town and within easy reach of Bodmin Moor, Tintagel Castle and the numerous moor and coastal walks around the area, Silvermoon provides guests with an ideal location from which to explore the vicinity and cyclists and walkers are welcome. Bedrooms are comfortable and well-equipped with two conveniently located on the ground floor.

FACILITIES: 3 en suite (2 GF) No smoking TVB tea/coffee No dogs (ex guide dogs) Cen ht TVL No children **PRICES:** s £22-£24; d £44-£48* **PARKING:** 5

CRACKINGTON HAVEN Map 02 SX19

♦♦♦ Coombe Barton

EX23 0JG ☎ 01840 230345 📠 01840 230788
e-mail: info@coombebartoninn.com
Dir: *turn off A39 at Wainhouse corner continue down lane to beach*

continued

Enjoying an enviable position overlooking the beach and surrounded by rugged cliffs, this long established, family run inn is popular with locals and visitors alike. An impressive range of Cornish real ales is a feature and a large selection of meals is available. The Sunday carvery is especially popular and booking is advisable. Bedrooms are attractive, comfortable and well equipped.

FACILITIES: 6 rms (3 en suite) (1 fmly) No smoking in 2 bedrooms No smoking in area of dining room No smoking in 1 lounge TV4B tea/coffee No dogs (ex guide dogs) Cen ht TVL Pool Table Dinner Last d 9.30pm **PRICES:** s £25-£30; d £50-£80* **LB MEALS:** Lunch £12.50-£18alc Dinner £12.50-£18alc* **PARKING:** 40 **NOTES:** Closed Nov-Feb **CARDS:**

CRANTOCK Map 02 SW76

♦♦♦ Carrek Woth

West Pentire Rd TR8 5SA ☎ 01637 830530 📠 01637 830086
Dir: *Take Crantock road off A3075 and go through Crantock. Carrek Woth is on way to Pentire*

Enjoying spectacular views across Crantock Bay and Goose Rock (from which Carrek Woth takes its Cornish name) this friendly home has been welcoming guests for years, and many return on a regular basis. Bedrooms are comfortably furnished, some on the ground floor and a number enjoying pleasant views. The bar offers local wines and ciders and fresh local produce is provided in the popular dining room.

FACILITIES: 10 en suite (3 fmly) (5 GF) No smoking in dining room No smoking in 1 lounge TVB tea/coffee Licensed Cen ht No coaches Dinner Last d 3pm **PRICES:** s fr £29.50; d fr £47* **LB PARKING:** 10

FALMOUTH Map 02 SW83

Premier Collection

♦♦♦♦♦ Dolvean Hotel

50 Melvill Rd TR11 4DQ ☎ 01326 313658 📠 01326 313995
e-mail: reservations@dolvean.co.uk
Dir: *on main road to Pendennis Castle & docks*

continued

This fine Victorian house, built as a gentleman's residence, is appropriately furnished to reflect its history and also features a collection of antique sewing machines. The attractive bedrooms are individually decorated, have comfortable beds and many thoughtful extras. There is an inviting lounge and delicious home-cooked breakfasts are served in the spacious dining room at individual tables.
FACILITIES: 11 en suite (3 GF) No smoking TVB tea/coffee No dogs (ex guide dogs) Licensed Cen ht TVL No children 12yrs No coaches **PRICES:** s £30-£40; d £55-£70✱ **LB PARKING:** 11 **CARDS:**

♦♦♦♦ Prospect House

1 Church Rd, Penryn TR10 8DA ☎ 01326 373198
📠 01326 373198
e-mail: prospecthouse@cornwall-selectively.co.uk
Dir: *turn off A39 at Treluswell rdbt onto B3292, past pub & through lights, after 50m turn right through white gates next to phone box*

Situated close to the waterside and set in pleasant grounds, Prospect House is an attractive building, which was built for a ship's captain around 1820. The original style and charm of the house has been carefully maintained. The bedrooms are attractively decorated and well equipped. A comfortable lounge is available and freshly cooked breakfasts are served in the elegant dining room.
FACILITIES: 4 rms (3 en suite) No smoking in bedrooms No smoking in dining room TVB tea/coffee Cen ht TVL No coaches **PRICES:** s £25-£35; d £55-£60✱ **LB PARKING:** 4 **CARDS:**

♦♦♦♦ Cotswold House Hotel

Melvill Rd TR11 4DF ☎ 01326 312077 📠 01326 319181
e-mail: ellis@cotswoldhousehotel.fsnet.co.uk
Dir: *A39 into Falmouth, follow signs for docks, beaches & Princess Pavillion. Hotel on right*
This smart Victorian house enjoys splendid views of the sea and is conveniently located a short walk from the town. The enthusiastic proprietors offer friendly and attentive service, whilst the dining room offers freshly cooked local produce. A bar and comprehensive wine list are available.
FACILITIES: 10 en suite (2 fmly) (1 GF) No smoking in 8 bedrooms No smoking in dining room No smoking in lounges TVB tea/coffee No dogs Licensed Cen ht TVL Dinner Last d 6.30pm **PRICES:** s £28-£32; d £56-£68 **LB PARKING:** 10 **CARDS:**

♦♦♦♦ Gayhurst

10 Pennance Rd TR11 4EA ☎ 01326 315161
e-mail: jfjgriffin@hotmail.com
Dir: *follow signs to beaches. At end of Western Terrace turn right at mini rndbt onto Pennance Rd. Gayhurst 100yds on right*
The friendly proprietors here at Gayhurst offer a warm welcome to guests, old and new. Their attractive home is located in a quiet residential area, yet close to the beaches and within easy strolling distance of the town centre. Spacious and comfortable rooms are provided, some with sea views. Breakfast is served in the bright dining room, which overlooks the attractive garden.
FACILITIES: 8 en suite (1 fmly) (2 GF) No smoking TVB tea/coffee No dogs (ex guide dogs) No children 5yrs **PRICES:** s £23-£30; d £40-£46✱ **PARKING:** 8 **NOTES:** Closed Nov-Etr

♦♦♦♦ Ivanhoe

7 Melvill Rd TR11 4AS ☎ 01326 319083 📠 01326 319083
e-mail: ivanhoe@enterprise.net
Dir: *on road leading to Pendennis Castle, docks and beaches, just before the Falmouth Hotel on the right*
A genuinely warm welcome is assured at this charming Edwardian guest house, which is conveniently located within walking distance of the town centre and the beaches. Bedrooms are generously equipped with practical extras as guest comfort is a priority here. The bright, cheerily decorated breakfast room provides an uplifting venue for the varied breakfast menu, which incorporates organic produce where possible.
FACILITIES: 6 rms (4 en suite) (1 fmly) (1 GF) No smoking TVB tea/coffee No dogs (ex guide dogs) Cen ht TVL No children 5yrs No coaches **PRICES:** s £20-£24; d £48-£54✱ **LB PARKING:** 4

♦♦♦♦ Melvill House Hotel

52 Melvill Rd TR11 4DQ ☎ 01326 316645 📠 01326 211608
e-mail: enquiries@melvill.eurobell.co.uk
Dir: *follow signs for Town Centre, Beaches & Docks, then Beaches & Docks via Dracaena Ave & Western Terrace, 1st hotel on the left in Melvill Rd*
Close to the beach, harbour and town centre Melvill House provides comfortable bedrooms, some with four-poster beds. Freshly prepared meals (dinner by prior arrangement) are a feature of the house, as is the friendly atmosphere.
FACILITIES: 7 en suite (2 fmly) (1 GF) No smoking TVB tea/coffee No dogs Licensed Cen ht TVL No coaches Dinner Last d Previous day **PRICES:** s £20-£26; d £40-£52✱ **LB PARKING:** 9 **NOTES:** Closed 23-27 Dec **CARDS:**

♦♦♦♦ Rosemary Private Hotel

22 Gyllyngvase Ter TR11 4DL ☎ 01326 314669
e-mail: rosemaryhotel@lineone.net
Dir: *A39 Melvill Rd signposted to beaches & seafront, right into Gyllyngvase Rd, then 1st left into Gyllyngvase Terrace*
Enjoying splendid views of Gyllyngvase beach from many rooms, this hotel is conveniently located for the town and harbour. Bedrooms are very well appointed, with comfortable furnishings and pleasant decor. Breakfast (and dinner in the summer) is taken in the smart dining room and guests can relax in the bar, comfortable lounge or pleasant garden.
FACILITIES: 10 en suite (2 fmly) No smoking in bedrooms No smoking in dining room TVB tea/coffee No dogs Licensed Cen ht TVL Dinner Last d 1pm **PRICES:** s fr £25; d fr £50✱ **LB PARKING:** 3 **NOTES:** Closed Nov-Dec rs May-Sept **CARDS:**

England

FALMOUTH continued

♦♦♦♦ Rosemullion Private Hotel

Gyllyngvase Hill TR11 4DF ☎ 01326 314690 📠 01326 210098
e-mail: gail@rosemullionhotel.demon.uk

This pleasant, friendly hotel is recognisable by its mock-Tudor exterior. Bedrooms, some on the ground floor, are comfortably furnished. Service and hospitality are a strong point here and guests are assured of a warm welcome and pleasant stay. Breakfast, served in the panelled dining room, is freshly cooked; and guests can relax in the well-appointed and comfortable lounge.
FACILITIES: 13 rms (11 en suite) (3 GF) No smoking TVB tea/coffee No dogs Cen ht No children No coaches **PRICES:** d £45-£57✱ **LB** **PARKING:** 18 **NOTES:** Closed 23-27 Dec

♦♦♦♦ Westcott Hotel

Gyllyngvase Hill TR11 4DN ☎ 01326 311309 📠 01326 311124
Dir: *A39 from Truro to Falmouth. Gyllyngvase Hill on right 600 yds before Princess Pavillion*
Close to Gyllyngvase beach and within walking distance of the town centre and attractions, this hotel provides a pleasant base from which to explore the region. Bedrooms, some of which have sea views, are comfortably furnished and well equipped. Fresh produce is served at dinner and breakfast in the spacious and airy dining room.
FACILITIES: 10 en suite No smoking TVB tea/coffee Licensed Cen ht TVL No children 16yrs Dinner Last d noon **PRICES:** s £22-£26.50; d £44-£53✱ **LB** **PARKING:** 8

♦♦♦ Clearwater

59 Melvill Rd TR11 4DF ☎ 01326 311344
e-mail: clearwater@lineone.net
Dir: *follow signs to main beaches and castle, straight over rdbt beside Green Lawns Hotel into Melvill Rd, on right after Fox Rosehill Gardens*
Situated close to the waterfront, beaches and town centre, this bright and stylish house provides comfortable accommodation. Ideal as a base for sporting enthusiasts, drying facilities are available for divers, sailors, walkers and cyclists. Freshly cooked breakfasts are served in the large dining room at separate tables.
FACILITIES: 10 rms (6 en suite) (2 fmly) (1 GF) No smoking in bedrooms No smoking in dining room TVB tea/coffee No dogs Licensed Cen ht **PRICES:** s £20-£25; d £40-£54✱ **PARKING:** 10 **NOTES:** Closed Xmas & New Year **CARDS:**

♦♦♦ Penwarren

3 Avenue Rd TR11 4AZ ☎ 01326 314216 📠 01326 314216
e-mail: penwarren@tinyworld.co.uk
An ideal base for the town centre, Gyllyngvase beach and other local attractions, Penwarren offers a very warm welcome. Bedrooms are comfortably furnished and well equipped. Breakfast is taken in the spacious dining room and there is also a cosy lounge for guest use. Ample off road parking is a bonus.
FACILITIES: 7 rms (6 en suite) (1 fmly) No smoking TVB tea/coffee Cen ht No coaches **PRICES:** s £19-£20; d £42-£44✱ **LB BB** **PARKING:** 10 **CARDS:**

♦♦♦ *Springfield*

69 Melvill Rd TR11 4DE ☎ 01326 311768
Dir: *opposite Fox Rosehill Gardens*
This secluded detached bungalow is an enchanting hideaway, which can justly lay claim to some of the best gardens in the area, as officially recognised by Britain in Bloom! The ground floor bedrooms are neatly furnished and decorated, and the annexe suite has its own sitting room. Breakfast is served in the conservatory-style dining room and enjoys views over the award winning garden.
FACILITIES: 2 en suite (1 fmly) No smoking TVB tea/coffee No dogs (ex guide dogs) Cen ht No children 5yrs No coaches **PARKING:** 3 **NOTES:** Closed Nov-Feb

♦♦♦ *Tregenna*

28 Melvill Rd TR11 4AR ☎ 01326 313881
e-mail: streggenna@aol.com
Dir: *A39 for Falmouth and the docks, 50 metres from the Princess Pavilion on right*
Conveniently located for the town centre and beaches Tregenna is a well run and welcoming home. A combined lounge/dining-room is available where freshly prepared breakfasts are served at individual tables. Guest rooms, some with views over the harbour, are comfortable and attractively decorated.
FACILITIES: 7 rms (5 en suite) (3 fmly) No smoking in 3 bedrooms No smoking in dining room No smoking in 1 lounge TVB tea/coffee Licensed Cen ht TVL No coaches **PARKING:** 8

FOWEY — Map 02 SX15

♦♦♦♦ Carnethic House

Lambs Barn PL23 1HQ ☎ 01726 833336 📠 01726 833296
e-mail: carnethic@btinternet.com
Dir: *off A3082, directly opposite 'Welcome to Fowey' sign*

A warm and friendly atmosphere awaits at this charming Regency house, situated in delightful gardens close to the seaside town of Fowey. Bedrooms are comfortable and spacious. The lounge benefits from a well stocked bar and fresh, enjoyable dinners, using local produce, are available in the dining room.
FACILITIES: 10 en suite (3 fmly) No smoking in bedrooms No smoking in dining room TVB tea/coffee Licensed Cen ht No coaches Outdoor swimming pool (heated) Tennis (grass) Croquet lawn Putting green Badminton, Bowls, Golf practice net, Dinner Last d 9pm **PRICES:** s £40-£55; d £75-£95✱ **LB** **PARKING:** 20 **NOTES:** Closed Dec-Jan **CARDS:**

♦♦♦♦ *King of Prussia*

Town Quay PL23 1AT ☎ 01726 832450 📠 01726 832450
(St Austell Brewery)
This atmospheric inn takes its name from an infamous local smuggler who operated around the nearby Prussia Cove. The cosy bedrooms, with modern en suite facilities, all enjoy wonderful

continued

estuary views and have tastefully co-ordinated decor. Good home-cooked meals and snacks are available in the convivial bar and hearty breakfasts are served in the dining room.
FACILITIES: 6 en suite (4 fmly) No smoking in bedrooms No smoking in dining room No smoking in lounges TVB tea/coffee No dogs (ex guide dogs) Cen ht No coaches Dinner Last d 9.30pm **CARDS:**

♦♦♦♦ *Trevanion*
70 Lostwithiel St PL23 1BQ ☎ 01726 832602 📠 01726 832602
e-mail: trefoy@globalnet.co.uk
Dir: *exit A390 onto B3269 signposted for Fowey, on descending the hill premises situated 200mtrs past turning for main car park*
A warm and genuine welcome is assured at this 16th-century merchant's house, conveniently located within easy walking distance of this historic town. The well equipped, comfortable bedrooms are decorated with pretty co-ordinated fabrics and the elegant dining room retains many original features. Hearty cooked breakfasts and alternatives are offered.
FACILITIES: 3 rms (2 en suite) (1 fmly) No smoking TVB tea/coffee No dogs (ex guide dogs) Cen ht No children 12yrs No coaches
PARKING: 3 **NOTES:** Closed Nov-Feb

GORRAN — Map 02 SW94

Tregerrick Farm B & B
PL26 6NF ☎ 01726 843418
At the time of going to press the Diamond classification for this establishment had not been confirmed. Please check the AA website www.theAA.com for up-to-date information.
FACILITIES: 2 en suite

GRAMPOUND — Map 02 SW94

♦♦♦ Perran House
Fore St TR2 4RS ☎ 01726 882066 📠 01726 882936
e-mail: perran.house@faxvia.net
Dir: *on A390 between St Austell and Truro*
Dating back to the 17th century, Perran House offers modern, comfortable accommodation. Rooms are brightly decorated and have pleasant co-ordinated fabrics. A short drive from both the Eden Project and Lost Gardens of Heligan, this is an ideal base from which to explore the area.
FACILITIES: 6 rms (3 en suite) No smoking TVB tea/coffee No dogs (ex guide dogs) Cen ht No coaches **PRICES:** s £17-£18; d £38-£40* **LB BB**
PARKING: 8 **CARDS:**

HARLYN BAY — Map 02 SW87

♦♦♦ Polmark Hotel
PL28 8SB ☎ 01841 520206 📠 01841 520206
e-mail: reception@polmarkhotel.co.uk
Dir: *off A30 towards St Mawgan (Newquay) airport, at rdbt exit for Wadebridge, next rdbt exit for Padstow on this road 5th exit left B3276 towards St Merryn, in 1.5m pass through village of Windmill next right to Harlyn pass beach Polmark 200yds on left*
Friendly service is offered at this extended 1920s Cornish stone property, just a short walk from the beautiful beach at Harlyn Bay. Bedrooms are well equipped, ranging from rooms in the original house to new bedrooms in a purpose-built wing.
FACILITIES: 5 en suite 8 en suite annexe (2 fmly) (5 GF) No smoking in dining room TVB tea/coffee Direct dial from bedrooms Licensed Cen ht TVL No coaches Outdoor swimming pool (heated) Pool Table Dinner Last d 6pm
PARKING: 20 **NOTES:** Closed Oct-Etr **CARDS:**

HAYLE — Map 02 SW53

♦♦♦♦ Beckside Cottage
Treeve Ln, Connor Downs TR27 5BN ☎ 01736 756751
e-mail: aa@becksidecottage.demon.co.uk
Dir: *A30 westbound to rdbt outskirts Hayle, 4th exit signed Hayle, in 100yds double mini rdbt, exit Portreath/Gwithian, in 0.5m at fork into Treeve Lane*
This 200-year-old cottage has been sympathetically restored to offer high standards of comfort, quality and a truly genuine welcome. Taking its name from the stream running through the garden, the house is opposite a nature reserve, and rare butterflies may often be seen. Advance bookings only, please.
FACILITIES: 2 en suite No smoking TVB tea/coffee No dogs Cen ht TVL No children 10yrs No coaches **PRICES:** d £45-£55* **PARKING:** 2

♦♦♦ Calize Country House
Prosper Hill, Gwithian TR27 5BW ☎ 01736 753268
📠 01736 753268
e-mail: calizebb@talk21.com
Dir: *B3301 (Hayle to Portreath), R in Gwithian at Pendarves Arms pub. House 350yds up hill on left*

Dating from the 1870s this house has splendid views across the countryside towards St Ives Bay and Godrevy Lighthouse. Ideally located for the beaches and coves of West Penrith, for walking, bird watching or as a base from which to visit the many gardens throughout the area. Calaize Country House is spacious and comfortable and the proprietors create a friendly and attentive atmosphere at their family home.
FACILITIES: 5 rms (3 en suite) No smoking tea/coffee Cen ht TVL No children 10yrs No coaches **PRICES:** s £26-£40; d £38-£46* **BB**
PARKING: 5

HELSTON — Map 02 SW62

♦♦♦♦ Colvennor Farmhouse *(SW683219)*
Cury TR12 7BJ ☎ 01326 241208 Mrs J Royds
e-mail: colvennor@aol.com
Dir: *A3083 Helston-Lizard, across rdbt at end of Airfield, next right to Cury/Poldhu Cove, follow road for 1.4m, farm on right at top of hill*
Quietly located in an acre of grounds, this Grade II listed former farmhouse is a charming base from which to explore the countryside, and is only a mile and a half from the nearest beach. Dating back to the 17th century the house offers comfort, modern facilities and a warm and friendly welcome.
FACILITIES: 3 en suite (1 GF) No smoking TVB tea/coffee No dogs Cen ht No children 10yrs **PRICES:** s £28-£30; d £42-£50* **LB**
PARKING: 4 **NOTES:** Closed 16 Dec-31 Jan

Places with this symbol are farmhouses.

England

HESSENFORD Map 02 SX35

♦♦♦ *Copley Arms*

PL11 3HJ ☎ 01503 240209

Dir: *From Plymouth, L off A38 at Trerulefoot rdbt towards Looe. Follow signs for Hessenford - inn is approx 2m on R. (St Austell Brewery)*

This popular village inn is just a short drive from Plymouth and provides an ideal base from which to explore East Cornwall. An extensive menu incorporates daily specials with al fresco dining popular on sunny summer evenings.

FACILITIES: 5 annexe en suite (1 fmly) No smoking in bedrooms No smoking in area of dining room STV TVB tea/coffee No dogs (ex guide dogs) Cen ht Pool Table Dinner Last d 9.15pm **PARKING:** 40
CARDS:

See advertisement on opposite page

LAUNCESTON Map 02 SX38

Premier Collection

♦♦♦♦♦ Stenhill Farm

North Petherwin PL15 8NN ☎ 01566 785686
01566 785686
e-mail: e.reddock@btinternet.com

Dir: *leave A30 at exit for Launceston, go 3/4 way round rdbt to go under A30 bridge. Follow signs for Bude & Tamar Otter Park, establishment 0.5m before Otter Park on left*

The perfect place for a relaxing break, Stenhill is set in 40 acres of grounds, gardens and farmland. This 500-year-old Devon long house has been lovingly restored, with authentic features - slate floors, oak beams and granite fireplaces - expertly retained. Bedrooms are beautifully decorated, some feature ornate four-poster beds. When possible, home-grown and local ingredients are included in breakfast (and dinner, by arrangement). Your hosts Phyllis and Eric will ensure your stay is a memorable one.

FACILITIES: 4 en suite No smoking TVB tea/coffee No dogs (ex guide dogs) Cen ht No children No coaches Fishing Croquet lawn Putting green Dinner Last d noon **PRICES:** d £58-£78* **PARKING:** 40

♦♦♦♦ Hurdon *(SX333828)*

PL15 9LS ☎ 01566 772955 Mrs M Smith

Dir: *leave A30 at 1st Launceston exit (A388), at rdbt take exit for Hospital, 2nd right signposted Trebullett, premises 1st on right*

Good-natured hospitality is assured at this delightful 18th-century granite farmhouse. The comfortable bedrooms are individually furnished and decorated and equipped with numerous extra facilities. Delicious dinners use only the best local produce, and are available by prior arrangement. Watch out for the home-made puddings and the farm-fresh clotted cream. Margaret Smith was a Top Twenty Finalist in the AA Landlady of the Year Award 2002-2003.

FACILITIES: 6 en suite (1 fmly) (2 GF) No smoking TVB tea/coffee No dogs (ex guide dogs) Cen ht TVL 400 acres mixed Dinner Last d 4.30pm **PRICES:** s £21-£25; d £42-£50* **PARKING:** 10 **NOTES:** Closed Nov-Apr

See advertisement on opposite page

♦♦♦♦ Tyne Wells House

Pennygillam PL15 7EE ☎ 01566 775810
e-mail: btucker@IC24.net

Dir: *A30 S, exit off dual carriageway left tp Launceston, 200mtrs to Pennygillam rdbt. Entrance to house directly off rdbt by B3254 exit*

Tyne Wells House enjoys panoramic views over the countryside. A relaxed and friendly atmosphere prevails and the cosy bedrooms are neatly furnished and well equipped. A hearty breakfast is served around a communal table in the dining room with evening meals available by prior arrangement.

continued

Tyne Wells House

FACILITIES: 3 en suite No smoking TVB tea/coffee No dogs (ex guide dogs) Cen ht No coaches Dinner Last d 11am **PRICES:** s £22-£27; d £40-£46* **LB** **PARKING:** 4

Withnoe Farm

Tavistock Rd PL15 9LG ☎ 01566 772523 & 07790 063975

At the time of going to press the Diamond classification for this establishment had not been confirmed. Please check the AA website www.theAA.com for up-to-date information.

FACILITIES: 3 rms (2 en suite) (1 fmly)

LELANT Map 02 SW53

♦♦♦♦ Badger

TR26 3JT ☎ 01736 752181 01736 759398
e-mail: www.marybadgerinn@aol.com

Dir: *take A3074 from Hayle by-pass towards St Ives, The Badger Inn in Lelant centre on right*

Conveniently situated for St Ives, this long-established inn offers good quality, spacious accommodation and a convivial atmosphere. A good selection of local produce is served in the restaurant and bar, including fresh seafood dishes and home-made puddings. An attractive patio and garden complete the picture, with al fresco dining popular in the summer.

FACILITIES: 6 en suite No smoking in dining room TVB tea/coffee Direct dial from bedrooms No dogs (ex guide dogs) Cen ht No children 12yrs No coaches Reduced fees at local golf course Dinner Last d 10.15pm **PRICES:** s £45-£50; d £65-£70* **PARKING:** 100 **CARDS:**

Super supper! this symbol shows that evening meals exceeded our Inspector's expectations.

LISKEARD Map 02 SX26

♦♦♦♦ Trecarne House

Penhale Grange, St Cleer PL14 5EB ☎ 01579 343543
📠 01579 343543
e-mail: trish@trecarnehouse.co.uk
Dir: *leave A38 at Liskeard onto A390 then B3254. Continue to St Cleer. Right at post office, 3rd left after church, 2nd right, house on the right*

A warm and friendly welcome awaits you at this large family home which is peacefully located on the edge of the village. The stylish, spacious bedrooms enjoy magnificent uninterrupted country views, and in addition to the exposed pine floors offer many thoughtful extras. A wide choice is available from the buffet-style breakfast which is taken in the dining room and sun-filled conservatory overlooking rolling countryside. Conveniently situated for the Eden Project.
FACILITIES: 3 en suite (2 fmly) No smoking TVB tea/coffee No dogs (ex guide dogs) Cen ht TVL No coaches table tennis, trampoline, small snooker table **PRICES:** s £40-£50; d £55-£66* **LB PARKING:** 6

♦♦♦♦ Tregondale *(SX294643)*

Menheniot PL14 3RG ☎ 01579 342407 📠 01579 342407
Mrs S Rowe
e-mail: tregondale@connectfree.co.uk
Dir: *E of Liskeard. Exit A38 for Menheriot at Hayloft Rest. 1.5m, through village, 1m left at junct. Signs on right. From A390 follow signs to Menheniot*
Located in a valley and surrounded by 210 acres of farmland, this working farm offers comfortable, individually decorated bedrooms with many thoughtful extras. Delicious meals, using homegrown produce, are served in the bright airy dining room. A conservatory and a lounge, with a log fire, are also provided for guests, as well as a tennis court and farm walks.
FACILITIES: 3 en suite No smoking TVB tea/coffee No dogs Cen ht TVL No children 2yrs Tennis (hard) Fishing Cycling, routes and maps avaliable 200 acres arable beef mixed sheep Dinner Last d 6pm **PRICES:** s fr £30; d £50-£56* **LB PARKING:** 3 **CARDS:**

♦♦♦ Elnor

1 Russell St PL14 4BP ☎ 01579 342472 📠 01579 345673
e-mail: elnor@btopenworld.com
Dir: *Turn off A38 from Plymouth and follow town centre, Elnor Guest house is on the right hand side opposite the Dairy Centre*
This well established guest house is located close to the town centre and railway station and is just a short drive from Bodmin Moor and other places of interest. Bedrooms are neatly presented and a guest lounge is also available.
FACILITIES: 6 rms (4 en suite) 3 annexe en suite (3 fmly) (4 GF) No smoking in 7 bedrooms No smoking in dining room TVB tea/coffee Direct dial from bedrooms No dogs (ex guide dogs) Licensed Cen ht TVL No coaches **PRICES:** s £20-£23; d £40-£46* **PARKING:** 8

England

LIZARD — Map 02 SW71

♦♦♦♦ *Penmenner House Hotel*

Penmenner Rd TR12 7NR ☎ 01326 290370

Dir: *at Helston take A3083 to Lizard Town, R at green in village centre by Top House pub. Follow rd to sea, last house on R*

Interesting history and tales abound at this Victorian house, splendidly located in a superb coastal setting. A friendly welcome is assured and bedrooms, some of which have magnificent sea views, are comfortably furnished and equipped with modern facilities. Excellent home cooked dinners, by arrangement, feature fresh and local ingredients.

FACILITIES: 6 rms (5 en suite) No smoking TVB tea/coffee Licensed Cen ht No coaches Dinner Last d 4pm **PARKING:** 10 **CARDS:**

LOOE — Map 02 SX25

Premier Collection

♦♦♦♦♦ St Aubyn's

Marine Dr, Hannafore, West Looe PL13 2DH

☎ 01503 264351 Fax 01503 263670

e-mail: welcome@staubyns.co.uk

Dir: *from Looe Bridge take West Quay road signed Hannafore 0.75m, carry onto Marine Drive, guest house is on right facing sea*

Standing in attractive gardens, this impressive Victorian house has uninterrupted sea views and is well located for the town, fishing harbour and local places of interest. Bedrooms are spacious, comfortable and well equipped with some having access to balconies. There is an elegantly furnished lounge, adjacent to the breakfast room.

FACILITIES: 8 rms (6 en suite) (3 fmly) No smoking TVB tea/coffee No dogs (ex guide dogs) TVL No children 5yrs No coaches **PRICES:** s £26-£28; d £46-£70* **LB PARKING:** 4 **NOTES:** Closed Nov-Etr Civ Wed **CARDS:**

♦♦♦♦ The Beach House

Marine Dr, Hannafore PL13 2DH ☎ 01503 262598

Fax 01503 262298

e-mail: enquiries@thebeachhouselooe.com

Dir: *From Looe town bridge turn left into West Looe Quay, follow road past church to Hannafore, and Marine Drive. At the Tom Sawyer Tavern either continue 50yds to front pedestrian gate or turn right to rear gate and car park.*

Set in a peaceful location, within easy strolling distance of the harbour, restaurants and town, the Beach House has splendid sea views. The charming proprietors provide friendly hospitality and attentive service. Bedrooms are well equipped and offer many extras. Breakfast is taken in the first floor dining room, where fresh appetising dishes provide a hearty start to the day.

continued

The Beach House

FACILITIES: 5 en suite (4 GF) No smoking TVB tea/coffee No dogs Cen ht No children 12yrs No coaches Video in all rooms & free film library **PRICES:** s £30-£47; d £50-£68 **LB PARKING:** 5 **NOTES:** Closed early Nov-mid Feb **CARDS:**

♦♦♦♦ Bucklawren Farm *(SX278540)*

St Martin-by-Looe PL13 1NZ ☎ 01503 240738

Fax 01503 240481 Mrs J Henly

e-mail: bucklawren@compuserve.com

Dir: *from Looe take B3253 to Plymouth. After 2m turn right to Monkey Sanctuary. After 1m turn right to Bucklawren. White farmhouse 0.5m on left*

This spacious 19th-century farmhouse is set in 500 acres of farmland with the beach just a mile away. Bedrooms are tastefully furnished and well equipped. Front-facing rooms enjoy spectacular views across fields to the sea beyond. Evening meals are available in the adjoining Granary Restaurant.

FACILITIES: 6 en suite (3 fmly) No smoking in bedrooms No smoking in dining room No smoking in lounges TVB tea/coffee No dogs (ex guide dogs) Licensed Cen ht TVL No children 5yrs Putting green 500 acres arable/beef Dinner Last d 8.30pm **PRICES:** s £26-£35; d £48-£52* **LB PARKING:** 6 **NOTES:** Closed Dec-Feb **CARDS:**

♦♦♦♦ *Coombe Farm Hotel*

Widegates PL13 1QN ☎ 01503 240223 Fax 01503 240895

e-mail: coombe_farm@hotmail.com

Dir: *on B3253 just S of Widegates village, 3.5m E of Looe*

Set in 10 acres with a heated swimming pool, Coombe Farm provides guests with a warm and friendly place in which to stay. Bedrooms are comfortable and spacious with three rooms located in a converted stone barn. A well-equipped games room is situated in another. Delicious four-course dinners are available by prior arrangement. Martin Eades was a Top Twenty Finalist in the AA Landlady of the Year Award 2002-2003.

FACILITIES: 7 en suite 3 annexe en suite (3 fmly) No smoking STV TVB tea/coffee Direct dial from bedrooms Licensed Cen ht TVL No coaches Outdoor swimming pool (heated) Pool Table Croquet lawn Table tennis Threequarter snooker table Dinner Last d 5pm **PARKING:** 20 **NOTES:** Closed Nov-14 Feb **CARDS:**

♦♦♦♦ Panorama Hotel

Hannafore Rd PL13 2DE ☎ 01503 262123 Fax 01503 265654

e-mail: panorama@looe.co.uk

Dir: *in West Looe overlooking pier & beach*

This splendidly located hotel certainly lives up to its name with spectacular views over the bay and port enjoyed from the comfortable bar and the private balconies of some rooms. All bedrooms are well furnished and equipped with many extra facilities. Dinners are available by prior arrangement during the summer season.

FACILITIES: 10 en suite (4 fmly) No smoking in bedrooms No smoking in dining room TVB tea/coffee No dogs Licensed Cen ht TVL No children 5yrs Dinner Last d 6.30pm **PRICES:** s £25.50-£41; d £46-£77* **LB PARKING:** 7 **CARDS:**

♦♦♦♦ *Trehaven Manor*

Station Rd PL13 1HN ☎ 01503 262028 📠 01503 262028
e-mail: enquiries@trehavenhotel.co.uk
Dir: *A387 onto B3263 at 'Widegates' after bearing left. On approaching Looe, turn left at T-junct, hotel is first driveway after Globe pub*

A charming former rectory, situated in a stunning location with magnificent views of the estuary. The proprietors are friendly and attentive, and many guests return to Trehaven on a regular basis. Many bedrooms have estuary views, and one is on the ground floor, are well equipped and attractively decorated. Breakfast is served in the spacious dining room and provides a memorable start to the day.
FACILITIES: 7 en suite (2 fmly) No smoking TVB tea/coffee No dogs Licensed Cen ht Dinner Last d 8.45pm **PARKING:** 10 **CARDS:**

♦♦♦♦ *Woodlands*

St Martins Rd PL13 1LP ☎ 01503 264405
Dir: *on B3253, 1m from St Martins Church*
This charming Victorian country house has views over the Looe river estuary and surrounding woodland areas and is within walking distance of the harbour and beaches. Bedrooms are cosy and well equipped. Public rooms include a guest lounge in addition to the elegant dining room where dinners are available by prior arrangement.
FACILITIES: 5 rms (4 en suite) No smoking TVB tea/coffee No dogs (ex guide dogs) Licensed Cen ht TVL No children 5yrs No coaches Dinner Last d breakfast **PARKING:** 6 **NOTES:** Closed Dec-Jan **CARDS:**

♦♦♦ Gulls Hotel

Hannafore Rd PL13 2DE ☎ 01503 262531
Dir: *A38 from Plymouth, A387 to Looe, cross bridge from E. Looe to W. Looe, L by river to seafront, turn R by pub & R again*
This friendly, family-run establishment is located in an elevated position with uninterrupted views of both East and West Looe. The bedrooms are neat and attractive. In warmer weather guests can relax on the terrace, and there is a comfortable lounge and cosy bar. Dinner is available by prior arrangement.
FACILITIES: 10 rms (4 en suite) (1 fmly) No smoking TVB tea/coffee Licensed Cen ht TVL No coaches Dinner Last d at breakfast **PRICES:** s £16-£19; d £32-£46* **LB BB PARKING:** 3 **NOTES:** Closed Nov-Etr rs New Years Eve.

Directions are provided by the proprietor, ask for more details when booking.

LOSTWITHIEL Map 02 SX15

♦♦♦♦ *Ship*

Lerryn PL22 0PT ☎ 01208 872374 📠 01208 872614
e-mail: shiplerryn@aol.com
Dir: *3m S off A390 at Lostwithiel*
This 17th century inn is full of traditional character with flagstone floors and beamed ceilings. The bar is well-stocked with traditional ales, malt whiskies and wine. The restaurant offers a range of dishes using local ingredients. Well furnished bedrooms are situated in an adjoining property, with one on the ground floor.
FACILITIES: 4 en suite No smoking in 2 bedrooms No smoking in dining room TVB tea/coffee Cen ht No coaches Pool Table Dinner Last d 9pm
CARDS:

MARAZION Map 02 SW53

♦♦♦ Glenleigh Hotel

Higher Fore St TR17 0BQ ☎ 01736 710308
Dir: *off A394 to Penzance, opposite the Fire Engine Inn*

Enjoying wonderful views towards St Michael's Mount, this proud granite house enjoys an elevated position. The proprietors have owned this welcoming home for more than 25 years and many guests return on a regular basis. Dinners, by prior arrangement, are served in the comfortable dining room and feature fresh and local produce where possible.
FACILITIES: 9 en suite (1 fmly) (1 GF) No smoking in dining room TVB tea/coffee No dogs Licensed Cen ht TVL No children 3yrs No coaches Dinner Last d noon **PRICES:** s £25.50-£26.50; d £51-£53* **LB PARKING:** 10 **NOTES:** Closed Nov-late Mar

MAWNAN SMITH Map 02 SW72

♦♦♦♦ Trevean Bed and Breakfast

Carwinion Rd TR11 5JD ☎ 01326 250100
e-mail: nicola.dugdale@btclick.com
Dir: *on entering village bear left at Red Lion Pub into Carwinion Rd. Trevean up hill on right.*
A warm welcome awaits guests to Trevean, which offers tasteful, recently redecorated accommodation. Set in mature gardens and close to the River Helford, the house is in an Area of Outstanding Natural Beauty. A hearty breakfast featuring fresh Cornish produce can be enjoyed in the comfortable dining room. For peace of mind, off road parking is also available.
FACILITIES: 2 en suite (1 fmly) No smoking TVB tea/coffee Cen ht No coaches **PRICES:** d £40-£58* **LB PARKING:** 3 **CARDS:**

England

MEVAGISSEY Map 02 SX04

♦♦♦♦ Kerryanna *(SX008453)*

Treleaven Farm, Valley Rd PL26 6SA ☎ 01726 843558
01726 843558 Mrs L Hennah
e-mail: linda.hennah@btinternet.com
Dir: *off B3273 on entrance to village, turn right by tennis courts*

Located peacefully on the outskirts of the town, Kerryanna is set in two acres of gardens, benefiting from outstanding views of the village, countryside and the sea. The bedrooms are comfortably furnished, with one room on the ground floor, suitable for the less mobile. A swimming pool is also available to guests.
FACILITIES: 6 en suite (1 fmly) No smoking TVB tea/coffee No dogs Cen ht TVL No children 5yrs Outdoor swimming pool (heated) Snooker Pool Table Putting green Games room 40 acres arable/ non-working **PRICES:** d £50-£60* **LB PARKING:** 7 **NOTES:** Closed Nov-Feb **CARDS:**

♦♦♦♦ Treleaven *(SX008454)*

Valley Rd PL26 6RZ ☎ 01726 842413 01726 842413
Mrs A Hennah
e-mail: stay@treleaven.co.uk
Dir: *turn right at foot of hill when entering Mevagissey, farm lane is between playing park and football pitch.*

Peacefully situated just outside the village, Treleaven enjoys views over the surrounding countryside and Mevagissey to the sea beyond. Bedrooms offer good standards of comfort. There is a licensed bar and the dining room serves an interesting menu featuring local produce. Leisure facilities include an outdoor pool, an 18-hole putting green and a games area in the barn.
FACILITIES: 6 en suite (1 fmly) No smoking TVB tea/coffee No dogs (ex guide dogs) Licensed Cen ht Outdoor swimming pool (heated) Pool Table Croquet lawn Putting green Games room 50 acres mixed Dinner Last d 7pm **PRICES:** d £52-£64* **LB PARKING:** 6 **NOTES:** Closed 15 Dec-7 Jan **CARDS:**

♦♦♦ Headlands Hotel

Polkirt Hill PL26 6UX ☎ 01726 843453 01726 844675
e-mail: headlandshotel@talk21.com
Dir: *follow one-way system through village & ascend towards Port Mellon, hotel on R 1m from village centre*
This charming hotel is set in an elevated position with spectacular views over the bay. The colourful bedrooms are comfortable and well equipped, with many benefiting from sea views. Public rooms include a stylish bar, lounge and dining room. Dinner is available by prior arrangement and offers an interesting selection of dishes.
FACILITIES: 13 rms (11 en suite) (1 fmly) (3 GF) No smoking in 4 bedrooms No smoking in dining room TVB tea/coffee Licensed Cen ht ch fac No coaches Dinner Last d 7pm **PRICES:** s £23; d £56-£60* **LB PARKING:** 10 **CARDS:**

♦♦♦ The Ship

Fore St PL26 6UQ ☎ 01726 843324
01726 844368
Dir: *Turn off A30 onto A391 to St Austell. Then take B3273 to Mevagissey. Ship Inn situated in central square on one way street (St Austell Brewery)*
Located in the centre of this delightful fishing village, the Ship Inn was built over 400 years ago. The popular bar, which has low beamed ceilings, flagstoned floors and a strong nautical feel, offers a choice of menu and blackboard specials. The pine-furnished bedrooms are attractively decorated.
FACILITIES: 5 en suite (2 fmly) No smoking in dining room TVB tea/coffee No dogs (ex guide dogs) Cen ht Dinner Last d 9pm **PRICES:** d £40-£55* **MEALS:** Lunch £4.25-£6.95 Dinner £10-£17* **CARDS:**

MOUSEHOLE Map 02 SW42

♦♦♦ *Ship Inn*

TR19 6QX ☎ 01736 731234 01736 732259
Dir: *follow A30 to Penzance thro Newlyn, L at bridge, follow road into village (St Austell Brewery)*
This smart harbour-side Inn is full of local charm and interest and friendly locals and staff provide a relaxed atmosphere. Bedrooms have views over the harbour and across Mounts bay towards the Lizard peninsula. Fresh Newlyn fish features on the menu in both the restaurant and in the bar.
FACILITIES: 2 en suite TVB tea/coffee No dogs (ex guide dogs) Cen ht Dinner Last d 9pm **CARDS:**

MULLION Map 02 SW61

♦♦♦♦ Alma House

Churchtown TR12 7BZ ☎ 01326 240509
e-mail: almahousehotel@aol.co.uk
Dir: *proceed into Mullion using the one way system and in centre of village turn left and Alma House is 200yds on right*
Alma House is a small privately owned Victorian hotel situated on the edge of the charming village of Mullion. The bedrooms are well presented and have excellent views across Mounts Bay. All are suitably equipped with many modern amenities. There is a well appointed lounge and bar. A choice of menus is offered at dinner, served in the attractive dining room, and Derek Gormley's cooking will not disappoint.
FACILITIES: 4 en suite No smoking in bedrooms No smoking in dining room TVB tea/coffee No dogs (ex guide dogs) Licensed Cen ht TVL No coaches Dinner Last d 9.30pm **PRICES:** s £30-£40; d £50* **LB PARKING:** 20 **CARDS:**

NEWQUAY Map 02 SW86

♦♦♦♦ Colan Barton *(SW867612)*
Colan TR8 4NB ☎ 01637 874395 📠 01637 881388
Mrs A Machin-Weaver
e-mail: colanbarton@yahoo.co.uk
Dir: *take A392 to Newquay. At hamlet of Mountjoy turn 2nd right signed Lady Nance & follow track for 1m, white-washed house on left*
Peace and tranquillity are assured at this 17th-century farmhouse, set in 11 acres and surrounded by lovely Cornish countryside. This non-working farm retains a great deal of character and combines charm and style with modern facilities. Bedrooms have pine furnishings and very comfortable beds. Breakfast features fresh home-produced eggs, local sausages, bacon and honey, and is not to be missed.
FACILITIES: 3 rms (1 en suite) No smoking TVB tea/coffee No dogs Cen ht 11 acres horses, chickens, geese, ducks **PRICES:** s £22-£27; d £34-£50* BB **PARKING:** 5 **NOTES:** Closed Oct-Mar

♦♦♦♦ *Degembris* *(SW852568)*
St Newlyn East TR8 5HY ☎ 01872 510555 📠 01872 510230
Mrs K Woodley
e-mail: kathy@degembris.co.uk
Dir: *from A30 turn left for Summercourt village, at crossroads turn right towards Newquay on A3058, take 3rd left to St Newlyn East, & 2nd left*

Parts of this delightful Grade II listed farmhouse date back to the 16th century. The house has a warm atmosphere and genuine hospitality. Bedrooms, complete with electric blankets, offer comfort, with lovely views across the valley. This is a great base for exploration. Fresh local produce and farmhouse cookery combine to provide pleasant dinners and breakfasts.
FACILITIES: 5 rms (3 en suite) (1 fmly) No smoking TVB tea/coffee No dogs Cen ht TVL Farm trail 165 acres arable Dinner Last d 10am
PARKING: 8 **NOTES:** Closed Xmas **CARDS:**

♦♦♦♦ Kallacliff Hotel
12 Lusty Glaze Rd TR7 3AD ☎ 01637 871704 📠 01637 871704
e-mail: jsavage@madasafish.com
Dir: *from A30 follow A392 signed Newquay. At Quintrell Downs turn right at mini rdbt for A3058 signposted St Columb Minor/Newquay/Porth. Upon reaching Newquay, continue ahead at 2 mini rdbts on A3058. Turn right at sign for hotel.*
Situated in a peaceful area, with stunning views of the Atlantic and coastal walks and beaches on the doorstep. Friendly proprietors provide attentive hospitality, and most of the spacious bedrooms have sea views. Guests can relax in the smart lounge bar while enjoying the views, and in the dining room freshly prepared dishes are offered at breakfast and dinner.
FACILITIES: 9 rms (7 en suite) (3 fmly) No smoking in bedrooms No smoking in dining room TVB tea/coffee No dogs Licensed No coaches Dinner Last d noon **PRICES:** s £18.50-£25; d £37-£50* LB BB
PARKING: 12 **NOTES:** Closed Nov-Mar **CARDS:**

♦♦♦♦ Kellsboro Hotel
12 Henver Rd TR7 3BJ ☎ 01637 874620
e-mail: kellsboro@cornwall-county.com
Dir: *take A30 to Bodmin, at Indian Queens turn right onto A392, via Henver Rd. Hotel on this road*
Conveniently located for the town and beaches, this popular hotel is spacious and comfortable, and offers friendly hospitality. A large bar and games area is provided for guest use and the indoor pool is also popular. Traditional well-cooked dinners are served in the attractive dining room.
FACILITIES: 14 en suite (8 fmly) No smoking in dining room No smoking in 1 lounge TVB tea/coffee Licensed Cen ht TVL Indoor swimming pool (heated) Pool Table Dinner Last d 7pm **PRICES:** s £30-£35; d £50-£60* LB **PARKING:** 25 **NOTES:** Closed Nov-Feb **CARDS:**

♦♦♦♦ Melancoose Mill *(SW861200)*
Colan TR8 4JS ☎ 01637 872811 📠 01637 854254
Mr & Mrs M Westmore
e-mail: westmore@melancoose.freeserve.co.uk
Dir: *A30/A392. At Mountjoy turn right to Colan, at T-junct turn left, follow lane for 2m and take first right. Pass entrance to reservoir, bottom of hill*

This picturesque old mill, with mill-pond and attractive gardens, is believed to date back to the Domesday Book and is now a working stable. Ideal as a base for walking breaks, this well-equipped and spacious house is only four miles from the many and varied attractions of Newquay. Local produce features on the breakfast menu.
FACILITIES: 2 en suite No smoking TVB tea/coffee No dogs (ex guide dogs) Cen ht TVL No children Riding 30 acres horses **PRICES:** s £27.50; d £55* LB **PARKING:** 2 **NOTES:** Closed Xmas

♦♦♦♦ *Pendeen Hotel*

7 Alexandra Rd, Porth TR7 3ND ☎ 01637 873521
🖹 01637 873521
e-mail: info@pendeenhotel.com
Dir: *turn off A30 onto A392 at Quinintrell Inn rdbt right onto A3058 after 2 miles turn right onto B3276 costal road, hotel 0.25m on right*

Pleasantly located opposite Porth beach, and having excellent views of the rugged Cornish coastline, Pendeen is a convenient place to stay. The friendly proprietors provide attentive service and comfortable rooms. In addition a well-stocked bar and lounge enjoy the sea views. Fresh local caught fish features on the menu.
FACILITIES: 15 en suite (2 fmly) No smoking in bedrooms No smoking in dining room TVB tea/coffee No dogs Licensed Cen ht No coaches Dinner Last d 4pm **PARKING:** 15 **CARDS:**

♦♦♦♦ Priory Lodge Hotel

30 Mount Wise TR7 2BN ☎ 01637 874111 🖹 01637 851803
e-mail: fiona@priorylodgehotel.fsnet.co.uk
Dir: *left at traffic lights in town centre onto Berry Rd, right onto Mount Wise B3282. Hotel approx 0.5m on right*
A short stroll from the town centre and beaches, this pleasant hotel offers an impressive range of facilities. Bedrooms, some with balconies and sea views, are spacious and comfortable. A pleasant range of choices, including vegetarian, are available at dinner and in the summer months, entertainment is provided in the bar most evenings.
FACILITIES: 22 rms (20 en suite) 4 annexe en suite (13 fmly) (1 GF) No smoking in 2 bedrooms No smoking in dining room TVB tea/coffee Direct dial from bedrooms No dogs Licensed Cen ht TVL Outdoor swimming pool (heated) Sauna Solarium Pool Table Jacuzzi Video machines Dinner Last d 7.30pm **PRICES:** s £30-£40; d £56-£76✻ **LB PARKING:** 30 **NOTES:** Closed 11-22 Dec, 4 Jan-early Mar rs Nov-Dec (Mon-Fri only) **CARDS:**

♦♦♦♦ Windward Hotel

Alexandra Rd, Porth Bay TR7 3NB ☎ 01637 873185
🖹 01637 873185
e-mail: enquiries@windwardhotel.co.uk
Dir: *approach Newquay on A3508, turn right onto B3276 Padstow rd, hotel 1m on right*

continued

Pleasantly located, close to the airport, and almost set on Porth Beach, Windward has spectacular views. Recently refurbished public areas now offer a terrace bar and conservatory restaurant where an exciting range of dishes featuring fresh local produce is served. Bedrooms, some now with balconies, are comfortable and spacious and are also well equipped.
FACILITIES: 14 en suite (1 fmly) (4 GF) No smoking TVB tea/coffee No dogs Licensed Cen ht TVL Dinner Last d 9pm **PRICES:** s £33-£53; d £48-£78✻ **LB PARKING:** 14 **CARDS:**

♦♦♦ *Hotel Trevalsa*

Whipsiderry Beach, Watergate Rd, Porth TR7 3LX
☎ 01637 873336 🖹 01637 878843
e-mail: graham-stevenson@lineone.net
Dir: *off A30 onto A392 follow signs for Porth Beach. 500 metres up hill, premises immediately on R.*
Pleasantly located and with views of Porth Beach, Trevalsa offers comfortable accommodation. Public rooms include a pleasant lounge and a cosy bar, and entertainment is available throughout the summer months. Bedrooms, many with sea views, are spacious and well equipped.
FACILITIES: 24 rms (20 en suite) (7 fmly) No smoking in 6 bedrooms No smoking in dining room No smoking in 1 lounge TVB tea/coffee Direct dial from bedrooms Licensed Cen ht TVL Dinner Last d 5pm
PARKING: 20 **NOTES:** Closed Nov-Mar **CARDS:** 

♦♦♦ Rolling Waves

Alexandra Rd, Porth TR7 3NB ☎ 01637 873236
🖹 01637 873236
e-mail: enquiries@rollingwaves.co.uk
Dir: *off A30 & join A3059 then onto B3276 into Porth, past beach, opposite pitch and putt on right*

This peaceful hotel is situated in a pleasant area and has an elevated position overlooking Porth Beach and the attractive coastline. The friendly proprietors are most attentive and many guests return to this welcoming and comfortable establishment. Dinner is taken in the bright and airy dining room and guests may relax with a drink from the bar and enjoy the panoramic views.
FACILITIES: 9 rms (8 en suite) (2 fmly) (5 GF) No smoking in 6 bedrooms No smoking in dining room No smoking in lounges TVB tea/coffee Licensed Cen ht TVL Dinner Last d 6pm **PRICES:** s £17-£22; d £38-£50✻ **LB BB PARKING:** 9 **NOTES:** Closed 19 Dec-28 Dec **CARDS:**

♦♦♦ Tir Chonaill Lodge

106 Mount Wise TR7 1QP ☎ 01637 876492
e-mail: tirchonaill@connexions.co.uk
Dir: *Mount Wise signposted from both boating lake rdbts on entering Newquay. Hotel is on Mount Wise above town centre*
Conveniently located close to the beaches and the town centre, the Tir Chonaill Lodge offers modern, spacious accommodation. A

continued

Tir Chonail Lodge Hotel

warm and genuine Celtic welcome, combined with attentive service are provided by the hosts who pride themselves on their home-cooked dinners and appetising breakfasts.
FACILITIES: 22 rms (21 en suite) (10 fmly) (1 GF) No smoking in 2 bedrooms No smoking in dining room TVB tea/coffee Licensed Cen ht TVL Dinner Last d 5pm **PRICES:** s £25-£35; d £50-£70✳ **LB PARKING:** 21 **CARDS:**

♦♦♦ Wenden

11 Berry Rd TR7 1AU ☎ 01637 872604 🖹 01637 872604
e-mail: wenden@newquay-holidays.co.uk
Dir: *take A392 into Newquay, proceed to railway station, with station on left, continue to traffic lights, 2nd on left around corner past lights*
Conveniently located for the beach and the town centre, this family-run guest house offers bright and modern accommodation. The bedrooms are tastefully decorated, and dinner and breakfast are taken in the pleasant conservatory-style dining room.
FACILITIES: 7 en suite No smoking in dining room TVB tea/coffee No dogs (ex guide dogs) Licensed Cen ht No children 16yrs No coaches Dinner Last d 6pm **PRICES:** d £30-£50✳ **LB BB PARKING:** 3 **CARDS:**

PADSTOW — Map 02 SW97

See also St Merryn

Premier Collection

♦♦♦♦♦ Cross House Hotel

Church St PL28 8AT ☎ 01841 532391 🖹 01841 533633
e-mail: info@crosshouse.co.uk
Dir: *turn off A30 onto B3274. Follow signs to Padstow, on reaching town take 3rd right. Follow one way street past church for 50 yds and take sharp left*

Located in the centre of town and within walking distance of the harbour, this charming Georgian property offers comfortable, spacious bedrooms that are stylishly designed

continued

and well-furnished with modern facilities. Two comfortable lounges are provided and the premises are licensed. A choice of full English or continental breakfast is served in the cosy dining room.
FACILITIES: 5 en suite 4 annexe en suite (2 fmly) No smoking in bedrooms No smoking in dining room No smoking in 1 lounge TVB tea/coffee Direct dial from bedrooms No dogs (ex guide dogs) Licensed Cen ht No coaches **PRICES:** d £60-£120✳ **LB PARKING:** 5 **CARDS:**

Premier Collection

♦♦♦♦♦ The Old Cabbage Patch

Trevone Rd, Trevone Bay PL28 8QX ☎ 01841 520956 🖹 01841 520956
e-mail: info@theoldcabbagepatch.co.uk
Dir: *from Padstow, take B3276 for approx 1.5m & turn right into Trevone Bay. Hotel in village centre*
A warm welcome is assured at this delightful, modern bungalow near the centre of Trevone Bay. The well equipped bedrooms are comfortable and stylishly decorated. Hearty, freshly cooked breakfasts are served in the well appointed dining room, which includes a sunny conservatory. An elegant lounge is also available for guests' use.
FACILITIES: 3 en suite No smoking STV TVB tea/coffee No dogs Cen ht No children 15yrs No coaches **PRICES:** d £56-£65✳ **LB PARKING:** 10 **NOTES:** Closed 2 Dec-30 Jan **CARDS:**

Premier Collection

♦♦♦♦♦ St Petroc's Hotel and Bistro

4 New St PL28 8EA ☎ 01841 532700 🖹 01841 532942
e-mail: reservations@rickstein.com
Dir: *A30-A38-A389 towards Padstow, continue 3m, right at T-junc, follow signs to Padstow town centre*
One of the oldest buildings in town, this charming establishment is located just up the hill from the picturesque harbour-side. Style, comfort and individuality are all great strengths here. Both dinner and breakfast reflect a serious approach to cuisine. There are lounges, a reading room and lovely gardens to complete the picture.
FACILITIES: 12 en suite No smoking in dining room TVB tea/coffee Direct dial from bedrooms Licensed Cen ht No coaches Dinner Last d 10pm **PRICES:** d £100-£160✳ **LB CONF:** Thtr 50 Board 18 **PARKING:** 22 **NOTES:** Closed 1 May & 22-27 Dec **CARDS:**

♦♦♦♦ Penjoly Cottage

Padstow Rd PL28 8LB ☎ 01841 533535 🖹 01841 532313
e-mail: penjolypadstow@btopenworld.com
Dir: *From A39 follow Padstow signs until Padstow signpost. Right towards St Issey & Little Petherick. Through St Issey & Little Petherick up hill to t-junct. Right onto A389 in approx 1m sign for Padstow Holiday Park, right just before sign*
Standing within an acre of grounds and approximately one mile from Padstow, this is an ideal location for those looking to explore the enduring beauty of North Cornwall. Attention to detail is a hallmark throughout public areas. Meals are served within the attractive dining room or conservatory, with a separate lounge also available.
FACILITIES: 3 en suite (3 GF) No smoking STV TVB tea/coffee No dogs Cen ht No children 16yrs No coaches Last d 10.30am **PRICES:** s £49.50-£54; d £55-£60✳ **LB PARKING:** 10

England

PADSTOW continued

♦♦♦♦ Roselyn

20 Grenville Rd PL28 8EX ☎ 01841 532756 📠 01841 532756
e-mail: padstowbbroselyn@bushinternet.com
Dir: *after passing 'Welcome to Padstow' sign, Grenville Road is 1st on left with new school on corner*
Situated just ten minutes' walk from the centre of this delightful fishing village, this charming small guest house is located in a quiet residential area and provides guests with smartly furnished and well-equipped bedrooms. The owners offer warm hospitality and a good choice of breakfast options are available.
FACILITIES: 3 en suite (1 fmly) No smoking TVB tea/coffee No dogs Cen ht No coaches **PRICES:** s £30-£35; d £45-£50✻ **LB PARKING:** 5

♦♦♦♦ Trevone Bay Hotel

Dobbin Close, Trevone PL28 8QS ☎ 01841 520243
📠 01841 521195
e-mail: webb@trevonebay.demon.co.uk
Dir: *off A39 onto A389 to Padstow, 0.5m before Padstow, left onto B3276, follow for 0.75m to Windmill, right to Trevone Bay, hotel signed*
Carole and Tony offer a warm welcome to all guests here at Trevone Bay, which is situated in the quiet village, just a short walk from the beach. Bedrooms, some of which enjoy super views of the coastline, are comfortable and practically furnished. Guests have the use of the spacious lounge and conservatory and dinner can be enjoyed in the pleasant dining room.
FACILITIES: 12 en suite (2 fmly) No smoking TVB tea/coffee No dogs (ex guide dogs) Licensed TVL No children 6yrs No coaches Dinner Last d 7.30pm **PRICES:** s £29.50-£35.50; d £51-£71✻ **LB**
PARKING: 12 **NOTES:** Closed end Oct-Feb school hol (open Xmas)
CARDS:

♦♦♦ *Newlands Hotel*

PL28 8QX ☎ 01841 520469
e-mail: newlandsho@aol.com
Dir: *Off B3276 Padstow to Newquay road at windmill. Hotel 100 metres left after village store*
This friendly family hotel, is a short walk from the beautiful sandy beach at Trevone Bay. There are two comfortable lounges and a cosy, well-stocked bar. Imaginative, home-cooked meals are served in the dining room. Bedrooms, some of which are on the ground floor, are light, airy and well equipped.
FACILITIES: 11 rms (10 en suite) (1 fmly) No smoking in dining room No smoking in 1 lounge TVB tea/coffee Licensed Cen ht TVL No children 6yrs No coaches Dinner Last d 4pm **PARKING:** 12 **NOTES:** Closed Nov-Dec rs Jan -Etr **CARDS:**

U Rick Stein's Cafe

Middle St PL28 8BY ☎ 01841 532700
At the time of going to press the Diamond classification for this establishment had not been confirmed. Please check the AA website www.theAA.com for up-to-date information.
FACILITIES: 3 en suite (1 fmly)

PENZANCE — Map 02 SW43

Premier Collection

♦♦♦♦♦ Chy-an-Mor

15 Regent Ter TR18 4DW ☎ 01736 363441
📠 01736 363441
e-mail: mikeandjan@chyanmor.co.uk
Dir: *A30 to Penzance. Follow road to rail station in left lane to Newlyn. Pass harbour, onto promenade, pass Jubilee Pool on left. Right at Stanley Hotel*

continued

Chy-an-Mor

The friendly and attentive hosts at this elegant Grade II listed Georgian house have provided a very comfortable and stylish home. Bedrooms are individually designed, well furnished and equipped with many thoughtful extras. Many have spectacular views of Mount's Bay. The sea views can also be enjoyed from the spacious lounge where guests are welcome to relax. Breakfast is served in the dining room where hearty breakfasts are cooked to order.
FACILITIES: 10 en suite (2 fmly) No smoking TVB tea/coffee No dogs Cen ht No children 10yrs No coaches **PRICES:** s £27.50-£35; d £50-£65✻ **LB PARKING:** 10 **NOTES:** Closed 20 Dec-10 Jan
CARDS:

Premier Collection

♦♦♦♦♦ Ennys Farm *(SW559328)*

Trewhella Ln, St Hilary TR20 9BZ ☎ 01736 740262
📠 01736 740055 Miss G Charlton
e-mail: ennys@ennys.co.uk

(For full entry see St Hilary)

Premier Collection

♦♦♦♦♦ The Summerhouse

Cornwall Ter TR18 4HL ☎ 01736 363744 📠 01736 360959
e-mail: summerhouse@dial.pipex.com
Dir: *enter Penzance on A30 drive along harbour past open air bathing pool follow promenade until Queens hotel, turn right immediately after Queens hotel, Summer house 30mtrs on left*

In a delightful residential location, the Summerhouse is close to the sea front and harbour. Stylishly decorated, the house has a real Mediterranean feel, with warm hospitality, attentive service and the freshest of local and Cornish produce, simply prepared to provide memorable dining from the daily changing menu. The walled garden also sets the scene with

continued

sub-tropical plantings and attractive blue tables and chairs where in warmer evenings dinner and drinks can be served.
FACILITIES: 5 en suite No smoking in bedrooms No smoking in dining room TVB tea/coffee No dogs Licensed Cen ht TVL No children 13yrs No coaches Dinner **PRICES:** s fr £60; d £65-£85* **LB PARKING:** 6 **NOTES:** Closed Jan & Feb **CARDS:**

♦♦♦♦ Blue Seas Hotel
13 Regent Ter TR18 4DW ☎ 01736 364744 📠 01736 330701
e-mail: blueseas@ukonline.co.uk
Dir: *A30, then at Penzance railway station follow road along harbour front in direction of Promenade. Opposite the Jubilee Bathing Pool, Regent Terrace 2nd right*

This comfortable Victorian house has excellent sea views from Mount's Bay towards Mousehole. Convenient for the ferry and Scillies heliport, the Blue Seas is only a short stroll from the centre and attractions. Bedrooms are very well equipped and tastefully decorated, a spacious lounge is provided with books and magazines and guests can also relax in the garden. The freshly prepared breakfast is a real pleasure and features local ingredients and home-made produce.
FACILITIES: 8 rms (7 en suite) (2 fmly) (3 GF) No smoking TVB tea/coffee No dogs (ex guide dogs) Cen ht No coaches **PRICES:** s £20-£24; d £42-£60 **PARKING:** 9 **NOTES:** Closed Dec-Feb **CARDS:**

♦♦♦♦ Camilla House Hotel
12 Regent Ter TR18 4DW ☎ 01736 363771 📠 01736 363771
e-mail: visitus@camillahouse-hotel.co.uk
Dir: *take seafront road to Promenade, Regent Terrace approx 30yds W of Jubilee Pool*
Rosemary and Bill Wooldridge offer a warm welcome at this attractive listed building. Set in a quiet terrace, parallel to the promenade, all the front-facing rooms benefit from delightful sea views. Bedrooms are tastefully furnished and well equipped, with a number of thoughtful extras such as fresh flowers. There is a comfortable television lounge and breakfast is served in the spacious dining room, where a varied choice is offered and vegetarians are catered for.
FACILITIES: 8 rms (4 en suite) No smoking TVB tea/coffee No dogs Licensed Cen ht TVL No children 10yrs **PRICES:** s £20-£25; d £40-£60* **LB PARKING:** 8 **NOTES:** Closed Nov-Feb **CARDS:**

♦♦♦♦ Dunedin
Alexandra Rd TR18 4LZ ☎ 01736 362652 📠 01736 360497
e-mail: info@dunedinhotel.co.uk
Dir: *from Penzance station follow seafront to mini rdbt, right into Alexandra Road*

Peacefully located a few minutes walk from the Promenade and town centre, Dunedin dates from 1886 and offers comfortable accommodation. Most of the well equipped bedrooms have been recently redecorated to a high standard. A good choice is offered at breakfast, which is taken in the garden level dining room. A cosy and inviting guest lounge is also available.
FACILITIES: 8 en suite (2 fmly) (2 GF) No smoking TVB tea/coffee No dogs (ex guide dogs) Licensed Cen ht TVL No children 3yrs **PRICES:** s £25-£35; d £40-£50 **LB NOTES:** Closed 10 Dec-10 Jan **CARDS:**

♦♦♦♦ Georgian House
20 Chapel St TR18 4AW ☎ 01736 365664 📠 01736 365664
Dir: *follow A30 into Penzance and then signs for town centre, with Lloyds Bank on the right turn left, premises 400yds on the right*

Conveniently situated close to the Scilly Isles ferry terminal, the seafront and town centre, this historic house was formerly the mayor's home and now offers spacious and comfortable accommodation. A pleasant bar is available where guests may relax. Breakfast is served in the Picasso and Matisse inspired dining room.
FACILITIES: 11 rms (9 en suite) (3 fmly) No smoking in 2 bedrooms No smoking in dining room TVB tea/coffee No dogs (ex guide dogs) Licensed Cen ht TVL Last d 8pm **PRICES:** s £23-£28; d £42-£46* **PARKING:** 11 **NOTES:** Closed Xmas & New year **CARDS:**

England

PENZANCE continued

♦♦♦♦ Hotel Minalto

Alexandra Rd TR18 4LZ ☎ 01736 362923 📠 01736 363463
Dir: *follow harbour to promenade end of seafront, turn right at mini rdbt. Alexandra Rd is at end of seafront. Hotel on left*

This spacious and elegant Victorian house is located in a quiet, tree-lined residential street, within easy walking distance of the centre of town. Bedrooms are well-equipped with little extras. There are two lounges, one with a small cocktail bar and the dining room, like the rest of the house, is bright and airy. Vegetarian breakfasts are a speciality. A no-smoking policy is enforced throughout.
FACILITIES: 11 rms (9 en suite) No smoking TVB tea/coffee Licensed Cen ht TVL No children 8yrs No coaches **PRICES:** s £19-£22.50; d £40-£55✳ **LB BB PARKING:** 9 **CARDS:**

♦♦♦♦ Rose Farm *(SW446290)*

Chyanhal, Buryas Bridge TR19 6AN ☎ 01736 731808
📠 01736 731808 Mrs P Lally
e-mail: lally@rosefarm.co.uk
Dir: *take A30 to Land's End, at Drift turn left (behind phone box), 0.75m down lane on left*

Situated in peaceful countryside only a short distance from Penzance, this working farm provides cosy accommodation. Bedrooms are attractively designed and well-equipped, and each room has its own private entrance. The barn room offers period furniture and a romantic four-poster bed. A hearty breakfast is served in the lounge/dining room at a farmhouse refectory table.
FACILITIES: 2 en suite 1 annexe en suite (1 fmly) (1 GF) No smoking in bedrooms No smoking in dining room TVB tea/coffee No dogs (ex guide dogs) Cen ht 23 acres beef **PRICES:** d £44-£50✳ **LB**
PARKING: 8 **NOTES:** Closed 24-27 Dec **CARDS:** 

Further details of AA rated B&Bs and hotels can be found on the AA website www.theAA.com

♦♦♦♦ *Tremont*

Alexandra Rd TR18 4LZ ☎ 01736 362614
Dir: *follow promenade towards Newlyn and at rdbt turn right into Alexandra Rd*

Pleasantly located close to the foreshore and town centre, Tremont is ideal for a short break or for a longer more relaxed stay. Modern well-furnished rooms are provided with a number of extra comforts, and guests can relax in the bright and pleasant lounge. Breakfast is taken in the lower-floor dining room.
FACILITIES: 10 en suite (1 fmly) No smoking in dining room TVB tea/coffee No dogs (ex guide dogs) Licensed Cen ht TVL No children 5yrs
PARKING: 5 **NOTES:** Closed 24 Dec-1 Jan

♦♦♦ Carlton Private Hotel

The Promenade TR18 4NW ☎ 01736 362081 📠 01736 362081
e-mail: carltonhotelpenzance@talk21.com
Dir: *from Railway/Bus/Coach Station, follow the signs for harbour and Newlyn. Hotel approx 0.75m on the right*

Situated on the promenade and enjoying fine sea views from many of its rooms, the Carlton is pleasantly located within easy strolling distance of Penzance's centre and amenities. Rooms are traditionally styled and are well equipped. A pleasant lounge and spacious dining room are provided.
FACILITIES: 12 rms (9 en suite) (6 fmly) No smoking in bedrooms No smoking in dining room TVB tea/coffee No dogs (ex guide dogs) TVL No coaches **PRICES:** s £18; d £40-£44✳ **LB BB CARDS:**

♦♦♦ Mount Royal Hotel

Chyandour Cliff TR18 3LQ ☎ 01736 362233 📠 01736 362233
e-mail: mountroyal@talk21.com
Dir: *on the old A30 entering Penzance*

This imposing part-Georgian, part-Victorian house offers well appointed spacious public rooms with wonderful views over Mount's Bay. Original features such as the fireplace and ornate sideboard can still be seen in the elegant dining room. Bedrooms are large, with some having the added benefit of sea views.
FACILITIES: 7 en suite (3 fmly) (1 GF) No smoking TVB tea/coffee No dogs Cen ht No coaches Pool Table **PRICES:** s £35; d £50-£55✳ **LB**
PARKING: 10 **NOTES:** Closed Nov-Feb

♦♦♦ Penalva

Alexandra Rd TR18 4LZ ☎ 01736 369060 📠 01736 369060
Dir: *follow seafront from railway station and along harbour to promenade, Alexandra Rd is at end of promenade on right*

Pleasantly located in a quiet area of Penzance, the Penalva offers comfortable and modern accommodation. Bedrooms are spacious and provide a number of extra items of comfort. The pleasant lounge features old photographs, many of which depict local shipwrecks. Pleasant breakfasts are served in the comfortable dining room where a collection of old artefacts are displayed.
FACILITIES: 5 en suite (3 fmly) No smoking TVB tea/coffee No dogs Cen ht TVL No children 3yrs No coaches **PRICES:** s £16-£22; d £32-£44✳ **BB**

♦♦♦ Pendennis

Alexandra Rd TR18 4LZ ☎ 01736 363823 📠 01736 363823
e-mail: ray@pendennishotel_freeserve.co.uk
Dir: *enter Penzance on A30 and at railway station take seafront road to small roundabout. Turn right into Alexandra Rd*

Located in a peaceful residential area, close to the town centre and seafront, this friendly home provides comfortable and well-equipped rooms. Two ground floor rooms are available for the less mobile. Good home cooked dinners and tasty breakfasts are taken in the attractive dining room.

FACILITIES: 8 rms (7 en suite) (5 fmly) No smoking in dining room TVB tea/coffee No dogs (ex guide dogs) Licensed Cen ht Dinner Last d 4.30pm
CARDS:

♦♦♦ Penmorvah Hotel

Alexandra Rd TR18 4LZ ☎ 01736 363711 📠 01736 363711
Dir: *from sea front, right at mini- rdbt into Alexandra Road, hotel on right, 250yds along*

Situated in a quiet tree-lined road only a short walk from the seafront and town centre and convenient for the ferry port, the Penmorvah provides a friendly and relaxing atmosphere. Bedrooms are well appointed, comfortable and equipped with many thoughtful extras. Well-cooked homemade dishes, with vegetarian options, are offered at dinner and breakfast.

FACILITIES: 8 en suite (2 fmly) (1 GF) No smoking in dining room TVB tea/coffee Licensed Cen ht Dinner Last d 6pm **PRICES:** s £18-£25; d £36-£50✱ LB BB **NOTES:** Closed Xmas **CARDS:**

♦♦♦ Southern Comfort

Seafront, 8 Alexandra Ter TR18 4NX ☎ 01736 366333
Dir: *follow seafront road for 0.75m. At 1st rdbt continue along seafront, after 0.25m 1st road on right after Lidl store, turn right. Large Victorian terrace, Establishment clearly marked*

This grand Victorian house has quiet location overlooking the bay and St Michael's Mount. A pleasant welcome awaits all guests and this is a convenient place for both the tourist or business visitor. Dinners, by arrangement, and breakfasts are served in the dining room and guests can take a drink either outside in summer months, or in the bar or lounge.

FACILITIES: 12 en suite (1 fmly) No smoking TVB tea/coffee Licensed Cen ht TVL No coaches Dinner Last d noon **PRICES:** s £20-£35; d £48-£84✱ LB **PARKING:** 6 **CARDS:**

♦♦♦ Estoril Hotel

46 Morrab Rd TR18 4EX ☎ 01736 362468 📠 01736 367471
e-mail: estorilhotel@aol.com

FACILITIES: 9 en suite No smoking TVB tea/coffee Direct dial from bedrooms No dogs Licensed Cen ht TVL No coaches **PRICES:** s £26-£29.50; d £48-£59✱ LB **PARKING:** 5 **NOTES:** Closed Xmas & New Year
CARDS:

♦♦ Coth'a Noweth

Catchall, Buryas Bridge TR19 6AQ ☎ 01736 810572
Dir: *follow A30 past Penzance towards Land's End. Establishment 0.25m beyond left turn to St Buryan on B3283*

This charming granite house is set within half an acre of delightful gardens and bordered by a trout stream, conveniently located in the country, close to the Minack Theatre and Land's End. A friendly welcome is assured at this comfortable home and the attractive bedrooms are furnished with pine and polished wood floors.

FACILITIES: 4 rms (2 fmly) No smoking in dining room No dogs (ex guide dogs) Cen ht TVL No coaches **PRICES:** d £32-£36✱ LB BB
PARKING: 8 **NOTES:** Closed Oct-Etr

PERRANUTHNOE — Map 02 SW52

Premier Collection

♦♦♦♦♦ Ednovean Farm *(SW538295)*

TR20 9LZ ☎ 01736 711883 Mr & Mrs C Taylor
e-mail: info@ednoveanfarm.co.uk
Dir: *from A394 Penzance/Helston turn off towards Perranuthnoe at Dynasty Cantonese Restaurant, farm drive on left on bend by post box*

Peace and tranquillity abound at this 17th-century farmhouse enjoying wonderful views across the countryside towards Mount's Bay. The bedrooms are individually styled and most comfortable. Designed in a Mediterranean style, the gardens are impressive. In addition to the sitting room there is also a garden room and several patio areas. Breakfast is served at a magnificent oak table.

FACILITIES: 3 en suite No smoking TVB tea/coffee No dogs Cen ht No children 16yrs 22 acres arable grassland horticultural **PRICES:** s £45-£65; d £60-£75✱ **PARKING:** 4 **CARDS:**

♦♦♦♦ Ednovean House

TR20 9LZ ☎ 01736 711071
e-mail: clive@ednoveanhouse.co.uk
Dir: *turn off A394 at Perran x-rds, between Penzance and Helston, just before Rosudgeon, then 1st lane on left and continue to very end of lane*

Ednovean House benefits from spectacular views over Mount's Bay and St Michael's Mount. The resident proprietors provide a friendly welcome and comfortable accommodation. A pleasant dining room, bar and two lounges are available for guest use. The lovingly tended gardens feature a putting green and a large terrace.

FACILITIES: 8 rms (6 en suite) No smoking tea/coffee Licensed Cen ht TVL No children 7yrs No coaches Putting green **PRICES:** s £24-£25; d £50-£54✱ **PARKING:** 12 **NOTES:** Closed Xmas & New Year **CARDS:**

England

PERRANUTHOE continued

♦♦♦ Quilkyns

1 St Pirans Way TR20 9NJ ☎ 01736 719141
e-mail: paul@quilkyns.co.uk
Dir: *turn off A30 at the A394 and follow road to Perran x-roads, turn right and follow road for about a quarter mile, left turn into St Pirans Way*
Just a short stroll from the sandy beach at Perran Sands, this family run establishment offers a warm and genuine welcome to all. Quietly located, there is easy access to the South West Coastal Path which runs through the village. The twin-bedded bedrooms, one with new en suite facilities and the other with a private bathroom, are spacious and thoughtfully equipped, with views across the garden to the sea beyond.
FACILITIES: 2 rms (1 en suite) (2 GF) No smoking TVB tea/coffee No dogs (ex guide dogs) Cen ht No coaches **PRICES:** s £25-£30; d £35-£40* **LB BB PARKING: NOTES:** Closed Dec & Jan

♦♦♦ The Victoria Inn

TR20 9NP ☎ 01736 710309 01736 710309
Dir: *Turn off A394 into Perranuthnoe, establishment 0.5m on right*
This friendly and popular village local is reputedly one of the oldest inns in Cornwall, dating back to the 12th century. Food comes highly recommended with an interesting choice of blackboard specials, using local produce wherever possible, with fine wines and real ales available to complement your meal. Conveniently located close to the beach and coastal path.
FACILITIES: 3 en suite No smoking in bedrooms No smoking in dining room TVB tea/coffee No dogs Cen ht Dinner Last d 9.30pm **PRICES:** s £35-£38; d £50-£55* **LB MEALS:** Lunch £16-£25alc Dinner £16-£25alc*
PARKING: 10 **CARDS:**

POLPERRO — Map 02 SX25

Premier Collection

♦♦♦♦♦ Trenderway *(SX214533)*

Pelynt PL13 2LY ☎ 01503 272214 01503 272991
Mrs L Tuckett
e-mail: trenderwayfarm@hotmail.com
Dir: *from Looe take A387 to Polperro, farm is signposted on main road, take 2nd sign turning*

Warm, genuine hospitality will be found at this delightful 16th-century farmhouse, set in 400 acres of beautiful countryside. The stylish bedrooms, (two in the farmhouse, and two in the adjacent barn), are luxuriously furnished and equipped. Hearty breakfasts, with free-range eggs from the farm, are served in the bright, airy conservatory. In the winter, guests can relax by an open fire in the comfortable sitting room. Self-catering accommodation is also available in The Meadow Barn.
FACILITIES: 2 en suite 2 annexe en suite (1 GF) No smoking TVB tea/coffee No dogs Cen ht No children 400 acres arable mixed sheep cattle **PRICES:** s £25-£45; d £60-£80* **LB PARKING:** 4 **NOTES:** Closed Xmas & New Year **CARDS:**

♦♦♦ Penryn House Hotel

The Coombes PL13 2RQ ☎ 01503 272157 01503 273055
e-mail: chrispidcock@aol.com
Dir: *follow A387 to Polperro, at mini-rdbt bear left down hill into village, ignoring restricted access sign. Establishment 200yds on left*

Located in the heart of this picturesque fishing village, this friendly, family run hotel provides well appointed comfortable bedrooms. After a gentle stroll in the village, guests may relax in the lounge or enjoy a drink in the well stocked bar. Breakfast is served in the bright and airy dining room.
FACILITIES: 12 en suite No smoking in bedrooms No smoking in dining room TVB tea/coffee Direct dial from bedrooms Licensed No coaches Dinner Last d 10pm **PRICES:** s £24-£31; d £42-£68* **LB PARKING:** 13
CARDS:

PORTHALLOW — Map 02 SW72

♦♦♦ Gallen Treath Guest House

TR12 6PL ☎ 01326 280400 01326 280400
e-mail: gallentreath@btclick.com
Dir: *A3083 from Helston. At rdbt left onto B3293 and right at next rdbt in Rosevear. Proceed past Goonhilly to St Keverne. Continue down road to Porthallow and round other side of valley, house on left*
Gallen Treath enjoys super views over the sea and the countryside from its elevated position above Porthallow. Bedrooms are individually decorated and feature many personal touches. For guest relaxation, there is a large and comfortable lounge complete with balcony. A hearty breakfast and dinner by arrangement can be enjoyed in the bright dining room.
FACILITIES: 5 rms (4 en suite) (1 fmly) (1 GF) No smoking in bedrooms No smoking in dining room TVB tea/coffee Licensed Cen ht TVL No children 2yrs Dinner Last d 6pm **PRICES:** s £22-£23; d £44-£46* **LB PARKING:** 6

PORTHCURNO — Map 02 SW32

♦♦♦♦ The Porthcurno Hotel

The Valley TR19 6JX ☎ 01736 810119 01736 810711
e-mail: porthcurnohotel@aol.com
Dir: *off A30 onto B3283, through St Buryan and after 3m turn left for Portucurno, hotel is on right as you go down the valley.*
FACILITIES: 12 rms (8 en suite) (1 fmly) (1 GF) No smoking in 2 bedrooms No smoking in dining room TV8B tea/coffee Licensed Cen ht TVL No coaches Dinner Last d 9pm **PRICES:** d £48-£80* **LB PARKING:** 18
CARDS:

PORTHLEVEN — Map 02 SW62

♦♦♦ *Harbour Inn*

Commercal Rd TR13 9JB ☎ 01326 573876 01326 572124
Dir: *left hand side of harbour (St Austell Brewery)*
This attractive inn is situated alongside the harbour, decked with flowers in summer months and inviting at all times of year. The spacious bar areas offer a wide range of local beers, wines and

continued

spirits, and dining also provides good choices of freshly cooked dishes. Bedrooms, many with harbour views, are comfortable and well equipped.
FACILITIES: 10 rms (8 en suite) (1 fmly) No smoking in dining room No smoking in 1 lounge STV TVB tea/coffee Direct dial from bedrooms No dogs (ex guide dogs) Cen ht TVL No coaches Pool Table Dinner Last d 9.15pm
PARKING: 10 **CARDS:**

PORT ISAAC Map 02 SW98

♦♦♦♦ The Corn Mill

Port Isaac Rd, Trelill PL30 3HZ ☎ 01208 851079
Dir: *between villages of Pendoggett and Trelill*

Dating from the 18th century, this former mill has been lovingly restored to provide a charming home, packed full of character. The bedrooms are individually styled and personal touches contribute to a wonderfully relaxed and homely atmosphere. The farmhouse kitchen is the venue for a delicious breakfast.
FACILITIES: 3 rms (2 en suite) (1 fmly) No smoking in bedrooms tea/coffee Cen ht No coaches **PRICES:** d £53-£56✳
PARKING: 3 **NOTES:** Closed 24 Dec-5 Jan

PORTREATH Map 02 SW64

♦♦♦♦ Benson's

1 The Hillside TR16 4LL ☎ 01209 842534 🖷 01209 843578
e-mail: bensons@portreath.fsbusiness.co.uk
Dir: *exit A30 for Portreath onto B3300 and turn left by Portreath school. Fork left by Glenfeadon Castle*

Benson's is a delightful place to stay and is ideally located for touring the area; from its peaceful and elevated position it enjoys splendid views over the bay. The friendly proprietors aim to

continued

provide 'total comfort and hospitality' and are attentive hosts. Breakfast is served buffet-style in the comfortable lounge conservatory.
FACILITIES: 4 en suite (4 GF) No smoking TVB tea/coffee No dogs Cen ht No children 12yrs No coaches **PRICES:** s £25; d £40✳
PARKING: 6 **NOTES:** Closed Oct-22 Jun

PRAA SANDS Map 02 SW52

♦♦♦♦ Gwynoon

Chy-an-Dour Rd TR20 9SY ☎ 01736 763508
e-mail: keithrallen@hotmail.com
Dir: *M5 junct 31 at Exeter, A30 to Penzance. A394 towards Helston,7m Germoe X-rds, right by golf club to Praa Sands, down hill past holiday village, 2nd left after post office to Chy-an-Dour Rd Guest house immediately left*
Gwynoon is ideally located in Praa Sands, which is considered one of Cornwall's best beaches. There are excellent views from the front bedrooms, balcony and well-tended gardens. Bedrooms are very comfortable, well furnished and are provided with many extras. The hosts are very attentive and provide a caring and peaceful atmosphere. The enjoyable breakfasts feature fresh and local produce.
FACILITIES: 2 en suite (2 fmly) No smoking TVB tea/coffee No dogs Cen ht No coaches **PRICES:** s £26; d £52✳ **PARKING:** 6

REDRUTH Map 02 SW64

♦♦♦♦ Aviary Court Hotel

Mary's Well, Illogan TR16 4QZ ☎ 01209 842256
🖷 01209 843744
e-mail: aviarycourt@connexions.co.uk
Dir: *off A30 at A3047 Camborne, Pool and Portreath sign. Follow Portreath and Illogan signs for 2m to Alexander Rd*
Friendly hospitality and a relaxing environment is provided at this family run Hotel, which is set in attractive gardens on the edge of Illogan Woods. Bedrooms are spacious and well equipped with many thoughtful extra touches. Dinner provides a highlight of any stay and features fresh Cornish produce, Sunday lunches are a speciality and booking is essential.
FACILITIES: 6 en suite (1 fmly) No smoking in dining room TVB tea/coffee Direct dial from bedrooms No dogs Licensed No children 3yrs No coaches Tennis (hard) **PRICES:** s £42.50-£45; d £62.50-£65✳ **PARKING:** 25
CARDS:

ROCK Map 02 SW97

♦♦♦ Roskarnon House Hotel

PL27 6LD ☎ 01208 862329 🖷 01208 862785
With fine views over the Camel Estuary towards Padstow, the same family has run this fine Edwardian house as a hotel for over 45 years. The majority of the public rooms and some bedrooms benefit from this view. Dinner is available by prior arrangement. A variety of water sports can be arranged locally.
FACILITIES: 12 rms (10 en suite) (5 fmly) No smoking in dining room TVB tea/coffee No dogs (ex guide dogs) Licensed TVL No coaches Dinner Last d 8pm **PRICES:** s fr £30; d fr £60✳ **LB PARKING:** 16 **NOTES:** Closed Nov-Feb **CARDS:**

England

ST AGNES Map 02 SW75

♦♦♦ Driftwood Spars Hotel

Trevaunance Cove TR5 0RT ☎ 01872 552428 & 553323
Fax 01872 553701
e-mail: driftwoodspars@hotmail.com
Dir: *off A30 at rdbt signed St Agnes, through village bear right past church, left at bottom of hill, hotel on right*

This romantic, historic inn is full of character and takes its name from the wrecked timbers it is built from. A good range of local produce is offered, from hand-pulled beers to a selection of delicious smoked fish. Bedrooms are attractively decorated in a fresh seaside style, with comfortable furnishings and many useful and interesting features.

FACILITIES: 9 en suite 6 annexe en suite (5 fmly) (4 GF) No smoking in dining room No smoking in 1 lounge TVB tea/coffee Direct dial from bedrooms Cen ht TVL Snooker Pool Table Sea fishing, surfing Dinner Last d 9.30pm **PRICES:** s £34-£45; d £68-£76* **CONF:** Thtr 40 Class 40 Board 20 **PARKING:** 81 **NOTES:** Closed 24-25 Dec **CARDS:**

♦♦ Penkerris

Penwinnick Rd TR5 0PA ☎ 01872 552262 Fax 01872 552262
e-mail: info@penkerris.co.uk
Dir: *A30 to B3277 to St Agnes for 3m. Penkerris is 1st house on right after village sign*

A creeper-clad Edwardian house on the edge of the village. The lounge is comfortable and homely, with a piano, magazines and videos, plus a real log fire. The breakfast room is full of blue glass and brassware and it is here that evening meals can be enjoyed, by prior arrangement.

FACILITIES: 6 rms (3 en suite) (3 fmly) TVB tea/coffee Licensed TVL ch fac No coaches Badminton, Volleyball, Swings Dinner Last d 10am
PRICES: s £20-£35; d £35-£50* **LB BB PARKING:** 9
CARDS:

> **LB** indicates that Leisure Breaks are offered by the establishment.

ST AUSTELL Map 02 SX05

Premier Collection

♦♦♦♦♦ Anchorage House

Nettles Corner, Tregrehan Mills PL25 3RH ☎ 01726 814071
e-mail: stay@anchoragehouse.co.uk
Dir: *2m E of St Austell on A390, turn at road signed Tregrehan and turn immediately left into drive leading to Anchorage House's courtyard*

This splendid house offers luxury and genuine friendliness. Bedrooms are spacious, comfortable, well-decorated and furnished to the highest standards with extra large beds, satellite television and numerous extra facilities. A lounge, conservatory and swimming pool are also available to guests. Dinners, which are available by prior arrangement, are taken house-party style with the very best use made of fresh Cornish produce. A wide choice is available at the buffet-style breakfast.

FACILITIES: 3 en suite No smoking STV TVB tea/coffee No dogs Cen ht No children 16yrs No coaches Outdoor swimming pool (heated) Jacuzzi Dinner Last d 24hr **PRICES:** s £60-£65; d £70-£84*
PARKING: 7 **NOTES:** Closed Dec-Feb **CARDS:**

♦♦♦♦ Lower Barn

Bosue, St Ewe PL26 6EU ☎ 01726 844881
e-mail: janie@bosue.co.uk
Dir: *A390 at St Austell. Follow directions for Mevagissey. After campsite, right at x-roads at top of hill, signed Gorran Haven. Follow road until sharp left bend, establishment signed, approx 1m on right.*

Tucked away in rolling Cornish landscape, this imaginatively transformed barn has much to offer. Stunningly designed - warm colours, wooden flooring, tiling and rugs all creating a Mediterranean feel. Bedrooms have great personality with many thoughtful extras; one room suitable for disabled access. Informality is the order of the day; breakfast is served at the huge table, or al fresco on the decked patio.

continued

FACILITIES: 3 en suite (3 fmly) No smoking TVB tea/coffee No dogs (ex guide dogs) Cen ht TVL No coaches Hot tub Dinner Last d lunchtime **PRICES:** s £50; d £65✳ **LB PARKING:** 7

♦♦♦♦ The Lodge at Carlyon Bay

91 Sea Rd, Carlyon Bay PL25 3SH ☎ 01726 815543
📠 01726 810070
e-mail: thelodge@carlyonbay.demon.co.uk
Dir: *A390 Liskeard/St Austell at St Blazey Gate turn left at 1st rdbt to Par Moor Rd, after 0.25m right onto Sea road. At sign to Carlyon Bay golf course, continue on this road, under railway bridge straight on at X-rds, Lodge first turn right.*

Hospitality and service are major strengths at this charming guest house, which stands in its own gardens close to Carlyon Bay. All of the spacious well-equipped bedrooms are on the ground floor and overlook the delightful grounds. There is residents' lounge, bar and dining room where delicious evening meals are available by prior arrangement.
FACILITIES: 6 en suite (2 fmly) No smoking TVB tea/coffee No dogs (ex guide dogs) Licensed Cen ht TVL No coaches Carlyon Bay golf club is opposite Dinner Last d at breakfast **PRICES:** s £50-£60; d £80-£90✳ **CONF:** Board 20 **PARKING:** 12 **CARDS:**

♦♦♦♦ Poltarrow *(SW998518)*

St Mewan PL26 7DR ☎ 01726 67111 📠 01726 67111
Mrs J Nancarrow
e-mail: enquire@poltarrow.co.uk
Dir: *A390 St Austell-Truro. 2m from St Austell turn right at St Mewan school. 2nd farm on left after 0.5m*

Set in 45 acres of gardens and pasture, many original features of this delightful farmhouse have been retained. The comfortable bedrooms are furnished and decorated with style. Breakfast is served in the conservatory/dining room overlooking the gardens. An impressive indoor pool is a recent addition.
FACILITIES: 3 en suite 2 annexe en suite (1 fmly) No smoking TVB tea/coffee No dogs (ex guide dogs) Cen ht TVL No children 5yrs Indoor swimming pool (heated) Fishing Pool Table 45 acres mixed **PRICES:** s £30-£40; d £50-£55✳ **LB PARKING:** 10 **NOTES:** Closed 16 Dec-5 Jan **CARDS:**

♦♦♦ Rashleigh Arms

Quay Rd, Charlestown PL25 3NX ☎ 01726 73635
📠 01726 73635
Dir: *A390, signposted on St Austell rdbt*

Located in the picturesque port village of Charlestown, a setting much in demand for films and TV series, The Rashleigh Arms is a popular traditional inn that offers comfortable accommodation in a convivial atmosphere. The two bars offer a range of real ales, with a lunch time carvery and evening meals also available.
FACILITIES: 5 rms (4 en suite) No smoking in 4 bedrooms TVB tea/coffee No dogs (ex guide dogs) Cen ht Pool Table Last d 10pm **PRICES:** s £40; d £55✳ **LB MEALS:** Lunch £5-£10&alc Dinner £5-£10&alc✳ **PARKING:** 120 **CARDS:**

♦♦♦ T'Gallants

6 Charlestown Rd, Charlestown PL25 3NJ ☎ 01726 70203
Dir: *exit A390 at rdbt signposted for Charlestown, premises at the bottom of hill*

Overlooking the historic port of Charlestown, with its fleet of square-rigged ships, this fine Georgian house has areas, which date from 1630. Bedrooms are generally spacious and well-maintained with one having a four-poster bed. Breakfast is served at separate tables, and often feature smoked haddock from a local smokery.
FACILITIES: 8 rms (6 en suite) No smoking in dining room No smoking in lounges TVB tea/coffee No dogs Licensed Cen ht No coaches **PRICES:** s £30; d £45-£48✳ **PARKING:** 16 **CARDS:**

ST BLAZEY — Map 02 SX05

Premier Collection

♦♦♦♦♦ Nanscawen Manor House

Prideaux Rd, Luxulyan Valley PL24 2SR ☎ 01726 814488
📠 01726 814488
e-mail: keith@nanscawen.com
Dir: *A38 from Plymouth, left at Dobwalls to A390-St Austell, in St Blazey turn right after railway, opposite garage, Nanscawen is 0.75m on right*

A beautifully renovated 14th-century manor house, offering a luxurious standard of accommodation. Bedrooms are elegant and bathrooms feature spa baths. There are extra touches throughout to pamper and delight the guest. The stylish lounge is spacious, with a well-stocked honesty bar. There are five acres of pleasant gardens with splendid views across woodlands, as well as a heated pool. Breakfast, served in the conservatory, features local fresh produce.
FACILITIES: 3 en suite No smoking TVB tea/coffee Direct dial from bedrooms No dogs Licensed Cen ht No children 12yrs No coaches Outdoor swimming pool (heated) Jacuzzi Whirlpool **PRICES:** s £70-£80; d £80-£90✳ **LB PARKING:** 8 **CARDS:**

ST HILARY Map 02 SW53

Premier Collection

♦♦♦♦♦ Ennys *(SW559328)*

Trewhella Ln, St Hilary TR20 9BZ ☎ 01736 740262
01736 740055 Miss G Charlton
e-mail: ennys@ennys.co.uk
Dir: *1m N of B3280, Leedstown to Goldsithney road*

Tucked away in a charming, secluded country setting, this is the perfect place to unwind. A friendly welcome awaits and afternoon tea, laid out in the kitchen, is presented 'compliments of the house'. Breakfast offers a wealth of fresh local ingredients including home-produced fresh eggs. The house, a 17th century Cornish manor, is spacious and very comfortable. Adorned with tasteful artwork and pictures, it is ideally placed to explore the region.
FACILITIES: 3 en suite 2 annexe en suite (2 fmly) (1 GF) No smoking in bedrooms No smoking in dining room TVB tea/coffee No dogs Cen ht No children 2yrs Outdoor swimming pool (heated) Tennis (grass) 20 acres Non-working **PRICES:** s £45-£65; d £65-£85* **PARKING:** 8 **NOTES:** Closed Nov-13 Feb **CARDS:**

ST IVES Map 02 SW54

♦♦♦♦ Beckside Cottage

Treeve Ln, Connor Downs TR27 5BN ☎ 01736 756751
e-mail: aa@becksidecottage.demon.co.uk
(For full entry see Hayle)

♦♦♦♦ Chy-an-Creet Private Hotel

Higher Stennack TR26 2HA ☎ 01736 796559 01736 796559
e-mail: stay@chy.co.uk
Dir: *on B3306 from harbour, opposite Leach Pottery*

High standards of comfort and quality can be found at this friendly, family-run guest house. Public areas are spacious and include a bar and separate lounge for relaxation. Bedrooms, including ground floor options, are well equipped and provided with many extra comforts. Bar snacks are available and breakfast, served in the dining room, includes home-made preserves.
FACILITIES: 8 en suite (2 fmly) (4 GF) No smoking in bedrooms No smoking in dining room No smoking in 1 lounge TVB tea/coffee Licensed TVL No coaches Last d 8.30pm **PRICES:** s £20-£56; d £40-£56* **LB** **PARKING:** 8 **NOTES:** Closed 1 Nov - Easter **CARDS:**

♦♦♦♦ Chy-Garth

Sea View Meadows, St Ives Rd, Carbis Bay TR26 2JX
☎ 01736 795677
e-mail: ann@chy-garth.demon.co.uk
Dir: *A30/A3074 follow signs to St Ives through Lelant and into Carbis Bay. Establishment on right opposite Post Office and Methodist Church*
Situated in delightful gardens and enjoying sea views, this attractive house is a short drive from the centre of St Ives. The tastefully decorated bedrooms are most comfortable and thoughtfully provided with many extra facilities. The resident proprietors create a friendly, attentive and relaxing atmosphere. At breakfast a splendid choice is offered with vegetarian or continental options also available.
FACILITIES: 8 rms (7 en suite) (1 fmly) (4 GF) No smoking TVB tea/coffee No dogs Cen ht No children 8yrs No coaches **PRICES:** s £25-£30; d £50-£60* **PARKING:** 8 **CARDS:**

♦♦♦♦ Kynance

The Warren TR26 2EA ☎ 01736 796636
e-mail: enquiries@kynance24.co.uk
Dir: *take A3074 into town centre, take sharp right turn before bus/coach terminus, into railway station approach road. Kynance 20yds on left*
Situated within a few yards level walking distance of the picturesque harbour and Porthminster Beach, Kynance is a charming old property in the heart of the town. The bedrooms are attractively decorated and well equipped, some have superb views. Guests can enjoy a varied choice at breakfast including a vegetarian option.
FACILITIES: 6 en suite (1 fmly) No smoking TVB tea/coffee No dogs Cen ht TVL No children 7yrs No coaches **PRICES:** d £44-£52* **PARKING:** 4 **NOTES:** Closed mid Nov-mid Mar **CARDS:**

♦♦♦♦ *Lyonesse Hotel*

5 Talland Rd TR26 2DF ☎ 01736 796315 01736 796315
Dir: *A3074 to St Ives fork left at Porthminster, left again at Albert Rd. Lyonesse 50yds on right*
This family run house provides comfortable and spacious accommodation, is conveniently located and has fine views of the harbour and sea and also has the benefit of some parking. Friendly and efficient service and hospitality are offered to all guests. Fresh, Aga-cooked breakfasts are served in the dining room at separate tables.
FACILITIES: 10 en suite (2 fmly) No smoking TVB tea/coffee No dogs Licensed Cen ht TVL No children 5yrs No coaches **PARKING:** 10 **NOTES:** Closed Oct-Mar **CARDS:**

♦♦♦♦ The Old Vicarage Hotel

Parc-an-Creet TR26 2ES ☎ 01736 796124 01736 796343
e-mail: holidays@oldvicaragehotel.com
Dir: *as 1st hill with shops in St Ives levels out, turn left at Nat West bank on B3306 to Land's End. 0.5m turn right into Parc-an-Creet*
Set in pleasant gardens, in a quiet part of St Ives, this Victorian rectory is convenient for the seaside and other attractions. Its Victorian atmosphere is enhanced by modern facilities. A good choice of local produce is offered at breakfast, including home-made yoghurt and preserves.
continued

FACILITIES: 7 en suite (4 fmly) No smoking in bedrooms No smoking in dining room No smoking in 1 lounge TVB tea/coffee Licensed Cen ht TVL No coaches Putting green **PRICES:** s £45; d £56✻ **PARKING:** 12 **NOTES:** Closed Nov-Easter **CARDS:**

♦♦♦♦ The Pondarosa

10 Porthminster Ter TR26 2DQ ☎ 01736 795875
01736 797811
e-mail: pondarosa.hotel@talk21.com
Dir: *approach town on A3074, fork left at Porthminster Hotel & follow road to left bend then take 1st left. Hotel 50yds on right*

Set high above the town, a short walk from the harbour, beaches and town centre, The Ponderosa is located in a quiet terrace. The proprietors create a relaxed and friendly atmosphere here. Bedrooms, some with sea views, are very comfortable. A new bar and an inviting lounge are available.

FACILITIES: 9 rms (8 en suite) (4 fmly) No smoking TVB tea/coffee No dogs Licensed Cen ht TVL **PRICES:** s £25-£30; d £46-£54✻ **LB** **PARKING:** 12 **CARDS:**

♦♦♦♦ *Regent Hotel*

Fernlea Ter TR26 2BH ☎ 01736 796195 01736 794641
e-mail: regent@mcmail.com
Dir: *in centre of town, close to bus & railway station*

This attractive hotel enjoys an enviable position looking over the town and across St Ives bay. The attentive hosts provide a friendly welcome. Bedrooms are well-equipped and some have spectacular sea views. A comfortable lounge and bar are available for guest use. Breakfast offers a wide selection including vegetarian choices.

FACILITIES: 9 rms (7 en suite) No smoking in 8 bedrooms No smoking in dining room TVB tea/coffee No dogs Licensed Cen ht TVL No children 9yrs No coaches Last d 7pm **PARKING:** 12 **CARDS:**

♦♦♦♦ Sloop

The Wharf TR26 1LP ☎ 01736 796584 01736 793322
e-mail: sloop@connexions.co.uk
Dir: *St Ives harbour by middle slipway*

continued

This attractive historic inn sits on the harbour-side with many rooms enjoying pleasant views. Each of the guest rooms are named with a nautical theme and all provide comfort and modern facilities. A good choice of dishes is offered at both lunch and dinner with an emphasis upon Cornish seafood.

FACILITIES: 14 rms (11 en suite) (3 fmly) No smoking in 2 bedrooms TVB tea/coffee No dogs (ex guide dogs) Cen ht No coaches Dinner Last d 8.45pm **PRICES:** d £65-£70✻ **LB** **MEALS:** Lunch £5-£10alc Dinner £6-£10alc✻ **CARDS:**

♦♦♦♦ Tregony

1 Clodgy View TR26 1JG ☎ 01736 795884 01736 798942
e-mail: info@tregony.com
Dir: *in St Ives left at Nat West. Past cinema, at mini rdbt right up Bullars Ln, right at T-junct. Straight on at next junct, house 100yds on right*

Close to the Tate and the town centre Tregony enjoys spectacular views of the coast, as it is set high above the town. Welcoming and attentive hosts, the owners provide a relaxed and friendly atmosphere. Bedrooms are comfortable and attractively decorated. Freshly cooked breakfasts can be enjoyed in the pleasant dining room and a stylish lounge is available for guests.

FACILITIES: 5 en suite (2 fmly) No smoking TVB tea/coffee No dogs Cen ht TVL No children 3yrs **PRICES:** s £26-£29; d £48-£56✻ **CARDS:**

♦♦♦♦ Tregorran Hotel

Headland Rd, Carbis Bay TR26 2NU ☎ 01736 795889
e-mail: book@carbisbay.com
Dir: *right at Carbis Bay to beach, along Porthrepta Rd. Take last right into Headland Rd, Tregorran Hotel halfway along*

Wonderful views of Carbis Bay and St Ives can be enjoyed from this friendly family-run hotel. Guests can relax in the garden, by the pool, use the games room or the gym. A pleasant bar is available as well as a comfortable lounge. Breakfast can be enjoyed in the airy dining room, which benefits from those superb views.

FACILITIES: 18 en suite (5 fmly) (4 GF) No smoking in bedrooms No smoking in dining room TVB tea/coffee Licensed Cen ht TVL No coaches Outdoor swimming pool (heated) Gymnasium Pool Table Games room **PRICES:** s £24-£44; d £48-£88✻ **LB** **PARKING:** 20 **NOTES:** Closed Nov-Easter **CARDS:**

England

ST IVES continued

♦♦♦♦ Treliska
3 Bedford Rd TR26 1SP ☎ 01736 797678 📠 01736 797678
e-mail: treliska.st.ives@ntlworld.com
Dir: *enter St Ives on A3074 to fork in road with Porthminster Hotel on right - take this road into town. At T-junct, Barclays Bank facing, turn left into Bedford Rd, house on right with pink sign*
The friendly proprietors make their guests most welcome at this pleasant house, which is situated close to the seafront, restaurants and galleries. The cosy bedrooms are well equipped and comfortable. Freshly cooked, enjoyable Cornish breakfast is served in the lounge/dining room.
FACILITIES: 5 en suite (1 fmly) No smoking TVB tea/coffee No dogs (ex guide dogs) Cen ht TVL No children 5yrs No coaches **PRICES:** s £30-£40; d £46-£52✱ **LB**

♦♦♦♦ Trewinnard
4 Parc Av TR26 2DN ☎ 01736 794168 📠 01736 798161
e-mail: sam.sears@btopenworld.com
Dir: *A3074 to St Ives, on entering town turn left at Nat West bank, then left at mini-rdbt. Pass car park & house 150yds on right*
Enjoying spectacular views over St Ives Bay, this impeccably maintained house has comfortable and well-equipped accommodation. The proprietors are very welcoming hosts, and guests are made to feel relaxed. A bar and lounge, which have views over the bay, are available and at breakfast, freshly cooked dishes are served in the adjoining dining room.
FACILITIES: 7 en suite (1 fmly) No smoking TVB tea/coffee No dogs Licensed Cen ht No children 6yrs No coaches **PRICES:** s £25-£35; d £50-£70✱ **PARKING:** 4 **NOTES:** Closed Nov-Mar **CARDS:**

♦♦♦ The Hollies Hotel
4 Talland Rd TR26 2DF ☎ 01736 796605 📠 01736 796605
e-mail: john@hollieshotel.freeserve.co.uk
Dir: *A30 to St Ives through Carbis Bay, down Trelyon Ave to Porthminster Hotel, fork left, 500yds, fork left, 50yds left again. Hotel 3rd on right*
Located in an elevated position within easy walking distance of town and harbour, this constantly improving hotel provides homely bedrooms and families are particularly welcome. Guests have the choice of light or full breakfast dependent on their budget and two sea view lounges are available.
FACILITIES: 10 en suite (4 fmly) No smoking in bedrooms No smoking in dining room No smoking in lounges TVB tea/coffee No dogs Licensed Cen ht TVL **PRICES:** s £17-£28✱ **LB BB PARKING:** 12 **NOTES:** Closed Dec-Feb (ex Xmas & New Year)

♦♦♦ Bay View
Headland Rd, Carbis Bay TR26 2NX ☎ 01736 796469
📠 01736 796469
Dir: *A3074 turn right Porthrepta Rd, 3rd right Headland Rd, 500 yds on right Bay View on corner of Headland Close*
Conveniently located close to the beach and within easy access of St Ives, this friendly home offers pleasantly decorated bedrooms with comfortable furnishings. A large homely lounge is available, with games and books. The bar, combined with dining room, offers traditional home cooked dinners and breakfast provides a hearty start to the day.
FACILITIES: 9 en suite (3 fmly) No smoking TVB tea/coffee No dogs (ex guide dogs) Licensed Cen ht TVL No children 5yrs No coaches Dinner Last d 1pm **PARKING:** 8 **NOTES:** Closed Nov-Feb

BB Great value! This indicates B&B for £19 and under, per person, per night.

♦♦♦ Channings Hotel
3 Talland Rd TR26 2DF ☎ 01736 799500 📠 01736 799500
e-mail: channings@tinyworld.co.uk
Dir: *on entering St Ives on A3074 fork left at Porthminster Hotel then 1st left & 1st left again into Talland Rd. 2nd hotel on right*
Located in a quiet residential area of the town, Channings Hotel is family run and offers a warm welcome to all guests. With impressive views over St Ives Bay, this spacious house provides homely accommodation. Traditional dishes are available at both dinner and breakfast in the comfortable dining room. Guests can also relax in the attractive lounge and bar.
FACILITIES: 10 en suite (4 fmly) No smoking in bedrooms No smoking in dining room No smoking in 1 lounge TVB tea/coffee No dogs Licensed Cen ht TVL Dinner Last d 2pm **PRICES:** s £25-£32; d £50-£64✱ **LB PARKING:** 9 **NOTES:** Closed Dec-Jan rs Nov, Feb-Mar **CARDS:**

♦♦♦ Chy-Roma
2 Seaview Ter TR26 2DH ☎ 01736 797539 📠 01736 797539
e-mail: jenny@omshanti.demon.co.uk
Dir: *on entering St Ives on A3074 fork left at Porthminster Hotel, then 1st left, 1st right, down slope 2nd guest house on left*
Quietly tucked away, this friendly home offers genuine hospitality provided by the attentive proprietors. Bedrooms are of mixed size, and are brightly decorated, some have delightful views over the harbour and St Ives Bay. Freshly prepared home cooked dinners and substantial breakfasts are served in the lounge/dining room.
FACILITIES: 7 rms (2 en suite) (2 fmly) No smoking in dining room No smoking in lounges TVB tea/coffee Cen ht TVL No children 5yrs No coaches Dinner Last d 4pm **PRICES:** s £21-£27; d £42-£54✱ **LB PARKING:** 5

♦♦♦ *Island View*
2 Park Av TR26 2DN ☎ 01736 795111
Dir: *A3074 to St Ives. On entering town turn left at NatWest bank, left at mini rdbt. Pass car park and house is 150yds on right*
Enjoying spectacular views towards the Atlantic and across the bay and harbour, the Island View has an elevated position close to the bus and railway stations. Bedrooms are comfortable and many have sea views. A cosy lounge is available and breakfast is taken in the dining room where hearty breakfasts are served at separate tables.
FACILITIES: 10 rms (5 en suite) (4 fmly) No smoking in 3 bedrooms No smoking in dining room No smoking in lounges TVB tea/coffee No dogs Cen ht No children 5yrs No coaches **NOTES:** Closed Nov-Feb

♦♦♦ Portarlington
11 Parc Bean TR26 1EA ☎ 01736 797278 📠 01736 797278
e-mail: Portarlington@btinternet.com
Situated in an elevated position and enjoying splendid views, this pleasant home is convenient for the town and beaches as well as the Tate Gallery. The friendly proprietors have been welcoming guests to their home for many years and some guests return on a regular basis. Bedrooms are well furnished and some have sea views. Guests can relax in the comfortable lounge and breakfast is taken in the attractive dining room.
FACILITIES: 4 en suite (3 fmly) No smoking in dining room TVB tea/coffee No dogs (ex guide dogs) Cen ht TVL No coaches **PRICES:** d £40-£44✱ **LB PARKING:** 4 **NOTES:** Closed Nov-Jan

♦♦♦ *Porthminster View*
13 Draycott Ter TR26 2EF ☎ 01736 795850 📠 01736 796811
e-mail: enquiry@porthminster.com
Dir: *leave A30 at rdbt W of Hayle onto A3074, establsihment 3.5m on seaward side of main road. Turn right into Draycott Terrace 300yds past Ford motor garage*

continued

England

Originally built around 1896, this relaxed and friendly establishment was formerly home to the local Station Master. Standing high above Porthminster Beach, the views are quite spectacular. Bedrooms are thoughtfully equipped and comfortable and, in addition, a well-appointed lounge is also available.
FACILITIES: 6 rms (3 en suite) (2 fmly) No smoking in dining room No smoking in lounges TVB tea/coffee No dogs (ex guide dogs) Cen ht **PARKING:** 1 **CARDS:**

♦♦♦ Primrose Valley Hotel

Primrose Valley, Porthminster Beach TR26 2ED
☎ 01736 794939 📠 01736 794939
e-mail: info@primroseonline.co.uk

This friendly and relaxing family run hotel enjoys a privileged position in St Ives, close to Porthminster Beach and only a short, level walk from town. Bedrooms are comfortable and many have been recently refurbished by the new owners. Dinner is available featuring daily home made specials and an interesting wine list.
FACILITIES: 10 en suite (4 fmly) No smoking in bedrooms No smoking in dining room No smoking in lounges TVB tea/coffee No dogs Licensed TVL No coaches Dinner Last d 6.30pm **PRICES:** s £24.50-£50; d £49-£80✱ **PARKING:** 10 **NOTES:** Closed Xmas **CARDS:**

♦♦♦ *Queens Tavern*

High St TR26 1RR ☎ 01736 796468 📠 01736 796468
Dir: *in town centre opposite Boots the Chemist on High Street (St Austell Brewery)*
This attractive inn with a mass of flower boxes is situated at the heart of St Ives. Traditional hospitality and attentive service are provided and rooms are comfortable and well-furnished. Lunch and dinner choices can be made from the menu and blackboard specials and dishes include local fish and fresh produce.
FACILITIES: 5 en suite (4 fmly) STV TVB tea/coffee No dogs (ex guide dogs) Cen ht Last d 8.30pm **CARDS:**

♦♦♦ Thurlestone Private Hotel

St Ives Rd, Carbis Bay TR26 2RT ☎ 01736 796369
e-mail: thurlestoneq@eclipse.co.uk
Dir: *off A30 follow A3074 St Ives signs. Through Lelant onto Carbis Bay, pass Spar and Londis stores on left. Hotel is 0.75m on left*
Built as a chapel in 1843, this granite house offers pleasant, modern accommodation while retaining much of the charm and style of the original building. There is an attractive lounge bar and some of the bedrooms have sea views. Thurlestone is within a short distance of the beaches.
FACILITIES: 7 rms (6 en suite) (3 fmly) No smoking in bedrooms No smoking in dining room No smoking in lounges TVB tea/coffee No dogs (ex guide dogs) Licensed Cen ht TVL No coaches **PRICES:** s £31-£35; d £42-£50✱ **PARKING:** 5 **NOTES:** Closed Nov & Jan
CARDS:

The Willows

5 Ayr Ter TR26 1ED ☎ 01736 794703
At the time of going to press the Diamond classification for this establishment had not been confirmed. Please check the AA website www.theAA.com for up-to-date information.
FACILITIES: 3 en suite

ST JUST (Near Land's End) — Map 02 SW33

♦♦♦ Wellington Hotel

Market Square TR19 7HD ☎ 01736 787319 📠 01736 787906
e-mail: wellingtonhotel@msn.com
Dir: *from A30 take A3071. St Just is 6m W of Penzance. Hotel overlooks Main Square*
Situated in the market square, this historic 14th-century inn is popular with locals and holidaymakers alike. Guest rooms are located in the main building with some rooms also available in the converted stables. Friendly hospitality, home-cooked food and local ales all making for a pleasant stay.
FACILITIES: 5 en suite 6 annexe en suite (4 fmly) (3 GF) No smoking in 1 bedrooms No smoking in area of dining room TVB tea/coffee Direct dial from bedrooms Cen ht TVL Pool Table Dinner Last d 9pm **PRICES:** s £27-£30; d £45-£50✱ **LB MEALS:** Lunch £7.50-£16alc Dinner £7.50-£16alc✱
CARDS:

ST KEVERNE — Map 02 SW72

♦♦♦ White Hart Hotel

The Square TR12 6ND ☎ 01326 280325 📠 01326 280325
e-mail: whitehart@easynet.co.uk
Dir: *from Helston, take A3083 towards the Lizard, at rdbt on exiting Culdrose turn L onto B3293 for approx 8m. Pass Goonhilly and enter village*
Peacefully located in the village square of this charming Cornish village, the White Hart is an ideal base. Guest rooms are spacious and offer modern comforts with many extra features. The restaurant and bar are traditional, with inglenook fireplaces and an exciting range of food, which features a daily specials board of fresh fish.
FACILITIES: 2 en suite No smoking in area of dining room TVB tea/coffee Direct dial from bedrooms Tennis (hard) Riding Pool Table Dinner Last d 9pm **PRICES:** s £35-£40; d £50-£60✱ **LB MEALS:** Lunch £12-£25alc Dinner £12-£25alc✱ **PARKING:** 10 **CARDS:**

England

ST MAWGAN Map 02 SW86

♦♦♦♦ The Falcon

TR8 4EP ☎ 01637 860225 🖹 01637 860884
e-mail: enquiries@falconinn.net
Dir: *from A30 follow signs to Newquay Airport, then St Mawgan village. Pub at bottom of hill in village centre*

This delightful 16th-century inn is opposite the village church in a quiet wooded valley. A warm and friendly atmosphere prevails with log fires blazing in the open hearth. Guest rooms vary in size and are comfortable and pleasantly furnished. A good choice is available at lunch and dinner, the menus featuring local fish and cheeses.
FACILITIES: 3 rms (2 en suite) No smoking in dining room TVB tea/coffee Direct dial from bedrooms Cen ht Dinner Last d 10pm **PRICES:** s £21-£38; d £50-£64✻ **MEALS:** Lunch £10-£18alc Dinner £12-£20alc✻ **PARKING:** 20 **CARDS:**

ST MERRYN Map 02 SW87

♦♦♦ *Farmers Arms*

PL28 8NP ☎ 01841 520303
(St Austell Brewery)
Located just South of Padstow, the Farmers Arms dates back to the 17th century. Sympathetically restored, many of its original features, which include beams, flagstone floors and an indoor well, have been retained. Bedrooms are comfortable and well-equipped with modern facilities. Meals are available in the two lively, spacious bars.
FACILITIES: 4 en suite (2 fmly)

ST NEOT Map 02 SX16

♦♦♦ London

St Neot PL14 6NG ☎ 01579 320263 🖹 01579 321642
e-mail: jpleisuregroup@compuserve.com
Dir: *turn off A30 at junct after Jamaica Inn signposted St Neot, follow Rd into St Neot and London Inn is situated next to the church*
You'll find a warm and friendly welcome from Stephen, Alison and the team here at the London Inn, which dates back to the 18th century and was the first coaching inn from Penzance to London. Public areas are charming and retain original character, with old beamed ceilings and flag stone floors. Bedrooms are comfortable with modern facilities. There is also a skittle alley.
FACILITIES: 3 en suite No smoking in bedrooms No smoking in dining room TVB tea/coffee No dogs (ex guide dogs) Dinner Last d 9pm **PRICES:** s £33-£38; d £45-£55✻ **MEALS:** Lunch £2.75-£6.95&alc Dinner £2.75-£6.95&alc✻ **PARKING:** 14 **CARDS:**

Prices may change during the currency of the Guide, please check when booking.

ST TEATH Map 02 SX08

Tregarthen Bed & Breakfast

PL30 3JX ☎ 01208 850603
At the time of going to press the Diamond classification for this establishment had not been confirmed. Please check the AA website www.theAA.com for up-to-date information.
FACILITIES: 3 en suite

SALTASH Map 02 SX45

♦♦♦♦ The Crooked Inn

Stoketon Cross, Trematon PL12 4RZ ☎ 01752 848177
🖹 01752 843203
e-mail: crooked.inn@virgin.net
Dir: *A38 to Tamar Bridge, cross & through tunnel. Straight over rdbt towards Liskeard. 2nd left (Trematon), immediate right to Inn*

The numerous friendly animals that freely roam the inn's courtyard add to the relaxed country style of this delightful inn. Bedrooms are comfortable, spacious and well-equipped. A good selection of freshly cooked dinners is available in either the bar or conservatory. Breakfast is served in the cottage-style dining room.
FACILITIES: 18 annexe rms (15 en suite) (5 fmly) (7 GF) No smoking in 7 bedrooms No smoking in area of dining room No smoking in 1 lounge TVB tea/coffee Cen ht Outdoor swimming pool Childrens play area Dinner Last d 9.30pm&10pm Fri/Sat **PRICES:** s £45; d £70✻ **MEALS:** Lunch £8.80-£20&alc Dinner £8.80-£20&alc✻ **PARKING:** 45 **CARDS:**

See advert on opposite page

♦♦♦♦ Weary Friar Inn

Pillaton PL12 6QS ☎ 01579 350238 🖹 01579 350238
Dir: *2m W of A388, between Saltash/Callington*
Built during the same period as the adjacent 12th century parish church in the village of Pillaton, this sympathetically extended inn retains many original features including open fires and a wealth of exposed beams. Bedrooms are homely and there is a good range of imaginative food offered.
FACILITIES: 12 en suite (1 fmly) No smoking in bedrooms No smoking in dining room TVB tea/coffee No dogs (ex guide dogs) Cen ht TVL No children 10yrs Dinner Last d 9.30pm **PRICES:** s £40-£45; d £50-£55✻ **LB MEALS:** Lunch £6-£15&alc Dinner £6-£15&alc✻ **PARKING:** 30 **CARDS:**

See advert on opposite page

♦♦♦ Holland Inn Motel

Hatt PL12 6PJ ☎ 01752 844044 🖹 01752 849701
Dir: *from A38 cross Tamar Bridge & through tunnel. Right at 1st rdbt onto A388 towards St Mellion/Callington. Inn 2m on right*
A traditional, country style inn, family orientated with an indoor play area and outdoor adventure castle. A wide choice of meals is provided in the bar area and more formal restaurant.

continued

Accommodation is in adjacent motel-style bedrooms, all of which are comfortably furnished and well equipped.
FACILITIES: 30 en suite (5 fmly) No smoking in 10 bedrooms No smoking in dining room No smoking in 1 lounge TVB tea/coffee Direct dial from bedrooms No dogs (ex guide dogs) Licensed Cen ht TVL Dinner Last d 9.30pm **PRICES:** s £44.99; d £49.99✻ **LB PARKING:** 30 **CARDS:**

SCILLY, ISLES OF

ST MARY'S — Map 02

♦♦♦♦ Carnwethers Country House

Carnwethers, Pelistry Bay TR21 0NX ☎ 01720 422415
Fax 01720 422415
Dir: *2.5m from Hugh Town, St Marys*
Carnwethers Country House is located in a quiet corner of this beautiful island. Bedrooms are bright, comfortably equipped and decorated with local watercolours and prints. There is a cosy lounge and well-stocked bar. Home-cooked meals are served in the smart dining room. Additional facilities include extensive gardens and an outdoor pool.
FACILITIES: 7 en suite 2 annexe en suite (2 fmly) (6 GF) No smoking in bedrooms No smoking in dining room No smoking in lounges TVB tea/coffee Licensed Cen ht TVL No children 10yrs No coaches Outdoor swimming pool (heated) Golf 9 Sauna Pool Table Croquet lawn Table tennis Dinner **PRICES:** d £100-£120✻ **LB PARKING:** 4 **NOTES:** Closed 30 Sep-16 April

♦♦♦♦ Crebinick House

Church St TR21 0JT ☎ 01720 422968
e-mail: aa@crebinick.co.uk
Dir: *If arriving by air - take the airport bus to Crebinick House. If arriving by sea, Crebinick House is 500m from quay through Hugh Town.*
Many guests return to this granite-fronted house dating back to 1760. Just a couple of minutes from the town centre and seafront, it is a convenient base for exploration. Bedrooms, which include two on the ground floor, are smartly presented and well-equipped. A quiet lounge is also available for guests to relax in.
FACILITIES: 6 en suite No smoking TVB tea/coffee No dogs Cen ht TVL No children 10yrs No coaches **PRICES:** d £58-£68 **NOTES:** Closed Nov-Mar

♦♦♦♦ The Wheelhouse

Little Porth TR21 0JG ☎ 01720 422719 Fax 01720 422719
Dir: *overlooking Portcressa Bay.*
FACILITIES: 9 en suite No smoking TVB tea/coffee No dogs Licensed Cen ht No children 15yrs No coaches Dinner Last d 6pm
PRICES: s £36-£48; d £72-£96✻ **LB**

SENNEN — Map 02 SW32

♦♦♦♦ Mayon Farmhouse

TR19 7AD ☎ 01736 871757 Fax 01736 871757
e-mail: mayonfarmhouse@fsmail.net
Dir: *enter Sennen on A30. Post office on right, opposite is driveway (100yds long) leading to establishment*
A warm welcome awaits at this farmhouse, as the new proprietors do their utmost to ensure guests have an enjoyable stay. Delightful views, a cosy lounge, a sunny conservatory and an open plan dining room are appealing features, whilst the bedrooms are comfortable and retain the charm of the old farmhouse.
FACILITIES: 3 en suite No smoking TVB tea/coffee Cen ht No children 16yrs No coaches **PRICES:** s £35-£40; d £46-£60✻ **LB PARKING:** 6

England

TINTAGEL Map 02 SX08

Premier Collection

♦♦♦♦♦ Old Borough House

Bossiney PL34 0AY ☎ 01840 770475 01840 779000
e-mail: theoldboroughhouse@hotmail.com
Dir: *off A39 signed Tintagel & Boscastle, situated on seaward side of B3263 in Bossiney*

Once the home of J B Priestly this engaging 15th century house has been sensitively and skilfully converted to combine modern comforts with oodles of character. Bedrooms are individually styled, with one located in a charming detached cottage. The hospitable hosts truly enjoy sharing their home with guests and many thoughtful extras abound to ensure a relaxed and enjoyable stay. Excellent dinners are available by prior arrangement.
FACILITIES: 3 en suite 1 annexe en suite (3 GF) No smoking TV5B tea/coffee No dogs (ex guide dogs) Licensed Cen ht No children 12yrs No coaches Tennis (hard) Dinner Last d by arrangement **PRICES:** s £37.50-£40; d £54-£70✱ **CONF:** Thtr 16 Class 16 Board 8 Del from £60 ✱ **PARKING:** 11 **NOTES:** Closed Dec-mid Feb **CARDS:**

♦♦♦♦ Pendrin House

Atlantic Rd PL34 0DE ☎ 01840 770560 01840 770560
e-mail: pendrin@tesco.net
Dir: *From A39 follow signs to Tintagel, through village past entrance to Tintagel Castle. Pendrin last house on right before Headlands caravan site*
Located close to coastal walks, Tintagel Castle and the town centre, Pendrin House provides comfortable accommodation with some rooms having views of the sea or surrounding countryside. Delicious evening meals, using fresh quality ingredients are available by prior arrangement. A cosy lounge is also provided for guests.
FACILITIES: 9 rms (4 en suite) (2 fmly) (1 GF) No smoking in bedrooms No smoking in dining room TVB tea/coffee No dogs (ex guide dogs) Cen ht TVL No coaches Dinner Last d 6pm **PRICES:** s £18; d £36-£40✱ **LB BB PARKING:** 6 **NOTES:** Closed Dec-Feb **CARDS:**

♦♦♦♦ Port William

Trebarwith Strand PL34 0HB ☎ 01840 770230 01840 770936
e-mail: william@eurobell.co.uk
Dir: *off B3263 from Camelford to Tintagel*
Just a short distance from Tintagel, this fascinating inn is perched on the side of a cliff, with spectacular views. The bedrooms are decorated to a high standard and all have views over the sea. Menus offer a wide range of good food, with the emphasis on locally caught fish. The traditional bar is furnished with old church pews and large wooden tables.

continued

Port William Inn

FACILITIES: 5 en suite (1 fmly) No smoking in bedrooms No smoking in area of dining room No smoking in 1 lounge TVB tea/coffee Direct dial from bedrooms Cen ht Dinner Last d 9.30pm **PRICES:** s £56-£63; d £73-£87✱ **LB MEALS:** Lunch £15-£25&alc Dinner £15-£30&alc✱ **PARKING:** 50 **CARDS:**

♦♦♦♦ *Tintagel Arms Hotel*

Fore St PL34 0DB ☎ 01840 770780
Dir: *from M5 take A30, R on B395, follow signs for Camelford. Hotel in Tintagel centre opposite Lloyds Bank*
Popular with locals and visitors alike, this Cornish stone property is centrally located in the village. Warm hospitality and comfortable accommodation is assured. A wide choice of meals, many with a Greek flavour, is provided in the dining area, next to the traditional bar. Ample parking is a bonus.
FACILITIES: 7 en suite No smoking in bedrooms No smoking in area of dining room TVB tea/coffee No dogs (ex guide dogs) Cen ht No children 6yrs Dinner Last d 9.30pm **PARKING:** 8 **CARDS:**

♦♦♦♦ The Cottage Teashop

Bossiney Rd PL34 0AH ☎ 01840 770639
e-mail: cotteashop@talk21.com
Dir: *off A30, 2m past Launceston junct onto A395. Follow signs to Camelford then Tintagel*
FACILITIES: 4 rms (3 en suite) TVB tea/coffee Licensed Cen ht No children 10yrs No coaches Dinner Last d 8.30pm **PRICES:** s £25-£30; d £40-£54✱ **LB PARKING:** 4 **NOTES:** Closed 24-26 Dec **CARDS:**

TORPOINT Map 02 SX45

♦♦♦ Edgcumbe Arms

Cremyll PL10 1HX ☎ 01752 822294 01752 822014
e-mail: edgcumbearms@btopenworld.com
Dir: *Travel towards Plymouth Head for Torpoint Ferry (runs 24hrs). Cross Ferry and head for Mount Edgcumbe House and Country Park, appox 12m (St Austell Brewery)*
Situated within the 800 acre Mount Edgcumbe Park Estate at the mouth of the River Tamar, this delightful character inn has wonderful views across Plymouth Sound. The spacious bedrooms offer good standards of comfort, whilst the timber-lined, flagstone-floored bar is the ideal venue for good food.
FACILITIES: 6 en suite (2 fmly) No smoking in bedrooms No smoking in area of dining room TVB tea/coffee No dogs (ex guide dogs) Cen ht Dinner Last d 9pm **PRICES:** s £35; d £60✱ **LB MEALS:** Lunch £2.95-£8.95 Dinner £8.95-£13.95alc✱ **CONF:** Class 40 Board 40 **PARKING:** 8 **NOTES:** rs Oct-Etr Civ Wed 40 **CARDS:**

An asterisk ✱ indicates that prices given are for 2002.

England

TRURO Map 02 SW84

Premier Collection

♦♦♦♦♦ Bissick Old Mill

Ladock TR2 4PG ☎ 01726 882557 01726 884057
e-mail: sonia.v@bissickoldmill.ndo.co.uk
Dir: *7m NE on B3275*

Dating back some 300 years, this charming old mill has an informal and friendly atmosphere. There is character in abundance here, with low ceilings, thick stone walls, beams and an impressive fireplace. The dining room provides an ideal setting for well prepared dishes, and the individually decorated bedrooms are spacious and well equipped. This is an ideal base from which to explore the area; the Eden Project is just a short drive away.
FACILITIES: 3 en suite 1 annexe en suite (1 GF) No smoking TVB tea/coffee Direct dial from bedrooms No dogs (ex guide dogs) Licensed Cen ht No children 10yrs No coaches Dinner Last d Noon **PRICES:** d £54-£74* **PARKING:** 6 **NOTES:** Closed Dec-Jan
CARDS:

♦♦♦♦ Manor Cottage

Tresillian TR2 4BN ☎ 01872 520212
e-mail: man.cott@cwcom.net
Dir: *2.5m from Truro on A390 St Austell road*
This establishment features a conservatory-style restaurant, open Thursday to Sunday evenings. Menus feature modern English-style cuisine, and use many local ingredients. Guest rooms have some interesting items of period furniture, and are comfortable and spacious. Manor Cottage is an ideal location for visiting many local attractions including the Eden Project and the Gardens of Heligan.
FACILITIES: 5 rms (3 en suite) (1 fmly) No smoking in 1 bedrooms No smoking in dining room TVB tea/coffee No dogs (ex guide dogs) Licensed Cen ht No coaches Dinner Last d 9pm **PRICES:** s £25-£50; d £50-£75* **LB PARKING:** 9 **NOTES:** Closed 24-26 Dec **CARDS:**

♦♦♦♦ Marcorrie Hotel

20 Falmouth Rd TR1 2HX ☎ 01872 277374 01872 241666
e-mail: marcorrie@aol.com
Dir: *A39 (A390) Truro ring rd, turn for city centre at Arch Hill rdbt (A39/A390 junct). Hotel 500mtrs towards city centre on L in Falmouth Rd*
Convenient for the city centre and ideal for either the business or touring guest, this hotel provides spacious accommodation. Personally run by the proprietors, the Marcorrie offers comfortable, well-equipped rooms. Traditional breakfasts are served in the dining room, and guests also have a comfortable lounge where they may relax.
FACILITIES: 9 en suite 3 annexe en suite (3 fmly) No smoking TVB tea/coffee Direct dial from bedrooms Licensed Cen ht TVL No coaches
PRICES: s £39.50-£47.50; d £49.50-£55* **LB PARKING:** 12
CARDS:

♦♦♦♦ Rock Cottage

Blackwater TR4 8EU ☎ 01872 560252 01872 560252
e-mail: rockcottage@yahoo.com
Dir: *take A30 to Chiverton rdbt, follow sign to Blackwater. Premises next to Red Lion Inn just past 2nd x-roads*
This former schoolmaster's home is a most pleasant and attractive house. The proprietors are attentive and friendly hosts and guests are made to feel at home. The comfortable bedrooms are very well-equipped and one room is located on the ground floor. Hearty breakfasts are served in the original kitchen in front of the Cornish range.
FACILITIES: 3 en suite (1 GF) No smoking TVB tea/coffee No dogs Cen ht TVL No children 18yrs No coaches **PRICES:** s £26-£28; d £44-£48* **LB PARKING:** 3 **NOTES:** Closed Xmas & New Year **CARDS:**

♦♦♦♦ Trevispian Vean *(SW850502)*

St Erme TR4 9AT ☎ 01872 279514 Nick & Jacqui Dymond
Dir: *from A30 take A39 for Truro, in 2.5m in Trispen village take 2nd left in 0.5m bear sharp left, farm entrance 500yds on left*
Set in peaceful countryside this busy working farm is convenient for visiting the areas many attractions. Many guests return to Trevispian on a regular basis and all are assured of a friendly welcome at this family run farmhouse. Freshly cooked traditional farmhouse breakfasts are served in the dining room at separate tables.
FACILITIES: 5 en suite (2 fmly) No smoking TVB tea/coffee No dogs (ex guide dogs) Licensed TVL Fishing Pool Table Table tennis 300 acres arable pigs Dinner Last d 4.30pm **PRICES:** s £21-£24; d £42* **LB PARKING:** 20 **NOTES:** Closed Oct, Dec-Jan

TYWARDREATH Map 02 SX05

♦♦♦♦ Elmswood

Tehidy Rd PL24 2QD ☎ 01726 814221 01726 814399
Dir: *turn off A390 at junct for Fowey, follow road for 3m B3269. Turn right at junct for Tywardreath & Par Hotel opposite St Andrew's Church*
Centrally located in a peaceful village, this fine gabled Victorian house provides a warm welcome. Bedrooms are well-equipped with quality furnishings and many extra facilities. The attractive dining room, lounge and bar overlook a beautiful award-winning garden. Home-cooked dinners featuring quality local produce are available by prior arrangement.
FACILITIES: 7 rms (6 en suite) (1 fmly) No smoking in dining room TVB tea/coffee No dogs (ex guide dogs) Licensed Cen ht TVL No coaches Dinner Last d noon **PRICES:** s £22.50-£30; d £46-£50* **PARKING:** 8
NOTES: Closed Dec-Jan

England

VERYAN Map 02 SW93

♦♦♦♦ Elerkey
Elerkey House TR2 5QA ☎ 01872 501261 📠 01872 501354
e-mail: anne.squire@btinternet.com
Dir: *A30 Exeter to St Austell, left fork B3287 to Tregary & St Mawes. Signposted Veryan after Esso garage (bear left to Veryan). Follow brown signs into villiage, Elerkey is 1st left after church & water gardens*

Situated in the heart of this charming village, and surrounded by attractive gardens, Elerkey is an ideal base from which to explore the delights of the area. The resident proprietors and their family provide exemplary hospitality and service and many guests return regularly to enjoy the comfort and charm of this delightful home. An extensive collection of the proprietor's artwork is available for sale in the adjoining gallery.
FACILITIES: 5 en suite (2 fmly) No smoking in bedrooms No smoking in dining room No smoking in 1 lounge TVB tea/coffee Direct dial from bedrooms No dogs Cen ht No coaches Art gallery & gift shop **PRICES:** s fr £23.50; d £47-£49✻ **LB PARKING:** 5 **NOTES:** Closed Xmas/New Year **CARDS:**

The New Inn
TR2 5QA ☎ 01872 501362
At the time of going to press the Diamond classification for this establishment had not been confirmed. Please check the AA website www.theAA.com for up-to-date information.
FACILITIES: 3 en suite

WADEBRIDGE Map 02 SW97

♦♦♦♦ *Swan Hotel*
9 Molesworth St PL27 7DD ☎ 01208 812526 📠 816479
(St Austell Brewery)
A popular, traditional inn, the Swan Hotel is situated in the centre of the town and still retains its beamed ceilings and wood-panelled walls. The well-furnished and equipped bedrooms provide many thoughtful extras. Bar meals are served at midday and during the evening. A delightful function room is also available.
FACILITIES: 6 en suite (1 fmly) STV TVB tea/coffee No dogs (ex guide dogs) Cen ht Pool Table Last d 9pm **CARDS:**

TVB means there are televisions in bedrooms
TVL means there's a television in the lounge
STV means satellite television.

CUMBRIA

ALSTON Map 12 NY74

See also Cowshill (Co Durham)

♦♦♦♦ Greycroft
Middle Park, The Raise CA9 3AR ☎ 01434 381383
e-mail: enquiry@greycroft.co.uk
Dir: *from Alston A686 for Penrith, over river 2nd junct right then 1st left signed Ward Way/Middle Park Greycroft 200yds on right at junction for Middle Park*
This bungalow, set in well tended and colourful gardens, is situated just outside the town, overlooking the fells. Comfortably furnished bedrooms are complemented by a welcoming lounge and spacious dining room with picture windows. A generous breakfast is served around one large table and dinner is available by arrangement. A warm welcome and helpful service can be expected.
FACILITIES: 2 en suite (2 fmly) (2 GF) No smoking TVB tea/coffee No dogs (ex guide dogs) Cen ht TVL No coaches Dinner Last d 2pm **PRICES:** s £27-£29; d £44-£48✻ **LB PARKING:** 3 **NOTES:** Closed Xmas & Apr

♦♦♦♦ Ivy House
Garrigill CA9 3DU ☎ 01434 382501 📠 01434 382660
e-mail: ivyhouse@garrigill.com
Dir: *from Penrith turn right off A686 2m before Alston. Signposted. From Alston, turn off B6277 after 2m. Signposted. Ivy House is opposite Church in the village centre.*
Animal lovers will be in their element at this converted 17th-century farmhouse, situated in the delightful village. Congenial hostess Laurie Humble will proudly introduce her pets, including the llamas, which are available for treks in the village and surrounding countryside. The house has a homely, welcoming atmosphere, and bedrooms are comfortable and well equipped. There is stabling for horses and cycle storage provided.
FACILITIES: 3 en suite (2 fmly) No smoking TVB tea/coffee Cen ht TVL No coaches Short, medium & long Llama treks Dinner Last d 24hr notice **PRICES:** s £27; d £44 **LB PARKING:** 11 **CARDS:**

AMBLESIDE Map 07 NY30

Premier Collection

♦♦♦♦♦ Grey Friar Lodge Country House Hotel
Clappersgate LA22 9NE ☎ 015394 33158 📠 015394 33158
e-mail: greyfriar@veen.freeserve.co.uk
Dir: *from M6 take A591 to Ambleside, then A593 to Coniston, 400 mtrs past Clappersgate*
Just a short drive from Ambleside, Grey Friar Lodge is a former Victorian vicarage. The hotel stands in its own grounds and has views overlooking the River Brathay. Bedrooms are tastefully decorated and furnished with an array of period and antique furnishings, the unusual beds are a particular feature. Guests can use the veranda in summer or enjoy a real log fire in one of the lounges during the winter.
FACILITIES: 9 en suite No smoking TVB tea/coffee No dogs Licensed Cen ht No children 12yrs No coaches Dinner Last d 10am **PRICES:** s £37-£96; d £54-£96✻ **LB PARKING:** 12 **NOTES:** Closed 11 Dec-9 Jan **CARDS:**

See advertisement on opposite page

England

Premier Collection

♦♦♦♦♦ Rowanfield Country House

Kirkstone Rd LA22 9ET ☎ 015394 33686 Fax 015394 31569
e-mail: email@rowanfield.com
Dir: *off A591 at button rdbt near Bridge House, signed 'Kirkstone 3', establishment is 0.75 mile on right*

This country house lies in lovely gardens high above the town, with delightful views across the valley towards Lake Windermere. Bedrooms are individually decorated and furnished; the stunning attic room is particularly spacious. The dining room has a modern style while retaining a country feel, with huge flagstones and a door leading to the garden. Guests are well looked after and are made to feel very much at home.
FACILITIES: 7 en suite (1 fmly) No smoking TVB tea/coffee No dogs Cen ht No children 8yrs No coaches **PRICES:** d £67-£100* **LB**
PARKING: 8 **NOTES:** Closed mid Nov-mid Mar (ex Xmas/New Year)
CARDS:

♦♦♦♦ Brathay Lodge

Rothay Rd LA22 0EE ☎ 015394 32000
e-mail: brathay@globalnet.co.uk
Dir: *M6 J36. Follow A591 to Ambleside. One-way system into town centre. Lodge on R opp church.*

Guests can indulge and relax at Brathay Lodge. Recently refurbished, accommodation consists of spacious comfortable bedrooms, all of which have en suite spa baths. Combining both traditional and contemporary styles, the property is immaculately decorated and furnished throughout. An extensive continental breakfast can be enjoyed either in the informal lounge or in the privacy of your room.
FACILITIES: 17 en suite 4 annexe en suite No smoking Cen ht TVL Jacuzzi
PARKING: 23 **CARDS:**

♦♦♦♦ Drunken Duck

Barngates LA22 0NG ☎ 015394 36347 Fax 015394 36781
e-mail: info@drunkenduckinn.demon.co.uk
Dir: *from Ambleside go towards Hawkshead, turn left on B5285 follow for 2.5m, turn right signposted Drunken Duck Inn, 0.5m up hill*

Enjoying stunning views, this former coaching inn dates back 400 years. Smartly furnished bedrooms are individually designed, thoughtfully equipped and include two luxury suites housed in an adjacent building. Carefully prepared meals are served in the popular bar or the more intimate restaurant. The pub has its own brewery that produces popular, award-winning beer.
FACILITIES: 8 en suite 3 annexe en suite No smoking in bedrooms No smoking in dining room TVB Direct dial from bedrooms No dogs (ex guide dogs) Cen ht No coaches Fishing Dinner Last d 9pm **PARKING:** 40
CARDS:

England

♦♦♦♦ Wateredge Inn
Waterhead Bay LA22 0EP ☎ 015394 32332 015394 31878
e-mail: rec@wateredgeinn.co.uk
Dir: *On A591, at Waterhead, 1m S of Ambleside. Wateredge situated at end of promenade by lake*

This smart modern inn enjoys an idyllic location nestling on the shores of Windermere at Waterhead Bay. The pretty bedrooms are particularly smart and generally spacious, all offering a high standard of quality and comfort. The open plan bar/restaurant has a light airy feel and opens directly onto the attractive gardens, with magnificent lake views. There is also a comfortable lounge.
FACILITIES: 15 en suite 6 annexe en suite (3 fmly) (3 GF) No smoking in 1 bedrooms No smoking in area of dining room No smoking in lounges TVB tea/coffee Cen ht Complimentary membership to nearby leisure club Dinner Last d 8.30pm **PRICES:** s £35-£45; d £70-£110* **MEALS:** Bar Lunch £10.40-£24.90alc Dinner £14.25-£24.90alc* **PARKING:** 40 **CARDS:**

♦♦♦♦ Easedale Lodge
Compston Rd LA22 9DJ ☎ 015394 32112 32112
e-mail: soar@easedaleambleside.co.uk
Dir: *on one way system going north through Ambleside - bottom of Compston Road on corner overlooking bowling & putting greens*
In a good central location, this charming, well-maintained guest house enjoys views over the park. Bedrooms are cosy and fresh and offer a host of thoughtful extras. There is a good choice at breakfast, served in the elegant dining room with conservatory extension. There is also a well presented lounge.
FACILITIES: 7 en suite (1 fmly) No smoking TVB tea/coffee No dogs Cen ht TVL No coaches **PRICES:** s fr £25; d fr £50* **LB NOTES:** Closed mid Nov-26 Dec & 5 Jan-mid Feb **PARKING:** 7

♦♦♦♦ Elterwater Park
Skelwith LA22 9NP ☎ 015394 32227
e-mail: enquiries@elterwater.com
Dir: *take A593 from Ambleside in direction of Coniston. 1m past Skelwith Bridge Hotel is a layby on right which fronts estate road to Elterwater Park. Signpost at gate*
A traditional Lakeland house, set high on the hills above Langdale. From the house and garden there are spectacular views, and the Cumbrian Way passes the door. Bedrooms are attractive, comfortably furnished and well equipped, with a ground floor bedroom and en suite specially fitted for disabled guests. Delicious evening meals and breakfasts are served at individual tables in the lounge/dining room.
FACILITIES: 5 en suite No smoking TVB tea/coffee No dogs (ex guide dogs) Cen ht No children 8 yrs No coaches **PRICES:** d £58-£70* **LB PARKING:** 8 **NOTES:** Closed 19-26 Dec & 3-31 Jan **CARDS:**

♦♦♦♦ Kent House
Lake Rd LA22 0AD ☎ 015394 33279 015394 31667
e-mail: info@kent-house.com
Dir: *from town centre, by post office in one way system 300yds on left on terrace above main road*

continued

Kent House

This traditional Lakeland house enjoys a super location sitting high above the main street overlooking the bustle of the town below. Kent House has lots of stylish touches, and those interested in good food beautifully cooked and presented will appreciate Richard's creative cooking at both dinner and breakfast. Bedrooms are very thoughtfully equipped.
FACILITIES: 6 en suite (2 fmly) No smoking TVB tea/coffee Direct dial from bedrooms Licensed Cen ht No coaches Dinner Last d noon **PRICES:** d £56-£70* **LB PARKING:** 2 **CARDS:**

♦♦♦♦ Stepping Stones
Under Loughrigg LA22 9LN ☎ 015394 33552 015394 33552
e-mail: info@steppingstonesambleside.com
Dir: *1m N of Ambleside on A591, turn left over hump backed bridge. Cross 2 cattle grids Stepping Stones approx. 50yds on right*
Just one mile from Ambleside, set in two acres of landscaped gardens, this beautiful historic Lakeland house (previously the home of the Wordsworth family) fronts the River Rothay, overlooking the famous 'Stepping Stones', and enjoys spectacular views of the fells and surrounding countryside. Bedrooms are spacious, attractively decorated and tastefully appointed. Hearty Cumberland breakfasts are served at individual tables.
FACILITIES: 3 en suite No smoking TVB tea/coffee No dogs (ex guide dogs) Cen ht No children No coaches **PRICES:** s £45-£65; d £50-£70*
PARKING: 8

♦♦♦♦ Compston House
Compston Rd LA22 9DJ ☎ 015394 32305
e-mail: compston@globalnet.co.uk
Dir: *in centre of village overlooking the park*
FACILITIES: 9 en suite No smoking TVB tea/coffee No dogs (ex guide dogs) Cen ht No children 14yrs No coaches **PRICES:** s £22-£35; d £44-£100* **LB PARKING:** 2 **CARDS:**

♦♦♦♦ Freshfields
Wansfell Rd LA22 0EG ☎ 015394 34469 015394 34469
e-mail: info@freshfieldsguesthouse.co.uk
Dir: *approach Ambleside on A591, through traffic lights at Waterhead, left opposite BP garage into Wansfell Rd.*
FACILITIES: 3 en suite No smoking TVB tea/coffee No dogs Cen ht No children 15 yrs No coaches **PRICES:** s £45; d £50-£60* **LB**
PARKING: 3 **NOTES:** Closed 24-26 Dec

♦♦♦ White Lion Hotel
Market Place LA22 9DB ☎ 015394 39901 015394 39902
Dir: *A591 towards Ambleside, round one-way system keeping to right, hotel on left opposite Post Office*
Situated in the centre of town, this traditional inn offers comfortable accommodation in generally spacious, thoughtfully equipped bedrooms. A varied menu offers a wide range of popular dishes, which can be enjoyed in the spacious bar, or in an area set-aside for residents. Staff are friendly and helpful.

continued

FACILITIES: 7 en suite (2 fmly) No smoking in bedrooms No smoking in area of dining room No smoking in 1 lounge TVB tea/coffee No dogs (ex guide dogs) Cen ht Pool Table Last d 8.45pm **PRICES:** s fr £35; d fr £50✻ **PARKING:** 10 **CARDS:**

♦♦♦ *2 Cambridge Villas*

Church St LA22 9DL ☎ 015394 32142

Near to the town centre, this small guest house offers a warm welcome and a relaxed atmosphere. Bedrooms are compact, modern and appropriately furnished. Decoration throughout is of a high standard, including the neat, bright dining room where hearty breakfasts are served.

FACILITIES: 5 rms (3 en suite) (1 fmly) No smoking in bedrooms No smoking in dining room TVB tea/coffee No dogs Cen ht TVL Last d 10.30am **NOTES:** Closed 30 Nov-1 Jan

♦♦♦ Chapel House Hotel

Kirkstone Rd LA22 9DZ ☎ 01539 433143 📠 01539 433143

Dir: *from S follow signs Keswick/Grasmere, leave shops in town centre & turn right off A591 just past little Bridge House along Smithy Brow into Kirkstone Rd. Hotel 200yds from bottom on right*

Old-world charm is retained at Chapel House Hotel. Located in the oldest part of Ambleside overlooking the village and fells, these former 16th century cottages have been sympathetically converted to provide clean, comfortable accommodation. Pre-dinner drinks are served in the cosy bar and delicious freshly prepared meals are served in the beamed dining room.

FACILITIES: 10 rms (4 en suite) (1 fmly) No smoking in bedrooms No smoking in dining room No dogs Licensed Cen ht No coaches Dinner Last d 5pm **PRICES:** (incl. dinner) s £45-£50; d £90-£100✻ **LB** **NOTES:** Closed Jan-Feb rs Nov-Dec

♦♦♦ Haven Cottage

Rydal Rd LA22 9AY ☎ 015394 33270 📠 015394 33270

e-mail: jon_elsabe@lineone.net

Dir: *400yds NW of the Bridge House, Ambleside on the left hand side of the A591*

Haven Cottage Guest House is situated just a five-minute walk from the town, perfect for those who just like to potter around. Low beamed ceilings and comfortable, pine furnished bedrooms create a cosy atmosphere and for those who wish to walk the fells, there is a drying room.

FACILITIES: 6 rms (4 en suite) (1 fmly) No smoking TVB tea/coffee No dogs (ex guide dogs) Cen ht **PRICES:** d £44-£54✻ **LB** **PARKING:** 8 **CARDS:**

♦♦♦ Meadowbank

Rydal Rd LA22 9BA ☎ 015394 32710 📠 015394 32710

e-mail: enquiries@meadowbank.org.uk

Dir: *M6 junct 36, South Lakes follow A591 to Ambleside, follow one way system through town, Meadowbank is last house on left*

On the edge of Ambleside, set in attractive grounds, this delightful family-run guest house offers comfortable, well-equipped accommodation. There is a cosy lounge and a large bright airy dining room where hearty traditional Cumbrian breakfasts are served at individual tables.

FACILITIES: 7 en suite (1 fmly) No smoking TVB tea/coffee Cen ht TVL **PRICES:** s £20-£32; d £40-£64✻ **PARKING:** 10 **CARDS:**

♦♦♦ Rysdale Hotel

Rothay Rd LA22 0EE ☎ 015394 32140 📠015394 33999

e-mail: info@rysdalehotel.co.uk

Dir: *leave M6 junct 36 to Ambleside on A591. Enter one-way system follow town centre signs, hotel opposite church & bowling green*

Overlooking the church and the park, this comfortable Lakeland house offers a warm and friendly welcome. Superb views of the Fells can be enjoyed from most of the tastefully decorated, well equipped bedrooms, and also from the dining room, home to an interesting collection of teapots. A cosy lounge with adjacent bar is also available.

FACILITIES: 9 rms (7 en suite) (3 fmly) No smoking TVB tea/coffee Licensed Cen ht TVL No children 8yrs No coaches **PRICES:** s £23-£35; d £38-£80✻ **LB** **BB** **PARKING:** 2

♦♦♦ Melrose

Church St LA22 0BT ☎ 015394 32500 📠 015394 31495

Dir: *Kendal to Windemere A591 past railway station to Ambleside left into one way system down Wansfell Road at bottom turn right then 2nd right to Kelswick road proceed around car park onto Church Street, Melrose at bottom on right*

FACILITIES: 8 en suite (3 fmly) No smoking TVB tea/coffee No dogs Cen ht **PRICES:** s £20-£27.50; d £40-£60✻

APPLEBY-IN-WESTMORLAND — Map 12 NY62

♦♦♦♦ Bongate House

Bongate CA16 6UE ☎ 017683 51245 📠 017683 51423

e-mail: Bongatehse@aol.com

Dir: *0.5m from town centre on B6542 signposted Brough*

A friendly welcome awaits guests at this lovely Georgian house, dating back to 1740. Bedrooms are comfortable, and the larger rooms have en suite facilities. The landscaped gardens and grounds are spacious and attractive. Hearty breakfasts and dinners by arrangement are served in the spacious dining room.

FACILITIES: 8 rms (5 en suite) (4 fmly) No smoking in bedrooms No smoking in dining room No smoking in 1 lounge TVB tea/coffee Licensed Cen ht No children 7yrs Croquet & putting lawn **PRICES:** s £20; d £40-£46✻ **LB** **PARKING:** 10

♦♦♦♦ Eden Grove Farmhouse

Bolton CA16 6AX ☎ 017683 62321

e-mail: edengrovecumbria@aol.com

Dir: *off A66 1.5m into village, pass villiage hall, 1st right 0.4 miles Edengrove right*

Charming and hospitable, this Victorian house is situated in pleasant gardens. The comfortable bedrooms are tastefully decorated and contain many thoughtful touches. Memorable breakfasts, served in the conservatory dinning room, boast local sausages and bacon, home-made bread and preserves, and free-range eggs. Eden Grove is no-smoking and unlicensed.

FACILITIES: 3 rms (2 en suite) No smoking TVB tea/coffee Direct dial from bedrooms No dogs (ex guide dogs) Cen ht TVL No children 12yrs No coaches Dinner Last d 4.30pm **PRICES:** s £21-£25; d £42-£50✻ **LB** **PARKING:** 3 **NOTES:** Closed Xmas/New Year

♦♦♦ *Clifton Cottage*

Bridge End, Warcop CA16 6PD ☎ 017683 41372

Dir: *turn off A66 onto B6259 into Warcop. Establishment approx 500yds beyond the church, turn left just before bridge, on right*

This is a terraced cottage that is located close to the green in the attractive village of Warcop. It is also situated just off the A66 and only a short drive from Appleby. There are two attractive bedrooms, which offer homely comforts. A friendly atmosphere prevails here.

FACILITIES: 2 rms (1 fmly) No smoking in 1 bedrooms No smoking in area of dining room tea/coffee No dogs (ex guide dogs) Cen ht No coaches Fishing permits for River Eden available Dinner Last d 5pm **PARKING:** 2

BB Great value! This indicates B&B for £19 and under, per person, per night.

England

ARNSIDE Map 07 SD47

♦♦♦♦ Willowfield Hotel

The Promenade LA5 0AD ☎ 01524 761354
e-mail: janet@willowfield.net1.co.uk
Dir: *turn off A6 at Milnthorpe traffic lights onto B5282, right at T-junction on entering village and right again at Albion public house*

Family run, this splendid Victorian house is set amidst gardens just off the promenade and boasts stunning views across the Morecambe Bay estuary to the distant Lake District, which is only a 30 minutes drive away. Bedrooms are attractively decorated and reception rooms extend to a comfortable lounge and a spacious conservatory dining room. Friendly hospitality is assured.

FACILITIES: 11 rms (10 en suite) (2 fmly) (1 GF) No smoking TVB tea/coffee Licensed Cen ht No coaches Dinner Last d 1pm
PRICES: s £25.50; d £53-£58* **LB PARKING:** 8
CARDS:

ASKHAM Map 12 NY52

♦♦♦ Queen's Head Inn

CA10 2PF ☎ 01931 712225 01937 712811
e-mail: d.nicholls@btconnect.com

This traditional 17th-century village inn is situated in the centre of the peaceful village of Askham. Bedrooms, including a spacious four-poster suite, are thoughtfully equipped and tastefully appointed. Public areas boast real fires, brass and copper memorabilia and original exposed beams. The bar and restaurant serve a wide range of dishes.

FACILITIES: 4 en suite (2 fmly) No smoking in bedrooms TVB tea/coffee Direct dial from bedrooms Cen ht Fishing Pool Table darts Dinner Last d 9pm **PRICES:** s £35-£40; d £55-£65* **LB MEALS:** Lunch £4.95-£11.95 Dinner £4.95-£11.95* **PARKING:** 22 **CARDS:**

BASSENTHWAITE LAKE Map 11 NY13

♦♦♦♦ Link House

CA13 9YD ☎ 017687 76291 017687 76670
e-mail: gfkerr@lineone.net
Dir: *A66 past Keswick & keep W of lake to N end then turn R onto B5291signed "Dubwath". Follow road to L.*

A warm welcome awaits guests at this attractive, well-maintained house, peacefully located at the northern end of the lake. Public rooms include an attractive cosy lounge, a bright conservatory with a residents' bar (where guests may smoke) and a smart dining room. Bedrooms vary in size and style but are all attractively decorated and smartly furnished.

FACILITIES: 9 rms (8 en suite) (1 fmly) No smoking in bedrooms No smoking in dining room No smoking in lounges TVB tea/coffee Licensed Cen ht TVL No children 7yrs No coaches Dinner Last d 10.30am
PRICES: s £23-£30; d £50-£58* **LB PARKING:** 11
CARDS:

BORROWDALE Map 11 NY21

Premier Collection

♦♦♦♦♦ Hazel Bank Country House

Rosthwaite CA12 5XB ☎ 017687 77248 017687 77373
e-mail: enquiries@hazelbankhotel.co.uk
Dir: *6m from Keswick on B5289 Seatoller road, turn left at sign just before Rosthwaite village*

In an elevated position, surrounded by four acres of well-tended lawns and woodland, this Victorian residence commands magnificent views of the Borrowdale valley. Bedrooms are well proportioned, thoughtfully equipped and tastefully decorated. Set four-course dinners, cooked with imagination and skill, and excellent breakfasts are served in the delightful dining room. Service is attentive and hospitality is warm, making guests feel very much at home.

FACILITIES: 8 en suite (2 GF) No smoking TVB tea/coffee No dogs Licensed Cen ht No children 10yrs No coaches Croquet lawn Dinner Last d 3pm **PRICES:** (incl. dinner) s £52.50-£77.50; d £105-£155*
PARKING: 12 **CARDS:**

♦♦♦♦ Greenbank

CA12 5UY ☎ 017687 77215
e-mail: jeanwwood@lineone.net
Dir: *3m S of Keswick on B5289*

This delightful Victorian house enjoys breathtaking views across to Derewentwater, and north to Skiddaw. The attractive bedrooms are comfortable and thoughtfully equipped. There is a choice of lounges, one of which has an honesty bar. Delicious evening meals and hearty Cumbrian breakfasts are served in the dining room. Bridge weekends and house parties are held.

FACILITIES: 10 en suite (1 fmly) (2 GF) No smoking in bedrooms No smoking in dining room No smoking in 1 lounge tea/coffee No dogs (ex guide dogs) Licensed Cen ht TVL No children 2yrs No coaches Dinner Last d 5pm **PRICES:** s £30-£35; d £60-£70* **LB PARKING:** 15 **NOTES:** Closed Xmas & Jan **CARDS:**

BOWNESS-ON-WINDERMERE

See **Windermere**

BRAITHWAITE Map 11 NY22

♦♦♦ The Royal Oak

Braithwaite CA12 5SY ☎ 017687 78533 017687 78533
e-mail: tpfranks@hotmail.com
Dir: *turn off A66 and follow Whinlatter Pass. Hotel in middle of Braithwaite.*

The Royal Oak, situated in the pretty village of Braithwaite, enjoys delightful views of Skiddaw and Barrow, and is an ideal base for tourists and walkers alike. Bedrooms, some of which are furnished with four-poster beds, are comfortable and well equipped. There is

continued

The Royal Oak

a restaurant where hearty evening meals and traditional Cumbrian breakfasts are served, and a well-stocked, atmospheric bar.
FACILITIES: 10 en suite (1 fmly) No smoking in bedrooms No smoking in dining room TVB tea/coffee Licensed Cen ht Tennis (hard & grass) Dinner Last d 9pm **PRICES:** s £35-£40; d £57-£70✻ **LB** **PARKING:** 20
CARDS:

BRAMPTON Map 12 NY56

See also Castle Carrock

Premier Collection

♦♦♦♦♦ *Cracrop (NY521697)*

Kirkcambeck CA8 2BW ☎ 016977 48245 016977 48333
Mrs M Stobart
e-mail: cracrop@aol.com
Dir: *At Brampton take A6071 (Longtown Rd) for 2m. After bridge, turn R, signed Walton/Roadhead. At Kirkcambeck over bridge, L at B&B sign, Cracrop is 1m on R.*
This delightful, friendly farmhouse forms part of a working farm dating back to 1847. Peacefully set in its own beautifully landscaped gardens it offers large, comfortable, tastefully appointed and thoughtfully equipped bedrooms. Spacious public areas include a fitness room and sauna and a smart, inviting lounge adjacent to the traditional dining room where hearty breakfasts are served.
FACILITIES: 4 en suite No smoking TVB tea/coffee No dogs (ex guide dogs) Cen ht TVL No children 10yrs Fishing Sauna Gymnasium Jacuzzi Marked farm trail 485 acres arable beef/sheep **PARKING:** 5
CARDS:

♦♦♦♦ Bush Nook

Upper Denton, Gilsland CA8 7AF ☎ 016977 47194
016977 47790
e-mail: info@bushnook.co.uk
Dir: *halfway between Brampton and Haltwhistle. Off the A69 signposted Spadeadam, Birdoswald & Bush Nook, 0.5m on right past wetland on left*

continued

Dating back to 1760, this charming farmhouse is thought to have been built using stones borrowed from the nearby Hadrian's Wall. Traditional bedrooms are comfortable and superbly equipped, and delicious home cooked dinners are available by arrangement. Tranquil rural views can be enjoyed from the conservatory lounge.
FACILITIES: 4 rms (2 en suite) 6 annexe en suite (1 fmly) (1 GF) No smoking TVB tea/coffee Licensed Cen ht No coaches Dinner Last d 6pm
PRICES: s £28-£33; d £46-£70✻ **LB** **PARKING:** 4 **CARDS:**

♦♦♦♦ Hullerbank

Talkin CA8 1LB ☎ *016977 46668* *016977 46668*
e-mail: info@hullerbank.freeserve.co.uk
Dir: *exit M6 junct 43 on to A69 to Brampton then B6413 (Castle Carrock Road) for approx. 2m, cross railway and pass golf club turn left to Talkin. Leave Talkin on Hallbankgate Road and follow signs to Hullerbank*
Dating from 1635, Hullerbank is a delightful Georgian farmhouse set in well tended gardens, convenient for Hadrian's Wall, the Lake District and the Scottish Borders. Bedrooms are comfortably proportioned, attractively decorated and well equipped. There is a cosy ground floor lounge and a separate dining room where hearty traditional breakfasts are served.
FACILITIES: 3 en suite No smoking TVB tea/coffee No dogs Cen ht TVL No children 12yrs No coaches **PRICES:** s £30; d £48✻ **PARKING:** 6
NOTES: Closed Dec-Jan **CARDS:**

♦♦♦ Diamonds are a guest's best friend!
The emphasis is on quality and guest care rather than extra facilities.

England

BRAMPTON continued

♦♦♦ The Blacksmiths Arms
Talkin Village CA8 1LE ☎ 016977 3452 016977 3396
e-mail: blacksmithsarmstalkin@yahoo.com
Dir: *A69 to Brampton, take B6413 to Castle Carrock, after railway level crossing take second left signposted Talkin*
This friendly country inn in the centre of Talkin village offers good home cooking and a selection of real ales. Bedrooms are comfortably furnished and thoughtfully equipped. An extensive menu as well as snacks and daily specials can be enjoyed in the cosy bar lounges or the smart panelled Old Forge restaurant.
FACILITIES: 5 en suite (2 fmly) No smoking in bedrooms No smoking in dining room No smoking in 1 lounge TVB tea/coffee No dogs (ex guide dogs) Cen ht No coaches Dinner Last d 9pm **PRICES:** s £30; d £45* **MEALS:** Lunch £10-£25alc Dinner £10-£25alc* **PARKING:** 20 **CARDS:**

See advertisement on page 89

BROUGH Map 12 NY71

Premier Collection

♦♦♦♦♦ Augill Castle
CA17 4DE ☎ 017683 41937
e-mail: enquiries@augillcastle.co.uk
Dir: *M6 junct 38, A685 through Kirkby Stephen. Continue through Brough Sowerby & right to South Stainmore. Castle 1m on left*
This Victorian neo-Gothic castle is peacefully located in the heart of the Eden Valley. Spacious bedrooms and bathrooms are individually and stylishly themed and lovingly furnished with period pieces. Public rooms include opulent lounges and a stunning Gothic dining room where hearty breakfasts and locally sourced dinners are taken around the huge oak table.
FACILITIES: 8 en suite 2 annexe en suite (3 fmly) (4 GF) No smoking TVB tea/coffee Licensed Cen ht No coaches Croquet lawn Dinner Last d same morning **PRICES:** s £50-£60; d £100-£120* **CONF:** Thtr 40 Board 20 Del £100 * **PARKING:** 12 **NOTES:** Closed Xmas Civ Wed 60 **CARDS:**

BROUGHTON IN FURNESS Map 07 SD28

♦♦♦♦ The Workshop Studios
The Workshop, Church St LA20 6HJ ☎ 01229 716159
 01229 716159
e-mail: workshop.accom@virgin.net
Dir: *M6 J36, A590 (Barrow-In-Furness) until Greenodd. A5092 (Millom). Right at High Cross Inn, Downhill, through traffic calming, 75 yds on left*

Aptly named, the Workshop studios' was originally used as a paint store for a decorating business and has been in the same family for over 100 years. The conversion now offers stylish modern bedrooms all of which have been individually decorated. Traditional Cumbrian breakfasts are served in the adjacent cottage.

continued

FACILITIES: 4 en suite (2 fmly) (4 GF) No smoking TVB tea/coffee Cen ht No coaches **PRICES:** s £25-£29.50; d £45-£49 **LB PARKING:** 4 **CARDS:**

CALDBECK Map 11 NY34

♦♦♦♦ Swaledale Watch Farm *(NY309396)*
Whelpo CA7 8HQ ☎ 016974 78409 016974 78409
Mr & Mrs Savage
e-mail: nan.savage@talk21.com
Dir: *1m SW of Caldbeck village on B5299*

This attractive farmhouse, with its own nature reserve, is peacefully located against a backdrop of picturesque fells. Bedrooms are spacious, well equipped and benefit from attractive en-suite facilities. Two rooms are housed in an adjacent converted farm building and share a comfortable sitting room. Dinner by arrangement, and hearty traditional breakfasts are served in the attractive dining room.
FACILITIES: 2 en suite 2 annexe en suite (2 fmly) (4 GF) No smoking TVB tea/coffee No dogs (ex guide dogs) Cen ht TVL Jacuzzi 100 acre Nature Reserve Pitch & putt 150 acres Sheep Dinner Last d 2pm **PRICES:** s £21-£25; d £38-£44* **BB PARKING:** 8 **NOTES:** Closed 24-26 Dec

CARLISLE Map 11 NY45

See also Brampton & Castle Carrock

Premier Collection

♦♦♦♦♦ Bessiestown Farm *(NY457768)*
Catlowdy CA6 5QP ☎ 01228 577219 & 577019
 01228 577219 Mr & Mrs J Sisson
e-mail: info@bessiestown.co.uk
Dir: *from Bush Hotel in Longtown, 6.5m to Bridge Inn, turn right onto B6318, 1.5m to Catlowdy, farm 1st on left*

The same owners have welcomed guests to this delightful farmhouse for the past thirty years. Stylish, comfortable bedrooms include family rooms and the luxury Dovecote Suite, with a king-sized four-poster bed, separate dressing

continued

room and spa bath. There is a choice of inviting lounges and a heated indoor swimming pool. Freshly prepared dinners and hearty breakfasts with home-made bread and preserves are served in the smart dining room.
FACILITIES: 5 en suite (1 fmly) (2 GF) No smoking TVB tea/coffee No dogs Licensed Cen ht TVL Indoor swimming pool (heated) 140 acres Dinner Last d 4pm **PRICES:** s £35; d £55-£65* **LB** **PARKING:** 10 **CARDS:**

♦♦♦♦ Angus Hotel & Almonds Bistro

14 Scotland Rd CA3 9DG ☎ 01228 523546 📠 01228 531895
e-mail: angus@hadrians-wall.fsnet.co.uk
Dir: *exit M6 at junct 44, on A7 at 8th set of traffic lights. Approx 2m from junct44 on left (The Independents)*
Just North of the city, this family-run hotel is ideal for both the business and leisure guest. A warm welcome is assured and the hotel offers comfortable, well-equipped accommodation. Almonds Bistro provides enjoyable food and home baking and there is also a lounge and large meeting room.
FACILITIES: 11 en suite (4 fmly) No smoking in 8 bedrooms No smoking in area of dining room TVB tea/coffee Direct dial from bedrooms Licensed Cen ht TVL No coaches Laptop points in bedrooms Dinner Last d 9pm **PRICES:** s £48; d £60* **LB** **CONF:** Thtr 25 Board 16 Del £65 * **PARKING:** 6 **CARDS:**

♦♦♦♦ Cambro House

173 Warwick Rd CA1 1LP ☎ 01228 543094 📠 01228 543094
e-mail: cambrohouse@amserve.net
Dir: *turn off M6 junct 43, down Warwick Rd, approx 1m on right before St Aidan's Church*
Cambro House is a smartly presented Victorian house which is conveniently situated close to both the town centre and the motorway network. The beautifully refurbished and spacious bedrooms are brightly decorated, smartly appointed and thoughtfully equipped. A hearty Cumbrian breakfast is served in the cosy morning room.
FACILITIES: 3 en suite (1 GF) No smoking TVB tea/coffee No dogs (ex guide dogs) Cen ht No children 5yrs No coaches **PRICES:** s £20-£25; d £36-£40* **LB** **BB** **PARKING:** 2 **CARDS:**

♦♦♦♦ Fern Lee

9 St Aidans Rd CA1 1LT ☎ 01228 511930 📠 01228 511930
Dir: *exit M6 junct 43 along Warwick Road. Right at 4th traffic lights onto Victoria Place. House 1st on left behind St Aidan's church*

The bedrooms are all recently redecorated and there are spacious public rooms at this conveniently located guest house. Mary and Geoffrey Bell do their best to ensure customers enjoy their stay and meals include good home cooking. Family room available.
FACILITIES: 8 en suite (2 fmly) (1 GF) No smoking in bedrooms No smoking in dining room No smoking in 1 lounge STV TVB tea/coffee No dogs (ex guide dogs) Cen ht TVL Dinner Last d 8pm **PRICES:** s £30-£40; d fr £45* **LB** **PARKING:** 10

♦♦♦♦ *Howard House*

27 Howard Place CA1 1HR ☎ 01228 529159 & 512550
📠 01228 512550
Dir: *M6 junct 43, main road to city centre past church on right, pedestrian crossing and then 1st right*
This late-Victorian town house enjoys a discreet position in a quiet tree lined street close to the city centre. Bedrooms are brightly decorated and smartly appointed. Public areas include an inviting lounge and a smart dining room. Guests interested in family history will enjoy chatting to Mr Fisher who specialises in genealogy.
FACILITIES: 5 rms (2 en suite) (2 fmly) No smoking in dining room TVB tea/coffee No dogs (ex guide dogs) Cen ht TVL Last d 2.30pm **CARDS:**

♦♦♦♦ Kingstown Hotel

246-248 Kingstown Rd CA3 0DE ☎ 01228 515292
📠 01228 515292
e-mail: akingstown-hotel@aol.com
Dir: *exit M6 junct 44, turn left onto A7 towards city centre. Hotel 0.25m on left*
On the northern side of the city, convenient for the lakes and Hadrian's Wall, this small and friendly hotel has a cosy and inviting atmosphere. Delicious home cooked meals are served in the steak house restaurant, and there is also an attractive lounge with residents bar. The pine furnished bedrooms are comfortable and suitably equipped.
FACILITIES: 8 en suite (1 fmly) (2 GF) No smoking in 7 bedrooms No smoking in dining room TVB tea/coffee No dogs (ex guide dogs) Licensed Cen ht TVL Dinner Last d 8.30pm **PARKING:** 14 **CARDS:**

♦♦♦♦ 🅰 Cornerways

107 Warwick Rd CA1 1EA ☎ 01228 521733
Dir: *1m from junct 43, opposite Our Lady and St Joseph's Church*
FACILITIES: 10 rms (3 en suite) (2 fmly) No smoking in dining room No smoking in lounges TVB tea/coffee **PRICES:** s £16-£20; d £28-£36* **BB** **PARKING:** 4 **NOTES:** Closed Xmas

♦♦♦♦ 🅰 Lynebank House

Westlington CA6 6AA ☎ 01228 792820 📠 01228 792693
e-mail: info@lynebank.co.uk
Dir: *off M6 at junct 44. 3m along A7 towards Longtown*
FACILITIES: 10 en suite (2 fmly) (3 GF) No smoking in bedrooms No smoking in dining room No smoking in 1 lounge TVB tea/coffee No dogs (ex guide dogs) Licensed Cen ht Fishing Dinner Last d 8.30pm **PRICES:** s £20-£26; d £36-£44* **LB** **BB** **CONF:** Class 36 Board 36 **PARKING:** 20 **CARDS:**

♦♦♦♦ 🅰 New Pallyards

Heathersgill CA6 6HZ ☎ 01228 577308 & 577182
📠 01228 577308
e-mail: info@newpallyards.freeserve.co.uk
Dir: *M6 N or A74 S to Longtown. In Longtown take Swan Street 1st right beyond speed limit zone signed Solport, follow road for 5.5m, New Pallyards signed*
FACILITIES: 3 en suite 2 annexe en suite (1 fmly) No smoking in 3 bedrooms No smoking in dining room No smoking in lounges TVB tea/coffee Licensed Cen ht TVL Tennis (grass) Fishing Riding Croquet lawn Dinner Last d 7.30pm **PRICES:** s fr £24; d £48-£84* **LB** **CONF:** Del from £49 * **PARKING:** 10 **CARDS:**

Smoking restrictions appear under the **FACILITIES** heading, please check when booking.

England

CARLISLE continued

♦♦♦ Cherry Grove

87 Petteril St CA1 2AW ☎ 01228 541942 📠 541942
e-mail: petteril87@aol.com
Dir: *M6 junct 43, 4th set of traffic lights, Cherry Grove is on left looking up towards M6*
Attractively decorated and meticulously maintained, this friendly house lies on the east side of the city. Nicely furnished bedrooms include one situated on the ground floor. The comfortable dining room is furnished with polished pine pieces and there is a small, cosy lounge upstairs.
FACILITIES: 4 en suite (2 fmly) No smoking in bedrooms No smoking in dining room STV TVB tea/coffee Cen ht No coaches **PRICES:** s £20-£25; d £38-£40✱ BB **PARKING:** 3

♦♦♦ *Blackwell Farm (NY401530)*

Blackwell, Durdar CA2 4SH ☎ 01228 524073
Mrs A Westmorland
e-mail: blackwellfarm@ukf.net
Dir: *M6 junct 42 towards Dalston. At Black Lion pub crossroads turn right for Carlisle. After 1.5m turn left at White Ox. House 50yds on right*
A relaxed and welcoming atmosphere prevails at this comfortable traditional farmhouse which is situated on the south side close to the racecourse. There are two comfortable bedrooms, one furnished in pine, the other in more traditional style. Hearty breakfasts are served around the communal table in the combined lounge/dining room.
FACILITIES: 2 rms (1 fmly) No smoking in bedrooms tea/coffee Cen ht TVL 120 acres dairy/beef **PARKING:** 4

♦♦♦ Craighead

6 Hartington Place CA1 1HL ☎ 01228 596767 📠 01228 593801
Dir: *M6 junct 43 through 4 sets of traffic lights, then 4th turn on right*

This smartly presented Grade II listed Victorian town house is conveniently located a short walk from the city centre. All bedrooms are individually styled and families are catered for. Breakfast is enjoyed at two separate tables located in the period style sitting room.
FACILITIES: 5 rms (1 en suite) (1 fmly) No smoking TVB tea/coffee Cen ht TVL No coaches **PRICES:** s £17-£19; d £35-£44✱ BB

♦♦♦ Dalroc

411 Warwick Rd CA1 2RZ ☎ 01228 542805
e-mail: margaret@dalroc.fsnet.co.uk
Dir: *midway between M6 exit 43 and city centre, beside Esso garage*
Guests are warmly greeted at this friendly house which is situated just off the M6 and a few minutes' drive from the city centre. Bedrooms are traditionally furnished and thoughtfully equipped. Guests have use of a comfortable lounge, whilst breakfast is served around one table in the smart dining room.
FACILITIES: 3 rms No smoking in bedrooms No smoking in dining room TV2B tea/coffee No dogs (ex guide dogs) Cen ht TVL No children 4yrs **PRICES:** s £17; d £34-£36✱ LB BB **PARKING:** 2

♦♦♦ East View

110 Warwick Rd CA1 1JU ☎ 01228 522112 📠 522112
Dir: *Approx. 1.25 miles from M6 J43. Guesthouse located on L going into Carlisle on junct of Lismore St/Warwick Rd*
East View Guest house is a friendly family run Victorian guesthouse lying some ten minutes walk from the city centre and the railway and bus station. Bedrooms, some of which are suitable for families are attractively decorated and equipped with modern facilities. There is an attractive dining room where traditional breakfasts are served at individual tables. Private car parking is available, as are street parking permits.
FACILITIES: 7 en suite (3 fmly) No smoking TVB tea/coffee No dogs (ex guide dogs) Cen ht **PRICES:** s £20-£25; d £40-£45✱ **PARKING:** 4

♦♦♦ Howard Lodge

90 Warwick Rd CA1 1JU ☎ 01228 529842
Dir: *M6 J43 into Carlisle, along Warwick Rd for 1m. Through 5 sets of lights, Howard Lodge on left*
Howard Lodge is a smart redbrick end-of-terrace house, with an adjoining secure car park, which is conveniently situated within easy walking distance of the town centre. The bedrooms are attractively decorated and well-equipped. Traditional home cooked breakfasts are served in the bright dining room.
FACILITIES: 6 en suite (2 fmly) No smoking in 1 bedrooms No smoking in dining room No smoking in lounges STV TVB tea/coffee Cen ht TVL No coaches Dinner Last d 3pm **PRICES:** s £20-£40; d £30-£50 BB
PARKING: 7

CARTMEL — Map 07 SD37

Premier Collection

♦♦♦♦♦ *Hill Farm (SD367792)*

LA11 7SS ☎ 01539 536477 📠 01539 536636
Mrs P Foulerton
e-mail: pafoulerton@btopenworld.com
Dir: *M6 junct 36, follow A590 to top of long steep hill. At 'Cartmel' sign go into centre of village, exit right signed 'Cartmel Village Store'. Follow 'cul-de-sac' signs and then signs to Hill Farm*
Enjoying an elevated position on the edge of this village, famous for its Sticky Toffee Pudding, Hill Farm dates from 1539, and has been sympathetically renovated to provide comfortable accommodation in a stunning location. Bedrooms retain much of their original character and are attractive and thoughtfully equipped, with many extra touches. A comfortable lounge, complete with log fires, is available, and delicious freshly-cooked breakfasts are served at a large table in the dining room.
FACILITIES: 3 en suite No smoking in bedrooms No smoking in dining room No smoking in 1 lounge TVB tea/coffee No dogs Cen ht TVL No children **PRICES:** s £25-£30; d £50-£60✱ LB
PARKING: 3 **NOTES:** Closed Nov-Jan

Premier Collection

♦♦♦♦♦ Uplands Hotel

Haggs Ln LA11 6HD ☎ 015395 36248 📠 015395 36848
e-mail: uplands@kencomp.net
Dir: *road signed to Grange opposite Pig & Whistle in Cartmel 0.75m onleft*
On the outskirts of Cartmel village, this pleasant country house enjoys super views towards the Duddon Estuary. The lounge is bright and comfortable, and ambitious cooking is served in the spacious restaurant. Bedrooms are comfortable and traditional in style, and staff are thoughtful and attentive.

continued

FACILITIES: 5 en suite No smoking in dining room TVB Direct dial from bedrooms Licensed Cen ht No children 8 yrs No coaches Dinner Last d 7.30pm **PRICES:** (incl. dinner) d £144-£164* **LB PARKING:** 18 **NOTES:** Closed Jan-Feb **CARDS:**

CASTLE CARROCK Map 12 NY55

♦♦♦ Gelt Hall Farm *(NY542554)*

CA8 9LT ☎ 01228 670260 📠 01228 670260 Mrs Annie Robinson
e-mail: robinson@gelthall.fsnet.co.uk
Dir: *B6413 to Castle Carrock*

This working farmhouse that retains much of its 17th-century character is located in the centre of the village. Spacious bedrooms are traditionally furnished and overlook the farmyard. There is a cosy TV lounge that houses a communal table where breakfast is served. Warm hospitality is a particular feature.

FACILITIES: 3 rms (1 en suite) (1 fmly) TV2B tea/coffee No dogs TVL 250 acres beef dairy sheep **PRICES:** s £17.50-£18; d £35-£37* **BB PARKING:** 7

COCKERMOUTH Map 11 NY13

♦♦♦♦ Highside Farmhouse *(NY163292)*

Embleton CA13 9TN ☎ 017687 76893 📠 017687 76893
Mr & Mrs J Winstanley
e-mail: highside@winstanley38.freeserve.co.uk
Dir: *A66 Keswick-Cockermouth, turn left at sign to Lorton/Buttermere, left at T-junction. After 300 mtrs turn right opposite church, farm at top of hill*

Warm hospitality, hearty breakfasts and panoramic views feature at this 17th-century farmhouse. Highside Farm, true to its name, is perched over 600 feet up Ling Fell, in a quiet haven of the National Park. The open-plan lounge and dining room are elegantly furnished with deep seating and fine antiques. Bedrooms are comfortable and thoughtfully equipped.

FACILITIES: 2 en suite No smoking TVB tea/coffee Cen ht No children 10yrs 2 acres non working **PRICES:** s £30-£32; d £50-£54 **LB PARKING:** 2

♦♦♦♦ Sundawn

Carlisle Rd, Bridekirk CA13 0PA ☎ 01900 822384
📠 01900 822885
e-mail: robert.hodge1@virgin.net
Dir: *1.5m from Cockermouth N on A595 towards Carlisle*

This smart Victorian house enjoys an elevated position with panoramic views out towards Skiddaw and the Lorton Valley. Bedrooms are stylishly appointed and comfortably furnished. Public areas include a smart lounge/dining room and a comfortably furnished sun lounge. Service and hospitality are warm and attentive.

FACILITIES: 3 rms (2 en suite) (1 fmly) No smoking TVB tea/coffee No dogs (ex guide dogs) Cen ht TVL No coaches **PRICES:** d £35-£40 **PARKING:** 6 **NOTES:** Closed 20 Dec-5 Jan

♦♦♦ *Rose Cottage*

Lorton Rd CA13 9DX ☎ 01900 822189 📠 01900 822189
Dir: *leave A66 at Cockermouth, follow signs to Lorton/Buttermere. Rose Cottage on R.*

This former inn on the edge of town has been carefully refurbished and transformed to provide attractive, modern accommodation. Smart bedrooms have en suite facilities and are brightly appointed. There is an inviting guest lounge and a smart dining room where home cooked dinners are a highlight.

FACILITIES: 7 en suite (2 fmly) No smoking in bedrooms No smoking in dining room TVB tea/coffee Licensed Cen ht Dinner Last d 8.30pm **PARKING:** 12 **NOTES:** Closed 24-27 Dec **CARDS:**

CONISTON Map 07 SD39

Premier Collection

♦♦♦♦♦ Coniston Lodge Hotel

Station Rd LA21 8HH ☎ 015394 41201 📠 015394 41201
e-mail: info@coniston-lodge.com
Dir: *at x-roads on A593, close to filling station, turn up hill at x-roads into Station Rd*

In the same family since 1911, Coniston Lodge is ideally situated for exploring the Lake District. The attractive bedrooms are well equipped and provide a host of thoughtful extras. Ambitious cooking can be sampled in the tastefully co-ordinated dining room, which might include home made pâté, local game and fish. The cosy lounge features a relief in local slate depicting an earlier guest, Donald Campbell, with his famous Campbell Bluebird.

FACILITIES: 6 en suite No smoking TVB tea/coffee Direct dial from bedrooms No dogs (ex guide dogs) Licensed Cen ht No children 10yrs No coaches Dinner Last d 12 noon **PRICES:** s £35-£52; d £70-£90 **LB PARKING:** 9 **CARDS:**

Premier Collection

♦♦♦♦♦ Wheelgate Country House Hotel

Little Arrow LA21 8AU ☎ 015394 41418 📠 015394 41114
e-mail: wheelgate@conistoncottages.co.uk
Dir: *1.5m S of Coniston, on W side of road*

Dating back to the 17th century, this charming farmhouse boasts original oak beams, panelling and low ceilings. An intimate bar, utility room and a comfortable lounge with open fire are provided. Views over the well-tended gardens and the beautiful Lakeland countryside are impressive, and a warm welcome can be expected.

FACILITIES: 4 en suite 1 annexe en suite No smoking in bedrooms No smoking in dining room No smoking in lounges TVB tea/coffee No dogs (ex guide dogs) Licensed Cen ht No children No coaches Free membership of Health Club with swimming pool **PRICES:** s £29-£32; d £50-£64* **LB PARKING:** 8 **NOTES:** Closed Jan-Feb rs Dec **CARDS:**

Super supper! this symbol shows that evening meals exceeded our Inspector's expectations.

England

CONISTON continued

♦♦♦♦ Arrowfield

Little Arrow, Torver LA21 8AU ☎ 015394 41741 📠 01539441275
e-mail: email@arrowfield-coniston.fsnet.co.uk
Dir: *1.5m from Coniston on A593*
Set in attractive gardens, this elegant Victorian house is peacefully located between Coniston and Torver. The brightly co-ordinated bedrooms are well-equipped, and the elegant lounge has deep, comfortable sofas and beautiful countryside views. Substantial breakfasts include local and home-made products, as do the packed lunches that are available on request.
FACILITIES: 5 en suite No smoking TVB tea/coffee No dogs (ex guide dogs) Licensed Cen ht TVL No coaches **PRICES:** s £24-£26; d £48-£52* **PARKING:** 6 **NOTES:** Closed Dec-Feb

♦♦♦♦ Browside

Browside, Little Arrow LA21 8AU ☎ 015394 41162
Dir: *on A593, 1.5m from Coniston on right, set in hillside*
Standing at the foot of the Coniston Old Man, this delightful bungalow offers delightful rural views towards the Lake. The two spacious bedrooms are comfortable and well equipped and one has its own private patio. Hearty breakfasts are cooked to order and served in the simply furnished dining room.
FACILITIES: 2 en suite No smoking TVB tea/coffee No dogs (ex guide dogs) Cen ht No coaches **PRICES:** s £22-£25; d £40-£45* **LB** **PARKING:** 6

♦♦♦ Wilson Arms

Torver LA21 8BB ☎ 015394 41237 📠 015394 41590
Dir: *at the junction of A5084 and A593*
FACILITIES: 7 en suite 1 annexe en suite No smoking in bedrooms No smoking in dining room No smoking in 1 lounge TVB tea/coffee No dogs (ex guide dogs) Licensed Cen ht No coaches Dinner Last d 8.45pm **PRICES:** s £30-£40; d £54-£60* **LB** **PARKING:** 20 **NOTES:** Closed 25-26 Dec **CARDS:**

CROSTHWAITE Map 07 SD49

♦♦♦♦ Crosthwaite House

LA8 8BP ☎ 01539 568264 📠 01539 568264
e-mail: bookings@crosthwaitehouse.co.uk
Dir: *M6 J36, A591 (Kendal), A590 (Barrow), right onto A5074, 4m take small through-road for Crosthwaite, 0.5m turn left*

Commanding stunning views across the Lyth Valley, this delightful Georgian house is a haven for peace and tranquillity. Bedrooms are spacious and offer a host of thoughtful extras. The reception rooms include a comfortable lounge and a pleasant dining room that has polished floorboards and individual tables. Hospitality is warm and friendly.
FACILITIES: 6 en suite No smoking TVB tea/coffee Licensed Cen ht TVL No coaches Dinner Last d 5pm **PRICES:** s £22-£25; d £44-£50* **PARKING:** 10 **NOTES:** Closed mid Nov-Dec rs Feb-Mar

GRANGE-OVER-SANDS Map 07 SD47

♦♦♦♦ Elton Hotel

Windermere Rd LA11 6EQ ☎ 015395 32838
Dir: *M6 J36, A590 follow signs to Grange-over-Sands, 2nd exit off rdbt by railway station. Hotel 500yds on left*
Friendly, attentive service is assured at The Elton Hotel. Just a short stroll from the town, this attractive Victorian house provides well-equipped bedrooms, two of which are on the ground floor. The spacious lounge is comfortable and boasts a stunning feature fireplace. Evening meals are available on request.
FACILITIES: 7 rms (5 en suite) (1 fmly) (2 GF) No smoking TVB tea/coffee Licensed Cen ht TVL Dinner Last d 10am **PRICES:** s £25-£30; d £40-£50* **LB** **NOTES:** Closed 1Dec-28 Feb

♦♦♦♦ Mayfields

3 Mayfield Ter, Kents Bank Rd LA11 7DW ☎ 015395 34730
Dir: *M6 J36, take A590 to Meathop rdbt, turn for Lindale. Left in Lindale at small rdbt to Grange, 1m S past rail station & fire station*
Enjoying views over the bay and located in a quiet part of the town, this small guest house offers a warm and friendly welcome. Hearty lunches and imaginative dinners are served in the attractive dining room, and there is a comfortably furnished lounge. Bedrooms are individually decorated and equipped with thoughtful extras.
FACILITIES: 3 rms (2 en suite) (2 GF) No smoking TVB tea/coffee No dogs Licensed Cen ht TVL No coaches Dinner Last d 6.30pm **PRICES:** s £25; d £50* **LB** **PARKING:** 3 **NOTES:** Closed 21 Dec- 6 Jan

GRASMERE Map 11 NY30

♦♦♦♦ Howbeck Vegetarian Guest House

Howbeck, Grasmere LA22 9RH ☎ 015394 35732
📠 015394 35553
e-mail: trevor.eastes@btinternet.com
Dir: *Leave A591 westwards, at the Swan Hotel towards Grasmere, Howbeck is 0.25m on right, opposite Rothay Garden Hotel, just after the bridge*
This delightful family run guest house in an acre of well-tended gardens is only minutes walk from the centre of the village. Brightly decorated, well appointed bedrooms are thoughtfully equipped and benefit from fully tiled, smart en-suites. There is a comfortable lounge/dining room with breathtaking mountain views where home cooked vegetarian dinners and breakfast are served.
FACILITIES: 2 en suite No smoking TVB tea/coffee No dogs (ex guide dogs) Cen ht Dinner Last d 10am **PRICES:** d £52-£58* **LB** **PARKING:** 2 **NOTES:** Closed Xmas & New Year

♦♦♦♦ Riversdale

White Bridge LA22 9RQ ☎ 015394 35619
e-mail: riversdalegrasmere@nascr.net
Dir: *turn off A591 into Swan Lane opposite Swan Hotel, signed to Grasmere village, Riversdale is on left just before bridge*
Built in 1830 this house has an excellent setting on the banks of the River Rothay with views towards Silver How and Easdale Tarn. Thoughtfully equipped bedrooms are tastefully decorated and comfortably furnished. Meals are served in the warm and bright dining room and breakfast features fresh, local produce.
FACILITIES: 3 en suite No smoking TVB tea/coffee No dogs Cen ht TVL No children 18yrs No coaches Dinner Last d 10.30am **PRICES:** d £50-£64* **LB** **PARKING:** 3

♦♦♦♦ Silverlea

Easedale Rd LA22 9QE ☎ 015394 35657 📠 015394 35657
e-mail: info@silverlea.com
Dir: *turn into Grasmere village off A591 and take Easedale Road opposite the Village Green (next to Heaton Cooper Studios). Silverlea is 300mtrs on right*

continued

A warm and friendly welcome is assured at this ivy-clad Lakeland stone guest house, situated just a short walk from the village. Delicious meals are home cooked using fresh produce and are served in the cosy cottage dining room. Bedrooms, one of which has its own sitting area, are fresh in appearance and very comfortable.
FACILITIES: 5 en suite (1 fmly) No smoking TVB tea/coffee No dogs Cen ht No children 11yrs Dinner Last d 12 hrs prior **PRICES:** (incl. dinner) s £38-£40; d £76-£88✻ **PARKING:** 5 **NOTES:** Closed Dec-Jan

♦♦♦♦ Woodland Crag

How Head Ln LA22 9SG ☎ 015394 35351 📠 015394 35351
e-mail: woodlandcrag@aol.com
Dir: *take A590/591 through Windermere and Ambleside to Grasmere. Just before mini rdbt entrance to village right into How Head Lane, continue to duck pond on left access via unmade road left of pond*
FACILITIES: 4 rms (3 en suite) No smoking TVB tea/coffee No dogs (ex guide dogs) Cen ht TVL No children 12yrs No coaches **PRICES:** s £25-£30; d £45-£70 **LB** **PARKING:** 4 **CARDS:**

♦♦♦ *Raise View*

White Bridge LA22 9RQ ☎ 015394 35215 📠 015394 35126
e-mail: john@raisevw.demon.co.uk
Dir: *turn off A591 opposite Swan Hotel. At corner of Swan Lane and Pye Lane*
Boasting unrestricted views over the fells and surrounding farmland, this cosy guest house extends a warm welcome to all guests. All bedrooms, although varying in size are comfortable, thoughtfully furnished and equipped. A daily-changing breakfast menu is offered and produce is freshly cooked to order. Public areas consist of a traditionally furnished lounge and a spacious dining room.
FACILITIES: 6 en suite No smoking TVB tea/coffee No dogs Cen ht No children 5yrs No coaches **PARKING:** 6 **NOTES:** Closed Dec-Jan

GRIZEDALE — Map 07 SD39

♦♦♦♦ Grizedale Lodge

LA22 0QL ☎ 015394 36532 📠 015394 36572
e-mail: enquiries@grizedale-lodge.com
Dir: *from M6 J36 follow signs to Windermere, Ambleside & Hawkshead. At Hawkshead follow signs to Grizedale, 2m on R*
Tranquilly situated in the heart of the Grizedale forest, this charming small hotel provides particularly well appointed bedrooms, some of which have fine four-poster beds and splendid views. There is an attractive dining room where hearty breakfasts and lunches are served and this leads on to a balcony where guests can relax on summer days.
FACILITIES: (1 fmly) No smoking in bedrooms No smoking in dining room TV8B tea/coffee Licensed Cen ht No children 5yrs No coaches **PRICES:** s £39.50-£42.50; d £70-£95✻ **PARKING:** 25 **CARDS:**

HAWKSHEAD — Map 07 SD39

See also Near Sawrey

Premier Collection

♦♦♦♦♦ Ees Wyke Country House

LA22 0JZ ☎ 015394 36393 📠 015394 36393
e-mail: eeswyke@aol.com

(For full entry see Near Sawrey)

♦♦♦♦ Sawrey Ground

Hawkshead Hill LA22 0PP ☎ 015394 36683 📠 015394 36683
e-mail: mail@sawreyground.com
Dir: *from Hawkshead take Coniston road 1m to Hawkshead Hill (B5285). Turn right immediately after Baptist Chapel, follow signs to Tarn Hows for 0.25m. Sawrey Ground on right*

In the heart of the lakes, this charming 17th-century farmhouse enjoys a superb rural setting on the doorstep of Tarn Hows. The flagstoned entrance hall leads to the relaxing sitting room with beamed ceiling, where on winter nights a real fire awaits. Hearty breakfasts featuring fresh fruit and home baked bread are served in the separate dining room. Bedrooms are comfortably traditional in style and are furnished in pine and oak.
FACILITIES: 3 en suite No smoking TVB tea/coffee No dogs (ex guide dogs) Cen ht No children 8yrs No coaches **PRICES:** s £32-£36; d £52-£64✻ **PARKING:** 6

England

HAWKSHEAD continued

♦♦♦♦ Sun
Main St LA22 0NT ☎ 015394 36236 015394 36155
e-mail: THESUNINN@hawkshead98.freeserve.co.uk
Dir: *from Windermere take A591 (Ambleside), B5286 (Hawkshead). In village centre opp 'Hawkshead Country Wear'*
A relaxed and welcoming atmosphere prevails at this charming 17th-century inn. Retaining many original characteristics, bedrooms feature stone walls, wood panelling and low-beamed ceilings. All are superbly equipped and one boasts a four-poster bed. Imaginative meals are served in the restaurant or lighter alternatives can be taken in the bar.
FACILITIES: 8 en suite (1 fmly) No smoking in bedrooms No smoking in dining room STV TVB tea/coffee Cen ht TVL Fishing Pool Table Dinner Last d 10pm **PARKING:** 8 **CARDS:**
See advertisement on page 95

♦♦♦♦ West Vale Country House
Far Sawrey LA22 0LQ ☎ 015394 42817 015394 45302
e-mail: enquiries@westvalecountryhouse.co.uk
Dir: *after crossing Lake Windemere by car ferry at Bowness, drive along B5285 for 1.25m to Far Sawrey. West Vale is on the left as you leave the village*
FACILITIES: 8 rms (7 en suite) (2 fmly) No smoking TVB tea/coffee No dogs (ex guide dogs) Licensed Cen ht TVL No children 7yrs No coaches Dinner Last d 5.30pm **PRICES:** s fr £40; d fr £56✳ **LB PARKING:** 8 **CARDS:**

♦♦♦ Kings Arms Hotel
LA22 0NZ ☎ 015394 36372 015394 36006
e-mail: info@kingsarmshawkshead.co.uk
Dir: *from Windermere take A591 to Ambleside then B5286 to Hawkshead, in main square*
A traditional Lakeland inn right in the heart of this conservation village. The cosy, thoughtfully equipped bedrooms retain their character and are traditionally furnished. A good choice of freshly prepared food is available in both the lounge bar and the neatly presented dining room.
FACILITIES: 9 rms (8 en suite) (4 fmly) No smoking in dining room No smoking in lounges TVB tea/coffee Direct dial from bedrooms Cen ht Fishing Dinner Last d 9.30pm **PRICES:** s £30-£40; d £50-£70✳ **LB MEALS:** Bar Lunch £6-£18alc Dinner £6-£18alc✳ **CARDS:**

HELTON Map 12 NY52

♦♦♦♦ Beckfoot Country House
CA10 2QB ☎ 01931 713241 01931 713391
e-mail: beckfoot@aol.com
Dir: *from S leave M6 junct 39 onto A6 to Shap. Through Shap & follow signs to Bampton, Beckfoot 2m down rd to Helton Village*
This delightful Victorian country house enjoys a peaceful location in well-tended gardens surrounded by beautiful open countryside, yet is only minutes drive from Penrith. Bedrooms are spacious, comfortable and particularly well-equipped. The stunning four-poster room is particularly impressive. Public areas include an elegant drawing room, an oak panelled dining room and a TV lounge.
FACILITIES: 7 en suite (1 fmly) No smoking in bedrooms No smoking in dining room STV TVB tea/coffee Licensed Cen ht TVL No coaches Dinner Last d 6pm **PRICES:** s £35-£45; d £70-£90✳ **LB PARKING:** 12 **NOTES:** Closed Dec-Feb **CARDS:**

IREBY Map 11 NY23

♦♦♦♦ Daleside Farm
CA7 1EW ☎ 016973 71268
e-mail: info@dalesidefarm.co.uk
Dir: *from Keswick, turn right in Ireby, after passing Sun Inn, at crossroads signposted Caldbeck. Farm on left on approaching T-junct. From Carlisle, proceed towards Caldbeck on B5299. After 3m take 2nd right signposted Ireby. Farm 100yds on right*
FACILITIES: 3 en suite (1 fmly) No smoking tea/coffee No dogs Cen ht TVL No coaches **PRICES:** s £30; d £50✳ **LB PARKING:** 12

KENDAL Map 07 SD59

Premier Collection

♦♦♦♦♦ Blaven Homestay
Middleshaw, Old Hutton LA8 0LZ ☎ 01539 734894
01539 727447
e-mail: enquiries@blavenhomestay.co.uk
Dir: *M6 J36, then A65 Skipton road, at 1st rdbt turn L. After approx 2m turn R at sign for Oxenholme Station. Turn R at t-junct opp station. Follow lane for approx 1.5m passing Station Inn on L. Continue to village of Old Hutton, turn L to Ewebank. Blaven is 200m on R*

Excellent hospitality and informal service ensure that guests are made to feel very much at home in this stunning barn conversion with its delightful garden. Hearty freshly cooked breakfasts are served in the dining room, or a lighter continental alternative can be taken in the comfort of your room.
FACILITIES: 2 en suite (1 fmly) (1 GF) No smoking TVB tea/coffee No dogs (ex guide dogs) Cen ht Dinner Last d 5pm **PRICES:** s £39.50-£46; d £59-£72✳ **LB PARKING:** 3 **CARDS:**

♦♦♦♦ Barrowfield Farm *(SD484908)*
Brigsteer LA8 8BJ ☎ 015395 68336 Mrs B Gardner
Dir: *4m on dual-carriageway, left after tourist info sign to T-junct, left to Brigsteer. Half way down hill on S-bend turn right. Over 4 cattlegrids*
This lovely stone farmhouse enjoys a peaceful location close to the village of Brigsteer; overlooking wonderful forest and farmland and reached via a mile long private track. Bedrooms retain original features and are traditionally furnished. Freshly cooked breakfasts are served in the comfortable guest lounge by the friendly attentive proprietors.
FACILITIES: 3 rms (1 fmly) No smoking No dogs Cen ht TVL 180 acres dairy sheep **PRICES:** d £38-£38✳ **BB PARKING:** 6
NOTES: Closed Nov-Mar

England

♦♦♦♦ Burrow Hall Country Guest House

Plantation Bridge LA8 9JR ☎ 01539 821711 01539 821711
e-mail: info@burrowhall.fsnet.co.uk
Dir: *on A591, between Kendal and Windermere, 1.5m after Crook rdbt on right*

Dating back to 1648, this charming country house has been sympathetically restored to provide comfortable, modern accommodation. Some bedrooms have lovely views of the fells, and all are neatly furnished and well equipped, with spacious en suites and direct access through a separate entrance.
FACILITIES: 3 en suite No smoking TVB tea/coffee No dogs (ex guide dogs) Cen ht TVL No children 12yrs No coaches **PRICES:** s £28-£30; d £48-£50✳ **PARKING:** 8 **NOTES:** Closed 23-26 Dec **CARDS:**

♦♦♦♦ Higher House Farm

Oxenholme Ln, Natland LA9 7QH ☎ 015395 61177
015395 61520
Dir: *exit M6 at junct 36, A65 to Kendal, at 2nd sign for Natland. Left onto Oxenholme Lane, premises at bottom of lane on right*

Excellent hospitality, hearty, freshly prepared breakfasts and comfortable, well equipped rooms all feature at this charming 17th century farmhouse. Peacefully located in the village of Natland, Higher House has large, well kept gardens which look towards the fells. There is a cosy lounge with an abundance of reading material, and a well-furnished dining room.
FACILITIES: 3 en suite No smoking TVB tea/coffee No dogs (ex guide dogs) Cen ht TVL No children 12yrs No coaches Golf 9 **PRICES:** d £49-£59✳ **LB PARKING:** 9 **NOTES:** Closed Xmas

♦♦♦♦ Low Jock Scar

Selside LA8 9LE ☎ 01539 823259 01539 823259
e-mail: philip@low-jock-scar.freeserve.co.uk
Dir: *6m N of Kendal on A6 turn L down a small side rd signposted to Low Jock Scar*
Peacefully located, this charming country guest house enjoys an idyllic riverside setting amid woodland gardens. Bedrooms are individual in style and comfortably furnished and a relaxing lounge is provided for guest use. Superb home cooked dinners and freshly prepared breakfasts are served in the conservatory dining room.
FACILITIES: 5 rms (3 en suite) No smoking tea/coffee Licensed Cen ht TVL No children 12yrs No coaches Dinner Last d 10am **PRICES:** s £34.50-£40; d £49-£60 **PARKING:** 7 **NOTES:** Closed Nov-Feb **CARDS:**

♦♦♦ Garnett House *(SD500959)*

Burneside LA9 5SF ☎ 01539 724542
01539 724542 Mrs S Beaty
e-mail: info@garnetthousefarm.co.uk
Dir: *exit A591 at Ratherheath crossroads, farm is on left on Burneside Rd*

Dating back to the 15th century, this working sheep and dairy farm enjoys a delightful country setting, within walking distance of the local amenities in the village of Burneside, and ideally located for Kendal and the Lakes. Bedrooms are traditionally furnished with an array of modern facilities. Breakfasts are freshly prepared.
FACILITIES: 5 en suite (2 fmly) No smoking TVB tea/coffee No dogs TVL 1000 acres Dairy Sheep **PRICES:** d £38-£45✳ **LB BB**
PARKING: 6 **NOTES:** Closed Xmas/New Year

♦♦♦ Gilpin Bridge

Bridge End, Levens LA8 8EP ☎ 015395 52206 015395 52444
e-mail: brewery@frederic-robinson.co.uk
Dir: *on A5074, 100mtrs from junct with A590 (Frederic Robinson)*
Situated just outside Levens, this modern, Tudor-style inn has a strong culinary theme and provides an extensive bar and restaurant menu. The modern bedrooms are stylishly decorated and offer practical accommodation with all expected amenities. There is also a games room and a function suite.
FACILITIES: 10 en suite No smoking in bedrooms No smoking in area of dining room No smoking in 1 lounge TVB tea/coffee Direct dial from bedrooms No dogs (ex guide dogs) Cen ht Pool Table Dinner Last d 9pm **PRICES:** s £40-£50; d £60-£80✳ **LB MEALS:** Lunch fr £6.25 Dinner fr £6.25&alc✳ **PARKING:** 100 **CARDS:**

♦♦♦ Martindales

9-11 Sandes Av LA9 4LL ☎ 01539 724028
Dir: *N on A6, before Victoria Bridge*
Close to the River Kent and just a short walk from the town centre, this double fronted guest house offers traditional accommodation. Modern bedrooms are cheerfully decorated and a welcoming lounge bar is available for guest use. Breakfast is served in the spacious dining room and light snacks are available by prior arrangement.
FACILITIES: 8 en suite No smoking in dining room TVB tea/coffee No dogs (ex guide dogs) Licensed Cen ht No children 8yrs No coaches
PRICES: s £30; d £47✳ **PARKING:** 7 **CARDS:**

England

KENDAL continued

♦♦♦ Millers Beck Country Guest House

Stainton LA8 0DU ☎ 015395 60877 📠 015395 60877

Dir: *exit M6 at junct 36 & take A65, then 1st left signed Crooklands/Endmoor. Millers Beck 3.5m on right*

The delightful sound of cascading water can be heard from this converted 16th-century corn mill. Situated in the countryside, close to Kendal, this charming guest house offers cosy, modern bedrooms. Public areas include a choice of two comfortable gallery lounges and hearty breakfasts are served in the airy conservatory dining room.

FACILITIES: 3 en suite No smoking in bedrooms No smoking in area of dining room No smoking in 1 lounge TVB tea/coffee No dogs Cen ht No coaches Dinner Last d 6pm **PRICES:** d £46-£49* **LB**
PARKING: 4 **NOTES:** Closed Jan-Feb

♦♦♦ The Glen

Oxenholme LA9 7RF ☎ 01539 726386
e-mail: greenintheglen@btinternet.com

Dir: *M6 J36, then A65 towards Crooklands, onto Oxenholme, R at sign to Oxenholme station, R at T-junct, 1st drive on R up hill*

FACILITIES: 5 en suite (1 fmly) No smoking TVB tea/coffee Cen ht TVL No children 7 yrs No coaches Jacuzzi Dinner Last d by arrangement
PRICES: s £25-£30; d £20-£50* **BB PARKING:** 10 **NOTES:** Closed Xmas & New Year.

♦♦♦ Sonata

19 Burneside Rd LA9 4RL ☎ 01539 732290 📠 01539 732290
e-mail: chris@sonataguesthouse.freeserve.co.uk

Dir: *A6 through Kendal follow signs for A591 Windermere. 300yds after leaving one-way system fork right at Union Tavern pub and establisment 100yds on right*

FACILITIES: 4 en suite (1 fmly) No smoking in 2 bedrooms No smoking in dining room No smoking in lounges TVB tea/coffee Cen ht TVL Dinner Last d 11am **PRICES:** s £32; d £46* **CARDS:**

KESWICK Map 11 NY22

See also Mungrisdale

Premier Collection

♦♦♦♦♦ Derwent Cottage

Portinscale CA12 5RF ☎ 017687 74838
e-mail: enquiries@dercott.demon.co.uk

Dir: *A66 to Portinscale, pass Farmers Arms, 200mtrs turn right after left bend*

Derwent Cottage, parts of which date back to the 18th century, is set back from the main road in lovely mature gardens, and enjoys splendid views across the valley to Skiddaw. Enthusiastically run, it is comfortably furnished and offers smart, cosy lounges and a small bar. The dining room is the venue for freshly prepared home-cooked meals and hearty Cumbrian breakfasts. Bedrooms are spacious, well furnished and include lots of personal touches.

FACILITIES: 5 en suite No smoking TVB tea/coffee No dogs (ex guide dogs) Licensed Cen ht No children 12yrs No coaches Croquet lawn Dinner Last d noon **PRICES:** d £54-£84* **LB**
PARKING: 10 **NOTES:** Closed Nov-Feb & last 2 wks Aug
CARDS:

Premier Collection

♦♦♦♦♦ Grange Country House

Manor Brow, Ambleside Rd CA12 4BA ☎ 017687 72500
📠 017687 72500
e-mail: info@grangekeswick.com

Dir: *leave M6 at junct 40 & take A66 into Keswick, then left on A591 towards Windermere for 0.5m. Take 1st right & house 200 mtrs on right*

This stylish, spacious Victorian residence is set in its own beautifully tended gardens just a short stroll from the town centre and offers guests a relaxed atmosphere and professional service. Spacious bedrooms are well equipped, some featuring bare beams and delightful views across the town to the distant mountains. Spacious lounges and ample parking are available for guests and advice available for local walks.

FACILITIES: 10 en suite No smoking TVB tea/coffee Direct dial from bedrooms No dogs (ex guide dogs) Licensed Cen ht No children 7yrs No coaches **PRICES:** s £31-£46; d £62-£82 **LB PARKING:** 11
NOTES: Closed mid Nov-Feb **CARDS:**

♦♦♦♦ Allerdale House

1 Eskin St CA12 4DH ☎ 017687 73891 📠 017687 74068
e-mail: allerdalechef@aol.com

Dir: *exit A66 towards Keswick town centre.L after Conservative club to Greta St joins Eskin St, house at far end.*

Located in a quiet residential area just a short stroll from the town centre, this smartly presented house offers well equipped, bedrooms with attractive soft furnishings and solid pine furniture. There is a comfortable lounge and an elegant dining room where traditional breakfasts and by prior arrangement delicious dinners are served.

FACILITIES: 6 en suite (2 fmly) No smoking TVB tea/coffee Direct dial from bedrooms Licensed Cen ht No children 5yrs No coaches Dinner Last d 5pm
PRICES: s £25-£27; d £50-£54* **LB PARKING:** 6 **CARDS:**

continued

England

♦♦♦♦ Amble House

23 Eskin St CA12 4DQ ☎ 017687 73288 📠 017687 80220
e-mail: info@amblehouse.co.uk
Dir: *M6 junct40, A66 to Keswick, 1st left signposted Keswick to T-junction, turn right onto A591 towards town centre. 5th turning is Greta St/Eskin St*
A warm and enthusiastic welcome awaits you at Amble House. This late Victorian mid-terrace, close to the town centre and local attractions, offers immaculately clean, comfortable accommodation. Co-ordinated bedrooms are thoughtfully equipped and pleasantly furnished in pine. Award-winning healthy breakfasts are served in the dining room. Judith Sharpe was a Top Twenty Finalist in the AA Landlady of the Year Award 2002-2003.
FACILITIES: 6 rms (4 en suite) No smoking TVB tea/coffee No dogs Licensed Cen ht No children 5yrs No coaches **PRICES:** s £17-£18; d £40-£42✳ **LB BB CARDS:**

♦♦♦♦ Avondale

20 Southey St CA12 4EF ☎ 017687 72735 📠 017687 75431
e-mail: enquiries@avondaleguesthouse.com
Dir: *A66 to Keswick,1st turn for Keswick onto A591 towards town centre, L at War Memorial into Station St, sharp L to Southey St, Avondale 100 yds R*
Friendly efficient service and a pristine appearance are features of this well-maintained terrace house; minutes walk from the town centre. Bright modern, well-equipped bedrooms come in a variety of sizes. Reception rooms extend to a cosy lounge with a collection of books and a light and airy dining room.
FACILITIES: 6 en suite No smoking TVB tea/coffee No dogs Licensed Cen ht No children 12yrs No coaches **PRICES:** s £23-£24.50; d £46-£49✳ **NOTES:** Closed Xmas **CARDS:**

♦♦♦♦ Badgers Wood

30 Stanger St CA12 5JU ☎ 017687 72621
e-mail: aa@badgers-wood.co.uk
Dir: *M6 junct40, left for Keswick. Past 1st Keswick turn off. Exit at rdbt for Keswick. Turn left. At T junct left. Over rdbt & left into Stanger Street*

A warm welcome awaits guests at this delightful Victorian terraced house, quietly located close to the town centre. Smartly decorated bedrooms are nicely furnished and well equipped. The attractive breakfast room at the front of the house overlooks the picturesque fells. The house is totally no-smoking and vegetarians are gladly catered for.
FACILITIES: 6 rms (4 en suite) No smoking TVB tea/coffee No dogs (ex guide dogs) Cen ht No children 12yrs No coaches **PRICES:** s £18; d £48✳ **LB BB NOTES:** Closed Xmas & New Year

♦♦♦♦ Charnwood

6 Eskin St CA12 4DH ☎ 017687 74111 07711 773925(mobile)
This listed Victorian building is situated close to the town centre and main attractions. Beautifully decorated, and furnished in keeping with the period of the house, the bedrooms here are both comfortable and well equipped. Delicious breakfasts and home-cooked evening meals (by arrangement) are served in the spacious dining room. There is also a comfortable lounge. *continued*

FACILITIES: 5 en suite (3 fmly) No smoking TVB tea/coffee No dogs (ex guide dogs) Licensed Cen ht No children 5yrs No coaches Dinner Last d 10am **PRICES:** d £44-£58✳ **LB NOTES:** Closed 24-25 Dec
CARDS:

♦♦♦♦ Claremont House

Chestnut Hill CA12 4LT ☎ 017687 72089 📠 017687 72089
e-mail: claremonthouse@btinternet.com
Dir: *SE on A591, about 1m from Keswick centre*
This well-maintained attractive house, the family home of Jackie and Peter Werfel, was built some 150 years ago, and is set in its own mature grounds overlooking the town. Bedrooms are smartly decorated, well equipped and all benefit from en suite bathrooms. There is a comfortable lounge and nearby a bright airy dining room where hearty traditional breakfasts are served.
FACILITIES: 4 en suite No smoking TVB tea/coffee No dogs (ex guide dogs) Cen ht TVL No children 12yrs No coaches **PRICES:** s £30; d £48-£52✳ **LB PARKING:** 6 **NOTES:** Closed Jan-Etr

♦♦♦♦ Craglands

Penrith Rd CA12 4LJ ☎ 017687 74406
e-mail: craglands@msn.com
Dir: *from A66, 1st exit signed Keswick and Windermere. 1m on right, past road junct*
Situated in an elevated position on the edge of town, this stylish Victorian house offers good value, comfortable accommodation. Bedrooms are attractively decorated and well equipped. For those wishing to relax after a busy day exploring the lakes, there is a cosy lounge next to the neat and tidy dining room where hearty, traditional breakfasts are served at individual tables.
FACILITIES: 7 rms (5 en suite) No smoking TVB tea/coffee No dogs (ex guide dogs) Cen ht TVL No children 8yrs No coaches **PRICES:** d £47-£50✳
PARKING: 6

♦♦♦♦ Dalegarth House Country Hotel

Portinscale CA12 5RQ ☎ 017687 72817 📠 017687 72817
e-mail: john@dalegarth-house.co.uk
Dir: *approach Portinscale from A66 pass Farmers Arms approx 100yds on left to hotel*

Memorable hospitality, attentive service and substantial imaginative meals are all strengths at Dalegarth House Hotel. Peacefully located in the village of Portinscale and enjoying views of the lake, this well maintained guesthouse offers comfortable accommodation. Spacious public areas include a delightful lounge and a well stocked bar.
FACILITIES: 10 en suite (1 fmly) No smoking TVB tea/coffee No dogs (ex guide dogs) Licensed Cen ht TVL No children 5yrs No coaches Dinner Last d 5.30pm **PRICES:** s £32-£34; d £64-£68 **LB PARKING:** 12
CARDS:

BB Great value! This indicates B&B for £19 and under, per person, per night.

England

KESWICK continued

♦♦♦♦ Goodwin House

29 Southey St CA12 4EE ☎ 017687 74634
e-mail: enquiries@goodwinhouse.co.uk
Dir: *from A591 signed town centre, left before traffic lights and sharp left into Southey St. House 0.75m on left at crossroads with Church St*
Originally built in 1890 by the Lowther family to resemble a New England villa with a mansard roof, this appealing house is on the corner of an attractive terrace just a short stroll from the town centre. The bedrooms vary in size and style but all are well equipped, comfortable and decorated in bright colours.
FACILITIES: 6 en suite No smoking TVB tea/coffee No dogs Licensed Cen ht No children 12yrs No coaches **PRICES:** s £23-£25; d £46-£50* **NOTES:** Closed Xmas day

♦♦♦♦ Greystones Hotel

Ambleside Rd CA12 4DP ☎ 017687 73108
e-mail: greystones@keslakes.freeserve.co.uk
Dir: *exit M6 junct 40, A66 to Keswick, A591 Windermere. 1st right Manor Brow, Greystones 0.5m on right*

Greystones is just a minute's walk from the town centre and local attractions. Individually styled, the spacious bedrooms are comfortable and thoughtfully equipped and some benefit from stunning views of the fells. The resident proprietors offer friendly hospitality and attentive service. Freshly cooked breakfasts are served in the dining room at individual tables.
FACILITIES: 8 rms (7 en suite) No smoking TVB tea/coffee No dogs Licensed Cen ht No children 10yrs No coaches **PRICES:** s £23-£26; d £46-£52* **LB PARKING:** 7 **NOTES:** Closed Dec **CARDS:**

♦♦♦♦ Hall Garth

37 Blencathra St CA12 4HX ☎ 017687 72627 📠 017687 72627
e-mail: tracyhallgarth@aol.com
Dir: *off A591, turning L by Millfield Nursing Home*
This friendly and welcoming family run guest house is situated in a peaceful residential area, within walking distance of the town centre. Bedrooms, all attractively decorated, are smart and modern. The pretty breakfast room is on the ground floor and is an appropriate setting for hearty Cumbrian breakfasts.
FACILITIES: 5 en suite No smoking TVB tea/coffee Cen ht
PRICES: d £39-£40* **CARDS:**

♦♦♦♦ Hazeldene Hotel

The Heads CA12 5ER ☎ 017687 72106 📠 017687 75435
e-mail: info@hazeldene-hotel.co.uk
Dir: *from A66 follow signs for Borrowdale and lake. Turn right into The Heads opposite central car park*
Situated in an elevated location overlooking Hope Park and enjoying views of Catbells, Causey Pike and Walla Crag this friendly family run guest house is within walking distance of the town centre. Bedrooms which vary in size are comfortably proportioned brightly decorated and well equipped. There are two comfortable lounges, one of which has a bar, a games room and a spacious dining room where dinners and hearty breakfasts are served at individual tables. There is a large car park.
FACILITIES: 18 rms (17 en suite) (4 fmly) TVB tea/coffee Direct dial from bedrooms Licensed TVL No coaches Pool Table Dinner Last d 7pm **PRICES:** s £25-£35; d £50-£70* **PARKING:** 12 **NOTES:** Closed Jan **CARDS:**

♦♦♦♦ Howe Keld Lakeland Hotel

5/7 The Heads CA12 5ES ☎ 017687 72417 📠 017687 72417
e-mail: david@howekeld.co.uk
Dir: *from town centre take rd to Borrowdale. Turn right opp main car park, 1st on left*
Offering modern accommodation throughout, this friendly, well-run hotel is close to the town and lakeside. Bedrooms are smartly decorated and furnished and the first floor lounge offers spectacular views of the fells. Breakfast is a particular highlight, with local and home-made produce featuring strongly on the menu. Dinner is available by prior arrangement.
FACILITIES: 15 en suite (3 fmly) (2 GF) No smoking in bedrooms No smoking in dining room No smoking in 1 lounge TVB tea/coffee Licensed Cen ht No coaches Dinner Last d Breakfast time **PRICES:** s £27-£30; d £54-£60* **LB PARKING:** 9 **NOTES:** Closed Xmas & Jan **CARDS:**

♦♦♦♦ Parkfield

The Heads CA12 5ES ☎ 017687 72328 📠 017687 71396
e-mail: enquiries@parkfieldkeswick.com
Dir: *from A66 take 2nd exit to Keswick and turn left. At T-junct turn left to mini rdbt, turn right and right again into The Heads*
This impeccably maintained guest house is quietly yet centrally located, just a couple of minutes' walk from the lake, town centre, bus station and New Theatre. The bedrooms include one on ground floor level, and are individually appointed and well equipped. Facilities include a very attractive lounge that overlooks the golf course to Grizedale and Causey Pikes. Separate tables are provided in the bright and pleasant breakfast room.
FACILITIES: 8 en suite No smoking TVB tea/coffee No dogs Cen ht No children 16yrs No coaches **PRICES:** s £30-£35; d £52-£56*
PARKING: 7 **NOTES:** Closed Dec-Jan ex open New Year **CARDS:**

♦♦♦♦ Rickerby Grange Country House Hotel

Portinscale CA12 5RH ☎ 017687 72344 📠 017687 75588
e-mail: val@ricor.co.uk
Dir: *bypass Keswick on A66 Cockermouth Rd, L at Portinscale sign, pass Farmer Arms Inn on L, 2nd lane to R*

Built at the turn of the last century by a local farmer, this small friendly hotel is peacefully situated in the village of Portinscale. Bedrooms are brightly decorated and include three on the ground floor. Public rooms are especially comfortable and include a

continued

spacious dining room, a bar and an inviting lounge. Five course evening meals, freshly prepared by the Chef/Proprietor, are a feature, including vegetarian meals by prior arrangement. There is a large private car park.
FACILITIES: 12 rms (11 en suite) (3 fmly) (2 GF) No smoking in bedrooms No smoking in dining room No smoking in lounges TVB tea/coffee Direct dial from bedrooms Licensed Cen ht No children 5yrs Dinner Last d 6pm **PRICES:** s £32-£34; d £64-£68✳ **LB** **PARKING:** 20 **CARDS:**

♦♦♦♦ Skiddaw Grove Country House

Vicarage Hill CA12 5QB ☎ 017687 73324 & 0800 2985693 017687 73324
e-mail: info@skiddawgrove.demon.uk
Dir: *exit M6 junct 40 then A66 W, turn off at Crosthwaite rdbt, A591 junct, into Keswick, immmediately right into Vicarage Hill. Hotel 20yds on left*

Just off the bypass and set in lovely gardens with an outdoor pool and magnificent views of both Bassenthwaite Lake and Skiddaw, this house offers comfortable, thoughtfully equipped bedrooms. In addition to a good breakfast, the host has a wealth of local knowledge and tourist information.
FACILITIES: 5 en suite (1 fmly) No smoking TVB tea/coffee No dogs Licensed Cen ht No coaches Outdoor swimming pool (heated) Table tennis **PRICES:** s £25-£27; d £50-£54✳ **LB** **PARKING:** 8 **NOTES:** Closed Xmas

♦♦♦♦ Stonegarth

2 Eskin St CA12 4DH ☎ 017687 72436
e-mail: info@stonegarth.com
Dir: *after BP station turn left, after 200 yds into Greta St and continue into Eskin St*
This large stone-built house is just a few minutes' walk from the town centre. Privately owned and personally run in a warm and friendly manner, it provides tastefully appointed, spacious and well equipped accommodation. Facilities include an elegant lounge and a very pleasant dining room, where separate tables are provided.
FACILITIES: 7 en suite (1 fmly) No smoking STV TVB tea/coffee Direct dial from bedrooms No dogs (ex guide dogs) Licensed Cen ht No children 5yrs No coaches **PRICES:** s £25-£40; d £50-£80✳ **LB** **PARKING:** 7 **CARDS:**

♦♦♦♦ Sunnyside

25 Southey St CA12 4EF ☎ 017687 72446
e-mail: enquiries@sunnysideguesthouse.com
Dir: *M6, A66 West, off at Keswick, right at T junct towards town centre, under railway bridge, left at war memorial, 100yds on left*
This stylishly decorated and inviting guest house is set in a quiet area close to the town centre. Bedrooms, including a family room, are comfortably furnished. There is a lounge with plenty of books and magazines. Breakfast is served in the light and airy dining room. Private parking is a bonus.
FACILITIES: 7 en suite (1 fmly) No smoking TVB tea/coffee No dogs (ex guide dogs) Cen ht No coaches **PRICES:** s £25; d £40-£50✳ **LB** **PARKING:** 9 **CARDS:**

♦♦♦♦ Tarn Hows

3-5 Eskin St CA12 4DH ☎ 017687 73217 017687 73217
e-mail: info@tarnhows.co.uk
Dir: *from Ambleside follow Keswick A591-town centre onto A5271. At Conservative Club, turn left into Greta St which continues into Eskin St*
This well maintained guest house consists of two interconnecting stone clad houses, recognisable in summer by the colourful garden and pretty hanging baskets. Bedrooms vary in size and style but all are smartly furnished and attractively decorated. Hearty traditional Cumbrian breakfasts are served at individual tables in the spacious dining room.
FACILITIES: 8 rms (5 en suite) No smoking TVB tea/coffee No dogs (ex guide dogs) Licensed Cen ht TVL No children 6yrs No coaches Dinner Last d 10am **PRICES:** s £26; d £52✳ **LB** **PARKING:** 8

♦♦♦♦ A Abacourt House

26 Stanger St CA12 5JU ☎ 017687 72967
e-mail: abacourt@btinternet.com
Dir: *off main street in town centre, 1st street on right after town hall*
FACILITIES: 5 en suite No smoking TVB tea/coffee No dogs No children No coaches **PRICES:** d £44✳ **PARKING:** 5 **NOTES:** Closed 25-26 Dec

♦♦♦♦ A Clarence House

14 Eskine St CA12 4DQ ☎ 017687 73186 017687 72317
e-mail: info@clarencehousekeswick.co.uk
Dir: *at BP garage 4th left into Greta St, cross 2 juncts into Eskine St*
FACILITIES: 8 en suite (3 fmly) No smoking TVB tea/coffee No dogs (ex guide dogs) **PRICES:** s £22-£27 d £44-£60✳ **CARDS:**

♦♦♦♦ A Paddock Guest House

Wordsworth St CA12 4HU ☎ 017687 72510 017687 72510
e-mail: val@thepaddock.info
Dir: *A591 through the lakes or A66 Penrith to join A591 at Keswick follow town centre, approach Keswick you pass "Twa Dogs Inn" go under rail bridge and take 3rd left into Wordsworth St. The Paddock is immediately on right*
FACILITIES: 6 en suite (1 fmly) No smoking TVB tea/coffee No dogs Licensed Cen ht TVL No coaches **PRICES:** d £38-£42✳ **LB** **BB** **PARKING:** 5 **CARDS:**

♦♦♦ Brierholme

21 Bank St CA12 5JZ ☎ 017687 72938
e-mail: enquiries@brierholme.co.uk
Dir: *on A591, 100yds from post office*
This period house enjoys a central location just minutes' walk from the main square. Bedrooms are traditionally furnished and thoughtfully equipped. Public areas include a first floor lounge with views over the town and surrounding peaks and a neatly appointed breakfast room where hearty breakfasts are served.
FACILITIES: 6 en suite (2 fmly) No smoking in bedrooms No smoking in dining room TVB tea/coffee No dogs (ex guide dogs) Licensed Cen ht No coaches **PRICES:** d £44-£60✳ **LB** **PARKING:** 6 **CARDS:**

♦♦♦ Cragside

39 Blencathra St CA12 4HX ☎ 017687 73344
e-mail: suetaylorparsons@hotmail.com
Dir: *A66, 1st L to Keswick, follow rd into town under rail bridge, L at Millfield House & follow rd to R, 1st house on R*
This small and very friendly guest house is located a short walk from the town centre and all the amenities. There are fine views of the surrounding fells from many rooms. Bedrooms are well equipped, and the pretty breakfast room overlooks the small front garden. Visually or hearing impaired guests are catered for.
FACILITIES: 4 en suite (2 fmly) No smoking TVB tea/coffee Cen ht No children 3yrs No coaches **PRICES:** d £40✳ **CARDS:**

England

KESWICK continued

♦♦♦ ***Dorchester House***
17 Southey St CA12 4EG ☎ 017687 73256
Dir: *turn off A66 at 1st Keswick junct. Follow road into town, turn left at war memorial into Southey St. House 50yds on left*
A warm and friendly welcome is assured at this smartly presented guest house, which is situated at the end of a Victorian terrace. Bedrooms are comfortably proportioned, brightly decorated and well-maintained. Substantial breakfasts are served at individual tables in the attractive ground floor dining room. This is a no-smoking establishment.
FACILITIES: 9 rms (5 en suite) (2 fmly) No smoking TVB tea/coffee No dogs Cen ht No coaches

♦♦♦ **Heatherlea**
26 Blencathra St CA12 4HP ☎ 017687 72430 017687 72430
e-mail: david@heatherleagh.fsnet.co.uk
Dir: *exit M6 onto A66 to Keswick, follow signs to Keswick, after petrol station take 2nd left*
Situated a short stroll from the town centre, this end-of-terrace Victorian house provides well equipped, tastefully decorated en-suite bedrooms. Guests can be assured of a warm and friendly welcome from proprietors David and Katie and substantial breakfasts are served in the dining room which has lovely views of the surrounding fells.
FACILITIES: 4 en suite (2 fmly) No smoking TVB tea/coffee Cen ht No children 5yrs No coaches **PRICES:** d £40-£44* **NOTES:** Closed Xmas

♦♦♦ ***The Mill Inn***
CA11 0XR ☎ 017687 79632 017687 79632
e-mail: the_mill_inn@compuserve.com
(For full entry see Mungrisdale)

♦♦♦ **Richmond House**
37-39 Eskin St CA12 4DG ☎ 017687 73965
e-mail: richmondhouse@tesco.net
Dir: *follow signs to town centre, turn 4th left after passing under bridge into Greta St which continues into Eskin St*
This small, friendly, privately owned and personally run guest house provides well equipped accommodation, equally suitable for tourists and business visitors. A family room is available. Facilities here include a cosy lounge, a lounge bar and a traditionally furnished dining room where separate tables are provided. The guest house is situated within walking distance of the town centre.
FACILITIES: 10 rms (9 en suite) (1 fmly) No smoking TVB tea/coffee No dogs Licensed Cen ht TVL No children 2yrs Dinner Last d 5pm **PRICES:** s £19-£25; d £38-£46* LB BB **NOTES:** Closed 25-26 Dec **CARDS:**

♦♦♦ **Swinside**
Newlands Valley CA12 5UE ☎ 017687 78253
e-mail: info@theswinsideinn.com
Dir: *A66 take turning for Portinscale/Grange and Newlands, proceed through Portinscale in 1m outside village right fork signed Stair/Buttermere, Swinside is 0.25m on right*
This historic 17th century traditional inn set in the scenic Newlands Valley boasts stunning views over the national park and is close to Keswick and Derwentwater. Extensive dinner menus are provided in the cosy beamed bar where a blazing fire burns on the cooler days. Bedrooms vary in size and all offer the expected modern facilities.
FACILITIES: 7 rms (4 en suite) (1 fmly) No smoking in bedrooms No smoking in dining room No smoking in 1 lounge TVB tea/coffee Cen ht Pool Table Dinner Last d 8.45pm **PRICES:** s £32-£42; d £44-£54* LB **MEALS:** Bar Lunch £3.25-£5.95 Dinner £12-£18alc* **PARKING:** 50 **CARDS:**

♦♦♦ **Watendlath**
15 Acorn St CA12 4EA ☎ 017687 74165 017687 74165
e-mail: info@watendlathguesthouse.co.uk
Dir: *M6 junct 40 then A66 to Keswick. 1st left and follow town centre signs, river and park on right turn immediately left before traffic lights into Southey St, go to end then left into Acorn St*
FACILITIES: 4 en suite (2 fmly) No smoking TVB tea/coffee No dogs Cen ht **PRICES:** d £36-£44* BB **NOTES:** Closed 15-26 Dec

KIRKBY LONSDALE — Map 07 SD67

♦♦ **The Copper Kettle**
3-5 Market St LA6 2AU ☎ 015242 71714
Dir: *M36 junct 36 follow signs to Kirkby Lonsdale (approx 5.5m) turn left at town centrte sign follow road to post office, turn in, drive down lane*
FACILITIES: 4 en suite (2 fmly) TVB Licensed Dinner Last d 9pm **PRICES:** s £17.50-£22; d £35-£41* LB BB **PARKING:** 3 **NOTES:** Closed 2 wks Jan, 1 wk Nov **CARDS:**

KIRKBY STEPHEN

Premier Collection

♦♦♦♦♦ **Augill Castle**
CA17 4DE ☎ 017683 41937
e-mail: enquiries@augillcastle.co.uk
(For full entry see Brough)

KIRKLINTON — Map 12 NY46

♦♦♦ **Clift House Farm**
CA6 6DE ☎ 01228 675237 01228 675237
e-mail: clifthousefarm@hotmail.com
FACILITIES: 3 en suite (1 fmly) No smoking TVB tea/coffee Cen ht TVL No coaches Fishing Dinner Last d prior arrangement **PRICES:** s £22-£25; d £44-£48* **PARKING:** 6 **NOTES:** Closed Xmas & New Year

LORTON — Map 11 NY12

Premier Collection

♦♦♦♦♦ **New House Farm**
CA13 9UU ☎ 01900 85404 01900 85412
e-mail: hazel@newhouse-farm.co.uk
Dir: *6m S of Cockermouth, on B5289 between Lorton and Loweswater*

A warm welcome awaits at this delightfully restored farmhouse. The inviting public areas and bedrooms have been stylishly decorated, yet retain many original features. Bedrooms offer large comfortable beds and are equipped with many thoughtful extras including home baked biscuits. A delicious five course daily-changing dinner menu and hearty breakfasts are a highlight.

England

FACILITIES: 4 en suite 1 annexe en suite (1 GF) No smoking tea/coffee Licensed Cen ht No children 6yrs No coaches Jacuzzi Dinner Last d 5pm **PRICES:** d £84-£92 **PARKING:** 30 **CARDS:**

Premier Collection

♦♦♦♦♦ Winder Hall Country House

CA13 9UP ☎ 01900 85107 📠 85107
e-mail: stay@winderhall.com
Dir: *from Keswick take A66 west & at Braithwaite take B5292 Whinlatter Pass to Lorton. 6m to junct with B5289, turn left, Winder Hall 0.5m on right*

Winder Hall is an impressive house dating back to the 14th century and features stone mullions, leaded windows and antiques. The lounge is luxuriously furnished and the elegant, spacious dining room is the ideal venue for skilfully prepared meals. Individually styled, smartly decorated bedrooms are thoughtfully equipped and all are furnished with fine antiques or pine. Two rooms benefit from beautiful four-poster beds.
FACILITIES: 6 en suite (2 fmly) No smoking TVB tea/coffee No dogs Licensed Cen ht No children 8yrs No coaches Dinner Last d 10am **PRICES:** d £92-£110✳ **LB** **PARKING:** 6 **CARDS:**

♦♦♦♦ Old Vicarage

Church Ln CA13 9UN ☎ 01900 85656
e-mail: enquiries@oldvicarage.co.uk
Dir: *turn off B5292 Whinlatter Road onto B5289 N of Lorton. Take first left signposted Church, house first on right*
Located in the peaceful Lorton Valley at the heart of the National Park, this delightful Lakeland Victorian house offers spacious accommodation. A converted barn offers two rooms with feature stone walls, and is ideal for families with young children. Bedrooms in the main house are well equipped and provide excellent views of distant mountains. Delicious home cooking can be enjoyed in the bright dining room.
FACILITIES: 6 rms (5 en suite) 2 annexe en suite No smoking TVB tea/coffee No dogs (ex guide dogs) Licensed Cen ht No coaches Last d 10am **PRICES:** s £60-£90✳ **LB** **PARKING:** 12 **CARDS:**

LOWESWATER — Map 11 NY12

♦♦♦♦ Kirkstile Inn

CA13 0RU ☎ 01900 85219 📠 01900 85239
e-mail: info@kirkstile.com
Dir: *From A66 towards Lorton via Whinlatter at Braithwaite. On entering Lorton tale left turn signposted to Buttermere. Follow road through village to t-junct turn left. Follow signs to Loweswater & turn left at sign for Kirkstile Inn*

continued

This delightful 16th-century inn enjoys a rural location and breathtaking views. Public areas include a bar, an elegant restaurant, a choice of lounges and a beer garden. Bedrooms have lots of original character and have been attractively refurbished. Annexe rooms comprise two spacious family suites, each with two bedrooms, a lounge and private bathroom.
FACILITIES: 7 en suite 2 annexe en suite (2 fmly) (2 GF) No smoking in bedrooms No smoking in dining room No smoking in lounges TV3B tea/coffee Cen ht No coaches Dinner **PRICES:** s £35-£37; d £60-£74✳ **LB** **MEALS:** Lunch £10-£15alc Dinner £11-£22.50alc✳ **PARKING:** 30 **CARDS:**

MARYPORT — Map 11 NY03

♦♦♦♦ The Retreat Hotel

Birkby CA15 6RG ☎ 01900 814056
e-mail: enquiries@retreathotel.co.uk
Dir: *situated in Birkby, just off A596, approx. 2m N of Maryport, 1m S of Crosby*
This spacious, Victorian house enjoys a peaceful yet convenient location in the hamlet of Birkby, just outside Maryport. Retaining many lovely original features it is tastefully furnished with antique and period pieces. Spacious, smartly decorated bedrooms offer all modern facilities. Public rooms include two separate lounges, one housing a well-stocked bar and an elegant restaurant.
FACILITIES: 3 en suite No smoking in bedrooms No smoking in dining room TVB tea/coffee No dogs (ex guide dogs) Licensed Cen ht No coaches Dinner Last d 8.15pm **PRICES:** s £38-£43; d £50-£55✳ **LB** **PARKING:** 12 **NOTES:** Closed 24-26 Dec & 1 Jan 60 **CARDS:**

MATTERDALE END — Map 11 NY32

♦♦♦♦ Bank House Farm

CA11 0LF ☎ 01768 482040 📠 01768 482040
e-mail: tjhargreaves@aol.com
Dir: *from M6 exit junct 40 onto A66 towards Keswick, pass Sportsman Inn on right next left A5091. In centre of Matterdale End opposite Brook House Farm turn right onto a No Through Road continue to top, Bank House last on left*

A genuine friendly welcome awaits guests at this delightful period farmhouse sitting in seven acres of grounds and enjoying splendid Lakeland views. En suite bedrooms are smartly decorated and furnished. There is a small comfortable lounge and home-cooked Aga breakfasts are served in the attractive dining room. The house is no-smoking.
FACILITIES: 3 en suite No smoking TVB tea/coffee No dogs Cen ht No children 18yrs No coaches **PRICES:** d £60✳ **PARKING:** 3 **NOTES:** Closed 20 Dec-6 Jan 60

England

MILLOM Map 07 SD18

♦♦♦♦ Duddon Pilot Hotel

Devonshire Rd LA18 4JT ☎ 01229 774116

Dir: *M6 junct 37 take A590 Barrow-in-Furness turn off at Greenodd onto A5092 Workington onto A595. Turn off onto A5093, leads you into Millom*

This friendly pub enjoys a coastal location on the edge of the village, and the welcoming Milligan family have a wealth of local knowledge to share with guests. Bedrooms are modern and well equipped, and public rooms are themed on the history of the local iron and shipping industries.

FACILITIES: 6 en suite (1 fmly) No smoking TVB tea/coffee Direct dial from bedrooms No dogs (ex guide dogs) Licensed Cen ht TVL Dinner Last d 9:30pm **PRICES:** s £25; d £50✱ **PARKING:** 32

♦♦♦♦ Pavilion Hotel

36 Duke St LA18 5BB ☎ 01229 770700 📠 01229 770700

e-mail: pavilionjb@aol.com

Dir: *leave M6 at junct 36, follow A590 towards Ulverston, at Greenodd turn right, A5092, at Grizebeck becomes A595 follow to junct with A5093 signed Millom. In Millom road bends right at Esso garage, hotel approx. 100yds on right*

FACILITIES: 5 en suite (1 fmly) No smoking TVB tea/coffee No dogs (ex guide dogs) Cen ht TVL Dinner Last d 7pm **PRICES:** s £20; d £40✱ **LB**

MUNGRISDALE Map 11 NY33

♦♦♦ *The Mill Inn*

CA11 0XR ☎ 017687 79632 📠 017687 79632

e-mail: the_mill_inn@compuserve.com

Dir: *M6 junct 40 Penrith follow A66 Keswick, after 10m right to Mungrisdale. The Mill Inn is 2m on this road on left*

Commanding splendid views, this 16th-century inn is set beside a tranquil stream against a woodland backdrop. The modern-style bedrooms provide good levels of comfort and facilities. A wide range of home-cooked dishes is provided in the spacious restaurant and bar. There is also a games room.

FACILITIES: 9 rms (7 en suite) (1 fmly) No smoking in bedrooms No smoking in dining room TVB tea/coffee Cen ht ch fac Pool table Darts Last d 9pm **PARKING:** 30 **NOTES:** Closed 25 Dec **CARDS:**

NEAR SAWREY Map 07 SD39

Premier Collection

♦♦♦♦♦ Ees Wyke Country House

LA22 0JZ ☎ 015394 36393 📠 015394 36393

e-mail: eeswyke@aol.com

Dir: *1.5m outside Hawkshead on B5285. On the road to the ferry across Windermere*

A genuine, warm welcome awaits at this elegant Georgian country house, nestling in its own grounds, with panoramic views over Lake Esthwaite and the beautiful Cumbrian countryside. Comfortable, thoughtfully equipped bedrooms have been decorated and furnished with care. There is a charming lounge, complete with real fire, and a splendid dining room, where a carefully prepared, daily-changing, five-course dinner is served. Breakfasts enjoy a fine reputation thanks to the superb use of local produce.

FACILITIES: 8 en suite No smoking in dining room No smoking in 1 lounge TVB tea/coffee Licensed Cen ht No children 10yrs No coaches Dinner Last d 7.15pm **PRICES:** (incl. dinner) s fr £67; d fr £134✱ **LB** **PARKING:** 12 **NOTES:** Closed Jan-Feb

Premier Collection

♦♦♦♦♦ Sawrey House Country Hotel

LA22 0LF ☎ 015394 36387 📠 015394 36010

e-mail: enquiries@sawrey-house.com

Dir: *from Ambleside take B5286 towards Hawkshead, left onto B5285. Hotel on right*

Set in three acres of gardens above Esthwaite Water, next door to Beatrix Potter's former home, this house dates back to 1830 and has been carefully and lovingly restored. Comfortable, well-equipped bedrooms all have delightful views, while the elegant lounge offers deep sofas, and a roaring fire in winter. Dinner is a highlight, with imagination, talent and flair clearly evident in the exquisitely presented food. Breakfasts are substantial and equally imaginative.

FACILITIES: 11 en suite (2 GF) No smoking TVB tea/coffee Direct dial from bedrooms Licensed Cen ht No children 10yrs Fishing Croquet lawn Dinner Last d 8pm **PRICES:** s £48-£60; d £100-£120✱ **LB** **CONF:** Thtr 25 Class 25 Del from £95 ✱ **PARKING:** 24 **NOTES:** Closed Jan rs Nov-Feb (weekends only), Xmas & New Year **CARDS:**

♦♦♦♦ Buckle Yeat

LA22 0LF ☎ 015394 36446 & 36538 📠 015394 36446

e-mail: info@buckle-yeat.co.uk

Dir: *M6 junct 36 towards Windermere & follow signs for Hawkshead via Ferry. Premises in 2nd village*

Close to Beatrix Potter's former home, Buckle Yeat is mentioned in some of the author's well-known tales. This charming 200-year-old cottage retains many original features including a beamed dining room where freshly cooked breakfasts and cream teas are served. Bedrooms are prettily decorated and an elegant lounge is provided.

continued

Buckle Yeat Guest House

FACILITIES: 7 en suite (1 fmly) No smoking in bedrooms No smoking in dining room TVB tea/coffee Cen ht TVL No coaches **PRICES:** s £27.50-£30; d £55-£60✻ **PARKING:** 9 **CARDS:**

♦♦♦ Beechmount Country House

LA22 0JZ ☎ 015394 36356
e-mail: beechmount@supanet.com
Dir: *from Hawkshead take B5285 for 2m to sign for 'Near Sawrey'- house opp*

Located in the peaceful village of Near Sawrey, this spacious Edwardian house enjoys delightful views over the lake and countryside. Decorated and furnished in an interesting mix of styles, bedrooms are comfortable and well-equipped. Breakfast is served at individual tables in the dining room, which also doubles as a lounge.
FACILITIES: 3 en suite (1 fmly) No smoking in 1 bedrooms No smoking in dining room No smoking in lounges TVB tea/coffee Cen ht TVL No coaches **PRICES:** s £30-£34; d fr £48✻ **PARKING:** 5

♦♦♦ High Green Gate

LA22 0LF ☎ 015394 36296
Dir: *on B5285 between Bowness & Hawkshead via ferry*
Located just a minute's walk from Hill Top, this converted 18th-century farmhouse sits within a colourful cottage garden in the heart of Near Sawrey. Afternoon tea is served either in the gardens or one of the cosy lounges and meals are taken in the well-appointed dining room. Warm hospitality is assured.
FACILITIES: 5 rms (4 en suite) (4 fmly) (1 GF) No smoking in dining room tea/coffee Cen ht TVL Dinner Last d 6pm **PRICES:** s £30-£40; d £48-£54✻ **PARKING:** 7 **NOTES:** Closed Nov-Mar

NEWBY BRIDGE — Map 07 SD38

♦♦♦♦ The Coach House

Hollow Oak LA12 8AD ☎ 015395 31622
e-mail: coachho@talk21.com
Dir: *2.5m W of Newby Bridge turn off A590 onto B5278 (signposted Cark) then immediately left into car park*

continued

Conveniently located for Lake Windermere this sympathetic conversion of an old coach house is set in delightful gardens. The modern bedrooms are light and airy and there is also a cosy lounge for visitor use. Breakfast is served a converted stable complete with stable style door.
FACILITIES: 3 rms (2 en suite) No smoking tea/coffee No dogs (ex guide dogs) Cen ht TVL No children 10yrs No coaches **PRICES:** s £30; d £45✻ **LB PARKING:** 3

♦♦♦♦ Hill Crest

Brow Edge LA12 8QP ☎ 015395 31766 📠 015395 31986
e-mail: enquiries@hillcrest.gbr.cc
Dir: *1m after Newby Bridge on A590 turn left into Brow Edge Rd, premises 0.75m on right*
A warm welcome is offered at this well-kept family home, which enjoys stunning views of the surrounding area. The Lakeland stone house is ideal for a quiet getaway, offering thoughtfully equipped bedrooms featuring pine furniture, and the pleasant lounge doubles as a breakfast room, where the breakfast menu makes good use of local produce.
FACILITIES: 3 en suite (1 fmly) (1 GF) No smoking TVB tea/coffee No dogs Cen ht TVL No coaches Free use of health & fitness club **PRICES:** s £30-£40; d £45-£50✻ **LB PARKING:** 4 **NOTES:** Closed 22-26 Dec

♦♦♦♦ The Knoll Country House

Lakeside LA12 8AU ☎ 015395 31347 📠 015395 30850
e-mail: info@theknoll-lakeside.co.uk
Dir: *leave M6 junct 36 and follow A590 to Newby Bridge, right after rdbt at Newby Bridge follow signs for lakeside steamers, the Knoll is 400mtrs on left after lakeside pier*
This late Victorian country house is set in attractive gardens a short walk from the pier at Lakeside. Accommodation, which varies in style, includes larger rooms, one with a four poster bed. High quality, fresh, local produce features on menus and is treated simply and with the respect it deserves. The lounge is elegantly furnished and includes a fully stocked bar.
FACILITIES: 8 en suite No smoking TVB tea/coffee Direct dial from bedrooms No dogs (ex guide dogs) Licensed Cen ht TVL No children No coaches Dinner Last d 4pm **PRICES:** s £36-£45; d £60-£90✻ **LB PARKING:** 8 **CARDS:**

♦♦♦♦ Lakes End

LA12 8ND ☎ 015395 31260 📠 015395 31260
e-mail: vjf.lakesend@virgin.net
Dir: *on A590 in Newby Bridge, premises 100mtrs from rdbt on left just before Newby bridge hotel*
In a sheltered, wooded setting away from the road, Lakes End is convenient both for the coast, lakes and other holiday attractions. Each of the comfortable bedrooms has been thoughtfully furnished and equipped, and one is located on the ground floor. Traditional English breakfasts are served and delicious home-cooked evening meals can be provided by prior arrangement.
FACILITIES: 4 en suite (2 fmly) (1 GF) No smoking TVB tea/coffee Licensed Cen ht TVL No coaches Dinner Last d 8pm **PRICES:** d £42-£46✻ **LB PARKING:** 8 **CARDS:**

♦♦♦♦ Old Barn Farm

Fiddler Hall LA12 8NQ ☎ 015395 31842
e-mail: peter@oldbarnfarm.com
Dir: *M6 junct 36 follow A591 to 1st turn off tp A590, keep on A590 through village of High Newton in further 1.5m turn left signed Cartmel Old Barn 200yds on left*
FACILITIES: 4 en suite (1 fmly) No smoking TVB tea/coffee No dogs (ex guide dogs) Cen ht **PRICES:** s £30; d £50✻ **LB PARKING:** 4

Places with this symbol are farmhouses.

England

PENRITH Map 12 NY53

♦♦♦♦ Beckfoot Country House
CA10 2QB ☎ 01931 713241 🖹 01931 713391
e-mail: beckfoot@aol.com

(For full entry see Helton)

♦♦♦♦ Brooklands
2 Portland Place CA11 7QN ☎ 01768 863395 🖹 01768 864895
e-mail: enquiries@brooklandsguesthouse.com
Dir: *M6 junct 40, follow tourist information signs. Left at town hall into Portland Place. Brooklands House 50yds on left*

A warm welcome awaits guests at this delightful Victorian terraced house, only minutes' walk from the town centre. Bedrooms are beautifully decorated and elegantly furnished and include rooms that are suitable for families. A hearty, freshly cooked breakfast is served in the attractive pine furnished dining room.
FACILITIES: 6 rms (4 en suite) (2 fmly) No smoking STV TVB tea/coffee No dogs (ex guide dogs) Cen ht **PRICES:** s £25-£40; d £40-£55* **LB** **PARKING:** 2

♦♦♦♦ Glendale
4 Portland Place CA11 7QN ☎ 01768 862579 🖹 01768 867934
e-mail: glendale@lineone.net
Dir: *M6 junct 40, follow signs for 'Tourist Information'. Follow road over mini-rdbts past rail station and ruined castle. Proceed downhill past supermarket, left at bottom onto one-way system and head into town. Take 1st left at Royal Pub/Town Hall, house on left*
Built in the Victorian era, this friendly family run guest house forms part of a terraced row only a short stroll from the town's centre and is convenient for the Lakes and Eden Valley. Bedrooms vary in size, but all are attractive, well equipped and presented. For those requiring them, drying facilities are available. Hearty breakfasts are served at individual tables in the charming ground floor dining room. Children and pets are welcome.
FACILITIES: 7 rms (5 en suite) (4 fmly) No smoking TVB tea/coffee Cen ht **PRICES:** s £25-£35; d £36-£45* **BB**

♦♦♦♦ 🅰 Roundthorn Country Hotel
Beacon Edge CA11 8SJ ☎ 01768 863952 🖹 01768 864100
e-mail: enquiries@roundthorn.co.uk
Dir: *from A686 to Alston turn left signed Roundthorn at T junct turn left*
FACILITIES: 10 en suite (2 fmly) No smoking in 4 bedrooms No smoking in dining room No smoking in 1 lounge TVB tea/coffee Direct dial from bedrooms Licensed Cen ht Dinner Last d 9.30pm **PRICES:** s £44.50-£49.50; d £59-£69* **LB** **CONF:** Thtr 200 Class 100 Board 50 Del from £75 * **PARKING:** 60 **NOTES:** Civ Wed 100 **CARDS:**

♦♦♦ Brandelhow
1 Portland Place CA11 7QN ☎ 01768 864470
Dir: *M6 junct 40 follow town centre signs, turn left into Portland Place at Town Hall*
This well-maintained terraced guest house is conveniently situated within easy walking distance of the town centre. All of the bedrooms are generally spacious, are all well co-ordinated. There are some rooms that are suitable for family use. Breakfast is served in the ground floor dining room.
FACILITIES: 5 rms (3 en suite) (3 fmly) No smoking TVB tea/coffee Cen ht No coaches **PRICES:** s fr £20; d £44* **LB** **PARKING:** 1 **NOTES:** Closed 24-25 Dec & 31 Dec

♦♦♦ Limes Country Hotel
Redhills, Stainton CA11 0DT ☎ 01768 863343 🖹 01768 867190
e-mail: jdhanton@aol.com
Dir: *M6 junct 40 onto A66, 0.5m W turn left immediately before Little Chef & follow rd for 0.25m. The Limes on right*
Conveniently situated for the motorway and for touring the northern Lakes, this Victorian house is peacefully situated in open countryside. Spacious bedrooms, some suitable for families, are traditionally furnished. There are plenty of games, books and magazines in the lounge and a substantial breakfast is served.
FACILITIES: 6 en suite (3 fmly) No smoking in 4 bedrooms No smoking in dining room TVB tea/coffee No dogs (ex guide dogs) Licensed Cen ht No coaches Dinner Last d 3pm **PRICES:** s £29-£30; d £48-£50 **LB** **PARKING:** 7 **CARDS:**

POOLEY BRIDGE Map 12 NY42

♦♦♦♦ Elm House
High St, Pooley Bridge CA10 2NH ☎ 017684 86334
🖹 017684 86851
e-mail: b&b@elmhouse.demon.co.uk
Dir: *turn left off A592 onto B5320 travel through village Elm House is last house on right adjacent to church*
A warm, friendly welcome awaits guests at this delightful sandstone house, conveniently located on the edge of the village, within easy reach of both the M6 and the Lake. Bedrooms are attractively decorated and thoughtfully equipped. Public rooms include an inviting guest lounge and a smart dining room where hearty Cumbrian breakfasts are served.
FACILITIES: 5 en suite No smoking TVB tea/coffee No dogs Cen ht TVL No children 12yrs No coaches **PRICES:** d £38-£49* **BB** **PARKING:** 5 **CARDS:**

RYDAL

See **Ambleside**

ST BEES Map 11 NX91

♦♦♦ *Queens Hotel*
Main St CA27 0DE ☎ 01946 822287 🖹 01946 822287
Dir: *turn off A595 S of Whitehaven, 1 mile south of whitehaven*
This bustling, friendly hostelry enjoys a convenient location in the centre of St Bees, just a short drive from Whitehaven. Public areas include a choice of bars, a cosy dining room and an airy conservatory. An extensive menu is offered both at lunch and dinner. The bedrooms are generously proportioned and furnished in pine.
FACILITIES: 14 en suite (1 fmly) No smoking in area of dining room STV TVB tea/coffee Licensed Cen ht No coaches Golf 9 Gymnasium Dinner Last d 9.30pm **PARKING:** 6 **CARDS:**

SEDBERGH Map 07 SD69

♦♦♦♦ Cross Keys Temperance Inn
Cautley LA10 5NE ☎ 015396 20284 Fax 015396 21966
e-mail: clowes@freeuk.com
Dir: *M6 junct 37 to A683 through Sedbergh. Hotel 4m north of Sedbergh on left*

Built in the 17th century, this charming inn retains many original features. No alcohol is sold at this 'Temperance' inn, however, guests may bring their own to complement the ambitious menu of home-cooked dishes. Bedrooms are traditionally presented and thoughtfully equipped. Delightful views of the Yorkshire Dales can be enjoyed from the conservatory.
FACILITIES: 2 en suite (1 fmly) No smoking tea/coffee Direct dial from bedrooms No dogs (ex guide dogs) Cen ht Riding Dinner Last d 9pm **PRICES:** s £32.50; d £65✻ **LB PARKING:** 9 **CARDS:**

SHAP Map 12 NY51

♦♦♦♦ Brookfield
CA10 3PZ ☎ 01931 716397 Fax 716397
Dir: *two minutes from M6 junct 39, turn right onto A6 towards Shap,1st accommodation off motorway*

This inviting house with its delightful garden enjoys a lovely, peaceful location yet is within minutes' of the M6. Bedrooms are smartly appointed and well-maintained. Public rooms include a comfortable lounge and a small bar area adjacent to the smart dinning room where substantial, home cooked breakfasts and dinners are served.
FACILITIES: 4 rms (3 en suite) (2 fmly) No smoking in bedrooms No smoking in dining room TVB tea/coffee No dogs Licensed Cen ht TVL No coaches Dinner Last d 7.30pm **PRICES:** s £20-£25; d £40-£50✻ **PARKING:** 34

Prices may change during the currency of the Guide, please check when booking.

SILLOTH Map 11 NY15

♦♦♦ Nith View
1 Pine Ter CA7 4DT ☎ 016973 31542 Fax 016973 31037
e-mail: nithview@aol.com
Dir: *B5302 into Silloth. At T-junct turn right for 200 metres. Overlooking tennis court & sea*
Popular with golfers, this smartly presented Victorian house enjoys panoramic views across the Solway Firth. Tastefully decorated throughout, there are several large bedrooms and those to the front benefit from sea views. A good choice is offered at breakfast.
FACILITIES: 6 rms (3 en suite) (3 fmly) No smoking in 3 bedrooms No smoking in dining room TVB tea/coffee Cen ht No coaches **PRICES:** s £17-£25; d £38-£44 **LB BB PARKING:** 6 **NOTES:** Closed Xmas

TEBAY Map 07 NY60

♦♦♦♦ Primrose Cottage
Orton Rd CA10 3TL ☎ 01539 624791 & 07778 520930
e-mail: primrosecottebay@aol.com
Dir: *exit M6 junct 38 turn right at rdbt, Primrose cottage 1st house on right).*
FACILITIES: 3 en suite (2 GF) No smoking TVB tea/coffee Cen ht TVL No coaches Jacuzzi Dinner Last d 24hrs prior **PRICES:** s £25-£35; d £45-£50✻ **LB PARKING:** 8

♦♦♦ Cross Keys
CA10 3UY ☎ 015396 24240 Fax 015396 24240
Dir: *M6 junct 38 turn right at rdbt onto A685 to Kendal. Establishment 0.25m*
In the centre of the village, only a few minutes away from the motorway this traditional coaching inn boasts original features such as low beamed ceilings and open fires. A wide selection of popular dishes is served in either the bar or the smart dining room. The bedrooms are comfortable.
FACILITIES: 6 rms (3 en suite) (1 fmly) (3 GF) No smoking in dining room TVB tea/coffee No dogs (ex guide dogs) Cen ht TVL Tennis (hard) Fishing Pool Table Pool darts Dinner Last d 9pm **PRICES:** s £25-£35; d £35-£45✻ **LB BB MEALS:** Lunch £18-£25&alc Dinner £18-£25&alc✻ **CONF:** Del from £45✻ **PARKING:** 30 **CARDS:**

THIRLMERE Map 11 NY31

♦♦♦ Stybeck Farm Experience *(NY319188)*
CA12 4TN ☎ 017687 73232 Mr & Mrs J Hodgson
e-mail: stybeckfarm@farming.co.uk
Dir: *on A591 near junction with B5322*

A traditional farmhouse with a delightful backdrop of Lakeland fells and crags. Three bedrooms, one of which is on the ground floor, are situated in the main house, whilst the other two are housed in a nearby delightful barn conversion. Both properties have their own dining room where hearty breakfasts are served.
FACILITIES: 3 en suite No smoking TVB tea/coffee No dogs Cen ht TVL No children 5yrs 200 acres dairy mixed sheep working **PRICES:** s £25-£26; d £40-£52✻ **LB PARKING:** 4 **NOTES:** Closed 25 Dec **CARDS:**

England

TROUTBECK (Near Keswick) Map 11 NY32

♦♦♦♦ *Lane Head Farm*

CA11 0SY ☎ 017687 79220 017687 79220
e-mail: b&b@laneheadfarm.freeserve.co.uk
Dir: *midway between Penrith and Keswick on A66*

This friendly guest house, dating back to the 1700s, enjoys a peaceful location and magnificent mountain views. Bedrooms vary in size and style; two are furnished with lovely four-poster beds. Public areas include a choice of lounges and a spacious dining room where hearty breakfasts and skilfully prepared dinners are served.
FACILITIES: 7 en suite No smoking TVB tea/coffee No dogs (ex guide dogs) Licensed Cen ht TVL No children 8 yrs No coaches Dinner Last d 5pm **PARKING:** 9 **NOTES:** Closed 6 Jan-15 Mar rs Nov-Dec **CARDS:**

TROUTBECK (Near Windermere) Map 07 NY40

♦♦♦♦ Queens Head Hotel

Town Head LA23 1PW ☎ 015394 32174 015394 31938
e-mail: enquiries@queensheadhotel.com
Dir: *M6 junct 36, take A590/591 W towards Windermere. Right at mini-rdbt onto A592 signed Penrith/Ullswater. Queens Head 2m on right*
This 17th-century-coaching inn enjoys stunning views of the Troutbeck Valley. The delightful bedrooms, several with four-poster beds, are furnished in keeping and equipped with modern facilities. Oak beams, flagstone floors, and a bar which was once an Elizabethan four-poster, provide a wonderful setting in which to enjoy the imaginative food, real ales and fine wines.
FACILITIES: 5 en suite 4 annexe en suite No smoking in bedrooms TV15B tea/coffee No dogs (ex guide dogs) Cen ht No coaches Dinner Last d 9pm **PRICES:** s £52.50-£62.50; d £70-£90✳ **LB MEALS:** Lunch £15.50&alc Dinner £15.50&alc✳ **PARKING:** 110 **NOTES:** Closed 25 Dec
CARDS:

WATERMILLOCK Map 12 NY42

♦♦♦ Brackenrigg

CA11 0LP ☎ 017684 86206 017684 86945
e-mail: enquiries@brackenrigginn.co.uk
Dir: *from M6 junct 40/A66, follow A66 W to next rdbt, follow A592 to Ullswater, at Lakeside turn right, continue to Watermillock, Brackenrigg is right*
This 18th-century coaching inn enjoys an elevated roadside position and superb views of Ullswater and the surrounding countryside. A good selection of freshly prepared dishes and daily specials are served in the traditional bar and restaurant. Bedrooms vary in size but all have Lakeland views and are equipped with modern facilities.

continued

Brackenrigg Inn

FACILITIES: 11 en suite (2 fmly) No smoking TVB tea/coffee No dogs Cen ht Dinner Last d 9pm **PRICES:** s £32-£37; d £54-£69✳ **LB MEALS:** Lunch £14.50-£21.40alc Dinner £17.95&alc✳ **CONF:** Del from £42 ✳
PARKING: 40 **CARDS:**

♦♦♦ Knotts Mill Country Lodge

Ullswater CA11 0JN ☎ 017684 86699 017684 86190
e-mail: relax@knottsmill.com
Dir: *M6 junct 40, then A66 (Keswick) after 0.5m take 2nd exit at rdbt, A592 to Ullswater for 3m until lake and at T junct right towards Patterdale. Follow lake road for 2.7m turn right into drive at sign*
FACILITIES: 9 en suite (3 fmly) (4 GF) No smoking TVB tea/coffee Licensed Cen ht Dinner Last d 5pm **PRICES:** d £45-£55✳ **LB PARKING:** 14
CARDS:

WHITEHAVEN Map 11 NX91

See also St Bees

♦♦♦♦ *Corkickle*

1 Corkickle CA28 8AA ☎ 01946 692073 01946 692073
e-mail: corkickle@tinyworld.co.uk
Dir: *take Southern Access road into Whitehaven from A595 at bottom of hill, left at lights by Esso garage, 1st left onto Corkickle, 1st house on left*
This delightful, beautifully maintained house enjoys an elevated position at the end of a Victorian terrace. There is an inviting lounge and a smart dining room where breakfasts and dinners (by request) are served round one large table. Well-equipped bedrooms are individually styled and smartly decorated.
FACILITIES: 6 rms (4 en suite) No smoking TVB tea/coffee Licensed Cen ht No coaches Dinner Last d 6pm **PARKING:** 2

WINDERMERE Map 07 SD49

Premier Collection

♦♦♦♦♦ Lakeshore House

Ecclerigg LA23 1LJ ☎ 015394 33202 015394 33213
e-mail: lakeshore@lakedistrict.uk.com
Dir: *A591-1m after Windermere signs for Brockhole Visitors Centre, the driveway for the house is the 2nd entrance on left. Take right fork to green gate*
A haven of luxury, this stunning property is the perfect place to relax and indulge. Modern, spacious bedrooms offer every conceivable extra, and either have a balcony or terrace to enjoy the splendid views of the gardens and Lake Windermere. Delicious breakfasts featuring the best of Cumbrian produce are served beside the swimming pool. Lakeshore House is AA Guest Accommodation of the Year for England 2002-2003.

continued

England

Lakeshore House

FACILITIES: 3 en suite No smoking TVB tea/coffee Direct dial from bedrooms No dogs (ex guide dogs) Cen ht TVL No children 12yrs No coaches Indoor swimming pool (heated) Sauna Putting/tennis/badminton on astroturf **PRICES:** s £75-£112.50✳ **LB** **PARKING:** 3 **CARDS:**

Premier Collection

♦♦♦♦♦ The Beaumont

Holly Rd LA23 2AF ☎ 015394 47075 📠 01539 447075
e-mail: thebeaumonthotel@btinternet.com
Dir: *follow town centre signs through one-way system then 2nd left into Ellerthwaite Rd & 1st left into Holly Rd*

A warm welcome awaits guests at this smart, traditional house, peacefully located just a short stroll from the town centre. Bedrooms, some with four poster beds, are all individually furnished to a high standard, as are the smart modern bathrooms. Public rooms include a spacious lounge and a smartly appointed dining room where hearty breakfasts are served.

FACILITIES: 10 en suite (3 GF) No smoking TVB tea/coffee No dogs (ex guide dogs) Licensed Cen ht TVL No children 10yrs No coaches Membership of Country Club **PRICES:** s £35-£45; d £65-£120✳ **LB** **PARKING:** 10 **CARDS:**

Premier Collection

♦♦♦♦♦ Howbeck

New Rd LA23 2LA ☎ 015394 44739 📠 015394 44739
e-mail: enquiries@howbeck.co.uk
Dir: *left off A591 through Windermere town centre 300yds on left. Main road to Bowness (The Independents)*

Howbeck is a delightful Victorian house, conveniently situated for both village and the lake. Beautiful bedrooms with rich soft furnishings are a real strength, and all are smartly furnished and well equipped. There is a bright airy lounge with a small bar and an attractive dining room where breakfast is served.

FACILITIES: 10 en suite (1 fmly) No smoking TVB tea/coffee No dogs Licensed Cen ht No children 5yrs No coaches **PRICES:** d £45-£90✳ **PARKING:** 12 **CARDS:**

If an establishment name appears in *italics*, details have not been confirmed for 2003.

WINDERMERE continued

Premier Collection

♦♦♦♦♦ Newstead

New Rd LA23 2EE ☎ 015394 44485
e-mail: info@newstead-guesthouse.co.uk
Dir: *0.5m from A591 between Windermere/Bowness*

This stylish and friendly Victorian home offers comfortable bedrooms, which retain original features such as fireplaces, woodwork, and beams. Furnished in pine, the bedrooms have many thoughtful extras and homely touches, and there are four-poster rooms available. The elegant day rooms include a comfortable lounge which looks out onto the neat garden. Freshly cooked breakfasts are served in the smart dining room.
FACILITIES: 7 en suite (1 fmly) No smoking TVB tea/coffee No dogs Cen ht No children 7yrs **PRICES:** s £30-£32.50; d £46-£65✱ **LB** **PARKING:** 10

♦♦♦♦ Alice Howe

3 The Terrace LA23 1AJ ☎ 015394 43325 📠 015394 43325
e-mail: info@alicehowe.co.uk
Dir: *turn off A591, 300yds beyond the Windermere town sign entering from the south*
Designed by Pugin, this delightful 1840s villa with mullion trefoil windows was one of the first houses to be built in Windermere. Today, the house provides comfortable, well-equipped bedrooms which are smartly presented with pine furnishings. Reception rooms include a cosy lounge and stylish dining room where the friendly resident proprietors serve delicious home cooked meals.
FACILITIES: 5 en suite No smoking TVB tea/coffee No dogs Cen ht No children 12yrs No coaches Dinner Last d 2pm **PRICES:** s £36; d £52-£64✱ **LB** **PARKING:** 7 **CARDS:**

♦♦♦♦ Belsfield House

4 Kendal Rd, Bowness-on-Windermere LA23 3EQ
☎ 015394 45823
Dir: *from A592 in Bowness, take 1st left after mini-rdbt, then at St Martins church turn left onto Kendal road, house on right*
In the heart of Bowness, just a minute's walk from Lake Windermere, this Victorian house offers attractive accommodation. Bedrooms are neatly decorated, generally spacious and some have views of the lake. Public areas include a cosy lounge and separate dining room, where hearty breakfasts are served. Guests also have free access to a local leisure complex.

continued

Belsfield House

FACILITIES: 9 en suite (4 fmly) (1 GF) No smoking in 5 bedrooms No smoking in dining room No smoking in lounges TVB tea/coffee No dogs (ex guide dogs) Cen ht No coaches **PRICES:** s £26-£30; d £50-£70✱ **LB** **PARKING:** 9

♦♦♦♦ Blenheim Lodge

Brantfell Rd, Bowness on Windermere LA23 3AE
☎ 015394 43440 📠 015394 43440
e-mail: blenheimlodge@supanet.com
Dir: *A591 Bowness village, across mini-rdbt, turn first left and left again, house is at the top*
Commanding stunning views over the Lake, Blenheim Lodge sits in a quiet location above the town of Bowness. Bedrooms are traditionally furnished and some have four-poster or half-tester beds. Public rooms include an elegant lounge, a cosy bar and a spacious dining room.
FACILITIES: 11 en suite (1 fmly) (2 GF) No smoking TVB tea/coffee No dogs Licensed Cen ht TVL No children 6yrs No coaches Membership of Country Club with sports facilities **PRICES:** s £37-£45; d £50-£90✱ **LB** **PARKING:** 12 **CARDS:**

♦♦♦♦ *Coach House*

Lake Rd LA23 2EQ ☎ 015394 44494 📠 015394 43476
e-mail: info@coachhouse.net1.co.uk
Dir: *leave M6 junct 36, take A590 then A591, in Windermere turn left towards Bowness. House 0.5m on right opposite St Herbert's church*
This stylish house has a chic, minimalist interior, with bright modern decor and cosmopolitan furnishings. There is a reception lounge and a contemporary dining room where hearty breakfasts are served. Light suppers are also available by prior arrangement. A relaxed and welcoming atmosphere prevails.
FACILITIES: 5 en suite (1 fmly) No smoking TVB tea/coffee No dogs (ex guide dogs) Licensed Cen ht No coaches Membership of local Health Club Dinner Last d 6pm previous day **PARKING:** 5 **CARDS:**

♦♦♦♦ *Dene House*

Kendal Rd LA23 3EW ☎ 015394 48236 📠 015394 48236
e-mail: jdene@globalnet.co.uk
Dir: *0.5m from Bowness on A5074 next to Burnside Hotel*
A friendly welcome awaits guests at this smart Victorian house, peacefully located just minutes walk from the centre of Bowness. Elegant bedrooms are generally spacious, individually decorated and are particularly well-equipped. Afternoon tea can be enjoyed on the patio, which overlooks the well-tended garden.
FACILITIES: 7 en suite (1 fmly) No smoking in bedrooms No smoking in dining room No smoking in lounges TVB tea/coffee No dogs (ex guide dogs) Cen ht No coaches Free use of adjacent leisure centre **PARKING:** 7

♦♦♦♦ Denehurst Guest House

Queens Dr LA23 3EL ☎ 015394 44710 📠 015394 44710
e-mail: denehurst@btconnect.com
Dir: *turn off A591 into Windermere village. Follow signs for Bowness and the lake, after 0.5m turn left onto Queens Dr*
Situated in a peaceful residential area, within walking distance of the lake at Bowness and Winderemere village, Denehurst is a comfortable, friendly family home. The attractively decorated bedrooms are cosy and well equipped with modern facilities. There is a stylish lounge in addition to the smart dining room where hearty Cumbrian breakfasts are served at individual tables.
FACILITIES: 6 en suite (1 fmly) No smoking TVB tea/coffee No dogs Cen ht No children 12yrs **PRICES:** s £26-£44; d £38-£60* **LB BB CARDS:**

♦♦♦♦ Fairfield

Brantfell Rd, Bowness-on-Windermere LA23 3AE
☎ 015394 46565 📠 015394 46565
e-mail: Ray&barb@the-fairfield.co.uk
Dir: *follow Bowness signs and at mini rdbt take rd to lake, turn left opp church & left again in front of Spinnery Restaurant, house up hill on right*

This welcoming house is located in a quiet lane above the town and within walking distance of the lake and Bowness. Bedrooms are comfortably furnished and thoughtfully equipped. Public rooms include an inviting lounge with adjacent residents' bar and an attractive dining room, overlooking the spacious, well-landscaped gardens.
FACILITIES: 9 rms (8 en suite) (2 fmly) (3 GF) No smoking TVB tea/coffee No dogs Licensed Cen ht TVL No coaches Corporate membership of leisure club **PRICES:** s £26-£33; d £52-£66* **LB PARKING:** 14 **NOTES:** Closed Dec-Jan **CARDS:**

♦♦♦♦ Fair Rigg

Ferry View LA23 5JB ☎ 015394 43941
e-mail: rtodd51257@aol.com
Dir: *proceed down the hill though Bowness to the mini-rdbt.. Left and left again at end of 1st parade of shops. Continue for 0.75m, house on left*
Built in the late 1800s this typical Lakeland house has been carefully and lovingly refurbished to provide spacious accommodation, while still retaining many of its original Victorian characteristics. Bedrooms are attractively decorated and well equipped. There is an elegant dining room, which enjoys delightful views up the lake to the mountains beyond, as do many of the bedrooms.
FACILITIES: 6 en suite No smoking TVB tea/coffee No dogs (ex guide dogs) Cen ht No children 12yrs No coaches **PRICES:** d £52-£67*
PARKING: 6

♦♦♦♦ Glencree Private Hotel

Lake Rd LA23 2EQ ☎ 015394 45822 📠 015394 45822
e-mail: h.butterworth@btinternet.com
Dir: *0.5m from Windermere town centre follow signs for Bowness & The Lake. Large wooded area on right. Glencree is 1st hotel on right after the wood*
Situated midway between Windermere and Bowness, there's plenty to do around Glencree, and the resident proprietor will be happy to offer advice and maps. Bedrooms, one of which is on the ground floor, are all individually furnished. Dinner (by prior arrangement) and breakfast make use of fresh local produce and are served in the charming dining room.
FACILITIES: 6 en suite (1 fmly) (1 GF) No smoking TVB tea/coffee No dogs (ex guide dogs) Licensed Cen ht TVL No coaches Dinner Last d 2.30pm
PRICES: s £35-£45; d £50-£65* **LB PARKING:** 7 **CARDS:**

♦♦♦♦ Hawksmoor

Lake Rd LA23 2EQ ☎ 015394 42110 📠 015394 42110
e-mail: enquiries@hawksmoor.com
Dir: *follow Windermere town centre one-way systemtowards Bowness for approx 0.5m to establishment on R opposite church*

Set back from the road and handy for both the Lake and the village, this inviting Victorian house provides spacious, traditional accommodation, warm hospitality and hearty breakfasts. The bedrooms vary in size and style and are decorated with attractive fabrics, two have four-poster beds and all have pleasant views.
FACILITIES: 10 en suite (3 fmly) (3 GF) No smoking TVB tea/coffee No dogs (ex guide dogs) Cen ht No children 6yrs No coaches Leisure facilities available nearby **PRICES:** s £30-£40; d £50-£75* **LB PARKING:** 11
CARDS:

♦♦♦♦ Hazel Bank

Hazel St LA23 1EL ☎ 015394 45486 📠 0153494 45486
e-mail: enquiries@hazelbank-guesthouse.co.uk
Dir: *from A591 turn into Windermere, through village (Crescent Road) turn up Oak Street and 2nd left is Hazel Street, Hazelbank at top on left*
A warm welcome is extended to all guests at this friendly, family run guesthouse. Situated on a quiet side road just a minute's walk from the centre of the village this Victorian home benefits from a pretty garden. The spacious bedrooms come equipped with a host of thoughtful extras. Breakfast is served in the brightly decorated dining room.
FACILITIES: 3 en suite (1 GF) No smoking TVB tea/coffee No dogs (ex guide dogs) Cen ht No coaches **PRICES:** s £30-£35; d £50-£60*
PARKING: 6 **NOTES:** Closed 23-30 Dec

England

WINDERMERE continued

♦♦♦♦ Laurel Cottage

St Martins Square, Kendal Rd LA23 3EF ☎ 015394 45594
🖹 015394 45594
e-mail: enquiries@laurelcottage-bnb.co.uk
Dir: *M6 junct 36, follow signs for Windemere. At Windemere Hotel turn left following signs for Bowness. At St Martin's church turn left onto Kendal Rd, cottage 30 mtrs on left*

Benefiting from a prime location in the centre of the village, this attractive cottage is less than a minute's walk from the lake and shops. The cottage dates back to the 17th century and the cosy bedrooms boast window seats. More spacious pine furnished rooms are available in the Victorian part of the house.
FACILITIES: 13 rms (11 en suite) (2 fmly) No smoking TVB tea/coffee No dogs (ex guide dogs) Cen ht TVL No coaches Membership to local leisure club **PRICES:** s £20-£27; d £44-£68✻ **LB** **PARKING:** 13 **CARDS:**

♦♦♦♦ The Old Court House

Lake Rd LA23 3AP ☎ 015394 45096
e-mail: aj@oldcourthouse2.fsnet.co.uk
Dir: *on Windermere/Bowness road on right at junct with Longlands Road*

Formerly a Victorian police station and courthouse, this attractive property retains many original feature and is centrally located in Bowness. Pine furnished bedrooms are comfortable and host fresh décor and a good range of extras. Freshly prepared dishes can be enjoyed in the bright breakfast room.
FACILITIES: 6 en suite (2 GF) No smoking TVB tea/coffee No dogs (ex guide dogs) Cen ht No children 7yrs No coaches **PRICES:** s £25-£30; d £45-£60✻ **LB** **PARKING:** 6

♦♦♦♦ White Lodge Hotel

Lake Rd LA23 2JJ ☎ 015394 43624 🖹 015394 44749
e-mail: enquiries@whitelodgehotel.com
Dir: *on main lake road, on right*
This stylish Victorian house lies in its own gardens at the north end of Bowness. The comfortable lounge and main dining room are furnished with antiques. The modern bedrooms offer a high level of comfort and make good use of quality pine furniture. There is a bright, attractive residents' bar that during the morning is used as a breakfast room.

White Lodge Hotel

FACILITIES: 12 en suite (3 fmly) No smoking in dining room No smoking in lounges TVB tea/coffee No dogs (ex guide dogs) Licensed Cen ht TVL No coaches Dinner Last d 6.30pm **PRICES:** s £29-£35; d £56-£68✻ **LB** **PARKING:** 14 **NOTES:** Closed Dec-Feb **CARDS:**

See advertisement on opposite page

♦♦♦♦ Woodlands Hotel

New Rd LA23 2EE ☎ 015394 43915 🖹 015394 43915
e-mail: enquiries@woodlandshotel.uk.net
Dir: *at Windermere railway station follow one-way system through village down New Road towards lake. Hotel on left, last building before war memorial clock*
Clean and comfortable bedrooms, together with welcoming hospitality and a relaxing atmosphere all ensure a memorable stay at this hotel. Stylishly decorated and furnished to a high standard, public areas include a spacious lounge, cosy residents' bar and an attractive dining room that overlooks the neat rear garden.
FACILITIES: 14 en suite (1 fmly) (2 GF) No smoking in bedrooms No smoking in dining room TVB tea/coffee No dogs (ex guide dogs) Licensed Cen ht No children 5yrs Free facilities at local leisure/sports club Last d 5pm **PRICES:** s £23-£30; d £50-£160✻ **LB** **PARKING:** 15 **CARDS:**

♦♦♦♦ 🅰 Fir Trees

Lake Rd LA23 2EQ ☎ 015394 42272 🖹 015394 42512
e-mail: enquiries@fir-trees.com
Dir: *0.5m below town centre on left towards the lake, 150yds past modern church also on left*
FACILITIES: 8 en suite (2 fmly) No smoking STV TVB tea/coffee No dogs (ex guide dogs) Cen ht No coaches Free use of local leisure club
PRICES: s £35-£45; d £48-£68✻ **LB** **PARKING:** 9
CARDS:

See advertisement on opposite page

♦♦♦♦ 🅰 Storrs Gate House

Longtail Hill LA23 3JD ☎ 015394 43272
e-mail: enquiries@storrsgatehouse.co.uk
Dir: *at junct of A592 and B5284, opposite Windermere Marina*
FACILITIES: 4 en suite (1 fmly) No smoking TVB tea/coffee No dogs (ex guide dogs) Licensed Cen ht TVL No children 5yrs No coaches Dinner Last d 12 midday **PRICES:** d £44-£64✻ **LB** **PARKING:** 6 **CARDS:**

♦♦♦ Broadlands

19 Broad St LA23 2AB ☎ 015394 46532 🖹 015394 46532
e-mail: broadlands@clara.co.uk
Dir: *from A591 to town centre follow one way system for 300mtrs to pelican crossing, Broad Street is next on the left*
Situated close to the shops and opposite the park and library, the proprietors of this attractively decorated Lakeland house extend a

continued

warm welcome to all guests. Bedrooms are pleasantly co-ordinated and comfortably furnished, and in the morning a freshly prepared breakfast can be enjoyed in the antique furnished dining room.
FACILITIES: 4 en suite (2 fmly) No smoking in 2 bedrooms No smoking in dining room No smoking in lounges TVB tea/coffee No dogs (ex guide dogs) Cen ht No children 5 yrs No coaches **PRICES:** d £40-£52✳
LB **NOTES:** Closed Xmas **CARDS:**

♦♦♦ Eagle & Child Inn

Kendal Rd, Staveley LA8 9LP ☎ 01539 821320
e-mail: info@eaglechildinn.co.uk
Dir: *M6 junct 36, follow A590 towards Kendal then A591 towards Windermere, take sign for Staveley, Kentmere pub is approx 500yds left*
Only a few minutes away from the beautiful Kentmere valley, this cosy village pub offers comfortable accommodation and good food. A wide selection of local ales are offered and can be enjoyed in either the tranquil riverside beer garden or spacious bar. Breakfast is served in the Redmond suite, which is also available for functions.
FACILITIES: 5 en suite (1 fmly) No smoking in bedrooms No smoking in area of dining room TVB tea/coffee No dogs (ex guide dogs) Cen ht Local Leisure Club facilities can be arranged Dinner Last d 8.45pm
PRICES: s £30-£35; d £40-£50✳ LB **MEALS:** Lunch £2.25-£8.50&alc Dinner fr £5.95&alc✳ **CONF:** Board 40 Del from £30 ✳ **PARKING:** 16
CARDS:

Directions are provided by the proprietor, ask for more details when booking.

England

WINDERMERE continued

♦♦♦ Elim House

Biskey Howe Rd LA23 2JP ☎ 015394 42021 & 0800 2985717
📠 015394 43430
e-mail: lakedistrict@elimhouse.freeserve.co.uk
Dir: *turn left off A5074 approx 150yds past police station - 1st house on left*
Just a minute's walk from the bustling village of Bowness and Lake Windermere, this attractive house is enhanced by a well-kept, colourful garden. Bedrooms vary in size and style, although all are suitably equipped and offer sound levels of comfort. A hearty Cumbrian breakfast is served in the cheerfully decorated breakfast room.
FACILITIES: 8 rms (6 en suite) 3 annexe rms (1 en suite) (2 fmly) No smoking in dining room TVB tea/coffee Cen ht No children 7yrs No coaches **PRICES:** s £20-£56; d £32-£80✳ **LB BB PARKING:** 7
CARDS:

♦♦♦ Firgarth

Ambleside Rd LA23 1EU ☎ 015394 46974 📠 015394 42384
e-mail: thefirgarth@netscapeonline.co.uk
Dir: *on A591, Windermere to Ambleside road, opposite Wynlass Beck Riding Stables*

This traditional guest house enjoys a convenient location on the main road between Windermere and Ambleside. Bedrooms are simply furnished with a mix of styles but all are thoughtfully equipped and rear rooms benefit from a pleasant, peaceful outlook. There is a cosy guest lounge, whilst hearty breakfasts are served in the adjacent breakfast room.
FACILITIES: 8 en suite (1 fmly) No smoking in 5 bedrooms No smoking in dining room TVB tea/coffee Licensed Cen ht No coaches **PARKING:** 10
CARDS:

♦♦♦ *Green Gables*

37 Broad St LA23 2AB ☎ 015394 43886
Dir: *leave A591 at Windermere town centre sign, follow one-way system through village and turn left at last shop into Broad Street*

Aptly named, Green Gables is a friendly family run guest house looking onto Elleray Gardens. Located just a short walk from the village centre, the house is pleasantly furnished and offers bright, fresh bedrooms. There is a comfortable bar/lounge and home cooked breakfasts are served in the adjacent dining room.
FACILITIES: 8 rms (3 en suite) (3 fmly) No smoking in bedrooms No smoking in dining room No smoking in 1 lounge TVB tea/coffee No dogs (ex guide dogs) Licensed Cen ht TVL No coaches Golf & riding can be arranged. Tours booked **PARKING:** 2

♦♦♦ The Haven

10 Birch St LA23 1EG ☎ 015394 44017
Dir: *on A5074, take 3rd left after entering one way system into Birch Street, post office on corner*
Built from Lakeland slate and stone, this Victorian house is located just a minute's walk form the village centre and shops. The bright, cheerful accommodation includes large bedrooms, one of which has an original brass bed. A hearty Cumbrian breakfast is served in the well-appointed dining room that also doubles as a lounge.
FACILITIES: 3 rms (1 en suite) (2 fmly) No smoking TVB tea/coffee No dogs (ex guide dogs) Cen ht No children 7yrs No coaches **PRICES:** d £36-£56✳ **BB PARKING:** 4

♦♦♦ Holly Lodge Guest House

6 College Rd LA23 1BX ☎ 015394 43873 📠 015394 43873
e-mail: doyle@hollylodge20.fsnet.co.uk
Dir: *from the A591 opp Windermere Hotel follow road downhill towards Bowness through village turn R into College Rd by bus shelter*
Just a short stroll from the village, this attractive Victorian house offers comfortable accommodation. Bedrooms vary in style, all are well equipped and many are suitable for families. Traditional home cooked breakfasts are served in the cosy dining room which also has a small bar. A lounge is also available.
FACILITIES: 10 rms (8 en suite) (4 fmly) No smoking in bedrooms No smoking in dining room TVB tea/coffee Licensed Cen ht No coaches
PRICES: s £19-£30; d £38-£54✳ **LB BB PARKING:** 7
CARDS:

♦♦♦ Montfort

Princes Rd LA23 2DD ☎ 015394 45671
e-mail: montfort@btconnect.com
Dir: *from A590 take A591 through Windermere, 4th left after pelican crossing by clock tower, then 1st right. House on right*
Personally run, this friendly Lakeland guest house is situated in a quiet residential area of the town. Bedrooms are comfortably modern in style and offer a good range of amenities; some have four-poster beds. Hearty breakfasts are served at individual tables in the bright dining room. This is a no-smoking establishment.
FACILITIES: 5 en suite No smoking TVB tea/coffee No dogs Cen ht No children No coaches Complimentary use of local country club
PRICES: d £36-£48✳ **LB BB CARDS:**

♦♦♦ Rosemount

Lake Rd LA23 2EQ ☎ 015394 43739 📠 015394 48978
e-mail: rosemt3739@aol.com
Dir: *turn off A591, through village & Rosemount is on left just beyond modern Catholic church*
This large Victorian property sits midway between Windermere and Bowness and is ideally located for the lake and local attractions. Hearty Cumbrian breakfasts freshly prepared using good-quality local produce are served in either the conservatory or dining room. Bedrooms are cheerfully decorated and an airy, modern lounge with a piano is provided for residents.
FACILITIES: 17 en suite (3 fmly) (3 GF) No smoking TVB tea/coffee No dogs Licensed Cen ht Golf can be arranged.Free use of local health club **PRICES:** s £20-£30; d £40-£80✳ **LB PARKING:** 14
CARDS:

England

♦♦♦ St Johns Lodge

Lake Rd LA23 2EQ ☎ 015394 43078
e-mail: mail@st-johns-lodge.co.uk
Dir: *on A5074 between Windermere village and Lake Windermere*
Ideally located between Windermere and Bowness, this large guest house offers a warm and friendly welcome. Bedrooms vary in size and are neatly and simply decorated and furnished. Freshly prepared meals are served in the well appointed basement dining room, and dinner is available by arrangement.
FACILITIES: 14 rms (12 en suite) (3 fmly) No smoking TVB tea/coffee Licensed Cen ht No children 4yrs No coaches Facilities at private leisure club **PRICES:** s £20-£32; d £38-£60* **LB BB PARKING:** 11
CARDS:

DERBYSHIRE

ALFRETON Map 08 SK45

♦♦♦ Oaktree Farm *(SK385566)*

Matlock Rd, Oakerthorpe, Wessington DE55 7NA
☎ 01773 832957 & 0780 3774079(mobile) Mrs K Prince
e-mail: oaktree_farm@talk21.com
Dir: *from M1 junct 28 onto A38 then A615 signed Matlock, fork left at Peacock Inn under bridge and past cottages for farmhouse on left*

Located in 22 acres which includes a coarse fishing lake, chicken run and kitchen garden, this mellow stone house provides thoughtfully equipped bedrooms complimented by modern efficient bathrooms. Breakfasts and dinners, by arrangement, are served in an attractive cottage style dining room and the pretty floral patio is an added benefit during the warmer months.
FACILITIES: 3 en suite No smoking STV TVB tea/coffee No dogs (ex guide dogs) Cen ht TVL Fishing 22 acres mixed **PRICES:** s £21-£24; d £40-£44*
PARKING: 10

ALKMONTON Map 07 SK13

♦♦♦♦ *The Courtyard*

Dairy House Farm DE6 3DG ☎ 01335 330187
01335 330187
e-mail: andy@dairyhousefarm.force9.co.uk
Dir: *off A50 at Foston, approx 3.5m up Woodyard Lane*
Surrounded by open countryside this is a delightful conversion of Victorian farm buildings in the Derbyshire Dales. The bedrooms are well furnished and thoughtfully equipped. A hearty breakfast is provided in the bright dining room and dinner is available by prior arrangement. Two rooms have been approved as providing suitable facilities for wheelchair users.
FACILITIES: 7 en suite (1 fmly) No smoking TVB tea/coffee No dogs (ex guide dogs) Cen ht No coaches Fishing Dinner Last d 4pm **PARKING:** 12
NOTES: Closed Xmas **CARDS:**

♦♦♦♦ Dairy House *(SK198367)*

Longford DE6 3DG ☎ 01335 330359 01335 330359
Mr A Harris
e-mail: andy@dairyhousefarm.org.co.uk
Dir: *3m up Woodyard Lane after turning off A50 at Foston*
This ancient farmhouse is full of character. The charming owners create a relaxed and friendly atmosphere. Freshly cooked farmhouse breakfasts and dinners are enjoyed communally at a large polished table. Another public area is the comfortable lounge in which guests can relax.
FACILITIES: 5 en suite No smoking TVB tea/coffee No dogs (ex guide dogs) Licensed Cen ht TVL No children 16yrs Croquet lawn Coarse fishing 18 acres stock grazing Dinner Last d 4pm **PRICES:** s £25* **LB**
PARKING: 8 **NOTES:** Closed 24-26 Dec

ASHBOURNE Map 07 SK14

See also Tissington and Waterhouses (Staffordshire)

Premier Collection

♦♦♦♦♦ Omnia Somnia

The Coach House, The Firs DE6 1HF ☎ 01335 300145
01335 300958
e-mail: alan@omniasomnia.co.uk
Dir: *from A52 Derby road, descend hill into Ashbourne. At lights sharp left into Old Hill. Turn first left into The Firs & follow sign for Omnia Somnia*

Within easy walking distance of the town, this delightfully furnished house offers guests every comfort. Bedrooms are very well furnished and two are located on the ground floor. Home-made dinners and substantial breakfasts are served in the delightful dining room, overlooking the sloping garden. There is also a cosy lounge with plenty of reading matter.
FACILITIES: 3 en suite (2 GF) No smoking TVB tea/coffee Licensed Cen ht TVL No children No coaches Dinner Last d 7pm
PRICES: s £50-£55; d £75-£85* **LB PARKING:** 3
CARDS:

♦♦♦ Diamonds are a guest's best friend!
The emphasis is on quality and guest care rather than extra facilities.

England

ASHBOURNE continued

Premier Collection

♦♦♦♦♦ Turlow Bank

Hognaston DE6 1PW ☎ 01335 370299 📠 01335 370299
e-mail: turlowbank@btinternet.com
Dir: *take turning to Hognaston village (signed Hognaston only) off B5035 Ashbourne to Wirksworth. Continue through village towards Hulland Ward. Turlow Bank right 0.5m out of village, look for clock tower*

Located in pretty grounds in a superb elevated position close to Carsington Water, this sympathetically extended 19th-century farmhouse provides high levels of comfort and facilities. Bedrooms are equipped with lots of thoughtful extras and quality modern bathrooms. Comprehensive breakfasts, which include free range chicken or duck eggs, are taken at one family table in the cosy dining room and a spacious guest lounge is also available.
FACILITIES: 2 en suite No smoking tea/coffee Cen ht No children 12yrs No coaches **PRICES:** s £32-£37; d £54-£58✳
PARKING: 6 **NOTES:** Closed 25-27 Dec

♦♦♦♦ Bramhall's

6 Buxton Rd DE6 1EX ☎ 01335 346158
e-mail: info@bramhalls.co.uk
Dir: *from the market square take the Buxton road N up the hill, Bramhall's is 30yds on left*
Located within the heart of this historic town, a sympathetic conversion of two former cottages and a period town house, this restaurant with rooms is gaining in popularity for imaginative food and attentive service. Bedrooms are filled with thoughtful extras and a warm welcome is assured.
FACILITIES: 10 rms (8 en suite) (1 fmly) (1 GF) No smoking in 5 bedrooms No smoking in area of dining room No smoking in 1 lounge TVB tea/coffee Licensed Cen ht No coaches Dinner Last d 9.30pm
PRICES: s £22.50; d £49.50-£55✳ **PARKING:** 6
CARDS:

♦♦♦♦ Common End Farm *(SK125485)*

Swinscoe DE6 2BW ☎ 01335 342342
Mr & Mrs Alan Hewitt
Dir: *from Ashbourne take A52 Stoke-on-Trent/Leek road for 4m to Swinscoe. House 500yds past Dog & Partridge Inn on right*

Located in the pretty hamlet of Swinscoe, between Ashbourne and Alton Towers, the property is a sympathetic conversion of former byres and a hayloft. The attractive pine furnished bedrooms are filled with thoughtful extras and modern efficient shower rooms compliment. A comfortable guest lounge is also available.
FACILITIES: 6 en suite (1 fmly) (4 GF) No smoking TVB tea/coffee No dogs Cen ht TVL ch fac 144 acres beef **PRICES:** s £29.50; d £45-£50✳ **LB**
PARKING: 8 **CARDS:**

♦♦♦♦ *Green Man*

St Johns St DE6 1GH ☎ 01335 345783 📠 01335 346613
Located in the heart of the historic town centre, this 17th-century former coaching inn retains many original features, and bedroom furnishing styles add to the feeling of a bygone age. Ground floor areas include a cosy traditional bar and a music and games room, very popular at weekends. The inn also offers extensive function facilities.

FACILITIES: 18 en suite (1 fmly) No smoking in dining room TVB tea/coffee Direct dial from bedrooms No dogs (ex guide dogs) Cen ht Pool Table Last d 8.30pm **PARKING:** 30 **CARDS:**

♦♦♦♦ Mercaston Hall *(SK279419)*
Mercaston DE6 3BL ☎ 01335 360263 📠 01335 361399
Mr & Mrs A Haddon
e-mail: mercastonhall@btinternet.com
Dir: *A52 Ashbourne/Derby road, in Brailsford left along Luke Lane, after 1m at 1st x-roads turn right. After Mugginton turn on left, house on right*
Located in a pretty rural hamlet, this historic property dates from the 11th century and many original features are retained including a wealth of exposed beams and an impressive inglenook fireplace within the spacious sitting room. Bedrooms are both practical and homely and additional facilities include an all weather tennis court and a livery service.
FACILITIES: 3 en suite No smoking TVB tea/coffee Cen ht No children 8yrs Tennis (hard) 60 acres mixed **PRICES:** s £30; d £48✳
PARKING: 3 **NOTES:** Closed Xmas

♦♦♦ Compton House
27-31 Compton DE6 1BX ☎ 01335 343100 📠 01335 348100
e-mail: jane@comptonhouse.co.uk
Dir: *A52 from Derby into Ashbourne, across lights at bottom of hill, house 100yds on left opposite garage*
Located within easy walking distance of all central attractions, this sympathetic conversion of three former period cottages has resulted in a house with good standards of comfort and facilities. Bedrooms are filled with both practical and homely extras and the cottage style dining room is the setting for comprehensive breakfasts.
FACILITIES: 5 en suite (2 fmly) No smoking TVB tea/coffee Direct dial from bedrooms Licensed TVL No coaches Dinner Last d 5pm **PRICES:** s £21-£28; d £42-£48✳ **LB PARKING:** 6 **CARDS:**

♦♦♦ Homesclose House
DE6 2DA ☎ 01335 324475
Dir: *A52 to Stoke-on-Trent, left to Stanton, 1.5m along narrow lane to middle of village*
Located in an elevated position at Stanton, this well maintained house has immaculate gardens and offers homely well equipped bedrooms with private facilities. English breakfasts are taken at one table in the cosy dining room which has a superb outlook over unspoilt countryside.
FACILITIES: 3 rms (2 en suite) (1 fmly) No smoking TVB tea/coffee Cen ht **PRICES:** s £18-£20; d £36-£40✳ **LB BB PARKING:** 4 **NOTES:** Closed Dec-Jan

♦♦♦ Millfields B & B
Fenny Bentley DE6 1LA ☎ 01335 350454
Dir: *take the A515 N out of Ashbourne towards Buxton, 2m out of Ashbourne on the left hand side B & B sign*
Located north of town at Fenny Bently, this extended chalet bungalow stands on a smallholding and free range duck or hen eggs are a feature of the memorable breakfasts. The homely bedrooms are filled with thoughtful extras and a warm welcome is assured.
FACILITIES: 2 en suite (1 fmly) No smoking in bedrooms No smoking in dining room No smoking in 1 lounge TVB tea/coffee No dogs Cen ht No coaches **PRICES:** s £22-£28; d £40-£44 **LB PARKING:** 5

♦♦♦ Stone Cottage
Green Ln, Clifton DE6 2BL ☎ 01335 343377 📠 01335 347117
e-mail: info@stone-cottagefsnet.co.uk
Dir: *1m out of Ashbourne on A52 from Leek-Uttoxeter. Left at signpost for Clifton, 2nd house on right*
This small family run, stone built guest house is situated just a short drive from Ashbourne. Each of the bedrooms is attractively appointed and well-equipped, with two of the rooms offering four-poster beds. Breakfast is served in the conservatory dining room, overlooking the garden, and dinner is available by prior arrangement.
FACILITIES: 3 en suite (1 fmly) No smoking STV TVB tea/coffee No dogs (ex guide dogs) Cen ht TVL No coaches Dinner Last d 9.30am
PRICES: s £25-£35; d £40-£50✳ **PARKING:** 4 **NOTES:** Closed 25 Dec
CARDS:

♦ Air Cottage Farm *(SK142523)*
Ilam DE6 2BD ☎ 01335 350475 Mrs J Wain
Mar-Nov
Dir: *from Ashbourne take A515, left at signpost Thorpe/Dovedale/Ilam. At Ilam turn right at Memorial Stone to Alstonfield. 1st cattlegrid gateway right*
Located in an elevated position with stunning views over the surrounding countryside, including the Dovedale, this 18th century farmhouse provides traditional standards of accommodation and is very popular with serious walkers and climbers visiting this lovely part of the Peak District.
FACILITIES: 3 rms (3 GF) No smoking in dining room No smoking in lounges tea/coffee No dogs (ex guide dogs) Cen ht TVL Resident beauty and holistic therapist available 320 acres beef cattle, sheep **BB PRICES:** s £19-£25; d £38-£50✳ **PARKING:** 4 **CARDS:**

BAKEWELL — Map 08 SK26

♦♦♦♦ Avenue House
Haddon Rd DE45 1EP ☎ 01629 812467
e-mail: awes912515@aol.com
Dir: *300yds from town centre on A6 towards Matlock*
Located a few minutes' walk from central attractions, this impressive Victorian house retains many original features which are complimented by the décor and furnishings throughout. Bedrooms have many thoughtful extras and the modern bathrooms contain power showers. Hearty English breakfasts are taken in a traditionally furnished dining room.
FACILITIES: 3 en suite No smoking TVB tea/coffee No dogs Cen ht TVL No coaches **PRICES:** d £40-£45✳ **LB PARKING:** 4 **NOTES:** Closed Nov-Jan

♦♦♦♦ Bene-Dorme
The Avenue DE45 1EQ ☎ 01629 813292 📠 01629 814208
e-mail: judithtwigg@callnetuk.com
Dir: *just off A6 near Rutland Recreation Ground*
A warm welcome is assured at this mellow stone house which is located on a peaceful road close to town centre. Quality modern en suite shower rooms cfeature in the cosy bedrooms and an attractive dining room is the setting for memorable breakfasts.
FACILITIES: 3 en suite No smoking TVB tea/coffee No dogs (ex guide dogs) Cen ht No children No coaches **PRICES:** s £36-£40; d £44-£50✳
PARKING: 4 **NOTES:** Closed 21-29 Dec

England

BAKEWELL continued

♦♦♦♦ Bourne House

The Park, Haddon Rd DE45 1ET ☎ 01629 813274
e-mail: atkinson@bakewellpark.freeserve.co.uk
Dir: *300mtrs from Bakewell town centre on A6 towards Matlock. Last house on left before park*
This former manse is situated in pleasant gardens, just a short walk from the town centre, and overlooking a large park and playing fields. Bedrooms are very well-appointed with many thoughtful touches. The spacious dining room, with individual tables, also looks out over the park. Guests have their own entrance and there is ample private parking.
FACILITIES: 3 en suite No smoking TVB tea/coffee No dogs Cen ht No children 7yrs No coaches Tennis (hard) Squash Nearby golf course. 9 hole course **PRICES:** d £46-£50* **PARKING:** 5 **NOTES:** Closed Dec-Feb

♦♦♦♦ Burre Close Cottage

2 Burre Close DE45 1GD ☎ 01629 812600
e-mail: greatstay@hotmail.com
Dir: *from main square take Baslow/Sheffield rd after 150yds over bridge take centre of rd & turn right into Station rd. After 100yds turn left into Burre Close. 1st house on right*
Set in a peaceful location, close to central attractions, and enjoying great views, this spacious detached house provides thoughtfully furnished bedrooms. Imaginative breakfasts are taken in a cosy dining room overlooking the pretty garden and the atmosphere is welcoming.
FACILITIES: 2 en suite No smoking TVB tea/coffee Cen ht No children No coaches **PRICES:** d £46-£50* **PARKING:** 3

♦♦♦♦ Croft Cottages

Coombs Rd DE45 1AQ ☎ 01629 814101 🖷 01629 815083
e-mail: croftco@btinternet.com
Dir: *Coombs Rd runs parallel with river on A619 side of Bakewell Bridge, first house on L*
This Derbyshire stone Grade II listed building sits close to the River Wye and the town centre. Thoughtfully equipped bedrooms are available in the main house or in the adjoining barn suite. Breakfast is taken in a separate dining room/lounge, which has a striking fireplace.
FACILITIES: 4 en suite (1 fmly) TVB tea/coffee Cen ht No coaches Riding **PRICES:** d £48-£60* LB **PARKING:** 3

♦♦♦♦ Holly House

The Avenue DE45 1EQ ☎ 01629 813207
e-mail: enquiries@hollyhouse.freeservers.com
Dir: *take A6 Matlock road. After petrol station turn right into The Avenue or turn left after petrol station if approaching from Matlock*
Located on a peaceful cul de sac within easy walking distance of central attractions, this impressive late Victorian house retains many original features highlighted by the quality furnishing and décor styles throughout. Bedrooms are filled with a wealth of thoughtful extras and a cosy guest lounge is also available
FACILITIES: 3 en suite No smoking TVB tea/coffee No dogs (ex guide dogs) Cen ht TVL No children 5yrs No coaches **PRICES:** d £48 **PARKING:** 6 **NOTES:** Closed Xmas

♦♦♦♦ Wyedale

25 Holywell DE45 1BA ☎ 01629 812845
Dir: *approaching Bakewell on A6 from Matlock turn left into Holywell immediately before pelican crossing, B&B directly ahead approximately 30mtrs*
Wyedale bed and breakfast is located close to the town centre and is an ideal base for relaxing or touring the surrounding area. The bedrooms are spacious and each is freshly decorated. Breakfast can be taken in the attractive dining room, which overlooks the rear patio.
continued

FACILITIES: 2 en suite No smoking TVB tea/coffee No dogs (ex guide dogs) Cen ht No children 14yrs No coaches **PRICES:** d £40-£44* **PARKING:** 3 **NOTES:** Closed 31 Dec rs Xmas Eve

♦♦♦ Barleycorn Croft

Sheldon DE45 1QS ☎ 01629 813636
Dir: *from A6 to Buxton, 1.5m from Bakewell take left turn 500yds past Ashford turning. House is last one on left in Sheldon, set back from green*
Barleycorn Croft is a pleasant barn conversion enjoying fine views. It has private access and offers one twin and one double bedroom, sharing bathroom facilities. However, rooms are only let to one party at a time, whether that be two or four people. Guests also have the use of a cosy lounge/dining room with colour TV.
FACILITIES: 2 rms No smoking tea/coffee No dogs (ex guide dogs) Cen ht TVL No children 12yrs No coaches **PRICES:** s £25-£30; d £39-£42* **PARKING:** 4

♦♦♦ White Lion

Main Rd, Great Longstone DE45 1TA ☎ 01629 640252
Dir: *turn off A6 onto B6465*
Set in a quiet location, yet within easy walking distance of the shops, restaurants and promenade. Bedrooms are attractively decorated and the beds are very comfortable. The bar, lounge, and dining room are all popular, with a variety of entertainment available.
FACILITIES: 2 en suite No smoking in bedrooms No smoking in dining room TVB tea/coffee No dogs Licensed Cen ht No children 12yrs Dinner Last d 9pm **PRICES:** s £25-£30; d £40-£50* LB **PARKING:** 6 **CARDS:**

♦♦♦ Wyeclose

5 Granby Croft DE45 1ET ☎ 01629 813702 🖷 01629 813702
e-mail: h.wilson@talk21.com
Dir: *from town centre take A6 Matlock rd at large rdbt, 1st left into Granby Rd, right into Granby Croft opposite Pine/Gift Centre. House left*
Located in a quiet cul-de-sac within the town centre, this Edwardian house provides traditionally furnished bedroom accommodation and an attractive dining room, the setting for comprehensive breakfasts. Original family art is a feature within the ground floor areas.
FACILITIES: 2 rms No smoking TVB tea/coffee No dogs (ex guide dogs) Cen ht No children 8 yrs No coaches Snooker **PRICES:** s fr £18; d fr £38* BB **PARKING:** 3 **NOTES:** Closed Xmas/New Year

♦♦♦ Castle Cliffe Guest House

Monsal Head DE45 1NL ☎ 01629 640258
e-mail: relax@castle-cliffe.com
Dir: *from Bakewell take A6 towards Buxton, after 1.5m turn right then first left into Ashford, turn right onto B6465, follow road for 1.5m. Castle Cliffe is on the right 100yds after Monsal Head hotel, opposite Ashford Arms.*
FACILITIES: 6 en suite (2 fmly) No smoking TVB tea/coffee No dogs (ex guide dogs) Licensed Cen ht TVL No coaches Last d 1wk prior **PRICES:** s £35-£40; d £50-£57.50* LB **PARKING:** 10 **NOTES:** Closed Xmas **CARDS:**

♦♦ George Hotel

Church St, Youlgreave DE45 1UW ☎ 01629 636292
🖷 01632 636292
Dir: *turn off A6 between Matlock & Bakewell onto B5056 Ashbourne road, and on to Youlgreave, hotel opposite church*
The public bars of this 17th century hotel are popular with locals and tourists alike. Bedroom styles vary, but all are attractively decorated and have en suite shower rooms. Breakfast is served in the lounge bar and a range of bar meals and snacks are available.
continued

George Hotel

FACILITIES: 3 en suite (1 fmly) TVB tea/coffee Cen ht Fishing Dinner Last d 8.30pm **PRICES:** s fr £29; d fr £48* **MEALS:** * **PARKING:** 12

BAMFORD Map 08 SK28

♦♦♦♦ The Outpost

Shatton Ln S33 0BG ☎ 01433 651400
e-mail: theoutpost@connectfree.co.uk
Dir: *turn off A625 between Bamford & Hope opposite High Peak Garden Centre, then 200yds on right*

Quietly situated in a mainly residential area this very pleasantly furnished house offers good comforts and fine hospitality. Bedrooms are homely and well equipped and superb breakfasts which include home baked bread and preserves are taken at one family table or in the attractive conservatory. A garden room is a recent addition.

FACILITIES: 3 rms (1 en suite) (1 fmly) No smoking TVB tea/coffee No dogs Cen ht TVL No coaches **PRICES:** s £25-£30; d £40-£54* **PARKING:** 3 **NOTES:** Closed 24 Dec-2 Jan

♦♦♦ The White House

Shatton Ln S33 0BG ☎ 01433 651487 📠 01433 651487
Dir: *A625 Hathersage to Hope, turn L opp High Peak Garden Centre into hamlet of Shatton. White House 250yds on L.*

Situated in a quiet lane among attractive gardens, this large detached house offers generally quite spacious, nicely laid out bedrooms. Breakfast is served around a large communal table in the neatly furnished dining room, which overlooks the garden. Guests also have the use of a cosy lounge with colour TV.

FACILITIES: 5 rms No smoking in bedrooms No smoking in dining room TVB tea/coffee Cen ht TVL No coaches **PRICES:** s £18-£20; d £36-£40* **BB** **PARKING:** 4

BASLOW Map 08 SK27

♦♦♦♦ Holly Cottage

Pilsley DE45 1UH ☎ 01246 582 245
e-mail: hollycottage.bnb@btopenworld.com
Dir: *in centre of Pilsley village, between Bakewell and Baslow follow signs for Chatsworth*

A warm welcome is assured at this mellow stone cottage, part of a combined post office and art and craft gallery in the conservation village of Pilsley, owned by the adjacent Chatsworth Estate. The cosy bedrooms are filled with a wealth of thoughtful extras, and comprehensive breakfasts, utilising quality local produce, are taken at one family table in an attractive dining room. Proprietors are also fluent Dutch speakers.

FACILITIES: 2 en suite No smoking TVB tea/coffee No dogs (ex guide dogs) Cen ht No coaches **PRICES:** s £30; d £40-£50* **PARKING:** 2 **CARDS:**

BELPER Map 08 SK34

Premier Collection

♦♦♦♦♦ Dannah *(SK314502)*

Bowmans Ln, Shottle DE56 2DR ☎ 01773 550273 & 550630 📠 01773 550590 Mrs J L Slack
e-mail: reservations@dannah.demon.co.uk
Dir: *from Belper A517 Ashbourne rd for approx 1.5m. After Hanging Gate pub on right, right to Shottle. 1m to village over x-rds turn right*

Located in a stunning, elevated position within the Chatsworth Estates at Shottle, this impressive Georgian house and outbuildings have been sympathetically renovated to provide high standards of comfort and facilities. Many original features have been retained, and are enhanced by quality décor and furnishings. The bedrooms are filled with a wealth of thoughtful extras. The 'Mixing Place' restaurant is the setting for imaginative dinners and memorable breakfasts, which make use of the finest local produce.

FACILITIES: 8 en suite (1 fmly) (2 GF) No smoking in bedrooms No smoking in dining room No smoking in 1 lounge TVB tea/coffee Direct dial from bedrooms No dogs (ex guide dogs) Licensed Cen ht Jacuzzi horse riding next door 128 acres mixed Dinner Last d 6.15pm **PRICES:** s £54-£65; d £75-£120* **LB** **CONF:** Thtr 14 Class 14 Board 14 Del from £100 * **PARKING:** 20 **NOTES:** Closed 24-26 Dec **CARDS:**

See advert under DERBY on page 123

♦♦♦♦ Chevin Green Farm *(SK339471)*

Chevin Rd DE56 2UN ☎ 01773 822328 📠 01773 822328 Mr & Mrs C Postles
Dir: *turn off A6 opposite Strutt Arms at Milford, onto Chevin Rd, 1.5m on left. From A517, turn off signed Milford, turn left (Milford), on right*

Guests can be sure of a warm welcome at this 300-year old farm which overlooks the Derwent valley. Bedrooms are nicely appointed and well-equipped. There is a comfortably appointed lounge, and breakfast is taken at separate tables in the dining room. This is a no-smoking establishment.

FACILITIES: 6 en suite (1 fmly) No smoking TVB tea/coffee No dogs Cen ht TVL 38 acres non-working **PARKING:** 6 **NOTES:** Closed Xmas/New Year **CARDS:**

BELPER continued

♦♦♦♦ Shottle Hall

Shottle DE56 2EB ☎ 01773 550276 & 550203 📠 01773 550276

Dir: *Leave A517 at x-roads with B5023, 200yds towards Wirksworth then turn R & proceed for 0.5m*

In a peaceful rural location and set in extensive gardens, this establishment is run by enthusiastic and friendly hosts and overlooks the Ecclestone Valley. The bedrooms are comfortably and stylishly furnished. Breakfast is taken in the elegant dining room and an interesting choice of dishes is available at dinner.

FACILITIES: 8 rms (6 en suite) (3 fmly) No smoking in bedrooms No smoking in dining room TV3B tea/coffee Licensed Cen ht TVL No coaches Croquet lawn Dinner Last d 6pm **PRICES:** s £30-£40; d £54-£70* **PARKING:** 30 **NOTES:** Closed Xmas & New Year

♦♦♦ The Hollins

45 Belper Ln DE56 2UQ ☎ 01773 823955

e-mail: hollins@belper.fslife.co.uk

Dir: *at Belper Mill, off A6 onto A517. After 300mtrs right into Belper Lane by the Talbot Hotel. The Hollins is 300mtrs up the hill*

Situated in a quiet residential area in easy striking distance of the town centre, this large detached house has two soundly furnished bedrooms that are well-maintained and share an adjacent bathroom. There is a neat dining room where guests can enjoy a freshly cooked breakfast seated at individual tables.

FACILITIES: 2 rms (1 fmly) No smoking TVB tea/coffee Cen ht No children 2yrs No coaches **PRICES:** s £22-£24; d £42-£44* **PARKING:** 1

BUXTON — Map 07 SK07

Premier Collection

♦♦♦♦♦ Grendon

Bishops Ln SK17 6UN ☎ 01298 78831 📠 01298 79257

e-mail: parkerh1@talk21.com

Dir: *0.75m from Buxton centre, just off A53, St John's Rd, behind Burbage Parish Church*

A warm welcome is assured at this no-smoking Edwardian house, set in immaculate grounds within a few minutes walk of the town centre. The spacious bedrooms are filled with extras, including fresh fruit and lots of local information. Stunning views of the surrounding countryside can be enjoyed from the elegant dining room, where imaginative dinners and memorable breakfasts are served.

FACILITIES: 3 en suite No smoking TVB tea/coffee Cen ht No children 10yrs No coaches Dinner Last d 6pm **PRICES:** s £25-£45; d £50-£66* **LB PARKING:** 8 **CARDS:**

LB indicates that Leisure Breaks are offered by the establishment.

♦♦♦♦ Buxton Wheel House Hotel

19 College Rd SK17 9DZ ☎ 01298 24869 📠 01298 24869

e-mail: lyndsie@buxton-wheelhouse.com

Dir: *A515 into Buxton. 1st left at lights onto Green Ln, 3rd on right onto College Rd.*

Bedrooms are very comfortable and well equipped at this tastefully furnished house set in a leafy part of town. There is a cosy lounge together with a well stocked bar. Good hospitality is provided by the resident owners and the hotel is within easy walking distance of all the town's amenities.

FACILITIES: 9 en suite (2 fmly) No smoking TVB tea/coffee No dogs Licensed Cen ht TVL **PRICES:** s £33-£45; d £52-£62* **LB PARKING:** 10 **NOTES:** Closed end Dec-early Jan **CARDS:**

♦♦♦♦ The Grosvenor House

1 Broad Walk SK17 6JE ☎ 01293 72439 📠 01298 214185

e-mail: grosvenor.buxton@btopenworld.com

Dir: *near Opera House overlooking Pavilion Gardens and the Crescent*

This Victorian house is centrally located overlooking the Pavilion Gardens and Opera House. Bedrooms are tastefully furnished and well equipped with many thoughtful extras provided. Comfortable seating is available in the period style sitting room, and freshly prepared breakfasts are served in the cosy dining room. There is coffee shop next to the property which is open during the summer months.

FACILITIES: 8 en suite (2 fmly) No smoking TVB tea/coffee No dogs (ex guide dogs) Licensed Cen ht No children 8yrs No coaches **PRICES:** s £45-£50; d £50-£75* **LB**

♦♦♦♦ Lakenham

11 Burlington Rd SK17 9AL ☎ 01298 79209

e-mail: lakenhamguesthouse@burlingtonroad11.freeserve.co.uk

Dir: *Burlington Rd is between B515 Macclesfield rd & A53 St Johns Rd*

Set back from the Market Square on a tree-lined avenue opposite the Pavilion Gardens, this Victorian house retains much of its original character. Bedrooms, including one on the ground floor, are smart, spacious and furnished in keeping within the style of the house. Breakfasts are served in the pleasant dining room.

FACILITIES: 6 en suite (2 fmly) (1 GF) No smoking in dining room STV TVB tea/coffee No dogs Licensed Cen ht No coaches **PRICES:** d fr £60* **LB PARKING:** 9

♦♦♦♦ Roseleigh Hotel

19 Broad Walk SK17 6JR ☎ 01298 24904 📠 01298 24904

e-mail: enquiries@roseleighhotel.co.uk

Dir: *A6 to Safeway rdbt, turn onto Dale Rd, right at lights, 100yds turn left by Swan pub, down hill & right into Hartington Rd*

An impressive stone building, overlooking the Pavilion Gardens and providing well maintained and spacious bedrooms. The public rooms also provide good comforts while excellent hospitality is offered by the resident owners.

See advertisement on opposite page

continued

FACILITIES: 14 en suite (3 fmly) No smoking TVB tea/coffee No dogs Licensed Cen ht No coaches **PRICES:** s £25-£56; d £52-£56✻ **PARKING:** 12 **NOTES:** Closed 16 Dec-10 Jan **CARDS:**

♦♦♦ Wellhead Farm

Wormhill SK17 8SL ☎ 01298 871023 📠 01298 872899
e-mail: yvonne4bunkntrough@lineone.net
Dir: *between Bakewell and Buxton. Take A6 then B6049 signposted Millers Dale/Tideswell then left to Wormhill*

This 16th-century farmhouse is in a peaceful location, with low beams and two comfortable lounges. The bedrooms, some with four poster beds, are all equipped with radios, beverage trays and many thoughtful extras. Barry and Yvonne Peirson provide friendly and attentive hospitality in their delightful home.

FACILITIES: 4 en suite (1 fmly) No smoking in bedrooms No smoking in dining room tea/coffee Cen ht TVL No coaches Dinner Last d 5pm **PRICES:** d £48-£58✻ **LB** **PARKING:** 4

♦♦♦ Hawthorn Farm

Fairfield Rd SK17 7ED ☎ 01298 23230 📠 01298 71322
e-mail: alan.pimblett@virgin.net
Dir: *on A6 Manchester/Stockport rd opposite St Peter's church*

A delightful Tudor farmhouse, set back from the Manchester road in attractive gardens. The lounge boasts a feature stone fireplace and many rooms display original beams. Some of the bedrooms are in converted farm buildings.

FACILITIES: 3 en suite 6 annexe rms (4 en suite) (1 fmly) (4 GF) No smoking TVB tea/coffee Cen ht TVL No coaches **PRICES:** s £25-£30; d £45-£50✻ **PARKING:** 12 **CARDS:**

♦♦♦ Old Manse

6 Clifton Rd, Silverlands SK17 6QL ☎ 01298 25638
📠 01298 25638
e-mail: old_manse@yahoo.co.uk
Dir: *from A6 approach Buxton via Safeway rdbt into Dale Rd B5059. 200yds before bridge turn right along Peveril Rd into Clifton Rd*

Close to the town centre, this large, semi-detached house offers comfortable, good-value accommodation in well-equipped bedrooms. There is a cosy sitting room, and the combined bar and dining room serves breakfast and set dinners.

FACILITIES: 7 en suite (2 fmly) No smoking in 4 bedrooms No smoking in dining room No smoking in lounges TVB tea/coffee Licensed Cen ht TVL No coaches Dinner Last d 5pm **PRICES:** s £18-£25; d £36-£50✻ **LB BB** **PARKING:** 4 **CARDS:**

♦♦♦ The Queen Anne

Great Hucklow SK17 8RF ☎ 01298 871246
e-mail: malcolm-hutton@bigfoot.com
Dir: *on A623, turn off at Anchor pub junct towards Bradwell, 2nd right to Great Hucklow*

Standing in the centre of the village, this delightful old inn offers a good range of interesting dishes. There are two modern bedrooms available to the rear.

FACILITIES: 2 en suite No smoking in bedrooms No smoking in 1 lounge TVB tea/coffee Cen ht Darts Dinner Last d 8.45pm **PRICES:** s £25; d £42-£50✻ **MEALS:** Bar Lunch £2.50-£13alc Dinner £9.50-£15alc✻ **PARKING:** 30 **CARDS:**

CALVER — Map 08 SK27

♦♦♦♦ Valley View

Smithy Knoll Rd S32 3XW ☎ 01433 631407 📠 01433 631407
e-mail: sue@a-place-2-stay.co.uk
Dir: *junct 29 M1, follow brown signs for Chatsworth house through Chesterfield on A619. From Baslow, take A623 towards Chapel-en-le Frith for 2m into Calver, take 3rd left onto Donkey Lane.*

This detached stone house is situated in the heart of the village close to all amenities. It is very well-furnished throughout and delightfully friendly service is provided by Mr & Mrs Stone. A hearty breakfast is provided in the cosy dining room.

FACILITIES: 3 en suite (1 fmly) No smoking TVB tea/coffee Cen ht No coaches **PRICES:** s £35; d £50✻ **LB** **PARKING:** 6

CARSINGTON — Map 08 SK25

♦♦♦♦ Henmore Grange

Hopton DE4 4DF ☎ 01629 540420 📠 01629 540720
e-mail: henmoregrange@hotmail.com
Dir: *from B5035 turn into Hopton, 1st left at Wirksworth end of by-pass*

This stone farmhouse has been tastefully restored and retains much of its original character. The spacious lounge has a stone fireplace and wood-burning stove. Breakfast is served in the farmhouse kitchen-style dining room. Bedrooms are comfortable and well appointed.

FACILITIES: 7 en suite (2 fmly) (2 GF) No smoking TVB tea/coffee No dogs (ex guide dogs) Cen ht TVL No coaches **PRICES:** s £31; d £55✻ **LB** **CONF:** Del from £40 ✻ **PARKING:** 14 **NOTES:** Closed 17 Dec-31 Dec

CASTLETON

See Hope

CHAPEL-EN-LE-FRITH — Map 07 SK08

◆◆ Craigside

4 Buxton Rd, Chinley, High Peak SK23 6DJ ☎ 01663 750604

Dir: *take A624 off A6 at Chapel-en-le-Frith for 1.5m then B6062 to Chinley, Craigside on left approaching village*

Located on a residential avenue in the village of Chinley, this house provides bedrooms equipped with homely extras and an attractive modern bathroom is also available. Hearty home cooked breakfasts are taken at one family table in a cosy dining room which also contains comfortable lounge seating and a colour television.

FACILITIES: 2 rms No smoking tea/coffee Cen ht TVL BB **PRICES:** s fr £25; d fr £36✳ **PARKING:** 2

CHESTERFIELD — Map 08 SK37

◆◆◆ Anis Louise

34 Clarence Rd S40 1LN ☎ 01246 235412

e-mail: neil@anislouise.co.uk

Anis Louise Guest House is conveniently located just a short walk from the town centre, and has ample rear car parking. A warm welcome and friendly attentive service is provided by the resident proprietors. Bedrooms vary in shape and size, and all are soundly appointed. Breakfast is taken in a neat dining room.

FACILITIES: 5 en suite (1 fmly) No smoking TVB tea/coffee No dogs Cen ht No children 8yrs No coaches **PRICES:** s £21-£25; d £36-£40✳ **LB** BB **PARKING:** 6 **CARDS:**

◆◆ The Beeches

280 Sheffield Rd, Stonegravels S41 7JQ ☎ 01246 550884

Dir: *junct 29 to Chesterfield, right on A61 at rdbt. Left to Stonegravels at Tesco rdbt. Left at next rdbt to Chesterfield. The Beeches is first on the right after the pelican crossing.*

Located on the outskirts close to the ring road, this early Edwardian red brick house offers value accommodation which includes freshly cooked English breakfasts.

FACILITIES: 4 rms (1 fmly) No smoking TVB tea/coffee No dogs (ex guide dogs) Cen ht No coaches **PRICES:** d fr £36✳ BB **PARKING:** 4

DERBY — Map 08 SK33

See also Belper & Melbourne

◆◆◆ Georgian House Hotel

32/36 Ashbourne Rd DE22 3AD ☎ 01332 349806

Fax 01332 349959

e-mail: mail@georgianhousehotel.org.uk

Dir: *A52 to Derby, follow signs A52 towards Ashbourne past Friargate, 500yds on right*

Located in historic Friargate, this Grade II listed inn retains many original features including fine oak paneling within the public areas. Bedrooms provide a range of both practical and homely extras and guests have the choice of an elegant a la carte restaurant or the more informal 'Mr Grundy's', both offering a range of imaginative food.

FACILITIES: 20 en suite (2 fmly) No smoking in 10 bedrooms No smoking in dining room TVB tea/coffee Direct dial from bedrooms Cen ht TVL ch fac Dinner Last d 9.30pm **PARKING:** 25 **CARDS:**

◆◆◆ The Longlands

Longlands Ln, Findern DE65 6AH ☎ 01283 702320

Fax 01283 701908

e-mail: bookings@thelonglands.com

Dir: *A50 junct4, take Willington turn, 1st left at Willington, immediately before Canal Bridge. After 0.75m turn left on entering Findern, opposite inn*

continued

This Georgian country house was formerly the home farmhouse to a group of neighbouring farms, and has a licensed bar, a comfortable lounge with wide-screen satellite television, and a separate dining room. The bedrooms vary in style and size, and each has a good range of facilities.

FACILITIES: 16 en suite (4 fmly) No smoking in 3 bedrooms No smoking in dining room No smoking in 1 lounge STV TVB tea/coffee Direct dial from bedrooms Licensed Cen ht TVL ch fac Dinner Last d 8.30pm **PARKING:** 24 **CARDS:**

◆◆◆ Rangemoor Park Hotel

67 Macklin St DE1 1LF ☎ 01332 347252 Fax 01332 369319

e-mail: res@rangemoorpark.freeserve.co.uk

Ideally located within easy walking distance of Pride Park Stadium, this commercial hotel has been in the same family ownership for a quarter of a century, providing traditional standards of service and hospitality. A range of standard and executive bedrooms is offered and the spacious secure car park is a real advantage.

FACILITIES: 24 rms (13 en suite) (3 fmly) No smoking in dining room STV TVB tea/coffee Direct dial from bedrooms Cen ht TVL **PRICES:** s £29.50-£46.50; d £46.50-£57.50✳ **LB** **PARKING:** 37 **NOTES:** Closed Xmas & New Year **CARDS:**

EDALE — Map 07 SK18

◆◆◆ Edale House

Hope Rd S33 7ZE ☎ 01433 670399 Fax 01433 670128

e-mail: edale.house@care4free.net

Built two hundred years ago and extended in Victorian times, this mellow stone detached house offers comfortable homely bedrooms all with fine views south over the River Noe to Black Tor and Hollins Cross. Tasty breakfasts are taken at one family table in the period hall.

FACILITIES: 3 rms (2 en suite) No smoking TV2B tea/coffee Cen ht No coaches **PRICES:** s £20-£30; d £50-£55✳ **PARKING:** 5

EYAM — Map 08 SK27

◆◆◆ Miners Arms

Water Ln S32 5RG ☎ 01433 630853 Fax 01433 639050

Dir: *off M1, J29, 10 miles from Chesterfield*

Located within this historic village, this 17th century inn is very much the focal point of local life with a strong following for both its imaginative food and well-stocked bars. Bedrooms are brightly decorated and comfortable, and public areas include an attractive restaurant, a cosy separate breakfast room and bars with polished brasses and ornaments.

FACILITIES: 7 en suite (1 fmly) (1 GF) No smoking in dining room No smoking in 1 lounge TVB tea/coffee Cen ht Dinner Last d 9pm **PRICES:** d £60-£80✳ **LB** **MEALS:** Lunch £8.95-£15.95alc Dinner £8.95-£15.95alc✳ **PARKING:** 75 **CARDS:**

England

FOOLOW Map 07 SK17

♦♦♦♦ *Bulls Head*

S32 5QR ☎ 01433 630873 01433 631738

Dir: *from junct 29 M1 follow signs to Bakewell. At Baslow take A623 Foolow is 3m after Stoney Middleton*

Located centrally in this peaceful village and popular with both locals and walkers, this inn has many of its original features and offers comfortable, well-equipped bedrooms. Full English breakfast and imaginative bar meals are served in the traditionally furnished dining room or cosy bar areas. Both local and guest ales are available.

FACILITIES: 3 en suite No smoking in bedrooms No smoking in dining room STV TVB tea/coffee No dogs Cen ht Dinner Last d 9.30pm **PARKING:** 20 **CARDS:**

FROGGATT Map 08 SK27

♦♦♦♦ The Chequers Inn

S32 3ZJ ☎ 01433 630 231 01433 631072

Dir: *on A625 between Sheffield & Bakewell*

A very popular 16th century roadside inn offering an extensive range of well-cooked food. The bedrooms are comprehensively equipped with all modern comforts and the hospitality is both professional and sincere. An ideal location for touring the Peak Park, Chatsworth and Derbyshire.

FACILITIES: 5 en suite TVB tea/coffee Direct dial from bedrooms Cen ht No coaches Dinner Last d 9.30pm **PRICES:** d £45-£75* **LB MEALS:** Lunch £13.65-£23.70alc Dinner £13.65-£23.70alc* **PARKING:** 45 **CARDS:**

GLOSSOP Map 07 SK09

♦♦♦♦ Brentwood

120 Glossop Rd, Charlesworth SK13 5HB ☎ 01457 869001

Dir: *on A626, 1m from A57 on road to Marple, next door but one to rugby field and garden centre*

This spacious family home is found on the edge of Charlesworth village and offers good value and fine hospitality. The bedrooms are well-equipped and pleasantly furnished while a comfortable lounge is provided for guests. Substantial breakfasts are served in the attractive dining room, which overlooks the large garden complete with a pond.

FACILITIES: 3 en suite (1 GF) No smoking TVB tea/coffee Cen ht TVL No coaches Golf 9 **PRICES:** s fr £20; d £40* **PARKING:** 6

England

GLOSSOP continued

♦♦♦♦ *Rock Farm (SK027907)*
Monks Rd SK13 6JZ ☎ 01457 861086 Mrs M Child
e-mail: pfc@rockfarm99.freeserve.co.uk
Dir: *2m S of Glossop on A624. Pass Grouse Inn on L, turn R into Monks Rd signed Charlesworth. After 1m farm signed on L, turn L, 2nd farm*
Rock farm is peacefully situated in a lovely position, with panoramic views overlooking Kinder Scout and the surrounding hills. The house has been lovingly furnished and provides extremely comfortable accommodation together with very friendly and attentive service. Fine hospitality is one of the keynotes to operation
FACILITIES: 2 rms No smoking TVB tea/coffee Cen ht 7 acres non-working **PARKING:** 3 **NOTES:** Closed 24-27 Dec

♦♦♦ Gables Hotel
87 Station Rd, Hadfield SK13 1AR ☎ 01457 868250
01457 858788
e-mail: welcome@gableshotel.com
Dir: *At Tintwistle turn off A628 to Hadfield, after 1m in village, go straight over mini rdbt, Gables 500m on left.*
This large detached house stands in the main street of the village and provides very good hospitality together with home-cooked dinners. The bedrooms are spacious and well equipped, and public rooms include a lounge, a bar and a pleasant dining room. Parking is found to the rear.
FACILITIES: 8 en suite (2 fmly) No smoking in dining room No smoking in lounges TVB tea/coffee Licensed Cen ht TVL No coaches Dinner Last d by arrangement **PRICES:** s £37; d £45* **LB** **PARKING:** 9 **CARDS:**

♦♦♦ Hollincross House
20 Hollincross Ln SK13 8JQ ☎ 01457 854587 & 0797 1264168
e-mail: renee@counseling.freeserve.co.uk
Dir: *off A57 from the W, right onto Victoria St, up street curving left. Sharp right at Crown pub onto Hollincross Ln. Pass church on left and house on right at junct with Hadfield St*
A warm welcome is assured at this early Victorian house, located within easy walking distance of central attractions and railway station, with its express service to Manchester. Bedrooms are filled with thoughtful extras and memorable breakfasts utilise home produced or local produce.
FACILITIES: 2 rms (2 fmly) No smoking TV1B tea/coffee No dogs (ex guide dogs) Cen ht TVL No children 2yrs **PRICES:** s £20; d £40*

♦♦♦ Peakdale Lodge
49-53 High St East SK13 8PN ☎ 01457 854109
01457 857080
Dir: *situated on A57 Manchester to Sheffield road, 100 yds on left from main traffic lights opposite Leisure Centre*
This well furnished guest house is situated in the centre of the town and offers friendly and polite hospitality. Bedrooms are well equipped and there is a bright dining room serving substantial breakfasts.
FACILITIES: 9 en suite (2 fmly) (1 GF) No smoking in bedrooms No smoking in dining room No smoking in 1 lounge TVB tea/coffee Cen ht **PRICES:** s fr £22; d fr £44*

♦♦♦ White House Farm
Padfield SK13 1ET ☎ 01457 854695 01457 854695
Dir: *from Sheffield A628 to Tintwistle, then signed to Padfield*
FACILITIES: 1 rms 2 annexe rms No smoking in 1 bedrooms No smoking in dining room TVB tea/coffee No dogs (ex guide dogs) Cen ht TVL No coaches **PRICES:** s £22; d £36* **BB** **PARKING:** 10

HARTINGTON — Map 07 SK16

♦♦♦ Bank House
Market Place SK17 0AL ☎ 01298 84465
Dir: *turn off A515 onto B5054, Hartington after 2m, establishment in centre of village on right*
Bank House is a listed Georgian building and stands in the main square of this delightful village. Bedrooms are neat and fresh in appearance, and guests have the use of a comfortable TV lounge. A hearty breakfast is taken in the ground-floor dining room.
FACILITIES: 5 rms (3 en suite) (3 fmly) No smoking TV3B tea/coffee No dogs (ex guide dogs) Cen ht TVL No coaches Dinner Last d noon **PRICES:** s £22-£27; d £42-£47* **LB** **PARKING:** 2 **NOTES:** Closed Xmas

HATHERSAGE — Map 08 SK28

♦♦♦♦ Highlow Hall *(SK218801)*
S32 1AX ☎ 01433 650393 01433 650393
Mr & Mrs B Walker
Dir: *take B6001 from Hathersage (signposted Bakewell), after 0.5m turn right opposite Plough Inn signposted Abney, house 1m on left*

Set in immaculate gardens overlooking the surrounding countryside, this splendid Tudor house (once belonging to the Eyre family), features a baronial hall with staircase, beams and inglenook fireplace. Bedrooms are well furnished and comfortable, one has an antique four-poster bed. Superb home-cooked breakfasts are taken in the panelled dining room and there is a comfortable sitting room.
FACILITIES: 3 en suite (1 fmly) No smoking tea/coffee No dogs Licensed Cen ht TVL No children 12yrs **PRICES:** s £40; d £60-£65*
PARKING: 10 **NOTES:** Closed Xmas and New Year **CARDS:**

♦♦♦♦ *Plough*
Leadmill Bridge S32 1BA ☎ 01433 650319 01433 651049
Dir: *1m SE of Hathersage on B6001. 150yds beyond bridge over River Derment at Leadmill*

This delightful 16th-century inn complete with beer garden enjoys an idyllic location by the River Derwent, one mile from Hathersage.
continued

England

A selection of real ales and imaginative food are served in the spacious public areas. Many original features such as open fires and exposed beams have been retained. Thoughtfully equipped, tastefully appointed bedrooms include two impressive suites.
FACILITIES: 3 en suite No smoking in bedrooms No smoking in dining room TVB tea/coffee Direct dial from bedrooms No dogs (ex guide dogs) Cen ht No coaches Dinner Last d 9.30pm **PARKING:** 50 **CARDS:**

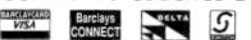

♦♦♦♦ Hillfoot Farm *(SK226815)*

Castleton Rd S32 1EG ☎ 01433 651673 Mrs J Wilcockson
e-mail: hillfootfarm@hotmail.com
Dir: *0.5m from Hathersage on right off A625 between Hathersage & Bamford*
This 16th century inn and tollhouse is at the bottom of the old jaggers' pack horse route. The farm has been extended to offer spacious and comfortable bedrooms and there is also a cosy lounge. Breakfast is served in adjacent beamed dining room. This is a non-smoking establishment.
FACILITIES: 4 en suite (1 fmly) (2 GF) No smoking TVB tea/coffee No dogs Cen ht No children 12yrs Last d day before **PRICES:** s £25-£50; d £40-£50* **LB PARKING:** 12

♦♦♦♦ Millstone

Sheffield Rd S32 1DA ☎ 01433 650258 📠 01433 651664
e-mail: jerry@millstone.fsbusiness.co.uk
Dir: *on A625 from Sheffield, 0.5m before reaching Hathersage*

In an elevated position affording magnificent views over the Hope Valley, this half-timbered stone inn offers comfortable well-equipped bedrooms, including one family suite. A large selection of dishes is served by friendly staff in the Granary Bar, and the brasserie/carvery, imaginatively themed with musical memorabilia, is available at busy periods and weekends.
FACILITIES: 7 en suite (2 fmly) No smoking in 5 bedrooms No smoking in area of dining room No smoking in 1 lounge STV TVB tea/coffee Direct dial from bedrooms Cen ht Dinner Last d 9.30pm **PRICES:** s £39.95-£49.95; d £59.95-£79.95* **LB MEALS:** Lunch £7-£15&alc Dinner £15-£30&alc* **CONF:** Thtr 40 Class 60 Board 40 Del from £49.95 * **PARKING:** 80 **CARDS:**

♦♦♦♦ Polly's

Moorview Cottage, Cannonfields, Jaggers Ln S32 1AG
☎ 01433 650110
Dir: *enter village on A625 & take 1st right after George Hotel into Jaggers Lane, then 1st left*
Quietly located on the former 'jaggers" or travelling drapers' route, this cottage has been lovingly renovated by Polly Fisher to provide three spacious bedrooms, all with modern facilities and lots of homely extras. Tasty English breakfasts are taken at one family table in the elegant dining room and a second floor guest lounge with superb views is also available
FACILITIES: 3 en suite (2 fmly) No smoking TVB tea/coffee No dogs (ex guide dogs) Cen ht No children 5yrs No coaches **PRICES:** s fr £35; d fr £45* **LB PARKING:** 3

♦♦♦♦ *Scotsman's Pack*

School Ln S32 1BZ ☎ 01433 650253 📠 01433 650253
Dir: *from A625 turn into School Ln, Inn 50yds, follow signs to church*

This comfortable inn is situated on the edge of the village and provides a wide range of well-prepared food. The bedrooms are well furnished and have been thoughtfully equipped while the open plan bar is delightful. Hearty breakfasts are served in the separate dining room, and the proprietors are very hospitable.
FACILITIES: 5 en suite No smoking in dining room No smoking in 1 lounge STV TVB tea/coffee Cen ht Dinner Last d 9pm **PARKING:** 15 **NOTES:** Closed 25 Dec **CARDS:**

♦♦♦ Moorgate

Castleton Rd S32 1EH ☎ 01433 650293
Dir: *on A6187 towards Hope/Castleton 100yds past George Hotel, on right just before railway bridge which crosses road*
This large Victorian house is set in its own attractive gardens and is just a few minutes walk from the village centre. Traditionally furnished spacious bedrooms are equipped with a host of interesting reading material. Breakfast is served in the lounge/dining room that overlooks the delightful front garden.
FACILITIES: 3 rms No smoking TVB tea/coffee No dogs Cen ht No coaches **PRICES:** s £18-£20; d £32* **BB PARKING:** 3

♦♦♦ *The Mount*

Castleton Rd S32 1EH ☎ 01433 650388 📠 01433 650388
e-mail: ward.themount@btinternet.com
Dir: *on A6187 200yds past George Hotel, towards Castleton, on R*
Located at the village edge in an elevated position overlooking the surrounding countryside, this stone Victorian house offers comfortable homely bedrooms and a second floor guest lounge filled with games and books. Hearty breakfasts are served at one family table in the attractive dining room.
FACILITIES: 3 rms (1 fmly) No smoking in bedrooms No smoking in dining room TV2B tea/coffee Cen ht TVL No coaches **PARKING:** 6

♦♦♦ Sladen Cottage

Castleton Rd S32 1EH ☎ 01433 650104
e-mail: colley@sladencottage.co.uk
Dir: *on A6187 towards Hope/Castleton, 200yds past George Hotel on right immediately before railway bridge*
From an elevated position overlooking the rolling countryside of the Hope Valley, the two smart bedrooms are contained in a private wing of the bungalow, which includes its own lounge/dining area. Friendly hospitality and care make this a special place, only two minutes' walk from the village centre.
FACILITIES: 2 en suite No smoking TVB tea/coffee No coaches **PRICES:** s £25-£35; d £42-£48* **PARKING:** 8

Directions are provided by the proprietor, ask for more details when booking.

England

HOPE Map 07 SK18

Premier Collection

♦♦♦♦♦ Underleigh House
Off Edale Rd S33 6RF ☎ 01433 621372 📠 01433 621324
e-mail: underleigh.house@btinternet.com
Dir: *from village church on A6187 (formerly A625) take Edale Road for 1m then left into lane*

Situated at the end of a private lane, in glorious scenery, Underleigh House was converted from a barn and cottage dating back to 1873, and now offers tastefully furnished and attractively decorated bedrooms with modern facilities. One room has a private lounge and others have access to the gardens. There is a spacious comfortable guest lounge with a welcoming log fire, and breakfast is served at one large table in the dining room.
FACILITIES: 6 en suite (2 GF) No smoking TVB tea/coffee Direct dial from bedrooms No dogs (ex guide dogs) Licensed Cen ht No children 12yrs No coaches **PRICES:** s £40-£49; d £64-£69 **LB**
PARKING: 6 **NOTES:** Closed Xmas & New Year **CARDS:**

♦♦♦♦ Stoney Ridge
Granby Rd, Bradwell S33 9HU ☎ 01433 620538 📠 01433 623154
e-mail: toneyridge@aol.com
Dir: *from N end of Bradwell turn up Town Lane, left uphill for 300yds. Sharp left (Granby Rd), house 4th on right*

This large, split-level bungalow sits in attractive mature gardens and grounds. Hens and ducks roam freely in the landscaped gardens, and their fresh eggs contribute towards the hearty breakfasts. Bedrooms are attractively furnished and thoughtfully equipped and guests have sole use of a spacious comfortable lounge and a superb indoor swimming pool.
FACILITIES: 4 en suite No smoking in dining room No smoking in 1 lounge STV TVB tea/coffee Cen ht TVL No children 10yrs No coaches Indoor swimming pool (heated) **PRICES:** s £33; d £59✻ **LB PARKING:** 3
CARDS:

♦♦♦ Round Meadow Barn *(SK189836)*
Parsons Ln S33 6RB ☎ 01433 621347 📠 621347
Mr & Mrs J G Harris
e-mail: rmbarn@bigfoot.com
Dir: *0.5m from Hope & N at staggered x-rds, 200yds over rail bridge. 200yds right into Hay barnyard, through gates, across 3 fields, house on left*
Mr and Mrs Harris's home is a converted barn, with original stone walls and exposed timbers, rurally situated in open fields in the picturesque Hope Valley. The bedrooms are large enough for families and there are two modern bathrooms for guests' use. Breakfast is served at one large table adjoining the family kitchen.
FACILITIES: 2 rms (2 fmly) No smoking TVB tea/coffee Golf Riding 4 acres non-working **PRICES:** s £26-£35; d £45-£46✻ **LB PARKING:** 8

ILKESTON Map 08 SK44

Premier Collection

♦♦♦♦♦ The Redhouse
Wharncliffe Rd DE7 5GF ☎ 0115 932 2965
📠 0115 932 1253
e-mail: info@theredhouse.net
Dir: *M1 junct 26/A610 (Matlock), then A6096 into Ilkeston, follow signs for Market Place*
Located on a leafy avenue close to the market square and central attractions, this elegant Victorian house (once the family residence of the lace manufacturing Maltby family) retains many original features including oak panelling, an impressive staircase and stained glass windows. Bedrooms, tastefully decorated with an individual 'artists' theme, are filled with a wealth of thoughtful extras and have modern efficient bathrooms. The spacious ground floor areas are furnished in keeping with the style of the building.
FACILITIES: 6 en suite (3 GF) No smoking in 1 bedrooms No smoking in dining room STV TVB tea/coffee Direct dial from bedrooms No dogs (ex guide dogs) Licensed Cen ht TVL No coaches **PRICES:** s £54; d £70✻ **PARKING:** 10 **CARDS:**

LONGFORD Map 07 SK23

♦♦♦♦ Russets
Off Main St DE6 3DR ☎ 01335 330874 📠 01335 330874
e-mail: geoffrey.nolan@virgin.net
Dir: *from A516 turn into Sutton Lane in Hatton. Follow this until 'T' junction, R onto Long Lane. Next R into Longford & R before telephone box on main st.*

A warm welcome is assured at this beautifully maintained extended bungalow, which is peacefully located in a residential area. Bedrooms are equipped with a wealth of thoughtful extras and have smart modern bathrooms. Comprehensive breakfasts are taken at one family table in a homely dining room and a guest lounge and indoor swimming pool are also available.

continued

FACILITIES: 2 en suite (1 fmly) No smoking STV TVB tea/coffee Cen ht TVL No coaches Indoor swimming pool (heated) **PRICES:** s £35-£45; d £50-£60✻ **PARKING:** 4 **NOTES:** Closed 3rd wk Dec-1st wk Jan

MATLOCK Map 08 SK36

♦♦♦♦ Glendon

Knowleston Place DE4 3BU ☎ 01629 584732

Dir: *M1 junct 28, take A615 Matlock road & premises on left past Total Service Station. Turn into car park just before Glendon B&B sign*

Glendon is set beside a park, and is just a short walk from the town centre. All of the bedrooms are spacious, pleasantly decorated and well-equipped. There is a comfortably appointed lounge on the third floor that has some lovely views out over Bentley Brook and the local church.

FACILITIES: 4 rms (2 en suite) (1 fmly) No smoking TVB tea/coffee No dogs Cen ht TVL No children 3 yrs No coaches **PRICES:** s £25-£28; d £43-£47 **PARKING:** 4 **NOTES:** Closed Dec

♦♦♦♦ Hearthstone Farm *(SK308583)*

Hearthstone Ln, Riber DE4 5JW ☎ 01629 534304
Fax 01629 534372 Mrs J Gilman
e-mail: bed_and_breakfast@hearthstonefarm.fsbusiness.co.uk

Dir: *A615 at Tansley 2m E of Matlock, turn opposite Royal Oak towards Riber, at gates to Riber Hall turn left into Riber Road and 1st left into Hearthstone Lane, farmhouse on left*

Located in a stunning elevated position on the edge of the historic village of Riber, this period stone house retains many original features and is stylish decorated throughout. Bedrooms are equipped with a wealth of homely extras and comprehensive breakfasts, which feature the farm's own organic produce, are served in an elegant dining room.

FACILITIES: 3 rms (2 en suite) (1 fmly) No smoking TVB tea/coffee Cen ht 150 acres Organic beef lamb pigs Dinner Last d 10am **PRICES:** s fr £30; d fr £50✻ **PARKING:** 6 **NOTES:** Closed Xmas & New Year

♦♦♦♦ Hodgkinsons Hotel

150 South Pde, Matlock Bath DE4 3NR ☎ 01629 582170
Fax 01629 584891
e-mail: enquiries@hodgkinsons-hotel.co.uk

Dir: *on A6 in centre of village*

This fine Georgian hotel was renovated in Victorian times and has many original and unusual features. Bedrooms are equipped with fine antique furniture and a wealth of thoughtful extras to enhance guest comfort. An elegant dining room is the setting for imaginative dinners and a comfortable lounge is also available.

FACILITIES: 7 en suite (1 fmly) No smoking in 1 bedrooms No smoking in dining room No smoking in 1 lounge TVB tea/coffee Direct dial from bedrooms Licensed Cen ht No children 6mnth No coaches Dinner Last d 9pm **PRICES:** s £38-£48; d £68-£95✻ **LB PARKING:** 6 **NOTES:** Closed 24-26 Dec **CARDS:**

♦♦♦♦ Littlemoor Wood Farm *(SK320580)*

Littlemoor Ln, Riber DE4 5JS ☎ 01629 534302
Fax 01629 534008 Mrs Gillian Groom
e-mail: gillygroom@ntlworld.com

Dir: *A615 to Tansley. Take road opposite Royal Oak (Alders Lane) signposted Riber. After 1m, turn left signposted Lea/Holloway. Farm on right after 500yds*

A charming farm with a large collection of rare livestock breeds. Guests are assured of a warm welcome at this house, surrounded by 20 acres of meadows with unspoilt views of the countryside. Bedrooms are attractively furnished, and there is a tastefully appointed dining room/study. Wholesome breakfasts feature farm produce.

FACILITIES: 2 en suite No smoking TVB tea/coffee No dogs (ex guide dogs) Cen ht No children 1yr 20 acres sheep, pigs Dinner Last d By arrangement **PRICES:** s £30-£40; d fr £50✻ **PARKING:** 10 **NOTES:** Closed Xmas/New Year **CARDS:**

♦♦♦♦ Manor House

Wensley DE4 2LL ☎ 01629 734360 & 07831 583300
Fax 01629 734360

Dir: *from A6, turn onto B5057 signed Wensley, past Square & Compass pub & continue up hill, house signposted on left 500yds after Wensley sign*

Located on four acres of immaculate landscaped grounds in the pretty village of Wensley, this mellow stone Georgian farm cottage has many original features and is furnished with a great deal of style. Breakfast is taken at one table in the cosy dining room and a comfortable lounge and conservatory offer stunning views of the surrounding countryside.

FACILITIES: 2 rms (3 GF) No smoking tea/coffee No dogs (ex guide dogs) Cen ht TVL No children 14yrs No coaches **PRICES:** s £25-£30; d £50-£54✻ **PARKING:** 6

♦♦♦♦ Old Sunday School

New St DE4 3FH ☎ 01629 583347 Fax 01629 583347
e-mail: davhpatrick@hotmail.com

Dir: *turn off A6 at Crown Square up Bank Rd (steep hill) to Derby County Council Office car park, New St. is directly opposite*

A warm welcome is assured at this sympathetic renovation of a mellow sandstone, early-Victorian former chapel, a few minutes' walk from central attractions. The comfortable, homely bedroom is complimented by a modern shower room, and the spacious open-plan living area includes a period dining table, the setting for comprehensive breakfasts and (by arrangement) imaginative dinners.

FACILITIES: 1 en suite (1 fmly) No smoking TVB tea/coffee No dogs Cen ht TVL No coaches Dinner Last d 5pm **PRICES:** s £20; d £40✻ **LB**

Places with this symbol are Inns.

England

MATLOCK continued

♦♦♦♦ The Red Lion
Matlock Green DE4 3BT ☎ 01629 584888
Dir: *A615 Alfreton/Matlock into Matlock, turn onto A632 to Chesterfield, car park 75mtrs on left*

This comfortable inn makes a good base for exploring Matlock and the surrounding Derbyshire countryside. Each bedroom is tastefully decorated, comfortable and suitably equipped. Public areas include a character bar and restaurant where a wide selection of meals are on offer.
FACILITIES: 6 en suite (1 fmly) No smoking in bedrooms No smoking in dining room No smoking in 1 lounge TVB tea/coffee No dogs (ex guide dogs) Cen ht Pool Table Dinner Last d 9pm **PRICES:** s £25; d £50✳ **MEALS:** Lunch £5-£10alc Dinner £3.50-£7alc✳ **PARKING:** 20 **CARDS:**

♦♦♦♦ Woodside
Stanton Lees DE4 2LQ ☎ 01629 734320
e-mail: kathpotter@stantonlees.freeserve.co.uk
Dir: *A6 Matlock/Bakewell in 2m 1st left at Red House Hotel, x-rds left onto B5057 into Darley Bridge, opposite pub right to Stanton Lees take right fork*
A neat stone-built cottage situated in the Peak District National Park overlooking the valley and hills beyond. The well-equipped bedrooms are attractively furnished. Hearty breakfasts are served in the spacious lounge/dining room, which is heated by a wood-burning stove in cooler weather.
FACILITIES: 3 en suite (3 GF) No smoking TVB tea/coffee No dogs Cen ht TVL No coaches **PRICES:** d £40-£48✳ **LB**

♦♦♦ Wayside *(SK324630)*
Matlock Moor DE4 5LZ ☎ 01629 582967 📠 01629 582967
Mrs J Hole
Dir: *from town centre take A632 to Chesterfield. Farm 2.5m on right*
Stunningly located on the outskirts, this 17th century farmhouse has been carefully restored to provide cottage style bedrooms filled with thoughtful extras and complimented by excellent modern bathrooms. Breakfast is taken in an attractive pine furnished conservatory and a cosy lounge with wood burning stove is also available. For families, a pets corner with childrens' play area is a special feature.
FACILITIES: 4 rms (3 en suite) (2 fmly) No smoking TVB tea/coffee No dogs (ex guide dogs) Cen ht TVL 35 acres mixed Dinner Last d 10am **PRICES:** s £25-£30; d £35-£50✳ **BB** **PARKING:** 10 **NOTES:** Closed Xmas & New Year

♦♦♦ Bradvilla
26 Chesterfield Rd DE4 3DQ ☎ 01629 57147 📠 01629 583021
Dir: *on A632 towards Chesterfield, below convent school, opposite Lilybank Hydro- nursing home*
This Victorian semi-detached house is situated in an elevated position on the edge of the town with a small private car park at the rear. Neat gardens and patios are also a feature. Bedrooms are comfortably furnished and include one suitable for families.
continued

FACILITIES: 2 rms (1 en suite) (2 fmly) No smoking TVB tea/coffee No dogs (ex guide dogs) Cen ht No coaches course nearby **PRICES:** d £40-£44✳ **PARKING:** 4 **NOTES:** Closed 22-28 Dec

♦♦♦ Farley *(SK294622)*
Farley DE4 5LR ☎ 01629 582533 & 07801 756409
📠 01629 584856 Mrs M Brailsford
e-mail: ericb@ukgateway.net
Dir: *A6 Buxton/Bakewell 1st R after rdbt in Matlock. Turn R at top of hill, then L up Farley Hill, 2nd farm on L*

Guests can expect a warm welcome at this traditional stone built farmhouse which dates back to the 12th century. The bedrooms are pleasantly decorated and equipped with many useful extras. Breakfast is served communally around one large table and dinner is available by prior arrangement.
FACILITIES: 2 en suite (3 fmly) No smoking in bedrooms No smoking in area of dining room TVB tea/coffee Cen ht TVL Riding 165 acres arable beef dairy Dinner Last d 5pm **PRICES:** s £25; d £40-£44✳ **LB**
PARKING: 8 **NOTES:** Closed Xmas & New Year

♦♦♦ Kensington Villa
84 Dale Rd DE4 3LU ☎ 01629 57627
e-mail: billgorman@virgin.net
Dir: *exit M1 junct 28, towards Matlock. On entering Matlock follow signs for A6 Bath/ Derby. Premises 120yds on right opposite Evans jewellers*
A warm welcome is assured at this terraced Victorian guest house. The bedrooms are of a good size, brightly and stylishly decorated. The dining room leads out onto a courtyard garden, and there are numerous guide books and maps of the Peak District that guests can use.
FACILITIES: 3 rms (3 GF) No smoking TVB tea/coffee No dogs (ex guide dogs) Cen ht No coaches **PRICES:** s £20-£22; d £40-£44✳ **PARKING:** 3

♦♦♦ Red House Carriage Museum
Old Rd, Darley Dale DE4 2ER ☎ 01629 733583
📠 01629 733583
Dir: *2m N of Matlock, L off A6, 200yds on L*
Located on pretty grounds within a famous working carriage museum, this detached house provides homely and thoughtfully equipped bedrooms, one of which is situated within a sympathetically renovated former stable. Comprehensive breakfasts are taken at one family table in an attractive dining room and a comfortable lounge is also available.
FACILITIES: 2 en suite 1 annexe en suite (1 fmly) (1 GF) No smoking TVB tea/coffee No dogs (ex guide dogs) Cen ht No coaches Riding Carriage & horses trips/tuition Horse riding **PRICES:** s £20-£30; d £40-£55
PARKING: 5

♦♦♦ Victoria House
65 Wellington St DE4 3GS ☎ 01629 55862
e-mail: amsmatlock@hotmail.com
Dir: *off A6 in town centre, into Bank Rd, bear right at T-junct, at top into Wellington St, 200yds on left*
continued

Located in an elevated position on the outskirts of town, this Victorian terraced house retains many original features. Bedrooms have many thoughtful extras and provide stunning views of the countryside. Imaginative dinners are served by arrangement and a guest lounge is also available.
FACILITIES: 2 rms (1 fmly) No smoking TVB tea/coffee No dogs (ex guide dogs) Cen ht TVL No coaches Dinner Last d day before **PRICES:** d fr £42* **PARKING:** 2

The Laurels
91 Wellington St DE4 3GW ☎ 01629 584137 & 07815 971343
At the time of going to press the Diamond classification for this establishment had not been confirmed. Please check the AA website www.theAA.com for up-to-date information.
FACILITIES: 3 rms

MELBOURNE Map 08 SK32

♦♦♦♦ The Coach House
69 Derby Rd DE73 1FE ☎ 01332 862338 📠 01332 862338
e-mail: GBT2000@hotmail.com
Dir: *from Derby take A514 then B587. From M42/M1 take A453 then B587*
Located within the heart of this conservation village and close to both Donnington Park and East Midlands Airport, this period cottage has been sympathetically restored to provide good standards of comfort and facilities. The thoughtfully furnished bedrooms, two of which are located within renovated former stables, have modern shower rooms, and a guest lounge is also available.
FACILITIES: 7 en suite (1 fmly) (4 GF) No smoking in bedrooms No smoking in dining room STV TVB tea/coffee No dogs (ex guide dogs) Cen ht TVL No coaches Dinner Last d 6pm **PRICES:** s £30; d £49* **LB** **PARKING:** 7

♦♦♦ Melbourne Arms
92 Ashby Rd DE73 1ES ☎ 01332 864949 📠 01332 865525
e-mail: info@melbournearms.com
Ideally located for both the airport and Donnington Park, this Grade II listed inn provides modern, thoughtfully equipped bedrooms, one of which is situated in sympathetic conversion of a former outbuilding. Ground floor areas include two bars, a coffee shop and an elegant Indian restaurant.
FACILITIES: 5 en suite (1 fmly) No smoking in bedrooms No smoking in area of dining room No smoking in 1 lounge TVB tea/coffee No dogs Cen ht TVL Dinner Last d 11pm **PRICES:** s £30-£35; d £50-£55; * **PARKING:** 52 **NOTES:** Closed 25 Dec **CARDS:**

MILLER'S DALE Map 07 SK17

♦♦♦ Dale Cottage
SK17 8SN ☎ 01298 872400 📠 01298 872400
e-mail: mik@dalecottage.freeserve.co.uk
Dir: *turn off A6 between Buxton & Bakewell onto B6049 signposted Millers Dale/Tideswell. Opposite Craft Supplies*
Quietly situated in a wooded valley, this 19th-century cottage is close to the Monsal Trail, Limestone Way and White Peak Trail. The proprietors keep maps of local walks for visitors to use. Bedrooms, both on the ground floor, are attractively furnished. Breakfast is a substantial affair served around one table, with views across the river.
FACILITIES: 2 rms No smoking TVB tea/coffee No dogs (ex guide dogs) Cen ht No coaches **PRICES:** s £30-£35; d £40-£44 **PARKING:** 3 **NOTES:** Closed Xmas & New Year

NEWHAVEN Map 07 SK16

Premier Collection

♦♦♦♦♦ The Smithy
SK17 0DT ☎ 01298 84548 📠 01298 84548
e-mail: thesmithy@newhavenderbyshire.freeserve.co.uk
Dir: *on A515, 10m S of Buxton, 10m N of Ashbourne. Adjacent to Biggin Lane, entrance via private driveway opposite Ivy House*
Set in a peaceful location close to the Tissington and High Peak trails, this 17th-century drovers' inn and blacksmith's workshop has been carefully renovated. Bedrooms, which are located in the former barn, are tastefully decorated and well equipped. Enjoyable breakfasts, which include free range eggs and home-made preserves, are taken in the forge, featuring the original working bellows to the vast open hearth. Excellent hospitality is provided by the resident owners.
FACILITIES: 4 en suite (1 fmly) (2 GF) No smoking TVB tea/coffee No dogs (ex guide dogs) Cen ht TVL No coaches **PRICES:** s fr £35; d fr £58* **LB** **CONF:** Thtr 15 Board 10 **PARKING:** 6

RISLEY Map 08 SK43

♦♦♦♦ Braeside
113 Derby Rd DE72 3SS ☎ 0115 9395885
Dir: *M1 junct 25, take 1st exit after A52, signed Risley, past Holiday Inn on right, at x-roads turn left into Risley, 2nd cottage on left past pub*
The enthusiastic hosts of this delightful property offer a very warm welcome to guests. Bedrooms are available within the main house and in a clever conversion of barns close to the house; all bedrooms are attractively appointed. Breakfast is served in the conservatory, with superb views over the colourful garden and adjacent fields.
FACILITIES: 4 en suite No smoking TVB tea/coffee No dogs (ex guide dogs) Cen ht No children 14yrs No coaches **PRICES:** d £48-£55* **PARKING:** 6 **NOTES:** Closed Dec-Jan

SOUTH NORMANTON Map 08 SK45

♦♦♦♦ *The Boundary Lodge*
Lea Vale, Broadmeadows DE55 3NA ☎ 01773 819066 📠 01773 819006
Dir: *turn off M1 junct 28 head towards South Normanton, turn left at mini rdbt, left at next rdbt follow road for 0.5m The Boundary Lodge is on left*
Located close to the M1, this establishment offers luxurious and very spacious accommodation; including a family room. There is a small breakfast room and a wide choice of meals is available in the adjoining pub. There is also a small meeting/conference room.
FACILITIES: 13 en suite (1 fmly) No smoking in 6 bedrooms No smoking in area of dining room No smoking in 1 lounge STV TVB tea/coffee Direct dial from bedrooms No dogs (ex guide dogs) Licensed Cen ht TVL Pool Table Jacuzzi Dinner Last d 9pm **CARDS:**

SWADLINCOTE Map 08 SK21

♦♦♦♦ Overseale House

Acresford Rd, Overseal DE12 6HX ☎ 01283 763741
e-mail: overseale house@hotmail.com
Dir: *situated on the main A444 leaving the village on route to Junct 11 M42*

Located in the village of Overseal, this well-proportioned Georgian mansion was built for a renowned industrialist. It retains many original features, which are enhanced by the quality décor and period furnishing schemes throughout the ground floor areas. Bedrooms are filled with thoughtful extras and a warm welcome is assured.
FACILITIES: 4 en suite (3 fmly) (1 GF) No smoking TVB tea/coffee Cen ht No coaches **PRICES:** s £25-£30; d £45-£55* **CONF:** Board 14 **PARKING:** 6 **NOTES:** Closed 20 Dec-6 Jan

TIDESWELL Map 07 SK17

♦♦♦ Greystones

Sunny Bank Ln SK17 8JY ☎ 01298 871591
Dir: *turn off A623 onto B6049 signposted Tideswell, turn right into Cherry Tree Square. Sunny Bank Lane runs up from the square*
A small, attractive private house built of Derbyshire stone, situated in an elevated position in a quiet lane close to the centre of the village. There are two bedrooms, one a single, the other a twin, both very tastefully decorated and comfortably furnished. Substantial breakfasts can be enjoyed in the downstairs dining room, which looks out over a pretty garden and patio.
FACILITIES: 2 rms No smoking TVB tea/coffee Cen ht No children 5yrs No coaches **PRICES:** s £20-£25; d £40-£44* **NOTES:** Closed Dec-Feb

♦♦♦ Jaret House

Queen St SK17 8JZ ☎ 01298 872470
Dir: *A6/A623-B6049, Jaret House in centre of village opposite Hills and Dales Tearooms*
This typical Derbyshire cottage offers traditionally furnished bedrooms, including one with a private adjacent bathroom. Friendly and attentive service is provided. A comfortable sitting room is warmed by a log fire during the cooler months, and a freshly prepared, substantial breakfast is served in the rear dining room.
FACILITIES: 3 en suite (1 fmly) No smoking TVB tea/coffee No dogs (ex guide dogs) Cen ht No coaches **PRICES:** s £25; d £45* **LB**

♦♦♦ Poppies

Bank Square SK17 8LA ☎ 01298 871083
e-mail: poptidza@dialstart.net
Dir: *Leave A623 onto B6049 Poppies 0.5m on right in centre of village opposite Nat West bank*
A friendly welcome is assured at this no-smoking house, located in the heart of a former lead mining and textile community, a few minutes' walk from the 14th century parish church. Bedrooms are

continued

homely and comfortable and the excellent breakfast features good vegetarian options.
FACILITIES: 3 rms (1 en suite) (1 fmly) No smoking TVB tea/coffee Cen ht Dinner Last d previous day **PRICES:** s £19-£21; d £38-£42* **BB**

TISSINGTON Map 07 SK15

♦♦♦ Bent *(SK177511)*

DE6 1RD ☎ 01335 390214 Fax 01335 390214 Mrs H Herridge
Dir: *A515 Ashbourne to Buxton rd, turn off at Tissington, through avenue of trees to village, past pond, Bent Farm 0.5m on left*
Set amidst rolling hills and open pastures this stone-built 17th-century Grade II listed farmhouse is still part of a working dairy farm. The spacious bedrooms are furnished to match the character of the house. Breakfast is served in the traditional dining room and there is a large, comfortable lounge.
FACILITIES: 2 en suite (1 fmly) No smoking tea/coffee No dogs (ex guide dogs) Cen ht TVL Farming activities 280 acres dairy **PRICES:** d £42-£45* **LB PARKING:** 6 **NOTES:** Closed Nov-Feb/Mar.

WESTON UNDERWOOD Map 08 SK24

Premier Collection

♦♦♦♦♦ Park View Farm *(SK293425)*

DE6 4PA ☎ 01335 360352 Fax 01335 360352 Mrs L Adams
e-mail: enquiries@parkviewfarm.co.uk
Dir: *6m NW of Derby off A38 1.5m Kedleston Hall National Trust property*

A delightful, early Victorian farmhouse surrounded by beautiful gardens and 370 acres of arable land. Each bedroom has an antique four-poster bed, attractive decor and period furniture. There is a spacious and comfortable sitting room in which to relax and a separate dining room where guests can enjoy a hearty breakfast.
FACILITIES: 3 en suite No smoking TVB tea/coffee No dogs Cen ht TVL No children 5 yrs 370 acres arable **PRICES:** s £38-£40; d £65-£70* **PARKING:** 10 **NOTES:** Closed 24 & 25 Dec

WIRKSWORTH Map 08 SK25

Premier Collection

♦♦♦♦♦ Old Lock-Up

North End DE4 4FG ☎ 01629 826272 Fax 01629 826272
e-mail: wheeler@theoldlockup.co.uk
Dir: *turn off A6 at Cromford, take B5036 and go up hill for Wirksworth, down into town, 1st turning left after infant school*
Located in the heart of the village, this early Victorian former magistrate's house retains many original features. Bedrooms,

continued

England

two of which are located in a former chapel and stable, are filled with a wealth of thoughtful extras and the modern bathrooms are supplemented by an aromatherapy spa bath. Other areas include a comfortable lounge and attractive dining room, the setting for imaginative dinners and hearty breakfasts.
FACILITIES: 2 en suite 2 annexe en suite (1 GF) No smoking TVB tea/coffee No dogs (ex guide dogs) Licensed Cen ht TVL No children No coaches Jacuzzi Air bath with aromatherapy oils Dinner Last d 6pm **PRICES:** s £40-£60; d £70-£120✱ **LB PARKING:** 5

YOULGREAVE Map 07 SK26

♦♦♦ The Old Bakery
Church St DE45 1UR ☎ 01629 636887
e-mail: croasdell@oldbakeryyoulgreave.freeserve.co.uk
Dir: *from A6 2m S of Bakewell, take the B5056 and follow signs to Youlgreave. The Old Bakery is 100mtrs on right after church*
Located in the centre of the village the Old Bakery is close to the church and a wonderful base for exploring the surrounding areas, which includes Chatsworth House. Rooms are comfortable and well equipped and breakfast is taken in the dining room, which used to be the old shop and retains some of the original features.
FACILITIES: 2 rms 1 annexe en suite No smoking No dogs (ex guide dogs) Cen ht TVL No coaches **PRICES:** s £22-£35; d £32-£54✱ **BB PARKING:** 2

DEVON

ASHBURTON Map 03 SX76

See also Bickington

♦♦♦♦ Greencott
Landscove TQ13 7LZ ☎ 01803 762649
Dir: *take A38 to Plymouth, then 2nd exit signed Landscove. At top of slip rd turn left, follow for 2m, keep village green on right, opposite village hall*
Greencott is peacefully located and has attractive views and gardens. A warm and friendly welcome is extended to all guests and a homely and relaxed atmosphere prevails. Bedrooms are comfortable and well equipped. Traditional country cooking is served at the oak dining table.
FACILITIES: 2 en suite No smoking in bedrooms No smoking in dining room tea/coffee No dogs (ex guide dogs) Cen ht No coaches Dinner Last d by arrangement **PRICES:** d £36✱ **LB BB PARKING:** 3 **NOTES:** Closed 25-26 Dec

♦♦♦♦ The Rising Sun
Woodland TQ13 7JT ☎ 01364 652544 01364 654202
e-mail: mail@risingsunwoodland.co.uk
Dir: *turn off A38 Exeter/Plymouth at sign for Woodland and Denbury (which is shortly after sign Plymouth 26m) continue down lane 1.5m Rising Sun is on left*
Pleasantly located in attractive countryside and an excellent base with the Devon Expressway just a short drive away. A friendly welcome is extended to all at the Rising Sun. Bedrooms are comfortable and very well equipped. Dinner and breakfast include organic and local produce. In addition local wines and quality ales also feature in the spacious bar.
FACILITIES: 2 en suite (2 GF) No smoking in bedrooms No smoking in dining room TVB tea/coffee Cen ht Dinner Last d 9.15pm **PRICES:** s £28-£35; d £53-£5✱ **BB MEALS:** Lunch £12-£20alc Dinner £12-£20alc✱ **PARKING:** 30 **CARDS:**

♦♦♦♦ Gages Mill
Buckfastleigh Rd TQ13 7JW ☎ 01364 652391 01364 652391
e-mail: moore@gagesmill.co.uk
Dir: *Take A38 towards Plymouth, 2nd exit to Ashburton, Peartree Junction, cross over A38, 1st left by Shell Garage. 1st property on left*

Set in delightful grounds and well-tended gardens, on the edge of Dartmoor National Park, Gages Mill is an attractive 14th century former wool mill. The proprietors Chris and Annie are welcoming hosts. Guests will feel relaxed and enjoy the home-from-home atmosphere. Dinner features fresh, local and many organic ingredients. Pleasant lounges and a well stocked bar are available for added enjoyment.
FACILITIES: 8 en suite (1 GF) No smoking in dining room tea/coffee No dogs (ex guide dogs) Licensed Cen ht TVL No children 12yrs No coaches Croquet lawn Dinner Last d day before **PRICES:** s £21-£30; d £42-£60✱ **LB PARKING:** 10 **NOTES:** Closed Dec-Feb

ATHERINGTON Map 02 SS52

Premier Collection

♦♦♦♦♦ Springfield Garden
EX37 9JA ☎ 01769 560034 01769 560034
e-mail: broadgdn@eurobell.co.uk
Dir: *A39 Bideford Rd, then A377 Crediton Rd, after 5m turn onto B3227 Atherington, 0.5m on right*
The countryside location provides Springfield Garden with lovely panoramic views across the Taw Valley. The pretty half-acre cottage garden contains many unusual plants. The two bedrooms are comfortably furnished, with many useful extras and views of the surrounding countryside or the garden. Enjoyable home cooked dinners are available by prior arrangement. A lounge is also available to guests.
FACILITIES: 3 en suite No smoking TVB tea/coffee Cen ht No children 13yrs No coaches Dinner Last d noon **PRICES:** s £18-£25; d £40-£50✱ **LB BB PARKING:** 3 **CARDS:**

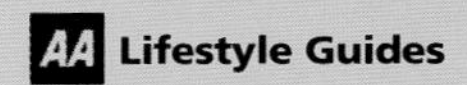

AXMINSTER Map 03 SY29

Premier Collection

♦♦♦♦♦ Kerrington House

Musbury Rd EX13 5JR ☎ 01297 35333
e-mail: jreaney@kerringtonhouse.com
Dir: *from Axminster town centre take A358 towards Seaton, Kerrington House on the left 0.5m from town centre*

This delightful period house, set in landscaped gardens, has been lovingly restored and sympathetically furnished. Bedrooms, decorated in soft neutral colours, are equipped with many thoughtful touches. The drawing room is light and airy, and antique pieces and personal treasures add to the feeling of well being. Dinner and breakfast are prepared with flair and imagination. Exclusive use for small house parties; whether friends, family or business.

FACILITIES: 5 en suite No smoking TVB tea/coffee Direct dial from bedrooms No dogs (ex guide dogs) Licensed Cen ht No coaches Dinner Last d 7pm **PRICES:** s £64-£75; d £88-£110* **LB**
CONF: Board 12 **PARKING:** 6 **CARDS:**

Premier Collection

♦♦♦♦♦ Lea Hill

Membury EX13 7AQ ☎ 01404 881881 🖷 01404 881890
e-mail: reception@leahill.co.uk
Dir: *from Chard A30 towards Honiton, in 3m turn left, follow signs through Membury village pass Trout Farm, Lea Hill is 0.5m on right. From Axminster take road signed Membury, out of Axminster over level crossing to Membury, as above*

Set in eight acres of stunning grounds and gardens, Lea Hill is the epitome of tranquillity. The annexes to the main house - a thatched Devon long house, which dates back to the 14th century - provide the accommodation. Bedrooms are furnished to a high standard and offer a thoughtful range of

continued

extras. Take tea on the terrace, or enjoy a game of golf on the 9-hole course. Breakfast is a highlight, with many ingredients sourced locally.

FACILITIES: 1 en suite 3 annexe en suite No smoking TVB tea/coffee Licensed Cen ht No children 16yrs No coaches **PRICES:** s £45-£50; d £70-£80* **PARKING:** 20

♦♦♦♦ Pump Farm *(ST261955)*

Whitford EX13 7NN ☎ 01297 552798 🖷 01297 552798
Mrs D Loud
e-mail: loud.pumpfarm@farmersweekly.net
Dir: *turn off A35 (Axminster-Honiton) at Kilmington, towards Whitford. Farmhouse on left at T junct in Whitford*

Situated in the peaceful village of Whitford between the A35 and Lyme Bay, this attractive 15th century thatched farmhouse has beams, wood panelling and an inglenook fireplace. It is convenient for the beach and coastal walks. The comfortable bedrooms are well appointed and a lounge is available for guest use. The farmhouse is no-smoking throughout.

FACILITIES: 2 en suite (1 fmly) no smoking TVB tea/coffee No dogs Cen ht TVL 180 acres organic/dairy/beef **PRICES:** s £20-£22; d £40-£44* **PARKING:** 4 **NOTES:** Closed Dec-Mar

♦♦♦♦ Shamwari

Musbury Rd, Abbey Gate EX13 8TT ☎ 01297 32838
🖷 01297 34465
e-mail: shamwariguesthouse@hotmail.com
Dir: *A35/A358 towards Musbury/Seaton, under bridge past large white house on left. Shamwari next on left around left bend next to layby*

Shamwari means 'my friend' and there is certainly a friendly welcome to be found here. Set in three acres with panoramic views of the Axe Valley, bedrooms are bright, comfortable and well equipped with numerous extras. Hearty breakfasts are served in the cosy dining room, where dinner is also available by prior arrangement. Pat Hicks was a Top Twenty Finalist in the AA Landlady of the Year Award 2002-2003.

FACILITIES: 3 en suite (1 GF) No smoking TVB tea/coffee Cen ht TVL No children 16yrs No coaches **PRICES:** s £21-£24; d £42-£48 **LB PARKING:** 3

♦♦♦♦ Goodmans House

Furley, Membury EX13 7TU ☎ 01404 881690 🖷 01404 881690
e-mail: p.a.spenceruk@yahoo.co.uk
Dir: *A30 at top of hill leaving Chard fork left signed Wambrook, after 3m (past Ferne Animal Sanctuary) turn right signed Stockland after 1m turn left signed Furley/Membury at T junct turn left signed Ford follow Goodmans sign*

FACILITIES: 2 en suite 5 annexe en suite (6 GF) No smoking TVB tea/coffee Cen ht No coaches Croquet lawn Dinner Last d 24 hrs **PRICES:** s fr £30; d £58-£66 * **LB PARKING:** 10 **NOTES:** Closed 15 Nov-24 Dec & 3 Jan-14 Feb

♦♦♦ Sellers Wood Farmhouse *(SY274941)*

Combpyne Rd, Musbury EX13 8SR ☎ 01297 552944
🖷 01297 552944 Mr & Mrs Pemberton
e-mail: sellerswood@hotmail.com
Dir: *A358 Axminster to Seaton road on reaching the Jet garage at Musbury turn left. At Musbury stores/post office turn right and along Combpyne Road for 0.75m heading out of village at the end of long Devon-stone wall turn left into driveway*

Situated on the edge of the village of Musbury between Axminster and Seaton, this delightful 16th-century farmhouse with its wealth of beams and flagstone floors, enjoys an elevated position with sweeping views over the Axe Valley to the cliffs of Beer. Tasty farmhouse dinners using home grown vegetables, are available by prior arrangement.

FACILITIES: 4 rms (1 fmly) No smoking tea/coffee Cen ht TVL No children 6yrs Croquet lawn 3 acres non-working Dinner Last d before 9am
PRICES: s £23-£27; d £42-£48* **LB PARKING:** 6

AMPTON Map 03 SS92

Premier Collection

♦♦♦♦♦ The Bark House

Oakford Bridge EX16 9HZ ☎ 01398 351236

Dir: *off M5 junct 27 onto A361. When this meets the A361 (N) take the A396 signposted to Minehead. The Bark house approx 8m N on A396*

Situated in the Exe Valley and surrounded by the picturesque countryside and pretty villages of Exmoor, this charming hotel offers a unique blend of deep comfort, delicious food and pampering hospitality and service. The owners know just what it takes to make guests feel special, and the house exudes character, with low beams, traditional furnishings and log fires. Dinner is lovingly prepared from fresh local produce and breakfast, with many house specialities, is also a memorable experience.

FACILITIES: 5 en suite (1 fmly) No smoking in bedrooms No smoking in dining room TVB Direct dial from bedrooms Licensed Cen ht No children No coaches Dinner Last d 7.45pm **PRICES:** s £45-£55; d £86-£110 **PARKING:** 15

♦♦♦♦ Newhouse Farm *(SS892228)*

X16 9JE ☎ 01398 351347 Mrs A Boldry

-mail: anne.boldry@btclick.com

ir: *5m W of Bampton on B3227. Do not go into Oakford village*

et in forty acres of rolling farmland this delightful farmhouse rovides guests with a warm, friendly, informal atmosphere. Smart ustic bedrooms are well-equipped with modern facilities. Delicious vell-prepared and imaginative, home-cooked dinners, using the est local produce are available by prior arrangement. Home-nade bread and preserves are a feature at breakfast.

ACILITIES: 3 en suite (1 fmly) (1 GF) No smoking TVB tea/coffee No dogs ex guide dogs) Cen ht TVL No children 10yrs Fishing 42 acres sheep Dinner ast d 4pm **PRICES:** s £25-£30; d £45-£50✻ **PARKING:** 3 **IOTES:** Closed Xmas

♦♦♦♦ Old Rectory

)akford EX16 9EW ☎ 01398 351486 🖷 01398 351486

-mail: prot@oakford57.fsnet.co.uk

ir: *B3227 to Oakford, in village turn right at shop, after 200yds left at 'olme Place. House on left at end of drive*

ocated on the edge of the village, this charming Victorian rectory set in several acres of gardens and vineyards. The spacious ooms are decorated and furnished with elegance. Enjoyable home ooking and a delightful location, together with the unobtrusive iendliness of the owners, ensure a pleasant stay.

ACILITIES: 2 rms (1 en suite) No smoking TVB tea/coffee No dogs Cen ht o children 15yrs No coaches Dinner Last d 5pm **PRICES:** s fr £30; d £40-50✻ **PARKING:** 3 **NOTES:** Closed Dec-Jan

ANTHAM Map 03 SX64

♦♦♦ Sloop

'Q7 3AJ ☎ 01548 560489 & 560215 🖷 01548 561940

ir: *from A379 at mini rdbt at Church Stow take Bantham Rd, 2.5m to 'llage, on left*

)nly a short distance from the beach this 16th-century smugglers' ın is well equipped with modern and comfortable facilities and ıe bedrooms have many thoughtful extra touches. The bar and estaurant have exposed beams and log-burning stoves where fine ining or lighter meals are available and feature seafood and fresh sh.

ACILITIES: 5 en suite (2 fmly) TVB tea/coffee Cen ht No coaches Dinner ast d 10pm **LB MEALS:** Lunch £11-£24.40alc Dinner £11-£24.40alc✻ **ARKING:** 35 **CARDS:**

BARNSTAPLE Map 02 SS53

See also Atherington

♦♦♦♦ *Home Park (SS553360)*

Lower Blakewell, Muddiford EX31 4ET ☎ 01271 342955 🖷 01271 342955 Mrs M Lethaby

e-mail: m-lethaby@gofornet.co.uk

Dir: *from Barnstaple take A39 Lynton rd, fork left on B3230 & take 2nd left to Home Park, continue to very end of no-through road*

With both rooms facing south, across the delightful North Devon countryside, Home Park Farm is peacefully located in award-winning gardens. The attractively presented bedrooms are comfortable with many personal touches. Guests have the use of the lovely conservatory as well as the inviting lounge.

FACILITIES: 2 en suite (1 fmly) No smoking TVB tea/coffee No dogs Cen ht TVL 70 acres non-working Dinner Last d previous day **PARKING:** 2 **NOTES:** Closed 21-31 Dec

♦♦♦♦ Yeo Dale Hotel

Pilton Bridge EX31 1PG ☎ 01271 342954 🖷 01271 344530

e-mail: stay@yeodalehotel.co.uk

Dir: *from A361 Barnstaple take A39 Lynton, hotel on left just after Pilton Park*

Deceptively spacious, this elegant Georgian town house is just a few minutes walk from the town centre across the River Yeo. Bedrooms at this fine old house, some dating back to the 17th century, are comfortable and well furnished. Breakfast is taken in the stylish new dining room, which has been recently redecorated by the new owners.

FACILITIES: 10 rms (4 en suite) (3 fmly) No smoking in 5 bedrooms No smoking in dining room No smoking in lounges TVB tea/coffee No dogs (ex guide dogs) Licensed Cen ht TVL No coaches **PRICES:** s £22.50-£30; d £43-£54✻ **CARDS:**

♦♦♦♦ A The Spinney Country Guest House

Shirwell EX31 4JR ☎ 01271 850282

e-mail: thespinney@shirwell.fsnet.co.uk

Dir: *3m from Barnstaple on A39 Lynton road. On left through village opposite shop*

FACILITIES: 5 rms (3 en suite) (2 fmly) No smoking TVB tea/coffee Licensed Cen ht TVL No coaches Dinner Last d 5pm **PRICES:** s £19-£23; d £38-£46✻ **LB BB PARKING:** 6

♦♦♦ Cresta

26 Sticklepath Hill EX31 2BU ☎ 01271 374022 🖷 01271 374022

Dir: *M5/A361, then B3233 towards Bideford, cross long bridge up Sticklepath Hill (main road) railway station on L, top of hill on R*

James and Judy provide warm and friendly hospitality, at this detached property on the outskirts of the town. The comfortable bedrooms are well equipped, with two available on the ground floor. A hearty breakfast is served in the recently redecorated dining room.

FACILITIES: 6 rms (4 en suite) (2 fmly) (2 GF) No smoking in dining room No smoking in lounges TVB tea/coffee Cen ht No coaches **PRICES:** s £16-£18; d £36✻ **BB PARKING:** 6 **CARDS:**

A indicates an Associate entry, which has been inspected and rated by the ETC or the RAC in England

England

BARNSTAPLE continued

♦♦♦ Rowden Barton *(SS538306)*

Roundswell EX31 3NP ☎ 01271 344365 Mrs J Dallyn

***Dir:** 2m South of Barnstaple on B3232*

With spectacular views of the surrounding countryside, a warm welcome awaits guests to Rowden Barton. Both of the comfortable bedrooms enjoy the rural views and share an adjoining bathroom. Dinner is available by prior arrangement in the bright and airy dining room. Delicious breakfasts, featuring fresh farm eggs, home-made bread and preserves provide a fine start to the day.

FACILITIES: 2 rms No smoking No dogs (ex guide dogs) Cen ht TVL No children 12yrs 90 acres beef & sheep **PRICES:** s fr £17; d fr £34* **BB**
PARKING: 4

♦♦♦ Twitchen Farm

Challacombe EX31 4TT ☎ 01598 763568
e-mail: holidays@twitchen.co.uk

***Dir:** exit M5 junct 27 onto A361 towards Barnstaple, A399 towards Combe Martin approx 10m on right B3358 to Challacombe, farm 0.5m on left after village*

FACILITIES: 2 en suite 6 annexe en suite (3 fmly) No smoking in bedrooms No smoking in dining room TVB tea/coffee Licensed Cen ht No coaches Dinner Last d 10am **PRICES:** s £27-£33; d £38-£52* **LB BB**
PARKING: 10 **CARDS:**

BEER — Map 03 SY28

♦♦♦ *Bay View*

Fore St EX12 3EE ☎ 01297 20489

***Dir:** Turn off A3052 & follow signs to Beer. Drive towards the sea, Bay View last building on left*

This delightful guest house is just a stone's throw from the beach in the centre of this charming fishing village. It is popular with walkers for its easy access to the Southwest Coastal Path. Bedrooms are bright and comfortably furnished. During the day, snacks and light meals are available in the adjacent tearooms.

FACILITIES: 6 rms (2 en suite) 2 annexe en suite (1 fmly) No smoking in dining room TVB tea/coffee Cen ht TVL **NOTES:** Closed Dec-Feb rs Nov & Mar

BICKINGTON (Near Newton Abbot) — Map 03 SX77

♦♦♦♦ Chipley Farm *(SX794726)*

TQ12 6JW ☎ 01626 821486 & 821947 📠 01626 821486
Mrs L Westcott
e-mail: louisa@chipleyfarmholidays.co.uk

***Dir:** From A38 take junct signed Newton Abbot. At Drum Bridges rdbt take 3rd exit (Bickington) & continue until the Toby Jug pub. Turn left, right, left and fork left. Follow lane past traditional Dutch Barn & Chipley Farm is 1st on right*

A genuinely warm and friendly welcome awaits at this working dairy farm. The hosts, with their pet dogs, make all guests feel like part of the family. Bedrooms, one of which has a four-poster bed, have modern facilities and many thoughtful extras. Dinner (by prior arrangement), and breakfast are taken either in the dining room, or in front of the Aga in the farmhouse kitchen, with Louisa and the family.

FACILITIES: 3 rms (1 en suite) (1 fmly) (2 GF) No smoking TVB tea/coffee No dogs Cen ht painting lessons 160 acres dairy Dinner Last d previous day
PRICES: d £50* **LB PARKING:** 6

♦♦♦♦ *Dartmoor Halfway Inn*

TQ12 6JW ☎ 01626 821270 📠 01626 821820

***Dir:** Leave A38 at Drumbridges Rdbt, signposted Ilsington/Bickington, in 3m turn L onto A383*

Recently converted, comfortable accommodation is at the rear of this character inn. With 12th century origins, the Dartmoor Halfway Inn is renowned for its extensive menu; food is served from breakfast until dinner. As its name suggests, the inn is located half way between Newton Abbot and Ashburton, and has a welcoming atmosphere.

FACILITIES: 4 annexe en suite No smoking in 2 bedrooms No smoking in area of dining room STV TVB tea/coffee Direct dial from bedrooms Cen ht ch fac Dinner Last d 10pm **PARKING:** 100 **CARDS:**

♦♦♦♦ East Burne *(SX799711)*

TQ12 6PA ☎ 01626 821496 📠 01626 821105
Mr & Mrs M Pallett
e-mail: info@eastburnefarm.screaming.net

***Dir:** 1.5m from A38 off A383*

Peacefully situated in 14 acres of countryside, this medieval hall-house is a comfortable family home. This is a non-working farm, with a pond and a stream, and the fields surrounding the house are ideal for walking. One bedroom has a four-poster bed, the other is on the ground floor, and both are delightfully furnished and many extra comforts. Breakfast features organic produce from the farm, as does dinner, available by prior arrangement.

FACILITIES: 2 en suite 1 annexe en suite (2 GF) No smoking TV2B tea/coffee TVL Outdoor swimming pool (heated) 14 acres non-working Last d by arrangement **PRICES:** s £30; d £50 **LB PARKING:** 8 **CARDS:**

BIDEFORD — Map 02 SS42

See also Westward Ho!

♦♦♦♦ Mount Hotel

Northdown Rd EX39 3LP ☎ 01237 473748 📠 01271 373813
e-mail: andrew@themountbideford.fsnet.co.uk

***Dir:** Bideford turning off A39, right after Rydon garage, premises 600 yards*

A warm welcome is assured at this delightful, centrally located Georgian property. Bedrooms are comfortably furnished and well equipped; a ground-floor room is available for less mobile guests. A hearty breakfast is served in the elegant dining room, and there is a cosy sitting room.

FACILITIES: 7 en suite (1 fmly) No smoking TVB tea/coffee No dogs (ex guide dogs) Licensed Cen ht TVL No coaches **PRICES:** s £26-£28; d £50-£54* **LB PARKING:** 5 **NOTES:** Closed Xmas **CARDS:**

♦♦♦♦ Pines at Eastleigh

The Pines, Eastleigh EX39 4PA ☎ 01271 860561
e-mail: pirrie@thepinesateastleigh.co.uk

***Dir:** turn off A39 Barnstaple/Bideford rd onto A386 signposted Torrington. After 0.75m turn left signposted Eastleigh, 2m to village, house on right*

This Grade II listed Georgian farmhouse is set in seven acres of lovingly tended gardens and surrounded by open countryside. Most of the comfortably furnished bedrooms are situated around a charming courtyard. Breakfast is served in the pleasant dining room and there is also a lounge for guest use.

continued

FACILITIES: 2 en suite 4 annexe en suite No smoking TVB tea/coffee Direct dial from bedrooms Licensed Cen ht No coaches Board games **PRICES:** s £28-£45; d £56-£90✻ **PARKING:** 12 **CARDS:**

♦♦♦ Sunset Hotel

Landcross EX39 5JA ☎ 01237 472962 📠 01237 422520
e-mail: hazellamb@hotmail.com
Dir: *from Bideford Town take A386, 1.5m to Landcross, hotel on left*

With glorious views over open countryside, this small, friendly hotel offers a warm welcome. The individually furnished and decorated bedrooms are comfortable and well equipped. A cosy lounge is available for guests and in the adjoining dining room, home-cooked dinners, which are available by prior arrangement, feature fresh local produce.
FACILITIES: 4 en suite (2 fmly) No smoking TVB tea/coffee No dogs Licensed Cen ht TVL No coaches Dinner Last d 7pm **PRICES:** s £50-£60; d £60-£70✻ **LB PARKING:** 6 **NOTES:** Closed Oct-Mar
CARDS:

BOVEY TRACEY — Map 03 SX87

Premier Collection

♦♦♦♦♦ Brookfield House

Challabrook Ln TQ13 9DF ☎ 01626 836181
📠 01626 836182
e-mail: brookfieldh@tinyworld.co.uk
Dir: *A38-A382 to Bovey Tracey. Left at 1st rdbt, then right at T-junct. After 300 yds turn left into Challabrook Lane. House is on the right after 75 yds*

With the benefit of panoramic views over Dartmoor, this charming Edwardian house is located on the edge of the attractive town. Set in two acres of park-like grounds, this is a perfect choice for those seeking peace, tranquillity and seclusion. The individually decorated bedrooms are comfortable and exceptionally well-equipped, with countryside views an added bonus. Breakfast features locally produced bacon and sausages and home-made breads and preserves. Dinner also comes highly recommended and is available by prior arrangement.
FACILITIES: 3 en suite No smoking TVB tea/coffee No dogs (ex guide dogs) Cen ht No children 12yrs No coaches **PRICES:** s £35-£42; d £50-£64✻ **LB PARKING:** 6 **NOTES:** Closed Dec & Jan
CARDS:

Premier Collection

♦♦♦♦♦ *Front House Lodge*

East St TQ13 9EL ☎ 01626 832202 📠 832202
e-mail: fronthouselodge@aol.com
Dir: *turn off A38 onto A382 into Bovey Tracey, through town centre, Front House Lodge is past the Town Hall on right*

continued

Front House Lodge

This delightful 16th-century home has historical connections with the Civil War and, from its central position in this lovely old town, offers comfortable accommodation with a unique style. Beamed ceilings and old fireplaces, combined with lovely old antique pieces and an abundance of china and other personal treasures, create a charming atmosphere. Supper is available by prior arrangement and fresh produce is used in the preparation of delicious breakfasts.
FACILITIES: 6 rms (5 en suite) (2 fmly) No smoking TVB tea/coffee No dogs Licensed Cen ht TVL Dinner Last d 10am **PARKING:** 6
CARDS:

♦♦♦♦ *Cromwell Arms Hotel*

Fore St TQ13 9AE ☎ 01626 833473 📠 01626 836873
e-mail: cromwell@transuk.co.uk
This historic inn dates back to the 17th century and is situated at the heart of the town. Guest rooms are stylish and provided with quality, comfortable furnishings, one room is suitable for families. A choice of dining is available in either the bar or restaurant and a no-smoking lounge is also available for guest use.
FACILITIES: 12 en suite (2 fmly) No smoking in dining room STV TVB tea/coffee Direct dial from bedrooms Cen ht Dinner Last d 9.30pm
PARKING: 25 **CARDS:**

♦♦♦♦ *Cleavelands*

TQ13 9SH ☎ 01647 277349 📠 01647 277349
Dir: *A382 Bovey Tracey/Moretonhampstead Rd, 5m L into Lustleigh, through village, turn L, to T-junct turn R, house on L*
Tucked away in rural tranquillity, this spacious and attractive country house is set in impressive gardens. Bedrooms are traditionally furnished and public areas are comfortable and feature work by local artists. Dishes such as freshly baked apples add an interesting and refreshing change at breakfast where menus feature fresh, local and organic produce.
FACILITIES: 3 en suite (1 fmly) No smoking TVB tea/coffee Cen ht No coaches Woodland walks/rides River & moor adjacent
PARKING: 7 **NOTES:** Closed Xmas

BRAUNTON — Map 02 SS43

♦♦♦♦ Denham House

North Buckland EX33 1HY ☎ 01271 890297
e-mail: info@denhamhouse.co.uk
Dir: *on A361 Barnstaple/Ilfracombe road, take 2nd left after Knowle signed North Buckland. House in centre of hamlet*
FACILITIES: 6 en suite (2 fmly) No smoking in bedrooms No smoking in dining room TVB tea/coffee No dogs Licensed Cen ht TVL No coaches Pool Table games room Dinner Last d 10am **PRICES:** s £30-£40; d £50-£60✻
LB PARKING: 8

England

BRIDESTOWE Map 02 SX58

♦♦♦♦ ***Week Farm (SX519913)***

EX20 4HZ ☎ 01837 861221 📠 01837 861221
Mrs Margaret Hockridge
e-mail: weekfarm@biscuits.win-uknet
Dir: *exit A30 at Sourton junct, turn right then left signposted Bridestowe, 2nd right, cross dual carriageway, left at x-roads, house 0.5m on right*
A delicious complimentary cream tea awaits guests to this 17th century farmhouse. Surrounded by undulating countryside, it is an ideal base from which to explore the area. In cool weather, log fires burn in the lounge and in the summer the heated pool is available. Traditional farmhouse breakfasts and dinner by prior arrangement can be enjoyed in the dining room. Bedrooms are furnished in traditional style, providing comfort and character.
FACILITIES: 5 en suite (2 fmly) No smoking TVB tea/coffee Cen ht TVL Outdoor swimming pool (heated) 180 acres sheep Dinner Last d 5pm **PARKING:** 10 **NOTES:** Closed Xmas **CARDS:**

BRIXHAM Map 03 SX95

♦♦♦ Harbour View Hotel

65 King St TQ5 9TH ☎ 01803 853052
Dir: *follow A380 onto A3022 Brixham rd to town centre/harbour, left at lights, right at T-junct, hotel on right of inner harbour*
This pleasant house overlooks the harbour and enjoys views across Tor Bay. The friendly proprietors provide comfortable and attractive accommodation. A pleasant lounge area is available for guests in the dining room where traditional well cooked and appetising breakfasts are served.
FACILITIES: 8 en suite (1 fmly) No smoking in 2 bedrooms No smoking in dining room TVB tea/coffee No dogs Cen ht No coaches **PRICES:** s £25-£29; d £40-£48* **LB PARKING:** 5 **CARDS:**

♦♦♦ ***Richmond House Hotel***

Higher Manor Rd TQ5 8HA ☎ 01803 882391 📠 01803 882391
e-mail: mail@therichmondhouse.co.uk
Dir: *into Brixham on A3022, 1st L after Golden Lion pub (Lower Manor Rd). House at junction of Lower & Higher Manor Rd*
Quietly located a few minutes walk from Brixham's historic harbour, this detached Victorian residence boasts fine south facing views over the town. The attractively decorated bedrooms are well equipped; one situated on the ground floor, suitable for the less mobile. Freshly-cooked breakfasts are served in the pleasant dining room, and there is a selection of board games and toys in the lounge.
FACILITIES: 6 en suite (2 fmly) No smoking in bedrooms No smoking in dining room TVB tea/coffee Cen ht TVL No coaches **PARKING:** 6 **CARDS:**

BUCKFAST Map 03 SX76

♦♦♦ Furzeleigh Mill Country Hotel

Old Ashburton Rd TQ11 0JR ☎ 01364 643476 📠 01364 643876
e-mail: enquiries@furzeleigh.co.uk
Dir: *Off Devon Expressway(A38) at Dartbridge junct, right at end of slip rd, right opposite Little Chef signposted Ashburton/Prince Town (do not cross River Dart bridge) Hotel 200yds right*
Conveniently close to the A38, yet set in open countryside, Furzeleigh Mill is an ideal base for touring the moorland and many of the nearby villages. A spacious family room is available as well as a separate lounge and bar. Good home-cooked dinners are served in the Mill Restaurant.
FACILITIES: 15 rms (14 en suite) (2 fmly) No smoking in 6 bedrooms No smoking in dining room No smoking in 1 lounge TVB tea/coffee Licensed Cen ht TVL No coaches Dinner Last d 8.10pm **PRICES:** s £23.50-£35.50; d £45-£62* **LB PARKING:** 32 **NOTES:** Closed 23 Dec-2 Jan **CARDS:**

BUCKFASTLEIGH Map 03 SX76

♦♦♦♦ Kilbury Manor

Colston Rd TQ11 0LN ☎ 01364 644079 📠 01364 644059
e-mail: accommodation@kilbury.co.uk
Dir: *off A38 at Dart Bridge junct onto B3380 (Buckfastleigh), L after 0.5m (Old Totnes Rd), R at bottom, Kilbury Manor sign on wall on L*
Friendly hospitality and excellent cuisine feature at this tranquil, comfortable country house, situated on the outskirts of the village and surrounded by six acres of gardens, orchards, pasture and a trout pond. Menus offer imaginative dishes, including vegetarian options, and use fresh vegetables from the farm garden. Cookery courses are available here.
FACILITIES: 4 en suite (1 fmly) No smoking in bedrooms No smoking in dining room No smoking in lounges TVB tea/coffee Cen ht No coaches Dinner Last d before 12pm **PRICES:** s £30-£35; d £54-£62* **PARKING:** 6

BUDLEIGH SALTERTON Map 03 SY08

♦♦♦♦ Long Range Hotel

5 Vales Rd EX9 6HS ☎ 01395 443321 📠 01395 442132
e-mail: info@thelongrangehotel.co.uk
Dir: *Turn off East Budleigh Road (on north east access to Budleigh Salterton) into Raleigh Rd, after 20yds turn right into Vales Rd. Hotel on left*
This charming hotel has a relaxed and friendly atmosphere, created by the welcoming proprietors. Set in quiet surroundings, the hotel is within walking distance of the town centre and the beach. Bedrooms are attractive and comfortable. There is a lounge and a conservatory-bar, with lovely views, where guests can enjoy a pre-dinner drink. Delightful home-cooked meals make good use of fresh local ingredients.
FACILITIES: 7 en suite (1 fmly) No smoking TVB tea/coffee No dogs Licensed Cen ht No children 10yrs No coaches Dinner Last d 8.45pm **PRICES:** s £30-£35; d £60-£70* **LB PARKING:** 7 **CARDS:**

♦♦♦♦ Lufflands

Yettington EX9 7BP ☎ 01395 568422 📠 01395 568810
e-mail: Lufflands@compuserve.com
Dir: *M5 junct 30, A376 for Exmouth, left onto B3179 at Clyst St George through Woodbury, straight across Four Firs x-roads to Yettington, on left*
This former farmhouse is situated in the pretty village of Yettington. Bedrooms are comfortably furnished; some have views of the delightful rear garden. The former kitchen, with its inglenook fireplace, is now the TV lounge and dining room where guests can start the day with a traditional English breakfast.
FACILITIES: 3 en suite (1 fmly) No smoking tea/coffee No dogs (ex guide dogs) Cen ht No coaches **PRICES:** s £19-£22; d £38-£44* **LB BB PARKING:** 10 **CARDS:**

CHAGFORD Map 03 SX78

Premier Collection

♦♦♦♦♦ Parford Well

Sandy Park TQ13 8JW ☎ 01647 433353
Dir: *A30 onto A382, after 3m turn left at Sandy Park towards Drewsteignton, house 50yds on left*
Set in delightful grounds, this attractive house is a restful and friendly home. Taste and style are combined in the comfortable, well-equipped accommodation. The lounge overlooks the well-tended gardens and in the two dining rooms, one smaller and more intimate, guests may take breakfast at fine tables dressed with silver and crisp linen. Freshly cooked breakfasts, made with quality fresh local ingredients, provide a delightful start to the day.

continued

Parford Well

FACILITIES: 3 en suite No smoking No dogs (ex guide dogs) Cen ht TVL No children 8yrs No coaches **PRICES:** s £30-£70; d £55-£70✻ **PARKING:** 4 **NOTES:** Closed Xmas

HAWLEIGH Map 03 SS71

♦♦♦ The Barn-Rodgemonts

odgemonts EX18 7ET ☎ 01769 580200
mail: pyerodgemonts@btinternet.com
ir: *from Exeter take A377 at Eggesford station (level crossing on left) turn ght B3042 to Chawleigh, in 1.5m at T junct left onto B3096 towards hulmleigh in 0.5m signed Chawleigh Week fork left after 250mtrs odgemonts drive on right*

is attractive house is set amid peaceful countryside and offers iendly hospitality and tranquillity. Bedrooms are located in the atched converted barn, each with views of the orchard, from hich the proprietors produce their own apple juice. Along with her home-made and local produce this features in the delightful eakfasts and (by prior arrangement) Aga-cooked dinners, served the farmhouse kitchen.
CILITIES: 2 en suite (1 fmly) No smoking TVB tea/coffee Cen ht No aches **PRICES:** s £23-£27; d £40-£44✻ **LB PARKING:** 3

HERITON BISHOP Map 03 SX79

♦ Holly Farm *(SX767943)*

X6 6JD ☎ 01647 24616 & 07778 917 409 📠 01647 24182
r G Sears
mail: graham.sears@lineone.net
ir: *turn off A30 at Cheriton Bishop, 0.5m into village, take the second rning right signed for Yeoford, farm 1m on left*
tuated in the heart of beautiful Mid-Devon countryside, yet nvenient for the A30, this working sheep farm and livery stables fers comfortable, practical accommodation, with a spacious unge offering TV, stereo and reading material. Riding, golf, ooting and escorted tours of the Moors can all be arranged.

continued

FACILITIES: 3 rms (3 GF) No smoking in bedrooms No smoking in dining room TV1B tea/coffee No dogs (ex guide dogs) Cen ht TVL No children 2yrs Outdoor swimming pool (heated) Riding can be arranged 50 acres sheep horses **PRICES:** s £20-£25; d £40-£45✻ **LB PARKING:** 6

CHILLATON Map 02 SX48

♦♦♦♦♦ Tor Cottage

PL16 0JE ☎ 01822 860248 📠 01822 860126
e-mail: info@torcottage.co.uk
Dir: *from A30 exit Lewdown through Chillaton towards Tavistock. Right 300mtrs after Post Office signed 'Bridlepath No Public Vehicular access' to end*

Tor Cottage, nestling in its own valley with 18 acres of grounds, is an escape from the rest of the world. Rooms are spacious and elegant - the cottage-wing bedroom has a separate sitting room and the garden rooms (expertly restored from former barns) have their own wood burners. The gardens are lovely, with a stream and many secluded little corners. An exceptional range of dishes is offered at breakfast, taken in the conservatory dining room or on the terrace.
FACILITIES: 1 en suite 3 annexe en suite (3 GF) No smoking TVB tea/coffee No dogs (ex guide dogs) Cen ht TVL No children 16yrs No coaches Outdoor swimming pool (heated) Riding,golf,fishing arranged locally. **PRICES:** s £89; d £94-£130✻ **LB PARKING:** 8 **NOTES:** Closed 17 Dec-7 Jan **CARDS:** 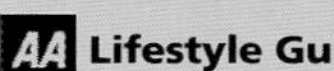

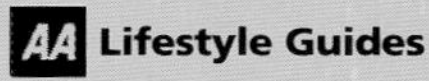

See advert under TAVISTOCK

England

CHUDLEIGH Map 03 SX87

♦♦♦♦ Farmborough House

Old Exeter Rd TQ13 0DR ☎ 01626 853258 📠 01626 853258
e-mail: holidays@farmborough-house.com
Dir: *B3344 to Chudleigh. At war memorial, turn into Old Exeter St, proceed for 1m. After bridge crossing A38, house on left*

Idyllically located in ten acres of grounds and gardens Farmborough House enjoys wonderful country views. The friendly proprietors are most welcoming hosts. Bedrooms are comfortably furnished and a thoughtful range of extra facilities is provided. Breakfast features good quality fresh and local ingredients including dry-cured bacon and pork and apple sausages. Dinner, all homemade, is available by prior arrangement.
FACILITIES: 3 en suite No smoking TVB tea/coffee No dogs Cen ht TVL No children 15yrs No coaches Dinner Last d 3pm **PRICES:** d £50-£56✻ **PARKING:** 6

CHULMLEIGH Map 03 SS61

♦♦♦♦ Old Bakehouse

South Molton St EX18 7BW ☎ 01769 580074 & 580137
📠 01769 580074
e-mail: theoldbakehouse@talk21.com
Dir: *off A377, onto B3096, proceed 2m to village, turn left into S Molton St, guest house is 100yds on left*

This 16th-century thatched house is situated in the centre of the medieval town. A cosy licensed restaurant, it offers fixed-price evening and lunch menus which feature local produce, and dishes are imaginative and carefully home-made. Of the accommodation on offer, some of the charming bedrooms are across a courtyard in the original village bakery.
FACILITIES: 3 en suite 1 annexe en suite (1 fmly) (1 GF) No smoking TVB tea/coffee No dogs (ex guide dogs) Licensed Cen ht No children 5yrs ch fac No coaches Painting holidays,Fishing,Riding,Golf all nearby. Dinner Last d 10am **PRICES:** s £28-£31.50; d £50-£55✻ LB
CARDS:

CLOVELLY Map 02 SS32

♦♦♦♦ Fuchsia Cottage

Burscott, Higher Clovelly EX39 5RR ☎ 01237 431398
e-mail: curtis@fuchsiacottage.fslife.co.uk
Dir: *turn onto B3237 from Clovelly Cross Rdbt. After approx 0.75m turn right into Burscott (signposted). Establishment approx 300yds on right*
Fuchsia Cottage is situated down a quiet country lane and is an ideal base for visiting the picturesque village of Clovelly. A modern house, it benefits from stunning views over the surrounding countryside. The comfortable bedrooms are delightfully decorated and well equipped with many extras. One room is available on the ground floor.
FACILITIES: 3 rms (2 en suite) No smoking TVB tea/coffee Cen ht No coaches **PRICES:** s £17; d £40✻ BB **PARKING:** 3

COLEFORD Map 03 SS70

♦♦♦♦ The New Inn

EX17 5BZ ☎ 01363 84242 📠 01363 85044
e-mail: new-inn@reallyreal-group .com
A 13th century listed inn, full of character, with cob and thatch, beams and a reassuring solidity. The chatty resident parrot, 'Captain', provides a somewhat unique welcome to all. A varied menu is augmented by excellent local fish from Brixham, and there is a stream-side patio for al fresco meals. Bedrooms are spacious and well appointed with contemporary comforts enhancing the original architectural features.
FACILITIES: 6 en suite (1 fmly) No smoking in bedrooms No smoking in dining room TVB tea/coffee Direct dial from bedrooms No dogs (ex guide dogs) Cen ht No coaches Dinner Last d 10pm **PRICES:** s £55-£65; d £65-£80✻ **MEALS:** Lunch £6.95-£14.95 Dinner £6.95-£14.95&alc✻
PARKING: 50 **NOTES:** Closed Xmas **CARDS:**

COLYFORD Map 03 SY29

♦♦♦♦ Lower Orchard

Swan Hill Rd EX24 6QQ ☎ 01297 553615
Dir: *on A3052 in Colyford, between Lyme Regis & Sidmouth*
Conveniently situated for Axminster, Sidmouth and Lyme Regis, this modern ranch-style family house enjoys fine rural views over the Axe Valley. Bedrooms are very spacious, well-equipped and located on the ground floor. Breakfast is served in the lounge/dining room, which has patio doors leading to a private sun terrace and splash pool.
FACILITIES: 2 en suite (1 fmly) (2 GF) No smoking TVB tea/coffee Cen ht TVL No coaches Outdoor swimming pool (heated) **PRICES:** s £35-£40; d £45-£50 **PARKING:** 3

COLYTON Map 03 SY29

♦♦♦♦ The White Cottage

Dolphin St EX24 6NA ☎ 01297 552401 📠 01297 553207
e-mail: info@colytoncottages.com
Dir: *turn left off A3052 towards Colyton, go through town centre towards Shute, cottage right after Kingfisher pub*
Centrally located in this picturesque village, these charming comfortable cottages have recently been converted from an old barn and still retain the character and beams of the original building. Each cottage includes lounge/dining room and fully equipped kitchen. Your hearty cooked breakfast will be delivered to your cottage.
FACILITIES: 4 en suite (2 GF) No smoking TVB tea/coffee Direct dial from bedrooms No dogs (ex guide dogs) Cen ht TVL No coaches **PRICES:** s £22.50-£27.50; d £45-£55✻ LB **PARKING:** 8

CREDITON Map 03 SS80

♦♦♦♦ Fircroft

George Hill EX17 2DS ☎ 01363 774224
e-mail: fircroftbb@talk21.com
Dir: *on A377 to Barnstaple at the green turn right. At x-roads straight over 1st on right*

Quietly located with views over the market town below, this delightful double-fronted Victorian home provides business and leisure guests alike with spacious bedrooms, thoughtfully equipped with numerous extra facilities. In warmer weather guests are welcome to relax in the South facing gardens.

FACILITIES: 2 en suite (2 fmly) No smoking TVB tea/coffee No dogs (ex guide dogs) Cen ht No coaches **PRICES:** s £35; d £46✳ **PARKING:** 6

CROYDE Map 02 SS43

♦♦♦♦ West Winds

Moor Ln EX33 1PA ☎ 01271 890489 📠 01271 890489
e-mail: chris@croydewestwinds.freeserve.co.uk
Dir: *in village centre turn left and 1st left again following signs to Croyde Bay*

With the spectacular backdrop of Croyde Beach, this is a small, personally-run establishment. Bedrooms are attractively decorated and very well equipped. In addition, the conservatory lounge benefits from similar views. Hearty, traditional breakfasts always prove popular; morning coffees and afternoon teas are also available.

FACILITIES: 5 en suite No smoking TVB tea/coffee Licensed Cen ht No coaches **PRICES:** s £26-£36; d £54-£72✳ **PARKING:** 6 **NOTES:** Closed Dec-Feb **CARDS:**

♦♦♦♦ The Whiteleaf

Croyde Rd EX33 1PN ☎ 01271 890266
Dir: *turn off A361 at Braunton for Croyde, Whiteleaf is on left at 'Road Narrows' sign*

This attractive house is within easy walking distance of both the pretty village of Croyde and the sandy, surfing beach. A warm family welcome awaits guests. Each of the well-equipped bedrooms has its own individual character and charm. Ambitious and imaginative dinners using fresh, seasonal produce are served each evening in the restaurant.

FACILITIES: 5 en suite (2 fmly) No smoking in 2 bedrooms No smoking in dining room No smoking in 1 lounge TVB tea/coffee Direct dial from bedrooms Licensed Cen ht No coaches Dinner Last d 9pm **PRICES:** s £35-£45; d £56-£68✳ **LB PARKING:** 10 **CARDS:**

CULLOMPTON Map 03 ST00

♦♦♦♦ Weir Mill Farm *(ST040108)*

Jaycroft, Willand EX15 2RE ☎ 01884 820803 📠 01884 820973
Mrs R Parish
e-mail: parish@weirmillfarm.freeserve.co.uk
Dir: *M5 junct 27, take B3181 to Willand. At Four Crossway rdbt, 1st left signed Uffculme. After 50yds take 1st right, further 50yds turn right into Jaycroft. Weir Mill 400yds on left*

Set in extensive farmland, this charming 19th century farmhouse offers comfortable accommodation in a relaxed and homely atmosphere. The spacious bedrooms are attractively decorated and equipped with an impressive range of thoughtful extras and accessories. A good choice of breakfast is offered in the well-appointed dining room. The farmhouse is now no-smoking throughout.

FACILITIES: 3 en suite (1 fmly) No smoking TVB tea/coffee No dogs (ex guide dogs) Cen ht 100 acres arable & beef **PRICES:** s fr £25; d fr £40✳ **PARKING:** 5 **NOTES:** Closed Xmas

DARTMEET Map 03 SX67

♦♦♦ Brimpts Barn *(SX668380)*

Brimpts Farm PL20 6SG ☎ 01364 631450 📠 01364 631450
Miss G Cross
e-mail: brimpts@btclick.com
Dir: *off A38 onto B3357. Follow signs to Dartmeet. Establishment signposted on R at top of hill*

A popular venue for walkers and lovers of the great outdoors, Brimpts is peacefully situated in idyllic surroundings and has been a Duchy of Cornwall farm since 1307. Bedrooms are all simply furnished, and many enjoy lovely views across Dartmoor. Dinner, served by prior arrangement, makes use of fresh, local produce.

FACILITIES: 10 en suite (1 fmly) No smoking in bedrooms No smoking in area of dining room No smoking in 1 lounge TV4B tea/coffee Licensed Cen ht TVL Sauna Pool Table Jacuzzi Abseiling/canoeing/riding etc can be arranged 700 acres beef Dinner **PRICES:** s £22.50; d £37-£45✳ **LB BB CONF:** Thtr 60 Class 40 Board 25 Del from £51 ✳ **PARKING:** 50 **CARDS:**

Super supper! this symbol shows that evening meals exceeded our Inspector's expectations.

England

DARTMOUTH Map 03 SX85

Premier Collection

♦♦♦♦♦ Nonsuch House

Church Hill, Kingswear TQ6 0BX ☎ 01803 752829
01803 752357
e-mail: enquiries@nonsuch-house.co.uk

AA Best Breakfast Award

Dir: *2m before Brixham on A3022 take A379. After rdbt, fork left on B3205 downhill through woods. Left up Higher Contour Rd, down Ridley Hill. Nonsuch on bend*

This delightful Edwardian property enjoys fabulous views across the River Dart estuary. Kit, Patricia and Geoffrey Noble are marvellous hosts, managing to combine warmth and friendliness with unobtrusive service. Bedrooms are spacious and superbly appointed, all with a spectacular panorama of the harbour. Fresh, locally-sourced ingredients - notably top-quality meat and fish, along with farmhouse cheeses - are treated with due respect at dinner, and a BYO policy applies to wine. Breakfast, taken on the terrace in good weather, features freshly squeezed juice, local sausages and home-baked bread. Kit Noble was a Top Twenty Finalist in the AA Landlady of the Year Award 2002-2003

FACILITIES: 3 en suite (1 GF) No smoking in bedrooms No smoking in dining room TVB tea/coffee No dogs (ex guide dogs) Cen ht No children 10yrs No coaches Dinner Last d 8pm **PRICES:** d £70-£90✳ LB **CARDS:**

Premier Collection

♦♦♦♦♦ Broome Court

Broomhill TQ6 0LD ☎ 01803 834275 833260

Dir: *A38 to A384, at Totnes right onto A381, left at Halwell onto A3122 to Dartmouth. At Sportsmans Arms turn right, then 3rd right*

Located in an Area of Outstanding Natural Beauty, Broome Court is peacefully tucked away at the end of a quiet country lane. The superbly converted farm buildings surround a pretty flower filled courtyard with a fountain. Bedrooms are comfortably furnished and decorated. Breakfasts, served in the old farmhouse kitchen, feature fresh local produce and are a highlight of the stay. Dinner is also available, by prior arrangement.

FACILITIES: 3 en suite No smoking in bedrooms TVB tea/coffee Cen ht TVL No children 12yrs No coaches Golf, tennis and riding available nearby Dinner Last d noon **PRICES:** s £45-£50; d £70-£90✳
PARKING: 6

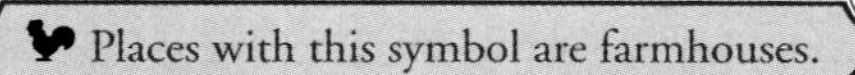
Places with this symbol are farmhouses.

Premier Collection

♦♦♦♦♦ Slide House

Hynetown Rd, Strete TQ6 0RS ☎ 01803 770378
01803 770197
e-mail: Bwood4@Aol.com

Dir: *Exeter to Plymouth turn off direction Totnes and follow to Dartmouth, pass Dartmouth Golf Course and turn right to Strete*

Magnificent views of the sea can be had from the sun deck at this delightful home. Dinner is available by prior arrangement, and the hosts, who serve evening drinks on the terrace, provide friendly and attentive hospitality. Breakfast features fresh and local produce and provides a further memorable aspect to a stay at Slide House.

FACILITIES: 3 en suite No smoking in bedrooms No smoking in dining room TVB tea/coffee No dogs Cen ht No children 12yrs No coaches **PRICES:** s £35-£37.50; d £45-£47.50✳
PARKING: 6 **NOTES:** Closed Dec-Jan

♦♦♦♦ Warfleet Lodge

Warfleet TQ6 9BZ ☎ 01803 834352

Dir: *from Dartmouth riverfront and hospital take Hanley Rd to Newcommon Rd-Southtown-Warfleet (all same road) in 0.5m driveway on right*

Just ten minutes stroll from the centre of historic Dartmouth, Warfleet Lodge, built in 1870 and frequented by Edward VII, is a relaxing retreat from everyday life. With fine views over Warfleet creek and the River Dart, accommodation is elegant and comfortable. Breakfast is a highlight, parking is a bonus and pets are welcome.

FACILITIES: 3 en suite TVB tea/coffee Cen ht **PRICES:** d £55-£75✳
PARKING: 4

♦♦♦♦ Captain's House

18 Clarence St TQ6 9NW ☎ 01803 832133
e-mail: enquiries@captainshouse.co.uk

Dir: *take B3122 Totnes to Dartmouth. Clarence Street is parallel with the river, one block removed*

Just a short walk from the quayside and town centre this house dates back to 1730 and retains many aspects of its original charm. Guestrooms are well equipped, comfortable and attractively decorated. Enjoyable breakfasts using local produce, and including quality preserves, are served in the dining room.

FACILITIES: 5 en suite No smoking in 2 bedrooms No smoking in dining room TVB tea/coffee No dogs (ex guide dogs) Cen ht No children 5yrs No coaches **PRICES:** s £26-£35; d £52-£67✳ LB **CARDS:**

♦♦♦♦ Cherub's Nest

15 Higher St TQ6 9RB ☎ 01803 832482

Dir: *from Lower Dartmouth ferry proceed along Lower St, take 2nd left into Smith Street, left again into Higher Street. Cherubs Nest 50 yds on left*

Dating back to 1710, this former Merchant's house is located in the very heart of Dartmouth. The well-appointed bedrooms vary in

continued

England

Cherub's Nest

size and each is equipped to meet the expectations of today's traveller. A choice of breakfasts is served in the cosy dining room.
FACILITIES: 3 en suite No smoking in dining room TVB tea/coffee Cen ht No children 10yrs No coaches **PRICES:** s £38.50-£44; d £51-£60✳ **LB**

♦♦♦♦ Courtyard House
10 Clarence Hill TQ6 9NX ☎ 01803 835967 📠 01803 835967
e-mail: ronandgail@courtyard-house.co.uk
The relaxing atmosphere of this small home is in keeping with its tranquil setting, peacefully located in Dartmouth's historic old town. Courtyard House is notable for its award winning floral displays and guests can relax on the patio amidst the flowers. Bedrooms are well equipped and provided with comfortable furnishings and one room has a four-poster bed. Freshly cooked, substantial breakfasts are served in the bright dining room.
FACILITIES: 1 en suite 3 annexe en suite No smoking TVB tea/coffee No dogs No children 10yrs No coaches **PRICES:** d £55-£75✳
PARKING: 4 **NOTES:** Closed 20-27 Dec

♦♦♦♦ Seale Arms
10 Victoria Rd TQ6 9SA ☎ 01803 832719 📠 01803 839366
e-mail: sealearms@hotmail.com
Dir: *turn off A38 at Buckfastleigh then A384 to Totnes. At Totnes take A381 to Halwell, then A3122 to Dartmouth*
This lively inn is conveniently located, only a few minutes level walk from the quayside. Bedrooms are spacious and very attractively decorated, with comfortable furnishings and a range of extras. In the bar, a good selection of freshly prepared dishes and daily specials are available. Breakfast is served in the first floor dining room.
FACILITIES: 4 en suite (2 fmly) No smoking in bedrooms No smoking in dining room TVB tea/coffee No dogs (ex guide dogs) Cen ht Pool Table Dinner Last d 8.30pm **PRICES:** d £50-£75✳ **CARDS:**

Hill View House
76 Victoria Rd TQ6 9DZ ☎ 01803 839372
At the time of going to press the Diamond classification for this establishment had not been confirmed. Please check the AA website www.theAA.com for up-to-date information.
FACILITIES: 5 en suite (1 fmly)

DOLTON — Map 02 SS51

♦♦♦♦ Union
Fore St EX19 8QH ☎ 01805 804633 📠 01805 804633
e-mail: union.inn@eclipse.co.uk
Dir: *from A3124 turn off at Beacon garage onto B3217 to Dolton 1m on R in village*
Originally built as a Devon longhouse, this delightful country inn has a quiet central village location. One of the comfortable bedrooms has a four-poster bed. Downstairs a fine selection of home cooked food and real ales are available for guests to enjoy, in either the cosy bar or restaurant.

continued

FACILITIES: 3 en suite No smoking in dining room TVB tea/coffee Cen ht No coaches Dinner Last d 9pm **PRICES:** s fr £35; d £55-£65✳ **LB**
MEALS: Bar Lunch £2.50-£7.50alc Dinner £12.50-£20alc✳
PARKING: 15 **NOTES:** Closed 1st 2wks Feb rs Oct-Etr **CARDS:**

EXETER — Map 03 SX99

See also Whimple

♦♦♦♦ Kerswell Grange Country House
Kennford EX6 7LR ☎ 01392 833660 📠 01392 833601
e-mail: kerswellgrange@hotmail.com
Dir: *M5 exit at Kennford. Turn left at junction exit, straight through village and out the other end. Before bridge essential to turn right, house 0.5m on left & signed*
Enjoying a peaceful rural setting, with sweeping views to the estuary of the River Exe, this large country house with its wealth of beams and open fires provides spacious accommodation for business and leisure guests alike. Hearty farmhouse breakfasts include fresh eggs from the owners' free-range hens and are served in the splendid dining room.
FACILITIES: 4 en suite No smoking TVB tea/coffee No dogs Cen ht TVL
PARKING: 6

♦♦♦♦ The Edwardian
30/32 Heavitree Rd EX1 2LQ ☎ 01392 276102 & 254699
📠 01392 253393
e-mail: michael@edwardianexeter.co.uk
Dir: *M5 J29. R at lights signed city centre. On Heavitree Rd after Exeter University, School of Education on L*

Situated just walking distance from the city centre, this attractive Edwardian terraced property offers stylish, tastefully decorated accommodation furnished in period style. All bedrooms feature personal touches and a number of rooms have four-poster beds. Books and local tourist information are provided in the comfortable lounge and resident proprietors Michael and Kay are on hand to help guests plan their stay in Devon.
FACILITIES: 12 en suite (4 fmly) (1 GF) No smoking in bedrooms No smoking in dining room TVB tea/coffee Direct dial from bedrooms Cen ht TVL No coaches **PRICES:** s £34-£48; d £54-£62✳ **LB**
PARKING: 3 **NOTES:** Closed Xmas **CARDS:** 

♦♦♦ Diamonds are a guest's best friend!
The emphasis is on quality and guest care rather than extra facilities.

England

EXETER continued

♦♦♦♦ Fairwinds Village House Hotel

Kennford EX6 7UD ☎ 01392 832911
e-mail: fairwindshotbun@aol.com
Dir: *4m S of Exeter, from M5 junct 31 onto A38, after 2m left for Kennford, 1st hotel on left*

This small and friendly hotel has been in the same ownership for many years and, from a position allowing easy access to the coast, the moors and the cities of Exeter and Plymouth, it offers comfortable and well equipped accommodation. Fairwinds is strictly a No Smoking establishment. Home-cooked food can be enjoyed in the bright dining room adjacent to the cosy bar.
FACILITIES: 6 en suite (1 fmly) (3 GF) No smoking TVB tea/coffee Direct dial from bedrooms No dogs Licensed Cen ht No coaches Dinner Last d 7.30pm **PRICES:** s £39-£42; d £54-£58✻ **LB PARKING:** 8 **NOTES:** Closed 18 Nov-Dec **CARDS:**

♦♦♦♦ *Gissons Arms*

Kennford EX6 7UD ☎ 01392 832444
Dir: *Along A38 towards Torquay, before fork in road, go up slip road on left hand side*
Situated within easy reach of Exeter, this delightful inn (parts of which date back to the 15th century) offers comfortable, well-equipped bedrooms, some with four-poster beds. The bars have wooden beams, panelling and a relaxed and friendly atmosphere. Daily specials, an extensive choice of dishes from the carvery and a tempting range of desserts are all on the menu.
FACILITIES: 6 en suite No smoking in area of dining room TVB tea/coffee Direct dial from bedrooms Cen ht Dinner Last d 10pm **PARKING:** 100 **CARDS:**

♦♦♦♦ Holbrook Farm *(SX991927)*

Clyst Honiton EX5 2HR ☎ 01392 367000 🖷 01392 367000
Mrs H Glanvill
e-mail: heatherglanvill@holbrookfarm.co.uk
Dir: *take A3052 Sidmouth road from M5, pass Westpont (county showground) and Cat and Fiddle pub. 500yds turn left at Hill Pond caravans. Follow B+B signs. Establishment 1m from main road*
This friendly farmhouse stands in lush rolling countryside and has spectacular views. The bedrooms have their own entrance and offer bright, attractive and spacious accommodation. Breakfast features the best local produce fresh from the farm and light suppers can be provided by arrangement. Ideally located for Exeter, the coast and moors.
FACILITIES: 3 en suite (1 fmly) (3 GF) No smoking TVB tea/coffee No dogs Cen ht 150 acres dairy Dinner Last d 10am **PRICES:** s £25-£35; d £42-£45✻ **LB BB PARKING:** 4 **CARDS:**

Smoking restrictions appear under the **FACILITIES** heading, please check when booking.

♦♦♦♦ Mill Farm *(SX959839)*

Kenton EX6 8JR ☎ 01392 832471 Mrs D Lambert
Dir: *from Exeter take A379 towards Dawlish, and bypassing Exminster, across mini rdbt by Swans Nest. Farm 1.5m on right*
Located just a short drive from the Powderham estate, this imposing working farmhouse is surrounded by pastureland. Each of the spacious bedrooms is comfortably furnished and has carefully co-ordinated decor, many benefiting from views across the countryside. Breakfast is served in the sunny dining room and a guest lounge is also provided.
FACILITIES: 5 en suite (3 fmly) No smoking in dining room No smoking in lounges TVB tea/coffee No dogs Cen ht 60 acres beef **PRICES:** s £25; d £40-£42✻ **LB PARKING:** 12 **NOTES:** Closed Xmas

♦♦♦♦ Rydon *(SX999871)*

Woodbury EX5 1LB ☎ 01395 232341 🖷 01395 232341
Mrs S Glanvill
e-mail: sallyglanvill@hotmail.com
Dir: *from Exeter A376, B3179 **(Woodbury)**, In village turn right 10yds before 30mph sign.*
The same family has owned this Devon long house for eight generations. The farmhouse provides spacious bedrooms, which are equipped with many useful extra facilities with one having a four-poster bed. There is a guest's TV lounge and a delightful garden in which to relax. Breakfast is served in front of an inglenook fireplace.
FACILITIES: 3 en suite (1 fmly) No smoking in bedrooms No smoking in dining room tea/coffee Cen ht TVL 350 acres dairy **PRICES:** s £27-£35; d £52-£58✻ **LB PARKING:** 3

♦♦♦♦ St Andrews Hotel

28 Alphington Rd EX2 8HN ☎ 01392 276784 🖷 01392 250249
Dir: *M5 exit junct 31 signposted Exeter, follow signs for city centre & Marsh Barton along Alphington road A377. Hotel on left*

Standards are high at this small and friendly hotel, situated within walking distance of the city centre, which has been in the same family ownership for over thirty years. Bedrooms are continually being upgraded, and each is equipped with modern comforts. Public rooms include a choice of sitting areas and a bright dining room where home-cooking is featured on the menu.
FACILITIES: 17 en suite (2 fmly) No smoking in 5 bedrooms No smoking in dining room STV TVB tea/coffee Direct dial from bedrooms No dogs (ex guide dogs) Licensed Cen ht No coaches Dinner **PRICES:** s £40-£51.50; d £55-£68✻ **LB PARKING:** 21 **NOTES:** Closed 24 Dec-1 Jan **CARDS:**

♦♦♦ Devon Arms

Fore St, Kenton EX6 8LD ☎ 01626 890213 🖷 01626 891678
e-mail: devon.arms@ukgateway.net
Dir: *on A379, halfway between Exeter and Dawlish*
About five miles from the city centre, in the village of Kenton, the Devon Arms provides comfortable accommodation. The village bar is popular with locals, offering pool, darts and skittles during the

continued

winter months. Bedrooms are comfortable and practically furnished and equipped. Both substantial meals and lighter options are available in the bar/lounge.

The Devon Arms

FACILITIES: 6 en suite (4 fmly) No smoking in 3 bedrooms No smoking in area of dining room TVB tea/coffee No dogs Cen ht No coaches Pool Table Dinner Last d 9pm **PRICES:** s £30-£35; d £45-£55✻ **LB** **PARKING:** 20 **CARDS:**

♦♦♦ Hotel Gledhills

32 Alphington Rd EX2 8HN ☎ 01392 430469 & 271439 📠 01392 430469

Dir: *M5 junct 31 onto A30 towards Okehampton, after 2m take A377 into Exeter, hotel 1m on left just before St Andrew Church on right*

Conveniently located for access from the motorway and within easy walking distance of the city centre, Hotel Gledhills offers friendly accommodation. Bedrooms are pleasantly decorated and comfortable. A cosy bar and comfortable lounge is provided, and hearty breakfasts are served in the separate dining room.

FACILITIES: 12 rms (10 en suite) (4 fmly) No smoking in 12 bedrooms No smoking in dining room TVB tea/coffee No dogs (ex guide dogs) Licensed Cen ht TVL No coaches **PRICES:** s £26-£37; d £45-£51✻ **PARKING:** 13 **NOTES:** Closed 22 Dec-20 Jan **CARDS:**

♦♦♦ Park View Hotel

8 Howell Rd EX4 4LG ☎ 01392 271772 📠 01392 253047
e-mail: philbatho@parkviewhotel.freeserve.co.uk

Dir: *M5 junct 29. follow signs A3015 City centre until clock tower rdbt, 3rd exit Elm Grove at end of road T-junct, turn left Howell Road*

This friendly family-owned guest house enjoys a peaceful situation overlooking Bury Meadow Park, close to the city centre. All bedrooms in this Grade II listed Georgian building are equipped with modern facilities. In addition, guests can relax in the comfortable sitting room and breakfast is taken in the bright and airy dining room.

continued

FACILITIES: 13 rms (11 en suite) (2 fmly) (1 GF) No smoking in 1 bedrooms No smoking in dining room TVB tea/coffee Direct dial from bedrooms No dogs (ex guide dogs) Cen ht TVL **PRICES:** s £24-£26; d £42-£55✻ **PARKING:** 6 **NOTES:** Closed Xmas-New Year **CARDS:**

♦♦♦ Sunnymede

24 New North Rd EX4 4HF ☎ 01392 273844

Dir: *from M5, junct 30, follow City Centre signs into one-way system. Pass Central Station in Queen St. At clocktower rdbt turn right. Sunnymede on left*

The Sunnymede enjoys a central location in the historic city of Exeter and is convenient for the college, shopping centre and tourist attractions. A compact guest house, it offers comfortable bedrooms, well suited for both business and leisure guests. A good choice is available at breakfast. The guest house is no-smoking throughout.

FACILITIES: 9 en suite (1 fmly) No smoking TVB tea/coffee No dogs (ex guide dogs) Cen ht TVL No coaches **PRICES:** s £20-£28; d £38-£42✻ **BB**

♦♦♦ Telstar Hotel

77 St Davids Hill EX4 4DW ☎ 01392 272466 📠 01392 272466
e-mail: reception@telstar-hotel.co.uk

Dir: *between city centre and St Davids railway station*

This family-run hotel occupies two adjacent houses located within walking distance of the city centre, railway station and the university. Bedrooms vary in size, though all are well equipped, and attractively furnished. There is a comfortable lounge for guests' use and a spacious dining room where traditional English breakfasts are served.

FACILITIES: 20 rms (11 en suite) (5 fmly) (3 GF) No smoking in bedrooms No smoking in dining room TVB tea/coffee No dogs (ex guide dogs) Cen ht TVL **PRICES:** s £22-£30; d £40-£60✻ **LB** **PARKING:** 9 **NOTES:** Closed 23-31 Dec **CARDS:**

♦♦ Dunmore Hotel

22 Blackall Rd EX4 4HE ☎ 01392 431643 📠 01392 431643
e-mail: Dunmorehtl@aol.com

Dir: *M5 junct 29 follow signs for city centre, through centre, at mini-rdbt turn right, house on left*

Conveniently located for the city centre, Exeter College and the railway station, the Dunmore Hotel provides guests with comfortable accommodation. The bedrooms are all well-presented and equipped. Traditional English breakfasts are served in the dining room.

FACILITIES: 8 rms (5 en suite) (3 fmly) No smoking in 3 bedrooms No smoking in dining room TVB tea/coffee No dogs (ex guide dogs) Cen ht TVL Dinner Last d noon **PRICES:** s £20-£26; d £36-£42✻ **LB** **BB** **CARDS:**

England

HARTLAND Map 02 SS22

♦♦♦ Fosfelle

EX39 6EF ☎ 01237 441273 Fax 01237 441273
Dir: *off A39 onto B3248 for 2m entrance on right*

Dating back to the 17th century, this delightful manor house offers comfortable accommodation close to the village of Hartland. It is set in six acres of gardens with two fishing lakes. Guests can enjoy pool or darts in the welcoming bar, and the restaurant offers a range of freshly prepared dishes.
FACILITIES: 7 rms (4 en suite) (2 fmly) No smoking in bedrooms TV6B tea/coffee No dogs (ex guide dogs) Licensed Cen ht TVL Fishing Pool Table Dinner Last d 9pm **PRICES:** s £24-£30; d £48-£58 **LB** **PARKING:** 20 **CARDS:**

HAYTOR Map 03 SX77

Premier Collection

♦♦♦♦♦ Bel Alp House

TQ13 9XX ☎ 01364 661217 Fax 01364 661292
Dir: *2.5m W of Bovey Tracey, A38 onto A382*
Breath-taking views of stunning countryside are a feature of this gracious Edwardian country mansion. Situated on a hillside on the south-eastern edge of Dartmoor, Bel Alp House is set in splendid gardens. All areas offer copious comfort, space and quality. By arrangement, a short, fixed-price dinner is available, featuring as much home-grown produce as possible.
FACILITIES: 8 en suite (2 fmly) (2 GF) No smoking in 1 bedrooms No smoking in dining room No smoking in 1 lounge TVB tea/coffee Direct dial from bedrooms Licensed Cen ht No coaches Snooker Croquet lawn Dinner Last d 6.30pm **PRICES:** s £60-£75; d £120-£150* **PARKING:** 20 **CARDS:**

HOLSWORTHY Map 02 SS30

♦♦♦♦ Clawford Vineyard

Clawton EX22 6PN ☎ 01409 254177 Fax 01409 254177
e-mail: john.ray@clawford.co.uk
Dir: *A388 Holsworth to Launceston road, turn left at Clawton crossroads, 1.5m to T-junct, turn left, then in 0.5m left again*
This working cider orchard and vineyard also has a number of lakes available for anglers. Bedrooms are spacious and comfortable, and most rooms have splendid views over the lakes and woods and the peaceful Claw Valley. Extensive choices are offered at the bar and also from the menu, and freshly cooked dishes are well prepared and attractively presented at both dinner and at breakfast.
FACILITIES: 11 en suite (7 fmly) No smoking TVB tea/coffee No dogs Licensed Cen ht TVL No children 6yrs Fishing Pool Table Coarse & game fishing Dinner Last d 9pm **PRICES:** s £33-£36; d fr £55* **LB** **PARKING:** 60 **CARDS:**

♦♦♦♦ Leworthy Farm House *(SS323012)*

Lower Leworthy, Nr Pyworthy EX22 6SJ ☎ 01409 259469 Mr & Mrs P Jennings
Dir: *leave Holsworthy via Bodmin St, in direction of North Tamerton, Leworthy is 3rd turning on left signed Leworthy/Southdown, approx 3m*

Located in an unspoilt area of North Devon with three acres of gardens, meadows, copse and fishing lake, this delightful farmhouse provides bright, comfortable accommodation with numerous extra facilities. Dinner is available by prior arrangement and like breakfast, is served in the large lounge/dining room. A self-contained cottage is also available.
FACILITIES: 4 en suite (1 fmly) No smoking TVB tea/coffee No dogs (ex guide dogs) TVL Fishing 3 acres non-working Dinner Last d 10am **PRICES:** s £25-£40; d £44-£50* **LB** **PARKING:** 8

♦♦♦ The Hollies Farm Guest House *(SS371001)*

Clawton EX22 6PN ☎ 01409 253770 Mr & Mrs G Colwill
e-mail: the-hollies-2001@hotmail.com
Dir: *on A388, turn left at Clawton village & follow vineyard signs, the Hollies in lane on left*
This sheep and dairy farm, set in 25 acres, offers comfortable accommodation in a family atmosphere. There are pleasant views across the countryside from most bedrooms, which are all well appointed and equipped with thoughtful extras. Breakfast is taken in the new conservatory and there is also a barbecue area, with gazebo for guest use.
FACILITIES: 3 en suite (3 fmly) No smoking TVB tea/coffee No dogs (ex guide dogs) Cen ht 25 acres beef sheep Dinner Last d early morning **PRICES:** s £18-£25; d £36-£42* **LB** **BB** **PARKING:** 6 **NOTES:** Closed 24-25 Dec

HONITON Map 03 ST10

Premier Collection

♦♦♦♦♦ West Colwell Farm

Offwell EX14 9SL ☎ 01404 831130 Fax 01404 831769
e-mail: stay@westcolwell.co.uk
Dir: *village signposted off A35 Honiton/Axminster road, at church go downhill, farm 0.5m on right*
Peacefully situated down a meandering country lane, in an Area of Outstanding Natural Beauty, West Colwell Farm offers stylishly decorated and comfortably furnished bedrooms in a converted dairy. The two rooms on the ground floor have direct access to their own terrace. Breakfast can be taken at tables outside or, when the weather is cooler, around a wood burning stove in the split level dining room.
FACILITIES: 3 en suite (2 GF) No smoking TVB tea/coffee No dogs (ex guide dogs) Cen ht No children 12yrs **PRICES:** s fr £32.50; d fr £65* **LB** **PARKING:** 3 **NOTES:** Closed Xmas **CARDS:**

♦♦♦♦ Atwell's at Wellington Farm

Wilmington EX14 9JR ☎ 01404 831885
e-mail: wilmington@btinternet.com
Dir: *3m from Honiton, take A35 towards Dorchester, approx 500 yds through village of Wilmington on the left*

A delightful Grade II listed farmhouse set in five acres, where a rescue centre is run for animals. Guests may visit hens, a goat, sheep and horses of varying sizes - from Shire to Shetland! This friendly guest house offers comfortable accommodation and a hearty breakfast using fresh local produce.

FACILITIES: 3 rms (1 en suite) (1 GF) No smoking TVB Cen ht TVL No coaches **PRICES:** s £18-£23; d £40-£46* BB **PARKING:** 10

♦♦♦♦ Courtmoor Farm *(ST207068)*

Upottery EX14 9QA ☎ 01404 861565 Mr & Mrs Buxton
e-mail: courtmoor.farm@btinternet.com
Dir: *off A30, 0.5m W of A30 and A303 merge, approx 4m from Honiton*

Conveniently accessed from the A30 and situated overlooking the attractive Otter Valley. Bedrooms all have views, and are spacious, comfortable and well equipped. Dinner, by prior arrangement, provides freshly cooked local produce, and the establishment is licensed. In addition to the attractive grounds guests have access to the leisure room, gym and sauna.

FACILITIES: 3 en suite (1 fmly) No smoking STV TVB tea/coffee No dogs (ex guide dogs) Licensed Cen ht Sauna Gymnasium 17 acres non-working Dinner Last d 10am **PRICES:** s £23.50-£28; d £40-£45*
PARKING: 20 **NOTES:** Closed 20 Dec-1 Jan **CARDS:**

♦♦♦♦ Old Forge

Wilmington EX14 9JR ☎ 01404 831297
e-mail: oldforge.wilmington@tesco.net
Dir: *At Honiton take A35 (Dorchester). Wilmington approx 3m from Honiton. Old Forge 100yds from Wilmington sign*

Parts of this thatched house, with its wealth of beams, date back to the 16th century. The pretty cottage-style bedrooms have been equipped with many personal touches. Delicious breakfasts, and dinners by prior arrangement, are served in the dining room, and there is an attractive sitting room with flagstone floor and woodburning stove.

FACILITIES: 3 rms (1 en suite) No smoking TVB tea/coffee Cen ht TVL ch fac No coaches Dinner Last d 5pm **PRICES:** s £25; d £44* LB
PARKING: 5

♦♦♦ The Crest

Moorcox Ln, Wilmington EX14 9JU ☎ 01404 831419
Dir: *3m E of Honiton on A35 at eastern end of village, after the river bridge turn left, The Crest is 100 metres on right*

A warm welcome awaits at The Crest, which enjoys delightful views across the Umborne Valley and its own gardens. The guest wing affords complete privacy with each room being equipped with modern comforts. Breakfast is served around one large table in the dining room and guests can also relax in the bright conservatory. Dinner is available by prior arrangement.

FACILITIES: 3 en suite (1 fmly) No smoking in bedrooms No smoking in dining room TVB tea/coffee Cen ht No coaches Dinner Last d previous day
PRICES: s £20-£26; d £40-£46* **PARKING:** 6

♦♦♦ Threshays

Awliscombe EX14 3QB ☎ 01404 43551 📠 01404 43551
e-mail: threshays@tesco.net
Dir: *A373 Honiton/Cullompton road, 2.5m from Honiton*

A converted threshing barn, situated on a non-working farm, Threshays enjoys wonderful views over open countryside. With tea and cake offered on arrival, this family run establishment offers comfortable accommodation in a friendly atmosphere. The lounge/dining room is light and airy, where a good breakfast can be enjoyed. Ample parking is a bonus.

FACILITIES: 2 rms (1 fmly) No smoking No dogs (ex guide dogs) Cen ht TVL No coaches **PRICES:** s £18; d £36* BB **PARKING:** 10

HORN'S CROSS — Map 02 SS32

Premier Collection

♦♦♦♦♦ Lower Waytown

EX39 5DN ☎ 01237 451787 📠 01237 451817
e-mail: colin-penny@beeb.net
Dir: *A39 from Bideford through Horns Cross, 0.5m past Hoops Inn, Roundhouse on left*

Converted from an old barn and roundhouse, this charming property is set in five acres of landscaped gardens. The unique lounge has exposed beams and an inglenook fireplace. Bedrooms are comfortable with many thoughtful extras. Breakfast is served around one large table in the dining room. There are also two self-catering, thatched cottages available and stabling for horses can be arranged.

FACILITIES: 3 en suite (1 fmly) (1 GF) No smoking TVB tea/coffee No dogs Cen ht TVL No children 12yrs No coaches Riding **PRICES:** s £39-£41; d £52-£57* LB **PARKING:** 8

ILFRACOMBE — Map 02 SS54

♦♦♦♦ *Southcliffe Hotel*

Torrs Park EX34 8AZ ☎ 01271 862958
Dir: *on A361 from Barnstaple, left at 1st set of lights, left at 2nd set, then immediately left. Hotel 400mtrs on left*

Peacefully located within walking distance of the seafront and town centre, this fully restored fine Victorian house has retained many original features and some bedrooms have four-poster beds. Evening meals are available by prior arrangement and served in the light and airy dining room. There is also a comfortable lounge and bar.

FACILITIES: 12 en suite No smoking TVB tea/coffee No dogs Licensed Cen ht TVL No children 16yrs No coaches Dinner Last d 5pm
PARKING: 10 **NOTES:** Closed Nov - Mar **CARDS:**

> ♦♦♦ Red Diamonds highlight the top establishments within the AA's rating 3, 4 and 5 Diamond ratings.

continued

England

ILFRACOMBE continued

♦♦♦♦ Strathmore Hotel

57 St Brannocks Rd EX34 8EQ ☎ 01271 862248
01271 862243
e-mail: strathmore@ukhotels.com
Dir: *on A361 approach into Ilfracombe, 1.5m from Mullacot Cross rndbt*

Situated within walking distance of the town centre and beach, this charming Victorian hotel offers a very warm welcome. Bedrooms are attractively decorated and comfortably furnished. Public areas include a well stocked bar, a cosy lounge and an elegant dining room, where meals prepared to the highest standards from fresh produce can be enjoyed.
FACILITIES: 9 rms (8 en suite) (3 fmly) No smoking in bedrooms No smoking in dining room No smoking in 1 lounge TVB tea/coffee Licensed Cen ht TVL No coaches Dinner Last d 7pm **PRICES:** s £30-£39; d £40-£58* **LB** **PARKING:** 7 **CARDS:**

♦♦♦♦ Varley House

13 Chambercombe Park Ter, Chambercombe Park EX34 9QW
☎ 01271 863927 01271 879299
e-mail: info@varleyhouse.co.uk
Dir: *A399 Combe Martin Rd, R at swimming pool , round L corner, on the inside of the R hand bend*

A charming Victorian house located within easy distance of the town centre and sea front. The well proportioned bedrooms are comfortably furnished and well equipped. There is a spacious lounge and a cosy bar. A home-cooked dinner and generous breakfast is served in the well appointed dining room.
FACILITIES: 8 en suite (2 fmly) (1 GF) No smoking in bedrooms No smoking in dining room TVB tea/coffee Licensed Cen ht TVL No children 5yrs No coaches Dinner Last d 4pm **PRICES:** s £26-£27; d £52-£54* **LB** **PARKING:** 8 **NOTES:** Closed Nov-Mar **CARDS:**

♦♦♦♦ *Waterloo House Hotel*

Waterloo Ter, Fore St EX34 9DJ ☎ 01271 863060
01271 863060
e-mail: info@waterloohousehotel.co.uk
Dir: *exit M5 J27, to A361 to Ilfracombe, along High St, after Cinema, filter left into Fore St, through No Entry signs, 1st terrace on right*

This charming, listed Georgian building was originally built to commemorate the battle of Waterloo and has been creatively transformed to provide a unique experience for guests. Every effort is made to facilitate a relaxed, enjoyable and memorable stay, typified by the 'negotiable' breakfast times. An imaginative dinner menu is offered in Bonapartes, dishes being skilfully prepared using fresh quality ingredients. A wedding licence is held and small receptions can be catered for.
FACILITIES: 9 rms (7 en suite) (2 fmly) No smoking in bedrooms No smoking in dining room TVB tea/coffee No dogs (ex guide dogs) Licensed Cen ht TVL No children 12yrs No coaches Dinner Last d 9pm **CARDS:**

♦♦♦ Collingdale Hotel

Larkstone Ter EX34 9NU ☎ 01271 863770 01271 863867
e-mail: collingdale@onet.co.uk
Dir: *on A339 travelling W from Combe Martin, 0.5m past Hele Bay on right. Travelling E through Ilfracombe, on left past B3230 turn off*

A friendly, family-run hotel located within easy walking distance of the town centre and seafront. Bedrooms, many with sweeping sea views, are well presented and equipped with modern facilities. The comfortable lounge also has wonderful views of the sea, and in addition there is a cosy bar. Dinner is available by prior arrangement.
FACILITIES: 8 rms (7 en suite) (2 fmly) No smoking in bedrooms No smoking in dining room TV7B tea/coffee No dogs (ex guide dogs) Licensed TVL Dinner Last d 2pm **PRICES:** d £42* **LB** **NOTES:** Nov-30 Mar **CARDS:**

♦♦♦ *Dedes Hotel*

1-3 The Promenade EX34 9BD ☎ 01271 862545
01271 862234
Dir: *on approach road into Ilfracombe follow signs to seafront, hotel on right*

Situated on the seafront with some rooms having sea views, this family-run hotel offers comfortable, suitably equipped accommodation. Guests have a choice of dining options with the formal restaurant offering both set and carte menus, whilst a good choice of bar meals are served in the Wheel House bar.
FACILITIES: 17 rms (12 en suite) (6 fmly) No smoking in area of dining room TVB tea/coffee Licensed Cen ht TVL Clay pigeon shooting Last d 9.45pm **PARKING:** 6 **NOTES:** Closed 23-26 Dec **CARDS:**

♦♦♦ Langleigh Park House

Langleigh Park EX34 8BG ☎ 01271 862158
e-mail: terrya@lineone.net
Dir: *turn into Church Hill at War Memorial. Go to end of Langleigh Rd. Turn right, 1st left (Langleigh Park). Lane 2nd left to hotel.*

The elevated position of this Victorian stone building set in 14 acres, provides guests with both country and sea views. Just 10 minutes walk from the town centre and beaches; Langleigh Park House offers comfortable bedrooms, some of which have four-poster beds. Home cooked evening meals are available by prior arrangement.
FACILITIES: 10 rms (7 en suite) (2 fmly) No smoking in 2 bedrooms No smoking in dining room No smoking in 1 lounge TV6B tea/coffee Licensed Cen ht TVL No coaches Pool Table Clay shooting,Mountain biking. Dinner Last d 9:30am **PRICES:** d £50-£60* **LB** **PARKING:** 8
NOTES: Closed Jan

If an establishment name appears in *italics*, details have not been confirmed for 2003.

♦♦♦ Norbury House Hotel

Torrs Park EX34 8AZ ☎ 01271 863888
e-mail: chrisdhewitt@talk21.com
Dir: *on entering Ilfracombe(A361) at 1st set of traffic lights turn left. At nxt set of lights left & left again into Torrs Park establishment on right*

Built as a gentleman's residence in 1870, Norbury House is quietly located in an elevated position overlooking the town, with views to the sea. Bedrooms are comfortable and well equipped. In addition to the inviting lounge, there is also a cosy bar. Evening meals are available by prior arrangement.
FACILITIES: 8 rms (6 en suite) (3 fmly) No smoking in bedrooms No smoking in dining room No smoking in 1 lounge TV7B tea/coffee Licensed Cen ht TVL No coaches Dinner Last d 5pm **PRICES:** s £20-£24; d £42-£52✱ **LB PARKING:** 6 **NOTES:** Closed Dec |
CARDS:

♦♦♦ The Towers Hotel

Chambercombe Park EX34 9QN ☎ 01271 862809
01271 879442
e-mail: info@thetowers.co.uk
Dir: *in Ilfracombe turn off A399 opposite the swimming pool*
FACILITIES: 8 rms (5 en suite) No smoking TVB tea/coffee Licensed Cen ht TVL No coaches Dinner Last d 5pm **PRICES:** s £21-£24; d £42-£48✱ **LB**
PARKING: 9 **NOTES:** Closed Nov-Feb **CARDS:**

♦♦ *Devonshire Moonta Hotel*

Capstone Crescent EX34 9BP ☎ 01271 862288 & 863774
01271 865276
e-mail: moontahotel@hotmail.com
Dir: *Follow signs to Barnstaple then Braunton and Ilfracombe. Follow Harbour signs down Wilder Road. Pass St James Church to T-junct 2 left turnings Capston Road*
Literally at the water's edge, the Devonshire Moonta Hotel is conveniently located for easy access to the town, harbour and beach. Friendly and relaxed family service is provided. By prior arrangement, hearty evening meals are available, while on the lower ground floor a cosy bar opens onto a patio overlooking the sea.
FACILITIES: 24 rms (19 en suite) No smoking in 5 bedrooms No smoking in dining room No smoking in 1 lounge TV20B tea/coffee No dogs (ex guide dogs) Licensed TVL Fishing Pool Table Dinner Last d 3.30pm
PARKING: 4 **NOTES:** Closed 2nd Nov - 20th April rs Nov-Mar
CARDS:

JACOBSTOWE — Map 02 SS50

♦♦♦♦ Higher Cadham *(SS585026)*

EX20 3RB ☎ 01837 851647 01837 851410 Mr & Mrs J King
e-mail: kingscadham@btopenworld.com
Dir: *from Jacobstowe take A3216 towards Hatherleigh/Bude, a few yards after church turn sharp right in front of Cottage Farm continue for 0.5m*
Guests have been returning to Higher Cadham Farm for over 25 years and the same excellent standard of welcome and hospitality awaits all visitors. A perfect location for either cycling or walking breaks; bicycles are available for hire. The working farm welcomes guests, and children will enjoy the animals and the large play area. Parents will appreciate the three comfortable lounges and bar.
FACILITIES: 4 rms 8 annexe en suite (3 fmly) (4 GF) No smoking in dining room No smoking in 1 lounge TV9B tea/coffee Licensed Cen ht TVL Nature Trail 139 acres Dinner Last d 6pm **PRICES:** s £20-£25✱ **LB**
PARKING: 10 **NOTES:** Closed Dec **CARDS:**

See advert under OKEHAMPTON

KINGSBRIDGE — Map 03 SX74

See also Bantham

♦♦♦♦ Staunton Lodge

Embankment Rd TQ7 1JZ ☎ 01548 854542 01548 854421
e-mail: miketreleaven@msn.com
Dir: *from Kingsbridge town centre take A381 along side the estuary, signposted Dartmouth, Lodge approx 0.25m on left.*
The proprietors at this delightful house provide a friendly and caring atmosphere, and guests will find the attentive and thoughtful service ensures a relaxing visit. Bedrooms are very well equipped and comfortably furnished, the bathrooms spacious and stylish. The waterside location means pleasant views can be enjoyed during the excellent breakfast, when freshly cooked local produce makes a memorable start to the day.
FACILITIES: 2 en suite No smoking STV TVB tea/coffee No dogs (ex guide dogs) Cen ht No children 8yrs No coaches **PRICES:** d £50✱ **LB**
PARKING: 4 **NOTES:** Closed 20 Dec-10 Jan rs 1 Nov-19 Dec & 11 Jan-28 Feb **CARDS:**

♦♦♦♦ Highwell House *(SX712457)*

Churchstow TQ7 3QP ☎ 01548 852131 Mrs A Pope
Dir: *turn off A379 at Churchstow opposite Church House Inn. after approx 30yds turn right following church wall. House on right*
Highwell House is a secluded country house set in extensive attractive gardens and with excellent views of the surrounding countryside. It is well situated to explore the many attractions and the beautiful coastline of the South Hams. Bedrooms are comfortably appointed and well equipped. In winter, breakfasts are served in the dining room and in summer in the conservatory.
FACILITIES: 3 en suite (1 fmly) No smoking TVB tea/coffee No dogs (ex guide dogs) Cen ht No children 4yrs Tennis (hard) Croquet lawn Badminton, Woodland Walk. 10 acres Sheep **PRICES:** s £32-£37; d £44-£52✱ **LB**
PARKING: 4 **NOTES:** Closed Xmas & New Year

♦♦♦♦ Ashleigh House

Ashleigh Rd TQ7 1HB ☎ 01548 852893 01548 852893
e-mail: reception@ashleigh-house.co.uk
Dir: *A381 from Kingsbridge in direction of Salcombe. Take 3rd L going up hill, after rdbt, proceed to Ashleigh Rd, house on L*
FACILITIES: 8 en suite (2 fmly) No smoking in bedrooms No smoking in dining room No smoking in 1 lounge TVB tea/coffee Licensed TVL No coaches Dinner Last d noon **PRICES:** s £26-£30; d £42-£50✱ **LB**
PARKING: 4 **NOTES:** rs Dec-Jan **CARDS:**

England

LEWDOWN Map 02 SX48

♦♦♦♦ Stowford House

EX20 4BZ ☎ 01566 783415 🖹 01566 783109
e-mail: alison@stowfordhouse.com
Dir: *turn off Lewdown-Lifton road at sign for Stowford. Downhill for 400yds, hotel on sharp left bend*

This delightful Georgian country house stands in secluded gardens and provides a peaceful, tranquil base from which to explore the surrounding area. There is a smart dining room where a hearty breakfast can be enjoyed and guests can relax in the elegant drawing room. Bedrooms offer good standards of comfort. Evening meals are available by prior arrangement.

FACILITIES: 4 en suite No smoking TVB tea/coffee No dogs (ex guide dogs) Licensed Cen ht TVL No children 14yrs No coaches **PRICES:** s £33-£40; d £46-£60✳ **LB** **PARKING:** 5 **NOTES:** Closed 21 Dec-Jan

LUSTLEIGH Map 03 SX78

Premier Collection

♦♦♦♦♦ Woodley House

Caseley Hill TQ13 9TN ☎ 01647 277214 🖹 01647 277126
Dir: *A38 from Exeter, take Plymouth route to rdbt A38/A382, then A382 to Bovey Tracey taking bypass. Follow Moretonhampstead and Lustleigh signs for 3m. After phone box 2nd left to Lustleigh. Into village, at T junct right to Caseley. House 2nd on left*

Set just a few minutes' stroll from the village pub, church and tea-room, Woodley House is a peaceful and tranquil retreat, with super views over the rolling countryside. A hearty breakfast, featuring as many as twelve home-made preserves, home-baked bread and a vast range of cooked breakfast options, can be enjoyed in the charming dining room. An ideal base for walkers, and dogs are welcome too.

FACILITIES: 2 en suite No smoking TVB tea/coffee Cen ht TVL No children 10yrs No coaches **PRICES:** s £38; d £52-£54✳ **PARKING:** 3

LYDFORD Map 02 SX58

Premier Collection

♦♦♦♦♦ Moor View House

Vale Down EX20 4BB ☎ 01822 820220 🖹 01822 820220
Dir: *turn off A30 at Sourton Cross onto A386 Tavistock road, hotel drive approx 4m on right*

Built around 1870, this charming house once changed hands over a game of cards! Retaining many original features, the bedrooms are elegant and beautifully decorated, furnished with an interesting collection of pieces. The two acres of

continued

Moor View House

moorland gardens have access to Dartmoor. Breakfast, and dinner by prior arrangement, are served house-party style at a large oak table.

FACILITIES: 4 en suite No smoking TVB tea/coffee Licensed Cen ht TVL No children 12yrs No coaches Bowls Croquet Dinner Last d 3pm **PRICES:** s fr £30; d fr £60✳ **LB** **PARKING:** 15

LYNMOUTH Map 03 SS74

Premier Collection

♦♦♦♦♦ Bonnicott House

Watersmeet Rd EX35 6EP ☎ 01598 753346
🖹 01598 753724
e-mail: bonnicott@hotmail.com
Dir: *A39, cross East Lyn River Bridge & turn left into Watersmeet Rd, 50yds on right, opposite Church*

With spectacular views over the harbour towards the sea and cliffs, Bonnicott House is set in attractive gardens. Bedrooms, most with sea views, are very well equipped, with comfortable furnishings and a host of thoughtful extra facilities. Dinner offers fresh local produce, imaginatively presented, and at breakfast hearty portions are served fresh from the Aga.

FACILITIES: 8 en suite No smoking TVB tea/coffee No dogs (ex guide dogs) Licensed Cen ht No children 12yrs No coaches Dinner Last d 5pm **PRICES:** d £46-£76✳ **NOTES:** Closed Xmas & New Year
CARDS:

♦♦♦♦ Countisbury Lodge Hotel

6 Tors Park, Countisbury Hill EX35 6NB ☎ 01598 752388
e-mail: maureenfrancis@countisburylodge.co.uk
Dir: *travelling W on A39 turn L at white sign for Countisbury Lodge on Countisbury hill, just before entering Lynmouth*

From its peaceful elevated position high above the town, this former Victorian vicarage enjoys spectacular views of the harbour

continued

and surrounding countryside. The atmosphere is friendly and informal but with attentive service. The comfortable bedrooms are suitably equipped. Breakfast is served in the pleasant dining room, and there is a well-appointed lounge and small bar.
FACILITIES: 6 en suite (1 fmly) No smoking in bedrooms No smoking in dining room tea/coffee Licensed Cen ht TVL No coaches **PRICES:** d £45-£56✱ **LB** **PARKING:** 8

♦♦♦♦ Glenville House

2 Tors Rd EX35 6ET ☎ 01598 752202
e-mail: tricia@glenvillelynmouth.co.uk
Dir: *turn left off A39 at the bottom of Countisbury Hill, 200 yds along Tors Road*
A friendly welcome awaits at this delightful Victorian house, overlooking the East Lyn River. The attractively decorated bedrooms feature co-ordinated soft furnishings. Traditional breakfasts are served at separate tables in the dining room. Also available is a comfortable first floor lounge, with river views and an attractive garden, where cream teas can be enjoyed in the summer months.
FACILITIES: 6 rms (3 en suite) (1 GF) No smoking tea/coffee No dogs Licensed Cen ht TVL No children 12yrs No coaches **PRICES:** s £23-£25; d £46-£56✱ **LB** **NOTES:** Closed mid Nov-mid Feb

♦♦♦♦ The Heatherville

Tors Park EX35 6NB ☎ 01598 752327 📠 01598 752634
Dir: *off A39 into Tors Rd, 1st left fork into Tors Park*

From a secluded and elevated south facing position, the Heatherville enjoys splendid views over Lynmouth and surrounding woodland. Recently redecorated, bedrooms are comfortable and well appointed. Enjoyable evening meals are provided in the dining room, by prior arrangement. In addition a cosy lounge with fireplace and a snug bar are available.
FACILITIES: 7 rms (5 en suite) No smoking TVB tea/coffee Licensed Cen ht No children 12yrs No coaches Dinner Last d breakfast **PRICES:** s £25; d £50-£64✱ **LB** **PARKING:** 7 **NOTES:** Closed Nov-Feb **CARDS:**

TVB means there are televisions in bedrooms
TVL means thereís a television in the lounge
STV means satellite television.

♦♦♦♦ Orchard House Hotel

12 Watersmeet Rd EX35 6EP ☎ 01598 753247 📠 01598 753855
e-mail: orchardhouse@lynmouth.fsnet.co.uk
Dir: *on A39, W side of East Lyn river bridge, adjacent to car park and church*
A warm and friendly welcome is offered here at Orchard House Hotel. A Grade II listed building it is conveniently positioned just a short stroll from Lynmouth High Street. Bedrooms are light and airy and thoughtfully equipped with practical extras. Tempting home cooked dinners are available by prior arrangement, in the pleasant dining room. A cosy bar and lounge are also available.

FACILITIES: 6 rms (5 en suite) (2 fmly) No smoking TVB tea/coffee No dogs (ex guide dogs) Licensed Cen ht TVL No children 12yrs Dinner Last d noon **PRICES:** s £35; d £48-£56✱ **NOTES:** Closed mid Dec-mid Jan **CARDS:**

♦♦♦♦ Rock House

Manor Grounds EX35 6EN ☎ 01598 753508 📠 01598 753508
e-mail: enquiries@rock-house.co.uk
Dir: *on A39, at the foot of Countisbury Hill*

With its stunning location at the entrance to the harbour, with the river on one side and the sea on the other, this Grade II listed hotel has breathtaking views. Of the comfortable bedrooms, one is on the ground floor and two have four poster beds. Guests can dine in either the restaurant or the bar.
FACILITIES: 6 en suite No smoking in bedrooms No smoking in dining room TVB tea/coffee Licensed Cen ht No coaches Dinner Last d 9pm **PRICES:** s £30; d £65-£76✱ **LB** **PARKING:** 6 **CARDS:**

LYNTON Map 03 SS74

Premier Collection

♦♦♦♦♦ Highcliffe House

Sinai Hill EX35 6AR ☎ 01598 752235 📠 01598 752235
e-mail: highcliffehotel@lycos.co.uk
Dir: *from A39 into Lynton 'Old Village' direction and turn right from Lydiate Lane.*

Eight hundred feet above sea level, Highcliffe House enjoys stunning views over the Exmoor hills and coastline, across to South Wales. Built in the 1870s as a gentleman's summer residence, this wonderful house is an ideal choice for those wishing to explore the surrounding area. Bedrooms are spacious and elegant, likewise the lounges and candlelit conservatory restaurant with its spectacular outlook. Dinner features an imaginative choice of home-made dishes. This is a totally no-smoking hotel.
FACILITIES: 6 en suite No smoking TVB tea/coffee No dogs Licensed Cen ht No children No coaches Dinner Last d Noon **PRICES:** s £39-£57; d £52-£76* **LB PARKING:** 7 **NOTES:** Closed 10 Dec-21 Jan
CARDS:

Premier Collection

♦♦♦♦♦ Victoria Lodge

Lee Rd EX35 6BS ☎ 01598 753203 📠 01598 753203
e-mail: info@victorialodge.co.uk
Dir: *Off A39 in centre of village, opposite Post Office*
Built in the 1880s, a warm welcome awaits at this elegant house in the heart of Lynton, with afternoon tea offered on arrival. Recently redecorated, rooms are individual and stylish. Antique brass beds, as well as a four-poster, a half-tester and various other canopied beds feature in the bedrooms, named after Queen Victoria's children and grandchildren. A super range of tempting home-made and local produce is available at breakfast, including home-made bread, muesli and Greek yoghurt. Jane Bennett was a Top Twenty Finalist in the AA Landlady of the Year 2002-2003.
FACILITIES: 9 en suite No smoking TVB tea/coffee No dogs Licensed Cen ht No coaches Dinner Last d 10am (Thu & wknds)
PRICES: s £43.50-£66; d £56-£88* **LB PARKING:** 7
NOTES: Closed Nov-Mar **CARDS:**

♦♦♦♦ *Alford House Hotel*

Alford Ter EX35 6AT ☎ 01598 752359 📠 01598 752359
e-mail: enquiries@alfordhouse.co.uk
Mid Feb-Mid Nov
Dir: *enter via Lynbridge and up hill past the Old Station then 2nd right into Normans Cleave*
A charming Georgian property, Alford House enjoys an elevated position and superb views over Lynton and the coastline. Bedrooms are well appointed and most benefit from the delightful views. Dinner, which features good home cooking, can be enjoyed in the dining room. Additional facilities include a lounge and a small, but well stocked bar.
FACILITIES: 8 rms (7 en suite) No smoking TVB tea/coffee Licensed Cen ht TVL No children 12yrs No coaches Last d 3pm **NOTES:** Closed Nov-Mid Feb
CARDS:

♦♦♦♦ Longmead House

9 Longmead EX35 6DQ ☎ 01598 752523 📠 01598 752523
e-mail: info@longmeadhouse.co.uk
Dir: *A39 Porlock into Lynmouth onto B3234 Lynton. Through village toward Valley of Rocks. Establishment on left*

Jacqueline and Nigel extend a warm and friendly welcome to all their guests at Longmead, an old Lynton house, with picturesque garden and croquet lawn. A relaxed and informal atmosphere prevails, with comfortable bedrooms, a spacious lounge and a well stocked bar all helping guests to unwind. Dinner (by arrangement) is a highlight, with a good choice of tempting dishes available.
FACILITIES: 7 en suite (1 fmly) No smoking TVB tea/coffee No dogs Licensed Cen ht TVL No coaches Croquet lawn Dinner Last d 2pm **PRICES:** s £28.50-£34.50; d £38-£46 **LB BB PARKING:** 7 **NOTES:** Closed 1 Dec-10 Feb **CARDS:**

♦♦♦♦ *Lynhurst Hotel*

Lyn Way EX35 6AX ☎ 01598 752241 📠 01598 752241
e-mail: enq@thelynhurst.co.uk
Dir: *garden entrance to hotel is located in far left corner of Lower Meadow car park, opp Royal Castle pub in town centre*
With spectacular views of the town, bay, or surrounding countryside all bedrooms are comfortably furnished and well-equipped with many extra facilities. By prior arrangement, delicious dinners are available in the charming dining room. Drinks can be enjoyed in the lounge bar and there is a delightful garden in which guests can relax.
FACILITIES: 7 rms (4 en suite) (1 fmly) No smoking in bedrooms No smoking in dining room No smoking in 1 lounge TVB tea/coffee Licensed No coaches Dinner Last d noon

♦♦♦♦ Pine Lodge

Lynway EX35 6AX ☎ 01598 753230
e-mail: info@pinelodgehotel.com
Dir: *A39 to Barbrook, turn onto B3234 direction Lynton/Lynmouth. In 0.25m keep right signed Lynmouth in further 0.25m Lynway on left opposite Bridge Inn*
This attractive house, set in a secluded position with views of the wooded West Lyn valley, provides comfortable and friendly accommodation. Bedrooms are spacious and well equipped with many thoughtful extras. The lounge is particularly appealing and comfortable. Breakfast (and dinner, by prior arrangement) offers freshly cooked home-made dishes.

continued

FACILITIES: 6 en suite (2 GF) No smoking TVB tea/coffee No dogs Licensed Cen ht No children 12yrs No coaches Dinner Last d breakfast **PRICES:** s £20-£23; d £40-£48* LB **PARKING:** 6 **CARDS:**

♦♦♦♦ St Vincent

Castle Hill EX35 6JA ☎ 01598 752244 📠 01598 752244

Dir: *approx midway between Barnstaple and Minehead, exit A39 to Lynton, premises located beside Exmoor Museum*

At this attractive Grade II listed house, guests are assured of a warm welcome. Bedrooms are individually furnished and decorated, all are well equipped and one ground floor room is available. Guests are able to enjoy a drink in the lounge, after a busy day exploring the many attractions the locality has to offer.
FACILITIES: 6 en suite (1 fmly) (1 GF) No smoking TVB tea/coffee Licensed Cen ht TVL No children 3yrs No coaches **PRICES:** d £46-£50* LB **NOTES:** Closed Dec-Jan

♦♦♦♦ Waterloo House

Lydiate Ln EX35 6AJ ☎ 01598 753391 📠 01598 753391
e-mail: relax@waterloohousehotel.com

Dir: *M5 junct 27 take A361 to Barnstaple at rdbt with Little Chef, turn right and follow A39. On entering Lynton, road bends to Lydiate Ln*

This family-run Georgian property has abundant character and period charm. Bedrooms are individually furnished and well-equipped, with a choice of lounges also available. The atmosphere is convivial, genuine and relaxed with every effort made to ensure an enjoyable stay. Authentic Thai cuisine is a unique feature, served within the hotel's elegant restaurant 'Thai-Lyn'.
FACILITIES: 8 en suite (3 fmly) No smoking in bedrooms No smoking in dining room No smoking in 1 lounge TVB tea/coffee No dogs (ex guide dogs) Licensed Cen ht TVL Dinner Last d 9.30pm **PRICES:** s £25; d £50-£56* LB **PARKING:** 3 **CARDS:**

♦♦♦ The Denes

15 Longmead EX35 6DQ ☎ 01598 753573 📠 01598 753573 (daytime only)
e-mail: j.e.mcgowan@btinternet.com

Dir: *from centre of Lynton follow signs for Valley of Rocks, last guest house on left by speed limit signs*

Guests will find an exceptionally warm and friendly welcome here at The Denes. Proprietors, Sally and John ensure a relaxing stay in their comfortable guest house, which enjoys a quiet location. Bedrooms are well appointed and an inviting lounge is also available. Enjoyable dinners (by arrangement) and breakfasts are taken in the dining room. Parking is a bonus.

continued

The Denes

FACILITIES: 5 rms (3 en suite) (3 fmly) No smoking TV3B tea/coffee No dogs Licensed Cen ht TVL No coaches Dinner Last d 6pm
PRICES: s £16-£22.50; d £32-£45* LB BB **PARKING:** 5
CARDS:

MORETONHAMPSTEAD — Map 03 SX78

Premier Collection

♦♦♦♦♦ Blackaller Hotel & Restaurant

North Bovey TQ13 8QY ☎ 01647 440322 📠 01647 441131
e-mail: peter@blackaller.fsbusiness.co.uk

Dir: *A38, A382 to Moretonhampstead, on entering Moretonhampstead take 1st L by newsagents to North Bovey*

Set in delightful countryside in the heart of the Dartmoor National Park, this 17th century woollen mill is named after the Black Alder trees which grow along the riverbanks. The bedrooms are spacious and comfortable, a pleasant sitting room and bar are available in which guests can relax. The dining room features an inglenook fireplace and exposed granite walls. The daily changing menus feature exclusive Devon produce and are prepared with flair and imagination.
FACILITIES: 5 en suite 1 annexe en suite No smoking TVB tea/coffee Licensed Cen ht No children 10yrs No coaches Fishing Riding Croquet lawn Bird watching Walking weekends Dinner Last d 8pm
PRICES: s £35; d £58-£60* LB **PARKING:** 6 **NOTES:** Closed Jan

England

MORETONHAMPSTEAD continued

Premier Collection

♦♦♦♦♦ Gate House

North Bovey TQ13 8RB ☎ 01647 440479 📠 01647 440479
e-mail: gatehouseondartmoor@talk21.com
***Dir:** A30, A382 to Moretonhampstead then B3212 to North Bovey*

The tranquil charm of this medieval Devon hall house is matched by the hospitality of the hosts and their splendid home cooking. Bedrooms reflect the elegance of this beautiful conservation village and are furnished with co-ordinated fabrics and luxury beds. Meals are served 'house party style' and feature local speciality produce. In the morning, the smell of freshly baked bread calls guests to breakfast. An outdoor swimming pool is available in the warmer months. Sheila Runham-Williams was a Runner-Up in the AA Landlady of the Year Award for 2002-2003.
FACILITIES: 3 en suite No smoking TVB tea/coffee Cen ht No children 15yrs No coaches Outdoor swimming pool Riding Fishing Guided walks Dinner Last d 3pm **PRICES:** s £36-£38; d £60✳ **LB PARKING:** 3

♦♦♦♦ Great Wooston Farm *(SX764890)*

TQ13 8QA ☎ 01647 440367 📠 01647 440367 Mrs M Cuming
e-mail: info@greatwoostonfarm.com
***Dir:** take Lime Street (opposite library) for 1.5 m over cattle grid. Fork left over 2nd cattle grid, 2nd house on right*
This peaceful country house, in the midst of Dartmoor's splendour, provides a convenient base from which to tour the area. Bedrooms, one with a four-poster, are comfortable and provided with many personal touches. Farmhouse breakfasts are served in the spacious dining room and guests are welcomed with tea on arrival.
FACILITIES: 3 en suite No smoking TVB tea/coffee No dogs (ex guide dogs) Cen ht TVL No children 8yrs 320 acres mixed **PRICES:** s £23-£25; d £40-£50✳ **LB PARKING:** 3 **CARDS:**

♦♦♦♦ Midfields

North Bovey Rd TQ13 8PB ☎ 01647 440462 📠 01647 440039
e-mail: sharon@ridgetor.freeserve.co.uk
***Dir:** From A30 onto A382 follow signs Moretonhampstead, left in centre of village, left opp supermarket into Pound Street. Midfields is on this lane 1m from Pound Street, on left at bottom steep hill.*
From its elevated position in the Dartmoor National Park, this hidden gem is an ideal base from which to explore. Genuine hospitality is at the heart of Midfields and this combined with thoughtfully equipped bedrooms make it a special place to stay. Breakfast is but one more highlight with home-made and local produce featuring on the menu.
FACILITIES: 3 en suite No smoking TVB tea/coffee No dogs (ex guide dogs) Cen ht No children 14yrs No coaches Riding Guided riding holidays with own horse, walks **PRICES:** d fr £50✳ **LB PARKING:** 60
NOTES: Closed Dec-Jan

♦♦♦♦ Moorcote

Chagford Cross TQ13 8LS ☎ 01647 440966
e-mail: moorcote@smartone.co.uk
***Dir:** A382 Chagford & Okehampton rd from Moretonhampstead for 350mtrs. Past hospital, Moorcote is on right*

Perched on a hill overlooking the town and surrounded by attractive mature country gardens, this Victorian house is an ideal base for exploring Dartmoor and only a short walk from the town centre. Friendly owners Pat and Paul Lambert extend a warm welcome to their guests, many of whom return on a regular basis.
FACILITIES: 5 rms (4 en suite) (2 fmly) No smoking TVB tea/coffee No dogs (ex guide dogs) Cen ht No children 5yrs No coaches **PRICES:** s £20-£26; d £40-£44✳ **LB PARKING:** 6 **NOTES:** Closed Nov-Jan

♦♦♦♦ Great Sloncombe

TQ13 8QF ☎ 01647 440595 📠 01647 440595
e-mail: hmerchant@sloncombe.freeserve.co.uk
***Dir:** from Moretonhampstead take A382 towards Chagford for 1.5m. At sharp double bend take left turning and farm is 0.5m up lane*
FACILITIES: 3 en suite No smoking TVB tea/coffee Cen ht No children 8yrs No coaches Dinner Last d 10am **PRICES:** d £48-£52✳ **PARKING:** 3

♦♦♦ Cookshayes Country Guest House

33 Court St TQ13 8LG ☎ 01647 440374 📠 01647 440374
e-mail: cookshayes@eurobell.co.uk
***Dir:** on B3213 Exeter/Princetown Rd, approx 400yds from x-roads in Moretonhampstead with A382 in direction of Princetown*
Set in nearly an acre of well tended gardens, this Victorian house has the benefit of distant views over Dartmoor. One of the comfortable bedrooms boasts a four-poster bed, while two rooms are located on the ground floor. Breakfast is served in the dining room at separate tables and dinner is available by prior arrangement. Guests can relax in the lounge which overlooks the attractive garden.
FACILITIES: 8 rms (6 en suite) (1 fmly) (2 GF) No smoking in 4 bedrooms No smoking in dining room No smoking in lounges TVB tea/coffee Licensed Cen ht TVL No children 5yrs No coaches Dinner Last d ordered when booking **PRICES:** s £19; d £38-£45✳ **LB BB CONF:** Class 10 Board 10 **PARKING:** 8 **NOTES:** Closed Xmas & New Year **CARDS:**

NEWTON ABBOT — Map 03 SX87

See also Widecombe in the Moor

♦♦♦♦ *Bulleigh Park (SX860660)*

Ipplepen TQ12 5UA ☎ 01803 872254 📠 01803 872254
Mrs A Dallyn
e-mail: bulleigh@lineone.net
***Dir:** turn off A381 for Compton at Jet garage follow for approx 1m. Signposted*
Bulleigh Park is a working farm that produces award-winning Aberdeen Angus beef. A friendly welcome is provided and guests

continued

are made comfortable in this family house. Breakfasts, notable for their wealth of fresh, local and homemade produce, are taken in the pleasant dining-room which enjoys fantastic views across the well tended gardens and open countryside beyond.
FACILITIES: 2 en suite 1 annexe en suite No smoking in bedrooms No smoking in dining room No smoking in 1 lounge TVB tea/coffee No dogs (ex guide dogs) Cen ht TVL ch fac Stabling available for own horse 60 acres beef,ponies,sheep **PARKING:** 6 **NOTES:** Closed Xmas

♦♦♦♦ Chipley Farm *(SX794726)*

TQ12 6JW ☎ 01626 821486 & 821947 📠 01626 821486
Mrs L Westcott
e-mail: louisa@chipleyfarmholidays.co.uk

(For full entry see Bickington)

♦♦♦♦ Sampsons Hotel & Restaurant

Preston TQ12 3PP ☎ 01626 354913 📠 01626 354913
e-mail: nigel@sampsonsfarm.com
Dir: *M5/A380/B3195 signed Kingsteignton. Pass Ten Tors Inn on left and take 2nd right signed B3193 to Chudleigh. At rdbt 3rd exit, left after 1m*
This charming 16th-century thatched farmhouse and converted stables have been tastefully restored to provide quality accommodation and dining. Bedrooms, many of which are on the ground floor and several with country views, are comfortably furnished. Accomplished cuisine can be enjoyed in the farmhouse restaurant; the menu offers a good choice of local produce, which is skilfully prepared.
FACILITIES: 5 rms (2 en suite) 6 annexe en suite (2 fmly) No smoking in bedrooms No smoking in dining room TVB tea/coffee Direct dial from bedrooms Licensed Cen ht No coaches Water colour classes Dinner Last d 9.15pm **PRICES:** s £30-£75; d £50-£120✻ **LB** **CONF:** Del from £90 ✻ **PARKING:** 20 **CARDS:**

♦♦♦ Walmer Towers

Moles Ln, South Whilborough, Kingkerswell TQ12 5LS
☎ 01803 872105 📠 01803 875477
Dir: *follow A380 from Newton Abbot. At first rdbt turn right, next rdbt turn left and then take 1st left, establishment 1m on right*
This pleasant house is peacefully located in the attractive Devon countryside and is convenient for Torquay and the many surrounding attractions. The proprietors, who are very friendly and helpful hosts, offer spacious and comfortable accommodation. The freshly prepared breakfast provides a very pleasant start to the day and includes home-made bread and preserves.
FACILITIES: 2 en suite (2 fmly) No smoking TVB tea/coffee No dogs (ex guide dogs) Cen ht No coaches **PRICES:** s £25-£28; d £40-£45✻ **LB**
PARKING: 6

OKEHAMPTON — Map 02 SX59

See also Holsworthy & Lewdown

England

OAKHAMPTON continued

♦♦♦♦ Luxridge *(SX561932)*

Hughslade Farm EX20 4LR ☎ 01837 52883 Mrs K C Heard

Dir: *from town centre follow B3260 for 2m past A30 recovery station. Climb hill and bungalow on right*

Glorious views over Dartmoor National Park and a warm welcome await guests at this charming farm bungalow. Both bedrooms are well equipped with comfortable, modern facilities. A hearty breakfast using local produce where possible is served in the airy conservatory. An elegant lounge is available for guests' use.

FACILITIES: 2 en suite No smoking in bedrooms No smoking in dining room TVB tea/coffee Cen ht TVL Snooker Games room 600 acres mixed **PRICES:** s fr £25; d fr £50* **PARKING:** 4 **NOTES:** Closed Xmas

See advertisement on page 153

♦♦♦♦ Pressland House

Hatherleigh EX20 3LW ☎ 01837 810871 📠 01837 810303

e-mail: accom@presslandhouse.co.uk

Dir: *from A30 take A386 towards Hatherleigh, after 5.5m Pressland House on right, 2m before Hatherleigh*

An acre of garden surrounds this fine Victorian house which benefits from distant views of Dartmoor. One of the spacious bedrooms has a four-poster bed with another on the ground floor, ideal for the less mobile. Dinner is available by prior arrangement. A large comfortable lounge and a cosy bar are provided for guests.

FACILITIES: 4 en suite 1 annexe en suite (1 GF) No smoking TVB tea/coffee No dogs (ex guide dogs) Licensed Cen ht TVL No children 12yrs No coaches Dinner Last d 6pm **PRICES:** s £35-£42; d £50-£70* LB **PARKING:** 10 **NOTES:** Closed 22 Dec-Mar **CARDS:**

♦♦♦ *Heathfield House*

Klondyke Rd EX20 1EW ☎ 01837 54211 📠 01837 54211

e-mail: Tim@tgibbins.freeserve.co.uk

Dir: *Okehampton Stn -under bridge 300yds up steep hill, through woods then straight ahead up drive into hotel car park*

Located in an elevated position above the town, with the Dartmoor National Park behind, this substantial Victorian property provides guests with comfortable, individually decorated bedrooms. In addition to the guest lounge there is also a bright conservatory which overlooks the outdoor pool. Evening meals are available by prior arrangement.

FACILITIES: 4 en suite (1 fmly) No smoking TVB tea/coffee Licensed Cen ht TVL No coaches Outdoor swimming pool (heated) Pool Table Pottery studio at additional cost Dinner Last d 7.30pm **PARKING:** 8 **NOTES:** Closed January **CARDS:**

♦♦♦ Meadowlea

65 Station Rd EX20 1EA ☎ 01837 53200 📠 01837 53200

Dir: *turn off A30 onto B3260. Take the left at the third set of traffic lights, Station Road, second left*

Within walking distance of the town centre, Meadowlea is a solid stone house in a quiet, residential area. The individually decorated bedrooms are comfortable and well equipped. Hearty breakfasts are served at separate tables in the rear dining room; evening meals are available by prior arrangement.

FACILITIES: 7 rms (4 en suite) (3 fmly) No smoking in dining room TVB tea/coffee Cen ht TVL No coaches Dinner **PRICES:** s £23; d £43* LB **PARKING:** 3

OTTERY ST MARY — Map 03 SY19

♦♦♦♦ Fairmile Inn

Fairmile EX11 1LP ☎ 01404 812827 📠 01404 815806

e-mail: leon.courtney@thefairmileinn.co.uk

Dir: *from Honiton, exit at Iron Bridge signs and follow road 3m. From motorway sliproad left at Fairmile sign. Inn 0.75m on left. From Exeter follow A30 to Fairmile sign on left. Follow signs to Fairmile Inn in village*

Located in the quiet village of Fairmile, this 400-year-old coaching house was given its name by Oliver Cromwell. Beams and inglenook fireplaces feature in the cosy restaurant and lounge bar, where delightful meals using fresh local produce are available. Bedrooms are comfortably furnished with many extras.

FACILITIES: 5 rms (3 en suite) No smoking in 4 bedrooms No smoking in dining room No smoking in 1 lounge TVB tea/coffee No dogs (ex guide dogs) Cen ht TVL No children 14yrs Pool Table Games bar Dinner Last d 9pm **PRICES:** s £19.50-£32.50; d £39-£45* LB **MEALS:** Lunch £8.65-£15 Dinner £11.35-£18.50alc* **PARKING:** 50 **CARDS:**

♦♦♦♦ Normandy House Hotel & Bistro

5 Cornhill EX11 1DW ☎ 01404 811088 📠 01404 811023

Dir: *M5 junct 29/A30 onto B3174. On approaching town centre bear left & follow directions for St Mary's church, hotel on right of church*

Under new ownership, Normandy House, a Grade II listed Georgian town house, enjoys an enviable position opposite St Mary's Church. Bedrooms are comfortable and well equipped. Breakfast is taken in the restaurant, which is well known locally for its bistro and carte menus, and interesting wine list.

FACILITIES: 5 en suite No smoking in bedrooms No smoking in dining room TVB tea/coffee Direct dial from bedrooms No dogs (ex guide dogs) Licensed Cen ht No coaches Dinner Last d 9.30pm **PRICES:** s £31.50-£37.50; d £60-£65* LB **NOTES:** Closed Jan **CARDS:**

continued

♦♦♦♦ Pitt Farm *(SY089966)*
Fairmile EX11 1NL ☎ 01404 812439 📠 01404 812439
Mrs S Hansford
e-mail: pittfarm@tiscall.co.uk
Dir: *from A30 follow signs for Fairmile, turn left at bottom of the hill (B3176) signed Cadhay House/Coombelake, 0.5m farm on left*

Situated in the picturesque Otter Valley, this charming 16th-century thatched farmhouse offers traditional hospitality and a relaxing, memorable stay. Surrounded by 185 acres of farmland, it is an ideal choice for those wishing to explore the rural delights of East Devon. Bedrooms are well equipped with many thoughtful extras.
FACILITIES: 5 rms (4 en suite) (2 fmly) No smoking in bedrooms No smoking in dining room TV4B tea/coffee No dogs TVL 190 acres mixed **PRICES:** s £22-£25; d £44-£50* **LB PARKING:** 6 **NOTES:** Closed Xmas & New year **CARDS:**

♦♦ Fluxton Farm
Fluxton EX11 1RJ ☎ 01404 812818 📠 01404 814843
Dir: *from Exeter/Honiton, off A30 at Daisymount junct for Ottery St Mary (B3174). Right at 1st set of x-rds at 30mph sign. Follow straight ahead for 1m*
Located just four miles from the coast in a peaceful farmland setting this interesting 16th-century Devon longhouse has a wealth of beams and open fireplaces. A haven for cat lovers, Fluxton Farm offers comfortable accommodation and features two lounges, a bar and a large garden complete with pond and ducks.
FACILITIES: 11 rms (10 en suite) (1 fmly) No smoking in dining room No smoking in 1 lounge TVB tea/coffee Licensed Cen ht TVL No children 8yrs No coaches Fishing Putting green Garden railway Dinner Last d 5pm **PRICES:** s £25; d £50* **LB PARKING:** 15

PAIGNTON — Map 03 SX86

♦♦♦♦ Beresford Private Hotel
5 Adelphi Rd TQ4 6AW ☎ 01803 551560 📠 01803 552776
e-mail: pat-beresford@lineone.net
Dir: *from A380 follow signs to town centre. Take Torbay Rd to seafront, right along esplanade, 1st right into Adelphi Rd, hotel 75yds on left*
This pleasant hotel is run by the resident proprietors who are welcoming and attentive hosts. Comfortable and spacious rooms are provided and are equipped with many thoughtful extra facilities. The Beresford is conveniently located for the town centre, the seafront and the many attractions.
FACILITIES: 8 en suite No smoking in 6 bedrooms No smoking in dining room TVB tea/coffee No dogs (ex guide dogs) Licensed Cen ht TVL No children 12yrs No coaches Dinner Last d noon **PRICES:** s £23-£47; d £36-£52* **LB BB PARKING:** 5 **CARDS:**

♦♦♦♦ The Clydesdale
5 Polsham Park TQ3 2AD ☎ 01803 558402
e-mail: info@theclydesdale.co.uk
Dir: *From A380 take ring road for Paignton. At 3rd rdbt turn left into Marldon Rd, continue to rdbt, bear left into Cecil Rd. At traffic lights turn left onto Torquay Rd 2nd right into Lower Polsham Rd & 2nd right into Polsham Park, establishment 50yds on left*
Conveniently located in a residential area, a level walk from the town centre and seafront. In the summer the colourful display of flowers is delightful. Bedrooms are comfortable, well maintained and equipped with modern facilities; two ground floor rooms are available. Home cooked evening meals are provided with prior arrangement; home made cakes are a speciality.
FACILITIES: 7 en suite (1 fmly) (2 GF) No smoking in dining room TVB tea/coffee No dogs Cen ht TVL No children 3yrs Free passes to local leisure centre Dinner Last d 4pm **PRICES:** s £17.50-£21.50; d £35-£43* **LB BB PARKING:** 5 **NOTES:** Closed 23 Dec-4 Jan **CARDS:**

♦♦♦♦ *Kingswinford Hotel*
32 Garfield Rd TQ4 6AX ☎ 01803 558358
e-mail: kingswinford@garfieldroad.freeserve.co.uk
Located just a short level stroll from the beach and pier, this friendly house offers comfortable accommodation. The attentive proprietors have been welcoming guests to their home for many years and some guests return on a regular basis. Dinner and breakfast are served in the attractive dining room and freshly prepared home cooked dishes are served daily. Guests can relax in the spacious lounge and a stylish bar is also available.
FACILITIES: 17 rms (14 en suite) (7 fmly) No smoking in dining room No smoking in lounges TVB tea/coffee Licensed Cen ht TVL Dinner Last d breakfast **NOTES:** Closed Nov & Jan

♦♦♦♦ Rosslyn Hotel
16 Colin Rd TQ3 2NR ☎ 01803 525578
Dir: *Turn left along sea front from Paignton town centre, road bends & Colin Road on left*

Within easy level strolling distance of the beach and town centre the Rosslyn Hotel is pleasantly situated. Bedrooms are well-equipped and comfortable, and the friendly proprietors are most welcoming and attentive. Dinner and breakfast are served in the beamed dining room, which also has a cosy bar. Guests can also relax in the inviting sitting room.
FACILITIES: 10 rms (7 en suite) (2 fmly) No smoking in 5 bedrooms No smoking in dining room No smoking in lounges TVB tea/coffee No dogs (ex guide dogs) Licensed Cen ht TVL Dinner Last d 3pm **PRICES:** s £18; d £36* **LB BB PARKING:** 10 **NOTES:** Closed Oct & Xmas **CARDS:**

England

PAIGNTON continued

♦♦♦♦ Torland Hotel

24 Sands Rd TQ4 6EJ ☎ 01803 558755 ✉ 01803 558707
e-mail: torlandhotel@hotmail.com
Dir: *Along Paignton seafront in southerly direction (Appollo Cinema on left) turn right at mini-rdbt into Sands Rd, hotel 50mtrs on left close to Belle Vue Rd*
Situated at the end of the seafront this traditional holiday hotel provides friendly and comfortable accommodation. The proprietors and their staff offer attentive service and the relaxed and homely atmosphere makes guests feel at ease. Rooms are pleasantly furnished and are equipped with many extra facilities. Dinner offers a good choice of freshly cooked traditional dishes, and at breakfast a delicious Devon breakfast is served.
FACILITIES: 15 en suite (4 fmly) (1 GF) TVB tea/coffee Licensed Cen ht TVL Dinner Last d 6.30pm **PRICES:** s £18.50-£22.50; d £33-£45* **LB BB PARKING:** 12 **NOTES:** Closed Nov-Etr **CARDS:**

♦♦♦♦ Bay Sands Hotel

14 Colin Rd TQ3 2NR ☎ 01803 524877
e-mail: enquiries@baysands.co.uk
Dir: *from M5 follow Torquay signs on A380 then follow Torbay road to seafront. When road turns into 2 way traffic turn 2nd right into Colin Rd*
FACILITIES: 9 en suite No smoking in dining room STV TVB tea/coffee No dogs (ex guide dogs) Licensed Cen ht TVL No children 2yrs No coaches Dinner Last d noon **PRICES:** s £16-£21; d £32-£42 **LB BB**
PARKING: 9 **NOTES:** Closed 29 Sep-23 Mar **CARDS:**

♦♦♦♦ Birchwood House Hotel

33 St. Andrews Rd TQ4 6HA ☎ 01803 551323 ✉ 01803 401301
e-mail: yates3048@aol.com
Dir: *proceed along seafront towards harbour. At rdbt turn right then 2nd left*
FACILITIES: 10 en suite (3 fmly) No smoking in 7 bedrooms No smoking in dining room No smoking in lounges TVB tea/coffee No dogs (ex guide dogs) Licensed Cen ht TVL No children 5yrs Dinner Last d 9pm **PRICES:** s £25-£30; d £50-£60* **LB PARKING:** 7 **CARDS:**

♦♦♦ Aquamarine Hotel

8 St Andrews Rd TQ4 6HA ☎ 01803 551193 ✉ 01803 403102
e-mail: aquahotel@aol.com
Dir: *from seafront proceed along esplanade with sea on left, turn right at mini rdbt into Sands Rd, St Andrews Rd 2nd on left*
This family-run, small hotel offers a friendly atmosphere and is within walking distance of both the town centre and the sea front. After a day exploring the many attractions locally, guests enjoy relaxing in the bar/lounge. Bedrooms are comfortable and well equipped. By prior arrangement, dinner is available.
FACILITIES: 9 en suite (3 fmly) No smoking in bedrooms No smoking in dining room No smoking in 1 lounge TVB tea/coffee No dogs (ex guide dogs) Licensed Cen ht TVL Dinner Last d 4pm **PRICES:** s £18-£22; d £36-£44* **LB BB PARKING:** 5 **CARDS:**

♦♦♦ Bay Cottage Private Hotel

4 Beach Rd TQ4 6AY ☎ 01803 525729 ✉ 01803 525729
e-mail: baycottage@hotmail.com
Dir: *75yds from seafront & green, between pier & cinema*
Bay Cottage, which offers friendly accommodation, is very convenient for the beach, theatre and shops. All of the bedrooms are comfortably furnished. Dinner, by prior arrangement, offers home-cooked food served in the pleasant surroundings of the pine-furnished dining room. There is also a comfortable lounge for guest use.
FACILITIES: 8 en suite (3 fmly) No smoking in dining room TVB tea/coffee Cen ht TVL Dinner Last d noon **PRICES:** s £17-£20; d £34-£40* **LB BB**

♦♦♦ Channel View Hotel

8 Marine Pde TQ3 2NU ☎ 01803 522432 ✉ 01803 528376
Dir: *from A380 Prestondown Rdbt follow signs Preston down hill to traffic lights, under railway bridge and turn left*
Situated on the edge of Paignton beach, this friendly hotel offers comfortable accommodation, with pleasantly furnished bedrooms, one on the ground floor. From the spacious sun lounge, guests enjoy splendid views over Torbay, and full evening meals are served in the combined bar and dining area. A 'dry' lounge is also available.
FACILITIES: 12 en suite (3 fmly) No smoking in dining room No smoking in 1 lounge STV TVB tea/coffee No dogs (ex guide dogs) Licensed Cen ht TVL No coaches Dinner Last d 12 noon **PRICES:** s £25-£35; d £50-£70* **LB**
PARKING: 10 **CARDS:**

♦♦♦ *Cherra Hotel*

15 Roundham Rd TQ4 6DN ☎ 01803 550723
e-mail: Lin_Toye@Lineone.net
Dir: *along seafront towards harbour, R at end along Sands Rd, 2nd L at church. Hotel at top of St Andrews Rd on corner of Roundham Rd*
In a quiet residential area of Paignton, the hotel is distinguished by its pleasant gardens, former winners of 'Torbay in Bloom'. The lounge is spacious and comfortable and contains a bar. Bedrooms, which include family rooms, vary in style and size and have modern facilities. Dinner is traditional and home-cooked.
FACILITIES: 11 rms (7 en suite) (3 fmly) No smoking in dining room TVB tea/coffee Licensed Cen ht TVL No children 3yrs Golf 9 Putting green Dinner Last d 9pm **PARKING:** 15 **CARDS:**

♦♦♦ The Haldon

6 Beach Rd TQ4 6AY ☎ 01803 551120
e-mail: peterearly@haldon68.fsnet.co.uk
Dir: *follow signs for Paignton Sea Front, Beach Road is off the Esplanade Road almost opposite Apollo Cinema*
This smart and tidy guest house, highly commended in a recent Paignton in bloom competition, provides comfortable accommodation. A friendly welcome is given to all guests by the resident proprietor and service is attentive. Bedrooms are well-equipped and have co-ordinated fabrics and colours. Well-cooked hearty breakfasts are freshly prepared and served at separate tables.
FACILITIES: 6 rms (3 en suite) (2 fmly) No smoking in dining room TVB tea/coffee Cen ht TVL No coaches **PRICES:** s £16-£20; d £32-£40* **LB BB**

♦♦♦ St Weonard's Private Hotel

12 Kernou Rd TQ4 6BA ☎ 01803 558842
Dir: *from Esplanade, Kernou Rd is between pier and cinema*
Guests are assured of a warm welcome at this friendly house, within easy, level walking distance of the seafront and the town centre. Bedrooms are attractively decorated and comfortable. Guests can relax in the lounge and a pleasant bar is provided in the dining room where bar-snacks are available; dinners and breakfast feature traditional home cooking.
FACILITIES: 8 rms (5 en suite) (2 fmly) No smoking TVB tea/coffee No dogs Licensed Cen ht TVL No coaches Dinner Last d 4.30pm **PRICES:** s £19; d £38-£44* **LB BB PARKING:** 2 **CARDS:**

♦♦♦ The Sealawn Hotel

Sea Front, 20 Esplanade Rd TQ4 6BE ☎ 01803 559031
Dir: *On Paignton seafront between Paignton pier and the cinema*
Ideally located on the seafront and having good parking, the Sealawn is a convenient and pleasant place to stay. Bedrooms are comfortable and well equipped, with some rooms located on the ground floor, and many have excellent views of Tor Bay. Dinner is served in the ground-floor dining room and at breakfast, hearty portions are served.

continued

FACILITIES: 12 en suite (3 fmly) (3 GF) No smoking in dining room TVB tea/coffee Direct dial from bedrooms No dogs Licensed Cen ht TVL No coaches Solarium Dinner Last d 5.30pm **PRICES:** s £24-£31; d £48-£52✳ LB **PARKING:** 13 **NOTES:** Closed 24 Dec-2 Jan **CARDS:**

♦♦♦ Wentworth Hotel

18 Youngs Park Rd, Goodrington TQ4 6BU ☎ 01803 557843
e-mail: ppriest@eurobell.co.uk
Dir: *from Paignton on B3199. Left at 1st rdbt, 1st right into Roundham Rd for 100mtrs. Right into Youngs Park Rd, hotel overlooks park on left*

This Victorian house overlooks Goodrington Park and is convenient for both the sea front and town centre. The recently refurbished bedrooms are comfortable and well equipped and feature many thoughtful extras. A choice of traditional English evening meals is available by prior arrangement. There is also a cosy bar and relaxing lounge.

FACILITIES: 10 en suite (3 fmly) No smoking in 6 bedrooms No smoking in dining room TVB tea/coffee Licensed Cen ht TVL No children 3yrs Dinner Last d 7pm **PRICES:** s £19-£22; d £36-£50✳ LB BB **PARKING:** 6

♦♦ *Torbay Sands Hotel*

16 Marine Pde, Preston Sea Front TQ3 2NU ☎ 01803 525568
Dir: *A380 to Torbay seafront, turn right & follow coast rd to Paington, after one-way system under rail bridge, straight ahead to Marine Parade*

This friendly family-owned hotel enjoys splendid views of Torbay and is within easy walking distance of the beach, pier and town centre. Bedrooms are comfortably furnished; one has a four-poster bed and some rooms are situated on the ground floor. Breakfast is taken in the dining room, which like the lounge, is spacious and pleasantly decorated.

FACILITIES: 13 rms (11 en suite) (4 fmly) No smoking in dining room TVB tea/coffee Licensed Cen ht TVL Dinner Last d 3pm **PARKING:** 5
CARDS:

PLYMOUTH — Map 02 SX45

♦♦♦♦ Berkeley's of St James

4 St James Place East, The Hoe PL1 3AS ☎ 01752 221654
📠 01752 221654
Dir: *from A38 toward city centre, left at sign The Hoe, straight through 7 sets of lights, left to Athenaum St, right to Crescent Ave, 1st left*

Conveniently located close to the Hoe and just a short walk from the City centre, this is an ideal choice for both business and leisure guests. Bedrooms are comfortably furnished and equipped with a number of thoughtful extras. A substantial breakfast using organic produce where possible is served in the dining room.

FACILITIES: 5 en suite (1 fmly) (1 GF) No smoking TVB tea/coffee No dogs (ex guide dogs) Cen ht No coaches **PRICES:** s £30-£35; d £45-£55✳ LB **PARKING:** 3 **NOTES:** Closed 23 Dec-1 Jan **CARDS:**

♦♦♦♦ Dudley Hotel

42 Sutherland Rd, Mutley PL4 6BN ☎ 01752 668322
📠 01752 673763
e-mail: butler@dudleyhotel.fsnet.co.uk
Dir: *A38 follow signs to city centre, before centre follow signs to rail stn, North Rd E for 200yds, left at traffic lights, left again, bear left. Down hill on right*

Located close to the city centre, university and railway station The Dudley Hotel provides guests with an ideal base for the city of Plymouth. Recently refurbished bedrooms offer good levels of comfort and are well equipped. A varied choice of breakfast is offered in the spacious dining room.

FACILITIES: 6 rms (5 en suite) (2 fmly) No smoking in bedrooms No smoking in dining room TVB tea/coffee Cen ht TVL **PRICES:** s £20-£30; d £40✳ **PARKING:** 1 **CARDS:**

♦♦♦♦ Jewell's

220 Citadel Rd, The Hoe PL1 3BB ☎ 01752 254760
📠 01752 254760
Dir: *A38 towards city centre, follow sign for Barbican, then The Hoe. Left at traffic lights, right at top of road onto Citadel Rd. Jewell's 0.25m*

This smartly decorated family-run hotel is only a short walk from the Hoe and is convenient for the city centre and the Barbican. Bedrooms offer a good standard of comfort and breakfast is served in the pleasant dining room. Secure parking is available.

FACILITIES: 10 rms (7 en suite) (5 fmly) No smoking in 3 bedrooms No smoking in dining room TVB tea/coffee Cen ht TVL **PRICES:** s £20-£25; d £40-£45✳ LB **PARKING:** 4 **CARDS:**

♦♦♦♦ *Squires*

7 St James Place East, The Hoe PL1 3AS ☎ 01752 261459
📠 01752 261459
Dir: *turn off A38 to city centre, 1st exit off rdbt, right at lights, left at next lights, 1st right, 1st left, Squires in left corner*

Tucked away in a quiet residential area, just a short walk from both the Hoe and the city centre, this family run establishment offers comfortable accommodation for both the business and leisure guest. Bedrooms are smartly presented and well equipped.

FACILITIES: 8 rms (6 en suite) (1 fmly) No smoking TVB tea/coffee No dogs (ex guide dogs) Cen ht No coaches **PARKING:** 4 **CARDS:**

A indicates an Associate entry, which has been inspected and rated by the ETC or the RAC in England

England

PLYMOUTH continued

♦♦♦ Hotel Royal
11 Elliot St, The Hoe PL1 2PP ☎ 01752 226222
01752 223499
e-mail: hotelroyal@virgin.co.uk
Dir: *from A38-A374, follow signs for city centre, then signs for Pavilions, turn left into Atheneum St, then straight into Elliot St, hotel half way up*

Situated just a short walk from the Hoe and Barbican and close to the city centre, this hotel is ideally located for both business and leisure use. Bedrooms are smartly presented and well equipped. A full cooked breakfast is served in the bright and cheerfully decorated dining room.
FACILITIES: 14 rms (11 en suite) (5 fmly) No smoking in dining room TVB tea/coffee No dogs Cen ht **PARKING:** 3 **CARDS:**

♦♦♦ Caraneal
12/14 Pier St, West Hoe PL1 3BS ☎ 01752 663589 & 212871
01752 663589
e-mail: caranealhotel@hotmail.com
Dir: *from A38 follow signs for city centre, then signs for 'The Hoe' & seafront. On seafront pass Plymouth Dome, turn right after Dome*
Within walking distance of the Hoe, city centre and numerous other attractions this small hotel offers stylish, well-equipped accommodation. Some rooms are located on the ground floor. A smart lounge and residents' bar are available to guests, whilst full English breakfasts are served in the dining room.
FACILITIES: 9 en suite (1 fmly) No smoking in 3 bedrooms No smoking in dining room TVB tea/coffee No dogs (ex guide dogs) Licensed Cen ht TVL No coaches **PRICES:** s £25-£30; d £40-£45* **PARKING:** 2
CARDS:

♦♦♦ Citadel House
55 Citadel Rd West, The Hoe PL1 3AU ☎ 01752 661712
01752 202190
e-mail: info@citadelhouse.co.uk
Dir: *from A38 follow The Hoe/Seafront signs to Notte St. Turn into Hoe approach rd to T-junct, turn right - Citadel Rd*
Just a short stroll from The Hoe, Barbican and the city centre, this delightful Victorian property offers warm and genuine hospitality and comfortable bedrooms. Breakfast is taken in the attractive front facing dining room, providing a hearty and tasty start to the day. Additional facilities include a guest lounge.
FACILITIES: 13 rms (7 en suite) (3 fmly) No smoking in dining room TVB tea/coffee No dogs (ex guide dogs) Cen ht TVL **PRICES:** s £15-£20; d £28-£44* **BB CARDS:**

♦♦♦ Cranbourne Hotel
278-282 Citadel Rd, The Hoe PL1 2PZ ☎ 01752 263858 & 224646 01752 263858
e-mail: cran.hotel@virgin.net
This attractive Georgian terraced house, a short walk from The Hoe, The Barbican and the city centre, has been extensively renovated. Bedrooms are neatly furnished and well equipped.

continued

Hearty breakfasts are served in the elegant dining room and there is also a cosy bar.
FACILITIES: 37 rms (25 en suite) (3 fmly) No smoking in dining room TVB tea/coffee Licensed Cen ht TVL **PRICES:** s £20-£35; d £40-£50*
PARKING: 14 **CARDS:**

♦♦♦ *Devonshire*
22 Lockyer Rd, Mannamead PL3 4RL ☎ 01752 220726
01752 220766
e-mail: phil@devshire.co.uk
Dir: *at Hyde Park public house on traffic island turn left into Wilderness Road. After 60mtrs turn left into Lockyer Rd*
This friendly Victorian town house is conveniently located close to the shopping area of Mutley Plain, and has a regular bus service to the city centre. The well-proportioned bedrooms are bright and attractive, and a comfortable lounge is available. Evening meals are provided by prior arrangement.
FACILITIES: 10 rms (4 en suite) (4 fmly) No smoking in 1 bedrooms No smoking in dining room STV TVB tea/coffee No dogs Licensed Cen ht TVL Dinner Last d 2pm **PARKING:** 6 **CARDS:**

♦♦♦ Four Seasons
207 Citadel Rd East, The Hoe PL1 2JF ☎ 01752 223591
01752 202192
e-mail: fourseasons1@talk21.com
Dir: *From A38 follow Hoe/Seafront signs to Notte St, turn left into Hoegate St, then right*
Full of charm, this professionally run small guest house is conveniently located for the Barbican and city centre. Many personal touches, such as fresh flowers, complement the friendly and hospitable atmosphere. A full English breakfast, or vegetarian option on request, is served in the cosy dining room.
FACILITIES: 8 rms (7 en suite) (3 fmly) No smoking in dining room TVB tea/coffee No dogs (ex guide dogs) Cen ht No coaches **PRICES:** d £32-£44* **LB BB NOTES:** Closed 25-31 Dec **CARDS:**

♦♦♦ Georgian House Hotel
51 Citadel Rd, The Hoe PL1 3AU ☎ 01752 663237
01752 253953
e-mail: georgianhousehotel@msn.com
Dir: *Citadel Rd opposite Plymouth Pavillion conference centre. House 500yds on left*
Providing comfortable accommodation this Georgian house is ideally located within walking distance of the city centre, the Hoe and Barbican. Bedrooms are well equipped, light and airy. Hear, traditional breakfasts are served in the pleasant dining room, and a smart lounge is available for guests.
FACILITIES: 10 en suite No smoking in 2 bedrooms No smoking in dining room TVB tea/coffee Direct dial from bedrooms No dogs (ex guide dogs) Cen ht No coaches **PRICES:** s £25-£31; d £37-£44* **BB NOTES:** Closed Dec-Jan **CARDS:**

♦♦♦ The Lamplighter Hotel
103 Citadel Rd, The Hoe PL1 2RN ☎ 01752 663855
01752 228139
e-mail: lamplighterhotel@ukonline.co.uk
Dir: *exit A38, follow signs to city centre, 1st exit at rdbt, left at 3rd traffic lights, right at 5th traffic lightsand take 2nd right*
Conveniently located with easy access to the Hoe, Barbican and city centre, this comfortable guest house is ideal for both leisure and business guests. Bedrooms, including family rooms are light and airy and vary in size. Breakfast is taken in the dining room, which has an adjoining lounge area.
FACILITIES: 9 en suite (2 fmly) No smoking in dining room TVB tea/coffee Cen ht TVL **PRICES:** s £22-£32; d £35-£42* **LB BB**
PARKING: 4 **NOTES:** Closed 25 Dec **CARDS:**

POSTBRIDGE Map 03 SX67

Premier Collection

♦♦♦♦♦ Lydgate House

PL20 6TJ ☎ 01822 880209 📠 01822 880202
e-mail: lydgatehouse@email.com
Dir: *M5/A30 take B3212 to Moretonhampstead & continue to Postbridge. Left down lane before bridge. From A386 Plymouth/Tavistock to Yelverton & Princetown on B3212 & onto Postbridge, right over bridge. House 500yds*

Set in a secluded valley, surrounded by 36 acres of moorland, with the East Dart River flowing through the fields below the house, this central Dartmoor location is ideal for walking the moors and exploring the many places of interest. Rooms and public areas are comfortable with numerous extra facilities. Lunches, afternoon cream teas and dinner are all available. A delightful lounge bar and sun terrace are also available.
FACILITIES: 7 en suite (1 GF) No smoking TVB tea/coffee Licensed Cen ht No children 12yrs No coaches Fishing Dinner Last d 8.30pm **PRICES:** s £37-£40; d £80-£100 **PARKING:** 10 **CARDS:**

SALCOMBE Map 03 SX73

See also Kingsbridge

♦♦♦♦ The Lodge Hotel

Higher Town, Malborough, Kingsbridge TQ7 3RN ☎ 01548 561405 📠 01548 561766
e-mail: info@thelodge.uk.com
Dir: *A381 from Kingsbridge to Salcombe. On reaching Malborough take 2nd turning on the bend opposite petrol station. 1st R into Lower Town rd. Towards the school, entrance 150yds on R*
This attractive house is a peaceful and comfortable place to stay. Guest rooms are stylishly decorated with stencilled walls, co-ordinated fabrics and pine furniture. Freshly cooked breakfasts, made with local ingredients, are served in the conservatory. There is a lounge and bar and guests may also use the pleasant garden.
FACILITIES: 8 en suite (1 fmly) (2 GF) No smoking TVB tea/coffee No dogs Licensed Cen ht No coaches Dinner Last d 3pm **PRICES:** s £24-£35; d £48-£58* LB **PARKING:** 8 **CARDS:**

SEATON Map 03 SY29

♦♦♦♦ Beach End Guest House

8 Trevelyan Rd EX12 2NL ☎ 01297 23388 📠 01297 625604
e-mail: beachendatseaton@aol.com
Dir: *turn off for Seaton from A3052 at eastern end of seafront near yacht club and harbour*

continued

Situated on the site of an old coastguard cottage, at the mouth of the River Axe, Beach End offers comfortable accommodation with wonderful sea views. Bedrooms are individually decorated and equipped with many thoughtful extras and personal touches. Breakfast is taken in the light and airy dining room.
FACILITIES: 3 en suite No smoking in dining room TVB tea/coffee No dogs (ex guide dogs) Cen ht No children No coaches **PRICES:** s £40; d £50* **PARKING:** 4 **NOTES:** Closed Nov-Mar **CARDS:**

♦♦♦♦ Mariners Hotel

Esplanade EX12 2NP ☎ 01297 20560 📠 01297 20560
Dir: *central of seafront*
This small, privately run hotel, situated on Seaton seafront, overlooks Lyme Bay. Bedrooms are comfortably furnished and feature thoughtful extras. There is a spacious and comfortable lounge, with an additional sea-facing sun lounge and adjacent bar. A choice of home-cooked meals is offered in the relaxed atmosphere of the dining room.
FACILITIES: 10 en suite (1 fmly) No smoking in dining room TVB tea/coffee Licensed Cen ht TVL No coaches Dinner **PRICES:** s £25-£30; d £42-£46* LB **PARKING:** 10 **CARDS:**

♦♦♦ Bay View

Trevelyan Rd EX12 2NL ☎ 01297 20400
e-mail: debbie.lindsey@members.v21.co.uk
Dir: *from M5 follow A358 Chard follow on through Axminster and Musbury, at staggered junct follow B3162 to Axmouth/Seaton, road runs parallel to River Axe, over bridge, Bay View 1st house on left overlooking harbour*
You'll find a warm welcome and homely atmosphere here at Bay View, a Victorian detached house that overlooks Axe Harbour and cliffs. Ideally located for the beach, town centre and local attractions, accommodation comprises of comfortably furnished and well-equipped bedrooms. Breakfast is taken around the communal table in the charming dining room.
FACILITIES: 3 rms (1 fmly) No smoking TVB tea/coffee No dogs (ex guide dogs) **PRICES:** d fr £40* LB **PARKING:** 3

U Beaumont

Castle Hill EX12 2QW ☎ 01297 20832
At the time of going to press the Diamond classification for this establishment had not been confirmed. Please check the AA website www.theAA.com for up-to-date information.
FACILITIES: 5 en suite (2 fmly)

SHALDON

See Teignmouth

England

SIDMOUTH Map 03 SY18

See also Ottery St Mary

Premier Collection

♦♦♦♦♦ The Old Farmhouse

Hillside Rd EX10 8JG ☎ 01395 512284

Dir: *from Exeter A3052 to Sidmouth, Bowd x-rds turn right, 2m, left at rdbt, left at mini-rdbt, next right, over humpback bridge, bear right on the corner*

This beautiful 16th-century thatched farmhouse has been lovingly restored to its former glory and is quietly located in a residential area, only a short stroll from the Esplanade and shops. Bedrooms are delightfully furnished and the public rooms are most charming with old beams and inglenook fireplaces. The welcoming proprietors delight in providing memorable dinners using old-fashioned recipes and fresh local ingredients.

FACILITIES: 3 en suite 4 annexe rms (3 en suite) (1 fmly) No smoking TV3B tea/coffee Licensed Cen ht TVL No coaches Dinner Last d am **PRICES:** s £24-£30; d £48-£60✱ **LB PARKING:** 4 **NOTES:** Closed Nov-Jan **CARDS:**

Premier Collection

♦♦♦♦♦ The Salty Monk

Church St, Sidford EX10 9QP ☎ 01395 513174
01395 514722
e-mail: andy@saltymonkhotelsidmouth.co.uk

Dir: *on A3052 in village of Sidford opposite church*

Dating back to the 16th century, this property is set in Sidford, about one mile from Sidmouth. Guests are assured of a warm welcome from the owners, who are responsible for producing the thoroughly enjoyable meals. Fresh produce, sourced locally and prepared with skill, ensures that the food is of a high standard. The well-presented bedrooms are comfortable, with many thoughtful extras; several rooms feature spa baths or special showers.

continued

FACILITIES: 5 en suite No smoking in bedrooms No smoking in dining room TVB tea/coffee Licensed Cen ht Pool Table Jacuzzi Dinner Last d 9pm **PRICES:** s £47.50-£59.50; d £75-£87✱ **LB PARKING:** 20 **CARDS:**

♦♦♦♦ Glendevon Hotel

Cotmaton Rd EX10 8QX ☎ 01395 514028
e-mail: enquiries@glendevon-hotel.co.uk

Dir: *M5 junct 30/A376 to rdbt, then A3052 for 12m, right for B3176 and follow road until it narrows to mini rdbt. Turn right, house 100m on right*

Located within a few minutes' walk of the town centre and beaches, this stylish Victorian house provides guests with neatly presented comfortable bedrooms, which are well-equipped with extra facilities. Guests are assured of a warm welcome from the resident owners, who provide friendly and attentive service and wholesome home-cooked evening meals, by prior arrangement.

FACILITIES: 8 en suite No smoking TVB tea/coffee No dogs Licensed Cen ht No children 10yrs No coaches Dinner Last d 4pm **PRICES:** s £24-£28; d £50-£56✱ **LB**

♦♦♦ Jubilee Cottage

75 Chapel St, Sidbury EX10 0RQ ☎ 01395 597295
e-mail: rd.coles@talk21.com

Dir: *on A375 between Honiton and Sidmouth, just past church in Sidbury*

This 16th-century, thatched cottage with exposed beams and period features, is centrally located in the peaceful village of Sidbury. Bedrooms are comfortably furnished and there is a cosy lounge for guests' use. Breakfast can be taken around the communal table in the dining room, or weather permitting, on the patio. German and Spanish spoken and Euros welcome.

FACILITIES: 3 rms No smoking TVB tea/coffee No dogs Licensed Cen ht TVL No children 9yrs No coaches **PRICES:** s fr £23; d fr £40✱ **LB NOTES:** Closed Xmas/New Year

SOUTH BRENT Map 03 SX66

Premier Collection

♦♦♦♦♦ *Coombe House*

North Huish TQ10 9NJ ☎ 01548 821277 01548 821277
e-mail: coombehouse@hotmail.com

Dir: *A38 from Exeter, exit at Ermington/Modbury/Yealmpton, take A3210, at x-rds onto B3196 towards Loddiswell. 2nd left & 2nd lane left*

This peaceful Georgian home is surrounded by meadows and woodland. Many bedrooms enjoy splendid views across the garden, which features a lake, pond and much wildlife. Bedrooms are individually furnished and bathrooms have recently been redecorated. The spacious, sumptuous lounge has an inviting log fire. Breakfast, and dinner (by arrangement) are taken in the elegant dining room.

continued

England

Ingredients used are local, organic and home-grown when possible. There is self-catering accommodation in the adjacent skilfully converted barns.
FACILITIES: 4 en suite (1 fmly) No smoking TVB tea/coffee No dogs (ex guide dogs) Cen ht No coaches Special arrangement with local golf club Dinner Last d 10am **PARKING:** 10

The Pack Horse
1 Plymouth Rd TQ10 9BH ☎ 01364 72283
At the time of going to press the Diamond classification for this establishment had not been confirmed. Please check the AA website www.theAA.com for up-to-date information.
FACILITIES: 3 en suite (1 fmly)

SOUTH MOLTON Map 03 SS72

Premier Collection

♦♦♦♦♦ Kerscott *(SS793255)*
Ash Mill EX36 4QG ☎ 01769 550262 01769 550910
Mrs T Sampson
e-mail: kerscott.farm@virgin.net
Dir: *6m east of South Molton on B3227. 1.5m from A361. Sign at bottom of lane*
Peacefully located on the edge of Exmoor National Park, this is a working farm, full of tradition and warmth. Mentioned in the Domesday Book of 1086, the present L-shaped house dates from the early 15th century. Full of beams, sloping floors, inglenook fireplaces, and log fires in the winter, it is beautifully furnished throughout with china and objets d'art. Dinner is available by prior arrangement.
FACILITIES: 3 en suite No smoking TVB tea/coffee No dogs Cen ht No children 14yrs 220 acres beef, sheep Dinner Last d 10am
PRICES: d £40-£46 **LB PARKING:** 4

♦♦♦♦ West Down *(SS749259)*
Whitechapel EX36 3EQ ☎ 01769 550373 01769 550839
Mr & Mrs R Savery
e-mail: Info@westdown.co.uk
Dir: *A361 turn right at rdbt sign posted Whitechapel, down slip road 100yds turn right into the drive*
Set in 34 acres and located on the southerly edge of Exmoor, West Down offers a warm welcome and comfortable accommodation. Bedrooms are spacious and equipped with many considerate extras. Using local produce whenever possible, Brenda's home-cooked dinners are available by prior arrangement. The enticing lounge features an open fire.
FACILITIES: 3 en suite (1 fmly) No smoking TVB tea/coffee No dogs (ex guide dogs) Cen ht TVL 34 acres racehorses Dinner Last d noon
PRICES: s £28-£30; d £44-£50✻ **LB PARKING:** 10

♦♦♦ Old Coaching Inn
Queen St EX36 3BJ ☎ 01769 572526
Dir: *leave A361 at roundabout signed to South Molton*
Situated in the bustling market town of South Molton, a warm welcome is assured at this popular inn which offers soundly appointed accommodation. An extensive menu provides a range of good value dishes served either within the bar area or separate restaurant. Additional facilities include a large function room.
FACILITIES: 6 en suite (2 fmly) TVB tea/coffee No dogs (ex guide dogs) Cen ht Sauna Pool Table Dinner Last d 9.30pm **PRICES:** s £25-£30; d £50✻
MEALS: Lunch £10-£15&alc Dinner £10-£15&alc✻ **PARKING:** 26
CARDS:

STOCKLAND Map 03 ST20

♦♦♦ The Kings Arms Inn
EX14 9BS ☎ 01404 881361 01404 881732
e-mail: info@kingsarms.net
Dir: *from centre of Honiton head for NE junct of A30 just before you join Stockland is signed right, straight ahead for 3m turn left downhill into village*
A convivial atmosphere prevails at this attractive village inn, where staff are helpful and attentive at all times. Bedrooms are spacious and comfortable, with high quality ensuite facilities. Food is a highlight, with an extensive and imaginative range of tempting homemade dishes to choose from. A garden is available and ample parking is a bonus.
FACILITIES: 3 en suite No smoking in dining room TVB tea/coffee Direct dial from bedrooms Cen ht TVL Dinner Last d 9pm **PRICES:** s fr £30; d fr £50✻ **MEALS:** Lunch £14.50-£23alc Dinner £14.50-£23alc✻
PARKING: 40 **NOTES:** Closed Xmas Day **CARDS:**

TAVISTOCK Map 02 SX47

Premier Collection

♦♦♦♦♦ Tor Cottage
PL16 0JE ☎ 01822 860248 01822 860126
e-mail: info@torcottage.co.uk

(For full entry see Chillaton)

TAVISTOCK continued

♦♦♦♦ April Cottage

12 Mount Tavy Rd PL19 9JB ☎ 01822 613280 ▤ 01822 613280
Dir: *from A30 take A386 to Tavistock continue over New Stannary Bridge, approx 100mtrs further approaching a mini rdbt April Cottage is on the right*
FACILITIES: 3 en suite (1 fmly) No smoking TVB tea/coffee Cen ht TVL No coaches Fishing Dinner Last d 5pm **PRICES:** s £30-£35; d £45-£50✳ LB **PARKING:** 5

♦♦♦ Coach House

PL19 8NS ☎ 01822 617515 ▤ 617515
e-mail: eddie@coachhouse1.supanet.com
Dir: *from Tavistock A390 W for 2m to Gulworthy Cross, turn right to chip shop. In village turn right to Ottery, 1st building on right*
Dating back to 1857, this building was constructed for the Duke of Bedford and sympathetically converted by the current owners. Some bedrooms are available on the ground floor and also in an adjacent barn conversion. Dinner is available in the cosy dining room or the newly constructed restaurant, which leads into the south-facing garden.
FACILITIES: 6 en suite 3 annexe en suite (1 fmly) (4 GF) No smoking in bedrooms No smoking in dining room TVB tea/coffee Direct dial from bedrooms Licensed Cen ht No children 5yrs Dinner Last d 9.30pm
PRICES: s £31; d £52✳ LB **PARKING:** 12 **NOTES:** Closed Jan-13 Feb
CARDS:

TEIGNMOUTH — Map 03 SX97

Premier Collection

♦♦♦♦♦ Thomas Luny House

Teign St TQ14 8EG ☎ 01626 772976
e-mail: alisonandjohn@thomas-luny-house.co.uk
Dir: *A381 to Teignmouth, at 3rd lights turn right to quay, 50yds turn left into Teign St, after 60yds turn right through white archway*

Built in the late 18th century by marine artist Thomas Luny this charming house offers unique and comfortable accommodation in the old quarter of Teignmouth. Bedrooms are individually decorated and furnished, all with a good range of thoughtful extras. An elegant drawing room with French windows leads into a walled garden with a terraced sitting area. Breakfast, featuring local produce, is served in the charming dining room.
FACILITIES: 4 en suite No smoking TVB tea/coffee Direct dial from bedrooms No dogs (ex guide dogs) Licensed Cen ht No children 12yrs No coaches **PRICES:** s £50-£57.50; d £60-£80✳ LB **PARKING:** 8
CARDS:

Potters Mooring

30 The Green, Shaldon TQ14 0DN ☎ 01626 873 225
At the time of going to press the Diamond classification for this establishment had not been confirmed. Please check the AA website www.theAA.com for up-to-date information.
FACILITIES: 6 en suite 2 annexe en suite (2 fmly)

TIVERTON — Map 03 SS91

Premier Collection

♦♦♦♦♦ Hornhill Farmhouse *(SS965117)*

Exeter Hill EX16 4PL ☎ 01884 253352 ▤ 01884 253352
Mrs B Pugsley
e-mail: hornhill@tinyworld.co.uk
Dir: *follow signs to Grand Western Canal, take right fork up Exeter Hill. Farmhouse on left at top of hill*

From its peaceful hilltop setting, Hornhill enjoys panoramic views of the town and the Exe Valley. Tasteful decor and antique furnishings enhance the character of the farmhouse, which dates in part from the 18th century. Bedrooms are equipped with modern facilities and there is a lovely sitting room with a log fire. Dinner is available by prior arrangement and guests take meals at one large table in the elegant dining room.
FACILITIES: 3 en suite (1 GF) No smoking TVB tea/coffee No dogs (ex guide dogs) No children 12yrs Croquet lawn 75 acres beef, sheep Dinner Last d 24hr in advance **PRICES:** s fr £25; d fr £45✳
PARKING: 5 **CARDS:**

♦♦♦♦ Lower Collipriest *(SS953117)*

EX16 4PT ☎ 01884 252321 ▤ 01884 252321 Mrs R Olive
e-mail: linda@lowercollipriest.co.uk
Dir: *off Great Western Way, approx 1m*
This delightful thatched farmhouse enjoys a pleasantly rural location in the Exe Valley, only one mile from Tiverton. Bedrooms are spacious, tastefully decorated and have many thoughtful extras. There is a lounge with an inglenook fireplace; and by prior arrangement, guests can enjoy home-cooked dinners around a large communal table.
FACILITIES: 3 en suite No smoking tea/coffee No dogs (ex guide dogs) Cen ht TVL No children 16yrs Fishing 220 acres dairy Dinner Last d noon
PRICES: s fr £25; d fr £50✳ LB **PARKING:** 6 **NOTES:** Closed Nov-Etr
CARDS:

♦♦♦ Lodge Hill *(SS945112)*

EX16 5PA ☎ 01884 251200 ▤ 01884 242090 Mr & Mrs B Reader
e-mail: checkin@lodgehill.co.uk
Dir: *1m S of town centre, off A396*
From its elevated position this large detached former farmhouse, set in well tended gardens, has good views over the surrounding countryside. The comfortable bedrooms are well equipped with many extras and the majority benefit from the delightful views. Guests may relax in the comfortable lounge or the charming bar. Ample parking is a bonus.
FACILITIES: 8 en suite (2 fmly) No smoking in bedrooms No smoking in dining room TVB tea/coffee Direct dial from bedrooms Licensed Cen ht TVL 3 acres non-working Dinner Last d 5pm **PRICES:** s fr £35; d fr £55✳ LB
PARKING: 12 **CARDS:**

♦♦♦ Angel

13 St Peter St EX16 6NU ☎ 01884 253392 📠 01884 251154
e-mail: cerimar@eurobell.co.uk
Dir: *from A361 exit at Gornhay Cross, follow signs to Bickleigh until reaching 5th rdbt, turn right then right again at next junct follow road round to left at triangle, Guest House 200mtrs on right*
Conveniently located in a quiet area close to the town centre, this personally run establishment offers a warm welcome to all guests. Bedrooms are neatly furnished and well-presented, whilst public areas include a comfortable guest lounge. There are a variety of local eateries within walking distance.
FACILITIES: 7 rms (3 en suite) (2 fmly) No smoking in dining room No smoking in lounges TVB tea/coffee No dogs (ex guide dogs) Cen ht TVL No coaches **PRICES:** s £18-£24; d £36-£44* BB

♦♦♦ Quoit-At-Cross *(ST923188)*

Stoodleigh EX16 9PJ ☎ 01398 351280 📠 01398 351351
Mrs L Hill
e-mail: quoit-at-cross@talk21.com
Dir: *A396 N for Bampton. After approx 3.5m turn left over blue bridge for Stoodleigh, into village, stone farmhouse on 1st junct*
A warm and friendly welcome is assured at this delightful stone-built working farmhouse with views over the rolling Devonshire countryside. The comfortable bedrooms are well-decorated and furnished, with many extra facilities provided. A lounge and pretty garden are also available to guests. Home cooked dinners are available by prior arrangement.
FACILITIES: 3 en suite No smoking TVB tea/coffee No dogs Cen ht TVL 160 acres organic mixed **PRICES:** s fr £22; d fr £44* **PARKING:** 3 **NOTES:** Closed Oct-Apr

TORBAY

See Brixham, Paignton and Torquay

TORQUAY Map 03 SX96

Premier Collection

♦♦♦♦♦ Colindale Hotel

20 Rathmore Rd, Chelston TQ2 6NY ☎ 01803 293947
e-mail: bronte@eurobell.co.uk
Dir: *From Torquay station 200mtr on left in Rathmore Rd*
Set in attractive and well-tended gardens, the Colindale Hotel is located in a quiet area, close to the seafront. This friendly home is stylish and elegant and service is most attentive. Guestrooms, some of which have views over Torbay, are comfortable and well appointed. Excellent dinners (by prior arrangement) and breakfast, feature freshly cooked, interesting dishes and provide a memorable dining experience not to be missed.
FACILITIES: 8 rms (6 en suite) (1 fmly) No smoking in bedrooms No smoking in dining room No smoking in lounges TVB tea/coffee No coaches Dinner Last d 12noon **PRICES:** s £25-£27; d £50-£54* LB **PARKING:** 6 **CARDS:**

♦♦♦ Red Diamonds highlight the top establishments within the AA's 3,4,and 5 Diamond ratings.

Premier Collection

♦♦♦♦♦ Mulberry House

1 Scarborough Rd TQ2 5UJ ☎ 01803 213639
Dir: *from Torquay seafront turn up Belgrave Rd, then 1st right up Scarborough Rd, premises on left*
More accurately described as a restaurant with rooms, this is a delightful Victorian property in a quiet residential area close to the seafront. Freshly prepared dishes are offered from a blackboard menu in the cosy restaurant, and a log fire burning on cooler evenings. The three attractively furnished and decorated bedrooms have an abundance of charm and character.
FACILITIES: 3 en suite No smoking TVB No dogs Licensed Cen ht Dinner Last d 9.30pm **PRICES:** s £35; d £50-£60* LB

♦♦♦♦ Atlantis Hotel

68 Belgrave Rd TQ2 5HY ☎ 01803 292917 📠 01803 292917
e-mail: simon.davies1@btinternet.com
Dir: *follow signs to Torquay seafront, turn left, left again at traffic lights into Belgrave Rd, straight through next lights, hotel on left*

The friendly proprietors are most attentive at this conveniently located hotel. Bedrooms are very well equipped with many personal touches and are comfortably furnished. Traditional breakfasts are served in the dining room and guests are invited to relax in the attractive lounge with a drink from the bar.
FACILITIES: 11 rms (9 en suite) (7 fmly) No smoking in bedrooms No smoking in dining room TVB tea/coffee No dogs (ex guide dogs) Licensed Cen ht TVL Dinner Last d 3pm **PRICES:** s £15-£20; d £40-£50* LB BB **PARKING:** 3 **CARDS:**

♦♦♦♦ Aveland Hotel

Aveland Rd, Babbacombe TQ1 3PT ☎ 01803 326622
📠 01803 328940
e-mail: avelandhotel@aol.com
Dir: *A380 to Torquay. Take A3022 following Torquay signs. 3rd traffic lights left signed Teignmouth, over next lights. Top of hill, over island along Hele Rd. Down hill to mini islands, left into Westhill Rd. After 0.5m at lights into Warbo Rd. Then 2nd left into Aveland Rd*
Set in well tended gardens and located in a peaceful area of Babbacombe, close to Cary Park and within easy walking distance of the town and Downs, this family-run hotel offers a warm, friendly and attentive service. Bedrooms are attractive and well equipped. A pleasant bar is available as well as two comfortable lounges. Members of the deaf community are especially welcome, the proprietors are both BSL signers.
FACILITIES: 10 en suite (3 fmly) No smoking in bedrooms No smoking in dining room No smoking in lounges tea/coffee No dogs Licensed Cen ht TVL No coaches Dinner Last d 5.30pm **PRICES:** s £18-£24; d £36-£48* LB BB **PARKING:** 10 **CARDS:**

England

TORQUAY continued

♦♦♦♦ Babbacombe Hall Hotel

17 Manor Rd, Babbacombe TQ1 3JX ☎ 01803 325668
01803 325668
e-mail: glyn.aida.rees@lineone.net
Dir: *A380 to Torquay. At Riviera rdbt head towards Torquay along Riviera Way until Courts store on left. Take slip road signed Babbacombe/St Marychurch into Hele Road. 2nd rdbt left, then right into Westhill Rd. Left at traffic lights into Manor Rd, hotel on right*

This family-run hotel provides friendly and attentive service. Bedrooms are very well-equipped and comfortable, and are decorated in colourful and tasteful style. The hotel offers many facilities and at dinner, traditional dishes are freshly prepared and something different is always on offer with the oriental cuisine provided by the resident proprietors.
FACILITIES: 7 en suite No smoking in bedrooms No smoking in dining room No smoking in lounges TVB tea/coffee No dogs Licensed Cen ht TVL No coaches Outdoor swimming pool (heated) Dinner Last d 6pm
PRICES: s £22-£30; d £44-£60✳ **LB** **PARKING:** 7
CARDS:

♦♦♦♦ Barclay Court Hotel

29 Castle Rd TQ1 3BB ☎ 01803 292791 01803 215715
e-mail: reservations@barclaycourt.co.uk
Dir: *from Newton Abbot into Torquay follow 'civic offices' signs. Continue until car park on right visible, then bear right. Immediately after pedestrian crossing left into Castle Rd, and hotel up hill on right*
The resident proprietors of this pleasant hotel are friendly and welcoming and provide an attentive service, including child minding. The hotel is within easy strolling distance of all the seaside attractions. Rooms are brightly decorated and comfortably furnished. A pleasant lounge is provided and there is also a spacious bar. Guests can also relax in the south-facing, well-tended garden.
FACILITIES: 5 en suite 9 annexe en suite (2 fmly) (4 GF) No smoking TVB tea/coffee Direct dial from bedrooms No dogs (ex guide dogs) Licensed TVL No coaches Dinner Last d before noon **PRICES:** s £28-£30; d £56-£60✳ **LB** **CONF:** Class 40 Board 20 Del from £45 ✳ **PARKING:** 8
CARDS:

♦♦♦♦ *Belmont Hotel*

66 Belgrave Rd TQ2 5HY ☎ 01803 295028 01803 211668
e-mail: belmont@murphytq2.fsnet.co.uk
Dir: *Follow signs to seafront, at seafront left at next traffic lights left into Belgrave Road up Belgrave Road, Hotel left past traffic lights.*
The friendly proprietors provide a comfortable and relaxing atmosphere at this conveniently located hotel. Bedrooms are well equipped and are provided with many extra facilities and comforts. Breakfast is served in the attractive dining room, which has many mementoes donated by thoughtful guests.
FACILITIES: 12 rms (8 en suite) (4 fmly) No smoking in dining room TVB tea/coffee No dogs Licensed Cen ht TVL No children 10yrs **PARKING:** 3
CARDS:

♦♦♦♦ Blue Haze Hotel

Seaway Ln TQ2 6PS ☎ 01803 607186 & 606205
01803 607186
e-mail: mail@bluehazehotel.co.uk
Mar-Oct
Dir: *follow signs to seafront, right to traffic lights by Grand Hotel. Right at lights, then immediately left into Hennapyn Rd. Turn right at crossroads with Seaway Lane. Blue Haze 200yds on right*
Surrounded by attractive and well-tended gardens and having splendid views towards the Bay, this delightful Victorian property is only 500 yards from the sea. Bedrooms are very comfortable, spacious and provided with a host of extra facilities and comforts. A relaxing lounge is available with an open fire in winter and guests are most welcome to use the garden in summer. Breakfast, not to be missed, provides a range of fresh and local produce, expertly cooked and attractively presented.
FACILITIES: 9 en suite (3 fmly) (2 GF) No smoking TVB tea/coffee No dogs Licensed Cen ht TVL No coaches **PRICES:** s £40-£45; d £60-£70 **LB**
PARKING: 20 **CARDS:**

♦♦♦♦ Cedar Court Hotel

3 St Matthews Rd, Chelston TQ2 6JA ☎ 01803 607851
01803 607851
Dir: *A3022, right lane at station signposted seafront, right at 2nd lights into Walnut Rd, right at church, located on the left*

Close to Cockington village and within easy strolling distance of the seafront, this friendly hotel is quietly located in a peaceful residential area. Bedrooms are individually decorated and very well equipped. Art and craft breaks are available, and many guests return on a regular basis. Dinner (by prior arrangement) and pleasant breakfasts are served in the attractive dining room.
FACILITIES: 8 en suite 2 annexe en suite (2 fmly) (1 GF) No smoking TVB tea/coffee No dogs (ex guide dogs) Cen ht TVL No coaches Dinner Last d 4.30pm **PRICES:** s £22-£28; d £44-£56✳ **LB** **PARKING:** 5
CARDS:

♦♦♦♦ Coombe Court Hotel

67 Babbacombe Downs Rd, Babbacombe TQ1 3LP
☎ 01803 327097 01803 327097
e-mail: pj@coombecourthotel.co.uk
Dir: *follow sign to St Marychurch and Babbacombe, through Hele, pass golf club & shops, 2nd turning left is Babbacombe Downs Rd, hotel on right*
There's a friendly atmosphere at this family run hotel, located close to Babbacombe's attractions. Bedrooms are spacious and comfortably furnished; some have access to the balcony and some are situated on the ground floor. A cosy bar is provided as well as a sunroom and lounge. Dinners are available by prior arrangement.
FACILITIES: 15 en suite (3 fmly) (2 GF) No smoking TVB tea/coffee No dogs Licensed Cen ht TVL No children 10yrs No coaches Pool Table Games room, 3/4 snooker table, darts Dinner Last d by arrangement
PRICES: s £26-£40; d £52-£64✳ **LB** **PARKING:** 15 **NOTES:** Closed Xmas/New Year rs Nov-Jan **CARDS:**

England

♦♦♦♦ *Court Prior*
St Lukes Rd South TQ2 5NZ ☎ 01803 292766 🖷 01803 292766
e-mail: courtprior@lineone.net
Dir: *A380 to Torquay, at Halfords on right, right at lights into Avenue Rd, proceed to seafront, left at next lights up Sheddon Hill St Lukes Rd*
Quietly located in a residential area yet in walking distance of the seafront and town centre, this charming house, built in 1860, offers comfortable accommodation. Rooms are spacious, well decorated and pleasantly furnished throughout. Traditional homemade dishes are served at dinner. There is also a large comfortable guest lounge.
FACILITIES: 10 en suite (3 fmly) No smoking in dining room TVB tea/coffee TVL No children 4yrs Last d 4pm **PARKING:** 10 **CARDS:**

♦♦♦♦ The Cranmore
89 Avenue Rd TQ2 5LH ☎ 01803 298488
e-mail: thecranmore@tesco.net
Dir: *A380 onto A3022, from Newton Abbot at Torre station turn right at traffic lights, premises 200yds on left*
A family run hotel, The Cranmore offers comfortable accommodation in a relaxed and friendly atmosphere. Conveniently located for the town centre and the seafront, bedrooms are attractive and well furnished, with family rooms available. Breakfast can be enjoyed in the pleasant dining room and special dietary requirements can also be catered for.
FACILITIES: 8 en suite (1 fmly) No smoking in 4 bedrooms No smoking in dining room No smoking in lounges TVB tea/coffee No dogs (ex guide dogs) Cen ht TVL No coaches **PRICES:** s £17-£22; d £34-£44✻ **LB BB**
PARKING: 4 **CARDS:**

♦♦♦♦ Crown Lodge
83 Avenue Rd TQ2 5LH ☎ 01803 298772 🖷 01803 291155
e-mail: crownlodgetqy@netscapeonline.co.uk
Dir: *A38 onto A380 through Kingkerswell onto A3022 passing The Willows on left. Pass traffic lights at Shiphay, at next traffic lights take right lane (harbour & seafront) Crown Lodge 200yds on left*
The new proprietors at this smart hotel are very friendly and welcoming and provide attentive and caring service. Crown Lodge is ideally located within level walking distance of the harbour and seafront and is close to the town centre attractions. The bedrooms are comfortably furnished and pleasantly spacious. An attractive lounge is available and well-cooked breakfasts, with a wide choice from the menu that includes healthy alternatives, provide a delightful start to the day.
FACILITIES: 5 en suite (1 fmly) (1 GF) No smoking in 2 bedrooms No smoking in dining room TVB tea/coffee No dogs (ex guide dogs) Cen ht TVL No children 8-14 yrs No coaches **PRICES:** s £23-£27.50; d £36-£45✻ **LB BB PARKING:** 7 **NOTES:** Closed 20 Dec-10 Jan **CARDS:**

♦♦♦♦ Elmdene Hotel
Rathmore Rd TQ2 6NZ ☎ 01803 294940 🖷 01803 294940
e-mail: elmdenehoteltorqy@amserve.net
Dir: *enter Torquay on A3022, follow seafront signs, turn right for Chelston & Cockington into Walnut Rd, hotel on corner of 1st right.*
A friendly welcome awaits guests to Elmdene, which is conveniently located close to the seafront and the railway station. Relax in the homely comfort of this pleasant establishment, which offers freshly prepared traditional dinners, enjoyed in the comfortable dining room. Bedrooms are well furnished and equipped with a good range of extra facilities.
FACILITIES: 11 rms (7 en suite) (4 fmly) No smoking in dining room No smoking in 1 lounge TVB tea/coffee No dogs (ex guide dogs) Licensed Cen ht TVL No children 10yrs Dinner Last d 4pm **PRICES:** s £20-£25; d £40-£50✻ **LB PARKING:** 12 **CARDS:**

♦♦♦♦ Everglades Hotel
32 St Marychurch Rd TQ1 3HY ☎ 01803 295389
🖷 01803 214357
e-mail: enquiries@evergladeshotel.co.uk
Dir: *A380 Newton Abbot to Torquay at rdbt follow A3022 for Torquay town centre, in 0.5m turn left at Courts into Hele Rd, straight over rdbt into Westhill Rd, right at traffic lights into St Mary Church Rd*
The Everglades offers comfortable accommodation and a warm welcome. The friendly proprietors are attentive and strive to ensure all guests feel at home. Well-appointed bedrooms feature a range of extras. The bright and spacious lounge, sun terrace and garden patio are all available to guests. Freshly cooked dinners are served in the airy dining room, from where guests can enjoy views over the town towards Torbay.
FACILITIES: 10 en suite (2 fmly) No smoking in 3 bedrooms No smoking in dining room No smoking in lounges TVB tea/coffee Direct dial from bedrooms No dogs Licensed Cen ht No children 3 yrs No coaches Dinner Last d 5pm **PRICES:** s £25-£28; d £50-£56✻ **LB PARKING:** 8
CARDS:

♦♦♦♦ *Gainsboro Hotel*
22 Rathmore Rd TQ2 6NY ☎ 01803 292032 🖷 01803 292032
e-mail: gainsboro@freeuk.com
Dir: *from seafront turn at traffic lights by Grand Hotel. Past cricket/rugby ground, fork left. Hotel 50mtrs from junction*
In a quiet location, a short level walk from the station, seafront and Tor Abbey gardens, this pleasant hotel is convenient and comfortable and many guests return regularly. Friendly, attentive proprietors ensure a homely atmosphere. A choice of dishes, including vegetarian option, are offered at dinner and well cooked traditional English breakfasts are served in the attractive dining room.
FACILITIES: 8 rms (6 en suite) No smoking TVB tea/coffee No dogs (ex guide dogs) Licensed Cen ht TVL No coaches Dinner Last d 2pm
PARKING: 5 **CARDS:**

♦♦♦♦ Glenorleigh Hotel
26 Cleveland Rd TQ2 5BE ☎ 01803 292135 🖷 01803 213717
e-mail: glenorleighhotel@btinternet.com
Dir: *follow A3022 Newton Abbot/Torquay road until traffic lights at Torre Station, bear right into Avenue Road A379 & Cleveland Road is 1st left*

Conveniently located in a residential area, Glenorleigh offers smartly decorated bedrooms, a number of which are on the ground floor. A host of other facilities such as solarium, outdoor pool and terrace and a convivial bar make this small family run hotel ideal for leisure or business use.
FACILITIES: 16 rms (13 en suite) (6 fmly) (6 GF) No smoking in bedrooms No smoking in dining room No smoking in 1 lounge TVB tea/coffee No dogs (ex guide dogs) Licensed Cen ht TVL No coaches Outdoor swimming pool (heated) Solarium Pool Table Darts, Board Games. Dinner Last d 2pm
PRICES: s £25-£36; d £50-£72✻ **LB PARKING:** 10 **CARDS:**

England

TORQUAY continued

♦♦♦♦ Harmony Hotel

67 Avenue Rd TQ2 5LG ☎ 01803 293918
e-mail: mike.harmonyhotel@amserve.net

This conveniently located detached property is within walking distance of the seafront and town centre. Bedrooms, including ground floor rooms, are comfortable and spacious. Facilities available to guests include a lounge, a bar and an ironing room. Off street parking is a bonus. Dinner is available by prior arrangement.

FACILITIES: 11 en suite (2 fmly) (5 GF) No smoking in 4 bedrooms No smoking in dining room TVB tea/coffee No dogs (ex guide dogs) Licensed Cen ht TVL No children 8yrs No coaches Dinner Last d 11am **PRICES:** s £23-£30; d £34-£48* LB BB **PARKING:** 11 **NOTES:** Closed Xmas & New Year **CARDS:**

♦♦♦♦ Headland View

37 Babbacombe Downs Rd, Babbacombe TQ1 3LN
☎ 01803 312612 01803 312612
e-mail: briangallimore@headlandview.freeserve.co.uk

Dir: *follow A379 coast road from A380, through Teignmouth and Shalden to Babbacombe and turn left onto seafront*

Spectacular views of Lyme Bay and the Downs can be had from this delightful hotel. A warm and friendly welcome is provided for all guests by the attentive proprietors. Bedrooms are attractively decorated and many feature sea-views, balconies or Four-poster beds. Breakfast features well-cooked quality ingredients and is a highlight.

FACILITIES: 11 rms (10 en suite) (2 fmly) (1 GF) No smoking in 5 bedrooms No smoking in dining room No smoking in lounges TVB tea/coffee No dogs (ex guide dogs) Cen ht TVL No children 3yrs No coaches Pool Table **PRICES:** d £32-£50* BB **PARKING:** 8 **NOTES:** Closed Nov-Mar

♦♦♦♦ Hotel Blue Conifer

Higher Downs Rd, The Seafront, Babbacombe TQ1 3LD
☎ 01803 327637

Dir: *follow signs for Babbacombe & seafront, hotel 500yds from model village*

Hotel Blue Conifer enjoys splendid views across the beaches, to Lyme Bay and provides a delightful place to stay. Surrounded by neatly tended gardens, this attractive hotel has a relaxing and friendly atmosphere. Bedrooms, many of which have sea views, are well-equipped and one is available on the ground floor. Dinner is highly recommended.

FACILITIES: 7 en suite (3 fmly) No smoking TVB tea/coffee Licensed Cen ht No coaches Dinner Last d midday **PRICES:** s £32-£39; d £48-£62* LB **PARKING:** 9 **NOTES:** Closed Nov-Feb

♦♦♦♦ Ingoldsby Hotel

1 Chelston Rd TQ2 6PT ☎ 01803 607497 01803 690463
e-mail: ingoldsby.hotel@virgin.net

Dir: *Head to Torquay seafront. At sea front t/lights right & then right again by Grand Hotel, left behind Grand Hotel, after r/way bridge bear left, right at next x-rds and 1st into Chelston Rd*

Located in the peaceful residential area of Chelston, this comfortable and friendly hotel is just a few minutes walk from the beach and railway station. Bedrooms are pleasantly decorated and well-equipped, whilst public areas include a sun lounge and convivial bar. Enjoyable dinners and breakfasts are served in the dining room, overlooking the attractive gardens.

FACILITIES: 14 rms (12 en suite) (3 fmly) (4 GF) No smoking in bedrooms No smoking in dining room No smoking in lounges TVB tea/coffee Licensed Cen ht TVL Dinner Last d 5pm **PRICES:** s £23-£25; d £50-£59* LB **PARKING:** 14 **CARDS:**

♦♦♦♦ Knowle Court Hotel

Kent Rd, Wellswood TQ1 2NN ☎ 01803 297076
01803 292980
e-mail: enquiries@knowle-court-hotel.co.uk

Dir: *Along the Strand past Debenhams, left into Torwood St, just before Saint Matthais church turn right then immediate right, then 2nd left into Kents Rd*

Situated in a peaceful residential area, this listed house is spacious and comfortable. Bedrooms are well equipped and attractively decorated. A lounge and pleasant dining room are provided and at breakfast guests can enjoy the view over the garden and swimming pool.

FACILITIES: 8 en suite (3 fmly) No smoking TVB tea/coffee No dogs (ex guide dogs) Licensed Cen ht TVL No coaches Outdoor swimming pool (heated) **PRICES:** s £22.50-£30; d £45-£60* LB **PARKING:** 4 **NOTES:** Closed 21 Dec-6 Jan **CARDS:**

♦♦♦♦ Manor Court Hotel

4 Manor Rd, Babbacombe TQ1 3JX ☎ 01803 327249
01803 327249
e-mail: stay@manorcourthotel.co.uk

Dir: *turn off A3022 onto B3199 Hele Road continue onto Westhill Road until traffic lights and xrds turn left into Manor Road, hotel 100yds on left*

Built in 1864 and once part of the Cary Estate, the family-run Manor Court Hotel is conveniently situated close to beaches and shops. Bedrooms are well appointed and attractively decorated, with premier rooms available. The swimming pool, well-stocked bar, elegant lounge and ample parking all add to guest comfort.

FACILITIES: 19 en suite (6 fmly) No smoking in bedrooms No smoking in dining room No smoking in 1 lounge TVB tea/coffee No dogs (ex guide dogs) Licensed Cen ht TVL Outdoor swimming pool (heated) Pool Table Dinner Last d 1pm **PRICES:** s £19.50-£24.50; d £39-£49* LB **PARKING:** 19 **CARDS:**

♦♦♦♦ Newton House

31 Newton Rd, Torre TQ2 5DB ☎ 01803 297520

Dir: *50yds on left hand side of junction of Newton Road and Avenue Road, opposite Torre Railway Station*

Close to the town centre and its main attractions, guests are assured a warm welcome at Newton House. Bedrooms are spacious, delightfully decorated and all benefit from extra little luxuries. Breakfast is taken in the very pleasant dining room and a separate, comfortably furnished lounge is available for guest relaxation.

FACILITIES: 9 en suite (2 fmly) (5 GF) No smoking TVB tea/coffee No dogs Cen ht No children 3yrs No coaches **PRICES:** s fr £25; d fr £40* **PARKING:** 9 **CARDS:**

♦♦♦♦ Norwood Hotel

60 Belgrave Rd TQ2 5HY ☎ 01803 294236 01803 294224
e-mail: enquiries@norwoodhoteltorquay.co.uk

Dir: *M5, follow signs to Torquay. At Torr station follow signs for Seafront which leads to Belgrave Rd, premises on right by traffic lights*

Guests are assured of a warm welcome at this centrally located hotel, with its prize winning floral displays. The new proprietors are keen to maintain the hotel's reputation with regular visitors. The well-equipped bedrooms are comfortable and public areas, spacious. By prior arrangement, enjoyable traditional dinners are served.

FACILITIES: 11 en suite (5 fmly) No smoking in 5 bedrooms No smoking in dining room No smoking in 1 lounge TVB tea/coffee No dogs (ex guide dogs) Licensed Cen ht TVL Dinner Last d 7pm **PRICES:** d £40-£60* LB **PARKING:** 3 **CARDS:**

♦♦♦♦ Oscars Hotel
56 Belgrave Rd TQ2 5HY ☎ 01803 293563 📠 01803 296685
e-mail: oscars@blodge.fsnet.co.uk
Dir: *from outskirts of Torquay at rdbt with garden sign English Riviera go straight onto Riviera Way then Newton Road, Halford store on right, right into Avenue Rd at 2nd traffic lights left into Falkland Rd, hotel 300mtrs on left corner*
Oscars Hotel is conveniently located within easy walking distance of the seafront and the shops. This attractive property offers comfortable, well-equipped accommodation and a relaxed and friendly atmosphere prevails throughout the property. Breakfast is served in the basement dining room, with a selection of cooked dishes available.
FACILITIES: 14 en suite (1 GF) No smoking in bedrooms No smoking in dining room No smoking in 1 lounge TVB tea/coffee Direct dial from bedrooms No dogs Licensed Cen ht TVL No children 12yrs No coaches Dinner Last d 4pm **PRICES:** s £25-£27.50; d £40-£48* **LB** **PARKING:** 4
CARDS:

♦♦♦♦ Robin Hill International Hotel
74 Braddons Hill Rd East TQ1 1HF ☎ 01803 214518
📠 01803 291410
e-mail: jo@robinhillhotel.co.uk
Dir: *from Torquay Harbour towards Babbacombe, on B3199 (Babbacombe Rd) take 4th turn on L, 1st hotel on R*
Jo and David welcome you to their attractive colonial-style residence, which was built in 1896. Ideally located in the heart of Torquay, it enjoys an elevated position overlooking the town. Bedrooms are constantly upgraded and pleasantly decorated. Dinner features freshly cooked produce, much of which is organic, and a good choice of dishes is offered at breakfast. Off road parking is a bonus.
FACILITIES: 18 en suite (3 fmly) (1 GF) No smoking in bedrooms No smoking in dining room TVB tea/coffee Direct dial from bedrooms Licensed Cen ht TVL No coaches Dinner Last d 6pm **PRICES:** s £24-£30; d £48-£60* **LB** **PARKING:** 16 **NOTES:** Closed Nov-Etr **CARDS:**

♦♦♦♦ Westgate Hotel
Falkland Rd TQ2 5JP ☎ 01803 295350 📠 01803 213710
e-mail: ann@westgatehotel.co.uk
Dir: *A380 turn right at Torre station into Avenue Rd, at 2nd lights left into Falkland Rd*
Conveniently situated for the beach and Torquay's many attractions, The Westgate continues to be a popular holiday venue. The neatly furnished bedrooms are well equipped and include one on the ground floor. Many guests return regularly to enjoy the relaxing atmosphere and the traditional home cooking. The large games room with darts, table tennis and a pool table opens onto a pretty outdoor terrace.
FACILITIES: 12 en suite (2 fmly) (1 GF) No smoking in 9 bedrooms No smoking in dining room No smoking in 1 lounge TVB tea/coffee No dogs Licensed TVL No children 5yrs Pool Table Games room, Table tennis, Darts Dinner Last d 7.30pm **PRICES:** s £21.50-£30; d £43-£60* **LB**
PARKING: 13 **CARDS:**

♦♦♦♦ Lindum Hotel
105 Abbey Rd TQ2 5NP ☎ 01803 292795 📠 01803 299358
e-mail: lindum@eurobell.co.uk
Dir: *on Abbey Rd (main road from town centre) at junct with Shedden Hill Rd*
FACILITIES: 17 en suite (2 fmly) (4 GF) No smoking in bedrooms No smoking in dining room No smoking in 1 lounge TVB tea/coffee No dogs Licensed Cen ht TVL No coaches Dinner Last d 7pm **PRICES:** s £22-£28; d £50-£56* **LB** **PARKING:** 14 **NOTES:** Closed Xmas & New Year
CARDS:

♦♦♦ Abberley Hotel
100 Windsor Rd, Babbacombe TQ1 1SU ☎ 01803 329797
📠 01803 329797
e-mail: enquiry@theabberley.co.uk
Dir: *off A3022 into Hele Rd, signed Teignmouth & Plainmoor. After 0.25m left then right at mini rdbt. Travel along Westhill Rd. After traffic lights take 6th right turn into Hingston Rd. At T junct left. Establishment on left*
This family-run hotel provides friendly and attentive service. Located in a quiet residential area, close to the town centre and within easy and level strolling distance of the beaches and attractions. The bedrooms, two of which are located on the ground floor and suitable for the less mobile, are comfortable and well equipped.
FACILITIES: 7 en suite (2 GF) No smoking TVB tea/coffee No dogs Cen ht TVL No coaches **PRICES:** s £18-£22; d £36-£44* **LB** **BB** **NOTES:** Closed Xmas/New Year **CARDS:**

♦♦♦ Arran Lodge
97 Avenue Rd TQ2 5LH ☎ 01803 292273 📠 01803 292273
e-mail: linda@arranlodge.co.uk
Dir: *from Exeter follow signs for Torbay, then Torquay centre, take right fork towards seafront. Arran Lodge 50mtrs on left*
The new proprietors at this pleasant and comfortable house provide a very warm welcome and their guests are made to feel at home. Bedrooms are attractively decorated and are provided with many extra conveniences and comforts. Dinner and breakfast is taken in the dining room where guests may relax after dinner.
FACILITIES: 6 en suite (2 fmly) No smoking TVB tea/coffee No dogs Cen ht No coaches Dinner Last d 10am **PRICES:** s £19-£22.50; d £38-£45* **LB** **BB** **PARKING:** 3

♦♦♦ Birdcage Hotel
St Lukes Rd TQ2 5NX ☎ 01803 212703 📠 01803 212703
e-mail: whitfield.s@talk21.com
Dir: *entering Torquay from Newton Abbot, right at Halfords traffic lights. At seafront traffic lights left. Next lights inside lane up Shedden hill, 2nd right into St Lukes Rd*
The new proprietors at this pleasant house are friendly and attentive to their guests and The Birdcage is set for further improvements to its present, well-provided accommodation. Ideally located and with views across Tor Bay this is a place for leisure and business guests alike. Dinner and hearty breakfasts provide traditional home cooked dishes and are most enjoyable.
FACILITIES: 7 en suite (3 fmly) (1 GF) No smoking in 2 bedrooms No smoking in dining room No smoking in lounges TVB tea/coffee Cen ht TVL No coaches Dinner Last d 11am **PRICES:** s £22-£27; d £36-£48* **BB**
PARKING: 5

♦♦♦ Burleigh House
25 Newton Rd TQ2 5DB ☎ 01803 291557
Dir: *Main approach road to Torquay A380, 4th house on left past Torre station*
Providing modern, comfortable accommodation, Burleigh House is conveniently located for Torquay's centre, and close to the beach and sea front. The bedrooms offer many extra facilities and are pleasantly furnished with quality pine furnishings; some rooms are on the ground floor. Secure parking is available on site.
FACILITIES: 8 en suite (2 fmly) TVB tea/coffee No dogs (ex guide dogs) Cen ht No coaches Last d 5pm **PRICES:** s £16-£18; d £36-£42* **BB**
PARKING: 11

An asterisk * indicates that prices given are for 2002.

England

TORQUAY continued

♦♦♦ *Devon Court Hotel*
Croft Rd TQ2 5UE ☎ 01803 293603 📠 01803 213660
e-mail: info@devoncourt.co.uk
Dir: *from A380 take A3022 to Avenue Rd, L at seafront. Cross lights & up Sheddon Hill. 1st L at church into Croft Rd, hotel 100yds on R*

Located in a quiet residential area close to the town centre and seafront, this attractive Victorian house offers comfortable, pleasantly decorated and well-equipped bedrooms. There is a no-smoking lounge, a spacious lounge/bar and dining room where dinner and full English breakfast are served. The property also benefits from a heated outdoor pool.
FACILITIES: 16 rms (11 en suite) (3 fmly) No smoking in bedrooms No smoking in dining room No smoking in 1 lounge TVB tea/coffee Licensed Cen ht TVL Outdoor swimming pool (heated) Dinner Last d 4pm
PARKING: 14 **CARDS:**

♦♦♦ *Fircroft*
69 Avenue Rd TQ2 5LG ☎ 01803 211634
Dir: *off A380 onto A3022. At Torre railway station take R fork and establishment 300/400yds on L*
Ideally located within easy strolling distance of the beach and town centre the Fircroft is a pleasant and comfortable home. Bedrooms, including one on the ground floor, are attractively decorated and provided with neat furnishings. Dinner and breakfast is served in the smart dining room and guests can also relax in the bright conservatory.
FACILITIES: 4 en suite No smoking in bedrooms No smoking in dining room TVB tea/coffee Cen ht TVL No children 12yrs No coaches Dinner Last d 2pm **PARKING:** 5 **CARDS:**

♦♦♦ Garlieston Hotel
5 Bridge Rd TQ2 5BA ☎ 01803 294050
e-mail: garliestonhotel@jridewood.fsnet.co.uk
Dir: *from seafront, go up Belgrave Rd, turn left after shops into Bampflyde Rd, then 1st right into Bridge Rd. Hotel on corner*
This small and friendly guest house offers comfortable accommodation and is ideally located for the town centre and is within easy strolling distance of the seafront. Bedrooms are neatly decorated and furnished. The resident proprietors have been welcoming guests for a number of years, many of whom return on a regular basis.
FACILITIES: 5 en suite (2 fmly) (1 GF) No smoking in dining room TVB tea/coffee No dogs (ex guide dogs) Cen ht TVL No coaches Dinner Last d 10am **PRICES:** s £15-£20; d £30-£40✻ **LB BB CARDS:**

♦♦♦ Green Park Hotel
25 Morgan Av TQ2 5RR ☎ 01803 293618 📠 01803 293618
This comfortable hotel is close to the town centre and provides an ideal place to stay. The friendly proprietors are most attentive and welcoming and create a homely environment. Dinners (by arrangement) offer good home-cooked meals; at breakfast generous portions, freshly cooked, give a pleasant start to the day.

continued

FACILITIES: 11 rms (8 en suite) (3 fmly) No smoking TVB tea/coffee No dogs (ex guide dogs) Licensed Cen ht No coaches Dinner Last d 11am
PRICES: s £18-£25; d £36-£50✻ **LB BB PARKING:** 7 **CARDS:**

♦♦♦ Grosvenor House Hotel
Falkland Rd TQ2 5JP ☎ 01803 294110
e-mail: grosvenorhse@eurobell.co.uk
Dir: *from Newton Abbot to Torquay. At Torre station turn right by Halfords. At 2nd traffic lights turn sharp left into Falkland Rd*
A warm welcome is assured at this owner managed hotel, which is located on a leafy avenue within easy walking distance of The Riveria Conference & Leisure Centre. The hotel is constantly improving; a choice of lounges is provided in addition to the attractive garden level dining room.
FACILITIES: 10 en suite (4 fmly) (3 GF) No smoking in bedrooms No smoking in dining room No smoking in 1 lounge TVB tea/coffee No dogs (ex guide dogs) Licensed Cen ht TVL Dinner Last d 4.30pm **PRICES:** s fr £21; d fr £42 **LB PARKING:** 7 **NOTES:** Closed Dec **CARDS:**

♦♦♦ The Palms Hotel
537 Babbacombe Rd TQ1 1HQ ☎ 01803 293970 📠 01803 293970
e-mail: grahamaward@yahoo.co.uk
Dir: *on B3199 Babbacombe Road 300yds from harbour opposite Torwood gardens*
The new owners here at Palms Hotel extend a very warm welcome to their guests. Family friendly, the hotel offers comfortable accommodation, with many books, games and videos available for the children. The Cyber café, a well stocked bar and light bar meals are welcome facilities. Breakfast is taken in the dining room, which overlooks Torwood Gardens.
FACILITIES: 9 en suite (4 fmly) No smoking in bedrooms No smoking in area of dining room No smoking in 1 lounge TVB tea/coffee No dogs (ex guide dogs) Licensed Cen ht No coaches Internet facilities in dry bar
PRICES: s £16.50-£22.50; d £33-£45✻ **LB BB PARKING:** 2
NOTES: Closed mid Dec-end Jan **CARDS:**

♦♦♦ Redlands
317 Babbacombe Rd TQ1 3TB ☎ 01803 298702
e-mail: ritaanddon@redlandsbb.freeserve.co.uk
Dir: *from Torquay harbour take B3199 signposted Babbacombe, 1.5m (Palace Hotel on right), Redlands on left just past Palace Hotel*
Situated in a peaceful and attractive area and with pleasant gardens, the Redlands is a convenient place for a restful break or short stay. Spacious and comfortable rooms are provided and a friendly welcome is given to all guests. Substantial breakfasts are served, freshly prepared dishes and home-made marmalade providing a pleasant start to the day.
FACILITIES: 3 en suite No smoking TVB tea/coffee Cen ht No children No coaches **PRICES:** d £38-£46✻ **BB PARKING:** 6 **NOTES:** Closed Nov-Etr

♦♦♦ Riviera Lodge Hotel
26 Croft Rd TQ2 5UE ☎ 01803 292614 📠 01803 292614
e-mail: riviera.lodge@virgin.net
Dir: *approach via M5, Newton Road will bring you to Torquay seafront, turn left onto seafront up Sheddon Hill, Croft Road is 1st left*
Providing a relaxed atmosphere, this personally run hotel is within walking distance of the promenade, shopping centre and the many attractions the town has to offer. Bedrooms vary in size, with the best use being made of the available space; all rooms being well-equipped. A choice of dishes is offered in the dining room.
FACILITIES: 24 en suite (5 fmly) No smoking in bedrooms No smoking in dining room TVB tea/coffee No dogs (ex guide dogs) Licensed Cen ht TVL Outdoor swimming pool (heated) Dinner Last d 7pm **PRICES:** s £32.50-£42.50; d £45-£59✻ **LB PARKING:** 20 **CARDS:**

England

♦♦♦ Stover Lodge Hotel

29 Newton Rd TQ2 5DB ☎ 01803 297287 📠 01803 297287
Dir: *Follow signs to Torquay town centre, at station/Halfords take left lane, Stover Lodge is 2nd hotel on left after traffic lights*

Conveniently located and close to the town centre and sea front, this family-run hotel has a relaxed and friendly atmosphere. Children and babies are welcome; a cot and high chair can be provided on request. Hearty breakfasts, with a vegetarian option, are served in the attractive dining room. Guests are welcome to use the garden in summer months.
FACILITIES: 10 rms (7 en suite) (3 fmly) (2 GF) No smoking in 3 bedrooms No smoking in dining room TVB tea/coffee Cen ht No coaches **PRICES:** s £16-£25; d £32-£44✳ **LB BB PARKING:** 10 **CARDS:**

♦♦♦ *Wayfarer*

37 Belgrave Rd TQ2 5HX ☎ 01803 299138 📠 01803 299138
e-mail: irene@wayfarer35.freeserve.co.uk
Dir: *M5, A380, A3022 into Torquay. Take rd to town centre past Kwikfit garage, R to seafront Belgrave Rd. L at traffic lights (Lucious Street). First L to Wayfarer car park.*
The friendly proprietors at this small home are most attentive to their guests and provide a welcoming atmosphere. Conveniently located for the town centre and seaside attractions, the Wayfarer is a pleasant place to stay. A bright and attractive lounge/dining room is available, and at breakfast very generous portions are served.
FACILITIES: 4 en suite (2 fmly) No smoking in dining room TVB tea/coffee TVL No coaches **PARKING:** 4

♦♦♦ Avenue Park

3 Avenue Rd TQ2 5LA ☎ 01803 293902 📠 01803 293902
e-mail: avenuepark@bushinternet.com
Dir: *from M5/A38 take A380 to Torquay, then A3022. Right fork at Halfords store, following seafront sign. Trough 1st traffic lights and Avenue Park on left before 2nd set of traffic lights*
FACILITIES: 8 en suite (3 fmly) (2 GF) No smoking in 2 bedrooms No smoking in dining room TVB tea/coffee No dogs (ex guide dogs) Cen ht
PRICES: s £17-£21; d £34-£42✳ **LB BB PARKING:** 4

♦♦ Athina

8 Vansittart Rd, Torre TQ2 5BT ☎ 01803 297547
Dir: *take Newton Abbott to Torquay road to Torre station. At traffic lights left fork to town centre, 1st turning off main road on right*
The Athina is quietly located in a residential area close to the centre and seaside attractions and provides value accommodation. Rooms are spacious and comfortable, and a cosy lounge is provided along with a car park. Traditional breakfasts are served in the dining room and provide a good start to the day.
FACILITIES: 3 rms No smoking in bedrooms No smoking in dining room No smoking in 1 lounge TVB tea/coffee No dogs Cen ht TVL No children No coaches **PRICES:** d £24-£32✳ **LB BB PARKING:** 4 **NOTES:** Closed mid Oct-Feb

♦♦ Tyndale

68 Avenue Rd TQ2 5LF ☎ 01803 380888
Dir: *A380 to Ring Rd, straight on A3022 from rdbt until Torre station, follow signs for Paignton & Harbour (Avenue Rd). At 1st traffic lights right Old Mill Rd and directly right into to car park*
This neatly presented establishment is conveniently located in a popular part of town, a level walk from the park and seafront. Bedrooms vary in size, all offering comfortable accommodation.
FACILITIES: 3 en suite (1 GF) No smoking in dining room TVB tea/coffee Cen ht TVL No coaches **PRICES:** d fr £32✳ **LB BB PARKING:** 5

TOTNES — Map 03 SX86

See also South Brent

♦♦♦♦ Durant Arms

Ashprington TQ9 7UP ☎ 01803 732240 📠 01803 732470
e-mail: info@thedurantarms.com
Dir: *from A38 take A384 or A385 to Totnes, at traffic lights take A381 for Kingsbridge. 1m turn left for Ashprington*

This delightful village inn, the focal point of the picturesque village of Ashprington, offers comfortable bedrooms which are very well appointed and attractively decorated. A range of carefully prepared dishes from blackboard menus can be enjoyed in the character bar or dining room and local ales, juices and wines are also specialities of the house.
FACILITIES: 3 en suite 4 annexe rms (2 GF) No smoking in bedrooms No smoking in dining room TV1B No dogs Cen ht Dinner Last d 9.15pm
PRICES: s £35-£40; d £60-£65✳ **LB MEALS:** Lunch £6.45-£7.25&alc Dinner £6.45-£7.25&alc✳ **PARKING:** 8 **CARDS:**

England

TOTNES continued

♦♦♦♦ The Old Forge at Totnes

Seymour Place TQ9 5AY ☎ 01803 862174 📠 01803 865385
e-mail: millier@supanet.com
Dir: *turn off A38 towards Totnes. From town centre cross river bridge and take 2nd right*

Located close to the town centre and Steamer Quay, this charming property is over 600 years old. Bedrooms vary from suites to cottage style, all of which have been equipped with many thoughtful extras. Public areas include a conservatory overlooking the gardens and a comfortable lounge. Breakfast is a leisurely and enjoyable affair; dinner is available by prior arrangement.
FACILITIES: 10 en suite (2 fmly) (3 GF) No smoking TVB tea/coffee Direct dial from bedrooms No dogs (ex guide dogs) Licensed Cen ht TVL No coaches Jacuzzi Dinner Last d Noon **PRICES:** s £44-£52; d £54-£74* **LB PARKING:** 9 **CARDS:**

♦♦♦♦ *Red Slipper*

Stoke Gabriel TQ9 6RU ☎ 01803 782315 📠 01803 782315
e-mail: clive@redslipper.co.uk
Dir: *from A385, take either of the two southbound turnings to Stoke Gabriel. Hotel is opp Church House Inn*
An ideal base for exploring the South Hams or just for a relaxing break, this delightful 1920s house is hidden away in the picturesque village of Stoke Gabriel. The tastefully furnished bedrooms have many extra facilities. Well cooked dinners are served by prior arrangement, and feature local produce.
FACILITIES: 3 en suite No smoking in bedrooms No smoking in dining room TVB tea/coffee Licensed Cen ht No coaches Dinner Last d 12am **PARKING:** 5 **CARDS:**

♦♦♦♦ Steam Packet Inn

St Peter's Quay TQ9 5EW ☎ 01803 863880 📠 01803 862754
e-mail: esther@thesteampacketinn-totnes.co.uk
Dir: *leave A38 at Totnes junct proceed to Dartington and Totnes. At 1st traffic lights straight on pass train station on left, follow signs for town centre at next rdbt. At mini rdbt straight across , River Dart on left the inn is 100yds on left*
An imposing Georgian building with its own private quay, set in a most attractive location on the banks of the river, the Steam Packet offers friendly hospitality and service. Bedrooms are well equipped and comfortable, and some have river views. Choices at both lunch and dinner offer interesting and well-cooked dishes, and at breakfast hearty traditional fare is served.
FACILITIES: 4 en suite (1 fmly) No smoking in bedrooms No smoking in area of dining room TVB tea/coffee No dogs (ex guide dogs) Cen ht Tennis (grass) Fishing Squash mooring facility for 4 boats Dinner **PRICES:** s £40; d £60-£65* **MEALS:** Lunch £13-£17 Dinner £13-£17&alc* **PARKING:** 18 **CARDS:**

♦♦♦♦ Four Seasons Guest House

13 Bridgetown TQ9 5AB ☎ 01803 862146 📠 01803 867779
e-mail: eecornford@msn.com
Dir: *from mini-rdbt at bottom of Fore St, go over bridge. Guest house 200yds on right*
FACILITIES: 7 en suite (1 fmly) (1 GF) No smoking in 1 bedrooms No smoking in dining room No smoking in 1 lounge TVB tea/coffee Licensed Cen ht TVL Dinner **PRICES:** s £25-£35; d £44-£46* **LB PARKING:** 6

TWO BRIDGES — Map 02 SX67

♦♦♦♦ *Cherrybrook Hotel*

PL20 6SP ☎ 01822 880260 📠 01822 880260
Dir: *on B3212*
Located on the high Moor in the centre of Dartmoor National Park, Cherrybrook has lovely views over the surrounding countryside. Over the years, this farmhouse has been extended, resulting in a selection of comfortable, well-equipped bedrooms and a cosy lounge with a bar. Delicious four-course dinners are available by prior arrangement.
FACILITIES: 7 en suite (2 fmly) No smoking in dining room No smoking in 1 lounge TVB tea/coffee Licensed Cen ht No coaches Dinner Last d 7.15pm **PARKING:** 12 **NOTES:** Closed 24 Dec-2 Jan

See advertisement on opposite page

WESTWARD HO! — Map 02 SS42

♦♦♦♦ Culloden House Hotel

Fosketh Hill EX39 1JA ☎ 01237 479421 📠 01237 475628
e-mail: culloden-house@ukgateway.net
Dir: *on A39 take turn for Westward Ho! at rdbt W of New Bridge at Bideford. House 1m from Welcome sign on L*
Located in an elevated position with sweeping views over the beach and surrounding coastline, guests to this detached Victorian property are assured of a warm welcome. By prior arrangement an imaginative three-course dinner is available. In addition to the cosy bar, there is a comfortable lounge available for guest use.
FACILITIES: 10 rms (8 en suite) (2 fmly) (1 GF) No smoking in 1 bedrooms No smoking in dining room TVB tea/coffee Licensed Cen ht TVL No coaches **PRICES:** s £30-£35; d £50-£55* **PARKING:** 12 **CARDS:**

WHIMPLE — Map 03 SY09

Premier Collection

♦♦♦♦♦ Woodhayes Country House & Cottage

EX5 2TD ☎ 01404 822237 📠 01404 822337
e-mail: info@woodhayes-hotel.co.uk
Dir: *Leave A30 Honiton/Exeter Road at Junct named Daisymount and follow the brown Woodhayes signs*
Once the home of the Whiteways Cider family, this charming, well-proportioned, Georgian house is located in four acres of gardens. The tastefully decorated dining room, lounge and country style bar with flagstone floor, all have open fires in winter. Bedrooms are spacious and comfortable with many extra facilities. Dinner is only available for house parties.
FACILITIES: 6 en suite (1 fmly) No smoking in bedrooms No smoking in dining room TVB tea/coffee Direct dial from bedrooms No dogs (ex guide dogs) Licensed Cen ht No coaches **PRICES:** s £65; d £75-£90* **PARKING:** 20 **CARDS:**

WIDECOMBE IN THE MOOR Map 03 SX77

♦♦♦♦ Manor Cottage

TQ13 7TB ☎ 01364 621218

Dir: *From A38 take junct signed for Bovey Tracey & Moretonhampstead (A382). At Bovey Tracey left on B3387 signed Haytor & Widecombe, continue across the moor to Widecombe. Cottage attached to post office*

Located in the centre of the historic village of Widecombe-in-the-Moor, this attractive home offers a friendly welcome to guests. Bedrooms are spacious and comfortable and have pleasant pine furnishings. Breakfast, and dinner by prior arrangement, are taken in the cosy dining room and feature good home cooking with fresh local produce.

FACILITIES: 3 rms (1 en suite) No smoking in bedrooms tea/coffee Cen ht TVL No children 15yrs No coaches **PRICES:** d £40✳ **PARKING:** 3 **NOTES:** Closed Xmas

WINKLEIGH Map 02 SS60

♦♦♦ The Old Parsonage

Court Walk EX19 8JA ☎ 01837 83772 01837 680074

Dir: *from Crediton turn left off A3124 and the Old Parsonage is on left behind Winkleigh parish church*

FACILITIES: 3 en suite (1 GF) No smoking TVB tea/coffee Cen ht No children 4yrs No coaches **PRICES:** s £30; d £43✳ **PARKING:** 4

WOOLACOMBE Map 02 SS44

♦♦♦♦ The Castle

The Esplanade EX34 7DJ ☎ 01271 870788 01271 870812
e-mail: john.david.frazier@amserve.net

Dir: *A361 from Barnstaple to Ilfracombe, turn right at Woolacombe sign*

Built in 1898 in the style of a castle, this Victorian stone folly has stunning views over the bay. The attractively decorated bedrooms comfortable and well equipped. The lounge has a carved-wood ceiling and interesting panelling. There is also a lounge/bar, and breakfast is served in the elegant dining room.

FACILITIES: 8 en suite (2 fmly) No smoking in bedrooms No smoking in dining room No smoking in lounges TVB tea/coffee No dogs (ex guide dogs) Licensed Cen ht TVL No children 5yrs No coaches **PRICES:** d £54-£60✳ **PARKING:** 8 **NOTES:** Closed Nov-Mar **CARDS:**

♦♦♦♦ Cleeve House Hotel

Mortehoe EX34 7ED ☎ 01271 870719 01271 870719
e-mail: info@cleevehouse.co.uk

Dir: *from A361 onto B3343 at Mullacott Cross. Turn right towards Mortehoe, then right at post office, hotel 300yds on left*

This friendly hotel provides attractively co-ordinated, well-equipped bedrooms with views of the sea, village or countryside; a ground floor room with wheelchair access is also available. After a day's exploration, why not enjoy a drink in the convivial bar before taking an imaginative dinner. Service is efficient and unobtrusive and every effort is made to ensure a pleasant and memorable stay.

FACILITIES: 7 en suite (1 fmly) (1 GF) No smoking in bedrooms No smoking in dining room No smoking in 1 lounge TVB tea/coffee No dogs (ex guide dogs) Licensed Cen ht No children 12yrs No coaches Dinner Last d 5.30pm **PRICES:** d £58-£64✳ LB **PARKING:** 9 **NOTES:** Closed Nov-Mar rs August, Tues in April and May **CARDS:**

♦♦♦♦ Ossaborough House

Ossaborough EX34 7HJ ☎ 01271 870297
e-mail: info@ossaboroughhouse.co.uk

Dir: *A361 onto B3343 at Mullacott Cross rdbt to Woolacombe. Past 'Once Upon a Time' attraction look for signs to Woolacombe village, 20yds on turn L hotel 0.25m down ln.*

Trevor and Rosie welcome you to their family run guest house. Steeped in history, the house boasts a beamed dining room and a lounge with inglenook fireplace and a rustic bar. Bedrooms are attractively decorated and provided with comfortable furnishings. Dinners, by prior arrangement, are freshly cooked and well presented. Guests also have the use of nearby swimming pools and tennis courts.

FACILITIES: 6 en suite (3 fmly) (2 GF) No smoking TVB tea/coffee Licensed Cen ht No coaches Dinner Last d noon **PRICES:** s £22-£35; d £48-£54✳ LB **PARKING:** 10 **CARDS:**

England

WOOLACOMBE continued

♦♦♦♦ Baycliffe Hotel
Chapel Hill, Mortehoe EX34 7DZ ☎ 01271 870393
01271 870393
e-mail: jane@baycliffehotel.fsnet.co.uk
Dir: *through Barnstaple on A361 towards Ilfracombe, in approx 7m take 1st exit off Mullacott Cross rdbt, signed Woolacombe/Morthoe, in approx. 3m turn right after sharp bend to Mortehoe continue through village hotel on left as you descend hill*
FACILITIES: 9 rms (7 en suite) (2 fmly) No smoking TVB tea/coffee No dogs Licensed Cen ht No coaches covered outdoor jacuzzi Dinner Last d 4pm **PRICES:** s £23-£27; d £46-£69* **LB** **PARKING:** 9 **NOTES:** Closed 10 Nov-9 Feb

♦♦♦ Holmesdale Hotel
Bay View Rd EX34 7DQ ☎ 01271 870335 01271 870335
e-mail: holmesdale@tinyworld.co.uk
Dir: *Barnstaple A361 to Ilfracombe, take Woolacombe exit at rdbt. R into Bay View Rd, parallel to the esplanade, hotel on R*
Enjoying an enviable position, overlooking the bay, this friendly, family run hotel provides comfortable and well-equipped accommodation. Bedrooms, which vary in size, are brightly decorated and furnished with modern pine furniture. A choice of menu is available at dinner and breakfast, and is served in the pleasantly appointed dining room, which benefits from delightful sea views.
FACILITIES: 15 rms (8 en suite) (10 fmly) No smoking in bedrooms No smoking in dining room TVB tea/coffee Licensed Cen ht TVL Dinner Last d 5.30pm **PRICES:** s £25-£28; d £50-£60* **LB** **PARKING:** 14 **NOTES:** Closed Feb **CARDS:**

YELVERTON — Map 02 SX56

♦♦♦♦ Harrabeer Country House Hotel
Harrowbeer Ln PL20 6EA ☎ 01822 853302 01822 853302
e-mail: reception@harrabeer.co.uk
Dir: *From Plymouth, A386 to Tavistock, 1st left on rdbt to Tavistock, 1st right into Grange Rd, turn right. The Harrabeer is on left*

A warm welcome awaits guests at this historic Devon longhouse on the edge of Dartmoor, which has been converted into an attractive hotel. Accommodation has all the expected modern comforts with a lounge, bar and dining room overlooking the garden. Dinners are available by prior arrangement with special diets catered for. Amanda Willats was a Top Twenty Finalist in the AA Landlady of the Year Award 2002-2003.
FACILITIES: 6 en suite (2 fmly) No smoking in bedrooms No smoking in dining room No smoking in lounges TVB tea/coffee Direct dial from bedrooms Licensed Cen ht TVL No coaches Dinner Last d mid day
PRICES: s £32-£39; d £54-£61* **LB** **CONF:** Board 20
PARKING: 8 **NOTES:** Closed 17 Dec-7 Jan
CARDS:

See advert under PLYMOUTH

♦♦♦♦ The Rosemont
Greenbank Ter PL20 6DR ☎ 01822 852175
e-mail: office@rosemontgh.fsnet.co.uk
Dir: *at Yelverton rdbt take the Princetown road and turn 1st left opposite Esso garage. Rosemont is in front of you.*
FACILITIES: 7 en suite (2 fmly) No smoking TVB tea/coffee Cen ht
PRICES: s £25-£35; d £45-£50* **PARKING:** 7 **NOTES:** Closed Xmas
CARDS:

DORSET

ABBOTSBURY — Map 03 SY58

♦♦♦ East Farm House *(SY578853)*
2 Rosemary Ln DT3 4JN ☎ 01305 871363 01305 871363 Mrs W M Wood
e-mail: wendy@eastfarmhouse.co.uk
Dir: *from Portesham turn right onto the B3157, 2m to Abbotsbury, on entering village Swan Inn on left, farmhouse 1st right into Rosemary Lane.*
This unspoilt farmhouse is located in the centre of the pretty village of Abbotsbury and has been in the owner's family since 1729. Traditionally furnished, with many personal touches, pictures, ornaments and dried flowers create a homely atmosphere. Hearty, farmhouse-style dinners are available by prior arrangement.
FACILITIES: 3 en suite No smoking TVB tea/coffee Cen ht No children 14yrs 20 acres stud Dinner Last d breakfast **PRICES:** d £50* **LB**
PARKING: 3

BEAMINSTER — Map 03 ST40

♦♦♦♦ Watermeadow House *(ST535001)*
Bridge Farm, Hooke DT8 3PD ☎ 01308 862619
01308 862619 Mrs P M Wallbridge
e-mail: enquiries@watermeadowhouse.co.uk
Dir: *off A356 approx 4m W of Maiden Newton signed Hooke. Left at crossroads signed Kingcombe. House approx 300yds on right*
A haven of peace and tranquillity, this Georgian style country house is on the edge of the village; guests are assured of a warm and friendly welcome here. Bedrooms feature several thoughtful extras, such as fridges and hot chocolate. Served in the sunroom overlooking the colourful garden, breakfast features local produce.
FACILITIES: 2 en suite (1 fmly) No smoking TVB tea/coffee No dogs (ex guide dogs) Cen ht 280 acres dairy beef **PRICES:** s £28-£32; d £44-£48*
LB **PARKING:** 6 **NOTES:** Closed Nov-Feb **CARDS:**

BLANDFORD FORUM

♦♦♦♦ Ramblers Cottage
DT11 8BY ☎ 01258 830528
e-mail: sworrall@ramblerscottage.fsnet.co.uk

(For full entry see Tarrant Launceston)

BOURNEMOUTH — Map 04 SZ09

♦♦♦♦ Alexander Lodge Hotel
21 Southern Rd, Southbourne BH6 3SR ☎ 01202 421662
01202 421662
e-mail: alexanderlodge@yahoo.com
Dir: *Southern rd turns off Southbourne Overcliff near the cliff lift*
A warm welcome and high levels of service are assured at this delightful family-run hotel located close to local beaches, the town centre, New Forest and other places of interest. The comfortable bedrooms have many useful extras and there is a lounge and a bar for guest's use. Evening meals are available by prior arrangement.

continued

England

Anne Clarke-Kehoe was a Top Twenty Finalist in the AA Landlady of the Year Award 2002-2003.

Alexander Lodge Hotel

FACILITIES: 6 en suite (2 fmly) No smoking TVB tea/coffee No dogs (ex guide dogs) Licensed Cen ht TVL No coaches Dinner Last d 5pm **PRICES:** s £24-£48; d £38-£54 LB BB **PARKING:** 7 **CARDS:**

♦♦♦♦ Amitie

1247 Christchurch Rd BH7 6BP ☎ 01202 427255
01202 427255
e-mail: b&b@amitie.co.uk
Dir: *On A35 near junct with A3060 at Iford.*

Well located in Boscombe, with good access for Bournemouth, Christchurch and Southbourne beach, this delightful guest house offers comfortable, neatly furnished bedrooms. A tasty breakfast is served in the dining room and extras, such as a fridge, are available to guests. Parking is an added bonus.

FACILITIES: 8 en suite (1 fmly) No smoking in 3 bedrooms No smoking in dining room No smoking in lounges TVB tea/coffee No dogs (ex guide dogs) Cen ht **PRICES:** s £25-£40; d £46-£80✻ LB **PARKING:** 8 **CARDS:**

♦♦♦♦ Balincourt Hotel

58 Christchurch Rd BH1 3PF ☎ 01202 552962
01202 552962
e-mail: rooms@balincourt.co.uk
Dir: *on A35*

Offering high standards of comfortable accommodation, this friendly hotel is located within easy reach of the town centre, beaches and attractions. In the evenings, a short fixed-price menu is offered. All bedrooms are well equipped and individually furnished and decorated; two ground-floor rooms are ideal for less mobile guests.

continued

The Balincourt Hotel

FACILITIES: 12 en suite No smoking TVB tea/coffee No dogs (ex guide dogs) Licensed Cen ht TVL No children 16yrs No coaches Use of nearby leisure centre Dinner Last d 6pm **PRICES:** s £32-£38; d £64-£76✻ LB **PARKING:** 11 **CARDS:**

♦♦♦♦ *The Boltons Hotel*

9 Durley Chine Rd South, West Cliff BH2 5JT ☎ 01202 751517
01202 751629
Dir: *from Wessex Way turn for West Cliff, R at 2nd rdbt (West Cliff Rd), 2nd R into Durley Chine Rd South*

Located in a quiet position close to the town centre, this fine Victorian property offers appealing public rooms, including a lounge, dining room and cosy residents' bar. There is a swimming pool in the secluded gardens. The comfortable bedrooms, which vary in size, are well equipped and furnished.

FACILITIES: 12 en suite (2 fmly) No smoking in bedrooms No smoking in dining room No smoking in 1 lounge TVB tea/coffee Direct dial from bedrooms Licensed Cen ht TVL Outdoor swimming pool (heated) Dinner Last d 5pm **PARKING:** 12 **CARDS:**

♦♦♦♦ Carisbrooke Hotel

42 Tregonwell Rd BH2 5NT ☎ 01202 290432 01202 310499
e-mail: info@carisbrooke.co.uk
Dir: *from direction of Ringwood, follow signs for BIC, past Wessex Hotel then 3rd left*

This comfortable hotel is conveniently located close to the town centre and beach. The bedrooms, which vary in size, are pleasantly furnished and well equipped. A good choice of breakfast is served in the attractive dining room. There is also a cosy bar and a lounge area.

FACILITIES: 22 rms (20 en suite) (8 fmly) (3 GF) No smoking in 4 bedrooms No smoking in dining room STV TV23B tea/coffee Direct dial from bedrooms Licensed Cen ht TVL Dinner Last d 4pm **PRICES:** s £22-£30; d £50-£66✻ LB **PARKING:** 18 **NOTES:** Closed 20 Dec-2 Jan **CARDS:**

♦♦♦♦ Cransley Hotel

11 Knyveton Rd, East Cliff BH1 3QG ☎ 01202 290067
01202 292977
e-mail: info@cransley.co.uk
Dir: *turn off A338 at St Paul's rdbt by ASDA Store, continue over next rdbt keeping Abbey Life building on right. Knyveton Rd 1st on left*

A warm welcome is assured at this delightful hotel situated in a peaceful tree lined avenue, conveniently located for all major road and rail links, town centre and beach. Traditional, home cooked meals are served in the south-facing dining room adjacent to the elegant lounge, both of which enjoy a garden outlook.

FACILITIES: 11 en suite (2 GF) No smoking TVB tea/coffee No dogs (ex guide dogs) Licensed Cen ht TVL No children 14yrs No coaches Dinner Last d 2pm **PRICES:** (incl. dinner) s £24-£30; d £48-£60✻ **PARKING:** 8 **CARDS:**

England

BOURNEMOUTH continued

♦♦♦♦ Fielden Court Private Hotel

20 Southern Rd, Southbourne BH6 3SR ☎ 01202 427459
📠 01202 427459
e-mail: fieldencourthotel@btinternet.com
Dir: *Southern Road is a turning off Southbourne Overcliff, close to cliff lift*

Located in Southbourne, close to the cliff top and lift and well located for Bournemouth, Christchurch and surrounding places of interest, this delightful guest house provides guests with comfortable, well appointed bedrooms. A charming lounge is also available for guests' use. By prior arrangement, home-cooked dinners using fresh ingredients are also available.
FACILITIES: 8 en suite (2 fmly) No smoking TVB tea/coffee No dogs Cen ht TVL No children 4yrs No coaches Dinner Last d 4pm **PRICES:** s £22-£26; d £44-£52✳ **LB PARKING:** 5

♦♦♦♦ The Lodge at Meyrick Park

Central Dr BH2 6LH ☎ 01202 786000 📠 01202 786020
e-mail: meyrickpark.lodge@clubhaus.com
Dir: *A338 into Bournemouth, take Richmond Hill exit and take the A347 to Wimborne (Wimborne Road), take first left (Bradley Road), at T-junction turn right. 50 metres on left*
An ideal location for the golfer, surrounded by a popular golf course, The Lodge offers very comfortably furnished bedrooms in a building adjacent to the main clubhouse. In addition to the golf course and shop, extensive leisure facilities are available as well as a café/bar offering a range of light snacks.
FACILITIES: 17 en suite (1 fmly) (12 GF) No smoking TVB tea/coffee Direct dial from bedrooms No dogs Licensed Indoor swimming pool (heated) Golf 18 Sauna Solarium Gymnasium Putting green Jacuzzi Aerobics classes Dinner Last d 8-9.30pm **PRICES:** d £69.50-£74.50✳ **LB**
PARKING: 145 **NOTES:** Closed 24 -26 Dec & 1 Jan
CARDS:

♦♦♦♦ Thanet Hotel

2 Drury Rd, Alum Chine BH4 8HA ☎ 01202 761135
📠 01202 761135
e-mail: thanethotel-bournemouth@hotmail.com
Dir: *follow signs for Alum Chine Beach. Hotel on corner of Alumhurst Rd & Drury Rd*

continued

A warm welcome is assured at this delightful Edwardian house, ideally located within easy walking distance of fashionable Westbourne and Alum Chine Beach. The bedrooms are filled with many homely extras. A lounge is also available to guests. Imaginative dinners and comprehensive breakfasts are served in the attractive dining room.
FACILITIES: 8 rms (5 en suite) (1 fmly) No smoking TVB tea/coffee No dogs (ex guide dogs) Licensed Cen ht No children 7yrs Dinner Last d 5pm
PRICES: s £19-£22.50; d £38-£49✳ **LB BB PARKING:** 6 **NOTES:** Closed Nov-Mar **CARDS:**

♦♦♦♦ *Tiffanys Hotel*

31 Chine Crescent, West Cliff BH2 5LB ☎ 01202 551424
📠 01202 318559
Feb-Nov
Conveniently situated for the town's many attractions, this detached property is set in attractive gardens with ample parking. The well decorated, spacious bedrooms are well equipped; some bedrooms are located on the ground floor. A continental breakfast is served in the stylish dining room.
FACILITIES: 15 en suite (2 fmly) No smoking in 3 bedrooms No smoking in dining room TVB tea/coffee Cen ht **PARKING:** 15 **CARDS:**

♦♦♦♦ Tudor Grange Hotel

31 Gervis Rd BH1 3EE ☎ 01202 291472 & 291463
📠 01202 311503
Dir: *follow signs for East Cliff*

Located on the East Cliff and close to the town centre, this fine Tudor-style house, set in attractive and well-maintained gardens, has retained many of its original features. The well-equipped bedrooms are thoughtfully decorated and furnished. Public rooms, which include a lounge and bar, provide guests with delightful areas in which to relax.
FACILITIES: 11 en suite (3 fmly) No smoking in dining room TVB tea/coffee Direct dial from bedrooms Licensed Cen ht TVL No coaches Use of indoor pool at neighbouring hotel **PRICES:** s £28-£37; d £56-£74✳ **LB**
PARKING: 11 **NOTES:** Closed 24 Dec-2 Jan **CARDS:**

♦♦♦♦ Westcotes House Hotel

9 Southbourne Overcliff Dr, Southbourne BH6 3TE
☎ 01202 428512
Dir: *from A338 onto A3060 to Christchurch, at 2nd rdbt turn right, 1m to traffic lights, left signed Southbourne Beaches in 1m right at Barclays Bank, down Grand Ave. to end and turn right*
Westcotes House is in a seafront location on the quieter side of Bournemouth overlooking the bay. Recently refurbished throughout, bedrooms provide guests with comfortable and well-

continued

England

Westcotes House Hotel

equipped facilities. Several rooms offer splendid sea views. Guests are welcome to use the conservatory sun lounge and enjoyable home-cooked dinners are available by prior arrangement.

FACILITIES: 6 en suite No smoking TVB tea/coffee No dogs (ex guide dogs) Cen ht TVL No children 10yrs No coaches Dinner Last d 5pm **PRICES:** s £33-£38; d £52-£62* **PARKING:** 6

♦♦♦♦ Whateley Hall Hotel

7 Florence Rd, Boscombe BH5 1HH ☎ 01202 397749
01202 397749
e-mail: whateleyhall.hotel@virgin.net

Dir: *A338 exit signed Boscombe, at small rdbt 3rd exit onto Holdenhurst Rd, left at traffic lights Ashley Rd, next rdbt 1st exit follow road round to left into Christchurch Rd next on right then 3rd on right is Florence Rd, hotel on left*

This family run hotel is well located between the beach and Boscombe and is ideal for those wishing to explore Bournemouth, Christchurch and the New Forest. Bedrooms are well appointed and brightly furnished with many extra facilities. There is a lounge and bar for guests' use, and dinner is available by prior arrangement.

FACILITIES: 10 en suite (3 fmly) No smoking TVB tea/coffee No dogs (ex guide dogs) Licensed Cen ht TVL No children 8yrs No coaches Dinner Last d noon **PRICES:** s £25-£28; d £50-£56* **LB PARKING:** 7 **CARDS:**

♦♦♦♦ Willowdene Hotel

43 Grand Av, Southbourne BH6 3SY ☎ 01202 425370
01202 425370
e-mail: willowdenehotel@aol.com

Dir: *turn off A338 onto A3060, left at lights, follow signs 'Southbourne' for 2m to Southbourne Grove. Right at Barclays Bank into Grand Avenue*

Ideally situated between the beach and the shopping areas of Southbourne and Boscombe, this small, family-run hotel offers comfortable, bright accommodation with many extra facilities. There is also a pleasant guests' lounge. Evening meals are available by prior arrangement and are served in the delightful dining room.

continued

Willowdene Hotel

FACILITIES: 6 en suite (2 fmly) No smoking TVB tea/coffee No dogs (ex guide dogs) Cen ht TVL No coaches Dinner Last d 6pm **PRICES:** s £23-£28; d £46-£56* **LB PARKING:** 5 **CARDS:**

♦♦♦♦ *Wood Lodge Hotel*

10 Manor Rd, East Cliff BH1 3EY ☎ 01202 290891
01202 290892

Dir: *leave A338 sign for Town Centre (East). Proceed across 2 rdbts & then turn immediately left into Manor Road. Hotel 300yrds on left*

Located in a pleasant tree-lined area of town, this hotel provides warm, friendly hospitality and comfortable well-appointed accommodation. Bedrooms are generally spacious and thoughtfully furnished with a range of modern comforts. There are two lounges, a small bar and well-tended garden. Traditional English meals are served in the attractive dining room.

FACILITIES: 14 en suite (4 fmly) No smoking in dining room No smoking in 1 lounge TVB tea/coffee Licensed Cen ht TVL No coaches Putting green 9 hole putting green 2 bowls rinks Dinner Last d 7pm **PARKING:** 10 **NOTES:** Closed Dec-Feb rs Mar & Nov (dinner by prior arrangement) **CARDS:**

♦♦♦♦ *Wychcote Hotel*

2 Somerville Rd, West Cliff BH2 5LH ☎ 01202 557898
e-mail: info@wychcote.co.uk

Dir: *from A338 ring road, at Bournemouth West rdbt take exit to West Cliff & Triangle, continue 400mtrs to St Michaels rdbt take 2nd exit onto Durley Chine Rd. 100mtrs 1st left into Somerville Rd*

Located in a quiet area of town and surrounded by its own gardens, the hotel is well positioned for conference delegates attending the BIC or for holiday makers wishing to enjoy all that the town has to offer. Bedrooms are comfortable, well appointed and equipped with many thoughtful extras.

FACILITIES: 12 en suite No smoking TVB tea/coffee No dogs Licensed Cen ht No children No coaches **PARKING:** 15 **NOTES:** Closed 16 Dec-28 Feb **CARDS:**

England

BOURNEMOUTH continued

♦♦♦♦ The Ventura Hotel

1 Herbert Rd BH4 8HD ☎ 01202 761265 📠 01202 757673
e-mail: enquiries@venturahotel.co.uk
Dir: *follow A338 (Wessex Way) until single carriageway at Frizzell House rdbt take 2nd exit signed Alum Chine, left at traffic lights into Western Road, 3rd exit off next rdbt Alumhurst Road, Hotel on corner of Alumhurst/Herbert Road*
FACILITIES: 8 en suite (2 fmly) No smoking TVB tea/coffee No dogs Cen ht No children 5yrs No coaches **PRICES:** d £46-£54✻ **LB** **PARKING:** 8 **CARDS:**

♦♦♦ *Alum Grange Hotel*

1 Burnaby Rd, Alum Chine BH4 8JF ☎ 01202 761195
📠 01202 760973
Dir: *M27 to A31, at Ringwood turn L onto A338, 2nd exit at Frizzel House rdbt, L at lights, R at next rdbt and L as sea comes into view*
Located between the town centres of Bournemouth and Poole, this spacious hotel is only a short stroll from the beautiful, sandy, Alum Chine Beach. All bedrooms are tastefully furnished and brightly decorated and one room has a four-poster bed. Guests can choose from the daily changing menu, served in the attractive open plan dining room/lounge bar.
FACILITIES: 14 en suite (7 fmly) No smoking in 4 bedrooms No smoking in dining room No smoking in 1 lounge TVB tea/coffee Licensed Cen ht TVL ch fac No coaches Dinner Last d mid afternoon **PARKING:** 11 **CARDS:**

♦♦♦ Cherry View Hotel

66 Alum Chine Rd BH4 8DZ ☎ 01202 760910
e-mail: enquiries@cherryview.co.uk
Dir: *at junct A35/A338 follow B3065 towards Alum Chine, 0.25m left at traffic lights into Western Road, Hotel across next rdbt*
Situated close to Alum Chine and with easy access for the town centres of Bournemouth and Westbourne, this family-run hotel provides its guests with comfortable well-equipped bedrooms. Public areas include a guest lounge and a cosy bar where guests can enjoy a pre-dinner drink. Dinner is available by prior arrangement.
FACILITIES: 11 en suite (1 fmly) (1 GF) No smoking in 6 bedrooms No smoking in dining room No smoking in 1 lounge TVB tea/coffee No dogs Licensed Cen ht TVL No children 7yrs Dinner Last d 4pm **PRICES:** s £35; d £50 **LB** **PARKING:** 11 **NOTES:** rs Nov-Mar

♦♦♦ Dorset House

225 Holdenhurst Rd, Springbourne BH8 8DD ☎ 01202 397908
Dir: *from W turn right off A338 or left if approaching from E, at rdbt adjacent to Asda. Take next left At St Paul's rdbt into Holdenhurst Rd. Establishment 400mtrs on left after passing railway station & Texaco garage*
Located close to the town centre, beaches and railway station, Dorset House offers comfortable accommodation and a warm, friendly atmosphere. Bedrooms are attractively decorated and equipped with a number of thoughtful extra touches. An evening meal is available by prior arrangement and is served in the well-appointed dining room.
FACILITIES: 5 en suite No smoking STV TVB tea/coffee No dogs Cen ht TVL No children Dinner Last d 5pm **PRICES:** s £22.50-£25; d £45-£50✻ **LB** **PARKING:** 5

♦♦♦ East Cliff Cottage Hotel

57 Grove Rd BH1 3AT ☎ 01202 552788 📠 01202 556400
e-mail: len@lwallen.freeserve.co.uk
Dir: *Wessex Way into Bournemouth, L at East Cliff Rd sign, R at next rdbt, L (Meyrick Rd), L (Grove Rd). (The Circle)*
Quietly located close to the town centre, East Cliff Lift, and just 300 yards from the seafront, this charming small hotel has comfortable bedrooms and a delightful garden in which guests can relax during the warmer months. A cosy lounge adjoins the large dining room where home cooked meals are served.
FACILITIES: 10 rms (7 en suite) (4 fmly) No smoking in dining room STV TVB tea/coffee Direct dial from bedrooms Licensed Cen ht TVL No coaches Dinner Last d 7.30pm **PRICES:** s £20-£35; d £50-£70✻ **LB** **PARKING:** 10 **CARDS:**

♦♦♦ Linwood House Hotel

11 Wilfred Rd, Boscombe BH5 1ND ☎ 01202 397818
📠 01202 397818
e-mail: linwood_house@lineone.net
Dir: *Wessex Way to Boscombe, follow signs to Shelley Museum*

Situated in a peaceful residential area, Linwood House is close to the beach and other local attractions. The comfortable bedrooms are equipped with many modern amenities. The spacious lounge overlooks the well-maintained garden, as does the dining room where breakfast is served. A set dinner using fresh, local produce is available by prior arrangement.
FACILITIES: 10 rms (8 en suite) (2 fmly) No smoking TVB tea/coffee No dogs Licensed Cen ht TVL No children 7yrs Dinner Last d breakfast **PRICES:** (incl. dinner) s £25-£35; d £50-£70✻ **LB** **PARKING:** 4

♦♦♦ Newlands Hotel

14 Rosemount Rd, Alum Chine BH4 8HB ☎ 01202 761922
e-mail: newlandshotel@totalise.co.uk
Dir: *follow A338 to the end at Frizzel rdbt, take 3rd exit marked Alum Chine. At turn left to small rdbt and turn right into Alum Hurst Rd, Rosemount Rd is 3rd on left*
Located in a quiet area near the beach and within easy driving distance of both Bournemouth and Poole town centres and other places of interest, this friendly, family run hotel offers comfortable accommodation. Home-cooked dinner is available by prior arrangement. There is a charming conservatory overlooking the garden for guests' use.
FACILITIES: 10 en suite (4 fmly) No smoking TVB tea/coffee No dogs Licensed Cen ht No coaches Dinner Last d breakfast **PRICES:** s £24-£30; d £48-£60✻ **LB** **PARKING:** 8 **NOTES:** Closed 21 Sept-1st week April (ex open Xmas)

♦♦♦ Denewood Hotel

1 Percy Rd BH5 1JE ☎ 01202 394493 📠 01202 391155
e-mail: res@denewood.co.uk
Dir: *follow Boscombe Pier signs from Bournemouth*
FACILITIES: 10 en suite (3 fmly) No smoking in dining room STV TVB tea/coffee Licensed Cen ht TVL No coaches Solarium health & beauty salon **PRICES:** s £20-£26; d £36-£48✻ **LB** **BB** **PARKING:** 14 **CARDS:**

U Fenn Lodge

11 Rosemount Rd, Alum Chine BH4 8HB ☎ 01202 761273
At the time of going to press the Diamond classification for this establishment had not been confirmed. Please check the AA website www.theAA.com for up-to-date information.
FACILITIES: 11 en suite (2 fmly)

BRIDPORT

Map 03 SY49

See also Chideock

♦♦♦♦ Britmead House

West Bay Rd DT6 4EG ☎ 01308 422941 📠 01308 422516
e-mail: britmead@talk21.com
Dir: *approaching Bridport on A35 follow signs for West Bay, Britmead House is 800yds S of A35*

With excellent views over the surrounding countryside, Britmead House is located south of Bridport, within easy reach of the town centre and West Bay harbour. Well-appointed, comfortable accommodation is provided for the predominantly leisure guests, many of whom return on a regular basis. A choice of breakfast is served in the light and airy dining room.
FACILITIES: 7 en suite (2 fmly) (1 GF) No smoking TVB tea/coffee Licensed Cen ht No coaches **PRICES:** s £26-£42; d £44-£64* **PARKING:** 12 **CARDS:**

♦♦♦ New House Farm *(SY483948)*

Mangerton Ln, Bradpole DT6 3SF ☎ 01308 422884 📠 01308 422884 Mrs C Greening
e-mail: jane@mangertonlake.freeserve.co.uk
Dir: *from Bridport take A3066 towards Beaminster. Leave town, straight over rdbt, then 1st right signed "Mangerton Mill, Powerstock, West Milton". Follow lane as if for Mill, farm 0.5m on left.*
This modern farmhouse offers spacious and comfortable accommodation. The Greening family welcome guests to their home, which nestles in the Dorset hills and is close to the seaside and World Heritage coastline. Breakfast and home-cooked dinners (available by arrangement) are taken in the newly redecorated dining room. A coarse fishing lake is on site.
FACILITIES: 2 en suite No smoking TVB tea/coffee No dogs Cen ht Fishing 50 acres beef Dinner Last d noon **PRICES:** s fr £25; d fr £50* **PARKING:** 3 **NOTES:** Closed Xmas

U The Travellers Rest

Dorchester Rd DT6 4PJ ☎ 01308 459503
At the time of going to press the Diamond classification for this establishment had not been confirmed. Please check the AA website www.theAA.com for up-to-date information.
FACILITIES: 3 rms

CASHMOOR

Map 03 ST91

♦♦♦♦ Cashmoor House

DT11 8DN ☎ 01725 552339 📠 01725 552291
e-mail: spencer.jones@ukonline.co.uk
Dir: *on A354 Salisbury-Blandford, 3m S of Sixpenny Handley rdbt just passed Inn on the Chase*
Situated virtually midway between Blandford and Salisbury, parts of Cashmoor House date back to the 17th century. Retaining its original character and charm, the whole property is attractively furnished and decorated, with a warm and homely farmhouse ambience. Traditional 'Aga' cooked breakfasts are served in the beamed dining room.
FACILITIES: 5 en suite (2 fmly) (2 GF) No smoking TVB tea/coffee Cen ht TVL **PRICES:** s fr £25; d fr £40* **PARKING:** 8

CHIDEOCK

Map 03 SY49

♦♦♦♦ Betchworth House

Chideock DT6 6JW ☎ 01297 489478 📠 01297 489932
e-mail: JllLdg@aol.com
Dir: *on A35, approx half way between Bridport and Lyme Regis*
Guests are assured of a warm and friendly welcome at this charming guest house. The comfortable bedrooms are well equipped and attractively decorated with many thoughtful extras such as flowers and toiletries. A hearty breakfast is served at separate tables in the delightful dining room. On sunny days, guests can relax in the attractive gardens at the rear of the property.
FACILITIES: 6 rms (5 en suite) (1 fmly) No smoking TVB tea/coffee No dogs Cen ht No children 10yrs No coaches fishing **PRICES:** s £30-£40; d £50-£60* **LB PARKING:** 6 **CARDS:**

♦♦♦♦ Rose Cottage

Main St DT6 6JQ ☎ 01297 489994
e-mail: suerosecottage@hotmail.com.
Dir: *on A35*
Conveniently located in the centre of Chideock, a charming Dorset village, this 300 year old cottage provides very well appointed, attractive accommodation. A friendly welcome is assured as Sue and Mick welcome you to their home. A delicious breakfast can be enjoyed around the communal table in the dining room and in finer weather guests may relax in the pretty garden.
FACILITIES: 2 en suite No smoking TVB tea/coffee Cen ht No children 14yrs No coaches **PRICES:** d fr £47* **PARKING:** 2

CHRISTCHURCH

Map 04 SZ19

Premier Collection

♦♦♦♦♦ Druid House

26 Sopers Ln BH23 1JE ☎ 01202 485615 📠 01202 473484
e-mail: reservations@druid-house.co.uk
Dir: *from A35 exit Christchurch main rdbt to Sopers Lane, establishment on left opposite recreation ground*
Overlooking the park, this delightful family-run establishment is conveniently situated in the heart of Christchurch and is just a short stroll from the main High Street, Priory and Quay. Bedrooms, including some with balconies, are very comfortably furnished and include many welcome extras. In addition to the pleasant rear garden, guests are welcome to use the relaxing lounge and bar areas. Evening meals are available by prior arrangement.
FACILITIES: 8 en suite (3 fmly) (4 GF) No smoking in 2 bedrooms No smoking in dining room STV TVB tea/coffee Direct dial from bedrooms No dogs (ex guide dogs) Licensed Cen ht No coaches Dinner Last d 8.30pm **PRICES:** s £28-£48; d £60-£80* **LB PARKING:** 8 **CARDS:**

LB indicates that Leisure Breaks are offered by the establishment.

continued

CHRISTCHURCH continued

Premier Collection

♦♦♦♦♦ The Lord Bute Hotel & Restaurant

181-185 Lymington Rd, Highcliffe on Sea BH23 4JS
☎ 01425 278884 📠 01425 279258
e-mail: @lordbute.co.uk

***Dir:** from A35 get onto A337 towards Highcliffe, the Lord Bute is approximately 1m along road opposite St Mark's church*

A smart, family-owned hotel in a converted lodge house, adjacent to its sister restaurant, where traditional favourites such as beef Wellington are served to residents and locals. Bedrooms are furnished to the highest standard, including spa baths and air-conditioning. Breakfast is served in the Orangery. A function room and residents' lounge is also available.

FACILITIES: 10 en suite (5 GF) No smoking in 2 bedrooms No smoking in dining room STV TVB tea/coffee Direct dial from bedrooms Licensed Cen ht No children 10yrs No coaches Air baths in each bedroom Dinner Last d 9.45pm **PRICES:** s £65-£75; d £80-£95* LB **CONF:** Thtr 25 Class 35 Board 14 **PARKING:** 15 **CARDS:**

♦♦♦♦ The Beech Tree

2 Stuart Rd, Highcliffe on Sea BH23 5JS ☎ 01425 272038

***Dir:** from Christchurch take A337 to New Milton, after 2m take 1st right past traffic lights in Highcliffe village*

Conveniently located for the New Forest, the coast and numerous places of interest, this delightful family-run guest house has bright comfortable bedrooms equipped with many extra facilities. A cosy lounge is also available for guests' use. Carefully presented breakfasts and evening meals (by prior arrangement) are served in the brightly decorated dining room.

FACILITIES: 6 en suite No smoking in bedrooms No smoking in dining room TVB tea/coffee No dogs (ex guide dogs) Cen ht TVL No children 12yrs No coaches **PARKING:** 9 **NOTES:** Closed 31 Dec~Jan 1

♦♦♦♦ Sea Corner

397 Waterford Rd BH23 5JN ☎ 01425 272731 📠 01425 272077
e-mail: marlene@seacorner.fsnet.co.uk

Situated within walking distance of the shops and beaches, this delightful establishment is just a short drive from Highcliffe Castle, Christchurch and the New Forest. The stylish, spacious bedrooms are well equipped with many extra facilities. The proprietors also run the delightful Italian restaurant on the ground floor where delicious evening meals are available.

FACILITIES: 4 rms (3 en suite) TVB tea/coffee No dogs (ex guide dogs) Licensed Cen ht No children 12yrs No coaches Dinner Last d 10am **PRICES:** d £45-£58* **PARKING:** 2 **CARDS:**

♦♦♦♦ Three Gables

11 Wickfield Av BH23 1JB ☎ 01202 481166 📠 01202 486171
e-mail: rfgill@3gables.fsnet.com.uk

***Dir:** M3 onto M27, W onto A31. Left onto A338 past Ringwood exit to Christchurch after 5m onto B3073*

Located a few minutes' walk from the town and the Quay, Three Gables is a relaxed, family-run home-from-home style guesthouse, where guests are encouraged to join in the banter with the proprietors, especially at breakfast. Bedrooms include one on the ground floor with its own small patio area.

FACILITIES: 3 en suite (1 GF) No smoking in dining room STV TVB tea/coffee No dogs (ex guide dogs) Cen ht No children 5yrs No coaches **PRICES:** s £20-£25; d £40-£58* **LB PARKING:** 5 **NOTES:** Closed Xmas & New Year

♦♦♦♦ White House

428 Lymington Rd, Highcliffe On Sea BH23 5HF
☎ 01425 271279 📠 01425 276900
e-mail: thewhitehouse@themail.co.uk

***Dir:** turn off A35 towards Highcliffe. Follow signs to Highcliffe. After rdbt The White House is about 200 yds on the right.*

This charming Victorian house is just a short drive from Highcliffe beach, the New Forest and the historic town of Christchurch. Comfortable, well appointed accommodation is provided, with all bedrooms being tastefully furnished and decorated. A generous, freshly cooked breakfast is served in the cosy dining room.

FACILITIES: 6 rms (5 en suite) No smoking STV TVB tea/coffee No dogs (ex guide dogs) Cen ht No coaches **PRICES:** s £28-£35; d £45-£54* LB **PARKING:** 8 **CARDS:**

See advertisement on opposite page

♦♦♦ Ashbourne

47 Stour Rd BH23 1LN ☎ 01202 475574 📠 01202 482905
e-mail: ashcroft.b@hotmail.com

***Dir:** leave A338 to Christchurch, follow signs to town centre, over railway bridge, right into Stour Rd, over traffic lights, Fourth House on right*

Conveniently located for the historic market town of Christchurch, the scenic River Stour and nearby New Forest and beaches, this delightful guest house provides a relaxed and friendly environment. Bedrooms and bathrooms are all neatly furnished and equipped with many extra facilities. Large cooked breakfasts are offered in the bright dining room.

FACILITIES: 7 rms (4 en suite) (2 fmly) No smoking in dining room No smoking in lounges STV TVB tea/coffee Cen ht No coaches **PRICES:** s £25-£35; d £40-£56* **LB PARKING:** 7

♦♦♦ Brantwood

55 Stour Rd BH23 1LN ☎ 01202 473446

***Dir:** Leave A31 follow A338 & signs for Christchurch follow along Hurn Rd/Fairmile Rd, turn right into Stour Rd, establishment through traffic lights on right*

Relaxed and friendly guest house where the proprietors encourage a home-from-home atmosphere. Bedrooms and bathrooms are all well decorated and comfortably furnished. The town centre is just a short stroll from the establishment and off-street parking is available.

FACILITIES: 5 en suite No smoking in dining room No smoking in lounges TVB tea/coffee No dogs (ex guide dogs) Cen ht No coaches **PRICES:** s fr £25; d fr £50* **PARKING:** 5

♦♦♦ Bure Farmhouse

107 Bure Ln, Friars Cliff BH23 4DN ☎ 01425 275498

***Dir:** A35 from Christchurch, continue into A337 towards Highcliffe and Lymington. At 1st roundabout turn right into 'The Runway'. Bure Farm House on left.*

A warm welcome is assured at this comfortable, family-run Edwardian farmhouse just a three minute walk from the beach and coastguard training station, situated between Christchurch and Highcliffe. Those wishing to explore the New Forest and numerous local places of interest will find the proprietors' local knowledge invaluable.

FACILITIES: 3 en suite No smoking TVB tea/coffee No dogs Cen ht No children 5yrs No coaches **PRICES:** s £25-£30; d £44-£50* LB **PARKING:** 3

♦♦♦ Lyndhurst Lodge

Lyndhurst Rd BH23 4SD ☎ 01425 276796 📠 01425 276499
e-mail: lynlodge1@aol.com

***Dir:** from M27 follow signs to Lyndhurst, then take A35 for Christchurch past Cat & Fiddle pub, down hill, GH on left 50yds past Toby Carvery pub*

This cosy family run guest house is ideally located close to beaches, the New Forest and other places of interest. Lyndhurst

continued

Lodge has brightly decorated and comfortable bedrooms. The garden and conservatory lounges (with patio doors) are ideal for rest and relaxation. Dinner is available by prior arrangement.
FACILITIES: 5 rms (3 en suite) (1 fmly) No smoking TVB tea/coffee No dogs (ex guide dogs) Cen ht TVL No coaches Dinner Last d noon
PRICES: s £23-£28; d £40-£56* LB **PARKING:** 8

♦♦♦ Number 19

19 Friars Rd, Friars Cliff BH23 4EB ☎ 01425 273323
01425 273323
Dir: *from A35/A337 to Lymington. After 0.5m turn right at Hoburne rdbt onto The Runway. Friars Rd is 0.5m on left, 50yds beyond Sandpiper pub*
Located in a quiet residential area, 100 metres from the sea and within walking distance of the Coast Guard training centre, this charming chalet bungalow provides guests with comfortable bedrooms. Every effort is made to ensure guests feel at home. There is a comprehensive local information centre in the hallway.
FACILITIES: 3 rms (1 fmly) No smoking in dining room STV TVB tea/coffee Cen ht No children 2yrs No coaches **PRICES:** s £13.50-£30; d £27-£48 BB
PARKING: 4

♦♦♦ Pines Hotel

39 Mudeford BH23 3NQ ☎ 01202 475121 01202 487666
e-mail: pineshotelcafe39@ic24.net
Dir: *turn off A35 at Somerford rdbt onto A337. Hotel on main rd through Mudeford opposite cricket ground*
Warm hospitality and an eclectic menu are features of this small hotel. Fresh, local produce is used extensively in both lunch and dinner options. Bedrooms are comfortable and bright and in addition a spacious lounge and bar are provided. During the summer months, meals may be served in the secluded garden.
FACILITIES: 15 rms (14 en suite) (3 fmly) (3 GF) No smoking in bedrooms No smoking in dining room No smoking in 1 lounge TVB tea/coffee Direct dial from bedrooms Licensed Cen ht TVL Sea fishing Sailing Windsurfing Dinner Last d 8pm **PRICES:** s £40-£45; d £60-£80* LB **CONF:** Class 12
PARKING: 12 **NOTES:** Closed 24 Dec-2 Jan **CARDS:**

♦♦♦ Stour Villa

67 Stour Rd BH23 1LN ☎ 01202 483379 01202 483379
e-mail: stourvilla@bushinternet.com
Dir: *on leaving Christchurch town centre heading towards Bournemouth on A35, left at lights to Stour Road, Villa approx 150 yds right.*
Well located for visiting the New Forest and local beaches, Stour Villa is situated just a five-minute walk from the town centre with its various attractions and restaurants. The bedrooms and bathrooms are neatly furnished and decorated. A substantial cooked breakfast is offered in the cosy dining room.
FACILITIES: 6 en suite (1 fmly) No smoking TVB tea/coffee Cen ht No coaches **PRICES:** s £19.50-£27.50; d £39-£54* LB **PARKING:** 7

U Grosvenor Lodge

53 Stour Rd BH23 1LN ☎ 01202 499008
At the time of going to press the Diamond classification for this establishment had not been confirmed. Please check the AA website www.theAA.com for up-to-date information.
FACILITIES: 7 rms (5 en suite) (4 fmly)

CORSCOMBE Map 03 ST50

♦♦♦♦ Fox

DT2 0NS ☎ 01935 891330 01935 891330
e-mail: dine@fox-inn.co.uk
Dir: *1 mile off A356, Crewkerne-Maiden Newton road or 5 miles off A37, Yeovil-Dorchester road*
Situated down winding lanes, this charming 17th-century thatched inn remains popular with locals and tourists alike. Guests are

continued

assured of warm and relaxed hospitality. The three spacious bedrooms have been thoughtfully furnished to a high standard and in keeping with the character of the building. Breakfast is served in the conservatory during the summer.
FACILITIES: 4 en suite No smoking in bedrooms No smoking in area of dining room TVB tea/coffee Cen ht Dinner Last d 9pm or 9.30 Fri/Sat
PRICES: s £55-£75; d £80-£100* **MEALS:** Lunch fr £15.75alc Dinner £15.75-£27alc* **PARKING:** 60 **CARDS:**

DORCHESTER Map 03 SY69

See also Sydling St Nicholas

Premier Collection

♦♦♦♦♦ Casterbridge Hotel

49 High East St DT1 1HU ☎ 01305 264043
01305 260884
e-mail: reception@casterbridgehotel.co.uk
Dir: *in town centre 75mtrs from town clock*
Within a short walk of the town centre, this Georgian property is equally suitable for both business and leisure travellers. Bedrooms are well-maintained and comfortable, some are situated off a concealed courtyard annexe at the rear of the property and ground floor rooms are available. Public areas consist of a bar/library, a gracious drawing room and a dining room and conservatory where a particularly good breakfast is provided.
FACILITIES: 9 en suite 5 annexe en suite (1 fmly) (2 GF) No smoking in 11 bedrooms No smoking in dining room No smoking in lounges TVB tea/coffee Direct dial from bedrooms No dogs (ex guide dogs) Licensed Cen ht **PRICES:** s £45-£60; d £75-£95* LB **NOTES:** Closed 25-26 Dec **CARDS:**

England

DORCHESTER continued

Premier Collection

♦♦♦♦♦ Yalbury Cottage

Lower Bockhampton DT2 8PZ ☎ 01305 262382
01305 266412
e-mail: yalburycottage@aol.com
Dir: *off A35 past Thomas Hardy's cottage, straight over x-rds, 400yds on L, past red telephone box, opp village pump*

Dating back some 300 years, this delightfully attractive, thatched property, in the rural hamlet of Lower Bockhampton, was originally the home of the local shepherd and keeper of the water meadows. The oak-beamed ceilings, inglenook fireplaces and stone walls are features in both the lounge and restaurant - the ideal venue in which to enjoy the hotel's award-winning cuisine. The well equipped bedrooms are comfortable and overlook either the colourful gardens or adjacent fields.
FACILITIES: 8 en suite (1 fmly) (6 GF) No smoking in bedrooms No smoking in dining room TVB tea/coffee Direct dial from bedrooms Licensed Cen ht Dinner Last d 8pm **PRICES:** s fr £58; d fr £90✻ **PARKING:** 16 **CARDS:**

♦♦♦♦ Westwood House Hotel

29 High West St DT1 1UP ☎ 01305 268018 01305 250282
e-mail: reservations@westwoodhouse.co.uk
Dir: *from A35 into town, hotel 100yds off 'Top o' Town' rdbt and car park (The Circle)*
Situated on the western side of the town, this fine, early 19th century building has been sympathetically restored. The thoughtfully furnished and equipped bedrooms are decorated in well-chosen, soft colour schemes. Hearty breakfasts are served in the conservatory/dining room at the rear of the property, in addition there is a comfortable lounge for guests.
FACILITIES: 6 en suite (1 fmly) No smoking in bedrooms No smoking in dining room TVB tea/coffee Direct dial from bedrooms No dogs (ex guide dogs) Cen ht TVL No coaches Jacuzzi **PRICES:** s £45-£65; d £55-£85✻
CARDS:

♦♦♦♦ Yellowham Farmhouse *(SY730330)*

Yellowham Wood DT2 8RW ☎ 01305 262892 01305 257707
Mrs K Birchenhough
e-mail: b&b@yellowham.freeserve.co.uk
Dir: *1.5m E of Dorchester, turn off A35. Farm situated on edge of Yellowham Wood*
Located on the East of the town and situated in the heart of Hardy Country with 130 acres of woodland at guests' disposal; peace is guaranteed. There are spectacular views and comfortable bedrooms, all of which are on the ground floor. Some guests may enjoy the special feature of seeing a hand-reared Roe deer.

continued

Yellowham Farmhouse

FACILITIES: 4 en suite (1 fmly) (4 GF) No smoking TVB tea/coffee No dogs (ex guide dogs) Licensed Cen ht No children 4yrs Tennis (hard) Croquet lawn 120 acres arable beef horse breeding Dinner Last d 10am
PRICES: s £30-£40; d £50-£60✻ **LB PARKING:** 8
CARDS:

♦♦♦♦ Maiden Castle Farm

DT2 9PR ☎ 01305 262356 01305 251085
e-mail: maidencastlefarm@euphony.net
Dir: *A35 to Dorchester then A354 to Weymouth, in 20yds turn up drive on right*
FACILITIES: 4 en suite (1 fmly) No smoking in bedrooms No smoking in dining room TVB tea/coffee Licensed Cen ht No coaches **PRICES:** s £26; d £52-£55✻ **LB PARKING:** 10 **CARDS:**

♦♦♦ Churchview

Winterbourne Abbas DT2 9LS ☎ 01305 889296
01305 889296
e-mail: stay@churchview.co.uk
Dir: *approach Winterbourne Abbas on A35, Churchview is in centre of village church*

An ideal base for touring the many attractions of 'Hardy Country', this friendly guest house retains many of its period features. Dating from the 17th century, the property has been sympathetically modernised, and offers comfortable, bright and well decorated bedrooms. During the summer months, good home cooked meals are served.
FACILITIES: 9 en suite (1 fmly) No smoking TVB tea/coffee Licensed Cen ht No children 4yrs No coaches Dinner Last d 7pm **PRICES:** s £28-£34; d £48-£60✻ **LB PARKING:** 9 **NOTES:** Closed 22 Dec-3 Jan rs Nov-Mar (no evening meals) **CARDS:**

♦♦♦ Lamperts Cottage

DT2 9NU ☎ 01300 341659 01300 341699
e-mail: nickywillis@tesco.net

(For full entry see Sydling St Nicholas)

England

♦♦♦ Long Barn House

1 Barton Mews, West Stafford DT2 8UB ☎ 01305 266899
e-mail: pessame@amserve.net
Dir: *follow A352 from A35, follow signs to west Stafford, on entering village turn L before church, follow signs*
Located in the heart of the picturesque village of West Stafford, this converted 19th-century granary is ideally situated for exploring the surrounding area made famous by the author Thomas Hardy. The historic towns of Dorchester and Weymouth are just a short drive away. Bedrooms are comfortable and well equipped.
FACILITIES: 2 en suite No smoking TVB tea/coffee Cen ht No children 8yrs **PRICES:** s fr £32; d fr £50✱ **PARKING:** 4 **NOTES:** Closed Dec

EVERSHOT Map 03 ST50

♦♦♦♦ Acorn

DT2 0JW ☎ 01935 83228 01935 83707
e-mail: stay@acorn-inn.co.uk
Dir: *off A37 or A356, in centre of village*
A delightful 16th-century coaching inn at the heart of this picturesque village. Bedrooms, each with a range of modern comforts, have been individually decorated and furnished. The public rooms have many original features and here interesting menus are complemented by a fine selection of wines.
FACILITIES: 9 en suite (1 fmly) No smoking in bedrooms No smoking in dining room TVB tea/coffee Direct dial from bedrooms Cen ht Dinner Last d 9pm or 9.30 Fri/Sat **PRICES:** s £55-£75; d £80-£120✱ **LB MEALS:** Lunch fr £15.75alc Dinner £22-£27&alc✱ **PARKING:** 40 **CARDS:**

FARNHAM Map 03 ST91

Premier Collection

♦♦♦♦♦ The Museum Inn

DT11 8DE ☎ 01725 516261 01725 516988
e-mail: themuseuminn@supanet.com
Dir: *12 miles south of Salisbury on A354*
This delightful part-thatched inn has recently been completely renovated, retaining all its original 17th-century charm and carefully combining it with modern facilities. The pub has an engaging buzz, and for those seeking somewhere quieter, there is a sumptuous sitting room with plenty of reading material. Bedrooms are deeply comfortable, with lots of thoughtful touches; bottled water, fresh flowers and home-baked biscuits. A varied menu is offered in the bar, while The Shed Restaurant is open for dinner on Fridays and Saturdays and Sunday lunch.
FACILITIES: 8 en suite No smoking TVB tea/coffee Direct dial from bedrooms Cen ht No children 8yrs Golf 18 Dinner Last d 9.30pm
PRICES: s fr £55; d £65-£120✱ **MEALS:** Lunch £22-£30 Dinner £22-£30✱ **PARKING:** 15 **NOTES:** Closed 25,26 & 31 Dec
CARDS:

IWERNE COURTNEY OR SHROTON Map 03 ST81

The Cricketers

Main St DT11 8QD ☎ 01258 860421
At the time of going to press the Diamond classification for this establishment had not been confirmed. Please check the AA website www.theAA.com for up-to-date information.
FACILITIES: 1 en suite

LYME REGIS Map 03 SY39

See also Axminster (Devon)

♦♦♦♦ Old Lyme

29 Coombe St DT7 3PP ☎ 01297 442929 01297 444652
e-mail: oldlyme.guesthouse@virgin.net
Guests' comfort is a high priority at this delightful 18th-century building which is just a short walk from the seafront. Bedrooms, varying in size, are all well equipped and include thoughtful extras. Served in the cheerfully decorated dining room, a wide choice is offered at breakfast including a daily special.
FACILITIES: 5 en suite (1 fmly) No smoking TVB tea/coffee No dogs Cen ht TVL No children 5yrs No coaches **PRICES:** d £44-£56✱ **LB**

♦♦♦♦ Albany

Charmouth Rd DT7 3DP ☎ 01297 443066
e-mail: albany@lymeregis.com
Dir: *on eastern main road into Lyme Regis. 50yds past car park on left and before Anning Rd*
Providing comfortable and well-appointed accommodation, this attractive house is located on the fringe of the town, within easy walking distance of the seafront. Bedrooms are spacious and have pleasant co-ordinating décor and soft furnishings. A choice of breakfasts is served in the smart dining room.
FACILITIES: 5 en suite (1 fmly) No smoking TVB tea/coffee No dogs Cen ht TVL No children 5yrs No coaches **PRICES:** s £30-£40; d £40-£52✱
PARKING: 6

England

LYME REGIS continued

♦♦♦♦ Coverdale

Woodmead Rd DT7 3AB ☎ 01297 442882 📠 01297 444673
e-mail: coverdale@tinyworld.co.uk
Dir: *off A35 onto B3165 through Uplyme, over mini-rdbt, 2nd left before Mariners Hotel*

Coverdale is located in a quiet residential area on the fringe of the town centre and within easy reach of the seafront. Bedrooms are brightly decorated and comfortably appointed. Sound English fare is provided at dinner and breakfast and is served in the light and airy dining room overlooking the garden.
FACILITIES: 9 en suite (5 fmly) (1 GF) No smoking TVB tea/coffee No dogs (ex guide dogs) Cen ht Dinner Last d 10am **PRICES:** s £25; d £50-£56* **PARKING:** 9

♦♦♦♦ The Orchard Country Hotel

Rousdon DT7 3XW ☎ 01297 442972 📠 01297 443670
e-mail: the.orchard@btinternet.com
Dir: *on A3052 follow brown signs from the centre of the village of Rousdon*

Delightfully located in the peaceful village of Rousdon, three miles west of Lyme Regis and set in attractive orchard gardens, this comfortable hotel is an ideal base from which to tour the area. Many guests return to this attractive hotel where service and hospitality are assured. Dinner features interesting and freshly prepared dished and vegetarian choices are always available. Bedrooms are very comfortable and are provided with a host of extras to enhance your stay.
FACILITIES: 12 en suite No smoking TVB tea/coffee No dogs (ex guide dogs) Licensed Cen ht TVL No children 8yrs No coaches Dinner Last d 6pm **PRICES:** s £26-£41; d £52-£78* **LB PARKING:** 15 **NOTES:** Closed Xmas & New Year **CARDS:**

♦♦♦♦ The White House

47 Silver St DT7 3HR ☎ 01297 443420
Dir: *on B3165 Axminster-Lyme Regis road approx 50mtrs from junct with A3052*
Conveniently located, this charming guesthouse dating back to 1770 has been thoroughly modernised. The bedrooms are cheerful and bright, and the best possible use has been made of the

continued

The White House

available space. There is a comfortable lounge and an attractive breakfast room where hearty breakfasts are served.
FACILITIES: 7 en suite No smoking in bedrooms No smoking in dining room TVB tea/coffee Cen ht TVL No children No coaches **PRICES:** d £42-£50* **PARKING:** 7 **NOTES:** Closed Nov-Mar

♦♦♦ Kent House Hotel

Silver St DT7 3HT ☎ 01297 443442 📠 01297 444626
e-mail: thekenthouse@talk21.com
Dir: *At Raymond's Corner turn off A35 onto B3165 to Lyme Regis. Pass through Yawl and Uplyme to mini rdbt. Cross onto Silver Street passing Queen Vic on left. Kent House is next right*
Guests are assured of a warm and friendly welcome at this detached hotel, on the edge of Lyme Regis. From its elevated position there are stunning views towards the Dorset coastline in the distance. Dinners and Sunday lunch are served by arrangement and a varied choice is offered.
FACILITIES: 9 rms (6 en suite) (1 fmly) No smoking TVB tea/coffee No dogs (ex guide dogs) Cen ht TVL No coaches Dinner Last d 8.30pm **PRICES:** s £35-£50; d £25-£40* **LB BB PARKING:** 8 **CARDS:**

♦♦♦ Lucerne

View Rd DT7 3AA ☎ 01297 443752
e-mail: lucerne@lineone.net
Dir: *A35 from Axminster follow signs for Lyme Regis. After mini rdbt take 2nd left (Woodmead Rd), 1st right (View Rd), 9th house on left*
A warm welcome is assured at this guest house, quietly set in an elevated position above the town, and only a few minutes' stroll to the sea. Bedrooms are comfortably furnished, and several have wonderful sea views. During the summer, the front of the house boasts a colourful display of pots and tubs.
FACILITIES: 5 en suite No smoking TVB tea/coffee No dogs (ex guide dogs) Cen ht No children 7yrs No coaches **PRICES:** s £23-£28; d £40-£46* **LB PARKING:** 6 **NOTES:** Closed 25-26 Dec

♦♦♦ Old Monmouth Hotel

12 Church St DT7 3BS ☎ 01297 442456 📠 01297 443577
e-mail: oldmonhotel@btinternet.com
Dir: *from E turn off A35 onto A3052, hotel 2m on right opposite parish church. From W and N turn off A35 onto B3165, hotel 4m on left*
This former coaching inn which dates back to 1630 and stands opposite the parish church, is just a few minutes walk from the harbour and the town centre. The bedrooms are spacious and neatly presented. The restaurant, which is open most evenings, offers an interesting range of dishes.
FACILITIES: 6 rms (5 en suite) (2 fmly) (1 GF) No smoking TV5B tea/coffee No dogs (ex guide dogs) Licensed Cen ht No coaches Dinner Last d 9.30pm **PRICES:** d £50* **LB NOTES:** Closed Xmas **CARDS:**

♦♦♦ *St Michael's Hotel*

Pound St DT7 3HZ ☎ 01297 442503

Dir: *Situated on main road into Lyme Regis, just before Langmoor Gardens on the same side*

Located just off the centre of this popular, historic resort town, St Michael's is a fine example of a three storey Georgian house. Many of the comfortable, well-equipped bedrooms have the benefit of spectacular views over Lyme Bay. Full English or Continental breakfast is served in the lofty, former billiards room.

FACILITIES: 6 rms (5 en suite) (2 fmly) No smoking TVB tea/coffee No coaches **PARKING:** 6

NETTLECOMBE — Map 03 SY59

♦♦♦♦ Marquis of Lorne

DT6 3SY ☎ 01308 485236 📠 01308 485666

e-mail: enquiries@marquisoflorne.com

Dir: *N from Bridport on A3066, after 1.5m after mini-rdbt turn right, through West Milton, straight over at junct, premises up hill*

Peacefully located amidst glorious Dorset countryside, this cosy inn is a short distance from the coastal town of Bridport. A choice of bars and dining areas, all retaining much of their original character, provide an ideal setting in which to enjoy the home-cooked dishes on offer. The individually decorated bedrooms are well equipped with modern facilities.

FACILITIES: 7 en suite No smoking in area of dining room No smoking in 1 lounge TVB tea/coffee Direct dial from bedrooms No dogs (ex guide dogs) Cen ht No children 10yrs Dinner Last d 9.30pm **PRICES:** s £45; d £70* **LB MEALS:** Lunch £12-£20alc Dinner £14-£22alc* **PARKING:** 50 **NOTES:** rs 24-26 Dec **CARDS:**

PIDDLETRENTHIDE — Map 03 SY79

♦♦♦♦ The Poachers

DT2 7QX ☎ 01300 348358 📠 01300 348153

e-mail: thepoachersinn@piddletrenthide.fsbusiness.co.uk

Dir: *8m from Dorchester on B3143, 2m into Piddletrenthide on left*

A warm welcome is assured at this friendly, family-run inn. The bar and dining areas retain much of their original 16th-century character and charm with fresh home cooked meals a key feature. Extensions have allowed for good-sized bedrooms, the majority of which are situated around the swimming pool, garden and adjacent stream.

FACILITIES: 3 en suite 15 annexe en suite (1 fmly) (13 GF) No smoking in area of dining room TVB tea/coffee Direct dial from bedrooms Cen ht Outdoor swimming pool (heated) Skittle alley Dinner Last d 9pm **PRICES:** s fr £35; d fr £60* **LB MEALS:** Lunch £10-£17alc Dinner £10-£17alc* **PARKING:** 40 **NOTES:** Closed 24-26 Dec **CARDS:**

See advert under DORCHESTER

POOLE — Map 04 SZ09

♦♦♦♦ Acorns

264 Wimborne Rd, Oakdale BH15 3EF ☎ 01202 672901 📠 01202 672901

e-mail: enquiries@acornsguesthouse.co.uk

Dir: *on A35, 0.5m from town centre, opposite Texaco garage*

With easy access to the town, ferry terminal, business parks, and various attractions, guests at this family run hotel are assured of a warm welcome. Bedrooms are decorated and furnished to a high standard. English breakfasts are served in the charming dining room and there is a cosy bar in which to relax.

FACILITIES: 6 en suite (1 GF) No smoking in bedrooms No smoking in dining room TVB tea/coffee No dogs Licensed Cen ht TVL No children 14yrs No coaches **PRICES:** s £30-£35; d £45-£48* **PARKING:** 7 **NOTES:** Closed 23 Dec-1 Jan **CARDS:**

♦♦♦♦ Blue Shutters Hotel

109 North Rd, Parkstone BH14 0LU ☎ 01202 748129 📠 01202 748129

e-mail: stay@blueshutters.co.uk

Dir: *0.5m from Poole Park and Civic Centre buildings*

This friendly, family-run hotel is close to the civic centre and offers brightly decorated, well equipped bedrooms with good levels of comfort. Sound home-cooked meals are served in the well presented dining room overlooking the attractive garden. There is also a well appointed lounge with bar facilities.

FACILITIES: 7 en suite (2 fmly) (1 GF) No smoking in bedrooms No smoking in dining room No smoking in 1 lounge TVB tea/coffee No dogs Licensed Cen ht TVL No children 5yrs No coaches Dinner Last d 7pm **PRICES:** s £30; d £50* **PARKING:** 7 **CARDS:**

♦♦♦♦ Sarnia Cherie

375 Blandford Rd, Hamworthy BH15 4JL ☎ 01202 679470 📠 01202 679470

e-mail: Criscollier@aol.com

Dir: *A350 leading to Poole Quay and Ferry Terminal*

This charming, well-maintained guest house is well-located for the ferry terminal and town centre. It offers comfortable, well-equipped bedrooms, spacious bathrooms and a warm welcome. A homely relaxed atmosphere prevails at all times with a hearty breakfast served in the cosy dining room.

FACILITIES: 3 en suite No smoking TVB tea/coffee Cen ht No coaches **PRICES:** s £25-£35; d £45* **PARKING:** 3

♦♦♦ *Burleigh Private Hotel*

76 Wimborne Rd BH15 2BZ ☎ 01202 673889 📠 01202 685283

Dir: *off A35 onto A349*

Located close to the town centre and ferry terminal, this well kept guest house is ideally suited to business and leisure guests. Bedrooms are decorated and fitted to a good standard and there is a small, attractive lounge available for guests' use. Breakfast is served at separate tables in the dining room.

FACILITIES: 8 rms (4 en suite) (1 fmly) No smoking in 3 bedrooms No smoking in dining room STV TVB tea/coffee Licensed Cen ht TVL **PARKING:** 5 **CARDS:**

England

POOLE continued

♦♦♦ Centraltown

101 Wimborne Rd BH15 2BP ☎ 01202 674080 📠 01202 674080
Dir: *A350 to town centre then take A349. Barclays International building on left, guest house 500mtrs further on*
This friendly and well-maintained guesthouse is within easy access of the town centre, ferry terminals, Speedway and many other attractions the area has to offer. Bedrooms are attractive and equipped with many useful extra facilities. Full English breakfast is served in the bright, cosy dining room.
FACILITIES: 4 en suite (2 fmly) No smoking in dining room No smoking in lounges TVB tea/coffee No dogs (ex guide dogs) Cen ht No coaches **PRICES:** s fr £35; d fr £50* **PARKING:** 6

♦♦♦ Harbour View

157 Longfleet Rd BH15 2HS ☎ 01202 672421
This small, friendly and well-run guest house benefits from its elevated position with fine views of Poole Harbour and Brownsea Island. The bright bedrooms are adequately furnished and equipped with modern en suite facilities. Hearty, well-presented, traditional choices are offered at breakfast in the cosy dining room.
FACILITIES: 3 en suite No smoking in 2 bedrooms No smoking in dining room No smoking in lounges TVB tea/coffee No dogs (ex guide dogs) Cen ht No coaches **PRICES:** s £25; d £50* **PARKING:** 4

♦♦♦ Lewina Lodge

225 Bournemouth Rd, Parkstone BH14 9HU ☎ 01202 742295
e-mail: Lewinalodge@hotmail.com
Dir: *exit A31 onto A338. Follow signs for Bournemouth. At the end of A338 (Liverpool Victoria) rdbt, take A35 towards Poole.*
This guest house which is well located between the town centres of Poole and Bournemouth, offers a warm and friendly atmosphere. Bedrooms are comfortable and equipped with all the essentials. A good choice of breakfast is served in the attractive dining room.
FACILITIES: 6 rms (3 en suite) (2 fmly) No smoking TVB tea/coffee No dogs (ex guide dogs) Cen ht No coaches **PRICES:** s £25-£35; d £38-£50* BB **PARKING:** 6

♦♦♦ Seacourt

249 Blandford Rd, Hamworthy BH15 4AZ ☎ 01202 674995
📠 01202 674995
Dir: *turn off A3049/A35 signposted to Hamworthy*
Within a short distance of the ferry port and town centre, this friendly establishment is well-maintained, and efficiently run. The comfortable bedrooms, some of which are located on the ground floor, are all well-decorated and equipped with useful extra facilities. A small lounge with TV and video is also available.
FACILITIES: 4 en suite (1 fmly) (2 GF) No smoking in 1 bedrooms TVB tea/coffee No dogs Cen ht TVL No coaches **PRICES:** s £30-£44; d £44*
PARKING: 4

♦♦♦ Towngate

58 Wimborne Rd BH15 2BY ☎ 01202 668552
e-mail: ann@towngatebandb.freeserve.co.uk
Dir: *take A349 towards centre of Poole. Guest house on left before town centre*
Guests are assured of a warm welcome at this centrally located guest house within walking distance of the town centre and harbour, and just a few minutes' drive from the ferry terminal. The well-equipped bedrooms are comfortable and nicely furnished with one room on the ground floor.
FACILITIES: 3 en suite No smoking in dining room TVB tea/coffee No dogs Cen ht No children No coaches **PRICES:** s £35; d £45-£48*
PARKING: 4 **NOTES:** Closed mid Dec-mid Jan

♦♦ Holly House

97 Longfleet Rd BH15 2HP ☎ 01202 677839 📠 01202 461722
e-mail: hol.house@tesconet.com
Dir: *just off A35*
Holly House is conveniently located for both the centre of town and the ferry terminal. It has a friendly and relaxed atmosphere. The comfortable bedrooms are simply furnished and ideal for those visiting the town for either business or pleasure.
FACILITIES: 4 en suite (1 fmly) No smoking in dining room No smoking in lounges TVB tea/coffee No dogs (ex guide dogs) Cen ht TVL **PRICES:** s £28-£35; d £46* **PARKING:** 7 **CARDS:**

PORTLAND — Map 03 SY67

♦♦♦♦ Queen Anne House

2/4 Fortuneswell DT5 1LP ☎ 01305 820028 📠 01305 824389
Dir: *A354 to Portland and then Fortuneswell. House on left 200mtrs past Royal Portland Arms*
Bedrooms are decorated and furnished with great elegance and style at this super Grade II listed building. Similarly both the sitting and dining rooms are also furnished to a high standard and decorated in keeping with the age of the house. At breakfast, guests are served around one large table, with a wide choice of options available.
FACILITIES: 3 en suite No smoking TVB tea/coffee No dogs (ex guide dogs) Cen ht TVL **PRICES:** d £35-£55* BB

♦♦♦ Alessandria Hotel

71 Wakeham Easton DT5 1HW ☎ 01305 822270 & 820108
📠 01305 820561
Dir: *off A354*
The bedrooms at Alessandria Hotel are compact but are neatly furnished. Most of the rooms have en suite facilities and some have sea views. There is a dining room, in which breakfast is served in addition to a comfortable sitting room, which is available for guest use.
FACILITIES: 15 rms (11 en suite) 1 annexe en suite (3 fmly) (2 GF) No smoking TVB tea/coffee No dogs Licensed Cen ht TVL Dinner Last d 8pm
PRICES: s £30-£50; d £55-£70* **LB PARKING:** 16 **CARDS:**

♦♦♦ Portland Lodge

Easton Ln DT5 1BW ☎ 01305 820265 📠 01305 860007
e-mail: allan@portlandlodge.fsnet.co.uk
Located high on Portland Bill, the property is well located for those wishing to explore, Weymouth, Chesil Beach and the other numerous places of interest that Dorset has to offer. Bedrooms and bathrooms have recently been refurbished and provide good levels of comfort. A full English breakfast is served at individual tables.
FACILITIES: 16 rms (11 en suite) (1 fmly) (5 GF) No smoking in bedrooms No smoking in dining room No smoking in 1 lounge TVB tea/coffee No dogs Cen ht **PRICES:** s £20-£25; d £40-£70* **PARKING:** 17 **CARDS:**

SHAFTESBURY — Map 03 ST82

♦♦♦♦ Grove Arms

SP7 9ND ☎ 01747 828328 📠 01747 828960
e-mail: info@dorsetaccomodation.com
(For full entry see Ludwell (Wiltshire))

♦♦♦♦ Old Forge

Chapel Hill, Compton Abbas SP7 0NQ ☎ 01747 811881
01747 811881
e-mail: theoldforge@hotmail.com

Dir: *A350 from Shaftsbury signed to Blandford, through Cann. Next village is Compton Abbas. Old Forge is 1st building on left*

The Old Forge has plenty of old world charm and is located close to an Area of Outstanding Natural Beauty. The bedrooms are delightfully decorated, have sloping ceilings and antique furnishings. Downstairs the dining/sitting room, with its log burning stove, is very inviting. Breakfast includes local, organic and homemade items.

FACILITIES: 3 rms (2 en suite) No smoking TVB tea/coffee No dogs (ex guide dogs) Cen ht No coaches **PRICES:** s £30-£40; d £45-£55✳ **PARKING:** 4 **NOTES:** Closed Xmas

SHERBORNE — Map 03 ST61

Premier Collection

♦♦♦♦♦ The Grange Hotel & Restaurant

Oborne DT9 4LA ☎ 01935 813463 01935 817464
e-mail: karen@thegrangehotel-dorset.co.uk

Dir: *Turn L off the A30, 0.75m out of Sherborne heading East signed The Grange, 0.5m through the village.*

This delightful country house nestles peacefully in impressive gardens, close to historic Sherborne. Bedrooms, some of which are situated in the Grange annexe, across the garden, are equipped with a range of modern facilities. The bar and restaurant feature log fires and exposed timbers and stonework and have a relaxed atmosphere.

FACILITIES: 4 en suite 6 annexe en suite (3 fmly) No smoking in bedrooms No smoking in dining room TVB tea/coffee Direct dial from bedrooms No dogs (ex guide dogs) Licensed Cen ht No children Dinner Last d 9pm **PRICES:** s £65-£75; d £85-£105✳ **LB CONF:** Thtr 40 Class 20 Board 20 **PARKING:** 30 **NOTES:** Closed 26 Dec- 10 Jan, 2 wks end Aug **CARDS:**

Premier Collection

♦♦♦♦♦ Munden House

Munden Ln, Alweston DT9 5HU ☎ 01963 23150
01963 23153
e-mail: sylvia@mundenhouse.demon.co.uk

Dir: *from Sherborne take A352, turn left onto A3030 to Alweston. Pass village shop on right and after 250 yds on left, look for bakery sign, turn left*

Munden House dates back to mid-Victorian times, and is peacefully located in the picturesque Blackmore Vale, within three miles of Sherborne. Sympathetically restored throughout, the bedrooms and bathrooms are elegantly

continued

Munden House

decorated and furnished. Breakfasts are yet another highlight of a stay here. Guests are encouraged to use the luxurious sitting room, with its splendid views over the surrounding countryside, and the well-tended gardens.

FACILITIES: 6 en suite 1 annexe en suite (2 GF) No smoking TVB tea/coffee Direct dial from bedrooms No dogs (ex guide dogs) Cen ht No coaches Table tennis **PRICES:** s £39-£49; d £72-£90✳ **PARKING:** 20 **CARDS:**

Premier Collection

♦♦♦♦♦ Old Vicarage

Sherborne Rd, Milborne Port DT9 5AT ☎ 01963 251117
01963 251515
e-mail: theoldvicarage@milborneport.freeserve.co.uk

Dir: *off A30*

Offering high quality accommodation, this charming, listed Victorian house is steeped in history. The guest lounge and conservatory are particularly pleasant and relaxing, overlooking the gardens and flood lit at night. Bedrooms in the main house are spacious and styled with considerable flair. Rooms in the adjacent coach house are smaller but very comfortable and stylish.

FACILITIES: 3 en suite 3 annexe en suite (3 fmly) No smoking in bedrooms No smoking in dining room TVB tea/coffee Direct dial from bedrooms No dogs (ex guide dogs) Licensed Cen ht No children 5yrs No coaches Dinner Last d 6pm **PRICES:** s £44-£74; d £59-£105✳ **LB PARKING:** 10 **NOTES:** Closed Jan **CARDS:**

Directions are provided by the proprietor, ask for more details when booking.

England

SHERBOURNE continued

♦♦♦♦ Cromwell House

Long St DT9 3BS ☎ 01935 813352

***Dir:** in centre of Sherborne, 200 yds from junction of Cheap St/Long St*

A stone's throw from the centre of town, this splendid old Georgian house has recently been lovingly restored to its former charm and elegance. Bedrooms, all furnished with pine pieces, offer modern comforts and smart bathrooms. In addition to the comfortable sitting room, the cosy dining room is an ideal pace to enjoy a hearty breakfast.

FACILITIES: 3 en suite No smoking TVB tea/coffee No dogs (ex guide dogs) Cen ht No children 8yrs **PRICES:** s £35-£40; d £55-£60✳ **CARDS:**

♦♦♦♦ The Alders

Sandford Orcas DT9 4SB ☎ 01963 220666 Fax 01963 220666
e-mail: jonsue@btinternet.com

***Dir:** from town take B3148 towards Marston Magna, after 2.5m take turn R signed 'Sandford Orcas', at T-junct in village turn left towards Manor House*

Set is a lovely walled garden in the charming conservation village of Sandford Orcas, this delightful property has bedrooms, which are attractively decorated and well-equipped. Charming watercolours, painted by the owner, are an added interest. The comfortable sitting room features a huge inglenook fireplace with a wood burning stove.

FACILITIES: 3 en suite No smoking TVB tea/coffee No dogs (ex guide dogs) Cen ht TVL No coaches **PRICES:** s £35-£40; d £45-£50✳ **PARKING:** 5

♦♦♦♦ Almshouse Farm *(ST651082)*

Hermitage, Holnest DT9 6HA ☎ 01963 210296
Fax 01963 210296 Mrs J Mayo

***Dir:** from Sherborne take A352 Dorchester rd for 5m, at Holnest crossrds turn right signed Hermitage for farm 1.2m on left*

This peacefully located farmhouse is part of a working dairy farm. The oldest part of the building is a former monastery, dating from the 16th century. Two of the spacious, well-equipped bedrooms overlook the pleasant garden. A hearty breakfast is served in the dining room, which has a magnificent inglenook fireplace

FACILITIES: 3 en suite No smoking in 2 bedrooms No smoking in dining room No smoking in lounges TVB tea/coffee No dogs (ex guide dogs) Cen ht TVL No children 10yrs Horse-riding, fishing and golf nearby 300 acres dairy **PRICES:** d £46-£50✳ **LB PARKING:** 6 **NOTES:** Closed Dec-Jan

♦♦♦ Venn *(ST684183)*

Milborne Port DT9 5RA ☎ 01963 250598 Fax 01963 250598
Mrs Pauline Tizzard

***Dir:** on A30, 3m E of Sherborne, on edge of village of Milborne Port*

An ideal location from which to explore West Dorset. This farm specialises in training National Hunt race horses. The individually furnished bedrooms are comfortable and bathrooms are fitted with power showers. Downstairs a farmhouse breakfast is served in the combined lounge and dining room. *continued*

FACILITIES: 3 en suite No smoking TVB tea/coffee No dogs (ex guide dogs) Cen ht TVL Golf Riding Golf, riding, swimming nearby 375 acres dairy/beef/arable/race horses **PRICES:** s fr £25; d fr £42✳ **PARKING:** 6 **NOTES:** Closed Xmas

SIXPENNY HANDLEY — Map 03 ST91

♦♦♦ Town Farm Bungalow

SP5 5NT ☎ 01725 552319 & 07885 407191 Fax 01725 552319
e-mail: townfarmbungalow@ukonline.co.uk

***Dir:** from Salisbury take A354 S towards Blandford Forum at Handley rdbt turn right to Sixpenny Handley B3081, 200yds on right*

Due to its quiet country location, wonderful rural views of the countryside are enjoyed from all rooms of this delightful bungalow where a warm welcome is guaranteed. Delicious dinners are available by prior arrangements and, like breakfast, are served around one large table. Log fires warm the cosy lounge in winter.

FACILITIES: 3 rms (2 en suite) No smoking in 2 bedrooms No smoking in dining room TV2B Cen ht TVL No coaches Dinner Last d 24 hrs prior **PRICES:** s £25-£35; d £38-£45✳ **BB PARKING:** 6

STURMINSTER NEWTON — Map 03 ST71

♦♦♦♦ Stourcastle Lodge

Goughs Close DT10 1BU ☎ 01258 472320 Fax 01258 473381
e-mail: enquiries@stourcastle-lodge.co.uk

***Dir:** small lane off town square opposite cross*

Down a narrow lane off the Market Square, this charming 18th century house is set in delightful gardens. Guests are assured of a warm, friendly welcome from the owners. Bedrooms are spacious, well presented and comfortably appointed; all equipped with modern facilities, including many useful extras. Fine home-cooked meals are provided at dinner and breakfast, served in the attractive dining room.

FACILITIES: 5 en suite No smoking in bedrooms No smoking in dining room TVB tea/coffee Direct dial from bedrooms No dogs (ex guide dogs) Cen ht No coaches Dinner Last d 7pm **PRICES:** s £42-£49; d £66-£80✳ **LB PARKING:** 8 **CARDS:**

SWANAGE — Map 04 SZ07

♦♦♦♦ The Gillan Hotel

5 Northbrook Rd BH19 1PN ☎ 01929 424548 Fax 01929 421696
e-mail: gillanhotel@free.uk.com

***Dir:** from Wareham follow road over railway bridge, continue down avenue until car park on right, hotel opposite. From Sandbanks Ferry right at clock tower on seafront through traffic lights hotel 50yds on right*

With its location close to the town centre and sea front this family run hotel provides guests with an ideal base from which to explore the Isle of Purbeck. Bedrooms are comfortable and well equipped. There is a bar adjacent to the bright spacious dining room where an extensive dinner menu is available. *continued*

FACILITIES: 9 en suite (3 fmly) No smoking in bedrooms No smoking in dining room No smoking in lounges TVB tea/coffee No dogs (ex guide dogs) Licensed Dinner Last d 8.30pm **PRICES:** s £30-£50; d £50-£60✻ **LB** **PARKING:** 8 **NOTES:** Civ Wed 80 **CARDS:**

♦♦♦♦ White Lodge Hotel

Grosvenor Rd BH19 2DD ☎ 01929 422696 📠 01929 425510
e-mail: whitelodge.hotel@virgin.net
Dir: *along seafront turn right before pier into Seymer Rd heading into Durlston Rd, hotel on corner of Durlston Rd & Grosvenor Rd*

Set in flower filled gardens in a quiet, elevated position, this welcoming, family-run hotel offers well-equipped bedrooms, some of which benefit from panoramic sea views. Breakfast and evening menus offer a varied choice using fresh, local produce. There are also two comfortable lounges, a large conservatory and a small bar where guests can relax.

FACILITIES: 13 en suite (3 fmly) (1 GF) No smoking in bedrooms No smoking in dining room No smoking in 1 lounge TVB tea/coffee No dogs Licensed Cen ht TVL No children 8yrs Dinner Last d 7.30pm **PRICES:** s £30-£45; d £60-£70✻ **LB** **PARKING:** 12 **CARDS:**

♦♦♦ Eversden Private Hotel

5 Victoria Rd BH19 1LY ☎ 01929 423276 📠 01929 427755
e-mail: Office@eversdenhotel.co.uk
Dir: *follow Swanage to Studland rd past Crows Nest pub. 2nd rd on R past Crows Nest*

Well-located for the beach and town centre, this substantial Victorian property is situated in a quiet residential area. The bedrooms are equipped with many extra facilities. There is a lounge and bar in which to relax and a dining room where evening meals are served by prior arrangement. Packed lunches are also available.

FACILITIES: 12 rms (11 en suite) (5 fmly) No smoking in bedrooms No smoking in dining room No smoking in lounges TVB tea/coffee No dogs (ex guide dogs) Licensed Cen ht TVL Dinner Last d 2pm **PRICES:** s £20-£30; d £44-£60✻ **LB** **PARKING:** 12 **CARDS:**

♦♦♦ Sandringham Hotel

20 Durlston Rd BH19 2HX ☎ 01929 423076 📠 01929 423076
e-mail: silk@sandhot.fsnet.co.uk
Dir: *follow signs for 'Durlston Country Park'*

Located in a peaceful elevated position high above the town, yet close to the beach and just half a mile from the beautiful Durlston Country Park, this delightful hotel offers attractive, well-equipped bedrooms and comfortable public rooms, which include a conservatory bar. Delicious home-cooked evening meals are available by prior arrangement.

FACILITIES: 11 rms (9 en suite) (5 fmly) (1 GF) No smoking in dining room TVB tea/coffee No dogs (ex guide dogs) Licensed Cen ht TVL No coaches Dinner Last d 6pm **PRICES:** s £27-£33; d £54-£66 **LB** **PARKING:** 8 **CARDS:**

SYDLING ST NICHOLAS — Map 03 SY69

♦♦♦ Lamperts Cottage

DT2 9NU ☎ 01300 341659 📠 01300 341699
e-mail: nickywillis@tesco.net
Dir: *Dorchester A37 turn right beyond Grimstone, follow valley rd to Sydling St Nicholas. Lamperts Cottage 1st thatched cottage on right*

Surrounded by Hardy Country, this quintessential 16th century, thatched cottage is situated by a stream in the village. The comfortable bedrooms are individually furnished and decorated; guests can enjoy the calm atmosphere created by the absence of televisions. Home produced eggs are served at breakfast in the cosy dining room; home-made jams also feature.

continued

Lamperts Cottage

FACILITIES: 3 rms (1 fmly) No smoking in 3 bedrooms No smoking in dining room No smoking in lounges tea/coffee Cen ht TVL No children 8yrs No coaches **PRICES:** s fr £25; d £42✻ **PARKING:** 3 **CARDS:**

TARRANT LAUNCESTON — Map 03 ST90

♦♦♦♦ Ramblers Cottage

DT11 8BY ☎ 01258 830528
e-mail: sworrall@ramblerscottage.fsnet.co.uk
Dir: *take A354 S from Salisbury towards Blandford Forum, at Tarrant Hinton turn left. Establishment 1m from main road on right just past farm on right*

Comfortable accommodation is provided at this charming 16th-century brick and flint cottage, with delightful rural views. Ideally located for touring the area, with bedrooms that are well presented bedrooms and a relaxed and friendly atmosphere. Guests take breakfast around one table in the dining room; the local pub, within strolling distance, serves a range of meals.

FACILITIES: 2 en suite (1 fmly) No smoking TVB tea/coffee Cen ht No children 12yrs No coaches **PRICES:** s £30; d £50✻ **PARKING:** 3

TARRANT MONKTON — Map 03 ST90

♦♦♦♦ The Langton Arms

DT11 8RX ☎ 01258 830225 📠 01258 830053
e-mail: info@thelangtonarms.co.uk
Dir: *Turn off A354 sign post for Tarrant Monkton in Tarrant Hinton*

Tucked away in the sleepy Dorset village of Tarrant Monkton, the Langton Arms offers the delights and charm of an old English inn and is an ideal base for touring this attractive area. Bedrooms, all situated in the modern annexe, are very well equipped and most comfortable. The bar is popular with locals and visitors alike, as is the restaurant, (open Wednesday till Sunday lunch) and both dining venues offer innovative and appetising dishes.

FACILITIES: 6 annexe en suite (6 fmly) No smoking in bedrooms No smoking in dining room TVB tea/coffee Direct dial from bedrooms Pool Table Dinner Last d 9pm **PRICES:** s fr £55; d fr £70✻ **LB** **MEALS:** Lunch £13.50-£20 Dinner £13.50-£20&alc✻ **PARKING:** 100 **NOTES:** Civ Wed 50 **CARDS:**

Super supper! this symbol shows that evening meals exceeded our Inspector's expectations.

England

THORNCOMBE Map 03 ST30

♦♦♦♦ Upperfold House

TA20 4PY ☎ 01460 30209
e-mail: pbatupperfold@onetel.net.uk
Dir: *from Crewkerne take A3165 (Lyme Regis road) and pass through Clapton. After x-roads follow signs to Thorncombe, down steep hill, 1st turning on left signed Saddle St, house on left.*

Peace and tranquillity are assured at this elegant Georgian country house, overlooking wonderfully lush Somerset countryside. A warm and genuine welcome is extended to all, with helpful advice on the area freely offered. One bedroom is in the main house, the other in the adjacent coach house, both offering good levels of comfort and quality. Dinner is available by prior arrangement. There are extensive gardens and an outdoor swimming pool.

FACILITIES: 1 en suite 1 annexe en suite No smoking TVB tea/coffee No dogs (ex guide dogs) Cen ht TVL No coaches Outdoor swimming pool (heated) Croquet lawn Dinner Last d 6pm **PRICES:** d fr £44* **LB** **PARKING:** 10 **NOTES:** Closed Xmas

WAREHAM Map 03 SY98

♦♦♦♦ Redcliffe *(SY932866)*

BH20 5BE ☎ 01929 552225 Mrs J E Barnes

This delightful home is situated on a turn in the River Frome and has delightful views. Only a short walk from Wareham, this is an ideal place for a peaceful holiday. One bedroom has wonderful river views. There is a large lounge and a cosy dining room with one large table where breakfast is served.

FACILITIES: 4 rms (2 en suite) No smoking TV1B tea/coffee No dogs (ex guide dogs) Cen ht TVL 250 acres dairy mixed **PRICES:** d fr £40* **PARKING:** 4 **NOTES:** Closed Xmas

WEYMOUTH Map 03 SY67

See also Portland

♦♦♦♦♦ Bay Lodge

27 Greenhill DT4 7SW ☎ 01305 782419 01305 782828
e-mail: barbara@baylodge.co.uk
Dir: *follow brown & white tourist signs to Sea Life Park. Hotel 200yds on town centre side of entrance on A353*

FACILITIES: 7 en suite No smoking in 2 bedrooms No smoking in dining room No smoking in lounges TVB tea/coffee Direct dial from bedrooms Cen ht TVL No coaches **PRICES:** s fr £49.50; d fr £72* **PARKING:** 18 **CARDS:**

♦♦♦♦ Esplanade Hotel

141 The Esplanade DT4 7NJ ☎ 01305 783129
01305 783129
e-mail: esplanadahotel@weymouth10.fsnet.co.uk
Dir: *E end of Esplanade, opposite pier bandstand*

With all 'front facing' public rooms enjoying the splendid sea views, this attractive Georgian property dates from 1835. Bedrooms are particularly well furnished and attractively decorated, including many thoughtful extras; some bedrooms having the benefit of sea-views. There is a first-floor lounge and a warm welcome is assured from the friendly owners.

FACILITIES: 11 en suite (2 fmly) (2 GF) No smoking TVB tea/coffee No dogs (ex guide dogs) Licensed Cen ht TVL No children 6yrs **PRICES:** s £25-£40; d £50-£70* **LB** **PARKING:** 9 **NOTES:** Closed Nov-Jan **CARDS:**

♦♦♦♦ *The Bay Guest House*

10 Waterloo Place DT4 7PE ☎ 01305 786289 01305 786289
Dir: *Weymouth seafront, from clock on esplanade with sea on right approx 200ydson left just before church*

Recently the subject of total renovation, this listed, terraced property is within easy walking distance of the beach and the town centre. Bedrooms vary in size and are comfortable, providing modern facilities. A hearty breakfast is served in the attractively presented dining room; in addition a well-presented lounge is available for guests' use.

FACILITIES: 6 rms (4 en suite) (2 fmly) No smoking TVB tea/coffee No dogs Cen ht No coaches **PARKING:** 8 **CARDS:**

♦♦♦♦ Bayview Hotel

35 The Esplanade DT4 8DH ☎ 01305 782083 782083
Dir: *from Dorchester take A354 to Weymouth and follow signs for ferry. Hotel on seafront 100yds before ferry terminal*

An elegant, family-run Victorian town house, beautifully refurbished with views over Weymouth Bay. Located on the sea front, the property is well situated to visit the town centre, old harbour, ferry port and the many other interesting attractions in the area. There is a delightful lounge where guests can relax.

FACILITIES: 8 en suite (1 fmly) (1 GF) No smoking in 1 bedrooms No smoking in dining room No smoking in lounges TVB tea/coffee No dogs Cen ht TVL No coaches Solarium **PRICES:** s £30-£40; d £55-£60* **LB** **PARKING:** 13 **NOTES:** Closed Dec-1 Feb rs Feb-Mar **CARDS:**

♦♦♦♦ Channel View

10 Brunswick Ter, The Esplanade DT4 7RW ☎ 01305 782527
01305 782527
e-mail: leggchannelview@aol.com
Dir: *From town centre proceed E along Esplanade, follow Dorchester road, right into Westerall Road, follow round 1st left at next traffic lights to Brunswick terrace.*

Just off the main Esplanade, this small guest house is literally 15 metres from the beach, occupying a superb spot, with all the many attractions within walking distance. Bedrooms, which are on three floors, vary in size with some having lovely views over the Bay, and all offering good levels of comfort and decor.

FACILITIES: 7 rms (4 en suite) (1 fmly) No smoking TVB tea/coffee No dogs Cen ht TVL No children 12yrs No coaches **PRICES:** s £21-£25; d £42-£50* **CARDS:**

♦♦♦♦ Cumberland Hotel

95 Esplanade DT4 7BA ☎ 01305 785644 01305 785644

An attractive sea front hotel, offering good levels of comfort and hospitality. Bedrooms are generally spacious, well-presented and well-equipped. A good choice is offered at breakfast, served in the pleasant lower ground floor dining room. A small archway leads to a comfortable, well-stocked bar, the ideal setting in which to enjoy a relaxing drink.

continued

FACILITIES: 12 en suite (2 fmly) (3 GF) No smoking in 6 bedrooms No smoking in dining room No smoking in lounges TVB tea/coffee No dogs Licensed Cen ht No children 10yrs Dinner Last d 2pm **PRICES:** s £30-£50; d £55-£90✱ LB **PARKING:** 2 **NOTES:** Closed 20-28 Dec
CARDS:

♦♦♦♦ Kingswood Hotel

55 Rodwell Rd DT4 8QX ☎ 01305 784926 📠 01305 767984
e-mail: robbie.f@virgin.net
Dir: *on the A354 up hill from inner harbour, on left after traffic lights*
This family friendly hotel is close to the Old Harbour and offers a convenient, relaxing style of accommodation. Bedrooms do vary in size, but the majority are spacious and the bathrooms offer a choice of bath or shower facilities. In addition to a pleasant garden there is a comfortable dining room, wide choice of meals and a bar.
FACILITIES: 9 en suite (3 fmly) TVB tea/coffee No dogs (ex guide dogs) Licensed Cen ht Dinner Last d 9.30pm **PRICES:** s £30; d £50
PARKING: 25 **CARDS:**

♦♦♦♦ The Seaham

3 Waterloo Place DT4 7NU ☎ 01305 782010
e-mail: stay@theseaham.co.uk
Dir: *Weymouth esplanade 200mtrs from St Johns church*
Ideally located on the sea front and close to the town centre, this conscientiously maintained establishment is an ideal base from which to explore. Bedrooms are attractively presented and equipped with many useful extras. The well-appointed open plan dining room has a comfortable adjoining lounge. The freshly cooked breakfasts are generous.
FACILITIES: 5 en suite No smoking TVB tea/coffee No dogs Licensed Cen ht No children No coaches **PRICES:** d £48-£64✱ LB **NOTES:** Closed 15 Dec-15 Jan **CARDS:**

♦♦♦♦ Suncroft Hotel

7 The Esplanade DT4 8EB ☎ 01305 782542 📠 01305 770071
e-mail: suncroft@cdr-i.net
Dir: *From Dorchester take A354 to Weymouth follow signs to ferry terminal, hotel on seafront 25yds before ferry terminal and Pavillion theatre*
With spectacular views over the beach, Esplanade and Weymouth Bay to the front and the harbour at the rear, this attractive, mid-terrace Georgian property is conveniently situated for the beach, ferry terminal, Pavilion Theatre and the town centre. The comfortable bedrooms offer well-appointed accommodation.
FACILITIES: 8 rms (6 en suite) (4 fmly) No smoking in 2 bedrooms No smoking in dining room No smoking in lounges TVB tea/coffee No dogs (ex guide dogs) Cen ht TVL No children 4yrs No coaches **PRICES:** s £20-£24; d £48-£52✱ **NOTES:** Closed Dec **CARDS:**

♦♦♦♦ Tamarisk Hotel

12 Stavordale Rd, Westham DT4 0AB ☎ 01305 786514
📠 01305 786514
e-mail: hilary@tamariskhotel.co.uk
Dir: *follow A354 to Westham rdbt, take 3rd exit left to Bridport & then immediately left into Stavordale Rd*
Situated in a quiet residential area, only a short walk from the harbour, this smartly presented hotel has well-equipped bedrooms. Home cooked dinners are served by prior arrangement in the elegant dining room. In addition there is a small comfortable lounge and bar. On-site parking is a definite bonus so close to the harbour and town centre.
FACILITIES: 14 en suite (5 fmly) (1 GF) No smoking in dining room TVB tea/coffee No dogs (ex guide dogs) Licensed Cen ht TVL Dinner Last d 4pm
PRICES: s £24-£35; d £48-£70✱ LB **PARKING:** 19 **NOTES:** Closed Nov-Feb **CARDS:**

♦♦♦ The Alendale

4 Waterloo Place DT4 7NX ☎ 01305 788817
e-mail: pat@thealendale.co.uk
This cosy guest house, located just fifty yards from the beach, provides guests with a warm homely environment with easy access to the town centre, ferry terminals and neighbouring places of interest. Bedrooms are well furnished and decorated and equipped with useful extras. Full English breakfasts are served at individual tables.
FACILITIES: 6 rms (4 en suite) (2 fmly) No smoking in dining room No smoking in lounges TVB tea/coffee Licensed Cen ht No coaches
PRICES: s £20-£25; d £40-£50✱ **PARKING:** 7
CARDS:

♦♦♦ Beachcomber

6 Waterloo Place DT4 7NZ ☎ 01305 783078 📠 01305 768254
e-mail: ray@cousins41.fsnet.co.uk
Dir: *on seafront 250mtrs from Jubilee clock*
A warm welcome is assured at this friendly family run guest house located close to the beach front and within easy walking distance of the town centre and various other places of interest. Bedrooms are cosy and well furnished. There is a guest lounge and tasty home-cooked evening meals are available by prior arrangement.
FACILITIES: 8 rms (6 en suite) (2 fmly) No smoking TVB tea/coffee No dogs Licensed TVL Dinner Last d 3pm **PRICES:** s £18-£26; d £34-£52✱ LB BB **PARKING:** 8 **CARDS:**

♦♦♦ Bedford House Hotel

17 The Esplanade DT4 8DT ☎ 01305 786995 📠 01305 786995
Dir: *proceed along Esplanade, seashore on left head towards harbour, turn right around amusement gardens (one way system) Bedford House on left*
Known locally as 'the Bear House', because of the ever growing collection of bears of every shape and description, Bedford House offers comfortable accommodation for guests. Guests are assured of a warm and friendly welcome and enjoy the relaxed atmosphere. Space in the stylishly decorated bedrooms is used to its full potential, with the front facing rooms always being in demand.
FACILITIES: 9 en suite (3 fmly) No smoking in dining room TVB tea/coffee No dogs (ex guide dogs) Licensed TVL No coaches **PRICES:** s £25-£30; d £40-£50✱ LB **NOTES:** Closed mid Nov-early Mar

♦♦♦ Letchworth

5 Waterloo Place, The Esplanade DT4 7NY ☎ 01305 786663
📠 01305 759203
e-mail: letchworth.hotel@virginnet.co.uk
Dir: *turn off A31 at Bere Regis to Weymouth, follow signs to seafront and esplanade*
Located on the sea front this well-maintained guest house provides guests with comfortable brightly decorated bedrooms that are thoughtfully equipped with many useful extras. A warm welcome is assured and dinner is available by prior arrangement. Guests also have use of a cosy lounge and bar.
FACILITIES: 6 rms (4 en suite) (2 fmly) No smoking in bedrooms No smoking in dining room TVB tea/coffee No dogs Licensed TVL No children 5yrs No coaches **PRICES:** s £20-£22; d £44-£50✱ LB **PARKING:** 6
CARDS:

♦♦♦ Diamonds are a guest's best friend!
The emphasis is on quality and guest care rather than extra facilities.

England

England

WEYMOUTH continued

♦♦♦ Sou'west Lodge Hotel

Rodwell Rd DT4 8QT ☎ 01305 783749

Guests are assured of a warm welcome at this small, family-run hotel. The smart bedrooms are neatly furnished; two ground-floor rooms are available for the less mobile. Traditional breakfasts are served in the dining room, in addition a comfortable bar/lounge is available for guests and a flower-filled patio.

FACILITIES: 8 en suite (2 fmly) (2 GF) No smoking in 3 bedrooms No smoking in dining room TVB tea/coffee No dogs Licensed Cen ht TVL No coaches Dinner Last d 5pm **PRICES:** s £30-£32; d £48-£64* **LB** **PARKING:** 12 **NOTES:** Closed 22 Dec-1 Jan **CARDS:**

♦♦♦ Tara

10 Market St DT4 8DD ☎ 01305 766235

Dir: *from Alexandra Gardens on the Esplanade turn R into Belle vue the R and L into Market Street*

Situated just back from the seafront at the harbour end of town, this welcoming guesthouse is neatly presented and provides a relaxed and friendly atmosphere. Bedrooms vary in scale, but all offer good levels of comfort. Please note that this is a strictly no-smoking establishment.

FACILITIES: 6 en suite (1 fmly) No smoking TVB tea/coffee No dogs Licensed Cen ht No coaches Dinner Last d breakfast **PRICES:** s £16-£20; d £32-£40* **LB BB**

♦♦♦ Trelawney Hotel

1 Old Castle Rd DT4 8QB ☎ 01305 783188 📠 01305 783181

e-mail: trelawney-hotel@talk21.com

Dir: *on leaving Harbourside follow signs Portland. Hotel 700yds on left*

This quiet, charming Victorian house is set in well-maintained gardens just a short walk from the town centre and beach. The accommodation provides spacious well-appointed bedrooms. Generous English breakfasts are offered in the light and airy dining room, a comfortable lounge is also available.

FACILITIES: 10 en suite (3 fmly) No smoking TVB tea/coffee No dogs (ex guide dogs) Licensed Cen ht TVL No coaches Putting green **PRICES:** s fr £40; d fr £59* **PARKING:** 13 **NOTES:** Closed Oct-April **CARDS:**

♦♦♦ Wadham Guesthouse

22 East St DT4 8BN ☎ 01305 779640

Dir: *from Jubilee clock on esplanade with sea on left drive towards ferry terminal turn right in front of Pavilion car park along Commercial Road. East St is 3rd turning right, Wadham House on right hand side*

Located in the centre of the town, this single fronted terraced property provides comfortable accommodation. Bedrooms vary in size and style. By prior arrangement, evening meals are served in the front facing dining room, in addition a dispense bar and a first floor lounge are available for guests. Parking permits are available during the summer.

FACILITIES: 9 en suite (3 fmly) (1 GF) No smoking in bedrooms No smoking in dining room TVB tea/coffee No dogs Licensed Cen ht TVL No children 2yrs No coaches Dinner Last d breakfast **PRICES:** s £17.50-£21; d £35-£42* **LB BB** **NOTES:** Closed Xmas

♦♦♦ Warwick Court Hotel

20 Abbotsbury Rd DT4 0AE ☎ 01305 783261 📠 01305 783261

e-mail: sharon@warwickcourtweymouth.co.uk

Dir: *right at Manor rdbt on Dorchester Road, onto Weymouth Way, left at Chafrey's rdbt, right at next rdbt into Abbotsbury Road. Hotel 150yds on right*

Within walking distance of the picturesque Radipole Lake and the swimming pool complex, this small, private hotel is also convenient for the town centre and sea front. Bedrooms vary in size, and all are well equipped with modern facilities. There is a cosy lounge for guests and hearty breakfasts are served in the front-facing, breakfast room.

continued

FACILITIES: 8 en suite (3 fmly) No smoking TVB tea/coffee No dogs Licensed Cen ht TVL No coaches **PRICES:** s £20-£27; d £36-£50* **LB BB** **PARKING:** 6 **NOTES:** Closed 24-26th Dec **CARDS:**

♦♦♦ Westwey Hotel

62 Abbotsbury Rd DT4 0BJ ☎ 01305 784564

Dir: *follow Esplanade towards Jubilee clock, right into King St, 2nd exit from island, continue to next island, 2nd exit into Abbotsbury Rd, pass lights, hotel on right*

Well located for the town centre and beach, this friendly hotel provides comfortable accommodation for both business and leisure guests. It offers comfortable and well-equipped bedrooms, a small lounge and a bar. Dinner and breakfast, both with a choice of menu, are served in the bright and pleasant dining room.

FACILITIES: 9 rms (7 en suite) (2 fmly) No smoking in bedrooms No smoking in dining room No smoking in lounges TVB tea/coffee No dogs (ex guide dogs) Licensed Cen ht TVL Dinner Last d 4.30pm **PRICES:** s £23.50-£28; d £47-£56 **PARKING:** 9 **CARDS:**

♦♦♦ 🅰 Hotel Kinley

98 The Esplanade DT4 7AT ☎ 01305 782264 & 0800 163794

e-mail: hotelkinley@hotmail.com

Dir: *centre of esplanade, opposite jubilee clock tower*

FACILITIES: 9 en suite (43 fmly) (1 GF) No smoking TVB tea/coffee No dogs Licensed Cen ht No coaches **PRICES:** d £50-£80* **LB** **PARKING:** 7 **NOTES:** Closed Xmas & New Year **CARDS:**

♦♦ Ferndown Guest House

47 Walpole St DT4 7HQ ☎ 01305 775228

e-mail: jean@ferndown47.freeserve.co.uk

Dir: *in town, pass church on 2-way traffic system, R into William St, over x-roads pass Waterloo pub & Scuba Centre. Ferndown opposite*

Just a short walk from both the seafront and the town centre, this neat, mid-terrace guest house provides comfortable accommodation. Rooms are simply furnished and pleasantly decorated, and downstairs there is a combined lounge-dining room where guests can enjoy breakfast.

FACILITIES: 6 rms No smoking TVB tea/coffee No dogs (ex guide dogs) TVL No coaches **PRICES:** s £15-£18; d £30-£35* **LB BB** **NOTES:** Closed Dec-Feb

🆄 Cavendish House

6 The Esplanade DT4 8EA ☎ 01305 782039

At the time of going to press the Diamond classification for this establishment had not been confirmed. Please check the AA website www.theAA.com for up-to-date information.

FACILITIES: 8 en suite (3 fmly)

🆄 The Chandlers Hotel

4 Westerhall Rd DT4 7SZ ☎ 01305 771341

At the time of going to press the Diamond classification for this establishment had not been confirmed. Please check the AA website www.theAA.com for up-to-date information.

FACILITIES: 9 en suite (2 fmly)

🆄 *A Room with a View*

7 Trinity Rd DT4 8TJ ☎ 01305 760048

At the time of going to press the Diamond classification for this establishment had not been confirmed. Please check the AA website www.theAA.com for up-to-date information.

FACILITIES: 1 en suite

Prices may change during the currency of the Guide, please check when booking.

WIMBORNE MINSTER Map 03 SZ09

♦♦♦♦ Ashton Lodge

10 Oakley Hill BH21 1QH ☎ 01202 883423 📠 01202 886180
e-mail: ashtonlodge@ukgateway.net
Dir: *from A31 S of Wimborne take A349 towards Poole, exit left at next rdbt signed Wimborne/Canford Magna. House on right after 200yds*

A warm welcome is assured at this delightful modern home where the comfortable bedrooms are stylishly furnished with attractively co-ordinated decor and fabrics. All are well-equipped with many extra facilities provided. Hearty breakfasts are served in the spacious dining room, which overlooks the pretty, well-maintained garden.
FACILITIES: 5 rms (3 en suite) (2 fmly) No smoking TVB tea/coffee No dogs Cen ht TVL No coaches **PRICES:** s £24; d £48-£52✻ **LB** **PARKING:** 4

CO DURHAM

BARNARD CASTLE Map 12 NZ01

♦♦♦♦ Greta House

89 Galgate DL12 8ES ☎ 01833 631193 📠 01833 631193
e-mail: gretahousebc@btclick.com
Dir: *on the west side of town going out on the main Darlington road*
At this spacious Victorian villa, constructed in 1870, very warm hospitality awaits you. Greta House is conveniently situated for The Bowes Museum, local antique shops, High Force and Raby Castle, a truly comfortable home from home. Bedrooms are comfortable and very well equipped.
FACILITIES: 3 en suite No smoking TVB tea/coffee No dogs (ex guide dogs) Cen ht No children 5yrs **PRICES:** s £30-£35; d £46-£52✻

♦♦♦♦ The Homelands

85 Galgate DL12 8ES ☎ 01833 638757
e-mail: homelands@barnard-castle.fsnet.co.uk
Dir: *400mtrs from town centre on A67*
Just 300 metres from the town, this stylish Victorian town house is a superb place to stay. Attractively decorated and well equipped bedrooms offer good levels of comfort. A hearty breakfast is served in the elegant dining room and tasty snacks are available by prior arrangement. There is also a comfortable lounge.
FACILITIES: 4 rms (3 en suite) 1 annexe en suite (1 GF) No smoking TVB tea/coffee Direct dial from bedrooms No dogs (ex guide dogs) Licensed Cen ht No children 5 No coaches Dinner Last d 8.15pm **PRICES:** s £25-£35; d £45-£55✻ **PARKING:** 5

♦♦♦♦ Wilson House *(NZ081124)*

Barningham DL11 7EB ☎ 01833 621218 📠 01833 621110
Mrs H Lowes
Dir: *turn off A66 at Greta Bridge, follow road to Barningham. Turn at 2nd farm on right*
For all those who seek a relaxing break, this attractive farmhouse offers an ideal retreat. It stands in 475 acres of land, among superb Pennine scenery and provides good home cooking and comfortable bedrooms which are flexible and ideal for families. Guests are free to wander around the farm and admire the spectacular views.
FACILITIES: 3 rms (2 en suite) (1 fmly) (1 GF) No smoking TVB tea/coffee No dogs (ex guide dogs) Cen ht TVL 475 acres mixed livestock Dinner Last d 2pm **PRICES:** s £20-£25; d £40-£50✻ **LB** **PARKING:** 5 **NOTES:** Closed 23-28 Dec

CHESTER-LE-STREET Map 12 NZ25

♦♦♦♦ Waldridge Fell Guest House

Old Waldridge Village DH2 3RY ☎ 0191 389 1908
e-mail: BBchesterlestreet@btinternet.com
Dir: *exit A167 at Chester Moor rdbt signed Waldridge. Turn L at next rdbt, house on L 0.75m up lane*
This former village chapel, fully renovated by the current owners, lies on the edge of the village, with fine views over the fells. Comfortably furnished bedrooms are complemented by a combined lounge/dining room, a substantial breakfast being served at the large table.
FACILITIES: 6 en suite (3 fmly) (1 GF) No smoking TVB tea/coffee No dogs (ex guide dogs) Cen ht TVL **PRICES:** s fr £28; d fr £48✻ **PARKING:** 8 **NOTES:** Closed Xmas/New Year

COWSHILL Map 12 NY84

♦♦♦♦ Low Cornriggs Farm *(NY845413)*

Cowshill-in-Weardale DL13 1AF ☎ 01388 537600
📠 01388 537777 Mrs J Elliott
e-mail: enquiries@lowcornriggsfarm.fsnet.co.uk
Dir: *at the head of Weardale, on A689 between Cowshill and Lanehead*
Enjoying stunning views across the upper Weardale valley, this old farmhouse has undergone considerable renovation. Original stone and stripped pine have combined to provide a conversion of real character. The excellent home-cooked dinners are taken in the conservatory during the summer. Bedrooms are attractive and thoughtfully equipped. There is a riding stable on the farm.
FACILITIES: 3 en suite (1 fmly) No smoking TVB tea/coffee Licensed Cen ht TVL Fishing Riding 42 acres sheep, ponies Dinner Last d 5pm **PRICES:** s £29; d £44✻ **LB** **PARKING:** 10 **NOTES:** Closed Dec-Jan

England

DARLINGTON Map 08 NZ21

Premier Collection

♦♦♦♦♦ Clow Beck House *(NZ281100)*

Monk End Farm, Croft on Tees DL2 2SW ☎ 01325 721075
01325 720419 Mr & Mrs D Armstrong
e-mail: heather@clowbeckhouse.co.uk
Dir: *take A167 to Northallerton from Darlington for 2m into village of Croft, over bridge & follow 3 brown directional signs to Clowbeck House*

A wide choice of bedrooms is available in this impressive hotel. Located in buildings separate from the main house, most are traditionally furnished but one has an oriental theme and another is more contemporary. However all benefit from a thoughtful selection of extras and delightful country and garden views. A luxurious lounge is provided in the house, and imaginative meals, using home-grown produce where possible, are taken in the stunning dining room.
FACILITIES: 13 annexe en suite (3 fmly) No smoking in 4 bedrooms No smoking in dining room TVB tea/coffee Direct dial from bedrooms No dogs (ex guide dogs) Licensed Cen ht TVL Fishing 2 acre award winning garden 90 acres mixed Dinner Last d by arrangement **PRICES:** s £55; d £85* **CONF:** Class 20 Board 20 Del £75 * **PARKING:** 15
CARDS:

♦♦♦ Balmoral

63 Woodland Rd DL3 7BQ ☎ 01325 461908 01325 461908
Dir: *exit A1(M) J58, premises on A68, opposite Memorial Hospital*
Well-established, this splendid Victorian townhouse retains many original features including stained glass windows and intricate coving. Bedrooms have pleasing colour schemes and are comfortably furnished; there is also a ground floor room. The dining room has a comfortable seating area.
FACILITIES: 9 rms (5 en suite) (2 fmly) No smoking TVB tea/coffee No dogs (ex guide dogs) Cen ht **PRICES:** s £23-£35; d £40-£46*
NOTES: Closed Xmas

DURHAM Map 12 NZ24

♦♦♦♦ Hillrise

13 Durham Rd West, Bowburn DH6 5AU ☎ 0191 377 0302
0191 377 0898
e-mail: enquiries@hill-rise.com
Dir: *A1 junct 61, Hillrise approx 200yds on left*
This small and friendly guest house offers comfortable accommodation. Bedrooms come in a variety of sizes and are very well equipped. Attractive public areas include a lounge with chunky leather chairs and a bright, spacious dining room where guests can enjoy delicious home-cooked breakfasts.
FACILITIES: 5 en suite (3 fmly) (2 GF) No smoking TVB tea/coffee No dogs (ex guide dogs) Cen ht TVL No coaches **PRICES:** s £25-£35; d £50*
CARDS:

♦♦♦♦ A Cathedral View Guest House

212 Gilesgate DH1 1QN ☎ 0191 386 9566
e-mail: cathedralview@hotmail.com
Dir: *exit from A1 for A690.Follow Durham sign onto dual carriageway, turn right at 1st rdbt. Guest House is 200yds on left*
FACILITIES: 6 en suite (1 fmly) (2 GF) No smoking TVB tea/coffee No dogs Cen ht No coaches **PRICES:** s £42-£50; d £60* **CARDS:**

♦♦♦ The Gables

10 South View, Middlestone Moor DL16 7DF ☎ 01388 817544
01388 812533
e-mail: thegablesghouse@aol.com
Dir: *7m S of Durham City off A688*
This Victorian house is situated close to the A1 and convenient for major commercial business and tourist destinations. Spacious bedrooms come with thoughtful extras and breakfast is taken in the bright dining room.
FACILITIES: 6 rms (3 en suite) (1 fmly) (4 GF) No smoking TVB tea/coffee Cen ht No coaches **PRICES:** s £27.50-£35; d £38-£46* BB
PARKING: 7 **NOTES:** Closed 23-27 Dec & 31 Dec-2 Jan
CARDS:

EGGLESTON Map 12 NY92

♦♦♦♦ Pine Ridge B & B

Folly Top DL12 0DH ☎ 01833 650777 01833 650877
e-mail: judy@chipchase.co.uk
Dir: *from Barnard Castle take B6278 Middleton-in-Teesdale Rd for 5m approx. at junct with B2679 Standrop Rd look for B & B sign on left 100yds*

This attractive bungalow is set in five acres of grounds in a peaceful yet convenient location. Spacious bedrooms are tastefully decorated and thoughtfully equipped. A stylish lounge offers panoramic views over three counties. A swim spa is available for a small charge. Hearty breakfasts feature homemade and local produce.
FACILITIES: 2 en suite No smoking TVB tea/coffee No dogs (ex guide dogs) Cen ht No children 7yrs No coaches swimming spa **PRICES:** s £28; d £42* **PARKING:** 6 **NOTES:** Closed Xmas & New Year

FIR TREE Map 12 NZ13

♦♦♦♦ Greenhead Country House Hotel

DL15 8BL ☎ 01388 763143 01388 763143
e-mail: info@thegreenheadhotel.co.uk
Dir: *on A68, turn right at Fir Tree Inn*
In the heart of rural Weardale this house was built in 1704. Bedrooms, one with a four poster bed, are spacious and comfortable and come with thoughtful extras. Public rooms include a 50ft-long beamed and stone-arched lounge with a well stocked bar at one end.

continued

Greenhead Country House Hotel

FACILITIES: 8 en suite (1 fmly) (2 GF) No smoking in bedrooms No smoking in dining room No smoking in 1 lounge TV7B tea/coffee No dogs (ex guide dogs) Licensed Cen ht TVL No children 13yrs No coaches Dinner Last d 5pm **PRICES:** s £45-£55; d £65-£75✳ **LB** **PARKING:** 20 **CARDS:**

♦♦♦♦ Duke of York Inn

DL15 8DG ☎ 01388 762848
e-mail: suggett@firtree-crook.fsnet.co.uk
Dir: *situated on A68, 0.5m S of junct with A689*
FACILITIES: 5 en suite (1 GF) TVB tea/coffee Direct dial from bedrooms No dogs (ex guide dogs) Licensed Cen ht TVL No children 10yrs Dinner Last d 9pm **PRICES:** s £52; d £69✳ **LB** **PARKING:** 50 **CARDS:**

MIDDLETON-IN-TEESDALE — Map 12 NY92

♦♦♦♦ Brunswick House

55 Market Place DL12 0QH ☎ 01833 640393
e-mail: enquiries@brunswickhouse.net
Dir: *on B6277 opposite St Mary's Church*

In the heart of the village and overlooking the marketplace, this charming stone-built house dates back to 1760. Many original features have been retained; there are beamed ceilings in the peaceful lounge and original Georgian fireplaces in several of the bedrooms. A good range of home-cooked food is served in the dining room.

FACILITIES: 5 en suite No smoking TVB tea/coffee No dogs (ex guide dogs) Licensed Cen ht No coaches Dinner Last d 7pm **PRICES:** s £35; d £50 **LB** **PARKING:** 5 **CARDS:**

SEDGEFIELD — Map 08 NZ32

♦♦♦ *Dun Cow*

High St TS21 3AT ☎ 01740 620894 📠 01740 622163
Dir: *Sedgefield is at junct of A177 and A689, premises in the centre of the village by village green and Parish church (Ramside)*

Parts of this typical English inn date from the 17th century. Spacious bedrooms are well appointed and come with a range of thoughtful extras. A good range of dishes can be enjoyed in the dining room, which is decorated with an interesting mix of local photographs and bric-a-brac.

FACILITIES: 6 en suite No smoking in lounges TVB tea/coffee Direct dial from bedrooms Cen ht Dinner Last d 9.45pm **PARKING:** 25 **CARDS:**

STANLEY — Map 12 NZ15

♦♦♦ Bush Blades Farm *(NZ168533)*

Harperley DH9 9UA ☎ 01207 232722 Mrs P Gibson
Dir: *leave A1(M) junct 63 for Stanley on A693. Follow sign for Consett, 0.5m after Stanley follow signs for Harperley. Farm on right 0.5m from crossroads*

continued

Bush Blades Farm

This farmhouse sits peacefully on a raised plateau of farming land to the west of Stanley. It has a friendly and relaxed atmosphere and the traditionally furnished bedrooms are comfortable and spacious.

FACILITIES: 3 rms (1 en suite) No smoking in 3 bedrooms No smoking in dining room No smoking in lounges TVB tea/coffee No dogs Cen ht TVL No children 12yrs 50 acres sheep **PRICES:** s £25-£30; d £37-£42✳ **LB** **BB** **PARKING:** 4 **NOTES:** Closed 20 Dec-2 Jan

STOCKTON-ON-TEES — Map 08 NZ41

♦♦♦ The Grange

33 Grange Rd, Norton TS20 2NS ☎ 01642 552541
Dir: *from A19 take A139 sliproad to Norton, over 1st rdbt with Red Lion Pub on right. Take 2nd left into Grange Rd*
FACILITIES: 8 rms (4 en suite) No smoking in 4 bedrooms No smoking in dining room No smoking in lounges TVB tea/coffee No dogs (ex guide dogs) Cen ht No coaches **PRICES:** s £22-£30; d £38-£45✳ **BB**
NOTES: Closed Xmas & New Year

WOLSINGHAM — Map 12 NZ03

♦♦♦ Old Barn *(NZ100375)*

Greenwell Farm DL13 4PH ☎ 01388 527248 📠 01388 526735
Ms L Vickers
e-mail: greenwell@farming.co.uk
Dir: *A68 to Tow Law. At war memorial take B6297 follow for 1.5m. Turn left, go 0.25m and fork right*

Enjoying panoramic views of Weardale's spectacular rolling countryside, this modern barn conversion hosts modern bedrooms of country cottage proportions. Benefiting from a real farmhouse ambience, guests are made to feel very much at home. Delicious dinners and breakfasts make excellent use of local produce.

FACILITIES: 4 en suite (1 fmly) (3 GF) No smoking TV3B tea/coffee No dogs (ex guide dogs) Cen ht TVL Farm nature trail and walk 450 acres mixed Dinner Last d 12hrs in advance **PRICES:** s £27.50; d £50✳ **LB** **CONF:** Thtr 30 Class 30 Board 20 Del from £100 ✳ **PARKING:** 12 **NOTES:** Closed 22 Dec-5 Jan **CARDS:**

England

ESSEX

BILLERICAY Map 05 TQ69

♦♦♦ 31 Mercer Road

31 Mercer rd CM11 1EP ☎ 01277 626547 Fax 01277 657500

Charming detached property situated on the outskirts of the town centre. The individually decorated bedrooms are pleasantly furnished and thoughtfully equipped. Breakfast is served seated around a large communal table in the elegant dining room.

FACILITIES: 3 rms No smoking TVB tea/coffee No dogs Cen ht No children No coaches **PRICES:** s £22; d £44* **PARKING:** 2 **NOTES:** Closed Xmas

BRAINTREE Map 05 TL72

♦♦♦♦ Spicers *(TL730293)*

Rotten End, Wethersfield CM7 4AL ☎ 01371 851021 Fax 01371 851021 Mr & Mrs B A Douse

e-mail: info@spicers-farm.co.uk

***Dir:** take B1053 from Braintree to Shalford. At Shalford turn right after civic amenity sign, farm is 2nd house on right over river*

Located north of the town in an elevated position with stunning views of the surrounding countryside, this impressive detached house offers comfortable homely bedrooms filled with thoughtful extras to enhance guest comfort. Breakfast is taken in the attractive conservatory which overlooks the immaculate gardens.

FACILITIES: 3 en suite No smoking TVB tea/coffee No dogs (ex guide dogs) Cen ht 72 acres arable **PRICES:** s £26-£30; d £40-£44* **LB** **PARKING:** 5 **NOTES:** Closed 24 Dec-2 Jan

♦♦♦ *Park Farmhouse* *(TL812223)*

Church Rd, Bradwell CM7 8EP

***Dir:** turn off A120 beside The Swan PH signposted Bradwell Village, continue for 0.5m, farmhouse set back from road on right*

Expect a warm friendly welcome at this lovely farmhouse which is located on the outskirts of Bradwell village. Bedrooms are comfortable and have many personal touches. Easily accessible for the historic town of Colchester, this farmhouse will appeal to the leisure and business traveller.

FACILITIES: 2 rms No smoking tea/coffee No dogs (ex guide dogs) Cen ht TVL No children 1 acres arable **PARKING:** 3 **NOTES:** Closed Xmas

CHELMSFORD Map 05 TL70

♦♦♦♦ Boswell House Hotel

118/120 Springfield Rd CM2 6LF ☎ 01245 287587 Fax 01245 287587

e-mail: SteveBoorman@aol.com

***Dir:** follow directions to Riverside Ice and Leisure Centre, over river, premises at junction with Victoria/Springfield Rd*

A warm welcome and attentive service can be expected from the caring hosts at this well maintained, privately owned hotel. The pleasantly decorated, thoughtfully equipped bedrooms have well chosen pine furnishings and co-ordinated soft fabrics. Breakfast and dinner are served at individual tables in the attractive dining room and pre-dinner drinks can be taken in the comfortable lounge bar.

FACILITIES: 13 en suite (2 fmly) (4 GF) No smoking in 11 bedrooms No smoking in dining room No smoking in 1 lounge TVB tea/coffee Direct dial from bedrooms No dogs (ex guide dogs) Licensed Cen ht TVL No coaches Dinner Last d 8.30pm **PRICES:** s £47-£50; d £65* **PARKING:** 15 **NOTES:** Closed 24 Dec-4 Jan **CARDS:**

♦♦♦ Beechcroft Private Hotel

211 New London Rd CM2 0AJ ☎ 01245 352462 or 250861 Fax 01245 347833

e-mail: enquiries@beechcrofthotel.com

***Dir:** exit A12 onto A414. Straight over 3 rdbts and L at the 4th. Hotel past 1st set of lights on the R*

Privately owned hotel conveniently situated just a few minutes' walk from the town centre. Bedrooms vary in size and style but all are pleasantly decorated and equipped with modern facilities. Breakfast is served at individual tables in the smart dining room and guests also have the use of a cosy lounge.

FACILITIES: 19 rms (13 en suite) (2 fmly) (5 GF) No smoking in 10 bedrooms No smoking in dining room TVB tea/coffee No dogs (ex guide dogs) Cen ht TVL **PRICES:** s £36-£44; d £52-£59* **LB** **PARKING:** 14 **CARDS:**

♦♦♦ Tanunda Hotel

217/219 New London Rd CM2 0AJ ☎ 01245 354295 Fax 01245 345503

Located a few minutes walk from the centre and county cricket ground, this double-fronted Victorian house offers a range of practical bedrooms suitable for all guests. Breakfasts are taken in the spacious dining room and a comfortable lounge overlooks the pretty rear garden. The private car park is an additional benefit.

FACILITIES: 20 rms (11 en suite) No smoking in area of dining room STV TVB tea/coffee Direct dial from bedrooms No dogs (ex guide dogs) Licensed Cen ht TVL **PRICES:** s £36-£60; d £52-£60* **PARKING:** 20 **NOTES:** Closed Xmas & New Year for 3 wks **CARDS:**

♦♦♦ Yew Tree Farm *(TL647158)*

CM3 1HX ☎ 01245 231229 Mrs G Tamlyn

e-mail: jktam@breathe.co.uk

(For full entry see Pleshey)

CHIPPING ONGAR Map 05 TL50

Premier Collection

♦♦♦♦♦ Diggins Farm

Fyfield CM5 0PP ☎ 01277 899303 Fax 01277 899015

***Dir:** A414 onto B184 for Great Dunmow, after 4m reach Fyfield and take next right after Black Bull pub, farm 0.75m on left*

This delightful 16th century Grade II listed farmhouse is set amidst open farmland in a rural location overlooking the Roding Valley. The property is ideally placed for access to Stansted Airport, which is just a short drive away. The spacious bedrooms are attractively decorated, tastefully furnished and well-equipped.

FACILITIES: 2 en suite No smoking TVB tea/coffee No dogs Cen ht No children 12yrs No coaches **PRICES:** s fr £30; d fr £50* **PARKING:** 20 **NOTES:** Closed 15 Dec-3 Jan

Places with this symbol are Inns.

continued

CLACTON-ON-SEA Map 05 TM11

♦♦♦ Sandrock Hotel

1 Penfold Rd, Marine Pde West CO15 1JN ☎ 01255 428215
Fax 01255 428215
Dir: *A12 to A120, to town/seafront, R at pier, signed Sandrock, 2nd rd on R*
Expect a warm welcome at this well maintained Victorian residence, which is situated just a short walk from the pier, seafront and town centre. Although the bedrooms vary in size and style each one is attractively decorated and thoughtfully equipped, some rooms have sea views. Breakfast is served in the smart restaurant/bar and guests also have the use of a cosy resident's lounge. Dinner is available by prior arrangement.
FACILITIES: 8 en suite (3 fmly) No smoking in 2 bedrooms No smoking in dining room TVB tea/coffee Licensed Cen ht No coaches Dinner Last d 5pm **LB PRICES:** s £35; d £53* **PARKING:** 6 **CARDS:**

COLCHESTER Map 05 TL92

See also Nayland (Suffolk)

♦♦♦ Globe Hotel

71 North Station Rd CO1 1RQ ☎ 01206 502502
Fax 01206 506506
Dir: *turn off A12 from London onto A133, at 3rd rdbt turn right, hotel 200yds on left*
This popular inn is ideally placed just a short walk from the town centre. Bedrooms vary in size and style; each is simply appointed and well equipped with the usual facilities. The open plan public rooms feature a cosy bar and a room with a pool table.
FACILITIES: 12 en suite (4 fmly) No smoking in dining room STV TVB tea/coffee No dogs (ex guide dogs) Cen ht TVL Last d 9pm **PRICES:** s £40-£50; d £50-£60* **PARKING:** 20 **CARDS:**

♦♦♦ Old Manse

15 Roman Rd CO1 1UR ☎ 01206 545154 Fax 01206 545153
e-mail: wendyanderson15@hotmail.com
Dir: *from High Street into East Hill, Roman Rd is 1st left after Castle, opposite St James' church*
Located a few minutes walk from the high street and castle, this late Victorian house offers comfortable homely bedrooms and a bright attractive dining room where tasty breakfasts are served. A warm welcome is assured from friendly proprietor Wendy Anderson.
FACILITIES: 3 en suite No smoking TVB tea/coffee No dogs (ex guide dogs) Cen ht No children 6yrs No coaches **PRICES:** s £30-£35; d £45-£52* **PARKING:** 1 **NOTES:** Closed 23-31 Dec

♦♦♦ Salisbury Hotel

112 Butt Rd CO3 3DL ☎ 01206 508508 Fax 01206 797265
This smartly presented inn is situated just a short walk from the centre of the historic garrison town. The bedrooms are comfortable and well equipped, and are pleasantly decorated throughout. The public rooms offer a wide choice of areas in which to relax.
FACILITIES: 11 rms (10 en suite) (2 fmly) No smoking in dining room STV TVB tea/coffee No dogs Cen ht TVL Dinner Last d 7pm **PRICES:** s £30-£50; d £50-£60* **PARKING:** 20 **CARDS:**

Fridaywood Farm

Bounstead Rd CO2 0DF ☎ 01206 573595
At the time of going to press the Diamond classification for this establishment had not been confirmed. Please check the AA website www.theAA.com for up-to-date information.
FACILITIES: 2 en suite

FELSTED Map 05 TL62

♦♦♦♦ Potash Farmhouse *(TL686196)*

Cobblers Green, Causeway End Rd CM6 3LX ☎ 01371 820510
Fax 01371 820510 Mr & Mrs R Smith
e-mail: rgspotash@compuserve.com
Dir: *from A120, take B1417 to Felsted village centre & turn into Chelmsford road, 0.5m to sign on left for Cobblers Green. Farm signed 400yds on left*
Situated on the outskirts of Felsted village and set in extensive, half-moated mature gardens, this 15th century Grade II listed house retains many original features including exposed beams and open fireplaces. The homely bedrooms are filled with thoughtful extras and are well equipped. All share one table in the spacious and attractive breakfast room. There is also a comfortable lounge plus a conservatory.
FACILITIES: 3 rms No smoking TVB tea/coffee No dogs Cen ht TVL No children 12yrs Croquet lawn 40 acres arable **PRICES:** s £25-£30; d £42-£46* **PARKING:** 6

FRINTON-ON-SEA Map 05 TM22

♦♦♦ Uplands

41 Hadleigh Rd CO13 9HQ ☎ 01255 674889 679232
e-mail: info@uplandsguesthouse.freeserve.co.uk
Dir: *Exit A12 onto A120, signed Harwich, then A133 signed Clacton, continue through Weeley onto B1033, Thorpe-le-Soken & Kirby Cross. Turn R into Frinton through level crossing gates, Hadleigh Rd is 3rd L, Uplands 250yds on L*
Located on a leafy residential avenue close to shops and seafront, this Edwardian house offers homely bedrooms, some with modern shower rooms. Breakfast is taken in the front-facing dining room which also contains a lounge section.
FACILITIES: 4 rms (2 en suite) No smoking tea/coffee No dogs (ex guide dogs) Cen ht No coaches **PRICES:** s £23-£28; d £46-£56* **LB PARKING:** 4

GREAT DUNMOW Map 05 TL62

♦♦♦♦ Homelye Farm *(TL648225)*

Homelye Chase, Braintree Rd CM6 3AW ☎ 01371 872127
Fax 01371 876428 Mr & Mrs N Pickford
e-mail: homelye@supanet.com
Dir: *follow A120 E from Dunmow for 1m. Turn left off main road at large water tower. Farm at bottom of Homelye Chase*
Located in peaceful rural surroundings within easy reach of Stansted Airport, this former livestock farm offers comfortable and well equipped bedrooms that are in fact sympathetic byre conversions. Breakfast is taken in a cosy dining room in the original farmhouse, where a warm welcome is assured.
FACILITIES: 9 en suite (1 fmly) (9 GF) No smoking TVB tea/coffee No dogs Cen ht 113 acres arable **PRICES:** s £30-£35; d £55* **PARKING:** 10 **NOTES:** Closed 24-27 Dec **CARDS:**

HARWICH

See also Manningtree

♦♦♦♦ New Farm House *(TM165289)*

Spinnel's Ln CO11 2UJ ☎ 01255 870365 Fax 01255 870837
Mr & Mrs B R Winch
e-mail: newfarmhouse@which.net

(For full entry see Wix)

England

LATCHINGDON Map 05 TL80

♦♦ *Neptune Cafe Motel*
Burnham Rd CM3 6EX ☎ 01621 740770 01621 740770
Dir: *A12 onto A414, B1010 to Latchingdon, in village turn right at mini roundabout at church, motel 300 yds*
Situated in rural Essex, this motel offers reasonably priced chalet style accommodation, which is comfortable and very well maintained. Two rooms are specifically adapted for the disabled. An ample breakfast is served in the adjoining café and there is a wide choice of cooked food available.
FACILITIES: 10 en suite (4 fmly) No smoking in 2 bedrooms No smoking in dining room TVB tea/coffee No dogs (ex guide dogs) Cen ht No coaches **PARKING:** 40 **NOTES:** Closed 24 Dec-3 Jan

MANNINGTREE

Premier Collection

♦♦♦♦♦ Dairy House *(TM148293)*
Bradfield Rd CO11 2SR ☎ 01255 870322 01255 870186
Mrs B Whitworth
e-mail: bridgetwhitworth@hotmail.com
(For full entry see Wix)

MARGARET RODING (Near Great Dunmow) Map 05 TL51

♦♦♦ Greys
Ongar Rd CM6 1QR ☎ 01245 231509
Dir: *in Margaret Roding turn off A1060, Bishops Stortford to Chelmsford rd, signed to Berners Roding. By telephone box, 2nd house on left approx 0.5m,*
Set in immaculate gardens, in a superb rural position, this sympathetic renovation of two period cottages retains many original features including a wealth of exposed beams. The traditionally furnished bedrooms are filled with thoughtful extras and a spacious comfortable lounge is also available.
FACILITIES: 3 rms No smoking No dogs Cen ht TVL No children 10yrs No coaches PRICES: s £25-£26; d fr £45✻ **LB PARKING:** 3 **NOTES:** Closed 24-26 Dec

PLESHEY Map 05 TL61

♦♦♦ Yew Tree Farm *(TL647158)*
CM3 1HX ☎ 01245 231229 Mrs G Tamlyn
e-mail: jktam@breathe.co.uk
Dir: *From A130 between villages of Barnston & Ford End, along road signed Onslow Green. Continue 1.5m, turn right at grass-triangle signed High Roding (ignore Pleshey) 400yds on sharp right bend, left into small lane. Yew Tree 200yds set back on right*
A warm welcome can be expected at this charming farmhouse, set in a peaceful rural location and handy for Stansted Airport. Bedrooms are attractively decorated and well equipped.
FACILITIES: 2 en suite No smoking TV1B tea/coffee Cen ht Croquet lawn PRICES: s £25; d £45✻ **PARKING:** 4

Egg cups for excellence!
This symbol shows that breakfast exceeded our Inspector's expectations.

SAFFRON WALDEN Map 05 TL53

Premier Collection

♦♦♦♦♦ The Bonnet
Overhall Ln, Stevington End, Ashdon CB10 2JE
☎ 01799 584955
e-mail: davjon12@yahoo.co.uk
Dir: *proceed through Ashdon (coming from Saffron Walden) and turn right into Camps Rd, turn right again at red telephone box*
Expect a warm welcome form the caring hosts at this charming property, which is situated in a peaceful rural location within easy driving distance of the town centre. This former inn has been lovingly restored by the present owners and offers a high standard of accommodation throughout. Bedrooms are attractively decorated, tastefully furnished and equipped with many thoughtful touches. Breakfast is served at a large table in the smart dining room and guests also have the use of a cosy lounge.
FACILITIES: 2 en suite No smoking TVB tea/coffee No dogs (ex guide dogs) Cen ht No coaches Dinner Last d by prior arrangement
PRICES: s £30-£35; d £55-£65✻ **PARKING:** 20 **CARDS:**

♦♦♦♦ Rowley Hill Lodge
Little Walden CB10 1UZ ☎ 01799 525975 01799 516622
e-mail: eh@clara.net
Dir: *1.25m N of town centre on B1052. On left of road - establishment has three tall chimneys & B+B sign*
Edward and Kate Haslam enjoy a regular international clientele at their extended Victorian lodge, which is situated in immaculate gardens. Bedrooms are both well-equipped and homely with pretty decor. Tasty English breakfasts are taken at one family table in the elegant dining room and a comfortable lounge is also available.
FACILITIES: 2 en suite No smoking in bedrooms No smoking in dining room TVB tea/coffee No dogs Cen ht TVL No coaches **PRICES:** s £30; d £50✻ **PARKING:** 4

♦♦♦♦ Yardleys
Orchard Pightle, Hadstock CB1 6PQ ☎ 01223 891822
01223 891822
e-mail: yardleys@waitrose.com
Dir: *M11 Northbound junct 9 take A11, at next junct A1307 for Haverhill. At Linton right onto B1052 past Zoo. At Hadstock left into Bartlow Rd, in 200mtrs left Moules Lane, left Bilberry End, left Orchard Pightle, house on left. M11 southbound junct 10, take A505 to A11 to A1307 then as above*
FACILITIES: 3 en suite No smoking TV1B tea/coffee No dogs Cen ht TVL No coaches Dinner **PRICES:** s £24-£35; d £48-£52✻
PARKING: 5 **NOTES:** Closed 16 Dec-5 Jan
CARDS:

♦♦♦ Cricketers' Arms
Rickling Green and Quendon CB11 3YG ☎ 01799 543210
01799 543512
e-mail: reservations@cricketers.demon.co.uk
Dir: *exit B1383 at Quendon, premises 300yds on left opposite cricket green*
Overlooking Rickling village green, parts of this inn date from the 16th century. A selection of real ales and imaginative food is available within the public rooms; a meeting room and courtesy Stansted airport car parking are also available. Bedrooms are comfortable and well-equipped; the four-poster room has lots of character and is very popular.
FACILITIES: 10 en suite (2 fmly) (3 GF) No smoking in area of dining room TVB tea/coffee Direct dial from bedrooms Cen ht Dinner Last d 9.30pm
PRICES: s £55-£75; d £70-£105✻ **MEALS:** Sunday Lunch £10-£21alc Dinner £10-£21alc✻ **CONF:** Thtr 40 Board 14 Del from £50 ✻
PARKING: 48 **CARDS:**

SOUTHEND-ON-SEA Map 05 TQ88

♦♦♦♦ Ilfracombe House Hotel

9-13 Wilson Rd SS1 1HG ☎ 01702 351000 🖹 01702 393989
e-mail: ilfracombe.hotel@alpine4.demon.co.uk
Dir: *A13 or A127 follow signs for town centre, from London Rd(A13) turn at Cricketers pub into Milton Rd, then 4th left into Cambridge Rd. Wilson Rd is on right just before a mini rdbt. Hotel car park at rear of hotel in Alexandra St*

This comfortably appointed private hotel is within Southend's conservation area, a short walk from the cliffs and gardens. Public rooms are tastefully appointed and comfortable. Breakfasts are taken in a separate, pleasant dining room. Bedrooms come in different styles, each is extremely well equipped; deluxe rooms have delightful bathrooms.
FACILITIES: 20 en suite (3 fmly) (2 GF) No smoking in 6 bedrooms No smoking in dining room No smoking in 1 lounge STV TVB tea/coffee Direct dial from bedrooms Licensed Cen ht TVL Dinner Last d 8pm
PRICES: s £39-£49; d £64-£79✳ **LB** **CONF:** Del from £54 ✳
PARKING: 9 **CARDS:**

♦♦♦ Mayflower Hotel

5-6 Royal Ter SS1 1DY ☎ 01702 340489 🖹 01702 340489
Dir: *overlooking pier and estuary. Approach from seafront*
Located in an elegant Regency terrace overlooking the Pier and a few minutes walk from the town centre, this well maintained hotel has been within the same family ownership for thirty years and offers homely bedrooms and a first floor lounge, which also contains a pool table. Breakfast is taken in the cosy basement dining room.
FACILITIES: 23 rms (8 en suite) (3 fmly) (3 GF) No smoking in dining room TVB tea/coffee Cen ht TVL Pool Table **PRICES:** s £25.85-£39.95; d £39.95-£49.35✳ **NOTES:** Closed 10 days Xmas & New Year

♦♦♦ Terrace Hotel

8 Royal Ter SS1 1DY ☎ 01702 348143 🖹 01702 348143
e-mail: lizbarrick@lizbarrick.totalserve.co.uk
Dir: *Royal Terrace can only be approached from Southend seafront, via Pier Hill, opposite the pier*
On a raised terrace above the main seafront promenade, this guest house has a comfortable, informal atmosphere. There is a cosy bar, elegant sitting room and breakfast room, and the spacious and well planned bedrooms consist of three en suite rear-facing rooms and six front-facing rooms which share two bathrooms.
FACILITIES: 9 rms (3 en suite) (3 fmly) No smoking in dining room No smoking in lounges TVB tea/coffee Licensed Cen ht TVL No coaches
PRICES: s £25.85-£39.95; d £39.95-£49.35✳ **NOTES:** Closed Xmas-New Year

Prices may change during the currency of the Guide, please check when booking.

♦♦♦ *Tower Hotel & Restaurant*

146 Alexandra Rd SS1 1HE ☎ 01702 348635 🖹 01702 433044
Dir: *turn off A13 at Cricketers Inn Pub into Milton Road. Take last turning left into Cambridge Road, then take 3rd right into Wilson Road, hotel on 1st right corner*
Family run Victorian hotel situated in a conservation area just a few minutes walk from the beach. Bedrooms are split between the main building and an adjacent annexe; they are pleasantly decorated and equipped with a good range of useful extras. Breakfast and dinner are served in the lower ground floor restaurant and guests have the use of a cosy lounge bar.
FACILITIES: 15 rms (14 en suite) 17 annexe en suite (4 fmly) TVB tea/coffee Direct dial from bedrooms Licensed TVL Membership sports/snooker club/fitness centre Dinner **PARKING:** 4 **CARDS:**

STANSTED AIRPORT

See *Bishops Stortford (Hertfordshire)*

THAXTED Map 05 TL63

♦♦♦♦ Crossways

32 Town St CM6 2LA ☎ 01371 830348
Dir: *on B184 in centre of town opposite Guildhall*
FACILITIES: 2 en suite No smoking TVB tea/coffee No dogs (ex guide dogs) Cen ht No coaches **PRICES:** s £38; d £56✳ **LB** **PARKING:** 2

THORPE BAY

See Southend-on-Sea

TOPPESFIELD Map 05 TL73

♦♦♦ Ollivers Farm *(TL754370)*

Toppesfield CO9 4LS ☎ 01787 237642 🖹 01787 237602
Mrs S R Blackie
e-mail: sueblackie@fsmail.net
Dir: *A1017 proceeding N, turn left after White Hart pub in Gt Yeldham, right if travelling S. Farm 1.5m on left, last driveway before T-junct to village*
Located on pretty gardens, this impressive 16th century farmhouse has a wealth of charm and character enhanced by many original features including exposed beams and a huge open fireplace in the reception hall. Bedrooms are comfortable, and furnishing styles and fine art enhance the charm of the interior. Breakfast is served in the elegant dining room.
FACILITIES: 2 en suite (4 GF) No smoking TVB tea/coffee No dogs No children 10yrs **PRICES:** s £35-£37.50; d £50-£55✳ **PARKING:** 4
NOTES: Closed 23 Dec-1 Jan

WESTCLIFF-ON-SEA

See Southend-on-Sea

WIX Map 05 TM12

Premier Collection

♦♦♦♦♦ Dairy House ***(TM148293)***
Bradfield Rd CO11 2SR ☎ 01255 870322 01255 870186
Mrs B Whitworth
e-mail: bridgetwhitworth@hotmail.com
Dir: *between Colchester & Harwich, turn off A120 into Wix. At crossroads take road signposted Bradfield and farm is 1m on left*
Set on 700 acres of arable land, with stunning views of the surrounding countryside, this Georgian house was extensively renovated in the Victorian era and retains many original features, including tiled decorative floors, moulded cornices and marble fireplaces. The spacious bedrooms are filled with thoughtful extras to create a real home from home feeling and an elegant antique furnished dining room is the setting for memorable breakfasts. A cosy guest lounge is also available.
FACILITIES: 2 en suite No smoking in bedrooms No smoking in dining room TVB tea/coffee No dogs (ex guide dogs) Cen ht TVL No children 12yrs Croquet 700 acres arable fruit **PRICES:** s £28-£30; d £44-£46* **PARKING:** 8

♦♦♦♦ New Farm House ***(TM165289)***
Spinnel's Ln CO11 2UJ ☎ 01255 870365 01255 870837
Mr & Mrs B R Winch
e-mail: newfarmhouse@which.net
Dir: *turn off A120 into Wix, at village crossroads take Bradfield road, under A120 to top of hill turn right New Farm House 200yds on left*
Expect a warm welcome at this impressive detached property, set amidst four acres of landscaped grounds with superb views over the countryside. Bedrooms are attractively decorated and equipped with many thoughtful extras. Public areas include a smartly appointed lounge, a cosy bar and a smart dining room.
FACILITIES: 5 rms (3 en suite) 6 annexe en suite (1 fmly) (6 GF) No smoking in bedrooms No smoking in dining room No smoking in 1 lounge TVB tea/coffee No dogs (ex guide dogs) Licensed Cen ht TVL 4 acres Non-working Dinner Last d 6.30pm **PRICES:** s £27-£32; d £44-£52* **LB**
PARKING: 20 **CARDS:**

GLOUCESTERSHIRE

ALMONDSBURY Map 03 ST68

♦♦♦♦ Abbotts Way
Gloucester Rd BS32 4JB ☎ 01454 613134 01454 613134
Dir: *7m S of M5 junct 14 on A38*
This large modern house is set in 12 acres of gardens, with panoramic views of the Severn Vale and the Severn Bridges. Bedrooms are well furnished. The lounge is a good place to relax and the cosy dining room and spacious conservatory are delightful settings in which to enjoy breakfast.
FACILITIES: 6 rms (5 en suite) (2 fmly) No smoking TVB tea/coffee No dogs (ex guide dogs) Cen ht TVL No coaches Indoor swimming pool (heated) Sauna **PRICES:** s £31-£33; d £50-£52* **PARKING:** 10
CARDS:

♦♦♦♦ *Hart's House*
Gloucester Rd BS32 4JB ☎ 01454 625494 01454 616665
Dir: *leave M5 jct 16 follow A38 towards Thornbury, Harts House is 1.5m from M5 just past Murco Petrol St on opp. side of A38*
Peacefully situated and yet conveniently located for easy access to the major road system, Hart's House is set in 10 acres of gardens and grounds. A warm welcome can be expected. Breakfast is taken around one large table and on cooler evenings a log fire burns in the spacious sitting room.

continued

FACILITIES: 5 rms (3 en suite) (1 fmly) No smoking TVB Cen ht TVL No coaches **PARKING:** 20 **CARDS:**

ARLINGHAM Map 03 SO71

♦♦♦♦ The Old Passage Inn
Passage Rd GL2 7JR ☎ 01452 740547 01452 741871
e-mail: oldpassage@ukonline.co.uk
Dir: *adjacent M5 junct 13 turn onto A38 South, then B4071 through Arlingham, the Inn is on the river bank*
A warm welcome is assured at this former Victorian inn stunningly located on the River Severn. Total sympathetic renovation has resulted in modern quality bedrooms with a wealth of practical and homely extras. The restaurant, specialising in seafood, enjoys a strong local clientele and guests can select fresh shellfish from a well-stocked tank.
FACILITIES: 3 en suite No smoking in dining room STV TVB tea/coffee Direct dial from bedrooms Cen ht No coaches Dinner Last d 9.30pm
PRICES: s £50-£55; d £80-£95* **MEALS:** Lunch £14-£40alc Dinner £14-£40alc* **PARKING:** 40 **NOTES:** Closed 24-31 Dec rs Sun pm & all day Mon **CARDS:**

BIBURY Map 04 SP10

♦♦♦♦ Cotteswold House
Arlington GL7 5ND ☎ 01285 740609 01285 740609
e-mail: cotteswold.house@btclick.com
Dir: *Bibury - on B4425 between Cirencester/Burford. Enter village from Cirencester, Cotteswold House on left*
Conveniently situated for exploration of the many and varied delights of this picturesque area, this welcoming house offers high levels of comfort and quality. Spacious bedrooms are equipped with thoughtful extras and guests also have exclusive use of a cosy lounge area, equipped with useful local information. Please note, this is a no-smoking establishment.
FACILITIES: 3 en suite (1 fmly) No smoking TVB tea/coffee No dogs (ex guide dogs) Cen ht No coaches **PRICES:** s fr £35; d fr £48* **LB**
PARKING: 3 **CARDS:**

BIRDWOOD Map 03 SO71

♦♦♦ Kings Head
GL19 3EF ☎ 01452 750348 01452 750348
Dir: *on A40 Gloucester to Ross on Wye*
Ideally located between Gloucester and Ross-on-Wye, this attractive roadside inn offers bright attractive bedrooms, two of which have individual patios. The spacious public areas are themed with a range of military memorabilia and a cosy dining room is the setting for breakfast and popular bar meals.
FACILITIES: 6 en suite (1 fmly) No smoking in dining room TVB tea/coffee No dogs (ex guide dogs) Cen ht TVL Pool table Dinner Last d 9pm
PRICES: s fr £30; d fr £40* **PARKING:** 100 **NOTES:** Closed 24-26 Dec
CARDS:

BLAKENEY Map 03 SO60

♦♦♦♦ Viney Hill Country
Lower Viney Hill GL15 4LT ☎ 01594 516000 01594 516018
e-mail: info@vineyhill.com
Dir: *2.5m from Lydney off A48 on unclassed road signposted 'Viney Hill'*
Located in pretty mature gardens and an ideal base for touring the Royal Forest of Dean and the Wye Valley, this 18th century house has been sympathetically renovated to provide comfortable homely bedrooms and a spacious elegant dining room where imaginative dinners and breakfasts are served. A choice of comfortable lounges is also available.

continued

England

Viney Hill County Guesthouse

FACILITIES: 4 en suite No smoking TVB tea/coffee No dogs (ex guide dogs) Licensed Cen ht TVL No coaches Dinner Last d 1pm **PRICES:** s £30-£40; d £48-£60✻ **LB** **PARKING:** 5 **NOTES:** Closed Xmas **CARDS:**

BLOCKLEY Map 04 SP13

Premier Collection

♦♦♦♦♦ Old Bakery

High St GL56 9EU ☎ 01386 700408 01386 700408

Dir: *turn off A44 at Bourton-on-the Hill onto B4479. Proceed to Blockley centre. Beyond Church Square, Old Bakery on corner of High St/School Lane*

Superb food and a warm welcome are assured at this mellow Cotswold stone property, a sympathetic conversion of four 200-year-old former cottages. Quality décor and furnishings, which include some fine period pieces, enhance the intrinsic charm of the house and the comfortable bedrooms provide a wealth of thoughtful extras. The elegant dining room is the setting for intimate dinners and a choice of lounges is also available.

FACILITIES: 3 en suite No smoking TVB tea/coffee No dogs (ex guide dogs) Licensed Cen ht No children 12yrs No coaches Dinner Last d 8.30pm **PRICES:** (incl. dinner) s £85-£105; d £130-£200✻ **PARKING:** 4 **NOTES:** Closed Dec-Jan & 2 wks Jun **CARDS:**

♦♦♦♦ Arreton House

Station Rd GL56 9DT ☎ 01386 701077 01386 701077

e-mail: bandb@arreton.demon.co.uk

Dir: *from A44 at Moreton-in-Marsh continue to Bourton-on-the Hill and take B4479 to Blockley. Arreton on left opposite Great Western pub*

Located in the heart of the historic village, this 17th-century mellow Cotswold stone house is constantly being improved by the caring proprietors. It provides homely bedrooms of quality filled with a wealth of thoughtful extras. Breakfasts, which include home-made and local produce, are taken in the cosy dining room or on the pretty patio.

continued

FACILITIES: 3 en suite (1 fmly) No smoking in bedrooms TVB tea/coffee No dogs Cen ht TVL No children 4yrs No coaches **PRICES:** s £30-£35; d £42-£46✻ **LB** **PARKING:** 6

BOURTON-ON-THE-WATER Map 04 SP12

♦♦♦♦ Coombe House

Rissington Rd GL54 2DT ☎ 01451 821966 01451 810477

e-mail: coombe.house@virgin.net

Dir: *exit A429, thru village. Combe House past model village on left; or exit A424 at Burford or Stow, continue into Bourton-on-the-Water, 0.5m on right*

A warm welcome is assured at this spotlessly clean, no-smoking mellow Cotswold- stone house set in immaculate gardens a few minutes' walk from the historic centre of Bourton. Bedrooms are equipped with a wealth of homely extras. There is a sun terrace and comfortable lounge in addition to an attractive breakfast room.

FACILITIES: 6 en suite (2 GF) No smoking TVB tea/coffee No dogs (ex guide dogs) Licensed Cen ht TVL No children 12yrs No coaches **PRICES:** s £40-£55; d £55-£65✻ **PARKING:** 6 **NOTES:** Closed Jan **CARDS:**

♦♦♦♦ Lansdowne Villa

Lansdowne GL54 2AR ☎ 01451 820673 01451 822099

e-mail: lansdownevilla@aol.com

Dir: *A429 (Cirencester/Stow-on-the-Wold), take Bourton-on-the-Water turning. Hotel 500yds on left, past garage*

Just a three minute stroll from the centre of this quintessentially Cotswold village, this family run establishment offers a warm and genuine welcome. Bedrooms combine comfort with quality and include both four poster and ground floor rooms. English breakfasts (and dinners by arrangement) are served in the bright attractive dining room and a cosy lounge and excellent car parking are additional features.

FACILITIES: 12 en suite (1 fmly) (2 GF) No smoking in bedrooms No smoking in dining room TVB tea/coffee No dogs (ex guide dogs) Licensed Cen ht TVL No coaches Dinner Last d 9.30am **PRICES:** s £32-£35; d £52-£58✻ **PARKING:** 14 **CARDS:**

♦♦♦ The Cotswold House

Lansdowne GL54 2AR ☎ 01451 822373

Dir: *turn off A429 into Landsdown & continue for 0.5m to Cotswold House on right opposite UK Garage*

A warm welcome is assured at this well maintained, mellow stone house. Just a few minutes walk from the church and the many attractions of this perennially popular village, this is a great base for touring the Cotswolds. Bedrooms are comfortably furnished, one of which is a self-contained conversion of the former village telephone exchange, set within the immaculate gardens.

FACILITIES: 3 en suite 1 annexe en suite (1 fmly) No smoking in dining room No smoking in 1 lounge TVB tea/coffee No dogs Cen ht No coaches **PRICES:** s £25-£35; d £40-£50✻ **LB** **PARKING:** 5

England

BOURTON-ON-THE-WATER continued

♦♦♦ Stepping Stone

Rectory Ln GL54 2LL ☎ 01451 821385 📠 01451 821008
e-mail: ststbandb@aol.com
Dir: *A40 between Oxford & Cheltenham, turn for Barringtons/Rissingtons. After 3m turn for Great Rissington. 200yds past Lamb, turn left*

Located on immaculate gardens in the pretty rural village of Great Rissington, this modern house provides thoughtfully equipped bedrooms, two of which are within sympathetically renovated outbuildings and can also be used for self-catering. An award-winning pub is just a few minutes walk from the property.

FACILITIES: 2 en suite 2 annexe en suite No smoking TVB tea/coffee No dogs (ex guide dogs) Cen ht No children 12yrs No coaches Dinner Last d on booking **PRICES:** s £27.50-£35; d £55-£60* **LB PARKING:** 9 **NOTES:** Closed Xmas **CARDS:**

♦♦♦ Chestnuts (Formerly Polly Perkins)

3 Chestnut Flats, High St GL54 2AN ☎ 01451 820244
📠 01451 820558
Dir: *turn off Fosse Way onto Landsdown & follow road to the village centre. B & B is opposite the village green.*

Situated in the heart of this picturesque Cotswolds village, this attractive listed building dates back some 300 years, and combines guest house accommodation with a restaurant and tea-rooms. Bedrooms are comfortable, well equipped and all with en suite facilities. A secure car park is an added feature.

FACILITIES: 6 en suite (2 fmly) No smoking TVB tea/coffee No dogs (ex guide dogs) Licensed Cen ht No coaches **PRICES:** d £50-£60* **LB PARKING:** 6 **NOTES:** Closed 24-26 Dec & 31 Dec-1 Jan **CARDS:**

BROOKTHORPE — Map 03 SO81

♦♦♦ Brookthorpe Lodge

Stroud Rd GL4 0UQ ☎ 01452 812645 📠 01452 812645
e-mail: enq@brookthorpelodge.demon.co.uk
Dir: *turn off A38 ring road onto A4173 Gloucester to Stroud Road for approx. 1.5m. The house is on the right just beyond Whaddon garage*

FACILITIES: 10 rms (6 en suite) (2 fmly) No smoking TVB tea/coffee Licensed Cen ht TVL No coaches Dinner Last d 5pm **PRICES:** s £22.50-£25; d £45-£50* **LB PARKING:** 15 **CARDS:**

CHELTENHAM — Map 03 SO92

Premier Collection

♦♦♦♦♦ Cleeve Hill Hotel

Cleeve Hill GL52 3PR ☎ 01242 672052 📠 679969
e-mail: gbtoncleevehill@aol.com
Dir: *on B4632 2.5m from Cheltenham between Prestbury and Winchcombe*

Located in an elevated position between Cheltenham and Broadway, this elegant Edwardian house provides comfortable, individually styled bedrooms, with both four-poster and ground floor rooms available. Attention to detail is a hallmark here, bedrooms featuring carefully chosen, practical and homely extras. The spacious lounges have deep sofas, superb décor and soft furnishings. A bar service is available and breakfasts are taken in the conservatory, with stunning views over the surrounding countryside and Malvern Hills.

FACILITIES: 9 en suite (1 fmly) (1 GF) No smoking TVB tea/coffee Direct dial from bedrooms No dogs (ex guide dogs) Licensed Cen ht No children 8 yrs No coaches **PRICES:** s £55-£60; d £75-£105* **PARKING:** 10 **CARDS:**

Premier Collection

♦♦♦♦♦ Georgian House

77 Montpellier Ter GL50 1XA ☎ 01242 515577
📠 01242 545929
e-mail: georgian_house@yahoo.com
Dir: *From M5 J11 head for town centre, keep on A40 into Montpellier Terrace. Georgian House on R after park*

Dating back to 1807, this impressive Georgian house is located in the fashionable area of Montpellier. Sympathetically renovated, original features are enhanced by quality decor and fine period furnishings. An extensive menu is offered at breakfast and this is served in the airy dining room. Warm hospitality and attentive service ensures a memorable stay.

FACILITIES: 3 en suite No smoking STV TVB tea/coffee Direct dial from bedrooms No dogs (ex guide dogs) Cen ht No children 16yrs No coaches **PRICES:** s £55; d £70-£85 **PARKING:** 2 **NOTES:** Closed Xmas/New Year **CARDS:**

♦♦♦♦ Beaumont House Hotel

56 Shurdington Rd GL53 0JE ☎ 01242 245986
📠 01242 520044
e-mail: rocking.horse@virgin.net
Dir: *SW side of town, on A46 (The Circle)*

Built as a private residence, Beaumont House continues to exude a refined and genteel charm. Breakfast is taken in the elegant dining room and there is a large, comfortable lounge in which to relax. The spacious, well-equipped bedrooms are named after racehorses and those situated to the rear of the building have views over Leckhampton Hill.

FACILITIES: 16 en suite No smoking STV TVB tea/coffee Direct dial from bedrooms No dogs Licensed Cen ht No children 10yrs No coaches **PRICES:** s £54-£69; d £75-£115 **PARKING:** 20 **CARDS:**

♦♦♦♦ Beechworth Lawn Hotel

133 Hales Rd GL52 6ST ☎ 01242 522583 📠 01242 574800
e-mail: beechworth.lawn@dial.pipex.com & info@beechworthlawnhotel.co.uk
Dir: *from A40 London Rd, turn into Hales Rd. Hotel approx 0.5m on right*

continued

Located in the residential area of Battledown, close to the racecourse, town centre and GCHQ, this elegant Victorian house offers thoughtfully furnished bedrooms, a light and airy breakfast room and a spacious guest lounge. Cooked breakfasts, with an emphasis on local produce, are a strong point.
FACILITIES: 6 en suite (2 fmly) (2 GF) No smoking in 4 bedrooms No smoking in dining room TVB tea/coffee Cen ht No coaches Dinner Last d noon **PRICES:** s £40-£45; d £55-£75✳ **LB CONF:** Thtr 12 Class 8 Board 12 **PARKING:** 10 **CARDS:**

♦♦♦♦ Moorend Park Hotel

Moorend Park Rd GL53 0LA ☎ 01242 224441 📠 01242 572413
e-mail: moorendpark@freeuk.com
Dir: *M5 J11A, A417 (Cirencester), A46 (Cheltenham). After 3m L at lights to enter hotel car park.*
This elegant early Victorian house is located a short distance from the town centre. Delicious breakfasts are served in the spacious dining room and there is a cosy bar with fireplace as well as a peaceful reading lounge. All nine rooms are tastefully decorated and well equipped. A warm welcome is assured.
FACILITIES: 9 en suite (2 fmly) No smoking TVB tea/coffee Direct dial from bedrooms No dogs (ex guide dogs) Licensed Cen ht No coaches **PRICES:** s £48-£52; d £58-£70 **LB PARKING:** 25 **NOTES:** Closed Xmas/New Year **CARDS:**

♦♦♦♦ Wishmoor House

147 Hales Rd GL52 6TD ☎ 01242 238504 📠 01242 226090
e-mail: wishmoor@aol.com
Dir: *from A40 turn into Hales Rd (B4075), 0.5m on right*

A warm welcome is assured at this immaculately maintained Victorian house which is located in a mainly residential area between the town centre and racecourse. Many original interior features are retained which are enhanced by the décor throughout and the elegant dining room overlooks a pretty patio garden.
FACILITIES: 11 rms (9 en suite) (1 fmly) No smoking in bedrooms No smoking in dining room TVB tea/coffee No dogs Cen ht No coaches **PRICES:** s £40; d £60-£65✳ **PARKING:** 8 **NOTES:** Closed 24 Dec-11 Jan **CARDS:**

♦♦♦♦ Stretton Lodge Hotel

Western Rd GL50 3RN ☎ 01242 570771 📠 01242 528724
e-mail: info@strettonlodge.co.uk
Dir: *M5 junct 11 through 2 rdbts then through traffic lights into Lansdown Rd, left at next lights into Christchurch Rd (Police HQ on right), through next lights to end Christchurch Road (T junct) left into Malvern Rd and Western Rd is 2nd on the right*
FACILITIES: 4 en suite (1 fmly) No smoking TVB tea/coffee Direct dial from bedrooms Licensed Cen ht TVL No coaches **PRICES:** s £45-£65; d £70-£98✳ **PARKING:** 7 **CARDS:**

♦♦♦ The Battledown

125 Hales Rd GL52 6ST ☎ 01242 233881 📠 01242 704219
e-mail: battledown125@hotmail.com
Dir: *turn off A40 onto B4075, hotel is 0.5m on right*
This elegant and well proportioned Grade II listed house offers comfortable accommodation in a convenient location close to the town centre and racecourse. Bedrooms are both practical and homely with many having direct access to gardens and the spacious car park. The recently refurbished dining room, which retains many attractive original features, is the setting for breakfast.
FACILITIES: 7 en suite (1 fmly) No smoking TVB tea/coffee No dogs (ex guide dogs) Cen ht No coaches **PRICES:** s £36; d £52✳ **LB PARKING:** 7 **NOTES:** Closed Xmas **CARDS:**

♦♦♦ Lonsdale House

Montpellier Dr GL50 1TX ☎ 01242 232379 📠 01242 232379
e-mail: lonsdalehouse@hotmail.com
Dir: *turn off A46 towards Stroud. 0.25m from town centre by Eagle Star building*
Conveniently located just a short walk from the town centre, this Regency house has been sympathetically renovated to provide a combination of quality and comfort. Bedrooms range in size, all featuring both practical and homely extras. Breakfast is taken in the bright and elegant dining room, adjacent to the well appointed guest lounge.
FACILITIES: 9 rms (3 en suite) (3 fmly) No smoking TVB tea/coffee No dogs Cen ht No coaches **PRICES:** s £23-£37; d £46-£56✳ **PARKING:** 6 **CARDS:**

♦♦♦ Montpellier Hotel

33 Montpellier Ter GL50 1UX ☎ 01242 526009
Dir: *M5 J11, follow A40 to rdbt at Montpellier, continue on A40, hotel 100mtrs on R beyond rdbt, overlooking tennis courts*
Part of a fine Georgian terrace overlooking the municipal gardens in Montpellier, this welcoming hotel is convenient for the shops, restaurants and local amenities. Bedrooms are comfortably furnished, and thoughtfully equipped with many practical extras and homely touches.
FACILITIES: 7 en suite (5 fmly) No smoking in 3 bedrooms No smoking in dining room STV TVB tea/coffee No dogs Licensed Cen ht TVL Dinner Last d 5pm **PRICES:** s £28-£38; d £48-£54✳

♦♦♦ Pardon Hill *(SO983298)*

Prescott, Gotherington GL52 9RD ☎ 01242 672468 & 07808 890467 📠 01242 672468 Mrs J Newman
e-mail: janet@pardonhillfarm.freeserve.co.uk
Dir: *off A435 Cheltenham to Evesham Rd towards Gotherington, through village,under railway bridge, farm 0.5m on R*
Located in an elevated position, north of the town and on the outskirts of the rural village of Gotherington, this impressive detached stone built house enjoys stunning views of the surrounding countryside. The thoughtfully furnished bedrooms are filled with homely extras and look out across the rolling fields. Breakfast is taken at one family table in the conservatory dining room.
FACILITIES: 3 en suite No smoking in bedrooms No smoking in dining room No smoking in 1 lounge TVB tea/coffee Cen ht Riding 300 acres mixed **PRICES:** s fr £30; d fr £50✳ **PARKING:** 6 **NOTES:** Closed Xmas

BB Great value! This indicates B&B for £19 and under, per person, per night.

England

CHELTENHAM continued

♦♦♦ Stray Leaves

282 Gloucester Rd GL51 7AG ☎ 01242 572303
Fax 01242 572303
Dir: *Adjacent to railway station. Take rear exit for access*
Stray Leaves Guest House is located on a mainly residential road within easy walking distance of a railway station. This extended semi-detached house provides a good selection of homely bedrooms. The hotels public rooms include a modern dining room, which overlooks the pretty rear garden and a separate lounge.
FACILITIES: 4 en suite (2 fmly) (2 GF) No smoking in dining room TVB tea/coffee No dogs (ex guide dogs) Cen ht TVL No coaches Dinner Last d 9am **PRICES:** s £25-£50; d £45-£70* **LB** **PARKING:** 6 **CARDS:**

♦♦♦ Ivydene House Hotel

145 Hewlett Rd GL52 6TS ☎ 01242 521726 Fax 01242 525694
e-mail: jvhopwood@ivydenehouse.freeserve.co.uk
Dir: *From A40 London Road follow into town, Hewlett Road is on right after lights & gardens*
FACILITIES: 9 rms (7 en suite) (2 fmly) No smoking TVB tea/coffee No dogs (ex guide dogs) Cen ht No coaches **PRICES:** s £27.50-£35; d £55-£65 **PARKING:** 6 **NOTES:** Closed 17-27 Dec **CARDS:**

CHIPPING CAMPDEN — Map 04 SP13

See also Blockley

♦♦♦♦ The Malt House

Broad Campden GL55 6UU ☎ 01386 840295 Fax 01386 841334
e-mail: enquiries@themalthousehotel.com
Dir: *A44 take A4081 to Chipping Campden, turn right to Broad Campden, hotel in 1m just after church on left*

This former malt house dates to the 16th century with many original features having been retained. Bedrooms are individual in style, with quality soft fabrics and English period furniture. Guests also have use of the comfortable lounge, entrance lounge/hall, elegant dining room and extensive grounds and gardens. Dinner is available by prior arrangement.
FACILITIES: 4 en suite 3 annexe en suite (3 fmly) No smoking TVB tea/coffee Licensed Cen ht No coaches Croquet lawn Dinner Last d 8.30pm **PRICES:** s £89.50-£92.50; d £112.50-£120.50* **PARKING:** 10 **NOTES:** Closed 22-28 Dec **CARDS:**

♦♦♦♦ Marnic House

Broad Campden GL55 6UR ☎ 01386 840014 & 841473
Fax 01386 840441
e-mail: marnic@zoom.co.uk
Dir: *turn off A44, take B4081 to Chipping Campden straight over T-junct for Broad Campden. Continue 0.75m, Marnic on left as entering village*
Located in immaculate gardens in the peaceful hamlet of Broad Campden, this very well maintained mellow-stone house provides comfortable bedrooms filled with a wealth of homely and thoughtful extras. Imaginative breakfasts are taken at an antique oak table in the elegant dining room and a spacious and relaxing lounge is also available.
FACILITIES: 3 en suite No smoking TVB tea/coffee No dogs Cen ht TVL No children No coaches **PRICES:** d £50-£55* **LB** **PARKING:** 4 **NOTES:** Closed 21 Dec-1 Jan

♦♦♦♦ Catbrook House

Catbrook GL55 6DE ☎ 01386 841499 Fax 01386 849248
e-mail: m.klein@virgin.net
Dir: *A44-B4081 to Chipping Campden,once there follow signs for Broad Campden until you reach Catbrook House on the right*
Enjoying stunning rural views and just a few minutes' walk across the meadow from the town centre, this mellow stone house provides bedrooms filled with both practical and homely extras and a comfortable, traditionally furnished dining room where imaginative breakfasts are served.
FACILITIES: 3 en suite No smoking TV1B tea/coffee No dogs Cen ht No children 9yrs No coaches **PRICES:** s fr £39; d fr £48* **PARKING:** 4 **NOTES:** Closed Xmas

♦♦♦♦ Holly House

Ebrington GL55 6NL ☎ 01386 593213 Fax 01386 593181
e-mail: hutsby@talk21.com
Dir: *from Chipping Campden take B4035 towards Shipston on Stour. After 0.5m turn left to Ebrington & follow signs*
In the heart of the pretty Cotswold village of Ebrington, this late Victorian house offers thoughtfully-equipped accommodation. Bedrooms are housed within buildings which were formerly home to the local wheelwright and offer seclusion and privacy. Quality English breakfasts are served in the light and airy dining room, where a range of local information is also available. For a meal and refreshment, the village pub is just a few minutes' walk away.
FACILITIES: 2 en suite 1 annexe en suite (1 fmly) (3 GF) No smoking TVB tea/coffee No dogs (ex guide dogs) Cen ht No coaches **PRICES:** s £35-£48; d £48-£50* **PARKING:** 5 **NOTES:** Closed Xmas

♦♦♦♦ Manor Farm *(SP124412)*

Weston-sub-Edge GL55 6QH ☎ 01386 840390 & 07889 108812
Fax 0870 1640638 Mrs L King
e-mail: lucy@manorfarmbnb.demon.co.uk
Dir: *on B4632 Stratford to Cheltenham rd, farm on left in Weston-sub-Edge*
Families with pets, including horses, are very welcome at this 17th century mellow Cotswold stone farmhouse, located in the pretty village of Weston-sub-Edge. The bedrooms are filled with thoughtful extras. A comfortable lounge is available in addition to an elegant dining room, where mouth-watering breakfasts are served.
FACILITIES: 3 en suite No smoking TVB tea/coffee Cen ht TVL g 800 acres arable cattle horses sheep **PRICES:** s £35-£50; d £50* **PARKING:** 8 **CARDS:**

♦♦♦♦ Primrose Cottage

3 The Bank, Broad Campden GL55 6US ☎ 01386 840921
Dir: *turn off A44 to Chipping Campden. As you approach thatched cottages look for right turn to Broad Campden - 1m turn right , towards end Bakers Arms pub on left, turn left to park by church, cottage opposite Church over bank.*
Part of a 200 year old mellow Cotswold stone terrace located opposite the village church in the pretty unspoilt hamlet of Broad Campden, a warm welcome is assured at this spotlessly clean cottage which provides homely bedrooms filled with thoughtful extras. Memorable breakfasts are taken at one table in the comfortable combined lounge dining room.
FACILITIES: 2 rms No smoking No dogs (ex guide dogs) Cen ht TVL No coaches **PRICES:** s £35-£39; d £39-£40* **LB** **NOTES:** Closed 24-27 Dec

continued

England

♦♦♦♦ Wyldlands

Broad Campden GL55 6UR ☎ 01386 840478 ℻ 01386 849031

Dir: *Chipping Campden centre opposite phone box, turn into Sheep St, left at top of rd for Broad Campden, hotel is 3rd house on right*

Located in the hamlet of Broad Campden, this mellow stone house offers thoughtfully equipped and homely bedrooms with superb rural views. English breakfasts are taken in the attractive dining room from which the multitude of birdlife can be watched busily enjoying the food provided. Of special mention is the immaculate country garden which has been featured on television's Flying Gardener series.

FACILITIES: 3 en suite No smoking TVB tea/coffee No dogs (ex guide dogs) Cen ht No coaches **PRICES:** s £35-£40; d £48-£50✳ **LB** **PARKING:** 4 **NOTES:** Closed Xmas

CIRENCESTER Map 03 SP00

♦♦♦♦ Smerrill Barns

Kemble GL7 6BW ☎ 01285 770907 ℻ 01285 770706

e-mail: gabi@smerillbarns.com

Dir: *off A429 from Cirencester towards Malmesbury, approx 3m SW of Cirencester*

This sympathetic conversion of two 17th-century barns offers comfortable accommodation with a unique style, combined with the relaxed atmosphere of a family home. Many original features have been retained and are further enhanced by carefully chosen furnishings. Bedrooms are cosy, and the open-plan public areas include a dining room and a sitting area.

FACILITIES: 7 en suite (1 fmly) No smoking TVB tea/coffee No dogs (ex guide dogs) Licensed Cen ht ch fac No coaches **PRICES:** s £45; d £55-£65✳ **PARKING:** 8 **CARDS:**

♦♦♦♦ Wimborne House

91 Victoria Rd GL7 1ES ☎ 01285 643653 ℻ 01285 653890

e-mail: wimborneho@aol.com

Dir: *with church in market place on left, head towards traffic lights, turn right into Victoria Rd, premises 300yrds on left*

Located a few minutes walk from central attractions, this impressive double fronted Victorian house offers spacious comfortable bedrooms filled with both practical and homely extras. Comprehensive breakfasts are offered in the elegant dining room and the rear car park is a real advantage.

FACILITIES: 6 en suite No smoking TVB tea/coffee No dogs Cen ht No children 8yrs No coaches **PRICES:** s fr £35; d fr £45✳ **LB** **PARKING:** 6 **NOTES:** Closed Xmas/New Year **CARDS:**

Places with this symbol are farmhouses.

♦♦♦ The Bungalow

93 Victoria Rd GL7 1ES ☎ 01285 654179 & 07714806202 ℻ 01285 656159

e-mail: CBEARD7@compuserve.com

Dir: *from town centre with church on left, go to the traffic lights, turn right into Victoria Rd, 2/3 down on the left hand side*

Located on a residential avenue, close to the historic centre, this carefully extended chalet bungalow offers comfortable, individually-styled bedrooms with a good range of facilities. Breakfast is taken in the pretty dining room and an adjoining conservatory lounge is available.

FACILITIES: 6 en suite (2 fmly) No smoking in 2 bedrooms No smoking in dining room STV TVB tea/coffee No dogs (ex guide dogs) Cen ht TVL No coaches Last d noon **PRICES:** s £35-£40; d £45-£55✳ **LB** **PARKING:** 10

♦♦♦ Masons Arms

Meysey Hampton GL7 5JT ☎ 01285 850164 ℻ 01285 850164

e-mail: jane@themasonsarms.freeserve.co.uk

Dir: *off A417 between Poulton and Fairford*

A focus of the rural community of Meysey Hampton, this well-maintained 17th century inn enjoys a good reputation for imaginative food, which can be taken either in the formal dining room or attractive bars. The cosy bedrooms have plenty of character and provide both practical and homely extras. Memorable breakfasts ensure a satisfying start to the day.

FACILITIES: 9 en suite (2 fmly) No smoking in dining room TVB tea/coffee Direct dial from bedrooms Cen ht No coaches Dinner Last d 9.15pm **PRICES:** s £45-£55; d £65-£85✳ **MEALS:** Lunch £5.95-£20.95alc Dinner £5.95-£20.95alc✳ **PARKING:** 6 **CARDS:**

DIDMARTON Map 03 ST88

♦♦♦♦ *Kings Arms*

The Street GL9 1DT ☎ 01454 238245 ℻ 01454 238249

e-mail: info@kadidmarton.com

Dir: *From J18 M4 head North on A46 signed for Stroud. After 8m turn right on A43 signed Didmarton. After 2m, Kings Arms on left side, in centre of village.*

Located on the fringes of the Beaufort Estate close to Westonbirt Arboretum, this 17th-century coaching inn retains many original features, which are highlighted by the furnishing and décor styles throughout. Imaginative food, including local game dishes, is served in the character bars or formal restaurant. Bedrooms are equipped with a range of thoughtful extras.

FACILITIES: 4 en suite No smoking in bedrooms No smoking in dining room No smoking in lounges TVB tea/coffee Direct dial from bedrooms No dogs (ex guide dogs) Cen ht No coaches adult pleasure garden with Boules pitch Dinner Last d 9.45pm **PRICES:** sfr £45; d fr £70-£80✳ **PARKING:** 28 **NOTES:** Closed 25 Dec (evening) **CARDS:**

England

FRAMPTON ON SEVERN Map 03 SO70

Premier Collection

♦♦♦♦♦ Old School House

Whittles Ln GL2 7EB ☎ 01452 740457 📠 01452 741721
e-mail: theoldies@f-o-s.freeserve.co.uk
Dir: *from A38 take right turn onto B4071, at village green turn left*

Frampton on Severn is a picturesque village, boasting the longest village green in England. Many original features have been retained here and the decor and furniture complement the character of the house. Bedrooms are spacious and comfortable with homely extras and modern facilities. The dining room, with its large polished table, is the setting for breakfast, and the spacious sitting room features many fine pieces of period furniture and an open fire for the cooler months.
FACILITIES: 2 en suite No smoking in bedrooms tea/coffee Cen ht TVL No children 10yrs No coaches **PRICES:** s £26.50; d £53✱ **PARKING:** 10 **NOTES:** Closed 21-31 Dec

GLOUCESTER

See **Blakeney**

GUITING POWER Map 04 SP02

Premier Collection

♦♦♦♦♦ Guiting Guest House

GL54 5TZ ☎ 01451 850470 📠 01451 850034
e-mail: info@guitingguesthouse.com
Dir: *A40, Andoversford lights R to Stow-on-the-Wold, 4m L to Lower Swell B4068, 1m L to Guiting Power. L into village, house in village centre*

Set in the heart of this unspoilt working rural village, the mellow Cotswold stone house is full of character, with many original features, and has been stylishly decorated throughout. Bedrooms are equipped with a wealth of thoughtful extras and have modern bathrooms. Ground floor areas include a comfortable lounge with open fire and a cosy dining room.
FACILITIES: 3 en suite 4 annexe rms (2 en suite) (2 GF) No smoking TVB tea/coffee Cen ht TVL No coaches Dinner Last d breakfast
PRICES: s £35; d £60✱ **PARKING:** 4 **CARDS:**

continued

♦♦♦ Hollow Bottom

Winchcombe Rd GL54 5UX ☎ 01451 850392 📠 01451 850945
e-mail: hollow.bottom@virgin.net
Dir: *M5 junct 11 follow A40 through Cheltenham. Ar Andoversford take A436 signed Stow-on-the-Wold, after 4m bear left for Guitings B4068, Guiting Power signed on left after approx. 2m*
Original features have been retained at this inn, located on the edge of this unspoilt Cotswold village and popular with followers of National Hunt racing. Rustic furniture and racing memorabilia all add to the atmosphere. A range of real ales and good food is complimented by warm hospitality.
FACILITIES: 3 en suite (1 fmly) TVB tea/coffee Cen ht Dinner Last d 9.30pmpm **PRICES:** s £30; d £50✱ **MEALS:** Lunch £17.50-£25.95alc Dinner £17.50-£29.95alc✱ **PARKING:** 12 **CARDS:**

LAVERTON Map 04 SP03

♦♦♦♦ Leasow House

Laverton Meadows WR12 7NA ☎ 01386 584526
📠 01386 584596
e-mail: leasow@clara.net
Dir: *from Broadway B4632 to Winchcombe for 2m, turn R to Wormington then 1st on R*

Located to the South of the village, this 16th century former farmhouse has been lovingly restored to provide high standards of comfort. Bedrooms are filled with a wealth of homely extras and an attractive dining room is the setting for comprehensive breakfasts. An elegant library lounge is also available and a warm welcome is assured.
FACILITIES: 5 en suite 2 annexe en suite (2 fmly) (1 GF) No smoking TVB tea/coffee Direct dial from bedrooms Cen ht No coaches **PRICES:** s £35-£45; d £55-£75✱ **PARKING:** 10 **NOTES:** Closed Xmas & New Year
CARDS:

TVB means there are televisions in bedrooms
TVL means there's a television in the lounge
STV means satellite television.

LECHLADE Map 04 SU29

♦♦♦♦ Cambrai Lodge

Oak St GL7 3AY ☎ 01367 253173 & 07860 150467
Dir: *from Swindon N on A361 through Highwoth to Lechlade. Proceed through village to Royal Oak pub on left and Cambrai Lodge is a few yards along*
FACILITIES: 4 en suite (1 fmly) (1 GF) No smoking TVB tea/coffee Cen ht No coaches **PRICES:** s £29-£37; d £48-£60S **PARKING:** 12

♦♦♦ Five Bells Broadwell

Broadwell GL7 3QS ☎ 01367 860076
e-mail: trevorcooper@skynow.co.uk
Dir: *2m N of Lechlade turn right towards Carterton. At Kings Lane turn right, at bottom turn left, 400mtrs on right*
Standing in immaculate gardens in the village of Broadwell, this 16th-century inn has many original features including polished stone floors, exposed beams and open fireplaces. Imaginative food is offered in the cosy bars or dining rooms and the separately located bedrooms offer a range of practical and homely extras.
FACILITIES: 5 en suite No smoking in bedrooms No smoking in dining room No smoking in 1 lounge TVB tea/coffee No dogs Cen ht No children 14yrs Dinner Last d 9pm **PRICES:** d £50-£55✱ **MEALS:** Lunch £11-£15&alc Dinner £11-£15&alc✱ **PARKING:** 30 **NOTES:** Closed 26-27 Dec & 14-29 Jan rs Closed Mondays **CARDS:**

MINCHINHAMPTON Map 03 SO80

♦♦♦♦ Hyde Wood House

Cirencester Rd GL6 8PE ☎ 01453 885504 📠 01453 885504
e-mail: info@hydewoodhouse.co.uk
Dir: *from Stroud A419 towards Cirencester, after village of Chalford at top of hill turn right signed Minchinhampton, House 1m on right. From Cirencester A419 towards Stroud, after approx 8m turn left, signed Minchinhampton, House 1m*

Located on extensive mature grounds, this well proportioned mellow stone house provides bedrooms filled with a range of practical and homely extras. Comprehensive breakfasts are taken in an elegant dining room and a spacious comfortable lounge is also available. A warm welcome is assured and afternoon tea includes delicious home-made cake.
FACILITIES: 2 en suite (3 fmly) No smoking TVB No dogs Cen ht TVL No children 14yrs **PRICES:** d £45-£50✱ **LB PARKING:** 6

MORETON-IN-MARSH Map 04 SP13

♦♦♦♦ Rigside

Little Compton GL56 0RR ☎ 01608 674128 📠 01608 674128
e-mail: rigside@lineone.net
Dir: *on A44 midway between Chipping Norton and Moreton-in-Marsh opposite the 'Oil Well' garage*
Located in immaculate gardens east of the historic town centre, this extended detached house provides a range of homely bedrooms complimented by modern efficient bathrooms. Breakfast is taken in the attractive dining room and a comfortable lounge is also available for guest use.
FACILITIES: 4 rms (2 en suite) (1 GF) No smoking in bedrooms No smoking in dining room TVB tea/coffee No dogs (ex guide dogs) Cen ht TVL No children 12yrs No coaches **PRICES:** s £24-£33✱ **PARKING:** 8

NAILSWORTH Map 03 ST89

♦♦♦♦ Aaron Farm

Nympsfield Rd GL6 0ET ☎ 01453 833598 📠 01453 833626
e-mail: aaronfarm@aol.com
Dir: *off A46 at Nailsworth mini rdbt into Spring Hill this continues into Nympsfield Rd. Farm is 1m on left at top of hill*

Located in an elevated semi-rural position on the town's outskirts, this mellow stone former farmhouse has been sympathetically extended to provide spacious bedrooms filled with thoughtful extras. Breakfasts, making use of local produce, are taken in the cosy dining room and a comfortable guest lounge is also available.
FACILITIES: 3 en suite No smoking TVB tea/coffee Cen ht No coaches **PRICES:** s £30-£32; d £42-£44✱ **PARKING:** 6

♦♦♦♦ Highlands

Shortwood GL6 0SJ ☎ 01453 832591 📠 01453 833590
Dir: *at rdbt on A46 in Nailsworth take Nympsfield road turn left, pass bus station. Fork left at Brittania Inn follow signs for Wallow Green. Hotel opposite church*

This mellow stone house is located outside of the town in a pretty rural hamlet. The tastefully furnished bedrooms are filled with both practical and homely extras. A comfortable lounge area is available in addition to the elegant dining room, where mouth-watering breakfasts are served.
FACILITIES: 3 en suite (1 fmly) No smoking TVB tea/coffee Direct dial from bedrooms No dogs (ex guide dogs) Cen ht TVL No children 2yrs No coaches Last d 5pm **PRICES:** s fr £24; d fr £45✱ **LB PARKING:** 3 **CARDS:**

continued

NEWENT Map 03 SO72

♦♦♦ George Hotel

Church St GL18 1PV ☎ 01531 820203 📠 01531 822899

***Dir:** between Gloucester and Ross-on-Wye off B4215*

FACILITIES: 9 rms (4 en suite) (2 fmly) No smoking in bedrooms No smoking in area of dining room No smoking in 1 lounge STV TVB tea/coffee Licensed Cen ht Dinner Last d 9pm **PRICES:** s £25-£35; d £35-£45* **LB BB PARKING:** 14 **CARDS:**

NEWNHAM Map 03 SO61

♦♦♦♦ Swan House Country Guest House

Swan House, High St GL14 1BY ☎ 01594 516504 📠 01594 516177

e-mail: enquiries@swanhousenewnham.co.uk

***Dir:** on service road set back from A48 between clock tower & Ship PH.*

A warm welcome is assured at this elegant property, parts of which date from the 17th century. Sympathetic restoration is planned to highlight the intrinsic charm of this lovely building. Bedrooms are filled with both practical and homely extras and a comfortable guest lounge with honesty bar is provided in addition to a cosy dining room. Elaine Sheldrake was a Top Twenty Finalist in the AA Landlady of the Year Award 2002-2003.

FACILITIES: 6 en suite (1 GF) No smoking in dining room TVB tea/coffee Licensed Cen ht No coaches Dinner Last d 6pm **PRICES:** s £25-£35; d £50-£70* **LB PARKING:** 5 **NOTES:** Closed Xmas & New Year **CARDS:**

NORTHLEACH Map 04 SP11

♦♦♦♦ Northfield

Cirencester Rd GL54 3JL ☎ 01451 860427 📠 01451 860427

e-mail: nrthfield0@aol.com

***Dir:** just off A429 Northleach to Cirencester road, 1m from Northleach traffic lights. Well signed from main road*

Located south of this historic town, this Cotswold stone house offers homely and tastefully furnished bedrooms, two of which have direct access to the immaculate gardens. Tasty breakfasts and imaginative dinners are served in the elegant dining room and a comfortable guest lounge is also available.

FACILITIES: 2 en suite 1 annexe en suite (1 fmly) (3 GF) No smoking TVB tea/coffee No dogs Licensed Cen ht TVL No coaches Dinner Last d 7pm **PRICES:** s £30-£40; d £48-£54* **LB PARKING:** 10 **NOTES:** Closed 23-31 Dec **CARDS:**

OLD SODBURY Map 03 ST78

♦♦♦♦ The Sodbury House Hotel

Badminton Rd BS37 6LU ☎ 01454 312847 📠 01454 273105

e-mail: sodburyhouse.hotel@virgin.net

***Dir:** M4 junct 18 take A46 N. After 2m left onto A432 to Chipping Sodbury. Hotel on left in 1m*

This comfortably furnished, 19th-century farmhouse stands in six acres of grounds. Bedrooms are very well-equipped and include some located on the ground floor, while others are in buildings adjacent to the main house. Breakfast offers a varied choice and is served in the spacious breakfast room.

FACILITIES: 8 en suite 9 annexe en suite (2 fmly) (10 GF) No smoking in 8 bedrooms No smoking in dining room TVB tea/coffee Direct dial from bedrooms No dogs (ex guide dogs) Licensed Cen ht TVL Croquet lawn Petanque Dinner **PRICES:** s £47.50-£54; d £65-£90* **LB CONF:** Thtr 25 Class 25 Board 20 **PARKING:** 30 **CARDS:**

STONEHOUSE Map 03 SO80

Premier Collection

♦♦♦♦♦ Grey Cottage

Bath Rd, Leonard Stanley GL10 3LU ☎ 01453 822515 📠 01453 822515

***Dir:** leave M5 junct 13 onto A419. After lights right - Leonard Stanley, at T-junct turn left, Grey Cottage on right*

Ideally located for Stroud and the M5, a warm and genuine welcome is assured at this beautifully maintained Victorian house, standing in immaculate gardens. Bedrooms are

continued

adorned with a wealth of thoughtful extras, creating a really special 'home from home' feeling. Public areas include a comfortable lounge and elegant dining room, the latter being the venue for impressive dinners and sumptuous breakfasts.
FACILITIES: 3 en suite No smoking in bedrooms No smoking in dining room No smoking in 1 lounge TVB tea/coffee No dogs Licensed Cen ht TVL No children 10yrs No coaches Dinner Last d on reservation **PRICES:** s £40-£45; d £54-£65✱ **PARKING:** 7

Rectory Farmhouse

FACILITIES: 3 en suite No smoking TVB tea/coffee No dogs Cen ht No children 16yrs No coaches **PRICES:** d £68-£80✱ **PARKING:** 6

♦♦♦♦ Oaktree Farm
Little Haresfield GL10 3DS ☎ 01452 883323
e-mail: jackie@oaktreefarm.fsn.co.uk
Dir: *at Hardwicks off A38 onto B4008, over M5 junct 12. 2nd left turning and farm 400yds on right*
FACILITIES: 2 en suite No smoking TVB tea/coffee No dogs Cen ht TVL No coaches **PRICES:** s £25-£30; d £40-£50✱ **PARKING:** 2 **NOTES:** Closed Dec & Jan

♦♦♦ *Rose & Crown*
Nympsfield GL10 3TU ☎ 01453 860240 Fax 01453 860900
Dir: *turn off B4066 at Uley Peak, 0.75m to village. Inn in village centre (The Circle)*

Located in the pretty rural village of Nympsfield, this 17th century inn retains many original features including a magnificent vaulted beamed ceiling within the attractive dining room. Bedrooms are fitted with a good range of practical extras and the bars, with open log fires create a warm and inviting atmosphere.
FACILITIES: 3 en suite (2 fmly) No smoking in bedrooms No smoking in dining room TVB tea/coffee Cen ht Dinner Last d 9.30pm **PARKING:** 20
CARDS:

♦♦♦♦ Kings Head Inn & Restaurant
The Green, Bledington OX7 6XQ ☎ 01608 658365
Fax 01608 658902
e-mail: kingshead@orr-ewing.com
Dir: *4m SE off B4450*

Located on the village green with its duck-populated river, in the pretty village of Bledington, this 15th century inn retains many original features, as well as rustic furniture and open fires. The spacious, thoughtfully furnished bedrooms are located in sympathetically converted outbuildings. The inn enjoys a good reputation for imaginative food.
FACILITIES: 6 en suite 6 annexe en suite No smoking in bedrooms No smoking in dining room No smoking in 1 lounge TVB tea/coffee Direct dial from bedrooms No dogs (ex guide dogs) Cen ht TVL No coaches Dinner Last d 9.30pm **PRICES:** s £50-£100; d £70-£100✱ **MEALS:** Dinner £14.50-£18.50&alc✱ **PARKING:** 24 **NOTES:** Closed 25-26 Dec
CARDS:

STOW-ON-THE-WOLD — Map 04 SP12

Premier Collection

♦♦♦♦♦ Rectory Farmhouse
Lower Swell GL54 1LH ☎ 01451 832351
e-mail: rectory.farmhouse@cw-warwick.co.uk
Dir: *from A429 at Stow-on-the-Wold. B4608 signed Lower Swell, left before Golden Ball Inn into a private Road. Farmhouse on right at far end of gravel drive*
Located in the pretty hamlet of Lower Swell, this 17th-century former farmhouse has been sympathetically renovated to provide comfortable accommodation with a host of thoughtful extras. Carefully chosen furnishings compliment the original features and a welcoming atmosphere prevails. Breakfast is served in the kitchen-dining room, or in summer, in the conservatory overlooking the gardens.

continued

♦♦♦♦ Crestow House
GL54 1JX ☎ 01451 830969 Fax 01451 832129
e-mail: Fsimonetti@btinternet.com
Dir: *at junct of A429 and B4068*
This beautiful Queen Anne house is peacefully located in its own delightful grounds close to the town centre. Spacious public rooms include an elegant drawing room, an adjacent conservatory and a lovely morning room where hearty breakfast are taken round one large table. Large, individually designed bedrooms are beautifully furnished and thoughtfully equipped.
FACILITIES: 4 en suite No smoking TVB tea/coffee No dogs Cen ht No children 15yrs No coaches Outdoor swimming pool (heated) Sauna Gymnasium Croquet lawn **PRICES:** s £45; d £60-£75✱
PARKING: 4 **NOTES:** Closed Jan **CARDS:**

England

STOW ON THE WOLD continued

♦♦♦♦ Aston House

Broadwell GL56 0TJ ☎ 01451 830475
e-mail: fja@netcomuk.co.uk
Dir: *from Stow-on-the-Wold take A429 towards Moreton-in-Marsh. Ignore 1st right turn; approx 1m further turn right to Broadwell at x-road. Aston house 1st on left, 0.5m from main road.*
FACILITIES: 3 en suite (1 GF) No smoking TVB tea/coffee No dogs Cen ht No children 10yrs No coaches **PRICES:** d £47-£50✳ **PARKING:** 3 **NOTES:** Closed Dec-Jan

♦♦♦ Corsham Field *(SP217249)*

Bledington Rd GL54 1JH ☎ 01451 831750 Mr R Smith
Dir: *take A436 out of Stow-on-the-Wold towards Chipping Norton. After 1m fork right onto B4450 Bledington road. 1st farm on right*
Located in an elevated position offering superb views of the surrounding countryside, modern practically equipped bedrooms are within two separate houses and the farm is popular with families and walking groups. Comprehensive breakfasts are taken in a spacious dining room, which also contains a lounge section.
FACILITIES: 7 rms (5 en suite) (3 fmly) (2 GF) No smoking in 3 bedrooms No smoking in dining room No smoking in lounges TVB tea/coffee Cen ht 100 acres arable **PRICES:** s £25-£35; d £40-£50✳ **LB PARKING:** 10

♦♦♦ Limes

Evesham Rd GL54 1EJ ☎ 01451 830034 📠 01451 830034
Dir: *turn off A429 towards Evesham on A424. The Limes 800yds on left*
Just a few minutes' walk from the village centre, this Victorian family house provides comfortable homely accommodation, including four-poster and ground floor bedrooms. A warm welcome is extended to all guests, many of whom return on a regular basis to enjoy the delights of this beautiful area. A spacious guest lounge is available and breakfast is served in the light and airy dining room.
FACILITIES: 4 en suite 1 annexe en suite (1 fmly) No smoking in bedrooms No smoking in dining room STV TVB tea/coffee Cen ht TVL No coaches **PRICES:** s £28-£44; d £44-£50✳ **PARKING:** 4 **NOTES:** Closed 24 Dec-2 Jan

♦♦♦ Woodlands

Upper Swell GL54 1EW ☎ 01451 832346
e-mail: stay@the-woodlands.co.uk
Dir: *1m from Stow-on-the-Wold, in Upper Swell on B4077*

For those wishing to explore the nearby Cotswold villages, this modern home located in the small hamlet of Upper Swell enjoys delightful rural views over the adjacent countryside and provides guests with comfortably appointed rooms. Breakfast is served at shared tables in the cosy dining room.
FACILITIES: 5 en suite (1 fmly) (1 GF) No smoking TVB tea/coffee No dogs Cen ht No children 12yrs No coaches **PRICES:** s fr £30; d fr £52✳ **PARKING:** 5

STROUD

Map 03 SO80

Premier Collection

♦♦♦♦♦ Hunters Lodge

Dr Browns Rd, Minchinhampton GL6 9BT
☎ 01453 883588 📠 01453 731449
Dir: *from Cirencester A419 Stroud. Left to Aston Down, over cattle grid take 3rd turn left, Lodge on right. From Stroud A46 towards Nailsworth. At rdbt left to T-junct. Turn right and lodge on right*

Located overlooking unspoilt Minchinhampton Common, this mellow Cotswold stone house stands in immaculate gardens. The fine period furniture and memorabilia all add to the building's intrinsic charm. Ground floor areas include an elegant dining room, a comfortable and superb conservatory. Bedrooms are filled with a wealth of thoughtful extras and proprietors have an extensive knowledge of the area and its many attractions.
FACILITIES: 3 en suite (1 fmly) No smoking TVB tea/coffee No dogs (ex guide dogs) Cen ht TVL No children 10yrs No coaches Golf 18 **PRICES:** s £30-£35; d £48-£50✳ **PARKING:** 8 **NOTES:** Closed Xmas

Premier Collection

♦♦♦♦♦ The Priory

Priory Fields, Horsley GL6 0PT ☎ 01453 834282 & 0800 0833484 📠 01453 833750
e-mail: theprioryhorsley@onetel.net.uk
Dir: *off A46 Cheltenham/Bath road in Nailsworth onto the B4058 signed Horsley in 1m turn left at Bell & Castle Pub in 180yds The Priory on the right through stone pillars*
Located in the rural hamlet of Horsley, this impressive Victorian house has been sympathetically renovated and provides bedrooms filled with a wealth of thoughtful extras. Public areas include a spacious drawing room with open fire, a cosy sitting room, and an elegant dining room where imaginative breakfasts are taken.
FACILITIES: 10 en suite (1 GF) No smoking in bedrooms No smoking in 1 lounge TVB tea/coffee Direct dial from bedrooms No dogs (ex guide dogs) Licensed Cen ht TVL No children 11yrs No coaches Pool Table outside kennels available for guests' dogs Dinner **PRICES:** s £45-£65; d £75-£95✳ **LB PARKING:** 18 **CARDS:**

♦♦♦♦ Hyde Crest

Cirencester Rd GL6 8PE ☎ 01453 731631
e-mail: HydeCrest@compuserve.com
Dir: *off A419, 7m (Cirencester to Stroud) at sign marked Minchinhampton and Aston Down. Hyde Crest 3rd house on right opposite Ragged Cot pub*
Hyde Crest sits on the edge of the picturesque village of Minchinhampton overlooking unspoilt commonland. Bedrooms

continued

Hyde Crest

are tastefully decorated and all are located on the ground floor, each with the added bonus of individual patio areas. Scrumptious breakfasts are served in the small dining room which also doubles as a lounge.

FACILITIES: 3 en suite (3 GF) No smoking TVB tea/coffee Cen ht TVL No children 7yrs No coaches **PRICES:** s fr £30; d fr £50✳ **PARKING:** 6

♦♦♦ Downfield Hotel

134 Caincross Rd GL5 4HN ☎ 01453 764496 📠 01453 753150
e-mail: info@downfieldhotel.co.uk
Dir: *1m W on A419 from Stroud, or 4m E from M5 junct 13*

Ideally located west of the town centre, close to the M5, this long established hotel is popular with both business and leisure travellers. A range of bedrooms to suit all requirements is available with a number of ground floor bedrooms offered. The open plan public areas include a comfortable lounge area, traditional restaurant and convivial bar offering a good range of wines by the glass.

FACILITIES: 21 rms (11 en suite) (4 fmly) No smoking in dining room TVB tea/coffee Direct dial from bedrooms Licensed Cen ht TVL Dinner Last d 8.15pm **PRICES:** s £28-£42; d £45-£60✳ **LB PARKING:** 25
CARDS:

♦♦♦ George

Frocester GL10 3TQ ☎ 01453 822302 📠 01453 791612
e-mail: enquiries@georgeinn.fsnet.co.uk
Dir: *M5 junct 13, onto A419 towards Stroud, at rdbt take Eastington exit. Through Eastington, turn left in front of Kings Head to Frocester. Pub is 400yds past railway bridge on right*

Located in the village of Frocester, this Georgian posting house retains many original features. Public areas include a superb function suite. Bedrooms are being steadily upgraded and the inn enjoys a good reputation for food, real ale and good old traditional hospitality!

FACILITIES: 9 rms (6 en suite) (4 fmly) No smoking in 3 bedrooms No smoking in area of dining room TVB tea/coffee Cen ht Pool Table Dinner Last d 9.30pm **PRICES:** s fr £39; d fr £59✳ **LB MEALS:** Lunch £12-£15alc Dinner £15-£20alc✳ **CONF:** Thtr 60 Class 40 Board 25 Del from £55 ✳
PARKING: 30 **CARDS:**

England

TEWKESBURY Map 03 SO83

♦♦♦ Willow Cottages

Shuthonger Common GL20 6ED ☎ 01684 298599
Fax 01684 298599
e-mail: robbrdl@aol.com

Dir: *1m N of Tewkesbury, on A38, right hand side or 1m S of M50 junct 1, on A38, left hand side*

Located north of Tewkesbury in pretty rural surroundings, this well maintained house offers comfortable homely bedrooms with efficient modern bathrooms and a cosy pine furnished breakfast room. An excellent base for those working in or visiting this picturesque area.

FACILITIES: 3 en suite (1 fmly) No smoking in bedrooms No smoking in dining room TVB tea/coffee Cen ht No coaches Dinner Last d noon **PRICES:** s fr £26; d fr £50 **LB PARKING:** 6

TIRLEY Map 03 SO82

♦♦♦ Town Street Farm

GL19 4HG ☎ 01452 780442 Fax 01452 780890
e-mail: townstreetfarm@hotmail.com

Dir: *M5 junct 9 to Tewkesbury. Take A387 towards Gloucester, then onto B4213 at traffic lights. 3m over River Severn, turn at x-rds towards Chaceley, 1st farm on right*

FACILITIES: 3 en suite (1 fmly) No smoking in dining room No smoking in lounges TVB tea/coffee Cen ht TVL No coaches Tennis (hard) **PRICES:** s fr £26; d fr £46* **PARKING:** 6

ULEY Map 03 ST79

♦♦♦♦ Hodgecombe Farm *(ST783993)*

GL11 5AN ☎ 01453 860365 Fax 01453 860365 Mrs C Bevan
e-mail: hodgecombe.farm@virgin.net

Dir: *In Uley on B4066 follow signs for Coaley via Fop Street, after approx. 1m take farm track on sharp left bend*

Located on the Cotswold Way and offering simply stunning views to the Malverns, River Severn and Forest of Dean, this impressive Victorian house has been sensitively renovated and has many original features, such as slate floors. Bedrooms are spacious and filled with thoughtful extras which typify the owners hospitable approach. Home-made bread and jam are features of the tasty breakfasts and imaginative dinners are available by prior arrangement.

FACILITIES: 3 rms (1 en suite) No smoking TV2B tea/coffee No dogs (ex guide dogs) Cen ht No children 5yrs 3 acres non-working Dinner Last d previous day **PRICES:** d £42-£46* **PARKING:** 6 **NOTES:** Closed Nov-Feb

WINCHCOMBE Map 03 SP02

Premier Collection

♦♦♦♦♦ Isbourne Manor House

Castle St GL54 5JA ☎ 01242 602281 Fax 01242 602281
e-mail: felicity@isbourne-manor.co.uk

Dir: *on B4632 between Cheltenham and Broadway. In centre of village turn into Castle St and house on left before bridge*

Tucked away in quiet gardens and bordered by the River Isbourne, this listed part-Georgian and part-Elizabethan house is just a couple of minutes' walk from both the Cotswold countryside and town amenities. Comfortable and elegant surroundings feature carefully chosen fine furnishings, creating a relaxed environment. Bedrooms are individual in character and include the thoughtful extras that reflect the attention to detail evident throughout. Breakfast makes use of local produce, with home-made marmalades and jams a speciality.

FACILITIES: 3 en suite No smoking TVB tea/coffee No dogs Cen ht No coaches **PRICES:** s £45-£70; d £60-£85 **LB PARKING:** 3 **NOTES:** Closed 25-26 Dec

♦♦♦♦ Postlip Hall Farm *(SP020280)*

GL54 5AQ ☎ 01242 603351 Fax 01242 603351
Mr & Mrs J Albutt
e-mail: val@postliphallfarm.free-online.co.uk

Dir: *leave Winchcombe on B4632 towards Cheltenham, 1m up hill on left sign for 'Farmhouse B&B'. Turn left and keep bearing left 0.75m up drive*

Located in an elevated position, this mellow Cotswold stone house and gardens are immaculately maintained. Stunning views of the surrounding countryside are a feature of the homely bedrooms and ground floor areas include a spacious sitting room, an elegant dining room and a magnificent conservatory with direct access to the grounds.

FACILITIES: 3 en suite No smoking TVB tea/coffee No dogs (ex guide dogs) Cen ht TVL Golf 18 Riding Riding Golf available nearby 300 acres beef sheep **PRICES:** s £25-£35; d £42-£50* **PARKING:** 8 **NOTES:** Closed Xmas

♦♦♦♦ Sudeley Hill Farm *(SP038276)*

GL54 5JB ☎ 01242 602344 Fax 01242 602344
Mrs B Scudamore
e-mail: scudamore4@aol.com

Dir: *turn off B4632 in Winchcombe into Castle St, White Hart Inn on corner. Farm 0.75m on left*

Located on an 800 acre mixed arable and sheep farm, this 15th century mellow stone house is full of original features including log fires and exposed beams. Genuine hospitality is always on offer here with a thoroughly relaxed and welcoming atmosphere. The comfortable bedrooms are filled with thoughtful extras and memorable breakfasts are taken in the elegant dining room overlooking the immaculate gardens.

FACILITIES: 3 en suite (1 fmly) No smoking in bedrooms No smoking in dining room TVB tea/coffee No dogs (ex guide dogs) Cen ht TVL 800 acres sheep arable **PRICES:** s fr £35 d £48-£50 **PARKING:** 10 **NOTES:** Closed Xmas

If an establishment name appears in *italics*, details have not been confirmed for 2003.

continued

♦♦♦♦ Wesley House
High St GL54 5LJ ☎ 01242 602366 01242 609046
e-mail: reservations@wesleyhouse.co.uk
Dir: *situated on the high street in the center of Winchcombe*

This splendid half-timbered15th century house takes its name from John Wesley, who is reputed to have stayed here in 1779. The charming bedrooms have many thoughtful extras and the elegant restaurant is the setting for excellent dinners and memorable breakfasts, making use of the finest of local produce.
FACILITIES: 5 en suite No smoking in bedrooms No smoking in dining room STV TVB tea/coffee Direct dial from bedrooms No dogs (ex guide dogs) Licensed Cen ht Dinner Last d 9.30pm **PRICES:** s £40-£55; d £70-£80✳ **LB CARDS:**

See advertisement on page 209

♦♦♦ 2 Dryfield Cottage
GL54 5AG ☎ 01242 676091 01242 663946
e-mail: plcook@ukonline.co.uk
Dir: *On B4632 towards Cheltenham, establishment signed on left. Pass through electric gates & follow the road left as far as possible*
Located two miles south of this historic town, the bedroom accommodation here is in a purpose-built extension which commands stunning views of the countryside. A generous breakfast is served in the family kitchen and a warm welcome is assured.
FACILITIES: 1 annexe en suite (1 fmly) No smoking TVB tea/coffee No dogs (ex guide dogs) Cen ht No coaches **PRICES:** s £25-£30; d £44-£50✳ **LB PARKING:** 2 **NOTES:** Closed 24-28 Dec

GREATER LONDON

London Plans 1 & 2 appear after the atlas section at the back of the guide.

BRENTFORD Plan 1 C3

Primrose House
56 Boston Gardens TW8 9LP ☎ 020 8568 5573
At the time of going to press the Diamond classification for this establishment had not been confirmed. Please check the AA website www.theAA.com for up-to-date information.
FACILITIES: 2 rms (1 en suite)

CRANFORD Plan 1 A3

See Heathrow Airport

CROYDON Map 04 TQ36

♦♦♦♦ Kirkdale Hotel
22 St Peter's Rd CR0 1HD ☎ 020 8688 5898 020 8680 6001
e-mail: reservations@kirkdalehotel.co.uk
Dir: *M25 junct 7 follow signs to Croydon on A23, straight over rdbt onto A235 to Croydon, at HSBC bank on right turn into Abredeen road. Hotel at top of road*
Close to the town centre, this late Victorian hotel is constantly being improved and restored with many original features still visible. Public areas include a small lounge bar and an attractive breakfast room. Bedrooms are well-equipped with good facilities, and there is a sheltered patio for the summer months.
FACILITIES: 19 en suite (4 fmly) (6 GF) No smoking in bedrooms No smoking in dining room TVB tea/coffee Direct dial from bedrooms No dogs Licensed Cen ht TVL No coaches **PRICES:** s £45-£75; d £58-£80✳ **PARKING:** 12 **NOTES:** Closed Xmas & New Year **CARDS:**

FELTHAM Plan 1 A2

See Heathrow Airport

HAYES Plan 1 A3

See Heathrow Airport.

HEATHROW AIRPORT Map 04 TQ07

See also Slough (Berkshire)

♦♦♦♦ The Cottage
150-152 High St, Cranford TW5 9WB ☎ 020 8897 1815
020 8897 3117
e-mail: bermuthecottage@tinyworld.co.uk
Dir: *leave M4 junct 3 onto A312 towards Feltham and continue to traffic lights & turn left. Continue and turn left after 1st pub on left Jolly Gardner*

This hotel is so peacefully situated, tucked away in a cul de sac behind the High Street, that it seems a million miles from Heathrow, but is in fact only 10 minutes away. Nearby attractions include Windsor Castle and Hampton Court. Accommodation is comfortable, attractively presented and there's secure parking.
FACILITIES: 17 en suite (2 fmly) (12 GF) No smoking TVB tea/coffee No dogs Cen ht TVL PRICES: s £49.50-£59.50; d £67✳ **PARKING:** 12
CARDS:

England

HEATHROW AIRPORT continued

♦♦♦♦ Harmondsworth Hall

Summerhouse Ln, Harmondsworth Village UB7 0BG
☎ 020 8759 1824 & 07713104229 📠 020 8897 6385
e-mail: Elaine@harmondsworthhall.com
Dir: *M4 junct 4 left onto A3044 Holloway Ln towards Harmondsworth. After 3rd rdbt into Harmondsworth village after Crown Pub on left next left into Summerhouse Ln*

Hidden away in the old part of the village, this guest house is ideally located for the airport and has convenient access to the motorways. Each bedroom is individually furnished and decorated and feature a good range of extra facilities. Breakfast is served in an attractive wood panelled dining room and there is a spacious lounge.

FACILITIES: 10 rms (8 en suite) (4 fmly) (2 GF) No smoking in 4 bedrooms No smoking in dining room No smoking in lounges TVB tea/coffee Direct dial from bedrooms Licensed Cen ht TVL No coaches Last d by arrangement **PRICES:** s £45-£55; d £55-£65✱ **LB CONF:** Board 12 **PARKING:** 8 **CARDS:**

♦♦♦ Longford

550 Bath Rd, Longford UB7 0EE ☎ 01753 682969
📠 01753 794189
Dir: *approx 1.5m from M25 junct 14*

Ideally located for the airport and only minutes away from the motorway network, this popular guest house dates back to the 17th century and retains many of its original features. Bedrooms are spacious and individually decorated. Downstairs there is a comfortable guest lounge and dining room.

FACILITIES: 5 rms No smoking in bedrooms No smoking in dining room TVB tea/coffee No dogs Cen ht TVL No children 10yrs No coaches **PRICES:** s fr £35; d fr £45✱ **PARKING:** 5 **NOTES:** Closed Xmas week **CARDS:**

♦♦♦ Shepiston Lodge

31 Shepiston Ln UB3 1LJ ☎ 020 8573 0266 📠 020 8569 2536
e-mail: shepistonlodge@aol.com
Dir: *leave M4 junct follow signpost for Hayes, from slip road onto Shepiston Lane. 50 yds from fire station and almost opposite Great Western pub*

Located close to Heathrow airport, this small private hotel offers bedrooms that are smartly presented and suitably equipped. Dinner is available on request and a freshly cooked breakfast is offered in the spacious dining room. Ample parking and an informal bar are additional features.

FACILITIES: 22 en suite (2 fmly) (9 GF) No smoking in dining room No smoking in 1 lounge TVB tea/coffee No dogs (ex guide dogs) Licensed Cen ht TVL Dinner Last d 6pm **PRICES:** s £46; d £65✱ **CONF:** Thtr 70 Class 50 Board 30 Del from £116.75 ✱ **PARKING:** 20 **CARDS:**

Places with this symbol are Inns.

♦♦ Lampton

47 Lampton Rd TW3 1JG ☎ 020 8570 0056 📠 020 8577 1220
e-mail: ppadda@talk21.com
Dir: *centre of Hounslow, 50yds from tube station, accesible from Bath Road from Heathrow Airport and A4 Great West Road at junct of Spring Grove Road*

This guest house is ideally situated in the centre of Hounslow and provides practical accommodation, all with en suite facilities. The breakfast area is quite compact and guests may sometimes need to share a table.

FACILITIES: 20 en suite (5 fmly) (4 GF) No smoking in dining room No smoking in lounges STV TVB tea/coffee Direct dial from bedrooms No dogs (ex guide dogs) Cen ht No children 4yrs **PRICES:** s £45-£48; d £55-£60✱ **PARKING:** 13 **CARDS:**

♦♦ Shalimar Hotel

215-223 Staines Rd TW3 3JJ ☎ 020 8577 7070 & 8572 281 & (free) 0500 238239 📠 020 8569 6789
e-mail: shalimarhotel@aol.com
Dir: *exit M4 junct 3, to Hounslow, at rdbt turn left, at next rdbt bear right, at 3rd traffic lights turn right, next lights turn left (The Independents)*

This centrally located hotel is well-situated for access to Heathrow Airport and the surrounding area. Shalimar Hotel offers simply decorated accommodation which is equipped to a good standard. The public areas include a smart open-plan restaurant, a bar and there is a lounge overlooking the garden.

FACILITIES: 39 rms (29 en suite) (5 fmly) No smoking in 2 bedrooms No smoking in area of dining room TVB tea/coffee Direct dial from bedrooms No dogs (ex guide dogs) Licensed Cen ht TVL **PRICES:** s £55; d £65✱ **LB CONF:** Thtr 150 Class 150 Board 150 **PARKING:** 20 **CARDS:**

♦♦ Skylark

297 Bath Rd TW3 3DB ☎ 020 8577 8455 📠 020 8577 8741
e-mail: info@skylark-66.com
Dir: *100yds from Hounslow tube station. Left at station, walk for 100yds, establishment on left. By car exit junct 3, follow A3006 towards Hounslow West, pass station 100 yds on left*

continued

Skylark Bed & Breakfast Guest House

The location of this guesthouse is ideal for access to London or Heathrow Airport, by road or by public transport. Bedrooms vary in size and are practical in style.

FACILITIES: 18 en suite (3 fmly) (9 GF) No smoking in 4 bedrooms STV TVB tea/coffee Direct dial from bedrooms No dogs (ex guide dogs) Cen ht Dinner Last d 6pm **PRICES:** s £39.95-£50; d £49.95-£65* LB **PARKING:** 8 **CARDS:**

♦♦ Civic Guest House

87/93 Lampton Rd TW3 4DP ☎ 020 8572 5107 & 8570 1851 Fax 020 8814 0203

e-mail: enquiries@civicguesthouse.freeserve.co.uk

Dir: *exit M4 junct 3 onto A306, left onto A4 towards Hounslow, right at BP station onto A3005 (Jersey rd) right at mini rdbt, left at Blackhorse Pub. Guest house 0.5m on the left handside*

FACILITIES: 28 rms (14 en suite) (9 fmly) No smoking in dining room STV TVB tea/coffee No dogs (ex guide dogs) Cen ht **PRICES:** s £45-£50; d £58-£65* **PARKING:** 12 **CARDS:**

HORNCHURCH — Map 05 TQ58

♦♦♦ Dorothea Bed & Breakfast

26 Wakerfield Close, Emerson Park RM11 2TH

☎ 01708 702063 Fax 01708 781305

e-mail: rrayment@cwctv.net

Dir: *from M25 junct 29 take A127 towards London (3m) left at 1st traffic lights (Kwikfit on corner). In 0.5m just past college left immediately behind college into Garland Way, keep right at pond into Wakerfield Close*

Expect a warm welcome from the caring hosts at this charming detached property situated just a short drive from the A127 and within easy walking distance of the town centre. The individually decorated bedrooms are tastefully furnished and thoughtfully equipped with many useful extras. Breakfast is served in the attractive dining room, which overlooks the garden, and guests have the use of a cosy lounge with plush furnishings.

FACILITIES: 5 rms (1 en suite) (1 fmly) No smoking in 3 bedrooms No smoking in dining room No smoking in lounges TVB tea/coffee No dogs (ex guide dogs) Cen ht No coaches Croquet lawn Jacuzzi **PRICES:** s £25-£30; d £50-£60* **PARKING:** 4

England

HOUNSLOW Plan 1 B2

See **Heathrow Airport**

ILFORD Plan 1 H5

♦♦♦ *Park Hotel*

327 Cranbrook Rd IG1 4UE ☎ 020 8554 9616 & 020 8554 7187 020 8518 2700
e-mail: parkhotelilford@netscapeonline.co.uk
Dir: *on A123 just south of junct with A12, Gantshill Rbt*
This family run guest house is located opposite Valentines Park and is close to the town centre. Bedrooms vary, but are simply furnished and suitably equipped. Guests have the use of a lounge and evening meals are available by prior arrangement.
FACILITIES: 20 rms (17 en suite) (3 fmly) STV TVB tea/coffee Licensed Cen ht TVL Dinner Last d 7.45pm **PARKING:** 23 **CARDS:**

♦♦♦ Woodville

10-12 Argyle Rd IG1 3BQ ☎ 020 8478 3779 020 8478 6282
e-mail: cass@woodville-guesthouse.co.uk
Dir: *M25-M11 Sthbound A12 towards Chelmsford/Southend, 1st rdbt 4th turning to Cranbrook Road, straight on past 2 sets traffic lights next right into Beal Road, 2nd left Argyle Road*

Woodville is a conversion of three large terraced houses located in a mainly residential road. The railway station, with its fast links to London, is within walking distance. The public rooms are comfortable and the bedrooms well-equipped.
FACILITIES: 16 rms (6 en suite) (5 fmly) No smoking in dining room STV TVB No dogs (ex guide dogs) Cen ht **PRICES:** s £35-£47; d £45-£60✱ **PARKING:** 11

See advertisement on opposite page

♦♦ Cranbrook Hotel

22-24 Coventry Rd IG1 4QR ☎ 020 8554 6544 & 4765 020 8518 1463
Dir: *exit A406 E onto A118, at top turn onto A123, second turning on right, at Ilford Station turn left, second right*

continued

Offering a relaxed atmosphere, this long-established hotel is situated close to the town centre and Gants Hill underground station. Public areas include a bar-lounge and a beamed dining room where a three-course set-price dinner menu is offered Monday to Thursday.
FACILITIES: 30 rms (26 en suite) (5 fmly) No smoking in 10 bedrooms No smoking in dining room STV TVB tea/coffee Direct dial from bedrooms Licensed Cen ht TVL **PRICES:** s £31-£45; d £42-£59✱ **LB CONF:** Class 35 Board 35 **PARKING:** 30 **CARDS:**

See advert under E4 (London)

NORTHWOOD Plan 1 A6

♦♦♦ Frithwood House

31 Frithwood Av HA6 3LY ☎ 01923 827864 01923 824720
e-mail: frithwood_31@hotmail.com
Dir: *A404 to Northwood. Off Watford Rd past RAF & NATO Headquarters*

This Edwardian guest house is located in quite residential surroundings and the style is very relaxed and informal, bedrooms vary in size and shape, all are well equipped and comfortable. Guests have the use of a TV lounge, and breakfast is served communally in the kitchen/dining room.
FACILITIES: 12 rms (9 en suite) (4 fmly) (3 GF) No smoking in bedrooms No smoking in dining room STV TVB Direct dial from bedrooms No dogs (ex guide dogs) Cen ht TVL **PRICES:** s £30-£40; d £50-£60✱ **PARKING:** 10 **CARDS:**

PURLEY Map 04 TQ36

♦♦♦ Arran Court

1 Briar Hill CR8 3LF ☎ 020 8645 9101 020 8645 9101
This large Tudor-style house is set in over an acre of well-presented gardens and caters for female guests only. The house is located in a peaceful residential area just a few minutes from the restaurants and amenities of Purley. Bedrooms are comfortably appointed and a continental breakfast is served around one table in the kitchen/dining room.
FACILITIES: 3 rms (1 en suite) No smoking TVB tea/coffee No dogs (ex guide dogs) Cen ht **PRICES:** s £38-£45; d £60✱ **PARKING:** 7
NOTES: Closed Xmas/New Year

ROMFORD Map 05 TQ58

♦♦♦ Havering Road Guest House

2 Havering Rd RM1 4QU ☎ 01708 732302
e-mail: vbuenavista2@aol.com
Dir: *off A12 onto B175, 1st bungalow on right*
Expect a warm welcome at this friendly, family run guest house situated just a short walk from the town centre and railway station. The attractive bedrooms have brightly co-ordinated soft furnishings and are thoughtfully equipped. Breakfast is served at individual tables in the smart dining room.
FACILITIES: 4 en suite TVB tea/coffee No dogs Cen ht No coaches **PRICES:** d £45✱ **PARKING:** 8

continued

♦♦♦ The Orchard Guest House

81 Eastern Rd RM1 3PB ☎ 01708 744099 Fax 01708 768881
e-mail: johnrt@globalnet.co.uk
Dir: *turn off main road into Junction Rd opposite Romford Police Station, Eastern Rd is 3rd turn on right*

This impressive Edwardian house is situated in a mainly residential area on the outskirts of town. The Orchard offers comfortable, homely bedrooms with modern facilities. There is a large, pretty garden available for guests' use during the summer.

FACILITIES: 5 rms (1 en suite) (2 fmly) TVB tea/coffee No dogs (ex guide dogs) Cen ht TVL No coaches **PRICES:** s £30-£40; d £45-£50* **PARKING:** 6

SURBITON — Plan 1 C1

♦♦ Warwick Lodge

319-321 Ewell Rd KT6 7BX ☎ 0208 296 0516 & 399 5837
Fax 0208 296 0517
e-mail: reception@warwicklodge.activehotels.com
Dir: *Turn off A3 onto A240 towards Kingston. Warwick Lodge is 0.5m on the right just before Police Station*

Warwick Lodge is conveniently located for access to the A3. This smart guest house offers a variety of rooms, many of which have been comfortably and smartly refurbished.

FACILITIES: 19 rms (12 en suite) (4 fmly) (6 GF) No smoking in 7 bedrooms No smoking in dining room TVB Direct dial from bedrooms No dogs (ex guide dogs) Cen ht TVL **PRICES:** s £38-£48; d £48-£58* **PARKING:** 19 **NOTES:** Closed 22 Dec-2 Jan **CARDS:**

SUTTON — Map 04 TQ26

♦♦♦ Ashling Tara Hotel

50 Rosehill SM1 3EU ☎ 020 8641 6142 Fax 020 8644 7872
Dir: *opposite Rose Hill Park, on A297 0.5m from Rosehill rdbt*

An established family run property, which has gained a loyal following over the years. Bedrooms are split between the main building and a separate house. All are smartly decorated and well-equipped. Spacious public areas include a cosy lounge, well-stocked bar and a bright dining room.

FACILITIES: 20 en suite (2 fmly) (11 GF) No smoking in 10 bedrooms No smoking in dining room TVB tea/coffee Direct dial from bedrooms No dogs Licensed Cen ht TVL Dinner Last d 8.45pm **PRICES:** s £45-£75; d £70-£85* **LB** **PARKING:** 25 **CARDS:**

10/12 Argyle Road, Ilford, Essex
Tel: 0208 478 3779 Fax: 0208 478 6282

A warm and friendly atmosphere pervades this family run business. The bedrooms are comfortable. A beamed dining room, a lovely garden and terrace make this a delightful stay. Rooms on ground floor and first floor and some rooms en suite. Families with children particularly welcome parking available.

WEMBLEY — Plan 1 C5

♦♦♦ Arena Hotel

6 Forty Ln HA9 9EB ☎ 020 8908 0670 & 020 8904 0019
Fax 020 8908 2007
e-mail: enquiry@arenahotel.fsnet.co.uk
Dir: *M1 North Circular close to stadium*

This constantly improving long-established hotel is located a few minutes drive from the North Circular Kingsbury turn off and is popular with commercial customers and visitors to the area's attractions. The bedrooms are practically equipped and there is a cosy lounge also available for guest use.

FACILITIES: 13 en suite (3 fmly) No smoking in dining room STV TVB tea/coffee Direct dial from bedrooms No dogs (ex guide dogs) Cen ht TVL **PRICES:** s £45-£49; d £55-£59* **PARKING:** 15 **CARDS:**

England

WEMBLEY continued

♦♦ Adelphi Hotel

4 Forty Ln HA9 9EB ☎ 020 8904 5629 📠 020 8908 5314
e-mail: adel@dial.pipex.com & enquiry@adelphihotel.fsnet.co.uk
Dir: *last exit of M1, right at rdbt onto A406 (N circular rd) for 1.5m. Upon reaching 2nd exit signposted Kingsbury turn off for Adelphi hotel*

Located a few minutes drive from the North Circular Road, this modernised hotel is popular with commercial contractors and visitors to the local conference centres.
FACILITIES: 13 rms (9 en suite) (2 fmly) No smoking in dining room STV TVB tea/coffee Direct dial from bedrooms No dogs Cen ht TVL No coaches **PRICES:** s £35-£42; d £45-£55* **PARKING:** 12 **CARDS:**

WEST DRAYTON Map 04 TQ04

See **Heathrow Airport**

GREATER MANCHESTER

ALTRINCHAM Map 07 SJ78

Premier Collection

♦♦♦♦♦ Ash Farm Country

Park Ln, Little Bollington WA14 4TJ ☎ 0161 929 9290
📠 0161 928 5002
e-mail: jan@ashfarm97.fsnet.co.uk
Dir: *turn off A56 beside Stamford Arms*

Peacefully located on a country lane, this 18th-century farmhouse is home to retired snooker player David Taylor and his wife Janice. Bedrooms boast handmade furniture - one has a huge seven foot bed. The many personal touches include home-made biscuits, fresh fruit, bathrobes and hot water bottles for cooler nights. The breakfast area is full of character, and breakfast is served at a large oak table.

continued

FACILITIES: 3 rms (2 en suite) No smoking TVB tea/coffee Direct dial from bedrooms No dogs (ex guide dogs) Cen ht No children 15yrs No coaches **PRICES:** s £45-£52; d £58-£70* **PARKING:** 6 **NOTES:** Closed 22 Dec-5 Jan **CARDS:**

♦♦♦♦ *The Old Packet House*

Navigation Rd, Broadheath WA14 1LW ☎ 0161 929 1331
📠 0161 233 0048
e-mail: theoldpackethouse@cheshireinns.co.uk
Dir: *on A56 Altrincham/Sale road at junct with Navigation Road*
This attractive black and white inn dates back to the 18th century. Bedrooms are modern, well furnished and equipped. Timbers and panelling are among the original features still on view in the bar and restaurant. An interesting range of food is served at lunch times and most evenings.
FACILITIES: 4 en suite No smoking in area of dining room STV TVB tea/coffee No dogs (ex guide dogs) Cen ht No coaches Dinner Last d 9pm **PARKING:** 10 **CARDS:**

BOLTON Map 07 SD70

♦♦♦♦ *Heron Lodge*

8 Bolton Rd, Turton Bottoms, Edgworth BL7 0DS
☎ 01204 852262 📠 01204 852262
e-mail: heronlodge@hotmail.com
Dir: *from M65 junct 5 take A6177 Haslington Rd for 1m. Turn right at Grey Mare signposted Edgworth. Lodge on left at bottom of Edgworth*
Enjoying a central village location, alongside the River Bradshaw, this delightful stone cottage is peacefully set back from the road. Bedrooms are attractively furnished and benefit from smart en suite facilities. There is an inviting lounge, and hearty breakfasts are served in the attractive dining room.
FACILITIES: 3 en suite No smoking tea/coffee No dogs (ex guide dogs) Cen ht TVL No children 15yrs No coaches **PARKING:** 6 **CARDS:**

♦♦♦ Broomfield Hotel

33-35 Wigan Rd, Deane BL3 5PX
☎ 01204 61570 📠 01204 650932
e-mail: chris@broomfield.force9.net
Dir: *M61 J5, take A58 to 1st set lights, straight on A676, hotel on R, 2m from M61*
A friendly relaxed atmosphere prevails at this conveniently located hotel, close to the motorway and west of the town centre. The bedrooms, some suitable for families, are equipped with modern facilities. Public areas include a bar, a lounge and a dining room, which offers good value meals.
FACILITIES: 20 en suite (2 fmly) No smoking in 4 bedrooms No smoking in dining room TVB tea/coffee Licensed Cen ht TVL Pool Table 3/4 Snooker table Dinner Last d 8.30pm **PRICES:** s fr £36; d fr £48* **PARKING:** 12 **CARDS:**

CHEADLE Map 07 SJ88

♦♦♦ Spring Cottage

60 Hulme Hall Rd, Cheadle Hulme SK8 6JZ
☎ 0161 485 1037 📠 0161 485 1037
Dir: *from M60 take Cheadle exit onto A34, turn left into Cheadle then right at 'White Hart' traffic lights. Follow road 2m crossing traffic lights onto Hulme Hall Rd*
FACILITIES: 6 rms (3 en suite) (1 fmly) No smoking in 1 bedrooms No smoking in dining room No smoking in lounges TVB tea/coffee Cen ht No coaches **PRICES:** s £25-£31; d £41-£45* **PARKING:** 5 **CARDS:**

England

DELPH Map 07 SD90

♦♦♦ Globe Farm

Huddersfield Rd, Standedge, Delph OL3 5LU ☎ 01457 873040
01457 873040
e-mail: globefarm@amserve.net
Dir: *on A62 between Oldham and Huddersfield, 0.75m after junct with A670 from Uppermill*
FACILITIES: 14 en suite (1 fmly) No smoking in 10 bedrooms No smoking in dining room No smoking in lounges TVB tea/coffee Licensed Cen ht ch fac No coaches **PRICES:** s fr £25; d fr £45✳ **PARKING:** 25 **NOTES:** Closed Xmas & New Year **CARDS:**

HYDE Map 07 SJ99

♦♦♦ Needhams *(SJ968925)*

Uplands Rd, Werneth Low, Gee Cross SK14 3AG
☎ 0161 368 4610 0161 367 9106 Mr & Mrs I Walsh
e-mail: charlotte@needhamsfarm.co.uk
Dir: *A560 at Gee Cross turn into Joel Lane, left at top of hill (Werneth Low Rd), 0.5m. Uplands Rd on right*

This old stone-built farmhouse has been extensively restored to provide modern accommodation. The bedrooms are well-equipped and include many personal touches. There is an open fire in the spacious lounge/dining room. Home cooking is served by arrangement and there is a small bar.
FACILITIES: 7 rms (6 en suite) (1 fmly) No smoking in bedrooms TVB tea/coffee Direct dial from bedrooms Licensed Cen ht TVL Golf 12 Riding 30 acres Non working Dinner Last d 8pm **PRICES:** s £20-£22; d £36-£40✳ **LB BB PARKING:** 14 **CARDS:**

MANCHESTER Map 07 SJ89

See also Altrincham

♦♦♦ *Crescent Gate Hotel*

Park Crescent, Victoria Park, Rusholme M14 5RE
☎ 0161 224 0672 0161 257 2822
e-mail: crescentgate@talk21.com
(The Circle)

Conveniently situated for the city centre but set in a quiet residential area, this house provides an ideal base for guests wishing to visit the many local universities and colleges. Bedrooms vary in size and style and day rooms include a bright dining room and a cosy lounge.
FACILITIES: 25 rms (20 en suite) (1 fmly) No smoking in 12 bedrooms No smoking in dining room STV TVB tea/coffee Direct dial from bedrooms Licensed Cen ht TVL **PARKING:** 14 **NOTES:** Closed Xmas/New Year **CARDS:**

♦♦♦ Thistlewood Hotel

203 Urmston Ln, Stretford M32 9EF ☎ 0161 865 3611
0161 866 8133
Dir: *leave M60 junct 7 towards Stretford, keep left, then left into Sandy Lane and left again into Urmston Lane*

This is a grand Victorian house that enjoys a residential location close to junction 7 of the M60, and within easy reach of Old Trafford football and cricket grounds. The bedrooms are well-equipped and public rooms, including a guests' lounge, are spacious and comfortable.

continued

Thistlewood Hotel

FACILITIES: 9 en suite (1 fmly) No smoking in dining room TVB tea/coffee No dogs Licensed Cen ht TVL No coaches Last d breakfast **PRICES:** s £33; d £46✳ **PARKING:** 12 **CARDS:**

♦♦♦ Victoria Park Hotel

4 Park Crescent, Victoria Park M14 5RE
☎ 0161 224 1399 0161 224 2219 0161 225 4949
e-mail: vph.manchester@claranet.co.uk
Dir: *A6010 to B5117 Park Cres directly off Wilmslow Rd*

A large Victorian House situated in a quiet crescent close to the city centre, university buildings and hospitals. Bedrooms are simply furnished and there is a comfortable guest lounge. Vegetarian continental breakfast is served in the attractive dining room. No alcohol is allowed on the premises.
FACILITIES: 20 rms (19 en suite) (5 fmly) (4 GF) No smoking in 14 bedrooms No smoking in dining room No smoking in lounges tea/coffee Direct dial from bedrooms No dogs Cen ht **PRICES:** s £38-£40; d £48-£50✳ **LB PARKING:** 40 **CARDS:**

MANCHESTER AIRPORT Map 07 SJ88

♦♦♦ Rylands Farm

Altrincham Rd SK9 4LT ☎ 01625 535646 & 548041
01625 255256
e-mail: info@rylandsfarm.com
Dir: *M56 J6 take A538 towards Wilmslow. Guest house 1.5m on left just past Wilmslow Moat House*

This well-maintained house is conveniently located for the airport and set in pleasant gardens. The modern conservatory houses a cosy sitting area and bar. Guests eat family style in the dining room. Bedrooms are in nearby buildings and are attractively decorated with pretty wallpapers and fabrics.
FACILITIES: 3 en suite 6 annexe en suite (3 fmly) (3 GF) No smoking TV6B tea/coffee Licensed Cen ht TVL No coaches **PRICES:** s £38; d £49.50* **PARKING:** 15 **NOTES:** Closed 24-25 Dec & 31 Dec-1 Jan **CARDS:**

MARPLE Map 07 SJ98

♦♦♦♦ Matteo's Bar & Country Hotel

Rock Tavern, Glossop Rd, Marple Bridge SK6 5RX
☎ 01457 852418 01457 852418
e-mail: matteo@freecall_uk.co.uk
Dir: *on A626*
A friendly, family-run restaurant with rooms, located high on the Cheshire/Derbyshire border, with panoramic views of delightful countryside. A good range of popular dishes is available from regularly changing menus, served by cheerful staff. Bedrooms are attractively decorated, with quality bathrooms and a range of useful facilities.
FACILITIES: 5 en suite (1 fmly) No smoking in bedrooms No smoking in dining room TVB tea/coffee Direct dial from bedrooms No dogs Cen ht TVL Dinner Last d 10pm **PARKING:** 100 **CARDS:**

OLDHAM Map 07 SD90

♦♦♦♦ Boothstead Farm

Rochdale Rd, Denshaw OL3 5UE ☎ 01457 878622
e-mail: boothsteadfarm@bushinternet.com
Dir: *turn of A672 onto A640 in Denshaw Village, Farmhouse 0.25m from x-road in village on the right hand side of the road*
FACILITIES: 2 rms (1 en suite) No smoking TVB tea/coffee Cen ht TVL No children 4yrs No coaches Dinner Last d 7pm **PRICES:** s £20-£25; d £40-£45* **LB PARKING:** 5 **NOTES:** Closed 24 Dec-1 Jan

♦♦ Farrars Arms

56 Oldham Rd, Grasscroft OL4 4HL ☎ 01457 872124
01457 820351
FACILITIES: 3 rms TVB tea/coffee Direct dial from bedrooms No dogs (ex guide dogs) Licensed Dinner **PRICES:** s fr £25; d fr £44* **PARKING:** 32

ROCHDALE Map 07 SD81

♦♦♦♦ Hindle Pastures

Highgate Ln, Whitworth OL12 0TS ☎ 01706 643310
01706 653846
e-mail: p-marshall@breathemail.net
Dir: *take A671 out of Rochdale, signposted Burnley. Over 3 mini rdbt onto dual carriageway. 1st right onto Towacliffe rd. Then right into Highgate Ln. At top of road 2nd left*
FACILITIES: 3 en suite No smoking in bedrooms No smoking in dining room TVB tea/coffee Direct dial from bedrooms No dogs (ex guide dogs) Cen ht TVL No children 12yrs No coaches Fishing Sauna Jacuzzi Dinner Last d 24 hrs **PRICES:** s £30-£35; d £45-£50* **PARKING:** 10

SALE Map 07 SJ79

♦♦♦♦ Brooklands Luxury Lodge

208 Marsland Rd M33 3NE ☎ 0161 973 3283 0161 282 0524
Dir: *on A6144, 1.5m from M60 junct 6, near Brooklands tram station*
This well-maintained, privately run hotel is ideally located for Manchester Airport, the city centre, Old Trafford and the Trafford Centre. Comfortably furnished accommodation includes many thoughtful extras. A complimentary breakfast is offered in all bedrooms, with a full English breakfast available if preferred in the dining room.
FACILITIES: 9 rms (5 en suite) (2 fmly) No smoking TVB tea/coffee No dogs (ex guide dogs) Cen ht No coaches Jacuzzi Dinner Last d 10am **PRICES:** s £28-£38; d £48-£50* **PARKING:** 6 **CARDS:**

STOCKPORT Map 07 SJ89

♦♦♦♦ Henry's Hotel

204-206 Buxton Rd, Davenport SK2 7AE ☎ 0161 292 0202
0161 355 6585
e-mail: enquiries@henryshotel.com
Situated on the main road a short way from the town, this family owned and run guest house offers fine hospitality. The bedrooms are modern and well equipped and a cosy lounge and separate bar are provided for guests' comforts.
FACILITIES: 10 en suite (1 fmly) No smoking in bedrooms No smoking in dining room No smoking in lounges tea/coffee No dogs (ex guide dogs) Licensed Cen ht TVL No children Solarium Dinner Last d noon **PRICES:** s £35.25-£41.13; d £47-£52.88* **PARKING:** 24 **CARDS:**

♦♦♦♦ *Red Lion Hotel*

112 Buxton Rd, High Ln SK6 8ED ☎ 01663 765227
01663 762170
e-mail: reservations@the-redlion-inn.co.uk
Dir: *on main A6, 0.5m from Lyme Park*
This busy roadside inn, hotel and café bar offers a wide selection of food together with very well equipped and comfortable bedrooms. Service is especially friendly and attentive.
FACILITIES: 6 en suite No smoking in area of dining room No smoking in 1 lounge STV TVB tea/coffee Direct dial from bedrooms No dogs Cen ht No coaches Dinner Last d 9.30pm **PARKING:** 200 **CARDS:**

Super supper! this symbol shows that evening meals exceeded our Inspector's expectations.

England

HAMPSHIRE

ALTON Map 04 SU73

♦♦♦ White Hart

London Rd, Holybourne GU34 4EY ☎ 01420 87654
01420 543982

Dir: *just off A31 into Alton. Establishment in centre of Holybourne*

An traditional inn which is very popular with locals and business guests. A choice of hand-pulled beers are available, and a good selection of meals are served in the bar or dining area; public rooms were being refurbished at the time of our last visit. The bedrooms are comfortable with smart shower rooms.

FACILITIES: 4 rms No smoking in bedrooms No smoking in dining room TVB tea/coffee Cen ht Pool Table 6 piste petanque terrain Dinner Last d 8.45pm **PRICES:** s £27; d £47✳ **MEALS:** Lunch £6.50-£12alc Dinner £6.50-£12alc✳ **PARKING:** 40 **CARDS:**

ANDOVER Map 04 SU34

♦♦♦♦ Tilehurst

Furzedown Ln, Amport SP11 8BW ☎ 01264 771437
01264 773651
e-mail: tilehurst@compuserve.com

Dir: *turn off A303 W of Andover in direction of Amport. At next T-junct turn right, right again at next T-junct. 4th house on left past St Mary's church*

Situated close to Thruxton race circuit on the A303 in the picturesque village of Amport, this delightful modern home provides guests with comfortably furnished bedrooms equipped with many thoughtful extras. Guests are welcome to use the attractive lounge and in summer, the swimming pool and secluded gardens may also be enjoyed.

FACILITIES: 3 en suite No smoking TVB tea/coffee No dogs Cen ht No children 16yrs No coaches Outdoor swimming pool Riding
PRICES: s £30-£35; d £60-£70 LB **PARKING:** 6

♦♦♦♦ Broadwater

Amport SP11 8AY ☎ 01264 772240 01264 772240
e-mail: carolyn@dmac.co.uk

Dir: *from A303 take turn for Hawk Conservancy/Amport. At T-junct, turn right, 1st road right, 1st cottage on right*

Situated in a quiet, picturesque village, this listed thatched cottage has an attractive garden. Broadwater is full of original character and is convenient for many major places of interest. The bedrooms are comfortable and homely. There is a combined lounge and dining room, where wholesome English breakfasts are served.

FACILITIES: 2 en suite No smoking in bedrooms No smoking in dining room TV1B tea/coffee No dogs Cen ht TVL No coaches **PRICES:** s £30-£35; d £60-£65✳ **PARKING:** 3 **NOTES:** Closed 20-31 Dec
CARDS:

♦♦♦♦ *Gunville House*

Grateley SP11 8JQ ☎ 01264 889206 01264 889060
e-mail: pct@onetel.net.uk

Dir: *leave A30 at Andover/Marlborough/Devizes junct, at rdbt follow signs for Grateley & Monxton. Through Monxton and after approx 2.5m pass Driving range then 70 metres on a track on right is signed Gunville House*

Located just South of the A303 and well-situated for exploring the Test Valley and surrounding countryside, this partly thatched 19th century home with its rural setting is also close to Thruxton race circuit. Bedrooms are comfortable and well-equipped with many useful extra facilities. Dinner is available by prior arrangement.

FACILITIES: 2 en suite (1 fmly) No smoking STV TVB tea/coffee Cen ht No children 5yrs No coaches Dinner Last d 24hrs prior

♦♦♦♦ Nether Cottage

The Green, Amport SP11 8BA ☎ 01264 772082
01264 772082

Dir: *A303 heading W, left at sign for Hawk Conservancy, continue to T-junct and turn right. At red telephone box on Amport village green, turn right onto track and continue to the end along gravel drive*

With a riverside frontage and an abundance of wildlife, this delightful property is located just off the village green. Being situated just South of the A303 it is close to Thruxton race circuit and numerous places of interest. The bedrooms are comfortable and stylish. Guests are able to relax in the peaceful garden or guest lounge.

FACILITIES: 3 rms No smoking TVB tea/coffee No dogs (ex guide dogs) Cen ht TVL No children 5yrs No coaches **PRICES:** s £25; d £40-£45✳
PARKING: 5 **NOTES:** Closed Nov

♦♦♦♦ New House Bed & Breakfast

Fullerton Rd, Wherwell SP11 7JS ☎ 01264 860817
01264 860817
e-mail: enquire@newhousebnb.co.uk

Dir: *from A303 take B3048 for Wherwell. Past White Lion pub towards Fullerton. House 50mtrs on left from junct*

FACILITIES: 3 rms (1 en suite) (2 fmly) No smoking TVB tea/coffee No dogs Cen ht ch fac **PRICES:** s £25; d £45-£55✳ **PARKING:** 4
NOTES: Closed 24-26 Dec

BARTON-ON-SEA Map 04 SZ29

Premier Collection

♦♦♦♦♦ Tower House

Christchurch Rd BH25 6QQ ☎ 01425 629508
01425 629508
e-mail: bandb@towerhouse-newforest.co.uk

Dir: *on A337,between Highcliff and New Milton*

A short drive from the town and just 900 metres from the sea, this fine Edwardian house offers a relaxed atmosphere and a warm welcome. Sympathetically upgraded, it retains many original features. Bedrooms are spacious, well equipped and comfortable. A good choice is served at breakfast, taken at a communal table in the elegant dining room.

FACILITIES: 3 en suite (1 fmly) (1 GF) No smoking TVB tea/coffee No dogs Cen ht No children 7yrs No coaches **PRICES:** d £50-£60✳ LB
PARKING: 10

BB Great value! This indicates B&B for £19 and under, per person, per night.

England

BARTON ON SEA continued

♦♦♦♦ Cleeve House

58 Barton Court Av BH25 7HG ☎ 01425 615211 📠 01425 615211
e-mail: cleeve.house@btinternet.com
Dir: *off A337*

Located in a quiet residential area, Cleeve House is within easy walking distance of the sea. Bedrooms are brightly decorated and comfortably furnished. There is a pleasant lounge and breakfast is served in the attractive dining room.
FACILITIES: 4 rms (2 en suite) (1 fmly) No smoking TVB tea/coffee No dogs Cen ht TVL No coaches **PRICES:** s £25; d £47-£50✳
PARKING: 8 **NOTES:** Closed Xmas/New Year

BASINGSTOKE — Map 04 SU65

See also Hook

♦♦♦♦ Fernbank Hotel

4 Fairfields Rd RG21 3DR ☎ 01256 321191 📠 01256 461467
e-mail: availability@fernbankhotel.co.uk
Dir: *M3 junct 6, 1st rdbt turn left, next rdbt right, signed Fairfields. Immediately left after Lamb pub on left, Fairfields Rd 2nd right*
This is a small and privately owned hotel, which is situated in a residential area and within walking distance of the town centre. The bedrooms are comfortably furnished and well-equipped. There is ample parking available to the rear of the building.
FACILITIES: 16 en suite (1 fmly) (3 GF) No smoking TVB tea/coffee Direct dial from bedrooms No dogs Licensed Cen ht **PRICES:** s £68-£76; d £80-£95✳ **PARKING:** 16 **NOTES:** Closed 2 wks at Xmas
CARDS:

♦♦♦♦ Hatchings

Woods Ln, Cliddesden RG25 2JF ☎ 01256 465279
Dir: *M3 junct 6, take Alton road A339 & pass under road bridge. Immediate right signed Cliddesden B3046, after 0.75m pass garage, take next right*
This lovely house is situated in the pretty village of Cliddesden and is very convenient for both Basingstoke and the M3. The comfortable bedrooms look out onto peaceful gardens and the extra touches are excellent. A hearty full English breakfast is served in the bedrooms and cereals, bread, jams, fruit and biscuits are freely available.
FACILITIES: 3 en suite No smoking TVB tea/coffee Direct dial from bedrooms Cen ht No children 10yrs No coaches **PRICES:** s £29.50-£32; d £50-£60✳ **PARKING:** 10

BISHOP'S WALTHAM — Map 04 SU51

Brent Villa

Winchester Rd SO32 1BD ☎ 01489 890188
At the time of going to press the Diamond classification for this establishment had not been confirmed. Please check the AA website www.theAA.com for up-to-date information.
FACILITIES: 10 rms

BRANSGORE — Map 04 SZ19

♦♦♦♦ *Tothill House*

Black Ln, off Forest Rd BH23 8EA ☎ 01425 674414
📠 01425 672235
Feb-Nov
Built for an admiral in 1908, Tothill House is perfectly located in the heart of the New Forest. The garden backs onto the forest where deer, ponies and other wildlife are frequent visitors. The attractive, spacious bedrooms are furnished to a high standard, reflecting the character of the house. There is an elegant library, and a generous breakfast is served in the dining room.
FACILITIES: 3 en suite No smoking TVB tea/coffee No dogs Cen ht No children 16yrs No coaches **PARKING:** 6

BROCKENHURST — Map 04 SU30

♦♦♦♦ The Cottage

Sway Rd SO42 7SH ☎ 01590 622296 📠 01590 623014
e-mail: terry_eisner@compuserve.com
Dir: *from Lyndhurst on A337,turn right at Careys Manor into Grigg Lane. Continue 0.5m to crossroads, straight over and cottage next to war memorial*

Located in the centre of the village and ideally positioned for exploring the New Forest, this delightful extended cottage dates back to the 18th century. The comfortable bedrooms are individually furnished with some featuring pieces of period furniture and items of memorabilia. Numerous extra facilities are provided to ensure guests' comfort.
FACILITIES: 6 en suite No smoking in bedrooms No smoking in dining room TVB tea/coffee Licensed Cen ht TVL No children 10yrs No coaches Dinner Last d 7pm **PRICES:** s £55-£85; d £70-£95✳ **PARKING:** 10
NOTES: Closed Dec-Jan **CARDS:**

♦♦♦ Bridge House

Lyndhurst Rd SO42 7TR ☎ 01590 623135 & 624760
📠 01590 623916
e-mail: jmub2@aol.com
Dir: *situated on A337*
Located in the Waters Green conservation area, this 18th-century house is set just off the main Brockenhurst to Lyndhurst road. Well positioned for easy access to the village and surrounding areas of the New Forest, the comfortably furnished bedrooms are equipped with many thoughtful extra facilities. Breakfast is a hearty affair.
FACILITIES: 3 en suite (1 fmly) No smoking TVB tea/coffee Cen ht No coaches **PRICES:** s £25-£40; d £50-£60✳ **LB PARKING:** 5
NOTES: Closed Xmas **CARDS:**

Directions are provided by the proprietor, ask for more details when booking.

England

♦♦♦ *Seraya*
8 Grigg Ln SO42 7RE ☎ 01590 622426 📠 01590 622426
e-mail: edwin.ward@nationwideisp.net
Dir: *exit Lymington-Lyndhurst road opposite Careys Manor Hotel. Now on Grigg Lane. 400 yds on right is Horlock Rd, house on corner Horlock Rd/Grigg Lane*
Well-located for visiting the New Forest and situated close to the centre of town with its multitude of eating options, this delightful guest house offers rooms that are quiet well-decorated and have a good selection of extra facilities. A hearty breakfast is served around the communal dining table.
FACILITIES: 3 rms (1 en suite) No smoking TVB tea/coffee Cen ht No coaches **PARKING:** 3

♦♦ Careys Cottages
11 Careys Cottages, Butts Lawn SO42 7TF ☎ 01590 622276
With its tranquil location overlooking a water splash, Careys Cottages is within walking distance of the main village and the New Forest. The two bedrooms share a shower-room. Freshly prepared breakfasts are served at one large table.
FACILITIES: 2 rms (1 fmly) No smoking Cen ht No children 5yrs No coaches **PRICES:** d fr £40✻ **PARKING:** 4

♦♦ Crossings
Lyndhurst Rd SO42 7RL ☎ 01590 622478 📠 01590 622478
Dir: *just before railway crossing on left coming from Lyndhurst A337*
Ideally situated for visiting the New Forest and the numerous local places of interest, Crossings is centrally situated to the towns facilities and is aptly named due to its close proximity to the station and level crossing. Rooms are comfortable and have secondary glazing so noise is minimised.
FACILITIES: 3 rms No smoking TVB tea/coffee No dogs (ex guide dogs) Cen ht No children 7yrs **PRICES:** s £21-£23; d £42-£46✻ **LB**
PARKING: 2

CADNAM — Map 04 SU31

♦♦♦♦ *Budds (SU310139)*
Winsor Rd, Winsor SO40 2HN ☎ 023 80812381
Mrs A M Dawe
Apr-Oct
Dir: *M27 junct 1 follow A336 signed Totton, at Hayway pub turn left, Budds Farm is 0.3m on right*
There is a lovely homely atmosphere at this charming thatched farmhouse located in the New Forest. The spacious bedrooms are comfortably appointed and suitably equipped. Guests have use of the cosy lounge. A generous English breakfast is served in the traditional dining room, overlooking the pretty cottage garden.
FACILITIES: 2 rms (1 en suite) (1 fmly) No smoking tea/coffee No dogs (ex guide dogs) Cen ht TVL No children 10yrs 200 acres beef dairy
PARKING: 3

♦♦♦♦ Walnut Cottage
Old Romsey Rd SO40 2NP ☎ 023 8081 2275 📠023 8081 2275
Dir: *At Cadnam rdbt take A3090, Old Romsey rd is first on left*
This charming 150-year-old cottage is located in an ideal position for those wishing to visit the New Forest or nearby business centres. The comfortable bedrooms are brightly decorated. A lounge is available to guests who can enjoy a full English breakfast around a large table in the cosy dining room.
FACILITIES: 3 rms (2 en suite) No smoking TVB tea/coffee No dogs (ex guide dogs) Cen ht TVL No children 14yrs No coaches **PRICES:** s £35; d £50✻ **PARKING:** 4 **NOTES:** Closed 24-26 Dec

♦♦♦ Kents *(SU315139)*
Winsor Rd, Winsor SO40 2HN ☎ 023 8081 3497
📠 023 8081 3497 Mrs A Dawe
Dir: *M27 junct 1, follow A336 signed Totton, at Haywain pub turn left, farm 0.3m on left*
This delightful thatched farmhouse forms part of a working dairy farm in the heart of the New Forest. Bedrooms overlook the pretty cottage garden and have quality furnishings. A hearty breakfast is served in the dining room, which like the lounge, has an inglenook fireplace and beams.
FACILITIES: 2 en suite (1 fmly) No smoking tea/coffee No dogs Cen ht TVL No children 8yrs 200 acres beef **PRICES:** d £46-£48✻
PARKING: 4 **NOTES:** Closed Nov-Mar

DAMERHAM — Map 04 SU11

♦♦♦ The Compasses
Damerham SP6 3HQ ☎ 01725 518231 📠 01725 518880
Dir: *centre of Fordingbridge at mini rdbt take rd marked Sandleheath/Damerham, 3m to Damerham. On L after garage.*
This friendly, 400-year-old traditional inn enjoys a peaceful village location just three miles from Fordingbridge and is an ideal base for exploring the surrounding area. The comfortable bedrooms are pleasantly furnished and well-equipped. The bars feature a selection of real ales and over 100 malt whiskies. Tasty meals are available at lunch and dinner.
FACILITIES: 6 en suite (1 fmly) No smoking in dining room No smoking in 1 lounge TVB tea/coffee Cen ht Pool Table Dinner Last d 9.30pm
PRICES: s £39.50-£45; d £69-£80✻ **LB MEALS:** Lunch £14-£25&alc Dinner £14-£25&alc✻ **PARKING:** 20 **CARDS:**

EAST TYTHERLEY — Map 04 SU22

♦♦♦♦ Star
SO51 0LW ☎ 01794 340225 📠 01794 340225
e-mail: info@starinn-uk.com
Dir: *N from Romsey on A3057, left on B3084 at Dukes head, left in Dunbridge at railway crossing right at end of road , follow rd for 1.5 m*

This charming old coaching inn offers bedrooms housed in a purpose-built block, separate from the main pub. These rooms are spacious, quiet and have high levels of quality and comfort. An environmentally friendly outdoor child's play area is also available. The inn has a loyal following of locals and visitors, with the award-winning food proving a particular attraction.
FACILITIES: 3 annexe en suite (3 GF) No smoking in bedrooms No smoking in dining room TVB tea/coffee No dogs Cen ht Skittle alley,Playground Dinner Last d 9pm **PRICES:** s fr £45; d fr £60✻
MEALS: Lunch £12-£35alc Dinner £12-£35alc✻ **CONF:** Thtr 24 Class 24 Board 30 **PARKING:** 50 **NOTES:** Closed 25-26 Dec **CARDS:**

England

FAREHAM Map 04 SU50

♦♦♦♦ Springfield Hotel

67 The Avenue PO14 1PE ☎ 01329 828325

***Dir:** leave M27 J9, take A27 signed Fareham, in 3m pub on right, through both sets of lights opp pub, hotel 1st building on right after lights*

This large attractive 1930s house is surrounded by gardens. The spacious bedrooms are well presented with co-ordinated furnishings and are equipped with many useful extras. The elegant dining room overlooks the garden, as does the delightful lounge where guests are welcome to relax.

FACILITIES: 6 en suite (1 fmly) No smoking in bedrooms No smoking in dining room TVB tea/coffee Direct dial from bedrooms No dogs Cen ht No coaches **PRICES:** s £45; d £55✳ **PARKING:** 10 **NOTES:** Closed 21Dec-1Jan **CARDS:**

♦♦♦ Avenue House Hotel

22 The Avenue PO14 1NS ☎ 01329 232175 📠 01329 232196

***Dir:** M27 junct 9 to Fareham West, A27on left after 5m, junct 11 through town bypass past railway stn on right after 500 mtrs*

Conveniently situated just west of the town centre, this well-presented hotel is ideally located for the continental ferry terminals and naval heritage sites. The comfortable bedrooms are spacious, attractive and well-equipped with one having a four-poster bed. Breakfast is served in the cosy conservatory dining room. Conference rooms are also available.

FACILITIES: 19 en suite (3 fmly) (6 GF) No smoking in 10 bedrooms No smoking in dining room No smoking in lounges TVB tea/coffee Direct dial from bedrooms Cen ht Dinner Last d 10pm **PRICES:** s £55; d £60-£65✳ **CONF:** Thtr 30 Class 30 Board 30 **PARKING:** 27 **CARDS:**

♦♦ Catisfield Cottage

1 Catisfield Ln PO15 5NW ☎ 01329 843301 📠 01329 841652

***Dir:** off A27 at Highlands Road traffic lights, Catisfield Lane 2nd on left*

FACILITIES: 6 rms (3 en suite) (2 fmly) No smoking in 1 bedrooms No smoking in dining room TVB tea/coffee Cen ht TVL No coaches **PRICES:** s £19-£27.50; d £40-£50✳ BB **PARKING:** 6 **NOTES:** Closed 24 Dec-5 Jan

FARNBOROUGH Map 04 SU85

♦♦♦♦ The White Residence

Farnborough Park, 76 Avenue Rd GU14 7BG

☎ 01252 375510 & 371817 📠 01252 655567

e-mail: info@countyapartments.com

***Dir:** from A325 (Farnborough rd) turn at Clockhouse rdbt into Rectory Rd. Avenue Rd is 4th on right at mini-rdbt*

This elegant house is situated in a quiet residential street not far from the centre of town. The four bedrooms are colour-themed and equipped with many thoughtful extras for the comfort of guests. Although evening meals are not available advice is always on hand. A warm welcome awaits all and parking is a welcomed bonus.

FACILITIES: 4 en suite No smoking STV TVB tea/coffee Direct dial from bedrooms No dogs Cen ht TVL No children 12yrs No coaches **PRICES:** s £65-£85; d £75-£95✳ **PARKING:** 6 **CARDS:**

FORDINGBRIDGE Map 04 SU11

Premier Collection

♦♦♦♦♦ Cottage Crest

Castle Hill, Woodgreen SP6 2AX ☎ 01725 512009

***Dir:** A338 Salisbury - Bournemouth, midway between Downton & Fordingbridge turn off at Breamore to Woodgreen. Right at post office/shop, last right*

Located in an elevated position, with breathtaking views over the River Avon and a backdrop of the New Forest, this charming guest house is set in five acres of garden. The comfortable and spacious bedrooms are equipped with many extra facilities and there is a garden suite with its own sitting room.

FACILITIES: 3 en suite No smoking TVB tea/coffee No dogs (ex guide dogs) Cen ht No children 8yrs No coaches **PRICES:** s £35; d £49✳ **PARKING:** 4

Premier Collection

♦♦♦♦♦ The Three Lions

Stuckton SP6 2HF ☎ 01425 652489 📠 01425 656144

e-mail: the3lions@btinternet.com

***Dir:** 0.5m E of Fordingbridge from A338 or B3078. At Q8 garage follow Three Lions tourist signs*

Situated a mile or so from the town the Three Lions dates from 1863 and is a popular and charming old inn. High levels of comfort and quality in bedrooms and a renowned restaurant are an attractive combination. The property also boasts a quiet garden to enjoy, complete with year-round hot tub.

FACILITIES: 3 en suite No smoking in bedrooms No smoking in dining room TVB tea/coffee No dogs (ex guide dogs) Cen ht No coaches Sauna Jacuzzi Whirlpool spa in garden Dinner Last d 9.45pm **PRICES:** s £59-£75; d £65-£85✳ LB **MEALS:** Lunch £14.50&alc Dinner £20-£30alc✳ **PARKING:** 50 **NOTES:** Closed 18 Jan-12 Feb rs Sun evening/Mon *(no meals)* **CARDS:**

♦♦♦♦ Ad Astra

18 Broomfield Dr, Alderholt SP6 3HY ☎ 01425 656735

e-mail: BettyGatherer@CompuServe.com

***Dir:** B3078 from Fordingbridge to Alderholt, left turn off S-bend into Hillbury Rd, 3rd right into Birchwood Dr, 5th left into Broomfield Dr*

continued

This hotel is conveniently located in a quiet residential area of the town. The bedrooms at Ad Astra offer guests comfortable accommodation with numerous extra facilities. A traditional cooked English breakfast is served in the charming cosy dining room overlooking the pretty rear garden.
FACILITIES: 2 en suite (2 GF) No smoking TVB tea/coffee No dogs Cen ht No children 5yrs No coaches **PRICES:** s fr £35; d £38-£44* BB **PARKING:** 4 **NOTES:** Closed Dec

♦♦♦♦ Alderholt Mill

Sandleheath Rd SP6 1PU ☎ 01425 653130 📠 01425 652868
e-mail: alderholt-mill@zetnet.co.uk
Dir: *M27 J1, B3078 through town, right fork (Damerham/Sandleheath). Left at x-roads in Sandleheath, 0.5m over bridge on right*

They grind their own flour at this delightful mill, and use it in their home-made bread. Guests can enjoy milling demonstrations, cream teas, barbecues by the river and private fishing. The bedrooms, lounge and dining room are all comfortable and well-appointed. Dinner is available by prior arrangement.
FACILITIES: 5 rms (4 en suite) No smoking TVB tea/coffee Cen ht No children 8yrs No coaches Fishing Dinner Last d 9am **PRICES:** s £20-£22.50; d £42-£50* LB **PARKING:** 10 **CARDS:**

FRITHAM — Map 04 SU21

♦♦♦♦ Fritham Farm *(SU243144)*

Fritham SO43 7HH ☎ 023 80812333 📠 023 80812333
Mrs P Hankinson
e-mail: frithamfarm@supanet.com
Dir: *leave M27 junct 1 and follow signs to Fritham, turn right at Fritham and Eyeworth only. Fritham Farm is 300m on right hand side*
This delightful 18th century farmhouse with its 51 acres is located in an unspoilt area of the New Forest and has attractive, traditionally furnished bedrooms. Guests enjoy freshly prepared farmhouse breakfasts around one large table in the cosy dining room. There is also a spacious, comfortable lounge with television and log fire.
FACILITIES: 3 en suite No smoking tea/coffee No dogs (ex guide dogs) Cen ht TVL No children 10yrs 51 acres mixed grass **PRICES:** d £43-£45* **PARKING:** 4 **NOTES:** Closed Nov-mid Feb

HOOK — Map 04 SU75

♦♦♦ Oaklea

London Rd RG27 9LA ☎ 01256 762673 📠 01256 762150
e-mail: oakleaguesthouse@amserve.net
Dir: *on A30, 200yds from centre of Hook,towards Basingstoke*
Just a few minutes drive from the M3, this attractive house offers tastefully decorated accommodation with good modern facilities. The residents' lounge is comfortably furnished and the large dining room also has a bar.

continued

FACILITIES: 11 en suite (1 fmly) No smoking in bedrooms No smoking in dining room TVB tea/coffee Licensed Cen ht TVL No coaches Dinner Last d noon **PRICES:** s £40; d £50* **PARKING:** 11 **CARDS:**

♦♦♦ Cedar Court Country

Reading Rd RG27 9DB ☎ 01256 762178 📠 01256 762178
Dir: *1m N of Hook on B3349*
A well-kept garden, sheltered by trees, surrounds this pretty bungalow. It is set in a quiet location with a private drive giving access from the road. Bedrooms are very comfortable and there are several pubs and restaurants in the area for evening meals.
FACILITIES: 6 rms (5 en suite) (6 GF) No smoking in dining room TVB tea/coffee No dogs (ex guide dogs) Cen ht TVL No coaches **PRICES:** s £30-£45; d £45-£65* **PARKING:** 6 **CARDS:**

♦♦♦ Cherry Lodge

Reading Rd RG27 9DB ☎ 01256 762532 📠 01256 766068
e-mail: cherrylodge@btinternet.com
Dir: *on B3349 Reading Road*
Cherry Lodge is an attractive brick built modern bungalow set back from the Reading road. Bedrooms are all en suite and very popular with business guests. Parking and a comfortable lounge are both available.
FACILITIES: 13 en suite (2 fmly) (13 GF) No smoking in 5 bedrooms No smoking in dining room No smoking in lounges STV TVB tea/coffee Direct dial from bedrooms No dogs (ex guide dogs) Cen ht TVL No coaches **PRICES:** s £40; d £55* **PARKING:** 20 **NOTES:** Closed Xmas & New Year **CARDS:**

ISLE OF WIGHT

See page 425

LYMINGTON — Map 04 SZ39

See also Milford-on-Sea

Premier Collection

♦♦♦♦♦ Efford Cottage

Everton SO41 0JD ☎ 01590 642315 📠 01590 641030
e-mail: effcottage@aol.com
Dir: *on A337, 2m W of Lymington*
This charming property, set in attractive well-maintained gardens, offers large comfortable bedrooms, which are well-furnished and equipped, and feature a host of thoughtful extras. There is a spacious lounge in which to relax. By previous arrangement, guests can enjoy a delicious evening meal featuring local and home-grown produce. The extensive breakfast menu also features home-made bread and other specialities.
FACILITIES: 3 en suite (1 fmly) No smoking in bedrooms No smoking in dining room TVB tea/coffee Direct dial from bedrooms Cen ht No children 14yrs No coaches Dinner Last d winter breaks only **PRICES:** d £50-£65* LB **PARKING:** 4

Premier Collection

♦♦♦♦♦ The Nurse's Cottage

Station Rd SO41 6BA ☎ 01590 683402 📠 01590 683402
e-mail: nurses.cottage@lineone.net

(For full entry see Sway)

LYMINGTON continued

Premier Collection

♦♦♦♦♦ The Olde Barn

Christchurch Rd, Downton SO41 0LA ☎ 01590 644939 & 07813 679757 Fax 01590 644939
e-mail: julie@theoldebarn.co.uk
Dir: *on A337 approx 3m from Lymington, approx 1m after Everton Nurseries on right near Royal Oak Pub*
A warm welcome awaits guests to this carefully converted 17th-century barn and associated buildings. Bedrooms are stylishly decorated and furnished, whilst the spacious bathrooms are equipped with power showers. There is a comfortable lounge where guests can relax. A traditional English breakfast is served around a farmhouse table in the attractive dining room.
FACILITIES: 3 en suite (1 fmly) No smoking STV TVB tea/coffee No dogs (ex guide dogs) Cen ht TVL No children 7yrs No coaches
PRICES: s £35-£60; d £50-£60 **PARKING:** 6

♦♦♦♦ Auplands

22 Southampton Rd SO41 9GG ☎ 01590 675944
Fax 01590 675944
e-mail: s.broomfield@btinternet.com
Dir: *on A337 just before town centre, almost opposite supermarket*
Conveniently located just a short walk from Lymington High Street, this friendly family-run guest house provides guests with comfortable, neatly decorated and well-equipped bedrooms. Hearty English breakfasts are served at individual tables in the attractive dining room. A small outdoor pool is also available in the warm weather.
FACILITIES: 3 en suite No smoking TVB tea/coffee No dogs (ex guide dogs) Cen ht No children No coaches **PRICES:** s £25-£50; d £40-£50✻ **LB**
PARKING: 8

♦♦♦♦ Harts Lodge

242 Everton Rd, Everton SO41 0HE ☎ 01590 645902
Dir: *at Everton turn off A337 into Everton Rd, 0.5m on L*
This large attractive bungalow is peacefully situated in three acres of gardens and paddocks. The bedrooms are furnished to a high standard and feature many thoughtful touches. One room has outside access. Public areas include a lounge and a pleasant breakfast room with views of the garden and wildlife pond.
FACILITIES: 3 en suite (1 fmly) (3 GF) No smoking TVB tea/coffee Cen ht TVL No coaches **PRICES:** s fr £28; d fr £48✻ **LB** **PARKING:** 6

♦♦♦♦ Jevington

47 Waterford Ln SO41 3PT ☎ 01590 672148 Fax 01590 672148
e-mail: jevingtonbb@lineone.net
Dir: *from High St, turn R at St Thomas Church into Church Lane. Take L fork into Waterford Lane*

Situated within walking distance of the town centre and marinas, Jevington offers attractively decorated bedrooms, furnished to a high standard and with well co-ordinated soft furnishings adding to the effect. An appetising breakfast is served at two tables in the open plan dining room, and the friendly proprietors are happy to suggest places for dinner.
FACILITIES: 3 en suite (1 fmly) No smoking TVB tea/coffee Cen ht No children 5 yrs No coaches **PRICES:** s £24-£35; d £48-£52✻ **PARKING:** 3

♦♦♦ *Kings Arms*

St Thomas St SO41 9NB ☎ 01590 672594
Dir: *from N approach Lymington on A337, bear left into St Thomas St, Kings Arms 50yds on right*
This friendly inn is located in the centre of town and provides comfortable accommodation. The bedrooms are tastefully appointed, well co-ordinated and equipped with smart en-suite facilities. The well-stocked bar features real ales, and evening meals are served in the cosy dining room. Secure parking is a real plus.
FACILITIES: 2 en suite No smoking in bedrooms No smoking in dining room No smoking in lounges TVB tea/coffee No dogs Cen ht No children 18yrs No coaches Dinner Last d 9.30pm **PARKING:** 8

♦♦♦ Passford Farm

Southampton Rd SO41 8ND ☎ 01590 674103
Dir: *opposite the Welcome to Lymington sign*
Parts of this delightful cottage date back seven hundred years. Passford Farm is full of character and charm and is located on the edge of Lyndhurst. The proprietors adopt a relaxed and friendly approach, ensuring guests feel comfortable to enjoy the facilities. Public areas include a pleasant garden and cosy lounge.
FACILITIES: 3 en suite (1 fmly) No smoking in bedrooms No smoking in dining room TVB tea/coffee No dogs (ex guide dogs) Cen ht No coaches half size snooker table **PRICES:** d £40-£44✻ **PARKING:** 30

♦♦♦ Victoriana

Victoria Mews, High St SO41 9FT ☎ 01590 688416
Fax 01590 688415
Dir: *Opposite Barclays Bank in Lymington High Street*
Tucked away in a small mews, in the centre of this busy little town The Victoriana provides guests with well-proportioned, comfortable rooms. Each is well-equipped and has a good range of facilities. Breakfast is served at individual tables, whilst the friendly atmosphere makes this an easy place, in which to relax.
FACILITIES: 3 rms (1 en suite) (1 fmly) No smoking in bedrooms TVB tea/coffee No dogs (ex guide dogs) Cen ht No coaches
PRICES: d £45-£55✻ **LB** **PARKING:** 3

LYNDHURST — Map 04 SU30

See also Fritham

♦♦♦♦ Bartley Farmhouse *(SU317129)*

Ringwood Rd, Bartley SO40 7LD ☎ 023 8081 4194
Fax 023 8081 4117 Mrs S Emberley
e-mail: emberley@amserve.net
Dir: *On A336, 1.5m from Cadnam rdbt, M27 junct 1 on left side, 1st property after very long layby*
Home from home hospitality is very much in evidence throughout any stay at this comfortably furnished farmhouse, which retains many of its original features. Bedrooms are cosy and guests are also invited to use the relaxing lounge or enjoy a drink by the open fire. There is even a paddock available should you decide to arrive by horse.
FACILITIES: 3 en suite No smoking No dogs (ex guide dogs) Cen ht TVL No children 12yrs Riding 3 acres non-working **PARKING:** 6
NOTES: Closed Xmas

continued

England

♦♦♦♦ *Heather House Hotel*

Southampton Rd SO43 7BQ ☎ 023 8028 4409
023 8028 4431
e-mail: enquiries@heatherhouse.co.uk
Dir: *from A31/junct1 M27 take A337 to Lyndhurst. At lights in centre of village turn left, establishment approx 800yds on left*

Located at the edge of town with views over the New Forest, this impressive double-fronted Edwardian house is well placed for those wishing to explore the area's many trails. Bedrooms are comfortable and well furnished, with many extra facilities. Light snacks are available in the evenings and there is also a cosy bar.
FACILITIES: 8 en suite No smoking in bedrooms No smoking in dining room TVB tea/coffee Direct dial from bedrooms No dogs (ex guide dogs) Licensed Cen ht TVL No coaches **PARKING:** 12 **CARDS:**

♦♦♦♦ Ormonde House

Southampton Rd SO43 7BT ☎ 023 8028 2806
023 8028 2004
e-mail: info@ormondehouse.co.uk
Dir: *off M27 onto A337, through Lyndhurst one-way system & leave village, then 400yds past fire station on L of A35*

Located just off the main Southampton-Lyndhurst road, this well presented property has spacious, comfortable bedrooms with co-ordinated furnishings and fabrics. Guests can relax in the bar or conservatory lounge which overlooks the gardens. Dinner is pre-ordered from a daily changing blackboard menu, which offers a wide range of fresh, home-cooked dishes.
FACILITIES: 19 en suite (1 fmly) (3 GF) No smoking in bedrooms No smoking in dining room No smoking in 1 lounge STV TVB tea/coffee Direct dial from bedrooms Licensed Cen ht No coaches Dinner Last d 5pm
PRICES: s £25-£40; d £50-£100✳ **LB PARKING:** 26 **NOTES:** Closed 8 days Xmas **CARDS:**

♦♦♦♦ Penny Farthing Hotel

Romsey Rd SO43 7AA ☎ 023 80284422 023 80284488
e-mail: stay@pennyfarthinghotel.co.uk
Dir: *from M27 junct 1 follow A337, hotel on left as coming into village (The Circle)*

continued

This small friendly hotel on the edge of town is ideally situated for exploring the New Forest and local attractions. Bedrooms, named after bicycles, are well equipped and attractively decorated with some being located in an adjacent cottage. There is a spacious breakfast room, a comfortable lounge bar and a bicycle store.
FACILITIES: 16 en suite 4 annexe en suite (2 fmly) (3 GF) No smoking in bedrooms No smoking in dining room No smoking in 1 lounge TVB tea/coffee Direct dial from bedrooms No dogs (ex guide dogs) Licensed Cen ht TVL No coaches **PRICES:** s £35-£45; d £59-£90✳ **PARKING:** 23
CARDS:

♦♦♦♦ Rufus House Hotel

Southampton Rd SO43 7BQ ☎ 023 8028 2930 8028 2200
023 8028 2930
e-mail: rufushousehotel@dcintra.fsnet.co.uk
Dir: *From centre of Lyndhurst turn towards Totton, on left opp. open forest*

Located on the edge of town, this delightful Victorian, family-run hotel is ideally situated for those wishing to explore the New Forest. Bedrooms have been appointed to a high standard with numerous extra facilities. Both the turret lounge and garden terrace are ideal places to relax.
FACILITIES: 11 en suite (2 GF) No smoking in bedrooms No smoking in dining room TVB tea/coffee No dogs (ex guide dogs) Cen ht TVL
PRICES: s £35-£40; d £55-£75✳ **LB PARKING:** 15
CARDS:

♦♦♦ Clarendon Villa

Gosport Ln SO43 7BL ☎ 023 80282803 023 80284303
e-mail: clarendonvilla@i12.com
Dir: *behind New Forest Visitor Information Centre, next to Gosport Lane entrance to car park*

This centrally located guest house provides guests with a warm and friendly environment from which to explore the New Forest. Bedrooms are bright, airy are neatly appointed with two rooms having video recorders and a library of films. A cooked breakfast is served in your room at a time of your choice.
FACILITIES: 3 en suite (1 fmly) No smoking TVB tea/coffee No dogs (ex guide dogs) Cen ht No coaches **PRICES:** s £35-£45; d £45-£60✳ **LB PARKING:** 3 **NOTES:** Closed 24-25 Dec **CARDS:**

♦♦♦ Stable End

Emery Down SO43 7FJ ☎ 023 8028 2504 023 8028 2504
e-mail: dibbenfam@aol.com
Dir: *follow A337 towards Lyndhurst & take 3rd turn on right. After 0.75m turn right at T-junction then immediately left into gravel entrance*

This charming country house in the New Forest has a warm, friendly atmosphere. It is an ideal base for touring the surrounding beauty spots. Bedrooms are brightly decorated, comfortably appointed and equipped with many thoughtful extras. The generous breakfast includes homemade preserves. A comfortable conservatory lounge is available to guests.
FACILITIES: 2 en suite No smoking TVB tea/coffee No dogs (ex guide dogs) Cen ht No children No coaches stabling nearby by prior arrangment
PRICES: d fr £50✳ **PARKING:** 4

England

LYNDHURST continued

♦♦♦ Whitemoor House Hotel

Southampton Rd SO43 7BU ☎ 023 8028 2186
e-mail: whitemoor@aol.com
Dir: *entering town from E on A35, hotel on right just past golf course*
Whitemoor House is an ideal base for touring the New Forest. The atmosphere is friendly and informal and a sound standard of accommodation is offered. Bedrooms are comfortable and brightly decorated. There is a cosy lounge and dinner is available by prior arrangement.
FACILITIES: 8 en suite (2 fmly) No smoking TVB tea/coffee Direct dial from bedrooms No dogs (ex guide dogs) Licensed Cen ht No coaches Dinner Last d 5pm **PRICES:** s £25-£40; d £50-£60✱ **LB** **PARKING:** 10
NOTES: Closed Xmas **CARDS:**

MILFORD ON SEA — Map 04 SZ29

♦♦♦♦ Alma Mater

4 Knowland Dr SO41 0RH ☎ 01590 642811 📠 01590 642811
e-mail: bandbalmamater@aol.com
Dir: *from Lymington on A337, L onto B3058 to Milford on Sea. Pass South Lawn Hotel, turn R into Manor Road, 1st L into Knowland Drive. Alma Mater is 3rd bungalow on R.*
Alma Mater is situated in a quiet residential area within walking distance of the village centre and beaches. The comfortable bedrooms are all well appointed with many extra touches. One room is on the ground floor and another has a small kitchen for long-staying guests. Dinner is available by prior arrangement.
FACILITIES: 3 en suite (1 fmly) No smoking TVB tea/coffee No dogs (ex guide dogs) Cen ht TVL No children 3yrs No coaches Dinner Last d 10am
PRICES: s £35-£38; d £45-£55✱ **LB** **PARKING:** 4

♦♦♦♦ Ha' Penny House

16 Whitby Rd SO41 0ND ☎ 01590 641210 📠 01590 641227
e-mail: info@hapennyhouse.co.uk
Dir: *from Lymington follow A337 towards Christchurch. At Everton turn left onto B3058 to Milford-on-Sea, pass through village and up the cliff road for approx. 0.25m, turn right into Cornwallis rd, R at T-junct into Whitby rd. Establishment 50yds on L*

This large double-fronted house is located in a quiet residential area, just a few minutes' walk from the cliff top of Milford-on-Sea with its sweeping views of the Isle of Wight and the Needles. Ideally situated for visiting coastal and New Forest attractions, the property offers bright, spacious, comfortable rooms with many extra facilities.
FACILITIES: 4 en suite No smoking TVB tea/coffee No dogs Cen ht TVL No children 8 No coaches **PRICES:** s £27-£32; d £44-£52✱ **LB** **PARKING:** 7

♦♦♦♦ Cherry Trees

Lymington Rd SO41 0QL ☎ 01590 643746
e-mail: cherrytrees@beeb.net
Dir: *at end of private lane between village centre and primary school just off B3058, between Manor Road and Church Hill*
This modern home is close to the village centre and ideally located for exploring Lymington and the New Forest. The proprietor is a qualified holistic therapist who has a treatment room on the premises. A traditional English breakfast is served at one large table.
FACILITIES: 2 en suite (1 fmly) No smoking TVB tea/coffee No dogs (ex guide dogs) Cen ht ch fac No coaches Holistic massage and beauty treatment room **PRICES:** s £25-£50; d £45-£58✱ **LB** **PARKING:** 4

NEW MILTON — Map 04 SZ29

♦♦♦♦ Cottage Bed & Breakfast

Appledore, Holmsley Rd, Wootton BH25 5PT ☎ 01425 629506
e-mail: mariette.jelley@ntlworld.com
Dir: *A35 from Lyndhurst towards Christchurch, after approx 9m turn left onto B3058, 0.25m on left*
Peacefully located in the New Forest, this delightful cottage has been refurbished to a high standard. Bedrooms are attractively decorated with colourful co-ordinated soft furnishings. A generous, freshly cooked breakfast is served in the attractive conservatory dining room overlooking the garden. Hospitality is warm and friendly, creating a relaxed atmosphere.
FACILITIES: 3 en suite (1 fmly) (1 GF) No smoking in bedrooms No smoking in dining room TVB tea/coffee Cen ht No coaches
PRICES: s £40-£50; d £50-£60 **LB** **PARKING:** 5

PETERSFIELD — Map 04 SU72

See also Rogate

♦♦♦♦ The Good Intent

40-46 College St GU31 4AF ☎ 01730 263838 📠 01730 302239
e-mail: pstuart@goodintent.freeserve.co.uk
Dir: *from A3(M) take A272 Midhurst turning. Turn right for town centre at roundabout on to one way system and keep right. Go all around one way system, pub on left before T-junction*
This cosy inn is full of character, with inglenook fireplaces and beams. Bedrooms are all en suite, comfortable and equipped with thoughtful extras. A popular à la carte menu is offered in the restaurant and simple snacks and real ales are also available.
FACILITIES: 2 en suite (1 fmly) No smoking in bedrooms No smoking in dining room TVB tea/coffee Licensed Cen ht No coaches Dinner Last d 9.30pm **PRICES:** s fr £45; d fr £60✱ **PARKING:** 10
CARDS:

A indicates an Associate entry, which has been inspected and rated by the ETC or the RAC in England.

PORTSMOUTH Map 04 SU60

♦♦♦♦ Hamilton House

95 Victoria Rd North, Southsea PO5 1PS ☎ 023 9282 3502
📠 023 9282 3502
e-mail: sandra@hamiltonhouse.co.uk
Dir: *M275 junct 12 into Portsmouth, at rdbt take 1st exit & follow road to right, then to left, cross 3 rdbts. 0.5m into Victoria Rd N*

This spacious Victorian property, carefully renovated by Graham and Sandra Tubb, provides bright, comfortable accommodation with many thoughtful extra facilities. The property is well located for exploring historic Portsmouth and is close to the University. A full cooked breakfast is available from 6.15am for those catching the cross channel ferry. Easy street parking is available.

FACILITIES: 9 rms (5 en suite) (3 fmly) No smoking TVB tea/coffee No dogs Cen ht TVL **PRICES:** s £25-£45; d £44-£50 **CARDS:**

♦♦♦♦ St Margarets

3 Craneswater Gate PO4 0NZ ☎ 023 9282 0097
📠 023 9282 0097
Dir: *follow signs to seafront through city. Head for South Parade Pier, at pier take left fork then 2nd left*

Ideally situated in a quiet residential location yet close to both the seafront and town centre. The bedrooms are attractively decorated, have co-ordinated soft furnishings and many thoughtful extras. Breakfast is taken in the smart dining room and guests also have the use of two lounges and a cosy bar.

FACILITIES: 13 en suite (1 fmly) No smoking in 5 bedrooms No smoking in dining room No smoking in 1 lounge TVB tea/coffee No dogs (ex guide dogs) Licensed Cen ht TVL No coaches **PRICES:** s £28-£37; d £44-£60✳ **LB PARKING:** 5 **NOTES:** Closed 21 Dec-2 Jan **CARDS:**

♦♦♦♦ Upper Mount House Hotel

The Vale, Clarendon Rd, Southsea PO5 2EQ ☎ 023 9282 0456
📠 023 9282 0456
e-mail: r.l.moth@uppermount.fsbusiness.co.uk
Dir: *exit M275, head for D-Day Museum, take road opposite museum, straight over crossroads, right at T-junct, right again*

Upper Mount House Hotel is peacefully located in a residential cul de sac. This impressive Victorian villa retains many original features, and the stylish furnishings throughout add to the character of the hotel. Public areas include a comfortable lounge bar featuring the proprietors' original art, and an elegant dining room where a fine collection of Venetian glassware is displayed. The bedrooms are spacious and well-equipped. continued

Upper Mount House Hotel

FACILITIES: 12 en suite (3 fmly) No smoking in 6 bedrooms No smoking in dining room STV TVB tea/coffee Direct dial from bedrooms No dogs (ex guide dogs) Licensed Cen ht TVL **PRICES:** s £28-£30; d £50-£57✳ **PARKING:** 12 **CARDS:**

♦♦♦ *Amberley Court*

97 Waverley Rd, Southsea PO5 2PL ☎ 023 92737473
📠 02392 356911
e-mail: nigelward@compuserve.com
Dir: *M275, 2nd exit of rdbt onto Kingston Cres, right into Kingston Rd, straight on at rdbt, straight on at lights, located on corner of first right*

Amberley Court Guest House enjoys a south-westerly aspect, ensuring the lounge and dining room are warm and bright. All rooms are decorated with bright modern co-ordinated fabrics providing comfortable rooms with good facilities.

FACILITIES: 9 rms (7 en suite) (4 fmly) No smoking TVB tea/coffee No dogs Cen ht TVL Dinner Last d 6.30pm **CARDS:**

♦♦♦ Bembell Court Hotel

69 Festing Rd, Southsea PO4 0NQ ☎ 023 9273 5915 & 9275 0497 📠 023 9275 6497
e-mail: keith@bembell.freeserve.co.uk
Dir: *road opposite Natural History Museum*

Located a few minutes' walk from the seafront, boating lake and Natural History Museum, this impressive ivy clad Victorian house has been sympathetically converted to provide a good standard of homely bedroom accommodation. Comprehensive breakfasts are taken in the attractive dining room and a stunning exterior floral display features in summer.

FACILITIES: 13 rms (10 en suite) (2 fmly) (2 GF) No smoking in 4 bedrooms No smoking in dining room No smoking in 1 lounge TVB tea/coffee No dogs (ex guide dogs) Licensed Cen ht TVL
PRICES: s £41.50-£43.50; d £54-£56 **LB PARKING:** 10
CARDS:

See advertisement on page 229

England

♦♦♦ Abbey Lodge
30 Waverley Rd, Southsea PO5 2PW ☎ 023 9282 8285
023 9287 2943
e-mail: linda@abbeylodge.co.uk
Dir: *follow seafront signs towards pier turn left into Granada, Clarendon or Burgoyne Rd to roundabout for Waverley Rd*
A warm welcome awaits at this attractive property which offers guests well equipped bedrooms along with the benefit of a guest lounge. It is close to the seafront and within walking distance of the shops. Breakfast is served in a small but cosy dining room at individual tables.
FACILITIES: 9 rms (3 en suite) (2 fmly) No smoking in dining room STV TVB tea/coffee No dogs Cen ht TVL No coaches **PRICES:** s £21-£25; d fr £42 **NOTES:** Closed Xmas & New Year **CARDS:**

♦♦♦ The Elms
48 Victoria Rd South, Southsea PO5 2BT ☎ 023 9282 3924
023 9282 3924
e-mail: theelmsgh@aol.com
Dir: *left at rdbt at end of M275, straight ahead at next 3 rdbts & traffic lights guest house 300yds on right*
This no-smoking Victorian property is conveniently located close to the shops and seafront. The bedrooms have been tastefully upgraded and all are air-conditioned. There is a comfortable lounge with cable TV. The traditional breakfast, which is served at individual tables, can be taken early for those wishing to catch ferries.
FACILITIES: 5 en suite (1 fmly) No smoking TVB tea/coffee No dogs (ex guide dogs) Cen ht TVL No children 4yrs No coaches **PRICES:** s £35-£48; d £42-£48 **PARKING:** 2 **CARDS:**

♦♦♦ The Festing Grove
8 Festing Grove, Southsea PO4 9QA ☎ 023 9273 5239
023 9286 3287
e-mail: thefestinggrove@aol.com
Dir: *follow signs to seafront, east along seafront to South Parade Pier, after pier immediate left, around lake 3rd left & 2nd right*

This is a very well-presented property that is situated in a quiet residential area conveniently close to the seafront and town. Owner Keith Newton continually upgrades the bedrooms to ensure that they reach high standards. The guests have use of a comfortable lounge.
FACILITIES: 6 rms (2 en suite) (3 fmly) No smoking TVB tea/coffee No dogs (ex guide dogs) Cen ht TVL No children No coaches **PRICES:** s £23-£30; d £35-£42✱ BB **CARDS:**

If an establishment name appears in *italics*, details have not been confirmed for 2003.

♦♦♦ Glencoe
64 Whitewell Rd, Southsea PO4 0QS ☎ 023 9273 7413
023 9273 7413
Dir: *at Southsea pier, left into Granada rd, then 1st right into Bembridge Cres. Then immediately right into Whitwell Rd*
Located in a quiet residential road close to the seafront, this late Victorian house has been carefully renovated to provide attractive homely bedrooms. Public areas include a bright dining room, and a comfortable lounge. A warm welcome is assured.
FACILITIES: 7 rms (5 en suite) (1 fmly) No smoking TVB tea/coffee No dogs Cen ht TVL No children 5yrs No coaches **PRICES:** s £23-£28; d £45-£48✱ **CARDS:**

♦♦♦ Norfolk Hotel
25/27 Granada Rd, Southsea PO4 0RD ☎ 023 9282 4162
e-mail: jbpnorfolk@ntlworld.com
Dir: *follow signs to Southsea, head for seafront and South Parade Pier. West along St Helens Parade, Granada Road is the 1st left*
Situated in a quiet road within walking distance of Southsea's many attractions the hotel is ideally suited to both business and leisure guests. Rooms are attractively decorated with a range of useful extras while some have a workspace. A guest lounge is also available.
FACILITIES: 13 en suite (2 fmly) (2 GF) No smoking in dining room TVB tea/coffee No dogs (ex guide dogs) Cen ht TVL **PRICES:** s £25; d £35-£45✱ BB **PARKING:** 9 **NOTES:** Closed Xmas **CARDS:**

♦♦ Collingham
89 St Ronans Rd, Southsea PO4 0PR ☎ 023 9282 1549
Dir: *follow signs for Southsea, at seafront E to canoe lake, take L fork, travel to Festing Rd at top turn L, L into St Ronans Rd*
This small and friendly guest house is situated a short distance from the shops and the seafront. The bedrooms are neatly decorated and a traditional cooked breakfast is served in the comfortable dining room.
FACILITIES: 6 rms (3 fmly) No smoking in 4 bedrooms No smoking in dining room No smoking in lounges TVB tea/coffee Cen ht TVL
PRICES: s £20-£22; d £36-£40✱ BB **NOTES:** Closed 25 Dec

♦♦ Fairlea
19 Beach Rd, Southsea PO5 2JH ☎ 023 9273 3090
023 9273 3090
Dir: *follow signs for seafront, then The Pyramids, facing E take 1st left and 2nd right onto Beach Rd*
Convenient located for both the town centre and the sea front, this neat and well maintained guest house is personally run. The bedrooms are bright and well appointed and breakfast is served in a pretty dining room.
FACILITIES: 4 rms (1 en suite) (2 fmly) No smoking in dining room No smoking in lounges TVB tea/coffee Cen ht TVL No coaches
PRICES: s fr £14; d fr £24; (room only) ✱ LB BB

♦♦ Sherwood
21 Beach Rd, Southsea PO5 2JH ☎ 023 9273 4108
023 9273 4108
e-mail: kev-lynne@sherwoodguesthouse.fsbusiness.co.uk
Dir: *leave M27 & take seafront road to The Pyramids, turn left into Florence Rd then 2nd right*
This small and friendly house is located a few minutes' walk from the seafront. Bedrooms are simply appointed and a hearty breakfast is served in the dining room. A warm welcome is assured.
FACILITIES: 6 rms (1 fmly) No smoking in dining room TVB tea/coffee No dogs Cen ht No coaches **PRICES:** s £17-£20; d £32-£38✱ BB
NOTES: Closed 25-26 Dec

RINGWOOD Map 04 SU10

Premier Collection

♦♦♦♦♦ Little Forest Lodge

Poulner Hill BH24 3HS ☎ 01425 478848 Fax 01425 473564

Dir: *1.5m E of Ringwood on A31*

This charming, friendly Edwardian house, set in two acres of gardens and woodland, offers high standards of hospitality and comfort. Bedrooms are pleasantly decorated and equipped with thoughtful extras. Enjoyable home-cooked meals, which make good use of fresh local produce, are served in the attractive wood-panelled dining room. There is also a delightful lounge overlooking the gardens, with a small bar and a wood-burning fire.

FACILITIES: 6 en suite (3 fmly) No smoking TVB tea/coffee Licensed Cen ht No coaches Croquet lawn clock golf, badminton Dinner Last d 8.30pm **PRICES:** s £35-£40; d £60-£70* **PARKING:** 10 **CARDS:**

♦♦♦♦ Old Cottage

Cowpitts Ln, North Poulner BH24 3JX ☎ 01425 477956 Fax 01425 477956

e-mail: forestgatewines@btinternet.com

Dir: *from A31 E/bound, 0.75m E of Ringwood. Left to Hangersley. 1st right, proceed for 0.5m to crossroads. Straight over, after 100yrds cottage on right*

Set in a beautiful garden with delightful views of the New Forest, this charming 17th-century thatched cottage retains its original characteristics including beams and an inglenook fireplace. The comfortable bedrooms are well-equipped with modern amenities, one has a four-poster bed. A freshly cooked breakfast is served in the elegant lounge/dining room.

FACILITIES: 2 en suite 1 annexe en suite (1 fmly) (1 GF) No smoking TVB tea/coffee No dogs (ex guide dogs) Cen ht TVL No children 8yrs No coaches Walking Cycling Bird watching **PRICES:** d £48-£56* **PARKING:** 3 **NOTES:** Closed Dec

♦♦♦♦ Amberwood

3/5 Top Ln BH24 1LF ☎ 01425 476615 Fax 01425 476615

e-mail: maynsing@aol.com

Dir: *off A31 & follow signs for Winkton/Sopley. Over 2 pelican crossings, left after 2nd into School Lane. Follow to top of rise, turn left to Top Lane. 3rd house on left*

This delightful Victorian home is situated in a quiet residential area within easy walking distance of the town centre. Bedrooms are attractively furnished and decorated with many thoughtful extras provided. A substantial breakfast is served around one large table in the conservatory which overlooks the well-tended garden. A guest lounge is also available.

FACILITIES: 2 en suite No smoking in bedrooms No smoking in dining room No smoking in 1 lounge TVB tea/coffee Direct dial from bedrooms No dogs (ex guide dogs) Cen ht TVL No children 12yrs No coaches **PRICES:** s £30; d £44-£48* **LB PARKING:** 2 **NOTES:** rs Xmas & New Year

♦♦♦♦ Old Stacks

154 Hightown Rd BH24 1NP ☎ 01425 473840 Fax 01425 473840

e-mail: oldstacksbandb@aol.com

Dir: *A31 W 1m before Ringwood, take slip road signed 'Hightown' & 'Owl Sanctuary'. Left into Eastfield Ln, after 0.5m turn right, Old Stacks 2nd on left*

This delightful bungalow is set in charming gardens. Of the two bedrooms, the twin bedded room has an en suite and its own garden entrance, whilst the double room has an adjoining bathroom. There is a comfortable lounge for guests' use whilst a hearty breakfast is served around a large table in the dining room.

FACILITIES: 2 en suite (2 GF) No smoking TVB tea/coffee No dogs (ex guide dogs) Cen ht TVL No children 12yrs No coaches **PRICES:** s £30-£35; d £42-£48* **LB PARKING:** 4 **NOTES:** Closed Xmas & New Year

England

RINGWOOD continued

◆◆◆◆ Picket Hill House
Picket Hill BH24 3HH ☎ 01425 476173 📠 01425 470022
e-mail: b+b@pickethill.freeserve.co.uk
Dir: *from Ringwood take A31 Southampton, in approx 2m left at Burley/Services, under A31 turn right A31 Ringwood 250yds turn left Hightown & Crow*

This is an ideal choice for those wishing to explore this beautiful area of the New Forest. The comfortable bedrooms are well-furnished with many extra facilities. Overlooking the delightful gardens there is a comfortable first floor lounge for guests' use. Delicious breakfasts are enjoyed at one large table in the dining room.
FACILITIES: 3 en suite No smoking in bedrooms No smoking in dining room No smoking in 1 lounge tea/coffee No dogs (ex guide dogs) Cen ht TVL No children 12yrs No coaches **PRICES:** s £30-£35; d £48-£56✻ **LB** **PARKING:** 6 **NOTES:** Closed 23 Dec-2 Jan **CARDS:**

◆◆◆ Fraser House
Salisbury Rd, Blashford BH24 3PB ☎ 01425 473958
📠 01425 473958
e-mail: fraserhouse@btinternet.com
Dir: *off A31 at Ringwood for A338 Salisbury Rd, guest house 1m on right*
FACILITIES: 4 en suite No smoking TVB tea/coffee Cen ht TVL No children 12yrs No coaches **PRICES:** s fr £30; d fr £48✻ **PARKING:** 6
CARDS:

ROMSEY Map 04 SU32

See also East Tytherley

◆◆◆◆ Country Accommodation
The Old Post Office, New Rd, Michelmersh SO51 0NL
☎ 01794 368739
Dir: *leave A3057 at Timsbury New Rd, Michelmersh, guest house at top of hill*

continued

This attractive guest house is decorated with many items of country memorabilia that reflect the previous uses of this delightful property. The comfortable bedrooms have excellent facilities and many useful extras. A freshly cooked English breakfast is served in the dining room, using home-produced eggs and homemade preserves.
FACILITIES: 3 annexe en suite No smoking in dining room TVB tea/coffee No dogs Cen ht No children 12yrs No coaches **PRICES:** s £30; d £50✻ **PARKING:** 5 **CARDS:**

◆◆◆◆ The Mill Arms
Barley Hill, Dunbridge SO51 0LF ☎ 01794 340401
📠 01794 340401
e-mail: info@themillarms.co.uk
Dir: *A3057 follow signs Awbridge/Kimbridge (opposite Bear & Ragged Staff) continue 1.5m to T-junct turn right & continue through village, in about 0.5m The Mill Arms on left*
Located in the Test Valley, this is a perfect base for those wishing to explore the area as walkers or cyclists or for those wanting to take fishing breaks. Bedrooms provide good levels of comfortable, well-furnished accommodation. An extensive blackboard menu provides an interesting range of meals at both lunch and dinner.
FACILITIES: 6 en suite (1 fmly) No smoking in bedrooms No smoking in dining room TVB tea/coffee No dogs (ex guide dogs) Cen ht Fishing Skittle alley Dinner Last d 9.30pm **PRICES:** s fr £50; d fr £55; (room only) ✻
MEALS: Bar Lunch £4-£13 Dinner £16-£25alc✻ **PARKING:** 30
CARDS:

◆◆◆◆ Springfields
Lyndhurst Rd, Landford SP5 2AS ☎ 01794 390093
(For full entry see Landford (Wiltshire))

ROWLAND'S CASTLE Map 04 SU71

◆◆◆◆ The Fountain Inn
34 The Green PO9 6AB ☎ 023 9241 2291 📠 023 9241 2291
e-mail: fountainsinnrc@aol.com
Dir: *A3(M) junct 2, follow B2149 for 2m, turn left at rdbt down Redlands Lane. Inn overlooks village green*

A charming coaching inn set back from the road and overlooking the village green. The well equipped bedrooms have been tastefully refurbished and have many thoughtful touches; one room has a lovely four-poster bed. Public areas consist of a popular local bar and a cosy Thai restaurant.
FACILITIES: 4 en suite (1 fmly) No smoking TVB tea/coffee Cen ht Dinner Last d 9.30pm **PRICES:** s £25-£40; d £50-£65✻ **LB**
MEALS: Sunday Lunch £8.50-£13.75&alc Dinner £13-£24.25&alc✻
CARDS:

SOUTHAMPTON Map 04 SU41

♦♦♦♦ Hunters Lodge Hotel

25 Landguard Rd, Shirley SO1 55DL ☎ 023 8022 7919
023 8023 0913
e-mail: hunterslodge.hotel@virgin.net
Located in a leafy residential area close to the city centre, this double fronted Victorian house provides business and leisure guests with comfortable well-equipped bedrooms. Full English breakfast is served at shared tables in the elegant dining room. There is also a TV lounge and a well-stocked bar.
FACILITIES: 14 en suite (1 fmly) (1 GF) No smoking in bedrooms No smoking in dining room No smoking in 1 lounge TVB tea/coffee Direct dial from bedrooms Licensed Cen ht TVL **PRICES:** s £35-£45; d £45-£55* **LB**
PARKING: 20 **CARDS:**

♦♦♦♦ Landguard Lodge

21 Landguard Rd SO15 5DL ☎ 023 8063 6904
023 8063 2258
e-mail: landguardlodge@141.com
Dir: *north of railway station between Hill Lane & Shirley Road*
Only a few minutes' walk from the railway station, this impressive Victorian house is well located in a quiet residential area. The bedrooms are bright, comfortable and well equipped with many thoughtful extras. The cosy lounge is available for guests' use.
FACILITIES: 10 en suite (1 GF) No smoking in bedrooms No smoking in dining room TVB tea/coffee No dogs (ex guide dogs) Cen ht No children 5yrs No coaches **PRICES:** s fr £29; d fr £49* **PARKING:** 3
CARDS:

♦♦♦ Alcantara

20 Howard Rd, Shirley SO15 5BN ☎ 023 8033 2966
023 8049 6163
e-mail: alcantara@supanet.com
Dir: *M3/A33, follow city centre signs to road with parkland on either side, turn 1st right after Cowherds pub into Northlands Rd, right at T-junct, straight at traffic lights*
Named after the ocean liner to reflect the property's close location to the city centre and its shipping connections, this efficiently run guest house offers comfortable accommodation. The bedrooms are well-decorated and have many thoughtful extras. A large car park is available for guest use at the rear of the building.
FACILITIES: 9 rms (3 en suite) (3 fmly) (2 GF) No smoking in dining room TVB tea/coffee No dogs (ex guide dogs) Cen ht No children 2yrs No coaches **PRICES:** s £25-£30; d £44-£60* **PARKING:** 7 **NOTES:** Closed 20 Dec-6 Jan **CARDS:**

♦♦♦ Ashelee Lodge

36 Atherley Rd, Shirley SO15 5DQ ☎ 023 8022 2095
023 8022 2095
Dir: *from M27 to Shirley High St, turn into Hill Lane, into Languard 4th left, 1st right into Atherley Rd*
This friendly guest house is located in a quiet residential area and is within easy reach of the city centre and university. The bedrooms are neatly decorated and comfortably furnished. Breakfast is served at individual tables in the nicely appointed dining room which opens into a comfortable lounge.
FACILITIES: 4 rms (1 en suite) (1 fmly) No smoking TVB No dogs Cen ht TVL No children 5yrs No coaches Outdoor swimming pool **PRICES:** s £20-£23; d £40-£46* **LB** **PARKING:** 3 **NOTES:** Closed 24 & 25 Dec
CARDS:

♦♦♦ Lodge

1 Winn Rd, The Avenue SO17 1EH ☎ 023 8055 7537
023 8055 3586
e-mail: Lodgehotel@faxvia.net
Dir: *take A33 into city and at end of Common, and at Cowherds pub turn left (The Independents)*
Located just over a mile from the city centre this hotel is even closer to the University. Bedrooms are mostly spacious and comfortably appointed. A choice of menu is offered at dinner and breakfast. The public rooms offer comfort and a relaxed atmosphere, and for guests' further enjoyment there is a small bar.
FACILITIES: 14 rms (8 en suite) (2 fmly) No smoking in dining room STV TVB tea/coffee Direct dial from bedrooms Licensed Cen ht TVL No coaches Dinner Last d 9pm **PRICES:** s £27-£37.50; d fr £49*
PARKING: 10 **NOTES:** Closed 23-27 Dec **CARDS:**

♦♦♦ The Fenland Guest House

79 Hill Ln SO15 5AD ☎ 023 8022 0360 023 8022 6574
Dir: *M3 take M27 E or W, take A33 Southampton exit at 1st rdbt proceed across to A33 Bassett Ave, next rdbt right onto Winchester Rd (A35) left at next rdbt then across mini rdbt into Hill Lane. After 2nd traffic lights Fen Lane on left*
FACILITIES: 7 rms (3 en suite) 1 annexe en suite (1 fmly) No smoking TVB tea/coffee Cen ht No coaches **PRICES:** s £23-£30; d £45-£50* **LB**
PARKING: 6 **CARDS:**

STOCKBRIDGE Map 04 SU33

♦♦♦♦ York Lodge

Nether Wallop SO20 8HE ☎ 01264 781313
e-mail: bradley@yorklodge.fslife.co.uk
Dir: *off A343 (Andover/Salisbury Rd) onto B7084 signed Romsey. 2nd left, single track road at bottom of hill. In 0.9m fork left, York Lodge 1st house on right with large wooden automatic gates*
Located in the picturesque village that was the setting for Agatha Christie's Miss Marple series, this recently built accommodation forms a self-contained addition to a charming modern single storey home set in beautiful peaceful gardens. Bedrooms are stylishly presented with many extra facilities. Delicious evening meals are available by prior arrangement.
FACILITIES: 2 en suite (2 GF) No smoking TVB tea/coffee Cen ht No children 8yrs No coaches Dinner Last d 24hrs prior
PRICES: s £30-£35; d £50-£60* **PARKING:** 4

♦♦♦ *Carbery*

Salisbury Hill SO20 6EZ ☎ 01264 810771
01264 811022
Dir: *on A30*
Situated in one acre of landscaped gardens overlooking the River Test, Carbery Guest House is within easy walking distance of the town centre. Dinner is available by prior arrangement. There is a guest lounge and separate games room with snooker table, and an outdoor pool is available in warmer months.
FACILITIES: 11 rms (8 en suite) No smoking in dining room TVB tea/coffee No dogs Licensed Cen ht Outdoor swimming pool (heated) Pool Table Croquet lawn Dinner Last d 6pm **PARKING:** 14 **NOTES:** Closed 2 wks Xmas **CARDS:**

England

SWAY Map 04 SZ29

Premier Collection

♦♦♦♦♦ The Nurse's Cottage

Station Rd SO41 6BA ☎ 01590 683402 📠 01590 683402
e-mail: nurses.cottage@lineone.net
Dir: *off B3055 in village next to post office*

This former District Nurse's cottage has been turned into luxury accommodation offering high levels of hospitality and service. Bedrooms are comfortable with many welcome extras whilst bathrooms have lovely toiletries and fluffy towels. The attractive Garden Room restaurant, also open to non-residents, has a range of carefully prepared dishes and a substantial wine list.
FACILITIES: 3 en suite (3 GF) No smoking TVB tea/coffee Direct dial from bedrooms Licensed Cen ht No children 10yrs No coaches Dinner Last d 8pm **PRICES:** s £62.50-£72.50; d £105 **LB** **CONF:** Thtr 29 Class 13 Board 13 Del from £95 ✻ **PARKING:** 8 **NOTES:** Closed 2wks Mar, 3wks Nov **CARDS:**

See advert inside front cover

♦♦♦ Forest Heath Hotel

Station Rd SO41 6BA ☎ 01590 682287 📠 01590 682626
Dir: *M27 junct 1. Take A337 to Lyndhurst, follow signs to Sway, turn right into village. Hotel 200 yds on right*
Located in the heart of this New Forest village, the inn dates from late Victorian times and is a popular meeting place for the local community. Bedrooms are both well-equipped and comfortable and a range of real ales and imaginative meals are offered in the bars and conservatory dining room.
FACILITIES: 7 en suite (2 fmly) No smoking in 1 bedrooms No smoking in area of dining room TVB tea/coffee Cen ht Petanque court Dinner Last d 9.30pm **PRICES:** s £35; d £65✻ **MEALS:** Lunch £6-£12.99alc Dinner £6.50-£12.99alc✻ **PARKING:** 20 **CARDS:**

THRUXTON Map 04 SU24

♦♦♦♦ May Cottage

SP11 8LZ ☎ 01264 771241 & 07768 242166 📠 01264 771770
e-mail: info@maycottage-thruxton.co.uk
Dir: *from A303 take sign Thruxton (village only), situated almost opposite George Inn*
Excellent customer care is assured at this 18th-century part thatched house which is located on pretty gardens in the heart of the village. Fine art and furnishing enhance the original internal features and bedrooms are filled with a wealth of thoughtful extras. Comprehensive breakfasts are taken in the attractive dining room.

continued

May Cottage

FACILITIES: 3 en suite No smoking STV TVB tea/coffee No dogs Cen ht TVL No children 6yrs No coaches **PRICES:** s £40-£45; d £55-£75✻ **LB** **PARKING:** 5 **NOTES:** Closed Xmas

WARSASH Map 04 SU40

♦♦♦♦ Dormy House Hotel

21 Barnes Ln, Sarisbury SO31 7DA ☎ 01489 572626
📠 01489 573370
e-mail: dormyhousehotel@warsash.globalnet.co.uk
Dir: *take A27 towards Fareham. At Sarisbury turn down Barnes Lane signposted Warsash, Dormy House Hotel sign at intersection of A27 & Barnes Lane*
With good access to major motor routes, this friendly hotel is popular with leisure and business guests alike. Bedrooms are neatly decorated and well-equipped with many extra facilities. Public rooms include a cosy lounge and attractive dining room, where evening meals are served by prior arrangement.
FACILITIES: 12 en suite (1 fmly) (6 GF) No smoking in 3 bedrooms No smoking in dining room TVB tea/coffee Direct dial from bedrooms No dogs (ex guide dogs) Licensed Cen ht TVL No coaches Dinner Last d when booking **PRICES:** s £46-£56; d £56-£66✻ **PARKING:** 18
CARDS:

♦♦♦♦ Solent View Hotel

33-35 Newtown Rd SO31 9FY ☎ 01489 572300
📠 01489 572300
Dir: *M27 junct 8 take A27 towards Fareham. After 1.75m right into Barnes Ln at top of hill. Travel 1m then right into Brook Lane, across rdbt, hotel 200yds on left*
This is a delightful Victorian house that is located just a few minutes' walk from the river. It has been extended to provide guests with comfortable well-equipped bedrooms. Public areas include an attractive dining room and a lounge with a well-stocked bar. Dinner is available by prior arrangement.
FACILITIES: 8 en suite (2 GF) No smoking in dining room TVB tea/coffee Direct dial from bedrooms Licensed Cen ht TVL No children 8yrs No coaches Dinner Last d 8am **PRICES:** s £47-£50; d £56-£60
PARKING: 10 **PRICES:** s £65-£85; d £75-£95✻ 2 wks Xmas, 1 wk Etr, 2 wks Aug
CARDS:

WINCHESTER Map 04 SU52

♦♦♦♦ Acacia

44 Kilham Ln SO22 5PT ☎ 01962 852259 📠 01962 852259
e-mail: amelia.shirley@btinternet.com
Dir: *M3 junct 11 follow signs for Oliver's Battery, at rdbt take A3040 for Winchester, left at lights into Kilham Lane. Acacia 200yds on right*
Acacia has a peaceful location on the outskirts of the city. The bedrooms are individually furnished and attractively decorated. A good selection of dishes is offered at breakfast, which is served in

continued

England

the bright conservatory/dining room. A comfortably appointed lounge overlooking the garden is also provided for guests' use.
FACILITIES: 3 en suite No smoking tea/coffee No dogs Cen ht TVL No children 10yrs No coaches **PRICES:** s £40-£45; d £50-£55* **PARKING:** 4 **NOTES:** Closed mid Nov-mid Mar.

♦♦♦♦ Shawlands
46 Kilham Ln SO22 5QD ☎ 01962 861166 📠 01962 861166
e-mail: kathy@pollshaw.u-net.com
Dir: *take A3090 from Winchester, straight over rdbt and right at 2nd traffic lights*

This attractive house is peacefully located on the outskirts of the City. Shawlands offers comfortable bedrooms, which are well co-ordinated and furnished with many extra facilities. Breakfast, with homemade bread and preserves, is enjoyed around one large table in the dining room, overlooking well-tended gardens.
FACILITIES: 5 rms (1 en suite) (2 fmly) No smoking TV4B tea/coffee Cen ht TVL No children 5yrs No coaches **PRICES:** s £30-£36; d £40-£52* **PARKING:** 5 **NOTES:** Closed 23 Dec-2 Jan **CARDS:**

♦♦♦♦ The Wykeham Arms
75 Kingsgate St SO23 9PE ☎ 01962 853834 📠 01962 854411
e-mail: doreen@wykeham.fsnet.co
Dir: *immediately south of the Cathedral, by Kingsgate and opposite Winchester College*

This is one of the oldest and best-loved public houses in Winchester and is situated just south of the cathedral. Bedrooms are sited in both the main house and annexe. All areas are furnished to a high standard with excellent facilities. Dining in the restaurant or bar is recommended - walls are adorned from top to bottom with every kind of memorabilia imaginable and the regularly changing menu uses fresh ingredients.
FACILITIES: 7 en suite 6 annexe en suite No smoking TV14B tea/coffee Direct dial from bedrooms Cen ht No children 14yrs No coaches Dinner Last d 8.45pm **PRICES:** d £50-£120* **MEALS:** Lunch £3.25-£13.50 Dinner £3.25-£13.50* **PARKING:** 12 **NOTES:** Closed 25 Dec
CARDS:

U 24 Clifton Road
SO22 5BU ☎ 01962 851620
At the time of going to press the Diamond classification for this establishment had not been confirmed. Please check the AA website www.theAA.com for up-to-date information.
FACILITIES: 1 en suite

HEREFORDSHIRE

ABBEY DORE — Map 03 SO33

♦♦♦♦ Tan House Farm *(SO385305)*
HR2 0AA ☎ 01981 240204 📠 01981 240204 Mrs G Powell
e-mail: jppowell@ereal.net
Dir: *turn right off A465 at Wormbridge and follow signs for Dore Abbey*
This stone-built farmhouse is close to the 12th-century Cistercian Dore Abbey in the beautiful Golden Valley. The traditionally furnished bedrooms have modern facilities. Breakfast is served family-style in the combined breakfast room and lounge, which has fine antique furnishings. Hospitality is warm and the welcome second to none.
FACILITIES: 3 en suite (2 GF) No smoking in bedrooms No smoking in dining room TVB tea/coffee No dogs (ex guide dogs) Cen ht TVL 350 acres arable cattle sheep horses **PRICES:** s fr £22; d fr £44* **PARKING:** 3

♦♦♦ The Nevill Arms
The Golden Valley HR2 0AA ☎ 01981 240319
Dir: *off A465 Abergavenny-Hereford rd onto B4347 at Pontrilas. Establishment 1m on left just before Abbey*
Although originally a 16th-century pub (The Griffin) which sold the local cider and perry, the name derives from its more recent use as a hunting lodge for the Neville family, who owned much of the surrounding land. In addition to the beautiful setting, the inn offers a bar and restaurant with fresh flowers and real fires, and two en suite rooms in a ground floor annexe.
FACILITIES: 2 annexe en suite (1 fmly) No smoking in bedrooms No smoking in dining room TV3B tea/coffee No children 4yrs Dinner
PRICES: d £50* **LB MEALS:** Bar Lunch £3.50-£8.50 Dinner £14*
PARKING: 30

BROCKHAMPTON — Map 03 SO53

U Ladyridge Farm
HR1 4SE ☎ 01989 740220
At the time of going to press the Diamond classification for this establishment had not been confirmed. Please check the AA website www.theAA.com for up-to-date information.
FACILITIES: 2 en suite

BROMYARD — Map 03 SO65

♦♦♦♦ Little Hegdon
Hegdon Hill, Pencombe HR7 4SL ☎ 01885 400263
e-mail: howardcolegrave@hotmail.com
Dir: *between villages of Pencombe & Risbury, at top of Hegdon Hill turn down a farm lane, property approx 500mtrs*
Located in a pretty hamlet, this fine period house has been sympathetically renovated to provide high standards of comfort. There are many original features, including exposed beams and open fires. Bedrooms are equipped with lots of thoughtful extras and provide stunning views of the surrounding countryside.
FACILITIES: 2 en suite No smoking in bedrooms No smoking in dining room No smoking in 1 lounge TVB tea/coffee No dogs (ex guide dogs) Cen ht Riding Pool Table Croquet lawn **PRICES:** s £25; d £50* **PARKING:** 4

BROMYARD continued

Linton Brook Farm
Malvern Rd, Bringsty WR6 5TR ☎ 01885 488875 & 01885 488875
At the time of going to press the Diamond classification for this establishment had not been confirmed. Please check the AA website www.theAA.com for up-to-date information.
FACILITIES: 3 en suite

FOWNHOPE Map 03 SO53

♦♦♦♦ Bowens Country House
HR1 4PS ☎ 01432 860430 📠 01432 860430
e-mail: thebowenshotel@aol.com
Dir: *6m SE of Hereford on B4224. In Fownhope, establishment opposite church*
Formerly a 17th-century farmhouse, Bowens has been provided with modern and comfortable facilities. Set in well tended grounds with a putting green and tennis court; the house is most peaceful and relaxing. Bedrooms have been attractively decorated and are provided with many extra touches. An honesty bar is available in the lounge and delicious home-cooked dishes are served in the dining room.
FACILITIES: 6 en suite 4 annexe en suite (3 fmly) (4 GF) No smoking in 6 bedrooms No smoking in dining room TVB tea/coffee Direct dial from bedrooms Licensed Cen ht No coaches Tennis (grass) 9 hole putting green Dinner Last d 8.30pm **PRICES:** s £32.50; d £50-£65* **LB PARKING:** 15
CARDS:

HEREFORD Map 03 SO54

See also Little Dewchurch

♦♦♦♦ Felton House
Felton HR1 3PH ☎ 01432 820366 📠 01432 820366
e-mail: bandb@ereal.net
Dir: *signposted off A417 between A49 and A465 beside Felton church*

This Victorian house, formerly a rectory, maintains many original charms and is full of character. Set in four acres of grounds with attractive gardens, there is a real air of peace and tranquillity. Bedrooms are most comfortable and the beds, including some four-posters, are a feature. Two lounges are provided where guests may relax. The award-winning breakfasts here offer a very impressive choice of local and specialist ingredients.
FACILITIES: 4 en suite No smoking tea/coffee Cen ht TVL ch fac No coaches **PRICES:** s £27; d £54* **LB PARKING:** 6 **NOTES:** Closed 24-28 Dec

♦♦♦♦ Grafton Villa Farm *(SO500361)*
Grafton HR2 8ED ☎ 01432 268689 📠 01432 268689
Mrs J Layton
e-mail: jennielayton@ereal.net
Dir: *2m S of Hereford, farm drive leads off A49 past Grafton Inn on right, from Ross-on-Wye 0.25m before Mercedes/Rover garage on left*

continued

Dating back to 1780, this farmhouse is full of character and is surrounded by well-kept gardens and farmland. Bedrooms are in keeping with the rest of the building and are tastefully decorated and thoughtfully equipped. There is a homely and comfortable lounge and a hearty breakfast can be taken in the dining room, which has a traditional feel and antique furniture.
FACILITIES: 3 en suite No smoking TVB tea/coffee No dogs (ex guide dogs) Cen ht TVL Riding Putting green 200 acres mixed **PRICES:** s £30-£35; d £45-£50* **LB PARKING:** 8 **NOTES:** Closed 20-28 Dec

♦♦♦♦ Sink Green *(SO542377)*
Rotherwas HR2 6LE ☎ 01432 870223 📠 01432 870223
Mr D E Jones
e-mail: sinkgreenfarm@email.msn.com
Dir: *on B4399 2m from junction with A49*
This charming 16th century farmhouse is set in attractive countryside. The bedrooms retain many original features with stone-flagged floors, exposed beamed ceilings and open fireplaces, and one room also has a four-poster bed. The proprietor is most friendly and the relaxed atmosphere places the guest at ease and leaves a lasting impression.
FACILITIES: 3 en suite No smoking TVB tea/coffee Cen ht TVL jacuzzi, summer house due to open late summer 2002 180 acres beef sheep
PRICES: s £23-£28; d £44-£50* **PARKING:** 10 **NOTES:** Closed Xmas

♦♦♦♦ Hedley Lodge
Belmont Abbey, Abergavenny Rd HR2 9RZ ☎ 01432 277475 📠 01432 277318
e-mail: hedleylodge@aol.com
Dir: *take Abergavenny Road S for 2m. Turn right 400mtrs after Tesco Stores and follow signs to Belmont Abbey.*
FACILITIES: 17 en suite (1 fmly) No smoking in 9 bedrooms No smoking in area of dining room No smoking in lounges TVB tea/coffee Direct dial from bedrooms No dogs (ex guide dogs) Licensed Cen ht Dinner Last d 8pm
PRICES: s £31.50-£35; d £53-£60* **PARKING:** 200
CARDS:

HOARWITHY Map 03 SO52

♦♦♦♦ Aspen House
HR2 6QP ☎ 01432 840353 & 07796 671749 📠 01432 840353
e-mail: hoarwithy@aol.com
Dir: *take A49 Hereford Road at its junct with A40 then 2nd turning on right signed Hoarwithy, proceed for 4m on entering village Aspen House is on left prior to New Harp Inn*
Set amidst the beautiful Herefordshire countryside with the River Wye meandering close by, Aspen House is a must for those seeking a relaxing stay or a more energetic walking holiday. The bedrooms are well equipped and quietly appointed whilst the public areas include a comfortable residents lounge and boast a wealth of original features.
FACILITIES: 3 en suite No smoking in 1 bedrooms No smoking in dining room TVB tea/coffee Cen ht TVL No coaches **PRICES:** s £25; d £40-£44* **LB PARKING:** 7

HOW CAPLE Map 03 SO63

♦♦♦ The Falcon
How Caple HR1 4TF ☎ 01989 740223
e-mail: falconguesthouse@tinyworld.co.uk
Dir: *M50 junct 3 follow signs Hereford B4221/B4224 continue for 5.5m over crossroads, pass Grange Hotel on left, then 0.7m down hill on left.*
FACILITIES: 4 en suite (1 fmly) No smoking TVB tea/coffee Cen ht Dinner Last d Breakfast **PRICES:** s £25; d £39* **PARKING:** 6

LEDBURY Map 03 SO73

♦♦♦♦ Bodenham Farm

Much Marcle HR8 2NJ ☎ 01531 660222
e-mail: bodenhamfarm@lineone.net
Dir: *M50 junct 4 follow A449 towards Ledbury, property 4m on left*

This impressive house, in well-tended gardens, is very attractive and dates back nearly 200 years. Many original features have been retained including exposed beams and four-poster beds, and now provides most comfortable accommodation along with modern facilities. The proprietors are welcoming and guests, who are made to feel very much at home, often make a return visit.
FACILITIES: 4 rms (3 en suite) No smoking TVB tea/coffee No dogs (ex guide dogs) Cen ht TVL No children 12yrs No coaches **PRICES:** s £30-£35; d £50-£60✱ **PARKING:** 8

LEOMINSTER Map 03 SO45

Premier Collection

♦♦♦♦♦ Hills Farm *(SO564638)*

Leysters HR6 0HP ☎ 01568 750205 01568 750306
Mrs J Conolly
e-mail: conolly@bigwig.net
Dir: *exit A4112 Leominster to Tenbury Wells rd. On edge of Leysters*

Peacefully located and enjoying views of the surrounding countryside, parts of this property date back to the 16th century. The attentive proprietors provide a relaxing and homely atmosphere and a very friendly welcome. Bedrooms, in the main house and converted barns, are attractively decorated, spacious and comfortable. Dinner and breakfast are served in the dining room and conservatory and feature fresh local produce. Both are excellent and should not be missed.
FACILITIES: 2 en suite 3 annexe en suite (1 GF) No smoking TVB tea/coffee No dogs (ex guide dogs) Cen ht No children 12yrs 120 acres arable Dinner Last d 3pm **PRICES:** s £39-£41; d £58-£62
PARKING: 8 **NOTES:** Closed Nov-Feb **CARDS:**

♦♦♦♦ Lawton Bury Farm Bed & Breakfast *(SO445594)*

Lawton HR6 9AX ☎ 01568 709285 01568 709285
Mrs E Lyke
Dir: *3m W of Leominster on B4529*
Largely 18th-century, this house is situated on a 180 acre farm and has been in the ownership of the present family for almost 100 years. The charming house has many original features such as exposed timbers and a huge fireplace in the spacious lounge. A warm welcome and tastefully appointed rooms complete the stay.
FACILITIES: 3 en suite (1 fmly) No smoking STV TVB tea/coffee No dogs (ex guide dogs) Cen ht 180 acres mixed Dinner Last d previous day
PRICES: s £30; d £40-£55✱ **LB** **PARKING:** 6 **NOTES:** Closed 2weeks Xmas

♦♦♦ Woonton Court Farm *(SO548613)*

Leysters HR6 0HL ☎ 01568 750232 01568 750232
Mrs E M Thomas
e-mail: thomas.woontoncourt@farmersweekly.net
Dir: *take A49, 2.5m from Leominster onto A4112. Through Kimbolton, R for Woonton before Leysters. Farm 0.5m down lane*
This attractive 15th century farmhouse is set in tranquil country. The house retains many original features and ancient beams and family mementoes abound. Bedrooms are well-equipped with comfortable furnishings and many extra facilities. Pleasant, freshly cooked breakfasts provide farm produced eggs, local sausage and homemade marmalade, served in the comfortable dining room.
FACILITIES: 3 en suite No smoking in 2 bedrooms No smoking in dining room No smoking in lounges TVB tea/coffee Cen ht TVL 250 acres mixed Dinner Last d previous day **PRICES:** s £22-£25; d £44-£46✱ **LB**
PARKING: 4 **NOTES:** Closed 22-27 Dec

LITTLE DEWCHURCH Map 03 SO53

♦♦♦♦ Cwm Craig *(SO535322)*

HR2 6PS ☎ 01432 840250 01432 840250 Mrs G Lee
Dir: *take A49 from Ross rdbt, take 2nd on right from rdbt, continue to Little Dewchurch, turn right in village. Cwm Craig is 1st farm on left*
This Georgian farmhouse is situated on the outskirts of the village amidst glorious countryside and offers spacious and delightfully proportioned accommodation. Bedrooms are tastefully furnished with period items and public areas consist of a games room and two dining rooms, one of which is offered for the use of families. A hearty breakfast is supplemented by eggs from the farm's own hens.
FACILITIES: 3 en suite (1 fmly) No smoking in bedrooms No smoking in dining room No smoking in 1 lounge TVB tea/coffee No dogs (ex guide dogs) Cen ht TVL Pool Table Snooker, Darts 190 acres arable beef
PRICES: d £36-£38✱ **BB** **PARKING:** 5

MORETON-ON-LUGG Map 03 SO54

♦♦♦♦ Upper House Farm

HR4 8AH ☎ 01432 760069 01432 761505
Dir: *on A49 3m N of Hereford*
In a peaceful setting with attractive gardens, conservatory and patio, this working farm just off the A49 boasts a heated outdoor swimming pool and a snooker room. Mr and Mrs Perkins are natural hosts - he's a mine of local knowledge (ideal for planning days out), while she's an accomplished cook, preparing the likes of home-made pâté, succulent roast chicken and strawberry pavlova (dinner by arrangement).
FACILITIES: 3 en suite No smoking TVB tea/coffee No dogs (ex guide dogs) Cen ht TVL No children No coaches Outdoor swimming pool (heated) Threequarter size snooker table Dinner Last d by prior arrangement **PRICES:** s £25; d £40✱ **PARKING:** 4

England

ROSS-ON-WYE Map 03 SO52

Premier Collection

♦♦♦♦♦ Trecilla Farm *(SO533212)*

Llangarron HR9 6NQ ☎ 01989 770647 or 07802 892456
Mrs C A Dew
e-mail: trecillafarm@hotmail.com
Dir: *A40 midway between Ross-on-Wye & Monmouth take A4137 towards Hereford. In approx 2m, at x-rds at top of hill. Signposted left to Llangarron. Exactly 1m Llangarron sign, Trecilla Farm is adjacent 2nd drive on right*

This delightful farmhouse, with exposed beams and an inglenook fireplace in the 'snug', dates back to the 16th century. Set in extensive and picturesque gardens, with a spring fed stream, it is quietly located in a rural area south west of Ross-on-Wye. The comfortable bedrooms are tastefully furnished with fine period pieces. Other facilities include a comfortable drawing room and an elegant dining room. Home cooked dinners are skilfully prepared on the Aga by Anne Dew.

FACILITIES: 3 en suite (8 GF) No smoking TVB tea/coffee No dogs (ex guide dogs) Cen ht TVL No children 12yrs Fishing Riding Pool Table Croquet lawn 3/4 size snooker table Games room 12 acres Horse livery & Sheep tack Dinner Last d by arrangement **PRICES:** s £30-£35; d £50-£70✻ **PARKING:** 10 **NOTES:** Closed 23 Dec-2 Jan

♦♦♦♦ Lumleys

Kern Bridge, Bishopswood HR9 5QT ☎ 01600 890040
🖷 0870 7062378
e-mail: helen@lumleys.force9.co.uk
Dir: *A40 turn off at Goodrich onto B4229 over Kern Bridge. Right at Inn On The Wye approx 400yds past inn opposite picnic ground*

This friendly guest house overlooks the River Wye and has been a hostelry since Victorian times, offering the character of a bygone era with modern comforts. Bedrooms are individually and carefully

continued

furnished and one has a four-poster bed and its own patio area. Public areas are comfortable and spacious and like the bedrooms are decorated to the owners' high standards.

FACILITIES: 3 en suite No smoking TVB tea/coffee Direct dial from bedrooms Cen ht No coaches Dinner Last d 7pm **PRICES:** s £30-£35; d £50-£60✻ **PARKING:** 15 **NOTES:** Closed Jan

♦♦♦♦ Brynheulog

Howle Hill HR9 5SP ☎ 01989 562051 🖷 01989 562051
Dir: *from Ross take B4234, left signed 'Howle Hill'. After 250yds take 1st right for Howle Hill, proceed to x-roads. Turn left, house past church*

This highly individual guest house has been lovingly designed and built by the owner to provide a high level of comfort throughout while benefiting from lovely views of open countryside. The bedrooms are all full of character and well equipped, with furniture built by a local craftsman. Two are in a self-contained wing with its own private lounge. Public areas consist of a tastefully decorated breakfast room and a relaxing lounge.

FACILITIES: 4 en suite (1 fmly) (2 GF) No smoking in 2 bedrooms No smoking in dining room No smoking in 1 lounge TV3B tea/coffee Cen ht TVL No coaches Jacuzzi Dinner **PRICES:** s £20-£30; d £40-£60✻ **LB** **PARKING:** 6

♦♦♦♦ Lea House

Lea HR9 7JZ ☎ 01989 750652 🖷 01989 750652
e-mail: enquiries@leahousebandb.com
Dir: *on A40, 4m SE of Ross-on-Wye*

This former 16th-century coaching inn is conveniently situated on the A40 into Ross on Wye and provides a relaxing base from which to explore the delightful Herefordshire countryside. Bedrooms are thoughtfully equipped and individually furnished, while hearty breakfasts can be enjoyed, family style, in the charming parlour.

FACILITIES: 3 en suite (1 fmly) No smoking TVB tea/coffee Cen ht No coaches Dinner Last d by prior arrangement **PRICES:** s £30; d £50-£60✻ **PARKING:** 4 **CARDS:**

♦♦♦♦ Sunnymount Hotel

Ryefield Rd HR9 5Ls ☎ 01989 563880 🖷 01989 566251
e-mail: sunnymount@tinyworld.co.uk
Dir: *M50 junct 4, at 1st rdbt follow signs for A449 Ross, at 2nd take A40 Gloucester turn, at 3rd turn right to Ross town centre, then take 2nd right*

This former 1920s residence is located in a quiet suburb on the outskirts of the town and has convenient access to the M50 and the A40. Immaculately maintained throughout, the bedrooms are well equipped and the public areas are spacious and comfortable. Diners are offered freshly prepared meals in the pleasant and airy dining room.

FACILITIES: 6 en suite No smoking in dining room No smoking in 1 lounge TVB tea/coffee No dogs (ex guide dogs) Licensed Cen ht TVL No coaches Dinner Last d 4pm **PRICES:** s £23-£28; d £46-£50✻ **LB** **PARKING:** 7 **CARDS:**

♦♦♦ The Whitehouse

Wye St HR9 7BX ☎ 01989 763572 🖷 01989 763572
Dir: *leave A40 onto A49 Ross-on-Wye, at Wilton rdbt, take 1st left after crossing river bridge, Whitehouse is 300yds on right*

This charming old house, part of a row of stone built properties, dates back to 1710. It is situated within easy reach of the town centre and is close to the River Wye. It has comfortable bedrooms of a good size and attractive style. Separate tables are provided in the traditionally furnished breakfast room.

FACILITIES: 6 en suite (2 fmly) TVB tea/coffee No dogs (ex guide dogs) Licensed No children 12yrs **PRICES:** s £40; d £58-£65✻ **CARDS:**

England

◆◆◆ The Arches
Walford Rd HR9 5PT ☎ 01989 563348 Fax 01989 563348
e-mail: the.arches@which.net
Dir: *take B4234 from town centre, heading towards Walford. Establishment is 0.5m on L, after childrens' play area*

Situated on the outskirts of town, this friendly guest house is a convenient base from which to explore the local countryside. Bedrooms are comfortable and thoughtfully equipped; public areas include a pleasant dining room where freshly-prepared breakfasts can be enjoyed, and a conservatory lounge which overlooks the large, well-maintained garden.
FACILITIES: 5 en suite (1 fmly) No smoking in bedrooms No smoking in dining room TVB tea/coffee Cen ht No coaches **PRICES:** s £25; d £50✳ **PARKING:** 5 **CARDS:**

◆◆◆ Brookfield House
Ledbury Rd HR9 7AT ☎ 01989 562188 Fax 01989 564053
e-mail: reception@brookfieldhouse.co.uk
Dir: *approaching town from M50 (via Ledbury rd) Brookfield House is on left at bottom of hill before town centre*
FACILITIES: 8 rms (3 en suite) No smoking in dining room TVB tea/coffee Licensed Cen ht TVL No children 5yrs No coaches **PRICES:** s £18-£27; d £33-£37; (room only) ✳ **LB BB PARKING:** 10 **NOTES:** Closed 3 days Xmas rs Dec-Jan **CARDS:**

◆◆ Raglan House
17 Broad St HR9 7EA ☎ 01989 768289
This listed Queen Anne property is located in the town centre. Pretty bedrooms are equipped with modern facilities, and there is a restaurant, open throughout the day for morning coffee and lunch but not for dinner. Public parking is close by.
FACILITIES: 7 en suite No smoking in dining room TVB tea/coffee No dogs (ex guide dogs) Licensed Cen ht Dinner Last d 6pm **PRICES:** s £20-£27.50; d £40-£45✳ **LB**

SYMONDS YAT (EAST) — Map 03 SO51

◆◆◆◆ Garth Cottage
HR9 6JL ☎ 01600 890364 Fax 01600 890364
Dir: *turn off A40 at Little Chef, Whitchurch & follow signs for Symonds Yat East*
The proprietors' serious approach to guest comfort is evident in this attractive 18th-century house. Bedrooms are well equipped and individually decorated and breakfast and dinner can be taken in the conservatory-style dining room whilst enjoying views over the River Wye. There is also a small, well stocked bar, and a sun lounge which also fronts the river.
FACILITIES: 4 en suite No smoking in bedrooms No smoking in dining room tea/coffee No dogs (ex guide dogs) Licensed Cen ht TVL No children 12yrs No coaches Fishing Dinner Last d 12noon **PRICES:** s £25-£45; d £50✳ **PARKING:** 9 **NOTES:** Closed Nov-Mar

SYMONDS YAT (WEST) — Map 03 SO51

◆◆◆◆ Norton House
Whitchurch, Symonds Yat HR9 6DJ ☎ 01600 890046
Fax 01600 890045
e-mail: norton@osconwhi.source.co.uk
Dir: *A40 sliproad for Whitchurch, right over A40, 1st left to T-junct, turn left, located 300yds on right past Memorial Hall*
Built as a farmhouse, Norton House dates back some 300 years. It has lots of character, with original features such as stone-flagged floors and beamed ceilings. The bedrooms, one with a four-poster, have modern facilities and are tastefully furnished in keeping with the style of the house. Log fires burn during cold weather in the comfortable lounge.
FACILITIES: 3 en suite No smoking TVB tea/coffee Cen ht TVL No children 12yrs No coaches Dinner Last d 9am **PRICES:** s £28-£32; d £44-£48✳ **PARKING:** 5 **NOTES:** Closed 25 Dec

WEOBLEY — Map 03 SO45

◆◆◆◆ *The Salutation Inn*
Market Pitch HR4 8SJ ☎ 01544 318443 Fax 01544 318216
e-mail: salutation@btclick.com
Dir: *situated off the A44 approx 8m SW of Leominster*

Located in the heart of this award-winning medieval village in an Area of Outstanding Natural Beauty, the inn is an intregal part of community life and enjoys a fine reputation for the imaginative food served in the informal dining room or elegant restaurant. Bedrooms are homely and comfortable and a warm welcome is assured.
FACILITIES: 3 en suite No smoking in bedrooms No smoking in dining room No smoking in 1 lounge STV TVB tea/coffee No dogs (ex guide dogs) Cen ht No children 10yrs No coaches Dinner Last d 9-9.30pm **PARKING:** 14 **CARDS:**

England

WEOBLEY continued

♦♦♦ Hill Top Farm *(SO419486)*
Wormsley HR4 8LZ ☎ 01981 590246 📠 01981 590246
Mrs R Jennings
e-mail: jennings.assoc@virgin.net
Dir: *from Hereford turn off A4103, Roman Road towards Weobley. After passing 2nd golf club follow B&B signs, turn left 0.5m after golf club. From Weobley take road marked Wormsley, in 2.5m right at brow of hill and follow B&B signs*

Located high in the Hereford hills, and enjoying splendid views over four counties. This traditional farmhouse offers comfortable accommodation and the informal atmosphere of the working farm enables guests to relax and enjoy the peaceful surroundings.
FACILITIES: 2 en suite (1 fmly) No smoking tea/coffee No dogs Cen ht TVL 250 acres arable, sheep **PRICES:** s fr £20; d £40-£44✻
PARKING: 6 **NOTES:** Closed Xmas

WIGMORE — Map 07 SO46

♦♦ *Compasses Hotel*
HR6 9UN ☎ 01568 770203 📠 01568 770705
This traditional village inn dates back to the 16th century and provides value-for-money accommodation. The bedrooms are equipped with modern facilities. There are two bars, a separate restaurant and a function room. The atmosphere is peaceful and relaxing and a good range of food is always available.
FACILITIES: 4 rms No smoking in 1 bedrooms No smoking in dining room TV3B tea/coffee Cen ht Dinner Last d 9.30pm **PRICES:** s £25; d £50✻
PARKING: 36 **CARDS:**

WINFORTON — Map 03 SO24

♦♦♦♦ Well Farm B & B *(SO296469)*
Well Farm HR3 6EA ☎ 01544 327278 📠 01544 327278
Mrs J Davies
e-mail: janet@wellfarm.fsworld.co.uk
Dir: *A438 on edge of Winforton village towards Brecon, farmhouse on left*
Well Farm is a large modern house which is situated on a 55 acre sheep rearing holding. It provides tastefully appointed accommodation. The facilities include a comfortable lounge and separate tables are provided in the conservatory breakfast room, which overlooks impressive views of the Black Mountains and Brecon Beacons.
FACILITIES: 4 en suite No smoking TV3B tea/coffee No dogs (ex guide dogs) Cen ht No children 14yrs 55 acres Beef/sheep
PRICES: s £25; d £50✻ **PARKING:** 6 **NOTES:** Closed Dec-Jan

YARKHILL — Map 03 SO64

♦♦♦♦ Garford Farm *(SO600435)*
HR1 3ST ☎ 01432 890226 📠 01432 890707 Mrs H Parker
e-mail: garfordfarm@lineone.net
Dir: *from Newtown x-rds where A417 crosses A4103 take A4103 towards Hereford, Garford is 1.5m on the left*
continued

This black and white timber-framed farmhouse dates back to the 17th century. Set on a large arable holding, it has a wealth of charm and character, enhanced by period furnishings and welcoming real fires which burn in the comfortable lounge during cold weather. The bedrooms, which include a family room, have modern equipment, and the one without en suite facilities has a private bathroom.
FACILITIES: 2 en suite (1 fmly) No smoking in dining room No smoking in lounges TVB tea/coffee Cen ht No children 2yrs Fishing Riding Croquet lawn 200 acres arable **PRICES:** s fr £23; d fr £42✻ **PARKING:** 6
NOTES: Closed 25-26 Dec

HERTFORDSHIRE

BERKHAMSTED — Map 04 SP90

♦♦ Laurel Cottage
31a Ashlyns Rd HP4 3BN ☎ 01442 876930
Dir: *Berkhamsted village, Kings Road 1st turning left after Collegiate school*
Located on a quiet residential road close to town centre, this attractive bungalow, surrounded by a laurel hedge, provides self-contained single accommodation in a purpose built annexe. The bedroom is equipped with both practical and homely extras and a room service continental breakfast is provided.
FACILITIES: 1 annexe en suite No smoking TVB tea/coffee No dogs Cen ht
PRICES: s £24✻ **PARKING:** 4 **NOTES:** Closed Xmas

BISHOP'S STORTFORD — Map 05 TL42

Premier Collection

♦♦♦♦♦ Harewood
Snakes Ln, Ugley CM22 6HW ☎ 01279 813907
📠 01279 647493
e-mail: susie-elmes@lineone.net
Dir: *M11 junct 8, A120 W to Puckeridge, B1383 N thru Stanstead Mountfitchet, approx 1m turn right to Elsenham & Ugley Green, right into Snakes Lane, Harewood approx 50yds on left*
Expect a warm welcome at this charming property, situated in a peaceful rural location, yet just 15 minutes drive from Stansted Airport. The house is surrounded by attractive well-tended gardens which include a pond and a summerhouse. The individually decorated bedrooms are tastefully furnished with well-chosen pieces and have many thoughtful touches. A wide choice of locally sourced items is available for breakfast, served at a large communal table in the elegant dining room.
FACILITIES: 2 en suite No smoking TVB tea/coffee Cen ht TVL No coaches Croquet lawn **PRICES:** s £35-£40; d £60✻ **PARKING:** 4
NOTES: Closed 21 Dec-1 Jan

♦♦♦♦ Anglesey
16 Grailands CM23 2RG ☎ 01279 653614
e-mail: jeanwindus@aol.com
Dir: *M11 junct 8, take A120 (Hertford), straight on at 2 rdbts, left at 3rd.Fork left immediately after Rugby Club & 2nd right*
Expect a warm welcome at this friendly family run guest house situated in a peaceful residential area just a short drive from the town centre. Bedrooms are attractively decorated and have a range of useful extras. Breakfast is served at a large table in the lounge/dining room, which overlooks the pretty garden.
FACILITIES: 3 rms (2 en suite) No smoking TVB tea/coffee No dogs Cen ht TVL No children 8yrs No coaches **PRICES:** d £50-£60✻ **LB PARKING:** 6
CARDS:

♦♦♦♦ Little Bullocks Farm

Hope End, Takeley CM22 6TA ☎ 01279 870464
🖷 01279 871430
e-mail: julie@waterman-farm.fsnet.co.uk
Dir: *M11, then A120 to Colchester cross traffic lights at x-rds 1st right to Hope End, left at Traingle Farm at bottom of lane on left*

A warm welcome is offered at this delightful family-run guest house, which is situated in a peaceful rural location. The property is ideally placed for the M11 and Stansted Airport. Bedrooms are smartly decorated, thoughtfully equipped and furnished with well-chosen pieces. A hearty continental breakfast is served at individual tables in the modern dining room.

FACILITIES: 3 en suite (2 fmly) (3 GF) No smoking TVB tea/coffee Cen ht No coaches **PRICES:** d £50-£55✳ **PARKING:** 15

♦♦♦♦ Nags Head

Wellpond Green SG11 1NL ☎ 01920 821424 🖷 01920 821424

(For full entry see Standon)

♦♦♦ Broadleaf Guest House

38 Broadleaf Av CM23 4JY ☎ 01279 835467
e-mail: paulabroadleaf63@freeserve.co.uk
Dir: *From M11 follow signs for Hertford (A120), straight over 6 rdbts at 7th turn left signed Bishop's Stortford over next rdbt then turn right at next rdbt, & right at next rdbt into Friedburge Ave. Broadleaf Ave 5th turning on right*

Close to the town centre and within easy driving distance of Stansted Airport and the M11. Attractive detached house situated in a quiet residential area at the end of a cul-de sac. The bedrooms are pleasantly decorated, tastefully furnished and well equipped. Breakfast is taken in the smart dining room, which overlooks the pretty garden.

FACILITIES: 1 rms (1 fmly) No smoking TVB tea/coffee Cen ht No coaches **PRICES:** s £25-£30; d fr £50✳ **PARKING:** 2

♦♦♦ *Pearse House*

Parsonage Ln CM23 5BQ ☎ 01279 757400 🖷 01279 506591
e-mail: pearsehouse@route56.co.uk
Dir: *from M11 take exit for A120 Bishop's Stortford.At next rdbt take A1250 B/Stortford.Turn right at next rdbt into Parsonage Lane. Take 1st left (The Independents)*

Detached half-timbered Victorian house situated on the edge of town just a few minutes drive from Stansted Airport. The extensive public areas include a bar, a lounge, a dining room and conference facilities. Bedrooms are smartly appointed and equipped with modern facilities.

FACILITIES: 13 en suite 24 annexe en suite (2 fmly) No smoking in bedrooms No smoking in dining room No smoking in lounges STV TVB tea/coffee Direct dial from bedrooms No dogs (ex guide dogs) Licensed Cen ht TVL Leisure room, Fitness room Dinner Last d 8pm **PARKING:** 100 **NOTES:** Closed Xmas/New Year
CARDS:

BUNTINGFORD — Map 05 TL32

♦♦♦♦ Buckland Bury Farm *(TL357336)*

Buckland Bury SG9 0PY ☎ 01763 272958 🖷 01763 274722
Mrs P Hodge
e-mail: buckbury@farmersweekly.net
Dir: *2nd house on right going north on the A10 in Buckland, white milk churn at the end of the road.*

A delightful 300-year-old farmhouse just a short drive from Buntingford. Public rooms retain much of their original character, with exposed beams, a communal table and a large open fireplace in the dining room. The individually furnished bedrooms are all well equipped and have a range of thoughtful extras.

FACILITIES: 3 rms (1 en suite) No smoking in bedrooms No smoking in dining room TVB tea/coffee No dogs (ex guide dogs) Lift Cen ht TVL 550 acres arable **PRICES:** s £25; d £45✳ **PARKING:** 12
CARDS:

HARPENDEN — Map 04 TL11

♦♦♦♦ Laurels

22 Leyton Rd AL5 2HU ☎ 01582 712226 🖷 01582 712226
Dir: *Follow A1081 to Harpenden. From N proceed through High St and straight over rdbt by Harpenden Arms keep in right lane. At next rdbt turn right into Leyton Rd, follow round to the right. House on left next to Day Nursery.*

Located within pretty gardens on the edge of the town, this well maintained house offers modern bedrooms with a range of practical extras and comprehensive breakfasts which are served in the cosy dining room.

FACILITIES: 8 en suite (2 fmly) No smoking TVB tea/coffee No dogs Cen ht No coaches **PRICES:** s £80; d £80✳ **PARKING:** 3 **NOTES:** Closed Xmas
CARDS:

HEMEL HEMPSTEAD — Map 04 TL00

♦♦♦ *Alexandra*

40/42 Alexandra Rd HP2 5BP ☎ 01442 242897
🖷 01442 211829
e-mail: alexhous@aol.com

This constantly improving well-managed guest house enjoys a regular commercial clientele and provides well-equipped bedrooms, which have practical extras. Breakfast is taken in the ground floor dining room, which also contains a lounge area. There is a good selection of tourist information provided.

FACILITIES: 16 rms (3 fmly) No smoking in 10 bedrooms No smoking in dining room STV TVB tea/coffee No dogs (ex guide dogs) Lift Cen ht TVL No children 2yrs **PARKING:** 6 **CARDS:**

England

HITCHIN Map 04 TL12

♦♦♦♦ Redcoats Farmhouse Hotel

Redcoats Green SG4 7JR ☎ 01438 729500 01438 723322
e-mail: sales@redcoats.co.uk

A delightful 14th-century property, ideally situated in four acres of mature landscaped grounds, yet only five minutes drive from the A1(M). The spacious bedrooms are split between the main house and a courtyard style annexe; each room is pleasantly decorated and very well equipped. Dinner and breakfast are served in the conservatory, which has superb views of the garden, and there is a cosy lounge as well as a smart bar.

FACILITIES: 5 rms (3 en suite) 9 annexe en suite (1 fmly) No smoking in 9 bedrooms No smoking in area of dining room TVB tea/coffee Direct dial from bedrooms Licensed Cen ht TVL No coaches Dinner Last d 9pm **PRICES:** s £55-£70; d £70-£115✻ **LB PARKING:** 30 **NOTES:** Closed 27 Dec-2 Jan & BH Mons rs Sun (dinner not served) Civ Wed 60 **CARDS:**

♦♦♦ The Greyhound

London Rd, St Ippollitts SG4 7NL ☎ 01462 440989
Dir: *on B656 1m S of Hitchin*

This popular inn stands in open farmland, but within striking distance of the town centre. Bedrooms are well-equipped with modern facilities, decorative with cheerful colour schemes and a variety of pictures and prints; two rooms are on the ground floor, with direct access from the car park. Service is both friendly and helpful within the bar and dining area; interesting meals are readily available.

FACILITIES: 4 en suite No smoking in dining room TVB tea/coffee Cen ht Dinner Last d 9:30pm **PRICES:** s £45-£55; d £60-£75✻ **LB MEALS:** Lunch £13.50-£24alc Dinner £13.50-£24alc✻ **PARKING:** 25 **CARDS:**

♦♦♦ Lord Lister Hotel

1 Park St SG4 9AH ☎ 01462 432712 & 459451
01462 438506
e-mail: info@lordlister.co.uk
Dir: *from junct 8 at A1(M), turn left to Hitchin. At 1st rdbt take sign to town centre. At bottom of hill at mini rdbt hotel on right*

The Lord Lister was built in the late 18th century and still has a number of its original features. The well-maintained bedrooms are comfortable, well-furnished and equipped. Guests have use of a lounge and cosy bar, whilst breakfast is served in the brightly decorated dining room; helpful advice is given on local eateries, with discounts at several.

FACILITIES: 16 en suite 4 annexe en suite (3 fmly) No smoking in 4 bedrooms No smoking in dining room No smoking in lounges TVB tea/coffee Direct dial from bedrooms No dogs Licensed Cen ht TVL **PRICES:** s £60-£70; d £70-£80✻ **PARKING:** 18 **CARDS:**

ST ALBANS Map 04 TL10

♦♦♦ Ardmore House

54 Lemsford Rd AL1 3PR ☎ 01727 859313 01727 859313

Located in immaculate grounds in a mainly residential area close to the town centre, this extended Edwardian house has been carefully renovated to provide a range of facilities, appreciated by a loyal commercial clientele. The practically furnished bedrooms offer a good range of facilities and the extensive public areas include a spacious conservatory dining room.

FACILITIES: 40 en suite (5 fmly) No smoking in 6 bedrooms No smoking in dining room No smoking in 1 lounge TVB tea/coffee Direct dial from bedrooms No dogs (ex guide dogs) Licensed Cen ht TVL Dinner Last d 8.30pm **PRICES:** s £45-£58; d £75-£95✻ **CONF:** Thtr 50 Class 40 Board 40 Del from £120 ✻ **PARKING:** 40 **NOTES:** rs 25-26 Dec & 1 Jan Civ Wed 150 **CARDS:**

STANDON Map 05 TL32

♦♦♦♦ Nags Head

Wellpond Green SG11 1NL ☎ 01920 821424 01920 821424
Dir: *Off A120 at sign for Wellford Grn, 0.5m down windy rd to junct. Nags Head on right*

A warm welcome and friendly service is just part of the appeal of this popular inn, situated in the quiet village of Wellpond Green. The spacious restaurant offers a good range of dishes, as does the local bar. Modern bedrooms are well-appointed and have good en suite showers.

FACILITIES: 5 en suite (1 fmly) No smoking in bedrooms No smoking in dining room TVB tea/coffee No dogs Cen ht Dinner Last d 9.15pm **PRICES:** s fr £45; d fr £65✻ **MEALS:** Lunch £16-£21alc Dinner £16-£21alc✻ **PARKING:** 25 **CARDS:**

WATFORD Map 04 TQ19

♦♦♦ Upton Lodge

26-28 Upton Rd WD18 0JP ☎ 01923 237316 01923 233109
e-mail: info@whitehousehotel.co.uk
Dir: *from M1 junct 5 take A4008 to Watford centre. Take junct 19 from M25 eastbound/junct 21A from M25 westbound*

Located within easy walking distance of the town centre, this careful renovation of two Edwardian houses provides a range of bedrooms equipped with lots of practical and homely extras. A cocktail bar and restaurant are situated in the White House Hotel opposite, which is under the same ownership and where registration also takes place.

FACILITIES: 26 annexe en suite (1 fmly) (7 GF) No smoking in 5 bedrooms No smoking in dining room No smoking in 1 lounge STV TVB tea/coffee Direct dial from bedrooms No dogs (ex guide dogs) Licensed Cen ht TVL Dinner Last d 9.45pm **PRICES:** s £64-£84; d £99; (room only) ✻ **PARKING:** 35 **CARDS:**

England

WELWYN GARDEN CITY Map 04 TL21

♦♦♦ Brocket Arms

Ayot St Lawrence AL6 9BT ☎ 01438 820250 01438 820068

Located in the pretty rural village of Ayot St Lawerence where George Bernard Shaw lived for forty years, this 14th century inn retains much of its original character including inglenook fireplaces and a wealth of exposed beams. Bedrooms, situated within the main building or converted outbuildings are homely and a range of imaginative food, featuring game in season, is served in the cosy restaurant.

FACILITIES: 3 en suite 3 annexe en suite (1 fmly) (3 GF) No smoking in bedrooms No smoking in dining room No smoking in lounges TVB tea/coffee No dogs (ex guide dogs) Cen ht Fishing Dinner Last d 9.30pm **PRICES:** s £70; d £80* **MEALS:** Lunch fr £6&alc Dinner fr £6&alc* **PARKING:** 4 **CARDS:**

WIGGINTON Map 04 SP91

♦♦♦♦ Rangers Cottage

Tring Park HP23 6EB ☎ 01442 890155 01442 827814

e-mail: rangerscottage@aol.com

Dir: *M25 junct 20 follow signs A41 Aylesbury, Tring exit, signposted Wigginton, up Oddy Hill at top right to Highfield Rd (letter box on corner) don't follow road round to left, go straight ahead into Tring Park, last house on track*

Close to the Ridgeway, in an area of outstanding natural beauty, this late 19th-century house was built for the Rothschild banking family's estate manager and has been sympathetically restored to provide thoughtfully furnished bedrooms accessed separately from the main house. A kitchen garden provides produce for the memorable breakfasts, taken at one family table in the dining room.

FACILITIES: 3 annexe en suite (1 fmly) (3 GF) No smoking TVB tea/coffee No dogs Cen ht No coaches **PRICES:** s £48-£53; d £60-£65* **PARKING: CARDS:**

KENT

APPLEDORE Map 05 TQ92

♦♦♦♦ *The Railway Hotel*

Station Rd TN26 2DF ☎ 01233 758253 758668 & 758785 01233 758705

e-mail: railwayhotel@enterprise.net

Dir: *leave M20 junct 10 follow A2070 for Brenzett. At rdbt in Brenzett turn right onto B2080 to Appledore. 2m, hotel on left*

Situated in rural surroundings with a good car park and beer garden, this extended Victorian hotel offers a range of comfortable public areas including cosy open plan bars, formal restaurant and a comfortable lounge. The bedrooms are located in a quality chalet block and all are equipped with a wide range of practical extras.

FACILITIES: 12 en suite (4 fmly) No smoking in 2 bedrooms No smoking in area of dining room TVB tea/coffee Direct dial from bedrooms Cen ht Fishing Dinner Last d 9.30pm **PARKING:** 47 **NOTES:** Closed 24 Dec-1 Jan **CARDS:**

ASHFORD Map 05 TR04

See also Challock

♦♦♦♦ *Bethersden Old Barn*

The Old Barn, Bridge Farm, Bethersden TN26 3LE

☎ 0870 740 1180 01233 820547

Dir: *south of Bethersden, on A28, over bridge by Bull Public House*

Located within a rural village community west of Ashford, this sympathetic conversion of an 18th century barn offers a self contained guest suite complete with cosy homely bedroom, private lounge and fully fitted modern kitchen. Guests are provided with a comprehensive breakfast within the main house or by room service.

FACILITIES: 2 rms (1 en suite) (1 fmly) No smoking TVB tea/coffee No dogs (ex guide dogs) Cen ht No coaches **PARKING:** 6 **CARDS:**

♦♦♦ Croft Hotel

Canterbury Rd, Kennington TN25 4DU

☎ 01233 622140 01233 635271

e-mail: crofthotel@btconnect.com

Dir: *approx 1.5m from M20 junct 9 or 10. Take A28 towards Canterbury (The Independents)*

Attractive 17th century redbrick house situated amidst two acres of landscaped grounds just a short drive from Ashford railway station. The generously proportioned bedrooms are located in pretty cottages with neat lawns; they are pleasantly decorated and thoughtfully equipped. Public rooms include a smart new restaurant, a bar and a cosy lounge.

FACILITIES: 15 en suite 13 annexe en suite (4 fmly) (12 GF) No smoking in 6 bedrooms No smoking in dining room No smoking in 1 lounge STV TVB tea/coffee Direct dial from bedrooms Licensed Cen ht TVL ch fac Dinner Last d 9.30pm **PRICES:** s £45-£65; d £58-£73* **LB CONF:** Del from £85 * **PARKING:** 30 **CARDS:**

♦♦♦ Vicky's

38 Park Rd North TN24 8LY ☎ 01233 631061 01233 640420

e-mail: vicky@ford27.freeserve.co.uk

A warm welcome is assured at this constantly improving terraced house, located a few minutes walk from the town centre. Bedrooms are filled with lots of thoughtful extras and comprehensive breakfasts are taken in an attractive dining room adjoining the cosy lounge.

FACILITIES: 4 rms (2 en suite) (1 fmly) No smoking in dining room TVB tea/coffee Cen ht Dinner Last d 9am **PRICES:** s £25; d £44* **PARKING:** 4 **NOTES:** Closed 24-26 Dec **CARDS:**

AYLESFORD Map 05 TQ75

♦♦♦♦ Wickham Lodge

73 High St ME20 7AY ☎ 01622 717267 01622 792855

e-mail: wickhamlodge@aol.com

Dir: *M20 junct 5 follow signs to Aylesford village. Wickham Lodge is in The Quay a small road beside Chequers Public House.*

FACILITIES: 3 en suite (1 fmly) (3 GF) No smoking TVB tea/coffee Cen ht No coaches **PRICES:** s fr £30; d fr £55* **PARKING:** 4 **CARDS:**

BIDDENDEN Map 05 TQ83

♦♦♦♦ *Bishopsdale Oast*

TN27 8DR ☎ 01580 291027 01580 292321

e-mail: drysdale@bishopsdaleoast.co.uk

Dir: *A28, Tenterden-Rolvenden road, first right after Tenterden into Cranbrook Rd, 2.5m to sign for B&B on left, turn left and follow signs*

Situated in a peaceful rural location amidst mature grounds, this property has been sympathetically restored and retains much of its original character. Bedrooms are cheerfully decorated with co-ordinated soft furnishings and equipped with many thoughtful touches. Public areas include a sitting room and a smartly appointed dining room. Imaginative home cooked dinners feature home-grown produce.

FACILITIES: 4 en suite (1 fmly) No smoking in bedrooms TVB tea/coffee No dogs (ex guide dogs) Cen ht TVL No coaches Dinner Last d before noon **PARKING:** 6 **CARDS:**

England

BROADSTAIRS Map 05 TR36

♦♦♦♦ Bay Tree Hotel

12 Eastern Esplanade CT10 1DR ☎ 01843 862502
📠 01843 860589

***Dir:** from rail station towards sea, take main road through town centre on leaving turn right into Rectory Road this leads to Eastern Esplanade, hotel on left*

The Bay Tree Hotel is a family run hotel that enjoys a prime sea-facing position on the East Cliff. It offers a good range of attractive, well-equipped bedrooms, the best with a balcony and sea view. There is a comfortable bar lounge and a separate front dining room that offers a good choice of menu at both breakfast and dinner.

FACILITIES: 10 en suite (1 GF) No smoking in bedrooms No smoking in dining room TVB tea/coffee No dogs Licensed Cen ht TVL No children 10yrs No coaches Dinner Last d breakfast **PRICES:** s £30-£34; d £60-£68 **LB** **PARKING:** 11 **NOTES:** Closed Xmas & New Year **CARDS:**

♦♦♦♦ Devonhurst Hotel

Eastern Esplanade CT10 1DR ☎ 01843 863010 📠 01843 868940
e-mail: info@devhotel@aol.com

***Dir:** in Broadstairs High Street, pass Barclays Bank take 3rd or 4th turning on right into Rectory Rd or Dickens Rd*

A warm welcome is assured at this small family run hotel, overlooking the sea and close to the town centre. Bedrooms are brightly decorated and comfortably furnished. There is a small cosy lounge linked to the attractive dining room. Guests are offered a choice of dishes at dinner and breakfast.

FACILITIES: 9 en suite (1 fmly) No smoking in bedrooms No smoking in dining room TVB tea/coffee No dogs (ex guide dogs) Licensed Cen ht TVL No children 5yrs No coaches Dinner Last d 5.30pm **PRICES:** s £30.50-£34; d £56-£65✻ **LB** **CARDS:**

♦♦♦♦ Oakfield Private Hotel

11 The Vale CT10 1RB ☎ 01843 862506 📠 01843 600659
e-mail: oakfield.hotel@lineone.net

***Dir:** half way down Broadstairs High Street turn right into Queens Road, 3rd right into The Vale. Hotel 50yds on right*

In a quiet residential area, close to the sea front and shops, this small family run hotel offers good hospitality and comfortable accommodation. Evening meals are readily available within the smart dining room, and there is also a comfortable lounge and a separate bar with a pool table.

FACILITIES: 10 en suite No smoking in bedrooms No smoking in dining room TVB tea/coffee Direct dial from bedrooms No dogs (ex guide dogs) Licensed Cen ht TVL No children 10yrs No coaches Pool Table Games room Dinner Last d 4.30pm **PRICES:** s £26-£30; d £52-£57✻ **LB** **PARKING:** 11 **CARDS:**

CANTERBURY Map 05 TR15

Premier Collection

♦♦♦♦♦ Magnolia House

36 St Dunstan's Ter CT2 8AX ☎ 01227 765121 & 0585 595970 📠 01227 765121
e-mail: magnolia_house_canterbury@yahoo.com

***Dir:** from A2 take turn for Canterbury. Left at 1st rdbt approaching the city (signposted University). 3rd turn on right*

Magnolia House is an attractive, personally run house, and combines a warm welcome with superbly appointed bedrooms. The pleasant lounge looks out over the front garden. Evening meals (by prior arrangement) are a delight, taken in the dining room overlooking the stunning walled garden. A wide choice is offered at breakfast, including fruit salad, hand-made sausages and locally smoked bacon.

continued

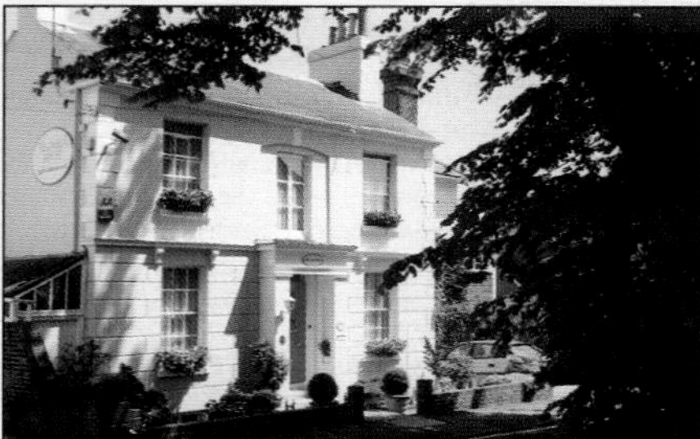

Magnolia House

FACILITIES: 7 en suite No smoking TVB tea/coffee No dogs Cen ht No children 12yrs No coaches Dinner Last d prebooked Nov-Feb **PRICES:** s £48-£55; d £85-£125✻ **LB** **PARKING:** 5 **CARDS:**

Premier Collection

♦♦♦♦♦ Thanington Hotel

140 Wincheap CT1 3RY ☎ 01227 453227 📠 01227 453225
e-mail: thanington@lineone.net

***Dir:** on A28, just outside city walls*

This fine Georgian property is close to the town centre and cathedral. The spacious and comfortable bedrooms are located in the main house or the smart modern extension, each with excellent facilities. Two bedrooms in the main house have four-posters. There is a spacious lounge, stunning dining room, games room and swimming pool overlooking the elegant courtyard. Secure parking is also a bonus.

FACILITIES: 16 rms (15 en suite) (2 fmly) (4 GF) No smoking in bedrooms No smoking in dining room TVB tea/coffee Direct dial from bedrooms No dogs (ex guide dogs) Licensed Cen ht TVL No coaches Indoor swimming pool (heated) Pool Table Threequarter size snooker table **PRICES:** s £55-£68; d £73-£110✻ **LB** **PARKING:** 13 **CARDS:**

See advertisement on opposite page

♦♦♦♦ *Yorke Lodge*

50 London Rd CT2 8LF ☎ 01227 451243 📠 01227 462006
e-mail: yorke-lg@dircon.co.uk

***Dir:** turn off A2 to Canterbury. At first rdbt bear left to the university into London Rd half way down on left*

This lovely house is decorated and run to the very highest of standards. The bedrooms are comfortable, spacious and very thoughtfully equipped. The rear garden is lovely and the cosy library has books, videotapes and newspapers. Breakfast is served in a stylish dining room, which features a display of household items from bygone days.

FACILITIES: 6 en suite (2 fmly) No smoking in dining room TVB tea/coffee No dogs Cen ht TVL No coaches **PARKING:** 6 **CARDS:**

♦♦♦♦ Beech Bank

Duckpit Ln, Waltham CT4 5QA ☎ 01227 700302
01227 700302
e-mail: beechbank@talk21.com
Dir: *B2068 from Canterbury for approx 4m, turn right into Petham and left into Duckpit Lane after The Oak Beamed House on left. House 2m on left*

This 15th century Tudor-style coach house has many architectural features, including a minstrels' gallery, and is set in landscaped

grounds and gardens with magnificent views and a rural setting, backing on to a Nature Reserve. Equipped with modern facilities, bedrooms have oak beams - one with a four-poster bed. Breakfast is served in the elegant Victorian conservatory, overlooking the Downs.

FACILITIES: 3 en suite (1 fmly) (2 GF) No smoking STV TVB tea/coffee No dogs Cen ht No coaches Tennis (grass) Croquet lawn Badminton Volleyball **PRICES:** s £35-£40; d £45-£49* **PARKING:** 8 **NOTES:** Closed 20 Dec-5 Jan

♦♦♦♦ Chislet Court Farm

Chislet CT3 4DU ☎ 01227 860309 01227 860444
e-mail: chisletcourtfarm@dial.pipex.com
Dir: *A28 Canterbury to Margate, left in Upstreet to Chislet. Farm on right 100yds past church. From London, M2 to A299 Margate road, signed*

In the pretty village of Chislet, just six miles from Canterbury, this early 18th century house retains a great deal of its original charm. All rooms in the house are huge, bedrooms included. Breakfast includes a fresh fruit selection and plentiful choice of both cereals and hot items. Service is warm and welcoming.

FACILITIES: 2 en suite No smoking TVB tea/coffee No dogs Cen ht No children 12yrs No coaches **PRICES:** s £30-£35; d £55-£60* **PARKING:** 4 **NOTES:** Closed Xmas

♦♦♦♦ Clare Ellen

9 Victoria Rd CT1 3SG ☎ 01227 760205 01227 784482
e-mail: loraine.williams@clareellenguesthouse.co.uk
Dir: *from A2 take A2050 to Canterbury. At 1st rdbt go straight over, right at 2nd at rdbt, right at 3rd rdbt (A28). 4th turning on left*

This comfortable, smart guest house offers attractive, well maintained accommodation, and is a pleasant walk from the city walls. Guests appreciate the secure car parking and breakfasts are freshly prepared and very enjoyable.

continued

FACILITIES: 6 en suite (2 fmly) No smoking in dining room No smoking in lounges STV TVB tea/coffee No dogs (ex guide dogs) Cen ht No coaches **PRICES:** s £28-£32; d £50-£58* **LB PARKING:** 9 **CARDS:**

♦♦♦♦ Ensigne Cottage

1 Ensigne Cottages, Shalmsford St, Chartham CT4 7RF
☎ 01227 738690
e-mail: pn72@dial.pipex.com
Dir: *off A28 Canterbury in direction of Ashford, at the Chelmsford St turning (ignore sign for Chartham) pass pub and post office turning is on right just beyond newsagents*

Charming cottage situated on the outskirts of Canterbury. A warm welcome, tea and homemade cake are to be expected on arrival at this friendly family run guest house. Bedrooms are attractively decorated, pleasantly furnished and thoughtfully equipped. Breakfast, which is served in the smart dining room, includes home made bread and preserves as well as free-range eggs.

FACILITIES: 3 rms (2 en suite) No smoking TVB tea/coffee No dogs Cen ht No coaches **PRICES:** s £25; d £45* **PARKING:** 3 **NOTES:** Closed 21-31Dec

♦♦♦♦ Waltham Court Hotel

Kake St, Petham CT4 5SB ☎ 01227 700413 01227 700127
e-mail: enquiries@walthamcourthotel.co.uk
Dir: *1.5m through Petham village towards Waltham.*

This striking Georgian house is set in a quiet, rural location, in its own attractive grounds. Chives restaurant is the hotel's focal point and has a strong local following, while the bar and lounge offer large inviting sofas. Bedrooms are beautifully appointed, bright and spacious, benefiting from modern en suites.

FACILITIES: 6 en suite (1 fmly) No smoking in area of dining room TVB tea/coffee No dogs (ex guide dogs) Licensed Cen ht No coaches Dinner Last d 9.30pm Wed-Sat **PRICES:** s £40-£45; d £65-£75* **LB CONF:** Thtr 60 Class 30 Board 25 Del from £55 * **PARKING:** 45 **NOTES:** Civ Wed 90 **CARDS:**

England

BROADSTAIRS continued

♦♦♦♦ The White House

6 St Peters Ln CT1 2BP ☎ 01227 761836
e-mail: WHWelcome@aol.com
Dir: *20yds off main shopping area inside old city walls. Follow car park signs for Marlowe Theatre, St Peter's Lane on right, just before bridge*

This attractive Regency house is situated in a quiet road close to the high street and offers comfortable and well maintained accommodation. The bedrooms all have modern en suite facilities and attractive co-ordinated decor. A traditional breakfast is served in the smart dining room.

FACILITIES: 9 en suite (2 fmly) No smoking in dining room No smoking in lounges TVB tea/coffee No dogs (ex guide dogs) Cen ht TVL No coaches **PRICES:** s £30-£40; d £50-£60✻ **LB**

♦♦♦ Canterbury Pilgrims Hotel

18 The Friars CT1 2AS ☎ 01227 464531 01227 762514
e-mail: pilgrimshotel@netscapeonline.co.uk
Dir: *follow signs for Marlowe Theatre, establishment opposite*

Located in the centre of historic Canterbury opposite the Marlowe Theatre, the Pilgrims Hotel has parts that date back some 350 years. Bedrooms are comfortably appointed and well equipped. Public areas include a spacious bar and an attractive restaurant. A good selection of dishes are available from the bar or restaurant menu.

FACILITIES: 15 en suite (1 fmly) No smoking in dining room TVB tea/coffee Direct dial from bedrooms No dogs (ex guide dogs) Cen ht Dinner Last d 9.30pm **PRICES:** s £45; d £65-£75✻ **PARKING:** 10 **CARDS:**

♦♦♦ Cathedral Gate Hotel

36 Burgate CT1 2HA ☎ 01227 464381 01227 462800
e-mail: cgate@cgate.demon.co.uk
Dir: *next to main gateway into cathedral precincts*

Built in 1438, the hotel is centrally located between the tranquillity of the cathedral and the bustle of the shopping precinct. Old beams, winding corridors and sloping floors attest to the age of the building, and all bedrooms are attractively furnished and equipped to modern standards. There is a comfortable guests' lounge and breakfasts are served either in the bedrooms or in the small breakfast room. Luggage may be unloaded at reception before parking in a local car park.

FACILITIES: 15 rms (2 en suite) 12 annexe rms (10 en suite) (5 fmly) No smoking in dining room TVB tea/coffee Direct dial from bedrooms Licensed Cen ht TVL Dinner Last d 9pm **PRICES:** s £24-£58; d £46.50-£88 **LB**
CARDS:

♦♦♦ *Ersham Lodge Hotel*

12 New Dover Rd CT1 3AP ☎ 01227 463174 & 768472
01227 455482
e-mail: ershamlod@aol.com
Dir: *From Canterbury ring road follow signs for Dover, after traffic lights by Blockbuster Videos, hotel on right*

This twin-gabled and galleried Victorian house is located close to the town and cathedral. The bedrooms vary in size and shape, but all are smartly presented and comfortable, some are situated on the ground floor. There is a cosy lounge bar and a spacious breakfast room which looks out onto the well kept patio and garden.

FACILITIES: 13 en suite (1 fmly) No smoking in 12 bedrooms No smoking in dining room No smoking in lounges TVB tea/coffee Direct dial from bedrooms No dogs (ex guide dogs) Licensed Cen ht **PARKING:** 15
CARDS:

♦♦♦ Upper Ansdore *(TR118498)*

Duckpit Ln, Petham CT4 5QB ☎ 01227 700672
01227 700840 Mr & Mrs R D Linch
e-mail: upperansdore@hotels.activebooking.com
Dir: *B2068 from Canterbury, right through village, left by telephone, after 1.5m right signed Ansdore*

This beautiful farmhouse once owned by a former Lord Mayor of London dates back to the 14th century. It is set in a peaceful rural location only 15 minutes drive from Canterbury and within easy reach of a number of pubs and restaurants. Bedrooms have en suite shower rooms and are comfortably furnished.

FACILITIES: 3 en suite (1 fmly) No smoking tea/coffee No dogs (ex guide dogs) Cen ht No children 5yrs Riding 4 acres mixed small holding
PRICES: d fr £45✻ **PARKING:** 5 **NOTES:** Closed Xmas
CARDS:

♦♦♦ Abberley House

115 Whitstable Rd CT2 8EF ☎ 01227 450265 01227 478626
e-mail: r.allcorn@virgin.net
Dir: *on left of A290 from Canterbury city*

FACILITIES: 3 rms (1 en suite) No smoking TVB tea/coffee No dogs Cen ht No children 8yrs No coaches **PRICES:** d £42-£48✻ **PARKING:** 3
NOTES: Closed 22 Dec-6 Jan

CHALLOCK Map 05 TR05

♦♦♦♦ Hegdale Farmhouse

Hegdale Ln, Pested TN25 4BE ☎ 01233 740224

Dir: *from A251 N of Challock rdbt towards Faversham, take 2nd right then 1st left into no through road. Farmhouse on left down narrow lane*

Expect a warm welcome from the caring host at this charming 16th century farmhouse set amidst four acres of grounds in the secluded Kent countryside. The bedrooms are attractively decorated, tastefully furnished and thoughtfully equipped. Breakfast is served at a large polished mahogany table in the lounge/dining room.

FACILITIES: 2 en suite (2 fmly) No smoking TVB tea/coffee No dogs Cen ht No coaches **PRICES:** s £22.50-£25.50; d £40-£45✳ **PARKING:** 3 **NOTES:** Closed 20 Dec-2 Jan

♦♦♦ Heycroft

Pested Ln TN25 4BD ☎ 01233 740423

Dir: *from A20 take A252 towards Canterbury, pass sign for Challock and at end of the Lees (large garden) turn right at sign for post office, last house on left*

Heycroft is an attractive detached property which is situated at the end of a private lane overlooking the green. The spacious bedrooms are pleasantly decorated, tastefully furnished and thoughtfully equipped. Breakfast is served at one large pine table, which has views onto the pretty gardens.

FACILITIES: 3 rms (1 en suite) (1 fmly) No smoking in bedrooms No smoking in dining room No smoking in 1 lounge TVB tea/coffee No dogs (ex guide dogs) Cen ht No coaches **PRICES:** s £20-£30; d £40-£45✳ **PARKING:** 4

CLIFTONVILLE

See **Margate**

CRANBROOK Map 05 TQ73

♦♦♦♦ Hallwood Farm Oast *(TQ755345)*

Hallwood Farm, Hawkhurst Rd TN17 2SP ☎ 01580 712416 Mrs S Wickham

e-mail: hallwoodfm@aol.com

Dir: *A229 S from Cranbrook 1m. Past Duke of Kent pub. Farm turning 400yds on right*

This delightful 17th century oasthouse located in beautiful rural surroundings between Cranbrook and Hawkhurst, has been sympathetically converted whilst retaining many original features. The spacious bedrooms are charmingly appointed and filled with many thoughtful and practical extras. Imaginative, carefully prepared breakfasts served in the attractive dining room are a highlight.

FACILITIES: 2 en suite No smoking TVB tea/coffee No dogs (ex guide dogs) No children 12yrs 230 acres fruit/ sheep/ arable **PRICES:** d £50-£60 **PARKING:** 6 **NOTES:** Closed Dec rs Jan

♦♦♦ Tolehurst Barn

Cranbrook Rd TN17 2BP ☎ 01580 714385 🖷 01580 714385

e-mail: info@tolehurstbarn.co.uk

Dir: *on A229 between Staplhurst/Cranbrook, 1.5m S of Staplehurst, on W side turn in where signed next to Bumbles Plant, along tarmac road to Barn*

FACILITIES: 3 en suite (1 fmly) No smoking TVB tea/coffee Cen ht No coaches Dinner Last d noon **PRICES:** s £25; d £40✳ **PARKING:** 6

DARTFORD Map 05 TQ57

♦♦♦ Rising Sun

Fawkham Green DA3 8NL ☎ 01474 872291 🖷 01474 872291

Dir: *from M20/M25 follow for A20 Brandshatch. Turn off old A20 into Scratchers Lane & follow until sign for Fawkham. Turn left (Brandshatch Rd) inn on left*

This popular inn is ideally situated just a short drive from Brands Hatch, the M25 and M20. Public rooms include a busy bar and restaurant as well as a patio for the warmer weather. The pleasantly decorated bedrooms are furnished with well chosen pieces and equipped with modern facilities.

FACILITIES: 5 en suite (1 fmly) No smoking TVB tea/coffee No dogs (ex guide dogs) Cen ht No coaches Dinner Last d 9.30pm **PRICES:** s £40-£50; d £65-£85✳ **MEALS:** Lunch £5-£15&alc Dinner £5-£15&alc✳ **PARKING:** 12 **NOTES:** Closed Xmas **CARDS:**

DEAL Map 05 TR35

Premier Collection

♦♦♦♦♦ Sutherland House Hotel

186 London Rd CT14 9PT ☎ 01304 362853 🖷 01304 381146

e-mail: info@sutherlandhouse.fsnet.co.uk

Dir: *on A258 Deal to Sandwich road, 200 yds from Deal Hospital*

This stylish hotel offers charming bedrooms which are decorated and furnished with great style and taste. The elegant dining room provides a charming venue for home cooked dinners and breakfasts and guests have the use of a comfortable lounge that is extremely well stocked with books and magazines.

FACILITIES: 4 en suite (1 GF) No smoking in bedrooms No smoking in area of dining room TVB tea/coffee Direct dial from bedrooms Licensed Cen ht No children 5yrs No coaches Dinner **PRICES:** s £45-£50; d £55-£60✳ **LB PARKING:** 7 **CARDS:**

♦♦♦♦ Sondes Lodge

14 Sondes Rd CT14 7BW ☎ 01304 368741 🖷 01304 368741

e-mail: sondeslodge@aol.com

Dir: *A258 Dover-Deal Road, along the Strand past Deal Castle, continue until last one-way street on right heading to seafront, 2nd guest house on right*

Expect a warm and friendly welcome at this Victorian terraced house, situated just off of the seafront and within walking distance of the town centre. Bedrooms are brightly decorated, pleasantly furnished and equipped with many useful extras. Breakfast is served in the elegant dining room seated at individual tables.

FACILITIES: 3 en suite No smoking in dining room TVB tea/coffee No dogs (ex guide dogs) Cen ht No children 10yrs No coaches **PRICES:** s £35; d £50-£60✳ **CARDS:**

England

DEAL continued

♦♦♦ The Hole in The Roof Hotel
42-44 Queen St CT14 6EY ☎ 01304 374839 01304 373768
e-mail: theholeintheroof@btopenworld.com
Dir: *off A2 onto A258 (7m to Deal). Follow Deal Station signs & hotel on junct of station*
FACILITIES: 8 en suite (2 fmly) No smoking in bedrooms No smoking in dining room STV TVB tea/coffee No dogs (ex guide dogs) Licensed Cen ht TVL Dinner Last d 9pm **PRICES:** s £40-£45; d £50-£60✳ **LB PARKING:** 2 **CARDS:**

DOVER Map 05 TR34

Premier Collection

♦♦♦♦♦ Old Vicarage
Chilverton Elms, Hougham CT15 7AS ☎ 01304 210668
01304 225118
e-mail: vicarage@csi.com
Dir: *M20/A20 towards Dover, exit at Hougham. At rdbt take B2011 signed West Hougham, then left. Through Hougham towards Dover, 1m on left*
Standing in immaculate grounds in a superb rural location offering stunning views of the surrounding countryside, this impressive early Victorian house retains many original features. Spacious bedrooms are filled with a wealth of thoughtful extras and have modern efficient bathrooms. Other areas include an elegant dining room, a sumptuous lounge and majestic staircase, enhanced by fine art and ornaments.
FACILITIES: 3 en suite (1 fmly) No smoking in bedrooms No smoking in dining room No smoking in 1 lounge TVB tea/coffee No dogs Cen ht TVL No coaches **PRICES:** d £70-£80✳ **PARKING:** 10 **CARDS:**

♦♦♦♦ Beulah House
94 Crabble Hill, London Rd CT17 0SA ☎ 01304 824615
828850
e-mail: owen@beulahhouse94.freeserve.co.uk
Dir: *on A256*
Located close to the town centre, this impressive redbrick Victorian house retains many original features, enhanced by the decor and furnishings. Bedrooms are spacious and comfortable, and public rooms include a sitting room and conservatory lounge. A full breakfast is served in the elegant dining room and the mature gardens feature fine, topiary examples.
FACILITIES: 9 rms (6 en suite) (2 fmly) No smoking TVB tea/coffee No dogs Cen ht TVL 1 acre gardens Dinner **PRICES:** s £30-£35; d £48-£56✳ **LB PARKING:** 11 **CARDS:**

♦♦♦♦ Number One
1 Castle St CT16 1QH ☎ 01304 202007 01304 214078
e-mail: res@number1guesthouse.co.uk
Dir: *exit A20 to castle, premises at bottom of Castle Hill. Or exit A2 at A258 into town & premises on corner on right before traffic lights*
The welcome is particularly warm at this early 19th-century former merchant banker's house, which sits just a few minutes' walk from the town's major attractions. Many original features remain in the public areas, whilst bedrooms are homely and well-equipped, complete with individual dining tables for private breakfasts.
FACILITIES: 4 en suite (1 fmly) No smoking in dining room No smoking in lounges TVB tea/coffee No dogs Cen ht No coaches **PRICES:** d £46-£52✳ **LB PARKING:** 6 **NOTES:** Closed Xmas

♦♦♦ Ardmore Private Hotel
18 Castle Hill Rd CT16 1QW ☎ 01304 205895
01304 208229
e-mail: res@ardmoreph.co.uk
Dir: *on A258 next to Dover Castle*
This delightful house dates back to 1796. It is situated in the leas of Dover Castle and within easy striking distance of the town centre. The no-smoking accommodation is attractively furnished, retaining its character and elegance. Public rooms include a sumptuous lounge and a well-appointed breakfast room.
FACILITIES: 4 en suite (1 fmly) No smoking TVB tea/coffee No dogs Cen ht **PRICES:** d £40-£50✳ **NOTES:** Closed Xmas
CARDS:

♦♦♦ Castle House
10 Castle Hill Rd CT16 1QW ☎ 01304 201656 01304 210197
e-mail: dimechr@aol.com
Dir: *A20 for Dover-over 4 rdbts, turn left at lights past BP petrol station, 1st right into Castle Hill Rd and premises are just below Dover Castle*
Attractive guest house conveniently situated close to the castle, eastern docks and town centre; off street parking provided. Bedrooms are bright and comfortably furnished. Breakfast is available from 6.00am, a real bonus for ferry travellers and is taken at individual tables in the dining room, which overlooks the pretty garden. Castle House is entirely no-smoking.
FACILITIES: 6 en suite (1 fmly) No smoking TVB tea/coffee Licensed Cen ht No coaches **PRICES:** s £25-£30; d £40-£50✳ **LB PARKING:** 7
CARDS:

♦♦♦ Dovers Restover
69 Folkestone Rd CT17 9RZ ☎ 01304 206031 01304 216052
e-mail: adamoum@aol.com
Dir: *on B2011 opposite Dover Priory Railway Station approx 300mtrs from town centre*
This late Victorian terraced house is situated opposite the railway station and close to the port and the town centre. Some refurbishment has enhanced the comfortable accommodation. Bedrooms are compact, homely and nicely decorated. Breakfast is taken in the cosy dining room from 6.45am.
FACILITIES: 6 rms (3 en suite) No smoking in 4 bedrooms No smoking in dining room TVB tea/coffee No dogs Cen ht No coaches **PRICES:** s £20-£28; d £32-£56✳ **BB PARKING:** 4 **CARDS:**

♦♦♦ *Gateway Hovertel*
149-156 Snargate St CT17 9BZ ☎ 01304 205479
01304 211504
e-mail: dspeters@hovertel.fsnet.co.uk
Dir: *opposite Dover Marina, beside A20 approach road into Dover*
This hotel overlooks the marina and is close to the ferry terminal, hoverport and cruise terminal. Friendly staff go out of their way to help - and will even serve continental breakfast from 3am. The bedrooms are bright and well presented. Public areas include a small lounge and bar. An alarm-secured car park is available.
FACILITIES: 27 en suite (7 fmly) No smoking in dining room TVB tea/coffee No dogs (ex guide dogs) Licensed Cen ht TVL
PARKING: 26 **NOTES:** Closed 23 Dec-6 Jan **CARDS:**

See advertisement on opposite page

An asterisk ✳ indicates that prices given are for 2002.

♦♦♦ Hubert House

9 Castle Hill Rd CT16 1QW ☎ 01304 202253 🖷 01304 210142
e-mail: huberthouse@btinternet.com
Dir: *at bottom of Castle Hill Rd leading to Dover Castle on A258*
A charming Georgian house within walking distance of the ferry port. Bedrooms are furnished in modern style and have remote control TV, clock radio alarm and tea tray. There is a small lounge and well appointed breakfast room. Families are especially welcome, full English and healthy breakfasts are provided.
FACILITIES: 8 en suite (4 fmly) No smoking in dining room TVB tea/coffee No dogs (ex guide dogs) Cen ht No coaches **PRICES:** s £30-£36; d £44-£50✳ **LB PARKING:** 7 **CARDS:**

♦♦♦ Kernow

189 Folkestone Rd CT17 9SJ ☎ 01304 207797
Dir: *turn off A20 onto B2011 & follow signs for Local Services. Establishment 3m from slip road on right*
A welcoming hotel, convenient for the ferries and train network. Accommodation is well maintained, neat and comfortable; rooms are not en suite but two bathrooms are available. There is adequate parking at the front of the property. Breakfast times can be arranged to suit travel arrangements.
FACILITIES: 3 rms TVB tea/coffee No dogs (ex guide dogs) Cen ht TVL No coaches **PRICES:** d £34-£38✳ **BB PARKING:** 4

♦♦♦ Longfield

203 Folkestone Rd CT17 9SL ☎ 01304 204716 🖷 01304 204716
e-mail: res@longfieldguesthouse.co.uk
Dir: *M20 to Dover, continue past junct 13, exit at Court Wood junction B2011. At rdbt turn left into Folkestone Rd. House 3m on right hand side*
This friendly, family run guest house is gradually being upgraded. Bedrooms are quite large and neatly appointed. Both Continental and English breakfasts are offered in the separate dining room. Secure car parking and garaging facilities are a real bonus.
FACILITIES: 8 rms (2 en suite) (2 fmly) (1 GF) No smoking in dining room No smoking in lounges TVB tea/coffee No dogs Cen ht No coaches Dinner Last d 4pm **PRICES:** s £18-£25; d £35-£50✳ **BB PARKING:** 11
NOTES: Closed Xmas/New Year **CARDS:**

♦♦♦ Penny Farthing

109 Maison Dieu Rd CT16 1RT ☎ 01304 205563
🖷 01304 204439
e-mail: pennyfarthing.dover@btinternet.com
This detached Victorian house is situated close the town centre. It provides airy, comfortable accommodation for the modern traveller. The bedrooms are spacious and all are well-equipped. Breakfast is taken in the separate dining room, which is filled with ornaments and plants.
FACILITIES: 6 rms (5 en suite) (2 fmly) No smoking TVB tea/coffee No dogs Cen ht No coaches **PRICES:** s £24; d £38-£42✳ **LB BB**
PARKING: 6

♦♦♦ Peverall House

28 Park Av CT16 1HD ☎ 01304 202573 🖷 01304 240034
e-mail: peverell_house@hotmail.com
Dir: *from A2 turn right at rdbt signed Dover Castle, take 2nd right (opposite Castle entrance), then 1st left*
Close to Connaught Park, this impressive Victorian house has a large, attractive garden. The pine-furnished accommodation includes an airy sun lounge and a breakfast room. Most bedrooms have a sunny aspect, and those on the top floor have views of the castle and town. The atmosphere is very informal and friendly.
FACILITIES: 7 rms (4 en suite) (4 fmly) No smoking in dining room TVB tea/coffee No dogs Cen ht No coaches **PRICES:** s £23-£32; d £36-£48✳ **LB BB PARKING:** 8 **CARDS:**

England

DOVER continued

♦♦♦ *St Albans Non-Smoking B&B*

71 Folkestone Rd CT17 9RZ ☎ 01304 206308 📠 01304 206888
e-mail: enquiries@accommodationdover.co.uk
Dir: *on B2011 (Old Dover/London road), opposite Priory railway station*
Situated opposite Priory Station and close to the town centre, this Victorian terraced house is adorned with pretty hanging baskets during the summer months. The friendly hosts are constantly improving the property, which is conveniently situated for the cross Channel traveller, with a free courtesy service to ports and the cruise liner terminal or for local attractions. Evening meals supplied by arrangement.
FACILITIES: 4 rms (3 en suite) No smoking STV TV6B tea/coffee No dogs Cen ht No coaches Dinner **CARDS:**

♦♦♦ St Martins

17 Castle Hill Rd CT16 1QW ☎ 01304 205938 📠 01304 208229
e-mail: res@stmartinsgh.co.uk
Dir: *on A258, by Dover Castle*
Expect a warm, friendly welcome at this small guest house which is ideally situated close to the castle, town centre and ferry terminal. The thoughtfully equipped bedrooms have pretty fabrics and decor, most rooms enjoy a sunny aspect. Other facilities include reception, an attractive pine-furnished breakfast room and a separate comfortable double-aspect lounge.
FACILITIES: 6 en suite (3 fmly) No smoking TVB tea/coffee No dogs Cen ht **PRICES:** s £30-£35; d £38-£48 **BB NOTES:** Closed Xmas **CARDS:**

♦♦♦ Swingate Inn & Hotel

Deal Rd CT15 5DP ☎ 01304 204043 📠 01304 204043
e-mail: terry@swingate.com
Dir: *turn off A2 onto 258 Deal road, hotel 0.25m on the right*
Ideal as a touring base, this inn offers modern accommodation with a relaxed and friendly atmosphere. Informal meals are served in the bar, whilst a la carte meals are offered in the pleasantly appointed restaurant; a spacious room with natural wood décor. Jazz evenings on Thursday prove particularly popular and family entertainment is provided on Sunday evenings.
FACILITIES: 11 en suite (2 fmly) No smoking in area of dining room No smoking in 1 lounge TVB tea/coffee No dogs (ex guide dogs) Cen ht Dinner Last d 9.45pm **PRICES:** s £42; d £50✳ **MEALS:** Lunch £20-£35alc Dinner £20-£35alc✳ **PARKING:** 60 **NOTES:** Civ Wed 200
CARDS:

See advertisement on page 247

DYMCHURCH — Map 05 TR12

♦♦♦♦ Waterside

15 Hythe Rd TN29 0LN ☎ 01303 872253 📠 01303 872253
e-mail: info@watersideguesthouse.co.uk
Dir: *on A259 5m W of Hythe*
An attractive well-maintained house with picturesque views, Waterside offers brightly decorated comfortably furnished bedrooms. A varied choice of popular dishes is offered for dinner and makes good use of home-grown produce. All meals are served in the cottage style dining room, and a small lounge and bar are also available.
FACILITIES: 5 en suite (1 fmly) No smoking in 3 bedrooms No smoking in dining room TVB tea/coffee No dogs Licensed Cen ht TVL No coaches Dinner Last d 7.30pm **PRICES:** s £25-£30; d £40-£45✳ **LB PARKING:** 7
CARDS:

Places with this symbol are farmhouses.

EASTCHURCH — Map 05 TQ97

♦♦♦ The Shurland

81 The High St ME12 4EH ☎ 01795 881100 📠 01795 880906
e-mail: reception@shurlandhotel.achivehotels.com
Dir: *Leave M2 /M20 via A249 towards Sheerness, over bridge to Isle of Sheppey,right at next rdbt towards Leysdown, straight ahead to Eastchurch village just past church*
This inn offers well-equipped accommodation for the discerning traveller; bedrooms are modern and bright with plenty of extra features. Guests have the use of the luxury fitness and leisure centre and can dine in the spacious restaurant which serves popular meals at both lunch and dinner. A further 11 bedrooms and a lift will become available during summer 2002.
FACILITIES: 9 rms (7 en suite) (1 fmly) No smoking in bedrooms No smoking in dining room No smoking in 1 lounge TVB tea/coffee Direct dial from bedrooms No dogs (ex guide dogs) Cen ht Squash Sauna Solarium Gymnasium Jacuzzi Aerobics,jacuzzi, gym, sunbed Dinner Last d 9.30pm **PRICES:** s £38.95-£50; d £55-£100✳ **LB PARKING:** 40 **NOTES:** rs 25 & 26 Dec **CARDS:**

EASTLING — Map 05 TQ95

♦♦♦ Carpenters Arms

The Street ME13 0AZ ☎ 01795 890234 📠 01795 890654
e-mail: carpenters-arms@lineone.net
Dir: *M2 junt 6 A251 to A2 1st left into Brosdale Rd 4m to Eastling. From M20, A2 to Lenham left on Hubbards Hill signed Warren St & Otterden, 5m to Eastling*
This delightful 14th-century village inn is full of character, with brick flooring, inglenook fireplaces and church pews. Bedrooms are located next door in Carpenters Cottage, and are all en suite and equipped with thoughtful extras. A popular à la carte menu is offered in the cosy candlelit restaurant.
FACILITIES: 3 en suite TVB tea/coffee No dogs (ex guide dogs) Cen ht No children 12yrs Dinner Last d 10pm **PRICES:** s £41.50; d £49.50-£52✳ **LB MEALS:** Lunch £15-£18&alc Dinner £15-£18&alc✳ **PARKING:** 20
CARDS:

EDENBRIDGE — Map 05 TQ44

♦♦♦♦ Ye Old Crown

74/76 The High St TN8 5AR ☎ 01732 867896 📠 01732 868316
Dir: *M25 junct 6, bear right onto A22 then onto A25, then B269 and B2026. Follow signs thereafter (The Circle)*

Popular inn dating back to the 13th-century, situated in the centre of town. Bedrooms are situated in a converted barn adjacent to the main building; each one is attractively decorated, tastefully furnished and equipped with many thoughtful extras. Breakfast is served in the upstairs restaurant and an interesting choice of home-made dishes are available for dinner.

continued

England

FACILITIES: 6 en suite (2 GF) No smoking in 2 bedrooms No smoking in area of dining room TVB tea/coffee Direct dial from bedrooms Cen ht Dinner Last d 10pm **PRICES:** s £59; d £74✱ **LB** **PARKING:** 12 **CARDS:**

FARNINGHAM Map 05 TQ56

Premier Collection

♦♦♦♦♦ Beesfield Farm

Beesfield Ln DA4 0LA ☎ 01322 863900 📠 01322 863900
e-mail: kim.vingoe@btinternet.com
Dir: *turn off A20 to A225 left to Beesfield Lane, farm 0.5m on left.*

Nestling in the lovely Kent countryside, this property also has easy access to major road networks and Brands Hatch. This delightful house offers individually appointed bedrooms with attention to detail and quality displayed throughout. Guests can enjoy good hospitality and home cooked breakfasts in the elegant and stylish lounge and dining room.
FACILITIES: 3 en suite No smoking TVB tea/coffee No dogs (ex guide dogs) Cen ht TVL No children 12yrs No coaches **PRICES:** d £80✱ **LB** **PARKING:** 10 **NOTES:** Closed 8 Dec-Jan

FAVERSHAM Map 05 TR06

♦♦♦♦ Preston Lea

Canterbury Rd ME13 8XA ☎ 01795 535266 📠 01795 533388
e-mail: preston.lea@which.net
Dir: *M2 junct 7/A2 signed Faversham, after approx 1 mile garage on right, establishment 200mtrs on right*

This Victorian mansion has three spacious bedrooms, each furnished in a traditional style creating a stylish and welcoming environment. Breakfast is served around a large oak table in the elegant dining room, whilst guests also have access to three comfortable lounges and impressive rear gardens.
FACILITIES: 3 en suite No smoking TVB tea/coffee No dogs Cen ht No children No coaches **PRICES:** s £35-£40; d £55-£60✱ **PARKING:** 11 **CARDS:**

FOLKESTONE Map 05 TR23

Premier Collection

♦♦♦♦♦ Harbourside Hotel

14 Wear Bay Rd CT19 6AT ☎ 01303 246824 & 01303 256528 📠 01303 241299
e-mail: joy@harboursidehotel.com
Dir: *M20 junct 13, follow signs to country park. Turn off A259, then A260 into Wear Bay Rd, hotel 1m*

This is a truly exceptional place to stay. No detail is overlooked in making guests feel comfortable and at home. Bedrooms are charmingly decorated and exceptionally well equipped. There is a lovely garden, three tasteful lounges, a hot tub and a small bar, where pride of place goes to the proprietor's MBE certificate. At the time of our last inspection, an adjacent building was being restyled to offer additional luxurious accommodation, including a ground-floor room for guests with disabilities.
FACILITIES: 6 en suite No smoking TVB tea/coffee No dogs Licensed Cen ht TVL No children 13yrs No coaches Sauna Jacuzzi
PRICES: s £35-£45; d £60-£110✱ **LB** **PARKING:** 2
CARDS:

♦♦♦ Chilton House Hotel

14-15 Marine Pde CT20 1PX ☎ 01303 249786 📠 01303 247525
e-mail: chiltonhousehotel@btinternet.com
Dir: *from M20 junct 13 follow Harbour signs to seafront, Chilton House along seafront on right*

This friendly hotel is situated on the seafront and is within walking distance of the town. Bedrooms are comfortably appointed, there's a lounge and breakfasts are served in the bright and spacious dining room.
FACILITIES: 16 en suite (1 fmly) No smoking in dining room No smoking in lounges TVB tea/coffee No dogs Licensed Cen ht No coaches cycle hire, scuba diving tuition arranged **PRICES:** s £23; d £38✱ **LB** **BB**
NOTES: Closed 21 Dec-14 Jan **CARDS:**

♦♦♦ The Cross Channel

11 Marine Pde CT20 1PX ☎ 01303 242805 📠 01303 242805
e-mail: janeandsteve@btconnect.com
Dir: *M20 junct 13 follow signs for harbour then to seafront, promenade*

This colourful property is located on the seafront and continues to undergo refurbishment. Bedrooms are well equipped and vary in size and style. Well-cooked breakfasts are served in the brightly decorated dining room.
FACILITIES: 9 rms (4 en suite) (4 fmly) No smoking in dining room No smoking in lounges TVB tea/coffee Licensed Cen ht No coaches
PRICES: s £16-£40; d £32-£55✱ **BB** **NOTES:** Closed 22 Dec-7 Jan

♦♦♦ The Rob Roy

227 Dover Rd CT19 6NH ☎ 01303 253341 📠 01303 770060
e-mail: RobRoyFolkestone@aol.com
Dir: *from M20 junct 13 follow signs to Folkstone Harbour (A259) then (A260) for 10mins, guest house is halfway down Dover Road hill on right.*
FACILITIES: 7 rms (3 en suite) (1 fmly) (1 GF) No smoking in 2 bedrooms No smoking in dining room No smoking in lounges TVB tea/coffee Cen ht TVL No coaches **PRICES:** s £23-£25; d £35-£40 **LB** **BB** **PARKING:** 4
CARDS:

♦♦♦ Red Diamonds highlight the top establishments within the AAs 3, 4 and 5 Diamond ratings

England

HADLOW Map 05 TQ65

♦♦♦♦ Leavers Oast

Stanford Ln TN11 0JN ☎ 01732 850924 📠 01732 850924
e-mail: denis@leavers-oast.freeserve.co.uk
Dir: *turn right off A26, 1m NE of Hadlow into Stanford Lane, continue 60mtrs passing 2 small drives together then Leavers Oast drive*
FACILITIES: 3 rms (1 en suite) No smoking TVB tea/coffee No dogs Cen ht No children 12yrs No coaches Dinner Last d 10am **PRICES:** s £35-£50; d £55-£62✻ **PARKING:** 4

HAWKHURST Map 05 TQ73

Premier Collection

♦♦♦♦♦ Southgate-Little Fowlers

Rye Rd TN18 5DA ☎ 01580 752526 📠 01580 752526
e-mail: Susan.Woodard@southgate.uk.net
Dir: *On A268, approx 0.25m from traffic lights in village eastwards on Rye Rd*

Expect a warm welcome at this wonderful 300-year-old former Dower house set in mature gardens. The property has been sympathetically renovated to provide attractive accommodation throughout. The spacious bedrooms are tastefully decorated and equipped with many thoughtful extras. A hearty breakfast is served at individual tables in the delightful Victorian conservatory.
FACILITIES: 2 en suite (1 fmly) No smoking TVB tea/coffee No dogs (ex guide dogs) Cen ht TVL No children 8yrs No coaches
PRICES: s £40-£45; d £54-£70✻ **PARKING:** 5
NOTES: Closed Nov-Feb

Premier Collection

♦♦♦♦♦ *Wrens Nest*

Hastings Rd TN18 4RT ☎ 01580 754919 📠 01580 754919
Dir: *turn off A229 and bear left onto B2244, 0.75m on left before Hawkhurst Fish Farm*

Expect a warm welcome at this friendly family run guesthouse. Bedrooms are situated in a converted annexe built in traditional Kentish style with oak beamed vaulted ceilings. They are attractively decorated, tastefully furnished and well equipped. Breakfast is served at individual pine tables in the main house.
FACILITIES: 3 en suite (1 fmly) No smoking TVB tea/coffee No dogs (ex guide dogs) Cen ht No children 12yrs No coaches Coarse fishing on adjoining land **PARKING:** 8

HEADCORN Map 05 TQ84

♦♦♦ Curtis *(TQ833422)*

Waterman Quarter TN27 9JJ ☎ 01622 890393
📠 01622 890393 *51 Miss M A Ray
Dir: *take A274 Maidstone, 1m S of Headcorn take 1st right at x-roads for Waterman Quarter, farm is 0.6m on left marked by Milk Marque & AA sign*
Situated in a rural location, one mile south of the town centre, Curtis Farm is close to the A274 between Sissinghurst Castle and Leeds Castle. The three bedrooms are pleasantly decorated and well equipped. Public areas include a cosy dining room where the hearty breakfast is served at individual tables.
FACILITIES: 3 en suite (1 fmly) No smoking TVB tea/coffee No dogs (ex guide dogs) Cen ht 58 acres dairy **PRICES:** s £20-£25; d £40-£50 **LB**
PARKING: 4

HERNE BAY Map 05 TR16

♦♦♦♦ Foxden

5 Landon Rd, off Beltinge Rd CT6 6HP ☎ 01227 363514
📠 01227 363514
e-mail: foxden@fsmail.net
Dir: *from A299 into Herne Bay, under railway arch, over small rdbt, turn right at crossroads up Beltinge Rd, take 8th right turn, 2nd house on left*
An immaculately maintained house in a quiet residential area, close to the town centre and beach. Recently refurbished bedrooms are well-appointed and comfortable with fine furniture, attractive paintings and interesting ornaments. The elegant breakfast room opens out onto a delightful sun terrace, bordered by a large lily pond and mature gardens.
FACILITIES: 4 rms (2 en suite) No smoking TVB tea/coffee No dogs (ex guide dogs) Cen ht No children 13yrs No coaches **PRICES:** s £22-£25; d £50-£55✻ **LB PARKING:** 3

HIGH HALDEN Map 05 TQ83

♦♦♦ Draylands

TN26 3JG ☎ 01233 850048 📠 01233 850048
e-mail: sallyrussell30@hotmail.com
Dir: *in centre of High Halden turn off A28 into Church Hill (signed Woodchurch) follow road past church and school. At bottom of hill keep to main road at junct/corner with Harbourne Lane. House on right 100yds after junct.*
A charming detached bungalow situated in a peaceful rural location amidst ten acres of mature grounds. The pleasantly decorated, well-equipped bedrooms are located in an annex that is adjacent to the main building. Freshly cooked breakfasts are served in the smart dining room seated around a large communal table.
FACILITIES: 2 annexe en suite No smoking TVB **PRICES:** d £46-£50✻
PARKING: 2

LB indicates that Leisure Breaks are offered by the establishment.

continued

MAIDSTONE Map 05 TQ75

See also Marden

Premier Collection

♦♦♦♦♦ Ringlestone Inn & Farmhouse Hotel

Ringlestone Hamlet, Harrietsham ME17 1NX
☎ 01622 859900 📠 01622 859966
e-mail: bookings@ringlestone.com

***Dir:** M20 junct 8 onto A20. At rdbt opp Great Danes Hotel take left to Hollingbourne. Through village, right at x-roads at top of hill (The Circle)*

This 16th-century inn, originally a hospice for monks, has delightful gardens, open grounds and features an inglenook fireplace, oak beams and brick and flint walls. Smart modern bedrooms are housed in the tastefully converted farmhouse opposite, each furnished with individual touches and very well equipped. Service is both attentive and friendly.

FACILITIES: 3 en suite No smoking in bedrooms TVB tea/coffee Direct dial from bedrooms No dogs (ex guide dogs) Cen ht TVL Day membership to local Health Club Dinner Last d 9.30pm **PRICES:** s £97-£117; d £119-£129* **LB MEALS:** Lunch £15-£20alc Dinner £20-£25alc* **CONF:** Thtr 50 Class 30 Board 24 Del from £139 * **PARKING:** 70 **NOTES:** Closed 25 Dec **CARDS:**

♦♦♦♦ Conway House

12 Conway Rd ME16 0HD ☎ 01622 688287 📠 01622 662589
e-mail: conwayhouse@ukgateway.net

***Dir:** exit M20 junct 5, left onto A20, at traffic lights/crossroads (with BP petrol station) right into Conway Rd*

Conway House is conveniently located in a quiet residential area with easy access to the motorway and town centre. A warm welcome is assured, and modern bedrooms are attractively presented and equipped with a range of useful facilities. Breakfast is taken around one large table in a pleasantly appointed dining room, which also has some lounge seating.

FACILITIES: 3 rms (1 en suite) (1 fmly) No smoking in dining room No smoking in lounges TVB tea/coffee No dogs (ex guide dogs) Cen ht TVL No coaches **PRICES:** s £35-£40; d £45-£50* **PARKING:** 5 **CARDS:** 

♦♦♦♦ Grove House

Grove Green Rd, Weavering St ME14 5JT ☎ 01622 738441
📠 01622 735927

***Dir:** M20 junct 7 follow signs to TV studios, right at rdbt, then left into Grovewood Dr, 2nd left past Tesco & left again into Grove Green Rd*

Situated in a quiet residential area close to the TV studios, this impressive modern house offers homely accommodation for the business or leisure traveller. Bedrooms are smartly presented and well-equipped with lots of little extras to make your stay more comfortable. *continued*

Grove House

FACILITIES: 3 rms (1 en suite) No smoking TVB tea/coffee No dogs Cen ht No children 10yrs No coaches **PRICES:** s £35; d £45-£50* **PARKING:** 6 **CARDS:**

♦♦♦♦ Langley Oast

Langley Park, Langley ME17 3NQ ☎ 01622 863523
📠 01622 863523
e-mail: margaret@langleyoast.freeserve.co.uk

***Dir:** From junct 6 follow signs to Maidstone town centre then Hastings. At Wheatsheaf traffic lights take the A274 to Tenterden. Past Parkwood Business Estate turn right into lane signposted Maidstone Golf Centre*

This traditional Kentish oast house has been delightfully modernised and converted. Bedrooms are spacious and well appointed, two of the rooms occupy the 24 feet diameter roundel towers. Breakfast is taken in the airy dining room that enjoys views of the garden and surrounding countryside.

FACILITIES: 3 rms (2 en suite) (1 fmly) No smoking TVB tea/coffee No dogs (ex guide dogs) Cen ht No coaches Jacuzzi in 1 bedroom **PRICES:** s £25-£50; d £45-£70* **PARKING:** 5 **NOTES:** Closed Xmas

♦♦♦♦ Scuffits *(TQ713486)*

Elphicks Farm, Hunton ME15 0SB ☎ 01622 820758
📠 01622 820754 Mr & Mrs S Day

***Dir:** from Maidstone take A229 S to Linton (signed to Hastings) turn right at lights, through Coxheath then 1st left signposted to Hunton & Yalding after 1.8m turn L into private drive through orchards to end*

Scuffits is a delightfully converted 16th-century oast house which sits in a peaceful location, surrounded by 180 acres of working orchards and farmland. Character bedrooms are pleasantly appointed and spacious, each occupying the 'roundels' of the oast house. Mrs Day is a charming and helpful host, who serves a tasty breakfast in the separate well-appointed dining room.

FACILITIES: 2 en suite (1 fmly) No smoking TVB tea/coffee No dogs (ex guide dogs) Cen ht No children 10yrs Fishing 180 acres arable/fruit **PRICES:** d £45-£65 **PARKING:** 6 **NOTES:** Closed Xmas

♦♦♦♦ King Street Hotel

74 King St ME14 1BH ☎ 01622 663266 📠 01622 663123
e-mail: reservations@kingstreethotel/maidstone.co.uk

***Dir:** exit junct 7 of M20, taking A249 Sittingbourne Road follow signs to town centre, turn right at large rdbt and take town centre lane. Hotel on left after pedestrian crossing*

FACILITIES: 13 en suite (1 fmly) (5 GF) No smoking in 4 bedrooms No smoking in dining room No smoking in 1 lounge TVB tea/coffee Direct dial from bedrooms No dogs (ex guide dogs) Licensed Cen ht TVL No coaches **PRICES:** s £47-£54; d £60-£72* **CONF:** Thtr 35 Class 16 Board 20 Del from £40 * **NOTES:** Closed 24 Dec-6 Jan **CARDS:**

If an establishment name appears in *italics*, details have not been confirmed for 2003.

England

MAIDSTONE continued

♦♦♦ Aylesbury Hotel

56-58 London Rd ME16 8QL ☎ 01622 762100 📠 01622 762100
e-mail: aylesbury@onetel.net.uk
Dir: *M20 junct 5, on A20 into Maidstone on left*

Conveniently located for the town centre, this well equipped and maintained establishment has a welcoming and friendly atmosphere. All the rooms are very comfortable and most have been refurbished to a high standard. The dining room overlooks the walled rear garden, and the hotel has its own car park.
FACILITIES: 8 rms (5 en suite) No smoking in 4 bedrooms No smoking in dining room TVB tea/coffee No dogs (ex guide dogs) Cen ht No coaches Leisure centre within 10 mins **PRICES:** s £42✻ **LB PARKING:** 8
NOTES: Closed 24-26 Dec, 31Dec-2 Jan **CARDS:**

♦♦♦ Rock House Hotel

102 Tonbridge Rd ME16 8SL ☎ 01622 751616 📠 01622 756119
Dir: *on A26, 0.5m from town centre*

Close to the town centre, this family run hotel has a friendly atmosphere, with breakfast taken in the separate conservatory dining room overlooking rear terrace and garden. Brightly decorated bedrooms offer sound standards of comfort.
FACILITIES: 14 rms (8 en suite) (4 fmly) No smoking in 4 bedrooms No smoking in dining room TVB tea/coffee No dogs (ex guide dogs) Cen ht TVL
PRICES: s £32-£43; d £40-£50✻ **PARKING:** 7 **CARDS:**

♦♦ A The Howard Hotel

22/24 London Rd ME16 8QL ☎ 01622 758778
📠 01622 609984
Dir: *from M20 take Junct 5 signed Aylesford South and Maidstone West, immediately join the A20 following the signs for Maidstone town centre.*
FACILITIES: 14 rms (2 GF) No smoking in dining room TVB tea/coffee No dogs (ex guide dogs) Licensed Cen ht TVL No coaches **PRICES:** s £29-£32; d £44-£48✻ **PARKING:** 15 **NOTES:** Closed 24 Dec-1 Jan
CARDS:

MARDEN — Map 05 TQ74

♦♦♦♦♦ Merzie Meadows

Hunton Rd TN12 9SL ☎ 01622 820500 📠 01622 820500
Dir: *from A229 Maidstone/Hastings rd, take B2079 towards Marden, 1st right into Underlyn Lane for 2.5m. Large Chainhurst sign, right into drive*
A unique detached property situated amidst 20 acres of mature gardens in the Kent countryside. The generously proportioned bedrooms are housed in two wings, which overlook a terrace with a swimming pool; each one is tastefully decorated, thoughtfully equipped and furnished with well-chosen pieces. The attractive breakfast room has an Italian tiled floor and superb views of the garden.
FACILITIES: 2 en suite (1 fmly) No smoking STV TVB tea/coffee No dogs Cen ht TVL No children 14yrs No coaches Outdoor swimming pool
PRICES: s £40-£45; d £50-£60✻ **PARKING:**
NOTES: Closed 15 Dec- 31st Jan

MARGATE — Map 05 TR37

♦♦♦♦ The Greswolde Hotel

20 Surrey Rd, Cliftonville CT9 2LA ☎ 01843 223956
📠 01843 223956
An attractive Victorian house located in a quiet residential area and close to the seafront, the Greswolde retains its period atmosphere and character, and is full of interesting memorabilia. Bedrooms are spacious, comfortably appointed and equipped with many useful extras. Breakfast is served in the dining room, and guests are welcome to relax in the cosy lounge.
FACILITIES: 5 en suite (2 fmly) No smoking in bedrooms No smoking in dining room TVB tea/coffee Licensed Cen ht No coaches
PRICES: s £28-£40; d £40-£46✻ **LB CARDS:**

♦♦♦ Elonville Hotel

70-72 Harold Rd, Cliftonville CT9 2HS ☎ 01843 298635
📠 01843 298635
e-mail: enquires@elonville-hotel.demon.co.uk
Dir: *from Margate clock tower stay on coastal road for 1m, Harold Rd is turn off on the right*
Elonville Hotel is situated within easy reach of the shops and beach. The atmosphere is warm and friendly and the accommodation comfortable, with well-appointed bedrooms. Evening meals and breakfast are served in the brightly decorated dining room overlooking the garden and there is a bar; entertainment is provided on some evenings.
FACILITIES: 16 rms (10 en suite) (2 fmly) (1 GF) No smoking in dining room TVB tea/coffee Licensed TVL Dinner Last d 4.30pm
CARDS:

♦♦♦ Westbrook Bay House

12 Royal Esplanade, Westbrook CT9 5DW
☎ 01843 292700
Dir: *from A28 turn left after going over railway bridge, turn right to seafront, 250yds along Royal Esplanade*
Expect a warm welcome at this friendly family-run guest house, which is situated overlooking the sandy bay and within easy reach of the town centre. Bedrooms are brightly decorated and well-appointed. Freshly prepared home cooked dinners are served in the smart dining room. Guests also have the use of a comfortably appointed lounge and bar.
FACILITIES: 10 rms (6 en suite) (4 fmly) No smoking in dining room TVB tea/coffee No dogs (ex guide dogs) Licensed Cen ht TVL No coaches
PRICES: s fr £17; d £34-£38✻ **LB BB**

RAMSGATE Map 05 TR36

♦♦♦ Belvidere

26 Augusta Rd CT11 8JS ☎ 01843 588809 📠 01843 588809

Dir: *take A253 into Ramsgate then A253 at Nether Coat Circle and either road to Ferry terminal or A253 to Victoria Rd*

A warm welcome is one of the strengths of this family-run guest house which sits close to the beach, ferry port and town centre. Refreshments are offered in the comfortable lounge on arrival, whilst breakfast is served in a smaller dining room. Bedrooms, of varying sizes, are soundly maintained and suitably appointed. Unrestricted street parking is available.

FACILITIES: 7 rms (3 en suite) (2 fmly) No smoking in dining room STV TVB tea/coffee No dogs (ex guide dogs) Lift Cen ht TVL No children 3yrs **PRICES:** s £15-£18; d £28-£36✻ **LB BB NOTES:** Closed 24 Dec-2 Jan

♦♦ Eastwood

28 Augusta Rd CT11 8JS ☎ 01843 591505 📠 01843 591505

Dir: *follow signs to Ramsgate, past harbour to east side and Augusta Road*

This family-run guest house is close to the beach, ferry port and town centre. The accommodation is in two houses, with the breakfast room in the main house. Bedrooms are bright and well-presented with modern furnishings and facilities. Evening meals are served in the main house by arrangement, and lock-up garages are available.

FACILITIES: 6 rms (3 en suite) 6 annexe en suite (6 fmly) No smoking in dining room No smoking in lounges TVB tea/coffee Cen ht TVL No coaches **PRICES:** s £20-£25; d £40-£45✻ **PARKING:** 8

SANDHURST Map 05 TQ82

♦♦♦ Hoads Farm *(TQ805282)*

Crouch Ln TN18 5PA ☎ 01580 850296 📠 01580 850296

Mrs A Nicholas

Dir: *on A268, 0.5m from Sandhurst turn right into Crouch Lane*

Situated in a peaceful rural location, this 16th century farmhouse still forms part of a working farm. Public rooms feature a spacious beamed lounge with a welcoming fireplace. Breakfast is served at a large table in the dining room, which overlooks the garden and dinner is available by prior arrangement. Hoads Farm also produce their own award wining wines.

FACILITIES: 3 rms tea/coffee No dogs Licensed Cen ht TVL 350 acres Apple Hops Vines Sheep Dinner Last d by arrangment **PRICES:** s £20; d £40✻ **PARKING:** 6 **CARDS:**

SEVENOAKS Map 05 TQ55

See also Farningham

♦♦♦ Barn Cottage

Seven Mile Ln, Borough Green TN15 8QY ☎ 01732 883384

e-mail: suzifilleul@aol.com

Dir: *from A20 take B2016 (Seven Mile Lane) for 1m. Over crossroads, Barn Cottage on left opposite sign for Viking Oak Kennels*

This pretty white-boarded cottage is set in a pleasant courtyard amidst attractive gardens. The bedrooms are neat and comfortably furnished. Breakfast is served in the flower-filled conservatory, which overlooks the garden. Guests also have use of a comfortably furnished lounge.

FACILITIES: 3 rms No smoking No dogs Cen ht No coaches Cycling **PRICES:** s £25; d £50✻ **PARKING:** 5

SHEERNESS Map 05 TQ97

♦ Sheppey Guest House

214 Queenborough Rd, Halfway ME12 3DF ☎ 01795 665950 📠 01795 661200

e-mail: mallas@btopenworld.com

Dir: *off M2 take A249 Sittingbourne/Sheerness, on Isle of Sheppey take A250 pass The Fields a small estate and guesthouse is on left*

FACILITIES: 9 en suite No smoking in dining room No smoking in lounges STV TVB tea/coffee Direct dial from bedrooms Licensed Cen ht TVL No coaches Indoor swimming pool (heated) Dinner Last d 10pm **PRICES:** s £20; d £30✻ **BB PARKING:** 9

SITTINGBOURNE Map 05 TQ96

Premier Collection

♦♦♦♦♦ Hempstead House

London Rd, Bapchild ME9 9PP ☎ 01795 428020 📠 01795 436362

e-mail: info@hempsteadhouse.co.uk

Dir: *on A2, 1.5m E of Sittingbourne opposite turning to Tonge*

Expect a warm welcome at this charming detached Victorian property which is situated amidst three acres of mature landscaped gardens. Bedrooms are attractively decorated with lovely co-ordinated fabrics, tastefully furnished and equipped with many thoughtful touches. Public rooms feature a choice of beautifully furnished lounges as well as a superb conservatory dining room.

FACILITIES: 15 en suite (3 fmly) No smoking in bedrooms No smoking in dining room No smoking in 1 lounge TVB tea/coffee Direct dial from bedrooms Licensed Cen ht TVL ch fac Outdoor swimming pool (heated) Croquet lawn Play area, free use of facilities at leisure club Dinner Last d 10pm **PRICES:** s £70; d £80✻ **LB CONF:** Thtr 70 Class 50 Board 50 Del £119.50 ✻ **PARKING:** 100 **NOTES:** Civ Wed 76 **CARDS:**

See advertisement on page 255

♦♦♦ Sandhurst Farm Forge

Seed Rd, Newnham ME9 0NE ☎ 01795 886854

e-mail: kate.charles@lineone.net

Dir: *in Newnham take Seed Rd by church & continue past Tun, Vine and Press Bistro for 1m. Establishment 3rd on right*

Expect a warm welcome at this friendly farmhouse, which is situated in a peaceful rural location. The bedrooms are spacious and smartly furnished in contemporary style. Breakfast is served in the dining room, which adjoins the bedrooms. At the Forge and gallery there is a range of decorative ironworks to view and for sale.

FACILITIES: 2 en suite (2 GF) No smoking TVB tea/coffee No dogs (ex guide dogs) Cen ht No coaches **PRICES:** s fr £25; d fr £47✻ **PARKING:** 6 **NOTES:** Closed 23 Dec-1 Jan

Egg cups for excellence!
This symbol shows that breakfast exceeded our Inspector's expectations.

England

SMARDEN Map 05 TQ84

♦♦♦♦ The Chequers Inn
The Street TN27 8QA ☎ 01233 770217
e-mail: charliebullock@lineout.net

Expect a warm welcome at this delightful 14th century inn, which has been tastefully renovated by the present owners. The individually decorated bedrooms are furnished with well-chosen pieces, one has a four poster bed. Public areas have a wealth of charm and character as well as many original features such as exposed beams and open fireplaces.
FACILITIES: 4 en suite (1 fmly) TVB tea/coffee Cen ht Dinner Last d 9.30pm **PRICES:** d £70-£80* **MEALS:** Lunch £15-£25alc Dinner £15-£25alc* **PARKING:** 13 **NOTES:** Closed 24-25 Dec **CARDS:**

TENTERDEN Map 05 TQ83

♦♦♦♦ Collina House Hotel
5 East Hill TN30 6RL ☎ 01580 764852 764004
01580 762224
e-mail: collina.house@dial.pipex.com
Dir: *turn off High Street in Tenterden, A28, onto Oaks Rd B2067, property will be found on the left opposite an orchard*
This attractive, sympathetically restored half-timbered Edwardian house enjoys a peaceful location just a few minutes' walk from the town centre. Smart en suite bedrooms are spacious and thoughtfully equipped. Public areas include a formal bar and elegant restaurant where imaginative dishes are served.
FACILITIES: 11 en suite 3 annexe en suite (8 fmly) No smoking in bedrooms No smoking in dining room TVB tea/coffee Direct dial from bedrooms No dogs (ex guide dogs) Licensed Cen ht Dinner Last d 8.30pm **PRICES:** s £35-£50* **LB PARKING:** 15 **NOTES:** Closed 21 Dec-11 Jan **CARDS:**

♦♦♦♦ White Lion
The High St TN30 6BD ☎ 01580 765077 01580 764157
e-mail: whitelion@lionheartinns.co.uk
Dir: *in centre of Tenterden High Street on A28 Ashford/Hastings road (The Circle)*

Delightful 15th-century coaching inn situated on the main high street of this historic town. Bedrooms are well appointed, thoughtfully equipped and some boast four-poster beds. Public rooms feature a popular bar; a separate lounge and an oak panelled restaurant serving an extensive range of dishes. There is also a small function and meeting room.
FACILITIES: 15 en suite (2 fmly) No smoking in dining room TVB tea/coffee Direct dial from bedrooms Cen ht Dinner Last d 10pm **PRICES:** s £35-£59; d £40-£74* **LB MEALS:** Lunch £7.75-£10.25&alc Dinner £7.75-£10.25&alc* **CONF:** Thtr 50 Class 30 Board 30 Del £79.50 * **PARKING:** 35 **CARDS:**

continued

TUNBRIDGE WELLS (ROYAL) Map 05 TQ53

Premier Collection

♦♦♦♦♦ Danehurst House
41 Lower Green Rd, Rusthall TN4 8TW ☎ 01892 527739
01892 514804
e-mail: danehurst@zoom.co.uk
Dir: *from Tunbridge Wells take A264 W, 1.5m turn right past Spa Hotel, right at crossroads, Lower Green Rd 200yds on left*

Situated in pretty gardens, in a quiet residential area, this late-Victorian gabled house is located west of the historic Spa town. The house retains many original features and is attractively decorated throughout, public areas include a comfortable lounge with a small bar. The homely bedrooms are equipped with a wealth of thoughtful extras. Excellent breakfasts are taken in the attractive conservatory.
FACILITIES: 4 en suite No smoking TVB tea/coffee No dogs Licensed Cen ht TVL No children 8yrs No coaches **PRICES:** s £45-£60; d £65-£80* **PARKING:** 6 **NOTES:** Closed Xmas, last week Aug **CARDS:**

Premier Collection

♦♦♦♦♦ The Old Parsonage
Church Ln, Frant TN3 9DX ☎ 01892 750773
01892 750773
e-mail: oldparson@aol.com
Dir: *2m S of Tunbridge Wells, off A267 in Frant. On reaching Frant sign, left into Church Ln. Parsonage on left just before church*
Superb 18th-century detached Georgian property set in three acres of mature landscaped grounds. The spacious bedrooms are attractively decorated and furnished to a very high standard. The elegant public rooms hold antique pieces; they include a comfortably appointed sitting room, a lovely dining room and an inviting conservatory, which overlooks the secluded gardens.

continued

The Old Parsonage

FACILITIES: 3 en suite No smoking in bedrooms No smoking in dining room No smoking in lounges TVB tea/coffee Cen ht TVL No children 7yrs No coaches Croquet lawn **PRICES:** s £49-£67; d £69-£87* **PARKING:** 12 **CARDS:**

◆◆◆ Hadleigh

69 Sandown Park TN2 4RT ☎ 01892 822760 Fax 01892 823170

Dir: *leave A21 S on A264 sign Tunbridge Wells, Paddock Wood, turn right over 2 rdbts approx 0.50m to school lights, turn right into Blackhurst Lane, immediately right Sandown park*

FACILITIES: 2 en suite (1 GF) No smoking TVB tea/coffee No dogs (ex guide dogs) Cen ht No coaches **PRICES:** s £22-£25; d £44* **PARKING:** 3

Bentham Hill Stables

Stockland Green Rd TN3 0TJ ☎ 01892 516602

At the time of going to press the Diamond classification for this establishment had not been confirmed. Please check the AA website www.theAA.com for up-to-date information.

FACILITIES: 3 en suite

WARREN STREET (NEAR LENHAM) Map 05 TQ95

◆◆◆ Harrow

Hubbards Hill, Warren St ME17 2ED ☎ 01622 858727 Fax 01622 850026

Dir: *Take Junct 8 off M20, follow A20 to Lenham turn off A20 marked Warren St, opposite Lenham, 1.25m Harrow Inn on right*

A popular inn situated high on the North Downs of Kent. The spacious bedrooms are soundly appointed and have modern facilities. The bar and restaurant offer a variety of good food; and a full English breakfast is served in the conservatory. The inn also caters for small functions and conferences.

FACILITIES: 14 en suite (6 fmly) No smoking in dining room TVB tea/coffee Direct dial from bedrooms No dogs (ex guide dogs) Cen ht jacuzzi in 4 poster room Dinner Last d 9.30pm **PRICES:** s £45-£50; d £70-£100* **LB** **PARKING:** 80 **NOTES:** Civ Wed 40 **CARDS:**

WESTGATE ON SEA Map 05 TR37

◆◆◆ Bridge Hotel

13-15 St Mildreds Rd CT8 8RE ☎ 01843 831023 Fax 01843 835564

e-mail: bridge@freedelta.net

Dir: *M2 to A299 coastal road, A299 to A28 towards Margate. After Birchington 3rd set of traffic lights turn left, signed shops & railway stn. Establishment 200yds on left (The Independents)*

This attractive old inn close to Westgate station offers spacious, comfortable accommodation. There are two cosy bars with pool

continued

tables, and an Italian restaurant provides a convenient eating option.

FACILITIES: 17 en suite (4 fmly) No smoking in 3 bedrooms No smoking in area of dining room No smoking in 1 lounge TVB tea/coffee Direct dial from bedrooms Licensed Cen ht Pool Table Dinner Last d 11pm **PRICES:** s £38.42-£42.60; d £54.52-£61* **LB** **PARKING:** 8 **CARDS:**

WEST MALLING Map 05 TQ65

◆◆◆◆ Eden Farm Accommodation *(TQ683582)*

Eden Farm Ln ME19 6HL ☎ 01732 843110 Fax 01732 843110

Mr K Kemsley

e-mail: edenfarm@beeb.net

Dir: *M20 junct 4 and follow signs to West Malling. In village 1st left into Swan St. After 400mtrs right by bridge over road, farm on right*

This delightful 18th-century farmhouse enjoys a tranquil setting surrounded by fields, yet is conveniently placed for the town centre. Bedrooms are decorated in bold modern colours, which harmonise well with the traditional style of the buildings. Service is attentive and friendly, and breakfast is taken around one large polished wooden table in the character dining room.

FACILITIES: 4 en suite (2 fmly) (2 GF) No smoking STV TVB tea/coffee No dogs (ex guide dogs) Cen ht No children 11yrs 56 acres horses/arable/grass/herbs **PRICES:** s £38-£50; d £48-£60* **LB** **PARKING:** 6

Prices may change during the currency of the Guide, please check when booking.

WHITSTABLE Map 05 TR16

♦♦♦♦ Windy Ridge
Wraik Hill CT5 3BY ☎ 01227 263506 📠 01227 771191
Dir: *from M2/A299, rdbt 3rd exit (A290), 2nd rdbt 2nd exit, and continue for 0.5m*
Jean and John Hawkins welcome guests to the Windy Ridge, which sits in a peaceful rural location with panoramic views of countryside and sea. Public rooms are a delight, and include a comfortably furnished character lounge. Bedrooms are well equipped, with one ground floor bedroom suitable for the less mobile.
FACILITIES: 10 en suite (3 fmly) (3 GF) No smoking in dining room No smoking in lounges TVB tea/coffee Direct dial from bedrooms Licensed Cen ht No coaches Dinner Last d 9am **PRICES:** s £30; d £50-£60✳ **PARKING:** 16 **NOTES:** Closed Xmas week Civ Wed 25 **CARDS:**

♦♦♦ Belmont House
74 Oxford St CT5 1DA ☎ 01227 266911
Dir: *Leave A229 onto B2205 continue for 0.5m into Whitstable under railway bridge Belmont House on left*
This Victorian house sits on the town's main street, within easy walking distance of all the attractions, pubs and restaurants. Bedrooms are individually appointed, well equipped and smartly maintained; freshly cooked breakfasts are served in the cosy ground floor dining room.
FACILITIES: 3 en suite (1 fmly) No smoking TVB tea/coffee No dogs (ex guide dogs) Cen ht No children 7yrs No coaches **PRICES:** s £35-£45; d £50-£60✳ **LB PARKING:** 3

LANCASHIRE

BLACKPOOL Map 07 SD33

Premier Collection

♦♦♦♦♦ The Old Coach House
50 Dean St FY4 1BP ☎ 01253 349195 📠 01253 344330
e-mail: blackpool@theoldcoachhouse.freeserve.co.uk
Dir: *at end of M55 follow signs for main car park, at 2nd mini rdbt turn right, at lights turn left, next lights left, Dean St 2nd on right*
This historic house has been lovingly restored. It is set in pretty, landscaped gardens, with its own outdoor spa bath. Thoughtfully equipped bedrooms, two with four-posters, are attractively furnished and tastefully decorated. The elegant restaurant is also open to non-residents, and there is a conservatory where guests can relax.
FACILITIES: 11 en suite No smoking in bedrooms No smoking in dining room TVB tea/coffee No dogs Licensed Cen ht No coaches Jacuzzi Dinner Last d 8.15pm **PRICES:** s £45-£80; d £70-£90 **CONF:** Board 30 **PARKING:** 12 **CARDS:**

♦♦♦♦ Briar Dene Hotel
56 Kelso Av, Thornton, Cleveleys FY5 3JG ☎ 01253 852312 📠 01253 851190
This friendly long-established family run hotel lies near the centre of Cleveleys, and is just a short drive or tram ride from Blackpool's many attractions. Bedrooms are equipped with modern facilities and many are suitable for families. Public areas are comfortably furnished, with a bar and a wide range of eating options available.
FACILITIES: 17 en suite (3 fmly) No smoking in area of dining room TVB tea/coffee Licensed Cen ht TVL Dinner Last d 9.30pm **PRICES:** s £32.50-£35; d £48-£60✳ **LB CONF:** Del from £60 ✳ **PARKING:** 12 **CARDS:**

♦♦♦♦ Burlees Hotel
40 Knowle Av FY2 9TQ ☎ 01253 354535 📠 01253 354535
e-mail: enquiries@burleeshotel.co.uk
Dir: *from Queens Promenade right at Uncle Toms Cabin into Knowle Av*
A friendly welcome awaits guests at this well-maintained house just a short stroll from the promenade. Smartly decorated bedrooms are thoughtfully equipped. There is a comfortable lounge overlooking the well-tended gardens in addition to a cosy bar lounge. Hearty breakfasts and home cooked meals are served in the pine-furnished dining room.
FACILITIES: 9 en suite (2 fmly) (1 GF) No smoking in bedrooms No smoking in dining room No smoking in lounges TVB tea/coffee No dogs Licensed Cen ht TVL No coaches **PRICES:** s £25-£28; d £50-£56 **LB PARKING:** 5 **NOTES:** Closed mid Nov-Feb **CARDS:**

♦♦♦♦ Sunray
42 Knowle Av, Queens Promenade FY2 9TQ ☎ 01253 351937 📠 01253 593307
e-mail: sunray_hotel@yahoo.co.uk
Dir: *from Blackpool Tower, head north along promenade for 1.75m, turn right at Uncle Toms Cabin, Sunray 300yds on left*
FACILITIES: 9 en suite (2 fmly) No smoking in dining room TVB tea/coffee Direct dial from bedrooms Cen ht TVL No coaches Dinner Last d 3pm **PRICES:** s £24-£30; d £48-£60✳ **LB PARKING:** 6 **NOTES:** Closed Dec-March **CARDS:**

♦♦♦ Sunny Cliff
98 Queens Promenade, Northshore FY2 9NS ☎ 01253 351155
Dir: *1.5m N of Tower on A584, just past Uncle Toms Cabin*
Good home-cooking is a highlight at this friendly, relaxed guest house overlooking the seafront. After four decades under the same ownership, it enjoys a loyal following of happy guests. The pretty bedrooms, some with sea views, are neatly furnished. Apart from a comfortable lounge and dining room, there is an atmospheric bar and a sun lounge that overlooks the promenade.
FACILITIES: 9 en suite (3 fmly) No smoking in dining room TVB tea/coffee No dogs Licensed Cen ht TVL No coaches Dinner Last d 5pm **PRICES:** s £22-£24; d £44-£48✳ **LB PARKING:** 6 **NOTES:** Closed 9 Nov-Etr

♦♦♦ Castlemere Hotel
13 Shaftesbury Av, North Shore FY2 9QQ ☎ 01253 352430 📠 01253 350116
e-mail: bookings@hotelcastlemere.co.uk
Situated in the quieter residential North Shore area, this friendly private hotel is just a short distance from many attractions. Bedrooms are pretty and well-equipped, with some suitable for families. There is a cosy resident's bar, and the provision of forecourt parking is a bonus. The owners create a relaxing atmosphere for their guests.
FACILITIES: 9 en suite (1 fmly) No smoking in dining room TVB tea/coffee No dogs (ex guide dogs) Licensed Cen ht TVL Dinner Last d noon **PRICES:** s £22-£25; d £44-£50✳ **LB PARKING:** 4 **CARDS:**

♦♦♦ The Colby Hotel
297 The Promenade FY1 6AL ☎ 01253 345845 📠 01253 345845
Dir: *on promenade midway between Blackpool Tower and Pleasure Beach*
This small hotel has a prime location facing the sea, between the pleasure beach and Central Pier. It offers a spacious lounge bar and a modern café/dining room, where meals can be taken. The thoughtfully equipped bedrooms include a family room, and one with a four-poster bed.
FACILITIES: 14 en suite (5 fmly) (1 GF) No smoking in dining room TVB tea/coffee Direct dial from bedrooms No dogs Licensed Cen ht No coaches Pool Table Dinner Last d 6pm **PRICES:** s £16.50-£25; d £33-£50✳ **BB PARKING:** 4 **NOTES:** Closed Nov-Etr rs Easter-Jun **CARDS:**

♦♦♦ Craigmore Hotel

3 Willshaw Rd, Gynn Square FY2 9SH ☎ 01253 355098
e-mail: blackpoolhotel@fsbdial.co.uk
Dir: *approx 1m N of the tower is a rdbt. Continue along promenade, take 1st R (Willshaw Rd) approx 100yds*

The Craigmore, which is owned and personally run, is attractively located overlooking Gynn Square and gardens, with the promenade and tram stops just yards away. Bedrooms are smart and modern, and include several suitable for families. There is a comfortable lounge and an additional sun lounge and patio area. The pretty dining room also contains a small bar.

FACILITIES: 9 en suite (3 fmly) No smoking in dining room TVB tea/coffee Licensed Cen ht TVL No coaches Dinner Last d 7pm **PRICES:** s £23-£25; d £40-£44✳ **LB** **NOTES:** Closed 6 Nov-21 Feb **CARDS:**

♦♦♦ Denely Private Hotel

15 King Edward Av FY2 9TA ☎ 01253 352757
Dir: *approximately 1m north of Blackpool Tower*

Just a short walk from the Promenade and Gynn Gardens, Denely Hotel offers comfortable accommodation. Simply furnished bedrooms are complemented by a spacious lounge and a bright dining room, where evening meals are available by prior arrangement. The resident owners provide friendly and attentive service.

FACILITIES: 9 rms (7 en suite) (3 fmly) No smoking in dining room TV5B tea/coffee No dogs (ex guide dogs) Cen ht TVL Dinner Last d 1pm **PRICES:** s £16.50-£25; d £33-£42✳ **LB** **BB** **PARKING:** 6 **NOTES:** Closed Dec-Jan **CARDS:**

♦♦♦ Fern Royd Hotel

35 Holmfield Rd, North Shore FY2 9TE ☎ 01253 351066
e-mail: info@fernroydhotel.co.uk

Located on a quiet side road just of the North Shore promenade, this family run hotel offers attentive service and friendly hospitality. Delicious home cooked meals are served in the wood panelled dining room and there is also a family bar complete with pool table and reading areas. Bedrooms are simply furnished and pleasantly co-ordinated.

FACILITIES: 10 en suite (2 fmly) No smoking in bedrooms No smoking in dining room No smoking in 1 lounge TVB tea/coffee No dogs (ex guide dogs) Licensed Cen ht TVL No coaches Pool Table Dinner **PRICES:** s £19-£25; d £38-£50✳ **LB** **BB** **PARKING:** 6 **CARDS:**

♦♦♦ Hartshead Hotel

17 King Edward Av FY2 9TA ☎ 01253 353133 & 357111
Dir: *off Promenade at Cliffs Hotel. Close to Gynn Square, North Shore*

Located 200 yards from the seafront, this owner-managed private hotel provides modern bedrooms of various sizes, equipped with a good range of practical extras. A verandah sitting room is available in addition to a comfortable lounge bar, and both breakfast and pre-theatre dinners are served in the attractive dining room.

FACILITIES: 10 en suite (3 fmly) No smoking in bedrooms No smoking in dining room TVB tea/coffee No dogs (ex guide dogs) Licensed Cen ht TVL No coaches Dinner Last d 3pm **PRICES:** s £17-£23; d £34-£46✳ **LB** **BB** **PARKING:** 6 **CARDS:**

♦♦♦ Mains Hall Hotel & Restaurant

Mains Ln, Little Singleton FY6 7LE ☎ 01253 885130
🖷 01253 894132
e-mail: enquiries@mainshall.co.uk
Dir: *M55 J3, take A585 signed Fleetwood for 5m. Mains Hall 0.5m beyond 2nd lights on R.*

This Grade II listed building, dating back to 1536, enjoys a tranquil location in its own grounds, within easy reach of both Blackpool and the M55. Public rooms include a cosy traditional bar, three differently themed dining rooms and a spacious conservatory.

continued

Bedrooms are individually styled, many with antique beds and period furnishings.

FACILITIES: 10 en suite No smoking in bedrooms No smoking in area of dining room TVB tea/coffee Direct dial from bedrooms Licensed Cen ht TVL No coaches Fishing Dinner Last d 10pm **PRICES:** s £45-£65; d £60-£100✳ **LB** **CONF:** Thtr 60 Class 40 Board 40 Del from £85 ✳ **PARKING:** 60 **CARDS:**

♦♦♦ Westdean Hotel

59 Dean St FY4 1BP ☎ 01253 342904 🖷 01253 342926
e-mail: mikeball@westdeanhotel.freeserve.co.uk
Dir: *along Promenade (from Pleasure Beach towards Blackpool Tower) take 1st right after South Pier into Dean St*

Well established, this small, private hotel is located within easy reach of the South Promenade attractions. The proprietors provide friendly hospitality and a welcoming atmosphere. Bedrooms are attractively decorated and all are equipped with modern facilities. Public areas include a comfortably furnished lounge, a cellar bar and a super games room for both adults and children.

FACILITIES: 11 rms (10 en suite) (3 fmly) No smoking in dining room TVB tea/coffee No dogs Licensed Cen ht TVL Pool Table Games room Dart board **PRICES:** s £20-£27; d £40-£54✳ **LB** **PARKING:** 2 **CARDS:**

♦♦♦ Wilmar

42 Osborne Rd FY4 1HQ ☎ 01253 346229
Dir: *From M55 follow 'Main Parking Area'. Turn right at Waterloo Rd exit, left at lights and left again at 2nd lights. Bear right at Grand Hotel & right again*

Conveniently located for the Pleasure Beach, Sandcastle and other resort attractions, this family run guest house extends a warm welcome. Well-maintained bedrooms are freshly decorated and offer modern facilities. A cosy lounge is provided and wholesome evening meals are served. A relaxing atmosphere prevails.

FACILITIES: 7 en suite (1 fmly) No smoking in dining room TVB tea/coffee No dogs (ex guide dogs) Licensed Cen ht No coaches Dinner Last d 10am **PRICES:** s £17.50-£25; d £35-£50✳ **LB** **BB** **NOTES:** Closed 23-27 Dec

BLACKPOOL continued

♦♦♦ Windsor Hotel

53 Dean St FY4 1BP ☎ 01253 400232 📠 01253 346886
e-mail: windsorhotel@btconnect.com
Dir: *M6 junct 32, M55 to large rdbt, straight on, at next mini rdbt turn right, follow road around supermarket to traffic lights turn left up and over bridge to next set of lights and turn left Dean Street second on right turning in front of Texaco garage, hotel on right*

A warm welcome and cup of tea awaits at this friendly, family run guest house. Close to the South Pier and Pleasure Beach with other resort attractions just a tram ride away. Cosy bedrooms are neatly decorated and some have stylish four-poster beds.
FACILITIES: 12 en suite (3 fmly) No smoking in 9 bedrooms No smoking in dining room TVB tea/coffee Direct dial from bedrooms No dogs (ex guide dogs) Licensed Cen ht TVL Dinner Last d noon **PARKING:** 8
CARDS:

♦♦♦ Windsor Park Hotel

96 Queens Promenade FY2 9NS ☎ 01253 357025 📠 01253 357076
e-mail: info@windsorparkhotel.net
Dir: *Queens Promenade, main road North shore*

Benefiting from stunning views, this attractive seafront hotel is located on the peaceful North Shore, however the main attractions are just a short tram ride away. Home cooked meals and substantial breakfasts are served in the elegant dining room. There is also a pleasant bar area and a sun lounge. Bedrooms offer modern amenities.
FACILITIES: 11 en suite (2 fmly) No smoking in bedrooms No smoking in dining room No smoking in 1 lounge TVB tea/coffee No dogs (ex guide dogs) Licensed Cen ht TVL No coaches Dinner Last d 4pm stairlift
PRICES: s fr £21; d fr £42✱ **LB PARKING:** 6 **NOTES:** Closed 8 Nov-Etr (ex Xmas/New Year) **CARDS:**

♦♦♦ 🅰 Ashcroft Hotel

42 King Edward Av FY2 9TA ☎ 01253 351538
e-mail: dave@ashcroftblackpool.freeserve.co.uk
Dir: *from promenade head N past the tower and N pier, in 0.75m at rdbt continue along promenade, take 3rd turning right into King Edward Avenue, cross x-rds establishment on left*
FACILITIES: 10 rms (7 en suite) (2 fmly) No smoking in dining room TVB tea/coffee No dogs (ex guide dogs) Licensed Cen ht TVL Dinner Last d breakfast **PRICES:** s £21-£23; d £42-£46✱ **LB**

♦♦ The New Central Hotel

64a Reads Av FY1 4DE ☎ 01253 623637 📠 01253 620857
e-mail: newcentral@hotmail.com
Dir: *A583 head towards town, until C.S.L. (showroom) next right*

Enjoying a central location, this large private hotel is just a short walk from the tower and promenade. Public areas are spacious and consist of a well stocked bar lounge, a games room and a large dining room where breakfast and dinner are served. Some four poster beds are available and there is also a night porter.
FACILITIES: 48 en suite (12 fmly) TVB tea/coffee No dogs (ex guide dogs) Licensed Lift Cen ht Dinner Last d 4pm **PRICES:** s £20-£59.95; d £39.95-£59.95✱ **LB PARKING:** 16 **CARDS:**

BOLTON-BY-BOWLAND — Map 07 SD74

♦♦♦♦ Middle Flass Lodge

Settle Rd BB7 4NY ☎ 01200 447259 📠 01200 447300
e-mail: joan@middleflasslodge.fsnet.co.uk
Dir: *A59 Skipton to Clitheroe rd, take turn for Sawley. Follow sign for Bolton-by-Bowland at Copynook, 2nd left signed Middle Flass Lodge 2m on right*

Set in beautiful countryside within the Forest of Bowland this smartly presented house provides a warm welcome to all. Stylishly converted from farm outbuildings, exposed timbers feature throughout, including the attractive restaurant and cosy lounge. Smart, modern bedrooms include family rooms. The restaurant is also popular with non-residents.
FACILITIES: 5 en suite 2 annexe en suite (1 fmly) No smoking TV5B tea/coffee No dogs Licensed Cen ht TVL No coaches Dinner Last d 6.30pm
PRICES: s £36-£40; d £48-£64✱ **LB PARKING:** 14
CARDS:

BURNLEY — Map 07 SD83

♦♦♦♦ Eaves Barn Farm *(SD787328)*

Hapton BB12 7LP ☎ 01282 771591 📠 01282 771591
Mrs M Butler
e-mail: mavis@eavesbarnfarm.co.uk
Dir: *M65 junct 9, turn right onto A679, at Hapton Inn turn right & after approx 1m left into lane between shop and houses*

continued

England

This delightful farmhouse is situated a short distance from Burnley and centrally located to tour other Lancashire towns. The attractive bedrooms are tastefully decorated, comfortably furnished and provide a host of thoughtful extras. Guests have the use of a conservatory, which overlooks the attractive garden and where breakfast is served, and there is also a very comfortable lounge.
FACILITIES: 3 en suite No smoking TVB tea/coffee No dogs Cen ht TVL No children 12yrs Fishing 38 acres sheep Dinner Last d 4pm
PRICES: s £27.50-£30; d £55-£60* **PARKING:** 12

♦♦♦ Ormerod Hotel
121/123 Ormerod Rd BB11 3QW ☎ 01282 423255
Dir: *from Burnley centre take A682, turn R 200mtrs after rdbt (Ormerod Rd), past Burnley College on L.Hotel 300mtrs on R*

This welcoming, privately owned hotel is situated a few minutes' walk from the town centre and is handy for Queens Park, Thompsons Park and Burnley FC. Accommodation is modern, bright and well-equipped. Separate tables are provided in the traditional wood panelled breakfast room and there is also a comfortably furnished lounge.
FACILITIES: 9 en suite (2 fmly) TVB tea/coffee Cen ht TVL
PRICES: s £26-£29; d £43* **PARKING:** 8

CARNFORTH Map 07 SD47

Premier Collection

♦♦♦♦♦ New Capernwray Farm
Capernwray LA6 1AD ☎ 01524 734284 01524 734284
e-mail: newcapfarm@aol.com
Dir: *M6 J35, follow signs for Over Kellet. Left at village green in Over Kellett, house on left after 1.7m*

A warm welcome is assured at this 17th-century, white-walled farmhouse. Bedrooms feature beamed ceilings and are all sumptuously furnished and equipped with thoughtful extras. Four course dinners and breakfast are taken in the dining room, formerly the dairy. The drawing room has views of the well-tended garden and peaceful countryside.

continued

FACILITIES: 3 en suite No smoking TVB tea/coffee Cen ht No children 9yrs No coaches Dinner Last d 5pm **PRICES:** s £45-£51; d £66-£78* **PARKING:** 4 **NOTES:** Closed Nov-Feb **CARDS:**

♦♦♦ The Redwell Inn
Arkholme LA6 1BQ ☎ 01524 221240 01524 221107
e-mail: julie@redwellinn.co.uk
Dir: *M6 junct 35, towards Kirkby Lonsdale. Through village of Kellet, Redwell Inn on left after approx 2m*
FACILITIES: 4 en suite (1 fmly) No smoking in bedrooms No smoking in dining room No smoking in 1 lounge STV TVB tea/coffee No dogs (ex guide dogs) Licensed Cen ht TVL Pool Table Dinner Last d 9pm **PRICES:** s fr £35; d £59.50* **PARKING:** 100 **CARDS:**

♦♦♦ The Silverdale Hotel
Shore Rd, Silverdale LA5 0TP ☎ 01524 701206
01524 702258
Dir: *from the M6 junct 35 take road to junct 35a and turn left to Carnforth. At traffic lights turn right to Warton, follow signs to Silverdale.*
FACILITIES: 7 en suite (2 fmly) No smoking in area of dining room TVB tea/coffee Direct dial from bedrooms Licensed Cen ht Pool table Dinner Last d 9pm **PRICES:** s £35; d £53* **LB PARKING:** 38 **CARDS:**

CHORLEY

See **Eccleston**

CLITHEROE Map 07 SD74

♦♦♦♦ Brooklyn
32 Pimlico Rd BB7 2AH ☎ 01200 428268 & 07971 917664
Dir: *M6, A59 to Clitheroe, take Clitheroe North turning, across rdbt, turn next left, 0.5m premises on left*
This elegant and welcoming Victorian town house is just a short stroll from the centre of town, and benefits from a peaceful, residential location. The smart bedrooms are neatly decorated, comfortably furnished and well-maintained. All offer a thoughtful range of extra facilities. A lounge with deep sofas is also available.
FACILITIES: 4 en suite No smoking TVB tea/coffee No dogs (ex guide dogs) Licensed Cen ht No coaches Dinner Last d noon **PRICES:** s fr £27; d fr £43* **CARDS:**

ECCLESTON Map 07 SD51

♦♦♦♦ Parr Hall Farm *(SD522173)*
Parr Ln PR7 5SL ☎ 01257 451917 01257 453749
Mrs K Motley
e-mail: parrhall@talk21.com
Dir: *from M6 junct 27 take A5209 for Parbold, then immediately right B5250 for Eccleston. After 5m Parr Lane on right, 1st property on left*
This attractive well-maintained farmhouse, located in a quiet corner of the village, dates back to the 17th century. Bedrooms are well equipped and smartly furnished in pine. Substantial breakfasts are served in the attractive dining room.
FACILITIES: 4 en suite (1 fmly) No smoking TVB tea/coffee No dogs Cen ht Croquet lawn 15 acres arable **PRICES:** s £30-£35; d £50-£60*
PARKING: 20 **CARDS:**

TVB means there are televisions in bedrooms
TVL means thereís a television in the lounge
STV means satellite television.

England

LANCASTER Map 07 SD46

Premier Collection

♦♦♦♦♦ New Capernwray Farm
Capernwray LA6 1AD ☎ 01524 734284 01524 734284
e-mail: newcapfarm@aol.com
(For full entry see Carnforth)

♦♦♦ Lancaster Town House
11/12 Newton Ter, Caton Rd LA1 3PB ☎ 01524 65527
01524 383148
e-mail: hedge-holmes@talk21.com
Dir: *1m from M6 junct 34, towards Lancaster, house on right*
FACILITIES: 7 en suite (1 fmly) No smoking in bedrooms No smoking in dining room TVB tea/coffee No dogs (ex guide dogs) Cen ht TVL No coaches **PRICES:** s £25-£32; d £42-£46 **CARDS:**

LONGRIDGE Map 07 SD63

♦♦♦♦ Jenkinsons *(SD611348)*
Alston Ln, Preston Rd PR3 3BD ☎ 01772 782624 Mrs E J Ibison
Dir: *off B6243 Preston to Longridge road - follow signs to Alston Hall College*
A warm welcome awaits guests at this beautiful Lancashire farmhouse, set in immaculate gardens with breathtaking views. Both public rooms and bedrooms are furnished to a high standard with antique pieces. Although bedrooms are not en-suite, the bathrooms are fitted to a very high standard. Breakfast is a substantial affair and utilises quality local produce.
FACILITIES: 6 rms No smoking tea/coffee No dogs (ex guide dogs) Cen ht TVL No children 12yrs 100 acres dairy, sheep **PRICES:** s £25-£30; d £45* **PARKING:** 10 **NOTES:** Closed 26 Dec-15 Jan

LYTHAM ST ANNES Map 07 SD32

♦♦♦ Endsleigh Private Hotel
315 Clifton Dr South FY8 1HN ☎ 01253 725622
01253 720072
Dir: *on A584 2.5m E of Blackpool, 1st hotel E of St Annes Sq shopping centre, opp main Post Office*
This friendly guest house is centrally located in the town and is just a short walk from the promenade. The accommodation is well-maintained and the bedrooms are thoughtfully equipped. Hearty breakfasts are taken in the bright dining room. Dinners are prepared by prior arrangement.
FACILITIES: 15 en suite (5 fmly) (2 GF) No smoking in 5 bedrooms No smoking in dining room No smoking in lounges TVB tea/coffee No dogs (ex guide dogs) Licensed Cen ht No coaches Dinner Last d 6pm
PRICES: s £23; d £46* **LB PARKING:** 8

♦♦♦ Strathmore Hotel
305 Clifton Dr South FY8 1HN ☎ 01253 725478
Dir: *on main Preston to Blackpool Rd at centre of St Annes opposite Post Office*
This friendly family run hotel enjoys a central location close to the Promenade. Well-equipped bedrooms are smartly furnished with neat decor. Recently refurbished public areas include an elegant, comfortable lounge where guests can enjoy a relaxing drink, and there is also a smartly presented dining room where good value home cooked meals are served.

continued

Endsleigh Private Hotel

FACILITIES: 8 rms (5 en suite) No smoking in dining room TVB tea/coffee No dogs Licensed Cen ht No children 9yrs No coaches Dinner Last d 5pm
PRICES: s £18-£24; d £36-£48* **LB BB PARKING:** 10

♦♦♦ Monarch Hotel
29 St Annes Rd East FY8 1TA ☎ 01253 720464
e-mail: churchill@monarch91.freeserve.co.uk
FACILITIES: 8 rms (7 en suite) (2 fmly) No smoking in 2 bedrooms No smoking in dining room TVB tea/coffee No dogs (ex guide dogs) Licensed Cen ht TVL No coaches aromatherapy & reflexology by appointment Dinner Last d noon **PRICES:** s £21-£27; d £42-£54* **LB PARKING:** 6
CARDS:

MORECAMBE Map 07 SD46

♦♦♦ Hotel Prospect
363 Marine Rd East LA4 5AQ ☎ 01524 417819 01524 417819
e-mail: peter@hotel-prospect.fsnet.co.uk
Dir: *exit M6 at junct 34/35, follow Morecombe Promenade, premises just before Gala Bingo*
Situated on Morecambe Promenade, this friendly family run hotel enjoys panoramic views over the bay to the Lakeland Hills beyond. Bedrooms are comfortably proportioned thoughtfully furnished and carefully decorated. The bright airy dining room extends into a small lounge area, which has its own well stocked bar and overlooks the sea. There is an enclosed car park, offering off road parking.
FACILITIES: 14 rms (13 en suite) (4 fmly) No smoking in 4 bedrooms No smoking in dining room TVB tea/coffee Licensed Cen ht Dinner Last d 3pm
PRICES: s £16-£18; d £32-£36 **LB BB PARKING:** 14 **CARDS:**

♦♦♦ Wimslow Private Hotel
374 Marine Rd East LA4 5AH ☎ 01524 417804
01524 417804
e-mail: morecambewimslow@aol.com
Dir: *400yds from Broadway Hotel, 300yds W of Town Hall*
Situated on the seafront, this small hotel offers fine views over the bay from the public areas and a number of the bedrooms. The public areas include a well-stocked bar and dining room where substantial evening meals are offered. Bedrooms, varying in size, are freshly decorated.
FACILITIES: 14 en suite (2 fmly) (3 GF) No smoking in dining room TVB tea/coffee No dogs (ex guide dogs) Licensed Cen ht No coaches Dinner Last d 4.30pm **PRICES:** s £18-£20; d £36-£40* **PARKING:** 9 **NOTES:** Closed 1 week Nov & 1 week Jan **CARDS:**

PRESTON Map 07 SD52

See also Longridge

Premier Collection

♦♦♦♦♦ Whitestake Farm

Pope Ln, Whitestake PR4 4JR ☎ 01772 613005 & 611146 📠 01772 611146
e-mail: marylou@airselet.co.uk
Dir: *M6 junct 29, follow signs Lytham St Annes on A582 until traffic lights, left for Longton into Wham Ln and 2nd right into Pope Ln*

A warm welcome awaits at this attractive white cottage, peacefully located just minutes from Preston and the M6, and within easy reach of Southport and Lytham. Beautifully appointed bedrooms and bathrooms are spacious and thoughtfully equipped. Carefully prepared, substantial breakfasts are taken around a huge table in the elegant dining room. There is an indoor swimming pool.

FACILITIES: 2 en suite (1 fmly) No smoking STV TVB Cen ht TVL No coaches Indoor swimming pool (heated) **PRICES:** d £70✳ **PARKING:** 2

♦♦♦♦ Tulketh Hotel

209 Tulketh Rd, Ashton-on-Ribble PR2 1ES ☎ 01772 726250 & 728096 📠 01772 723743
Dir: *from M6 junct 31, turn left onto A59 Preston then right onto A5085 towards Blackpool. Left at St Andrews Church after 3m onto Tulketh Rd*

This friendly, privately run hotel is situated in a leafy area, minutes from the town centre. Many original features have been retained including an impressive Edwardian hallway. Individually styled, smartly decorated bedrooms are thoughtfully equipped and include a four-poster room. There is a comfortable lounge bar and spacious dining room.

FACILITIES: 13 en suite (4 GF) No smoking in 5 bedrooms No smoking in dining room TVB tea/coffee Direct dial from bedrooms No dogs (ex guide dogs) Licensed Cen ht TVL No coaches Dinner Last d 6pm **PRICES:** s £37.50-£40; d £49.50-£60✳ **PARKING:** 12 **NOTES:** Closed 20 Dec-4 Jan **CARDS:**

♦♦♦ Withy Trees

175-177 Garstang Rd, Fulwood PR2 8JQ ☎ 01772 717693 📠 01772 511087
e-mail: info@withytrees.co.uk
Dir: *from M6 junct 32 turn left on A6 direction of Preston. Guest House approx. 1.5m on right*

Conveniently located on the A6 Garstang road, this friendly yet relaxed private hotel is only minutes from the town centre and from the M55 and M6 motorways. Bedrooms are well-equipped and offer modern facilities. A comfortably furnished lounge is provided and substantial breakfasts served in the airy dining room.

FACILITIES: 9 en suite (2 fmly) (2 GF) No smoking in 5 bedrooms No smoking in dining room TVB tea/coffee Cen ht TVL No coaches Dinner Last d by arrangement **PRICES:** s £35; d £45✳ **PARKING:** 7

WHITEWELL Map 07 SD64

♦♦♦♦ The Inn at Whitewell

Forest Of Bowland, Nr Clitheroe BB7 3AT ☎ 01200 448222 📠 01200 448298
Dir: *from Clitheroe take B6243 and follow signs for Whitewell*

This famous old inn is located deep in the beautiful Forest of Bowland, alongside the River Hodder. A wide range of food is available in the relaxed bar and also in the elegant restaurant. Bedrooms are particularly well equipped and furniture includes many fine antique and period pieces. Four excellent new Coach House suites have been added. *continued*

FACILITIES: 13 en suite 4 annexe en suite (10 fmly) STV TVB tea/coffee Direct dial from bedrooms Cen ht Fishing Clay pigeon shooting by arrangement Dinner Last d 9.30pm **PRICES:** s £63-£99; d £87-£125✳ **MEALS:** Bar Lunch £13.50-£21.10alc Dinner £21.10-£32.30alc✳ **PARKING:** 60 **CARDS:**

YEALAND CONYERS Map 07 SD57

Premier Collection

♦♦♦♦♦ The Bower

LA5 9SF ☎ 01524 734585 📠 01524 730710
e-mail: info@thebower.co.uk
Dir: *leave M6 junct 35, follow A6 towards Milnthorpe for 0.75m, under narrow bridge, take next left & bear left at end*

Located in an Area of Outstanding Natural Beauty and within walking distance of Leighton Moss RSPB Reserve, The Bower is a stylishly furnished Georgian country house. Spacious bedrooms are very comfortable and the opulent day rooms are relaxing. Convivial, candlelit kitchen suppers are available as lighter alternatives to formal dinners. Excellent hospitality and attentive service are assured.

FACILITIES: 2 en suite (1 fmly) No smoking TVB tea/coffee No dogs (ex guide dogs) Cen ht TVL No children 12yrs No coaches Croquet lawn Bridge games/lessons Dinner Last d 24hrs **PRICES:** s £39.50; d £59-£69 **PARKING:** 6 **CARDS:**

LEICESTERSHIRE

ASHBY-DE-LA-ZOUCH

See Coalville

BARKESTONE-LE-VALE Map 08 SK73

♦♦♦♦ Woodside Farm *(SK797336)*

NG13 0HQ ☎ 01476 870336 Mrs D Hickling
e-mail: hickling-woodside@supanet.com
Dir: *from A52 at Bottesford, exit towards Harby and Belvoir Castle. After passing x-roads signposted 'Belvoir Castle' lane leading to Woodside Farm on left.*

A warm welcome awaits guests at this friendly working farm, peacefully located on the Belvoir Castle estate in the Vale of Belvoir: Nottingham and Grantham are within easy reach. Bedrooms are smartly appointed and enjoy beautiful views over the local countryside. Hearty breakfasts are served in the lounge/dinning room and packed lunches are available on request.

FACILITIES: 2 rms No smoking tea/coffee No dogs Cen ht Cycle storage available 340 acres dairy/arable **PRICES:** s £24; d £40✳ **LB PARKING:** 2

England

BOTTESFORD Map 08 SK83

♦♦♦♦ The Old Whitehouse

Market St NG13 0BW ☎ 01949 842244

***Dir:** follow A52 to centre of village. Establishment next to telephone box opposite cross and stocks*

This delightful house is conveniently located just off the A52 in the heart of the Vale of Belvoir. The A1, Nottingham and Belvoir Castle are all within easy reach. Accommodation includes attractive, individually styled bedrooms and spacious public rooms. Hearty breakfasts are served either in the cosy breakfast room or in the oak beamed lounge/dinning room.

FACILITIES: 4 rms (1 en suite) (1 fmly) No smoking TVB tea/coffee No dogs (ex guide dogs) Cen ht TVL No coaches **PRICES:** s £25-£30; d £44-£55* **PARKING:** 6

♦♦♦♦ The Thatch Hotel & Restaurant

26 High St NG13 0AA ☎ 01949 842330 & 844407

01949 843421

e-mail: thatch.hotelrestaurant@btinternet.com

***Dir:** turn off A1 onto A52 approx 5m off A52 turn right into Bottesford village or A52 from Nottingham to Grantham 1st turn left signed Bottesford*

This lovely thatched cottage enjoys a prominent location in the centre of the village, just off the A52. The hub of the operation is a busy restaurant offering carefully prepared imaginative dishes. There is a comfortable bar lounge and an attractive rear garden. Bedrooms are smartly appointed and well equipped.

FACILITIES: 3 en suite (1 fmly) No smoking in bedrooms No smoking in dining room TVB tea/coffee No dogs (ex guide dogs) Licensed Cen ht TVL No children 5yrs No coaches Dinner Last d 9.30pm **PRICES:** s £36-£40; d £48-£56* **PARKING:** 6 **NOTES:** Closed 24-30 Dec **CARDS:**

BRUNTINGTHORPE Map 04 SP68

♦♦♦♦ Knaptoft House Farm & The Greenway *(SP619894)*

Bruntingthorpe Rd, Bruntingthorpe LE17 6PR ☎ 0116 247 8388

Mrs A T Hutchinson

e-mail: info@knaptoft.com

***Dir:** at Bruntingthorpe/Saddington x-roads turn off A5199 (former A50) for Bruntingthorpe, premises on left after 1m, beyond Shearsby Bath Hotel*

This family run farmhouse and modern bungalow stands in well kept grounds and enjoys beautiful views of the countryside. Bedrooms are attractively decorated, thoughtfully furnished and equipped. Each building has a comfortably appointed lounge with wood burning stove and freshly cooked breakfasts are served in a cheerful dining room.

continued

Knaptoft House Farm & The Greenway

FACILITIES: 3 rms (2 en suite) 3 annexe en suite No smoking TVB tea/coffee No dogs Cen ht No children 5yrs Fishing 145 acres sheep **PRICES:** s fr £30; d £46-£50* **PARKING:** 10 **NOTES:** Closed Xmas/New Year **CARDS:**

CASTLE DONINGTON

See East Midlands Airport

COALVILLE Map 08 SK41

♦♦♦♦ Church Lane Farm House

Ravenstone LE67 2AE ☎ 01530 810536 & 811299

01530 811299

e-mail: annthorne@ravenstone-guesthouse.co.uk

***Dir:** at A511/A447 junct, follow signs for Ibstock . Church Lane 1st right, establishment 2nd house on left*

Located in the heart of Ravenstone village, this Queen Anne house retains many original features that are complemented by fine period furniture and artefacts. Bedrooms are individually appointed and comfortable. Breakfasts are taken in the beamed dining room, which also contains an honesty bar; imaginative dinners are available by prior arrangement.

FACILITIES: 3 en suite No smoking TV4B tea/coffee Licensed Cen ht TVL No children 18yrs No coaches Painting tuition Dinner Last d noon **PRICES:** s £31.50-£35; d £50-£63* LB **PARKING:** 6 **NOTES:** Closed Xmas **CARDS:**

EAST MIDLANDS AIRPORT Map 08 SK42

Premier Collection

♦♦♦♦♦ Kegworth House

42 High St DE74 2DA ☎ 01509 672575 01509 670645

e-mail: tony@kegworthhouse.co.uk

***Dir:** M1 junct 23A, onto A6 to Derby/Nottingham, after 0.75ml, follow sign to 'Kegworth Village Only'. In village, follow church steeple ahead, it disappears into roof of 3 storey house, this is Kegworth House*

continued

Ideally located for major road links and East Midlands Airport, this impressive Georgian town house with an immaculate walled garden has been lovingly restored. The individually styled luxury bedrooms are equipped with a wealth of thoughtful extras. An elegant dining room is the setting for memorable dinners and wholesome breakfasts, featuring local produce, are served in the attractive kitchen.
FACILITIES: 10 en suite (2 fmly) No smoking TVB tea/coffee Direct dial from bedrooms No dogs (ex guide dogs) Licensed Cen ht TVL Dinner Last d 7.30pm **PRICES:** s fr £70.50; d fr £87* **PARKING:** 20 **NOTES:** Closed 20 Dec-1Jan **CARDS:**

♦♦♦♦ Donington Park Farmhouse Hotel

Melbourne Rd, Isley Walton DE74 2RN ☎ 01332 862409
01332 862364
e-mail: info@parkfarmhouse.co.uk
Dir: *on A453 at Isley Walton take Melbourne turn, premises 0.5m on right (The Circle)*

Located adjacent to Donington Park and convenient for East Midlands Airport, this 17th century former farmhouse has been sympathetically renovated to provide high standards. The tastefully furnished bedrooms, some of which are located in converted outbuildings, are equipped with a range of both practical and homely extras. Imaginative dinners, served in the attractive kitchen dining room, make use of home grown produce.
FACILITIES: 8 en suite 8 annexe en suite (3 fmly) No smoking in 4 bedrooms No smoking in dining room TVB tea/coffee Direct dial from bedrooms Licensed Cen ht Caravan site with play area. Dinner Last d 9.30pm **PRICES:** s £60-£85; d £70-£100* LB **CONF:** Thtr 50 Class 16 Board 16 Del from £80 * **PARKING:** 20 **NOTES:** Closed Xmas **CARDS:**

HINCKLEY

Map 04 SP49

♦♦♦♦ *Ambion Court Hotel*

The Green, Dadlington CV13 6JB ☎ 01455 212292
01455 213141
e-mail: stay@ambionhotel.co.uk
Dir: *from Hinckley Police Station take Stoke Golding Rd past Safeway Superstore. At Stoke Golding turn right into Dadlington*

This smart guest house was originally a group of cottages and stable blocks and overlooks the village green. The individually decorated bedrooms are located in a courtyard-style annexe. The spacious public areas feature a beamed dining room, where delicious dinners and breakfasts are served, a cosy lounge bar and a sitting room.
FACILITIES: 2 en suite 5 annexe en suite (1 fmly) No smoking in bedrooms No smoking in dining room No smoking in 1 lounge TVB tea/coffee Direct dial from bedrooms No dogs (ex guide dogs) Licensed Cen ht TVL No coaches Dinner Last d 8:30pm **PARKING:** 12 **CARDS:**

♦♦♦♦ *Badgers Mount*

6 Station Rd, Elmesthorpe LE9 7SG ☎ 01455 848161
01455 848161
e-mail: info@badgersmount.com
Dir: *on B581*

This large detached house is located in a quiet setting. Bedrooms are spacious, comfortable, and individual in design with many thoughtful touches as standard. Extensive grounds include an outdoor heated swimming pool, well-kept gardens and a chicken run, which provides fresh eggs for breakfast.
FACILITIES: 12 en suite (3 fmly) No smoking in bedrooms No smoking in dining room No smoking in 1 lounge TVB tea/coffee No dogs Licensed Cen ht TVL No coaches Outdoor swimming pool (heated) Dinner Last d 7.30pm **PARKING:** 20 **CARDS:**

KEGWORTH

See East Midlands Airport

England

LEICESTER Map 04 SK50

♦♦♦ Stoneycroft Hotel

5-7 Elmfield Av LE2 1RB ☎ 0116 270 7605 📠 0116 270 6067
e-mail: reception@stoneycrofthotel.co.uk
Dir: *near city centre on A6 to Market Harborough*
This large hotel provides comfortable accommodation and helpful service. The bedrooms have modern fittings, which include desks and suitable chairs. The public areas include a foyer lounge area, breakfast room and conference facilities. There is also a large restaurant/bar area, which serves a good selection of freshly cooked dishes.
FACILITIES: 41 en suite (4 fmly) No smoking in bedrooms No smoking in dining room TVB tea/coffee Direct dial from bedrooms No dogs (ex guide dogs) Licensed Cen ht TVL Pool Table Dinner Last d 9.30pm **PRICES:** s £39; d £49✻ **PARKING:** 20 **CARDS:**

LOUGHBOROUGH Map 08 SK51

♦♦♦ De Montfort Hotel

88 Leicester Rd LE11 2AQ ☎ 01509 216061 📠 01509 233667
e-mail: thedemontforthotel@amserve.com
Dir: *situated on A6, 4 mins from town centre, opposite Southfields Park & Fairfield School*
A Victorian hotel, retaining many original features. Comfortable bedrooms have been attractively decorated with bright colours. Downstairs, guests can relax in the cosy bar; there is a separate lounge, and meals are served in the well-appointed dining room. Parking is available next to the school opposite.
FACILITIES: 9 rms (7 en suite) (3 fmly) No smoking in dining room TVB tea/coffee No dogs Licensed Cen ht TVL Dinner Last d 6pm
PRICES: s £35-£40; d £45-£50✻ **CARDS:**

♦♦♦ Garendon Park Hotel

92 Leicester Rd LE11 2AQ ☎ 01509 236557 📠 01509 265559
e-mail: info@gardenparkhotel.co.uk
Dir: *M1 J23, A512 to Loughborough, at 2nd island turn R, at 5th island turn L, at lights turn L. Hotel is on R just before next lights*
Located a few minutes' walk from the town centre, this late Victorian house offers well-equipped accommodation, most of which has modern en suite facilities. English breakfasts, and dinners by arrangement, are taken in the pleasantly appointed dining room. There is also a lounge available for guests to use.
FACILITIES: 9 en suite (4 fmly) No smoking in bedrooms No smoking in dining room STV TVB tea/coffee Licensed Cen ht TVL Dinner Last d 6pm
PRICES: s £35-£40; d £45-£55✻ **CARDS:**

♦♦♦ 🅰 Croft

21 Hall Croft, Shepshed LE12 9AN ☎ 01509 505657
📠 0870 052 2266
e-mail: ray@croftguesthouse.demon.co.uk
Dir: *W of M1 J23 - A512 take right at traffic lights after J23 (B5330). At the centre of Shepshed take 2nd exit on rdbt right at mini rdbt 1st right at Red Lion Pub and sharp right again*
FACILITIES: 10 rms (5 en suite) (2 fmly) No smoking in bedrooms No smoking in dining room TVB tea/coffee Cen ht TVL Pool Table
PRICES: s £20-£32; d £40-£45✻ **NOTES:** Closed 24 Dec - 2 Jan
CARDS:

LUTTERWORTH Map 04 SP58

♦♦♦ *The Old Rectory B & B*

Church St, North Kilworth LE17 6EZ ☎ 01858 881130
e-mail: janewestaway@beeb.net
Dir: *In village take road next to Swan pub. Bear right across green, pass War Memorial & continue down hill, left at bottom. Sharp right before heading uphill towards church, entrance to right of church gates*

continued

The Old Rectory is located in the peaceful rural village of North Kilworth, conveniently placed for access to major road networks. A warm welcome is assured from Jane Westaway and her family. Bedrooms are suitably appointed, each with compact en suite shower rooms, and breakfast is served in the separate open plan lounge and dining area, whilst guests also have access to the adjacent small kitchenette.
FACILITIES: 3 annexe en suite (1 fmly) No smoking No dogs (ex guide dogs) Cen ht **PARKING:** 4 **NOTES:** Closed Xmas

MARKET HARBOROUGH Map 04 SP78

♦♦♦♦ 🅰 Hunters Lodge

By Foxton Locks, Gumley LE16 7RT ☎ 0116 279 3744
📠 0116 279 3855
e-mail: info@hunterslodgefoxton.co.uk
Dir: *M1 junct 20, A4304 for Market Harborough, after 8m in village of Lubenham take 2nd left signed Foxton, next left signed Laughton pass village hall and out of village for 1.5m over hump backed bridge next right Gumley in 200yds right signed Foxton*
FACILITIES: 2 en suite (1 fmly) (2 GF) No smoking STV TVB tea/coffee Cen ht TVL No coaches **PRICES:** s fr £24.99; d fr £39.99✻ **PARKING:** 5
CARDS:

MELTON MOWBRAY Map 08 SK71

♦♦♦♦ Bryn Barn

38 High St, Waltham-on-the-Wolds LE14 4AH
☎ 01664 464783 & 07790 963542 📠 01664 464138
e-mail: glenarowlands@onetel.net.uk
Dir: *off A607 onto High St between Marquis of Granby pub and church, Bryn Barn 200mtrs on R*
A warm welcome is offered at this charming barn and stable conversion set in secluded cottage gardens within a picturesque conservation village in the Belvoir Vale. There is a comfortable lounge and separate breakfast room, and dinner can be taken at one of the nearby village pubs.
FACILITIES: 4 rms (3 en suite) (2 fmly) (1 GF) No smoking TVB tea/coffee Cen ht TVL No coaches **PRICES:** s £25-£30; d £40-£45✻ **LB**
PARKING: 4 **NOTES:** Closed 21 Dec - 4 Jan

♦♦♦♦ 🅰 Amberley Gardens

4 Church Ln, Asfordby-by-the-Wreake LE14 3RU
☎ 01664 812314 📠 01664 813740
e-mail: doris@amberleygardens.net
Dir: *Asfordby is on the A6006, 3m W of Melton Mowbray. Look for Church Steeple turn down road opposite petrol Stn, bear left, proceed right across the church yard past church entrance, Amberley is on the right.*
FACILITIES: 3 en suite No smoking TVB tea/coffee No dogs (ex guide dogs) Cen ht No children 14yrs No coaches Fishing
PRICES: s £20-£25; d £40-£50✻ **PARKING:** 6

NARBOROUGH Map 04 SP59

♦♦♦♦ Fossebrook

Coventry Rd, Croft LE9 3GP ☎ 01455 283517 📠 01455 283517
Dir: *M1 junct 20 through Lutterworth, left to Broughton Astley, at T-junction right onto B4114. Right at end of dual carriageway, house 100yds opposite Highways Depot*
This friendly guest house enjoys a quite rural location and good access from road networks. Bedrooms are spacious, very comfortable and offer an excellent range of facilities including videos in all rooms. Breakfast is served in the bright dining room, which overlooks pleasant grounds.
FACILITIES: 5 en suite (1 fmly) No smoking in bedrooms TVB tea/coffee No dogs Cen ht No coaches Riding **PRICES:** s £40; d £40✻
PARKING: 16

LINCOLNSHIRE

ASWARBY — Map 08 TF03

◆◆◆ Tally Ho

NG34 8SA ☎ 01529 455205 01529 309024

Dir: *3m S of Sleaford, on A15*

Bedrooms at this delightful inn are in an adjacent building, and all are bright and well-equipped. A wide range of snacks and meals are available at lunch and dinner. Guests can sit in the bar or dine in the restaurant where service is very friendly and attentive.

FACILITIES: 6 annexe en suite No smoking in dining room TVB tea/coffee Cen ht No coaches Dinner Last d 10pm **PRICES:** s £35; d £50* **LB** **MEALS:** Sunday Lunch £10.65-£15.30&alc Dinner £15.35-£21alc* **PARKING:** 40 **CARDS:**

BARTON-UPON-HUMBER — Map 08 TA02

◆◆◆ Tobias House

Market Place, Cross Hill, Barrow-upon-Humber DN19 7BW ☎ 01469 531164

Dir: *leave A15 at Humber Bridge rdbt to Barton, then A1077 to Barrow upon Humber, turn right at rdbt follow A1077 to bottom of hill turn left & 1st right*

Set in the Victorian market square of this charming village, this guest house has ample public parking, four comfortable bedrooms, and a small bar and dining room. Hospitality is very caring and sincere.

FACILITIES: 4 en suite (1 fmly) No smoking in bedrooms No smoking in dining room TVB tea/coffee No dogs (ex guide dogs) Licensed Cen ht No coaches Last d 7pm **PARKING:** 4

BOSTON — Map 08 TF34

◆◆◆◆ Boston Lodge

Browns Drove, Swineshead Bridge PE20 3PX ☎ 01205 820983 01205 820512

e-mail: info@bostonlodge.co.uk

Dir: *adjacent to A1121, 300yds from the juction with A17*

This attractive, ivy clad hotel is ideally situated within easy striking distance of the historic town of Boston. The bedrooms are pleasantly furnished and equipped with many useful extras. Breakfast is served at individual tables in the open plan lounge/dining room; the lounge offers comfortable seating and TV.

FACILITIES: 9 en suite (2 fmly) (3 GF) No smoking STV TVB tea/coffee Cen ht TVL No children 1yr No coaches **PRICES:** s £24; d £39.50* **LB** **PARKING:** 16 **CARDS:**

BRACEBY — Map 08 TF03

◆◆◆◆ Saddleback Cottage

Main St NG34 0SZ ☎ 01529 497353

e-mail: waiter@onetel.net.uk

Dir: *from A52 Boston/Spalding road, take road to Ropsley, 1m on right after B6403/A52 junct, at Ropsley turn left signed Braceby, cottage is last on left*

This peacefully located house is found on the edge of the small hamlet of Braceby and stands is mature and well-cared for grounds. The house is very comfortably furnished with guests also having the use of a cosy lounge. Good home cooking is also a feature.

FACILITIES: 2 rms (3 GF) No smoking TVB tea/coffee No dogs (ex guide dogs) No coaches **PRICES:** s £40; d £45* **PARKING:** 2

NOTES: Closed 20 Dec-7 Jan

BRIGG — Map 08 TA00

◆◆◆ Hamsden Garth

Cadney Rd LN7 6LA ☎ 01652 678703 01652 678703

e-mail: reservations@hamsden.co.uk

Dir: *from Brigg, A1084 for 2m then B1434, at Howsham turn R into Cadney Rd, 400yds on right*

The friendly proprietors here welcome guests to their home, offering contemporary bedrooms which share a modern general bathroom with separate shower and bath. Guests are welcome to use the lounge, and breakfast is taken around a large table in a separate dining room, overlooking the rear garden.

FACILITIES: 2 rms No smoking TVB tea/coffee Cen ht TVL No coaches **PRICES:** s £20; d £35* **BB** **PARKING:** 10

CLEETHORPES — Map 08 TA30

◆◆◆◆ *Adelaide Hotel*

41 Isaac's Hill DN35 8JT ☎ 01472 693594 01472 329717

e-mail: robert.callison@ntlworld.com

Dir: *Isaac's Hill lies at end of A180 and A46. Hotel located on right hand side at bottom of hill*

This very well-presented house offers well-equipped bedrooms together with comfortable public rooms. Good home cooking is also provided and hospitality is a major strength of the operation. Secure car parking is readily available.

FACILITIES: 5 rms (3 en suite) (1 fmly) No smoking STV TVB tea/coffee No dogs (ex guide dogs) Licensed Cen ht TVL No children 4yrs Dinner Last d 12pm **PARKING:** 6 **CARDS:**

◆◆◆◆ Clee House

31-33 Clee Rd DN35 8AD ☎ 01472 200850 01472 200850

e-mail: clee.house@btinternet.com

Dir: *on entering town from Grimsby, turn right onto Clee Rd at Isaac's Hill rndbt. 50mtrs house in own grounds on left*

Close to the town centre, this detached Victorian house retains many of its original features. Tasty breakfasts and imaginative evening meals are served in the cosy dining room, while a comfortable lounge with a well-stocked bar is also available for residents. Bedrooms are spacious and very well equipped, and there are several ground floor bedrooms with disabled facilities.

FACILITIES: 10 en suite (6 fmly) (4 GF) No smoking in bedrooms No smoking in dining room STV TVB tea/coffee Direct dial from bedrooms No dogs (ex guide dogs) Licensed Cen ht TVL ch fac Dinner Last d 9pm **PRICES:** s £29.50-£37.50; d £49.50-£65.50* **LB** **PARKING:** 14 **CARDS:**

◆◆◆◆ Comat Hotel

26 Yarra Rd DN35 8LS ☎ 01472 694791 & 591861 01472 592823

e-mail: comat-hotel@ntlworld.com

Dir: *from Grimsby Rd, follow signs for seafront. Continue along Alexandra Rd to library, turn right on left-hand side. Hotel 50yds on right*

Located a few minutes' walk from the shops and seafront, this comfortable establishment is friendly and welcoming and offers cosy well-equipped bedrooms. Tasty English breakfasts and home cooked dinners are taken in the bright attractive dining room. A quiet sitting room and bar with pool table are also available for guest use.

FACILITIES: 6 en suite (2 fmly) No smoking in dining room TVB tea/coffee No dogs (ex guide dogs) Licensed Cen ht TVL No coaches Dinner Last d noon **PRICES:** s £22; d £44-£48* **LB** **CARDS:**

England

CLEETHORPES continued

♦♦♦♦ Tudor Terrace

11 Bradford Av DN35 0BB ☎ 01472 600800 📠 01472 501395
e-mail: tudor.terrace@btinternet.com
Dir: *from sea front, turn into Bradford Ave, guest house is first property on left*

The Tudor Terrace Guest House offers attractive bedrooms, which are thoughtfully designed and furnished to a high standard. The hotel has a pleasant patio and a well-maintained garden. Very caring and friendly service is provided and the house is strictly no-smoking.

FACILITIES: 6 rms (4 en suite) (1 GF) No smoking TVB tea/coffee Cen ht TVL No coaches Dinner Last d 2pm **PRICES:** s £17-£25; d £39-£45* LB BB **PARKING:** 3 **CARDS:**

♦♦♦ Burlington Guest House

2-4 Albert Rd DN35 8LX ☎ 01472 699071 📠 01472 699071
e-mail: burlington2_4@btopenworld.com
Dir: *on the upper Prom, next to library*

A welcoming establishment in a quiet location, with private rear car parking. Bedrooms are neatly presented with some ground floor rooms. There is a comfortably appointed residents' bar, and breakfast is served in a pleasant dining room.

FACILITIES: 12 rms (2 en suite) (3 fmly) (2 GF) No smoking in dining room TVB tea/coffee Licensed Cen ht TVL No coaches **PRICES:** s £15; d £28-£36* BB **PARKING:** 8 **NOTES:** Closed 24 Dec-1 Jan **CARDS:**

♦♦♦ Holmhirst Hotel

3 Alexandra Rd DN35 8LQ ☎ 01472 692656 📠 01472 692656
e-mail: holmhirst@aol.com
Dir: *from M180 take A180 to Cleethorpes, along seafront to council offices*

Ideally located overlooking the sea and pier, this Victorian terraced house offers comfortable well equipped bedrooms many with en suite shower rooms. Tasty English breakfasts and a range of both lunchtime and evening meals are served in the attractive front-facing dining room and a well stocked bar is also available.

FACILITIES: 8 rms (5 en suite) No smoking in dining room No smoking in 1 lounge TVB tea/coffee No dogs (ex guide dogs) Licensed Cen ht TVL No children 3yrs No coaches Dinner Last d 8pm **PRICES:** s £20-£25; d £42* **NOTES:** Closed 27 Dec-12 Jan **CARDS:**

♦♦♦ Shellys

15 Princes Rd DN35 8AW ☎ 01472 690153
e-mail: elaine@shellyb-b.fsnet.co.uk
Dir: *Turn off Grimsby Rd at Isacc's Hill rdbt, guest house on left-hand side*

This relaxed and very friendly guest house is informal and welcoming, and the accommodation is well equipped. Hearty breakfasts are served in the cosy combined dining room/lounge.

FACILITIES: 8 rms (1 en suite) (2 fmly) No smoking in bedrooms No smoking in dining room TVB tea/coffee Cen ht TVL No coaches **PRICES:** s £15; d £30* LB BB **PARKING:** 6

♦♦♦ Ginnies

27 Queens Pde DN35 0DF ☎ 01472 694997 📠 01472 316799
e-mail: kimkwood@aol.com
Dir: *along seafront on Alexander Rd past small rdbt onto Highcliff Rd then onto Kingsway. At next small rdbt right into Queens Parade, Ginnies 30yds on left*

FACILITIES: 7 en suite (3 fmly) No smoking TVB tea/coffee No dogs (ex guide dogs) Cen ht **PRICES:** s £16-£20; d £32-£36* LB BB **PARKING:** 2 **NOTES:** Closed 25 Dec-1 Jan

♦♦ Dovedale Hotel

14 Albert Rd DN35 8LX ☎ 01472 692988 📠 01472 313121

This family run guest house is found just off the promenade in a quiet side road. It offers modern bedrooms and some bathrooms with spa baths. There is a cosy dining room and a small bar.

continued

FACILITIES: 19 rms (15 en suite) (6 fmly) (47 GF) No smoking in dining room TVB tea/coffee Licensed Cen ht Jacuzzi **PRICES:** s £18-£39; d £34-£69* BB **PARKING:** 12 **CARDS:**

GAINSBOROUGH

See **Marton**

GRANTHAM — Map 08 SK93

♦♦♦ The Roost

82 Harrowby Rd NG31 9DS ☎ 01476 560719 📠 01476 563303
e-mail: stobbs@theroost.fsnet.co.uk
Dir: *Harrowby Rd off A52 (S side of town), opposite Crematorium (well signposted from all parts of town)*

A friendly welcome is provided at this pleasant guest house, which is located in a quiet residential area of the town. There are four attractive bedrooms, which host a range of thoughtful extras. Public areas include a cosy dining room where breakfast is served.

FACILITIES: 4 rms (2 en suite) No smoking in dining room No smoking in lounges TVB tea/coffee No dogs (ex guide dogs) Cen ht TVL No children 14yrs No coaches **PRICES:** s £25-£30; d £35-£45* BB **PARKING:** 2 **NOTES:** Closed 10 days in January

GRIMSBY — Map 08 TA21

♦♦♦ Peaks Top Farm

Hewitts Av, New Waltham DN36 4RS ☎ 01472 812941 📠 01472 812941
e-mail: lmclayton@tinyworld.co.uk
Dir: *turn off A16 onto A1098 after 0.25m, through traffic lights, farm entrance is on the left*

FACILITIES: 5 en suite 1 annexe en suite (2 fmly) No smoking TVB tea/coffee No dogs (ex guide dogs) Cen ht No coaches **PRICES:** s £20-£25; d £40-£45* LB **PARKING:** 6 **NOTES:** Closed Xmas-New Year

HOLBEACH — Map 08 TF32

♦♦♦♦ Elloe Lodge

37 Barrington Gate PE12 7LB ☎ 01406 423207 📠 01406 423207
e-mail: bandbholbeach@lineone.net
Dir: *in town centre take Church Street from traffic lights then 2nd left*

This large detached house is also a family home and it stands in well tended and spacious gardens. The bedrooms are pleasantly furnished and comfortable while the guests' lounge is a delightful room. Good breakfasts are served in the rear dining room around a large table enjoying fine views over the lovely gardens.

FACILITIES: 3 en suite (1 fmly) No smoking tea/coffee No dogs Cen ht TVL No coaches **PRICES:** s £25; d £40* LB **PARKING:** 10 **NOTES:** Closed 18 Dec-5 Jan

♦♦♦♦ Pipwell Manor

Washway Rd, Saracens Head PE12 8AY ☎ 01406 423119
📠 01406 423119
e-mail: honnor@pipwellmanor.freeserve.co.uk
Dir: *turn off A17 into Washway Road. 0.25m on left, just past garage and pub*

This period farmhouse sits in beautiful grounds, featuring a miniature railway with original steam engines. Public rooms include an attractive dining room and a comfortable lounge with books and TV. The bedrooms are attractively decorated and delightfully furnished with well chosen pieces, and a thoughtful range of extras.

FACILITIES: 4 en suite No smoking tea/coffee No dogs Cen ht TVL No children 12yrs No coaches Free use of cycles Garden railway
PRICES: s £35; d £46* **PARKING:** 4 **NOTES:** Closed 24 Dec-1 Jan

HORNCASTLE — Map 08 TF26

♦♦♦♦ *Greenfield Farm (TF175745)*

Minting LN9 5PJ ☎ 01507 578457 & 07768 368829
📠 01507 578457 Mrs J Bankes Price
e-mail: greenfieldfarm@farming.co.uk
Dir: *from Lincoln, A158 through Wragby. After 3m turn right at Midge Pub, farm 1m on right*

Ideally located on the outskirts of Minting village, this impressive spacious red brick house enjoys fine views over its gardens across the Lincolnshire countryside. The house offers comfortable en suite bedrooms together with a cosy lounge. Excellent hospitality is provided.

FACILITIES: 3 en suite No smoking tea/coffee No dogs (ex guide dogs) Cen ht TVL No children 10yrs Tennis (grass) 387 acres arable
PARKING: 12 **NOTES:** Closed Xmas & New Year

HOUGH-ON-THE-HILL — Map 08 SK94

♦♦♦♦ *Brownlow Country Restaurant*

Grantham Rd NG32 2AZ ☎ 01400 250234 📠 01400 250772
Dir: *Turn off A607 from Grantham to Seaford at sign for Hough on the Hill. Follow road for approx 2.5m to village. Hotel is on right.*

Set in an unspoilt village, this creeper clad 16th-century building was extended in early Victorian times resulting in a house full of charm and character. Bedrooms are spacious and well equipped while the lounges and restaurant are very comfortably furnished. The cooking shows much flair and imagination.

FACILITIES: 7 en suite (1 fmly) No smoking in area of dining room No smoking in 1 lounge TVB tea/coffee Direct dial from bedrooms Cen ht TVL ch fac Dinner Last d 9.45pm **PARKING:** 50 **CARDS:**

LINCOLN — Map 08 SK97

See also Horncastle, Marton & Swinderby

Premier Collection

♦♦♦♦♦ *Minster Lodge Hotel*

3 Church Ln LN2 1QJ ☎ 01522 513220 📠 01522 513220
e-mail: minsterlodge@cs.com
Dir: *A15 & A46*

This delightful no-smoking house enjoys a wonderful location on the edge of Lincoln, close to the castle and the cathedral. Bedrooms are comfortable and beautifully furnished, all have well appointed, spacious bathrooms. There is an inviting guest lounge with deep cushioned sofas and an attractive dining room where impressive Aga-cooked breakfasts are served. Hospitality and service are warm and attentive.

FACILITIES: 6 en suite (2 fmly) No smoking TVB tea/coffee Direct dial from bedrooms No dogs (ex guide dogs) Licensed Cen ht TVL No coaches **PARKING:** 6 **CARDS:**

♦♦♦♦ St Clements Lodge

21 Langworth Gate LN2 4AD ☎ 01522 521532 📠 01522 521532
Dir: *approx 350yds to E of Lincoln Cathedral, down Eastgate into Langworthgate, 1st house on left 50yds past Bull & Chain pub*

Guests at this delightful house can be assured of a warm welcome from Janet Turner - a previous AA Landlady of the Year Top Twenty finalist. Bedrooms are stylishly appointed and equipped with a host of thoughtful extras. There is a comfortable, inviting lounge and an elegant dining room where super breakfasts are served.

FACILITIES: 3 en suite (1 fmly) No smoking TVB tea/coffee No dogs Cen ht No coaches **PRICES:** s £35-£36; d £50-£56 **LB** **PARKING:** 3

England

LINCOLN continued

♦♦♦♦ Abbottsford House

5 Yarborough Ter LN1 1HN ☎ 01522 826696 📠 01522 826696
e-mail: abbotsfordhouse@ntlworld.co.uk
Dir: *Left off A1102. A15 North, establishment 1m from A46 bypass & A57 into city*

This charming no-smoking guest house is situated just a short walk from the city centre. Attractive bedrooms are beautifully decorated and thoughtfully equipped. There is a smartly appointed dining room/lounge with individual tables and comfortable seating, and guests also have use of a patio area in the delightfully landscaped garden.

FACILITIES: 3 en suite (1 fmly) No smoking TVB tea/coffee No dogs (ex guide dogs) Cen ht No children 3yrs No coaches **PRICES:** s £30-£35; d £44✳ **PARKING:** 5 **NOTES:** Closed 23 Dec-5 Jan

♦♦♦♦ Carholme

175 Carholme Rd LN1 1RU ☎ 01522 531059 📠 01522 511590
e-mail: farrelly@talk21.com
Dir: *turn off A46 bypass, house situated on A57 past Lincoln Racecourse*

Situated just a short walk from the Marina and Lincoln University is this small family-run guest house. Bedrooms are attractively decorated, well-maintained and equipped with many useful extras. Breakfast is served in the smart dining room seated at a large communal pine table. Guests also have the use of a neat lounge and undercover parking.

FACILITIES: 5 en suite (1 fmly) (1 GF) No smoking TVB tea/coffee No dogs Cen ht No coaches **PRICES:** s £23-£25; d £40-£42✳ **LB PARKING:** 20

♦♦♦♦ Carline

1-3 Carline Rd LN1 1HL ☎ 01522 530422 📠 01522 530422
Dir: *left off A1102, A15 N. Premises 1m from A46 bypass & A57 into city*

This smart double-fronted Edwardian house enjoys a convenient location within easy walking distance of the castle and the cathedral. Bedrooms are particularly smartly appointed and benefit from a host of useful extras. Breakfast is served at individual tables in the spacious dining room.

FACILITIES: 8 en suite (3 GF) No smoking TVB tea/coffee No dogs (ex guide dogs) Cen ht No children 3yrs No coaches **PRICES:** s £30-£35; d £44✳ **LB PARKING:** 6 **NOTES:** Closed Xmas & New Year

♦♦♦♦ D'Isney Place Hotel

Eastgate LN2 4AA ☎ 01522 538881 📠 01522 511321
e-mail: info@disneyplacehotel.co.uk
Dir: *100yds from Lincoln Cathedral. Nearest main roads - A15 & A46*

This charming period town house is located minutes' walk from the cathedral and the historic area of the city. Individually designed bedrooms include rooms with four-poster or half-tester beds and come equipped with every conceivable extra. Breakfasts make use of quality ingredients and are served in bedrooms, or weather permitting, in the delightful rear garden.

continued

D'Isney Place Hotel

FACILITIES: 17 en suite (2 fmly) (8 GF) No smoking in 10 bedrooms TVB tea/coffee Direct dial from bedrooms Cen ht **PRICES:** s £55-£75; d £86-£106✳ **LB PARKING:** 4 **CARDS:**

♦♦♦♦ Eagles

552A Newark Rd, North Hykeham LN6 9NG ☎ 01522 686346
Dir: *turn off A46 onto A1434, 0.5m on right*

This large detached house is very convenient for the bypass and has been well-furnished and thoughtfully equipped. The bedrooms are bright and fresh, and a conservatory has been added for guests' use. Substantial breakfasts are served in the pleasant dining room while excellent hospitality is provided.

FACILITIES: 5 en suite (2 fmly) No smoking TVB tea/coffee Cen ht No coaches **PRICES:** s £25-£30; d £40✳ **LB PARKING:** 6

♦♦♦♦ Orchard House

119 Yarborough Rd LN1 1HR ☎ 01522 528795
e-mail: orchardhouse50@hotmail.com
Dir: *on A57 follow road to junct, keep in left lane up hill , on right halfway up hill*

Close to the shopping centre and cathedral, this detached Edwardian house is situated in immaculate gardens complete with an apple orchard and hens that provide fresh eggs for breakfast. Bedrooms are well equipped and homely, whilst the bright, attractive dining room has wonderful views over the valley.

FACILITIES: 3 en suite (2 fmly) No smoking in bedrooms No smoking in dining room TVB tea/coffee Cen ht TVL No coaches **PRICES:** d £42-£46✳ **LB PARKING:** 6

♦♦♦♦ Tennyson Hotel

7 South Park LN5 8EN ☎ 01522 521624 📠 01522 521355
e-mail: tennyson.hotel@virgin.net
Dir: *S of city centre on A15, nr South Park Common*

This smart house is conveniently located just a mile from the city centre. Bedrooms are attractively appointed and benefit from a host of thoughtful extras. There is a comfortable guest lounge and a smart dining room where impressive breakfasts are served.

continued

FACILITIES: 8 en suite (2 GF) No smoking in dining room No smoking in lounges TVB tea/coffee Direct dial from bedrooms No dogs Licensed Cen ht No coaches **PRICES:** s £33-£37; d £45-£47✻ **PARKING:** 8 **CARDS:**

♦♦♦♦ 30 Bailgate

LN1 3AP ☎ 01522 521417

Dir: *on main tourist route close to Cathedral and Castle*

A delightfully presented Georgian house in the centre of the city offering two very comfortable and thoughtfully furnished bedrooms. There are also two cosy lounges and a fine breakfast is served in the dining room, which overlooks the garden. Hospitality is very good and parking is available.

FACILITIES: 2 en suite No smoking TVB tea/coffee No dogs Cen ht No children 14yrs **PRICES:** s £35; d £45✻ **PARKING:** 2

♦♦♦♦ Westlyn Guest House

67 Carholme Rd LN1 1RT ☎ 01522 537468 📠 01522 537468

e-mail: westlynbblincoln@hotmail.com

Dir: *follow Lincoln central signs onto A57 Westlyn is approx 1m on left*

Situated within walking distance of the city, this friendly guesthouse offers well-furnished and comfortable bedrooms. There is a cosy guests lounge and a hearty breakfast is served in the pleasant dining room.

FACILITIES: 4 en suite (1 fmly) No smoking TVB tea/coffee Cen ht No children 5yrs No coaches **PRICES:** s £20-£25; d £40-£42✻ **PARKING:** 5

♦♦♦♦ 🅰 The Gables

546 Newark Rd, North Hykeham LN6 9NG ☎ 01522 829102 📠 01522 850497

e-mail: gary.burnett@ntlworld.com

Dir: *turn off A1 take A46 signed Lincoln. Nxt rdbt A1434 0.5m on R just beyond McDonald's*

FACILITIES: 4 rms (2 en suite) No smoking STV TVB tea/coffee Cen ht No coaches Sauna Pool Table **PRICES:** s £25-£35; d £40-£50✻ **LB** **PARKING:** 8 **CARDS:**

♦♦♦♦ 🅰 Savill

203 Yarborough Rd LN1 3NQ ☎ 01522 523261

e-mail: vvn@themail.co.uk

Dir: *off A15 to Yarborough Cresent, next rdbt leads to Yarborough Rd. After 500mtrs house on left*

FACILITIES: 4 en suite 1 annexe en suite (1 fmly) No smoking in bedrooms No smoking in dining room TVB tea/coffee Cen ht TVL No children 10yrs No coaches **PRICES:** d £42-£45✻ **LB** **PARKING:** 7 **CARDS:**

♦♦♦ Ashlin House Hotel

132 West Pde LN1 1LD ☎ 01522 531307 📠 01522 569648

e-mail: ashlinhouse@talk21.com

Dir: *first turn left on approach to Lincoln centre off A57 Hewson Rd, follow road round to West Parade*

Located a few minutes walk from the main shopping area, this large late Victorian House retains many of its original features. Ashlin House offers homely comfortable bedrooms, most of which have modern facilities. Comprehensive English breakfasts are taken in the spacious dining room, which features shipping memorabilia.

FACILITIES: 9 rms (6 en suite) (2 fmly) (2 GF) No smoking TVB tea/coffee No dogs (ex guide dogs) Cen ht No coaches **PRICES:** s £25-£30; d £40-£48✻ **LB** **PARKING:** 6 **CARDS:**

♦♦♦ Elma

14 Albion Crescent, Off Long Leys Rd LN1 1EB ☎ 01522 529792 📠 01522 529792

e-mail: ellen@elma-guesthouse.freeserve.co.uk

Dir: *from A51 turn onto Longleys rd signposted to St Georges Hospital. 1m along turn L onto Albion Crescent*

This friendly family-run guest house enjoys a peaceful location in a quiet residential area, within walking distance of the city centre. Attractive bedrooms are comfortably furnished and thoughtfully equipped. Breakfast is served around a large communal table in the dining room and guests have use of a shared lounge.

FACILITIES: 4 rms No smoking in bedrooms No smoking in dining room TVB tea/coffee No dogs Cen ht TVL No coaches Dinner Last d breakfast **PRICES:** s fr £18; d fr £36✻ **LB BB** **PARKING:** 5

♦♦♦ The Hollies Hotel

65 Carholme Rd LN1 1RT ☎ 01522 522419 📠 01522 522419

e-mail: holhotel@aol.com

Dir: *Approach town centre on A57, Hotel left of main road just before entering town.*

This well furnished hotel is within easy walking distance of the city. It offers well equipped bedrooms, a comfortable lounge and a cosy dining room, in addition to friendly hospitality and good standards of service.

FACILITIES: 8 en suite (1 fmly) No smoking in bedrooms No smoking in dining room TVB tea/coffee Direct dial from bedrooms No dogs (ex guide dogs) Licensed Cen ht TVL No coaches **PARKING:** 8 **NOTES:** Closed 24Dec-2Jan **CARDS:**

♦♦♦ New Farm *(SK960740)*

Burton LN1 2RD ☎ 01522 527326 📠 01522 576572

Mrs P Russon

Dir: *off A57 onto Fen Lane at sign for Burton (3m from Lincoln), 3rd left. Or leave Lincoln on B1398, left at traffic lights, through village, on right*

A warm welcome is offered at this peaceful farm, a spacious modern bungalow just North of Lincoln. Genuine hospitality, relaxed service and good wholesome home-cooking are real strengths here. There are delightful countryside views from the lounge.

FACILITIES: 2 rms (1 en suite) (2 GF) No smoking TV1B tea/coffee No dogs Cen ht TVL No children 5yrs Fishing 328 acres dairy arable Dinner Last d 12 hrs notice **PRICES:** s £24; d £40✻ **LB** **PARKING:** 3 **NOTES:** Closed 30 Nov-1 Mar

♦♦♦ Newport

26-28 Newport Rd LN1 3DF ☎ 01522 528590 📠 01522 542868

e-mail: info@newportguesthouse.co.uk

Dir: *on A15 going N, 200mtrs on R past Radio Lincs. Or S, 0.5m from ring rd just before Newport Arch*

Located in the upper part of the city and just a few minutes walk from the cathedral. This double fronted terraced house offers well-equipped and comfortable bedrooms. The pleasing public areas include a bright and attractive dining room, and a very comfortable sitting room.

FACILITIES: 8 en suite (2 GF) No smoking TVB tea/coffee Cen ht TVL No children 8yrs No coaches **PRICES:** s £28-£35; d £40-£50✻ **PARKING:** 4 **NOTES:** Closed Xmas rs New Year **CARDS:**

England

LINCOLN continued

♦♦ Edward King House

The Old Palace, Minster Yard LN2 1PU ☎ 01522 528778
 01522 527308
e-mail: enjoy@ekhs.org.uk
Dir: *follow directions to cathedral. Located within Old Palace site. Entrance through archway in SE corner of Minster Yard*

Once the residence of the Bishops of Lincoln, this historic house lies in the lea of the cathedral and next to the old palace. The bedrooms are pleasantly furnished and suitably equipped. Public areas include a television lounge and a spacious dining room where a hearty breakfast is served.
FACILITIES: 17 rms (1 fmly) No smoking tea/coffee Licensed Cen ht TVL Dinner Last d 48 hours **PRICES:** s £19-£21; d £37-£41✻ **BB CONF:** Thtr 80 Class 30 Board 30 Del £38 ✻ **PARKING:** 12 **NOTES:** Closed Xmas/New Year **CARDS:**

♦♦ Jaymar

31 Newland St West LN1 1QQ ☎ 01522 532934
 01522 820182
e-mail: ward.jaymar4@ntlworld.com
Dir: *turn off A1onto A46, proceed to junct with A57 turn right to Lincoln Central. At 1st set of traffic lights turn left into Gresham Street then take 2nd right by off licence, Jaymar approx. 500mtrs on left*
Situated within easy walking distance of the city, this small friendly guest house offers three well-equipped bedrooms. Served in the cosy dining room (and available from 5am on request) breakfast includes full English and vegetarian options. Pets and children welcome. Guests can be collected from the bus or railway stations if required.
FACILITIES: 3 rms (1 fmly) No smoking TVB tea/coffee No coaches **PRICES:** s £17; d £32✻ **LB BB**

See advertisement on opposite page

LOUTH — Map 08 TF38

♦♦♦ Masons Arms

Cornmarket LN11 9PY ☎ 01507 609525 0870 7066450
e-mail: justin@themasons.co.uk
Dir: *from N - M180/A18 past Humberside Airport to Laceby, A146 junction take A18/A16 to Louth*
This is a popular coaching inn situated in the corner of a market place. The first floor restaurant is spacious and can also be used as a meeting room. The bars have a lively atmosphere while all of the bedrooms are comfortably furnished and thoughtfully equipped.
FACILITIES: 10 rms (5 en suite) No smoking in area of dining room TVB tea/coffee No dogs (ex guide dogs) Cen ht Cycling Nature Trail Dinner Last d 9.00pm **PRICES:** s £23-£38; d £38-£52✻ **LB BB MEALS:** Lunch £3.95-£8.95&alc Dinner £4.95-£12.95&alc✻ **CONF:** Class 80 Board 20 **PARKING:** 3 **CARDS:**

MARKET RASEN — Map 08 TF18

♦♦♦♦ Blaven

Walesby Hill, Walesby LN8 3UW ☎ 01673 838352
e-mail: blaven@amserve.net
Dir: *from Market Rasen take A46 towards Grimsby, turn right at junct with A1103 then left at T-junct, Blaven 100yds on right*
On the edge of the village of Walesby, this smart house offers comfortable bedrooms with many thoughtful extras. The beautifully appointed shared bathroom benefits from a separate power shower. Freshly prepared breakfasts are served round one table in the smart dining room whilst there is a large conservatory lounge overlooking the immaculate gardens.
FACILITIES: 2 rms No smoking TVB tea/coffee No dogs (ex guide dogs) Cen ht No children 8yrs No coaches **PRICES:** s £28; d £42 **PARKING:** 4

♦♦♦♦ Chuck Hatch

Kingerby Rd, West Rasen LN8 3NB ☎ 01673 842947
 01673 842947
e-mail: chuck.hatch@btinternet.com
Dir: *A631 West Rasen follow signs Osgodby and North Owersby, house 0.5m on left*

Chuck Hatch sits in open countryside and was built in 1780. Bedrooms are tastefully appointed, each individually styled and well equipped. Public rooms include a lounge and a breakfast room, which looks out over the lake and grounds beyond. Smoking is not permitted in the house.
FACILITIES: 4 en suite No smoking TVB tea/coffee No dogs Cen ht TVL No children 6yrs No coaches Fishing Jacuzzi **PRICES:** s £30-£35; d £45-£70✻ **LB PARKING:** 6

MARTON (Village) — Map 08 SK88

♦♦♦♦ Black Swan Guest House

21 High St DN21 5AH ☎ 01427 718878 01427 718878
e-mail: reservations@blackswan-marton.co.uk
Dir: *on A156, at junct with A1500, 12m from Lincoln, 5m from Gainsborough*

continued

Centrally located in the village of Marton, this former 18th-century coaching inn retains many original features and offers homely bedroom accommodation, all with modern facilities. Tasty breakfasts are taken in the cosy dining room and a comfortable lounge is also available for guest use. Good hospitality is provided and transport to nearby pubs and/or restaurants can be provided.
FACILITIES: 6 en suite 2 annexe en suite (3 fmly) (2 GF) No smoking TVB tea/coffee No dogs (ex guide dogs) Licensed Cen ht TVL No coaches Golf 18 Riding **PRICES:** s £30-£40; d £50-£60✱ **LB PARKING:** 10
CARDS:

SKEGNESS Map 09 TF56

♦♦♦ Crawford Hotel

104 South Pde PE25 3HR ☎ 01754 764215 📠 01754 764215
This friendly family-run guest house enjoys a prime location, overlooking the putting green and the seafront beyond. Spacious public areas include a choice of comfortable lounge areas, a heated indoor swimming pool, Jacuzzi and sauna. Bedrooms are neatly decorated and well equipped and include a number of rooms suitable for families.
FACILITIES: 20 en suite (8 fmly) No smoking in dining room TVB tea/coffee No dogs (ex guide dogs) Licensed Lift Cen ht TVL Indoor swimming pool (heated) Sauna Pool Table Jacuzzi Dinner Last d 5pm
PRICES: s £31.50-£38; d £50-£66✱ **LB NOTES:** Closed 1 Nov-24 Dec
CARDS:

SLEAFORD

See Aswarby

STAMFORD Map 08 TF00

See also Maxey (Cambridgeshire)

Premier Collection

♦♦♦♦♦ Rock Lodge

1 Empingham Rd PE9 2RH ☎ 01780 481758
📠 01780 481757
e-mail: rocklodge@innpro.co.uk
Dir: *off A1 at A606, signed Oakham, follow signs into Stamford for 1.25m. Rock Lodge on left before junct with B1087*
Philip and Jane Sagar are well experienced in managing and operating luxury hotels and offer guests a warm welcome to their imposing 1900 town house. It is conveniently located for access to the town and has private off-street parking. Bedrooms are individually furnished and attractively appointed, equipped with a good range of useful extras and facilities. Character public rooms have been sympathetically furnished, especially notable in the oak-panelled breakfast room with its mullion windows.
FACILITIES: 4 en suite (1 fmly) No smoking STV TVB tea/coffee No dogs (ex guide dogs) Cen ht TVL No coaches **PRICES:** s £50-£90; d £65-£90✱ **PARKING:** 7 **CARDS:**

♦♦♦ Diamonds are a guest's best friend! The emphasis is on quality and guest care rather than extra facilities.

SUTTON-ON-SEA Map 09 TF58

♦♦♦ Athelstone Lodge Hotel

25 Trusthorpe Rd LN12 2LR ☎ 01507 441521
Dir: *on A52 N of vilage*
Athelstone Lodge is situated between Mablethorpe and Skegness in the small seaside resort of Sutton-on-Sea. Bedrooms are pleasantly decorated, soundly maintained and equipped with many useful extras. Breakfast is served in the dining room and guests also have the use of a bar and lounge. A variety of enjoyable home cooked dinners are available.
FACILITIES: 6 rms (5 en suite) (2 fmly) No smoking in dining room TVB tea/coffee Licensed Cen ht TVL No coaches Dinner Last d 4.30pm
PRICES: s £19-£22; d £38-£44✱ **LB BB PARKING:** 6
NOTES: Closed Nov-Feb **CARDS:**

SWINDERBY Map 08 SK86

♦♦♦ Halfway Farm Motel & Guest House

Newark Rd, A46 LN6 9HN ☎ 01522 868749 📠 01522 868082
Dir: *8m N of Newark on A46, 2m from Lincoln ring road*
This 300-year-old farmhouse enjoys a prime position set back from the A46, midway between Lincoln and Newark. Spacious bedrooms range from traditional in the main house to motel-style rooms located round a courtyard to the rear. There is a bright, airy dining room and a comfortable residents' lounge.
FACILITIES: 7 rms (5 en suite) 10 annexe en suite (3 fmly) (10 GF) No smoking in 4 bedrooms No smoking in dining room TVB tea/coffee Direct dial from bedrooms No dogs (ex guide dogs) Cen ht **PRICES:** s £35; d £42✱ **PARKING:** 20 **CARDS:**

England

WOODHALL SPA Map 08 TF16

See also Horncastle

♦♦♦♦ Village Limits Motel

Stixwould Rd LN10 6UJ ☎ 01526 353312 📠 01526 353312

Dir: *from large sign for Pettwood Hotel, 'Village Limits' is approx 500yds further, on same road*

This smartly presented former farmhouse offers warm friendly hospitality and freshly prepared home cooking. The attractive restaurant and bar are housed in the main building whilst bedrooms are located in a separate block, motel style around a courtyard. Rooms are thoughtfully equipped and pleasantly furnished in pine.

FACILITIES: 8 annexe en suite (1 fmly) No smoking in 4 bedrooms No smoking in dining room TVB tea/coffee Cen ht 1m from EGU HQ. Hotchkin/Bracken course Dinner Last d 9pm **PRICES:** s £37.50; d £60✳ **LB** **MEALS:** Lunch £8.50-£11.50&alc Dinner £10-£14&alc✳ **PARKING:** 30 **CARDS:**

♦♦♦ The Vale

50 Tor-O-Moor Rd LN10 6SB ☎ 01526 353022
📠 01526 354949
e-mail: thevale@amserve.net

Dir: *E on B1191 from Woodhall Spa central x-roads towards Horncastle. Take 3rd right (Tarleton Av) opposite golf club car park, Tor-O-Moor Road on right*

Just a short walk from the famous Woodhall Spa Golf Club, this Edwardian villa stands in one acre of mature grounds. The public rooms look out over the gardens, and include a cosy lounge and a separate dining room where breakfasts are taken around one large table. This is a no-smoking establishment.

FACILITIES: 3 en suite (1 fmly) (1 GF) No smoking TVB tea/coffee Cen ht TVL No coaches Fishing **PRICES:** s £25-£27; d £36-£40✳ **LB** **BB** **PARKING:** 4

♦♦ *Claremont*

9/11 Witham Rd LN10 6RW ☎ 01526 352000

Dir: *on B1191 Horncastle/Kirkstead Bridge Rd, at the centre of Woodhall Spa close to mini rdbt*

This large guest house is located close to the town centre, and has been owned and run by Mrs Brennan for a number of years. The bedrooms are generally quite spacious, traditionally furnished and well-equipped. The public areas are pleasant and include a breakfast room.

FACILITIES: 10 rms (5 en suite) (5 fmly) No smoking in 4 bedrooms No smoking in dining room TVB tea/coffee No coaches **PARKING:** 5

LONDON

London Plans 1 & 2 appear after the atlas section at the back of the guide.

E4 Plan 1 G6

♦♦♦ Ridgeway Hotel

115/117 The Ridgeway, North Chingford E4 6QU
☎ 020 8529 1964 📠 020 8524 9130

Dir: *M25 junct 25, A10 Gt Cambridge Rd, left onto A110 Southbury Rd to Chingford, right opposite police station onto B169. Hotel 0.25m on left*

Privately owned hotel, within easy reach of the North Circular and M25. Bedrooms vary in size and style and are all nicely decorated and well equipped. Breakfast is served at individual tables in the smart dining room, overlooking the well-tended garden. Guests also have the use of a lounge bar.

FACILITIES: 20 en suite (6 fmly) STV TVB tea/coffee Direct dial from bedrooms No dogs (ex guide dogs) Licensed Cen ht TVL Jacuzzi Dinner Last d 9pm **PRICES:** s £50-£52; d £65✳ **PARKING:** 9 **CARDS:**

E18 London Plan 1 G6

♦♦♦ Grove Hill Hotel

38 Grove Hill, South Woodford E18 2JG ☎ 020 8989 3344 & 8530 5286 📠 020 8530 5286

Dir: *off A11 London Rd, close to South Woodford tube station. Grove Hotel is off A11 just beyond The George pub*

Privately-owned hotel dating back to 1884, originally built as a family house for a naval officer. Ideally situated in a quiet side road within easy walking distance of the tube station (20 minutes to Liverpool Street). Bedrooms vary in size and style but all are comfortably furnished and well equipped. Breakfast is served at individual tables in the smart dining room.

FACILITIES: 21 rms (12 en suite) (2 fmly) No smoking in dining room STV TVB tea/coffee Licensed Cen ht TVL **PRICES:** s £33-£45; d £58-£61✳ **PARKING:** 12 **CARDS:**

See advertisement on opposite page

N1 Plan 1 F4

♦♦♦ Kandara

68 Ockendon Rd N1 3NW ☎ 020 7226 5721 📠 020 7226 3379
e-mail: admin@kandara.co.uk

Dir: *at Highbury corner rdbt on A1 take St Pauls Road for 0.5m then turn right at junction into Essex Road, Ockendon Road is 4th on left.*

FACILITIES: 9 rms 2 annexe rms (4 fmly) (2 GF) No smoking TVB tea/coffee No dogs (ex guide dogs) Cen ht No coaches **PRICES:** s £41-£49; d £51-£62✳ **CARDS:**

N4 Plan 1 F5

Premier Collection

♦♦♦♦♦ Mount View

31 Mount View Rd N4 4SS ☎ 020 8340 9222
📠 020 8342 8494
e-mail: mountviewbb@aol.com

Dir: *A406, A1 to Highgate tube station, left into Shepherds Hill, end of road turn right, through Crouch End, left fork by Nat West bank*

This delightful guest house is situated in a quiet, tree-lined side road and is convenient for the city. The bedrooms have been very carefully furnished and thoughtfully equipped while a comfortable guests lounge is also provided. Excellent breakfasts are served around a large table and very friendly hospitality is provided by the resident owners.

FACILITIES: 3 rms (2 en suite) No smoking TVB tea/coffee No dogs Cen ht No coaches **PRICES:** s £40-£60; d £50-£70✳ **CARDS:**

♦♦♦ *Majestic Hotel* Plan 1 F5

392/394 Seven Sisters Rd, Finsbury Park N4 2PQ
☎ 020 8800 2022 8802 4131
e-mail: Hotelmaj@aol.com

Dir: *nearest tube: Manor House, Piccadilly Line*

Located near Manor House tube station, this bed and breakfast offers convenient access to the City and the West End. The public areas are well presented, the newly refurbished guest lounge is particularly smart and comfortable; breakfast is served in an attractive dining room. Rooms are well appointed and individually decorated. The availability of free car parking is a bonus; some secure parking available.

FACILITIES: 36 rms (16 en suite) (13 fmly) No smoking in 6 bedrooms No smoking in dining room TVB tea/coffee No dogs Cen ht TVL Use of local leisure club **PARKING:** 25 **CARDS:**

♦♦♦ Ossian House

Plan 1 F5

20 Ossian Rd N4 4EA ☎ 020 8340 4331 📠 020 8340 4331
e-mail: ann@ossianguesthouse.co.uk

Dir: *A406 A1 to Highgate tube station, left into Shepherds Hill, right at end, left fork at Nat West Bank, then left, onto Mount View Road. First right down hill, 1st left Ossian Road*

This pleasant guest house is quietly located, just north of the city. Bedrooms are tastefully decorated and furnished, offering a very good range of extra facilities and accessories. One room also features a spa bath. Breakfast is served in the attractive dining room, which can also double as a sitting room.

FACILITIES: 3 en suite (1 fmly) No smoking TVB tea/coffee No dogs (ex guide dogs) Cen ht TVL No coaches Jacuzzi **PRICES:** s £55; d £65* **LB PARKING:**

N8

Plan 1 E5

♦♦♦ White Lodge Hotel

1 Church Ln, Hornsey N8 7BU ☎ 020 8348 9765
📠 020 8340 7851

Dir: *A406 follow sign to Bounds Green, Hornsey High Rd and Church Lane*

This friendly, quiet and well-presented guest house is centrally located and provides smart accommodation. Guests have the use of a small but attractive lounge to relax in and breakfast is served in the spacious dining room.

FACILITIES: 16 rms (8 en suite) (5 fmly) (1 GF) No smoking in 4 bedrooms No smoking in dining room No smoking in 1 lounge TVB tea/coffee No dogs (ex guide dogs) Cen ht TVL No coaches Dinner Last d at breakfast **PRICES:** s £30-£34; d £40-£50* **CARDS:** 

England

NW1 Plan 2 B4

♦♦♦♦ Four Seasons Hotel

173 Gloucester Place, Regents Park NW1 6DX ☎ 020 7724 3461 & 020 7723 9471 020 7402 5594
e-mail: fourseasons@dial.pipex.com
Dir: *from Marylebone Rd, left into Gloucester Place. Follow Gloucester Rd up to no. 173. establishment on left*
FACILITIES: 28 en suite (2 fmly) (2 GF) No smoking in 12 bedrooms No smoking in dining room STV TVB Direct dial from bedrooms No dogs Cen ht **PRICES:** s £80-£95; d £105-£115✻ **CARDS:**

See advertisement on page 273

♦♦♦ *Euston Square Hotel* Plan 2 C5

152-156 North Gower St NW1 2ND ☎ 020 7388 0099
Situated close to Euston Square station, this hotel is ideal for both business and leisure guests. Bedrooms are functional and have smart facilities. There are conference facilities, a modern reception area and Java Joe's, where breakfast and light snacks are offered.

NW3 Plan 2 E5

♦♦♦ Langorf Hotel

20 Frognal, Hampstead NW3 6AG ☎ 020 7794 4483
020 7435 9055
e-mail: langorf@aol.com
Dir: *approx 3m N of Oxford St and 3m S of M1, just off A41 Finchley Rd*

This elegant Edwardian building has been thoughtfully and tastefully furnished and decorated throughout. The bedrooms are smartly presented with colourful decor, and include extras such as 24-hour room service, telephones and hairdryers. Public areas include a small cosy reception lounge and an attractive dining room.
FACILITIES: 31 en suite (4 fmly) (3 GF) No smoking in area of dining room STV TVB tea/coffee Direct dial from bedrooms No dogs Licensed Lift Cen ht TVL No coaches **PRICES:** s £82-£90; d £98-£110✻ **CARDS:**

♦♦♦ Quality Hampstead Plan 2 E5

5 Frognal, Hampstead NW3 6AL ☎ 020 7794 0101
020 7794 0100
e-mail: quality-H@lth-hotels.com
Dir: *turn off Finchley Rd into Frognal, hotel on left (Quality Franchise)*
This modern, purpose-built hotel benefits from its own car park and enjoys a prime location just off the Finchley Road, minutes walk from the tube, just three stops from the West End. Recently refurbished, the bedrooms are smart and well equipped. Public areas include an open-plan bar/lounge and a smart basement restaurant.

continued

Quality Hampstead

FACILITIES: 57 en suite (10 fmly) No smoking in 27 bedrooms STV TVB tea/coffee Direct dial from bedrooms Licensed Lift TVL **PRICES:** s £70-£85; d £75-£89✻ **LB CONF:** Thtr 10 Class 6 Board 8 **PARKING:** 20 **CARDS:**

♦♦♦ Swiss Cottage Hotel Plan 2 E4

4 Adamson Rd, Swiss Cottage NW3 3HP ☎ 020 7722 2281
020 7483 4588
e-mail: reservations@swisscottagehotel.co.uk
Dir: *On A41 go around Swiss Cottage pub to far left lane, at lights left, next lights left to Winchester road, hotel at end of road right. (Best Western)*

This attractive, Victorian hotel is set in a peaceful residential area a short walk from Swiss Cottage tube station. Accommodation is comfortable and well appointed, with a number of family rooms available; bedrooms have recently been refurbished and upgraded, and offer a good range enhanced facilities. Lounge/Room service and bar are available, and a hot breakfast buffet is served in the lower ground floor dining room.
FACILITIES: 59 en suite (8 fmly) (11 GF) No smoking in 24 bedrooms No smoking in dining room STV TVB tea/coffee Direct dial from bedrooms No dogs (ex guide dogs) Licensed Lift Cen ht Dinner Last d 9.45pm **PRICES:** s £97.50-£122.50; d £115-£140✻ **CONF:** Thtr 40 Board 25 Del £145 ✻ **PARKING:** 4 **CARDS:**

♦♦♦ La Gaffe Plan 2 E5

107-111 Heath St NW3 6SS ☎ 020 7435 4941 & 7435 8965
020 7794 7592
e-mail: la-gaffe@msn.com
Dir: *at top end of Heath St, 3mins walk from Hampstead Underground*
This guest house on Hampstead High Street offers character and warm hospitality. The Italian restaurant, open for lunch and dinner is popular with locals. Bedrooms are compact but all en suite.
FACILITIES: 18 annexe en suite (1 fmly) (2 GF) No smoking in bedrooms TVB tea/coffee Direct dial from bedrooms No dogs (ex guide dogs) Licensed Cen ht No coaches Dinner Last d 11.30pm **PRICES:** s £60-£100; d £90-£125✻ **CARDS:**

See advertisement on opposite page

England

NW6 Plan 1 E4

♦♦♦♦ Dawson House Hotel

72 Canfield Gardens NW6 3ED ☎ 020 7624 0079 & 7624 6525
020 7644 6321
e-mail: dawsonhtl@aol.com

This small hotel is situated in a quiet residential area of South Hampstead, close to the Finchley Road tube station. The accommodation is comfortable and well-equipped, each bedroom is complete with modern en suite facilities. Public areas include a guest lounge and an attractive garden to the rear.

FACILITIES: 15 en suite (2 fmly) No smoking in dining room No smoking in lounges TVB tea/coffee Direct dial from bedrooms No dogs Cen ht TVL No children 3yrs No coaches **PRICES:** s £40-£45; d £65-£70✳
CARDS:

NW11 Plan 1 D5

♦♦♦ Anchor Hotel

10 West Heath Dr, Golders Green NW11 7QH ☎ 020 8458 8764
020 8455 3204
e-mail: reservations@anchor-hotel.co.uk

Dir: *North Circular A406 onto A598 Finchley Rd. At tube turn left then 1st right*

This friendly and privately owned guest house is located close to Golders Green tube station (on the Northern line) and the town centre. Bedrooms are comfortably appointed and suitably equipped.

FACILITIES: 11 rms (8 en suite) (3 fmly) (3 GF) No smoking in dining room No smoking in lounges TVB tea/coffee Direct dial from bedrooms No dogs (ex guide dogs) Cen ht TVL No coaches **PRICES:** s £35-£52; d £53-£70✳ **PARKING:** 5 **CARDS:**

♦♦♦ Central Hotel

Plan 1 D5

35 Hoop Ln, Golders Green NW11 8BS ☎ 020 8458 5636
020 8455 4792

Dir: *M11/M40 to A406 E, turn right at Finchley Rd onto A598, hotel near 1st traffic lights*

This privately owned and run commercial hotel is located close to Golders Green underground station. Bedrooms are practical, with good levels of space and well equipped with en suite facilities. Parking is available.

FACILITIES: 26 en suite TVB Direct dial from bedrooms No dogs Cen ht **PRICES:** s £50; d £70 **PARKING:** 8 **CARDS:**

SE9 Plan 1 H2

♦♦♦ Yardley Court

18 Court Rd, Eltham SE9 5PZ ☎ 020 8850 1850
020 8488 1509
e-mail: yardleycourt@aol.com

Dir: *leave M25 junct 3 onto A20 to London, turn right at traffic lights at Court Rd, Mottingham 0.5m on left*

This friendly Victorian villa enjoys an ideal location just one mile from the A20 and within walking distance of the station with its fast links to London. Bedrooms are generally spacious and are well equipped, with modern well-appointed bathrooms. Breakfast is served in the modern dining room, overlooking the pretty rear garden.

FACILITIES: 9 en suite (1 fmly) (1 GF) No smoking in dining room No smoking in lounges TVB tea/coffee Direct dial from bedrooms No dogs Cen ht **PRICES:** s £40; d £59✳ **PARKING:** 9
NOTES: Closed 23 Dec-1 Jan **CARDS:**

SE10 Plan 1 G3

♦♦♦ The Pilot Inn

68 Riverway, Greenwich SE10 0BE ☎ 020 8858 5910
020 8293 0371
e-mail: marron@thepilotinn.fsnet.co.uk

Dir: *turn into John Harrison Way, then left into West Park Side, then 1st right into Riverway*

There is a friendly atmosphere at this popular inn situated close to the river, right next to the Millennium Dome. The bedrooms, which are located in an adjacent annexe, are furnished in a modern style, with bright decor and colourful soft furnishings. Sound British meals are offered, plus a generous breakfast.

FACILITIES: 7 rms (1 fmly) TVB tea/coffee No dogs (ex guide dogs) Cen ht Dinner Last d 8.45pm **PRICES:** s £45; d £65✳
CARDS:

England

SE20 Plan 1 F1

♦♦♦♦ Melrose House Hotel

89 Lennard Rd SE20 7LY ☎ 020 8776 8884 📠 020 8325 7636
e-mail: melrose.hotel@virgin.net
Dir: *corner of Courtenay Road/Lennard Road between Penge High St and Sydenham High St, off the A234 via Kent House Road*

There's a warm welcome to all at this attractive Victorian house. Bedrooms are comfortably furnished, very well equipped and feature extra touches such as books and luxury toiletries. Breakfast is served in a pleasant dining room around a communal table, whilst the adjacent spacious conservatory overlooks the pretty rear garden.
FACILITIES: 3 en suite No smoking STV TV4B tea/coffee Direct dial from bedrooms No dogs (ex guide dogs) Cen ht No coaches **PARKING:** 6 **NOTES:** Closed 23 Dec-2 Jan **PRICES:** s £35-£45; d £50-65✱ **CARDS:**

SW1 Plan 2 B1

♦♦♦♦ The Willett

32 Sloane Gardens, Sloane Square SW1W 8DJ
☎ 020 7824 8415 📠 020 7730 4830
e-mail: willett@eeh.co.uk
Dir: *off Sloane Square opposite tube station*

This nicely presented Victorian town house, situated in a tree-lined street just off Sloane Square, provides comfortable accommodation. Staff are friendly, attentive and welcoming. Room service is available throughout the day and night, whilst breakfast is served in the lower ground floor dining room.
FACILITIES: 19 en suite (6 fmly) (3 GF) No smoking in dining room STV TVB tea/coffee Direct dial from bedrooms No dogs (ex guide dogs) Cen ht No coaches **PRICES:** s £102-£118; d £118-£170✱ **CARDS:**

An asterisk ✱ indicates that prices given are for 2002.

♦♦♦♦ Windermere Hotel

Plan 2 C-D1

142/144 Warwick Way, Victoria SW1V 4JE
☎ 020 7834 5163 & 7834 5480 📠 020 7630 8831
e-mail: reservations@windermere-hotel.co.uk
Dir: *from coach stn on Buckingham Palace Rd - opposite the stn turn left onto Elizabeth Bridge, then 1st right, take Hugh St to Alderney St, hotel on corner*

This relaxed and informal family-run hotel is within easy reach of Victoria Station and many of the capital's attractions. Bedrooms vary in size, and are smart and well-equipped. The Pimlico restaurant serves delicious evening meals and a good quality breakfast. There is a comfortable ground floor lounge/ reception area.
FACILITIES: 22 rms (20 en suite) (3 fmly) No smoking in 7 bedrooms No smoking in dining room No smoking in lounges STV TVB tea/coffee Direct dial from bedrooms No dogs (ex guide dogs) Licensed Cen ht TVL Dinner Last d 10.30pm **PRICES:** s £69-£96✱ **CARDS:**

♦♦♦ Blades Hotel

Plan 2 C-D1

122 Belgrave Rd, Victoria SW1V 2BL ☎ 020 7976 5552
📠 020 7976 6500
Situated close to Victoria station, this friendly family run hotel is ideal for both business and leisure guests. Bedrooms are comfortably appointed and feature smart en suite facilities. There is a first floor conservatory style lounge, and continental breakfasts are served in the attractive dining room.
FACILITIES: 24 en suite (3 fmly) No smoking in dining room TVB No dogs (ex guide dogs) Cen ht TVL **PRICES:** s £60; d £75✱
CARDS:

♦♦♦ Melbourne House Hotel

Plan 2 C-D1

79 Belgrave Rd, Victoria SW1V 2BG ☎ 020 7828 3516
📠 020 7828 7120
e-mail: melbourne.househotel@virgin.net
Dir: *exit Pimlico tube stn onto Rampayne St. On Lypus St right into St George's Sq which continues into Belgrave Rd*
This family-run private hotel is situated within easy walking distance of Victoria Station and close to Pimlico tube station. The bedrooms have all been refurbished in a modern style and are equipped with many useful extras. There are also rooms available for family use.
FACILITIES: 17 rms (15 en suite) (2 fmly) (2 GF) No smoking TVB tea/coffee Direct dial from bedrooms No dogs Cen ht TVL
PRICES: s fr £62; d fr £85✱ **CARDS:**

♦♦♦ Sidney Hotel

Plan 2 C-D1

68-76 Belgrave Rd SW1V 2BP ☎ 020 7834 2738
📠 020 7630 0973
e-mail: reservations@sidneyhotel.com
Dir: *follow Central London & Victoria signs. Take A23 Vauxhall Bridge road, turn into Charlwood St. Hotel in corner of Charlwood St and Belgrave Rd*
This smart hotel enjoys a convenient location close to Victoria station and many local attractions. The brightly decorated

continued

bedrooms are well-equipped and are comfortably furnished. There are several rooms available that are suitable for family use. The public areas include a bar lounge and an airy breakfast room.
FACILITIES: 81 rms (80 en suite) (13 fmly) (9 GF) No smoking in 30 bedrooms No smoking in dining room No smoking in lounges STV TVB tea/coffee Direct dial from bedrooms No dogs (ex guide dogs) Licensed Lift Cen ht TVL **PRICES:** s £62-£78; d £68-£94✳
CARDS:

♦♦♦ Victoria Inn — Plan 2 C-D1

65-67 Belgrave Rd, Victoria SW1V 2BG
☎ 020 7834 6721 & 7834 0182 📠 020 7931 0201
e-mail: welcome@victoriainn.co.uk

Two fine Victorian houses located just a short walk from Victoria station and coach terminal. The modern accommodation is well-equipped and popular with both business people and tourists. There is also a small lounge available to guests. A cooked breakfast is not provided although a limited self-service buffet is available in the basement breakfast room.

continued

FACILITIES: 43 en suite (7 fmly) No smoking in dining room STV TVB tea/coffee Direct dial from bedrooms No dogs (ex guide dogs) Lift Cen ht No coaches **PRICES:** s £50-£64; d £65-£79✳
CARDS:

♦♦♦ Winchester Hotel — Plan 2 C-D1

17 Belgrave Rd SW1V 1RB ☎ 020 7828 2972 📠 020 7828 5191
Dir: *3min/300 yds from Victoria Station just before Warwick Way*
On four floors, this terraced establishment is in a less frenetic area near Victoria coach/railway stations. The accommodation offers bright and comfortable rooms, which all benefit from en suite facilities. A helpful team is willing to advise on tourist ideas.
FACILITIES: 18 en suite (2 fmly) (2 GF) No smoking in dining room No smoking in lounges TVB No dogs Cen ht No children 5yrs No coaches
PRICES: d £70-£85✳

♦♦ Central House Hotel — Plan 2 C-D1

39 Belgrave Rd SW1V 2BB ☎ 020 7834 8036 📠 020 7834 1854
e-mail: reception@centralhouse.demon.co.uk
Dir: *walking distance from Victoria station*
Located just a short walk from Victoria Station, the Central House offers sound accommodation. Bedroom sizes vary, and each room is suitably appointed, with en suite compact modular shower rooms. Continental breakfast is served in the lower ground floor dining room; full English cooked breakfast is available at an extra charge.
FACILITIES: 54 en suite (4 fmly) TVB tea/coffee Direct dial from bedrooms No dogs Lift Cen ht TVL **PRICES:** s £66-£83; d £83-£104✳ **LB**
CARDS:

England

◆◆ Carlton Hotel — Plan 2 C-D1
90 Belgrave Rd SW1V 2BJ ☎ 020 7976 6634 Fax 020 7821 8020
e-mail: info@cityhotelcarlton.co.uk
FACILITIES: 17 en suite (2 fmly) No smoking in 3 bedrooms No smoking in dining room No smoking in lounges TVB tea/coffee Direct dial from bedrooms No dogs Cen ht No coaches **PRICES:** s £49-£59; d £59-£69* **CARDS:**

◆◆ Dover Hotel — Plan 2 C-D1
42-44 Belgrave Road, Victoria SW1V 1RG ☎ 020 7821 9085
Fax 020 7834 6425
e-mail: reception@dover-hotel.co.uk
FACILITIES: 33 rms (29 en suite) (8 fmly) STV TVB tea/coffee Direct dial from bedrooms No dogs Cen ht No coaches **PRICES:** s £55-£65; d £65-£75* **CARDS:**

◆◆ Stanley House Hotel — Plan 2 C-D1
19-21 Belgrave Rd, Victoria SW1V 1RB
☎ 020 7834 5042 & 7834 7292 Fax 020 7834 8439
e-mail: cmahotel@aol.com
Dir: *behind Victoria railway station*
FACILITIES: 44 rms (32 en suite) (7 fmly) (8 GF) No smoking in dining room TVB Direct dial from bedrooms No dogs Cen ht TVL No children 4yrs **PRICES:** s £40-£50; d £50-£60* **LB CARDS:**

◆ Colliers Hotel — Plan 2 C1
97 Warwick Way SW1V 1QL ☎ 020 7828 0210 & 020 7834 6931 Fax 020 7828 7111
e-mail: colliershotel@aol.com
Dir: *from Victoria Stn take Wilton Rd, turning right from 2nd traffic lights iinto Warwick Way*
FACILITIES: 19 rms (3 en suite) (1 fmly) (5 GF) No smoking in dining room No smoking in lounges TVB Cen ht **PRICES:** s £28-£35; d £38-£45* **BB CARDS:**

SW3 — Plan 2 B2

◆◆◆◆ The Claverley Hotel
13-14 Beaufort Gardens, Knightsbridge SW3 1PS
☎ 020 7589 8541 Fax 020 7584 3410
e-mail: reservations@claverleyhotel.co.uk
Dir: *take M4/A4 into London. East on Brompton Rd, Beaufort Gdns is 6th on right after Victoria & Albert Museum*

In a quiet tree-lined cul-de-sac, the Claverley Hotel is only a stroll from Harrods. Each bedroom has an individual style and character. Some have four-poster beds and all have TV and telephone. The reading room has comfortable leather Chesterfields, the day's newspapers and tea and coffee making facilities.
FACILITIES: 30 rms (27 en suite) (7 fmly) (2 GF) No smoking in 20 bedrooms No smoking in dining room STV TVB Direct dial from bedrooms No dogs (ex guide dogs) Lift Cen ht No coaches **PRICES:** s £85-£120; d £120-£205* **LB CARDS:**

SW5 — Plan 1 D3

◆◆◆ Maranton House Hotel
14 Barkston Gardens, Earls Court SW5 0EN ☎ 020 7373 5782
Fax 020 7244 9543
e-mail: marantonhotel@hotmail.com
Dir: *Round corner from Earls Court tube station*
Overlooking an attractive garden square close to Earls Court, this small, friendly, family-run hotel has been recently refurbished. Bedrooms are stylishly furnished, well-equipped and all feature particularly smart en suite facilities. Public areas include a spacious reception, a modern bar and a dining room, where substantial continental breakfasts are offered.
FACILITIES: 16 en suite No smoking in 6 bedrooms No smoking in area of dining room No smoking in lounges TVB tea/coffee Direct dial from bedrooms Licensed Cen ht TVL **PRICES:** s £65-£75; d £85-£95* **NOTES:** Closed 25 Dec **CARDS:**

◆◆◆ My Place Hotel — Plan 1 D3
1-3 Trebovir St SW5 9LS ☎ 020 7373 0833 Fax 020 7373 9998
e-mail: info@myplacehotel.co.uk
Dir: *M4 becomes A4 (West Cromwell Road) turn right into Earls Court Road, then 3rd turning on the right*

This recently refurbished Victorian house sits in a quiet residential street close to Earls Court station and provides easy access to the West End. Breakfast is served in the attractive restaurant and light snacks are also available. The smartly presented bedrooms vary in size and have an extremely good range of modern facilities.
FACILITIES: 50 en suite (6 fmly) No smoking in 9 bedrooms No smoking in area of dining room STV TVB Direct dial from bedrooms No dogs (ex guide dogs) Licensed Lift Cen ht TVL Night Club Dinner Last d 11pm
PRICES: s £60-£100; d £75-£135* **LB CONF:** Thtr 100 Class 100 Board 50 Del from £90 * **CARDS:**

◆◆◆ Henley House Hotel — Plan 1 D3
30 Barkston Gardens, Earls Court SW5 0EN
☎ 020 7370 4111 Fax 020 7370 0026
e-mail: reservations@henleyhousehotel.com

continued

England

Dir: *turn off A4 Cromwell Rd at junction with A3220, S for 0.4km. Barkston Gardens on left past underground*

Close to the bustle of Earls Court yet situated in the relative peace of Barkston Gardens, this Victorian townhouse has been tastefully and carefully decorated to provide modern comforts. There is a pleasant foyer lounge to relax in and breakfast is taken in the conservatory-style dining room. The well-equipped bedrooms have a welcoming and homely feel to them.

FACILITIES: 20 en suite (2 fmly) No smoking in dining room STV TVB tea/coffee Direct dial from bedrooms No dogs (ex guide dogs) Lift Cen ht No coaches **PRICES:** s £65-£75; d £75-£92 **CARDS:**

♦♦♦ Rushmore Hotel — Plan 1 D3

11 Trebovir Rd, Earls Court SW5 9LS
☎ 020 7370 3839 & 020 7370 6505 📠 020 7370 0274
Dir: *turn off A4 onto A3220 (Earls Court Road) and take the 3rd street on right Trebovir Road.The hotel is 50mtrs on the right*

This smart private hotel is conveniently located close to the exhibition halls and a short stroll from the tube station. Multilingual staff are friendly and helpful and the reception is staffed 24 hours. Individually themed bedrooms are well-equipped and include rooms suitable for families. A continental breakfast room is served in the modern conservatory.

FACILITIES: 22 en suite (3 fmly) No smoking in 4 bedrooms No smoking in dining room STV TVB tea/coffee Direct dial from bedrooms No dogs Cen ht TVL **PRICES:** s £49-£59; d £69-£79✳ **CARDS:**

♦♦♦ Swiss House Hotel — Plan 2 A1

171 Old Brompton Rd, South Kensington SW5 0AN
☎ 020 7373 2769 & 7373 9383 📠 020 7373 4983
e-mail: recep@swiss-hh.demon.co.uk
Dir: *from A4 turn right down Earls Court Rd, at Old Brompton Rd turn left, pass traffic lights, hotel on right*

This delightful private hotel enjoys a prime location in the heart of South Kensington, within easy reach of London's main attractions, shops and exhibition centres. Smart bedrooms are furnished in pine and are particularly thoughtfully equipped. A continental buffet breakfast is served in the cosy dining room, where a supplementary freshly cooked breakfast is also available.

FACILITIES: 16 rms (15 en suite) (7 fmly) (1 GF) No smoking in 4 bedrooms No smoking in dining room No smoking in lounges STV TVB Direct dial from bedrooms Cen ht TVL No coaches Last d 9.30pm
PRICES: s £50-£71; d £89-£104✳
CARDS:

Places with this symbol are Inns.

SW7

♦♦♦♦ The Gallery — Plan 2 A1

8-10 Queensberry Place, South Kensington SW7 2EA
☎ 020 7915 0000 📠 020 7915 4400
e-mail: gallery@eeh.co.uk
Dir: *turn off Cromwell Rd opposite Natural History Museum into Queensberry Place in South Kensington*

This stylish hotel is close to Kensington and Knightsbridge, and has individually designed bedrooms. Recently refurbished public rooms include a choice of lounges and the refined bar. 24-hour room service is available and at breakfast guests have the option of English or continental breakfast served in the elegant breakfast room. Staff are friendly and services are attentive.

FACILITIES: 36 en suite No smoking in dining room No smoking in 1 lounge STV TVB tea/coffee Direct dial from bedrooms No dogs (ex guide dogs) Licensed Lift Cen ht No coaches **PRICES:** s £141-£152; d £152-£258✳ **CONF:** Board 12 **CARDS:**

♦♦♦♦ Five Sumner Place Hotel — Plan 2 A1

5 Sumner Place, South Kensington SW7 3EE
☎ 020 7584 7586 📠 020 7823 9962
e-mail: reservations@sumnerplace.com
Dir: *300yds from South Kensington underground station, take second left off Old Brompton Road from South Kensington Station*

This elegant Victorian terraced house is located in a residential area set back from the Fulham Road. All the bedrooms are individually designed and tastefully decorated. Guests can take breakfast or drinks in the bright conservatory. The hotel provides complimentary newspapers and magazines to its guests.

FACILITIES: 13 en suite (4 fmly) No smoking in 10 bedrooms No smoking in dining room No smoking in lounges STV TVB tea/coffee Direct dial from bedrooms No dogs Lift Cen ht TVL No coaches **PRICES:** s £85-£99; d £130-£153✳ **CARDS:**

England

♦♦♦♦ The Gainsborough — Plan 2 A1

7-11 Queensberry Place, South Kensington SW7 2DL
☎ 020 7957 0000 Fax 020 7957 0001
e-mail: gainsborough@eeh.co.uk
Dir: *off Cromwell Rd, opposite Natural History Museum in South Kensington*

Located on a quiet street near the Natural History Museum in South Kensington, this smart mid-Georgian townhouse is ideally placed. Bedrooms vary in size and are individually designed and decorated in fine fabrics, quality furnishings and carefully co-ordinated colours. Guests are offered a choice of breakfast, served in the very attractive dining room. There is a small lounge and 24-hour room service is available.
FACILITIES: 49 en suite (5 fmly) No smoking in dining room STV TVB tea/coffee Direct dial from bedrooms No dogs (ex guide dogs) Licensed Lift Cen ht No coaches **PRICES:** s £78-£141; d £141-£258✱
CARDS:

SW15 — Plan 1 D2

♦♦♦♦ The Lodge Hotel

52-54 Upper Richmond Rd, Putney SW15 2RN
☎ 020 8874 1598 Fax 020 8874 0910
e-mail: res@thelodgehotellondon.com
(Best Western)
This spacious hotel is conveniently located close to East Putney tube station, the mainline station and the A3. Attractively public areas include a choice of lounges, a smart bar with satellite TV and conference and banqueting facilities. An impressive buffet breakfast is served in the garden conservatory. Thoughtfully equipped, comfortable bedrooms include a selection of executive rooms and suites.
FACILITIES: 64 en suite (10 fmly) STV TVB tea/coffee Direct dial from bedrooms Licensed Cen ht TVL **PRICES:** s £88-£99; d £110-£130✱ **LB**
PARKING: 30 **NOTES:** Civ Wed 80 **CARDS:**

SW19 — Plan 1 D1

♦♦♦ Worcester House Hotel

38 Alwyne Rd, Wimbledon SW19 7AE ☎ 020 8946 1300
Fax 020 8946 9120
e-mail: janet@worcesterhouse.demon.co.uk
Dir: *turn off A3, to Worple Rd & follow to end, turn left & 2nd right to Alwyne Rd*
Located in a quiet residential area, just a few minutes from Wimbledon town, this small friendly hotel extends a warm welcome to guests. Attractively decorated and furnished throughout, the comfortable bedrooms are well-equipped with direct dial phones and televisions. Delicious breakfasts are served in the pine-furnished dining room.
FACILITIES: 9 en suite (2 fmly) (2 GF) No smoking in dining room TVB tea/coffee Direct dial from bedrooms No dogs (ex guide dogs) Cen ht No coaches **PRICES:** s £49.50-£54; d £70✱ **CARDS:**

♦♦ Trochee Hotel — Plan 1 D1

21 Malcolm Rd, Wimbledon SW19 4AS ☎ 020 8946 1579
Fax 020 8946 1579
e-mail: info@trocheehotel.co.uk
Dir: *turn off A3 to Worple Rd, and before road ends left into Malcolm Rd*
This is a friendly hotel, which is located in a quiet residential area, and is in easy walking distance of the shops and Wimbledon station. The bedrooms are sensibly equipped. Guests will find that en suite rooms are located in a separate building.
FACILITIES: 17 rms (2 fmly) (5 GF) TVB tea/coffee No dogs (ex guide dogs) Cen ht TVL **PRICES:** s £44-£47; d £59-£62✱ **PARKING:** 6
CARDS:

See advertisement on opposite page

♦♦ Wimbledon Hotel — Plan 1 D1

78 Worple Rd, Wimbledon SW19 4HZ
☎ 020 8946 9265 & 8946 1581 Fax 020 8946 9265
Dir: *M25, A3, Merton exit*

Situated within walking distance of the centre and transport links, this double-fronted Victorian house provides simple but well-equipped accommodation. English breakfasts are taken in the bright, modern dining room and a small television lounge is available.
FACILITIES: 14 rms (11 en suite) (6 fmly) No smoking in dining room TVB tea/coffee Direct dial from bedrooms No dogs Cen ht TVL **PRICES:** s £45; d £65✱ **PARKING:** 10 **CARDS:**

W1 — Plan 2 C4

♦♦♦♦ Mermaid Suite Hotel

3-4 Blenheim St W1S 1LA ☎ 020 7629 1875 Fax 020 7499 9475
e-mail: info@mermaidsuite.com
The Mermaid Suite Hotel provides excellent accommodation in one of the best shopping areas of London. The bedrooms are all smartly presented and well-equipped. There is also a popular restaurant serving authentic Italian food.
FACILITIES: 30 rms (29 en suite) (4 fmly) No smoking in 3 bedrooms STV TVB tea/coffee Direct dial from bedrooms No dogs Licensed Cen ht Dinner Last d 10pm **PRICES:** s £50-£70; d £70-£90✱ **CARDS:**

See advertisement on opposite page

♦♦♦♦ St George Hotel — Plan 2 B4

49 Gloucester Place W1U 8JE ☎ 020 7486 8586 & 020 7486 6567 Fax 020 74866567
e-mail: reservations@stgeorge-hotel.net
This attractive, Grade II listed house is situated in the heart of the West End and is close to Baker Street tube station. Bedrooms are furnished to a high standard and feature an excellent range of in-room facilities, including modem points, safes, hair dryers and mini fridges. Breakfasts are served in the smart breakfast room and the friendly staff offer a very warm welcome.
FACILITIES: 19 en suite (3 fmly) (3 GF) No smoking in 6 bedrooms No smoking in dining room No smoking in 1 lounge STV TVB tea/coffee Direct

continued

dial from bedrooms No dogs (ex guide dogs) Cen ht No coaches **PRICES:** s £70-£85; d £90-£125✱ **LB CARDS:**

♦♦♦♦ 22 Plan 2 B4

22 York St W1U 6PX ☎ 020 7224 2990 & 7224 3990
020 7224 1990
e-mail: mc@22yorkstreet.prestel.co.uk
Dir: *From Marylebone Road go South into Baker Street towards Oxford Street, York Street is the second turning on the right.*

This elegant town house is within walking distance of Oxford Street and very close to the Tube, so an ideal base for shopping, theatre-going and sightseeing. A splendid staircase leads up to the bedrooms and comfortable first-floor lounge. All rooms are high-ceilinged and decorated and furnished to enhance the Georgian architecture. Continental breakfast is served around a large table in the open-plan kitchen/dining room where the friendly proprietors and their staff extend a warm welcome.

FACILITIES: 6 en suite 6 annexe en suite (2 fmly) (4 GF) No smoking TVB Direct dial from bedrooms No dogs Cen ht No children 5yrs No coaches
PRICES: s £82.25; d £100✱ **CARDS:**

England

♦♦♦ Bryanston Court Plan 2 B4

50-60 Great Cumberland Place W1H 8DD ☎ 020 7262 3141
020 7262 7248
e-mail: info@bryanstonhotel.com
Dir: *central London 2mins from Marble Arch and Oxford St*

This terrace of Georgian townhouses has been converted to provide accommodation ideally placed for central London. The public areas consist of a bar with spacious seating and an elegant breakfast room. Bedrooms vary in size, some being compact, but are all en suite with good facilities.

FACILITIES: 54 en suite (4 fmly) No smoking in dining room STV TVB tea/coffee Direct dial from bedrooms No dogs (ex guide dogs) Licensed Lift Cen ht No coaches **PRICES:** s £75-£95; d £100-£120✳ **CARDS:**

♦♦♦ Georgian House Hotel Plan 2 B4

87 Gloucester Place, Baker St W1U 6JF ☎ 020 7486 3151
020 7486 7535
e-mail: info@georgian-hotel.demon.co.uk
Dir: *parallel to Baker St, N of Oxford St, short walk from Marble Arch*

This privately owned hotel is ideally located for touring the sights of London, just minutes walk from Baker Street tube station. Bedrooms suitably equipped for both leisure and business guests vary in size and include some rooms suitable for families. A cold buffet breakfast is available in the smartly appointed dining room.

FACILITIES: 19 en suite (4 fmly) (3 GF) No smoking in dining room No smoking in lounges TVB tea/coffee Direct dial from bedrooms No dogs Lift Cen ht No children 5yrs No coaches **PRICES:** s fr £70✳ **CARDS:**

♦♦♦ Hart House Hotel Plan 2 B4

51 Gloucester Place, Portman Sq W1U 8JF ☎ 020 7935 2288
020 7935 8516
e-mail: reservations@harthouse.co.uk
Dir: *just off Oxford St behind Selfridges, nearest underground is Baker St or Marble Arch*

Hart House Hotel is an elegant Georgian building, part of a terrace of mansions that were home to the French emigré nobility during the French Revolution. The building has been restored and retains much of its original character, offering modern bedrooms with a good range of facilities. Breakfast is served in the cosy dining room.

FACILITIES: 16 en suite (4 fmly) (4 GF) No smoking in bedrooms No smoking in dining room No smoking in lounges TVB tea/coffee Direct dial from bedrooms No dogs Cen ht TVL No coaches **PRICES:** s £65-£70; d £85-£105✳ **CARDS:**

♦♦♦ The Regency Hotel Plan 2 C4

19 Nottingham Place W1U 5LQ ☎ 020 7486 5347
020 7224 6057
e-mail: enquiries@regencyhotelwestend.co.uk
Dir: *A40 into Marylebone Rd, turn right at Baker St, left into Crawford St which leads into Nottingham Place*

continued

The Regency Hotel

The Regency Hotel is located close to Baker Street tube station and West End shops. The accommodation at this hotel is well-equipped. Breakfast is taken in a brightly appointed breakfast room that is located in the basement. There is some parking available near to the hotel.

FACILITIES: 20 en suite (2 fmly) No smoking in 2 bedrooms No smoking in dining room No smoking in 1 lounge STV TVB tea/coffee Direct dial from bedrooms No dogs (ex guide dogs) Licensed Lift Cen ht Dinner Last d 9pm **PRICES:** s £60-£68; d £80-£89✳ **LB CARDS:**

See advertisement on opposite page

♦♦♦ Wigmore Court Hotel Plan 2 B4

23 Gloucester Place W1U 8HS ☎ 020 7935 0928
020 7487 4254
e-mail: info@wigmore-court-hotel.co.uk
Dir: *turn off A40 onto Baker St, turn right at George St, turn right at Gloucester Place*

The Wigmore Court Hotel offers its guests comfortable accommodation. The bedrooms are all suitably equipped. Additional facilities at this hotel include laundry and kitchen facilities, which are available on request. Public areas include a nicely appointed dining room in which breakfast is served.

FACILITIES: 18 rms (16 en suite) (4 fmly) (4 GF) TVB tea/coffee Direct dial from bedrooms No dogs (ex guide dogs) Cen ht TVL **PRICES:** s £50-£75; d £70-£95✳ **LB CARDS:**

♦♦ Lincoln House Hotel Plan 2 B4

33 Gloucester Place W1U 8HY
☎ 020 7486 7630 & 0500 007 208 020 7486 0166
e-mail: reservations@lincoln-house-hotel.co.uk
Dir: *enter Oxford St from Marble Arch end, left into Portman St. Continue forward Gloucester Place. Hotel on left after George St*

This friendly, family run Georgian town house has been impressively renovated and restored and is ideally located close to Oxford Street. Bedrooms vary in size but are all thoughtfully equipped for both business and leisure guests. A full English breakfast is served in the basement cottage style dinning room, whilst continental fare can also be served in bedrooms.

continued

FACILITIES: 23 en suite (5 fmly) (6 GF) STV TVB tea/coffee Direct dial from bedrooms No dogs (ex guide dogs) **PRICES:** s £59-£75; d £69-£79
CARDS:

♦♦ Bentinck House Plan 2 C4

20 Bentinck St W1U 2EU ☎ 020 7935 9141 020 7224 5903
e-mail: b.hh@virgin.net
Dir: *follow Marylebone Lane from Oxford St. 3rd right into Bentinck St. Establishment on right*
FACILITIES: 17 rms (12 en suite) (5 fmly) (3 GF) No smoking in 3 bedrooms No smoking in dining room STV TVB Direct dial from bedrooms Cen ht **PRICES:** s £40-£68; d £75-£95✱ **LB CARDS:**

♦♦ Marble Arch Inn Plan 2 B3

49-50 Upper Berkeley St, Marble Arch W1H 5QR
☎ 020 7723 7888 020 7723 6060
e-mail: sales@marblearch-inn.co.uk
Dir: *near Marble Arch rdbt, take A5 leading N 3rd turning right*
FACILITIES: 29 rms (23 en suite) (9 fmly) STV TVB tea/coffee Direct dial from bedrooms No dogs Cen ht No coaches **PRICES:** s £45-£75; d £65-£75✱ **CARDS:**

W2 Plan 2 A3

♦♦♦♦ Mornington Hotel

12 Lancaster Gate W2 3LG ☎ 020 7262 7361 020 7706 1028
e-mail: london@mornington.co.uk
Dir: *north of Hyde Park, off A40-Bayswater Road (Best Western)*

This fine Victorian building is located in a quiet road close to Lancaster Gate station for easy access to the West End. The bedrooms have been upgraded to provide comfortable, stylish accommodation. There are two lounges and an attractive dining room where an extensive Scandinavian-style breakfast is served.
FACILITIES: 66 en suite (6 fmly) No smoking in 27 bedrooms No smoking in dining room STV TVB tea/coffee Direct dial from bedrooms Licensed Lift Cen ht No coaches **PRICES:** s fr £120; d fr £130-£165✱
CARDS:

♦♦♦♦ Norfolk Plaza Hotel Plan 2 A4

29/33 Norfolk Square, Paddington W2 1RX ☎ 020 7723 0792
020 7224 8770
e-mail: carolina@norfolkplazahotel.co.uk
Dir: *300mtrs from Paddington station. Inside Norfolk Sq, off London St*
This popular hotel in the heart of Paddington is located in a quiet residential square, within easy walking distance of the West End. Bedrooms are thoughtfully furnished, particularly well equipped and include a number of split level suites. The public areas include a smart well appointed bar and lounge, plus an attractive restaurant where breakfast is served.
FACILITIES: 87 en suite (6 fmly) (8 GF) No smoking in 5 bedrooms No smoking in dining room No smoking in 1 lounge STV TVB tea/coffee Direct

continued

dial from bedrooms No dogs (ex guide dogs) Licensed Lift Cen ht TVL
PRICES: s £95-£105; d £120-£130✱ **CONF:** Thtr 15 Board 10 Del from £150 ✱ **CARDS:**

♦♦♦♦ Norfolk Towers Hotel Plan 2 A4

34 Norfolk Place W2 1QW ☎ 020 7262 3123 020 7224 8687
e-mail: norfolktowers@dial.pipex.com
Dir: *From Paddington Station walk down Praed Street in the direction of St Mary's hospital and Edgeware Road. Turn right into Norfolk Place*
This elegant Victorian building is located close to the West End and provides comfortable and well-equipped accommodation. Breakfast is served in the spacious dining room and Cads café/bar is available for meals until 11pm. The public areas feature a modern, attractive lounge and bar facilities.
FACILITIES: 85 en suite (3 fmly) TVB tea/coffee Direct dial from bedrooms No dogs (ex guide dogs) Licensed Lift Cen ht **PRICES:** s £63-£85; d £82-£110✱ **CARDS:**

♦♦♦ Blakemore Hotel Plan 2 A3

30 Leinster Gardens W2 3AN ☎ 020 7262 4591
020 7724 1472
e-mail: info@starcrown.com
Dir: *In the direction of Marble Arch, just off Bayswater Rd. Turn into Leinster Terrace, which leads into Leinster Gardens*
Enjoying a quiet yet central position, this large hotel is just minutes from Hyde Park. The bedrooms are neatly decorated and the executive rooms have been refurbished to a high standard. The spacious public areas include a bar lounge, smart foyer and attractive restaurant, which offers a range of popular dishes.
FACILITIES: 164 en suite TVB tea/coffee Direct dial from bedrooms No dogs (ex guide dogs) Licensed Lift Cen ht TVL Dinner Last d 9pm
PRICES: s £63-£85; d £82-£110✱ **CONF:** Thtr 50 Class 30 Board 30 Del £130 ✱ **CARDS:**

England

♦♦♦ Byron Hotel Plan 2 A3

36-38 Queensborough Ter W2 3SH ☎ 020 7243 0987
020 7792 1957
e-mail: byron@capricornhotels.co.uk
Dir: *off Bayswater Rd close to Queensway. From Marble Arch follow signs to Notting Hill*

This charming terraced house has been thoughtfully restored to provide comfortable accommodation, and to retain a number of original features. Bedrooms vary in size but all are tastefully decorated and equipped with modern facilities. Breakfast is served in the attractive dining room and there is an elegant guest lounge.

FACILITIES: 45 en suite (5 fmly) No smoking in dining room STV TVB tea/coffee Direct dial from bedrooms No dogs Licensed Lift Cen ht TVL **PRICES:** s £60-£78; d £75-£120* **CARDS:**

♦♦♦ Comfort Inn Plan 2 A3

5-7 Princes Square, Bayswater W2 4NP ☎ 0207 792 1414
0207 792 0099
e-mail: cib@lth-hotels.com
Dir: *from Shepherds Bush follow signs to West End through Notting Hill Gate. Left into Queens Way, 2nd left into Porchester Gardens through to Princes Square (Quality Franchise)*

The hotel is located in a quiet square near Bayswater tube station, and on- street parking is easily available. Bedrooms, all with en suite, are compact but comfortable. Public areas include two breakfast rooms and a bar.

FACILITIES: 67 en suite (5 fmly) No smoking in 22 bedrooms No smoking in dining room No smoking in 1 lounge TVB tea/coffee Direct dial from bedrooms Licensed Lift Cen ht TVL **PRICES:** s £65-£88; d £79-£115* **CONF:** Thtr 20 Class 12 Board 12 **CARDS:**

♦♦♦ Averard Hotel Plan 2 A3

10 Lancaster Gate W2 3LH ☎ 020 7723 8877 020 7706 0860
e-mail: sales@averard.com
Dir: *opposite Hyde Park & Kensington Gdns, 2 mins walk from Lancaster Gate tube stn/10 mins walk from Paddington main line stn*

This is a friendly hotel that sees a continuing programme of upgrading to provide modern, comfortably furnished and well-equipped bedrooms. The public rooms include a comfortable lounge, a bar area and a smartly appointed breakfast room.

FACILITIES: 52 en suite (5 fmly) (2 GF) TVB Direct dial from bedrooms Licensed Lift Cen ht **NOTES:** Closed 22-30 Dec **CARDS:**

♦♦♦ Camelot House Hotel Plan 2 A3/4

18-20 Sussex Gardens W2 1UL ☎ 020 7723 2219
020 7402 3412
e-mail: reception@camelot-house.co.uk

Camelot House is located close to the Edgware Road. Bedrooms, all of which have been refurbished, vary in size, with most benefiting from en suite facilities. Limited parking is also an asset.

FACILITIES: 24 rms (14 en suite) (4 fmly) (4 GF) No smoking in 4 bedrooms No smoking in dining room TVB tea/coffee Direct dial from bedrooms No dogs (ex guide dogs) Cen ht No coaches **PRICES:** s £45-£60; d £65-£85* **LB PARKING:** 8 **CARDS:**

♦♦♦ Kingsway Park Hotel Plan 2 A3/4

139 Sussex Gardens W2 2RX ☎ 020 7723 5677 & 7724 9346
020 7402 4352
e-mail: kingswaypark@hotmail.com

This centrally located hotel provides good value accommodation in well co-ordinated rooms that vary in size. Modern and interesting art work features in all areas including the basement dining room.

FACILITIES: 22 en suite (5 fmly) No smoking in 8 bedrooms No smoking in dining room No smoking in 1 lounge STV TVB tea/coffee Direct dial from bedrooms No dogs Licensed Cen ht TVL Dinner Last d 7pm **PRICES:** s £48-£60; d £60-£85* **LB PARKING:** 3 **CARDS:**

♦♦♦ Mitre House Hotel Plan 2 A3/4

178-184 Sussex Gardens, Hyde Park W2 1TU ☎ 020 7723 8040
020 7402 0990
e-mail: reservations@mitrehousehotel.com
Dir: *Sussex Gardens is parallel to Bayswater Road*

This family-run hotel, conveniently situated for the West End and Paddington rail and transport links, is a comfortable and friendly establishment. Bedrooms, some on the ground floor, are pleasantly appointed and suitably equipped. A lounge and bar are available for guests' use.

FACILITIES: 70 rms (64 en suite) (3 fmly) (6 GF) No smoking in 10 bedrooms No smoking in area of dining room STV TVB Direct dial from bedrooms No dogs (ex guide dogs) Licensed Lift Cen ht TVL No coaches **PRICES:** s £60-£70; d £80* **PARKING:** 25 **CARDS:**

See advert inside back cover
See advertisement on opposite page

♦♦♦ *Park Lodge Hotel* Plan 2 A3

73 Queensborough Ter, Bayswater W2 3SU ☎ 020 7229 6424
020 7221 4772
e-mail: smegroup.kfc@mcmail.com
Dir: *Queensborough Terrace is just off Bayswater Rd.*

Ideally located within a few minutes walk of Kensington Gardens and fashionable Queensway, this former town house has been sympathetically converted to provide good practically equipped bedrooms, which have the benefit of bathrooms with power showers. An English breakfast, included in the room price, is taken in a cosy basement dining room.

FACILITIES: 29 en suite (2 fmly) No smoking in 5 bedrooms No smoking in dining room No smoking in lounges STV TVB tea/coffee Direct dial from bedrooms No dogs (ex guide dogs) Lift Cen ht Last d noon
CARDS:

♦♦ Barry House Hotel Plan 2 A3/4

12 Sussex Place, Hyde Park W2 2TP
☎ 020 7723 7340 & 0845 126 7856 020 7723 9775
e-mail: hotel@barryhouse.co.uk
Dir: *follow Paddington signs into Sussex Gardens, then turn into Sussex Place*

continued

This is a smartly presented and family-run property that offers comfortable and well-equipped accommodation. Barry House Hotel is conveniently located close to Hyde Park and the rail links. It is an ideal choice for tourist and business guests alike.
FACILITIES: 18 rms (15 en suite) (5 fmly) (2 GF) No smoking in 3 bedrooms No smoking in dining room No smoking in lounges TVB tea/coffee Direct dial from bedrooms No dogs Cen ht **PRICES:** s £38-£54; d £75-£86* **CARDS:**

◆◆ *Kingsway Hotel* — Plan 2 A4

27 Norfolk Square, Hyde Park W2 1RX
☎ 020 7723 7784 & 020 7723 5569 Fax 020 7723 7317
e-mail: kngswyh@aol.com
Dir: *follow sign to Hyde Park/Marble Arch, then Paddington Station*
In a square of town houses close to Paddington and the Bayswater Road side of Hyde Park, the hotel provides comfortable, reasonably priced accommodation. Traditional breakfasts are served in the dining room.
FACILITIES: 33 rms (30 en suite) (8 fmly) No smoking in dining room TVB tea/coffee Direct dial from bedrooms No dogs (ex guide dogs) Lift Cen ht TVL **CARDS:**

W4 — Plan 1 D3

◆◆◆ 🅰 Chiswick Lodge

104 Turnham Green Ter W4 1QN ☎ 020 8994 9926
Fax 020 8742 8238
e-mail: chishot@clara.net
Dir: *at end of M4 continue on A4, left at Hogarth rdbt onto A316 and into Chiswick High Rd. Left onto A315 at next lights, right onto Turnham Green Terrace, lodge on right next to tube station*
FACILITIES: 9 en suite No smoking in dining room STV TVB tea/coffee No dogs (ex guide dogs) Cen ht **PRICES:** s £50-£55; d £70-£75* **CARDS:**

England

W6 Plan 1 D3

♦♦ Hotel Orlando

83 Shepherds Bush Rd W6 7LR ☎ 020 7603 4890
020 7603 4890
e-mail: hotelorlando@btconnect.com

A small, privately-owned hotel, situated within easy walking distance of Hammersmith underground station in a Victorian terrace. Although the bedrooms vary in size and style they are all soundly furnished and well-maintained. Breakfast is served in the smart basement dining room, seated at individual tables.

FACILITIES: 14 en suite (3 fmly) No smoking in dining room No smoking in lounges TVB tea/coffee Direct dial from bedrooms No dogs Cen ht
PRICES: s £40; d £52* **CARDS:**

W8 Plan 1 D3

♦♦♦ Atlas-Apollo Hotel

18-30 Lexham Gardens, Kensington W8 5JE ☎ 020 7835 1155
020 7370 4853
e-mail: reservations@atlas-apollo.com
Dir: *A4 into London, onto Cromwell Rd, 1st on left after Cromwell Hospital. Hotel on right (The Independents)*

This popular hotel is conveniently placed for access to the museums and the centre. Bedrooms consist of different room types and sizes, all of the same quality and with a range of facilities. Breakfasts are served in the downstairs dining room. There is also a cosy bar.

FACILITIES: 99 rms (91 en suite) (14 fmly) TVB Direct dial from bedrooms No dogs (ex guide dogs) Licensed Lift Cen ht No coaches **PRICES:** s £75; d £90-£100* **CARDS:**

W14 Plan 2 D3

♦♦♦♦ Avonmore Hotel

66 Avonmore Rd W14 8RS ☎ 020 7603 4296 & 3121
020 7603 4035
e-mail: reservations@avonmorehotel.co.uk
Dir: *off Hammersmith Road opposite Olympia Exhibition Centre*

continued

This guest house, ideally placed for access to Olympia and within reach of central London is well presented and efficiently run. All rooms, most of which are en suite, are well appointed with co-ordinated fabrics and thoughtful facilities. The breakfast room is attractive with a small bar available for guests' use.

FACILITIES: 9 rms (7 en suite) (3 fmly) No smoking in 2 bedrooms TVB tea/coffee Direct dial from bedrooms No dogs Licensed Cen ht TVL
PRICES: s £73-£95; d £95-£105* **LB CARDS:**

♦♦♦ *Aston Court Hotel* Plan 2 D3

25/27 Matheson Rd, West Kensington W14 8SN
☎ 020 7602 9954 020 7371 1338

This large corner property is situated in a peaceful residential area, not far from West Kensington tube station and Olympia exhibition halls. Bedrooms are comfortable and well-equipped. Public areas include a small comfortable lounge bar and a conservatory where tasty English breakfasts are served.

FACILITIES: 29 en suite (3 fmly) No smoking in 14 bedrooms STV TVB tea/coffee Direct dial from bedrooms No dogs (ex guide dogs) Licensed Lift Cen ht TVL **CARDS:**

See advertisement on page 285

WC1 Plan 2 D5

♦♦♦ Euro Hotel

51-53 Cartwright Gardens, Russell Square WC1H 9EL
☎ 020 7387 4321 020 7383 5044
e-mail: reception@eurohotel.co.uk
Dir: *M1 junct 1 to Edgeware Rd/Marylebone Rd/Euston Rd, right into Judd St, right into Leigh St, over Marchmont St into Cartwright Gdns*

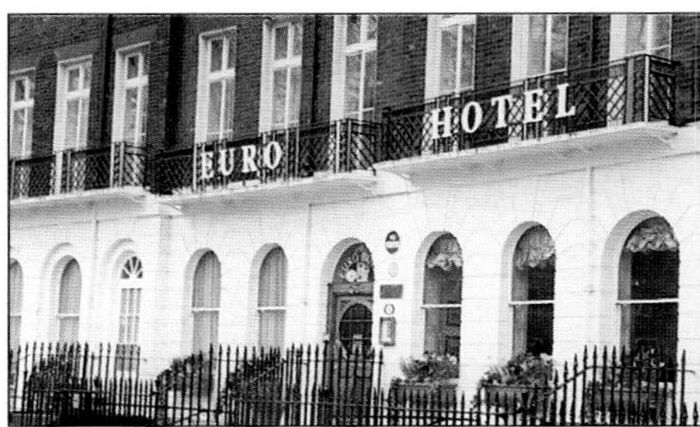

Set in a Georgian crescent, this bed and breakfast offers an excellent location and quality accommodation at reasonable prices. Continued redecoration is resulting in a constant improvement of the well-equipped bedrooms. Breakfast can be taken in an attractive dinning area with wooden floors and individual tables.

FACILITIES: 34 rms (10 en suite) (9 fmly) No smoking in dining room STV TVB tea/coffee Direct dial from bedrooms No dogs (ex guide dogs) Cen ht Tennis (hard) **PRICES:** s £49-£70; d £69-£89* **CARDS:**

♦♦♦ Mentone Hotel Plan 2 D5

54-56 Cartwright Gardens, Bloomsbury WC1H 9EL
☎ 020 7387 3927 & 7388 4671 020 7388 4671
e-mail: mentonehotel@compuserve.com
Dir: *Between Euston Rd and Russell Square*

This impressive Victorian terrace overlooking pleasant gardens is located close to many central London attractions and only minutes walk from Russell Square tube station. Most bedrooms are en suite and provide a very useful range of extra facilities. Breakfast is taken in the smart downstairs dining room and free Internet access is available for residents.

continued

FACILITIES: 43 en suite (14 fmly) No smoking in dining room TVB tea/coffee Direct dial from bedrooms No dogs Cen ht Tennis (hard)
CARDS:

♦♦ Guilford House Hotel — Plan 2 D5

6 Guilford St WC1N 1DR ☎ 020 7430 2504 020 7430 0697
e-mail: guilford-hotel@lineone.net
Dir: *A40, pass Marylebone flyover, under Euston underpass. At Kings Cross follow Grays Inn Rd signs. Guilford St at junct with Grays Inn Rd*
FACILITIES: 14 en suite (5 fmly) No smoking in 2 bedrooms No smoking in dining room No smoking in lounges TVB tea/coffee No dogs Cen ht **PRICES:** s £35-£39; d £49-£54* **CARDS:**

MERSEYSIDE

BILLINGE — Map 07 SD50

♦♦♦ Woodside

44 Tennyson Dr WN5 7EJ ☎ 01942 519647
Dir: *M6 junct 26, signed Billinge, left at traffic lights onto A577, next lights onto B5206, right after 1.5m opp hospital, 2nd left, 1st right*
This large semi-detached house is situated in a quiet residential area near Houghwood Golf Club. Friendly hospitality is offered and the accommodation consists of one room. Guests have use of their own private lounge and combined dining room. Evening meals can be provided.
FACILITIES: 1 en suite TVB tea/coffee No dogs (ex guide dogs) Cen ht TVL No children 10yrs No coaches Dinner Last d before noon **PRICES:** s £25; d £40* **PARKING:** 2 **NOTES:** Closed Dec-Jan

LIVERPOOL — Map 07 SJ39

♦♦♦ Aachen Hotel

91 Mount Pleasant L3 5TB ☎ 0151 709 3477 & 709 3633
0151 709 1126
e-mail: f.pwaachen@netscapeonline.co.uk
Dir: *from M62, M56, M57, M53 or M58 follow signs for city centre to Mount Pleasant car park*
This friendly private hotel is conveniently located within easy walking distance of the cathedrals, university and the city centre. It provides pretty and well equipped bedrooms and there is a cosy lounge bar for residents.
FACILITIES: 17 rms (11 en suite) (6 fmly) (3 GF) No smoking in 10 bedrooms No smoking in dining room STV TVB tea/coffee Direct dial from bedrooms No dogs (ex guide dogs) Licensed Cen ht TVL Snooker Pool Table Dinner Last d 8.30pm **PRICES:** s £28-£38; d £46-£54* **LB PARKING:** 2 **NOTES:** Closed 22 Dec-2 Jan **CARDS:**

♦♦♦ Blenheim Lodge

37 Aigburth Dr, Sefton Park L17 4JE ☎ 0151 727 7380
0151 727 5833
Dir: *turn off A561 into Sefton Park, 1st house on left in park*
Once the home of Stuart Sutcliffe of Beatles fame, this large Victorian house lies on the edge of Sefton Park. Bedrooms are modern and provide good-value accommodation. Public rooms extend to a comfortable lounge bar, air conditioned function room and a bright dining room where hearty breakfasts and evening meals are served.
FACILITIES: 17 rms (8 en suite) (4 fmly) No smoking in dining room STV TVB tea/coffee No dogs Licensed Cen ht TVL Dinner Last d 8pm
CONF: Thtr 120 Class 100 Board 40 Del from £50 * **PRICES:** s fr £25.50; d fr £39.50* **PARKING:** 20 **CARDS:**

SOUTHPORT — Map 07 SD31

Premier Collection

♦♦♦♦♦ Cambridge Town House Hotel

4 Cambridge Rd PR9 9NG ☎ 01704 538372
01704 547183
e-mail: info@cambridgehousehotel.co.uk
Dir: *on A565, close to Hesketh Park*
Every aspect of guest comfort is considered at this stylish hotel. From the spacious bedrooms which are individually decorated and furnished, and offer countless extras facilities, to the lavish public areas that extend to a cosy bar, elegant lounge or choice of dining rooms. Attentive service and delicious food also ensure a memorable stay.
FACILITIES: 16 en suite (2 fmly) No smoking in bedrooms No smoking in dining room No smoking in lounges TVB tea/coffee Direct dial from bedrooms No dogs (ex guide dogs) Licensed Cen ht No coaches Dinner Last d 8pm **PRICES:** s £55-£60; d £69-£77* **LB PARKING:** 20 **CARDS:**

♦♦♦♦ Ambassador Private Hotel

13 Bath St PR9 0DP ☎ 01704 543998
e-mail: ambassador.walton@virgin.net
Dir: *turn W off Lord St by the monument, Bath St is 2nd on the right*
This friendly, well-maintained hotel is conveniently situated in the heart of town only minutes walk from the seafront. The neatly decorated, well-equipped bedrooms provide comfortable accommodation, suitable for families, leisure or business guests. The hotel also benefits from its own attractive bar.
FACILITIES: 8 en suite (2 fmly) (1 GF) No smoking in 5 bedrooms No smoking in dining room TVB tea/coffee No dogs Licensed Cen ht TVL Dinner Last d 10am **PRICES:** d £58-£60* **LB BB PARKING:** 6 **NOTES:** Closed 22 Dec-2 Jan **CARDS:**

♦♦♦♦ Rosedale Hotel

11 Talbot St PR8 1HP ☎ 01704 530604 01704 530604
e-mail: info@rosedalehotelsouthport.co.uk
Dir: *from A570, into Southport, & left into Talbot St*
This friendly, smartly maintained hotel enjoys a prime location in a quiet street, only minutes walk from all the town's main attractions. Bedrooms are brightly appointed and thoughtfully equipped. Public rooms include a smart lounge, a cosy bar and a lovely South facing rear garden available for guest use.
FACILITIES: 9 en suite (2 fmly) No smoking in dining room No smoking in 1 lounge TVB tea/coffee No dogs (ex guide dogs) Licensed Cen ht TVL **PRICES:** s £25-£29; d £50-£58* **LB PARKING:** 6 **NOTES:** Closed 21 Dec-3 Jan **CARDS:**

♦♦♦♦ Whitworth Falls Hotel

16 Lathom Rd PR9 0JH ☎ 01704 530074
e-mail: whitworthfalls@rapid.co.uk
Dir: *from Southport town centre take Lord St towards Preston, straight over rdbt, 2nd left into Alexandra Rd, 4th right is Lathom Rd*
Just a short walk from key attractions, this hotel benefits from a peaceful, residential location. Public areas are extensive and include a TV lounge and a spacious bar. Many bedrooms have benefited from tasteful refurbishment.
FACILITIES: 12 en suite (2 fmly) No smoking in 7 bedrooms No smoking in dining room No smoking in lounges TVB tea/coffee Direct dial from bedrooms Licensed Cen ht TVL Dinner Last d 12noon **PRICES:** s £20-£30; d £40-£60* **LB PARKING:** 8

England

SOUTHPORT continued

♦♦♦ Edendale Hotel

83 Avondale Rd North PR9 0NE ☎ 01704 530718
📠 01704 547299
Dir: *at end of A570 turn right at traffic lights follow to rdbt straight over, then 3rd road on left (Leyland Rd), then 2nd on left (Avondale Rd North), hotel on corner on left*
This smart Victorian house enjoys a peaceful location in a leafy residential road; minutes walk from the promenade and the town centre. Bedrooms are individually styled and all benefit from a host of thoughtful facilities. There is a comfortable bar lounge adjacent to the smart dining room where imaginative evening meals and freshly cooked breakfasts are served
FACILITIES: 8 en suite (2 fmly) No smoking TVB tea/coffee Direct dial from bedrooms Licensed Cen ht n Dinner Last d 4pm **PRICES:** s £24.50-£30; d £40-£50* **PARKING:** 8 **CARDS:**

♦♦♦ Sidbrook Hotel

14 Talbot St PR8 1HP ☎ 01704 530608 📠 01704 530608
e-mail: sidbrookhotel@tesco.net
Dir: *from Liverpool, take A565 into Southport, at Scarisbrick Hotel turn right onto A570 (Eastbank St), 3rd right (Talbot St). Hotel 50yds on right*
This friendly private hotel is conveniently situated for Lord Street and all of the town centre's major attractions. Rooms are brightly appointed, well equipped and include one with a four-poster bed. There is a secluded garden and a comfortable lounge bar. Breakfast is taken in the brightly decorated dining room.
FACILITIES: 8 en suite (1 fmly) No smoking in bedrooms No smoking in dining room TVB tea/coffee No dogs (ex guide dogs) Licensed Cen ht Pool Table **PRICES:** s £27-£31; d £42-£52* **LB PARKING:** 8 **CARDS:**

♦♦♦ The White Lodge Private Hotel

12 Talbot St PR8 1HP ☎ 01704 536320 📠 01704 536320
Dir: *A570/A565 to town centre, then off Eastbank St into Talbot St. White lodge 50yds on right*
A short stroll from the town centre, this friendly, family-run guest house offers a warm welcome. Bedrooms, including one on the ground floor, are thoughtfully equipped. Public areas feature a comfortably furnished lounge and a bar, which has a good atmosphere. Evening meals are available by arrangement.
FACILITIES: 8 rms (6 en suite) (2 fmly) No smoking in bedrooms No smoking in dining room TVB tea/coffee No dogs (ex guide dogs) Licensed Cen ht Dinner Last d 6pm **PRICES:** s £24-£30; d £50-£60 **LB PARKING:** 6

♦♦ Lyndhurst

101 King St PR8 1LQ ☎ 01704 537520 & 07759 526864
Dir: *off A570 at McDonalds on corner of King St, guest house 100yds on left*
This well maintained, friendly guest house is situated just a short walk from Lord Street and the town's main attractions. It offers brightly decorated accommodation and comfortable residents' lounge leading into the breakfast room.
FACILITIES: 7 rms TVB tea/coffee No dogs (ex guide dogs) Licensed Cen ht TVL No children 5yrs No coaches Last d noon **PRICES:** s £17; d £34* **LB BB PARKING:** 2

A indicates an Associate entry, which has been inspected and rated by the ETC or the RAC in England.

NORFOLK

ATTLEBOROUGH Map 05 TM09

♦♦♦ Conifers

27 The Street, Rockland All Saints NR17 1TR ☎ 01953 483385
📠 01953 488444
e-mail: dave.hedger@btinternet.com
Dir: *from Attleborough take B1077 signed Watton pass through Gt Ellingham and continue to Rocklands pass Rigeons builders merchants on right take next left into The Street, Conifers is at junct of Mill Lane opposite village hall*
Linda and Dave Hedger welcome guests to their home, a bungalow set in the small quiet village of Rockland All Saints, just a short drive from Attleborough. The two east facing bedrooms have recently been refurbished, and guests share one general bathroom. Friendly and helpful service is one of the strengths here and a freshly cooked breakfast is served in a pleasant separate dining room. Holistic and Beauty treatments are available by prior arrangement.
FACILITIES: 2 rms No smoking No dogs (ex guide dogs) Cen ht No children 18yrs No coaches **PRICES:** d fr £40* **PARKING:** 3
NOTES: Closed Oct-Mar

BACTON Map 09 TG33

♦♦♦ A Keswick Hotel & Restaurant

Walcott Rd NR12 0LS ☎ 01692 650468 📠 01692 650788
e-mail: bookings@keswickhotelbacton.co.uk
Dir: *from King's Lynn take A148 to Cromer, left at lights onto B1159 through Bacton, hotel is on the left*
FACILITIES: 9 en suite (2 fmly) No smoking in 6 bedrooms No smoking in dining room TVB tea/coffee Direct dial from bedrooms No dogs (ex guide dogs) Licensed Cen ht No children 11yrs Dinner Last d 9pm **PRICES:** s £28.50-£33.50; d £49-£68.50* **LB CONF:** Thtr 30 Class 30 Board 30 Del from £50 * **PARKING:** 50 **CARDS:**

BARNEY Map 09 TF93

♦♦♦♦ The Old Brick Kilns

Little Barney Ln, Barney NR21 0NL
☎ 01328 878305 & 0870 3018877 📠 01328 878948
e-mail: enquire@old-brick-kilns.co.uk
Dir: *6m NE of Fakenham turn off A148 towards Barney, then towards Little Barney*
Expect a friendly welcome at this small country house, which is set in its own peaceful grounds. Three separate cottages have been carefully converted to provide tastefully decorated accommodation. An attractive lounge features a log fire and comfortable sofas. Breakfast is served at a large communal table in the dining room; dinner is available by prior arrangement.
FACILITIES: 3 en suite No smoking TVB tea/coffee Direct dial from bedrooms No dogs (ex guide dogs) Licensed Cen ht TVL No coaches Fishing Croquet lawn Table tennis, Boules & Giant chess Dinner Last d 10am
PRICES: s £25; d £50* **PARKING:** 15 **CARDS:**

BINHAM Map 09 TF93

♦♦♦ Chequers

45 Front St NR21 0AL ☎ 01328 830297
Dir: *turn off A148 Fakenham-Holt-Cromer Road at Thursford, signposted Hindringham & Binham. 4m to Binham, inn on left of village centre*
Traditional 17th-century inn situated in the heart of this rural village. A range of real ales is available in the popular bar, which has many original features including exposed beams and open fires. An interesting choice of freshly prepared dishes is offered in

continued

England

the cosy restaurant. The pleasantly decorated bedrooms are popular with visiting bird watchers.
FACILITIES: 2 en suite No smoking in bedrooms No smoking in dining room No smoking in 1 lounge TVB tea/coffee No dogs No children 14yrs Dinner Last d 9pm **PRICES:** s fr £30; d fr £50* **MEALS:** Lunch fr £16 Dinner fr £18* **PARKING:** 20 **NOTES:** Closed Xmas/New Year
CARDS:

BRISTON Map 09 TG03

♦♦♦ John H Stracey
West End NR24 2JA ☎ 01263 860891 862984
e-mail: thejohnhstracey@btinternet.com
Dir: *located 3m S of Holt, through Hunworth to Briston crossroads onto B1354 towards Saxthorpe, turn left, continue for 0.5m*

The hosts at this country inn are extremely hospitable. There are a range of bedrooms, which are neatly furnished, homely and comfortable. Public areas include a bar and a dining room where a wide range of well-cooked food is served to guests.
FACILITIES: 3 rms (1 en suite) No smoking in bedrooms No smoking in dining room No smoking in lounges TVB tea/coffee Cen ht Dinner Last d 9.15pm **PRICES:** s £22.50-£30.50; d £45-£61* **LB PARKING:** 30
CARDS:

BROOKE Map 05 TM29

♦♦♦♦ Old Vicarage
48 The Street NR15 1JU ☎ 01508 558329
Dir: *from Norwich follow B1332 signed Bungay. Approx 7m to Brooke. Left at crossroads at village sign, left at fork with duck pond on right, house 1.25m*
Set in its own mature gardens in a peaceful location and within easy driving distance of Norwich city centre. The individually decorated bedrooms are tastefully furnished and thoughtfully equipped, one of the rooms has a lovely four-poster bed. Public rooms include an elegant dining room and a cosy lounge. Dinner is available by prior arrangement.
FACILITIES: 2 en suite No smoking tea/coffee No dogs Cen ht TVL No children 15yrs No coaches Dinner Last d day before **PRICES:** s fr £21; d fr £42* **LB PARKING:** 4

BURNHAM MARKET Map 09 TF84

♦♦♦♦ Staffordshire House
Station Rd, Docking PE31 8LS ☎ 01485 518709
e-mail: enquiries@staffordshirehouse.com
Dir: *located on B1153 (Station Rd) next door but one to duck pond, approx 300yds from church and diagonally opposite Post Office*
This charming, detached property is situated in the centre of the quiet rural village of Docking, ideally placed for exploring Burnham Market and the North Norfolk coastline. The individually decorated bedrooms are tastefully furnished and thoughtfully equipped with many useful extras. The property also features an 'antique and interiors' shop, which is in a separate part of the building.

continued

FACILITIES: 3 rms No smoking in bedrooms No smoking in dining room TVB tea/coffee No dogs (ex guide dogs) Cen ht No coaches **PRICES:** s £32; d £48-£52S **LB PARKING:** 4 **CARDS:**

♦♦♦♦ Whitehall Farm *(TF856412)*
Burnham Thorpe PE31 8HN ☎ 01328 738416 & 07050 247390 01328 730937 Mrs V Southerland
e-mail: barrysoutherland@aol.com
Dir: *from Lord Nelson pub in Burham towards Holkam/Wells. Farmhouse last building on R on leaving village*
Set on an arable farm with large landscaped gardens and a menagerie of animals, this country house has a relaxing and informal atmosphere. An unusual asset is the Southerland's private airstrip, and other amateur pilots are welcome to fly in by arrangement. Communal hearty breakfasts are served in the cosy dining room.
FACILITIES: 3 en suite (1 fmly) No smoking in bedrooms TVB tea/coffee No dogs (ex guide dogs) Cen ht TVL 560 acres arable **PRICES:** s £35-£45; d £45* **PARKING:** 7

♦♦♦ *North Farmhouse* *(TF765372)*
Station Rd, Docking PE31 8LS ☎ 01485 518493 Mr Roberts
e-mail: NorthFarmshouse@aol.com
Dir: *off A148 onto B1153, 10m to Docking, at church follow B1153 towards Brancaster. Farmhouse 400yds on R*
This flint and brick farmhouse is peacefully situated and provides an excellent base for touring around the North Norfolk coast. Fairly spacious bedrooms are pleasantly appointed and public areas feature a separate lounge and a dining room, where breakfast is served around a large polished wood table.
FACILITIES: 2 en suite No smoking TV1B tea/coffee Cen ht 1 acres non working **PARKING:** 5 **NOTES:** Closed 15 Dec-13 Jan

CLEY NEXT THE SEA Map 09 TG04

Premier Collection

♦♦♦♦♦ Old Town Hall House
Coast Rd NR25 7RZ ☎ 01263 740284
Dir: *on A149, coast road between Blakeney/Salthouse, opposite old telephone box*

Expect a warm welcome from the caring hosts at this delightful guest house, which overlooks the world famous bird reserve of Cley Marshes and perfectly placed for touring this lovely area. The attractively decorated bedrooms are thoughtfully equipped with many useful extras. An imaginative choice is available for breakfast, served at individual tables in the smart dining room.
FACILITIES: 3 en suite No smoking TVB tea/coffee No dogs Cen ht No children 12yrs No coaches **PRICES:** d £55-£70* **LB NOTES:** Closed Xmas & New Year

England

COLTISHALL Map 09 TG21

♦♦♦♦ The Hedges
Tunstead Rd NR12 7AL ☎ 01603 738361 01603 738983
e-mail: thehedges@msn.com
Dir: *B1150 from Norwich, through Horstead over hump-back bridge, right onto B1354, opposite river turn left into White Lion Rd at top take right fork (Tunstead Rd).*
A warm welcome can be expected at this delightful family-run guest house, situated close to the Norfolk Broads and within easy driving distance of the Bure Valley Railway and Wroxham town centre. Breakfast is served at individual tables in the dining room, which overlooks the garden, and there is a lounge with a log burning fire. The well-maintained bedrooms are comfortably furnished and equipped with many thoughtful extras.
FACILITIES: 5 en suite (2 fmly) (2 GF) No smoking TVB tea/coffee No dogs (ex guide dogs) Licensed Cen ht TVL Dinner Last d 9pm **PRICES:** s £23-£30; d £46-£49 **LB PARKING:** 10 **CARDS:**

♦♦♦ *Kings Head*
26 Wroxham Rd NR12 7EA ☎ 01603 737426 01603 736542
Dir: *Norwich ring road onto B1150 towards North Walsham. In Coltishall, right at petrol station. Follow road past church on right, next to car park*
Popular 17th century inn situated on the banks of the River Bure just a short walk from the village centre. The inn has a local following and is well known for its interesting range of freshly prepared dishes. The bedrooms are attractively decorated, pleasantly furnished and thoughtfully equipped.
FACILITIES: 4 rms (2 en suite) (1 fmly) No smoking in dining room TVB tea/coffee No dogs (ex guide dogs) Cen ht No coaches Dinner Last d 9.30pm **PARKING:** 20 **CARDS:**

CROMER Map 09 TG24

♦♦♦♦ Beachcomber Guest House
17 Macdonald Rd NR27 9AP ☎ 01263 513398
Dir: *take the Runton road from Cromer, 1st left after Cliftonville Hotel (opposite putting green)*
Located adjacent to the seafront, a few minutes walk from the town centre, this very well maintained Edwardian house has been sympathetically renovated to provide homely bedrooms, filled with lots of thoughtful extras. English breakfasts are taken in the cosy dining room and a spacious comfortable guest lounge is also available.
FACILITIES: 6 rms (5 en suite) (1 fmly) No smoking in bedrooms No smoking in dining room TVB tea/coffee No dogs (ex guide dogs) Cen ht TVL No children 4yrs **PRICES:** d £42-£50* **LB NOTES:** Closed Xmas

♦♦♦♦ Bon Vista
12 Alfred Rd NR27 9AN ☎ 01263 511818 01263 512306
e-mail: jcramshaw@lineone.net
Dir: *from pier follow 148 copast road for 400yds, turn left into Alfred rd*
Close to the seafront and town centre, this Victorian terraced house retains many original features, enhanced by pretty decor and soft furnishings. The well-equipped bedrooms have a homely feel. Breakfast is taken in the attractive dining room, and a spacious sitting room is available. The friendly, considerate hosts have a good knowledge of the area.
FACILITIES: 6 rms (3 en suite) (1 fmly) No smoking TVB tea/coffee No dogs (ex guide dogs) Cen ht TVL No coaches Dinner Last d breakfast **PRICES:** s £21; d £36-£46* **LB BB PARKING:** 3

♦♦♦♦ Brightside
19 Macdonald Rd NR27 9AP ☎ 01263 513408
e-mail: bright-side@supanet.com
Dir: *off the seafront on Runton Rd (A149) 1st left after Cliftonville Hotel*
A friendly family-run guest house situated close to the seafront and within easy walking distance of the town centre. The attractively decorated bedrooms come in a variety of sizes and are well equipped. Breakfast is served in the smart dining room at individual tables and guests also have the use of a comfortable lounge.
FACILITIES: 6 en suite (3 fmly) No smoking TVB tea/coffee No dogs Cen ht No children 4yrs No coaches **PRICES:** d £39-£50* **LB**

♦♦♦♦ *Morden House*
20 Cliff Av NR27 0AN ☎ 01263 513396
e-mail: rosemary@broadland.com
Dir: *last road on right before traffic lights on A140, Norwich to Cromer*
Located in a quiet residential avenue, close to the centre and seafront, a warm welcome is assured at this impressive Victorian house, which stands in mature grounds and retains many original features, including open fires, moulded cornices and a fine staircase. The spacious bedrooms are filled with lots of thoughtful extras and imaginative dinners are preceded by complimentary sherry.
FACILITIES: 6 rms (4 en suite) (1 fmly) No smoking in bedrooms No smoking in dining room No smoking in lounges TVB tea/coffee Licensed Cen ht TVL No coaches Dinner Last d 6pm **PARKING:** 3

♦♦♦♦ Shrublands Farm *(TG246393)*
Church St, Northrepps NR27 0AA ☎ 01263 579297
01263 579297 Mrs A Youngman
e-mail: youngman@farming.co.uk
Dir: *turn off A149 to Northrepps, 2m from Cromer. Through village, past Foundry Arms on right for 50yds, cream house on left behind trees*

Situated in an area of outstanding natural beauty, this 18th-century farmhouse is a working family farm, set in mature gardens amid 300 acres of arable farmland. Old fashioned hospitality is a distinguishing feature, with good farmhouse cooking from the Aga. Dinner is available October to March by prior arrangement (bring your own wine). An ideal place from which to explore the coastline and countryside of north Norfolk.
FACILITIES: 3 en suite No smoking TVB tea/coffee No dogs (ex guide dogs) Cen ht TVL No children 12yrs 300 acres arable **PRICES:** s £29-£31; d £48-£52* **PARKING:** 5 **NOTES:** Closed 23 Dec-1 Jan

England

♦♦♦♦ Westgate Lodge Private Hotel

10 MacDonald Rd NR27 9AP ☎ 01263 512840

Dir: *proceed along sea front and turn left after the Cliftonville Hotel, Westgate Lodge is 50yds on the right hand side*

Delightful guest house situated just a short walk from the beach and town centre. Although the bedrooms vary in size and style they are all pleasantly decorated and equipped with many useful extras. Breakfast and dinner are served at individual tables in the smart dining room and guests also have the use of a cosy lounge.

FACILITIES: 11 en suite (3 fmly) No smoking in dining room TVB tea/coffee No dogs (ex guide dogs) Licensed Cen ht No children 3yrs No coaches Dinner **PRICES:** d £44-£58* **LB** **PARKING:** 12 **NOTES:** Closed Xmas & New Year **CARDS:**

♦♦♦♦ White Cottage

9 Cliff Dr NR27 0AW ☎ 01263 512728

e-mail: jboocockwhitecottagecromer.freeserve.co.uk

Occupying a wonderful position overlooking the beach with panoramic views of the sea. The property offers spacious tastefully decorated well-equipped bedrooms equipped with many thoughtful extras. Breakfast is served seated around a large communal table in the cosy dining room. Please note this is a no-smoking establishment.

FACILITIES: 3 en suite No smoking TVB tea/coffee No dogs (ex guide dogs) Cen ht No children 18yrs No coaches **PRICES:** d £54-£58* **LB BB** **PARKING:** 3 **NOTES:** Closed Xmas

♦♦♦ Chellow Dene

23 MacDonald Rd NR27 9AP ☎ 01263 513251

Dir: *off main coastal rd between Cromer & Sheringham, opp putting green, Sandcliff Hotel on corner of A140, Chellow Dene on left*

Situated a short walk from the beach, this small family-run guest house offers a friendly welcome. Bedrooms are tastefully decorated and well equipped. There is a cosy ground floor lounge and a set breakfast and dinner are served in the pleasant dining room.

FACILITIES: 7 rms (5 en suite) (2 fmly) No smoking in dining room TVB tea/coffee Licensed Cen ht TVL No coaches Dinner Last d 5pm **PRICES:** s £20-£25; d £40-£55* **LB** **PARKING:** 6

♦♦♦ Glendale

33 Macdonald Rd NR27 9AP ☎ 01263 513278

e-mail: glendalecromer@aol.com

Dir: *from Tourist Information Centre take A149 coast road, Macdonald Road 4th on left*

Located on a peaceful side street, this Victorian property is just a short walk from the seafront and town centre. Bedrooms are pleasantly decorated, well maintained and thoughtfully equipped. Breakfast is served at individual tables in the smart dining room.

FACILITIES: 5 rms (1 en suite) No smoking TVB tea/coffee No coaches **PRICES:** s £19-£25; d £38-£50* **LB BB** **PARKING:** 4 **NOTES:** Closed 21 Oct - 28 Feb 2003 **CARDS:**

♦♦♦ Sandcliff Private Hotel

Runton Rd NR27 9AS ☎ 01263 512888 Fax 01263 512888

e-mail: sandcliff@btclick.com

Dir: *on seafront towards Sheringham*

Friendly family run hotel situated on the seafront overlooking the promenade and beach. Bedrooms are pleasantly decorated, well maintained and thoughtfully equipped; some rooms have lovely sea views. Public rooms include a large lounge bar and a smartly appointed restaurant serving home cooked food.

FACILITIES: 22 rms (16 en suite) (10 fmly) (3 GF) No smoking in dining room TVB tea/coffee Licensed Dinner Last d 6pm **PRICES:** s £27; d £48-£60* **LB** **PARKING:** 10 **NOTES:** Closed 21 Dec-4 Jan

♦♦♦ Birch House

34 Cabbell Rd NR27 9HX ☎ 01263 512521

Dir: *off A140 Holt Rd and take 2nd left after station*

FACILITIES: 8 rms (3 en suite) No smoking STV TVB tea/coffee No dogs (ex guide dogs) Licensed No coaches Dinner **PRICES:** s fr £19; d £38-£44* **LB BB** **PARKING:** 1 **NOTES:** Closed annual holiday & winter time **CARDS:**

DEREHAM — Map 09 TF91

♦♦♦ Yaxham Mill

Norwich Rd, Yaxham NR19 1RP ☎ 01362 693144 Fax 01362 699801

Dir: *from A47 at Dereham, follow signs for Wymondham into Yaxham, follow signs for Mattishal, hotel on right*

Popular inn situated in a rural location amidst open countryside but within easy striking distance of East Dereham. Public rooms feature a comfortable lounge bar, a further seating area and a smart restaurant. The bedrooms are situated in an annexe adjacent to the main building; each room has attractive pine furnishings and many thoughtful touches.

FACILITIES: 5 en suite 2 annexe en suite (1 fmly) (2 GF) No smoking in dining room No smoking in 1 lounge TVB tea/coffee No dogs (ex guide dogs) Cen ht TVL Outdoor swimming pool Pool Table Badminton court, Boules, Cycle hire Dinner Last d 9.30pm **PRICES:** s £30-£35; d £39.50-£45* **LB** **MEALS:** Lunch fr £5.95 Dinner fr £6.95* **PARKING:** 30 **CARDS:**

DISS — Map 05 TM18

♦♦♦♦ Jasmine House

3 Bungay Rd, Scole IP21 4HH ☎ 01379 740482

e-mail: BradleyJasmineBB@aol.com

Dir: *S of Scole village at A140 rdbt take A143 to Yarmouth by-passing Scole, establishment is 0.75m from rdbt in a lone group of houses on the left at the top of the hill*

Expect a warm welcome at this charming property on the Norfolk and Suffolk borders overlooking the Waveney Valley. The individually decorated bedrooms are tastefully furnished and thoughtfully equipped. Breakfast is served at a large pine table in the attractive dining room.

FACILITIES: 2 en suite No smoking TVB tea/coffee No dogs Cen ht No children 14yrs No coaches **PRICES:** d £46-£56* **PARKING:** 3

Egg cups for excellence!
This symbol shows that breakfast exceeded our Inspector's expectations.

England

DOWNHAM MARKET Map 05 TF60

♦♦♦♦ The Dial House

12 Railway Rd PE38 9EB ☎ 01366 388358
e-mail: bookings@thedialhouse.co.uk
Dir: *A10 follow sign for Downham Market, at lights turn left & 1st right, follow signs for Rail Station, at T-junct turn left, house 100yds on right*

A warm, friendly welcome is offered at this delightful 17th-century house. The bedrooms are attractively decorated and have well co-ordinated soft furnishings and fabrics. Public rooms include a spacious ground floor lounge and separate dining room with a large communal table. Home-made bread and preserves are a house speciality.
FACILITIES: 3 rms (2 en suite) No smoking TVB tea/coffee No dogs (ex guide dogs) Cen ht TVL No coaches Dinner Last d noon **PRICES:** s £28-£36; d £38-£48✻ **LB BB CONF:** Board 16 **PARKING:** 5

FAKENHAM Map 09 TF92

See also Barney

♦♦♦♦ Holly Tree

40 Sandy Ln NR21 9EZ ☎ 01328 851955 🖷 01328 851955
e-mail: gartcarving@aol.com
Dir: *Turn off A1065 at Shell garage or from A148, across rdbt and 1st right past Shell garage, into Sandy Lane, Holly Tree 200 yds on left.*
Expect a friendly welcome at this small family run guest house, which is situated in a quiet road on the outskirts of town. Bedrooms are smartly decorated, have co-ordinated soft furnishings and many useful extras. Breakfast is served around the large communal table in the attractive dining room which overlooks the neat well tended gardens.
FACILITIES: 2 en suite No smoking TVB tea/coffee No dogs Cen ht No children 10yrs No coaches **PRICES:** s £30; d £40✻ **PARKING:** 2

♦♦♦ Abbott Farm *(TF975390)*

Walsingham Rd, Binham NR21 0AW ☎ 01328 830519 & 07986 041715 🖷 01328 830519 Mrs E Brown
e-mail: abbot.farm@btinternet.com
Dir: *leave A148 at Thursford (Crawfish Thai Restaurant) towards Hindringham, then 4m to Binham, in village L on B1388 to Walsingham, farm 1m on L*
This detached red-brick dormer house is situated in a peaceful rural location amid 150 acres of arable farmland. The spacious bedrooms are pleasantly decorated and thoughtfully equipped, the ground floor room features a very spacious en suite shower. Breakfast is taken in the attractive conservatory, which has superb views across the surrounding countryside.
FACILITIES: 2 en suite (1 GF) No smoking TVB tea/coffee Cen ht 160 acres arable **PRICES:** s £20-£25; d £40-£50✻ **PARKING:** 20

♦♦♦ White Horse

Fakenham Rd, East Barsham NR21 0LH ☎ 01328 820645 🖷 01328 820645
e-mail: rsteele@btinternet.com
Dir: *turn off A148 onto B1105 towards Walsingham, inn 2m on left just before Barsham Manor*
Delightful inn situated in a peaceful rural location just to the north of Fakenham town centre. An interesting choice of dishes are served in the small dining room and guests also have the use of a cosy well-stocked lounge bar. Bedroom are pleasantly decorated and thoughtfully equipped.
FACILITIES: 3 en suite (1 fmly) No smoking in bedrooms No smoking in dining room TVB tea/coffee No dogs (ex guide dogs) Cen ht Dinner Last d 9.30pm **PRICES:** s £35; d £54-£75✻ **PARKING:** 50 **CARDS:**

GREAT ELLINGHAM Map 05 TM09

♦♦♦♦ Aldercarr Hall

Attleborough Rd NR17 1LQ ☎ 01953 451255 🖷 01953 457993
e-mail: bedandbreakfast@aldercarr-limited.com
Dir: *turn of A11 to Attleborough follow Walton road, Wayland Hospital is on left Aldercarr Hall is 2m on right*
Comfortable modern accommodation is provided at Aldecarr Hall, which stands in its own grounds in quiet rural surroundings on the edge of Great Ellingham, with easy access to the A11. Service is friendly and helpful, and public rooms include a comfortably appointed conservatory and a delightful dining room where breakfast is taken around a large communal table. A new health, beauty and hairdressing studio was due to open shortly after our visit, and there is also an indoor swimming pool and a snooker room within the grounds.
FACILITIES: 2 en suite 3 annexe en suite No smoking TVB tea/coffee No dogs (ex guide dogs) Cen ht TVL No children 10yrs Indoor swimming pool (heated) Snooker Pool Table Jacuzzi **PRICES:** s £29.99-£39.99; d £49.99-£59.99✻ **PARKING:** 200 **CARDS:**

GREAT YARMOUTH Map 05 TG50

♦♦♦♦ Barnard House

2 Barnard Crescent NR30 4DR ☎ 01493 855139 🖷 01493 843143
e-mail: barnardhouse@btinternet.com
Dir: *follow signs to Caister, through 3 sets of traffic lights, house on right after last set of lights*
Fronted by pretty mature gardens on a leafy road in a residential area of the town, this homely and comfortable house provides bedrooms filled with thoughtful extras, and memorable breakfasts, which are served at one family table in the elegant hall dining room.
FACILITIES: 3 en suite No smoking STV TVB tea/coffee Cen ht TVL No coaches Dinner Last d 4pm **PRICES:** s £25-£30; d £48-£52✻ **PARKING:** 3

♦♦♦♦ Ship Hotel

71 Avondale Rd, Gorleston on Sea NR31 6DJ ☎ 01493 662746 🖷 01493 650025
e-mail: grahambb@aol.com
Dir: *off A12*
A warm welcome is offered at this small privately owned hotel situated close to the seafront and town centre. The property has been totally refurbished by the current owners and provides attractive accommodation throughout. The well-equipped bedrooms are tastefully decorated and have pretty soft furnishings; some rooms have sea views and four-poster beds.

continued

FACILITIES: 8 en suite (3 fmly) No smoking in bedrooms No smoking in dining room No smoking in 1 lounge TVB tea/coffee No dogs (ex guide dogs) Licensed Cen ht TVL No coaches **PRICES:** s £28-£40; d £50-£60* **LB PARKING:** 5 **CARDS:**

◆◆◆◆ The Ryecroft

91 North Denes Rd NR30 4LW ☎ 01493 844015
01493 856096
e-mail: TheRyecroft@aol.com
Dir: *from seafront proceed past 'Waterways' on right. Left into Beaconsfield Rd, right at x-rds and Ryecroft in 15mtrs on right*
FACILITIES: 8 rms (5 en suite) (3 fmly) No smoking in 1 bedrooms No smoking in dining room No smoking in 1 lounge TVB tea/coffee Licensed Cen ht TVL Dinner Last d 12 noon **PRICES:** s £19-£28; d £38-£46* **LB BB PARKING:** 5 **CARDS:**

◆◆◆ Andover Hotel

28-30 Camperdown NR30 3JB ☎ 01493 843490
01493 843490
Dir: *follow directions for seafront. Turn right onto Marine Pde, turn right at Wellington Pier this road runs into Camperdown*
Situated in a quiet side road just off the seafront and within easy walking distance of the town centre, this small privately owned hotel has a wide range of amenities which include, a children's play room, sun bed and pool room. Breakfast is served at individual tables in the basement dining room and home cooked dinners are also available.
FACILITIES: 25 en suite (10 fmly) (1 GF) No smoking in dining room No smoking in 1 lounge TVB tea/coffee No dogs (ex guide dogs) Licensed Cen ht TVL Sauna Solarium Pool Table Small amount exercise equipment Dinner **PRICES:** s £25-£30; d £38-£45* **LB BB NOTES:** Closed 2 Jan-Mar

◆◆◆ Avalon Private Hotel

54 Clarence Rd, Gorleston-on-Sea NR31 6DR ☎ 01493 662114
01493 661521
e-mail: avalonhotel@gorleston54.freeserve.co.uk
Dir: *from A12 follow seafront signs, Clarence Rd is at right angle to Marine Parade*

Edwardian terrace house situated just a short stroll from the promenade and beach. Bedrooms are pleasantly decorated, thoughtfully furnished and well-equipped. Breakfast is served at individual tables in the smart dining room and four-course dinners are available. Guests also have the use of a cosy lounge bar and a games room.
FACILITIES: 9 rms (8 en suite) (5 fmly) No smoking in 2 bedrooms No smoking in dining room TVB tea/coffee Licensed Cen ht TVL Pool Table Darts and games room Dinner Last d 2pm **PRICES:** s £18-£25; d £36-£50* **LB BB CARDS:**

◆◆◆ *Church Farm*

Church Rd, Burgh Castle NR31 9QG ☎ 01493 780251
01493 780251
e-mail: F.snellcff@aol.com
200-year-old Grade II listed farmhouse nestling beside Breydon waters where the rivers Waveney and Yare meet. Bedrooms are pleasantly decorated and thoughtfully equipped, some rooms have superb views. Public rooms include a large lounge bar, games room, restaurant and pool room.
FACILITIES: 6 rms (5 en suite) (2 fmly) No smoking in bedrooms No smoking in area of dining room TVB tea/coffee Direct dial from bedrooms No dogs (ex guide dogs) Cen ht TVL Fishing Pool Table Dinner Last d 9.30pm **PARKING:** 100 **CARDS:**

◆◆◆ Harbour Hotel

20 Pavilion Rd, Gorleston on Sea NR31 6BY ☎ 01493 661031
01493 661031
e-mail: jeffchambers@harbourhotel.freeserve.co.uk
Dir: *A12 to Gorleston on Sea town centre, follow signs to beach. Hotel 20yds from lighthouse*
Situated near the harbour overlooking the sandy beach and sea beyond. Although the bedrooms vary in size and style they are all pleasantly decorated and thoughtfully equipped, many rooms have lovely sea views. Breakfast is served at individual tables in the spacious dining room and snacks are offered in the lounge bar during the evening.
FACILITIES: 8 rms (4 en suite) (6 fmly) No smoking in dining room tea/coffee No dogs Licensed Cen ht TVL No coaches **PRICES:** s £25-£35; d £40-£46* **LB PARKING:** 2

◆◆◆ Jennis Lodge

63 Avondale Rd, Gorleston-on-Sea NR31 6DJ ☎ 01493 662840
01493 662840
Dir: *from A12 follow signs for sea front, Avondale Rd off Marine Parade*
Friendly, family run guest house situated just off the sea front and close to the town centre. The cosy bedrooms are pleasantly decorated and well equipped. Breakfast is served in the smart dining room/bar and guests have the use of a comfortable lounge. Dinner is available by arrangement.
FACILITIES: 10 rms (5 en suite) (3 fmly) No smoking in 2 bedrooms No smoking in dining room TVB tea/coffee No dogs (ex guide dogs) Licensed Cen ht TVL Dinner Last d 4pm **PRICES:** s £20-£26; d £40-£52* **LB CARDS:**

◆◆◆ Winchester Private Hotel

12 Euston Rd NR30 1DY ☎ 01493 843950 01493 843950
Dir: *follow A12 to A47, follow signs for seafront, left at Sainsburys through lights. Hotel 400mtrs on right*
Located close to the seafront this impressive Victorian villa retains many original features, which are enhanced by the furnishing and décor styles throughout. Bedrooms, some of which are situated on the ground floor, are equipped with practical and homely extras.
FACILITIES: 14 en suite (2 fmly) No smoking in dining room TVB tea/coffee No dogs Cen ht TVL No children 12yrs No coaches Dinner Last d 5pm **PRICES:** s £20-£25; d £40-£50* **LB PARKING:** 14 **NOTES:** Closed Dec-Feb

England

HARLESTON Map 05 TM28

♦♦♦♦ Heath Farmhouse

Homersfield IP20 0EX ☎ 01986 788417

Dir: *turn off A143 onto B1062 towards Flixton, over bridge past 'Suffolk' sign & take 2nd farm entrance on left at AA sign*

Located on spacious gardens, which include a croquet lawn, this 16th century former farmhouse retains many original features including a wealth of exposed beams and open fireplaces with roaring wood burners. The homely bedrooms are filled with thoughtful extras and quality furnishings, memorabilia and original art enhance the intrinsic charm.

FACILITIES: 2 rms (1 fmly) No smoking in bedrooms No smoking in dining room No smoking in 1 lounge tea/coffee No dogs (ex guide dogs) Cen ht TVL No coaches Croquet lawn Table tennis Dinner Last d 10am **PRICES:** s £28; d £42* **PARKING:** 8

HINDRINGHAM Map 09 TF93

Premier Collection

♦♦♦♦♦ Field House

Moorgate Rd NR21 0PT ☎ 01328 878726 01328 878955

e-mail: wendyfieldhouse@lineone.net

Dir: *A148 from Fakenham to Thursford, left at the Crawfish follow signs to Hindringham, through the village. Right into Moorgate Road at Lower Green and Field House is 1st on the left.*

Field House stands in lovely gardens on the edge of the peaceful village and enjoys fine views of the Norfolk countryside. Luxury bedrooms are available offering many thoughtful extras while the lounge and dining room are quite superbly furnished. Quality home cooking is provided, with dinner being a highlight.

FACILITIES: 2 en suite No smoking TVB tea/coffee No dogs (ex guide dogs) Cen ht No children 8yrs No coaches Croquet lawn Croquet Lawn Dinner Last d when booking **PRICES:** s £40-£45; d £60-£70* **LB** **PARKING:** 3 **NOTES:** Closed 25 & 26 Dec

HOLT Map 09 TG03

♦♦♦♦ The Old Telephone Exchange

The Old Telephone Exchange, 37 New St NR25 6JH

☎ 01263 712992

Dir: *turn off A148 into Holt High St. Take New St - beside Barclays Bank. Establishment approx 200yds on left*

Expect a friendly welcome at this small family run guest house, which is situated in a quiet side road close to the town centre. Bedrooms are smartly decorated, well maintained and equipped with many useful extras. Public rooms feature a comfortably appointed open plan lounge/dining area with a wide screen television, books and games.

FACILITIES: 3 en suite No smoking TVB tea/coffee No dogs (ex guide dogs) Cen ht TVL No children 5yrs **PRICES:** s £30; d £34-£40* **LB** **BB** **PARKING:** 2

HORSHAM ST FAITH Map 09 TG21

♦♦♦♦ Elm Farm Country House

55 Norwich Rd NR10 3HH ☎ 01603 898366 01603 897129

e-mail: pmpbelmfarm@aol.com

Dir: *on A140 Cromer road from Norwich, pass airport, take right turn into village*

A charming detached property in the heart of the village and just a short drive from Norwich and the airport. Bedrooms are located in an adjacent farm building which dates back to the 17th century. Breakfast is served in the main farmhouse restaurant, which is also open to non-residents for morning coffee, lunch and afternoon tea.

FACILITIES: 9 annexe en suite (2 fmly) (9 GF) No smoking TVB tea/coffee Direct dial from bedrooms No dogs (ex guide dogs) Licensed Cen ht TVL **PRICES:** s £33-£38; d £54-£58* **LB** **PARKING:** 20 **CARDS:**

HUNSTANTON Map 09 TF64

♦♦♦♦ The Gables

28 Austin St PE36 6AW ☎ 01485 532514

e-mail: bbatthegables@aol.com

Dir: *from A149 into Austin St, cross Church St, Gables at bottom of road on right at junct of Northgate/Austin St*

Expect a warm welcome at this friendly, family run guest house, situated just a short walk from the seafront and town centre. The individually decorated bedrooms are tastefully furnished and equipped with many useful extras. Breakfast is served at individual tables in the panelled dining room and guests have the use of an elegant sitting room.

FACILITIES: 5 en suite (4 fmly) No smoking STV TVB tea/coffee No dogs Cen ht TVL No coaches Dinner Last d 2pm **PRICES:** s £25; d £40-£54* **LB** **CARDS:**

♦♦♦♦ Claremont

35 Greevegate PE36 6AF ☎ 01485 533171

Dir: *off A149, turn left at Greevegate, opposite recreation ground. House is 300mtrs on right before St Edmunds church*

Spacious, family run Victorian guest house situated in a central position close to the shops, beach and gardens. The individually decorated bedrooms are tastefully furnished and have a good range of useful extras. There is a ground floor room with disabled access as well as two feature rooms, one with a four-poster, and the other a canopied bed.

FACILITIES: 7 en suite (1 fmly) (1 GF) No smoking TVB tea/coffee Cen ht TVL No children 5yrs No coaches **PRICES:** s £23-£25; d £46-£50* **LB** **PARKING:** 4 **NOTES:** Closed Xmas & New year

England

♦♦♦♦ Green Shutters

44 Cliff Pde PE36 6EH ☎ 01485 533240 Fax 01485 534874
e-mail: chris@thegreenshutters.co.uk
Dir: *exit A147 into Cliff Parade at lighthouse lane, premises 350yds past lighthouse on the left*
A warm welcome is offered at this small family run guest house situated in a wonderful location, with magnificent views of the sea and within easy walking distance of the town centre. Public rooms are decorated in warm Mediterranean colours and feature a smart dining room where breakfast is served at individual tables. The bedrooms are individually decorated, with co-ordinated soft furnishings and many thoughtful extras.
FACILITIES: 4 en suite No smoking in dining room No smoking in lounges TVB tea/coffee No dogs Cen ht No children 10yrs No coaches **PRICES:** s £35-£60; d £40-£60* **LB** **PARKING:** 4 **NOTES:** Closed 23 Dec-2 Jan **CARDS:**

♦♦♦♦ Narara House

9 Lincoln Square PE36 6DW ☎ 01485 534290
Dir: *from A149 take coast road & turn off almost opposite bowling greens into Lincoln Square*
Delightful detached Edwardian property built in traditional carrstone and dating back to 1903. Ideally placed for the beach, town centre and local amenities. The spacious bedrooms are attractively decorated and equipped with many thoughtful touches. Public rooms feature a smart lounge/dining room where freshly prepared breakfasts are served at individual tables.
FACILITIES: 5 en suite No smoking TVB tea/coffee No dogs Cen ht No children 9yrs No coaches **PRICES:** s £26-£27; d £48-£50* **LB** **PARKING:** 3 **NOTES:** Closed Xmas & New Year

♦♦♦♦ The Priory

2 Lower Lincoln St PE36 6DD ☎ 01485 532737
e-mail: mikenal@swootton86.freeserve.co.uk
Dir: *on entering Hunstanton proceed on the main A149. Opposite the entrance to the Recreation Ground turn into Greevegate, then 2nd right into Northgate. Lower Lincoln St 2nd on right, The Priory on corner overlooking Lincoln Square.*
Delightful family run guest house situated just a short walk from the sea front and town centre. The well-furnished bedrooms are pleasantly decorated, have co-ordinated soft fabrics and many thoughtful touches, some rooms have lovely sea views. Breakfast is served at individual tables in the smart dining room.
FACILITIES: 3 en suite (1 fmly) No smoking TVB tea/coffee No dogs Cen ht No children 2yrs **PRICES:** s £23-£30; d £40-£50 **LB**

♦♦♦ The White Cottage

19 Wodehouse Rd PE36 6JW ☎ 01485 532380
Charming detached cottage situated in a quiet side road in Old Hunstanton. The property has been owned and run by Mrs Burton for over 25 years. The spacious bedrooms are attractively decorated and well equipped, some rooms have lovely sea views. Dinner is served at individual pine tables in the smart dining room and guests have the use of a cosy sitting room with TV.
FACILITIES: 3 rms (1 en suite) No smoking in dining room No smoking in lounges TV1B Cen ht TVL No children 3yrs No coaches Dinner Last d 6.30pm **PRICES:** s fr £19; d fr £38* **LB** **BB** **PARKING:** 11

♦♦♦ *Richmond House Hotel*

6-8 Westgate PE36 5AL ☎ 01485 532601
Dir: *A149 Hunstanton, take 2nd exit at 1st rdbt, next mini island turn right, next jct, 3rd property on right*
Large well-maintained privately owned hotel ideally situated for the seafront and town centre. Bedrooms vary in size and style but all are pleasantly decorated and well equipped, some rooms have superb sea views. Public rooms feature a smartly appointed restaurant and a cosy lounge bar. continued

FACILITIES: 13 rms (5 en suite) No smoking in dining room TVB tea/coffee No dogs Licensed Lift Cen ht No children 14yrs **NOTES:** Closed Nov-Etr

♦♦♦ Sutton House Hotel

24 Northgate PE36 6AP ☎ 01485 532552 Fax 01485 532552
e-mail: mikeemsden@totalise.co.uk
Dir: *turn left off A149 into Greevegate, 2nd turn on right by Nat West Bank. Hotel 300yds on right*
Friendly guest house, situated in a peaceful residential area close to the sea front and town centre. Bedrooms are pleasantly decorated and thoughtfully equipped, some have superb sea views. Breakfast is served at individual tables in the smart dining room and there is a cosy bar as well as a separate lounge. Dinner is available by prior arrangement.
FACILITIES: 8 en suite (2 fmly) No smoking in bedrooms No smoking in dining room TVB tea/coffee No dogs (ex guide dogs) Licensed Cen ht TVL No coaches Dinner Last d 12pm **PRICES:** s £40; d £56* **LB** **PARKING:** 5 **CARDS:**

♦♦♦ Rosamaly

14 Glebe Av PE36 6BS ☎ 01485 534187
e-mail: vacancies@rosamaly.co.uk
Dir: *from Kings Lynn take A149 to Hunstanton. At rdbt take 3rd exit staying on A149 towards Cromer. In 1m telephone box on left, Glebe Ave next left, Rosamaly is 50mts on left*
FACILITIES: 6 en suite (2 fmly) No smoking in bedrooms No smoking in dining room STV TVB tea/coffee Cen ht TVL No coaches Dinner Last d 1pm **PRICES:** s £25-£46; d £44-£46* **LB** **NOTES:** Closed 24 Dec-1 Jan

KING'S LYNN — Map 09 TF62

Premier Collection

♦♦♦♦♦ Wallington Hall

PE33 0EP ☎ 01553 811567 Fax 01553 810661
e-mail: luddington@wallingtonhall.co.uk
Dir: *Off A10 left heading North 3.5 miles from Downham Market*

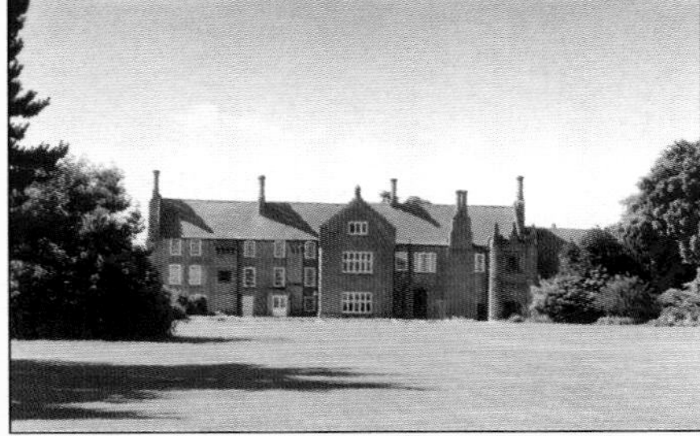

Impressive Tudor house with landscaped gardens situated in a peaceful rural location. The individually decorated bedrooms are extremely spacious, have attractive co-ordinated soft furnishings and an abundance of useful extras. Breakfast is served at a large communal table in the panelled dining room.
FACILITIES: 3 en suite (2 fmly) No smoking in bedrooms No smoking in dining room No smoking in 1 lounge TVB tea/coffee No dogs (ex guide dogs) Cen ht TVL No coaches Outdoor swimming pool (heated) Tennis (hard) Fishing Riding Croquet lawn badminton **PRICES:** s £50; d £80* **PARKING:** 10 **CARDS:**

If an establishment name appears in *italics*, details have not been confirmed for 2003.

England

KING'S LYNN continued

♦♦♦♦ Fairlight Lodge

79 Goodwins Rd PE30 5PE ☎ 01553 762234 📠 01553 770280
e-mail: joella@nash42.freeserve.co.uk
Dir: *from A17/A10/A47 rdbt turn off into Vancouver Ave via South Gate rdbt. Lodge across mini rdbt into Goodwins Rd, house 700yds on left*
Conveniently located on the outskirts of King's Lynn, in its own attractive gardens, this well maintained Victorian guest house offers bedrooms with carefully appointed well co-ordinated soft furnishings. Public areas are limited to a small dining room, in which freshly prepared and tasty breakfasts are served; service is both friendly and attentive.
FACILITIES: 5 rms (1 en suite) 3 annexe en suite (1 fmly) (4 GF) No smoking TVB tea/coffee Cen ht No coaches **PRICES:** s £22-£27; d £38-£44* BB **PARKING:** 6 **NOTES:** Closed 24 Dec-2 Jan

♦♦♦ Guanock Hotel

South Gate PE30 5QJ ☎ 01553 772959 📠 01553 772959
Dir: *follow signs to town centre, hotel immediately on right of South Gates*
A friendly, family run guest house situated just inside the town gate, within easy walking distance of the shops. Although bedrooms vary in size and style they are all suitably equipped. Public areas include a comfortable lounge bar, a pool room and a cheerful dining room where breakfast and evening meals are served.
FACILITIES: 17 rms (5 fmly) No smoking in 8 bedrooms No smoking in dining room STV TVB tea/coffee No dogs (ex guide dogs) Licensed Cen ht Pool Table Dinner Last d on booking **PRICES:** s £22-£25; d £38-£40* BB **PARKING:** 12 **CARDS:**

♦♦♦ Maranatha Guest House

115/117 Gaywood Rd PE30 2PU ☎ 01553 774596
📠 01553 763747
Formerly two separate dwellings, this Victorian house is located opposite King Edward School, a few minutes' walk from the town centre. A selection of practically equipped bedrooms is provided and breakfasts are taken in an attractive dining room, which also contains a lounge area.
FACILITIES: 10 rms (6 en suite) (3 fmly) No smoking in 5 bedrooms No smoking in dining room No smoking in lounges TVB tea/coffee Cen ht TVL Pool Table **PRICES:** s fr £20; d £36-£44* BB **PARKING:** 12
CARDS:

MUNDESLEY — Map 09 TG33

♦♦♦ Manor Hotel

Beach Rd NR11 8BG ☎ 01263 720309 📠 01263 721731
Dir: *at junct of B1150 & B1159*
Late Victorian property ideally situated on the clifftop with superb views of the sea. The hotel has been owned and run by the same family for over 30 years and retains many of its original features in the public rooms. There is a choice of bars and lounges as well as the traditionally furnished restaurant offering a wide range of imaginative dishes. The comfortable bedrooms are pleasantly decorated and equipped with modern facilities.
FACILITIES: 23 en suite 4 annexe en suite (3 fmly) No smoking in dining room No smoking in 1 lounge TVB tea/coffee Cen ht TVL Outdoor swimming pool (heated) Dinner Last d 8.50pm **PRICES:** s £50-£52; d £75-£80* **CONF:** Thtr 40 Board 20 Del from £100 * **PARKING:** 40 **NOTES:** Closed 2-18 Jan **CARDS:**

NEATISHEAD — Map 09 TG32

♦♦♦♦ Regency

The Street NR12 8AD ☎ 01692 630233 📠 01692 630233
e-mail: wrigleyregency@talk21.com
Dir: *Neatishead is 1m off A1151, between Wroxham & Stalham*
A warm welcome is to be expected at this charming 17th-century property, situated in the heart of this picturesque village close to the Norfolk Broads. Bedrooms are attractively decorated with co-ordinated soft furnishings and many thoughtful touches. Breakfast is served at individual tables in the smart dining room and guests also have the use of two comfortable lounges.
FACILITIES: 5 rms (3 en suite) (1 fmly) No smoking in dining room No smoking in lounges TVB tea/coffee No coaches **PRICES:** s £30-£35; d £44-£50* LB **PARKING:** 6

NORTH WALSHAM — Map 09 TG22

Premier Collection

♦♦♦♦♦ White House Farm *(TG302341)*

NR28 0RX ☎ 01263 721344 📠 01263 721344
Mr & Mrs C Goodhead
e-mail: goodhead@whfarm.swinternet.co.uk
Dir: *take B1145 from North Walsham towards Mundsley. In Knapton after sharp right bend, farm is on the left opposite the water tower.*
Expect a warm welcome from the caring hosts at this delightful 18th-century house, which is set in a peaceful rural location sur rounded by open farmland. The house has been sympathetically restored and retains many original features. Bedrooms are attractively decorated, tastefully furnished and equipped with many thoughtful touches. Breakfast is served in the smart dining room and guests also have the use of a cosy lounge.
FACILITIES: 3 en suite (1 fmly) No smoking TVB tea/coffee No dogs (ex guide dogs) Cen ht TVL 400 acres arable Dinner Last d 10am **PRICES:** s £30; d £40-£48* LB **PARKING:** 6 **CARDS:**

♦♦♦♦ Green Ridges

104 Cromer Rd NR28 0HE ☎ 01692 402448 📠 01692 402448
e-mail: admin@greenridges.com
Dir: *on A149 Cromer Rd out of North Walsham directly opposite left onto B1145 to Aylsham*
Expect a warm welcome from the caring host at this delightful detached property, situated on the edge of the town centre. Bedrooms are pleasantly decorated, attractively furnished and thoughtfully equipped. Breakfast is served at individual tables in the smart dining room and imaginative home cooked dinners are available by prior arrangement.
FACILITIES: 3 en suite (1 fmly) No smoking in bedrooms No smoking in dining room No smoking in lounges TVB tea/coffee Cen ht No coaches **PRICES:** s £20-£30; d £40-£50* **PARKING:** 6

NORWICH — Map 05 TG20

See also Stoke Holy Cross

Premier Collection

♦♦♦♦♦ Catton Old Hall

Lodge Ln, Old Catton NR6 7HG ☎ 01603 419379
📠 01603 400339
e-mail: enquiries@catton-hall.co.uk
Dir: *from A11 take signs for airport. Keep on road until B1150 on left. Follow road over traffic lights. Left into White Woman Ln. At traffic lights left into Lodge Ln*
Expect a warm welcome from the caring hosts at this delightful Jacobean house, which is ideally placed for the city centre and airport. The property has an abundance of original features such as flint, oak timbers and reclaimed Caen stone. The individually decorated bedrooms are tastefully appointed, offer a high degree of comfort and a wealth of personal touches. The elegant public areas include a lovely dining room and a cosy lounge with plush furnishings.

continued

FACILITIES: 7 en suite No smoking in bedrooms No smoking in dining room STV TVB tea/coffee Direct dial from bedrooms No dogs Licensed Cen ht TVL No children 12yrs No coaches Jacuzzi Dinner Last d 6pm **PRICES:** s £65-£70; d £70-£120✳ **LB PARKING:** 11 **NOTES:** Closed 15 Dec-5 Jan **CARDS:**

♦♦♦♦ Beaufort Lodge

62 Earlham Rd NR2 3DF ☎ 01603 627928 📠 01603 440712
e-mail: beaufortlodge@aol.com
Dir: *A11 left into Unthank road (1st turning on leaving dual carriageway) follow for 2m to 3rd set of lights, straight to Earlham road, Beaufort Lodge 0.25m ahead on left*

This attractive Victorian property is situated within easy walking distance of the city centre. The spacious bedrooms are tastefully decorated with co-ordinated soft furnishings and have many thoughtful touches. Public rooms feature a smart dining room where breakfast is served at individual tables. Please note: this is a no-smoking establishment.
FACILITIES: 4 en suite No smoking TVB tea/coffee No dogs Cen ht No children 18yrs No coaches **PRICES:** s £40-£45; d £50-£55✳ **PARKING:** 6 **NOTES:** Closed 28 Dec-2 Jan rs Xmas

♦♦♦♦ Gables

527 Earlham Rd NR4 7HN ☎ 01603 456666 📠 01603 250320
Dir: *turn off Southern bypass onto B1108, follow signs to University of East Anglia, 300yds on left pass Fiveways rdbt, towards city centre*

Friendly family run guest house ideally situated close to the University of East Anglia and just a short drive from the new hospital. The spacious bedrooms are individually decorated, comfortably furnished and thoughtfully equipped. Public rooms include an attractive conservatory dining room, a lounge and first floor games room with a full sized snooker table.
FACILITIES: 11 en suite (1 fmly) (5 GF) No smoking TVB tea/coffee Direct dial from bedrooms No dogs (ex guide dogs) Cen ht TVL No coaches **PRICES:** s £42-£47; d £62-£67 **PARKING:** 11 **NOTES:** Closed 20 Dec-1 Jan **CARDS:**

♦♦♦♦ Old Thorn Barn

Corporation Farm, Wymondham Rd, Hethel NR14 8EU
☎ 01953 607785 📠 08707 066409
e-mail: enquires@oldthornbarn.co.uk
Dir: *6m S of Norwich & 3m E of Wymondham on B1135. Follow signs for Lotus Cars from A11 or B1113*

A warm welcome is offered at this charming Grade II listed barn situated in a peaceful rural location, just a short drive from the city centre. The property has been sympathetically converted and features attractively decorated, thoughtfully equipped bedrooms with polished wood floors and antique pine furniture. Breakfast is served at individual oak tables in the open plan long barn, which also has a wood-burning stove and a cosy lounge area.
FACILITIES: 5 en suite (5 GF) No smoking TVB tea/coffee No dogs (ex guide dogs) Cen ht TVL No coaches **PRICES:** s £31-£35; d £48-£50✳ **PARKING:** 10 **CARDS:**

♦♦♦♦ Carr House

Low Rd, Strumpshaw NR13 4HT ☎ 01603 713041
e-mail: margotdunham@supanet.com
Dir: *from Norwich on A47 towards Gt Yarmouth turn right to Brundall, follow signs for RSPB to Low Rd. Right & follow by-way sign 100yds to House*

Ideally situated amidst attractive well-tended gardens and only 15 minutes from the city centre and Norfolk Broads. Bedrooms are cheerfully decorated and thoughtfully equipped with many useful extras. Breakfast is served in the attractive dining room overlooking the garden and private fishing lake. Guests also have the use of a cosy sitting room.
FACILITIES: 3 en suite (1 fmly) No smoking in bedrooms No smoking in dining room TVB tea/coffee Cen ht No coaches Fishing Bird watching Boat hire **PRICES:** s £25-£35; d £40-£50 **PARKING:** 6

♦♦♦♦ *Earlham*

147 Earlham Rd NR2 3RG ☎ 01603 454169 📠 01603 454169
e-mail: earlhamgh@hotmail.com
Dir: *from southern by-pass A47 take B1108 & follow City Centre signs. Over 2 rbts, guest house on left after Earlham House Shopping Centre*

A welcoming, attractive Victorian house which is situated just a short walk from the city centre. The smartly decorated bedrooms are well equipped and come in a variety of styles. Breakfast is served at individual tables in the dining room and guests also have the use of a small first-floor lounge.
FACILITIES: 7 rms (2 en suite) (1 fmly) No smoking TVB tea/coffee No dogs Cen ht TVL No children 10yrs No coaches **NOTES:** Closed 23-26 Dec **CARDS:**

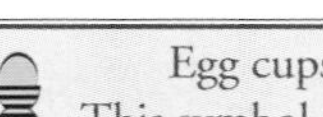

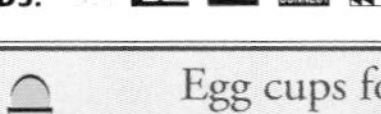

Egg cups for excellence!
This symbol shows that breakfast exceeded our Inspector's expectations.

NORWICH continued

◆◆◆◆ Arbor Linden Lodge

Linden House, 557 Earlham Rd NR4 7HW ☎ 01603 451303 01603 250641
e-mail: info@guesthousenorwich.com
Dir: *off A47 onto B1108 towards Norwich centre. Through 2 sets of traffic lights, over next rdbt. Guest house 1st left immediately over rdbt*
FACILITIES: 6 en suite (1 fmly) (1 GF) No smoking TVB tea/coffee Direct dial from bedrooms No dogs Cen ht **PRICES:** s £32-£38; d £47-£52* **LB PARKING:** 6 **CARDS:**

◆◆◆◆ Marsham Arms Inn

Holt Rd NR10 5NP ☎ 01603 754268 01603 754839
e-mail: nigelbradley@marshamarms.co.uk
Dir: *follow signs from Norwich to Norwich Airport. Past airport at rdbt Left onto B1149 to Horsford. Through Hornsford, after 2m establishment on right*
FACILITIES: 10 annexe en suite (8 fmly) No smoking in 8 bedrooms No smoking in dining room TVB tea/coffee Direct dial from bedrooms No dogs (ex guide dogs) Cen ht Dinner Last d 9.30pm **PRICES:** s £45-£50; d £65-£75* **LB MEALS:** Lunch £15-£20&alc Dinner £15-£20&alc*
PARKING: 100 **CARDS:**

◆◆◆ Arrandale Lodge

431 Earlham Rd NR4 7HL ☎ 01603 250150 01603 250150
Expect a friendly welcome at this detached property set in well-tended gardens just a short drive from the city centre. The smartly decorated bedrooms are generally quite spacious, pleasantly furnished and thoughtfully equipped. Breakfast is served at individual tables in the attractive dining room.
FACILITIES: 7 rms (4 en suite) (3 GF) No smoking TVB tea/coffee No dogs (ex guide dogs) Cen ht No coaches **PRICES:** s £25; d £45*
PARKING: 12 **NOTES:** Closed Xmas

◆◆◆ Chesters Restaurant & Guesthouse

Main Rd, Swardeston NR14 8AD ☎ 01508 570373 01508 570373
Dir: *off A147 onto B1113 establishment in 1st village*
This is a popular seafood restaurant with rooms situated just a short drive from the city centre. The smartly appointed public rooms include a large restaurant and a comfortable lounge/bar with leather Chesterfields. The pleasantly decorated bedrooms are generally quite spacious and equipped with modern facilities.
FACILITIES: 4 en suite (3 fmly) No smoking TVB tea/coffee No dogs (ex guide dogs) Licensed Cen ht TVL Dinner Last d 9pm **PRICES:** s £29.50; d £39.50* **LB PARKING:** 50 **CARDS:**

◆◆◆ Church Farm

Church St, Horsford NR10 3DB ☎ 01603 898020 01603 891649
e-mail: churchfarmguesthouse@btopenworld.co.uk
Dir: *from A11 take signs for airport, turn left onto B1149, then at 1st x-rds (Yeast & Feast PH on corner) turn into Church St*
Expect a friendly welcome at this large detached property situated in a peaceful rural location just a short drive from the airport and city centre. The spacious bedrooms are smartly decorated and equipped with many thoughtful extras. Breakfast is served at individual tables in the attractive dining room and guests also have the use of a comfortable TV lounge.
FACILITIES: 9 en suite (2 fmly) No smoking in dining room TVB tea/coffee No dogs (ex guide dogs) Cen ht TVL No coaches **PRICES:** s £25-£30; d £45-£50* **PARKING:** 20 **CARDS:**

◆◆◆ The Larches

345 Aylsham Rd NR3 2RU ☎ 01603 415420 01603 414422
Dir: *on A140 500yds past ring road, on left adjacent to Lloyds Bank*
Modern, detached property situated just off the outer ring road yet within easy driving distance of the city centre and airport. The cheerfully decorated bedrooms are generally quite spacious; each room is pleasantly furnished and thoughtfully equipped. Public rooms include a cosy lounge and a smart dining room with additional lounge seating. Dinner is available by prior arrangement.
FACILITIES: 4 en suite (1 fmly) No smoking in area of dining room No smoking in 1 lounge STV TVB tea/coffee Cen ht TVL No coaches Dinner Last d 8pm **PRICES:** s fr £29.50; d fr £39.50* **PARKING:** 10 **CARDS:**

◆◆◆ Harvey House

50 Harvey Ln NR7 0AQ ☎ 01603 436575 01603 436575
e-mail: harvey.house@which.net
Dir: *from Norwich Thorpe station take A1242 towards Gt. Yarmouth. At 1st main road junct turn left at traffic lights into Harvey Ln, 0.5m on right*
Expect a warm welcome at this friendly, family-run guest house, which is situated close to the city centre. Bedrooms are pleasantly decorated, thoughtfully equipped and offer a good degree of comfort. Breakfast is taken at individual tables in the smart dining room and guests have use of a cosy lounge. Please note this is a no-smoking establishment.
FACILITIES: 4 en suite No smoking TVB tea/coffee No dogs (ex guide dogs) Cen ht No children 3yrs No coaches **PRICES:** s £23-£26; d £39-£43*
LB PARKING: 6

◆◆◆ Marlborough House Hotel

22 Stracey Rd, Thorpe Rd NR1 1EZ ☎ 01603 628005 01603 628005
Dir: *adjacent to Norwich railway station on A47, Thorpe to Yarmouth rd*
Conveniently situated for the railway station and football ground yet just a short walk from the city centre. Bedrooms are pleasantly decorated, soundly maintained and equipped with modern facilities. Public rooms feature an open plan lounge-dining area with a corner bar. Dinner is available by prior arrangement.
FACILITIES: 12 rms (7 en suite) (2 fmly) (1 GF) No smoking in 3 bedrooms No smoking in area of dining room No smoking in 1 lounge TVB tea/coffee Licensed Cen ht TVL Dinner Last d 4.30pm **PRICES:** s £26-£36; d £45-£48* **LB PARKING:** 5

◆◆ Rosedale

145 Earlham Rd NR2 3RG ☎ 01603 453743 01603 259887
e-mail: drcbac@aol.com
Dir: *from city centre on B1108, just passed St Thomas church on right*
FACILITIES: 6 rms (2 fmly) No smoking TVB tea/coffee No dogs Cen ht No children 4yrs **PRICES:** s £20-£25; d £38-£44* **BB CARDS:**

SAXLINGHAM THORPE — Map 05 TM29

◆◆◆◆ Foxhole Farm *(TM218971)*

Foxhole NR15 1UG ☎ 01508 499226 01508 499226
Mr & Mrs J N O Spear
e-mail: foxholefarm@hotmail.com
Dir: *Foxhole is signposted 100yds S of village of Newton Flotman & immediately prior to the Mill Inn on A140, Norwich-Ipswich road. The farm is 0.75m east off A140.*
Delightful farmhouse set amidst its own pretty gardens in a peaceful rural location surrounded by open farmland. The attractive bedrooms have co-ordinated soft furnishings and are thoughtfully equipped with many useful extras. Freshly cooked breakfast is taken at a large communal table in the smart dining room.
FACILITIES: 2 en suite No smoking TVB tea/coffee No dogs Cen ht No children 14yrs Barn games room 5 acres non-working **PRICES:** s £25; d £38-£42* **BB PARKING:** 8 **NOTES:** Closed 15 Dec-1 Jan

SHERINGHAM Map 09 TG14

♦♦♦♦ Fairlawns

26 Hooks Hill Rd NR26 8NL ☎ 01263 824717 📠 01263 824115

Dir: *from A149 turn into Holt Road opposite Police Station then 2nd left and at T-junct turn right*

This charming Victorian guest house sits in attractive grounds in a secluded cul-de-sac, just a few minutes from the town centre and the beach. Bedrooms are well equipped, with a good range of useful extras. Public areas include a comfortable lounge with a small corner bar. There is also a lovely garden with a croquet pitch. As Fairlawns has a Heartbeat award, guests are assured of a healthy cooked breakfast, dinner is also available by prior arrangement.

FACILITIES: 5 en suite No smoking in bedrooms No smoking in dining room TVB tea/coffee No dogs (ex guide dogs) Licensed Cen ht TVL No coaches Croquet lawn Putting green Dinner Last d noon **PRICES:** s £25-£42; d £50-£60* **LB PARKING:** 6 **NOTES:** Closed Dec-Jan rs Feb & Nov

♦♦♦♦ Highfield

5 Montague Rd NR26 8LN ☎ 01263 825524

Dir: *leave A148, left at mini r/about, then first right. Turn left at the church, then left into South St, which becomes Montague Rd. House is on left*

Highfield Guest House is situated in a quiet side road and is just a short walk from the town centre and beach. This delightfully furnished house offers well-equipped bedrooms and a hearty breakfast. The charming Mrs Caldwell provides good hospitality to her guests.

FACILITIES: 7 rms (6 en suite) (3 fmly) No smoking TVB tea/coffee No dogs (ex guide dogs) Cen ht TVL No children 7yrs **PRICES:** s fr £30; d £46-£50* **LB PARKING:** 4 **NOTES:** Closed 2 wks in Nov

♦♦♦♦ Homefield Guest House

48 Cromer Rd, West Runton NR27 9AD ☎ 01263 837337 📠 0870 134 2544

e-mail: bandb-norfolk@icscotland.net

Dir: *on the A149 Sheringham to Cromer road. Just past shops at West Runton, on the right, corner of A149 and Rosebury Rd*

Imposing detached property dating back to 1890 situated on the A149 in the village of West Runton. Bedrooms are cheerfully decorated in pastel shades, have attractive co-ordinated fabrics and well-chosen furniture, some rooms have superb sea views. Breakfast is served in the smart dinning room seated at individual tables and traditional Russian cuisine is available for dinner.

FACILITIES: 6 en suite (1 fmly) No smoking in bedrooms No smoking in dining room TVB tea/coffee No dogs (ex guide dogs) Cen ht TVL Dinner Last d 7pm **PRICES:** s £30; d £50* **LB PARKING:** 14

♦♦♦♦ Knollside Lodge

43 Cliff Rd NR26 8BJ ☎ 01263 823320 📠 01263 823320

e-mail: millar@knollside.free-online.co.uk

Dir: *A148-A1082 towards sea over rdbt. Turn right into Wyndham St, Cliff Rd is opposite on a staggered junct. Hotel on left before putting green*

continued

Guests can expect a warm welcome at this Victorian house, which sits above the beach. Bedrooms are generally spacious and have many useful extras. Breakfast is served in the elegant dining room and includes locally sourced and home-made products. The cosy lounge has a range of books and games and a small bar lounge is planned.

FACILITIES: 3 en suite (1 fmly) No smoking TVB tea/coffee No dogs Cen ht No children 2yrs No coaches Dinner **PRICES:** s £55-£60* **LB PARKING:** 3

♦♦♦♦ Providence Place

6 The Boulevard NR26 8LJ ☎ 01263 821034 📠 01263 824477

e-mail: providenceplace@btinternet.com

Dir: *off A148 signposted Sheringham. Down hill, straight over at rdbt, 1st left into Railway Approach, 2nd right into St Peters Rd and continue over next junct into The Boulevard. Providence Place is on corner of Morris St*

A very well maintained and welcoming Victorian house, located close to the seafront. Many original internal features have been retained, and these are enhanced by the quality furnishing and décor styles throughout. The homely bedrooms include a magnificent four-poster suite and a ground floor room.

FACILITIES: 3 en suite No smoking TVB tea/coffee No dogs Cen ht No children 8yrs No coaches **PRICES:** s £40-£45; d £50-£70* **PARKING:** 3 **NOTES:** Closed Xmas & New Year

♦♦♦♦ The Birches

27 Holway Rd NR26 8HW ☎ 01263 823550

Dir: *on A1082 into Sheringham. Next to Baptist church, 3 mins walk from railway station*

Expect a warm, family welcome at this small guest house, situated within easy walking distance of the beach, railway station and town centre. The bedrooms are attractively decorated, well equipped and feature many personal touches. Breakfast is served in the dining room/lounge and evening meals are available by prior arrangement.

FACILITIES: 2 en suite No smoking TVB tea/coffee No dogs (ex guide dogs) Cen ht No children 12yrs No coaches Dinner **PRICES:** s £30; d £52* **PARKING:** 2 **NOTES:** Closed Oct-Apr

♦♦♦♦ Willow Lodge

6 Vicarage Rd NR26 8NH ☎ 01263 822204 📠 01263 822204

Dir: *From A148 Holt to Cromer road, A1082 to Sheringham town, rdbt left on A149 towards Weybourne/Blakeney. 1st left B1157 signed Upper Sheringham, 2nd left to Vicarage Road.*

This detached house is set in a quiet and leafy part of the town and yet only a short walk from all amenities. Willow Lodge is very well-furnished throughout and public areas include an extremely comfortable lounge. The house provides smart and well-equipped bedrooms.

FACILITIES: 5 en suite (2 fmly) (1 GF) No smoking TVB tea/coffee No dogs Cen ht TVL No children 5yrs No coaches **PRICES:** d £50-£56* **PARKING:** 7 **CARDS:**

England

SHERINGHAM continued

♦♦♦ Bayleaf
10 Saint Peters Rd NR26 8QY ☎ 01263 823779
📠 01263 820041
e-mail: thebayleaf@bushinternet.com
Dir: *A148 onto A1082, turn left into Station Approach, house opposite steam railway platform*
A short walk from Sheringham golf course, the steam railway and town centre, this pleasant Victorian house offers a warm welcome. There is a popular bar and breakfast is served in the dining room overlooking the patio. The proprietors are keen golfers and are happy to take golfing parties.
FACILITIES: 7 en suite (2 fmly) (2 GF) No smoking TVB tea/coffee No dogs (ex guide dogs) Licensed Cen ht TVL No children 8yrs **PRICES:** d £50-£55* **LB** **PARKING:** 4 **NOTES:** Closed Xmas

♦♦♦ Camberley House
62 Cliff Rd NR26 8BJ ☎ 01263 823101 📠 01263 821433
e-mail: graham@camberleyguesthouse.co.uk
Dir: *head towards seafront, turn right at Lobster Pub into Wyndham St, continue down street into Cliff Rd & entrance opposite putting green*
FACILITIES: 4 en suite (2 fmly) No smoking in dining room TVB tea/coffee No dogs Cen ht TVL No coaches **PRICES:** s £25-£32; d £40-£54* **LB** **PARKING:** 6 **NOTES:** Closed Xmas & New year

SNETTISHAM — Map 09 TF63

♦♦♦♦ Rose & Crown
Old Church Rd PE31 7LX ☎ 01485 541382 📠 01485 543172
e-mail: roseandcrown@btclick.com
Dir: *N from King's Lynn on A149 signed to Hunstanton. Inn in centre of Snettisham between market square & church*
A delightful 14th-century inn situated close to some of west Norfolk's most beautiful beaches. Public rooms include a choice of dining areas as well as a family room and no-smoking bar. The individually decorated bedrooms have co-ordinated soft furnishings and many thoughtful touches. A range of real ales and good wines complement the interesting choice of dishes available in the restaurant. There is an outside play area, pet menagerie and a special children's menu available.
FACILITIES: 11 en suite (2 fmly) No smoking in bedrooms No smoking in area of dining room No smoking in lounges TVB tea/coffee Direct dial from bedrooms Cen ht Dinner Last d 9pm **PRICES:** s £60; d £90* **LB** **MEALS:** Lunch £15; Dinner £25* **PARKING:** 75 **CARDS:**

STOKE HOLY CROSS — Map 05 TG20

♦♦♦ Salamanca *(TG235022)*
NR14 8QJ ☎ 01508 492322 Mr & Mrs Harrold
Dir: *at A47/A140 junction take minor road to Caistor St Edmunds, then 1st right, farm approx 1m on left*
Smart red brick farm house, parts of which date back to the 16th century, and ideally situated within easy driving distance of Norwich. The spacious bedrooms are pleasantly decorated, comfortably furnished and well equipped. Breakfast is served in a large dining room at individual tables, and guests also have the use of a cosy lounge.
FACILITIES: 3 rms (2 en suite) 1 annexe en suite No smoking TV1B tea/coffee No dogs Cen ht TVL No children 6yrs 165 acres beef mixed **PRICES:** s £26-£30; d £48-£56* **LB** **PARKING:** 7 **NOTES:** Closed 15 Dec-15 Jan & Etr

SWAFFHAM — Map 05 TF80

♦♦♦♦ Corfield House
Sporle PE32 2EA ☎ 01760 723636
e-mail: info@corfieldhouse.co.uk
Dir: *3m E of Swaffham on S edge of village, 0.5m from A47*

continued

Situated in immaculate gardens, this extended 19th century house retains many original features. Bedrooms are cosy and have the benefit of modern en suite facilities. Local produce is a feature of the comprehensive breakfast selection. A quiet lounge is available for guest use. Good levels of customer care and exemplary housekeeping are definite strengths here.
FACILITIES: 4 en suite (1 GF) No smoking TVB tea/coffee No dogs (ex guide dogs) Cen ht No coaches **PRICES:** s £30; d £49* **PARKING:** 5 **NOTES:** Closed mid Dec-mid Feb

♦♦♦ Red Lion Hotel
87 Market Place PE37 7AQ ☎ 01760 721022 📠 01760 720664
e-mail: gwhoare@aol.com
Dir: *leave A47 at Swaffham sign, to Market Place. Red Lion next to Woolworths*
This popular public house in the centre of the bustling market town has colourfully furnished, well equipped bedrooms that are located in a motel-style block to the rear of the main building. Some of the rooms are designed to take family groups. A range of snacks and meals is available in the lounge bar.
FACILITIES: 9 annexe en suite (9 GF) No smoking in dining room TVB tea/coffee No dogs (ex guide dogs) Cen ht Dinner Last d 9.30pm **PRICES:** s £30-£35; d £40-£45* **MEALS:** Lunch £4-£10.75 Dinner £4-£10.75* **PARKING:** 8 **CARDS:**

THETFORD — Map 05 TL88

♦♦♦♦ The Chequers Inn
Griston Rd IP24 1PX ☎ 01953 483360 📠 01953 488092
e-mail: themcdowalls@barbox.net
Dir: *from A11 at Thetford left to Watton at main rdbt. After 10m take 2nd left to Thompson and Inn 1m on right*
FACILITIES: 3 annexe en suite (1 fmly) No smoking in 2 bedrooms No smoking in area of dining room TVB tea/coffee Direct dial from bedrooms Licensed Cen ht Fishing Dinner Last d 9.15pm **PRICES:** s £40; d £60* **PARKING:** 35 **CARDS:**

THURNING — Map 09 TG02

♦♦ Rookery *(TG078307)*
NR24 2JP ☎ 01263 860357 Mrs A M Fisher
Dir: *leave A148 at Thursford onto B1354, through Briston, pass Green Man pub, bear right then left, then left. Farm is 1st on left after 1m*
Guests can expect a friendly welcome at this delightful 300-year-old red brick farmhouse. The accommodation features an extremely large bedroom and a further single room and is therefore ideally suited to families. The public rooms comprise a large sitting and breakfast room.
FACILITIES: 2 rms (1 en suite) (1 fmly) No smoking tea/coffee No dogs (ex guide dogs) TVL 400 acres arable Dinner Last d By arrangement **PRICES:** s £19-£20; d £38-£40* **BB** **NOTES:** Closed Dec-Jan

THURSFORD GREEN — Map 09 TF93

Premier Collection

♦♦♦♦♦ Holly Lodge
The Street NR21 0AS ☎ 01328 878465 📠 01328 878465
e-mail: hollyguestlodge@talk21.com
Dir: *leave the A148 at the Crawfish Pub, then follow signs for Thursford Green. Pass the museum. Holly Lodge is 2nd on left after Village Green*
Expect a warm welcome at this charming 18th-century property situated in a picturesque location surrounded by open farmland. The stylish bedrooms are housed in a

continued

England

Holly Lodge

converted stable block; each room is individually decorated, beautifully furnished and equipped with many useful extras. Public rooms are attractively appointed and have a wealth of charm and character, with their flagstone floors, oak beams and open fireplaces.
FACILITIES: 3 en suite No smoking TVB tea/coffee No dogs (ex guide dogs) Cen ht TVL No children 14yrs No coaches **PRICES:** s £50-£70; d £60-£80 **LB** **PARKING:** 6 **NOTES:** Closed 18 Dec-18 Mar

WALCOTT — Map 09 TG33

Premier Collection

♦♦♦♦♦ Holly Tree Cottage
Walcott Green, Walcott NR12 0NS ☎ 01692 650721
Dir: *from Walcott church B1159 towards Stalham, straight on at x-roads, 1st left at Hollyhocks Nursery, then 2nd left, right at pond, house on right*

Charming cottage set in a peaceful countryside setting within easy driving distance of the Norfolk Broads and the seaside. The bedrooms are spacious and attractively decorated throughout. Breakfast is served in the smart dining room and there is also a cosy snug with a wood-burning stove.
FACILITIES: 3 en suite No smoking TVB tea/coffee No dogs Cen ht No children 18yrs No coaches **PRICES:** s £29; d £48 **PARKING:** 4 **NOTES:** Closed Oct-mid Apr

WELLS-NEXT-THE-SEA — Map 09 TF94

♦♦♦ Branthill Farm *(TF900407)*
NR23 1SB ☎ 01328 710246 01328 711524 Mrs Maufe
e-mail: branthill.farms@appleonline.net
Dir: *A1065 (Fakenham-Cromer), turn left for Wells and then first left. After 6m, Dalgety Arable on left, after 0.75m take second turning on left*
A friendly family run farmhouse situated in a peaceful rural

continued

location just a short drive from Wells-next-the-Sea. A hearty breakfast is served at the large communal table in the attractive dining room. The one letting bedroom is equipped with many useful extras and offers a good degree of comfort.
FACILITIES: 1 en suite No smoking TVB tea/coffee No dogs Cen ht No children 12yrs Outdoor swimming pool (heated) Tennis (hard) 1000 acres arable **PRICES:** d £43-£45✳ **PARKING:** 2

WROXHAM — Map 09 TG31

♦♦♦♦ Bramble House
Cats Common, Norwich Rd, Smallburgh NR12 9NS
☎ 01692 535069 01692 535069
e-mail: bramblehouse@tesco.net
Dir: *A1151 to Wroxham, follow signs to Stalham, 1m past Beeston St Lawrence church enter layby on left for Cats Common. House 150mtrs on left*
Delightful detached property, situated in a peaceful rural location just a short drive from the busy town centre. The individually decorated bedrooms are tastefully furnished and thoughtfully equipped, one room has a private sauna. Breakfast, which includes home produced free-range eggs and locally sourced items, is served at individual tables in the smart dining room.
FACILITIES: 3 en suite (1 fmly) No smoking TVB tea/coffee No dogs (ex guide dogs) Cen ht TVL No coaches Sauna **PRICES:** s £30-£35; d £46-£50✳ **LB** **PARKING:** 6 **NOTES:** Closed Xmas/New Year

♦♦♦♦ Park Lodge
142 Norwich Rd NR12 8SA ☎ 01603 782991
e-mail: prklodge@nascr.net
Dir: *take A1151 from Norwich, once in Wroxham pass Shell garage on left, over pelican crossing and lodge on left*
FACILITIES: 3 en suite No smoking in bedrooms No smoking in dining room TVB tea/coffee Cen ht No coaches **PRICES:** s £22-£28; d £40-£48✳ **PARKING:** 4 **NOTES:** Closed early Nov

♦♦♦ Beech Tree House
Wroxham Rd, Rackheath NR13 6NQ
☎ 01603 781419 & 07889 152063 01603 781419
e-mail: beechtree@talk21.com
Dir: *leave Norwich on A1151 towards Wroxham, house on right after approx 4m opposite Green Man public house*
Detached property surrounded by open farmland just a short drive from Wroxham Broads and Norwich City centre. The spacious bedrooms are pleasantly decorated with co-ordinated soft furnishings and many useful extras. Breakfast is served in the sunny conservatory, which overlooks the extensive well-tended gardens.
FACILITIES: 3 rms (1 en suite) (3 fmly) No smoking in bedrooms No smoking in dining room No smoking in lounges TVB tea/coffee Cen ht TVL No coaches Tennis (grass) Jacuzzi **PRICES:** s £25; d £30✳ **LB BB** **PARKING:** 5 **NOTES:** Closed 23 Dec-1 Jan

WYMONDHAM — Map 05 TG10

♦♦♦♦ Witch Hazel
Church Ln, Wicklewood NR18 9QH ☎ 01953 602247
01953 602247
Dir: *from A11 exit B1135 East Dereham (not Mulbarton). Follow signs for B1135 cross rail bridge, fork left immediately after humped back bridge, along this rd past Cherry Tree PH, then next right at the X-rds. Establishment approx 200mtrs on right*
FACILITIES: 3 en suite No smoking TVB tea/coffee No dogs Cen ht No children 15yrs Dinner Last d 10.30am **PRICES:** s £26-£28; d £40-£44✳ **PARKING:** 3

NORTHAMPTONSHIRE

CORBY — Map 04 SP88

♦♦♦♦ Thatches on the Green

School Ln, Weldon NN17 3JN ☎ 01536 266681
01536 266659
e-mail: tom@thatches-on-the-green.fsnet.co.uk
Dir: *on old A43 opposite "The Woolpack" on village green*

Located at Weldon, by the village green, this former 16th cenrury inn and adjoining cottages has been sympathetically renovated to provide comfortable thoughtfully equipped bedrooms, one of which has two en suite shower rooms. Breakfast and imaginative dinners are taken in the attractive dining room, which also contains a small bar.

FACILITIES: 10 rms (9 en suite) (1 fmly) (4 GF) No smoking in bedrooms No smoking in dining room TVB tea/coffee Licensed Cen ht TVL Dinner Last d by arrangement **PRICES:** s £30-£45; d £60-£70✳ **LB PARKING:** 15 **CARDS:**

♦♦ Raven Hotel

Rockingham Rd NN17 1AG ☎ 01536 202313 01536 203159
e-mail: ravenhotel@hotmail.com
Dir: *A6003 towards Rockingham right into Rockingham Road hotel right after shopping parade.*

A haven for music lovers, the public areas consist of Peppers bar, filled with a wealth of Beatles memorabilia and a spacious comfortable Piano bar where a wide range of popular drinks and bar meals are served. Bedrooms are modern in style and popular with contractors and weekend sports groups.

FACILITIES: 17 rms (5 en suite) (3 fmly) No smoking in 2 bedrooms No smoking in area of dining room TVB tea/coffee No dogs (ex guide dogs) Cen ht TVL Pool Table Dinner Last d 8.45pm **PRICES:** s £30-£50; d £35-£55; (room only) ✳ **BB MEALS:** Bar Lunch £2.75-£6 Dinner £9-£15✳ **PARKING:** 40 **CARDS:**

KETTERING — Map 04 SP87

♦♦♦♦ Wold Farm

Old Village NN6 9RJ ☎ 01604 781258 01604 781258
Dir: *from A14 take A43 towards Northampton, right at 1st rdbt , signed Old, then 1st left into village, house on corner of village green*

FACILITIES: 2 rms (1 en suite) 3 annexe en suite (1 GF) No smoking TV2B tea/coffee Cen ht TVL No coaches **PRICES:** s £25-£28; d £50-£56✳ **PARKING:** 6

♦♦♦ Pennels

175 Beatrice Rd NN16 9QR ☎ 01536 481940 & 07713 899508 01536 410798
e-mail: pennelsgh@aol.com
Dir: *A14 J7, A43 (Corby/Stamford), at rdbt follow signs to Kettering. 1st left past football ground. 1st left again. House at top of hill*

Located within easy walking distance of the town centre and football ground, this constantly improving guest house provides a range of thoughtfully equipped bedrooms, some of which have direct access to the immaculate walled garden. Comprehensive breakfasts are taken in a cosy dining room and a warm welcome is assured.

FACILITIES: 7 rms (5 en suite) (2 fmly) No smoking in bedrooms No smoking in dining room No smoking in lounges STV TVB tea/coffee No dogs (ex guide dogs) Cen ht TVL No coaches Dinner Last d 6pm **PRICES:** s £25-£35; d £45-£50✳ **LB CONF:** Class 10 Del from £40 ✳ **PARKING:** 10 **CARDS:**

NORTHAMPTON — Map 04 SP76

♦♦♦♦ Green Park Hotel

477 Wellingbrough Rd NN3 3HN ☎ 01604 716777
01604 719888
e-mail: info@greenpark-hotel.co.uk
Dir: *end of Wellingborough Rd, 1m from town centre facing Abington Park, 300yds E from County Cricket ground*

Located opposite Abington Park a few minutes walk from the County Cricket Ground, this totally refurbished hotel offers comfortable bedrooms with a range of practical facilities. Ground floor areas include an attractive dining room and a guest lounge with vending bar. An illuminated rear car park and automatic lift are additional benefits.

FACILITIES: 24 rms (21 en suite) (8 fmly) No smoking in area of dining room TVB tea/coffee No dogs (ex guide dogs) Licensed Lift Cen ht TVL **PRICES:** s £45; d £60✳ **LB PARKING:** 7 **CARDS:**

♦♦♦♦ Poplars Hotel

33 Cross St, Moulton NN3 7RZ ☎ 01604 643983
01604 790233
e-mail: thepoplars.hotel@btopenworld.com
Dir: *off A43 into Moulton & follow signs for Moulton College*

Located north of the city in the pretty village of Moulton, this ivy clad period house provides traditional standards of service and hospitality. Bedrooms, some of which are located in a quality chalet extension, are filled with a good range of practical extras and character public areas include a cottage style dining room where imaginative dinners are served.

FACILITIES: 16 rms (12 en suite) (7 fmly) (5 GF) No smoking in 11 bedrooms No smoking in dining room No smoking in 1 lounge TVB tea/coffee Direct dial from bedrooms Licensed Cen ht TVL No coaches Dinner Last d 7.45pm **PRICES:** s £25-£69.50; d £55-£79.50✳ **CONF:** Thtr 16 Board 12 Del from £85 ✳ **PARKING:** 16 **NOTES:** Closed Xmas & New Year rs No dinner available Fri-Sun **CARDS:**

See advertisement on opposite page

OUNDLE Map 04 TL08

♦♦♦ Ship

18-20 West St PE8 4EF ☎ 01832 273918 📠 01832 270232
e-mail: enquiries@theshipinn-oundle.co.uk
Dir: *turn off A1 junct 17 onto A605, 9m to Oundle*
This traditional inn, centrally situated on historic Oundle's main street, has lots of atmosphere and a busy taproom with plenty of character. Bedrooms are in three buildings to the rear of the pub. Older rooms are more traditionally furnished, whilst the newer ones benefit from bright bold fabrics.
FACILITIES: 14 rms (11 en suite) (1 fmly) No smoking in area of dining room TV11B tea/coffee Cen ht TVL Dinner Last d 9pm **PRICES:** s £30-£50; d £40-£60✳ **PARKING:** 70 **CARDS:**

TITCHMARSH Map 04 TL07

♦♦♦ Wheatsheaf Inn & Hotel

1 North St NN14 3DH ☎ 01832 732203 📠 01832 731103
e-mail: wheatsheaf@clara.co.uk
Dir: *exit A14 at junct 13 signed Peterborough A605, follow Titchmarsh signs for 1m, turn right into village, Wheatsheaf is 0.5m on left*

Located in the heart of this rural village the inn and adjacent buildings date from the 17th century and retain many original features including a wealth of exposed beams. Bedrooms are sympathetically renovated from former barns or cottages and one was formally the community post office.
FACILITIES: 9 en suite 5 annexe en suite (2 fmly) (7 GF) No smoking in 10 bedrooms No smoking in dining room TVB tea/coffee No dogs (ex guide dogs) Cen ht Pool Table Dinner Last d 9.15pm **PRICES:** s £40; d £45✳ **MEALS:** Sunday Lunch £6.95-£9.95 Dinner £6.95-£10.95✳ **PARKING:** 24 **CARDS:**

WELLINGBOROUGH Map 04 SP86

♦♦♦ *Oak House Private Hotel*

8-11 Broad Green NN8 4LE ☎ 01933 271133 📠 01933 271133
Dir: *from A45 take A509 towards Kettering, hotel on edge of town near cenotaph (The Independents)*
Located within walking distance of the town centre, this conversion of three former Victorian cottages provides practically equipped bedrooms popular with a regular commercial clientele. Two separate lounges are available and both dinner and breakfast are served in the cottage-style dining room.
FACILITIES: 16 rms (15 en suite) (2 fmly) No smoking in 6 bedrooms No smoking in area of dining room No smoking in 1 lounge TVB tea/coffee Licensed Cen ht TVL Dinner Last d noon **PARKING:** 7 **NOTES:** Closed Xmas **CARDS:**

Places with this symbol are Inns.

NORTHUMBERLAND

ALNWICK Map 12 NU11

♦♦♦ Bondgate House Hotel

Bondgate Without NE66 1PN ☎ 01665 602025
📠 01665 602025
e-mail: bondgatehouse@tiscali.co.uk
Dir: *turn off A1 for town centre, hotel 200yds past war memorial on right*
Originally the doctor's house, this Georgian building stands by the old gate which leads into the town centre. Bedrooms are well maintained, furnished with quality pine, and several have attractive window seats. There is a spacious dining room and a comfortable lounge.
FACILITIES: 8 rms (5 en suite) (3 fmly) No smoking in dining room TVB tea/coffee No dogs (ex guide dogs) Licensed Cen ht TVL **PRICES:** s £25-£30; d £47-£49✳ **PARKING:** 8 **CARDS:**

BAMBURGH Map 12 NU13

♦♦♦♦ Hillside

25 Lucker Rd NE69 7BS ☎ 01668 214674 📠 01668 214674
Dir: *A1 onto B1341 follow for 5m into Bamburgh, Mizen Hotel on left Hillside opposite*
This pleasant house is located in the heart of the village within easy walking distance of the castle. Accommodation is provided in brightly decorated, attractive rooms, all of which are spacious. Hospitality is warm and hearty breakfasts can be enjoyed in the airy dining room.
FACILITIES: 3 rms (2 en suite) No smoking in bedrooms TVB tea/coffee No dogs No children 2yrs **PRICES:** s fr £25; d fr £50

England

BEADNELL Map 12 NU22

♦♦♦♦ Low Dover

Harbour Rd NE67 5BJ ☎ 01665 720291 📠 01665 720291
e-mail: kathandbob@lowdover.co.uk
Dir: *from S leave A1 at Alnwick onto B1340 to Beadnell, from N leave A1 at Belford onto B1342 through Seahouses and on towards Beadnell. Follow signpost to Beadnell Harbour, Low Dover is the last house on right, adjacent to beach*
Low Dover is just a few steps from a sandy beach and the harbour, but it is the attractive gardens, which are a blaze of colour in the summer, that first take the eye. The owners are friendly and attentive, and each bedroom has its own external entrance - patio doors leading into the garden.
FACILITIES: 2 en suite No smoking TVB tea/coffee No dogs Cen ht No children 12yrs No coaches **PRICES:** d £54-£70* **LB PARKING:** 2 **CARDS:**

BELFORD Map 12 NU13

♦♦♦♦ Market Cross

1 Church St NE70 7LS ☎ 01668 213013
e-mail: details@marketcross.net
Dir: *off A1 signposted Belford, establishment 0.5m on R next to post office*
Situated on the main village street, this fine period house offers a high standard of accommodation in rooms adorned with extra comforts. Breakfast is a delightful feature, with an excellent choice of dishes, which may include kedgeree, pancakes and griddle scones.
FACILITIES: 3 en suite No smoking TVB tea/coffee Cen ht No coaches Special rates at local golf courses **PRICES:** s £25-£45; d £45-£60* **LB PARKING:** 3 **CARDS:**

BERWICK-UPON-TWEED Map 12 NT95

♦♦♦♦ Dervaig Guest House

1 North Rd TD15 1PW ☎ 01289 307378 📠 01289 307378
e-mail: dervaig@talk21.com
Dir: *turn off A1 at A1167 (North Road) to town, last house on right before railway bridge*
Overlooking an immaculate rear garden, this detached Victorian house is located just a few minutes walk from the town centre. Bedrooms are well proportioned and tastefully furnished. The bright breakfast room features an interesting collection of plates.
FACILITIES: 5 en suite (3 fmly) No smoking in bedrooms No smoking in dining room TVB tea/coffee Cen ht No coaches **PRICES:** s £25-£40; d £50-£55* **LB PARKING:** 8 **CARDS:**

♦♦♦♦ High Steads

Lowick TD15 2QE ☎ 01289 388689 📠 01289 388689
e-mail: highstead@aol.com
Dir: *A1/B6353 to Lowick, L at Post Office, 0.5m then 1st R, house 0.5m on L*
Close to Holy Island and St Cuthbert's Way, this 18th-century Grade II listed farmhouse enjoys breathtaking views of the Cheviots and is set in four acres of Borders countryside. The house has a relaxing atmosphere. A wide choice offered at breakfast, which is taken downstairs at a large antique table. French and German are spoken.
FACILITIES: 2 en suite No smoking in bedrooms No smoking in dining room No smoking in lounges tea/coffee No dogs (ex guide dogs) Cen ht TVL No children 8yrs No coaches Croquet lawn **PRICES:** d £46-£55 **LB PARKING:** 14

♦♦♦♦ The Old Vicarage

Church Rd, Tweedmouth TD15 2AN ☎ 01289 306909
📠 01289 309052
e-mail: enquiries@oldvicarageberwick.co.uk
Dir: *from S through Tweedmouth, right at Queens Head pub, 1st left. From N through Berwick, over bridge to Tweedmouth, left at Angel Inn, 1st right*
Furnished with antiques, period pieces and stripped pine, this imposing 19th-century house has well-tended gardens and is situated in a quiet part of town. Comfortable bedrooms vary in size and contain many thoughtful touches. There is a cosy lounge with reading material and a spacious, elegant dining room.
FACILITIES: 6 rms (4 en suite) (1 fmly) (1 GF) No smoking in dining room No smoking in lounges TV7B tea/coffee Cen ht TVL **PRICES:** s £18-£20; d £36-£54* **BB PARKING:** 5 **NOTES:** Closed Xmas & New Year

CORBRIDGE Map 12 NY96

♦♦♦♦ Priorfield

Hippingstones Ln NE45 5JP ☎ 01434 633179 📠 01434 633179
e-mail: nsteenberg@btinternet.com
Dir: *from village centre through market place along Watling St past Wheatsheaf pub, 2nd right into St Helens Ln. 1st left into Hippingstones Ln, last house on right*
Jill and Nick Steenberg's Edwardian family home lies in attractive gardens, minutes from the historic village centre. The house is a showpiece for Jill's flair for interior design, which is prominent in the stylishly decorated bedrooms. Both rooms are en suite, the twin room can accommodate a family, and the double bedroom features a relaxing airbath. Hearty breakfasts include local produce. Off road parking and cycle storage is available.
FACILITIES: 2 en suite (1 fmly) No smoking TVB tea/coffee No dogs Cen ht No coaches Jacuzzi Cycle store **PRICES:** s £28-£38; d £48-£58 **PARKING:** 2

♦♦♦♦ Riverside

Main St NE45 5LE ☎ 01434 632942 📠 01434 633883
e-mail: david@theriversideguesthouse.co.uk
Dir: *turn off A68 or A69 into Corbridge. In village centre Riverside overlooks bridge, opp garage*
An 18th-century house, enjoying a prominent position in the centre of the village, with spectacular views over the River Tyne and the bridge. Providing personal hospitality from Margaret and David Fairbairn ground-floor bedrooms and family rooms are available. Breakfast is served in a spacious dining room, and there are ample parking facilities.
FACILITIES: 10 rms (7 en suite) (2 fmly) (4 GF) No smoking TVB tea/coffee Direct dial from bedrooms Cen ht No coaches **PRICES:** s £28-£44; d £45-£60* **LB PARKING:** 7 **CARDS:**

♦♦♦ The Hayes

Newcastle Rd NE45 5LP ☎ 01434 632010 📠 01434 632010
e-mail: mjct@mmatthews.fsbusiness.co.uk
Dir: *A69 or A68 to Styford rdbt take Corbridge turn off in 2m. Guest House on left, just beyond 30mph sign).*
FACILITIES: 4 rms (2 en suite) (2 fmly) No smoking in dining room No smoking in lounges TVB tea/coffee No dogs (ex guide dogs) Lift Cen ht TVL Croquet lawn **PRICES:** s £21-£35; d £42-£50* **LB PARKING:** 15 **NOTES:** Closed 23 Dec-1 Jan

England

CORNHILL-ON-TWEED Map 12 NT83

Premier Collection

♦♦♦♦♦ Ivy Cottage

1 Croft Gardens, Crookham TD12 4SY ☎ 01890 820667 Fax 01890 820667

Dir: *A697, 10m N of Wooler, R into Crookham village, 0.5m on R past village hall.*

Modern living blends with traditional home comforts at Ivy Cottage. A twin and a double room are available, both of which are furnished in antique pine and adorned with thoughtful touches. Delicious breakfasts are served either in the farmhouse style kitchen or cosy dining room, and dinner is available by prior arrangement.

FACILITIES: 2 en suite No smoking TVB tea/coffee Cen ht No children 5yrs No coaches Dinner Last d am same day **PRICES:** s £26.50-£28.50; d £53-£57✳ **LB** **PARKING:** 2

CRASTER Map 12 NU22

♦♦♦ Cottage

Dunstan Village NE66 3SZ ☎ 01665 576658 Fax 01665 576788

e-mail: enquires@cottageinnhotel.co.uk

Dir: *follow coastal route signs to Craster from A1 at Alnwick*

In the heart of Northumbrian countryside, yet just a few minutes from the sea and the fishing village of Craster, The Cottage Inn offers comfortable, en suite, ground floor accommodation. Hearty meals are served either in the bar, conservatory, or the restaurant, which has been decorated by a local artist.

FACILITIES: 10 en suite (10 GF) No smoking in area of dining room TVB tea/coffee Direct dial from bedrooms No dogs (ex guide dogs) Cen ht Pool Table Dinner Last d 9.30pm **PRICES:** s £35; d £63✳ **LB** **CONF:** Del from £37 ✳ **PARKING:** 60 **CARDS:**

FALSTONE Map 12 NY78

♦♦♦♦ Pheasant

Stannersburn NE48 1DD ☎ 01434 240382 Fax 01434 240382

e-mail: thepheasantinn@kielderwater.demon.co.uk

Dir: *A68 onto B6320, follow signs for Kielder Water. From A69, B6079, B6320, follow signs to Kielder Water (The Circle)*

This charming establishment has everything one would want from a traditional country inn; character, good food, warm hospitality, modern accommodation and magnificent scenery. Bedrooms are comfortable, with co-ordinating furnishings and many useful extras. The bar features stone walls and low beamed ceilings. Delicious home-cooked meals are served either there or in the stylish dining room.

FACILITIES: 11 annexe en suite (1 fmly) (5 GF) No smoking TVB tea/coffee Cen ht No coaches Pool Table Dinner Last d 8.50pm **PRICES:** s £30-£40; d £55-£65✳ **LB** **MEALS:** Lunch £15-£20&alc Dinner £18-£22&alc✳ **PARKING:** 40 **CARDS:**

♦♦♦ Blackcock

NE48 1AA ☎ 01434 240200 Fax 01434 240200

e-mail: blackcock@falstone.fsbusiness.co.uk

Dir: *off C200 road from Bellingham which can be accessed off A68 or B6320*

This traditional family-run inn, with comfortable bedrooms, lies close to Kielder Water, magnificent scenery and excellent walking. A cosy pub, it boasts exposed beams and a roaring fire burns in the bar in season. Tasty home-cooked meals are served in both the bar and little restaurant.

FACILITIES: 4 en suite (1 fmly) No smoking in bedrooms No smoking in dining room TVB tea/coffee Cen ht Pool Table Dinner Last d 8.30pm **PRICES:** s £28; d £50✳ **LB** **MEALS:** Lunch £3.95-£9.95&alc Dinner £7.95-£14.85&alc✳ **PARKING:** 20 **CARDS:**

GREENHEAD Map 12 NY66

♦♦♦♦ Holmhead

Thirlwall Castle Farm, Hadrians Wall CA8 7HY

☎ 016977 47402 Fax 016977 47402

e-mail: Holmhead@hadrianswall.freeserve.co.uk

Dir: *from B6318 turn between Ye Olde Forge Tea Rooms & Youth Hostel beside phone box, over bridge, premises 0.25m along Farm Rd*

An old farmhouse in a sheltered valley. The cosy bedrooms have modern facilities; some have views of the ruins of Thirlwall Castle. The lounge contains an abundance of books, board games and toys. A set dinner menu is available, and breakfast can be chosen from "the longest breakfast menu in the world".

FACILITIES: 4 en suite 1 annexe en suite (1 fmly) No smoking tea/coffee No dogs Licensed Cen ht TVL Table tennis Badminton Dinner Last d 3pm **PRICES:** d fr £59✳ **LB** **PARKING:** 6 **NOTES:** Closed 19 Dec-9 Jan rs Nov-Estr **CARDS:**

England

HALTWHISTLE Map 12 NY76

♦♦♦♦ Vallum Lodge

Military Rd, Twice Brewed, nr Bardon Mill NE47 7AN
☎ 01434 344248 📠 01434 344488
e-mail: vallum.lodge@ukonline.co.uk
Dir: *on B6318, 400yds W of Once Brewed National Park visitors centre*

Set in the Northumberland National Park, this house provides easy access to Hadrian's Wall. Spotlessly maintained, it offers comfortable cottage-style accommodation all on ground floor level. It has a natural spring water supply, and there is a choice of lounges, one containing a residents' bar, whilst freshly prepared home-cooked meals are provided in the dining room.
FACILITIES: 7 rms (4 en suite) (1 fmly) (7 GF) No smoking in bedrooms No smoking in dining room tea/coffee Licensed Cen ht TVL No children 3yrs No coaches Dinner Last d 6.30pm **PRICES:** s £22-£25; d £44-£56✱ **LB PARKING:** 25 **NOTES:** Closed Nov-Feb **CARDS:**

HEXHAM Map 12 NY96

Premier Collection

♦♦♦♦♦ Montcoffer

Bardon Mill Village NE47 7HZ ☎ 01434 344138
📠 01434 344730
e-mail: john-dehlia@talk21.com
Dir: *turn left off A69 4m W of Haydon Bridge signed Bardon Mill. House 0.25m into village on left .*
A stylish conversion of a former stable block in the heart of the village. Bedrooms have been tastefully decorated and both have headboards made from reclaimed timber from the chapel at Bagshot House, home of the Earl and Countess of Wessex. Breakfasts make use of fresh, local produce including eggs from the owners' ducks. An interesting collection of signs is to be found in the lovely gardens.
FACILITIES: 2 en suite (1 fmly) No smoking TVB tea/coffee No dogs Cen ht No coaches Fishing Riding **PRICES:** s £32; d £52-£58✱ **LB PARKING:** 12

♦♦♦♦ Dene House

Juniper NE46 1SJ ☎ 01434 673413 📠 01434 673413
e-mail: margaret@denehouse-hexham.co.uk
Dir: *4m S of Hexham, take B6306, 1st right fork, then 1st left, both signed Dye House. Follow road for 3.5m, Dene House 100yds past Juniper sign*
A warm welcome awaits guests at this lovely cottage in Juniper, on the outskirts of Hexham. Bedrooms are attractively furnished and smartly decorated whilst spacious public areas include a comfortable lounge with a real fire, a bright conservatory and an elegant dining room. Aga-cooked breakfasts that include home-made bread and preserves are enjoyed in the farmhouse kitchen.

continued

Dene House

FACILITIES: 3 rms (2 en suite) No smoking tea/coffee Cen ht TVL No children 10yrs No coaches **PRICES:** s £22.50; d £45✱ **PARKING:** 4 **CARDS:**

♦♦♦♦ Peth Head Cottage

Juniper NE47 0LA ☎ 01434 673286 📠 01434 673038
e-mail: tedliddle@compuserve.com
Dir: *B6306 out of Hexham for 200yds, take right fork, then next left. Continue for 3.5mls. After Juniper sign, house is 400yds on the right*

This lovely sandstone cottage is peacefully located in the village of Juniper, ideal for visiting Hexham, Hadrian's Wall, Durham and Newcastle. Guests can enjoy home-made biscuits on arrival as well as home-baked bread and preserves at breakfast. Attractive bedrooms are comfortable and benefit from spacious en suite facilities.
FACILITIES: 2 en suite No smoking tea/coffee No dogs (ex guide dogs) Cen ht TVL No coaches **PRICES:** s £20; d £40✱ **LB PARKING:** 2 **CARDS:**

♦♦♦♦ Rye Hill *(NY958580)*

Slaley NE47 0AH ☎ 01434 673259 📠 01434 673259
Mrs E A Courage
e-mail: enquiries@consult-courage.co.uk
Dir: *5m S of Hexham, off B6306, 1st right after Travellers Rest pub then 1st farm road right*
Enjoying delightful panoramic views, Rye Hill offers a real farm-stay experience, complete with wake up calls from the sheep. Accommodation is contained in two converted barns in the main courtyard. There is a cosy lounge area with tourist information and a games room. Meals are taken at two pine tables overlooking the garden.

continued

BB Great value! This indicates B&B for £19 and under, per person, per night.

England

Rye Hill

FACILITIES: 6 en suite (2 fmly) No smoking in bedrooms No smoking in dining room TVB tea/coffee Licensed Cen ht TVL Games room, Skittle alley 30 acres sheep Dinner Last d 6pm **PRICES:** s £28; d £45✱ **PARKING:** 6 **CARDS:**

♦♦♦ Loughbrow House

NE46 1RS ☎ 01434 603351 01434 609774
e-mail: patricia@loughbrow.fsnet.co.uk
Dir: *take B6303 signed Blanchland. 0.25 mile up hill, take right hand fork. After 0.25 mile, the drive to the house located between the fork in the road*
Advance booking is required at Loughbrow House, which lies in extensive grounds and well-tended gardens at the end of a long driveway. There are views across the valley from its elevated position outside the town. Meals, (which must be pre-booked and for a minimum of four) are taken house-party style in the original dining room.
FACILITIES: 5 rms (3 en suite) (3 fmly) (5 GF) No smoking in bedrooms TV1B tea/coffee No dogs Cen ht TVL No coaches Dinner Last d 3 days prior to meal **PRICES:** s £30; d £50-£60✱ **PARKING:** 4 **NOTES:** Closed 20 Dec-6 Jan

♦♦♦ Rose & Crown

Main St, Slaley NE47 0AA ☎ 01434 673263 01434 673305
e-mail: rosecrowninn@supanet.com
Dir: *exit A68 onto B6306 signposted Slaley, premises 4m on left*
The Rose & Crown lies high above Hexham in the village of Slaley, amidst open countryside. Delicious home-cooked meals can be enjoyed in the restaurant as well as both bar areas, where good real ale is also on tap. Upstairs, the pine-furnished bedrooms are attractively decorated and thoughtfully equipped.
FACILITIES: 3 en suite No smoking in bedrooms No smoking in area of dining room No smoking in 1 lounge TVB tea/coffee No dogs (ex guide dogs) Cen ht No coaches Fishing Riding Dinner Last d 9.45pm **PRICES:** s £29.50-£35; d £45-£50✱ **MEALS:** Lunch £10.50-£15 Dinner £11.50-£16&alc✱ **PARKING:** 35 **CARDS:**

U The Sun Inn

Main St, Acomb NE46 4PW ☎ 01434 602934
At the time of going to press the Diamond classification for this establishment had not been confirmed. Please check the AA website www.theAA.com for up-to-date information.
FACILITIES: 4 rms (2 en suite)

ROCHESTER Map 12 NY89

♦♦♦♦ Redesdale Arms Hotel

NE19 1TA ☎ 01830 520668 01830 520063
e-mail: redesdalehotel@hotmail.com
Dir: *on A68 between villages of Otterburn & Rochester*
FACILITIES: 10 en suite (3 fmly) TVB tea/coffee Direct dial from bedrooms

continued

Licensed Lift Cen ht Fishing Pool Table Dinner Last d 9pm **PRICES:** s £38-£43; d £60-£70✱ **LB PARKING:** 60 **NOTES:** Closed 25 Dec **CARDS:**

ROTHBURY Map 12 NU00

♦♦♦♦ Orchard

High St NE65 7TL ☎ 01669 620684
e-mail: jpickard@orchardguesthouse.co.uk
Dir: *turn off A697 onto B6334 to Orchard Guest House on right side of village, opposite arts centre*

Despite being over 200 years old, this charming guest house has every modern convenience. On arrival, guests are welcomed with a cup of tea in the lounge, which is stocked with a wealth of local information. Bedrooms are comfortable and well-equipped, and the surrounding countryside includes many spectacular views, the new Alnwick Garden, and Cragside House.
FACILITIES: 6 en suite (1 fmly) No smoking TVB tea/coffee No dogs Cen ht No coaches **PRICES:** s £25-£30; d £46-£50✱

ROTHBURY continued

♦♦♦♦ Katerina's
High St NE65 7TQ ☎ 01669 620691
e-mail: cath@katerinasguesthouse.co.uk
Dir: *from A1 take A597 (N of Morpeth) signed Coldstream. After 8m further N, take B6344 to Rothbury. Katerina's 100yds past row of shops on village's main street*
FACILITIES: 3 en suite No smoking TVB tea/coffee No dogs Licensed Cen ht No coaches Dinner Last d 7pm **PRICES:** s £30; d £44-£46✱

♦♦♦♦ Whitton Farm Hotel
NE65 7RL ☎ 01669 620811 01669 620811
e-mail: whittonfarmhotel@supanet.com
Dir: *N on A1, take A697 at Morpeth, take B6344 at Wheldon Bridge to village of Rothbury, take 1st major road opposite bank, right after river bridge, follow road to top of hill, left at T junct, hotel car park 400yds*
FACILITIES: 3 en suite No smoking TVB tea/coffee Licensed Cen ht No coaches Dinner Last d breakfast **PRICES:** s £24-£28; d £48-£56✱ **LB**
PARKING: 10 **NOTES:** Closed Nov-Mar

♦♦♦ Newcastle Hotel
NE65 7UT ☎ 01669 620334 01669 620334
Dir: *turn off A1 onto A697 at Morpeth then turn onto B6344 at Weldon then 6m to Hotel in centre of the village of Rothbury*
FACILITIES: 8 rms (3 en suite) (1 fmly) No smoking in dining room TVB tea/coffee Licensed Cen ht TVL Dinner Last d 8.30pm **PRICES:** s £24-£30; d £48-£60✱ **LB** **CARDS:**

SEAHOUSES Map 12 NU23

♦♦♦♦ Railston House
133 Main St, North Sunderland NE68 7TS ☎ 01665 720912
Dir: *exit A1 N of Alnwick signed Seahouses & Beadnell. L at 1st rdbt after Beadnell, house 400yds on L*

This charming Georgian house has been imaginatively restored, and many of the original features have been retained. Bedrooms are furnished with pine and traditional pieces and enhanced with thoughtful personal touches. The room without an en suite has sole use of a super bathroom. Breakfast is taken round the one large table in the period dining room.
FACILITIES: 3 en suite No smoking TVB tea/coffee Cen ht No coaches
PRICES: d £46-£52✱ **PARKING:** 2 **NOTES:** Closed Nov-Mar

WOOLER Map 12 NT92

Premier Collection

♦♦♦♦♦ The Old Manse
New Rd, Chatton NE66 5PU ☎ 01668 215343
01668 21343
e-mail: chattonbb@aol.com
Dir: *from A697 Wooler, take B6348 to Chatton. From A1 13m N of Alnwick take B6348 to Chatton*

continued

Built in 1875 this imposing former manse is situated on the edge of the village with commanding views over the open countryside. Both bedrooms are spacious and one has a private sitting room and its own patio. The house is set in extensive gardens, including a wildlife pond and an area for exercising dogs. Hospitality is caring, and breakfasts are hearty.
FACILITIES: 2 en suite (1 fmly) No smoking TVB tea/coffee Cen ht TVL No children 2 yrs **PRICES:** s £26-£42; d £52-£60✱ **LB**
PARKING: 4

NOTTINGHAMSHIRE

BINGHAM Map 08 SK73

♦♦♦♦ Yeung Sing Hotel & Restaurant
Market St NG13 8AB ☎ 01949 831831 & 01949 831222
01949 838833
Dir: *At junction of A52/A46 midway between Nottingham & Grantham*
This family run hotel is part of the highly successful Yeung Sing restaurant, which is centrally situated in the market town of Bingham. All of the bedrooms are comfortably appointed and well-equipped and each room has modern en suite facilities. The ground floor restaurant serves a fine selection of Cantonese and regional Chinese dishes.
FACILITIES: 15 en suite (2 fmly) No smoking in area of dining room No smoking in 1 lounge TVB tea/coffee Direct dial from bedrooms No dogs Licensed Lift Cen ht TVL Dinner Last d 9.30pm **CONF:** Thtr 100 Class 30 Board 30 **PARKING:** 30 **NOTES:** Closed 25-26 Dec
CARDS:

COTGRAVE Map 08 SK63

♦♦♦♦ Jerico Farm *(SK654307)*
Fosse Way NG12 3HG ☎ 01949 81733 01949 81733
Mrs S Herrick
e-mail: info@jericofarm.co.uk
Dir: *9m SE of Nottingham city centre. Jerico Farm on lane off A46- 1m N of A46/A606 junction*
In a peaceful rural setting, this 150 acre working farm is in an ideal location for both the business and leisure guest. The spacious bedrooms are well furnished and equipped with a range of both practical and homely extras. Comprehensive breakfasts are taken in the bright and attractive dining room overlooking the well tended garden and a comfortable lounge is also available.
FACILITIES: 3 en suite (1 fmly) No smoking TVB tea/coffee No dogs Cen ht TVL No children 5yrs Fishing 150 acres mixed **PRICES:** s £35-£40; d £50-£60✱ **PARKING:** 4 **NOTES:** Closed Xmas week
CARDS:

FARNSFIELD Map 08 SK65

♦♦♦ Grange Cottage
Main St NG22 8EA ☎ 01623 882259 01623 883300
01623 883300
e-mail: bedandbreakfast@grange-cottage.co.uk
Dir: *off A614 (Ollerton/Doncaster) at White Post rdbt, 3rd exit to Farnsfield. Through village to Plough Inn, house opp Plough Inn car park*
Grange Cottage is a charming 18th-century Georgian building set in two acres of gardens. The bedrooms are comfortable and homely, and each is individually furnished, with lots of family touches. Breakfast is taken at one large table in the elegant dining room.

continued

FACILITIES: 3 rms (1 en suite) (1 fmly) No smoking TVB tea/coffee Cen ht No coaches **PRICES:** s £22.50-£25; d £45-£85* **PARKING:** 6

HOLBECK Map 08 SK57

Premier Collection

♦♦♦♦♦ Browns

The Old Orchard Cottage, Holbeck S80 3NF
☎ 01909 720659 Fax 01909 720659
e-mail: browns@holbeck.fsnet.co.uk
Dir: *6m from M1 junct 30, 0.5m off A616 Sheffield/Newark road turn for Holbeck at crossroads*

Located amidst beautifully tended gardens which feature ponds and a dovecote, this Queen Anne cottage offers a tranquil place to stay. Breakfasts are taken in the elegant dining room, and the bedrooms, situated in former farm buildings, are comfortable and homely. Friendly and caring services are provided by the owners, including courtesy transport to a nearby restaurant.

FACILITIES: 3 annexe en suite No smoking TVB tea/coffee No dogs (ex guide dogs) Cen ht TVL No children 12yrs No coaches **PRICES:** d £46-£55* **PARKING:** 3 **NOTES:** Closed Xmas week

MANSFIELD Map 08 SK56

♦♦♦♦ Appleby Guest House

Chesterfield Rd, Pleasley NG19 7PF ☎ 01623 810508
Fax 01623 810508
e-mail: gordon@applebyhouse53.fsnet.co.uk
Dir: *M1 junct 29, A617 for Mansfield. Appleby House 3.5m on left*

Appleby Guest House stands in its own well-tended grounds. This well-furnished country house offers spacious and well-equipped bedrooms. Public areas include a comfortable lounge in which guests can relax and a delightful dining room where substantial breakfasts are served.

FACILITIES: 5 rms (3 en suite) (2 fmly) No smoking in bedrooms No smoking in dining room TVB tea/coffee No dogs Cen ht No coaches Outdoor swimming pool (heated) Croquet lawn **PRICES:** s £20-£30; d £36-£45* BB **PARKING:** 8 **NOTES:** Closed 23 Dec-2 Jan **CARDS:**

♦♦♦ Parkhurst

28 Woodhouse Rd NG18 2AF ☎ 01623 627324
Fax 01623 621855
e-mail: philfletcher@parkhurst28.freeserve.co.uk
Dir: *A60 from Mansfield towards Warsop/Worksop, 0.25m from town centre turn right onto Park Avenue*

This well furnished Victorian property is only ten minutes' walk from the centre of town. Bedrooms are well equipped and comfortable. A cosy bar is provided for guests, and good breakfasts are served in the traditional style dining room.

FACILITIES: 11 rms (6 en suite) (4 fmly) No smoking in dining room No smoking in lounges TVB tea/coffee No dogs (ex guide dogs) Cen ht TVL **PRICES:** s £22-£27; d £38-£44* LB BB **PARKING:** 9 **CARDS:**

NOTTINGHAM Map 08 SK54

See also Barkestone-le-Vale (Leics), Bottesford (Leics), Cotgrave & Ilkeston (Derbyshire)

♦♦♦♦ *Beech Lodge*

222 Porchester Rd, Mapperley NG3 6HG ☎ 0115 952 3314
Dir: *turn off A684 into Porchester Road. Take 8th road on left, with Punchbowl PH on right corner. Beech Lodge is on left corner.*

A warm welcome and good levels of customer care are strengths of Beech Lodge. The modern accommodation is well-presented and suitably equipped, whilst the ground floor residents' lounge is particularly comfortable. Breakfast is taken in the open plan dining area, and offers a good choice.

FACILITIES: 4 en suite (1 fmly) No smoking in bedrooms No smoking in dining room No smoking in 1 lounge TVB tea/coffee No dogs (ex guide dogs) Cen ht TVL No children 8yrs No coaches Dinner Last d 24hrs prior **PARKING:** 6

♦♦♦ Acorn Hotel

4 Radcliffe Rd, West Bridgford NG2 5FW ☎ 0115 981 1297
Fax 0115 981 7654
e-mail: reservations@acorn-hotel.co.uk
Dir: *turn off A60 onto A6011, hotel adjacent to Trent Bridge cricket ground*

This pleasant guest house is an excellent base for those visiting nearby Trent Bridge cricket ground. The comfortable public rooms include a relaxing lounge, a spacious dining room and a downstairs bar serving a small range of hot meals. The well-planned bedrooms come in a variety of sizes and shapes.

FACILITIES: 12 en suite (2 fmly) (1 GF) No smoking in 4 bedrooms No smoking in dining room No smoking in lounges TVB tea/coffee Direct dial from bedrooms No dogs (ex guide dogs) Licensed Cen ht TVL No coaches Pool Table **PRICES:** s £35-£40; d £50-£75* **PARKING:** 12 **CARDS:**

♦♦♦ Fairhaven Private Hotel

19 Meadow Rd, Beeston NG9 1JP ☎ 0115 922 7509
Fax 0115 840 3655
e-mail: bookings@fairhaven.ssnet.co.uk
Dir: *from A52 take B6005 for Beeston Railway Station. Hotel 200yds after bridge*

This is a well-established private hotel, situated in a quiet area of Beeston on the outskirts of Nottingham. The bedrooms vary in style and size and all are comfortably equipped. The public rooms include a spacious and comfortably furnished lounge with a small honesty bar, and a cosy breakfast room.

FACILITIES: 13 rms (6 en suite) (2 fmly) No smoking in 2 bedrooms No smoking in area of dining room No smoking in 1 lounge TVB tea/coffee Licensed Cen ht TVL **PRICES:** s £23-£36; d £38-£44* BB **CONF:** Class 10 Board 10 Del from £40 * **PARKING:** 13

Super supper! this symbol shows that evening meals exceeded our Inspector's expectations.

England

NOTTINGHAM continued

♦♦♦ Gallery Hotel

8-10 Radcliffe Rd, West Bridgford NG2 5FW
☎ 0115 981 3651 & 981 1346 📠 0115 981 3732
Dir: *on A52, 20 mins from M1 junct 24*
This smartly maintained Victorian property is located minutes' walk from Trent Bridge and many major local sports venues. Beautifully decorated cosy bedrooms are smartly furnished and well equipped. Public areas include an inviting elegant lounge and a spacious basement bar, featuring a host of interesting memorabilia reflecting the proprietor's career as an international footballer.
FACILITIES: 16 en suite (3 fmly) No smoking TVB tea/coffee No dogs Licensed Cen ht TVL Pool Table **PRICES:** s £28-£36; d £49-£56* **PARKING:** 35 **CARDS:**

♦♦♦ Grantham Hotel

24-26 Radcliffe Rd, West Bridgford NG2 5FW
☎ 0115 981 1373 📠 0115 981 8567
Dir: *follow signs for Nottingham South/Trent Bridge/National Water Sports Centre. Hotel 0.75km from A52*
This double fronted house is ideally located within a few minutes' walk of the county cricket ground. It offers well-equipped bedrooms and bright attractive public areas including a comfortable lounge and a dining room where freshly cooked English breakfasts are served.
FACILITIES: 22 rms (15 en suite) No smoking in bedrooms No smoking in dining room TVB tea/coffee No dogs (ex guide dogs) Licensed Cen ht TVL No coaches **PRICES:** s £24-£33; d £48* **PARKING:** 7 **NOTES:** Closed Xmas **CARDS:**

♦♦♦ Hall Farm House *(SK679475)*

Gonalston NG14 7JA ☎ 0115 966 3112 📠 0115 966 4844
Mrs A R Smith
Dir: *A612 towards Southwell from Lowdham rdbt. After 1.5m left at Hovering/Gonalston X-Rds, then 1st right after post box, Hall Farm on left after 150 yds*
Tucked away behind mature trees and shrubs in this small village, Hall Farm House has a heated outdoor swimming pool and tennis court, and the comfortable bedrooms and lounges are full of character. Evening meals are not served but there are several pubs close by where guests can enjoy excellent food.
FACILITIES: 4 rms (2 en suite) (1 fmly) No smoking TV3B tea/coffee No dogs Cen ht TVL Outdoor swimming pool (heated) Croquet lawn Large playroom with piano and table tennis 22 acres sheep **PRICES:** s £25-£30; d £45-£50* **LB PARKING:** 5 **NOTES:** Closed 20 Dec-2 Jan

♦♦♦ Andrews Private Hotel

310 Queens Rd, Beeston NG9 1JA ☎ 0115 925 4902
📠 0115 9178839
e-mail: andrews.hotel@ntlworld.com
Dir: *from A52 take B6006 to Beeston, turn right at 4th traffic lights into Queens Rd, hotel 200mtrs on right*
This pleasant establishment is close to shops and facilities, and is popular with business people and tourists alike. Although the well-kept bedrooms do vary in size they are all suitably decorated and equipped. Guests also have the use of a comfortable lounge and dining room.
FACILITIES: 10 rms (3 en suite) (1 fmly) No smoking in 5 bedrooms No smoking in dining room TVB tea/coffee Cen ht TVL No coaches
PRICES: s £23-£30; d £35-£40* **BB PARKING:** 6

♦♦ Tudor Lodge Hotel

400 Nuthall Rd NG8 5DS ☎ 0115 924 9244 📠 0115 924 9243
e-mail: sales@commodoreinternational.co.uk
Dir: *A610 3miles from junction 26 M1 towards Nottingham*
Tudor Lodge is conveniently located for the M1 and the city centre. Accommodation is bed and breakfast only and bedrooms come in a variety of sizes and styles. The ground floor en suite room is particularly suitable for the less mobile. Breakfast is served in the cosy dining room/lounge.
FACILITIES: 7 rms (5 en suite) (2 fmly) (3 GF) No smoking in area of dining room No smoking in 1 lounge TVB tea/coffee No dogs (ex guide dogs) Cen ht TVL No coaches Dinner Last d 9.30pm **PRICES:** s £45.50; d £52.50* **PARKING:** 10 **CARDS:**

WORKSOP — Map 08 SK57

♦♦♦♦ Acorn Lodge

85 Potter St S80 2HL ☎ 01909 478383 📠 01909 500037
e-mail: russ@acornlodge.fsbusiness.co.uk
Dir: *from town centre near Market Place take rd to Retford, B6040 straight across mini-rdbt. Guest house on L next to Post Office.*
The unremarkable exterior is immediately offset by bright, attractively appointed accommodation. Well-equipped bedrooms with smart modern en suite shower rooms are provided. The attractively refurbished public rooms offer a separate comfortable lounge and a pleasantly appointed breakfast room. Private car parking to the rear is a bonus, as is a small patio area.
FACILITIES: 7 en suite (3 fmly) No smoking in 4 bedrooms No smoking in dining room No smoking in lounges STV TVB tea/coffee Direct dial from bedrooms No dogs (ex guide dogs) Cen ht TVL **PRICES:** s £35; d £45* **PARKING:** 16 **CARDS:**

♦♦♦♦ The Dukeries Park

29 Park St S80 1HW ☎ 01909 476674
e-mail: dukeries@supanet.com
Dir: *100yds from Market square on left*
A warm welcome and friendly service is assured at this carefully restored Victorian building, which is only a minute's walk from the market and the town centre. Quality accommodation is complimented by smart public areas, and these include a well-appointed lounge bar and attractive breakfast room.
FACILITIES: 6 en suite (2 fmly) No smoking in bedrooms No smoking in dining room TVB tea/coffee No dogs (ex guide dogs) Licensed Cen ht No children 2yrs No coaches **PRICES:** s £30-£35; d £45-£50* **PARKING:** 8 **CARDS:**

OXFORDSHIRE

ABINGDON — Map 04 SU49

♦♦♦♦ Rafters

Abingdon Rd OX13 6NU ☎ 01865 391298 📠 01865 391173
e-mail: b&b@graw.fsnet.co.uk
Dir: *from A34 take A415 towards Witney. Rafters on A415 in Marcham by 1st street light on right*
A warm welcome is assured at this impressive half-timbered house standing in immaculate gardens. Bedrooms are equipped with a range of practical and homely extras. Memorable breakfasts include home-made bread and preserves.
FACILITIES: 3 en suite No smoking TVB tea/coffee No dogs (ex guide dogs) Cen ht No coaches **PRICES:** s £30-£48; d £40-£60* **PARKING:** 3 **CARDS:**

♦♦♦♦ Dinckley Court

Burcot OX14 3DP ☎ 01865 407763 📠 01865 407010
e-mail: annette@dinckleycourt.co.uk
Dir: *from M40 junct 7 take A329, right onto A4074 Oxford rd, then A415 to Abingdon*
Located in Burcot in ten acres of grounds, which include river frontage, this former farmhouse has been sympathetically

continued

refurbished to provide bedrooms filled with both practical and thoughtful extras. Memorable breakfasts and imaginative dinners are served in the cosy kitchen and a spacious lounge is also available.

Dinckley Court

FACILITIES: 4 en suite (1 fmly) No smoking TVB tea/coffee No dogs (ex guide dogs) Cen ht TVL No coaches Fishing Boating Close to watersports, skiing **PRICES:** s £49; d £65✻ **LB** **PARKING:** 10 **CARDS:**

ASTHALL Map 04 SP21

♦♦♦ Maytime

OX18 4HW ☎ 01993 822068 🖷 01993 822635

Dir: *0.25m N of A40, between Witney & Burford*

Situated in the centre of this pretty village between Witney and Burford. The inn has been owned and run by Mr & Mrs Morgan for over 25 years. The tastefully furnished, well-equipped bedrooms are housed in an annexe constructed from attractive Cotswold stone. Public rooms include a smart restaurant, a lounge bar and a function room.

FACILITIES: 6 annexe en suite (6 GF) No smoking in area of dining room TVB tea/coffee Direct dial from bedrooms Cen ht Dinner Last d 9.15pm **PRICES:** s £52.50; d £69.50✻ **LB** **MEALS:** alc **PARKING:** 100 **CARDS:**

BAMPTON Map 04 SP30

♦♦♦ *Romany*

Bridge St OX18 2HA ☎ 01993 850237 🖷 01993 852133

e-mail: romany@barbox.net

Dir: *located on the A4095 Witney/Faringdon Road in centre of Bampton*

Very much a focal point of the village, which dates from the Saxon period, this Georgian inn retains many interesting characteristics and sympathetic modernisation has provided comfortable bedrooms. A wide range of imaginative food and real ales are offered in the cosy bar areas or dining room.

FACILITIES: 7 en suite 3 annexe en suite (4 fmly) No smoking in bedrooms No smoking in dining room TVB tea/coffee Direct dial from bedrooms Cen ht TVL Darts Dinner Last d 9.30pm **PARKING:** 6 **CARDS:**

BANBURY Map 04 SP44

♦♦♦♦ La Madonette Country Guest House

North Newington Rd OX15 6AA ☎ 01295 730212

🖷 01295 730363

e-mail: lamadonett@aol.com

Dir: *from M40 junct 11 follow signs to Banbury Cross. Take B4035 (Shipston-on-Stour) for approx 2.5m then right for North Newington*

Many original features are retained in this 17th-century former miller's house, which is set in immaculate gardens in a peaceful rural location. Bedrooms are tastefully furnished, with pretty co-ordinating fabrics and modern bathrooms. Ground floor areas

continued

include a comfortable lounge bar and reproduction French style dining room, the setting for imaginative breakfasts and dinners by prior arrangement.

La Madonette Country Guest House

FACILITIES: 6 en suite (2 fmly) No smoking in bedrooms No smoking in dining room TVB tea/coffee Direct dial from bedrooms No dogs (ex guide dogs) Licensed Cen ht TVL No coaches Outdoor swimming pool (heated) Dinner Last d prebooked Oct-Apr **PRICES:** s £45-£50; d £67-£95✻ **LB** **CONF:** Thtr 25 Board 12 Del £74 ✻ **PARKING:** 20 **CARDS:**

♦♦♦ *Lampet Arms*

Main St, Tadmarton OX15 5TB ☎ 01295 780070

🖷 01295 788066

e-mail: lampet@compuserve.com

Dir: *take B4035 (west) to Tadmarton from Banbury Cross, Banbury*

Located on the Shipston-on-Stour road, west of Banbury, this popular village inn enjoys a strong local following for its range of real ales, home-cooked food and fine wines, taken in the warm and inviting public areas, which retain many original features. The spacious throughtfully furnished bedrooms are situated in a sympathetic conversion of the former coaching house.

FACILITIES: 4 annexe en suite (2 fmly) No smoking in dining room TVB tea/coffee Direct dial from bedrooms No dogs (ex guide dogs) Cen ht Dinner Last d 9.30pm **PARKING:** 14 **CARDS:**

♦♦♦ *The Blinking Owl*

Main St, North Newington OX15 6AE ☎ 01295 730650

Dir: *B4035 form Banbury,2miles sharp bend, road on right to village of North Newington.Inn opposite the green.*

An important part of the community in the pretty village of North Newington, this former 17th-century inn retains many original features. Simple food and a range of real ales are served in the beamed bar lounges. A converted barn, houses the bedrooms and a restaurant, open at weekends.

FACILITIES: 3 en suite No smoking in 1 bedrooms No smoking in area of dining room TVB tea/coffee No dogs (ex guide dogs) Cen ht Dinner Last d 9pm **PARKING:** 14

BANBURY continued

♦♦♦ *Calthorpe Lodge*

4 Calthorpe Rd OX16 5HS ☎ 01295 252325
Dir: *head S from Banbury Close on A4260. Take 3rd turning left. Immediately after St Johns Church turn into St Johns Rd, turn 2nd right*
Located in a residential road within a few minutes' walk from Banbury Cross, this period terraced town house offers a range of practically furnished bedrooms complemented by modern bathroom facilities. Breakfast is taken in a ground floor dining room, which also contains some lounge seating.
FACILITIES: 6 rms (4 en suite) (1 fmly) No smoking TVB tea/coffee Cen ht No coaches **PARKING:** 6 **CARDS:**

♦♦♦ Fairlawns

60 Oxford Rd OX16 9AN ☎ 01295 262461 Fax 01295 261296
e-mail: fairlawnsgh@aol.com
Dir: *M40 junct 11 towards Banbury, left at 2nd island signposted 'town centre'. T-junct after 2m, house opposite*
Ideally located, this extended Edwardian house retains some interesting original features and offers a range of bedrooms, including some with direct access to the car park. A comprehensive breakfast is taken in the traditionally furnished dining room and a selection of soft drinks and snacks is also available.
FACILITIES: 15 rms (14 en suite) 3 annexe en suite (5 fmly) No smoking in dining room No smoking in lounges TVB tea/coffee Direct dial from bedrooms Cen ht **PRICES:** s £40; d £50✻ **PARKING:** 18 **CARDS:**

♦♦♦ *Roebuck Inn*

Stratford Rd, Drayton OX15 6EN ☎ 01295 730542
Fax 01295 730542
Dir: *exit M40 junct 11, premises on A442*
Located on the town's outskirts in an ideal rural touring location, this 16th century inn has many original features which are enhanced by the furnishing styles throughout. An attractive conservatory dining room is the setting for imaginative food and a wealth of memorabilia adds additional character to the cosy bars.
FACILITIES: 2 rms No smoking in bedrooms No smoking in dining room TVB tea/coffee No dogs Cen ht Dinner Last d 9.30pm
PARKING: 20 **NOTES:** Closed Dec **CARDS:**

BURFORD — Map 04 SP21

Premier Collection

♦♦♦♦♦ Burford House Hotel

99 High St OX18 4QA ☎ 01993 823151 Fax 01993 823240
e-mail: stay@burfordhouse.co.uk
Dir: *turn off A40 between Cheltenham & Oxford, following signs for Burford. Burford House on High St*

In the heart of this famous Cotswold town, Burford House, with its half-timbered and mellow stone exterior, is a haven for travellers. Bedrooms are charming and include thoughtful, homely extras. Two comfortable lounges with roaring log fires create a welcoming feeling and superb breakfasts and light meals are served in the dining room. The Hentys are caring and attentive hosts who ensure that a visit to their home is a happy and memorable one.
FACILITIES: 8 en suite No smoking in bedrooms No smoking in dining room TVB Direct dial from bedrooms No dogs (ex guide dogs) Licensed Cen ht No coaches **PRICES:** s £75-£110; d £95-£130✻ **LB**
CARDS:

Premier Collection

♦♦♦♦♦ Jonathan's at the Angel

14 Witney St OX18 4SN ☎ 01993 822714 Fax 01993 822069
e-mail: jo@theangel-uk.com
Dir: *from A40 turn off at Burford rdbt and go down the hill, turn 1st right into Swan Lane, 1st left to Pytts Lane and left at the end into Witney Street*

Peacefully located a few minutes' walk from main attractions, this mellow Cotswold stone, 16th-century former coaching inn retains a wealth of exposed beams and many other original features. Individually-themed bedrooms are filled with practical and homely extras and a cosy guest lounge is also available. Rustically-furnished ground floor areas are the setting for imaginative, award-winning food.
FACILITIES: 3 en suite No smoking in bedrooms No smoking in dining room TVB tea/coffee Direct dial from bedrooms No dogs (ex guide dogs) Cen ht No children 9yrs No coaches Dinner Last d 9.30pm
PRICES: s £65-£75; d £85-£95✻ **NOTES:** Closed 18 Jan-8 Feb
CARDS:

CHINNOR

See Bledlow (Buckinghamshire)

CHIPPING NORTON — Map 04 SP32

See also Long Compton (Warwickshire)

♦♦♦♦ The Forge House

Church Rd, Churchill OX7 6NJ ☎ 01608 658173
Fax 01608 659262
e-mail: jon@theforge.co.uk
Dir: *exit M40 junct 11, A361 to Chipping Norton, B4450 to Churchill, premises next to village green on B4450*
This 200 year old honey-coloured stone house is in the pretty village of Churchill, recorded in the Domesday Book as Cercelle.

continued

England

Bedrooms, many of which have four-poster beds, are filled with a wealth of thoughtful extras and a spacious lounge is available in addition to the cottage style dining room.
FACILITIES: 6 en suite (1 GF) No smoking STV TVB tea/coffee No dogs (ex guide dogs) Cen ht TVL No children 12yrs One bedroom with jacuzzi **PRICES:** s £45-£55; d £55-£65* **PARKING:** 6 **CARDS:**

CHISLEHAMPTON Map 04 SU59

♦♦♦ Coach & Horses

Watlington Rd OX44 7UX ☎ 01865 890255 📠 01865 891995
e-mail: david-mcphillips@lineone.net
Dir: *beside B480*

Located within easy reach of Oxford centre, this 16th-century inn retains many original features including exposed beams and open fires, and furniture styles enhance the intrinsic character of the building. A wide range of imaginative food is served and the practically equipped chalet-style bedrooms have lovely rural views.
FACILITIES: 9 en suite TVB tea/coffee Direct dial from bedrooms Cen ht Club fishing 200yds, Riding stable (1m) Dinner Last d 9.45pm **PRICES:** s £49.50-£51; d £60-£70* **LB MEALS:** Lunch £13.50&alc Dinner £13.50&alc* **PARKING:** 30 **CARDS:**

CHOLSEY Map 04 SU58

♦♦♦ The Well Cottage

Caps Ln OX10 9HQ ☎ 01491 651959
e-mail: thewellcottage@talk21.com
Dir: *M4 junct 8 to Henley. A4130 to Oxford at Crowmarsh Gifford rdbt left onto Wallingford By pass, right at next rdbt over Thames, left at 1st of double rdbts one mile on right is Caps Lane*
FACILITIES: 2 annexe en suite (2 fmly) (2 GF) No smoking in area of dining room No smoking in 1 lounge TVB tea/coffee No dogs (ex guide dogs) Cen ht No coaches **PRICES:** s £20-£40; d £40-£60* **PARKING:** 5

HENLEY-ON-THAMES Map 04 SU78

Premier Collection

♦♦♦♦♦ Lenwade

3 Western Rd RG9 1JL ☎ 01491 573468 & 0374 941629
📠 01491 573468
e-mail: lenwadeuk@aol.com
Dir: *leaving Henley town centre, take Reading road, right into St Andrews Rd over crossroads, next left into Western Rd, Lenwade on left*

This Victorian family house is quietly situated, close to the centre of Henley. Attractive, comfortable bedrooms are well-equipped and include many thoughtful extras. Breakfast is served around one large table and there is a comfortable lounge with satellite TV and an open fire. Children are welcome.
FACILITIES: 3 en suite No smoking STV TVB tea/coffee Direct dial from bedrooms No dogs Cen ht No children No coaches
PRICES: s £45-£50; d £55-£60* **PARKING:** 2

♦♦♦ Diamonds are a guest's best friend! The emphasis is on quality and guest care rather than extra facilities.

Premier Collection

♦♦♦♦♦ Thamesmead House Hotel

Remenham Ln RG9 2LR ☎ 01491 574745 📠 01491 579944
e-mail: thamesmead@supanet.com
Dir: *M4 junct 8, follow signs for Henley-on-Thames, just before Henley bridge at bottom of Remenham Hill, house is signposted on right overlooking Henley Cricket Ground*

Located beside the cricket pitch, a few minutes' walk from the river and town centre, a warm welcome is assured at this impressive Victorian house, which retains many original

features including stained glass and marble fireplaces. Minimalist décor enhances the quality soft furnishings, art and Scandinavian-style furniture, and superb beds ensure a comfortable night's rest. Organically sourced produce is a feature of the comprehensive breakfasts, and light meals with a drinks service are also available. Tricia Thorburn-Muirhead was a Top Twenty Finalist in the AA Landlady of the Year 2002-2003.
FACILITIES: 6 en suite No smoking STV TVB tea/coffee Direct dial from bedrooms No dogs Licensed Cen ht No children 10yrs No coaches **PRICES:** s £95-£105; d £115-£140* **LB PARKING:** 6
CARDS:

♦♦♦♦ The Knoll

Crowsley Rd, Shiplake RG9 3JT ☎ 0118 940 2705
📠 0118 940 2705
e-mail: theknollhenley@aol.com
Dir: *from Henley take A4155 towards Reading, after 2m left at war memorial, then 1st right into Crowsley Rd, 3rd house on right*

The Knoll is set in a quiet residential area, just two miles from Henley on Thames. One of the two bedrooms has a second room off it for children. Both are traditionally furnished and comfortably equipped. Breakfast includes a delicious array of fresh fruit, muffins, home-made preserves and fresh juices. Beautiful secure gardens are also a delight.
FACILITIES: 3 rms (2 en suite) (1 fmly) (3 GF) No smoking in bedrooms No smoking in dining room No smoking in 1 lounge TVB tea/coffee No dogs (ex guide dogs) Cen ht TVL No coaches **PRICES:** s £45; d £56-£59*
LB PARKING: 5

♦♦♦ Slater's Farm

Peppard Common RG9 5JL ☎ 01491 628675 📠 01491 628675
Dir: *leave Henley via Gravel Hill, at junction with B481 turn left. 0.25m after The Dog pub fork left. Farm 200yds on right*
FACILITIES: 3 rms (1 en suite) No smoking TVB No dogs (ex guide dogs) Cen ht TVL No coaches Tennis (hard) Dinner Last d at breakfast
PRICES: s fr £30; d fr £50* **PARKING:** 5

IDBURY Map 04 SP21

♦♦♦♦ Bould Farm *(SP244209)*

OX7 6RT ☎ 01608 658850 01608 658850 Mrs L Meyrick
e-mail: meyrick@bould-farm.fsnet.co.uk

Dir: *leave A424 Burford/Stow-on-the-Wold rd signed Idbury, through village, farm on right. Or B4450 from Chipping Norton, left after rail bridge signed Idbury*

Located in pretty formal gardens between Stow-on-the-Wold and Burford, this constantly improving 17th-century house retains many original characteristics, enhanced by the quality furniture and décor styles throughout. The homely spacious bedrooms offer stunning views of the countryside and a cast iron stove and flagstone floor are features within the cosy breakfast room.

FACILITIES: 3 en suite (1 fmly) TVB tea/coffee No dogs (ex guide dogs) Cen ht TVL 400 acres arable sheep **PRICES:** s £30-£50; d £50* **PARKING:** 6 **NOTES:** Closed Dec-Jan

KIDLINGTON Map 04 SP41

♦♦♦ *Bowood House Hotel*

238 Oxford Rd OX5 1EB ☎ 01865 842288 01865 841858

Dir: *on A4260, 4m N of Oxford, opposite Thames Valley Police HQ*

This constantly improving commercial hotel offers spacious practically equipped bedrooms, some of which are located in a wing surrounding a pretty patio garden. A choice of lounges is provided and dinner is available in an elegant formal dining room.

FACILITIES: 10 rms (8 en suite) 12 annexe en suite (4 fmly) No smoking in 10 bedrooms No smoking in dining room STV TVB tea/coffee Direct dial from bedrooms Licensed Cen ht TVL Golf 18 Jacuzzi Dinner Last d 8.30pm **PARKING:** 26 **NOTES:** Closed 24 Dec-4 Jan **CARDS:**

See advert under OXFORD

KINGSTON BLOUNT Map 04 SU79

♦♦♦♦ *Lakeside Town Farm (SP737996)*

Brook St OX39 4RZ ☎ 01844 352152 01844 352152
Mr & Mrs J Clark
e-mail: townfarmcottage@oxfree.com

Dir: *M40 junct 6, 2m on B4009 towards Princes Risborough. 1st left in Kingston Blount, in 300 yds turn right to Brook St, immediately left down drive to last house set in farmyard*

Located in immaculate grounds which include sweeping lawns, mature shrubs and a duck pond, this impressive red brick and timber house was constructed thirteen years ago from reclaimed materials and is adjacent to the family livestock farm. All interiors are filled with a wealth of thoughtful extras and breakfasts feature own produce including home-baked bread and free-range eggs.

FACILITIES: 2 en suite No smoking TVB tea/coffee No dogs Cen ht TVL No children 8yrs 400 acres arable beef sheep **CARDS:**

MOULSFORD Map 04 SU58

♦♦♦♦ White House

OX10 9JD ☎ 01491 651397 01491 652560
e-mail: mwatsham@hotmail.com

Dir: *from M4 junct 12 take A4 towards Newbury. At Theale rdbt take A340 to Pangbourne, A329 through Streatley. Over x-roads, 4th left*

Excellent customer care is assured at this spotlessly clean, no-smoking house, which stands in immaculate mature gardens close to Goring and the River Thames. The bedrooms are equipped with a wealth of thoughtful extras and imaginative breakfasts are served at one table in an elegant dining room.

continued

FACILITIES: 3 rms (3 GF) No smoking TVB tea/coffee No dogs Cen ht No coaches Croquet lawn Dinner Last d on booking **PRICES:** s £30-£35; d £50* **PARKING:** 6 **NOTES:** Closed Xmas/New Year

OXFORD Map 04 SP50

See also Wheatley & Yarnton

Premier Collection

♦♦♦♦♦ Burlington House

374 Banbury Rd, Summertown OX2 7PP ☎ 01865 513513
01865 311785
e-mail: stay@burlington-house.co.uk

Dir: *at Peartree rdbt follow signs to Oxford. Next rdbt 2nd exit (A40). After approx 0.5m next rdbt, 3rd exit. On corner of 4th road on left*

Located within easy walking distance of restaurants in fashionable Summertown, this constantly improving, immaculately maintained Victorian house retains many original features, and is very stylishly decorated. Bedrooms, two overlooking a pretty patio garden, are filled with a wealth of thoughtful extras. Memorable breakfasts include home-made preserves, fruit breads, and Granola, and excellent coffee.

FACILITIES: 9 rms (7 en suite) 2 annexe en suite No smoking TVB tea/coffee Direct dial from bedrooms No dogs (ex guide dogs) Cen ht No children 12yrs No coaches **PRICES:** s £55; d £75-£80* **PARKING:** 5 **NOTES:** Closed 23 Dec-3 Jan **CARDS:**

Premier Collection

♦♦♦♦♦ Chestnuts

45 Davenants Rd, off Woodstock Rd OX2 8BU
☎ 01865 553375 01865 513712
e-mail: stay@chestnutsguesthouse.co.uk

Dir: *M40 junct 8 signed Oxford/Aylesbury. Stay on dual carriageway to Heddington rdbt/Oxford ring road, in 4m next rdbt exit left Banbury Rd immediate right Davenant Road. From M40/A34 leave dual carriageway at Oxford junct, at lower rdbt 1st left, next rdbt 3rd exit Woodstock Rd, 900yds on left*

Located on a residential avenue, this constantly improving and well-maintained house stands on immaculate gardens. The pretty patio is overlooked by the elegant dining room, where memorable breakfasts are taken. The cosy bedrooms are filled with a wealth of thoughtful extras and shower rooms are modern and efficient. The house is no-smoking.

FACILITIES: 6 en suite (1 fmly) No smoking TVB tea/coffee No dogs (ex guide dogs) Cen ht TVL No children 12yrs No coaches **PRICES:** s £50; d £70-£80* **PARKING:** 12 **CARDS:**

England

Premier Collection

◆◆◆◆◆ Cotswold House

363 Banbury Rd OX2 7PL ☎ 01865 310558
📠 01865 310558
e-mail: d.r.walker@talk21.com
Dir: *exit A40 onto A423 into Oxford city centre, following signs to Summertown, 0.5m on right*

Ideally situated in a leafy avenue close to the northern ring road and Summertown, this well maintained house offers comfortable, well equipped bedrooms and a friendly welcome. Enjoy a traditional, hearty English breakfast or vegetarian choice, including home made muesli and fresh fruit, served in the bright attractive dining room. For evening meals, there is a wide range of pubs and restaurants in the area.
FACILITIES: 7 en suite (2 fmly) (1 GF) No smoking TVB tea/coffee No dogs Cen ht No children 6yrs No coaches **PRICES:** s £50-£55; d £70-£75✳ **PARKING:** 6 **CARDS:**

◆◆◆◆ Gables

6 Cumnor Hill OX2 9HA ☎ 01865 862153 📠 01865 864054
e-mail: stay@gables-oxford.co.uk
Dir: *M40 junct 9 take A34 towards Newbury, at junct with A420 exit A34 to rdbt, take Oxford/Botley turn off, turn right at T-junct, then 500yds on right*

Located in a residential area a few minutes drive from the city and A34, a warm welcome is assured at this Victorian house which has been sympathetically renovated to provide high levels of comfort throughout. Bedrooms are filled with a wealth of thoughtful extras and ground floor areas include a cosy dining room and conservatory lounge overlooking the immaculate enclosed rear garden.
FACILITIES: 6 en suite No smoking STV TVB tea/coffee Direct dial from bedrooms No dogs Cen ht TVL No coaches Pool Table special arrangements with local lesiure centre **PRICES:** s £30-£32; d £50-£55✳ **LB PARKING:** 6 **NOTES:** Closed 24 Dec-1 Jan **CARDS:**

◆◆◆◆ Galaxie Private Hotel

180 Banbury Rd OX2 7BT ☎ 01865 515688 📠 01865 556824
e-mail: info@galaxie.co.uk
Dir: *1m N from centre of Oxford. Hotel on right just before shops in Summertown*

Located close to bars and restaurants in fashionable Summertown, this hotel enjoys a strong clientele of both commercial and leisure guests. A range of bedrooms is provided including a very attractive honeymoon suite. Comprehensive breakfasts are taken in a modern conservatory dining room overlooking the pretty garden.
FACILITIES: 32 rms (28 en suite) (3 fmly) No smoking in bedrooms No smoking in dining room STV TV31B tea/coffee Direct dial from bedrooms No dogs (ex guide dogs) Lift Cen ht TVL **PRICES:** s £45-£58; d £74-£84✳ **LB PARKING:** 30 **CARDS:**

◆◆◆◆ Marlborough House

321 Woodstock Rd OX2 7NY ☎ 01865 311321 📠 01865 515329
e-mail: enquiries@marlbhouse.win-uk.net
Dir: *from A34/A44 junction, N of city, follow city centre signs into Woodstock Rd. Hotel on right by traffic lights*

Purpose built in the last decade, this establishment offers excellent standards of bedroom accommodation with a combination of practical facilities and comfort. Continental breakfasts are provided within each individual room kitchenette and a coffee lounge is also available, where smoking is permitted.
FACILITIES: 12 en suite 4 annexe en suite (2 fmly) (4 GF) No smoking in bedrooms STV TVB tea/coffee Direct dial from bedrooms No dogs Licensed Cen ht No children 5yrs No coaches **PRICES:** s £70; d £84✳ **PARKING:** 6 **CARDS:**

A indicates an Associate entry, which has been inspected and rated by the ETC or the RAC in England.

England

OXFORD continued

♦♦♦♦ Pickwicks

15-17 London Rd, Headington OX3 7SP ☎ 01865 750487
01865 742208
e-mail: pickwicks@tiscali.co.uk
Dir: *from A40 Shotover rdbt, E of Oxford, take exit to Headington. Follow signs to Oxford city centre. Pickwicks approx 1.5m on right at junct with Sandfield Road*

Pickwicks Guest House is located a few minutes' walk from the bustling community of Headington. This double fronted Edwardian house has been sympathetically converted to provide good standards of overall comfort. Bedrooms offer a useful range of facilities and the attractive breakfast room overlooks the pretty gardens.
FACILITIES: 15 rms (13 en suite) (5 fmly) (4 GF) No smoking in bedrooms No smoking in dining room No smoking in 1 lounge TVB tea/coffee Direct dial from bedrooms Licensed Cen ht TVL **PRICES:** s £30-£50; d £65-£70✳ **PARKING:** 12 **NOTES:** Closed 25 Dec **CARDS:**

♦♦♦♦ Sandfield House

19 London Rd, Headington OX3 7RE ☎ 01865 762406
01865 762406
e-mail: stay@sandfieldguesthouse.co.uk
Dir: *M40 junct 8 onto A40 towards Oxford. At Headington rdbt follow signs city centre/Headington hospitals. After 4th traffic lights, over pedestrian lights, Sandfield immediately on right corner of London Rd & Sandfield Rd*
A warm welcome is assured at this beautifully maintained no-smoking house ideally located for Oxford Brookes University and hospitals. The tastefully furnished spacious bedrooms are filled with a wealth of thoughtful extras and comprehensive breakfasts are taken in an elegant dining room overlooking the immaculate landscaped gardens.
FACILITIES: 4 en suite No smoking TVB tea/coffee No dogs Cen ht No children 6yrs No coaches **PRICES:** s £38-£48; d £62-£74✳ **LB** **PARKING:** 5 **NOTES:** Closed 23 Dec-3 Jan **CARDS:**

♦♦♦♦ Victoria House Hotel

29 George St OX1 2AY ☎ 01865 727400 01865 727402
e-mail: info@victoriahouse-hotel.co.uk
Dir: *M40 junct 8, 2nd exit off Green Rd rdbt. Along London Rd to St Clements St, 3rd exit at rdbt on to High St. Left at traffic lights into Longwall St, continue to St Giles. Left at lights then right on Board St towards George St*
Located close to the bus station in the heart of the city centre, this hotel provides modern, thoughtfully equipped bedrooms complimented by smart efficient bathrooms. Breakfast is available in the ground floor café bar there are several public car parks within a few minutes' walk.

continued

Victoria House Hotel

FACILITIES: 14 en suite (1 fmly) No smoking TVB tea/coffee Direct dial from bedrooms No dogs Licensed Cen ht No children 7yrs **PRICES:** s £60-£75; d £70-£95; (room only) ✳ **LB** **CARDS:**

♦♦♦ Highfield

91 Rose Hill OX4 4HT ☎ 01865 774083
e-mail: highfield.house@tesco.net
Dir: *on A4158*
This attractive detached house stands in immaculate gardens close to Cowley and provides comfortable homely bedrooms, which are equipped with quality pine furniture. An attractive front facing dining room is the setting for comprehensive breakfasts and there is a spacious lounge available for guests to relax in.
FACILITIES: 7 rms (5 en suite) No smoking TVB tea/coffee No dogs Cen ht TVL **PRICES:** s £26-£33; d £56-£60✳ **NOTES:** Closed weekends/Xmas **CARDS:**

♦♦♦ Pine Castle Hotel

290/292 Iffley Rd OX4 4AE ☎ 01865 241497 01865 727230
e-mail: stay@pinecastle.co.uk
Dir: *off Ring Rd onto A4158, 1.5m guest house on left after traffic lights*
This double fronted late Victorian house is located between city centre and Southern ring road system, and provides a range of practically equipped bedrooms stocked with a wide selection of thoughtful extras. English breakfast is taken in an attractive dining room and a comfortable lounge with bar is also available.
FACILITIES: 8 en suite (1 fmly) No smoking in bedrooms No smoking in dining room TVB tea/coffee Direct dial from bedrooms No dogs (ex guide dogs) Licensed Cen ht TVL No coaches **PRICES:** s £57-£60; d £71-£74✳ **PARKING:** 6 **CARDS:**

♦♦♦ All Seasons

63 Windmill Rd, Headington OX3 7BP ☎ 01865 742215
01865 432691
e-mail: admin@allseasonsguesthouse.com
Dir: *from Ring Road take exit at Headington rdbt towards city centre. After 2m, at t/lights take left turn into Windmill Road*
Within easy walking distance of the suburb of Headington, this constantly improving double fronted Victorian house provides comfortable homely bedrooms equipped with both practical and thoughtful extras. The elegant dining room features an original fireplace and secure parking is available to rear of property.
FACILITIES: 6 rms (4 en suite) No smoking TVB tea/coffee No dogs Cen ht No children 6yrs Thai Massage, Reflexology, Shiatsu, Reiki **PRICES:** s £35-£50; d £55-£70✳ **PARKING:** 6 **CARDS:**

♦♦♦ *Beaumont*

234 Abingdon Rd OX1 4SP ☎ 01865 241767 01865 241767
e-mail: info@beaumont.sagehost.co.uk
Dir: *at Kennington rdbt, on south ringroad, follow signs for city centre. Beaumont is 1m on left, one block after Duke of Monmouth pub*
A warm welcome is assured at this constantly improving Victorian terraced house, located a few minutes' walk from city centre. The

continued

bedrooms are filled with many thoughtful extras. Comprehensive breakfasts are taken in the attractive front facing dining room, which also contains lots of local information.
FACILITIES: 5 rms (1 en suite) (1 fmly) No smoking TVB tea/coffee No dogs Cen ht No coaches **CARDS:**

♦♦♦ Brown's

281 Iffley Rd OX4 4AQ ☎ 01865 246822 ▤ 01865 246822
e-mail: brownsgh@hotmail.com
Dir: *from city centre take High St over Magdalen Bridge, Iffley Rd 3rd exit on roundabout*
Located between the city and southern ring road system, this Victorian house has been totally refurbished to provide tastefully furnished bedrooms some with smart modern en suite shower rooms. Ground floor areas include a choice of cosy dining rooms and an attractive conservatory lounge overlooking the pretty enclosed rear garden.
FACILITIES: 9 rms (4 en suite) (1 fmly) No smoking TVB tea/coffee No dogs (ex guide dogs) Licensed Cen ht TVL No coaches **PRICES:** s £34; d £54-£68✳ **PARKING:** 4 **CARDS:**

♦♦♦ *Conifer*

116 The Slade, Headington OX3 7DX ☎ 01865 763055
▤ 01865 742232
e-mail: info@coniferguesthouse.co.uk
Dir: *turn off ring road at Green Rd/Headington rdbt towards city centre. Left at Windmill Rd and past hospital. Hotel on left*
Located on a mainly residential avenue, close to the hospitals, this impressive Edwardian house has been totally renovated in recent years to provide attractive pine furnished bedrooms equipped with thoughtful extras. Breakfast is taken in an attractive front facing dining room and the extensive rear garden has the benefit of a swimming pool.
FACILITIES: 8 en suite No smoking TVB tea/coffee No dogs (ex guide dogs) Cen ht No coaches Outdoor swimming pool (heated) **PARKING:** 8 **CARDS:**

♦♦♦ Green Gables

326 Abingdon Rd OX1 4TE ☎ 01865 725870 ▤ 01865 723115
e-mail: green.gables@virgin.net
Dir: *exit Oxford ring rd, S side, at Kennington Rbt, towards city centre. Green Gables 0.5m on left*

A warm welcome is assured at this Edwardian house, located within easy walking distance of the city centre. Bedrooms are equipped with a range of practical and homely extras, and the cosy dining room is the setting for a comprehensive breakfast.
FACILITIES: 11 en suite (5 fmly) (4 GF) No smoking TVB tea/coffee Direct dial from bedrooms No dogs (ex guide dogs) Cen ht TVL No coaches **PRICES:** s £48-£54; d £57-£68✳ **PARKING:** 9 **NOTES:** Closed 23-31 Dec **CARDS:**

♦♦♦ Heather House

192 Iffley Rd OX4 1SD ☎ 01865 249757 ▤ 01865 249757
Dir: *A40 S onto A4142 to Littlemore rdbt and onto A4158 Iffley Rd. House 1.25m on left just past pelican crossing*
Located within easy walking distance of central attractions, this Edwardian house provides a range of practically furnished bedrooms with modern shower rooms. Breakfast is taken in a traditionally furnished dining room and a separate guest lounge is also available.
FACILITIES: 6 en suite (2 fmly) No smoking TVB tea/coffee Direct dial from bedrooms No dogs (ex guide dogs) Cen ht TVL No coaches **PRICES:** s £27-£35; d £54-£66✳ **PARKING:** 4 **NOTES:** Closed Xmas/New Year **CARDS:**

♦♦♦ River Hotel

17 Botley Rd OX2 0AA ☎ 01865 243475 ▤ 01865 724306
e-mail: reception@riverhotel.co.uk
Dir: *1m towards city and railway station, off ring rd at W exit (off A34) onto A420. Hotel on right by Osney Bridge, car park at rear*
Ideally located beside the Thames, a few minutes walk from the railway station and central attractions, this impressive Victorian hotel provides comfortable bedrooms, some of which are located in a period house opposite. Enjoyable breakfasts are taken in the ground floor dining room and additional benefits include a lounge bar and car park.
FACILITIES: 13 en suite 7 annexe en suite (5 fmly) No smoking in dining room TVB tea/coffee Direct dial from bedrooms No dogs (ex guide dogs) Licensed Cen ht TVL No coaches **PRICES:** s £60-£67.50; d £76-£86✳ **CONF:** Thtr 30 **PARKING:** 20 **NOTES:** Closed Xmas & New Year **CARDS:**

England

OXFORD continued

♦♦♦ Newton House

82-84 Abingdon Rd OX1 4PL ☎ 01865 240561
Fax 01865 244647
e-mail: newton.house@btinternet.com
Dir: *on A4144 Abingdon Rd*
FACILITIES: 13 en suite (4 fmly) (4 GF) No smoking STV TVB tea/coffee Direct dial from bedrooms No dogs (ex guide dogs) Cen ht **PRICES:** s £34-£48; d £44-£68* **LB PARKING:** 8 **CARDS:**

♦♦ *Acorn*

260/262 Iffley Rd OX4 1SE ☎ 01865 247998 Fax 01865 247998
Dir: *from ring road take A4158 north for 1m. On left opposite VW garage*
This double fronted Edwardian house is conveniently located between the northern ring road and the city centre, and offers good value accommodation. There is also an automatic lift to one wing of the property. The guest lounge gives direct access to the quiet enclosed rear garden.
FACILITIES: 12 rms (4 en suite) (3 fmly) No smoking in 8 bedrooms No smoking in dining room No smoking in lounges TVB tea/coffee No dogs Lift Cen ht No children 9yrs **PARKING:** 11 **NOTES:** Closed Xmas-New Year **CARDS:**

♦♦ Casa Villa

388 Banbury Rd OX2 7PW ☎ 01865 512642 Fax 01865 512642
e-mail: stoya@casavilla.fsnet.co.uk
Dir: *on Banbury Rd - A4165. 1.75m N of city centre, 200yds from A40 link to M40*
This pleasantly appointed modern property is well placed for major road links and the many shops and restaurants of Summertown. Accommodation is comfortable and well equipped.
FACILITIES: 9 rms (8 en suite) (1 fmly) (2 GF) No smoking TVB tea/coffee No dogs Cen ht TVL **PRICES:** s £35-£49; d £69* **PARKING:** 5 **CARDS:**

♦♦ Kings Guest House

363 Iffley Rd OX4 4DP ☎ 01865 205333 Fax 01865 711544
Dir: *exit M40 junct 9 follow ring road towards A34 turn right on 2nd rdbt*
Located on a residential avenue leading to the city centre, this property is enthusiastically run by friendly hosts who provide a range of practically equipped bedrooms complimented in some cases by modern shower rooms. Breakfast is taken at separate tables in a traditionally furnished dining room.
FACILITIES: 7 rms (4 en suite) (2 fmly) No smoking TVB tea/coffee No dogs (ex guide dogs) Cen ht TVL Dinner Last d 8pm **PRICES:** s £22-£28; d £45-£60* **PARKING:** 10 **CARDS:**

STADHAMPTON — Map 04 SU69

♦♦♦♦ *The Crazy Bear Hotel*

Bear Ln OX44 7UR ☎ 01865 890714 Fax 01865 400481
Dir: *M40 junct 7 signposted Thame & Wallingford - left onto A329. 5m & turn left immediately after petrol station & left again*
Bedrooms at this stylishly refurbished 17th-century inn are furnished with artefacts from all corners of the globe and have impressive bathrooms. The two restaurants, one offering high quality Thai food and one modern British, have a huge local following. Travel weary guests can now book a Thai massage in their room.
FACILITIES: 12 en suite (2 fmly) No smoking in area of dining room No smoking in 1 lounge STV TVB No dogs Cen ht No coaches Dinner Last d 10pm **PARKING:** 50 **CARDS:**

STEEPLE ASTON — Map 04 SP42

♦♦♦♦ Westfield Farm Motel

The Fenway OX25 4SS ☎ 01869 340591 Fax 01869 347594
e-mail: info@westfieldmotel.u-net.com
Dir: *off A4260, 0.5m into village*

A focal point of the rural community, this constantly improving motel provides spacious, comfortable bedrooms all with direct access to the pretty courtyard. Imaginative food is offered in the cosy dining room and the extensive immaculate grounds include woodlands and pretty wild flower areas.
FACILITIES: 7 en suite (2 fmly) No smoking in 5 bedrooms No smoking in dining room STV TVB tea/coffee Direct dial from bedrooms Licensed Cen ht TVL No coaches Dinner Last d 8.30pm **PRICES:** s fr £55; d fr £75* **LB PARKING:** 12 **CARDS:**

TETSWORTH — Map 04 SP60

♦♦♦♦ Little Acre Bed & Breakfast

4 High St OX9 7AT ☎ 01844 281423 Fax 01844 281423
e-mail: julia@little-acre.co.uk
Dir: *M40 junct 6 from S, or 8a from N. From Oxford take A40 turn off at Wheatley and follow A418 towards Thame, in 1m turn right onto A40 to Tetsworth, in 2m at 30mph sign Little Acre is on right*

Ideally located two miles from M40 in twenty acres of mature grounds, this impressive cottage style house provides individually themed comfortable bedrooms filled with a wealth of thoughtful extras. Mouth watering breakfasts are taken in a period furnished dining room which overlooks the pretty enclosed patio garden.
FACILITIES: 3 rms (2 en suite) (1 fmly) No smoking in 2 bedrooms No smoking in dining room No smoking in lounges TVB tea/coffee Cen ht No coaches **PRICES:** d £40-£45* **LB PARKING:** 4

THAME — Map 04 SP70

See also Kingston Blount

Premier Collection

♦♦♦♦♦ The Dairy

Moreton OX9 2HX ☎ 01844 214075
e-mail: thedairy@freeuk.com
Dir: *M40 junct 8 left to Thame, right at rdbt, 400yds left to Moreton, left at War Memorial, left again after 150yds*

continued

Located in the pretty village of Moreton, a gentle stroll across the fields from Thame, this former milking parlour, standing in four acres of immaculate grounds, has been sympathetically renovated to provide high standards of comfort and facilities. The spacious bedrooms are filled with a wealth of both practical and homely extras and have luxury modern bathrooms. Breakfasts are memorable and a warm welcome is assured.
FACILITIES: 3 en suite (3 GF) No smoking TVB tea/coffee No dogs Cen ht TVL No children 12yrs No coaches **PRICES:** s fr £62; d fr £86✻
PARKING: 8 **CARDS:**

WANTAGE Map 04 SU38

♦♦♦♦ Star

Watery Ln, Sparsholt OX12 9PL ☎ 01235 751539 & 751001
01235 751539
e-mail: thestarinn@sparsholt111.fsnet.co.uk
Dir: *from B4507, 4m W of Wantage turn right to Sparsholt. The Star Inn is signposted*
Located in Sparsholt village and very much a part of the rural community, this 17th century inn retains many original features including exposed beams and a polished flagstone floor in the attractive dining room. The modern bedrooms are in a sympathetic conversion of a former barn and stable block.
FACILITIES: 8 annexe en suite (1 fmly) (5 GF) No smoking in bedrooms No smoking in dining room TVB tea/coffee No dogs (ex guide dogs) Cen ht Riding Stabling for guests horses Bar Billiards Dinner Last d 9pm **PRICES:** d £60; (room only) ✻ **MEALS:** Lunch £12.95-£21.65 Dinner £12.95-£21.65✻ **PARKING:** 18 **CARDS:**

♦♦♦ *Stanford Park House*

Park Ln, Stanford in the Vale SN7 8PF ☎ 01367 710702
01367 710329
Dir: *travelling from Oxford towards Swindon on the A420 turn left onto A417, pass through Stanford-in-the-Vale and turn left into Park Lane, house is 0.75m on right hand side*
Located in 17 acres of mature gardens on the outskirts of Stanford in the Vale, this impressive red-brick house offers spacious, comfortable bedrooms. English breakfasts are served at the family table in the elegant dining room, and a large lounge with a conservatory extension is also available to guests.
FACILITIES: 5 rms (1 en suite) (1 fmly) No smoking TVB tea/coffee No dogs (ex guide dogs) Cen ht TVL No coaches **PARKING:** 5

WHEATLEY Map 04 SP50

♦♦♦ Bat & Ball

28 High St, Cuddesdon OX44 9HJ ☎ 01865 874379
01865 873363
e-mail: tony@batandball.fsbusiness.co.uk
Dir: *from M4 through Wheatley towards Garsington. After 1m turn left into Cuddesdon*
Located in a quiet village a short drive from Oxford, this inn offers well equipped bedroom accommodation, all with modern en suite shower rooms. Comprehensive meals are available in the attractive conservatory dining room or bars where cricketing memorabilia is said by some to be more extensive than in the Long Room at Lords!
FACILITIES: 7 en suite (1 fmly) No smoking in dining room TVB tea/coffee No dogs (ex guide dogs) Cen ht Dinner Last d 9.45pm **PRICES:** s £49; d £60✻ **LB MEALS:** Lunch £5-£30alc Dinner £5-£30alc✻
PARKING: 20 **NOTES:** Closed Dec26th **CARDS:**

WOODSTOCK Map 04 SP41

♦♦♦♦ Kings Head Inn & Restaurant

Chapel Hill, Wootton OX20 1DX ☎ 01993 811340
01993 813131
e-mail: t.fay@kings-head.co.uk
Dir: *1m N of Woodstock on A44, turn right (signposted Wootton). Inn located in village centre close to church*

Set in the pretty village of Wootton, this mellow stone inn retains many original features including exposed beams and open fireplaces, and decorated in keeping with the style of the building. The homely bedrooms, including one in a sympathetic barn conversion, are equipped with good practical extras; and imaginative food is offered in the spacious, open-plan public areas.
FACILITIES: 2 en suite 1 annexe en suite (1 fmly) No smoking in bedrooms No smoking in dining room No smoking in lounges TVB tea/coffee No dogs (ex guide dogs) Cen ht No children 12yrs No coaches Dinner Last d 8.30pm
PRICES: s £60-£75; d £80-£100✻ **LB MEALS:** Lunch £16-£22alc Dinner £20-£30alc✻ **PARKING:** 8 **CARDS:**

♦♦♦♦ The Laurels

40 Hensington Rd OX20 1JL ☎ 01993 812583 01993 810041
e-mail: malnikk@aol.com
Dir: *from A44 turn into Hensington Rd by the Punchbowl PH, The Laurels is approx 500yds on right opposite Catholic church*
Peacefully located a few minutes walk from the historic centre and its many attractions, this late Victorian house has been sympathetically renovated to provide high standards of overall comfort. Bedrooms are filled with lots of homely extras and modern efficient bathrooms compliment. A period furnished dining room is the setting for imaginative breakfasts.
FACILITIES: 3 en suite No smoking TVB tea/coffee No dogs Cen ht No children 10yrs No coaches **PRICES:** s £40-£48; d £48-£58✻
PARKING: 3 **NOTES:** Closed Xmas **CARDS:**

♦♦♦♦ The Townhouse

15 High St OX20 1TE ☎ 01993 810843 01993 810843
e-mail: info@woodstock-townhouse.com
Dir: *take A44 to Woodstock, Townhouse is in High Street*
Located in the heart of an historic Cotswold town, this 18th-century mellow stone terraced house has been sympathetically renovated to provide bedrooms filled with thoughtful and practical extras. Breakfast is taken in the attractive combined kitchen dining room or on the enclosed patio during the warmer months.
FACILITIES: 5 en suite (1 fmly) No smoking TVB tea/coffee Direct dial from bedrooms Cen ht No coaches Dinner Last d 5pm **PRICES:** d £65-£75✻ **LB**
CARDS:

England

WOODSTOCK continued

♦♦♦ *Crown*

31 High St OX20 1TE ☎ 01993 811117 📠 01993 813339

Dir: *from Oxford take A44 towards Evesham. Crown Inn 1st establishment on entering town, 150yds beyond Blenheim Palace gates*

Located in the heart of this historic town, the Crown has been sympathetically refurbished and provides comfortable well equipped bedrooms and attractive public areas which include a conservatory restaurant.

FACILITIES: 9 rms (4 en suite) (1 fmly) No smoking in bedrooms No smoking in dining room STV TVB tea/coffee No dogs Cen ht TVL Dinner Last d 9.30pm **CARDS:**

♦♦♦ Punchbowl Inn

12 Oxford St OX20 1TR ☎ 01993 811218 📠 01993 811393

e-mail: info@punchbowl-woodstock.co.uk

Dir: *on A44 from Oxford, in centre of Woodstock*

FACILITIES: 10 en suite (1 fmly) No smoking in 2 bedrooms No smoking in dining room TVB tea/coffee No dogs Licensed Cen ht Dinner Last d 7.30pm **PRICES:** s £50; d £65* **PARKING:** 12 **CARDS:**

WOOLSTONE Map 04 SU28

♦♦♦♦ The White Horse

SN7 7QL ☎ 01367 820726 📠 01367 820566

e-mail: WHorseUffington@aol.com

Dir: *establishment ion middle of village*

In the heart of Oxfordshire countryside, Woolstone is a 16th century village offering a real taste of 'Olde England'. Full of character, the inn has an inviting ambience, with beams, an open fire and a fine collection of malt whiskies. Smart bedrooms and bathrooms are located in the annexe.

FACILITIES: 6 annexe en suite (1 fmly) No smoking in 2 bedrooms No smoking in area of dining room STV TVB tea/coffee Direct dial from bedrooms No dogs (ex guide dogs) Cen ht Last d 10pm **PRICES:** s £50; d £65* **LB MEALS:** Lunch £15-£17.95&alc Dinner £15-£17.95&alc* **PARKING:** 60 **CARDS:**

YARNTON Map 04 SP41

♦♦♦♦ Eltham Villa

148 Woodstock Rd OX5 1PW ☎ 01865 376037 📠 01865 376037

Dir: *on A44, between Oxford and Woodstock*

Located a few minutes drive from Peartree intersection, this well maintained house offers comfortable homely bedrooms and a choice of cosy lounges. Imaginative breakfasts are taken in the cottage style dining room, which features a large collection of decorative china teapots. Proprietors have a good knowledge of local attractions including Blenheim Palace.

FACILITIES: 7 en suite (2 fmly) No smoking TVB tea/coffee No dogs Cen ht TVL No children 5yrs No coaches **PRICES:** s £25-£35; d £45-£50* **PARKING:** 10 **NOTES:** Closed Xmas & New year **CARDS:**

RUTLAND

OAKHAM Map 08 SK80

♦♦♦♦ Kirkee House

35 Welland Way LE15 6SL ☎ 01572 757401 📠 0870 0569418

e-mail: carolbeech@kirkeehouse.demon.co.uk

Located on a leafy avenue within a few minutes' walk of the town centre, this immaculately maintained modern house provides comfortable bedrooms filled with both practical and homely extras. Comprehensive breakfasts are taken in the elegant conservatory extended dining room, which overlooks the pretty garden.

FACILITIES: 2 en suite No smoking TVB tea/coffee No dogs Cen ht No coaches **PRICES:** d fr £44* **PARKING:** 2

WING Map 04 SK80

♦♦♦♦ Kings Arms Inn & Restaurant

Top St LE15 8SE ☎ 01572 737634 📠 01572 737255

e-mail: enquiries@thekingsarms-wing.co.uk

Dir: *1m off A6003 between Uppingham and Oakham*

The Kings Arms, dating back to 1649, has open fires, real ales, blackboards of appetising fare, low beams and flagstone floors. The recently restyled restaurant has a contrasting feel, with warm colour schemes and modern table appointments. The cottage-style, well-equipped bedrooms are spacious and relaxing, split between the Old Bakehouse and Granny's Cottage.

FACILITIES: 8 en suite (4 fmly) No smoking in bedrooms No smoking in dining room No smoking in 1 lounge TVB tea/coffee Direct dial from bedrooms No dogs (ex guide dogs) Cen ht Dinner Last d 9pm **PRICES:** s £50-£100; d £60-£100* **LB MEALS:** Lunch £10-£25alc Dinner £13.50-£30alc* **CONF:** Thtr 25 Class 20 Board 16 Del from £59.50 * **PARKING:** 30 **CARDS:**

SHROPSHIRE

ALBRIGHTON Map 07 SJ80

♦♦♦♦ Parkside Farm *(SJ822021)*

Holyhead Rd WV7 3DA ☎ 01902 372310 📠 01902 375013

Mrs M Shanks

e-mail: jmshanks@farming.co.uk

Dir: *M54 junct 3/A41 for Wolverhampton. Take A464 (Holyhead Rd), farm left after 1.5m*

This is a busy working farm conveniently located for business and tourist attractions. Bedrooms are attractively decorated and well equipped and public areas are cosy and well furnished. This farm has been the proprietors' home for many years and they offer a genuinely warm and friendly welcome to their guests.

FACILITIES: 3 en suite (1 fmly) No smoking TVB tea/coffee No dogs (ex guide dogs) Cen ht Fishing Croquet lawn 600 acres arable working **PRICES:** s £27-£30; d £50-£60* **PARKING:** 4

BISHOP'S CASTLE Map 07 SO38

♦♦♦ The Boar's Head

Church St SY9 5AE ☎ 01588 638521 📠 630126

e-mail: sales@boarsheadhotel.co.uk

Dir: *from A488 follow signs to livestock market, continue past market. Inn on L at x-roads (The Circle)*

Located in the heart of this ancient borough, the inn retains many original features including flag stone floors, exposed beams and open fireplaces. Thoughtfully equipped bedrooms are situated in a sympathetic conversion and a wide range of real ales and imaginative food is available in a non-smoking restaurant.

continued

FACILITIES: 4 en suite (1 fmly) No smoking in dining room No smoking in 1 lounge STV TVB tea/coffee Direct dial from bedrooms Cen ht TVL Pool Table Dinner Last d 9.30pm **PRICES:** s £35-£40; d £60-£70* **LB** **MEALS:** Lunch £10-£15&alc Dinner £10-£15&alc* **PARKING:** 20 **CARDS:**

♦♦♦ The Old Brick Guesthouse

7 Church St SY9 5AA ☎ 01588 638471
e-mail: oldbrick@beeb.net
Dir: *from A488, turn by Community College into Bishops Castle, follow road past church into town, 100yds on left*
Located in the centre of the historic town, this early 18th-century town house retains many original features highlighted by the furnishing and décor styles. Bedrooms are equipped with many homely extras. Public areas include a comfortable guest lounge and a traditionally furnished dining room. Breakfast includes homemade preserves.
FACILITIES: 4 en suite (1 fmly) (1 GF) No smoking in dining room TVB tea/coffee Licensed Cen ht No coaches **PRICES:** s £29; d £50* **LB** **PARKING:** 5 **NOTES:** Closed Xmas & New Year **CARDS:**

BRIDGNORTH — Map 07 SO79

See also Cleobury North

♦♦♦♦ Oldfield Cottage

Oldfield WV16 6AQ ☎ 01746 789257 Fax 01746 789257
e-mail: oldfield.cottage@talk21.com
Dir: *B4364 from Bridgnorth, after 3m pass Down Inn, 2nd L signposted Oldfield, 0.25m on R*
This delightful cottage, in the pretty hamlet of Oldfield, provides two bedrooms with modern facilities in a converted building close by. Both breakfast room and sitting area are in the cottage and on warmer days breakfast can be taken in the conservatory.
FACILITIES: 2 annexe en suite No smoking TVB tea/coffee Cen ht TVL No children 10yrs No coaches **PRICES:** d £45* **LB** **PARKING:** 3 **NOTES:** Closed 24-25 Dec

♦♦ Wyndene

57 Innage Rd WV16 4HS ☎ 01746 764369 & 0797 794 3074
e-mail: wyndene@bridgnorth2000.freeserve.co.uk
Dir: *exit Bridgnorth bypass (A458) for town centre. Turn right at T junct & left into Victoria Road, then right into Hookfield through to Innage Lane*
Situated within walking distance of the centre of Bridgnorth, this small guest house provides a home from home. Bedrooms are comfortable and tastefully decorated, one with a four-poster bed. Home cooked breakfasts are served in an attractive dining room and parking space is available.
FACILITIES: 4 rms (1 en suite) No smoking TVB tea/coffee No dogs Cen ht Dinner Last d 3pm **PRICES:** s £22; d £44-£46* **PARKING:** 3

CHURCH STRETTON — Map 07 SO49

Premier Collection

♦♦♦♦♦ Jinlye

Castle Hill, All Stretton SY6 6JP ☎ 01694 723243
Fax 01694 723243
e-mail: info@jinlye.co.uk
Dir: *from Shrewsbury on A49 turn onto B4370 to All Stretton. In village, turn by red telephone box onto Castle Hill & proceed 1m to top*

Stunningly located in immaculate grounds, this 200-year-old property retains many original features. Sympathetic renovation has resulted in high standards of comfort. Quality décor and fine period furniture add to the charm of the house. Spacious bedrooms contain a wealth of practical and homely extras. Public areas include an elegant dining room and a choice of comfortable sitting rooms.
FACILITIES: 8 rms (7 en suite) No smoking in bedrooms No smoking in dining room No smoking in 1 lounge TVB tea/coffee No dogs Licensed Cen ht TVL No children 12yrs No coaches Mountain bikes for hire **PRICES:** s £42-£50; d £54-£70* **LB** **PARKING:** 8 **CARDS:**

Premier Collection

♦♦♦♦♦ Willowfield *(SO459979)*

Lower Wood, All Stretton SY6 6LF ☎ 01694 751471
Fax 01694 751471 Mr & Mrs P W Secrett
e-mail: wgh@care4free.net
Dir: *turn off A49 at lower wood turning 0.25m S of Leebotwood, 0.5m up lane on left*

Located in an elevated position in immaculate gardens, this sympathetic Edwardian conversion provides high standards of comfort. Bedrooms are filled with practical extras and offer stunning views. Stylish décor and period furnishings all add to the charm and a guest lounge with honesty bar is available in addition to two elegant dining rooms.
FACILITIES: 6 en suite (1 GF) No smoking TVB tea/coffee Direct dial from bedrooms No dogs Licensed Cen ht Dinner Last d noon **PRICES:** d £56-£64* **LB** **PARKING:** 6 **NOTES:** Closed Nov-Feb

♦♦♦♦ Belvedere

Burway Rd SY6 6DP ☎ 01694 722232 Fax 01694 722232
e-mail: belv@bigfoot.com
Dir: *turn W off A49 at Church Stretton & continue for 0.25m past war memorial*
Located on the lower slopes of the Long Mynd, this well-proportioned impressive Edwardian house provides a range of homely bedrooms also equipped with a range of practical extras and complimented by modern efficient bathrooms. Ground floor areas include a cottage style dining room, overlooking the pretty garden and a choice of guest lounges.
FACILITIES: 12 rms (6 en suite) (2 fmly) No smoking in dining room tea/coffee Licensed Cen ht TVL No coaches Last d 6pm **PRICES:** s £26-£34; d £52-£58* **LB** **PARKING:** 10 **CARDS:**

England

CHURCH STRETTON continued

♦♦♦♦ Gilberries Hall Farm *(SO514938)*
Gilberries Ln SY6 7HZ ☎ 01694 771253 📠 01694 771253
Mrs C J Hotchkiss
Dir: *from A49 in village turn at lights onto B4371 for Much Wenlock, after 4m pass Plough Inn on right. Left at sign for Gretton, house first on the left*
Peacefully located and offering stunning views of the surrounding countryside, this well-proportioned house stands on pretty mature gardens and has the additional benefit of a large indoor swimming pool. Bedrooms are filled with both practical and homely extras and modern efficient bathrooms compliment. Public areas include an elegant dining room and a guest lounge.
FACILITIES: 3 en suite (1 fmly) (1 GF) No smoking TVB tea/coffee No dogs (ex guide dogs) Cen ht TVL No children 10yrs Indoor swimming pool (heated) 320 acres dairy arable **PRICES:** s £28-£32; d £48-£54* **PARKING:** 6 **NOTES:** Closed Dec-Jan

♦♦♦♦ Rectory Farm *(SO452985)*
Woolstaston SY6 6NN ☎ 01694 751306 📠 01694 751306
Mrs A Rodenhurst
e-mail: rectoryfarm@woolstation.fsnet.co.uk
Dir: *1.5m from A49 Shrewsbury to Ludlow road,turn by Copper Kettle*

This impressive timber-framed farmhouse lies in the pretty hamlet of Woolstaston. It dates back to the early 17th century and has fine views of the attractive gardens. Exposed beams and oak panelling feature in both the public areas and the spacious bedrooms.
FACILITIES: 3 en suite No smoking TVB tea/coffee No dogs (ex guide dogs) Cen ht TVL No children 12yrs 10 acres non-working **PRICES:** s fr £35; d fr £50* **PARKING:** 6

♦♦♦ Malt House Farm *(SO459979)*
Lower Wood SY6 6LF ☎ 01694 751379 Mr & Mrs D Bloor
Dir: *from Church Stretton turn off A49 after 3m signed Lower Wood, 0.5m to farm*

Located in an elevated position North of the town centre, this period house was 'modernised' in 1772 and has retained many original features. Modern bathrooms compliment the homely bedrooms. Comprehensive breakfasts, which include free-range eggs, are served in the cosy dining room and a guest lounge is also available.

continued

FACILITIES: 3 en suite No smoking TVB tea/coffee No dogs Licensed Cen ht No children 100 acres beef sheep Dinner Last d 9am
PRICES: s fr £18.50; d fr £37* **PARKING:** 3 **NOTES:** Closed Dec-Jan

♦♦♦ Brookfields
Watling St North SY6 7AR ☎ 01694 722314 📠 01694 722314
e-mail: paulangie@brookfields51.fsnet.co.uk
Dir: *on reaching Church Stretton on A49 turn onto the B4371 Much Wenlock road at traffic lights. After a few yards turn left into Watling Street North and Brookfields is short distance along on the left.*
FACILITIES: 5 en suite (1 fmly) No smoking TVB tea/coffee No dogs (ex guide dogs) Licensed Cen ht No coaches Dinner Last d 10am
PRICES: s £30-£35; d £45-£55* **LB PRICES:** s £25-£27.50; d £50-£55*
PARKING: 8

CLEOBURY MORTIMER Map 07 SO67

♦♦♦♦ *Crown*
Hopton Wafers DY14 0NB ☎ 01299 270372 📠 01299 271127
e-mail: desk@crownathopton.co.uk
Dir: *off A4117, 2m W of Cleobury Mortimer*

Set in extensive gardens with a duck pond, this 16th-century inn retains many original features including exposed beams and roaring log fires. Bedrooms are individually furnished and well equipped with modern facilities. Public areas include an elegant restaurant and spacious areas where a good selection of real ales and imaginative food is served.
FACILITIES: 7 en suite No smoking in bedrooms No smoking in dining room TVB tea/coffee Direct dial from bedrooms No dogs (ex guide dogs) Cen ht Dinner Last d 9.15pm **PARKING:** 40 **CARDS:**

♦♦♦♦ Old Bake House
46-47 High St DY14 8DQ ☎ 01299 270193
e-mail: old-bake-house@amserve.com
Dir: *on A4117 from Kidderminster. 100yds past church on right*
This family home dates back to the 18th century and lies near the centre of town. It provides traditionally furnished bedrooms and the lounges are comfortable. Freshly and thoughtfully prepared meals can be enjoyed around one table in the separate dining room.
FACILITIES: 2 en suite No smoking in bedrooms No smoking in dining room No smoking in 1 lounge tea/coffee Cen ht TVL No coaches Dinner Last d 7pm **PRICES:** s £25-£27.50; d £50-£55* **PARKING:** 2

♦♦♦ Red Diamonds highlight the top establishments within the AA's 3, 4 and 5 Diamond ratings.

England

CLEOBURY NORTH Map 07 SO68

Premier Collection

♦♦♦♦♦ Cleobury Court

WV16 6RW ☎ 01746 787005 📠 01746 787005
e-mail: info@cleoburycourthotel.co.uk
Dir: *from Bridgenorth bypass turn onto B4364 signed Ludlow. Cleobury North is 8m along B4364, from Ludlow B4117 to Kidderminster after 1m turn left onto B4364*
Located between the ancient market town of Bridgenorth and gastronomic Ludlow, this former dower house to the Boyne estate has been lovingly restored, and provides the highest standards of comfort and facilities. Quality décor and soft furnishings, antiques, art and memorabilia add to the many original features, and the spacious bedrooms have many thoughtful extras. Ground floor areas include an elegant dining room, sumptuous lounge, fitness room and a billiards room.
FACILITIES: 3 en suite No smoking TVB tea/coffee No dogs (ex guide dogs) Cen ht No children 12yrs No coaches Snooker Gymnasium Croquet lawn boules Dinner Last d 24hrs notice **PRICES:** d £75-£99✻ **PARKING:** 10 **CARDS:**

CLUN Map 07 SO38

♦♦♦♦ Birches Mill

SY7 8NL ☎ 01588 640409 📠 01588 640224
e-mail: gill@birchesmill.fsnet.co.uk
Dir: *from Clun take A488 N for Bishops Castle. Leaving village 1st left for Bicton. In Bicton 2nd left for Mainstone. Pass farm, take 1st right*
Located in pretty mature gardens beside a river in an area of outstanding natural beauty, this stylishly decorated 17th-century former mill retains many original features. Bedrooms are filled with lots of thoughtful extras and a comfortable lounge is available in addition to the elegant dining room.
FACILITIES: 3 en suite No smoking tea/coffee No dogs Cen ht TVL No children 8yrs No coaches Dinner Last d 24hrs **PRICES:** d £58-£62✻ **PARKING:** 4 **NOTES:** Closed Nov-Mar

♦♦♦ Hurst Mill *(SO318811)*

SY7 0JA ☎ 01588 640224 📠 01588 640224 Mrs J Williams
e-mail: hurstmillholidays@tinyworld.co.uk
Dir: *1m E of Clun, signed from B4368, turn right into drive or turn off A49 at Craven Arms, onto B4368 and continue 7.5m, turn left at Hurst Mill Farm sign and continue up driveway.*
This farm is quietly located in a picturesque valley about a mile east of the village. Bedrooms are brightly and cheerfully decorated. In addition to the comfortable lounge, there is a conservatory overlooking the garden. Guests share one table in the pleasant dining room. Three self-catering cottages are also available.
FACILITIES: 3 rms (1 en suite) (1 fmly) No smoking in bedrooms No smoking in dining room No smoking in 1 lounge TV2B tea/coffee Cen ht TVL Fishing Clay pigeon shooting 100 acres mixed Dinner Last d 6.30pm **PRICES:** s £25; d £46-£48✻ **LB** **PARKING:** 6

CRAVEN ARMS Map 07 SO48

♦♦♦♦ The Firs

Norton SY7 9LS ☎ 01588 672511 📠 01588 672511
e-mail: thefirs@go2.co.uk
Dir: *leave A49 at Craven Arms and proceed E on B4368 towards Bridgnorth. After approx 2m turn right at x-roads and follow B & B sign to Norton. Pass farm on left to next left turn, house 100mtrs on left*
Located in an elevated position in the rural hamlet of Norton, this impressive Victorian house retains many original features highlighted by the period furnishings and quality décor throughout. Bedrooms are filled with a wealth of thoughtful extras and provide stunning views of the surrounding countryside. Breakfast makes use of local produce and is taken in an elegant dining room. A lounge is also available.
FACILITIES: 3 en suite No smoking TVB tea/coffee Cen ht TVL **PRICES:** s £25-£35; d £50-£65✻ **PARKING:** 5

♦♦♦♦ Strefford Hall Farm *(SO444856)*

Strefford SY7 8DE ☎ 01588 672383 📠 0870 132 3818
Mrs C Morgan
e-mail: streffordhallfarm@farmersweekly.net
Dir: *0.25m off A49. 1st house on right*
Original features have been retained at this well-proportioned Victorian house, located at the foot of Wenlock Edge. Spacious bedrooms filled with both practical and homely extras, offer stunning views of the surrounding countryside. Breakfast is taken in the elegant dining room and a comfortable lounge is also available.
FACILITIES: 3 en suite No smoking TVB tea/coffee No dogs (ex guide dogs) Cen ht TVL 350 acres arable,beef,sheep,pigs **PRICES:** s £24-£28; d £46-£48 **LB** **PARKING:** 3 **NOTES:** Closed Xmas & New Year

♦♦♦ *Stokesay Castle Inn*

School Rd SY7 9PE ☎ 01588 672304 📠 01588 673877
e-mail: stokesaycastleinn@go2.co.uk
Dir: *on outskirts of Craven Arms, 200yds off A49 Hereford-Shrewsbury road*
Located on the edge of town, next to the Secret Hills Discovery Centre, this hospitable, privately owned inn is ideally situated for exploring the countryside. Bedrooms are modern, well equipped and brightly decorated. The public rooms include a spacious bar/lounge serving real ales and an elegant oak-panelled dining room.
FACILITIES: 12 en suite (1 fmly) No smoking in bedrooms No smoking in dining room STV TVB tea/coffee Direct dial from bedrooms No dogs (ex guide dogs) Cen ht Golf/fishing/gliding/shooting can be arranged Last d 9am **PARKING:** 30 **CARDS:**

DORRINGTON Map 07 SJ40

♦♦♦♦ Ashton Lees

Ashton Lees SY5 7JW ☎ 01743 718378
Dir: *from Shrewsbury, 6m S on A49, establishment on right upon entering village of Dorrington*
Located in immaculate mature gardens on the edge of this rural community, the well-proportioned mid 20th-century house has been renovated to provide high standards of comfort and facilities. Bedrooms are filled with thoughtful extras. Public areas include a cosy dining room with comfortable lounge section and a separate sitting room, both offering blazing open fires.
FACILITIES: 3 rms (2 en suite) No smoking TVB tea/coffee No dogs (ex guide dogs) Licensed Cen ht TVL No coaches Dinner Last d 9am
PRICES: s £22-£25; d £44-£50✻ **LB** **PARKING:** 6
NOTES: Closed Dec-Jan

HADNALL Map 07 SJ52

♦♦♦ Hall Farm House

Shrewsbury Rd SY4 4AG ☎ 01939 210269
e-mail: hallfarmhouse1@whsmithnet.co.uk
Dir: *on A49 at Hadnall, 3m north of Shrewsbury*
FACILITIES: 2 en suite No smoking TVB tea/coffee No dogs (ex guide dogs) Cen ht No coaches **PRICES:** s £25; d £40✻ **LB** **PARKING:** 6

HODNET Map 07 SJ62

♦♦♦ The Grange

Hopton TF9 3LQ ☎ 01630 685579 🖷 01630 685579

Dir: *turn off A53 for Lee Brockhurst, the Grange is 0.5m on left hand side*

In a rural location close to the West Midlands Shooting Range, this sandstone house has been sympathetically renovated, and the cosy bedroom is furnished in quality pine complimented by pretty soft fabrics. Breakfast is taken in a private combined dining and sitting room which overlooks the pretty garden.

FACILITIES: 2 en suite No smoking tea/coffee No dogs Cen ht TVL **PRICES:** s fr £40; d fr £60✻ **PARKING:** 6 **NOTES:** Closed 25-26 Dec

IRONBRIDGE Map 07 SJ60

Premier Collection

♦♦♦♦♦ The Library House

11 Severn Bank TF8 7AN ☎ 01952 432299 🖷 01952 433967

e-mail: info@libraryhouse.com

Dir: *50yds from the Iron Bridge*

A warm welcome is assured at this sympathetically renovated Georgian town house, once the local library. Bedrooms are filled with a wealth of thoughtful extras. The immaculate gardens and hanging baskets are stunning during spring and summer. Memorable breakfasts are served in the pine and copper furnished dining room.

FACILITIES: 4 en suite (1 fmly) No smoking TVB tea/coffee Licensed Cen ht TVL No children 10yrs No coaches **PRICES:** s £50; d £60✻

♦♦♦ Broseley

The Square, Broseley TF12 5EW ☎ 01952 882043 🖷 01952 882043

e-mail: roshavard@netscapeonline.co.uk

Dir: *from Telford take the A442 to Bridgenorth, A4169 to Ironbridge, B4373 to Broseley turn right into Church Street, Establishment is in village Square at centre of Broseley*

Located in the heart of the pretty village of Broseley, this impressive early Victorian town house retains many original features and the proprietors plan to return the property to its former glory. Bedrooms are equipped with both practical and homely extras and comprehensive breakfasts are taken in an elegant dining room.

FACILITIES: 4 en suite (2 fmly) (1 GF) No smoking TVB tea/coffee No dogs (ex guide dogs) Cen ht No children 5yrs **PRICES:** s £28-£35; d £40-£52✻ **LB**

♦♦♦ *Grove Inn & Fat Frog Restaurant*

10 Wellington Rd, Coalbrookdale TF8 7DX ☎ 01952 433269 & 432240 🖷 01952 433269

e-mail: frog@fat-frog.co.uk

Dir: *M4 J6, follow Ironbridge Gorge signs to Jiggers rdbt, take 2nd exit, at bottom of hill on R*

continued

Grove Inn & Fat Frog Restaurant

Located a few minutes' walk from the Coalbrookdale Museum, the interior of this inn has a continental flavour with attractive murals, and both formal and informal dining rooms provide an intimate setting to enjoy the imaginative food. Bedrooms are homely and attentive service is assured.

FACILITIES: 4 en suite (1 fmly) No smoking in bedrooms No smoking in dining room No smoking in 1 lounge TVB tea/coffee Cen ht TVL Dinner Last d 9.30pm **PARKING:** 15 **CARDS:**

♦♦♦ Woodlands Farm Guest House

Beech Rd TF8 7PA ☎ 01952 432741 🖷 01952 432741

Dir: *in Ironbridge, turn into Church Hill from small rdbt with tree in middle, follow this road into Beech Rd, house is approx. 0.5m on the right down small private lane*

Located on four acres in mature grounds, which include a well-stocked fishing lake, this extended Victorian bungalow is constantly being upgraded to provide a range of homely bedrooms filled with both practical and thoughtful extras. A comprehensive breakfast is taken in the cosy dining room, overlooking the pretty formal garden.

FACILITIES: 4 en suite (2 fmly) (4 GF) No smoking TVB tea/coffee Cen ht No children 5yrs No coaches Fishing 4 acres of grounds with Lake **PRICES:** s £15-£30; d £40-£50✻ **LB BB** **PARKING:** 8 **NOTES:** Closed 24 Dec-1 Jan

KNOCKIN Map 07 SJ32

♦♦♦♦ Top Farm House *(SJ334214)*

SY10 8HN ☎ 01691 682582 🖷 01691 682070

Mrs P A Morrissey

e-mail: p.a.m@knockin.freeserve.co.uk

Dir: *in Knockin, past Bradford Arms & shop, past turning for Kinnerley, large black & white house on left*

This impressive black-and-white 16th century house, located in pretty gardens, retains many original features including a wealth of exposed beams and open fires. Bedrooms are filled with lots of thoughtful extras and the open plan ground floor area includes a comfortable sitting room and elegant dining section, the setting for imaginative comprehensive breakfasts.

FACILITIES: 3 en suite (1 fmly) No smoking in dining room TVB tea/coffee Cen ht TVL **PRICES:** s £28-£35; d £46-£50✻ **LB** **PARKING:** 6 **CARDS:**

England

LLANFAIR WATERDINE Map 07 SO27

Premier Collection

♦♦♦♦♦ The Waterdine

LD7 1TU ☎ 01547 528214 📠 01547 529992

Dir: *turn right off B4335 in Lloyney opposite Lloynyey inn, 0.5 into village. Establishment last property on left before church*

Standing in pretty, mature gardens and located within an area of outstanding natural beauty, which includes part of Offa's Dyke, this former 16th century drovers' inn retains much of its original charm and character. Bedrooms are filled with a wealth of thoughtful extras and have modern efficient bathrooms. Public areas include a cosy lounge bar and an elegant restaurant, the setting for imaginative dinners which make use of quality seasonal local produce.

FACILITIES: 3 en suite No smoking in bedrooms No smoking in dining room TVB tea/coffee No dogs Cen ht No children 12yrs No coaches Dinner Last d 9.30pm **PRICES:** s £50; d £80✳ **MEALS:** Lunch £18-£25alc Dinner £20-£25alc✳ **PARKING:** 12 **NOTES:** Closed 1wk Autumn 1 wk Spring **CARDS:**

LONGNOR Map 07 SJ40

♦♦♦♦ Cobblers Cottage

SY5 7PP ☎ 01743 718443 📠 01743 719177

e-mail: n.rigg@btinternet.com

Dir: *turn off A49 at Longnor, keep right at next junct, on right 200yds past school*

Set in pretty gardens, this delightful timber framed, black and white cottage dates back to 1625. Many original features remain; the comfortable lounge has an inglenook fireplace where log fires burn in winter. Bedrooms are charming and very pretty, and one is on the ground floor. Dinner is not served but light suppers are available.

FACILITIES: 3 en suite (1 fmly) (1 GF) No smoking TVB tea/coffee No dogs (ex guide dogs) Cen ht TVL No coaches **PRICES:** d £46✳ **PARKING:** 3

LUDLOW Map 07 SO57

See also Cleobury North

Premier Collection

♦♦♦♦♦ Line Farm *(SO494668)*

Tunnel Ln, Orleton SY8 4HY ☎ 01568 780400

📠 01568 780995 Mrs C Lewis

e-mail: linefarm@lineone.net

Dir: *signposted from A49 in Ashton. Follow the B&B signs in Tunnel Lane to Line Farm*

A warm welcome is assured at this well-maintained no-smoking farmhouse, which is set in immaculate gardens to the south of Ludlow. Bedrooms are filled with a wealth of thoughtful extras and have modern efficient bathrooms. Comprehensive breakfasts are taken in an elegant dining room and a spacious comfortable lounge is also available for guests' use.

FACILITIES: 3 en suite No smoking TVB tea/coffee Direct dial from bedrooms No dogs (ex guide dogs) Cen ht TVL No children 54 acres mixed **PRICES:** d £55-£60✳ **PARKING:** 6 **NOTES:** Closed Nov-Feb

Premier Collection

♦♦♦♦♦ Number Twenty Eight

28 Lower Broad St SY8 1PQ ☎ 01584 876996 & 0800 081 5000 📠 01584 876860

e-mail: ross@no28.co.uk

Dir: *just off B4361. Over Ludford St, forward 20yds on R*

Situated in the Georgian/early Victorian area of this historic town, this hotel is a combination of separate houses, all retaining original features and enhanced by period furnishings. A relaxed and friendly atmosphere prevails and a freshly prepared breakfast, which relies heavily on local produce, is served in the cosy dining room.

FACILITIES: 9 en suite No smoking TVB tea/coffee Direct dial from bedrooms Licensed Cen ht No coaches **PRICES:** d £75-£99✳

CARDS:

England

LUDLOW continued

♦♦♦♦ The Marcle

Brimfield SY8 4NE ☎ 01584 711459 Fax 01584 711459
e-mail: marcle@supanet.com
Dir: turn left off A49 in centre of village, opposite post office
This delightful 16th-century house lies in the centre of the pretty village of Brimfield. The elegantly furnished lounge and other areas are impeccably maintained and decorated. There are just three bedrooms, decorated with pretty wallpapers and equipped with modern facilities. Well tended lawns and gardens surround the house.
FACILITIES: 3 en suite No smoking TVB tea/coffee No dogs (ex guide dogs) Cen ht No children 12yrs No coaches Dinner Last d by arrangement **PRICES:** s £40-£55 d £55-£65* **PARKING:** 6 **NOTES:** Closed Jan-Feb

♦♦♦♦ *Moor Hall*

SY8 3EG ☎ 01584 823209 & 823333 Fax 01584 823387
This very impressive Georgian house is surrounded by extensive gardens and farmland. The bedrooms are richly decorated and well equipped, and one room has its own sitting area. Public areas are spacious and elegantly furnished. There is a choice of sitting rooms and a well-stocked bar. Guests dine family-style in the dining room.
FACILITIES: 3 en suite No smoking in bedrooms No smoking in dining room TVB tea/coffee Licensed Cen ht TVL No coaches Fishing Archery Clay shooting Boules Croquet **PARKING:** 12

See advertisement on page 325

♦♦♦♦ *Red Roofs*

Little Hereford, Nr Ludlow SY8 4AT ☎ 01584 711439
Dir: on A456 1.5m from A49, 3m W of Tenbury Wells
Set in impressive grounds this pleasant house is most welcoming with friendly and attentive hospitality. This is a lovely area, and Red Roofs is conveniently located for the attractions of the three counties. Bedrooms are well-equipped, spacious and comfortable. Breakfast is taken in the attractive dining room, which looks out on the gardens.
FACILITIES: 2 en suite (1 fmly) No smoking TVB tea/coffee No dogs Cen ht TVL No coaches **PARKING:** 5 **NOTES:** Closed Xmas

♦♦♦♦ Roebuck

Brimfield SY8 4NE ☎ 01584 711230 Fax 01584 711654
e-mail: dave@roebuckinn.demon.co.uk
Dir: in centre of Brimfield, just off A49 between Leominster & Ludlow
This 15th-century country inn maintains its traditional atmosphere, which it combines with modern style and quality. Bedrooms are comfortable and attractive, and friendly and relaxing hospitality is provided. Fresh local produce is used to brilliant effect in the dining room, with choices from either the blackboard specials or the carte menu.
FACILITIES: 3 en suite No smoking in bedrooms No smoking in dining room TVB tea/coffee Direct dial from bedrooms Cen ht Dinner Last d 9.30pm **PRICES:** s £45; d £70* **LB MEALS:** Lunch £23-£27alc Dinner £23-£27alc* **PARKING:** 18 **CARDS:**

♦♦♦♦ Ravenscourt Manor

Wooferton SY8 4AL ☎ 01584 711905 Fax 01584 711905
Dir: A49 Ludlow rd, pass Ashford Bowdler on left, over bridge, round bend on left
FACILITIES: 3 en suite No smoking in bedrooms TVB tea/coffee No dogs Cen ht TVL **PRICES:** s £35-£40; d £45-£60* **PARKING:** 10
NOTES: Closed xmas & Jan

♦♦♦ Charlton Arms

Ludford Bridge SY8 1PJ ☎ 01584 872813 Fax 01584 879120
Dir: from A49 Ludlow bypass, follow signs for 'livestock market'. On approaching town centre, premises on L before bridge
Located to the South of the historic centre, on the banks of the River Teme beside the 13th-century Ludford Bridge, this popular inn provides a range of practically equipped bedrooms, some with river views. Imaginative food and a wide range of real ales are taken in the open plan public areas.
FACILITIES: 6 en suite TVB tea/coffee No dogs (ex guide dogs) Cen ht Fishing Pool Table Dinner Last d 8.30pm **PRICES:** s £30; d £50-£55* **MEALS:** Lunch £10-£20alc Dinner £10-£20alc* **PARKING:** 20 **CARDS:**

♦♦♦ Church Inn

The Buttercross SY8 1AW ☎ 01584 872174 Fax 01584 877146
e-mail: Reception@thechurchinn.com
Dir: in Ludlow town centre at top of Broad St
Located in the heart of the historic centre, this Grade II listed building retains many original features, which are enhanced by the décor and furnishing styles throughout. Bedrooms are equipped with a range of homely extras and imaginative food and a wide beer range is available in the cosy public areas.
FACILITIES: 9 en suite (1 fmly) No smoking in area of dining room No smoking in 1 lounge TVB tea/coffee Direct dial from bedrooms Cen ht No coaches Dinner Last d 9pm **NOTES:** Closed 25 Dec **CARDS:**

♦♦♦ Haynall Villa *(SO543674)*

Little Hereford SY8 4AY ☎ 01584 711589 Fax 01584 711589
Mrs R Edwards
e-mail: rachelmedwards@hotmail.com
Dir: leave Ludlow on A49 S, turn L onto A456 towards Kidderminster at Woofferton. At Little Hereford turn R onto lane signed Leysters, 1m on R
Located on immaculate gardens in the pretty hamlet of Little Hereford, this stylishy decorated early Victorian house has many original features. Bedrooms are filled with lots of homely extras and a guest lounge with open fire is also available.
FACILITIES: 3 rms (1 en suite) (1 fmly) No smoking tea/coffee Cen ht TVL No children 6yrs Fishing 72 acres cows sheep Dinner Last d 3pm **PRICES:** s fr £20; d £38-£44* BB **PARKING:** 3 **NOTES:** Closed mid Dec-mid Jan

MARKET DRAYTON — Map 07 SJ63

♦♦♦♦ *Mickley House (SJ615325)*

Faulsgreen, Tern Hill TF9 3QW ☎ 01630 638505
Fax 01630 638505 Mrs P Williamson
e-mail: mickleyhouse@hotmail.com
Dir: A41 to Tern Hill rdbt, then A53 towards Shrewsbury, 1st right for Faulsgreen, 4th house on right
Recommended for its warmth and hospitality, this comfortable farmhouse is surrounded by an acre of beautiful landscaped gardens. Original beams and oak doors reflect the character of the property. Bedrooms are individually designed - two are on the ground floor, and one has an impressive Louis XV bed. There is a spacious and comfortable drawing room for guests.
FACILITIES: 3 en suite (1 fmly) No smoking TVB tea/coffee No dogs Cen ht TVL No children 125 acres beef **PARKING:** 10 **NOTES:** Closed Xmas

♦♦♦ The Four Alls Inn

Woodseaves TF9 2AG ☎ 01630 652995 Fax 01630 653930
e-mail: inn@thefouralls
Dir: 1m from Market Drayton on the A529 towards Hinstock. Hotel on the right just before turning for Tyrley Locks
This friendly country inn is situated conveniently close to Market Drayton. The well-equipped accommodation is located in a separate annexe. A wide range of meals is served in the comfortable bar and there is also a separate function room.
FACILITIES: 9 annexe en suite (4 fmly) (9 GF) No smoking in 4 bedrooms TVB tea/coffee Direct dial from bedrooms No dogs (ex guide dogs) Dinner Last d 2pm **PRICES:** s fr £37.50; d fr £47* **LB MEALS:** Lunch £5.25-£15 Dinner £5.25-£15* **CONF:** Del from £50 * **PARKING:** 60 **NOTES:** Closed 24-26 Dec **CARDS:**

MINSTERLEY Map 07 SJ30

♦♦♦♦ Woodhouse Farm *(SJ388053)*
Malehurst Bank SY5 0BS ☎ 01743 791762 📠 01743 791762
Mr & Mrs R Bromley
e-mail: rogro@woodhousefarm.junglelink.co.uk
Dir: *from A5 onto A488 for 6m, through Pontesbury, farm 0.75m on left*
This fine old farmhouse is surrounded by pretty gardens and lovely Shropshire countryside. Two bedrooms are in a tastefully converted barn, which is also available as a self-catering cottage. Another attractively appointed and well-equipped bedroom is located in the house. A wood-burning stove heats the comfortable lounge, and meals are taken in the welcoming dining room.
FACILITIES: 2 en suite (1 fmly) No smoking TVB tea/coffee No dogs Cen ht 40 acres sheep cattle/ grazing Dinner Last d by arrangement **PRICES:** s £25-£27.50; d £45-£50* **LB PARKING:** 6 **NOTES:** Closed Dec-Feb

MUCH WENLOCK Map 07 SO69

♦♦♦ Gaskell Arms
Bourton Rd TF13 6AQ ☎ 01952 727212 📠 01952 728505
e-mail: maxine@gaskellarms.co.uk
Dir: *on A458 between Shrewsbury & Bridgnorth*
A former posting house on the Shrewsbury to Bath route, this 17th century inn retains many original features including a wealth of exposed beams and open fireplaces. Bedrooms are filled with both practical and homely extras and the pretty walled garden is an additional benefit during the warmer months.
FACILITIES: 13 rms (6 en suite) (2 fmly) (1 GF) No smoking in bedrooms No smoking in dining room TVB tea/coffee Direct dial from bedrooms No dogs (ex guide dogs) Cen ht TVL ch fac Dinner Last d 9.30pm **PRICES:** s £40-£50; d £60-£80* **MEALS:** Lunch £12.95 & alc Dinner £10&alc* **CONF:** Del £70 * **PARKING:** 22
CARDS:

MUNSLOW Map 07 SO58

♦♦♦♦ Crown Country Inn
SY7 9ET ☎ 01584 841205 📠 01584 841255
e-mail: info@crowncountryinn.co.uk
Dir: *A49, turn on to B4368 at Craven Arms, 7m on left, car park opposite*
Located between Much Wenlock and Craven Arms, this impressive half timbered Tudor inn is full of character and charm, with stone floors, a wealth of exposed beams and blazing log fires during the cooler months. Smart pine furnished bedrooms are located in a sympathetic conversion of the former stable block and spacious public areas include two dining rooms, the setting for imaginative food, utilising quality local produce.
FACILITIES: 3 en suite (1 fmly) (1 GF) No smoking in bedrooms No smoking in dining room TVB tea/coffee Cen ht Dinner Last d 8.45pm **PRICES:** s £35; d £55-£65* **MEALS:** Lunch £15-£25alc Dinner £15-£25alc* **CONF:** Thtr 30 Class 30 Board 20 Del from £65 * **PARKING:** 20
CARDS:

NEWPORT Map 07 SJ71

♦♦♦ Norwood House Hotel
Pave Ln TF10 9LQ ☎ 01952 825896 📠 01952 825896
e-mail: tony@norwoodhse.freeserve.co.uk
Dir: *off A41 Wolverhampton-Whitchurch road, close to Lilleshall National Sports Centre*
Located in the quiet village of Pave Lane, this family managed house provides comfortable homely bedrooms and a popular restaurant offering a range of imaginative dishes.
FACILITIES: 5 en suite (1 fmly) No smoking in dining room TVB tea/coffee Licensed Cen ht Dinner Last d 9pm **PRICES:** s £37.50-£39.50; d £47.50-£49.50* **PARKING:** 30 **CARDS:**

♦♦♦ Adams House Hotel & Restaurant
7 High St TF10 7AR ☎ 01952 820085 📠 01952 811144
e-mail: enquiries@adamshousehotel.com
Dir: *M54 junct 3, take Whitchurch A41 exit. Continue 5m, take Newport sign. At rdbt 3rd exit to town centre, hotel is next to Guild Hall on left*
Located in the heart of this historic town, this impressive Georgian property has been sympathetically renovated to provide a range of homely bedrooms and spacious ground floor areas which include a popular local reataurant.
FACILITIES: 8 rms (4 en suite) (2 fmly) No smoking in 6 bedrooms No smoking in dining room No smoking in 1 lounge TVB tea/coffee Direct dial from bedrooms Licensed Cen ht TVL Tennis (hard) Dinner Last d 8.30pm **PRICES:** s £29.50-£39.50; d £49.50-£59.50* **LB PARKING:** 15 **CARDS:**

OSWESTRY Map 07 SJ22

♦♦♦♦ Bradford Arms Hotel
Llanymynech SY22 6EJ ☎ 01691 830582 📠 01691 830728
e-mail: info@bradfordarmshotel.com
Dir: *located in centre of village on A483*
Formally a coaching inn on the Earl of Bradford's estate, this sympathetically renovated hotel provides a range of tastefully furnished bedrooms, filled with a wealth of thoughtful extras. The elegant ground floor areas include lounges, attractive bars and a choice of formal or conservatory restaurants, settings for imaginative food which justifies a strong local following.
FACILITIES: 5 en suite (1 fmly) No smoking in bedrooms No smoking in dining room TVB tea/coffee Direct dial from bedrooms No dogs (ex guide dogs) Cen ht No coaches Dinner Last d 10pm **PRICES:** s £35-£60; d £55-£80* **MEALS:** Lunch £13.95-£22.95alc Dinner £13.95-£26.95alc*
PARKING: 20 **NOTES:** Closed 1st 2wks Jan,last 2wks Sep & 25-26 Dec
CARDS:

♦♦♦♦ Bear Hotel
Salop Rd SY11 2NR ☎ 01691 652093 📠 01691 679996
e-mail: accom@bearhotel.net
Dir: *from A5 take Oswestry road from Mile End Services. Follow town centre signs. Hotel on left approx 25yds beyond right turn into Sainsburys*
Located close to the historic centre, this early 18th century inn enjoys a strong local following for its imaginative food and is also a popular stopping point for travellers on the London to Holyhead route. Bedrooms are both practical and homely and the bar selection includes over 130 different whiskies including an excellent single malt range.
FACILITIES: 10 rms (5 en suite) (1 fmly) TVB tea/coffee Cen ht Dinner Last d 9.30pm **PRICES:** s £25-£47.50; d £40-£70* **LB MEALS:** Lunch £6-£14alc Dinner £10-£20alc* **PARKING:** 30 **NOTES:** Closed 24 Dec-1 Jan
CARDS:

♦♦♦♦ Elgar House
16 Elgar Close SY11 2LZ ☎ 01691 661323 & 07879 462813
e-mail: dennis.harding@amserve.com
Dir: *take Oswestry rd. Take 1st turning on right at end junct left & then 1st right. 2nd left & then 1st right into Elgar Close. On right at end of road*
Located in a quiet cul-de-sac, this much-extended modern house is a short distance from the town centre. Bedrooms are very well equipped and the comfortable lounges and conservatories are tastefully decorated with film and musical memorabilia. There is a bar, and outside an extensive terraced garden with barbecue area. Den Harding is an entertaining host and dinner is available by arrangement.
FACILITIES: 3 en suite (2 fmly) No smoking in bedrooms No smoking in dining room No smoking in 1 lounge TVB tea/coffee No dogs (ex guide dogs) Cen ht TVL No coaches Dinner Last d 3pm **PRICES:** s £25-£35; d £40-£60* **LB PARKING:** 6 **CARDS:**

England

OSWESTRY continued

♦♦♦♦ *The Hawthorns*

Weston Ln SY11 2BG ☎ 01691 657678
e-mail: thehawthornsuk@yahoo.co.uk
Dir: *exit A5 at Little Chef rdbt to Oswestry. After 1m fork left after humpback bridge. Left at lights, 2nd left, establishment on right*
Located in a peaceful residential area, this Victorian house retains some original features and is stylishly decorated throughout. Bedrooms are equipped with thoughtful extras and a cosy lounge is available in addition to an elegant dining room, the setting for comprehensive breakfasts that makes good use of home-made and local produce.
FACILITIES: 2 en suite No smoking TVB tea/coffee No dogs Cen ht No children No coaches **PARKING:** 4

♦♦♦♦ Old Vicarage

Llansilin SY10 7PX ☎ 01691 791345
e-mail: pam@vicarage-guests.co.uk
(For full entry see Llansilin (Powys))

♦♦♦♦ The Pentre

Trefonen SY10 9EE ☎ 01691 653952
e-mail: helen@thepentre.com
Dir: *turn off Oswestry/Trefonen/Treflach Rd into New Well Lane & follow signs for The Pentre*
This 400-year-old stone built farmhouse is in a remote locatation in beautiful border country near Offa's Dyke and there are breathtaking views over the surrounding countryside. The house has a wealth of charm and character with original features such as beamed ceilings and an impressive inglenook fireplace. Bedrooms are comfortably furnished and modern equipment is provided.
FACILITIES: 2 en suite (2 fmly) No smoking TVB tea/coffee No dogs (ex guide dogs) Cen ht TVL No coaches Dinner Last d 9pm **PRICES:** s £30; d £44✻ **LB PARKING:** 10

♦♦♦♦ Top Farm House *(SJ334214)*

SY10 8HN ☎ 01691 682582 🖷 01691 682070
Mrs P A Morrissey
e-mail: p.a.m@knockin.freeserve.co.uk
(For full entry see Knockin)

♦♦♦♦ Ashfield Farmhouse

Maesbury SY10 8JH ☎ 01691 653589 🖷 01691 653589
e-mail: marg@ashfieldfarmhouse.co.uk
Dir: *approx 1m from A5/A483 roads. Turn off A5 at Aston Gates junction and stay on road for approx 300 hundred yds. Bear left and stay on lane to farmhouse next to white church*
FACILITIES: 3 en suite (2 fmly) No smoking in bedrooms No smoking in dining room TVB tea/coffee Cen ht TVL No coaches pony & chicks for children to feed **PRICES:** s £28-£38; d £44-£54✻ **LB PARKING:** 6
CARDS:

PONTESBURY Map 07 SJ30

♦♦♦♦ Gatten Lodge

SY5 0SJ ☎ 01743 790038 🖷 01743 790068
Dir: *From Shrewsbury take A488 to Pontesbury, before Red Lion left to Habberley. Form Habberley, at grass triangle, right signed Westcott & Bridges. In 1m, right at grass triangle. In 2m, over 2 grids lodge on left*
Located in an elevated position offering stunning views of the surrounding unspoilt countryside, this elegant well-proportioned house is also the setting for point to point racehorse training and game luncheons. Bedrooms are equipped with thoughtful extras and a spacious drawing room with open log fire is available in addition to a formal dining room.
FACILITIES: 3 en suite No smoking in bedrooms TVB tea/coffee No dogs Licensed Cen ht No children 14yrs No coaches Fishing Dinner Last d 9pm
PRICES: s fr £34; d fr £58✻ **LB PARKING:** 6

RUYTON-XI-TOWNS Map 07 SJ32

♦♦♦ Brownhill House

SY4 1LR ☎ 01939 261121 🖷 01939 260626
e-mail: brownhill@eleventowns.co.uk
Dir: *leave A5 onto B4397, 2m to Ruyton-XI-Towns. Through village. Brownhill House on left on a right bend*
This very friendly guest house dates back to the 18th century and has a lot of charm and character. Its large terraced garden has been painstakingly created on the side of a steep hill above the River Perry, and guests are welcome to explore. Bedrooms all have modern facilities, including workstations suitable for PCs. Guests dine together in the kitchen.
FACILITIES: 3 en suite (1 GF) No smoking in bedrooms No smoking in dining room tea/coffee No dogs (ex guide dogs) Cen ht TVL No coaches Fishing Croquet lawn Canoeing Dinner Last d noon **PRICES:** s £20.50-£24; d £35-£46 **LB BB PARKING:** 5 **CARDS:**

U Top House Inn

SY4 1LA ☎ 01939 260793
At the time of going to press the Diamond classification for this establishment had not been confirmed. Please check the AA website www.theAA.com for up-to-date information.
FACILITIES: 3 en suite

SHREWSBURY Map 07 SJ41

See also Criggion (Powys), Longnor, Ruyton-X1-Towns, Wem & Westbury

♦♦♦♦♦ Meole Brace Hall

Meole Brace SY3 9HF ☎ 01743 235566 🖷 01743 236886
e-mail: hathaway@meolebracehall.co.uk
Dir: *from traffic island S of town where A49 from Church Stretton runs N and crosses A5 bypass, go N to town centre until large island with traffic lights, take 2nd exit then 2nd left into Upper Road, into 1 way system 1st left then immediately right into Church Lane*
FACILITIES: 3 en suite No smoking TVB tea/coffee No dogs (ex guide dogs) Cen ht TVL No children 10 yrs No coaches Outdoor swimming pool (heated) Tennis (hard) **PRICES:** s fr £39; d fr £59✻
PARKING: 10 **NOTES:** Closed Xmas & New Year

♦♦♦♦ Fieldside

38 London Rd SY2 6NX ☎ 01743 353143
🖷 01743 354687
e-mail: robrookes@btinternet.com
Dir: *from A5 take A5064, premises 1m on left*

Parts of this delightful house date back to 1825. Standing in a large and attractive garden, it is conveniently located for the town centre. The well-equipped bedrooms have period

continued

furnishings and all are pleasantly decorated. Breakfast is served at individual tables in the spacious dining room.
FACILITIES: 4 en suite No smoking TVB tea/coffee No dogs (ex guide dogs) Cen ht No coaches **PRICES:** s £35; d £50-£55✳ **PARKING:** 8

♦♦♦♦ Abbey Court
134 Abbey Foregate SY2 6AU ☎ 01743 364 416
📠 01743 358559
e-mail: info@abbeycourt.org
Dir: *on M54 untill you reach rdbt, 1st exit on M54/A5. At nxt rdbt take exit signed Town Centre/Crematorium. At nxt rdbt take Shirehall exit. Establishment 200yrds on left*
Ideally located within easy walking distance from central attractions, this Grade II listed house has been sympathetically refurbished to provide a range of homely bedrooms, some of which are located in an attactive extension. Comprehensive breakfasts are served in a cosy dining room and a warm welcome is assured.
FACILITIES: 6 rms 4 annexe en suite (2 fmly) No smoking in dining room No smoking in lounges TVB tea/coffee Direct dial from bedrooms No dogs (ex guide dogs) Cen ht **PRICES:** s £23-£25; d £40-£48✳ **LB**
PARKING: 10 **NOTES:** Closed 23-27 Dec **CARDS:**

♦♦♦♦ The Day House *(SJ465104)*
Nobold SY5 8NL ☎ 01743 860212 📠 01734 860212
Mrs P A Roberts
Dir: *exit A5 towards Shrewsbury at rdbt with Esso service stn, follow signs for Nuffield Hospital, continue for 0.5m past hospital, turn right into drive*

Peacefully located on pretty mature gardens within a few minutes' drive from major road links. This impressive 18th-century house, extended in early Victorian times, retains many original features. The spacious bedrooms are equipped with homely extras and a comfortable sitting room is available in addition to an elegant dining room.
FACILITIES: 3 en suite (3 fmly) No smoking in 2 bedrooms No smoking in dining room TVB tea/coffee No dogs (ex guide dogs) Cen ht Rough & game shooting 400 acres arable dairy **PRICES:** s £32-£36; d £52-£56✳
PARKING: 11 **NOTES:** Closed Xmas & New Year

♦♦♦♦ Sandford House Hotel
St Julians Friars SY1 1XL ☎ 01743 343829 📠 01743 343829
e-mail: sandfordhouse@lineone.net
Dir: *cross River Severn over 'English Bridge' & take 1st sharp left*
Located a few minutes walk from historic centre and English Bridge, this Georgian house is full of original features including decorative plaster work and sympathetic refurbishment has resulted in a good range of modern facilities. Bedrooms are both practical and homely and an elegant lounge is available in addition to the pretty dining room.
FACILITIES: 10 en suite (4 fmly) No smoking in 6 bedrooms No smoking in dining room No smoking in lounges TVB tea/coffee Licensed Cen ht TVL
PRICES: s £40; d £55-£65✳ **PARKING:** 3 **CARDS:**

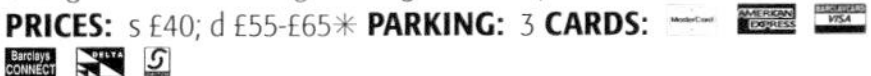

♦♦♦♦ Tudor House
2 Fish St SY1 1UR ☎ 01743 351735
Dir: *enter town via English Bridge, ascend Wyle Cop after 50yds 1st right*
Located on a restored cobbled street within the heart of the historic centre, this fine 15th century town house retains many original features including a wealth of exposed beams and open fireplaces. Bedrooms are filled with thoughtful extras and a cosy lounge is available, in addition to the elegant dining room where breakfast is served.
FACILITIES: 3 rms (2 en suite) No smoking in 2 bedrooms No smoking in dining room TVB No dogs Cen ht TVL No children 12yrs No coaches
PRICES: s £28-£35; d £46-£52✳ **NOTES:** Closed 23-26 Dec

♦♦♦ Lythwood Hall Bed & Breakfast
2 Lythwood Hall, Lythwood, Bayston Hill SY3 0AD
☎ 07074 874747 📠 01743 874747
e-mail: lythwoodhall@amserve.net
Dir: *A49 at Bayston Hill signed Lythwood, 2nd right Lythwood Rd, through village not right but straight ahead for 100yds, then left by rd hump sign, keep right*
This friendly guest house is part of 18th century Lythwood Hall. Set in peaceful rural surroundings while still close to main routes to and from Shropshire. Bedrooms are well equipped, the comfortable sitting room overlooks a lovely walled garden, and the attractive dining room has period furnishings.
FACILITIES: 2 en suite No smoking tea/coffee No dogs (ex guide dogs) Cen ht TVL No coaches kennel and run for dogs Dinner Last d 6pm
PRICES: s £20-£25; d £40-£45✳ **LB PARKING:** 3

Prices may change during the currency of the Guide, please check when booking.

England

SHREWSBURY continued

♦♦♦ Stiperstones
18 Coton Crescent, Coton Hill SY1 2NZ
☎ 01743 246720 & 350303 Fax 01743 350303
e-mail: thestiperstones@aol.com
Dir: *from town centre take A528 for Ellesmere. Left at sign for Baschurch B5067. Next right. At x-rds, house opposite on right*

Located in a mainly residential area within easy walking distance from central attractions, this Edwardian house provides homely thoughtfully equipped bedrooms, three of which are situated in an adjacent separate cottage. Comprehensive breakfasts are taken in an attractive dining room and a warm welcome is assured.

FACILITIES: 3 rms 3 annexe rms (1 fmly) (1 GF) No smoking in 1 bedrooms No smoking in dining room No smoking in lounges TVB tea/coffee No dogs (ex guide dogs) Cen ht No coaches **PRICES:** s £22.50; d £38* **BB** **PARKING:** 6 **CARDS:** [CARDS]

♦♦♦ Sydney House Hotel
Coton Crescent, Coton Hill SY1 2LJ ☎ 01743 354681
Fax 01743 354681
e-mail: sydneyhouseshrews@talk21.com
Dir: *junct of A528/B5067*

This family run hotel provides well equipped, modern accommodation and benefits from a prime location - minutes' walk from the town centre. Facilities include an oak-panelled lounge bar with a feature embossed-plaster ceiling. Meals are freshly prepared and can be taken at separate tables in the smartly appointed dining room.

FACILITIES: 6 en suite (1 fmly) No smoking in 2 bedrooms No smoking in dining room TVB tea/coffee No dogs (ex guide dogs) Licensed TVL No children 10yrs Dinner Last d 6.30pm **PARKING:** 7 **CARDS:** [CARDS]

U Glyndene
Abbey Foregate SY2 6BL ☎ 01743 352488

At the time of going to press the Diamond classification for this establishment had not been confirmed. Please check the AA website www.theAA.com for up-to-date information.

FACILITIES: 3 en suite

TELFORD — Map 07 SJ60

♦♦♦♦♦ Bridge House
Buildwas Rd TF8 7BN ☎ 01952 432105 Fax 01952 432105
e-mail: janethedges@talk21.com
Dir: *at the bottom of Buildwas Bank (A4169) turn left then next left into car park*

FACILITIES: 4 en suite (1 fmly) No smoking in dining room TVB tea/coffee No dogs Cen ht TVL No coaches Fishing **PRICES:** s £42-£45; d £58-£65* **PARKING:** 6 **NOTES:** Closed Xmas-New Year

♦♦♦♦ Shray Hill
Shray Hill TF6 6JR ☎ 01952 541260 Fax 01952 541260
Dir: *turn off A442 at Crudgington cross roads onto B5062 towards Newport. Shray Hill House 2m on left*

Located in four acres of immaculate grounds in an area of outstanding natural beauty, this impressive 19th-century house retains many original features. The spacious bedrooms are filled with lots of thoughtful extras and have modern efficient shower rooms. Ground floor areas include an elegant dining room and sumptuous guest lounge.

FACILITIES: 4 en suite No smoking TVB tea/coffee No dogs (ex guide dogs) Cen ht TVL No coaches **PRICES:** s £25-£28.50; d £50*
PARKING: 7

♦♦♦♦ Avenue Farm *(SJ599099)*
Uppington TF6 5HW ☎ 01952 740253 Fax 01952 740401
Mrs M Jones
e-mail: jones@avenuefarm.fsnet.co.uk
Dir: *from M54 junct 7 take B5061 for Atcham, 2nd left signed Uppington pass sawmill, turn right farm 400yds on right*

Located within the pretty rural hamlet of Uppington, this impressive house stands in immaculate mature gardens. The many period features add to the building's charm. Bedrooms offer a balance between practicality and homeliness and a comfortable guest sitting room is also available.

FACILITIES: 3 en suite (1 fmly) No smoking in bedrooms No smoking in dining room TV1B tea/coffee No dogs (ex guide dogs) Riding 430 acres arable **PRICES:** s £25-£30; d £45-£50* **PARKING:** 4
NOTES: Closed Xmas

♦♦♦♦ Church Farm
Wrockwardine Village, Wellington TF6 5DG ☎ 01952 244917
Fax 01952 244917
e-mail: jo@churchfarm.freeserve.co.uk
Dir: *in centre of village, opposite church*

Located opposite the church in the pretty village of Wrockwardine. With many original features, such as exposed beams and open fireplaces, this is an impressive Grade II listed house. The comfortable bedrooms, one located in a separate building, are filled with thoughtful extras, and memorable breakfasts are taken at one family table in the elegant dining room.

FACILITIES: 5 rms (2 en suite) 1 annexe en suite (1 fmly) (2 GF) No smoking in dining room TVB tea/coffee Cen ht TVL No children 10yrs No coaches **PRICES:** s fr £26; d £48-£58* **LB** **PARKING:** 10
CARDS: [CARDS]

WEM — Map 07 SJ52

♦♦♦♦ *Lowe Hall Farm*
SY4 5UE ☎ 01939 232236 Fax 01939 232236
e-mail: bandb@lowehallfarm.demon.co.uk
Dir: *enter Wem on B5476, turn left at church and immediately right after garage up Lowe Hill Rd. After approx 1m, Lowe Hall opposite T-junct*

Lowe Hall is a 16th-century listed farmhouse set in a large garden with a moat. The interior includes a Jacobean staircase, Charles II fireplace and antique furniture and paintings. The tastefully decorated bedrooms are well furnished and are equipped with many useful extras and accessories including refrigerators, bathrobes and hairdryers. Downstairs there is a comfortable lounge.

FACILITIES: 3 en suite (1 fmly) No smoking TVB tea/coffee No dogs Cen ht TVL Fishing **PARKING:** 6

♦♦♦♦ Soulton Hall *(SJ543303)*
Soulton SY4 5RS ☎ 01939 232786 Fax 01939 234097
Mrs A P Ashton
e-mail: j.ashton@soultonhall.com
Dir: *turn off A49 onto B5065 towards Wem, 2m on left after small bridge*

Located on 500 acres in the historic town centre, this fine Tudor house was home to Lord Mayor of London Thomas Hill, has been sympathetically renovated to provide high levels of comfort. Bedrooms are equipped with both practical and homely extras and ground floor areas include a spacious hall sitting room, lounge bar and attractive dining room.

continued

England

Soulton Hall

FACILITIES: 4 en suite 3 annexe en suite (2 fmly) (3 GF) No smoking TVB tea/coffee Direct dial from bedrooms Licensed Cen ht Fishing Croquet lawn Birdwatching in 50 acre woodland 560 acres arable Dinner Last d 8.30pm **PRICES:** s £37-£47.50; d £70-£80✻ **LB** **CONF:** Del from £80 ✻ **PARKING:** 52 **CARDS:**

See advertisement on page 329

WESTBURY Map 07 SJ30

♦♦♦♦ Barley Mow House

Aston Rogers SY5 9HQ ☎ 01743 891234
e-mail: colinrigby@astonrogers.fsnet.co.uk
Dir: *off A5 onto B4386, signposted Montgomery. 2m after Westbury, turn right to Aston Rogers. House is 400yds on left, opposite Aston Hall*

Parts of this charming old property date back to the 17th century. Extended about 200 years ago, it was a pub until 1992. Now tastefully restored and converted, it provides comfortable accommodation with modern equipment and facilities, including a bedroom on ground floor level. The guest house is located in a peaceful rural area and is surrounded by extensive gardens.

FACILITIES: 3 en suite (1 fmly) (1 GF) No smoking TVB tea/coffee No dogs (ex guide dogs) Cen ht TVL No coaches **PRICES:** s fr £24; d fr £40✻ **LB** **PARKING:** 4 **NOTES:** Closed Dec-Feb

WHITCHURCH Map 07 SJ54

Premier Collection

♦♦♦♦♦ Dearnford Hall *(SJ543389)*

Tilstock Rd SY13 3JJ ☎ 01948 662319 Fax 01948 666670
Charles & Jane Bebbington
e-mail: dearnford_hall@yahoo.com
Dir: *at Tilstock rdbt on S Whitchurch by-pass take B5476 to Tilstock. Establishment 0.5m on L*

Located in immaculate mature grounds, this elegant, well-proportioned house retains many original features. The very spacious bedrooms are filled with a wealth of thoughtful extras and have modern efficient bathrooms. Ground floor rooms include a cosy sitting room and a superb dining room, the setting for memorable mouth-watering breakfasts. Outdoor activities include boules and a well-stocked fly fishing lake.

FACILITIES: 2 en suite No smoking TVB tea/coffee No dogs Cen ht TVL No children 15yrs Fishing Trout lake, hot air ballooning 500 acres Arable/Wildflower Meadow **PRICES:** s £45-£55; d £80-£90✻ **LB** **CONF:** Board 10 **PARKING:** 10 **NOTES:** Closed Xmas **CARDS:**

SOMERSET

BATH Map 03 ST76

For other locations surrounding Bath see also Box (Wiltshire), Bradford on Avon (Wiltshire), Combe Hay, Frome, Stanton Prior, and Trowbridge (Wiltshire)

Premier Collection

♦♦♦♦♦ Ayrlington

24/25 Pulteney Rd BA2 4EZ ☎ 01225 425495
Fax 01225 469029
e-mail: mail@ayrlington.com
Dir: *M4 junct 18, A46 then A4 to Bath. Follow signs for A367 Wells/Exeter, hotel on right 100mtrs beyond St Mary's church*

The splendour and charm of this impressive Victorian house is apparent from the attractive exterior and throughout the rooms, many of which feature oriental artefacts and pictures. Bedrooms, some of which have spa-baths, four-poster beds and views over Bath cricket ground, are tastefully decorated and comfortable. Breakfast is taken in the elegant dining room and guests can enjoy the views while eating.

FACILITIES: 12 en suite (3 fmly) No smoking TVB tea/coffee Direct dial from bedrooms No dogs (ex guide dogs) Licensed Cen ht No coaches Unlimited free golf at local golf club **PRICES:** d £75-£145✻ **PARKING:** 14 **NOTES:** Closed 2 weeks at Xmas **CARDS:**

See advertisement on page 333

Premier Collection

♦♦♦♦♦ Apsley House Hotel

Newbridge Hill BA1 3PT ☎ 01225 336966
Fax 01225 425462
e-mail: info@apsley-house.co.uk
Dir: *on A431 1m west of city*

Built in 1830 as a country house for the Duke of Wellington, Apsley House is conveniently located a short stroll from the city. The house is extremely stylish and elegant, and the spacious bedrooms (one of which has a king size four-poster bed) have pleasant views. A delightful bar is available and guests can also relax in the lounge. Breakfast is a feast, and a range of choices are offered.

FACILITIES: 9 en suite (3 fmly) No smoking in 9 bedrooms No smoking in dining room No smoking in 1 lounge STV TVB tea/coffee Direct dial from bedrooms No dogs (ex guide dogs) Licensed Cen ht No children 5yrs **PRICES:** s £60-£90; d £65-£140✻ **LB** **PARKING:** 10 **NOTES:** Closed 1 wk Xmas **CARDS:**

A indicates an Associate entry, which has been inspected and rated by the ETC or the RAC in England.

England

BATH continued

Premier Collection

♦♦♦♦♦ Athole Guest House

33 Upper Oldfield Park BA2 3JX ☎ 01225 334307
01225 320009
e-mail: info@atholehouse.co.uk
Dir: *follow signs A367 Radstock, road leads around city ctr and turns left at large rdbt towards Radstock (Wellsway). Upper Oldfield Park is 1st right in approx 300yds*

Recently refurbished to offer very high standards of quality and comfort, this quietly located traditional detached house has modern, highly equipped bedrooms and bathrooms. A varied menu is available at breakfast including fresh fruit salad and home-made bread. Secure car parking via electronic gates is a further addition.

FACILITIES: 3 en suite (1 fmly) No smoking STV TVB tea/coffee Direct dial from bedrooms No dogs (ex guide dogs) Cen ht No coaches
PRICES: s £48-£58; d £65-£90* LB **PARKING:** 7
CARDS:

Premier Collection

♦♦♦♦♦ Bath Lodge

Warminster Rd BA2 7NH ☎ 01225 723040
01225 723737
e-mail: info@bathlodge.com

(For full entry see Norton St Philip)

Premier Collection

♦♦♦♦♦ Cheriton House

9 Upper Oldfield Park BA2 3JX ☎ 01225 429862
01225 428403
e-mail: cheriton@which.net
Dir: *south of Bath, 0.5m on A367. Take 1st right hand turn into Upper Oldfield Park. Cheriton House is 200yds along on the left*

A few minutes' stroll from the city centre, this well maintained house enjoys lovely views over the Georgian architecture of Bath. Guest rooms, one of which has a four-poster bed, are tastefully decorated. A comfortable lounge leads to a bright conservatory that is an ideal setting for breakfast.

FACILITIES: 11 en suite (1 fmly) No smoking TVB tea/coffee Direct dial from bedrooms No dogs (ex guide dogs) Cen ht No children 12yrs No coaches **PRICES:** s £50-£66; d £66-£95* LB **PARKING:** 11
CARDS:

See advertisement on opposite page

Premier Collection

♦♦♦♦♦ Dorian House

1 Upper Oldfield Park BA2 3JX ☎ 01225 426336
01225 444699
e-mail: info@dorianhouse.co.uk
Dir: *leave A367 & turn right into Upper Oldfield Park, 3rd building left*

This elegant Victorian property, situated within walking distance of the city centre, enjoys lovely views. The atmosphere is welcoming and the accommodation is of high quality. Two of the rooms have fine wooden four-poster beds and all offer an excellent range of extra facilities. There is an attractive lounge with honesty bar, fresh flowers and reading material.

FACILITIES: 12 en suite (1 fmly) (2 GF) No smoking TVB tea/coffee Direct dial from bedrooms No dogs (ex guide dogs) Licensed Cen ht No coaches **PRICES:** s £47-£85; d £72-£140* **PARKING:** 11
CARDS:

Premier Collection

♦♦♦♦♦ Haydon House

9 Bloomfield Park BA2 2BY ☎ 01225 444919 & 427351
01225 444919
e-mail: stay@haydonhouse.co.uk
Dir: *follow signs for A367 Exeter. At large rdbt turn left. After 0.75m right at shopping centre, fork right then 2nd right for 200yds*

This charming house offers excellent standards of comfort and hospitality. The delightful rooms include four-poster and canopied beds and are tastefully decorated with Laura Ashley fabrics, as well as being very well equipped and provided with many thoughtful extras. Special rates are available between November and March. Breakfast is excellent - an interesting feature is the Scotch whisky or rum porridge.

FACILITIES: 5 en suite (1 fmly) No smoking TVB tea/coffee Direct dial from bedrooms No dogs (ex guide dogs) Cen ht No coaches Sun Terrace **PRICES:** s £50-£70; d £75-£105 LB **PARKING:** 1
CARDS:

BATH continued

Premier Collection

♦♦♦♦♦ Holly Lodge

8 Upper Oldfield Park BA2 3JZ ☎ 01225 424042 & 339187 📠 01225 481138
e-mail: stay@hollylodge.co.uk
Dir: *0.5m SW of city centre off A367*

Set in delightful gardens and just a few minutes walk from Bath's many attractions, Holly Lodge enjoys splendid views over the city. Bedrooms, including one on the ground floor, are well appointed with comfortable furnishings and many charming features. Two rooms have four-poster beds, one in a most impressive Egyptian style. The freshly cooked breakfasts provide a good start to the day. Ample parking is a bonus.

FACILITIES: 7 en suite No smoking STV TVB tea/coffee Direct dial from bedrooms No dogs (ex guide dogs) Cen ht No coaches **PRICES:** s £48-£55; d £79-£97✻ **LB PARKING:** 8 **CARDS:**

See advertisement on opposite page

Premier Collection

♦♦♦♦♦ Kennard Hotel

11 Henrietta St, off Great Pulteney St BA2 6LL
☎ 01225 310472 📠 01225 460054
e-mail: reception@kennard.co.uk
Dir: *from A4 London Road turn left onto A36 over river turn right past fire station. Kennard is top right on Henrietta Street (The Circle)*

A very attractive Georgian house, dating back to 1794. With parking available the house is convenient for the city centre, which is just a short stroll away. Bedrooms and public areas alike are luxuriously appointed and very stylish. Silver-service breakfast is taken in the dining room, and freshly squeezed orange juice and 'Kennard' chutneys are just two of the many delights.

FACILITIES: 13 rms (11 en suite) (2 fmly) No smoking STV TVB tea/coffee Direct dial from bedrooms No dogs (ex guide dogs) Cen ht No children 12yrs No coaches **PRICES:** s £54-£58; d £88-£120 **NOTES:** Closed Xmas & New Year **CARDS:**

Premier Collection

♦♦♦♦♦ Leighton House

139 Wells Rd BA2 3AL ☎ 01225 314769 📠 01225 443079
e-mail: welcome@leighton-house.co.uk
Dir: *leave A36 at Churchill Bridge in town centre & take A367, 600mtrs & house on left, at junction with Hayesfield Park*

This splendid Victorian house overlooks the city and is within easy walking distance of Bath's many attractions, with ample parking available. The elegance of the house has been retained while modern facilities provide excellent levels of comfort. Two bedrooms are on the ground floor and all rooms overlook the delightful gardens. Breakfast is taken in the attractive dining room.

FACILITIES: 8 en suite (1 fmly) (2 GF) No smoking TVB tea/coffee Direct dial from bedrooms No dogs (ex guide dogs) Cen ht No children 7yrs No coaches **PRICES:** s £50-£95; d £65-£95✻ **LB PARKING:** 8 **CARDS:**

Premier Collection

♦♦♦♦♦ Monkshill

Shaft Rd, Monkton Combe BA2 7HL ☎ 01225 833028
📠 01225 833028
e-mail: monks.hill@virgin.net
Dir: *Join A36 (Pulteney Road) towards Bristol. Turn L into A3062 (Prior Park Rd) towards Combe Down. At top of hill turn L (North Road). 2nd R into Shaft Rd. Pass fields, down hill, Monkshill is 100m on R*

Monkshill is an elegant family home, enjoying uninterrupted views over the Limpley Stoke Valley. The city of Bath is just a short drive away and other local attractions are also within easy reach. Classically furnished throughout, this appealing house has a great deal of charm. Guests take breakfast around one large table in the dining room, and afternoon tea may be taken in the delightful sitting room.

FACILITIES: 3 rms (2 en suite) (1 fmly) No smoking TVB tea/coffee Cen ht No coaches Croquet lawn Bowling **PRICES:** s £55-£70; d £70-£85 **PARKING:** 8 **NOTES:** Closed 2 wks Xmas & New Year **CARDS:**

Premier Collection

♦♦♦♦♦ Monmouth Lodge

BA2 7LH ☎ 01373 834367

(For full entry see Norton St Philip)

Premier Collection

♦♦♦♦♦ Paradise House Hotel

Holloway BA2 4PX ☎ 01225 317723 📠 01225 482005
e-mail: info@paradise-house.co.uk
Dir: *from A36 (Bristol/Warminster road) at Churchill Bridge rdbt take A367, then 3rd left, down hill into cul-de-sac, house 200yds on left*

Set in half an acre of lovely walled gardens, this Georgian house, built in 1720 from mellow Bath stone, is within walking distance of the city centre. Many bedrooms have fine views

continued

over the city, and all are decorated in opulent style. Furnishings are elegant and facilities modern. The lounge is comfortable and relaxing and breakfast is served in the smart dining room. Hospitality and service here are friendly and professional.
FACILITIES: 11 en suite (2 fmly) No smoking TV10B tea/coffee Direct dial from bedrooms No dogs Licensed Cen ht No coaches Croquet lawn Boules pitch **PRICES:** s £55-£89; d £70-£150✳ **LB**
PARKING: 6 **NOTES:** Closed 3 days Xmas
CARDS:

Premier Collection

♦♦♦♦♦ The County Hotel

18-19 Pulteney Rd BA2 4EZ ☎ 01225 425003
01225 466493
e-mail: reservations@county-hotel.co.uk
This fine house offers delightful accommodation. Guest rooms are very comfortably furnished; many have fine views of the city, and one has a four-poster bed. A traditional bar, bright conservatory and charming lounge are provided. At breakfast, served overlooking the delightful green towards the Abbey, an impressive selection featuring fresh and local produce is available.
FACILITIES: 22 en suite No smoking in bedrooms No smoking in dining room STV TVB tea/coffee Direct dial from bedrooms No dogs Licensed Cen ht No children 15yrs No coaches **PRICES:** s £60-£70; d £100-£185✳ **PARKING:** 45 **NOTES:** Closed 22 Dec-15 Jan
CARDS:

See advertisement on page 337

Premier Collection

♦♦♦♦♦ Widbrook Grange

Trowbridge Rd, Widbrook BA15 1UH ☎ 01225 864750 & 863173 01225 862890
e-mail: stay@widbrookgrange.com

(For full entry see Bradford on Avon (Wiltshire))

♦♦♦♦ Badminton Villa

10 Upper Oldfield Park BA2 3JZ ☎ 01225 426347
01225 420393
e-mail: badmintonvilla@blueyonder.co.uk
Dir: *from city centre take A367 towards Radstock. 1st right 600yds up hill into Upper Oldfield Park. Premises 300yds on right*
Large comfortable rooms and friendly, welcoming proprietors provide a relaxing base from which to explore the many attractions of Bath. This charming Victorian house is located in a quiet residential area and delightful views over the city can be enjoyed from some of the bedrooms. Breakfast is served in the pleasant dining room and in summer months guests are also welcome to use the conservatory and attractive gardens.
FACILITIES: 4 en suite (1 fmly) No smoking TVB tea/coffee No dogs (ex guide dogs) Cen ht No children 8yrs No coaches **PRICES:** s £50-£52; d £68-£75 **LB** **PARKING:** 5 **NOTES:** Closed 24 Dec-30 Jan
CARDS:

England

BATH continued

♦♦♦♦ Brocks

32 Brock St BA1 2LN ☎ 01225 338374 🖷 01225 334245
e-mail: marion@brocksguesthouse.co.uk
Dir: *leave M4 junct 18 onto A46, Brocks is just off A4 between Circus & Royal Crescent*

This delightful Georgian property, located very close to the famous Royal Crescent, is within easy walking distance of the city centre. Marion Dodd is a natural when it comes to making guests feel welcome, and all the rooms display the comfortable elegance that reflects the Georgian era. A traditional breakfast is offered in the charming dining room where guests can also relax in easy chairs.
FACILITIES: 6 en suite (2 fmly) No smoking TVB tea/coffee No dogs (ex guide dogs) Cen ht No coaches **PRICES:** s £45-£55; d £63-£78✳ **LB PARKING:** 2 **NOTES:** Closed Xmas **CARDS:**

♦♦♦♦ The Plaine

Bell Hill BA2 7LT ☎ 01373 834723 🖷 01373 834101
e-mail: theplaine@easynet.co.uk

(For full entry see Norton St Philip)

♦♦♦♦ St Leonards

Warminster Rd BA2 6SQ ☎ 01225 465838 🖷 01225 442800
e-mail: stleon@dircon.co.uk
Dir: *M4 J18, take A4 towards Bath. L onto A36 Warminster Rd. Up hill, 200yds on L past Bathampton sign.*

St Leonards is an impressive Victorian house, which is close to the city's many attractions. Superb views and friendly and attentive proprietors provide a peaceful and memorable setting. Bedrooms and bathrooms are stylish and spacious and very are very comfortable. A full English breakfast is served in the attractive dining room.
FACILITIES: 6 en suite (2 fmly) (2 GF) No smoking TVB tea/coffee Cen ht No coaches **PRICES:** s £30-£65; d £55-£88✳ **LB PARKING:** 10 **CARDS:**

♦♦♦♦ Tasburgh House Hotel

Warminster Rd BA2 6SH ☎ 01225 425096 🖷 01225 463842
e-mail: hotel@bathtasburgh.co.uk
Dir: *on N side of A36 - adjacent to Bathampton Ln junct - approx 0.5m from Bathwick St rdbt & Sydney Gdns*

Set in seven acres of well tended gardens this delightful Victorian property enjoys panoramic views and is just a fifteen-minute stroll from the city. The comfortable bedrooms have been individually furnished and are particularly well-equipped. Public rooms include an elegant lounge leading into a bright conservatory and an attractive dining room where imaginative evening meals can be enjoyed.
FACILITIES: 12 en suite (3 fmly) (2 GF) No smoking TVB tea/coffee Direct dial from bedrooms No dogs Licensed Cen ht TVL No coaches Croquet lawn Dinner Last d 8pm **PRICES:** s £57-£67; d £82-£112✳ **PARKING:** 16 **CARDS:**

♦♦♦♦ Villa Magdala Hotel

Henrietta Rd BA2 6LX ☎ 01225 466329 🖷 01225 483207
e-mail: office@VillaMagdala.co.uk
Dir: *turn left off A4 following signs for A36 to Warminster. Henrietta Rd is 2nd on right, opposite Henrietta Park*

A gracious and stylish Victorian town house, Villa Magdala is a short walk from the many and varied city sights. Pleasant views can be enjoyed from the attractively furnished and spacious bedrooms, all of which are equipped to meet the demands of any visitor. The charming lounge and dining room overlook one of Bath's delightful parks. On site car parking is a definite bonus.
FACILITIES: 17 en suite (4 fmly) No smoking TVB tea/coffee Direct dial from bedrooms No dogs (ex guide dogs) Cen ht No children 7yrs No coaches **PRICES:** s £65-£85; d £85-£140✳ **LB PARKING:** 17 **CARDS:**

♦♦♦♦ *Ainsborough Hotel*

Weston Ln BA1 4AB ☎ 01225 311380 🖷 01225 447411
e-mail: ainsboroughhotel@aol.com
Dir: *W from Queens Square on A4 for 1m, right into Park Lane by park corner & left at top for 600yds. Hotel approx 0.25m from main hospital gates*

continued

Close to Bath's Royal Crescent and city attractions this hotel is ideal as a base for visiting the city or for the business guest. Friendly service is provided and rooms are well-equipped, comfortable and spacious. An attractive lounge and a bar are available and overlook the secluded well-tended gardens.

FACILITIES: 17 en suite (3 fmly) No smoking in 10 bedrooms No smoking in dining room No smoking in lounges STV TVB tea/coffee Direct dial from bedrooms No dogs Licensed Cen ht No coaches **PARKING:** 18 **CARDS:**

♦♦♦♦ Anchor Farm *(ST745604)*

BA2 7EE ☎ 01225 832124 Mr & Mrs R Saker-Harper

(For full entry see Combe Hay)

♦♦♦♦ Aquae Sulis Hotel

174/176 Newbridge Rd BA1 3LE ☎ 01225 420061 & 339064 Fax 01225 446077

e-mail: enquiries@aquaesulishotel.com

Dir: *Leave Queens Square in city centre along Upper Bristol Road (A4) towards Bristol. Fork left onto Newbridge Rd, at 2nd set of traffic lights after Victoria Park, Hotel on the right*

Located within easy reach of the city centre, this attractive Edwardian house offers a warm and genuine welcome. Bedrooms are of a good size and well equipped with many modern facilities such as Internet/e-mail access. There are two inviting lounges, one with a small but well stocked bar. Breakfast is taken in the comfortable dining room and a good selection of meals is available in the evening.

FACILITIES: 13 en suite (5 fmly) No smoking in bedrooms No smoking in dining room No smoking in 1 lounge STV TVB tea/coffee Direct dial from bedrooms Licensed Cen ht TVL Free use of local golf course & club provided

continued

Aquae Sulis Hotel

Dinner Last d 6pm **PRICES:** s £45-£59; d £55-£95✻ **LB PARKING:** 12 **CARDS:**

See advertisement on page 339

♦♦♦♦ Armstrong House

41 Crescent Gardens, Upper Bristol Rd BA1 2NB

☎ 01225 442211 Fax 01225 460665

e-mail: tony@armstronghouse.junglelink.co.uk

Dir: *on A4 in central Bath, 30yds on right at bottom of Charlotte St, leaving Queens Square*

This delightful Victorian property is just a short walk from Bath's many attractions. The proprietor is a welcoming host and, by prior request, can arrange parking, a great benefit in this busy city. The spacious bedrooms are comfortably furnished and tastefully decorated. A substantial continental-style breakfast is served in the bedrooms.

FACILITIES: 4 en suite (1 fmly) No smoking TVB tea/coffee No dogs (ex guide dogs) Cen ht No children 6yrs No coaches **PRICES:** d £50-£65✻ **LB PARKING:** 4 **NOTES:** Closed 24 Dec-1 Jan

See advertisement on page 339

England

BATH continued

♦♦♦♦ Ashley Villa Hotel

26 Newbridge Rd BA1 3JZ ☎ 01225 421683 🖷 01225 313604
e-mail: ashleyvilla@clearface.co.uk
Dir: *leaving Bath on A4 west, Upper Bristol Rd, take left fork at 2nd traffic lights into Newbridge Rd, hotel 200yds on right*

Ideally located a short walk from the city centre, Ashley Villa has much to offer the guest. Comfortable accommodation is provided and some rooms are of a superior standard. The friendly and relaxing atmosphere provides makes this an ideal base, and new corporate facilities offer the business guest a good range of services. Dinner features fresh produce from the proprietor's smallholding.

FACILITIES: 13 en suite 5 annexe en suite (5 fmly) No smoking in 12 bedrooms No smoking in dining room STV TVB tea/coffee Direct dial from bedrooms No dogs (ex guide dogs) Licensed Cen ht TVL Outdoor swimming pool Dinner Last d 8.30pm **PRICES:** s £49-£69; d £59-£130✱ **LB** **PARKING:** 18 **CARDS:**

♦♦♦♦ Beckfords

59 Upper Oldfield Park BA2 3LB ☎ 01225 334959
🖷 01225 334959
e-mail: post@beckford-house.com
Dir: *turn off A36 (Bristol-Warminster rd) at Green Park Tavern & 3rd left*

This Victorian house is set in a quiet location a short walk from the city centre and its many attractions. Spacious bedrooms are contemporary in style and offer thoughtful extra touches. Local and organic produce is a feature of breakfast served in the well-appointed dining room.

FACILITIES: 2 en suite No smoking TVB tea/coffee No dogs Cen ht No children No coaches **PRICES:** s £48; d £65-£75✱ **LB** **PARKING:** 2 **NOTES:** Closed Xmas

♦♦♦♦ Brompton House

St John's Rd BA2 6PT ☎ 01225 420972 🖷 01225 420505
e-mail: bromptonhouse@btinternet.com
Dir: *off M4 junct 18, A46 to Bath, A4 to city centre, turn left onto A36, cross Cleveland Bridge, 1st right into St Johns Rd*

This attractive and peaceful hotel is pleasantly located close to Bath's many attractions. Surrounded by well-tended gardens, with private parking, Brompton House offers attractively decorated bedrooms with comfortable modern facilities. A relaxing sitting room is provided and the elegant dining room offers a good choice at breakfast.

Brompton House

FACILITIES: 16 en suite (1 fmly) No smoking TVB tea/coffee Direct dial from bedrooms No dogs Licensed Cen ht No children 15yrs No coaches **PRICES:** s £36-£55; d £60-£95✱ **LB** **PARKING:** 20 **NOTES:** Closed Xmas & New Year **CARDS:**

See advertisement on opposite page

♦♦♦♦ Cranleigh

159 Newbridge Hill BA1 3PX ☎ 01225 310197 🖷 01225 423143
e-mail: cranleigh@btinternet.com
Dir: *on A431, west side of city*

This pleasant Victorian house is quietly located close to the city centre. Bedrooms, some of which are on the ground floor and two of which have four posters, are comfortable and decorated in styles sympathetic to the period. Breakfast is served in the elegant lounge/dining-room, and guests are welcome to make use of the attractive gardens.

FACILITIES: 8 en suite (3 fmly) (2 GF) No smoking TVB tea/coffee No dogs (ex guide dogs) Cen ht No children 5yrs No coaches free golf at local course **PRICES:** s £45-£55; d £65-£85✱ **LB** **PARKING:** 5 **CARDS:**

♦♦♦♦ Devonshire House

143 Wellsway BA2 4RZ ☎ 01225 312495 🖷 01225 335534
e-mail: info@devonshire-house-bath.co.uk
Dir: *1m from city centre on A367 out of Bath*

This charming house maintains its Victorian style and is conveniently located within strolling distance of the centre of Bath. Secure car parking is available and the friendly proprietors make every effort to ensure your stay is pleasant and memorable. Bedrooms are attractively decorated and provided with many extra facilities. Freshly cooked breakfast is served in the dining room and special diets can be catered for.

continued

England

Devonshire House

FACILITIES: 3 en suite (1 fmly) No smoking TVB tea/coffee No dogs Cen ht No children 6yrs No coaches **PRICES:** s £38-£55; d £55-£75✻ **LB** **PARKING:** 6 **CARDS:**

♦♦♦♦ Eagle House

Church St, Bathford BA1 7RS ☎ 01225 859946
📠 01225 859430
e-mail: jonap@eagleho.demon.co.uk

Dir: *from A4 take A363 for 150yds towards Bradford-on-Avon, fork left into Bathford Hill, 1st right into Church St. House 200yds on right*

This delightful Georgian house, set in attractive gardens is pleasantly located on the outskirts of the city. Bedrooms are spacious and comfortable, and each is provided with a thoughtful range of extra facilities. The lounge is most impressive and is adorned with attractive pictures. The dining room and lounge have views of the grounds.

FACILITIES: 6 en suite 2 annexe en suite (2 fmly) (2 GF) No smoking in 2 bedrooms TVB tea/coffee Direct dial from bedrooms Cen ht Tennis (grass) Croquet lawn Childrens play area & treehouse **PRICES:** s £42-£56; d £54-£86✻ **LB** **CONF:** Thtr 20 Class 20 Board 14 **PARKING:** 10 **NOTES:** Closed 20 Dec-3 Jan **CARDS:**

England

BATH continued

♦♦♦♦ Grove Lodge

11 Lambridge BA1 6BJ ☎ 01225 310860 01225 429630
e-mail: grovelodge@bath24.fsnet.co.uk
Dir: *M4 junct 18 follow signs for Bath (10m). Establishment 500mtrs after city sign, on right.*

This fine Georgian house lies within easy reach of the city centre and is accessed by a winding stone path through a neat garden surrounded by trees. Spacious bedrooms reflect the style of the architecture and all are well equipped. There is an attractive breakfast room and parking is available in nearby side streets.
FACILITIES: 5 en suite (1 GF) No smoking TVB tea/coffee No dogs (ex guide dogs) Licensed Cen ht No children 6 yrs No coaches
PRICES: s £32-£40; d £56-£66✻ **LB NOTES:** Closed Xmas & New Year
CARDS:

♦♦♦♦ Highways House

143 Wells Rd BA2 3AL ☎ 01225 421238 01225 481169
e-mail: stay@highwayshouse.co.uk
Dir: *on A367 to Radstock*

This elegant house is conveniently located only 10 minutes walk from the centre of town, and has the benefit of good parking. The bedrooms are pleasantly decorated, well-equipped and most comfortable. An attractive lounge is provided for guests, and breakfast is served in the bright dining room, which features the impressive floral artwork of the proprietor.
FACILITIES: 6 en suite (1 GF) No smoking TVB tea/coffee No dogs (ex guide dogs) Cen ht No children 3 yrs No coaches **PRICES:** s £40-£50; d £60-£75✻ **LB PARKING:** 8 **CARDS:**

♦♦♦♦ Laura Place Hotel

3 Laura Place, Great Pulteney St BA2 4BH ☎ 01225 463815
01225 310222
Dir: *turn left off A4 at 1st traffic lights over Cleveland Bridge, past fire station then turn right along Henrietta Rd into Laura Place*
Ideally located at the heart of the city, with its own parking, this beautiful Georgian house overlooks the Laura Place fountain and offers splendid style and comfort. Bedrooms are elegantly furnished and attractively decorated. Breakfast is taken in the delightful dining room, where freshly cooked dishes provide a good start to the day.

Laura Place Hotel

FACILITIES: 8 rms (7 en suite) (1 fmly) (2 GF) No smoking TVB tea/coffee Direct dial from bedrooms No dogs (ex guide dogs) Cen ht No children 11yrs No coaches **PRICES:** d £72-£93✻ **LB PARKING:** 10 **NOTES:** Closed 22 Dec-Feb **CARDS:**

♦♦♦♦ Marlborough House

1 Marlborough Ln BA1 2NQ ☎ 01225 318175
01225 466127
e-mail: mars@manque.dircon.co.uk
Dir: *on corner of A4 & Marlborough Lane. W of Queen Square in city centre*

This elegant town house, situated opposite Royal Victoria Park, is ideally placed for the city centre. The combination of American hospitality, antique furnishings - some of the rooms have four poster beds - and globally inspired vegetarian cuisine using organic ingredients, make this a must for those looking for something out of the ordinary.
FACILITIES: 7 en suite (3 fmly) No smoking TVB tea/coffee Direct dial from bedrooms Licensed Cen ht No coaches Dinner Last d 11am **PRICES:** s £45-£70; d £65-£85✻ **LB CONF:** Del from £100 ✻ **PARKING:** 3 **CARDS:**

♦♦♦♦ North Lodge Guest House

Sulis Manor Rd, Odd Down BA2 2AL ☎ 01225 837782
01225 837782
e-mail: stay@northlodge.co.uk
Dir: *from A4 take A367 Exeter road for approx 2m. Left at Odd Down Park & Ride, then left into Sulis Manor Rd. 100yds to Lodge*
As its name may suggest, this was originally the lodge of a local manor and has been converted to provide three comfortable bedrooms, one on the ground floor. A range of options is available at breakfast, served in the cosy conservatory overlooking the walled garden which provides a pleasant sun-trap in summer.

continued

North Lodge Guest House

FACILITIES: 6 en suite (2 fmly) (3 GF) No smoking TVB tea/coffee Cen ht TVL **PRICES:** s £25-£35; d £40-£60✳ LB **PARKING:** 7 **CARDS:**

♦♦♦♦ Oakleigh House

19 Upper Oldfield Park BA2 3JX ☎ 01225 315698
Fax 01225 448223
e-mail: oakleigh@which.net
Dir: *off A367*

This large Victorian house, built from honey-coloured Bath stone, offers friendly and spacious accommodation. Bedrooms are very well equipped with comfortable pine furnishings and a host of extra facilities. A pleasant lounge offers the daily papers and lots of books, games and local information, and freshly cooked breakfasts are served in the attractive dining room.

FACILITIES: 3 en suite No smoking TVB tea/coffee No dogs (ex guide dogs) Cen ht No children 18yrs No coaches **PRICES:** s £50-£60; d £68-£78✳ LB **PARKING:** 4 **CARDS:**

♦♦♦♦ Owl House

Lower Kingsdown Rd, Kingsdown SN13 8BB ☎ 01225 743883
Fax 01225 744450
e-mail: venus@zetnet.co.uk

(For full entry see Box (Wiltshire))

♦♦♦♦ The Parade Park and Lambrettas Bar

8,9,10 North Pde BA2 4AL ☎ 01225 463384 Fax 01225 442322
e-mail: info@paradepark.co.uk
Dir: *opposite Parade Gardens*

Formerly the home of William Wordsworth, this attractive, centrally located Georgian property offers modern facilities. Sympathetically restored rooms are well equipped and brightly decorated.
A modern, Lambretta-themed bar is open to the public. A traditional breakfast is served in the impressive, panelled, first-floor dining room.

FACILITIES: 33 rms (27 en suite) (5 fmly) No smoking in bedrooms No smoking in dining room No smoking in lounges TVB tea/coffee No dogs (ex guide dogs) Licensed Cen ht Pool Table **PRICES:** s £35-£65; d £50-£80✳ LB **CARDS:**

♦♦♦♦ *Victoria House*

40 Crescent Gardens, Upper Bristol Rd BA1 2NB
☎ 01225 312812
e-mail: victoriahousebath@hotmail.com
Dir: *M4 junct 18 A46 to Bath, through Bath on A4-London Road following signs for A4 Bristol. Around three sides of Queen Sq and out onto Charlotte St down to junct with Upper Bristol Rd Victoria House on right*

Style and elegance abound at this delightful home which convenient for the theatre and restaurants. Hospitality and service are memorable aspects of a stay here, as are the impressive bedrooms and bathrooms which are most comfortable and restful. Breakfast is excellent and offers delightful quality dishes, attractively presented and freshly prepared.

continued

FACILITIES: 2 en suite No smoking TVB tea/coffee No dogs Cen ht No children 12yrs No coaches **PARKING:** 2 **CARDS:**

♦♦♦♦ Wheatsheaf Inn

BA2 7EG ☎ 01225 833504 Fax 01225 833504
e-mail: silkwinp@aol.com

(For full entry see Combe Hay)

♦♦♦ Bailbrook Lodge

35/37 London Rd West BA1 7HZ ☎ 01225 859090
Fax 01225 852299
e-mail: hotel@bailbrooklodge.co.uk
Dir: *M4 junct 18, take A46 Bath exit at rdbt. Turn left signposted Batheaston, hotel on left. From Bath, take A4 Chippenham. At A46 rdbt go straight on to Batheaston. Hotel on left (The Circle)*

This imposing Georgian building, with sun terrace, is set in extensive gardens on the eastern edge of the city. The well-equipped bedrooms include some with four-poster beds and period furniture. The comfortable lounge with its honesty bar, is the ideal place to relax at the end of a busy day

FACILITIES: 12 en suite (4 fmly) No smoking in 4 bedrooms No smoking in area of dining room TVB tea/coffee No dogs (ex guide dogs) Licensed Cen ht TVL **PRICES:** s £39-£50; d £60-£70✳ LB **CONF:** Board 8 **PARKING:** 12 **CARDS:**

♦♦♦ Aran House Number Ninety Three

93 Wells Rd BA2 3AN ☎ 01225 317977
Dir: *A367 Wells road, within 0.25m of centre of Bath*

A warm welcome is offered at this Victorian terraced house, conveniently situated just a short walk from the city centre. Parking is available for guests by prior arrangement and is a particular benefit in this busy location. Bedrooms are attractively decorated and well equipped.

FACILITIES: 4 en suite (1 fmly) No smoking TVB tea/coffee No dogs Cen ht No coaches **PRICES:** s £25-£45; d £40-£65✳ LB

♦♦♦ Arney

99 Wells Rd BA2 3AN ☎ 01225 310020
Dir: *on A367*

Pleasant accommodation and a friendly welcome are provided at this conveniently located house which is within easy walking distance of the city centre. Breakfast is taken in the bright dining room and provides a good start to the day.

FACILITIES: 3 rms (1 fmly) No smoking in dining room No smoking in lounges TV2B tea/coffee No dogs (ex guide dogs) Cen ht No coaches **PRICES:** s £25-£30; d £46-£50✳

Egg cups for excellence!
This symbol shows that breakfast exceeded our Inspector's expectations.

England

BATH continued

♦♦♦ *Ashgrove*

39 Bathwick St BA2 6PA ☎ 01225 421911 📠 01225 461287
e-mail: ashgroveguesthouse@talk21.com
Dir: *from M4 junct 18, to city centre on London Rd, follow rd to left into Bathwick St. Fire & ambulance station on left, house on right after garage*
A very conveniently located Georgian terraced property, being a six-minute level walk from the city centre. Bedrooms, all of which are neatly and brightly decorated, combine traditional furnishings with modern facilities. Breakfast is served in the cheerful dining room.
FACILITIES: 9 rms (6 en suite) (1 fmly) No smoking in 3 bedrooms No smoking in dining room No smoking in lounges TVB tea/coffee No dogs (ex guide dogs) **PARKING:** 6 **NOTES:** Closed 21 Dec-Jan **CARDS:**

♦♦♦ Cairngorm

3 Gloucester Rd, Lower Swainswick BA1 7BH ☎ 01225 429004 📠 01225 429004
e-mail: cairn-gorm@supanet.com
Dir: *M4 junct 18, take A46 for 7.5m turn left signposted Swainswick, turn left after bridge 0.5m on left*
Pleasantly situated within a short distance from the city centre, the Cairngorm is set in a quiet residential location and enjoys splendid views over the city. Guest rooms are bright and comfortably furnished and the resident proprietors provide a pleasant home-from-home atmosphere.
FACILITIES: 3 en suite (1 fmly) No smoking TVB tea/coffee No dogs (ex guide dogs) Cen ht No children 1yr No coaches **PRICES:** s £27-£38; d £38-£48 **LB BB PARKING:** 3 **NOTES:** Closed Nov-Feb

♦♦♦ Dolphin House

8 Northend, Batheaston BA1 7EN ☎ 01225 858915 📠 01225 858915
Dir: *on A4, 2m E of Bath. Take turning to northend from Batheaston High Street. Hotel situated 100yds on right*

A detached Georgian Grade II listed house, conveniently located for the city centre. There is a delightful terraced walled garden. Bedrooms, one of which is a private suite with lounge, twin bedroom and large bathroom, are very attractive with tasteful period décor. Continental breakfast is served in the bedrooms or on the terrace.
FACILITIES: 2 en suite No smoking TVB tea/coffee No dogs (ex guide dogs) Cen ht No children 12yrs No coaches **PRICES:** d £55-£65✳ **PARKING:** 2 **NOTES:** Closed Xmas rs 24-27 Dec

♦♦♦ Edgar Hotel

64 Great Pulteney St BA2 4DN ☎ 01225 420619 📠 01225 466916
e-mail: edgar-hotel@pgen.net
Dir: *A46 onto A4 for 1m. Left at lights, over bridge, after rdbt take 2nd right in to Edgar Hotel.*

continued

Edgar Hotel

This pleasant, small hotel offers comfortable and smart accommodation and is convenient for either the business or touring guest. Bedrooms are attractively furnished and decorated. A small lounge, which looks over the garden, is available for guests and the smart dining room provides a relaxed atmosphere where English breakfasts are served.
FACILITIES: 18 en suite (1 fmly) No smoking in bedrooms No smoking in dining room No smoking in lounges TVB tea/coffee No dogs (ex guide dogs) Cen ht TVL **PRICES:** s £35-£50; d £50-£75✳ **LB**
CARDS:

♦♦♦ Henrietta Hotel

32 Henrietta St BA2 6LR ☎ 01225 447779 📠 01225 444150
e-mail: edgar-hotel@pgen.net
Dir: *M4 junct 18, then A46 on A4 for 1m. Left at lights over bridge then 2nd turning on right*

Conveniently located just off Great Pulteney Street, this informal hotel is a short walk from the city centre. Bedrooms, including one with four poster bed are well equipped and make good use of space. Helpful, friendly staff are pleased to provide information on nearby attractions.
FACILITIES: 10 en suite (3 fmly) (2 GF) No smoking TVB tea/coffee No dogs (ex guide dogs) Cen ht TVL **PRICES:** s £35-£50; d £50-£75✳ **LB**
CARDS:

♦♦♦ Hermitage

Bath Rd SN13 8DT ☎ 01225 744187 📠 01225 743447
e-mail: hermitage@telecall.co.uk
(For full entry see Box (Wiltshire))

♦♦♦ Hotel St Clair

1 Crescent Gardens, Upper Bristol Rd BA1 2NA ☎ 01225 425543 📠 01225 425543
e-mail: hotel-st-clair@ukonline.co.uk
Dir: *on A4, Bristol side of Bath*
Guests are assured of a relaxed atmosphere at this friendly hotel, which is also conveniently situated within walking distance of the city centre. There is a small and comfortable lounge off reception; whilst breakfast and dinner can be taken in the dining room on the

continued

lower ground floor. A public 'pay and display' car park is avaialble at the rear of the property.
FACILITIES: 18 rms (16 en suite) (4 fmly) No smoking in 9 bedrooms No smoking in dining room No smoking in lounges TVB tea/coffee Direct dial from bedrooms No dogs (ex guide dogs) Licensed Cen ht Dinner Last d 4pm **CARDS:**

♦♦♦ Ko Ryu
7 Pulteney Gardens BA2 4HG ☎ 01225 337642
01225 337642
e-mail: japanesekoryu@aol.com
Ko Ryu means 'sunshine' in Japanese and that is exactly the style in this pleasant establishment with its bright, clean decor. In keeping with Japanese tradition, guests are asked to remove their shoes whilst in this charming home. Bedrooms are comfortably furnished. Breakfast is taken in the sunny dining room around a large communal table.
FACILITIES: 5 en suite (1 fmly) No smoking TVB tea/coffee No dogs Cen ht No coaches **PRICES:** s £30-£33; d £50-£55✻ **PARKING:** 6

♦♦♦ Lamp Post Villa
3 Crescent Gardens, Upper Bristol Rd BA1 2NA
☎ 01225 331221 01225 426783
Dir: *on A4, Bristol side of city*
Pleasantly located for the city's many attractions, Lamp Post Villa offers comfortable modern facilities and the benefit of residents' parking. A lounge and attractive dining room offer further comfort for guests, and the freshly cooked breakfast provides a good start to the day.
FACILITIES: 4 en suite (1 fmly) No smoking in bedrooms No smoking in dining room TVB tea/coffee Direct dial from bedrooms Cen ht TVL No coaches **PRICES:** s £35-£45; d £45-£55✻ **PARKING:** 4
NOTES: Closed 24-26 Dec **CARDS:**

♦♦♦ Lynwood
6 Pulteney Gardens BA2 4HG ☎ 01225 426410
Dir: *at end of A4 turn left onto A36. Follow signs for Bristol/Exeter & Wells for 0.5m to traffic lights at railway bridge, then 2nd left*
This pleasant house has attractive plantings in the garden and is only a short walk from Bath's city centre and the picturesque towpath of the Kennet and Avon canal. Bedrooms are individually decorated and comfortably appointed. A spacious lounge is available and a warm and friendly welcome is assured to guests.
FACILITIES: 6 rms (3 en suite) (2 fmly) No smoking in dining room TVB tea/coffee Cen ht TVL No coaches **PRICES:** s £27-£30; d £54-£60✻
PARKING: 2 **NOTES:** Closed 2 Jan-6 Feb

♦♦♦ *Mendip View*
133 Bradford Rd, Combe Down BA2 5BS ☎ 01225 835897
01225 835897
Dir: *from M4 take A4 to city centre then A367 for 1m, left to St Martins Hospital on B3110. Pass hospital, left at double rdbt onto A3062*
The friendly and welcoming proprietors at this attractive home are most attentive and provide comfortable accommodation and a homely atmosphere. Guestrooms are very well-equipped with many useful extra facilities. A pleasant lounge is provided and a good choice of freshly cooked dishes is served at breakfast.
FACILITIES: 4 rms (2 en suite) No smoking in dining room TVB tea/coffee Cen ht TVL **PARKING:** 4

♦♦♦ Old Red House
37 Newbridge Rd BA1 3HE ☎ 01225 330464 01225 331661
e-mail: oldredhouse@amserve.net
Dir: *1m W of city centre along Upper Bristol Rd, situated on left just past The Weston pub*
This attractive building, an old bakery, stands out among the surrounding honey-coloured Bath stone, with imposing stained glass windows and period features. A short, level distance from the centre of town, this is a friendly home and many guests return on a regular basis. Bedrooms are delightfully furnished and pleasantly decorated.

Old Red House

FACILITIES: 4 en suite (1 fmly) (2 GF) No smoking TVB tea/coffee No dogs Cen ht TVL No children 4yrs No coaches **PRICES:** s £30-£55; d £50-£75✻
LB PARKING: 4 **NOTES:** Closed Jan **CARDS:**

♦♦♦ *Orchard Lodge*
Warminster Rd (A36), Bathampton BA2 6XG ☎ 01225 466115
01225 446050
e-mail: orchardlo@aol.com
Dir: *1m from city centre on A36 Warminster road*
Orchard Lodge is a well-equipped modern establishment, purpose-built to provide spacious accommodation. Ideally located only one mile from Bath's centre, with good parking, Orchard Lodge is an ideal base for touring the area. Breakfast is served in the bright dining room, which has spectacular views overlooking the Avon Valley.
FACILITIES: 14 en suite (3 fmly) No smoking in 4 bedrooms No smoking in dining room No smoking in lounges TVB tea/coffee Direct dial from bedrooms Cen ht **PARKING:** 16 **CARDS:**

♦♦♦ The White Guest House
23 Pulteney Gardens BA2 4HG ☎ 01225 426075
01225 426075
e-mail: thewhiteguesthouse@zoom.co.uk
Dir: *from M4 take A4 to Bath, turn left onto A36, follow signs to Bristol/ Wells for 0.5m, under railway bridge, 2nd turning on left*
Conveniently located only a short walking distance from Bath's many attractions this pleasant house offers cosy and comfortable accommodation. The resident proprietors provide a friendly and relaxed atmosphere and a tasty breakfast is served in the country style dining room. Free permits are available for guests to use the residential parking in the surrounding area.
FACILITIES: 3 en suite No smoking TVB tea/coffee No dogs Cen ht No coaches **PRICES:** s £30-£35; d £48-£55✻ **LB**

♦♦ Waltons
17-19 Crescent Gardens, Upper Bristol Rd BA1 2NA
☎ 01225 426528 1225 420350
Dir: *on A4*
Waltons is situated within strolling distance of the centre of Bath and offers value accommodation. Bedrooms are pleasantly furnished and are attractively decorated. Guests will receive a friendly and relaxed approach from the host. A traditional English breakfast is served in the cosy dining room.
FACILITIES: 15 rms (3 fmly) No smoking in dining room TVB tea/coffee Direct dial from bedrooms No dogs (ex guide dogs) Cen ht
PRICES: s £27-£30; d £47-£50✻ **PARKING:** 2

continued

England

BATH continued

Highfields
207 Bailbrook Ln, Batheaston BA1 7AB ☎ 01225 859782
At the time of going to press the Diamond classification for this establishment had not been confirmed. Please check the AA website www.theAA.com for up-to-date information.
FACILITIES: 3 en suite

Roman City
18 Raby Place, Bathwick Hill BA2 4EH ☎ 01225 463668 & 07899777953
At the time of going to press the Diamond classification for this establishment had not been confirmed. Please check the AA website www.theAA.com for up-to-date information.
FACILITIES: 4 rms (1 fmly)

BECKINGTON — Map 03 ST85

♦♦♦♦ Pickford House
23 Bath Rd BA11 6SJ ☎ 01373 830329 01373 830329
e-mail: ampritchar@aol.com
Dir: *off A36 (Texaco rdbt) signposted Beckington, follow road for 300yds to 30mph signs by village hall, turn right then immediately left*

This Regency-style house is set in secluded walled gardens. The proprietors are both welcoming and attentive, and many guests visit this pleasant house on a regular basis. Dinner is an enjoyable experience with a 'pot luck' menu, (unless you require vegetarian or special dietary dishes) and, along with the impressive wine list, provides fine dining.
FACILITIES: 2 rms 3 annexe en suite (2 fmly) (1 GF) No smoking in 2 bedrooms No smoking in dining room TVB tea/coffee Licensed Cen ht No coaches Outdoor swimming pool Dinner Last d 9pm **PRICES:** s £20-£25; d £34-£44* **LB BB PARKING:** 15 **NOTES:** Closed Xmas

BEERCROCOMBE — Map 03 ST32

Premier Collection

♦♦♦♦♦ Whittles *(ST324194)*
TA3 6AH ☎ 01823 480301 01823 480301
Mr & Mrs Mitchem
e-mail: dj.cm.mitchem@themail.co.uk
Dir: *turn off A358 follow signs to Hatch Beauchamp, then through Beercrocombe. 0.75m from village*
Situated between the Quantock and Blackdown Hills, this 16th-century farmhouse is an ideal base for a relaxing break. The friendly and attentive owners have been accommodating guests here for 20 years and all are assured of a caring and genuine welcome. Guests have their own drawing room, dining and sitting room, and bedrooms are spacious and comfortable. Freshly prepared suppers, featuring local produce and farmhouse cheeses, are offered by prior arrangement.

continued

FACILITIES: 3 en suite No smoking in bedrooms No smoking in dining room No smoking in 1 lounge TVB tea/coffee No dogs Licensed Cen ht No children 16yrs 200 acres beef dairy Dinner Last d 6.30pm(previous day) **PRICES:** s £35-£38; d £50-£54*
PARKING: 4 **NOTES:** Closed Dec & Jan

BLUE ANCHOR — Map 03 ST04

♦♦♦ The Langbury
TA24 6LB ☎ 01643 821375 01643 822012
e-mail: post@langbury.co.uk
Dir: *from Taunton/Bridgwater (M5) take A39 to Carhampton turn R - signed 'Blue Anchor'*
This small friendly hotel is just two-minutes walk from the beach and the Blue Anchor Steam Railway Station and provides comfortable accommodation in relaxed surroundings. A hearty breakfast is served at separate tables in the dining room, and there is a lounge and bar for guest's use. An outdoor swimming pool is also available.
FACILITIES: 5 en suite (1 fmly) (1 GF) No smoking TVB tea/coffee Licensed Cen ht No coaches Outdoor swimming pool **PRICES:** s fr £30; d fr £44*
PARKING: 15 **NOTES:** Closed Dec-Jan **CARDS:**

BRIDGWATER — Map 03 ST33

♦♦♦♦ Model Farm
Perry Green, Wembdon TA5 2BA ☎ 01278 433999
e-mail: info@modelfarm.com
Dir: *M5 J23/24, A38 into Bridgwater. A39 Minehead, proceed 1m past garage on R. Down hill, at double bend turn R (Wembdon). Turn L (Perry Green). At T-junct, follow sign No Through Road. Farm 2nd drive on L.*

Model Farm is in a peaceful rural setting, ideal for business and leisure guests alike. The imposing Victorian house has glorious country views from virtually every window. Bedrooms are comfortable and guests are assured of a warm welcome. By arrangement, imaginative three course dinners are served at one large table.
FACILITIES: 3 en suite (1 fmly) No smoking tea/coffee Licensed Cen ht TVL No children 3yrs No coaches Dinner Last d 6pm **PRICES:** s £40; d £60*
PARKING: 6 **CARDS:**

♦♦♦ The Boat & Anchor Inn
Huntworth TA7 0AQ ☎ 01278 662473 01278 662542
e-mail: boatand.anchorinn@virgin.net
Dir: *M5 junct 24, take Huntworth turning, through village of Huntworth, approx 0.5m out of village cross canal bridge.*
This popular canalside inn offers easy access to the M5 and makes an ideal stopover en route for the many attractions of Somerset, Devon and Cornwall. Bedrooms vary in size and style and are

continued

situated above the busy bars where an impressive selection of dishes is offered from blackboard menus.

The Boat & Anchor Inn

FACILITIES: 8 en suite (2 fmly) No smoking in bedrooms TVB tea/coffee Cen ht Dinner Last d 9pm **PRICES:** s £42.50-£55; d fr £55* LB **PARKING:** 100 **CARDS:**

♦♦♦ Chinar

17 Oakfield Rd TA6 7LX ☎ 01278 458639
e-mail: rosie.lea@ic24.net
Dir: *exit M5 J23, follow signs for Minehead, left at lights past Safeway onto West St, past School, Oakfields Rd next on right, establishment on left*

A warm welcome awaits guests to Chinar, which is situated in a quiet residential area on the edge of the town. The bedrooms are comfortable and well equipped, and there is an inviting lounge. A good choice is available at breakfast, including muffins, pancakes, scrambled eggs with smoked salmon, as well as a traditional English breakfast.

FACILITIES: 2 en suite No smoking in bedrooms TVB tea/coffee Cen ht TVL No children 6yrs No coaches **PRICES:** s £23-£25; d £42-£46* **PARKING:** 2

♦♦♦ Phoenicia

31 Liney Rd, Westonzoyland TA7 0EU ☎ 01278 691385
Dir: *take A372 from Bridgwater, at Westonzoyland through village past St Mary's church & turn off A372. After approx 200yds into Liney Rd*

A warm welcome can be found at Phoenicia, which is quietly located on the edge of this pleasant village. Just a short drive from the M5, it is an ideal base from which to explore the local area. Bedrooms have been recently refurbished. Two of the three bedrooms are interconnecting and can be rearranged as required, ideal for family use.

FACILITIES: 3 rms (2 en suite) (1 fmly) No smoking TV2B tea/coffee No dogs Cen ht No children 10yrs No coaches **PRICES:** s £21-£22.50; d £42-£45* **PARKING:** 3 **NOTES:** Closed Xmas/New Year

♦♦♦ Rockfield House

Puriton Hill, Puriton TA7 8AG ☎ 01278 683561
📠 01278 683561
e-mail: rockfieldhouse@talk21.com
Dir: *just off M5 junct 23 on A39 at top of hill on right*

With easy access to the M5 and just 3 miles from Bridgwater, guests are assured of a warm welcome at this large family home set in a two-acre garden. Bedrooms are comfortable and well equipped. Hearty breakfasts are served in the attractive dining room, where freshly cooked dinners are also available by prior arrangement.

FACILITIES: 2 rms (1 en suite) 1 annexe en suite (1 fmly) No smoking TVB tea/coffee No dogs Cen ht TVL No coaches Dinner Last d 4pm **PRICES:** s £17.50; d £35-£45* BB **PARKING:** 5 **NOTES:** Closed 25-31 Dec

BROMPTON REGIS — Map 03 SS93

♦♦♦♦ Holworthy Farm *(SS978308)*

TA22 9NY ☎ 01398 371244 📠 01398 371244 Mrs G Payne
e-mail: holworthyfarm@aol.com
Dir: *off M5 at Tiveston, follow signs to Wimbleball Lake*

Close to Exmoor, this 200-year-old working livestock farm has spectacular views over Wimbleball Lake. Bedrooms in the main house are traditionally furnished, while the newer bedrooms are more spacious and decorated in bold colour schemes. The attractive dining room overlooks the garden and provides a pleasant setting for breakfast, dinner is available by prior arrangement.

FACILITIES: 5 en suite (2 fmly) (1 GF) TVB tea/coffee No dogs (ex guide dogs) Cen ht TVL Fishing in resevoir overlooking farm,Riding 200 acres beef sheep Dinner **PRICES:** s fr £27; d fr £54* LB **PARKING:** 8

England

BROMPTON REGIS continued

♦♦♦ Bruneton House
TA22 9NN ☎ 01398 371224
e-mail: brunetonhouse@hotmail.com
Dir: *turn off A396 onto Watchet Rd at Machine Cross. Follow signs for Brompton Regis, after 3m establishment at bottom end of churchyard*
The warmest of welcomes will be received at this 17th-century family home in the Exmoor National Park. Doubling as both village store and tea room, this is somewhere to experience a true taste of the joys of rural life. Bedrooms are spacious and comfortable, and a bright lounge is available for guests. Wonderful views can be enjoyed from the cottage garden.
FACILITIES: 3 en suite No smoking in dining room tea/coffee No dogs (ex guide dogs) Cen ht TVL ch fac No coaches Dinner Last d 5pm
PRICES: s £22.50-£25; d £45-£50* **PARKING:** 4 **NOTES:** Closed Xmas rs Sep-Etr (limited availability)

BRUTON Map 03 ST63

♦♦♦♦ Gants Mill
BA10 0DB ☎ 01749 812393
e-mail: shingler@gantsmill.co.uk
Dir: *0.5m SW of Bruton, signed off A359*
FACILITIES: 3 rms (2 en suite) (2 fmly) No smoking TVB tea/coffee No dogs (ex guide dogs) Cen ht No children 12yrs No coaches
PRICES: s £25; d £50* **PARKING:** 6 **NOTES:** Closed Xmas & New Year
CARDS:

BUCKLAND ST MARY Map 03 ST21

♦♦♦♦ Hillside
TA20 3TQ ☎ 01460 234599 & 07703 633770
e-mail: royandmarge@hillsidebsm.freeserve.co.uk
Dir: *A303, approx 4m S of the Ilminster turning, turn right at the Eagle Tavern pub, take next left (water tower on corner) and Hillside approx 500yds on left*
Enjoying splendid views of the surrounding countryside this peaceful house is set in approximately one acre of attractive gardens. Bedrooms are spacious and decorated to a high standard and provided with many thoughtful extra items. Hearty breakfasts are served fresh from the Aga in the bright dining room which overlooks the garden.
FACILITIES: 4 rms (2 en suite) No smoking TVB tea/coffee No dogs (ex guide dogs) Cen ht TVL No coaches **PRICES:** s £22.50-£25; d £40-£50* **LB PARKING:** 4 **NOTES:** Closed Xmas & New Year

BURNHAM-ON-SEA Map 03 ST34

♦♦♦ Somewhere House
68 Berrow Rd TA8 2EZ ☎ 01278 795236
e-mail: di@somewherehouse.com
Dir: *M5 junct 22 follow Burnham signs then Berrow Brean signs into Berrow Road. Establishment 100mtrs past zebra crossing on right.*
FACILITIES: 5 en suite (3 fmly) (1 GF) No smoking TVB tea/coffee No dogs Cen ht TVL No coaches **PRICES:** s £26; d £40* **PARKING:** 7
NOTES: Closed Xmas & New Years Day **CARDS:**

BURROWBRIDGE Map 03 ST33

Premier Collection

♦♦♦♦♦ Saltmoor House
Saltmoor TA7 0RL ☎ 01823 698092
e-mail: saltmoorhouse@amserve.net
Dir: *from M5 J24 through Huntworth Moorland towards Burrowbridge*
In the heart of the Somerset Levels, Saltmoor House is a Grade II listed property dating back to the 18th century. Set in 15 acres of gardens and grounds, overlooking the River Parrett

Saltmoor House

and open countryside, it offers stylish bedrooms and spacious public areas. Breakfast may be taken in the dining room or the garden room, with french doors opening onto the walled garden. An imaginative dinner is available by prior arrangement.
FACILITIES: 3 en suite No smoking No dogs Cen ht TVL No children 18yrs No coaches Dinner Last d 4.30pm **PRICES:** s £45; d £90*
PARKING: 6

BUTLEIGH Map 03 ST53

♦♦♦ Court Lodge
Sub Rd BA6 8SA ☎ 01458 850575
Dir: *from the Yeovilton (Podimore) rdbt on the A303. Take A37, after 1.5m 1st left through Charlton Macrell. After 1m over crossroads 3rd right signposted Butleigh. Court Lodge is last house on right.*
Situated at the entrance to Butleigh Court and surrounded by pleasant gardens, this charming and attractive house offers comfortable accommodation. Guests are assured of a friendly welcome and made to feel relaxed. Two lounges are available, and at breakfast traditional fare is provided at the single dining table.
FACILITIES: 4 rms No smoking TV2B Cen ht TVL No coaches
PRICES: s fr £16.50; d fr £33* **BB PARKING:**

CASTLE CARY Map 03 ST63

♦♦♦♦ Clanville Manor *(ST618330)*
BA7 7PJ ☎ 01963 350124 & 07966 512732 01963 350719
Mrs S Snook
e-mail: info@clanvillemanor.co.uk
Dir: *turn off A371 onto B3153, entrance to Clanville Manor is via white gate & cattle grid under bridge 0.75m along B3153*
Built in 1743, Clanville Manor Farm has been owned by the Snook family since 1898, and remains a welcoming family home. A polished oak staircase leads up to the individually decorated bedrooms, which retain a great deal of their original character. The dining room looks out over open meadows.
FACILITIES: 3 en suite (1 fmly) No smoking TVB tea/coffee No dogs Cen ht TVL Outdoor swimming pool (heated) Croquet lawn 200 acres dairy
PRICES: s £25-£30; d £50-£60* **LB PARKING:** 6 **NOTES:** Closed 21 Dec - 2 Jan **CARDS:**

♦♦♦ The Horse Pond Inn & Motel
The Triangle BA7 7BD ☎ 01963 350318 & 351762
01963 351764
e-mail: horsepondinn@aol.com
Dir: *turn off A303, at Wincanton from E, or Sparkford from W. Inn at bottom of main road*
Situated opposite the Horse Pond, where in times past horses were washed and watered, the inn now offers spacious modern accommodation. Ideally located for local touring or the business

continued

traveller, and offering pleasant dining in either the restaurant or bar, this traditional inn has a friendly, welcoming atmosphere.
FACILITIES: 4 en suite (2 fmly) No smoking in dining room TVB tea/coffee Direct dial from bedrooms Cen ht Pool Table Dinner Last d 9pm **PRICES:** s £35-£45; d £50-£55; (room only) * **LB MEALS:** Lunch £6.80-£8 Dinner £4.50-£6.95&alc* **PARKING:** 24 **CARDS:**

CATCOTT Map 03 ST33

♦♦♦♦ Honeysuckle

King William Rd TA7 9HU ☎ 01278 722890
Dir: *from Glastonbury take A39 to Bridgwater, after 8m turn right to Catcott, past King William pub. House 200yds on right*
Situated in the centre of the village, Honeysuckle is a delightful modern house conveniently located for visiting the many attractions of the area. Bedrooms are comfortable and tastefully decorated, and in addition to the spacious lounge guests may also use the charming garden.
FACILITIES: 3 rms (1 en suite) No smoking TV2B tea/coffee No dogs (ex guide dogs) Cen ht No children 5yrs **PRICES:** s £16; d £36-£50* **BB**
PARKING: 3 **NOTES:** Closed 20 Dec-3 Jan

CHARD Map 03 ST30

See also Buckland St Mary

Premier Collection

♦♦♦♦♦ Bellplot House Hotel

High St TA20 1QB ☎ 01460 62600 📠 01460 62600
e-mail: info@bellplothouse.co.uk
Dir: *located in the centre of Chard, 500yrds from Guildhall*
This splendid Georgian property is ideally situated in the centre of town and is well positioned for both business and holiday visitors. All areas are stylishly decorated to reflect the property's past; the comfortable bedrooms are well equipped with many thoughtful extras. An innovative menu is available in the elegant restaurant.
FACILITIES: 7 en suite (1 fmly) (2 GF) No smoking in dining room STV TVB tea/coffee Direct dial from bedrooms No dogs (ex guide dogs) Licensed Cen ht No coaches Pool Table Use of leisure club & golf course Dinner Last d 9pm **PRICES:** s £47.50-£57.50; d £57.50-£67.50; (room only) * **PARKING:** 12 **CARDS:**

Premier Collection

♦♦♦♦♦ Higher Beetham Farm *(ST277120)*

Whitestaunton TA20 3PZ ☎ 01460 234460
📠 01460 234450 Mrs H Cumming
Dir: *leave Ilminster on A303 towards Honiton/Exeter, left after 4.5m at x-rds, signed Whitestaunton & Cricklease, 0.5m down country lane farm is 2nd gateway on right*
Located in a quiet rural setting with sweeping views over adjacent fields and countryside, this is a haven of peace and tranquillity. Every effort is made to ensure an enjoyable and relaxing stay and guests can be assured of a warm and friendly welcome. The comfortable, well-furnished accommodation comes with all manner of thoughtful touches and extra facilities. Meals are delicious with dinner being available by prior arrangement.
FACILITIES: 1 en suite (2 GF) No smoking tea/coffee No dogs (ex guide dogs) Cen ht TVL No children 12yrs 22 acres non-working Dinner Last d noon **PRICES:** s £25-£32.50; d £50-£65* **LB**
PARKING: 3 **NOTES:** Closed Xmas & New Year

♦♦♦ Bere *(ST377058)*

Winsham TA20 4JQ ☎ 01460 30207 📠 01460 30850
Mr & Mrs T Jeffery
e-mail: info@berefarm.com
Dir: *A30 between Crewkerne & Chard, left (Winsham), left in village centre, church on right down hill. Under bridge, farm on right*

Originally part of the Ford Abbey Estate, this attractive farm is peacefully located in beautiful, rural surroundings. Bedrooms are individually furnished and have thoughtful extra facilities. Traditional breakfasts are served around a large table in the dining room, which looks over the garden.
FACILITIES: 2 en suite (2 fmly) No smoking TVB tea/coffee Table tennis, Childrens play area. 8 acres non working **PRICES:** s £35; d £50* **LB PARKING:** 6 **CARDS:**

♦♦♦ Watermead

83 High St TA20 1QT ☎ 01460 62834 📠 01460 67448
e-mail: trudy@watermeadguesthouse.co.uk
Dir: *on A30 through the High St continue up the hill from shopping centre*
This family-run house provides pleasant and comfortable accommodation. Conveniently located, this is ideal as a base from which to explore the area. All guests are attentively served and made to feel at home and relaxed. Hearty breakfasts are served in the spacious dining room, which overlooks the attractive garden.
FACILITIES: 9 rms (6 en suite) 1 annexe en suite (1 fmly) No smoking in 8 bedrooms No smoking in dining room No smoking in lounges TVB tea/coffee Cen ht TVL No coaches **PRICES:** s £20-£32; d £47*
PARKING: 10

England

CHEDDAR Map 03 ST45

See also Draycott

♦♦♦♦ Tor Farm *(ST455534)*

Nylund BS27 3UD ☎ 01934 743710 📠 01934 743710
Mrs C Ladd
e-mail: bcjbkj@aol.com
***Dir:** take A371 from Cheddar towards Wells, after 2m turn right towards Nyland. Tor Farm 1.5m on right*

Tucked away in the Somerset countryside, this comfortable guest house has many welcome extras including its own heated swimming pool. Smartly furnished bedrooms, including several on the ground floor, benefit from wonderful views. Guests can relax in the cosy lounge, or in summer months, enjoy barbecues in the garden.
FACILITIES: 7 en suite (2 fmly) (4 GF) No smoking in bedrooms No smoking in dining room No smoking in 1 lounge TVB tea/coffee No dogs Licensed Cen ht TVL Outdoor swimming pool (heated) 33 acres beef Dinner **PRICES:** d £50-£60* **LB PARKING:** 12 **CARDS:**

♦♦♦ Market Cross Hotel

Church St BS27 3RA ☎ 01934 742264 📠 01934 741411
e-mail: annefieldhouse@aol.com
***Dir:** on A371 opposite market cross in village*
This is an attractive Regency property in the heart of Cheddar. Bedrooms are comfortable and there is also a cosy lounge/bar. The dining room is spacious and home cooked dinners are available by prior arrangement.
FACILITIES: 6 rms (3 en suite) (2 fmly) No smoking in bedrooms No smoking in dining room TVB tea/coffee Direct dial from bedrooms No dogs (ex guide dogs) Licensed Cen ht TVL ch fac No coaches Dinner Last d 6pm **PRICES:** s £21.50-£30; d £43-£56* **LB PARKING:** 6
CARDS:

CHURCHINFORD Map 03 ST21

♦♦♦ The York Inn

Honiton Rd TA3 7RF ☎ 01823 601333
e-mail: wdatheyorkinn@aol.com
***Dir:** M5 J26, (Wellington) for 0.5m, 1st left at rdbt, 1m left into Ford St, 2m left at top of hill, 4m to phone box, right to Inn*
Located amidst the Blackdown Hills, this traditional inn with its low ceilings, oak beams and an impressive fireplace, has inter-connecting bars and dining areas with an impressive display of china cups. An extensive blackboard menu features fresh fish and imaginative dishes. The bedrooms are well equipped and comfortably furnished.
FACILITIES: 2 en suite 1 annexe en suite (1 fmly) (1 GF) No smoking in dining room TVB tea/coffee Direct dial from bedrooms Cen ht No coaches Pool Table Dinner Last d 9.30pm **PRICES:** s £35-£40; d £50-£60*
MEALS: Lunch £12.50&alc Dinner £16.50&alc* **PARKING:** 15
CARDS:

CLUTTON Map 03 ST65

U The Hunters Rest

King Ln, Clutton Hill BS39 5QL ☎ 01761 452303
At the time of going to press the Diamond classification for this establishment had not been confirmed. Please check the AA website www.theAA.com for up-to-date information.
FACILITIES: 4 en suite (1 fmly)

COMBE HAY Map 03 ST75

♦♦♦♦ Anchor Farm *(ST745604)*

BA2 7EE ☎ 01225 832124 Mr & Mrs R Saker-Harper
***Dir:** from A46 into Bath take A367 signed Exeter, then 1st exit at 2nd rdbt (pay and ride) and immediately right to Combe Hay. Establishment is 1st on right after pub & out of village*
Anchor Farm enjoys an idyllic setting and the proprietors devote their attention to providing friendly and relaxing accommodation for their guests. The farm has delightful country views and is just a short walk from the local pub. Organic produce is a speciality, and features at breakfast, where a splendid choice of well preepared dishes is offered.
FACILITIES: 1 annexe en suite No smoking TVB tea/coffee No dogs Cen ht No children Riding 20 acres organic cattle sheep PRICES: d £55-£65*
PARKING: 2 **NOTES:** Closed 23 Dec-5 Jan

♦♦♦♦ Wheatsheaf Inn

BA2 7EG ☎ 01225 833504 📠 01225 833504
e-mail: silkwinp@aol.com
***Dir:** take A367 Exeter road from Bath to Oddown and left at Park and Ride for Combe Hay. Follow lane for approx 2m to thatched cottage and turn left*

Originally built in 1576, this typical country inn, with its wooden beams and log fire, is set in large terraced gardens. Spacious, comfortable, pine furnished bedrooms are housed in the converted stable block. The Wheatsheaf specialises in traditional English fare to compliment the wide selection of local ales and beers.
FACILITIES: 3 en suite (1 fmly) (3 GF) No smoking in bedrooms No smoking in area of dining room TVB tea/coffee No dogs Cen ht No coaches Dinner Last d 9.30pm **PRICES:** s £50; d £75* **PARKING:** 100 **NOTES:** Closed Xmas/New Year **CARDS:**

COMPTON MARTIN Map 03 ST55

♦♦♦ *Haydon Grange Farm* *(ST525542)*

BS40 6LE ☎ 01761 221258 Mrs B Harris
Situated at the very heart of the Mendips, this farmhouse has been upgraded to comfortable modern standards over the last few years. The bedrooms enjoy splendid views over the surrounding countryside. A hearty breakfast is served at separate tables in the dining room which at other times guests are welcome to use as a lounge.

continued

FACILITIES: 3 en suite (1 fmly) No smoking in bedrooms No smoking in dining room No smoking in 1 lounge TVB tea/coffee No dogs (ex guide dogs) Cen ht TVL 1000 acres beef sheep **PARKING:** 30

CREWKERNE — Map 03 ST40

♦♦♦♦ Manor Farm *(ST409071)*

Wayford TA18 8QL ☎ 01460 78865 & 0776 7620031
01460 78865 Mr & Mrs A Emery
Dir: *from Crewkerne take B3165 to Lyme Regis, after 3m in Clapton turn right into Dunsham Lane, 0.5m up hill Manor Farm on right*

Off the beaten track, this fine Victorian country house has extensive views over Clapton towards the Axe Valley. The comfortably furnished bedrooms are well equipped; front-facing rooms enjoy splendid views. Breakfast is served at separate tables in the dining room. A spacious lounge is provided.
FACILITIES: 3 en suite 1 annexe en suite No smoking STV TVB tea/coffee No dogs Cen ht TVL Fishing Riding 20 acres breeding beef **PRICES:** s £25-35; d £44-£50* **PARKING:** 14

♦♦♦♦ Shores Farm

Frogs St, Lopen TA13 5JR ☎ 01460 240587 & 07788 186616
e-mail: ARouston@compuserve.com
Dir: *turn off A303 at South Petherton rdbt & take turn signed Lopen, continue to next rdbt & turn left into village, thatch house on right*
Built of local Hamstone, this 17th-century thatched farmhouse has a real feeling of solidity with many of its original features retained, including beautiful oak beams and inglenook fireplaces. The well equipped bedrooms are comfortable and traditionally styled. Breakfast is served around a large table in the dining room; a spacious guest lounge is also provided.
FACILITIES: 4 rms (2 en suite) (1 fmly) No smoking TVB tea/coffee No dogs Cen ht No coaches Dinner Last d 24 hrs notice **PRICES:** s £25-£30; d £46-£50 **LB** **PARKING:** 4 **NOTES:** Closed Xmas & New Year

♦♦♦ Manor Arms

North Perrott TA18 7SG ☎ 01460 72901 01460 72901
e-mail: info@manorarmshotel.co.uk
Dir: *from A30 take A3066, signed Bridport. 1m to Manor Arms in North Perrott (The Circle)*

Dating back to the 16th century, this Grade II listed building offers a wide selection of freshly cooked meals in the 'olde worlde' bars, which have exposed stone walls and an inglenook fireplace. Most of the rooms are in the converted coach house at the rear of the property, while the rest are in the main building.
FACILITIES: 8 en suite (1 fmly) (3 GF) No smoking in bedrooms No smoking in dining room No smoking in 1 lounge TVB tea/coffee No dogs (ex guide dogs) Cen ht No coaches Dinner Last d 9pm **PRICES:** s £42; d £54-£69* **LB** **MEALS:** Lunch fr £7.50&alc Dinner £15-£21alc* **CONF:** Thtr 24 Class 12 Board 12 Del from £65 * **PARKING:** 22
CARDS:

CROSCOMBE — Map 03 ST54

♦♦♦ Bull Terrier

BA5 3QJ ☎ 01749 343658
e-mail: barry.vidler@bullterrierpub.co.uk
Dir: *midway between Wells & Shepton Mallet on A371. By village cross*
Ideally located in the centre of the village, this attractive country inn has a relaxed and friendly atmosphere. The public areas are particularly enjoyable, as the character of the inn has been retained with the flagstone floors and inglenook fireplace. Bedrooms are brightly decorated and well equipped. Freshly prepared lunches and dinners are available.
FACILITIES: 2 en suite No smoking in bedrooms No smoking in area of dining room TVB tea/coffee No dogs (ex guide dogs) Cen ht No children 10yrs Dinner Last d 9pm **PRICES:** s £30; d £50-£54*
MEALS: Lunch £9-£23&alc Dinner £9-£23&alc* **PARKING:** 3
CARDS:

CROWCOMBE — Map 03 ST13

♦♦♦♦ Home Leigh House

Leigh Ln TA4 4BL ☎ 01984 618 439
Dir: *M5 junct 25, take A358 towards Taunton for approx 10m. Pass sign for Crowcombe. Left at Stogumber sign. Continue uphill and take 1st left downhill signed Lower Vexford. Pass x-roads and over level crossing, house at bottom of hill on right.*
An exceptionally warm welcome awaits guests here. Close to the Quantocks, the Steam Railway and the coast, and convenient for Taunton and Bridgwater, Home Leigh is the perfect base for walkers, train enthusiasts and business travellers alike. Bedrooms are very comfortable and enjoy views over the surrounding countryside. A hearty breakfast, and dinner, (by arrangement) can be enjoyed around the communal table in the dining room.
FACILITIES: 2 en suite No smoking TVB tea/coffee No dogs (ex guide dogs) Cen ht No coaches Dinner Last d before noon **PRICES:** s £25; d £44* **LB** **PARKING:** 8

England

DINDER Map 03 ST54

♦♦♦ Crapnell Farm *(ST597457)*
BA5 3HG ☎ 01749 342683 📠 01749 342683 Mrs P J Keen
e-mail: pamkeen@yahoo.com

A peacefully located farmhouse with pleasant views of the surrounding countryside. The hosts create a relaxed and friendly atmosphere, and bedrooms are attractively decorated and comfortable. The lounge has an open fire in colder months and the garden is smart and well tended. Traditional breakfasts are served in the dining room.
FACILITIES: 3 en suite (1 fmly) No smoking TVB tea/coffee No dogs Cen ht TVL 3/4 size snooker table Splash pool **PRICES:** s £20-£25; d £40-£45* **PARKING:** 8 **NOTES:** Closed 18 Dec-3 Jan

DITCHEAT Map 03 ST63

♦♦♦♦ Manor House Inn
BA4 6RB ☎ 01749 860276
e-mail: manorhouse@onetel.net.uk
Dir: *At Shepton Mallet take A371 (Castle Carey/Wincanton). R after 3m for Ditcheat. Inn in middle of village*

This pleasant inn has many features which combine to provide a most relaxing environment. Friendly locals, good food, fine wines and real ales, flag-stoned floors and cosy gas lighting in the bar, all contribute to a memorable stay. Guestrooms are delightfully decorated in a bright and tasteful style and are most spacious and comfortable.
FACILITIES: 3 en suite (1 fmly) (3 GF) No smoking in bedrooms No smoking in dining room TVB tea/coffee Cen ht Dinner Last d 9.30pm PRICES: s £45-£50; d £65-£75* **LB MEALS:** Bar Lunch £3.25-£7.95alc Dinner £17.20-£26alc* **PARKING:** 25 **CARDS:**

Places with this symbol are farmhouses.

DRAYCOTT Map 03 ST45

♦♦♦♦ Oakland House
Wells Rd BS27 3SU ☎ 01934 744195 📠 01934 744195
e-mail: peterandmarcia@oaklandhouse.fsworld.co.uk
Dir: *M5 junct 22, follow signs into Cheddar on A371. Draycott is 2.5m & house last on right before market garden*
Situated a short distance from Cheddar, this warm and friendly home provides comfortable and spacious accommodation. Splendid views of the Somerset Moors and Glastonbury Tor can be had from the sun lounge and guest bedrooms, which are well appointed and attractively furnished. Dinner features fresh fruit and vegetables from the garden.
FACILITIES: 3 en suite (1 fmly) No smoking in 1 bedrooms No smoking in dining room No smoking in 1 lounge STV TVB tea/coffee No dogs (ex guide dogs) Cen ht No coaches Pool Table Dinner Last d 24 hrs notice **PRICES:** s £30-£40; d £45-£60* **LB PARKING:** 6 **NOTES:** Closed late Dec-mid Jan

DULVERTON Map 03 SS92

See also Winsford

Premier Collection

♦♦♦♦♦ Highercombe
TA22 9PT ☎ 01398 323451 📠 01398 323451
e-mail: highercombe@btconnect.com
Dir: *from Dulverton take B3223 towards Lynton, premises are approx 2.5m on right after sharp left bend*
With delightful views over Exmoor, this charming Grade II listed former hunting lodge and farmhouse, is set in eight acres of parkland and landscaped gardens. Bedrooms are spacious and comfortably furnished with many extra facilities. The lounge and dining room are furnished to reflect the style and character of the house.
FACILITIES: 3 rms (2 en suite) (1 fmly) No smoking TVB tea/coffee Cen ht TVL No coaches Fishing Riding **PRICES:** s £35-£37.50; d £70-£75* **PARKING:** 6 **CARDS:**

♦♦♦♦ *Higher Langridge Farm* *(SS903245)*
Exbridge TA22 9RR ☎ 01398 323999 📠 01398 323999
Mrs G Summers
e-mail: gill.langridge@ukf.net
Dir: *off A396 between Exbridge & Oldways End*
Straddling the Somerset/Devon border, just a short drive from Exmoor National Park, this 17th-century farmhouse has been home to the Summers family for six generations. Comfortable bedrooms have lovely views and are tastefully furnished, and the cosy dining/sitting room has a wood-burning stove. Resident hens provide eggs for breakfast, and red deer can often be glimpsed in nearby fields. Freshly prepared evening meals, featuring local produce where possible, are available by prior arrangement.
FACILITIES: 3 rms (2 en suite) (1 fmly) No smoking tea/coffee Cen ht TVL 375 acres beef sheep Dinner Last d 10am **PARKING:** 5 **NOTES:** Closed 1 Dec - 31 Jan **CARDS:**

♦♦♦♦ Threadneedle
EX16 9JH ☎ 01398 341598
Dir: *on Devon/Somerset border just off B3227 between Oldways End & East Anstey*
Threadneedle is built in the style of a Devon Longhouse, and situated on the edge of Exmoor near Dulverton. The spacious, well appointed family home offers guests comfortable en suite

continued

accommodation. Traditional West Country dishes are served in the light airy dining room which overlooks the garden and surrounding countryside.
FACILITIES: 2 en suite (1 fmly) No smoking in bedrooms TVB tea/coffee Cen ht No coaches Dinner Last d 10am **PRICES:** d £50-£52✳ **LB** **PARKING:** 12

♦♦♦♦ Town Mills

High St TA22 9HB ☎ 01398 323124
e-mail: townmills@onetel.net.uk
Dir: *Dulverton is on B3222, Town Mills 200 yds on left after crossing River Barle next to the Mill Leat*
This attractive Georgian mill house is ideally situated for those wishing to explore Exmoor. Two of the comfortable, well-equipped bedrooms have log fires, with one room located on the ground floor. Each bedroom has easy chairs and a dining table, where guests can enjoy their choice of continental or cooked breakfast.
FACILITIES: 5 en suite (1 GF) TVB tea/coffee No dogs (ex guide dogs) Cen ht No coaches **PRICES:** d £48-£56✳ **PARKING:** 5 **NOTES:** Closed Xmas **CARDS:**

DUNSTER — Map 03 SS94

See also Roadwater

♦♦♦♦ Conygar House

2A The Ball TA24 6SD ☎ 01643 821872 📠 01643 821872
e-mail: bale-dunster@virgin.net
Dir: *from A39 turn left at traffic lights for Dunsterand proceed uphill. Take right turn past Dunster Visitor Centre (The Ball). House 150mtrs on right*
Tucked away in an elevated position in the fascinating medieval village of Dunster, this delightful house provides an excellent base from which to explore the picturesque surroundings. Bedrooms are of a very high standard and comfort is clearly of paramount importance. A lounge is available, and the immaculately presented gardens have a number of quiet seating areas in which to relax and unwind.
FACILITIES: 3 en suite No smoking TVB tea/coffee No dogs Cen ht TVL No coaches **PRICES:** s fr £30; d fr £50 **NOTES:** Closed Dec-Jan

♦♦♦♦ Buttercross

56 St Georges St TA24 6RS ☎ 01643 821413
e-mail: megabucks@buttercross39.freeserve.co.uk
Dir: *turn off A39 into Dunster, right immediately after traffic lights into St Georges St, pass school and church. Last white house on right*
Located at the edge of the village, this charming family home is just a short walk from Dunster Castle and the other interesting sights that the village has to offer. The spacious accommodation is tasteful, well equipped and has lovely views. A hearty breakfast is available to set you up for the day.
FACILITIES: 1 en suite (1 fmly) No smoking TVB tea/coffee No dogs Cen ht No children 5yrs No coaches **PRICES:** d £40-£48✳ **LB** **NOTES:** Closed 21-27 Dec

♦♦♦♦ Dollons House

10-12 Church St TA24 6SH ☎ 01643 821880
e-mail: jmott@onetel.net.uk
Dir: *exit A39 at traffic lights, follow A396 through High Street into Church Street*
Centrally situated in medieval Dunster, this charming Grade II listed property, once the village pharmacy now operates as a gift shop as well as offering comfortable, high quality guest accommodation. Bedrooms have lots of character, being individually furnished and attractively decorated; two of which overlook the castle. The tasty breakfast includes a complimentary fruit basket for each guest.

continued

Dollons House

FACILITIES: 3 en suite No smoking TVB tea/coffee No dogs Cen ht TVL No children 16yrs No coaches **PRICES:** s £37.50; d £55✳ **NOTES:** Closed 25-26 Dec **CARDS:**

FITZHEAD — Map 03 ST12

♦♦♦ Fitzhead Inn

TA4 3JP ☎ 01823 400667
Dir: *off A3065 Taunton to Wiveliscombe road just after Preston Bowyer*
Overflowing with character, this delightful old inn with its exposed beams and log fires in the winter is centrally located in the village of Fitzhead. The charming bedrooms have been converted from an adjacent barn and are equipped with all modern facilities. Delicious lunches and dinners are served in the cosy bar.
FACILITIES: 4 en suite (4 GF) No smoking in bedrooms TVB tea/coffee Cen ht Dinner Last d 9.30pm **PRICES:** d fr £60✳ **MEALS:** Lunch £7.45-£10.65&alc Dinner £7.45-£10.65&alc✳

FROME — Map 03 ST74

♦♦♦♦ Garden House

30 Fromefield BA11 2HE ☎ 01373 301951
Dir: *A361 from Bath. 1m from Frome follow B3090 for 1m, turning right at fork for Town center. Establishment is 150mtrs on left*

This peaceful Georgian house is full of charm and elegance. Bedrooms are comfortable, and a host of extra items such as CD players, sherry and chocolates are provided. Dinners, by prior arrangement, feature local fresh produce and are taken in the smart dining room, where a well cooked and carefully prepared breakfast is also presented in style.
FACILITIES: 2 en suite No smoking TVB tea/coffee No dogs Cen ht TVL No children No coaches Dinner Last d flexible **PRICES:** d £55-£65✳
PARKING: 3

Places with this symbol are Inns.

FROME continued

♦♦♦♦ The Fox & Hounds Inn

Bulls Quarry Rd, Tytherington BA11 5BN ☎ 01373 473902
01373 465152
e-mail: foxandhounds@btinternet.com
This traditional inn offers friendly and comfortable accommodation and is conveniently located for the attractive countryside and within driving distance of Wells and Glastonbury. Bedrooms are well-equipped and offer good levels of comfort. Good choices can be made at dinner where Thai and Indonesian specialities are offered along with traditional fare.
FACILITIES: 3 en suite No smoking in bedrooms No smoking in dining room TVB tea/coffee No dogs (ex guide dogs) Cen ht No children 5yrs Dinner Last d 9-9.30pm **PARKING:** 60 **CARDS:**

♦♦♦♦ Olde Bath Arms Hotel & Restaurant

1 Palmer St BA11 1DS ☎ 01373 465045
e-mail: oldebatharms@tinyonline.co.uk
Dir: *A361 to Frome town centre, car park entrance is on main road, Bath St, next to traffic lights opposite St John's Church*
An excellent base from which to tour the area or ideal for the business guest, the Olde Bath Arms is steeped in history and has interesting architectural features. The friendly proprietors provide comfortable rooms and attentive service. Good home cooked lunches and dinners and freshly prepared breakfasts are served in the spacious dining room and guests can also relax in the well stocked bar.
FACILITIES: 3 en suite 2 annexe en suite No smoking in bedrooms No smoking in dining room No smoking in lounges TVB tea/coffee No dogs (ex guide dogs) Licensed Cen ht TVL No children No coaches Dinner Last d 8pm **PRICES:** s £40; d £55✻ **PARKING:** 6 **CARDS:**

♦♦♦♦ The Talbot 15th Century Coaching Inn

Mells BA11 3PN ☎ 01373 812254 01373 813599
e-mail: roger@talbotinn.com
Dir: *A36 Bath to Warminster Rd, R into Frome, A362 to Radstock, follow signs for Mells (The Circle)*
Located in the peaceful village of Mells, this unique inn retains many original features including flagstone floors and a wealth of exposed beams. Sympathetic renovation has resulted in bedrooms well equipped for the modern traveller and public areas, furnished in rustic style, are full of character and offer a relaxed informal setting for the enjoyment of food and real ales.
FACILITIES: 8 en suite No smoking in area of dining room TVB tea/coffee Direct dial from bedrooms Dinner Last d 9.15pm **PRICES:** s £45-£55; d £75✻ **LB MEALS:** Lunch £15-£20alc Dinner £20-£27alc✻
CONF: Board 16 **PARKING:** 10 **CARDS:**

♦♦♦ Brookover Farm *(ST775514)*

Orchardleigh BA11 2PH ☎ 01373 462806 Mrs E M J White
Dir: *1.5m from Frome on Radstock road A362*
This 18th-century farmhouse is located in a delightfully tranquil setting, convenient for surrounding attractions. Bedrooms are spacious and attractively decorated, and the welcoming and helpful hosts provide a relaxing atmosphere. Generous breakfasts are served in the combined lounge and dining room.
FACILITIES: 3 en suite No smoking TVB tea/coffee No dogs Cen ht Fishing Riding 40 acres **PRICES:** s fr £35; d £50✻ **LB PARKING:** 8
NOTES: Closed 23-31 Dec

♦♦ Highview

Buckland Dinham BA11 2QP ☎ 01373 464539
Dir: *A362 from Frome to Buckland Dinham, on right of main rd adjacent to side rd leading to 14-th century Church*
Peacefully located and enjoying outstanding country views this pleasant home offers comfortable accommodation. Bedrooms are attractively decorated, comfortably furnished and traditionally equipped, and Highview is ideal for either the business or leisure traveller. Hearty breakfast is served around a single table and dinner is available at the nearby 16th century village pub.
FACILITIES: 2 rms (2 GF) No smoking TV1B tea/coffee No dogs Cen ht TVL No children 12yrs No coaches **PRICES:** s £25; d £42-£46✻
PARKING: 2 **NOTES:** Closed mid Dec-mid Jan

GLASTONBURY — Map 03 ST53

See also Butleigh, Catcott, Somerton & West Pennard

♦♦♦♦ Cradlebridge *(ST477385)*

BA16 9SD ☎ 01458 831827 Mrs J Tinney
Dir: *take A39 south from Glastonbury, after Morlands factory take 2nd right . Cradlebridge Farm is signposted on left after 1m*
Located in quiet countryside, Cradlebridge Farm is a 200-acre dairy farm with pleasant views over the Somerset Levels. Bedrooms are comfortably furnished and spacious. Ideal as a base for touring the area or for a more relaxing break, many guests regularly return to Cradlebridge. Breakfast is served at a communal table and features local bacon and the farm's own sausages.
FACILITIES: 2 annexe en suite (2 fmly) No smoking TVB tea/coffee No dogs Cen ht No children 3yrs 200 acres dairy **PRICES:** s £35; d £50✻
PARKING: 6

♦♦♦♦ Greenacres

Barrow Ln, North Wootton BA4 4HL ☎ 01749 890497
e-mail: harvie.greenacres@talk21.com
Dir: *A39 Wells-Glastonbury, turn at Browns gdn centre, follow campsite signs. A361 Shepton Mallet-Glastonbury, turn at Steanbow, follow campsite signs*
Quietly located within sight of Glastonbury Tor this friendly home offers pleasant accommodation. The bright and comfortable bedrooms share adjacent bath and shower. A separate lounge is provided. Breakfast is served in the conservatory and guests are welcome to use the well-tended garden.
FACILITIES: 2 rms No smoking TVB tea/coffee No dogs (ex guide dogs) Cen ht TVL No children No coaches **PRICES:** d £40✻ **PARKING:** 4

♦♦♦♦ 100 Boundary Way

BA6 9PH ☎ 01458 834311
e-mail: chris@cdalexander.freeserve.co.uk
Dir: *on estate opposite B&Q rdbt*
A warm welcome is assured at this delightful modern home located in a residential estate on the edge of town and yet within walking distance of the Abbey, town centre and Tor. The comfortable bedroom and bathroom are well decorated, presented and equipped, with many useful extras.
FACILITIES: 1 en suite No smoking TVB tea/coffee No dogs Cen ht No children **PRICES:** d fr £50✻ **PARKING:** 1 **NOTES:** Closed NOv-feb

♦♦♦♦ Wearyall Hill House

78 The Roman Way BA6 8AD ☎ 01458 835510
e-mail: enquiries@wearyallhillhouse.co.uk
Dir: *on leaving Glastonbury take A39 to Street. After the rdbt (B & Q on right) take 1st left (Roman Way). House is 8th on left, after front fencing turn sharp left into a private drive*
Situated on the edge of town and close to the numerous places of interest in the area, the elevated position enjoyed by this delightful Victorian residence provides guests with sweeping views of the surrounding area. Restored to its former glory by the present owners, the property is appropriately decorated and furnished with many extra facilities.

continued

Wearyall Hill House

ACILITIES: 3 en suite No smoking STV TVB tea/coffee No dogs Cen ht No hildren 10yrs **PRICES:** s £35-£48; d £48-£58* **PARKING:** 8

♦♦♦♦ Wood Lane House

utleigh BA6 8TR ☎ 01458 850354

ir: *A37 to Bristol, at Lydford on Fosse turn at lights for Keinton Mandeville, ght to Barton St David, Wood Lane opposite Rose & Portcullis pub*

urrounded by very pleasant gardens and farmland, Wood Lane louse offers guests a relaxing base from which to visit the many ttractions of the area. The owners provide a warm and friendly velcome and many guests return on a regular basis. Breakfast, erved at one large table, makes an enjoyable start to the day.

ACILITIES: 3 en suite (2 GF) No smoking TVB tea/coffee No dogs (ex uide dogs) Cen ht TVL No coaches **PRICES:** s £28; d £48* **ARKING:** 3 **NOTES:** Closed Xmas/New Year

♦♦♦ Barrow Farm *(ST553416)*

orth Wootton BA4 4HL ☎ 01749 890245 01749 890245

Ars M White

ir: *A361, turn right after Pilton, onto North Wootton, at T-junct in village ırn left, house 1.5m on left*

his 15th-century working farm is pleasantly located in an ttractive setting. Welcoming, well-maintained bedrooms are rovided and guests are made to feel at home in the relaxed and riendly atmosphere. The lounge and dining room are both omfortable and fresh local produce and good cooking all ontribute to a memorable stay.

ACILITIES: 3 rms (1 fmly) No smoking in dining room No smoking in 1 ounge TVB tea/coffee No dogs (ex guide dogs) TVL 150 acres working dairy)inner Last d 9am **PRICES:** s fr £24; d £36-£40* BB **ARKING:** 4 **NOTES:** Closed Dec-Jan

♦♦ Melrose

7 Bere Ln BA6 8BD ☎ 01458 832016 & 07866 693731

-mail: deeperry@globalnet.co.uk

)ir: *on A361*

friendly welcome is given to guests at this family home, which is vithin strolling distance of the town centre. Bedrooms are astefully decorated and are comfortably furnished. Guests are nade to feel at home and can use the open plan lounge and lining room where views of the garden and Glastonbury Abbey in he background.

ACILITIES: 2 en suite (2 fmly) No smoking tea/coffee No dogs Cen ht TVL lo coaches **PRICES:** s £18-£25; d £36-£50* BB

HINTON ST GEORGE — Map 03 ST41

♦♦♦♦ The Lord Poulett Arms

High St TA17 8SE ☎ 01460 73149 01460 76400

e-mail: lordpoulett@aol.com

Dir: *from A303 take Sth Petherton off, through Watergore and turn left at rdbt onto Lopen road, through Lopen turn right by white house and right at cross road in village*

This delightful thatched inn offers comfortable well-appointed accommodation in the heart of the village. A wide range of hearty homecooked meals is available at both lunch and dinner. A restaurant, beer garden and private meeting/dining room are also available.

FACILITIES: 4 en suite (1 fmly) No smoking in bedrooms TVB tea/coffee No dogs (ex guide dogs) Cen ht Beer garden with swings Dinner Last d 9pm **PRICES:** s fr £28; d fr £45* **CONF:** Board 14 **PARKING:** 15 **CARDS:**

ILMINSTER — Map 03 ST31

See also Buckland St Mary & Chard

Premier Collection

♦♦♦♦♦ Old Rectory

Cricket Malherbie TA19 0PW ☎ 01460 54364

01460 57374

e-mail: theoldrectory@malherbie.freeserve.co.uk

Dir: *from rdbt junct A358/A303 take A358 S towards Chard. After Donyatt turn left towards Ilminster, right to Cricket Malherbie, Old Rectory on left*

Set in secluded gardens, this is an enchanting stone cottage. Unobtrusive yet high levels of hospitality and service are the order of the day. Bedrooms are furnished with comfort in mind and provide beautiful views over the garden and countryside beyond. Dinner is available by prior arrangement with only the finest fresh ingredients being used.

FACILITIES: 5 en suite No smoking TVB tea/coffee No dogs (ex guide dogs) Licensed Cen ht No children 16yrs No coaches Dinner Last d 10am **PRICES:** s £50; d £80-£90 LB **PARKING:** 5 **NOTES:** Closed 23-27 Dec **CARDS:**

England

KEYNSHAM Map 03 ST66

♦♦♦♦ Grasmere Court Hotel

22-24 Bath Rd BS31 1SN ☎ 0117 986 2662 Fax 0117 986 2762
e-mail: grasmerecourt@aol.com
Dir: *on B3116 just off A4 between Bristol and Bath*

This very friendly family-run hotel is conveniently located between the cities of Bath and Bristol. Bedrooms vary in size and are spacious and equipped with modern comforts; one has a four-poster bed. A comfortable lounge is available as well as a cosy bar. Good value, freshly prepared food is served in the attractive dining room.
FACILITIES: 16 en suite (2 fmly) No smoking in bedrooms No smoking in dining room STV TVB tea/coffee Direct dial from bedrooms No dogs Licensed Cen ht TVL No coaches Dinner Last d 7.30pm **PRICES:** s £40-£56; d £56-£66* **LB PARKING:** 18 **CARDS:**

KILVE Map 03 ST14

♦♦♦♦ *Hood Arms Hotel*

TA5 1EA ☎ 01278 741210 Fax 01278 741477
e-mail: mattbri@tinyworld.co.uk
Dir: *12m W of Bridgwater on the A39*
Centrally located in the village of Kilve, this former 17th-century coaching inn offers comfortable bedrooms that are well equipped with a good range of facilities. In the beamed bars, blackboard menus offer a wide range of dishes; on Fridays and Saturdays a carte menu is available in the restaurant.
FACILITIES: 6 en suite (1 fmly) No smoking in bedrooms No smoking in dining room TVB tea/coffee Direct dial from bedrooms Cen ht Pool Table Dinner Last d 9.30pm **PARKING:** 8 **CARDS:**

LANGPORT Map 03 ST42

The Old Pound Inn

Aller TA10 0RA ☎ 01458 250469
At the time of going to press the Diamond classification for this establishment had not been confirmed. Please check the AA website www.theAA.com for up-to-date information.
FACILITIES: 6 en suite (1 fmly)

MARTOCK Map 03 ST41

♦♦♦♦ Higher Farm

Bladon Hill, Kingsbury Episcopi TA12 6BJ ☎ 01935 823099
Dir: *turn off A303, signposted Kingsbury Episcopi, through villages of Ash and Coat. When entering village, turn left at Wyndham Arms pub, farm right*
Peacefully located in the picturesque village of Kingsbury Episcopi, Higher Farm provides comfortable, well-equipped accommodation within a relaxed and friendly environment. Breakfast is served in the pleasant dining room, which opens onto the rear garden and patio area. Two local pubs serving evening meals are just a five-minute stroll in either direction.
FACILITIES: 2 en suite (2 fmly) (5 GF) No smoking TVB tea/coffee No dogs (ex guide dogs) Cen ht No children 7yrs No coaches **PRICES:** d £40-£45*
PARKING: 6

♦♦♦♦ Wychwood

7 Bearley Rd TA12 6PG ☎ 01935 825601 Fax 01935 825601
e-mail: wychwoodmartock@yahoo.co.uk
Mar-Nov
Dir: *exit A303 to centre of Martock by post office, continue up East St from Post Office, Bearley Rd on left opposite Nags Head*
A warm welcome is assured at this delightful family home. A comfortable lounge and flower-filled conservatory overlook the pretty garden with its abundance of wildlife. Bedrooms are equipped with many thoughtful extras. Breakfast features organic produce when possible and the proprietors are pleased to recommend local restaurants and pubs for evening meals.
FACILITIES: 3 en suite No smoking TVB tea/coffee No dogs Cen ht TVL No children No coaches **PRICES:** s £36-£38; d £48-£52* **PARKING:** 4
CARDS:

♦♦♦♦ White Hart Hotel

East St TA12 6JQ ☎ 01935 822005 Fax 01935 822056
e-mail: j&mpc@whitehartthotel
Dir: *turn off A303 signed Martock.*
FACILITIES: 10 rms (9 en suite) No smoking in bedrooms No smoking in dining room TVB tea/coffee Direct dial from bedrooms No dogs (ex guide dogs) Licensed Cen ht TVL No children 5yrs Dinner Last d 8.45pm
PRICES: s £30-£50; d £45-£70* **LB PARKING:** 15
CARDS:

MINEHEAD Map 03 SS94

See also Dunster

Premier Collection

♦♦♦♦♦ Glendower Hotel

32 Tregonwell Rd TA24 5DU ☎ 01643 707144
Fax 01643 708719
Dir: *A39 into Minehead. Take last exit at mini-rdbt, 200yds right by school into Ponsford Rd/Tregonwell Rd. Hotel on left*
Conveniently located, just a short walk from the seafront and town, this well run, friendly hotel is set in an attractive residential area. Furnished in keeping with the period of the property, the public areas include a spacious bar/lounge and a well appointed dining room. The comfortable bedrooms are impeccably maintained, attractively decorated and equipped with all modern comforts.
FACILITIES: 14 en suite (2 fmly) (3 GF) No smoking in 3 bedrooms No smoking in dining room TVB tea/coffee Licensed Cen ht TVL No coaches Golf 18 **PRICES:** s £25-£28; d £40-£56*
PARKING: 14 **CARDS:**

♦♦♦♦ Gascony Hotel

The Avenue TA24 5BB ☎ 01643 705939 Fax 01643 709926
Dir: *on The Avenue at corner of Tregonwell Rd*
Situated between the town centre and the seafront, this comfortable Victorian hotel is considered by many regular guests, as a second home by the sea. The spacious bar/lounge is well furnished and decorated, whilst in the dining room, a short fixed-price menu features home-cooked dishes, complemented by an interesting wine list.

continued

ACILITIES: 13 en suite (2 fmly) (1 GF) No smoking in dining room TVB a/coffee No dogs (ex guide dogs) Licensed Cen ht No coaches Dinner Last 5.30pm **PRICES:** s £29.50-£31.50; d £52-£54* **LB PARKING:** 15 **OTES:** Closed Dec-Feb rs Nov **CARDS:**

♦♦♦ Red House

eriton Rd TA24 8DT ☎ 01643 706519 📠 01643 706519
ir: 1m from Alcombe rdbt on A39 (Minehead to Porlock road)
eally located and enjoying excellent views towards the sea this tractive house is comfortable, spacious and full of charm. Many uests return to Red House due to the relaxed atmosphere and omely, comfortable style. Breakfast is taken in the dining room, hich overlooks the smart gardens and provides a pleasant start the day.
ACILITIES: 3 en suite No smoking TVB tea/coffee No dogs (ex guide ogs) Cen ht TVL No children 12yrs No coaches **PRICES:** s £25; d £50* **B PARKING:** 5 **NOTES:** Closed Dec

♦♦ The Old Ship Aground

uay St TA24 5UL ☎ 01643 702087 📠 01643 709066
mail: enquiries@oldshipaground.co.uk
ir: turn R towards Butlins at 1st rdbt after Dunster lights, turn L at rdbt on afront, proceed to harbour with sea on R, on front
ocated at the edge of the harbour and enjoying views of the bay, the ld Ship Aground offers traditional, friendly hospitality. Bedrooms re spacious and thoughtfully equipped. An extensive choice is vailable from the menu in the bar and a separate restaurant which ecialises in fish dishes, is available from Thursday to Saturday.
ACILITIES: 13 en suite (3 fmly) No smoking in area of dining room STV /B tea/coffee Cen ht Pool Table Dinner Last d 9.30pm **PRICES:** s £25-£30; £40-£45* **MEALS:** Lunch £3-£12 Dinner £3-£12* **PARKING:** 10 **ARDS:**

ETHER STOWEY — Map 03 ST13

♦♦♦♦ Castle of Comfort

A5 1LE ☎ 01278 741264 📠 01278 741144
mail: reception@castle-of-comfort.co.uk
ir: on A39, approx 1.3m from Nether Stowey on left
ating in part from the 16th century, this former inn is situated on e northern slopes of the Quantock Hills in an Area of utstanding Natural Beauty. Bedrooms are well equipped and the ublic rooms are smart and comfortable. In addition to the naginative dinner, served by prior arrangement, morning coffees nd cream teas are available.
ACILITIES: 6 rms (5 en suite) (1 fmly) (1 GF) No smoking TVB tea/coffee irect dial from bedrooms Licensed Cen ht No coaches Outdoor swimming ool (heated) Dinner Last d 6pm **PRICES:** s £33-£76; d £87-£117 **LB ONF:** Thtr 20 Class 20 Board 12 Del from £69 * **PARKING:** 10 **ARDS:**

ORTH CURRY — Map 03 ST32

♦♦♦ Banana Cottage

Greenway, North Curry TA3 6NJ ☎ 01823 490100
-mail: enquiries@bananacottage.co.uk
ir: From A358 onto A378 at Thornfalcon traffic lights, through Wrantage ass Wrantage mill animal feed warehouse. After 0.5m left at Newport & orth Curry sign. Cottage 0.5m on right
his charming cottage, located in a quiet rural setting, is full of haracter - watch out for low beams! Bedrooms are cosy and omfortable. There is a delightful TV lounge/dining room available or guests to relax in while the large cottage garden is a picture in he warmer months.
ACILITIES: 3 rms (2 en suite) No smoking No dogs Cen ht TVL No hildren 6yrs No coaches **PRICES:** s £25-£28; d £39-£41* **LB ARKING:** 4 **NOTES:** Closed 23 Dec-6 Jan

NORTH PETHERTON — Map 03 ST23

♦♦♦ *Lower Clavelshay Farm (ST254309)*

TA6 6PJ ☎ 01278 662347 📠 01278 662347 Mrs S M Milverton
e-mail: sue.milverton@lineone.net
***Dir:** in North Petherton, turn off A38 beside bakery, to end of rd and Cliff Rd. After 0.5m R signed Clavelshay for 2m. L beside Old Orchard Cottage*
Set in 260 acres with wonderful views, this delightful 17th-century farmhouse offers visitors a taste of 'a real farm'. Guests are encouraged to wander around the farm, watch the cows being milked, feed the pigs and collect the eggs. Home-cooked evening meals can be provided by prior arrangement.
FACILITIES: 3 en suite (1 fmly) No smoking tea/coffee Cen ht TVL 260 acres dairy Dinner Last d 5pm **PARKING:** 4 **NOTES:** Closed Dec-Feb

NORTON ST PHILIP — Map 03 ST75

Premier Collection

♦♦♦♦♦ Bath Lodge

Warminster Rd BA2 7NH ☎ 01225 723040 📠 01225 723737
e-mail: info@bathlodge.com
***Dir:** 7m S of Bath on A36, S of junction with A366*
This impressive property with its castellated stone architecture is set in five acres of gardens and woodland. The bedrooms continue the theme of the house, with a selection of four-poster beds, circular showers and heraldic shields. Breakfast is served in the conservatory. Dinner is available on Saturday evenings by prior arrangement.
FACILITIES: 6 en suite 1 annexe en suite (1 fmly) No smoking STV TVB tea/coffee Direct dial from bedrooms No dogs Licensed Cen ht No children 10yrs No coaches Dinner Last d 5pm **PRICES:** s £40-£95; d £75-£120* **LB PARKING:** 25 **CARDS:**

Premier Collection

♦♦♦♦♦ Monmouth Lodge

BA2 7LH ☎ 01373 834367
***Dir:** leave Bath on A36, after 7m right onto A366 to Norton St Philip*
This delightful lodge offers friendly and spacious accommodation. Only a ten-minute drive from the outskirts of Bath, the historic village is a peaceful and charming setting. Bedrooms are comfortably furnished and two have king-size beds; one room leads onto a garden terrace. Breakfast is a delight, and for dinner, the magnificent George Inn is only a short walk away.
FACILITIES: 3 en suite (1 fmly) No smoking TVB tea/coffee No dogs Cen ht No children 5yrs No coaches **PRICES:** s £55-£65; d £65-£75* **PARKING:** 5 **NOTES:** Closed 20 Dec-2 Jan **CARDS:**

♦♦♦♦ The Plaine

Bell Hill BA2 7LT ☎ 01373 834723 📠 01373 834101
e-mail: theplaine@easynet.co.uk
***Dir:** from A36 Bath to Warminster rd turn right onto A366 signed Radstock, house at x-rds in village*
Only 15 minutes from Bath, this charming 16th century home provides comfortable accommodation, all rooms have four-poster beds and are equipped with many thoughtful extra touches. A number of good inns are within strolling distance and offer excellent dining. Breakfasts are taken around the large table.
FACILITIES: 3 en suite No smoking TVB tea/coffee No dogs (ex guide dogs) Cen ht No children 3yrs No coaches **PRICES:** s fr £52; d fr £58* **PARKING:** 5 **NOTES:** Closed 24-26 Dec
CARDS:

England

PORLOCK Map 03 SS84

Premier Collection

♦♦♦♦♦ Dunster Steep House

TA24 8EU ☎ 01643 863008

e-mail: johnbishop@dunstersteep.freeserve.co.uk

Dir: *A39 forks at Porlock, turn off A39 at signpost Bossington, 100yds on left*

Standing in an acre of mature gardens, this house enjoys wonderful views towards the coastline. The elegant interior includes many fine furnishings and antiques, collectively evoking the atmosphere of the Edwardian era. This is somewhere to relax and unwind, either in the comfortable lounge, conservatory or flower-filled gardens. Bedrooms combine comfort with quality and include many thoughtful extras.

FACILITIES: 3 en suite No smoking TVB tea/coffee No dogs Cen ht No children 14yrs No coaches **PRICES:** d £80* **LB PARKING:** 4

ROADWATER Map 03 ST03

♦♦♦♦ Wood Advent Farm *(ST037374)*

TA23 0RR ☎ 01984 640920 01984 640920 Mr & Mrs Brewer

Dir: *M5 junct 23, take A39 to Williton, left in Washford by hairdressers & 1st right in front of White Horse pub. Into Roadwater, left after shop*

Surrounded by the beautiful rolling hills of Exmoor, this working farm has been in the same family for generations. The spacious bedrooms are well equipped and comfortable; guests have the choice of two charming sitting rooms, with log fires burning on cooler evenings. By prior arrangement, home-cooked dinners are available.

FACILITIES: 4 en suite (1 fmly) No smoking in bedrooms No smoking in dining room No smoking in lounges STV TVB tea/coffee No dogs Licensed Cen ht TVL No children 11yrs Outdoor swimming pool (heated) Tennis (grass) Riding Clay pigeon shooting 350 acres arable beef sheep Dinner Last d 8pm **PRICES:** s £25-£35; d £45-£55* **LB PARKING:** 10 **CARDS:**

SIMONSBATH Map 03 SS73

♦♦♦♦ Barkham

Sandyway EX36 3LU ☎ 01643 831370 01643 831370

e-mail: adie.exmoor@btinternet.com

Dir: *exit A361 to North Molton, through village & onto moor signed Sandyway, left at crossroads signed Simonsbath, 400mtrs turn right*

Tucked away in a secret wooded valley at the top of Exmoor, this wonderfully restored Georgian farmhouse is set in 12 acres of pasture with streams and waterfalls. Bedrooms are comfortable and attractively furnished. Traditional breakfasts and tempting dinners (which are available by prior arrangement) are served in the impressive oak-panelled dining room. There is also a spacious drawing room for guest use.

continued

FACILITIES: 3 en suite No smoking No dogs Licensed Cen ht TVL No children 12yrs No coaches Croquet lawn Tree house. Dinner Last d 9am **PRICES:** s fr £30; d £32-£35* **BB PARKING:** 6 **CARDS:**

SOMERTON Map 03 ST4

Premier Collection

♦♦♦♦♦ Lydford House

Lydford-on-Fosse TA11 7BU ☎ 01963 240217

01963 240413

e-mail: lynn@jamesribbons.demon.co.uk

Dir: *A303 to Podimore rdbt take A37 Bath/Bristol after 3m crossroads B3153. Lydford House on left after traffic lights*

Built in 1860 as a gentleman's residence, this delightful home now provides comfortable, elegant accommodation, with part of the house being used as an antique shop. The spacious bedrooms are attractively decorated and have quality furnishings. The sitting/dining area is furnished with style and panache; and breakfast is served around one large table.

FACILITIES: 4 en suite No smoking in bedrooms TVB tea/coffee No dogs (ex guide dogs) Cen ht TVL No coaches **PRICES:** s £40-£50; d £60* **PARKING:** 35 **CARDS:**

♦♦♦♦ Lower Farm *(ST527309)*

Kingweston TA11 6BA ☎ 01458 223237 01458 223276 Mrs J Sedgman

e-mail: lowerfarm@kingweston.demon.co.uk

Dir: *A303 take A37 N towards Shepton Mallet to traffic lights at Lydford-on Fosse, left onto B3153 through Keinton Mandeville & onto Kingweston. Farm on right*

Set within a conservation area with spectacular rural views, this Grade II listed stone farmhouse has been occupied by the same family for several generations. Furnished in cottage style, the cosy bedrooms combine old-world charm with modern comforts. Guests are served a hearty breakfast in the attractive dining room.

FACILITIES: 3 en suite (1 fmly) No smoking TVB tea/coffee No dogs (ex guide dogs) Cen ht Badminton net 500 acres Arable **PRICES:** s £27.50-£40; d £55* **PARKING:** 8 **NOTES:** Closed Xmas/New Year **CARDS:**

♦♦♦♦ Somerton Court Country House

TA11 7AH ☎ 01458 274694 01458 274693

e-mail: owen@newopaul.freeserve.co.uk

Dir: *turn off A303 at Podimore rdbt onto A372. 2m turn right A3165 to Somerton rd in 3m at bad right bend turn left & follow B&B signs*

Dating back to the 17th century and set in 55 acres of gardens and grounds, Somerton Court Country House offers a tranquil haven for guests wishing to escape the pressures of modern life. The comfortable bedrooms offer lovely views. Breakfast is served in the delightful dining room that overlooks the gardens.

FACILITIES: 6 en suite (2 fmly) No smoking TVB tea/coffee No dogs (ex guide dogs) Licensed Cen ht Riding **PRICES:** s fr £40; d fr £60* **CONF:** Thtr 100 **PARKING:** 30 **NOTES:** Closed Xmas & New Year Civ Wed 100 **CARDS:**

♦♦♦ Home Farm

Kingweston TA11 6BD ☎ 01458 223268

Dir: *from Somerton take B3153, on approaching Kingweston turn left on sharp right bend in 300yds farm is on left*

Quietly located at the edge of the village, Home Farm offers guest accommodation with its own sitting area in a delightful barn conversion, adjacent to the original stone farmhouse where a traditional breakfast is served. A warm welcome is assured, and friendly proprietors are happy to help you plan your exploration of the area.

continued

ACILITIES: 1 annexe en suite (1 fmly) No smoking TVB tea/coffee No ogs (ex guide dogs) **PRICES:** d £44✱ **PARKING:**

♦♦ *Church Farm*

ompton Dundon TA11 6PE ☎ 01458 272927 🖹 01458 272927

ir: *turn off B3151 in Compton Dundon into Hayes, follow road to church. hurch Farm on left*

et in peaceful, rural surroundings, this charming 17th-century atched cottage offers well equipped, comfortable bedrooms hich have all been upgraded; the majority of rooms are located the converted barn. The owners are friendly and welcoming, and any guests return regularly to enjoy the home cooked dinner, erved by prior arrangement only.

ACILITIES: 1 en suite 4 annexe en suite (2 fmly) No smoking TVB a/coffee Licensed Cen ht TVL No coaches Fishing Dinner Last d 10am **ARKING:** 5 **NOTES:** Closed 8 Dec-6 Jan

TANTON DREW — Map 03 ST56

♦♦♦ Greenlands

S39 4ES ☎ 01275 333487 🖹 01275 331211

mail: greenlands.bandb@virgin.net

ir: *off A37 onto B3130, establishment on right before 'Round House' and anton Drew Garage*

ituated near the ancient village of Stanton Drew in the heart of e Chew Valley, Greenlands is conveniently located to explore oth the surrounding countryside and cities of Bath, Bristol and Vells. The recently renovated accommodation includes omfortable well-equipped bedrooms and a separate downstairs uest lounge. Breakfast is a definite highlight of any stay here.

ACILITIES: 4 en suite No smoking in bedrooms No smoking in dining oom STV TVB tea/coffee Cen ht TVL No children 12yrs No coaches **RICES:** s fr £22.50; d fr £40✱ **PARKING:** 8

♦♦♦♦ Valley Farm *(ST595631)*

andy Ln BS39 4EL ☎ 01275 332723 & 07799 768161

🖹 01275 332723 Doreen & John Keel

-mail: highmead.gardens@virgin.net

ir: *A37 from Bristol to B3130 at Pensford. Left at garage into Stanton rew, over bridge 400yds on right Sandy Ln*

eacefully located along a quiet country lane in the village of tanton Drew, Valley Farm offers a relaxed and friendly standard of ccommodation. All bedrooms are comfortable and well equipped nd each enjoys pleasant views over the surrounding countryside. Although dinner is not available, the village pub is just a short stroll way.

continued

Valley Farm

FACILITIES: 3 en suite (1 fmly) (1 GF) No smoking TVB tea/coffee No dogs Cen ht TVL No children 8yrs 25 acres **PRICES:** s £22-£25; d £42-£45✱ **LB** **PARKING:** 6 **NOTES:** Closed 24-26 Dec

STANTON PRIOR — Map 03 ST66

♦♦♦ Poplar Farm *(ST679630)*

Stanton Prior BA2 9HX ☎ 01761 470382 🖹 01761 470382

Mrs V Hardwick

e-mail: poplarfarm@talk21.com

Dir: *from Bath take A4 (Bath/Bristol). At 1st rdbt take A39, 2m turn left opposite Wheatsheaf pub. Farm 1st on left in village*

A warm welcome is assured at this delightful 17th-century farmhouse, ideally located for the sights of Bath and the surrounding area. The bedrooms are spacious, and there is a cosy sitting/dining room. Guests take a hearty breakfast around a large table by the splendid inglenook fireplace.

FACILITIES: 2 rms (1 en suite) 1 annexe en suite (1 fmly) No smoking TV1B tea/coffee No dogs (ex guide dogs) Cen ht TVL 400 acres arable/beef **PRICES:** s £20-£30; d £50-£60 **LB** **PARKING:** 10

STAPLE FITZPAINE — Map 03 ST21

♦♦♦♦ Greyhound

TA3 5SP ☎ 01823 480227 🖹 01823 481117

Dir: *M5 junct 25 take A358 Yeovil road after 4m, follow signs to Staple Fitzpaine*

Set in an area of outstanding natural beauty, this picturesque village inn with its flagstone floors and open fires was formerly a hunting lodge. An imaginative choice of freshly prepared dishes is offered in the bars, and the more formal restaurant. The delightful bedrooms are comfortable and well equipped with many extra facilities.

FACILITIES: 4 en suite No smoking in bedrooms No smoking in dining room No smoking in lounges TVB tea/coffee No dogs No children 12yrs No coaches Pool room, Skittle Alley Dinner Last d 9pm **PRICES:** s £45; d £60-£69.90✱ **LB** **PARKING:** 60 **CARDS:**

England

STOGUMBER Map 03 ST03

♦♦♦♦ *Northam Mill*

Water Ln TA4 3TT ☎ 01984 656916 & 656146 01984 656144
e-mail: bmsspicer@aol.com

Dir: *A358 approx 11m NW of Taunton. L at 1st sign Stogumber, down lane, pass 1st lane L in dip, uphill, downhill, next L, 100yds on R into Water Ln*

Set in an area of Outstanding Natural Beauty, this delightful 16th century former mill house is full of character and timeless charm. Two of the thoughtfully equipped bedrooms are in the main house, while those in the Garden Suite are just a stone's throw away. Dinner, which is by arrangement, features imaginative dishes prepared from local ingredients. The Old Mill Barn Apartment is available for self-catering.

FACILITIES: 2 en suite 4 annexe en suite No smoking in bedrooms No smoking in dining room No smoking in 1 lounge TVB tea/coffee Direct dial from bedrooms No dogs (ex guide dogs) Licensed Cen ht TVL No children No coaches Riding Croquet lawn Shooting arranged Dinner Last d 8pm **PARKING:** 12 **CARDS:**

STOKE ST GREGORY Map 03 ST32

♦♦♦♦ Meare Green Farm

Meare Green TA3 6HT ☎ 01823 490759 01823 490759
e-mail: jane@kiteconsulting.com

Dir: *M5 junct 25 take A358 through Henlade up dual carriageway to traffic lights and garage, turn left onto A378 in 100yds fork left for North Curry, in 1.5m from centre North Curry farm on left opposite greystone barn*

FACILITIES: 2 en suite No smoking TVB tea/coffee Cen ht TVL No coaches Fishing Riding **PRICES:** s £28-£30; d £48-£50* **LB PARKING:** 3

STREET Map 03 ST43

♦♦♦ Kasuli

71 Somerton Rd BA16 0DN ☎ 01458 442063 01458 441423

Dir: *A39 to main rdbt in Street, then B3151 for Somerton. House 400m past Street Inn on left*

A warm and friendly welcome is assured at this charming family home located close to Clarke's Shopping Village and with easy access to local places of historical interest. Bedrooms are comfortable and neat with a lounge available for guests' use. An enjoyable, traditional breakfast is served at the family dining table.

FACILITIES: 2 rms No smoking TVB tea/coffee No dogs (ex guide dogs) Cen ht No coaches **PRICES:** s £18.50-£20; d £35-£38 **BB PARKING:** 2

TAUNTON Map 03 ST22

See also Burrowbridge, Churchinford, Staple Fitzpaine & Stogumber

Premier Collection

♦♦♦♦♦ Heathfield Lodge

Heathfield, Nr Hillcommon TA4 1DN ☎ 01823 432286
01823 433566
e-mail: heathfieldlodge@tinyworld.co.uk

Dir: *from Taunton take B3227 W towards Wiveliscombe, through Norton Fitzwarren & approx 2.5m. Past sign to Heathfield, then 1st entrance on right*

This elegant Regency house, nestling in five acres of landscaped gardens and grounds, is just ten minutes drive from the centre of Taunton and within easy reach of Exmoor National Park and the coast. Sue and Phil Thornton delight in

continued

Heathfield Lodge

sharing their home with guests, and many return to savour the peaceful surroundings. Individually furnished and decorated bedrooms are equipped with many thoughtful touches. With prior arrangement, imaginative home-cooked dinners are available, vegetarian and special diets catered for.

FACILITIES: 3 en suite (2 GF) No smoking TVB tea/coffee No dogs (ex guide dogs) Cen ht No children 16yrs No coaches Snooker Croquet lawn Dinner Last d noon **PRICES:** s £32; d £55* **LB**
PARKING: 6 **NOTES:** Closed 20 Dec-2 Jan

♦♦♦♦ Cutsey House

Cutsey, Trull TA3 7NY ☎ 01823 421705 01823 421294

Dir: *M5 junct 26, take West Buckland turn. Follow Lane into village, turn right at T junction. Take 2nd left, at junct take right fork. At next junct take right fork and house 200yds on right*

Cutsey House is set in over 20 acres of gardens and grounds; parts of the building date back to the 15th and 16th centuries. From the spacious, comfortable bedrooms there are glorious views of the surrounding countryside towards the Blackdown Hills. By prior arrangement dinner is available, with guests taking drinks in the library.

FACILITIES: 3 en suite No smoking in 1 bedrooms No smoking in dining room TVB No dogs Cen ht TVL No coaches Riding Snooker Dinner Last d 5pm **PRICES:** s £35-£40; d £50-£60* **PARKING:** 11 **NOTES:** Closed Xmas-Etr

♦♦♦♦ Blorenge House

57 Staple Grove Rd TA1 1DG ☎ 01823 283005
01823 283005
e-mail: enquiries@blorengehouse.co.uk

Dir: *M5 junct 25 towards cricket ground on left. Through traffic lights, at 2nd lights turn left, right at next lights, hotel 300yds on left*

This fine old Victorian property is conveniently situated within walking distance of the town centre. The individually furnished bedrooms are well equipped; with some having four-poster beds. A bar-lounge, garden and outdoor swimming pool are available fo guests, with evening meals being provided by prior arrangement.

FACILITIES: 23 rms (18 en suite) (4 fmly) (3 GF) No smoking in 15 bedrooms No smoking in dining room TVB tea/coffee Licensed Cen ht TVL Outdoor swimming pool (heated) **PRICES:** s £29-£42; d £48-£69 **LB**
PARKING: 23 **CARDS:**

♦♦♦♦ Brookfield

16 Wellington Rd TA1 4EQ ☎ 01823 272786 01823 272786
e-mail: info@brookfieldguesthouse.uk.com

Dir: *from town centre follow signs to Musgrove Hospital into Wellington R (A38). House on right hand side opposite turning to hospital*

This Grade II listed Georgian house is a five minute level walk from the centre of town. It is a family home where great pride is taken i the standard of guest care. Bedrooms are brightly decorated and well equipped. There is an attractive dining room where a choice i offered from a traditional breakfast menu.

continue

England

ACILITIES: 7 en suite (1 fmly) (1 GF) No smoking TVB tea/coffee No dogs ex guide dogs) Cen ht No children 5 yrs No coaches **PRICES:** s £35-£38; £45-£55✳ **PARKING:** 8

♦♦♦♦ Creechbarn

/icarage Ln, Creech-St-Michael TA3 5PP ☎ 01823 443955
01823 443509
-mail: mick@somersite.co.uk
ir: *exit M5 junct 25 onto A358. Turn to Creech St Michael via Ruishton. ollow canal boat signs to end of Vicarage Lane*

ocated next to the canal and on the Sustrans cycle route, this omerset Longbarn was lovingly converted by the current owners. edrooms are comfortable and there is a spacious sitting room vith books, television and table tennis. Food is carefully prepared - ree-range eggs for breakfast, for example (set dinner is available y prior arrangement) - and the dining room opens out onto the atio.

ACILITIES: 3 rms (2 en suite) No smoking in bedrooms No smoking in lining room TV1B tea/coffee Cen ht TVL No coaches bird watching Dinner ast d breakfast **PRICES:** s £27-£29; d £40-£44✳ **PARKING:** 4
IOTES: Closed 20 Dec-6 Jan

♦♦♦♦ Gatchells

Angersleigh TA3 7SY ☎ 01823 421580 & 07808 164276
-mail: gatchells@somerweb.co.uk
ir: *from Trull just S of Taunton, turn right signed Angersleigh into Dipford d, follow for 2m. Gatchells marked on right, take country track to cottage t end*

his delightful early 15th-century thatched former farmhouse estles at the foot of the Blackdown Hills. Gatchells is surrounded y peaceful cottage gardens, which boast a super outdoor pool. he accommodation is comfortable and retains many original eatures. Dinner, by prior arrangement, is served in the onservatory.

ACILITIES: 3 en suite (1 fmly) No smoking in bedrooms No smoking in lining room TVB tea/coffee TVL No coaches Outdoor swimming pool Dinner Last d 10am **PRICES:** s £30-£35; d £44-£54✳ **LB** **PARKING:** 3
CARDS:

♦♦♦♦ Higher Dipford *(ST216205)*

Trull TA3 7NU ☎ 01823 275770 01823 257916
Mrs M Fewings
Dir: *from County Hall Taunton signed Trull, pass Queens College on Honiton/Trull Rd, right to Dipford Rd, before fork Higher Dipford Farm on left*

Three miles from town, this Grade II listed, 600 year-old long-house is part of a working dairy farm. The exceptionally well equipped bedrooms are comfortable and individually decorated. There is an honesty bar and a spacious lounge. Excellent, home-cooked dinners are served in the dining room, where guests sit at one table.

FACILITIES: 3 en suite No smoking in bedrooms No smoking in dining room No smoking in 1 lounge STV TVB tea/coffee No dogs (ex guide dogs) Licensed Cen ht TVL Pool Table 120 acres beef dairy Dinner Last d 8pm
PRICES: s £30-£35; d £50-£60✳ **LB** **PARKING:** 6

Super supper! this symbol shows that evening meals exceeded our Inspector's expectations.

♦♦♦♦ Lower Farm *(ST281241)*

Thornfalcon TA3 5NR ☎ 01823 443549 01823 443549
Mrs D Titman
e-mail: lowerfarm@talk21.com
Dir: *2m SE from M5 junct 25, on A358 Ilminster/Yeovil road, turn left opposite Nags Head PH. Lower Farm in 1m on left, signed on driveway*

Only three miles from Taunton, this charming thatched 15th-century farmhouse is set in lovely gardens and is surrounded by open countryside. A hearty breakfast, taken in the farmhouse kitchen, features home-produced eggs. Imaginative, home-cooked dinners are also available (by prior arrangement). There is a comfortable sitting room with a log fire. New bedrooms are located in the recently renovated former granary, some on the ground floor.

FACILITIES: 3 en suite 5 annexe rms (3 en suite) (4 fmly) (3 GF) No smoking TV6B tea/coffee No dogs Cen ht TVL 10 acres beef cows poultry Dinner Last d 11am **PRICES:** s fr £30; d £50-£60✳ **LB** **PARKING:** 8

England

♦♦♦♦ Lower Manor Farm

Thornfalcon TA3 5NR ☎ 01823 443634 & 443222
e-mail: marion@lowermanorfarm.co.uk
Dir: *M5 junct 25, onto A358 signed Chard and Yeovil. Through Henlade onto dual carriageway. Ignore 1st left to Thornfalcon, take next left in 0.25m at x-rds opposite Nags Head Inn. Follow lane 0.5m, keep left by War Memorial, Farm next right*

In its delightful rural setting, Lower Manor Farm provides guests with a high standard of comfortable, well-furnished accommodation. All bedrooms are dual aspect, with views across the surrounding countryside. Tempting breakfasts, which feature home produce when available, are served at individual tables in a cosy dining room.

FACILITIES: 3 rms (2 en suite) (1 fmly) No smoking TVB tea/coffee No dogs Cen ht No children 7yrs No coaches **PRICES:** s £25-£30; d £50✳ **LB** **PARKING:** 10

♦♦♦♦ Meryan House Hotel

Bishop's Hull TA1 5EG ☎ 01823 337445 📠 01823 322355
e-mail: meryanhousehotel@btclick.com
Dir: *from Taunton take A38 towards Wellington. After crematorium on left take 1st right & house approx 600yds*

Located in a pretty village setting just over a mile from the centre of town, this 17th-century property has delightful individually furnished rooms. The comfortable bedrooms feature many antiques along with all modern facilities. Interesting and varied dishes are available at dinner. There is also a cosy bar and a spacious lounge.

FACILITIES: 12 en suite (2 fmly) (2 GF) No smoking in 4 bedrooms No smoking in dining room No smoking in 1 lounge STV TVB tea/coffee Direct dial from bedrooms Licensed Cen ht TVL No coaches Dinner Last d 7.30pm **PRICES:** s £45-£55; d £50-£65✳ **LB** **CONF:** Thtr 25 Class 25 Board 18 **PARKING:** 17 **CARDS:**

♦♦♦♦ The Spinney

Curland TA3 5SE ☎ 01460 234362 📠 01460 234362
e-mail: bartlett.spinney@zetnet.co.uk
Dir: *off A358, Taunton to Ilminster road*

A warm welcome awaits at this delightful family home, set in well-tended gardens, surrounded by open countryside and commanding magnificent views from the Blackdowns to the Quantock and Mendip Hills. Bedrooms are attractively decorated and equipped with modern comforts; one is suitable for the less mobile. Using the best local produce, delicious dinners are available by prior arrangement. Although unlicensed, guests may bring their own wine.

FACILITIES: 3 en suite (2 fmly) No smoking TVB tea/coffee No dogs (ex guide dogs) Cen ht TVL No coaches Dinner Last d 4pm **PRICES:** s £35; d £48-£50✳ **PARKING:** 5

♦♦♦♦ Yallands Farmhouse

Staplegrove TA2 6PZ ☎ 01823 278979 📠 01823 278983
e-mail: mail@yallands.co.uk
Dir: *from A358, 2m NW of Taunton town centre, turn S at rdbt into Silk Mills Lane. Left into Bindon Rd, left into Hudson Way, left into Darwin Cl & left into Speke Cl*

This 16th century farmhouse offers an unexpected 'oasis' of peace and tranquillity with mature trees and well-kept gardens. The comfortable and well-equipped bedrooms are individually furnished and decorated; a ground floor room is available. In addition to the freshly cooked, English breakfast, a range of lighter options is served.

FACILITIES: 7 en suite (2 fmly) (1 GF) No smoking in bedrooms No smoking in dining room TVB tea/coffee No dogs (ex guide dogs) Cen ht TVL No coaches **PRICES:** s £32-£35; d £50-£58✳ **LB** **PARKING:** 7 **CARDS:**

♦♦♦♦ West View

Minehead Rd, Bishops Lydeard TA4 3BS ☎ 01823 432223
e-mail: westview@pattemoore.freeserve.co.uk
Dir: *from Taunton turn off A358 at Bishops Lydeard signs, follow road into village. Straight over x-rds and West View is 1st detached house on right*

FACILITIES: 3 rms (2 en suite) No smoking TVB tea/coffee Cen ht TVL No children 3yrs No coaches **PRICES:** s £20-£35; d £42-£50✳ **LB** **PARKING:** 4

♦♦♦ *Lower Marsh Farm (ST224279)*

Kingston St Mary TA2 8AB ☎ 01823 451331 📠 01823 451331
Mr & Mrs J Gothard
e-mail: mail@lowermarshfarm.co.uk
Dir: *0.25m from northern edge of Taunton town on the Taunton to Kingston-St-Mary Rd*

Located at the foot of the Quantock Hills, this delightful family-run working farm provides bright comfortable rooms with many extra facilities. Evening meals are available by prior arrangement and like breakfast, are served at one large table in the dining room. A lounge is also available for guests' use.

FACILITIES: 3 en suite (1 fmly) No smoking TVB tea/coffee No dogs Cen ht TVL 300 acres arable Dinner Last d noon **PARKING:**

♦♦♦ Pare Mill

Hagley Bridge, Hagley, Waterrow TA4 2AS ☎ 01984 623865
e-mail: r.sargent@btinternet.com

A warm welcome is offered to guests in this former mill house. The neatly furnished and decorated bedrooms overlook the garden and during cooler months, a log fire is a great attraction in the charming sitting room. Breakfast, served around a large table is made from local produce including home-produced marmalade and honey.

FACILITIES: 3 rms No smoking in bedrooms No smoking in dining room tea/coffee Cen ht TVL No coaches Fishing bird-watching **PRICES:** s £20; d £36✳ **LB** **BB** **PARKING:** 7 **NOTES:** Closed Dec-Feb

England

VASHFORD Map 03 ST04

♦♦♦ Washford

TA23 0PP ☎ 01984 640256 01984 641288

Dir: on A39 Taunton-Minehead road

As well as being close to the North Somerset coastline, this country inn is just a stone's throw from the West Somerset Steam Railway. Bedrooms are equipped with modern comforts and all reflect consistent standards of presentation. In the open-plan bar lounge, a popular range of meals is available at lunch and during the evening.

FACILITIES: 7 en suite (1 fmly) No smoking in 2 bedrooms No smoking in area of dining room TVB tea/coffee Direct dial from bedrooms No dogs (ex guide dogs) Cen ht Pool Table Skittles Dinner Last d 9pm **PARKING:** 30 **CARDS:**

VATCHET Map 03 ST04

♦♦♦♦ The Georgian House

28 Swain St TA23 0AD ☎ 01984 639279

Dir: A39 over railway bridge into Watchet main street

This elegant Georgian house is situated in the heart of this increasingly popular coastal resort within a short walk of the impressive new marina. Refurbished with considerable care and attention to detail, there is comfort and character in abundance here with bedrooms combining quality and individuality. Breakfast and dinner (by prior arrangement) are served in the well appointed dining room with additional facilities including a guest lounge area and garden.

FACILITIES: 3 rms (1 en suite) No smoking in bedrooms TVB No dogs (ex guide dogs) Cen ht Dinner Last d 9pm **PRICES:** s £30; d £55✳ **LB**

VATERROW Map 03 ST02

♦♦♦ The Rock

TA4 2AX ☎ 01984 623293 01984 623293

Dir: on B3227 14m W of Taunton

Located in the beautiful Tone Valley, this 16th-century inn, as its name suggests, is built against the rock face. Public areas retain much of the original character and charm, the bar featuring the rock wall. An extensive range of freshly prepared meals is available in the bar or restaurant. In addition to the comfortable, well-equipped bedrooms, there is a spacious first floor lounge.

FACILITIES: 7 en suite (1 fmly) No smoking in 2 bedrooms TVB Direct dial from bedrooms Cen ht TVL Pool Table Dinner Last d 10pm **PARKING:** 25 **CARDS:**

VELLS Map 03 ST54

See also Compton Martin & Croscombe

Premier Collection

♦♦♦♦♦ Beaconsfield Farm *(ST515475)*

Easton BA5 1DU ☎ 01749 870308 & 870754

01749 870308 Mrs C Lloyd

e-mail: carol@beaconsfieldfarm.co.uk

Dir: *2.5m from Wells on A371, on right just before village of Easton*

Pleasantly located in well-tended gardens and surrounded by the lovely countryside of the Mendip Hills, Beaconsfield Farm is conveniently situated for visiting this attractive area. The welcoming hosts are most friendly and attentive and many guests return on a regular basis. Bedrooms, which are very comfortable and equipped with many extra facilities, are delightfully decorated with co-ordinated colours and fabrics. A choice of well-cooked dishes featuring fresh local produce is offered at breakfast.

continued

Beaconsfield Farm

FACILITIES: 3 en suite No smoking in bedrooms No smoking in dining room TVB tea/coffee Direct dial from bedrooms No dogs (ex guide dogs) Cen ht TVL No children 8yrs 4 acres non-working **PRICES:** s £35-£45; d £45-£55✳ **PARKING:** 10 **NOTES:** Closed 22 Dec-24 Jan

England

WELLS continued

Premier Collection

♦♦♦♦♦ Old Farmhouse

62 Chamberlain St BA5 2PT ☎ 01749 675058
01749 675058
e-mail: theoldfarmhouse@talk21.com
Dir: *from Bath or Bristol on A39 follow signs for city centre, fork right at lights into Chamberlain St. Old Farmhouse on right opposite Almshouses*

The Old Farmhouse has secure parking and is in the centre of Wells so everything is within easy walking distance. Elegant decoration and a relaxed, friendly atmosphere are the hallmarks of this charming 17th-century house, set in its own pretty walled garden. The quality of the furnishings, including the comfortable beds, is super. Excellent Cordon Bleu dinners, available by prior arrangement, should not be missed.
FACILITIES: 2 en suite No smoking TVB tea/coffee No dogs Cen ht No children 12yrs No coaches Library Dinner Last d By Arrangement
PRICES: s £45-£50; d £50-£60* **PARKING:** 4

Premier Collection

♦♦♦♦♦ Riverside Grange

Tanyard Ln, North Wootton BA4 4AE ☎ 01749 890761
e-mail: riversidegrange@hotmail.com
Dir: *take A39 towards Glastonbury. On leaving Wells take 1st left signed North Wootton, through village to T-junct, turn left & 2nd left*

A delightful restored tannery, built in 1853, the foundations of which actually sit in the River Redlake, which runs alongside the house. A warm welcome is guaranteed from the friendly proprietors, who are most attentive and make every effort to make their guests feel at home. The house, furnished throughout with rosewood, is most comfortable and guests can relax in the attractive garden in summer months.
FACILITIES: 2 en suite No smoking TVB tea/coffee No dogs (ex guide dogs) Cen ht No children 10yrs **PRICES:** s £30-£35; d £45-£49*
PARKING: 6

♦♦♦♦♦ Beryl

Hawkers Ln BA5 3JP ☎ 01749 678738 01749 670508
e-mail: stay@beryl-wells.co.uk
Dir: *leave or approach Wells on Radstock Rd, B3139. Follow signs to The Horringtons or hospital. Turn into Hawkers Ln opposite Shell Garage. At top of lane*
FACILITIES: 8 en suite No smoking in bedrooms No smoking in dining room TVB tea/coffee Direct dial from bedrooms Licensed Cen ht TVL No coaches Outdoor swimming pool (heated) Croquet lawn Dinner Last d 24hrs prior **PRICES:** s £50-£65; d £65-£95* **LB**
PARKING: 20 **NOTES:** Closed 23-27 Dec **CARDS:**

♦♦♦♦ Bekynton House

7 St Thomas St BA5 2UU ☎ 01749 672222 01749 672222
e-mail: reservations@bekynton.freeserve.co.uk
Dir: *St Thomas Street (B3139 from Wells to Radstock) signed The Horringtons*

Set in one of the oldest streets in the city, Bekynton House is just a few minutes' walk from the cathedral and the rest of Wells and offers comfortable, well-furnished bedrooms. A comprehensive breakfast is served in the elegant, antique-furnished dining room, and the lounge has several hundred books. The atmosphere is friendly and welcoming, and many guests return year after year. Secure parking is a bonus.
FACILITIES: 4 en suite (1 fmly) No smoking TVB tea/coffee No dogs (ex guide dogs) Cen ht TVL No children 5yrs No coaches **PRICES:** d £53-£55*
PARKING: 5 **NOTES:** Closed 24-26 Dec **CARDS:**

♦♦♦♦ *Canon Grange*

Cathedral Green BA5 2UB ☎ 01749 671800
e-mail: canongrange@email.com
Dir: *On entering Wells follow signs for Hospital A&E onto the 'Liberty'. At east end of Liberty enter St Andrews Street. House is opposite the cathedral*

Facing the cathedral green and enjoying views of the West Front of the cathedral, parts of Canon Grange were renewed in 1545. This attractive house is conveniently located for the town centre attractions and restaurants. Bedrooms are spacious and comfortable and are well-equipped. Breakfast offers vegetarian

continued

and vegan choices, by arrangement, and provides a good start to the day.
FACILITIES: 5 rms (4 en suite) (2 fmly) No smoking TVB tea/coffee No dogs (ex guide dogs) Cen ht No children 3yrs No coaches Cathedral and Palace opposite Dinner Last d One day in advance

♦♦♦♦ Double-Gate Farm *(ST484424)*

Godney BA5 1RX ☎ 01458 832217 📠 01458 835612
Mrs H Millard
e-mail: doublegatefarm@aol.com
Dir: *from Wells A39 towards Glastonbury, at Polsham turn right signed Godney/Polsham, approx 2m to x-roads, continue to farmhouse on left after Inn*

Surrounded by the Somerset Levels and enjoying splendid views to the Mendips, this farm provides a warm and friendly welcome. Bedrooms are very attractively decorated and are most comfortable, with one room particularly well suited for the less mobile. Breakfast is served at two refectory style tables where guests can choose from an interesting and extensive menu. Double-Gate Farm was a Top Twenty Finalist in the AA Accessible Hotel of the Year Awards 2002-2003.
FACILITIES: 3 en suite 3 annexe en suite (1 fmly) (1 GF) No smoking TVB tea/coffee No dogs (ex guide dogs) Cen ht TVL Snooker Table tennis, darts 100 acres mixed **PRICES:** d £50-£55* **PARKING:** 9 **NOTES:** Closed Dec & Jan **CARDS:**

♦♦♦♦ Furlong House

Lorne Place, St Thomas St BA5 2XF ☎ 01749 674064
e-mail: johnhowardwells@aol.com
Dir: *Lorne Place is a mews turning on south side of St Thomas St (B3139), 0.25m E of Cathedral*

Pleasant views of the cathedral, National Trust woodland, and Glastonbury Tor to the west, can be seen from this Grade II listed Georgian house. Situated in delightful grounds and gardens only a five-minute stroll from the cathedral and Wells' many attractions, Furlong House provides comfortable and friendly accommodation.
FACILITIES: 3 en suite No smoking TVB tea/coffee No dogs (ex guide dogs) Cen ht No coaches **PRICES:** s £30-£40; d £46-£50
PARKING: 4 **NOTES:** Closed Sun **CARDS:** 

♦♦♦♦ Garden Cottage

60 Southover BA5 1UH ☎ 01749 676348
Dir: *Garden Cottage is in Southover via St Johns St. Or the turning nxt to Shelston pub*
A warm welcome is assured at this delightful home ideally located for the cathedral and the town centre. The pleasant bedrooms are comfortably furnished and attractively decorated and provided with many extra facilities and accessories. Guests are welcome to relax in the large attractive garden. A substantial breakfast is served at a communal table.
FACILITIES: 2 en suite (2 GF) No smoking TVB tea/coffee No dogs (ex guide dogs) Cen ht No coaches **PRICES:** d £44* **PARKING:** 2 **NOTES:** Closed 16-31 Dec

♦♦♦♦ *Highcroft*

Wells Rd, Priddy BA5 3AU ☎ 01749 678264
e-mail: spencerjrussell@yahoo.com
Dir: *turn off A368 (towards Weston-Super-Mare) onto B3134 signed Burrington, continue for approx. 8m, straight on at x-roads, right at 2nd x-roads, Highcroft approx 500mtrs on right*
Highcroft offers a range of facilities for the sporting guest, with stabling and a 'wet-room'. The house is situated in a pretty village and only a short drive from Wells. Bedrooms are comfortable and have many extra facilities. A good choice of local eateries are close by for dinner, while generous breakfasts are served in the dining room.
FACILITIES: 3 rms (1 en suite) No smoking tea/coffee No dogs Cen ht TVL ch fac No coaches **PARKING:** 5

♦♦♦♦ Highfield

93 Portway BA5 2BR ☎ 01749 675330
Dir: *enter Wells & follow signs for A371 Cheddar. Highfield on Portway, just after last traffic lights at top of hill*
Just a short walk from the city and cathedral, this delightful home maintains its Edwardian style and provides comfortable accommodation. A warm welcome is assured and many guests return on a regular basis. Bedrooms are well furnished and attractively designed with co-ordinated fabrics. Breakfast is served at one large table in the smart dining room, which overlooks the large garden.
FACILITIES: 3 en suite (1 fmly) No smoking in bedrooms TVB tea/coffee No dogs Cen ht No children 2yrs **PRICES:** s £25-£35; d £42-£45* **LB**
PARKING: 7 **NOTES:** Closed 23 Dec-1 Jan

♦♦♦♦ Hollow Tree Farm *(ST051428)*

Launcherley BA5 1QJ ☎ 01749 673715 Mrs J Coombes
Dir: *from Wells take A39 Glastonbury road, take 1st left at Brownes Garden Centre & farm approx 0.75m on right*
Delightfully appointed rooms with bright, cheery colour schemes and comfortable furnishings are provided at this non-working farm. Spectacular views of Wells Cathedral and Glastonbury Tor can be seen and delightful flower-filled gardens add to the charm. The friendly hosts are most welcoming and attentive. Home-baked bread, jams and marmalade are only a part of the delicious breakfast.
FACILITIES: 3 en suite (1 fmly) No smoking TVB tea/coffee No dogs (ex guide dogs) Cen ht No children 12yrs 27 acres Grazing **PRICES:** s £20; d £34* **BB** **PARKING:** 4 **NOTES:** Closed mid Dec-mid Jan

Smoking restrictions appear under the **FACILITIES** heading, please check when booking.

England

WELLS continued

♦♦♦♦ Infield House

36 Portway BA5 2BN ☎ 01749 670989 Fax 01749 679093
e-mail: infield@talk21.com
Dir: *from city centre, on right of A371, driveway immediately after traffic lights at junction with Strawberry Way*

This charming Victorian house offers comfortable, spacious rooms of elegance and style. The friendly hosts are very welcoming and provide a relaxing home from home. Guests may bring their pets, by prior arrangement. Dinners, also by prior arrangement, are served in the pleasant dining room where good home cooking ensures an enjoyable and varied range of options.
FACILITIES: 3 en suite No smoking TVB tea/coffee Cen ht TVL No coaches Jacuzzi Dinner Last d 10.30am **PRICES:** d £42-£49* **LB PARKING:** 3 **CARDS:**

♦♦♦♦ Littlewell Farm

Coxley BA5 1QP ☎ 01749 677914
Dir: *1m from centre on A39 towards Glastonbury*

This non-working farm is a quaint and comfortable home with many interesting features and dates back over 200 years. Pleasantly located between Wells and Glastonbury, it sits in well-tended gardens with splendid views of the countryside. Dinners, by prior arrangement, feature fresh produce and are served in the smart dining room.
FACILITIES: 5 en suite (1 GF) No smoking TVB tea/coffee No dogs (ex guide dogs) Licensed Cen ht No children 10yrs No coaches Riding Dinner Last d 3pm **PRICES:** s £24-£29; d £46-£52* **PARKING:** 10

♦♦♦♦ Manor Farm

Old Frome Rd, East Horrington BA5 3DP ☎ 01749 679832
Fax 01749 679849
e-mail: info@somersetbed.co.uk
Dir: *B3139 from Wells, into St Thomas St proceed into Bath Rd. After 0.5m turn right by Wells Golf Club into Old Frome Rd. Farm 1m on left, opposite church*

continued

Manor Farm is in a peaceful village setting and convenient for Wells, Bath, Cheddar and Glastonbury. Surrounded by large, well-tended gardens, the 14th-century Grade II listed building retains many period features and provides light, spacious accommodation. Dinner (available by prior arrangement) is an enjoyable and memorable aspect of a stay here.
FACILITIES: 2 en suite (1 fmly) No smoking in bedrooms No smoking in area of dining room No smoking in 1 lounge TVB tea/coffee No dogs Cen ht TVL ch fac No coaches Pool Table Croquet lawn Boules, Darts, BBQ, Games Room Dinner Last d 12noon **PRICES:** s £35; d £55* **LB CONF:** Class 6 Board 6 Del from £175 * **PARKING:** 2

♦♦♦♦ Tynings House

Harters Hill Ln, Coxley BA5 1RF ☎ 01749 675368
Fax 01749 675368
e-mail: b+b@tynings.co.uk
Dir: *A39 to Coxley from Wells or Glastonbury. Turn off at Coxley Church School, take 4th left onto private road over cattle grid to house*

Situated only a short driving distance from both Wells and Glastonbury, this 17th century house is set in peaceful countryside. The charming hosts are most attentive and welcoming, and bedrooms are very well-equipped and comfortable, many with views over the surrounding countryside. Delightful home-cooked dinners are available by prior arrangement.
FACILITIES: 3 en suite (1 fmly) No smoking TVB tea/coffee Direct dial from bedrooms No dogs Cen ht TVL No coaches Dinner Last d morning
PRICES: d £50-£60* **LB PARKING:** 7 **NOTES:** Closed Xmas

♦♦♦♦ The Old Stores

Westbury-Sub-Mendip BA5 1HA ☎ 01749 870817
Fax 01749 870980
e-mail: moglin980@aol.com
Dir: *Westbury-Sub-Mendip is on A371 midway between Wells & Cheddar. The Old Stores is opposite Westbury Inn, in the centre of the village.*
FACILITIES: 3 en suite No smoking TVB tea/coffee Cen ht TVL No coaches
PRICES: s £22; d £44* **PARKING:** 3 **CARDS:**

♦♦♦ Number One Portway

1 Portway BA5 2BA ☎ 01749 678864 & 07786 217624
Dir: *enter Wells on A37 from Bristol/Bath, right at first traffic lights, left at second right at mini rdbt. House opposite Little Theatre*
This attractive late Victorian town house offers comfortable, tasteful accommodation. Conveniently located within walking distance of the cathedral and other attractions, Number One Portway is an excellent base for a short stay or for a longer relaxing break. Breakfast features fresh local produce and is freshly cooked, providing a pleasant start to the day.
FACILITIES: 2 rms (1 en suite) (2 fmly) No smoking TVB tea/coffee No dogs (ex guide dogs) Cen ht No coaches **PRICES:** s £22-£25; d fr £39*

♦♦♦ *Amber House*

Coxley BA5 1QZ ☎ 01749 679612

Dir: *on A39 Wells to Glastonbury rd. In village 0.25m past Pound Inn on right*

Located just a short drive from the centre of Wells, this comfortable home offers guests a pleasant place to stay. The friendly proprietors are most welcoming and maintain a relaxed atmosphere. Bedrooms are well equipped and guests can relax in the snug dining room which doubles as a lounge. A pleasant garden is also available.

FACILITIES: 3 rms (1 en suite) No smoking TVB tea/coffee No dogs (ex guide dogs) Cen ht No coaches **PARKING:** 3

♦♦♦ Birdwood House

Birdwood, Bath Rd BA5 3EW ☎ 01749 679250

e-mail: s_crane_@hotmail.com

Dir: *from town centre follow signs on one-way system to the Horringtons. Take B3139 for 1.5m, last house on left near double bend sign*

Set in delightful grounds just a short drive from the town centre, this imposing detached house dates back to the 1850s. The comfortable bedrooms are simply furnished with a number of extra facilities. A conservatory and lounge are also available to guests, while breakfast is taken in the pleasant dining room.

FACILITIES: 4 rms (1 en suite) (1 fmly) No smoking TVB tea/coffee No dogs (ex guide dogs) Cen ht TVL No coaches **PRICES:** s £20; d £40-£50* **PARKING:** 12 **NOTES:** Closed Xmas & New Year

♦♦♦ 19 St Cuthbert Street

BA5 2AW ☎ 01749 673166

Dir: *at bottom of High Street opposite St Cuthberts Church*

Guests are assured of a friendly welcome at this charming terraced home, providing comfortable accommodation. The house is conveniently located a short stroll from the cathedral, restaurants and the bus station. Breakfast features home made Seville marmalade.

FACILITIES: 2 rms TVB tea/coffee No dogs Cen ht TVL No children 7yrs No coaches **PRICES:** d £38-£40* **BB**

♦♦♦ Sedgemoor House

5 Glebe Paddock, Wookey BA5 1LH ☎ 01749 675211

Dir: *from Wells take A371 towards Cheddar. Outside city limits fork left towards Wookey on B3139. In Wookey turn right by Burcott Inn, 1st left into Glebe Paddock*

Just a short drive from the historic city of Wells, this smart and quietly located establishment offers bedrooms that are simply furnished and practically equipped. Breakfast is taken in the dining room, next to the guests' conservatory. The pretty garden leads down to a small stream.

FACILITIES: 2 rms No smoking TVB tea/coffee No dogs (ex guide dogs) Cen ht No children 6yrs No coaches **PRICES:** s £19-£20; d £38-£40* **BB** **PARKING:** 3 **NOTES:** Closed 19 Dec-8 Jan

WEST BAGBOROUGH — Map 03 ST13

Premier Collection

♦♦♦♦♦ Bashfords Farmhouse *(ST172333)*

TA4 3EF ☎ 01823 432015 Fax 0870 167 1587

Mr & Mrs C Ritchie

e-mail: info@bashfordsfarmhouse.co.uk

Dir: *follow main road through village for approx 1.5m. Bashfords 3rd on left after pub*

On the southern slopes of the Quantocks, this period farmhouse is situated in the centre of the village. Bedrooms are attractively decorated and furnished, and feature thoughtful extras. Meals are taken around a large pine table in the dining room. Dinner is available by prior arrangement.

FACILITIES: 3 en suite No smoking TVB tea/coffee No dogs Cen ht No children 10yrs Dinner Last d by arrangment **PRICES:** s £30-£32.50; d £50-£55* **PARKING:** 4

Premier Collection

♦♦♦♦♦ Tilbury Farm *(ST177334)*

Cothelstone TA4 3DY ☎ 01823 432391 Mrs P Smith

Dir: *take A358 towards Minehead, 0.75m after 2nd railway bridge take sharp right towards West Bagborough. Through village, on left up steep hill*

Said to be the highest dwelling on the Quantocks, this delightful farmhouse has stunning views over Taunton Vale. The resident proprietors have taken enormous care in renovating their home. Bedrooms are tastefully decorated and furnished and have comfortable beds. Dinner is available by prior arrangement, served around an impressive 17th-century table.

FACILITIES: 3 en suite No smoking TVB tea/coffee No dogs Cen ht TVL No children 8yrs Riding Stabling 20 acres none working **PRICES:** s £30; d £50* **PARKING:** 20

WESTON-SUPER-MARE — Map 03 ST36

Premier Collection

♦♦♦♦♦ Church House

27 Kewstoke Rd, Kewstoke BS22 9YD ☎ 01934 633185

e-mail: chapman1@euphony.net

Situated at the foot of Monk's Hill, adjacent to the old village church, this lovingly restored family home offers quality accommodation. Wonderful views over the Bristol Channel can be enjoyed, with Wales visible on clear days. Style and comfort are the hallmarks here, with bedrooms and public areas elegantly furnished. Breakfast provides a taste of local produce, an enjoyable and satisfying start to the day.

FACILITIES: 5 en suite No smoking TVB tea/coffee No dogs Cen ht No coaches **PRICES:** s £50; d £65* **PARKING:** 10 **CARDS:**

continued

WESTON-SUPER-MARE continued

♦♦♦♦ Ashcombe Court
17 Milton Rd BS23 2SH ☎ 01934 625104 📠 01934 625104
e-mail: ashcombecourt@tinyonline.co.uk
Dir: *Milton Rd is one of the main roads into Weston-Super-Mare from motorway. Ashcombe Court is near cemetary at top of Ashcombe Rd*
Hospitality and friendliness are at the heart of this delightful Victorian family home, situated within walking distance of the town centre and all the seafront attractions. Delightfully appointed bedrooms, one on the ground floor, offer a host of thoughtful extras, and there is an attractive sitting room. Home-cooked meals are available by prior arrangement.
FACILITIES: 6 en suite (1 fmly) No smoking in bedrooms No smoking in dining room TVB tea/coffee No dogs Cen ht TVL No children 11yrs No coaches Dinner Last d 9am **PRICES:** s £30; d £46* **LB**
PARKING: 6 **NOTES:** Closed 2 Dec-Jan

♦♦♦♦ Braeside
2 Victoria Park BS23 2HZ ☎ 01934 626642 📠 01934 626642
e-mail: braeside@tesco.net
Dir: *with sea on left, take 1st right after Winter Gardens then 1st left into Lower Church Rd. Victoria Park on right after left bend*

This small, quietly located hotel is a short stroll from the town centre and sea front. Some of the comfortably furnished and well-equipped bedrooms have fine views over Weston Bay. In addition to a well-laid out dining room, there is a comfortable lounge. Unrestricted on-street parking is available.
FACILITIES: 9 en suite (3 fmly) No smoking in 2 bedrooms No smoking in dining room No smoking in lounges TVB tea/coffee Licensed Cen ht No coaches **PRICES:** s £26; d £52* **LB NOTES:** Closed Xmas & New Year

♦♦♦♦ *Milton Lodge*
15 Milton Rd BS23 2SH ☎ 01934 623161 📠 01934 623210
e-mail: vallen@miltonlodge.freeserve.co.uk
Dir: *M4 junct 21 to town centre, take B3440, right at mini-rdbt for Milton & Sea Front North, at lights left into Milton Rd*
Conveniently located with off-street parking this comfortable guest house offers spacious, attractive and well-equipped bedrooms, including one on the ground floor. The atmosphere is relaxed and friendly and the town centre and all the attractions of the sea front are within walking distance. There is a comfortable lounge and attractive dining room.
FACILITIES: 6 en suite (1 fmly) No smoking in dining room No smoking in lounges TVB tea/coffee No dogs (ex guide dogs) Cen ht TVL No children 16yrs No coaches Dinner Last d 7pm **PARKING:** 6 **NOTES:** Closed Nov-Dec

♦♦♦♦ *Seafarers*
12 Victoria Park BS23 2HZ ☎ 01934 632013 📠 01934 414716
e-mail: francesca@timbertop.freeserve.co.uk
Dir: *travel north towards seafront and harbour, pass pier and gardens, right after Cabot Bars, 1st left into Lower Church Rd, 2nd right is Victoria Park*

continued

Located in a quiet cul-de-sac close to the seafront and Winter Gardens, this totally refurbished property provides the highest standards of hospitality, service and comfort. The four en suite bedrooms are all attractively decorated and very well-equipped. In addition to a comfortable guest lounge, a substantial buffet-style breakfast is offered in the spacious dining room.
FACILITIES: 4 en suite (1 fmly) No smoking in dining room TVB tea/coffee No dogs (ex guide dogs) Cen ht TVL No coaches **PARKING:** 4 **CARDS:**

♦♦♦ Bella Vista Hotel
19 Upper Church Rd BS23 2DX ☎ 01934 631931
📠 01934 620126
Dir: *from M5 junct 21, take A370 to town and sea front, turn right past Grand Pier. Right after 300 mtrs into Upper Church Rd and right at x-roads*
A terraced establishment, with an attractive patio at the front, situated close to the seafront and the town centre. Now refurbished throughout, the rooms are prettily decorated and have TVs and courtesy trays. There is a cosy dining room and large, comfortably furnished guest lounge.
FACILITIES: 8 en suite (3 fmly) No smoking in dining room TVB tea/coffee No dogs (ex guide dogs) Cen ht TVL **PRICES:** d £40-£48* **LB**

♦♦♦ Baymead Hotel
Longton Grove Rd BS23 1LS ☎ 01934 622951 📠 01934 628110
Close to the town and seafront, this friendly hotel is suitable for both holidaymakers and business travellers. The bedrooms, while not large, are well equipped and attractively decorated. The bar has a dance floor and entertainment three nights a week. There is a spacious dining room where meals including dinner are available.
FACILITIES: 33 rms (30 en suite) (3 fmly) No smoking TVB tea/coffee Licensed Lift Cen ht TVL Half size snooker table Dinner Last d 6pm **PRICES:** s £23-£26; d £40-£46* **LB PARKING:** 12

♦♦♦ Beverley
11 Whitecross Rd BS23 1EP ☎ 01934 622956
e-mail: beverley11@hushmail.com
Dir: *follow town centre/railway stn signs. With station on left, turn left, past stn then 2nd left into Ellenborough Park Rd leading to Whitecross Rd*
This quietly located Victorian guest house offers well-equipped and attractively decorated rooms in a relaxed atmosphere. It is well located for the seafront, close to the railway station and within walking distance of the town centre. Good home-cooked breakfasts are served in the dining room.
FACILITIES: 5 en suite (3 fmly) (1 GF) No smoking TVB tea/coffee No dogs (ex guide dogs) Cen ht No coaches **PRICES:** s £23-£25; d £40-£44*
LB NOTES: Closed Xmas **CARDS:**

♦♦♦ Clifton Lodge
48 Clifton Rd BS23 1BN ☎ 01934 629357
Dir: *follow main road to sea front, Clifton Rd is 1st turning on left past the Tropicana*
Located within walking distance of the seafront, town centre and other amenities, this charming house is ideal for tourists. A relaxed and informal atmosphere is created. Bedrooms vary in size but all are well-equipped and include a number of thoughtful extras.
FACILITIES: 5 rms (3 en suite) (1 fmly) No smoking in bedrooms No smoking in dining room TVB tea/coffee No dogs (ex guide dogs) Cen ht No children 3yrs No coaches **PRICES:** (incl. dinner) s £20-£21; d £40-£42*
LB PARKING: 2

♦♦♦ Corbiere Hotel
24 Upper Church Rd BS23 2DX ☎ 01934 629607
e-mail: corbierehotel@aol.com
Dir: *facing Grand Pier turn right, along seafront for approx 400yds. Right at Knightstone harbour into Upper Church Rd. Right at x-roads, 1st hotel on right*

continued

This attractive Victorian house is situated in easy walking distance to the sea front and town centre. It offers comfortable, neatly decorated bedrooms, which although compact, are thoughtfully appointed. Good home cooking is offered at dinner, and served in the pleasant dining room; there is a small bar and a lounge.
FACILITIES: 10 en suite (4 fmly) (2 GF) No smoking in dining room No smoking in lounges TVB tea/coffee No dogs (ex guide dogs) Cen ht TVL No coaches Dinner Last d 1pm **PRICES:** s £17-£25; d £34-£50* **LB BB**

♦♦♦ Goodrington
23 Charlton Rd BS23 4HB ☎ 01934 623229
e-mail: vera.bishop@talk21.com
Dir: *from A370 follow signs to seafront. Left at end of beach lawns, then 3rd left and establishment 50yds on left*
Quietly tucked away in a residential area, Goodrington is a charming Victorian house where the owners make every effort to ensure their guests enjoy their stay. Bedrooms are spacious and comfortably furnished, and there is also an attractive lounge. Families are especially welcome and this is an ideal base for holidays.
FACILITIES: 3 rms (2 en suite) (1 fmly) No smoking TVB tea/coffee No dogs (ex guide dogs) Cen ht TVL No coaches Dinner Last d 24hr notice **PRICES:** s £19-£22; d £36-£42* **BB NOTES:** rs Oct-Mar

♦♦♦ Oakover
25 Clevedon Rd BS23 1DA ☎ 01934 620125
e-mail: info@oakover.co.uk
Dir: *from M5 junct 21 follow signs for seafront. Over 4 rdbts. At 5th rdbt take turn left then 2nd right into Brighton Rd follow into Clevedon Rd*
Oakover is a substantial Victorian property, situated a short level walk from the town centre and sea front. Bedrooms are comfortable and well equipped. Substantial breakfasts are served in the bright dining room. The establishment is run in an easy going and friendly manner by the resident proprietor.
FACILITIES: 7 en suite (1 fmly) (2 GF) No smoking in dining room STV TVB tea/coffee No dogs (ex guide dogs) Cen ht **PRICES:** s £20-£23; d £40-£50 **PARKING:** 7 **CARDS:**

♦♦♦ Sarnia Hotel
28 Upper Church Rd BS23 2DX ☎ 01934 629696
01934 629696
Dir: *facing Grand Pier, turn right along seafront. Upper Church Rd 0.5m on right after Pavilion Bar. Hotel on right*
This friendly, family-run guest house is located close to the seafront and within easy walking distance of the town centre. The compact bedrooms are well furnished and equipped. A generous breakfast is served in the brightly decorated dining room and guests are welcome to use the lounge bar.
FACILITIES: 8 rms (5 en suite) (4 fmly) No smoking in bedrooms No smoking in dining room TVB tea/coffee No dogs (ex guide dogs) Licensed Cen ht TVL No coaches **PRICES:** s £18-£25; d £36-£50* **LB BB**

♦♦♦ The Weston Bay Hotel
2-4 Clevedon Rd BS23 1DG ☎ 01934 628903 01934 417661
e-mail: westonbayhotel@btinternet.com
Dir: *exit M5 junct 21, 15 min to Weston Bay Hotel follow signs for seafront. Hotel opposite the Sea life center on the seafront.*
Located on the seafront, this welcoming family run hotel provides spacious well-equipped bedrooms, all of which have modern en suite facilities. There is a comfortable lounge for the use of guests, and an attractive dining room where Mr and Mrs Hui serve breakfast. Evening meals are available by prior arrangement.
FACILITIES: 9 en suite (5 fmly) No smoking in 2 bedrooms No smoking in dining room STV TVB tea/coffee No dogs (ex guide dogs) Cen ht TVL No coaches Last d 7.30pm **PARKING:** 11 **NOTES:** Closed Dec-Feb
CARDS:

WEST PENNARD — Map 03 ST53

♦♦♦ Ashcombe Farm *(ST573398)*
Stean Bow BA6 8ND ☎ 01749 890153 Mrs D Frayne
Dir: *between Glastonbury and Shepton Mallet on A361, 4m from Glastonbury opposite Apple Inn*
Guests are warmly welcomed at this country home which is just a few miles from Glastonbury and Wells. The spacious bedrooms are most comfortable, and have pleasant country views. A relaxing lounge is provided and from the dining room, guests can enjoy traditional breakfasts and views of the large garden. For dinner, there are a number of good pubs close by and one just across the road.
FACILITIES: 3 en suite No smoking in dining room No smoking in lounges TVB tea/coffee No dogs (ex guide dogs) Cen ht TVL No children 5yrs 6 acres non-working **PRICES:** s £22-£25; d £38-£44 **BB PARKING:** 6
NOTES: Closed 8 Dec-28 Feb

WHEDDON CROSS — Map 03 SS93

♦♦♦♦ Rest and be Thankful Inn
Wheddon Cross TA24 7DR ☎ 01643 841222 01643 841813
e-mail: enquiries@restandbethankful.co.uk
Dir: *on crossroads of A396 & B3224, 5m S of Dunster*
Situated in the highest village on Exmoor, The Rest and be Thankful overlooks Dunkery Beacon. The comfortable bedrooms are extremely well equipped with extras such as fridges and trouser presses. Popular with locals and visitors alike, the convivial bar, complete with log fires, is just the place to relax prior to a wholesome meal in the restaurant. Service is professional and warm hospitality always assured.
FACILITIES: 5 en suite No smoking in bedrooms No smoking in dining room TVB tea/coffee Direct dial from bedrooms No dogs (ex guide dogs) Cen ht No children 11yrs Pool Table Pool Darts Skittle alley Dinner Last d 10pm **PRICES:** s £26-£30; d £52-£60* **CONF:** Del from £40 *
PARKING: 35 **NOTES:** Closed 24-26 Dec
CARDS:

WINSFORD — Map 03 SS93

♦♦♦♦ Karslake House
Halse Ln TA24 7JE ☎ 01643 851242 01643 851242
e-mail: karslakehouse@aol.com
Dir: *leave A396 (Winsford). In village turn L beyond village stores signed Karslake Hse. Around corner 50yds on R*
This small country hotel is situated in a peaceful Exmoor village, making it an ideal base for touring the area. Bedrooms have been thoughtfully furnished and a number of extra touches have been added. Public rooms feature original beams and fireplaces and include a dining room where interesting menus offer a selection of delicious meals.
FACILITIES: 6 rms (5 en suite) (1 GF) No smoking in bedrooms No smoking in dining room No smoking in lounges TVB tea/coffee Licensed Cen ht No children 12yrs No coaches Riding, shooting, fishing on request Dinner Last d 8.15pm **PRICES:** s £50-£65; d £65-£100*
PARKING: 15 **NOTES:** Closed Feb and Mar
CARDS:

♦♦♦ Red Diamonds highlight the top establishments within the AA's 3, 4 and 5 Diamond ratings.

England

YEOVIL Map 03 ST51

See also Crewkerne

Premier Collection

♦♦♦♦♦ *Holywell House*
Holywell, East Coker BA22 9NQ ☎ 01935 862612
01935 863035
e-mail: b&b@holywellhouse.freeserve.co.uk
Dir: *leave Yeovil on A30 Crewkerne road, 2m turn left past Yeovil Court Hotel signed East Coker, down lane & Holywell House is on right*
Set in three acres of peaceful award winning gardens, with tennis and croquet lawns, this imposing 18th-century house is a relaxing place to stay. Hospitality is a real strength, with every effort made to ensure guests feel at home. Breakfast is taken around a large table in the attractive dining room and is a most pleasant start to the day.
FACILITIES: 3 en suite No smoking in dining room No smoking in lounges TVB tea/coffee No dogs (ex guide dogs) Cen ht ch fac No coaches Tennis (hard) Croquet lawn Garden games
PARKING: 12 **NOTES:** Closed Xmas & New Year

♦♦♦♦ Helyar Arms
Moor Ln, East Coker BA22 9JR ☎ 01935 862332
01935 864129
e-mail: info@helyar-arms.co.uk
Dir: *Take A358 Yeovil, then A303, then A3088. Approaching Yeovil, follow the A37 Dorchester - on the Yeovil outskirts look for sign to East Coker. Turn at junction with Post Office and The Helyar Arms is on this rd*

Centrally located in the picturesque village of East Coker, this 15th-century inn is full of character and charm. A wealth of beams and an inglenook fireplace add charm to the bar and restaurant where a wide range of meals is available. Bedrooms are comfortably furnished and exceedingly well equipped.
FACILITIES: 6 en suite (3 fmly) No smoking in bedrooms No smoking in dining room No smoking in 1 lounge TVB tea/coffee Direct dial from bedrooms No dogs Cen ht Dinner Last d 9pm **PRICES:** s £45-£59; d £50-£70✳ **LB MEALS:** Lunch fr £12alc Dinner fr £18alc✳
PARKING: 40 **CARDS:**

YEOVILTON Map 03 ST52

♦♦♦♦ Cary Fitzpaine Farm *(ST549270)*
BA22 8JB ☎ 01458 223250 01458 223372 Mrs S Crang
e-mail: acrang@aol.com
Dir: *from J A303/A37 at Podimore take A37 (Bristol/Shepton Mallet) for 1m. Take 1st R (Cary Fitzpaine), follow rd to farm*
Surrounded by 600 acres of mixed farmland, this charming farmhouse dates back to Georgian times. The comfortable bedrooms are well equipped and fitted with modern facilities. Breakfast is served at separate tables, and on sunny mornings can be enjoyed on the verandah.

continued

FACILITIES: 3 en suite (1 fmly) No smoking TVB tea/coffee No dogs (ex guide dogs) Cen ht TVL Fishing 600 acres arable beef horses sheep
PRICES: s £28; d £50-£55✳ **LB PARKING:** 6 **NOTES:** Closed 23-26 Dec
CARDS:

STAFFORDSHIRE

ABBOTS BROMLEY Map 07 SK02

♦♦♦ Marsh *(SK069261)*
WS15 3EJ ☎ 01283 840323 Mrs M K Hollins
Dir: *1m N on B5013 of Abbots Bromley*
Guests at this working farm are welcome to walk around the fields and watch the activities. The farmhouse has been extensively modernised and offers lovely bedrooms, furnished in keeping with the style of the house. Breakfasts are generous, and afternoon tea is also available.
FACILITIES: 2 rms (1 fmly) No smoking in dining room TVB tea/coffee Cen ht 64 acres mixed **PRICES:** s £21-£23✳ **PARKING:** 8
NOTES: Closed Dec

ALTON Map 07 SK04

♦♦♦♦ Farriers Cottage & Mews at Woodhouse Farm *(SK079398)*
Nabb Ln, Croxden ST14 5JB ☎ 01889 507507 Mrs D Ball
e-mail: ddeb@lineone.net
Dir: *from A50 take B5030 at Uttoxeter. Turn left onto Hollington Rd at Rocester. Nabb Lane is 1.5m on right*

This delightful old farmhouse dates back to the 18th century. It has been tastefully modernised to provide well-equipped accommodation, including ground floor bedrooms, two of which are located in cleverly converted mews. The house stands in delightful gardens and is quietly situated, less than two miles from Alton and Alton Towers theme park.
FACILITIES: 5 en suite (1 fmly) (3 GF) No smoking TVB tea/coffee No dogs Cen ht No children 5yrs 105 acres sheep **PRICES:** s fr £29; d £40-£60✳ **LB PARKING:** 6 **CARDS:**

♦♦♦ *Bull's Head*
High St ST10 4AQ ☎ 01538 702307 702065
e-mail: janet@alton.freeserve.co.uk
Dir: *from A50 follow signs for Alton Towers into the village of Alton*
This popular old village inn is ideally situated for visitors to Alton Towers and the Staffordshire Moors. It provides well-equipped modern accommodation and has public areas of some character. The traditional bar has an inglenook fireplace, and the separate dining room is attractively decorated.
FACILITIES: 6 en suite (2 fmly) No smoking in dining room TVB tea/coffee No dogs (ex guide dogs) Cen ht No coaches Dinner Last d 9pm
PARKING: 12 **CARDS:**

BETLEY Map 07 SJ74

♦♦♦♦ Betley Court Farm *(SJ753484)*

CW3 9BH ☎ 01270 820229 Fax 01270 829077 Mrs J Speed

Dir: *leave M6 junct 16 onto A500 towards Crewe & to 2nd rdbt, then A531, farm in 2.5m on right*

Host to the Annual Village Show and Betley Bonfire, this early Victorian house stands on 250 acres which includes a mere. Many original features are retained within the interior, enhanced by quality furnishing and décor styles and memorable breakfasts include farm produce, including home-made preserves.

FACILITIES: 3 en suite (1 fmly) No smoking TVB tea/coffee No dogs (ex guide dogs) Cen ht Fishing Riding Croquet lawn birdwatching, walking 220 acres mixed Dinner **PARKING:**

BOBBINGTON Map 07 SO89

♦♦♦♦ Blakelands Country House

Halfpenny Green DY7 5DP ☎ 01384 221000 Fax 01384 221585

e-mail: info@blakelands.com

Dir: *4m from A449 at Himley, B4176 towards Bridgnorth at Himley after 3m left fork towards Halfpenny Green & Bobbington straight on approx 1.5m establishment signed. From Bridgnorth A454 towards Wolverhampton then B4176 at Fudge Heath follow signs*

Blakelands is an imposing country house set in several acres of its own grounds and with its own fishing lake. Accommodation is set in various buildings and rooms are attractive and well equipped. There is a spacious restaurant where an extensive menu is available and there are also conference and wedding facilities.

FACILITIES: 15 en suite (2 fmly) No smoking in bedrooms TVB tea/coffee No dogs (ex guide dogs) Dinner Last d 9pm **PRICES:** s £50; d £67 **LB PARKING:** 60 **NOTES:** Closed 25Dec-2Jan

CARDS:

BURTON UPON TRENT Map 08 SK22

♦♦♦♦ Delter Hotel

5 Derby Rd DE14 1RU ☎ 01283 535115 Fax 01283 845261

e-mail: delterhotel@burtonontrenthotels.co.uk

Dir: *from A511 turn into Derby Rd (A5121)at roundabout, hotel 50 yards on left. From A38, A5121, at Stretton straight over 2 rdbts, hotel 0.5m from rdbt*

This comfortable and relaxing guest house is situated on the outskirts of Burton upon Trent, close to the famous Bass Museum. Bedrooms are well and thoughtfully equipped and tastefully decorated whilst the public areas consist of the Delter bar and an airy breakfast room.

FACILITIES: 6 en suite No smoking in lounges TVB tea/coffee No dogs (ex guide dogs) Licensed Cen ht No coaches Dinner Last d 5pm

PRICES: s £35-£38; d £47-£50✱ **PARKING:** 8 **NOTES:** Closed 25-26 Dec

CARDS:

♦♦♦♦ Edgecote Hotel

179 Ashby Rd DE15 0LB ☎ 01283 568966 Fax 01283 740118

e-mail: edgecote@tesco.net

Dir: *on A511, Leicester side of town*

Edwardian style hotel ideally situated on the outskirts of town. Although the bedrooms vary in size and layout they are tastefully decorated, soundly appointed and well equipped. The comfortable sitting room features beautiful stained glass windows and in the oak-panelled dining room guests can enjoy a freshly cooked breakfast.

FACILITIES: 11 rms (5 en suite) (1 fmly) No smoking in bedrooms No smoking in dining room TVB tea/coffee No dogs (ex guide dogs) Licensed Cen ht TVL Dinner Last d 6pm **PRICES:** s £42-£48; d £58✱

PARKING: 6 **CARDS:**

CHEADLE Map 07 SK04

See also Froghall

♦♦♦ The Grange

Oakamoor Rd ST10 4QR ☎ 01538 754093

Dir: *B5417 1 mile east of Cheadle*

Dating from the 16th century and extended in Victorian times, this impressive detached property which stands on immaculate landscaped grounds, retains many original features which are enhanced by the décor and furnishing schemes throughout. The homely bedrooms are filled with thoughtful extras and a warm welcome is assured.

FACILITIES: 2 en suite (2 fmly) No smoking in bedrooms No smoking in lounges TVB tea/coffee No dogs (ex guide dogs) Cen ht No coaches

PRICES: d £40✱ **LB PARKING:** 10 **NOTES:** Closed Nov-2 wks before Etr

CHEDDLETON Map 07 SJ95

Premier Collection

♦♦♦♦♦ Choir Cottage and Choir House

Ostlers Ln ST13 7HS ☎ 01538 360561

e-mail: ELAINE.SUTCLIFFE@ic24.net

Dir: *turn off A520 opposite Red Lion into Hollow Ln pass church & left into Ostlers Ln. Cottage on right at top of hill*

Located in a residential area on pretty grounds, this 17th-century property retains many original features, which are enhanced by the quality furnishing styles throughout. Bedrooms are equipped with lots of thoughtful extras and have modern bathrooms. Spacious comfortable lounge areas are available in an adjacent house in addition to an attractive dining room.

FACILITIES: 1 en suite 2 annexe en suite (1 fmly) (2 GF) No smoking TVB tea/coffee Direct dial from bedrooms No dogs (ex guide dogs) Cen ht No children 4yrs No coaches **PRICES:** s £35-£39; d £57-£60✱

LB PARKING: 5 **NOTES:** Closed Xmas

CHURCH EATON Map 07 SJ81

♦♦♦♦ Slab Bridge Cottage

Little Onn ST20 0AY ☎ 01785 840220 Fax 01785 840220

Dir: *from Stafford take A518 signed Newport, left at Haughton signed Church Eaton, right along Main Street, left along Little Onn Road, over canal bridge 300yds on left signed Lapley/Stretton cottage on left*

FACILITIES: 2 en suite No smoking TVB tea/coffee Cen ht TVL No coaches Fishing Dinner Last d noon **PRICES:** s £30-£32.50; d £50-£55

PARKING: 8 **NOTES:** Closed Xmas & New Year

CODSALL Map 07 SJ80

♦♦♦ Moors Farm & Country Hotel *(SJ859048)*

Chillington Ln WV8 1QF ☎ 01902 842330 Fax 01902 847878

Mrs D E Moreton

e-mail: enquiries@moorsfarm-hotel.co.uk

Dir: *between Codsall & Codsall Wood, down Chillington Lane to T-junction & turn right*

Located to the north of Codsall village and within easy reach of the M54 motorway, this working farm provides friendly hospitality and traditionally furnished, well-equipped accommodation. A self-catering apartment is also available. Meals are served in the spacious, traditional style dining room.

FACILITIES: 7 rms (4 en suite) (1 fmly) No smoking TVB tea/coffee No dogs Licensed Cen ht No children 4yrs 100 acres mixed Dinner Last d 2pm

PRICES: s £30-£40; d £55-£65✱ **LB PARKING:** 20

CARDS:

ELLASTONE Map 07 SK14

♦♦♦♦ Cross Farm

Main Rd DE6 2GZ ☎ 01335 324668 📠 01335 324039
e-mail: janecliffe@hotmail.com
Dir: *turn off A50 at Uttoxeter proceed along B5030 for 6m into village of Ellastone, Cross Farm is on right*
FACILITIES: 3 en suite (1 fmly) No smoking in bedrooms No smoking in dining room No smoking in lounges TV2B tea/coffee No dogs Cen ht No coaches **PRICES:** s £20-£24; d £36-£40✱ **BB PARKING:** 6

FROGHALL Map 07 SK04

♦♦♦ *Hermitage Working Farm (SK037497)*

ST10 2HQ ☎ 01538 266515 📠 01538 266155 Mrs W Barlow
e-mail: wilma@hermitagefarm.co.uk
Dir: *turn off A52 in Frognall onto B5053, farm 0.5m on left at top of hill*
Parts of this charming old sandstone-built house date back to the 16th century. It is quietly located in an elevated position with impressive panoramic views. There is traditionally furnished accommodation in the main house as well as a recently converted barn, which offers rooms suitable for families. Convenient for visiting Alton Towers.
FACILITIES: 3 en suite 6 annexe en suite (3 fmly) No smoking in bedrooms No smoking in area of dining room No smoking in 1 lounge TVB tea/coffee Direct dial from bedrooms No dogs (ex guide dogs) Cen ht TVL ch fac Riding shooting 75 acres beef, sheep, poultry **PARKING:** 12
CARDS:

LEEK Map 07 SJ95

♦♦♦ *Abbey*

Abbey Green Rd ST13 8SA ☎ 01538 382865 📠 01538 398604
e-mail: martin@abbeyinn.co.uk
Dir: *off A523, N of town take turn signed Meerbrook, bear right at T-junction. Inn on left*
Dating from the turn of the 18th-century, this local sandstone inn is located in a rural position a few minutes drive from the town centre. Bedrooms, which are located in former stables, provide good levels of comfort and the attractive character bar areas and restaurant enjoy a strong local following.
FACILITIES: 5 annexe en suite No smoking in area of dining room TVB tea/coffee Direct dial from bedrooms No dogs (ex guide dogs) Cen ht No children 14yrs No coaches Dinner Last d 9pm **PARKING:** 60
CARDS:

LICHFIELD Map 07 SK10

♦♦♦♦ Stone House Farm

Farewell WS13 8DS ☎ 01543 682575 📠 01543 682575
Dir: *in Lichfield take A51 signed Rugeley/Stafford, take 2nd lane on left signposted Farewell. After 2m bear left (signed Chorley) 2nd cottage on right*
This cottage was built with stone from the Farwell nunnery, which was destroyed during the Reformation, and retains many original features. It is set in pretty gardens and offers well equipped and homely bedrooms.
FACILITIES: 4 rms (1 en suite) No smoking TVB tea/coffee No dogs Cen ht TVL No children 5yrs No coaches Riding **PRICES:** s £20-£30; d £36-£48✱ **BB PARKING:** 2

♦♦♦ Coppers End

Walsall Rd, Muckley Corner WS14 0BG ☎ 01543 372910
📠 01543 360423
Dir: *on A461, 100yds from Muckley Corner rdbt off A5*
Formerly the local police station, this family run guest house now provides smart modern accommodation. Bedrooms, two of which are on the ground floor, are well equipped. There is a comfortable lounge for guests to enjoy, and breakfast is served in a modern conservatory overlooking pretty rear gardens.
FACILITIES: 6 rms (4 en suite) (2 GF) No smoking in bedrooms No smoking in area of dining room TVB tea/coffee No dogs (ex guide dogs) Licensed Cen ht TVL No coaches **PRICES:** s £26-£34; d £41-£50✱ **LB PARKING:** 12 **NOTES:** Closed Xmas New Year **CARDS:**

♦♦♦ *Little Pipe Farm (SK078106)*

Little Pipe Ln, Farewell, Chorley WS13 8BS ☎ 01543 683066
Mrs E Clewley
Dir: *A51 N from Lichfield, from Bowling Gr. Island 1st left into Abnalls Lane follow Chorley signs, 1st right Dark Lane, 1st left Little Pipe Lane. Farm Drive first on right*
Home of the friendly Clewley family for many years, this 19th-century house is very much part of a working arable and beef farm. Guests are made to feel very welcome, bedrooms are neat and freshly decorated and the breakfast room is full of character.
FACILITIES: 3 rms (1 fmly) No smoking in bedrooms TVB No dogs Cen ht TVL Fishing 230 acres arable beef Dinner Last d by arrangement
PRICES: s £18-£25; d £36-£50✱ **BB PARKING:** 16

♦♦♦ Park View

Shaw Ln WS13 7AG ☎ 01543 256166
Dir: *from city centre follow signs to cathedral, follow road for approx 200yds & left into Shaw Lane, bungalow on right*
Ideally located on the edge of Beacon Park and within a few minutes' walk of the cathedral, this well maintained modern guest house provides comfortable, well equipped bedrooms both with modern en suite facilities and the luxury of breakfast room service.
FACILITIES: 2 en suite (2 GF) No smoking TVB tea/coffee No dogs Cen ht No children No coaches **PRICES:** s £25; d £45✱ **PARKING:** 6
NOTES: Closed 22-26 Dec

♦♦ Main View

18 Burton Rd DE13 7BB ☎ 01283 790725
e-mail: bb@main-view.fsnet.co.uk
Dir: *on A38 northbound 0.25m from A513, 200yds past British Legion Club*
Mrs Conrad has established a fine reputation over the past fifteen years in this large detached house which is located between Lichfield and Burton-on-Trent. Bedrooms are well equipped and homely and hearty breakfasts are taken in the conservatory which overlooks the well tended garden.
FACILITIES: 3 rms (1 en suite) No smoking in dining room TVB tea/coffee No dogs (ex guide dogs) Cen ht TVL No coaches **PRICES:** s £19-£20; d £38-£40✱ **BB PARKING:** 6 **NOTES:** Closed 24 Dec-2 Jan

Moat Cottage

29 Gaia Ln WS13 7LW ☎ 01543 255230
At the time of going to press the Diamond classification for this establishment had not been confirmed. Please check the AA website www.theAA.com for up-to-date information.
FACILITIES: 1 en suite (1 GF)

England

LOYNTON Map 07 SJ72

♦♦♦♦ The Lodge

Loynton Lodge ST20 0QA ☎ 01785 284113 📠 01785 284113
e-mail: janet.shakespear@blackwhitemortgageco.co.uk
Dir: *on A519 3m E of Newport*
This friendly guest house is a converted and extended gatekeeper's lodge and offers comfortable, modern accommodation throughout. The bedrooms, both on the ground floor, are well equipped and furnished to a high standard while breakfast is taken in the dining/lounge area in the hallway, where there is also a jukebox for guests' use.
FACILITIES: 2 rms No smoking TVB tea/coffee No dogs (ex guide dogs) Cen ht No coaches **PRICES:** s £25; d £45* **PARKING:** 6

OAKAMOOR Map 07 SK04

Premier Collection

♦♦♦♦♦ Bank House

Farley Ln ST10 3BD ☎ 01538 702810 📠 01538 702810
e-mail: john.orme@dial.pipex.com
Dir: *from Cheadle take B5417. In Oakamoor pass church, then pub. Right After 80yds. House 0.75m right.*

A warm welcome is assured at this former farmhouse, which stands in immaculate landscaped gardens. Bedrooms feature a wealth of thoughtful extras and public areas include an elegant dining room and spacious comfortable lounge with a welcoming log fire. Memorable breakfasts (and dinners, by arrangement) are provided, making use of quality local produce.
FACILITIES: 3 en suite (2 fmly) No smoking TVB tea/coffee Direct dial from bedrooms Licensed Cen ht TVL No coaches **PRICES:** s £45-£54; d £60-£78* **LB PARKING:** 6 **NOTES:** Closed Xmas week
CARDS:

♦♦♦♦ The Beehive Guest House

Churnet View Rd ST10 3AE ☎ 01538 702420 📠 01538 702420
e-mail: thebeehiveoakamoor@btinternet.com
Dir: *A50 onto A522 signed Cheadle, in Cheadle straight on at 1st rdbt, right at mini rdbt, follow road to Oakamoor. Turn left at Cricketers pub, left at Lord Nelson pub, immediate left turn into Churnet View Road, house on right*
Standing in the centre of the village and close to the river, this spacious detached house offers thoughtfully equipped and comfortable bedrooms. There is also a comfortable lounge dining room where substantial breakfasts are served. Hospitality is a strength here.
FACILITIES: 5 en suite (2 fmly) No smoking TVB tea/coffee No dogs (ex guide dogs) Cen ht TVL No coaches **PRICES:** s £30-£40; d £44-£50* **PARKING:** 6 **CARDS:**

♦♦♦♦ Crowtrees Farm

Eaves Ln ST10 3DY ☎ 01538 702260
e-mail: crowtrees@fenetre.co.uk
Dir: *A52 from Stoke-on-Trent towards Ashbourne, at Whiston turn right into Eaves Lane towards Oakamoor, approx 1.5miles on right*
This impeccably maintained 200-year old farmhouse is conveniently located for the Potteries and Alton Towers, and provides well equipped bedrooms. It is still very much a working farm with sheep and cattle, as well as a collection of pets. The friendly owners create a relaxing atmosphere for their guests.
FACILITIES: 3 en suite 1 annexe en suite (2 fmly) No smoking TVB tea/coffee No dogs (ex guide dogs) Cen ht No coaches **BB**
PARKING: 6 **NOTES:** Closed 25-26 Dec **CARDS:**

♦♦♦♦ Ribden Farm *(SK075471)*

Three Lows, Oakamoor ST10 3BW ☎ 01538 702830
📠 01538 702830 Mrs C Shaw
e-mail: ribdenfarm@aol.com
Dir: *on B5417 Cheadle/Ashbourne road, on right 0.5m before junction with A52*
This 18th-century farmhouse on the Staffordshire Moors is near Alton Towers. Tastefully modernised, it provides well-furnished bedrooms, including some with four-poster beds and some in a converted farm building. Breakfast is taken in the pine-furnished dining room overlooking the pretty gardens. There is a children's play area in the grounds.
FACILITIES: 6 rms (5 en suite) (4 fmly) No smoking in bedrooms No smoking in dining room No smoking in 1 lounge TVB tea/coffee No dogs Cen ht TVL 100 acres sheep **PRICES:** d fr £48* **PARKING:** 6
NOTES: Closed mid Nov-mid Mar **CARDS:**

♦♦♦♦ Tenement Farm

Three Lows, Ribden, Oakamoor ST10 3BW ☎ 01538 702333
📠 01538 703603
e-mail: stanleese@aol.com
Dir: *turn left off A52 from Ashbourne onto B5417 then first drive on left. Signed*
Families are particularly welcome at this non-smoking former farmhouse, which has been sympathetically renovated to provide high standards of comfort throughout. Popular with visitors to Alton Towers, bedrooms are equipped with both practical and homely extras and public areas include a comfortable lounge with honesty bar, an attractive dining room and children's' play room.
FACILITIES: 8 en suite (6 fmly) (2 GF) No smoking TVB tea/coffee Direct dial from bedrooms No dogs (ex guide dogs) Licensed Cen ht TVL No coaches Dinner Last d 6.30pm **PRICES:** s £25-£27.50; d £50-£55* **LB**
PARKING: 12 **NOTES:** Closed Nov-Feb **CARDS:**

STAFFORD Map 07 SJ92

♦♦♦♦ Yew Tree Inn & Restaurant

Long Compton, Ranton ST18 9JT ☎ 01785 282278
📠 01785 282278
Dir: *take A518 Stafford-Newport road, on entering Haughton take right turn opposite Shropshire Inn into Station Rd, after 2.5m inn on right*
This delightful inn started life as a farmhouse in the 17th century. Character filled bars still display many original features. Bedrooms are attractively decorated and neatly furnished. As well as a good range of bar food, there is a restaurant serving a range of international dishes.
FACILITIES: 3 en suite (1 fmly) No smoking in bedrooms No smoking in dining room No smoking in 1 lounge TVB tea/coffee Cen ht Fishing Dinner Last d 9.15pm **PRICES:** s £40-£50; d £60-£80* **LB MEALS:** Lunch £5.95-£12.95&alc Dinner £12.95-£18.95&alc* **CONF:** Thtr 20 Class 20 Board 20 Del from £65 * **PARKING:** 100 **CARDS:**

England

STAFFORD continued

♦♦♦ Bailey Hotel
63 Lichfield Rd ST17 4LL ☎ 01785 214133 Fax 01785 227920
Dir: *on A34 1m south of town centre*
This large, well-maintained house offers smart and well decorated bedrooms with modern facilities. There is a room at ground floor level suitable for less mobile visitors. A traditional lounge and a cosy dining room are provided.
FACILITIES: 10 rms (4 en suite) (1 fmly) No smoking in dining room TVB tea/coffee Direct dial from bedrooms Licensed Cen ht No coaches Dinner Last d 6.45pm **PRICES:** s £20-£32; d £40-£49* **PARKING:** 11 **NOTES:** Closed 20 Dec-2 Jan **CARDS:**

♦♦♦ Leonards Croft Hotel
80 Lichfield Rd ST17 4LP ☎ 01785 223676
Dir: *M6 junct 13 follow A449 for 2m. Right at Esso Garage then left onto A34, on right after railway bridge*
Located south of the town centre, this well-proportioned late Victorian house has been carefully renovated to provide a range of practically furnished bedrooms, two of which are situated on the ground floor. A range of popular evening dishes is available in addition to comprehensive breakfasts and a spacious lounge is also available.
FACILITIES: 9 en suite (4 fmly) (2 GF) No smoking in bedrooms No smoking in dining room TVB tea/coffee Licensed Cen ht TVL No coaches Dinner Last d 6pm **PRICES:** s £30-£40; d £50-£60*
PARKING: 11 **NOTES:** Closed Xmas **CARDS:**

♦♦♦ Old School
Newport Rd, Haughton ST18 9JH ☎ 01785 780358
Fax 01785 780358
e-mail: info@theoldsc.co.uk
Dir: *from centre of Stafford take A518 for 3m towards Telford. Old School is next to church in centre of Haughton, parking at rear*
Located in the heart of Haughton village, this Grade II former early Victorian school has been sympathetically renovated to provide a range of modern bedrooms equipped with thoughtful extras. Breakfast is taken at one family table in a cosy dining room, which also contains lounge seating.
FACILITIES: 3 rms (3 GF) No smoking TVB tea/coffee No dogs (ex guide dogs) Cen ht No coaches **PRICES:** s £20; d £40* **PARKING:** 3

♦♦ Windsor Hotel
69 Lichfield Rd ST17 4LW ☎ 01785 258531 Fax 01785 246875
Dir: *M6 junct 13 to Stafford, right at Esso garage to mini rdbt, follow Silkmore lane till 2nd rdbt, 2nd exit to town centre, 0.25m right*
This hotel is popular with contractors and overseas students. It provides a range of practically equipped bedrooms and has the benefit of a large car park. Breakfast is taken in the dining room of the adjacent Abbey Hotel, which is under the same ownership.
FACILITIES: 14 rms (2 en suite) No smoking in dining room No smoking in 1 lounge STV TVB tea/coffee No dogs (ex guide dogs) Licensed Cen ht TVL No coaches Dinner Last d 8.30pm **PRICES:** s £23-£25; d £40-£42*
PARKING: 16 **CARDS:**

STOKE-ON-TRENT — Map 07 SJ84

See also Cheddleton & Leek

♦♦♦ A The Limes
Cheadle Rd, Blythe Bridge ST11 9PW ☎ 01782 393278
Dir: *from Stoke on Trent take A50 S for 5m, exit onto A521 to Blythe Bridge. Continue 1m and Cheadle Rd 2nd left after railway crossing*
FACILITIES: 3 rms (2 en suite) (1 fmly) No smoking in bedrooms No smoking in dining room No dogs Cen ht TVL No children 5yrs No coaches **PRICES:** s £24-£25; d £39* **PARKING:** 5 **NOTES:** Closed 25 Dec

♦♦♦ A Victoria Hotel
4 Roundwell St, Tunstall ST6 5JJ ☎ 01782 835964
Fax 01782 835964
e-mail: victoria_hotel@tunstall51-fsnet.co.uk
Dir: *from M6 junct 15 take A500 then A527 to Tunstall. At main rdbt left and at T-junct turn right. Hotel 25yds on left*
FACILITIES: 9 rms (4 en suite) (2 fmly) (2 GF) TVB tea/coffee No dogs (ex guide dogs) Cen ht TVL No coaches **PRICES:** s £20-£23; d £34-£40 **BB**
PARKING: 6 **NOTES:** Closed Xmas **CARDS:**

STONE — Map 07 SJ93

♦♦♦ Field House
59 Stafford Rd ST15 0HE ☎ 01785 605712 Fax 01785 605712
e-mail: fieldhouse@ntlworld.com
Dir: *A34 exit with Shell garage, head for Stone town centre, turn right into Stafford Rd, house on right opposite Walton Grange*

This family home is close to the town centre but in quiet, pretty gardens convenient for the A34. A Georgian house, it offers traditionally furnished bedrooms with family pieces in some rooms. Guests breakfast together in a combined lounge/dining room. Hospitality is warm and welcoming.
FACILITIES: 3 rms (1 en suite) (2 fmly) No smoking in bedrooms No smoking in dining room No smoking in 1 lounge TVB tea/coffee No dogs Cen ht TVL No coaches Art tuition on request **PRICES:** s £25-£34; d £35-£44* **LB BB PARKING:** 4

STRETTON — Map 07 SJ81

♦♦♦ Woodlands House
Cottage Garden Roses ST19 9LG ☎ 01785 840217
Fax 01902 850193
e-mail: teresa@cottagegardenroses.com
Dir: *M6 junct 12, A5 towards Telford, after 0.5m Gailey Island rdbt , after 2m follow brown tourist signs for cottage*
This charming old house dates back to the mid 18th century. The delightful garden is given over to the commercial production of old varieties of roses. Rose based toiletries and beauty products are produced on the premises. At the time of our last inspection, there was one traditionally furnished twin bedroom, with its own bathroom and sitting room/dining room. A second similar room was expected to be available in 2002.
FACILITIES: 1 en suite No smoking TVB tea/coffee Cen ht TVL Dinner Last d 8pm (day before) **PRICES:** s £35-£50; d £50-£75* **LB PARKING:** 4
CARDS:

If an establishment name appears in *italics*, details have not been confirmed for 2003.

England

TAMWORTH Map 04 SK20

Premier Collection

♦♦♦♦♦ Oak Tree Farm *(SK180047)*

Hints Rd, Hopwas B78 3AA ☎ 01827 56807
01827 56807 Mrs S Purkis
Dir: *take A51 Lichfield to Tamworth rd & turn into Hints Rd at Tame Otter pub. Last house on left where road divides*

This beautifully restored farmhouse nestles in delightful gardens in the Staffordshire countryside. Bedrooms are attractively furnished and comfortable, with many thoughtful extras. Rooms are located in the main house and a converted farm building. Additional features include a spacious lounge, a breakfast room and a small swimming pool. Mrs Purkis is an attentive and caring hostess.
FACILITIES: 2 en suite 5 annexe en suite (2 GF) No smoking TVB tea/coffee Direct dial from bedrooms Cen ht No children 16yrs Indoor swimming pool (heated) Fishing Croquet lawn Steam room 4 acres non-working **PRICES:** s £57-£60; d £100* **CONF:** Thtr 14 Class 6 Del from £95 * **PARKING:** 10 **NOTES:** Closed Xmas & New Year
CARDS:

♦♦♦♦ Harlaston Post Office

Main Rd, Harlaston B79 9JU ☎ 01827 383324 01827 383746
Dir: *turn off M42/A42 at junct 11 onto B5453 to No Man's Heath, turn right for Clifton Campville & straight on for Haunton & Harlaston*
This is a well-kept guest house that is situated just opposite the church in this idyllic hamlet. The individually styled bedrooms are attractive and provide a range of modern facilities. Hearty cooked breakfasts can be enjoyed around a large table in the bright and comfortable dining room.
FACILITIES: 4 en suite (1 fmly) (1 GF) No smoking STV TVB tea/coffee Direct dial from bedrooms No dogs (ex guide dogs) Cen ht TVL No coaches
PRICES: s £22-£25; d £40-£45* **PARKING:** 3

♦♦♦♦ The Old Rectory

Churchside, Harlaston B79 9HE ☎ 01827 383583
01827 383583
Dir: *in the centre of Harlaston, 4.5m N of Tamworth*
This former Victorian rectory stands in the heart of this pretty, award-winning village. Bedrooms are furnished in pine and are neatly presented, with many thoughtful extras. Well-cooked breakfasts feature home-made bread and preserves and can be taken in the spacious kitchen or sunny breakfast room, overlooking the garden.

FACILITIES: 4 rms (3 en suite) No smoking TVB tea/coffee Cen ht No coaches Croquet lawn **PRICES:** s £22-£24; d £42-£44* **PARKING:** 7

♦♦♦♦ Middleton House Farm

Tamworth Rd, Middleton B78 2BD ☎ 01827 873474
01827 872246
e-mail: rob.jane@tinyonline.co.uk
Dir: *from M42 junct 9 take A446 to Lichfield, in 1m take A4091 at rdbt, travel 1m farm on right just past lay-by on left*
FACILITIES: 6 en suite No smoking TVB tea/coffee No dogs Cen ht TVL No children 12yrs No coaches **PRICES:** s £40; d £55-£75* **PARKING:** 8
NOTES: Closed Xmas & New Year **CARDS:**

♦♦♦ The Sleepy Owl

20 Church Ln, Edingale B79 9JD ☎ 01827 383436 & 383853
e-mail: irene@sleepyowlbb.freeserve.co.uk
Dir: *from Tamworth take Wigginton Rd to Harlaston & left at White Lion pub for Edingale, right over bridge, left at Black Horse pub*
This modern detached house is in a cul-de-sac in the peaceful village of Edingale, not far from Tamworth. Bedrooms are smartly presented and are thoughtfully equipped. There is a spacious lounge, plus a breakfast room overlooking a pleasant garden.
FACILITIES: 2 rms No smoking TVB tea/coffee Direct dial from bedrooms No dogs (ex guide dogs) Cen ht TVL No children 8yrs No coaches Dinner Last d 8pm **PRICES:** s £23-£26; d £36-£38* **LB BB PARKING:** 3

UTTOXETER Map 07 SK03

♦♦♦ *Hillcrest*

3 Leighton Rd ST14 8BL ☎ 01889 564627 01889 564627
e-mail: mridge@hillcrest.fsnet.co.uk
Dir: *follow Racecourse signs along A518 to B5017, right at mini-rdbt on B5017 400m, right Wood Leighton right again Leighton Rd, end on right*
This long-established, family-run guest house is within easy reach of Alton Towers. Bedrooms are equipped with modern facilities and extras such as hairdryers and radios. Some rooms are suitable for families and one is on the ground floor. There is a spacious, comfortable lounge and an attractive parquet-floored dining room.
FACILITIES: 7 en suite (5 fmly) No smoking TVB tea/coffee No dogs (ex guide dogs) Licensed Cen ht TVL No coaches Dinner Last d 2pm
PARKING: 12 **NOTES:** Closed 25 Dec **CARDS:**

England

UTTOXETER continued

♦♦♦ *Oldroyd Guest House & Motel*

18-22 Bridge St ST14 8AP ☎ 01889 562763 Fax 01889 568916
e-mail: jim@oldroyd-guesthouse.com
Dir: *situated on the A518, close to Uttoxeter Race Course*

This privately owned and personally run guest house is conveniently close to the town centre and only eight miles from Alton Towers. Bedrooms have modern facilities, and some family and ground-floor rooms are available. Breakfast is served at separate tables in the bright and pleasant breakfast room.
FACILITIES: 12 rms (10 en suite) 3 annexe en suite (7 fmly) No smoking TVB tea/coffee Cen ht TVL **PARKING:** 20 **CARDS:**

♦♦♦ Parkbrook Lodge

Hollington Rd, Stubwood ST14 5HX ☎ 01889 590695
Fax 01889 590964
e-mail: emma-titterton@yahoo.co.uk
Dir: *turn off B5030 by JCB factory into Hollington Road, Parkbrook Lodge 0.5m on right at junct of Hollington Road and Stubwood Lane*
Convenient for both Uttoxeter and Alton Towers this large Victorian house offers spacious bedrooms, all with their own facilities. Many rooms are suitable for children and have views of the Staffordshire countryside. Breakfast is served in the dining room, and there is also a conservatory.
FACILITIES: 7 en suite (5 fmly) No smoking in bedrooms No smoking in dining room No smoking in 1 lounge TVB tea/coffee No dogs Cen ht
PRICES: d £45-£50* **LB PARKING:** 14 **CARDS:**

WATERHOUSES — Map 07 SK05

♦♦ Ye Olde Crown

ST10 3HL ☎ 01538 308204
Dir: *in centre of village, on A523*
Ye Olde Crown is a busy village inn which is full of character. There is a friendly atmosphere and the food draws in a lot of local custom. Bedrooms all have modern facilities, and some are in nearby cottages.

FACILITIES: 3 rms (2 en suite) 4 annexe en suite (2 fmly) (2 GF) TVB tea/coffee No dogs (ex guide dogs) Cen ht Dinner Last d 9.30pm **PRICES:** s £15-£25; d £40* **BB MEALS:** Lunch £7-£15alc Dinner £7-£15alc*
PARKING: 50 **CARDS:**

SUFFOLK

BADINGHAM — Map 05 TM36

♦♦♦♦ Colston Hall *(TM316672)*

IP13 8LB ☎ 01728 638375 Fax 01728 638084
Mr & Mrs Bellefontaine
e-mail: 112john@colstonhall.com
Dir: *from Ipswich A12 to Lowestoft, turn left onto A1120 at Yoxford. Continue to Badingham, brown sign for Colston Hall*
Expect a warm welcome at this friendly, family-run farmhouse, situated in a peaceful rural location in the heart of Suffolk countryside. The property dates back over 400 years and has been sympathetically restored to retain much of the original character with exposed beams and flint walls. Bedrooms are pleasantly decorated with co-ordinated soft furnishings. Breakfast is served at individual tables in the smart dining room and guests have the use of a cosy lounge.
FACILITIES: 3 en suite 3 annexe en suite No smoking tea/coffee No dogs Cen ht TVL No children 12yrs Fishing Indoor bowls 27 acres sheep
PRICES: s £35-£45; d £55-£75* **LB PARKING:** 18
CARDS:

BARNINGHAM — Map 05 TL97

♦♦♦♦ College House Farm

Bardwell Rd, Barningham IP31 1DF ☎ 01359 221512
Fax 01359 221512
e-mail: jackie.brightwell@talk21.com
Dir: *A14/A143/B1111 to Garboldisham and Barningham. In village turn left at 1st crossroad by village store, immediately left again into Bardwell Rd*
Charming Grade II listed Jacobean property situated in a peaceful rural location yet within easy striking distance of Bury St Edmunds. The building has been sympathetically converted to retain much of its original character, which are enhanced by some fine period furnishings. Breakfast is taken at a large communal table in the elegant dining room and guests also have the use of a cosy lounge.
FACILITIES: 4 rms (1 en suite) 2 annexe en suite (4 fmly) No smoking TVB tea/coffee No dogs (ex guide dogs) Cen ht No children 5yrs No coaches Croquet lawn Jacuzzi Dinner Last d by arrangement **PRICES:** s £25-£27.50; d £50-£55* **LB CONF:** Del from £52.50 * **PARKING:** 8 **CARDS:**

BEYTON — Map 05 TL96

Premier Collection

♦♦♦♦♦ Manorhouse

The Green IP30 9AF ☎ 01359 270960
e-mail: manorhouse@beyton.com
Dir: *Beyton is signposted off A14, 4m E of Bury St Edmunds*
Set in immaculate gardens, opposite the village green, this 15th-century Suffolk longhouse retains many original features, including a wealth of exposed beams and roaring log fires. Bedrooms, two of which are in a sympathetic barn conversion, are very spacious and filled with quality furnishings and lots of thoughtful extras. Memorable breakfasts are taken in the elegant dining room, which also contains a relaxing lounge section.

continued

Manorhouse

FACILITIES: 2 en suite 2 annexe en suite (2 GF) No smoking TVB tea/coffee No dogs Cen ht No children 12 yrs No coaches Last d by arrangement **PRICES:** s £40-£50; d £50-£58 **PARKING:** 6 **NOTES:** Closed Xmas

BOXFORD — Map 05 TL94

♦♦♦♦ Cox Hill House

CO10 5JG ☎ 01787 210449 Fax 01787 211590
e-mail: coxhillhouse@hotmail.com
Dir: *off A134 onto A1071, take 2nd sign left to Boxford, next right to Kersey. House 0.5m at top of Cox Hill*

Expect a warm welcome at this friendly family run guest house. The property is situated in a peaceful rural location overlooking a delightful. Bedrooms are pleasantly decorated, furnished with well chosen pieces and thoughtfully equipped. Public rooms feature an attractive dining room where breakfast is served at a large communal table.

FACILITIES: 3 en suite (1 GF) No smoking TVB tea/coffee No dogs (ex guide dogs) Cen ht No children 12yrs No coaches Golf arrangement with two courses **PRICES:** s £30-£35; d £45-£50* **PARKING:** 20 **NOTES:** Closed 24-26 Dec

♦♦♦♦ Hurrells Farmhouse *(SU960402)*

Boxford Ln CO10 5JY ☎ 01787 210215 Fax 01787 211806
Dr & Mrs A K Deb
e-mail: hurrellsf@aol.com
Dir: *From Colchester take A134 towards Sudbury. 4m before Sudbury turn R onto A1071 towards Ipswich. Farmhouse 1m on A1071 on L*

Expect a warm welcome at this friendly, family-run farmhouse, which is situated on the Essex/Suffolk border. The attractively decorated bedrooms are tastefully furnished and equipped with many thoughtful little extras. Breakfast is served in the elegant dining room seated at a large communal table and guests also have the use of a cosy television lounge.

FACILITIES: 3 rms No smoking TVB tea/coffee Cen ht TVL No children 10yrs 4 acres non-working **PRICES:** s £25; d £40* **PARKING:** 6

BRANDON — Map 05 TL78

♦♦ Riverside Lodge

78 High St IP27 0AU ☎ 01842 811236 Fax 01842 811236
Dir: *from A11 at Barton Mills rdbt, take A1065 to Brandon. Establishment by river bridge in High St, parking at rear & entrance*

A 16th-century Grade II listed merchant's house set in 12 acres of landscaped gardens. Bedrooms are spacious, pleasantly decorated and well equipped. The public rooms feature a bright, cheerful dining room and a comfortably appointed lounge on the first floor.

FACILITIES: 3 en suite (1 fmly) No smoking in bedrooms No smoking in dining room No smoking in 1 lounge TVB tea/coffee No dogs (ex guide dogs) Licensed Cen ht TVL Fishing **PRICES:** s £25-£40* **LB** **PARKING:** 12 **CARDS:**

BUNGAY — Map 05 TM38

♦♦♦♦ Earsham Park Farm *(TM304883)*

Harleston Rd, Earsham NR35 2AQ ☎ 01986 892180
Fax 01986 894796 Mrs B Watchorn
e-mail: aa@earsham-parkfarm.co.uk
Dir: *3m SW of Bungay on A143, on right side of road in SW direction*

Located in a superb elevated position on land once part of the Duke of Norfolk's deer park, this impressive Victorian house retains many original features which are enhanced by the quality furnishing styles throughout. Bedrooms are filled with thoughtful homely extras and the pretty décor styles, which include imaginative stencilling, create a warm and inviting atmosphere. Evening meals available in winter only.

FACILITIES: 3 en suite No smoking TVB tea/coffee Cen ht 589 acres arable pigs Dinner Last d 24hrs prior **PRICES:** s £35-£40; d £48-£60 **PARKING:** 11 **CARDS:**

BURY ST EDMUNDS — Map 05 TL86

♦♦♦♦ Orchard Crescent

16 Short Brackland IP33 1EL ☎ 01284 749221 Fax 01284 724769
e-mail: htthomas@nildram.co.uk
Dir: *from A14 take 2nd Bury exit fro Bury Central, towards town centre, at next rdbt left into Northgate St after phone box right into Cadney Lane then left up Cannon St to top of hill, across junct guest house on right*

Guests can expect a warm welcome at this charming terraced property, which is situated just a short walk from the town centre. Bedrooms are tastefully furnished with well-chosen pieces, have bright co-ordinated soft furnishings and many thoughtful touches. Breakfast includes locally sourced produce and is served at a large table in the neat dining room.

FACILITIES: 2 en suite (2 fmly) No smoking TVB tea/coffee No dogs (ex guide dogs) Cen ht No coaches **PRICES:** s £38; d £48* **PARKING:** 1 **CARDS:**

England

BURY ST EDMUNDS continued

♦♦♦♦ The Three Kings

Hengrave Rd, Fornham All Saints IP28 6LA ☎ 01284 766979
01284 723308
e-mail: c.conway@tinyworld.co.uk
Dir: *from West exit A14 at 1st BSE sign, follow sign for Fornham, after approx 1m left at mini rdbt onto B1106 (Mildenhall). Establishment on left*

This attractive inn is situated in the pleasant village of Farnham All Saints. Bedrooms are housed in a new building adjacent to the main property and each is tastefully decorated and furnished, and equipped with an excellent range of facilities. Public rooms include a smart lounge bar, a conservatory, and a comfortable restaurant.

FACILITIES: 9 annexe en suite (2 fmly) TVB tea/coffee Direct dial from bedrooms No dogs (ex guide dogs) Cen ht Pool Table Dinner Last d 9pm **PRICES:** s £60; d £85✳ **LB MEALS:** Lunch fr £11.40 Dinner fr £11.40✳ **PARKING:** 30 **CARDS:**

♦♦♦♦ Ash Cottage

59 Whiting St IP33 1NP ☎ 01284 755098 & 0585 038797
01284 755098
e-mail: ashcottage@freebie.net
Dir: *2nd exit off A14 from Cambridge & Ipswich. Follow for centre. R at T junct, next R after Angel Hotel, 3rd L into Whiting St*

Charming 16th century half timbered townhouse situated just a short walk from the town centre. The property has been sympathetically restored to retain much of its original character. Breakfast is taken at a large table in the attractive dining room, which overlooks the pretty garden. Guests also have use of the comfortable lounge.

FACILITIES: 2 en suite No smoking TVB tea/coffee Cen ht TVL No coaches

♦♦♦♦ The Chantry Hotel

8 Sparhawk St IP33 1RY ☎ 01284 767427 01284 760946
e-mail: chantryhotel-bse@faxvia.net
Dir: *S from Cathedral (on L), take next L, into R lane, turn R, hotel on R*

Expect a friendly welcome at this lovely Georgian house which stands on the site of a 12th-century chantry chapel. Bedrooms are attractively decorated, tastefully furnished and thoughtfully equipped. Public rooms include a smart restaurant and a cosy lounge bar with plush furnishings.

FACILITIES: 13 en suite 3 annexe en suite (1 fmly) No smoking in 8 bedrooms No smoking in dining room TVB tea/coffee Direct dial from bedrooms Licensed Cen ht No coaches Dinner Last d 7pm **PRICES:** s £49.50-£69; d £69-£79✳ **LB PARKING:** 16 **CARDS:**

♦♦♦♦ 83 Whiting Street

83 Whiting St IP33 1NX ☎ 01284 704153
e-mail: gordon@83whitingst.fsnet.co.uk
Dir: *Town centre.*

Attractive three story terrace property conveniently placed for exploring this historic town. The spacious, individually decorated bedrooms are furnished with pine pieces and thoughtfully equipped with modern facilities. Breakfast is served in the beamed dining room that features an open fireplace and a wall painting that dates back to 1530. This is a non-smoking establishment.

FACILITIES: 3 en suite No smoking TVB tea/coffee No dogs (ex guide dogs) Cen ht No coaches **PRICES:** s £35; d £54✳

♦♦♦♦ Maypole Green Barns

Fox and Hounds, Felsham Rd, Bradfield St George IP30 0AB
☎ 01284 386379
e-mail: fox.hounds@talk21.com
Dir: *5m from Bury St Edmunds. Turn off A14 at Bury St Edmunds East sign/Sudbury, take A134 Sudbury road. At Sicklesmere turn onto unclassified road signed Little Welnetham/Bradfield St George, in approx. 2.5m The Fox & Hounds on left*

continued

This is a converted barn set amidst open countryside to the rear of the Fox and Hounds pub. The spacious bedrooms are tastefully furnished in pine and have a good range of useful extras. Public areas include a smart restaurant, a cosy bar and a small conservatory.

FACILITIES: 2 en suite (2 GF) No smoking TVB tea/coffee No dogs (ex guide dogs) Licensed Cen ht No children No coaches Dinner Last d 9.30pm **PRICES:** d £49.95✳ **PARKING:** 30 **CARDS:**

♦♦♦♦ Old Cannon Brewery

86 Cannon St IP33 1JR ☎ 01284 768769 01284 701137
e-mail: rej@btinternet.com
Dir: *Take A14 towards town centre. At rdbt after Tesco turn L then immediately R into Cadney Lane. At end turn L into Cannon St, B&B on L*

Renovated red brick Victorian building, originally built as a beer house and brewery. The present owner has reopened the brewery and the finished products are served in the bar, which also features a unique, specially constructed mirror-polished stainless steel mash tun and boiler. The individually decorated bedrooms have attractive soft furnishings and many thoughtful touches.

FACILITIES: 5 en suite No smoking TVB tea/coffee No dogs (ex guide dogs) Licensed Cen ht No children 14yrs Dinner Last d 9.30pm **PRICES:** s £44-£49; d £62✳ **PARKING:** 6 **CARDS:**

♦♦♦♦ The Six Bells Country Inn

The Green, Bardwell IP31 1AW ☎ 01359 250820
01359 250820
e-mail: sixbellsbardwell@aol.com
Dir: *A143, take turn marked Bardwell Windmill/Six Bells. Inn 1m on L before village green (The Circle)*

Charming 16th century inn situated in a peaceful rural location. Bedrooms are housed in a carefully converted stable block; each one is comfortably furnished and well-equipped. Public rooms have a wealth of original character such as, exposed beams and open fireplaces. A range of real ales and imaginative food is also available.

FACILITIES: 10 en suite (1 fmly) (10 GF) No smoking TVB tea/coffee Direct dial from bedrooms Cen ht Dinner Last d 9pm **PRICES:** s £40-£55; d £55-£85 **LB MEALS:** Dinner £17.50-£22.50 **PARKING:** 40 **NOTES:** Closed 25 & 26 Dec rs restaurant closed Sun evening winter **CARDS:**

♦♦♦♦ South Hill House

43 Southgate St IP33 2AZ ☎ 01284 755650 01284 752718
e-mail: southill@lineone.net
Dir: *turn off A14 at Bury St Edmunds East, proceed in direction of Sudbury, at 2nd rdbt just after garden centre and BP garage turn right, South Hill House is 100 mtrs on right*

FACILITIES: 3 en suite No smoking TVB tea/coffee No dogs Cen ht No coaches **PRICES:** s £30.60-£39; d £42.30-£54✳ **PARKING:** 4 **CARDS:**

♦♦♦ The Abbey Hotel

35 Southgate St IP33 2AZ ☎ 01284 762020 01284 724770
e-mail: reception@theabbeyhotel.demon.co.uk
Dir: *take east exit off A14 & follow signs for Bury St Edmunds, pass BP garage on right at rdbt take last exit into Southgate St, hotel 400yds*

Privately owned hotel ideally placed for visiting this historic town centre. The property is split between several buildings, which date from 1150 to 1680. Public rooms are situated within the Tudor inn section and feature a comfortable lounge as well as an informal dining area. Bedrooms vary in size and style but all are comfortably furnished and well equipped.

FACILITIES: 9 en suite 3 annexe en suite (2 fmly) No smoking in 7 bedrooms No smoking in dining room TVB tea/coffee Direct dial from bedrooms No dogs (ex guide dogs) Licensed Cen ht No children 3yrs No coaches **PRICES:** s £45-£55; d £55-£68✳ **PARKING:** 9 **CARDS:**

♦♦♦ Brambles Lodge

Welham Ln, Risby IP28 6QS ☎ 01284 810701 📠 01284 811542
Dir: *E along A14, turn off at sign for Saxham Business Park/Saxham/Risby. Turn left into village & past Crown & Castle pub into Welham Lane*

Located in the peaceful village of Risby, this constantly improving house offers high levels of homely comfort. Memorable breakfasts are taken in the attractive conservatory overlooking the picturesque gardens which include a well inhabited duck pond.
FACILITIES: 3 rms (1 en suite) 1 annexe en suite (1 fmly) No smoking TVB tea/coffee No dogs (ex guide dogs) Cen ht No children 6yrs No coaches **PRICES:** s £25-£35; d £45-£55✻ **PARKING:** 5

♦♦♦ Hamilton House

4 Nelson Rd IP33 3AG ☎ 01284 703022 📠 01284 703022
Dir: *Exit A14 onto A1302. follow rd for 1m, across rdbt, right after Lloyds Bank. establishment on left*
A warm welcome awaits at this comfortable family home, an Edwardian villa in a quiet road a short walk from the centre. Bedrooms are light and pleasantly appointed, and most are of good, comfortable proportions, with modern facilities. Breakfast is taken at a communal table in the dining room, which also has lounge seating for guests.
FACILITIES: 4 rms (2 en suite) No smoking TVB tea/coffee Cen ht No coaches **PRICES:** s £22; d £45✻

♦♦♦ St Andrews Lodge

30 St Andrews St North IP33 1SZ ☎ 01284 756733
e-mail: di.groves@thelodge30.freeserve.co.uk
Dir: *turn off A14 at Bury St Edmunds Central, take town centre direction straight across next 2 rdbts at next rdbt left into St Andrews St Nth, St Andrews Lodge on right*
This small guest house is conveniently close to both the A14 and the town centre. It provides well equipped, modern bedrooms, all of which are located on the ground floor of a separate purpose-built building to the rear of the house. Separate tables are provided in the traditionally furnished breakfast room.
FACILITIES: 3 en suite No smoking TVB tea/coffee No dogs (ex guide dogs) Cen ht **PRICES:** s £35; d £50✻ **PARKING:** 3 **NOTES:** Closed Xmas & New Year **CARDS:**

♦♦♦ St Vincent

109 Fornham Rd IP32 6AS ☎ 01284 705884 📠 01284 705884
e-mail: janetbacchus@aol.com
Dir: *leave A14 at Bury St Edmunds central exit, follow signs to town centre, next rdbt 3rd exit signed Mildenhall, this is Fornham Road continue under 2 bridges St Vincent on left*
A cheerful welcome and friendly service await at the St Vincent Guest House, which is located just a short walk from the railway station and local inns, and approximately a 15 minute walk from the town centre. Bedrooms are of comfortable proportions and suitably equipped, while a hearty breakfast is served in the pleasant ground floor dining room.

continued

FACILITIES: 4 rms (1 en suite) (2 fmly) No smoking TVB tea/coffee No dogs Cen ht No coaches **PRICES:** s £25; d £48-£60✻ **PARKING:** 2 **CARDS:**

♦♦♦ 🅰 Dunston Guest House Hotel

8 Springfield Rd IP33 3AN ☎ 01284 767981 📠 01284 764574
Dir: *from A14 towards Cambridge, take 1st slip road onto A1302. In 1.5m after pedestrian crossing turn left into Springfield Rd*
FACILITIES: 11 rms (6 en suite) 6 annexe rms (2 en suite) (5 fmly) No smoking in 4 bedrooms No smoking in dining room No smoking in lounges TVB tea/coffee No dogs Licensed Cen ht TVL **PRICES:** s £25-£45; d £50-£60✻ **PARKING:** 10

♦♦ Avery House

2 Newmarket Rd IP33 3SN ☎ 01284 755484
Dir: *1m from Bury St Edmunds West, junct off A14 heading to town centre*

Located on the outskirts within easy walking distance of major attractions, this purpose built accommodation is popular with business travellers for its value for money policy. The practically equipped bedrooms offer acceptable comfort and a full English breakfast is provided in the cafeteria style dining room.
FACILITIES: 6 en suite (1 fmly) (3 GF) No smoking in dining room No smoking in lounges TVB tea/coffee No dogs Cen ht **PRICES:** s £30; d £40✻ **PARKING:** 8

CLARE — Map 05 TL74

♦♦♦ Ship Stores

22 Callis St CO10 8PX ☎ 01787 277834
e-mail: shipclare@aol.com
Dir: *M11 junct 9, A11/A1307 to Haverhill, left onto A1092 to Stoke by Clare, then Clare, left onto B1063, past church, 100mtrs on right*
Located in the heart of this historic market town, the Ship Stores adjoins the village shop and tea rooms. Visitors can enjoy homely, thoughtfully equipped bedrooms, some of which are situated in sympathetically converted former stables. Many of the 17th century characteristics are retained and the attractive breakfast room is particularly warm and inviting.
FACILITIES: 4 en suite 2 annexe en suite (1 fmly) No smoking in bedrooms No smoking in dining room TVB tea/coffee No dogs Cen ht TVL No coaches Dinner Last d breakfast **PRICES:** s £25-£45; d £45-£50✻ **LB** **PARKING:** 3 **CARDS:**

England

CRETINGHAM Map 05 TM26

♦♦♦♦ Shrubbery Farmhouse

Chapel Hill IP13 7DN ☎ 01473 737494 01473 737312
e-mail: sm@marmar.co.uk
Dir: *left at T junct after Otley agricultural college, right at Otley post office. In 2.5m turn right at 2nd right signed Monewen 350yds up hill right onto farm track*

Dating back in parts to the 16th century, this building has been sympathetically restored to retain much of its original character. Bedrooms are pleasantly furnished and equipped with many thoughtful extras. Breakfasts includes home-grown produce and free range eggs. Additional facilities include a very comfortable lounge, a croquet lawn, a gymnasium and a tennis court.

FACILITIES: 3 rms (1 en suite) (1 fmly) No smoking STV TVB tea/coffee No dogs (ex guide dogs) Cen ht TVL ch fac No coaches Tennis (hard) Gymnasium Croquet lawn Dinner Last d breakfast **PRICES:** s £39-£45; d £59.50-£78✻ **PARKING:** 7

ELMSWELL Map 05 TL96

♦♦♦ Kiln Farm

Kiln Ln IP30 9QR ☎ 01359 240442
e-mail: Barry-Sue@kilnfarm.fsnet.co.uk
Dir: *at junct A14/A1088 to roundabout, take Ipswich exit, farm 0.5m on left, along Kiln Lane*

FACILITIES: 4 en suite (1 fmly) (4 GF) No smoking in 3 bedrooms No smoking in dining room No smoking in lounges TVB tea/coffee Cen ht No coaches **PRICES:** s £25-£40; d £48-£50✻ **PARKING:** 8

EYE Map 05 TM17

♦♦♦ Gislingham Westview House

High St, Gislingham IP23 8HS ☎ 01379 783975
e-mail: reesengland@clara.net
Dir: *A140 from Ipswich, left at White Horse signed Finningham. At 4 Horseshoes rightR signed Gislingham. Left after 1.25m into High St. House on left after village hall*

Expect a warm welcome at this delightful 16th-century Suffolk long house. The property has been carefully restored to retain much of its original character including inglenook fireplaces and exposed beams. Breakfast includes home-produced, free-range eggs as well as locally sourced items, and is served at a large communal table.

FACILITIES: 2 rms No smoking TVB tea/coffee Cen ht TVL No children 2yrs No coaches **PRICES:** s £30; d £40✻ **LB PARKING:** 4

♦♦♦ White Horse

Stoke Ash IP23 7ET ☎ 01379 678222 01379 678557
e-mail: whitehorse@stokeash.fsbusiness.co.uk
Dir: *on A140 midway between Ipswich/Norwich*

Popular 17th century coaching inn situated on the A140 in the village of Stoke Ash. The modern bedrooms are located in an annexe adjacent to the main building; each one is pleasantly decorated, attractively furnished and well equipped. An interesting choice of dishes is offered in the smartly decorated restaurant, which features exposed beams and inglenook fireplaces.

FACILITIES: 7 annexe en suite (1 fmly) No smoking in 1 bedrooms No smoking in dining room TVB tea/coffee Direct dial from bedrooms No dogs (ex guide dogs) Cen ht Dinner Last d 10pm **PRICES:** s £39.95; d £54.95✻ **LB CONF:** Thtr 50 **PARKING:** 60 **CARDS:**

See advert under IPSWICH

FELIXSTOWE Map 05 TM33

♦♦♦ *Dorincourt*

41 Undercliff Rd West IP11 2AH ☎ 01394 270447
01394 270447
All apart from holidays.
Dir: *on A14 follow signs for Leisure Centre/Seafront. Dorincourt on seafront opp Leisure Centre*

Imposing Victorian villa situated in a prominent position opposite the leisure centre overlooking the promenade and the sea. Bedrooms are pleasantly decorated and equipped with modern facilities. Breakfast and dinner are served in the smart conservatory dining room and guests have the use of a comfortable TV lounge.

FACILITIES: 9 rms (3 en suite) (1 fmly) No smoking STV TVB tea/coffee Licensed Cen ht TVL No coaches Dinner Last d 2pm **PARKING:** 4 **NOTES:** Closed Xmas & New Year **CARDS:**

FRAMLINGHAM Map 05 TM26

♦♦♦♦ Bridge House

Earl Soham IP13 7RT ☎ 01728 685473 01728 685289
e-mail: bridgehouse46@hotmail.com

A warm welcome is to be expected at this charming cottage which dates back to the 16th century. Set amidst pretty landscaped gardens in the heart of the village, the house has been sympathetically refurbished to maintain much of its original character. The individually decorated bedrooms are equipped with many thoughtful extras. Freshly cooked breakfasts are served at a large communal table and guests also have the use of a comfortable lounge.

FACILITIES: 3 en suite No smoking TVB tea/coffee No dogs (ex guide dogs) Cen ht No coaches Dinner Last d by prior arrangment **PRICES:** s fr £28; d fr £50✻ **PARKING:** 5

♦♦♦♦ Woodlands Farm

Brundish IP13 8BP ☎ 01379 384444
e-mail: woodlandsfarm@hotmail.com
Dir: *from A1120 at Dennington, take B1116 towards Laxfield, then 4th on left. Follow lane for 0.5m and turn left into No Through Road*

Peacefully located north of the town, this 16th century house retains many original features which are enhanced by the furnishing and decor styles throughout. Bedrooms are filled with homely extras and both tasty breakfasts and dinners, by arrangement, are taken at one family table in the elegant dining room.

FACILITIES: 3 en suite No smoking tea/coffee No dogs (ex guide dogs) Cen ht TVL No children 10yrs No coaches **PRICES:** s £27.50; d £42-£46✻ **PARKING:** 6 **NOTES:** Closed 24 Dec-2 Jan

♦♦♦♦ Fieldway

Saxtead Rd, Dennington IP13 8AP ☎ 01728 638456
01728 638456
e-mail: dianaturan@hotmail.com
Dir: *on A1120 tourist route in centre of Dennington opposite church and village green*

FACILITIES: 3 rms (1 en suite) (2 fmly) No smoking tea/coffee No dogs (ex guide dogs) Cen ht TVL No children 10yrs No coaches Croquet lawn Dinner Last d am **PRICES:** s £30; d £45-£46✻ **LB PARKING:** 6

♦♦♦ Church Farm *(TM605267)*

Church Rd, Kettleburgh IP13 7LF ☎ 01728 723532 Mrs A Bater
e-mail: jbater@suffolkonline.net
Dir: *from A12 northbound take 2nd left to Wickham market, follow signs to Easton Farm Park then to Kettleburgh 1.25m, house behind church*

Charming 300-year-old farmhouse situated close to the village church amid superb grounds that feature a duck pond, mature

continued

shrubs and sweeping lawns. The property has been sympathetically converted and retains exposed beams and open fireplaces. Bedrooms are pleasantly decorated and equipped with a good range of useful extras, a ground floor bedroom is available.
FACILITIES: 3 rms (1 en suite) (1 GF) No smoking in bedrooms No smoking in dining room tea/coffee No dogs Cen ht TVL Fishing Clay pigeon shooting 70 acres arable mixed Dinner Last d 7.30pm **PRICES:** s £23-£25; d £46-£50 **PARKING:** 10

FRESSINGFIELD — Map 05 TM27

Premier Collection

♦♦♦♦♦ Chippenhall Hall
IP21 5TD ☎ 01379 588180 & 586733
e-mail: info@chippenhall.co.uk
Dir: *8m E of Diss: 1.5m outside Fressingfield on B1116 to Framlingham*
This charming country house which dates back to the Saxon period offers great hospitality. The property has a wealth of original features and the spacious, individually decorated bedrooms are tastefully furnished. Breakfast and imaginative home cooked dinners are served in the elegant dining room. Guests also have the use of cosy lounge.
FACILITIES: 4 en suite No smoking in bedrooms No smoking in dining room No smoking in 1 lounge tea/coffee No dogs Cen ht TVL No children 14yrs No coaches Outdoor swimming pool (heated) Croquet lawn Clay pigeon shooting Dinner Last d 4.30pm **PRICES:** s £80-£90; d £85-£95✳ **PARKING:** 20 **CARDS:**

HADLEIGH — Map 05 TM04

♦♦♦♦ Edgehall Hotel
2 High St IP7 5AP ☎ 01473 822458 📠 01473 827751
e-mail: r.rolfe@edgehall-hotel.co.uk
Dir: *5m N of Colchester, left onto B1070, continue 5.5m to Hadleigh. 1st property in High St on right*

This privately owned hotel dates back to the 16th century. The spacious bedrooms are attractively decorated, thoughtfully equipped and tastefully furnished in period style; one room has a superb four poster bed. Breakfast and dinner are served in the elegant dining room and guests have the use of a comfortably furnished lounge.
FACILITIES: 8 rms (6 en suite) (2 fmly) (1 GF) No smoking in 6 bedrooms No smoking in dining room No smoking in lounges TVB tea/coffee Licensed Cen ht No coaches Dinner Last d 7.30pm **PRICES:** s £40-£50; d £50-£85✳ **LB PARKING:** 20

HARTEST — Map 05 TL85

Premier Collection

♦♦♦♦♦ The Hatch
Pilgrims Ln, Cross Green IP29 4ED ☎ 01284 830226
📠 01284 830226
Dir: *6m from Bury St Edmunds, take A143 towards Haverhill, then B1066 to Glemsford. 1st road on left on entering village*
Located on a medieval pilgrims' way, this 15th century former hall house retains many original features including a wealth of exposed beams and inglenook fireplaces. High standards of comfort and hospitality are assured and the fine period furniture throughout adds to the intrinsic charm of the house.
FACILITIES: 2 en suite (1 fmly) No smoking TVB tea/coffee Direct dial from bedrooms No dogs (ex guide dogs) Cen ht TVL No children 9yrs No coaches **PRICES:** s £35-£45; d £60-£70✳ **PARKING:** 3

IPSWICH

See advertisement above

England

KEDINGTON Map 05 TL74

Premier Collection

♦♦♦♦♦ The White House

Silver St CB9 7QG ☎ 01440 707731 🖷 01440 707731

Dir: *from A143, Haverhill to Bury St Edmunds rd, take B1061 into Kedington, then 3rd left, King's Hill. House at bottom of hill opposite pub*

A Grade II listed, timber-framed, 17th-century house with exposed beams. Sympathetically extended in the Victorian era, this delightful house has been tastefully furnished and restored by enthusiastic proprietors, Toby and Chrissy Barclay. The charming, individually furnished bedrooms offer many creature comforts and personal touches.

FACILITIES: 3 en suite No smoking TVB tea/coffee No dogs Licensed Cen ht No children 12yrs No coaches Shooting tuition Dinner Last d 24 hrs notice **PRICES:** s £40-£60; d £60✳ **PARKING:** 5

LAVENHAM Map 05 TL94

See also Boxford

Premier Collection

♦♦♦♦♦ Lavenham Priory

Water St CO10 9RW ☎ 01787 247404 🖷 01787 248472

e-mail: mail@lavenhampriory.co.uk

Dir: *A1141 to Lavenham, turn by side of Swan into Water St & right after 50yds into private drive*

A warm welcome awaits at this superb Grade I listed building, which dates back to the 13th century. The property once belonged to Benedictine monks and has been lovingly restored so as to maintain much of its original character. The individually-decorated bedrooms are very spacious; each is beautifully furnished and thoughtfully equipped. Breakfast is served in the spectacular Merchants room or in the sheltered courtyard herb garden and guests also have use of the Great Hall, with inglenook fireplace, and an adjoining lounge.

FACILITIES: 6 en suite No smoking TVB tea/coffee No dogs Licensed Cen ht TVL No children 10yrs No coaches **PRICES:** s £59-£79; d £78-£126✳ **PARKING:** 11 **NOTES:** Closed 21 Dec-2 Jan

CARDS:

continued

♦♦♦♦ Wood Hall

Little Waldingfield CO10 0SY ☎ 01787 247362 🖷 01787 248326

e-mail: susan@woodhallbnb.fsnet.co.uk

Dir: *turn off A1141 onto B1115 into Little Waldingfield, pass Swan PH on left. Wood Hall is approx. 200yds on left, parking at rear*

Expect a warm welcome from the caring host at this delightful 15th century Suffolk hall that is situated just a short drive from the historic town of Lavenham. The spacious, individually decorated bedrooms are tastefully furnished and thoughtfully equipped with many useful extras. Breakfast is taken at a large communal table in the elegant dining room, which features a superb inglenook fireplace with a wood burning stove.

FACILITIES: 2 en suite No smoking TVB tea/coffee No dogs (ex guide dogs) Cen ht No children 10yrs No coaches Croquet lawn Dinner Last d 48 hr before meal **PRICES:** s £30-£70; d £60-£70✳ **PARKING:** 4 **NOTES:** Closed 21 Dec-2 Jan

♦♦♦♦ A Anchor House

Prentice St CO10 9RD ☎ 01787 249018 🖷 01787 249018

e-mail: Suewade1@aol.com

Dir: *B1115 from Sudbury to Lavenham. After Swan Hotel take next right into Market Lane. Straight across Market Place into Prentice Street. Establishment is last on right*

FACILITIES: 1 annexe en suite No smoking TVB No dogs Cen ht TVL No coaches **PRICES:** d £65-£70✳

LEISTON Map 05 TM46

♦♦♦♦ Field End

1 Kings Rd IP16 4DA ☎ 01728 833527 🖷 01728 833527

e-mail: pwright@fieldend-guesthouse.co.uk

Dir: *A12/A1094, turn left after 3m onto B1069. After Leiston town sign turn right at Aldeburgh/Leisure Centre sign, last house on right*

Large detached Edwardian house refurbished to a high standard by the present owners. Ideally placed for visiting the Suffolk coastline and close to several RSPB reserves. Bedrooms are tastefully decorated, have well co-ordinated soft furnishings and many thoughtful touches. Breakfast is taken in the attractive dining room, which has a large sofa as well as a range of puzzles and games.

FACILITIES: 5 en suite (1 fmly) No smoking TVB tea/coffee No dogs (ex guide dogs) Cen ht No children 6mths No coaches **PRICES:** s £30-£37; d £50-£60✳ **PARKING:** 5

England

LOWESTOFT Map 05 TM59

Premier Collection

♦♦♦♦♦ *Abbè House Hotel*
322 London Rd South NR33 0BG ☎ 01502 581083
01502 514327
e-mail: abbehouseh@hotmail.com
Dir: *on A12 (London rd) northbound - Hotel on right. Approx 1.5m from town outskirts*
Expect a warm, friendly welcome, as well as tea and home made cake from the caring hosts at this small, family-run hotel. Bedrooms vary in size and style, and are tastefully decorated and well-equipped. There is an attractive lounge with a small bar and a smart dining room. An excellent choice is offered at breakfast, including lots of local produce.
FACILITIES: 3 rms (2 en suite) No smoking TVB tea/coffee No dogs (ex guide dogs) Licensed Cen ht TVL No children No coaches
PARKING: 1

♦♦♦♦ Albany Hotel
400 London Rd South NR33 0BQ ☎ 01502 574394
01502 581198
e-mail: geoffrey.ward@btclick.com
Dir: *on A12 to Lowestoft from S. Hotel on right just after entering one-way system from Pakefield*

Expect a warm welcome at this delightful hotel, which is close to the beach and town centre. The individually decorated bedrooms are furnished with well-chosen pieces and equipped with many thoughtful extras. Public rooms feature a tastefully appointed lounge with a corner bar. Breakfast is served at individual tables in the smart dining room.
FACILITIES: 8 rms (6 en suite) (3 fmly) No smoking in bedrooms No smoking in dining room TVB tea/coffee Licensed Cen ht TVL No coaches Dinner Last d 2pm **PRICES:** s £21.50-£27.50; d £44-£56✱ **LB**
PARKING: 1 **CARDS:**

♦♦♦♦ Kingsleigh
44 Marine Pde NR33 0QN ☎ 01502 572513
Dir: *on A12 southbound from Lowestoft town centre. House on right, approx 0.25m from Harbour Bridge*
Expect a friendly welcome at this delightful Victorian property which is situated on the south side of town just a short walk from the shops. The bedrooms are attractively decorated in pastel shades, have co-ordinated soft furnishings and many thoughtful touches, most rooms have superb sea views.
FACILITIES: 5 rms (3 en suite) No smoking TVB tea/coffee Cen ht
PRICES: s £20-£25; d £40-£45✱

♦♦♦♦ *Longshore*
7 Wellington Esplanade NR33 0QQ ☎ 01502 565037
01502 582032
e-mail: longshore@7wellington.fsnet.co.uk
Dir: *on A12 going south overlooking sea*
Grade II listed building situated on the south side of town overlooking the award winning beach and sea beyond. Bedrooms come in a variety of sizes, all are pleasantly decorated and equipped with modern facilities, and some have lovely sea views. Breakfast is served at individual tables in the smart dining room.
FACILITIES: 6 en suite (1 fmly) No smoking in dining room No smoking in lounges TVB tea/coffee Cen ht No coaches **PARKING:** 5 **NOTES:** Closed 20 Dec-1 Jan **CARDS:**

♦♦♦ Hotel Katherine
49 Kirkley Cliff Rd NR33 0DF ☎ 01502 567858
01502 581341
e-mail: beauthaikatherine@amserve.net
Dir: *situated on seafront, opposite Kensington Garden*
Charming privately owned hotel situated close to the beach at the southern end of town overlooking Kensington Gardens. Public areas feature a cosy lounge bar and the Beau Thai Restaurant where freshly prepared traditional Thai cuisine is available for dinner. The spacious bedrooms are attractively decorated, tastefully furnished and thoughtfully equipped.
FACILITIES: 10 en suite (5 fmly) No smoking in 4 bedrooms No smoking in area of dining room No smoking in 1 lounge TVB tea/coffee Direct dial from bedrooms Licensed Cen ht TVL Dinner Last d 10pm **PRICES:** s £35-£45; d £55-£60✱ **LB PARKING:** 3 **CARDS:**

♦♦♦ Coventry House
8 Kirkley Cliff NR33 0BY ☎ 01502 573865
Dir: *0.25m from harbour bridge on s'bound A12 (sea front). On R-hand side opp Claremont pier*
A warm welcome is offered at this impressive Victorian terrace house, which is ideally situated overlooking the pier and seafront. Bedrooms are pleasantly decorated, comfortably furnished and well-equipped; many rooms have superb sea views. Breakfast and dinner is served in the tastefully furnished dining room. Guests also have the use of a comfortable lounge.
FACILITIES: 7 rms (5 en suite) (3 fmly) (1 GF) No smoking in 3 bedrooms No smoking in dining room TVB tea/coffee Cen ht TVL No coaches Dinner Last d breakfast **PRICES:** s £20-£26; d £42-£45✱ **LB**
PARKING: 4 **NOTES:** Closed Xmas

♦♦♦ Edingworth
395/7 London Rd South NR33 0BJ ☎ 01502 572051
01502 572051
Dir: *on the left side of the A12 thro' Lowestoft towards Great Yarmouth*
Friendly, family run guest house situated within easy walking distance of the town centre and seafront. Bedrooms are generally quite spacious and thoughtfully equipped with modern facilities. Breakfast is taken at individual tables in the dining room and guests have the use of a comfortable TV lounge. Dinner is available by prior arrangement.
FACILITIES: 10 en suite (9 fmly) (1 GF) No smoking in dining room TVB tea/coffee No dogs (ex guide dogs) Cen ht TVL Dinner Last d noon
PRICES: s £20-£22; d £40-£42✱ **LB PARKING:** 4
NOTES: Closed 24-26 Dec

England

LOWESTOFT continued

♦♦♦ Fairways

398 London Rd South NR33 0BQ ☎ 01502 572659
e-mail: amontali@netmatters.co.uk
Dir: *S of town centre on A12, 1m from railway and bus station*

Expect a friendly welcome at this family run guest house situated at the southern end of town. Bedrooms come in a variety of sizes and styles; each one is pleasantly decorated and well equipped. Breakfast is served at individual tables in the dining room and guests also have the use of a cosy lounge.

FACILITIES: 7 rms (4 en suite) (2 fmly) No smoking in bedrooms No smoking in dining room TVB tea/coffee Licensed Cen ht TVL **PRICES:** s £18-£25; d £38-£40✻ **BB PARKING:** 2 **CARDS:**

♦♦♦ Seavilla Hotel

43 Kirkley Cliff Rd NR33 0DF ☎ 01502 574657
01502 574657
Dir: *A12 into town, right at South Beach, 300yds past Clarment Pier*

Friendly, privately owned hotel situated on the southern side of town, overlooking the beach and sea beyond. The smartly decorated, well-maintained bedrooms are equipped with many useful extras; some rooms have superb sea views. Breakfast is served at individual tables in the attractive dining room and guests also have the use of a cosy lounge bar.

FACILITIES: 9 rms (5 en suite) No smoking in bedrooms No smoking in dining room No smoking in 1 lounge TVB tea/coffee No dogs Licensed Cen ht TVL No coaches Dinner Last d before lunch **PRICES:** s £20-£35; d £40-£50✻ **LB PARKING:** 3 **CARDS:**

♦♦♦ Somerton House

7 Kirkley Cliff NR33 0BY ☎ 01502 565665 01502 501176
e-mail: hotel@somerton.screaming.net
Dir: *On A12 southbound on seafront 100yds from Claremont pier*

Victorian Grade II listed terraced house situated at the quieter end of town overlooking the sea. Bedrooms are pleasantly decorated and attractively furnished in a period style, some rooms have four poster or half tester beds. Guests have the use of a comfortably furnished lounge bar and meals are served in the smart dining room.

FACILITIES: 6 en suite (1 fmly) (1 GF) No smoking in 2 bedrooms No smoking in dining room STV TVB tea/coffee Licensed Cen ht TVL No coaches Dinner Last d 12pm **PRICES:** s £30; d £45✻ **LB CARDS:**

♦♦♦ Wavecrest

31 Marine Pde NR33 0QN ☎ 01502 561268 01502 512287
e-mail: sue@wave-crest.freeserve.co.uk
Dir: *Located on Southbound A12 just S of Lowestoft Bridge*

This Victorian terrace property is situated within easy walking distance of the town centre and overlooks the award-winning beach. The bedrooms are smartly decorated, each with co-ordinated soft furnishings and modern facilities. Public areas feature an elegant dining room where breakfast is served at individual tables. *continued*

FACILITIES: 4 en suite (2 fmly) No smoking in 2 bedrooms No smoking in dining room No smoking in lounges TVB tea/coffee No dogs (ex guide dogs) Cen ht No coaches **PRICES:** s £22-£27; d £40-£50✻ **PARKING:** 2 **NOTES:** Closed 24-31 Dec **CARDS:**

MENDHAM Map 05 TM28

♦♦♦♦ Weston House *(TM292828)*

IP20 0PB ☎ 01986 782206 01986 782414 Mrs J E Holden
e-mail: holden@farmline.com
Dir: *from A143 or B1123 follow signs for Mendham then follow signs from centre of village*

An attractive 17th-century farmhouse situated in the heart of the Waveny valley amidst 300 acres of open farmland. The individually decorated bedrooms are generally quite spacious, thoughtfully furnished and well equipped. Breakfast is served in the dining room which overlooks the garden. Dinner is available by prior arrangement.

FACILITIES: 3 en suite (1 GF) No smoking TVB tea/coffee No dogs (ex guide dogs) Cen ht TVL 600 acres Mixed Dinner Last d 2pm **PRICES:** s £25-£30; d £40-£50✻ **PARKING:** 6 **NOTES:** Closed Dec-Feb **CARDS:**

NAYLAND Map 05 TL93

♦♦♦♦ White Hart Inn

High St CO6 4JF ☎ 01206 263382 01206 263638
e-mail: nayhart@aol.com
Dir: *M25 junct 28 to A12 then onto A133 to Colchester centre. At rdbt take A134 to Nayland*

A warm welcome is assured at this delightful 15th century coaching inn which is situated in the heart of this charming village, surrounded by colourwashed timber framed houses. The individually decorated bedrooms are tastefully furnished and have many thoughtful touches. An interesting menu featuring quality local produce is served in the smart restaurant and guests also have the use of a small lounge.

FACILITIES: 6 en suite No smoking in bedrooms TVB tea/coffee Direct dial from bedrooms No dogs (ex guide dogs) Cen ht Dinner Last d 9pm **PRICES:** s £69; d £82✻ **MEALS:** Lunch £9.95-£12.95&alc Dinner £17.50-£21.50&alc✻ **PARKING:** 20 **NOTES:** Closed 26 Dec-9 Jan rs Mon Civ Wed 70 **CARDS:**

♦♦♦♦ Hill House

Gravel Hill CO6 4JB ☎ 01206 262782
e-mail: heigham.hillhouse@rdplus.net
Dir: *enter village from A134 into Bear St, continue past T-junct into Birch St, Gravel Hill is 100yds on left. Hill House 50yds on right*

Set in secluded grounds, in a peaceful location on the edge of Constable country, this 16th-century, Grade II listed, timber-framed building has a wealth exposed beams, a flagstone hall and inglenooks. The tasteful bedrooms are well equipped and overlook the pretty garden. Breakfast is served around a large communal table in the attractive beamed dining room.

FACILITIES: 2 en suite (1 fmly) No smoking TVB tea/coffee No dogs Cen ht No children 12yrs No coaches **PRICES:** s £28-£30; d £48-£52✻ **LB PARKING:** 4 **NOTES:** Closed 20 Dec-1 Jan

♦♦♦♦ Gladwins Farm

Harper's Hill CO6 4NU ☎ 01206 262261 01206 263001
e-mail: gladwinsfarm@compuserve.com
Dir: *on A134 between Colchester/Sudbury, N of Nayland on left at top of hill*

FACILITIES: 3 rms (2 en suite) No smoking TV2B tea/coffee Direct dial from bedrooms No dogs Cen ht TVL No children 8yrs No coaches Indoor swimming pool (heated) Tennis (hard) Fishing Sauna Croquet lawn Dinner Last d 6.30pm **PRICES:** s £23.30-£25; d £58.30-£60✻ **LB**

continued

PARKING: 17 **NOTES:** Closed Xmas & New Year **CARDS:**

NEEDHAM MARKET — Map 05 TM05

♦♦♦♦ Pipps Ford *(TM109537)*

Norwich Rd rdbt IP6 8LJ ☎ 01449 760208 📠 01449 760561
Mrs Hackett-Jones
e-mail: b&b@pippsford.co.uk
Dir: *entrance off rdbt junct A14/A140*

Charming 16th-century farmhouse set amidst its own attractive grounds and surrounded by meadowland. Bedrooms come in a variety of styles, traditional with antique furnishings in the main house and brighter rooms with pine pieces in the converted barn. Breakfast is served in the stylish dining room or conservatory; dinner is available by prior arrangement.

FACILITIES: 3 en suite 4 annexe en suite (4 GF) No smoking in bedrooms No smoking in dining room No smoking in 1 lounge tea/coffee No dogs (ex guide dogs) Licensed Cen ht TVL No children 5yrs Fishing 8 acres non-working Dinner Last d 5pm **PRICES:** d £65-£75* **LB CONF:** Thtr 35 Board 20 Del £90 * **PARKING:** 20 **NOTES:** Closed 21 Dec-5 Jan **CARDS:**

NEWMARKET — Map 05 TL66

See also Kirtling (Cambridgeshire)

♦♦♦♦ Birdcage Walk

2 Birdcage Walk CB8 0NE ☎ 01638 669456 📠 01638 669456
Dir: *from A14 drive into Newmarket town Establishment is on slip road adjacent to A1303 Newmarket to Cambridge rd.*

A warm welcome awaits guests at this delightful house located close to the racecourse and only minutes' walk from the town centre. Bedrooms and bathrooms are smartly appointed and thoughtfully equipped with a host of thoughtful extra touches. A hearty breakfast is served in the elegant dining room, overlooking the well-tended garden.

FACILITIES: 2 en suite No smoking TVB tea/coffee No dogs Cen ht No children 12yrs **PRICES:** s fr £35; d fr £55* **PARKING:** 5

SAXMUNDHAM — Map 05 TM36

♦♦♦♦♦ A Church Farm

Yoxford Rd, Sibton IP17 2LX ☎ 01728 660101
📠 01728 660102
e-mail: dixons@church-farmhouse.demon.co.uk
Dir: *from A12 at Yoxford onto A1120. Church Farm is located on the left after the Sibton Green sign).*

FACILITIES: 3 en suite No smoking TVB tea/coffee No dogs Cen ht TVL No children 6 yrs No coaches **PRICES:** s £33-£40; d £55-£65*
PARKING: 4 **NOTES:** Closed 24-28 Dec

> **A** indicates an Associate entry, which has been inspected and rated by the ETC or the RAC in England.

SHIMPLING — Map 05 TL85

♦♦♦♦ Gannocks House

Old Rectory Ln IP29 4HG ☎ 01284 830499 📠 01284 830191
e-mail: gannocks-house@lineone.net
Dir: *from A14 exit for Sudbury A134, just before Long Melford at Bridge St turn right at Rose & Crown, continue up hill turn right into Aveley Lane for 2m. B & B sign on white iron bridge, into Old Rectory Ln*

Detached Victorian house situated amidst lovely landscaped gardens with superb views across open farmland. The property is ideally placed for touring the Suffolk countryside. The spacious bedrooms are pleasantly decorated, tastefully furnished and thoughtfully equipped. Public rooms include a smart breakfast room and a sunny conservatory.

FACILITIES: 3 en suite (2 fmly) No smoking TVB tea/coffee No dogs Cen ht No children 8yrs No coaches **PRICES:** s £30-£45; d £45-£55* **LB PARKING:** 5 **CARDS:**

STOKE-BY-NAYLAND — Map 05 TL93

♦♦♦♦ The Angel Inn

Polstead St CO6 4SA ☎ 01206 263245 📠 01206 263373
Dir: *off A12 midway between Colchester and Ipswich onto B1068*

This charming inn is well known for its food and has been welcoming guests since the 16th century. The property has been carefully restored and retains much of its original character. The attractively decorated bedrooms are equipped with many useful extras and offer a good degree of comfort throughout.

FACILITIES: 5 en suite 1 annexe en suite No smoking in bedrooms No smoking in area of dining room TVB tea/coffee Direct dial from bedrooms No dogs (ex guide dogs) Cen ht No children 8yrs No coaches Dinner Last d 9pm **PRICES:** s fr £54.50; d fr £69.50* **MEALS:** Lunch £14-£21.35alc Dinner £14-£24.65alc* **PARKING:** 25 **NOTES:** Closed 25-26 Dec & 1 Jan **CARDS:**

SUDBURY — Map 05 TL84

♦♦♦♦ A The Plough

Gages Rd CO10 7BT ☎ 01787 278882
e-mail: info@theplough-belchamp.co.uk
Dir: *from centre of Clare take A1092 towards Haverhill. Turn left signed The Belchamps, past priory, then 1st left to Belchamp St. Paul. Past Half Moon Pub and Plough 300mtrs on left*

FACILITIES: 2 rms (1 en suite) 1 annexe en suite No smoking TVB tea/coffee No dogs (ex guide dogs) Cen ht No children 6yrs No coaches **PRICES:** s £28-£35; d £45-£50* **LB PARKING:** 6

♦♦♦ *Old Bull Hotel & Restaurant*

Church St CO10 2BL ☎ 01787 374120 📠 01787 379044
Dir: *on A131 Halstead Rd. 0.25m from town centre*

Charming 16th-century coaching inn situated just a short walk from the town centre. The property has recently been refurbished by the current owners and now offers attractively appointed accommodation throughout. Public rooms include a cosy residents' lounge with plush furnishings and a small bar leading through to a smart bistro style restaurant. Bedrooms are pleasantly decorated and equipped with many thoughtful extras.

FACILITIES: 7 en suite 3 annexe en suite (4 fmly) No smoking in 3 bedrooms No smoking in dining room No smoking in 1 lounge TVB tea/coffee Direct dial from bedrooms Licensed Cen ht TVL No coaches Jacuzzi Dinner Last d 8.45pm **PARKING:** 15 **CARDS:**

England

WHEPSTEAD Map 05 TL85

♦♦♦♦ Folly House Bed & Breakfast

Folly Ln IP29 4TJ ☎ 01284 735207 🖷 01284 735207
e-mail: lowerlinda@hotmail.com
Dir: *B1066 turn left after post office into Rectory Rd in 1.5m at T junct turn right, turn into Folly Lane*

The original house dates back to the 1830s, when it was an alehouse. It has been extended in recent times to provide tastefully appointed, good quality accommodation. The house is quietly situated in a rural area and stands in its own extensive grounds and gardens. Facilities include an elegant dining room where all share one table, a bright conservatory lounge and an indoor swimming pool.

FACILITIES: 3 rms (1 en suite) (1 fmly) No smoking TVB tea/coffee No dogs (ex guide dogs) Cen ht TVL No coaches Indoor swimming pool (heated) Croquet lawn Dinner Last d 9am **PRICES:** s £25-£35; d £40-£48✳ **PARKING:** 10

WOODBRIDGE Map 05 TM24

♦♦♦ *Grove House*

39 Grove Rd IP12 4LG ☎ 01394 382202 🖷 01394 380652
e-mail: reception@grovehousehotel.com
Dir: *on A12, 400yds beyond junct with B1079*

A warm welcome is offered at this small, privately owned guest house. Bedrooms are tastefully furnished and thoughtfully equipped. Breakfast is served at individual tables in the smart dining room. Guests also have the use of a small lounge with an honesty bar. Dinner is available by prior arrangement.

FACILITIES: 11 en suite (1 fmly) No smoking in 4 bedrooms No smoking in dining room TVB tea/coffee Licensed Cen ht TVL No coaches Dinner Last d 7.30pm **PARKING:** 14 **CARDS:**

SURREY

ALBURY Map 04 TQ04

♦♦♦ Drummond Arms

The Street GU5 9AG ☎ 01483 202039 🖷 01483 205361
Dir: *off A25 between Guildford & Dorking, take A248 signed Albury, Godalming. Establishment 1m on right*

The old inn is centrally located in this picturesque village, with attractive gardens running down to a small river at the rear of the property. Well appointed and comfortable bedrooms all with en suite facilities are a strength, while the separate restaurant offers a set-priced menu; a good selection of traditional pub food is also available in the popular bar.

continued

FACILITIES: 7 en suite 4 annexe en suite (1 fmly) No smoking in area of dining room TVB tea/coffee Direct dial from bedrooms No dogs (ex guide dogs) Cen ht No children 14yrs No coaches Sauna & spa bath in one room Dinner Last d 9.30pm **PRICES:** s £50-£65; d £65-£80✳ **MEALS:** Lunch £12.50-£25alc Dinner £12.50-£25alc✳ **PARKING:** 70 **CARDS:**

See advert on opposite page

CHARLWOOD

See Gatwick Airport (Sussex, West)

ELSTEAD Map 04 SU94

♦♦♦♦ The White House

Thursley Rd GU8 6LW ☎ 01252 702272 702747
🖷 01252 702747
e-mail: johnhn@globalnet.co.uk
Dir: *from A3, take B3001 to Elstead. At village green, fork left - signed Churt, follow road for 1m. After 40mph sign house short distance on left*

A warm welcome awaits at the White House, set in this village just a few miles from Farnham and Godalming. There is an elegant comfortable lounge for guests' use and the traditional breakfast is made with quality local produce. Bedrooms are comfortably furnished with many thoughtful touches included, such as bath robes, mineral water and biscuits.

FACILITIES: 4 rms No smoking tea/coffee No dogs (ex guide dogs) Cen ht TVL No children 10yrs No coaches **PRICES:** s £22.50-£25; d £45-£50✳ **PARKING:** 8 **NOTES:** Closed 25 Dec

EPSOM Map 04 TQ26

♦♦♦♦ *The White House*

Downs Hill Rd KT18 5HW ☎ 01372 722472 🖷 01372 744447
e-mail: hopkins.epsom@virgin.net
Dir: *0.25m from A24*

This substantial Edwardian house has undergone an almost complete refurbishment. Bedrooms have been fitted out, with new beds, carpets and pine dressing tables in most. There is a spacious bar/dining room with parquet floor where both dinner and breakfast are served. Ample parking is available.

FACILITIES: 15 rms (7 en suite) (1 fmly) No smoking in area of dining room TVB tea/coffee Direct dial from bedrooms No dogs (ex guide dogs) Licensed Cen ht TVL Dinner Last d 8.30pm **PARKING:** 15 **CARDS:**

See advertisement on opposite page

♦♦♦ Epsom Downs Hotel

9 Longdown Rd KT17 3PT ☎ 01372 740643 🖷 01372 723259
e-mail: e.d.h@dial.pipex.com
Dir: *M25 junct 9, at rdbt take A243 to BP Garage on right, turn right at lights, and cont into rd signed Upper High St for 1.5m, then 4th left*

This small hotel is located in a quiet residential area, not far from the famous racecourse. Public rooms include a comfortable bar, restaurant, and a leather-furnished lounge area by the reception desk. Bedrooms are all en suite with good facilities.

FACILITIES: 13 en suite (1 GF) No smoking in bedrooms No smoking in dining room No smoking in lounges TVB tea/coffee Direct dial from bedrooms No dogs (ex guide dogs) Licensed Cen ht TVL Dinner Last d 9pm **PRICES:** s £65-£85; d £75-£95✳ **PARKING:** 11 **NOTES:** Closed 20 Dec-4 Jan **CARDS:**

England

EWELL Map 04 TQ26

♦♦♦ Nonsuch Park Hotel

355/357 London Rd KT17 2DE ☎ 020 8393 0771
020 8393 1415
e-mail: nonsuch@tinyworld.co.uk
Dir: *M25 junc 10 onto A3. Tolworth r/about onto A240, down to lights, turn left onto A24, London Rd*

Conveniently located on the A24 this hotel provides comfortable accommodation. The bedrooms are attractively decorated with good facilities. Public areas include a small bar area, a dining room and a lounge and patio area. Evening meals are served and some car parking is provided.

FACILITIES: 11 rms (7 en suite) (2 fmly) (4 GF) No smoking in 4 bedrooms No smoking in dining room TVB tea/coffee Direct dial from bedrooms No dogs (ex guide dogs) Licensed Cen ht TVL Dinner Last d 8.30pm **PRICES:** s £55-£75; d £69.50-£85✳ **PARKING:** 11 **NOTES:** Closed 2-3 wks Xmas
CARDS:

FARNHAM Map 04 SU84

♦♦♦ Sandiway

24 Shortheath Rd GU9 8SR ☎ 01252 710721 01252 710721
e-mail: john@shortheath.freeserve.co.uk
Dir: *take A287 Hindhead. At top of hill traffic lights turn right into Ridgway Rd, past green on left. Sandiway is 300yds on the right*

In a quiet residential area, this property has the added benefit of being close to the centre of Farnham. The bedrooms are nicely presented with comfortable furnishings and good facilities.

FACILITIES: 3 rms No smoking tea/coffee No dogs (ex guide dogs) Cen ht TVL No coaches **PRICES:** s £22.50-£25; d £40-£45✳
PARKING: 3 **NOTES:** Closed Xmas/New Year

England

GUILDFORD Map 04 SU94

See also advert on page 385

♦♦♦ Blanes Court Hotel

Albury Rd GU1 2BT ☎ 01483 573171 01483 532780
e-mail: reservations@blanes.demon.co.uk

Dir: *exit A3 signposted Burpham, cross 4 rdbts at 5th rdbt take 1st exit. At traffic light turn right to town centre, after 0.5km turn left into Albury rd, Establishment half way*

This large Edwardian house is located in a quiet residential area, close to the town centre. Bedrooms vary in shape and size, each is individually decorated and all offer a useful range of in-room facilities. Public areas include a small seating area with a bar and a light and airy conservatory overlooking the attractive back garden.

FACILITIES: 18 rms (15 en suite) (3 fmly) (4 GF) No smoking in dining room No smoking in lounges TVB tea/coffee No dogs (ex guide dogs) Licensed Cen ht No coaches Small heated outdoor pool **PRICES:** s £45-£58; d £78-£84✳ **LB PARKING:** 22 **NOTES:** Closed 1wk Xmas **CARDS:**

HASLEMERE Map 04 SU93

♦♦♦ Wheatsheaf

Grayswood Rd, Grayswood GU27 2DE ☎ 01428 644440
01428 641285
e-mail: thewheatsheaf@hotmail.com

Dir: *turn off A3 at Milford Junction, follow signs A286 Haslemere. Proceed for 7 miles, inn in Grayswood Village opposite Rover Dealer*

Conveniently situated just outside of Haslemere in the small village of Grayswood, this well presented inn has a warm and friendly atmosphere. A smart conservatory restaurant is a recent addition, and complements the attractive dining area and informal bar, which is a popular meeting place. Bedrooms are similar in style and all furnished to a good standard.

FACILITIES: 7 en suite No smoking in bedrooms No smoking in dining room TVB tea/coffee Direct dial from bedrooms Cen ht No coaches Dinner Last d 9.45pm **PRICES:** s £55; d £75✳ **PARKING:** 21
CARDS:

HORLEY

See Gatwick Airport (Sussex, West)

LIGHTWATER Map 04 SU96

♦♦♦♦ Carlton

63-65 Macdonald Rd GU18 5XY ☎ 01276 473580
01276 453595
e-mail: carltongh@aol.com

Dir: *M3 junct 3, S on A322, after 300yds filter right into Guildford Rd. After 500yds, next to newsagent right into MacDonald Rd*

FACILITIES: 13 rms (9 en suite) (5 GF) No smoking TVB tea/coffee Direct dial from bedrooms No dogs Licensed Lift Cen ht TVL No children No coaches **PRICES:** s £40-£50; d £50-£60✳ **PARKING:** 15
CARDS:

REDHILL Map 04 TQ25

♦♦♦♦ Ashleigh House Hotel

39 Redstone Hill RH1 4BG ☎ 01737 764763 01737 780308

Dir: *on A25 Redhill to Sevenoaks, 500yds from Redhill railway station*

An attractive and well-established guest house conveniently located for the mainline railway station and town centre shops. Bedrooms are tastefully furnished and decorated, featuring a good range of modern facilities. The breakfast room overlooks the well-tended gardens.

continued

FACILITIES: 8 rms (6 en suite) (2 fmly) No smoking TVB tea/coffee No dogs (ex guide dogs) Cen ht No coaches **PRICES:** s £40-£55; d £56-£60✳ **PARKING:** 9 **NOTES:** Closed Xmas **CARDS:**

See advertisement on page 385

♦♦♦ Hillside Cottage *(TQ313498)*

Coopers Hill Rd, Nutfield RH1 4HX ☎ 01737 822916
01737 822916 Mr J Bader
e-mail: jurgen@hillsidecott.co.uk

Dir: *off A25 between Redhill & Godstone. Turn into Coopers Hill Rd at Crown public house. Cottage 0.5m on left. Close to Gatwick Airport*

This charming farmhouse in its peaceful setting is surprisingly convenient for Gatwick Airport and has easy access to main road networks. Bedrooms have a homely feel and are individually decorated. At breakfast guests share one large table to enjoy an extensive continental breakfast. During the summer guests can relax in the colourful garden.

FACILITIES: 3 rms No smoking TVB tea/coffee No dogs (ex guide dogs) Cen ht 5 acres non-working **PRICES:** s £30-£36; d £45-£50✳
PARKING: 4

♦♦♦ Lynwood House

50 London Rd RH1 1LN ☎ 01737 766894 & 762804
01737 778253
e-mail: lynwoodguesthouse@yahoo.co.uk

Dir: *500yds from railway station, adjacent to memorial park*

A large, friendly Victorian house located close to the town centre and railway station. Bedrooms are spacious and provide comfortable accommodation either en suite or with in-room showers.

FACILITIES: 9 rms (4 fmly) No smoking in 4 bedrooms No smoking in dining room No smoking in lounges TVB tea/coffee No dogs Cen ht TVL **PRICES:** s £32-£35; d £52-£55✳ **PARKING:** 8 **NOTES:** Closed 24 Dec-2 Jan **CARDS:**

RICHMOND UPON THAMES Map 04 TQ17

♦♦♦ Hobart Hall Hotel

43-47 Petersham Rd TW10 6UL ☎ 020 8940 0435
020 8332 2996
e-mail: hobarthall@aol.com

Dir: *on A307, 200yds from Richmond Bridge*

Originally built around 1690, this friendly hotel is on the banks of the Thames, close to Richmond Bridge. Many of the spacious bedrooms have views of the river and public areas include an impressive reception, comfortable lounge and attractive breakfast room. There is also a fine meeting room which can accommodate up to 60 people and overlooks the river.

FACILITIES: 33 rms (21 en suite) (4 fmly) (2 GF) No smoking in bedrooms No smoking in dining room TVB tea/coffee Direct dial from bedrooms No dogs Cen ht TVL **PRICES:** s £65; d £90✳ **PARKING:** 14
CARDS:

England

SUSSEX, EAST

ARLINGTON — Map 05 TQ50

Premier Collection

♦♦♦♦♦ Bates Green *(TQ553077)*
BN26 6SH ☎ 01323 482039 01323 482039
Mrs C McCutchan
e-mail: batesgreen@nlconnect.co.uk
Dir: *2m W of A22 towards Arlington turn right Old Oak Inn*

Expect a warm welcome at this restored 18th-century gamekeeper's cottage. The property is set amid two acres of attractive landscaped grounds in a peaceful rural location. Individually decorated bedrooms are tastefully furnished and have many thoughtful extras, such as local mineral water. Public rooms feature a comfortable lounge and a cosy dining room.
FACILITIES: 3 en suite No smoking TVB tea/coffee No dogs Cen ht No children 12yrs Tennis (hard) 130 acres sheep **PRICES:** d £65-£70* **PARKING:** 3 **NOTES:** Closed 22-27 Dec

BATTLE — Map 05 TQ71

♦♦♦♦ Fox Hole Farm *(TQ694166)*
Kane Hythe Rd TN33 9QU ☎ 01424 772053 01424 772053
Mr & Mrs P Collins
Dir: *off A271 onto B2096 farm 0.75m from junct on R*
18th-century woodcutter's cottage set amidst 40 acres of grounds just a short drive from the historic town of Battle. The individually decorated bedrooms are traditionally furnished and equipped with modern facilities. Breakfast is served at individual tables in the charming dining room and guests also have the use of a cosy sitting room with exposed beams and an inglenook fireplace.
FACILITIES: 3 en suite No smoking TVB tea/coffee Cen ht No children 10yrs 40 acres beef/chickens/sheep Dinner Last d 11am **PRICES:** s £33-£39; d £54-£59* **PARKING:** 6 **CARDS:**

♦♦♦♦ Farthings Farm *(TQ734149)*
Catsfield TN33 9BA ☎ 01424 773107 Mr & Mrs J Rodgers
e-mail: Penny.Rodgers@btopenworld.com
Dir: *from Battle on A271. Turn left onto B2204 towards Catsfield for 1m. Farm on left of sharp S-bend & farmhouse 0.5m down farm lane*
Superbly located in seventy acres of unspoilt countryside, this Edwardian farmhouse retains many original features. The sympathetically renovated guest wing comprises a thoughtfully furnished bedroom and private comfortable lounge, and you can eat breakfast on the patio during the warmer months.
FACILITIES: 1 en suite No smoking tea/coffee No dogs Cen ht TVL No children 70 acres cows/dairy Dinner Last d 24 hrs notice **PRICES:** s £30; d £50-£55* **PARKING:** 1

BEXHILL — Map 05 TQ70

♦♦♦♦ The Arosa
6 Albert Rd TN40 1DG ☎ 01424 212574 & 0800 748041
01424 212574
Dir: *from seafront turn N onto Devonshire Rd, 1st left, 1st left onto Albert Rd, premises on right*

A warm welcome is assured at this well maintained house, located within the Edwardian Conservation Area close to seafront and shops. Bedrooms are equipped with lots of thoughtful extras and complimented by modern efficient bathrooms. A comfortable guest lounge is available in addition to an attractive dining room, the setting for memorable breakfasts and dinners by arrangement.
FACILITIES: 9 rms (6 en suite) (3 fmly) No smoking in 2 bedrooms No smoking in dining room TVB tea/coffee Direct dial from bedrooms No dogs (ex guide dogs) Cen ht TVL No coaches Dinner Last d 5.30pm
CARDS:

♦♦♦ Park Lodge
16 Egerton Rd TN39 3HH ☎ 01424 216547 & 215041
01424 217460
Dir: *from A259 coast road, follow signs for town cntr and De La Warr Pavillion. Hotel is 100mts W of De La Warr Pavillion in Egerton Road*
FACILITIES: 10 rms (8 en suite) (2 fmly) (2 GF) No smoking in bedrooms No smoking in dining room TVB tea/coffee Direct dial from bedrooms Licensed Cen ht TVL Dinner Last d noon **PRICES:** s £21-£33; d £44-£48S **LB** **PARKING:** 5 **CARDS:**

BRIGHTON & HOVE — Map 04 TQ30

♦♦♦♦ Adelaide Hotel
51 Regency Square BN1 2FF ☎ 01273 205286 01273 220904
e-mail: adelaide@pavilion.co.uk
Dir: *on seafront square opposite West Pier (The Circle)*
This attractive, well-kept Grade II listed Regency house is located in a quiet garden square just off the seafront and close to the town centre. Bedrooms are individually decorated and feature a good range of useful extras. Guests have the use of an elegant period-style lounge, and breakfast is taken in the cheerful downstairs dining room.
FACILITIES: 12 en suite (1 fmly) No smoking in dining room TVB tea/coffee Direct dial from bedrooms No dogs Licensed Cen ht No children 12yrs No coaches **PRICES:** s £35-£45; d £70-£92* **LB** **NOTES:** Closed 25 & 26 Dec
CARDS:

Prices may change during the currency of the Guide, please check when booking.

BRIGHTON & HOVE continued

♦♦♦♦ Ainsley House Hotel

28 New Steine BN2 1PD ☎ 01273 605310 01273 688604
e-mail: ahhotel@fastnet.co.uk

Rooms have been pleasantly furnished and have extras such as sweets and bottled water. A good choice of breakfast is offered in the spacious dining room, overlooking New Steine square. Guests can also take advantage of a comfortable lounge. The resident proprietors are happy to advise guests on where to dine in the area.
FACILITIES: 11 rms (8 en suite) (3 fmly) No smoking in 3 bedrooms No smoking in dining room TVB tea/coffee Direct dial from bedrooms No dogs (ex guide dogs) Cen ht TVL No children 8 yrs **PRICES:** s £25-£34; d £46-£80✻ **LB NOTES:** Closed 24-27 Dec **CARDS:**

♦♦♦♦ Ambassador Hotel

22-23 New Steine, Marine Pde BN2 1PD ☎ 01273 676869
01273 689988
e-mail: ambassadorhoteluk@hotmail.com
Dir: *from M23 to Brighton. At rdbt opposite Brighton Pier, turn left into Marine Parade. New Steine is along this road on left*

This well-established property with a friendly and relaxing atmosphere is located on a seafront square. Bedrooms vary in size, and are attractively decorated, with a range of extra facilities. There is a small lounge, separate bar and a spacious, bright dining room.
FACILITIES: 21 en suite (8 fmly) No smoking in 7 bedrooms No smoking in dining room No smoking in lounges TVB tea/coffee Direct dial from bedrooms No dogs (ex guide dogs) Licensed Cen ht TVL **PRICES:** s £28-£40; d £60-£80✻ **LB CARDS:**

See adverisement on opposite page

♦♦♦♦ Amblecliff Hotel

35 Upper Rock Gardens BN2 1QF ☎ 01273 681161
01273 676945
e-mail: amblecliff.brighton@virgin.net
Dir: *at end of A23 opposite Palace Pier turn left along Marine Parade, left at 2nd traffic lights into Lower Rock, cross traffic lights*

continued

Amblecliff Hotel

This delightful Victorian guest house is within easy walking distance of the seafront and the town centre. Each bedroom is individually furnished and decorated to a high standard and a range of thoughtful extras are provided. A substantial and appetising breakfast is served in the well-appointed downstairs dining room.
FACILITIES: 8 en suite (3 fmly) No smoking TVB tea/coffee No dogs (ex guide dogs) Licensed Cen ht No children 4yrs No coaches
PRICES: s £35-£50; d £55-£90✻ **LB PARKING:** 5
CARDS:

♦♦♦♦ Arlanda Hotel

20 New Steine BN2 1PD ☎ 01273 699300 01273 600930
e-mail: arlanda@brighton.co.uk
Dir: *from Brighton Pier 400yds E along Marine Parade, New Steine is on left*

A Georgian townhouse, conveniently located near the seafront and town centre. The comfortable lounge boasts a pair of fine period fireplaces with ornaments adding to the homely feel. Breakfast is served in the well designed dining room, and light refreshments can be provided throughout the day.
FACILITIES: 14 en suite (4 fmly) No smoking in bedrooms No smoking in dining room TVB tea/coffee Direct dial from bedrooms No dogs (ex guide dogs) Licensed Cen ht Arrangements made for sports facilities
PRICES: s £30-£48; d £60-£120✻ **NOTES:** Closed 18 - 27 Dec
CARDS:

♦♦♦♦ Ascott House Hotel

21 New Steine, Marine Pde BN2 1PD ☎ 01273 688085
01273 623733
e-mail: welcome@ascotthousehotel.com
Dir: *from Brighton Pier E along Marine Parade for 400yds & New Steine is on left*

A warm welcome awaits all in this well-kept hotel, set just off the seafront and within easy reach of the town centre. Bedrooms vary in shape and size and are all individually designed with excellent facilities. Extra touches include light refreshments, available throughout the day. A wide choice at breakfast includes homemade pancakes, full English or vegetarian.

continued

Ascott House Hotel

FACILITIES: 12 en suite (3 fmly) No smoking in bedrooms No smoking in dining room TVB tea/coffee Direct dial from bedrooms No dogs Licensed Cen ht TVL No children 2yrs No coaches **PRICES:** s £25-£40; d £60-£120* LB **CARDS:**

♦♦♦♦ Brighton House Hotel

52 Regency Square BN1 2FF ☎ 01273 323282
e-mail: enquiries@brightonhousehotel.co.uk
Dir: *on sea front opposite West Pier*

Located in Regency Square just off the seafront, this property offers smart new bedrooms. The attractive decor and some thoughtful extras ensure guests have a comfortable stay. A substantial continental breakfast is provided and served in the spacious elegant dining room.

FACILITIES: 12 en suite (8 fmly) No smoking TVB tea/coffee No dogs (ex guide dogs) Licensed Cen ht No children 5yrs No coaches
PRICES: s £35-£85; d £50-£105* **LB CONF:** Thtr 20 Class 12 Board 18
NOTES: Closed 25 & 26 Dec **CARDS:**

♦♦♦♦ Brighton Pavilions

7 Charlotte St BN2 1AG ☎ 01273 621750 🖹 01273 622477
e-mail: sanchez-crespo@lineone.net
Dir: *take A23 to Brighton Pier, sharp left onto A259 signed Rottingdean, Charlotte St is 15th turning on left*

This well-run operation is located in one of the Regency streets minutes walk from the sea front and town centre. Bedrooms are being refurbished with elegant and stylish themes such as Titanic and Pompeii. The cosy dining room has a nautical theme and is well-appointed.

FACILITIES: 10 rms (5 en suite) No smoking TVB tea/coffee Direct dial from bedrooms Cen ht No children 2yrs No coaches **PRICES:** s £42-£45; d £72-£110* **CARDS:**

Egg cups for excellence!
This symbol shows that breakfast exceeded our Inspector's expectations.

♦♦♦♦ Hotel Pelirocco

10 Regency Square BN1 2FG ☎ 01273 327055 🖹 01273 733845
e-mail: info@hotelpelirocco.co.uk
Dir: *Off A23 right towards Hove, along sea front. Regency Square is situated at bottom of West pier.*

Situated in a prime location close to the seafront, Pelirocco provides imaginative accommodation, which tends to defy convention. All rooms are comfortable and individually themed with names such as Betty's Boudoir. In room facilities reflect the style of the rooms and all include a PlayStation. A funky bar doubles as a breakfast room and there's also a contemporary styled meeting room.

FACILITIES: 18 en suite (1 fmly) (2 GF) No smoking in 17 bedrooms No smoking in dining room No smoking in 1 lounge TVB tea/coffee Direct dial from bedrooms No dogs (ex guide dogs) Licensed Lift Cen ht TVL Spa bath in 1 bedroom, playstations in rooms **PRICES:** s £50-£55; d £85-£125*
CONF: Thtr 14 Board 9 **NOTES:** Closed 24-26 Dec & 3-7 Jan
CARDS:

♦♦♦♦ Hotel Twenty One

21 Charlotte St, Marine Pde BN2 1AG
☎ 01273 686450 & 681617 🖹 01273 695560
e-mail: the21@pavilion.co.uk
Dir: *turn off A23 onto A259 towards Newhaven, 0.5m & Charlotte St on left*

This well-established small hotel is conveniently placed for both the town centre and the seafront. Bedrooms are all individually decorated with good facilities including telephones and refrigerators. Guests can enjoy traditional breakfasts, including vegetarian options, in the bright dining room.

FACILITIES: 8 en suite No smoking in dining room No smoking in lounges TVB tea/coffee Direct dial from bedrooms No dogs Cen ht No children 12yrs
PRICES: s £30-£35; d £60-£95* **LB CARDS:**

England

BRIGHTON & HOVE continued

♦♦♦♦ New Steine Hotel

12a New Steine, Marine Pde BN2 1PB ☎ 01273 681546
🖹 01273 679118
e-mail: newsteine@hotel-brighton.fsnet.co.uk
Dir: *A27 ends opposite Brighton Pier, turn left along Marine Parade. Approx 300 yards along on the left is the New Steine*

Situated in an impressive Regency square close to the town and seafront, this hotel has much to offer. Rooms are individually decorated and comfortably furnished, and those that are en suite have good shower rooms. There is a lounge and a dining room which serves French cuisine in the evenings.
FACILITIES: 11 rms (7 en suite) No smoking in dining room TVB tea/coffee No dogs (ex guide dogs) Licensed Cen ht TVL No children 12yrs No coaches Dinner Last d 5pm **PRICES:** s £25-£35; d £47-£90✳ **LB**
CARDS:

♦♦♦♦ *Nineteen*

19 Broad St BN2 1TJ ☎ 01273 675529 🖹 01273 675531
Dir: *left at Brighton Pier. Broad Street is 3rd on the left*

This stylish, modern hotel is located near Brighton Pier. Bedrooms are decorated with a fresh new approach; white walls, pale wood floors and chrome blinds, some rooms have illuminated glass brick beds. Contemporary works of art, champagne breakfasts and a small rear courtyard help to create that special experience.
FACILITIES: 7 en suite No smoking TVB Direct dial from bedrooms No dogs (ex guide dogs) Cen ht No children 18yrs No coaches
CARDS:

♦♦♦♦ Paskins Town House

18/19 Charlotte St BN2 1AG ☎ 01273 601203 🖹 01273 621973
e-mail: welcome@paskins.co.uk
Dir: *A23 to pier, turn left, Charlotte Street on left (The Independents)*
Located in a quiet residential area and within walking distance of the seafront and town centre. This environmentally friendly town house offers bedrooms that are individually designed with thoughtful facilities. Breakfast is the speciality with items such as home-made vegetarian sausages, all served in the tastefully decorated dining room.

continued

Paskins Town House

FACILITIES: 19 rms (16 en suite) (2 fmly) No smoking in area of dining room TVB tea/coffee Direct dial from bedrooms Licensed Cen ht **PRICES:** s £25-£40; d £55-£110✳ **LB CARDS:**

♦♦♦♦ Penny Lanes

11 Charlotte St BN2 1AG ☎ 01273 603197 🖹 01273 689408
e-mail: welcome@pennylanes.co.uk
Dir: *from Brighton Pier go towards "Marina". after 2nd set of traffic lights 4th left (at "The Lanes" hotel on Seafront) establishment is at top on right*
This small and friendly guest house is situated in a quiet road not far from the seafront and the centre of Brighton. Bedrooms are smart in appearance and well equipped. Breakfast is served in the wooden panelled dining room.
FACILITIES: 12 rms (7 en suite) (1 fmly) No smoking in 5 bedrooms No smoking in dining room No smoking in lounges TVB tea/coffee No dogs (ex guide dogs) Cen ht No coaches **PRICES:** s £25-£35; d £50-£90✳ **LB**
CARDS:

♦♦♦♦ Regency Hotel

28 Regency Square BN1 2FH ☎ 01273 202690
🖹 01273 220438
e-mail: enquiries@regencybrighton.co.uk
Dir: *opposite West Pier*

A large town house situated opposite the West Pier with views of the sea. Bedrooms, of various sizes and styles, are sympathetically decorated, tastefully furnished and well-equipped. One room has an antique half-tester bed. The hotel boasts an elegant dining room and lounge, as well as a bar, and there are many restaurants nearby.
FACILITIES: 13 rms (10 en suite) (1 fmly) No smoking in bedrooms No smoking in dining room TVB tea/coffee Direct dial from bedrooms No dogs (ex guide dogs) Licensed Cen ht TVL No children 7yrs No coaches Golf, riding & tennis can be arranged **PRICES:** s £55-£65; d £85-£100✳ **LB**
CONF: Thtr 20 Class 10 Board 10 Del from £120 ✳
CARDS:

♦♦♦♦ Topps Hotel
17 Regency Square BN1 2FG ☎ 01273 729334 🖷 01273 203679
e-mail: toppshotel@aol.com
Dir: *opposite West Pier*

An attractive Regency town house located in one of the seafront squares. Most bedrooms are particularly spacious with comfortable sofas, fireplaces, mini-bars and many extra touches. The dining room has a warm atmosphere with large tables and a good quality breakfast is served; service is both helpful and attentive.

FACILITIES: 15 en suite (3 fmly) No smoking in 2 bedrooms No smoking in dining room TVB tea/coffee Direct dial from bedrooms No dogs (ex guide dogs) Licensed Lift No coaches Dinner Last d 4pm **PRICES:** s £40-£49; d £84-£129* **NOTES:** Closed Last 2wks Dec **CARDS:**

♦♦♦♦ Trouville Hotel
11 New Steine, Marine Pde BN2 1PB ☎ 01273 697384
Dir: *A259 approx 300yds from Palace Pier*

The Trouville is an attractive Grade II listed building situated in a Regency seafront square. The bedrooms are individually decorated and designed to provide comfortable and well appointed accommodation. Well-cooked breakfasts are served in the bright open-plan lounge/dining room.

FACILITIES: 8 rms (6 en suite) (2 fmly) No smoking in dining room TVB tea/coffee No dogs Licensed Cen ht TVL No coaches **PRICES:** s £29-£45; d £59-£65* **NOTES:** Closed Xmas & Jan **CARDS:**

♦♦♦ Prince Regent Hotel
29 Regency Square BN1 2FH ☎ 01273 329962 🖷 01273 748162
e-mail: princeregent@ukonline.co.uk
Dir: *turn off A23 on to seafront Road at Brighton Pier (A259)*

Close to both the seafront and to the many town centre attractions the Prince Regent offers a warm welcome and mostly spacious bedrooms.

FACILITIES: 20 en suite No smoking in dining room TVB tea/coffee Direct dial from bedrooms No dogs Licensed Cen ht No children 16yrs No coaches **PRICES:** s £45-£50; d £85-£175* **LB CARDS:**

♦♦♦ Adastral Hotel
8 Westbourne Villas BN3 4GQ ☎ 01273 888800
🖷 01273 883839
e-mail: info@adastralhotel.co.uk
Dir: *from Brighton Pier, sea on left, proceed for 2.25 miles to King Alfred Leisure Centre, over traffic lights, Westbourne Villas 3rd right*

Located just off the Hove sea front, this double fronted Victorian villa offers a variety of well-equipped bedrooms, many of which are suitable for family use. Public areas include a small lounge/bar area and a restaurant serving breakfast and evening meals.

FACILITIES: 18 en suite (10 fmly) (2 GF) No smoking in dining room STV TVB tea/coffee Direct dial from bedrooms Licensed Cen ht Dinner Last d 9pm **PRICES:** s £50; d £98* **PARKING:** 2 **CARDS:**

♦♦♦ Allendale Hotel
3 New Steine BN2 1PB ☎ 01273 675436 🖷 01273 602603
e-mail: allendalehotel@tinyworld.co.uk
Dir: *Once in Brighton follow signs to seafront. At seafront turn L, New Steine is 8th on L. The Allendale is 1st hotel on L*

Located in an attractive Regency square just off the front, this hotel offers sea views and bedrooms of varying sizes. Some superior rooms are available, and all provide a good range of facilities. An English breakfast is served in the smart dining room, and there is a small lounge area.

FACILITIES: 13 rms (9 en suite) (3 fmly) No smoking in bedrooms No smoking in dining room TVB tea/coffee Direct dial from bedrooms No dogs (ex guide dogs) Licensed Cen ht TVL No coaches Dinner Last d 4pm **NOTES:** Closed Dec **CARDS:**

England

BRIGHTON & HOVE continued

♦♦♦ Alvia Hotel

36 Upper Rock Gardens BN2 1QF ☎ 01273 682939
01273 626287
e-mail: enquires@alviahotel.co.uk
Dir: *from Brighton Pier rdbt turn left, approx 500yds on left are traffic lights, turn left into Lower Rock Gdns continue to Upper Rock Gdns*
Located a short walk from the sea front and town centre. This fine Victorian house offers a choice of comfortable and suitably equipped bedrooms. A choice of English and vegetarian breakfast is offered and is served in the bright dining room. There is some parking available.
FACILITIES: 10 rms (7 en suite) (2 fmly) No smoking TVB tea/coffee No dogs (ex guide dogs) Cen ht **PRICES:** s £20-£45; d £60-£90* **LB PARKING:** 5 **CARDS:**

♦♦♦ Brighton Marina House Hotel

8 Charlotte St BN2 1AG ☎ 01273 605349 01273 679484
e-mail: rooms@jungs.co.uk
Located on a period street within easy walking distance of town and seafront, this constantly improving house provides a range of bedrooms, many individually themed with fine Asian fabrics and quality art. Breakfast is served in an attractive garden level dining room and evening meals are available by prior arrangement.
FACILITIES: 10 rms (7 en suite) (3 fmly) No smoking TVB tea/coffee No dogs Cen ht TVL No coaches Dinner Last d 4pm **PRICES:** s fr £25; d fr £45* **LB CARDS:**

See advertisement on page 391

♦♦♦ Gullivers

10 New Steine BN2 1PB ☎ 01273 695415 & 622663
01273 622663
e-mail: gulliversh@aol.com
Dir: *A23 to Brighton to seafront & pier. Turn left onto Marine Parade towards the Marina. New Steine on left directly after Wentworth St*
A bright, attractive establishment situated close to the seafront in one of Brighton's Regency squares. The spacious bedrooms are well equipped and some offer a view of the sea. The lounge/dining room can be used by guests all day.
FACILITIES: 9 rms (5 en suite) (3 fmly) No smoking in 4 bedrooms No smoking in dining room No smoking in lounges TVB tea/coffee Direct dial from bedrooms No dogs (ex guide dogs) Cen ht TVL No coaches **PRICES:** s £25-£35; d £60-£70* **LB CARDS:**

♦♦♦ *Kempton House Hotel*

33/34 Marine Pde BN2 1TR ☎ 01273 570248 01273 570248
Dir: *A23, towards London, to roundabout by Brighton Pier, left onto Marine Parade, A259, premises 250yds on left*
This hotel enjoys a good location opposite Brighton Pier offering stunning views from the front bedrooms. The rooms, though not large, are attractively furnished and equipped with extensive facilities. Breakfast is served in the dining room, which also overlooks the sea.
FACILITIES: 12 en suite (4 fmly) STV TVB tea/coffee Direct dial from bedrooms Licensed Cen ht No coaches Last d 9am **CARDS:**

♦♦♦ Westbourne Hotel

46 Upper Rock Gardens BN2 1QF ☎ 01273 686920
01273 686920
e-mail: mail@westbournehotel.net
Dir: *A23 to Brighton, turn left at rdbt by Brighton Pier to Marine Parade going towards Marina, 100yds turn left at lights, hotel is up rd on right*
Just a short walk from the seafront, this Victorian house is run by friendly owners. Bedrooms are attractively decorated and well furnished, while public rooms include a comfortable lounge with huge sofas and a breakfast room which houses a small bar.
FACILITIES: 10 rms (6 en suite) (4 fmly) No smoking TVB tea/coffee No dogs Licensed Cen ht No children 3yrs No coaches **PRICES:** s £28-£50; d £55-£60* **CARDS:**

♦♦♦ Cavalaire Hotel

34 Upper Rock Gardens BN2 1QF ☎ 01273 696899
01273 600504
e-mail: cavalaire.hotel@virgin.net
Dir: *follow A259 towards Newhaven, turn left at 2nd traffic lights*
FACILITIES: 10 en suite (2 fmly) No smoking TVB tea/coffee No dogs (ex guide dogs) Licensed Cen ht No children 5yrs No coaches **PRICES:** s £29-£55; d £49-£70* **LB PARKING:** 3 **CARDS:**

♦♦♦ Hotel Seafield

23 Seafield Rd BN3 2TP ☎ 01273 735912 01273 323525
e-mail: brighton.co.uk./hotels/seafield
Dir: *from M25 to M23 bypass to Hove, take A27 coastal road west. Texaco garage on sea side opposite Seafield Road.*
FACILITIES: 14 rms (12 en suite) (4 fmly) No smoking in 4 bedrooms No smoking in area of dining room TVB tea/coffee Cen ht TVL **PRICES:** s £35-£50; d £75-£90* **PARKING:** 15 **NOTES:** Closed 22-27 Dec
CARDS:

♦♦ *The Brighton Beach Hotel*

41 Marine Pde BN2 1PE ☎ 01273 681435 01273 624186
e-mail: Brightonbeach@aol.com
Dir: *towards seafront Brighton Pier and rdbt from A23 turn left on seafront*
Situated in a prime location on the sea front, this guest house is undergoing refurbishment, currently it provides modest accommodation with bedrooms of varying sizes and styles; a good range of facilities in each. Breakfasts are served in the lower ground floor restaurant, which is bright and airy. There is some parking available.
FACILITIES: 25 rms (23 en suite) (3 fmly) No smoking in dining room No smoking in lounges STV TVB tea/coffee Direct dial from bedrooms No dogs (ex guide dogs) Cen ht TVL No coaches **PARKING:** 12 **CARDS:**

♦♦ The Shalimar Hotel

23 Broad St BN2 1TJ ☎ 01273 694314 01883 623222
Dir: *A23 to Brighton Pier, 1st exit on rdbt, 1st right turnoff at lights, end of road turn right, Broad Street is 2nd on right, hotel is on left*
This small and friendly hotel is positioned on a side street just off the seafront. Bedrooms are functional and well kept and breakfast is served in the basement dining room.
FACILITIES: 8 rms (5 en suite) (1 fmly) No smoking in dining room TVB tea/coffee No dogs (ex guide dogs) Licensed Cen ht No coaches
PRICES: s £30-£35; d £45-£60*

♦♦ Chatsworth Hotel

9 Salisbury Rd BN3 3AB ☎ 01273 737360 01273 737360
Dir: *from London Road take right at Brighton Pier along seafront into Hove. Turn right at 1st avenue, right again at Church Road opposite St Johns Church, Salisbury Road. Chatsworth is halfway up on left.*
FACILITIES: 8 rms (4 en suite) (2 fmly) No smoking in dining room No smoking in lounges TVB tea/coffee Cen ht TVL No coaches
PRICES: s £26.50-£35; d £55-£75* **CARDS:**

♦♦ Sandpiper Guest House

11 Russell Square BN1 2EE ☎ 01273 328202 & 329974
01273 329974
e-mail: sandpiper@brighton.co.uk
Dir: *after conference centre on King's Rd, right into Cannon Place. Russel Sq at end of street*
FACILITIES: 6 rms (1 fmly) No smoking in 3 bedrooms No smoking in dining room No smoking in lounges TVB tea/coffee No dogs (ex guide dogs) Cen ht **PRICES:** s £18-£28; d £36-£56* **LB BB**
CARDS:

BURWASH Map 05 TQ62

♦♦♦♦ Judins

Heathfield Rd TN19 7LA ☎ 01435 882455 Fax 01435 883775
e-mail: sandra.jolly@virgin.net

Dir: *A265 to Burwash, through village, past BP station on right, house 0.5m on left. Or from A22 at Uckfield/B2102/A265 to Burwash Common, house on right*

A warm welcome is offered at this charming 300-year old country house which is set amidst 70 acres of grounds. The spacious bedrooms are tastefully decorated, thoughtfully equipped and pleasantly furnished. Public rooms include an attractive conservatory, a comfortable lounge and a smart dining room where evening meals are available by prior arrangement.

FACILITIES: 3 en suite No smoking STV TVB tea/coffee No dogs Cen ht TVL No coaches Outdoor swimming pool (heated) Dinner Last d 9pm **PRICES:** d £60-£70✻ **LB PARKING:** 8 **CARDS:**

CROWBOROUGH Map 05 TQ53

♦♦♦♦ Plough & Horses

Walshes Rd TN6 3RE ☎ 01892 652614 Fax 01892 652614

Dir: *from Tunbridge Wells left at Boars Head rdbt into green lane (1st exit) to end. Cross over Crowborough Hill into Tollwood. Inn on right at end of Tollwood*

A warm welcome is offered at this popular inn which has been owned and run by the Newton family for two decades. The attractively decorated bedrooms are thoughtfully equipped and have well chosen pine furniture. Public rooms include a traditional style bar, a restaurant and a further lounge bar.

FACILITIES: 15 en suite (3 fmly) No smoking in bedrooms No smoking in area of dining room TVB tea/coffee Cen ht TVL Dinner Last d 10pm **PRICES:** s £28-£37; d £48-£52✻ **PARKING:** 40 **NOTES:** Closed 24-25 Dec **CARDS:**

EASTBOURNE Map 05 TV69

See also Wilmington

Premier Collection

♦♦♦♦♦ Pinnacle Point

Foyle Way, Upper Duke's Dr BN20 7XL ☎ 01323 726666
Fax 01323 643946
e-mail: info@pinnaclepoint.co.uk

Dir: *take A22 past rail station, follow signs to seafront, west along promenade towards South Downs. At foot of hill immediately after St Bedes prep school turn left Pinnacle Point is 80m beyond metal gate*

In a desirable location - overlooking Eastbourne from the Pinnacle point, this superb modern establishment has all the quality touches that ensure an enjoyable, relaxing stay. Bedrooms are spacious, fitted out with quality fabrics, and room facilities are extensive. There are verandahs and an open-plan lounge dining room. The hosts offer a warm welcome.

FACILITIES: 3 en suite No smoking STV TVB tea/coffee No dogs (ex guide dogs) Cen ht TVL No children 10yrs No coaches Outdoor swimming pool (heated) **PRICES:** s £50-£60; d £80-£100✻ **PARKING:** 4 **NOTES:** Closed Xmas & New Year

♦♦♦♦ Beachy Rise

5 Beachy Head Rd BN20 7QN ☎ 01323 639171

Dir: *take the A22 into Eastbourne, turn right just before the sign post to Beachy Head*

Charming family-run guest house situated in a peaceful residential location close to Meads Village. Bedrooms are attractively decorated with co-ordinated soft furnishings and have many useful extras. Breakfast is served in the smart dining room/lounge, which overlooks the garden and guests also have the use of a range of board games.

FACILITIES: 4 en suite (2 fmly) No smoking in 2 bedrooms No smoking in dining room No smoking in lounges TVB tea/coffee No dogs (ex guide dogs) Cen ht No coaches **PRICES:** s £25-£40; d £45-£60✻

♦♦♦♦ Bella Vista

30 Redoubt Rd BN22 7DH ☎ 01323 724222
e-mail: bellavistauk@aol.com

Dir: *from A22 take A2021 to the seafront, turn right at Redoubt Fortress, take Redoubt Road Bella Vista on left*

Situated on the east side of town, just off the seafront, the Bella Vista is a friendly and attractive flint covered house. Bedrooms are generally spacious and neatly appointed with modern facilities. There is a comfortable guest lounge and parking is a bonus.

FACILITIES: 10 en suite (3 GF) No smoking TVB tea/coffee No dogs (ex guide dogs) Licensed TVL No coaches Dinner Last d 4pm **PRICES:** d £50-£56✻ **PARKING:** 10

England

EASTBOURNE continued

♦♦♦♦ Brayscroft Hotel

13 South Cliff Av BN20 7AH ☎ 01323 647005 🖹 01323 725705
e-mail: brayscroft@hotmail.com
Dir: *B2103 (Grand Parade) from pier in direction of Beachy Head, pass Grand Hotel, then take right incline up South Cliff & 1st right into South Cliff Avenue*

This small and charming hotel is located close to the seafront and was formerly an Edwardian family house. Bedrooms are tastefully decorated and include many extra touches as a standard. A comfortable lounge is made available for guest use and evening meals are also available by arrangement.
FACILITIES: 5 en suite (2 fmly) No smoking TVB tea/coffee Licensed Cen ht No children 12yrs No coaches Dinner Last d 10am **PRICES:** s £27-£29.50; d £54-£59✳ **LB CARDS:**

♦♦♦♦ *Chalk Farm Hotel & Restaurant*

Coopers Hill, Willingdon BN20 9JD ☎ 01323 503800
🖹 01323 520331
Dir: *1m S of Polegate crossroads turn right off A22, immediately after traffic lights*
Expect a warm welcome at this 17th century Grade II listed farmhouse situated in a peaceful location. The charming bedrooms have a wealth of original features such as exposed beams and open fireplaces; they are pleasantly decorated and thoughtfully equipped. Public rooms include a bar, a choice of lounges and a smart restaurant.
FACILITIES: 9 rms (8 en suite) (2 fmly) No smoking in bedrooms No smoking in dining room No smoking in 1 lounge TVB tea/coffee Direct dial from bedrooms Licensed Cen ht No coaches Cycle hire Last d 8.45pm
PARKING: 15 **CARDS:**

♦♦♦♦ St Omer Hotel

13 Royal Pde BN22 7AR ☎ 01323 722152 🖹 01323 723400
e-mail: st.omer@lineone.net
Dir: *on seafront, 0.25m from pier & town centre*
A warm welcome is offered at this friendly family-run hotel, which is situated on the seafront. Although the bedrooms vary in size and style they are all smartly decorated and thoughtfully equipped. Breakfast and dinner are served at individual tables in the large oak-panelled dining room. Public areas include a comfortable lounge bar and small conservatory.
FACILITIES: 12 rms (11 en suite) (1 fmly) (1 GF) No smoking TVB tea/coffee No dogs (ex guide dogs) Licensed TVL No children 12yrs No coaches Dinner Last d 6pm **PRICES:** s £22-£25; d £44-£50✳ **LB**
CARDS:

♦♦♦♦ Southcroft Hotel

15 South Cliff Av BN20 7AH ☎ 01323 729071
e-mail: southcroft@eastbourne34.freeserve.co.uk
Quietly set on a terraced hillside away from the crowds, this charming little hotel has attractively presented, carefully maintained en suite bedrooms. The cosy lounge offers comfort and relaxation and the standard of breakfast is high. Dinner is also available on request.
FACILITIES: 4 en suite No smoking TVB tea/coffee No dogs Licensed Cen ht TVL No children No coaches Dinner Last d noon **PRICES:** s £27-£35; d £54-£58✳ **LB CARDS:**

♦♦♦♦ Cromwell Private Hotel

23 Cavendish Place BN21 3EJ ☎ 01323 725288
🖹 01323 725288
e-mail: cromwell-hotel@lineone.net
Dir: *follow seafront signs. Cavendish Place opposite pier, hotel 50mtrs on right before traffic lights*
FACILITIES: 8 en suite (2 GF) No smoking TVB tea/coffee No dogs Licensed Cen ht TVL No children 14yrs No coaches Dinner Last d 3pm
PRICES: s £22-£24; d £44-£48✳ **LB NOTES:** Closed Nov-Etr **CARDS:**

♦♦♦ Arden Hotel

17 Burlington Place BN21 4AR ☎ 01323 639639
🖹 01323 639639
e-mail: mail@ardenhoteleastbourne.co.uk
Dir: *50 yds from seafront, near bandstand*
This friendly hotel enjoys a central location and is close to the seafront. Bedrooms are spacious and smartly appointed. Public areas are tastefully decorated and include a luxurious guest lounge and a spacious dining room where hearty breakfasts are served.
FACILITIES: 11 en suite (2 GF) No smoking TVB tea/coffee Licensed Cen ht TVL **PRICES:** s £25-£30; d £50-£60✳ **LB PARKING:** 6 **NOTES:** Closed Xmas/New Year **CARDS:**

♦♦♦ Bay Lodge Hotel

61-62 Royal Pde BN22 7AQ ☎ 01323 732515 🖹 01323 735009
e-mail: beryl@mnewson.freeserve.co.uk
Dir: *A22, A2021 to junct with B2103 seafront road, right, 300yds & pedestrian crossing directly outside premises*

Friendly family run hotel situated in an ideal location on the seafront, opposite the pavilion gardens and Redoubt lawns. Bedrooms are attractively decorated and thoughtfully equipped, many rooms have superb sea views. Breakfast and dinner is served in the smart dining room and guests also have the use of a sun lounge and cosy bar.
FACILITIES: 12 rms (9 en suite) (2 GF) No smoking in dining room No smoking in 1 lounge TVB tea/coffee No dogs Licensed Cen ht TVL No coaches Dinner Last d lunchtime **PRICES:** s £22-£30; d £44-£60✳ **LB**
PARKING: 2 **CARDS:**

♦♦♦ Birling Gap Hotel

Seven Sisters Cliffs, Birling Gap, East Dean BN20 0AB
☎ 01323 423197 🖹 01323 423030
e-mail: Info@birlinggaphotel.co.uk
Dir: *turn off A259 Coast Road at Eastdean Village (4 m W of Eastbourne) onto Gilberts Drive towards Birling Gap. approx 1.5m (The Circle)*

continued

Friendly, family run hotel situated in a superb clifftop location with superb views of the sea. Bedrooms are pleasantly decorated and well equipped with many rooms having lovely sea views. Public rooms include a spacious lounge bar and restaurant, which offers a wide range of popular dishes. The hotel also has a coffee shop that is open throughout the day.
FACILITIES: 9 en suite (3 fmly) No smoking in area of dining room STV TVB tea/coffee Direct dial from bedrooms No dogs (ex guide dogs) Licensed Cen ht Pool Table Beach,golf,riding,swim,nearby, sea fishing Dinner Last d 9.30pm **PRICES:** s fr £30; d £40-£70✳ **LB CONF:** Thtr 150 Class 100 Board 80 **PARKING:** 100 **CARDS:**

♦♦♦ Camelot Lodge
35 Lewes Rd BN21 2BU ☎ 01323 725207 📠 01323 722799
Dir: *exit A22 onto A2021, premises approx 0.5m after General Hospital*
This delightful, family-run Edwardian hotel is located within walking distance of the seafront and local amenities. Bedrooms are attractively decorated and feature a range of extra facilities. Guests have the use of a spacious lounge/bar area in which to relax and meals are served in the bright conservatory dining room. Dinner is available by prior arrangement.
FACILITIES: 7 en suite (2 fmly) No smoking in dining room TVB tea/coffee No dogs (ex guide dogs) Licensed Cen ht No coaches Dinner Last d 24hr notice **PRICES:** s fr £25; d fr £50✳ **LB PARKING:** 10

♦♦♦ Far End Hotel
139 Royal Pde BN22 7LH ☎ 01323 725666
Dir: *1m E of Pier on the seafront*
This popular guest house is located at the 'far end' of the Eastbourne seafront. Most bedrooms have sea views. Guests have the use of a comfortable first floor lounge, a bright sunny dining room and a cosy residents-only bar. Dinner is by prior arrangement and may be accompanied by the hotel's own-label wine.
FACILITIES: 10 rms (4 en suite) No smoking in dining room No smoking in lounges TVB tea/coffee Licensed Cen ht No children 4yrs No coaches Dinner Last d 1pm **PRICES:** s £19-£27; d £38-£60✳ **LB BB**
PARKING: 8 **NOTES:** Closed Nov-1 Mar rs Mar

♦♦♦ Halcyon Hotel
8 South Cliff BN20 7AF ☎ 01323 723710 📠 01323 411743
e-mail: mail@halcyonhoteleastbourne.freeserve.co.uk
Dir: *follow A22 to Eastbourne, go to western end of seafront, hotel just past Grand Hotel opposite Wish Tower Gardens*
Privately owned hotel situated in an elevated position overlooking the beach and sea beyond. Bedrooms are smartly appointed and well equipped with telephones and remote control TV/video. Public rooms include a spacious lounge bar with plush sofas and evening meals are served in the comfortable downstairs dining room.
FACILITIES: 15 en suite (1 fmly) (2 GF) No smoking TVB tea/coffee Direct dial from bedrooms No dogs (ex guide dogs) Licensed Cen ht TVL
PRICES: s fr £26; d fr £52 **LB NOTES:** Closed 1st 2 weeks Jan
CARDS:

♦♦♦ Mowbray Hotel
2 Lascelles Ter BN21 4BJ ☎ 01323 720012 📠 01323 720253
e-mail: info@mowbrayhotel.freeserve.co.uk
Dir: *A22 to seafront, R past pier/bandstand, R off seafront, hotel 50yds on L*
Located a few minutes' walk from the seafront and Devonshire Theatre, this constantly improving late Victorian hotel provides good practical bedroom accommodation, which is served by a lift. Breakfast, and dinner by arrangement, is served in an attractive lower-ground floor dining room and a guest lounge is also available.
FACILITIES: 14 en suite (2 fmly) (1 GF) No smoking in dining room TVB tea/coffee Lift Cen ht Dinner Last d 4pm **PRICES:** s £25-£29; d £50-£58✳ **LB CARDS:**

♦♦♦ Sheldon Hotel
9-11 Burlington Place BN21 4AS ☎ 01323 724120
📠 01323 430406
e-mail: gmeyer@sheldonhotel.fs.businesses.co.uk
Dir: *100yds from seafront, 500yds W of pier, and opp bandstand*

This is an impressive late Victorian house, which is situated in a quiet side road just off the seafront. The bedrooms are cheerfully decorated with co-ordinated soft furnishings and are equipped with modern facilities. Public rooms include a smart dining room, a bar and a spacious comfortably furnished lounge.
FACILITIES: 24 en suite (4 fmly) No smoking in bedrooms No smoking in dining room STV TVB tea/coffee Direct dial from bedrooms Licensed Lift Cen ht TVL No coaches Dinner Last d 6pm **PRICES:** s £26-£30; d £52-£60✳ **LB PARKING:** 15 **CARDS:**

♦♦♦ *Westways*
10 Rylstone Rd BN22 7HN ☎ 01323 639709
Westways Guest House is tucked away in a peaceful side road just off the seafront and close to the bowling greens. The individually decorated bedrooms are comfortably furnished and well-equipped. Traditional English breakfasts are served in the attractive dining room at individual tables.
FACILITIES: 7 rms (4 en suite) (1 fmly) No smoking in dining room TVB tea/coffee Licensed Cen ht TVL Last d day before

HARTFIELD — Map 05 TQ43

Premier Collection

♦♦♦♦♦ Bolebroke Watermill
Perry Hill, Edenbridge Rd TN7 4JP ☎ 01892 770425
📠 01892 770425
e-mail: b&b@bolebrokemill.demon.co.uk
mid Feb-wknd prior Xmas
Dir: *turn off A264 onto B2026. 1m on left pass Perryhill Nurseries turn left down unsurfaced farm road follow B & B sign 400yds*
Dating partly to the 11th century, and sympathetically converted by David and Christine Cooper. Two rooms are in the original mill, at the top of steep stairs through trap doors, and have a shared lounge on the ground floor (with much of the original mill machinery still visible). The other bedrooms (two with four-poster beds) are in the Barn. The nearby Winnie the Pooh walk takes in the sites of A.A. Milne's famous books.
FACILITIES: 5 en suite (1 GF) No smoking TVB tea/coffee No dogs Cen ht No children 8yrs No coaches **PRICES:** d £66-£79✳ **CONF:** Board 12 **PARKING:** 10 **CARDS:**

 Places with this symbol are farmhouses.

England

HASTINGS & ST LEONARDS Map 05 TQ80

Premier Collection

♦♦♦♦♦ Parkside House

59 Lower Park Rd TN34 2LD ☎ 01424 433096
01424 421431
Dir: *follow town centre signs, turn right off A21 at rdbt then 1st right into Lower Park Rd*

Situated in an elevated position overlooking Alexandra Park, this attractive Victorian house offers individually decorated bedrooms, tastefully furnished with beautiful antique pieces and equipped with many useful little extra touches. The atmosphere is friendly, welcoming and informal. Breakfast is served at individual tables in the elegant dining room and guests also have the use of a cosy inviting lounge with plush furniture. The house is no-smoking throughout.

FACILITIES: 5 rms (4 en suite) (1 fmly) No smoking TVB tea/coffee No dogs (ex guide dogs) Licensed Cen ht TVL No coaches **PRICES:** s £25-£35; d £50-£70* LB **CARDS:**

♦♦♦♦ *Lionsdown House*

116 High St TN34 3ET ☎ 01424 420802
Dir: *along seafront A259, turn left into High Street. We are situated at top on left hand side*

Delightful medieval Grade II listed property situated near the top of the hill, in the older part of town. The house has been lovingly restored to a very high standard and retains many of its original features such as, exposed timbers and Tudor fireplaces. Bedrooms are individually decorated, well-furnished and equipped with many thoughtful touches.

FACILITIES: 3 en suite No smoking TVB tea/coffee No dogs (ex guide dogs) Cen ht TVL No coaches **CARDS:**

♦♦♦♦ Tower House Hotel

26-28 Tower Rd West TN38 0RG ☎ 01424 427217 & 421217
01424 427217
e-mail: enquiries@Towerhousehotel.com
Dir: *from E - At lights after pier right up London Rd, Tower Rd West about 0.5m on left). From W turn left at traffic lights (A21to London) turn left then immediately right into Charles Rd. West at crossroads. Turn left into Tower Road West.*

Located in an elevated position within a residential area, this elegant double fronted Victorian house has been sympathetically renovated to provide high standards of comfort and facilities. Bedrooms are tastefully furnished and equipped with a wealth of thoughtful extras to enhance guest comfort. Ground floor areas include a sumptuous lounge, a formal bar and a superb conservatory dining room with direct access to immaculate gardens.

continued

FACILITIES: 10 en suite (2 fmly) No smoking in bedrooms No smoking in dining room TVB tea/coffee Direct dial from bedrooms No dogs Licensed Cen ht TVL No coaches Dinner Last d 4pm **PRICES:** s £42-£45; d £60-£70* LB **CARDS:**

♦♦♦♦ Eagle House

Pevensey Rd TN38 0JZ ☎ 01424 430535 & 441273
01424 437771
e-mail: info@eaglehousehotel.com
Dir: *turn off seafront onto London Rd, premises adjacent to St Leonards Shopping Centre.*

Attractive Victorian property situated in a peaceful residential area within easy walking distance of the shops and seafront. The spacious bedrooms are traditionally decorated and equipped with many useful extras. Dinner is served in the elegant dining room and guests also have the use of a cosy lounge.

FACILITIES: 20 en suite (2 fmly) No smoking in 10 bedrooms No smoking in dining room TVB tea/coffee Direct dial from bedrooms No dogs (ex guide dogs) Licensed Cen ht No coaches Dinner Last d 8.30pm
PRICES: s £30-£33; d £48-£52* **PARKING:** 13
CARDS:

♦♦♦♦ Filsham Farmhouse *(TQ784096)*

111 Harley Shute Rd TN38 8BY ☎ 01424 433109
01424 461061 Mrs B Yorke
e-mail: filshamfarmhouse@talk21.com
Dir: *off A21 at speed limit sign into Old Harrow Rd, house 1.5m on R after railway bridge*

Guest can expect a warm welcome at this charming 17th century house. Public rooms are elegantly appointed with fine period furniture and memorabilia. The individually decorated bedrooms are attractively furnished and thoughtfully equipped; some have superb sea views. Breakfast is served in the delightful dining room, which features a magnificent inglenook fireplace.

FACILITIES: 3 en suite No smoking in bedrooms No smoking in 1 lounge TVB tea/coffee Cen ht TVL No children 5yrs 1 acres non-working
PRICES: s £25-£35; d £40-£60* **PARKING:** 4
CARDS:

♦♦♦♦ White Cottage

Battery Hill, Fairlight TN35 4AP ☎ 01424 812528
01424 812285
e-mail: JuneandJohn@whitecottagebb.fsnet.co.uk
Dir: *A259 Hastings-Rye, signposted Fairlight*

This modern house is set amidst mature gardens on the outskirts of the peaceful village of Fairlight between Hastings and Rye. White Cottage offers pleasantly decorated, thoughtfully furnished and well-equipped bedrooms throughout. Breakfast is served at a large communal table in the open-plan lounge/dining area.

continued

White Cottage

FACILITIES: 3 en suite (1 GF) No smoking TVB tea/coffee No dogs Cen ht No children 12yrs No coaches **PRICES:** s £25-£30; d £45-£50✻ LB **PARKING:** 4 **NOTES:** Closed Nov-Feb

♦♦♦♦ Seaspray

54 Eversfield Place TN37 6DB ☎ 01424 436583
e-mail: jo@seaspray.freeserve.co.uk
Dir: *from London A21 follow signs to town centre/seafront. Seaspray is 100mts W of the pier.*
FACILITIES: 9 rms (7 en suite) (3 fmly) No smoking TVB tea/coffee No dogs Cen ht TVL No coaches **PRICES:** s £18-£22; d £40-£50✻ LB BB

♦♦♦♦ Summerfields House

Bohemia Rd TN34 1EX ☎ 01424 718142 Fax 01424 718142
e-mail: liz.orourke@totalise.co.uk
Dir: *from M25 junct 5 Sthbound onto A21 towards Hastings town centre. At Silverhill junct. stay in left lane into Bohemia Road. Summerfields House on left after passing the Fire Station*
FACILITIES: 3 en suite (3 fmly) No smoking TVB tea/coffee Cen ht No coaches jacuzzi 1 rm only Dinner Last d morning of meal
PRICES: d £40-£56✻ LB **PARKING:** 6 **NOTES:** Closed 24-26 Dec

♦♦♦ Beechwood

59 Baldslow Rd TN34 2EY ☎ 01424 420078
e-mail: beechwoodhastings@talk21.com
Dir: *from A21 onto A2101, left at rdbt then 1st left*
FACILITIES: 12 rms (5 en suite) (3 fmly) (4 GF) No smoking in dining room TV3B tea/coffee Licensed Cen ht TVL **PRICES:** s £16-£27; d £30-£42✻ LB BB **PARKING:** 6

HEATHFIELD — Map 05 TQ52

Premier Collection

♦♦♦♦♦ Old Corner Cottage

Little London Rd TN21 0LT ☎ 01435 863787
Fax 01435 863787
e-mail: hamishcjbrown@aol.com
Dir: *A267 towards Heathfield take 1st right past Cross in Hand pub, signposted Horam & Eastbourne into Little London Rd*
Charming 300-year old cottage set amongst pretty gardens. The property has been sympathetically extended to retain much of its original character and provides comfortable, homely accommodation. Breakfast is served in the attractive dining room at a large oak table. Guests also have the use of a conservatory lounge with plush seating.
FACILITIES: 3 en suite (1 GF) No smoking TVB tea/coffee No dogs (ex guide dogs) Cen ht TVL No coaches **PRICES:** s £25-£30; d £45-£55
PARKING: 8

♦♦♦♦ Iwood Bed & Breakfast

Mutton Hall Ln TN21 8NR ☎ 01435 863918 Fax 01435 868575
e-mail: iwoodbb@aol.com
Dir: *A265 through Heathfield High St towards Burwash. At top of hill sharp left at traffic lights into Mutton Hall Lane, last house on left b&b sign above gate*
FACILITIES: 3 rms (2 en suite) (1 fmly) (1 GF) No smoking TVB tea/coffee No dogs Cen ht TVL No coaches **PRICES:** s £20-£25; d £40-£45✻
PARKING: 2 **NOTES:** Closed Xmas & New Year

HERSTMONCEUX — Map 05 TQ61

Premier Collection

♦♦♦♦♦ Wartling Place

Wartling Place, Wartling BN27 1RY ☎ 01323 832590
Fax 01323 831558
e-mail: accom@wartlingplace.prestel.co.uk
Dir: *take A271 signed Herstmonceux after Windmill Hill turn right continue following signs, at Wartling village, Wartling Place is on right, opposite St Mary Magdalane church*
This beautifully appointed Grade II listed country home is set in two acres of well-tended gardens. Bedrooms are luxurious and individually decorated, two have four-poster beds. A thoughtful range of facilities adds further to guest comfort. This is an ideal base for exploring the castles, gardens and National Trust houses of Sussex and Kent.
FACILITIES: 4 en suite (1 fmly) No smoking TVB tea/coffee No dogs (ex guide dogs) Cen ht No coaches Dinner Last d 24hrs in advance
PRICES: s £58-£75; d £72-£105✻ LB **PARKING:** 10
CARDS:

LEWES — Map 05 TQ41

Premier Collection

♦♦♦♦♦ Nightingales

The Avenue, Kingston BN7 3LL ☎ 01273 475673
Fax 01273475673
e-mail: nightingales@totalise.co.uk
Dir: *A23 S/A27 E signposted Lewes. At 1st rdbt take 3rd exit, right at 30mph sign, establishment 2nd from end on right*

Nightingales is surrounded by beautifully kept gardens and grounds. Mrs Hudson is a charming and caring host who offers tea on arrival to her guests, taken in either the conservatory or the comfortably appointed lounge. Bedrooms are very comfortably furnished and come with a wide range of thoughtful extras, including fresh fruits and sherry.
FACILITIES: 2 en suite (2 GF) No smoking TVB tea/coffee Cen ht TVL No children No coaches **PRICES:** d £50-£58✻ **PARKING:** 2
CARDS:

England

LEWES continued

♦♦♦♦ Holly Cottage

Lewes Rd, Laughton BN8 6BL ☎ 01323 811309
01323 811106
e-mail: hollycottage@tinyworld.co.uk
Dir: *from Lewes, take A26 towards Uckfield. On outskirts of Lewes take B2192 to Ringmer then B2124 to Laughton. Pass Roebuck Inn on left, Holly Cottage 300 yds on left*

Holly cottage is a delightful house set in this quiet village. The spacious and cheerful bedrooms are well equipped with thoughtful extras and all enjoy pleasant views of the gardens. Well-cooked breakfasts are served in the main house.

FACILITIES: 3 rms (2 en suite) (2 fmly) No smoking TVB tea/coffee No dogs (ex guide dogs) Cen ht TVL **PRICES:** s fr £35; d £48-£52* **PARKING:** 4 **NOTES:** Closed Xmas

♦♦♦♦ No. 6

6 Gundreda Rd BN7 1PX ☎ 01273 472106 01273 472106
e-mail: jacquelinelucas@yahoo.co.uk
Dir: *A27 from Brighton, left at rdbt to Lewes town. At traffic lights left onto A275 to Haywards Heath. After hospital on left turn right into Prince Edwards Rd, then 3rd left into Gundreda Rd*

This attractive house is located in a quiet residential area not far from the centre of Lewes. Bedrooms are smartly presented and offer many thoughtful extras. Breakfast is served in the conservatory, which enjoys pleasant views of the garden.

FACILITIES: 3 en suite (1 fmly) No smoking TVB tea/coffee No dogs (ex guide dogs) Cen ht **NOTES:** Closed Xmas
CARDS:

PETT — Map 05 TQ81

Premier Collection

♦♦♦♦♦ Pendragon Lodge

Watermill Ln TN35 4HY ☎ 01424 814051 01424 812499
e-mail: pendragon_lodge@hotmail.com
Dir: *A259 from Hastings, turn right opposite Beefeater inn into minor road signed Pett Rd. Proceed 1m, pass shops on right, 2nd turning left, house right*

This impressive Edwardian house, located in rural surroundings, offers spotless accommodation. The tastefully furnished bedrooms, including one four-poster, are filled with lots of thoughtful extras. A spacious lounge overlooks the immaculate gardens and imaginative breakfasts, which include home baked bread, are served at one family table.

FACILITIES: 3 en suite (1 fmly) No smoking TVB tea/coffee No dogs (ex guide dogs) Cen ht No coaches **PRICES:** s fr £35; d £57-£64* **LB** **PARKING:** 5 **CARDS:**

PEVENSEY — Map 05 TQ60

♦♦♦♦ Priory Court Hotel

Castle Rd BN24 5LG ☎ 01323 763150 01323 769030
e-mail: priorycourthotel@aol.com
Dir: *at rdbt junct A27/A259 take Pevensey exit and follow main road through traffic lights hotel on right opposite Pevensey Castle*

Located directly opposite the Roman castle, this 15th century inn retains many original features, enhanced by the furnishing and décor styles throughout. Bedrooms are equipped with thoughtful extras and a wide range of imaginative dishes is available in either a formal cottage style restaurant or attractive bars.

FACILITIES: 9 rms (7 en suite) 1 annexe en suite (2 fmly) (2 GF) No smoking in dining room TVB tea/coffee Direct dial from bedrooms Licensed Cen ht Dinner Last d 9.30pm **PRICES:** s £40-£50; d £53-£85* **LB** **CONF:** Thtr 26 Class 12 Board 18 Del from £99.50 * **PARKING:** 40 **CARDS:**

The Sandcastle

46 Val Prinseps Rd BN24 6JG ☎ 01323 743706

At the time of going to press the Diamond classification for this establishment had not been confirmed. Please check the AA website www.theAA.com for up-to-date information.

FACILITIES: 4 en suite

ROBERTSBRIDGE — Map 05 TQ72

♦♦♦♦ Swallowfield Farm

Brightling TN32 5HB ☎ 01424 838225 01424 838885
e-mail: jssp@swallowfieldfarm.freeserve.co.uk
Dir: *situated 2.5m from A21 at Robertsbridge*

FACILITIES: 3 en suite (1 fmly) No smoking TVB tea/coffee No dogs Cen ht Riding Croquet lawn Dinner Last d by prior arrangement
PRICES: s £25-£30; d £50* **PARKING:** 20

RYE — Map 05 TQ92

See also Pett

Premier Collection

♦♦♦♦♦ *The Benson*

15 East St TN31 7JY ☎ 01797 225131 01797 225512
e-mail: info@bensonhotel.co.uk
Dir: *in direction of town centre & High Street, through Landgate arch & continue 200mtrs to High St. East St is 1st on left*

Situated in a quiet side road just off the high street in the heart of this bustling town centre. The spacious bedrooms are individually decorated, tastefully furnished and equipped with

continued

England

The Benson

modern facilities. Breakfast is served in the attractive dining room seated at individual tables and guests have the use of a lounge and sunny conservatory which overlooks the terraced garden and River Rother beyond.
FACILITIES: 4 en suite (1 fmly) No smoking in dining room No smoking in lounges TVB tea/coffee Direct dial from bedrooms No dogs (ex guide dogs) Licensed Cen ht No coaches **CARDS:**

Premier Collection

♦♦♦♦♦ Durrant House Hotel

Market St TN31 7LA ☎ 01797 223182 01797 226940
e-mail: kingslands@compuserve.com
Dir: *follow signs for town centre. Pass under Landgate Arch and up East Cliff into High St. Take 1st left into East St, hotel located at top of street*

A warm welcome is assured at this town house, 100 yards from the historic parish church. Dating from the time of the Spanish Armada, the building was extended in the Georgian period. The homely bedrooms are thoughtfully equipped and imaginative breakfasts are offered in either the cosy dining room or pretty garden during the warmer months.
FACILITIES: 6 en suite (2 fmly) No smoking TVB tea/coffee Licensed Cen ht No coaches Dinner Last d 4pm **PRICES:** s £40-£60; d £60-£85* **LB NOTES:** Closed 5-31 Jan **CARDS:**

Premier Collection

♦♦♦♦♦ Jeake's House

Mermaid St TN31 7ET ☎ 01797 222828 01797 222623
e-mail: jeakeshouse@btinternet.com
Dir: *within the cobbled medieval town centre, approached either from High St or from The Strand Quay*
Built as wool store in 1689, converted in 1853 to a Baptist school and finally used as a private dwelling in 1909, the house stands on an ancient cobbled street in one of the most beautiful parts of this small, bustling town. Bedrooms combine traditional elegance and comfort with modern amenities and many thoughtful extras. Public rooms include an oak-beamed lounge and a book-lined bar furnished with the old chapel pews. Breakfast is served in the galleried dining room.

FACILITIES: 12 rms (10 en suite) (2 fmly) No smoking in dining room No smoking in 1 lounge TVB tea/coffee Direct dial from bedrooms Licensed Cen ht No children 12yrs No coaches **PRICES:** s £34; d £84-£110* **PARKING:** 21 **CARDS:**

See advertisement on page 401

Premier Collection

♦♦♦♦♦ King Charles II Guest House

4 High St TN31 7JE ☎ 01797 224954
Dir: *centrally in Rye High St*

Charming 14th century building situated on the main high street in the heart of the town centre. The public rooms feature a wealth of old black beams and ancient brick fireplaces adorned with flowers. Tastefully decorated bedrooms have been carefully converted to retain much of their original character.
FACILITIES: 3 en suite No smoking TVB tea/coffee No dogs Licensed Cen ht **PRICES:** s £55-£65; d £80-£95*

England

RYE continued

Premier Collection

♦♦♦♦♦ Little Orchard House
West St TN31 7ES ☎ 01797 223831 🖷 01797 223831
Dir: *follow one way system to town centre, through Landgate Arch into High St. West St is third turning on left, house on left hand side*

Delightful property set in peaceful surroundings and ideally placed for the town centre. The house has been tastefully renovated and retains a good deal of original character. The bedrooms are attractively decorated, thoughtfully equipped and comfortable. Breakfast is served at one large table in the elegant dining room and guests also have the use of a lounge and a reading room.
FACILITIES: 2 en suite No smoking in bedrooms No smoking in dining room No smoking in 1 lounge TVB tea/coffee No dogs (ex guide dogs) Cen ht No children 12yrs No coaches **PRICES:** s £45-£65; d £64-£90✻ **LB PARKING:** 2 **CARDS:**

Premier Collection

♦♦♦♦♦ Manor Farm Oast
Workhouse Ln TN36 4AJ ☎ 01424 813787 🖷 01424 813787
e-mail: manor.farm.oast@lineone.net
Dir: *A259 Rye to Hastings road, from Rye in Icklesham pass church on left, turn left at crossroads into Workhouse Lane. After sharp left bend turn left into Orchards*

A warm welcome and memorable food is assured at this 19th century oast house which retains much of its original charm and character. The individually styled, spacious bedrooms have many thoughtful extras and ground floor areas include a comfortable lounge with roaring fire and an elegant dining room; the setting for tasty breakfasts and Kate Mylrea's imaginative dinners.
FACILITIES: 3 en suite (1 fmly) No smoking TVB tea/coffee No dogs (ex guide dogs) Licensed Cen ht No children 11yrs No coaches Croquet lawn Steam bath & Garden quoits Dinner Last d 7.30pm **PRICES:** s £38-£43; d £60-£70✻ **LB PARKING:** 8 **NOTES:** Closed 28 Dec-1 Jan **CARDS:**

Premier Collection

♦♦♦♦♦ The Old Vicarage Guesthouse
66 Church Square TN31 7HF ☎ 01797 222119
🖷 01797 227466
e-mail: oldvicarageryе@tesco.net
Dir: *from A259 follow town centre signs, enter town via Landgate Arch, 3rd left in High St into West St, by St Mary's Church footpath to Vicarage*

Guests can expect a warm welcome at this delightful detached Georgian property, situated adjacent to the church. Individually decorated bedrooms have attractive soft furnishings and many extras such as home-made biscuits and fudge. Breakfast is served in the attractive dining room, which overlooks the walled garden, and includes home-made preserves, breads and scones.
FACILITIES: 4 en suite (1 fmly) No smoking TVB tea/coffee No dogs (ex guide dogs) Cen ht TVL No children 8yrs No coaches **PRICES:** s £45-£70; d £56-£104✻ **LB PARKING:** 4 **NOTES:** Closed 24-26 Dec

Premier Collection

♦♦♦♦♦ Playden Cottage
Military Rd TN31 7NY ☎ 01797 222234
Dir: *leave Rye in direction of Appledore, Playden Cottage is last house on left, at the speed-limit sign*

Located on the outskirts of Rye, with fine views over the River Rother and Romney Marsh, this impressive early 19th century house retains its original charm and a warm welcome is assured. The spacious bedrooms are filled with thoughtful extras and the Long Sitting Room, with its roaring log fire, creates a warm and inviting atmosphere. Breakfasts are truly memorable, featuring long forgotten dishes, many of which are produced locally.
FACILITIES: 3 en suite (1 fmly) No smoking in 2 bedrooms No smoking in dining room No smoking in 1 lounge tea/coffee No dogs (ex guide dogs) Cen ht TVL No children 12yrs No coaches Dinner Last d by arrangement **PRICES:** d £60-£68✻ **LB PARKING:** 5 **CARDS:**

Premier Collection

♦♦♦♦♦ *White Vine House*

24 High St TN31 7JF ☎ 01797 224748 & 227768
01797 223599
e-mail: irene@whitevinehouse.freeserve.co.uk
Dir: *Rye is at junction of A259/A268. Follow signs to town centre and enter through Landgate Arch. Follow road into High Street and hotel is on right*

A warm welcome is assured at this impressive town house, originally a 16th century inn and extensively rebuilt in Georgian times. Many original features have been retained, including exposed beams and carved fireplaces, which are enhanced by the quality furnishings throughout. Bedrooms vary in size, and all are equipped with a wealth of homely extras. Comprehensive English breakfasts are served in addition to light meals during the day.
FACILITIES: 7 en suite (1 fmly) No smoking in dining room TVB tea/coffee Licensed Cen ht TVL No coaches **NOTES:** Closed 1-7 Jan
CARDS:

♦♦♦♦ The Strand House

The Strand, Winchelsea TN36 4JT ☎ 01797 226276
01797 224806
e-mail: strandhouse@winchelsea98.fsnet.co.uk
Dir: *2m W of Rye in the direction of Hastings on A259, 1st building on left after passing town sign*
Dating from the 15th century, this fine harbour-side house retains many original features including inglenook fireplaces and exposed beams. Bedrooms are full of quality furnishings, thoughtful extras and the ground floor areas include a comfortable lounge, cosy dining room and an honesty bar.
FACILITIES: 10 en suite (1 fmly) (1 GF) No smoking TVB tea/coffee No dogs Licensed Cen ht No children 2yrs No coaches **PRICES:** s £36-£42; d £52-£76✳ **LB PARKING:** 12 **NOTES:** Closed 25-27 Dec
CARDS:

♦♦♦♦ Old Borough Arms Hotel

The Strand TN31 7DB ☎ 01797 222128 01797 222128
e-mail: info@oldborougharms.co.uk
Dir: *turn off A259 into the Strand. Hotel is situated at foot of Mermaid Street overlooking Strand Quay*
Expect a warm welcome at this former sailor's inn. The property is in an elevated position in a peaceful setting, yet just minutes from town. Bedrooms come in a variety of sizes and styles, are pleasantly decorated and thoughtfully equipped. Breakfast is served in the charming dining room and guests can use the cosy lounge bar.
FACILITIES: 9 en suite (1 fmly) (4 GF) No smoking TVB tea/coffee No dogs (ex guide dogs) Licensed Cen ht TVL **PRICES:** s £30-£40; d £50-£80✳
PARKING: 10 **CARDS:**

♦♦♦♦ A Layces Bed & Breakfast

Chitcombe Rd, Broad Oak Brede TN31 6EU ☎ 01424 882836
01424 882281
e-mail: stephens@layces.co.uk
Dir: *on B2086 W of Rye, 200mtrs W of intersection of B2089 with A28 at Broad Oak x-rds*
FACILITIES: 3 en suite (1 GF) No smoking TVB tea/coffee No dogs Cen ht No coaches **PRICES:** s £27; d £40✳ **PARKING:** 5 **CARDS:**

♦♦♦ Cliff Farm *(TQ933237)*

Military Rd, Iden Lock TN31 7QD ☎ 01797 280331
01797 280331 Mrs P Sullivin
e-mail: pat@cliff-farm.freeserve.uk
Mar-Oct
Dir: *2m along the Military Road to Appledore turn left at hanging milk churn*
A detached property situated in a peaceful rural location surrounded by open countryside. The bedrooms are pleasantly decorated, comfortably furnished and thoughtfully equipped. Breakfast is served at individual tables in the dining room and guests also have the use of a cosy sitting room with a wood burning stove.
FACILITIES: 3 rms (1 fmly) No smoking tea/coffee Cen ht TVL 6 acres smallholding **PRICES:** d £34-£36✳ **LB BB PARKING:** 6

A indicates an Associate entry, which has been inspected and rated by the ETC or the RAC in England.

RYE continued

♦♦♦ Little Saltcote

22 Military Rd TN31 7NY ☎ 01797 223210 📠 01797 224474
e-mail: littlesaltcote.rye@virgin.net
Dir: *turn off A268 onto Military Rd, signposted to Appledore. House 300mtrs on left*

Friendly, family run guest house situated on the outskirts of town yet within walking distance. Bedrooms are pleasantly decorated and equipped with modern facilities. Breakfast is served at individual tables in the smart dining room.

FACILITIES: 5 rms (3 en suite) (3 fmly) (1 GF) No smoking in 2 bedrooms No smoking in dining room TVB tea/coffee Cen ht **PRICES:** s £25-£28; d £40-£50✳ **LB** **PARKING:** 3 **CARDS:**

♦♦♦ Old Vicarage

Rye Harbour TN31 7TT ☎ 01797 222088
e-mail: johnathan@oldvicarageryeharbour.fsnet.co.uk

Located in the medieval port of Rye, this house retains a great deal of original charm, which is enhanced by the décor and furniture throughout. Bedrooms are filled with thoughtful extras and the dining room has a real Victorian atmosphere, with memorabilia in abundance.

FACILITIES: 2 rms No smoking in 1 bedrooms No smoking in dining room TVB tea/coffee Cen ht No coaches **PRICES:** s £25-£40; d £39-£55✳ **LB** **PARKING:** 3

SEAFORD — Map 05 TV49

♦♦♦♦ Avondale Hotel

Avondale Rd BN25 1RJ ☎ 01323 890008 📠 01323 490598
Dir: *from Seaford town centre take A259 towards Eastbourne. Avondale is on left opposite town memorial*

A warm welcome is offered by the caring owners at this friendly, family run hotel which is ideally placed for the Newhaven to Dieppe Seacat ferry service. The bedrooms are attractively decorated, pleasantly furnished and thoughtfully equipped. Breakfast and dinner are served in the attractive dining room and guests also have the use of a cosy lounge.

FACILITIES: 16 rms (10 en suite) (4 fmly) No smoking TVB tea/coffee No dogs (ex guide dogs) Lift Cen ht No coaches Golf Seaford leisure centre is nearby Dinner Last d 10am **PRICES:** s £20-£38; d £38-£60✳ **BB**
CARDS:

♦♦♦♦ Silverdale

21 Sutton Park Rd BN25 1RH ☎ 01323 491849
📠 01323 891131
e-mail: silverdale@mistral.co.uk
Dir: *on A259 in the centre of Seaford, close to Memorial*

Expect a warm welcome at this friendly family run hotel, which is ideally situated for the town centre and seafront. Bedrooms are pleasantly decorated, tastefully furnished and equipped with many useful extras. Breakfast and dinner are served in the smart dining room and guests also have the use of a cosy well-stocked lounge bar.

continued

FACILITIES: 8 rms (6 en suite) (2 fmly) (1 GF) No smoking in 3 bedrooms No smoking in area of dining room No smoking in lounges TVB tea/coffee Direct dial from bedrooms Licensed Cen ht No coaches Dinner Last d 6pm
PRICES: s £28-£35; d £38-£65✳ **LB** **BB** **PARKING:** 6
CARDS:

UCKFIELD — Map 05 TQ42

Premier Collection

♦♦♦♦♦ Hooke Hall

250 High St TN22 1EN ☎ 01825 761578 📠 01825 768025
e-mail: a.percy@virgin.net
Dir: *N end of Uckfield High St*

An elegant Queen Anne town house, beautifully furnished with antique pieces, fine paintings and ornaments to create a wonderful country house feel. The property was built in the early 18th century and has been lovingly restored by the present owners. The individually decorated bedrooms are very stylish and have a good range of modern facilities. Guests can relax in the comfortable panelled study, which has an open fire.

FACILITIES: 10 en suite No smoking in dining room STV TVB tea/coffee Direct dial from bedrooms No dogs Licensed Cen ht No children 10yrs No coaches **PRICES:** s £55-£85; d £85-£135✳
PARKING: 8 **NOTES:** Closed 23 Dec-6 Jan **CARDS:**

WADHURST — Map 05 TQ63

♦♦♦ Spring Cottage

Best Beech Hill TN5 6JH ☎ 01892 783896 & 785752
📠 01892 784866
e-mail: penny@southerncrosstravel.co.uk
Dir: *from Tunbridge Wells take A267 to Mark Cross, turn left onto B2100. Cottage 2m up hill on left*

FACILITIES: 2 rms (1 en suite) (1 fmly) No smoking TVB tea/coffee No dogs (ex guide dogs) Cen ht No coaches **PRICES:** s £21-£35; d £50-£56✳ **LB** **PARKING:** 4 **NOTES:** Closed 24-27 Dec

♦♦ *Four Keys*

Station Rd TN5 6RZ ☎ 01892 782252 📠 01892 784113

Situated on the edge of this popular town and ideally placed for the railway station, this property comprises the main building and a motel style building which lies adjacent. Bedrooms are located in the latter and breakfast and evening meals are served at individual tables in the main building.

FACILITIES: 7 annexe en suite (1 fmly) TVB tea/coffee Direct dial from bedrooms Cen ht Last d 10pm **PARKING:** 24 **CARDS:**

WILMINGTON — Map 05 TQ50

Premier Collection

♦♦♦♦♦ Crossways Hotel

Lewes Rd BN26 5SG ☎ 01323 482455 📠 01323 487811
e-mail: stay@crosswayshotel.co.uk
Dir: *on A27 between Lewes and Polegate, 2m E of Alfriston rdbt*

A well-established restaurant with a good local reputation is the focus for this attractive property. Bedrooms are all individually decorated with taste and style with superior rooms available. Guest comfort is paramount with excellent facilities and hospitality that ensures guests return frequently.

continued

England

FACILITIES: 7 en suite No smoking in dining room TVB tea/coffee Direct dial from bedrooms No dogs (ex guide dogs) Licensed Cen ht No children 12yrs No coaches Dinner Last d 8.45pm **PRICES:** s £52; d £80-£90✱ **LB** **PARKING:** 30 **NOTES:** Closed 24 Dec-23 Jan **CARDS:**

SUSSEX, WEST

AMBERLEY Map 04 TQ01

♦♦♦♦ Woody Banks

Crossgates BN18 9NR ☎ 01798 831295

Dir: *turn off B2139 into village of Amberley then right at the Black Horse pub. Continue for 0.5m. Woody Banks is on left just past Sportsman pub*

Located four miles from Arundel in an elevated position with stunning views over the Wildbrooks, this immaculately maintained house and gardens are very popular with walkers and provides comfortable homely bedrooms filled with thoughtful extras. Imaginative breakfasts are taken in the panoramic dining room, which also contains a lounge area.

FACILITIES: 2 rms No smoking TVB tea/coffee No dogs (ex guide dogs) Cen ht TVL No coaches Croquet lawn **PRICES:** d fr £40✱ **LB** **PARKING:** 3 **NOTES:** Closed 24 Dec-2 Jan

ARDINGLY Map 05 TQ32

Premier Collection

♦♦♦♦♦ Avins Bridge Restaurant

College Rd RH17 6SH ☎ 01444 892393

e-mail: enquiries@theavinsbridge.co.uk

Dir: *M23 J10/A264 towards East Grinstead, at Dukes Head rdbt take B2028 to Ardingly. At end of village take B2112 for 1m*

This attractive Victorian property is set in a peaceful location in the Sussex countryside. Bedrooms are decorated to a high standard with a bright modern feel offering a range of facilities. The two attractive dining rooms serve breakfasts and evening meals using mainly organic and local produce. The hosts provide a warm friendly welcome.

FACILITIES: 5 en suite (1 fmly) No smoking in bedrooms No smoking in area of dining room TVB tea/coffee Direct dial from bedrooms Licensed Cen ht No children 6yrs No coaches Dinner Last d 9.30pm **PRICES:** s £40-£65; d £60-£65✱ **LB** **PARKING:** 20 **NOTES:** Closed 24-30 Dec rs Sun-Mon (restaurant closed) **CARDS:**

ARUNDEL Map 04 TQ00

Premier Collection

♦♦♦♦♦ Bonham's Country House

Main Rd, Yapton BN18 0DX ☎ 01243 551301

01243 551301

e-mail: bonhams@compass-rose.org.uk

Dir: *from A27 between Fontwell/Arundel turn onto B2132. Turn right at T-junct by Black Dog pub onto B2233 100mtrs on right (The Independents)*

Built in 1746, this delightful house provides a warm, friendly welcome. Spacious bedrooms are attractively decorated with thoughtful extras. Guests can relax in the comfortable lounge and enjoy good home cooked breakfasts in the traditional dining room. Evening meals are not served but there are many local restaurants and pubs. A tennis court, an exercise pool and a landscaped garden are all for guests to enjoy. Sailing on a yacht can also be arranged.

Bonham's Country House

FACILITIES: 3 en suite (1 fmly) No smoking TVB tea/coffee No dogs (ex guide dogs) Cen ht TVL No coaches Indoor swimming pool (heated) Tennis (hard) Pool Table Croquet lawn Luxury yacht hire (1day-2wks) 1/4 snooker table **PRICES:** s £40-£50; d £50-£70✱ **LB** **CONF:** Thtr 18 Class 12 Board 12 Del £70 ✱ **PARKING:** 8

♦♦♦♦ Blakehurst Farm *(TQ046066)*

BN18 9QG ☎ 01903 882632 01903 889562

Claire & Alex Lock

e-mail: alex.lock@farmline.com

Dir: *3m E of Arundel, N off the A27 dual carriageway, signed Blakehurst*

This fine Georgian property is situated on a working farm and enjoys good views of rural Britain. Bedrooms are spacious and cheerfully decorated. Guests have use of the comfortable lounge and breakfast is taken around a single table. Dinner is available on request and mountain bikes are also available for hire.

FACILITIES: 2 rms No smoking TVB tea/coffee No dogs (ex guide dogs) Cen ht TVL 1000 acres arable horses **PRICES:** s £30-£35; d £45-£50✱ **PARKING:** 3 **NOTES:** Closed Xmas

♦♦♦♦ Pindars

Lyminster BN17 7QF ☎ 01903 882628 01903 882628

Dir: *turn S off A27, onto A284 signed Lyminster/Littlehampton. After 1m Guest house immediately on left after sharp right bend*

FACILITIES: 3 rms (1 en suite) No smoking TVB tea/coffee No dogs (ex guide dogs) Cen ht TVL No children 10yrs No coaches Outdoor swimming pool (heated) Dinner Last d 10am **PRICES:** d £40-£50✱ **PARKING:** 4 **NOTES:** Closed Xmas & New Year **CARDS:**

continued

England

ARUNDEL continued

♦♦♦ Arden
4 Queens Ln BN18 9JN ☎ 01903 882544
This well-maintained, non-smoking Victorian guest house is situated by the River Arun and only a few minutes walk from all of the central attractions. The house has excellent standards of housekeeping and accommodation includes good practical bedrooms. Comprehensive breakfasts are served in the bright and attractive dining room.
FACILITIES: 8 rms (3 en suite) (2 GF) No smoking TVB tea/coffee No dogs (ex guide dogs) Cen ht No children 5yrs No coaches **PRICES:** s £25-£30; d £40-£44✻ **PARKING:** 4

BOGNOR REGIS Map 04 SZ99

♦♦♦♦ Old Priory
80 North Bersted St PO22 9AQ ☎ 01243 863580
🖷 01243 826597
e-mail: old.priory@mcmail.com
Dir: *from Chichester take A259 to North Bersted, Old Priory sign is on left. From Fontwell proceed along A29 to b/b sign after Robin Hood pub*

Located in the mainly residential area of North Bersted, this 400-year old property retains many original features, which are highlighted by the decor and furniture styles throughout the building. Bedrooms are well-equipped and homely. There is an outdoor pool and attractive grounds, perfect in the summer months and dinner is also a treat.
FACILITIES: 3 en suite No smoking in lounges STV TVB tea/coffee No dogs (ex guide dogs) Licensed Cen ht TVL No coaches Outdoor swimming pool Jacuzzi Dinner Last d noon **PARKING:** 4 **CARDS:**

♦♦♦ Jubilee
5 Gloucester Rd PO21 1NU ☎ 01243 863016 & 07702 275967
🖷 01243 868017
e-mail: JubileeGuestHouse@breathemail.net
Dir: *from A27 to seafront, house opposite Day Entrance to Butlins Family Entertainment Resort*

This property is close to Butlin's, the seafront and the town centre. The brightly decorated and well-equipped bedrooms vary in size, and all have clock radios and hairdryers. A generous and freshly cooked breakfast, including provision for vegetarians, is served in the attractive dining room.
FACILITIES: 6 rms (2 en suite) (2 fmly) No smoking in dining room TVB tea/coffee No dogs Cen ht No coaches **PRICES:** s £22-£35; d £44-£70✻ LB **PARKING:** 4 **NOTES:** Closed Xmas & Jan **CARDS:**

♦♦♦ Regis Lodge
3 Gloucester Rd PO21 1NU ☎ 01243 827110 🖷 01243 827110
e-mail: frank@regislodge.fsbusiness.co.uk
Dir: *Opposite Southcoast World Holiday Camp - Day Visitors entrance*
Located within easy walking distance to the sea front, this family run guest house offers a high standard of hospitality. Bedrooms vary in size but are well presented and suitably equipped. The brightly decorated dining room has separate tables and a good choice of breakfast is offered.
FACILITIES: 12 en suite (8 fmly) No smoking in dining room TVB tea/coffee No dogs Cen ht No children 5yrs No coaches **PRICES:** s £25-£35; d £40-£60✻ LB **PARKING:** 9 **NOTES:** Closed Nov-Mar

BOSHAM Map 04 SU80

Premier Collection

♦♦♦♦♦ Kenwood
Off A259 PO18 8PH ☎ 01243 572727 🖷 01243 572738
Dir: *400m W of Bosham roundabout on A259*
Kenwood is an impressive Victorian house, set in pleasant gardens with views across the harbour. Some bedrooms have views over the gardens. Breakfast is served in the bright conservatory, which also contains a fridge and microwave for guests who wish to cater for themselves in the evening. An elegant lounge is also available for guest use with a pool table in the adjacent room.
FACILITIES: 3 en suite (1 fmly) No smoking in bedrooms No smoking in dining room No smoking in 1 lounge TVB tea/coffee Direct dial from bedrooms No dogs (ex guide dogs) Cen ht TVL No coaches Indoor swimming pool (heated) Croquet lawn Fitness equipment Pool table, Archery **PRICES:** s £27; d £54✻ **PARKING:** 14

♦♦♦♦ White Barn
Crede Ln PO18 8NX ☎ 01243 573113 🖷 01243 573113
e-mail: whitebarn@compuserve.com
Dir: *A259 Bosham rdbt, turn S signed Bosham Quay, 0.5m to T-junct, left signed White Barn, 0.25m turn left signed White Barn, 50yds turn right*

This delightful single storey property is close Bosham Harbour, Goodwood Race Circuit, Chichester and Portsmouth, and has cosy bedrooms with colour co-ordinated soft furnishings and many thoughtful extras. The open plan dining room overlooks an attractive garden. Four course dinners are available by prior arrangement.

continued

FACILITIES: 2 en suite 1 annexe en suite (1 fmly) (3 GF) No smoking TVB tea/coffee No dogs Cen ht No children 12yrs No coaches Dinner Last d breakfast **PRICES:** s £35-£50; d £60-£80* LB **PARKING:** 3 **CARDS:**

BURGESS HILL — Map 04 TQ31

♦♦♦♦ The Homestead

Homestead Ln, Valebridge Rd RH15 0RQ
☎ 01444 246899 & 0800 064 0015 Res 🖹 01444 241407
e-mail: homestead@burgess-hill.co.uk
Dir: *from A23, Hickstead, take A2300 signed Burgess Hill. On approaching town, follow signs at every rdbt to Wivelsfield Station. Left into Valebridge Rd. Homestead Lane 0.5m on right. at end of lane*

The Homestead enjoys a country setting, in 7 acres of garden and woodland, but just a short distance from the town centre. Bedrooms vary in size, all are well appointed and equipped with modern facilities. A good choice of breakfast is offered including vegetarian options. The attractive dining room overlooks a garden and there is a comfortable conservatory lounge area.
FACILITIES: 4 en suite (2 GF) No smoking STV TVB tea/coffee No dogs (ex guide dogs) Cen ht No children 12yrs No coaches **PRICES:** s £25-£30; d £50-£60* **PARKING:** 50 **CARDS:**

CHARLTON — Map 04 SU81

♦♦♦♦ Woodstock House Hotel

PO18 0HU ☎ 01243 811666 🖹 01243 811666
e-mail: info@woodstockhousehotel.co.uk
Dir: *take A286 heading S towards Chichester, on reaching village of Singleton turn left and follow road for 1m to Charlton. Hotel immediately on left.*

Peacefully located accommodation in the pleasant village of Charlton, close to a range of recommended inns and restaurants together with all the attractions of Chichester and Goodwood. Bedrooms are individually decorated and well equipped with many useful extras. Several rooms overlook the pleasant rear garden. The proprietors here offer an especially friendly welcome.
FACILITIES: 12 en suite No smoking in bedrooms No smoking in dining room No smoking in lounges TVB tea/coffee Direct dial from bedrooms Licensed Cen ht No coaches **PRICES:** s £45-£48.50; d £68-£82 **PARKING:** 12 **CARDS:**

CHICHESTER — Map 04 SU80

See also Bosham & Chilgrove

♦♦♦♦ Cedar House

8 Westmead Rd PO19 3JD ☎ 01243 787771 🖹 01243 538316
e-mail: mel.judi@talk21.com
Dir: *from 'Fishbourne' rdbt on A27 W of city, proceed for city centre. Then 1st left into Fishbourne Rd East, right into Clay Lane, 1st right*

continued

Cedar House

Conveniently located for the Sussex coast and many places of interest, Cedar House, with its brightly decorated rooms, is situated in a quiet residential area to the west of the city, just 12 minutes walk from the centre of town. A full English breakfast is served in the cosy dining room.
FACILITIES: 4 rms (2 en suite) No smoking TVB tea/coffee No dogs Cen ht TVL No coaches **PRICES:** s £20-£25; d £50* **PARKING:** 4

♦♦♦♦ Chichester Lodge

Oakwood PO18 9AL ☎ 01243 786560 🖹 01243 784525
Dir: *3m W of Chichester off the B2178. Establisment 170 metres on left after Salthill Road*

A delightful Victorian gate lodge in a peaceful location amidst secluded grounds, yet only two miles form the city centre. The spacious bedrooms are attractively decorated and tastefully furnished with well-chosen pieces. Breakfast is served in the elegant dining room and guests also have the use of a lovely conservatory.
FACILITIES: 2 en suite No smoking TVB tea/coffee No dogs Cen ht No children No coaches **PRICES:** d £50-£60* **PARKING:** 3

♦♦♦♦ Downfields

Level Mare Ln, Eastergate PO20 6SB ☎ 01243 542012
Dir: *Southern side of A27 From Fontwell rdbt 2nd turning on left on the westbound carriageway, Downfields on right side.*

Downfields is set in a quiet rural location and provides comfortable and homely accommodation. The single bedroom is spacious and well-equipped. The public areas here include a bright and comfortable dining room where English breakfast is served and the surrounding garden is a delight.
FACILITIES: 1 en suite No smoking in bedrooms TVB tea/coffee No dogs Cen ht No children 10yrs No coaches **PRICES:** d £50-£60* LB BB **PARKING:** 6 **NOTES:** Closed 21 Dec-4 Jan

> TVB means there are televisions in bedrooms
> TVL means thereís a television in the lounge
> STV means satellite television.

England

CHICHESTER continued

♦♦♦♦ Old Chapel Forge

Lower Bognor Rd, Lagness PO20 1LR ☎ 01243 264380
Fax 01243 261649
e-mail: cfbarnes@breathemail.net
Dir: *from A27 Chichester By-Pass, exit on Bognor rdbt signed Pagham/Runcton, in S direction. At rdbt turn left onto B2166 Pagham Rd, continue to Royal Oak PH on right. Left onto Lower Bognor Rd for 0.75m Old Chapel Forge on right*

Old Chapel Forge is located in beautiful rural surroundings and overlooks sweeping fields. The accommodation takes the form of a self-contained suite, which includes its own dining area, comfortable lounge and en suite bedroom. Breakfast is substantial and of a high quality.

FACILITIES: 1 en suite (1 fmly) No smoking TVB tea/coffee Cen ht TVL No coaches Croquet lawn Dinner Last d prior to stay **PRICES:** s £30-£45; d £50-£75✳ **LB PARKING:** 5

♦♦♦♦ Wilbury House

Main Rd, Fishbourne PO18 8AT ☎ 01243 572953
Fax 01243 572953
e-mail: jackie.penfold@talk21.com
Dir: *from A27 Chichester by-pass, take A259 W to Fishbourne and Bosham, 1m on left from Tesco roundabout*

This modern and well-appointed house is located on the edge of the village surrounded by countryside. Personally supervised by the charming owner, the atmosphere is warm and friendly. Bedrooms are individually decorated, nicely furnished and well-equipped. A generous English breakfast is served in the kitchen or in the dining room.

FACILITIES: 4 en suite (1 fmly) (2 GF) No smoking TVB tea/coffee Cen ht TVL No children 6yrs No coaches **PRICES:** s £30-£35; d £50-£60✳ **PARKING:** 7 **NOTES:** Closed mid Dec-mid Jan

CHILGROVE Map 04 SU81

Premier Collection

♦♦♦♦♦ Forge Hotel

PO18 9HX ☎ 01243 535333 Fax 01243 535363
e-mail: enquiries@forgehotel.com
Dir: *off B2141, adjacent to White Horse Inn, 6m NW of Chichester*

Set in tranquil surroundings, this hotel offers quality throughout. Good hospitality is supported by character bedrooms, all of which have private or en suite facilities. Attractive quality décor, thoughtful extras and well-designed bathrooms are all features of the rooms. The evening meals and breakfasts are freshly prepared to a high standard.

FACILITIES: 5 en suite No smoking in bedrooms No smoking in dining room TVB Direct dial from bedrooms Licensed Cen ht No children 14yrs No coaches Croquet lawn Dinner Last d 9pm **PRICES:** s £40-£55; d £90-£150✳ **LB CONF:** Thtr 12 Class 12

continued

Forge Hotel

Board 12 **PARKING:** 10 **NOTES:** Closed last wk Oct & 1 wk Feb
CARDS:

CRAWLEY

See **Gatwick Airport**

FINDON Map 04 TQ10

♦♦♦ Village House Hotel

Findon BN14 0TE ☎ 01903 873350 Fax 01903 877931
Dir: *Turn off A24 into Findon village by the Black Horse pub, hotel on main X-road in village*

Located in the heart of the village, this 16th-century inn offers well-equipped bedrooms with modern bathrooms. A wide range of imaginative dishes is offered in either the formal dining room or the spacious bars, which are furnished with character and style.

FACILITIES: 6 en suite (1 fmly) No smoking in area of dining room TVB tea/coffee No dogs Cen ht No coaches Dinner Last d 9pm **PRICES:** s fr £30; d fr £50✳ **MEALS:** Lunch £6.25-£11.75&alc Dinner £6.25-£11.75&alc✳ **PARKING:** 8 **CARDS:**

GATWICK AIRPORT (London) Map 04 TQ24

♦♦♦♦ Corner House Hotel

72 Massetts Rd RH6 7ED ☎ 01293 784574 Fax 01293 784620
e-mail: info@thecornerhouse.co.uk
Dir: *M23 junct 9, 1st rdbt 2nd exit, next rdbt 4th exit to Redhill join A23 to next rdbt 3rd exit, 2nd turn on right, Massetts Rd Cornerhouse on left*

Ideally located for Gatwick Airport and with a 24 hour courtesy transfer service, this constantly improving hotel provides a range of thoughtfully furnished bedrooms, some of which are situated in a separate elegant house. Ground floor areas include an attractive dining room and comfortable lounge bar.

FACILITIES: 13 en suite 12 annexe en suite (6 fmly) No smoking in bedrooms No smoking in dining room No smoking in 1 lounge TVB tea/coffee Direct dial from bedrooms No dogs (ex guide dogs) Licensed Cen ht TVL Membership to local sports centre Dinner Last d 9pm

continued

England

PRICES: s £36-£59; d £59-£69✱ **PARKING:** 40
CARDS:

♦♦♦♦ Cumberland House

39 Brighton Rd RH6 7HH ☎ 01293 825800 📠 01293 825017
e-mail: info@cumberlandhs.com
Dir: *from rdbt at Gatwick Nth terminal, take 4th exit. Follow sign to A23. at next rdbt take 3rd exit onto A23. on A23 first left Church Rd Cumberland House is on corner.*
This attractive and well-run guest house is conveniently located for travelling to Gatwick Airport. The bedrooms are comfortable and tastefully decorated and all offer a good range of room facilities. Breakfast is served in an attractive first floor dining room and there is ample off-road parking.
FACILITIES: 7 en suite (1 fmly) (1 GF) No smoking TVB tea/coffee No dogs (ex guide dogs) Cen ht No coaches **PRICES:** s £39.50; d £49.50✱
PARKING: 20 **CARDS:**

♦♦♦♦ The Lawn

30 Massetts Rd RH6 7DE ☎ 01293 775751 📠 01293 821803
e-mail: info@lawnguesthouse.co.uk
Dir: *M23 J9, follow signs to A23 (Redhill), at rdbt by Esso garage take 3rd exit, Massetts Rd 300yds on right*

Ideally situated for Gatwick Airport, this fine detached Victorian house offers brightly decorated bedrooms, equipped with many thoughtful extras. A choice of breakfast is provided and served in the attractive dining room. There is even an Internet facility available to guests.
FACILITIES: 12 en suite (4 fmly) No smoking TVB tea/coffee Direct dial from bedrooms Cen ht No coaches **PRICES:** s £40-£45; d £55✱
PARKING: 15 **CARDS:**

♦♦♦♦ Rosemead

19 Church Rd RH6 7EY ☎ 01293 784965 📠 01293 430547
e-mail: info@rosemeadguesthouse.co.uk
Dir: *exit M23 junct 9, follow A23 Redhill signs, through 3 rdbts, Church Rd is 4th on right, premises 3rd house on right*
This well established hotel enjoys a central position on the seafront and is only minutes away from the high street. Bedrooms are modern in style and equipped with a good range of facilities. The public areas are tastefully decorated and include a comfortable cocktail bar and spacious restaurant.
FACILITIES: 6 en suite (2 fmly) No smoking STV TVB tea/coffee Cen ht No coaches **PRICES:** s £35-£40; d £50✱ **PARKING:** 40 **CARDS:**

♦♦♦♦ *Trumbles*

Stan Hill RH6 0EP ☎ 01293 862925 & 863418
📠 01293 862925
e-mail: trumbles.gatwick@tesco.net
Dir: *junct 8 M25 A217 to Gatwick, turn right at rdbt to Charlwood Village, through village bear right to Leigh, 1st left into Stanhill, Trumbles 300yds on right*

continued

This attractive house, within easy reach of Gatwick, enjoys a quiet and secluded setting in this charming village. Bedrooms are spacious with a good range of facilities. The conservatory offers an ideal environment for guests to relax and enjoy the continental breakfasts. Parking is also available.
FACILITIES: 4 en suite No smoking STV TVB tea/coffee No dogs (ex guide dogs) Cen ht No children 5yrs No coaches **PARKING:** 20
CARDS:

♦♦♦♦ Vulcan Lodge

27 Massetts Rd RH6 7DQ ☎ 01293 771522 📠 01293 786206
e-mail: reservations@vulcan-lodge.com
Dir: *M23 J9, follow signs A23 Redhill. At 4th rdbt exit right. Take 2nd right signposted Horley Town Centre. Premises 25mtrs on right).*

A particularly warm and friendly welcome is offered by the hosts of this charming period house, which sits back from the main road and is convenient for Gatwick Airport. Bedrooms are all individually decorated, well equipped and feature many thoughtful extras. A choice of breakfast is offered, including vegetarian, and is served in a delightful dining room.
FACILITIES: 4 en suite (1 fmly) No smoking TVB tea/coffee No dogs (ex guide dogs) Cen ht TVL No coaches **PRICES:** s £36-£40; d £55✱
PARKING: 13 **CARDS:**

♦♦♦♦ Wayside Manor Farm

Norwood Hill RH6 0ET ☎ 01293 862692 📠 01293 863417
e-mail: info@wayside-manor.com
Dir: *M25 junct 8, S on A217 through Reigate follow Gatwick signs. 2m S of Reigate right onto Ironsbottom 2nd right Collendean Ln, to x-rds Norwood Hill. House on X-rds opp pub*

A delightful Edwardian farmhouse situated in a peaceful country setting within easy reach of Gatwick Airport. The spacious bedrooms offer good levels of comfort and are well equipped with modern amenities. The elegant public rooms are tastefully appointed and breakfast is served in the charming dining room, guests sharing one large table.
FACILITIES: 3 en suite No smoking in bedrooms No smoking in dining room TVB tea/coffee No dogs Cen ht No coaches **PRICES:** s £50; d £60✱
PARKING: 20

England

GATWICK AIRPORT continued

♦♦♦♦ The Beeches

60 Massetts Rd RH6 7DS ☎ 01293 823457 01293 415595
e-mail: val@beechesguesthouse.com
Dir: *exit M23 junct 9, pass Gatwick airport onto A23, continue on A23 into Horley take 2nd right, the Beeches approx. 200mtrs on left*
FACILITIES: 5 en suite (2 fmly) No smoking TVB tea/coffee No dogs (ex guide dogs) Cen ht **PRICES:** s fr £35; d fr £50* **PARKING:** 9
CARDS:

♦♦♦ April Cottage

10 Langley Ln, Ifield Green RH11 0NA ☎ 01293 546222
01293 518712
e-mail: aprilcottage.guesthouse@tesco.net
Dir: *M23 junct 10, follow signs to Crawley. At 1st rdbt signed Horsham. At 3rd rdbt right to Ifield. Over 2 mini rdbts then next left (Ifield Green). After pub next left. Cottage 4th on right*
An attractive cottage on the edge of the town offering a cosy atmosphere in a strictly no smoking environment. Bedrooms are homely with some thoughtful extras. Breakfast is served by your friendly hosts in a central dining room area with home-made preserves on offer.
FACILITIES: 3 rms (1 en suite) 1 annexe en suite (1 fmly) No smoking TVB tea/coffee No dogs (ex guide dogs) Cen ht No coaches
PRICES: d £50-£60* **PARKING:** 12 **CARDS:**

♦♦♦ Gainsborough Lodge

39 Massetts Rd RH6 7DT ☎ 01293 783982 01293 785365
e-mail: enquiries@gainsborough-lodge.co.uk
Dir: *2m NE of airport adjacent A23*
Close to Gatwick, this fine Edwardian house offers a courtesy service to and from the airport. The bedrooms are comfortably appointed with bright decor. A fine selection is offered at breakfast, including a vegetarian option, and is served in the bright conservatory dining room. There is an attractive lounge.
FACILITIES: 18 rms (16 en suite) 7 annexe en suite (4 fmly) No smoking in 19 bedrooms No smoking in dining room TVB tea/coffee Direct dial from bedrooms No dogs Cen ht TVL No coaches Free membership of local sports centre **PRICES:** s fr £41; d fr £55* **PARKING:** 20 **CARDS:**

♦♦♦ *Gatwick Belmont*

46 Massetts Rd RH6 7DS ☎ 01293 820500 01293 783812
e-mail: stay@gatwickbelmont.com
Dir: *off A23 into Massetts Rd, half way down on left*
Located within easy walking distance from town centre and one mile from Garwick Airport, this constantly improving Edwardian house offers a range of practically furnished bedrooms, some of which have direct access to car parks. Spacious ground floor areas include a comfortable lounge bar and a courtesy airport bus service is also provided.
FACILITIES: 15 rms (13 en suite) (2 fmly) No smoking in 9 bedrooms No smoking in dining room TVB tea/coffee Direct dial from bedrooms No dogs Cen ht **PARKING:** 15 **CARDS:**

♦♦♦ Gatwick White House Hotel

50-52 Church Rd RH6 7EX ☎ 01293 402777 01293 424135
e-mail: stay@gatwickwhitehouse.com
Dir: *from M23 junct 9, pass Gatwick Airport (Sth Terminal) follow signs for A23 London/Redhill, through 2rdbts, at Longbridge rdbt turn right into Horley in 500yds Church Rd on right*
Conveniently located for the Airport and road networks, this hotel provides smart and well-equipped accommodation. A bar, restaurant and good parking also feature.
FACILITIES: 27 rms (22 en suite) No smoking in bedrooms No smoking in dining room TVB tea/coffee Direct dial from bedrooms Licensed Cen ht TVL Dinner Last d 3.30pm **PRICES:** s £30-£40; d £50-£65* **PARKING:** 50
CARDS:

♦♦♦ Prinsted

Oldfield Rd RH6 7EP ☎ 01293 785233 01293 820624
e-mail: kendall@prinstedguesthouse.co.uk
Dir: *M23 junct 9, follow signs for Airport. At Airport rdbt take A23 & continue to Texaco Garage, turn right immediately into Woodroyd Ave, on left*
This well established family-run business is a popular choice. Courtesy cars to the airport are provided. A variety of bedroom types is available; all are thoughtfully furnished. Many original features have been retained and add character to the property.
FACILITIES: 8 rms (6 en suite) No smoking TVB tea/coffee No dogs (ex guide dogs) Cen ht No coaches **PRICES:** s fr £32; d £37-£47* BB
PARKING: 12 **NOTES:** Closed 23-26 Dec **CARDS:**

♦♦♦ *Springwood Guest House*

58 Massetts Rd RH6 7DS ☎ 01293 775998 01293 823103
e-mail: ernest@springwood58.u-net.com
Dir: *Leave A23 into Massetts Rd which is approx 200yds from junct of A23/A217*
This large Victorian house is ideally located for the airport and services are well suited to meet these requirements. The bedrooms vary is size and all offer comfortable accommodation with good facilities. Breakfasts are served in the bright dining room, which has separate tables.
FACILITIES: 11 rms (10 en suite) (2 fmly) No smoking in 5 bedrooms No smoking in dining room No smoking in lounges TVB tea/coffee Direct dial from bedrooms Cen ht TVL No coaches **PARKING:** 14
CARDS:

HAYWARDS HEATH — Map 05 TQ32

♦♦♦♦ Sliders Farm *(TQ404257)*

Furners Green, Danehill TN22 3RT ☎ 01825 790258
01825 790258 Mr & Mrs D Salmon
e-mail: jeananddavidsalmon@sliders.freeserve.co.uk
Dir: *Intersection A22 South/A275 , 1m S of Danehill village on A275, signposted at small crossroads, turn right into Sliders Lane, second on right*
A 16th-century farmhouse situated in a peaceful rural location. Bedrooms are tastefully furnished and decorated. They are also equipped with many thoughtful extras including a comprehensive guide to walks and other nearby attractions. The spacious lounge boasts an inglenook fireplace, and a snooker table. There is also a beamed breakfast room. Self-catering accommodation is available.
FACILITIES: 3 en suite (1 fmly) No smoking in bedrooms No smoking in dining room TVB tea/coffee No dogs Cen ht Outdoor swimming pool (heated) Tennis (hard) Fishing Snooker Croquet lawn 3 quarter pool table 30 acres non working Dinner **PRICES:** s £34-£40; d £55-£65*
PARKING: 12 **NOTES:** Closed 21-28 Dec

HORSHAM — Map 04 TQ13

Premier Collection

♦♦♦♦♦ Random Hall

Stane St, Slinfold RH13 0QX ☎ 01403 790558
01403 791046
e-mail: nigel@randomhall.fsnet.co.uk
Dir: *on A29 London/Bognor Rd. Close to A281 Horsham/Guildford road.*
This property combines plenty of character with good quality accommodation; bedrooms have excellent facilities. Exposed beams, flagstones and quality fabrics add style to the attractive bar and public areas. There is a wide range to choose from at breakfast, including fruit and bakery items. Dinner is served to residents Monday to Thursday.

continued

England

Random Hall

FACILITIES: 13 en suite No smoking in 6 bedrooms No smoking in dining room STV TVB tea/coffee Direct dial from bedrooms No dogs Licensed Cen ht No coaches Dinner Last d 9pm **PRICES:** s £76; d £86✳ **CONF:** Thtr 30 Class 16 Board 16 Del £130 ✳ **PARKING:** 50 **NOTES:** Closed last wk Aug 2 wks Xmas **CARDS:**

♦♦♦♦ The Willows

Wimlands Ln RH12 4SP ☎ 01293 851030 📠 01293 852466
e-mail: stay@the-willows.co.uk
Dir: *M23 junct 11 A264 Horsham Cross, cross 1st rdbt, left at 2nd rdbt, right at 3rd rdbt Faygate village, pass garage, Holmbush Inn 0.25m, turn left on brow of hill into Wimlands Lane 0.25m to the Willows*
FACILITIES: 4 en suite No smoking TVB tea/coffee No dogs (ex guide dogs) Cen ht TVL No coaches **PRICES:** s £35; d £50✳ **PARKING:** 26

HORSTED KEYNES — Map 05 TQ32

♦♦♦ *The Croft*

Lewes Rd RH17 7DP ☎ 01825 790546
e-mail: thecroftbandb@aol.com
Dir: *M23 junct 10 turn right at 2nd rdbt (B2028), through Turners Hill/Ardingly, 2nd left Horsted Keynes, right into Lewes Road*
A modern building located in a quiet residential area. The bedrooms are attractively decorated, nicely furnished and provide useful extras. The freshly cooked breakfast includes several organic options together with fresh fruit and juices.
FACILITIES: 2 rms No smoking TVB tea/coffee Cen ht No coaches Dinner Last d 24 hours previous **PARKING:** 4

LINDFIELD — Map 05 TQ32

Premier Collection

♦♦♦♦♦ Pilstyes

106-108 High St RH16 2HS ☎ 01444 484101
e-mail: bnbuk@pavilion.co.uk
Dir: *from Gatwick travel S on B2028 to Lindfield, past church on left. From Haywards Heath take B2028 to Lindfield passing pond on left. The Pilstyles is on right*
A warm welcome is assured at this charming Grade II listed Elizabethan cottage that dates to around 1575. Self-contained and appointed to a very high standard, with an antique pine four-poster bed and comfortable sitting room, the cottage is in the picturesque village of Lindfield, just North of Haywards Heath and convenient for Gatwick Airport.
FACILITIES: 2 en suite No smoking TVB No dogs Cen ht TVL No children 8yrs No coaches **PRICES:** s £50-£90; d £75-£95✳ **PARKING:** 1 **CARDS:**

MIDHURST — Map 04 SU82

See also Rogate

♦♦♦♦ Amberfold

Amberfold, Heyshott GU29 0DA ☎ 01730 812385
📠 01730 812842
Dir: *from Midhurst follow A286 towards Chichester, pass Royal Oak pub on left Greyhound pub on right, next left signed Graffham/Heyshott follow for 2m, pass turning for Heyshott village, continue past village pond, in 1km Amberfold on left*
A delightful 17th century listed cottage, set in mature and attractive gardens in peacefully idyllic countryside. The accommodation is provided in two very different self-contained units, a cottage annexe and an ultra-modern open-plan lodge. Each has its own dining area, where guests help themselves to a self-service continental breakfast. Each bedroom is nicely appointed and very well equipped with thoughtful extras.
FACILITIES: 1 en suite 1 annexe en suite No smoking TVB tea/coffee No dogs (ex guide dogs) **PRICES:** s fr £40; d fr £55✳ **PARKING:** 2

♦♦♦♦ Whincote

Redford GU29 0QF ☎ 01428 741355 📠 01428 741017
e-mail: philip@whincote.freeserve.co.uk
Dir: *leave Midhurst on A272 westwards in the direction of Petersfield. After 400 yds take right turn signposted to Woolbeding and Redford. After 4m 'Redford' village sign with petrol station on left, house 250 yds on left.*
A friendly family home, Whincote is located in rural surroundings in the Milland Valley; the house is surrounded by mature National Trust common land. A warm welcome is assured, and guests are offered refreshments on arrival. There are attractive rear gardens, and a heated outdoor swimming pool is available in summer months. The private sitting room has satellite TV, video and a large collection of books. The sole bedroom is comfortably appointed and has an adjacent private bathroom.
FACILITIES: 1 en suite No smoking tea/coffee No dogs (ex guide dogs) Cen ht TVL No children No coaches Outdoor swimming pool (heated) Croquet lawn **PRICES:** d £60✳ BB **PARKING:** 5 **NOTES:** Closed 16 Oct-14 Mar

PULBOROUGH — Map 04 TQ01

♦♦♦ Harkaway

8 Houghton Ln, Bury RH20 1PD ☎ 01798 831843
e-mail: carol.clarke@tinyworld.co.uk
Dir: *5m S of Pulborough turn left just before Squire and horse pub. After 200mtrs right into Houghton Ln signed Houghton. Harkaway on left past turning to Coombe Crescent*
Located north of Arundel in the pretty village of Bury, once the home of John Galsworthy, this well maintained no smoking house provides comfortable homely bedrooms and comprehensive breakfasts, taken in the attractive dining room which overlooks the pretty garden, where a variety of wild birds are encouraged by selective feeding.
FACILITIES: 4 rms (1 en suite) (1 GF) No smoking No dogs Cen ht TVL No children 6yrs No coaches **PRICES:** s £18-£20; d £36-£40✳ BB **PARKING:** 2

♦♦♦ Red Diamonds highlight the top establishments within the AA's 3, 4 and 5 Diamond ratings.

England

ROGATE Map 04 SU82

Premier Collection

♦♦♦♦♦ Mizzards *(SU803228)*

GU31 5HS ☎ 01730 821656 01730 821655
Mrs J C Francis
e-mail: julian.francis@hemscott.net
Dir: *from x-rds in Rogate S for 0.5m, cross river, 300yds then turn right, signed Mizzards Farm*

This charming 16th-century house is set in two acres of landscaped gardens, leading to a lake. Guests are able to relax in either the conservatory or split-level drawing room. The largest bedroom has a canopied bed and large marble bathroom. Public areas include a dining room and a swimming pool is available during the summer.
FACILITIES: 3 en suite No smoking TVB tea/coffee No dogs Cen ht No children 9yrs Outdoor swimming pool (heated) Croquet lawn 13 acres sheep non-working **PRICES:** d £60-£70* **PARKING:** 12
NOTES: Closed Xmas

RUSTINGTON Map 04 TQ00

♦♦♦♦ Kenmore

Claigmar Rd BN16 2NL ☎ 01903 784634 01903 784634
e-mail: kenmoreguesthouse@amserve.net
Dir: *A259 follow signs for Rustington turn for Claigmar Rd between War Memorial & Alldays Shop. Kenmore on right as Claigmar Rd bends*
A warm welcome is assured at this Edwardian house located close to the sea and convenient for touring West Sussex. Spacious bedrooms, all individually decorated, are provided with many useful extras. There is a comfortable lounge in which to relax and a bright dining room where a good choice of breakfast is served.
FACILITIES: 7 rms (6 en suite) (2 fmly) No smoking TVB tea/coffee Cen ht TVL No coaches **PRICES:** s £23.50-£26; d £47-£52* **PARKING:** 7
CARDS:

SELSEY Map 04 SZ89

♦♦♦♦ St Andrews Lodge Hotel

Chichester Rd PO20 0LX ☎ 01243 606899 01243 607826
e-mail: info@standrewslodge.co.uk
Dir: *turn off A27 onto the B2145 for 7 miles. Hotel is on right past Police Station just before the church (The Independents)*
Located close to the town centre the hotel provides comfortable accommodation and a warm welcome. Bedrooms are bright and spacious and all have a range of useful extras. There are five rooms in an annexe at the back of the house, and one is adapted for disabled use. Dinner is available by prior arrangement.
FACILITIES: 5 en suite 5 annexe en suite (3 fmly) No smoking in bedrooms No smoking in dining room TVB tea/coffee Direct dial from bedrooms Licensed Cen ht TVL No coaches Dinner Last d breakfast

continued

PRICES: s £30-£60; d £60-£90* **LB PARKING:** 12
NOTES: Closed 20 Dec-1 Jan **CARDS:**

STEYNING Map 04 TQ11

♦♦♦♦ Springwells Hotel

9 High St BN44 3GG ☎ 01903 812446 & 812043
01903 879823
e-mail: contact@springwells.co.uk
Dir: *from A283 by-pass, take main road through village. House on right opposite Methodist Church*
Located within the heart of the historic village, this former Georgian merchant's house retains many original features highlighted by the furnishing and décor styles throughout. Bedrooms are individually designed and offer a good balance between practicality and homeliness with lots of thoughtful extras to enhance guest comfort. Ground floor areas include an elegant dining room and an attractive conservatory lounge overlooking the imaculate mature gardens.
FACILITIES: 10 rms (8 en suite) (1 fmly) No smoking in 1 lounge TVB tea/coffee Direct dial from bedrooms Licensed Cen ht TVL No coaches Outdoor swimming pool (heated) Sauna **PRICES:** s £34-£49; d £58-£93* **LB CONF:** Thtr 25 Class 12 Board 12 **PARKING:** 6 **NOTES:** Closed 24 Dec-1 Jan **CARDS:**

WORTHING Map 04 TQ10

♦♦♦♦ The Conifers

43 Parkfield Rd BN13 1EP ☎ 01903 265066 & 0794 7321096
e-mail: conifers@hews.org.uk
Dir: *From A24 or A27 turn onto A2031. At Offington r/about. Straight on at lights. Parkfield Rd is the fifth on the right*
A warm welcome is assured at this impressive detached house which stands on immaculate gardens within a residential area on the town's outskirts. Bedrooms are equipped with lots of home extras and a comfortable lounge is available in addition to an attractive dining room, the setting for comprehensive breakfasts.
FACILITIES: 2 rms No smoking TVB tea/coffee No dogs Cen ht No children 5yrs No coaches Dinner Last d 24hrs notice **PRICES:** s £30-£33.50; d £50-£57* **PARKING:** 2

♦♦♦♦ Moorings

4 Selden Rd BN11 2LL ☎ 01903 208882 01903 236878
e-mail: annette@mooringshotel.fsnet.co.uk
Dir: *on A259 towards Brighton, pass indoor swimming pool on right and hotel opposite car showroom*

Ideally placed for access to the seafront and town centre, this Victorian house is to be found in a quiet residential area. Bedrooms are well co-ordinated in bright colours and the recently refurbished dining room is smartly appointed. There is a small lounge for guests where magazines and games are provided.
FACILITIES: 6 en suite (2 fmly) No smoking TVB tea/coffee Direct dial from bedrooms No dogs Cen ht No coaches **PRICES:** s £25-£27; d £45-£50*
NOTES: Closed 19 Dec-4 Jan **CARDS:**

England

TYNE & WEAR

NEWCASTLE UPON TYNE Map 12 NZ26

♦♦♦♦ Imperial

194 Station Rd, Wallsend NE28 8RD ☎ 0191 236 9808
Fax 0191 236 9808
e-mail: enquiries@imperialguesthouse.co.uk
Dir: *opposite Trinity Methodist Church on Station Rd*

A deceptively plain mid-Victorian terrace house which contains a mixed assortment of Victoriana and collectibles adorning the two comfortable lounges. There are two bedrooms and each contains many thoughtful extras. Service is attentive and friendly. Nearby is the start of the Roman Wall.

FACILITIES: 2 rms (1 en suite) (2 GF) No smoking in bedrooms No smoking in dining room No smoking in 1 lounge TVB tea/coffee Direct dial from bedrooms No dogs (ex guide dogs) Cen ht No children 11yrs No coaches **PRICES:** s £24-£35; d £55✳

♦♦♦ Chirton House Hotel

46 Clifton Rd, Grainger Park Rd NE4 6XH ☎ 0191 273 0407
Fax 0191 273 0407
Dir: *exit A1 at Newcastle West junct, take A186 for 2m, right at General Hospital into Grainger Park Rd, left into Clifton Rd*

Chirton House is situated in a quiet residential suburb close to Newcastle General Hospital and every effort is made to ensure you are looked after. Public areas include a comfortable lounge and a well-stocked bar. The bedrooms are well-equipped and a full breakfast is served every morning. The hotel boasts good car parking facilities.

FACILITIES: 11 rms (6 en suite) (3 fmly) No smoking in 1 bedroom No smoking in dining room No smoking in 1 lounge TVB tea/coffee Licensed Cen ht TVL **PRICES:** s £26-£36; d £39-£49✳ **LB CONF:** Board 15 Del from £46 ✳ **PARKING:** 12 **CARDS:**

SOUTH SHIELDS Map 12 NZ36

♦♦♦ Beach Haven

63 Ocean Rd NE33 2JJ ☎ 0191 4568129 Fax 0191 4544470
e-mail: beachhavenguesthouse@fsmail.net
Dir: *head towards Town Centre, through lights to mini rdbt. At rdbt turn left. Straight over the following rdbt. At next rdbt turn right. 500yrds on left*

Set in a terraced row, on a main route from the town centre to the beach, this guest house is well located near the town centre. It is attractively decorated throughout and offers modern, well-equipped bedrooms and a smart breakfast room.

continued

Beach Haven

FACILITIES: 8 rms (7 en suite) (1 fmly) (1 GF) No smoking in dining room STV TVB tea/coffee No dogs (ex guide dogs) Cen ht **PRICES:** s £25; d £40✳ **PARKING:** 1 **CARDS:**

WHITLEY BAY Map 12 NZ37

♦♦♦♦ Marlborough Hotel

20-21 East Pde, Central Promenade NE26 1AP
☎ 0191 251 3628 Fax 0191 252 5033
e-mail: reception@marlborough-hotel.com
Dir: *A19 follow signs for Tynemouth/Whitley Bay. From S A1058 to seafront turn N into Whitley Bay. From N A186 to seafront, turn S along Bay*

With an Edwardian sandstone façade, this attractive and well-maintained hotel enjoys a beachfront and promenade location. The smart, modern bedrooms, two of which are on the ground floor, offer a good standard of accommodation. Some of the larger rooms have seating areas from which to enjoy splendid sea views.

FACILITIES: 17 rms (14 en suite) (4 fmly) No smoking in 10 bedrooms No smoking in dining room TVB tea/coffee Direct dial from bedrooms Licensed TVL Dinner Last d 5.30pm **PRICES:** s £22-£40; d £45-£65✳ **LB PARKING:** 7 **NOTES:** Closed Xmas and New Year **CARDS:** 

♦♦♦♦ A York House Hotel & Studios

30 Park Pde NE26 1DX ☎ 0191 252 8313 Fax 0191 251 3953
e-mail: reservations@yorkhousehotel.com
Dir: *A19 onto A193 & turn left at Baptist Church*

FACILITIES: 14 en suite 14 annexe en suite (6 fmly) (5 GF) No smoking in 2 bedrooms No smoking in dining room STV TVB tea/coffee Direct dial from bedrooms Licensed Cen ht TVL Gymnasium Dinner Last d 7.30pm **PRICES:** s £40; d £55-£65✳ **LB CONF:** Thtr 40 Class 30 Board 20 Del £60 ✳ **PARKING:** 12 **CARDS:**

♦♦♦ *Cherrytree House*

35 Brook St NE26 1AF ☎ 0191 251 4306 Fax 0191 2514306
e-mail: cherrytreehouse@cherrytreehouse.free-online.co.uk
Dir: *A19 follow signs for Tynemouth/Whitley Bay. Then for seafront, turn into Whitley Bay. 1st on left past Marlborough Hotel*

Conveniently situated between the seafront and the town centre, this large Edwardian house is situated in a quiet residential area. Traditionally furnished bedrooms are comfortable, and there is also a homely lounge available for guest use. Hearty breakfasts are cheerfully served at individual tables in the pleasant dining room.

FACILITIES: 4 rms (3 en suite) No smoking in dining room TVB tea/coffee Cen ht TVL No coaches Dinner **PARKING:** 1

England

WARWICKSHIRE

ALDERMINSTER Map 04 SP24

♦♦♦♦ The Bell

Shipston Rd CV37 8NY ☎ 01789 450414 01789 450998
e-mail: thebellald@aol.com
Dir: *on A3400 3m S of Stratford-upon-Avon on Shipston-Oxford road*

A focal part of the local community, this former coaching house retains many original features which are enhanced by the quality décor and furnishing styles throughout the public areas. The inn specialises in gastronomic festivals throughout the year and the homely bedrooms are located in a sympathetically renovated separate house, accessed via the immaculate gardens.

FACILITIES: 5 annexe rms (3 en suite) (2 fmly) (2 GF) No smoking in bedrooms No smoking in dining room No smoking in lounges TVB tea/coffee Cen ht ch fac Dinner Last d 9.30pm **PRICES:** s £25-£50; d £40-£85✱ LB **MEALS:** Lunch fr £6.30&alc Dinner £12-£25alc✱ **CONF:** Thtr 15 Class 10 Board 12 **PARKING:** 70 **CARDS:**

ARMSCOTE Map 04 SP24

♦♦♦♦ Willow Corner

CV37 8DE ☎ 01608 682391
e-mail: willowcorner@compuserve.com
Dir: *from Stratford, on A3400 turn after church in Newbold to Armscote, follow lane into Armscote, house is 100 yds on left beyond public house.*

This 300-year-old thatched cottage was once the village smithy and retains many original features, low beamed ceilings, and a magnificent inglenook. Bedrooms have many thoughtful extras, and the delicious breakfasts include home-made produce. The village inn is just a stroll away, and the pretty hamlet of Armscote is convenient for Stratford-upon-Avon, Warwick and the Cotswolds.

FACILITIES: 3 en suite No smoking TVB tea/coffee No dogs Cen ht No children 15 yrs No coaches **PRICES:** s £42; d £58-£60✱ LB **PARKING:** 3 **NOTES:** Closed Xmas/New Year

ATHERSTONE Map 04 SP39

♦♦♦♦ Mythe Farm

Pinwall Ln, Sheepy Magna CV9 3PF ☎ 01827 712367
01827 715738
e-mail: info@mythefarm.co.uk
Dir: *3.5m from junct 10 of M42 N of Atherstone between the villages of Sheepy Magna and Ratcliffe Culey*

Elegant Regency farmhouse with spacious interior and attractive bedrooms. Set in lovely countryside, in the heart of the Midlands, within 20 miles of Birmingham, Leicester and Coventry, and close to Hinckley, Tamworth, Nuneaton and Atherstone. Beautiful riverside walks, and interesting things to see on this friendly working farm.

continued

Mythe Farm

FACILITIES: 2 en suite (1 fmly) No smoking TVB tea/coffee Cen ht TVL Fishing Riding Dinner Last d 24hrs prior **PRICES:** s £25-£35; d £50-£65✱ LB **PARKING:** 15

COLESHILL Map 04 SP28

♦♦♦ The Old Vicarage

Shawbury Ln, Shustoke B46 2LA ☎ 01675 481331
01675 481331
e-mail: jbhawk@doctors.org.uk
Dir: *leave A446 at B4114 for Coleshill, B4114 Coleshill/Nuneaton Rd for Shustoke, 0.5m after Shustoke village turn right on apex tight left bend (at Griffin Inn) then immediately left towards Church*

Opposite the magnificent church of St Cuthberts at the edge of Shustoke, this impressive house stands in pretty mature gardens. Retaining many original features, the house is stylishly decorated and furnished throughout. Bedrooms are filled with a wealth of thoughtful extras and superb breakfasts are taken in an elegant dining room.

FACILITIES: 3 rms (1 en suite) No smoking TVB tea/coffee No dogs Cen ht No coaches Dinner Last d 24hrs prior **PRICES:** s £25-£30; d £44-£49✱ **PARKING:** 6 **NOTES:** Closed Xmas

♦♦♦ Ye Olde Station

Church Rd, Shustoke B46 2AX ☎ 01675 481736
01675 481736
e-mail: yeoldestationguestho@talk21.com
Dir: *M6 junct14 onto A446. After 1m right at rdbt onto B4114. After 3.5m, through Shustoke village, guest house located 300yds past Griffin public house*

A sympathetic conversion of a former Victorian railway station, this house has been modernised to provide a range of practically furnished bedrooms complimented by efficient bathrooms. Ground floor areas include an open plan lounge dining room and a separate games room with pool table.

FACILITIES: 9 en suite (1 fmly) No smoking in bedrooms TVB tea/coffee Cen ht TVL Pool Table **PRICES:** s £35-£40; d £55-£65✱ **PARKING:** 16 **CARDS:**

DUNCHURCH Map 04 SP47

♦♦♦♦ Toft Hill

CV22 6NR ☎ 01788 810342

Dir: *from traffic lights in Dunchurch take A426 towards Southam. Exactly 0.5m from lights Toft Hill is behind white gates on right*

FACILITIES: 3 rms (1 en suite) (1 fmly) No smoking in dining room No smoking in lounges TVB tea/coffee Cen ht No coaches

PRICES: s £22.50; d £45✳ **PARKING:** 10

ETTINGTON Map 04 SP24

♦♦♦ The Houndsmill

Banbury Rd CV37 7NS ☎ 01789 740267 & 740936

01789 740075

Dir: *4m S of Stratford-upon-Avon. 1m N of Ettington village on the A422.*

FACILITIES: 8 en suite (2 fmly) TVB tea/coffee Direct dial from bedrooms Licensed Cen ht Dinner Last d 9.30 pm **PRICES:** s fr £40; d fr £60✳

PARKING: 50 **NOTES:** Closed 25-28 Dec

CARDS:

FILLONGLEY Map 04 SP28

♦♦♦♦ Bourne Brook Lodge

Mill Ln CV7 8EE ☎ 01676 541898 01676 541898

Dir: *from Fillongley Village, take B4098 Tamworth rd towards Tamworth for 1m. Mill Lane is on left, Bourne Brook 200mtrs on right*

FACILITIES: 4 rms (4 GF) No smoking TVB tea/coffee No dogs (ex guide dogs) TVL No children 0 No coaches **PRICES:** s £25-£35; d £50-£55 **LB**

PARKING: 7

HENLEY-IN-ARDEN Map 07 SP16

♦♦♦♦ Ashleigh House

Whitley Hill B95 5DL ☎ 01564 792315 01564 794126

e-mail: enquiries@ashleigh-house.fsbusiness.co.uk

Dir: *leave A3400 at lights on High St. Along A4189 towards Warwick, Ashleigh House, 1m from lights*

Set in two acres, on the outskirts of Henley, this impressive Edwardian house offers well equipped, comfortable bedrooms. The tastefully decorated dining room has an array of period furniture, and offers a varied breakfast as well as dinner by arrangement. The lounge is the perfect setting for a pre-dinner drink or for relaxing.

FACILITIES: 6 en suite 5 annexe en suite (2 fmly) (5 GF) No smoking in bedrooms No smoking in dining room No smoking in lounges TVB tea/coffee Direct dial from bedrooms Licensed Cen ht No coaches Dinner Last d before noon **PRICES:** s £47-£52; d £59.50-£74✳ **LB CONF:** Class 4 Board 24 **PARKING:** 17 **CARDS:**

KENILWORTH Map 04 SP27

♦♦♦♦ Victoria Lodge Hotel

180 Warwick Rd CV8 1HU ☎ 01926 512020 01926 858703

e-mail: info@victorialodgehotel.co.uk

Dir: *0.25m S on A452, opposite St Johns Church*

On the fringe of this historic town, within easy walking distance of the castle and restaurants, this refurbished Victorian house has been extended to provide excellent accommodation. There is a beautiful walled garden, and off street parking is available. Conveniently located for the NEC, NAC, IAC, golf courses and the Cotswolds.

continued

Victoria Lodge Hotel

FACILITIES: 9 en suite (2 GF) No smoking TVB tea/coffee Direct dial from bedrooms No dogs (ex guide dogs) Licensed Cen ht No coaches

PRICES: s £42-£52; d £64✳ **LB PARKING:** 9 **NOTES:** Closed Xmas/ New Year **CARDS:**

♦♦♦ Hollyhurst

47 Priory Rd CV8 1LL ☎ 01926 853882 01926 855211

e-mail: admin@hollyhurstguesthouse.co.uk

Dir: *from A46,onto A452 follow signs for Kenilworth town centre.Enter Warwick Rd then right into Waverley Rd, follow A452 to Priory Rd, guest house 150 mtrs on right*

This attractive house is just a short walk from the castle and town centre, and is a most friendly and comfortable place to stay. Rooms are well-equipped and pleasantly decorated. Guests can relax in the comfortable lounge and a bar is also available. Traditional English breakfasts are freshly cooked and most enjoyable.

FACILITIES: 7 rms (3 en suite) (1 fmly) No smoking TVB tea/coffee No dogs Licensed Cen ht TVL No coaches Last d 0 **PRICES:** s £25-£30; d £40-£45✳ **PARKING:** 7 **NOTES:** Closed Xmas/New Year

LEAMINGTON SPA (ROYAL) Map 04 SP36

♦♦♦♦ Bubbenhall House

Paget's Ln CV8 3BJ ☎ 02476 302409 02476 302409

e-mail: wharrison@bubbenhallhouse.freeserve.co.uk

Dir: *approaching Bubbenhall from Leamington on A445, village on left, Pagets Lane on right. 1m on single track lane (sleeping policeman)*

Located on extensive mature grounds between Royal Leamington Spa and Coventry, this impressive late Edwardian house, once the home of the Mini's designer, contains many interesting features including a fine Jacobean staircase. Thoughtful extras are provided in the comfortable bedrooms and public areas include an elegant dining room and choice of sumptuous lounges.

FACILITIES: 3 en suite No smoking in bedrooms No smoking in dining room TVB tea/coffee No dogs (ex guide dogs) Cen ht TVL No coaches Tennis (hard) Croquet lawn Petanque **PRICES:** s £29-£35; d £49-£60✳ **LB**

PARKING: 12

♦♦♦♦ Hill *(SP343637)*

Lewis Rd, Radford Semele CV31 1UX ☎ 01926 337571

Mrs R Gibbs

e-mail: rebecca@hillfarm3000.fsnet.co.uk

Dir: *2m from Leamington Spa on A425, in village turn right into Lewis Rd & continue to bottom*

Peacefully located within the village of Radford Semele, this Victorian house provides thoughtfully equipped bedrooms complimented by modern efficient bathrooms. Ground floor areas include an attractive dining room, a guest lounge and the immaculate mature garden is ablaze with colour during the warmer months.

FACILITIES: 4 en suite No smoking TVB tea/coffee No dogs Cen ht TVL 350 acres arable mixed sheep **PRICES:** s £25-£30; d £50✳

PARKING: 6 **NOTES:** Closed Xmas & New Year

England

LEAMINGTON SPA (ROYAL) continued

♦♦♦♦ Lansdowne Hotel

87 Clarendon St CV32 4PF ☎ 01926 450505 📠 01926 421313
e-mail: thelansdowne@cwcom.net

Dir: *M40 junct 13, follow signs to Leamington City Centre. Take A425 to Warwick St. Hotel at junct with Clarendon St (The Circle)*

An established friendly family guest house located close to the centre of town with comfortable well-equipped bedrooms. There is a small bar, guests' lounge and meals are available by arrangement.

FACILITIES: 14 rms (11 en suite) (2 fmly) (2 GF) No smoking in 5 bedrooms No smoking in dining room No smoking in 1 lounge TVB tea/coffee Direct dial from bedrooms No dogs Licensed Cen ht TVL No coaches Dinner Last d 8pm **PRICES:** s £49.95-£54.95; d £60-£68✻ **PARKING:** 12 **CARDS:**

♦♦♦♦ Milverton House Hotel

1 Milverton Ter CV32 5BE ☎ 01926 428335 📠 01926 428335
e-mail: anne-stephen@milvertonhousehotel.fsnet.co.uk

Dir: *200yds from fire station*

Located a few minutes' walk from the Parade, this Victorian house retains many original features which are enhanced by the decor and furnishing styles, especially within the spacious public areas. Bedrooms are well-equipped and comfortable and the majority have the benefit of modern en suite facilities. Ann & Steve Kinzett are friendly and caring hosts.

FACILITIES: 10 rms (7 en suite) (1 fmly) No smoking in dining room No smoking in lounges TVB tea/coffee Direct dial from bedrooms No dogs (ex guide dogs) Licensed Cen ht No children 5yrs No coaches **PRICES:** s £28-£45; d £46-£62✻ **LB PARKING:** 6 **CARDS:**

LIGHTHORNE — Map 04 SP35

♦♦♦ Redlands *(SP334570)*

Banbury Rd CV35 0AH ☎ 01926 651241 📠 01926 651241
Mrs J Stanton

Dir: *off B4100, 5m S of Warwick*

Quietly located in pretty gardens close to major attractions, this house dates in part from the 16th century. Bedrooms are spacious and homely. Tasty cooked English breakfasts are taken in a cosy dining room. The comfortable lounge with its open fire is a real attraction during winter.

FACILITIES: 3 rms (1 en suite) (1 fmly) No smoking TVB tea/coffee No dogs (ex guide dogs) Cen ht TVL Outdoor swimming pool 100 acres arable **PRICES:** s £20-£30; d £45-£50✻ **PARKING:** 7 **NOTES:** Closed Xmas

LONG COMPTON — Map 07 SP23

♦♦♦♦ Ashby House

Clarks Ln CV36 5LB ☎ 01608 684286
e-mail: e.p.field@fieldashby.demon.co.uk

Dir: *midway on A3400 between Oxford and Stratford-on-Avon. S end of village, 600yds opposite Red Lion Hotel*

Located close to the Rollright Stones in the pretty rural village of Long Compton, this early Victorian house retains many original features highlighted by the quality décor and furnishing schemes throughout. Bedrooms are equipped with thoughtful extras and have private bathrooms. An elegant dining room is the setting for memorable breakfasts and a comfortable guest lounge is also available.

FACILITIES: 2 en suite (1 fmly) No smoking TV1B tea/coffee No dogs (ex guide dogs) Cen ht TVL No coaches Dinner Last d 8.30pm **PRICES:** s £25-£35; d £38-£44✻ **LB BB PARKING:** 3 **NOTES:** Closed 24-27 Dec

♦♦♦♦ Tallett Barn B & B

Yerdley Farm CV36 5LH ☎ 01608 684248 📠 01608 684248
e-mail: talletbarn@btinternet.com

Dir: *16m S of Stratford upon Avon on A3400, once in village turn into Vicarage Lane directly opposite stores/PO. Entrance 3rd on right*

Located in the heart of this pretty village, bedrooms are a sympathetic conversion of a former stable and grain store, providing an excellent combination of character and comfort. Super breakfasts are taken within the main house in the beamed dining room, which also contains a comfortable lounge area.

FACILITIES: 2 annexe en suite (1 fmly) (1 GF) No smoking TVB tea/coffee No dogs (ex guide dogs) Cen ht No children 6yrs No coaches **PRICES:** s £30; d £42-£45✻ **PARKING:** 3

NUNEATON — Map 04 SP39

Premier Collection

♦♦♦♦♦ Leathermill Grange

Leathermill Ln, Caldecote CV10 0RX ☎ 01827 714637
📠 01827 716422
e-mail: davidcodd@leathermillgrange.co.uk

Dir: *from A5, take turning for Hartshill, at give way sign go under railway bridge follow road towards Nuneaton. Leathermill Ln 400yds on left*

Located in stunning rural surroundings, in five acres of mature grounds that includes a well stocked koi carp lake, this impressive Victorian house has been sympathetically renovated to provide high standards of accommodation. It is conveniently close to major road networks and historical attractions. Décor styles enhance the many original features. Imaginative dinners are served in the elegant dining room. Excellent hospitality is assured.

FACILITIES: 3 en suite No smoking TVB tea/coffee No dogs Licensed Cen ht No children 16yrs No coaches Fishing Pool Table Croquet lawn Exercise machine Dinner Last d 24hr prior **PRICES:** s £60-£70; d £80-£90✻ **PARKING:** 20 **CARDS:**

OXHILL — Map 04 SP34

♦♦♦♦ Nolands Farm *(SP312470)*

CV35 0RJ ☎ 01926 640309 📠 01926 641662 Mrs S Hutsby
e-mail: inthecountry@nolandsfarm.co.uk

Dir: *1m E of Pillarton Priors on A422*

This pleasant farm provides spacious and comfortable accommodation in a peaceful and attractive countryside location. Bedrooms are well-equipped, most are on the ground floor and provide access for the less able guest. Breakfast is served buffet style, in the flagstone-floored dining room and provides a hearty start to the day.

FACILITIES: 8 annexe en suite (2 fmly) (7 GF) No smoking in bedrooms No smoking in dining room No smoking in 1 lounge TVB tea/coffee No dogs (ex guide dogs) Licensed Cen ht No children 7yrs Fishing Clay shooting, Bike hire, Hot air ballooning 200 acres arable Dinner Last d 24hrs notice **PRICES:** s £30-£46; d £44-£56 **LB PARKING:** 12 **NOTES:** Closed Xmas & New Year **CARDS:**

England

RUGBY Map 04 SP57

♦♦♦ The White Lion Inn

Coventry Rd, Pailton CV23 0QD ☎ 01788 832359
01788 832359
Dir: exit Rugby via A426.Under railway bridge, 1st left off rdbt onto B4112. In Pailton village turn left, Inn 200 yrds further on
FACILITIES: 9 rms (5 en suite) (2 fmly) No smoking in 6 bedrooms TVB tea/coffee Direct dial from bedrooms Licensed Cen ht TVL Dinner Last d 10pm **PRICES:** s £22.50-£32.50; d £39.50-£49.50* **PARKING:** 60 **CARDS:**

SHIPSTON ON STOUR Map 04 SP24

♦♦♦♦ The Red Lion Hotel

Main St, Long Compton CV36 5JS ☎ 01608 684221
01608 684221
e-mail: redlionhot@aol.com
Dir: Long Compton is on A3400 between Chipping Norton & Shipston on Stour

Located within the pretty rural village of Long Compton, this mid 18th century posting house retains many original features which are highlighted by the rustic furniture and furniture styles throughout the warm and inviting public areas. Bedrooms are furnished with a good range of practical facilities and food provided utilises quality local produce.
FACILITIES: 5 en suite (1 fmly) No smoking in area of dining room TVB tea/coffee Cen ht No coaches Pool Table Traditional pub games Dinner Last d 9pm **PRICES:** s £30; d £50* **MEALS:** Lunch £11-£20alc Dinner £11-£20alc* **PARKING:** 60 **CARDS:**

Crab Mill

Grump St, Ilmington CV36 4LE ☎ 01608 682233
At the time of going to press the Diamond classification for this establishment had not been confirmed. Please check the AA website www.theAA.com for up-to-date information.
FACILITIES: 2 rms

STRATFORD-UPON-AVON Map 04 SP25

See also Alderminster

Premier Collection

♦♦♦♦♦ Glebe Farm House *(SP248533)*

Stratford Rd, Loxley CV35 9JW ☎ 01789 842501
01789 841194 Mrs K M McGovern
e-mail: scorpiolimited@msn.com
Dir: S from Stratford, cross River Avon, turn immediately left onto B4086 Tiddington rd, then immediately right onto Loxley rd. Farm 2.5m on left

continued

Glebe Farm House

Set in the middle of its own farmland and yet very convenient for nearby Stratford upon Avon, guests can expect a warm welcome and a relaxing stay at Glebe Farm. Luxurious décor and high quality furnishings, together with real fires in colder weather, add to the comfort. Award-winning meals can be taken in the conservatory dining room, which often include the farm's home-reared, organic produce.
FACILITIES: 3 en suite No smoking TVB tea/coffee No dogs Licensed Cen ht TVL No children 30 acres rare breed, fully organic Dinner Last d 10pm **PRICES:** s £72; d £105* LB **PARKING:** 40 **CARDS:**

♦♦♦♦ Loxley Farm *(SP273553)*

Loxley CV35 9JN ☎ 01789 840265 01789 840645
Mr & Mrs R P K Horton
Dir: Loxley is signposted off A422 Stratford-Banbury rd, 4m from Stratford on left. Through village to bottom of hill. Turn left, 3rd house on right

Set in a lovely cottage garden, this thatched, former farmhouse offers homely, well-equipped bedrooms in a converted 17th century shieling or cart barn. Private sitting rooms in both help to make this a relaxing venue and breakfast is taken in the atmospheric, period dining room around a family table in the main farmhouse.
FACILITIES: 2 en suite No smoking in bedrooms No smoking in dining room No smoking in lounges TVB tea/coffee Cen ht TVL 6 acres
PRICES: s fr £45; d fr £64* **PARKING:** 10 **NOTES:** Closed Xmas & New Year

England

STRATFORD UPON AVON continued

♦♦♦♦ *Aidan*

11 Evesham Place CV37 6HT ☎ 01789 292824 📠 01789 269072
e-mail: john2aidan@aol.com
***Dir:** M40 junct 15, A46 for 4m and enter on A3400. At lights turn right along A4390, Ardan St, then Grove Rd to Evesham Place*
Within a short walk of the theatre and other attractions, this Victorian property is most picturesque with its prize winning frontage. The hosts are very friendly and warmly welcome guests to their home. Bedrooms are comfortable and well appointed with modern facilities. The dining room offers many interesting features and artefacts, and at breakfast freshly cooked dishes provide an appetising start to the day.
FACILITIES: 6 en suite (1 fmly) No smoking STV TVB tea/coffee Direct dial from bedrooms No dogs Cen ht **PARKING:** 9 **CARDS:**

♦♦♦♦ Ambleside

41 Grove Rd CV37 6PB ☎ 01789 297239 📠 01789 295670
e-mail: ruth@amblesideguesthouse.com
***Dir:** from Railway station right at traffic lights to Grove Road, guest house is 250 yds on right, opposite Firs Park*
This attractive, friendly and well maintained guest house is situated close to the Market Square and the town centre. Bedrooms are tastefully decorated and well appointed. Hearty breakfasts are served in the light airy dining room.
FACILITIES: 8 rms (4 en suite) (2 fmly) No smoking STV TVB tea/coffee No dogs (ex guide dogs) Cen ht **PRICES:** s £20-£26; d £40-£64✱ **PARKING:** 8 **CARDS:**

♦♦♦♦ *Brook Lodge*

192 Alcester Rd CV37 9DR ☎ 01789 295988 📠 01789 295988
e-mail: brooklodgeguesthouse@btinternet.com
***Dir:** W on A422 opposite turning to Anne Hathaway's Cottage*

Located within easy walking distance of Anne Hathaway's Cottage, this beautifully maintained modern house offers beautifully maintained bedroom accommodation filled with thoughtful extras. Ground floor areas include an open plan living area with cosy lounge section and attractive dining area, the setting for imaginative breakfasts.
FACILITIES: 7 en suite (2 fmly) No smoking TVB tea/coffee No dogs (ex guide dogs) Cen ht TVL No children 6yrs No coaches **PARKING:** 10 **CARDS:**

♦♦♦♦ Craig Cleeve House

67-69 Shipston Rd CV37 7LW ☎ 01789 296573
📠 01789 299452
e-mail: craigcleev@aol.com
***Dir:** follow A3400 out of Stratford towards Oxford. Hotel 150yds on right*
A constantly improving impressive double fronted Victorian house, bedroom accommodation offers a good balance between practicality and homeliness. Ground floor areas include a comfortable sitting room, lounge bar and an attractive split level dining room overlooking the immaculate secluded rear garden.

continued

FACILITIES: 14 en suite (2 fmly) (5 GF) No smoking in bedrooms No smoking in dining room No smoking in 1 lounge TVB tea/coffee No dogs (ex guide dogs) Licensed Cen ht TVL **PRICES:** s £45-£54; d £54-£62✱ **LB** **PARKING:** 15 **CARDS:**

♦♦♦♦ Eastnor House Hotel

Shipston Rd CV37 7LN ☎ 01789 268115 📠 01789 551133
e-mail: enquiries@eastnorhouse.com
***Dir:** follow A3400 Shipston Rd. Hotel 1st on right, close to Clopton Bridge*
A Victorian townhouse offering modern comforts, tasteful décor and 21st century technology in the form of a computer and e-mail facilities for residents. Whether guests are staying for business or leisure The Eastnor is ideally located for Stratford's many attractions and restaurants.
FACILITIES: 10 en suite (3 fmly) No smoking TVB tea/coffee Direct dial from bedrooms No dogs (ex guide dogs) Cen ht No coaches **PRICES:** s £45-£55; d £66-£80✱ **LB** **PARKING:** 10 **NOTES:** Closed Xmas day **CARDS:**

♦♦♦♦ *Eversley Bears*

37 Grove Rd CV37 6PB ☎ 01789 292334 📠 01789 292334
e-mail: eversleybears@btinternet.com
***Dir:** behind Police Station. 4mins walk from Railway Station and town centre*
Situated close to town centre and attractions, this semi-detached guest house offers good value accommodation. Bedrooms are comfortable, well equipped and maintained with double-glazing throughout. Public rooms include a tastefully appointed dining room and a quiet, comfortable lounge; the house is well known for its large collection of teddy bears (now numbering well over 700) which are found throughout this no-smoking establishment.
FACILITIES: 6 rms (2 en suite) (2 fmly) No smoking TVB tea/coffee No dogs (ex guide dogs) Cen ht **PARKING:** 4 **CARDS:**

♦♦♦♦ The Fox & Goose Inn

Armscote CV37 8DD ☎ 01608 682293 📠 01608 682293
***Dir:** head S from Stratford-upon-Avon on A3400 and follow for 7m, as you leave the village of Newbold on Stour, turn right at Church (signed Armscote 1m) bear right in village*
A sympathetic conversion of two cottages and a blacksmith's forge, this inn retains many original features, which are enhanced by the quality furnishing and décor throughout. Bedrooms are designed with individual flair and imaginative, award-winning food is served in the attractive and intimate public areas.
FACILITIES: 4 en suite No smoking in 1 bedrooms No smoking in area of dining room TVB tea/coffee No dogs (ex guide dogs) Cen ht No coaches Dinner Last d 9.30pm **PRICES:** s £35-£40; d £70-£80✱ **MEALS:** Lunch £5-£15alc Dinner £12-£20alc✱ **CONF:** Thtr 20 Class 20 Board 20 **PARKING:** 16 **NOTES:** Closed 25-26 Dec **CARDS:**

♦♦♦♦ Gravelside Barn

Binton CV37 9TU ☎ 01789 750502 📠 01789 750502
e-mail: gravelside@hotmail.com
***Dir:** B439 from Stratford-on-Avon, 3.5m turn right to Binton. Through village Gravelside Barn up private drive signposted on left*
On the outskirts of Binton with some stunning views, Gravelside is a converted early 19th-century barn, which provides quality accommodation close to major attractions. Bedrooms are comfortable, tastefully furnished, well equipped and include mini bars and modern en suite shower rooms with power showers. The ground floor area contains a comfortable sitting area and a dining section where English breakfasts are served.
FACILITIES: 3 en suite No smoking TVB tea/coffee No dogs (ex guide dogs) Cen ht No children 12yrs No coaches Golf 18 Tennis (hard) **PRICES:** s £40-£50; d £50-£60✱ **PARKING:** 6 **CARDS:**

England

♦♦♦♦ Hardwick House
1 Avenue Rd CV37 6UY ☎ 01789 204307 📠 01789 296760
e-mail: hardwick@waverider.co.uk
Dir: *turn right off A439 at St Gregory's Church into St Gregory's Rd, Hardwick House 200yds on right*

Situated in a residential area a few minutes from the river and Shakespeare's birthplace, this late-Victorian property offers warm hospitality. Bedrooms are comfortable and well equipped, each with modern en suite or private facilities. Much of the decor in public areas focuses on cricket memorabilia, collected by ex-professional Mr Wooton.

FACILITIES: 14 rms (13 en suite) (3 fmly) No smoking in bedrooms No smoking in dining room TVB tea/coffee No dogs (ex guide dogs) Licensed Cen ht No children 5yrs No coaches **PRICES:** s £32-£38; d £50-£75 **LB** **PARKING:** 12 **CARDS:**

♦♦♦♦ Melita Private Hotel
37 Shipston Rd CV37 7LN ☎ 01789 292432 📠 01789 204867
e-mail: info@melitahotel.co.uk
Dir: *200yds from the Clopton bridge on the A3400 S, establishment on right*

A spacious Victorian house offering pleasant accommodation with friendly service. Bedrooms are varied in style but all are well equipped with useful extras. The public areas include a breakfast room overlooking the pretty garden and a lounge with feature fireplace and an honesty bar.

FACILITIES: 12 en suite (2 fmly) (3 GF) No smoking in bedrooms No smoking in dining room No smoking in 1 lounge TVB tea/coffee Direct dial from bedrooms Licensed Cen ht TVL **PRICES:** s £37-£57; d £49-£82✳ **LB** **PARKING:** 12 **NOTES:** Closed 20 Dec-2 Jan **CARDS:**

♦♦♦♦ Monk's Barn *(SP206516)*
Shipston Rd CV37 8NA ☎ 01789 293714 📠 01789 205886
Mrs R M Meadows
e-mail: rmeadows@hotmail.com
Dir: *on A3400 approx 2m S*

Situated south of the town and enjoying fine country views, this very friendly and welcoming red brick house has been carefully renovated to provide comfortable accommodation. The well

continued

equipped bedrooms all benefit from modern facilities, and breakfast is served in the cosy dining room.

FACILITIES: 4 rms (3 en suite) 3 annexe en suite No smoking TVB tea/coffee No dogs (ex guide dogs) Cen ht TVL 75 acres mixed **PRICES:** s £19.50-£22; d £36-£40✳ **BB** **PARKING:** 7 **NOTES:** Closed 25-26 Dec

♦♦♦♦ Moonraker House
40 Alcester Rd CV37 9DB ☎ 01789 267115 📠 01789 295504
e-mail: moonrakerleonard@aol.com
Dir: *north-west on A422, house located on right*

Ideally located a few minutes walk from railway station and central attractions, this constantly improving establishment provides a range of homely and tastefully furnished bedrooms, located within two separate adjacent houses. An elegant dining room is the setting for imaginative breakfasts and the attractive exterior is enhanced by a magnificent floral display during the warmer months.

FACILITIES: 6 en suite 4 annexe en suite (2 fmly) (5 GF) No smoking TVB tea/coffee No dogs Cen ht No children 5yrs No coaches **PRICES:** s £40-£55; d £55-£80✳ **PARKING:** 10 **CARDS:**

England

STRATFORD UPON AVON continued

♦♦♦♦ Sequoia House Private Hotel

51-53 Shipston Rd CV37 7LN ☎ 01789 268852
🖹 01789 414559
e-mail: info@sequoiahotel.co.uk
Dir: *on A3400 close to Clopton Bridge*

This elegant Victorian house retains many original features highlighted by the quality furnishing and décor schemes throughout. Bedrooms, some of which are located within a sympathetic conversion of former outbuildings, are equipped with both practical and homely extras. A spacious modern air-conditioned restaurant overlooks the immaculate gardens from which guests have direct access to the river and town centre.
FACILITIES: 18 en suite 5 annexe en suite (2 fmly) (3 GF) No smoking in bedrooms No smoking in dining room No smoking in 1 lounge TVB tea/coffee Direct dial from bedrooms No dogs Licensed Cen ht TVL No children 5yrs **PRICES:** s £45-£59; d £59-£89✳ **LB CONF:** Thtr 30 Class 20 Board 20 **PARKING:** 26 **NOTES:** Closed 21-27 Dec **CARDS:**

♦♦♦♦ Twelfth Night

Evesham Place CV37 6HT ☎ 01789 414595
Dir: *on B439. Town centre approx 200mtrs from police station*

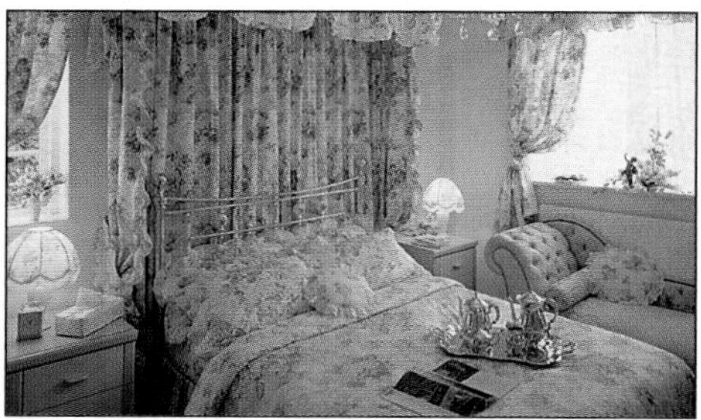

This well-presented Victorian villa is just a short walk from the town. Bedrooms are tastefully decorated and each room has a thoughtful range of high quality facilities and extra personal touches, some rooms have half-tester or brass beds. The comfortably appointed lounge and dining room feature smart period furnishings and good quality fittings.
FACILITIES: 6 en suite No smoking TVB tea/coffee No dogs Cen ht No children 12yrs No coaches **PRICES:** d £54-£68✳ **PARKING:** 8
CARDS:

Smoking restrictions appear under the **FACILITIES** heading, please check when booking.

♦♦♦♦ Victoria Spa Lodge

Bishopton Ln, Bishopton CV37 9QY ☎ 01789 267985
🖹 01789 204728
e-mail: ptozer@victoriaspalodge.demon.co.uk
Dir: *1.5m N on A3400/A46 junct. 1st exit left Bishopton Lane, 1st house on right*

This attractive, early Victorian house is peacefully located on the outskirts of the town. The dramatic lounge, with its stripped hardwood floor, offers many period features. The spacious bedrooms are well equipped with stylish fabrics, quality furnishings and welcome extra touches. This house is no-smoking throughout.
FACILITIES: 7 en suite (3 fmly) No smoking TVB tea/coffee No dogs Cen ht No coaches **PRICES:** s £50; d £60-£65✳ **PARKING:** 12
CARDS:

See advertisement on opposite page

♦♦♦ The Dylan

10 Evesham Place CV37 6HT ☎ 01789 204819
e-mail: dylanguesthouse@lineone.net
Dir: *from A439 Evesham road, pass Shell Garage and continue over traffic island. Guest house 200yds towards Stratford on L*

This Victorian house is situated close to Market Square and the birthplace of Shakespeare. Staff offer a warm and friendly welcome. It retains many original features including moulded cornices and marble fireplaces, enhanced by the fine reproduction furniture. Bedrooms are all well-equipped with modern facilities.
FACILITIES: 5 en suite (2 fmly) (1 GF) No smoking TVB tea/coffee No dogs (ex guide dogs) Cen ht No children 6yrs No coaches **PRICES:** s £25-£28; d £46-£56✳ **LB PARKING:** 5

♦♦♦ Highcroft

Banbury Rd CV37 7NF ☎ 01789 296293 🖹 01789 415236
e-mail: Suedavies_highcroft@hotmail.com
Dir: *on A422 from Stratford towards Banbury, 2m from river bridge on left*

A warm welcome is assured at this creeper-clad red-brick house which is set in immaculate gardens on the town's outskirts. Bedrooms are homely, well equipped and one is located in the converted 18th-century barn. Breakfasts are taken at one table in the spacious open-plan living room.
FACILITIES: 1 en suite 1 annexe en suite (1 fmly) No smoking TVB tea/coffee Cen ht TVL No coaches Tennis (hard) **PRICES:** s £25-£30; d £45-£50✳ **PARKING:** 5

♦♦♦ Avon Lodge

Ryon Hill, Warwick Rd CV37 0NZ ☎ 01789 295196
Located on the town's outskirts in pretty gardens, this red brick detached house offers homely bedrooms some with modern en suite facilities. Tasty breakfasts are taken in the cottage-style dining room and Joan Hampshire provides friendly and attentive services.
FACILITIES: 6 en suite (1 fmly) No smoking TV5B tea/coffee Cen ht TVL No coaches **PRICES:** s fr £25; d fr £50✳ **PARKING:** 7

♦♦♦ Clomendy

10 Broad Walk CV37 6HS ☎ 01789 266957

Dir: *turn off Evesham Place on B439 and establishment is white house on left*

Clonmendy is a small family run house, just a short walk away from the river and the theatre. Mr and Mrs Jones provide a friendly warm welcome. The quiet bedrooms are pretty and comfortable and overlook the garden as does the dining room where hearty breakfasts are taken.

FACILITIES: 2 en suite No smoking TVB tea/coffee No dogs (ex guide dogs) Cen ht No children 5yrs No coaches **PRICES:** s £30; d £40-£46✳ **LB** **PARKING:** 1

♦♦♦ Compton House

22 Shipston Rd CV37 7LP ☎ 01789 205646 📠 01789 205646

e-mail: carteratcomptonhouse@talk21.com

Dir: *follow A3400 out of Stratford-Upon-Avon towards Oxford. Compton House 75mtrs on left, close to Clopton Bridge and River Avon*

A warm welcome is offered at this no smoking establishment - just a short walk over the river from the town centre - where genuine hospitality is a real strength. Bedrooms vary in size and style; several have modern en suite shower rooms. A hearty, freshly-cooked breakfast is served in a ground floor breakfast room overlooking the mature gardens.

FACILITIES: 6 rms (5 en suite) (2 fmly) (2 GF) No smoking TVB tea/coffee No dogs (ex guide dogs) Cen ht No coaches **PRICES:** s £20-£32; d £38-£64✳ **BB** **PARKING:** 8

♦♦♦ The Croft

49 Shipston Rd CV37 7LN ☎ 01789 293419 📠 01789 552986

e-mail: croft.stratford_uk@virgin.net

Dir: *on A3400, 400 yds from Clopton Bridge*

Extended Victorian guest house situated close to Clopton Bridge and with access to the swimming pool. Although the bedrooms come in a variety sizes and styles they are all well equipped to the same high standard. Breakfast is served in the dining room at individual tables and guests also have the use of a smart lounge.

FACILITIES: 9 en suite (5 fmly) No smoking in 2 bedrooms No smoking in dining room TVB tea/coffee Licensed Cen ht TVL Outdoor swimming pool (heated) **PRICES:** s £28-£46; d £50-£68✳ **PARKING:** 4 **CARDS:**

♦♦♦ Curtain Call

142 Alcester Rd CV37 9DR ☎ 01789 267734 📠 01789 267734

e-mail: curtaincall@btinternet.com

Dir: *from A46 take A422 towards Stratford. Curtain Call on brow of hill, just past turn off for Shottery & Anne Hathaway's Cottage*

Curtain Call Guest House is within easy walking distance of Anne Hathaway's Cottage. This semi-detached house has a relaxed atmosphere and staff offer a very warm welcome. The homely bedrooms are all well-equipped homely and individually themed. Each bedroom is filled with many thoughtful extras.

continued

FACILITIES: 6 rms (4 en suite) (1 fmly) No smoking TVB tea/coffee No dogs (ex guide dogs) Cen ht Dinner Last d 11am **PRICES:** s fr £20; d fr £45✳ **LB** **PARKING:** 6 **CARDS:**

♦♦♦ Hollies

'The Hollies', 16 Evesham Place CV37 6HQ ☎ 01789 266857 📠 01789 266857

This former Victorian school is within easy walking distance of the town centre. Hollies Guesthouse offers comfortable bedrooms and boasts a private car park, which is an additional benefit. A comprehensive English breakfast can be taken in the elegant dining room.

FACILITIES: 6 rms (3 en suite) (4 fmly) No smoking TVB tea/coffee No dogs (ex guide dogs) Cen ht TVL **PRICES:** d £35-£45✳ **BB** **PARKING:** 6 **CARDS:**

♦♦♦ Hunters Moon

150 Alcester Rd CV37 9DR ☎ 01789 292888 📠 01789 204101

e-mail: thehuntersmoon@ntlworld.com

Dir: *M40 junct 15 take A46 for 3 rdbts. On 3rd take A422 to town centre. Hunter's Moon is 0.5m further, on brow of slight incline on left*

Guests can benefit from the proximity to Anne Hathaway's Cottage and other tourist attractions on the northern side of Stratford whilst staying at The Hunters Moon. Accommodation is comfortable and well equipped and some bedrooms have views over the well-tended garden

FACILITIES: 6 en suite 1 annexe en suite (3 fmly) No smoking TVB tea/coffee No dogs (ex guide dogs) Cen ht **PRICES:** s £25-£32; d £42-£56✳ **LB** **PARKING:** 6 **NOTES:** Closed 25 Dec **CARDS:**

England

STRATFORD UPON AVON continued

♦♦♦ Marlyn

3 Chestnut Walk CV37 6HG ☎ 01789 293752 📠 01789 293752
e-mail: evansmarlynhotel@aol.com
Dir: *Evesham Road A439 towards town centre, 2nd right after rdbt*
An easy walk from the old part of the town centre and theatre, and with unrestricted parking opposite, Marlyn offers cheery bedrooms and breakfast room, and a cosy lounge. In summer, guests have use of the rear gardens. Aromatherapy/reflexology can be arranged.
FACILITIES: 8 rms (4 en suite) (2 fmly) (1 GF) No smoking in 2 bedrooms No smoking in dining room TVB tea/coffee Licensed Cen ht No coaches Aromatherapy & reflexology treatment Dinner Last d breakfast/midday **PRICES:** s £20-£22; d £40-£52* **CARDS:**

♦♦♦ Parkfield

3 Broad Walk CV37 6HS ☎ 01789 293313 📠 01789 293313
e-mail: parkfield@btinternet.com
Dir: *from Stratford take B439. Parkfield just off B439 on left, immediately before first rdbt*
This attractive Victorian house stands in a quiet road close to the town centre. Much of its original character has been maintained and bedrooms offer comfortable accommodation. A good range of hearty breakfast dishes includes pancakes.
FACILITIES: 7 en suite (1 fmly) No smoking TVB tea/coffee No dogs (ex guide dogs) Cen ht No children 5yrs No coaches **PRICES:** s £25-£26; d £43-£48* **LB PARKING:** 8 **CARDS:**

♦♦♦ Stretton House Hotel

38 Grove Rd CV37 6PB ☎ 01789 268647 📠 01789 268647
e-mail: skyblues@strettonhouse.co.uk
Dir: *A39 central Stratford-upon-Avon road behind police station*
This attractive Edwardian terraced house is within easy walking distance of both the railway station and Shakespeare's birthplace. Bedrooms are tastefully decorated, well equipped and many have modern en suite shower rooms. The pretty front garden is a very welcoming feature.
FACILITIES: 7 rms (4 en suite) (2 fmly) No smoking TVB tea/coffee No dogs (ex guide dogs) Cen ht No children 8yrs **PRICES:** s £28-£40; d £30-£56* **BB PARKING:** 6

♦♦♦ *Travellers Rest*

146 Alcester Rd CV37 9DR ☎ 01789 266589 📠 01789 266589
e-mail: travellersrest146@hotmail.com
Dir: *on A422 1/2 mile from town centre, past railway station on brow of hill.*
Located on the Alcester Road with easy access to town centre, this attractive semi-detached house provides cosy bedrooms, filled with thoughtful extras complimented by modern shower rooms. Breakfast is taken in an attractive front facing dining room and a warm welcome is assured.
FACILITIES: 3 en suite (1 fmly) No smoking TVB tea/coffee No dogs (ex guide dogs) Cen ht No coaches **PARKING:** 5 **NOTES:** Closed 24-26 & 31 Dec

♦♦♦ 🅰 Whitchurch Farm

Whitchurch, Wimpstone CU37 8NS ☎ 01789 450359
📠 01789 450359
Dir: *from Stratford-upon-Avon travel 4m S on A3400 . Take right turn for Wimpstone then left at telephone box in Wimpstone, 0.25m to Whitchurch Farm.*
FACILITIES: 3 en suite (2 fmly) No smoking TVB tea/coffee No dogs (ex guide dogs) Cen ht TVL No children 10 yrs No coaches Dinner Last d 10.30am **PRICES:** s £22-£25; d £44-£50* **PARKING:** 4
NOTES: Closed Xmas & New Year

TEMPLE GRAFTON — Map 04 SP15

♦♦♦ 🅰 The Blue Boar Inn

B49 6NR ☎ 01789 750010 📠 01789 750635
e-mail: blueboar@covlink.co.uk
Dir: *turn off A46 towards Binton and Temple Grafton, Inn is on 1st x-rds reached*
FACILITIES: 15 en suite (5 fmly) No smoking in bedrooms STV TVB tea/coffee Direct dial from bedrooms No dogs (ex guide dogs) Cen ht TVL Dinner Last d 10pm **PRICES:** s £45; d £65* **PARKING:** 50 **CARDS:**

WARWICK — Map 04 SP26

See also Lighthorne

♦♦♦♦ The Hare On The Park

3 Emscote Rd CV34 4PH ☎ 01926 491366
e-mail: prue@thehareonthepark.co.uk
Dir: *off A46 at A425 Warwick. Follow signs to town centre to T-junct. At traffic lights left towards Leamington. Establishment 0.5m on left. From M40 junct 15 through town to park, through traffic lights, over rdbt into Smith St. 0.5m down road on left*
Ideally located for both Warwick and Royal Leamington Spa, this sympathetically restored Victorian house, retains many original features which are highlighted by the quality décor and furnishing styles throughout. Bedrooms are filled with a wealth of thoughtful extras and a comprehensive imaginative breakfast selection includes locally sourced organic produce.
FACILITIES: 3 en suite No smoking in bedrooms No smoking in dining room No smoking in 1 lounge TVB tea/coffee Cen ht TVL No children 7yrs No coaches **PRICES:** s £40; d £65* **PARKING:** 2 **CARDS:**

♦♦♦♦ Agincourt Lodge Hotel

36 Coten End CV34 4NP ☎ 01926 499399 📠 01926 499399
e-mail: enquiries@agincourtlodge.co.uk
Dir: *2m from M40 junct 15 on A429 North*
Located within easy walking distance of the centre and its many attractions, this impressive Victorian house has been sympathetically renovated to provide a range of bedrooms furnished with style and flair. An elegant dining room is the setting for imaginative breakfasts and a spacious lounge with bar is also available.
FACILITIES: 6 en suite (1 fmly) No smoking in bedrooms No smoking in dining room TVB tea/coffee No dogs (ex guide dogs) Licensed Cen ht TVL No coaches **PRICES:** d £52-£70* **PARKING:** 9 **CARDS:**

♦♦♦♦ Croft

Haseley Knob CV35 7NL ☎ 01926 484447 📠 01926 484447
e-mail: david@croftguesthouse.co.uk
Dir: *from Warwick by-pass take A4177 towards Solihull, 4.5m turn R signed M6 Stonebridge then 0.5m turn R to Haseley Knob follow B&B signs*

continued

Set in a peaceful countryside location, and convenient for Warwick and the NEC, this attractive house offers comfortable accommodation. The friendly proprietors provide a home from home atmosphere. Spacious and well-kept gardens are overlooked from the dining room where fresh eggs from the house's own chickens are used for well-cooked English breakfasts.
FACILITIES: 7 en suite (2 fmly) (2 GF) No smoking TVB tea/coffee Cen ht TVL No coaches **PRICES:** s £35-£40; d £48-£55✻ **PARKING:** 8 **NOTES:** Closed Xmas wk **CARDS:**

◆◆◆◆ Dockers Barn Farm

Oxhill Bridle Rd, Pillerton Hersey CV35 0QB ☎ 01926 640475
📠 01926 641747
e-mail: jwhoward@onetel.net.uk
Dir: *A422 Stratford-upon-Avon to Banbury, turn left in Pillerton Priors to Pillerton Hersey, 1st right in village onto Oxhill Bridle Rd for 0.75m. Or M40 junct 12 onto B4451 to Pillerton Hersey, after 6m turn left by village seat onto Oxhill Bridle Rd*

Superbly located in an area of outstanding natural beauty, this former 18th century threshing barn retains many original features including a wealth of exposed beams and flagstone floors. Bedrooms, one of which is situated within a sympathetic conversation of a granary, are equipped with lots of thoughtful extras and the open plan ground floor areas are furnished with style and quality.
FACILITIES: 3 en suite (1 fmly) (1 GF) No smoking TVB tea/coffee Cen ht No children 8yrs No coaches **PRICES:** s £28-£35; d £42-£50✻ **PARKING:** 9 **NOTES:** Closed Xmas rs Daily

◆◆◆ Austin House

96 Emscote Rd CV34 5QJ ☎ 01926 493583 📠 01926 493679
e-mail: mike@austinhouse96.freeserve.co.uk
Dir: *from M40 junct 15 take A429 N, proceed to A445 Warwick to Leamington Spa road*
FACILITIES: 7 rms (5 en suite) (2 fmly) (1 GF) No smoking in 5 bedrooms No smoking in dining room No smoking in lounges TVB tea/coffee No dogs Cen ht No coaches **PRICES:** s £20-£25; d £38-£46 BB **PARKING:** 6 **NOTES:** Closed Xmas **CARDS:**

WEST MIDLANDS

BIRMINGHAM Map 07 SP08

Premier Collection

◆◆◆◆◆ Westbourne Lodge

25-31Fountain Rd, Edgbaston B17 8NJ ☎ 0121 429 1003
📠 0121 429 7436
e-mail: info@westbournelodge.co.uk
Dir: *50 mtrs from A456. 2 km from Five Ways*

This privately-owned hotel has been personally run by the same family for 30 years. The soundly maintained, no smoking accommodation is well equipped and includes family rooms and bedrooms on ground floor level. Facilities include a comfortable lounge, a bar with access to the patio and garden, and a pleasant dining room.
FACILITIES: 24 en suite (6 fmly) (3 GF) No smoking in bedrooms No smoking in area of dining room TVB tea/coffee Direct dial from bedrooms Licensed Cen ht TVL Dinner Last d 8.30pm **PRICES:** s £35-£55; d £45-£75✻ **PARKING:** 12 **NOTES:** Closed 24 Dec-1 Jan **CARDS:**

◆◆◆◆ Black Firs

113 Coleshill Rd, Marston Green B37 7HT ☎ 0121 779 2727
📠 0121 7792727
e-mail: julie@b-firs.co.uk
Dir: *Birmingham airport 1.5m follow signs for Marston Green*

This establishment is ideally placed for access to the NEC or the city itself. The bedrooms are compact with colourful fabrics that have been carefully chosen. Breakfasts are served in the light and airy conservatory overlooking the well-kept gardens. At the front of the house parking is available.
FACILITIES: 6 en suite No smoking TVB tea/coffee No dogs Cen ht No coaches **PARKING:** 6

◆◆◆◆ Bridge House Hotel

49 Sherbourne Rd, Acocks Green B27 6DX ☎ 0121 706 5900
📠 0121 624 5900
e-mail: emailenquiries@bridgehousehotel.co.uk

This private hotel offers comfortable accommodation convenient for the city centre and the NEC. Bedrooms are attractively presented and well equipped. Public areas include a lounge bar, a comfortable sitting area and a spacious restaurant. There is also a split level function room.
FACILITIES: 51 en suite (1 fmly) No smoking in 50 bedrooms No smoking in dining room No smoking in 1 lounge STV TVB tea/coffee Direct dial from bedrooms No dogs (ex guide dogs) Licensed Cen ht TVL Dinner Last d 9pm **PRICES:** s £59.95; d £80✻ **CONF:** Thtr 100 Class 50 Board 50 **PARKING:** 70 **NOTES:** Closed Xmas **CARDS:**

◆◆◆ Diamonds are a guest's best friend! The emphasis is on quality and guest care rather than extra facilities.

England

BIRMINGHAM continued

♦♦♦♦ Olton Cottage

School Ln, Old Yardley Village, Yardley B33 8PD
☎ 0121 783 9249 📠 0121 789 6545
e-mail: olton.cottage@virgin.net
Dir: *M42 junct 5 at NEC/airport take A45 to central Birmingham, turn off A45 onto A4040 to Yardley/Stechford for 1m, turn right into Vicarage Rd, at top of rd right into Church Rd. Left into School Ln*
A warm welcome is assured at this tastefully renovated early Victorian house located in a peaceful residential area yet close to city centre. Cosy bedrooms contain a wealth of thoughtful extras and ground floor areas include a cottage style dining room and comfortable lounge overlooking the pretty enclosed garden.
FACILITIES: 6 rms (2 en suite) (1 fmly) No smoking in 2 bedrooms No smoking in dining room No smoking in lounges TVB tea/coffee No dogs (ex guide dogs) Cen ht TVL **PRICES:** s £24-£30; d £44* **PARKING:** 2

♦♦♦ Ashdale House Hotel

39 Broad Rd, Acock's Green B27 7UX ☎ 0121 706 3598
📠 0121 707 2324
e-mail: ashdalehouse@talk21.com
Dir: *M42 J5/A41 towards Solihull, approx 4.5m to Acock's Green Centre. At rdbt take 2nd exit for B4217, 400yds, turn into Broad Rd*
Located opposite a park with easy walking distance of Acock's Green centre, this sympathetically renovated Victorian house provides a range of bedrooms equipped with period pine furniture and homely extras. Breakfast is taken in a cosy dining room and a comfortable guest lounge is also available.
FACILITIES: 9 rms (5 en suite) (2 fmly) No smoking in 4 bedrooms No smoking in dining room No smoking in 1 lounge TVB tea/coffee Cen ht No coaches **PRICES:** s £22-£30; d £40-£48* **PARKING:** 4 **CARDS:**

♦♦♦ Cape Race Hotel

929 Chester Rd, Erdington B24 OHJ ☎ 0121 373 3085
📠 0121 373 3085
Dir: *on A452, 2m from juncts 5 and 6 of M6, between A38 & A5127*
The friendly proprietors provide a comfortable and homely environment at this attractive house. Convenient for many of the city's attractions and located in an attractive tree-lined avenue this is a pleasant place to stay. Bedrooms are well equipped and comfortable, and guests can relax in the cosy lounge and the bar.
FACILITIES: 9 rms (8 en suite) No smoking in 4 bedrooms No smoking in dining room TVB tea/coffee Direct dial from bedrooms No dogs (ex guide dogs) Licensed Cen ht TVL No coaches Outdoor swimming pool (heated) Dinner Last d 8pm **PRICES:** s £28-£33; d £46* **PARKING:** 9 **CARDS:**

♦♦♦ Central

1637 Coventry Rd, South Yardley B26 1DD ☎ 0121 706 7757
📠 7067757
e-mail: mmou826384@aol.com
Dir: *off M42 at NEC junct, A45, continue past McDonalds and row of shops, pull in after houses on left*
The friendly and attentive proprietors at this comfortable house provide a real home-from-home for their guests. Bedrooms are equipped with many extra facilities. The guests are welcome to relax in the attractive garden. Situated between the airport and city centre this proves a convenient place to stay.
FACILITIES: 5 en suite (1 fmly) No smoking in dining room TVB tea/coffee Cen ht No coaches **PRICES:** s £20-£25; d £40-£45* **PARKING:** 4

♦♦♦ Charde

289 Mackadown Ln, The Cross B33 0NH ☎ 0121 785 2145
📠 0121 785 2149
e-mail: chardeguesthouse@talk21.com
Dir: *M42 to A45 till Wheatsheaf, right next island right pass garage on left,next left Mackadown Lane, end of road guest house right.*

continued

Charde Guest House is a friendly home-from-home establishment just outside the city centre. The well-planned bedrooms are comfortable and all benefit from suitably equipped en suite bathrooms. Off road parking is available.
FACILITIES: 7 rms (5 en suite) (2 fmly) (3 GF) No smoking in 4 bedrooms TVB tea/coffee No dogs (ex guide dogs) Cen ht ch fac Dinner Last d by arrangement **PRICES:** s £21.50-£27.50; d £45-£55* **LB PARKING:** 7 **CARDS:**

♦♦♦ Comfort Inn

Station St B5 4DY ☎ 0121 643 1134 📠 0121 643 3209
e-mail: comfort.inn@talk21.com
Dir: *off M6 junct 6 onto A38 into city centre to Smallbrook Queens Way, turn into Hill St, then into Station St, nr Pallasades shopping centre (Quality Franchise)*
Situated opposite New Street railway station in the heart of the city, this hotel offers well equipped bedrooms, all with modern facilities. Breakfast is taken the attractive basement dining room.
FACILITIES: 40 rms (39 en suite) (2 fmly) No smoking in 8 bedrooms No smoking in dining room No smoking in 1 lounge STV TVB tea/coffee Direct dial from bedrooms No dogs (ex guide dogs) Lift Cen ht Dinner Last d 9.15pm **PRICES:** s £40-£60; d £50-£75* **LB MEALS:** Dinner £6-£15alc*
CONF: Thtr 60 Class 30 Board 25 Del from £50 *
CARDS:

♦♦♦ La Caverna Restaurant & Hotel

2327-2329 Coventry Rd, Sheldon B26 3PG ☎ 0121 743 7917
📠 0121 7223307
Dir: *From M42 junct 6 (NEC airport junct), take A45 towards Birmingham city centre, Sheldon is approx 2m, hotel next to Texaco petrol station*
Situated on the outskirts of Birmingham this family run hotel and restaurant offers authentic Italian cuisine, genuine hospitality and comfortable accommodation for both business and leisure markets.
FACILITIES: 19 en suite (2 fmly) STV TVB tea/coffee Direct dial from bedrooms No dogs Licensed Cen ht TVL Dinner Last d 10.30pm
PARKING: 19 **CARDS:**

♦♦♦ Lyndhurst Hotel

135 Kingsbury Rd, Erdington B24 8QT ☎ 0121 373 5695
📠 0121 373 5697
e-mail: info@lyndhurst-hotel.co.uk
Dir: *from M6 junct 6 follow A5127 then take right fork, signed Minworth, into Kingsbury Rd for hotel on right*

Convenient for the M6 and many of the city's attractions and facilities, this peaceful hotel is situated in a pleasant residential area. Bedrooms are well appointed and comfortable with some located on the ground floor. A spacious restaurant overlooks the attractive garden and guests may relax in the bar or cosy lounge.
FACILITIES: 14 rms (13 en suite) (3 fmly) (5 GF) No smoking in bedrooms No smoking in dining room No smoking in 1 lounge TVB tea/coffee No

continued

dogs (ex guide dogs) Licensed Cen ht TVL No coaches Dinner Last d 8.15pm **PRICES:** s £35-£46; d £46-£58 **PARKING:** 15 **NOTES:** Closed Xmas **CARDS:**

◆◆◆ Robin Hood Lodge Hotel

142 Robin Hood Ln, Hall Green B28 0JX
☎ 0121 778 5307 & 0121 608 6622 0121 608 6622
Dir: *on A4040, 5m from city centre*

This family-run hotel is conveniently located for the motorway links and easy access to the city centre and many guests choose it as a regular base. Bedrooms are well-equipped and spacious, and provide value-for-money accommodation. A good choice is available in the restaurant and guests may wish to relax in the comfort of the bar.
FACILITIES: 9 rms (5 en suite) (1 fmly) No smoking in dining room TVB tea/coffee Licensed Cen ht TVL No coaches Dinner Last d 8pm **PRICES:** s £33-£38; d £42-£49* **PARKING:** 11 **CARDS:**

◆◆◆ Tri-Star Hotel

Coventry Rd, Elmdon B26 3QR ☎ 0121 782 1010 & 0121 782 6131 0121 782 6131
Dir: *on A45*
This attractive small hotel has recently been refurbished and provides modern and comfortable rooms, which are well-equipped and spacious. Convenient for the NEC, airport and city centre, the Tri-Star is a pleasant and friendly establishment. A lounge and games room are available and traditional breakfasts are served in the dining room, which overlooks the countryside.
FACILITIES: 15 en suite (2 fmly) No smoking in 10 bedrooms No smoking in dining room TVB tea/coffee No dogs Licensed Cen ht TVL games room Dinner Last d 8pm **PRICES:** s fr £49; d fr £59* **PARKING:** 25 **CARDS:**

◆◆◆ The Old Barn

Birmingham Rd, Coleshill B64 1DP ☎ 01675 463692
01675 466275
Dir: *from M6 junct 4 turn onto A446 towards Coleshill. Straight on at first rdbt left at next rdbt onto B4114, bear left at rdbt Old Barn 200yds past rdbt on left after layby*
FACILITIES: 11 rms (9 en suite) (3 fmly) (6 GF) No smoking in bedrooms No smoking in dining room TVB tea/coffee No dogs Licensed Cen ht TVL Indoor swimming pool (heated) Pool Table Pool table **PRICES:** s £37.50-£40; d £63.50-£68.50* **PARKING:** 25 **NOTES:** Closed Xmas & New Year **CARDS:**

◆◆ Awentsbury Hotel

21 Serpentine Rd, Selly Park B29 7HU ☎ 0121 472 1258
0121 472 1258
e-mail: ian@awentsbury.com
Dir: *A38 from city centre, at end of dual carriageway & just after fire station, take 1st L, L again & 1st R*
This large Victorian house is quietly located in a residential area, yet conveniently close to the University, city centre and motorway links. The bedrooms are simply furnished and many have en suite showers. Breakfast is taken in the dining room, which overlooks the garden.
FACILITIES: 16 rms (7 en suite) (1 fmly) No smoking in dining room TVB tea/coffee Direct dial from bedrooms Cen ht Dinner Last d 7pm
PRICES: s £38-£48; d £52-£60* **PARKING:** 12
CARDS:

◆◆ Elston

749-751 Washwood Heath Rd, Ward End B8 2JY
☎ 0121 327 3338 688 0781
e-mail: enquiries@elstonguesthouse.co.uk
Dir: *on A47/A4040 crossroads, 1.5m from M6 junct 5/6*
Ideally located for major road links this conversion of two Edwardian houses provides a range of practically equipped bedrooms popular with contractors and weekend groups. A selection of restaurants and pubs is within easy walking distance and the spacious rear car park is an additional advantage.
FACILITIES: 12 rms (2 en suite) (2 fmly) (4 GF) No smoking in 1 bedrooms No smoking in dining room No smoking in lounges TVB tea/coffee Cen ht TVL No coaches safe garden with toys for children **PRICES:** s £20; d £35-£40* BB **PARKING:** 13 **CARDS:**

◆◆ Rollason Wood Hotel

130 Wood End Rd, Erdington B24 8BJ ☎ 0121 373 1230
0121 382 2578
e-mail: rollwood@globalnet.co.uk
Dir: *M6 J6, exit Birmingham Rd. At island take A5127 to Sutton & Erdington for 1m, at island turn R onto A4040, hotel 0.25m on L*

This commercial hotel offers simply appointed rooms which are both comfortable and well-equipped and is convenient for the major road links and Erdington's centre. A popular bar is available as well as a spacious garden and good parking. A good range of bar-snacks as well as dinner choices are available.
FACILITIES: 35 rms (11 en suite) (5 fmly) No smoking in 7 bedrooms No smoking in area of dining room TVB tea/coffee Licensed Cen ht TVL Pool Table Games room & darts Dinner Last d 8.30pm **PRICES:** s £18-£38; d £32-£49.50* BB **PARKING:** 35 **CARDS:**

BIRMINGHAM (National Exhibition Centre)

See **Hampton-in-Arden & Solihull**

England

COVENTRY Map 04 SP37

♦♦♦♦ Acacia
11 Park Rd, Cheyles More CV1 2LE ☎ 024 7663 3622
024 7663 3622
e-mail: acaciaguesthouse@hotmail.com
Dir: *Coventry ring road exit 6 into railway stn and turn left for 250 yds*

This friendly welcoming guest house offers immaculately maintained accommodation; all rooms have en suite bathrooms. Ground floor public areas combine a comfortable lounge with bar and a spacious dining room. Evening meals and snacks are readily available. Located close to city centre.
FACILITIES: 11 en suite (4 fmly) No smoking in 4 bedrooms TVB tea/coffee No dogs (ex guide dogs) Licensed Cen ht TVL Dinner Last d 8.30pm **PRICES:** s fr £27.50; d fr £42✳ **PARKING:** 12

♦♦♦ Ashleigh House
17 Park Rd CV1 2LH ☎ 024 76223804 024 76223804
Easily located from the major road links and convenient for the city centre, this attractive house has the benefit of secure parking. Efficient and friendly service is provided and guests have the use of a bar and a lounge, and at dinner a good choice of freshly prepared and appetising dishes are available.
FACILITIES: 10 en suite (5 fmly) TVB tea/coffee No dogs Licensed Cen ht TVL No coaches Dinner Last d 8.45pm **PRICES:** s £25.50-£27.50; d £40-£46✳ **PARKING:** 12 **NOTES:** Closed 23 Dec-1 Jan

♦♦♦ Croft on the Green
23 Stoke Green, off Binley Rd CV3 1FP ☎ 024 7645 7846
024 7645 7846
e-mail: croftonthegreen@aol.com
Dir: *fromA428 Coventry City Centre towards Rugby on Binley Rd, turn off onto Stoke Green signed, towards Aldermoor House*
This Victorian detached house is situated close to the city centre in a quiet conservation area. Five of the bedrooms have full en suite facilities and the accommodation has been recently redecorated by the new owners. The spacious public areas include a comfortable dining room with an adjacent lounge and a separate bar.
FACILITIES: 12 rms (9 en suite) (2 fmly) No smoking in bedrooms No smoking in dining room TVB tea/coffee No dogs (ex guide dogs) Licensed Cen ht TVL **PRICES:** s £25-£35; d £45-£65 **CONF:** Class 25 Del from £45 ✳ **PARKING:** 12 **CARDS:**

♦♦♦ A Ashdowns
12 Regent St CV1 3EP ☎ 024 7622 9280
Dir: *off junct6 onto ring road, follow sign 2 train stn. Straight over rdbt before ring road 1st left into Grosvenor rd. R into Westminster rd. Turn R at bottom of Westminster rd into Regent street.*
FACILITIES: 8 rms (7 en suite) (3 fmly) No smoking TVB tea/coffee No dogs (ex guide dogs) Cen ht TVL No children 13yrs
PRICES: s £25-£36; d £45-£48✳ **LB PARKING:** 8

HAMPTON-IN-ARDEN Map 04 SP28

♦♦♦ The Cottage
Kenilworth Rd B92 0LW ☎ 01675 442323 01675 443323
Dir: *on A452, 2m from M42, 4m from M6*
This delightful cottage is an ideal base from which to visit the NEC or to explore the area. A friendly atmosphere and attentive service provide a relaxing environment and many guests return. Freshly cooked traditional breakfasts are served in the cottage dining room and provide a good start to the day.
FACILITIES: 9 en suite No smoking in dining room TVB tea/coffee Cen ht TVL **PRICES:** s fr £30; d fr £46✳ **PARKING:** 14 **NOTES:** Closed Xmas

♦♦♦ A The Hollies Guest House
Kenilworth Rd B92 0LW ☎ 01675 442681 01675 442941
e-mail: thehollies@hotmail.com
Dir: *M42 junct 6 onto A45 towards Coventry, exit left onto A452 to Lemington/Balsall Common. Right at rdbt, over next rdbt. Establishment 1m on right, next door to Trade Car Sales*
FACILITIES: 10 en suite (1 fmly) No smoking in 4 bedrooms No smoking in dining room No smoking in lounges TVB tea/coffee Cen ht TVL **PRICES:** s fr £30; d £45-£60✳ **PARKING:** 10 **NOTES:** Closed 21 Nov-5 Jan

MERIDEN Map 04 SP28

♦♦♦ Meriden Hotel
155 Main Rd CV7 7NH ☎ 01676 522005 01676 523744
e-mail: meridenhotel@aol.com
Dir: *A45/B4104 signposted to Nuneaton & Meriden. At rdbt take second exit, continue for exactly 1m, hotel on left beyond manor*

This commercial hotel is situated in pleasant village surroundings and is with easy driving distance of the NEC. Bedrooms are well equipped and comfortable. A lounge is available and also a pleasant small bar. Breakfast is served in the attractive dining room.
FACILITIES: 16 en suite (2 fmly) (3 GF) No smoking in dining room TVB tea/coffee Direct dial from bedrooms Licensed Cen ht TVL Dinner Last d 9pm **PRICES:** s £45; d £70✳ **PARKING:** 20
CARDS:

ROWLEY REGIS Map 07 SO98

♦♦ Highfield House Hotel
1 Holly Rd, Blackheath B65 0BH ☎ 0121 559 1066
0121 561 2424
Dir: *M5 junct 2, take A4034 (Birchfield Road) towards to Blackheath, joining Oldbury Road, right into Henderson Way, join High St, then Powke Lane, left into Holly Road at 1st traffic lights*
This extended Victorian house offers simply appointed, well maintained accommodation. It has the benefit of a comfortable lounge and bar service. Most bedrooms share bathrooms.

continued

FACILITIES: 14 rms (2 en suite) (2 fmly) No smoking in dining room TVB tea/coffee No dogs (ex guide dogs) Licensed Cen ht TVL No coaches **PRICES:** s £20-£30; d £35-£40✱ **BB** **PARKING:** 10
CARDS:

SOLIHULL — Map 07 SP17

♦♦♦ The Gate House

Barston Ln, Barston B92 0JN ☎ 01675 443274 📠 01675 442938
e-mail: gatehouse@jjemmett.fsnet.co.uk
Dir: *A4141 Warwick 1.2m to Hampton Rd, left at Wilson Arms, 2m to Wyevale Gdn Cntr. Turn right into Barston Ln, The Gate House on right*
This elegant Victorian building is set in peaceful grounds, which have the benefit of secure parking, and is within easy driving distance of the NEC. The resident proprietor is most welcoming, and spacious and comfortable accommodation is provided. Breakfast is served in the dining room, which looks out over the garden.
FACILITIES: 4 rms (2 en suite) No smoking TVB tea/coffee No dogs (ex guide dogs) Cen ht TVL No coaches **PRICES:** s £25-£35; d £50-£60✱ **PARKING:** 20

♦♦♦ Ivy House

Warwick Rd, Heronfield, Knowle B93 0EB ☎ 01564 770247 📠 01564 778063
e-mail: john@ivy-guest-house.freeserve.co.uk
Dir: *3m from junct 5 of M42, on A4141 heading towards Warwick*
Ivy House is set in peaceful countryside and only a short walk of the bustling canal and it's riverside Inn, yet within easy driving from the NEC, this friendly family-run house provides comfortable accommodation. Hearty breakfasts are served in the comfortable dining room at separate tables.
FACILITIES: 8 en suite (1 fmly) No smoking TVB tea/coffee Cen ht TVL Fishing **PRICES:** s £35-£40; d £50-£60✱ **PARKING:** 20

SUTTON COLDFIELD — Map 07 SP19

♦♦♦♦ Standbridge Hotel

138 Birmingham Rd B72 1LY ☎ 0121 354 3007 📠 0121 354 6373
e-mail: enquires@standbridgehotel.co.uk
Dir: *1m S on A5127*
Located on a mainly residential avenue within a few minutes walk from the town centre, this constantly improving Edwardian house provides cosy bedrooms equipped with quality soft furnishings. Breakfast is taken in a bright attractive conservatory overlooking the immaculate rear garden and a guest lounge is also available.
FACILITIES: 10 en suite (3 fmly) (1 GF) No smoking TVB tea/coffee No dogs (ex guide dogs) Licensed Cen ht TVL No children 5yrs No coaches **PRICES:** s £29.50-£33; d £46-£50✱ **LB** **PARKING:** 12 **CARDS:**

♦♦♦♦ Windrush

337 Birmingham Rd, Wylde Green B72 1DL ☎ 0121 384 7534
e-mail: windrush59@hotmail.com
Dir: *on A5127 to Sutton Coldfield from Birmingham. House immediately before doctors' surgery, 'The Hawthorns' on right*
Lynne Bridgwater provides a home-from-home atmosphere for both business and leisure guests. Situated between Sutton Coldfield and Birmingham, this property offers comfortable, well equipped and attractively decorated rooms, with lots of thoughtful extras. The main bathroom offers both bath and shower.
FACILITIES: 3 rms (1 en suite) No smoking STV TVB tea/coffee No dogs Cen ht No children 16yrs No coaches Dinner Last d 10am **PRICES:** s £25-£35; d £50-£65✱ **PARKING:** 5 **NOTES:** Closed 19 Dec-3 Jan

WIGHT, ISLE OF

BONCHURCH — Map 04 SZ57

U Winterbourne

Bonchurch Village Rd PO38 1RQ ☎ 01983 852535
At the time of going to press the Diamond classification for this establishment had not been confirmed. Please check the AA website www.theAA.com for up-to-date information.
FACILITIES: 7 en suite

See advertisement on page 427

CHALE — Map 04 SZ47

♦♦♦♦ The Old House

Gotten Manor, Gotten Ln PO38 2HQ ☎ 01983 551368 📠 0870 1369453
e-mail: aa@gottenmanor.co.uk
Dir: *0.5m S of Chale Green on B3399 after village turn left at Gotten Lane (opp Chapel) house at end of lane*
Peacefully located close to the coastal road, parts of this historic building date from the Saxon period. Sympathetic restoration has created comfortable, homely bedrooms equipped with antique bathtubs within the sleeping area. Comprehensive breakfasts make use of the finest ingredients and are taken in the cosy dining room; there is a spacious lounge with open fire.
FACILITIES: 2 en suite No smoking STV TVB tea/coffee No dogs Cen ht No children 12yrs Croquet lawn **PRICES:** d £60-£80✱ **LB** **PARKING:** 4

U Chale Bay Farm

Military Rd PO38 2JF ☎ 01983 730950
At the time of going to press the Diamond classification for this establishment had not been confirmed. Please check the AA website www.theAA.com for up-to-date information.
FACILITIES: 8 en suite (2 fmly)

COWES — Map 04 SZ49

♦♦♦ Windward House

69 Mill Hill Rd PO31 7EQ ☎ 01983 280940 & 07771 573580 📠 01983 280940
Dir: *A320 Cowes-Newport, halfway up Mill Hill Rd on right from floating bridge from E Cowes (Red Funnel Ferries)*
A friendly atmosphere prevails at this comfortable Victorian house, located close to the centre of Cowes. Bedrooms are bright and neat whilst downstairs there is a spacious lounge, well-equipped with satellite TV, video and music systems. Breakfast is served in a separate dining room around a shared table.
FACILITIES: 6 rms (3 en suite) (2 fmly) No smoking in dining room TVB tea/coffee Cen ht TVL No coaches Jacuzzi **PRICES:** s £20-£30; d £40-£60✱ **PARKING:** 4

NEWPORT — Map 04 SZ48

♦♦♦♦ Redway Cottage

East Ln, Herstone PO30 3DJ ☎ 01983 533929 📠 01983 533929
e-mail: gem@merstone.fsnet.co.uk
Dir: *on A3056. right turn approx. 4m from Newport, through Merstone, turn left onto Bury Lane Establishment at top of junct with East Lane*
Located in the centre of the island in a tranquil rural setting surrounded by fields, Redway Cottage is ideal for those wishing to enjoy countryside walks and escape from the hustle and bustle of everyday life. Bedrooms are comfortable, well decorated and equipped with many extra facilities. Breakfast is served at individual tables.
FACILITIES: 2 rms No smoking TVB tea/coffee No dogs Cen ht No children No coaches **PRICES:** s £46-£54; d £92-£108✱ **LB** **PARKING:** 2
NOTES: Closed Nov-Feb

England

NEWPORT continued

♦♦♦ Elizabeth House

21 Carisbrooke Rd PO30 1BU ☎ 01983 521389
🖷 01983 521389
Dir: *on a Victorian Mall on outskirts of Newport*
A warm friendly welcome is assured at this fine Victorian house located within easy walking distance of the town centre. Bedrooms are spacious, comfortably furnished and suitably equipped. Breakfast is served in the cosy dining room with guests sharing one large table.
FACILITIES: 4 rms (2 en suite) (1 fmly) No smoking TVB tea/coffee No dogs (ex guide dogs) Cen ht No coaches **PRICES:** s £20; d £40✻ **PARKING:** 4

NITON — Map 04 SZ57

♦♦♦♦ Pine Ridge Country House

Niton Undercliff PO38 2LY ☎ 01983 730802 🖷 01983 731001
e-mail: pine_ridge@lineone.net
Dir: *on A3055 Niton to Ventor Rd, just after garage on right, opposite green at bottom of hill*
This attractive country house is set in well maintained gardens in a peaceful setting with excellent views. Bedrooms are comfortably appointed and well equipped with one having a four-poster bed. An interesting supper menu and choice of breakfasts are available. Guests also have use of a smart lounge and bar.
FACILITIES: 7 en suite (3 fmly) No smoking in 2 bedrooms No smoking in dining room No smoking in 1 lounge TVB tea/coffee Direct dial from bedrooms Licensed Cen ht TVL No coaches Dinner Last d 8pm
PRICES: s £35-£62.50; d £65-£100✻ **LB PARKING:** 10
NOTES: Closed 25 Dec **CARDS:**

RYDE — Map 04 SZ59

Premier Collection

♦♦♦♦♦ Little Upton Farm *(SZ578900)*

Gatehouse Rd, Upton, Ashey PO33 4BS ☎ 01983 563236
🖷 01983 563236 Mr & Mrs H Johnson
e-mail: web@littleuptonfarm.co.uk
Dir: *from E Cowes/Fishbourne follow signs to Ryde. At mini rdbt at top of rise turn right along Newnham Rd, signed Havenstreet/Brickfields Horsecountry, pass Brickfields on right, take junct on left, left immediately into Stroudwood Rd at mini rdbt turn right, farm on left in 0.25m*
Little Upton Farm is set in a beautiful rural location on a 200-acre dairy farm close to Ryde. The farmhouse is a listed 17th century building, furnished with antiques and carefully restored with all its original charm, featuring exposed timbers and inglenook fireplaces, where cosy log fires burn in winter. It provides very well furnished bedrooms, all with garden views, together with ample, comfortable public rooms.
FACILITIES: 2 en suite No smoking TVB tea/coffee No dogs (ex guide dogs) Cen ht TVL No children 12yrs 200 acres sheep, pigs & chickens
PRICES: s £25-£35; d £56-£60✻ **PARKING:** 4
NOTES: Closed Xmas & New year

Premier Collection

♦♦♦♦♦ Newnham Farm *(SZ569915)*

Newnham Ln, Binstead PO33 4ED ☎ 01983 882423
🖷 01983 882423 Mrs D Cleaver
e-mail: newnhamfarm@talk21.com
Dir: *off A3054 (Ryde to Newport) at top of Binstead Hill, mini rdbt into Newnham Road, 0.5m turn right into Newnham Lane, 0.5m to Newnham Farm*

Newnham Farm

A warm welcome is assured at this delightful old stone farmhouse situated in forty acres of pasture and woodlands where an abundance of wildlife can be encountered during cross-country walks. Lawns and mature trees surround a duck lake where guests are welcome to sit and relax. The spacious, comfortable bedrooms are equipped with many thoughtful extras. A substantial English breakfast is served at one large table in the charming dining room. Diana Cleaver was a Top Twenty Finalist in the AA Landlady of the Year Award 2002-2003.
FACILITIES: 2 en suite (1 fmly) No smoking TVB tea/coffee No dogs Cen ht TVL 320 acres arable, sheep, horses **PRICES:** s £33-£45; d £56-£70✻ **LB PARKING:** 6

♦♦♦♦ Eleanor Cottage

Carpenters Rd PO33 1YG ☎ 01983 873979 🖷 01983 873979
Dir: *off A3055 signed Bembridge/St Helens. Cottage approx 1m on right*
Located close to the village green of St Helens and within a short distance of the coast, Bembridge and Ryde, this delightful cottage provides guests with comfortable well equipped rooms one of which has a four-poster bed. In the morning guests share a table where a full English breakfast is served.
FACILITIES: 3 rms (1 fmly) No smoking TV2B tea/coffee No dogs Cen ht No coaches **PRICES:** s £20; d £40✻ **PARKING:** 3

♦♦♦ Abingdon Lodge Hotel

20 West St PO33 2QQ ☎ 01983 564537 🖷 01983 566722
e-mail: sandyandlarry@abingdonlodge.freesave.co.uk
Dir: *Take through traffic signs. Establishment is opposite 1st set of traffic lights*
Abingdon Lodge has a loyal clientele who return for the friendly hospitality that is provided. Bedrooms are fully en suite and equipped with thoughtful and useful extras. A bright conservatory dining room and bar are recent additions.
FACILITIES: 11 en suite (1 fmly) No smoking in 4 bedrooms TVB tea/coffee Direct dial from bedrooms No dogs (ex guide dogs) Licensed Cen ht TVL No children 5yrs No coaches Dinner Last d by arrangement
PRICES: s £20-£25; d £40-£46✻ **LB PARKING:** 7 **CARDS:**

U Grange Farm B&B

Grange Farm, Staplers Rd, Wootton PO33 4RW ☎ 01983 882147
At the time of going to press the Diamond classification for this establishment had not been confirmed. Please check the AA website www.theAA.com for up-to-date information.
FACILITIES: 2 en suite

SANDOWN — Map 04 SZ58

♦♦♦ Carisbrooke House Hotel

11 Beachfield Rd PO36 8NA ☎ 01983 402257 🖷 01983 402295
e-mail: carisbrookehotel@aol.com
Dir: *follow signs through Sandown town centre and through High Street onto Beachfield Road, hotel 200yds past Post Office on right*

continued

England

Located within walking distance of the town centre and sea front this delightful family-run hotel provides guests with a warm welcome and comfortable bedrooms. There is a large dining room where full English breakfasts are served at individual tables. There is also a well-stocked bar which leads through to a cosy television lounge.
FACILITIES: 10 rms (7 en suite) (4 fmly) No smoking in bedrooms No smoking in dining room No smoking in lounges TVB tea/coffee Licensed Cen ht TVL Dinner Last d noon **PRICES:** s £18-£25; d £36-£50* **LB BB**
CARDS:

♦♦♦ Chester Lodge Hotel
7 Beachfield Rd PO36 8NA ☎ 01983 402773 📠 01983 402773
e-mail: chesterlodgehotel@bigwig.net
Dir: *turn off A3055 (Broadway, Sandown) into Melville St. 1st right into Royal Crescent. Right at end into Beachfield Rd. Hotel 30yrds on right*
Located within walking distance of the seafront and shops, this family run hotel offers neatly decorated and appropriately equipped bedrooms, some of which are on the ground floor. There is a spacious bar lounge where regular entertainment is provided. Evening meals, which are available by prior arrangement, are served in the brightly appointed dining room.
FACILITIES: 16 rms (15 en suite) (5 fmly) (7 GF) No smoking in bedrooms No smoking in dining room TVB tea/coffee No dogs Licensed Cen ht TVL Dinner Last d 5.45pm **PRICES:** s £21-£25; d £42-£50*
PARKING: 15 **NOTES:** Closed Jan-Feb rs Oct-Etr (mainly groups)
CARDS:

♦♦♦ Culver Lodge Hotel
Albert Rd PO36 8AW ☎ 01983 403819 01983 402902
📠 01983 403819
e-mail: culverlodge@lowholidays.fsnet.co.uk
Dir: *turn off The Broadway into Station Rd and left into Albert Rd*
This well-kept hotel is located in a quiet residential area, a short walk from the seafront and town centre. Public areas are spacious with an attractive lounge, bar and games room. Bedrooms are well presented and equipped. The pool and terrace are ideal areas to enjoy the sun; evening meals are also available.
FACILITIES: 22 en suite (5 fmly) (4 GF) No smoking in dining room TVB tea/coffee No dogs (ex guide dogs) Licensed Cen ht TVL Outdoor swimming pool Bar Billards,Table Football Dinner Last d 6pm **PRICES:** s £22-£28; d £44-£56* **LB PARKING:** 20 **NOTES:** Closed Nov-Etr
CARDS:

♦♦♦ The Philomel Hotel
21 Carter St PO36 8BL ☎ 01983 406413 📠 0870 094061
e-mail: philomel@tiscali.co.uk
Dir: *From Ryde on A3055, on entering Sandown, 1st rdbt take B3329 Avenue Rd approx 0.25m left is "Caulkheads" pub, right opposite pub to Carter St, hotel left opposite church.*
This is a family owned and run hotel, which is located close to the town centre. The bedrooms at this smart guesthouse are all well-decorated. Public areas include a cosy lounge and a pleasant dining room in which hearty breakfasts are served.
FACILITIES: 9 rms (6 en suite) (2 fmly) No smoking in bedrooms No smoking in dining room tea/coffee No dogs (ex guide dogs) Licensed TVL No coaches Dinner Last d 4pm **PRICES:** s £17-£19; d £38-£42* **BB**
PARKING: 5

♦♦♦ Lyndhurst Hotel
8 Royal Crescent PO36 8LZ ☎ 01983 403663 📠 01983 403663
Dir: *from Ryde A3055 to Sandown, right at rdbt into the Broadway, 7th turning left (Melville St), then 1st right Royal Crescent. From Newport A3056 left at lights in Lake to Sandown, up Lake Hill over traffic lights 2nd right Melville St 1st right Melville Crescent*

continued

FACILITIES: 10 en suite (4 fmly) (5 GF) No smoking in bedrooms No smoking in dining room TVB tea/coffee No dogs (ex guide dogs) Licensed Cen ht TVL Dinner Last d 1pm **PRICES:** s £18-£45; d £36-£50* **LB BB**
CARDS:

Lawns Hotel
72 Broadway PO36 9AA ☎ 01983 402549
At the time of going to press the Diamond classification for this establishment had not been confirmed. Please check the AA website www.theAA.com for up-to-date information.
FACILITIES: 15 rms (10 en suite) (5 fmly)

SEAVIEW Map 04 SZ69

♦♦♦ Northbank Hotel
Circular Rd PO34 5ET ☎ 01983 612227 📠 01983 612227
e-mail: northbank@netguides.co.uk
Dir: *B3330 from Ryde to Seaview, take right into Nettlestone Green, left down the hill into Seaview, hotel on right of High St into Circular Road*
The views from Northbank across The Solent to the mainland are stunning, while its delightful gardens run down to a sandy beach. The hotel contains some lovely objets d'art which add to the ambience of this fine Victorian home. There is a games room, television room, library and bar for guests to enjoy.
FACILITIES: 18 rms (6 fmly) No smoking in dining room No smoking in lounges TV16B tea/coffee No dogs (ex guide dogs) Licensed TVL Snooker Dinner Last d 8pm **PRICES:** s £35-£40; d £70-£80*
PARKING: 12 **NOTES:** Closed Oct-Etr **CARDS:**

England

SHANKLIN Map 04 SZ58

♦♦♦♦ Bedford Lodge Hotel

4 Chine Av PO37 6AQ ☎ 01983 862416 📠 01983 868704
e-mail: aa@bedfordlodge.co.uk
Dir: *A3055 from Sandown. At traffic lights take Queens Rd to end. Right onto Chine Avenue, hotel opposite Tower Cottage Gardens*
A warm welcome is assured at this delightful property located in its own grounds and within walking distance of the beach and town centre. Bedrooms are comfortable and well equipped. A full English breakfast is served at individual tables in the charming dining room. There is also a guest lounge and bar.
FACILITIES: 12 en suite (4 fmly) No smoking in dining room TVB tea/coffee Licensed Cen ht TVL No coaches **PRICES:** s £35-£55; d £50-£60✻ **LB**
PARKING: 8 **CARDS:**

♦♦♦♦ St Georges House Hotel

2 St Georges Rd PO37 6BA ☎ 01983 863691 📠 01983 861597
e-mail: info@stgeorgesiow.com
Dir: *turn left off A3055 (Sandown to Shanklin road) at Cross St (Conservative Club on corner), then left into Palmerston Rd and 1st left into St Georges Rd. Hotel on corner.*
A warm welcome is assured at this delightful family run hotel located in a quiet area between the town centre and cliff top. Bedrooms are comfortable and well appointed. There is also a lounge, bar and patio for guests to enjoy. Tasty dinners are available by prior arrangement.
FACILITIES: 8 rms (7 en suite) (2 fmly) No smoking in bedrooms No smoking in dining room No smoking in lounges TVB tea/coffee No dogs (ex guide dogs) Licensed Cen ht TVL No coaches Dinner Last d 24hr notice
PRICES: s £25-£30; d £44-£54✻ **LB** **PARKING:** 8
CARDS:

♦♦♦ Hayes Barton Hotel

7 Highfield Rd PO37 6PP ☎ 01983 867747 📠 01983 862104
e-mail: williams.2000@virgin.net
Dir: *A3055 from Ryde or Cowes, turn off on to A3020. High St, Shanklin into Victoria Av, Highfield Rd is 3rd turning on left, hotel on right*
Hayes Barton enjoys the relaxed atmosphere of a family home and also provides well equipped bedrooms and a range of comfortable public areas. Dinner, available from a short selection of home-cooked dishes, is a treat and there is a cosy bar lounge. The Old Village, the beach and the promenade are within walking distance.
FACILITIES: 10 en suite (9 fmly) No smoking in bedrooms No smoking in dining room TVB tea/coffee Licensed Cen ht TVL No coaches Indoor swimming pool Dinner **PRICES:** (incl. dinner) s £29-£36; d £58-£72✻ **LB**
PARKING: 10 **NOTES:** Closed Nov-1 March

♦♦♦ Holly Lodge

29 Queens Rd PO37 6DQ ☎ 01983 863604
e-mail: coliwat@freeuk.com
Dir: *on A3055 at traffic lights at bottom of Arthur's hill take 2nd left into Queens rd*
A warm welcome is assured at this charming family-run guest house located close to the centre of town, the seafront and Shanklin Old Village. Bedrooms are comfortable, brightly decorated and equipped with many extra facilities. A full English breakfast is served at individual tables.
FACILITIES: 4 rms (2 en suite) No smoking TVB tea/coffee No dogs (ex guide dogs) Cen ht No children 12yrs No coaches **PRICES:** d £40-£46✻
PARKING: 1 **NOTES:** Closed Nov-Feb

♦♦♦ Mount House Hotel

20 Arthurs Hill PO37 6EE ☎ 01983 862556 📠 01983 867551
e-mail: mount-house@netguides.co.uk
Dir: *take A3055 towards Sandown, on outskirts of town on corner of Clarence Road*

continued

A warm welcome awaits guests to this family run hotel with a homely atmosphere. Bedrooms are bright with modern extras and neatly kept en suite bathrooms. There is a spacious dining room where home cooked dinners and breakfast are served. The town centre, cliffs and beach are all within easy walking distance.
FACILITIES: 9 en suite (2 fmly) (1 GF) No smoking in dining room TVB tea/coffee Licensed Cen ht TVL No coaches Dinner Last d 5pm
PRICES: s £19-£22; d £38-£44✻ **BB** **PARKING:** 5
NOTES: Closed 1Feb-21Dec **CARDS:**

♦♦♦ Norfolk House Hotel

19 Esplanade PO37 6BN ☎ 01983 863023 📠 01983 863023
e-mail: gcking@talk21.com
Dir: *A3055 Sandown-Shanklin at Arthurs Hill traffic light junct (leaving Lake) turn left onto Hope Road, signed Esplanade, Hotel on right opposite Victorian clock tower*
A warm welcome is assured at this friendly, family-run hotel, located on the sea front with the beach across the road. Bedrooms are comfortable with many extras provided. There is also a bar, lounge and garden for guests' use. The Restaurant is open to non-residents with lunches and afternoon teas also available.
FACILITIES: 11 rms (9 en suite) (2 fmly) No smoking in bedrooms No smoking in dining room No smoking in lounges TVB tea/coffee Licensed Cen ht TVL Dinner Last d 5.30pm **PRICES:** s £25-£30; d £50-£60✻ **LB**
PARKING: 8 **NOTES:** Closed mid Jan-mid Feb **CARDS:**

♦♦♦ The Richmond Hotel

23 Palmerston Rd PO37 6AS ☎ 01983 862874 📠 01983 862874
e-mail: richmondhotel.shanklin@virgin.net
Dir: *off Shanklin High Street at Conservative Club and hotel 100mtrs ahead*
A warm and friendly welcome awaits at this delightful hotel located in the centre of town yet just a couple of minutes walk from the beach. Rooms are well furnished and maintained with many extra facilities provided. Dinner is available by prior arrangement and a guest lounge and bar are also available.
FACILITIES: 10 rms (9 en suite) (2 fmly) No smoking in bedrooms No smoking in dining room TVB tea/coffee No dogs (ex guide dogs) Licensed Cen ht TVL No coaches Dinner Last d 3pm **PRICES:** s £25; d £50✻ **LB**
PARKING: 5 **NOTES:** Closed Nov-mid Mar rs Mar-Apr & Oct
CARDS:

♦♦♦ Rowborough Hotel

32 Arthurs Hill PO37 6EX ☎ 01983 866072 & 863070
📠 01983 867703
Dir: *1m S of Lake at junct of A3055/A3056*
Located on the main road into town, this charming family-run hotel provides guests with comfortable bedrooms that include many extra facilities. There is a conservatory overlooking the garden for non-smokers, along with a guests' lounge and bar. Dinner is available by prior arrangement.
FACILITIES: 9 en suite (2 fmly) (1 GF) No smoking in 2 bedrooms No smoking in dining room No smoking in 1 lounge TVB tea/coffee Licensed Cen ht TVL No coaches Dinner Last d 6.30pm **PRICES:** d £42-£56✻ **LB**
PARKING: 5 **CARDS:**

♦♦♦ The Triton Hotel

23 Atherley Rd PO37 7AU ☎ 01983 862494 📠 01983 861281
e-mail: jackie@tritonhotel.freeserve.co.uk
Located within easy walking distance of the town centre, Shanklin Old Village and the sea front, this charming friendly hotel provides guests with comfortable well appointed rooms, a guest lounge and bar. Some rooms are available on the ground floor. Tasty home cooked dinners are available by prior arrangement.
FACILITIES: 17 rms (9 en suite) (4 fmly) No smoking in 2 bedrooms No smoking in dining room No smoking in 1 lounge TVB tea/coffee Licensed Cen ht TVL Dinner Last d 1pm **PRICES:** s £18-£22; d £36-£48✻ **LB** **BB**
CARDS:

♦♦♦ White House Hotel

Eastcliff Promenade PO37 6AY ☎ 01983 862776 & 867904
📠 01983 865980
e-mail: white_house@netguides.co.uk
Dir: *A3055 from Sandown, at 1st traffic lights, take B3328, 2nd on left, at top of hill turn right into Park Rd*

With its cliff top position, this friendly hotel commands wonderful views over Shanklin Bay. The comfortable bedrooms are equipped with many extra facilities. The public areas are spacious and include a sun lounge, bar and TV lounge. Home-cooked meals are available in the dining room overlooking the garden.

FACILITIES: 11 en suite (3 fmly) No smoking in dining room TVB tea/coffee Direct dial from bedrooms No dogs (ex guide dogs) Licensed Cen ht TVL No coaches Dinner Last d 5pm **LB PRICES:** d fr £56 **PARKING:** 12 **NOTES:** Closed Nov **CARDS:**

♦♦♦ The Hazelwood

14 Clarence Rd PO37 7BH ☎ 01983 862824 📠 01983 862824
e-mail: barbara.tubbs@thehazelwood.free-online.co.uk
Dir: *A3055 Sandown/Shanklin road from Ryde. On entering Shanklin, Clarence Road is the 3rd on right past Texaco garage.*

FACILITIES: 8 en suite (2 fmly) (2 GF) No smoking in dining room TVB tea/coffee Cen ht TVL No children 5yrs No coaches Dinner Last d 6pm **PRICES:** s £19-£21; d £38-£42✱ **BB PARKING:** 3 **NOTES:** Closed Xmas & New Year **CARDS:**

The Clarendon Hotel Shanklin Ltd

20 North Rd PO37 6DB ☎ 01983 866252

At the time of going to press the Diamond classification for this establishment had not been confirmed. Please check the AA website www.theAA.com for up-to-date information.

FACILITIES: 6 en suite (4 fmly)

Clifton Hotel

Queens Rd PO37 6AN ☎ 01983 863015

At the time of going to press the Diamond classification for this establishment had not been confirmed. Please check the AA website www.theAA.com for up-to-date information.

FACILITIES: 17 rms (15 en suite)

Jasmine Lodge Hotel

156 Sandown Rd PO37 6HF ☎ 01983 863296

At the time of going to press the Diamond classification for this establishment had not been confirmed. Please check the AA website www.theAA.com for up-to-date information.

FACILITIES: 4 en suite (1 fmly)

St Brelades Hotel

15 Hope Rd PO37 6EA ☎ 01983 862967

At the time of going to press the Diamond classification for this establishment had not been confirmed. Please check the AA website www.theAA.com for up-to-date information.

FACILITIES: (4 fmly)

Shoreside Hotel

39 The Esplanade PO37 6BG ☎ 01983 863169

At the time of going to press the Diamond classification for this establishment had not been confirmed. Please check the AA website www.theAA.com for up-to-date information.

FACILITIES: 17 rms (12 en suite) (5 fmly)

> **BB** Great value! This indicates B&B for £19 and under, per person, per night.

TOTLAND BAY — Map 04 SZ38

♦♦♦♦ Sandford Lodge

61 The Avenue PO39 0DN ☎ 01983 753478 📠 01983 753478
e-mail: sandfordlodge@cwcom.net
Dir: *from Yarmouth travel W on A3054 to Totland and turn left onto A3055 signposted Freshwater and house immediately on right*

This delightful Edwardian property is located on the quieter side of the Island about halfway between Totland and Freshwater with the Needles Rocks, Colwell and Totland Bays being close by. Bedrooms are attractively decorated and well equipped whilst an attractive beamed dining room, comfortable lounge, patio and delightful rear garden are also available to guests.

FACILITIES: 5 en suite (2 fmly) No smoking TVB tea/coffee Licensed Cen ht TVL No coaches Dinner Last d 3pm **PRICES:** s £22-£24; d £44-£48✱ **LB PARKING:** 6 **NOTES:** Closed Nov-Feb **CARDS:**

♦♦♦ Frenchman's Cove

Alum Bay Old Rd PO39 0HZ ☎ 01983 752227 📠 01983 755125
e-mail: boatfield@frenchmanscove.co.uk
Dir: *off B3322, signposted to Freshwater Bay. Hotel 500yds on right*

Frenchman's Cove occupies a wonderfully peaceful location close to The Needles. The simply furnished bedrooms are decorated in fresh colours. Some have splendid views over The Solent and there are two suites with two separate bedrooms. There is a bar, lounge and garden available for guests' use. Dinners are available by prior arrangement.

FACILITIES: 10 en suite (6 fmly) (4 GF) No smoking TV12B tea/coffee No dogs (ex guide dogs) Licensed Cen ht TVL No coaches Badminton Table tennis Volleyball Dinner Last d 6pm **PRICES:** s £40-£50; d £50-£70 **LB PARKING:** 15 **CARDS:**

VENTNOR — Map 04 SZ57

♦♦♦♦ The Old Rectory

Ashknowle Ln, Whitwell PO38 2PP ☎ 01983 731242
📠 01983 731288
e-mail: rectory@ukonline.co.uk
Dir: *next to church at S end of Whitwell, on corner of Whitwell High Street and Ashknowle Ln*

Located in the centre of the village of Whitwell, this fine stone Victorian country house set in its own grounds, was built nearly 150 years ago as a Rectory to the neighbouring church. Now fully restored and refurbished this delightful property provides guests with spacious bedrooms, which are equipped with numerous extra facilities.

FACILITIES: 2 en suite No smoking TVB tea/coffee Direct dial from bedrooms No dogs (ex guide dogs) Cen ht TVL No children 14yrs No coaches **PRICES:** s £40-£45; d £50-£60✱ **LB PARKING:** 12 **CARDS:**

England

VENTNOR continued

♦♦♦♦ Lake Hotel

Shore Rd, Bonchurch PO38 1RF ☎ 01983 852613
e-mail: enquiries@lakehotel.co.uk
Dir: *opposite Bonchurch pond in village*
A warm friendly welcome is assured at this family run hotel set in two acres of very attractive and well-tended gardens close to the sea. Bedrooms are comfortably appointed and equipped with modern facilities. The elegant public rooms offer a high standard of comfort. A choice of menus is offered at dinner and breakfast.
FACILITIES: 11 en suite 9 annexe en suite (7 fmly) (4 GF) No smoking in 14 bedrooms No smoking in dining room No smoking in 1 lounge TVB tea/coffee Licensed Cen ht TVL No children 3yrs No coaches Dinner Last d 6.30pm **PRICES:** s £26-£30; d £52-£60* **LB PARKING:** 20
NOTES: Closed Nov-Feb

♦♦♦ Cornerways

39 Madeira Rd PO38 1QS ☎ 01983 852323
e-mail: cornerwaysventnor@btopenworld.com
Dir: *turn off Trinity Rd (main south coast road) near Trinity Church into Madeira Rd, house on left.*
Quietly located between Bonchurch and the town centre, yet only a short stroll from the beach, shops and numerous places of interest, this charming family run guest house provides comfortable well-equipped rooms. There is also a lounge and a cosy bar where guests can relax. Full English breakfasts are served at individual tables.
FACILITIES: 6 en suite (3 fmly) No smoking in bedrooms No smoking in dining room No smoking in lounges TVB tea/coffee No dogs Licensed TVL No coaches **PRICES:** s £20-£52; d £40-£52* **LB PARKING:** 4
NOTES: Closed Nov-Feb **CARDS:**

♦♦♦ Picardie Hotel

Esplanade PO38 1JX ☎ 01983 852647 🖷 01983 852647
Superbly located overlooking the beach, this early Victorian villa is being carefully improved by Marcia Forsyth-Grant to provide homely bedrooms. Guests can enjoy tasty English breakfasts, and dinners by arrangement in the pleasant dining room. There is a comfortable sitting room also available.
FACILITIES: 10 en suite (2 fmly) No smoking TVB tea/coffee No dogs (ex guide dogs) Licensed Lift Cen ht TVL Dinner Last d 7pm **PRICES:** s £22.50-£30; d £50-£70* **LB CONF:** Class 15 Board 15 Del from £12 *

♦♦♦ St Andrews Hotel

Belgrave Rd PO38 1JH ☎ 01983 852680 🖷 01983 852612
e-mail: navayoung@aol.com
Dir: *from town centre left from Pier St to Church St signposted Niton/Blackgang, past St Catherine's church, hotel on left in Belgrave Rd*
A central location means this hotel is well placed for exploring Ventnor. The hillside location ensures magnificent sea views from some rooms. Bedrooms vary in size; all are en suite with bright fabrics and thoughtful facilities. A smart new conservatory creates an attractive seating area for guests. Car parking is also available.
FACILITIES: 10 en suite (3 fmly) No smoking TVB tea/coffee No dogs Licensed Cen ht TVL Dinner Last d 4.30pm **PRICES:** s £31-£37; d £42-£51* **LB PARKING:** 8 **NOTES:** Closed mid Oct-mid Nov rs beginning Oct & mid Nov-Mar **CARDS:**

♦♦♦ Little Span Farm

Rew Ln, Wroxall PO38 3AU ☎ 01983 852419 🖷 01983 852419
e-mail: info@spanfarm.co.uk
Dir: *from A3020 (Shanklin road) turn onto B3327 to Wroxall. By post office turn into West Street out of village up hill around sharp bend. Ignore next right turning, farm on right 300yds from bend).*
FACILITIES: 3 en suite 1 annexe en suite (3 fmly) No smoking in bedrooms No smoking in dining room No smoking in lounges STV TVB tea/coffee Cen ht TVL No coaches **PRICES:** d £36-£50* **LB BB PARKING:** 4

♦♦ Llynfi Hotel

23 Spring Hill PO38 1PF ☎ 01983 852202 🖷 01983 852202
Dir: *A3055 from Shanklin, right before sharp S-bend into St Boniface Rd. Next left into Spring Hill. Hotel 200yds on right*

A warm welcome is offered to guests at this family run hotel located just a short way up the hill from the High Street. Bedrooms are bright and comfortably appointed. Extensive public areas include a sunny conservatory with adjoining terrace, cosy bar and dining room. Dinner is available by prior arrangement.
FACILITIES: 9 en suite (5 fmly) No smoking in 2 bedrooms No smoking in dining room TVB tea/coffee No dogs (ex guide dogs) Licensed Dinner Last d 6pm **PRICES:** s £20-£25; d £40-£50* **PARKING:** 7
CARDS:

Troubadour Hotel

24 High St PO38 1RZ ☎ 01983 856537
At the time of going to press the Diamond classification for this establishment had not been confirmed. Please check the AA website www.theAA.com for up-to-date information.
FACILITIES: 5 en suite

WOOTTON Map 04 SZ59

♦♦ Island Charters

"Sea Urchin", 26 Barge Ln PO33 4LB ☎ 01983 882315
🖷 01983 882315
Accommodation is provided in two adjacent converted static barges. Cabins vary in size, with some having limited facilities. There is a saloon area with a TV and a large well-equipped galley with sun deck where guests can enjoy refreshments. Breakfast is served in the galley on board one of the boats.
FACILITIES: 5 rms (1 fmly) No smoking TV2B No dogs Cen ht No children 10yrs No coaches lake fishing, canoeing **PRICES:** s £18; d £36* **LB BB PARKING:** 10 **NOTES:** Closed Nov

YARMOUTH Map 04 SZ38

♦♦♦ Medlars

Halletts Shute PO41 0RH ☎ 01983 761541 🖷 01983 761541
Dir: *from Yarmouth Ferry turn right over bridge and bear left up Halletts Shute. At 'Savoy Holiday Village' sign turn left into drive with stone pillars. Medlars second house on right*
Located just to the south-west of Yarmouth and well situated for the Lymington to Yarmouth ferry, from which guests can be collected if required. This delightful converted barn provides guests with comfortable accommodation which is full of character. Bedrooms are well furnished and equipped; one has a four-poster bed with adjoining private bathroom. Guests share a table for a full cooked breakfast.
FACILITIES: 2 rms (1 en suite) No smoking TVB tea/coffee Cen ht No children 6yrs **PRICES:** d £50* **PARKING:** 2

England

WILTSHIRE

AMESBURY Map 04 SU14

♦♦♦♦ *Mandalay*

15 Stonehenge Rd SP4 7BA ☎ 01980 623733 📠 01980 626642
Dir: *A303/A345 signposted Amesbury. Through traffic lights, right at mini rdbt, left at Lloyds Bank, past church & over river, bear right*
Quietly located on the outskirts of town, yet within easy reach of Stonehenge and the cathedral, this delightful property provides guest with tasteful, individually decorated rooms that are equipped with many thoughtful extras. Freshly cooked breakfasts can be enjoyed in the airy breakfast room, overlooking the landscaped gardens.
FACILITIES: 5 en suite (1 fmly) No smoking TVB tea/coffee No dogs Cen ht TVL No coaches **PARKING:** 5 **CARDS:**

♦♦♦♦ Park House Motel

SP4 0EG ☎ 01980 629256 📠 01980 629256
Dir: *at junction of A303/A338*
A warm welcome awaits at this family-run establishment. Bedrooms are comfortable with modern facilities, and come in a variety of sizes - some in the main house, and the remainder around the courtyard. There is a large dining room where dinner is served during the week, and a cosy bar in which to relax.

FACILITIES: 33 rms (23 en suite) (5 fmly) No smoking in 5 bedrooms No smoking in dining room No smoking in lounges STV TVB tea/coffee Licensed Cen ht TVL Dinner Last d 8.30pm **PRICES:** s £32-£46; d £52-£58✳ **PARKING:** 40 **CARDS:**

♦♦♦ Catkin Lodge

93 Countess Rd SP4 7AT ☎ 01980 624810 & 622139
📠 01980 622139
e-mail: info@catkinlodge.fsnet.co.uk
Dir: *from rdbt on A303 at Amesbury, take A345 Marlborough rd, about 400mtrs on left.*

continued

Popular with business people and close to Stonehenge, Catkin Lodge is easy to find and offers off-road parking. The three bedrooms offer good levels of comfort and can accommodate children if required. One room has an en suite while the other two are located on the ground floor.
FACILITIES: 3 rms (1 en suite) (1 fmly) No smoking TVB tea/coffee No dogs (ex guide dogs) Cen ht No children 5yrs No coaches **PRICES:** s £25-£40; d £44-£64✳ **PARKING:** 7

BOX Map 03 ST86

Premier Collection

♦♦♦♦♦ Spinney Cross

Lower Kingsdown Rd, Kingsdown SN13 8BA
☎ 01225 742019 01225 461518
e-mail: dotcom@spinneycross.co.uk
Dir: *from Bath A4 towards Chippenham, at Bathford take A353 to Bradford on Avon. Under railway bridge, left at Crown PH uphill to Kingsdown, left at Swan PH bear right at bottom of hill. Spinney Cross 500yds on left*
Set in a delightful location in the quiet village of Kingsdown, views from this guest house are absolutely lovely. Guests staying here will feel pampered and relaxed within moments of arrival. A varied range of options is available at breakfast with scrambled eggs and smoked salmon proving a popular choice.
FACILITIES: 3 rms (2 en suite) (1 fmly) (3 GF) No smoking in bedrooms No smoking in dining room No smoking in lounges TVB tea/coffee No dogs Cen ht No coaches **PRICES:** s £40-£70; d £70-£80✳ **LB PARKING:** 6 **CARDS:**

Premier Collection

♦♦♦♦♦ White Smocks

Ashley SN13 8AJ ☎ 01225 742154 📠 01225 742212
e-mail: whitesmocksashley@hotmail.com
Dir: *on A4 1m W of Box take road opposite Northy Arms, after 200yds at T junct White Smocks is to right of thatched cottage*

Quietly located property in the pleasant village of Ashley, and just a short drive from Bath and many local attractions. White Smocks offers a relaxing escape where guests are encouraged to enjoy the pleasant garden in the summer, real fires in the winter and the jacuzzi all year round. The two bedrooms and bathrooms are immaculately presented and very comfortably furnished. Guests are also welcome to use the lounge.
FACILITIES: 2 en suite (1 fmly) No smoking TVB tea/coffee No dogs (ex guide dogs) Cen ht TVL No coaches Jacuzzi **PRICES:** s £40-£45; d £65-£70✳ **LB PARKING:** 3 **CARDS:**

England

BOX continued

♦♦♦♦ Lorne House

London Rd SN13 8NA ☎ 01225 742597
e-mail: lornehousebandb@aol.com
Dir: *on A4. 100mtrs after zebra crossing on left travelling from Bath*

This attractive house was once the home of Reverend Awdry, author of the 'Thomas the Tank Engine' stories. The rooms are comfortable and well equipped, and decorated with bright and pleasant colours and fabrics. The proprietors are attentive to their guests and offer a good choice of freshly prepared dishes at breakfast.
FACILITIES: 4 en suite (1 fmly) No smoking in bedrooms TVB tea/coffee No dogs (ex guide dogs) Cen ht TVL No coaches Jacuzzi **PRICES:** s £30-£35; d £45-£50✳ **PARKING:** 6 **CARDS:**

♦♦♦♦ Owl House

Lower Kingsdown Rd, Kingsdown SN13 8BB ☎ 01225 743883
01225 744450
e-mail: venus@zetnet.co.uk
Dir: *M4 junct18/A46, approx 8m to A4, proceed to rdbt, turn right on A363 to Bradford-On-Avon, under bridge, left into Bathford, left after Swan pub*
Enjoying a peaceful country location with excellent views of the surrounding countryside, Owl House is a convenient base for touring the area or for visiting the many attractions of Bath. The bedrooms have been individually decorated and equipped with some thoughtful extras. In summer months breakfast is taken in the conservatory which overlooks the attractive garden.
FACILITIES: 3 en suite (1 fmly) No smoking TVB tea/coffee No dogs (ex guide dogs) Cen ht TVL No children 8yrs No coaches **PRICES:** s £38; d £68✳ **PARKING:** 4 **CARDS:**

♦♦♦ Hermitage

Bath Rd SN13 8DT ☎ 01225 744187 01225 743447
e-mail: hermitage@telecall.co.uk
Dir: *5m from Bath on A4 towards Chippenham, Hermitage is 1st drive on left after 30mph signs*

Pleasantly located in the countryside, not too far from the centre of Bath, this 16th-century house is set in delightful gardens with a heated swimming pool. Bedrooms are spacious and comfortably furnished with two rooms available in a small adjacent cottage. Breakfast is taken in the dining hall.
FACILITIES: 3 en suite 2 annexe en suite (2 fmly) No smoking in 3 bedrooms No smoking in dining room No smoking in lounges TVB tea/coffee No dogs (ex guide dogs) Cen ht No coaches Outdoor swimming pool (heated) **PRICES:** s £35-£40; d £50-£55✳ **PARKING:** 6
NOTES: Closed 22 Dec-6 Jan

BRADFORD-ON-AVON Map 03 ST86

Premier Collection

♦♦♦♦♦ Bradford Old Windmill

4 Masons Ln BA15 1QN ☎ 01225 866842
01225 866648
e-mail: aa@distinctlydifferent.co.uk
Dir: *enter Bradford on A363, at mini-rdbt at Castle pub turn to town centre, after 50yds turn left into private drive immediately beside 1st roadside house. No sign or number*

A unique property, having been sympathetically restored retaining many original features. Bedrooms are individually decorated and include a number of interesting options such as a round room, a waterbed or a suite with minstrels' gallery. An extensive breakfast menu offers a range of alternatives from devilled mushrooms or passion fruit pancakes to the more traditional. A comfortable lounge is also available for guests to enjoy.
FACILITIES: 3 en suite No smoking TVB tea/coffee No dogs Cen ht No children 6yrs No coaches Dinner Last d previous day **PRICES:** s £59-£99; d £69-£109✳ **PARKING:** 3 **NOTES:** Closed Jan-Feb
CARDS:

Premier Collection

♦♦♦♦♦ Widbrook Grange

Trowbridge Rd, Widbrook BA15 1UH ☎ 01225 864750 & 863173 01225 862890
e-mail: stay@widbrookgrange.com
Dir: *1m from Bradford-on- Avon on the A363 Trowbridge road*
A beautiful former farmhouse, built as a model farm in the 18th century, now tastefully renovated and equipped with modern comforts. Bedrooms, some in the main house and the majority in adjacent courtyard buildings, offer all the character and charm of old converted buildings. Guests can enjoy an aperitif in one of two elegant drawing rooms prior to dinner. Other attractions include a large indoor heated swimming pool and a spacious conference suite.

continued

Widbrook Grange

FACILITIES: 5 rms (4 en suite) 15 annexe en suite (4 fmly) (13 GF) No smoking in 6 bedrooms No smoking in dining room No smoking in 1 lounge TVB tea/coffee Direct dial from bedrooms No dogs (ex guide dogs) Licensed Cen ht No coaches Indoor swimming pool (heated) Tennis (hard) Gymnasium Croquet lawn Dinner Last d 8pm **PRICES:** s fr £65; d fr £110✻ **CONF:** Thtr 50 Class 20 Board 24 Del from £141 ✻ **PARKING:** 50 **NOTES:** Closed 24-31 Dec rs Fri & Sun **CARDS:**

♦♦♦♦ *Home Farm*

Farleigh Rd, Wingfield BA14 9LG ☎ 01225 764492
📠 01225 764492

Dir: *exit A36 onto A366 to Fairleigh Hungerford, pass castle into Wingfield, gate to premises after three cottages*

The rooms at this delightful renovated farmhouse are most comfortable and provided with many interesting and useful features. The friendly proprietors are most hospitable and many guests return on a regular basis. Guests are welcome to use the immaculate gardens, which have wonderful views over the neighbouring farmland.

FACILITIES: 3 en suite (1 fmly) No smoking STV TVB tea/coffee No dogs (ex guide dogs) Cen ht TVL No coaches **PARKING:** 30 **CARDS:**

♦♦♦♦ Midway Cottage

Farleigh Wick BA15 2PU ☎ 01225 863932 📠 01225 866836
e-mail: midway_cottage@hotmail.com

Dir: *on A363 midway between Bathford & Bradford-on-Avon next to Fox & Hounds pub*

This charmingly restored Victorian cottage is located midway between Bradford-on-Avon and Bath. Bedrooms are very comfortable rooms and a variety of thoughtful extras are provided. Hospitality and service are particularly memorable aspects of a stay here, Mrs Lindsay is a most friendly and welcoming hostess, and a Top Twenty Finalist in the AA Landlady of the Year Award 2002-2003. A pleasant garden is available for guests. Breakfast is taken in the lounge/dining room.

continued

FACILITIES: 3 en suite No smoking TVB tea/coffee Direct dial from bedrooms Cen ht No coaches **PRICES:** s £25-£30; d £45-£50✻ **LB PARKING:** 3

♦♦♦♦ Serendipity

19f Bradford Rd, Winsley BA15 2HW ☎ 01225 722380
📠 01225 723415
e-mail: vanda.shepherd@tesco.net

Dir: *turn off A36 Bath/Warminster road onto B3108 turn right after 1.5m into Winsley. Establishment on right on main road*

Located in a quiet residential area, convenient for touring the Somerset/Wiltshire borders as well as Bath. The rooms are brightly decorated, comfortably furnished and equipped with a range of extra facilities. Breakfast is taken in the conservatory, which overlooks the well-tended garden. The resident proprietors are welcoming and attentive, making their guests feel at home.

FACILITIES: 3 en suite (1 fmly) No smoking TVB tea/coffee No dogs (ex guide dogs) Cen ht No coaches Croquet lawn **PRICES:** s £30-£45; d £38-£49 **LB BB PARKING:** 5 **CARDS:**

BROAD CHALKE — Map 04 SU02

Premier Collection

♦♦♦♦♦ Ebblesway Courtyard

High Rd SP5 5EF ☎ 01722 780182 📠 01722 780482
e-mail: enquiries@ebblesway courtyard.co.uk

Feb-Nov

Dir: *from Salisbury A354 signed Blandford. In 3m take 1st turn right as you come into the village of Coombe Bissett, (signed Stratford Tony, Bishopstone & Broad Chalke), continue for 3m and establishment on right behind Stoke Manor.*

Well located for visiting Salisbury, the racecourse and Stonehenge, this delightful barn, with its wealth of beams and views across neighbouring farmland, has recently been converted to provide guests with very comfortable, elegant accommodation with numerous extra facilities. Delicious breakfasts are served around one large table in the spacious dining room.

FACILITIES: 4 en suite No smoking TVB tea/coffee No dogs (ex guide dogs) Cen ht No children 10yrs No coaches Hire of bicycles
PRICES: s £31.50-£35; d £54-£65✻ **LB PARKING:** 6
CARDS:

CALNE — Map 03 ST97

Premier Collection

♦♦♦♦♦ *Chilvester Hill House*

SN11 0LP ☎ 01249 813981 & 815785 📠 01249 814217
e-mail: gill.dilley@talk21.com

Dir: *A4 from Calne towards Chippenham, after 0.5m take right turn marked Bremhill, drive of house immediately on right*

This elegant Victorian house, built of Bath stone, stands in well kept gardens and grounds. Dr and Mrs Dilley ensure a warm and genuinely friendly welcome. Bedrooms are spacious, comfortable and well equipped, with many thoughtful extras. A set dinner is available (by arrangement), served at one large table in the dining room. Mrs Dilley checks with guests for likes and dislikes. Dishes are freshly prepared from the best local produce and many of the fruit and vegetables used are home-grown.

FACILITIES: 3 en suite No smoking in dining room No smoking in 1 lounge TVB tea/coffee No dogs (ex guide dogs) Licensed Cen ht TVL No children 12yrs No coaches Stables and golf course avaliable locally Dinner Last d 11am **PARKING:** 8 **CARDS:**

England

CALNE continued

♦♦♦♦ *Maundrell House*
Horsebrook, The Green SN11 8DL ☎ 01249 821267
01249 821267
e-mail: liz@maundrell.bigwig.net
Dir: *from A4 Calne to Marlborough road, turn left at White Hart Inn into The Green, straight ahead to Horsebrook. 1st house on left*
Built in the 17th century, this attractive Grade II listed house is situated in a quiet corner of Calne. All rooms are decorated in keeping with the style of the building and furnishing is elegant. Guests can relax in the lovely, spacious lounge with its open fire. An excellent breakfast is served around one large table in the dining room.
FACILITIES: 2 en suite No smoking TVB tea/coffee No dogs (ex guide dogs) Cen ht TVL No children 15yrs No coaches **NOTES:** Closed 23 Dec-2 Jan

♦♦♦♦ The White Horse
Compton Bassett SN11 8RG ☎ 01249 813118 01249 811595
e-mail: white.horse.inn@btclick.com
Dir: *M4 junct 16 2nd left to Wooton Bassett, through High St over bridge left to Bushton then follow signs Compton Bassett. M4 junct 17 take A350 towards Chippenham through town and leave by A4, through Calne and Quemerford, left signed Cherhill continue to Compton Bassett*
Located in the heart of the village of Compton Bassett, this fine old inn with its beams and open fires provides guests with a good base for exploring the local countryside and nearby towns of Swindon, Chippenham and Marlborough. Bedrooms are located in a purpose built annexe, and some rooms have balconies or patios.
FACILITIES: 7 annexe en suite (2 fmly) No smoking in 3 bedrooms No smoking in dining room TVB tea/coffee Cen ht Dinner Last d 9.30pm **PRICES:** s fr £45; d fr £65✱ **MEALS:** Lunch £12.50-£25alc Dinner £12.50-£25alc✱ **PARKING:** 75 **NOTES:** Closed 25 Dec **CARDS:**

CASTLE COMBE — Map 03 ST87

♦♦♦♦ Fairfield Farm
Upper Wraxall SN14 7AG ☎ 01225 891750 01225 891050
e-mail: mcdonoug@globalnet.co.uk
Dir: *M4 junct 18. Follow A46 to Bath. After approx 4m left at 1st rdbt onto A420 towards Chippenham. Upper Wraxall signed after 4m, farm on left*
FACILITIES: 2 en suite (1 fmly) No smoking TVB tea/coffee No dogs Cen ht TVL **PRICES:** s £25-£30; d £45✱ **PARKING:** 6 **NOTES:** Closed 20 Dec - 7 Jan

CHICKLADE — Map 03 ST93

♦♦♦♦ Old Rectory
SP3 5SU ☎ 01747 820226 01747 820783
e-mail: vbronson@old-rectory.co.uk
Dir: *Situated on the A303 immediately behind the lay-by*
This delightful old Rectory dates from the 17th century and is set in mature gardens. Bedrooms are spacious and comfortable. Downstairs the lounge/dining room can be used by guests at all times whilst tea or coffee is available on request at any time. Delicious dinners can be provided by prior arrangement.
FACILITIES: 3 rms (1 fmly) No smoking No dogs (ex guide dogs) Cen ht TVL No coaches Dinner Last d 9.45pm **PRICES:** s fr £30; d fr £55✱ LB **PARKING:** 6 **NOTES:** Closed 18 Dec-Jan

CHIPPENHAM — Map 03 ST97

See also Calne & Corsham

♦♦♦♦ Home Farm *(ST860720)*
Home Farm, Harts Ln, Biddestone SN14 7DQ ☎ 01249 714475
01249 701488 Mr & Mrs I Smith
e-mail: audrey.smith@homefarmbandb.co.uk
Dir: *from A4 between Bath & Chippenham, at Corsham turn off to Biddestone at lights. In village take 1st right off village green, farm signposted*
The Smith family welcome guests to their home, a traditionally run farm of 200 acres, near the pretty village of Biddestone. Bedrooms are filled with thoughtful extras and are brightly decorated. There is a comfortable lounge, and breakfast, using the freshest ingredients, is served at one large table in dining room.
FACILITIES: 4 en suite (2 fmly) (1 GF) No smoking TVB tea/coffee No dogs (ex guide dogs) Cen ht TVL 200 acres arable/Beef **PRICES:** s £27; d £45-£50✱ **PARKING:** 4 **NOTES:** Closed Xmas & New Year **CARDS:**

♦♦♦♦ Pickwick Lodge Farm *(ST857708)*
Guyers Ln SN13 0PS ☎ 01249 712207 01249 701904
Mrs G Stafford
e-mail: b&b@pickwickfarm.freeserve.co.uk
(For full entry see Corsham)

♦♦♦ Home From Home
Grathie Cottage, 72 Marshfield Rd SN15 1JR ☎ 01249 650306
Dir: *Situated on A420. From town centre, under railway bridge, on junct of 2nd left turning*
Convenient for the M4 and within walking distance of the town centre and train station, Home From Home provides comfortable, well-kept accommodation. A warm welcome and well cooked breakfast are assured, and guests dine around one table in the breakfast room. Parking is available to the rear of the house.
FACILITIES: 4 rms (2 en suite) (1 GF) No smoking in dining room No smoking in lounges TVB tea/coffee No dogs (ex guide dogs) Cen ht No coaches **PRICES:** s £20-£22; d £40-£46✱

CORSHAM — Map 03 ST87

♦♦♦♦ Pickwick Lodge Farm *(ST857708)*
Guyers Ln SN13 0PS ☎ 01249 712207 01249 701904
Mrs G Stafford
e-mail: b&b@pickwickfarm.freeserve.co.uk
Dir: *turn off A4, Bath side of Corsham, into Guyers Lane. Follow lane to end, farmhouse on right at end*

This Grade II listed, 17th-century farmhouse is peacefully located on a 300-acre beef and arable farm, within easy reach of Bath. The spacious bedrooms are well-equipped with modern facilities and many thoughtful extras. A hearty breakfast using the best local produce is served at one large table in the dining room.

continued

FACILITIES: 3 en suite (1 fmly) No smoking TVB tea/coffee No dogs (ex guide dogs) Cen ht TVL 300 acres arable beef **PRICES:** s £25-£30; d £45-£50✻ **LB PARKING:** 6 **NOTES:** Closed Xmas & New Year

♦♦♦♦ Church Farm

Hartham SN13 0PU ☎ 01249 715180 01249 715572
e-mail: kmjbandb@aol.com
Dir: *M4 junct 17, A350 bypass Chippenham, A4 towards Bath for 3m until Corsham. At Cross Keys x-rds stay on A4 take next right turn into Hartham Lane 500yds on left before church*
FACILITIES: 2 en suite 2 annexe en suite (3 fmly) (2 GF) No smoking TVB tea/coffee Cen ht No children 6mths No coaches **PRICES:** s £28-£40; d £45-£55 **LB PARKING:** 10 **NOTES:** Closed Xmas & New Year

CRICKLADE Map 04 SU09

♦♦♦ *Upper Chelworth Farm*

Upper Chelworth SN6 6HD ☎ 01793 750440
Dir: *from M4 junct 15 take A419 to Cricklade, left at T-junct next right & into B4040 for 1.5 m to Ashton Keynes/Chelworth crossroads turn left*

Near to the M4 and Swindon, Upper Chelworth Farm provides neat, comfortable bedrooms of varying sizes with smart bathrooms. There is a spacious lounge with wood-burning stove, games room with pool table and a lovely garden. Breakfast is served in the farmhouse dining room.

FACILITIES: 7 rms (6 en suite) (1 fmly) No smoking in 2 bedrooms No smoking in dining room STV TV6B tea/coffee No dogs (ex guide dogs) Licensed Cen ht TVL No coaches Pool Table **PARKING:** 10
NOTES: Closed mid Dec-mid Jan **CARDS:**

DEVIZES Map 03 SU06

Premier Collection

♦♦♦♦♦ Blounts Court Farm *(SU996583)*

Coxhill Ln, Potterne SN10 5PH ☎ 01380 727180
Mr & Mrs C Cary
e-mail: blountscourtfarm@tinyworld.co.uk
Dir: *A360 to Potterne turn into Coxhill Lane opposite George & Dragon, at fork turn left and follow drive to farmhouse*

A working arable farm in a tranquil setting, overlooking the cricket field. The old barn and cider press have been renovated to provide two attractive, comfortable bedrooms on the ground floor, one of which has a four-poster bed. Décor throughout is elegant and stylish, in keeping with the exposed beams and charm of the house. Breakfast, featuring local produce, is served in the farmhouse dining room and hot dishes are cooked to order on the Aga.

FACILITIES: 2 en suite No smoking TVB tea/coffee No dogs (ex guide dogs) Cen ht TVL No children 8yrs 200 acres arable **PRICES:** s £32-£38; d £52-£58✻

♦♦♦♦ Greenfields

Bath Rd SN10 1QG ☎ 01380 729315 & 07763 935993
01380 729315
e-mail: reservations@greenfields-devizes.co.uk
Dir: *Greenfields on left just after entering town limits. Or from town centre take A361 Trowbridge road*

With private access to the Kennet and Avon Canal at the top of the world-famous Caen Hill flight of locks, this attractive Victorian home is popular with walkers and cyclists. The well-decorated bedrooms have high quality furnishings and thoughtful touches throughout. Breakfast is cooked to order and served at separate tables in the dining room.

FACILITIES: 3 en suite (1 fmly) No smoking TVB tea/coffee No dogs (ex guide dogs) Cen ht No coaches **PRICES:** s fr £27; d fr £48✻
PARKING: 4

♦♦♦♦ *Littleton Lodge*

Littleton Panell (A360), West Lavington SN10 4ES
☎ 01380 813131 01380 816969
e-mail: stay@littletonlodge.co.uk
Dir: *from Stonehenge on A360, at crossroads with B3098 at Dauntsey's School continue, establishment 500mtrs on right. From Devizes, 4m S on A360, on left 500 mtrs after railway bridge*

Convenient for Stonehenge and for touring the many attractions of this pleasant area, Littleton Lodge offers spacious and comfortable accommodation. The friendly proprietors provide a relaxing and welcoming home. Breakfast is taken in the stylish dining room and freshly cooked dishes provide a pleasant start to the day.

FACILITIES: 3 en suite No smoking TVB tea/coffee No dogs Cen ht No coaches badminton **PARKING:** 4 **CARDS:**

♦♦♦ Eastcott Manor

Easterton SN10 4PL ☎ 01380 813313
Dir: *on B3098 between Urchfont & Easterton, S of Devizes between A360 Salisbury & A342 Andover*

This 16th-century farmhouse offers comfortable accommodation in a rural setting. Bedrooms vary in size and are suitably furnished and equipped. Breakfast and evening meals are served in the delightful dining room, guests sharing one large table. A pleasant lounge and conservatory are also available to guests.

FACILITIES: 4 en suite No smoking in bedrooms No smoking in dining room No smoking in lounges TVB tea/coffee TVL No coaches Stabling Chair lift Dinner Last d 24hrs in advance **PRICES:** s £25; d £58✻
PARKING: 6 **NOTES:** Closed 23 Dec-1 Jan

Super supper! this symbol shows that evening meals exceeded our Inspector's expectations.

DEVIZES continued

♦♦ Craven House

Station Rd SN10 1BZ ☎ 01380 723514 🖷 01380 723514
e-mail: shawg640@aol.com
Dir: *Town Centre/Market Square. Looking at the Bear Hotel on right is Corn Exchange. on right of Corn Exchange is Station Rd, establishment 50 yds on left*

Conveniently located guest house being literally two minutes' walk to the historic centre of Devizes with its interesting attractions and restaurants. Service here is relaxed and friendly with breakfast times very flexible. Rooms offer a choice of two en suite or two with shared bathroom. Nearby car-parking is also available.

FACILITIES: 4 rms (2 en suite) No smoking in dining room No smoking in lounges TVB tea/coffee No dogs (ex guide dogs) Cen ht No coaches **PRICES:** s £25; d £35-£40✱ **LB BB**

HANNINGTON — Map 04 SU19

♦♦♦♦ The Jolly Tar

Queens Rd SN6 7RP ☎ 01793 762245 🖷 01793 762247
e-mail: thejollytar@btopenworld.com
Dir: *From A419 at Blunsdon follow B4019 towards Highworth, left at Freke Arms, follow road for Hannington for 1m. Jolly Tar located in centre of village.*

Traditional, warm hospitality can be expected at this delightful country inn. Bedrooms and bathrooms have high standards of quality and comfort. In addition to locally brewed beer, guests can enjoy a selection of delicious home cooked food either in the cosy lounge complete with oak beams and log fire or in the Cotswold stone conservatory.

FACILITIES: 4 annexe en suite (1 fmly) (1 GF) No smoking in bedrooms No smoking in dining room TVB tea/coffee No dogs (ex guide dogs) Cen ht No coaches Dinner Last d 9pm **PRICES:** s £50; d £65✱ **MEALS:** Lunch £12-£16alc Dinner £18-£24alc✱ **PARKING:** 40 **CARDS:**

HOLT — Map 03 ST86

♦♦♦ The Coppers Bed & Breakfast

21b Leigh Rd BA14 6PW ☎ 01225 783174
e-mail: coppersb/b@holtwiltsl.freeserve.co.uk
Dir: *from M4 junct 18 A46 to Bath then A363 to Bradford-on-Avon and B3107 Holt/Melksham. On entering village 1st left opposite Toll Gate Inn into Leigh Road, Coppers is 1st left signed*

Quietly located just a few minutes' stroll to the pleasant village of Holt, with its choice of local inns. Run in a relaxed and friendly manner, this guest house offers two neatly furnished bedrooms, one en suite and one with its own private facilities. After breakfast, the dining room may be used as a lounge.

FACILITIES: 2 en suite (1 fmly) (2 GF) No smoking TVB tea/coffee Cen ht ch fac No coaches Dinner Last d breakfast **PRICES:** s £35-£45; d £45-£55✱ **PARKING:** 8

LACOCK — Map 03 ST96

Premier Collection

♦♦♦♦♦ At the Sign of the Angel

6 Church St SN15 2LB ☎ 01249 730230 🖷 01249 730527
e-mail: angel@lacock.co.uk
Dir: *M4 J17, follow Chippenham signs, 3m S of Chippenham on A350 Lacock signed L, follow 'local traffic' sign*

Guests cannot fail to be impressed by the historic character of this 15th-century, former wool merchant's house in the National Trust village of Lacock. Bedrooms vary in size and style from the atmospheric older rooms of the main house to others in a newer adjacent building. Award-winning dinners

continued

At the Sign of the Angel

and breakfasts are served in the beamed dining rooms. Guests are also welcome to use the first-floor lounge and the pleasant rear garden.

FACILITIES: 6 en suite 4 annexe en suite (1 fmly) No smoking in bedrooms TVB tea/coffee Direct dial from bedrooms Licensed Cen ht No coaches Dinner Last d 9pm **PRICES:** s £68-£85; d £99-£137.50✱ **PARKING:** 7 **NOTES:** Closed 23 Dec-30 Dec Civ Wed 30 **CARDS:**

LANDFORD — Map 04 SU21

♦♦♦♦ Springfields

Lyndhurst Rd, Landford SP5 2AS ☎ 01794 390093
Dir: *M27 J1, B3078 to Brook then B3079 through Bramshaw into Landford. On left 0.5m after Landford perimeter sign*

This modern detached house located in a peaceful rural setting, is an ideal base from which to tour the New Forest. Bedrooms are spacious, attractively decorated and comfortably furnished. Breakfast is served in the light and airy dining room overlooking the garden. There is also a well-appointed lounge in which to relax.

FACILITIES: 3 rms (4 GF) No smoking TVB tea/coffee Cen ht TVL No coaches Dinner Last d breakfast **PRICES:** s £25-£30; d £38-£42✱ **BB** **PARKING:** 6 **NOTES:** Closed 10-24 Nov rs Xmas & New Year

LONGLEAT — Map 03 ST84

♦♦♦♦ Sturford Mead *(ST834456)*

Corsley BA12 7QU ☎ 01373 832213 🖷 01373 832213
Mrs L N Corp
e-mail: lynn_sturford.bed@virgin.net
Dir: *on A362 half way between Warminster & Frome*

Situated in an area of outstanding natural beauty, Sturford Mead Farm is well placed for visitors to Longleat, Bath, Glastonbury and Salisbury. The proprietors provide a friendly and welcoming atmosphere and guests are made to feel comfortable in the attractive rooms. Breakfast, served in the dining room, features home-made preserves and freshly cooked Wiltshire bacon.

continued

FACILITIES: 3 en suite No smoking TVB tea/coffee No dogs (ex guide dogs) Cen ht TVL 5 acres non-working **PARKING:** 10

LUDWELL — Map 03 ST92

♦♦♦♦ Grove Arms

SP7 9ND ☎ 01747 828328 01747 828960
e-mail: info@dorsetaccomodation.com
Dir: *On main A30 Shaftesbury - Salisbury Road*

This well-presented landmark on the A30 is a popular destination for guests in search of comfortable accommodation, home cooked food and a relaxed and friendly atmosphere. All bedrooms have desks, hairdryers and other extra facilities, including excellent showers. Lunch and dinner feature imaginative dishes and some 'old favourites'.
FACILITIES: 6 en suite No smoking in bedrooms No smoking in area of dining room TVB tea/coffee No dogs Cen ht TVL No children 14yrs No coaches Dinner Last d 9pm **PARKING:** 70 **CARDS:**

MALMESBURY — Map 03 ST98

Premier Collection

♦♦♦♦♦ Horse & Groom

The Street, Charlton SN16 9DL ☎ 01666 823904
01666 823390
Dir: *exit M4 junct 17, towards Malmesbury, at 2nd rdbt take B4040. Premises through village on left*

Located in a pretty village, this 16th-century inn has been sympathetically renovated to provide spacious comfortable bars and a restaurant. Bedrooms are spacious and feature thoughtful extras such as fresh fruit, mineral water and bathrobes. In the summer, sit in the garden for drinks or meals, in the winter the bars and lounges have open fires.
FACILITIES: 3 en suite TVB tea/coffee Direct dial from bedrooms No dogs (ex guide dogs) Cen ht Dinner Last d 10pm **PRICES:** s fr £60; d fr £80✻ **MEALS:** Lunch £4.95-£15alc Dinner £4.95-£15alc✻
PARKING: 25 **CARDS:**

♦♦♦♦ Lovett Farm *(ST974850)*

Little Somerford SN15 5BP ☎ 01666 823268 01666 823268
Mrs S Barnes
e-mail: lovettfarm@btinternet.com
Dir: *3m from Malmesbury on B4042 (Wootton Bassett/Swindon road) on left opposite 2nd signpost to the Somerfords*
Guests are assured of a warm welcome at this modern, working farmhouse with lovely views over Dauntsey Vale. Bedrooms are comfortable and well-equipped with many extras. A traditional home cooked breakfast is served at one large table in the sunny guest lounge. Stabling for horses can be arranged.
FACILITIES: 2 en suite No smoking TVB tea/coffee No dogs Cen ht No children 2yrs 70 acres beef **PRICES:** s £27-£32; d £47-£52✻
PARKING: 5 **CARDS:**

♦♦♦♦ *Manby's Farm (ST981931)*

Oaksey SN16 9SA ☎ 01666 577399 01666 577241
Mrs A Shewry-Fitzgerald
e-mail: manbys@oaksey.junglelink.co.uk
Dir: *M4 junct 15 take A419 to Cirencester approx 13m, left onto B4696 signed Cotswold Water Park, in 6m at Oaksey left at mini-rdbt, 1st entrance on left*
Mamby's Farm is the ideal 'rural retreat', set in the glorious countryside of the Wiltshire/Gloucestershire borders and conveniently located for the Cotswold Water Park. Accommodation is well-equipped and comfortable, and all rooms enjoy the splendid views. A lounge with inglenook open fire is available, along with the indoor pool and snooker room.
FACILITIES: 3 en suite (1 fmly) No smoking TVB tea/coffee No dogs Cen ht TVL Indoor swimming pool (heated) Snooker Mini Golf & Boule Area. 46 acres grassland Dinner Last d 9am **PARKING:** 6
CARDS:

MARLBOROUGH — Map 04 SU16

♦♦♦♦ The Vines

High St SN8 1HJ ☎ 01672 515333 01672 515338
e-mail: IVY.HOUSE@btconnect.com
Dir: *on High Street, approx 150yds from Marlborough College*
Situated on the High Street in the lovely market town of Marlborough, this hotel provides a high standard of accommodation, with pleasantly decorated bedrooms and bathrooms including many modern facilities. Dinner can be taken across the road in the sister hotel's restaurant, where breakfast is also served.
FACILITIES: 7 en suite (1 fmly) No smoking in 3 bedrooms No smoking in dining room No smoking in lounges TVB tea/coffee No dogs (ex guide dogs) Licensed Cen ht Dinner Last d 9.15pm **PRICES:** s £50; d £60-£65✻
PARKING: 36 **CARDS:**

♦♦♦ Merlin Hotel

36-39 High St SN8 1LW ☎ 01672 512151 01672 515310
e-mail: info@merlinhotel.co.uk
Dir: *on A4 in High St, nearly opposite Boots the Chemist*
Standing at one end of the High Street, the Merlin Hotel is a Grade II listed building with plenty of character. Bedrooms vary in size, each being individually decorated and well equipped. Although there are no public areas, guests can enjoy the added comfort of breakfast offered in bedrooms.
FACILITIES: 15 rms (13 en suite) (1 fmly) TVB tea/coffee Cen ht No coaches **PRICES:** s £40-£45; d £60-£70; (room only) ✻
CARDS:

If an establishment name appears in *italics*, details have not been confirmed for 2003.

England

MERE Map 03 ST83

♦♦♦♦ Chetcombe House

Chetcombe Rd BA12 6AZ ☎ 01747 860219 📠 860111
e-mail: mary.butchers@lineone.net
Dir: *located off A303 when heading westbound*

Chetcombe House enjoys wonderful views across its acre of well-tended gardens towards Gillingham and the Blackmore Vale. The house, built in 1937, provides elegance and charm, is pleasantly spacious and very comfortable. The bedrooms are well equipped and are provided with many extra facilities. Breakfast is taken in the attractive dining room and provides a good start to the day.
FACILITIES: 5 en suite (1 fmly) No smoking TVB tea/coffee Direct dial from bedrooms No dogs (ex guide dogs) Cen ht **PRICES:** s £30; d £55✻
PARKING: 10

♦♦♦ Talbot Hotel

The Square BA12 6DR ☎ 01747 860427 📠 01747 861978
Dir: *off A303 signed Mere. Hotel in centre facing the square & clock tower*
Located in the centre of the town square, friendly service is assured at this attractive 16th century inn where a choice of dining is available in either the restaurant or character bar with inglenook fireplace. Bedrooms are comfortable and decorated in keeping with the style of this historic inn.
FACILITIES: 7 en suite (4 fmly) No smoking in bedrooms No smoking in dining room No smoking in 1 lounge TVB tea/coffee No dogs Cen ht Pool Table Dinner Last d 9pm **PRICES:** s fr £37.50; d £50-£65✻ **LB**
MEALS: Lunch £15-£20alc Dinner £15-£22alc✻ **PARKING:** 24
CARDS:

MIDDLE WINTERSLOW Map 04 SU23

Premier Collection

♦♦♦♦♦ Beadles

Middleton SP5 1QS ☎ 01980 862922 📠 01980 863565
e-mail: winterbead@aol.com
Dir: *leave A30 at Pheasant Hotel to Middle Winterslow. Enter village, turn 1st right to West Winterslow and right at end, 1st right after "Trevano" down unmade drive*
Guests are assured of a warm and friendly welcome to this delightful home with rural views in a village location just eight miles from Salisbury. Bedrooms have high levels of comfort and all feature antique furniture and many thoughtful extras. Delicious dinners are available by prior arrangement and are served in the attractive dining room. Guests have access to a very comfortable lounge and conservatory and may use the garden in summer.
FACILITIES: 3 en suite No smoking TVB tea/coffee Direct dial from bedrooms No dogs (ex guide dogs) Cen ht No children 12yrs No coaches Dinner Last d 24 hrs **PRICES:** d £55-£65✻ **PARKING:** 5
CARDS:

NETTLETON Map 03 ST87

♦♦♦♦ Fosse Farmhouse Country Hotel

Nettleton Shrub SN14 7NJ ☎ 01249 782286 📠 01249 783066
e-mail: caroncooper@compuserve.com
Dir: *off B4039, 1.5m past Castle Combe race circuit take 1st left at Gib Village for farm 1m on right*
Set in the quiet Wiltshire countryside close to Castle Combe, this small hotel has well equipped bedrooms decorated in an individual and interesting style, in keeping with its 18th-century origins. Excellent dinners are served in the farmhouse and cream teas can be enjoyed in the old stables.
FACILITIES: 3 en suite No smoking in 1 bedrooms No smoking in dining room TVB tea/coffee Licensed Cen ht Golf 18 Dinner Last d 8.30pm
PRICES: s £55-£65; d £85-£135✻ **LB CONF:** Thtr 10 Class 10 Board 10 Del from £100 ✻ **PARKING:** 10 **CARDS:**

NOMANSLAND Map 04 SU21

♦♦♦♦ Clovenway House

Forest Rd SP5 2BN ☎ 01794 390620 📠 01794 390620
Dir: *off A36 at Landford Poacher pub onto B3079, travel to Nomansland x-roads. Turn right into Forest Rd, to cattle grid, 4th house on right*
Quietly located on the edge of Nomansland village in the heart of the New Forest, this delightful modern guest house has a superb situation. The comfortable bedrooms are well-furnished and equipped with many extra facilities. Full cooked breakfasts are served at individual tables and a guest lounge is also provided.
FACILITIES: 3 rms (2 en suite) (1 fmly) No smoking TVB tea/coffee Cen ht TVL No children 5yrs No coaches **PRICES:** s £27-£30; d £36-£40✻ **LB BB**
PARKING: 4 **NOTES:** Closed Xmas & New Year

PEWSEY Map 04 SU16

♦♦♦♦ Three Horseshoes Cottage

Three Horseshoes, Enford SN9 6AW ☎ 01980 670459
e-mail: jcjonkler@aol.com
Dir: *on A345 between Salisbury & Marlborough*
As the former village inn, blacksmiths and butcher's shop, Three Horseshoes cottage retains much of its charming character with well-preserved original features such as beams, inglenook fireplaces and the old forge. Bedrooms are cosy but comfortable and breakfast is served around the farmhouse kitchen table where genuine hospitality and informality are hallmarks.
FACILITIES: 2 rms (1 en suite) No smoking in bedrooms STV TVB tea/coffee No dogs (ex guide dogs) Cen ht No coaches
PRICES: s fr £25; d fr £50✻ **PARKING:**

SALISBURY Map 04 SU12

See also **Amesbury, Sixpenny Handley (Dorset), Stoford & Winterbourne Stoke**

Premier Collection

♦♦♦♦♦ Beadles

Middleton SP5 1QS ☎ 01980 862922 📠 01980 863565
e-mail: winterbead@aol.com

(For full entry see Middle Winterslow)

Egg cups for excellence!
This symbol shows that breakfast exceeded our Inspector's expectations.

Premier Collection

♦♦♦♦♦ Ebblesway Courtyard
High Rd SP5 5EF ☎ 01722 780182 01722 780482
e-mail: enquiries@ebbleswaycourtyard.co.uk
(For full entry see Broad Chalke)

Premier Collection

♦♦♦♦♦ Newton Farmhouse
Southampton Rd SP5 2QL ☎ 01794 884416
01794 884416
e-mail: reservations@newtonfarmhouse.co.uk
(For full entry see Whiteparish)

♦♦♦♦ Clovelly
17-19 Mill Rd SP2 7RT ☎ 01722 322055 01722 327677
e-mail: clovelly.hotel@virgin.net
Dir: *approx 5 mins from Market Square & Cathedral, & 2 mins from station*

Centrally located with easy access to the cathedral, railway station and city centre, the Clovelly provides quality accommodation and service. The proprietor is a Blue Badge Guide and offers personalised driving tours around Wessex. The bedrooms are smartly decorated with well co-ordinated and attractive furnishings. Public areas include a delightful lounge and breakfast room.
FACILITIES: 14 en suite (3 fmly) No smoking TVB tea/coffee No dogs (ex guide dogs) Licensed Cen ht No children **PRICES:** s £40-£60; d £55-£70✻ LB **PARKING:** 15 **CARDS:**

♦♦♦♦ The Old House
161 Wilton Rd SP2 7JQ ☎ 01722 333433 01722 335551
Dir: *on A36 between Wilton & Salisbury, close to police station*

Conveniently located close to the city centre, this historic property dates back to the 17th-century. The cosy cellar bar is the only place in the house where smoking is permitted. Bedrooms, including two on the ground floor, have been tastefully decorated and are equipped with modern facilities; one has a four-poster bed.
FACILITIES: 7 en suite (1 fmly) No smoking in bedrooms No smoking in dining room No smoking in 1 lounge TVB tea/coffee No dogs (ex guide dogs) Licensed Cen ht TVL No coaches Games room Table tennis
PRICES: s £30-£35✻ LB **PARKING:** 10

England

SALISBURY continued

♦♦♦♦ Websters

11 Hartington Rd SP2 7LG ☎ 01722 339779 01722 421903
e-mail: websters.salis@eclipse.co.uk
Dir: *from city centre take A360 Devizes road. Hartington Rd is 500yds from St Pauls rdbt on left*

A warm and friendly welcome is assured at this delightful property located in a quiet cul-de-sac close to the city centre. The charming, comfortable and well-presented bedrooms are equipped with numerous extras. There is one ground-floor room with easy access, also suitable for wheelchair users. The guests' lounge also has an e-mail facility. Dinner is available by prior arrangement. Websters was a Top Twenty Finalist in the AA Accessible Hotel of the Year Awards 2002-2003.

FACILITIES: 5 en suite No smoking in bedrooms No smoking in dining room TVB tea/coffee No dogs (ex guide dogs) Cen ht No children 12yrs No coaches **PRICES:** s £32-£36; d £42-£45✳ **LB PARKING:** 5
CARDS:

♦♦♦♦ Briden House

West St, Barford St Martin SP3 4AH ☎ 01722 743471
01722 743471
e-mail: bridenhouse@barford25.freeserve.co.uk
Dir: *close to village church on B3089 in Barford St Martin*

This charming Grade II listed property, situated not far from Salisbury, has been restored to its former glory. Bedrooms are pleasantly furnished and well equipped. There is also a ground floor garden bedroom with its own sitting room. Breakfast is served in the delightful beamed dining room.

FACILITIES: 4 en suite No smoking in dining room No smoking in lounges TVB tea/coffee Cen ht No coaches **PRICES:** s £40-£45; d £50-£60✳
PARKING: 6 **CARDS:**

♦♦♦♦ Cathedral Hotel

Milford Place, 7-9 Milford St SP1 2AJ ☎ 01722 343700
01722 343701
e-mail: cathedralhotel@regent-inns.plc.uk
Dir: *M3, follow signs to Salisbury/ South West (Junct 8). Follow A303 to A338, then take A30 to Salisbury. At Ring Road follow signs to the city. At Exeter St rdbt turn R into Exeter St. Follow one way along St John and Catherine Street. Turn R into Milford St*

Good purpose built accommodation right in the centre of the city. The comfortable bedrooms vary in size although all are fitted with workstations and telephones. The busy bar on the ground floor offers food and refreshments throughout the day from breakfast to dinner.

FACILITIES: 21 en suite (4 fmly) No smoking in 11 bedrooms No smoking in dining room No smoking in lounges TVB tea/coffee Direct dial from bedrooms No dogs (ex guide dogs) TVL Dinner Last d 9pm
PRICES: s £46.90-£56.95; d £53.85-£63.85 ✳ **CONF:** Thtr 20 Class 20 Board 16 **CARDS:**

♦♦♦♦ The Edwardian Lodge

59 Castle Rd SP1 3RH ☎ 01722 413329 01722 503105
e-mail: richardwhite@edlodge.freeserve.co.uk
Dir: *0.5m N of city centre on A345 or 300mtrs N of A345 rdbt on main ring road. Turn into Victoria Rd to access car park at back of property*

Located close to the city centre, this fine Edwardian home is ideally situated for all local places of interest. It has spacious, comfortably furnished and well-equipped bedrooms, some of which are located on the ground floor. Breakfast is taken in the bright conservatory.

FACILITIES: 7 en suite (1 fmly) No smoking TVB tea/coffee No dogs (ex guide dogs) Cen ht No children 6mnths **PRICES:** s £30-£37.50; d £45-£55✳ **PARKING:** 7 **NOTES:** Closed 20th-28th Dec **CARDS:**

♦♦♦♦ Glen Lyn

6 Bellamy Ln, Milford Hill SP1 2SP ☎ 01722 327880
01722 327880
e-mail: glen.lyn@btinternet.com
Dir: *from A36 turn into Tollgate Rd, at lights turn R (Milford Hill). Bellamy Ln at top on L*

This attractive Victorian house, located in a quiet area close to the city centre, offers high levels of hospitality and service. Breakfast is served in the pleasant dining room and a traditional dinner is available by prior arrangement. There is a spacious lounge with books, maps and tourist information.

FACILITIES: 7 rms (4 en suite) (1 fmly) No smoking TVB tea/coffee Licensed Cen ht No children 12yrs No coaches **PRICES:** s £35-£48; d £47-£64✳ **PARKING:** 5 **CARDS:**

♦♦♦♦ Malvern

31 Hulse Rd SP1 3LU ☎ 01722 327995 01722 327995
e-mail: malvern_gh@madasafish.com
Dir: *from A30 follow Amesbury sign at 2nd rdbt, then 1st left into Butts Rd, then 1st left*

Situated in a peaceful cul-de-sac, this guest house is within easy walking distance of the city centre. The comfortable lounge has a relaxing, homely atmosphere. Bedrooms are individually furnished and attractively decorated with numerous little extras. Breakfast is served in the bright conservatory dining room overlooking the well-maintained garden.

FACILITIES: 3 en suite No smoking TVB tea/coffee No dogs (ex guide dogs) Cen ht TVL No children 10yrs No coaches **PRICES:** d £45✳
PARKING: 3

continued

♦♦♦♦ *Salisbury Old Mill House*

Warminster Rd, South Newton SP2 0QD ☎ 01722 742458
📠 01722 742458
e-mail: salisburymill@yahoo.com
Dir: *1m from Wilton roundabout on A36 to Warminster, property on left by 30mph South Newton sign*

A sympathetic restoration of this historic watermill and millpond has ensured that the old mill machinery is on view to guests. Friendly and welcoming, the property offers well appointed comfortable bedrooms, guests' lounge with wood -burning stove and a dining area, where delicious dinners are available by prior arrangement.
FACILITIES: 4 rms (3 en suite) (1 fmly) No smoking TVB tea/coffee No dogs (ex guide dogs) Licensed Cen ht No coaches Fishing Dinner Last d 24hr prior **PARKING:** 10 **NOTES:** Closed 25 Dec & 1 Jan

♦♦♦♦ Stratford Lodge

4 Park Ln, off Castle Rd SP1 3NP ☎ 01722 325177
📠 01722 325177
e-mail: enquires@stratfordlodge.co.uk
Dir: *take A345 Castle Rd past St Francis Church on right & Victoria Park on left. Park Lane is an unadopted road between park & Alldays store (The Circle)*

Close to the city centre, Stratford Lodge benefits from a peaceful setting, being tucked away in a lane overlooking Victoria Park. One of the spacious bedrooms has a four-poster bed. Home-prepared dinners using fresh local ingredients are served in the cosy dining room or taken in the conservatory where breakfast is also served.
FACILITIES: 8 en suite (2 fmly) No smoking TVB tea/coffee No dogs (ex guide dogs) Licensed Cen ht TVL No children 5yrs Dinner Last d 8.30pm **PRICES:** s £45-£50; d £65-£70✳ **LB PARKING:** 12 **CARDS:**
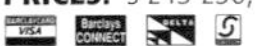

♦♦♦♦ Wyndham Park Lodge

51 Wyndham Rd SP1 3AB ☎ 01722 416517 📠 01722 328851
e-mail: enquiries@wyndhamparklodge.co.uk
Dir: *on rdbt with A345 Amesbury Salisbury ring road (Churchill Way West) take Exit to City Centre (Castle street). Under railroad bridge, Wyndham rd 2nd left.* continued

Located close to the centre of the city, Wyndham Park Lodge provides good access to the cathedral and numerous surrounding tourist attractions. Decorated with co-ordinated furnishings in keeping with its Victorian heritage, bedrooms are comfortable and equipped with numerous extra facilities. A full English breakfast is served at individual tables.
FACILITIES: 3 en suite 1 annexe en suite (1 fmly) No smoking TVB tea/coffee No dogs Cen ht No coaches **PRICES:** s £30-£35; d £40-£45✳
PARKING: 3 **CARDS:**

♦♦♦ The Butt of Ale

Sunnyhill Rd SP1 3QJ ☎ 01722 327610
Located in a quiet residential area just a short drive from the city centre, the cathedral, Stonehenge and various other places of interest, this modern pub provides guests with a warm welcome and a good choice of dinner menu. Bedrooms are comfortable and there is a large beer garden adjoining.
FACILITIES: 2 rms (1 en suite) (1 fmly) No smoking in bedrooms No smoking in area of dining room TVB tea/coffee No dogs (ex guide dogs) Cen ht Pool Table Dinner Last d 9pm **PRICES:** s fr £20; d fr £40✳
MEALS: Lunch £5.25-£9.95 Dinner £5.25-£9.95✳ **PARKING:** 40
CARDS:

♦♦♦ Byways House

31 Fowlers Rd SP1 2QP ☎ 01722 328364 📠 01722 322146
e-mail: byways@stonehenge-uk.com
Dir: *from A30 follow A36 Southampton signs then follow 'Youth Hostel' signs to the hostel. Fowlers Rd is directly opposite*
Located in a quiet street with off road parking, Byways is situated within walking distance of the town centre. Two bedrooms have been decorated in a Victorian style and another two have four-poster beds. All rooms offer good levels of comfort, with one being adapted for less mobile guests.
FACILITIES: 23 rms (19 en suite) (5 fmly) No smoking in dining room No smoking in lounges STV TVB tea/coffee Licensed Cen ht **PRICES:** s £35-£60; d £55-£70✳ **LB PARKING:** 15 **NOTES:** Closed Xmas & New Year
CARDS:

♦♦♦ Hayburn Wyke

72 Castle Rd SP1 3RL ☎ 01722 412627 📠 01722 412627
e-mail: hayburn.wyke@tinyonline.co.uk
Dir: *0.5m N on A345 from Salisbury town centre, on the left*
Located close to the city centre, Victoria Park, and numerous places of interest, this charming guest house provides visitors with a friendly and comfortable base from which to explore the area. Bedrooms are bright and airy and equipped with many useful extras. One bedroom is located on the ground floor allowing for easy access.
FACILITIES: 7 rms (4 en suite) (3 fmly) (1 GF) No smoking in 2 bedrooms No smoking in dining room No smoking in lounges TVB tea/coffee No dogs (ex guide dogs) Cen ht TVL **PRICES:** s £32-£58; d £42-£60✳
PARKING: 7 **CARDS:**

♦♦♦ Richburn

25 Estcourt Rd SP1 3AP ☎ 01722 325189 📠 01722 325189
Dir: *from A30 at St Marks rdbt, take 3rd exit to Estcourt Rd towards town centre. House at junct of Estcourt Rd & College St*
A warm welcome awaits at this attractive Victorian property, just a few minutes' walk from the city centre. It is well-located for the cathedral, Stonehenge and other places of interest. The cosy bedrooms are comfortably furnished and there is a spacious dining room where tasty breakfasts are served.
FACILITIES: 4 en suite (1 fmly) No smoking TVB tea/coffee No dogs (ex guide dogs) Cen ht No children 10yrs No coaches **PRICES:** s £20-£35; d £38-£60✳ **BB PARKING:** 4 **NOTES:** Closed Xmas & New Year

England

SALISBURY continued

♦♦ Holmhurst
Downton Rd SP2 8AR ☎ 01722 410407 📠 01722 323164
e-mail: holmhurst@talk21.com
Dir: *follow ring road around city taking A338-South coast route*
Holmhurst is conveniently located on the outskirts of town, yet within walking distance of the city centre and the cathedral. This family-run hotel provides guests with bedrooms that are comfortable and well-equipped and each has modern facilities. A traditional breakfast is served in the brightly appointed dining room.
FACILITIES: 5 rms (4 en suite) (2 fmly) No smoking in 2 bedrooms No smoking in dining room No smoking in lounges TVB tea/coffee No dogs (ex guide dogs) Cen ht **PRICES:** s £25-£35; d £40-£48✱ **PARKING:** 9 **CARDS:**

STOFORD Map 04 SU03

♦♦♦ Swan
SP2 0PR ☎ 01722 790236 📠 01722 790115
e-mail: info@theswanatstoford.co.uk
Dir: *from A303 join A360, after 3m right at x-roads, after 1m establishment on right at T-junc of A36*
In a good location for people wishing to tour the region, this family-run establishment, besides attractively furnished and comfortable bedrooms, offers a skittle alley and fishing on a private stretch of river. Tasty home-cooked meals are available at lunch and dinner in either the popular pub bar or in the restaurant.
FACILITIES: 9 en suite (2 fmly) No smoking in bedrooms No smoking in dining room TVB tea/coffee No dogs Cen ht Fishing Pool Table Skittle alley Dinner Last d 9.15pm **PRICES:** s £35-£60; d £45-£65✱ **CONF:** Thtr 20 Class 30 Board 15 **PARKING:** 50 **CARDS:**

SWINDON Map 04 SU18

♦♦♦♦ Parklands Hotel
High St, Ogbourne St George SN8 1SL ☎ 01672 841555
📠 01672 841533
e-mail: enquiries@parklandshoteluk.co.uk
Dir: *M4 junct 15, towards Marlborough. After 4m turn left at Ogbourne Downs golf club. Right at T-junct, 1st right & hotel on right, signed by brown tourist signs*

A short distance from both Swindon and Marlborough, Parklands Hotel provides a peaceful and pleasant location whether visiting on business or for pleasure. The dining room has plenty of character retained from the 17th century origins and there is a pleasant adjoining bar/lounge area. Bedrooms are well furnished and include a number of welcome extra facilities.
FACILITIES: 10 en suite No smoking in bedrooms No smoking in dining room TVB tea/coffee Direct dial from bedrooms Licensed Cen ht Dinner Last d 9.15pm **PRICES:** s £45-£60; d £70✱ **LB CONF:** Thtr 16 Class 16 Board 16 Del £76.50 ✱ **PARKING:** 11 **CARDS:**

♦♦♦ Grove Lodge
108 Swindon Rd, Stratton St Margaret SN3 4PT
☎ 01793 825343 📠 01793 825343
Dir: *turn off A417 to Stratton St Margaret, follow to Swindon town centre, house on right after 1m*
Within easy reach of the M4, this family run guest house provides comfortable accommodation whether for business or leisure guests. Rooms vary in size but all are well maintained and satellite TV is a plus.
FACILITIES: 10 en suite (2 fmly) No smoking in 3 bedrooms No smoking in dining room No smoking in lounges STV TVB tea/coffee Cen ht Dinner Last d At breakfast **PARKING:** 12

♦♦♦ Portquin
Highworth Rd, Broadbush, Broad Blunsdon SN26 7DH
☎ 01793 721261 📠 01793 721261
e-mail: portquin@msn.com
Dir: *turn off A419 at Blunsdon onto B4019 signposted Highworth, 0.5m from A419*

Close to Swindon and with views of the Berkshire Downs, this friendly guest house offers a warm welcome. The comfortable rooms offer a considerable range of shapes and sizes – six are in the main house and three in an adjacent annexe. Public areas include a pleasant open-plan dining room and comfortable lounge.
FACILITIES: 6 en suite 3 annexe en suite (2 fmly) (4 GF) No smoking STV TVB tea/coffee Direct dial from bedrooms Cen ht No coaches **PRICES:** s £35-£40; d £50-£60✱ **PARKING:** 12 **CARDS:**

TISBURY Map 03 ST92

♦♦♦♦ The Beckford Arms
Fonthill Gifford SP3 6PX ☎ 01747 870385 📠 01747 870385
Dir: *Off A303 to B3089, arrive at Fonthill Bishop right 1st left under Fonthill estate arch, through park to crossroads.*
Located in immaculate mature gardens within the peaceful hamlet of Fonthill Gifford, this impressive Regency inn retains many original features, which are enhanced by the rustic period furniture styles and memorabilia throughout the public areas. Bedrooms are thoughtfully equipped and a warm welcome with imaginative food is assured.
FACILITIES: 8 rms (5 en suite) (1 fmly) No smoking in bedrooms TVB tea/coffee Cen ht Pool Table Dinner Last d 9.15-9.45pm
PARKING: 30 **NOTES:** Closed X-mas **CARDS:**

TROWBRIDGE Map 03 ST85

♦♦♦ Watergardens
131 Yarnbrook Rd, West Ashton BA14 6AF ☎ 01225 752045
📠 01225 719427
e-mail: lucy@heard28.freeserve.co.uk
Dir: *Watergardens on A350, 200mtrs from A350/A363 junction at Yarnbrook rdbt (Hungry Horse pub/garage)*

continued

Watergardens

Conveniently located for touring the area, this house offers comfortable and modern accommodation. The friendly proprietors ensure guests are made to feel at home and the well-equipped rooms are spacious and attractive. Freshly cooked breakfast is served in either the dining room or the conservatory, which overlooks the water gardens.
FACILITIES: 2 en suite (1 fmly) No smoking TVB tea/coffee No dogs (ex guide dogs) Cen ht No coaches **PRICES:** s £20-£30; d £40-£45✱ **PARKING:** 4 **NOTES:** Closed 21 Dec-2 Jan

WARMINSTER Map 03 ST84

See also Wylye

Premier Collection

♦♦♦♦♦ The Angel

Upton Scudamore BA12 0AG ☎ 01985 213225
01985 218182
Dir: *follow signs to Upton Scudamore from either A36 or A350, inn in centre of village*

Centrally located in the quiet village of Upton Scudamore, this charming and delightfully restored 16th-century coaching inn offers individually furnished bedrooms, some of which are situated in an adjacent cottage. There is a busy bar and restaurant with cosy sitting area. An extensive selection of imaginative dishes is available at lunch and dinner.
FACILITIES: 4 en suite 6 annexe en suite (3 GF) No smoking in bedrooms No smoking in area of dining room TVB tea/coffee Direct dial from bedrooms No dogs (ex guide dogs) Cen ht No coaches Dinner Last d 9.30pm **PRICES:** s £55; d £75✱ **MEALS:** Lunch £16.50-£30alc Dinner £16.50-£30alc✱ **PARKING:** 30 **NOTES:** Closed 24 Dec-2 Jan **CARDS:**

♦♦♦♦ Granary

Manor Farm, Upton Scudamore BA12 0AG
☎ 01985 214835 01985 214835
Dir: *from Granada Services rdbt take A350, 1st left after railway bridge then 1st right. The Granary is 2nd house on left*

Delightfully located in a peaceful village and enjoying pleasant views over the countryside, the Granary is a charming establishment. Bedrooms are stylishly decorated with co-ordinated fabrics and comfortable furnishings, and are provided with many thoughtful extras, including a fridge to cool the wine. Breakfast is served in the rooms, each of which has a private terrace.
FACILITIES: 2 annexe en suite (2 GF) No smoking TVB tea/coffee No dogs Cen ht No children 12yrs No coaches **PRICES:** s £40; d £50✱ **LB** **PARKING:** 3 **NOTES:** Closed 20 Dec-3 Jan

♦♦♦♦ The Angel Coaching Inn

High St, Heytesbury BA12 0ED ☎ 01985 840330
01985 840931
e-mail: angelheytesbury@aol.com
Dir: *From Cotley Hill rdbt on A36, E of Warminster, follow signs for village, The Angel is at eastern end of main street*

Centrally situated, parts of this delightful coaching inn date back to 1400. Public areas include a comfortable guest lounge and the bedrooms are spacious and well-decorated. Guests can choose from a range of real ales, wines and a varied blackboard menu and can dine in either the characterful bar or more formal dining room.
FACILITIES: 6 en suite 2 annexe en suite (1 fmly) (2 GF) No smoking in bedrooms No smoking in dining room TVB tea/coffee Direct dial from bedrooms Cen ht Dinner Last d 9pm **PRICES:** s £50; d £65-£75✱ **CONF:** Thtr 40 Class 30 Board 24 **PARKING:** 9 **CARDS:**

♦♦♦♦ *The Barn*

The Marsh, Longbridge Deverill BA12 7EA ☎ 01985 841138
01985 841138
Dir: *A36 Salisbury/Bath, then A350 into Longbridge Deverill, turn 300yds past BP garage on left, house 1st right*

Built in the 19th century and originally a milking parlour, The Barn is now an attractive, spacious home which retains a great deal of character. Bedrooms are spacious and attractively decorated in soft colours, with comfortable furnishings. Generous breakfasts are taken in the kitchen at a large pine table, family style, and the atmosphere is welcoming.
FACILITIES: 2 en suite No smoking in bedrooms No smoking in dining room TVB tea/coffee Cen ht No coaches **PARKING:** 5

♦♦♦♦ The Dove Inn

Corton BA12 0SZ ☎ 01985 850109 01985 851041
e-mail: info@thedove.co.uk
Dir: *From A36 N of Salisbury signed to Corton & Boyton, cross railway line, turn right at x-rds. Corton approx 1m, The Dove at entrance of village*

This peaceful village is a relaxing and tranquil place to stay. Rooms are well equipped and tastefully decorated and are most comfortable. Dinner, not to be missed, offers imaginative dishes and interesting choices and menus feature fresh and seasonal produce along with vegetarian choices.
FACILITIES: 5 annexe en suite (1 fmly) (4 GF) No smoking in area of dining room TVB tea/coffee Cen ht Dinner Last d 9.30pm **PRICES:** s fr £49.50; d fr £70✱ **MEALS:** Lunch £15-£18 Dinner £18-£28alc✱ **PARKING:** 22 **NOTES:** Closed 25 & 26 Dec **CARDS:**

Places with this symbol are Inns.

England

WARMINSTER continued

♦♦♦♦ George
Longbridge Deverill BA12 7DG ☎ 01985 840396
01985 841333
Dir: *situated on the A350 towards Blandford*
Located in the village of Longbridge Deverill, The George Inn combines a friendly village pub atmosphere with the comfort of recently refurbished well-equipped bedrooms. In addition to the pleasant bar and separate restaurant, guests also have the benefit of their own lounge and the delightful river garden.
FACILITIES: 10 en suite (1 fmly) No smoking in 5 bedrooms No smoking in dining room TVB tea/coffee Direct dial from bedrooms No dogs Cen ht Dinner Last d 9.30pm **PRICES:** s £40; d £60✻ **LB CONF:** Thtr 100 Class 40 Board 30 Del from £75 ✻ **PARKING:** 50 **CARDS:**

♦♦♦♦ White Lodge
22 Westbury Rd BA12 0AW ☎ 01985 212378 01985 212378
e-mail: carol@lioncountry.co.uk
Dir: *from centre of Warminster take Portway road signed for Westbury from the High St. House 0.75m on this road, situated on left*
Conveniently located for the many attractions of Wiltshire and Somerset, this attractive house is notable for its Art Deco features, including an impressive stairway and hall. Bedrooms are spacious and pleasantly decorated and breakfast is taken in the dining room, overlooking the delightful gardens.
FACILITIES: 3 en suite (1 fmly) No smoking TVB tea/coffee No dogs (ex guide dogs) Cen ht No children 5yrs No coaches **PRICES:** s £40; d £50-£55✻ **PARKING:** 8 **NOTES:** Closed Xmas

♦♦♦ Deverill End
Sutton Veny BA12 7BY ☎ 01985 840356
e-mail: riversgreathead@amserve.net
Dir: *from A36 at Heytesbury rdbt take exit to Sutton Veny, 3km. Straight over crossroads, establishment 200mtrs on left*
Stonehenge, Longleat and Stourhead are all within easy reach of this property being conveniently located midway between Bath and Salisbury. The well-equipped comfortable bedrooms have spectacular southern views and in the summer the flower-filled garden is the ideal place in which to relax.
FACILITIES: 3 en suite (3 GF) No smoking TVB tea/coffee No dogs Cen ht TVL No children 10yrs No coaches **PRICES:** d £50-£55✻ **PARKING:** 4

WESTBURY — Map 03 ST85

♦♦♦♦ Glenmore Farm *(ST862524)*
Ham Rd BA13 4HQ ☎ 01373 865022 Mr & Mrs G R A Painter
e-mail: stay@glenmorefarm.freeserve.co.uk
Dir: *A350 N from Westbury, at Heywood turn left into village and left at end of village. Farm on right after West Wilts Trading Estate*

Within two miles of the famous 'White Horse', this detached farmhouse is situated on 145 acres of farmland. Bedrooms are very well furnished and equipped, two having four-poster beds. A smart lounge and sunny conservatory are also available for guests.

continued

FACILITIES: 3 rms (2 en suite) (1 fmly) No smoking TVB tea/coffee No dogs Cen ht TVL Riding 300 acres horses **PRICES:** s £22-£45; d £40-£45✻ **LB PARKING:** 21

♦♦♦ Birchanger Farm *(ST898521)*
Bratton Rd BA13 4TA ☎ 01373 822673 01373 822673
Mrs C Knight
e-mail: carolknight@birchangerfarm03.freeserve.co.uk
Dir: *M4 junct 17 southbound, take A350 towards Warminster. In Westbury turn left onto B3098 to Bratton. Farm 1m on left after White Horse Monument*
Located close to the familiar chalk White Horse, this 18th-century farmhouse offers a range of comfortable, well-equipped bedrooms including one on the ground floor. A hearty breakfast is served in the cosy dining room. Service is friendly and relaxed.
FACILITIES: 3 rms (2 en suite) (2 GF) No smoking in dining room TV4B tea/coffee No dogs Cen ht TVL 40 acres arable **PRICES:** s £20-£25; d £40-£45✻ **PARKING:** 6 **NOTES:** Closed Xmas

♦♦ Duke at Bratton
Melbourne St, Bratton BA13 4RW ☎ 01380 830242
01380 831239
Dir: *from Westbury follow B3098 signed White Horse & Bratton. From Devizes A360 towards Salisbury, 7m to West Lavington, then right to B3098 to Bratton*
Only a short distance from the famous White Horse of Westbury, this inn offers friendly hospitality and comfortable rooms, one of which has a four-poster bed. Dinners are taken in either the restaurant or bar with an enjoyable selection of home cooking.
FACILITIES: 3 rms No smoking in dining room No smoking in 1 lounge TVB tea/coffee Cen ht No children 14yrs No coaches Dinner Last d 9pm **PRICES:** s £30; d £50✻ **MEALS:** Lunch £17.15-£28.90alc Dinner £17.15-£28.90alc✻ **PARKING:** 30 **CARDS:**

WHITEPARISH — Map 04 SU22

Premier Collection

♦♦♦♦♦ Newton Farmhouse
Southampton Rd SP5 2QL ☎ 01794 884416
01794 884416
e-mail: reservations@newtonfarmhouse.co.uk
Dir: *Just S of Salisbury- 6 miles, on A36 1m S of junct with A27*

This delightful farmhouse dates from the 16th century and was gifted to Lord Nelson's family as part of the Trafalgar estate. Close to Salisbury and on the fringe of the New Forest, the house has been thoughtfully restored. Bedrooms, most with four-poster beds, have been equipped with numerous extra touches. Delicious home cooked meals, which are a speciality, are available by prior arrangement. At breakfast home-made yoghurt, bread and preserves feature along with traditional dishes.

continued

England

FACILITIES: 8 en suite No smoking TVB tea/coffee No dogs (ex guide dogs) Cen ht TVL No coaches Outdoor swimming pool Dinner Last d 24hrs notice **PRICES:** s £30-£35; d £40-£60✻ **PARKING:** 10

See advert under SALISBURY

WINTERBOURNE STOKE Map 04 SU04

♦♦♦♦ Scotland Lodge

SP3 4TF ☎ 01980 620943 📠 01980 621403
e-mail: scotland-lodge@virgin.net
Dir: *from Salisbury A360 to junct with A303, left to Winterbourne Stoke. 1.25m W of village beyond turn to Berwick St James - only house on right*
Well-situated for those wishing to visit Stonehenge and the cathedral cities of Salisbury and Winchester, this fine Victorian home has spacious, comfortable bedrooms equipped with a number of thoughtful extras. An English breakfast is served at one large table in the attractive dining room. There is also a cosy sitting room.
FACILITIES: 3 en suite (1 fmly) No smoking TVB tea/coffee No dogs (ex guide dogs) Cen ht No coaches **PRICES:** s £25-£30; d £45-£55✻ **LB CONF:** Board 16 **PARKING:** 5

♦♦♦♦ Scotland Lodge Farm

SP3 4TF ☎ 01980 621199 📠 01980 621188
e-mail: william.lockwood@bigwig.net
Dir: *entrance on A303, W of Winterbourne Stoke, just beyond turning to Berwick St James, immediately after Scotland Lodge on R*

Set in 46 acres of paddocks and grassland the farm provides guests with comfortable well-appointed rooms featuring numerous thoughtful extra touches. Full English breakfasts are served at the large farmhouse table in the conservatory/lounge overlooking the paddocks. The proprietors are keen horse lovers and are happy to offer stabling. Dogs are welcome by prior arrangement.
FACILITIES: 3 en suite (1 fmly) (2 GF) No smoking TV2B tea/coffee Cen ht TVL No coaches **PRICES:** s £27-£30; d £48-£50✻ **PARKING:** 5
CARDS:

WOODFALLS Map 04 SU12

♦♦♦♦ *Woodfalls*

The Ridge SP5 2LN ☎ 01725 513222 📠 01725 513220
e-mail: woodfallsi@aol.com
Dir: *on B3080 (The Circle)*
This welcoming, attractive inn is located in a quiet village, within easy reach of Salisbury and the New Forest. Bedrooms are well-furnished and comfortable with co-ordinated decor and soft furnishings. Two bedrooms have four-poster beds. There are public and lounge bars and a cosy restaurant, whilst breakfast is served in the airy conservatory.
FACILITIES: 10 en suite (1 fmly) No smoking in bedrooms No smoking in dining room No smoking in 1 lounge TVB tea/coffee Direct dial from bedrooms Cen ht Bike hire Dinner Last d 9.30pm **PARKING:** 30
CARDS:

WOOTTON BASSETT Map 04 SU08

♦♦♦♦ *Little Cotmarsh Farm (SU090797)*

Broad Town SN4 7RA ☎ 01793 731322 Mrs M A Richards
Dir: *from Wootton Bassett take the Broad Hinton road (opposite town hall) for approx 2.5m, turn left into Cotmarsh, bear left at T junction. 2nd right*
A few minutes from Wootton Bassett and also convenient for Swindon, this is a lovely Grade II listed farmhouse. Bedrooms are comfortable and two have very smart shower rooms. Character and quality abound in the dining room with its fireplace and wood burning stove. Breakfast is cooked to order using good quality produce.
FACILITIES: 3 en suite (1 fmly) No smoking TVB tea/coffee No dogs (ex guide dogs) Cen ht 108 acres beef **PARKING:** 6 **NOTES:** Closed Dec-Jan

WYLYE Map 03 SU03

♦♦♦ Bell

High St BA12 0QP ☎ 01985 248338
e-mail: lk.thebell@wylye2.freeserve.co.uk
Dir: *next to church in centre of village of Wylye. Two exits off A303, one at either end of the village, village being next to A36*
Dating back nearly 700 years this charming inn retains much of its original character and offers modern and comfortable accommodation. Excellent choices are available from the menu, which features local and seasonal produce and provides interesting and well-prepared dishes. Rooms are stylish and well-equipped and feature attractive co-ordinated fabrics.
FACILITIES: 3 en suite No smoking in area of dining room TVB tea/coffee Cen ht No coaches Dinner Last d 9.30pm **PRICES:** s £30; d £45-£60✻
MEALS: Lunch £17.85-£24.85&alc Dinner £17.85-£24.85&alc✻
PARKING: 40 **CARDS:**

YATTON KEYNELL Map 03 ST87

♦♦♦♦ The Crown Inn

Giddea Hall SN14 7ER ☎ 01249 782229 📠 01249 782337
e-mail: enquiries@crown-at-giddeahall.co.uk
Dir: *turn off M4 at junct. 18 follow signs for A420 Chippenham and Castle Combe. Giddea Hall is approx 4m W of Chippenham*

Situated with easy access to Chippenham and Castle Combe race circuit, this delightful inn, full of character, has rooms named after racing cars and feature motoring memorabilia. Bedrooms are well equipped with many extra facilities and two have four-poster beds. Tasty meals are served at lunch and dinner.
FACILITIES: 8 annexe en suite No smoking in bedrooms No smoking in area of dining room STV TVB tea/coffee Direct dial from bedrooms No dogs (ex guide dogs) Cen ht Dinner Last d 9pm **PRICES:** s fr £55; d fr £65✻
MEALS: Lunch £3.75-£14.50&alc Dinner £3.75-£14.50&alc✻ **CONF:** Thtr 18 Class 18 Board 18 **PARKING:** 40 **CARDS:**

England

WORCESTERSHIRE

ABBERLEY Map 03 SO76

♦♦♦ Manor Arms Country Inn & Hotel

WR6 6BN ☎ 01299 896507 📠 01299 896723
e-mail: themanorarms@btconnect.com
Dir: *village located between Tenbury Wells and Worcester on A443. Leave A443 at Abberley and follow signs to Norman Church/Abberley Village, inn on left*

Located in the heart of this pretty rural village opposite the Norman church, this 17th-century inn retains many original features including a wealth of exposed beams and open log fires. Bedrooms are filled with practical extras and three have direct access to the pretty gardens. A range of popular dishes is available in the cosy bars or the restaurant.
FACILITIES: 8 en suite (1 fmly) No smoking in bedrooms No smoking in dining room STV TVB tea/coffee Direct dial from bedrooms No dogs (ex guide dogs) Cen ht Dinner Last d 9pm **PRICES:** s fr £40; d fr £54✻ **LB MEALS:** Lunch £4-£9 Dinner £12-£20alc✻ **PARKING:** 16
CARDS:

♦♦♦ Whoppets Wood

WR6 6BU ☎ 01299 896545
e-mail: whoppets@breathemail.net
Dir: *1.3m from 'Shavers End' signpost off A451 between Dunley and Great Witley at Dick Brook Bridge*

A warm welcome is assured at this former farmhouse, located in an elevated position close to major walking paths. Stunning views over the surrounding countryside can be seen from the homely bedrooms; breakfasts are memorable.
FACILITIES: 3 rms (2 en suite) (1 fmly) No smoking TV2B tea/coffee No dogs Cen ht No children 4yrs No coaches **PRICES:** s fr £20; d fr £35✻ **LB BB PARKING:** 3 **NOTES:** Closed Dec-1 Jan

Places with this symbol are farmhouses.

ALVECHURCH Map 07 SP07

♦♦♦ Alcott Farm

Icknield St, Weatheroak B48 7EH ☎ 01564 824051
📠 01564 829799
Dir: *M42 junct 3 take A435 towards Birmingham. Take left slip road signed Weatheroak. At x-rds left down steep hill, then left past pub. Farm 0.5m on right up long drive*
FACILITIES: 4 en suite No smoking in bedrooms No smoking in dining room TVB tea/coffee Cen ht TVL No children 10yrs No coaches
PRICES: s £35; d £55✻ **PARKING:**

BEWDLEY Map 07 SO77

♦♦♦ Bank House

14 Lower Park DY12 2DP ☎ 01299 402652 📠 01299 402652
e-mail: fleur.nightingale@virgin.net
Dir: *from Kidderminster follow signs Bewdley A456, over bridge into main street (Load Street) continue until St Annes church, turn left into the high street. Continue until Lax Lane junct on left, Bank House after this junction on left*
Once a private bank, this Georgian town house retains many original features and offers comfortable accommodation. The cosy dining room is the setting for tasty English breakfasts served at one family table. Owner Mrs Nightingale has a comprehensive knowledge of the town and its history.
FACILITIES: 3 rms (1 fmly) No smoking TVB tea/coffee No dogs Cen ht No coaches **PRICES:** s £22; d £44✻ **PARKING:** 2 **NOTES:** Closed 24-26 Dec rs 27-31 Dec

BROADWAY Map 04 SP03

Premier Collection

♦♦♦♦♦ Mill Hay House

Snowshill Rd WR12 7JS ☎ 01386 852498 📠 01386 858038
e-mail: millhayhouse@aol.com
Dir: *turn off A44 (at Broadway Main Green) towards Snowshill. House 0.75m on right*
Set in three acres of immaculate grounds beside a 12th-century water mill, this impressive mellow-stone Queen Anne house retains many original features which are complemented by quality décor, period furniture and works of art. Bedrooms are spacious, filled with thoughtful extras and one has a balcony. Imaginative breakfasts are served in the elegant dining room and there is a comfortable drawing room.
FACILITIES: 3 en suite No smoking in bedrooms No smoking in dining room No smoking in 1 lounge TVB tea/coffee Direct dial from bedrooms No dogs Cen ht TVL No children 12yrs No coaches 3 acre garden with medieval pond & moat **PRICES:** s £108-£144; d £120-£160✻ **PARKING:** 15 **CARDS:**

♦♦♦♦ *Bowers Hill Farm (SP086420)*

Bowers Hill, Willersey WR11 5HG ☎ 01386 834585
📠 01386 830234 Mr & Mrs M Bent
e-mail: sarah@bowershillfarm.com
Dir: *from A44 Broadway-Evesham, follow signs to Willersey. At village, turn L, at mini rdbt signed Badsey. Farm 2m on R by postbox*
Located in immaculate gardens, on a diverse farm, where point-to-point horses are also bred, this impressive Victorian house has been sympathetically renovated to provided very comfortable and homely bedrooms complimented by modern bathrooms. Breakfast is taken in the elegant dining room or magnificent conservatory and a guest lounge with open fire is also available.

continued

FACILITIES: 3 en suite (1 fmly) No smoking in bedrooms No smoking in dining room No smoking in 1 lounge TVB tea/coffee No dogs Cen ht TVL ch fac Walking on farm. 80 acres mixed **PARKING:** 5 **CARDS:**

♦♦♦♦ Leasow House

Laverton Meadows WR12 7NA ☎ 01386 584526
01386 584596
e-mail: leasow@clara.net
(For full entry see Laverton (Gloucestershire))

♦♦♦♦ Cowley House

Church St WR12 7AE ☎ 01386 853262
Dir: *off A44*

A warm welcome is assured at this mellow Costwold stone house, located a few minutes' walk from the village green. Fine period furniture enhances the original interior features, including the polished flagstone floor in the elegant hall, and the homely bedrooms include an Elizabethan four-poster suite.
FACILITIES: 3 en suite No smoking TVB No dogs Cen ht TVL No children 10yrs No coaches **PRICES:** s fr £35; d £40-£75✻ **PARKING:** 6

♦♦♦♦ Lower Field Farm *(SP098406)*

Willersey WR11 7HF ☎ 01386 858273 01386 854608
Mrs J Hill
e-mail: info@lowerfield-farm.co.uk
Dir: *from A44 at Broadway follow signs to Willersey. At mini rdbt in Willersey follow sign to Badsey. Lower Field Farm 0.5m on right.*

Peacefully located in immaculate grounds close to Willersey, this impressive house, originally built in the 17th century, has been sympathetically renovated to provide spacious and homely bedrooms with stunning views of the surrounding countryside. Memorable breakfasts, and dinners by arrangement, are served in the attractive dining room or farmhouse kitchen.
FACILITIES: 3 en suite (1 fmly) No smoking TVB tea/coffee Cen ht TVL 300 acres sheep, arable Dinner Last d 9am **PRICES:** d £50-£80 **LB**
PARKING: 8 **CARDS:**

♦♦♦♦ Milestone House

122 Upper High St WR12 7AJ ☎ 01386 853432
01386 853432
e-mail: milestone.house@talk21.com
Dir: *from Broadway by-pass(A44) follow signs to Broadway. House on left at Upper High St*

Located on the upper high street, close to antique shops and art galleries, this Grade II listed 17th-century mellow stone town house has been sympathetically renovated to provide comfortable homely bedrooms, one of which is accessed directly from the pretty, enclosed garden. There is an attractive conservatory dining room and choice of lounges.
FACILITIES: 4 en suite No smoking TVB tea/coffee No dogs (ex guide dogs) Cen ht No coaches **PRICES:** s fr £45; d fr £56✻ **LB** **PARKING:** 5
CARDS:

♦♦♦♦ Mount Pleasant Farm *(SP056392)*

Childswickham WR12 7HZ ☎ 01386 853424 01386 853424
Mrs H Perry
e-mail: helen@mount-pleasant.fslife.co.uk
Dir: *at end of Broadway village turn left onto B4632 to Winchcombe, after 50yds right for Childswickham for 3m. Establishment on left 1.5m after Childswickham pub*
Located in immaculate, mature grounds, in a pretty rural hamlet, this impressive Victorian house provides spacious, traditionally furnished bedrooms which have modern bathrooms. Comprehensive breakfasts are taken in an elegant dining room and a comfortable guest lounge is also available.
FACILITIES: 3 en suite (1 fmly) No smoking in bedrooms No smoking in dining room No smoking in lounges TVB tea/coffee No dogs Cen ht No children 5yrs **PRICES:** s £35; d £50✻ **PARKING:** 10 **CARDS:**

♦♦♦♦ Olive Branch Guest House

78 High St WR12 7AJ ☎ 01386 853440 01386 859070
e-mail: davidpam@theolivebranch-broadway.fsnet.co.uk
Dir: *off A44 onto Leamington Rd. At mini-rdbt on High St, proceed into Upper High St. Establishment 60mtrs on left*
Located at the peaceful upper end of the High Street, this mellow stone 16th-century house retains many original features including flag stone floors and exposed beams. Bedrooms are filled with both practical and homely extras and memorable breakfasts, which include home-baked bread, are taken in an elegant cottage-style dining room
FACILITIES: 8 en suite (2 fmly) (1 GF) No smoking STV TVB tea/coffee Cen ht TVL ch fac Dinner Last d 24hr notice **PRICES:** s £40-£65; d £58-£75✻
PARKING: 7 **CARDS:**

BROADWAY continued

♦♦♦♦ Southwold House

Station Rd WR12 7DE ☎ 01386 853681 Fax 01386 854610
e-mail: sueandnick.southwold@talk21.com
Dir: *on B4632 opposite turning signposted to Winchcombe*
Located a few minutes walk from the village centre, this impressive Edwardian house has been sympathetically renovated to provide high levels of comfort and facilities. The homely bedrooms are filled with a wealth of thoughtful extras and a comfortable guest lounge is available in addition to an attractive dining room, which overlooks the immaculate garden.
FACILITIES: 8 en suite (1 fmly) No smoking TVB tea/coffee Cen ht TVL **PRICES:** s fr £29; d fr £48✱ **PARKING:** 8 **CARDS:**

♦♦♦♦ Whiteacres

Station Rd WR12 7DE ☎ 01386 852320
e-mail: whiteacres@btinternet.com
Dir: *at junct of A44 and B4632*
Located a few minutes walk from the centre of this award winning Cotswold village, this late Victorian house has been sympathetically refurbished to provide comfortable homely bedrooms filled with lots of thoughtful extras. Comprehensive breakfasts are taken in the cosy dining room and a guest lounge is also available.
FACILITIES: 5 en suite (1 fmly) No smoking TVB tea/coffee Cen ht TVL No children 5yrs No coaches Dinner **PRICES:** s £35-£40; d £50-£65✱ **PARKING:** 8

♦♦♦♦ Windrush House

Station Rd WR12 7DE ☎ 01386 853577 Fax 853790
e-mail: richard.pinder@virgin.net
Dir: *from A44 take turn for Broadway, Windrush House is opp junction with B4632*
Located in immaculate gardens, a short walk from the village centre, this constantly improving elegant Edwardian house provides comfortable homely bedrooms, some with stunning views of the surrounding countryside. Comprehensive breakfasts are taken in the attractive dining room, which also contains a cosy lounge area with a fine collection of original art.
FACILITIES: 5 en suite No smoking TVB tea/coffee Cen ht TVL Dinner Last d 1pm **PRICES:** s £40-£55; d £55-£70✱ **LB** **PARKING:** 7 **CARDS:**

♦♦♦♦ Barn House

152 High St WR12 7AJ ☎ 01386 858633 Fax 01386 858633
e-mail: barnhouse@btinternet.com
Dir: *In the Upper High Str of Broadway (now a cul de sac)*
FACILITIES: 4 rms (3 en suite) (1 fmly) TVB tea/coffee Cen ht No coaches Outdoor swimming pool (heated) **PRICES:** s £35-£55; d £58-£75✱ **PARKING:** 8

♦♦♦ *Pathlow*

82 High St WR12 7AJ ☎ 01386 853444 Fax 01386 853444
e-mail: pathlow@aol.com
Dir: *from A44 take Evesham road at new rdbt until bypass, road then becomes Broadway High Street*
Peacefully located on the now bypassed upper high street, this 18th-century mellow stone house retains many original features. One of the cosy bedrooms has direct access to the pretty enclosed garden and the attractive dining room is a perfect setting for wholesome breakfasts, light meals and cream teas.
FACILITIES: 6 rms (4 en suite) 1 annexe en suite (2 fmly) No smoking TVB tea/coffee Cen ht TVL Dinner Last d 6pm **PARKING:** 8

BROMSGROVE — Map 07 SO97

Premier Collection

♦♦♦♦♦ Rosa Lodge

38 Station Rd B60 1PZ ☎ 0121 445 5440 Fax 0121 445 5440
e-mail: sandra@rosalodge.co.uk
Dir: *at junct of M42 with A38 take B4096, signposted Burcot, after 1.25m turn left up Green Hill. 1st right into Station Rd. Take drive on right before rail bridge*

Located in a quiet residential area, a few minutes' drive from the town centre, this red brick Edwardian house retains many original features, complemented by the décor throughout. Bedrooms are equipped with a wealth of thoughtful extras and the smart modern bathrooms offer a wide range of toiletries including aromatherapy products. Imaginative dinners are provided in the dining room and a spacious, elegant lounge is also available.
FACILITIES: 3 en suite No smoking in bedrooms No smoking in dining room No smoking in 1 lounge TVB tea/coffee No dogs (ex guide dogs) Cen ht TVL No children 12yrs No coaches Dinner Last d 7.15pm **PRICES:** s £35; d £60✱ **PARKING:** 7

♦♦♦ Lower Bentley *(SO962679)*

Lower Bentley B60 4JB ☎ 01527 821286 Fax 01527 821193
Mr & Mrs A Gibbs
e-mail: AJ.Gibbs@farmline.com
Dir: *A38/B4091 (Hanbury) past Navigation Pub, left signed Woodgate. 1st right into Woodgate Rd, 3rd left (Lower Bentley Ln).*
Located a few minutes drive from major road links, this impressive red brick Victorian house is full of original features, and stylishly furnished and decorated throughout. Bedrooms are filled with lots of thoughtful extras and a comfortable lounge is provided in addition to an elegant dining room, the setting for memorable breakfasts.
FACILITIES: 3 rms (2 en suite) No smoking in dining room No smoking in lounges TVB tea/coffee Cen ht TVL 346 acres dairy beef
PRICES: s £27-£29; d £45✱ **PARKING:** 5

EVESHAM — Map 04 SP04

♦♦♦♦ Buttercup House

Long Hyde Rd, South Littleton WR11 5TH ☎ 01386 830724
e-mail: mary@buttercup-house.com
Dir: *leave Evesham on B4035, left to Offenham (B4510), continue for 3m & turn right at sign for Bennetts Hill opposite Oakfield Nursery, house on hill*
Located on pretty gardens, which include an orchard in a superb elevated position overlooking the Vale of Evesham, this red brick Edwardian house retains many original features and furnishing styles create a real home from home feeling. Bedrooms are filled with thoughtful extras and welcoming tea with home baked cake is provided on arrival.

continued

FACILITIES: 2 en suite No smoking tea/coffee No dogs Cen ht TVL No coaches **PRICES:** s £32-£42; d £39.75-£49.75✻ **LB PARKING:** 5

FLYFORD FLAVELL Map 03 SO95

♦♦♦♦ Boot Inn

Radford Rd WR7 4BS ☎ 01386 462658 📠 01386 462547
e-mail: thebootinn@yahoo.com
Dir: *signposted, off main road by brown tourist sign*
Rebuilt in the Georgian period, an inn has occupied this site since the 13th century and a sympathetic modernisation has ensured that immense charm and character have been retained. Bedrooms are equipped with both practical and homely extras and have modern bathrooms. A range of ales, wines and imaginative food is provided in the cosy public areas.
FACILITIES: 5 en suite (2 GF) No smoking in bedrooms No smoking in dining room No smoking in lounges TVB tea/coffee Direct dial from bedrooms No dogs (ex guide dogs) Cen ht Dinner Last d 9.50pm **PRICES:** s £45; d £55-£75✻ **LB PARKING:** 31 **CARDS:**

KEMPSEY Map 03 SO84

♦♦♦ Walter de Cantelupe Inn

Main Rd (A38) WR5 3NA ☎ 01905 820572 📠 01905 820572
e-mail: walter.depub@fsbdial.co.uk
Dir: *4m S of Worcester town centre on E side of A38 in middle of village*
Ideally located for both M5 and Worcester, this old English inn provides comfortable cosy bedrooms complimented by smart efficient bathrooms. The intimate, open plan public areas are the setting for a range of real ales and imaginative food featuring local produce and a fine British cheese selection.
FACILITIES: 2 en suite (1 fmly) No smoking in bedrooms No smoking in area of dining room TVB tea/coffee No dogs Cen ht No coaches Dinner Last d 9pm Fri/Sat 10pm **PRICES:** s £29-£40; d £40-£60✻ **LB MEALS:** Lunch £12-£19alc Dinner £12-£19alc✻ **PARKING:** 24 **NOTES:** Closed Xmas & last half Jan **CARDS:**

KIDDERMINSTER Map 07 SO87

♦♦♦ Victoria Hotel

15 Comberton Rd DY10 1UA ☎ 01562 67240
e-mail: victoriakidderminster@yahoo.co.uk
Dir: *on A448, 0.5m from town centre, 200yds from Kidderminster Station*
Situated close to the railway station and the famous Severn Valley Steam Railway, this large semi-detached house offers bedrooms of varying size and style, all with modern equipment. Family-bedded rooms are also available and separate tables are provided in the traditionally furnished breakfast room.
FACILITIES: 7 rms (5 en suite) (2 fmly) No smoking TVB tea/coffee No dogs (ex guide dogs) Cen ht No children 2yrs No coaches **PRICES:** s £27-£30; d £49 **PARKING:** 5 **CARDS:**

MALVERN Map 03 SO74

♦♦♦♦ The Dell House

Green Ln, Malvern Wells WR14 4HU ☎ 01684 564448
📠 01684 893974
e-mail: diana@dellhouse.co.uk
Dir: *2m S of Great Malvern on A449. Turn left off A449 into Green Ln & Dell House at top of this road on the right*
Located in immaculate mature grounds, this impressive well-proportioned early Victorian house retains many unique features, which were introduced by the resident scholar and vicar during its period as a rectory. The spacious bedrooms are filled with thoughtful extras and a comfortable sitting room is available in addition to the elegant dining room.

continued

FACILITIES: 3 en suite No smoking TVB tea/coffee No dogs Cen ht No children 10yrs No coaches 2 acre grounds **PRICES:** s £30-£45; d £54-£60✻ **PARKING:** 6

♦♦♦♦ Hills Reach

Chase Rd, Upper Welland WR14 4JY ☎ 01684 578157
📠 01684 578157
e-mail: hillsreach@netscapeonline.co.uk
Dir: *turn off A449 between Ledbury/Malvern onto A4104 (signed Upton-upon-Severn). In approx 1m turn left to Upper Welland, in village turn right opposite Post Office into Chase Road*
This picturesque house is pleasantly situated in a quiet village with superb views of the Malvern Hills. The bedrooms are well equipped and thoughtfully provided with extras whilst breakfast is taken in the conservatory extension from spring onwards.
FACILITIES: 2 rms (1 en suite) (1 fmly) No smoking STV TVB tea/coffee No dogs (ex guide dogs) Cen ht No coaches **PRICES:** s £25-£30; d £45-£50✻ **LB PARKING:** 4 **NOTES:** Closed 24 Dec-2 Jan

♦♦♦♦ St Just

169 Worcester Rd WR14 1EU ☎ 01684 562023
e-mail: stjust@lineone.net
Dir: *M5 junct 7 follow A449 for 5m through Malvern Link Shopping Ctr. 350yds on, turn right into Albert Pk Rd, right into green gates*
Located in pretty, mature gardens close to Malvern Link, this impressive early Victorian house retains many original features, and is stylishly decorated and furnished throughout. Bedrooms are filled with a wealth of thoughtful extras and comprehensive breakfasts are taken in an elegant dining room. Secure parking is a bonus.
FACILITIES: 3 en suite No smoking TVB tea/coffee No dogs (ex guide dogs) Cen ht No children 7yrs No coaches **PRICES:** d £50-£60✻ **LB PARKING:** 8 **NOTES:** Closed Xmas

♦♦♦♦ Bredon House Hotel

34 Worcester Rd WR14 4AA ☎ 01684 566990 📠 01684 575323
e-mail: suereeves@bredonhousehotel.co.uk
Dir: *On A449 (main Malvern to Worcester Rd), 100mtrs from Malvern centre. Look out for large fir tree in front car park.*
Superbly located and offering stunning views of the Cotswold Escarpment, this elegant Regency house has many original features, which are enhanced by the quality furniture and décor styles throughout. The spacious bedrooms offer many practical and homely extras, and a comfortable guest lounge is also available.
FACILITIES: 9 en suite (2 fmly) No smoking in 1 bedrooms No smoking in dining room TVB tea/coffee Direct dial from bedrooms Licensed Cen ht No coaches Quiet secluded garden Dinner Last d 8pm **PRICES:** s £35-£45; d £60-£70✻ **PARKING:** 9 **NOTES:** Closed 21 Dec-4 Jan **CARDS:**

♦♦♦♦ Link Lodge

3 Pickersleigh Rd WR14 2RP ☎ 01684 572345 📠 01684 572345
e-mail: barbara@linklodge.co.uk
Dir: *A449 from Worcester, straight through main lights in Malvern Link. Take 1st L. Establishment is 1st house on L*
Sir Edward Elgar was once the visiting music teacher at this impressive Grade II Queen Anne house sympathetically extended in a Palladian style during the Georgian period. Bedrooms are filled with thoughtful extras and a choice of sumptuous lounges is available in addition to the cosy kitchen where mouth-watering breakfasts are served.
FACILITIES: 3 en suite No smoking TVB tea/coffee Cen ht TVL No coaches Croquet lawn Large landscaped gardens **PRICES:** s £25-£40; d £50-£55✻ **LB PARKING:** 5

England

MALVERN continued

♦♦♦♦ Pembridge Hotel

114 Graham Rd WR14 2HX ☎ 01684 574813 🖷 01684 566885
e-mail: pembridgehotel@aol.com
Dir: *M5 junct 7, follow signs to Malvern to join A449. Through Malvern link, at 5th set of traffic lights turn left into Graham Rd*
Located on a leafy residential road close to town centre, this impressive Victorian house retains many original features including a superb staircase. Bedrooms are both practical and homely. Other areas include a comfortable sitting room and an elegant dining room.
FACILITIES: 8 en suite (1 GF) No smoking in bedrooms No smoking in dining room TVB tea/coffee Direct dial from bedrooms No dogs (ex guide dogs) Licensed Cen ht No children 7yrs No coaches Dinner Last d 8pm **PRICES:** s £38-£48; d £60-£68✻ **LB PARKING:** 7 **NOTES:** Closed 22 Dec - 5 Jan **CARDS:**

♦♦♦♦ Woodpeckers

66 Peachfield Rd, Malvern Wells WR14 4AL ☎ 01684 562827
e-mail: woodpeckers@cmail.co.uk
Located in an unspoilt wooded hollow close to the Three Counties Showground, this attractive bungalow standing in pretty, mature gardens provides a homely twin bedroom with private adjacent bathroom. Breakfast is served in the cosy dining room with a glass wall, overlooking the garden, which backs on to golf course. The interior is enhanced by the proprietor's fine original art and sculpture.
FACILITIES: 1 en suite (1 GF) No smoking TVB tea/coffee No dogs Cen ht No children 8 yrs No coaches **PRICES:** s £21-£25; d £42-£50✻ **BB PARKING:** 1 **NOTES:** Closed Xmas

♦♦♦ Chestnut Hill

Oaklands, Off Green Ln WR14 4HU ☎ 01684 564648
e-mail: patorr@chestnuts.enta.net
Dir: *take B4209 in either direction. On reaching telephone kiosk turn up Green Ln & then turn left past houses to end of road & take 2nd right*
This timber clad detached house is located in extensive mature grounds in a peaceful area. It provides practically equipped bedrooms with stunning views of the surrounding countryside. Breakfast is taken in the cottage style dining room and a spacious and comfortable guest lounge is also available.
FACILITIES: 5 rms (3 en suite) No smoking TV1B tea/coffee No dogs Cen ht TVL No children 14 No coaches Riding Outdoor riding arena **PRICES:** s £18-£22; d £36-£44✻ **LB BB PARKING:** 4 **NOTES:** Closed Jan-Feb

♦♦♦ Hillside

113 Worcester Rd WR14 1ER ☎ 01684 565287 🖷 01684 565287
Dir: *on A449 from Worcester. Hillside on right at link top opposite common*
Located opposite the common on the town's outskirts, this attractive stone-faced Victorian house offers spacious homely bedrooms, and modern efficient bathrooms. Breakfast is taken in an attractive dining room and a small comfortable sitting room, which holds lots of local information, is available for guest use.
FACILITIES: 3 en suite No smoking in bedrooms No smoking in dining room TVB tea/coffee No dogs (ex guide dogs) Cen ht No children 10yrs No coaches **PRICES:** s £30-£44; d £44-£50✻ **NOTES:** Closed 14 Dec-4 Jan

♦♦♦ Sidney House Hotel

40 Worcester Rd WR14 4AA ☎ 01684 574994 🖷 01684 574994
Dir: *alongside A449 approx 200yds from town centre*
Located close to centre and offering commanding views over the Cotswolds, this constantly improving detached Georgian house offers comfortable, thoughtfully equipped bedrooms and a guest lounge with honesty bar.
FACILITIES: 8 rms (5 en suite) (1 fmly) No smoking in dining room TVB tea/coffee Licensed Cen ht TVL No coaches **PRICES:** s £20-£40; d £50-£60✻ **PARKING:** 9 **NOTES:** Closed 24 Dec - 3 Jan **CARDS:**

MARTLEY — Map 03 SO76

♦♦♦♦ Admiral Rodney Inn

Berrow Green WR6 6PL ☎ 01886 821375 🖷 01886 821375
e-mail: admiral@biimember.net
Dir: *turn off A44 at Knightwick onto B4197, Admiral Rodney approx 2m on left*
Located in the pretty village of Berrow Green, this 16th-century inn has been sympathetically renovated to provide high standards of comfort and facilities. Spacious, tastefully furnished bedrooms are complimented by luxurious modern bathrooms and ground floor areas include a unique tiered and beamed restaurant, where imaginative dishes are served.
FACILITIES: 3 en suite No smoking in dining room No smoking in 1 lounge TVB tea/coffee Direct dial from bedrooms No dogs (ex guide dogs) Cen ht No coaches Dinner Last d 9pm **PRICES:** d £55-£64✻ **MEALS:** Lunch £5-£14 Dinner £6-£15&alc✻ **PARKING:** 40 **CARDS:**

WORCESTER — Map 03 SO85

♦♦♦ Burgage House

4 College Precincts WR1 2LG ☎ 01905 25396 🖷 01905 25396
Dir: *M5 junct 7 towards city centre, at 5th traffic lights (inc. pedestrian crossings) turn left into Edgar St, College Precinct is pedestrian only street on the right*

Ideally located adjacent to the cathedral and many historical attractions, this impressive Georgian town house retains many original features which are enhanced by the décor and furnishing styles throughout. Bedrooms, one of which is located on the ground floor, are spacious and homely and an elegant dining room is the setting for comprehensive English breakfasts.
FACILITIES: 4 en suite (1 fmly) (1 GF) No smoking TVB tea/coffee No dogs Cen ht **PRICES:** s £30; d £55✻ **NOTES:** Closed 23-30 Dec

♦♦♦ Croft Guest House

WR6 5JD ☎ 01886 832227 🖷 01886 830037
Dir: *on A4103, 4m from Worcester, take Leigh/Alfrick exit from Bransford rdbt, drive is on left*
Ideally located for both city centre and the Malverns, parts of this cottage style property date from the 16th century and bedrooms provide a good balance between practicality and homeliness. Pretty gardens include a water feature and dogs are welcome, subject to current vaccination certificate.
FACILITIES: 5 rms (3 en suite) (1 fmly) No smoking in bedrooms TVB tea/coffee Licensed Cen ht TVL No coaches Arrangement with opposite golf course Dinner Last d 10am **PRICES:** s £22-£32; d £40-£55✻ **LB PARKING:** 5 **CARDS:**

♦♦♦ *Park House Guest Accommodation*

.2 Droitwich Rd WR3 7LJ ☎ 01905 21816

ir: *M5 junct 6, follow signs for Worcester North, after 4m take sharp left urn at 1st traffic lights. House 100yds on right*

.ocated within easy walking distance of the city centre, this large letached Victorian house is being steadily improved to highlight its original features. Bedrooms are practically equipped and a guest ounge is provided.

ACILITIES: 6 rms (3 en suite) (1 fmly) No smoking in bedrooms STV TVB ea/coffee No dogs (ex guide dogs) Licensed Cen ht TVL No coaches **PARKING:** 8

♦♦♦ Wyatt

0 Barbourne Rd WR1 1HU ☎ 01905 26311 📠 01905 26311

-mail: wyatt.guest@virgin.net

Dir: *M5 junct 6 follow signs for city centre (A449). At junction with A38 turn ight, house approx 0.25m on left*

.ocated within a few minutes walk from the city centre, this constantly improving Victorian house offers comfortable homely bedrooms, equipped with lots of thoughtful extras. Other areas nclude a traditionally furnished breakfast room and guest lounge.

ACILITIES: 8 rms (7 en suite) (4 fmly) (1 GF) No smoking in 2 bedrooms No smoking in dining room STV TVB tea/coffee Cen ht TVL **PRICES:** s £25-35; d £44-£48✱ **CARDS:**

YORKSHIRE, EAST RIDING OF

BEVERLEY — Map 08 TA03

See also Leven

Premier Collection

♦♦♦♦♦ Burton Mount Country House

Malton Rd, Cherry Burton HU17 7RA ☎ 01964 550541 📠 01964 551955

e-mail: pg@burtonmount.co.uk

Dir: *from M62 take South Cave route B1230 to Walkington, at traffic lights left for Matton. At rdbt take B1248 to Matton, at x-rds turn right, establishment 10yds on left*

A charming country house just two miles from Beverley, set in extensive gardens, and offering luxurious accommodation. Bedrooms are well equipped and have thoughtful extra touches. The spacious drawing room has a blazing fire in the cooler months, and an excellent, Aga-cooked Yorkshire breakfast is served in the morning room. Pauline Greenwood is renowned locally for her focused customer care, culinary skills and warm hospitality.

FACILITIES: 3 en suite No smoking STV TVB tea/coffee Cen ht No children 8yrs No coaches Croquet lawn Putting green Dinner Last d 4.30pm **PRICES:** s £59-£75; d £86-£106✱ **LB PARKING:** 20

♦♦♦ The Eastgate

7 Eastgate HU17 0DR ☎ 01482 868464 📠 01482 871899

Dir: *200yds from Beverley Minster*

This family run hotel provides modern decor and well-equipped bedrooms, together with comfortable public rooms. The helpful staff, who are always on hand, provides very friendly service. Please phone in advance for details of local parking facilities.

continued

The Eastgate Guest House

FACILITIES: 16 rms (7 en suite) (5 fmly) No smoking in bedrooms No smoking in dining room TVB tea/coffee Cen ht TVL **PRICES:** s £15-£33; d £30-£47✱ **LB BB**

BRIDLINGTON — Map 08 TA16

♦♦♦♦ Marton Grange

Flamborough Rd, Marton cum Sewerby YO15 1DU

☎ 01262 602034 📠 01262 602034

Dir: *on B1255, 600yds from Links golf club*

Surrounded by three acres of gardens, this substantial detached Georgian house has two elegant lounge areas and two dining rooms, one of which has an inglenook fireplace. All recently refurbished, the modern bedrooms vary in style, and all are spacious, have good beds and are suitably equipped. Staff are friendly and attentive.

FACILITIES: 11 en suite (2 fmly) (3 GF) No smoking TVB tea/coffee Licensed Lift Cen ht No children 12yrs No coaches Dinner Last d 10am **PRICES:** s £32-£40; d £52-£62 **PARKING:** 11

♦♦♦♦ The Mount Hotel

2 Roundhay Rd YO15 3JY ☎ 01262 672306 📠 01262 672306

Dir: *from the Spa South along South Marine Drive, after approx 100yds right along Belgrave Rd, at the end turn left. Hotel on right.*

A good night's sleep and a full stomach are both guaranteed at this substantial Victorian hotel. Bedrooms are clean, comfortable and prettily furnished. Home cooked five course meals are served in the bright dining room, and afterwards guests can relax in the lounge or enjoy a drink at the bar.

FACILITIES: 8 en suite (2 fmly) No smoking in dining room TVB tea/coffee No dogs (ex guide dogs) Licensed Cen ht TVL No coaches Dinner Last d 2pm **PRICES:** s £20-£23; d £40-£46✱ **LB PARKING:** 2

♦♦♦♦ Royal Hotel

1Shaftesbury Rd YO15 3NP ☎ 01262 672433 📠 01262 672433

Dir: *from Howden, A164 to Bridlington, South Bay Rd to Hull Road. Left towards Bridlington South Bay, past Broadacres pub on left, right at X-rds into Shaftesbury Road*

Family-run, this well established hotel extends a warm welcome to all guests. Stylishly furnished and decorated throughout, it has a spacious TV lounge, a well stocked bar and a large dining room with a conservatory extension. Bedrooms are clean, fresh and modern and some benefit from stunning sea views. Home-cooked meals are a highlight.

FACILITIES: 12 en suite 3 annexe en suite (3 fmly) No smoking in bedrooms No smoking in dining room No smoking in 1 lounge TVB tea/coffee No dogs (ex guide dogs) Licensed Cen ht TVL ch fac Pool Table Dinner Last d 6.30pm **PRICES:** s £26-£36; d £52✱ **LB CONF:** Class 34 Board 34 Del from £39 ✱ **PARKING:** 8

England

BRIDLINGTON continued

♦♦♦♦ Ryburn Hotel

31 Flamborough Rd YO15 2JH ☎ 01262 674098
📠 01262 674098

Dir: *in Bridlington follow signs to Leisure World. Past Leisure World and church on right Ryburn Hotel is on left*

This attractive Tudor style hotel sits in a prominent position just a short walk from the town centre. A variety of rooms are available, some are very large and are suitable for families, one is on the ground floor and two have private balconies. Public areas include a dining room and an attractive lounge.

FACILITIES: 10 rms (8 en suite) (4 fmly) (1 GF) No smoking TVB tea/coffee No dogs Licensed Cen ht No coaches Dinner Last d 1pm **PRICES:** s £22; d £50* **LB PARKING:** 4 **NOTES:** Closed Nov rs Nov-Etr

♦♦♦ Bay Ridge Hotel

Summerfield Rd YO15 3LF ☎ 01262 673425

Dir: *towards Bridlington off A614/A165 go to southside seafront. Premises in Summerfield Rd, off South Marine Drive which is the main south side seafront*

Family run and offering value for money accommodation, this very friendly guest house is located on a side road just off the sea front. Public areas are comfortable and consist of a spacious bar lounge, separate sitting room and well appointed dining room. The modern bedrooms are generously equipped and comfortable.

FACILITIES: 14 rms (12 en suite) (5 fmly) No smoking in dining room TVB tea/coffee No dogs (ex guide dogs) Licensed Cen ht TVL ch fac Bar billiards Library Darts Dinner Last d 5.45pm **PRICES:** s £22.50-£28.50; d £45-£57* **LB PARKING:** 6 **CARDS:**

♦♦♦ Langdon Hotel

13-16 Pembroke Ter YO15 3BX ☎ 01262 400124 & 673065
📠 01262 605377

Dir: *on a terrace facing sea between the harbour and Spa Royal Hall & Theatre*

Located opposite the Spa Theatre on the seafront, this family owned hotel offers pleasantly decorated, comfortable bedrooms. The reception rooms extend to a small garden porch, cosy bar and lounge where regular evening entertainment is held. Home cooked meals are served in the cheerful dining room.

FACILITIES: 30 en suite (10 fmly) No smoking in dining room TVB tea/coffee No dogs (ex guide dogs) Licensed Lift Cen ht Dinner Last d 4pm **PRICES:** s £20-£27; d £40-£58* **LB PARKING:** 5 **CARDS:**

♦♦♦ *Lansdowne House*

33 Lansdowne Rd YO15 2QT ☎ 01262 604184
e-mail: cynthbroadway@btinternet.com

Dir: *look for signs for Bridlington North Beach, then follow signs for Leisure World and opposite is a PH, The Greyhound, take road at side of Greyhound (Lansdowne Road) last house on left.*

Located in a residential area, not far from the town centre, Lansdowne House is a small and friendly guest house. Bedrooms are cosy and neatly decorated and a number of single rooms are available. Meals are served in the airy dining room and generous portions are guaranteed.

FACILITIES: 9 rms (4 en suite) (3 fmly) No smoking in dining room TVB tea/coffee No dogs (ex guide dogs) Cen ht TVL Dinner Last d 3pm

♦♦♦ Sandra's Guest House

6 Summerfield Rd, South Marine Dr YO15 3LF ☎ 01262 677791

Dir: *from town centre,2nd right turn off South Marine drive past Spa Royal Hall*

Close to both the South beach and the Spa Theatre this friendly guest house has been totally refurbished and offers immaculate accommodation and good home cooking. There is a comfortable lounge and the dining room includes a residents' bar.

continued

FACILITIES: 7 rms (6 en suite) (1 fmly) No smoking in dining room No smoking in 1 lounge TVB tea/coffee Licensed Cen ht TVL No coaches Dinner Last d 2pm **PRICES:** s £19.50-£24.50; d fr £39* **LB**

♦♦♦ Southdowne Hotel

78 South Marine Dr YO15 3NS ☎ 01262 673270

Benefiting from fine coastal views, this sea front hotel offers fresh, comfortable bedrooms that are simply furnished. English breakfasts and home cooked dinners are served in the bright and cheerful dining room and drinks from the bar can be enjoyed in the spacious lounge.

FACILITIES: 12 rms (8 en suite) (2 fmly) No smoking TV8B tea/coffee No dogs Licensed Cen ht TVL No coaches Dinner Last d 5.30pm **PRICES:** s fr £24; d fr £48* **PARKING:** 10

♦♦♦ Thiswilldo

31 St Hilda St YO15 3EE ☎ 01262 678270

Dir: *turn right off A166 onto A165, take town centre sign, after coach park on left take 2nd right into Windsor Crescent leading to St Hilda Street*

Pam Smith and Don Bashforth offer a warm and friendly welcome to this traditional guest house, which offers excellent value for money and sits in a residential area close to the shops. Bedrooms sizes vary, all are clean and comfortable. Substantial evening meals and breakfasts are served in the pleasant dining room adjacent to the cosy lounge.

FACILITIES: 5 rms (2 fmly) No smoking in dining room TVB tea/coffee No dogs (ex guide dogs) Licensed Cen ht TVL No coaches Dinner **PRICES:** s £15; d £30* **BB**

♦♦ Pembroke

6 Pembroke Ter YO15 3BX ☎ 01262 675643 📠 01262 678181

Dir: *between the harbour and the Spa Theatre*

Located in a prime position midway between the Spa and the harbour, this well established seaside guest house offers traditional accommodation. A variety of bedrooms are available and spectacular sea views can be enjoyed from the lounge. Meals are served in the basement dining room that also has a bar.

FACILITIES: 10 rms (8 en suite) No smoking in dining room TVB tea/coffee No dogs Licensed TVL Dinner Last d noon **PRICES:** s £20-£21; d £40-£42* **LB CARDS:**

HUGGATE — Map 08 SE85

♦♦♦ The Wolds Inn

Driffield Rd YO42 1YH ☎ 01377 288217 📠 01377 288217
e-mail: huggate@woldsinn.freeserve.co.uk

Dir: *follow signs to Huggate off A166, also brown signs to Wold Inn*

Nestling at the end of the highest village in the Yorkshire Wolds, and midway between York and the coastline, this ancient inn offers a rural haven beside the Wolds Way walk. Substantial meals are served in the dining room and a good range of well kept beers in the bar. Bedrooms, which vary in size, are well equipped and comfortable.

FACILITIES: 3 en suite TVB tea/coffee Cen ht Dinner Last d 9pm **PRICES:** s fr £25; d £35-£37; (room only) * **BB MEALS:** Lunch £8.95 Dinner £13.75-£20.10alc* **PARKING:** 50 **CARDS:**

HULL — Map 08 TA02

♦♦♦ Earlesmere Hotel

76/78 Sunnybank, Spring Bank West HU3 1LQ
☎ 01482 341977 📠 01482 473714
e-mail: su@earlsmerehotel.karoo.co.uk

Dir: *M62, under Humber bridge, left after 4m at Infirmary turn off, straight over 1st rdbt and traffic lights, turn left at next 2 T-juncts then 2nd street on left, Earlsmere is at the bottom*

continued

This friendly and comfortable small hotel is situated in a quiet location overlooking a college sports field. Bedrooms are well appointed and most have en suite facilities. There is a comfortable lounge and an attractive breakfast room. Ample street parking outside the hotel.
FACILITIES: 10 rms (7 en suite) (6 fmly) (2 GF) No smoking in dining room No smoking in lounges TVB tea/coffee Licensed Cen ht TVL
PRICES: s £20-£30; d £40-£45✱ **LB** **CARDS:**

LEVEN — Map 08 TA14

♦♦♦ The New Inn

44 South St HU17 5NZ ☎ 01964 542223 ℻ 01964 549828
Dir: *off A1035, 6m NE of Beverley*

A red brick inn built in the early 19th century, situated in the centre of the village. Three new modern bedrooms have been added, and all rooms are en suite. There is an attractive breakfast room and bars serving traditional ales. The property has ample car parking.
FACILITIES: 7 en suite (1 fmly) No smoking in 1 bedrooms No smoking in area of dining room TVB tea/coffee Cen ht TVL Golf 18 Dinner Last d 9pm
PRICES: s £23; d £35✱ **BB** **MEALS:** Dinner £5-£8✱ **PARKING:** 55
CARDS:

MARKET WEIGHTON — Map 08 SE84

♦♦♦ Robeanne House

Driffield Ln, Shiptonthorpe YO43 3PW ☎ 01430 873312
℻ 01430 873312
e-mail: robert@robeanne.freeserve.com
Conveniently located beside the A614, but set far enough back to be a quiet location, this delightful modern family home was built as a farmhouse. Dogs, cats and horses abound, and bedrooms include a large family room built over outbuildings.
FACILITIES: 3 en suite (2 fmly) No smoking in dining room No smoking in lounges TVB tea/coffee Cen ht No coaches Dinner Last d 24hrs prior
CARDS:

SLEDMERE — Map 08 SE96

♦♦♦ Triton

YO25 3XQ ☎ 01377 236644
e-mail: thetritoninn@sledmere.fsbusiness.co.uk
Dir: *leave A166 at Garton-on-the-Wolds onto B1252 signed Sledmere House. Inn on left opposite road junct to Luttons & adjacent to Sledmere House*
Dating back to the 18th-century this delightful coaching inn is situated in the centre of the village, close to Sledmere House. Public areas include an oak-panelled bar, a poolroom and a cosy dining room where a good selection of home-made food is available. The service is friendly and attentive.

continued

FACILITIES: 5 rms (2 en suite) No smoking in bedrooms No smoking in dining room TVB tea/coffee No dogs (ex guide dogs) Cen ht Pool Table Dinner Last d 9pm **PRICES:** s £24-£29; d £44-£52✱ **LB** **MEALS:** Lunch £8.35-£14.50alc Dinner £10.65-£18.70alc✱ **PARKING:** 35
CARDS:

SOUTH CAVE — Map 08 SE93

♦♦♦♦ The Fox and Coney Inn

52 Market Place HU15 2AT ☎ 01430 422275 ℻ 01430 421552
e-mail: foxandconey@aol.com
Dir: *At eastern end of M62 follow A63 to 1st junct, left off junct into South Cave, hotel on right after clock tower.*
Standing in the centre of the village, this friendly inn provides modern, attractive bedrooms, which vary in size and are split between the main building and the adjoining annexe. An extensive range of food is available, either in the bar or in the dining room. The pleasant staff create a relaxed, informal atmosphere.
FACILITIES: 12 en suite (3 fmly) No smoking in 6 bedrooms No smoking in dining room No smoking in 1 lounge STV TVB tea/coffee Direct dial from bedrooms Cen ht Dinner Last d 9.30pm **PRICES:** s fr £42; d fr £55✱ **LB**
MEALS: Lunch £4-£6 Dinner £4-£20✱ **PARKING:** 21
CARDS:

♦♦♦♦ Rudstone Walk

South Cave HU15 2AH ☎ 01430 422230 ℻ 01430 424552
e-mail: office@rudstone-walk.co.uk
Dir: *M62 junct 38, take A1034 to South Cave. Turn right onto B1230. Rudstone Walk 200yds on left*

A delightful complex, in which there is a very comfortable lounge, a charming little bar and a beautiful farmhouse dining room. Dinner is available by prior arrangement. Comfortable and very tastefully furnished bedrooms have been converted from some of the old stables. There is a walled courtyard garden. One room has special facilities for the disabled.
FACILITIES: 14 en suite (3 fmly) (10 GF) No smoking in 10 bedrooms No smoking in dining room STV TVB tea/coffee Direct dial from bedrooms Licensed Cen ht Dinner Last d 7pm **PRICES:** s £40-£46; d £55-£59✱ **LB**
CONF: Thtr 50 Class 30 Board 26 Del from £80 ✱ **PARKING:** 50
NOTES: rs 24 Dec-2 Jan **CARDS:**

Super supper! this symbol shows that evening meals exceeded our Inspector's expectations.

England

WINESTEAD Map 08 TA22

♦♦♦ *Farm House B & B (TA293240)*
Park Farm HU12 0NJ ☎ 01964 630348 📠 01964 630348
Mr B R Croft
e-mail: brcroftson@winstead.fslife.co.uk
Dir: *A1033 from Hull to Withernsea Road, travel East through village of Ottringham, pass Red Hall Engineering on right, approx. 0.5m further 1st right*
To stay on a working farm such as this is a rare opportunity. The Croft family offer a friendly welcome and the bedrooms are comfortable and quiet. There is a comfortable lounge/breakfast room, and a fully equipped resident's kitchen/utility room. An ideal location for twitchers, fishing, city shopping, and the nearby seaside or ferry terminals.
FACILITIES: 3 rms (1 en suite) (1 fmly) No smoking TVB tea/coffee No dogs (ex guide dogs) Cen ht TVL No children 5yrs Tennis (grass) Fishing 300 acres mixed **PARKING:** 6

WOLD NEWTON Map 08 TA07

Premier Collection

♦♦♦♦♦ The Wold Cottage *(TA042723)*
YO25 3HL ☎ 01262 470696 📠 01262 470696 Mrs K Gray
e-mail: katrina@woldcottage.com
Dir: *from B1249 towards Wold Newton, turn right by pond, round double bend, 1st right, past bungalow, 200yds to farmhouse*

Enjoying extensive views across Wolds countryside, this skilfully restored Georgian farmhouse is delightfully furnished throughout. Bedrooms are comfortable - one has a four-poster bed and spa bath - and the two rooms in the barn conversion are very spacious. The lounge has a log fire, TV and music centre. Freshly cooked breakfasts and evening meals (by arrangement) are served in the charming dining room. A monument in the grounds marks the spot where a meteorite landed in 1795.
FACILITIES: 5 rms (3 en suite) (1 fmly) (1 GF) No smoking tea/coffee No dogs Cen ht TVL Croquet lawn Jacuzzi 450 acres arable sheep beef Dinner Last d Day before **PRICES:** d £52-£70 **LB** **PARKING:** 6
CARDS:

A indicates an Associate entry, which has been inspected and rated by the ETC or the RAC in England.

YORKSHIRE, NORTH

AMPLEFORTH Map 08 SE57

Premier Collection

♦♦♦♦♦ Shallowdale House
West End YO62 4DY ☎ 01439 788325 📠 01439 788885
e-mail: stay@shallowdalehouse.demon.co.uk
Dir: *from Thirsk on A19, through Coxwold & Wass. Or B1363 from York turn left at Brandsby. Or A170 (Thirsk to Helmsley) turn 4m from Sutton Bank*

An outstanding example of an architect-designed 1960s house, Shallowdale lies in two acres of hillside gardens. Stunning views are enjoyed from every room, and the elegant public rooms include a choice of lounges. Spacious bedrooms blend their 60s style with vibrant soft furnishings and traditional home comforts. Dinner is a freshly cooked four-course meal.
FACILITIES: 3 en suite No smoking TVB tea/coffee No dogs (ex guide dogs) Licensed Cen ht No children 12yrs No coaches Dinner Last d noon **PRICES:** s £45-£55; d £70-£84 **LB** **PARKING:** 3
NOTES: Closed Xmas/New Year 70 **CARDS:**

ASKRIGG Map 07 SD99

♦♦♦♦ Whitfield
Helm DL8 3JF ☎ 01969 650565 📠 01969 650565
e-mail: empsall@askrigg.yorks.net
Dir: *off A684 at Bainbridge by Rose & Crown Hotel, signed Askrigg, over river to T-junc, 150mtrs to No Through Road sign, left up hill for 0.5m*
Formerly a barn built from Yorkshire limestone, this traditionally furnished house enjoys a peaceful fell side location. Both bedrooms are well equipped and comfortable and enjoy stunning views of the Yorkshire countryside. Hearty breakfasts are served around a communal table in the inviting open-plan lounge/dining room.
FACILITIES: 2 en suite No smoking TVB tea/coffee Cen ht TVL No coaches **PRICES:** s £21-£24; d £48✳ **LB** **PARKING:** 1 **NOTES:** Closed 23 - 27 Dec. 70 **CARDS:**

AYSGARTH Map 07 SE08

♦♦♦♦ Stow House Hotel
DL8 3SR ☎ 01969 663635
e-mail: info@stowhouse.co.uk
Dir: *7m W of Leyburn on A684, 0.6m before Aysgarth village*
Nestling in its own grounds, set back from the road, this imposing Victorian house is delightfully furnished and decorated throughout. Bedrooms, most with fabulous views of the Yorkshire Dales, are bright and homely. The smart dining room is the venue for hearty, carefully prepared breakfasts. Dinner is available by prior arrangement.

continued

FACILITIES: 9 en suite (1 GF) No smoking in bedrooms No smoking in dining room TVB tea/coffee Licensed Cen ht No coaches Tennis (grass) Croquet lawn Dinner Last d 4pm **PRICES:** s £33-£41; d £66-£74 **LB** **PARKING:** 10 **CARDS:**

BEDALE

Map 08 SE28

Premier Collection

♦♦♦♦♦ Elmfield Country House

Arrathorne DL8 1NE ☎ 01677 450558 📠 01677 450557
e-mail: stay@elmfieldhouse.freeserve.co.uk
Dir: *from A1 follow A684 through Bedale towards Leyburn. After Patrick Brompton turn right towards Richmond. Premises 1.5m on right*

Originally a gamekeeper's cottage, and now tastefully extended, Elmfield enjoys uninterrupted views of the surrounding countryside. The modern bedrooms are generally spacious and superbly equipped. The attractive public rooms are also well-proportioned and offer an elegant lounge with a small corner bar, as well as a conservatory/games room. Outdoor activities can also be arranged.
FACILITIES: 11 en suite (2 fmly) (4 GF) No smoking in 6 bedrooms No smoking in dining room STV TVB tea/coffee Direct dial from bedrooms No dogs (ex guide dogs) Licensed Cen ht Fishing Solarium Pool Table Paintballing, Quads, Gdn Chess, play area, 4 wd Dinner Last d before noon **PRICES:** s £37.50; d £55-£70✻ **LB** **CONF:** Board 40 **PARKING:** 20 **CARDS:**

♦♦♦♦ Upsland Farm *(SE267818)*

Kirklington DL8 2PA ☎ 01845 567709 📠 01845 567709
Mr & Mrs L Hodgson
Dir: *from A1 take B6267 towards Masham, farm 2.2m from A1 on B6267 on L. Set back from road.*
A warm welcome awaits guests at this delightful farmhouse, peacefully located in its own beautiful grounds, within easy reach of Masham and Beadle. There is a spacious, inviting lounge and a smart dining room where hearty breakfasts are served. Stylish bedrooms are all and smartly appointed and benefit from stunning views.
FACILITIES: 3 en suite No smoking TVB tea/coffee Cen ht TVL Fishing Croquet lawn 45 acres mixed Dinner Last d noon **PRICES:** d fr £55✻ **LB** **PARKING:** 4 **NOTES:** Closed Xmas

♦♦♦♦ Castle Arms

Snape DL8 2TB ☎ 01677 470270 📠 01677 470837
e-mail: castlearms@aol.com
Dir: *A1 to Leeming Bar, then A684 to Bedale and B6268 to Masham. After 2m turn left signed Thorp Perrow Arboretum. 1m past arboretum left into Snape*
This inn dates from the 14th century and is located in the heart of the quiet village of Snape. Bright bedrooms, with pine furnishings, are housed in a converted barn, complete with wooden beams.
continued

Dinner and breakfast are taken in the bar where a wide range of real ales can be enjoyed.

Castle Arms

FACILITIES: 9 annexe en suite No smoking in bedrooms No smoking in dining room TVB tea/coffee Cen ht No coaches Dinner Last d 8.30pm **PRICES:** s £47.50; d £62.50 **LB** **MEALS:** Lunch £12-£18alc Dinner £12-£25alc **PARKING:** 15 **CARDS:**

♦♦♦ Southfield

96 Southend DL8 2DS ☎ 01677 423510
Dir: *A1 northbound, at Leeming Motel take A684 to Bedale. Turn left at White Bear pub. 400yds on right, fronted by white stones*
Located in a residential area on the edge of town, this family run guesthouse extends a warm and friendly welcome to all guests. Bedrooms are traditionally furnished and decorated, and are equipped with many thoughtful touches. Guests are free to enjoy the delightful lounge and neatly tended garden. This is a no-smoking house.
FACILITIES: 4 rms (2 en suite) No smoking tea/coffee No dogs (ex guide dogs) Cen ht TVL No coaches **PRICES:** s £22; d £44✻ **PARKING:** 4

BOROUGHBRIDGE

Map 08 SE36

♦♦♦ The Crown Inn

Roecliffe YO51 9LY ☎ 01423 322578 📠 01423 324060
e-mail: crownroecliffe@btinternet.com
Dir: *A1 junct 48 take Boroughbridge exit, at 1st rdbt take A1 Dishforth/Ripon. In 1m at next rdbt exit to Roecliffe. Inn on village green*
Lying in a quiet village just a mile off the A1, this old inn boasts modern, well appointed bedrooms which will appeal to the business traveller as well as the tourist. Imaginative menus are served in both the bar and restaurant.
FACILITIES: 3 en suite 6 annexe en suite (2 fmly) (3 GF) No smoking in 3 bedrooms No smoking in dining room TVB tea/coffee Direct dial from bedrooms TVL Pool Table Dinner Last d 9.30pm **PRICES:** s £30-£35; d £45-£80✻ **LB** **PARKING:** 30 **CARDS:**

BURNSALL

Map 07 SE06

♦♦♦ Burnsall Manor House Hotel

Main St BD23 6BW ☎ 01756 720231 📠 720231
e-mail: joe@manorhouseuk.co.uk
Dir: *on B6160. Village between Grassington & Bolton Abbey*
A warm welcome awaits you at this 19th-century house, situated on the River Wharfe. Bedrooms are traditionally furnished and have delightful views. The freshly prepared meals can be enjoyed in the spacious dining room. There is also a cosy bar, TV lounge, and in the warmer months, the large garden provides a peaceful venue in which to relax.
FACILITIES: 8 rms (7 en suite) No smoking tea/coffee Licensed Cen ht TVL Fishing Croquet lawn Dinner Last d 5pm **PRICES:** d £49-£57✻ **LB** **PARKING:** 9 **CARDS:**

England

BURNT YATES Map 08 SE26

♦♦♦♦ The New Inn

Pateley Bridge Rd HG3 3EG ☎ 01423 771070 📠 01423 771070
e-mail: enquiries@newinnburntyates.co.uk
Dir: *from Harrogate take A61 to Ripon. Go through Killinghall to Ripley. At 2nd Ripley rdbt follow sign for Pately Bridge (B6165) after approx 2.5m New Inn on right at Clint Bank x-roads*

FACILITIES: 8 en suite (1 fmly) No smoking in bedrooms No smoking in dining room TVB tea/coffee Direct dial from bedrooms No dogs (ex guide dogs) Licensed Cen ht Dinner Last d 8.30 pm **PRICES:** s fr £50; d fr £60✱ **LB PARKING:** 40 **CARDS:**

CARPERBY Map 07 SE08

♦♦♦ Wheatsheaf Hotel

DL8 4DF ☎ 01969 663216 📠 01969 663019
e-mail: wheatsheaf@paulmit.globalnet.co.uk
Dir: *from A1 take west route on A684 to Wensley, right turn signposted Castle Bolton. Next village is Carperby*

The Wheatsheaf is a typical Dales hotel and offers comfortable accommodation. The bedrooms are pleasantly furnished and include two with attractive four-poster beds. The comfortable lounge features a 17th-century stone fireplace. Guests can enjoy good home cooking, from extensive menus in either the cosy bar or the dining room.

FACILITIES: 8 en suite (1 fmly) No smoking in 1 bedrooms No smoking in dining room TVB tea/coffee Licensed Cen ht No coaches Fishing Dinner Last d 9pm **PRICES:** s £27.50; d £55-£65✱ **LB PARKING:** 40 **CARDS:**

CATTERICK Map 08 SE29

♦♦♦ Rose Cottage

26 High St DL10 7LJ ☎ 01748 811164
Dir: *5m S of Scotch Corner, take A6136 off A1 into Catterick Village. House opp newsagents*

Convenient for the Dales and Moors, this small and friendly stone built guest house lies in the middle of Catterick Village. The neatly decorated bedrooms are simply furnished and offer good levels of comfort. Breakfast is served in the cottage style dining room; dinner can be arranged during the summer months.

FACILITIES: 4 rms (2 en suite) (1 fmly) No smoking in dining room TVB tea/coffee Cen ht No coaches Dinner Last d 9.30am **PRICES:** s £24-£29; d £39-£45 **PARKING:** 4 **NOTES:** Closed 24-26 Dec

CLOUGHTON Map 08 TA09

♦♦♦ *Blacksmiths Arms*

High St YO13 0AE ☎ 01723 870244
Dir: *6m N of Scarborough on A171 towards Whitby*

Within easy reach of Scarborough, this inn features attractive, smartly furnished bedrooms, four of which are in converted stone buildings and have their own private entrances. A good range of dishes is served in the bar and dining room.

FACILITIES: 6 en suite (1 fmly) No smoking in bedrooms TVB tea/coffee No dogs (ex guide dogs) Cen ht No coaches Last d 9.45pm **PARKING:** 35 **CARDS:**

DARLEY Map 08 SE25

♦♦♦♦ Elsinglea Guest House

Sheepcote Ln HG3 2RW ☎ 01423 781069 📠 01423 780189
Dir: *A59 towards Skipton, leave A59 onto B6451 towards Pateley Bridge, the 2nd right into Sheepcote Lane & 1st house on the right*

"Small is beautiful" aptly describes Elsinglea, set amidst rolling countryside yet just a short drive from Harrogate. Recently converted from a barn, many original features have been retained to offer a charming country cottage style. Bedrooms are not large but are full of character, with super en suites. Hospitable owners offer tea with homemade cakes.

FACILITIES: 3 en suite (1 GF) No smoking TVB tea/coffee No dogs Cen ht No children 15 **PRICES:** s £30-£35; d £45-£48✱ **PARKING:** 5

EASINGWOLD Map 08 SE56

♦♦♦ Stillington Mill

Mill Ln, Stillington YO61 1NG ☎ 01347 810161
📠 01347 810265
Dir: *from York on A19 towards Easingwold, R & 4m to Stillington. Or on B1363, in Sutton-on-the-Forest R to Stillington, R at garage - Farlington, Mill 0.2m.*

In a rural setting on the edge of Stillington village, this renovated mill has been modernised, retaining many original features. Good family accommodation is available and hearty breakfasts are served overlooking the millpond, which is a haven for wildlife. Guests have the use of a covered swimming pool and a tennis court in the summer.

FACILITIES: 4 en suite (2 fmly) No smoking TVB tea/coffee No dogs Cen ht TVL No coaches Indoor swimming pool (heated) Tennis (hard) Pool Table Games room Half size snooker Dinner Last d before 10am
PRICES: d £40✱ **LB PARKING:** 5

ESCRICK Map 08 SE64

♦♦♦♦ Church Cottage

York Rd YO19 6EX ☎ 01904 728462 📠 01904 728896
e-mail: churchcottage@rgm.co.uk
Dir: *A19, S of York, 5m from A64 York ringroad. 1st property on right on entering Escrick*

In its own stunning grounds, next to the church, this attractive stone guest house boasts well-equipped accommodation of generous proportions. There is a modern, airy lounge where guests can enjoy pre-dinner drinks from the bar, before dining in the Thai restaurant. Conveniently situated for York and Leeds.

continued

FACILITIES: 7 en suite (3 fmly) No smoking TVB tea/coffee No dogs (ex guide dogs) Licensed Cen ht No coaches Dinner **PRICES:** s £50-£60; d £75-£85* **PARKING:** 20 **CARDS:**

♦♦♦ Black Bull Inn

Main St YO19 6JP ☎ 01904 728245 📠 01904 728154

Dir: *from York follow A19 S for 5m, enter Escrick, take 2nd left up main street, premises on left*

Just a few miles from York in the picturesque village of Escrick, the Black Bull Inn is popular with both locals and visitors. Freshly cooked meals can be taken in the main bar area, while breakfast is served in an adjacent dining room. All bedrooms are well equipped. One has a sunken bath, while another boasts a superb four-poster bed.

FACILITIES: 10 en suite (2 fmly) No smoking in bedrooms No smoking in dining room TVB tea/coffee No dogs (ex guide dogs) Cen ht TVL Dinner Last d 9.30pm **PRICES:** s £40-£42* **LB MEALS:** Lunch £6.50-£10alc Dinner £10.75-£18.50alc* **PARKING:** 15 **CARDS:**

FILEY — Map 08 TA18

♦♦♦♦ Gables

Rutland St YO14 9JB ☎ 01723 514750

e-mail: kate_gables@talk21.com

Dir: *leave A165 at Filey, right in town centre into West Ave, 2nd left into Rutland St. On corner opp church*

Located in a quiet residential area, just a short stroll from the centre and promenade, this smart Edwardian house extends a warm welcome to all guests. Bedrooms are brightly decorated and well-equipped and some are suitable for families. Breakfasts are substantial and a varied evening meal menu is available.

FACILITIES: 5 en suite (1 fmly) No smoking in 2 bedrooms No smoking in dining room TVB tea/coffee Cen ht No coaches Tennis (hard) Dinner Last d 3pm **PRICES:** s £25; d £40* **LB PARKING:** 3 **CARDS:**

♦♦♦ Abbots Leigh

7 Rutland St YO14 9JA ☎ 01723 513334

e-mail: barbara_abbots@yahoo.com

Dir: *from A165 follow signs for town centre, then turn right at church clock tower, then 2nd left*

Located on a quiet Victorian terrace, within a minute's walk of the Promenade, this cosy guest house offers modern bedrooms that are comfortable and well equipped. A small lounge is also provided. Friendly hospitality and service are assured and housekeeping is very good.

FACILITIES: 6 en suite (1 fmly) No smoking in bedrooms No smoking in dining room No smoking in 1 lounge TVB tea/coffee No dogs (ex guide dogs) Licensed Cen ht TVL No children 3yrs No coaches Dinner Last d noon **PRICES:** s £23.50-£25.50; d £37-£41* **LB BB PARKING:** 4 **CARDS:**

♦♦♦ Seafield Hotel

9/11 Rutland St YO14 9JA ☎ 01723 513715

Dir: *exit A64 signposted to Filey, at crossroads in town centre turn right, 2nd left into Rutland St*

Just a short stroll from the seafront, this attractive mid-terraced hotel offers bright and freshly decorated bedrooms. A residents' bar/lounge and a second lounge are provided as well as a dining room adorned with a number of paintings and photographs. Good home-cooking is served.

FACILITIES: 15 en suite (7 fmly) (1 GF) No smoking in bedrooms No smoking in dining room No smoking in 1 lounge TVB tea/coffee No dogs Licensed Cen ht TVL No coaches Dinner Last d 4pm **PRICES:** s £18.50-£20.50; d £37-£41* **LB BB PARKING:** 8 **CARDS:**

FLIXTON — Map 08 TA07

♦♦♦♦ Orchard Lodge

Ness Cottage, North St YO11 3UA ☎ 01723 890202 📠 01723 890202

e-mail: don.pummell@onyxnet.co.uk

Dir: *on A64 from York, take A1039 Filey Road at Staxton rdbt. Flixton is 1st village on this road. At T junct in the centre take left turning, Orchard Lodge is on left*

Just off the main road through Flixton, this B&B offers newly built, spacious and comfortable bedrooms. In an ideal location for touring the coast or the Wolds, yet only five miles from the centre of Scarborough. Connie's home-made preserves crown a hearty breakfast. Orchard Lodge is a no-smoking residence.

FACILITIES: 6 en suite No smoking TVB tea/coffee No dogs (ex guide dogs) Cen ht No children No coaches **PRICES:** s fr £40; d fr £50* **LB PARKING:** 8 **NOTES:** Closed Jan **CARDS:**

GIGGLESWICK — Map 07 SD86

♦♦♦ Black Horse Hotel

32 Church St BD24 0BE ☎ 01729 822506 📠 01729 822506

e-mail: blackhorse@giggleswick.freeserve.co.uk

Dir: *off A65 Giggleswick to Settle. Inn next to St Alkelda church in village centre*

Nestling peacefully beside the church, this popular inn offers comfortable, homely bedrooms. A roaring log fire provides a welcoming focal point in the bar at cooler times of the year. There is a wood-panelled dining room that has a good reputation for freshly prepared meals.

FACILITIES: 3 en suite No smoking in bedrooms No smoking in dining room TVB tea/coffee No dogs Cen ht No coaches Dinner Last d 8.45pm **PRICES:** s £32-£38; d £52-£72* **MEALS:** Lunch £15-£25alc Dinner £15-£25alc* **PARKING:** 15 **CARDS:**

♦♦♦ *Woodlands*

The Mains BD24 0AX ☎ 01729 822058 📠 01729 822058

Standing on the edge of the village, and benefiting from stunning views, Woodlands is ideally situated for the scenic Settle to Carlisle railway. The simply furnished bedrooms are thoughtfully equipped, and there is combined lounge and dining room where home cooked meals are served.

FACILITIES: 3 en suite (1 fmly) No smoking in dining room No smoking in lounges TVB tea/coffee Licensed Cen ht TVL Dinner Last d 10am **PARKING:** 10 **NOTES:** Closed Xmas

England

GOATHLAND Map 08 NZ80

♦♦♦ Fairhaven Country Hotel

The Common YO22 5AN ☎ 01947 896361 📠 01947 896099
e-mail: royellis@thefairhavenhotel.co.uk
Dir: *from A169 follow signs for Goathland. Fairhaven is on road that runs through village, between North Yorkshire Moors Railway station and St Marys Church*

In the centre of 'Heartbeat' country, this family-run, Edwardian hotel stands in the village of Goathland. Public areas are extensive and include a spacious lounge, separate bar and well appointed dining room where good home cooking is a feature. Bedrooms vary in size and style and are all comfortable with private facilities.
FACILITIES: 9 en suite (4 fmly) No smoking TV7B tea/coffee Licensed Cen ht TVL No coaches Dinner Last d noon **PRICES:** s £26-£27; d £56* **PARKING:** 9 **CARDS:**

GRASSINGTON Map 07 SE06

Premier Collection

♦♦♦♦♦ Ashfield House Hotel

Summers Fold BD23 5AE ☎ 01756 752584
📠 01756 752584
e-mail: info@ashfieldhouse.co.uk
Dir: *take B6265 to village centre then turn left off Main St into Summers Fold*

Guests are greeted like old friends at this beautifully maintained 17th-century house, peacefully tucked away a few yards from the village square. Smartly presented lounges offer a high level of comfort where guests can relax or enjoy pre-dinner drinks from an honesty bar. A freshly prepared four-course dinner is available by arrangement (except for Saturdays) and is a highlight of any stay. Bedrooms are attractively decorated, well furnished and thoughtfully equipped.

continued

FACILITIES: 7 en suite No smoking TVB tea/coffee No dogs (ex guide dogs) Licensed Cen ht No children 5yrs No coaches Dinner Last d 3pm **PRICES:** s £35-£60; d £70 **LB** **PARKING:** 7 **NOTES:** Closed Xmas & 1 wk Mar rs Jan & early Feb **CARDS:**

Premier Collection

♦♦♦♦♦ Grassington Lodge

8 Wood Ln BD23 5LU ☎ 01756 752518 📠 01756 752518
e-mail: relax@grassingtonlodge.co.uk
Dir: *take B6265 North from Skipton, after 8m turn right in Threshfield, continue for 1m then left at garages, located 100yds on right*

This impressive house was built in 1898 and is now the thoughtfully furnished and welcoming home of Sandra and Michael Wade. The stylish bedrooms are comfortably and attractively furnished and are equipped with a host of thoughtful extras. On chilly days a log fire blazes in the guest lounge; Sandra's excellent breakfasts are served in the separate dining room. Grassington Lodge is a no-smoking establishment.
FACILITIES: 7 en suite No smoking TVB tea/coffee No dogs (ex guide dogs) Cen ht No children 7yrs No coaches **PRICES:** s fr £32; d £64-£72* **LB** **BB** **PARKING:** 8 **NOTES:** Closed Xmas

GREAT AYTON Map 08 NZ51

♦♦♦ *Royal Oak Hotel*

123 High St TS9 6BW ☎ 01642 722361 & 723270
📠 01642 724047

Well-equipped and cosy bedrooms are provided at this 18th-century former coaching inn, which is very popular with the locals. An extensive range of food is available and is served in the bar or the dining room.
FACILITIES: 5 rms (4 en suite) TVB tea/coffee Direct dial from bedrooms Cen ht Dinner Last d 9.30pm **CARDS:**

GREAT BARUGH Map 08 SE77

Barugh House

YO17 6UZ ☎ 01653 668615
At the time of going to press the Diamond classification for this establishment had not been confirmed. Please check the AA website www.theAA.com for up-to-date information.
FACILITIES: 2 en suite

HARROGATE Map 08 SE35

Premier Collection

♦♦♦♦♦ *Ruskin Hotel*

1 Swan Rd HG1 2SS ☎ 01423 502045 01423 506131
e-mail: ruskin.hotel@virgin.net
Dir: *off A61, Ripon road. Turn L opposite The Majestic*

This delightful hotel has bedrooms that are stylishly decorated and furnished with Victorian pine; one has a beautiful four-poster bed and another its own separate entrance. The drawing room looks out over the neatly maintained garden and the elegant dining room opens out onto the terrace. Delicious light suppers are available by prior arrangement.
FACILITIES: 7 en suite (2 fmly) No smoking in bedrooms No smoking in dining room TVB tea/coffee Direct dial from bedrooms Licensed Cen ht No coaches Arrangement for guests to use local leisure centre Dinner Last d 7pm **PARKING:** 9 **CARDS:**

♦♦♦♦ Kimberley Hotel

11-19 Kings Rd HG1 5JY ☎ 01423 505613 01423 530276
e-mail: info@thekimberley.co.uk
Dir: *follow signs for Harrogate International Centre or Kings Rd, premises on left approx 150yds past the centre*
This is a large hotel located on Kings Road close to the conference centre. Facilities include a well-stocked bar, cosy lounge and choice of conference rooms. There is also a lift to each floor. Bedrooms have an impressive range of accessories and larger suites are available. Breakfast is served buffet style.
FACILITIES: 48 en suite (3 fmly) (15 GF) No smoking in 2 bedrooms No smoking in dining room STV TVB tea/coffee Direct dial from bedrooms No dogs (ex guide dogs) Licensed Lift Cen ht **PRICES:** s £60-£74.50; d £70-£94.50; (room only) ✳ **LB** **CONF:** Thtr 40 Class 16 Board 26 Del £95 ✳ **PARKING:** 50 **CARDS:**

♦♦♦♦ Acacia Lodge

21 Ripon Rd HG1 2JL ☎ 01423 560752 01423 503725
Dir: *on A61, 600yds N of town centre*
Old paintings and antiques characterise this charming Victorian house. The comfortable bedrooms are very well-appointed, and include a separate two bedroom family suite that benefits from its own private entrance. Delicious breakfasts use local produce and are served in the oak-furnished dining room. Acacia Lodge is ideally located for the conference centre, town and valley gardens.
FACILITIES: 6 en suite (3 fmly) No smoking TVB tea/coffee No dogs (ex guide dogs) Cen ht TVL No children 10yrs No coaches **PRICES:** s £50-£68; d £64-£75✳ **PARKING:** 7 **NOTES:** Closed 6 Dec-6 Jan

♦♦♦♦ Alexa House & Stable Cottages

26 Ripon Rd HG1 2JJ ☎ 01423 501988 01423 504086
e-mail: alexahouse@msn.com
Dir: *on A61, 0.25m from junction of A59/A61*
This busy hotel offers stylish, well-equipped bedrooms, boasting mini-bars and thick duvets, while rooms in converted stables provide extra space and comfort. Memorable, skilfully prepared dinners are served, and the hearty cooked breakfasts have a fine reputation. Opulent day rooms include an elegant lounge with honesty bar, and a bright dining room. Hands-on proprietors ensure high levels of customer care at every turn.
FACILITIES: 9 en suite 4 annexe en suite (2 fmly) No smoking in bedrooms No smoking in dining room TVB tea/coffee Direct dial from bedrooms No dogs (ex guide dogs) Licensed Cen ht TVL No coaches Dinner Last d 10am on the day **PRICES:** s £45-£55; d £65-£80✳ **LB** **PARKING:** 10 **CARDS:**

♦♦♦♦ April House

3 Studley Rd HG1 5JU ☎ 01423 561879 01423 548149
e-mail: info@aprilhouse.com
Dir: *Follow signs for Harrogate International Centre. Moat House Hotel adjoins. Alexandra Road opposite, April House at top of road on right.*
Located in a quiet residential area, although just a short walk from the Conference Centre, this impeccably maintained, late-Victorian house retains many original features. Bedrooms are comfortable and include an array of homely touches. Breakfast is served in the attractively appointed dining room.
FACILITIES: 5 en suite (1 fmly) No smoking TVB tea/coffee No dogs (ex guide dogs) TVL No coaches **PRICES:** s £25-£30; d £50-£65✳ **LB** **CARDS:**

♦♦♦♦ Ashley House Hotel

36-40 Franklin Rd HG1 5EE ☎ 01423 507474 01423 560858
e-mail: ashleyhousehotel@btinternet.com
Dir: *on entering Harrogate follow signs for conference centre. Opposite centre turn into Strawberry Dale Ave, left into Franklin Rd, premises on right*
Stylishly decorated and furnished throughout, this immaculate hotel has been sympathetically converted from three Victorian townhouses. Attractive bedrooms are superbly equipped and public areas extend to an attractive lounge with leather armchairs and tartan bar lounge that boasts an extensive collection of whiskies. Its quiet location is in close proximity to the town and conference centre.
FACILITIES: 18 en suite (1 fmly) (2 GF) No smoking in 5 bedrooms No smoking in dining room No smoking in lounges TVB tea/coffee Direct dial from bedrooms Licensed Cen ht Dinner Last d by prior arrangement **PRICES:** s £42.50-£75; d £65-£85✳ **LB** **PARKING:** 4 **CARDS:**

England

HARROGATE continued

♦♦♦♦ Ashwood House

7 Spring Grove HG1 2HS ☎ 01423 560081 📠 01423 527928
e-mail: ashwoodhouse@aol.com
Dir: *off A61, from Ripon Rd turn into Springfield Ave, 3rd left into Spring Grove, premises on left*

Delightfully decorated and furnished throughout, this substantial Edwardian house is situated in a quiet area of town. The spacious, well-appointed bedrooms are all individually furnished and thoughtfully equipped and one has a four-poster bed. There is a cosy lounge and an elegant dining room, in which full English breakfasts are served.
FACILITIES: 6 en suite (1 fmly) No smoking TVB tea/coffee No dogs Cen ht TVL No children 7yrs No coaches **PRICES:** s £35-£37; d £55-£58✻ **LB**
PARKING: 5 **NOTES:** Closed Xmas/New Year

♦♦♦♦ Britannia Lodge

16 Swan Rd HG1 2SA ☎ 01423 508482 📠 01423 526840
e-mail: info@britannia.harrogate.co.uk
Dir: *from S follow signs for Town Centre, down hill, through lights and 1st left to Swan Rd*
Recently refurbished throughout, this Grade II listed townhouse combines traditional elegance with modern design. In the main house the airy, spacious bedrooms, many of which boast king sized beds, are individually decorated and tastefully furnished with many period pieces. A lower floor self contained suite is available for families or colleagues. Breakfast is served around a communal table.
FACILITIES: 3 en suite 2 annexe en suite No smoking TVB tea/coffee No dogs (ex guide dogs) Licensed Cen ht No coaches **PRICES:** d £80-£100✻
CARDS:

♦♦♦♦ Camberley Hotel

52-54 Kings Rd HG1 5JR ☎ 01423 561618 📠 01423 536360
e-mail: camberley-hotel@virgin.net
Dir: *opposite Harrogate International Centre*
Ideally located directly opposite the conference centre, this delightful Victorian house offers extensively equipped, individually styled bedrooms. Breakfast is served in the Victorian themed dining room, complete with original Yorkshire Range. There is a well-stocked bar and a spacious, comfortable lounge. Service and hospitality are particularly friendly and attentive.
FACILITIES: 8 en suite (1 fmly) No smoking in bedrooms TVB tea/coffee Direct dial from bedrooms No dogs (ex guide dogs) Licensed Cen ht No coaches **PRICES:** s fr £30; d fr £60✻ **PARKING:** 10
CARDS:

♦♦♦♦ Cavendish Hotel

3 Valley Dr HG2 0JJ ☎ 01423 509637 📠 01423 504434
Dir: *in centre of Harrogate beside The Valley Gardens*
This welcoming hotel is only a short walk from the conference centre and town. The Cavendish offers comfortable, well-equipped bedrooms with a multitude of extras. The resident proprietors provide a warm and friendly service. Snacks or drinks are served in the beautiful lounge, whilst breakfast is served in the well-appointed dining room.
FACILITIES: 9 en suite No smoking in bedrooms No smoking in dining room TVB tea/coffee Direct dial from bedrooms No dogs (ex guide dogs) Licensed Cen ht No coaches **PRICES:** s £35-£45; d £55-£70✻
CARDS:

♦♦♦♦ Dales Hotel

101 Valley Dr HG2 0JP ☎ 01423 507248
e-mail: dales.hotel@virgin.net
Dir: *entering Harrogate on A61 from Leeds, Turn left before Betty's on Parliament St, to rndbt, 2nd exit, then left into Valley Drive*
Enjoying a peaceful, residential location, overlooking Valley Gardens, this cosy hotel has been delightfully decorated and includes well-equipped bedrooms all with either en suite or private facilities. The sunny, stylish lounge also contains a bar. Quality breakfasts are provided in the adjacent dining room. Service is friendly and attentive.
FACILITIES: 8 en suite (1 fmly) No smoking in 2 bedrooms No smoking in dining room TVB tea/coffee No dogs (ex guide dogs) Licensed Cen ht TVL No coaches **PRICES:** s £33-£37; d £55-£60✻ **LB** **CARDS:**

♦♦♦♦ Delaine Hotel

17 Ripon Rd HG1 2JL ☎ 01423 567974 📠 01423 561723
Dir: *on A61, 0.25m from The Royal Hall*

An attractive property owned and managed by 1970s Liverpool and England football star Peter Thompson. The house is surrounded by award-winning gardens and within an easy walk of the town. Bedrooms are elegantly furnished and equipped and comfortable family accommodation is available in a converted coach house. A large collection of football memorabilia proves popular with many guests.
FACILITIES: 8 en suite 2 annexe en suite (2 fmly) No smoking in bedrooms No smoking in dining room TVB tea/coffee Direct dial from bedrooms Licensed Cen ht TVL No coaches **PRICES:** s £40-£45; d £60-£62✻
PARKING: 10 **CARDS:**

♦♦♦♦ Fountains Hotel

27 Kings Rd HG1 5JY ☎ 01423 530483 📠 01423 705312
e-mail: dave@fountains.fsworld.co.uk
Dir: *A1 (M) junct 47 onto A661 to Harrogate. Take A59 off Skipton/Knaresborough/Ripon rdbt. Continue down A59 for approx. 1.5m turn left into Kings Rd, Fountains approx. 0.75m on right*
On the same road as the conference centre, this delightful small hotel offers comfortable accommodation. Tastefully decorated throughout, bedrooms are simply furnished and enhanced by co-ordinated soft fabrics. An elegant lounge is available and there is a neatly presented dining room where substantial breakfasts are served.
FACILITIES: 10 en suite (2 fmly) (2 GF) No smoking TVB tea/coffee No dogs (ex guide dogs) Cen ht TVL No children 6yrs No coaches **PRICES:** s £30-£35; d £55-£58✻ **PARKING:** 8 **CARDS:**

England

♦♦♦♦ Grafton Hotel

1-3 Franklin Mount HG1 5EJ ☎ 01423 508491
01423 523168
e-mail: enquiries@graftonhotel.co.uk
Dir: *Follow signs to conference centre, along Kings rd with centre on L for approx 400yds, R into Franklin mount*

Family-run, this delightful small hotel is situated in a quiet location, only a few minutes from the conference centre and town. Bedrooms are particularly well-appointed, tastefully decorated and comfortably furnished throughout. There are two relaxing lounges, one of which contains a small bar. Breakfast is served in the charming dining room, which overlooks the garden.
FACILITIES: 17 en suite (3 fmly) No smoking in bedrooms No smoking in dining room TVB tea/coffee Direct dial from bedrooms No dogs (ex guide dogs) Licensed Cen ht TVL **PRICES:** s £35-£48; d £60-£78* **LB**
PARKING: 3 **NOTES:** Closed 10 Dec-5 Jan
CARDS:

♦♦♦♦ Valley Hotel

93-95 Valley Dr HG2 0JP ☎ 01423 504868 01423 531940
e-mail: valley@harrogate.com
Dir: *Close to the exhibition/conference site over looking and opposite the Valley Gardens*
This family-run hotel enjoys a delightful location opposite Valley Gardens, in the heart of Harrogate's spa area. Bedrooms are individually styled, comfortably furnished and particularly well-equipped with every conceivable extra. Public areas include a spacious lounge bar and a well-appointed dining room where hearty breakfasts that include locally made sausages, are served.
FACILITIES: 17 en suite (4 fmly) No smoking in 8 bedrooms No smoking in dining room TVB tea/coffee Direct dial from bedrooms Licensed Lift Cen ht Free use of local leisure/health club **PRICES:** s £35-£45; d £65-£75* **LB**
PARKING: 2 **NOTES:** Closed 22 Dec-3 Jan
CARDS:

♦♦♦♦ Wynnstay House

60 Franklin Rd HG1 5EE ☎ 01423 560476 01423 562539
e-mail: wynnstay.house@ukgateway.net
Dir: *in town centre turn into Strawberry Dale opposite the conference centre left at the end of the road, top of road on right*
Located in a residential area, only a short distance from the conference centre, shops and local attractions, this friendly guest house is ideal for both business and leisure. A passion for historic ruined castles exists at Wynnstay House; the comfortable, well-equipped bedrooms are all attractively furnished and each is named after a once-spectacular fortress.
FACILITIES: 6 en suite No smoking TVB tea/coffee No dogs Cen ht No children 1yr No coaches **PRICES:** s £30-£54; d £55-£70* **LB**
CARDS:

♦♦♦ *The Albany Hotel*

22-23 Harlow Moor Dr HG2 0JY ☎ 01423 565890
01423 565890
Dir: *follow signs for 'Valley Gardens'. Take road on left side of Gardens (Valley Drive). Harlow Moor Drive is a continuation of this road*
Overlooking the Valley Gardens just a short walk from the town centre, this house provides modern, well equipped bedrooms, and a spacious lounge. Breakfast is served in the pleasant dining room. Friendly service is provided by the resident proprietors.
FACILITIES: 14 en suite (3 fmly) No smoking in dining room TVB tea/coffee No dogs (ex guide dogs) Licensed Cen ht **CARDS:**

♦♦♦ Aston Hotel

7-9 Franklin Mount HG1 5EJ ☎ 01423 564262
01423 505542
e-mail: astonhotel@btinternet.com
Dir: *from town centre, at bottom of Parliament Street, right onto Kings Rd, straight on at lights, then 3rd road on right*
Situated just a short walk from the town centre and Exhibition Centre, the Aston Hotel is comfortable and well appointed with a welcoming and relaxed atmosphere. Bedrooms are smartly decorated and generally spacious. Japanese cuisine is served by appointment in the cosy cellar restaurant.
FACILITIES: 14 en suite (1 fmly) No smoking in 7 bedrooms TVB tea/coffee Direct dial from bedrooms Licensed Cen ht TVL Dinner
PRICES: s fr £35; d fr £65* **CARDS:**

England

HARROGATE continued

♦♦♦ Azalea Court Hotel

56-58 Kings Rd HG1 5JR ☎ 01423 560424 📠 01423 505662
Dir: *from town centre, at bottom of Parliament Street, right onto Kings Road, hotel is opposite conference centre on right*

This traditional house enjoys a central location next to the conference centre. Bedrooms are bright, comfortable and well equipped. Parking to the rear is a real bonus in the area.

FACILITIES: 12 en suite (2 fmly) No smoking in 6 bedrooms TVB tea/coffee Cen ht **PRICES:** s fr £25; d fr £45✱ **PARKING:** 8 **CARDS:**

♦♦♦ Gillmore Hotel

98 Kings Rd HG1 5HH ☎ 01423 503699 & 507122
📠 01423 563223
e-mail: gillmore.hotel@tiscali.co.uk
Dir: *from town centre turn into Kings Rd pass conference centre hotel approx 200yds on right*

This large family-run guest house is situated within easy reach of the town centre and the conference and exhibition hall. Public areas include an inviting bar lounge complete with large screen TV and a small function room. Traditionally furnished bedrooms vary in size and style, are all well-equipped and include several rooms suitable for families.

FACILITIES: 18 rms (7 en suite) (8 fmly) No smoking in dining room TVB tea/coffee Licensed Cen ht TVL Dinner **PRICES:** s £26-£35; d £48-£70✱ **PARKING:** 13 **CARDS:**

♦♦♦ Glenayr

19 Franklin Mount HG1 5EJ ☎ 01423 504259 📠 504259
Dir: *from A61, right into Kings Rd, pass conference centre, through traffic lights, 2nd road on right*

Situated in a pleasant tree-lined avenue only a few minutes' walk from the Conference Centre and shops, this small and friendly guest house is very welcoming. Bedrooms are comfortably furnished and well-equipped and substantial English breakfasts are served in the dining room. There is also a comfortable lounge for guests' use.

FACILITIES: 6 rms (5 en suite) No smoking in dining room TVB tea/coffee No dogs (ex guide dogs) Licensed Cen ht TVL No coaches **PRICES:** s £25-£30; d fr £48✱ **LB PARKING:** 3 **CARDS:**

♦♦♦ Pigeon Olde Farm

Bilton Hall Dr HG1 4DW ☎ 01423 868853
e-mail: maureen@tatemd.fsnet.co.uk
Dir: *from A1 take A59 to Knaresborough, through town, past 'Mother Shipton's Cave', Farm on right in Bilton Hall Drive opposite Golf Club*

A warm friendly welcome awaits guests at this delightful guest house, lovingly converted from farm buildings and barns. Enjoying a peaceful location opposite Harrogate Golf Club, both Knaresborough and Harrogate town centre are within easy reach. The bedrooms are smartly appointed and are attractively furnished in pine.

FACILITIES: 2 en suite (2 GF) No smoking TVB tea/coffee No dogs Cen ht No children No coaches **PRICES:** d £48✱ **PARKING:** 10

♦♦♦ Princes Hotel

7 Granby Rd HG1 4ST ☎ 01423 883469 📠 01423 881417
Dir: *off A59 at Empress roundabout*

Convenient for the Yorkshire Showground, this Victorian townhouse hotel is situated on the edge of town. Traditionally furnished, the comfortable accommodation comprises a mix of double, single and family rooms. The elegant dining room has a feature grandfather clock and overlooks the gardens.

FACILITIES: 6 en suite (2 fmly) No smoking in 1 bedrooms No smoking in dining room TVB tea/coffee Direct dial from bedrooms Cen ht No children 3yrs No coaches **PRICES:** s £22-£32; d £44-£55✱ **PARKING:** 1

♦♦♦ Roxanne

12 Franklin Mount HG1 5EJ ☎ 01423 569930 📠 01423 527545
e-mail: pims@annedwards.plus.com
Dir: *A661 towards Harrogate, over rdbt onto Skipton Rd for 1m turn left onto King's Rd for 0.5m turn left into Franklin Mount*

This small and friendly guest house benefits from an attractive front garden. Situated in a quiet residential area just a short walk from the town and the conference centre, Monkgate's location is ideal for business and leisure guests alike. The bedrooms are attractively decorated and well equipped and there is a cosy lounge dining room.

FACILITIES: 5 rms (1 fmly) No smoking in bedrooms No smoking in dining room No smoking in lounges TVB tea/coffee No dogs (ex guide dogs) Cen ht TVL **PRICES:** s £22.50-£25; d £45-£50✱ **PARKING:** 2
NOTES: Closed Xmas week

♦♦♦ Shelbourne

78 Kings Rd HG1 5JX ☎ 01423 504390 📠 01423 504390
e-mail: sue@shelbourne house.co.uk
Dir: *on entering Harrogate follow signs for conference centre, through traffic lights by Moat House Hotel, premises on right*

Conveniently situated opposite the conference centre, this Victorian guest house is well established and family run. Bedrooms are all individually decorated and offer good levels of comfort. The newly refurbished lounge is bright and spacious and combines traditional furnishings with contemporary style. Breakfasts are freshly cooked to order.

FACILITIES: 8 rms (6 en suite) (2 fmly) No smoking TVB tea/coffee Licensed Cen ht TVL No coaches Last d previous day **PRICES:** s fr £28; d £42-£50✱ **LB PARKING:** 1 **CARDS:**

♦♦♦ Wharfedale House

28 Harlow Moor Dr HG2 0JY ☎ 01423 522233
Dir: *alongside the Valley Gardens in central Harrogate*

During the summer months, this well-established guest house boasts a colourful display of hanging baskets. It overlooks the beautiful Valley Gardens and is in a peaceful part of town just a few minutes away from the main shops and amenities. Guests have their own lounge and a separate dining room in which to savour hearty breakfasts.

FACILITIES: 8 en suite (2 fmly) No smoking in bedrooms No smoking in dining room TVB tea/coffee Direct dial from bedrooms Licensed Cen ht Dinner Last d 10am **PRICES:** s fr £32; d fr £54✱ **LB PARKING:** 3

See advertisement on page 461

HAWES Map 07 SD88

♦♦♦♦ Steppe Haugh

Town Head DL8 3RH ☎ 01969 667645
e-mail: steppehaugh@talk21.com
Dir: *on A684, west side of Hawes, next to petrol staion*

Dating back over 350 years, this characterful stone built guest house retains much of its traditional charm. The thoughtfully

continued

England

furnished bedrooms are cosy, well-equipped and prettily decorated and spacious seating is also available. Located in the pretty town of Hawes, the Dales are on the doorstep and the Lakes are just a short drive away.
FACILITIES: 5 rms (4 en suite) No smoking TVB tea/coffee Licensed Cen ht TVL No children 7yrs No coaches **PRICES:** s £26-£28; d £52-£56✳ **LB PARKING:** 5

♦♦♦ Board Hotel
Market Place DL8 3RD ☎ 01969 667223 & 667970 📠 01969 667970
e-mail: theboardhotel1@netscapeonline.co.uk
Dir: *from A1, take A684 to Hawes, through the one-way system, last public house on right*

Conveniently located in the centre of the town this traditional inn provides a warm welcome. The modern accommodation also offers hearty cooking and a pleasant, relaxed atmosphere. The staff are extremely friendly and keen to please.
FACILITIES: 3 en suite No smoking in dining room TVB tea/coffee Cen ht Dinner Last d 6.30pm **PRICES:** d £50✳ **LB PARKING:** 10
CARDS:

HAWNBY Map 08 SE58

♦♦♦♦ Laskill Grange *(SE562007)*
Hawnby YO62 5NB ☎ 01439 798268 📠 01439 798498
Mrs S Smith
e-mail: suesmith@laskillfarm.fsnet.co.uk
Dir: *6m N of Helmsley on B1257*

Country lovers will adore this charming 19th-century farmhouse, whether opting for a walk in the surrounding countryside or fishing the River Seph which runs through the grounds. Comfortable bedrooms are divided between the main house and converted farm buildings, all are neatly furnished and have many useful extras.
FACILITIES: 2 en suite 4 annexe en suite No smoking TVB tea/coffee Licensed Cen ht Fishing Riding 600 acres beef sheep **PRICES:** s £30-£35; d £60-£64✳ **LB PARKING:** 20 **NOTES:** Closed 25 Dec
CARDS:

HELMSLEY Map 08 SE68

See also Hawnby

Premier Collection

♦♦♦♦♦ Shallowdale House
West End YO62 4DY ☎ 01439 788325 📠 01439 788885
e-mail: stay@shallowdalehouse.demon.co.uk
(For full entry see Ampleforth)

♦♦♦♦ Plumpton Court
High St, Nawton YO62 7TT ☎ 01439 771223 📠 01439 771223
e-mail: chrisandsarah@plumptoncourt.com
Dir: *entering Beadlam & Nawton from Helmsley on A170, take 3rd turn on left (establishment signed), Plumpton Court 60yds on left*
Located in the village of Nawton in the foothills of the North Yorkshire Moors, this characteristic 17th-century stone built house extends a warm welcome to all guests. The cosy lounge bar hosts an open fire, and good home cooking is served in the pleasant dining room. Bedrooms are comfortable, modern and well equipped.
FACILITIES: 7 en suite (1 GF) No smoking TVB tea/coffee No dogs Licensed Cen ht No children 12yrs No coaches Dinner Last d 9.30am
PRICES: s £40; d £48-£54✳ **PARKING:** 7

♦♦♦♦ The Carlton Lodge
Bondgate YO62 5EY ☎ 01439 770557 📠 01439 770623
e-mail: aaenquiries@carlton-lodge.com
Dir: *on A170 Thirsk to Scarborough Road, 400mtrs from Market Sq*
FACILITIES: 8 rms (6 en suite) (1 fmly) (2 GF) No smoking in 6 bedrooms No smoking in dining room No smoking in lounges TVB tea/coffee Direct dial from bedrooms Licensed Cen ht No coaches **PRICES:** s £25-£35; d £50-£70✳ **LB PARKING:** 10 **CARDS:**

HOVINGHAM Map 08 SE67

♦♦ Sedgwick Country Guest House
Park St YO62 4JZ ☎ 01653 628740 📠 01653 628740
e-mail: sedgwick.ges-ho@amserv.net
Dir: *from York take A64 Malton Rd, turn N into Castle Howard Rd to B1257 and turn left again. 2m to Hovingham, house on left overlooking village green*
Standing in the centre of this lovely village, a stone built house providing decent practical accommodation, ample private parking, and hearty breakfasts. A good centre for touring and there are good places to eat nearby.
FACILITIES: 6 en suite (2 fmly) No smoking TVB tea/coffee No dogs (ex guide dogs) Licensed Cen ht **PRICES:** s £26-£30; d £42-£50✳ **LB PARKING:** 6

England

HUBY Map 08 SE56

♦♦♦ *The New Inn Motel*

Main St YO61 1HQ ☎ 01347 810219 📠 01347 810219
Dir: *approach village from A19, L onto Main St. Hotel on L. The inn is behind the pub*

Nestling behind the New Inn, this modern motel style accommodation has a quiet location in the village of Huby, nine miles north of York. Comfortable bedrooms are neatly furnished, and breakfast is served in the cosy dining room. The reception area hosts an array of tourist information and the resident owners provide a friendly and helpful service.
FACILITIES: 8 en suite (3 fmly) No smoking in 2 bedrooms No smoking in dining room TVB tea/coffee Cen ht No coaches **PARKING:** 8
NOTES: Closed part of Nov & Mar

HUNTON Map 07 SE19

♦♦♦♦ The Countryman's Inn

Hunton, Bedale DL8 1PY ☎ 01677 450554 📠 01677 450570
e-mail: contactus@thecountrymansinn.co.uk
Dir: *just off A684 Bedale/Leyburn road between Patrick Brompton and Constable Burton*
This recently refurbished inn is also the only pub in this quiet village on the edge of the North York Moors. Bright, modern décor is a feature of the simple yet elegant accommodation. The restaurant, popular with locals, provides carefully prepared meals using local produce.
FACILITIES: 5 en suite No smoking in bedrooms No smoking in dining room TVB tea/coffee No dogs (ex guide dogs) Cen ht No children Dinner Last d 9pm **PRICES:** s £30-£40; d £50-£60✱ **LB** **MEALS:** Lunch £14-£25&alc Dinner £5.95-£12alc✱ **PARKING:** 12
CARDS:

HUTTON-LE-HOLE Map 08 SE79

♦♦♦♦ Moorlands of Hutton-le-Hole

YO62 6UA ☎ 01751 417548 📠 01751 417760
e-mail: welcome@moorlandshouse.com
Dir: *on the A170 between Thirsk/Scarborough, turning for Hutton-le-Hole head N from A170 approx. 1m E of Kirkby Moorside, as you enter village keep to main road, Moorlands is on left*
At the edge of this moorland village, ideally located for stunning scenery and the Ryedale Folk Museum. Comfortable spacious lounges with log fires if cold, good food and a cottage garden bordering the village stream.

continued

Moorlands of Hutton-le-Hole

FACILITIES: 4 en suite No smoking TVB tea/coffee No dogs (ex guide dogs) Licensed Cen ht No children 15yrs Tennis (hard) Croquet lawn Green bowls Dinner Last d 24hr prior **PRICES:** s fr £40; d £65✱ **LB**
PARKING: 6 **CARDS:**

INGLETON Map 07 SD67

♦♦♦♦ Ferncliffe Country

55 Main St LA6 3HJ ☎ 015242 42405
e-mail: ferncliffe@hotmail.com
Dir: *off A65 by the Bridge pub, onto B6255, 75yds on R*

This attractive stone built house overlooks Ingleborough and is therefore a superb base for walkers. All bedrooms are tastefully furnished and boast bright imaginative décor. A selection of books and videos can be found in the cosy lounge and substantial breakfasts are served in the adjacent dining room. Dinner is available by prior arrangement.
FACILITIES: 5 en suite No smoking in bedrooms No smoking in dining room TVB tea/coffee Cen ht TVL No children No coaches Dinner Last d midday **PRICES:** s fr £30; d £48-£50✱ **LB** **PARKING:** 5
NOTES: Closed Xmas **CARDS:**

See advertisement on opposite page

♦♦♦ Inglenook

20 Main St LA6 3HJ ☎ 015242 41270
e-mail: inglenook20@hotmail.com
Dir: *turn off A65 towards village at Bridge Inn, house 300yds on left*
Close to the River Greta with lovely views of Ingleborough peak, this comfortable Victorian house extends a warm and friendly welcome. Bedrooms are freshly decorated and well equipped with a host of comforts. Home cooked four course dinners are available by prior arrangement and are served in the spacious dining room. A guest lounge is also available.
FACILITIES: 4 en suite 1 annexe en suite No smoking TVB tea/coffee No dogs Cen ht TVL No children 5yrs No coaches Dinner Last d previous evening **PRICES:** d £44✱ **LB** **NOTES:** Closed Xmas
CARDS:

♦♦♦ *Seed Hill*
Village Centre LA6 3AB ☎ 015242 41799 📠 015242 41799
e-mail: adrianseedhill@hotmail.com
Dir: *Ingleton is on A65 between Skipton/Kendal. Follow village centre signs under railway viaduct, pass Church on left, Seed Hill is on right in village centre, parking at rear*
Exuding charm and character, no two walls are straight at this cottage style B&B. Sympathetically restored and furnished bedrooms are cosy and comfortable. Freshly cooked breakfasts are served in the dining room, which in the summer doubles as a tea-room, where one can enjoy delicious cream teas. Genuine hospitality is assured.
FACILITIES: 2 en suite No smoking TVB tea/coffee Cen ht **PARKING:** 4

KETTLEWELL — Map 07 SD97

♦♦♦♦ Littlebeck
The Green BD23 5RD ☎ 01756 760378 📠 01756 760378
e-mail: stay@little-beck.co.uk
Dir: *on entering Kettlewell on B6160 from Skipton, turn right at the Old Smithy shop, carry straight onto the Maypole. Littlebeck on left*
Located in the glorious upper valley of Wharfedale this refurbished Georgian house stands on the village green, with its maypole, and has a fast flowing beck to the rear. It provides well-equipped and comfortable bedrooms together with two delightful lounges. Genuine hospitality and attentive service are great strengths here.
FACILITIES: 3 en suite No smoking TVB tea/coffee No dogs Cen ht No children No coaches **PRICES:** d £50-£54✳ **LB PARKING:** 4
NOTES: Closed Xmas

KEXBY — Map 08 SE75

♦♦♦ Ivy House *(SE691511)*
YO41 5LQ ☎ 01904 489368 📠 01904 489368 Mrs K R Daniel
e-mail: kevin-jayne-daniel@supanet.com
Dir: *On A1079 approx 5m from York*
Part of a working farm, this Victorian farmhouse has belonged to the same family for over a hundred years. Hospitality is friendly and sincere, and bedrooms are pleasantly decorated and equipped. A freshly prepared Yorkshire breakfast is served in the cosy dining room.
FACILITIES: 3 rms (2 en suite) (1 fmly) No smoking in bedrooms No smoking in dining room TVB tea/coffee No dogs (ex guide dogs) Cen ht TVL 132 acres mixed **PRICES:** s £22; d £32-£36✳ **BB PARKING:** 5

KILBURN — Map 08 SE57

♦♦♦ *Forresters Arms Hotel*
YO61 4AH ☎ 01347 868386 & 868550 📠 01347 868386
Dir: *from Thirsk take A170 for 2m then turn right for Kilburn. Follow road for 3m into village (The Circle)*
Situated beneath the famous White Horse, and next door to the 'Mouseman' furniture, this traditional inn was built by the Normans in the 12th century. Bedrooms are well equipped and comfortable and a wide range of popular food is served either in the dining room or one of the cosy, characterful bars.
FACILITIES: 10 en suite (2 fmly) No smoking in dining room TVB tea/coffee Direct dial from bedrooms Cen ht Pool Table Dinner Last d 9pm
PARKING: 40 **CARDS:**

♦♦♦ Red Diamonds ahighlight the top establishments within the AA's 3, 4 and 5 Diamond ratings.

KILNSEY — Map 07 SD96

♦♦♦♦ Kilnsey Old Hall
BD23 5PS ☎ 01756 753887
e-mail: oldhall.kilnsey@virgin.net
Dir: *take B6265 Skipton to Threshfield, then B6160 Threshfield to Kilnsey, immediately after Kilnsey Trout farm left up hill last house on right.*
Built in 1648 this historic hall has been painstakingly restored and many of the original features blend seamlessly with the modern, stylish conversion. The bedrooms vary in size but all are well equipped with a host of thoughtful extras, including TVs with VCRs, and are furnished with classic furniture. Breakfast is served and enjoyed in the central hall.
FACILITIES: 3 en suite No smoking TVB tea/coffee Cen ht No children 14yrs No coaches **PRICES:** s £30; d £55-£65✳ **PARKING:** 5
NOTES: Closed Xmas week

KIRKBYMOORSIDE — Map 08 SE68

♦♦♦♦ Appletree Court
9 High Market Place YO62 6AT ☎ 01751 431536
Dating to around 1750, this delightful stone house, once a farm, retains a number of original features. Today this friendly guest house offers individually decorated, well equipped bedrooms.
FACILITIES: 5 en suite (2 fmly)

U Brickfields Farm
Kirby Mills YO62 6NS ☎ 01751 433074
At the time of going to press the Diamond classification for this establishment had not been confirmed. Please check the AA website www.theAA.com for up-to-date information.
FACILITIES: 3 en suite

KNARESBOROUGH Map 08 SE35

♦♦♦♦ Newton House Hotel

5-7 York Place HG5 0AD ☎ 01423 863539 📠 01423 869748
e-mail: newtonhouse@btinternet.com
Dir: *on A59, 2.5m from A1 turn off*

This delightful coaching inn is located only two minutes from the river, castle and market square. The hotel is entered through its own archway into a courtyard. The attractively decorated and well-equipped bedrooms include some four-posters and king-sized doubles. Guests have a lounge with small dispense bar and a set menu is served in the dining room.

FACILITIES: 9 en suite 3 annexe en suite (3 fmly) (3 GF) No smoking in 5 bedrooms No smoking in dining room TVB tea/coffee Direct dial from bedrooms Licensed Cen ht TVL No coaches Dinner Last d 11am **PRICES:** s £40-£65; d £60-£90* **LB PARKING:** 9 **NOTES:** Closed Xmas **CARDS:**

♦♦♦ *The Villa*

47 Kirkgate HG5 8BZ ☎ 01423 865370 📠 01423 867740
Dir: *Turn off A1 N onto A59 Harrogate/Knaresborough. Just off Knaresborough High Street at Spar Supermarket onto Kirkgate*

Enjoying spectacular views over the River Nidd, this delightful Tudor building boasts comfortable accommodation. Located next to the railway station, the Market Square and castle are within easy walking distance. The bedrooms are very well-equipped, one has a beautiful hand-carved four-poster bed and another has a small balcony.

FACILITIES: 5 en suite (1 fmly) No smoking in dining room TVB tea/coffee Direct dial from bedrooms Licensed Cen ht TVL No coaches

LEYBURN Map 07 SE19

The Old Horn Inn

Spennithorne DL8 5PR ☎ 01969 622370

At the time of going to press the Diamond classification for this establishment had not been confirmed. Please check the AA website www.theAA.com for up-to-date information.

FACILITIES: 2 en suite

MALHAM Map 07 SD96

♦♦♦♦ River House Hotel

BD23 4DA ☎ 01729 830315 📠 01729 830672
e-mail: info@riverhousehotel.co.uk

FACILITIES: 9 en suite No smoking in bedrooms No smoking in dining room No smoking in 1 lounge TVB tea/coffee No dogs (ex guide dogs) Licensed Dinner Last d 7.30pm **PRICES:** s £38-£55; d £59-£69* **LB PARKING:** 4 **CARDS:**

MALTON Map 08 SE77

♦♦♦♦ The Wentworth Arms

111 Town St, Old Malton YO17 7HD ☎ 01653 692618
📠 01653 600061
e-mail: wentwortharms@btinternet.com
Dir: *turn left off A64 from York onto B1248 signed Malton. Wentworth Arms 400yds on right*

This friendly inn, which stands in the centre of the village, has a 'home from home' atmosphere. It has comfortable, well-equipped bedrooms. Generous, home cooked meals can be taken either in the smart dining room with its exposed stone walls and old beams, or in the popular bar. The inn has undergone much refurbishment by its enthusiastic new owners.

continued

FACILITIES: 5 en suite No smoking in area of dining room TVB tea/coffee No dogs (ex guide dogs) Cen ht No children 10yrs Dinner Last d 9pm **PRICES:** s £25-£33; d £56* **MEALS:** Lunch £10-£20alc Dinner £10-£20alc* **PARKING:** 20 **CARDS:**

♦♦♦ The Brow

25 York Rd YO17 6AX ☎ 01653 693402
Dir: *turn off A64 into Malton, houses start on right hand side with high stone wall, 1st drive when wall changes to brick*

Once the home of Malton's oldest brewing family, and set in a commanding position overlooking the Derwent Valley, this fine Georgian house retains many original features including moulded cornices and open fireplaces. Public areas include a spacious dining room overlooking the landscaped gardens and a child-free sitting room, furnished with fine period pieces.

FACILITIES: 5 rms (4 en suite) (1 fmly) No smoking in bedrooms No smoking in lounges TVB tea/coffee No dogs Cen ht TVL No coaches **PRICES:** s £25-£35; d £50-£65* **PARKING:** 6 **NOTES:** Closed 2wks Xmas/New Year

MASHAM Map 08 SE28

♦♦♦♦ Bank Villa

HG4 4DB ☎ 01765 689605 📠 01765 689605
Dir: *on A6108 from Ripon, premises 100yds after 30mph sign on right on entering Masham*

A charming Georgian house lovingly cared for, set in a charming walled garden which guests are free to relax in. Individually decorated bedrooms feature stripped pine, period furniture and crisp white linen. Public rooms have character, there are a choice of lounges, whilst good home-cooked meals are served in the attractive dining room.

FACILITIES: 6 en suite (1 fmly) No smoking tea/coffee No dogs (ex guide dogs) Licensed Cen ht TVL No children 5yrs No coaches Dinner Last d 24hrs before meal **PRICES:** s £35-£52; d £46-£52* **PARKING:** 6

MIDDLESBROUGH Map 08 NZ41

♦♦♦♦ The Grey House Hotel

79 Cambridge Rd, Linthorpe TS5 5NL ☎ 01642 817485
📠 01642 817485
e-mail: dwattis@fsmail.net
Dir: *turn off from A19 heading for Middlesbrough on A1130*

The Grey House is a small hotel occupying a large corner site in a quiet residential area, which has its own attractive gardens. All of the bedrooms are spacious and comfortable. Downstairs, there is a large inviting lounge and an airy dining room where a hearty breakfast is served.

FACILITIES: 9 en suite (1 fmly) No smoking in bedrooms No smoking in dining room No smoking in 1 lounge TVB tea/coffee Direct dial from bedrooms Cen ht No coaches **PRICES:** s £40-£50; d £55-£60* **PARKING:** 10 **CARDS:**

MUKER
Map 07 SD99

♦♦♦♦ Oxnop Hall *(SD931973)*
Low Oxnop, Gunnerside DL11 6JJ ☎ 01748 886253
Fax 01748 886253 Mrs A Porter
Dir: *off B6270 between the villages Muker and Gunnerside*

Nestling in beautiful Swaledale scenery, this smartly presented 17th-century farmhouse has been furnished with thought and care. The attractive bedrooms are well-equipped and some boast original exposed beams and mullion windows. Good home cooking, using local produce where possible, is served in the country dining room which is adjacent to the cosy lounge.
FACILITIES: 5 rms (4 en suite) 1 annexe en suite (1 fmly) No smoking TV5B tea/coffee No dogs (ex guide dogs) Licensed Cen ht No children 5yrs 1000 acres beef sheep hill farming Dinner Last d 6.30pm **PRICES:** s £26-£32; d £52-£64* **PARKING:** 10 **NOTES:** Closed Xmas

NORTHALLERTON
Map 08 SE39

♦♦♦♦ Porch House
68-70 High St DL7 8EG ☎ 01609 779831 Fax 01609 778603
Dir: *A684 from A1 or A19. Porch House on A167 opposite All Saints Church*
This charming house dates from the 16th century with floorboards and beams made of wood plundered from the Spanish Armada. Charles I was held prisoner here until a £400,000 ransom was paid for his release. Décor throughout is tasteful and comfortable bedrooms are equipped with quality period furnishings, one has an antique American bed. Breakfast is served in the attractive dining room with its original stone flooring.
FACILITIES: 6 en suite No smoking TVB tea/coffee No dogs (ex guide dogs) Licensed Cen ht No children 12yrs No coaches **PRICES:** s £38-£40; d £56-£58* **PARKING:** 6 **NOTES:** Closed 24 Dec-9 Jan
CARDS: MasterCard, Barclaycard Visa, Delta

♦♦♦ The Windsor Guest House
56 South Pde DL7 8SL ☎ 01609 774100
Dir: *on A684 at southern end of High Street*
Within ten minutes walking distance from the town centre, a friendly welcome awaits you at this Victorian town house. Accommodation consists of bright and cheerful bedrooms and a cosy lounge. Home cooking is served in the dining room that overlooks the garden.
FACILITIES: 6 rms (5 en suite) No smoking TVB tea/coffee No dogs (ex guide dogs) Licensed Cen ht TVL No coaches Dinner Last d am
PRICES: s £25; d £43* **CARDS:** MasterCard, Barclaycard Visa, Barclays Connect, Delta, Switch

OSMOTHERLEY
Map 08 SE49

♦♦ Queen Catherine Hotel
7 West End DL6 3AG ☎ 01609 883209
e-mail: info@queencatherinehotel.co.uk
Dir: *turn off A19 onto A168 signposted to Osmotherley-Northallerton and follow signs to Osmotherley. Approx 0.5m from junct*
This traditionally styled inn nestles in the heart of the picturesque village. Bedrooms are compact, but are comfortably equipped and decorated. The cosy bar offers imaginative menus and the hearty breakfasts make good use of fresh local produce.
FACILITIES: 5 en suite No smoking in bedrooms No smoking in dining room TVB tea/coffee No dogs (ex guide dogs) Cen ht TVL Dinner Last d 9pm **PRICES:** s fr £22.50; d fr £45* **CARDS:** MasterCard, Barclaycard Visa, Barclays Connect, Delta, Switch

PATELEY BRIDGE
Map 07 SE16

Central House
Glasshouses, Nidderdale HG3 5QY ☎ 01423 711371
At the time of going to press the Diamond classification for this establishment had not been confirmed. Please check the AA website www.theAA.com for up-to-date information.
FACILITIES: 2 en suite (1 fmly)

PICKERING
Map 08 SE88

Premier Collection

♦♦♦♦♦ Moorlands
Levisham YO18 7NL ☎ 01751 460229 Fax 01751 460470
e-mail: ronaldoleonardo@aol.com
Dir: *A169 from Pickering to Whitby, travel approx 6m to Fox & Rabbit pub on right. After 0.25m turn left at sign for Lockton, follow road to Levisham*

Standing on the edge of the peaceful village of Levisham, the property commands stunning views over the North York Moors National Park, and "Heartbeat Country". Stylishly decorated and tastefully furnished throughout, this country house offers luxury accommodation and genuine hospitality. Bedrooms have been very thoughtfully equipped and there is also a comfortable lounge. A hearty breakfast is served in the elegant dining room.
FACILITIES: 7 en suite No smoking TVB tea/coffee No dogs (ex guide dogs) Licensed Cen ht TVL No children 14yrs **PRICES:** s £35-£45; d £70-£90* **LB PARKING:** 10 **NOTES:** Closed Nov-Feb

England

PICKERING continued

♦♦♦♦ Fox & Hounds Country

Main St, Sinnington YO62 6SQ ☎ 01751 431577
01751 432791
e-mail: foxhoundsinn@easynet.co.uk
Dir: *3m W of Pickering, off A170*

An attractive village inn offering smart, well-equipped bedrooms. The public areas include a bar, a cosy lounge and a restaurant which offers an impressive range of well presented and well cooked dishes.

FACILITIES: 10 en suite (4 GF) No smoking in bedrooms No smoking in dining room TVB tea/coffee Direct dial from bedrooms Cen ht No coaches Dinner Last d 9pm **PRICES:** s £44-£50; d £60-£80✻ **LB PARKING:** 40
CARDS:

♦♦♦♦ Old Manse

19 Middleton Rd YO18 8AL ☎ 01751 476484 01751 477124
Dir: *from A169, left at rdbt, through lights, 1st right into Potter Hill. Follow rd to left. From A170 left at 'local traffic only'*

Within walking distance of the town, this former minister's home offers comfortable accommodation. Bedrooms are pleasantly decorated and thoughtfully equipped. There is a cosy lounge and separate dining room where delicious breakfasts are served. Dinner is also available. Warm and friendly hospitality is provided by the resident owners.

FACILITIES: 10 en suite (2 fmly) (2 GF) No smoking TVB tea/coffee Licensed Cen ht TVL No children 10yrs No coaches Dinner Last d 7pm
PRICES: s £28-£30; d £52-£60✻ **CONF:** Thtr 20 Class 12 Board 10 Del from £65 ✻ **PARKING:** 12 **CARDS:**

♦♦♦ Warrington

Whitbygate, Thornton-Le-Dale YO18 7RY ☎ 01751 475028
e-mail: amanda@brennano.fsnet.co.uk
Dir: *from Pickering take A170 to Scarborough. In Thornton-le- Dale at village green/x-roads turn left signposted Dalby Forest, 2nd building on left*

This attractive stone built guest house includes a teashop together with cosy bedrooms, which are simply furnished along modern lines. Enjoying a central village location, the teashop offers a wide range of home cooked dishes during the day, and special diets are catered for.

continued

FACILITIES: 8 rms (4 en suite) (1 fmly) No smoking in bedrooms No smoking in area of dining room TVB tea/coffee No dogs (ex guide dogs) Licensed Cen ht **PRICES:** s £19-£24; d £38-£48✻ **LB BB PARKING:** 2

RAVENSCAR — Map 08 NZ90

♦♦♦♦ Smugglers Rock Country

YO13 0ER ☎ 01723 870044 01723 870044
e-mail: info@smugglersrock.co.uk
Dir: *leave A171 towards Ravenscar. Guest house 0.5m before Ravenscar, opposite an old stone windmill*

FACILITIES: 8 en suite (3 fmly) No smoking TVB tea/coffee No dogs (ex guide dogs) Licensed Cen ht TVL No coaches Pool Table **PRICES:** s £27-£31; d £48-£52✻ **LB PARKING:** 12 **NOTES:** Closed Nov-Jan
CARDS:

REDCAR — Map 08 NZ62

♦♦♦ Claxton Hotel

196 High St TS10 3AW ☎ 01642 486745 01642 486522
e-mail: enquiries@claxtonhotel.co.uk
Dir: *leave A174 at double rdbt signed Redcar continue across railway crossing, right at lights by St Peter's Church hotel rear car park on lef*

This friendly, family-owned commercial hotel overlooking the sea is a popular venue for local functions. Bedrooms, although compact, are bright and fresh with practical modern furnishings. Public areas include a recently extended lounge and an attractive dining room.

FACILITIES: 28 rms (26 en suite) (2 fmly) (6 GF) No smoking in dining room No smoking in 1 lounge TVB tea/coffee Licensed Cen ht TVL Dinner Last d 9pm **PRICES:** s £22.32-£25.85; d £38.77-£41.12✻ **PARKING:** 10
CARDS:

REETH — Map 07 SE09

♦♦♦♦ Arkleside Hotel

DL11 6SG ☎ 01748 884200 01748 884200
e-mail: info@arklesidehotel.co.uk
Dir: *follow B6160 then B6270 from Richmond to Reeth. Hotel on top right corner of village green*

Overlooking the beautiful Swaledale scenery this delightful hotel is located just off the village green. Bedrooms are attractively decorated and well-equipped and there is a suite available. Public areas extend to large conservatory, a cosy lounge, a bar and well-kept gardens and terrace. Delicious candlelit dinners can be enjoyed in the dining room.

FACILITIES: 10 en suite No smoking in bedrooms No smoking in dining room No smoking in lounges TVB tea/coffee Licensed Cen ht TVL No children 10yrs No coaches Riding Walking & painting trips arranged Dinner Last d 6.30pm **PRICES:** s £37.50-£47.50; d £74-£84✻ **LB PARKING:** 6
NOTES: Closed Jan-9 Feb **CARDS:**

♦♦♦♦ Charles Bathurst

Arkengarthdale DL11 6EN ☎ 01748 884058 & 884567
01748 884599
e-mail: info@cbinn.co.uk
Dir: *A1 Catterick to Richmond, follow A6108 to Reeth, at Buck Hotel turn right to Langthwaite, pass church on right, inn on right 0.5m past church*

Surrounded by magnificent scenery, this delightful inn has been completely refurbished by Dales craftsmen using local hardwood and stone. Stylishly decorated bedrooms are comfortable, well-equipped and some are furnished with fine period pieces. The open fires in the bar and dining room create a relaxing atmosphere.

FACILITIES: 18 en suite (2 fmly) No smoking in bedrooms No smoking in area of dining room TVB tea/coffee Direct dial from bedrooms Cen ht

continued

Fishing Pool Table Dinner Last d 9pm **PRICES:** d £52.50-£75✳ **LB** **MEALS:** Lunch £13-£16 Dinner £14-£24✳ **PARKING:** 35 **CARDS:**

RICHMOND Map 07 NZ10

See also Reeth and Thwaite

♦♦♦♦ *Old Brewery*

29 The Green DL10 4RG ☎ 01748 822460 Fax 01748 825561

Dir: *A6108 to Richmond, turn at 2nd roundabout along Victoria Rd, then 2nd left into Cravengate leading to The Green*

Recognised by its hanging baskets and award winning gardens, The Old Brewery Guest House is located in the oldest part of this historic town, enjoying views of the castle. Bedrooms are comfortable and there is a cosy lounge. Homemade muffins at breakfast coupled with delicious local produce provide a hearty start to the day.

FACILITIES: 5 en suite No smoking TVB tea/coffee No dogs Cen ht TVL No children 10yrs No coaches Puzzles Needlepoint Books **NOTES:** Closed Dec-Jan **CARDS:**

♦♦♦♦ Whashton Springs *(NZ149046)*

DL11 7JS ☎ 01748 822884 Fax 01748 826285 Mrs M F Turnbull
e-mail: whashton@turnbullg.f.freeserve.co.uk

Dir: *in Richmond turn right at traffic lights towards Ravensworth, 3m down steep hill farm at bottom on left*

A warm welcome can be expected at this attractive Georgian farmhouse, situated high in the hills, amongst 600 acres of farmland. The courtyard bedrooms are contemporary in style, whilst those in the main house are more traditional. Hearty Yorkshire breakfasts are served in the spacious dining room, overlooking the lawns.

FACILITIES: 3 en suite 5 annexe en suite (2 fmly) No smoking in 5 bedrooms No smoking in dining room No smoking in lounges TVB tea/coffee Direct dial from bedrooms No dogs (ex guide dogs) Licensed Cen ht No children 5yrs 600 acres arable beef mixed sheep **PRICES:** s £30; d £50-£54✳ **PARKING:** 10 **NOTES:** Closed late Dec-Jan

♦♦♦ Pottergate

4 Pottergate DL10 4AB ☎ 01748 823826

Dir: *A1608 to Richmond straight over 1st rdbt through traffic lights, establishment 50yds on left*

Dating back to the 1800s, this attractive mid-terrace guest house is a short walk from the market place. Bedrooms are modern in style, and mostly furnished in pine. There is a small cosy lounge as well as a separate dining room with bar. Evening meals are available by prior arrangement.

FACILITIES: 7 rms (1 fmly) No smoking TVB tea/coffee No dogs (ex guide dogs) Licensed Cen ht TVL No coaches Dinner Last d morning **PRICES:** s £20; d £38✳ **LB BB PARKING:** 5

RIPON Map 08 SE37

♦♦♦♦ *Bay Tree (SE263685)*

Aldfield HG4 3BE ☎ 01765 620394 Fax 01765 620394
Mrs V Leeming

Dir: *approx 4m W, take unclass road S off B6265*

Enjoying a tranquil, rural setting, this delightful farmhouse lies close to Fountains Abbey and offers a high standard of hospitality. A converted barn, it retains many original features, and the thoughtfully equipped bedrooms are comfortable and generally spacious. Wholesome home-cooked food is served and there is a comfortable lounge with log-burning fire.

FACILITIES: 6 en suite (1 fmly) No smoking TVB tea/coffee Licensed Cen ht 400 acres beef, arable Dinner Last d 10am **PARKING:** 10 **CARDS:**

♦♦♦♦ St George Court *(SE237697)*

Old Home Farm, Grantley HG4 3EU ☎ 01765 620618 Fax 01765 620618 Mrs S Gordon
e-mail: stgeorgescourt@bronco.co.uk

Dir: *from Ripon take B6265, pass Fountains Abbey and right hand sign to Grantley & Wiwitsley, up hill for 1m past 'Risplith' sign & next right*

This charming farmhouse is the perfect location to 'get away from it all', being set in delightful countryside close to Fountains Abbey. Attractive, well-equipped ground floor bedrooms are located around a central courtyard. Hearty breakfasts are served in the conservatory dining room, which has splendid views of the surrounding countryside.

FACILITIES: 5 en suite (1 fmly) No smoking TVB tea/coffee Cen ht 20 acres beef sheep **PRICES:** s fr £40; d £50-£60✳ **LB PARKING:** 12 **CARDS:**

♦♦♦ Diamonds are a guest's best friend! The emphasis is on quality and guest care rather than extra facilities.

England

RIPON continued

♦♦♦♦ Moor End Farm

Knaresborough Rd, Littlethorpe HG4 3LU ☎ 01765 677419
e-mail: pspensley@ukonline.co.uk
Dir: *from A61 Ripon bypass take sign for Bishop Monkton (ignore sign for Littlethorpe), Moor End is approx 1.5m on the left.*
FACILITIES: 3 rms (2 en suite) No smoking TVB tea/coffee No dogs Cen ht TVL No children 15yrs No coaches **PRICES:** d £45-£50* **LB**
PARKING: 5 **NOTES:** Closed Xmas & New Year

Ravencroft B & B

Moorside Av HG4 1TA ☎ 01765 602543
At the time of going to press the Diamond classification for this establishment had not been confirmed. Please check the AA website www.theAA.com for up-to-date information.
FACILITIES: 2 en suite (1 fmly)

ROBIN HOOD'S BAY — Map 08 NZ90

♦♦♦♦ Flask

Robin Hoods Bay, Fylingdales YO22 4QH
☎ 01947 880305 & 880692 01947 880592
e-mail: flaskinn@aol.com
Dir: *on A171 11m from Scarborough, 7m from Whitby*

The Flask was originally a 16th-century monks' hostel, and is now a comfortable inn offering a good range of well produced food. The bedrooms are split between the inn and a separate lodge and are all furnished in pine and thoughtfully equipped. The bar is spacious and has a friendly atmosphere.
FACILITIES: 6 en suite 6 annexe en suite (3 fmly) (6 GF) No smoking in dining room TVB tea/coffee No dogs Cen ht TVL No coaches Dinner Last d 9pm **PRICES:** s £25-£30; d £50* **LB PARKING:** 20
CARDS:

ROSEDALE ABBEY — Map 08 SE79

♦♦♦♦ Sevenford House

YO18 8SE ☎ 01751 417283 01751 417505
e-mail: sevenford@aol.com
Dir: *off A170 at sign for Rosedale Abbey, in village turn sharp left at Coach & Horses Restaurant & right at White Horse*

continued

Nestling in the heart of the National Park, this elegant Victorian house stands in its own peaceful grounds far from the crowds but within walking distance of the village. The well-proportioned bedrooms are comfortable, well equipped and benefit from stunning views. There is also an inviting lounge and a spacious breakfast room with grand piano.
FACILITIES: 3 en suite (1 fmly) No smoking TVB tea/coffee No dogs (ex guide dogs) Cen ht No coaches **PRICES:** s £30-£35; d £45-£50* **LB**
PARKING: 6 **NOTES:** Closed Xmas day

SCARBOROUGH — Map 08 TA08

♦♦♦♦ Croft Hotel

87 Queens Pde YO12 7HT ☎ 01723 373904 01723 350490
e-mail: crofthotel@btinternet.com
Dir: *follow North Bay Sea Front tourist signs. Head along front towards castle headland. Take only right turn up cliff. Right at top, 1st hotel on left*
A flexible approach to guests' needs are a key feature of this friendly hotel. Set in a prime position overlooking the bay, guests can enjoy the view from either the comfortable lounge or in better weather from the patio. A very pleasant bar is provided, and meals are served either here, or in the well-appointed dining room.
FACILITIES: 6 en suite (4 fmly) No smoking in bedrooms No smoking in dining room No smoking in lounges TVB tea/coffee No dogs (ex guide dogs) Licensed Cen ht TVL Golf arranged at local courses Dinner Last d 6.30pm **PRICES:** s £20-£22; d £40-£44* **LB PARKING:** 5
CARDS:

♦♦♦♦ Hotel Columbus

124 Columbus Ravine YO12 7QZ ☎ 01723 374634
e-mail: hotel.columbus@lineone.net
Dir: *A64 into town centre. Left at lights, proceed over next set. Police Station on left. Follow main road across R at rdbt past cemetery across 2nd rdbt at bottom of hill 2nd hotel on L*
Yorkshire hospitality at its best is experienced here, and Bonnie Purchon is a welcoming hostess. Ideally located for both the beach and major attractions. Bedrooms, although compact, are well-equipped and homely. A very comfortable lounge is provided, in the dining room a good breakfast is served, and evening meals during the main season.
FACILITIES: 11 en suite (2 fmly) No smoking TVB tea/coffee No dogs Licensed Cen ht TVL Dinner Last d noon **PRICES:** s £25-£30; d £50-£70*
LB PARKING: 8 **CARDS:**

♦♦♦♦ Interludes

32 Princess St YO11 1QR ☎ 01723 360513 01723 368597
e-mail: interludes@ntlworld.com
Dir: *from harbour take narrow road between Princess Cafe & Newcastle Packet Pub. Princess St 2nd on left. Interludes on right set back from road*
A charming well proportioned Georgian house which retains much of its original character. It has been sympathetically renovated with a theatrical theme to provide a balance of quality and comfort. Bedrooms are comfortable and well equipped, and on-street parking is available nearby.
FACILITIES: 5 rms (4 en suite) No smoking TVB tea/coffee No dogs Licensed Cen ht No children 16yrs No coaches Dinner Last d breakfast
PRICES: s £29-£34; d £50-£60* **LB NOTES:** Closed Owners holidays
CARDS:

♦♦♦♦ Paragon Hotel

123 Queens Pde YO12 7HU ☎ 01723 372676 01723 372676
e-mail: derek@paragon-hotel.demon.co.uk
Dir: *on A64, follow signs for North Bay. Hotel on cliff top*
This welcoming Victorian terraced house has been carefully renovated to provide stylishl, superbly equipped, non-smoking accommodation. Hearty English breakfasts and four course dinners

continued

are served in the attractive dining room and there is also a lounge bar with a fabulous sea view.
FACILITIES: 14 en suite (1 fmly) No smoking in bedrooms No smoking in dining room TVB tea/coffee Direct dial from bedrooms No dogs (ex guide dogs) Licensed Cen ht No children 3yrs No coaches Dinner Last d 6pm **PRICES:** s £25-£30; d £48-£52✻ **LB** **PARKING:** 6 **NOTES:** Closed Nov-24 Jan **CARDS:**

♦♦♦♦ The Ramleh

135 Queens Pde YO12 7HY ☎ 01723 365745 01723 365745
e-mail: Johncramlehhotel@aol.com
Dir: *from A64 left at station, right at traffic lights, left at rdbt, 2nd right, 1st left*
Overlooking North Bay, this terraced house provides a friendly atmosphere. Freshly decorated bedrooms are bright, modern and comfortable. Delicious home-cooked meals are served in the spacious dining room, which also boasts a well stocked bar. A guest lounge is also available.
FACILITIES: 8 annexe en suite (3 fmly) No smoking in bedrooms No smoking in dining room TVB tea/coffee No dogs (ex guide dogs) Licensed Cen ht TVL No coaches Dinner Last d 1pm **PRICES:** d fr £42✻ **LB** **PARKING:** 6 **NOTES:** Closed 24-26 Dec
CARDS:

♦♦♦♦ The Whiteley Hotel

99/101 Queens Pde YO12 7HY ☎ 01723 373514
01723 373007
e-mail: whiteleyhotel@bigfoot.com
Dir: *follow signs to North Bay. By Alexander Bowls Centre turn into Queens Parade. Hotel on cliff top*

Benefiting from an elevated position on the sea front, this small family-run hotel is immaculately maintained. The bedrooms are brightly decorated, well co-ordinated and equipped with many useful extras. Good home cooking is served in the cosy, traditional dining room and there is also a well-stocked bar and choice of lounges.
FACILITIES: 10 en suite (3 fmly) No smoking TVB tea/coffee No dogs (ex guide dogs) Licensed Cen ht TVL No coaches Dinner Last d 2pm
PRICES: s £26.50-£28; d £43-£50✻ **PARKING:** 10
NOTES: Closed 30 Nov-Jan **CARDS:**

♦♦♦♦ Lonsdale Villa Hotel

Lonsdale Rd YO11 2QY ☎ 01723 363383
e-mail: lonsdalevilla@talk21.com
Dir: *from A64 turn onto B1427 (Queen Margaret Road), at mini rdbt right onto A165 (Filey) turn 2nd left into Granville Rd/ Lonsdale Road*
FACILITIES: 10 en suite No smoking in bedrooms No smoking in dining room No smoking in 1 lounge TVB tea/coffee No dogs (ex guide dogs) Licensed Cen ht TVL No coaches Dinner Last d 10am **PRICES:** s £20-£25; d £40-£50✻ **LB** **NOTES:** Closed Nov-Feb

♦♦♦♦ Mount House Hotel

33 Trinity Rd, South Cliff YO11 2TD ☎ 01723 362967
e-mail: bookings@mounthouse-hotel.co.uk
Dir: *off A64 into Valley Rd(direction SPA, Park&Ride), at 2nd mini-rdbt take 2nd exit, Westbourne Grove, 1st R in Trinity Rd. Hotel 300 yds on R*
FACILITIES: 8 rms (7 en suite) (1 fmly) No smoking TVB tea/coffee No dogs (ex guide dogs) Licensed Cen ht TVL No coaches Dinner Last d 9am
PRICES: s £26.50-£39; d £53-£56✻ **LB** **PARKING:** 3
NOTES: Closed Dec-Jan **CARDS:**

♦♦♦ Argo Hotel

134 North Marine Rd YO12 7HZ ☎ 01723 375745
Dir: *close to Scarborough Cricket Ground main entrance*
A haven for cricket fans, this pleasant hotel offers comfortable bedrooms - those at the rear overlook the championship ground - and tasty breakfasts. The resident proprietors provide friendly and caring services. A residents' bar and cosy lounge are also provided.
FACILITIES: 8 rms (5 en suite) (2 fmly) No smoking in 2 bedrooms No smoking in dining room TVB tea/coffee No dogs Licensed Cen ht TVL No coaches Dinner Last d 3pm **PRICES:** s £16-£17; d £38-£40✻ **LB**
BB **NOTES:** Closed Dec

♦♦♦ Hotel Danielle

9 Esplanade Rd, South Cliff YO11 2AS ☎ 01723 366206
e-mail: hoteldanielle@yahoo.co.uk
Dir: *A64 to Scarborough, past B&Q, right at mini island to Queen Margarets Rd, next island on Filey Rd turn right, immediately left Avenue Victoria, straight across at x-rds to Esplanade. Left 50 yds left Esplanade Rd hotel on right.*
A comfortable family run guest house situated just off the South Cliff Esplanade, so many rooms have sea views down the bay. Rooms are well equipped and hospitality is kind and caring.
FACILITIES: 9 rms (7 en suite) (4 fmly) No smoking in dining room TVB tea/coffee No dogs (ex guide dogs) Licensed Cen ht TVL No children 2yrs Dinner Last d 10am **PRICES:** s £20-£24; d £44-£54✻ **LB**
NOTES: Closed Dec-mid Feb

♦♦♦ Lysander Hotel

22 Weydale Av YO12 6AX ☎ 01723 373369
e-mail: joy-harry@lysanderhotel.freeserve.co.uk
Dir: *between Peasholm Park & Northstead Manor Gardens*
Close to the North Shore attractions, in a quiet residential area, this well maintained hotel offers comfortable accommodation. Bedrooms have attractive soft furnishings and are well equipped. There is a cosy lounge bar that often hosts evening entertainment, and a bright dining room where good home cooked food is served. The resident owners provide friendly service.
FACILITIES: 18 rms (15 en suite) (3 fmly) No smoking in dining room TVB tea/coffee No dogs (ex guide dogs) Licensed Cen ht TVL Dinner Last d 7pm
PRICES: s £21-£26; d £42-£52✻ **LB** **PARKING:** 10 **NOTES:** Closed Jan-Feb rs 24-28 Dec & 30 Dec-2 Jan **CARDS:**

♦♦♦ North End Farm Country

88 Main St, Seamer YO12 4RF ☎ 01723 862965
Dir: *turn off A64 onto B1261 at new rdbt, continue through Seamer Village. Farmhouse adjacent to 2nd rdbt on B1261*
Located in Seamer, a village inland from Scarborough, this 18th century farmhouse contains comfortable, well equipped bedrooms, all with en suite facilities. Breakfast is served at individual tables in the smart dining room, and the cosy lounge has colour TV.
FACILITIES: 3 en suite No smoking TVB tea/coffee No dogs (ex guide dogs) Cen ht TVL No coaches **PRICES:** s £26-£32; d £40-£44 **PARKING:** 6

England

SCARBOROUGH continued

♦♦♦ Parmelia Hotel

17 West St YO11 2QN ☎ 01723 361914
e-mail: parmaliehotel@btinternet.com
Dir: *turn right off A64 at The Mere, up Queen Margarets Rd, left at next circle (A165) down Ramshill Rd, turn right - Esplanade Gdns Rd*
Only a short walk from the Esplanade on the south cliff, this large guest house provides modern co-ordinated bedrooms. Cheerful hospitality is extended to all guests who are made to feel at home. There is an attractive lounge to relax in and a spacious lounge bar.
FACILITIES: 14 rms (12 en suite) (4 fmly) (1 GF) No smoking in bedrooms No smoking in dining room No smoking in 1 lounge TVB tea/coffee No dogs (ex guide dogs) Licensed Cen ht TVL No children 4yrs Dinner Last d 3pm **PRICES:** s £19.50-£29.50; d £39-£43* **LB NOTES:** Closed Nov-Feb

♦♦♦ Plane Tree Cottage Farm *(SE999984)*

Staintondale YO13 0EY ☎ 01723 870796 Mrs M A Edmondson
Dir: *7m N of Scarborough*
The Edmondson family are welcoming hosts and their rare breeds farm is an interesting and pleasant venue for a tranquil stay in a secluded setting. The good home-cooking, comfortable bedrooms and cosy lounge and dining room all make a stay here memorable.
FACILITIES: 2 en suite No smoking tea/coffee No dogs Cen ht TVL No children 60 acres sheep hens Dinner Last d 10am **PRICES:** d £42*
PARKING: 2 **NOTES:** Closed Nov-Feb

♦♦♦ Premier Hotel

66 Esplande, South Cliffe YO11 2UZ ☎ 01723 501062
01723 501112
e-mail: trevor@twynn.freeserve.co.uk
Dir: *on the Esplanade, just prior to clock tower and putting green*
Located on the Esplanade overlooking the south bay, this large Victorian hotel retains many of its original features. Well-equipped bedrooms are stylishly decorated, and many have splendid sea views. Friendly hospitality and attentive service ensure a relaxing stay. There is an elegant, comfortable lounge, a well stocked bar lounge, and careful home cooking is enjoyable.
FACILITIES: 18 en suite (2 fmly) No smoking in dining room TVB tea/coffee Licensed Lift Cen ht No children 12yrs No coaches Dinner Last d breakfast
PRICES: s £35; d £70-£92* **LB PARKING:** 5 **NOTES:** Closed Dec-Jan
CARDS:

♦♦♦ Stewart Hotel

15 St Nicholas Cliff YO11 2ES ☎ 01723 361095
01723 350442
Dir: *follow A64 to town centre lights, right then left at the next lights. Over next set & straight on at rdbt. 2nd right, opposite Grand Hotel*
This imposing Georgian terrace house commands a central location in the town and is close to the beach. Bedrooms vary in size and style and those on the top (fourth) floor boast excellent views of the sea and castle. Decor is bright and cheerful, with a smart lounge and basement dining room.
FACILITIES: 14 en suite (2 fmly) No smoking in 1 bedrooms No smoking in dining room TVB tea/coffee No dogs (ex guide dogs) Licensed Cen ht TVL No coaches **PRICES:** d £50-£60* **LB CARDS:**

♦♦♦ Brincliffe Edge Hotel

105 Queens Pde YO12 7HY ☎ 01723 364834
e-mail: brincliffeedgehotel@yahoo.co.uk
Dir: *from North Marine Road by Alexander Bowls Centre, take road right, follow round into Queens Parade, hotel on right overlooking sea*
FACILITIES: 10 rms (7 en suite) (3 fmly) No smoking in 4 bedrooms No smoking in dining room TVB tea/coffee No dogs (ex guide dogs) Licensed Cen ht TVL No children 5yrs No coaches **PRICES:** s £19-£23; d £44-£50*
LB BB PARKING: 8 **NOTES:** Closed Dec-Jan
CARDS:

♦♦♦ Kenways

9 Victoria Park Av YO12 7TR ☎ 01723 365757 01723 365757
Dir: *from North Bay Beach follow road to rdbt where Peasholm Park is, take left turning along side of park until you come to Peasholm Hotel and shops. Victoria Park Avenue is between the two on the left*
FACILITIES: 7 en suite (2 fmly) No smoking in bedrooms No smoking in dining room TVB tea/coffee TVL No coaches Dinner Last d noon
PRICES: s £17.50-£18; d £35-£36* **BB NOTES:** Closed 22 Dec-5 Jan

♦♦♦ Sefton Hotel

18 Prince of Wales Ter YO11 2AL ☎ 01723 372310
Dir: *turn off A64 South Bay. Sefton Hotel 0.5m*
FACILITIES: 10 en suite No smoking in 8 bedrooms No smoking in dining room No smoking in lounges No dogs (ex guide dogs) Licensed Lift Cen ht TVL No children No coaches Dinner Last d 6pm **PRICES:** s £22-£23; d £44-£46* **NOTES:** Closed Nov-Feb

♦♦ Jalna House Hotel

168 North Marine Rd YO12 7HZ ☎ 01723 360668
01723 360668
e-mail: jalna@btconnect.com
Dir: *enter Scarborough on A64 and drive in town centre at T-junction (railway station on right). Turn left, through traffic lights, over 2 roundabouts to Peasholm Park. Turn right, right again and hotel on right*
A former gentleman's residence close to Peasholme Park and within walking distance of both the North Beach and the town centre. Compact bedrooms are comfortable, there is a cosy lounge and a dining room serving tasty home cooked meals.
FACILITIES: 10 rms (6 en suite) (6 fmly) No smoking in dining room TVB tea/coffee Licensed Cen ht TVL Dinner Last d noon
PRICES: s £17; d £34* **BB**

♦♦ Kerry Lee (Non Smoking) Private Hotel

60 Trafalgar Square YO12 7PY ☎ 01723 363845
Dir: *In Scarborough follow signs to North Bay Leisure Parks, at Peasholm Park rdbt take North Marine Rd turning, turn right at Post Office on the corner*
A warm and friendly welcome is offered at this value for money, non-smoking, guest house which is located in quiet residential square close to the cricket ground. Meals are served in a cosy dining room, which has a bar, and there is a very comfortable lounge
FACILITIES: 8 rms (2 en suite) (4 fmly) No smoking TVB tea/coffee Licensed TVL Dinner Last d 4pm **PRICES:** s £13-£16; d £26-£32* **LB BB**
CARDS:

♦♦ Lyness

145 Columbus Ravine YO12 7QZ
☎ 01723 375952 07966 404219
Dir: *A64 to Scarborough. Follow North Bay signs to Peasholm Park, we are situated 200yds away from the park on the opposite side of the road.*
Substantial breakfasts are served at this friendly guest house and evening meals are available by prior arrangement. Guests are also free to use the comfortable and inviting lounge. The well maintained bedrooms are all en suite and are cheerfully decorated.
FACILITIES: 8 rms (6 en suite) (2 fmly) No smoking in 4 bedrooms No smoking in dining room No smoking in lounges TVB tea/coffee Licensed Cen ht TVL Dinner Last d 4pm **PRICES:** s £18-£20; d £36-£40* **LB BB**

Smoking restrictions appear under the **FACILITIES** heading, please check when booking.

SCOTCH CORNER Map 08 NZ20

♦♦♦ Vintage Hotel
DL10 6NP ☎ 01748 824424 & 822961 01748 826272
Dir: *leave A1 at Scotch Corner and take A66 towards Penrith, hotel is 200yds on left*
FACILITIES: 8 rms (5 en suite) TVB tea/coffee Direct dial from bedrooms No dogs (ex guide dogs) Licensed Cen ht TVL Dinner Last d 9pm
PRICES: s £23.50-£35.50; d £29.50-£42.50; (room only) * **LB BB**
CONF: Thtr 40 Class 30 Board 20 **PARKING:** 40
CARDS:

SETTLE Map 07 SD86

♦♦♦♦ Golden Lion
5 Duke St BD24 9DU ☎ 01729 822203 01729 824103
e-mail: goldenlion@yorks.net
Dir: *in town centre opposite Barclays Bank*

This former traditional coaching inn is located centrally within the town. The Golden Lion provides a wide range of freshly prepared meals, which are served in either the character bar or the spacious restaurant. Most of the bedrooms have been stylishly refurbished to compliment the sparkling new bathrooms.
FACILITIES: 12 rms (10 en suite) (2 fmly) No smoking in dining room TVB tea/coffee No dogs (ex guide dogs) Cen ht Pool Table Dinner Last d 10pm
PRICES: s £25.50-£33; d £50-£62* **LB MEALS:** Lunch fr £9.95&alc Dinner £12.50-£18.50alc* **PARKING:** 11 **CARDS:**

♦♦♦♦ Liverpool House
Chapel Square BD24 9HR ☎ 01729 822247
Dir: *turn off B6480 by side of police station (Chapel Street) and take 2nd turning on right*
This Grade II listed building, within walking distance of the town centre, was originally a gatehouse for an intended waterway link to the Leeds-Liverpool Canal. Its character is shown in the top floor beamed bedrooms which are all comfortably furnished. A cosy TV lounge is available and a substantial breakfast is served in the dining room. Proprietors are very friendly and nothing is too much trouble.
FACILITIES: 7 rms (2 en suite) No smoking tea/coffee No dogs (ex guide dogs) Licensed Cen ht TVL No coaches **PRICES:** s £20-£22; d £40-£48* **LB PARKING:** 8 **CARDS:**

♦♦♦ The Oast Guest House
5 Pen-y-Ghent View, Church St BD24 9JJ ☎ 01729 822989
01729 822989
e-mail: king@oast2000.freeserve.co.uk
Dir: *N from Settle (Shambles & Market Place on right/Shell petrol station on left.) premises 100yds on left*
This friendly guest house provides a range of accommodation and many bedrooms enjoy delightful views of the surrounding hills.
continued
Home-cooked dinners are available by arrangement, and vegetarians are provided for with specially prepared dishes. Guests are invited to relax in the comfortable sitting room to study the wealth of local information.
FACILITIES: 5 rms (3 en suite) (1 fmly) No smoking TVB tea/coffee No dogs (ex guide dogs) Licensed Cen ht TVL No coaches Golf Fishing Riding Dinner Last d noon **PRICES:** s £30-£40; d £42-£48* **LB PARKING:** 4

♦♦♦ Whitefriars Country Guesthouse
Church St BD24 9JD ☎ 01729 823753
e-mail: info@whitefriars-settle.co.uk
Dir: *from A65 follow signs through Settle market place, premises signposted 50 yds on left, north of market place.*
This friendly, family run house can be found in peaceful gardens just a short stroll from the town centre. Bedrooms, some quite spacious, are attractively furnished and thoughtfully equipped. Good standards of home cooking are offered in the beamed dining room where dishes are freshly prepared from a daily changing menu.
FACILITIES: 9 rms (6 en suite) (2 fmly) No smoking TVB tea/coffee No dogs (ex guide dogs) Licensed Cen ht TVL No coaches Dinner Last d 10am
PRICES: s £19.50; d £39-£50* **PARKING:** 9 **NOTES:** Closed Xmas Day

SKIPTON Map 07 SD95

♦♦♦♦ Low Skibeden Farmhouse ***(SD013526)***
Skibeden Rd BD23 6AB ☎ 01756 793849 & 07050 207787
01756 793804 Mrs H Simpson
e-mail: skibhols.yorksdales@talk21.com
Dir: *at E end of Skipton bypass off A65/59*

A warm welcome awaits guests at this lovely stone farmhouse set in lovingly tended gardens on the outskirts of town. Heather Simpson is the perfect host and offers all guests afternoon tea, suppertime drinks and good hearty breakfasts. A range of well-equipped accommodation is available including spacious family rooms.
FACILITIES: 5 rms (4 en suite) (3 fmly) No smoking tea/coffee No dogs Cen ht TVL No children 10yrs 40 acres Beef & sheep **PRICES:** s £30-£40; d £44-£52 **LB PARKING:** 6 **CARDS:**

♦♦♦ Brylie House
48 Keighley Rd BD23 2NB ☎ 01756 700860 01756 791454
e-mail: keith@bryliehouse.fsnet.co.uk
Dir: *Skipton town centre take A629 to Keighley. Over Canal bridge with Eastwoods fish restaurant on L. Brylie House is 200 yds up rd on R.*
A warm welcome is assured at this small guest house which is situated just a few minutes walk from the town centre. In keeping with the period of the property, bedrooms are elegantly decorated and furnished. Substantial breakfasts are cooked to order and served in the ground floor dining room.
FACILITIES: 3 en suite No smoking TVB tea/coffee No coaches
PRICES: s £20-£40; d £32-£40* **LB BB**

England

♦♦♦ Cravendale

57 Keighley Rd BD23 2LX ☎ 01756 795129

Dir: *A629 out of Skipton, over canal bridge. Cravendale Guest House is on the left*

This family run, friendly guest house is situated within easy walking distance of the town centre. Bedrooms vary in size and style. A substantial Yorkshire breakfast is offered in the cosy dining room and service is friendly and attentive.

FACILITIES: 3 en suite (2 fmly) No smoking TVB tea/coffee No dogs Licensed TVL No coaches Dinner Last d noon **PRICES:** s fr £21.50; d fr £37✳ BB

♦♦♦ Craven House

56 Keighley Rd BD23 2NB ☎ 01756 794657 🖷 01756 794657

e-mail: info@craven-house.co.uk

Dir: *from Keighley, Craven House is on A629 into Skipton just past Esso garage*

Situated just a short stroll from the market square, this double fronted late Victorian house offers well-equipped, homely bedrooms and hearty English breakfasts. Chris and Joanne Rushton are friendly and caring hosts.

FACILITIES: 7 rms (3 en suite) No smoking in dining room No smoking in lounges TVB tea/coffee Cen ht **PRICES:** s fr £20; d fr £30✳ **PARKING:** 3 **NOTES:** Closed 25 Dec-3 Jan **CARDS:**

♦♦♦ Herriots Hotel, Bar & Dining Rooms

Broughton Rd BD23 1RT ☎ 01756 792781 🖷 01756 793967

e-mail: herriots@mgrleisure.com

Dir: *off A59, opposite railway station*

Close to the centre of the town and on the doorstep of the Yorkshire Dales National Park, this friendly hotel offers brightly decorated, modern equipped bedrooms. The stylish open-plan brasserie is a relaxing place in which to dine from the varied menu. Meals and snacks are also available in the bar. Entertainment is normally provided on Sunday evenings.

FACILITIES: 13 en suite (2 fmly) No smoking in bedrooms TVB tea/coffee Direct dial from bedrooms Dinner **PRICES:** s £50-£60; d £55-£65✳ LB **MEALS:** Lunch £5-£8 Dinner £10-£15✳ **CONF:** Thtr 20 Class 15 Board 14 Del from £65 ✳ **PARKING:** 25 **CARDS:**

♦♦♦ Rockwood House

14 Main St, Embsay BD23 6RE ☎ 01756 799755 🖷 01756 799755

e-mail: jstead@btclick.com

Dir: *take A59 Harrogate Road from Skipton, pass the castle and continue for 250yds turn left to Embsay at the Elmtree Inn.Road bears right, car park 50yds on left, Rockwood House opposite*

This end terrace Victorian house enjoys a peaceful location in the village of Embsay. Bedrooms are thoughtfully furnished, individually styled and reassuringly comfortable. The traditionally styled dining room sets the venue for hearty breakfasts. Hospitality is a feature here; the warmth of welcome being genuine and friendly.

continued

FACILITIES: 3 en suite (1 fmly) (1 GF) No smoking TVB tea/coffee No dogs (ex guide dogs) Cen ht TVL No coaches **PRICES:** s £20-£25; d £38-£42✳ LB BB **PARKING:** 3 **CARDS:**

♦♦♦ Westfield House

50 Keighley Rd BD23 2NB ☎ 01756 790849

Dir: *from S: M1 take A650 J41 to Bradford and Keighley - A629 Skipton - past Esso garage on left. Westfield house 200 yds on left in Keighley Road*

Just a short stroll from the town centre, this friendly guest house provides smart, well-equipped accommodation. Bedrooms are well-presented and some have king sized beds. Thoughtful accessories including bathrobes are also provided. A hearty breakfast is served in the cosy dining room. Hospitality here is very good and nothing is too much trouble.

FACILITIES: 5 rms (4 en suite) No smoking STV TVB tea/coffee No dogs Cen ht No children No coaches **PRICES:** s £22-£23; d £42-£44✳

STEARSBY — Map 08 SE67

♦♦♦♦ The Granary

YO61 4SA ☎ 01347 888652 🖷 01347 888652

e-mail: roberttur1@thegranary.org.uk

Dir: *Off A1237 onto B1363 towards Helmsley, on reaching Brandsby village turn right before Post Office heading for Stearsby & Sherrif Hutton, 2m on to small x-rds Stearsby on left*

Renovated farm buildings sitting in large gardens on open farmland, this is a haven for peace and tranquillity, yet only minutes from Ampleforth, Helmsley, or York. Guests may use the outdoor heated swimming pool in summer, and expect warm hospitality all the year round.

FACILITIES: 1 en suite 2 annexe en suite (2 GF) No smoking in bedrooms No smoking in dining room No smoking in 1 lounge TVB tea/coffee Cen ht TVL No coaches Outdoor swimming pool (heated) **PRICES:** s £30-£35; d £50-£55✳ **PARKING:** 6 **NOTES:** Closed Nov-Jan

THIRSK — Map 08 SE48

♦♦♦♦ The Old Manor House

27 Front St, Sowerby YO7 1JQ ☎ 01845 526642 🖷 01845 526568

Dir: *from town centre take road for Ripon, at 1st mini-rdbt take left signed Sowerby. Past St Oswalds Church on left & take next house on green, after walled field is The Old Manor House*

Reputedly the oldest house in Thirsk, the Old Manor House's origins can be traced to at least the beginning of the 17th century. Bedrooms are well equipped and comfortable, with views of the garden and hills beyond at the back and the village green at the front. Two of the three suites have an adjacent breakfast room. The third is larger and incorporates a breakfast area as part of the room.

FACILITIES: 3 en suite (2 fmly) No smoking TVB tea/coffee Cen ht No coaches **PRICES:** s fr £35; d fr £45✳ **PARKING:** 3 **NOTES:** Closed Xmas **CARDS:**

♦♦♦♦ **Spital Hill**
York Rd YO7 3AE ☎ 01845 522273 01845 524970
e-mail: spitalhill@amserve.net
Dir: *from A1(M) take A168, then A170, at rdbt take A19 to York for 1m. House set back 600yds from road on right, drive marked by 2 white posts*

Set in gardens this substantial Victorian country house is delightfully furnished. Spacious bedrooms are thoughtfully equipped with many extras - one even has a piano - but no TVs or kettles, the proprietor preferring to offer tea as a service. Delicious meals feature local and home-grown produce and are served house party style around one table in the interesting dining room.
FACILITIES: 3 en suite 2 annexe en suite No smoking Direct dial from bedrooms No dogs (ex guide dogs) Licensed Cen ht TVL No children 12yrs No coaches Croquet lawn Dinner Last d 2pm **PRICES:** s £50-£54; d £80-£90 **LB** **PARKING:** 6 **CARDS:**

THORNTON LE DALE — Map 08 SE88

Premier Collection

♦♦♦♦♦ **Allerston Manor House**
YO18 7PF ☎ 01723 850112 01723 850112
e-mail: aa@allerston-manor.com
Dir: *from A64, E of Malton, take B1258. On leaving Yedingham, turn left, then immediately right to Allerston. In Allerston, the driveway on right after Church Ln*
A Queen Anne house which overlooks the village church, it built around a 14th-century Knights Templar Hall. This beautifully furnished home offers guests fine hospitality. Bedrooms have been thoughtfully equipped and furnished, and the spacious drawing room offers every comfort. Dinner, which features the best of seasonal local produce, is served around one large table, and guests are invited to bring their own wine.
FACILITIES: 3 en suite No smoking TVB tea/coffee No dogs Cen ht No children 12yrs No coaches Croquet lawn Dinner Last d by arrangement
PRICES: s £50-£70; d £70-£90* **LB** **PARKING:** 7
CARDS:

THWAITE — Map 07 SD89

♦♦♦ **Kearton Country Hotel**
DL11 6DR ☎ 01748 886277 01748 886590
e-mail: jdanton@aol.com
Ideal for both walkers and visitors, this stone built guest house is located in the heart of the dales in the delightful village of Thwaite. Comfortable accommodation is complemented by a popular a tearoom and restaurant where an extensive range of food is served. There is also a spacious lounge.

continued

FACILITIES: 13 rms (12 en suite) (2 fmly) No smoking in dining room tea/coffee No dogs (ex guide dogs) Licensed Cen ht Last d 6.30pm
PRICES: (incl. dinner) s fr £31.50; d fr £63* **PARKING:** 50
CARDS:

WESTOW — Map 08 SE76

♦♦♦♦ **Woodhouse Farm** *(SE749637)*
YO60 7LL ☎ 01653 618378 01653 618378 Mrs S Wardle
e-mail: woodhousefarm@farmersweekly.net
Dir: *from A64 turn to Kirkham Priory and continue to Westow. Right at T-junct and 0.5m out of village, farmhouse on right*
A young farming family who open their home and offer caring hospitality. Home made bread, jams and farm produce turn breakfast into a feast, and the views from the house across the open fields are splendid.
FACILITIES: 2 en suite (1 fmly) No smoking in bedrooms No smoking in dining room TVB tea/coffee No dogs (ex guide dogs) Cen ht 350 acres arable/beef **PRICES:** s £18.50-£25; d £37-£40 **LB** **BB** **PARKING:** 12
NOTES: Closed Nov-Apr

♦♦♦ **Blacksmith Arms**
Main St, Westow YO60 7NE ☎ 01653 618365 & 618343
01653 618365
e-mail: blacksmithsinn@clycom.net
Dir: *turn right off A64 between York and Malton onto unclassified road signposted Kirkham Priory and Westow for 1.5m*
Retaining many of its original 18th-century features, this traditional public house is popular with both locals and tourists. A comprehensive range of well-cooked dishes is available in the bar and there is also a games room. Bedrooms are located in the carefully restored outbuildings and all are comfortable and well equipped with nice compact en suites.
FACILITIES: 6 annexe en suite No smoking in bedrooms No smoking in dining room TVB tea/coffee Direct dial from bedrooms No dogs (ex guide dogs) Cen ht TVL Dinner Last d 9.30pm **PRICES:** s fr £22.50; d £45-£50*
MEALS: Lunch £5-£10 Dinner £5-£10* **PARKING:** 18
NOTES: Closed Xmas **CARDS:**

WEST TANFIELD — Map 08 SE27

♦♦♦ **Bruce Arms**
Main St HG4 5JJ ☎ 01677 470325 01677 470796
Dir: *turn off A1 northbound, onto B6267 at sign for Masham/Thirsk, follow signs for Lightwater Valley, approx 4.5m to West Tanfield*
At the heart of this quiet village, this stone built inn dates from the 1700s and is a popular bistro/pub serving quality food. The three bedrooms are smartly furnished in pine and are both comfortable and very well-equipped. The resident owners provide warm hospitality.
FACILITIES: 3 en suite No smoking in bedrooms TVB tea/coffee No dogs (ex guide dogs) Cen ht No coaches Dinner Last d 9.30pm
PRICES: s fr £40; d fr £60* **LB** **PARKING:** 22 **NOTES:** Closed 2 wks Jan rs lunch Sat & Sun. Dinner Tue-Sat **CARDS:**

♦♦♦ ***Bull***
Church St HG4 5JQ ☎ 01677 470678 01677 470678
e-mail: cwba@bullinn.demon.co.uk
Dir: *6m from Ripon on A6108*
Benefiting from a private river frontage, this 17th-century inn is peacefully located within the pretty village of West Tanfield. The well-equipped comfortable bedrooms boast modern en suite facilities. There are a range of appetising bar meals which are served in the cosy bar lounge.
FACILITIES: 5 en suite (2 fmly) No smoking in bedrooms No smoking in dining room TVB tea/coffee Cen ht Dinner Last d 9pm **PARKING:** 20
CARDS:

England

WHITBY Map 08 NZ81

♦♦♦♦ Chiltern

13 Normanby Ter, West Cliff YO21 3ES ☎ 01947 604981 🖷 01947 604981
e-mail: john@chilternguesthouse.fsnet.co.uk
Dir: *In Whitby follow signs to West Cliff. Proceed until you pass Pavilion Theatre on L. Next R Crescent Avenue, then 2nd L.*

A warm welcome is assured at this well maintained Victorian terraced house which is located in a mainly residential road a few minutes' walk from the town and historic port. Many of the homely bedrooms have the benefit of small, modern en suite facilities.

FACILITIES: 8 rms (5 en suite) (2 fmly) No smoking in 4 bedrooms No smoking in dining room TVB tea/coffee Cen ht TVL
PRICES: s fr £20; d fr £45✱ LB BB

♦♦♦♦ Corra Lynn

28 Crescent Av YO21 3EW ☎ 01947 602214 🖷 01947 602214
Dir: *corner of A174 & Crescent Avenue*

Within walking distance of the town and the picturesque harbour, this friendly guesthouse is ideally situated on the West Cliff. The well-equipped bedrooms are comfortable and are cheerfully decorated. Breakfasts are hearty and the menu changes according to the season. You can be assured of warm hospitality.

FACILITIES: 5 en suite (1 fmly) No smoking in dining room No smoking in lounges TVB tea/coffee Licensed Cen ht TVL No children 5yrs No coaches **PRICES:** s fr £21; d fr £48✱ **PARKING:** 5 **NOTES:** Closed 21Dec-01Feb rs Nov-Apr

See advertisement on opposite page

♦♦♦♦ Crescent House

6 East Crescent YO21 3HD ☎ 01947 600091 🖷 01947 600091
e-mail: janet@whitby.fsbusiness.co.uk
Dir: *follow signs for Whitby town centre, straight ahead at rdbt, left lane at lights to go ahead into one way system. House 0.5m along on left*

As the name suggests, this friendly house is situated in an elegant crescent and has four rooms, each with a fine sea view. The bedrooms and bathrooms at Crescent House are smart and modern, and a number of the rooms have king-size beds.

FACILITIES: 6 en suite (2 fmly) No smoking TVB tea/coffee No dogs Cen ht TVL No coaches **PRICES:** s £42; d £46 **NOTES:** Closed mid Nov-Mid Mar

♦♦♦♦ Kimberley House Hotel

7 Havelock Place YO21 3ER ☎ 01947 604125 🖷 01947 606147
e-mail: enquiries@kimberleyhousehotel.co.uk
Dir: *on the W cliff of Whitby, at the corner of Havelock Place and Hudson Street*

A 19th century town house built for a local seafaring family, in a quiet residential area within walking distance of the West Cliff promenades and the historic town centre. Bedrooms are well equipped and comfortable, and a wide choice of breakfasts is available. Julie and Stephen are warm and friendly hosts.

continued

FACILITIES: 8 en suite (2 fmly) (1 GF) No smoking TVB tea/coffee No dogs (ex guide dogs) Cen ht **PRICES:** s £20-£30; d £44✱ LB
NOTES: Closed 17 Dec-1 Feb

♦♦♦♦ Seacliffe Hotel

North Promenade, West Cliff YO21 3JX ☎ 01947 603139 🖷 01947 603139
e-mail: julie@seacliffe.fsnet.co.uk
Dir: *follow signs for West Cliff & West Cliff car park, hotel on seafront*

Enjoying fine sea views, this holiday hotel on the West Cliff has an attractive beamed restaurant where an extensive menu is served. Bedrooms may be compact but are comfortably furnished and superbly equipped. The residents' lounge is adjacent to the bar which leads out onto a sunny, summer patio.

FACILITIES: 19 en suite (4 fmly) No smoking in 3 bedrooms No smoking in dining room STV TVB tea/coffee Direct dial from bedrooms Licensed Cen ht TVL Pool Table Dinner Last d 8.45pm **PRICES:** s £42.50-£49.50; d £67-£71✱ LB **PARKING:** 8 **CARDS:**

See advertisement on opposite page

♦♦♦♦ The Waverley

17 Crescent Av YO21 3ED ☎ 01947 604389 🖷 01947 604389
e-mail: the.waverley@virgin.net
Dir: *follow signs to West Cliff, hotel 200yds from Crescent Gardens*

A warm welcome from the friendly owners awaits guests to this comfortable family home. Within easy reach of the seafront, harbour and shops, The Waverley offers bright, fresh bedrooms with modern appointments. In addition to the sitting room there is a cosy lounge bar and enjoyable home cooking and hearty breakfasts are served at individual tables in a pleasant dining room.

FACILITIES: 6 rms (5 en suite) (2 fmly) No smoking in dining room TVB tea/coffee No dogs Licensed Cen ht TVL No children 5yrs No coaches Dinner Last d 1pm **PRICES:** s £19-£21; d £46-£50✱ BB
PARKING: 3 **NOTES:** Closed 9 Nov-8 Feb
CARDS:

♦♦♦ *Sandbeck Hotel*

2 Crescent Ter, West Cliff YO21 3EL ☎ 01947 604012 🖷 01947 606402
e-mail: dysonsandbeck@tesco.net
Dir: *on West Cliff, opposite the theatre and Pavilion booking office*

Enjoying spectacular views from all front rooms this family run hotel provides comfortable and spacious accommodation. Within strolling distance of Whitby's many attractions, the Sandbeck is quietly located on the West Cliff. An attractive lounge and pleasant dining room are provided and at breakfast, an extensive choice is offered including vegetarian and children's menus.

FACILITIES: 15 en suite (6 fmly) No smoking in dining room No smoking in lounges TVB tea/coffee Licensed Cen ht TVL No coaches
NOTES: Closed Dec **CARDS:**

♦♦♦ Ye Olde Beehive Inn

Newholm YO21 3QY ☎ 01947 602703

Dir: *between Whitby and Sandsend on A174 is Whitby Golf Course, Newholm is 1m inland. Or 0.5m from A171*

The exterior walls are whitewashed, and inside this 15th century inn there are old oak beams and a host of interesting features. Bedrooms are equipped with modern conveniences and hospitality is informal and friendly, particularly in the bar where the locals congregate.

FACILITIES: 3 en suite No smoking in bedrooms TVB tea/coffee Cen ht TVL No children Dinner Last d 9pm **PRICES:** d fr £50 **PARKING:** 30 **CARDS:**

♦♦♦ Rosslyn

11 Abbey Ter YO21 3HQ ☎ 01947 604086 01947 604086

e-mail: rosslynhouse@bushinternet.com

Dir: *from A169 or A171 follow Westcliff car park signs then turn right past car park entrance then 1st left into Hudson St, Rosslyn on left*

FACILITIES: 6 en suite (2 fmly) (1 GF) No smoking in 3 bedrooms No smoking in dining room TVB tea/coffee No dogs Cen ht TVL No children 6 months No coaches Dinner Last d 12 hrs before meal **PRICES:** s £25; d £39-£42 **LB PARKING:** 2 **NOTES:** Closed mid Dec-mid Jan **CARDS:**

YORK

Map 08 SE65

See also Kexby

Premier Collection

♦♦♦♦♦ Alexander House

94 Bishopthorpe Rd YO23 1JS ☎ 01904 625016

e-mail: info@alexanderhouseyork.co.uk

Dir: *from A64 take A1036 York West into city centre, turn right at Scarcroft Rd at the end turn right Alexander House 100yds on left*

Guests are made to feel very much at home at this Victorian terraced house, which is located just a short walk from the city centre. Stylishly decorated and furnished throughout, the owners take delight in sharing their beautiful home with guests and have created four superbly equipped comfortable rooms. Delicious breakfasts featuring quality local produce are served in the well-appointed dining room.

FACILITIES: 4 en suite (1 fmly) No smoking TVB tea/coffee No dogs (ex guide dogs) Cen ht No children 9yrs No coaches **PRICES:** s £45-£49; d £55-£69✱ **LB PARKING:** 3 **NOTES:** Closed Xmas-New Year **CARDS:**

England

YORK continued

♦♦♦♦ Arndale Hotel

290 Tadcaster Rd YO24 1ET ☎ 01904 702424 📠 01904 709800

Dir: *turn off A64 onto A1036 towards city centre for 2m. Hotel on left overlooking racecourse*

Situated opposite the racecourse, this delightful Victorian house has been carefully restored to provide elegantly furnished accommodation. Several of the bedrooms have antique beds and three rooms are peacefully located in converted buildings at the far end of the garden. The breakfast menu is extensive and the spacious drawing room includes a well-stocked bar.

FACILITIES: 12 en suite (1 fmly) No smoking in bedrooms No smoking in dining room TVB tea/coffee Direct dial from bedrooms No dogs (ex guide dogs) Licensed Cen ht No coaches **PRICES:** s £50; d £80✻ **LB PARKING:** 20 **NOTES:** Closed Xmas & New Year **CARDS:**

♦♦♦♦ Hazelwood

24-25 Portland St, Gillygate YO31 7EH ☎ 01904 626548 📠 01904 628032

Dir: *approaching York from north on A19 turn left before City Gate and take 1st turning left*

An elegant Victorian town house quietly situated in the heart of the ancient city, only 400 yards from York Minster. The bedrooms are individually styled and tastefully fitted to very high standards using designer fabrics. Wide choice of breakfasts, including vegetarian, ranging from traditional English to croissants and Danish pastries. The car park is a real bonus in this central location.

FACILITIES: 14 en suite (2 fmly) (2 GF) No smoking TVB tea/coffee No dogs Licensed Cen ht No children 8yrs No coaches **PRICES:** s £49-£95; d £75-£100✻ **LB PARKING:** 9 **CARDS:**

♦♦♦♦ Ascot House

80 East Pde YO31 7YH ☎ 01904 426826 📠 01904 431077

e-mail: j&k@ascot-house-york.demon.co.uk

Dir: *From A1 or M1 take A64 for York. Stay on A64 ring-road to eastern side of city and take A1036 into York. After 30mph signs, take 2nd exit from rdbt signed Heworth, at traffic lights turn right into East Parade*

continued

Ascot House

This house dates from 1869 and stands in its own grounds. June and Keith Wood provide friendly service in Ascot House. Bedrooms are thoughtfully equipped; many with four poster or canopy beds and many other period pieces of furniture, the wide staircase has an impressive stained-glass window. Reception rooms include a comfortable lounge also retaining original features.

FACILITIES: 15 rms (12 en suite) (3 fmly) (2 GF) No smoking in dining room TVB tea/coffee Licensed Cen ht TVL Sauna **PRICES:** s £22-£50; d £44-£60✻ **LB PARKING:** 14 **CARDS:**

♦♦♦♦ Ashbourne House

139 Fulford Rd YO10 4HG ☎ 01904 639912 📠 01904 631332

e-mail: ashbourneh@aol.com

Dir: *on A19, follow signs to York city centre, through Fulford, after 2 traffic lights, establishment on right*

Aileen and David Minns extend a friendly welcome to their home, located just outside of the city centre. The bedrooms at Ashbourne house are thoughtfully equipped and suitably comfortable. Public areas include a lounge and a breakfast room, which are both practical and spacious.

FACILITIES: 7 en suite (2 fmly) No smoking TVB tea/coffee Direct dial from bedrooms No dogs (ex guide dogs) Licensed Cen ht No coaches **PRICES:** s £35-£45; d £40-£60✻ **LB PARKING:** 7 **NOTES:** Closed 24 Dec - 1 Jan **CARDS:**

♦♦♦♦ Brontë House

22 Grosvenor Ter, Bootham YO30 7AG ☎ 01904 621066 📠 01904 653434

e-mail: info@bronte-guesthouse.com

Dir: *from A19 north follow signs for city centre, take left turn immediately after Churchill Hotel into Grosvenor Terrace*

Beautifully decorated throughout, this warm and friendly guest house offers comfortable individually styled bedrooms; some with fine period furniture. Hearty breakfasts are served in the spacious dining room and special diets can also be catered for. A cosy residents' lounge is available.

continued

England

FACILITIES: 5 en suite (1 fmly) No smoking TVB tea/coffee No dogs (ex guide dogs) Cen ht No coaches **PRICES:** s £32-£40; d £54-£60 **LB** **PARKING:** 1 **NOTES:** Closed 23-29 Dec
CARDS:

♦♦♦♦ City Guest House

68 Monkgate YO31 7PF ☎ 01904 622483
e-mail: jeff@cityguesthouse.co.uk
Dir: *from A1 take A64 to York, at rdbt take A1036 to York in 2.5m blue sign on left*

Just a minutes walk from the historic Monkbar, City Guest house is superbly located for business, shopping or sightseeing. The thoughtfully furnished bedrooms boast stylish interior design and come equipped with a host of thoughtful touches. The smart dining room is the venue for the carefully cooked breakfasts.
FACILITIES: 7 en suite (1 fmly) No smoking TVB tea/coffee No dogs Cen ht No children 8 yrs No coaches **PRICES:** s £30-£35; d £54-£58✳ **PARKING:** 6 **NOTES:** Closed 20 Dec - 1 Feb
CARDS:

♦♦♦♦ Curzon Lodge and Stable Cottages

23 Tadcaster Rd, Dringhouses YO24 1QG ☎ 01904 703157
🖹 01904 703157
Dir: *from A64 take A1036 towards city centre, 2m on right between York Holiday Inn & York Marriott Hotel*

Close to York's famous Knavesmire Racecourse, this charming 17th-century Grade II listed house sits in gardens on the grand Royal route into the city. Comfortable, pine furnished bedrooms are located either in the main house or in the converted coach house and stables. Breakfast is served in the cottage-style dining room.
FACILITIES: 5 en suite 5 annexe en suite (1 fmly) No smoking TVB tea/coffee No dogs Cen ht No children 7yrs No coaches **PRICES:** s £39-£49; d £55-£70✳ **LB PARKING:** 16 **NOTES:** Closed 24-26 Dec
CARDS:

♦♦♦♦ The Granary

YO61 4SA ☎ 01347 888652 🖹 01347 888652
e-mail: robertturl@thegranary.org.uk
(For full entry see Stearsby)

♦♦♦♦ The Heathers

54 Shipton Rd, Clifton - Without YO30 5RQ ☎ 01904 640989
🖹 01904 640989
e-mail: thghyork@globalnet.co.uk
Dir: *north of York on A19 York/Thirsk rd, midway between A1237 ring road & York city centre*

Lying back off a main road just North of the city, this friendly family-run guest house extends a warm welcome to all guests. The modern bedrooms, some of which are on the ground floor, are neatly decorated and furnished. Hearty breakfasts are served in the pleasant breakfast room that looks out onto the gardens.
FACILITIES: 8 rms (5 en suite) (3 fmly) No smoking TVB tea/coffee No dogs Cen ht No children 10yrs No coaches **PRICES:** s £36-£104; d £40-£108 **PARKING:** 9 **NOTES:** Closed Xmas & Jan
CARDS:

♦♦♦♦ *Hobbits*

9 St Peters Grove, Clifton YO30 6AQ ☎ 01904 624538
🖹 01904 651765
e-mail: admin@ecsyork.co.uk
Dir: *A1237/A19 junct into York, to traffic lights at Clifton Green, after 500yds at footbridge over A19, turn left into St Peter's Grove*
Located in a quiet cul-de-sac, this large Victorian semi-detached house is just a short stroll from the city. Bedrooms, some of which are in an annexe, vary in size and are superbly equipped and decorated with modern fabrics and furniture. The stylish lounge boasts deep leather seating, and the dining room has a well-stocked bar.
FACILITIES: 9 en suite 10 annexe en suite (7 fmly) No smoking in 9 bedrooms No smoking in dining room No smoking in 1 lounge STV TVB tea/coffee Direct dial from bedrooms Licensed Cen ht TVL No coaches Dinner Last d 4pm **PARKING:** 15 **CARDS:**

♦♦♦ Diamonds are a guest's best friend!
The emphasis is on quality and guest care rather than extra facilities.

YORK continued

♦♦♦♦ Holly Lodge

204-206 Fulford Rd YO10 4DD ☎ 01904 646005

Dir: *on A19 south side, 1.5m on left from A64/A19 junct, or follow A19 Selby signs from city centre to Fulford Rd*

Just a few minutes walk from the city walls; this pleasant Georgian hotel offers co-ordinated bedrooms that are comfortable and well equipped. The spacious lounge comes complete with a grand piano and hearty breakfasts are served in the cosy dining room. Guests can also make use of the delightful walled garden.

FACILITIES: 5 en suite (1 fmly) No smoking TVB tea/coffee No dogs (ex guide dogs) Cen ht No coaches **PRICES:** d £58-£78✻ **PARKING:** 6 **NOTES:** Closed 24-27 Dec **CARDS:** 

♦♦♦♦ Holmwood House Hotel

114 Holgate Rd YO24 4BB ☎ 01904 626183 🖹 01904 670899

e-mail: holmwood.house@dial.pipex.com

Dir: *on A59, on the Harrogate to York road on L 300yds past The Fox pub*

With ample parking, a 15-minute walk from this delightful Victorian town house will take you into the centre of York. Elegantly styled bedrooms are richly decorated and smartly furnished with many antiques. There is a delightful lounge and a substantial breakfast is served in the pleasant dining room.

FACILITIES: 14 en suite (2 fmly) (4 GF) No smoking TVB tea/coffee Direct dial from bedrooms No dogs Licensed Cen ht No children 8yrs No coaches Jacuzzi **PRICES:** s £37.50-£65; d £65-£105✻ **LB** **CONF:** Class 20 Board 12 **PARKING:** 10 **CARDS:**

♦♦♦♦ Nunmill House

85 Bishopthorpe Rd YO23 1NX ☎ 01904 634047

🖹 01904 655879

e-mail: info@nunmill.co.uk

Dir: *400yds outside City Wall at SE corner between Scarcroft rd & Southlands Chapel*

This elegant Victorian house is set back from the road in a well tended garden. Co-ordinated bedrooms are individually styled and all have the expected modern comforts. There is a comfortably furnished residents' lounge, and a well-appointed dining room where a wide choice is offered for breakfast.

continued

FACILITIES: 8 en suite (1 fmly) No smoking TVB tea/coffee No dogs Cen ht No coaches **PRICES:** s £45-£50; d £50-£65 **PARKING:** 4 **NOTES:** Closed Dec-Jan

See advertisement on opposite page

♦♦♦ Bedford

108/110 Bootham YO30 7DG ☎ 01904 624412

🖹 01904 632851

e-mail: info@bedfordhotelyork.co.uk

Dir: *5mins walk north of York Minster*

Recognisable by its Tudor façade, the Bedford Hotel is well maintained throughout and offers spacious, co-ordinated bedrooms with modern amenities. A residents' bar is provided as well as a separate lounge and an attractive dining room, and freshly prepared meals are served. Ample parking is a bonus, as the city is just a few minutes' walk away.

FACILITIES: 17 en suite (5 fmly) No smoking in bedrooms No smoking in dining room No smoking in 1 lounge TVB tea/coffee No dogs (ex guide dogs) Licensed Cen ht TVL No coaches Pool Table Dinner Last d 3pm **PRICES:** d £56-£70 **PARKING:** 17 **NOTES:** Closed Xmas-New Year **CARDS:**

♦♦♦ Adams House Hotel

5 Main St, Fulford YO10 4HJ ☎ 01904 655413 🖹 01904 643203

e-mail: bob.cook@virgin.net

Dir: *turn left off A64 onto A19, hotel is 1m on right just beyond St Oswalds Church & traffic lights*

Situated approximately one and a half miles from York centre in the suburban village of Fulford, this Tudor style building offers comfortable accommodation. It has many fine period features, pleasant, well-proportioned bedrooms and an attractive dining room with fresh flowers on every table. The resident owners offer friendly and attentive service.

FACILITIES: 8 rms (7 en suite) (4 fmly) (2 GF) No smoking in dining room TVB tea/coffee No dogs (ex guide dogs) Licensed Cen ht Dinner Last d 2pm **PRICES:** s £25-£30; d £55-£60✻ **LB** **PARKING:** 8 **CARDS:**

♦♦♦ Beech House

6-7 Longfield Ter, Bootham YO30 7DJ ☎ 01904 634581

Dir: *from A64, A1237, A19, follow city centre signs for 1.5m, under pedestrian flyover, 2nd right into Bootham Ter which leads into Longfield Ter*

Located within easy walking distance of both the Minster and the Railway Museum (free entry). This extended Victorian villa is comfortable, homely with well-equipped bedrooms, and free parking. Breakfast is served in the spacious dining room and there is also a cosy lounge with piano and feature fireplace.

FACILITIES: 10 en suite No smoking in dining room No smoking in lounges TVB tea/coffee Direct dial from bedrooms No dogs Cen ht No children 10yrs No coaches **PRICES:** s £31-£35; d £52-£56✻ **LB** **PARKING:** 5 **NOTES:** Closed Dec-Jan

England

◆◆◆ Blue Bridge Hotel

Fishergate YO10 4AP ☎ 01904 621193 🖷 01904 671571
e-mail: info@bluebridgehotel.co.uk
Dir: *Exit A64 at 3rd exit for York signposted to city centre/A19,hotel is 2 miles on right*

This comfortable hotel has been remodelled in a modern style and is just five minutes walk from the centre of the city. A wide range of rooms from self contained suites to budget twins. A restaurant, which enjoys a local trade, two comfortable lounge bars, and ample parking are additional benefits.

FACILITIES: 15 rms (13 en suite) 3 annexe en suite (5 fmly) No smoking in 2 bedrooms No smoking in dining room TVB tea/coffee Direct dial from bedrooms Licensed Cen ht TVL Dinner Last d 9pm **PRICES:** s £45-£50; d £55-£90✳ **LB CONF:** Del from £79.50 ✳ **PARKING:** 15
CARDS: MasterCard, Barclaycard VISA, Barclays Connect, Switch

◆◆◆ *Cavalier Private Hotel*

39 Monkgate YO31 7PB ☎ 01904 636615 🖷 01904 636615
Dir: *on A1036 (A64) York to Malton rd, 250mtrs from York inner ring road & city wall (Monkgate)*

Only a minute's walk from Monk Bar, a gateway to the city with a working portcullis, this early Georgian house is ideal for sightseeing in York. The cosy bedrooms are comfortable and well equipped and English breakfast is served in the elegant dining room. Parking is available.

FACILITIES: 10 rms (7 en suite) (4 fmly) No smoking TVB tea/coffee No dogs (ex guide dogs) Cen ht TVL No children 5yrs No coaches Sauna
PARKING: 6 **CARDS:** MasterCard, Barclaycard VISA, Switch

85 Bishopthorpe Road, York, YO23 1NX
Tel: 01904 634047
Fax: 01904 655879
E-mail: info@nunmill.co.uk
Web: www.nunmill.co.uk

AA ◆◆◆◆

Nunmill House is an elegant Victorian residence lovingly restored to enhance the original architectural features now offers Bed and Breakfast and the benefit of an easy walk to all of York's historic attractions. Each bedroom, individually furnished and smoke-free is for those looking for comfortable yet affordable accommodation and includes tea/coffee facilities, colour TV, etc.

PLEASE VISIT OUR WEBSITE.

Greenside

124 Clifton, York. Tel: York (01904) 623631
Martyn & Lynne Tattersall

Greenside is a charming detached conservation house fronting on to Clifton Green.
Situated in a most convenient location just outside the city walls, close to the many attractions that York has to offer.
Spacious fully equipped large bedrooms are all situated on ground or first floor, all have tea/coffee facilities, colour TV and central heating. En suite rooms available but there are also ample bath, shower and WC facilities. Enclosed car park. First class English breakfast and evening meals. Licensed. Fire certificate.
Winter Break Specials.
Registered with English Tourist Council.

THE CAVALIER

The Cavalier is open all year and offers every modern comfort in a beautiful old building only 200 yards from the ancient city walls and five minutes from the Minster and City centre. Car Parking
Bed and Breakfast – colour TV's, coffee and tea facilities in all rooms. Central Heating – Sauna, most rooms with en-suite facilities.

Julia Woodland, The Cavalier
39 Monkgate, York YO31 7PB
Fax/Telephone (01904) 636615
Web: www.cavalierhotel.co.uk
E-mail: julia@cavalierhotel.fsnet.co.uk

VISA MasterCard

England

YORK continued

♦♦♦ Cumbria House

2 Vyner St, Haxby Rd YO31 8HS ☎ 01904 636817
e-mail: reservation@cumbriahouse.freeserve.co.uk
Dir: *from ring road A1237, take B1363 towards town centre, past hospital, sharp left at traffic lights. 400yds on L*

A warm welcome can be expected at this family run guest house which is located within a reasonable walk of the centre. Bedrooms are attractively decorated and well furnished and equipped with many useful extras. Freshly cooked breakfasts are served in the smart dining room at individual tables.

FACILITIES: 6 rms (2 en suite) (2 fmly) No smoking TVB tea/coffee No dogs (ex guide dogs) Cen ht **PRICES:** s £22-£25; d £40-£50✻ **LB** **PARKING:** 5 **CARDS:**

♦♦♦ Farthings Hotel

5 Nunthorpe Av YO23 1PF ☎ 01904 653545 🖹 01904 628355
e-mail: farthings@york181.fsbusiness.co.k

Originally a Victorian family residence, now Bill and Barbara Dickson offer sincere hospitality in well equipped and smart bedrooms. Freshly cooked breakfasts are served in a bright and airy dining room. Approximately ten minutes walk to the city centre.

FACILITIES: 9 rms (5 en suite) (2 fmly) No smoking TVB tea/coffee No dogs Cen ht No coaches **PRICES:** s £25-£35; d £40-£50✻ **LB** **CARDS:**

♦♦♦ Greenside

124 Clifton YO30 6BQ ☎ 01904 623631 🖹 01904 623631
Dir: *approach city centre on A19 N, at traffic lights straight on for Greenside, on the L opp Clifton Green*

Overlooking Clifton Green, this detached house is just within walking distance of the city centre. Accommodation consists of simply furnished bedrooms together with a cosy lounge and a dining room, where dinners by arrangement and traditional breakfasts are served. It is a family home, and families are welcome.

FACILITIES: 6 rms (3 en suite) (2 fmly) (3 GF) No smoking in dining room No smoking in lounges TVB tea/coffee Licensed Cen ht TVL Children's play area Dinner Last d 6pm **PRICES:** s fr £22; d fr £38✻ **LB BB** **PARKING:** 6

See advertisement on page 481

♦♦♦ Hillcrest

110 Bishopthorpe Rd YO23 1JX ☎ 01904 653160
e-mail: hillcrest@accommodation.gbr.fm
Dir: *follow signs A1036 for city centre and take 1st right after Marriot Hotel and at T-junct turn left*

Ideally situated for the racecourse and city, this well established guest house provides thoughtfully furnished bedrooms. The lounge offers a comfortable place in which to relax and hearty English breakfasts are served in the small, bright dining room. The resident proprietors are helpful and friendly, and there is a private car-park.

FACILITIES: 13 rms (7 en suite) (4 fmly) (1 GF) No smoking TVB tea/coffee No dogs (ex guide dogs) Cen ht TVL **PRICES:** s £21-£28; d £40-£60✻ **LB** **PARKING:** 8 **CARDS:**

♦♦♦ *Holgate Bridge Hotel*

106-108 Holgate Rd YO24 4BB ☎ 01904 635971 & 647288
🖹 01904 670049
e-mail: info@holgatebridge.co.uk
Dir: *on A59 close to Holgate Bridge*

Converted from an early Victorian town house, Holgate Bridge Hotel provides accommodation, which is suitable for business and leisure travellers, and has convenient parking. English breakfasts are served in the cosy dining room, and dinner is available by prior arrangement.

FACILITIES: 13 rms (10 en suite) (4 fmly) No smoking in dining room TVB tea/coffee Direct dial from bedrooms Licensed Cen ht TVL Dinner Last d 6pm **PARKING:** 14 **NOTES:** Closed 24-26 Dec **CARDS:**

♦♦♦ Linden Lodge Hotel

Nunthorpe Av, Scarcroft Rd YO23 1PF ☎ 01904 620107
🖹 01904 620985
e-mail: bookings@lindenlodge.yorkshire.net
Dir: *A64 take York West, follow signs for city centre, past racecourse on right, then 2nd right into Scarcroft Rd, & 2nd right into Nunthorpe Ave*

Friendly service is provided at this well furnished, comfortable house, in a quiet side road a short walk from the city. The bedrooms are well equipped and there is a comfortable lounge with small bar.

FACILITIES: 13 rms (10 en suite) (2 fmly) (1 GF) No smoking TVB tea/coffee No dogs (ex guide dogs) Licensed Cen ht TVL No coaches **PRICES:** s £24-£27.50; d £48-£52✻ **LB** **CARDS:**

♦♦♦ Moat Hotel

Nunnery Ln YO23 1AA ☎ 01904 652926
Dir: *from outer ring W follow signs city center for 2m to mediaeval archway. R at lights before archway into Nunnery Lane. Establishment adjacent to city walls on L*

Aptly named, this delightful, family run hotel sits beside the city walls, only a few minutes' walk from the city attractions. The tastefully decorated bedrooms boast a splendid array of antique furniture and some rooms have half-tester beds. Breakfast is served in the elegant dining room, and ample private parking is a bonus.

FACILITIES: 8 en suite No smoking TVB tea/coffee No dogs (ex guide dogs) Cen ht TVL No children 7ys No coaches **PRICES:** s £35-£45; d £56-£65✻ **PARKING:** 10 **NOTES:** Closed X-mas **CARDS:**

See advertisement on opposite page

♦♦♦ Priory Hotel & Garth Restaurant

126-128 Fulford Rd YO10 4BE ☎ 01904 625280
🖹 01904 637330
e-mail: reservations@priory-hotelyork.co.uk
Dir: *On S side of city, on A19 (Selby). From Leeds, take 3rd turning off A64 to York signed Fulford & Designer Centre. Located 2m on L*

continued

This well-established hotel has been run by the same family for over four generations. Reception rooms include a dining room, lounge and cosy bar, decorated in keeping with the period of the house. Bedrooms are designed in modern style and provide a high standard of comfort. Ancient Gothic arches lead to the beautifully landscaped gardens.
FACILITIES: 16 en suite (5 fmly) STV TVB tea/coffee Direct dial from bedrooms Licensed Cen ht TVL Dinner Last d 9.15pm **PRICES:** s fr £45; d fr £70* **LB PARKING:** 25 **NOTES:** Closed Xmas
CARDS:

♦♦♦ St Denys Hotel

St Denys Rd YO1 9QD ☎ 01904 622207 & 646776
01904 624800
e-mail: info@stdenyshotel.co.uk
Dir: *from A64 turn off A1079 York/Hull straight on approx 2.5m, through lights, through Walmgate, left after 500yds. Hotel opposite St Denys Church*
Formerly a vicarage, this small hotel is located in the heart of the city centre. En suite bedrooms are comfortably furnished with all modern facilities. The neatly appointed dining room leads through to a conservatory lounge with a well stocked bar.
FACILITIES: 13 en suite (3 fmly) No smoking in 2 bedrooms No smoking in dining room TVB tea/coffee Direct dial from bedrooms Licensed Cen ht TVL
PRICES: s £40-£50; d £55-£80* **LB PARKING:** 9
CARDS:

♦♦♦ St Georges Hotel

6 St Georges Place, Tadcaster Rd YO24 1DR ☎ 01904 625056
01904 625009
e-mail: sixstgeorg@aol.com
Dir: *from A64 take A1036, as racecourse finishes, St Georges Place is on left*
Conveniently located near the racecourse, this family-run private hotel is also within walking distance of the city. Bedrooms are attractively decorated and are equipped with modern facilities, some rooms have four-poster beds and other can accommodate families. A cosy lounge is available for residents and hearty breakfasts are served in the delightful dining room.
FACILITIES: 10 en suite (5 fmly) No smoking in dining room TVB tea/coffee Licensed Cen ht No coaches Dinner Last d 7pm **PRICES:** s £35-£50; d £48-£57.50 **LB PARKING:** 7 **CARDS:**

♦♦♦ *Wellgarth House*

Wetherby Rd, Rufforth YO23 3QB ☎ 01904 738592
Dir: *A64-A1237 York outer ring road, left at 2nd rdbt onto B1224 signposted Rufforth, after 1m 1st house on left on entering village immediately after Rufforth sign*
Overlooking open countryside on the edge of Rufforth village, this modern house offers comfortable, fresh bedrooms; one of which has a four-poster bed. Substantial Yorkshire breakfasts are served in the dining room which overlooks the garden and there is also a cosy lounge for residents to use. Conveniently situated for York Park and Ride.
FACILITIES: 7 en suite No smoking TVB tea/coffee No dogs (ex guide dogs) Cen ht No children 16yrs No coaches **PARKING:** 8
CARDS:

♦♦♦ A Bishopgarth

3 Southlands Rd YO23 1NP ☎ 01904 635220 01904 635220
Dir: *from A1(M) take A64 eastbound. Leave at 2nd York exit and take A1036 (city centre). Pass York racecourse turn right into Scarcroft Road, 3rd right into Millfield Road leading to Southlands Road.*
FACILITIES: 5 en suite (2 fmly) No smoking TVB tea/coffee No dogs (ex guide dogs) Cen ht No coaches Dinner Last d noon **PRICES:** s £18-£46; d £36-£48 **LB BB CARDS:**

England

YORK continued

♦♦♦ Fourposter Lodge Hotel

68-70 Heslington Rd YO10 5AU ☎ 01904 651170
01904 651170
e-mail: fourposter.lodge@virgin.net
Dir: *turn off A64 onto A19 towards York through Fulford, in 1m turn into Cemetry Rd then right at traffic lights into Hestington Road Hotel 100mtrs on left.*
FACILITIES: 10 en suite (2 fmly) (3 GF) No smoking in 8 bedrooms No smoking in dining room No smoking in lounges TVB tea/coffee Licensed Cen ht No coaches Dinner Last d 1pm **PRICES:** s £40-£50; d £55-£80* **LB PARKING:** 6 **NOTES:** Closed Xmas **CARDS:**

♦♦ Bootham Bar Hotel

4 High Petergate YO1 7EH ☎ 01904 658516 01904 634573
e-mail: boothambar@hotmail.com
Dir: *High Petergate is the continuation of Bootham - A19 towards York Minster. Through Botham Bar Gateway on left - 100yds from York Minster*

Situated in a narrow lane, yards away from the Minster and within the city wall, this friendly house offers accommodation right in the heart of the City. Secure parking can be arranged by prior notice, and a secluded rear garden affords fine views of the Minster and is adjacent to the city wall.
FACILITIES: 14 rms (11 en suite) (2 fmly) No smoking TVB tea/coffee No dogs (ex guide dogs) Cen ht No coaches **PRICES:** s £25-£55; d £60-£76 **LB PARKING:** 6 **NOTES:** Closed 22 Dec-09 Jan
CARDS:

See advertisement on page 483

♦♦ Crescent

77 Bootham YO30 7DQ ☎ 01904 623216 01904 623216
Dir: *approach city on A1237 outer ring road along A19 from north. Situated on A19, 5 mins walk from Bootham Bar*
Ideally located only five minutes walk from the city walls, this guest house offers well-equipped bedrooms with thoughtful extra facilities. Breakfast is taken in the first floor dining room and there is a small lounge with comfortable seating.
FACILITIES: 10 rms (8 en suite) (4 fmly) No smoking in dining room TVB tea/coffee Direct dial from bedrooms No dogs (ex guide dogs) Cen ht TVL No coaches **PRICES:** s £22-£26; d £40-£50* **LB PARKING:** 2
CARDS:

Smoking restrictions appear under the **FACILITIES** heading, please check when booking.

YORKSHIRE, SOUTH

BARNSLEY — Map 08 SE30

♦♦♦♦ Churchills Hotel

1 High St, Wombwell S73 0DA ☎ 01226 340099
01226 211126
e-mail: churchillshotel@btconnect.com
Churchills is in Wombwell, near Barnsley, and offers good accommodation and a friendly welcome. There is a relaxed atmosphere in the bar areas on the ground floor, where a good range of meals and snacks is available; and there is entertainment on some evenings during the week. Bedrooms are of good comfortable proportions and are well equipped. The secure car park is a real bonus for residents.

FACILITIES: 16 en suite No smoking in area of dining room No smoking in 1 lounge STV TVB tea/coffee Direct dial from bedrooms Cen ht Pool Table Dinner Last d 8.45pm **CONF:** Thtr 50 Class 30 Board 20 Del £70 *
PARKING: 66 **CARDS:**

DONCASTER — Map 08 SE50

♦♦♦♦ Canda Lodge

Hampole Balk Ln, Skellow DN6 8LF ☎ 01302 724028
01302 727999
Dir: *adjacent to A1 South, 6m S off M62 junction with A1. 5m N of junction with M18*
Very conveniently located for the A1, this stone-built house has its own well-tended gardens and spacious parking. Garden bedrooms are attractively decorated, well equipped and delightfully furnished. The public areas consist of a pleasant breakfast room with individual tables and a small lounge area; service is both friendly and caring.
FACILITIES: 3 rms 6 annexe en suite (2 fmly) No smoking TVB tea/coffee Direct dial from bedrooms No dogs (ex guide dogs) Cen ht TVL No children No coaches **PRICES:** s fr £35; d fr £40* **PARKING:** 20
CARDS:

♦♦♦ Balmoral Hotel

129 Thorne Rd DN2 5BH ☎ 01302 364385 364385
e-mail: thebalmoralhotel@blueyonder.co.uk
Dir: *M18 junct 3, straight on at racecourse rdbt, 2nd left into Leicester Ave. Through traffic lights onto Thorne Rd. Left and hotel on right*
Conveniently situated on a main road and within easy walking distance of the hospital, racecourse and the town, this well cared for guesthouse provides a mix of bedroom styles. There is a comfortable lounge and hearty breakfasts are served in the well-furnished dining room. Hospitality is strength here.
FACILITIES: 10 rms (4 en suite) 1 annexe en suite (3 fmly) (2 GF) No smoking in 6 bedrooms No smoking in dining room No smoking in 1 lounge TVB tea/coffee Cen ht TVL Dinner Last d noon
PRICES: s £20-£35; d £36-£46* **BB PARKING:** 12
CARDS:

England

ROTHERHAM Map 08 SK49

♦♦♦ Stonecroft

138 Main St, Bramley S66 2SF ☎ 01709 540922
📠 01709 540922

Dir: *M18 junct 1, towards Rotherham on A631, after 300yds turn right at Ball Inn, continue through village to Stonecroft on right after 400yds*

This small hotel offers accommodation both in the main house and the annexe of mews-style bedrooms, set around a courtyard and garden. They are pleasantly furnished and include many extras. Breakfast is served at individual tables in the smart dining room. A bar has been recently added to the lounge, and bar meals are available.

FACILITIES: 3 en suite 5 annexe en suite (1 fmly) (4 GF) No smoking in bedrooms No smoking in dining room No smoking in 1 lounge TVB tea/coffee Licensed Cen ht TVL No coaches **PRICES:** s £39.95-£43.95; d £52.95-£56.95✱ **PARKING:** 10 **CARDS:**

SHEFFIELD Map 08 SK38

Premier Collection

♦♦♦♦♦ Westbourne House Hotel

25 Westbourne Rd, Broomhill S10 2QQ ☎ 0114 266 0109
📠 0114 266 7778
e-mail: guests@westbournehousehotel.com

A former Victorian gentleman's residence situated in beautiful gardens close to the university and hospitals. There is an attractive licensed restaurant where carefully prepared imaginative meals are served by prior arrangement. Bedrooms are modern in style, individually furnished and decorated, and extremely well equipped. There is also a comfortable lounge that overlooks the terrace and garden.

FACILITIES: 10 rms (9 en suite) (2 fmly) No smoking in bedrooms No smoking in dining room No smoking in 1 lounge TVB tea/coffee Direct dial from bedrooms No dogs (ex guide dogs) Licensed Cen ht Jacuzzi Dinner Last d 2pm **PRICES:** s £45-£75; d £74-£95✱ **CONF:** Thtr 15 Class 15 Board 15 **PARKING:** 12 **CARDS:**

♦♦♦♦ Quarry House

Rivelin Glen Quarry, Rivelin Valley Rd S6 5SE
☎ 0114 234 0382 📠 0114 234 7630
e-mail: penelopeslack@aol.com

Dir: *turn onto A6101 Rivelin Valley Road from Hillsborough/Malin Bridge. In approx. 1m just after sharp bend road warning turn right at end of row of old cottages. There is a lone street lamp at bottom of drive, uphill to car park*

A warm welcome is given to guests at this delightful stone built Quarry Master's house in the Rivelin Valley. Service is attentive and helpful. Tasty evening meals and comprehensive breakfasts are sure to be appreciated by all guests. Bedrooms are well-appointed and thoughtfully equipped. Public rooms include a comfortable cosy lounge and a smart dining room.

FACILITIES: 3 rms (2 en suite) (1 fmly) (1 GF) No smoking STV TVB tea/coffee Cen ht TVL No coaches Dinner Last d 10pm **PRICES:** s £25; d £50✱ **PARKING:** 8 **NOTES:** Closed 24 Dec-1 Jan

♦♦♦ Critchleys

6 Causeway Head Rd, Dore S17 3DT ☎ 0114 236 4328
📠 0114 236 4328

Dir: *accessed off of the A621 Sheffield/Bakwell road or the A625 Sheffield/Castleton road*

Located above shops in the residential area of Dore, this sympathetically converted maisonette provides comfortable bedroom accommodation, which includes both practical and homely extras. Quality English breakfasts are served at one table in the cosy dining room. You can be assured of a very warm welcome.

FACILITIES: 3 en suite No smoking in dining room No smoking in lounges TVB tea/coffee Cen ht **PRICES:** s £25-£45; d £35-£45✱ BB
CARDS:

♦♦♦ Hunter House Hotel

685-691 Ecclesall Rd S11 8TG ☎ 0114 266 2709
📠 0114 268 6370
e-mail: ma@hunterhousehotel.freeserve.co.uk

Dir: *on A625 overlooking Endcliffe Park, 1m from City Centre*

This popular hotel, part of which is a tollhouse that dates back 250 years, offers friendly service from polite staff. The well-equipped, spacious bedrooms have facilities geared towards the business guest. The public rooms include a cosy bar and an attractive breakfast room.

FACILITIES: 24 rms (11 en suite) (9 fmly) (2 GF) No smoking in 1 bedrooms No smoking in dining room TVB tea/coffee Direct dial from bedrooms Licensed Cen ht TVL Free use of Hallamshire Leisure Club Dinner Last d 8.30pm **PRICES:** s £32-£45; d £50-£55✱ **CONF:** Thtr 30 Class 30 Board 20 **PARKING:** 8 **NOTES:** Closed 24 Dec-2Jan
ARDS:

♦♦♦ *Lindrick Hotel*

226 Chippinghouse Rd S7 1DR ☎ 0114 258 5041
📠 0114 255 4758
e-mail: reception@thelindrick.co.uk

Dir: *off A621 Abbydale Rd into Chippinghouse Rd. Hotel 200yds on R*

This is a spacious private hotel, which is situated in a leafy residential area to the South of the city centre. Public areas include a television lounge and a cosy bar. The modern breakfast room is large and bright and all of the bedrooms are well-equipped.

FACILITIES: 21 rms (13 en suite) (2 fmly) No smoking in dining room TVB tea/coffee Direct dial from bedrooms Licensed Cen ht TVL Dinner Last d 8.30pm **PARKING:** 20 **NOTES:** Closed 24 Dec-first Sat in Jan
CARDS:

WORTLEY Map 08 SK39

♦♦♦ Wortley Cottage Guest House

Park Av S35 7DB ☎ 01142 881864 📠 01142 881095

Dir: *M1 junct 35A/36,ON A629 To Wortley situated in villiage square 5 mins from M1*

Situated opposite the village church, this intimate guest house offers good comforts and fine hospitality. Bedrooms are well equipped and a hearty breakfast is served in the cosy dining room. It is also part of the village Post Office, shop and includes an art gallery. An ideal location for touring South Yorkshire.

FACILITIES: 4 rms (3 en suite) No smoking TVB tea/coffee Cen ht No children 1yr No coaches Golf 12 Tennis (hard) Fishing Riding
PRICES: s £27.50-£30; d £55-£60✱ **PARKING:** 4
NOTES: Closed 25-27 Dec 1-2 Jan **CARDS:**

England

YORKSHIRE, WEST

BINGLEY Map 07 SE13

♦♦♦♦ Five Rise Locks
Beck Ln BD16 4DD ☎ 01274 565296 📠 01274 568828
e-mail: 101731.2134@compuserve.com
Dir: *off A650 at Dacre, Son and Hartley turn onto Park Rd, at x-roads sign turn L, hotel on L*

Enjoying fine views over the Aire valley and the canal locks from which the hotel draws its name, this imposing house offers well equipped bedrooms. The new bistro is the venue for imaginative meals using fresh, local produce.

FACILITIES: 7 en suite 2 annexe en suite (2 fmly) (2 GF) No smoking in bedrooms No smoking in dining room No smoking in 1 lounge TVB tea/coffee Direct dial from bedrooms Licensed Cen ht No coaches Dinner Last d 9pm **PRICES:** s fr £45; d £62-£67* **LB CONF:** Thtr 16 Class 10 Board 12 **PARKING:** 17 **CARDS:**

GUISELEY Map 07 SE14

♦♦♦ Moor Valley Park Motel
Moor Valley Park, Mill Ln, Hawksworth LS20 8PQ
☎ 01943 876083 📠 01943 870335
Dir: *from A65 near Harry Ramsden's take 2nd left into Thorpe Ln, right at golf club through Hawksworth then left into Mill Ln*

Part of a holiday park, some bedrooms at Moor Valley are motel-style and others are in cabins around the extensive grounds. All are well furnished and thoughtfully equipped with lots of useful features. The main building houses the bar and dining area where an English breakfast can be enjoyed by prior arrangement.

FACILITIES: 10 annexe en suite (2 fmly) (10 GF) STV TVB tea/coffee Direct dial from bedrooms No dogs (ex guide dogs) Licensed Cen ht No coaches Dinner Last d 9.30pm **PRICES:** s £35; d £42.50* **LB PARKING:** 100 **CARDS:**

HALIFAX Map 07 SE02

♦♦♦♦ Shibden Mill
Shibden Mill Fold, Shibden HX3 7UL ☎ 01422 365840
📠 01422 362971
e-mail: shibdenmillinn@zoom.co.uk
Dir: *off A58*

Nestling in a fold of the Shibden Valley this 17th-century inn features beams and open fire. One can dine well in both the bars and restaurant and also outside in summer. Bedrooms come in a variety of sizes; all are thoughtfully equipped and have access to a free video library. Service is friendly and obliging.

continued

FACILITIES: 12 en suite No smoking in 2 bedrooms STV TVB tea/coffee Direct dial from bedrooms No dogs (ex guide dogs) Cen ht Free use of gym and leisure facilities nearby Dinner Last d 9.30pm PRICES: s £60-£85; d £72-£100* **MEALS:** Lunch £20-£30alc Dinner £20-£30alc* **CONF:** Thtr 50 Class 21 Board 24 Del £63.95 * **PARKING:** 100 **NOTES:** Civ Wed 70 **CARDS:**

♦♦♦ Pinfold
Dewsbury Rd, Upper Edge, Elland HX5 9JU
☎ 01422 372645 📠 01422 374713
e-mail: debbie@dlsbusiness.fsnet.co.uk
Dir: *M62 junct 24, 3rd turning at major rdbt (Hilton on the Hill), follow A643 towards Brighouse. After 1m turn left at lights, 0.25m on left*

This genuinely friendly guesthouse enjoys an elevated position and boasts super, panoramic views from front facing rooms. Offering good all round comforts, bedrooms are tastefully furnished and thoughtfully equipped. Hearty breakfasts are served in the bright and fresh dining room and an inviting lounge is also provided.

FACILITIES: 7 en suite (1 fmly) No smoking in dining room STV TVB tea/coffee No dogs (ex guide dogs) Cen ht TVL Library Dinner Last d 12 noon **PRICES:** s £26; d £38* **LB BB PARKING:** 10

HAWORTH Map 07 SE03

♦♦♦♦ Aitches
11 West Ln BD22 8DU ☎ 01535 642501
e-mail: aitches@talk21.com
Dir: *enter Haworth, pass steam railway station carry on for 0.5m, pass Edinburgh Wool shop next left into Brontë Museum car park, Aitches is to the right of steps to main street*

This stone built Victorian house enjoys a central location on the cobbled main street, just one minute's walk from the Brontë Parsonage. Bedrooms are attractively styled, thoughtfully equipped and come in a variety of sizes. Hearty breakfasts are not to be missed; dinners are available but must be pre-booked.

FACILITIES: 4 en suite No smoking TVB tea/coffee No dogs (ex guide dogs) Licensed Cen ht Dinner Last d 3pm **PRICES:** d £50-£60* **CARDS:**

♦♦♦♦ Old Registry
4 Main St BD22 8DA ☎ 01535 646503 📠 01535 646503
e-mail: oldregistry.haworth@virgin.net
Dir: *M62 exit 26 M606 (Bradford) follow Brontë Country signs*

A friendly welcome awaits guests at this delightful 100-year-old house centrally located on Haworth's main street. Each bedroom has been carefully themed and well-equipped with many thoughtful extras. Almost every room has an individually chosen four poster bed. Hearty Yorkshire breakfasts are served in the airy breakfast room.

FACILITIES: 10 en suite (1 fmly) (1 GF) No smoking TVB tea/coffee No dogs (ex guide dogs) Cen ht **PRICES:** s £30-£50; d £45-£70* **PARKING:** 2 **CARDS:**

HEBDEN BRIDGE Map 07 SD92

♦♦♦♦ Redacre Mill
Redacre, Mytholmroyd HX7 5DQ
☎ 01422 881569 & 885563 📠 01422 885563
e-mail: peters@redacremill.freeserve.co.uk
Dir: *on A646 westbound at Mytholmroyd turn right after fire station, cross hump-back bridge & turn right. Redacre Mill on canal side*

Situated alongside the Rochdale Canal, this former cotton warehouse retains many original features such as the winch used to lift the cotton bales. The delightful owners are warm and welcoming and take pride in serving imaginative home cooked meals. Bedrooms are comfortably furnished and attractively decorated.

continued

Redacre Mill

FACILITIES: 4 en suite (1 fmly) No smoking TVB tea/coffee No dogs (ex guide dogs) Licensed Cen ht No coaches Fishing Dinner Last d 6.45pm **PRICES:** s £39; d £59* LB **PARKING:** 8 **CARDS:**

HOLMFIRTH Map 07 SE10

♦♦♦♦ Holme Castle Country Hotel

The Village, Holme HD9 2QG ☎ 01484 680680
01484 686764
e-mail: info.holmecastle@virgin.net
Dir: *2m SW of Holmfirth on A6024 (The Circle)*

This former mill owners' residence enjoys superb views over the countryside. Bedrooms vary, but all are comfortable and spacious. Public areas include an oak panelled lounge and stylish dining room, which doubles as a gallery for local artists. Dinner is available by arrangement and quality breakfasts are served around a large table. As an added benefit the house boasts a textile-weaving studio for which residential courses are available.
FACILITIES: 7 rms (5 en suite) (2 fmly) No smoking TVB No dogs (ex guide dogs) Licensed Cen ht No coaches Childrens climbing frame, swing & slide Dinner Last d when booking **PRICES:** s £35-£60; d £55-£80* LB **CONF:** Class 12 Board 12 Del from £6 * **PARKING:** 12 **CARDS:**

HUDDERSFIELD Map 07 SE11

♦♦♦♦ Weavers Shed Restaurant with Rooms

Knowl Rd, Golcar HD7 4AN ☎ 01484 654284 01484 650980
e-mail: info@weaversshed.co.uk
Dir: *from Huddersfield A62 Oldham Rd, right into Milnsbridge. Left into Scar Lane at Kwiksave, then to top of hill, establishment on right before church. Follow Colne Valley Museum signs.*

This converted house offers spacious and comfortable bedrooms. All are extremely well equipped. An inviting bar/lounge leads into the well-established restaurant where fresh produce, much of it from the kitchen gardens, is used.
FACILITIES: 5 en suite No smoking in dining room TVB tea/coffee Direct dial from bedrooms No dogs (ex guide dogs) Licensed Cen ht No coaches Dinner Last d 9pm Tue 10pm Sat **PRICES:** s £40-£50; d £55-£65* LB **CONF:** Board 16 **PARKING:** 25 **NOTES:** Closed Xmas/New Year **CARDS:**

A indicates an Associate entry, which has been inspected and rated by the ETC or the RAC in England.

ILKLEY Map 07 SE14

♦♦♦♦ Grove Hotel

66 The Grove LS29 9PA ☎ 01943 600298 0870 7065587
e-mail: res@grovehotel.org
Dir: *from A65 Leeds/Skipton rd, turn left at main lights by parish church into Brook St, at top turn right into The Grove. Hotel 300mtrs on right*

Centrally situated in the town, this well maintained hotel offers a comfortable lounge and a snug bar. Bedrooms, some quite spacious and suitable for families, are attractively furnished and equipped to meet the needs of business and leisure travellers alike. Services are provided with a smile and a hearty breakfast is served.

FACILITIES: 6 en suite (2 fmly) No smoking in dining room No smoking in 1 lounge TVB tea/coffee Direct dial from bedrooms No dogs (ex guide dogs) Licensed Cen ht TVL No coaches Free use of health club opposite the hotel **PRICES:** s £47-£54; d £64-£69* **PARKING:** 5 **CARDS:**

KEIGHLEY Map 07 SE04

♦♦♦ Bankfield

1 Station Rd, Cross Hills BD20 7EH ☎ 01535 632971
Dir: *turn off A650/A629 Aire Valley Rd at Kildwick rdbt, take weight-limit restriction rd towards Cross Hills. 0.5m on right*

A real 'home from home' atmosphere prevails in this delightful house. Popular as a starting point for a tour of the Dales, the house is close to all major transport links. Susan Dowgill is a welcoming hostess who prepares a hearty breakfast, served family style. The neatly decorated bedrooms are spacious and there is a homely sitting room and convenient parking to the rear.
FACILITIES: 3 rms (2 en suite) (1 fmly) No smoking in bedrooms No smoking in dining room TVB tea/coffee Cen ht TVL No coaches **PRICES:** s £25; d £42* **PARKING:** 5

LEEDS Map 08 SE33

♦♦♦ Ash Mount Hotel

22 Wetherby Rd, Oakwood LS8 2QD
☎ 0113 265 8164 & 265 4263 0113 265 8164
e-mail: bookings@ashmounthotel.co.uk
Dir: *on E outskirts of city, just off A58*

This delightful Victorian house is peacefully yet conveniently located, close to Roundhay Park and the Canal Gardens yet within easy access of Leeds city centre and the motorway network. Bedrooms are tastefully decorated, and thoughtfully equipped. Public areas include a beautifully appointed lounge and a smart dining room that overlooks the landscaped leafy garden.
FACILITIES: 12 rms (9 en suite) (2 fmly) No smoking in 3 bedrooms No smoking in dining room TVB tea/coffee Direct dial from bedrooms No dogs (ex guide dogs) Licensed Cen ht TVL No coaches **PRICES:** s £26-£35; d £55* **PARKING:** 8 **CARDS:**

England

LEEDS continued

♦♦♦ Merevale Hotel
16 Wetherby Rd, Oakwood LS8 2QD
☎ 0113 265 8933 & 273 7985 Fax 0113 265 8933
e-mail: office@merevalehotel.co.uk
Dir: *A58 towards Wetherby from city centre, at 1st rdbt on dual-carriageway turn left into Oakwood Lane, right at traffic lights into Wetherby Rd*
Interesting stained glass windows prove an inspiring feature in this friendly Victorian house. Well-equipped bedrooms are provided in a range of styles, with many boasting modern showers. Breakfast is served in the stylish dining room that overlooks the well-tended gardens. A feature ceiling has been retained in the comfortable, elegant lounge.
FACILITIES: 12 rms (7 en suite) (1 fmly) (1 GF) No smoking TVB tea/coffee Direct dial from bedrooms No dogs (ex guide dogs) Licensed Cen ht TVL No children 3yrs No coaches **PRICES:** s £25-£38; d £39-£50* **PARKING:** 9 **NOTES:** Closed Xmas & Etr
CARDS:

♦♦♦ Trafford House & Budapest Hotel
18 Cardigan Rd, Headingley LS6 3AG
☎ 0113 275 2034 & 275 6637 Fax 0113 274 2422
Dir: *off A660 Otley Rd*
A haven for cricket enthusiasts, this large hotel overlooks Headingley cricket ground - home of Yorkshire and test match cricket. Accommodation comprises of three adjacent Victorian villas which offer a variety of bedrooms including ground-floor rooms, family units and rooms with balconies. Breakfast is taken at individual tables in the large bright dining room, and dinner is available by arrangement.
FACILITIES: 27 rms (4 en suite) (4 fmly) (6 GF) No smoking in 10 bedrooms No smoking in dining room TVB tea/coffee Direct dial from bedrooms No dogs (ex guide dogs) Licensed Cen ht TVL Dinner Last d noon **PRICES:** s £28-£44; d £42-£60* **PARKING:** 30 **NOTES:** Closed 24 & 25 Dec **CARDS:**

♦♦ Highbank Hotel
83 Harehills Ln, Chapelallerton LS7 4HA
☎ 0113 262 2164 & 08707 456744 Fax 0113 237 4436
e-mail: highbankhotel@hotmail.com
Dir: *opposite Potternewton Park*
This traditional hotel enjoys an elevated position with views across the city. There is a pleasantly appointed dining room, in which breakfast and evening meals are served. Other public areas include a lounge bar and a separate guests' lounge.
FACILITIES: 20 rms (8 en suite) (4 fmly) (3 GF) No smoking in 4 bedrooms No smoking in dining room No smoking in 1 lounge TVB tea/coffee Direct dial from bedrooms No dogs (ex guide dogs) Licensed Cen ht TVL Pool Table Croquet lawn Games room with pool table Dinner Last d 8pm-8.30pm **PRICES:** s £25-£38; d £40-£55* **LB CONF:** Thtr 60 Class 30 Board 30 Del from £18 * **PARKING:** 32 **CARDS:**

OSSETT — Map 08 SE22

♦♦♦♦ Mews Hotel
Dale St WF5 9HN ☎ 01924 273982 Fax 01924 279389
e-mail: enquiries@mews-hotel.co.uk
Dir: *from M1 junct 40 towards Dewsbury from rdbt. 200yds on left take slip rd signed Flushdyke/Ossett. 0.75m & Dale St on left. Hotel 200yds on right*
This friendly family hotel provides comfortable public rooms together with well furnished and thoughtfully equipped bedrooms. Hand-pulled ales are served in the bar and a good variety of meals are on offer.

continued

FACILITIES: 14 en suite (1 fmly) (5 GF) TVB tea/coffee Direct dial from bedrooms Cen ht Dinner Last d 9.30pm **PRICES:** s £40-£46; d £55-£60* **MEALS:** Lunch £12-£25 Dinner £12-£25* **CONF:** Thtr 30 Class 25 Board 16 **PARKING:** 40 **CARDS:**

PONTEFRACT — Map 08 SE42

♦♦♦♦ Wentvale
Great North Rd, Knottingley WF11 8PF ☎ 01977 676714
Fax 01977 676714
e-mail: wentvale@aol.com
Dir: *A1 S, junct of A645 for Pontefract & Goole turn immediately right. Wentvale on the left*
This welcoming Victorian house has some pleasing original features such as wood panelling in the hall, and a decorative stained glass front door. Double-glazed windows in the attractively furnished, comfortable bedrooms provide effective sound insulation. Public rooms include a comfortable lounge and separate breakfast room.
FACILITIES: 4 en suite 3 annexe en suite No smoking TVB tea/coffee No dogs (ex guide dogs) Cen ht TVL No children 12yrs **PRICES:** s fr £25; d fr £45* **PARKING:** 10 **NOTES:** Closed Xmas & New Year
CARDS:

♦♦♦ Southmoor Hotel
Union House, 55 Southmoor Rd WF9 4LX ☎ 01977 625526
Fax 01977 625170
e-mail: enquiries@southmoorhotel.com
Dir: *S of Pontefract on the B6273 Rotherham Road and 2 mins by foot to Hemsworth Market*
Near to the open market in the centre of the town, pleasant well-equipped bedrooms, a comfortable lounge and a small bar make this a convenient location for touring the area. The staff are all very helpful and the car park is secured at night.
FACILITIES: 15 rms (14 en suite) (4 fmly) No smoking in 10 bedrooms No smoking in dining room No smoking in lounges STV TVB tea/coffee Licensed Lift Cen ht TVL Dinner Last d 2pm **PRICES:** s £20-£25; d fr £40* **LB PARKING:** 18 **CARDS:**

SHIPLEY — Map 07 SE13

♦♦♦♦ Beeties
7 Victoria Rd, Saltaire Village BD18 3LA
☎ 01274 595988 581718 Fax 01274 582118
e-mail: info@beeties.co.uk
Dir: *A650 to Saltaire Village, Beeties is on left along Victoria Rd in the heart of the village opposite Salts Mill*
Part of the model industrial village constructed by Titas Salt and nominated for a World Heritage Award in 2002, this Grade II listed retailer's shop has modern, well-equipped bedrooms above, and is an ideal centre for sightseeing or touring further afield. An extensive range of skilfully prepared food is available all day.
FACILITIES: 5 en suite (1 fmly) No smoking in bedrooms No smoking in area of dining room No smoking in 1 lounge TVB tea/coffee Direct dial from bedrooms No dogs (ex guide dogs) Licensed Cen ht No children 10yrs No coaches Dinner Last d 9.30pm **NOTES:** Closed 27-30 Dec
CARDS:

TODMORDEN — Map 07 SD92

♦♦♦ Staff of Life
550 Burnley Rd, Knotts OL14 8JF ☎ 01706 812929
Fax 01706 813773
e-mail: Staff.of.life@talk21.com
Dir: *on A646 Halifax to Burnley rd, approx 1.5m from Todmorden centre toward Burnley, on right*

continued

Situated on the edge of the town, this stone-built inn offers value-for-money accommodation in a friendly ambience. The comfortable bedrooms are pleasingly decorated and the bar, serving real ales, is full of character. There is also a small panelled dining room in which breakfast is served. The food is good and bar menus offer a wide choice of traditional and ethnic dishes.
FACILITIES: 3 en suite No smoking in dining room TVB tea/coffee Cen ht Dinner Last d by arrangement **PRICES:** s £26; d £38✱ **BB**
MEALS: Lunch £7-£20alc Dinner £9-£20alc✱ **PARKING:** 26
CARDS:

WAKEFIELD — Map 08 SE32

♦♦♦ Kirklands Hotel

605 Leeds Rd, Outwood WF1 2LU ☎ 01924 826666
Fax 01924 826682
Dir: *from M1 junct 41, take A650 signed Wakefield. At 2nd rdbt take A61. Hotel approx 1.5m on left next to parish church*
This friendly well-furnished inn is conveniently located only a short distance from the city. The bedrooms are modern in style and all are well equipped. The pub is well known locally for its real ales, and a good range of food is served in the bar.
FACILITIES: 6 en suite (1 fmly) (1 GF) TVB tea/coffee Direct dial from bedrooms No dogs (ex guide dogs) Cen ht Dinner Last d 8.30pm **PRICES:** s £40; d £50✱ **MEALS:** Lunch fr £8.50&alc Dinner £8.25-£15.50alc✱ **PARKING:** 30 **CARDS:**

♦♦♦ Stanley View

226-230 Stanley Rd WF1 4AE ☎ 01924 376803
Fax 01924 369123
e-mail: enquiries@stanleyviewguesthouse.co.uk
Dir: *2m off M62 junct 30 on A642 to York, close to city centre. Or 3m off M1 junct 41 on A640*
Set in an attractive terrace this pleasant family-run guest house with private parking at the rear is situated a short distance from the city centre. The well-equipped bedrooms are brightly and freshly decorated and there is also a comfortable lounge. Hearty home-cooked meals are served in the attractive dining room.
FACILITIES: 17 rms (12 en suite) (6 fmly) No smoking in bedrooms STV TVB tea/coffee Direct dial from bedrooms Licensed Cen ht TVL Dinner Last d 8pm **PRICES:** s £22.30-£42.30; d £42.30✱ **PARKING:** 10
CARDS:

WETHERBY — Map 08 SE44

♦♦♦ Broadleys

39 North St LS22 6NU ☎ 01937 585866
Dir: *turn off A1 into Wetherby, Broadleys is situated on the main street*
FACILITIES: 2 en suite (1 fmly) No smoking in bedrooms No smoking in dining room TVB tea/coffee Cen ht TVL No coaches **PRICES:** s £40-£45; d £50✱ **PARKING:** 2 **NOTES:** Closed 2 wks in Jan
CARDS:

♦♦ Prospect House

8 Caxton St LS22 6RU ☎ 01937 582428
Dir: *A1 to Wetherby rdbt, turn left to Wetherby, through 1st traffic lights, at 2nd lights turn left, continue to Kwiksave on left, house on corner*
This is privately owned guest house, which is close to the town centre. It offers clean and comfortable bedrooms. Public areas include a lounge/dining room, and rooms are adorned with home-worked tapestries. Service from the owners is caring and hospitable.
FACILITIES: 6 rms (4 en suite) TV1B tea/coffee Cen ht TVL No coaches
PRICES: s £25; d £50✱ **PARKING:** 6

CHANNEL ISLANDS

GUERNSEY

FOREST

♦♦♦♦ Maison Bel Air Guest House

La Chene GY8 0AL ☎ 01481 238503 Fax 01481 239403

In a peaceful setting with delightful gardens in which to relax, Maison Bel Air is also well located for the airport, coastal walks and numerous places of interest around the island. The attractive bedrooms and bathrooms are comfortable, bright and airy. A guest lounge is also available.
FACILITIES: 6 en suite (1 fmly) No smoking TVB tea/coffee No dogs Cen ht No children 3yrs **LB** **PRICES:** s fr £35; d fr £56✱ **PARKING:** 8

ST PETER PORT

♦♦♦ *Marine Hotel*

Well Rd GY1 1WS ☎ 01481 724978 Fax 01481 711729
Dir: *just off Glategny Esplanade, opposite Queen Elizabeth II Marina*
A family-run hotel 30 metres from the seafront and just a short walk from the centre of St Peter Port. It provides well decorated bedrooms and a comfortable guest lounge. There is an attractive sun terrace with the island's only functioning red telephone box. Breakfast is served in a smart dining room.
FACILITIES: 11 en suite (3 fmly) No smoking in 9 bedrooms No smoking in dining room No smoking in lounges TVB tea/coffee No dogs (ex guide dogs) Cen ht TVL No coaches **CARDS:**

JERSEY

GREVE DE LECQ BAY

♦♦♦ Hotel Des Pierres

JE3 2DT ☎ 01534 481858 Fax 01534 485273
e-mail: despierres@jerseyhols.com
Dir: *from airport drive east, left at rdbt, continue along A12 St Ouen's Rd for 0.25m, at fork turn right to Mont de La Greve de Lecq , near foot of hill is the hotel*
Located to the north of the island at the pleasant Greve De Lecq Bay, this friendly and relaxed guest house is very popular and has many regularly returning guests. Bedrooms and bathrooms are neatly furnished, and some enjoy views over the bay. A regularly changing menu provides guests with many options both at dinner and breakfast.
FACILITIES: 16 en suite (4 fmly) No smoking in bedrooms No smoking in dining room No smoking in lounges TVB tea/coffee No dogs Licensed Cen ht Cycling Dinner Last d 8pm **PRICES:** s £33.50-£36.50✱ **LB**
PARKING: 13 **NOTES:** Closed 15 Dec-15 Jan
CARDS:

England

GROUVILLE

♦♦♦ Lavender Villa Hotel

La Rue A Don JE3 9DX ☎ 01534 854937 Fax 01534 856147

Dir: *approx 3m from St Helier on East Coast Road just off A3*

Set in a peaceful location overlooking the Royal Jersey Golf course, this comfortable hotel offers a warm and friendly welcome to guests old and new. Bedrooms are spacious and pleasantly decorated and some are located on the ground floor. The beamed dining room offers freshly cooked dinners each evening and guests may relax in the cosy bar or comfortable lounge.

FACILITIES: 21 en suite (3 fmly) (6 GF) No smoking in dining room No smoking in lounges TVB tea/coffee No dogs Licensed Cen ht TVL No children 3yrs No coaches Outdoor swimming pool Dinner Last d 7.45pm **PRICES:** s £22-£32; d £44-£64* **LB PARKING:** 20 **NOTES:** Closed late Nov-mid Mar **CARDS:**

ST AUBIN

♦♦♦♦ The Panorama

La Rue du Crocquet JE3 8BZ ☎ 01534 742429 Fax 01534 745940

e-mail: info@panoramajersey.com

Dir: *overlooking St Aubins Bay, and out to sea, situated in the village of St Aubin*

This establishment has spectacular views over St Aubin's Bay to St Helier from front-facing rooms and the terrace garden. The well-equipped bedrooms vary in standard, but the superior rooms are much in demand for their quality and style. Public areas, which also enjoy the best of the view, are noteworthy for their antique fireplaces. Home-baked cream teas are served, mainly at the weekends during the summer months, and breakfast is excellent.

FACILITIES: 17 en suite (4 GF) No smoking STV TVB tea/coffee No dogs Cen ht No children 16yrs No coaches **PRICES:** s £20-£50; d £40-£100 **NOTES:** Closed early Nov-mid Mar **CARDS:**

♦♦♦ Peterborough House

La Rue Du Croquet JE3 8BZ ☎ 01534 741568 Fax 01534 746787

e-mail: fernando@localdial.com

Dir: *from St Helier turn right (sign Red Houses) 400mtrs before St Aubin, take 1st left and follow road until cobbles. House on left*

Situated on the old St Aubin high street, this well presented guests house dates back to 1690. The well-maintained bedrooms are comfortable; the sea facing rooms are always popular. Two lounge areas are available, one with a bar, and the outdoor terrace provides an ideal area to enjoy the views.

FACILITIES: 14 rms (12 en suite) No smoking in bedrooms No smoking in dining room No smoking in 1 lounge TVB tea/coffee No dogs Licensed Cen ht TVL No children 12yrs No coaches **PRICES:** s £24-£34.75 **LB NOTES:** Closed Nov-Feb **CARDS:**

Directions are provided by the proprietor, ask for more details when booking.

ST CLEMENT

♦♦♦♦ *Bon Air Hotel*

Coast Rd, Pontac JE2 6SE ☎ 01534 855324 Fax 01534 857801

With a warm and welcoming atmosphere, this attractive, small hotel offers comfortable bedrooms, of varying sizes, all furnished and decorated to good modern standards. Public areas include a cosy bar, with a separate lounge and no-smoking area, and a beamed dining room. The covered, heated swimming pool opens onto a patio.

FACILITIES: 18 en suite (3 fmly) No smoking in dining room TVB tea/coffee No dogs (ex guide dogs) Licensed Cen ht TVL No coaches Indoor swimming pool (heated) Pool Table Games room **PARKING:** 20 **NOTES:** Closed Nov-Feb

ST HELIER

♦♦♦♦ Millbrook House

Rue de Trachy, Millbrook JE2 3JN ☎ 01534 733036 Fax 01534 724317

e-mail: millbrook.house@jerseymail.co.uk

Dir: *1.5m W of town off A1*

This pleasant Georgian mansion is set in ten acres of attractive and well tended grounds is peacefully located, within a short drive of St Helier. Bedrooms are spacious and comfortable, the majority with delightful views of the gardens and some having sea views. Dinner provides an interesting choice of home cooked dishes enhanced with an impressive range of wines.

FACILITIES: 27 en suite (2 fmly) (6 GF) No smoking in dining room No smoking in 1 lounge TVB tea/coffee Direct dial from bedrooms No dogs Licensed Lift TVL No coaches Golf 5 Dinner Last d 7pm **PRICES:** s £34-£38; d £68-£76* **LB PARKING:** 20 **NOTES:** Closed 6 Oct-5 May **CARDS:**

♦♦♦ *Cliff Court Hotel*

St Andrews Rd, First Tower JE2 3JG ☎ 01534 734919 Fax 01534 766715

Enjoying an elevated position in the First Tower area with easy access to the centre, this family run hotel offers spacious bedrooms, some of which are located on the ground floor. The public rooms include a bar with pool table, a comfortable red plush lounge are plus a separate TV lounge. Freshly cooked dinners and breakfasts are served in the ground floor dining room.

FACILITIES: 17 en suite (3 fmly) No smoking in area of dining room TVB tea/coffee No dogs (ex guide dogs) Licensed Cen ht TVL No coaches Outdoor swimming pool (heated) Last d 7.30pm **PARKING:** 14 **NOTES:** Closed Nov-Mar **CARDS:**

ST SAVIOUR

Premier Collection

♦♦♦♦♦ *Champ Colin*

Rue du Champ Colin JE2 7UN ☎ 01534 851877 Fax 01534 854902

Dir: *from airport, signs to St Helier, through tunnel. 1st L to lights/middle lane, up Mont Millais. B28 to Hougue Bie, then Rue du Champ Colin*

Dating back to 1815 this Jersey granite-built house is a charming home set in attractive gardens in the tranquillity of the countryside. A friendly welcome is provided by the resident family who are most attentive and helpful hosts. The elegant and spacious bedrooms are impressive; with two rooms having half-tester beds and all having period furnishings. Freshly cooked breakfast featuring local produce is served in the well-appointed breakfast room, which has a magnificent fireplace.

continued

Champ Colin

FACILITIES: 3 en suite (1 fmly) No smoking TVB tea/coffee Cen ht No children 5yrs **PARKING:** 10 **NOTES:** Closed 18 Dec-5 Jan
CARDS:

SARK

SARK

♦♦♦♦ Hotel Petit Champ

GY9 0SF ☎ 01481 832046 01481 832469
e-mail: hpc@island-of-sark.co.uk
Dir: *from Methodist Chapel take lane, signposted, towards sea & turn left*
Guests here are assured of a high level of hospitality and service. Most of the bedrooms, the gardens and lounges have wonderful views of the sea and neighbouring islands. A five-course dinner is included in the half board terms and a well stocked wine cellar and bar add to the enjoyment. Caroline Robins was a Top Twenty Finalist in the AA Landlady of the Year Award 2002-2003.
FACILITIES: 13 en suite (2 fmly) (2 GF) No smoking in dining room No smoking in 1 lounge No dogs (ex guide dogs) Licensed Cen ht TVL No children 7yrs Outdoor swimming pool (heated) Croquet lawn Putting green Dinner Last d 8.30pm **PRICES:** (incl. dinner) s £53.50-£62; d £103-£120 **LB**
NOTES: Closed Nov-Etr **CARDS:**

MAN, ISLE OF

DOUGLAS Map 06 SC37

Premier Collection

♦♦♦♦♦ Engelwood Lodge

105 King Edward Rd IM3 2AS ☎ 01624 616050
01624 616051
e-mail: info@engelwood.co.im
Dir: *1m N from the Promenade. In King Edward Road on left after Churchill of India Restaurant. Private road parallel to main road over railway line*

continued

This large, modern detached house situated at Onchan Head commands superb panoramic views of Douglas Bay, the promenade and harbour. The accommodation is luxurious and well equipped. There is a choice of spacious and comfortable lounges, one overlooking the pleasant garden. There is also a very attractive breakfast room. Genuinely friendly and caring hospitality is offered by Linda Lister, who goes out of her way to make guests feel welcome.
FACILITIES: 3 en suite No smoking STV TVB tea/coffee No dogs (ex guide dogs) Cen ht TVL No children 14yrs No coaches Pool Table
PRICES: s fr £38.50; d fr £65* **LB** **PARKING:** 3 **NOTES:** Closed Nov-Feb

♦♦♦♦ Dreem Ard

Ballanard Rd IM2 5PR ☎ 01624 621491 01624 621491
Dir: *From St Ninian's Church/School traffic lights travel along Ballanard Rd for approx 1m, straight on through Johnny Watterson Lane x-rds, past old old farm on left. Dreem Ard just ahead on left, look for red post box on corner*
Dreem Ard offers a relaxing sanctuary of comfort and good food, with superb views over the glens just to the North of Douglas. Bedrooms are spacious and well-equipped with caring hosts who genuinely make a difference. Both dinner and breakfast are served around a large table, where good food and company go hand in hand.
FACILITIES: 3 en suite (1 fmly) (2 GF) No smoking STV TVB tea/coffee No dogs (ex guide dogs) Cen ht No children 8yrs No coaches Dinner Last d breakfast **PRICES:** d £40-£50* **LB** **PARKING:** 6

♦♦♦ All Seasons

11 Clifton Ter, Broadway IM2 3HX ☎ 01624 676323
01624 676323
e-mail: allseasons@hotels.activebooking.com
Dir: *turn off Central Promenade Villa Marina. Premises in 1st row of hotels on left*
This pleasant, friendly guest house is centrally located just a few minutes walk from the promenade. Bedrooms are well equipped and soundly maintained. There is a lounge bar reserved for residents and a separate lounge where guests can relax. The jet stream pool and exercise bicycles are popular with guests.
FACILITIES: 6 rms (4 en suite) No smoking TVB tea/coffee No dogs (ex guide dogs) Licensed Cen ht No coaches Indoor swimming pool (heated) Dinner Last d 6pm **PRICES:** s fr £22.50; d fr £45* **LB**
CARDS:

♦♦♦ Chesterfield Hotel

4 Mona Dr IM2 4LG ☎ 01624 675105 01624 675105
Dir: *from ferryport along promenade straight through traffic lights left at zebra crossing onto Mona Drive. Establishment 30 yrds on right*
This hotel is set just back from the sea front offering fine views over the bay. The hotel has recently reopened following refurbishment and nothing is too much trouble for the friendly, attentive hosts. Bedrooms are well equipped and comfortable with many benefiting from en suite bathrooms. Public rooms include a lounge and bar.
FACILITIES: 13 rms (5 en suite) (1 fmly) No smoking in dining room tea/coffee No dogs Licensed TVL **PRICES:** s £18; d £36-£42* **BB**
CARDS:

♦♦♦ Diamonds are a guest's best friend! The emphasis is on quality and guest care rather than extra facilities.

England

♦♦♦ Rosslyn Guest House
3 Empire Ter, Central Promenade IM2 4LE ☎ 01624 676056
🖷 01624 674122
This personally run, friendly guest house is conveniently situated just a few yards from the promenade. Bedrooms are neatly decorated and thoughtfully equipped. There is a comfortable first floor lounge and hearty breakfasts are served in the traditionally furnished dining room.
FACILITIES: 12 rms (6 en suite) No smoking in 4 bedrooms No smoking in dining room No smoking in lounges TV6B tea/coffee No dogs (ex guide dogs) Licensed Cen ht TVL No children 5yrs **PRICES:** s fr £20; d £40-£50✻ **LB NOTES:** Closed Dec-1 Jan

PORT ERIN — Map 06 SC16

Premier Collection

♦♦♦♦♦ Rowany Cottier
Spaldrick IM9 6PE ☎ 01624 832287 🖷 01624 835685
Dir: *on entering Port Erin, proceed up promenade, passing hotels, road levels off and dips down to Spaldrick. House on right opposite path to Bradda Glen*
This large and impressive house stands in its own spacious garden, overlooking Port Erin Bay. The tastefully appointed accommodation is equally suitable for business guests and holidaymakers. One bedroom is located on the ground floor and has a walk-in shower with wheelchair access.
FACILITIES: 5 en suite (1 GF) No smoking TVB tea/coffee No dogs (ex guide dogs) Cen ht No children 12yrs No coaches **PRICES:** s £26.50-£42; d £53-£65 **LB PARKING:** 5

PORT ST MARY — Map 06 SC26

Premier Collection

♦♦♦♦♦ Aaron House
The Promenade IM9 5DE ☎ 01624 835702
e-mail: aaron_house_iom@yahoo.com
Dir: *Follow signs for South & Port St Mary, turn left at post office, Aaron House in middle of promenade*

Aaron House is truly individual; from the arrival in the Victorian parlour, through to the cast iron baths, the house has been restored to more than its former glory. The family work hard to offer the best quality, whether in bedroom luxury and comfort, or through to the home-made cakes on arrival.
FACILITIES: 3 en suite No smoking tea/coffee No dogs Cen ht No children 16yrs No coaches **PRICES:** s £30-£35; d £60-£70✻
NOTES: Closed 21 Dec-3 Jan

RAMSEY — Map 06 SC49

Premier Collection

♦♦♦♦♦ *River House*
IM8 3DA ☎ 01624 816412 🖷 01624 816412

A beautiful Georgian house, standing in extensive mature gardens beside the River Sulby. The accommodation is comfortable and spacious with luxurious facilities and the bedrooms overlook the river. There is a delightful separate breakfast room also overlooking the river and Cordon Bleu dinners can be arranged, Sunday to Thursday.
FACILITIES: 3 en suite STV TVB tea/coffee No dogs (ex guide dogs) Cen ht No coaches Last d morning **PARKING:** 12

Scotland

Nether Underwood, Symington

Scotland

SCOTLAND

ABERDEEN CITY

ABERDEEN Map 15 NJ90

♦♦♦♦ The Jays Guest House

422 King St AB24 3BR ☎ 01224 638295 📠 01224 638295
e-mail: alice@jaysguesthouse.co.uk
Dir: *A90 from S to Main St - Union St, continue on A92 to King St N*
Guests are warmly welcomed to this attractive granite house on the north side of the city. Maintained in first class order throughout, it offers attractive bedrooms, smartly furnished to appeal to business guests as well as tourists. Freshly prepared breakfasts are enjoyed in the tastefully appointed dining room.
FACILITIES: 10 en suite (1 GF) No smoking STV TVB tea/coffee No dogs Cen ht No children 12yrs No coaches **PRICES:** s £35-£40; d £60-£80✻ **PARKING:** 9 **CARDS:**

♦♦♦♦ Strathisla

408 Gt Western Rd AB10 6NR ☎ 01224 321026
e-mail: elza@strathislaguesthouse.co.uk
Dir: *follow A90, over Dee Bridge, straight over rdbt, on dual-carriageway, over 2nd rdbt to lights, then right into Great Western Rd*
A comfortable granite-built terraced house on the west side of the city, Strathisla boasts attractive bedrooms, all individual and inviting, with added touches such as alarm clocks and a complimentary slice of cake with the beverage facilities. Vegetarian options are available at breakfast.
FACILITIES: 5 en suite (1 fmly) No smoking TVB tea/coffee Cen ht No coaches **PRICES:** s £26-£32; d £40-£44✻ **PARKING:** 1 **CARDS:**

♦♦♦ Corner House Hotel

385 Great Western Rd AB10 6NY ☎ 01224 313063 📠 01224 313063
e-mail: cornerhouse.hotel@virgin.net
Dir: *on A93, 1m from city centre*
There is a welcoming atmosphere at this comfortable family-run hotel just west of the city centre. Bedrooms come in a variety of sizes - some huge - all being thoughtfully laid out and with a good range of amenities. Public rooms include an attractive lounge and bright airy dining room.
FACILITIES: 17 en suite (3 fmly) (1 GF) No smoking in 8 bedrooms No smoking in dining room TVB tea/coffee Direct dial from bedrooms No dogs (ex guide dogs) Licensed Cen ht TVL No coaches Dinner Last d 8pm **PRICES:** s £38-£58; d £52-£60✻ **LB PARKING:** 12 **CARDS:**

♦♦♦ *Arkaig*

43 Powis Ter AB25 3PP ☎ 01224 638872 📠 01224 622189
e-mail: arkaig@netcomuk.co.uk
Dir: *on A96/A956 Inverness-Aberdeen road, 0.5m N of city centre, close to university & hospital*
Good value accommodation is offered at this comfortable friendly guesthouse, situated on the north side of the city close to the University. Bedrooms are bright and well-equipped, with the best use made of all available space. Hearty breakfasts are served at individual tables in the ground floor dining room.
FACILITIES: 9 rms (7 en suite) (1 fmly) No smoking in dining room No smoking in lounges STV TVB tea/coffee Direct dial from bedrooms Cen ht TVL No coaches Videos available Dinner Last d 6pm **PARKING:** 10 **CARDS:**

♦♦♦ Bimini

69 Constitution St AB24 5ET ☎ 01224 646912 📠 01224 647006
e-mail: info@bimini.co.uk
Dir: *5 mins walk from town centre, 15-20 mins walk from Rail/Bus station, near University*
A welcoming atmosphere prevails at this guest house which is situated north of the city centre and close to the seafront. Bedrooms contain a very useful guest information directory. Most have smart en suites, but the two without offer the greater space. There is a cosy lounge adjoining the dining room.
FACILITIES: 8 rms (6 en suite) (1 fmly) No smoking TVB tea/coffee No dogs (ex guide dogs) Cen ht TVL No coaches **PRICES:** s £35-£37; d £50-£55✻ **PARKING:** 7 **CARDS:**

♦♦♦ Kildonan

410 Great Western Rd AB10 6NR ☎ 01224 316115 📠 01224 316115
e-mail: dey@kildonan.fsbusiness.co.uk
Dir: *100mtrs from junct of A90, A93 & A96*
An end-of-terrace house which is attractively presented both inside and out. Bedrooms come in various sizes and are enhanced by cheerful co-ordinated décor and modern shower rooms.
FACILITIES: 7 rms (6 en suite) (2 fmly) (3 GF) No smoking TVB tea/coffee No dogs (ex guide dogs) Cen ht No coaches **PRICES:** s £26-£32; d £40-£44✻ **PARKING:** 3 **NOTES:** Closed Xmas & New Year **CARDS:**

♦♦♦ Manorville

252 Gt Western Rd AB10 6PJ ☎ 01224 594190 📠 01224 594190
Situated in the west end of the city, Manorville is an immaculate granite-built house set in attractive gardens. Bedrooms combine cheerful colour schemes with comfortable modern furnishings. Public areas include a relaxing lounge and separate dining room where breakfasts are served at individual tables.
FACILITIES: 3 en suite (2 fmly) No smoking in dining room TVB tea/coffee No dogs (ex guide dogs) Cen ht No coaches **PRICES:** s fr £25; d fr £42✻ **PARKING:** 4 **CARDS:**

A Crown Private Hotel

10 Springbank Ter AB11 6LS ☎ 01224 586842 📠 01224 573787
e-mail: crown_hotel@yahoo.co.uk
FACILITIES: 9 rms (7 en suite) (2 fmly) No smoking in dining room No smoking in lounges TVB tea/coffee Cen ht No coaches **PRICES:** s £20-£34; d £36-£42✻ **BB NOTES:** ★★★ **CARDS:**

ABERDEENSHIRE

BALLATER Map 15 NO39

♦♦♦♦ Glen Lui Hotel

Invercauld Rd AB35 5PP ☎ 013397 55402 📠 013397 55545
e-mail: infos@glen-lui-hotel.co.uk
Dir: *Invercauld Rd is off A93 in Ballater, turn at the Auld Kirk - drive to end of road*
This friendly hotel lies secluded in its own landscaped grounds with views across the golf course to mountains beyond. Inviting public areas include a cosy bar, restaurant and a choice of tastefully appointed lounges. Bedrooms are smartly presented and very well equipped; the chalet rooms are popular with outdoor sports guests and pet owners.

continued

Glen Lui Hotel

FACILITIES: 10 en suite 9 annexe en suite (2 fmly) (9 GF) No smoking in bedrooms No smoking in dining room No smoking in 1 lounge TVB tea/coffee Direct dial from bedrooms Licensed Cen ht TVL Croquet lawn Dinner Last d 9pm **PRICES:** s £25-£45; d £50-£122✻ **LB CONF:** Thtr 32 Board 24 Del from £68 ✻ **PARKING:** 30 **CARDS:**

♦♦♦♦ Belvedere

Station Square AB35 5QB ☎ 013397 55996 📠 013397 55110
e-mail: flora-ingram@freeuk.com
Dir: *town centre, opposite old station, adjacent to Albert & Victoria Halls*

Set in the centre of the village opposite the old railway station, Belvedere is an attractive guest house with all amenities on first and second floors. Bedrooms are comfortable and equipped with extras including complimentary sherry. Breakfasts are served at individual tables in a delightful dining room.

FACILITIES: 4 en suite (1 fmly) No smoking STV TVB tea/coffee No dogs (ex guide dogs) Cen ht No coaches **PRICES:** s £25; d £40-£46✻ **PARKING:** 4

♦♦♦♦ Inverdeen House

11 Bridge Square AB35 5QJ ☎ 013397 55759 📠 013397 55993
e-mail: info@inverdeen.com
Dir: *on A93, near bridge over River Dee, as you approach Ballater from Aberdeen*

Friendly attentive service will be found at this Georgian house, set close to the River Dee on the west side of the village. Bedrooms reflect the character of the house, two having neat en suite shower rooms. The new owners are making a feature of breakfast, with hearty and healthy options on offer.

FACILITIES: 4 en suite (1 fmly) No smoking STV TVB tea/coffee No dogs Cen ht TVL No coaches Golf, Fishing, Beauty treatment, Shooting arranged **PRICES:** s £20-£28; d £40-£50✻ **LB PARKING:** 2 **CARDS:**

♦♦♦♦ Moorside

Braemar Rd AB35 5RL ☎ 013397 55492 📠 013397 55492
e-mail: moorside.house@virgin.net
Dir: *on left of main road on entering Ballater on A93 from SW*

A relaxed welcoming atmosphere is assured at this guest house which stands in attractive gardens beside the Braemar Road. Carefully maintained throughout, it offers bright airy bedrooms and comfortable public rooms which include an inviting lounge and well-proportioned dining room.

FACILITIES: 9 en suite (3 fmly) (1 GF) No smoking in bedrooms No smoking in dining room TVB tea/coffee No dogs (ex guide dogs) Cen ht No coaches **PRICES:** d £40-£44✻ **PARKING:** 10 **NOTES:** Closed Nov-Feb **CARDS:**

BANFF — Map 15 NJ66

♦♦♦♦ Morayhill

Bellevue Rd AB45 1BJ ☎ 01261 815956 📠 01261 818717
e-mail: morayhill@aol.com
Dir: *turn off A947 onto A97 towards Aberchirder, 2nd on right, 3rd house on left*

Guests get a warm welcome at this fine Victorian house set in mature gardens in a residential area close to the town centre. Meticulously maintained, it offers comfortable bedrooms, an inviting lounge and bright airy dining room overlooking the garden. An impressive starter buffet is a feature of breakfast.

FACILITIES: 3 rms (2 en suite) (2 fmly) No smoking in bedrooms TVB tea/coffee Cen ht TVL No coaches **PRICES:** s £22-£25; d £38-£42✻ **LB BB PARKING:** 5

BRAEMAR — Map 15 NO19

♦♦♦♦ Callater Lodge Hotel

9 Glenshee Rd AB35 5YQ ☎ 013397 41275 📠 013397 41345
e-mail: mariaaa@hotel-braemar.co.uk
Dir: *adjacent to A93, 300yds S of Braemar centre*

Set in grounds at the south end of the village, this Victorian lodge is well presented throughout. There is a comfortable lounge and attractive dining room. Bedrooms come in a range of sizes, many being well proportioned, all individual in style and thoughtfully equipped.

FACILITIES: 7 rms (6 en suite) No smoking TVB tea/coffee Licensed Cen ht TVL No children 4yrs No coaches Dinner Last d noon **PRICES:** s £24-£30; d £48-£60✻ **LB PARKING:** 7 **CARDS:**

OLDMELDRUM — Map 15 NJ82

A Cromlet Hill

South Rd AB51 0AB ☎ 01651 872315 📠 01641 872164
e-mail: john.isabel@tinyworld.co.uk
Dir: *from Aberdeen turn off A947 onto A920 signed Inverurie/town centre, Cromlet Hill is 200yds on the right. From Inverurie through town square on Aberdeen Road, Cromlet Hill is 200 yds on left*

FACILITIES: 3 en suite (1 fmly) No smoking in bedrooms No smoking in dining room TVB tea/coffee Direct dial from bedrooms No dogs (ex guide dogs) Cen ht TVL No coaches **PRICES:** s £28-£40; d £44-£65✻ **PARKING:** 4 **NOTES:** ★★★★

A Associate entries with stars have been ★ inspected and rated by the ★ Welsh Tourist Board or Scottish Tourist Board.

Scotland

Scotland

STONEHAVEN — Map 15 NO88

♦♦♦♦ Arduthie House

Ann St AB39 2DA ☎ 01569 762381 📠 01569 766366
e-mail: arduthie@talk21.com

Dir: *A90 from S, turn into Stonehaven at traffic lights, turn left, then 2nd right (Ann St). House 100yds on left. A90 from N, turn right at lights*

Set in attractive gardens, Arduthie House is meticulously maintained. The delightful public areas are graced with personal touches and include two inviting lounges. Bedrooms and bathrooms feature thoughtful extras. Breakfast is well presented and offers an impressive selection.

FACILITIES: 6 rms (5 en suite) (1 fmly) No smoking in bedrooms No smoking in dining room No smoking in 1 lounge TVB tea/coffee No dogs (ex guide dogs) Cen ht TVL No coaches **PRICES:** s £18; d £48-£52✳ **LB BB**

♦♦♦♦ Woodside Of Glasslaw

AB39 3XQ ☎ 01569 763799 📠 01569 763799
e-mail: douton@globalnet.co.uk

Dir: *Heading N leave A90 at 1st sign for Stonehaven. At end of sweeping bend turn right, take next road on left*

A relaxed and welcoming atmosphere prevails at this modern bungalow set in gardens amidst farmland. Bedrooms are comfortably furnished and attractively decorated. There is also a combined lounge/dining room where hearty breakfasts are served at individual tables.

FACILITIES: 6 en suite (1 fmly) (4 GF) No smoking in bedrooms No smoking in dining room TVB tea/coffee Cen ht TVL No coaches **PRICES:** s £22-£25; d £40-£44✳ **PARKING:** 5

🅰 Alexander

36 Arduthie Rd AB39 2DD ☎ 01569 762265 📠 0870 1391045
e-mail: marion@alexanderguesthouse.com

Dir: *from market square traffic lights in Stonehaven town centre, turn into Evan St. Arduthie Road is 5th street on right. Guesthouse on right*

FACILITIES: 7 rms (5 en suite) (3 fmly) No smoking TVB tea/coffee Licensed Cen ht TVL No coaches **PRICES:** s £20-£30; d £48-£52✳ **NOTES:** ★★★ **CARDS:**

ANGUS

ARBROATH — Map 12 NO64

♦♦ Kingsley

29 Marketgate DD11 1AU ☎ 01241 873933 📠 01241 873933
e-mail: kingsleyarbroath@aol.com

Dir: *from A92 follow sign for harbour then 1st left 100mtrs from harbour*

Situated a short walk from the harbour and central amenities, this family-run guesthouse offers good value accommodation. The bedrooms vary in size and are brightly decorated, with modern furnishings and the expected amenities.

FACILITIES: 15 rms (8 en suite) (3 fmly) (2 GF) No smoking in dining room STV TVB No dogs Licensed Cen ht TVL Pool Table Childrens play ground Dinner **PRICES:** s £20-£25; d £36-£44✳ **BB PARKING:** 4 **CARDS:**

TVB means there are televisions in bedrooms
TVL means thereís a television in the lounge
STV means satellite television.

CARNOUSTIE — Map 12 NO53

♦♦♦♦ Park House

12 Park Av DD7 7JA ☎ 01241 852101 📠 01241 852101
e-mail: parkhouse@bbcarnoustie.fsnet.co.uk

Dir: *turn off A92 onto A930 Muirdrum road*

A warm friendly welcome is assured at this delightful Victorian villa, which stands in its own well-tended grounds. The attractive bedrooms, one of which has a Jacuzzi bath, are comfortably furnished and well-quipped. Freshly prepared breakfasts are served in the smart ground floor dining room, which is situated opposite the comfortable lounge.

FACILITIES: 3 en suite No smoking TVB tea/coffee No dogs (ex guide dogs) Cen ht TVL No coaches BBQ area **PRICES:** s £26-£40; d £52✳ **PARKING:** 5 **NOTES:** Closed Xmas & New Year **CARDS:**

GLENISLA — Map 15 NO26

♦♦♦ The Glenisla Hotel

PH12 8PH ☎ 01575 582223 📠 01575 582203
e-mail: glenisla.hotel@btinternet.com

Situated in glorious countryside the Glenisla Hotel offers comfortable good value accommodation and delicious food. Bedrooms which vary in size, are attractive and well equipped. There is an elegant dining room and a beamed well-stocked bar and dining area where a log fire blazes on the cooler evenings. Evening meals can be chosen from the bar or restaurant menu, and feature almost forgotten dishes from the days of the "Auld Alliance". For those who enjoy outdoor pursuits a drying room is available.

FACILITIES: 6 en suite (1 fmly) No smoking in bedrooms No smoking in dining room tea/coffee Cen ht Games room Dinner **PRICES:** s £20-£25; d £40-£50✳ **PARKING:** 10 **NOTES:** Closed 25 Dec **CARDS:**

MONTROSE — Map 15 NO75

♦♦♦ Oaklands

10 Rossie Island Rd DD10 9NN ☎ 01674 672018
📠 01674 672018
e-mail: oaklands@altavista.net

Dir: *on A92, S end of town*

The Merckaert family takes pleasure in welcoming guests old and new to their comfortable home, a detached house situated on the South side of the town. Bedrooms are attractively decorated, comfortably furnished and well-equipped. There is a relaxing lounge located on the ground floor adjacent to the dining room where hearty breakfasts are served.

FACILITIES: 7 en suite (1 fmly) (1 GF) No smoking in 2 bedrooms No smoking in dining room TVB tea/coffee Cen ht TVL No coaches **PRICES:** s £25; d £40-£50✳ **PARKING:** 8 **CARDS:**

ARGYLL & BUTE

ARDRISHAIG — Map 10 NR88

🅰 Fascadale House

Tarbert Rd PA30 8EP ☎ 01546 603845 📠 01546 602152
e-mail: info@fascadale.com

Dir: *from Lochilphead take A83 S to Campbletown, through Ardrishaig, cross Crinan Canal swing Bridge and Fascadale is 1m on right*

FACILITIES: 4 en suite (1 fmly) No smoking TVB tea/coffee No dogs (ex guide dogs) Cen ht TVL No coaches Fishing Snooker Croquet lawn Mooring available Dinner Last d 6pm **PRICES:** s £30-£50; d £60-£80✳ **LB PARKING:** 10 **NOTES:** ★★★★ **CARDS:**

Scotland

ARROCHAR Map 10 NN20

♦♦♦ *Bemersyde*

Tarbet, Loch Lomond G83 7DE ☎ 01301 702230

Dir: *on A82*

This extended bungalow offers comfortable, good value accommodation. Two rooms are located on the first floor. A ground floor bedroom is also available, and is suitable for guests with limited mobility. There is a cosy lounge and hearty breakfasts are served at individual tables in the separate dining room.

FACILITIES: 3 en suite (1 fmly) No smoking TV1B tea/coffee Cen ht TVL No coaches **PARKING:** 3 **NOTES:** Closed Nov-Feb

CAMPBELTOWN Map 10 NR72

♦♦♦ Westbank

Dell Rd PA28 6JG ☎ 01586 553660 📠 01586 553660

Dir: *A83 to Campbeltown turn right at T-junct follow signs for Southend, B842, through S-bend, Heritage centre on left, 1st right Dell Rd*

Located in a quiet residential area close to the town centre, this smartly presented Victorian house offers guests old and new a warm and friendly welcome. Public areas include a relaxing lounge and separate dining room where hearty breakfasts are served.

FACILITIES: 7 rms (6 en suite) No smoking in dining room TVB tea/coffee Cen ht TVL No coaches **PRICES:** s £23-£28; d £38-£48* **LB BB**
CARDS:

CARDROSS Map 10 NS37

Premier Collection

♦♦♦♦♦ Kirkton House

Darleith Rd G82 5EZ ☎ 01389 841951 📠 01389 841868
e-mail: AA@kirktonhouse.co.uk

Dir: *0.5m N of village, turn N off A814 into Darleith Rd at W end of village. Kirkton House 0.5m on right (The Circle)*

This delightful converted 18th-century farmstead enjoys lovely views of the River Clyde. Inviting public areas have a comfortable traditional feel, with a welcoming open fire in the relaxing lounge. Bedrooms are individual in style with lots of extra amenities provided, and home cooked meals are served in the rustic dining room.

FACILITIES: 6 en suite (4 fmly) No smoking in dining room TVB tea/coffee Direct dial from bedrooms Licensed Cen ht No coaches Riding Dinner Last d 7.30pm **PRICES:** s £42-£47.50; d £61-£75 **LB**
PARKING: 12 **NOTES:** Closed Dec-Jan **CARDS:**

CLADICH Map 10 NN02

♦♦♦ Rockhill *(NN072219)*

PA33 1BH ☎ 01866 833218 📠 01866 833218
Mr & Mrs Whalley

Dir: *from Inverary or Dalmally take A819, then onto B840 at Cladich for 3m to Rockhill*

A warm welcome awaits guests at this cottage-style farmhouse overlooking Loch Awe to Ben Cruchan. Bedrooms are comfortably traditional in style and offer the expected amenities. Public areas include a relaxing lounge with ample reading material and a separate dining room where enjoyable home-cooked fare is served at individual tables.

FACILITIES: 5 en suite (3 fmly) (2 GF) No smoking in dining room No smoking in lounges TVB tea/coffee Licensed No children 8yrs Fishing 200 acres horses Dinner Last d 7pm **PRICES:** (incl. dinner) d £70-£78*
PARKING: 8 **NOTES:** Closed Nov-Apr

CONNEL Map 10 NM93

♦♦♦♦ *Kilchurn*

PA37 1PG ☎ 01631 710581
e-mail: kilchurn@msn.com

Dir: *on A85*

Situated on the eastern edge of the village, overlooking Loch Etive, this elegant Victorian house offers a warm and friendly welcome. The pretty bedrooms are comfortably proportioned and well-equipped. There is an attractive, peaceful guest lounge and a smart dining room where hearty Scottish breakfasts are served.

FACILITIES: 3 en suite No smoking TVB tea/coffee No dogs No children 12yrs No coaches **PARKING:** 3 **NOTES:** Closed Nov-Etr

♦♦♦♦ Ards House

PA37 1PT ☎ 01631 710255
e-mail: ardsconnel@aol.com

Dir: *on A85, 4m N of Oban*

A delightful Victorian villa, situated on the approaches to Loch Etive and enjoying stunning views over the Firth of Lorn and the Morven Hills beyond. The individually decorated bedrooms are well equipped and offer many thoughtful extras. There is a spacious drawing room with a real fire on cooler evenings and an abundance of games and books. The attractive dining room is an appropriate setting for delicious five-course dinners and hearty breakfasts, featuring the best of fresh local produce.

FACILITIES: 5 en suite (2 fmly) No smoking TV1B tea/coffee Licensed Cen ht TVL No children 10yrs No coaches **PRICES:** s £25-£30; d £40-£60* **LB**
PARKING: 12 **CARDS:**

♦♦♦♦ Loch Etive House Hotel

Connel Village, By Oban PA37 1PH ☎ 01631 710400
📠 01631 710680
e-mail: frankwop@btinternet.com

Dir: *turn off A85 in Connel, 5m from Oban, 50yds from St Orons Kirk (The Circle)*

Conveniently located in the centre of the village, Loch Etive House is a family run establishment where a warm friendly welcome is assured. Bedrooms are comfortably furnished and well equipped. A combined lounge/dining room is available where delicious evening meals and freshly cooked breakfasts are served at individual tables.

FACILITIES: 5 rms (3 en suite) (3 fmly) No smoking TVB tea/coffee Licensed Cen ht TVL No coaches Dinner Last d 9.30am
PRICES: s £18.50-£27.50; d £37-£55* **LB BB PARKING:** 6
CARDS:

Scotland

CONNEL continued

♦♦♦♦ Ronebhal Guest House

PA37 1PJ ☎ 01631 710310 & 710813 Fax 01631 710310
e-mail: ronebhal@btinternet.com
Dir: *on A85 Oban road. 4th house past turn off for Fort William*

The Strachan family extends a warm friendly welcome to guests to their lovely detached home which enjoys stunning views over Loch Etive. Bedrooms, with attractive colour schemes, are comfortably furnished in mixed modern styles. Public areas include a relaxing sitting room and an attractive dining room where hearty traditional breakfasts are served at individual tables.

FACILITIES: 5 rms (4 en suite) (1 fmly) (1 GF) No smoking TVB tea/coffee No dogs Cen ht No children 7yrs No coaches **PRICES:** s £20-£25; d £40-£60* **LB PARKING:** 6 **NOTES:** Closed Dec-Jan
CARDS:

DUNOON — Map 10 NS17

Premier Collection

♦♦♦♦♦ The Anchorage

Sandbank PA23 8QG ☎ 01369 705108 Fax 01369 705108
e-mail: long@anchorage.uk.com
Dir: *1.5m from Hunters Key Ferry Terminal on Loch side driving North*

This delightful small hotel overlooking the Holy Loch is under new ownership and continues to offer high levels of personal attention. Bedrooms are tastefully decorated, furnished in pine, and have a good range of amenities, one has a four-poster bed. Public areas include a relaxing sitting room and a cosy bar and dining room, where the short menu offers dishes made with carefully prepared quality ingredients. This is a non-smoking house.

FACILITIES: 5 en suite No smoking TVB tea/coffee No dogs (ex guide dogs) Licensed Cen ht No children 12yrs No coaches Dinner Last d 9pm **PRICES:** s £27.50-£30; d £55-£60* **LB PARKING:** 10
CARDS:

♦♦♦ Lyall Cliff Hotel

141 Alexandra Pde, East Bay PA23 8AW ☎ 01369 702041 Fax 01369 702041
e-mail: lyallcliff@talk21.com
Dir: *0.5m N of Dunoon Pier, on main promenade (A815)*

Situated on the East Bay Promenade and enjoying lovely views of the Firth of Clyde, Lyall Cliff is a family-run hotel where a friendly welcome is assured. Bedrooms are attractive and well equipped, with three on the ground floor offering partial disabled facilities including an access ramp and special parking bays. The public areas include a spacious lounge, library and dining room where meals are served at individual tables. There is also a large car park.

FACILITIES: 10 en suite (2 fmly) No smoking in 8 bedrooms No smoking in dining room No smoking in lounges TVB tea/coffee No dogs (ex guide dogs) Licensed Cen ht TVL No children 4yrs No coaches Dinner Last d 4pm **PRICES:** s £24-£32; d £42-£52 **LB PARKING:** 9
NOTES: Closed Nov-26 Dec **CARDS:**

Egg cups for excellence!
This symbol shows that breakfast exceeded our Inspector's expectations.

HELENSBURGH — Map 10 NS28

See also Cardross

♦♦♦♦ Lethamhill

West Dhuhill Drive G84 9AW ☎ 01436 676016 Fax 01436 676016
e-mail: Lethamhill@talk21.com
Dir: *turn off A82 onto B831, left onto B832, follow sign for Hillhouse. Take 2nd right after 30mph sign, over minor x-road, 3rd entrance on right*

From the red telephone box in the garden to the old typewriters and slot machines inside, this fine house is an Aladdin's cave of collectibles and memorabilia. Beyond this unique insight into British heritage is a house offering spacious, comfortable bedrooms with superb bathrooms. The home-cooked breakfasts and delicious baking earn much praise, and are served around the communal table in the elegant dining room.

FACILITIES: 3 en suite No smoking TVB tea/coffee No dogs Cen ht TVL No coaches Jacuzzi **PRICES:** s £35-£45; d £55-£70* **LB PARKING:** 6
CARDS:

INVERARAY — Map 10 NN00

See Cladich

Claonairigh House

Bridge of Douglas PA32 8XT ☎ 01499 302160 Fax 01499 302774
e-mail: fiona@argyll-scotland.demon.co.uk
Dir: *4m from Inveraray on the A38 (Campbeltown/Lochgilphead). Turn left at layby with B&B sign and AA phone box, 300yds up the forest road on the left*

FACILITIES: 3 en suite No smoking STV TVB tea/coffee Cen ht TVL No coaches Fishing **PRICES:** s £20-£25; d £36-£50* **LB BB**
PARKING: 5 **NOTES:** ★★★ Closed Xmas & New Year rs winter months

KILMARTIN — Map 10 NR89

♦♦♦♦ Dunchraigaig House

PA31 8RG ☎ 01546 605209
e-mail: dunchraig@aol.com
Dir: *from Lochgilphead take A816 Oban Rd, 7m on right opposite Ballymeanoch Standing Stones, 1m S of Kilmartin*

Guests are assured of a warm welcome at this delightful home. The smart bedrooms are bright and airy and furnished in both modern and traditional styles. There is an inviting lounge with well stocked bookshelves and a separate dining room where hearty breakfasts and, by prior arrangement, home-cooked evening meals are served.

FACILITIES: 5 en suite (1 fmly) No smoking TVB tea/coffee No dogs (ex guide dogs) Licensed Cen ht No coaches Dinner **PRICES:** s £25-£30; d £44-£50* **PARKING:** 8 **CARDS:**

OBAN Map 10 NM83

♦♦♦♦ Glenbervie House

Dalriach Rd PA34 5NL ☎ 01631 564770 📠 01631 566723

Dir: *on reaching Oban via A82, left at Kings Knoll Hotel. Straight through x-roads. Tennis courts & swimming pool on left. Glenbervie on right*

A warm and friendly welcome is given at this elegant Victorian house. The bedrooms are of various sizes; all are attractively decorated and well-equipped. A comfortable lounge offers breath-taking views over to the Islands of Kerrera and Mull. Delicious home-cooked meals and hearty Scottish breakfasts can be enjoyed in the charming dining room.

FACILITIES: 8 rms (6 en suite) (1 fmly) No smoking TVB tea/coffee No dogs (ex guide dogs) Licensed Cen ht TVL No children No coaches Dinner Last d 4pm **PRICES:** d £44-£60✳ **LB PARKING:** 8

♦♦♦♦ Glenburnie Private Hotel

The Esplanade PA34 5AQ ☎ 01631 562089 📠 01631 562089

e-mail: graeme.strachan@btinternet.com

Dir: *directly on Oban seafront, follow signs for Ganavan*

This elegant Victorian house, situated on the sea front, has been lovingly restored to a high standard. Bedrooms (which include a four-poster room and a mini suite) are beautifully decorated and well-equipped. There is a cosy ground floor lounge and a smart dining room where hearty traditional breakfasts are served.

FACILITIES: 14 en suite No smoking TVB tea/coffee No dogs (ex guide dogs) Cen ht No children 12yrs No coaches **PRICES:** s £28-£35; d £56-£70✳ **PARKING:** 12 **NOTES:** Closed Nov-Mar **CARDS:**

♦♦♦♦ Braeside

Kilmore PA34 4QR ☎ 01631 770243 📠 01631 770343

e-mail: braeside.guesthouse@virgin.net

Dir: *S from Oban on A816 for 3m. On left on entering village of Kilmore*

Situated in the village of Kilmore, this delightful family-run house stands in landscaped grounds and enjoys stunning views towards Loch Feochan. Bedrooms are bright and airy, comfortably furnished and well equipped. There is a lounge/dining room with a dispense bar, which is an appropriate setting for delicious home cooked dinners and breakfasts. All rooms are on ground level and suitable for guests with limited mobility.

continued

FACILITIES: 6 en suite (6 GF) No smoking TVB tea/coffee Direct dial from bedrooms No dogs Licensed Cen ht No children 10yrs Dinner Last d 6.30pm **PRICES:** s £25-£27.50; d £50-£55✳ **LB PARKING:** 10 **NOTES:** Closed Nov-Feb

♦♦♦♦ Greencourt

Benvoullin Ln, off Benvoullin Rd PA34 5EF ☎ 01631 563987 📠 01631 571276

e-mail: relaxation@greencourt-oban.fsnet.co.uk

Dir: *On reaching Oban, left at Kings Knoll Hotel. At x-roads straight over & follow Dalriach Rd. Pass Leisure Centre and Bowling Green on left then turn left. Turn left again and hard left into lane, Greencourt is the 2nd house on the left*

In an elevated position, overlooking the bowling green and leisure centre, this delightful detached house is the welcoming family home of Joanie and Michael Garvin. The pretty bedrooms vary in size and are comfortable and well equipped. Freshly prepared breakfasts are served in the bright airy dining room, which enjoys lovely views of the surrounding area.

FACILITIES: 8 en suite (6 GF) No smoking TVB tea/coffee No dogs Cen ht No children 12yrs No coaches **PRICES:** s £23-£30; d £46-£60✳ **LB PARKING:** 8 **CARDS:**

♦♦♦♦ Roseneath

Dalriach Rd PA34 5EQ ☎ 01631 562929 📠 01631 567218

e-mail: quirkers@aol.com

Dir: *approaching Oban from A85 turn left at King's Knoll Hotel & follow signs for swimming pool & leisure centre. Roseneath is 300mtrs beyond the leisure complex*

This delightful Victorian villa is situated in an elevated position and commands stunning views over Oban Bay to the Sound of Kerrera beyond. The attractive bedrooms, some with sea views, are comfortable and well equipped, and two have their own sitting rooms. There is a relaxing first-floor lounge with ample books and magazines. The hearty breakfasts are made using the best local produce.

FACILITIES: 8 en suite (1 GF) No smoking TVB tea/coffee Cen ht **PRICES:** s £25-£30; d £42-£56✳ **LB PARKING:** 8 **NOTES:** Closed Nov-Jan **CARDS:**

♦♦♦♦ Thornloe

Albert Rd PA34 5JD ☎ 01631 562879 📠 01631 562879

e-mail: thornloeoban@aol.com

Dir: *from A85, turn left at King's Knoll Hotel and pass swimming pool, last house on right*

Enjoying stunning views from its elevated position overlooking Oban Bay, Thornloe is an impressive Victorian house which been completely refurbished by attentive new owners and is now no smoking. Bedrooms are comfortable with attractive furnishings and decoration. The public areas comprise a bright dining room where hearty breakfasts are served. A conservatory lounge should be completed by 2003.

FACILITIES: 7 en suite (2 fmly) No smoking TV8B tea/coffee No dogs (ex guide dogs) Cen ht **PRICES:** s £21-£26; d £42-£54✳ **PARKING:** 4 **CARDS:**

♦♦♦ Red Diamonds highlight the top establishments within the AA's 3, 4 and 5 Diamond ratings.

Scotland

OBAN continued

♦♦♦ *Corriemar House*
6 Corran Esplanade PA34 5AQ ☎ 01631 562476
01631 564339
e-mail: corriemar@tinyworld.com
Dir: *Follow A85 to Oban. Proceed down hill in the right hand lane & follow sign for Gamavan at mini-rdbt onto Esplanade*
This impressive Victorian detached house enjoys unobstructed views across Oban Bay and on a fine day Duart Castle on the Isle of Mull can be seen from some rooms. Bedrooms are beautifully decorated, furnished in period style and well equipped. The attractive ground floor dining room is an appropriate setting for hearty traditional breakfasts.
FACILITIES: 9 en suite 4 annexe en suite (3 fmly) No smoking TVB tea/coffee No dogs (ex guide dogs) Cen ht **PARKING:** 9
CARDS:

Scotland

♦♦♦ Wellpark House
Esplanade PA34 5AQ ☎ 01631 562948 01631 565808
e-mail: enquiries@wellparkhouse.co.uk
Dir: *A85 to Oban seafront, turn right 200yds to Wellpark Hotel*
A welcoming family-run guest house situated on the Esplanade, with a lovely outlook over the bay to the Isle of Mull beyond. Bedrooms are well equipped and furnished in a modern style. Excellent views can be enjoyed from the first floor lounge and hearty breakfasts are served at individual tables in the ground floor dining room.
FACILITIES: 19 en suite (2 fmly) (4 GF) No smoking in 8 bedrooms No smoking in dining room TVB tea/coffee Direct dial from bedrooms Cen ht No coaches **PRICES:** s £26-£30; d £42-£70 **LB PARKING:** 16
NOTES: Closed Nov-Mar rs Etr **CARDS:**

A Rhumor
Drummore Rd PA34 4JL ☎ 01631 563544 01631 563544
e-mail: rhumor@vacations-scotland.co.uk
Dir: *from A85 follow signs for George St to rdbt, turn left at A816 onto Soroba Rd, approx 100yds after service station turn left into Drummore Rd*
FACILITIES: 3 en suite (1 fmly) No smoking TVB tea/coffee Cen ht TVL No coaches **PRICES:** d £36-£40✳ **BB PARKING:** 4 **NOTES:** ★★★
Closed Dec

TARBERT Map 10 NR86

♦♦♦♦ The Victoria Hotel
Barmore Rd PA29 6TW ☎ 01880 820236 01880 820638
e-mail: victoria.hotel@lineone.net
Dir: *follow A83 from Glasgow to Lochgilphead & follow road S to Tarbert. Hotel 1st on left upon entering Tarbert*
A small hotel that enjoys fine views over the harbour - and none better than that from its conservatory restaurant. As well as offering good fresh food, it also features stunning furniture crafted from elm wood and wrought iron. One can also eat well in the spacious bar. Bedrooms are smart and well equipped.
FACILITIES: 5 en suite (2 fmly) No smoking in dining room TVB tea/coffee Direct dial from bedrooms Cen ht Pool Table Dinner Last d 8.55pm
PRICES: d £64✳ **NOTES:** Closed 25 Dec **CARDS:**

CITY OF EDINBURGH

EDINBURGH Map 11 NT27

See also East Calder (West Lothian)

Premier Collection

♦♦♦♦♦ Elmview
15 Glengyle Ter EH3 9LN ☎ 0131 228 1973
e-mail: marny@elmview.co.uk
Dir: *take A702 S up Lothian Rd, turn 1st left past Kings Theatre into ValleyField St, one-way system leading to Glengyle Terrace*
Occupying the lower ground level of a fine Victorian terraced house, Elmview offers stylish accommodation. The tastefully furnished bedrooms and smart bathrooms are comfortable and extremely well equipped, with many thoughtful extras such as fridges with fresh milk and water. Breakfasts are excellent and are taken at one large, elegantly appointed table.
FACILITIES: 3 en suite (3 GF) No smoking TVB tea/coffee Direct dial from bedrooms No dogs Cen ht No children 15yrs No coaches
PRICES: s £60-£75; d £75-£95✳ **PARKING:** 2 **CARDS:**

Premier Collection

♦♦♦♦♦ Newington Cottage
15 Blacket Place EH9 1RJ ☎ 0131 668 1935
0131 667 4644
e-mail: fmickel@newcot.demon.co.uk
Dir: *driving from N, S, or from the airport, approach from city bypass exiting at Straiton junct. Follow city centre signs until you reach Minto Hotel on your right, take next turning right*

Newington Cottage, situated in a quiet residential area is built on classical Italian lines and is deceptively spacious. Combining elegance with a friendly atmosphere, it offers superb public rooms adorned with flowers and plants. The spacious bedrooms are attractively decorated, well equipped and include fridge, CD player, fresh fruit and a decanter of sherry.
FACILITIES: 3 en suite No smoking TVB tea/coffee No dogs Cen ht TVL No children 13yrs No coaches **PRICES:** s £60-£75; d £80-£110✳
LB CARDS:

Premier Collection

♦♦♦♦♦ Bonnington
202 Ferry Rd EH6 4NW ☎ 0131 554 7610 Fax 0131 554 7610
e-mail: bonningtongh@btinternet.com
Dir: *located on A902*

The resident proprietors at this delightful Georgian house extend a warm and friendly welcome. Bedrooms vary in style and all are comfortable. The cosy ground floor lounge has a grand piano. Carefully prepared breakfasts offer an excellent choice and are served in the attractive dining room.
FACILITIES: 6 rms (4 en suite) (3 fmly) No smoking in bedrooms No smoking in dining room TVB tea/coffee Cen ht TVL No coaches
PRICES: s £38-£48; d £50-£80* **PARKING:** 9
CARDS:

Premier Collection

♦♦♦♦♦ Dunstane House Hotel
4 West Coates, Haymarket EH12 5JQ
☎ 0131 337 6169 & 337 5320 Fax 0131 337 6169
e-mail: reservations@dunstanehousehotel.co.uk
Dir: *on A8 between Murrayfield Stadium and Haymarket railway station. 5 mins from city centre 15 mins from airport*
A splendid Victorian villa which combines architectural grandeur (crow step gables, archers' windows and ornate open fireplaces) with an intimate country house atmosphere, this small hotel offers comfortable bedrooms and is conveniently situated for the city centre. The Skerries restaurant features fish from the proprietors' native Orkney Islands, with lighter meals and a wide selection of malt whisky also offered in the Stane bar.
FACILITIES: 16 en suite (4 fmly) No smoking in bedrooms No smoking in dining room TVB tea/coffee Direct dial from bedrooms No dogs (ex guide dogs) Licensed Cen ht TVL Dinner Last d 2pm
PRICES: s £40-£65; d £78-£110* **LB CONF:** Thtr 35 Class 18 Board 20 Del from £105.95 * **PARKING:** 12
CARDS:

Scotland

EDINBURGH continued

Premier Collection

♦♦♦♦♦ Kildonan Lodge Hotel

27 Craigmillar Park EH16 5PE ☎ 0131 667 2793
📠 0131 667 9777
e-mail: info@kildonanlodgehotel.co.uk
Dir: *from city by pass (A720), exit A701 city centre, continue approx 2.75m to large rdbt straight on, located 6 buildings on right hand side*

This is a delightful Victorian house, carefully restored to provide very high standards of accommodation. Bedrooms are beautifully decorated and very well appointed, some have splendid four-poster beds. Super hospitality is provided and nothing is too much trouble. Imaginative dinners can be enjoyed in the popular 'Potters Fine Dining Restaurant', while pre-dinner drinks can be enjoyed from the honesty bar in the stylish, elegant lounge.
FACILITIES: 12 en suite (2 fmly) No smoking in bedrooms No smoking in dining room TVB tea/coffee Direct dial from bedrooms No dogs (ex guide dogs) Licensed Cen ht Jacuzzi Dinner Last d 9.30pm **PRICES:** s £55-£79; d £78-£140* **LB PARKING:** 16 **NOTES:** Closed Xmas **CARDS:**

Premier Collection

♦♦♦♦♦ The Lodge Hotel

6 Hampton Ter, West Coates EH12 5JD ☎ 0131 337 3682
📠 0131 346 1573
e-mail: jeanandsteve@thelodgehotel.co.uk
Dir: *on A8, 0.75m W of Princess Street*

This charming Georgian house lies in Edinburgh's West End, within easy walking distance of the city centre and also on the main bus route. Bedrooms are beautifully decorated and presented. There is a comfortable lounge and an atmospheric bar; delicious evening meals by prior arrangement, and hearty breakfasts are served at individual tables in the dining room.

continued

FACILITIES: 9 en suite (1 fmly) (3 GF) No smoking TVB tea/coffee Direct dial from bedrooms No dogs Licensed Cen ht TVL Dinner Last d 7.30pm **PRICES:** s £35-£65; d £60-£110* **LB PARKING:** 10 **CARDS:**

Premier Collection

♦♦♦♦♦ The Stuarts

17 Glengyle Ter EH3 9LN ☎ 0131 229 9559
📠 0131 229 2226
e-mail: gloria@the-stuarts.com
Dir: *E of A702, between the Kings Theatre and Bruntsfield Links*
In a central location, overlooking a tree filled park, this welcoming guest house offers spacious, immaculately maintained bedrooms with luxury en suite bathrooms. Bedrooms are extremely well equipped with many thoughtful extras, such as hi-fi and video player (CDs and videos available), fridge with wine, trouser press and ironing centre. The dining room overlooks the lovely courtyard garden.
FACILITIES: 3 en suite No smoking TVB tea/coffee Direct dial from bedrooms No dogs Cen ht No coaches **PRICES:** d £95* **NOTES:** Closed Xmas **CARDS:**

♦♦♦♦ Kew House

1 Kew Ter, Murrayfield EH12 5JE ☎ 0131 313 0700
📠 0131 313 0747
e-mail: kewhouse@ednet.co.uk
Dir: *on A8 Glasgow road, 1m W of city centre, close to Murrayfield Rugby Stadium*

Forming part of a listed Victorian terrace, Kew House lies west of the city centre and is convenient for Murrayfield Rugby Stadium. Meticulously maintained throughout, it offers attractive bedrooms in a variety of sizes, all thoughtfully equipped to suite both business and tourist guests. There is a comfortable lounge offering a supper and snack menu.
FACILITIES: 6 en suite (1 fmly) (2 GF) No smoking TVB tea/coffee Direct dial from bedrooms Licensed Cen ht No coaches Dinner Last d 8pm **PRICES:** s £50-£55; d £70-£100* **LB PARKING:** 6 **CARDS:**

♦♦♦♦ *Acorn Lodge*

26 Pilrig St EH6 5AJ ☎ 0131 555 1557 📠 0131 555 4475
e-mail: info@acornlodge.co.uk
This Georgian terraced house is situated just off Leith Walk, a short distance to the north of the city centre. Bedrooms are stylishly decorated, comfortably furnished and extremely well equipped for both business and leisure guests. Newspapers are provided in the smartly appointed dinning room where high teas and hearty breakfasts are served.

continued

FACILITIES: 7 en suite (2 fmly) No smoking TVB tea/coffee Direct dial from bedrooms No dogs (ex guide dogs) Cen ht Dinner Last d 6.45pm
CARDS:

♦♦♦♦ *Adam Hotel*

19 Lansdowne Crescent EH12 5EH ☎ 0131 337 1148
🖹 0131 337 1729
e-mail: welcome@adam-hotel.co.uk
Dir: *from Airport follow City Centre signs, on reaching Haymarket Terrace turn left opp Station car park & follow road which bears right*
This fine Georgian terraced house lies in a quiet residential crescent in the West End of the city. Period features retained in the elegant public areas include ornate ceilings, marble fireplaces and varnished paper panels in the entrance hallway. Bedrooms vary in size and are all attractively decorated and comfortably furnished.
FACILITIES: 13 en suite (3 fmly) No smoking TVB tea/coffee Direct dial from bedrooms No dogs (ex guide dogs) Licensed Cen ht TVL ch fac No coaches Last d 7.30pm **CARDS:**

♦♦♦♦ Arden

126 Old Dalkeith Rd EH16 4SD ☎ 0131 664 3985
🖹 0131 621 0866
e-mail: dot@baigan.freeserve.co.uk
Dir: *on A7*
Colourful flowering baskets adorn the front of this welcoming, personally run guest house situated on the South side of the city, convenient for both the leisure and business traveller to Edinburgh. The modern bedrooms enjoy a superb range of facilities including cable TV. Traditional Scottish breakfasts are served at individual tables in the conservatory dining room.
FACILITIES: 8 en suite (3 fmly) (3 GF) No smoking in 2 bedrooms No smoking in dining room No smoking in lounges STV TVB tea/coffee Cen ht
PRICES: s £25-£60; d £36-£80* **LB BB PARKING:** 8
CARDS:

♦♦♦♦ *Ashgrove House*

12 Osborne Ter EH12 5HG ☎ 0131 337 5014 🖹 0131 313 5043
e-mail: info@theashgrovehouse.com
Dir: *on A8 between Murrayfield & Haymarket opposite Donaldson's College for Deaf, (under 1m to Princes Street)*
A well-proportioned detached Victorian house; bedrooms are comfortably furnished in modern style and equipped with many extras. Freshly prepared breakfasts and evening meals, by prior arrangement, are served at individual tables in the stylish dining room. A sun lounge overlooking the rear garden is the only area where smoking is permitted.
FACILITIES: 7 en suite (2 fmly) No smoking TVB tea/coffee Direct dial from bedrooms No dogs (ex guide dogs) Cen ht TVL No coaches Dinner Last d 11am **PARKING:** 10 **NOTES:** Closed 23-26 Dec
CARDS:

♦♦♦♦ Ben Doran

11 Mayfield Gardens EH9 2AX ☎ 0131 667 8488
🖹 0131 667 0076
e-mail: info@ben-doran.co.uk
Dir: *from east side of Princes Street, take A701, Ben Doran on left, approx 1m*
This smart guest house enjoys a convenient location close to the city centre on a major bus route. Stylish, well-equipped bedrooms and impressive bathrooms reflect a very discerning approach to interior design. Hearty breakfasts and dinner by prior request are served in the smartly appointed dining room. Packed lunches are also available.
FACILITIES: 10 rms (6 en suite) No smoking TVB tea/coffee Direct dial from bedrooms No dogs (ex guide dogs) Cen ht No children 12yrs Dinner Last d 11am **PRICES:** s £35-£120; d £55-£175* **LB PARKING:** 10
CARDS:

See advertisement on page 505

EDINBURGH continued

♦♦♦♦ Dorstan Private Hotel

7 Priestfield Rd EH16 5HJ ☎ 0131 667 6721 & 667 5138
Fax 0131 668 4644
e-mail: reservations@dorstan-hotel.demon.co.uk
Dir: *turn off A68 at Priestfield Road, just before Commonwealth Swimming Pool*

A warm welcome is assured at this beautiful Victorian villa, set in a residential area on the south side of the city. Bedrooms vary in size, are thoughtfully equipped and enhanced by quality fabrics and individual styling. There is an inviting lounge, and by prior arrangement, good value dinners are served in the cosy dining room.

FACILITIES: 14 rms (12 en suite) (2 fmly) (3 GF) No smoking TVB tea/coffee Direct dial from bedrooms No dogs (ex guide dogs) Cen ht No coaches Dinner Last d 10am **PRICES:** s £34-£50; d £72-£86* **LB PARKING:** 8 **CARDS:**

See advertisement on opposite page

♦♦♦♦ Ellesmere House

11 Glengyle Ter EH3 9LN ☎ 0131 229 4823 Fax 0131 229 5285
e-mail: celia@edinburghbandb.co.uk
Dir: *central Edinburgh off A702 overlooking Bruntsfield Links*

This delightful terraced house hotel overlooks Bruntsfield Links, and is convenient for the city centre. The attractive bedrooms, which vary in size are comfortable and very well equipped, with many thoughtful extra touches. Breakfast features the best of local produce and can be enjoyed in the elegant combined lounge/dining room.

FACILITIES: 6 en suite (1 fmly) (2 GF) No smoking in dining room TVB tea/coffee No dogs (ex guide dogs) Cen ht TVL No children 10yrs No coaches **PRICES:** s £28-£38; d £56-£76*

♦♦♦♦ Greenside Hotel

9 Royal Ter EH7 5AB ☎ 0131 557 0022 & 557 0121
Fax 0131 557 0022
e-mail: greensidehotel@ednet.co.uk
Dir: *follow A1 into London Rd, Royal Terrace at end of London Rd, turning left at rdbt*

This comfortable private hotel is set in an elegant Georgian terrace with pretty gardens to the rear. The newly refurbished bedrooms vary in size - several are particularly spacious - and are attractively decorated and well equipped. The dining room has a small bar; evening meals are available by prior arrangement.

FACILITIES: 15 rms (14 en suite) (5 fmly) (1 GF) No smoking in dining room TVB tea/coffee Direct dial from bedrooms No dogs (ex guide dogs) Licensed Cen ht TVL Arrangement with 4 star hotel to use facilities Dinner Last d 4pm **PRICES:** s £25-£45; d £45-£95* **LB CARDS:**

♦♦♦♦ Grosvenor Gardens Hotel

1 Grosvenor Gardens EH12 5JU ☎ 0131 313 3415
Fax 0131 346 8732
e-mail: info@stayinedinburgh.com
Dir: *from A8, continue towards city centre. Turn left before Haymarket Station into Roseberry Crescent and hotel on left on corner with Grosvenor Gardens*

Generally spacious bedrooms are a feature of this Victorian town house, quietly situated in the west end of the city. Attractively furnished and equipped to meet the needs of business travellers and tourists alike, they even offer a welcoming decanter of Scotch whisky. A hearty breakfast is served in the brightly decorated dining room.

FACILITIES: 9 en suite (4 fmly) No smoking in 7 bedrooms No smoking in dining room No smoking in lounges TVB tea/coffee Direct dial from bedrooms No dogs (ex guide dogs) Cen ht No coaches **PRICES:** s £35-£55; d £50-£135* **LB CARDS:**

♦♦♦♦ International

37 Mayfield Gardens EH9 2BX ☎ 0131 667 2511
Fax 0131 667 1112
e-mail: intergh@easynet.co.uk
Dir: *1.5m S of Princes St on A701 (4m from Straiton Junction on Edinburgh City by-pass)*

Guests are assured of a warm and friendly welcome at this attractive Victorian terraced house situated to the south of the city centre. The smartly presented bedrooms are thoughtfully decorated and comfortably furnished. Hearty Scottish breakfasts are served at individual tables in the traditionally styled dining room, which boasts a beautiful ornate ceiling.

FACILITIES: 9 en suite (3 fmly) No smoking in 4 bedrooms No smoking in dining room No smoking in lounges STV TVB tea/coffee Direct dial from bedrooms No dogs (ex guide dogs) Cen ht TVL **PRICES:** s £30-£50; d £50-£90* **LB PARKING:** 3 **CARDS:**

BB Great value! This indicates B&B for £19 and under, per person, per night.

continued

Scotland

♦♦♦♦ Priory Lodge
The Loan EH30 9NS ☎ 0131 331 4345 📠 0131 331 4345
e-mail: calmyn@aol.com

(For full entry see South Queensferry)

♦♦♦♦ Ravensdown
248 Ferry Rd EH5 3AN ☎ 0131 552 5438 📠 0131 552 7559
e-mail: len@ravensdown.freeserve.co.uk
Dir: *A1-A199 Leith & Granton, N side of Princes St, round corner from Royal Botanic Gardens and up from Royal Yacht Britannia*
This substantial end-of-terrace house enjoys wonderful views of the city skyline. Immaculately maintained, it offers comfortable, individually styled bedrooms with smart bathrooms. Guests are welcome to use the music centre and piano in the inviting lounge. Freshly prepared breakfasts are served at individual tables in the dining room which features a working collection of old radio sets.
FACILITIES: 7 en suite (4 fmly) No smoking TVB tea/coffee No dogs Licensed Cen ht TVL **PRICES:** s £30-£40; d £46-£70✳ **PARKING:** 4

The AA Restaurant Guide **2003**

The right choice every time with this invaluable guide for food lovers.

Lifestyle Guides *www.theAA.com*

Ben Doran Guest House
11 Mayfield Gardens, Edinburgh EH9 2AX
Tel: 0131 667 8488 Fax: 0131 667 0076
E-mail: info@bendoran.com
Website: www.bendoran.com

Ben Doran is a handsome listed centrally located Georgian townhouse, yet with private off-street parking. Edinburgh Castle and City Centre are less than one mile. We are close to all historical attractions, Olympic standard swimming pool and panoramic hillwalks. Transport is not a problem; Ben Doran is on a bus route. An excellent accommodation is offered, where comfort and elegance are combined. Most rooms ensuite; all rooms have colour television, clock/radios, central heat, complimentary coffee/tea and full Scottish breakfast cooked to your liking. Ben Doran is popular, family run, and proud of its cleanliness and service.

EDINBURGH

DORSTAN

PRIVATE HOTEL

7 Priestfield Road, Edinburgh, EH16 5HJ
Tel: 0131 667 6721 / 5138 Fax: 0131 668 4644
E-mail: reservations@dorstan-hotel.demon.co.uk
www.dorstan-hotel.demon.co.uk

A tastefully furnished Victorian house, The Dorstan offers a warm welcome and comfortable accommodation. Situated in a quiet southside residential area conveniently located for bypass and city centre. Come and enjoy the friendly personal service of this family run hotel. Guest car park.

Proprietor: **Mairae Campbell.** **Send for colour brochure.**

EDINBURGH continued

♦♦♦♦ Six Mary's Place

6 Mary's Place, Raeburn Place, Stockbridge EH4 1JH
☎ 0131 332 8965 📠 0131 624 7060
e-mail: info@sixmarysplace.co.uk
***Dir:** From Waverley Station head west on Princes Street, right onto Fredrick Street and continue to Howe Street taking left onto Circus Place. Guest House 0.5 mile on left before rugby grounds.*

A relaxed and friendly environment is found at this terraced Georgian house, situated a short distance from the city centre. The attractive bedrooms are comfortably proportioned and well equipped including Internet access. There is a lounge and a delightful conservatory dining room; they both look out on to the neat garden and patio where a buffet breakfast can be enjoyed at individual tables.
FACILITIES: 8 en suite (1 fmly) No smoking TVB tea/coffee Direct dial from bedrooms No dogs (ex guide dogs) Cen ht TVL Internet Access
PRICES: s £30-£48; d £60-£96✳ **CARDS:**

♦♦♦♦ Southside

8 Newington Rd EH9 1QS ☎ 0131 668 4422 📠 0131 667 7771
e-mail: fionasouthside@aol.com
***Dir:** Straiton junct, A701 for Borton Brae, Mayfield Rd then Newington Rd Establishment on L at top of Newington Rd*

Southside is an elegant blonde sandstone town house. The attractive bedrooms, including two suites, are individually designed, comfortable and well-equipped. Dinners and hearty Scottish breakfasts are served in the bright Café South, which is open throughout the day.
FACILITIES: 8 en suite (2 fmly) (1 GF) No smoking TVB tea/coffee No dogs (ex guide dogs) Licensed Cen ht Coffee shop **PRICES:** s £32.50-£50; d £65-£150✳ **LB CARDS:**

♦♦♦ Abbotsford

36 Pilrig St EH6 5AL ☎ 0131 554 2706 📠 0131 555 4550
e-mail: info@abbotsfordguesthouse.co.uk
Situated just of Leith Walk and within walking distance of the city centre, this charming guest house offers individually decorated, pleasantly furnished and thoughtfully equipped bedrooms. Breakfast is taken at individual tables in the attractive ground floor dining room.
FACILITIES: 8 rms (5 en suite) No smoking STV TVB tea/coffee No dogs (ex guide dogs) Cen ht **PRICES:** s £25-£50; d £50-£50✳
CARDS:

♦♦♦ Eglinton Hotel

29 Eglinton Crescent EH12 5DB ☎ 0131 337 2641
📠 0131 337 4495
e-mail: reservations@eglinton-hotel.co.uk
***Dir:** from A720 (city bypass) turn R at Glasgow rdbt onto A8. After approx 3m turn L after Donaldson college then 1st R establishment 50 yds on L*
Occupying a fine Georgian property in the west end of the city, the Eglington provides stylish and attractive accommodation. The smart well-equipped bedrooms vary in size, the larger ones being extremely elegant and comfortable. The breakfast room highlights the period features of the house, and there is a small residents' bar.
FACILITIES: 12 en suite (4 fmly) No smoking in dining room TVB tea/coffee Direct dial from bedrooms No dogs (ex guide dogs) Licensed Cen ht
PRICES: s £40-£70; d £60-£120✳ **LB NOTES:** Closed Xmas
CARDS:

♦♦♦ Ivy House

7 Mayfield Gardens EH9 2AX ☎ 0131 667 3411
📠 0131 620 1422
e-mail: don@ivyguesthouse.com
***Dir:** on A701 1.5m S of Princes Street*
Handy for the city centre, this friendly guest house forms part of an elegant terraced Victorian property. Bedrooms vary in size, and are generally spacious and attractively decorated. A substantial breakfast is served at individual tables in the attractively furnished dining room.
FACILITIES: 8 en suite (4 fmly) No smoking in bedrooms No smoking in dining room TVB tea/coffee Cen ht **PRICES:** s £25-£70; d £36-£75✳ **LB BB PARKING:** 7

♦♦♦ The Newington

18 Newington Rd EH9 1QS ☎ 0131 667 3356 📠 0131 667 8307
e-mail: newington.guesthouse@dial.pipex.com
***Dir:** between A7 & A68 (routes into Edinburgh)*
Situated a short distance from the city centre, this delightful house offers comfortable, well-equipped bedrooms, some with lovely antique furnishings. An elegant ground floor lounge/dining room features Far Eastern memorabilia and is a charming setting for traditional breakfasts served at individual tables.
FACILITIES: 9 rms (6 en suite) (1 fmly) No smoking TVB tea/coffee Licensed Cen ht **PRICES:** s £35-£45; d £47-£65✳ **PARKING:** 3
CARDS:

♦♦♦ Sandaig

5 East Hermitage Place, Leith Links EH6 8AA
☎ 0131 554 7357 & 554 7313 📠 0131 467 6389
e-mail: marina-ferbej@msn.com
***Dir:** once in Edinburgh follow signs for Leith. Establishment is located facing Leith Links Park*
Sandaig Guest House occupies a terraced row overlooking Leith Links. It offers comfortable bedrooms in various sizes and styles. Public areas include the attractive dining room and inviting lounge, which are in keeping with the period character of the house.
FACILITIES: 10 rms (7 en suite) (2 fmly) No smoking in 6 bedrooms No smoking in dining room TVB tea/coffee Direct dial from bedrooms No dogs (ex guide dogs) Cen ht **PRICES:** s £25-£40; d £40-£85✳ **LB**
CARDS:

◆◆◆ Adria Hotel
11-12 Royal Ter EH7 5AB ☎ 0131 556 7875 📠 0131 558 7782
e-mail: manager@adriahotel.co.uk
Dir: *E end of city centre, round corner from Playhouse theatre. Nearest main roads - Leith Walk & London Rd*
This delightful Georgian townhouse retains many original features including stunning skylights, high ceilings with cornices and beautiful tiled fireplaces. The generally spacious bedrooms are comfortable. Breakfast is served in the neatly appointed dining room, and its convenient location close to the city means there are numerous restaurants within walking distance.
FACILITIES: 23 rms (9 en suite) (6 fmly) (1 GF) No smoking in bedrooms No smoking in dining room TV10B tea/coffee No dogs (ex guide dogs) Cen ht TVL No coaches **PRICES:** s £25-£45; d £42-£70✱ **NOTES:** Closed Dec-Jan **CARDS:**

◆◆◆ *Ailsa Craig Hotel*
24 Royal Ter EH7 5AH ☎ 0131 556 1022 📠 0131 556 6055
e-mail: ailsacraighotel@ednet.co.uk
Forming part of a fine Georgian terrace this comfortable Hotel enjoys views Northwards towards the Firth of Forth and Fife beyond. The bedrooms are all spacious and well-equipped. There is a lounge bar and an adjoining room where traditional breakfasts are served at individual tables.
FACILITIES: 18 rms (15 en suite) (6 fmly) TVB tea/coffee Direct dial from bedrooms No dogs (ex guide dogs) Licensed Cen ht TVL Dinner Last d 2pm **CARDS:**

◆◆◆ Airport Bed & Breakfast
Ingliston Park Lodge, Glasgow Rd, Ingliston EH28 8NB
☎ 0131 335 3437
Dir: *on main A8 1m from Edinburgh Airport Terminal*
This friendly B&B caters mainly for guests using Edinburgh Airport which is just a couple of minutes' drive away. Attractively presented both outside and in, it provides a self-service continental breakfast only, from 7am in the cosy dining room. Payment is on arrival so guests can leave when they please.
FACILITIES: 3 en suite No smoking TVB tea/coffee No dogs (ex guide dogs) Cen ht No children 8yrs No coaches **PRICES:** s £40-£45; d £49-£60✱ **PARKING:** 3

◆◆◆ *Boisdale Hotel*
9 Coates Gardens EH12 5LG ☎ 0131 337 1134
📠 0131 313 0048
A popular and welcoming, personally run guest house, part of a terraced row close to Haymarket station. The bedrooms have smart furniture and beds are very comfortable. Freshly prepared breakfasts and by prior arrangement, home cooked evening meals, are offered in the smart basement dining room.
FACILITIES: 11 en suite (6 fmly) TVB tea/coffee Licensed Cen ht TVL Last d 7pm

◆◆◆ Classic House
50 Mayfield Rd EH9 2NH ☎ 0131 667 5847 📠 0131 662 1016
e-mail: info@classichouse.demon.co.uk
Dir: *turn off by-pass onto A701. Establishment 0.5m on left just after Kings Building*
This is a charming Victorian terraced house which has well-equipped and attractively appointed bedrooms. Hearty breakfasts are served at individual tables in the pretty conservatory, which overlooks the well-tended rear garden. Another public area is the adjacent, comfortable lounge.
FACILITIES: 7 rms (6 en suite) No smoking TVB tea/coffee No dogs Cen ht TVL **PRICES:** s £20-£45; d £40-£60✱ **CARDS:**

◆◆◆ Corstorphine
188 St Johns Rd, Corstorphine EH12 8SG
☎ 0131 539 4237 📠 0131 539 4945
e-mail: corsthouse@aol.com
Dir: *from M8 take city by-pass north towards city centre for 1m along A8. Guest house on left*
This is a detached Victorian house that is convenient for both the airport and central amenities. Bedrooms vary in size and are tastefully decorated. There is a cosy lounge and a bright airy conservatory dining room where traditional, continental, or vegetarian breakfasts can be enjoyed.
FACILITIES: 5 en suite (2 fmly) No smoking STV TVB tea/coffee No dogs (ex guide dogs) Cen ht TVL **PRICES:** s £25; d £39✱ **LB** **PARKING:** 8 **CARDS:**

◆◆◆ *Ecosse International*
15 McDonald Rd EH7 4LX ☎ 0131 556 4967 📠 0131 556 7394
e-mail: erlinda@ecosseguesthouse.fsnet.co.uk
Dir: *E end Princes St exit to Leith St. Down past rdbt, Playhouse Theatre on right. Turn left at service station, McDonald Rd on right*
Situated just off Leith Walk to the north, and within easy walking distance of the city centre, this well maintained guest house offers comfortable and cheerful accommodation. The cosy lounge area, and the adjacent dining room where hearty breakfasts are served at individual tables, is situated on the lower ground floor.
FACILITIES: 5 en suite (3 fmly) No smoking TVB tea/coffee No dogs (ex guide dogs) Cen ht TVL No coaches **CARDS:**

◆◆◆ Elder York
38 Elder St EH1 3DX ☎ 0131 556 1926 📠 0131 624 7140
e-mail: morag@elderyork.co.uk
Dir: *from Princes St onto Queen St, then York Place*
Occupying the third and fourth floors of a terraced building, this guest house offers good value accommodation and is ideally situated for Princess Street and the major attractions. An on-going refurbishment programme has resulted in smartly furnished bedrooms and a freshly prepared breakfast is served in the spacious dining room.
FACILITIES: 13 rms (8 en suite) (1 fmly) No smoking TVB tea/coffee No dogs (ex guide dogs) Cen ht **PRICES:** s £30; d £50✱ **LB** **CARDS:**

◆◆◆ Galloway
22 Dean Park Crescent EH4 1PH ☎ 0131 332 3672
📠 0131 332 3672
e-mail: galloway-theclarks@hotmail.com
Dir: *0.5m from Princes St, west end on A9*
Smart, comfortable and thoughtfully equipped bedrooms and well-presented breakfasts feature at this friendly terraced guesthouse which was built in 1890 and restored to its former glory in 1990. It is situated in a residential area close to shops and bistros North of the city centre, but within easy reach of the major tourist attractions.
FACILITIES: 11 rms (7 en suite) (6 fmly) (1 GF) TV10B tea/coffee Cen ht **PRICES:** s £30-£45; d £40-£60✱ **LB** **CARDS:**

Smoking restrictions appear under the **FACILITIES** heading, please check when booking.

EDINBURGH continued

♦♦♦ Heriott Park

256 Ferry Rd, Goldenacre EH5 3AN ☎ 0131 552 3456
e-mail: accommodation@parkviewvilla.com
Dir: *turn off M8 and follow signs for Leith, this will take you along Ferry Rd, Heriott Park is 300 mtrs after Goldenacre traffic lights on the left*

This welcoming guest house lies on the north side of the city and enjoys lovely panoramic views of the skyline with the Castle and Arthur's Seat prominent. Bedrooms are served by excellent en suites and general bathrooms. Breakfast is noted for its choice.
FACILITIES: 7 rms (3 en suite) (2 fmly) (1 GF) No smoking TVB tea/coffee No dogs Cen ht **PRICES:** s £25-£60; d £40-£80✻
CARDS:

♦♦♦ *Hermitage*

16 East Hermitage Place, Leith Links EH6 8AB
☎ 0131 555 4868 🖹 0870 124 9537
e-mail: info@guesthouse-edinburgh.com
Dir: *follow signs for Edinburgh East & Leith*
This friendly guest house is set in a terraced row overlooking Leith Links and has bright cheerfully decorated bedrooms. There is a spacious dining room, where traditional breakfasts are served at individual tables. There are also business facilities available for guest use.
FACILITIES: 6 en suite (2 fmly) No smoking TVB tea/coffee No dogs (ex guide dogs) Cen ht **CARDS:**

♦♦♦ MacKenzie

2 East Hermitage Place, Leith Links EH6 8AA
☎ 0131 554 3763 🖹 0131 554 0853
e-mail: info@mackenzieguesthouse.co.uk
Dir: *at bottom of Leith Walk turn right at lights, then left at rdbt. House on right opp park*
This attractively maintained guest house lies in a peaceful terraced row overlooking Leith Links. Bedrooms vary in size, but are all well equipped and comfortable. The ground floor dining room is an appropriate setting for delicious home cooked breakfasts featuring the best of local produce.
FACILITIES: 5 rms (3 en suite) (3 fmly) No smoking TVB tea/coffee No dogs (ex guide dogs) Cen ht **PRICES:** s £25-£35; d £44-£70✻
CARDS:

♦♦♦ Mayville

5 Minto St, Newington EH9 1RG ☎ 0131 667 6103
🖹 0131 667 6103
e-mail: mayville@ebbpp.com
Dir: *from Edinburgh City by pass at Straiton junct. Follow signs for City Centre/Newington (main route A701 then A7) at end of long straight climb, almost at junct. Between Minto St and Newington Rd Guest house on right*
With a secluded garden to the rear, this substantial Victorian house offers spacious, comfortable, accommodation including smart, modern, en suite bathrooms.

continued

FACILITIES: 6 rms (4 en suite) (3 fmly) (2 GF) No smoking TVB tea/coffee No dogs Cen ht No coaches **PRICES:** s £25-£50; d £40-£80✻
PARKING: 10 **NOTES:** Closed 25-26 Dec **CARDS:**

♦♦♦ Parklands

20 Mayfield Gardens EH9 2BZ ☎ 0131 667 7184
🖹 0131 667 2011
e-mail: reservations@parklands-guesthouse.co.uk
Dir: *1.5m S of Princes Street on A7/A701*

This friendly, long-established family run guest house lies on the South side of the city, on the main bus route convenient for Edinburgh's many tourist attractions and the city centre. The comfortable bedrooms are attractively decorated and well-equipped. Hearty traditional breakfasts are served at individual tables in the elegant ground floor dining room.
FACILITIES: 6 rms (5 en suite) (1 fmly) No smoking in 1 bedrooms No smoking in dining room No smoking in lounges TVB tea/coffee No dogs (ex guide dogs) Cen ht No coaches **PRICES:** s £25-£40; d £40-£64✻
PARKING: 1

♦♦♦ Quaich

87 St John's Rd EH12 6NN ☎ 0131 334 4440 🖹 0131 476 9002
e-mail: reservations@quaichguesthouse.com
Dir: *M74 to M8 & A8 to Edinburgh, pass airport, through underpass at Gogar rdbt, through Maybury traffic lights into Glasgow Rd & into St John's Rd*
The Quaich offers guests good value, comfortable accommodation in a friendly family environment. Bedrooms, some of which are very generously proportioned, are bright and cheerful. Breakfast is served in the attractive ground floor dining room.
FACILITIES: 6 rms (4 en suite) (4 fmly) (2 GF) No smoking TVB tea/coffee No dogs (ex guide dogs) Cen ht **PRICES:** s £22-£32; d £44-£64✻
PARKING: 8 **CARDS:**

♦♦♦ Rowan

13 Glenorchy Ter EH9 2DQ ☎ 0131 667 2463 🖹 0131 667 2463
e-mail: angela@rowan-house.co.uk
Dir: *just off A701, L at Bright's Crescent, 1.5m S of Princes St*
A friendly, welcoming guesthouse in a peaceful residential terrace on the city's south side. Bedrooms are comfortable and well furnished, in keeping with the traditional elegance of the property. Hearty breakfasts, which include delicious home made scones, are served at individual tables in the smart dining room.
FACILITIES: 9 rms (3 en suite) (2 fmly) No smoking TVB tea/coffee Cen ht **PRICES:** s £26-£32; d £46-£70✻ **PARKING:** 2 **CARDS:**

♦♦♦ Sherwood

42 Minto St EH9 2BR ☎ 0131 667 1200 🖹0131 667 2344
e-mail: sherwdedin@aol.com
Dir: *1m up North Bridge from Princes St on A701*
This friendly family run guest house is situated on the South side of the city on the main bus route and within easy reach of the major tourist attractions. Sherwood Guest House offers well-equipped

continued

Scotland

and comfortable bedrooms. Hearty breakfasts are served at individual tables in the attractive dining room.
FACILITIES: 6 en suite (2 fmly) (1 GF) No smoking TVB tea/coffee No dogs Cen ht **PRICES:** s £35-£60; d £50-£70✻ **LB** **PARKING:** 3 **NOTES:** Closed 20-29 Dec **CARDS:**

♦♦♦ Terrace Hotel

37 Royal Ter EH7 5AH ☎ 0131 556 3423 📠 0131 556 2520
e-mail: Terracehotel@btinternet.com
Dir: *from Waverley Station/Princes St, E along Regent Rd turn left Regent Terrace - leads into Royal Terrace*
This well proportioned property is part of an impressive Georgian terrace just off the city centre. Bedrooms are comfortably proportioned, attractive and well equipped. There is an elegant lounge and a bright airy dining room where breakfast is served at individual tables.
FACILITIES: 14 rms (11 en suite) (7 fmly) No smoking in bedrooms No smoking in dining room TVB tea/coffee No dogs Cen ht No coaches **PRICES:** s £30-£40; d £45-£85✻ **CARDS:**

♦♦♦ *Thistle Court Hotel*

5 HamptonTerrace EH12 5JD ☎ 0131 313 5500 📠 0131 313 5511
e-mail: info@thistlecourt.co.uk
Situated at the West End of the city, on the main bus route, and within walking distance of the city centre, this friendly hotel offers good value accommodation. Bedrooms are comfortable and well equipped. There is a bright sunny conservatory that opens onto the neat rear garden and the newly appointed Bistro where meals can be enjoyed.
FACILITIES: 15 en suite (3 fmly) No smoking in bedrooms TVB tea/coffee Direct dial from bedrooms No dogs (ex guide dogs) Licensed Lift Cen ht TVL Dinner Last d 9.30pm **PARKING:** 8
CARDS:

Scotland

EDINBURGH continued

♦♦♦ The Walton Hotel

79 Dundas St EH3 6SD ☎ 0131 556 1137 Fax 0131 557 8367
e-mail: enquiries@waltonhotel.com

Situated in Edinburgh's Georgian New Town only minutes from the world famous Princes Street, Princes Street gardens and Edinburgh Castle, The Walton Hotel offers comfortable, good value accommodation in a friendly relaxed atmosphere. Bedrooms are comfortably furnished and well equipped. Traditional breakfasts are served at individual tables in the stylish dining room. There is a small car park.

FACILITIES: 10 en suite (4 fmly) No smoking TVB tea/coffee No dogs (ex guide dogs) Cen ht **PRICES:** s £30-£80; d £60-£160* **PARKING:** 8
CARDS:

♦♦ Averon City Centre

44 Gilmore Place EH3 9NQ ☎ 0131 229 9932
Fax 0131 228 9265
e-mail: info@averon.co.uk
Dir: *turn left at the west end of Princes Street and follow A702 and turn right at Kings Theatre*

Situated within easy walking distance of the town centre this popular guesthouse continues to offer good value accommodation. Bedrooms come in a variety of sizes. There is a car park to the rear of the establishment.

FACILITIES: 10 rms (6 en suite) (3 fmly) No smoking in dining room TVB tea/coffee No dogs Cen ht **PRICES:** s £32; d £34* **BB PARKING:** 19
CARDS:

See advertisement on page 509

♦♦ Kariba

10 Granville Ter EH10 4PQ ☎ 0131 229 3773 Fax 0131 229 4968
e-mail: karibaguesthouse@hotmail.com

Good value accommodation is provided at this family-run guesthouse, which is situated in a south-side residential area within easy reach of the Kings Theatre. Bedrooms come in varying sizes with modern appointments. Public areas include a comfortable lounge and separate breakfast room.

FACILITIES: 9 rms (8 en suite) (3 fmly) No smoking in dining room No smoking in lounges TVB tea/coffee Cen ht TVL No coaches
PRICES: s £25-£50; d £36-£56* **BB PARKING:** 6 **CARDS:**

See advertisement on page 509

Adam Drysdale House

42 Gilmore Place EH3 9NQ ☎ 0131 228 8952
Fax 0131 228 8952
e-mail: ad-drysdale@drysdale57.fsnet.co.uk

FACILITIES: 2 en suite (1 GF) No smoking TVB tea/coffee No dogs (ex guide dogs) Cen ht No coaches **PRICES:** d £36-£56* **LB BB**
PARKING: 3 **NOTES:** ★★

Brae Lodge

30 Liberton Brae EH16 6AF ☎ 0131 672 2876 Fax 0131 672 3956
e-mail: lynda@braelodge.freeserve.co.uk
Dir: *on main A701 2m from city bypass (Straiton junct) on left.*

FACILITIES: 6 en suite (2 fmly) (2 GF) No smoking TVB tea/coffee Cen ht
PRICES: s £30-£60; d £50-£84* **LB PARKING:** 5 **NOTES:** ★★★
CARDS:

Dukes of Windsor Street

17 Windsor St EH7 5LA ☎ 0131 556 6046 Fax 0131 556 6046
e-mail: info@dukesofwindsor.com
Dir: *E-end of Princes St onto Leith St. Pass Playhouse theatre R onto London Rd, Windsor St is 1st L*

FACILITIES: 8 en suite (1 fmly) No smoking TVB tea/coffee Cen ht
PRICES: s £25-£50; d £50-£100* **NOTES:** ★★★ Closed 23-27 Dec
CARDS:

Gildun

9 Spence St EH16 5AG ☎ 0131 667 1368 Fax 0131 668 4989
e-mail: gildun.edin@btinternet.com
Dir: *A720 city bypass to Sheriffhall rdbt onto A7 for 4m to Cameron Toll rdbt go under railway bridge follow A7 sign onto Dalkeith Road, Spence Street is 4th on left opposite church*

FACILITIES: 8 rms (6 en suite) (5 fmly) (2 GF) No smoking in 6 bedrooms No smoking in dining room TVB tea/coffee Cen ht No coaches
PRICES: s £20-£35; d £40-£65* **LB PARKING:** 4 **NOTES:** ★★★
CARDS:

The St Valery

36 Coates Gardens, Haymarket EH12 5LE ☎ 0131 337 1893
Fax 0131 346 8529
e-mail: thestvalery@cs.com
Dir: *from M8 & M9 take A8 towards City Centre, pass Donalson school on left and two streets before Haymarket station on the left*

FACILITIES: 11 en suite (3 fmly) (1 GF) No smoking in 2 bedrooms No smoking in dining room No smoking in lounges STV TVB tea/coffee Direct dial from bedrooms Cen ht **PRICES:** s £25-£42; d £45-£76*
NOTES: ★★★ **CARDS:**

Salisbury

45 Salisbury Rd EH16 5AA ☎ 0131 667 1264 Fax 0131 667 1264
e-mail: Brenda.Wright@btinternet.com
Dir: *left off A7 - opposite Royal Commonwealth Pool*

FACILITIES: 8 en suite (1 fmly) (3 GF) No smoking TVB tea/coffee No dogs (ex guide dogs) Licensed Cen ht TVL No children 5yrs No coaches
PRICES: s £28-£38; d £50-£68* **LB PARKING:** 12
NOTES: ★★★ Closed Xmas, New Year & Jan **CARDS:**

SOUTH QUEENSFERRY Map 11 NT17

♦♦♦♦ Priory Lodge

The Loan EH30 9NS ☎ 0131 331 4345 Fax 0131 331 4345
e-mail: calmyn@aol.com
Dir: *just off High St, at the westerly end*

This charming guest house has been purpose built and enjoys a dramatic location between the two Forth Bridges. The attractive bedrooms are maintained to a high standard, comfortably furnished in antique pine and adorned with many thoughtful extras. There is a small lounge complete with video and stereo, and a lovely conservatory style dining room. Guests are welcome to use the modern kitchen facilities. Calmyn Lamb was a Top Twenty Finalist in the AA Landlady of the Year Award 2002-2003.

FACILITIES: 5 en suite (3 fmly) No smoking TVB tea/coffee No dogs Cen ht TVL No coaches **PRICES:** s £40-£50; d £54-£60* **PARKING:** 5
CARDS:

Places with this symbol are Inns.

CITY OF GLASGOW

GLASGOW Map 11 NS56

See also Eaglesham

♦♦♦ Hotel Enterprise

144 Renfrew St G3 6RF ☎ 0141 332 8095 Fax 0141 332 8095

Dir: *leave M8 at Charing Cross. Straight along Sauchiehall St, L into Scott St, R into Renfrew St.*

A friendly, hospitable, small hotel situated in a Victorian terrace close to the Art school and Sauchiehall Street. It is easily identified by the two trees and the two period lamp posts that stand in its forecourt. Bedrooms are modern and very well equipped, and guests will enjoy the hearty breakfasts served in the small, downstairs dining room.

FACILITIES: 6 en suite (2 fmly) (4 GF) No smoking in 1 bedrooms No smoking in dining room TVB tea/coffee Direct dial from bedrooms Licensed Cen ht TVL No children No coaches **PRICES:** s £40-£50; d £50-£60✻ **LB CARDS:**

♦♦♦ Kelvingrove Hotel

944 Sauchiehall St G3 7TH ☎ 0141 339 5011 Fax 0141 339 6566

e-mail: kelvingrove.hotel@business.ntl.com

Dir: *0.25m W of Charing Cross, M8 J18, follow signs for Kelvingrove*

This private, well-maintained hotel lies in a terrace row just west of the city centre. Bedrooms, including several rooms suitable for families, are particularly well-equipped and those that are en suite have smart fully tiled bathrooms. There is a bright breakfast room and a reception lounge that is manned 24 hours.

FACILITIES: 25 rms (24 en suite) (7 fmly) (4 GF) No smoking STV TVB tea/coffee Direct dial from bedrooms Cen ht TVL **PRICES:** s £33-£38; d £48-£58✻ **CARDS:**

♦♦♦ Victorian House

212 Renfrew St G3 6TX ☎ 0141 332 0129 Fax 0141 353 3155

e-mail: kdmcmillan@msn.com

Dir: *turn L into Garnet st at 1st set of traffic light on Sauchiehall St E of Charing Cross. Take R into Renfrew St hotel is 100 yds on L*

continued

Close to the Art School and Sauchiehall Street, this raised terraced house has been sympathetically extended to offer a range of well-equipped bedrooms. Some rooms have polished floors and bright modern décor, whilst others are more traditional. There is a comfortable lounge area leading into the breakfast room, which serves buffet style meals.

FACILITIES: 57 rms (49 en suite) (6 fmly) No smoking in dining room TVB tea/coffee Direct dial from bedrooms Cen ht **PRICES:** s £30-£35; d £40-£52✻ **LB CARDS:**

♦♦ *Belgrave*

2 Belgrave Ter, Hillhead G12 8JD

☎ 0141 337 1850 & 337 1741 Fax 0141 337 1741

e-mail: belgraveguesthse@hotmail.com

Dir: *from M8 take junct 17 onto Gt Western Rd, GH approx 1m on left side*

A warm and friendly welcome is assured at this guesthouse which forms part of a Victorian Terrace. The comfortably proportioned bedrooms are smartly decorated and offer modern furnishings; this contrasts with the simple appointment of the older rooms. Hearty traditional breakfasts are served at individual tables in the ground floor dining room.

FACILITIES: 11 rms (2 en suite) (3 fmly) No smoking in 3 bedrooms No smoking in dining room No smoking in lounges TVB tea/coffee No dogs (ex guide dogs) Cen ht No coaches **PARKING:** 12 **CARDS:**

♦♦ Kelvin Private Hotel

15 Buckingham Ter, Great Western Rd, Hillhead G12 8EB

☎ 0141 339 7143 Fax 0141 339 5215

e-mail: norman@kelvin-lomond.freeserve.co.uk

Dir: *M8 J17, A82 Kelvinside/Dumbarton, 1m from motorway on right before Botanic Gardens*

Two substantial Victorian terraced houses on the west side of the city have been combined to create this friendly private hotel, close to the Botanical Gardens. Bedrooms range from compact singles to more spacious en suite rooms. This is the sister of the Lomond Hotel just along the terrace.

FACILITIES: 21 rms (9 en suite) (5 fmly) No smoking in dining room TVB tea/coffee Cen ht **PRICES:** s £24-£39; d £40-£58✻ **PARKING:** 5 **CARDS:**

♦♦ Lomond Hotel

6 Buckingham Ter, Great Western Rd, Hillhead G12 8EB

☎ 0141 339 2339 Fax 0141 339 5215

e-mail: norman@kelvin-lomond.freeserve.co.uk

Dir: *M8 J17. Follow A82 Dumbarton, 1m from motorway, on R before Botanic Gardens*

Situated in the west end of the city, part of a tree-lined Victorian terrace, a sound standard of comfort is offered at this well maintained small friendly hotel. Hearty breakfasts are served at individual tables in the bright dining room.

FACILITIES: 17 rms (6 en suite) (6 fmly) TVB tea/coffee Cen ht **PRICES:** s £24-£35; d £46-£52✻ **CARDS:**

Scotland

GLASGOW continued

♦♦ McLays

264/276 Renfrew St, Charing Cross G3 6TT
☎ 0141 332 4796 📠 0141 353 0422
e-mail: info@mclays.com
Dir: *exit at junct 18 on the M8 going into Sauchiehall St, turn left into Garnet or Rose St then 3rd left into Buccleuch St this leads into Renfrew St*

Popular with the budget tourist market and commercial guests this large guesthouse provides well equipped good value accommodation close to the city centre and local attractions.
FACILITIES: 62 rms (39 en suite) (14 fmly) No smoking in 20 bedrooms No smoking in dining room No smoking in 1 lounge STV TVB tea/coffee Direct dial from bedrooms No dogs (ex guide dogs) Lift Cen ht TVL
CARDS:

♦ Georgian House Hotel

29 Buckingham Ter, Great Western Rd, Kelvinside G12 8ED
☎ 0141 339 0008
e-mail: thegeorgianhouse@yahoo.com
Dir: *M8 junct 17 N follow signs to A82 (Dumbarton) Great Western Rd & the hotel is 1.8m on your right just before junction with Queen Maragret Drive & Byres Rd at Royal Botanic Gdns*
Located at the West End of the city and peacefully situated in a tree-lined Victorian terrace, this friendly private hotel offers good value accommodation. Bedrooms vary in size and are furnished in modern style. Breakfast is served in the first floor combined lounge/dining room.
FACILITIES: 12 rms (10 en suite) (4 fmly) No smoking in 6 bedrooms No smoking in dining room No smoking in lounges TVB tea/coffee No dogs (ex guide dogs) Cen ht Dinner Last d 6pm **PRICES:** s £20-£37; d £38-£70✱ **LB BB PARKING:** 9 **CARDS:**

🅰 Craigielea House B&B

35 Westercraigs G31 2HY ☎ 0141 554 3446
e-mail: craigielea.b-b@amserve.net
Dir: *M8 junct 15, left at filter light into Cathedral St, at lights turn right into Castle St. Through next lights, left at next lights into Duke St, pass Tennents Brewery and turn left at lights into Westercraigs*
FACILITIES: 4 rms (2 GF) No smoking TVB tea/coffee No dogs (ex guide dogs) Cen ht No children 3yrs No coaches **PRICES:** d £34-£36✱ **BB PARKING:** 3 **NOTES:** ★★

CLACKMANNANSHIRE

TILLICOULTRY — Map 11 NS99

♦♦♦♦ Westbourne House

10 Dollar Rd FK13 6PA ☎ 01259 750314 📠 01259 750642
e-mail: odellwestbourne@compuserve.com
Dir: *A91 to St Andrews. Establishment on left just past mini-rdbt*
A friendly welcome is assured at this former mill owner's home which lies secluded in wooded gardens on the edge of the village. It is adorned with a stunning collection of memorabilia, objets d'art and items gathered by the owners during their time abroad. Breakfast is served house party style and offers an excellent choice.
FACILITIES: 3 rms (1 GF) No smoking TVB tea/coffee Cen ht TVL No coaches Croquet lawn **PRICES:** s £25-£27; d £44-£48✱ **PARKING:** 3 **NOTES:** Closed Xmas-New Year **CARDS:**

DUMFRIES & GALLOWAY

AUCHENCAIRN — Map 11 NX75

♦♦♦♦ Balcary Mews

Balcary Bay DG7 1QZ ☎ 01556 640276 📠 01556 640272
Dir: *leave A711 at Auchencairn. Follow shore road 2m to the end. Turn left under archway into Balcary Mews*

Set close to the shore, this fine residence enjoys spectacular views across the bay to distant hills. Spacious and well-maintained, it offers bright modern accommodation and a splendid sitting room with picture window and patio doors leading into the gardens. The breakfasts draw praise with home made preserves - including delicious lemon curd.
FACILITIES: 3 en suite (1 GF) No smoking TVB tea/coffee No dogs (ex guide dogs) Cen ht No children 12yrs No coaches **PRICES:** s £35; d £54✱ **LB PARKING:** 8

CANONBIE — Map 11 NY37

🅰 T&C Four Oaks

DG14 0TF ☎ 013873 71329
Dir: *1st turning to Canonbie on right off A7 onto B7021, Carlisle to Edinburgh road*
FACILITIES: 2 en suite No smoking in bedrooms No smoking in dining room tea/coffee No dogs (ex guide dogs) Cen ht TVL No coaches
PRICES: s £20-£22; d £40-£44✱ **PARKING:** 3 **NOTES:** ★★★ Closed Xmas & New Year

CASTLE DOUGLAS — Map 11 NX76

Premier Collection

♦♦♦♦♦ Craigadam *(NX797728)*

Craigadam DG7 3HU ☎ 01556 650233 & 650100
📠 01556 650233 Ms C Pickup
e-mail: enquiry@craigadam.com
Dir: *leave Castle Douglas E on A75 to Crocketford. In Crocketford turn left on A712 for 2m. house on hill*
Set on a working farm, this elegant country house offers gracious living in a relaxed environment. The large bedrooms - most of which are set around a courtyard to the rear - are all individual in style and very comfortable. Public areas include a delightful lounge and panelled dining room featuring a magnificent 15-seater table.

continued

Craigadam

FACILITIES: 8 en suite (2 fmly) (4 GF) No smoking in bedrooms No smoking in area of dining room No smoking in 1 lounge TVB tea/coffee Licensed Cen ht Fishing Snooker Croquet lawn Jacuzzi Shooting 700 acres sheep Dinner Last d 8am **PRICES:** s £35-£45; d £70 **CONF:** Del from £70 ✻ **PARKING:** 12 **NOTES:** Closed Xmas & New Year Civ Wed 22 **CARDS:**

Premier Collection

♦♦♦♦♦ Longacre Manor

Ernespie Rd DG7 1LE ☎ 01556 503576 🖷 01556 503886
e-mail: ball.longacre@btinternet.com
Dir: *Leave A75 at rdbt signed Castle Douglas A745, continue 0.75m, Manor on left*

This fine Edwardian country house lies secluded in wooded gardens, overlooking green fields, and is within walking distance of the town. Features such as oak panelling and antique furniture combine with a relaxed atmosphere. Bedrooms mirror the style of the house, including two particularly spacious rooms and also a twin room featuring single four-poster beds. All rooms are very well-equipped and include decanters of sherry on arrival. Meals are taken around one large antique table.

FACILITIES: 4 en suite No smoking in bedrooms No smoking in dining room No smoking in 1 lounge TVB tea/coffee Direct dial from bedrooms No dogs (ex guide dogs) Licensed Cen ht No children 10yrs No coaches Dinner Last d 6.30pm **PRICES:** s £35-£50; d £60-£90✻ **LB CONF:** Board 18 Del from £80 ✻ **PARKING:** 10 **NOTES:** Closed Xmas/New year (ex for party of 8 people) **CARDS:**

DALBEATTIE Map 11 NX86

Premier Collection

♦♦♦♦♦ Auchenskeoch Lodge

DG5 4PG ☎ 01387 780277 🖷 01387 780277
e-mail: Brmsmth@aol.com
Dir: *5m SE off B793*

This fine Victorian shooting lodge stands in 20 acres of grounds, including a vegetable garden, croquet lawn and small fishing loch. The house is full of charm and graced with antiques. A set, four-course dinner is served house-party style and there is an honesty bar in the billiard room.

FACILITIES: 3 en suite (1 GF) No smoking in dining room TVB tea/coffee Licensed Cen ht No children 12yrs No coaches Fishing Snooker Croquet lawn Dinner Last d 8pm **PRICES:** s £37-£39; d £59-£64✻ **LB PARKING:** 22 **NOTES:** Closed Nov-Etr **CARDS:**

♦♦♦ Pheasant Hotel

1 Maxwell St DG5 4AH ☎ 01556 610345 🖷 01556 612362
e-mail: reception@pheasanthotel.co.uk
Dir: *A74 onto A75 (Dumfries) onto A711, hotel at junct of A711/High St*

Friendly service and good value meals feature at the Pheasant Hotel. The range of bedrooms are modern and very well-equipped, all have direct dial telephones. The popular restaurant is on the first floor and provides a wide selection of dishes, including daily specials.

FACILITIES: 8 en suite (3 fmly) TVB tea/coffee Direct dial from bedrooms Cen ht TVL Ideal for outdoor pursuits Dinner Last d 9pm **PRICES:** s fr £22.50; d fr £45✻ **CARDS:**

DUMFRIES Map 11 NX97

♦♦♦♦ Southpark Country House

Quarry Rd, Locharbriggs DG1 1QG
☎ 01387 711188 & 0800 9701588 🖷 01387 711155
e-mail: ewan@southparkhouse.co.uk
Dir: *A75/A701 (Edinburgh, Glasgow & Dumfries), past Curries European Transport, left into Quarry Rd, house last on left*

This renovated guest house enjoys superb country views, yet is still convenient for the town. The comfortable bedrooms are attractively furnished, and decorated. Friendly proprietor Ewan Maxwell officiates personally over the hearty Scottish breakfasts served in the bright open-plan dining room

FACILITIES: 4 rms (3 en suite) (1 fmly) No smoking TVB tea/coffee No dogs Cen ht TVL No coaches **PRICES:** s £25✻ **LB PARKING:** 23 **CARDS:**

Scotland

ESKDALEMUIR — Map 11 NY29

♦♦♦♦ Hart Manor

DG13 0QQ ☎ 013873 73217
e-mail: visit@hartmanor.co.uk
Dir: *from junct17 On M74 (Lockerbie) take B723 to Eskdalemuir, Hart Manor is 1m past the village on the Langholm road*
Quietly located in the picturesque hamlet of Eskdalemuir, this small hotel has been completely refurbished to provide a bright, comfortable, modern style that is in symphony with the surroundings. The food is especially an attraction with good honest home cooked dishes accompanied by an energetic, enthusiastic and attentive host. Kath Leadbetter was a Top Twenty Finalist in the AA Landlady of the Year Award 2002-2003.
FACILITIES: 4 en suite No smoking TVB tea/coffee Licensed Cen ht No children 10yrs No coaches Fishing Dinner Last d 8.30pm **PRICES:** s £61.50-£71.50; d £123-£129 **LB PARKING:** 10 **CARDS:**

GRETNA (With Gretna Green) — Map 11 NY36

♦♦♦ The Mill

Grahams Hill, Kirkpatrick Fleming DG11 3BQ ☎ 01461 800344 📠 01461 800255
e-mail: info@themill.co.uk
Dir: *A74 N'bound exit 0.5m after services N of Gretna, R at end of sliproad. A74 S'bound exit junct 21 Canonbie/Kirkpatrick Fleming, follow hotel signs*
This attractive complex has evolved from farm buildings, the original 18th-century barn has been transformed into The Barn Restaurant. Bedrooms are in chalet-type accommodation set around several courtyards and gardens. Some rooms have four-poster beds, and one is adapted for less mobile guests. This is a popular venue for weddings and a 'chapel' has now been added.
FACILITIES: 27 annexe en suite (10 fmly) No smoking in area of dining room TVB tea/coffee Licensed Cen ht Dinner Last d 8.45pm **PRICES:** s £48; d £68✳ **PARKING:** 50 **CARDS:**

♦♦♦ Surrone House

Annan Rd DG16 5DL ☎ 01461 338341 📠 01461 338341
e-mail: enquiries@surronehouse.co.uk
Dir: *exit M74 onto B721, turn onto B7076, town centre 500yds on right*
Guests are assured of a warm and friendly welcome at this well maintained guesthouse, which sits in attractive grounds well back from the road. Bedrooms, including a delightful honeymoon suite, are neatly decorated. There is a comfortable ground floor lounge, and a choice of menus and a full wine list are available at dinner.
FACILITIES: 7 rms (6 en suite) (4 fmly) (2 GF) TVB tea/coffee No dogs (ex guide dogs) Licensed Cen ht TVL No coaches Dinner Last d 8pm **PRICES:** s £40; d £50✳ **PARKING:** 10 **CARDS:**

KIRKCUDBRIGHT

See Twynholm

LANGHOLM — Map 11 NY38

♦♦♦ Reivers Rest

81 High St DG13 0DJ ☎ 01387 381343
e-mail: mail@reivers-rest.co.uk
Dir: *adjacent to Town Hall on A7, 20m N of Carlisle*
Situated in the heart of this historic town the Reivers Rest is a friendly, family-run establishment, which dates back to the 1800s. Bedrooms are comfortable, well-equipped, and offer many thoughtful extras. Guests can relax in the cosy lounge bar, where a log fire burns on the colder evenings. A no smoking policy is in operation.
FACILITIES: 5 en suite (1 fmly) No smoking TVB tea/coffee No dogs (ex guide dogs) Licensed Cen ht No children 12yrs No coaches Golf 9 Tennis (hard) Gymnasium Dinner Last d 8pm **PRICES:** s fr £36; d fr £59✳ **LB CARDS:**

LOCKERBIE — Map 11 NY18

♦♦♦♦ Rosehill

Carlisle Rd DG11 2DR ☎ 01576 202378 📠 01576 202378
Dir: *south end of town*
This immaculately maintained detached Victorian house provides a warm and friendly welcome to all. Bedrooms are generally spacious and boast attractive soft furnishings and good levels of comfort. Day rooms include an inviting lounge and hearty breakfasts are taken in the elegant dining room.
FACILITIES: 5 en suite (1 fmly) No smoking TVB tea/coffee Cen ht TVL No coaches **PRICES:** s fr £25; d fr £44 **PARKING:** 5

MOFFAT — Map 11 NT00

♦♦♦♦ Hartfell House

Hartfell Crescent DG10 9AL ☎ 01683 220153
e-mail: mary.whitsell@virgin.net
Dir: *exit A74(M) junct 15, A701, to town centre. At clock tower turn right up Well St. Straight on into Old Well Rd. 1st right is Hartfell Crescent*
Enjoying delightful country views, this fine Victorian house nestles high above the town. Beautifully maintained and retaining all its original character, the house boasts bedrooms that offer a high degree of quality and comfort. There is a charming lounge on the first floor, and guests can enjoy delicious low fat home-cooked meals in the elegant dining room.
FACILITIES: 8 rms (7 en suite) (2 fmly) (1 GF) No smoking TVB tea/coffee Licensed Cen ht No coaches Dinner Last d previous day **PRICES:** s £25; d £48✳ **PARKING:** 6 **NOTES:** Closed Xmas & New year

♦♦♦♦ Limetree House

Eastgate, off Dickson St DG10 9AE ☎ 01683 220001 📠 01683 220001
e-mail: limetree-house@btconnect.com
Dir: *off M74 at junct 15, Moffat is just over 1m further on B7076. In Moffat turn up Well Street, at top turn left into Eastgate Limetree House 100yds*
A warm welcome and typical Scottish hospitality is assured at this guesthouse, quietly situated off the main high street. Bedrooms are bright, attractive and well equipped. There is a comfortable ground floor lounge and an airy dining room where traditional Scottish breakfasts are served at individual tables.
FACILITIES: 6 en suite (1 fmly) (1 GF) No smoking TVB tea/coffee Cen ht No coaches **PRICES:** s £22.50-£30; d £40-£50✳ **LB PARKING:** 7 **NOTES:** Closed Jan-Feb

♦♦♦♦ Queensberry House

12 Beechgrove DG10 9RS ☎ 01683 220538 📠 01683 221521
e-mail: queensberryhouse@amserve.net
Dir: *M74 junc 15 into Moffat. On the High Street turn right after the school into Beechgrove. The house is on the right opposite tennis courts*
Queensberry House is set in a quiet location opposite the tennis courts and bowling greens. Guests occupy the ground floor of this attractive white Victorian house, which has a comfortable and homely lounge in addition to the cosy dining breakfast room with its pine furniture. Bedrooms are stylish and well-equipped.
FACILITIES: 3 en suite No smoking TVB tea/coffee Cen ht TVL No coaches **PRICES:** s £23-£25; d £40✳ **LB NOTES:** Closed 24-26 Dec

♦♦♦ Barnhill Springs Country

DG10 9QS ☎ 01683 220580
Dir: *leave A74(M) junct 15, Barnhill Rd is first on right, 50m from the rdbt on the A701 towards Moffat*

continued

This Victorian country house enjoys fine views of the Annan Valley. Bedrooms are well proportioned and although none have en suite bathrooms, one room on the ground floor has the use of its own private shower room. Both the lounge and dining room are comfortable, and dinner is available by prior arrangement.
FACILITIES: 5 rms (1 en suite) (1 fmly) (1 GF) No smoking in dining room tea/coffee Licensed Cen ht TVL No coaches Dinner Last d 9am
PRICES: s £23-£24; d £46-£48 **PARKING:** 10

MONIAIVE Map 11 NX79

♦♦♦♦ *Auchencheyne (NX751876)*

DG3 4EW ☎ 01848 200589 📠 01848 200589 Mr N Gourlay
e-mail: ngourlay@aol.com
Dir: *take A702 out of Moniaive (left at Criagdarroch Hotel) establishment is 3m on left*
Built in 1901 and situated in the stunning Glencairn Valley, this spacious country house is a working beef and sheep farm. Traditional hospitality is assured, with every effort made to ensure a stay here is relaxing and enjoyable. The surrounding mature well-tended gardens include a tennis court. Evening meals and hearty breakfasts featuring the best of home-grown produce are served in one of the two dining rooms. Accommodation can also be let on a self-catering basis.
FACILITIES: 3 rms (1 en suite) No smoking in bedrooms No dogs Cen ht TVL Tennis (hard) Fishing Hillwalking, Cycling,Rough shooting, Birdwatching 5000 acres mixed/beef/sheep Dinner Last d noon **PARKING:** 12

NEW GALLOWAY Map 11 NX67

♦♦♦♦ Kalmar

Balmaclellan DG7 3QF ☎ 01644 420685
e-mail: kalmar@dial.pipex.com
Dir: *from Dumfries take A75 N then A712. Establishment situated in village of Balmaclellan*
Quietly situated on the edge of the Forest Park, this modern house offers comfortably furnished bedrooms. A terraced rear garden is the backdrop to a combined lounge and dining room, where hearty meals are served around a communal table. Service is attentive and warm hospitality is a particular feature.
FACILITIES: 2 en suite No smoking in bedrooms TVB tea/coffee No dogs (ex guide dogs) Cen ht TVL No children No coaches Dog run in garden Dinner Last d 7pm **PRICES:** s fr £29; d fr £44* **LB** **PARKING:** 4
CARDS:

PORTPATRICK Map 10 NX05

♦♦♦♦ Blinkbonnie

School Brae DG9 8LG ☎ 01776 810282 📠 01776 810792
Dir: *Follow A77. Once entering Portpatrick Town, pass the parish church on the left. Take the next road on left into School Brae. 2nd house on left*
This detached villa stands in pretty, well-kept gardens in an elevated position overlooking the town and harbour. Mrs Robinson is a super host and ensures all her guests are well looked after. The neat bedrooms are thoughtfully equipped and both the delightful lounge and cosy dining room enjoy fine sea views
FACILITIES: 5 en suite No smoking TVB tea/coffee No dogs Cen ht TVL No coaches **PRICES:** s £26-£27; d £39-£41* **PARKING:** 10
NOTES: Closed Dec

STRANRAER Map 10 NX06

♦♦♦♦ Glenotter

Leswalt Rd DG9 0EP ☎ 01776 703199
e-mail: glenotterBB@aol.com
Dir: *enter town from A77/A75, follow signs for ferry. From Stena ferry terminal follow sign for A718 for 1m along seafront. House on left*

continued

Set in well-tended gardens, this semi-detached house is spotlessly maintained, both inside and out. The attractive bedrooms are well-equipped and have smart bathrooms. There is a comfortable lounge, whilst hearty breakfasts are enjoyed in the nicely appointed dining room.
FACILITIES: 3 en suite (1 fmly) No smoking TVB tea/coffee No dogs Cen ht TVL No coaches **PRICES:** s £25-£37; d £42-£48* **PARKING:** 5
CARDS:

♦♦♦ Balyett Bed & Breakfast

Cairnryan Rd DG9 8QL ☎ 01776 703395 📠 01776 703395
e-mail: balyettbb@talk21.com
Dir: *0.5m N of Stranraer on A77 overlooking Loch Ryan*
Set within farmland at the head of Lochryan, this traditional house is convenient for both ferry terminals. Bedrooms are all on the first floor and are attractively furnished and decorated and have all of the expected facilities. There is a comfortable lounge on the ground floor in addition to the cosy dining room where guests will enjoy a wholesome breakfast at a communal table.
FACILITIES: 3 en suite (1 fmly) No smoking TVB tea/coffee Cen ht TVL Fishing **PRICES:** s fr £25; d £30-£40* **LB BB** **PARKING:** 6

♦♦♦ Fernlea

Lewis St DG9 7AQ ☎ 01776 703037 📠 01776 703037
e-mail: fernlea@btinternet.com
Dir: *when entering Stranraer from A75 or A757, follow directions for Ryan Leisure Centre, Fernlea is adjacent*
Conveniently situated for the town centre and Ferry Terminal, Fernlea Guest House offers good value accommodation in a friendly family environment. Bedrooms are prettily decorated, well equipped and all have en suite bathrooms. Hearty traditional breakfasts are served at individual tables in the elegant ground floor dining room.
FACILITIES: 3 en suite No smoking TVB tea/coffee No dogs Cen ht TVL No coaches childrens play area **PRICES:** s £22-£26; d £36-£40* **LB BB**
PARKING: 5 **NOTES:** Closed 24-27 Dec & 31 Dec-2 Jan

THORNHILL Map 11 NX89

♦♦♦♦ Gillbank House

8 East Morton St DG3 5LZ ☎ 01848 330597 📠 01848 330597
e-mail: giilbankhouse@aol.com
Dir: *14m N of Dumfries on A76*
Gillbank House was originally built for a wealthy Edinburgh Merchant. Convenient for the many outdoor pursuits enjoyed in this area, such as fishing and golfing, this delightful house offers comfortable bedrooms and smart en suite bathrooms. Breakfast is served at individual tables in the bright airy dining room, which is situated adjacent to the comfortable lounge.
FACILITIES: 6 en suite (3 fmly) (1 GF) No smoking in bedrooms No smoking in dining room tea/coffee Cen ht **PRICES:** s fr £27; d fr £44* **LB**
PARKING: 8 **CARDS:**

TWYNHOLM Map 11 NX65

♦♦♦♦ *Fresh Fields*

Arden Rd DG6 4PB ☎ 01557 860221
Dir: *turn off A75 into Twynholm, continue past church, turn R into Arden Rd, 0.5m on L*
A gabled white house with neat gardens and surrounded by meadows. Bedrooms are comfortably furnished and tastefully decorated and, with the exception of one single room, have modern en suite facilities. Public areas include a TV lounge and a panelled dining room. A feature of Fresh Fields is the genuine hospitality and the high standard of cooking.
FACILITIES: 5 en suite 1 annexe en suite No smoking in 2 bedrooms No smoking in dining room No smoking in lounges tea/coffee Licensed Cen ht TVL No coaches Dinner Last d 4pm **PARKING:** 8 **NOTES:** Closed Nov-Jan

Scotland

Scotland

DUNDEE CITY

DUNDEE — Map 11 NO43

♦♦♦♦ Anlast Three Chimneys

379 Arbroath Rd DD4 7SQ ☎ 01382 456710 🖷 01382 456710
e-mail: angus.three.chimneys@talk21.com
Dir: *turn off A90 onto A92, house 200yds on right, next to tennis court*
A warm and friendly greeting is extended to all guests at this immaculately maintained, family run guest house, situated on the northeast side of town. The comfortable bedrooms are attractively decorated and well equipped. Hearty breakfasts are served around a communal table in the lovely dining room.
FACILITIES: 3 en suite No smoking TVB tea/coffee No dogs Cen ht No coaches **PRICES:** s £25-£35; d £45-£50✳ **PARKING:** 6

♦♦♦♦ Beach House Hotel

22 Esplanade, Broughty Ferry DD5 2EN
☎ 01382 775537 & 776614 🖷 01382 480241
Lovely views over the River Tay can be enjoyed from this welcoming family-run hotel, which stands on the Broughty Ferry esplanade. The bedrooms combine pretty colour schemes with comfortable modern furnishings and offer a wide range of amenities. The ground floor dining room is an appropriate setting for hearty breakfasts.
FACILITIES: 5 en suite (1 fmly) No smoking in 2 bedrooms No smoking in dining room TVB tea/coffee Direct dial from bedrooms Licensed Cen ht TVL No coaches **PRICES:** s £35-£40; d £46-£50✳ **PARKING:** 1
CARDS:

♦♦♦♦ *Homebank*

9 Ellieslea Rd, Broughty Ferry DD5 1JH ☎ 01382 477481
🖷 01382 477481
This delightful Victorian house, set in its own well tended grounds, in a peaceful residential area offers all guests a friendly relaxed atmosphere. Bedrooms are comfortable and tastefully decorated. There is an elegant first floor sitting room, which enjoys lovely views of the garden and an attractive dining room where breakfast is served around a large communal table.
FACILITIES: 4 rms (2 en suite) No smoking TVB tea/coffee No dogs (ex guide dogs) Cen ht TVL No children No coaches **PARKING:** 6

♦♦♦♦ Invermark House

23 Monifeith Rd, Broughty Ferry DD5 2RN ☎ 01382 739430
🖷 01382 739430
e-mail: invermarkhouse@onetel.net.uk
Dir: *3m E A930*
Guests are assured of a warm and friendly welcome at this comfortable detached Victorian villa set in well-tended grounds. Bedrooms are tastefully decorated and offer comfortable modern furnishings, and a good range of amenities. There is an inviting ground floor lounge, and a smartly furnished breakfast room where hearty traditional breakfasts are served.
FACILITIES: 4 en suite (1 fmly) No smoking TVB tea/coffee No dogs (ex guide dogs) Licensed Cen ht TVL **PRICES:** s £25-£30; d £40-£45✳ **PARKING:** 16 **NOTES:** Closed 23 Dec-3 Jan **CARDS:**

EAST AYRSHIRE

DALRYMPLE — Map 10 NS31

♦♦♦ Kirkton Inn Hotel

1 Main St KA6 6DF ☎ 01292 560241 🖷 01292 560835
e-mail: kirkton@cqm.co.uk
Dir: *between A77 and A713 approx 5m from Ayr, signed from both roads. In centre of village large black and white building with red roof (The Circle)*

continued

This friendly village inn has a good reputation for its food, popular with locals and visitors alike. There is a separate bar with a selection of malt whiskies. Accommodation comprises three comfortable bedrooms, and self-catering units are also available. The inn is well situated for exploring Burns country and nearby Ayr.
FACILITIES: 3 en suite No smoking in area of dining room TVB tea/coffee Cen ht Pool Table Dinner Last d 8.45pm **PRICES:** s £35-£45; d £45-£70✳ **LB MEALS:** Lunch £3-£12.95&alc Dinner £12.95&alc✳
CONF: Class 30 Board 15 Del from £30 ✳ **PARKING:** 40
CARDS:

KILMARNOCK — Map 10 NS43

♦♦♦♦ Burnside Hotel

18 London Rd KA3 7AQ ☎ 01563 522952 🖷 01563 573381
e-mail: djd@burnsidehotel.co.uk
Dir: *on main road opposite Dick Institute, Library and Museum*

Located within a conservation area, this detached Victorian house hosts elegantly furnished public areas which consist of an inviting lounge and a stylish dining room where good home cooking and hearty breakfasts are served. Bedrooms vary from comfortable singles to larger family units, and all offer the expected amenities. Service is attentive and professional.
FACILITIES: 10 rms (7 en suite) (2 fmly) No smoking in bedrooms No smoking in dining room TVB tea/coffee No dogs (ex guide dogs) Cen ht TVL No coaches Dinner Last d noon **PRICES:** s £25-£35; d £50-£70✳ **LB**
PARKING: 10 **CARDS:**

♦♦♦ *Aulton Farm (NS386422)*

Kilmaurs KA3 2PQ ☎ 01563 538208 & 01294 211584
Mrs A Hawkshaw
Dir: *Irvine to Stewarton road A769. 1st right past Cunningham Head crossroads, 1st farm on left*
Aulton Farm is a well-maintained farmhouse that offers comfortable and attractively furnished bedrooms. Public areas include a pleasant lounge. It has a home-from-home atmosphere and the owners' hospitality will make a stay here memorable.
FACILITIES: 4 rms (1 fmly) No smoking TVB tea/coffee No dogs Cen ht TVL ch fac Riding 22 acres beef **PARKING:** 6

Laigh Langmuir Farmhouse

Irvine Rd, Kilmaurs KA3 2NU ☎ 01563 538270
e-mail: asteel_laighlangmuir@talk21.com
Dir: *off A77 at Fenwick Hotel onto B751 for Kilmaurs. In Kilmaurs village take B769 for Irvine. Laigh Langmuir is 0.5m on right*
FACILITIES: 4 en suite (2 fmly) No smoking TVB tea/coffee Cen ht TVL
PRICES: s £20-£22; d £36-£40✳ **BB PARKING:** 20
NOTES: ★★★ Closed 24-25 Dec

EAST LOTHIAN

EAST LINTON Map 12 NT57

Premier Collection

♦♦♦♦♦ Kippielaw Farmhouse
EH41 4PY ☎ 01620 860368 Fax 01620 860368
e-mail: info@kippielawfarmhouse.co.uk
Dir: *leave A1 at E Linton, follow Traprain sign 0.75m, take single track road on right after farm. Establishment 0.5m on left opposite CP*
Kippielaw is in an elevated position, sheltered by delightful well-tended gardens, and enjoys views of the picturesque Tyne Valley. Country-cottage style bedrooms are prettily decorated and well equipped. There is a peaceful lounge with an open staircase and log fire; excellent meals are served in the elegantly appointed dining room, overlooking the attractive courtyard.
FACILITIES: 2 en suite No smoking TVB tea/coffee No dogs Cen ht No children 13yrs No coaches Dinner Last d 10am **PRICES:** s £35-£36; d £50-£52✳ **PARKING:** 4 **CARDS:**

GULLANE Map 12 NT48

♦♦♦♦ Faussetthill House
20 Main St EH31 2DR ☎ 01620 842396 Fax 01620 842396
e-mail: faussetthill@talk21.com
Dir: *on A198, from A1 follow A198 to Gullane*
This is a delightful Edwardian House standing in its own well-tended gardens. Immaculately maintained, the house is both comfortable and inviting. The well-proportioned bedrooms are tastefully decorated and a first floor lounge has well-stocked bookshelves. Breakfast is served at a large table in the elegant dining room.
FACILITIES: 3 en suite No smoking tea/coffee No dogs Cen ht TVL No children 12yrs No coaches **PRICES:** s £40-£45; d £56-£60✳ **PARKING:** 4 **NOTES:** Closed Nov-Mar **CARDS:**

HADDINGTON Map 12 NT57

Eaglescairnie Mains
By Gifford EH41 4HN ☎ 01620 810491 Fax 01620 810491
e-mail: williams.eagles@btinternet.com
Dir: *leave A1 at Haddington(1st exit signed N 2nd signed going S) traffic lights- straight across & out of town on B6368 signed Humbie & Bolton, in 3m through Bolton at top of hill fork left signed Eaglescairnie & Gifford. 0.5m up on left.*
FACILITIES: 4 en suite No smoking in bedrooms No smoking in dining room tea/coffee Cen ht TVL No coaches Tennis (hard) **PRICES:** s £25-£35; d £50-£60 **PARKING:** 10 **NOTES:** ★★★★ Closed Xmas
CARDS:

NORTH BERWICK Map 12 NT58

♦♦♦♦ Glentruim
53 Dirleton Av EH39 4BL ☎ 01620 890064 Fax 01620 890434
e-mail: glentruim@aol.com
Dir: *diagonally opposite Golf Hotel*
Built around 1895, Glentruim is a traditional sandstone house, sympathetically restored to retain many original features while providing all the comforts of modern life. Just a five minute walk from the High Street, beach, golf course and railway station, and Edinburgh is easily accessible by car or train. There is a spacious drawing room and an elegant dining room where traditional breakfasts are served.

continued

FACILITIES: 3 rms (2 en suite) No smoking TVB tea/coffee No dogs (ex guide dogs) Cen ht No coaches **PRICES:** s £30-£35; d £50-£60✳
PARKING: 6 **CARDS:**

EAST RENFREWSHIRE

EAGLESHAM Map 11 NS55

♦♦♦♦ New Borland
Glasgow Rd G76 0DN ☎ 01355 302051 Fax 01355 302051
e-mail: newborland@dial.pipex.com
Dir: *9m S of Glasgow city centre, 0.8m from lights at junction of B764 & B767*
Just outside the village in landscaped gardens, New Borland is a smart barn conversion with comfortable bedrooms, contemporary in style. Relaxing public rooms include a cosy lounge with a wood burning stove, a games/exercise room and a comfortable dining room where appetising breakfasts are served around a large table.
FACILITIES: 4 rms (2 en suite) No smoking TVB tea/coffee No dogs (ex guide dogs) Cen ht TVL No children 12yrs No coaches Gymnasium Table tennis Mountain biking **PRICES:** s £22.50-£30; d £48 **PARKING:** 10

FALKIRK

FALKIRK Map 11 NS88

♦♦♦♦ Ashbank
105 Main St, Redding FK2 9UQ ☎ 01324 716649
Fax 01324 712431
e-mail: ashbank@guest-house.freeserve.co.uk
Dir: *from junct5 off M5 go to rdbt take turn signed Falkirk/Polmont. Turn L after Brewsters uphill to Crossroads. straight through turn 2nd R. Establishment on R*
Enjoying lovely views of the Forth Valley, the Ochill Hills and the ancient Kingdom of Fife this detached house was built in 1896, and lies to the east of Falkirk, some twenty three miles from Edinburgh and is convenient for Central Scotland's motorway and rail network. Bedrooms are comfortably proportioned, tastefully decorated and well equipped. Breakfast, and by prior arrangement evening meals are served in the attractive dining room.
FACILITIES: 4 en suite (1 fmly) No smoking TVB tea/coffee No dogs (ex guide dogs) Cen ht TVL No coaches Dinner Last d 11am **PRICES:** s £30-£35; d £44-£50✳ **LB PARKING:** 7 **CARDS:**

FIFE

ANSTRUTHER Map 12 NO50

Premier Collection

♦♦♦♦♦ Beaumont Lodge
43 Pittenweem Rd KY10 3DT ☎ 01333 310315
e-mail: info@beaumontlodge.co.uk
Dir: *B9131 from St Andrews to Anstruther, right at x-roads, Beaumont Lodge on left past hotel*
Julia Anderson extends a warm welcome to her comfortable detached home, ideally located for the many golf courses in the area. Immaculately maintained throughout it offers mainly spacious bedrooms, including some with sea views. Delicious home-cooked fare, featuring the best of local produce and freshly baked bread, is served at individual tables in the attractive dining room.
FACILITIES: 4 en suite (1 fmly) No smoking TVB tea/coffee No dogs (ex guide dogs) Cen ht No children 14yrs No coaches Dinner Last d 4pm **PRICES:** s £30-£35; d £50-£60✳ **LB PARKING:** 10
CARDS:

Premier Collection

♦♦♦♦♦ The Grange

45 Pittenweem Rd KY10 3DT ☎ 01333 310842
📠 01333 310842
e-mail: pamela@thegrangeanstruther.fsnet.co.uk
Dir: *in Anstruther proceed along Shore St, then up Rodger St to mini rdbt. Turn left along A917, pass Craws Nest Hotel on left and the Grange slightly further on*

The Grange is an impressive building, within easy walking distance of the centre of this picturesque village, and convenient for the many golf courses in the area. Bedrooms are attractively decorated and well equipped, with many thoughtful extra touches. There is a spacious, comfortable lounge, and a charming dining room where delicious breakfasts are served at a large communal table.

FACILITIES: 4 rms (2 en suite) No smoking tea/coffee No dogs Cen ht TVL No children 10yrs **PRICES:** s £25-£30; d £54-£60✱ **PARKING:** 3 **CARDS:**

♦♦♦♦ The Spindrift

Pittenweem Rd KY10 3DT ☎ 01333 310573 📠 01333 310573
e-mail: info@thespindrift.co.uk
Dir: *from W 1st building on left on entering town. From E last building on right when leaving*

Guests are assured of a warm and friendly welcome at the Spindrift, an imposing detached Victorian house on the western fringe of the village. The brightly decorated bedrooms are individually furnished and offer a wide range of amenities. The Captain's Room, a replica of a cabin, is a particular feature. The attractive lounge, with its honesty bar, invites relaxation, and enjoyable home cooked fare is served at individual tables in the dining room.

FACILITIES: 8 en suite (2 fmly) No smoking TVB tea/coffee Direct dial from bedrooms Licensed Cen ht TVL No children 10yrs No coaches Dinner Last d noon **PRICES:** d £53-£62✱ **LB PARKING:** 12 **CARDS:**

COWDENBEATH — Map 11 NT19

♦♦♦ Struan Bank Hotel

74 Perth Rd KY4 9BG ☎ 01383 511057 📠 01383 511057
Dir: *M90 junct 2a Northbound onto A909 to Cowdenbeath. Through town centre and up hill. M90 junct 4 Southbound follow Cowenbeath Hotel signs on left before High St*

Struan Bank Hotel is a friendly, family-run guest house that lies at the North side of the town and provides good value accommodation. The bedrooms are all well equipped, attractively presented and comfortably proportioned. Drinks are available in the lounge and enjoyable home cooked fare is served in the adjacent dining room.

continued

FACILITIES: 9 rms (6 en suite) (2 fmly) No smoking in 3 bedrooms No smoking in dining room TVB tea/coffee No dogs (ex guide dogs) Licensed Cen ht TVL No coaches Dinner Last d 8.30pm **PRICES:** s £26-£31; d £44-£52✱ **PARKING:** 6 **CARDS:**

CRAIL — Map 12 NO60

♦♦♦ *Selcraig House*

47 Nethergate KY10 3TX ☎ 01333 450697 📠 01333 451113
e-mail: margaretselcraigcrail@compuserve.com
Dir: *opposite the Marine Hotel*

This charming 18th-century stone-built, semi-detached house has been enthusiastically and sympathetically restored by friendly and welcoming owner, Margaret Carstairs. The pretty bedrooms are comfortably individual in style, with the two top floor rooms having private sitting areas. Freshly prepared breakfasts are served in the Edwardian-style dining room, which has a lovely conservatory extension.

FACILITIES: 6 en suite (1 fmly) No smoking TVB tea/coffee Cen ht No coaches **PARKING:** 2

CUPAR — Map 11 NO31

Premier Collection

♦♦♦♦♦ Todhall House

Dairsie KY15 4RQ ☎ 01334 656344 📠 01334 650791
e-mail: todhallhouse@ukgateway.net
Dir: *located 2m east of Cupar and 0.5m before the village Dairsie. Head east and look for sign to Todhall House at road end. House is 0.5m fom main rd. 7m W of St Andrews*

John and Gill Donald delight in welcoming guests to their charming home, a traditional Scottish country house set in landscaped gardens, with lovely views over the Eden Valley. Bedrooms are furnished to a high standard and come equipped with thoughtful extras. Freshly prepared breakfasts and, by prior arrangement, enjoyable home-cooked evening meals, are served around the communal table in the sunny dining room.

FACILITIES: 3 en suite No smoking TVB tea/coffee No dogs (ex guide dogs) Cen ht No children 10yrs No coaches **PRICES:** d £56-£70✱ **PARKING:** 5 **NOTES:** Closed Nov-mid Mar **CARDS:**

A Associate entries with stars have been ★ inspected and rated by the ★ Welsh Tourist Board or Scottish Tourist Board.

Premier Collection

♦♦♦♦♦ Westfield House

Westfield Rd KY15 5AR ☎ 01334 655699 📠 01334 650075
e-mail: westfieldhouse@standrews4.freeserve.co.uk
Dir: *off A91 opposite Cupar Police Station into Westpark Road, left at top into Westfield Road 200yds on left*

Built in 1748, this delightful house is set in well-tended grounds, in a peaceful residential area within easy walking distance of the town centre. Hospitality is very special here, with nothing being too much trouble. Bedrooms are spacious, comfortable and well equipped. There is a bright airy lounge for guests' use and a charming dining room where delicious breakfasts are served at a large communal table.
FACILITIES: 3 en suite No smoking TVB tea/coffee No dogs Cen ht TVL No children 12yrs No coaches **PRICES:** s £40-£50; d £60-£80✳ **PARKING:** 10

♦♦♦ Rathcluan Country House

Carslogie Rd KY15 4HY ☎ 01334 650000 📠 01334 650000
e-mail: info@rathcluanch.co.uk
Dir: *situated on A91 at W entrance to Cupar between Elmwood College and Police Station*

A friendly welcome is assured at this impressive country house, set in well-tended grounds on the edge of town. Bedrooms are comfortable and attractively decorated. There is a spacious lounge, and a charming breakfast room. A varied selection of popular dishes is available in the evening.
FACILITIES: 10 rms (8 en suite) (1 fmly) No smoking in bedrooms No smoking in dining room No smoking in lounges TVB tea/coffee No dogs Licensed Cen ht TVL No children 8yrs No coaches Dinner Last d 8.30pm **PRICES:** s £30-£45; d £65-£80✳ **LB CONF:** Del from £50 ✳ **PARKING:** 27 **NOTES:** Civ Wed 50 **CARDS:**

DUNFERMLINE — Map 11 NT08

♦♦♦♦ Clarke Cottage

139 Halbeath Rd KY11 4LA ☎ 01383 735935 📠 01383 623767
e-mail: clarkecottage@ukonline.co.uk
Dir: *exit M90 junct 3, follow signs for Dunfermline on A907, pass Halbeath Retail Park. Clarke Cottage on the left after 2nd set of traffic lights*
This delightful Victorian home is situated in a residential area on the east side of town. The comfortable bedrooms are bright and airy and offer an excellent range of facilities. Hearty breakfasts are served at individual tables in the conservatory dining room, which is situated adjacent to the cosy lounge. This is a non-smoking establishment.
FACILITIES: 9 en suite (9 GF) No smoking TVB tea/coffee No dogs (ex guide dogs) Licensed Cen ht No coaches **PRICES:** s £25-£29; d £48-£52✳ **PARKING:** 11 **CARDS:**

♦♦♦♦ Hillview House

9 Aberdour Rd KY11 4PB ☎ 01383 726278 📠 01383 726278
e-mail: info@hillviewhousedunfermline.co.uk
Dir: *from Edinburgh exit M90 junct 2 & follow A823 for Dunfermline, after 3rd rbt turn right at traffic lights into Aberdour Road for Hillview House 200m on the right*
Situated in a peaceful residential area, this welcoming family run home offers good value bed and breakfast accommodation. Bedrooms, all of which are en suite, are smartly decorated, comfortably furnished and well-equipped. Freshly prepared breakfasts are served at individual tables in the bright dining room, which overlooks the secure car park.
FACILITIES: 4 en suite No smoking TVB tea/coffee Direct dial from bedrooms No dogs (ex guide dogs) Cen ht No children 12yrs No coaches Video library **PRICES:** s £25-£27; d £42-£46✳ **PARKING:** 4 **CARDS:**

♦♦♦♦ Hopetoun Lodge

141 Halbeath Rd KY11 4LA ☎ 01383 620906
e-mail: bhast10021@aol.com
Dir: *exit M90 junct 3, 1.5m & through Halbeath, past Retail Park on right, over rdbt & 2 traffic lights. Lodge on left after Kwik-Fit*
Situated on the East side of the town within easy reach of the M90, this comfortable family-run guest house offers all guests a warm and friendly welcome. The attractive bedrooms are varied in size and well-equipped. A combined lounge/dining room is available and is the setting for hearty home-cooked breakfasts.
FACILITIES: 3 rms (1 en suite) (1 fmly) (3 GF) No smoking TVB tea/coffee No dogs (ex guide dogs) Cen ht TVL No coaches **PRICES:** s £24-£28; d £48-£52✳ **PARKING:** 4 **NOTES:** Closed 25-26 Dec, 1-2 Jan

♦♦♦♦ Pitreavie

3 Aberdour Rd KY11 4PB ☎ 01383 724244 📠 01383 724244
e-mail: Info@pitreavie.com
Dir: *at west end of Aberdour Rd at junct with A823. 0.5m S of Dunfermline town centre*
A warm and friendly welcome awaits guests at this comfortable semi-detached house at the junction of the Aberdour Road and the A823. Bedrooms are attractively decorated, comfortably furnished in pine and offer a good range of amenities including videos. Hearty breakfasts and, by arrangement, evening meals are served in the combined lounge/dining room
FACILITIES: 5 rms (4 en suite) (1 fmly) No smoking TVB tea/coffee Direct dial from bedrooms No dogs (ex guide dogs) Cen ht TVL No coaches Dinner Last d 4pm **PRICES:** s £25-£30; d £45-£50✳ **LB PARKING:** 6 **CARDS:**

Scotland

INVERKEITHING Map 11 NT18

♦♦♦♦ The Roods

16 Bannerman Av KY11 1NG ☎ 01383 415049 📠 01383 415049
e-mail: bookings@theroods.com
Dir: *off A90/M90 onto B981*

This charming house is located in a secluded well-tended garden setting, yet is still close to the station and central amenities. Bedrooms are individually furnished and graced with many thoughtful personal touches and a wide range of amenities. There is an inviting lounge, and a pretty conservatory, where breakfast is served at individual tables.
FACILITIES: 2 en suite (2 GF) No smoking TVB tea/coffee Direct dial from bedrooms No dogs (ex guide dogs) Cen ht TVL No coaches Dinner Last d 9am **PRICES:** s £22-£25; d £44-£50✻ **LB PARKING:** 4 **CARDS:**

♦♦♦ Forth Craig Private Hotel

90 Hope St KY11 1LL ☎ 01383 418440
Dir: *off A90 at 1st exit after Forth Bridge, signed Inverkeithing, for hotel in 0.5m on right next to church*
Situated at the South end of the village, this friendly family-run guest house enjoys views over the Firth of Forth. The modern styled no-smoking bedrooms are comfortable and offer the expected amenities. Breakfast is served at individual tables in the airy dining room and there is a dispense bar.
FACILITIES: 5 en suite No smoking in bedrooms No smoking in dining room TVB tea/coffee Licensed Cen ht No coaches Dinner Last d 6pm **PRICES:** s fr £30; d fr £50✻ **PARKING:** 8 **CARDS:**

LEVEN Map 12 NO30

Sandilands

20 Leven Rd, Lundin Links KY8 6AH ☎ 01333 329881
📠 01333 329881
e-mail: bandb.atsandilands@tesco.net
Dir: *in centre of village on Fife coastal tourist route (A915) 12m from St Andrews and 2m from Leven*
FACILITIES: 3 en suite (1 fmly) No smoking TVB tea/coffee No dogs (ex guide dogs) Cen ht No children 5yrs No coaches **PRICES:** s £22-£30; d £40-£50 **PARKING:** 3 **NOTES:** ★★★ Closed 4-20 Apr & 10-27 Oct **CARDS:**

MARKINCH Map 11 NO20

♦♦♦♦ Town House Hotel

1 High St KY7 6DQ ☎ 01592 758459 📠 01592 755039
e-mail: townhouse@ecosse.net
Dir: *opposite railway station in Markinch*
This comfortable small hotel on the edge of the village offers guests a warm friendly welcome. Bedrooms have pleasing colour schemes, modern furnishings and a good range of accessories and facilities. The attractive restaurant and bar serves a varied, competitively priced supper menu, and is popular with locals.

continued

FACILITIES: 4 rms (3 en suite) (1 fmly) No smoking in bedrooms No smoking in area of dining room No smoking in 1 lounge TVB tea/coffee Cen ht No coaches Dinner Last d 9pm **PRICES:** s £35-£40; d £60-£65✻ **MEALS:** Lunch £8.50-£10.50 Dinner £14.50-£17.50alc✻ **CONF:** Thtr 20 Class 15 Board 15 Del from £71.50 ✻ **NOTES:** Closed 25-26 Dec & 1-2 Jan **CARDS:**

ROSYTH Map 11 NT18

♦♦♦♦ Backmarch House

54A Norval Place KY11 2RJ ☎ 01383 412997 📠 01383 414318
e-mail: info@backmarchhouse.com
Dir: *from N exit M90 junct 1, signposted 'Admiralty interchange' turn right signposted 'Kincardine', go straight ahead at rdbt, 1st right, house on right. From S exit M40 junct 1, signposted 'Kincardine', take left ahead at roundabout, first right, house on right*
Dating from 1829, Backmarch House is centrally located in Rosyth and convenient for Edinburgh city centre and airport, Dunfermline's business parks and the many tourist attractions in this lovely area. This peaceful Georgian farmhouse has been beautifully renovated to provide attractive and extremely well equipped accommodation. Breakfasts, featuring the best of local produce, are served in the elegant ground floor dining room. There is also ample car parking.
FACILITIES: 2 en suite No smoking TVB tea/coffee No dogs (ex guide dogs) Cen ht TVL No coaches **PRICES:** s £25-£30; d £40-£50✻ **PARKING:** 4 **CARDS:**

ST ANDREWS Map 12 NO51

Premier Collection

♦♦♦♦♦ *Fossil House*

12-14 Main St, Strathkinness KY16 9RU ☎ 01334 850639
📠 01334 850639
e-mail: the.fossil@virgin.net
Dir: *follow A91 towards St Andrews, Strathkinness signposted. Fossil House at top end of village close to pub*

Wonderful hospitality coupled with memorable breakfasts are the hallmarks of any visit to this charming house. Two of the attractive bedrooms are in the house, and two in the adjacent cottage, which has its own lounge and conservatory. The family room has a sun lounge extension featuring lots of thoughtful extras for children. Kornelia's delicious breakfasts continue to attract much praise - she has won a Golden Spurtle award for her porridge.
FACILITIES: 2 en suite 2 annexe en suite (1 fmly) No smoking TVB tea/coffee No dogs (ex guide dogs) Cen ht TVL No coaches Croquet lawn **PARKING:** 5 **CARDS:**

♦♦♦♦ Craigmore

3 Murray Park KY16 9AW ☎ 01334 472142 01334 477963
e-mail: enquiries@standrewscraigmore.com
Dir: *on A91 from Cupar direction, straight across 2 mini-rdbts, 1st left down Golf Place, 1st right then 1st right again to top of street*
Situated close to the seafront, the famous Old Course and central amenities, this immaculately maintained guest house forms part of a Victorian terraced row. The stylish bedrooms are attractively decorated and well-equipped. The tempting breakfast menu offers hot and cold items served at individual tables in the elegant lounge/dining room.
FACILITIES: 7 en suite (4 fmly) (1 GF) No smoking TVB tea/coffee No dogs Cen ht TVL No coaches **PRICES:** d £50-£72✻ **LB**
CARDS:

♦♦♦♦ *Hazlebank Private Hotel*

28 The Scores KY16 9AS ☎ 01334 472466 01334 472466
e-mail: michael@hazelbank.com
A friendly atmosphere prevails at this personally run hotel which overlooks the bay and is close to the famous Old Course. Bedrooms, with attractive colour schemes, are comfortably modern in style and offer a good range of amenities. Freshly prepared breakfasts are served at individual tables in the ground floor dining room. This is a no-smoking house.
FACILITIES: 10 en suite (4 fmly) No smoking in bedrooms No smoking in dining room STV TVB tea/coffee Direct dial from bedrooms No dogs (ex guide dogs) Licensed Cen ht TVL No coaches Last d 6.45pm
NOTES: Closed 16 Dec-6 Jan **CARDS:**

♦♦♦♦ The Larches

7 River Ter, Guardbridge KY16 0XA ☎ 01334 838008
01334 838008
e-mail: thelarches@aol.com
Dir: *A91 to Guardbridge from St Andrews, turn left before bridge at far end of village by phone and post box, house 50yds on left*
Situated in a village just Northwest of St Andrews, this comfortable, family run guest house, formerly the memorial hall stands in mature colourful gardens close to the River Eden. It has a welcoming atmosphere and offers modern comfortably proportioned, well-equipped bedrooms, a spacious lounge supplied with books and board games, and an attractive conservatory dining room.
FACILITIES: 4 rms (2 en suite) No smoking TVB tea/coffee No dogs (ex guide dogs) Cen ht TVL No coaches **PRICES:** s fr £30; d fr £50✻
PARKING: 10

♦♦♦♦ Lorimer House

19 Murray Park KY16 9AW ☎ 01334 476599 01334 476599
e-mail: lorimersta@talk21.com
Dir: *A91 to St Andrews, turn left into Golf Place, turn right into The Scores, turn right into Murray Park*
A warm welcome is assured at this delightful Victorian terraced townhouse, situated within easy reach of the Old Course, the sea front and the town centre. Bedrooms are comfortably furnished and well equipped. Freshly prepared Scottish breakfasts are served in the attractive dining room, which also has a lounge area.
FACILITIES: 6 en suite (2 fmly) No smoking STV TVB tea/coffee No dogs (ex guide dogs) Cen ht TVL No children 12yrs No coaches
PRICES: s £25-£35; d £50-£70 **CARDS:**

♦♦♦♦ *Riverview*

Edenside KY16 9SQ ☎ 01334 838009 01334 839944
e-mail: kenny@riverviewguesthouse.freeserve.co.uk
Dir: *on A91 3m N of St Andrews*
The Paton family provide friendly relaxed hospitality in their detached home overlooking the River Eden estuary. The bedrooms are comfortably proportioned and well-equipped, with access through individual patio doors, from either the terrace or balcony. Hearty breakfasts, and by prior arrangement evening meals are served in the cheery dining room.
FACILITIES: 7 en suite (2 fmly) No smoking TVB tea/coffee No dogs (ex guide dogs) Cen ht No coaches Last d 10am **PARKING:** 8
CARDS:

♦♦♦♦ Spinkstown Farmhouse *(NO541144)*

KY16 8PN ☎ 01334 473475 01334 473475 Mrs A E Duncan
e-mail: anne-duncan@lineone.net
Dir: *2m E of St Andrews on A917 coast road to Crail, 3rd farmhouse on right*
This immaculately maintained modern farmhouse is situated two miles from the town and is surrounded by gently rolling countryside. Bedrooms are spacious, with attractive colour schemes and are well-equipped. The comfortable lounge, complete with baby grand piano, overlooks the well-tended rear garden. Breakfast is served around a communal table in the peaceful dining room.
FACILITIES: 3 en suite No smoking TVB tea/coffee No dogs Cen ht TVL 250 acres arable/cattle/sheep **PRICES:** s £25; d £46-£50✻ **PARKING:** 3

♦♦♦ West Park House

5 St Mary's Place KY16 9UY ☎ 01334 475933 01334 476634
e-mail: rosemary@westparksta.freeserve.co.uk
Dir: *to the W end of Market St, just beyond Hope Park Church*
This attractive Georgian house is situated within walking distance of the famous university and golf course, and has a welcoming and friendly atmosphere. The pretty, spacious bedrooms are comfortably modern in style and well-equipped. The relaxing sitting room overlooks the delightful garden and freshly prepared breakfasts are served in the elegant dining room.
FACILITIES: 4 rms (3 en suite) (1 fmly) No smoking TVB tea/coffee No dogs (ex guide dogs) Cen ht TVL No coaches **PRICES:** s £32.50-£35; d £46-£55✻ **NOTES:** Closed Jan **CARDS:**

♦♦♦ Annandale

23 Murray Park KY16 9AW ☎ 01334 475310 01334 475310
e-mail: brian@dcs.st-and.ac.uk
Dir: *A91 to St Andrews. Straight over 1st rdbt to mini-rdbt, straight over at 2nd rdbt, then 1st left, 1st right onto one-way system, right again, 1st guest house on left*
This is a welcoming and comfortable family-run guest house, which forms part of a terraced row and is positioned conveniently for the seafront and central amenities. Bedrooms have pleasing colour schemes and are furnished in both modern and traditional styles. Hearty breakfasts are served in the combined lounge/dining room.
FACILITIES: 5 en suite (2 fmly) No smoking TVB tea/coffee No dogs (ex guide dogs) Cen ht No children 8yrs **PRICES:** d £44-£68
CARDS:

Scotland

ST ANDREWS continued

♦♦♦ Edenside House

Edenside KY16 9SQ ☎ 01334 838108 Fax 01334 838493
e-mail: yreid19154@aol.com
Dir: *clearly visible from A91, 2m W of St Andrews directly on estuary shore*

Overlooking the Eden estuary and nature reserve, this modernised 18th century house is family-run and offers a friendly home from home atmosphere. Bedrooms are comfortable, bright and cheerful, and are for the most part accessed externally. There is a cosy lounge and a pretty dining room where hearty breakfasts are served.
FACILITIES: 2 en suite 6 annexe en suite (1 fmly) (6 GF) No smoking TVB tea/coffee Cen ht No coaches Dinner Last d 9pm **PRICES:** s £25-£38; d £40-£60* **PARKING:** 10 **CARDS:**

♦♦♦ Yorkston House

68 & 70 Argyle St KY16 9BU ☎ 01334 472019 Fax 01334 470351
e-mail: yorkstonhouse@aol.com
Dir: *400yds from petrol station and West Port travelling W*
This welcoming and friendly family-run guest house lies close to the West Port and the town centre. The comfortable bedrooms are tastefully decorated and well equipped. A good selection of books, magazines and games are provided in the airy first floor lounge, with hearty traditional breakfasts served at individual tables in the attractive dining room.
FACILITIES: 10 rms (6 en suite) (2 fmly) No smoking TVB tea/coffee No dogs Licensed Cen ht No coaches **PRICES:** s £25-£35; d £50-£76* **NOTES:** Closed Dec-Jan

UPPER LARGO — Map 12 NO40

♦♦♦♦ Monturpie

Monturpie KY8 5QS ☎ 01333 360254 Fax 01333 360850
e-mail: enquiries@monturpie.co.uk
Dir: *from Edinburgh exit M90 junct 2A continue on A92 to Kirkcaldy, at rdbt signed Kirkcaldy East take exit for St Andrews A915 until Upper Largo turn left A915 St Andrews and Monturpie is 2nd property on right after leaving village*
A traditional stone-built farmhouse situated in an elevated position with magnificent views over the Firth of Forth towards Edinburgh. Easy access to varied attractions and many golf courses including the Old Course at St Andrews. Bedrooms are attractive, comfortably proportioned and well equipped. There is a spacious lounge and a peaceful dining room where hearty breakfasts (and evening meals by prior arrangement) can be enjoyed. Ample off road parking is available.
FACILITIES: 4 en suite (1 fmly) No smoking TVB tea/coffee No dogs Licensed Cen ht TVL No coaches Dinner Last d 6.30pm **PRICES:** s £22-£25; d £44-£50* **PARKING:** 12 **NOTES:** Closed 15 Dec-15 Jan
CARDS:

HIGHLAND

AULTBEA — Map 14 NG88

♦♦♦♦ Mellondale

47 Mellon Charles IV22 2JL ☎ 01445 731326 Fax 01445 731326
e-mail: mellondale@lineone.net
Dir: *A835 N from Inverness to Braemore junct, left on A832, at Aultbea/Mellon Charles sign turn right and right again at Aultbea Hotel, 3m on left*
This modern guest house enjoys spectacular views of Loch Ewe from its elevated position. Bedrooms are prettily decorated, very well equipped and include thoughtful touches. The atmosphere in the house is warm and friendly and the home-cooked meals are delicious. There is also a homely lounge for guests to relax in.
FACILITIES: 4 en suite (2 GF) No smoking in bedrooms No smoking in dining room TVB tea/coffee No dogs Cen ht TVL No coaches Dinner
PRICES: s fr £26; d fr £52* **LB PARKING:** 6 **NOTES:** Closed Nov-Mar
CARDS:

AVIEMORE — Map 14 NH81

Premier Collection

♦♦♦♦♦ The Old Minister's House

Rothiemurchus PH22 1QH ☎ 01479 812181
Fax 01479 812181
e-mail: theoldministershouse@tinyworld.co.uk
Dir: *from Aviemore take B970 signed Glenmore & Coylumbridge, establishment 0.75m from Aviemore at Inverdruie*
Built as a manse in 1906 The Old Minister's House stands in its own well-tended grounds. The house is beautifully furnished and immaculately maintained. Bedrooms are spacious, attractively decorated and well-equipped. There is a comfortable lounge and an elegant dining room where hearty breakfasts are served.
FACILITIES: 4 en suite No smoking TVB tea/coffee No dogs Cen ht No children 4yrs No coaches **PRICES:** s £28-£35; d £56-£70*
PARKING: 8 **CARDS:**

♦♦♦ Cairngorm

Grampian Rd PH22 1RP ☎ 01479 810630 Fax 01479 810630
e-mail: conns@lineone.net
Dir: *off A9 at Aviemore junct, then left at B9152. On N side of Main Rd, opposite war memorial*
A true highland welcome is assured at the Cairngorm guest house. It is an extended detached house, set in its own grounds. All of the bedrooms are bright and comfortable. There is a relaxing lounge with log burning fire and a selection of games. Breakfasts are served at individual tables in the airy dining room.
FACILITIES: 10 en suite (2 fmly) (5 GF) No smoking in bedrooms No smoking in dining room No smoking in 1 lounge TVB tea/coffee No dogs (ex guide dogs) Cen ht TVL No coaches **PRICES:** s £25-£45; d £40-£60*
LB PARKING: 12 **CARDS:**

♦♦♦ Ravenscraig

Grampian Rd PH22 1RP ☎ 01479 810278 Fax 01479 812742
e-mail: ravenscrg@aol.com
Dir: *at north end of Main St on left. 250mtrs N of Police Station*
This friendly, family-run guest house is located on the North side of the village beside the main road. Bedrooms, including those in the adjacent annexe, are comfortably furnished and well-equipped. There is a relaxing residents' lounge and separate dining room, where freshly prepared breakfasts are served at individual tables.

continued

Ravenscraig

FACILITIES: 6 en suite 6 annexe en suite (2 fmly) (6 GF) No smoking in bedrooms No smoking in dining room TVB tea/coffee No dogs (ex guide dogs) Cen ht TVL Membership to local golf/leisure club available
PRICES: s £18-£26; d £36-£52 BB **PARKING:** 15
CARDS:

BALLACHULISH Map 14 NN05

Premier Collection

♦♦♦♦♦ Ballachulish House

Ballachulish House PH49 4JX ☎ 01855 811266
01855 811498
e-mail: McLaughlins@btconnect.com
Dir: *off A82 onto A825 Oban road. Establishment 0.25m on left, just beyond Ballachullish Hotel*

Peacefully situated in two acres of well-tended grounds in a stunning setting, this historic 17th-century Laird's house has been lovingly restored to provide something very special. Bedrooms are tastefully decorated and well equipped, with many thoughtful touches, and the atmosphere is friendly and welcoming. There is an elegant sitting room with an open fire and a sophisticated dining room where delicious, award-winning meals are served.
FACILITIES: 8 en suite (2 fmly) No smoking tea/coffee Direct dial from bedrooms No dogs (ex guide dogs) Licensed TVL No children 10yrs Golf 9 Fishing Croquet lawn Putting green Badminton Dinner Last d 7pm **PRICES:** s £50-£70; d £80-£140✳ **LB CONF:** Board 12 Del from £80 ✳ **PARKING:** 10 **CARDS:**

♦♦♦♦ *Fern Villa*

Loanfern PH49 4JE ☎ 01855 811393 01855 811727
e-mail: aa@fernvilla.com
Dir: *leave A82 & take left turn on entering village, house 150yds on left*
A warm and friendly welcome is assured at Fern Villa, the elegant Victorian home of June and Kenneth Chandler. The bedrooms are well-equipped and maintained, and offer all the expected

continued

amenities. There is a comfortable lounge with a selection of board games, and an attractive dining room where June's delicious home cooking can be enjoyed.

Fern Villa

FACILITIES: 5 en suite No smoking TVB tea/coffee No dogs (ex guide dogs) Licensed Cen ht TVL No children 10yrs No coaches Dinner Last d 5pm
PARKING: 5 **CARDS:**

♦♦♦♦ Lyn-Leven

West Laroch PH49 4JP ☎ 01855 811392 01855 811600
e-mail: lynleven@amserve.net
Dir: *off A82 signed on left West Lorroch*

Genuine Highland hospitality and high standards are part of the appeal of this comfortable guest house. The attractive bedrooms vary in size, are well-equipped and offer many thoughtful extra touches. There is a spacious lounge and a smart dining room where delicious home cooked evening meals and breakfasts are served at individual tables.
FACILITIES: 8 en suite 4 annexe en suite (1 fmly) (12 GF) No smoking in 1 bedrooms TVB tea/coffee Licensed Cen ht TVL Dinner Last d 7pm
PRICES: s £22-£30; d £40-£50✳ **LB PARKING:** 12 **NOTES:** Closed Xmas
CARDS:

BEAULY Map 14 NH54

♦♦♦♦ Heathmount

Station Rd IV4 7EQ ☎ 01463 782411
Dir: *20mtrs from Post Office*
This delightful and traditional Victorian residence, set in a well-tended garden offers a friendly atmosphere and good value accommodation. The bedrooms are spacious and well-maintained. There is a comfortable ground floor lounge which invites relaxation, and a bright airy dining room where hearty breakfasts are served at individual tables.
FACILITIES: 5 rms (2 fmly) No smoking in bedrooms No smoking in dining room TVB tea/coffee Cen ht TVL No coaches **PRICES:** s £20; d £40✳
PARKING: 5 **NOTES:** Closed Xmas & New Year **CARDS:**

Scotland

Scotland

BONAR BRIDGE Map 14 NH69

◆◆◆ Kyle House

Dornoch Rd IV24 3EB ☎ 01863 766360 Fax 01863 766360
e-mail: kylehouse360@msn.com
Dir: *on A949, 4th house on left after newsagents going north bound out of village*

A spacious old house, with splendid views of the Kyle of Sutherland and the hills beyond. Bedrooms are furnished in traditional style. There is a guest lounge and hearty breakfasts are enjoyed in the spacious dining room.

FACILITIES: 6 rms (3 en suite) (2 fmly) No smoking in bedrooms No smoking in dining room TVB tea/coffee No dogs (ex guide dogs) Licensed Cen ht TVL No children 5yrs No coaches **PRICES:** s £22-£25; d £44-£50* **PARKING:** 6 **NOTES:** Closed Dec-Jan rs Oct & Apr

BRORA Map 14 NC90

Premier Collection

◆◆◆◆◆ Glenaveron

Golf Rd KW9 6QS ☎ 01408 621601 Fax 01408 621601
e-mail: glenaveron@hotmail.com
Dir: *from S, cross bridge in middle of Brora, turn right off A9 into Golf Rd, take 2nd on left. 2nd house on right*

Glenaveron sits in landscaped gardens a short distance from the beach and golf course. It is both a delightful house and a family home and the friendly and relaxing atmosphere will create a lasting impression. Two bedrooms are pine-furnished and one is graced with period pieces. There is an inviting guest lounge. Excellent breakfasts are served house party style in the elegant dining room.

FACILITIES: 3 en suite (1 fmly) No smoking TVB tea/coffee No dogs Cen ht No coaches Paid use of leisure facilities at adjacent hotel **PRICES:** s £25-£35; d £50-£56* **PARKING:** 6 **CARDS:**

◆◆◆◆ Lynwood

Golf Rd KW9 6QS ☎ 01408 621226 Fax 01408 621226
Dir: *turn off A9 by river bridge onto Golf Rd, 500yds on left*

This welcoming family home stands in pretty gardens close to the golf course. Bedrooms are comfortably furnished, with one room having external access from the garden. There is a homely lounge, an attractive dining room and a conservatory extension where breakfast is served.

FACILITIES: 3 en suite No smoking TVB tea/coffee No dogs (ex guide dogs) Cen ht TVL No coaches Dinner Last d day before **PRICES:** s £28-£30; d £46-£56* **LB PARKING:** 4 **NOTES:** Closed Jan & Feb **CARDS:**

CARRBRIDGE Map 14 NH92

◆◆◆◆ Carrmoor

Carr Rd PH23 3AD ☎ 01479 841244 Fax 01479 841244
e-mail: christine@carrmoorguesthouse.co.uk
Dir: *drive to centre of village & turn into Carr rd opposite church & village hall. Carrmoor on left in Carr Rd*

A welcoming atmosphere prevails at this immaculately maintained guest house. Bedrooms, where the best use has been made of available space, have pretty colour schemes and are comfortably modern in appointment. There is an inviting lounge where guests can relax. In the dining room, quality fresh ingredients are used. Vegetarian and children's options are also available.

continued

Carrmoor Guest House

FACILITIES: 6 en suite (1 fmly) (1 GF) No smoking in bedrooms No smoking in dining room tea/coffee Licensed Cen ht TVL No coaches Dinner Last d 8pm **PRICES:** s £22.50-£27; d £40-£44* **PARKING:** 6 **CARDS:**

◆◆◆ Pines Country House

Duthil PH23 3ND ☎ 01479 841220 Fax 01479 841220 *51
e-mail: Lynn@thepines-duthil.fsnet.co.uk
Dir: *A9 to Carrbridge, turn onto A938 Grantown-on-Spey road, 2m to Duthil. 5th house on left*

A warm and friendly welcome is assured at this comfortable home which enjoys a delightful rural setting. The bright bedrooms are comfortably furnished and offer the expected amenities. Enjoyable home cooked fare is served around a communal table. In the conservatory lounge guests can watch squirrels feed by the wood.

FACILITIES: 4 en suite (1 fmly) (1 GF) No smoking in 1 bedrooms No smoking in dining room No smoking in lounges STV TVB tea/coffee Cen ht No coaches Dinner Last d 4pm **PRICES:** s £25; d £40* **LB PARKING:** 5 **CARDS:**

DALCROSS Map 14 NH7

◆◆◆◆ *Easter Dalziel Farmhouse*

Easter Dalziel Farm, Dalcross IV2 7JL ☎ 01667 462213 Fax 01667 462213
e-mail: aa@easterdalzielfarm.co.uk
Dir: *from Inverness A96 for 5m, left onto B9039 signed Castle Stuart & Fort George, after 2m farm is signed on right, Farmhouse 300yds*

A warm and friendly welcome awaits guests to Margaret Pottie's early Victorian farmhouse, which stands amid wooded countryside near Inverness Airport. Bedrooms are comfortably furnished in both period and traditional styles. There is a relaxing lounge with a piano, stereo and television, and breakfasts are served at a communal table in the adjacent dining room.

FACILITIES: 3 rms No smoking in dining room tea/coffee TVL Dinner Last d 24hrs **PARKING:** 10 **NOTES:** Closed 20 Dec-6 Jan rs 1-20 Dec & 6 Jan-28 Feb **CARDS:**

DINGWALL Map 14 NH5

Braelangwell House

Balblair IV7 8LQ ☎ 01381 610353 Fax 01381 610467
e-mail: braelangwell@btinternet.com
Dir: *from Inverness & A9 turn onto B9161. Right onto A832 for approx 8m then left at Balblairs onto B9160, 3m to mount high. Turn left off bend through gates*

FACILITIES: 3 en suite No smoking TVB tea/coffee Cen ht No coaches Snooker Croquet lawn Putting green **PRICES:** s £35-£50; d £50-£80* **PARKING:** 40 **NOTES:** ★★★★ Closed Nov-Feb Civ Wed 150

ᴐORNOCH Map 14 NH78

♦♦♦♦ Inistore House
ᴐastle St IV25 3SN ☎ 01862 811263
-mail: theAA@inistore.co.uk
Dir: on left hand side of main street, 200mtrs before cathedral
ssentially a restaurant with rooms, Inistore House compliments he fine dining of the 2 Quail Restaurant. The bedrooms are ttractively decorated and well-equipped. There is a comfortable ounge situated adjacent to the bedrooms, in which you can relax fter a busy day.
ACILITIES: 2 en suite (1 fmly) No smoking in bedrooms No smoking in ining room TVB tea/coffee No dogs (ex guide dogs) Licensed Cen ht No hildren 8yrs No coaches Dinner Last d by arrangement **PRICES:** s fr £50; £60-£80✱ **LB CARDS:**

♦♦♦ Achandean
ᴐhe Meadows IV25 3SF ☎ 01862 810413 🖹 01862 810413
-mail: basilhellier@amserve.net
Dir: from A9 (N) approx 1.5m past Dornoch Firth Bridge. Right onto A949 ᴐ Dornoch, right opposite Eagle Hotel, 1st left and house on left opposite re station

ᴐhis modern bungalow lies secluded in well tended gardens just ᴐehind the main street. The proprietors are friendly hosts and varmly welcome all their guests, old and new. The bedrooms are vell equipped and comfortable, two being particularly spacious.
ACILITIES: 3 en suite (3 GF) No smoking in bedrooms No smoking in lining room TVB tea/coffee Cen ht TVL No children No coaches Dinner Last l on request **PRICES:** s £28-£30; d £36-£44✱ **LB BB**
ARKING: 3 **NOTES:** Closed mid Oct-Feb rs March 150

ᴐRUMNADROCHIT Map 14 NH52

♦♦♦♦ Beechwood
Marchfield, Balnain IV63 6TJ ☎ 01456 476377 🖹 01456 476377
-mail: cdou793101@aol.com
Dir: A82 to Drumnadrochit then bear right on A831 signed Cannich for .5m. Right at T-junct called Upperton and 1st right again for Beechwood
n an elevated location overlooking Loch Meikle in beautiful Glen Jrquhart, Beechwood offers pretty bedrooms, spacious and well equipped, with many thoughtful extra touches. There is a comfortable first floor lounge, which enjoys lovely views of the surrounding countryside and a bright airy ground floor dining room where traditional Scottish breakfasts are served.
FACILITIES: 2 en suite (1 fmly) No smoking TVB tea/coffee No dogs (ex guide dogs) Cen ht TVL No coaches **PRICES:** s fr £25; d fr £46✱ **LB**
PARKING: 4

♦♦♦♦ Glen Rowan
West Lewiston IV63 6UW ☎ 01456 450235 🖹 01456 450817
e-mail: glenrowan@loch-ness.demon.co.uk
Dir: from Inverness, A82 to Fort William, through Drumnadrochit, then to Lewiston, turn right after Esso Garage. Glen Rowan 600yds on left
The Harrod family extends a warm and friendly welcome to guests visiting their comfortable family home, which stands in well-tended gardens beside the River Coiltie. The attractive bedrooms are well-equipped and offer all the expected amenities, and many thoughtful extras. Hearty Scottish breakfasts are served at individual tables in the combined lounge/ dining room.
FACILITIES: 3 en suite No smoking STV TVB tea/coffee No dogs Cen ht No coaches **PRICES:** s £25-£50; d £35-£50✱ **BB PARKING:** 3
NOTES: Closed 28 Nov-1 Feb **CARDS:**

♦♦♦ Riverbank
West Lewiston IV63 6UW ☎ 01456 450274 & 07752 108862
🖹 01456 450274
e-mail: river.bank@virgin.net
Dir: on entering village, follow road through village to Petrol Station. 1st right, house 500yds on left
Guests are assured of a warm and friendly welcome at Riverbank, the comfortable home of the Cridge family, which is situated in a peaceful residential area close to all local amenities. The pretty bedrooms, all on the ground floor, are well equipped and offer all the expected facilities. The attractive dining room, which enjoys lovely views of the pretty garden, is an appropriate setting for hearty Scottish breakfasts.
FACILITIES: 4 en suite (4 GF) No smoking TVB tea/coffee Cen ht No coaches Dinner Last d 7pm **PRICES:** s £17-£18; d £35-£40✱ **BB**
PARKING: 6 **CARDS:**

DULNAIN BRIDGE Map 14 NH92

♦♦♦ Bydand
PH26 3LU ☎ 01479 851278
e-mail: stewart.crabb@virgin.net
Dir: 10m N of Aviemore, take A938. House is 200mtrs on right
Betty and Stewart Crabb enjoy welcoming guests to their home, a detached house set in wooded grounds to the South of the village. Bedrooms are cosy and offer a homely atmosphere. Guests are welcome to share the owners comfortable ground floor lounge. Enjoyable home cooked fare is served at individual tables in the dining room.
FACILITIES: 2 rms No smoking in bedrooms No smoking in dining room Cen ht TVL No coaches Dinner Last d 8.30pm **PRICES:** d £32-£35✱ **BB**
PARKING: 6 **CARDS:**

Scotland

Scotland

FORT WILLIAM Map 14 NN17

See also Spean Bridge

Premier Collection

♦♦♦♦♦ The Grange

Grange Rd PH33 6JF ☎ 01397 705516 🖷 701595
e-mail: jcampbell@grangefortwilliam.com
Dir: *leave Fort William on A82 S-300yds from rdbt take left onto Ashburn Ln. The Grange is at top on left*

Situated in immaculately maintained gardens in an elevated position this lovely Victorian villa enjoys beautiful views of Loch Linnhe. Attractive décor and pretty fabrics have been used to good effect in the charming bedrooms, two of which have loch views. There is ample provision of books and fresh flowers in the tasteful and comfortably furnished lounge, and the elegant dining room is a lovely setting for hearty breakfasts.
FACILITIES: 4 en suite No smoking TVB tea/coffee No dogs (ex guide dogs) Cen ht TVL No children 13yrs **PRICES:** d £80-£94✻ **LB** **PARKING:** 4 **NOTES:** Closed Nov-Mar

Premier Collection

♦♦♦♦♦ Ashburn House

8 Achintore Rd PH33 6RQ ☎ 01397 706000 🖷 01397 702024
e-mail: ashburn.house@tinyworld.co.uk
Dir: *junct A82 and Ashburn Ln 500yds from large rbt at south end of High St or 400yds on right after entering 30mph zone from S*

This elegant Victorian villa, which enjoys wonderful views overlooking Loch Linnhe, has been lovingly restored to its former glory. The charming bedrooms are spacious, individually decorated and offer an extensive range of amenities. There is a sunny conservatory lounge and an attractive dining room, which is an appropriate setting for the delicious breakfast.

continued

FACILITIES: 7 en suite (1 fmly) (2 GF) No smoking TVB tea/coffee No dogs (ex guide dogs) Cen ht No coaches **PRICES:** s £30-£40; d £60-£90✻ **LB** **PARKING:** 8 **NOTES:** Closed Dec-Jan
CARDS:

♦♦♦♦ Distillery House

Nevis Bridge, North Rd PH33 6LR ☎ 01397 700103
🖷 01397 702980
e-mail: disthouse@aol.com
Dir: *from S A82 3rd rdbt on left. From N A82 just before Glen Nevis rdbt, on right*

Situated in the grounds of the former Glenlochy Distillery, this friendly guest house was once the distillery manager's home. Bedrooms vary in size and are comfortably furnished offering a wide range of amenities. There is a comfortably furnished lounge and a bright airy dining room where traditional Scottish breakfasts are served at individual tables.
FACILITIES: 7 en suite (1 fmly) No smoking TVB tea/coffee No dogs (ex guide dogs) Cen ht Fishing **PRICES:** d £45-£70✻ **PARKING:** 15
CARDS:

♦♦♦♦ Mansefield House

Corpach PH33 7LT ☎ 01397 772262 🖷 01397 772262
e-mail: mansefield@aol.com
Dir: *turn off A82 onto A830 , establishment 2m from junct on left on corner of Hill View Drive*
Mansefield House is a friendly family run guest house. The comfortable lounge has been carefully refurbished to reflect its Victorian character, with a roaring coal fire on the colder evenings. Bedrooms are prettily decorated and well-equipped. An attractive dining room with individual tables is the setting for delicious home cooked evening meals and breakfasts.
FACILITIES: 6 rms (5 en suite) (2 fmly) No smoking TVB tea/coffee No dogs (ex guide dogs) Cen ht No children 12yrs No coaches Dinner Last d Noon **PRICES:** d £40-£55✻ **LB** **PARKING:** 6 **NOTES:** Closed 24-28 Dec
CARDS:

♦♦♦♦ Seangan Croft

Seangan Bridge, Banavie PH33 7PB
☎ 01397 773114 & 01397 772228
e-mail: seangan-chalets@fortwilliam59.freeserve.co.uk
Dir: *take A82 2m N of Fort William at traffic lights and turn left onto A830. After 1m turn right onto B8004 (Gairlochy), House 2m further than Moorings Hotel opposite Crann Restaurant.*
This modern bungalow on the northside of the Caledonian Canal offers stunning views of Ben Nevis and the ski slopes of Aonach Mor. The bedrooms are contemporary in style and guests have use of a spacious and comfortable lounge. Full breakfasts are served in the neat dining room and if dinner is required guests can eat at the An Crann (The Plough) restaurant across the road, also run by Siné Ross.

continued

FACILITIES: 3 en suite No smoking TVB tea/coffee No dogs (ex guide dogs) Licensed Cen ht TVL ch fac No coaches Dinner Last d 9pm **PRICES:** s £25; d £36-£50* **LB BB PARKING:** 6 **NOTES:** Closed Nov-Feb **CARDS:**

♦♦♦ Benview
Belford Rd PH33 6ER ☎ 01397 702966
e-mail: benview@gowanbrae.co.uk
Dir: *A82 Glasgow-Inverness Road, near town centre*
Good value accommodation is offered at this friendly guesthouse which stands at the northern end of town. Bedrooms combine tasteful décor with comfortable modern appointments. There is a choice of lounges and a bright airy dining room where traditional breakfasts are served at individual tables.
FACILITIES: 11 rms (9 en suite) No smoking TVB tea/coffee No dogs (ex guide dogs) Cen ht TVL **PRICES:** s £18-£28; d £36-£54* **LB BB PARKING:** 20 **NOTES:** Closed Nov-Mar

♦♦♦ Glenlochy
Nevis Bridge PH33 6PF ☎ 01397 702909
e-mail: glenlochyguesthouse@hotmail.com
Dir: *0.5m N on A82*

Situated beside the A82 on the north side of town, the garden of this friendly family-run guesthouse marks the end of the West Highland Way. Bedrooms are comfortable and well-equipped. There is a cosy first floor lounge and a bright airy ground floor dining room, where hearty breakfasts are served at individual tables.
FACILITIES: 10 rms (8 en suite) (2 fmly) No smoking in bedrooms No smoking in dining room TVB tea/coffee No dogs (ex guide dogs) Cen ht TVL No coaches **PRICES:** s £20-£30; d £32-£56* **LB BB PARKING:** 14 **CARDS:**

Lochan Cottage
Lochyside PH33 7NX ☎ 01397 702695
At the time of going to press the Diamond classification for this establishment had not been confirmed. Please check the AA website www.theAA.com for up-to-date information.
FACILITIES: 6 en suite

Berkeley House
Belford Rd PH33 6BT ☎ 01397 701185
e-mail: berkeleyhouse67@hotmail.com
Dir: *on A82 at N end of town adjacent to St Mary's Church*
FACILITIES: 4 en suite (1 fmly) No smoking TVB tea/coffee No dogs Cen ht No coaches **PRICES:** s £20-£30; d £36-£50* **BB PARKING:** 6 **NOTES:** ★★★ Closed 23-27 Dec **CARDS:**

Lochview
Heathercroft, Argyll Rd PH33 6RE ☎ 01397 703149
01397 706138
e-mail: info@lochview.co.uk
Dir: *up hill at rdbt at West End Hotel on A82. Left into Argyll Terrace & 1st right up Heathercroft Road & follow to top*

continued

FACILITIES: 6 en suite No smoking TVB tea/coffee No dogs Cen ht No coaches **PRICES:** s £25-£35; d £40-£52* **PARKING:** 6 **NOTES:** ★★★ Closed Oct-Apr **CARDS:**

FOYERS — Map 14 NH42

♦♦♦♦ Foyers Bay House
Lochness IV2 6YB ☎ 01456 486624 01456 486337
e-mail: carol@foyersbay.co.uk
Dir: *from Inverness B862 to Dores, right (B852) 10m to Foyers. From Ft Augustus A82 onto B862 10m then left onto B852 to Foyers. House in Lower Foyers*
Situated in its own grounds featuring wooded pine slopes and abundant rhododendrons, this delightful Victorian villa enjoys stunning views of Loch Ness. The pretty bedrooms vary in size, but all are well equipped and comfortable. Delicious meals and snacks are served in the bright and airy plant filled café conservatory.
FACILITIES: 5 en suite No smoking in bedrooms TVB tea/coffee Direct dial from bedrooms No dogs (ex guide dogs) Licensed Cen ht TVL No coaches Dinner Last d 8pm **PRICES:** s £29-£40; d £48-£60* **LB PARKING:** 6 **CARDS:**

GAIRLOCH — Map 14 NG87

♦♦♦♦ The Old Inn
Flowerdale Glen IV21 2BD ☎ 01445 712006 01445 712445
e-mail: nomadscot@lineone.net
Dir: *from Inverness take A9 N over Kessock Bridge, at Tore rdbt take A835 to Garve. N of Garve A835 to Achnasheen, continue on A832 at Achnasheen rdbt to Gairloch Inn on right side of A832 opposite Gairloch harbour*
Situated close to the harbour, this well established and lively inn has an idyllic location overlooking the burn and the old bridge. As well as serving real ales, a good range of meals, featuring many seafood dishes, are served in the bars and dining areas (and at picnic tables outside on the finer days). Live music is also a feature on several evenings. Bedrooms are well equipped and attractively decorated.
FACILITIES: 14 en suite (3 fmly) No smoking in bedrooms No smoking in dining room STV TVB tea/coffee Direct dial from bedrooms Cen ht No coaches Dinner Last d 9.30pm **PRICES:** s £27.50-£40; d £49-£69* **LB MEALS:** Lunch £11.10-£21.95&alc Dinner £11.10-£21.95&alc* **PARKING:** 40 **NOTES:** Civ Wed 40 **CARDS:**

GLENBORRODALE — Map 13 NM66

Feorag House
PH36 4JP ☎ 01972 500248 01972 500285
e-mail: admin@feorag.demon.co.uk
Dir: *take corran ferry from A82 8m S of Fort William. Follow A830 to Salen then onto B8007 to Glenborrodale. Feorag House is 300yds on left beyond primary school*
FACILITIES: 3 en suite No smoking TVB tea/coffee Direct dial from bedrooms Cen ht No children 10yrs No coaches Private sea fishing Dinner Last d 8pm **PRICES:** s £80-£90; d £130-£150* **PARKING:** 4 **NOTES:** ★★★★★ **CARDS:**

GLENCOE — Map 14 NN15

♦♦♦♦ *Fern Villa*
Loanfern PH49 4JE ☎ 01855 811393 01855 811727
e-mail: aa@fernvilla.com

(For full entry see Ballachulish)

Scotland

GLENCOE continued

♦♦♦♦ Lyn-Leven
West Laroch PH49 4JP ☎ 01855 811392 📠 01855 811600
e-mail: lynleven@amserve.net

(For full entry see Ballachulish)

♦♦♦ Scorrybreac
PH49 4HT ☎ 01855 811354 📠 01855 811354
e-mail: info@scorrybreac.fsnet.co.uk
Dir: *off A82 just outside village, 500mtrs from Bridge of Coe*
This welcoming family-run guesthouse stands on a hillside above the village overlooking the loch. The individual bedrooms are comfortably furnished and offer all the expected amenities. Books and board games are provided in the lounge and enjoyable breakfasts are served at individual tables in the attractive dining room.
FACILITIES: 6 en suite (6 GF) No smoking TVB tea/coffee Cen ht No coaches Permits available for fishing 500m **PRICES:** s £20-£40; d £36-£50✳ **LB BB PARKING:** 8 **NOTES:** Closed 1 Nov-26 Dec
CARDS:

Scotland

GRANTOWN-ON-SPEY Map 14 NJ02

Premier Collection

♦♦♦♦♦ Ardconnel House
Woodlands Ter PH26 3JU ☎ 01479 872104 📠 01479 872104
e-mail: enquiry@ardconnel.com
Dir: *from SW & A95 to town, premises on left near Craiglynne Hotel*

Barbara and Michel Bouchard extend a warm and friendly welcome to guests at their delightful Victorian villa, set in spacious gardens and conveniently located within walking distance of the town centre and River Spey. Bedrooms are tastefully decorated, well equipped and beautifully furnished. There is an elegant and comfortable lounge and an atmospheric dining room where Michel's delicious meals, which combine Gallic flair and the best of local ingredients, can be enjoyed at individual tables.
FACILITIES: 6 en suite (2 fmly) No smoking TVB tea/coffee No dogs Licensed Cen ht No children 8yrs No coaches Dinner Last d by arrangement **PRICES:** s £28-£35; d £56-£70✳ **PARKING:** 6 **NOTES:** Closed Nov-Mar **CARDS:**

BB Great value! This indicates B&B for £19 and under, per person, per night.

Premier Collection

♦♦♦♦♦ The Pines
Woodside Av PH26 3JR ☎ 01479 872092 📠 01479 872092
e-mail: info@thepinesgrantown.co.uk
Dir: *at lights follow Elgin signs, then take 1st R*
This large, elegant Victorian house has been sympathetically and lovingly restored to offer extremely comfortable, well-equipped bedrooms, all individually decorated. There is a choice of lounges, including a small library packed with books and local information, and the house is full of fine period pieces, objets d'art, and paintings. The substantial breakfasts and dinners contain the best of local produce whenever possible.
FACILITIES: 8 en suite (1 GF) No smoking TVB tea/coffee Licensed Cen ht TVL No children 12yrs No coaches Dinner Last d noon **PRICES:** s £38-£48; d £66-£90✳ **LB PARKING:** 9 **NOTES:** Closed Nov-Feb
CARDS:

♦♦♦♦♦ Ravenscourt House Hotel
Seafield Av PH26 3JG ☎ 01479 872286 📠 01479 873260
Dir: *turn off A9 at Avimore onto A95 to Grantown-on-Spey, pass through traffic lights in town centre take 1st right into Seafield Avenue. Hotel is 150mtrs on right*
FACILITIES: 8 rms (7 en suite) (2 fmly) No smoking in bedrooms No smoking in dining room No smoking in 1 lounge TVB tea/coffee No dogs (ex guide dogs) Licensed Cen ht TVL No coaches Dinner Last d noon **PRICES:** s £27.50-£35; d £50-£70✳ **PARKING:** 8 **NOTES:** Closed Dec-Feb

♦♦♦♦ Garden Park
Woodside Av PH26 3JN ☎ 01479 873235 📠 01479 873235
e-mail: gardenpark@tiscali.co.uk
Dir: *turn off High Street at Forest Road, Garden Park at junction of Forest Rd & Woodside Ave*
Many guests have become regular visitors to Garden Park, a lovely Victorian villa that stands in landscaped gardens in a residential part of the town. Bedrooms vary in size and are well equipped and comfortably furnished. The relaxing lounge has a log-burning stove, while breakfast is served in the stylish dining room. Evening meals are served by arrangement.
FACILITIES: 5 en suite (1 GF) No smoking in dining room TV4B tea/coffee No dogs Licensed Cen ht TVL No children 12yrs No coaches Dinner Last d 5pm **PRICES:** s £24-£25; d £48-£50✳ **PARKING:** 8 **NOTES:** Closed Nov-Feb

♦♦♦♦ Rossmor
Woodlands Ter PH26 3JU ☎ 01479 872201 📠 01479 872201
e-mail: johnsteward.rossmor@lineone.net
Dir: *take A95 from Aviemore to Grantown-on-Spey. Left at rdbt on approach to town through pine woods, Rossmor on left opposite park*
A delightful Victorian villa situated in a quiet and slightly elevated position in a residential area close to the town centre. Bedrooms are comfortably proportioned and well equipped. The breakfast room at the front of the house is attractively appointed and enjoys lovely views of the surrounding country, as does the cosy lounge.
FACILITIES: 6 en suite (2 fmly) No smoking TVB tea/coffee No dogs Cen ht No children 16yrs No coaches **PRICES:** s £25-£28; d £46-£50✳ **LB PARKING:** 6 **CARDS:**

INVERGARRY Map 14 NH30

♦♦♦♦ Craigard

PH35 4HG ☎ 01809 501258

***Dir:** off A82 onto A87. House 1m on right*

A warm and friendly welcome awaits at this delightful family run guesthouse which stands in a well-tended garden at the edge of the village. Bedrooms are spacious and well equipped; several retain their original fireplaces. The comfortable lounge is an ideal place to relax and enjoy a wide selection of reading material. Breakfasts and, by prior arrangement, evening meals are served in the attractive dining room, which has a dispense bar.

FACILITIES: 7 rms (3 en suite) No smoking STV TVB tea/coffee No dogs (ex guide dogs) Licensed TVL No children 12yrs No coaches Dinner Last d 24hrs notice **PRICES:** s £22; d £37-£44* BB **PARKING:** 10 **CARDS:**

♦♦♦ Forest Lodge

South Laggan PH34 4EA ☎ 01809 501219 🖹 01809 501476

e-mail: info@flgh.co.uk

***Dir:** 3m SW off Invergarry on north side of A82*

Standing in its own well-tended garden south of the village, this family-run guesthouse provides a friendly and welcoming atmosphere. Well-maintained bedrooms are in both modern and traditional styles. There is a choice of comfortable lounges and a bright airy dining room where hearty Scottish breakfasts and evening meals are served at individual tables.

FACILITIES: 7 en suite (2 fmly) (3 GF) No smoking tea/coffee No dogs (ex guide dogs) Cen ht TVL No coaches Dinner Last d 6.30pm **PRICES:** d £40-£48* LB **PARKING:** 10 **CARDS:**

INVERNESS Map 14 NH64

See also Dalcross

Premier Collection

♦♦♦♦♦ Ballifeary House Hotel

10 Ballifeary Rd IV3 5PJ ☎ 01463 235572 🖹 01463 717583

e-mail: info@ballifearyhousehotel.co.uk

***Dir:** off A82, 0.5m from town centre, turn left into Bishops Rd & sharp right into Ballifeary Rd*

Situated in a peaceful residential area, close to the Eden Court Theatre and within easy walking distance of the city centre, this delightful detached house set in its own well-tended grounds offers lovely, comfortably appointed and well equipped bedrooms. There is an elegant lounge and an attractive dining room, where delicious breakfasts featuring the best of local produce are served at individual tables.

continued

Ballifeary House Hotel

FACILITIES: 5 en suite (1 GF) No smoking TVB tea/coffee No dogs (ex guide dogs) Licensed Cen ht No children 15yrs No coaches **PRICES:** s £36-£39; d £72-£78* LB **PARKING:** 8 **NOTES:** Closed 21 Dec- 31 Jan **CARDS:**

Premier Collection

♦♦♦♦♦ Moyness House

6 Bruce Gardens IV3 5EN ☎ 01463 233836

🖹 01463 233836

e-mail: stay@moyness.co.uk

***Dir:** off A82 Fort William road, almost opposite Highland Regional Council headquarters*

Situated in a quiet residential area just minutes from the city centre, this elegant Victorian villa dates from 1880 and offers beautifully decorated, comfortable bedrooms and well-fitted bathrooms. There is an attractive sitting room and an inviting dining room where traditional Scottish breakfasts are served. Guests are welcome to use the secluded and well-maintained back garden.

FACILITIES: 7 en suite (2 GF) No smoking TVB tea/coffee Cen ht No coaches **PRICES:** s £33-£37; d £66-£74* LB **PARKING:** 10 **CARDS:**

♦♦♦ Red Diamonds highlight the top establishments within the AA's 3, 4 and 5 Diamond ratings.

Scotland

INVERNESS continued

Premier Collection

♦♦♦♦♦ Trafford Bank

96 Fairfield Rd IV3 5LL ☎ 01463 241414 & 221178
e-mail: traff@pop.cali.co.uk
Dir: *Turn off A82, 2nd road on L is Fairfield Rd, 600yds on L*

This impressive Victorian villa stands in its own well-tended gardens in a quiet residential area close to the canal. Bedrooms are furnished with many attractive pieces of restored, traditional furniture, and also offer thoughtful extras. Dinner, available on request, is home-cooked by owner Peter McKenzie and served at a communal table in the elegant dining room, where outstanding breakfasts are also enjoyed.
FACILITIES: 5 en suite No smoking TVB tea/coffee Cen ht No coaches Dinner Last d 12am **PARKING:** 8 **CARDS:**

♦♦♦♦ Culduthel Lodge

14 Culduthel Rd IV2 4AG ☎ 01463 240089 📠 01463 240089
e-mail: AA@culduthel.com
Dir: *follow B861 Castle St from town centre*

Enjoying an elevated location overlooking the town, this elegant Georgian villa has been carefully restored and sympathetically extended. Bedrooms are individually decorated and furnished to a high standard, with many thoughtful extras. Public areas include a drawing room and a dining room in which freshly prepared dishes can be enjoyed.
FACILITIES: 12 en suite (1 fmly) (4 GF) No smoking in bedrooms No smoking in dining room TVB tea/coffee Direct dial from bedrooms Licensed Cen ht No coaches Dinner Last d 7pm **PRICES:** s £45-£55; d £80-£105✻ **PARKING:** 13 **CARDS:**

♦♦♦♦ Acorn House

2A Bruce Gardens IV3 5EN ☎ 01463 717021 & 240000
📠 01463 714236
e-mail: enquiries@acorn-house.freeserve.co.uk
Dir: *Acorn House is on west side of Inverness, Bruce Gdns is just as you leave Tomnahurich St on the A82. House is 5 min walk from town centre*

A friendly welcome awaits guests at this attractive detached house, only a short walk from the town centre. There is a strong Scottish theme, with bold use of tartan in decor and fabrics. Bedrooms are comfortable and well equipped. For those wishing to relax there is a Sauna and Jacuzzi available. Breakfast and dinner are served in the bright, pretty dining room, followed by coffee served in the comfortable lounge.

continued

Acorn House

FACILITIES: 6 en suite (3 fmly) No smoking in bedrooms No smoking in dining room STV TVB tea/coffee Cen ht TVL Sauna Jacuzzi Dinner Last d 8pm **PRICES:** s £35-£50; d £58-£65✻ **LB PARKING:** 7
CARDS:

♦♦♦♦ Taransay Lower Muckovie Farm *(NH707436)*

Lower Muckovie Farm IV2 5BB ☎ 01463 231880
📠 01463 231880 Mrs A Munro
e-mail: aileen@munro2.freeserve.co.uk
Dir: *A9, B9177, past Drumossie Hotel, down hill, yellow B&B sign at end of farm rd on R*

This comfortable modern home, adjacent to the family farm on the outskirts of town, offers stunning views of the Moray Firth. Attractively decorated bedrooms are cleverly designed to make good use of space, and are well equipped. There is a comfortable lounge and an adjacent dining room where substantial breakfasts are served around a communal table.
FACILITIES: 2 en suite (1 fmly) No smoking TVB tea/coffee No dogs (ex guide dogs) Cen ht TVL 170 acres dairy **PRICES:** d fr £38 **PARKING:** 3

♦♦♦♦ Westbourne

50 Huntly St IV3 5HS ☎ 01463 220700 📠 01463 220700
e-mail: richard@westbourne.org.uk
Dir: *off A9 to A82 at football stadium, straight across 3 rdbts & Friars Bridge, 1st left from bridge into Wells St, & right into Huntley St*

Westbourne Guest House lies on the banks of the River Ness, looking across to the town centre. Immaculately maintained, it offers bright modern bedrooms of varying size, all furnished in pine and well-equipped to include hair dryer and trouser press.
FACILITIES: 10 en suite (6 fmly) No smoking TVB tea/coffee Cen ht No coaches **PRICES:** s £25-£40; d £50-£80✻ **LB PARKING:** 6
CARDS:

♦♦♦ Craigside Lodge

4 Gordon Ter IV2 3HD ☎ 01463 231576 📠 01463 713409
e-mail: craigsidelodge@amserve.net
Dir: *from town centre take Castle St, then 1st on left (Old Edinburgh Rd), then take 3 1st left turns*

continued

Situated within easy walking distance of the city centre, this delightful Georgian house enjoys superb views of Inverness Castle and Ben Wyvis. Bedrooms are bright, well-equipped and comfortable. There is an elegant lounge with well-stocked bookshelves and an attractive dining room where hearty Scottish breakfasts are served at individual tables.
FACILITIES: 5 en suite No smoking in bedrooms No smoking in dining room TVB tea/coffee No dogs (ex guide dogs) Cen ht No coaches
PRICES: s fr £25; d fr £44✳ **PARKING:** 4 **CARDS:**

♦♦♦ Brae Ness Hotel
17 Ness Bank IV2 4SF ☎ 01463 712266 📠 01463 231732
e-mail: braenesshotel@aol.com
Dir: *0.25m along river bank below Inverness Castle, on B862 from town centre towards Dores*
Brae Ness is situated in a pleasant area by the riverside. It offers bedrooms that are mainly of a good size and has an attractive, front-facing dining room and a first floor lounge.
FACILITIES: 10 en suite (2 fmly) No smoking in bedrooms No smoking in dining room TVB tea/coffee No dogs (ex guide dogs) Licensed Cen ht No coaches Dinner Last d 6pm **PRICES:** s £36-£42; d £60-£68✳ **LB**
PARKING: 7 **NOTES:** Closed 14 Oct-20 May
CARDS:

♦♦♦ Hawthorn Lodge
15 Fairfield Rd IV3 5QA ☎ 01463 715516 📠 01463 221578
e-mail: ann@hawthorn-lodge.com
Dir: *from town centre, turn up Waterside to bridge. Over bridge onto Kenneth St & 2nd left into Fairfield Rd*
This charming detached house is situated in a quiet residential area, within walking distance of the town centre. The attractively decorated bedrooms, some of which are suitable for families, offer all the expected amenities. Breakfast is served at individual tables in the smart dining room.
FACILITIES: 5 rms (2 en suite) (3 fmly) No smoking in 2 bedrooms No smoking in dining room No smoking in lounges STV TVB tea/coffee No dogs Cen ht **PARKING:** 6 **CARDS:**

♦♦♦ Park
51 Glenurquhart Rd IV3 5PB ☎ 01463 231858
e-mail: hendry.robertson@connectfree.co.uk
Dir: *on A82 leaving town centre, on W side of river*

A substantial, welcoming Victorian villa with distinctive ivy-clad frontage and a neat front garden. The bedrooms are comfortable, attractively decorated and well equipped. There is a comfortable ground floor lounge and a cheerful breakfast room where traditional breakfasts are served at individual tables.
FACILITIES: 6 rms (3 en suite) (3 fmly) No smoking TVB tea/coffee Cen ht TVL No coaches **PRICES:** s £17.50-£25; d £35-£50✳ **LB BB PARKING:** 6
CARDS:

♦♦♦ St Ann's House
37 Harrowden Rd IV3 5QN ☎ 01463 236157 📠 01463 236157
e-mail: stannshous@aol.com
Dir: *at Telford Street rdbt junct A82 & A862 at W side of Friars Shott Bridge*
Just a ten-minute walk from the town centre, this small family-run hotel offers guests a warm and friendly welcome. Bedrooms are comfortable, well equipped and maintained. There is a relaxing lounge where refreshments can be enjoyed and a bright airy dining room where hearty breakfasts are served at individual tables.
FACILITIES: 6 rms (5 en suite) (1 fmly) (1 GF) No smoking in bedrooms No smoking in dining room TVB tea/coffee No dogs Licensed Cen ht TVL No coaches Board games **PRICES:** s £20-£30; d £46-£50✳ **LB**
PARKING: 4 **NOTES:** Closed Nov-Feb

♦♦♦ *Sunnyholm*
12 Mayfield Rd IV2 4AE ☎ 01463 231336 📠 01463 715788
e-mail: ago7195587@aol.com
Dir: *From town centre proceed up Castle St, continue up hill, at lights turn left into Mayfield Road, Sunnyholm is half way along on right*

Situated in a peaceful residential area within easy walking distance of the city centre, Sunnyholm offers guests comfortably proportioned well-equipped bedrooms with all the expected amenities supplied. There is an attractive lounge, and a bright airy dining room, which overlooks the well-tended colourful rear garden.
FACILITIES: 4 en suite No smoking TVB tea/coffee No dogs (ex guide dogs) Cen ht No children 3yrs No coaches **PARKING:** 6

A *Ardmuir House*
16 Ness Bank IV2 4SF ☎ 01463 231151 📠 231151
e-mail: hotel@ardmuir.com
Dir: *on E bank of river, opposite the cathedral*
FACILITIES: 11 en suite (2 fmly) No smoking in 8 bedrooms No smoking in dining room TVB tea/coffee Direct dial from bedrooms No dogs (ex guide dogs) Licensed Cen ht No coaches **PARKING:** 4 **NOTES:** ★★★
CARDS:

A Cedar Villa
33 Kenneth St IV3 5DH ☎ 01463 230477 📠 01463 230477
e-mail: cedarvilla@guesthouseinverness.co.uk
Dir: *turn off A9 onto A82 continue across Friars Bridge. At Telford St rdbt take 2nd exit into Kenneth St*
FACILITIES: 6 rms (4 en suite) (3 fmly) No smoking in dining room No smoking in lounges TVB tea/coffee No dogs (ex guide dogs) Cen ht
PRICES: s £20-£25; d £36-£50✳ **LB BB NOTES:** ★★ Closed 19-29 Dec
CARDS:

INVERNESS continued

Melrose Villa
35 Kenneth St IV3 5DH ☎ 01463 233745
e-mail: info@melrosevilla.com
Dir: *from A9 take A82 signed Fort William. Kenneth Street is part of the A82, and runs parallel with the River Ness on the West side. From Fort William approx. 2m from Inverness town centre road crosses the canal, left at traffic lights after canal bridge. into Kenneth Street.*
FACILITIES: 9 rms (7 en suite) (2 fmly) No smoking in 4 bedrooms No smoking in dining room No smoking in lounges TVB tea/coffee Cen ht No coaches **PRICES:** s £20-£25; d £36-£50* BB **NOTES:** ★★★ Closed 15-28 Dec **CARDS:**

JOHN O'GROATS Map 15 ND37

♦♦♦ Bencorragh House
Upper Gills, Canisbay KW1 4YD ☎ 01955 611449 📠 01955 611449
e-mail: bartonsandy@hotmail.com
Dir: *A99 (3m S of John O'Groats), signed to Canisbay. 2nd turn left after 3.5m, 2nd house on L*
From it high position, this working croft enjoys superb panoramic views over the Pentland Firth. This is home to a variety of animals and livestock including ducks, cats and Irish Setters. The house is most attractive, with nicely appointed bedrooms and a choice of lounges, one a conservatory that doubles as the dining room.
FACILITIES: 3 en suite (1 fmly) (3 GF) No smoking tea/coffee Cen ht TVL No coaches Dinner Last d 7pm **PRICES:** s £25-£30; d £42-£44 **PARKING:** 4 **NOTES:** rs Dec-Feb **CARDS:**

KINGUSSIE Map 14 NH70

Premier Collection

♦♦♦♦♦ Osprey Hotel
Ruthven Rd PH21 1EN ☎ 01540 661510 📠 01540 661510
e-mail: aileen@ospreyhotel.co.uk
Dir: *turn of A9 into Kingussie, hotel at the S end of main street*

This smartly presented, family-run house close to the centre of the village has a well-deserved reputation for fine food and warm hospitality. Dinner is a lavish affair that makes excellent use of local ingredients whilst hearty breakfasts include home-baked breads and preserves. Bedrooms vary in size and style and all are comfortable.
FACILITIES: 8 en suite (2 GF) No smoking in 6 bedrooms No smoking in dining room No smoking in 1 lounge TVB tea/coffee Licensed Cen ht TVL No coaches Dinner Last d 6.30pm **PRICES:** s £45-£59; d £84-£112* **LB CARDS:**

♦♦♦♦ Avondale House
Newtonmore Rd PH21 1HF ☎ 01540 661731 📠 01540 662362
e-mail: avondalehouse@talk21.com
Dir: *turn off A9 to Kingussie/Newtonmore, pass through Newtonmore, Avondale House is on main road at S side of town*
Built in 1907, this delightful Edwardian house stands in its own well-tended gardens to the south of the village. Bedrooms, which include a ground floor room are tastefully decorated and furnished. There is a comfortable lounge and an attractive dining room where delicious evening meals and breakfasts are served at individual tables.
FACILITIES: 4 en suite (3 fmly) (1 GF) No smoking TVB tea/coffee Cen ht Drying facilities, storage/workshop for bikes/skis Dinner Last d noon **PRICES:** s £19-£25; d £38-£50* **LB** BB **CONF:** Class 8 **PARKING:** 11 **NOTES:** Closed Xmas **CARDS:**

♦♦♦♦ Columba House Hotel & Restaurant
Manse Rd PH21 1JF ☎ 01540 661402 📠 01540 661652
e-mail: reservations@columbahousehotel.co.uk
Dir: *exit A9 at Kingussie/Kincraig onto A86. Turn onto Manse Road, hotel is 2nd on left*
Myra Shearer delights in welcoming guests old and new to this comfortable small hotel, standing in its own grounds on the northern edge of town. Bedrooms include two four-poster rooms and a family suite, and are comfortably furnished and offer a good range of amenities and thoughtful personal touches. The lounge, with its welcoming open fire, invites relaxation and enjoyable home cooked fare is served in the attractive dining room overlooking the garden. At the time of our visit work had just started on the new restaurant extension.
FACILITIES: 5 en suite 5 annexe en suite (3 fmly) No smoking in 4 bedrooms No smoking in dining room TVB tea/coffee Direct dial from bedrooms Licensed Cen ht TVL ch fac No coaches Dinner **PRICES:** s £35-£50; d £60-£70* **LB CONF:** Thtr 60 Class 40 Board 40 Del from £45 * **PARKING:** 30 **CARDS:**

Arden House
Newtonmore Rd PH21 1HE ☎ 01540 661369 📠 01540 661369
e-mail: ardenhouse@tiscali.co.uk
Dir: *250yds S of traffic lights in centre of town, on right hand side, opposite Catholic Church*
FACILITIES: 5 rms (3 en suite) (1 fmly) (1 GF) No smoking TVB tea/coffee Cen ht TVL No coaches Dinner Last d 5pm **PRICES:** s £22-£26; d £38-£46* **LB** BB **PARKING:** 6 **NOTES:** ★★★ **CARDS:**

KINLOCHBERVIE Map 14 NC25

♦♦♦ Old School Hotel
Inshegra IV27 4RH ☎ 01971 521383 📠 01971 521383
Dir: *from A838 at Rhiconich take B801 to Kinlochbervie, 2m on L*
This former schoolhouse lies between Rhiconich and Kinlochbervie and enjoys stunning sea loch views from its elevated position. Now a pleasant restaurant, it retains much of its original character. The attractive well-equipped bedrooms are contained in a modern house, whilst a cosy single room is set on its own behind the main building.
FACILITIES: 6 annexe rms (4 en suite) (1 fmly) (6 GF) No smoking in dining room No smoking in 1 lounge TVB tea/coffee Direct dial from bedrooms Licensed Cen ht No coaches Dinner Last d 8pm **PRICES:** s £24-£29; d £48-£58* **PARKING:** 10 **NOTES:** Closed 25 Dec & 1 Jan **CARDS:**

KYLE OF LOCHALSH — Map 13 NG72

♦♦♦♦ The Old Schoolhouse
Tigh Fasgaidh, Erbusaig IV40 8BB ☎ 01599 534369
01599 534369
e-mail: cuminecandJ@lineout.net
Dir: *turn right in Kyle of Lochalsh towards Plockton. Follow road for 2m to arrive at Erbusaig. Do not enter village on left but continue for 0.25m, house on right*
Situated in the quiet hamlet of Erbusaig, just north of The Skye Bridge, this former school has been skilfully converted to a family home and guesthouse. Bedrooms are homely and well equipped and the lounge is very cosy, with a real fire and small dispense bar. The spacious dining room provides a pleasant environment to enjoy chef/patron Calum Cumine's carefully prepared and tasty dinners.
FACILITIES: 3 en suite No smoking in dining room TVB tea/coffee Licensed Cen ht No coaches Dinner Last d 5pm **PRICES:** s £35-£40; d £50-£58* **PARKING:** 15 **NOTES:** Closed 11 Oct-21 Oct & 22 Dec-12 Jan
CARDS:

KYLESKU — Map 14 NC23

♦♦♦♦ Newton Lodge Hotel
IV27 4HW ☎ 01971 502070 01971 502070
e-mail: newtonlge@aol.com
Dir: *1.5m S on A894*
Situated in an elevated position well back from the road, south of Kylesku Bridge, this imposing purpose built private hotel commands breathtaking loch and mountain views. The delightful lounge and bright airy conservatory make the most of the spectacular panorama, whilst the dining room is an attractive setting, where dinner might feature locally caught seafood. The comfortable bedrooms are well equipped and smartly furnished.
FACILITIES: 7 en suite (3 GF) No smoking TVB tea/coffee Licensed Cen ht TVL No children 13yrs No coaches Dinner Last d 7.30pm
PRICES: d fr £90* **PARKING:** 10 **NOTES:** Closed Oct-Apr
CARDS:

MELVICH — Map 14 NC86

Premier Collection

♦♦♦♦♦ Sheiling
KW14 7YJ ☎ 01641 531256 531256
e-mail: thesheiling@btinternet.com
Dir: *17m W of Thurso, on A836 coastal road*
Enjoying an elevated position to the east of the village, the Sheiling enjoys glorious and unobstructed sea views. The attractive bedrooms are comfortable and are equipped with a host of thoughtful extras. There are two lounges available for guest use, and both offer a good range of leisure pursuits. Hearty breakfasts are served in the elegant dining room.
FACILITIES: 3 en suite No smoking tea/coffee No dogs (ex guide dogs) Cen ht TVL No children 5yrs No coaches **PRICES:** d £52* **PARKING:** 5 **NOTES:** Closed Nov-Mar **CARDS:**

Prices may change during the currency of the Guide, please check when booking.

PORTNANCON — Map 14 NC46

♦♦♦♦ Port-Na-Con House
Loch Eriboll IV27 4UN ☎ 01971 511367 01971 511367
e-mail: portnacon70@hotmail.com
Dir: *0.25m off A838, on shore of loch, 6m SE of Durness*
Great food and hospitality are all part of the appeal at this haven of tranquillity, set on the shores of Loch Eriboll. Bedrooms, the conservatory extension and the lounge all have delightful views. Downstairs, fresh produce is the order of the day, where both the dinner menu and wine list offer an impressive choice.
FACILITIES: 3 en suite (1 fmly) No smoking tea/coffee Licensed Cen ht No coaches Golf 9 Dinner Last d 5pm **PRICES:** s £27-£28; d £38-£40* BB
PARKING: 6 **CARDS:**

SPEAN BRIDGE — Map 14 NN28

♦♦♦♦ Corriechoille Lodge
PH34 4EY ☎ 01397 712002 01397 712002
e-mail: enquiry@corriechoille.com
Dir: *off A82, signed Corriechoille, for 2.25m, keeping left at road fork at 10mph sign. At end of tarmac road, turn right up hill & then left*
This fine country house is set above the River Spean. Magnificent views towards the Nevis Range and surrounding mountains can be enjoyed from the comfortable first floor lounge and some of the spacious and well appointed bedrooms. Friendly and attentive service is provided, as are traditional breakfasts and delicious evening meals (by prior arrangement).
FACILITIES: 5 en suite (2 fmly) (1 GF) No smoking TVB tea/coffee No dogs (ex guide dogs) Licensed Cen ht No children 7yrs No coaches Dinner Last d noon **PRICES:** s £30-£34; d £46-£54* **PARKING:** 7 **NOTES:** Closed Nov-Feb **CARDS:**

♦♦♦♦ Distant Hills
PH34 4EU ☎ 01397 712452 01397 712452
e-mail: enquiry@distanthills.com
Dir: *turn off A82 from Fort William to Inverness onto A86 at junct in village of Spean Bridge. Establishment 0.5m on right*
A warm and friendly welcome is assured at this family-run guesthouse set in its own well-tended garden. Bedrooms are maintained to a high standard with tasteful modern appointments. There is a spacious split-level lounge, which enjoys access to the large garden. Enjoyable home cooked evening meals and hearty Scottish breakfasts are served at individual tables.
FACILITIES: 7 en suite (1 fmly) No smoking in bedrooms No smoking in dining room TVB tea/coffee Cen ht TVL No coaches Dinner Last d 2pm
PRICES: s £20-£30; d £40-£50 **PARKING:** 10 **NOTES:** Closed Xmas rs Nov-Jan **CARDS:**

♦♦♦♦ The Smiddy House
Roy Bridge Rd PH34 4EU ☎ 01397 712335 01397 712043
e-mail: accommodation@smiddyhouse.com
Dir: *At junct of A82 Inverness & A86 Newtonmore*
The atmosphere at this house hotel is relaxed and friendly, with the attractive lounge offering good levels of comfort. In the evenings delicious food is served in the lively Bistro. The bedrooms are tastefully decorated, comfortably furnished in pine and well equipped.
FACILITIES: 4 en suite (1 fmly) No smoking in bedrooms No smoking in area of dining room TVB tea/coffee Licensed Cen ht No coaches Golf 9 Dinner Last d 9.30pm **PRICES:** s £25-£45; d £45* LB **PARKING:** 20
CARDS:

Scotland

STRATHPEFFER Map 14 NH45

Premier Collection

♦♦♦♦♦ Craigvar

The Square IV14 9DL ☎ 01997 421622 📠 01997 421796
e-mail: craigvar@talk21.com

Craigvar is an elegant Victorian house that occupies an elevated position overlooking the Square of the historic Highland Spa town. Two bedrooms, one of which has a four-poster bed, are on the first floor, with the third on the ground floor. There is a comfortable lounge and a delightful breakfast room where traditional Scottish breakfasts featuring the best of local produce are served.

FACILITIES: 3 en suite No smoking TVB tea/coffee Direct dial from bedrooms No dogs (ex guide dogs) Cen ht No coaches
PARKING: 7 **NOTES:** Closed Xmas & New Year **CARDS:**

♦♦♦♦ Dunraven Lodge

Golf Course Rd IV14 9AS ☎ 01997 421210
e-mail: sandra.iddon@ntlworld.com
Dir: *from Inverness take A9 N to roundabout and take 2nd exit (A835) to Dingwall. At next rdbt take A862 through Dingwall, at traffic lights turn left onto A834 to Strathpeffer. Turn right after shops into Golf Course Rd, 2nd house on right past Holly Lodge Hotel*

Built between 1899-1901 for two sisters, on land gifted to them by the Earl of Cromerty, this delightful house stands in extensive grounds overlooking Strathpeffer. Bedrooms are spacious, comfortable and well equipped, with large French windows opening onto balconies that enjoy stunning views. There is a peaceful ground floor dining room where delicious traditional Scottish breakfasts are served at individual tables.

FACILITIES: 3 en suite (1 fmly) No smoking STV TVB tea/coffee Cen ht No coaches Snooker Children's play area in garden **PRICES:** s £27-£32; d £45-£54 **LB** **PARKING:** 5 **CARDS:**

♦♦♦ Inver Lodge

IV14 9DL ☎ 01997 421392
e-mail: derbyshire@inverlg.fsnet.co.uk
Dir: *from A834 through Strathpeffer centre, turn beside Spa Pavilion signed Bowling Green. Inver Lodge on right*

Guests are assured of a warm welcome at this Victorian lodge, which is situated within easy walking distance of the town centre. Bedrooms are comfortable and well equipped. Imaginative breakfasts, and by prior arrangement, enjoyable home-cooked evening meals, are served at a communal table.

FACILITIES: 2 rms (1 fmly) No smoking TVB tea/coffee No dogs Cen ht No coaches Fishing and riding can be arranged Last d 4pm **PRICES:** s £21-£25; d £32-£34* **LB** **BB** **PARKING:** 2 **NOTES:** Closed mid Dec-Feb
CARDS:

STRATHY POINT Map 14 NC86

♦♦♦♦ Catalina

Aultivullin KW14 7RY ☎ 01641 541395 📠 0870 124 7960
e-mail: jane@catalina72.freeserve.co.uk
Dir: *turn off A836 at Strathy onto Strathy Point Rd, 1.5m then turn left & follow 1m to end*

Enjoying a stunning setting close to the sea and remote enough to inspire peace and tranquillity, this former croft house provides the ultimate getaway location for those who wish to simply relax. The only guest bedroom is self-contained in a wing that includes a dining room, a cosy lounge with TV and lots of reading material. Meal times are flexible, as Jane and Pete believe in providing dinner and breakfast at times suitable to their guests.

FACILITIES: 1 en suite (1 GF) No smoking TVB tea/coffee No dogs Cen ht TVL No children No coaches Bird watching Dinner Last d any time
PRICES: s £20-£30; d £34-£40* **BB** **PARKING:** 2

TAIN Map 14 NH78

♦♦♦♦ Golf View House

13 Knockbreck Rd IV19 1BN ☎ 01862 892856 📠 01862 892172
e-mail: golfview@btinternet.com
Dir: *1st right off A9 at Tain (B9174), follow for 0.5m, house signposted on right*

Formerly a manse, Golf View House enjoys stunning views across the nearby golf course to the Dornoch Firth beyond. Bedrooms are attractively decorated and comfortably appointed in both modern and traditional styles. There is a comfortable lounge, and the dining room, with individual beech tables, is the setting for traditional breakfasts featuring the best of local produce.

FACILITIES: 5 rms (3 en suite) (1 fmly) No smoking STV TVB tea/coffee No dogs (ex guide dogs) Cen ht TVL No coaches **PRICES:** s £25-£35; d £46-£50* **PARKING:** 7 **NOTES:** Closed Dec-Jan **CARDS:**

♦♦♦♦ Aldie House

IV19 1LZ ☎ 01862 893787 📠 01862 893787
e-mail: info@aldiehouse.co.uk
Dir: *from Inverness, 500yds before Tain on A9, turn left and follow private road*

continued

Spacious bedrooms and comfortable public areas are a feature of Aldie House, set in 10 acres of attractive grounds, with views across rolling fields. A substantial freshly cooked breakfast is offered and the proprietors genuinely welcome guests to their home.
FACILITIES: 3 en suite (2 fmly) No smoking TVB tea/coffee No dogs (ex guide dogs) Cen ht No coaches **PRICES:** s £30-£32; d £48-£52* **LB**
PARKING: 7 **CARDS:**

ULLAPOOL Map 14 NH19

♦♦♦♦ Dromnan

Garve Rd IV26 2SX ☎ 01854 612333 📠 01854 613364
e-mail: info@dromnan.co.uk
Dir: *from A835 S, on entering town turn left at 30mph sign*
This charming house is situated in well-tended gardens on the outskirts of the fishing village of Ullapool. Bedrooms are attractive, comfortable and well equipped; the ground floor bedroom is suitable for those with limited mobility. Traditional Scottish breakfasts are served at individual tables in the tastefully furnished open plan dining room.
FACILITIES: 7 en suite (2 fmly) No smoking TVB tea/coffee No dogs (ex guide dogs) Cen ht TVL **PRICES:** d £48-£54* **PARKING:** 7
CARDS:

WICK Map 15 ND35

♦♦♦♦ The Clachan

13 Randolph Place, South Rd KW1 5NJ ☎ 01955 605384
e-mail: enquiry@theclachan.co.uk
Dir: *1st house on right on S side of Wick*
A warm welcome is assured at this immaculately maintained detached home by the main road on the edge of the town. Though not spacious, the bright airy bedrooms (all on the ground floor) are tastefully decorated and offer lots of thoughtful touches. Breakfast is served at individual tables in the attractive lounge/dining room.
FACILITIES: 3 en suite (3 GF) No smoking TVB tea/coffee No dogs Cen ht TVL No children 12yrs **PRICES:** s £25-£30; d £40-£44*
PARKING: 3 **NOTES:** Closed Xmas & New Year

MIDLOTHIAN

GOREBRIDGE Map 11 NT36

Ivory House

14 Vogrie Rd EH23 4HH ☎ 01875 820755 📠 01875 823345
e-mail: barbara@ivory-house.co.uk
Dir: *A7 S from Edinurgh, left into B704 pass Inn Garage, 1st left, 1st right, 300mtrs on right. From A68 onto B6372 into Gorebridge 3rd right turning, 200mtrs on left.*
FACILITIES: 4 en suite (1 fmly) No smoking TVB tea/coffee No dogs Cen ht TVL **PRICES:** s £35-£45; d £60-£90* **LB PARKING:** 6 **NOTES:** ★★★★
CARDS:

ROSLIN Map 11 NT26

♦♦♦ *Olde Original Rosslyn*

4 Main St EH25 9LE ☎ 0131 440 2384 📠 0131 4402514
This delightful village inn offers a good range of eating options. In addition to the attractive Victorian restaurant, both the lounge and conservatory provide a comprehensive selection of bar meals. Bedrooms, four of which have four-poster beds, are all well equipped and comfortable.

continued

Olde Original Rosslyn Inn

FACILITIES: 6 en suite STV TVB tea/coffee Cen ht Last d 10pm
PARKING: 14 **CARDS:**

MORAY

ELGIN Map 15 NJ26

Premier Collection

♦♦♦♦♦ The Croft

10 Institution Rd IV30 1QX ☎ 01343 546004 📠 546004
e-mail: thecroft_elgin@etn.org
Dir: *turn off A96 at Safeway and down Queen St turn right at bottom*
Built in 1848 this distinguished Victorian mansion is set in attractive gardens a short distance from the town centre. The pretty bedrooms are spacious, comfortable and well-equipped. There is an elegant lounge, which overlooks the delightful rear garden, and a peaceful dining room where hearty breakfasts are served at a well-appointed communal table.
FACILITIES: 3 en suite (1 fmly) No smoking TVB tea/coffee No dogs Cen ht No coaches **PRICES:** d £52-£56* **PARKING:** 6

♦♦♦♦ Lodge

20 Duff Av IV30 1QS ☎ 01343 549981 📠 01343 540527
e-mail: thelodgeguesthouse@talk21.com
Dir: *from A96 Aberdeen turn L at 3rd rdbt & 5th road on R*
Built in 1895 for a wealthy tea merchant, the Lodge is an impressive establishment set in its own well-tended grounds. Bedrooms are well-equipped and attractively decorated. The spacious lounge is comfortable and enjoys lovely views from the turret window to the garden. Traditional breakfasts are served at individual tables in the dining room.
FACILITIES: 8 en suite (1 fmly) No smoking in bedrooms No smoking in dining room TVB tea/coffee Cen ht TVL No coaches **PRICES:** s £25-£40; d £48-£50* **PARKING:** 9 **CARDS:**

The Pines

East Rd IV30 1XG ☎ 01343 552495 📠 01343 552495
e-mail: thepines@talk21.com
Dir: *East end of Elgin on the A96 rd between Inverness & Aberdeen*
FACILITIES: 6 en suite (1 fmly) No smoking TVB tea/coffee No dogs (ex guide dogs) Cen ht No coaches **PRICES:** s £30-£45; d £44-£48*
PARKING: 10 **NOTES:** ★★★★ Closed 23 Dec-7 Jan
CARDS:

Scotland

FOCHABERS — Map 15 NJ35

♦♦♦ Castlehill Farm *(NJ310600)*

Blackdam IV32 7LJ ☎ 01343 820351 Fax 01343 821856
Mrs A Shand
Feb-Nov
Dir: *6m E of Elgin & 3m W of Fochabers on A96.*
Castlehill Farm is situated in gently rolling countryside close to the River Spey, convenient for a number of local golf courses, distilleries and castles. Bedrooms, both of which are situated on the ground floor are attractively decorated and well-equipped. There is a cosy lounge/dining room complete with roaring coal fire.
FACILITIES: 2 rms (1 en suite) No smoking tea/coffee No dogs (ex guide dogs) Cen ht TVL No children 224 acres mixed **PRICES:** d £32-£44* **LB BB** **PARKING:** 4

FORRES — Map 14 NJ05

♦♦♦♦ Knockomie Lodge

IV36 2SG ☎ 01309 676785 Fax 01309 676785
e-mail: welcome@knockomie.com
Dir: *A940, Forres to Grantown-on-Spey road, 1m from Forres on right*
Knockomie Lodge is a former gatehouse set in a pretty rural location, within easy reach of the town centre. The well-equipped bedrooms are attractively decorated and comfortably proportioned. Public areas include a relaxing lounge and a smart dining room, where hearty Scottish breakfasts are served.
FACILITIES: 3 en suite (1 fmly) (1 GF) No smoking TVB tea/coffee No dogs (ex guide dogs) Cen ht No coaches Dinner Last d 3pm **PRICES:** s £25-£35; d £38-£45* **BB** **PARKING:** 6 **CARDS:**

GLENLIVET — Map 15 NJ12

♦♦♦ Roadside Cottage

Tomnavoulin AB37 9JL ☎ 01807 590486 Fax 01807 590486
Dir: *on B9008 Tomintoul to Dufftown Rd, 0.75m S of Tomnavoulin*
A relaxed and friendly atmosphere is offered at this comfortable roadside cottage. Bedrooms are bright and airy with mixed modern furnishings and offer the expected amenities. Public areas include a cosy lounge and enjoyable home cooked fare is served in the open plan kitchen.
FACILITIES: 2 rms (1 fmly) TVB tea/coffee Cen ht No coaches Dinner Last d on request **PRICES:** s £16-£18; d £32-£36* **LB BB** **PARKING:** 9 **NOTES:** Closed 20 Dec-6 Jan **CARDS:**

HOPEMAN — Map 15 NJ16

♦♦♦♦ Ardent House

43 Forsyth St IV30 5SY ☎ 01343 830694 Fax 01343 830694
e-mail: normaardent@aol.com
Dir: *A9 to Inverness, A96 to Elgin, B9012 to Hopeman. Ardent House on main road opposite Bowling Green*
Norma MacPherson takes great pleasure in welcoming guests to her delightful home, which stands in a lovely walled rose garden. The attractive bedrooms are modern in style and well equipped, with many thoughtful extra touches. Breakfast, which includes home-smoked fish, fresh garden produce and delicious home-baking, is an excellent start to the day.
FACILITIES: 3 rms (1 en suite) (1 GF) No smoking TVB tea/coffee No dogs (ex guide dogs) Cen ht TVL No coaches **PRICES:** s £19-£30; d £32-£44* **BB** **PARKING:** 4 **NOTES:** Closed 13 Dec-3 Jan

KEITH — Map 15 NJ45

♦♦♦♦ The Haughs

AB55 6QN ☎ 01542 882238 Fax 01542 882238
e-mail: jiwjackson@aol.com
Apr-Oct
Dir: *0.5m from Keith off A96, signed Inverness*

A warm welcome is assured at this comfortable farmhouse on the outskirts of town. The bright airy bedrooms are spacious and have a good range of accessories. Public areas include a relaxing lounge and separate dining room overlooking the garden.
FACILITIES: 3 en suite (1 fmly) No smoking in bedrooms No smoking in dining room TVB tea/coffee No dogs (ex guide dogs) Cen ht TVL No coaches Dinner Last d 3pm **PRICES:** s £25-£27* **PARKING:** 10

LOSSIEMOUTH — Map 15 NJ27

♦♦♦ Carmania

45 St Gerardines Rd IV31 6JX ☎ 01343 812276
e-mail: jennifertoye@btinternet.com
Dir: *enter town from Elgin A941, branch left up hill. House on left just over brow*
Carmania is a smart detached bungalow, set in a well-tended garden in an elevated position. Bedrooms, both of which are on the ground floor are attractively decorated and well-maintained. The combined lounge/dining room is the setting for hearty breakfasts featuring the best of local produce served at a large communal table.
FACILITIES: 2 en suite (2 GF) No smoking TVB tea/coffee No dogs (ex guide dogs) Cen ht TVL No children 12yrs No coaches **PRICES:** d fr £37* **BB** **PARKING:** 2 **NOTES:** Closed Nov-Mar

♦♦♦ Lossiemouth House

33 Clifton Rd IV31 6DP ☎ 01343 813397 Fax 813397
e-mail: frances@lossiehouse.freeserve.co.uk
Dir: *enter town from Elgin on A941, house on right before police station by the East Beach*
There's a friendly welcoming atmosphere at this 16th-century dower house which stands in its own beautifully tended walled garden, close to the beach. The comfortable bedrooms are individual in style. There is a relaxing lounge with a wide range of tourist information. Breakfast is served in the separate dining room.
FACILITIES: 4 rms (2 en suite) (2 fmly) No smoking in 2 bedrooms No smoking in dining room No smoking in lounges TVB tea/coffee Cen ht TVL No coaches Last d noon **PRICES:** s £18-£22; d £32-£40* **BB** **PARKING:** 6

Scotland

NORTH AYRSHIRE

BEITH Map 10 NS35

♦♦♦ Shotts Farm *(NS363500)*
KA15 1LB ☎ 01505 502273 Fax 01505 502273 Mrs J Gillan
e-mail: gurlston@hotmail.com
Dir: *A736/A737 take B706 to Barnhill/Greenhills, follow B&B signs*
A relaxed and friendly atmosphere prevails at this working dairy farm, which is situated in peaceful rolling countryside. Bedrooms are comfortable, well-appointed and equipped. There is a separate guest lounge, but most guests prefer to meet and chat in the spacious lounge/dining room that overlooks the pretty garden.
FACILITIES: 3 rms (1 en suite) (1 fmly) (2 GF) TVB tea/coffee No dogs Cen ht TVL 200 acres dairy Dinner Last d 10am **PRICES:** s fr £15; d fr £30* **BB**
PARKING: 3

LARGS Map 10 NS25

♦♦♦♦ Lea-Mar
20 Douglas St KA30 8PS ☎ 01475 672447 Fax 01475 672447
e-mail: leamar.guesthouse@fsbdial.co.uk
Dir: *take A78, on reaching town turn left at sign for Brisbane Glen/Inverclyde Sports Centre. Lea-Mar 100yds on right*
A friendly welcome awaits guests at this well maintained detached house located in a quiet residential street, close to the seafront. Pine-furnished en suite bedrooms are thoughtfully equipped. There is a smartly furnished guest lounge with TV and video. Hearty breakfasts are served at individual tables in the separate dining room.
FACILITIES: 4 en suite No smoking TVB tea/coffee No dogs (ex guide dogs) Cen ht TVL No children 12yrs No coaches **PRICES:** d £46-£50* **LB**
PARKING: 4 **NOTES:** Closed Feb, Xmas & New Year
CARDS:

♦♦♦♦ South Whittlieburn *(NS218632)*
Brisbane Glen KA30 8SN ☎ 01475 675881 Fax 01475 675080
Mrs M Watson
e-mail: largsbandb@southwhittlieburnfarm.freeserve.co.uk
Dir: *2m NE of Largs town centre, off road signed Brisbane Glen, just past leisure complex*
This comfortable and welcoming farmhouse on a working sheep farm lies two miles from town and is surrounded by gently rolling countryside. Bedrooms are attractively decorated and well-equipped, with many thoughtful extras. There is a spacious ground floor lounge and a bright airy dining room where delicious breakfasts are served.
FACILITIES: 3 en suite (1 fmly) No smoking in bedrooms No smoking in dining room TVB tea/coffee No dogs (ex guide dogs) Cen ht TVL farming activities 155 acres sheep/horses **PRICES:** s fr £21.50; d fr £43* **LB**
PARKING: 10

♦♦♦♦ Whin Park
16 Douglas St KA30 8PS ☎ 01475 673437 Fax 01475 687291
e-mail: enquiries@whinpark.co.uk
Dir: *off A78 at Brisbane Glen sign*
Situated a short stroll from the seafront, this comfortable bungalow takes its name from the gorse bushes which grow in profusion on the surrounding hillsides. Bedrooms, one of which is on the ground floor are attractively decorated and well-equipped. There is an elegant lounge and a lovely dining room.
FACILITIES: 5 en suite (1 fmly) (1 GF) No smoking in bedrooms No smoking in dining room TVB tea/coffee No dogs (ex guide dogs) No coaches **PRICES:** s fr £25; d fr £50* **PARKING:** 4 **NOTES:** Closed Feb
CARDS:

SALTCOATS Map 10 NS24

♦♦♦♦ Lochwood Farm Steading *(NS265450)*
KA21 6NG ☎ 01294 552529 Fax 01294 553315 Mrs E Murdoch
e-mail: elaine@lochwoodfarm.fsbusiness.co.uk
Dir: *1m off the Saltcoats/Dalry road*
Set in rolling countryside this immaculately maintained offers warm and friendly hospitality coupled with delicious food. The attractive bedrooms are comfortably furnished and well-equipped. There is a cosy lounge, which overlooks the surrounding countryside, and a spacious dining room where hearty farmhouse fare is served at a well appointed, large communal tables.
FACILITIES: 4 en suite (4 GF) No smoking in bedrooms No smoking in dining room No smoking in 1 lounge TVB tea/coffee No dogs (ex guide dogs) Cen ht Pool Table Jacuzzi 200 acres Beef & Dairy Dinner Last d 12hr notice **PRICES:** s £25-£29; d £40-£48* **LB PARKING:** 8
CARDS:

Scotland

NORTH LANARKSHIRE

AIRDRIE Map 11 NS76

♦♦♦♦ Easter Glentore Farm *(NS803717)*
Slamannan Rd, Greengairs ML6 7TJ ☎ 01236 830243
Fax 01236 830243 Mrs E C Hunter
e-mail: hunter@glentore.freeserve.co.uk
Dir: *A73 onto B803 to Greengairs and Slamannan, continue for 3.5m, farm is on the right between the 2 villages*
This lovely 18th-century farmhouse is situated between Stirling and Glasgow and is convenient for the new Falkirk Wheel. The comfortable and well-equipped bedrooms are all located on the ground floor. The attractive dining room is an appropriate setting for delicious farmhouse breakfasts and the spacious lounge is a conceivable and comfortable room giving fine views over rolling countryside towards the northern mountains.
FACILITIES: 3 en suite No smoking TVB tea/coffee No dogs Cen ht TVL 240 acres sheep **PRICES:** s £30-£35; d £42-£48* **LB PARKING:** 6
CARDS:

AIRDRIE continued

♦♦♦♦ Shawlee Cottage

108 Lauchope St, Chapelhall ML6 8SW ☎ 01236 753774
📠 01236 749300
e-mail: cathy@csaitken.fsbusiness.co.uk
Dir: *M8 junct 6, head for Aidrie on A73. First village is Chapelhall. Left at traffic lights onto the B799. Shawlee 600yds on right*

Shawlee Cottage, the family home of Sandy and Cathy Aitken, is ideally located for the motorway and rail networks, and within easy reach of Edinburgh and Glasgow. This delightful cottage dates back to the 1800s and has comfortable, well-equipped bedrooms, suitable for guests with limited mobility, benefiting from wide doors and a wheelchair ramp at the entrance. Scottish breakfasts (and dinner by prior arrangement) are served in the attractive dining room.
FACILITIES: 5 en suite (5 GF) No smoking TVB tea/coffee Direct dial from bedrooms No dogs (ex guide dogs) Cen ht No coaches Dinner **PRICES:** s £30-£35; d £45-£50✻ **PARKING:** 6 **CARDS:**

♦♦♦ Rosslee

107 Forrest St ML6 7AR ☎ 01236 765865 📠 01236 748535
e-mail: alanrgh@blueyonder.co.uk
Dir: *1m E on A89*
In neat gardens set well back from the road on the eastern edge of the town, this licensed guesthouse offers modern-style bedrooms in a variety of sizes. There is an inviting lounge and an attractive dining room where breakfast is served at individual tables.
FACILITIES: 6 rms (4 en suite) (2 fmly) No smoking in dining room TVB tea/coffee Licensed Cen ht TVL No coaches **PRICES:** s £20-£25; d £40-£50✻ **PARKING:** 8

A Calder

13 Main St, Calderbank ML6 9SG ☎ 01236 769077
📠 01236 750506
e-mail: calderguesthouse@blueyonder.co.uk
Dir: *Travelling from E take M8 which runs onto small section of A8 take B802 cut off to Calderbank. From W, take cut off to B799 then B802 off motorway. Calderhouse is next to primary school on main street of Calderbank village*
FACILITIES: 4 rms (1 en suite) (1 fmly) No smoking TVB tea/coffee Cen ht TVL No coaches Pool Table **PRICES:** s £25; d £50✻
PARKING: 6 **NOTES:** ★★★

COATBRIDGE — Map 11 NS76

♦♦♦ Auchenlea

153 Langmuir Rd, Bargeddie G69 7RT
☎ 0141 771 6870 & 07775 791381 📠 0141 771 6870
Dir: *turn off A8 onto A752, 0.5m on right before A89*
Backing onto farmland, yet only a short distance from the motorway, this cottage-style house is well placed for both Glasgow and Edinburgh. Satisfying, well-cooked breakfasts are served at the communal table in the dining room and there is a summerhouse in the garden where guests can relax. The comfortable bedrooms are modern in style.
FACILITIES: 5 en suite (1 fmly) (5 GF) No smoking in bedrooms No smoking in dining room No smoking in lounges TVB tea/coffee No dogs (ex guide dogs) Cen ht TVL **PRICES:** s fr £25; d fr £40✻ **PARKING:** 8

PERTH & KINROSS

BLAIR ATHOLL — Map 14 NN86

♦♦♦♦ Dalgreine Guest House

Bridge of Tilt PH18 5SX ☎ 01796 481276 📠 01796 481276
Dir: *turn off A9 at Blair Atholl sign. Pass Esso garage on left, next left, then left again Dalgreine 20yds on right*

This pretty guest house sits in its own well-tended gardens, close to the heart of the village and Blair Castle. Bedrooms, with pretty colour schemes, are comfortably furnished and offer all the expected amenities. A comfortable lounge is available for guests' relaxation, and enjoyable home cooked fare is served in the adjacent dining room.
FACILITIES: 6 rms (3 en suite) (1 fmly) No smoking tea/coffee No dogs (ex guide dogs) Cen ht TVL No coaches Dinner Last d 10am **PRICES:** s £18; d £36-£44✻ **BB** **PARKING:** 6

BLAIRGOWRIE — Map 15 NO14

♦♦♦♦ Duncraggan

Perth Rd PH10 6EJ ☎ 01250 872082 📠 01250 872098
Dir: *on A93 from Perth pass small garage on left, 2 bungalows, Duncraggon on corner of Essendy and Perth road*
Guests are assured of a warm and friendly welcome from Christine McClement on arrival at her delightful turreted home which stands in well-tended gardens that include putting greens. Bedrooms, one of which has a four-poster, are comfortably proportioned. Breakfast, light suppers and, by prior arrangement, evening meals are served in the smart dining room.
FACILITIES: 4 rms (3 en suite) No smoking TV3B tea/coffee No dogs Cen ht TVL No coaches 9 hole putting Dinner Last d 5pm **PRICES:** s £18.50-£20; d £40✻ **LB** **BB** **PARKING:** 6 **NOTES:** Closed mid Oct-Feb

♦♦♦♦ Gilmore House

Perth Rd PH10 6EJ ☎ 01250 872791 📠 01250 872791
e-mail: jill@gilmorehouse.co.uk
Dir: *on A93 from Perth. On outskirts of Blairgowrie*
This attractive detached house stands in well kept gardens south of town. The pretty bedrooms are comfortably furnished in antique pine, and are well equipped. There are two lounges were guests can relax and unwind, one of which offers lovely views of the surrounding countryside. Hearty traditional breakfasts are served in the attractive dining room.

continued

FACILITIES: 3 en suite No smoking TVB tea/coffee Cen ht TVL No coaches **PRICES:** d £36-£44✻ BB **PARKING:** 3 **NOTES:** Closed X-mas

COMRIE Map 11 NN72

♦♦♦ Mossgiel

Burrell St PH6 2JP ☎ 01764 670567 📠 01764 670567
e-mail: mossgielcomrie@hotmail.com
Dir: *on A85 opposite Parish Church*
Situated on the main road at the west side of the village, this welcoming guesthouse offers guests comfortable well-equipped accommodation. Public areas include a cosy TV lounge and separate dining room where hearty traditional breakfasts are served.
FACILITIES: 3 en suite No smoking tea/coffee No dogs Cen ht TVL No children 5yrs No coaches Golf packages, Physical therapy clinic **PRICES:** s £20-£25; d £40-£44✻ LB **PARKING:** 6 **NOTES:** Closed Dec-Feb

CRIEFF Map 11 NN82

♦♦♦♦ Comely Bank

32 Burrell St PH7 4DT ☎ 01764 653409
e-mail: bookings@comelybank.demon.co.uk
Dir: *on A822*
The White family delight in welcoming guests to their comfortable home, a smart terraced house situated within easy access to central amenities. Bedrooms are bright and airy with attractive soft furnishings and offer comfortable modern furnishings; one room is suitable for less mobile guests. The lounge invites relaxation and, with prior arrangement, enjoyable home cooking is provided in the tastefully appointed dining room.
FACILITIES: 5 rms (3 en suite) (2 fmly) (1 GF) No smoking in bedrooms No smoking in dining room TVB tea/coffee Licensed Cen ht TVL No coaches **PRICES:** s £17-£18; d £34-£40✻ BB

♦♦♦♦ Gwydyr House Hotel

Comrie Rd PH7 4BP ☎ 01764 653277 📠 01764 653277
e-mail: enquiries@gwdyrhouse.co.uk
Dir: *on A85, Comrie Road, 0.25m from town centre, on right opposite Macrosty Park entrance*
Lovely views over the surrounding countryside can be enjoyed from this impressive detached Victorian house. Most of the well-maintained bedrooms are generously proportioned and furnished in both modern and traditional styles. There is a comfortable sitting room, where guests can relax with a drink from the dispense bar. On Friday and Saturday a carte menu is offered in the smart dining room, with a short set-price menu on the other days.
FACILITIES: 8 en suite (2 fmly) No smoking in 4 bedrooms No smoking in dining room TVB tea/coffee Licensed Cen ht No coaches Dinner Last d 6.30pm **PRICES:** s fr £40; d £60-£80✻ **PARKING:** 12 **CARDS:**

♦♦♦♦ Merlindale

Perth Rd PH7 3EQ ☎ 01764 655205 📠 01764 655205
e-mail: merlin.dale@virgin.net
Dir: *Leave A9 take A822 through Greenloaning/Braco/Muthill to Crieff. Follows signs for town centre on A85, 500yds on right Tower Hotel straight past Houseproud on right Merlindale 4th house on left*
Situated in a quiet residential area, within walking distance of the town centre, this delightful detached house stands in well-tended grounds and offers a warm welcome. The pretty bedrooms are attractively decorated, comfortably furnished and well equipped. There is a spacious ground floor lounge, an impressive library and an elegant dining room, which is an ideal setting for delicious evening meals and traditional breakfasts.
FACILITIES: 3 en suite (1 fmly) No smoking TVB tea/coffee No dogs Cen ht No coaches Jacuzzi Dinner Last d 24 hrs in advance **PRICES:** s £35-£45; d £50-£70✻ **PARKING:** 3 **NOTES:** Closed 9 Dec-19 Jan

♦♦♦♦ Number Five B&B

5 Duchlage Ter PH7 3AS ☎ 01764 653516 📠 01764 653516
e-mail: number5@ecosse.net
Dir: *off A85, Perth to Crieff road, into Church St (2nd left after Crieff Hotel) then 1st right into Addison Terrace, B&B on left.*
Set in a residential area close to the town centre, and enjoying lovely views over Strathearn, this friendly family-run establishment provides comfortable, individually styled bedrooms. There is an inviting lounge that overlooks the neat, colourful garden and a smart dining room where evening meals and hearty breakfasts are served at individual tables.
FACILITIES: 3 en suite (1 fmly) No smoking TVB tea/coffee Cen ht TVL No coaches Dinner Last d 11am **PRICES:** s £18-£20; d £36-£40✻ BB **PARKING:** 2 **NOTES:** Closed 22 Dec-5 Jan

DUNKELD Map 11 NO04

Waterbury

Murthly Ter PH8 0BG ☎ 01350 727324 📠 01350 727023
e-mail: brian@waterbury-guesthouse.co.uk
Dir: *exit A9 to Birnam/Dunkeld, on main street next to church & post office*
FACILITIES: 8 rms (6 en suite) (2 fmly) No smoking in bedrooms No smoking in dining room TVB tea/coffee Licensed Cen ht No coaches **PRICES:** s £20-£23; d £40-£46✻ LB **PARKING:** 3 **NOTES:** ★★★ **CARDS:**

GLENSHEE (Spittal of), Map 15 NO17

♦♦♦♦ Dalhenzean Lodge

PH10 7QD ☎ 01250 885217
e-mail: mikepurdie@wwmail.co.uk
Dir: *located on the main Blairgowrie/Braemar Road A93, 2m S of Spittal of Glenshee*
Dalhenzean Lodge was built in 1715, and is situated in the shadow of Meall Uaine, overlooking Shee Water. Some seven miles from the ski slopes at the Cairnwell, it is ideally located for fishing, hill walking and climbing, with the Cateran Trail nearby. Bedrooms are beautifully decorated and well equipped with many thoughtful extras. Hearty breakfasts feature the best of local produce.
FACILITIES: 2 en suite No smoking in dining room STV TVB tea/coffee No dogs (ex guide dogs) Cen ht TVL No coaches **PRICES:** d £35-£45✻ LB BB **PARKING:** 2

KINROSS Map 11 NO10

♦♦♦ Muirs Inn Kinross

49 Muirs KY13 8AU ☎ 01577 862270 📠 01577 862270
e-mail: themuirsinn@aol.com
Dir: *off M90 junct 6 and follow signs for A922 at T-junct. Inn diagonally opposite on right*
A relaxed atmosphere prevails at this superb Scottish inn. Public areas include a choice of bars, boasting a tempting range of cask-conditioned ales and an impressive selection of malt whiskies. Home cooked fare is served in the attractive restaurant. The comfortable bedrooms are well-equipped and offer many useful extras.
FACILITIES: 4 en suite (1 fmly) No smoking in bedrooms No smoking in area of dining room STV TVB tea/coffee No dogs (ex guide dogs) Cen ht Dinner Last d 9pm **PRICES:** s fr £45; d fr £70✻ **PARKING:** 10 **CARDS:**

BB Great value! This indicates B&B for £19 and under, per person, per night.

Scotland

KINROSS continued

Burnbank

79 Muirs KY13 8AZ ☎ 01577 861931 Fax 01577 861931
e-mail: bandb@burnbank-kinross.co.uk
Dir: *M90 junct 6, A922 towards Kinross. Take left signed Milnathort into Springfield Road. At T junct left on to Muirs,3rd right signed Kinnesswood and turn right into Burnbank entrance*
FACILITIES: 3 en suite (1 fmly) No smoking TVB tea/coffee No dogs Cen ht No coaches **PRICES:** s £25-£33; d £44-£50* **PARKING:** 6
NOTES: ★★★★ **CARDS:**

KIRKMICHAEL Map 15 NO05

♦♦♦♦ Cruachan Country Cottage

Cruachan PH10 7NZ ☎ 01250 881226
e-mail: cruachanaa@kirkmichael.net
Dir: *on A924, approx 300yds beyond village of Kirkmichael*
A detached, period cottage, set in a quiet location on the edge of Kirkmichael, but within walking distance of all local amenities. Equidistant from Pitlochry and Blairgowrie, it is ideally situated for touring the Scottish Highlands. Bedrooms, one of which has a four-poster bed, are well-equipped and attractive. There is a lounge, and a pretty, well-tended garden, with off-road parking and drying facilities available. Delicious evening meals and breakfasts featuring Scottish produce are served in the panelled dining room.
FACILITIES: 3 en suite (2 fmly) No smoking in bedrooms No smoking in dining room TVB tea/coffee Cen ht No children 5yrs No coaches Dinner Last d 7pm **PRICES:** s £24.50-£29.50; d £39-£49* **PARKING:** 6
CARDS:

PERTH Map 11 NO12

Premier Collection

♦♦♦♦♦ Over Kinfauns

Kinfauns PH2 7LD ☎ 01738 860538 Fax 01738 860803
e-mail: b&b@overkinfauns.co.uk
Dir: *from A90 Perth/Dundee Road take Kinfauns exit (not Kinfauns Castle). Drive uphill for 0.25m turn left straight uphill to gates on left*

An ideal base for exploring central Scotland and Perthshire, this delightful house enjoys lovely views over the River Tay to the Ochil hills beyond. The spacious and comfortable bedrooms are furnished with antiques and equipped with many thoughtful extras. A relaxing lounge complete with deep sofas is available for guests and lies adjacent to the bright airy conservatory. Delicious evening meals and breakfasts are served around a large table in the elegant dining room.
FACILITIES: 3 en suite No smoking TVB tea/coffee No dogs Cen ht TVL No children 10yrs No coaches Croquet lawn Dinner Last d 8hrs prior **PRICES:** s £38-£43; d £60-£70 **PARKING:** 7 **NOTES:** Closed 24-26 Dec **CARDS:**

♦♦♦♦ Adam

6 Pitcullen Crescent PH2 7HT ☎ 01738 627179 Fax 01738 627179
Dir: *from town centre, over bridge onto A94 Coupar/Angus road. A few minutes' drive & guest house on left*
This well maintained friendly, family run guesthouse is situated beside the Coupar Angus Road. Bedrooms, all of which are en suite are attractively decorated and well equipped. There is a relaxing ground floor lounge and a peaceful dining room where traditional breakfasts are served at individual tables.
FACILITIES: 4 en suite (1 fmly) (1 GF) No smoking in bedrooms No smoking in dining room TVB tea/coffee Cen ht TVL **PRICES:** s £20-£27.50; d £40-£46* **LB** **PARKING:** 6 **CARDS:**

♦♦♦♦ Kinnaird

5 Marshall Place PH2 8AH ☎ 01738 628021 Fax 01738 444056
e-mail: tricia@kinnaird-gh.demon.co.uk
Dir: *From Edinburgh on M90 junct 10, follow signs for Perth City Centre. At 2nd set of traffic lights turn left for guesthouse on right (Relais et Chateaux)*

Situated overlooking South Inch Park, this charming guesthouse forms part of a Georgian terrace and offers friendly traditional hospitality. Bedrooms are attractively decorated, comfortably furnished and offer a good range of amenities. There is a comfortable lounge and a smart dining room where hearty breakfasts are served at individual tables.
FACILITIES: 7 en suite No smoking TVB tea/coffee No dogs Cen ht No children 12yrs No coaches **PRICES:** s £25-£30; d £45-£50*
PARKING: 7 **NOTES:** Closed 15 Dec-21 Jan **CARDS:**

♦♦♦♦ Park Lane Guest House

17 Marshall Place PH2 8AG ☎ 01738 637218 Fax 01738 643519
e-mail: stay@parklane-uk.com
Dir: *Exit at junct 10 on M90, enter Town on A912, cross park & turn left at traffic lights. Park Ln on right opposite park*

Built in 1807, this delightful terraced Georgian house overlooks the South Inch Park, close to the town centre and within walking distance of the golf course. The elegant lounge/dining room features a pleasing selection of paintings and is an appropriate setting for freshly prepared breakfasts, which utilise the best of local produce.

continued

ACILITIES: 6 en suite (1 fmly) No smoking TVB tea/coffee No dogs (ex uide dogs) Cen ht TVL **PRICES:** s £24-£28; d £46-£52✳ **LB**
ARKING: 8 **NOTES:** Closed Dec-20 Jan
ARDS:

♦♦♦ *Westview*
9 Dunkeld Rd PH1 5RP ☎ 01738 627787 📠 01738 627787
ir: 2nd exit at Inveralmond roundabout off A9. Establishment 1m on left pposite Royal Bank of Scotland
nthusiastic owner Angie Livingstone assures guests of a warm elcome. Angie is a Victoriana fan, and her house is a time warp of at period, not to mention the teddies on the stairs. Best use has een made of available space in the bedrooms, which are full of naracter. Public areas include an inviting lounge and a separate ning room.
ACILITIES: 5 rms (3 en suite) (1 fmly) No smoking in 3 bedrooms No noking in dining room No smoking in lounges STV TVB tea/coffee Cen ht /L No coaches Last d 4pm **PARKING:** 4 **CARDS:**

♦♦♦ Clunie
2 Pitcullen Crescent PH2 7HT ☎ 01738 623625
01738 623625
mail: ann@clunieguesthouse.co.uk
ir: on A94 opposite side of river from town
ving on the East Side of the town on the A94, this family run uesthouse has a welcoming atmosphere. The attractive bedrooms ary in size, and are well-equipped. Dinner, by prior arrangement, nd breakfast are served at individual tables in the ground floor ning room, which leads to a comfortable lounge.
ACILITIES: 7 en suite (3 fmly) No smoking in 5 bedrooms No smoking in ning room No smoking in lounges TVB tea/coffee Cen ht No coaches inner Last d by arrangement **PRICES:** s £19-£27; d £38-£46✳ **BB**
ARKING: 8 **CARDS:**

♦♦ Anglers Inn
Main Rd, Guildtown PH2 6BS ☎ 01821 640329
01821 640329
ir: 7m N of Perth on A93
relaxed and welcoming atmosphere is a feature of this country n set in the heart of the village. The spacious bar/dining room ffers a good selection of dishes from high teas to steak suppers nd is popular with locals and tourists alike. Attractive fabrics have een used to good effect in the modern, well-equipped bedrooms.
ACILITIES: 4 en suite (1 fmly) TVB tea/coffee Licensed Cen ht Pool Table inner Last d 9pm **PRICES:** s fr £30; d fr £50✳ **PARKING:** 30
ARDS:

♦♦ Castleview
56 Glasgow Rd PH2 0LY ☎ 01738 626415 📠 01738 626415
ir: A93, 1m from Broxden rdbt on left
tuated on the edge of the city, this Victorian house lies within ndscaped gardens. Comfortably furnished bedrooms are brightly ecorated and freshly prepared breakfasts are served around one rge table in the dining room.
ACILITIES: 3 en suite (1 fmly) No smoking in 2 bedrooms No smoking in ning room No smoking in lounges TVB tea/coffee Cen ht No coaches inner Last d 5pm **PRICES:** s £20-£30; d fr £40✳ **PARKING:** 6
OTES: Closed 25th Dec-Feb

PITLOCHRY
Map 14 NN95

Premier Collection

♦♦♦♦♦ Dunfallandy House
Logierait Rd, Dunfallandy PH16 5NA ☎ 01796 472648
📠 01796 472017
e-mail: dunfalhse@aol.com
Built around 1800 for the Chief of the Clan McFergus of Atholl, Dunfallandy House is a secluded Georgian mansion, set in an elevated location in several acres of well-tended grounds. Lovingly restored, the house retains many original features. Bedrooms are individually decorated and furnished, and all enjoy lovely views. There is an elegant drawing room, and delicious evening meals and breakfasts are served at individual tables in the spacious dining room.
FACILITIES: 8 en suite No smoking TVB tea/coffee No dogs Cen ht No children 12yrs No coaches **PRICES:** d £50-£90✳ **PARKING:** 20
CARDS:

♦♦♦♦ Craigroyston House
2 Lower Oakfield PH16 5HQ ☎ 01796 472053 📠 01796 472053
e-mail: reservations@craigroyston.co.uk
Dir: *in town centre just above Information Centre car park*
The Maxwell family delight in welcoming guests to their home, a detached Victorian house set in its own garden. The bedrooms have pretty colour schemes and are comfortably furnished in period style. Relaxing public areas include an inviting sitting room. Scottish breakfasts are served in the attractive dining room. This is a no-smoking house.
FACILITIES: 8 en suite (1 fmly) (1 GF) No smoking TVB tea/coffee No dogs (ex guide dogs) Cen ht No coaches **PRICES:** d £40-£56✳ **LB**
PARKING: 9

♦♦♦♦ Arrandale House
Knockfarrie Rd PH16 5DN ☎ 01796 472987 📠 01796 472987

This elegant Victorian villa, situated in an elevated position enjoys delightful views of the Tummel Valley. Bedrooms are tastefully decorated, comfortably furnished and offer all the expected amenities. The attractive ground floor dining room is an appropriate setting for hearty traditional breakfasts, which are served at individual tables.
FACILITIES: 6 rms (5 en suite) (3 fmly) No smoking TV7B tea/coffee No dogs Cen ht No coaches **PRICES:** s £20-£25; d £40-£50✳
PARKING: 9 **NOTES:** Closed Nov-Mar

Scotland

PITLOCHRY continued

♦♦♦♦ Dundarave House

Strathview Ter PH16 5AT ☎ 01796 473109 📠 01796 473109
e-mail: dundarave.guesthouse@virgin.net
Dir: *from Pitlochry main street turn into West Moulin Rd, 2nd left into Strathview Terrace*

Built in the 19th century and set in an elevated position a short stroll from the town centre, Dundarave House offers comfortable accommodation in friendly surroundings. Bedrooms are attractively decorated and well equipped. Substantial breakfasts and, by prior arrangement, evening meals are served at individual tables in the airy dining room.
FACILITIES: 7 rms (5 en suite) (1 fmly) (1 GF) No smoking TVB tea/coffee No dogs (ex guide dogs) Cen ht No coaches Dinner Last d 2pm **PRICES:** s £18-£22; d £36-£48✻ **LB BB PARKING:** 7 **CARDS:**

♦♦♦♦ Torrdarach Hotel

Golf Course Rd PH16 5AU ☎ 01796 472136 📠 01796 473733
e-mail: torrdarach@msn.com
Dir: *turn off Athol Road to Golf Course, Torrdarach is last hotel before Golf Course, Red House*

Enjoying stunning views over the Tummel valley, this substantial detached Victorian home lies in a secluded spot, close to the golf course. Owners Dave and Beryl are great hosts and provide hospitality that is second to none. Bedrooms are comfortable and well-appointed. Delicious home cooked fare is served at individual tables in the delightful dining room.
FACILITIES: 7 en suite (1 GF) No smoking TVB tea/coffee No dogs (ex guide dogs) Licensed Cen ht No children 12yrs No coaches
PRICES: s £20-£28; d £40-£56✻ **LB PARKING:** 8 **NOTES:** Closed Jan-Feb **CARDS:**

♦♦♦♦ *The Well House*

11 Toberargan Rd PH16 5HG ☎ 01796 472239 📠 01796 472239
e-mail: enquiries@wellhouseandarrochar.co.uk
Dir: *close to town centre on road running parallel to main street*

Colourful tubs and flowering baskets adorn the exterior of this delightful family home. The pretty bedrooms are comfortably furnished, attractively decorated and well equipped with video recorders and extensive video library. There is a spacious, tastefully appointed lounge - the ideal setting in which to relax, and an inviting dining room where enjoyable home-cooked fare is served.
FACILITIES: 6 en suite (1 fmly) No smoking in bedrooms No smoking in dining room TVB tea/coffee Licensed Cen ht No coaches Dinner Last d 5.30pm **PARKING:** 6 **NOTES:** Closed Dec-Feb **CARDS:**

♦♦♦ Wellwood House

West Moulin Rd PH16 5EA ☎ 01796 474288 📠 01796 474299
e-mail: croft@loan1.fsnet.co.uk
Dir: *off A9 into Pitlochry town centre, right into West Howlin Rd. Pass Supermarket. Establishment on left opposite town hall*

Wellwood House is a Victorian building of immense presence and character, occupying an elevated position within easy walking distance of the town centre. The stunning views of the Vale of Atholl and the beautiful grounds can be enjoyed from most rooms The atmospheric dining room is an appropriate setting for delicious breakfasts.
FACILITIES: 10 rms (8 en suite) (1 fmly) No smoking in dining room TVB tea/coffee Cen ht **PRICES:** s £22-£26; d £38-£50✻ **LB BB PARKING:** 20 **NOTES:** Closed Jan-Mar

RENFREWSHIRE

GLASGOW AIRPORT — Map 11 NS46

Premier Collection

♦♦♦♦♦ East Lochhead

Largs Rd PA12 4DX ☎ 01505 842610 📠 01505 842610
e-mail: eastlochhead@aol.com

(For full entry see Lochwinnoch)

Premier Collection

♦♦♦♦♦ Myfarrclan

146 Corsebar Rd PA2 9NA ☎ 0141 884 8285
📠 0141 581 1566
e-mail: myfarrclan_qwest@compuserve.com
Dir: *M8 junct 29 take A726 to Paisley. At BP Garage mini rdbt, turn right and follow Hospital signs. Pass Royal Alexandra Hospital on left, house 0.5m up hill on right, with tall evergreen hedge*

A warm and friendly welcome awaits guests at this delightful bungalow, located in a leafy suburb on the south side of town. Bedrooms offer quality furnishings and fittings, as well as a wide range of useful extras. There is a cosy sitting room and a conservatory lounge overlooking the pretty back garden. Hearty breakfasts (and evening meals by prior arrangement) are served at the communal table in the bright dining room.
FACILITIES: 3 en suite No smoking STV TVB tea/coffee No dogs (ex guide dogs) Cen ht TVL No coaches Dinner Last d 11am **PRICES:** s £50-£60; d £70-£80✻ **LB PARKING:** 2 **CARDS:**

JOHNSTONE — Map 10 NS46

Premier Collection

♦♦♦♦♦ Nether Johnstone House

Off Barochan Rd, Nether Johnstone PA5 8YP
☎ 01505 322210 & 325055 📠 01505 324004
e-mail: bookings@netherjohnstone.co.uk
Dir: *M8, then A737 (Irvine), after Glasgow Airport take Johnstone exit. From A737 turn left towards Johnstone then immediate right into private lane*

continued

Nether Johnstone House

Situated within easy reach of Glasgow city centre, Glasgow Airport and the main motorway network, this delightful house lies in a peaceful, well tended mature garden. Bedrooms are comfortable and well equipped, with many thoughtful extras. A tranquil lounge is available, and traditional breakfasts featuring the best of local produce, are served at individual tables in the breakfast room.

FACILITIES: 7 en suite No smoking TVB tea/coffee Direct dial from bedrooms No dogs (ex guide dogs) Licensed Cen ht No children 12yrs No coaches **PRICES:** s £38-£48; d £66-£76 **PARKING:** 9 **CARDS:**

LOCHWINNOCH Map 10 NS35

Premier Collection

♦♦♦♦♦ East Lochhead

Largs Rd PA12 4DX ☎ 01505 842610 01505 842610
e-mail: eastlochhead@aol.com

***Dir:** from Glasgow take M8 junct 28a for A737 Irvine. At Roadhead rdbt turn right on A760. Premises 2m on left*

A relaxed country-house atmosphere prevails at this former farmhouse, that dates back over 100 years. Sitting in its own grounds amidst delightful countryside the house boasts magnificent views over Barr Loch. The stylishly furnished bedrooms are all superbly equipped and enjoyable home cooking is served around a communal table in the combined dining room/lounge. A barn has been tastefully converted into five self-contained units with their own private entrances, however these are also available on a serviced basis. A separate barn hosts a conference/function room.

FACILITIES: 3 en suite (1 fmly) (1 GF) No smoking TVB tea/coffee Cen ht TVL ch fac No coaches Cycle track Dinner Last d 2pm **CONF:** Del from £75 ✱ **PARKING:** 24 **CARDS:** 

♦♦♦ Belltrees Beild *(NS376584)*

PA12 4JN ☎ 01505 842376 Mr & Mrs A Mackie

***Dir:** from Glasgow take M8 junct 28A for A737 in direction of Irvine, left into Belltrees Rd*

Set on a working farm, this large detached bungalow, in an elevated position, has fine views over the loch and hills beyond. Guests are also free to wander through the adjacent woodland. Bedrooms are practical in layout and there is a spacious lounge. Genuine hospitality is assured.

FACILITIES: 2 rms (1 en suite) (1 fmly) (2 GF) No smoking in bedrooms No smoking in dining room No smoking in lounges TVB tea/coffee No dogs (ex guide dogs) Cen ht TVL 220 acres mixed **PRICES:** s £18-£20; d £35-£40✱ **BB PARKING:** 4

PAISLEY

See **Glasgow Airport (Renfrewshire)**

SCOTTISH BORDERS

BROUGHTON Map 11 NT13

♦♦♦♦ Glenholm Centre

ML12 6JF ☎ 01899 830408 01899 830408
e-mail: glenholm@dircon.co.uk

***Dir:** A701, 1m S of Broughton, turn right signposted Glenholm. Follow road for 1m, centre on right near road, before cattlegrid*

Surrounded by peaceful farmland, this former schoolhouse has a distinct African theme and provides bright and airy bedrooms that are superbly equipped. The home-cooked meals and baking have received much praise and are served in the spacious open-plan dining room/lounge. Service is attentive yet informal and guests are made to feel very much at home. A computer training course may also be taken.

FACILITIES: 4 en suite (1 fmly) No smoking TVB tea/coffee Direct dial from bedrooms Licensed Cen ht TVL No coaches Dinner Last d 6pm **PRICES:** s fr £28; d fr £50✱ **LB CONF:** Class 20 Del from £43.50 ✱ **PARKING:** 14 **NOTES:** Closed Jan **CARDS:**

♦♦♦♦ Over Tweed

ML12 6QH ☎ 01899 830455 01899 830455
e-mail: over_tweed@cableinet.co.uk

***Dir:** From Edinburgh Ring Road (A720) follow directions to Penicuik and Moffat A701. 30m to Over Tweed going S*

Guests are very well looked after in this modern house which is surrounded by hills and overlooks the River Tweed. The bedrooms are bright, spacious and furnished in pine, and one is available on the ground floor. Breakfast is enjoyed at a shared table in the spacious entrance hall.

FACILITIES: 3 en suite No smoking TVB tea/coffee No dogs Cen ht No children 18yrs No coaches Cycling **PRICES:** s £30; d £50✱ **PARKING:** 4 **CARDS:**

Scotland

Scotland

CRAILING Map 12 NT62

♦♦♦♦ Crailing Old School B&B
TD8 6TL ☎ 01835 850382 01835 850382
e-mail: jean.player@virgin.net
***Dir:** off A698 Jedburgh to Kelso road on B6400 signposted Nisbet, Harestanes visitor centre.Crailing Old School also signed*

Built in 1887 as the village school, this delightful house has comfortable and tastefully appointed accommodation. Bedrooms, one of which is en suite, are immaculately maintained, and well-equipped. Breakfast is served in an elegant combined lounge/dining room. Evening meals are by prior arrangement featuring the best of local produce. Jean Player was a Top Twenty Finalist in the AA Landlady of the Year Award 2002-2003.
FACILITIES: 4 rms (1 en suite) No smoking TVB tea/coffee No dogs TVL No children 6yrs Dinner Last d 7.30pm **PRICES:** s £20-£22; d £44-£50* **LB PARKING:** 7 **NOTES:** Closed 24-27 Dec & 2wks Feb and Nov
CARDS:

GALASHIELS Map 12 NT43

♦♦♦ Ashlyn
7 Abbotsford Rd TD1 3DP ☎ 01896 752416 01896 752416
e-mail: phyllis@ashlynguesthouse.fsnet.co.uk
A warm welcome awaits at this substantial period house. Attractive bedrooms have modern en suite shower rooms, and two are particularly spacious. There is a well proportioned lounge and an attractive breakfast room.
FACILITIES: 3 en suite No smoking TVB tea/coffee Cen ht TVL No coaches **PRICES:** s £25-£35; d £40-£50* **PARKING:** 3

♦♦♦ Island House
65 Island St TD1 1PA ☎ 01896 752649
e-mail: irene@islandguesthouse.co.uk
***Dir:** opposite B&Q store*
Just a short walk from the town centre, Island House is conveniently located and provides comfortable accommodation. The modern bedrooms are attractively decorated and one is located on the ground floor. There is a spacious lounge, and breakfast is served in the cosy, pine furnished dining room. Warm hospitality is assured.
FACILITIES: 3 rms (2 en suite) No smoking in bedrooms No smoking in dining room TVB tea/coffee Cen ht TVL **PRICES:** s £28-£35; d £56* **PARKING:** 2 **NOTES:** Closed 24 Dec-4 Jan

INNERLEITHEN Map 11 NT33

♦♦♦ *Traquair Arms Hotel*
Traquair Rd EH44 6PD ☎ 01896 830229 01896 830260
e-mail: traquair.arms@scottishborders.com
***Dir:** from A72 Peebles to Galashiels road take B709 for St Mary's Loch & Traquair*
continued

The Traquair Arms offers simply furnished bedrooms in a variety of sizes, including a two-bedroom family suite on the top floor. All are very well equipped. Meals are served either in the dining room or cosy bar, where open fires burn and there are real ales on tap. A residents' only lounge is also provided.
FACILITIES: 10 en suite (2 fmly) No smoking in dining room No smoking in 1 lounge TVB tea/coffee Direct dial from bedrooms Cen ht TVL Fishing Dinner Last d 9pm **PARKING:** 10 **NOTES:** Closed 25-26 Dec, 1-2 Jan
CARDS:

Caddon View
14 Pirn Rd EH44 6HH ☎ 01896 830208
e-mail: caddonview@aol.com
***Dir:** 6m S of Peebles on A72. Signposted on A72, turn right into Hasburgh St, hotel entrance 100mtrs on right*
FACILITIES: 8 en suite (3 fmly) (2 GF) No smoking in bedrooms No smoking in dining room TVB tea/coffee Direct dial from bedrooms Licensed Cen ht No coaches Dinner Last d 5pm **PRICES:** s £38-£55; d £56-£70* **LB PARKING:** 6 **NOTES:** ★★★★ Closed Mar
CARDS:

JEDBURGH Map 12 NT62

Premier Collection

♦♦♦♦♦ The Spinney
Langlee TD8 6PB ☎ 01835 863525 01835 864883
e-mail: thespinney@btinternet.com
***Dir:** 2m S of Jedburgh on A68*
Two cottages have been transformed into this attractive modern home set in mature landscaped gardens, surrounded by scenic countryside. The spacious bedrooms have contemporary furnishings and all sorts of thoughtful touches have been added to ensure a comfortable stay. A wide choice of dishes is available at breakfast, which is served in the luxurious dining room.
FACILITIES: 3 en suite No smoking TVB tea/coffee No dogs (ex guide dogs) Cen ht TVL No coaches **PRICES:** d £46* **PARKING:** 8 **NOTES:** Closed Dec-Feb **CARDS:**

♦♦♦♦ Glenfriars House
The Friars TD8 6BN ☎ 01835 862000 01835 862112
e-mail: glenfriars@edenroad.demon.co.uk
***Dir:** from A68 onto road directly in front of Abbey, follow to T-junct turn right then immediate left between the Wishing Well shop and hairdressers in 100yds hard right into road marked Friarsgate. House 0.25m on left (The Circle)*
Picturesquely situated on the high slopes overlooking Jedburgh, yet only a short stroll from the town, Glenfriars House is a substantial Victorian house offering comfortable accommodation. Bedrooms, some of which have four poster beds are mostly spacious and have numerous extra facilities. Public areas include an elegant dining room and a bright guest lounge.
FACILITIES: 6 en suite (3 fmly) No smoking TVB tea/coffee Licensed Cen ht TVL No coaches Dinner Last d by arrangement **PRICES:** s £30; d £50* **LB PARKING:** 6 **NOTES:** Closed 22 Dec-7 Jan
CARDS:

♦♦♦ Bridge House
5 Bridge St TD8 6DW ☎ 01835 863405
***Dir:** in Jedburgh, just off A68, by the Jed Water & opposite Baptist church*
Formerly a tollhouse, this friendly family home extends a warm welcome to all guests. Neatly appointed bedrooms are clean, comfortable and benefit from large en suite bathrooms with double showers. Public areas include a guest lounge and a conservatory dining room, where well-prepared breakfasts are served.
continued

FACILITIES: 2 en suite (1 GF) No smoking tea/coffee No dogs (ex guide dogs) Cen ht TVL No coaches **PRICES:** s £20; d £40✳ **NOTES:** Closed 24 Dec-3 Jan rs Nov-Mar

♦♦♦ Ferniehirst Mill Lodge

TD8 6PQ ☎ 01835 863279 863279
e-mail: ferniehirstmill@aol.com
Dir: *2.5m S on A68, at the end of a private track directly off A68*
Forming part of a riding centre this modern chalet-style lodge enjoys a secluded setting beside the River Jed. A tremendously friendly atmosphere prevails and guests are made to feel extremely welcome. Excellent home-cooked dinners and hearty breakfasts are served in the pine-furnished dining room. Bedrooms are small and functional, and there is a bright, spacious lounge.
FACILITIES: 9 en suite No smoking in dining room tea/coffee Direct dial from bedrooms Licensed Cen ht TVL No coaches Fishing Riding Dinner Last d 5pm **PRICES:** s fr £23; d fr £46✳ **PARKING:** 10 **CARDS:**

♦♦ Kenmore Bank Hotel

Oxnam Rd TD8 6JJ ☎ 01835 862369 01835 862112
e-mail: kenmore@edenroad.demon.co.uk
Dir: *off A68 entering town from S, take 1st right by church, house is 500yds on left*
Enjoying fine views of the abbey from its position high above the Jed Water this cosy guest house is just a five minutes walk from the town. Hearty breakfasts provide a perfect start to the day and are served in the spacious dining room at individual tables. A large guest lounge is also provided.
FACILITIES: 6 en suite (2 fmly) No smoking TVB tea/coffee Licensed Cen ht TVL No coaches **PRICES:** s fr £32; d fr £46✳ **LB PARKING:** 5 **NOTES:** Closed 23 Dec-4 Jan **CARDS:**

MELROSE — Map 12 NT53

Premier Collection

♦♦♦♦♦ Fauhope House

Gattonside TD6 9LU
☎ 01896 823184 & 822245 01896 820188
e-mail: tauhope@bordernet.co.uk
Dir: *right off A68 at the B6360 to Gattonside. At 30mph sign, turn right, then right again and go up a long drive which leads to Fauhope*

Off the beaten track, Fauhope is peacefully situated amid well-tended gardens. In keeping with the period of the house, public areas are elegantly decorated and furnished, and enhanced by beautiful floral arrangements. The dining room is particularly stunning. Bedrooms are a haven of luxury, all individual in style, generous in size and superbly equipped.
FACILITIES: 3 en suite No smoking TVB tea/coffee No dogs (ex guide dogs) Cen ht No coaches Tennis (hard) Riding **PRICES:** d £50-£60✳ **LB PARKING:** 10 **CARDS:**

♦♦♦♦ Dunfermline House

Buccleuch St TD6 9LB ☎ 01896 822148 01896 822148
e-mail: bestaccom@dunmel.freeserve.co.uk
Dir: *opposite Abbey car park - Melrose is 2m from both A7 and A68*
Rooms at the front of this delightful Victorian house offer glimpses of the abbey and those at the rear overlook the well-kept terraced garden. All bedrooms are comfortable, attractively decorated and superbly equipped. There is a cosy lounge and smart dining room, where praiseworthy breakfasts are served.
FACILITIES: 5 en suite No smoking TVB tea/coffee No dogs Cen ht TVL No coaches **PRICES:** s £25; d £50✳ **LB**

♦♦♦♦ Kilkerran House

12 High St TD6 9PA ☎ 01896 822122 01896 820118
e-mail: stay@kilkerranhouse
Dir: *turn off A68 or A7 and follow bypass to Melrose. All roads lead to main High St, house situated half way next to delicatessen 'The Cooks Privilege'*
Situated in the heart of historic Melrose, within easy walking distance of the ancient Abbey and convenient for the local amenities, Kilkerran House offers extremely comfortable accommodation in friendly, peaceful surroundings. Bedrooms are attractively decorated and well equipped with lovely soft furnishings. There is a delightful combined sitting and dining room where delicious breakfasts are served.
FACILITIES: 3 en suite (1 fmly) No smoking TVB tea/coffee No dogs Cen ht No children 14yrs No coaches **PRICES:** s fr £35; d fr £50✳ **CARDS:**

PEEBLES — Map 11 NT24

♦♦♦♦ Venlaw Farm *(NT254416)*

EH45 8QG ☎ 01721 722040 Mrs S Goldstraw
e-mail: louisewalker@clara.co.uk
Dir: *turn off A703 opposite David Harrisons Garage & drive up Tarmacadam private road for 0.33m*
Located amid peaceful farmland, the only noise that can be heard is that of the cows! A warm and friendly welcome awaits at this modern farmhouse bungalow. Bedrooms are thoughtfully equipped and the well proportioned lounge is inviting and enjoys views of the neatly tended gardens. Breakfast is taken round the one table in the traditional dining room.
FACILITIES: 3 rms (2 en suite) (1 fmly) (3 GF) No smoking TVB tea/coffee No dogs Cen ht 100 acres beef sheep **PRICES:** d £40✳ **PARKING:** 7 **NOTES:** Closed Nov-Mar

TIBBIE SHIELS INN — Map 11 NT22

♦♦♦ Tibbie Shiels

TD7 5LH ☎ 01750 42231 01750 42302
Dir: *just off A708 between Moffat and Selkirk*
Standing by St Mary's Loch, this historic drovers' inn has played host to many famous people such as Robert Louis Stevenson and Walter Scott. Today, the inn's hospitality and stunning location attract visitors from all round the world. Original features have been retained where possible, and bright cheery bedrooms contribute to a comfortable stay.
FACILITIES: 5 en suite (2 fmly) (4 GF) No smoking in area of dining room No smoking in 1 lounge tea/coffee No dogs (ex guide dogs) Cen ht TVL Fishing Dinner Last d 8.15pm **PRICES:** s £30; d £52✳ **MEALS:** Lunch £8.95-£13.55alc Dinner £10.30-£22alc✳ **PARKING:** 30 **NOTES:** Closed Nov-Etr rs Mon-Wed **CARDS:**

Scotland

SOUTH AYRSHIRE

AYR Map 10 NS32

See also Dalrymple (East Ayrshire) & Dunure

♦♦♦♦ Craggallan

8 Queens Ter KA7 1DU ☎ 01292 264998
e-mail: craggallan@aol.com
Dir: *from A70 or A77 take town centre signs, A19 through Wellington Square to beach, off seafront*
This immaculately maintained and comfortable guest house lies in a quiet residential street just off the sea front, within easy walking distance of the town centre. Bedrooms, most of which are spacious, are attractively decorated and comfortably furnished. Overseas golfing visitors will feel especially welcome with the owner providing some very useful services aimed at this market.
FACILITIES: 5 rms (4 en suite) (2 fmly) No smoking TVB tea/coffee No dogs (ex guide dogs) Cen ht No coaches Pool Table Jacuzzi Dinner Last d 7pm **PRICES:** s £20-£30; d £40-£60✳ **LB PARKING:** 4
CARDS:

♦♦♦♦ Daviot House

12 Queens Ter KA7 1DU ☎ 01292 269678 01292 880567
e-mail: thedaviot@aol.com
Dir: *into Ayr by A71(N) or A77(S). Take town centre signs, left at Esso petrol station, right at traffic lights. Next left, right at next lights, 2nd left and 2nd right*

This well-maintained Victorian house sits in a peaceful location close to the shore and town centre. Bedrooms are all modern in style and well-equipped. Public areas include a comfortable lounge and dining room, where enjoyable home cooked evening meals and hearty breakfasts are served.
FACILITIES: 5 en suite (3 fmly) No smoking TVB tea/coffee Cen ht TVL No coaches Dinner Last d 5pm **PRICES:** s £22-£30; d £40-£48✳ **LB**
PARKING: 2

♦♦♦♦ *Glenmore*

35 Bellevue Crescent KA7 2DP ☎ 01292 269830
01292 269830
Dir: *on A77 from S or A71 from N. Take town centre turn, left at Tourist Information, left at lights, 1st right then left into Bellevue Crescent*
Marie Mitchell's fine Victorian house lies in a peaceful tree lined terrace within easy reach of the town centre and the beach. Bedrooms are stylishly decorated, and graced with quality period furniture. There is a comfortable lounge and a neat dining room where hearty traditional breakfasts are served.
FACILITIES: 5 en suite (2 fmly) No smoking in dining room No smoking in lounges TVB tea/coffee No dogs (ex guide dogs) Cen ht TVL No coaches

♦♦♦♦ Greenan Lodge

39 Dunure, Doonfoot KA7 4HR ☎ 01292 443939
Dir: *2m S on A719, coastal route*
Situated in a quiet area just outside the town, this smart modern bungalow has fine views over the coastline. Attractively furnished bedrooms offer numerous extras and the spacious lounge is an inviting area in which to relax. Generous Scottish breakfasts are served and guests are made to feel truly welcome.
FACILITIES: 3 en suite (3 GF) No smoking TVB tea/coffee Cen ht TVL No children 7yrs No coaches **PRICES:** s £35; d £54-£60✳ **PARKING:** 10

♦♦♦ Belmont

15 Park Circus KA7 2DJ ☎ 01292 265588 01292 290303
e-mail: belmontguesthouse@btinternet.com
Dir: *off A77 onto A70 Holmston road. At double rdbt follow Town Centre signs. Over railway bridge and left at traffic lights. After next lights turn right into Bellevue Rd. At end of street right into Park Circus establishment on right*
Belmont Guest House is a pleasant terraced house in an attractive tree-lined conservation area, close to the town centre. The public areas are spacious, and the hosts are very hospitable. The bedrooms are well-equipped and comfortable each with many thoughtful additional services.
FACILITIES: 5 en suite (3 fmly) (2 GF) TVB tea/coffee Cen ht TVL No coaches **PRICES:** s £23-£25; d £40-£44✳ **PARKING:** 5
NOTES: Closed Xmas & New Year **CARDS:**

♦♦♦ Dargill

7 Queens Ter KA7 1DU ☎ 01292 261955 01292 290535
e-mail: info@dargil.co.uk
Dir: *take A79 through Prestwick into Ayr, over bridge into Sandgate, right into Fort St, 1st left Charlotte St, left into Queens Terrace*
This guest house forms part of a terrace of attractively painted Victorian properties close to the town centre. It backs onto the promenade and has fine views over the garden towards the Firth of Clyde and Isle of Arran. There is a spacious and comfortable lounge and a pine-furnished dining room. Bedrooms are brightly decorated and well equipped.
FACILITIES: 5 rms (3 en suite) (3 fmly) No smoking in bedrooms No smoking in dining room TVB tea/coffee Cen ht No coaches
PRICES: s £20-£35; d £40-£50✳ **LB PARKING:** 5
NOTES: Closed 22 Dec-2 Jan **CARDS:**

♦♦♦ Windsor Hotel

6 Alloway Place KA7 2AA ☎ 01292 264689
e-mail: windsorhotel.ayreukonline.co.uk
Dir: *from centre of Ayr, take A19 through Wellington Square. Hotel 1st on right.*
A friendly private hotel, within easy walking distance of the seafront and town centre. Bedrooms, several of which are on the ground floor, with many suitable for families are comfortable, well equipped and attractive. The inviting dining room is an appropriate setting for Ann Hamilton's delicious home cooked fare.
FACILITIES: 10 rms (7 en suite) (4 fmly) (3 GF) No smoking in dining room TVB tea/coffee Cen ht TVL No coaches Dinner Last d 10am
PRICES: s £23-£25; d £46-£50✳ **LB NOTES:** Closed Xmas & New Year
CARDS:

Coila

10 Holmston Rd KA7 3BB ☎ 01292 262642 01292 285439
e-mail: hazel@coila.co.uk
Dir: *A77 S from Glasgow, past Kilmarnock continue S on A77, follow signs for Ayr & Stranraer, turn right onto A70, at Holmston rdbt continue for 1m towards town. Coila is on the left just before next rdbt*
FACILITIES: 4 en suite No smoking TVB tea/coffee No dogs Cen ht No coaches **PRICES:** s £25-£35; d £40-£50✳ **LB PARKING:** 7
NOTES: ★★★ **CARDS:**

BALLANTRAE Map 10 NX08

Premier Collection

♦♦♦♦♦ Cosses Country House

Cosses KA26 0LR ☎ 01465 831363 📠 01465 831598
e-mail: cosses@compuserve.com
Dir: *S of Ballantrae on A77, take inland road at caravan sign, house 2m on the right*

A delightful country house, set in twelve acres of woodland and gardens. Two of the bedrooms have their own lounges, and all rooms are on the ground floor. Guests meet for pre-dinner drinks with hosts Robin and Susan in the lounge, and award-winning dinners, served at an elegant communal table, will include home-grown and local produce, Scottish cheese and fine wines. Breakfast offers a choice of dishes, home-made yoghurt, preserves and bread.
FACILITIES: 3 en suite (2 fmly) No smoking in bedrooms No smoking in dining room TVB tea/coffee Licensed Cen ht No children 6yrs No coaches Snooker Pool Table Games room Table tennis Dinner Last d 7pm **PRICES:** s £42-£48; d £64-£76* **PARKING:** 8
NOTES: Closed Nov-Feb **CARDS:**

DUNURE Map 10 NS21

Premier Collection

♦♦♦♦♦ Dunduff

Dunure KA7 4LH ☎ 01292 500225 📠 01292 500222
e-mail: gemmelldunduff@aol.com
Dir: *on A719, 400yds past village school on left*

A working farm, parts of which date back to the 15th and 17th centuries, which from its elevated position enjoys stunning views across the River Clyde towards Arran and the Mull Of Kintyre beyond. All of the bedrooms are stylish, well-equipped and modern in design. A comfortable lounge is provided for guests to relax in, and it is here where genuine Scottish hospitality can be enjoyed. Breakfast includes specialities such as locally smoked kippers.
FACILITIES: 3 rms (2 en suite) (2 fmly) No smoking TVB tea/coffee No dogs (ex guide dogs) Cen ht TVL No coaches Fishing
PRICES: s £35-£40; d £50-£57* **LB PARKING:** 10 **NOTES:** Closed Nov-Feb **CARDS:**

PRESTWICK Map 10 NS32

♦♦♦♦ Golf View Hotel

17 Links Rd KA9 1QG ☎ 01292 671234 📠 01292 671244
e-mail: welcome@golfviewhotel.com
Dir: *from Prestwick Airport take A79 to town centre 'Prestwick Cross'. Take outside lane at 1st set of traffic lights. Turn right, under railway bridge, Golf View is 200yds on left*

Golf View Hotel overlooks the historic Old Prestwick Golf Club where the first 'Open' Championship was played in 1860. It is situated only 200 yards from the beach and Esplanade, and within walking distance of the town. Bedrooms, all of which are attractively decorated, are comfortable and well-equipped. A spacious first floor lounge is available and offers delightful views over the Firth of Clyde. Traditional Scottish breakfasts are served in the elegant ground floor dining room.
FACILITIES: 6 en suite (1 fmly) No smoking in bedrooms No smoking in dining room TVB tea/coffee No dogs (ex guide dogs) Licensed Cen ht No coaches **PRICES:** s £36; d £70* **PARKING:** 8
CARDS:

♦♦♦ *Fernbank*

213 Main St KA9 1LH ☎ 01292 475027 📠 01292 678944
e-mail: bandb@fernbank.co.uk
Dir: *from Prestwick Airport, follow A79 S. After 200yds turn right at rdbt into Prestwick. Fernbank 0.5m on left by church with large tower*

This well maintained house is situated close to the town centre, the railway station (just ten minutes on foot) and the airport (five minutes by car). Fernbank Guest House offers attractive well-equipped bedrooms. The dining room is situated on the ground floor and is an appropriate setting for hearty Scottish breakfasts.
FACILITIES: 6 en suite (1 fmly) No smoking TVB tea/coffee No dogs (ex guide dogs) Cen ht TVL No children 2yrs No coaches **PARKING:** 8
CARDS:

♦♦♦ Kincraig Private Hotel

39 Ayr Rd KA9 1SY ☎ 01292 479480 📠 01292 479480
e-mail: iain@kincraig.demon.co.uk
Dir: *follow A77 onto A79 and continue for 1m past Prestwick Airport*

Lying between Prestwick and Ayr, and convenient for both the golf course and the airport, this substantial red sandstone house offers a variety of bedroom, all of which are comfortable and well-equipped. A small bungalow at the rear provides an apartment with two single rooms, ideal for two golfers sharing.
FACILITIES: 6 rms (5 en suite) 2 annexe en suite (1 fmly) (1 GF) No smoking in bedrooms No smoking in dining room TVB tea/coffee No dogs (ex guide dogs) Licensed Cen ht TVL No coaches Dinner Last d prior arrangement **PRICES:** s £20-£30; d £50-£60* **LB PARKING:** 7
CARDS:

Scotland

Scotland

SYMINGTON Map 10 NS33

Premier Collection

♦♦♦♦♦ Nether Underwood Country House

KA1 5NG ☎ 01563 830666 830777
e-mail: netherund@aol.com
Dir: *A77 S of Kilmarnock pass signs to Symington. Left after Hansel village signed Underwood. Left at next 2 juncts. After 1.5m turn left into lane*

Set amongst the splendours of the Ayrshire countryside, Nether Underwood is a delightful country house, which features charming, elegant well-equipped bedrooms. A comfortable lounge is available for guests, and there is a striking dining room, where delicious home-cooked evening meals and Scottish breakfasts are served. This is a non-smoking house. Nether Underwood Country House is the Guest Accommodation of the Year for Scotland 2002-2003.
FACILITIES: 3 en suite No smoking TVB Direct dial from bedrooms No dogs Cen ht TVL No children 16yrs No coaches Croquet lawn Dinner Last d prior arrangement **PRICES:** s £55; d £90✱ **PARKING:** 6 **NOTES:** Closed 23 Dec-4 Jan **CARDS:**

SOUTH LANARKSHIRE

KIRKMUIRHILL Map 11 NS74

♦♦♦ Dykecroft *(NS776419)*

ML11 0JQ ☎ 01555 892226 Mrs I H McInally
e-mail: dykecroftbandb@talk21.com
Dir: *from S M74 junct 10 (from N junct 9), take B7078 for 2m, then B7086 to Strathaven for 1.5m, past Boghead, 1st bungalow on left*
A warm and friendly welcome is assured at this modern bungalow that is situated in an open rural location on the road to Strathaven. The bedrooms are traditionally furnished and comfortable. There is a bright airy lounge/dining room, which enjoys lovely views of the surrounding countryside.
FACILITIES: 3 rms (3 GF) No smoking tea/coffee Cen ht TVL 60 acres sheep **PRICES:** s £22-£24; d £39-£40✱ **PARKING:** 4

STRATHAVEN Map 11 NS74

♦♦ Avonlea

46 Millar St, Glassford ML10 6TD ☎ 01357 521748
Dir: *from Strathaven turn into Commercial Rd, continue for approx 2m, Avonlea is 3rd terraced house on left*
Formerly a weaver's cottage, Avonlea is a comfortable home in which guests are made to feel very welcome. The spacious bedrooms are restful and have many homely touches. Traditional Scottish breakfasts are served in the conservatory dining room overlooking the well-tended rear garden.

continued

FACILITIES: 2 rms No smoking TVB tea/coffee No dogs Cen ht No children 7yrs No coaches **PRICES:** s £22-£25; d £34-£38✱ BB **NOTES:** Closed Dec

♦♦ Springvale Hotel

18 Lethame Rd ML10 6AD ☎ 01357 521131 01357 521131
Dir: *from M74 junct 8 take Kilmarnock (A71) for 5m bypassing Stonehouse*
A friendly atmosphere prevails at this family-run guesthouse. The bedrooms are thoughtfully equipped and all are sensibly furnished. There is residents' lounge and a dining room (also open to non-residents) which is popular for its high teas and enjoys views over the well-tended garden.
FACILITIES: 12 en suite (2 fmly) (3 GF) TVB tea/coffee Licensed Cen ht TVL Dinner Last d 6.45pm **PRICES:** s £27-£30; d £40-£45✱ **PARKING:** 8 **NOTES:** Closed 26-27 Dec & 1-3 Jan **CARDS:**

STIRLING

CALLANDER Map 11 NN60

Premier Collection

♦♦♦♦♦ Leny House

Leny Estate FK17 8HA ☎ 01877 331078 01877 331335
e-mail: res@lenyestate.com
Dir: *leave Callander going N on A84, just beyond town outskirts, look right for sign to Leny Estate*

Set in extensive parkland, this splendid building with its imposing entrance tower dates in part from 1513 and offers outstanding quality and comfort throughout. Tapestries, Victorian prints and baronial surroundings all add to the atmosphere. Bedroom are in the Victorian wing, some have original fireplaces that are used in the colder months, and all have luxury bathrooms. There is a delightful lounge, and breakfast is served house-party style.
FACILITIES: 3 en suite No smoking TVB tea/coffee No dogs (ex guide dogs) Cen ht TVL No children 12yrs No coaches **PRICES:** d £100-£110✱ **PARKING:** 15 **NOTES:** Closed Nov-Etr **CARDS:**

♦♦♦♦ Arden House

Bracklinn Rd FK17 8EQ ☎ 01877 330235 01877 330235
e-mail: ardenhouse@onetel.net.uk
Dir: *from A84 into Callander from Stirling turn right into Bracklinn Rd, signposted to golf course & Bracklinn Falls. House 200yds on left*
This large Victorian villa lies in a quiet part of the village, and enjoys lovely views. It featured in the TV series 'Dr. Finlay's Casebook' and is a friendly, welcoming establishment. Bedrooms are comfortable, well equipped with many thoughtful extras, and are complemented by a stylish lounge and a bright airy dining room where traditional breakfasts are served.

continued

Arden House

FACILITIES: 6 en suite (2 GF) No smoking TVB tea/coffee No dogs Cen ht No children 14yrs No coaches Putting green **PRICES:** s £30-£40; d £60-£65✻ **LB** **PARKING:** 10 **NOTES:** Closed Nov-30 Mar **CARDS:**

♦♦♦♦ Brook Linn Country House

Leny Feus FK17 8AU ☎ 01877 330103 📠 01877 330103
e-mail: derek@blinn.freeserve.co.uk
Dir: *A84 through Callander from Stirling, right at Pinewood Nursing Home (Leny Feus). right up hill at 'Brook Linn' sign*

Brook Linn Country House is a delightful Victorian villa which stands in two acres of well-tended gardens, in an elevated position overlooking the town. Bedrooms are smartly decorated and have a comfortable traditional feel. There is a relaxing lounge and a separate dining room where freshly prepared breakfasts are served at individual tables.

FACILITIES: 6 en suite (1 GF) No smoking TVB tea/coffee Cen ht No children No coaches **PRICES:** s £25-£27; d £50-£62✻ **PARKING:** 10 **NOTES:** Closed Nov-Etr **CARDS:**

♦♦♦♦ Easter Tarr Farmhouse *(NS636007)*

FK8 3QL ☎ 01786 850225 📠 01786 850225 Mr D Lubiewski
e-mail: trudi@eastertarr.freeserve.co.uk

(For full entry see Thornhill)

♦♦♦♦ Lubnaig House

Leny Feus FK17 8AS ☎ 01877 330376
e-mail: info@lubnaighouse.co.uk
Dir: *W on A84 through main street of Callander to western outskirts, turn 1st right into Leny Feus after Poppies sign*

Lubnaig House, located on the western outskirts of Callander but within five minutes walk of the town centre, is set in a delightful tree lined secluded garden. The house, built in 1864, has been modernised to provide comfortable well appointed bedrooms, some of which are located on the ground floor. There are two cosy lounges and an impressive dining room where hearty traditional breakfasts are served at individual tables.

FACILITIES: 6 en suite 4 annexe en suite No smoking in bedrooms No smoking in dining room No smoking in 1 lounge TVB tea/coffee No dogs Cen ht No children 7yrs No coaches **PRICES:** s £25-£45; d £50-£64✻ **PARKING:** 10 **NOTES:** Closed Nov-Mar **CARDS:**

♦♦♦ Annfield

18 North Church St FK17 8EG ☎ 01877 330204
📠 01877 330674
e-mail: janet-greenfield@amserve.com
Dir: *A84 into Callander, R before pedestrian crossing (North Church St), at top on R.*

Situated within easy reach of the town centre, this welcoming family-run guesthouse offers good value comfortable accommodation. The spacious bedrooms are attractively decorated

continued

and well equipped. An elegant first floor lounge invites peaceful relaxation, while hearty breakfasts are served at individual tables in the pretty dining room.

FACILITIES: 7 rms (5 en suite) (1 fmly) No smoking tea/coffee Cen ht TVL No children 10yrs No coaches **PRICES:** s £25; d £42✻ **PARKING:** 9 **NOTES:** Closed 19 Dec-5 Jan **CARDS:**

♦♦♦ *Abbotsford Lodge*

Stirling Rd FK17 8DA ☎ 01877 330066 📠 01877 339363
e-mail: sam@abbotsfordlodge.fsnet.co.uk
Dir: *off A84 eastern approach to town*

This family-run Victorian villa stands in its own well-tended grounds; it offers a relaxed and welcoming atmosphere. The comfortable bedrooms are varied in size and have mixed furnishings. There are two relaxing lounges, one of which has a bar and a fire for cold evenings. The adjacent dining room is a pleasant setting for delicious home-cooked fare.

FACILITIES: 17 rms (12 en suite) (7 fmly) No smoking in dining room tea/coffee Licensed Cen ht TVL Dinner Last d 7pm **PARKING:** 20 **CARDS:**

CRIANLARICH — Map 10 NN32

♦♦♦♦ The Lodge House

FK20 8RU ☎ 01838 300276 📠 01838 300276
e-mail: admin@lodgehouse.co.uk

A superbly located guest house. The well-proportioned bedrooms are comfortable, and the adjacent Scandinavian-style chalet is ideal for family use. A cosy bar adjoins the stylish and relaxed lounge, both of which have open fires in the winter months. Set meals are served in the attractive dining room that enjoys stunning views of the surrounding mountains.

FACILITIES: 5 en suite 1 annexe en suite (1 fmly) No smoking TVB tea/coffee No dogs (ex guide dogs) Licensed Cen ht No coaches Dinner Last d 5pm **PRICES:** s £30-£45; d £50-£60✻ **LB** **PARKING:** 12 **CARDS:**

♦♦♦ Ben More Lodge Hotel

FK20 8QS ☎ 01838 300210 📠 01838 300218
e-mail: info@ben-more.co.uk
Dir: *300yds out of Crianlarich on A85 (The Circle)*

A relaxed and informal atmosphere prevails at this small roadside hotel on the eastern edge of the village. The compact bedrooms are contained in timber lodges, each having its own verandah. Traditional meals and refreshments are served in the main complex adjacent.

FACILITIES: 11 annexe en suite (2 fmly) No smoking in dining room No smoking in lounges TVB tea/coffee Cen ht Fishing Dinner Last d 8.45pm **PRICES:** s £30-£42; d £50-£66✻ **LB** **MEALS:** Lunch £10.95-£18alc Dinner £10.95-£18alc✻ **PARKING:** 50 **NOTES:** Closed Xmas rs Nov-Mar **CARDS:**

Scotland

DRYMEN Map 11 NS48

♦♦♦♦ Croftburn Cottage

Croftamie G63 0HA ☎ 01360 660796 📠 01360 661005
e-mail: johnreid@croftburn.fsnet.co.uk
Dir: *2m S of Drymen on A809 adjacent to Dalnair House*

This former keeper's cottage is set in spacious gardens with views of the Campsie Fells. Attractive public areas include a spacious and comfortable lounge with French windows giving access to the patio. Meals are served around a communal table in the dining room. Bedrooms are cheerfully decorated, comfortably furnished, and thoughtfully equipped.

FACILITIES: 3 rms (2 en suite) No smoking in bedrooms No smoking in dining room TVB tea/coffee Cen ht TVL No children 12yrs No coaches Croquet lawn Dinner Last d 10am **PRICES:** s £25-£30; d £42-£46✱ **LB PARKING:** 12 **CARDS:**

DUNBLANE Map 11 NN70

Premier Collection

♦♦♦♦♦ Rokeby House

Doune Rd FK15 9AT ☎ 01786 824447 📠 01786 821399
e-mail: rokeby.house@btconnect.com
Dir: *M9 N, Dunblane exit, then next turn to Doune along Doune Road. Premises 0.5m on left*

This charming, detached Edwardian home stands in carefully tended gardens on the western edge of the village. The spacious bedrooms are comfortable and modern in style, offering a good range of amenities. Public areas include a relaxing lounge on the ground floor. Delicious evening meals and breakfasts are served at individual tables in the elegant dining room.

FACILITIES: 3 en suite (1 fmly) No smoking TVB tea/coffee No dogs Licensed Cen ht No children 14yrs No coaches Dinner Last d 8pm **PRICES:** s £55-£75; d £80-£110✱ **PARKING:** 10 **CARDS:**

KILLIN Map 11 NN53

♦♦♦♦ Fairview House

Main St FK21 8UT ☎ 01567 820667 📠 01567 820667
e-mail: info@fairview-killin.co.uk
Dir: *off A58 onto A827 to Killin (approx 2m). Once over bridge on Falls of Dochart Rd and bear right. House 300 yds on left*

Situated in the centre of the village, there are fine views of the surrounding hills from the comfortable lounge and from most bedrooms. A warm welcome is assured from the friendly proprietors and dinner, by prior arrangement, is a particular feature. Comfortably furnished bedrooms include accommodation for families.

continued

FACILITIES: 6 en suite (1 fmly) No smoking TV1B tea/coffee Cen ht TVL No coaches Dinner Last d noon **PRICES:** s £25-£30; d £44-£50✱ **PARKING:** 9

LOCHEARNHEAD Map 11 NN52

♦♦♦♦ Mansewood Country House

FK19 8NS ☎ 01567 830213 & 830485 📠 01567 830485
e-mail: katiestalker@aol.com
Dir: *turn onto A84 at Stirling. Travel through Callender and Strathyre to Lochearnhead. 1st building on the left*

A charming 250-year-old former manse, set in its own well tended grounds on the south side of the village. Bedrooms have been attractively decorated to offer high standards of comfort. Drinks can be enjoyed in the cosy bar or the elegant and comfortable lounge, and meals, which are prepared with flair by Katie Stalker, are served in the attractive restaurant.

FACILITIES: 6 en suite No smoking in bedrooms No smoking in dining room No smoking in lounges TVB tea/coffee Licensed Cen ht No coaches Dinner Last d 5pm **PRICES:** s £30; d £40-£50 **PARKING:** 10 **CARDS:**

STIRLING Map 11 NS79

♦♦♦♦ XI Victoria Square

Kingspark FK8 2RA ☎ 01786 475545 & 446045
e-mail: iain.galloway@btinternet.com
Dir: *turn S of A911 (Dumbarton rd/ Albert Place) at Smith gallery in Victoria place 2nd left into south-side of Victoria Sq, XI is 1st on right*

A spacious and comfortable Victorian family home, within easy walking distance of the town centre and golf course. Built on land that was once part of a 15th-century Royal hunting ground, the house offers fine views of some of Stirling's historic landmarks. Bedrooms are spacious, well equipped and individually decorated. Public areas include the Oriental dining room where superb breakfasts, featuring the best of local produce and seasonal fruits, are served.

FACILITIES: 3 en suite (1 fmly) No smoking TVB tea/coffee No dogs (ex guide dogs) Cen ht No coaches Bechstein grand piano **PRICES:** s £45-£60; d £60-£70✱ **PARKING:** 5

♦♦♦♦ Castlecroft

Ballengeich Rd FK8 1TN ☎ 01786 474933 📠 01786 466716
e-mail: billsalmond@aol.com
Dir: *M9 junct 10 toward Stirling, turn 1st right into Raploch Rd. At fire station, turn left at Back'O'Hill then immediatley right*

From its elevated position on the hillside, in the shadow of the castle, Castlecroft enjoys lovely views over the countryside. Bedrooms are fresh and bright with comfortable modern furnishings. There is a spacious first floor lounge, complete with picture windows on three sides, which takes full advantage of the stunning view, and a ground floor dining room where hearty breakfasts are served.

FACILITIES: 6 en suite (1 fmly) No smoking in bedrooms No smoking in dining room TVB tea/coffee Lift Cen ht No coaches **PRICES:** s £30-£45; d fr £50✱ **PARKING:** 9 **NOTES:** Closed Xmas & New Year **CARDS:**

THORNHILL Map 11 NN60

♦♦♦♦ Easter Tarr Farmhouse *(NS636007)*

FK8 3QL ☎ 01786 850225 📠 01786 850225 Mr D Lubiewski
e-mail: trudi@eastertarr.freeserve.co.uk
Dir: *M9 junct 10,off A84 onto A873 just past safari park. Through Thornhill village. Establishment 2m on left*

Just a few miles from Callander, Easter Tarr provides a relaxing atmosphere and a friendly welcome. This stylish property has a

continued

relaxed and friendly farmhouse ambience. Breakfast is served in the bright airy conservatory, with the stylish bedrooms well-equipped and thoughtfully and attractively furnished in pine.
FACILITIES: 2 en suite (1 fmly) No smoking TVB tea/coffee Cen ht TVL 10 acres Chickens sheep horses **PRICES:** s £30; d £44-£50 **PARKING:** 10

WEST DUNBARTONSHIRE

BALLOCH Map 10 NS38

♦♦♦♦ Willowdale B & B
12 Old Luss Rd G83 8QP ☎ 01389 756481
e-mail: willowdale@blueyonder.co.uk
Dir: *turn off A82 at Stonymullen rdbt (turn right), left at next rdbt Big Mac on corner, in 20 yds left at next rdbt, 3rd house on right*
This charming bungalow is set in quiet cul-de-sac yet is handy for all local facilities and major routes. The two lovely bedrooms, one on the first floor and suitable for families, are very well equipped and decorated and have many thoughtful facilities. Ample breakfasts are served in the neat and cosy breakfast room, with caring attention from Iona Hull.
FACILITIES: 2 en suite No smoking TVB tea/coffee No dogs (ex guide dogs) Cen ht No coaches **PRICES:** s £25-£40; d £44* **PARKING:** 3
CARDS:

♦♦♦ Sunnyside
35 Main St G83 9JX ☎ 01389 750282
Dir: *3rd exit on A82 bypass, then A813 to Balloch, bridge on left, head straight on, house is on right 400yds from bridge*
Set in its own grounds back from the road that runs from Balloch, by Loch Lomond, this attractive traditional detached house, part of which is over 170 years old, has been extended to provide attractive modern accommodation. Bedrooms are comfortably proportioned and well-equipped. Wholesome breakfasts are served in the spacious combined lounge/dining room.
FACILITIES: 3 en suite (1 fmly) No smoking TVB tea/coffee Cen ht No coaches **PARKING:** 6

DUMBARTON

See **Cardross (Argyll & Bute)**

WEST LOTHIAN

EAST CALDER Map 11 NT06

Premier Collection

♦♦♦♦♦ Ashcroft Farmhouse *(NT095682)*
EH53 0ET ☎ 01506 881810 📠 01506 884327
Mr & Mrs D Scott
e-mail: scottashcroft7@aol.com
Dir: *on B7015, off A71, 0.5m E of East Calder, near to Almondell Country Park*
With over 35 years experience of caring for their guests, Derek and Elizabeth Scott ensure a stay at Ashcroft will be memorable. Their modern home sits in lovely landscaped gardens and provides ground floor bedrooms. The comfortable residents lounge includes a video library. Breakfast features home-made sausages and the best of local produce.

Ashcroft Farmhouse

FACILITIES: 6 en suite (2 fmly) (6 GF) No smoking TVB tea/coffee No dogs (ex guide dogs) Cen ht TVL No children 5yrs 5 acres Arable
PRICES: s £40-£50; d £60* **PARKING:** 8
CARDS:

See advert under EDINBURGH

continued

♦♦♦♦ Whitecroft
7 Raw Holdings EH53 0ET ☎ 01506 882494 📠 01506 882598
e-mail: lornascot@aol.com
Dir: *turn off A71 onto B7015, establishment on right*

A relaxed and friendly atmosphere prevails at this charming guesthouse. The bedrooms, all of which are on the ground floor, are attractively colour co-ordinated, well-equipped and contain many thoughtful extra touches. Breakfast is served to guests at individual tables in the smart dining room.
FACILITIES: 3 en suite No smoking TVB tea/coffee No dogs (ex guide dogs) Cen ht No children 12yrs No coaches **PRICES:** s £30-£35; d £50* **PARKING:** 5 **NOTES:** Closed 24-26 Dec **CARDS:**

Scotland

Scotland

EAST CALDER continued

♦♦♦ Overshiel Farm *(NT099689)*

EH53 0HT ☎ 01506 880469 Fax 01506 883006 Mrs J Dick
e-mail: jandic5@aol.com
Dir: *W from Edinburgh on A71, onto B7015, then 2nd right, 0.5m on right*

Situated in sheltered gardens adjacent to the farm, this Victorian farmhouse offers guests a friendly welcome. Two of the bedrooms are at ground floor level, have external access and are suitable for guests with limited mobility. All bedrooms are comfortable and offer the expected amenities. There is a spacious lounge adjacent to the attractive dining room.
FACILITIES: 1 rms 2 annexe en suite No smoking TVB tea/coffee No dogs (ex guide dogs) Cen ht 340 acres mixed **PRICES:** s £25-£30; d £36-£40 BB
PARKING: 6

LINLITHGOW Map 11 NS97

♦♦♦♦ Bomains Farm *(NS990791)*

by Bo'Ness EH49 7RQ ☎ 01506 822188 & 822861
Fax 01506 824433 Mrs B Kirk
e-mail: bomains.farmhouse@euphony.net
Dir: *M9 junct 3, left to Linlithgow, take A706 for Boness Drive, 1.5m to golf course x-roads, turn left, first farm on right*

From its elevated position this friendly farmhouse enjoys delightful views across the Firth of Forth. There is an elegant lounge, which invites peaceful relaxation, and an attractive dining room where home-cooked fare is served. Bedrooms vary in size but the smart, modern fitted-furniture makes excellent use of space and is enhanced by quality fabrics.
FACILITIES: 3 en suite No smoking TVB tea/coffee Cen ht TVL 180 acres Arable Dinner Last d 5.30pm **PRICES:** s fr £30; d fr £50✱ **PARKING:** 8

♦♦♦♦ Thornton

Edinburgh Rd EH49 6AA ☎ 01506 844693 Fax 01506 844876
e-mail: inglisthornton@hotmail.com
Dir: *A803 into Linlithgow High Street. At rdbt take B9080. Pass garage on left, turn R at end of high stone wall house 1st R in lane*
Built in the 1870s this delightful house is situated within easy reach of the centre of the historic town of Linlithgow, the birthplace of Mary, Queen of Scots. Bedrooms are comfortably proportioned, well-equipped and offer many thoughtful touches. The spacious combined lounge/dining room overlooks the lovely rear garden and is supplied with interesting books and newspapers.

FACILITIES: 2 en suite (2 GF) No smoking TVB tea/coffee No dogs (ex guide dogs) Cen ht TVL No children 12yrs No coaches **PRICES:** s £28-£30; d £50-£60✱ **PARKING:** 2 **NOTES:** Closed mid Dec-mid Jan
CARDS:

♦♦♦ Belsyde House

Lanark Rd EH49 6QE ☎ 01506 842098 Fax 01506 842098
e-mail: belsyde.guesthouse@virgin.net
Dir: *1.5m SW on A706, 1st left after crossing Union Canal*

This welcoming farmhouse is peacefully situated in lovely grounds above the Union Canal. Though varied in size, the bright airy bedrooms are all comfortable and well equipped. Hearty farmhouse breakfasts are served at individual tables in the smart dining room, next to the relaxing sitting room.
FACILITIES: 4 rms (1 en suite) (1 fmly) No smoking TVB tea/coffee No dogs (ex guide dogs) Cen ht TVL Nearby Leisure centre
PRICES: s fr £20; d fr £40✱ **PARKING:** 10 **NOTES:** Closed Xmas
CARDS:

LIVINGSTON

♦♦♦♦ Whitecroft

7 Raw Holdings EH53 0ET ☎ 01506 882494 🖷 01506 882598
e-mail: lornascot@aol.com

(For full entry see East Calder)

ARRAN, ISLE OF

BRODICK Map 10 NS03

♦♦♦♦ Dunvegan House

Dunvegan Shore Rd KA27 8AJ ☎ 01770 302811
🖷 01770 302811

Dir: *turn right from ferry terminal, 500yds along Shore Road*

Dunvegan is a delightful detached home overlooking the bay towards Brodick Castle with Goat Fell beyond. Bedrooms have pretty colour schemes and are comfortably furnished in pine. Guests can relax in the cosy lounge; evening meals during the season and breakfasts are provided in bright dining room, which has lovely views.

FACILITIES: 9 en suite (1 fmly) (3 GF) No smoking in 2 bedrooms No smoking in dining room TVB tea/coffee No dogs (ex guide dogs) Licensed Cen ht TVL No coaches Dinner Last d 4pm **PRICES:** s £35; d £60✳ **PARKING:** 10 **NOTES:** Closed Xmas & New Year

♦♦♦ Allandale

KA27 8BJ ☎ 01770 302278

Dir: *2 mins from Brodick Pier, turn left at junct follow sign to Lamlash, up hill take 2nd left at Corriegills sign Allandale on corner of main rd*

A comfortable guest house on the southern edge of town, close to the ferry terminal. Relax with a drink in the lounge before moving to the dining room to sample some home-cooked fare. Bedrooms vary in size and have pleasing colour schemes, offering mixed modern furnishings along with the expected amenities.

FACILITIES: 4 en suite 2 annexe en suite (4 fmly) No smoking in dining room No smoking in 1 lounge TVB tea/coffee Licensed Cen ht Last d 7pm **PRICES:** s £25-£30; d £50-£60✳ **LB PARKING:** 6 **NOTES:** Closed Nov-Dec **CARDS:**

BUTE, ISLE OF

ASCOG Map 10 NS16

🅰 Balmory Hall

PA20 9LL ☎ 01700 500669 🖷 01700 500669
e-mail: enquiries@balmoryhall.com

Dir: *from main ferry terminal turn left & follow coast road S for approx 3m. Immediately after leaving 30mph zone, turn right into Balmory Rd. Balmory Hall is at top of road*

FACILITIES: 3 en suite No smoking TVB tea/coffee No dogs (ex guide dogs) Cen ht No children 12yrs No coaches Croquet lawn **PRICES:** d £80-£130✳ **PARKING:** 20 **NOTES:** ★★★★★ **CARDS:**

MULL, ISLE OF

DERVAIG Map 13 NM45

♦♦♦ Bellachroy Hotel

PA75 6QW ☎ 01688 400314 🖷 01688 400314
e-mail: enquiries@bellachroy.co.uk

Dir: *from Craignure ferry turn right and follow signs to Tobermory. Through Salen village to left turn signed Dervaig at Aros Bridge, take turn, proceed for 12m until T junct by church and turn right hotel in 100mtrs on left*

A warm welcome is assured at this hotel, parts of which date back to 1608. Built as a drovers' inn, it is reputedly the oldest continuously inhabited building in Mull. Bedrooms are comfortable and well equipped, there is a spacious, comfortable lounge, and a bright airy dining room where delicious home-cooked evening meals and Scottish breakfasts are served. Bar meals are also available. Permits for river and loch fishing are available, and there are mountain bikes for hire.

FACILITIES: 7 rms (4 en suite) (2 fmly) No smoking in dining room No smoking in lounges tea/coffee Licensed TVL No coaches Fishing Pool Table Fishing, Riding, Bike hire and Boat trips arranged Dinner Last d 8pm (9.30pm Summer) **PRICES:** s £18-£22; d £36-£56✳ **LB BB PARKING:** 15 **CARDS:**

SALEN Map 10 NM54

Premier Collection

♦♦♦♦♦ Gruline Home Farm

Gruline PA71 6HR ☎ 01680 300581 Fax 01680 300573
e-mail: aa@gruline.com
Dir: *from Craignure ferry turn right and travel 10m to Salen. In village turn left on B8035 and drive for 2m, keep left at fork, past church, farm left*

Peacefully situated in the heart of the island, this former farmhouse has been lovingly restored and converted by Mr and Mrs Boocock, who warmly welcome visitors to their charming home. Bedrooms have elegant period furnishings and luxurious bathrooms. The inviting lounge has been tastefully decorated and the smart conservatory overlooks the well-tended garden with waterfall and pond. Hearty breakfasts and carefully prepared five-course dinners are served around a communal table in the attractive dining room.

FACILITIES: 2 en suite No smoking TVB tea/coffee No dogs Cen ht No children 16yrs No coaches Dinner Last d 7pm **PRICES:** s fr £57; d fr £64✳ LB **PARKING:** 6 **CARDS:**

SHETLAND

LERWICK Map 16 HU44

♦♦♦♦ *Glen Orchy House*

20 Knab Rd ZE1 0AX ☎ 01595 692031 Fax 01595 692031
e-mail: glenorchy.house@virgin.net
Dir: *adjct to coastguard station*

Formerly a convent, this welcoming hotel sits high above the town. Most of the modern bedrooms are in the smart new extensions. There is a selection of inviting lounges, one with an honesty bar, and all have a range of books and board games. Enjoyable three-course dinners and substantial breakfasts are served.

FACILITIES: 22 en suite (5 fmly) No smoking in 7 bedrooms No smoking in dining room No smoking in 1 lounge STV TVB tea/coffee Licensed Cen ht No coaches Dinner Last d 2pm **PARKING:** 10 **CARDS:**

SKYE, ISLE OF

EDINBANE Map 13 NG35

♦♦♦♦ Shorefield House

Edinbane IV51 9PW ☎ 01470 582444 Fax 01470 582414
e-mail: shorefieldhouse@aol.com
Dir: *approx 12m from Portree and 8m from Dunvegan, turn off A850 into Edinbane, house 1st on right.*

Shorefield is a modern house with a range of rooms, including family rooms and specially adapted ground floor rooms suitable for disabled guests and those with limited mobility. There is a charming conservatory adjoining the dining room, and a large child-friendly garden. The village has a choice of venues for an evening meal.

FACILITIES: 5 en suite (3 fmly) (4 GF) No smoking tea/coffee No dogs Cen ht TVL No coaches **PRICES:** s £25-£32; d £45-£58✳ LB **PARKING:** 10 **CARDS:**

PORTREE Map 13 NG44

♦♦♦♦ Quiraing

Viewfield Rd IV51 9ES ☎ 01478 612870 Fax 01478 612870
Dir: *on A87 from S - Bridge End - pass BP filling station & guest house 400mtrs on right*

This stylishly furnished bungalow stands in its own well-tended garden, on the southern approach to the town, which is only a four-minute walk away. Bedrooms are bright airy and immaculately maintained. There is a comfortable lounge and an attractive dining room where hearty traditional breakfasts are served at individual tables.

FACILITIES: 6 en suite (2 fmly) No smoking in bedrooms No smoking in dining room No smoking in 1 lounge TVB tea/coffee No dogs (ex guide dogs) Cen ht TVL No coaches **PRICES:** d £44-£48✳ **PARKING:** 8 **CARDS:**

♦♦♦ Craiglockhart

Beaumont Crescent IV51 9DF ☎ 01478 612233

A genuinely welcoming guesthouse with delightful views over Portree Harbour, Craiglockhart provides attractively decorated, well-equipped bedrooms. Family photographs create a homely atmosphere in the lounge, and hearty breakfasts featuring the best of local produce are served at shared tables.

FACILITIES: 9 rms (3 en suite) No smoking TVB tea/coffee No dogs Cen ht TVL No coaches **PRICES:** s £18-£20; d £40-£50✳ BB **PARKING:** 4 **NOTES:** Closed Dec

Egg cups for excellence!
This symbol shows that breakfast exceeded our Inspector's expectations.

Wales

The Talkhouse, Caersws

WALES

ANGLESEY, ISLE OF

AMLWCH — Map 06 SH49

Penycefn House
Salem St LL68 9DD ☎ 01407 832122 📠 01407 832122
e-mail: joancadden@amserve.com
Dir: *travel over Brittania Bridge 2nd exit A5025 to Amlwch. 17m to Amlwch cross rdbt in approx. 200yds signed Town cntr. House on right).*
FACILITIES: 5 rms (1 fmly) (2 GF) No smoking in dining room TVB tea/coffee Cen ht TVL No coaches **PRICES:** s £16; d £32✳ BB
PARKING: 6 **NOTES:** ★★ Closed 23 Dec-3 Jan
CARDS:

CEMAES BAY — Map 06 SH39

♦♦♦♦ Hafod Country House
LL67 0DS ☎ 01407 710500 📠 01407 710055
e-mail: hirst.hafod@tesco.net
Dir: *off A5025, turning for Llanfechell, opposite renovated windmill*
This fine Edwardian house is set on the edge of a pretty fishing village and lies in an acre of attractive lawns and gardens with a wildlife pond. The three smart, modern bedrooms are attractively decorated and well equipped. A spacious drawing room is provided and breakfast, including home-made preserves and fresh juices when in season, is served in a separate dining room. Evening meals can be obtained at a pub a short stroll away.
FACILITIES: 3 en suite No smoking TVB tea/coffee No dogs (ex guide dogs) Licensed Cen ht No children 7yrs No coaches Croquet lawn
PRICES: d £45-£47✳ LB **PARKING:** 5 **NOTES:** Closed Oct-Feb
CARDS:

HOLYHEAD — Map 06 SH28

♦♦♦♦ *Yr Hendre*
Porth-y-Felin Rd LL65 1AH ☎ 01407 762929 📠 01407 762929
e-mail: rita@yr-hendre.freeserve.co.uk
Dir: *from A5 in town centre turn left at War Memorial. Take next left, up steep hill, straight on X-roads, house on right facing park*
A short walk from the promenade lies this delightful house, once the local manse. It is convenient for travellers on the nearby Ireland-bound ferries. Bedrooms are attractively decorated with rich fabrics and wallpapers and all are thoughtfully equipped. Reception rooms also offer stylish comfort. A freshly prepared breakfast relies heavily on local produce.
FACILITIES: 3 en suite No smoking TVB tea/coffee No dogs (ex guide dogs) Cen ht TVL No coaches Dinner Last d 3pm **PARKING:** 7

♦♦♦ Wavecrest
93 Newry St LL65 1HU ☎ 01407 763637 📠 01407 764862
e-mail: cwavecrest@aol.com
Dir: *at end of A55 turn left. After 600yds turn by railings, premises 100yds up hill on right*
Conveniently located for the Irish ferry terminals and within easy walking distance of the town centre, the Wavecrest is proving to be a popular overnight staging post. Pretty bedrooms are equipped with satellite television and other modern facilities. There is a comfortable lounge and evening meals may be booked in advance.
FACILITIES: 4 rms (2 en suite) (3 fmly) No smoking STV TVB tea/coffee Cen ht TVL No coaches Dinner Last d 3pm **PRICES:** s £20-£30; d £38-£45✳ BB **PARKING:** 1 **NOTES:** Closed 24-31 Dec

Places with this symbol are farmhouses.

LLANERCHYMEDD — Map 06 SH48

♦♦♦♦ *Tre-Wyn (SH454851)*
Maenaddwyn LL71 8AE ☎ 01248 470875 Mrs N Bown
e-mail: nia@trewyn.fsnet.co.uk
Dir: *A5025 to Benllech Bay, B5108 to Brynteg x-roads, take LLannerch-y-medd road 3m to Maenaddwyn. Right after 6 houses, 0.5m to farm*
An extremely warm and friendly welcome is extended to guests at this spacious farmhouse. Rooms are well equipped and attractively furnished. Both the dining room and the relaxing lounge with its real log fire offer wonderful views across the gardens and rural countryside to Bodafon Mountain.
FACILITIES: 3 en suite (1 fmly) No smoking TVB tea/coffee No dogs (ex guide dogs) Cen ht TVL 240 acres arable beef sheep **PARKING:** 5

Llwydiarth Fawr
LL71 8DF ☎ 01248 470321 & 470540
e-mail: llwydiarth@hotmail.com
Dir: *take the A55 to Anglesey, turning off for Llangefni A5114. At Llangefni follow signs for Oriel Ynys & the B5111 to Llanermymedd, turn right in village square for Amlwch (B5111) Llwydiarth Fawr is 0.5m on the right*
FACILITIES: 4 rms (3 en suite) (4 fmly) No smoking TVB tea/coffee No dogs (ex guide dogs) Cen ht TVL No coaches Fishing Dinner Last d 6.30pm **PRICES:** s £25-£30; d £50✳ **PARKING:** 9
NOTES: ★★★★ **CARDS:**

LLANFACHRAETH — Map 06 SH38

♦♦♦ Holland Hotel
LL65 4UH ☎ 01407 740252 📠 01407 741344
e-mail: info@holland-hotel.co.uk
Dir: *on A5025, in centre of village. 3 m from A55.*
A friendly, traditional 18th-century village inn ideally located only 7 miles from Holyhead for the ferry to Ireland. Bedrooms offer a high standard of comfort and meal specialities include local Anglesey shellfish, which can be accompanied by drinks from the extensive range of beers, wines and spirits.
FACILITIES: 4 en suite (1 fmly) No smoking in 4 bedrooms No smoking in area of dining room TVB tea/coffee Direct dial from bedrooms Cen ht Dinner Last d 8.30pm **PRICES:** s fr £30; d fr £60✳ **MEALS:** Bar Lunch £3.95-£7.95alc Dinner £3.95-£7.95alc✳ **PARKING:** 30
CARDS:

LLANGEFNI — Map 06 SH47

Doldir
Glanhwfa Rd LL77 7EN ☎ 01248 723938 📠 01248 723938
e-mail: doldirguesthouse@amstrad.com
Dir: *turn off A5 to Llangefni, in 1.5m Doldir is on right nect to Chapel/Court House*
FACILITIES: 4 rms (3 en suite) (2 fmly) No smoking TVB tea/coffee No dogs (ex guide dogs) Cen ht TVL No coaches **PRICES:** s £20-£25; d £40-£45✳
NOTES: ★★★ **CARDS:**

MENAI BRIDGE — Map 06 SH57

♦♦♦♦ Wern Farm *(SH550740)*
Pentraeth Rd LL59 5RR ☎ 01248 712421 📠 01248 712421
Mr & Mrs P Brayshaw
e-mail: wernfarmanglesey@onetel.net.uk
Dir: *from A5/A55 take 2nd exit after crossing Britannia Bridge signed A5025 Amlwch/Benllech. After rdbt pass large garage, farm on right*
This immaculately maintained farm guest house lies two miles north east off the Amlwch road. It provides modern and very well equipped bedrooms that are attractively decorated and comfortably furnished. An elegant lounge is available for guests and breakfast is served in the modern conservatory.

continued

FACILITIES: 3 rms (2 en suite) (2 fmly) No smoking TVB tea/coffee No dogs Cen ht TVL Tennis (hard) Croquet lawn 3/4 snooker table, Boules, Whirlpool bath 235 acres mixed **PRICES:** d £46-£56* **PARKING:** 10 **NOTES:** Closed Nov-Feb **CARDS:**

PENTRAETH Map 06 SH57

Premier Collection

♦♦♦♦♦ Parc-yr-Odyn *(SH510785)*

Parc-yr-Odyn LL75 8UL ☎ 01248 450566 Mrs H Thomas
e-mail: parcyrodyn@yahoo.com
Dir: *from Brittania bridge take A5025 to Amlwch. When you reach Reihracht to Talwrn in centre of village. Follow B5109 to Talwren drive on for 1m, establishment is on left*

The owners built this large modern house in 1996. It is quietly located on a sheep-rearing holding about a mile from Pentraeth. Bedrooms are comfortable, tastefully appointed and well equipped. There is an attractive lounge with an adjacent dining area. Separate tables can be provided if preferred.

FACILITIES: 2 en suite No smoking TVB tea/coffee No dogs (ex guide dogs) Cen ht No children 150 acres sheep/mixed **PRICES:** d £25-£28* **LB BB**

TREARDDUR BAY Map 06 SH27

♦♦♦ Moranedd

Trearddur Rd LL65 2UE ☎ 01407 860324 01407 860324
Dir: *from Bangor take A5 to Valley x-roads. L onto B4545 for 3.1 m. Past gardens on R, take 2nd R, Moranedd is 50yds on L.*

Moranedd has a slightly elevated location and there are good views over the area from many rooms. Bedrooms are fresh and attractively decorated, some are suitable for families. A relaxing lounge is provided and there is also a small sun terrace that looks out over the well tended gardens.

FACILITIES: 6 en suite (1 fmly) No smoking in bedrooms No smoking in dining room TVB tea/coffee No dogs (ex guide dogs) Licensed Cen ht No coaches Golf 18 **PRICES:** s £25-£27.50; d £45-£55* **PARKING:** 6

BRIDGEND

PORTHCAWL Map 03 SS87

♦♦♦♦ Penoyre

29 Mary St CF36 3YN ☎ 01656 784550 01656 784550
Dir: *Near seafront opp car park. From M4 J37, follow signs to prothcrawl seafront , 1st R before Grand Pavilion*

Located a few minutes walk from seafront and main shopping centre, this Edwardian terraced house is constantly being improved and bedrooms are both practical and homely. Imaginative breakfasts and dinners by arrangement, are taken in an attractive dining room, which also contains a bar and lounge area.

FACILITIES: 5 en suite (5 fmly) No smoking TVB tea/coffee Licensed Cen ht TVL No coaches **PRICES:** s £22.50-£25; d £42-£48* **LB NOTES:** Closed Xmas & New Year **CARDS:**

♦♦♦ Glenaub Hotel

50 Mary St CF36 3YA ☎ 01656 788242 01656 773649
e-mail: welcome@glenaubhotel.co.uk
Dir: *exit M4 junct 37 to Porthcawl. Hotel in town center, adjacent to Somerfields supermarket. Car park on side street next to Somerfields.*

continued

This hotel offers comfortable and simply appointed accommodation. All of the bedrooms benefit from full en suite bathrooms, and include many useful extra facilities. Public areas include a bar and a lounge, which offer a cheerful place in which to relax and enjoy a drink.

FACILITIES: 15 en suite TVB tea/coffee Direct dial from bedrooms Cen ht No coaches Dinner Last d 5.30pm **PRICES:** s £25-£32.50; d £40-£42.50* **CARDS:**

♦♦♦ Minerva Hotel

52 Esplanade Av CF36 3YU ☎ 01656 782428 01656 772055
Dir: *2.5m from M4 junct 37 take A4229 to seafront. Hotel next to Grand Pavilion Theatre*

The Minerva is an attractive and friendly hotel. Located just a short stroll from the seafront it is convenient for the theatre and other attractions. Comfortable rooms are provided and there is also a peaceful lounge and pleasant bar. Dinner is available from Monday to Thursday by arrangement.

FACILITIES: 9 rms (8 en suite) (2 fmly) No smoking in 2 bedrooms No smoking in dining room TVB tea/coffee Direct dial from bedrooms No dogs (ex guide dogs) Licensed Cen ht TVL No coaches Dinner Last d 6.30pm **PRICES:** s £26-£29; d £38-£40* **BB NOTES:** Closed 19 Dec-4 Jan rs weekends (no evening meals) **CARDS:**

CAERPHILLY

CAERPHILLY Map 03 ST18

♦♦♦ The Cottage

Pwllypant CF83 3HW ☎ 029 2086 9160
e-mail: thecottage@tesco.net
Dir: *at rdbt junct of A468 & A469, take exit to Energlyn*

A mulberry tree planted in the reign of Charles II stands in the front garden of this house, which was previously used as a vicarage and the first girls' school in Wales. Many original features are retained which are enhanced by the quality décor and furnishing schemes throughout.

FACILITIES: 3 en suite No smoking TVB tea/coffee No dogs (ex guide dogs) Cen ht No coaches **PRICES:** s £29; d £45* **PARKING:** 8 **NOTES:** Closed Xmas

CARDIFF

CARDIFF Map 03 ST17

♦♦♦♦ Annedd Lon

157 Cathedral Rd, Pontcanna CF11 9PL ☎ 029 2022 3349 029 2064 0885
Dir: *From Cardiff Castle, W across the river Taff. First right is Cathedral Road. On left hand side just after 4th side street*

Located within easy walking distance of both Sophia Gardens and the Millennium Stadium, this impressive Victorian house retains many original features and is attractively furnished. The public areas include a comfortable lounge as well as a cosy dining room.

FACILITIES: 6 rms (5 en suite) (2 fmly) No smoking TVB tea/coffee No dogs (ex guide dogs) Cen ht TVL No coaches **PRICES:** s fr £30; d fr £50 **PARKING:** 7 **NOTES:** Closed Xmas-New Year's Eve **CARDS:**

Places with this symbol are Inns.

Wales

CARDIFF continued

♦♦♦♦ Big Sleep Hotel

Bute Ter CF10 2FE ☎ 029 2063 6363 📠 029 2063 6364
e-mail: bookings.cardiff@thebigsleephotel.com
Dir: *opposite Cardiff International Arena*

Part of Cardiff's skyline, this city centre hotel offers modern style, technology and convenience and is ideal for both the business traveller and tourist. The bedrooms have spectacular views over the city towards the bay and all are very well equipped. A range of rooms is available, from penthouse to standard. There is a bar on the ground floor and also secure parking. Continental breakfast is served or as an alternative for the traveller wishing to make an early start 'Breakfast to go'.

FACILITIES: 81 en suite (6 fmly) No smoking in 40 bedrooms STV TVB tea/coffee Direct dial from bedrooms No dogs (ex guide dogs) Lift Cen ht **PRICES:** d £45-£99✳ **LB** **PARKING:** 30
CARDS:

♦♦♦♦ *Marlborough*

98 Newport Rd CF24 1DG ☎ 029 2049 2385
📠 029 2046 5982

This family run guest house is just a few minutes from the city centre and has a warm and friendly atmosphere. Bedrooms are mostly spacious and all are well furnished and equipped. Bathrooms are particularly well fitted. A comfortably furnished lounge is available for residents and hearty breakfasts are served in the pleasant breakfast room.

FACILITIES: 8 rms (5 en suite) (2 fmly) No smoking in bedrooms No smoking in dining room STV TVB tea/coffee No dogs Licensed Cen ht TVL ch fac Last d 7pm **PARKING:** 8

♦♦♦♦ Tanglewood

4 Tygwyn Rd, Penylan CF23 5JE
☎ 029 2047 3447 & 07971546812 📠 029 2047 3447
e-mail: reservations@tanglewoodguesthouse.com
Dir: *Head for Cardiff E & Docks. 3rd exit at rdbt. Next rdbt 1st exit. Left at lights. Turn right just past next lights. Establishment 120yds on right*

continued

A spacious and well-kept former Edwardian residence, Tanglewood is situated in a quiet suburban area in its own attractive gardens. The bedrooms are pleasantly decorated and thoughtfully equipped and there is a comfortable lounge overlooking the gardens in which to relax.

FACILITIES: 4 rms (1 en suite) No smoking TVB tea/coffee No dogs (ex guide dogs) Cen ht TVL No coaches **PRICES:** s fr £28; d £54-£56✳ **PARKING:** 8 **NOTES:** Closed 15 Dec-10 Jan

Courtfield Hotel

101 Cathedral Rd CF11 9PH ☎ 029 2022 7701 📠029 2022 7701
e-mail: courtfield@ntlworld.com
Dir: *from city centre/Cardiff Castle cross bridge over River Taff and turn 1st right into Cathedral Road*

FACILITIES: 10 rms (6 en suite) (1 fmly) (1 GF) No smoking in dining room No smoking in lounges TVB tea/coffee Direct dial from bedrooms No dogs (ex guide dogs) Licensed Cen ht TVL No children 7yrs No coaches **PRICES:** s £25-£40; d £55-£80✳ **NOTES:** ★★ Closed 24-31 Dec
CARDS:

CARMARTHENSHIRE

BRECHFA Map 02 SN53

♦♦♦♦ Glasfryn

SA32 7QY ☎ 01267 202306 📠0870 1341770
e-mail: joyce.glasfryn@clara.co.uk
Dir: *M4 junct 49 onto A48 to Cross Hands, towards Carmarthen for approx 1m, turn 2nd left onto B4310 past gardens over the A40. Continue on B4310 for approx 6m into Brechfa*

Located close to a riverside walk in the heart of the village, this late Victorian house has been sympathetically renovated to provide comfortable bedrooms with the added benefit of power showers. The spacious dining room, which overlooks a pretty patio, is the setting for imaginative dinners using fresh local produce.

FACILITIES: 3 en suite No smoking in bedrooms No smoking in dining room TVB tea/coffee Licensed Cen ht TVL Mountian Bike Cycle hire Dinner Last d 9pm **PRICES:** s £25-£30; d £45-£50✳ **PARKING:** 12
CARDS:

BURRY PORT Map 02 SN40

♦♦♦♦ The George

Stepney Rd SA16 0BH ☎ 01554 832211
Dir: *turn off A484 at traffic lights, at Achddu Post Office look for town centre sign, near railway station at lower end of Stepney Road*

The George is a very pleasant place to stay with welcoming hospitality and attentive service that make guests, old and new, feel entirely at home. The bar and restaurant areas celebrate Burry Port's aeronautical connections from Amelia Earhart's landing to its more recent connections with Concorde. Bedrooms are comfortable and very well equipped. Well-cooked dinners offer a wide range of choices and, as at breakfast, hearty portions are served.

FACILITIES: 5 en suite 4 annexe rms (3 en suite) (2 fmly) (1 GF) TVB tea/coffee No dogs (ex guide dogs) Cen ht No children 6yrs No coaches Dinner Last d 9.30pm **PRICES:** s £19.50-£36.50; d £38-£47✳ **BB**
MEALS: Lunch £5.40-£18.90alc Dinner £8.35-£22.90alc✳

BB Great value! This indicates B&B for £19 and under, per person, per night.

CARMARTHEN Map 02 SN42

See also Brechfa & Cwmduad

♦♦♦♦ Sarnau Mansion

Llysonnen Rd SA33 5DZ ☎ 01267 211404 📠 01267 211404
e-mail: fernihough@so1405.force9.co.uk

Dir: *From Carmarthen on A40 W, turn right after 4m to Bancyfelin. After 0.5m, Hafod Bakery is on the right and 150yds past the bakery on the right is the entrance to Sarnau Mansion*

Located west of the town on sixteen acres which include a tennis court and walled garden, this impresive late Georgian house retains much of its original character and is stylishly decorated. Ground floor areas include a lounge with log fire, a dining room and the spacious bedrooms offer stunning rural views.

FACILITIES: 3 en suite No smoking TVB tea/coffee No dogs Cen ht TVL No coaches Tennis (hard) Dinner Last d by arrangement
PRICES: s £28-£35; d £45-£55* **PARKING:** 10

♦♦♦♦ Capel Dewi Uchaf Country House *(SN485203)*

Capel Dewi SA32 8AY ☎ 01267 290799 📠 01267 290003
Mrs F Burns
e-mail: uchaffarm@aol.com

Dir: *from M4 junct 49, A48 to exit for National Botanical Garden for Wales. Take B4310 to junct with B4300. Turn left. Establishment approx 1m on right*

Located in 30 acres of grounds with stunning views and private fishing in the River Towy, this Grade II listed 16th-century house has retained many magnificent features. Home-grown produce is a feature of the memorable dinners and generous Welsh breakfasts. Ideally located for the National Botanic Gardens.

FACILITIES: 3 en suite No smoking TVB tea/coffee No dogs Licensed Cen ht TVL Fishing Riding 34 acres non-working Dinner Last d 10am
PRICES: s £40; d £56* **LB PARKING:** 10 **NOTES:** Closed Xmas
CARDS:

♦♦♦♦ Glôg Farm *(SN371154)*

Llangain SA33 5AY ☎ 01267 241271 Mrs H E Rodenhurst

Dir: *leave Carmarthen on A40 W, turn left onto B4312 signposted Llanstephan, through Llangain turn right signed Llangynog/Glog, farm 0.75m on right*

Located 4 miles from the sandy beach and castle at Llanstephan, this Welsh longhouse has been sympathetically renovated to provide attractive homely bedrooms, some ideal for family use. A comfortable lounge with wood burner is also available and breakfast is taken in the cosy dining room, which contains an antique pine chicken coop dresser.

Glôg Farm

FACILITIES: 4 en suite (2 fmly) No smoking in dining room tea/coffee No dogs (ex guide dogs) Cen ht TVL 40 acres beef Dinner Last d noon
PRICES: s £25; d £40* **LB PARKING:** 10

CWMDUAD Map 02 SN33

♦♦♦♦ Neuadd-Wen

SA33 6XJ ☎ 01267 281438 📠 01267 281438
e-mail: goodbourn@neuaddwen.plus.com

Dir: *alongside A484, 9m N of Carmarthen*

Excellent customer care is assured at this combined post office and house situated in pretty gardens within an unspoilt village in the Duad Valley. Bedrooms are filled with thoughtful extras and there is a choice of guest lounges in addition to an attractive dining room where imaginative dinners are served utilising fresh local produce. Elizabeth Goodbourn was a Top Twenty Finalist in the AA Landlady of the Year Award 2002-2003.

FACILITIES: 8 rms (6 en suite) (2 fmly) (2 GF) No smoking in dining room No smoking in 1 lounge TVB tea/coffee Direct dial from bedrooms Licensed Cen ht TVL Dinner Last d 6pm **PRICES:** s £18-£22; d £36-£44 **LB BB**
PARKING: 12 **CARDS:**

LLANDDAROG Map 02 SN51

Coedhirion Farm

Fferm Coedhirion SA32 8BH ☎ 01267 275666
e-mail: welshfarmhouse@hotmail.com

Dir: *along A48 dual carriageway 9m W junct 49 M4, 6m E of Carmarthen. 0.5m from LLanddarog*

FACILITIES: 3 en suite (1 fmly) (1 GF) No smoking TVB tea/coffee No dogs Cen ht No coaches **PRICES:** s £25-£30; d £40-£45* **LB PARKING:** 10
NOTES: ★★

Wales

LLANELLI Map 02 SN50

♦♦ Awel Y Mor

86 Queen Victoria Rd SA15 2TH ☎ 01554 755357
Fax 01554 755357

Dir: *follow A484 town centre signs until Asda is on the right, half circle around Asda, at traffic lights straight through lights. Go over mini rdbt, establishment 300yds on right*

This friendly and relaxed guest house is situated close to the town centre and offers bright accommodation. There are some family rooms available. Public areas include a lounge and dining room, which are open-plan, and there is an enclosed rear car park for guest use.

FACILITIES: 12 rms (8 en suite) (3 fmly) (2 GF) No smoking in dining room TVB tea/coffee No dogs (ex guide dogs) Licensed Cen ht TVL Dinner Last d 5pm **PRICES:** s £20-£25; d £35-£40* **LB BB PARKING:** 11
CARDS:

Ffynnon Rhosfa

Llwynteg, Llannon SA14 8JN ☎ 01269 845874 Fax 01269 831500
e-mail: ffynnon.rhosfa@virgin.net

Dir: *M4 westbound junct 48, turn right to Hendy then left onto B4306 after 3.1m turn right pass telephone box on left next house on the right*

FACILITIES: 3 en suite (7 fmly) No smoking in bedrooms TVB tea/coffee Cen ht TVL No coaches Dinner Last d noon
PRICES: s £20-£25; d £40-£50* **LB PARKING:** 6 **NOTES:** ★★

NANTGAREDIG Map 02 SN42

Dolau

Felingwn Isaf SA32 7PB ☎ 01267 290464

At the time of going to press the Diamond classification for this establishment had not been confirmed. Please check the AA website www.theAA.com for up-to-date information.

FACILITIES: 3 en suite

RHANDIRMWYN Map 03 SN74

♦♦♦ The Royal Oak

SA20 0NY ☎ 01550 760201 Fax 01550 760332
e-mail: royaloak@rhandirmwyn.com

Dir: *follow signs to Rhandirmwyn from A40 at Llandovery*

Located North of Llandovery in an area of outstanding natural beauty, this 17th-century former hunting lodge for the Cawdor Estate offers a wealth of character within its public areas. There are a wide range of real ales and imaginative food served. Comfortable bedrooms are equipped with both practical and homely extras.

FACILITIES: 5 rms (3 en suite) (1 fmly) TV3B tea/coffee Pool table Clay pigeon wknds Last d 9.30pm **PRICES:** s £20-£22.50; d £50-£56*
MEALS: Lunch £2.99-£10.49alc Dinner £2.99-£10.49alc* **PARKING:** 20
CARDS:

CEREDIGION

ABERAERON Map 02 SN46

♦♦♦♦ Arosfa

Harbourside SA46 0BU ☎ 01545 570120
e-mail: arosfabandb@aol.com

Dir: *at pedestrian crossing on A487 coast road in middle of town, take Market St towards sea, 150mtrs to car park with Arosfa alongside, painted green*

A warm welcome is assured at this sympathetically renovated Georgian house, located adjacent to the harbour in this historic town. Bedrooms are filled with thoughtful extras and smart modern bathrooms compliment. Other areas include a cosy lounge, stairways enhanced by quality art and memorabilia and a bright attractive dining room, the setting for imaginative award winning Welsh breakfasts.

continued

Arosfa Guesthouse

FACILITIES: 3 en suite 1 annexe en suite (1 fmly) (1 GF) No smoking TVB tea/coffee No dogs Cen ht No coaches **PRICES:** s £25-£38; d £46-£60* **LB**

ABERPORTH Map 02 SN25

♦♦♦ Ffynonwen Country

SA43 2HT ☎ 01239 810312

Dir: *turn off A487 at Gogerddan Arms towards Aberporth, sign to Ffynonwen 1m on L*

Located on twenty acres of grounds, one mile from the sea, this 17th-century former farmhouse provides comfortable accommodation. The bedrooms are homely and public areas are very spacious. These include a dining room and a separate bar, in addition to a guest lounge.

FACILITIES: 5 en suite (3 fmly) (2 GF) TVB tea/coffee Licensed Cen ht No coaches Games Room Dinner Last d 10am **PRICES:** s £22; d £44*
PARKING: 30

ABERYSTWYTH Map 06 SN58

♦♦♦♦ Glyn-Garth

South Rd SY23 1JS ☎ 01970 615050 Fax 01970 636835
e-mail: glyngarth@aol.com

Dir: *from A487 take 1st left into South Rd, Glyn-Garth on right close to South Promenade*

Close to the sea front and run by the same family for over 40 years, Glyn-Garth offers bedrooms with modern facilities. A comfortable lounge, family rooms and a ground floor bedroom are provided. Freshly cooked breakfast is served at individual tables.

FACILITIES: 10 rms (6 en suite) (2 fmly) No smoking STV TVB tea/coffee No dogs Cen ht TVL No coaches **PRICES:** s £21-£22; d £42-£56*
PARKING: 2 **NOTES:** Closed 2 wks Xmas & New Year

♦♦♦♦ Llety Ceiro Country House

Peggy Ln, Llandre, Bow St SY24 5AB ☎ 01970 821900
Fax 01970 820966

Located close to Aberystwyth this country house has been tastefully converted in modern style. Bedrooms all have their own facilities, are comfortably furnished and very well equipped. The attractive dining room has views across the valley and there is an adjacent conservatory where guests can relax and enjoy the tranquillity. Llety Ceiro was a Top Twenty Finalist in the AA Accessible Hotel of the Year Awards 2002-2003.

FACILITIES: 10 en suite (2 fmly) (3 GF) No smoking in 1 bedrooms No smoking in dining room STV TVB tea/coffee Direct dial from bedrooms Licensed Cen ht Dinner Last d 8pm **PRICES:** s £30-£40; d £45-£75* **LB**
PARKING: 21 **NOTES:** Civ Wed 45 **CARDS:**

♦♦♦♦ Yr Hafod
1 South Marine Ter SY23 1JX ☎ 01970 617579 📠 01970 636835
e-mail: johnyrhafod@aol.com
Dir: *on south promenade between harbour and castle*
A small, friendly guest house on the promenade of this university town, with well equipped, modern bedrooms and cosy public areas. Many rooms have sea views, overlooking the bay.
FACILITIES: 7 rms (3 en suite) No smoking TVB tea/coffee No dogs Cen ht TVL No coaches **PRICES:** s £21-£22; d £42-£54* **PARKING:** 1
NOTES: Closed Xmas & New Year

♦♦♦ *Llety Gwyn Hotel*
Llanbadarn Fawr SY23 3SR ☎ 01970 623965
Dir: *1m E A44*
A private hotel, run by the friendly Jones family for many years. It has a large public bar and extensive function rooms. Bedrooms have modern facilities, some are suitable for families and many are in a nearby building reached from the car park. Pets are very welcome and there are ten acres of grounds to explore.
FACILITIES: 8 rms (4 en suite) 6 annexe rms (4 en suite) TVB tea/coffee Licensed Cen ht TVL Pool Table Football Pitch Dinner Last d 12.30pm
PARKING: 40 **CARDS:**

♦♦♦ *Queensbridge Hotel*
Promenade, Victoria Ter SY23 2DH ☎ 01970 612343 615025
📠 01970 617452
Dir: *N end of promenade, near Constitution Hill Cliff Railway*
A friendly private hotel on the promenade. The bedrooms, some suitable for families, are well equipped with modern facilities and many have fine sea views. A comfortable lounge is available and a lift serves all floors.
FACILITIES: 15 en suite (6 fmly) No smoking in 6 bedrooms No smoking in dining room TVB tea/coffee Direct dial from bedrooms No dogs (ex guide dogs) Licensed Lift Cen ht TVL **NOTES:** Closed 1 wk Xmas
CARDS:

Mount Pleasant Guest House
Devil's Bridge SY23 4QY ☎ 01970 890219 📠 01970 890239
e-mail: relax@mpleasant.co.uk
Dir: *from A44 turn off at Ponterwyd to Devils Bridge, drive through village on A4120, Mount Pleasant is last house on the left. From A487 coast road take A4120 to Devil's Bridge 1st house on right*
FACILITIES: 2 en suite 1 annexe en suite No smoking TVB tea/coffee No dogs (ex guide dogs) Licensed Cen ht No children 11yrs No coaches Dinner Last d 5pm **PRICES:** d £40-£50* **PARKING:** 3 **NOTES:** ★★★ Closed Xmas & New Year

CARDIGAN — Map 02 SN14

♦♦♦ Brynhyfryd
Gwbert Rd SA43 1AE ☎ 01239 612861 📠 01239 612861
e-mail: g.arcus@btinternet.com
Dir: *on B4548 in Cardigan signposted Gwbert. From Town Centre turn right, keep left. Follow straight on. After Spar Shop take next left. 100yds on left*
Located within easy walking distance of central attractions, this elegant Victorian house has been sympathetically renovated to provide a range of homely bedrooms, complimented by smart modern bathrooms. Breakfast is taken in an attractive ground floor dining room and the house has a guest lounge and the benefit of unrestricted street parking.
FACILITIES: 7 rms (3 en suite) (1 fmly) No smoking in bedrooms No smoking in dining room STV TVB tea/coffee No dogs Cen ht No children 5yrs No coaches Dinner Last d 11am
PRICES: s £16-£18; d £36-£40* **LB BB**

♦♦♦ *Webley Waterfront Hotel*
Poppit Sands, St Dogmaels SA43 3LN ☎ 01239 612085
📠 01239 612085
Dir: *from A484 from Carmarthen to Cardigan. Then take B4546 from Cardigan to St Dogmaels to Poppit Sands*
A very friendly riverside inn, overlooking the Teifi Estuary near Poppit Sands. There are lovely views from many of the bedrooms, which are smart and modern with good facilities. The bar is popular locally and good value meals are usually on offer. There is a small cosy lounge for residents.
FACILITIES: 8 rms (5 en suite) No smoking in dining room TV5B tea/coffee No dogs Cen ht TVL Dinner Last d 9pm **PARKING:** 53

LAMPETER — Map 02 SN54

♦♦♦ *Dremddu Fawr (SN554529)*
Creuddyn Bridge SA48 8BL ☎ 01570 470394
Mrs M A Williams Jones
Dir: *take A482 towards Aberaeron then 2nd right opposite second-hand car forecourt over bridge. Turn sharp left follow road for approx 300yds*

Located four miles north of Lampeter in a secluded rural area, this Edwardian farmhouse offers two cosy, well equipped and homely bedrooms and a traditional dining room where delicious home cooked dinners are served by arrangement.
FACILITIES: 2 en suite No smoking STV TVB tea/coffee No dogs (ex guide dogs) Cen ht 205 acres beef/sheep Dinner Last d 7pm **PARKING:** 2
CARDS:

♦♦♦ Haulfan
6 Station Ter SA48 7HH ☎ 01570 422718
Dir: *from N A485/A482, follow signs for Lampeter, left at 1st x-rds near university. From S, M4/A485, through town centre, right by fountain, right again*
Very popular with visitors to the nearby university, this Victorian town house provides bedrooms filled with practical and homely extras. Generous breakfasts are taken in the cosy dining room and a warm welcome is assured from proprietors who have an excellent knowledge of the area.
FACILITIES: 3 rms (1 en suite) (1 fmly) No smoking STV TVB tea/coffee Cen ht TVL No coaches **PRICES:** s £19-£21; d £36-£40* **LB BB**
NOTES: Closed 20 Dec-mid Jan

♦♦♦ Red Diamonds highlight the top establishments within the AA's 3, 4 and 5 Diamond ratings.

Wales

LLANDYSUL Map 02 SN44

♦♦♦♦ Plas Cerdin

Ffostrasol SA44 4TA ☎ 01239 851329 🖷 01239 851329
e-mail: plascerdin@talk21.com
Dir: *from Llandysul take A486 to New Quay through Bwlch-y-Groes. R into private rd*

Located north of the town in an elevated position that offers stunning views of the Cerdin Valley and Cambrian mountains, this very well maintained house, standing on lovely gardens, provides homely and thoughtfully furnished bedrooms one of which is ideal for family use. A guest lounge is also available.
FACILITIES: 3 en suite (1 fmly) (1 GF) No smoking in bedrooms No smoking in dining room TVB tea/coffee Cen ht TVL No children 3yrs No coaches Dinner Last d 11am **PRICES:** s £25-£30; d £45-£50✳
PARKING: 4 **NOTES:** Closed Dec & Jan

NEW QUAY Map 02 SN35

♦♦♦ Brynarfor Hotel

New Rd SA45 9SB ☎ 01545 560358 🖷 01545 561204
e-mail: enquiries@brynarfor.co.uk
Dir: *exit A487 at Llanina junct, take B4342 towards New Quay, premises 2m on left*

In an elevated position on sloping landscaped gardens, close to the harbour and attractions, this constantly improving owner-managed hotel provides a range of practical homely bedrooms. The excellent dinner choice features good vegetarian options and the public areas are spacious.
FACILITIES: 5 en suite 2 annexe en suite (3 fmly) No smoking in dining room No smoking in 1 lounge TVB tea/coffee No dogs (ex guide dogs) Licensed Cen ht TVL ch fac No coaches Pool Table Games room Exercise machines Dinner Last d 6pm **PRICES:** s £32-£35; d £50-£70✳ **LB**
PARKING: 11 **NOTES:** Closed Nov-Feb **CARDS:** 

CONWY

BETWS-Y-COED Map 06 SH75

♦♦♦♦ Aberconwy House

Lon Muriau LL24 0HD ☎ 01690 710202 🖷 01690 710800
e-mail: welcome@aberconwy-house.co.uk
Dir: *on A470, 0.5m N from A5/A470 junction*

This large Victorian house has splendid views over the Llugwy and Conwy Valleys from many rooms. The attractive bedrooms are comfortably furnished. There is a bright and cheerful lounge and breakfast is served at individual tables in the spacious breakfast room. Much thought has been put into providing local information.
FACILITIES: 8 en suite (1 fmly) (1 GF) No smoking TVB tea/coffee No dogs (ex guide dogs) Licensed Cen ht No children 6yrs No coaches
PRICES: s £28-£44; d £46-£52✳ **LB** **PARKING:** 10
CARDS:

See advertisement on opposite page

♦♦♦♦ Afon View Non Smokers Guest House

Holyhead Rd LL24 0AN ☎ 01690 710726 🖷 01690 710726
e-mail: k.roobottom@which.net
Dir: *situated on A5 approx. 150mtrs E of HSBC Bank*

This house, a short walk from the village centre, offers walkers and tourists alike a warm welcome. Guided walks, together with information on local places of interest are also available. Bright bedrooms are thoughtfully furnished and equipped. Reception rooms extend to a comfortable lounge and a pine furnished breakfast room.
FACILITIES: 7 en suite No smoking TVB tea/coffee No dogs Cen ht TVL No children 10yrs **PRICES:** s £25-£30✳ **LB** **PARKING:** 8
NOTES: Closed 24-26Dec **CARDS:**

♦♦♦♦ Coed-y-Fron

Vicarage Rd LL24 0AD ☎ 01690 710365
e-mail: welcome@coedyfron.co.uk
Dir: *enter Betws-y-Coed on A5 (Bangor), pass traffic lights & post office. Immediately after St Mary's Church turn into Vicarage Rd*

continued

A warm welcome is assured at this stone fronted non-smoking Victorian house, which is centrally located in an elevated position with stunning views of the historic centre and surrounding countryside. The homely, comfortable bedrooms are complimented by smart modern bathrooms and local produce is a feature of the Welsh breakfasts, which are taken in an attractive front facing dining room.
FACILITIES: 4 rms (2 en suite) No smoking TVB tea/coffee No dogs Cen ht No children 7yrs **PRICES:** s £21-£29; d £42-£58* **LB**

♦♦♦♦ Ferns Non Smokers Guest House

Holyhead Rd LL24 0AN ☎ 01690 710587 📠 01690 710587
e-mail: ferns@betws-y-coed.co.uk
Dir: *on A5 close to Waterloo Bridge*

Situated near the centre of the village, this guest house offers guests friendly hospitality. The bedrooms are neatly decorated and all are equipped with modern facilities. Some of the beds have attractive canopies. Breakfast can be taken in the dining room, which looks out onto the garden and valley.
FACILITIES: 9 en suite (2 fmly) No smoking TVB tea/coffee No dogs Licensed Cen ht TVL No children 7yrs No coaches **PRICES:** s £28-£40; d £44-£48* **LB PARKING:** 9 **CARDS:**

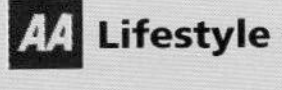

♦♦♦♦ Fron Heulog Country House

LL24 0BL ☎ 01690 710736 📠 01690 710920
e-mail: jean&peter@fronheulog.co.uk
Dir: *In Betws-y-Coed turn N off A5 onto B5106 over Pont y Pair bridge. Over bridge immediately left Fronheulog 150 mtrs ahead*
Superbly located by the river within a few minutes' walk from central attractions, this impressive Victorian house has been restored to provide a range of thoughtfully equipped bedrooms. Memorable breakfasts, featuring home made or local produce, are served in an attractive spacious dining room and a choice of guest lounges is also available.
FACILITIES: 3 en suite No smoking STV TVB tea/coffee No dogs (ex guide dogs) Cen ht TVL No children No coaches **PRICES:** d £44-£60* **LB PARKING:** 3

Wales

BETWS-Y-COED continued

♦♦♦♦ Henllys

Old Church Rd LL24 0AL ☎ 01690 710534 01690 710884
e-mail: henllys@betws-y-coed.co.uk
Dir: *A5 into Betws-y-Coed pass two petrol stations on left then turn 1st right into Old Church Rd from south or from north A5 pass Royal Oak Hotel, village green & turning for railway station then turn left into Old Church Rd*

Superbly located in immaculate gardens beside the river, this Victorian former police station and magistrates' court has been sympathetically renovated to provide bedroom accommodation of immense charm. One room is located in a former cell. Memorable breakfasts are taken in the original courtroom and a warm welcome is assured.
FACILITIES: 9 en suite (1 fmly) (3 GF) No smoking TVB tea/coffee No dogs (ex guide dogs) Licensed Cen ht No coaches **PRICES:** s £27-£30; d £54-£60* **LB** **PARKING:** 10 **CARDS:**

See advertisement on page 563

♦♦♦♦ Ty Gwyn

LL24 0SG ☎ 01690 710383 01690 710383
e-mail: mratel1050@aol.com
Dir: *junct of A5/A470, by Waterloo Bridge*
Situated on the edge of the village, close to the Waterloo Bridge, this old coaching inn retains much of its original character. Rooms including the bar and restaurant have many exposed timbers. The bar meals and the daily-changing carte are both very popular. Bedrooms are attractively decorated and some have four-poster or half-tester beds.
FACILITIES: 12 rms (10 en suite) (2 fmly) No smoking in 1 bedrooms No smoking in dining room TVB tea/coffee Cen ht TVL Dinner Last d 9pm **PRICES:** s £17-£50; d £34-£90* **LB** **BB** **MEALS:** Lunch £7.95-£22alc Dinner £7.95-£22alc* **PARKING:** 14 **NOTES:** Closed Mon-Wed in Jan **CARDS:**

♦♦♦♦ White Horse

Capel Garmon LL26 0RW ☎ 01690 710271 01690 710721
e-mail: whitehorse@supanet.com
Dir: *from Llanwrst to Betws main road turn left at Snowdonia and Capel Garmon sign*
This 16th-century inn has a wealth of charm and character, enhanced by original features - exposed timbers, stone walls and log fires. The bars feature an impressive collection of pottery and china. A good selection of home-cooked food is available, served in either the bars or in the cottage-style restaurant. The no smoking bedrooms are compact and nicely furnished, with modern facilities.
FACILITIES: 6 en suite No smoking in bedrooms No smoking in dining room TVB tea/coffee No dogs Cen ht No children 12yrs Pool Table Dart board Dinner Last d 9pm **PRICES:** s £35; d £58-£66* **LB**
MEALS: Sunday Lunch £6-£11alc Dinner £6-£11alc* **PARKING:** 30
NOTES: Closed 25 Dec **CARDS:**

♦♦♦ Bryn Llewelyn Non Smokers Guest House

Holyhead Rd LL24 0BN ☎ 01690 710601 710601
e-mail: bryn.llewelyn@tiscali.co.uk
Dir: *travelling W on A5, 300yds past Royal Oak Hotel on left*
This friendly and popular guest house offers a warm welcome and good-value accommodation. The pretty bedrooms are equipped with modern facilities and some are suitable for families. There is a cosy lounge and a separate breakfast room, where a wide choice is offered at breakfast.
FACILITIES: 7 en suite (3 fmly) No smoking TVB tea/coffee Cen ht TVL No children 3yrs No coaches **PRICES:** s £18.50-£45; d £35-£60* **LB** **BB**
PARKING: 9

♦♦♦ Church Hill House

Vicarage Rd LL24 0AD ☎ 01690 710447 01690 710447
e-mail: church_hill@compuserve.com
Dir: *turn off A5 between post office and church, house just ahead*
This is a friendly guest house that stands in an elevated position overlooking the church and the village green. The bedrooms are attractively decorated and modern facilities are provided. There is a comfortable lounge, a small bar and an attractive dining room where evening meals are served.
FACILITIES: 7 rms (5 en suite) 6 annexe en suite (1 fmly) No smoking in 9 bedrooms No smoking in dining room No smoking in lounges TVB tea/coffee No dogs Licensed Cen ht No coaches Dinner Last d noon
PRICES: s £19-£24; d £38-£48* **LB** **BB** **PARKING:** 12
CARDS:

Summer Hill Non Smokers Guesthouse

Coed Cynhelier Rd LL24 0BL ☎ 01690 710306 01690 710306
Dir: *turn off A5 opposite 'Ultimate Outdoors' shop, cross bridge, turn left, through car park. Summer Hill 50yds on right*
FACILITIES: 7 rms (4 en suite) (1 fmly) No smoking TVB tea/coffee Licensed Cen ht TVL No children 3yrs No coaches Mountain biking
PRICES: s £21.50-£23.50; d £35.90-£39.90* **LB** **BB**
PARKING: 6 **NOTES:** ★★ **CARDS:**

COLWYN BAY Map 06 SH87

Premier Collection

♦♦♦♦♦ Plas Rhos Hotel

Cayley Promenade, Rhos-on-Sea LL28 4EP
☎ 01492 543698 01492 540088
e-mail: enquiries@destination.wales.co.uk
Dir: *off A55 junct 20. Turn right twice to rdbt and take 2nd turning. Then 4th turning at next rdbt. 3rd left turn to hotel on left*
Stunning sea views are a feature of this sympathetically renovated late Victorian house which provides high standards of comfort and hospitality. Bedrooms are filled with a wealth of thoughtful extras and have smart modern bathrooms. Ground floor areas include a choice of sumptuous lounges featuring fine original art and memorabilia, and comprehensive breakfasts are taken in an attractive dining room, decorated in delightful pastel shades, which overlooks the pretty, enclosed patio garden.
FACILITIES: 9 en suite (2 fmly) No smoking in 2 bedrooms No smoking in dining room No smoking in 1 lounge TVB tea/coffee No dogs (ex guide dogs) Licensed Cen ht TVL No coaches Dinner Last d 8pm **PRICES:** s £26.50-£33.50; d £53-£67* **LB** **PARKING:** 5
CARDS:

♦♦♦♦ Whitehall Hotel

51 Caley Promenade, Rhos-on-Sea LL28 4EP ☎ 01492 547296
e-mail: mossd.cymru@virgin.net

Dir: *From A55 E or W use exit to Old Colwyn. At T-junct turn down to Promenade. Turn left at Promenade and travel W for 1.9m to Rhos on Sea. Turn Left at Puppet Theatre. Hotel 5th on right*

Overlooking the Rhos-on-Sea promenade, this popular and friendly family-run hotel is convenient for shopping and other local amenities. It offers pretty bedrooms that include some suitable for families. Radios and hairdryers are provided in the rooms. A bar and separate lounge cater for residents and the menu offers hearty, home-cooked meals. Bar snacks are also available.

FACILITIES: 12 en suite (4 fmly) No smoking in dining room No smoking in lounges TVB tea/coffee Direct dial from bedrooms No dogs (ex guide dogs) Licensed Cen ht TVL Dinner Last d 4.30pm **PRICES:** s fr £24.50; d £49-£55✳ **LB PARKING:** 5 **CARDS:**

♦♦♦ Cabin Hill Private Hotel

College Av, Rhos-on-Sea LL28 4NT ☎ 01492 544568

Dir: *exit A55 at Rhos-on-Sea, signed to promenade, through Rhos village, L at Rhos Fynach pub. 3rd R (College Ave).*

Cabin Hill lies in a quiet residential area within walking distance of the sea-front and local shops. Bedrooms are neatly decorated and thoughtfully furnished and equipped. There is a foyer bar for residents and a separate lounge which is comfortably furnished. Meals are available in the spacious dining room.

FACILITIES: 10 rms (7 en suite) (2 fmly) No smoking in dining room TVB tea/coffee Cen ht TVL Dinner Last d 4.30pm
PRICES: s £18; d £36 **BB PARKING:** 2

♦♦♦ Crossroads

15 Coed Pella Rd LL29 7AT ☎ 01492 530736
e-mail: aae@crossroadsguesthouse.co.uk

Dir: *Coed Pella Rd is W of Town centre, HTV and job centre on corner of road*

Ideally situated for touring North Wales. Although tucked away in a quiet residential street, this hotel is only a short walk from the town centre and shops. The bedrooms are decorated with care and come in a variety of sizes, including family rooms. The lounge is large and comfortable.

FACILITIES: 5 rms (2 en suite) (1 fmly) No smoking in dining room TVB tea/coffee No dogs (ex guide dogs) Cen ht TVL No children 3yrs No coaches
PRICES: s £13-£25; d £26-£40✳ **LB BB PARKING:** 3
NOTES: Closed 24 Dec-2 Jan

♦♦♦ Northwood Hotel

47 Rhos Rd, Rhos-on-Sea LL28 4RS ☎ 01492 549931
🖹 01492 549931
e-mail: mail@northwoodhotel.co.uk

Dir: *exit A55 at Rhos-on-Sea, signed to Prom. Turn up Rhos Rd (opposite building with clock), hotel 200yds on left before church*

A short walk away from the seafront and shops, a warm and friendly atmosphere prevails at Northwood Hotel, which welcomes back many regular guests. Bedrooms are furnished in modern style and freshly prepared meals can be enjoyed in the spacious dining room/bar with light refreshments offered in the lounge.

FACILITIES: 12 rms (11 en suite) (3 fmly) (2 GF) No smoking in dining room No smoking in lounges TVB tea/coffee Licensed Cen ht TVL No coaches Dinner Last d 7pm **PRICES:** s £24; d £48✳ **LB PARKING:** 12
CARDS:

CONWY — Map 06 SH77

Premier Collection

♦♦♦♦♦ Sychnant Pass House

Sychnant Pass Rd LL32 8BJ ☎ 01492 596868
🖹 01492 596868
e-mail: bresykes@sychnant-pass-house.co.uk

continued

Dir: *follow signs to Conwy Town Centre. Past visitor centre then 2nd left into Uppergate St. Continue out of town for 0.75m on right near top of hill*

Sychnant Pass House

Located on three acres of landscaped grounds, this sympathetically extended Edwardian house offers high standards of comfort. Bedrooms, which include some suites, are filled with a wealth of thoughtful extras and the spacious, tastefully furnished lounges include a music room. Imaginative food using locally sourced produce is offered in the intimate dining room.

FACILITIES: 9 en suite (4 fmly) (3 GF) No smoking in bedrooms No smoking in dining room No smoking in 1 lounge TVB tea/coffee Licensed Cen ht TVL No coaches Riding Croquet lawn All rooms with video, up to date films available Dinner Last d 8.30pm
PRICES: s £50-£100; d £70-£120✳ **LB PARKING:** 30
CARDS:

Wales

CONWY continued

♦♦♦♦ Gwern Borter Country Manor

Barkers Ln LL32 8YL ☎ 01492 650360 Fax 01492 650360
e-mail: mail@snowdoniaholidays.co.uk
Dir: *from Conwy take B5106 for 2.25m, turn right onto unclass road towards Rowen for 0.5m then right (Gwern Borter) 0.5m on left*
A delightful creeper-clad mansion in several acres of lawns and gardens. Children are very welcome and there is a rustic play area, games room and many farmyard pets. Bedrooms are furnished with period or antique pieces and equipped with modern facilities. One has an Edwardian four-poster bed. There is an elegant lounge and Victorian-style dining room, where freshly cooked breakfasts are served.
FACILITIES: 3 en suite (1 fmly) No smoking in dining room TVB tea/coffee Cen ht TVL No coaches Riding Sauna Gymnasium Cycle hire Games room Pets corner **PRICES:** s £35-£38; d £52-£58✻ **LB PARKING:** 16
CARDS:

♦♦♦ Bryn Derwen

Woodlands LL32 8LT ☎ 01492 596134
Dir: *on B5106, approx 800yds from castle*
Sympathetically restored, and retaining many of its original Victorian features, Bryn Derwen is in an elevated position with views of Conwy. Bedrooms offer modern facilities and are brightly decorated. The breakfast room overlooks the garden, and guests also have use of the period style lounge.
FACILITIES: 6 en suite (1 fmly) No smoking in dining room No smoking in lounges TVB tea/coffee No dogs (ex guide dogs) Cen ht
PRICES: d fr £40✻ **LB PARKING:** 6

♦♦♦ Glan Heulog

Llanrwst Rd, Woodlands LL32 8LT ☎ 01492 593845
e-mail: glanheulog@no1guesthouse.freeserve.co.uk
Dir: *from Conwy Castle take B5106, house approx 0.25m on left*
This late 19th-century house lies in an elevated location with fine views over the town and castle from many rooms. Bedrooms are decorated with pretty wallpapers and are well equipped. One has a four-poster bed. A pleasant breakfast room is provided and hospitality from the proprietors is warm and friendly.
FACILITIES: 6 rms (5 en suite) (1 fmly) No smoking TVB tea/coffee Cen ht TVL No coaches Dinner Last d 9.30am **PRICES:** s £17-£25; d £34-£44✻ **LB BB PARKING:** 7 **CARDS:**

LLANDUDNO Map 06 SH78

Premier Collection

♦♦♦♦♦ Abbey Lodge

14 Abbey Rd LL30 2EA ☎ 01492 878042 Fax 01492 878042
e-mail: enquiries@abbeylodgeuk.com
Dir: *from promenade (sea on right) at T-junct L. Straight on at rdbt, 3rd right into Clement Ave, at top turn Right into Abbey Rd*

continued

Located on a leafy avenue within easy walking distance of the Promenade, this impressive Victorian villa has been lovingly restored, and the stylish décor and furniture throughout add to its charm. Bedrooms are filled with a wealth of thoughtful extras and there is a choice of sumptuous lounges in addition to an elegant dining room.
FACILITIES: 4 en suite No smoking TVB tea/coffee No dogs Licensed Cen ht TVL No children 12yrs No coaches Dinner Last d 4pm
PRICES: s £40-£50; d £55-£65✻ **LB PARKING:** 8
NOTES: Closed Xmas/New Year

Premier Collection

♦♦♦♦♦ Bryn Derwen Hotel

34 Abbey Rd LL30 2EE ☎ 01492 876804 Fax 01492 876804
e-mail: brynderwen@fsbdial.com
Dir: *from A55 onto A470, left at promenade to cenotaph, turn left, straight on at rdbt, 4th right into York Rd, hotel at top*
The hotel was built as a gentleman's residence in 1878 and has been converted with impeccable taste by Stuart and Valerie Langfield. Stuart's intuitive cooking has gained a fine reputation. Bedrooms are individually designed and imaginative use is made of rich colours and matching fabrics. Public rooms are elegantly furnished; a beauty salon and a sauna are available.
FACILITIES: 10 en suite No smoking TVB tea/coffee No dogs Licensed Cen ht TVL No children 12yrs No coaches Solarium fully equipped beauty salon, aromatherapy Dinner Last d noon **PRICES:** s £45-£55; d £70-£88✻ **LB PARKING:** 9 **NOTES:** Closed Nov-Feb
CARDS:

♦♦♦♦ Brigstock Hotel

1 St David's Place LL30 2UG ☎ 01492 876416
e-mail: mtajmemory@brigstock58.fsnet.co.uk
Dir: *Turn off A55 & onto Promenade at St George, left into St David's Road & left into St David's Place*
This friendly hotel is located in a quiet residential area, within easy walking distance of the sea front. Bedrooms are attractively decorated and very well equipped. A comfortable lounge is provided and meals and packed lunches are available by arrangement.
FACILITIES: 9 rms (8 en suite) (1 fmly) No smoking TVB tea/coffee No dogs (ex guide dogs) Licensed Cen ht TVL No children 12yrs No coaches Dinner Last d 2pm **PRICES:** s £20-£24; d £40-£48✻ **PARKING:** 6
CARDS:

♦♦♦♦ Carmel Private Hotel

17 Craig-y-Don Pde, The Promenade LL30 1BG
☎ 01492 877643 Fax 01492 871783
Dir: *on main promenade between the Great and Little Ormes*
This impeccably maintained private hotel stands at the eastern end of the promenade, overlooking the sea. It is conveniently close to the theatre and most of Llandudno's other facilities and attractions are within easy reach. Most of the modern equipped bedrooms are en suite. There is a pleasant lounge and an attractively appointed dining room.
FACILITIES: 9 rms (6 en suite) (2 fmly) No smoking TVB tea/coffee No dogs Cen ht TVL No children 4yrs Dinner Last d 6pm
PRICES: s £22-£26; d £34-£42✻ **LB BB PARKING:** 6

♦♦♦♦ The Concord

35 Abbey Rd LL30 2EH ☎ 01492 875504 📠 01492 873768
e-mail: theconcord@amserve.com
Situated in a quiet side road only short walk from the town, this family owned and run hotel offers well equipped and comfortable bedrooms together with delightful public rooms. It boasts an attractive front garden all year round.
FACILITIES: 11 en suite (6 fmly) No smoking TVB tea/coffee No dogs Licensed Cen ht TVL No coaches Dinner Last d 4pm
PRICES: s £24-£27; d £48-£51* **PARKING:** 11

♦♦♦♦ Cornerways Hotel

2 St Davids Place LL30 2UG ☎ 01492 877334 📠 01492 873324
e-mail: cornerwayshotel@btinternet.com
Dir: *turn off A55 at Llandudno sign onto A470, on entering town turn left after railway station at traffic lights. 4th right into St Davids Place, then 1st right is St Davids Place*
Located in a quiet mainly residential area a few minutes walk from the town centre, this well proportioned Edwardian house provides spacious comfortable bedrooms equipped with a wide range of practical and homely extras. Ground floor areas include an attractive dining room, a comfortable guest lounge and a pretty patio during the warmer months.
FACILITIES: 7 en suite No smoking TVB tea/coffee No dogs (ex guide dogs) Licensed Cen ht TVL No coaches Dinner Last d 4pm
PRICES: s £20-£25; d £40-£50* **LB** **PARKING:** 4

♦♦♦♦ Cranberry House

12 Abbey Rd LL30 2EA ☎ 01492 879760 📠 01492 879760
e-mail: cranberryhse@aol.com
Dir: *from A470, along Conway Rd to Mostyn St, turn left at end rdbt, 2nd right up Arvon Ave, left at T junct, 5th house on right*

Ideally located for all attractions, this elegant Victorian house has been lovingly renovated to provide a range of thoughtfully equipped bedrooms complimented by luxurious modern bathrooms. A comfortable guest lounge is available in addition to an antique furnished dining room where comprehensive breakfasts are served.
FACILITIES: 5 en suite No smoking TVB tea/coffee No dogs (ex guide dogs) Cen ht No children 8yrs No coaches
PRICES: s £30-£56; d £48-£56* **PARKING:** 5
NOTES: Closed Dec-Jan rs Feb **CARDS:**

♦♦♦♦ Lynton House Hotel

80 Church Walks LL30 2HD ☎ 01492 875057 & 875009
📠 01492 875057
e-mail: jfair75440@aol.com
Dir: *along promenade towards pier turn left at rdbt immediately after pier, hotel on right*
This immaculately maintained private hotel lies under the Great Orme just off the sea-front. Bedrooms are smart and modern, with well chosen decor, and two have four-posters. There is a comfortable lounge for residents and hospitality is warm and welcoming.

Lynton House Hotel

FACILITIES: 14 en suite (4 fmly) (1 GF) No smoking in dining room TVB tea/coffee Direct dial from bedrooms Licensed Cen ht TVL No coaches
PRICES: s £31; d £52-£62* **LB** **PARKING:** 7 **NOTES:** Closed 20-27 Dec
CARDS:

continued

♦♦♦♦ Sefton Court Hotel

49 Church Walks LL30 2HL ☎ 01492 875235 📠 01492 875235
e-mail: seftoncourt@aol.com
Dir: *A55 from Chester, follow signs for LLandudno Promenade, proceed to the pier and turn left into Church Walks, Sefton Court on the right*

An imposing private hotel located under the Great Orme, within easy walking distance of the resort centre and north and south shores. Bedrooms provide all modern comforts and many have good views over the area. A comfortable lounge featuring an honesty bar is provided for residents and families can be accommodated.
FACILITIES: 11 en suite (3 fmly) No smoking in dining room TVB tea/coffee No dogs Cen ht **PRICES:** s £23-£25; d £46-£50* **LB** **PARKING:** 11
NOTES: Closed Dec-Feb

♦♦♦♦ White Lodge Hotel

9 Neville Crescent, Central Promenade LL30 1AT
☎ 01492 877713
Dir: *Llandudno main promenade*
This friendly and relaxing hotel is located on the promenade with all local amenities within easy walking distance. Many bedrooms enjoy good seafront views and have pretty canopies over the beds. Guests also have the use of a lounge and separate bar.
FACILITIES: 12 en suite (4 fmly) No smoking in bedrooms No smoking in dining room No smoking in lounges TVB tea/coffee No dogs (ex guide dogs) Licensed Cen ht Dinner Last d 10pm **PRICES:** s £35-£40; d £56* **LB**
PARKING: 15

Wales

LLUNDUDNO continued

♦♦♦ Beach Cove

8 Church Walks LL30 2HD ☎ 01492 879638 📠 01492 860522
e-mail: david@beachcove.freeserve.co.uk
Dir: *from promenade proceed towards the pier, at rdbt turn left into Church Walks. Beach Cove approx 100yds on left*

Nestling beneath the Great Orme, a short distance from the Promenade, Beach Cove offers a combination of comfort, convenience and warm hospitality. Attractive bedrooms are well equipped and include a four-poster and a ground floor room.
FACILITIES: 7 rms (5 en suite) No smoking in dining room TVB tea/coffee No dogs (ex guide dogs) Cen ht No coaches **PRICES:** s £18; d £34-£48✳ **BB** **PARKING:** 4 **CARDS:**

♦♦♦ Bodnant

39 St Mary's Rd LL30 2UE ☎ 01492 876936
e-mail: dyfrig.williams@talk21.com
Dir: *A470 to Llandudno town centre, take left fork past station, left at lights, 2nd right into St Marys Rd, Bodnant on right*
Peacefully located on a residential avenue within easy walking distance of central attractions, this Edwardian house provides a range of bedrooms equipped with thoughtful extras. Wholesome breakfasts are taken in an attractive traditionally furnished dining room, which also contains comfortable lounge seating.
FACILITIES: 4 en suite No smoking TVB tea/coffee No dogs (ex guide dogs) Cen ht No coaches **PRICES:** s £19-£21; d £38-£42✳ **BB**

♦♦♦ Britannia Hotel

Promenade, 15 Craig-y-Don Pde LL30 1BG ☎ 01492 877185
e-mail: guswebster8@aol.com
Dir: *close to North Wales Theatre & 100yds from Texaco garage and Llandudno Conference Centre*
Situated towards the Little Orme end of the promenade, this hospitable private hotel is being constantly upgraded. Bedrooms are comfortably furnished and equipped. A freshly prepared breakfast can be enjoyed at separate tables in the breakfast room.
FACILITIES: 10 rms (8 en suite) (5 fmly) No smoking in dining room TVB tea/coffee No dogs (ex guide dogs) Cen ht No coaches Dinner Last d 5pm **PRICES:** d £34-£50✳ **LB** **BB** **NOTES:** Closed 22 Nov-14 Feb

♦♦♦ Minion Private Hotel

21-23 Carmen Sylva Rd, Craig-y-Don LL30 1EQ
☎ 01492 877740
Dir: *exit A55 onto A470 proceed to promenade turn right then right again at Carmen Sylva Rd. estabishment 150yds on right*
The friendly Buet family have been welcoming visitors here for over 50 years. It is a private hotel and lies at the western end of the promenade. Bedrooms are smart and comfortable; two are located on ground floor level. There is a cosy bar and a separate lounge.
FACILITIES: 10 en suite (1 fmly) (2 GF) No smoking in dining room tea/coffee Licensed TVL No children 2yrs No coaches Dinner Last d 4pm **PRICES:** s £17-£18.50✳ **BB** **PARKING:** 8 **NOTES:** Closed Nov-Mar

♦♦♦ Quinton Hotel

36 Church Walks LL30 2HN ☎ 01492 876879 📠 01492 876879
The Quinton Hotel is conveniently located for the town centre and both beaches. Personally run by the same owners for over 25 years, it provides warm and friendly hospitality and value for money. Bedrooms are well equipped and include one on the ground floor.
FACILITIES: 9 en suite (3 fmly) No smoking in dining room TVB tea/coffee Direct dial from bedrooms Licensed Cen ht TVL No children Pool Table Dinner Last d 7pm **PRICES:** s £18.50✳ **LB** **BB** **PARKING:** 12

♦♦♦ *Sunnyside Private Hotel*

Llewelyn Av LL30 2ER ☎ 01492 877150
Set in a quiet location, yet within easy walking distance of the shops, restaurants and promenade. Bedrooms are attractively decorated and the beds are very comfortable. The bar, lounge, and dining room are all popular, with a variety of entertainment available.
FACILITIES: 25 en suite (4 fmly) No smoking in 1 bedrooms No smoking in dining room TVB tea/coffee Licensed Cen ht TVL Last d 6.30pm
NOTES: Closed mid Oct-Etr

♦♦♦ Tudno Lodge

66 Church Walks LL30 2HG ☎ 01492 876174 & 0800 0349496
e-mail: tudnolodge@supanet.com
Dir: *turn off A55 at Llandudno junct head for Llandudno 4m, main street Mostyn Street drive to top of Mostyn Street facing you will be facing the Empire Hotel, turn left Tudno Lodge is on right*
Peacefully located a few minutes walk from pier, beach and shops, this Victorian villa retains many features and sympathetic improvements have resulted in homely thoughtfully equipped bedrooms, some with fine sea views. Breakfast and dinners are served in an attractive front facing dining room and a first floor lounge with open fire is also available.
FACILITIES: 7 rms (4 en suite) (3 fmly) No smoking in bedrooms No smoking in dining room TVB tea/coffee TVL No coaches Dinner Last d 4pm **PRICES:** s £16-£21; d £32-£38✳ **LB** **BB** **PARKING:** 7 **NOTES:** Closed Dec-Jan **CARDS:**

♦♦♦ The Victoria Town House

5 Church Walks LL30 2HD ☎ 01492 876144
Dir: *at bottom of Church Walks (opposite pier on North Shore) approx 80yds on left*
Located a few minutes walk from pier and main shops, this Victorian terraced house has been sympathetically renovated to provided modern comfortable facilities. Bedrooms are homely and other areas include a cosy dining room, guest lounge and games room. Inclusive dinner tariffs are available - meals being taken at the adjacent pub restaurant.
FACILITIES: 6 en suite (1 fmly) No smoking in dining room TVB tea/coffee No dogs Cen ht TVL No coaches **PRICES:** s fr £18; d fr £42 **LB** **BB**

♦♦♦ Vine House

23 Church Walks LL30 2HG ☎ 01492 876493
e-mail: barryharris@bigfoot.com
Dir: *by Great Orme tram station*
Vine House is a nicely maintained family-run guest house lying just a short walk from the sea front and pier. It is located under the Great Orme opposite the tram station and all rooms have views of the sea or of the Orme. Pretty bedrooms are equipped with modern facilities and hospitality is warm and welcoming.
FACILITIES: 6 rms (3 en suite) (1 fmly) No smoking TVB tea/coffee Cen ht **PRICES:** s £15-£17; d £29-£30✳ **LB** **BB** **NOTES:** Closed Dec-Feb **CARDS:**

Wales

♦♦♦ Wedgwood Hotel

6 Deganwy Av LL30 2YB ☎ 01492 878016 ▤ 01492 870014
e-mail: yvonne@wedgwoodhotel.fsnet.co.uk
Set in a quiet location, yet within easy walking distance of the shops, restaurants and promenade. Bedrooms are attractively decorated and the beds are very comfortable. The bar, lounge, and dining room are all popular, with a variety of entertainment available.
FACILITIES: 10 en suite (2 fmly) No smoking in bedrooms No smoking in dining room TVB tea/coffee Licensed Cen ht TVL Dinner Last d 3pm
PRICES: s £20; d £40* **LB PARKING:** 7 **NOTES:** Closed Nov-Mar
CARDS:

Bryn Arthur

Tabor Hill, Great Orme LL30 2QW ☎ 01492 876278
e-mail: amanda1evanas@supanet.com
Dir: *travel along Moyston Street until facing the Empire Hotel bear right into Ty Gwyn Road. Follow up the hill for 500 yds. Bryn Arthur is on left hand side.*
FACILITIES: 6 rms (2 en suite) (1 fmly) No smoking in bedrooms No smoking in lounges TVB tea/coffee Cen ht No children 3yrs No coaches Dinner Last d 1pm **PRICES:** s £25-£35; d £39-£48* **NOTES:** ★★
CARDS:

RHOS-ON-SEA

See **Colwyn Bay**

DENBIGHSHIRE

CORWEN Map 06 SJ04

♦♦♦♦ Powys Country House

Bonwm LL21 9EG ☎ 01490 412367
e-mail: PowysHouse@aol.com
Dir: *from A5 Corwen to Llangollen road, premises approx 1m on left after leaving Corwen*
This delightful country house is peacefully located in three acres of gardens and woodland. The impressive entrance hall is wood-panelled and there is a relaxing lounge and separate dining room. Bedrooms are equipped with modern facilities and one room has a four-poster bed. Dinner is available by arrangement and hospitality is warm and welcoming. Self-catering cottages are also available.
FACILITIES: 7 rms (6 en suite) (2 fmly) No smoking in bedrooms No smoking in dining room TV6B tea/coffee No dogs (ex guide dogs) Licensed Cen ht No children 2yrs No coaches Tennis (grass) Croquet lawn Dinner Last d at breakfast **PRICES:** s £27.50-£30; d £48-£50* **LB PARKING:** 10
NOTES: Closed Xmas

DENBIGH Map 06 SJ06

♦♦♦♦ Bach-Y-Graig *(SJ075713)*

Tremeirchion LL17 0UH ☎ 01745 730627 ▤ 01745 730971
Mrs A Roberts
e-mail: anwenroberts@bachygraig.fsnet.co.uk
Dir: *from A55 take A525 to Trefnant. At traffic lights turn left A541 to x-roads with white railings, turn left down hill, over river bridge, turn right*
Dating from the 16th century this listed building was the first brick-built house in Wales. Bedrooms are furnished with fine period pieces, and equipped with modern facilities. The larger of the two lounges displays exposed timbers, an inglenook fireplace and magnificent dining table where breakfast is served. The farm extends to 200 acres and contains a woodland trail.

continued

Bach-Y-Graig

FACILITIES: 3 en suite (1 fmly) No smoking TVB tea/coffee No dogs Cen ht TVL Fishing Woodland trail 200 acres dairy **PRICES:** s fr £30; d fr £54* **LB**
PARKING: 3 **NOTES:** Closed Xmas & New Year

♦♦♦ Cayo

74 Vale St LL16 3BW ☎ 01745 812686
Dir: *off A525 into town, at lights turn up hill, supermarket on right. Guest house up hill on left*
This creeper-clad guest house is situated on the main street, just a short walk from the town centre. Bedrooms are comfortably and thoughtfully furnished. Good home cooking is provided by arrangement in a Victorian themed dining room and there is a cosy basement lounge.
FACILITIES: 6 rms (4 en suite) No smoking TVB tea/coffee Licensed Cen ht TVL No coaches Dinner Last d 2pm **PRICES:** s £19; d £38* **BB**
NOTES: Closed Xmas **CARDS:**

LLANGOLLEN Map 07 SJ24

See also **Corwen**

♦♦♦♦ Oakmere

Regent St LL20 8HS ☎ 01978 861126
e-mail: oakmeregh@aol.com
Dir: *300yds on right from A5 traffic lights in Llangollen, towards Shrewsbury/Oswestry*

This impressive Victorian house is set in terraced grounds with fine views across the valley to Dinas Bran Castle and the mountains beyond. Bedrooms are attractively decorated and well equipped, and there is a comfortable lounge. The house has been carefully restored and improved and offers a friendly and relaxing atmosphere.
FACILITIES: 6 en suite (2 fmly) No smoking TVB tea/coffee No dogs Cen ht No coaches Tennis (hard) **PRICES:** s £35-£45; d £45-£50*
PARKING: 10

Wales

LLANGOLLEN continued

♦♦♦♦ Tyn Celyn Farmhouse *(SJ218412)*

Tyndwr LL20 8AR ☎ 01978 861117 📠 01978 861771
Mrs J Bather
e-mail: j.m.bather-tyncelyn@talk21.com
Dir: *A5 to Llangollen, pass golf club on right, take next left signed Youth Hostel. After 0.5m sharp left onto Tyndwr Rd, left past youth hostel*

This 300-year old farmhouse is located above the Vale of Llangollen with splendid views over the area. It provides nicely furnished bedrooms (including one on the ground floor) which are equipped with modern facilities. One room has an attractive four-poster bed. Spacious public areas include a traditionally furnished breakfast room and cosy lounge.
FACILITIES: 3 en suite (1 fmly) (1 GF) No smoking TVB tea/coffee No dogs (ex guide dogs) Cen ht TVL **PRICES:** s £35; d £45-£46* **LB** **PARKING:** 5

♦♦♦♦ *Whitegate*

Grange Rd LL20 8AP ☎ 01978 860960 📠 01978 861699
Dir: *no car access on Grange Rd. Proceed up Hill St (behind Grapes Hotel on A5) and past Plas Newydd on left. Whitegate is on right after short narrow road.*
This impressive Edwardian family house is a short walk from the centre of town and has its own gardens where guests can relax. All rooms have there own facilities and are traditionally furnished. Two have fine views over the Vale of Llangollen. There is a comfortable lounge and at breakfast the emphasis is on using fresh local produce.
FACILITIES: 3 en suite No smoking tea/coffee No dogs (ex guide dogs) Cen ht TVL No coaches **PARKING:** 8

PRESTATYN Map 06 SJ08

♦ Roughsedge House

26-28 Marine Rd LL19 7HD ☎ 01745 887359 📠 01745 852883
e-mail: roughsedge@ykubler.fsnet.co.uk
Dir: *on A548, coast road, opposite fire station & Llys Nant Day Care Centre*
This little guest house is located on the eastern end of the town, not far from the golf course. Bedrooms are very well equipped with modern facilities. Family and ground floor rooms are available. There is a cosy lounge for residents and the attractive pine-furnished dining room has a small dispense bar.
FACILITIES: 9 rms (3 en suite) (2 fmly) (1 GF) No smoking TVB tea/coffee Direct dial from bedrooms No dogs Licensed Cen ht TVL No coaches Dinner Last d 2pm **PRICES:** s £17.50-£25; d £35-£40* **LB BB PARKING:** 2 **NOTES:** Closed Xmas & last 2wks in Mar & Oct **CARDS:**

RHYL Map 06 SJ08

♦♦♦♦ Barratts Restaurant

Ty'n Rhyl, 167 Vale Rd LL18 2PH ☎ 01745 344138 & 07730954994 📠 01745 344138
e-mail: sbarratt@freeuk.com
Dir: *from A55, take the Rhyl slip Rd. Take A525 to Rhyl, pass Sainsburys and B&Q. Then Garden Centre on left, Barratts 400yds on right*

This delightful 16th-century house lies in a secluded location surrounded by attractive gardens. It is really a restaurant with rooms and the quality of food reflects the skill of owner/chef. Public areas are smartly furnished and include a panelled lounge and separate bar. Bedrooms are comfortable and have many extra facilities and creature comforts.
FACILITIES: 3 en suite No smoking in bedrooms No smoking in dining room TVB tea/coffee No dogs (ex guide dogs) Licensed Cen ht TVL Croquet lawn Dinner Last d 9pm **PRICES:** s £35; d £70* **LB** **PARKING:** 20
CARDS:

♦♦♦ Pier Hotel

23 East Pde LL18 3AL ☎ 01745 350280 📠 01745 350280
e-mail: gherndlhofer@hotmail.com
Dir: *on promenade between Sea Life and bowling greens*
The friendly proprietors of this sea side hotel have been welcoming guests for over 27 years. The Pier is near the town centre, Sun Centre and other amenities. Bedrooms are decorated with pretty wallpapers and many have good sea views. There is a cosy bar and separate lounge for residents.
FACILITIES: 8 rms (7 en suite) (3 fmly) TVB tea/coffee Licensed Cen ht TVL No coaches **PRICES:** s £19-£21; d £34-£38* **BB PARKING:** 2
NOTES: Closed 22-31 Dec **CARDS:**

♦♦♦ Tremorfa Hotel

38 Marine Dr LL18 3AY ☎ 01745 334444
Dir: *from A55, follow signs for Sun Centre/town centre. Located on right hand side of Marine Drive*
Located close to the beach, this comfortable guesthouse offers a convenient base for exploring North Wales and the surrounding countryside. Some bedrooms are en suite and all are freshly decorated and equipped with TV and courtesy trays. Downstairs there is a comfortable lounge/bar and breakfast is served in the attractive dining room.
FACILITIES: 7 rms (3 en suite) (2 fmly) No smoking in bedrooms No smoking in dining room No smoking in 1 lounge TVB tea/coffee Licensed Cen ht TVL No coaches **PRICES:** s £20; d £35-£40* **LB BB PARKING:** 5

RUTHIN Map 06 SJ15

♦♦♦♦ Eyarth Station

Llanfair Dyffryn Clwyd LL15 2EE ☎ 01824 703643
01824 707464
e-mail: stay@eyarthstation.com
Dir: *off A525, 1 m S Ruthin. Take lane on right - 600metres to Eyarth Station*

Until 1964 and the Beeching cuts, this was a sleepy country station. A comfortable lounge and outdoor swimming pool occupy the space once taken up by the railway and platforms. Bedrooms are tastefully decorated and full of thoughtful extras. Family rooms are available, and two rooms are in the old station master's house adjoining the main building.

FACILITIES: 6 en suite 1 annexe en suite (2 fmly) (4 GF) No smoking in bedrooms No smoking in dining room No smoking in 1 lounge TV1B tea/coffee Licensed Cen ht TVL No coaches Outdoor swimming pool (heated) Riding walking riding golf shooting nearby Dinner Last d 7pm **PRICES:** s £30-£46; d £50-£54* **LB PARKING:** 6 **NOTES:** Closed Jan-Feb & 2 wks in Nov **CARDS:**

♦♦♦♦ Tyddyn Chambers *(SJ102543)*

Pwllglas LL15 2LS ☎ 01824 750683 Mrs E Williams
e-mail: williams@tyddynchambers.fsnet.co.uk
Dir: *from Ruthin take A494 for Bala for 3m to Pwllglas, turn right after the Fox & Hounds PH, establishment signposted*

This charming little farmhouse has recently been extended to provide tastefully appointed, modern accommodation, which includes a family bedded room. Separate tables are provided in the pleasant, traditionally furnished breakfast room and there is also a comfortable lounge. Quietly located, the house stands in an elevated position, overlooking panoramic views.

FACILITIES: 3 en suite (1 fmly) No smoking TVB tea/coffee No dogs Cen ht TVL 180 acres Beef, dairy, sheep Dinner Last d 2pm **PRICES:** s £25; d fr £44* **LB PARKING:** 3

FLINTSHIRE

FLINT Map 07 SJ27

Oakenholt Farm Country Guest House

Chester Rd, Oakenholt CH6 5SD ☎ 01352 733264
01352 733264
e-mail: jenny@oakenholt.freeserve.co.uk
Dir: *just off A548, 1.5m W of Flint, 1.5m E of Connahs Quay. Drive entrance on dual carriageway look for large B&B sign on left coming from Connahs Quay direction.*

FACILITIES: 4 en suite No smoking TVB tea/coffee Cen ht TVL No coaches Dinner Last d 7.30pm **PRICES:** s £20-£30; d £40-£45* **LB PARKING:** 10 **NOTES:** ★★★

HOLYWELL Map 07 SJ17

♦♦♦ Greenhill Farm *(SJ186776)*

CH8 7QF ☎ 01352 713270 Mrs M Jones
e-mail: mary@greenhillfarm.fsnet.co.uk
Dir: *from Holywell follow sign to St Winefrid's Well. 200yds beyond well turn left opposite Royal Oak, follow road up hill to end*

This 16th-century house is situated on a dairy farm high above the Dee Estuary and enjoys superb views over the area. Exposed timbers are a feature and there is an unusual window only visible from inside the property. The bedrooms are traditionally furnished. There is a comfortable lounge and a games room.

FACILITIES: 4 rms (2 en suite) (1 fmly) No smoking in 1 bedrooms TVB tea/coffee No dogs (ex guide dogs) Cen ht TVL Snooker Childrens play area, dart board, indoor games 120 acres dairy mixed Dinner Last d 9am **PRICES:** s £20-£22; d £40-£44 **PARKING:** 6 **NOTES:** Closed Dec-Feb

MOLD Map 07 SJ26

See also Nannerch

♦♦♦ Heulwen

Maes Bodlonfa CH7 1DR ☎ 01352 758785
Dir: *follow road which crosses Mold high street at traffic lights at top of Kings St, down Earl Rd past post office, turn left at bottom*

This family-run hotel is located in a quiet residential area with pretty gardens extending to open fields at the rear. Guests breakfast family-style in a cosy dining room and a comfortable lounge is also provided. Families can be accommodated and hospitality is warm and friendly.

FACILITIES: 2 rms (1 fmly) No smoking TVB tea/coffee No dogs (ex guide dogs) Cen ht No coaches **PRICES:** s £20-£25; d £40* **PARKING:** 3

NANNERCH Map 07 SJ16

♦♦♦♦ The Old Mill

Melin-Y-Wern, Denbigh Rd CH7 5RH ☎ 01352 741542
e-mail: welcome@old-mill.co.uk

A cleverly and tastefully converted stone-built former stable block, which was part of a Victorian watermill complex. The site also includes a craft and art gallery and a restaurant and wine bar. Now a personally run private hotel, it offers modern, comfortable and well equipped bedrooms with private bathrooms, equally suitable for tourists and business people alike; smoking is not permitted throughout the hotel.

FACILITIES: 6 en suite (2 fmly) No smoking TVB tea/coffee Direct dial from bedrooms Licensed Cen ht No coaches **PRICES:** s £45; d £65* **LB PARKING:** 12 **CARDS:**

NORTHOP HALL Map 07 SJ26

Brookside House

Brookside Ln CH7 6HN ☎ 01244 821146
e-mail: christine@brooksidehouse.fsnet.co.uk
Dir: *exit A55 Connahs Quay to T junct. right onto B5126 next right onto B5125 follow lane into village, right in front of Londis shop into Brookside in 200yds right into lane. Brookside house on the left. From A55 eastbound exit Northop Hall bear left 100yds turn left Brookside on left*

FACILITIES: 3 en suite (1 fmly) No smoking TVB tea/coffee No dogs (ex guide dogs) Cen ht TVL No coaches **PRICES:** s £25-£30; d £42-£44* **PARKING:** 10 **NOTES:** ★★★ Closed 23 Dec - 2 Jan

GWYNEDD

ABERDYFI Map 06 SN69

♦♦♦♦ Cartref

LL35 0NR ☎ 01654 767273 📠 01654 767000
e-mail: moeran@globalnet.co.uk
Dir: *W on A493 opp Station Rd which leads to Aberdovey Station*

Situated on the edge of the village, close to both the golf course and bowling green, this detached Edwardian-style villa is an easy walk from the sandy beach. Bedrooms are quite spacious and well-equipped and family accommodation is available. There is also a comfortable well-furnished lounge.
FACILITIES: 8 rms (4 en suite) (3 fmly) No smoking TVB tea/coffee Cen ht TVL **PRICES:** s £19-£24; d £38-£48* **LB BB PARKING:** 8
CARDS:

ABERSOCH Map 06 SH32

♦♦♦♦ Riverside Hotel

LL53 7HW ☎ 01758 712419 📠 01758 712671
e-mail: info@riversideabersoch.co.uk
Dir: *situated on the A499 overlooking the harbour just before entering the village of Abersoch*
Located close to harbour and town centre on a river bank garden which offers seating for wildfowl observation, this constantly improving hotel provides many thoughtfully equipped bedrooms, some of which have good family facilities and direct access to gardens. Other areas include a Mediterranean themed restaurant, a spacious lounge bar and covered heated swimming pool.
FACILITIES: 12 en suite (5 fmly) (3 GF) No smoking in bedrooms No smoking in dining room No smoking in 1 lounge TVB tea/coffee Licensed Cen ht Indoor swimming pool (heated) Fishing Dinner **PRICES:** s £49-£59; d £72-£94* **LB PARKING:** 20 **CARDS:**

BALA Map 06 SH93

♦♦♦♦ Erw Feurig

Cefnddwysarn LL23 7LL ☎ 01678 530262 & 0780 1320419
📠 01678 530262
e-mail: erwfeurig@yahoo.com

continued

Dir: *on the A494, Bala to Corwen road, 2nd on left after telephone kiosk at Cefnddwysarn*
This farm cottage has been extended and modernised, and enjoys fine views of the Berwyn Mountains. The bedrooms are well-equipped and there is one that is situated on the ground floor. Guests also have use of a cosy lounge.
FACILITIES: 4 en suite (2 fmly) No smoking TVB tea/coffee No dogs Cen ht TVL No coaches Fishing **PRICES:** s fr £25; d £40-£44* **LB PARKING:** 6
NOTES: Closed Xmas period

♦♦♦♦ Pen-Y-Bryn Farmhouse *(SH928363)*

Sarnau LL23 7LH ☎ 01678 530389 📠 01678 530389
Mrs E Jones
e-mail: jonespenbryn@lineone.net
Dir: *3m NE of Bala on A494. Pass red telephone box on left at Cefnddwysarn, 2nd left, green B&B sign, 2nd Farm*

A warm welcome is assured at this late-Victorian stone built house, located in a superb elevated position overlooking Sarnau and the surrounding mountains. Bedrooms are homely and have the benefit of modern en suite or private facilities. Comprehensive breakfasts are taken in the attractive conservatory and a comfortable sitting room is also available.
FACILITIES: 3 en suite No smoking tea/coffee No dogs Cen ht TVL Fishing Bird watching 200 acres mixed **PRICES:** s £25; d £44-£46* **LB PARKING:** 6 **NOTES:** Closed 25-26 Dec

BANGOR Map 06 SH57

♦♦♦♦ Gors-yr-Eira Country Guest House

Mynydd Llandegai, Bethesda LL57 4DZ ☎ 01248 601353
📠 01248 601353
e-mail: einir@gors-yr-eira.freeserve.co.uk
Dir: *A5 to town of Bethesda, on leaving take next junct R (B4409) over bridge and bear R. 1st L at bus shelter, turn L up hill to chapel, R over river. House on L up hill*
Situated on the edge of Snowdonia National Park this modern house offers tastefully decorated, well-equipped bedrooms and there is a comfortable lounge with an open fire. Dinner is available by arrangement and meals are served in the conservatory overlooking the garden.
FACILITIES: 3 en suite (1 fmly) No smoking STV TVB tea/coffee Cen ht No coaches Dinner Last d previous day **PRICES:** s £22.50; d £40* **LB PARKING:** 8

♦♦♦♦ Nant y Fedw

Trefelin, Llanedgai LL57 4LH ☎ 01248 351683
e-mail: nantyfedw.fsnet.co.uk
Dir: *take A5122 to Bangor, turn onto road signed Llandegai/Tal-y-Bont at mini rdbt at Penrhyn Castle, 100mtrs down hill, turn R to large gates, turn R.*
Nant y Fedw was built in 1834 as two adjoining cottages, to house the artisans working at nearby Penrhyn Castle. It has a lovely garden, and many exposed beams and timbers still feature throughout the house. Two bedrooms are available and one is

continued

Wales

ocated at ground floor level. The one without an en suite bathroom has its own private facility.

Nant y Fedw

FACILITIES: 2 en suite (1 GF) No smoking in bedrooms No smoking in dining room STV TVB tea/coffee No dogs (ex guide dogs) Cen ht TVL No coaches **PRICES:** s £25; d £40* **PARKING:** 4

♦♦♦ Goetre Isaf Farmhouse *(SH557697)*

Caernarfon Rd LL57 4DB ☎ 01248 364541 01248 364541
Mr & Mrs Whowell
e-mail: wer@fredw.com
Dir: *2m W of Bangor on north side of A4087*

This 18th-century farmhouse lies in several acres enjoying some superb views of the surrounding countryside. Rooms are traditionally presented with a choice of lounges. Meals rely on local and home-made produce, especially the cheeses, and dinners are available by prior arrangement.

FACILITIES: 3 rms (1 en suite) (1 fmly) No smoking in bedrooms No smoking in area of dining room No smoking in 1 lounge Direct dial from bedrooms Cen ht TVL 10 acres sheep horses bees Dinner **PRICES:** s fr £20; d £35-£45* **LB BB PARKING:** 10

BARMOUTH — Map 06 SH61

♦♦♦♦ Llwyndu Farmhouse *(SH599185)*

Llanaber LL42 1RR ☎ 01341 280144 01341 281236
Mr P Thompson
e-mail: Intouch@llwyndu-farmhouse.co.uk
Dir: *A496 towards Harlech. Where street lights end, on outskirts of Barmouth, take next R*

A converted 16th century farmhouse with inglenook fireplaces, exposed beams and timbers. There is a cosy lounge for residents and meals can be enjoyed at individual tables in the characterful dining room. Bedrooms are modern and well equipped, some have four-poster beds. Four rooms are in nearby buildings.

FACILITIES: 3 en suite 4 annexe en suite (2 fmly) No smoking TVB tea/coffee Licensed Cen ht TVL 4 acres non-working Dinner Last d 6.30pm **PRICES:** d £64-£70* **LB PARKING:** 10 **NOTES:** Closed 25-26 Dec rs Sundays **CARDS:**

BEDDGELERT — Map 06 SH54

♦♦♦♦ Sygun Fawr Country House

LL55 4NE ☎ 01766 890258 01766 890258
e-mail: sygunfawr@aol.com
Dir: *signposted from A498 on Capel Curig side of village, turn off road over river at sign and the lane leads to hotel*

Sygun Fawr is set in a spectacular location within the Snowdonia National Park, where the surrounding countryside is a mass of colour in the spring. Bedrooms are neat and pretty and many have superb views. Stone walls and exposed timbers abound and a cosy bar is provided in addition to several comfortable sitting rooms.

FACILITIES: 9 en suite (1 fmly) (1 GF) No smoking in bedrooms No smoking in dining room No smoking in 1 lounge tea/coffee Licensed Cen ht TVL Dinner Last d 8pm **PRICES:** s £47; d £64-£74* **LB PARKING:** 20 **NOTES:** Closed Jan **CARDS:**

BETWS GARMON — Map 06 SH55

♦♦♦♦ Betws Inn

LL54 7YY ☎ 01286 650324
e-mail: pag@betwsinn.freeserve.co.uk
Dir: *on A4085 from Caernarfon to Beddgelert, opp Bryn Gloch Caravan Park*

Located close to Mount Snowdon, this former coaching inn dates from 1630 and has been tastefully converted. The bedrooms are spacious and well appointed. Downstairs there is a comfortable lounge with an inglenook fireplace, and dinner is available by arrangement. There is also a large attractive garden which guests are welcome to enjoy.

FACILITIES: 3 rms (1 en suite) No smoking in bedrooms No smoking in dining room tea/coffee TVL No coaches Dinner Last d 2pm
PRICES: s £15-£20; d £30-£40* **BB PARKING:** 3

A Associate entries with stars have been ★ inspected and rated by the ★ Welsh Tourist Board or Scottish Tourist Board.

Wales

CAERNARFON Map 06 SH46

See also Clynnog Fawr & Penygroes

♦♦♦♦ Hafoty *(SH504584)*

Rhostryfan LL54 7PH ☎ 01286 830144 & 07880 702 684
01286 830441 Mrs M Davies
e-mail: hafoty@btinternet.com
Dir: *off A487 Caernarfon/Porthmadog road, 2.5m from Caernarfon follow B road signposted Rhostryfan. On reaching village 1st left after 30mph sign, pass school, go to the top of lane, Hafoty on the left*

Hafoty has been cleverly created from a former farm cottage and buildings. Enjoying panoramic views towards Anglesey and Caernarfon Castle, it provides well-equipped modern accommodation with spacious bedrooms, one in a nearby building with its own kitchen. The main house has a comfortably furnished, lounge and a pleasant breakfast room, with separate tables. Self-catering cottages are also available.

FACILITIES: 3 en suite 1 annexe en suite (1 fmly) No smoking in bedrooms No smoking in dining room TVB tea/coffee No dogs (ex guide dogs) Licensed Cen ht TVL 17 acres sheep **PRICES:** s £28; d £48-£52✳ **LB PARKING:** 14 **NOTES:** Closed Dec-Feb **CARDS:**

♦♦♦♦ Pengwern *(SH459587)*

Saron LL54 5UH ☎ 01286 831500 01286 830741
Mr & Mrs G Rowlands
e-mail: pengwern@talk21.com
Dir: *from Caernarfon take A487 S, pass supermarket on right, take 1st right turn after bridge 2m to Saron, through x-roads, farm is 1st drive on right*

A delightful farmhouse surrounded by 130 acres of farmland, running down to Foryd Bay, which is noted for its birdlife. Bedrooms are generally spacious, and all are well equipped with modern facilities. A comfortable lounge is provided and good home cooking is served.

FACILITIES: 3 en suite No smoking TVB tea/coffee No dogs Cen ht Car hire 130 acres beef sheep Dinner Last d 12pm **PRICES:** s £35-£38; d £48-£56 **LB PARKING:** 4 **NOTES:** Closed Dec & Jan
CARDS:

♦♦♦ Menai View Guest House & Restaurant

North Rd LL55 1BD ☎ 01286 674602 01286 674602
e-mail: info@menaiview.co.uk
Dir: *N on A487. Main Rd into Caernarfon from Bangor overlooking Menai Straits*

Located on the approach to the town centre from Bangor, this guest house enjoys fine views over the Menai Straits. The first floor lounge, which also contains a small bar, benefits from the views, as do some of the bedrooms. These are equipped with modern facilities, and include one on the ground floor and others suitable for families.

FACILITIES: 9 rms (8 en suite) (3 fmly) No smoking in bedrooms No smoking in dining room TVB tea/coffee Licensed Cen ht TVL Jacuzzi Dinner

continued

Menai View Guest House & Restaurant

Last d 6.30pm **PRICES:** s £30-£35; d fr £45✳ **LB**
CARDS:

Caer Menai

15 Church St LL55 1SW ☎ 01286 672612 01286 672612
e-mail: khlardner@talk21.com
Dir: *within Old Town walls*

FACILITIES: 7 rms (3 en suite) (2 fmly) No smoking TVB tea/coffee No dogs (ex guide dogs) TVL No coaches **PRICES:** s £24-£30; d £37-£46✳ **LB BB NOTES:** ★★★ Closed Dec-Feb

CLYNNOG FAWR Map 06 SH44

♦♦♦♦ Bryn Eisteddfod Country House Hotel

LL54 5DA ☎ 01286 660431
e-mail: bryn.eisteddfod@virgin.net
Dir: *approx 9m S of Caernarfon on A499*

This tastefully converted Victorian house, near the Lleyn Peninsula and Snowdonia, offers comfort to tourists and travellers alike and is popular with golfers. The traditionally furnished bedrooms are tastefully decorated and well-equipped. There is a comfortable lounge and a large attractive conservatory bar/dining room, where a wide selection of dishes is available.

FACILITIES: 8 en suite (3 fmly) No smoking TVB tea/coffee No dogs (ex guide dogs) Licensed Cen ht No coaches Dinner Last d by arrangement **PRICES:** s £28-£32; d £46-£60✳ **LB PARKING:** 25
CARDS:

CRICCIETH Map 06 SH43

♦♦♦♦ Abereistedd Hotel

West Pde LL52 0EN ☎ 01766 522710 01766 523526
e-mail: info@abereistedd.co.uk
Dir: *take A487 through Criccieth towards Pwllheli. 400yds after Elf petrol station on left, turn left following signs for beach. On left at seafront*

An extremely warm welcome is offered at this seafront hotel that has uninterrupted mountain and coastal views. Attractive bedrooms are all very well-equipped and downstairs there is a comfortable lounge and a well-stocked bar. Meals, which feature fresh local produce, are served in the bright and airy dining room.

continued

FACILITIES: 12 en suite (3 fmly) No smoking in 6 bedrooms No smoking in dining room No smoking in lounges TVB tea/coffee Direct dial from bedrooms Licensed Cen ht Dinner Last d 6.30pm **PRICES:** s £25-£29; d £50-£58✳ **LB PARKING:** 10 **NOTES:** Closed Dec-Feb rs Mar & Nov **CARDS:**

♦♦♦♦ Glyn-Y-Coed Hotel

Portmadoc Rd LL52 0HP ☎ 01766 522870 01766 523341
e-mail: glyn-y-coedhotel@amserve.net
Dir: *on A497 on right, out of Porthmadoc last hotel overlooking Castle & Gorgoe sea*

This small, family-run hotel is in a south-facing, elevated position, with views to the Berwyn Mountains and Criccieth Castle. Bedrooms are attractive and comfortable; two have four-poster beds and several have all-new bathrooms. Meals are freshly prepared and served in the dining room with views over Cardigan Bay.
FACILITIES: 9 en suite 1 annexe en suite (2 fmly) (1 GF) No smoking TVB tea/coffee Direct dial from bedrooms No dogs (ex guide dogs) Licensed Cen ht TVL Dinner Last d 5pm **PARKING:** 16
CARDS:

♦♦♦♦ Min y Gaer Hotel

Porthmadog Rd LL52 0HP ☎ 01766 522151 01766 523540
e-mail: info@minygaer.co.uk
Dir: *on A497 400yds E of junct with B4411*

A family-run private hotel with superb views from many rooms. Bedrooms are smart, modern and attractively pine furnished. The proprietors are friendly and welcoming, a bar is provided and there is a traditionally furnished lounge.
FACILITIES: 10 en suite (3 fmly) No smoking in bedrooms No smoking in dining room TVB tea/coffee No dogs (ex guide dogs) Licensed Cen ht TVL No coaches **PRICES:** d £45-£47✳ **LB PARKING:** 12 **NOTES:** Closed Nov-Feb **CARDS:**

U Bron Rhiw Hotel

Caernarfon Rd LL52 0AP ☎ 01766 522257
At the time of going to press the Diamond classification for this establishment had not been confirmed. Please check the AA website www.theAA.com for up-to-date information.
FACILITIES: 9 en suite (2 fmly)

DOLGELLAU

Map 06 SH71

Premier Collection

♦♦♦♦♦ Tyddynmawr Farmhouse *(SH704159)*

Islawrdref LL40 1TL ☎ 01341 422331 Mr & Mrs Evans
Dir: *from town centre branch left at top of square, then turn left at garage into Cader Rd for approx 3m. 1st farm on left after Gwernan Lake*

This 18th-century farmhouse, lies at the foot of Cader Idris in breathtaking scenery. The bedrooms are spacious, with Welsh Oak furniture, the upper one has a balcony and the ground-floor room has a patio area. Bathrooms are large and luxurious. Superb breakfasts are a feast of home-made items, bread, preserves, muesli or smoked fish, the choice is excellent. Self-catering cottages are also on the farm.
FACILITIES: 3 en suite No smoking TV2B tea/coffee No dogs Cen ht TVL No children Fishing 800 acres beef sheep **PRICES:** d £50✳
PARKING: 8 **NOTES:** Closed Nov-17 Mar

♦♦♦ Clifton House Hotel

Smithfield Square LL40 1ES ☎ 01341 422554 01341 423580
e-mail: info@clifton-house-hotel.co.uk
Dir: *in Dolgellau join one-way system. Follow round to street directly facing hotel*

For many years the county gaol, this historic building now provides a friendly welcome and smart, well-equipped bedrooms. Close to the town centre, it is a convenient base for exploring the region. The character dining room, featuring exposed stone walls and low ceilings, offers imaginative dishes. The bread pudding is very special.
FACILITIES: 7 rms (4 en suite) (1 GF) No smoking TVB tea/coffee No dogs (ex guide dogs) Licensed Cen ht No coaches Dinner Last d 6.30pm
PRICES: s £20-£39; d £40-£50✳ **LB PARKING:** 2 **CARDS:**

Wales

DOLGELLAU continued

♦♦♦ *Ivy House*

Finsbury Square LL40 1RF ☎ 01341 422535 📠 01341 422689
e-mail: ivy.hse.dolgellau@ic24.net
Dir: *from A470 or A494, follow town centre signs to main square. Drive straight across top of square, out other side, house on left after bend*
Friendly hospitality is offered at this house, situated in the centre of Dolgellau, at the foot of the Cader Idris. Bedrooms are brightly decorated and are thoughtfully equipped. Downstairs there is a comfortable lounge and a small bar in the dining room, where a wide selection of dishes is available.
FACILITIES: 6 rms (3 en suite) (1 fmly) No smoking in dining room TVB tea/coffee Licensed Cen ht TVL No coaches Dinner Last d 8pm
NOTES: Closed 24-26 Dec **CARDS:**

FFESTINIOG — Map 06 SH74

♦♦♦ *Morannedd*

Blaenau Rd LL41 4LG ☎ 01766 762525 & 762734
📠 01766 762734
e-mail: morannedd@talk21.com
Dir: *at edge of village on A470 towards Blaenau Ffestiniog*
This guest house is set in the Snowdonia National Park and is ideally located for touring North Wales. A warm and friendly welcome is offered and the atmosphere is relaxed and informal. Bedrooms are smart and modern with a cosy lounge available for residents. Hearty home-cooking can be enjoyed here.
FACILITIES: 4 en suite No smoking TVB tea/coffee Cen ht No coaches Dinner Last d 4pm **NOTES:** Closed Xmas

♦♦♦ Ty Clwb

The Square LL41 4LS ☎ 01766 762658
e-mail: tyclwb@talk21.com
Dir: *on B4391 in centre of Ffestiniog, opp church, 100mtrs from A470*
This impeccably maintained guest house overlooks the village square, and has particularly picturesque views from the back of the house. Although fully modernised, it still manages to retain a lot of original character. Bedrooms are smart and attractively decorated, and the lounge has a fine south facing balcony.
FACILITIES: 3 en suite No smoking tea/coffee Cen ht TVL No coaches
PRICES: d £40-£48

HARLECH — Map 06 SH53

♦♦♦♦ ⊛ Castle Cottage Restaurant with Rooms

Pen Llech LL46 2YL ☎ 01766 780479 📠 01766 781251
e-mail: glyn@castlecottageharlech.co.uk
Dir: *exit B4573 to Harlech castle*
This delightful old property dates back to the 16th century and much of the original charm and character has been retained. Hospitality is warm and friendly and the restaurant has a well deserved reputation for its cuisine. Bedrooms are attractively furnished in pine, and are well designed and cosy. Facilities include a comfortable lounge where real fires burn in winter.
FACILITIES: 6 rms (4 en suite) No smoking in bedrooms No smoking in dining room tea/coffee No dogs Licensed Cen ht TVL No coaches Dinner Last d 9pm **PRICES:** s £30-£45; d £65✳ **LB NOTES:** Closed 3 wks Feb
CARDS:

♦♦♦♦ Gwrach Ynys Country

Talsarnau LL47 6TS ☎ 01766 780742 📠 01766 781199
e-mail: aa@gwrachynys.co.uk
Dir: *2m N of Harlech on A496*
This well maintained Edwardian house is set in pretty lawns and gardens. Bedrooms have pretty wallpapers and modern facilities. Two comfortably furnished lounges are provided and hospitality is warm and welcoming. Dinner is available by arrangement and hearty meals can be enjoyed at separate tables in the dining room.

continued

FACILITIES: 7 rms (6 en suite) (2 fmly) No smoking TVB tea/coffee Direct dial from bedrooms No dogs (ex guide dogs) Cen ht TVL Dinner Last d noon **PRICES:** s £22; d £44-£56✳ **LB PARKING:** 10
NOTES: Closed Nov-Feb

🅰 Morlyn

Llandanwg LL46 2SB ☎ 01341 241 298 📠 01341 241559
e-mail: info@northwales-holidays.com
Dir: *0.25m from A496 at Llandanwg, 1m S of Harlech*
FACILITIES: 1 en suite 2 annexe en suite (1 fmly) No smoking in dining room TVB tea/coffee Licensed No children 3yrs No coaches Dinner Last d 9pm **PRICES:** s £31; d £45-£59✳ **LB PARKING:** 7
NOTES: ★★★★ Closed Nov-Etr **CARDS:**

🅰 Noddfa

Ffordd Newydd LL46 2UB ☎ 01766 780043 📠 01766 780043
e-mail: val@thepaddock.info
Dir: *turn off A496 (lower road) guest house is opposite golf course).*
FACILITIES: 6 en suite No smoking in bedrooms No smoking in dining room No smoking in 1 lounge TVB tea/coffee No dogs (ex guide dogs) Licensed Cen ht No children 7yrs No coaches Dinner Last d 5pm
PRICES: s £24-£26; d £48-£52✳ **PARKING:** 12 **NOTES:** ★★★
CARDS:

LLANBEDR — Map 06 SH52

♦♦♦♦ Pensarn Hall Country House

Pensarn LL45 2HS ☎ 01341 241236
e-mail: welcome@pensarn-hall.co.uk
Dir: *S on A496 past Harlech. After 1.75m establishment on left*

This lovely Victorian country house stands in its own spacious gardens, overlooking the Artro Estuary and Shell Island. The house has an interesting history, including connections with David Lloyd-George. It provides warm and friendly hospitality as well as thoughtfully equipped accommodation, including a room with a four-poster bed.
FACILITIES: 7 en suite (1 fmly) No smoking TVB tea/coffee Licensed Cen ht TVL No children 2yrs No coaches **PRICES:** s £26-£35; d £52-£70✳
PARKING: 8 **CARDS:**

♦♦♦♦ Victoria

LL45 2LD ☎ 01341 241213 📠 01341 241644
e-mail: jbarry@currantbun.com
Dir: *Village centre (Frederic Robinson)*
This fine old coaching inn lies on the banks of the River Artro in the centre of a very pretty village. Many original features remain, including the Settle bar with its flagged floor, black polished fireplace and unusual circular wooden settle. The menu is extensive and is supplemented by blackboard specials. Bedrooms are attractively pine-furnished and are equipped with modern facilities.

continued

FACILITIES: 5 en suite No smoking in bedrooms No smoking in dining room STV TVB tea/coffee No dogs (ex guide dogs) Cen ht Dinner Last d 9.30pm **PRICES:** s £42.50; d £72.50✳ **LB PARKING:** 75
CARDS:

Bryn Artro Country House

LL45 2LE ☎ 01341 241619
At the time of going to press the Diamond classification for this establishment had not been confirmed. Please check the AA website www.theAA.com for up-to-date information.
FACILITIES: 6 en suite (3 fmly)

LLANBERIS — Map 06 SH56

♦♦♦♦ Plas Coch

High St LL55 4HB ☎ 01286 872122 📠 01286 872648
e-mail: reservations@plas-coch.co.uk
Dir: *from A4086 turn into Llanberis. Guest house is on main street near Spa shop*

A fine stone-built house set in attractive lawns and gardens. The Snowdon train service starts a short walk away. Smart bedrooms are decorated with pretty papers and equipped with period furniture. A comfortable lounge is provided and many authentic Welsh dishes are served by friendly owner Tracey Rogers.
FACILITIES: 8 rms (7 en suite) (3 fmly) (1 GF) No smoking tea/coffee No dogs (ex guide dogs) Cen ht TVL No coaches Dinner Last d 3pm
PRICES: s £20-£24.50; d £40-£49✳ **LB PARKING:** 7

LLANFACHRETH — Map 06 SH72

♦♦♦♦ Cors-y-Garnedd

LL40 2EH ☎ 01341 422627 📠 01341 421062
e-mail: marie@welshmountain.co.uk
Dir: *N of Dolgellau town centre, cross Afon Union Bridge, turn R, pass Kwik Save, L along minor rd signed Llanfachreth, through village, 0.5m further as rd turns R, L through farm gate*

continued

This beautiful Grade II listed longhouse, dating from 1550, oozes character and charm with a plethora of timbers and panelling. Its elevated position, 4 miles from Dolgellau, gives panoramic views. Rooms are tastefully decorated, and thoughtfully furnished and equipped. Freshly prepared meals can be enjoyed around one table, and an inglenook fireplace is the focal point of the comfortable lounge.
FACILITIES: 3 en suite No smoking tea/coffee No dogs (ex guide dogs) Cen ht TVL No children 10yrs No coaches Pottery/painting courses available Dinner Last d noon **PRICES:** s £23; d £51✳ **PARKING:** 4
NOTES: Closed Dec-Mar **CARDS:**

♦♦♦♦ *Ty Isaf*

LL40 2EA ☎ 01341 423261 📠 01341 423261
e-mail: raygear@tyisaf78.freeserve.co.uk
Dir: *from Dolgellau, cross river & turn right onto A494 towards Bala, pass Kwiksave store on right then next left signed LLanfachreth & up hill*

This delightful 16th-century long house was a working farm until recently, and chickens still provide fresh eggs each morning. Bedrooms are fitted with stripped pine furniture and comfortable beds. There is a television lounge and separate reading room for guests. The pretty grounds are home to pet llamas.
FACILITIES: 3 en suite No smoking tea/coffee No dogs (ex guide dogs) Cen ht TVL No children 13yrs No coaches Dinner Last d 3pm
PARKING: 5 **NOTES:** Closed Xmas & New Year

PENYGROES — Map 06 SH45

♦♦♦ Llwyndu Mawr *(SH475536)*

Carmel Rd LL54 6PU ☎ 01286 880419 📠 01286 880845
Mr E Williams
Dir: *A487 to Penygroes, in middle of village turn onto B4418. After 500yds L for Carmel, 500yds up hill after cemetery, 1st L*
Origins of this hillside farmhouse date back to the 19th century. Home from home hospitality is provided and guests are welcome to take part in the life of this working sheep farm. Prettily decorated bedrooms offer views over the Menai Straits and toward Snowdonia. Fresh, hearty meals can be enjoyed in the conservatory style dining room.
FACILITIES: 4 rms (1 en suite) (1 fmly) No smoking in bedrooms No smoking in dining room No smoking in 1 lounge tea/coffee Cen ht TVL 98 acres sheep Dinner Last d 4pm **PRICES:** s £16-£20; d £32-£40✳ **LB BB**
PARKING: 7 **NOTES:** Closed 20 Dec-6 Jan

A Associate entries with stars have been ★ inspected and rated by the ★ Welsh Tourist Board or Scottish Tourist Board.

Wales

PORTHMADOG Map 06 SH53

♦♦♦♦ Tyddyn-Du Farm Holidays *(SH691398)*

Gellilydan LL41 4RB ☎ 01766 590281 📠 01766 590281
Mrs P Williams
e-mail: paula@snowdonia-farm.com
Dir: *1st farmhouse on L after junct of A487/A470 near Gellilydan*

Superbly located in an elevated position with stunning views of the surrounding countryside, this constantly improving 400 year old stone built property provides a range of beautifully furnished and equipped bedrooms, sympathetically renovated from former stables and barns. Superb breakfasts are taken in a cosy pine furnished dining room within the main house and a guest lounge with log fire is also available.
FACILITIES: 4 en suite (4 fmly) No smoking TVB tea/coffee Cen ht TVL ch fac Tennis (grass) Jacuzzi Large garden suitable for outdoor games 150 acres sheep Dinner Last d 5pm **PRICES:** s £40; d £58-£80 **PARKING:** 10

♦♦ Owen's Hotel

71 High St LL49 9EU ☎ 01766 512098
e-mail: johnbull@ukonline.co.uk
Dir: *on A487*
Offering friendly hospitality, Owen's Hotel is located in the centre of this bustling market and tourist town. It also operates a busy café business from the ground floor. Bedrooms are comfortable, well equipped, and family rooms are available.
FACILITIES: 10 rms (7 en suite) (3 fmly) No smoking in dining room No smoking in lounges TVB tea/coffee Licensed Cen ht TVL
PRICES: s £25-£30; d £40-£50✻ **PARKING:** 9 **CARDS:**

TYWYN Map 06 SH50

♦♦♦♦ Eisteddfa *(SH651055)*

Eisteddfa, Abergynolwyn LL36 9UP ☎ 01654 782385
📠 01654 782228 Mrs G Pugh
Dir: *on B4405 between Abergynolwyn and Dolgoch Falls*
Eisteddfa is a modern, stone-built bungalow situated less than a mile from Abergynolwyn, and is an ideal spot for walking or for visiting the local railway. Rooms are comfortable and well equipped, and the lounge and dining room have views over the valley. Evening meals are by arrangement and ceoliac diets are catered for.
FACILITIES: 3 rms (2 en suite) (3 GF) TVB tea/coffee Cen ht TVL 1200 acres mixed **PRICES:** d £36-£40✻ **LB BB NOTES:** Closed Dec-Feb

Smoking restrictions appear under the **FACILITIES** heading, please check when booking.

MERTHYR TYDFIL

MERTHYR TYDFIL Map 03 SO00

♦♦♦♦ Penrhadw Farm

Pontsticill CF48 2TU ☎ 01685 723481 722461 📠 01685 721591
e-mail: info@penrhadwfarm.co.uk
Dir: *5m N of Merthyr Tydfil*
In an elevated position in the Brecon Beacons National Park, this Victorian former farmhouse has been sympathetically renovated to provide excellent, spacious bedroom accommodation equipped with a range of practical and homely extras. An elegant lounge is available in addition to the cosy breakfast room.
FACILITIES: 5 en suite No smoking in bedrooms No smoking in dining room STV TVB tea/coffee No dogs (ex guide dogs) Cen ht TVL Dinner Last d by arrangement **PRICES:** s £42-£46; d £55-£65✻ **LB PARKING:** 12
CARDS:

♦♦♦♦ Llwyn Onn

Cwmtaf CF48 2HT ☎ 01685 384384 📠 01685 359310
e-mail: reception@llwynonn.co.uk
Dir: *off A470 2m N of Cefn Coed.*
This delightful house is in a splendid location overlooking Llwyn-Onn reservoir and is ideal for either the business guest or for those touring the area. This is a comfortable and relaxing home where the bedrooms are pleasantly spacious and well furnished. The friendly proprietors are attentive hosts and a stay here will be a memorable experience.
FACILITIES: 4 rms (3 en suite) No smoking in bedrooms No smoking in dining room STV TVB tea/coffee No dogs Cen ht TVL No coaches **PRICES:** s £22-£30; d £50✻ **LB PARKING:** 4 **CARDS:**

♦♦ *Tredegar Arms Hotel*

66 High St, Dowlais Top CF48 3PW ☎ 01685 377467
📠 01685 377467
Dir: *turn onto A4102 at Junction / rdbt of A465 / A4060, A470*
Located on the outskirts in the village of Dowlais, the Tredegar Arms offers practically equipped bedrooms. The inn enjoys a good local reputation for a range of ales and traditional meals, which are available in the bars or dining room.
FACILITIES: 8 en suite (2 fmly) TVB tea/coffee Cen ht TVL No coaches Pool Table Dinner Last d 10.30pm **PARKING:** 9
CARDS:

MONMOUTHSHIRE

ABERGAVENNY Map 03 SO21

Premier Collection

♦♦♦♦♦ Oak Meadows

Old Monmouth Rd NP7 8BG ☎ 01873 850927
📠 01873 850927
Dir: *from Abergavenny take B4233 signed Rockfield, after 2m field gate signed Oak Meadows on left*
This delightful house has been created by tastefully converting an early 19th-century barn. A haven of peace and tranquillity, it stands in extensive grounds and attractive gardens, overlooking panoramic views of the surrounding countryside, including the Sugar Loaf Mountain. Bedrooms include one on the ground floor, and are attractively appointed, modern and well equipped. Facilities include a pleasant lounge area and a bright breakfast room, where all guests share one table.
FACILITIES: 3 en suite No smoking TVB tea/coffee No dogs Cen ht No children 10yrs **PRICES:** s £25; d £45✻ **LB PARKING:** 6
NOTES: Closed Nov-Etr

♦♦♦♦ Hardwick Farm *(SO306115)*

NP7 9BT ☎ 01873 853513 & 01873 854238 01873 854238
Mrs C Jones
e-mail: carol.hardwickfarm@virgin.net
Dir: *1m from Abergavenny, off A4042, farm sign on R*

Pleasantly located in peaceful countryside this traditional farmhouse provides warm and friendly hospitality. The spacious bedrooms are pleasantly comfortable and well equipped. Traditional farmhouse breakfasts are served in the dining room at separate tables.
FACILITIES: 2 en suite (1 fmly) No smoking TVB tea/coffee Cen ht 230 acres dairy mixed **PRICES:** s £27-£30; d £40-£45✳ **LB**
PARKING: 2 **NOTES:** Closed Xmas

♦♦♦♦ Llanwenarth House

Govilon NP7 9SF ☎ 01873 830289 01873 832199
e-mail: info@welsh-hotel.co.uk
Dir: *E of Abergavenny follow A465 towards Merthyr Tydfil for 3.5m to next rdbt. Take 1st exit to Govilon, drive 150yds on right 0.5m long*

The ancestors of Sir Henry Morgan, the infamous privateer who eventually became Governor of Jamaica, built this spacious and beautiful manor house. Elegance and charm abound in all rooms. Interesting and innovative dishes feature at dinner and fresh fruits and vegetables from the garden add a further memorable aspect to dining here.
FACILITIES: 5 en suite (1 fmly) (1 GF) No smoking in bedrooms No smoking in dining room TVB tea/coffee Licensed Cen ht No children 8yrs No coaches Croquet lawn Dinner Last d 6pm **PRICES:** s £62-£68; d £84-£88✳
PARKING: 6

Super supper! this symbol shows that evening meals exceeded our Inspector's expectations.

♦♦♦ Penyclawdd *(SO291173)*

Llanvihangel Crucorney NP7 7LB ☎ 01873 890591
01873 890591 Mrs A Davies
e-mail: davies@penyclawdd.freeserve.co.uk
Dir: *take road signed Pantygelli from A465, Hereford/Abergavenny*
This attractive modern house is located on immaculate gardens off the Abergavenny to Hereford road. It offers homely bedrooms filled with many thoughtful extras. A traditionally furnished dining room is the setting for imaginative breakfasts and a comfortable lounge with wood burner is also available.
FACILITIES: 2 rms (2 fmly) No smoking TVB tea/coffee No dogs (ex guide dogs) Cen ht TVL 160 acres sheep beef, working farm **PRICES:** s fr £22; d fr £40✳ **PARKING:** 6 **NOTES:** Closed 24-25 Dec

CALDICOT — Map 03 ST48

♦♦♦♦ Penylan *(ST429905)*

St Brides Netherwent NP26 3AS ☎ 01633 400267
01633 400997 Mrs A Arthur
e-mail: johnann@penylan267.freeserve.co.uk
Dir: *M4 junct 23A, turn left just before village of Magor into St Brides Rd. North 2m, 100yds past Carrow Hill turning*
Many original features are retained at this Elizabethan house which is located in a commanding elevated position close to main road links. Bedrooms are filled with homely extras and memorable breakfasts are served in the attractive conservatory, which offers stunning views. A comfortable guest lounge with inglenook fireplace and indoor swimming pool are also available.
FACILITIES: 3 rms (2 en suite) (1 fmly) No smoking TVB tea/coffee No dogs (ex guide dogs) Cen ht Indoor swimming pool (heated) Croquet lawn 150 acres non working **PRICES:** s £25-£30; d fr £50✳
PARKING: 6 **NOTES:** Closed Dec-mid Mar

CHEPSTOW

See **Caldicot & Tintern**

LLANDOGO — Map 03 SO50

♦♦♦ The Sloop

NP25 4TW ☎ 01594 530291 01594 530935
Dir: *on A466 between Monmouth & Chepstow in centre of village*
Centrally located between Monmouth and Chepstow in a valley of outstanding natural beauty, this inn offers traditional standards of food, hospitality and comfort. The spacious bedrooms are equipped for both the business and leisure traveller.
FACILITIES: 4 en suite (1 fmly) TVB tea/coffee Cen ht Pool Table Dinner Last d 9pm **PRICES:** s £29; d £49-£60✳ **MEALS:** Lunch £12-£21alc Dinner £12-£21alc✳ **PARKING:** 30 **CARDS:**

MONMOUTH — Map 03 SO51

♦♦♦ Church Farm

Mitchel Troy NP25 4HZ ☎ 01600 712176
Dir: *from A40 S, L onto B4293 for Trelleck before tunnel, 150yds turn L & follow signs to Mitchel Troy. GH on main rd, on L 200 yds beyond campsite*
Located in the village of Mitchel Troy, this 16th century former farmhouse retains many original features including exposed decorative beams and open fireplaces. A range of bedrooms is provided and a spacious lounge is available in addition to the traditionally furnished dining room where breakfast is served.
FACILITIES: 8 rms (6 en suite) (2 fmly) No smoking tea/coffee Cen ht TVL No coaches Dinner Last d noon **PRICES:** s £22-£30; d £44-£50✳
PARKING: 12

Wales

TINTERN Map 03 SO50

♦♦♦ Fountain Inn
Trellech Grange NP16 6QW ☎ 01291 689303 📠 01291 689303
e-mail: dmaachi@aol.com
Dir: *A466 turn left just before Royal George Hotel, signed Raglan continue until next signpost for Raglan on right take this turn & follow road bearing right towards Trellech*
Located in a peaceful valley north of Tintern, this 17th-century inn retains many original features that are enhanced by the rustic-style furniture throughout the public areas. Bedrooms are cosy and homely. A range of popular dishes is available at dinner.
FACILITIES: 5 rms (2 en suite) No smoking in bedrooms No smoking in dining room TVB tea/coffee Cen ht Dinner Last d 10pm
PRICES: s £30; d £40-£46* **MEALS:** Bar Lunch £12-£20 Dinner £12-£25*
CONF: Board 20 **PARKING:** 25 **CARDS:**

USK Map 03 SO30

♦♦♦♦ Ty-Gwyn Farm *(SO389044)*
Cold Harbour, Gwehelog NP15 1RT ☎ 01291 672878
📠 01291 672878 Mr & Mrs J Arnett
Dir: *M4 junct 24. Take A449-A472 to Usk, turn right after last 30mph signs to Gwehelog. 2.5m, bear left at Coldharbour sign and left again at Ty Gwyn sign.*
Located in the pretty hamlet of Cold Harbour, this well-maintained house provides fine views of the surrounding countryside including the Black Mountains. Bedrooms are comfortable and homely and modern efficient bathrooms compliment. Breakfast, which includes free-range eggs and home made preserves, is taken at one family table overlooking secluded lawns. The local pub is within walking distance for evening meals or nearby Usk also provides restaurants and pubs.
FACILITIES: 2 en suite (1 fmly) No smoking TVB tea/coffee No dogs Cen ht TVL No children 4yrs 20 acres Mixed **PRICES:** s £28-£30; d £44-£48* LB **PARKING:** 3 **NOTES:** Closed 24-27 Dec

NEATH PORT TALBOT

NEATH Map 03 SS79

Premier Collection

♦♦♦♦♦ Green Lanterns
Hawdref Ganol Farm, Cimla SA12 9SL ☎ 01639 631884
📠 01639 899550
e-mail: caren.jones@btinternet.com
Dir: *M4 J43 towards Neath. Take B4287 signposted Cimla & R at x-roads 300yds past comprehensive school, AA signposted*

This 18th-century farmhouse is part of a 46-acre equestrian and pony-trekking centre and has superb views over the area. Bedrooms are spacious, decorated in keeping with the style of the house, and equipped with modern facilities. An impressive lounge is provided for residents and this features an enormous inglenook fireplace. Meals are taken family style in the attractive dining room.
FACILITIES: 4 en suite (2 fmly) No smoking in bedrooms No smoking in dining room TVB tea/coffee Licensed Cen ht TVL Riding
Dinner Last d 7pm **PRICES:** d £54* LB **PARKING:** 6
CARDS:

♦♦♦♦ Cwmbach Cottages
Cwmbach Rd, Cadoxton SA10 8AH ☎ 01639 639825 & 641436
e-mail: cwmbachcottages@guesthouse25.fsnet.co.uk
Dir: *north of Neath come off A465 - signed Aberdulais and Tonna. At rdbt follow signs for Cadoxton. Turn right opposite church, guest house is signposted*

Originally a terrace of farm labourers' cottages, this family-run guest house is located on a pretty wooded hillside. The modern bedrooms are spacious and well-equipped. One ground floor room has been designed for the convenience of disabled guests. Public areas include a dining room and a lounge that overlooks the gardens. Self-catering accommodation is also available.
FACILITIES: 5 en suite (1 fmly) No smoking in bedrooms No smoking in dining room TVB tea/coffee No dogs (ex guide dogs) Cen ht TVL No coaches Biking **PRICES:** s £28; d £42-£46* LB **PARKING:** 7

NEWPORT

NEWPORT Map 03 ST38

Premier Collection

♦♦♦♦♦ The Inn at the Elm Tree
St Brides Wentlooge NP10 8SQ ☎ 01633 680225
📠 01633 681035
e-mail: inn@the-elm-tree.co.uk
Dir: *off A48, 300yds after leaving M4 junct 28. At 1st rdbt proceed 0.75m to Morgan Way, turn right. At T-junct with B4239, turn right. Proceed for 2.5m*
Located on Wentlooge Flats and on the site of a former ancient barn, the inn provides high standards of comfort. The spacious bedrooms are all individually styled, offering excellent standards of comfort complimented by modern bathrooms, some with spa facilities. Award winning food is served in the elegant restaurant and a comfortable lounge bar is available.
FACILITIES: 10 en suite (3 fmly) (2 GF) No smoking in 4 bedrooms No smoking in dining room TVB tea/coffee Direct dial from bedrooms Cen ht No children 12yrs No coaches Croquet lawn Jacuzzi Dinner Last d 10pm **PRICES:** s £70-£100; d £80-£120* LB **MEALS:** Lunch £14.50&alc Dinner £14.50&alc* **CONF:** Thtr 30 Class 30 Board 20 Del £125 * **PARKING:** 30 **CARDS:**

continued

♦♦♦♦ Crescent Guest House
11 Caerau Crescent NP20 4HG ☎ 01633 776677
01633 761279
Dir: *M4 junct 27 towards town centre. Through traffic lights with Handpost pub on right. After 50yds left into Caerau Crescent*
Located on a quiet residential avenue within easy walking distance of the centre, this elegant Victorian house retains many original features including a fine tiled hall and stained glass windows. Bedrooms are comfortable, filled with thoughtful extras and modern efficient bathrooms compliment. Breakfasts use quality local produce and are taken in an attractive dining room.
FACILITIES: 7 en suite (2 fmly) (2 GF) No smoking TVB tea/coffee No dogs (ex guide dogs) Cen ht **PRICES:** s fr £30; d fr £45* **PARKING:** 5
CARDS:

♦♦♦♦ Kepe Lodge
46a Caerau Rd NP20 4HH ☎ 01633 262351 01633 262351
Dir: *exit M4 junct 27, follow town centre signs, at 2nd traffic lights turn left, premises on right*
Situated in a quiet residential area and set in pleasant gardens, Kepe Lodge offers comfortable and well equipped bedrooms. Breakfast is taken in the dining room overlooking the garden.
FACILITIES: 8 rms (3 en suite) No smoking TVB tea/coffee No dogs (ex guide dogs) Cen ht No children 10yrs No coaches Dinner Last d before noon **PRICES:** s £23; d £46* **PARKING:** 12

♦♦♦♦ Rising Sun Hotel
1 Cefn Rd, Rogerstone NP10 9AQ ☎ 01633 895126
01633 891020
Dir: *M4 junct 27, take 3rd turning L of rdbt onto B4581 signposted Roserstone. Establishment 0.5m on L*
Located a few minutes' drive from the M4 in the residential community of Rogerstone, this impressive detached Edwardian inn benefits from spacious ground floor areas which are enhanced by a superb split level conservatory overlooking the surrounding countryside. The modern tastefully furnished bedrooms are comfortable and a wide range of real ales and popular food is offered.
FACILITIES: 6 en suite (1 fmly) No smoking in area of dining room No smoking in 1 lounge TVB tea/coffee No dogs (ex guide dogs) Cen ht Pool Table Children's play area Dinner Last d 9pm **PRICES:** s £37; d £47*
MEALS: Lunch £8.70-£9 Dinner £12.35-£19.45alc* **PARKING:** 200
CARDS:

Chapel Guest House
Church Rd, St Bridges Wentloog NP10 8SN ☎ 01633 681018
01633 681431
e-mail: chapelguesthouse@hotmail.com
Dir: *exit M4 at junct28, take A48 towards Newport, at rdbt 3rd exit signed B4239 St Brides, follow for approx 3m into center of village, right into Church Rd, then 1st left into car park of Church House Inn*
FACILITIES: 3 en suite (1 fmly) No smoking TVB tea/coffee Cen ht No coaches **PRICES:** s £25-£30; d £44-£46* **LB PARKING:** 6
NOTES: ★★★ **CARDS:**

Egg cups for excellence!
This symbol shows that breakfast exceeded our Inspector's expectations.

REDWICK Map 03 ST48

♦♦♦♦ Brickhouse
North Row NP26 3DX ☎ 01633 880230 01633 882441
e-mail: brickhouse@compuserve.com
Dir: *from M4 junct 23A follow steel works road for 1.5m. Turn left after sign for Redwick, 1.5m to Brickhouse on left*
This impressive country house is peacefully located and set in attractive and well-tended gardens. The friendly hosts are most attentive and provide a relaxing atmosphere for their guests. Bedrooms are spacious and well furnished and there is a choice of lounges where guests may relax. Dinner features local and home produced ingredients and is a delight not to be missed
FACILITIES: 7 rms (5 en suite) (1 fmly) No smoking TVB No dogs Licensed Cen ht TVL No children 10yrs No coaches Dinner Last d Noon
PRICES: s £40; d £50* **PARKING:** 7

PEMBROKESHIRE

FISHGUARD Map 02 SM93

♦♦♦♦ Erw-Lon *(SN028325)*
Pontfaen SA65 9TS ☎ 01348 881297 Mrs L McAllister
Dir: *on B4313 between Fishguard and Maenclochog*

Located in the Pembrokeshire National Park, with stunning views of the Gwaun Valley, this attractive house has been sympathetically converted to provide bedrooms filled with a wealth of homely extras. A warm welcome is assured and memorable dinners feature the finest local produce.
FACILITIES: 3 rms (2 en suite) No smoking TVB tea/coffee No dogs (ex guide dogs) Cen ht TVL No children 10yrs Jacuzzi 128 acres beef sheep Dinner Last d 24hrs in advance **PRICES:** s £25-£30; d £50-£60* **LB**
PARKING: 5 **NOTES:** Closed Dec-Feb

♦♦♦ Stanley House
Quay Rd, Goodwick SA64 0BS ☎ 01348 873024
e-mail: stanleyhouse@btinternet.com
In a commanding position overlooking the harbour and surrounding countryside, this well maintained Victorian house with its pretty landscaped rear garden offers cosy homely bedrooms and an attractive dining room, which also contains a lounge area.
FACILITIES: 3 rms (1 en suite) (1 fmly) No smoking TVB tea/coffee No dogs (ex guide dogs) Cen ht No coaches **PRICES:** s £20.50; d £35-£41* **BB**
PARKING: 3

Wales

HAVERFORDWEST Map 02 SM91

See also Narberth

♦♦♦♦ Lower Haythog Farm *(SM996214)*

Spittal SA62 5QL ☎ 01437 731279 01437 731279
Mrs N M Thomas
e-mail: nesta@lowerhaythogfarm.co.uk
Dir: *5m N off B4329, continue along this road until railway bridge, farmhoues entrance on right*

Located north of the town, this sympathetically renovated farmhouse dates from the 14th century and furniture styles and décor enhance its intrinsic charm. Bedrooms, three of which are located in converted farm buildings, are filled with a wealth of homely extras and the beamed dining room is a charming setting for breakfast and imaginative dinners, featuring local produce.

FACILITIES: 6 en suite (2 fmly) No smoking TVB tea/coffee Cen ht TVL Fishing Pony rides 250 acres dairy Dinner **PRICES:** s fr £25; d £50-£60* **LB PARKING:** 5

U College

93 Hill St, St Thomas Green SA61 1QL ☎ 01437 763710

At the time of going to press the Diamond classification for this establishment had not been confirmed. Please check the AA website www.theAA.com for up-to-date information.

FACILITIES: 8 en suite (2 fmly)

MILTON Map 02 SN00

A Milton Manor

SA70 8PG ☎ 01646 651398 01646 650010
e-mail: info@milton-manor.co.uk
Dir: *on the A477 5m E of Pembroke Dock in the village of Milton*

FACILITIES: 11 en suite 5 annexe en suite (8 fmly) No smoking in bedrooms No smoking in dining room No smoking in 1 lounge TVB tea/coffee Licensed Cen ht TVL Riding Snooker Pool Table Putting green **PRICES:** s £30-£35; d £52-£57* **CONF:** Class 30 **PARKING:** 50 **NOTES:** ★★★ Closed 21 Dec-30 Jan **CARDS:**

NARBERTH Map 02 SN11

♦♦♦ *Highland Grange*

Robeston Wathen SA67 8EP ☎ 01834 860952 01834 860952
e-mail: info@highlandgrange.co.uk
Dir: *22m W of Carmarthen, A40 to hilltop village Robeston Wathen, property last on right before Bush Inn. 8m E of Haverfordwest.*

This modern house standing on pretty gardens provides homely bedroom accommodation popular with international visitors on the Ireland Fishguard route. Imaginative dinners using home-grown produce are a feature in addition to a comprehensive Welsh breakfast.

FACILITIES: 3 rms (2 en suite) (1 fmly) No smoking in bedrooms No smoking in dining room TVB tea/coffee No dogs (ex guide dogs) Licensed Cen ht TVL No coaches Dinner Last d 5pm **PARKING:** 6

See advert on opposite page

PEMBROKE Map 02 SM90

See also Narberth

♦♦♦♦ Poyerston Farm *(SM027025)*

Cosheston SA72 4SJ ☎ 01646 651347 01646 651347
Mrs S Lewis
e-mail: poyerstonfarm@btinternet.com
Dir: *from Carmarthen take A40 to St Clears rdbt, then continue on A447 towards Pembroke Dock, drive through Milton. Poyerston 0.75m on the left opposite Vauxhall garage*

continued

Situated on 300 acres, close to local attractions, this delightful Victorian house offers comfortable homely bedrooms, some of which are located in the adjacent former dairy. Ground floor areas include a choice of cosy lounges and an elegant dining room, which extends into a conservatory with direct access to the gardens.

Poyerston

FACILITIES: 6 en suite (2 fmly) (3 GF) No smoking TVB tea/coffee No dogs (ex guide dogs) Cen ht TVL No children 2yrs Farm walks, Stables 10 min walk 350 acres arable beef dairy Last d 10am **PRICES:** s £25-£30; d £45-£55* **LB PARKING:** 12 **NOTES:** Closed 20-27 Dec

ST DAVID'S Map 02 SM72

See also Solva

♦♦♦♦ Ramsey House

Lower Moor SA62 6RP ☎ 01437 720321 & 720332
01437 720025
e-mail: info@ramseyhouse.co.uk
Dir: *from A487 in centre of St David's bear left in front of HSBC Bank signposted Porthclais, house 0.5m on left*

Surrounded by unspoilt countryside, this house provides thoughtfully furnished bedrooms that include a wealth of homely extras. Imaginative dinners featuring authentic Welsh produce and recipes ensure a memorable visit. Room price includes dinner. Ramsey House caters exclusively for non-smoking adults.

FACILITIES: 6 en suite (3 GF) No smoking TVB tea/coffee Licensed Cen ht No children 14yrs No coaches Dinner Last d 7pm **PRICES:** (incl. dinner) s £32-£70; d £64-£70 **LB PARKING:** 6 **CARDS:**

♦♦♦♦ Y-Gorlan

77 Nun St SA62 6NU ☎ 01437 720837 & 07974 108029
01437 721148
e-mail: mikebohlen@aol.com
Dir: *in centre of St David's*

Located close to major attractions, with superb rural views from the comfortable first floor lounge, this immaculately maintained house provides cosy bedrooms filled with lots of thoughtful extras and home cooked dinners by prior arrangement.

continued

FACILITIES: 5 en suite (1 fmly) No smoking in bedrooms No smoking in dining room STV TVB tea/coffee No dogs (ex guide dogs) Licensed Cen ht TVL No coaches Dinner Last d 6pm **PRICES:** s £26-£30; d £50-£60✳
PARKING: 2 **CARDS:**

♦♦♦ Coach House

15 High St SA62 6SB ☎ 01437 720632
Dir: *centre of St Davids, opposite city hall*
This Georgian townhouse is located near the cathedral and other local attractions. It provides smart modern bedrooms, including some suitable for families. A good choice of dishes is available for breakfast, served in a pretty dining room that doubles as a coffee shop during the day.
FACILITIES: 7 rms (5 en suite) (1 fmly) No smoking TVB tea/coffee No dogs (ex guide dogs) TVL **PRICES:** s £15-£25; d £40-£50✳ **BB**
CARDS:

♦♦♦ Y Glennydd Hotel

51 Nun St SA62 6NU ☎ 01437 720576 📠 01437 720184
Mar-Oct
Dir: *on one-way system next to the fire station*
Located close to the cathedral, this impressive Georgian town house has been sympathetically modernised to provide homely bedroom accommodation furnished to enhance the building's intrinsic charm. Ground floor areas include a choice of lounges and a restaurant which enjoys a strong local following.
FACILITIES: 10 rms (8 en suite) (4 fmly) No smoking in 5 bedrooms No smoking in dining room TVB tea/coffee No dogs (ex guide dogs) Licensed Cen ht TVL Dinner Last d 8.45pm **PRICES:** s £22-£28; d £38-£44✳ **BB**
PARKING: 5 **CARDS:**

SAUNDERSFOOT — Map 02 SN10

♦♦♦♦ Vine Cottage

The Ridgeway SA69 9LA ☎ 01834 814422
e-mail: helen@caple4.freeserve.co.uk
Dir: *at Kilgetty rdbt on A477 take exit A478 Saundersfoot/Tenby, in village of Pentlepoir left opp Fountain Head Inn. B4316 signed Saundersfoot continue 0.5m under railway bridge turn right signed Saundersfoot (Ridgeway) Cottage on left 100mtrs*
Located in extensive mature gardens, a few minutes' walk from major attractions, this 200-year-old former farmhouse provides homely bedrooms, some of which are equipped for families. Other areas include a very comfortable lounge with large screen TV and a cosy dining room where breakfast and dinner are served.
FACILITIES: 5 en suite (2 fmly) No smoking TVB tea/coffee Cen ht TVL No children 6yrs No coaches **PRICES:** s £30-£35; d £50-£56✳ **LB**
PARKING: 10

♦♦♦ Woodlands Hotel

St Brides Hill SA69 9NP ☎ 01834 813338 📠 01834 811480
e-mail: woodlands.hotel@virgin.net
Dir: *located in the village of Saundersfoot 200yds from beach*
Located in an elevated position within easy walking distance to harbour and beaches, this friendly owner managed hotel provides comfortable homely bedrooms, some suitable for family use. Breakfast and dinners by arrangement are taken in the cottage style dining room and the comfortable lounge bar has direct access to the pretty garden.
FACILITIES: 10 en suite (3 fmly) No smoking in bedrooms No smoking in dining room TVB tea/coffee No dogs Licensed Cen ht TVL No coaches Dinner Last d 8pm **PRICES:** s £30-£35; d £45-£55✳ **LB**
PARKING: 14 **NOTES:** Closed Nov-Feb
CARDS:

SOLVA — Map 02 SM82

Premier Collection

♦♦♦♦♦ Lochmeyler Farmhouse *(SM855275)*

Llandeloy SA62 6LL ☎ 01348 837724 📠 01348 837622
Mrs M Jones
e-mail: stay@lochmeyler.co.uk
Dir: *from Haverfordwest A487 St Davids Rd to Penycwm, turn R, follow road to village of Llandeloy.*

Located on a 200-acre working dairy farm, this sympathetically renovated 16th-century house provides superbly comfortable, spacious bedrooms with many homely extras. Comprehensive Welsh breakfasts and imaginative dinners are taken in the elegant dining room and guests have the benefit of four separate lounges. The pretty gardens are quiet and secluded.
FACILITIES: 14 en suite (14 fmly) No smoking in bedrooms No smoking in dining room No smoking in 1 lounge TVB tea/coffee Direct dial from bedrooms Licensed Cen ht TVL 220 acres dairy
PRICES: s £20-£37.50; d £40-£55✳ **LB PARKING:** 14
NOTES: Closed Nov-Feb **CARDS:**

Wales

TENBY Map 02 SN10

♦♦♦♦ Giltar Grove Country House

Penally SA70 7RY ☎ 01834 871568
e-mail: giltarbnb@aol.com
Dir: *from Tenby, take A4139 towards Manorbier/Pembroke. Pass petrol station, after 2m reach railway bridge on bend, second right after bridge*

Just a few minutes' walk from the spectacular Pembrokeshire Coastal Path, this impressive Victorian farmhouse retains many original features. Bedrooms are filled with homely extras and public areas include a cosy sitting room, an elegant dining room and spacious conservatory.

FACILITIES: 6 en suite (1 fmly) (2 GF) No smoking TVB tea/coffee No dogs (ex guide dogs) Cen ht TVL No children 5yrs No coaches Croquet lawn **PRICES:** s £20-£25; d £40-£50✻ **PARKING:** 10 **NOTES:** Closed Xmas & New Year

♦♦♦♦ Gwynne House

Bridge St SA70 7BU ☎ 01834 842862 📠 01834 842862
e-mail: gwynnehouse@msn.com
Dir: *From A478 continue until 'Welcome to Tenby' sign, then turn left. Head towards the harbour and take left turn. 3rd house on the left*

Located in a superb position overlooking the historic harbour, this impressive Georgian house retains many original features, enhanced by the quality furnishing and décor schemes throughout. Bedrooms are filled with thoughtful extras and a very comprehensive breakfast selection is offered in the elegant dining room, which provides stunning sea views.

FACILITIES: 5 en suite (5 fmly) No smoking in 2 bedrooms No smoking in dining room TVB tea/coffee No dogs (ex guide dogs) Cen ht No coaches **PRICES:** s £30-£40; d £40-£60✻ **LB** **PARKING:** 1 **CARDS:**

♦♦♦♦ Rosendale Park

Rosendale Park, Lydstep SA70 7SQ ☎ 01834 870040
e-mail: rosendalewales@yahoo.com
Dir: *at Tenby take B4139 towards Pembroke, establishment 4m on right hand side after Lydstep village*

continued

A warm and friendly welcome can be expected at Rosendale Park, which is conveniently located for exploring South Pembrokeshire. Rooms, all recently refurbished to a high standard, have an impressive provision of facilities. Special dietary requirements can be accommodated and activities including fishing, golf and horse riding can be arranged locally.

FACILITIES: 4 en suite (1 fmly) No smoking TVB tea/coffee Cen ht No children 2yrs No coaches **PRICES:** s £20-£24; d £40-£48✻ **LB** **PARKING:** 6 **NOTES:** Closed Jan

♦♦♦♦ Weybourne

14 Warren St SA70 7JU ☎ 01834 843641
Dir: *On entering Tenby, take the first left under Railway bridge. At top of hill take first right into Green Hill Ave, at the end you will be in Warren St. Weybourne on right.*

Located a few minutes' walk from the railway station and historic centre, this sympathetically converted townhouse provides comfortable homely bedrooms, one of which is very suitable for families. Imaginative breakfasts are taken in the attractive dining room, which is themed with lots of framed sepia postcards and original Titanic advertising memorabilia.

FACILITIES: 4 en suite (2 fmly) No smoking in dining room No smoking in lounges TVB tea/coffee No dogs Cen ht No children 2yrs **PRICES:** s £16-£25; d £32-£50✻ **LB BB CARDS:**

♦♦♦ Castle View Private Hotel

The Norton SA70 8AA ☎ 01834 842666
Dir: *1st left after 'Welcome to Tenby' sign pass coach park, hotel on right before zebra crossing*

This attractive, family run hotel offers friendly hospitality and attentive service. Delightful sea views from the first-floor lounge can be enjoyed and also from some of the bedrooms. There is a cosy bar and traditional dinners and well-cooked breakfasts are served in the spacious dining room.

FACILITIES: 10 en suite (4 fmly) No smoking in 3 bedrooms No smoking in dining room No smoking in 1 lounge TVB tea/coffee No dogs Licensed TVL **PRICES:** s £25-£38; d £44-£56✻ **LB** **PARKING:** 7

♦♦♦ Clarence House Hotel

Esplanade SA70 7DU ☎ 01834 844371 📠 01834 844372
e-mail: clarencehotel@freeuk.com
Dir: *follow South Parade by old town walls to Esplanade and turn right*

Enjoying an elevated position with superb views, this hotel has been owned by the same family for over 50 years. Many of the bedrooms have sea views and are all comfortably furnished. There is a sheltered rose garden, which leads from the bar and in addition, a number of lounges are available for guests; entertainment is provided in the high season.

FACILITIES: 68 en suite (6 fmly) No smoking in 30 bedrooms No smoking in dining room No smoking in 1 lounge TVB tea/coffee Licensed Lift Cen ht TVL Pool Table In house entertainment, live music Dinner Last d 7.30pm **PRICES:** s £15-£39; d £30-£86✻ **LB BB** **NOTES:** Closed 18-28 Dec **CARDS:**

See advertisement on opposite page

Wales

♦♦♦ *Gumfreston Private Hotel*

Culver Park SA70 7ED ☎ 01834 842871 📠 01834 842871
e-mail: gumf@supanet.com
Dir: *50yds from Rectory car park, 150yds from South Beach*

A few minutes' walk from South Beach and the town centre, this period house offers comfortable homely bedrooms, some with family facilities. Ground floor areas include a cosy lounge, intimate basement bar and an attractive dining room where generous Welsh breakfasts are served. Dinner is available by arrangement.

FACILITIES: 9 en suite (2 fmly) No smoking in bedrooms No smoking in dining room TVB tea/coffee No dogs (ex guide dogs) Licensed Cen ht TVL No coaches Dinner Last d 4pm **NOTES:** Closed 25-26 Dec
CARDS:

St Teresa's Old Convent

South Pde SA70 7DL ☎ 01834 844495

At the time of going to press the Diamond classification for this establishment had not been confirmed. Please check the AA website www.theAA.com for up-to-date information.

FACILITIES: 3 en suite

TREFIN — Map 02 SM83

♦♦♦♦ Awel-Mor

Penparc SA62 5AG ☎ 01348 837865 📠 01348 837865
e-mail: robin.jill@awel-mor.freeserve.co.uk
Dir: *from Fishguard on A487, turn right about 300yds past the Square and Compass pub into road signed Treffin. After 100yds take the 2nd left and Awel Mor is on left*

Set in immaculate mature gardens, in an elevated position which offers stunning views of the National Park and coastline, this guesthouse provides comfortable homely bedrooms filled with thoughtful extras. Superb breakfasts and imaginative dinners are provided in the spacious dining room, which also contains a lounge section.

FACILITIES: 3 rms (2 en suite) (1 GF) No smoking TVB tea/coffee No dogs Licensed Cen ht TVL No children 7yrs No coaches Dinner Last d by arrangement **PRICES:** s £24-£29; d £48-£58✱ **LB PARKING:** 6
NOTES: Closed Nov-Mar **CARDS:**

POWYS

BRECON — Map 03 SO02

See also Sennybridge

♦♦♦♦ Llanddetty Hall *(SO124205)*

Talybont-on-Usk LD3 7YR ☎ 01874 676415 📠 01874 676415
Mrs H E Atkins
Dir: *7m SE off B4558*

This impressive 16th-century listed farmhouse is very attractive and located amidst the beautiful scenery and tranquillity of the Usk Valley. The friendly proprietors ensure their guests are comfortable and service is attentive. Bedrooms are most pleasant and, in the style of the house, feature exposed timbers and polished floorboards.

FACILITIES: 3 en suite 1 annexe en suite (1 GF) No smoking TV1B tea/coffee No dogs (ex guide dogs) Cen ht TVL No children 12yrs 48 acres sheep Dinner Last d day before **PRICES:** s fr £28; d £42-£48✱
PARKING: 6 **NOTES:** Closed 16 Dec-14 Jan rs Mar-Apr

♦♦♦♦ The Usk

Station Rd, Talybont-on-Usk LD3 7JE ☎ 01874 676251
📠 01874 676392
e-mail: stay@uskinn.co.uk
Dir: *just off the A40 6m E of Brecon. 10m W of Abergavenny*

This delightful inn is located in the village of Talybont-on-Usk. It is personally run in a warm and friendly manner and has been renovated to a very high standard. Thoughtfully equipped and appointed bedrooms include rooms with four-poster beds. Public areas have a wealth of charm and the inn has a well deserved reputation for its food.

FACILITIES: 11 en suite (1 fmly) No smoking in bedrooms No smoking in area of dining room TVB tea/coffee Direct dial from bedrooms No dogs (ex guide dogs) Cen ht Dinner Last d please give notice
PRICES: s £35-£50; d £65-£90✱ **LB MEALS:** Lunch fr £10&alc Dinner £17.95-£22.95&alc✱ **CONF:** Board 10 Del from £85 ✱ **PARKING:** 30
NOTES: Closed 25-27 Dec **CARDS:**

Places with this symbol are farmhouses.

POWYS continued

◆◆◆ Cherrypicker House

9 Orchard St LD3 8AN ☎ 01874 624665
e-mail: info@cherrypickerhouse.co.uk
Dir: *from town centre follow signs to Llandovery A40, cross bridge over Usk. In 200mtrs through traffic lights house approx. 20mtrs on right*
Just a short walk from the town centre, a hospitable and warm welcome is assured at Cherrypicker House. Rooms are comfortably furnished and thoughtful extras are provided. The guest house is conveniently placed for the Brecon Beacons National Park, mid Wales and the A40 and A470 main roads.
FACILITIES: 3 rms (1 en suite) No smoking in bedrooms No smoking in dining room No smoking in lounges TVB tea/coffee No dogs (ex guide dogs) Cen ht TVL No coaches **PRICES:** s £20-£30; d £40-£50✳ **PARKING:** 3

◆◆◆ Beacons

16 Bridge St LD3 8AH ☎ 01874 623339 Fax 01874 623339
e-mail: beacons@brecon.co.uk
Dir: *turn off junct of A40/A470 onto B4601, 0.5m on left opposite Christ College school*

Located West of the historic centre, this former 17th century riverside farm has been sympathetically renovated to provide a range of homely bedrooms, some of which are housed in former barns and outbuildings. The traditionally furnished dining room is the setting for imaginative dinners and a cosy bar and comfortable lounges are also available.
FACILITIES: 11 rms (8 en suite) 3 annexe en suite (3 fmly) (3 GF) No smoking in bedrooms No smoking in dining room No smoking in lounges TVB tea/coffee Licensed Cen ht TVL Dinner Last d 9pm **PRICES:** s £30-£35; d £38-£60✳ BB **PARKING:** 21 **CARDS:**

◆◆◆ Borderers

47 The Watton LD3 7EG ☎ 01874 623559
e-mail: ian@borderers.com
Dir: *E on B4601, on right 200mtrs past pedestrian crossing opposite church. From west on A40 200mtrs past mini rdbt on left*
Originally a 17th-century drover's inn. The courtyard, now a car park, is surrounded by many of the bedrooms. A former winner of the Brecon in Bloom competition, pretty hanging baskets are seen everywhere. Bedrooms are attractively decorated, with rich floral fabrics used to good effect.
FACILITIES: 4 rms (2 en suite) 5 annexe en suite (3 fmly) (4 GF) No smoking TVB tea/coffee Cen ht No coaches **PRICES:** s £30-£40; d £40-£50✳ **PARKING:** 6 **CARDS:**

◆◆◆ The Old Ford Inn

Llanhamlach LD3 7YB ☎ 01874 665220 Fax 01874 665220 (phone first)
e-mail: enquiries@theoldfordinn.co.uk
Dir: *East of Brecon on main A40 Brecon to Abergavenny Rd. From rdbt junct of A40 & A470 head towards Abergavenny (A40) Inn is on right 300yds past end of dual carriageway*

continued

Parts of this former drover's inn date back to the 11th century. The bedrooms have modern facilities and most look out towards the Brecon Beacons. Public areas have a wealth of charm and character and include a choice of bars and a quaint cottage-style dining room. A wide range of wholesome dishes is available.
FACILITIES: 8 en suite (2 fmly) No smoking in bedrooms No smoking in dining room No smoking in lounges TVB tea/coffee Cen ht Dinner Last d 9.30pm (9pm Sun) **PRICES:** s £26; d £48-£50✳ **PARKING:** 16 **CARDS:**

The Flag and Castle

11 Orchard St, Llanfaes LD3 8AN ☎ 01874 625860
e-mail: flagandcastle@btinternet.com
Dir: *W of Brecon on the B4601 opposite Christ College*
FACILITIES: 3 en suite (1 fmly) No smoking TVB tea/coffee No dogs Cen ht TVL No coaches **PRICES:** s fr £25; d fr £40✳ **PARKING:** 2 **NOTES:** ★★★ Closed 14 Dec-14 Jan

Ty Newydd

Cambrian Cruisers, Pencelli LD3 7LJ ☎ 01874 665315 Fax 01874 665315
e-mail: cambrian@talk21.com
Dir: *off A40, on B4558, 3m SW of Brecon*
FACILITIES: 3 en suite No smoking TVB tea/coffee No dogs Cen ht No children No coaches Narrowboat hire **PRICES:** s £28; d £48✳ **PARKING:** 6 **NOTES:** ★★★ Closed Nov-Feb **CARDS:**

BUILTH WELLS — Map 03 SO05

◆◆◆◆ *Woodlands*

Hay Rd LD2 3YL ☎ 01982 552354 Fax 01982 552354
e-mail: heskethn@aol.com
Dir: *just S of Builth Wells on side of A470, entrance by lay-by*
This imposing, former Edwardian residence is situated on the outskirts of town in its own wooded grounds. Inside the proprietor has gone to great lengths to retain the feel and ambience of yesteryear but with the comforts of modern facilities. Bedrooms are light, airy and thoughtfully furnished while the public areas include a comfortable lounge.
FACILITIES: 4 en suite No smoking TVB tea/coffee No dogs Cen ht No children 13yrs No coaches **PARKING:** 4

CAERSWS — Map 06 SO09

Premier Collection

◆◆◆◆◆ The Talkhouse

Ty Siarad, Pontdolgoch SY17 5JE ☎ 01686 688919 Fax 01686 689134
e-mail: info@talkhouse.co.uk
Dir: *from Caersws follow A470 to Machynlleth, inn on left*
This delightful 19th-century inn has been completely refurbished over recent years. The lounge, a cosy room filled with sofas, is the ideal place to while away an hour with a glass of wine or cup of tea, while the bar centres around the large fireplace. Bedrooms have been restored to an excellent standard, and offer luxury in every area. The emphasis here is on food, with fine use made of both local produce and home made items. The Talkhouse is the Guest Accommodation of the Year for Wales 2002-2003.
FACILITIES: 3 en suite No smoking in bedrooms No smoking in dining room No smoking in lounges TVB tea/coffee No dogs Cen ht No children 14yrs No coaches Dinner Last d 9pm **PRICES:** s £65; d £75-£95✳ **MEALS:** Lunch £10-£15alc Dinner £20-£25alc✳ **PARKING:** 30 **NOTES:** Closed 1wk Spring,1wk Autumn, 25-26 Dec & 1 Jan **CARDS:**

Wales

♦♦♦♦ *Lower Ffrydd (SO000916)*
SY17 5QS ☎ 01686 688269 Fax 01686 688269
Mr & Mrs J Evans
e-mail: loffrydd@dircon.co.uk
Dir: *from Caersws, take road for Trefeglwys opposite garage. Follow road for 2m to sign on left for Upper and Lower Ffrydd, 1st left off small road*
Lower Ffrydd is a lovely half-timbered, 16th-century farmhouse which has been tastefully restored and extended. It has delightful views of the surrounding hills and valleys and is close to Newton and the historic market town of Llanidloes, making it a useful base for touring Mid Wales. Bedrooms are very well equipped with thoughtful extras. Downstairs there are comfortable lounges with inglenooks and beams. Dinner is available by arrangement.
FACILITIES: 3 en suite (1 fmly) No smoking in bedrooms No smoking in dining room TVB tea/coffee No dogs Cen ht TVL 110 acres beef sheep Dinner Last d 10am **PARKING:** 4

CHURCH STOKE Map 07 SO29

♦♦♦♦ The Drewin *(SO261905)*
SY15 6TW ☎ 01588 620325 Fax 01588 620325 Mrs C Richards
e-mail: ceinwen@drewin.freeserve.co.uk
Dir: *from Churchstoke take A489 towards Newtown. Left onto B4385. After 1m take 1st right for Cwm/Pantglas. Next right and then next left, follow up hill. Take left fork to Mainstone. 1st on left*
This delightful 17th-century farmhouse lies close to Offa's Dyke and attracts many walkers as a result. Very much a working farm, it is in an elevated location and commands superb views. Many original features remain with an abundance of exposed timbers and inglenook fireplaces. Two sitting rooms are provided and bedrooms are well equipped and comfortable. Ceinwen and Robert Richards are the very friendly owners who go out of their way to make their guests feel welcome. Ceinwen is responsible for the hearty Welsh breakfasts on offer.
FACILITIES: 2 en suite (1 fmly) No smoking TVB tea/coffee No dogs (ex guide dogs) Cen ht TVL 102 acres mixed Dinner Last d 5pm
PRICES: s £25; d £42-£44* **PARKING:** 6 **NOTES:** Closed Nov-Mar

CRICKHOWELL Map 03 SO21

Premier Collection

♦♦♦♦♦ Glangrwyney Court
NP8 1ES ☎ 01873 811288 Fax 01873 810317
e-mail: glangrwyne@aol.com
Dir: *3m from Abergavenny on A40 towards Brecon, first right after Powys county change on left*
Located on extensive mature grounds this impressive Georgian house has been sympathetically renovated to provide high standards of comfort and facilities. The spacious bedrooms are equipped with a range of both practical and homely extras, and bathrooms include a Jacuzzi or steam shower. The interior has been decorated with style and flair. Comprehensive breakfasts are taken at one table in the elegant dining room and a sumptuous lounge is also provided.
FACILITIES: 5 rms (4 en suite) (1 fmly) No smoking in bedrooms No smoking in dining room No smoking in 1 lounge STV TVB tea/coffee Direct dial from bedrooms Licensed Cen ht TVL No coaches Croquet lawn Boules Dinner Last d 24hrs notice **PRICES:** s £42-£65; d £54-£70* **LB PARKING:** 12 **CARDS:** 

CRIGGION Map 07 SJ21

♦♦♦♦ Brimford House *(SJ310150)*
SY5 9AU ☎ 01938 570235 Fax 01938 570235 Mrs Dawson
e-mail: info@brimford.co.uk
Dir: *At Shrewsbury take A458 (Welshpool), through Ford, right on B4393. Left after Crew Green for Criggion, on left after pub*
This impressive 16th-century farmhouse lies in lovely open countryside and is a convenient base for touring Mid Wales and the Marches. Bedrooms are spacious and comfortably furnished to high standards. A relaxing lounge is available for residents and a cheery log fire burns here during colder weather. Hospitality is warm and friendly and the atmosphere throughout is peaceful and relaxing.
FACILITIES: 3 en suite No smoking TVB tea/coffee Cen ht TVL Fishing 250 acres dairy **PRICES:** d fr £45* **LB PARKING:** 4

DYLIFE Map 06 SN89

♦♦♦ *Star*
SY19 7BW ☎ 01650 521345
Dir: *off B4518, 9m NW of Llanidloes*
This friendly Inn is set in beautiful countryside and is an ideal place to relax from life's hustle and bustle, or for the more active walking, cycling and bird watching are popular. The inn is a most historic establishment and is a popular watering hole. A wide range of choice is available from the menu and bedrooms are clean and comfortable.
FACILITIES: 7 rms (2 en suite) (1 fmly) No smoking in dining room No smoking in 1 lounge tea/coffee Cen ht TVL Last d 10.30pm
PARKING: 30 **CARDS:**

Wales

GLASBURY Map 03 SO13

♦♦♦♦ Ffforddfawr *(SO192398)*

HR3 5PT ☎ 01497 847332 📠 01497 847003 Mrs B Eckley
e-mail: barbara@ffordd-fawr.co.uk
Dir: *from Hay-on-Wye take B4350 towards Brecon, farm 3m on right*

Dating from the 17th century this attractive farmhouse is set in well-tended gardens which, join the River Wye. The friendly proprietors are most welcoming and provide a home from home atmosphere. Bedrooms are spacious and comfortable and one room is suitable for families. Traditional farmhouse breakfast is served in the dining room.
FACILITIES: 3 en suite (1 fmly) No smoking TVB tea/coffee No dogs (ex guide dogs) Cen ht TVL No children 8yrs Fishing 280 acres mixed
PRICES: s £32-£34; d £42-£46✻ **PARKING:** 10 **NOTES:** Closed Dec-Feb

HAY-ON-WYE Map 03 SO24

See also Glasbury

♦♦♦♦ Tinto House

Broad St HR3 5DB ☎ 01497 820590 📠 01497 821058
e-mail: john@tintohouse.co.uk
Dir: *centre of Hay-on-Wye opposite clock tower on B4350*

Centrally located in the town and also ideal as a base from which to tour the Welsh borders, this fine Georgian house offers comfortable and well-equipped rooms. A pleasant lounge is provided and the impressive gardens, which front onto the river, are ideal places to relax. Delightful breakfasts are served and feature home-made preserves and freshly cooked dishes.
FACILITIES: 3 en suite 1 annexe en suite (2 fmly) (1 GF) No smoking TVB tea/coffee No dogs (ex guide dogs) Cen ht TVL No coaches
PRICES: s £30; d £50-£60✻ **PARKING:** 2 **NOTES:** Closed 23-26 Dec
CARDS:

♦♦♦♦ York House

Hardwick Rd, Cusop HR3 5QX ☎ 01497 820705
📠 01497 820705
e-mail: roberts@yorkhouse59.fsnet.co.uk
Dir: *on B4348 0.5m from main car park in Hay-on-Wye*

This fine Victorian house lies in its own extensive gardens, just half a mile from Hay town centre. Olwen and Peter Roberts offer a friendly welcome to their guests. Bedrooms are attractively decorated and well equipped with modern facilities. There is a comfortable lounge for residents, and a lovely garden.
FACILITIES: 4 en suite (1 fmly) No smoking TVB tea/coffee Cen ht No children 8yrs No coaches Dinner Last d noon
PRICES: s £26-£38; d £52-£56 **LB** **PARKING:** 8
NOTES: Closed 24-26 Dec **CARDS:**

LLANDRINDOD WELLS Map 03 SO06

♦♦♦♦ Guidfa House

Crossgates LD1 6RF ☎ 01597 851241 📠 01597 851875
e-mail: guidfa@globalnet.co.uk
Dir: *3m N, at junct of A483/A44*

Guests are assured of a relaxed and pampered stay at this elegant Georgian house situated just outside the town. Comfort is the keynote here whether in the attractive and well-equipped bedrooms or in the homely lounge, which has a real fire burning in colder weather. Food is also a highlight, where the proprietor's skilful touch has earned a dinner award.

FACILITIES: 6 en suite No smoking in bedrooms No smoking in dining room TVB tea/coffee No dogs (ex guide dogs) Licensed Cen ht No children 10yrs Dinner Last d noon **PRICES:** s £33.50-£39.50; d £55-£60✻ **LB**
PARKING: 10 **CARDS:**

♦♦♦♦ Holly *(SO045593)*

Holly Farm, Howey LD1 5PP ☎ 01597 822402 📠 01597 822402
Mrs R Jones
e-mail: hollyfarm@ukworld.net
Dir: *2m S on A483 near Howey*

This working farm dates back to Tudor times and is surrounded by its own fields. Bedrooms are homely and full of character, and

continued

public areas include a period dining room where local produce and traditional home cooking can be sampled and a comfortable lounge with a log fire in cooler months.
FACILITIES: 3 en suite (1 fmly) TVB tea/coffee No dogs Cen ht TVL Walking, cycling & bird watching 70 acres beef sheep Dinner Last d 5pm **PRICES:** s £22-£26; d £40-£50* **LB** **PARKING:** 4 **CARDS:**

♦♦♦ The Drovers Arms
Howey LD1 5PT ☎ 01597 822508
e-mail: info@drovers-arms.co.uk
Dir: *1m S of Llandrindod Wells. Turn off A483 into Howey Village. Inn adjacent to shop and post office*
Located in the pretty rural village of Howey, this red brick Victorian inn has been sympathetically renovated to provide homely bedrooms complimented by smart modern shower rooms. Imaginative dinners are a feature in the attractive dining room and a warm welcome is assured.
FACILITIES: 3 en suite No smoking in bedrooms No smoking in dining room No smoking in lounges TVB tea/coffee No dogs Cen ht No children 12yrs No coaches concessionary green fees at local golf clubs Dinner Last d 8.45pm **PRICES:** s £40-£45; d £50-£60* **LB** **MEALS:** Lunch £11.70-£12.90alc Dinner £16.45-£18.95alc* **PARKING:** 4
CARDS:

♦♦♦ *Kincoed Hotel*
Temple St LD1 5HF ☎ 01597 822656 📠 01597 824660
Dir: *on A483 50yds beyond the hospital*
Located close to the town centre, this friendly guest house offers well equipped bedrooms. There is a snug lounge and freshly prepared meals are served in the bay fronted dining room. Here guests can enjoy substantial breakfasts and home-cooked evening meals.
FACILITIES: 10 rms (5 en suite) (3 fmly) No smoking in 2 bedrooms TVB tea/coffee Direct dial from bedrooms Licensed Cen ht TVL No coaches **PARKING:** 10 **CARDS:**

Brynllys
High St LD1 6AG ☎ 01597 823190
Dir: *from N: enter town turn right opposite Hodges P.O. over level crossing and left along Waterloo Rd, past station into High St guest house on right. From S follow sign for Rhayader into town, HSBC on right over Railway Bridge right into High St guest house on left*
FACILITIES: 3 en suite No smoking TVB tea/coffee No dogs Licensed Cen ht TVL No coaches Dinner Last d 9pm
PRICES: s £18-£22; d £36-£40* **BB** **NOTES:** ★★

LLANGURIG — Map 06 SN97

♦♦♦♦ Old Vicarage
SY18 6RN ☎ 01686 440280 📠 01686 440280
e-mail: theoldvicarage@llangurig.fslife.co.uk
Dir: *5m from Llanidloes towards Aberystwyth. At rdbt take A44 into Llangurig take 1st R, Old Vicarage is 100yds on L*
The Old Vicarage, set in the heart of Llangurig, offers attractively furnished bedrooms, with improvements being made all the time. Downstairs, a small bar serves the dining room and both lounges. Wonderful collections of porcelain and antiques provide a talking point. Evening meals and afternoon teas make good use of local produce.
FACILITIES: 4 en suite (2 fmly) No smoking in bedrooms No smoking in dining room No smoking in 1 lounge TVB tea/coffee Licensed Cen ht TVL No coaches Dinner Last d 6.30pm **PRICES:** s £25-£30; d £42-£46* **LB**
PARKING: 5

LLANIDLOES — Map 06 SN98

♦♦♦ *Mount*
China St SY18 6AB ☎ 01686 412247 📠 01686 412247
e-mail: mountllani@aol.com
Dir: *off A470*
Dating back to the 14th century, the inn is believed to occupy the site of a previous motte and bailey castle and started life as a coaching inn. Traditional bars are full of character, with exposed beams and timbers as well as cobbled flooring and log fires. A games room and children's play area is provided.
FACILITIES: 3 en suite (1 fmly) TVB tea/coffee Cen ht TVL Pool Table Play area for children Dinner Last d 9pm **PARKING:** 10
CARDS:

LLANSILIN — Map 07 SJ22

♦♦♦♦ Old Vicarage
Llansilin SY10 7PX ☎ 01691 791345
e-mail: pam@vicarage-guests.co.uk
Dir: *centre of village, follow B4580 from Oswestry, entrance near red telephone box by Give Way sign*
Set in well-tended, secluded gardens and enjoying splendid views of the countryside this former Victorian vicarage dates back to 1792. The proprietors provide a friendly welcome and are caring and attentive hosts. Bedrooms are spacious, comfortable and attractively decorated. Traditional breakfasts are served in the dining room and feature freshly cooked dishes and home-made preserves.
FACILITIES: 3 en suite No smoking tea/coffee No dogs Cen ht TVL No children 12yrs No coaches All sports can be arranged
PRICES: s £30-£46; d £46-£52* **LB** **PARKING:** 4 **NOTES:** Closed Xmas

LLANYMYNECH — Map 07 SJ22

♦♦♦ *The Manse*
SY22 6EN ☎ 01691 831108
e-mail: themillers@mansewales.freeserve.co.uk
Situated in this border village, The Manse offers traditionally presented bedrooms that have modern facilities. The warm and friendly hospitality ensures that guests feel at home, and a freshly cooked, substantial breakfast can be enjoyed in the pine-furnished dining room.
FACILITIES: 3 rms. No smoking in bedrooms, dining room, lounges. TVB tea/coffee Cen ht TVL **PRICES:** s £26; d £45* **PARKING:** 6

LLOWES — Map 03 SO14

♦♦♦♦ Ty-Bach
HR3 5JE ☎ 01497 847759 📠 01479 847940
e-mail: j.bradfield@btinternet.com
Dir: *turn off A438 opposite Radnor Arms pub, through Llowes villages and up hill. After 0.5 rd forks establishment drive in middle of fork*
Situated on the outskirts of the village of Llowes, this large house provides tastefully appointed and well-equipped accommodation. Facilities include a spacious and comfortable lounge with an adjoining conservatory. Surrounded by fourteen acres of grounds and gardens, there are panoramic views across the River Wye towards Hay-on-Wye and the Black Mountains.
FACILITIES: 2 en suite (1 fmly) No smoking in bedrooms No smoking in dining room TVB tea/coffee No dogs (ex guide dogs) Cen ht No children No coaches Dinner Last d noon **PRICES:** s £30-£40; d £45-£50* **LB**
PARKING: 6 **NOTES:** Closed 16Dec-31Jan

LLYSWEN Map 03 SO13

♦♦♦ *Oakfield*

Llyswen LD3 0UR ☎ 01874 754301

Dir: *off A470*

This fine house dates back to 1914 and lies in pleasant lawns and gardens near the village centre. Bedrooms are fresh and equipped with comfortable beds and pretty fabrics. Guests dine family style in the smart breakfast room, which also has a small sitting area with a conservatory. Oakfield is a no-smoking establishment.

FACILITIES: 2 rms (1 en suite) No smoking tea/coffee No dogs (ex guide dogs) Cen ht TVL No coaches **PARKING:** 6 **NOTES:** Closed Nov-Feb

MACHYNLLETH Map 06 SH70

♦♦♦ Maenllwyd

Newtown Rd SY20 8EY ☎ 01654 702928 📠 01654 702928

e-mail: maenlwyd@dircon.co.uk

Dir: *on A489 opposite the hospital*

This Victorian house lies on the outskirts of the historic town of Machynlleth, a short walk from local amenities. A warm welcome has been offered to guests here for many years and friendly hospitality can be enjoyed. Bedrooms are attractively decorated with modern facilities provided. There is a comfortable lounge for residents with a separate dining room.

FACILITIES: 8 en suite (1 fmly) No smoking in bedrooms No smoking in dining room TVB tea/coffee Cen ht TVL No coaches **PRICES:** d £44-£50✳ **PARKING:** 11 **NOTES:** Closed 25 & 26 Dec **CARDS:**

U *Yr Hen Felin (The Old Mill)*

Abercegir SY20 8NR ☎ 01650 511818

At the time of going to press the Diamond classification for this establishment had not been confirmed. Please check the AA website www.theAA.com for up-to-date information.

FACILITIES: 3 en suite

MONTGOMERY Map 07 SO29

♦♦♦♦ Little Brompton *(SO244941)*

SY15 6HY ☎ 01686 668371 📠 01686 668371 Mrs G M Bright

e-mail: gaynor.brompton@virgin.net

Dir: *2m E on B4385, 0.5m W off A489*

A warm welcome is assured at this 17th-century farmhouse, which lies on a working farm crossed by Offa's Dyke. The house is full of character and boasts exposed beams and timbers with the comfortable lounge housing an inglenook fireplace. Aga-cooked meals can be enjoyed in the traditional dining room.

FACILITIES: 3 en suite (1 fmly) No smoking TVB tea/coffee No dogs (ex guide dogs) Cen ht TVL 100 acres arable beef mixed sheep Dinner Last d 5pm **PRICES:** s £25; d £46-£48✳ **LB PARKING:** 4

NEWTOWN Map 06 SO19

♦♦♦♦ Yesterdays

Severn Square SY16 2AG ☎ 01686 622644 📠 01686 625992

e-mail: yesterdayshotel@compuserve.com

Dir: *from the junct of Broad St and High St proceed from Barclays Bank along Severn Street for 80yds into Severn Square*

Dating back to the 17th century, this attractive restaurant with rooms provides comfortable, spacious and well-equipped accommodation with many thoughtful extras. The friendly hosts provide a genuine welcome and attentive service. Good choices are available at lunch and dinner, and dishes feature local specialities and produce, some vegetarian.

continued

FACILITIES: 4 en suite 1 annexe en suite (2 fmly) (1 GF) No smoking TVB tea/coffee No dogs (ex guide dogs) Licensed Cen ht No coaches Dinner Last d 8.30pm **PRICES:** s £30; d £45✳ **NOTES:** Closed 2/3 wks in Jan **CARDS:**

PRESTEIGNE Map 03 SO36

A Gumma Farm

Discoed LD8 2NP ☎ 01547 560243

e-mail: anne.owens@farming.co.uk

Dir: *from Presteigne head west, signposted Whitton B4356. After 1m brown- Gumma farm B&B sign on left hand turn towards Discoed follow signs.*

FACILITIES: 2 en suite TVB tea/coffee No dogs Cen ht No coaches Croquet lawn Dinner Last d 24hrs **PRICES:** d £42-£45✳ **LB PARKING:** 20 **NOTES:** ★★★ Closed Dec-Feb

SENNYBRIDGE Map 03 SN92

♦♦♦ Maeswalter *(SN932237)*

Heol Senni LD3 8SU ☎ 01874 636629 Mrs M J Mayo

e-mail: maeswalter@talk21.com

Dir: *exit A470 onto A4215, after 2.5m turn left for Heol Senni. Farm 1.5m on right over cattle grid*

Set in a peaceful country location with splendid views of the Senni Valley, this 17th century farmhouse offers a friendly and relaxing place to stay. Bedrooms are well-equipped with comfortable furnishings and are attractively decorated. A combined lounge and dining room are provided and guests can take freshly cooked farmhouse breakfast in a relaxing atmosphere.

FACILITIES: 4 rms (2 en suite) (1 fmly) (5 GF) No smoking TVB tea/coffee No dogs (ex guide dogs) Cen ht TVL No children 5yrs 1 acres Non-working Dinner Last d Noon **PRICES:** s £20-£25; d £40-£50✳ **LB PARKING:** 11

TALGARTH Map 03 SO13

♦♦♦ Castle Inn

Pengenffordd LD3 0EP ☎ 01874 711353 📠 01874 711353

e-mail: castlepen@aol.com

Dir: *4m S Talgarth alongside A479*

Located in the heart of the Black Mountains this inn is a convenient place to stay. The proprietors, staff and locals provide a friendly and relaxed atmosphere, to which many guests return. Bedrooms are smart and well decorated with modern facilities. Good breakfasts are served in the spacious dining room and there is a popular bar.

FACILITIES: 4 en suite (1 fmly) No smoking in bedrooms TVB tea/coffee No dogs (ex guide dogs) Cen ht Pool Table Dinner Last d 9.30pm **PRICES:** d £46✳ **MEALS:** Lunch £4.50-£8alc Dinner £8-£12alc✳ **PARKING:** 50 **CARDS:**

WELSHPOOL Map 07 SJ20

See also Criggion

♦♦♦♦ Heath Cottage *(SJ239023)*
Kingswood, Forden SY21 8LX ☎ 01938 580453
01938 580453 Mr & Mrs M C Payne
e-mail: heathcot@bushinternet.com
Dir: *behind Forden Old P.O. off A490 Welshpool/Churchstoke road, opposite Parrys Garage*
Located to the south of Welshpool, this early 18th-century farmhouse retains many original features, which are highlighted by the furnishing and décor styles throughout. Bedrooms offer stunning views of the countryside and a choice of guest lounges, one with log fire, is available. Memorable breakfasts include free-range eggs and home made preserves.
FACILITIES: 3 en suite (1 fmly) No smoking tea/coffee No dogs Cen ht TVL 6 acres poultry sheep **PRICES:** s £22; d £44* **PARKING:** 4
NOTES: Closed Nov-Etr

♦♦♦♦ Lower Trelydan *(SJ225105)*
Lower Trelydan, Guilsfield SY21 9PH ☎ 01938 553105
01938 553105 Mrs Sue Jones
e-mail: stay@lowertrelydan.com
Dir: *A490 N from Welshpool, after 1.5m turn right onto B4392, 0.5m turn right at 30mph sign, 500yds on the left*
A warm welcome is assured at this 16th century farmhouse, once home to John Gwyn, Royalist and Diarist of the Civil War. Quality furnishings and décor enhance the many original features which include a wealth of exposed beams and open fires. The property also contains self-catering cottages and a livery service is available.
FACILITIES: 3 en suite (1 fmly) No smoking TVB tea/coffee No dogs Licensed Cen ht TVL Children's play area 350 acres beef dairy sheep Dinner Last d 10am **PRICES:** s fr £30* **LB PARKING:** 10
NOTES: Closed Xmas & New Year

♦♦♦♦ Moat *(SJ214042)*
SY21 8SE ☎ 01938 553179 01938 553179 Mr & Mrs W Jones
e-mail: ewjones@freenetname.co.uk
Dir: *on A483, 0.5m from junct with A490 on the left hand side set 100mtrs from A483*
Enjoying splendid views, peacefully located and set in attractive gardens, the friendly proprietors have owned and run this working farm for many years. The house is over 400 years old and exposed beams and period furnishings maintain the style in the comfortable, pretty rooms. Traditional breakfasts are served in the spacious dining room.
FACILITIES: 3 en suite (1 fmly) No smoking STV TVB tea/coffee No dogs Cen ht 260 acres dairy **PRICES:** s £26-£30; d £44-£52*
PARKING: 3 **NOTES:** ★★★ Closed Dec-Jan

> **A** Associate entries with stars have been ★ inspected and rated by the ★ Welsh Tourist Board or Scottish Tourist Board.

A Orchard House
Leighton SY21 8HN ☎ 01938 553624 01938 553624
e-mail: pearce@orchardhouse-leighton.fsnet.co.uk
FACILITIES: 3 en suite (1 GF) No smoking TVB tea/coffee Cen ht TVL No coaches **PRICES:** s £22-£25; d £44-£46* **LB PARKING:** 3
NOTES: ★★★ Closed Xmas & New Year **CARDS:**

SWANSEA

FELINDRE Map 02 SN60

♦♦♦ *Coynant Farm* *(SN648070)*
SA5 7PU ☎ 01269 595640 Mr F Jones
Dir: *4m N of Felindre off unclass rd linking M4 junct 46 and Ammanford*
Remotely located on the mountains to the North of Swansea, this 200-acre holding includes deer, llamas, emus and rare waterfowl. Private fishing for trout and carp is also available and both breakfast and dinner uses own produce, where possible. Bedrooms are homely and a cosy lounge with wood burning stove is also available.
FACILITIES: 7 en suite (2 fmly) No smoking in bedrooms No smoking in dining room STV TVB tea/coffee No dogs (ex guide dogs) Licensed Cen ht Fishing Riding Games room 200 acres mixed Last d 7pm **PARKING:** 10
CARDS:

OXWICH Map 02 SS48

♦♦♦♦ Woodside
SA3 1LS ☎ 01792 390791
e-mail: david@oxwich.fsnet.co.uk
Dir: *from A4118 from Penmaen after 1m turn left for Oxwich and Slade, premises at crossroads*

Located close to beach and nature reserve, this sympathetically converted period cottage with adjoining barn provides comfortable homely bedrooms, three of which are situated at ground floor level. Other areas include a cosy bar with open fire and a spacious conservatory dining room, which also contains a lounge section.
FACILITIES: 5 en suite (1 fmly) (3 GF) No smoking in dining room No smoking in lounges TVB tea/coffee No dogs Licensed Cen ht No coaches
PRICES: s £30-£46; d £40-£62* **PARKING:** 8 **NOTES:** Closed Dec-Jan rs Nov & Feb

Wales

PARKMILL (Near Swansea) Map 02 SS58

♦♦♦ *Parc-le-Breos House (SS529896)*

SA3 2HA ☎ 01792 371636 ▤ 01792 371287 Mrs O Edwards

Dir: *at village turn right 300yds after Shepherds shop, then next left, signposted. Follow private road to end*

At the end of a forest drive and set in 70 acres of delightful grounds, this imposing country house dates back to the early 19th century. Much of the charm and many of the original features of the building have been retained in the public rooms, which include a lounge and a games room. In the bedrooms, many of which are suitable for family occupancy, comfortable furnishings are provided.

FACILITIES: 10 rms (8 en suite) (7 fmly) TVB tea/coffee No dogs (ex guide dogs) Cen ht TVL Riding Games room 65 acres arable horses pigs chickens Dinner Last d 3pm **PARKING:** 12

SWANSEA Map 03 SS69

See also Felindre

♦♦♦♦ Grosvenor House

Mirador Crescent, Uplands SA2 0QX ☎ 01792 461522 ▤ 01792 461522

e-mail: grosvenor@ct6.com

Dir: *off A4118 in the uplands area of Swansea*

This pleasant house is located in the fashionable and attractive Uplands district and is convenient for touring the Gower Peninsular and Mumbles. The hosts who provide comfortable and attractive accommodation ensure a warm and friendly welcome. Secure parking, a pleasant lounge and an attractive dining room complement the facilities of this attractive home.

FACILITIES: 7 en suite (2 fmly) No smoking TVB tea/coffee No dogs (ex guide dogs) Cen ht TVL No children 4 yrs No coaches **PRICES:** s £30-£34; d £50-£56 **PARKING:** 3 **NOTES:** Closed 23 Dec-3 Jan **CARDS:**

♦♦♦ Cefn Bryn

6 Uplands Crescent SA2 0PB ☎ 01792 466687

e-mail: enquiries@cefnbryn.co.uk

Dir: *on A4118, 1m from Swansea Railway Station*

This impressive Victorian house retains many original features including fireplaces and ornate decorative ceilings to public rooms. Bedrooms are equipped with both practical and homely extras and a comfortable guest lounge is available in addition to the elegant dining room.

FACILITIES: 7 en suite (2 fmly) No smoking TVB tea/coffee No dogs (ex guide dogs) No coaches **PRICES:** s £29; d £50-£55*
NOTES: Closed 22-31 Dec & 1-2 Jan

♦♦♦ Alexander Hotel

3 Sketty Rd, Uplands, Sketty SA2 0EU ☎ 01792 470045 & 476012 ▤ 01792 476012

e-mail: alexander.hotel@swig-online.co.uk

Dir: *on A4118, 1m from city centre on road to Gower Peninsula*

Located in fashionable Uplands between Gower and the city centre, this Victorian house has been sympathetically modernised to provide good levels of comfort and facilities. Bedrooms are filled with practical extras and other areas include a cosy dining room, lounge bar and games room.

FACILITIES: 7 rms (6 en suite) (4 fmly) No smoking in 3 bedrooms No smoking in dining room TVB tea/coffee Direct dial from bedrooms No dogs (ex guide dogs) Licensed Cen ht No children 5yrs No coaches Pool Table Weights, Exercise bike, Darts **PRICES:** s £25-£38; d £56-£60* **NOTES:** Closed 24 Dec-1 Jan **CARDS:**

♦♦♦ Crescent

132 Eaton Crescent, Uplands SA1 4QR ☎ 01792 466814 ▤ 01792 466814

e-mail: conveyatthecrescent@compuserve.com

Dir: *1st left off A4118 after St James Church travelling W*

Located on a leafy avenue close to restaurants, bars and shops, this Edwardian house has been sympathetically converted to provide comfortable bedrooms suitable for all guests. Breakfast is taken in the cosy dining room and the spacious lounge offers stunning views of Swansea Bay.

FACILITIES: 6 en suite (1 fmly) No smoking in bedrooms No smoking in dining room TVB tea/coffee No dogs (ex guide dogs) Cen ht TVL No coaches **PRICES:** s £30-£31; d £48-£50* **PARKING:** 5 **NOTES:** Closed 23 Dec-1 Jan **CARDS:**

TORFAEN

PONTYPOOL Map 03 SO20

♦♦♦♦ Mill Farm *(SO271049)*

Cwmafon NP4 8XJ ☎ 01495 774588 ▤ 01495 774588 Mrs C Jayne

Dir: *between Pontypool and Blaenavon on A4043, 0.5m S of Cwmafon Village, turn E into Denbridge Rd, after 100 mtrs right over river, 400mtrs to house*

Located in a stunning elevated position, in mature grounds, which include an ancient woodland, croquet lawn and boules piste, this delightful property dates from Tudor times and has many original features. Bedrooms are filled with homely extras. Public areas include an elegant dining room and choice of lounges, one of which contains a heated swimming pool.

FACILITIES: 3 en suite 1 annexe en suite No smoking in bedrooms No smoking in dining room No smoking in 1 lounge tea/coffee No dogs Cen ht TVL No children Indoor swimming pool (heated) Croquet lawn Boules 30 acres sheep **PRICES:** s £25-£30; d £50* **PARKING:** 5 **NOTES:** Closed 16 Dec-2 Jan

Further details of AA rated B&Bs and hotels can be found on the AA website www.theAA.com

♦♦♦♦ Ty-Cooke *(SO310052)*
Mamhilad NP4 8QZ ☎ 01873 880382 📠 01873 880382
Mrs M Price
e-mail: tycookefarm@hotmail.com
Dir: *turn off A4042 to Mamhilad at Du Pont factory, follow road for 2m, 1st farm on left past Horseshoe Inn*
This working farm is located in a most attractive setting and has lovely views. It is reputed to date back to at least 1700 and provides traditionally furnished, farmhouse accommodation. Refurbishment has ensured that bedrooms are well equipped. There is a breakfast room and a very comfortable lounge, with a log fire, available to residents.
FACILITIES: 3 en suite (1 fmly) No smoking TVB tea/coffee No dogs (ex guide dogs) Cen ht TVL 135 acres beef sheep **PRICES:** s £30; d £50✻

VALE OF GLAMORGAN

COWBRIDGE — Map 03 SS97

Crossways House
CF71 7LJ ☎ 01446 773171 📠 01446 771707
e-mail: enquiries@crosswayshouse.co.uk
Dir: *from A48 W of Cardiff, exit for Cowbridge. At end of high street turn left signed St Donats. 0.5m opposite Cross Inn*
FACILITIES: 4 en suite (1 fmly) No smoking TVB tea/coffee Cen ht No coaches Tennis (hard) Pool Table **PRICES:** s £30-£35; d £50-£60✻ **LB**
PARKING: 12 **NOTES:** ★★★ **CARDS:**

PENARTH — Map 03 ST17

♦♦ Westbourne
8 Victoria Rd CF64 3EF ☎ 029 20707268 📠 029 20708265
e-mail: westbourne.gh@btinternet.com
Located 3 miles from Cardiff city centre and the Millennium Stadium, and a few minutes walk from Penarth's centre and attractions, this detached Victorian house has been in the same ownership for fourteen years and provides traditionally furnished accommodation. Comprehensive breakfasts are taken in the spacious dining room which also contains a bar.
FACILITIES: 9 rms (3 en suite) (1 fmly) No smoking in 4 bedrooms No smoking in dining room No smoking in lounges TVB tea/coffee No dogs (ex guide dogs) Licensed Cen ht No coaches **PRICES:** s £25-£35; d £45-£58✻
LB PARKING: 4 **CARDS:**

Wales

Ireland

Ballywarren House, Cong

NORTHERN IRELAND

CO ANTRIM

CUSHENDUN Map 01 D6

♦♦♦♦ GH *Drumkeerin*

201A Torr Rd BT44 0PU ☎ 028 2176 1554 📠 028 2176 1556
e-mail: drumkeerin@zoom.co.uk
Dir: *Cushendun to Ballycastle via Torr Road, approx 50yds on left on bend turn into lane, house is 0.25m along this road*

High above the village in rolling countryside, this haven of peace and tranquillity enjoys views of the Antrim coast and Irish Sea towards Scotland. The bedrooms are attractively decorated, and there is a comfortable lounge whose focus is a bay window overlooking the glen and harbour. Breakfasts are substantial and make excellent use of organic produce and delicious home-baked delicacies. Mary and Joe McFadden are very welcoming and hospitable hosts and Mary is the winner of the 2002-2003 Landlady of the Year Award.

FACILITIES: 3 rms (1 en suite) No smoking TV1B No dogs (ex guide dogs) Cen ht TVL Painting tuition available **PARKING:** 4

♦♦♦ GH The Villa Farm House

185A Torr Rd BT44 0PU ☎ 028 2176 1252 📠 028 2176 1252
e-mail: maggiescally@amserve.net
Dir: *turn right onto Torr Road after leaving village of Cushendun on B92. At T junct turn right and travel 0.5m, Villa Farmhouse is 3rd road on left marked by black and white sign*

This Tudor-style two-storey farmhouse with its well-kept garden provides stunning views of the Bay of Cushendun, the Antrim Coast and over the Irish Sea towards Scotland. Bedrooms are traditional in style, some are suitable for families and are well equipped. Good service and freshly cooked meals are assured.

FACILITIES: 3 en suite (2 fmly) No smoking TVB tea/coffee No dogs (ex guide dogs) Cen ht TVL Riding Dinner Last d noon **PRICES:** s £25; d £40✱ **LB** **CONF:** Board 20 Del from £18 ✱ **PARKING:** 25

LARNE Map 01 D5

♦♦♦♦ GH Manor

23 Older Fleet Rd, Harbour Highway BT40 1AS
☎ 028 2827 3305 📠 028 2826 0505
e-mail: welcome@themanorguesthouse.com
Dir: *2 minutes walk from Larne Ferry Terminal & Harbour Train Station*

This traditionally styled Victorian town house continues to prove popular with travellers thanks to its convenient location; just a short stroll from the ferry terminal. There is an elegant sitting room and a separate cosy breakfast room. The well-equipped bedrooms vary in size and are furnished in modern or period style. Hospitality is very good.

FACILITIES: 8 en suite (2 fmly) No smoking TVB tea/coffee No dogs (ex guide dogs) Cen ht Jacuzzi **PRICES:** s £22.50-£25; d £40-£44 **PARKING:** 6 **NOTES:** Closed 25-26 Dec **CARDS:**

♦♦♦ GH Derrin

2 Prince's Gardens BT40 1RQ ☎ 028 2827 3269 & 2827 3762
📠 028 2827 3269
e-mail: info@derrinhouse.co.uk
Dir: *off A8 (Harbour Highway) for A2 coastal route, after lights at Main St, take 1st road on left*

Just a short walk from the town centre, and a minute's drive from the harbour, this comfortable Victorian house offers smartly decorated modern bedrooms with a wide range of amenities. The spacious lounge invites peaceful relaxation, whilst hearty breakfasts are offered in the stylish dining room.

FACILITIES: 6 rms (4 en suite) (2 fmly) No smoking in bedrooms No smoking in dining room TVB tea/coffee Cen ht TVL No coaches **PRICES:** s £20-£25; d £34-£40✱ **BB** **PARKING:** 5 **NOTES:** Closed 25 & 26 Dec **CARDS:**

MARTINSTOWN Map 01 D6

♦♦♦ GH Caireal Manor

90 Glenravel Rd, Glen's of Antrim BT43 6QQ ☎ 028 2175 8465
📠 028 2175 8465
Dir: *on A43, 6m N of Ballymena*

Caireal Manor offers smartly furnished, well-equipped bedrooms. There are two ground floor bedrooms, one fully designed for disabled guests. Breakfast is served in the bright dining room, and a taxi service is provided to the proprietor's restaurant a few miles down the road.

FACILITIES: 5 en suite (4 fmly) (2 GF) No smoking in 2 bedrooms No smoking in area of dining room No smoking in lounges STV TVB tea/coffee Licensed Cen ht TVL Leisure complex nearby Dinner Last d 8.45pm **PRICES:** s £25; d £50✱ **LB** **PARKING:** 7 **NOTES:** Closed 24-26 Dec **CARDS:**

CO BELFAST

BELFAST Map 01 D5

♦♦♦ GH *Malone*

79 Malone Rd BT9 6SH ☎ 028 9066 9565 📠 028 9022 3020
Dir: *exit M1 at Balmoral, enter Stockmans Lane, turn left after 5th traffic lights, after 3rd traffic lights*

There is a welcoming atmosphere at this detached red-brick Victorian house, situated close to the university. Bedrooms are simply and smartly presented, and well maintained, whilst charming day rooms include an inviting lounge and a separate dining room.

FACILITIES: 8 en suite No smoking in bedrooms No smoking in dining room TVB tea/coffee No dogs Cen ht No children 12yrs No coaches **PARKING:** 9 **NOTES:** Closed 24 Dec-6 Jan

CO DOWN

BANGOR Map 01 D5

A GH Hebron House

59 Queens Pde BT20 3BH ☎ 028 9146 3126 📠 028 9127 4178
e-mail: reception@hebron-house.com
Dir: *from Belfast A2 to Bangor town centre, turn left at lights located at bottom of main street, continue with marina on right, take 2nd exit at mini rdbt and immediate 1st right, at end of Somerset Ave right at T junct. Hebron on right*

FACILITIES: 3 rms (1 fmly) No smoking STV TVB tea/coffee Direct dial from bedrooms No dogs Cen ht TVL No coaches **PRICES:** s £30-£45; d £40-£45✱ **NOTES:** Closed 22 Dec-1 Jan **CARDS:**

Ireland

BANGOR continued

GH Tara

49/51 Princeton Rd BT20 3TA ☎ 028 9146 8924 & 9145 8820
028 9146 9870
e-mail: taraguesthouse@lineone.net
Dir: *A2 to Bangor,down Main Street, turn left onto Queens Parade and continue to mini rdbt (Gray Hill) turn right into Princetown Road*
FACILITIES: 10 en suite (3 fmly) No smoking in 1 lounge TVB tea/coffee Direct dial from bedrooms Cen ht TVL Dinner Last d 8pm **PRICES:** s £30; d £45* **NOTES:** Closed 25-30 Dec **CARDS:**

COMBER Map 01 D5

GH The Old Schoolhouse Inn

Castle Espie BT23 6EA ☎ 028 9754 1182
At the time of going to press the Diamond classification for this establishment had not been confirmed. Please check the AA website www.theAA.com for up-to-date information.
FACILITIES: 12 en suite

DOWNPATRICK Map 01 D5

Premier Collection

♦♦♦♦♦ Pheasants Hill Country House

(J4493483)
37 Killyleagh Rd BT30 9BL ☎ 028 44838707
028 4461 7246 Mrs J Bailey
e-mail: info@pheasantshill.com
Dir: *on A22, 3m N of Downpatrick*

This modern farmhouse enjoys a rural setting on the border of The Quoile Pondage, just north of the town. Surrounded by fields this working farm houses pigs and horses and grows organic crops. The stylish bedrooms feature country-style furniture and there is a comfortable lounge.
FACILITIES: 4 en suite No smoking TVB tea/coffee No dogs (ex guide dogs) Cen ht TVL 20 acres rare breeds **PRICES:** s £39-£45; d £56-£60 LB **PARKING:** 10 **NOTES:** Closed 1Nov-28Feb
CARDS:

HOLYWOOD Map 01 D5

Premier Collection

♦♦♦♦♦ GH Beech Hill

23 Ballymoney Rd, Craigantlet BT23 4TG ☎ 028 9042 5892
028 9042 5892
e-mail: info@beech-hill.net
Dir: *leave Belfast on A2 (Bangor) bypassing Holywood, 1.5m from bridge at Ulster Folk Museum, right along Ballymoney Rd. House 1.75m on left*

continued

Beech Hill Country House

Nestling high in the rolling Holywood Hills, this delightful Georgian-style house enjoys panoramic views of the surrounding countryside. The classically styled bedrooms, all on the ground floor, include many useful extras and a host of homely touches. Public areas include a large conservatory, a comfortable lounge and a dining room where a generous breakfast is served.
FACILITIES: 3 en suite (3 GF) No smoking in bedrooms No smoking in dining room TVB tea/coffee Direct dial from bedrooms Cen ht TVL No children 10yrs No coaches Croquet lawn boules **PRICES:** s fr £40; d fr £60* **PARKING:** 6 **CARDS:**

♦♦♦♦ GH Braeside Country House

10 Brown's Brae, Croft Rd BT18 0HL
☎ 028 9042 6665 & 9042 6065 028 9042 6665
e-mail: info@braesidecountryhouse.com
Dir: *A2 Belfast-Bangor road. After Holywood sign, continue on A2. Exit at 3rd set of t/lights, cross over carriageway & bear sharp left into Croft Rd. Continue for 1.5m, house on left*

As one of the area's best kept secrets, Braeside enjoys an idyllic elevated location and enjoys panoramic views across Belfast Lough. Stylish, comfortable bedrooms are available in a ground floor wing or on the first floor of the main house. A substantial breakfast is served at a communal table in the attractive lounge/breakfast room.
FACILITIES: 4 en suite (2 GF) No smoking in bedrooms No smoking in dining room No smoking in 1 lounge TVB tea/coffee No dogs (ex guide dogs) Cen ht TVL No coaches Summer house and large garden
PRICES: s fr £40; d fr £60* **CONF:** Del £60 * **PARKING:** 6
CARDS:

Prices may change during the currency of the Guide, please check when booking.

NEWTOWNARDS Map 01 D5

Premier Collection

♦♦♦♦♦ GH Edenvale House

130 Portaferry Rd BT22 2AH ☎ 028 9181 4881
028 9182 6192
e-mail: edenvalehouse@hotmail.com
Dir: *between Newtownards and Greyabbey, 2m from Newtownards on A20*

A smartly presented Georgian house, set back from the road in seven acres of peaceful gardens and paddock. Traditional bedrooms are decorated and furnished in period style. Breakfast is served around a communal table in the dining room, and there are two lounges, one with delightful views across Strangford Lough towards the Mountains of Mourne.
FACILITIES: 3 en suite (2 fmly) No smoking in bedrooms No smoking in dining room No smoking in 1 lounge TVB tea/coffee Cen ht No coaches Riding Croquet lawn **PRICES:** s fr £35; d fr £55✻ **PARKING:** 15 **NOTES:** Closed 24-26 Dec **CARDS:**

Premier Collection

♦♦♦♦♦ GH Ballynester House

1a Cardy Rd, (Off Mount Stewart Rd) BT22 2LS
☎ 028 4278 8386 028 4278 8986
e-mail: geraldine.bailie@virgin.net
Dir: *A20 S from Newtownards to Greyabbey, or A20 N from Portaferry to Greyabbey, signposted at Greyabbey rdbt*

Nestling in the rolling hills above Strangford Lough this stylish, modern house provides a haven of peace and tranquillity. Geraldine Bailie provides the warmest of welcomes and ensures that guests are cosseted at every turn. Smart day rooms make the most of the super views; hearty wide-ranging breakfasts are served at a communal table in the bright dining room. Richly furnished bedrooms include a host of thoughtful extras. Geraldine Bailie was a runner up in the AA Landlady of the Year Awards 2002-2003.
FACILITIES: 3 en suite (1 fmly) (3 GF) No smoking TVB tea/coffee No dogs (ex guide dogs) Cen ht TVL No coaches Aromatherapy Reflexology **PRICES:** s £35; d £55✻ **LB PARKING:** 9 **CARDS:**

PORTAFERRY Map 01 D5

♦♦♦♦ GH The Narrows

8 Shore Rd BT22 1JY ☎ 028 4272 8148 028 4272 8105
e-mail: reservations@narrows.co.uk
Dir: *follow A20 & continue to shore & turn left, The Narrows is on left*

Built around an 18th-century courtyard and enjoying a delightful quayside location on the shores Strangford Lough, this converted family home offers spacious, recently refurbished bedrooms, a comfortable first floor sitting room and a small kitchen for guests use. The restaurant has a fine reputation for serving imaginitive, skillfuly prepared menus.
FACILITIES: 13 en suite (3 fmly) No smoking in bedrooms No smoking in dining room TVB tea/coffee Direct dial from bedrooms No dogs (ex guide dogs) Licensed Lift Cen ht TVL Dinner Last d 9.15pm **PRICES:** s £50-£60; d £70-£90✻ **LB CONF:** Thtr 50 Class 24 Board 24 Del from £75 ✻ **PARKING:** 5 **CARDS:**

continued

Ireland

CO FERMANAGH

ENNISKILLEN Map 01 C5

♦♦♦♦ GH Arch Tullyhona Farm

Marble Arch Rd, Florencecourt BT92 1DE ☎ 028 6634 8452
e-mail: tullyguest60@hotmail.com
Dir: *through Enniskillen follow A4, Sligo road for 2.5m then A32 & follow signs for Marble Arch Caves. Turn right at NT sign for Florencecourt*

This welcoming house nestles in a peaceful setting very close to the Marble Arch Caves and the National Trust property at Florencecourt. Tullyhona's restaurant is open for all-day breakfasts, as well as a range of traditional evening meals. The bedrooms are pleasant and offer modern comforts.

FACILITIES: 4 en suite (4 fmly) No smoking in bedrooms No smoking in dining room No smoking in 1 lounge TVB Cen ht TVL ch fac Riding Farm tours, BBQ, trampoline, swings, table tennis Dinner Last d 5.30pm
PRICES: d £40-£44✱ LB **PARKING:** 8 **CARDS:**

♦♦♦♦ GH Dromard House

Tamlaght BT74 4HR ☎ 028 6638 7250
Dir: *2m from Enniskillen, on A4 (Belfast Rd)*

This smartly presented house enjoys its own woodland trail down to the shores of Lough Erne. The attractively decorated bedrooms, with separate access, are located in a converted stable block. Hearty breakfasts are taken in the main house.

FACILITIES: 4 annexe en suite No smoking TVB tea/coffee Cen ht No coaches Fishing Woodland trail to Lough shore **PRICES:** s £25; d £40✱ **PARKING:** 4 **NOTES:** Closed 24-26 Dec

♦♦♦ GH Aghnacarra House

Carrybridge, Lisbellaw BT94 5HX ☎ 028 6638 7077
🖷 028 6638 5811
e-mail: normaensor@talk21.com
Dir: *turn off A4 Belfast/Enniskillen onto B514 to Carrybridge. Turn left at Carrybridge. 500yds on right. Sign at bridge*

continued

Enjoying an idyllic location on the shores of Lough Erne, this delightful house is a haven of peace and quiet, especially for fishermen, who may fish from the grounds. Bedrooms are well maintained, and day rooms include an elegent lounge, bright dining room and a spacious games room equipped with a pool table.

FACILITIES: 7 en suite (2 fmly) (5 GF) No smoking in 2 bedrooms No smoking in 1 lounge tea/coffee No dogs Licensed Cen ht TVL No children No coaches Pool Table Games room-Pool TV Video Dinner Last d 10am **PRICES:** s £23-£24; d £36-£38✱ LB BB **PARKING:** 8 **NOTES:** Closed Nov-Mar **CARDS:**

CO LONDONDERRY

COLERAINE Map 01 C6

Premier Collection

♦♦♦♦♦ GH Greenhill House

24 Greenhill Rd, Aghadowey BT51 4EU ☎ 028 7086 8241
🖷 028 7086 8365
e-mail: greenhill.house@btinternet.com
Dir: *from Coleraine take A29 south for 7m turn left onto B66 Greenhill Rd for approx 300yds. House on right, AA sign at front gate*

Situated in the Bann Valley, overlooking the Antrim Hills, this delightful Georgian house nestles in well-tended gardens. Public rooms are traditionally styled and include a lounge and a tastefully appointed dining room, where home cooking is offered by arrangement. The pleasant bedrooms vary in size and style and are well equipped with a host of thoughtful extras.

FACILITIES: 6 en suite (2 fmly) No smoking in dining room No smoking in lounges TVB tea/coffee Direct dial from bedrooms No dogs (ex guide dogs) Cen ht TVL Dinner Last d previous day
PRICES: s fr £35; d fr £55✱ **PARKING:** 10
NOTES: Closed Nov-Feb **CARDS:**

GH Camus Country Guest House

27 Curragh Rd, Castleroe BT51 3RY ☎ 028 7034 2982
Dir: *in Coleraine at Lodge Rd rdbt follow sign Londonderry, cross river Bann toStrand Rd rdbt, take 1st left on A54 to Kilrea, through village of Castleroe in 100yds 1st left pass Spanboard factory, forest on left 1m, wide entrance with stones NTTB sign Camus House*

FACILITIES: 3 rms (1 fmly) No smoking in 2 bedrooms No smoking in dining room No smoking in lounges TVB tea/coffee No dogs (ex guide dogs) Cen ht TVL No coaches Fishing Putting green
PRICES: s fr £25; d fr £45✱ **PARKING:** 12

LONDONDERRY Map 01 C5

GH Arkle House
2 Coshquin Rd BT48 0ND ☎ 028 7127 1156 & 7127 1157
028 7137 7262
e-mail: arklehse@tinyonline.co.uk
Dir: *off Northland rd at Aileach rdbt, Coshquin rd immediately on right. Establishment 1st on left*
FACILITIES: 4 en suite (2 fmly) No smoking in dining room TVB No dogs Cen ht No coaches **PRICES:** s £25; d £38✳ **LB BB**
PARKING: 8 **CARDS:**

GH Clarence House
15 Northland Rd BT48 7HY ☎ 028 7126 5342 028 7126 5342
e-mail: clarencehouse@zoom.co.uk
Dir: *from Belfast A6 next to University opposite Fire Station & Radio Foyle*
FACILITIES: 9 rms (7 en suite) (2 fmly) No smoking in 6 bedrooms No smoking in dining room TVB tea/coffee Direct dial from bedrooms No dogs (ex guide dogs) Cen ht TVL Dinner Last d in advance
PRICES: s £25-£30; d £40-£50✳ **CARDS:**

CO TYRONE

DUNGANNON Map 01 C5

Premier Collection

♦♦♦♦♦ **GH Grange Lodge**
7 Grange Rd BT71 7EJ ☎ 028 8778 4212 028 8778 4313
e-mail: grangelodge@nireland.com
Dir: *1m from M1 junct 15 on A29 Armagh, take sign for 'Grange' then 1st right & 1st white walled entrance on right*

Nestling in twenty acres of well-tended grounds, Grange Lodge continues to set the highest of standards. Summer visits allow guests to sample award-winning cooking in the bright and airy extension while home-baked afternoon teas can be enjoyed in the sumptuous drawing room. This is a fine house where you will enjoy hospitality and food at their best.
FACILITIES: 5 en suite No smoking in bedrooms No smoking in dining room No smoking in 1 lounge STV TVB tea/coffee Direct dial from bedrooms No dogs (ex guide dogs) Licensed Cen ht TVL No children 12yrs No coaches Snooker table Golf & Stables locally Dinner Last d 1pm previous day **PRICES:** s £50-£59; d £72-£79✳
PARKING: 12 **NOTES:** Closed 21 Dec-9 Jan
CARDS:

OMAGH Map 01 C5

♦♦♦♦ **GH Hawthorn House**
72 Old Mountfield Rd BT79 7EN ☎ 028 8225 2005
028 8225 2005
e-mail: hawthorn@lineone.net
Dir: *A5 to Omagh, on entering town go through 3 sets of traffic lights, turn right at 4th set & right again at 5th set. House on left, just past Omagh Leisure Centre*

Situated on the edge of the town in well-tended grounds, this stylish Victorian house provides well equipped, modern accommodation and a spacious restaurant and cosy bar. Dinner is the highlight of any visit, with exciting, contemporary cooking of a high standard. The hearty breakfasts are also very enjoyable.
FACILITIES: 5 en suite (4 fmly) No smoking in 2 bedrooms No smoking in area of dining room STV TVB tea/coffee Direct dial from bedrooms No dogs (ex guide dogs) Licensed Cen ht TVL Dinner Last d 9.30pm
PRICES: s £40; d £60✳ **LB CONF:** Thtr 80 Class 50 Board 30
PARKING: 65 **CARDS:**

REPUBLIC OF IRELAND

CO CARLOW

BAGENALSTOWN Map 01 C3

♦♦♦♦ **GH *Orchard Grove***
Wells ☎ 0503 22140
e-mail: orchardgrove@eircom.net
Dir: *on N9 road midway between Carlow and Kilkenny*
Lovely gardens with a play area surround this child-friendly house, which offers comfortable bedrooms and evening meals by arrangement. Inclusive packages can be arranged, and the house is close to Goresbridge bloodstock, fishing, golf, and walking routes.
FACILITIES: 4 rms (3 en suite) (3 fmly) No smoking TVB tea/coffee No dogs Cen ht TVL No coaches Pool Table Childrens play area Dinner Last d 3pm **PARKING:** 8 **NOTES:** Closed Dec **CARDS:**

Ireland

CARLOW Map 01 C3

Premier Collection

♦♦♦♦♦ GH *Barrowville Town House*
Kilkenny Rd ☎ 0503 43324 📠 0503 41953
Dir: *North-on N9 50mtrs before 1st lights, South-on N59 50mtrs after 4th lights*
Marie and Randal Dempsey are the friendly owners of this elegantly restored 18th-century town house. Comfortable bedrooms are mostly spacious, the cosy single room being more compact. The gracious drawing room has a grand piano and there is a smoking room, a conservatory breakfast room with lovely views and ample parking.
FACILITIES: 7 en suite No smoking in bedrooms No smoking in dining room STV TVB tea/coffee Direct dial from bedrooms No dogs (ex guide dogs) Cen ht TVL No children 15yrs No coaches
PARKING: 11 **CARDS:**

♦♦♦♦ GH Carlow Guest House
Green Ln, Dublin Rd ☎ 0503 36033 & 36034 📠 0503 36033
e-mail: carlowguesthouse@eircom.net
Dir: *From Dublin on N9 go through 2 rdbts, Carlow Guest House 700 m on left before Statoil garage on right*
A corner house with a new wing of colourfully decorated bedrooms. There are two comfortable lounges, with a separate area for smokers. Five minutes' walk from the town centre and Carlow Golf Course, and a good area for anglers. Off street parking available.
FACILITIES: 9 en suite (1 fmly) No smoking in bedrooms No smoking in dining room No smoking in lounges STV TVB tea/coffee Direct dial from bedrooms No dogs (ex guide dogs) Cen ht TVL Dinner Last d 24hr prior
PRICES: s €38 - €80; d €70 - €100✱ **LB PARKING:** 20
CARDS:

Ireland

RATHVILLY Map 01 D3

♦♦♦ Baile Ricead *(S 845836)*
☎ 0503 61120 Mrs M Corrigan
e-mail: minacorrigan@eircom.net
Dir: *N9 from Dublin, left at Castle Inn, left at next junct. 2nd rd on right before Graney Bridge. Left after water pump. GH on bend*
This modern house stands in a rural position, on farmland just three miles from Rathvilly. Bedrooms are comfortable and furnished to a good standard. There is a choice of lounge areas. The conservatory is ideal for admiring the gardens and the view to the distant Wicklow Mountains.
FACILITIES: 4 rms (2 en suite) (1 fmly) No smoking TVB tea/coffee Cen ht TVL 66 acres mixed **PRICES:** s €26; d €56✱ **PARKING:** 6
NOTES: Closed Nov-16 Mar

CO CLARE

BALLYVAUGHAN Map 01 B3

Premier Collection

♦♦♦♦♦ GH Drumcreehy
☎ 065 7077377 📠 065 7077379
e-mail: b&b@drumcreehyhouse.com
Dir: *At Hyland's Hotel in the village of Ballyvaughan, turn onto N67 in direction of Galway. House on right approx 1m outside village*
A detached house surrounded by attractive gardens, situated in the famous Burren area of County Clare. Facilities include comfortable sitting and dining rooms, where evening meals are served by arrangement. Home-baking is a feature, and the hosts are friendly and attentive. There are village pubs and restaurants nearby, as well as golf and hill walking.
FACILITIES: 10 en suite (2 fmly) (2 GF) No smoking in bedrooms No smoking in dining room STV TVB Direct dial from bedrooms Licensed Cen ht Last d noon **PRICES:** s €44 - €54; d €56 - €76✱
PARKING: 12 **CARDS:**

♦♦♦♦ GH Rusheen Lodge
☎ 065 7077092 📠 065 7077152
e-mail: rusheen@iol.ie
Dir: *on N67 1km from Ballyvaughan*
A charming house nestling in the valley of the Burren Mountains, an area famous for its Arctic and Alpine plants in the spring and summer. The McGann family were founders of the famous Aillwee Caves and have a wealth of local folklore. The bedrooms are large and well equipped, with attractive decor and extras which ensure a comfortable visit. Patio gardens lead out from the cosy dining room.
FACILITIES: 9 en suite (3 fmly) No smoking STV TVB tea/coffee Direct dial from bedrooms No dogs (ex guide dogs) Cen ht TVL
PRICES: s €50 - €65; d €70 - €95✱ **LB PARKING:** 12
NOTES: Closed Dec-14 Feb **CARDS:**

BUNRATTY Map 01 B3

♦♦♦♦ T&C Park House
Low Rd ☎ 061 369902 📠 061 369903
e-mail: parkhouse@eircom.net
Dir: *From the N18 take the exit for Bunratty, turn left at the castle, drive pass the Folk Park, Park House is the 4th house on the left*
A purpose built guest house with spacious bedrooms. There is a comfortable guest lounge and a lovely garden, and Mairead Bateman's home baking can be sampled on arrival. Within walking distance of the castle.
FACILITIES: 6 en suite (1 fmly) No smoking STV TVB tea/coffee No dogs (ex guide dogs) Cen ht **PRICES:** s €40 - €45; d €56 - €64✱
PARKING: 6 **NOTES:** Closed mid Dec-Jan **CARDS:**

COROFIN Map 01 B3

♦♦♦ T&C Fergus View
Kilnaboy ☎ 065 6837606 📠 065 6837192
e-mail: deckell@indigo.ie
Dir: *3km N of Corofin en route to Kilfenora, past ruins of Kilnaboy Church on left side of road*
Sensitively renovated to provide an excellent standard of comfort, this fourth generation family home is an attractive farmhouse, centrally located for touring the Burren area. Mary Kelleher enjoys cooking and wherever possible uses home-grown vegetables to prepare the meals.
FACILITIES: 6 rms (5 en suite) (1 fmly) No smoking in bedrooms No smoking in dining room No smoking in 1 lounge No dogs Licensed Cen ht TVL No coaches Dinner Last d noon **PRICES:** s €46 - €49; d €68✱
PARKING: 8 **NOTES:** Closed Oct-Etr

continued

DOOLIN Map 01 B3

♦♦♦ GH *Cullinan's*

☎ 065 7074183 📠 065 7074239
e-mail: cullinans@eircom.net
Dir: *centre of Doolin at crossroads between McGann's Pub & O'Connors Pub*

Charming pine-furnished bedrooms, with attractive decor, are a feature of this detached house, whose grounds run down to the River Aille. Chef patron James features locally caught fresh fish on his dinner menu, along with steaks, lamb and vegetarian dishes. Other facilities include a residents' lounge, a patio and gardens.

FACILITIES: 6 en suite (2 fmly) No smoking in bedrooms No smoking in dining room tea/coffee Direct dial from bedrooms No dogs (ex guide dogs) Cen ht TVL Dinner Last d 9pm **PARKING:** 15 **NOTES:** Closed 23-26 Dec **CARDS:**

ENNIS Map 01 B3

♦♦♦♦ GH *Cill Eoin House*

Killadysert Cross, Clare Rd ☎ 065 6841668 & 6828311
📠 065 6841669
e-mail: cilleoin@iol.ie
Dir: *100yds off N18 on R473 Killadysert road*

This smart purpose-built house stands a short distance from the town centre. It is attractively furnished and comfortable with well-equipped en suite bedrooms. A hospitable owner is always available to attend to guests' needs.

FACILITIES: 14 en suite (2 fmly) No smoking TVB tea/coffee Direct dial from bedrooms Cen ht TVL Tennis (hard) Dinner Last d 4pm **PARKING:** 14 **NOTES:** Closed 22 Dec-9 Jan **CARDS:**

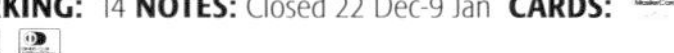

♦♦♦♦ GH Fountain Court

Lahinch Rd ☎ 065 6829845 📠 065 6845030
e-mail: kyran@fountain-court.com
Dir: *2m from Ennis on N85 on left*

Set in four acres of mature gardens on an elevated site, this comfortable guest house is family run. The majority of bedrooms are spacious and tastefully decorated. Guests can relax in the elegant lounge which has an honesty bar. There is also a games room.

FACILITIES: 18 en suite (4 fmly) No smoking in bedrooms No smoking in area of dining room No smoking in 1 lounge STV TVB tea/coffee Direct dial from bedrooms No dogs (ex guide dogs) Licensed Cen ht Pool Table **PRICES:** s €40 - €50; d €65 - €90 **LB PARKING:** 25 **NOTES:** Closed 21 Dec-5 Jan **CARDS:**

ENNISTYMON Map 01 B3

♦♦♦♦ GH Grovemount House

Lahinch Rd ☎ 065 7071431 & 7071038 📠 065 7071823
e-mail: grovmnt@indigo.gofree.ie
Dir: *Take N85 from Ennis to Ennistymon. Govemount House situated 1km from Ennistymon on the Lahinch Rd, on right approx 90mtrs from main rd on elevated site*

A smart purpose-built house, enjoying an elevated position on the outskirts of Ennistymon near The Burren, ideally located for touring County Clare. Bedrooms are en suite and well equipped. The friendly and hospitable owners will gladly recommend local restaurants and traditional pubs, or arrange golf or lake fishing for guests.

FACILITIES: 8 en suite (1 fmly) No smoking TVB tea/coffee Direct dial from bedrooms No dogs Cen ht TVL **PRICES:** s €38 - €45; d €58 - €76 **PARKING:** 20 **NOTES:** Closed Nov-Apr **CARDS:**

KILRUSH Map 01 B3

♦♦♦♦ T&C Hillcrest View

Doonbeg Rd ☎ 065 9051986 📠 065 9051986
e-mail: ethnahynes@eircom.net
Dir: *off N67 Kilkee road, on Doonbeg road*

This pink house is within walking distance of the town centre and five minutes' drive from the Killimer ferry. The new bedrooms are spacious and well appointed. There is an open plan sitting/dining room with a conservatory and a patio where guests can relax in the pretty garden. Mrs Hynes serves a fine breakfast.

FACILITIES: 6 en suite (2 fmly) No smoking STV TVB tea/coffee No dogs (ex guide dogs) Cen ht TVL No coaches **PRICES:** s €40 - €45; d €56 - €64✱ **PARKING:** 7 **CARDS:**

♦♦♦ T&C Bruach-na-Coille

Killimer Rd ☎ 065 9052250 📠 065 9052250
e-mail: clarkekilrush@hotmail.com
Dir: *from Kilrush, left at Credit Union onto Moore St, right at Spar supermarket onto Killimer Rd (N67). From ferry, turn left (N67), 8km to house*

This house, overlooking Kilrush Forest, offers accommodation with views of the Shannon Estuary. All rooms are well equipped and guests can look forward to a warm welcome, an enjoyable breakfast and helpful information about the local area.

FACILITIES: 4 rms (2 en suite) No smoking in bedrooms No smoking in dining room No smoking in 1 lounge TVB tea/coffee No dogs (ex guide dogs) Cen ht TVL Dinner **PRICES:** s fr €38; d €51 - €61 **PARKING:** 8 **NOTES:** Closed 25 Dec

LAHINCH Map 01 B3

Premier Collection

♦♦♦♦♦ GH Moy House

☎ 065 708 2800 📠 065 708 2500
e-mail: moyhouse@eircom.net
Dir: *follow signs for Lahinch/Ennistymon, N85 on reaching Ennistymon take left over bridge & follow road to Lahinch. House is situated 2m out of Lahinch on Miltown Malbay Rd, signed from Lahinch*

This 18th-century house has been sensitively restored and overlooks Lahinch's world famous surfing beach and championship links golf course. Individually designed bedrooms are decorated with luxurious fabrics and fine antique furniture. The elegant drawing room has an open turf fire and enjoys breathtaking views. Dinner is served every night, guests choosing from a carefully selected menu.

FACILITIES: 8 en suite (1 fmly) No smoking in bedrooms No smoking in dining room TVB Direct dial from bedrooms No dogs (ex guide dogs) Licensed Cen ht Dinner Last d 8.45pm **PRICES:** s €127 - €152; d €190 - €229✳ **CONF:** Board 16 **PARKING:** 30
NOTES: Closed 24 Dec-16 Jan **CARDS:**

LISDOONVARNA Map 01 B3

♦♦♦♦ GH Kincora House Country Inn & Restaurant

☎ 065 7074300 📠 065 7074490
e-mail: kincorahotel@eircom.com
Dir: *From Lisdoonvarna town centre take the the Doolin Rd. House situated on the 1st t-junction 200 mtrs from town*

Built in 1860 on the outskirts of this famous spa town on the edge of the Burren. Carefully restored, it retains the original floorboards and has a traditional bar with turf fire and a restaurant. The attractive dining room looks out over the award winning gardens, and the bedrooms are comfortable, individually decorated and furnished with locally made pine furniture.

FACILITIES: 14 en suite (1 fmly) (3 GF) No smoking in bedrooms No smoking in dining room STV TVB Direct dial from bedrooms No dogs Licensed Cen ht No children 10yrs Feature Garden/ Art Gallery Dinner Last d 9pm **PRICES:** s €50 - €110; d €80 - €130✳ **LB** **PARKING:** 15
NOTES: Closed Nov-Feb **CARDS:**

OGONNELLOE Map 01 B3

♦♦♦ GH Lantern House

☎ 061 923034 & 923123 📠 061 923139
e-mail: phil@lanternhouse.com
Dir: *From Birdhill N7 turn onto 463 to Ballina/ Killalue. Cross bridge and turn right. Lantern House is approx 6m on left hand side*

Situated overlooking Lough Derg, in a very scenic setting, this comfortable house offers nicely furnished and decorated

continued

bedrooms, together with a popular restaurant. The well tended gardens provide a marvellous view of the lake.

FACILITIES: 6 en suite (2 fmly) (2 GF) No smoking in bedrooms No smoking in area of dining room TVB Direct dial from bedrooms No dogs (ex guide dogs) Licensed Cen ht TVL No coaches Dinner Last d 9pm
PRICES: s €36 - €42; d €64 - €70 **PARKING:** 25
NOTES: Closed Nov-Mar **CARDS:**

CO CORK

BALLINHASSIG Map 01 B2

♦♦ T&C *Blanchfield House*

Rigsdale ☎ 021 4885167 📠 021 4885305
e-mail: blanchfield@eircom.net
Dir: *N71 Cork/Bandon rd between Innishannon Village and Halfway Village rdbt*

This guest house is in a quiet yet convenient location, within easy reach of the airport and ferry. Proprietor Patricia Blanchfield offers good home cooking. Private salmon and trout fishing are available.

FACILITIES: 6 rms (2 en suite) (2 fmly) No smoking in bedrooms No smoking in area of dining room No dogs (ex guide dogs) Licensed Cen ht TVL Dinner Last d noon **PARKING:** 20 **NOTES:** Closed 9-31 Dec
CARDS:

BANDON Map 01 B2

♦♦♦♦ T&C Glebe Country House

Ballinadee ☎ 021 4778294 📠 021 4778456
e-mail: glebehse@indigo.ie
Dir: *exit N71 at Innishannon Bridge signposted Ballinadee, 8km along river bank, left after sign for village*

This lovely old guest house stands in well kept gardens, and is run with great attention to detail. Antique furnishings predominate throughout this comfortable house, which has a guest lounge and an elegant dining room. An interesting breakfast menu offers unusual options, and a country-house style dinner is available by reservation.

FACILITIES: 4 en suite (2 fmly) No smoking in bedrooms No smoking in dining room tea/coffee Direct dial from bedrooms Cen ht TVL outdoor badminton Dinner Last d noon **PRICES:** d €70 - €100✳ **LB**
PARKING: 30 **NOTES:** Closed 21 Dec-3 Jan **CARDS:**

BANTRY Map 01 B2

♦♦♦ T&C Mill

Glengarriff Rd, New Town ☎ 027 50278 📠 027 50278
e-mail: bbthemill@eircom.net
Dir: *situated on N71 Bantry-Glengarriff Rd, 0.5m from town centre*

Colourful gardens are the setting for this well maintained double bungalow, a few minutes' drive from Bantry. Well appointed bedrooms are equipped with good showers, and a spacious dining/sitting room forms the heart of the house; decor throughout reflects the owner's ebullient personality and enthusiasm. Facilities include laundry service, bicycle hire and ample car parking - and Dutch is spoken here.

FACILITIES: 6 en suite (3 fmly) (6 GF) No smoking STV TVB No dogs (ex guide dogs) Cen ht No coaches **PRICES:** s €40; d €60✳ **PARKING:** 10
NOTES: Closed Nov-Mar

Prices in the Republic of Ireland are shown in Euros.

BLARNEY Map 01 B2

Premier Collection

♦♦♦♦♦ T&C Ashlee Lodge

Tower ☎ 021 4385346 📠 021 4385726
e-mail: info@ashleelodge.com
Dir: *4kms from Blarney on R617*

Ashlee Lodge is a purpose-built guest house, set close to Blarney Castle and within walking distance of pubs and restaurants. Bedrooms are decorated with comfort and elegance in mind, some have whirlpool baths and canopy beds. The breakfast menu is extensive and fresh baked bread is a speciality. Unwind in the sauna and roof-top garden complete with outdoor Canadian hot tub. Many golf courses nearby. Transfers to Cork Airport and station can be arranged.
FACILITIES: 10 en suite (2 fmly) (6 GF) No smoking in bedrooms No smoking in dining room STV TVB tea/coffee Direct dial from bedrooms No dogs (ex guide dogs) Cen ht TVL No children 12yrs Sauna Jacuzzi **PRICES:** s €100 - €164; d €100 - €164* **LB PARKING:** 12
CARDS:

♦♦♦♦ T&C Blarney Vale House

Cork Rd ☎ 021 4381511
e-mail: info@blarneyvale.com
Dir: *on R617 adjacent to golf driving range on approach to town*
A dormer bungalow, located in an elevated position above the Cork Road, surrounded by landscaped gardens. Everything is of an excellent standard. Ann and Ray Hennessy are enthusiastic hosts, and a pleasant lounge offers guests a chance to relax in the evening.
FACILITIES: 4 en suite (2 fmly) (1 GF) No smoking TVB tea/coffee No dogs Cen ht **PRICES:** s fr €50; d fr €60 **PARKING:** 9 **NOTES:** Closed Dec-Jan

♦♦♦♦ GH Killarney House

Station Rd ☎ 021 4381841 📠 021 4381841
e-mail: killarneyhouseblarney@eircom.net
Dir: *turn off N20 onto R617, immediately beyond Blarney Filling Station turn right, 1km up Statin Road on right*
A non-smoking house with four ground floor bedrooms in a new extension, and two on the first floor. Caroline Morgan is a charming, attentive hostess whose comfortable house is very well appointed. There is a TV lounge, drying facilities for wet gear, and off street parking. Golf available nearby.
FACILITIES: 6 en suite (2 fmly) No smoking TVB tea/coffee No dogs Cen ht **PRICES:** s €40 - €50; d €58 - €70* **LB PARKING:** 8

♦♦♦♦ T&C White House

Shean Lower ☎ 021 4385338
e-mail: info@thewhitehouseblarney.com
Dir: *on R617, Cork/Blarney road*
Conveniently situated near to the town, in an elevated position, with views of Blarney Castle, this carefully maintained bungalow is set in its own grounds. Bedrooms, with modern facilities, are well appointed and have comfortable armchairs. There is a TV lounge and a breakfast room. A private car park is also available.
FACILITIES: 6 en suite (1 fmly) No smoking STV TVB tea/coffee No dogs Cen ht **PRICES:** s €40 - €50; d €56 - €62* **PARKING:** 7

CLONAKILTY Map 01 B2

♦♦♦♦ *An Garran Coir (W 332358)*

Rathbarry, Rosscarbery Coast Route ☎ 023 48236 📠 023 48236
Mr & Mrs M Calnan
e-mail: angarrancoir@eircom.net
Dir: *signposted at Maxol Service Station in Clonakilty, 4m W of town, off N71 1m on right*
Situated on the coast road to Rosscarbery, close to sandy beaches and award-winning village, this luxurious split-level home boasts panoramic views. Some bedrooms contain jacuzzi baths. There are spacious gardens, tennis courts, cycling and walking tours by arrangement. An extensive breakfast menu is available, making use of organic produce.
FACILITIES: 5 en suite (2 fmly) No smoking in bedrooms No smoking in dining room No smoking in lounges TVB No dogs Cen ht Tennis (hard) Jacuzzi Local leisure club available - rates negotiated Last d 3pm
PARKING: 5 **CARDS:**

♦♦♦♦ Duvane *(W 349405)*

Ballyduvane ☎ 023 33129 📠 33129 Mrs N McCarthy
Dir: *2km SW on N71*

About a mile from Clonakilty stands this well kept house decorated in cheerful colours. Comfortable throughout, one bedroom has a four-poster bed, and two are on the ground floor and share a bathroom, ideal for family groups. Guests have their own sitting room, and the dining room serves a wide choice at breakfast. Dinner is available by arrangement. Local amenities include beaches, riding and golf.
FACILITIES: 4 en suite (1 fmly) No smoking in bedrooms No smoking in dining room TV3B tea/coffee No dogs (ex guide dogs) Cen ht TVL Fishing Pool Table Putting green Swimming Facilities,tennis,fishing,golf 100 acres beef Last d 4pm **PRICES:** s €40 - €43; d €60 - €66* **LB**
NOTES: Closed Nov-Mar

CLONAKILTY continued

♦♦♦♦ Springfield House *(W 330342)*

Kilkern, Rathbarry, Castlefreke ☎ 023 40622 023 40622
Mr & Mrs J Callanan
e-mail: jandmcallanan@eircom.net
Dir: *take Skibbereen N71 exit road from Clonakilty. Turn left approx 0.25m beyond Pike Bar and follow signs for 3m*

A Georgian-style farmhouse in a picturesque rural setting. Maureen and John Callanan are genuine and welcoming hosts, and their home is very comfortable, with well appointed bedrooms and lovely gardens. Guests are welcome to watch the cows being milked. Home cooking is a speciality, and dinner is available by arrangement.
FACILITIES: 4 rms (3 en suite) (2 fmly) No smoking in bedrooms No smoking in dining room No smoking in 1 lounge TV3B No dogs Cen ht TVL 130 acres dairy/beef Dinner Last d 3pm **PARKING:** 8
NOTES: Closed Xmas & Etr

♦♦ Desert House *(W 390411)*

Coast Rd ☎ 023 33331 023 33048 Mrs D Jennings
e-mail: deserthouse@eircom.net
Dir: *signposted on N71, 1km E of Clonakilty, at 1st rdbt*
This Georgian farmhouse, overlooking Clonakilty Bay, is an ideal centre for touring West Cork and Kerry.
FACILITIES: 5 rms (4 en suite) STV TVB tea/coffee Cen ht 100 acres dairy mixed **PARKING:** 10 **CARDS:**

CORK Map 01 B2

♦♦♦♦ GH Crawford House

Western Rd ☎ 021 4279000 021 4279927
e-mail: crawford@indigo.ie
Dir: *0.5m from city on main Cork-Killarney road(N22)directly opposite University College Cork*

Two adjoining Victorian houses form this friendly guest house, close to the university and city centre. Sympathetically refurbished in a contemporary style, the bedrooms have refreshing natural colour schemes. The attractive dining room and conservatory overlook a colourful patio. An interesting breakfast menu is available and there is ample secure parking.

continued

FACILITIES: 12 en suite (2 fmly) No smoking in 6 bedrooms No smoking in dining room STV TVB tea/coffee Direct dial from bedrooms No dogs (ex guide dogs) Cen ht Jacuzzi **PRICES:** s €70 - €80; d €88 - €100✻
PARKING: 12 **NOTES:** Closed 22-27 Dec **CARDS:**

♦♦♦♦ GH *Fairylawn*

Western Rd ☎ 021 4543444 021 4544337
e-mail: fairylawn@holidayhound.com
Dir: *At Capitol Cineplex right at lights to Washington St, straight out past college gates on right hand side before next lights*
Imposing cream coloured period residence close to the University. Recently extended and refurbished to a high standard, all areas are attractively decorated and bedrooms are spacious and comfortable.
FACILITIES: 14 en suite (5 fmly) No smoking in bedrooms No smoking in dining room STV TVB tea/coffee Direct dial from bedrooms No dogs (ex guide dogs) Cen ht TVL **PARKING:** 14 **CARDS:**

♦♦♦♦ GH Garnish House

1 Aldergrove, Western Rd ☎ 021 4275111 021 4273872
e-mail: garnish@iol.ie
Dir: *Opposite Cork University College*

A stay in Garnish House is a memorable one. Tastefully appointed rooms, with optional en suite jacuzzi and extensive breakfast menu. Convenient for the ferry and airport, the guest house has 24 hour reception for enquiries, reservations, departures and late arrivals. Five minutes walk to the city centre.
FACILITIES: 13 en suite (4 fmly) (1 GF) No smoking in 5 bedrooms STV TVB tea/coffee Direct dial from bedrooms No dogs (ex guide dogs) Cen ht TVL **PRICES:** s €44 - €90; d €80 - €140✻ **PARKING:** 10
CARDS:

♦♦♦♦ GH Lancaster Lodge

Lancaster Quay, Western Rd ☎ 021 4251125 021 4251126
e-mail: info@lancasterlodge.com
Dir: *Located alongside Jurys hotel on the Western Road*
Just five minutes from the city centre, this purpose-built guest house overlooks the River Lee. Public rooms include a guest lounge with TV. Bedrooms are spacious and come equipped with safes. Two ground floor rooms are fitted for wheelchair users. A wide choice is offered for breakfast.
FACILITIES: 39 en suite (3 GF) No smoking in dining room No smoking in lounges STV TVB tea/coffee Direct dial from bedrooms No dogs (ex guide dogs) Lift Cen ht TVL **PRICES:** s €70 - €100; d €90 - €130✻
PARKING: 40 **NOTES:** Closed 24-27 Dec
CARDS:

♦♦♦ GH Antoine House

Western Rd ☎ 021 4273494 021 4273092
Dir: *0.5km from city centre on the Cork-Macroom-Killarney road*
This converted four-storey house is close to the University and caters for both tourist and commercial clientele.

continued

Ireland

FACILITIES: 7 en suite TVB tea/coffee No dogs (ex guide dogs) Cen ht TVL **PRICES:** s €40 - €60; d €60 - €100✳ **PARKING:** 8
CARDS:

♦♦♦ GH *Killarney*

Western Rd ☎ 021 4270290 📠 021 4271010
e-mail: killarneyhouse@iol.ie
Dir: *from N22 (Cork city to Killarney road), premises just opposite University College*

Mrs O'Leary is the welcoming owner of this well equipped guest house which stands near Cork University on the N22. The bedrooms all have TVs, telephones and tea/coffee making facilities. A lounge is available to guests and there is a large car park behind the house.

FACILITIES: 19 en suite (3 fmly) No smoking in 10 bedrooms No smoking in dining room STV TVB tea/coffee Direct dial from bedrooms No dogs Cen ht TVL Jacuzzi **PARKING:** 15 **NOTES:** Closed 24-25 Dec
CARDS:

♦♦♦ GH Lough Mahon House

Tivoli ☎ 021 4502142 📠 021 4501804
e-mail: info@loughmahon.com
Dir: *1m from city centre on N8*

This family-run Georgian terraced house is situated on the outskirts of the city. Bedrooms are comfortable and well equipped. There is a cosy sitting room and a separate breakfast room, where guests can enjoy home-baking and hearty breakfasts made using local produce.

FACILITIES: 6 en suite (1 fmly) No smoking in bedrooms No smoking in dining room STV TVB tea/coffee Direct dial from bedrooms Cen ht TVL No coaches **PRICES:** s €44.50 - €57; d €70 - €84✳ **PARKING:** 10 **NOTES:** Closed 24-27 Dec **CARDS:**

♦♦♦ GH Roserie Villa

Mardyke Walk, off Western Rd ☎ 021 4272958 📠 021 4274087
e-mail: info@roserievilla.com
Dir: *take N22 from city centre, pass Jury's Hotel on left, turn right at University College gates, right again for hotel on right*

This family-run guest house stands just ten minutes' walk from the city centre. The en suite bedrooms are well appointed and equipped with TVs, telephones and tea/coffee making facilities. Off-street parking is available.

FACILITIES: 16 en suite (4 fmly) No smoking in dining room STV TVB tea/coffee Direct dial from bedrooms No dogs (ex guide dogs) Cen ht TVL **PARKING:** 8 **CARDS:**

♦♦ GH Brazier's Westpoint House

Western Rd ☎ 021 4275526 & 4274091 📠 021 4251955
e-mail: info@braziersguesthouse.com
Dir: *Leave Cork city centre via Washington St, pass Jury's Hotel, Western Rd on left. Through traffic lights at UCC Gates, Brazier's on right*

A Victorian red brick house, located just ten minutes' walk from the city and opposite University College Cork. Rooms vary in size, and all are en suite with modern facilities. Private lock-up parking is available.

FACILITIES: 8 en suite (5 fmly) No smoking TVB tea/coffee Direct dial from bedrooms No dogs (ex guide dogs) Cen ht TVL No coaches **PRICES:** s €42 - €48; d €68 - €76✳ **PARKING:** 9 **NOTES:** Closed 23 Dec-2 Jan **CARDS:**

FERMOY

Map 01 B2

Premier Collection

♦♦♦♦♦ T&C Ballyvolane House

Castlelyons ☎ 025 36349 📠 025 36781
e-mail: ballyvol@iol.ie
Dir: *from N8, turn off onto R628 and follow signs*

An Italianate country house, originally built in 1728, which enjoys a magnificent setting in parkland and well known gardens (open to the public in May). The Greens are exceptionally welcoming and friendly hosts. Public areas are spacious, and bedrooms are comfortable. Dinner is available, served around a fine table. There are three lakes, one stocked with brown trout.

FACILITIES: 6 en suite No smoking in bedrooms No smoking in dining room No smoking in 1 lounge TVB tea/coffee No dogs (ex guide dogs) Licensed Cen ht Fishing Croquet lawn Dinner Last d noon **PRICES:** d €130 - €160✳ **PARKING:** 25 **NOTES:** Closed 23-31 Dec
CARDS:

♦♦♦♦ GH *Glanworth Mill Country Inn*

Glanworth ☎ 025 38555 📠 025 38560
e-mail: glanworth@iol.ie
Dir: *turn off N8 between Fermoy and Mitchelstown at Kilworth/Glanworth junction. Travel 5m to Glanworth to narrow stone bridge - mill facing*

An oasis of tranquillity in the shadows of a Norman castle on the banks of the River Funcheon, Glanworth Mill is a 200-year-old woollen mill, tastefully and attractively restored, with two restaurants, a library and a newly built craft shop. Bedrooms are furnished and decorated in the style of various authors with local connections. Georgian elegance in Anthony Trollope, country style in Alice Taylor. Relax and watch the swans glide past, or the heron fish the river. Staff are friendly and welcoming.

FACILITIES: 10 en suite (1 fmly) No smoking in bedrooms No smoking in area of dining room tea/coffee Direct dial from bedrooms No dogs Licensed Cen ht No coaches Fishing Croquet lawn Summer season only Dinner Last d 9.30pm **PARKING:** 30 **NOTES:** rs Xmas, New Year & Good Fri
CARDS:

Ireland

GOLEEN

Map 01 A1

♦♦♦♦ T&C Carraig-Mor House

Toormore Bay ☎ 028 28410 📠 028 28410
e-mail: carraigmorhouse@eircom.net
Dir: *from Cork take N71 to Ballydehob then R592 to Schull and on to Toormore, Carraig-Mor is 2nd house on right past Altar Church*

Situated on the edge of Toormore Bay on the West Cork coast. The house is very attractively decorated and offers comfortable bedrooms and a conservatory lounge where guests can relax and enjoy the views across the bay. Fresh local ingredients feature at dinner, which is served nightly (booking essential), and packed lunches can be provided. A 24-hour mini bus service is available for airport, ferry or pub collection. Off-season painting weekends with artist Dor Sievers can be arranged.

FACILITIES: 5 en suite (2 fmly) No smoking TVB tea/coffee No dogs Cen ht TVL No children 6yrs Dinner Last d noon **PRICES:** s €34; d €56✻ **LB** **PARKING:** 8 **NOTES:** Closed 24-25 Dec **CARDS:**

♦♦♦♦ T&C Heron's Cove

The Harbour ☎ 028 35225 📠 028 35422
e-mail: suehill@eircom.net
Dir: *turn left down to harbour in middle of Goleen (75m from Cork city)*

This big white house lies in a sheltered cove on Ireland's most south-westerly point, near to Mizen Head. A warm, friendly atmosphere is created by glowing fires at either end of the lounge, in which there is also a wine bar. The restaurant is run by the award-winning chef/patron Sue Hill. Bedrooms are comfortable, and some rooms, with balconies, enjoy a view over the harbour.

FACILITIES: 5 en suite (2 fmly) No smoking in bedrooms STV TVB tea/coffee Direct dial from bedrooms No dogs (ex guide dogs) Licensed Cen ht No coaches Dinner Last d 9.30pm **PRICES:** s €35; d €70✻ **PARKING:** 10 **NOTES:** Closed Xmas & New Year **CARDS:**

See advertisement on opposite page

KANTURK

Map 01 B2

Premier Collection

♦♦♦♦♦ GH *Assolas Country House*

☎ 029 50015 📠 029 50795
e-mail: assolas@eircom.net
Dir: *5.5km NE, off N72*

Ideally situated for touring the south west, this 17th-century manor house enjoys a sylvan setting on a tributary of the River Blackwater, surrounded by prize-winning gardens, parkland and rolling country. Home to the Bourke family for several generations, guests can expect a warm and friendly welcome, magnificent public rooms with log fires, and fresh garden and local produce creatively presented in the restaurant.

continued

FACILITIES: 6 en suite 3 annexe en suite (3 fmly) No smoking in bedrooms No smoking in dining room Direct dial from bedrooms No dogs (ex guide dogs) Licensed Cen ht No coaches Tennis (grass) Fishing Croquet lawn Jacuzzi Boating Gardens Dinner Last d 7.30pm **PARKING:** 20 **NOTES:** Closed 2 Nov-16 Mar **CARDS:**

KILLEAGH

Map 01 C2

♦♦♦ T&C Tattans

☎ 024 95173 📠 024 95173
e-mail: Tattans@eircom.net
1 Mar-31 Oct
Dir: *on N25, between Midleton and Youghal on Cork Rosslare route*

This 18th-century house, set in the picturesque village of Killeagh and just 25 minutes from Cork, is an excellent touring base with golf, fishing and beaches nearby. It offers comfortable bedrooms, a TV lounge, large attractive gardens and a tennis court. Bar snacks are served throughout the day and evening meals are also available.

FACILITIES: 5 rms (4 en suite) (2 fmly) No smoking in bedrooms No smoking in dining room TVB tea/coffee Licensed Cen ht TVL Tennis Dinner Last d 8.00 **PRICES:** s €35.50; d €58.40 - €63.46✻ **PARKING:** 12 **NOTES:** Closed Nov-Feb **CARDS:**

KINSALE

Map 01 B2

Premier Collection

♦♦♦♦♦ GH Old Bank House

11 Pearse St ☎ 021 4774075 📠 021 4774296
e-mail: oldbank@indigo.ie
Dir: *on main road into Kinsale from Cork Airport (R600). House on right at start of Kinsale, next to post office*

Under the personal supervision of Marie and Michael Riese, this delightful Georgian house has been restored to its former elegance. The en suite bedrooms, with period furniture and attractive decor, combine charm with modern comforts. Sailing, deep sea fishing and horse riding can be arranged. Irish, French and German spoken.

FACILITIES: 17 en suite (2 fmly) No smoking in dining room No smoking in lounges STV TVB Direct dial from bedrooms Licensed Lift Cen ht No children 7yrs No coaches **PRICES:** s €170 - €270; d €170 - €270✻ **NOTES:** Closed 23-26 Dec **CARDS:**

♦♦♦♦ T&C Chart House Luxury Accommodation

6 Denis Quay ☎ 021 4774568 📠 021 4777907
e-mail: charthouse@eircom.net
Dir: *On Pier Rd between Actons & Trident Hotels. Turn right after Actons Hotel onto Denis Quay, last house on right*

This Georgian house in 1790 was once a sea captain's residence. It has been lovingly restored to its original style and the comfortable bedrooms are furnished with period pieces and fitted to a high standard. There is a cosy lobby lounge and dining room where guests can enjoy Mary O'Connor's delicious breakfasts that include home-made breads. Being in the gourmet capital, dinner reservations are arranged and golfing and touring trips organised.

FACILITIES: 3 en suite No smoking STV TVB Direct dial from bedrooms No dogs Cen ht No children **PRICES:** s €78-£115; d €90 - €196✻ **NOTES:** Closed Xmas **CARDS:**

♦♦♦♦ T&C Desmond House

42 Cork St ☎ 021 4773575 📠 021 4773575
e-mail: desmondhouse@compuserve.com
Dir: *R600 into Kinsale, left at White House Hotel, 2nd right at police station, Desmond House on right after 30mtrs*

A refurbished Georgian townhouse, where hospitality is a priority of the welcoming owners. Large bedrooms are inviting and very comfortable, and an excellent choice of dishes is offered on the breakfast menu. Dinner is by arrangement, booking is essential.
FACILITIES: 4 en suite (2 fmly) No smoking TVB tea/coffee No dogs (ex guide dogs) Cen ht Dinner Last d 24hrs notice **PRICES:** s €125 - €150; d €125 - €170✳ **CONF:** Class 12 Board 12 **PARKING:** 2
NOTES: Closed Xmas & New Year **CARDS:**

♦♦♦♦ GH Long Quay House

Long Quay ☎ 021 4774563 & 4773201 📠 021 4774563
e-mail: longquayhouse@eircom.net
Dir: *on right immediately after entering town centre from R600, before Super Valu supermarket. House covered in Virginia Creeper*

Centrally located overlooking the inner harbour and yacht marina, Long Quay House is a restored Georgian town house with very comfortable bedrooms and a large conservatory lounge. Local amenities include sailing, fishing, golf and sandy beaches.
FACILITIES: 7 en suite (2 fmly) No smoking in area of dining room TVB tea/coffee Direct dial from bedrooms No dogs (ex guide dogs) Cen ht TVL No coaches **PRICES:** s €50 - €70; d €76 - €100✳
NOTES: Closed 15 Nov-26 Dec **CARDS:**

♦♦♦♦ T&C Old Presbytery

43 Cork St ☎ 021 4772027 📠 021 4772166
e-mail: info@oldpres.com
Dir: *from Cork Rd to end of Pearse St, turn left, 1st right & 1st right again, establishment on right opposite parish church*

This charming period house, situated on a quiet street in the centre of the town, offers a comfortable, elegant lounge and a delightful breakfast room. Bedrooms are traditional, with pine furnishings, brass beds and interesting memorabilia. One bedroom has external access via a staircase and is very peaceful. Sailing and sea fishing are available and there are plenty of excellent restaurants nearby. Booking is advised.
FACILITIES: 6 en suite (1 fmly) No smoking STV TVB tea/coffee Direct dial from bedrooms No dogs (ex guide dogs) Cen ht TVL No coaches
PRICES: s €45 - €55; d €70 - €140✳ **PARKING:** 6
NOTES: Closed 1Dec-14 Feb **CARDS:**

♦♦♦♦ T&C *Rivermount House*

Knocknabinny, Barrells Cross ☎ 021 4778033 &4778225
📠 021 4778225
e-mail: rivermnt@iol.ie
Dir: *take R600 west towards Old Head of Kinsale, turn right at Barrels Cross (3km from Kinsale)*

This charming house is surrounded by lovely gardens, a patio and a children's play area. Attractive bedrooms are well equipped and furnished to a high standard, and there is a fine, large sitting room with a sun lounge. Evening meals and packed lunches can be provided on request. The house overlooks the River Bandon, near a superbly sited new golf course, the Old Head Golf Links. Sea angling and bicycle hire can be arranged.
FACILITIES: 6 en suite (3 fmly) No smoking in bedrooms No smoking in dining room No smoking in 1 lounge TVB tea/coffee Direct dial from bedrooms No dogs (ex guide dogs) Cen ht TVL **PARKING:** 10
NOTES: Closed 2 Dec-30 Jan **CARDS:**

♦♦♦♦ GH Toddies

Eastern Rd ☎ 021 4777769
e-mail: toddies@eircom.net
Dir: *Kinsale Road from airport. On entering Kinsale Texaco garage on right. Toddies is 4th on left yellow building looking onto harbour*

This Victorian-style house overlooks the famous harbour of Kinsale on the edge of town. Guests can enjoy lovely views from the luxuriously furnished bedrooms. A private art collection hangs in the dining room, where chef-proprietor Pearse provides dinner nightly, while Mary welcomes guests. Drinks are served in the Library or on the patio.
FACILITIES: 3 en suite (1 fmly) No smoking in bedrooms TVB Direct dial from bedrooms Licensed Cen ht No coaches Dinner Last d 10.30pm
PRICES: s €100 - €145; d €145 - €170✳ **LB PARKING:** 10
NOTES: Closed 2 Jan-12 Feb **CARDS:**

♦♦♦♦ T&C Waterlands

Cork Rd ☎ 021 4772318 087 276 7917 📠 021 4774873
e-mail: info@collinsbb.com
Dir: *follow R600 to Kinsale, turn off at 'Welcome to Kinsale' sign, Waterlands sign at this junct, turn right - house 140mtrs from junct*

This house, located in an elevated position, provides luxury accommodation. A south-facing conservatory breakfast room overlooks the picturesque gardens and serves an extensive breakfast menu. The comfortable, well decorated en suite bedrooms have electric blankets, hairdryers and clock radios.
FACILITIES: 4 en suite (2 fmly) No smoking TVB tea/coffee No dogs Cen ht TVL No coaches **PRICES:** s €50; d €56 - €64✳ **PARKING:** 10
NOTES: Closed Nov-Feb **CARDS:**

♦♦♦ GH Kilcaw House

☎ 021 4774155 📠 021 4774755
e-mail: kilcawhouse@hotmail.com
Dir: *on R600 road from Cork to Kinsale. 1km NE of Kinsale town*
A modern house in a rural location where friendly owners are hospitable and attentive. Facilities include a sitting room, breakfast room, and comfortable, attractively decorated bedrooms; surrounded by well-tended gardens and grounds with ample parking. Close to golf and all the amenities of Kinsale.
FACILITIES: 5 en suite (2 fmly) No smoking in bedrooms No smoking in dining room No smoking in 1 lounge TVB tea/coffee No dogs (ex guide dogs) Cen ht TVL **PRICES:** s €38 - €63; d €57 - €82✳ **LB** **PARKING:** 20 **NOTES:** Closed 23-27 Dec **CARDS:**

MALLOW — Map 01 B2

♦♦♦♦ T&C *Greenfield House*

Navigation Rd ☎ 022 50231
e-mail: greenfieldhouse@hotmail.com
Dir: *turn off N20 at Mallow rdbt onto N72 Killarney Rd, establishment 300m last house on left*
A purpose-built house, designed and furnished to the highest standards. Large, airy rooms look out over open country and all are luxuriously appointed with quality en suite facilities. Conveniently situated, within walking distance of the town centre, station and Cork Racecourse. Good parking facilities.
FACILITIES: 6 en suite (3 fmly) No smoking in 3 bedrooms No smoking in dining room STV TVB tea/coffee No dogs (ex guide dogs) Cen ht TVL **PARKING:** 10 **CARDS:**

♦♦♦ T&C *Oaklands House*

Springwood ☎ 022 21127 📠 022 21127
e-mail: oaklands@eircom.net
Dir: *turn off Killarney road (N72) at railway bridge (signposted)*
Situated in a quiet residential area on the edge of town, Winifred O'Donovan's home is inviting and attractively decorated throughout. The atmosphere is particularly tranquil, with a dining room overlooking the lovely gardens where guests can enjoy Winifred's cooking.
FACILITIES: 4 en suite (1 fmly) No smoking in bedrooms STV TVB tea/coffee No dogs Cen ht TVL **PARKING:** 6 **NOTES:** Closed Nov-Mar **CARDS:**

MIDLETON — Map 01 C2

♦♦♦♦ T&C *Old Parochial House*

Castlemartyr ☎ 021 4667454 📠 021 4667429
e-mail: enquiries@oldparochial.com
Dir: *at Castlemartyr on N25 take turn for Garryvoe/Ballycotton, 1st on left*
Kathy and Paul Sheehy are welcoming hosts and they make guests feel instantly at ease, in this lovely, restored Georgian house. The drawing room and dining room are furnished with antiques and have open fires. Two of the attractive bedrooms have four-poster beds and all have good facilities.
FACILITIES: 3 en suite (3 fmly) No smoking in bedrooms No smoking in dining room STV TVB tea/coffee No dogs (ex guide dogs) Cen ht No coaches **NOTES:** Closed Nov-Jan **CARDS:**

SHANAGARRY — Map 01 C2

Premier Collection

♦♦♦♦♦ GH *Ballymaloe House*

Ireland's Blue Book

☎ 021 4652531 📠 021 4652021
e-mail: res@ballymaloe.ie
Dir: *Ballymaloe House is on L35 from Midleton, 3km beyond Cloyne on Ballycotton Road*

continued

This charming country house stands on a 400-acre farm, part of the old Geraldine Castle estate. Bedrooms are split between the main house and the adjacent courtyard buildings, such as the 16th-century gatehouse. All of the rooms are comfortable, well furnished and equipped with hairdryers. Other facilities include a craft shop and a fine restaurant which makes good use of farm produce.
FACILITIES: 22 en suite 10 annexe en suite (1 fmly) No smoking in area of dining room Direct dial from bedrooms No dogs (ex guide dogs) Licensed Cen ht TVL Outdoor swimming pool (heated) Golf 7 Tennis (hard) Croquet lawn Putting green Craft & Kitchen shop Dinner Last d 9pm **PARKING:** 30 **NOTES:** Closed 23-26 Dec rs 27 Dec **CARDS:**

SKIBBEREEN — Map 01 B2

♦♦♦ T&C Ilenroy House

10 North St ☎ 028 22751 & 22193 📠 028 23228
e-mail: ilenroyhouse@oceanfree.net
Dir: *90mtrs from main street on N71 Clonakilty Road*
A three-storey streetside house. All bedrooms are en suite and equipped to a high standard. This is an excellent base from which to tour South West Cork and the Sherkin Islands.
FACILITIES: 6 rms (5 en suite) (1 fmly) STV TVB tea/coffee Direct dial from bedrooms No dogs (ex guide dogs) Cen ht **PRICES:** s €25 - €30; d €50 - €60✳ **CARDS:**

YOUGHAL — Map 01 C2

See also Killeagh

Premier Collection

♦♦♦♦♦ GH Ahernes

Ireland's Blue Book

163 North Main St ☎ 024 92424 📠 024 93633
e-mail: ahernes@eircom.net
Dir: *rdbt on edge of town, N25. Take sign for Town Centre*
In the same family since 1923, Ahernes offers a warm welcome, with turf fires and a traditional atmosphere. Spacious bedrooms are furnished to the highest standard and include antiques and modern facilities. There is a restaurant, well known for its daily-changing menu of the freshest seafood specialities, in addition to which guests can use the cosy drawing room.
FACILITIES: 13 en suite (3 GF) No smoking in area of dining room STV TV12B Direct dial from bedrooms No dogs (ex guide dogs) Licensed Cen ht Dinner Last d 9.30pm **PRICES:** s €105 - €110; d €140 - €180✳ **LB** **PARKING:** 12 **NOTES:** Closed 20-28 Dec **CARDS:**

CO DONEGAL

ARDARA — Map 01 B5

♦♦♦ T&C *Bay View Country House*

Portnoo Rd ☎ 075 41145
e-mail: chbennett@eircom.net
Dir: *off N56 at top of town in Ardara, straight down for 0.5m on road to Portnoo, situated on right overlooking the bay and Owenea River*
This large, modern bungalow on the outskirts of a small town, overlooks the sea.
FACILITIES: 6 en suite (2 fmly) No smoking in bedrooms No smoking in dining room STV TV3B tea/coffee No dogs Cen ht TVL Dinner Last d noon **PARKING:** 20 **NOTES:** Closed 1-27 Dec & 3-31 Jan **CARDS:**

Ireland

BALLYLIFFIN Map 01 C6

♦♦♦♦ T&C Rossaor House

☎ 077 76498 📠 077 76498
e-mail: rossaor@gofree.indigo.ie
Dir: *from Derry City take A2 towards Muff, continue on R238 to Quigleys Point, left to Carndonagh R240, left to Ballyliffin R238*

Set in lovely mature gardens in peaceful location on the Inishowen Peninsula, this is a delightful house. The elegant sitting room has marvellous panoramic views of Pollen Bay and Malin Head, Ireland's most northerly point, and overlooks the Ballyliffen links golf course. Of the luxuriously appointed bedrooms, four are in the main house and the others in cottages in the grounds. Breakfast is served in the conservatory.
FACILITIES: 4 en suite (3 fmly) (3 GF) No smoking in dining room STV TVB tea/coffee Direct dial from bedrooms No dogs (ex guide dogs) Cen ht No coaches **PRICES:** s fr €45; d fr €70✻ **PARKING:** 10
CARDS:

BALLYSHANNON Map 01 B5

♦♦♦♦ GH Dún Na Sì

Bundoran Rd ☎ 072 52322 52072
e-mail: dun-na-si@oceanfree.net
Dir: *on N50, 0.25m from Ballyshannon on Bundoran road, adjacent to Donegal Parian China showrooms*

A smart purpose-built guest house set back from the road and within walking distance of the town. The spacious bedrooms are comfortable and well equipped, and one of the two ground floor rooms is suitable for the less mobile.
FACILITIES: 7 en suite (2 fmly) No smoking in bedrooms No smoking in dining room STV TVB tea/coffee Direct dial from bedrooms No dogs (ex guide dogs) Cen ht **PRICES:** s €32 - €40.50; d €56 - €62✻
PARKING: 15 **CARDS:**

CARRIGANS Map 01 C5

♦♦♦♦ T&C Mount Royd Country Home

☎ 074 40163 📠 074 40400
e-mail: jmartin@mountroyd.com
Dir: *off N13 & N14 on road 236, from Derry city take A40*

Set in mature gardens, Mount Royd is an attractive creeper-clad house with the River Foyle running along the back boundary. The friendly Martins have brought hospitality to new heights - nothing is too much trouble for them. Breakfast is a feast of choices. Bedrooms are very comfortable, with lots of personal touches.
FACILITIES: 4 en suite (3 fmly) No smoking in bedrooms No smoking in dining room STV TVB tea/coffee No dogs (ex guide dogs) Cen ht TVL No children 10yrs **PRICES:** s €38.50; d €54 - €56✻ **LB PARKING:** 7

DONEGAL Map 01 B5

♦♦♦♦ T&C *Ardeevin*

Lough Eske, Barnesmore ☎ 073 21790 📠 073 21790
e-mail: seanmcginty@eircom.net
Dir: *take N15 (Derry road) from Donegal Town for 5km, turn left at junction for Ardeevin and Lough Eske and follow signs for 'Ardeevin'*
This comfortable homely house enjoys a lovely location high above Lough Eske and with superb views of lake and mountain. Well appointed bedrooms have en suite facilities.
FACILITIES: 6 en suite (2 fmly) No smoking STV TVB tea/coffee No dogs Cen ht TVL No children 9yrs No coaches **PARKING:** 10
NOTES: Closed Nov-Mar

FAHAN Map 01 C6

Premier Collection

♦♦♦♦♦ GH St John's Country House & Restaurant

☎ 077 60289 📠 077 60612
e-mail: stjohnsrestaurant@eircom.net
Ireland's Blue Book
A comfortable and spacious 18th century home with panoramic views across Lough Swilly to Inch Island. Food takes pride of place and local lamb and seafood feature on the menu. Bedrooms vary in size, and there is a cosy bar with a turf fire. Just half an hour's drive from the Giant's Causeway, the house is ideally located for exploring this area.
FACILITIES: 4 en suite (2 fmly) No smoking TVB tea/coffee Direct dial from bedrooms No dogs (ex guide dogs) Licensed Cen ht TVL Dinner Last d 7pm **PRICES:** s fr €61; d €112 - €180✻ **LB PARKING:** 60
CARDS:

Ireland

LETTERKENNY Map 01 C5

♦♦♦♦ T&C *Pennsylvania House*
Curraghleas, Mountain Top ☎ 074 26808 📠 074 28905
e-mail: pennsylvania.house@indigo.ie

The Donegal hills make a stunning setting for this distinctive, purpose-built guest house. A sense of space, warm colours and personal touches contribute to the inviting atmosphere and accommodation includes a fine sitting room and a dining room. The Duddys, recently returned from running a B&B in the USA, are welcoming hosts.
FACILITIES: 5 en suite No smoking STV TV6B Direct dial from bedrooms No dogs Cen ht TVL No children 12yrs Many facilities are available nearby **PARKING:** 10 **NOTES:** Closed 20-26 Dec **CARDS:**

♦♦♦ GH Ballyraine
Ramelton Rd ☎ 074 24460 & 20851 📠 074 20851
e-mail: ballyraineguesthouse@eircom.net
Dir: *N13 onto R245*

This purpose-built guest house, 5 km from the town centre, is ideally located for touring the Fanad and Inishowen Peninsula. Bedrooms are spacious and pleasantly decorated, some are suitable for families. There is a comfortable lounge and an attractive breakfast room.
FACILITIES: 8 en suite (1 fmly) No smoking STV TVB tea/coffee Direct dial from bedrooms No dogs (ex guide dogs) Cen ht TVL
PRICES: s €30 - €38; d €52 - €60✳ **PARKING:** 12
CARDS:

ROSSNOWLAGH Map 01 B5

♦♦♦♦ T&C *Smugglers Creek*
☎ 072 52366 📠 072 22000
e-mail: smugcreek@eir.net
Set on a hilltop, overlooking Donegal Bay, this splendid inn has a timeless atmosphere of warmth and conviviality. En suite bedrooms are cosy and the award-winning bar features stripped-pine furnishings and a turf fire. There is also an intimate restaurant.
continued

The hospitality and attention to detail are simply excellent. There is a superb panorama of miles of sandy beaches and coves, and this is a well known surfing area.

FACILITIES: 5 en suite No smoking in dining room Direct dial from bedrooms Licensed Cen ht TVL No coaches Stabling for own horses Dinner Last d 9.30pm **PARKING:** 25 **NOTES:** Closed 18 Nov-26 Dec rs Oct-Etr (closed Mon & Tue) **CARDS:**

CO DUBLIN

DUBLIN Map 01 D4

See also Howth

Premier Collection

♦♦♦♦♦ GH Aberdeen Lodge
53 Park Av, Ballsbridge ☎ 01 2838155 📠 01 2837877
e-mail: aberdeen@iol.ie
Dir: *from city centre take the Merrion road towards Sydney Parade Dart Station and then 1st left into Park Avenue*

This particularly fine early Edwardian house stands on one of Dublin's most prestigious roads near to the main hotel and Embassy suburb. Bedrooms are well equipped and there are suites with air-spa baths. It is only minutes away from the centre by DART or bus, as well as being easily accessible from the airport and car ferries. Dinner is served and a Christmas Programme is available.
FACILITIES: 16 en suite (8 fmly) No smoking in 8 bedrooms No smoking in area of dining room No smoking in lounges STV TVB tea/coffee Direct dial from bedrooms No dogs Licensed Cen ht Jacuzzi
PRICES: s €90 - €114; d €109 - €149✳ **LB CONF:** Thtr 50 Class 40 Board 40 Del from €104 ✳ **PARKING:** 16
CARDS:

Ireland

Premier Collection

♦♦♦♦♦ GH Ariel House

50-54 Lansdowne Rd, Ballsbridge ☎ 01 6685512
📠 01 6685845
e-mail: reservations@ariel-house.com

Gracious Victorian residence in a useful location, close to all amenities. Staff are friendly and professional. There is a choice of bedrooms, either luxurious premier rooms or the more contemporary standard ones. Breakfast includes healthy and vegetarian options. Secure parking available.

FACILITIES: 37 en suite (4 fmly) (6 GF) No smoking in bedrooms No smoking in dining room TVB tea/coffee Direct dial from bedrooms No dogs Licensed Cen ht TVL Aromotherapist/Reflexologist
PRICES: s €65 - €140; d €80 - €200* **PARKING:** 30
CARDS:

Premier Collection

♦♦♦♦♦ GH Blakes Townhouse

50 Merrion Rd, Ballsbridge ☎ 01 6688324 📠 01 6684280
e-mail: blakestownhouse@iol.ie
Dir: *minutes from city centre by DART, or by car take Merrion Rd S to Ballsbridge, Blakes is opposite RDS Convention Centre*

Luxurious town house which has been completely refurbished to a very high standard. Some of the spacious, air-conditioned bedrooms have four-poster beds, others have balconies overlooking the gardens, plus all the expected facilities. Parking available.

FACILITIES: 13 en suite (1 fmly) No smoking in 5 bedrooms No smoking in dining room No smoking in lounges STV TVB tea/coffee Direct dial from bedrooms No dogs Licensed Cen ht No coaches Jacuzzi **PRICES:** s €90 - €114; d €109 - €149* **LB PARKING:** 6
CARDS:

Premier Collection

♦♦♦♦♦ GH Brownes Townhouse & Brasserie

22 St Stephen's Green ☎ 01 6383939 📠 01 6383900
e-mail: info@brownesdublin.com
Dir: *northside of St Stephens Green*

A gracious Georgian town house located on Dublin's most prestigious square, close to Trinity College. Bedrooms are luxuriously decorated and there is also a comfortable sitting room and a meeting room. Reservations are advisable at the popular brasserie where good food is served.

continued

FACILITIES: 12 en suite (1 fmly) No smoking in 8 bedrooms No smoking in area of dining room STV TVB tea/coffee Direct dial from bedrooms No dogs (ex guide dogs) Licensed Lift Cen ht No coaches Dinner Last d 10.30pm **PRICES:** s €170; d €235*
CONF: Thtr 24 **NOTES:** Closed 21 Dec-5 Jan rs Good Fri
CARDS:

Premier Collection

♦♦♦♦♦ GH *Butlers Town House*

44 Lansdowne Rd, Ballsbridge ☎ 01 6674022
📠 01 6673960
e-mail: info@butlers-hotel.com
Dir: *on junct of Lansdowne and Shelbourne*

This fine Victorian house, in the heart of Dublin's Embassy belt, has been beautifully restored and retains the charm of a gracious family home. Accommodation is air-conditioned and all bedrooms are individually furnished to the highest standard. Rich fabrics create a restful ambience in the drawing room, where afternoon tea is served. There is also a charming conservatory breakfast room, where a selection of hot and cold dishes is offered.

FACILITIES: 19 en suite No smoking in dining room STV TVB Direct dial from bedrooms No dogs (ex guide dogs) Cen ht Dinner Last d 8.45pm **PARKING:** 9 **NOTES:** Closed 23 Dec-8 Jan
CARDS:

Premier Collection

♦♦♦♦♦ GH *Cedar Lodge*

98 Merrion Rd, Ballsbridge ☎ 01 6684410 📠 01 6684533
e-mail: info@cedarlodge.ie
Dir: *opposite the British Embassy*

A lovely old house, with a modern extension, set back from the Dunlaoghaire Road and opposite the new British Embassy. Cedar Lodge offers comfortable, fully equipped bedrooms. There is ample parking with a secure area to the rear and full access for the disabled.

FACILITIES: 15 en suite (3 fmly) No smoking in bedrooms No smoking in dining room STV TVB tea/coffee Direct dial from bedrooms No dogs Cen ht No children 5yrs **PARKING:** 18 **NOTES:** Closed 23-27 Dec **CARDS:**

Premier Collection

♦♦♦♦♦ GH *Eglinton Manor*

83 Eglinton Rd, Donnybrook ☎ 01 2693273 📠 01 2697522

A fine Victorian town house, set in attractive gardens, close to the city centre. The accommodation has been totally refurbished, with the best of the original features retained, and now offers elegant decor, antique furnishings and beautiful objet d'art in the charming reception rooms. Very comfortable bedrooms are all individually styled with attractive colour schemes, large armchairs and smart new bathrooms.

FACILITIES: 8 en suite (2 fmly) No smoking STV TVB tea/coffee Direct dial from bedrooms No dogs (ex guide dogs) Cen ht TVL

Ireland

DUBLIN continued

Premier Collection

♦♦♦♦♦ GH Glenogra

64 Merrion Rd, Ballsbridge ☎ 01 6683661 📠 01 6683698
e-mail: glenogra@indigo.ie
Dir: *opposite Royal Dublin's Showgrounds and Four Seasons Hotel*
This fine gabled house run by Cherry and Seamus McNamee is not far from Dublin's centre and stands in a pleasant suburb opposite the RDS Centre. The house offers comfort with more than a touch of elegance, and the atmosphere is exceptionally welcoming.
FACILITIES: 13 en suite (1 fmly) No smoking STV TVB tea/coffee Direct dial from bedrooms No dogs (ex guide dogs) Cen ht TVL No coaches **PRICES:** s €75 - €85; d €99 - €120✳ **LB PARKING:** 10 **NOTES:** Closed 21 Dec-12 Jan **CARDS:**

Premier Collection

♦♦♦♦♦ GH Merrion Hall

54-56 Merrion Rd, Ballsbridge ☎ 01 6681426
📠 01 6684280
e-mail: merrionhall@iol.ie
Dir: *Ballsbridge is approx 2m along main route from Dublin city centre to Dun Laoghaire Port. Situated between British & US Embassies*

Elegant town house in Ballsbridge, ideally located and convenient for all amenities. Reception rooms are spacious, and the breakfast room overlooks the gardens. Bedrooms have recently been enlarged and air conditioning fitted. Some rooms have balconies and parking is available.
FACILITIES: 24 en suite (4 fmly) No smoking in 10 bedrooms No smoking in area of dining room No smoking in lounges STV TVB tea/coffee Direct dial from bedrooms No dogs Licensed Cen ht Jacuzzi **PRICES:** s €90 - €114; d €109 - €149✳ **LB CONF:** Thtr 50 Class 40 Board 40 Del from €104 ✳ **PARKING:** 10
CARDS:

Premier Collection

♦♦♦♦♦ GH Pembroke Town House

90 Pembroke Rd, Ballsbridge ☎ 01 6600277 📠 01 6600291
e-mail: info@pembroketownhouse.ie
Dir: *after Trinity College continue on to Nassan St and then Northumberland Rd. Service station on right before traffic lights. Take lane to right of service station and establishment 200mtrs on right*
Near the city centre, three Georgian houses have been carefully restored and interlinked to produce this luxurious guest house. A marble-tiled reception foyer and a luxurious lounge with big, comfortable easy chairs create a great first impression, enhanced by the friendly, attentive staff. The bedrooms are varied and interesting, some containing a mezzanine floor. The Landsdowne Rugby Grounds are nearby.
FACILITIES: 48 en suite (4 fmly) (10 GF) No smoking in 12 bedrooms No smoking in dining room TVB tea/coffee Direct dial from bedrooms No dogs (ex guide dogs) Lift Cen ht TVL **PRICES:** s €76 - €132; d €102 - €196✳ **LB PARKING:** 20 **NOTES:** Closed 22 Dec-2 Jan
CARDS:

Premier Collection

♦♦♦♦♦ GH *Waterloo House*

8-10 Waterloo Rd, Ballsbridge ☎ 01 6601888 📠 01 6671955
e-mail: waterloohouse@eircom.net
Dir: *S on St Stephens Green for 1m. Take next right. After Baggot Street, situated on left*
On a tree-lined avenue, ten minutes from the city centre, these two adjoining Georgian town houses have been refurbished to a high standard. Bedrooms and bathrooms are very comfortable and the varied breakfast menu is especially popular with guests.
FACILITIES: 17 en suite (2 fmly) No smoking STV TVB tea/coffee Direct dial from bedrooms No dogs Lift Cen ht TVL
PARKING: 8 **NOTES:** Closed Xmas Week **CARDS:**

♦♦♦♦ GH *Raglan Lodge*

10 Raglan Rd, Ballsbridge ☎ 01 6606697 📠 01 6606781
Dir: *from city centre, at American Embassy turn left into Elgin Rd, left at rdbt into Raglan Rd*

A charming Victorian lodge, situated on a tree-lined residential road in the suburb of Ballsbridge, close to the US Embassy, the RDS centre and with easy access to the city centre. Owner Helen Moran puts great effort into ensuring guests' comfort. The elegant drawing room invites relaxation around the fire, while breakfast is served in the cosy dining room. The bedrooms are all en suite, some are very spacious, and all are well equipped.
FACILITIES: 7 en suite (4 fmly) No smoking in 4 bedrooms No smoking in dining room STV TVB tea/coffee Direct dial from bedrooms Cen ht TVL No coaches **PARKING:** 12 **NOTES:** Closed 23 Dec-6 Jan
CARDS:

♦♦♦♦ T&C Aaron House

152 Merrion Rd, Ballsbridge ☎ 01 2601644 & 2601650
📠 01 2601651
e-mail: aaronhouse@indigo.ie
Dir: *4km south of City Centre, 550mtrs past the R.D.S*
Located near the city centre in the residential suburb of Ballsbridge this comfortable house is well equipped and tastefully decorated. The Dunn family have been involved in the business for many years and guests return frequently to experience their hospitality and friendliness.
FACILITIES: 6 en suite (1 fmly) No smoking in bedrooms No smoking in dining room tea/coffee Direct dial from bedrooms No dogs Cen ht TVL
PRICES: s €53 - €75; d €76 - €120✳ **LB PARKING:** 6
NOTES: Closed 24-26 Dec **CARDS:**

Ireland

♦♦♦♦ GH *Aaronmor House*

1b-1c Sandymount Av, Ballsbridge ☎ 01 6687972
🖹 01 6682377
e-mail: aaronmor@indigo.ie

One of a terrace of red brick Victorian houses, Aaronmor has a guest TV lounge, a breakfast room, and a secure car park at the rear of the house.

FACILITIES: 19 en suite (4 fmly) No smoking in 4 bedrooms No smoking in dining room No smoking in 1 lounge TVB tea/coffee Direct dial from bedrooms No dogs (ex guide dogs) Lift Cen ht TVL **PARKING:** 12
NOTES: Closed 23-27 Dec & 31 Dec-2 Jan **CARDS:**

♦♦♦♦ GH Abrae Court

9 Zion Rd, Rathgar ☎ 01 4922242 🖹 01 4923944
e-mail: abrae@eircom.net

Abrae Court is a redbrick Victorian house built in 1864. It combines original features with modern comforts. The bedrooms are attractively decorated and well appointed, and there is a spacious guest sitting room with an open fire.

FACILITIES: 14 en suite (2 fmly) No smoking in dining room STV TVB tea/coffee Direct dial from bedrooms No dogs Cen ht Sightseeing tours available **PRICES:** s fr €54; d fr €99✳ **LB PARKING:** 15
NOTES: Closed Xmas **CARDS:**

♦♦♦♦ GH Charleville Lodge

268/272 North Circular Rd, Phibsborough ☎ 01 8386633
🖹 01 8385854
e-mail: charleville@indigo.ie
Dir: *250mtrs from St Peters Church*

Situated close to the city centre near Phoenix Park, this elegant terrace of Victorian houses has been tastefully restored to a high standard. The two interconnecting lounges are welcoming and the smart dining room offers a choice of breakfasts. Bedrooms are very comfortable with pleasant decor and there is a secure car park for guests' use.

FACILITIES: 30 en suite (2 fmly) (1 GF) STV TVB Direct dial from bedrooms No dogs Cen ht TVL **PRICES:** s €45 - €80; d €75 - €150✳
LB CONF: Thtr 20 Class 20 Board 20 **PARKING:** 18 **NOTES:** Closed 21-26 Dec **CARDS:**

♦♦♦♦ GH Eliza Lodge

23/24 Wellington Quay, Temple Bar ☎ 01 6718044
🖹 01 6718362
e-mail: info@dublinlodge.com

Very smart accommodation in a completely refurbished building situated at the foot of the Millennium Bridge. Inviting, comfortable bedrooms are well equipped, and there is a lounge with a hospitality centre, and a fully licensed restaurant.

FACILITIES: 18 en suite (2 fmly) No smoking in bedrooms No smoking in area of dining room STV TVB tea/coffee Direct dial from bedrooms No dogs (ex guide dogs) Licensed Lift Cen ht TVL **PRICES:** s €76 - €95; d €152 - €177✳ **LB NOTES:** Closed 23 Dec-2 Jan
CARDS:

♦♦♦♦ GH Ferryview House

96 Clontarf Rd, Clontarf ☎ 01 8335893 🖹 01 8532141
e-mail: ferryview@oceanfree.net
Dir: *follow coast road from city centre via Fairview heading N to Clontarf Rd, just beyond Yacht Pub. On left hand side, 2.5m from City Centre*

Situated on the coast road 2.5 miles from the city centre on the 130 bus route, this house is conveniently located between Dublin Airport, the Point Theatre and the city centre. Tastefully refurbished to provide relaxing and cheerful accommodation, equipped with all facilities. Free secure parking provided. Local amenities i nclude the Bull Island Bird Sanctuary, Dollymount Beach and three golf courses.

FACILITIES: 8 en suite (3 fmly) (2 GF) No smoking in bedrooms No smoking in dining room No smoking in 1 lounge STV TVB tea/coffee Direct dial from bedrooms No dogs (ex guide dogs) Cen ht TVL
PRICES: s €57 - €76; d €70 - €100✳ **PARKING:** 12
NOTES: Closed 23 Dec-3 Jan **CARDS:**

DUBLIN continued

♦♦♦♦ GH Glenshandan Lodge

Dublin Rd, Swords ☎ 01 8408838 📠 01 8408838
e-mail: glenshandan@eircom.net

Family and dog-friendly house, where the hospitable owners are attentive and offer good facilities including e mail access. Bedrooms are comfortable and one is adapted for wheelchair users. Secure parking available. Close to pubs, restaurants, golf, airport and the Kennel Club.

FACILITIES: 9 en suite (5 fmly) No smoking in dining room TVB tea/coffee Cen ht TVL **PRICES:** s €65; d €90* **PARKING:** 10 **CARDS:**

♦♦♦♦ GH Harrington Hall

69-70 Harcourt St ☎ 01 4753497 📠 01 4754544
e-mail: harringtonhall@eircom.net

Dir: *approach from O'Connell St, then St Stephen's Green via O'Connell St, in Earlsfort Terrace pass National Concert Hall and turn right into Hatch St then right into Harcourt St*

Restored Georgian house on a one-way street, adjoining St Stephen's Green in the centre of the city. A lovely plasterwork ceiling adorns the luxurious dining room. Spacious bedrooms and bathrooms are very comfortable and include two junior suites with galleried bedroom areas, and a full suite. Elevator, porter service and car parking.

FACILITIES: 28 en suite (3 fmly) (3 GF) No smoking STV TVB tea/coffee Direct dial from bedrooms No dogs (ex guide dogs) Licensed Lift Cen ht **PRICES:** s €127 - €165; d €165 - €380* **LB CONF:** Thtr 20 Class 6 Board 12 **PARKING:** 8 **CARDS:**

♦♦♦♦ T&C *Hazelhurst*

166 Stillorgan Rd, Donnybrook ☎ 01 2838509 📠 01 2600346

Dir: *on N11, 1km from Donnybrook Village, 3km from city centre*

Stone eagles on the gateposts make Hazelhurst an easy place to spot. Inside there are two comfortable lounges, and well appointed en suite bedrooms. Close to the city centre and other local attractions.

FACILITIES: 6 en suite (1 fmly) No smoking in bedrooms No smoking in dining room No smoking in 1 lounge STV TVB tea/coffee No dogs (ex guide dogs) Cen ht TVL **PARKING:** 6 **NOTES:** Closed 15 Dec-15 Jan rs Xmas **CARDS:**

♦♦♦♦ GH Kilronan House

70 Adelaide Rd ☎ 01 4755266 📠 01 4782841
e-mail: info@dublinn.com

Dir: *situated adjacent to National Concert Hall, Conrad Hotel and Eye and Ear Hospital*

Ideally located just five minutes south of St Stephen's Green this fine period town house has comfortable, well appointed bedrooms that vary in size. A smart dining room and guest lounge are available. Personally run by Rose and Terry Masterson, there is secure car parking at the rear.

continued

FACILITIES: 12 en suite (1 fmly) No smoking TVB tea/coffee Direct dial from bedrooms No dogs (ex guide dogs) Cen ht TVL **PRICES:** s €76; d fr €100* **LB PARKING:** 8 **CARDS:**

♦♦♦♦ GH *Kingswood Country House*

Old Kingswood, Naas Rd, Clondalkin ☎ 01 4592428 & 4592207 📠 01 4592428
e-mail: kingswoodcountryhse@tinet.ie

Dir: *turn left off M50 heading south, premises 1.5km on left past Green Isle Hotel*

This Georgian house offers attractive en suite bedrooms, a cosy sitting room and an intimate restaurant specialising in good home cooking. The proprietors make guests feel very welcome here and there are also well maintained gardens.

FACILITIES: 7 en suite (2 fmly) No smoking in area of dining room TVB Direct dial from bedrooms No dogs (ex guide dogs) Licensed Cen ht No coaches Last d 10.30pm **PARKING:** 60 **NOTES:** Closed 25-28 Dec & Good Fri **CARDS:**

♦♦♦♦ GH *Merrion Square Manor*

31 Merrion Square North ☎ 01 6628551 📠 01 6628556
e-mail: merrionmanor@eircom.net

Dir: *centre of the City, close to National Gallery and Trinity College*

Ideally situated in the heart of the city, close to the National Gallery and Trinity College, this Georgian house has been tastefully restored, and the two reception rooms have retained their original plaster work. Bedrooms are all en suite and vary in size. Breakfast is a highlight, with a wide-ranging menu on offer.

FACILITIES: 18 en suite (4 fmly) No smoking in bedrooms No smoking in dining room STV TVB tea/coffee Direct dial from bedrooms No dogs (ex guide dogs) Cen ht TVL No coaches **PARKING:** 5 **NOTES:** Closed 23 Dec-1 Jan **CARDS:**

♦♦♦♦ T&C No 66 Townhouse

Northumberland Rd, Ballsbridge ☎ 01 6600333 & 6600471 📠 01 6601051

Dir: *1m from Trinity College on Northumberland Rd. Opposite Czech Embassy*

This imposing house has six comfortable bedrooms all fully equipped to a very high standard. Attractive public areas include a dining room and two comfortable lounges, one in a lovely conservatory. It is very convenient for the city, Landsdowne Road and the RDS showgrounds.

FACILITIES: 8 en suite (2 fmly) No smoking in dining room No smoking in lounges STV TVB tea/coffee Direct dial from bedrooms No dogs (ex guide dogs) Cen ht TVL No coaches **PRICES:** s €70 - €120; d €95 - €190* **PARKING:** 6 **CARDS:**

See advertisement on opposite page

♦♦♦♦ GH Trinity Lodge

12 South Frederick St ☎ 01 6795044 & 6795182 📠 01 6795223
e-mail: trinitylodge@eircom.net

Dir: *from N end of Grafton St along Nassau St past Dawson St. South Frederick St is next right*

This listed Georgian townhouse has been restored and converted to provide excellent accommodation right in the heart of the city centre. Accommodation consists of en suite, quality bedrooms and three luxury suites in annexe accommodation across the street, all beautifully appointed and fully equipped. The many facilities include air conditioning and a personal safe. Most of the city's attractions are within walking distance.

FACILITIES: 13 en suite (5 fmly) (1 GF) No smoking in 8 bedrooms No smoking in dining room STV TVB tea/coffee Direct dial from bedrooms No dogs (ex guide dogs) Cen ht No coaches **PRICES:** s €85 - €220; d €135 - €320* **PARKING:** 2 **NOTES:** Closed 22-28 Dec **CARDS:**

♦♦♦ GH Ardagh House

1 Highfield Rd, Rathgar ☎ 01 4977068 📠 01 4973991
e-mail: enquiries@ardagh-house.ie
Dir: *S of city centre through Rathmines*

This large, former hotel has been greatly refurbished and upgraded by Mary and Willie Doyle. Some of the airy, comfortable en suite rooms look out over the attractive rear garden.

FACILITIES: 19 en suite (4 fmly) (1 GF) No smoking in 10 bedrooms No smoking in dining room STV TVB tea/coffee Direct dial from bedrooms No dogs (ex guide dogs) Cen ht TVL **PRICES:** s €51 - €90; d €80 - €130✳ **PARKING:** 20 **NOTES:** Closed 22-28 Dec **CARDS:**

♦♦♦ T&C *Askill*

86 Stillorgan Grove, Stillorgan ☎ 01 2884514 📠 01 2780426
e-mail: harraghy@tinet.ie
Dir: *S from Dublin on N11, pass Stillorgan Park Hotel, in 1km take left turn for Stillorgan Park. Right turn before rdbt, house on right*

Askill is near the Smurfit Business School and Dun Laoghaire. The house has a car park and there are good bus services. Its attractively decorated en suite bedrooms are equipped with good modern amenities. Lounge and dining room are combined, and the cooked breakfasts are a speciality of the house. Mr and Mrs Harraghy are friendly hosts.

FACILITIES: 5 en suite (3 fmly) No smoking in bedrooms No smoking in 1 lounge STV TVB tea/coffee Direct dial from bedrooms No dogs Cen ht **PARKING:** 5 **CARDS:**

♦♦♦ GH *Belgrave*

8-10 Belgrave Square, Rathmines ☎ 01 4963760 & 4962549 📠 01 4979243
Dir: *from canal into Rathmines Rd to Swan Shopping Centre, turn left and at next traffic lights turn right for Belgrave Square*

Interlinked early Victorian houses in a residential suburb on the south side of the city and on direct bus routes. Restored and modernised to a high standard with plenty of lounge space, a well appointed dining room and pleasant gardens. The en suite bedrooms are all well equipped and some are on the ground floor. The resident proprietors are very helpful and friendly.

FACILITIES: 24 en suite (2 fmly) No smoking in area of dining room TVB tea/coffee Direct dial from bedrooms No dogs (ex guide dogs) Cen ht TVL No coaches **PARKING:** 7 **NOTES:** Closed 23-31 Dec **CARDS:**

♦♦♦ T&C Charleston Manor

15/16 Charleston Rd, Ranelagh ☎ 01 4910262 📠 01 4966052
Dir: *on main road between Ranelagh & Rathmines*

Conveniently situated ten minutes from the city centre, two red-brick houses have been restored to give Charleston Manor five bedrooms at ground floor level. They are attractively decorated and well equipped. The dining room has individual tables where full Irish breakfast is served.

FACILITIES: 14 en suite No smoking in dining room TV5B tea/coffee Direct dial from bedrooms No dogs Cen ht TVL **PRICES:** s €50; d €95✳ **PARKING:** 8 **NOTES:** Closed 23 Dec-1 Jan **CARDS:**

♦♦♦ T&C *Clifden*

32 Gardiner Place ☎ 01 8746364 📠 01 8746122
e-mail: bnb@indigo.ie
Dir: *From north end of O'Connell St, around 3 sides of Parnell Sq, exit at church into Gardiner Row, through lights. House 4th on right*

This city centre house is just a few minutes' walk from O'Connell Street, and close to all amenities. Facilities include a comfortable sitting room, cheerfully appointed breakfast room and a car park at the rear of the house.

continued

FACILITIES: 14 en suite (4 fmly) No smoking in dining room No smoking in lounges STV TVB tea/coffee Direct dial from bedrooms No dogs Cen ht TVL No coaches **PARKING:** 12 **CARDS:**

♦♦♦ GH The Fitzwilliam

41 Upper Fitzwilliam St ☎ 01 6600448 📠 01 6767488
e-mail: fitzwilliamguesthouse@eircom.net
Dir: *junct of Fitzwilliam St upper & Baggot St lower. 5mins walk to St Stephen's Green*

This beautifully restored Georgian townhouse is just a few minutes' walk from St Stephen's Green and the main shopping area. The well-proprtioned rooms, with their fine drapes and soft furnishings, recreate the charm of the Georgian period, while lovely bathrooms complete the picture of modern comfort and elegance.

FACILITIES: 12 en suite (1 fmly) STV TVB Direct dial from bedrooms Licensed Cen ht TVL Dinner Last d 10.30pm **PRICES:** s €70 - €76; d €101 - €127✳ **PARKING:** **NOTES:** Closed 21 Dec-3 Jan **CARDS:**

♦♦♦ T&C Pairc na Bhfuiseog

55 Lorcan Crescent, Santry ☎ 01 8421318 📠 01 8423371
e-mail: rpjd@eircom.net
Dir: *N1 Dublin Airport, Swords Rd to Santry, over the flyover turn left at sharp U-turn continue to top of road turn right into Lorcan Crescent*

An extended, modern semi-detached house, very nicely appointed throughout, with excellent en suite facilities. Convenient for Dublin Airport, ferries and city centre. The owners Ronald and Colette Downey provide a homely atmosphere and lots of local information.

FACILITIES: 4 rms (3 en suite) (1 fmly) (1 GF) No smoking STV TVB No dogs (ex guide dogs) Cen ht No coaches **PRICES:** s €33 - €35; d €66 - €70✳ **PARKING:** 4 **NOTES:** Closed 21 Dec-1 Jan **CARDS:**

DUBLIN continued

♦♦♦ GH St Aiden's

32 Brighton Rd, Rathgar ☎ 01 4902011 📠 01 4920234
e-mail: staidens@eircom.net
Dir: *turn off M50 junct 11 towards city centre. Premises 3rd left after traffic lights in Terenure village*

A fine Victorian house situated in a residential tree-lined road just 15 minutes from the city centre. The well-proportioned reception rooms are comfortable and relaxing, and a hospitality trolley is available for guests. Bedrooms vary in size from spacious family rooms to snug singles, and all offer modern comforts.

FACILITIES: 8 en suite (3 fmly) No smoking in 3 bedrooms No smoking in dining room STV TVB Direct dial from bedrooms No dogs Cen ht No coaches **PRICES:** s €50 - €75; d €75 - €99✱ **LB PARKING:** 8 **CARDS:**

♦♦ GH Antrim Arms

27 Upper Drumcondra Rd ☎ 01 8375356 📠 01 8378769
Dir: *off A50 at Eastern End. Take N1 to Dublin city. At the end of N1, after 1m onto Drumcondra Rd and house nxt door to Jury Skylon Hotel*

This fine, detached guest house is conveniently situated within ten minutes' drive of Dublin Airport, ferry port and the city centre. Attractively decorated bedrooms, which vary in size, include some large family rooms and one room adapted for wheelchair users. There is also a comfortable lounge and a separate dining room.

FACILITIES: 24 en suite (3 fmly) No smoking in dining room TVB tea/coffee Cen ht TVL No children 16yrs **PRICES:** s €54 - €60; d €72 - €80✱ **PARKING:** 17 **CARDS:**

♦♦ T&C Aran House

5 Home Farm Rd, Drumcondra ☎ 01 8367395 📠 01 8367395
Dir: *From city centre head for airport/Drumcondra road. Past St Patrick's College and Cat & Cage pub. 1st left after Skylon Hotel*

This redbrick terraced house is conveniently situated just off the main airport road. It has a friendly, homely atmosphere and bedrooms are fresh and bright. The house is a short walk from local shops and pubs and on a bus route to the city centre and airport.

FACILITIES: 4 en suite (2 fmly) No smoking TVB tea/coffee Cen ht TVL
PRICES: d €80✱

♦♦ GH Lyndon

26 Gardiner Place ☎ 01 8786950 📠 01 8787420
e-mail: lyndonh@gofree.indigo.ie
Dir: *top end of O'Connell St off Parnell Sq. Top right-hand corner of Parnell Sq or off Gardiner St by Mountjoy Sq*

A fine old Georgian townhouse, close to the city centre, in an area enjoying something of a revival. The house has been completely restored in tasteful style with rich modern colours throughout. Bedrooms are all en suite and uniformly furnished to a high standard.

FACILITIES: 9 en suite (4 fmly) No smoking STV TVB tea/coffee No dogs Cen ht No coaches **PRICES:** s fr €45; d fr €90✱ **PARKING:** 2
CARDS:

DUN LAOGHAIRE — Map 01 D4

♦♦♦♦ T&C *Cumberland Lodge*

54 York Rd ☎ 01 2809665 📠 01 2843227
e-mail: cumberlandlodge@tinet.ie
Dir: *going S from city centre follow Dun Laoghaire car ferry signs, on approaching Georges St turn right at Cumberland Inn into York Rd*

Convenient to the ferryport and DART rapid railway, only 15 minutes from Dublin Central, this charming Regency house has been beautifully restored. Elegant reception rooms are furnished and decorated in keeping with the period, with richly coloured fabrics and rugs, and polished wooden floors. Comfortable bedrooms include two on the ground floor. There is a very large enclosed garage which can accommodate a mini-coach as well as cars.

FACILITIES: 4 en suite (1 fmly) No smoking in bedrooms No smoking in area of dining room No smoking in 1 lounge TVB tea/coffee Direct dial from bedrooms No dogs (ex guide dogs) Cen ht TVL **PARKING:** 3
CARDS:

HOWTH — Map 01 D4

♦♦♦♦ T&C Inisradharc

Balkill Rd ☎ 01 8322306 📠 01 8322306
e-mail: jimmcn@gofree.indigo.ie
Dir: *turn right off R105 past Howth Yacht Club up Abbey St. Keep right of church in the middle of the road. House 0.25m up hill on right*

This modern hotel is situated overlooking Dublin Bay and Ireland's Eye in its own parkland golf courses. The spacious well-equipped bedrooms have spectacular views. The Four Earls Restaurant is famous for fresh fish from Howth Harbour, and there is a lively bar and bistro. There is a Leisure Centre, all-weather tennis courts and a choice of four golf courses nearby.

FACILITIES: 3 en suite (1 fmly) No smoking TVB tea/coffee No dogs Cen ht TVL No children 4yrs **PRICES:** d €66✱ **PARKING:** 3 **NOTES:** Closed 21 Dec-2 Jan **CARDS:**

LUSK — Map 01 D4

♦♦♦ T&C Brookfield Lodge

Blakescross ☎ 01 8430043 📠 01 8430177
e-mail: trishb@indigo.ie
Dir: *10 mins N of Dublin Airport N. Ignore signs for Lusk and cont past Esso garage for 400 mtrs. Located on junct of N1/R129.*

Set in an acre of gardens, this modern bungalow offers first-class hospitality and spacious, well appointed rooms. Breakfasts are served in a conservatory-style dining room and there is also a comfortable lounge.

FACILITIES: 4 en suite (2 fmly) No smoking STV TVB tea/coffee No dogs Cen ht TVL **PRICES:** s €45 - €65; d €65 - €102✱ **PARKING:** 10
CARDS:

SKERRIES — Map 01 D4

♦♦♦♦ GH Redbank House & Restaurant

6 & 7 Church St ☎ 01 8491005 & 8490439 📠 01 8491598
e-mail: redbank@eircom.net
Dir: *N1 north past the airport & bypass Swords. 3m N at end of dual carriageway at Esso station right towards Rush, Lusk & Skerries*

A comfortable period town house adjacent to the well known restaurant of the same name, this is the latest venture of chef/patron Terry McCoy and his wife Margaret who is responsible for the tasteful refurbishment of the house. Double fronted, with two reception rooms, en suite bedrooms and a secluded garden, there is also secure parking. Convenient for Dublin airport and the ferry port.

continued

Ireland

FACILITIES: 7 en suite 5 annexe en suite (12 fmly) (4 GF) No smoking in 7 bedrooms No smoking in area of dining room No smoking in 1 lounge STV TVB tea/coffee Direct dial from bedrooms No dogs (ex guide dogs) Licensed Cen ht TVL No coaches Dinner Last d 9.45pm **PRICES:** s €50 - €60; d €80 - €100* **LB PARKING:** 4 **NOTES:** Closed 24-28 Dec
CARDS:

CO GALWAY

CARNA — Map 01 A4

♦♦♦♦ T&C Hillside House B&B

Kylesalia, Kilkieran ☎ 095 33420 📠 095 33624
e-mail: hillsidehouse@oceanfree.net
Dir: *off N59 at Maam Cross or Recess onto R340 or follow coast road from Galway R336*

At the foot of Mordan Mountain, this house is ideally located for touring. Bedrooms are comfortable, there are lovely gardens and secure parking. Snack service available. Near fishing and beach.
FACILITIES: 4 en suite (4 fmly) No smoking STV TVB tea/coffee No dogs Cen ht No coaches **PRICES:** s €38.50 - €44; d €51 - €60* **PARKING:** 8
NOTES: Closed Nov-mid Mar **CARDS:**

CLIFDEN — Map 01 A4

Premier Collection

♦♦♦♦♦ GH Byrne's Mal Dua House

Galway Rd ☎ 095 21171 & 0800 904 7532 📠 095 21739
e-mail: info@maldua.com
Dir: *on N59, Galway Rd, 1km from Clifden*

Set in the heart of Connemara, this house offers a relaxed atmosphere of luxury, with warm hospitality, excellent food and peace and quiet paramount. The dining room overlooks the manicured landscaped gardens, and afternoon tea is served in the drawing room. Courtesy minibus, bicycles for hire and Internet access available.
FACILITIES: 14 en suite (2 fmly) (3 GF) No smoking STV TVB tea/coffee Direct dial from bedrooms No dogs (ex guide dogs) Licensed Cen ht TVL ch fac Croquet lawn Bicycles for rent Dinner Last d 7pm **PRICES:** s €44 - €63; d €88 - €126* **LB PARKING:** 20
CARDS:

Premier Collection

♦♦♦♦♦ GH *O'Grady's Sunnybank House*

Church Hill ☎ 095 21437 📠 095 21976
Dir: *N59 from Galway, turn right at Esso station & 1st left past R C Church*

Set in mature grounds beside the tennis court and swimming pool, Sunnybank is a refurbished period house with elegant reception rooms and comfortable bedrooms. The two-bedroomed private suite has its own sitting room with a turf fire. One of two sitting rooms offers use of the Internet and there is a large car park.
FACILITIES: 8 en suite (4 fmly) No smoking in 1 bedrooms No smoking in dining room No smoking in 1 lounge STV TVB Direct dial from bedrooms No dogs Cen ht TVL No children 7yrs Outdoor swimming pool (heated) Tennis (hard) Sauna **PARKING:** 12
NOTES: Closed Dec-Feb **CARDS:**

♦♦♦♦ GH Buttermilk Lodge

Westport Rd ☎ 095 21951 📠 095 21953
e-mail: buttermilk@anu.ie
Dir: *N59 from Galway. Right at Esso Station onto Westport Rd, Lodge 400mtrs from junct on left. From Westport, Lodge on right, 100mtrs after Clifden sign*

Tastefully decorated and appointed bedrooms, all with luxury bath and shower en suite, along with many personal touches, can be expected at this large house on the edge of town. Cathriona and Patrick O'Toole are welcoming hosts who offer fresh baking, tea and coffee when guests arrive.
FACILITIES: 11 en suite (2 fmly) (4 GF) No smoking in 8 bedrooms No smoking in dining room No smoking in 1 lounge STV TVB Direct dial from bedrooms No dogs (ex guide dogs) Cen ht No children 5yrs farmland available for walking and hill-climbing **PRICES:** s €35 - €50; d €60 - €80* **LB PARKING:** 14 **NOTES:** Closed 7-31 Jan **CARDS:**

♦♦♦♦ Ardmore House *(L 730495)*

Sky Rd ☎ 095 21221 📠 095 21100 Mr & Mrs J Mullen
e-mail: info@ardmore-house.com
Apr-Sep
Dir: *5km W of Clifden,from Clifden follow signs for Sky Rd, pass bank onto the Abbey Glen Castle, Ardmore house is signed 3.5m*

Ardmore is set amongst the wild scenery of Connemara between hills and the sea. Bedrooms are attractively decorated and the house is very comfortable throughout. A pathway leads from the house to the coast.
FACILITIES: 6 en suite (3 fmly) No smoking STV TVB tea/coffee No dogs (ex guide dogs) Cen ht 25 acres non-working Dinner Last d 3pm
PRICES: s €37 - €40; d €54 - €60* **LB PARKING:** 8
NOTES: Closed Oct-Mar

♦♦♦♦ GH *Dun Ri*

Hulk St ☎ 095 21625 📠 095 21635
e-mail: dunri@anu.ie
Dir: *on entering Clifden via N59 turn left before Statoil service station, signed*

This large, guest house stands in a quiet street close to the town centre. All the rooms are furnished to the same high standard and are equipped with modern comforts. Guests enjoy the amenity of a comfortable lounge and a separate dining room.
FACILITIES: 10 en suite (2 fmly) No smoking in bedrooms No smoking in dining room STV TVB Direct dial from bedrooms No dogs (ex guide dogs) Cen ht TVL No children 4yrs **PARKING:** 10 **NOTES:** Closed 3 Nov-Feb
CARDS:

CLIFDEN continued

♦♦♦♦ *Faul House (L 650475)*
Ballyconneely Rd ☎ 095 21239 📠 095 21998 Mrs K Conneely
15 Mar-Oct
Dir: *1m from town, turn right at Connemara Pottery and follow signs*

A fine modern farmhouse stands on a quiet and secluded road overlooking Clifden Bay. It is smart and comfortable with large en suite bedrooms, all well furnished and with good views.
FACILITIES: 6 en suite (3 fmly) No smoking in 3 bedrooms No smoking in dining room No smoking in 1 lounge No dogs (ex guide dogs) Cen ht TVL 28 acres sheep, ponies **PARKING:** 10

♦♦♦♦ T&C Mallmore House
Ballyconneely Rd ☎ 095 21460
e-mail: info@mallmorecountryhouse.com
Dir: *1.5km from Clifden towards Ballyconneely, turn right at Connemara Pottery*
A charming Georgian-style house set in 35 acres of woodland overlooking Clifden Bay, is situated one mile from Clifden on the Ballyconneely road, close to the Rock Glen Hotel. Alan and Kathy Hardman have tastefully restored the house, with parquet flooring and some favourite antiques, together with turf fires providing warmth and atmosphere.
FACILITIES: 6 en suite (2 fmly) (6 GF) No smoking in bedrooms No smoking in dining room tea/coffee No dogs (ex guide dogs) Cen ht TVL No coaches 35 acres of mature woodland **PRICES:** s €25 - €50; d €50 - €60* **PARKING:** 15 **NOTES:** Closed Oct-15Mar

♦♦♦ GH *Ben View House*
Bridge St ☎ 095 21256 📠 095 21226
e-mail: benviewhouse@ireland.com
Dir: *enter town on N59, opposite Esso petrol station*
This town-centre house offers good quality accommodation at a moderate cost making it an ideal touring base.
FACILITIES: 10 rms (9 en suite) (3 fmly) No smoking in 2 bedrooms No smoking in dining room TV9B No dogs (ex guide dogs) Cen ht TVL
CARDS:

♦♦♦ *Dan O'Hara's Farmhouse (L 730495)*
Lettershea ☎ 095 21246 & 21808 📠 095 22098
Mr & Mrs M Walsh
e-mail: danohara@eircom.net
Dir: *well signposted on N59 (main Galway/Clifden road), 8km from Clifden next to Connemara Heritage History Centre. 45m from Galway city*
This smart country residence is part of the Connemara Heritage and History Centre, situated on a 50-acre traditional working farm, set in the foothills of the Twelve Pins Mountains. Bedrooms are attractively decorated with pine furnishings and good facilities. There's a tea room, craft shop, comfortable sitting room, patio garden and a large car park.
FACILITIES: 4 en suite (6 fmly) No smoking in bedrooms No smoking in dining room TVB tea/coffee Direct dial from bedrooms No dogs Cen ht 200 acres mixed **PARKING:** 30 **NOTES:** Closed Nov-Mar
CARDS:

♦♦♦ T&C Failte
Ardbear, Ballyconneely Rd ☎ 095 21159 📠 095 21159
e-mail: kelly-failte@iol.ie
Dir: *from Clifden take Ballyconneely road, 1.5km from Clifden take 1st right at pottery, hotel 400mtrs from pottery*
A modern bungalow in a scenic location on edge of Clifden features excellent standards of comfort, has welcoming hosts and is an ideal touring centre.
FACILITIES: 5 rms (2 en suite) (2 fmly) (2 GF) No smoking in dining room No smoking in 1 lounge No dogs (ex guide dogs) Cen ht TVL **PRICES:** s €25 - €38; d €46 - €50* **PARKING:** 15
NOTES: Closed Oct-Mar **CARDS:**

♦♦♦ T&C Kingstown House
Bridge St ☎ 095 21470 📠 095 21530
Dir: *enter Clifden on N59(W) onto one-way system, 2nd house on right*
Situated just off Clifden's main street and centrally located close to all amenities, this pleasant guest house offers a warm welcome from the friendly proprietors Mary and Joe King, who provide comfortable accommodation.
FACILITIES: 8 rms (7 en suite) (2 fmly) No smoking TVB tea/coffee No dogs (ex guide dogs) Cen ht TVL **PRICES:** s €25 - €27; d €50 - €54*
NOTES: rs 23-28 Dec **CARDS:**

CRAUGHWELL Map 01 B3

Premier Collection

♦♦♦♦♦ GH *St Clerans*
☎ 091 846555 📠 091 846600
e-mail: stcleran@iol.ie
Dir: *off N6 between Loughrea and Craughwell. Turn right 1m outside Loughrea, signposted St Clerans/Athenry. Follow road for 3.5m, at x-roads turn left*

IRELAND'S BLUE BOOK

A lovely 18th-century Georgian manor house, set in 45 acres, with some intriguing showbusiness connections. Previously owned by American film director, John Houston, it is now owned by US TV personality, Merv Griffin. Public areas include a drawing room, a dining room, a library and a study. Coarse fishing, riding, croquet and golf are available in the grounds, and the whole house can be hired for weddings.
FACILITIES: 12 en suite (2 fmly) No smoking in dining room STV TVB Direct dial from bedrooms No dogs (ex guide dogs) Licensed Cen ht TVL Fishing Riding Croquet lawn Putting green Dinner Last d 9pm
PARKING: 13 **CARDS:**

Ireland

GALWAY Map 01 B3

Premier Collection

♦♦♦♦♦ T&C Killeen House

Killeen, Bushypark ☎ 091 524179 📠 091 528065
e-mail: killeenhouse@ireland.com
Dir: *on N59 midway between the city and Moycullen village*

This charming 19th-century house stands in 25 acres of grounds stretching down to the shores of the loch. The interior is beautifully appointed with antique furnishings, hand-woven carpets, fine linen and exquisite crystal. Bedrooms reflect the character of the house and are well equipped. Guests have use of two reception rooms and a breakfast room overlooking the garden. The hosts are genuinely hospitable.
FACILITIES: 5 en suite (1 fmly) (1 GF) No smoking in dining room STV TVB tea/coffee Direct dial from bedrooms No dogs Lift Cen ht No children 12yrs No coaches **PRICES:** s €80 - €100; d €120 - €140✳ **PARKING:** 6 **NOTES:** Closed 23-28 Dec **CARDS:** 

♦♦♦♦ T&C Almara House

2 Merlin Gate, Merlin Park, Dublin Rd ☎ 091 755345 & 771585 📠 091 771585
e-mail: matthewkiernan@eircom.net
Dir: *located beside N6 & N18 junct beside Corrib Great Southern Hotel & Galway Irish Chrystal Factory. Follow signs for Merlin Park*

A purpose built red brick house on the outskirts of Galway, a bus to the town centre stops just outside. Attractively decorated bedrooms are comfortable with lots of extras. Breakfast includes freshly baked bread and pork and bacon from the proprietors' own butchers shop. There is pleasant sitting room and ample off street parking.
FACILITIES: 4 en suite (1 fmly) No smoking STV TVB tea/coffee No dogs (ex guide dogs) Cen ht TVL **PRICES:** s €40 - €50; d €60 - €90✳ **LB** **PARKING:** 8 **NOTES:** Closed 23-29 Dec
CARDS:

♦♦♦♦ GH Ardawn House

31 College Rd ☎ 091 568833 & 564551 📠 091 563454
e-mail: ardawn@iol.ie
Dir: *take Galway East exit off dual-carriageway near Galway, follow signs for city centre, 1st guest house on right after Galway greyhound track*

This friendly and hospitable hotel is conveniently situated for the city centre. Breakfasts are a feature here, offering a wide variety of home-baked breads, fruit yogurt, cheese and cereal. Bedrooms are all en suite, with colour co-ordinated furnishings.
FACILITIES: 8 en suite (2 fmly) No smoking in bedrooms No smoking in dining room STV TVB Direct dial from bedrooms No dogs (ex guide dogs) Cen ht No children 12yrs **PRICES:** s €50 - €90; d €90 - €120✳ **LB** **PARKING:** 8 **NOTES:** Closed 21-26 Dec **CARDS:**

♦♦♦♦ T&C Atlantic Heights

2 Cashelmara, Knocknacarra Cross, Salthill
☎ 091 529466 & 528830 📠 091 529466
e-mail: atlanticheights@galway.iol.ie
Dir: *1km from Salthill Promenade in upper Salthill on coast road to Barna & Spiddal - R336. 0.25m on right after Spinnaker House Hotel, before t-junc*

This fine balconied house overlooks Galway Bay, where enthusiastic hosts, Robbie and Madeline Mitchell, take great pride in their home. All bedrooms have TV, tea and coffee making facilities, telephone, hairdryer and many thoughful extras. An extensive breakfast menu, served late if required, features home baking. Laundry service available.
FACILITIES: 6 en suite (3 fmly) No smoking in bedrooms No smoking in dining room No smoking in lounges STV TVB tea/coffee Direct dial from bedrooms Cen ht **PRICES:** s €32 - €55; d €56 - €84 **LB** **PARKING:** 6 **NOTES:** Closed 22-26 Dec **CARDS:**

♦♦♦♦ GH Corrib Haven

107 Upper Newcastle ☎ 091 524171 & 524711 📠 091 524171
e-mail: corribhaven@eircom.net
Dir: *from Galway on N59, follow signs for Clifden until Westwood House Hotel on left side of T-junct. Turn right at junct, Corrib Haven on right*

A new, purpose-built guest house on the N9 route to Connemara, close to the university. The excellent bedrooms all have private bathrooms, and ample car parking is provided.
FACILITIES: 9 en suite No smoking STV TVB Direct dial from bedrooms No dogs Cen ht TVL No children 12yrs **PRICES:** s €32 - €80; d €50 - €80✳ **PARKING:** 13 **CARDS:**

♦♦♦♦ T&C Four Winds Lodge

Gentian Hill, Salthill ☎ 091 526026
e-mail: fourwindslodge@ireland.com
Dir: *Galway golf club on right, pass Statoil petrol station on right, next turning right next to Gentian Villas apartments*

A large, old world home set in its own grounds overlooking lovely gardens. Bernie Power very much enjoys looking after her guests and has created a delightful ambience in her very inviting conservatory. Bedrooms all have new bathrooms and there is off-street parking.
FACILITIES: 4 en suite (3 fmly) No smoking STV TVB tea/coffee No dogs (ex guide dogs) Cen ht **PRICES:** d €46 - €80✳ **LB** **PARKING:** 5 **NOTES:** Closed 24-27 Dec **CARDS:**

Super supper! this symbol shows that evening meals exceeded our Inspector's expectations.

GALWAY continued

♦♦♦♦ GH *Marian Lodge*

Knocknacarra Rd, Salthill Upper ☎ 091 521678 📠 091 528103
e-mail: celine@iol.ie

Dir: *from Galway proceed to Salthill R336. Through Salthill, take 1st right after Spinnaker Hotel into Knocknacarra Rd. Marian Lodge 1st on left*

A large modern house only 50 yards from the seafront on Knocknacarra Road in Upper Salthill. The fully equipped bedrooms have orthopedic beds and en suite facilities. There is also a lounge and separate breakfast room available.

FACILITIES: 6 en suite (4 fmly) No smoking STV TVB tea/coffee Direct dial from bedrooms No dogs Cen ht TVL **PARKING:** 10 **NOTES:** Closed 23-28 Dec **CARDS:**

♦♦♦♦ T&C *Sunrise Lodge*

3 Ocean Wave, Dr Colohan Rd, Salthill ☎ 091 527275 📠 091 583130
e-mail: kheery@eircom.net

Dir: *entrance beside Cois Cuan apartments before Seapoint*

A luxurious new house looking out over Galway Bay and the eastern end of the promenade at Salthill. All rooms are en suite and decorated and furnished to a very high standard with balconies where guests can sit and enjoy the sea views.

FACILITIES: 6 annexe en suite (2 fmly) No smoking in bedrooms No smoking in dining room No smoking in 1 lounge STV TVB tea/coffee Direct dial from bedrooms No dogs (ex guide dogs) Cen ht TVL **PARKING:** 10 **CARDS:**

♦♦♦ T&C Four Seasons

23 College Rd ☎ 091 564078 📠 091 569765
e-mail: 4season@gofree.indigo.ie

Dir: *from E or S take left turn off motorway, following signs for Galway City East, then city centre. 5th house right after sports ground/greyhound track*

This comfortable house adjacent to the city centre is the family home of Eddie and Helen Fitzgerald who will immediately make you feel at home and help you with itineraries, sight seeing and will recommend restaurants for evening meals.

FACILITIES: 5 en suite 2 annexe en suite (3 fmly) No smoking in 3 bedrooms No smoking in dining room No smoking in lounges STV TVB tea/coffee No dogs (ex guide dogs) Cen ht TVL **PRICES:** s €40 - €65; d €70 - €90✳ **PARKING:** 7 **CARDS:**

♦♦♦ T&C *Rhondda*

Barna Rd ☎ 091 526561

Dir: *from Salthill Promenade travel 400mtrs to T-junct and turn left, house 250mtrs on right*

This handsome, yellow-painted house is set back at a layby from the Barna road, near the Salthill road. A new extension houses bedrooms with modern shower rooms, and most have sea views. The dining room, with separate tables, is adjacent to a comfortable lounge, and there is ample parking in front of and behind the hotel.

continued

Rhondda

FACILITIES: 4 en suite (1 fmly) No smoking in 2 bedrooms No smoking in dining room No smoking in lounges STV TVB tea/coffee No dogs (ex guide dogs) Cen ht TVL **PARKING:** 8 **NOTES:** Closed Nov-Est

♦♦♦ T&C Woodhaven Lodge

20 Woodhaven, Merlin Park, Dublin Rd ☎ 091 753806
e-mail: woodhavenlodge@eircom.net

Dir: *off N6, between Corrib Great Southern Hotel and Merlin Park Hospital*

A large modern redbrick building offering comfortable en suite accommodation with a pleasing outlook. Guests can relax in one of the two inviting lounges.

FACILITIES: 4 en suite (1 fmly) No smoking STV TVB tea/coffee No dogs (ex guide dogs) Cen ht TVL No children 3yrs **PRICES:** s €38.50 - €55; d €45 - €80✳ **PARKING:** 4 **NOTES:** Closed 21-29 Dec **CARDS:**

♦ T&C *Swallow*

98 Fr Griffin Rd ☎ 091 589073 📠 091 589175

A large modern house with annexe to the rear, in a quiet residential area close to the city centre, that offers comfortable en suite rooms. The breakfast room opens onto a patio, where guests can eat outdoors on fine summer mornings.

FACILITIES: 6 en suite 4 annexe en suite (2 fmly) No smoking in area of dining room STV TVB tea/coffee No dogs (ex guide dogs) Cen ht **PARKING:** 7 **CARDS:**

KYLEMORE — Map 01 A4

♦♦♦ T&C Kylemore House

☎ 095 41143 📠 095 41143
e-mail: kylemorehouse@eircom.net

Dir: *turn off N59 from Galway at Recess onto R344*

Standing on the shores of Lake Kylemore, protected by the Twelve Pins Mountains, this comfortable house has fishing rights on three lakes in a very scenic area of Connemara. Owner Mrs Naughton takes pride in her cooking and serves evening meals by prior arrangement.

FACILITIES: 6 en suite (1 fmly) No smoking in bedrooms No smoking in dining room No smoking in 1 lounge tea/coffee No dogs (ex guide dogs) Licensed Cen ht TVL No children 10yrs Fishing Boat hire for fishing Dinner Last d 4pm **PRICES:** s €38.50 - €45; d €56 - €68✳ **PARKING:** 8 **NOTES:** Closed Nov-Mar **CARDS:**

LEENANE — Map 01 A4

♦♦♦♦ GH Killary Lodge

☎ 095 42276 & 42245 📠 095 42314
e-mail: lodge@killary.com

Dir: *From Leenane, take N59 towards Clifden for approx 3m. As the road turns away from Killary Harbour, there is a sign for Killary Lodge in the trees on the right. Turn R and it's approx 0.75m to lodge*

continued

In a spectacular setting, overlooking the only fjord in Ireland, Killary Lodge features hand-crafted beech furniture and home cooking in an informal, relaxed atmosphere. A wide range of outdoor pursuits is available nearby, including archery, tennis, orienteering, hill walking, and sailing.
FACILITIES: 12 en suite 9 annexe en suite (8 fmly) (3 GF) No smoking in dining room Direct dial from bedrooms No dogs (ex guide dogs) Licensed Cen ht Tennis (hard) Sauna Mountain biking Rock climbing sailing kayaking Dinner Last d 8pm **PRICES:** s €41 - €75; d €82 - €100* **LB**
CONF: Class 35 Del from €98 * **PARKING:** 30 **CARDS:**

OUGHTERARD Map 01 B4

Premier Collection

♦♦♦♦♦ GH River Run Lodge
Glann Rd ☎ 091 552697 📠 091 552669
e-mail: rivrun@indigo.ie
Dir: *N59 from Galway turn right in Oughterard Square into Camp St. 250yds turn left across Owenriff Bridge. Lodge 2nd on right after 250yds*

The airy and well equipped bedrooms at this newly-built lodge offer comfortable armchairs, luxurious bath/shower rooms and lots of thoughtful extras. An intimate restaurant serves a range of interesting dishes and the lovely landscaped gardens are edged by the river.
FACILITIES: 8 en suite (3 fmly) (2 GF) No smoking in bedrooms No smoking in dining room No smoking in 1 lounge STV TVB tea/coffee Direct dial from bedrooms No dogs (ex guide dogs) Licensed Cen ht TVL No coaches Dinner Last d 9.30pm **PRICES:** s €45 - €52; d €65 - €110* **LB PARKING:** 20 **NOTES:** Closed 24-28 Dec rs Jan
CARDS:

Premier Collection

♦♦♦♦♦ T&C Waterfall Lodge
☎ 091 552168
e-mail: kdolly@eircom.net
Dir: *on N59, 1st house on left after Sweeneys Hotel*
An elegant period residence beside a river and waterfall, with private fishing. Set in an idyllic location, yet close to the village, the house has antique furnishings, wooden floors, and log fires. The en suite bedrooms are all well appointed and equipped, and the owner, Mrs Dolly, ensures a warm welcome. Activities available nearby include pony trekking, mountain climbing, golf and fishing, and there are plenty of pubs and restaurants.
FACILITIES: 6 en suite (2 fmly) No smoking TVB No dogs Cen ht TVL No coaches Fishing **PRICES:** d €64* **PARKING:** 8

♦♦♦ GH The Boat Inn
The Square ☎ 091 552196 📠 091 552694
e-mail: info@theboatinn.com
Dir: *on N59 Galway to Clifden road in centre of Oughterard*
This popular guest house, bar and bistro is located in the centre of the village close to the famous Lough Corrib. Excellent sea, lake and river fishing is available in the area, which also offers a choice of golf courses and other outdoor pursuits. In season, live Irish music is provided most evenings.
FACILITIES: 11 en suite (4 fmly) TVB tea/coffee Direct dial from bedrooms No dogs (ex guide dogs) Licensed Cen ht TVL Dinner Last d 9pm **PRICES:** s €39 - €45; d €64 - €76* **LB PARKING:** 5
NOTES: Closed 25 Dec **CARDS:**

♦♦♦ T&C *Lakeland Country House*
Portacarron Bay ☎ 091 552121 & 552146 📠 091 552146
e-mail: mayfly@eircom.net
Dir: *off N59 20 mins from Galway take 2nd right after Oughterard Golf Club sign. From Maam Cross through Oughterard, pass Gateway Hotel next left, house on lake shore*
Situated on the shores of the lough, this comfortable house offers a spacious TV lounge, and a fine dining room with views across the water. Fishing and boat trips can be arranged, and dinner is available.
FACILITIES: 9 rms (8 en suite) (3 fmly) No smoking in bedrooms No smoking in dining room tea/coffee No dogs Licensed Cen ht TVL Fishing
PARKING: 20 **NOTES:** Closed 10 Dec-16 Jan **CARDS:**

ROUNDSTONE Map 01 A4

♦♦♦♦ T&C Ivy Rock House
Letterdyfe ☎ 095 35872 📠 095 35959
e-mail: ivyrockhouse@eircom.net
Overlooking Bertraghboy Bay this yellow-painted house has been decorated to a high standard and provides comfortable accommodation. Public rooms include two adjoining reception rooms and a first floor sitting room. Bedrooms are of a good size. There are good restaurants nearby.
FACILITIES: 6 en suite (4 fmly) No smoking TV4B No dogs Cen ht TVL Riding locally Last d 3pm **PARKING:** 10 **NOTES:** Closed Oct-Mar **CARDS:**

SPIDDAL Map 01 B3

♦♦♦♦ T&C Ardmor Country House
Greenhill ☎ 091 553145 📠 091 553596
e-mail: ardmor@yahoo.com
Dir: *on R336 coast road out of Galway. 1km west of Spiddal*

A luxury, split-level bungalow with superb views of Galway Bay and the Aran Islands. That offers spacious en suite bedrooms. There are two fine lounges, a well stocked library and a pleasant garden that guests may use. Mrs Feeney has won awards for her breakfasts.
FACILITIES: 7 en suite (4 fmly) No smoking TVB tea/coffee No dogs Cen ht TVL **PRICES:** s €40 - €45; d €56 - €60* **PARKING:** 20
NOTES: Closed Jan-Feb **CARDS:**

Ireland

SPIDDAL continued

♦♦♦♦ T&C Suan Na Mara

Stripe, Furbo ☎ 091 591512 🖷 091 591632
e-mail: brian@suannamara.com
Dir: *R336 coastal route from Salthill via Barna village, turn right at Furbo church, 200mtrs on left*

This modern house stands next to a church between the villages of Furbo and Spiddal. There are two comfortable ground-floor rooms, with family rooms occupying the first floor. The adjoining sitting and dining rooms look out towards Galway Bay in the distance; booking in advance for dinner is appreciated. There are beaches and golf courses nearby, and ferries to the Aran Islands.

FACILITIES: 4 en suite (1 fmly) No smoking STV TVB tea/coffee No dogs (ex guide dogs) Cen ht Dinner Last d 2pm **PRICES:** s €50; d €75✻ **LB PARKING:** 10 **NOTES:** Closed 23 Dec-Jan **CARDS:**

♦♦♦♦ T&C Tuar Beag

Tuar Beag ☎ 091 553422 🖷 091 553010
e-mail: tuarbeagbandb@eircom.net
Dir: *on western edge of Spiddal on R336 coastal road*

Tuar Beag is a prominent house, much extended from the original 19th-century cottage where four generations of the proprietor's family grew up. The original stone walls and fireplace have been retained and the house now offers excellent accommodation overlooking Galway Bay and the Aran Islands. Breakfast is a notable feature.

FACILITIES: 6 en suite (6 fmly) No smoking in bedrooms No smoking in dining room TVB tea/coffee No dogs Cen ht TVL No children 2yrs **PRICES:** s €25.50 - €40; d €51-€56✻ **PARKING:** 20 **NOTES:** Closed 16 Nov-Jan

♦♦♦ T&C Ard Aoibhinn

☎ 091 553179 🖷 091 553179
e-mail: aoibhinn@gofree.indigo.ie
Dir: *1km west of Spiddal village on R336 coast road*

This establishment is a modern bungalow set back from the road in a lovely garden. Fine views are to be seen over Galway Bay and to the Aran Islands.

FACILITIES: 5 en suite (3 fmly) (5 GF) No smoking TVB tea/coffee No dogs (ex guide dogs) Cen ht TVL **PRICES:** d €51✻ **LB PARKING:** 6 **CARDS:**

♦♦♦ GH *Tigh Chualain*

Kilroe East ☎ 091 553609 & 553725 🖷 091 553049
Dir: *on R336 coast road out of Galway. 3 km West of Spiddal village*

This family-run guest house is attatched to a pub, where Irish music sessions take place during the season. Bedrooms are spacious and comfortable, most enjoying spectacular sea views. There is a comfortable lounge and guests can enjoy a hearty breakfast in the cosy dining room.

FACILITIES: 9 en suite (7 fmly) No smoking TVB Direct dial from bedrooms No dogs (ex guide dogs) Cen ht TVL No coaches **PARKING:** 20 **NOTES:** Closed Nov-Mar

CO KERRY

CAHERDANIEL — Map 01 A2

♦♦♦ T&C Derrynane Bay House

☎ 066 9475404 🖷 066 9475436
e-mail: derrynanebayhouse@eircom.net
Dir: *1km on Waterville side of Caherdaniel village on N70 overlooking Derrynane Bay*

Set back from the main road, this meticulously maintained house is in an elevated position with views over Derrynane Bay. Tastefully furnished throughout, there is a comfortable sitting and dining room and attractive bedrooms. The owner is very welcoming and offers a good breakfast menu. Walking, watersports, good beaches, fishing and golf are all nearby.

FACILITIES: 6 en suite (2 fmly) (4 GF) No smoking in bedrooms No smoking in dining room STV TVB tea/coffee Direct dial from bedrooms No dogs (ex guide dogs) Cen ht TVL No coaches Various facilities available locally Dinner Last d noon **PRICES:** s €40; d €60-€66✻ **PARKING:** 10 **NOTES:** Closed 24-29 Dec rs 30 Dec-mid Mar **CARDS:**

CAMP — Map 01 A2

♦♦♦♦ T&C *Barnagh Bridge Country House*

☎ 066 7130145 🖷 066 7130299
e-mail: bbguest@eircom.net
Dir: *leave N86 Tralee/Dingle road at Camp. Follow Conor Pass road for 1km*

Barnagh Bridge is in a perfect position to enjoy the northern side of the Dingle peninsula with its unspoilt beaches, ancient sites and powerful natural beauty. The house is cleverly designed to take full advantage of the views of Tralee Bay. The bedrooms are named after flowers of the area and their colours are reflected in the decor. Local amenities include golf, hill walking, fresh water and deep sea angling.

FACILITIES: 5 en suite (2 fmly) No smoking in bedrooms No smoking in dining room STV TVB tea/coffee Direct dial from bedrooms No dogs (ex guide dogs) Cen ht TVL No children 10yrs No coaches **PARKING:** 7 **NOTES:** Closed Nov-mid Mar **CARDS:**

♦♦♦♦ GH Suan Na Mara

Lisnagree, Castlegregory Rd ☎ 066 7139258 🖷 066 7139258
e-mail: suanmara@eircom.net
Dir: *leave N86 Tralee/Dingle road at Camp and follow the Conor Pass road for 2.5km*

This beautifully appointed Laura Ashley-style home is maintained to a very high standard. Situated on the Atlantic coast, set between mountains and unspoilt sandy beaches, it offers cosy, comfortable bedrooms and an excellent and extensive breakfast menu. Local restaurants, hill walking, forest walks, pony trekking and windsurfing are all available nearby.

FACILITIES: 7 en suite No smoking TV6B tea/coffee No dogs (ex guide dogs) Cen ht TVL Putting green **PRICES:** s €36 - €41; d €58 - €65✻ **PARKING:** 8 **NOTES:** Closed Nov-16 Mar **CARDS:**

CASTLEGREGORY — Map 01 A2

Premier Collection

♦♦♦♦♦ T&C *Shores Country House*

Cappatigue ☎ 066 7139196 🖷 066 7139196
e-mail: theshores@eircom.net
Dir: *on Connor Pass Rd, 1.5m W of Stradbally*

This charming house enjoys panoramic views of the Dingle Peninsula. Bedrooms, one with a balcony, are tastefully decorated. Guests can relax in the comfortable lounge and library and afternoon tea is served on the patio. An interesting home-cooked dinner menu, served in the attractive dining room, features fresh local produce.

FACILITIES: 6 en suite (2 fmly) No smoking TVB tea/coffee Direct dial from bedrooms No dogs Cen ht TVL Library Dinner Last d 6pm **PARKING:** 8 **NOTES:** Closed Dec & Jan **CARDS:**

Ireland

♦♦♦♦ T&C Sea-Mount House

Cappatigue, Conor Pass Rd ☎ 066 7139229 📠 066 7139229
e-mail: seamount@unison.ie
Dir: *On Conor Pass road, 1.5m W of Stradbally Village*
This house, between Tralee and Dingle on the Conor Pass road, overlooks Brandon Bay and is an ideal base for touring the Dingle Peninsula. Bedrooms are attractively decorated and the cosy sitting area enjoys spectacular views. Tea and home-baking are served in the garden on arrival.
FACILITIES: 3 en suite (1 fmly) (2 GF) No smoking TVB tea/coffee No dogs (ex guide dogs) Cen ht TVL No coaches **PRICES:** s €40 - €45; d €60 - €66✱ **LB PARKING:** 5 **NOTES:** Closed Dec-Feb **CARDS:**

♦♦♦♦ T&C Strand View House

Kilcummin, Conor Pass Rd ☎ 066 7138131 📠 066 7138386
e-mail: strandview@eircom.net
Dir: *20m from Tralee on the Dingle, Conor Pass road 1.5m W of Stradbally*
A superb brick house two miles west of Stradbally on the Castlegregory to Conor Pass road. Luxury bedrooms enjoy panoramic sea views over Kilcummin beach, and there is a terraced rock garden to the rear in which to relax. Mrs Lynch is a charming hostess who loves to entertain her guests.
FACILITIES: 5 en suite (2 fmly) (1 GF) No smoking STV TVB tea/coffee No dogs (ex guide dogs) Cen ht TVL No coaches **PRICES:** s €35 - €50; d €58 - €60✱ **PARKING:** 12 **CARDS:**

♦♦♦ Griffin's Tip-Top Country Farmhouse *(Q 525085)*

Goulane, Conor Pass Rd ☎ 066 7139147 📠 066 7139073
Mrs Catherine Griffin
e-mail: griffinstiptopfarmhouse@eircom.net
Dir: *1m from Stradbally village*
Situated only a short distance from a golf club and a Blue Flag beach, one of the many unspoilt beaches along the coastline of the Dingle Peninsula. Mrs Griffin believes in a warm welcome, good beds and home baking to keep her guests happy. The dining room offers a panorama of Tralee Bay.
FACILITIES: 8 rms (6 en suite) (3 fmly) No smoking Cen ht TVL 150 acres sheep **PRICES:** s fr €38; d fr €64✱ **PARKING:** 10 **NOTES:** Closed 2 Nov-Feb **CARDS:**

DINGLE — Map 01 A2

Premier Collection

♦♦♦♦♦ GH Emlagh House

Emlagh House ☎ 066 9152345 & 9152353 📠 066 9152369
e-mail: info@emlaghhouse.com
Dir: *N72/R563/R561 Emlagh House is just past petrol station at entrance to town turn left & house ahead*
Impressive Georgian-style house, set in its own grounds. Attention to detail and luxury combine to make a stay here memorable. Superb drawing room and dining room overlook the harbour, where Dingle's famous dolphin, Fungie, may appear. Bedrooms and bathrooms are excellent, some have private patios. Parking available.
FACILITIES: 10 en suite (1 fmly) (4 GF) No smoking in bedrooms STV TVB Direct dial from bedrooms No dogs Licensed Lift Cen ht No children 8yrs **PRICES:** s €125 - €135; d €180 - €210✱ **PARKING:** 20 **NOTES:** Closed mid Dec-mid Feb **CARDS:**

Premier Collection

♦♦♦♦♦ GH *Milltown House*

Milltown ☎ 066 9151372 📠 066 9151095
e-mail: milltown@indigo.ie
Dir: *1.5km W of Dingle on Slea Head road, cross Milltown Bridge and turn left*
Situated on a sea channel to the west of town, the house has been elegantly refurbished and has a warm inviting atmosphere, Mr Kerry making guests feel really welcome. Bedrooms are all en suite, have attractive decor and are well equipped. There is also a cosy sitting room leading to a conservatory.
FACILITIES: 10 en suite (1 fmly) No smoking STV TVB tea/coffee Direct dial from bedrooms No dogs (ex guide dogs) Cen ht No children 5yrs No coaches **PARKING:** 10 **NOTES:** Closed Dec & Jan
CARDS:

Premier Collection

♦♦♦♦♦ GH *Gormans Clifftop House & Restaurant*

Glaise Bheag, Ballydavid ☎ 066 9155162 📠 066 9155162
e-mail: gormans@eircom.net
Dir: *From Dingle, take Harbour road to rdbt W of town, straight across signed An Feothanach 8m to coast*
In a superb location overlooking Smerwick Harbour, this traditional stone-fronted building offers marvellous hospitality and comfort. The lounges and restaurant enjoy stunning views, and the food is excellent. Bedrooms are most inviting, and one is adapted for the less mobile.
FACILITIES: 9 en suite (2 fmly) No smoking in bedrooms No smoking in dining room TVB Direct dial from bedrooms No dogs (ex guide dogs) Licensed Cen ht Jacuzzi Dinner Last d 9pm
PARKING: 15 **NOTES:** Closed 11 Jan-Feb **CARDS:**

Premier Collection

♦♦♦♦♦ GH Greenmount House

☎ 066 9151414 📠 066 9151974
e-mail: mary@greenmounthouse.com
Dir: *on entering town turn right at rdbt & next right at T-junct*
Greenmount has a reputation for comfort and hospitality, and offers a splendid extension containing six mini-suites, all overlooking Dingle Harbour. These bedrooms are spacious, with split-level lounge areas, and quality furnishings and decor. The original bedrooms are just as comfortable. A conservatory-style dining room and two sitting rooms are provided for guests, and the town centre is only a five minute walk away.
FACILITIES: 12 en suite No smoking in bedrooms No smoking in dining room No smoking in 1 lounge STV TVB tea/coffee Direct dial from bedrooms No dogs (ex guide dogs) Cen ht TVL No children 8yrs No coaches **PRICES:** s €50; d €75 - €125✱ **PARKING:** 12
NOTES: Closed 21-26 Dec **CARDS:**

DINGLE continued

Premier Collection

♦♦♦♦♦ GH *Pax House*

Upper John St ☎ 066 9151518 & 9151650 📠 066 9152461
e-mail: paxhouse@iol.ie
Dir: *turn right off N86 at Pax House finger sign, establishment 1km on left*

Pax House is a peaceful detached house in a acre of ground with stunning views of Dingle Bay. The patio off the sitting room is very popular with guests, with a hospitality trolley nearby and fine garden views. Bedrooms are very comfortable and the bathrooms are excellent. Above all, the hospitality and generosity of Joan and Ron Brosnan-Wright will make guests wish to return.
FACILITIES: 12 en suite (2 fmly) No smoking in bedrooms No smoking in dining room No smoking in 1 lounge STV TVB tea/coffee Direct dial from bedrooms Licensed Cen ht **PARKING:** 14 **NOTES:** Closed Dec & Jan **CARDS:**

♦♦♦♦ GH *Heatons*

The Wood ☎ 066 9152288 📠 066 9152324
e-mail: heatons@iol.ie

A family run guest house located on the waterfront and near the town. Most bedrooms have views of Dingle Bay and are very comfortable and well appointed. Guests can also enjoy the views and relax in the spacious foyer lounge. The breakfast room is brightly decorated and offers an impressive carte.
FACILITIES: 16 en suite (2 fmly) No smoking in bedrooms No smoking in dining room STV TVB tea/coffee Direct dial from bedrooms No dogs Cen ht No children 8yrs **PARKING:** 16 **CARDS:**

♦♦♦♦ T&C Alpine

Mail Rd ☎ 066 9151250 📠 066 9151966
e-mail: alpinedingle@eircom.net
Dir: *on right on N86 at entrance to town*

On the edge of Dingle, this large, attractive three-storey guest house is run by the O'Shea family, who maintain excellent standards. The elegantly furnished bedrooms have large, spacious bathrooms. There is a private car park, and the guest house is just two minutes walk from the town centre.
FACILITIES: 10 en suite (3 fmly) No smoking in bedrooms No smoking in dining room STV TVB tea/coffee Direct dial from bedrooms No dogs (ex guide dogs) Cen ht TVL No children 5yrs No coaches **PRICES:** s €30 - €65; d €60 - €100 **PARKING:** 15 **CARDS:**

♦♦♦♦ T&C Bambury's

Mail Rd ☎ 066 9151244 📠 066 9151786
e-mail: info@bamburysguesthouse.com
Dir: *on left on entering Dingle town on N86, past Shell Station*

Set on the edge of Dingle, this pink house is eyecatching on the outside and attractive on the inside with pretty decor and comfortable appointments. There is a cosy lounge and a spacious dining room. En suite bedrooms are excellent with pine furnishings, pottery lamps, tea/coffee trays and big showers.
FACILITIES: 12 en suite (1 fmly) No smoking in bedrooms No smoking in dining room No smoking in 1 lounge STV TVB tea/coffee Direct dial from bedrooms No dogs Cen ht TVL No children 4yrs **PRICES:** s €35 - €60; d €64 - €90✳ **PARKING:** 12 **CARDS:**

♦♦♦♦ GH *Cleevaun*

Lady's Cross, Milltown ☎ 066 9151108 📠 066 9152228
e-mail: cleevaun@aol.ie
Dir: *R559 from Tralee to Dingle follow sign for Slea Head scenic route*

Overlooking Dingle Bay, this luxurious bungalow offers attractive bedrooms with pine furniture, and the opportunity of enjoying Mrs Cluskey's breakfast menu which caters for a wide range of tastes. The house is about seven minutes' drive from town.
FACILITIES: 9 en suite No smoking STV TVB tea/coffee Direct dial from bedrooms No dogs (ex guide dogs) Cen ht TVL No children 3yrs **PARKING:** 9 **NOTES:** Closed mid Dec-mid Jan **CARDS:**

♦♦♦♦ GH *Doyles Town House*

Ireland's Blue Book

4 John St ☎ 066 9151174 📠 066 9151816
e-mail: cdoyles@iol.ie
Dir: *in the heart of Dingle town*

A charming town house, with spacious well equipped bedrooms, all tastefully styled with period furnishings and marble-tiled bathrooms. The owners' seafood restaurant adjoins the house.
FACILITIES: 8 en suite No smoking in bedrooms No smoking in area of dining room STV TVB tea/coffee Direct dial from bedrooms No dogs (ex guide dogs) Licensed Cen ht Dinner Last d 10pm **NOTES:** Closed mid Nov-mid Mar **CARDS:**

♦♦♦♦ T&C Mount Eagle Lodge

Ventry ☎ 066 9159754 📠 066 9159754
e-mail: lodging@iol.ie
Dir: *at 2nd rdbt in Dingle take R559 Slea Head Drive, follow coastal road for 3.9m. Lodge on right, with eagles on gate posts*

This welcoming home commands spectacular views of Ventry Bay from bedrooms, the sun lounge and the dining room. A tranquil setting where a relaxed stay is guaranteed, together with an enjoyable breakfast. Local maps and guide books are available for guests' use.
FACILITIES: 4 en suite (3 fmly) (1 GF) No smoking TVB tea/coffee No dogs (ex guide dogs) Cen ht TVL No children 5yrs No coaches **PRICES:** s €38.50 - €45; d €60 - €80✳ **PARKING:** 10 **NOTES:** Closed Nov-Etr **CARDS:**

♦♦♦ T&C *Dingle Heights*

Ballinaboola ☎ 066 9151543
e-mail: dingleheights@hotmail.com
Dir: *up main street for 1km to hospital, 180mtrs - house 4th on right*

Set high overlooking Dingle Bay, this house features comfortable, well-appointed accommodation and the charming hospitality of owner Mrs Fitzgerald.

continued

FACILITIES: 4 en suite (4 fmly) No smoking in bedrooms No smoking in dining room No smoking in 1 lounge No dogs Cen ht TVL **PARKING:** 10

♦♦♦ Hurleys *(Q 392080)*

An Dooneen, Kilcooley ☎ 066 9155112 Ms Mary Hurley
e-mail: andooneen@eircom.net

Hurleys Farm is tucked away behind the church in Kilcooley, a mile from the beach and sheltered by Mount Brandon, a popular place for hill walkers. Accommodation includes a cosy TV room, dining room and comfortable en suite bedrooms, graced by some special pieces of high quality furniture. The whole area is rich in early historic and prehistoric relics: ogham stones, ring forts and the famous dry-stone masonry 'beehive' huts. Dingle and Tralee are within walking distance.

FACILITIES: 4 en suite No smoking in bedrooms No smoking in dining room No smoking in 1 lounge No dogs (ex guide dogs) Cen ht TVL 32 acres mixed **PRICES:** s €27 - €35; d €54 - €60* **PARKING:** 6 **NOTES:** Closed Nov-Etr

♦♦ T&C *Ballyegan House*

Upper John St ☎ 066 9151702

Dir: *on entering Dingle from Killarney/Tralee road turn right at rdbt & right at next junct. Premises at top of John St on left, overlooking Dingle Bay*

This large, two-storey house enjoys a quiet position just a short walk of the town centre, and has spectacular views to the front over Dingle Bay. Bedrooms and public areas are comfortable, and there is a large private car park.

FACILITIES: 6 en suite (4 fmly) No smoking TVB No dogs Cen ht TVL No coaches **PARKING:** 8

GLENBEIGH — Map 01 A2

♦♦♦♦ T&C Ocean Wave

☎ 066 9768249 Fax 066 9768412
e-mail: oceanwave@iol.ie

Dir: *on N70 from Killorglin, 1km before Glenbeigh, on left*

An impressive dormer bungalow set in landscaped gardens overlooking Dingle Bay. Bedrooms are comfortable and well appointed, and the large first floor lounge enjoys delightful panoramic views across the bay.

FACILITIES: 6 en suite No smoking in bedrooms No smoking in dining room STV TVB tea/coffee No dogs Cen ht TVL No coaches **PRICES:** s €45; d €70* **PARKING:** 6 **NOTES:** Closed Nov-Feb **CARDS:**

KENMARE — Map 01 B2

Premier Collection

♦♦♦♦♦ T&C *Sallyport House*

Glengarriff Rd ☎ 064 42066 Fax 064 42067
e-mail: port@iol.ie

Dir: *400mtrs S on N71*

continued

A superbly refurbished house, built for the Arthur family in 1932 and still owned by the family. Set in its own grounds and luxuriously appointed, the house is just a few minutes' walk from the town. Guests will appreciate the tranquil atmosphere of a house which has attractively decorated bedrooms, furnished with antiques, including a four-poster room. The comfortable sitting room has a roaring fire during the winter months.

FACILITIES: 5 en suite (2 fmly) No smoking STV TVB tea/coffee Direct dial from bedrooms No dogs (ex guide dogs) Cen ht No children 10yrs **PARKING:** 10 **NOTES:** Closed Nov-Mar

♦♦♦♦ GH Davitts

Henry St ☎ 064 42741 Fax 064 42757
e-mail: info@davitts-kenmare.com

Dir: *N22 Cork-Killarney rd. Take Kenmare junct (R569). Centrally located in town of Kenmare*

Newly refurbished to a high standard, this town centre guest house offers contemporary, well appointed bedrooms. The restaurant and bar are popular venues, serving a ranges of meals until 9.30pm daily. There is a car park at the rear, and directions will be given on booking.

FACILITIES: No smoking in bedrooms No smoking in area of dining room No smoking in lounges STV TV available Direct dial from bedrooms No dogs (ex guide dogs) Licensed Cen ht Dinner Last d 9.50pm **PRICES:** s €45 - €60; d €68 - €90* **CARDS:**

♦♦♦♦ GH Sea Shore Farm

Tubrid ☎ 064 41270 & 41675 Fax 064 41270
e-mail: seashore@eircom.net

Dir: *1m from Kenmare on Sneem Rd N70. Signposted at N70/N71 junct, Ring of Kerry-Killarney road*

Lovely views of Kenmare Bay can be enjoyed from the spacious rooms of this modern bungalow, which stands in its own grounds on the edge of town. One bedroom has a drive-in shower suitable for wheelchair users. There is a large comfortable sitting room and also a new fitness/steam room.

FACILITIES: 6 en suite (2 fmly) (2 GF) No smoking TVB tea/coffee Direct dial from bedrooms No dogs (ex guide dogs) Cen ht Tennis Private shore **PRICES:** d €80 - €120* **PARKING:** 10 **NOTES:** Closed 21Nov-28Feb **CARDS:**

♦♦♦ GH Ashberry Lodge

Sneem Rd (N70) ☎ 064 42720
e-mail: ashberry@iolfree.ie

Dir: *take N71 out of Kenmare town, left onto N70 (Sneem Rd) 2nd on left after Kenmare Bay*

A newly built family-run guest house, just two km from the town centre, on a two acre site with a pond and pretty garden. Bedrooms are spacious and well appointed. The guest sitting room and dining room are attractively decorated and an interesting breakfast menu is offered. Ideally located at the beginning of the famous Ring of Kerry.

FACILITIES: 8 en suite (1 fmly) No smoking in bedrooms No smoking in dining room TVB tea/coffee No dogs (ex guide dogs) Cen ht **PRICES:** s €37.50 - €42.50; d €55 - €65* **PARKING:** 10 **CARDS:**

Prices may change during the currency of the Guide, please check when booking.

Ireland

KENMARE continued

♦♦♦ T&C *Harbour View*

Castletownbere Rd, Dauros ☎ 064 41755 📠 064 42611
e-mail: maureenmccarthy@eircom.net
Dir: *from Kenmare towards Glengurriffe take Castletownbere Haven Rd 571, 1st right after bridge, Harbour View 4m on left on seashore*

A dormer-style house on the seashore, with lovely views of Kenmare Bay and the mountains beyond. Mrs Maureen McCarthy is a cheerful, caring hostess with infectious enthusiasm, and her attention to detail is evident throughout this house. Bedrooms are attractively decorated, and are either en suite or have sole use of a bathroom. Dinner is available when pre-booked, and the home-baking is excellent.

FACILITIES: 4 en suite (3 fmly) No smoking in 1 bedrooms No smoking in dining room STV TVB tea/coffee No dogs Cen ht TVL Dinner Last d 8pm
PARKING: 6 **NOTES:** Closed Nov-Feb

KILGARVAN — Map 01 B2

♦♦♦♦ T&C Birchwood

Church Ground ☎ 064 85473 📠 064 85570
e-mail: info@birchwood-kilgarvan.com
Dir: *500mtrs E of Kilgarvon on R569*

Situated in 1.5 acres of gardens, facing a natural forest and backed by the Mangerton Mountains in an area ideal for hill-walking and touring. The MacDonnells are caring hosts in this tranquil location who offer comfortable and attractively decorated bedrooms. Dinner is available, and the nearby Rivers Roughty and Slaheny provide good salmon and trout fishing.

FACILITIES: 5 en suite (3 fmly) No smoking TVB tea/coffee No dogs (ex guide dogs) Cen ht TVL Fishing Dinner Last d 6.30pm
PRICES: s €33; d €52* **PARKING:** 6

KILLARNEY — Map 01 B2

Premier Collection

♦♦♦♦♦ GH Earls Court House

Woodlawn Junction, Muckross Rd ☎ 064 34009
📠 064 34366
e-mail: info@killarney-earlscourt.it
Dir: *on Muckross Road turn off at traffic lights*

A distinctive yellow building, contemporary in design and purpose-built, with the added facility of balconies adjoining most bedrooms. Elegance and luxury can be seen in the decor and the antique furnishings throughout the house. There is a comfortable lounge where rich fabrics have been used to create a setting for relaxation.

FACILITIES: 19 en suite (3 fmly) No smoking in bedrooms No smoking in dining room No smoking in 1 lounge STV TVB tea/coffee

continued

Earls Court House

Direct dial from bedrooms Licensed Cen ht TVL **PRICES:** s €75 - €110; d €90 - €130* **PARKING:** 19 **NOTES:** Closed 13Nov-11Feb rs 6 Nov-28 Feb (group bookings 8+ only) **CARDS:**

Premier Collection

♦♦♦♦♦ GH Foleys Town House

22/23 High St ☎ 064 31217 📠 064 34683
Dir: *in town centre on right, midway between main street & traffic lights, northbound towards Tralee*

Charming bedrooms with stripped-pine furniture and co-ordinated colour schemes are a feature of this delightful town house, which also offers a cosy lounge, a bar and private car park. It is run by Carol Hartnett who is also head chef at her popular adjoining seafood restaurant.

FACILITIES: 28 en suite No smoking in 5 bedrooms No smoking in area of dining room STV TVB tea/coffee Direct dial from bedrooms No dogs Licensed Cen ht TVL Jacuzzi Dinner Last d 10.30pm
PRICES: s €70 - €85; d €118 - €126* **PARKING:** 60
NOTES: Closed 6 Nov-16 Mar **CARDS:**

Premier Collection

♦♦♦♦♦ GH Kathleen's Country House

Tralee Rd ☎ 064 32810 📠 064 32340
e-mail: info@kathleens.net
Dir: *on N22 3km N*

An exclusive, modern, purpose-built guest house is set in its own lovely gardens one mile from the town centre on the Tralee road. Family-run, luxury accommodation in scenic countryside makes this an ideal touring centre. Bedrooms are elegantly furnished, with antique pine, and excellent bathrooms, and there are five sitting rooms, all enjoying different views. Breakfast is served in the elegant dining room which overlooks the gardens.

continued

Ireland

FACILITIES: 17 en suite (2 fmly) No smoking STV TVB tea/coffee Direct dial from bedrooms No dogs Licensed Cen ht No children 5yrs Croquet lawn Reflexology, Massage aromatheraphy **PRICES:** d €90 - €130 **LB PARKING:** 20 **NOTES:** Closed mid Oct-mid Mar **CARDS:**

Premier Collection

♦♦♦♦♦ GH Old Weir Lodge

Muckross Rd ☎ 064 35593 064 35583
e-mail: oldweirlodge@eircom.net
Dir: *on main Muckross Rd, 500mtrs from Killarney*

Welcoming, purpose-built Tudor-style lodge, set in attractive gardens. Maureen loves to cook and home-baking is a feature of the breakfasts; evening meals, are also available by prior arrangement. Dermot will help with leisure activities such as boat trips on the Killarney Lakes or golf and fishing. The comfortable bedrooms are equipped to a high standard and there is a delightful sitting room overlooking the gardens. There is also a drying room and ample off-street parking.
FACILITIES: 30 en suite (7 fmly) (6 GF) No smoking in 12 bedrooms No smoking in dining room No smoking in lounges STV TVB tea/coffee Direct dial from bedrooms No dogs Licensed Lift Cen ht TVL Dinner Last d 8pm **PRICES:** s €55 - €72; d €76 - €96✳ **PARKING:** 30 **NOTES:** Closed 23-26 Dec **CARDS:**

♦♦♦♦ T&C Applecroft House

Woodlawn Rd ☎ 064 32782
e-mail: applecroft@eircom.net
Dir: *from Killarney take Muckross Rd N71 for 500mtrs, turn left at Shell Filling Station, down Woodlawn Rd for 500 mtrs, signpost on left*
Applecroft is a family home tucked away in a residential area, with beautiful landscaped gardens. Bedrooms are spacious and there is great attention to detail in the decoration. Guests can relax in the lounge or on the patio. The breakfast room overlooks the garden.
FACILITIES: 5 en suite (2 fmly) No smoking in bedrooms No smoking in dining room No smoking in 1 lounge STV TVB No dogs (ex guide dogs) Cen ht TVL **PRICES:** s €38.50 - €50; d €58 - €66✳ **LB PARKING:** 5 **NOTES:** Closed Dec-Feb **CARDS:**

♦♦♦♦ T&C Crystal Springs

Ballycasheen ☎ 064 33272 & 35518 064 35518
e-mail: crystalsprings@eircom.net
Dir: *from Killarney town turn right off Cork Rd at 1st lights & Texaco. Left into Rookery Rd, to end & Crystal Springs is across road at T-junct*
This luxurious purpose-built house stands on the banks of the River Flesk. It overlooks an old historic mill, and is surrounded by the mountains and lakes of Killarney's National Park. All the en suite bedrooms are attractively decorated and very well equipped.

continued

Guests can enjoy fishing and there are three golf courses in Killarney to choose from.

Crystal Springs

FACILITIES: 6 en suite (3 fmly) (3 GF) No smoking in bedrooms No smoking in dining room No smoking in 1 lounge STV TVB tea/coffee Direct dial from bedrooms No dogs Cen ht TVL Fishing All activities within 1mile Dinner Last d 3pm **PRICES:** s €40 - €5; d €60 - €76✳ **LB PARKING:** 10 **CARDS:**

♦♦♦♦ GH *Glena House*

Muckross Rd ☎ 064 32705 & 34284 064 35611
e-mail: glena@iol.ie
Dir: *at Friary church on N22 turn left & left again at cinema. Glena House 550mtrs on right*
Only a few minutes from the town centre, this comfortable guest house offers attractively decorated bedrooms, with pine furnishings and modern facilities. There is a large dining room with an adjoining Wine Bar, and a separate lounge for relaxation.
FACILITIES: 26 en suite (6 fmly) No smoking in 10 bedrooms No smoking in area of dining room STV TVB tea/coffee Direct dial from bedrooms No dogs (ex guide dogs) Licensed Cen ht TVL Library Last d 9pm **PARKING:** 26 **CARDS:**

♦♦♦♦ T&C Killarney Villa

Cork-Mallow/Waterford Rd (N72) ☎ 064 31878 064 31878
e-mail: killarneyvilla@eircom.net
Dir: *N22 from Killarney, through 1st rdbt, continue after 2nd rdbt on N22/N72 (Cork/Mallow road) for 1.3m. Turn left at signpost for Mallow, Killarney Villa 300 mtrs*
A luxurious country home with roof-top conservatory offering complimentary tea/coffee/biscuits from 7am to 11pm daily. Situated in the heart of the beautiful Killarney Lake District and just a few minutes' drive from the town centre. Family run and equipped with all modern comforts, this makes an ideal holiday destination.
FACILITIES: 6 en suite No smoking STV TVB tea/coffee No dogs (ex guide dogs) Cen ht TVL No children 6yrs **PRICES:** s €40; d €60✳ **LB PARKING:** 20 **NOTES:** Closed Nov-Etr **CARDS:**

♦♦♦♦ T&C Shraheen House

Ballycasheen, Off Cork Rd (N22) ☎ 064 31286 064 37959
e-mail: info@shraheenhouse.com
Dir: *on Ballycasheen/Woodlawn road, 1m off N71 turn at Shell station. 0.25m off N22 Cork Rd turn at White Bridge sign*
Located on a quiet road, this large modern house is set in two acres. The bedrooms are all well equipped and have attractive soft furnishings. The quiet gardens and the pleasant sun lounge are very relaxing. Within easy reach of three golf courses or local fishing.
FACILITIES: 6 en suite (2 fmly) No smoking STV TVB tea/coffee No dogs Cen ht TVL **PRICES:** s €40 - €50; d €56 - €62✳ **PARKING:** 8 **NOTES:** Closed Xmas & New Year

KILLARNEY continued

♦♦♦ GH Ashville

Rock Rd ☎ 064 36405 🖷 064 36778
e-mail: ashvillehouse@eircom.net
Dir: *on N22*
Two minutes' walk from the town centre, this inviting house is conveniently situated for all amenities and is easy to find near the approach to the N22 Tralee road. Accommodation is new and purpose-built, offering all the comforts thay make for a pleasant stay, with a relaxing sitting room furnished with deep sofas. There is a private car park behind the house. Tours can be arranged on request.
FACILITIES: 10 en suite (3 fmly) (4 GF) No smoking in 6 bedrooms No smoking in dining room No smoking in lounges STV TVB tea/coffee Direct dial from bedrooms No dogs Cen ht TVL **PRICES:** s €40 - €65; d €56 - €78 **PARKING:** 13 **NOTES:** Closed 18-30 Dec **CARDS:**

♦♦♦ GH *Coffey's Loch Lein*

Golf Course Rd, Fossa ☎ 064 31260 🖷 064 36151
e-mail: ecoffey@indigo.ie
Dir: *take N72 W towards Killorglin. At Fossa Village look for sign immediately after church on left*
A comfortable, well kept bungalow set in its own peaceful grounds and overlooking Killarney's Lower Lake. Mrs Coffey has a keen interest in interior decorating and has used her skills successfully in the sitting and dining rooms, both of which have panoramic views of the lake.
FACILITIES: 16 en suite (12 fmly) No smoking in dining room No smoking in lounges STV TVB Direct dial from bedrooms No dogs (ex guide dogs) Cen ht TVL **PARKING:** 20 **NOTES:** Closed 27 Oct-15 Mar
CARDS:

♦♦♦ T&C Gorman's

Tralee Rd ☎ 064 33149 🖷 064 33149
e-mail: mgorman@eircom.net
Dir: *on N22 Tralee Rd, up main street onto Tralee Rd on left, Gorman's 3.5m*
A large and attractive bungalow set in well-cultivated gardens. It offers magnificent views from comfortable en suite bedrooms. Open fire in the lounge and satellite TV is available. Separate breakfast menu. Discount for senior citizens. Special off-season rates.
FACILITIES: 5 en suite (2 fmly) No smoking in 3 bedrooms No smoking in dining room STV TVB tea/coffee Cen ht TVL No children 4yrs Gardens Last d 6pm **PRICES:** s €41.50; d €51✳ **LB PARKING:** 7
NOTES: Closed 1Nov-16Mar **CARDS:**

♦♦♦ GH *Hussey's Bar & Townhouse*

43 High St ☎ 064 37454 🖷 064 33144
e-mail: husseys@iol.ie
Dir: *on High Street northern end towards Tralee Rd*
In a quiet location on the north-west side of town, with its own pub next door, this is a friendly place where guests and locals mingle. There is a separate breakfast room, and also a TV lounge on the first floor. Bedrooms are attractively decorated, comfortable and well maintained. The car park is at the rear of the house. There are some good restaurants in the neighbourhood.
FACILITIES: 5 en suite No smoking in bedrooms No smoking in dining room STV TVB tea/coffee Direct dial from bedrooms No dogs Licensed Cen ht No children 10yrs No coaches **PARKING:** 5
NOTES: Closed 30 Oct-21 Mar **CARDS:**

♦♦♦ T&C *Nashville*

Tralee Rd ☎ 064 32924 🖷 064 32924
e-mail: nashville@eircom.net
Dir: *3km from Killarney on N22 Dublin/Limerick road*
A comfortable country home surrounded by lovely gardens. Situated in the heart of the beautiful Killarney Lake district, three minutes' drive from Killarney Town. The large bedrooms are bright and cheerful.

continued

FACILITIES: 6 en suite (2 fmly) No smoking in 3 bedrooms TVB tea/coffee No dogs Cen ht TVL Golf Fishing Horse riding available within 3km
PARKING: 10 **NOTES:** Closed Dec-Feb **CARDS:**

♦♦♦ *O'Donovans Farm & Muckross Riding Stables (V 977878)*

Mangerton Rd, Muckross ☎ 064 32238 Mrs M O'Donovan
Dir: *from Killarney on N71 for 1m to Muckross Park Hotel, directly left after hotel for 0.5m*
This modern farm bungalow has panoramic views of Killarney's National Park and Mangerton Mountain where groups can go on horse riding treks. Five of the bedrooms are en suite and one has sole use of a separate bathroom. The dining room overlooks the valley and there is a comfortable guest lounge.
FACILITIES: 6 en suite (2 fmly) No smoking tea/coffee No dogs (ex guide dogs) Cen ht TVL Riding 20 acres horses sheep Dinner Last d 5pm
PARKING: 20 **NOTES:** Closed 11 Nov-Feb

♦♦ GH *Green Acres*

Fossa ☎ 064 31454
Dir: *2km on T67 Killorglin road*
This modern house is situated on the Ring of Kerry 1.5 miles outside town.
FACILITIES: 8 rms (6 en suite) (2 fmly) No smoking in bedrooms No smoking in dining room No smoking in 1 lounge No dogs Cen ht TVL
PARKING: 10 **NOTES:** Closed Dec-9 Jan

♦♦ GH *McCarthy's Town House*

19 High St ☎ 064 35655 🖷 064 35745
Dir: *in town centre*
Town centre accommodation next door to the Crock of Gold bar and restaurant, and run by the same owners. Comfortable new en suite bedrooms are available on the first and second floors - the latter with large roof windows but no views. Guests can relax in the TV lounge. A rear car park offers off-street parking.
FACILITIES: 8 en suite (2 fmly) No smoking in bedrooms No smoking in dining room No smoking in 1 lounge TVB Direct dial from bedrooms No dogs Licensed Cen ht TVL Dinner Last d 9pm **PARKING:** 10
CARDS:

♦♦ T&C *Sliabh Luachra House*

Loretto Rd ☎ 064 32012
Dir: *off Muckross Road or National Park Road. 1st turn after Glen Eagle Hotel from town side. 1st right after Lake Hotel from Kenmare side*

A fine modern house in delightful gardens on a quiet residential road off Muckross Road about 1.5 miles from the town centre. Rooms vary in size, but all are furnished to the same degree of comfort. Private parking is available.
FACILITIES: 6 en suite (1 fmly) No smoking in bedrooms No smoking in dining room No smoking in 1 lounge tea/coffee No dogs (ex guide dogs) Cen ht TVL No children 12yrs **PARKING:** 6 **NOTES:** Closed Oct-Mar
CARDS:

KILLORGLIN Map 01 A2

Premier Collection

♦♦♦♦♦ T&C Carrig House Country House & Restaurant

Caragh Lake ☎ 066 9769100 📠 066 9769166
e-mail: info@carrighouse.com

This charming, meticulously restored Victorian house is set on the shores of Caragh Lake, in beautiful mature gardens and natural woodlands. The restaurant overlooks the lake and serves fresh, locally produced food. Bedrooms are spacious, elegant and individually decorated. There is a private jetty, and a boat and fishing tackle are available for guests.
FACILITIES: 16 en suite No smoking in bedrooms No smoking in dining room Direct dial from bedrooms Licensed Cen ht TVL No children 8yrs No coaches Fishing Croquet lawn Dinner Last d 9.15pm **PRICES:** s €120 - €140; d €150 - €190✳ **LB** **PARKING:** 20

♦♦♦♦ T&C *Grove Lodge*

Killarney Rd ☎ 066 9761157 📠 066 9762330
e-mail: groveldg@iol.ie
Dir: *800mtrs from Killorglin Bridge on Killarney road-N72*
A lovely riverside house extended and developed to a high standard, with all the rooms en suite and fully equipped. Mrs Foley is an enthusiastic host who likes to please her guests and for those who just want to relax there is a patio seating area in the garden by the river.
FACILITIES: 10 en suite (4 fmly) No smoking in bedrooms No smoking in dining room STV TVB tea/coffee Direct dial from bedrooms No dogs (ex guide dogs) Cen ht **PARKING:** 15 **NOTES:** Closed Dec
CARDS:

♦♦♦ Dromin Farmhouse *(V 806902)*

Milltown Post Office ☎ 066 9761867 Mrs M Foley
e-mail: drominfarmhouse@yahoo.com
Dir: *3km from Killorglin. Turn off N70 approx 1km from Killorglin at signpost after factory. Straight on for 2km to house*
Set on a sheep and cattle farm with fantastic mountain views, this elevated bungalow is conveniently near to local beaches, golf, fishing and horse-riding. A private TV lounge is available for guests, and babysitting can be arranged. Evening meals are served, but reservations are appreciated.
FACILITIES: 4 rms (3 en suite) (2 fmly) No smoking in dining room No smoking in lounges TVB tea/coffee No dogs Cen ht TVL 42 acres dairy sheep Dinner Last d mid-day **PRICES:** s €35 - €40; d €50 - €56✳ **PARKING:** 10 **NOTES:** Closed Nov-16 Mar **CARDS:**

♦♦♦ T&C O'Regan's Country Home

Bansha ☎ 066 9761200 📠 066 9761200
e-mail: jeromeoregan@eircom.net
Dir: *1m from Killorglin, on N70, turn right, beside Killorglin golf club*
This dormer bungalow is set in colourful-award-winning gardens just off the N70, adjacent to Killorglin Golf Club. The bedrooms are comfortable, and there is an inviting breakfast room and a guest lounge that overlooks the beautiful garden.
FACILITIES: 4 rms (3 en suite) (1 fmly) No smoking TVB tea/coffee No dogs Cen ht TVL Last d noon **PRICES:** s fr €38.50; d fr €27.50 **LB** **PARKING:** 8 **NOTES:** Closed 11-31 Dec

TAHILLA Map 01 A2

♦♦♦♦ GH *Tahilla Cove*

☎ 064 45204 📠 064 45104
Dir: *just off Ring of Kerry road N70*
Set in 13 acres of quiet seashore estate overlooking Kenmare Bay, Tahilla Cove has lawns and terraces that sweep down to the water's edge, where there is a private pier. The comfortable and well appointed bedrooms are located in two houses and most have views of the bay. The Waterhouse family take pride in cooking with fresh local produce and dinner is available to residents. This is an ideal base for golfing, hill walking, fishing and bathing.
FACILITIES: 3 en suite 6 annexe en suite (4 fmly) No smoking in dining room TVB Direct dial from bedrooms Licensed Cen ht TVL No coaches Last d 9.30am **PARKING:** 20 **NOTES:** Closed Nov-Etr rs Tues evenings
CARDS:

TRALEE Map 01 A2

♦♦♦♦ T&C Brianville

Clogherbrien, Fenit Rd ☎ 066 7126645 📠 066 7126645
e-mail: michsmit@gofree.indigo.ie
Dir: *R558 Tralee-Fenit road, 1.25m from Tralee. Bungalow on right*
This welcoming large yellow bungalow, situated on the road to Fenit on the outskirts of Tralee, is within easy reach of beaches, golf and the Aqua Dome. Bedrooms vary in size and are attractively furnished with hand-crafted pine. Breakfast is served in the bright sitting/dining room overlooking the well tended garden.
FACILITIES: 5 en suite (1 fmly) No smoking STV TVB tea/coffee No dogs (ex guide dogs) Cen ht TVL **PRICES:** (incl. dinner) d €60 - €70✳ **PARKING:** 10 **CARDS:**

♦♦♦♦ Heatherville *(Q 816118)*

Blennerville ☎ 066 7121054 📠 066 7121054
Hanna & Ann Kerins
e-mail: heatherville@eircom.net
Dir: *exit N86 Dingle Rd at Blennerville, premises 0.5m on left*
A luxury modern farmhouse just off the Tralee to Dingle road. Mrs Hanna Kerins and her daughter, Ann, extend a warm welcome to their guests and ensure their comfort. Close to the restored Blennerville Windmill and steam railway.
FACILITIES: 6 en suite (2 fmly) No smoking TVB tea/coffee Direct dial from bedrooms No dogs Cen ht TVL 40 acres Beef **PRICES:** d €58 - €70✳ **PARKING:** 8 **NOTES:** Closed Nov-Feb **CARDS:**

♦♦♦ Red Diamonds highlight the top establishments within the AA's 3, 4 and 5 Diamond ratings.

Ireland

TRALEE continued

♦♦♦ GH Tralee Townhouse
1-2 High St ☎ 066 718111 📠 066 7181112
e-mail: townhouse@iolfree.ie
Conveniently located in Tralee town centre, close to pubs, shops, restaurants and Splash World, this friendly guest house offers well equipped bedrooms, and there is a lift to all floors. Guests can relax in the comfortable lounge and Eleanor Collins serves a variety of breakfast dishes and home baked breads.
FACILITIES: 19 en suite (2 fmly) No smoking in 9 bedrooms No smoking in dining room STV TVB tea/coffee Direct dial from bedrooms No dogs (ex guide dogs) Lift Cen ht TVL **PRICES:** s €38 - €55; d €59 - €76* **LB** **CARDS:**

WATERVILLE Map 01 A2

♦♦♦♦ GH Brookhaven House
New Line Rd ☎ 066 947 4431 📠 066 947 4724
e-mail: brookhaven@esatclear.ie
Dir: *on N70, on Ring of Kerry, 1km N of Waterville*
A new and imposing two storey house in an acre of garden, overlooking the Waterville Golf Course and the Atlantic Ocean. Bedrooms are spacious and individually decorated, with spectacular views. The lounge has an open turf fire and plenty of books.
FACILITIES: 5 en suite (5 fmly) No smoking TVB tea/coffee Direct dial from bedrooms No dogs (ex guide dogs) Cen ht TVL **PRICES:** s €60-€70; d €70-€80* **LB PARKING:** 16 **NOTES:** Closed Dec-Feb **CARDS:**

♦♦♦ T&C *Klondyke House*
New Line Rd ☎ 066 9474119 📠 066 9474666
e-mail: klondykehouse@eircom.net
Dir: *on N70, beside Waterville craft market*
An attractive house at the western end of the village, extended and refurbished to high standards. The sun lounge to the front has views over Waterville Bay. Bedrooms are comfortable with semi-orthopaedic beds and en suite showers. Breakfast features an excellent choice including fruit fresh fruit yoghurts and homebaked breads.
FACILITIES: 6 en suite (1 fmly) TVB tea/coffee Direct dial from bedrooms No dogs (ex guide dogs) Cen ht TVL Tennis (hard) **PARKING:** 10 **CARDS:**

CO KILDARE

ATHY Map 01 C3

Premier Collection

♦♦♦♦♦ T&C Coursetown House
Stradbally Rd ☎ 0507 31101 📠 0507 32740
Dir: *turn off N78 at Athy or N80 at Stradbally on to R428. 9km from Stradbally, 3km from Athy*

This charming Victorian country house is set on a 250-acre tillage farm and bird sanctuary two miles from Athy on the Stradbally Road. It has been extensively refurbished, and all bedrooms are furnished to the highest standards. Convalescent or disabled guests are especially welcome, and Iris and Jim Fox are happy to share their knowledge of the Irish countryside and its wildlife.
FACILITIES: 5 en suite No smoking TVB tea/coffee Direct dial from bedrooms No dogs (ex guide dogs) Cen ht TVL No children 8yrs No coaches **PRICES:** s €60; d €100* **PARKING:** 22 **CARDS:**

CLANE Map 01 C4

♦♦♦ T&C *Ashley*
Richardstown ☎ 045 868533 📠 045 868533
This charming bungalow is set in a quiet wooded area about half a mile from the main Celbridge/Clane road (R403). Colm and Evelyn Ryan have earned an enviable reputation for their hospitality which brings them many returning visitors. A complimentary car service can be provided for guests attending local weddings and functions.
FACILITIES: 4 rms (2 en suite) (1 fmly) No smoking in bedrooms TV1B tea/coffee No dogs (ex guide dogs) Cen ht TVL Dinner Last d 5pm **PARKING:** 9 **NOTES:** Closed 18 Dec-1 Jan

♦♦♦ *Silverspring House (N 863272)*
Firmount ☎ 045 868481 📠 045 892246 Mr & Mrs J Phelan
Dir: *N7 to Naas from Dublin or N4 from Galway to Clane*
A modern farmhouse situated in its own grounds, one mile from Clane. There is a TV lounge and separate dining room for the guests to use. Peaceful gardens surround the house, complete with free-range chickens that provide the eggs for breakfast. Nearby is a model racing circuit and racecourses; canoeing and fishing are also close at hand.
FACILITIES: 4 en suite (2 fmly) No smoking in bedrooms No smoking in dining room TVB tea/coffee No dogs Cen ht TVL 25 acres beef sheep **PARKING:** 12 **NOTES:** Closed Dec-Feb **CARDS:**

KILCULLEN Map 01 C3

♦♦♦ T&C Chapel View Country Home
Gormanstown ☎ 045 481325
This large modern house is set in stud-farm country and run in friendly style by Daniel and Breda O'Sullivan who offer their guests good company as well as good cooking. Soda bread is often on the breakfast menu and dinners can be pre-booked. There is a spacious TV lounge, large dining room overlooking the gardens and plenty of room for parking.
FACILITIES: 6 en suite (2 fmly) No smoking No dogs Licensed Cen ht TVL Dinner Last d 2pm **PRICES:** s €40 - €50; d €60 - €70* **PARKING:** 20 **NOTES:** Closed 2 Nov-Feb **CARDS:**

NEWBRIDGE Map 01 C3

♦♦♦♦ GH Gables
Ryston, Kilcullen Rd ☎ 045 435330 📠 045 435355
e-mail: gablesguesthse@ireland.com
Dir: *from Dublin exit M7 junct 8, 200yds on left Kilcullen Road from Newbridge*
The River Liffey curves gently by this well appointed house. Lovely views can be had from the dining room, and the pool, sauna and jacuzzi all make for a very relaxing stay.
FACILITIES: 9 en suite (2 fmly) STV TV11B tea/coffee Direct dial from bedrooms No dogs (ex guide dogs) Cen ht TVL Indoor swimming pool (heated) Fishing Sauna Gymnasium Jacuzzi Jacuzzi, steam bath

continued

GH Gables

PRICES: s €38 - €45; d €76 - €90✳ **LB** **PARKING:** 40 **NOTES:** Closed 23-2 Jan **CARDS:**

STRAFFAN Map 01 D4

♦♦♦ T&C Woodside Lodge

Barberstown ☎ 01 6273499
e-mail: woodsidelodge@ireland.com
Dir: *Turn off M4 onto R406 to Straffan or turn off N7 at Kill junct & follow signs to Straffan, Woodside Lodge 0.25m from Straffan village on Maynooth road*

New dormer-style house in a quiet area close to the K Club Golf Course, with attractive gardens and off-street parking. Modern bedrooms are all en suite and one is adapted for wheelchair users. Home made bread and jams plus free range eggs feature at breakfast.
FACILITIES: 5 annexe en suite (2 fmly) (2 GF) No smoking STV TVB tea/coffee No dogs (ex guide dogs) Cen ht No coaches **PRICES:** s €38; d €64✳ **PARKING:** 6 **CARDS:**

CO KILKENNY

KILKENNY Map 01 C3

♦♦♦♦ T&C Alcantra

Maidenhill, Kells Rd ☎ 056 61058 📠 056 61058
e-mail: alcantra@tinet.ie
Dir: *on R697, 400mtrs from junction with R910 (N10) 1km from Kilkenny city centre*
An impressive new house close to the city centre. Public rooms include a pleasant lounge and conservatory with a separate dining room, all well decorated.
FACILITIES: 4 en suite (2 fmly) No smoking STV TVB No dogs Cen ht TVL No coaches **PRICES:** d €56 - €68 **LB** **PARKING:** 4 **NOTES:** Closed 23-30 Dec **CARDS:**

♦♦♦♦ GH Butler House

Patrick St ☎ 056 65707 & 22828 📠 056 65626
e-mail: res@butler.ie
Dir: *follow signs for city centre. Located in centre near Kilkenny Castle*

continued

Once the dower house of Kilkenny Castle, this fine Georgian building fronts onto the main street with secluded gardens at the rear, through which guests stroll to have full breakfast in Kilkenny Design Centre. Continental breakfast is served in bedrooms, which feature contemporary décor. There is a comfortable foyer lounge and conference/banqueting suites.
FACILITIES: 13 en suite (4 fmly) No smoking in 5 bedrooms STV TVB tea/coffee Direct dial from bedrooms No dogs (ex guide dogs) Licensed Cen ht No coaches **PRICES:** s €87.50 - €125.50; d €125.50 - €239.50✳ **LB** **CONF:** Thtr 120 Class 40 Board 40 **PARKING:** 24 **NOTES:** Closed 24-29 Dec
CARDS:

♦♦♦♦ T&C Shillogher House

Callan Rd ☎ 056 63249 & 64865 📠 056 64865
e-mail: shillogherhouse@tinet.ie
Dir: *on N76 Callan/Clonmel/Cork Road, approx 1km south of Kilkenny*
A lovely new house that is set back from the Callen/Clonmel road and within walking distance of Kilkenny, tastefully decorated and furnished. The breakfast menu includes vegetarian options as well as a hearty Irish breakfast.
FACILITIES: 6 en suite (1 fmly) No smoking STV TVB tea/coffee Direct dial from bedrooms No dogs (ex guide dogs) Cen ht **PRICES:** s €38 - €55; d €65 - €90✳ **PARKING:** 10 **CARDS:**

♦♦♦ T&C *Auburn Lodge*

Bennettsbridge Rd ☎ 056 65119 📠 056 70008
e-mail: pat-dunphy@tinet.ie
Dir: *from rdbt on Castle Rd 1 mile, 1st B&B on left, striaght through rdbt towards Bennetts Bridge*
Auburn Lodge is a modern house set in well kept gardens. It is attractively decorated throughout and the bedrooms are cheerful. There is a comfortable guest lounge and a breakfast room where excellent meals are served in the morning.
FACILITIES: 5 rms (3 en suite) (4 fmly) No smoking TVB tea/coffee No dogs Cen ht Tennis (hard) **PARKING:** 6

THOMASTOWN Map 01 C3

♦♦♦♦ T&C *Abbey House*

Jerpoint Abbey ☎ 056 24166 📠 056 24192
Dir: *on N9 from Dublin directly opposite Jerpoint Abbey*
Standing on the banks of the Little Argile River, this historic house was once part of the Jerpoint Abbey estates. The bedrooms are well equipped and tea trays and TVs are available on request. A comfortable sitting room overlooks the river banks, and dinner can be taken by arrangement in a separate dining room. There is trout fishing on the river and golf can be played nearby; the area is also known for its local crafts.
FACILITIES: 6 en suite (2 fmly) No smoking in bedrooms No smoking in dining room No smoking in 1 lounge TVB Direct dial from bedrooms Cen ht TVL Fishing Last d noon **PARKING:** 30 **NOTES:** Closed 21-30 Dec
CARDS:

♦♦♦ T&C Carrickmourne House

New Ross Rd ☎ 056 24124 📠 056 24124
Dir: *from Thomastown follow signs to New Ross/Inistioge, after 2km turn left, house is signed, 1km up hill on left*
In a peaceful rural position not far from Thomastown, this split-level house is set on an elevated site. The dining room has picture windows overlooking the gardens, there is a comfortable TV lounge and the accommodation is provided in five attractively decorated bedrooms.
FACILITIES: 5 en suite (2 fmly) No smoking STV TVB tea/coffee No dogs Cen ht TVL **PRICES:** s €36 - €40; d €51 - €74✳ **PARKING:** 9
CARDS:

CO LAOIS

PORTLAOISE Map 01 C3

Premier Collection

♦♦♦♦♦ T&C Ivyleigh House
Bank Place ☎ 0502 22081 🖷 0502 63343
e-mail: dinah@ivyleigh.com
Dir: *opposite town centre multi-storey car park*
This gracious Georgian town house, close to the station and theatre, has been completely refurbished. There is an elegant drawing room, and breakfast is served in the attractive dining room, where the wide-ranging breakfast menu includes freshly-baked bread. The luxurious bedrooms boast wonderfully comfortable beds, armchairs and power showers. Lovely decor and warm hospitality makes a visit to Ivyleigh a memorable one.
FACILITIES: 4 en suite No smoking STV TVB tea/coffee Direct dial from bedrooms No dogs Cen ht TVL No children 8yrs No coaches **PRICES:** s €70; d €105✻ **PARKING:** 6 **NOTES:** Closed 20 Dec-4 Jan **CARDS:**

♦♦ T&C O'Sullivan
8 Kelly Ville Park ☎ 0502 22774
Dir: *in town centre 50mtrs from Tourist Office beside town car park*
This period semi-detatched house is situated on the outskirts of town and is family run, with a homely atmosphere. Bedrooms are comfortable and all with en suite facilities. Secure parking is available.
FACILITIES: 6 en suite (1 fmly) (2 GF) STV TVB No dogs (ex guide dogs) Cen ht TVL **PRICES:** s €50; d €70✻ **PARKING:** 8

STRADBALLY Map 01 C3

♦♦♦♦ Tullamoy House *(S 608911)*
☎ 0507 27111 🖷 0507 27111 Mr & Mrs P Farrell
e-mail: tullamoy@indigo.ie
Dir: *just off N80 3m S of Stradbally*
This pleasant limestone farmhouse was built in 1871, and is located just south of Stradbally on the Carlow Road. Caroline and Pat Farrell and their children welcome guests and offer tea and homebaking, served beside the fire in the sitting room. Local produce and home produced beef are served at dinner, available on request. Bedrooms vary in size and are comfortably furnished and attractively decorated.
FACILITIES: 4 en suite (1 fmly) No smoking in bedrooms No smoking in dining room No dogs (ex guide dogs) Cen ht TVL 250 acres beef Dinner Last d noon **PRICES:** s €42; d €64✻ **LB PARKING:**

CO LIMERICK

ADARE Map 01 B3

♦♦♦♦ T&C Adare Lodge
Kildimo Rd ☎ 061 396629 🖷 061 395060
Dir: *in village turn right at bank*
A charming modern house, recently extended and suitable for wheelchair users, stands on a quiet street off the main N21 road in a picturesque village famous for its thatched cottages. Its comfortable en suite bedrooms are well equipped. Guests also have the use of a spacious lounge.
FACILITIES: 6 en suite (3 fmly) No smoking in bedrooms No smoking in dining room No smoking in 1 lounge TVB tea/coffee No dogs Cen ht TVL **PRICES:** s fr €60; d fr €65✻ **PARKING:** 6 **CARDS:**

♦♦♦♦ T&C Berkeley Lodge
Station Rd ☎ 061 396857 & 396957 🖷 061 396857
e-mail: berlodge@iol.ie
Dir: *take N21 (Limerick-Kerry), in village centre turn right at rdbt (Lenas bar), pass petrol station on right, 5th house on right*
Situated just off the main street of this pretty village, Berkeley Lodge offers comfortable, well equipped amd tastefully decorated accommodation. The guest lounge leads on to an attractive conservatory style breakfast room, which offers a wide ranging menu.
FACILITIES: 6 en suite (2 fmly) (1 GF) No smoking TVB tea/coffee No dogs Cen ht TVL **PRICES:** s €50 - €58; d €65 - €70✻ **LB PARKING:** 6 **CARDS:**

♦♦♦♦ T&C Coatesland House
Tralee/Killarney Rd, Graigue ☎ 061 396372 🖷 061 396833
e-mail: coatesfd@indigo.ie
Dir: *from Adare follow Killarney road N21 for less than 1km, Coatesland House on left beside W W Doherty's Garage*

Coatesland House, situated on the main Killarney road five minutes from Adare village, is a very well appointed house featuring attractive bedrooms, all with en suite facilities. Proprietors Florence and Donal Hogan are welcoming and friendly and give superb attention to detail. Dinner is available. Nearby activities include hunting, fishing, golf and there is also an equestrian centre.
FACILITIES: 6 en suite (2 fmly) No smoking in bedrooms No smoking in dining room STV TVB tea/coffee Direct dial from bedrooms Cen ht TVL ch fac Garden **PARKING:** 20 **NOTES:** Closed 23-26 Dec
CARDS:

♦♦♦ T&C Avona House
Kildimo Rd ☎ 061 396323 🖷 061 396323
e-mail: avona@eircom.net
Dir: *exit N21 at rdbt in village. Premises 150mtrs on left from main street*
This well appointed modern house stands just 100 yards from the main street of a pretty village. Attractive en suite bedrooms, all with colour TV, reflect the owners' careful attention to detail. A courtesy tray for guests to help themselves to tea and coffee is provided in the lounge and there is a separate breakfast room.
FACILITIES: 4 en suite (1 fmly) No smoking TVB No dogs (ex guide dogs) Cen ht TVL **PRICES:** s €40 - €45; d €60 - €64 **PARKING:** 5
NOTES: Closed Nov-Feb **CARDS:**

BRUREE Map 01 B3

♦♦♦♦ Ballyteigue House *(R 524313)*
Rockhill ☎ 063 90575 🖷 063 90575 Mr & Mrs R Johnson
e-mail: ballyteigue@eircom.net
Dir: *southbound on N20 pass O'Roukes & take next right, pass Rockhill Church, 1m and premises are signposted*
This country house, surrounded by gardens and fields, stands in a rural area not far from Charleville Golf Course. Margaret and Richard Johnson are welcoming hosts who have created a very pleasant

continued

Ireland

atmosphere for guests, with period furnishings, comfortable accommodation and a relaxing sitting room and dining room where evening meals can be served by prior request. Horse riding, hunting and fishing can all be arranged in the neighbourhood.
FACILITIES: 5 rms (4 en suite) (2 fmly) No smoking tea/coffee No dogs (ex guide dogs) Cen ht TVL 30 acres cattle horses Dinner Last d 12am
LB NOTES: Closed 20 Dec-mid Feb rs Winter months-book in advance
CARDS:

KILMALLOCK Map 01 B3

Premier Collection

♦♦♦♦♦ Flemingstown House *(R 629255)*

063 98093 063 98546 Mrs I Sheedy-King
e-mail: flemingstown@keltec.ie
Dir: *on Kilmallock/Fermoy R512 road, establishment 2m from Kilmallock*

A lovely 18th-century farmhouse which has been modernised to provide stylish en suite facilities throughout. Public rooms include a comfortably furnished sitting room with antiques, and a dining room with beautiful stained glass windows. At breakfast much of the produce comes from the owners' own farm. Dinner is available by arrangement. The area is excellent for walkers, riders, anglers and golfers.
FACILITIES: 5 en suite (2 fmly) No smoking TVB tea/coffee No dogs (ex guide dogs) Cen ht Riding 102 acres dairy beef Dinner Last d 3pm
PRICES: d €80 - €100✳ **PARKING:** 12 **NOTES:** Closed Nov-Feb
CARDS:

LIMERICK Map 01 B3

♦♦♦ GH Clifton House

Ennis Rd 061 451166 061 451224
e-mail: michaelpowell@eircom.net
Dir: *on N18 towards Shannon Airport, opposite Woodfield House Hotel*
Providing well equipped, attractive and very comfortable bedrooms has been the aim of the refurbishment of Michael and Mary Powell's guest house. Complimentary tea and coffee are available in the spacious, relaxing lounge.
FACILITIES: 16 en suite No smoking in dining room STV TVB Direct dial from bedrooms No dogs (ex guide dogs) Cen ht TVL
PARKING: 22 **NOTES:** Closed 21 Dec-2 Jan **PRICES:** s fr €45; d fr €70✳ **CARDS:**

♦♦♦ T&C White House B & B

Raheen 061 301709 061 301709
Dir: *Beside Church at Rahleen Rdbt 0.25,m from regional hospital*
This welcoming, family-run house offers bright and airy ground floor bedrooms. A comfortable lounge is available for relaxation, and freshly prepared breakfasts are served in the separate dining room. There is ample off-street car parking available in the front garden.
FACILITIES: 5 en suite (3 fmly) No smoking in bedrooms No smoking in dining room TVB tea/coffee No dogs (ex guide dogs) Cen ht TVL Dinner Last d noon **PRICES:** s €40 - €53; d €60 - €70✳ **PARKING:** 7
CARDS:

CO LONGFORD

DRUMLISH Map 01 C4

♦♦♦♦ Longford Country House-Cumiskeys *(N 173808)*

Ennybegs 043 23320 043 23516 Ms P Cumiskey
e-mail: kc@iol.ie

A hospitable, Tudor-style house. The parlour has a wrought iron spiral stairway to the library loft, as well as a cosy sitting room with turf fire and a dining room where dinner is served by prior arrangement. Other facilities include a games room and pitch and putt. Self-catering cottages are also available.
FACILITIES: 6 rms (5 en suite) (2 fmly) No smoking in bedrooms No smoking in dining room No smoking in 1 lounge TVB tea/coffee No dogs Licensed Cen ht TVL Pitch & putt course Games room Aromatherapy Last d noon **PRICES:** d fr €52✳ **LB PARKING:** 20 **NOTES:** rs Nov-14 Dec & 16 Jan-Feb (prior booking) **CARDS:**

GRANARD Map 01 C4

♦♦♦ *Toberphelim House (N 356810)*

043 86568 043 86568 Mr & Mrs Smyth
e-mail: tober2@eircom.net
Dir: *from Belfast take N55 from Cavan, left at Statoil, right at next junct, house on left*
A large Georgian country house stands at the end of a long driveway. Children are well catered for with a private playground and a chance to see the various farmyard animals and activities. A separate lounge is also available.
FACILITIES: 3 rms (2 en suite) (3 fmly) No smoking No dogs (ex guide dogs) Cen ht TVL Pool Table Children's playground Stables for guests horses 200 acres beef sheep **PARKING:** 10 **NOTES:** rs 21 Sep-Apr
CARDS:

Ireland

CO LOUTH

CARLINGFORD Map 01 D4

Premier Collection

♦♦♦♦♦ T&C *Beaufort House*
Ghan Rd ☎ 042 9373878/9 📠 042 9373878
e-mail: michaelcaine@beauforthouse.net
Dir: *located on the shore of Carlingford Lough, to the south of the East Pier of Carlingford harbour*
Situated on the coast road, this newly built house has spacious and well equipped bedrooms which enjoy views of the lough. An interesting breakfast menu, including fresh fish as well as traditional fare, is served in the dining room. Dinner is available for large parties by prior arrangement.
FACILITIES: 5 en suite (2 fmly) No smoking in bedrooms No smoking in dining room No smoking in 1 lounge TVB tea/coffee Direct dial from bedrooms No dogs (ex guide dogs) Licensed Cen ht No children 7yrs No coaches Tennis (hard) Dinner Last d 8pm **PARKING:** 20
CARDS:

DROGHEDA Map 01 D4

Premier Collection

♦♦♦♦♦ T&C Boynehaven House
Dublin Rd ☎ 041 9836700 📠 041 9836700
e-mail: taramcd@ireland.com
Dir: *2km S of Drogheda on N1 opposite Europa Hotel*
A modern bungalow off the Dublin Road, well-screened from noise and view of the road outside. This recently-extended house offers excellent standards of comfort, with fully-equipped en suite bedrooms. Hospitality is also guaranteed, and there is a cosy lounge and interesting breakfast menu.
FACILITIES: 4 en suite (4 GF) No smoking in bedrooms No smoking in dining room TVB tea/coffee No dogs (ex guide dogs) Cen ht TVL No children 12yrs **PRICES:** s €45 - €55; d €65 - €80✳ **PARKING:** 20
CARDS:

Premier Collection

♦♦♦♦♦ T&C Tullyesker Country House
Tullyesker, Monasterboice ☎ 041 9830430 & 9832624
📠 041 9832624
e-mail: mcdonnellfamily@ireland.com
Dir: *5km N on the old Drogheda/Belfast road (N1) on right at Tullyesker hill just past Papel Cross*
Situated in a spectacular site on Tullyesker Hill, overlooking the Boyne Valley and Drogheda, this large family-run house is set in 3 acres of lovely gardens and wooded grounds. An extensive breakfast menu is offered, and bedrooms (many of which overlook the gardens) are comfortable and well equipped.
FACILITIES: 5 en suite (2 fmly) No smoking in bedrooms No smoking in dining room STV TVB tea/coffee No dogs Cen ht TVL No children 10yrs **PRICES:** d €60 - €70✳ **PARKING:** 20
NOTES: Closed Dec-Jan

DUNDALK Map 01 D4

♦♦♦♦ T&C *Rosemount*
Dublin Rd ☎ 042 35878
Dir: *on N1, 2kms S of Dundalk*
This handsome bungalow stands in beautiful gardens north of the Belfast by-pass with attractive views over surrounding farmland. The nicely furnished bedrooms all have en suite showers and there is a comfortable lounge available for guests.
FACILITIES: 6 annexe en suite (4 fmly) No smoking in bedrooms No smoking in dining room No smoking in 1 lounge TV2B No dogs (ex guide dogs) Cen ht TVL **PARKING:** 8

CO MAYO

ACHILL ISLAND Map 01 A4

♦♦♦♦ T&C *Finncorry House*
Breanascill Bay, Atlantic Dr ☎ 098 45755 & 086 8252998
📠 098 45755
e-mail: achill_island@hotmail.com
Dir: *N59 onto R319 into Achill. Pass through Achill Sound village then left for Atlantic Drive. House 1.5m, right turn after shop with petrol pump*
Peacefully located overlooking Breanaskill Bay, in an area popular with artists for its marvellously clear light, this pleasant house has been purpose built to a high standard. Close by are good beaches and a deserted village. Achill, joined to the mainland by a bridge, is the most westerly inhabited island in Europe.
FACILITIES: 6 en suite (2 fmly) No smoking in bedrooms No smoking in dining room No smoking in 1 lounge STV TVB No dogs (ex guide dogs) Cen ht TVL ch fac Jacuzzi bath available Last d 2pm **NOTES:** Closed Nov-Feb **PARKING:** 6 **CARDS:**

♦♦♦♦ GH Gray's
Dugort ☎ 098 43244 & 43315
Dir: *towards Castlebar, Newport, Mulrany, Achill Sound and then Dugort*

This welcoming guest house is in Dugort, on the northern shore of the island, at the foot of the Slievemore Mountains. There is a smart conservatory and various lounges. Dinner is served nightly in the cheerful dining room, and the cosy bedrooms all have orthopædic beds. A self-contained villa, ideal for families, is also available.
FACILITIES: 5 en suite 10 annexe en suite (4 fmly) No smoking in dining room No smoking in 1 lounge TVB tea/coffee Licensed Cen ht TVL Pool Table Croquet lawn Table tennis Dinner Last d 6pm **PRICES:** s €46; d €80✳ **PARKING:** 30 **NOTES:** Closed 25 Dec

♦♦♦ T&C Lavelles Seaside House

Dooega ☎ 098 45116 & 01 2828142
e-mail: celiamlavelle@hotmail.com
Dir: *R319 from Achill Sound, 2.5m NW of Achill Sound turn left, continue for a further 2.5m to village of Dooega*

Friendliness and good food are offered at this comfortable guest house, where facilities include a guest lounge, breakfast room and adjoining pub. Parking is available opposite the house.

FACILITIES: 14 en suite (5 fmly) No smoking in dining room tea/coffee No dogs Licensed Cen ht TVL Dinner Last d 6.30pm **PRICES:** d €60 - €80 **LB NOTES:** Closed 2 Nov-14 Mar **PARKING:** 20 **CARDS:**

♦♦♦ T&C West Coast House

School Rd, Dooagh ☎ 098 43317 098 43317
e-mail: westcoast@anu.ie
Dir: *turn off N59 onto R319 onto Achill Island continue to Keel & then Dooagh, West Coast House signed*

This smart new house is in an elevated position giving superb views over Dooagh to the sea. Recent renovations have resulted in en suite facilities to all bedrooms. Guests can take full advantage of the panoramic views from the comfortable sitting room and adjacent dining room. Achill is Ireland's largest island, now connected to the mainland by a bridge, and offers magnificent scenery and long sandy beaches.

FACILITIES: 5 en suite (1 fmly) No smoking TVB tea/coffee No dogs (ex guide dogs) Cen ht TVL No children 8yrs Dinner Last d 6pm **PRICES:** s €35 - €50; d €50 - €60✻ **LB PARKING:** 10 **CARDS:**

CONG — Map 01 B4

Premier Collection

♦♦♦♦♦ T&C Ballywarren House

Ballymacgibbon North, Cross ☎ 092 46989 092 46989
e-mail: ballywarrenhouse@eircom.net
Dir: *R334 (Headford to Ballinrobe), take R346 at Cross, 0.75m down Cong Road on right*

Situated in its own grounds in a scenic rural area. A lot of care and attention to detail has gone into this gracious country house. Bedrooms have all the little extras that make a difference, and Diane and David Skelton are friendly, generous hosts whose priorities are comfort and good food. Pre-booking for dinner is essential. Ballywarren House is the Guest Accommodation of the Year for Ireland 2002-2003.

FACILITIES: 3 en suite No smoking in bedrooms No smoking in dining room No smoking in 1 lounge TVB Direct dial from bedrooms Licensed Cen ht No children 12 yrs No coaches Fishing Croquet lawn Dinner Last d 9am **PRICES:** s €92 - €98; d €124 - €140✻ **PARKING:** 4 **CARDS:**

WESTPORT — Map 01 B4

Premier Collection

♦♦♦♦♦ GH Knockranny Lodge

Knockranny ☎ 098 28595 098 28805
e-mail: knockranny@anu.ie
Dir: *approaching Westport on N5 arrive at speed limit sign (30mph) turn left off main road then 2nd left, Knockranny Lodge signed on the right*

Luxurious house situated in a quiet cul-de-sac, just 5 minutes from the town and their sister hotel, where guests have full use of the Leisure Centre. Bedrooms are comfortable, and public areas include a lounge and separate breakfast room. Other facilities include a tennis court and easy parking.

FACILITIES: 16 en suite (1 fmly) (5 GF) No smoking in bedrooms No smoking in dining room No smoking in 1 lounge STV TVB Direct dial from bedrooms No dogs (ex guide dogs) Cen ht TVL Tennis (hard) **PRICES:** s €65 - €80; d €80 - €110✻ **LB PARKING:** 16 **NOTES:** Closed Dec-Jan **CARDS:**

♦♦♦♦ T&C Carrabaun House

Carrabaun, Leenane Rd ☎ 098 26196 098 28466
e-mail: carrabaun@anu.ie
Dir: *on N59 S to Leenane, Clifden and Galway. On this road leave Westport town for 1m pass Maxol petrol station on left, house 200mtrs*

Friendly hosts, attractively furnished bedrooms and stunning views are all features here. Pilgrimage mountain Croagh Patrick, and Clew Bay beneath, are framed by picture windows in the sitting and dining rooms. There is private parking, and gardens surround the house.

FACILITIES: 6 en suite (6 fmly) (2 GF) No smoking TVB tea/coffee No dogs Cen ht TVL **PRICES:** s €40; d €54 - €58✻ **PARKING:** 12 **NOTES:** Closed 16-31 Dec **CARDS:**

♦♦♦ Bertra House *(L 903823)*

Thornhill, Murrisk ☎ 098 64833 098 64969 Mrs M Gill
e-mail: bertrahse@anu.ie
Dir: *0.25m off R335 Westport to Louisburgh Road. Im after Croagh Patrick*

This attractive bungalow overlooks Bertra Blue Flag beach. Four bedrooms have en suite facilities and the fifth has sole use of a bathroom. Breakfast is generous and Mrs Gill offers tea and home baked cakes on arrival, served in the cosy guest lounge.

FACILITIES: 5 rms (4 en suite) (3 fmly) No smoking TVB tea/coffee No dogs Cen ht TVL 42 acres beef and sheep **PRICES:** d €52 - €56✻ **PARKING:** 7 **NOTES:** Closed Jan-Feb **CARDS:**

♦♦♦ T&C Riverbank House

Rosbeg, Westport Harbour ☎ 098 25719
Dir: *on R335, 2km from Westport on Louisburgh Coast Road. Turn left 300 metres past Quays pub.*

This peaceful country house is close to Westport harbour and within walking distance of pubs and restaurants. Bedrooms are freshly decorated, and reception rooms are large and welcoming. Mrs O'Malley is an enthusiastic hostess who enjoys baking, so her guests can enjoy home made scones and tarts.

FACILITIES: 8 rms (7 en suite) (1 fmly) No smoking in bedrooms No smoking in dining room STV TV1B No dogs Cen ht TVL **PARKING:** 8 **NOTES:** Closed Nov-Mar **CARDS:**

> ♦♦♦ Red Diamonds highlight the top establishments within the AA's 3, 4 and 5 Diamond ratings.

WESTPORT continued

♦♦♦ GH Seabreeze

Kilsallagh ☎ 098 66548
e-mail: seabreeze@eircom.net
A genuine warm welcome awaits you at this comfortable and friendly home. Close to pubs, restaurants and Croagh Patrick.
FACILITIES: 3 en suite (3 fmly) (2 GF) No smoking in bedrooms No smoking in dining room TV1B No dogs Cen ht TVL Dinner Last d 7pm
PRICES: s □ 30 - □ 38; d □ 54✳ **LB** **CARDS:**

♦♦♦ *Seapoint House (L 972897)*

Kilmeena ☎ 098 41254 📠 098 41903 M O'Malley
May-Oct
Dir: *signposted on main Westport/Newport road N59, 6km N of Westport turn left & continue for 2.5km*
Seapoint View is a large and luxurious modern two-storey farmhouse set in 40 acres on Clew Bay.
FACILITIES: 6 en suite (4 fmly) No smoking TV2B tea/coffee No dogs Cen ht TVL Jacuzzi Sea angling, walking 40 acres mixed **PARKING:** 8
CARDS:

CO MEATH

BETTYSTOWN Map 01 D4

Premier Collection

♦♦♦♦♦ T&C Lis-Maura

☎ 041 9828387 📠 041 9828396
Dir: *from Dublin take N1 to Drogheda, turn right at Julianstown for Laytown/Bettystown (R151), drive through Laytown past church and school and 2nd entrance on right*
A restored Georgian house set in three acres, with private access to the beach. The attentive hosts have refurbished Lis-Maura to a very high standard. Breakfast is served at a communal table and there is a sitting room as well as a board room. Luxurious bedrooms are individually styled with antique furnishings and marble-tiled bathrooms.
FACILITIES: 4 en suite No smoking TVB Direct dial from bedrooms No dogs Cen ht No children 12yrs No coaches Tennis (hard) Croquet lawn
PRICES: s □ 50 - □ 65; d □ 100 - □ 130✳ **PARKING:** 5
NOTES: Closed 22 Dec-2 Jan

NAVAN Map 01 C4

♦♦♦♦ T&C Killyon

Dublin Rd ☎ 046 71224 📠 046 72766
Dir: *on N3, River Boyne side, opposite Ardboyne Hotel*
This luxurious house enjoys fine views over the River Boyne from its balcony, and is located on the Dublin Road opposite the Ardboyne Hotel. Comfortable, well-appointed bedrooms and an inviting attractive lounge make this a popular place to stay. Owner Mrs Fogarty offers a wide range of home cooking.
FACILITIES: 6 en suite (1 fmly) (1 GF) No smoking in 2 bedrooms No smoking in dining room No smoking in lounges STV TVB Direct dial from bedrooms No dogs (ex guide dogs) Cen ht TVL **PRICES:** s □ 45 - □ 50; d □ 70 - □ 80 **PARKING:** 12 **CARDS:**

CO MONAGHAN

EMYVALE Map 01 C5

♦♦♦♦ T&C *Fortsingleton*

☎ 047 86054 📠 047 86120
e-mail: fortsingleton@eircom.net
Dir: *N2 Dublin - Donegal. Fortsingleton 400mtrs off N2, 0.75miles N of Emyvale*
An ideal stop-off point between Donegal and Dublin, this Georgian house enjoys a tranquil setting in six acres of woodland, and has been carefully restored. Bedrooms are comfortable and feature fascinating memorabilia. Dinner is served around one large table (advance bookings requested).
FACILITIES: 7 en suite (1 fmly) No smoking in bedrooms No smoking in dining room No smoking in 1 lounge TVB tea/coffee No dogs Cen ht TVL Fishing Dinner Last d noon **PARKING:** 30
NOTES: Closed 23-26 Dec **CARDS:**

CO SLIGO

BALLYSADARE Map 01 B5

♦♦♦ T&C Seashore House

Lisduff ☎ 071 67827 📠 071 67827
e-mail: seashore@oceanfree.net
Dir: *turn off N4 at Ballisadore and take N59 W for 4km, Seashore sign is visible, turn right 600mtrs to house*
Attractive dormer bungalow in a quiet seashore location, just 2.5 miles from the village. A comfortable lounge with open turf fire and sunny conservatory dining room looking out over attractive landscaped gardens to sea and mountain scenery. Bedrooms are attractively appointed and comfortable, and there is also a tennis court and bicycle storage.
FACILITIES: 4 en suite (2 fmly) No smoking STV TVB No dogs Cen ht TVL No children Tennis (hard) Solarium Jacuzzi **PRICES:** s □ 35 - □ 40; d □ 60 - □ 64✳ **LB** **PARKING:** 6 **CARDS:**

GRANGE Map 01 B5

♦♦♦ T&C Rowanville Lodge

☎ 071 63958
e-mail: rowanville@hotmail.com
Dir: *on N15, 1m past Grange village on main road driving from Sligo*
A friendly house in a wonderfully scenic area, directly opposite Benbulben. The conservatory is the heart of the house where excellent breakfasts are served. There is an Equestrian Centre nearby, and also hill/mountain climbing.
FACILITIES: 3 en suite (3 fmly) No smoking in bedrooms No smoking in dining room No smoking in 1 lounge STV TVB tea/coffee No dogs Cen ht TVL No coaches **PRICES:** s □ 38; d □ 52 - □ 56✳ **PARKING:** 8
NOTES: Closed Oct-Apr **CARDS:**

SLIGO Map 01 B5

♦♦♦ T&C Aisling

Cairns Hill ☎ 071 60704 📠 071 60704
e-mail: aislingsligo@eircom.net
Dir: *approach Sligo on N4 right at 1st set of traffic lights, travelling south from Sligo pass Esso S/Sta turn left at traffic lights*
This well cared for modern bungalow stands only a short distance from the town centre. Bedrooms offer all modern comforts and there is a pleasant sitting room with a dining area, where at breakfast time guests can enjoy mountain views.
FACILITIES: 5 rms (3 en suite) (2 fmly) No smoking STV TVB tea/coffee No dogs Cen ht TVL No children 6yrs **PRICES:** s □ 37 - □ 40; d □ 54 - □ 60✳
PARKING: 6 **NOTES:** Closed 24-28 Dec **CARDS:**

♦♦♦ T&C *Chestnut Lawn*

Cummeen, Strandhill Rd ☎ 071 62781 📠 071 62781
Dir: *from Sligo follow signs for airport. Premises on right 3km from town on main airport/Strandhill road*

A modern dormer-style house set in its own gardens with private parking space. The house is comfortable, and the bedrooms are attractively decorated and very well maintained. Convenient for the beach, golf course, and the nearby megalithic tombs.

FACILITIES: 3 en suite (1 fmly) No smoking in bedrooms No smoking in dining room TVB tea/coffee No dogs (ex guide dogs) Cen ht TVL No coaches **PARKING:** 4 **NOTES:** Closed 21 Dec-21 Jan **CARDS:**

TOBERCURRY Map 01 B4

♦♦♦ T&C Cruckawn House

Ballymote/Boyle Rd ☎ 071 85188 📠 071 85188
e-mail: cruckawn@esatclear.ie
Dir: *300mtrs off N17 on R294 on right, overlooking golf course*

Overlooking the golf course, just a few minutes walk from the town centre, Cruckawn House offers friendly hospitality. The dining room adjoins the comfortable sun lounge, and there is also a TV lounge. Salmon and coarse fishing, riding and mountain climbing are all available nearby and the area is renowned for traditional Irish music.

FACILITIES: 5 en suite (2 fmly) No smoking in bedrooms No smoking in dining room No smoking in 1 lounge TVB No dogs (ex guide dogs) Cen ht TVL Gymnasium Game & coarse fishing, bike hire Dinner Last d 6pm
PRICES: s €35 - €40; d €56 - €64✳ **LB PARKING:** 8
NOTES: Closed Nov-Feb **CARDS:**

CO TIPPERARY

BANSHA Map 01 C3

♦♦♦♦ Bansha House *(R 962320)*

☎ 062 54194 📠 062 54215 Mr & Mrs J Marnane
e-mail: banshahouse@eircom.net
Dir: *turn off N24 in Bansha opposite Esso filling station*

Old world Georgian atmosphere on 100 acres of farmland, where brood mares and foals roam freely. Riding can be arranged at the nearby Equestrian Centre. This comfortable house is noted for its excellent home baking, and the hosts are friendly and hospitable. Dinner is available by request.

FACILITIES: 8 rms (5 en suite) (1 fmly) (2 GF) No smoking No dogs (ex guide dogs) Licensed Cen ht TVL Fishing Riding 100 acres horses cattle Dinner Last d 7pm **PRICES:** s €36 - €40; d €72 - €80✳ **LB**
PARKING: 10 **NOTES:** Closed 21-31 Dec **CARDS:**

CASHEL Map 01 C3

♦♦♦♦ GH Aulber House

Deerpark ROI ☎ 062 63713
e-mail: beralley@eircom.net

A newly-built guest house, set in landscaped gardens just five minutes' walk from the Rock of Cashel and town centre. Spacious bedrooms are thoughtfully furnished and equipped, and include one fitted for the less mobile. Relax by the open fire in the sitting room, or enjoy views of the surrounding countryside and the Rock from the first floor lounge.

FACILITIES: 12 en suite (2 fmly) No smoking in bedrooms No smoking in dining room No smoking in 1 lounge STV TVB tea/coffee Direct dial from bedrooms No dogs (ex guide dogs) Cen ht TVL Jacuzzi
PRICES: s €40; d €80✳ **NOTES:** Closed 23-27 Dec
CARDS:

♦♦♦♦ GH *Baileys of Cashel*

Main St ☎ 062 61937 📠 062 62038
e-mail: info@baileys-ireland.com

This listed building in the town centre dates back to 1709. Sensitively restored to its original splendour, it offers modern comforts, bedrooms varying in size, some with views of the Rock of Cashel. All are attractively decorated, comfortable and well appointed. The Cellar Bistro serves lunch and dinner.

FACILITIES: 9 en suite No smoking STV TVB Direct dial from bedrooms Licensed Cen ht Modem lines in bedrooms Dinner Last d 8.30pm
PARKING: 15 **NOTES:** Closed 24-28 Dec
CARDS:

Ireland

CASHEL continued

♦♦♦♦ Dualla House *(S 120430)*

Dualla ☎ 062 61487 📠 062 61487 Mrs M Power
e-mail: duallahse@eircom.net
Dir: *from Kilkenny (R691), 1m from Dualla village on right. From Cashel, travel up Main St from Cork, right at lights, left at church.*
Located in the Golden Vale of Tipperary, this 200-year-old house is on a 300-acre sheep farm. Period furniture graces the spacious rooms which include a sitting room with turf fire, dining room and comfortable en suite bedrooms. Big breakfasts are a speciality.
FACILITIES: 4 en suite (4 fmly) No smoking TVB tea/coffee No dogs (ex guide dogs) Cen ht TVL 300 acres sheep arable **PARKING:** 6
NOTES: Closed 15 Nov-Feb **CARDS:**

♦♦♦♦ GH *Legend's Townhouse & Restaurant*

The Kiln ☎ 062 61292
e-mail: info@legendsguesthouse.com
Dir: *turn off N8 onto R660 in direction of Thurles, establishment 30yds on left, signed*
This distinctive house has been purpose built to blend in with its dramatic location beneath the Rock of Cashel. The restaurant enjoys mystical floodlit views and diners will experience an atmosphere of almost eerie magic in the evening. A guests' lounge and very comfortable bedrooms complete the picture of this smart house on the edge of the town centre.
FACILITIES: 7 en suite (2 fmly) No smoking in bedrooms No smoking in dining room No smoking in 1 lounge STV TVB tea/coffee Direct dial from bedrooms No dogs Licensed Cen ht Dinner Last d 9.30pm
PARKING: 7 **NOTES:** Closed 23-26 Dec rs 19 Feb-9 Mar
CARDS:

♦♦♦♦ T&C Thornbrook House

Dualla Rd ☎ 062 62388 📠 062 61480
e-mail: thornbrookhouse@eircom.net
Dir: *1st turn right after Tourist Information Office onto Friar St. Next turn left after Church onto R691. Thornbrook House is 1km on right signed at entrance*
Visitors to Thornbrook will relish the combined skills of the Kennedys. Mary runs this attractively appointed bungalow with great attention to detail, while the superbly landscaped gardens are the handiwork of Willie Kennedy. Comfortable lounge and bedrooms, ample parking.
FACILITIES: 5 rms (3 en suite) (1 fmly) (5 GF) No smoking TVB tea/coffee No dogs (ex guide dogs) Cen ht **PRICES:** s €38 - €45; d €60 - €64✻
PARKING: 8 **NOTES:** Closed 17 Nov-Mar **CARDS:**

♦♦♦ T&C Ashmore House

John St ☎ 062 61286 📠 062 62789
e-mail: ashmorehouse@eircom.net
Dir: *turn off N8 in centre of town onto John St, house 100yds on right*
Ashmore House is set in a pretty walled garden in the town centre with an enclosed car park. Guests have use of a large sitting and dining room, and bedrooms come in a variety of sizes from big family rooms to a more compact double.
FACILITIES: 5 en suite (2 fmly) No smoking in bedrooms No smoking in dining room STV TVB tea/coffee No dogs Cen ht TVL **PRICES:** s €32 - €38; d €52 - €64✻ **PARKING:** 6 **CARDS:**

♦♦♦ *Knock-Saint-Lour House* *(S 074390)*

☎ 062 61172 Mr E O'Brien
Knock-Saint-Lour is a homely and comfortable house with spacious lounge and dining room, all nicely appointed. Bedrooms are spacious and comfortable.
FACILITIES: 7 en suite (2 fmly) tea/coffee No dogs (ex guide dogs) Cen ht TVL 30 acres mixed **PARKING:** 20 **NOTES:** Closed Nov-Mar

CLONMEL Map 01 C2

♦♦♦ T&C Farrenwick Country House

Poulmucka, Curranstown ☎ 052 35130 📠 052 35377
e-mail: kayden@clubi.ie
Dir: *from N24, Clonmel-Cahir road turn right onto R687, guest house 2m on L*
Close to many local beauty spots, this modern bungalow offers compact, well equipped accommodation, convenient for the historic towns of Cahir, Cashel, Clonmel and Kilkenny. Kay and Denis Fahy are very friendly hosts with a wide knowledge of the area and amenities. Guided tours and parking available.
FACILITIES: 4 rms (3 en suite) (4 fmly) (1 GF) No smoking STV TVB tea/coffee Direct dial from bedrooms No dogs (ex guide dogs) Cen ht TVL **PRICES:** s €32 - €35; d €51 - €70✻ **LB PARKING:** 11
NOTES: Closed 1 Dec-8 Jan **CARDS:**

NENAGH Map 01 B3

♦♦♦ T&C Ashley Park House

Ashley Park ☎ 067 38223 & 06738013 📠 067 38013
e-mail: margaret@ashleypark.com
Dir: *on N52, 4m N of Nenagh on left across lake*

An attractive, colonial style Georgian farmhouse, built in 1770. Set in gardens which run down to Lake Orna, it offers comfortable, spacious bedrooms, with quality antique furnishings. Breakfast is served in the dining room overlooking the lake, and dinner can be taken by prior arrangement.
FACILITIES: 6 rms (5 en suite) (3 fmly) No smoking in bedrooms No smoking in dining room No smoking in 1 lounge TV2B tea/coffee Licensed Cen ht TVL Golf 18 Fishing Snooker Dinner Last d 9pm **PRICES:** s fr €55; d fr €90✻ **CONF:** Board 30 Del from €145 ✻ **PARKING:** 30
NOTES: Civ Wed 90

♦♦♦ T&C *Williamsferry House*

Fintan Lalor St ☎ 067 31118 📠 067 31256
e-mail: williamsferry@eircom.net
Dir: *From N7 take sign for Nenagh off of motorway. From Limerick, drive through 1st rdbt as you enter the town, and take right turn at Centra foodstore*
This refurbished period house is ideally situated close to local amenities including water sports and cruising on the River Shannon. Facilities include a comfortable television lounge and breakfast room. Two of the bedrooms are located on the ground floor.
FACILITIES: 6 en suite No smoking in dining room TVB tea/coffee No dogs Cen ht TVL **PARKING:** 10 **NOTES:** Closed Xmas/New Year
CARDS:

ROSCREA Map 01 C3

♦♦♦ T&C Tower Guest House & Restaurant
Church St ☎ 0505 21774 & 21189 📠 0505 22425
e-mail: thetower@eircom.net
Dir: *on N7 Dublin to Limerick road alongside Round Tower. Take town centre rdbt on the outskirts of the town*
This comfortable guest house, restaurant and bar is fronted by a smart yellow and burgundy façade. The en suite bedrooms feature locally crafted furniture, attractive decor and a high standard of equipment. The Refectory Restaurant is open for breakfast, lunch and dinner; bar lunches and snacks are available in the West Gable Bar.
FACILITIES: 10 en suite (2 fmly) No smoking in area of dining room TVB tea/coffee Direct dial from bedrooms No dogs (ex guide dogs) Licensed Cen ht Dinner Last d 8.45pm **PRICES:** s €32 - €40; d €52 - €70✱ **PARKING:** 30 **NOTES:** Closed 25-26 Dec **CARDS:**

TEMPLEMORE Map 01 C3

♦♦♦♦ T&C Saratoga Lodge
Barnane ☎ 0504 31886 📠 0504 31491
Dir: *N7 to Roscra then N6 to Templemore, then R510 to Borrisoleigh for approx 2m. Turn right before 'Red Flag' complex. left at end of road. House beside Barnane Stud.*
Excellent hospitality from Valerie Beamish in a very comfortable house, beautifully located in a rural setting. Spacious bedrooms are attractively decorated, the sitting room has an open fire, and evening meals are available by arrangement. Convenient for golf, trekking, traditional music pubs, restaurants and hill climbing.
FACILITIES: 3 rms (2 en suite) (3 GF) No smoking in bedrooms tea/coffee No dogs (ex guide dogs) Cen ht TVL No coaches Dinner Last d 4pm **PRICES:** s €30 - €40; d €60 - €80✱ **CONF:** Del from €85 ✱ **PARKING:** 6 **NOTES:** Closed 23-30 Dec

THURLES Map 01 C3

Premier Collection

♦♦♦♦♦ T&C The Castle B & B
Two Mile Borris ☎ 0504 44324 📠 0504 44352
e-mail: b&b@thecastletmb.com
A fascinating historic house, sheltered by the 16th century castle tower house, and which has been in the Duggan family for two hundred years. Very comfortable, with big bedrooms and bathrooms, a luxurious lounge and dining room and very friendly and welcoming hosts. Golf, fishing, hill walking, and traditional pubs and restaurants nearby.
FACILITIES: 4 en suite (3 fmly) No smoking TVB tea/coffee No dogs (ex guide dogs) Cen ht TVL Fishing Pool Table Croquet Lawn **PRICES:** s €38 - €40; d €56 - €60✱ **PARKING:** 30 **CARDS:**

Premier Collection

♦♦♦♦♦ GH Inch House Country House & Restaurant
☎ 0504 51348 & 51261 📠 0504 51754
e-mail: inchhse@iol.ie
Dir: *turn off N8 at Turnpike for Thurles, through town, turn right at top of square for Nenagh Rd and 6.5km further*
This lovely Georgian house was built in 1720 by John Ryan, a landed Catholic gentleman, whose descendants lived there until the current owners bought it in 1985. The property has been greatly restored and decorated throughout and also

continued

boasts a restaurant. The elegant drawing room ceiling is particularly outstanding in the grandly decorated public rooms.
FACILITIES: 5 en suite (2 fmly) No smoking in dining room TVB tea/coffee Direct dial from bedrooms No dogs (ex guide dogs) Licensed Cen ht TVL Dinner Last d 9.30pm **PRICES:** s €60; d €105✱ **PARKING:** 40 **CARDS:**

TIPPERARY Map 01 C3

♦♦♦ GH Ach-na-Sheen
Clonmel Rd ☎ 062 51298 📠 062 80467
e-mail: gernoonan@eircom.net
Dir: *0.5m from Tipperary town on Clonmel Rd*
This large, modern bungalow, stands only five minutes' walk from main street of Tipperary and offers sound, comfortable accommodation.
FACILITIES: 10 rms (7 en suite) (1 fmly) No smoking in bedrooms No smoking in area of dining room STV TVB tea/coffee No dogs (ex guide dogs) Cen ht TVL **PRICES:** s €28 - €38; d €54 - €70✱ **PARKING:** 13 **NOTES:** Closed 11 Dec-8 Jan **CARDS:**

CO WATERFORD

ANNESTOWN Map 01 C2

Premier Collection

♦♦♦♦♦ T&C Annestown House
☎ 051 396160 📠 051 396474
e-mail: relax@annestown.com
Dir: *9.5km W of Tramore on R675 coast road*
This period house stands in an elevated position, overlooking a sandy cove with private access to the beach. The bedrooms are well equipped and successfully combine period furnishings and contemporary bathrooms. Public areas comprise a spacious sitting room, a library, billiards room and a dining room serving dinner by arrangement. The house has pleasant gardens and is less than an hour and a half's drive from Rosslare.
FACILITIES: 5 en suite No smoking in bedrooms tea/coffee Direct dial from bedrooms No dogs (ex guide dogs) Licensed Cen ht TVL No coaches Tennis (grass) Snooker Croquet lawn Private beach Dinner Last d 10pm previous day **PRICES:** s €65 - €80; d €100 - €125 **PARKING:** 10 **NOTES:** Closed 1 Nov-1 Mar **CARDS:**

ARDMORE Map 01 C2

♦♦♦♦ GH *Newtown Farm Guesthouse*
Grange ☎ 024 94143 & 086 2600799 📠 024 94143
e-mail: newtownfarm@eircom.net
Dir: *on N25 Dungarvan to Youghal road, turn left at Flemings public house*
Guests can be sure of a warm welcome at this comfortable modern farmhouse. Bedrooms look out over the dairy farm, and guests are welcome to stroll about, looking at the animals and farm activities. There is a play area and room for children, and home baking is a feature.
FACILITIES: 6 annexe en suite (3 fmly) No smoking in bedrooms No smoking in dining room STV TVB tea/coffee Direct dial from bedrooms Cen ht TVL Tennis (hard) Snooker Last d 6pm **PARKING:** 12 **CARDS:**

BALLYMACARBRY Map 01 C2

Premier Collection

♦♦♦♦♦ **Glasha** *(S1104106)*
Glasha ☎ 052 36108 📠 052 36108 Mr & Mrs P O'Gorman
e-mail: glasha@eircom.net
Dir: *8m from Clonmel on 671, turn right at Glasha Accommodation sign and 1km further*

Excellent accommodation and a warm welcome are assured at this comfortable country house. Two of the bedrooms are on the ground floor and all rooms are individually styled with tasteful furnishings and lots of personal touches. Home-cooking is a speciality and trout fishing is available on the river which runs through the grounds.
FACILITIES: 8 en suite (5 fmly) (2 GF) No smoking TVB tea/coffee No dogs Cen ht TVL Fishing 150 acres dairy Dinner Last d 5.30pm
PRICES: s €45; d €90* **PARKING:** 10
NOTES: Closed 1 Dec-1 Feb **CARDS:**

Premier Collection

♦♦♦♦♦ **GH Hanoras Cottage**
Nire Valley ☎ 052 36134 36442 📠 052 36540
e-mail: hanorascottage@eircom.net
Dir: *From Clonmel or Dungarvan (R672) to Ballymacarbry at Melodys Bar turn into Nire Valley. Establishment by bridge, beside Nire Church*

Nestling in the beautiful Nire Valley, Hanora's Cottage offers spacious bedrooms with jacuzzi baths. Lounge areas are very comfortable and the award winning restaurant serves fresh local produce. Mrs Wall's breakfasts are a real feast and deserve to be savoured at leisure!
FACILITIES: 10 en suite No smoking in bedrooms No smoking in dining room No smoking in 1 lounge TVB tea/coffee Direct dial from bedrooms No dogs Licensed Cen ht No children No coaches Jacuzzi Conservatory with hot spa tub Dinner Last d 8.30pm

continued

PRICES: d €150 - €250* **LB** **PARKING:** 15 **NOTES:** Closed Xmas wk rs Sun **CARDS:**

CAPPOQUIN Map 01 C2

Premier Collection

♦♦♦♦♦ **GH Richmond House**
☎ 058 54278 📠 058 54988
e-mail: info@richmondhouse.net
Dir: *on N72, 1km from Cappoquin on Dungarvan road*
An 18th-century Georgian country house with an award-winning restaurant and private parkland. Set in the heart of the Blackwater Valley, this splendid building has been carefully restored and renovated and is an ideal location for fishing, golfing and walking holidays. Each room is inviting and relaxing with nice antique pieces to suit each room, and modern comforts provided for guests' enjoyment.
FACILITIES: 9 en suite (2 fmly) No smoking in area of dining room TVB tea/coffee Direct dial from bedrooms No dogs Licensed Cen ht Dinner Last d 9pm **PRICES:** s €50 - €80; d €95 - €140* **LB**
PARKING: 20 **NOTES:** Closed 23 Dec-20 Jan
CARDS:

CHEEKPOINT Map 01 C2

♦♦♦ **GH *Three Rivers***
☎ 051 382520 📠 051 382542
e-mail: mail@threerivers.ie
Dir: *from Waterford follow R684 towards Dunmore East then follow signs for Cheekpoint*
This charming house is superbly located overlooking the rivers Barrow, Noire and Suir, within sight of the twinkling lights of Passage East where a ferry provides quick access to Rosslare port. There are well appointed bedrooms, attractive gardens and a sunny balcony. The lounge and dining room are sited to take full advantage of the magnificent views. The house stands within five minutes of Faithlegg Golf Course.
FACILITIES: 14 en suite (1 fmly) No smoking in bedrooms No smoking in dining room tea/coffee Direct dial from bedrooms No dogs (ex guide dogs) Cen ht TVL ch fac Golf 18 Golf Fishing and Riding all close by
PARKING: 20 **NOTES:** Closed 20 Dec-7 Jan **CARDS:**

DUNGARVAN Map 01 C2

Premier Collection

♦♦♦♦♦ **Castle Country House** *(S 192016)*
Millstreet, Cappagh ☎ 058 68049 📠 058 68099
Mrs J Nugent
e-mail: castlefm@iol.ie
Dir: *N72, take R671 for 3.5m, right at Millstreet, house 200yds on right*
This delightful house is to be found in the west wing of a 15th century castle. Guests are spoilt by host Joan Nugent who loves to cook and hunt out antiques for her visitors to enjoy. She is helped by her husband Emmett who enjoys showing off his high-tech dairy farm and is a fount of local knowledge. Bedrooms are spacious and enjoy lovely views. There is a river walk and a beautiful garden to relax in.
FACILITIES: 5 en suite (1 fmly) No smoking TVB tea/coffee Licensed Cen ht TVL Fishing 170 acres dairy & beef **PRICES:** s €60 - €70; d €80 - €90* **LB** **PARKING:** 11 **NOTES:** Closed Nov-mid Mar
CARDS:

Premier Collection

♦♦♦♦♦ GH Powersfield House

Ballinamuck West ☎ 058 45594 📠 058 45550
e-mail: powersfieldhouse@cablesurf.com
Dir: *take the Killarney/Clonmel R672 out of Dungarvan, Powersfield House is 2nd turn left 1st house on right*

The warmth of Eunice Powers' welcome is matched by her cooking skills, charming bedrooms and very high standards. A Georgian-style residence in its own grounds, with a comfortable sitting room - the ideal place for afternoon tea or drinks beside the fire.

FACILITIES: 6 en suite (3 fmly) (1 GF) No smoking in bedrooms STV TVB Direct dial from bedrooms No dogs (ex guide dogs) Licensed Cen ht Dinner Last d 9.30pm **PRICES:** s €50 - €55; d €80 - €90✻ **LB**
PARKING: 12 **CARDS:**

♦♦♦♦ GH An Bohreen

Killineen West ☎ 051 291010 📠 051 291011
e-mail: mulligans@anbohreen.com

A purpose-built bungalow, commanding panoramic views over Dungarvan Bay and the Commeragh Mountains. Bedrooms are comfortable and individually decorated, two have balconies. Open plan, contemporary public areas take advantage of the wonderful scenery. The Mulligans are passionate about their business, Ann cooking each evening, (booking advised) and home baking is her speciality. Jim will organise trips and make bookings for golf at the many nearby Championship courses.

FACILITIES: 4 en suite No smoking Licensed Cen ht TVL No children 6yrs No coaches Dinner **PRICES:** s €50; d €64✻ **PARKING:** 6
NOTES: Closed Nov-14 Mar **CARDS:**

♦♦♦♦ Gortnadiha House *(X 259890)*

Ring ☎ 058 46142 📠 058 46444 Mrs E Harty
e-mail: ringcheese@tinet.ie
Dir: *turn off N25 onto R674, 1st left on this road, 2nd house on right*

Set in a woodland garden on a dairy farm in the heart of the Ring Irish-speaking area, this elegant country house offers gracious living in a relaxed environment. The bedrooms are individual in style and very comfortable. Afternoon tea is served in the elegant drawing room and breakfast, chosen from an extensive menu, is taken at the large mahogany table.

FACILITIES: 3 en suite No smoking in bedrooms No smoking in dining room No smoking in 1 lounge TV1B tea/coffee No dogs (ex guide dogs) Cen ht TVL Riding 300 acres dairy **PRICES:** s €30 - €40; d €70 - €80✻
PARKING: 4 **NOTES:** Closed Xmas & New Year rs Nov-Mar
CARDS:

♦♦♦♦ Sliabh gCua Farmhouse *(S 191057)*

Touraneena, Ballinamult ☎ 058 47120 Mrs B Cullinan
e-mail: breedacullinan@sliabhgcua.com
Dir: *from Dungarvan take R672 off N25 towards Clonmel for 15km. Farmhouse signposted on left and 1km off main road beside Touraneena*

This comfortable farmhouse offers a home from home on a dairy farm in the shadow of the Knockmealdown and Comeragh mountains. There are lovely views and splendid gardens in which to sit and relax. A popular feature is the well equipped play room provided for young children and Mrs Breeda Cullinan is a truly welcoming hostess.

continued

Sliabh gCua Farmhouse

FACILITIES: 3 en suite (1 fmly) No smoking tea/coffee No dogs (ex guide dogs) Cen ht TVL Pool Table private woodland nature walks, playground, treehouse 200 acres dairy beef arable forrestry **PRICES:** s €30; d €60 **LB**
PARKING: 6 **NOTES:** Closed Nov-Mar

TRAMORE — Map 01 C2

♦♦♦♦ T&C Glenorney

Newtown ☎ 051 381056 📠 051 381103
e-mail: glenoney@iol.ie
Dir: *on R675 opposite the Tramore Golf Club*

A beautifully spacious and luxurious home with spectacular views of Tramore Bay, located opposite a championship golf course. Great attention has been paid to detail and there is an extensive breakfast menu. Bedrooms are tastefully decorated and the lounge is comfortably furnished, there is also a sun room, patio and private garden for guests.

FACILITIES: 6 en suite (2 fmly) No smoking TVB tea/coffee Direct dial from bedrooms No dogs (ex guide dogs) Cen ht TVL **PRICES:** s €50 - €60; d €70 - €80✻ **PARKING:** 6 **NOTES:** Closed Xmas
CARDS:

Ireland

TRAMORE continued

♦♦♦♦ T&C Cliff House

Cliff Rd ☎ 051 381497 & 391296 🖷 051 381497
e-mail: hilary@cliffhouse.ie
Dir: *just off R675, turn left at Ritz thatched pub*

A comfortable and spacious home with panoramic views of Tramore Bay and secure private parking. All bedrooms are decorated to a high standard, with modern facilities, and most rooms have sea views. The extensive breakfast menu offers many delicious choices. This is an ideal base for touring, and further developments planned for mid-2003 include rooms with private balconies overlooking the bay.
FACILITIES: 6 en suite (3 fmly) (3 GF) No smoking STV TVB tea/coffee No dogs Cen ht TVL No children 6yrs **PRICES:** d fr €70✻ **LB** **PARKING:** 10 **NOTES:** Closed Jan **CARDS:**

♦♦♦♦ T&C *Sea View Lodge*

Seaview Park ☎ 051 381122 🖷 051 381122
e-mail: seaviewlodge@eircom.net
Dir: *from Waterford, take R675 to Tramore. On entering Tramore, turn right after 'Welcome' sign. Onto small rdbt & turn left then right. Lodge signposted*
A large bungalow with panoramic sea views of Tramore Bay from the dining room and a sun lounge overlooking the garden. Bedrooms are attractively decorated and a pleasant conservatory has been built at the front of the house. An extensive breakfast menu is on offer. Close to the golf course, and the beach, and horse riding is available nearby.
FACILITIES: 5 en suite (3 fmly) No smoking STV TVB tea/coffee No dogs Cen ht TVL No children 6yrs Jacuzzi Last d by arrangement **PARKING:** 7 **NOTES:** Closed Nov-Apr **CARDS:**

WATERFORD — Map 01 C2

See also Cheekpoint

Premier Collection

♦♦♦♦♦ Foxmount Country House *(S 659091)*

Passage East Rd, Dunmore Rd ☎ 051 874308
🖷 051 854906 Mrs M Kent
e-mail: foxmount@iol.ie
Dir: *from Waterford take Dunmore East road, after 1.5m take left fork towards Passage East for 0.5m. Right at next T-junct*
This charming 17th-century country house is set on a busy dairy farm amid beautiful lawns and gardens with screening trees and a hard tennis court. Tastefully modernised, it offers en suite bedrooms and attentive service from the charming hostess. The farm and gardens provide most of the raw materials for the carefully prepared evening meals.

continued

Foxmount Country House

FACILITIES: 5 en suite (1 fmly) No smoking in bedrooms No smoking in dining room No dogs (ex guide dogs) Cen ht TVL Tennis (hard) Table tennis 200 acres dairy Dinner Last d 6pm **PRICES:** s €60; d €90✻ **LB** **PARKING:** 6 **NOTES:** Closed early Nov-early Mar

Premier Collection

♦♦♦♦♦ T&C Sion Hill House & Gardens

Sion Hill, Ferrybank ☎ 051 851558 🖷 051 851678
e-mail: sionhill@eircom.net
Dir: *take Rosslare road from Waterford Bridge rdbt, rail station on left, next left entrance after Jury's Hotel on N25 (Wexford/Rosslare road*

Although close to the city this 18th-century residence has extensive and peaceful gardens, that are gradually being restored to their 1870 design. Rare plants, a walled garden, a meadow and woodlands are all to be found here. Flanked by two pavillions, the house has also undergone major refurbishment resulting in two fine reception rooms and comfortable en suite bedrooms. This is a gracious house where the friendly owners like to mix with their guests, as the visitors' book shows, their hospitality is much appreciated.
FACILITIES: 4 en suite (4 fmly) No smoking STV TVB tea/coffee No dogs (ex guide dogs) Cen ht TVL No coaches **PRICES:** s €45 - €62.50; d €70 - €88 **LB** **PARKING:** 16 **NOTES:** Closed mid Dec-early Jan **CARDS:**

Ireland

♦♦♦♦ GH Arlington Lodge
John's Hill ☎ 051 878584 📠 051 878127
e-mail: info@arlingtonlodge.com
A charming house dating from the early 18th century. From 1871 it was the residence of the Catholic Bishops of Waterford. Extensively and sympathetically restored and extended, it now provides all the amenities of a luxurious country house, with a fine restaurant, a cocktail bar and an elegant drawing room. Bedrooms are individually decorated and furnished with style.
FACILITIES: 20 en suite No smoking in bedrooms No smoking in area of dining room STV TVB tea/coffee Direct dial from bedrooms No dogs (ex guide dogs) Licensed Lift Cen ht Dinner Last d 9pm **PRICES:** s €80 - €140; d €140 - €220* **LB CONF:** Thtr 40 Class 40 Board 20
PARKING: 40 **NOTES:** Closed 24-27 Dec **CARDS:**

♦♦♦♦ T&C *Brown's Town House*
29 South Pde ☎ 051 870594 📠 051 871923
e-mail: info@brownstownhouse.com
Dir: *off N25 at the mall and turn into Catherine St, which becomes South Parade. Brown's 800mtrs on right*
This late Victorian house in the centre of Waterford offers a convivial atmosphere. Impeccable bedrooms feature big power showers with plenty of hot water, while the comfortable sitting room invites relaxation. Home-made breads and jams are part of the generous breakfasts served around the dining table. Local golf courses, beaches and the Waterford Glass complex are nearby.
FACILITIES: 6 en suite (2 fmly) No smoking STV TVB tea/coffee Direct dial from bedrooms No dogs Cen ht TVL No coaches
NOTES: Closed 20 Dec-29 Jan **CARDS:**

♦♦♦♦ GH Coach House
Butlerstown Castle, Butlerstown, Cork Rd ☎ 051 384656 📠 051 384751
e-mail: coachhse@iol.ie
Dir: *N25 towards Cork (pass Holycross pub) for 3m from Waterford Crystal Factory until crossroads with sign for Coach House. Turn left, house on right*

Built in 1870 as the coach house to Butlerstown Castle, this comfortable house has been skilfully refurbished. There is a fine lounge and the bedrooms are well equipped and furnished in traditional pine; a sauna is available.
FACILITIES: 7 en suite (1 fmly) No smoking in bedrooms No smoking in dining room TVB tea/coffee Direct dial from bedrooms No dogs (ex guide dogs) Licensed Cen ht No coaches Sauna **PRICES:** s €48.50 - €60; d €71 - €95* **PARKING:** 15 **NOTES:** Closed 20 Dec-1 Feb
CARDS:

Super supper! this symbol shows that evening meals exceeded our Inspector's expectations.

♦♦♦♦ GH Diamond Hill
Diamond Hill, Slieverue ☎ 051 832855 📠 051 832254
e-mail: diamondhill29@hotmail.com
Dir: *1.2km from Waterford city off Rosslare/Waterford road N25*

Extensive refurbishment has been carried out to a very high standard at this friendly house. These include spacious new bedrooms, comfortable lounges and a private car park. Diamond Hill is a welcoming home with lovely gardens and a sun terrace.
FACILITIES: 18 en suite (6 fmly) (10 GF) No smoking STV TVB tea/coffee Direct dial from bedrooms No dogs (ex guide dogs) Cen ht TVL
PRICES: s €35 - €45; d €64 - €80* **PARKING:** 20
NOTES: Closed 22-27 Dec **CARDS:**

♦♦♦ Ashbourne House *(S6631140)*
Slieverue ☎ 051 832037 📠 051 833783 Mrs A Forrest
e-mail: ashburne@gofree.indigo.ie
Dir: *2.5m E of Waterford, off N25 Waterford/Wexford Rd, signposted*
A comfortable ivy-clad house in a quiet residential area where the charming owner serves tea and fresh home-made scones on arrival. There is a hospitality tray in the first-floor sitting room and the welcoming bedrooms are all en suite, with one ground floor bedroom.
FACILITIES: 7 en suite (6 fmly) (1 GF) No smoking in dining room STV TVB tea/coffee Cen ht TVL 25 acres beef **PRICES:** s €39.50; d €60*
PARKING: 7 **NOTES:** Closed Dec-Mar **CARDS:**

♦♦♦ T&C Belmont House
Belmont Rd, Rosslare Rd, Ferrybank ☎ 051 832174
e-mail: belmonthouse@eircom.net
Dir: *on Waterford to Rosslare road N25, 2km from Waterford city*
A dormer bungalow that is conveniently situated for the Waterford Glass Factory, golf clubs and the city centre. Guests can make use of tea and coffee making facilities in the sitting room and from the dining room they can enjoy views of the garden to the countryside beyond. Bedrooms are comfortably furnished.
FACILITIES: 4 en suite No smoking No dogs Cen ht TVL No children 7yrs
PRICES: d €52 - €58* **PARKING:** 6 **NOTES:** Closed Nov-Apr

♦♦♦ GH O'Gradys
Cork Rd ☎ 051 378851 📠 051 374062
e-mail: info@ogradyshotel.ie
Dir: *on the main Cork Road N25, midway between crystal factory and city centre*
Midway between the city centre and the Crystal Factory, O'Grady's is an old Gothic-style gatehouse. Bedrooms vary in size, with singles available, and excellent food is served in attractive surroundings. Off street parking is available.
FACILITIES: 9 en suite (1 fmly) No smoking in bedrooms No smoking in area of dining room TVB tea/coffee Direct dial from bedrooms No dogs Licensed Cen ht TVL Dinner Last d 9.30pm **PRICES:** s €40 - €50; d €80 - €90* **LB PARKING:** 30 **NOTES:** Closed 1st 2wks Nov & Xmas, New Year **CARDS:**

CO WESTMEATH

ATHLONE — Map 01 C4

♦♦♦♦ T&C *Riverview House*

Galway Rd, Summerhill ☎ 0902 94532 📠 0902 94532
e-mail: riverviewhouse@hotmail.com
Dir: *on N6, 2km from town centre*

Three curved red-brick archways distinguish this pleasant house which is well positioned close to the town centre. Carmel Corbett is a friendly owner who offers modern en suite accommodation in attractively decorated and comfortable bedrooms. Other facilities include a cosy lounge, and a breakfast room that opens on to the gardens. Nearby Lough Ree attracts anglers, who are well catered for with a bait and tackle shop, and there is ample off-street parking.

FACILITIES: 4 en suite (3 fmly) No smoking STV TVB tea/coffee No dogs Cen ht TVL **PARKING:** 10 **NOTES:** Closed 18 Dec-1 Mar
CARDS:

♦♦♦♦ T&C Shelmalier House

Retreat Rdy, Cartrontroy ☎ 0902 72245 & 72145 📠 0902 73190
e-mail: shelmal@iol.ie

Shelmalier is a modern house in a residential area, set in well-kept gardens. The decor is very attractive, and bedrooms offer good quality furnishings and facilities. There is a comfortable lounge and a breakfast room.

FACILITIES: 7 en suite (2 fmly) No smoking STV TVB tea/coffee Direct dial from bedrooms No dogs (ex guide dogs) Cen ht TVL **PRICES:** s €39; d €52* **PARKING:** 10 **NOTES:** Closed 20 Dec-31 Jan
CARDS:

HORSELEAP — Map 01 C4

♦♦♦ Woodlands Farm *(N 286426)*

Streamstown ☎ 044 26414 Mrs M Maxwell
Dir: *from Dublin take N6 and continue through Kilbeggan to Horseleap, turn right at filling station. Farm 2.5m signposted "Woodlands Farm"*

continued

Comfortable farmhouse set in 120 acres. The spacious sitting and dining rooms are very relaxing, and a new addition is the hospitality kitchen, where tea and coffee are available at all times. Dinner is served by prior arrangement.

FACILITIES: 6 rms (3 en suite) (2 fmly) (3 GF) No smoking in bedrooms No smoking in dining room No smoking in 1 lounge Cen ht TVL 120 acres mixed Last d 5pm **PRICES:** s fr €35; d fr €52* LB
NOTES: Closed Nov-Feb

MOATE — Map 01 C4

Premier Collection

♦♦♦♦♦ *Temple Country House & Spa* *(N 267395)*

Horseleap ☎ 0506 35118 📠 0506 35008
Mr & Mrs D Fagan
e-mail: templespa@spiders.ie
Dir: *0.5m off N6, signposted*

A Georgian house with 100 acres, built on the site of an early monastery, this sympathetically refurbished farmhouse offers accommodation in very comfortable en suite bedrooms. The spa building offers treatment rooms and hydrotherapy, as well as a relaxation room. Dinner features produce from the farm and gardens, and is taken round a hunting table, then guests can relax by the fire. Activity packages (golf, riding, cycling or walking) can be arranged here.

FACILITIES: 3 en suite 5 annexe en suite (1 fmly) No smoking in 5 bedrooms No smoking in dining room No smoking in 1 lounge TVB tea/coffee Direct dial from bedrooms No dogs (ex guide dogs) Licensed Cen ht Sauna Spa facilities, beauty treatments 96 acres cattle sheep Dinner Last d 10am **NOTES:** Closed Dec-Jan **CARDS:**

MULLINGAR — Map 01 C4

Premier Collection

♦♦♦♦♦ GH *Crookedwood House*

Ireland's Blue Book

Crookedwood ☎ 044 72165 📠 044 72166
e-mail: info@crookedwoodhouse.com
Dir: *from Dublin take second exit off Mullingar Bypass, continue to Crookedwood village, at Wood Pub turn right, and continue for 2km*

As charming as its name, this beautifully restored old rectory overlooks Lake Derravaragh and offers exceptionally comfortable bedrooms. There is also an inviting lounge where tea is served and a bar for drinks before dinner. The evening meals are the highlight of a stay here and have earned great praise for chef/patron Niall Kenny.

FACILITIES: 8 en suite No smoking in 4 bedrooms No smoking in dining room TVB Direct dial from bedrooms Licensed Cen ht Tennis (hard) Croquet lawn Dinner Last d 9.30pm **NOTES:** Closed 4 days at Xmas **CARDS:**

♦♦♦♦ T&C Hilltop Country House
Delvin Rd, Rathconnell ☎ 044 48958 📠 044 48013
e-mail: casean@tinet.ie
Dir: *take 2nd exit off Mullingar by-pass road (N4) and follow N52 sign for Delvin, Hilltop sign is 1km from exit rdbt*
This is a charming country house in glorious gardens, where flowers and shrubs fill every available space, the creative work of owner, Sean Casey. South facing, the house is well designed, elevated reception rooms have an attractive patio garden adjacent to them. The bedrooms are very comfortable with good en suite showers. The breakfast menu is excellent with an extensive choice. Dinner is by advance reservation only. Dymphna and Sean Casey will do everything posible to ensure happy visits to their home.
FACILITIES: 5 en suite No smoking STV TVB No dogs Cen ht TVL No children 15yrs No coaches **PRICES:** s €40 - €42; d €60 - €64✳ LB **PARKING:** 6 **NOTES:** Closed Dec & Jan **CARDS:**

CO WEXFORD

ARTHURSTOWN Map 01 C2

♦♦♦♦ T&C Glendine Country House
☎ 051 389258 📠 051 389677
e-mail: glendinehouse@eircom.net
Dir: *from Rosslare on N25 for 5m, at 1st & 2nd rdbts turn left, R733, 32km towards Wellingtonbridge*
A Georgian house in its own grounds overlooking the estuary in Arthurstown, and next to the village of Ballyhack where the local ferry crosses to and from Passage East in Waterford. Glendine is a well-maintained house with attractive gardens, a play area for children, and plenty of car parking space. Inside there is a spacious sitting room with TV, a separate dining room, and comfortable en suite bedrooms, one of which has a second bedroom attached which is useful for family or friends.
FACILITIES: 4 en suite (1 fmly) No smoking in bedrooms No smoking in dining room No smoking in 1 lounge TVB tea/coffee Cen ht TVL small cafe **PRICES:** s €50 - €60; d €80 - €90✳ LB **PARKING:** 20
NOTES: Closed 15 Dec-15 Jan **CARDS:**

BALLYHACK Map 01 C2

♦♦♦♦ T&C Marsh Mere Lodge
☎ 051 389186
e-mail: stay@marshmerelodge.com
Dir: *from Rosslare Harbour take N25 to Wexford then take R733 to Ballyhack*
This charming house is situated a few minutes' walk from the Ballyhack ferry overlooking Waterford harbour. The house is full of the friendly proprietor's personal touches. Bedrooms are delightful and a fine tea is served on the flower-filled verandah.
FACILITIES: 4 en suite No smoking in bedrooms No smoking in dining room No smoking in 1 lounge No dogs (ex guide dogs) Cen ht TVL Pony trap rides available on request **PRICES:** s fr €50; d fr €80 LB
PARKING: 5 **CARDS:**

Super supper! this symbol shows that evening meals exceeded our Inspector's expectations.

CAMPILE Map 01 C2

Premier Collection

♦♦♦♦♦ T&C Kilmokea Country Manor & Gardens
Great Island ☎ 051 388109 📠 051 388776
e-mail: kilmokea@indigo.ie
Dir: *from New Ross take R733 S towards Campile, before village turn right for Great Island and Kilmokea Gardens. 12km from New Ross*
A gracious 18th-century, stone-built rectory, recently restored. Nestling in wooded gardens (open to the public), where peacocks wander and trout fishing is available on the lake. Comfortable bedrooms and public rooms are richly furnished, and a 'country house' style dinner is served nightly (booking essential). Take breakfast in the conservatory and tea overlooking the beautiful gardens.

FACILITIES: 4 en suite 2 annexe en suite (1 fmly) (2 GF) No smoking in bedrooms No smoking in dining room No smoking in lounges tea/coffee Cen ht ch fac Fishing Dinner Last d noon **PRICES:** s €80 - €115; d €140 - €190✳ **CONF:** Board 25 **PARKING:** 12
NOTES: Closed 6 Nov-Feb **CARDS:**

CARRIGBYRNE Map 01 D3

♦♦♦ T&C Woodlands House
☎ 051 428287 📠 051 428287
e-mail: woodwex@eircom.net
Dir: *on N25 between Wexford and New Ross, 0.25m from Cedar Lodge Hotel towards New Ross*

Commanding panoramic views, this is a recently rerfurbished bungalow with pretty gardens. It is only half an hour's drive to Rosslare Harbour. Snacks are available, and dinner by arrangement. Bedrooms vary in size, though all are very comfortable. There is a guest sitting room.
FACILITIES: 4 en suite (4 GF) No smoking in bedrooms No smoking in dining room TVB tea/coffee No dogs Cen ht No children 5yrs No coaches Dinner Last d 10am **PRICES:** s €38.50; d €55✳ LB **PARKING:** 6
NOTES: Closed Nov-14 Mar **CARDS:**

Ireland

ENNISCORTHY

Map 01 D3

Premier Collection

♦♦♦♦♦ Ballinkeele House *(T 030334)*
Ballymurn ☎ 053 38105 053 38468 Mr & Mrs J Maher
e-mail: info@ballinkeele.com
Dir: *from Wexford N11 N to Oilgate, right at sign post & follow signs. From Enniscorthy take N11 S to Oilgate, left at signpost & follow signs*

Set amid 350 acres of farmland, this classical house - built in 1840 and a fine example of the work of Daniel Robertson - retains its original features while adding modern comforts. The fine portico leads to the entrance hall, where a blazing fire creates a warm, hospitable atmosphere. Carefully cooked dinners are served round an elegant table in the fine dining room, and particularly inviting bedrooms welcome guests with a decanter of sherry. Easy parking.
FACILITIES: 5 en suite No smoking in bedrooms No smoking in dining room No smoking in 1 lounge No dogs (ex guide dogs) Licensed Cen ht TVL No children 3yrs Fishing Croquet lawn Bicycles 360 acres arable, forestry Dinner Last d 10am **PRICES:** s €85 - €105; d €130 - €170✱ **LB PARKING:** 20 **NOTES:** rs 13 Nov-Feb
CARDS:

♦♦♦♦ T&C *Lemongrove House*
Blackstoops ☎ 054 36115 054 36115
Dir: *1km N of Enniscorthy at roundabout on Dublin to Rosslare road (N11)*

A large house in its own grounds on an elevated site surrounded by gardens and plenty of parking space. Lemongrove House offers en suite bedrooms which are all individually decorated in warm, cheerful colour schemes, and there is a comfortable sitting room and breakfast room.
FACILITIES: 9 en suite (3 fmly) No smoking STV TVB tea/coffee No dogs (ex guide dogs) Cen ht TVL **PARKING:** 12 **NOTES:** Closed 20-31 Dec
CARDS:

FERNS

Map 01 D3

♦♦♦♦ Clone House *(T 022484)*
☎ 054 66113 Mrs B Breen
e-mail: tbreen@e-merge.ie
Dir: *2m SE off N11. From Dublin left at chemist and from Wexford right at Dunbars*
The hospitable Mrs Breen takes great pride in her farmhouse. Fine furniture from past generations enhances the modern day comforts and the prize-winning gardens are a delight.
FACILITIES: 5 en suite (4 fmly) No smoking in bedrooms No smoking in dining room No smoking in 1 lounge TV3B No dogs (ex guide dogs) Licensed Cen ht TVL Fishing Pool Table 280 acres mixed working Dinner Last d 4pm **PRICES:** s €39 - €47; d €76✱ **PARKING:** 37
NOTES: Closed Oct-May

GOREY

Map 01 D3

Premier Collection

♦♦♦♦♦ Woodlands Country House *(T 163648)*
Killinierin ☎ 0402 37125 37133 0402 37133
Philomena O'Sullivan
e-mail: info@woodlandscountryhouse.com
Dir: *signposted 3m N of Gorey off N11*
One hour's drive from Dublin, Wexford and Kilkenny, and an ideal location for touring Wicklow. This country house, built in 1836, is set in 1.5 acres of mature gardens and courtyard of old stone buildings. The O'Sullivan family offer warm hospitality to guests. Three rooms have balconies. Homemade scones served on arrival.
FACILITIES: 6 en suite (3 fmly) No smoking STV TVB tea/coffee No dogs (ex guide dogs) Licensed Cen ht TVL Tennis (hard) Children's play room 8 acres mixed **PRICES:** d €80 - €90✱ **LB**
PARKING: 10 **NOTES:** Closed Oct-Feb **CARDS:** 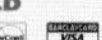

♦♦♦♦ T&C *Hillside House*
Tubberduff ☎ 055 21726 & 22036 055 22567
e-mail: hsh@eircom.net
Dir: *from Dublin turn left off N11, 1.5km after Toss Byrnes pub, signposted Hillside House. From Rosslare turn right off N11 2km after Gorey Town*

A pristine house with pretty gardens, set in a lovely rural location commanding panoramic views of mountains and the sea - only three km from Ballymoney beach. Ann Sutherland is a good cook, providing guests with a variety of home baking for the evening meal. Both reception rooms are big with large windows to take advantage of the beautiful setting. Bedrooms are very comfortable, decorated in attractive colour tones and have good beds.
FACILITIES: 6 en suite (4 fmly) No smoking in bedrooms No smoking in dining room STV TVB tea/coffee No dogs (ex guide dogs) Licensed Cen ht TVL Dinner Last d 6pm **PARKING:** 6 **NOTES:** Closed 20-28 Dec
CARDS:

Ireland

KILMORE QUAY — Map 01 D2

♦♦♦♦ GH *Quay House Guest House & Restaurant*

☎ 053 29988 Fax 053 29808
e-mail: kilmore@esatclear.ie
Dir: *turn off N25 onto R739 following sign to Kilmore Quay, house on left past Hotel Saltees*

Situated on the main street in this fishing village that is only 15 minutes from Rosslare Harbour. Comfortable accommodation is provided by the friendly and hospitable owners. Local attractions include fishing, bird-watching and island cruises. Private parking available.
FACILITIES: 8 en suite (6 fmly) No smoking in dining room TVB tea/coffee No dogs (ex guide dogs) Licensed Cen ht Angling and diving facilities Dinner Last d 9.30pm **PARKING:** 16 **CARDS:**

NEW ROSS — Map 01 C3

♦♦♦♦ T&C Oakwood House

Ring Rd, Mountgarrett ☎ 051 425494 Fax 051 425494
e-mail: susan@oakwoodhouse.net
Dir: *on ring road(N30) of New Ross Town, close to Stat Petrol station*
Purpose-built red brick house, surrounded by lovely gardens and just 15 minutes walk from the town centre. The friendly owners are helpful and attentive, bedrooms are comfortable, and facilities include a TV lounge and breakfast room, and off-street parking. Golf, swimming pool, pubs and restaurants are all nearby.
FACILITIES: 4 en suite (1 fmly) No smoking TVB tea/coffee No dogs Cen ht TVL No children 6yrs No coaches **PRICES:** s €40 - €45; d €60 - €64✳ LB **PARKING:** 10 **NOTES:** Closed Nov-Mar **CARDS:**

ROSSLARE HARBOUR — Map 01 D2

Premier Collection

♦♦♦♦♦ GH Churchtown House

☎ 053 32555 Fax 053 32577
e-mail: info@churchtownhouse.com
Dir: *take R736 from N25 at Tagoat, turn between Cushens pub and church. House 0.5m on left*
A charming period house, set in mature grounds on a link road between Rosslare Harbour and Rosslare Strand. Patricia and Austin Cody are excellent hosts who have spent a lot of time and energy restoring and extending their home. Bedrooms are varied, attractive and comfortable. The reception rooms are spacious and elegant and the Codys are always pleased to help guests plan their itinerary.
FACILITIES: 12 en suite (1 fmly) (5 GF) No smoking TVB Direct dial from bedrooms No dogs (ex guide dogs) Licensed Cen ht TVL No coaches Croquet lawn Dinner Last d noon **PRICES:** s fr €75; d fr €120✳ LB **PARKING:** 14 **NOTES:** Closed 15 Nov-Feb
CARDS:

♦♦♦♦ T&C Oldcourt House

☎ 053 33895 & 086 3742568
e-mail: oldcrt@gofree.indigo.ie
Dir: *turn off N11 at St Patricks Church - establishment approx 700yds on left*
An impressively large, modern house on the quiet shoreside road overlooking Rosslare Bay, just 200 yards beyond Hotel Rosslare,and convenient for the car ferry, beaches and golf courses. The en suite bedrooms are large, airy and furnished to a high standard. There is a comfortable lounge and separate dining room. An ideal base for small golfing parties.
FACILITIES: 6 en suite No smoking in bedrooms No smoking in dining room STV TVB No dogs (ex guide dogs) Cen ht TVL **PRICES:** s €30 - €35; d €50 - €60✳ LB **PARKING:** 10 **NOTES:** Closed Dec-Feb
CARDS:

♦♦♦ GH *Euro Lodge*

☎ 053 33118 33994 Fax 053 33120
e-mail: eurolodge@eircom.net
Dir: *600mtrs from port on N25, on left past church*
This purpose built guest house is ideally situated for access to the port terminal and can be booked on a room only rate. Breakfast is served in the restaurant. The bedrooms are spacious and well appointed and there is a guest sitting room.
FACILITIES: 38 en suite (1 fmly) No smoking in 30 bedrooms TVB tea/coffee Direct dial from bedrooms No dogs (ex guide dogs) Cen ht TVL **PARKING:** 54 **NOTES:** Closed Nov-Mar **CARDS:**

♦♦♦ T&C *Kilrane House*

☎ 053 33135 Fax 053 33739
Dir: *on N25 opposite pub/restuarant, in the village of Kilrane, 2km from Rosslare Harbour ferry port. Bus stop outside house*
This period house has been restored and all bedrooms now have private bathrooms. There are many original features, open fires and a superb guest lounge. Early breakfasts can be served if required.
FACILITIES: 6 en suite (2 fmly) No smoking in bedrooms No smoking in dining room TV4B tea/coffee No dogs (ex guide dogs) Cen ht TVL **PARKING:** 10 **NOTES:** Closed 25-28 Dec **CARDS:**

♦♦♦ T&C *The Light House*

Main Rd ☎ 053 33214 Fax 053 33214
A contemporary styled bungalow set in its own grounds, The Light House makes an ideal stopover for ferry users or for those who want to relax near a beach and golf club. There is a TV lounge and breakfast room in addition to the bedrooms, all of which have excellent en suite shower rooms.
FACILITIES: 4 en suite No smoking TVB tea/coffee No dogs Cen ht TVL No children 18yrs **PARKING:** 6 **NOTES:** Closed 2 Oct-Feb
CARDS:

Ireland

WEXFORD Map 01 D3

♦♦♦♦ *Clonard House (T 021199)*

Clonard Great ☎ 053 43141 & 47337 📠 053 43141
Mr & Mrs J Hayes
e-mail: clonardhouse@indigo.ie
Dir: *signposted on R733/N25 roundabout. Take R733 S for 500mtrs, 1st road on left and 1st entrance on left*

This lovely old farmhouse is an outstanding example of a well maintained Georgian house. Public rooms include an attractive and comfortable lounge with a large open fire, and some of the bedrooms have four-poster beds with beautiful antique lace. Furnishings include many period pieces and all the bedrooms enjoy views of gardens and farmland.
FACILITIES: 9 en suite (4 fmly) No smoking in bedrooms No smoking in dining room No smoking in 1 lounge TVB No dogs (ex guide dogs) Licensed Cen ht TVL No children 5yrs 120 acres dairy Dinner Last d 6pm **PARKING:** 10 **NOTES:** Closed 5 Nov-16 Mar **CARDS:**

♦♦♦♦ T&C Darral House

Spawell Rd ☎ 053 24264 📠 053 24284
Dir: *take N11 from Dublin after Ferrycarrig Hotel. Proceed to rdbt turn left. Racecourse on right, Hospital on left near Hill Rd. Left into Hill St and left at hill. House 50yds on left*
A period town house which has been completely refurbished to a very high standard by friendly owners Kathleen and Sean Nolan. Fine high ceilings are a feature of the elegant sitting and dining room, and comfort is the keynote in the en suite bedrooms which are attractively decorated. Guests are offered a wide range of choices at breakfast, including fresh fruit, fish and other tempting dishes.
FACILITIES: 4 en suite No smoking in bedrooms No smoking in dining room TVB tea/coffee No dogs Cen ht **PRICES:** s €40 - €50; d €65 - €70✳ **PARKING:** 6 **NOTES:** Closed 20 Dec-1 Jan **CARDS:**

♦♦♦♦ Killiane Castle *(T 058168)*

Drinagh ☎ 053 58885 & 58898 📠 053 58885
Mr & Mrs J Mernagh
e-mail: killiane@yahoo.com
Dir: *off N25 between Wexford and Rosslare*

continued

Set in 230 acres of pastureland, this guest house is adjacent to a 13th-century castle. The comfortable sitting and dining rooms are on the ground floor, and there is also a hospitality area where tea and coffee are available at all times. Bedrooms are furnished in keeping with the period of the house. There are hard tennis courts in the grounds.
FACILITIES: 8 en suite (2 fmly) No smoking TVB No dogs Licensed Cen ht TVL Tennis (hard) 230 acres dairy Dinner Last d noon **PRICES:** s €45; d €66✳ **NOTES:** Closed Dec-Feb **CARDS:**

♦♦♦♦ T&C Maple Lodge

Castlebridge ☎ 053 59195 & 59062 📠 053 59195
e-mail: sreenan@tinet.ie
Dir: *on R741 Dublin to Wexford Road, on the outskirts of Castlebridge village, pink house on left*
This imposing pink house, set in one acre of maturing gardens, is in a peaceful location close to Curracloe Beach, just 5 kms north of Wexford town and 15km from Rosslare Euro-Port. Eamonn and Margaret Sreenan offer warm hospitality in their comfortable and tastefully decorated home. A varied breakfast menu and home-baking are available. Secure parking.
FACILITIES: 4 en suite (3 fmly) No smoking STV TVB No dogs Cen ht TVL No children 4yrs No coaches **PRICES:** s €39 - €45; d €56 - €64✳ **LB** **PARKING:** 5 **NOTES:** Closed Nov-Feb **CARDS:**

♦♦♦♦ T&C *McMenamin's Town House*

3 Auburn Ter, Redmond Rd ☎ 053 46442 📠 053 46442
e-mail: mcmem@indigo.ie
Dir: *at west end of town opposite railway and bus station*
This charming late Victorian residence is owned by Seamus and Kay McMenamin, who offer warm and caring hospitality. The en suite rooms have some fine antique beds and are well equipped. A wide choice of breakfast dishes is served in the attractively furnished dining room, and there is a pleasant guests' sitting room. Nearby attractions include golf, swimming, beaches, a heritage centre, and an opera house.
FACILITIES: 6 en suite (1 fmly) No smoking in 3 bedrooms No smoking in dining room No smoking in 1 lounge TVB tea/coffee No dogs Cen ht No coaches **PARKING:** 9 **NOTES:** Closed 20-30 Dec **CARDS:**

♦♦♦♦ T&C Mount Auburn

1 Auburn Ter, Redmond Rd ☎ 053 24609 📠 053 24609
e-mail: mountauburn@eircom.net
Dir: *from Dublin direction on N11, turn left at Ferrycarrig Bridge. House 3km on right*
Conveniently placed for the station and city centre, Mount Auburn offers attractive and comfortable bedrooms with all modern facilities. There is a residents' lounge and a dining room where evening meals are served by arrangement.
FACILITIES: 6 en suite (3 fmly) No smoking TVB tea/coffee No dogs (ex guide dogs) Cen ht TVL No coaches **PRICES:** s €34 - €44; d €56 - €70✳ **PARKING:** 6 **NOTES:** Closed 20-28 Dec **CARDS:**

♦♦♦♦ T&C O'Briens Auburn House

2 Auburn Ter, Redmond Rd ☎ 053 23605 📠 053 42725
e-mail: mary@obriensauburnhouse.com
Dir: *opposite railway station and Savoy Cinema and adjactent to Dunnes Stores*
This attractive late Victorian town house has been extensively and tastefully renovated. Bedrooms are well equipped and spacious, and guests can relax in the evening in a large and comfortable lounge. Secure parking provided.
FACILITIES: 5 en suite (2 fmly) No smoking TVB tea/coffee No dogs (ex guide dogs) Cen ht TVL No coaches **PRICES:** s €35 - €45; d €60 - €65✳ **PARKING:** 5 **NOTES:** Closed 18 Dec-2 Jan **CARDS:**

♦♦♦♦ GH *Slaney Manor*
Ferrycarrig ☎ 053 20051 & 20144 🖷 053 20510
Dir: *on N25 0.5m W of N11 junction*
This attractive period manor house stands in 60 acres of woodland overlooking the River Slaney. Completely restored by the owners, the house retains many fine features. The elegant, high-ceilinged drawing room and dining room have views of the river, and four-poster beds feature in all bedrooms. The rooms in the converted Coach House can be reserved on a room only basis for those travelling on the Rosslare ferry.
FACILITIES: 8 en suite (2 fmly) No smoking TVB tea/coffee Direct dial from bedrooms No dogs (ex guide dogs) Licensed Lift Cen ht TVL Dinner Last d noon **PARKING:** 30 **NOTES:** Closed Xmas week
CARDS:

♦♦♦ T&C Rathaspeck Manor
Rathaspeck ☎ 053 42661
Dir: *signposted on N25, near Johnstone Castle*
Standing in its own grounds, which feature an 18-hole par-3 golf course, this 300-year-old Georgian country house is half a mile from Johnstone Castle. The comfortable, spacious bedrooms are en suite and the public rooms are appointed with period furnishings. Hospitable Mrs Cuddihy will provide dinner by arrangement.
FACILITIES: 6 en suite (3 fmly) No smoking in dining room No smoking in 1 lounge TVB tea/coffee No dogs TVL No children 10yrs Golf 18 Tennis (hard) **PRICES:** s €38; d €64✳ **PARKING:** 8 **NOTES:** Closed 8 Nov-May

CO WICKLOW

ASHFORD — Map 01 D3

♦♦♦♦ Ballyknocken House *(T 246925)*
☎ 0404 44627 & 44614 🖷 0404 44696 Mrs C Fulvio
e-mail: cfulvio@ballyknocken.com
Dir: *turn right after Texaco garage in Ashford (N11). House 3m from Ashford on right*
In the foothills of the Wicklow mountains, this farmhouse offers great hospitality, very good food and excellent accommodation. Refurbished bedrooms have smart new bathrooms, and there are two relaxing sitting rooms. Catherine Fulvie is an enthusiastic hostess. Dinner reservations necessary. Walking holidays can be arranged.
FACILITIES: 7 en suite (1 fmly) No smoking in bedrooms No smoking in dining room No smoking in 1 lounge TVB tea/coffee Direct dial from bedrooms No dogs Licensed Cen ht No children 2 yrs Tennis (hard) 350 acres sheep/mixed Dinner Last d Noon **PRICES:** s €75 - €85; d €88 - €99 **LB PARKING:** 8 **NOTES:** Closed Dec&Jan **CARDS:**

AVOCA — Map 01 D3

♦♦♦♦ GH Sheepwalk House & Cottages
Beech Rd ☎ 0402 35189 🖷 0402 35789
e-mail: sheepwalk@eircom.net
Dir: *turn off N11 at Arklow/Redcross junct, take sliproad towards Arklow, right at Rover Garage towards Avoca, 2m to Sheepwalk House*
An historic 18th-century Georgian house, two miles from Avoca and with lovely views across Arklow Bay. The cosy, comfortably-furnished bedrooms are equipped with every thoughtful extra. Guests can breakfast in the informal sun lounge which commands sea views, and owner Jim McCabe is a mine of information on golfing, shooting and fishing holidays.

continued

Sheepwalk House & Cottages

FACILITIES: 6 en suite TVB tea/coffee No dogs (ex guide dogs) Cen ht No coaches **PRICES:** s €47; d €70 - €76✳ **PARKING:** 12 **NOTES:** Closed Nov-Feb **CARDS:**

♦♦♦ T&C Ashdene
Knockanree Lower ☎ 0402 35327 🖷 0402 35327
e-mail: burns@ashdeneavoca.com
Dir: *turn off R752 into village. House 1.5km on right beyond Avoca Handweavers on Avoca/Redcross road*
Set two miles from Avoca, Ashdene represents an ideal centre for touring Co Wicklow. Mrs Burns is very enthusiastic in her care of guests, and takes pride in her breakfast menu.
FACILITIES: 5 rms (4 en suite) (2 fmly) No smoking TVB No dogs (ex guide dogs) Cen ht TVL No coaches Tennis (grass) **PRICES:** s €36 - €38.50; d €50 - €56✳ **PARKING:** 5 **NOTES:** Closed Nov-Mar
CARDS:

♦♦♦ T&C *Cherrybrook Country Home*
☎ 0402 35179 🖷 0402 35179
e-mail: cherrybandb@tinet.ie
Set in the village made famous by TV series 'Ballykissangel' Cherrybrook has fine gardens with a barbeque area. It is a well presented house with a guest lounge and dining room. Bedrooms are attractively decorated. Evening meals are available by prior arrangement.
FACILITIES: 4 en suite (2 fmly) No smoking in bedrooms No smoking in dining room TVB tea/coffee No dogs (ex guide dogs) Cen ht TVL ch fac Last d noon **PARKING: CARDS:**

♦♦♦ T&C Old Coach House
Meeting of the Waters ☎ 0402 35408 🖷 0402 35408
e-mail: avocacoachhouse@eircom.net
Dir: *turn off N11 at Rathnew for Rathdrum, take Woodenbridge Rd from Rathdrum, Coach House is 300 yds past The Meeting of the Waters on the Avoca/Woodenbridge Rd*
A black and white coaching inn set in the picturesque Vale of Avoca, close to the Meeting of the Waters. The comfortable bedrooms vary in size and are attractively decorated. There is a warm and inviting atmosphere and guests can relax in the restful lounge. Dinner is available by prior arrangement.
FACILITIES: 6 en suite (1 fmly) No smoking in bedrooms No smoking in dining room TVB tea/coffee No dogs (ex guide dogs) Cen ht Dinner Last d noon **PRICES:** s €45; d €70 - €80 **PARKING:** 10 **NOTES:** Closed Xmas

Further details of AA rated B&Bs and hotels can be found on the AA website www.theAA.com

Ireland

BRAY Map 01 D3

♦♦♦ T&C *Woodville*
Ballywaltrim Ln ☎ 01 2863103 📠 01 2863103
e-mail: catherik@gofree.indigo.ie
An attractively designed bungalow, tucked away at the end of a cul de sac, to the south of Bray town and convenient for the ferry port of Dun Laoghaire. Bedrooms are comfortable and well appointed. There is a relaxing lounge with a hostess trolley, where guests can help themselves to tea or coffee. The garden is well maintained and there is a security gate with ample car parking.
FACILITIES: 4 en suite (1 fmly) No smoking in bedrooms No smoking in dining room TVB No dogs Cen ht No children 3yrs No coaches
PARKING: 6 **NOTES:** Closed 15 Dec-7 Jan

DUNLAVIN Map 01 C3

♦♦♦♦ Tynte House *(N 870015)*
☎ 045 401561 📠 045 401586 Mr & Mrs J Lawler
e-mail: info@tyntehouse.com
***Dir:** N81 at Hollywood Cross, right at Dunlavin, follow finger signs for Tynte House, past market house in centre of town*

A gracious 19th-century farmhouse standing in the square of this quiet country village. The friendly hosts have carried out a lot of restoration and facilities now include bedrooms, self-catering apartments in an adjoining courtyard, a laundry, tennis courts, children's play area and indoor games room.
FACILITIES: 7 en suite (2 fmly) No smoking in 2 bedrooms No smoking in area of dining room TVB tea/coffee Direct dial from bedrooms Cen ht TVL Golf 18 Tennis (hard) Pool Table Playground games room with table tennis 200 acres arable beef Dinner Last d Noon **PRICES:** s fr €44; d fr €70 **LB**
PARKING: 16 **NOTES:** Closed 23 Dec-2 Jan **CARDS:**

GLENDALOUGH Map 01 D3

♦♦♦♦ T&C Pinewood Lodge
☎ 0404 45437 📠 0404 45437
e-mail: pwlodge@gofree.indigo.ie
***Dir:** right after Laragh Village on Glendalargh Rd, the 2nd house on right after school & church*
Set in one acre and bordered by forests, Pinewood Lodge is comfortable and well appointed. The bedrooms are attractively decorated and there is a spacious lounge and a breakfast room for guests. There are pubs and restaurants nearby.
FACILITIES: 6 en suite (3 fmly) No smoking tea/coffee Cen ht TVL No children 4yrs No coaches **PRICES:** s fr €41; d fr €60✱ **PARKING:** 10

KILTEGAN Map 01 D3

♦♦♦♦ T&C Barraderry House
☎ 0508 73209 📠 0508 73209
e-mail: jo.hobson@oceanfree.net
***Dir:** take N81 Dublin-Baltinglass, then left on R747 for 4.5m to entrance on right*

A granite stone gateway is the entrance to this restored Georgian house half a mile from Kiltegan. The drawing room is adjacent to the TV study, and breakfast is served in the dining room. Light evening meals are available if booked in advance. The bedrooms are all furnished in keeping with the period of the house and have new en suite bathrooms.
FACILITIES: 4 en suite (2 fmly) No smoking TVB tea/coffee No dogs (ex guide dogs) Cen ht TVL **PRICES:** s €40 - €45; d €70 - €80✱ **LB**
PARKING: 12 **NOTES:** Closed mid Dec-mid Jan **CARDS:**

RATHDRUM Map 01 D3

♦♦♦ GH Avonbrae
☎ 0404 46198 📠 0404 46198
e-mail: info@avonbrae.com
***Dir:** 180mtrs on Laragh Road after leaving village*
Lovely rose gardens surround this peaceful rural retreat in the Wicklow Hills. Owner Paddy Geoghegan has spent the last few years refurbishing the house to a very high standard. Bedrooms, with pine furniture, are attractively decorated and residents can enjoy the comfort of a charming sitting room and spacious dining room.
FACILITIES: 7 rms (6 en suite) (2 fmly) No smoking in dining room tea/coffee Direct dial from bedrooms Licensed Cen ht TVL No coaches Indoor swimming pool (heated) Tennis (grass) Games room, table tennis Dinner Last d noon **PRICES:** s fr €41; d fr €66✱ **LB** **PARKING:** 7
NOTES: Closed Nov-Feb **CARDS:**

Ireland

County Maps

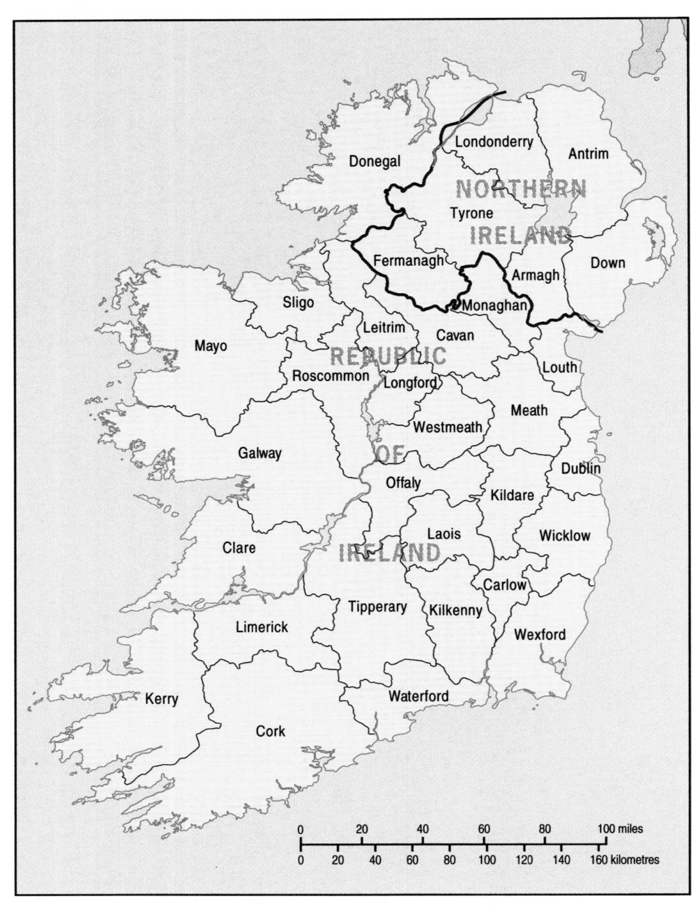

England

1 Bedfordshire
2 Berkshire
3 Bristol
4 Buckinghamshire
5 Cambridgeshire
6 Greater Manchester
7 Herefordshire
8 Hertfordshire
9 Leicestershire
10 Northamptonshire
11 Nottinghamshire
12 Rutland
13 Staffordshire
14 Warwickshire
15 West Midlands
16 Worcestershire

Scotland

17 City of Glasgow
18 Clackmannanshire
19 East Ayrshire
20 East Dunbartonshire
21 East Renfrewshire
22 Perth & Kinross
23 Renfrewshire
24 South Lanarkshire
25 West Dunbartonshire

Wales

26 Blaenau Gwent
27 Bridgend
28 Caerphilly
29 Denbighshire
30 Flintshire
31 Merthyr Tydfil
32 Monmouthshire
33 Neath Port Talbot
34 Newport
35 Rhondda Cynon Ta
36 Torfaen
37 Vale of Glamorgan
38 Wrexham

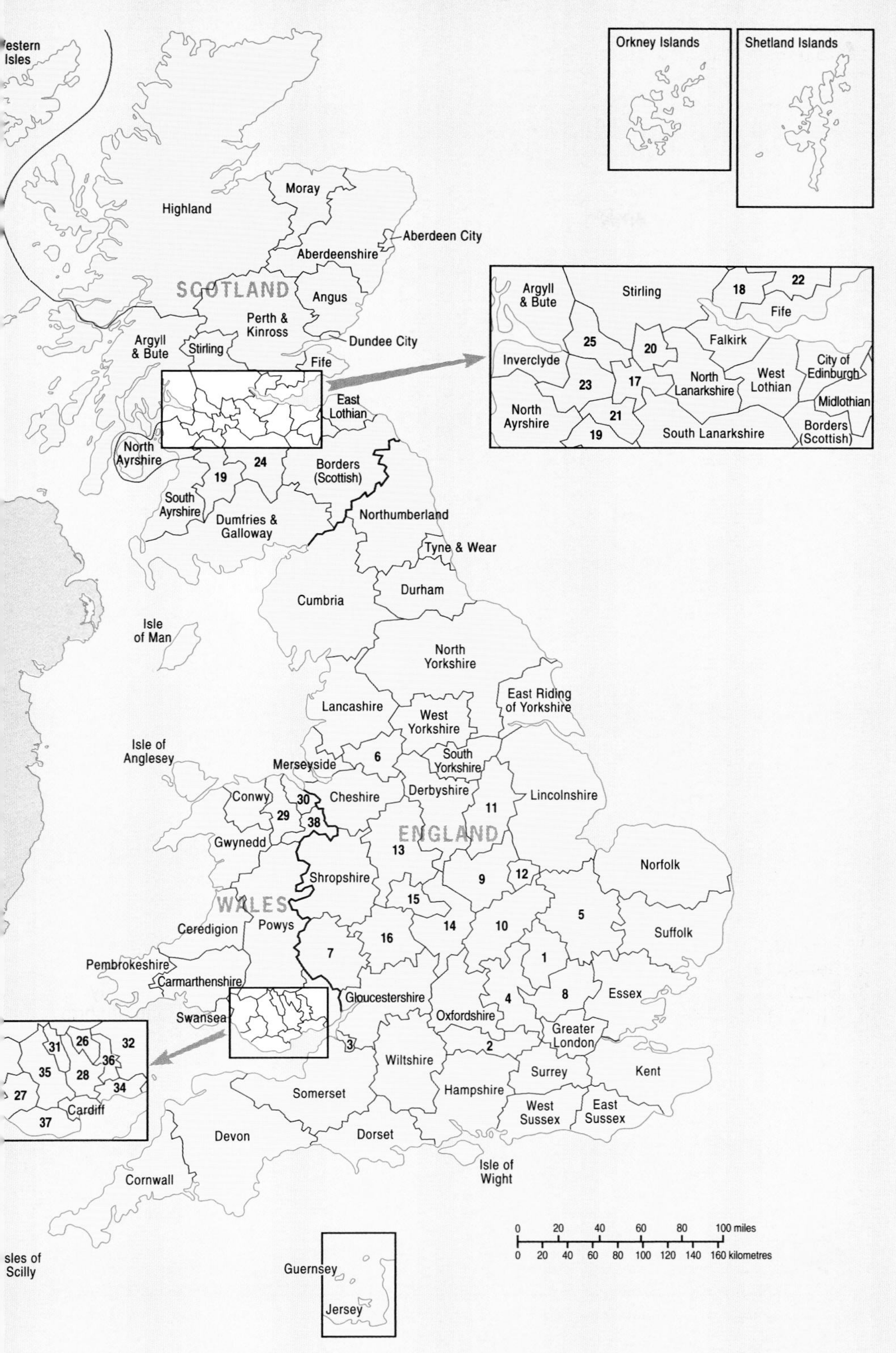

Western Isles
Orkney Islands
Shetland Islands
Moray
Highland
Aberdeen City
Aberdeenshire
SCOTLAND
Angus
Perth & Kinross
Argyll & Bute
Stirling
Dundee City
Fife
East Lothian
North Ayrshire
24
19
Borders (Scottish)
South Ayrshire
Dumfries & Galloway
Northumberland
Tyne & Wear
Durham
Cumbria
Isle of Man
North Yorkshire
East Riding of Yorkshire
Lancashire
West Yorkshire
Isle of Anglesey
6
South Yorkshire
Merseyside
Conwy
30
Cheshire
Derbyshire
Lincolnshire
29
38
11
Gwynedd
ENGLAND
13
Norfolk
Shropshire
9
12
WALES
15
5
Ceredigion
Powys
14
10
Suffolk
16
7
1
Pembrokeshire
Carmarthenshire
Gloucestershire
8
Essex
4
Swansea
Oxfordshire
Greater London
3
2
Wiltshire
Surrey
Kent
Somerset
Hampshire
West Sussex
East Sussex
Devon
Dorset
Isle of Wight
Cornwall
Isles of Scilly
Guernsey
Jersey
Argyll & Bute
Stirling
18
22
Fife
25
20
Falkirk
Inverclyde
City of Edinburgh
23
17
North Lanarkshire
West Lothian
Midlothian
North Ayrshire
21
19
South Lanarkshire
Borders (Scottish)
31
26
32
36
35
28
34
27
Cardiff
37
0 20 40 60 80 100 miles
0 20 40 60 80 100 120 140 160 kilometres

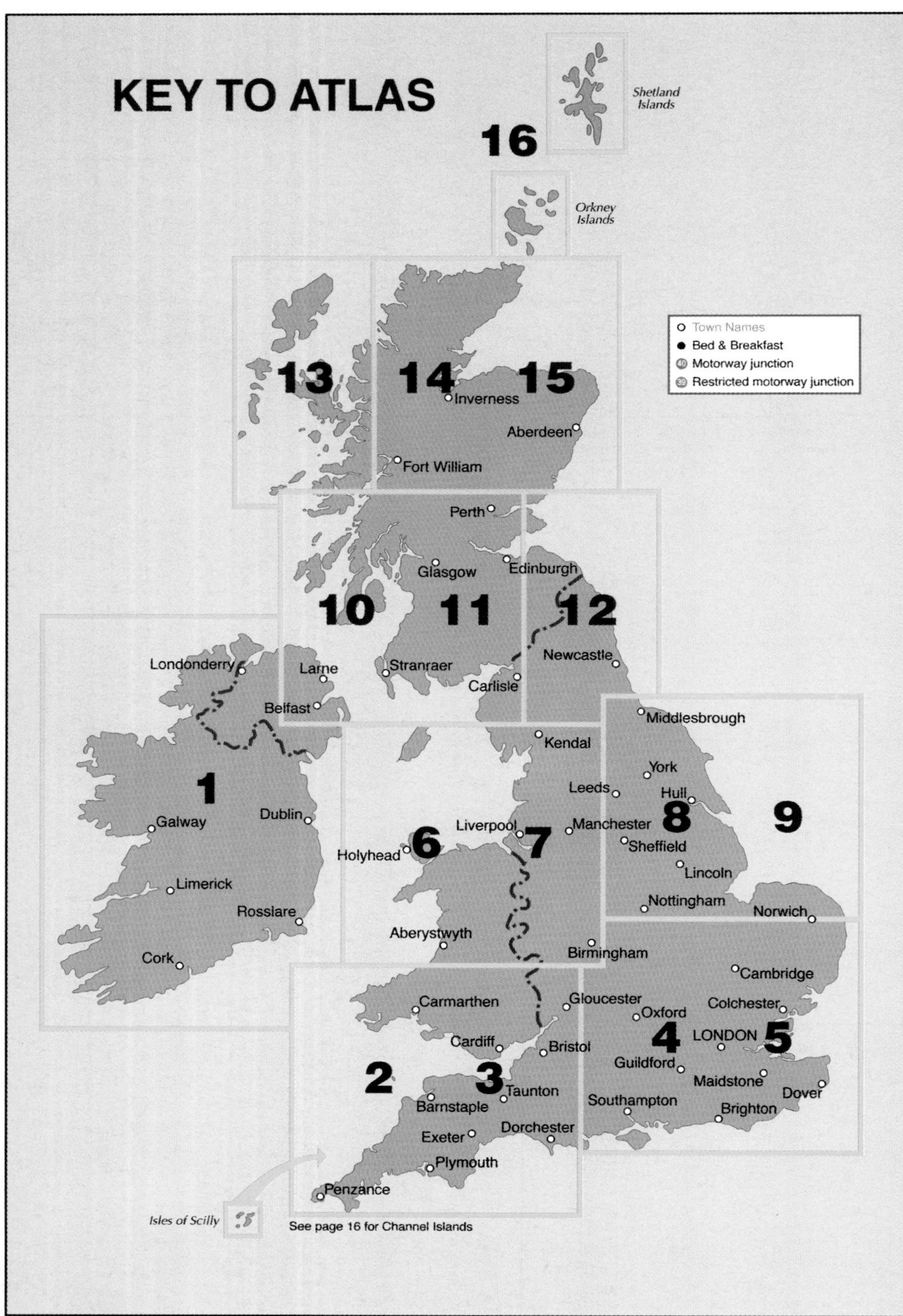
KEY TO ATLAS
16
Shetland Islands
Orkney Islands
13
14
15
Inverness
Aberdeen
Fort William
Town Names
Bed & Breakfast
Motorway junction
Restricted motorway junction
Perth
Glasgow
Edinburgh
10
11
12
Londonderry
Larne
Stranraer
Newcastle
Carlisle
Belfast
Middlesbrough
Kendal
York
1
Leeds
Hull
Galway
Dublin
Liverpool
Manchester
8
9
Holyhead
6
7
Sheffield
Lincoln
Limerick
Nottingham
Rosslare
Norwich
Aberystwyth
Cork
Birmingham
Cambridge
Carmarthen
Gloucester
Colchester
Oxford
Cardiff
Bristol
4
LONDON
5
2
3
Guildford
Maidstone
Taunton
Dover
Barnstaple
Southampton
Brighton
Exeter
Dorchester
Plymouth
Penzance
Isles of Scilly
See page 16 for Channel Islands

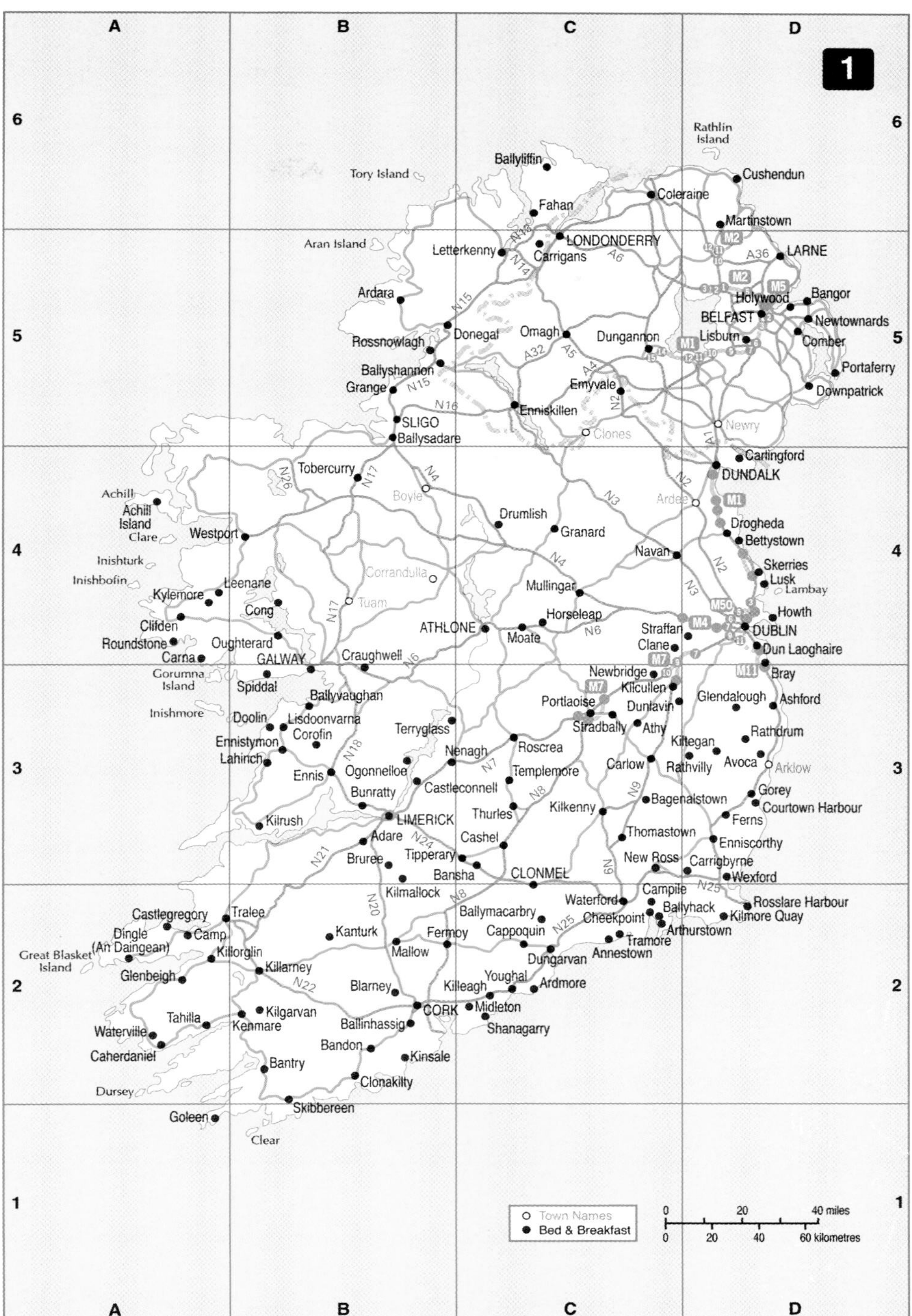
A
B
C
D
1
6
5
4
3
2
1
Rathlin Island
Tory Island
Ballyliffin
Cushendun
Coleraine
Fahan
Martinstown
Aran Island
LONDONDERRY
Letterkenny
Carrigans
LARNE
M2
A36
A6
N13
N14
Ardara
N15
M2
M5
Holywood
Bangor
BELFAST
Newtownards
Donegal
Omagh
Dungannon
Lisburn
Comber
Rossnowlagh
M1
A5
A32
A4
Portaferry
Ballyshannon
Emyvale
Grange
N15
N2
Downpatrick
N16
Enniskillen
SLIGO
Newry
Ballysadare
Clones
A1
Carlingford
N26
Tobercurry
N17
N4
DUNDALK
Achill
Achill Island
Clare
Boyle
N2
Ardee
M1
N3
Drumlish
Granard
Drogheda
Westport
Bettystown
Inishturk
N4
Navan
N2
Skerries
Inishbofin
Leenane
Corrandulla
Lusk
Kylemore
Mullingar
N3
Lambay
Cong
Tuam
N17
M50
Howth
Clifden
Horseleap
M4
Straffan
DUBLIN
ATHLONE
N6
Roundstone
Oughterard
Moate
Clane
Dun Laoghaire
Carna
GALWAY
Craughwell
N6
M7
Gorumna Island
Bray
Newbridge
M11
Spiddal
Kilcullen
M7
Ballyvaughan
Glendalough
Ashford
Portlaoise
Dunlavin
Inishmore
Doolin
Lisdoonvarna
Stradbally
Athy
Corofin
Terryglass
Rathdrum
Ennistymon
N18
Kiltegan
Roscrea
Lahinch
Nenagh
Carlow
Rathvilly
Avoca
Arklow
Ennis
Ogonnelloe
N7
Templemore
Gorey
N9
Castleconnell
Bunratty
N8
Kilkenny
Bagenalstown
Courtown Harbour
Kilrush
LIMERICK
Thurles
Ferns
Adare
N24
Cashel
Thomastown
Enniscorthy
N21
Bruree
Tipperary
New Ross
Carrigbyrne
Bansha
CLONMEL
Wexford
N9
N20
Kilmallock
N25
N8
Waterford
Campile
Rosslare Harbour
Castlegregory
Tralee
Ballymacarbry
Ballyhack
Kilmore Quay
Cheekpoint
Dingle (An Daingean)
Camp
Kanturk
Fermoy
Cappoquin
N25
Arthurstown
Great Blasket Island
Killorglin
Tramore
Mallow
Dungarvan
Annestown
Killarney
Glenbeigh
N22
Youghal
Ardmore
Blarney
Killeagh
Tahilla
Kilgarvan
CORK
Midleton
Waterville
Kenmare
Ballinhassig
Shanagarry
Caherdaniel
Bandon
Kinsale
Bantry
Clonakilty
Dursey
Skibbereen
Goleen
Clear
Town Names
Bed & Breakfast
0
20
40 miles
0
20
40
60 kilometres

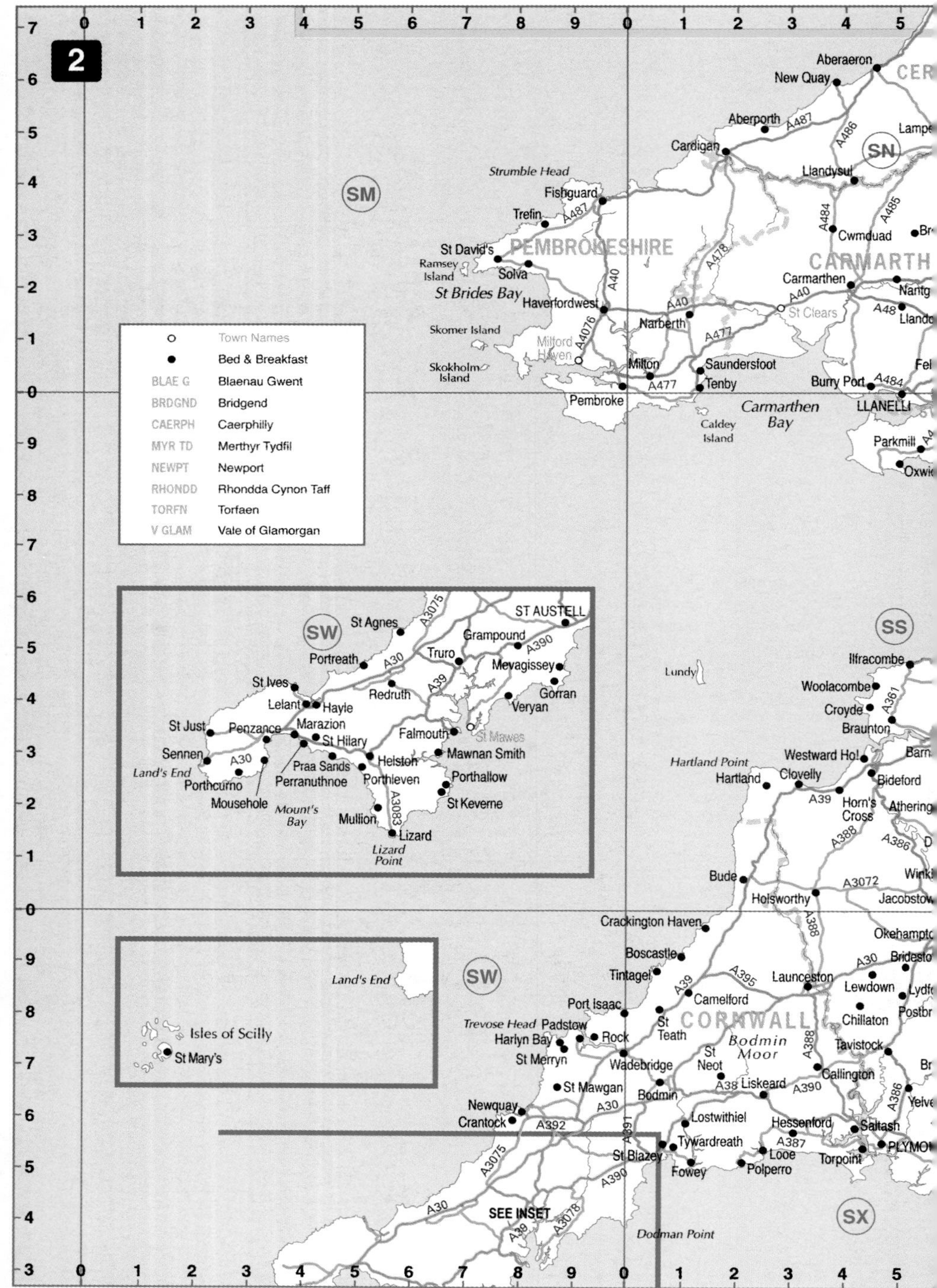

For continuation pages refer to numbered arrows

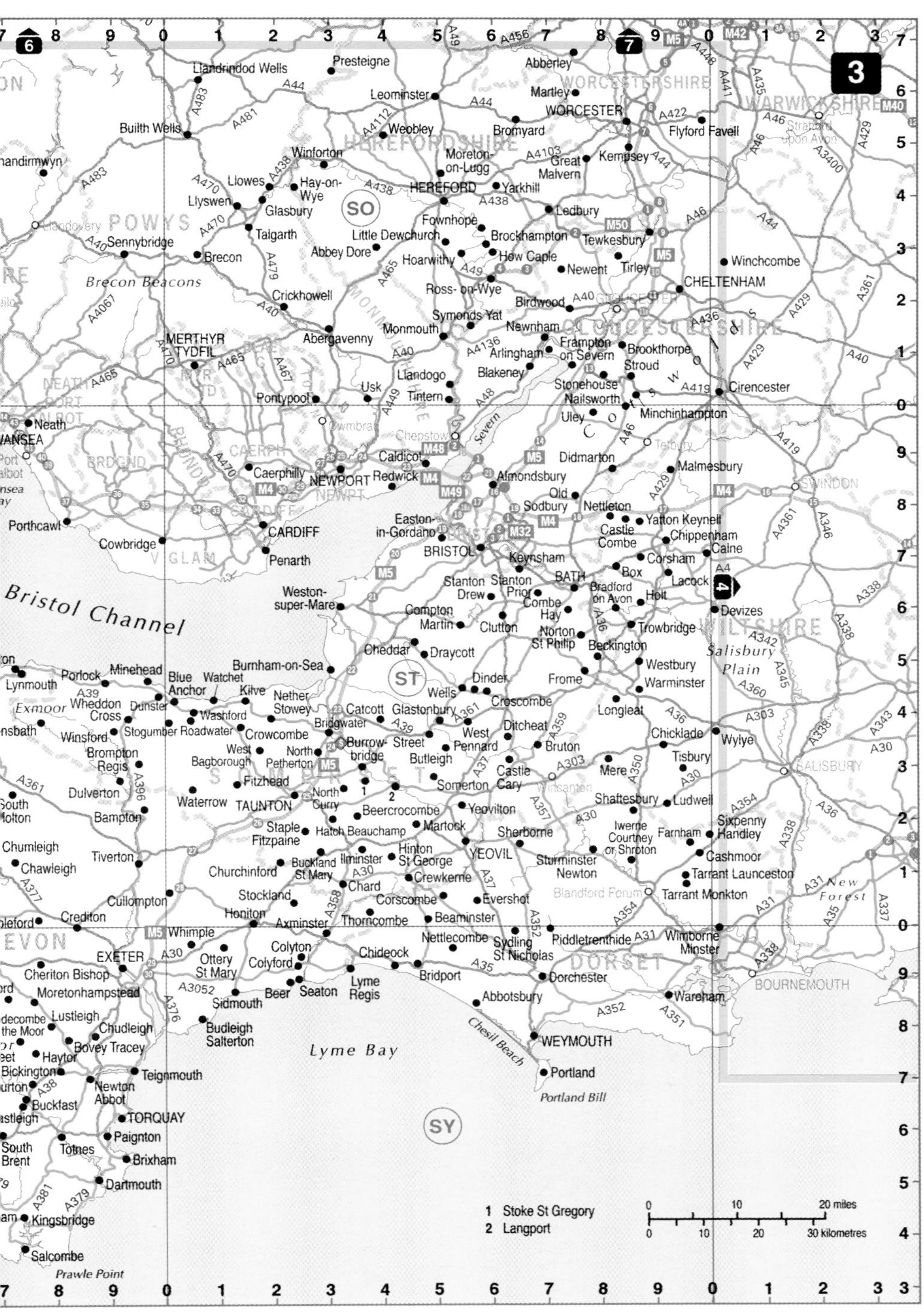

3
6
7
4
WORCESTERSHIRE
WARWICKSHIRE
HEREFORDSHIRE
POWYS
MONMOUTHSHIRE
GLOUCESTERSHIRE
Cotswolds
WILTSHIRE
SOMERSET
DORSET
DEVON
SO
ST
SY
Llandrindod Wells
Presteigne
Abberley
Leominster
Martley
WORCESTER
Flyford Favell
Stratford upon Avon
Builth Wells
Weobley
Bromyard
Winforton
Moreton-on-Lugg
Great Malvern
Kempsey
Llowes
Hay-on-Wye
HEREFORD
Yarkhill
Llyswen
Glasbury
Ledbury
Llandovery
Fownhope
Talgarth
Little Dewchurch
Brockhampton
Tewkesbury
Sennybridge
Abbey Dore
Hoarwithy
How Caple
Brecon
Newent
Tirley
Winchcombe
Brecon Beacons
Ross-on-Wye
CHELTENHAM
Crickhowell
Birdwood
GLOUCESTER
Symonds Yat
Newnham
Monmouth
Abergavenny
MERTHYR TYDFIL
Frampton on Severn
Brookthorpe
Arlingham
Stroud
Llandogo
Blakeney
Stonehouse
Cirencester
Usk
Tintern
Nailsworth
Pontypool
Uley
Minchinhampton
Neath
SWANSEA
Cwmbran
Chepstow
Severn
Tetbury
Caldicot
Didmarton
Malmesbury
Caerphilly
NEWPORT
Redwick
Almondsbury
SWINDON
Old Sodbury
Nettleton
Porthcawl
CARDIFF
Easton-in-Gordano
Yatton Keynell
Castle Combe
Chippenham
Cowbridge
BRISTOL
Keynsham
Corsham
Calne
Penarth
BATH
Box
Lacock
Bristol Channel
Weston-super-Mare
Stanton Drew
Stanton Prior
Combe Hay
Bradford on Avon
Holt
Devizes
Compton Martin
Clutton
Norton St Philip
Trowbridge
Cheddar
Draycott
Beckington
Salisbury Plain
Burnham-on-Sea
Westbury
Porlock
Minehead
Blue Anchor
Watchet
Kilve
Dinder
Frome
Warminster
Lynmouth
Wells
Croscombe
Exmoor
Wheddon Cross
Dunster
Nether Stowey
Catcott
Glastonbury
Longleat
Washford
Bridgwater
West Pennard
Ditcheat
Chicklade
Wylye
Winsford
Stogumber
Roadwater
Crowcombe
Burrow-bridge
Street
Bruton
Brompton Regis
West Bagborough
North Petherton
Butleigh
Castle Cary
Mere
Tisbury
SALISBURY
Fitzhead
Somerton
Wincanton
Dulverton
Waterrow
TAUNTON
North Curry
Shaftesbury
Ludwell
South Molton
Bampton
Beercrocombe
Yeovilton
Staple Fitzpaine
Hatch Beauchamp
Martock
Sherborne
Iwerne Courtney or Shroton
Farnham
Sixpenny Handley
Chumleigh
Hinton St George
YEOVIL
Cashmoor
Chawleigh
Tiverton
Buckland St Mary
Ilminster
Sturminster Newton
Tarrant Launceston
Churchinford
Chard
Crewkerne
New Forest
Cullompton
Stockland
Corscombe
Evershot
Blandford Forum
Tarrant Monkton
Crediton
Honiton
Axminster
Thorncombe
Beaminster
Whimple
Nettlecombe
Sydling St Nicholas
Piddletrenthide
Wimborne Minster
EXETER
Ottery St Mary
Colyton
Colyford
Chideock
Bridport
Dorchester
Cheriton Bishop
BOURNEMOUTH
Moretonhampstead
Sidmouth
Beer
Seaton
Lyme Regis
Abbotsbury
Wareham
Widecombe in the Moor
Lustleigh
Budleigh Salterton
Chudleigh
Bovey Tracey
Haytor
Chesil Beach
Lyme Bay
WEYMOUTH
Bickington
Teignmouth
Newton Abbot
Portland
Buckfast
Portland Bill
TORQUAY
Paignton
South Brent
Totnes
Brixham
Dartmouth
Kingsbridge
Salcombe
Prawle Point
1 Stoke St Gregory
2 Langport
20 miles
30 kilometres

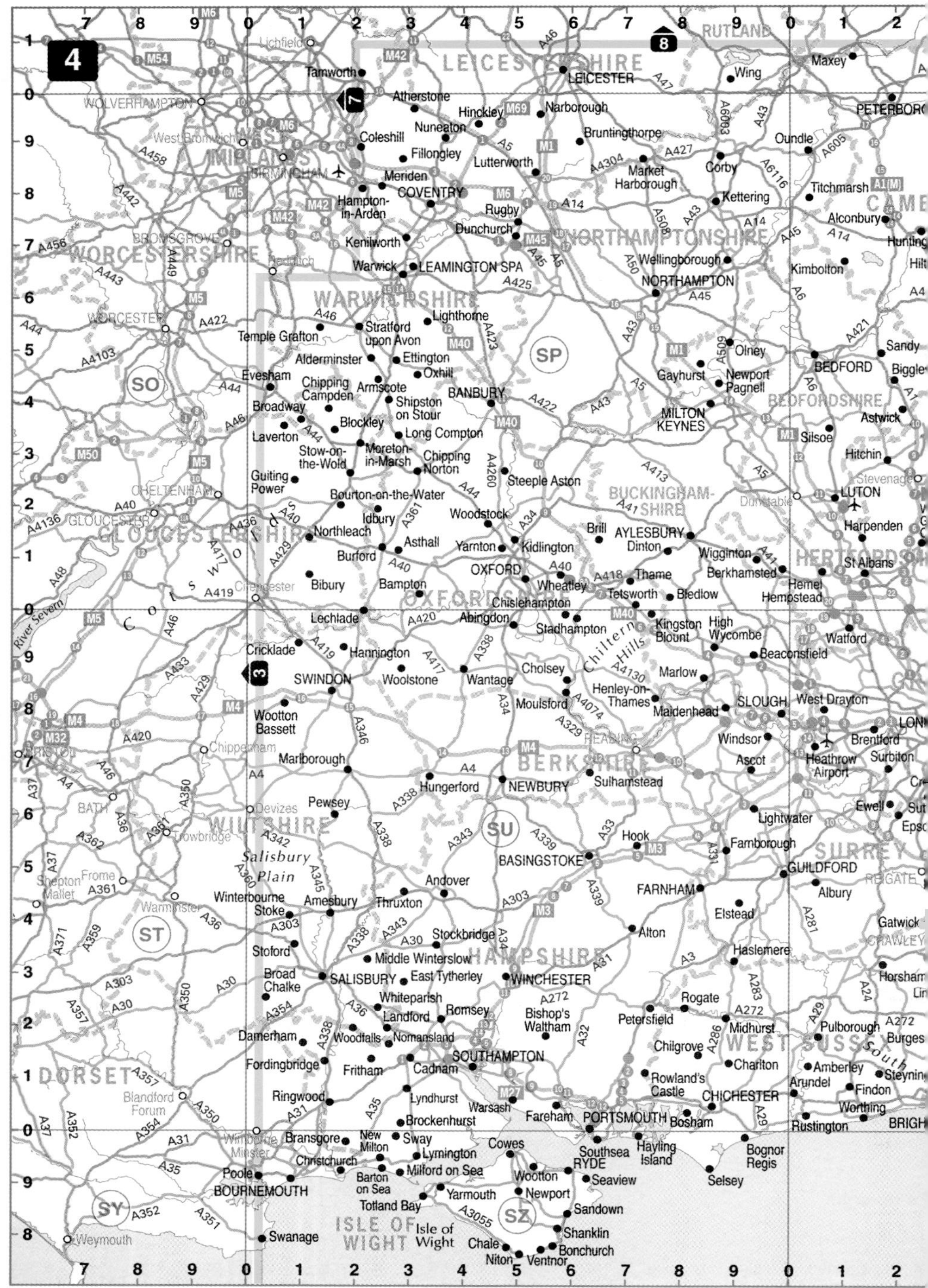

For continuation pages refer to numbered arrows

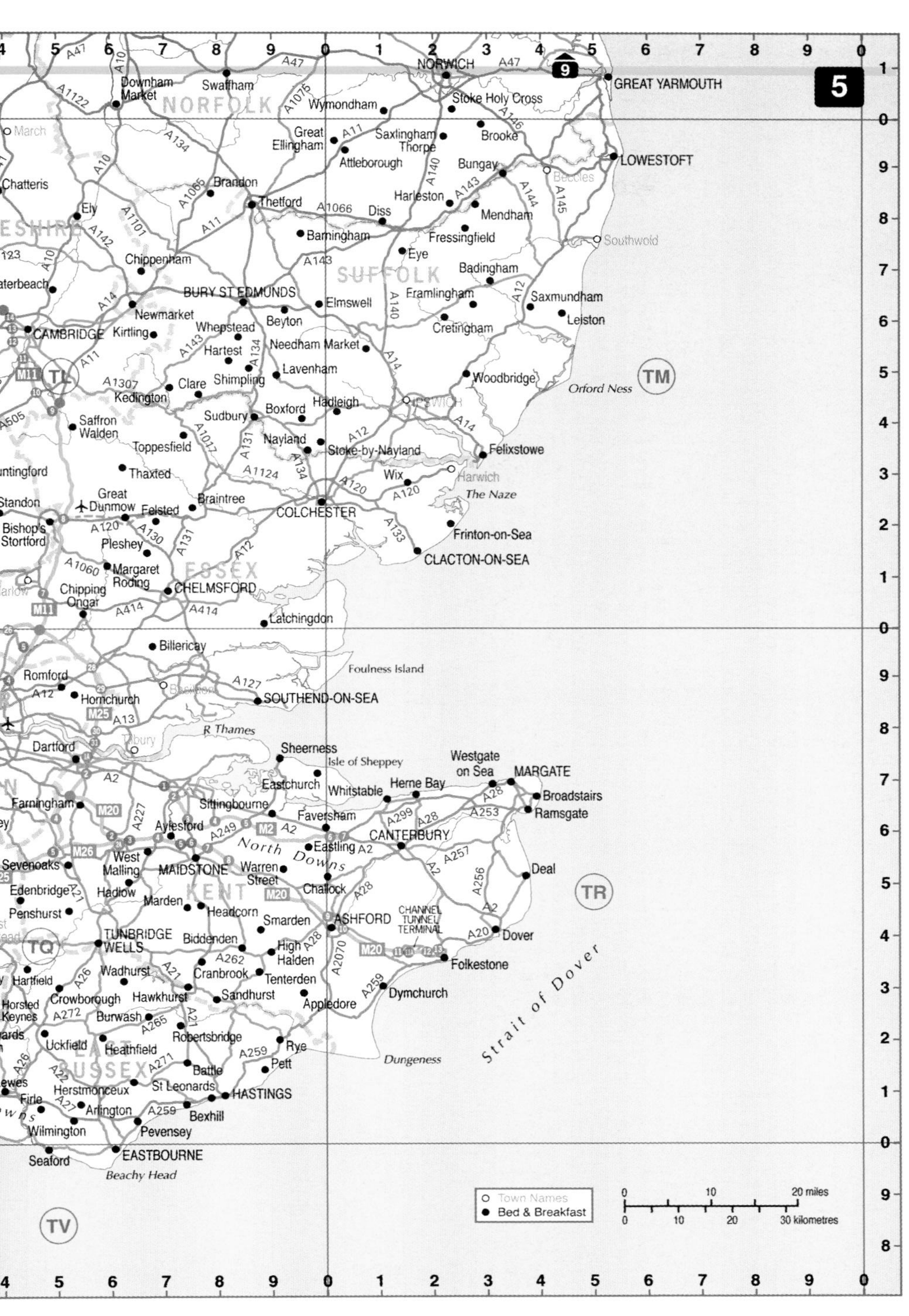
5
NORWICH
GREAT YARMOUTH
Downham Market
Swaffham
NORFOLK
Wymondham
Stoke Holy Cross
March
Great Ellingham
Saxlingham Thorpe
Brooke
Attleborough
LOWESTOFT
Bungay
Beccles
Chatteris
Brandon
Thetford
Harleston
Ely
Diss
Mendham
Barningham
Fressingfield
Southwold
Eye
Chippenham
SUFFOLK
Badingham
Waterbeach
BURY ST EDMUNDS
Elmswell
Framlingham
Saxmundham
Newmarket
Beyton
Leiston
Whepstead
Cretingham
CAMBRIDGE
Kirtling
Needham Market
Hartest
Lavenham
Woodbridge
TL
TM
Shimpling
Clare
Orford Ness
Kedington
Hadleigh
Ipswich
Boxford
Sudbury
Saffron Walden
Toppesfield
Nayland
Stoke-by-Nayland
Felixstowe
Thaxted
Wix
Harwich
The Naze
Great Dunmow
Felsted
Braintree
Standon
COLCHESTER
Bishop's Stortford
Frinton-on-Sea
Pleshey
CLACTON-ON-SEA
ESSEX
Margaret Roding
Chipping Ongar
Harlow
CHELMSFORD
Latchingdon
Billericay
Foulness Island
Romford
Hornchurch
Basildon
SOUTHEND-ON-SEA
R Thames
Tilbury
Dartford
Sheerness
Isle of Sheppey
Westgate on Sea
MARGATE
Eastchurch
Whitstable
Herne Bay
Broadstairs
Farningham
Sittingbourne
Ramsgate
Faversham
Aylesford
CANTERBURY
North Downs
Eastling
West Malling
Sevenoaks
MAIDSTONE
Warren Street
Deal
Edenbridge
Hadlow
KENT
Chilham
TR
Marden
Headcorn
Penshurst
Smarden
ASHFORD
CHANNEL TUNNEL TERMINAL
TUNBRIDGE WELLS
Biddenden
Dover
TQ
High Halden
Folkestone
Hartfield
Wadhurst
Cranbrook
Tenterden
Crowborough
Hawkhurst
Sandhurst
Dymchurch
Horsted Keynes
Burwash
Appledore
Strait of Dover
Uckfield
Heathfield
Robertsbridge
Rye
EAST SUSSEX
Battle
Pett
Dungeness
Lewes
Herstmonceux
St Leonards
HASTINGS
Firle
Arlington
Bexhill
Wilmington
Pevensey
Seaford
EASTBOURNE
Beachy Head
TV
Town Names
Bed & Breakfast
0 10 20 miles
0 10 20 30 kilometres

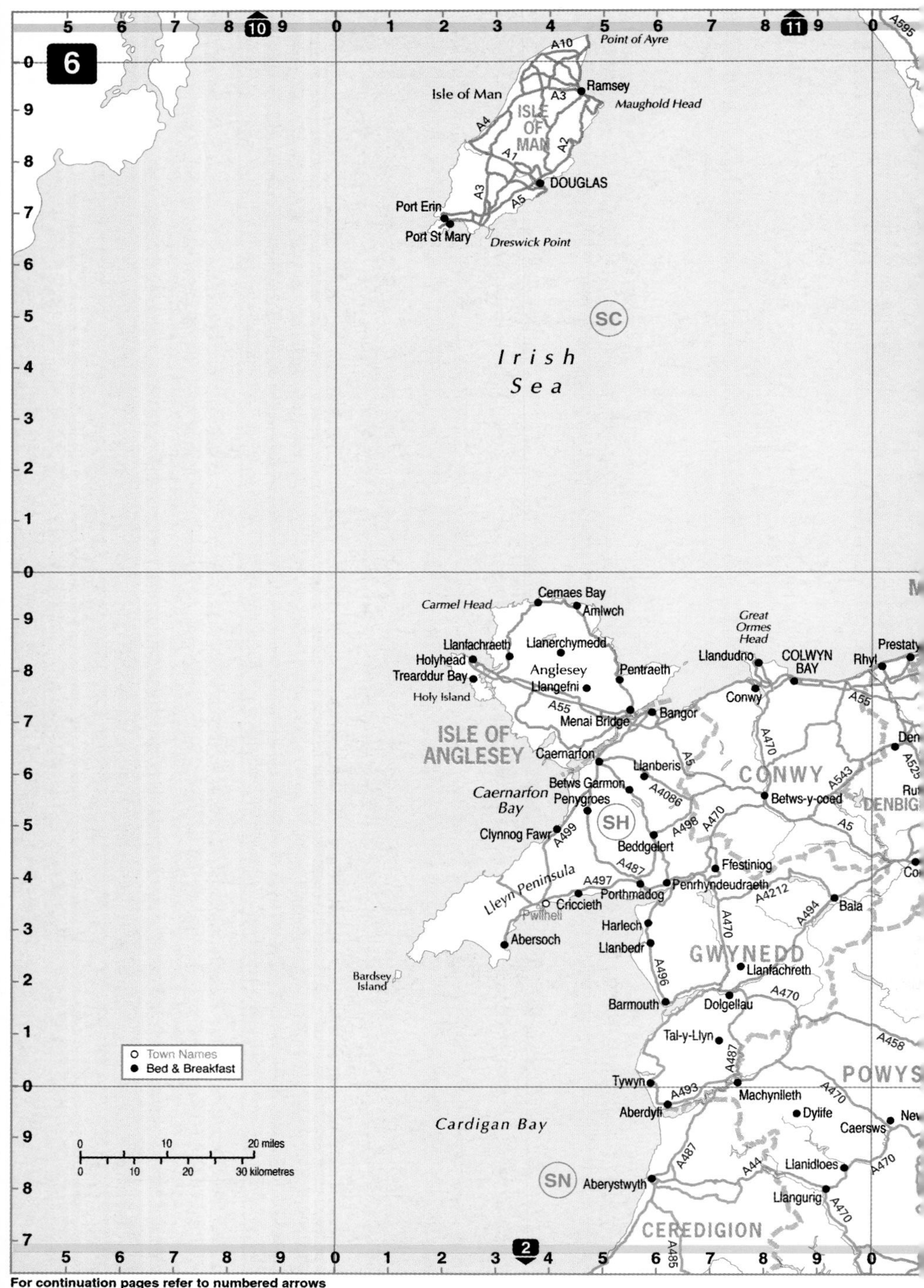

For continuation pages refer to numbered arrows

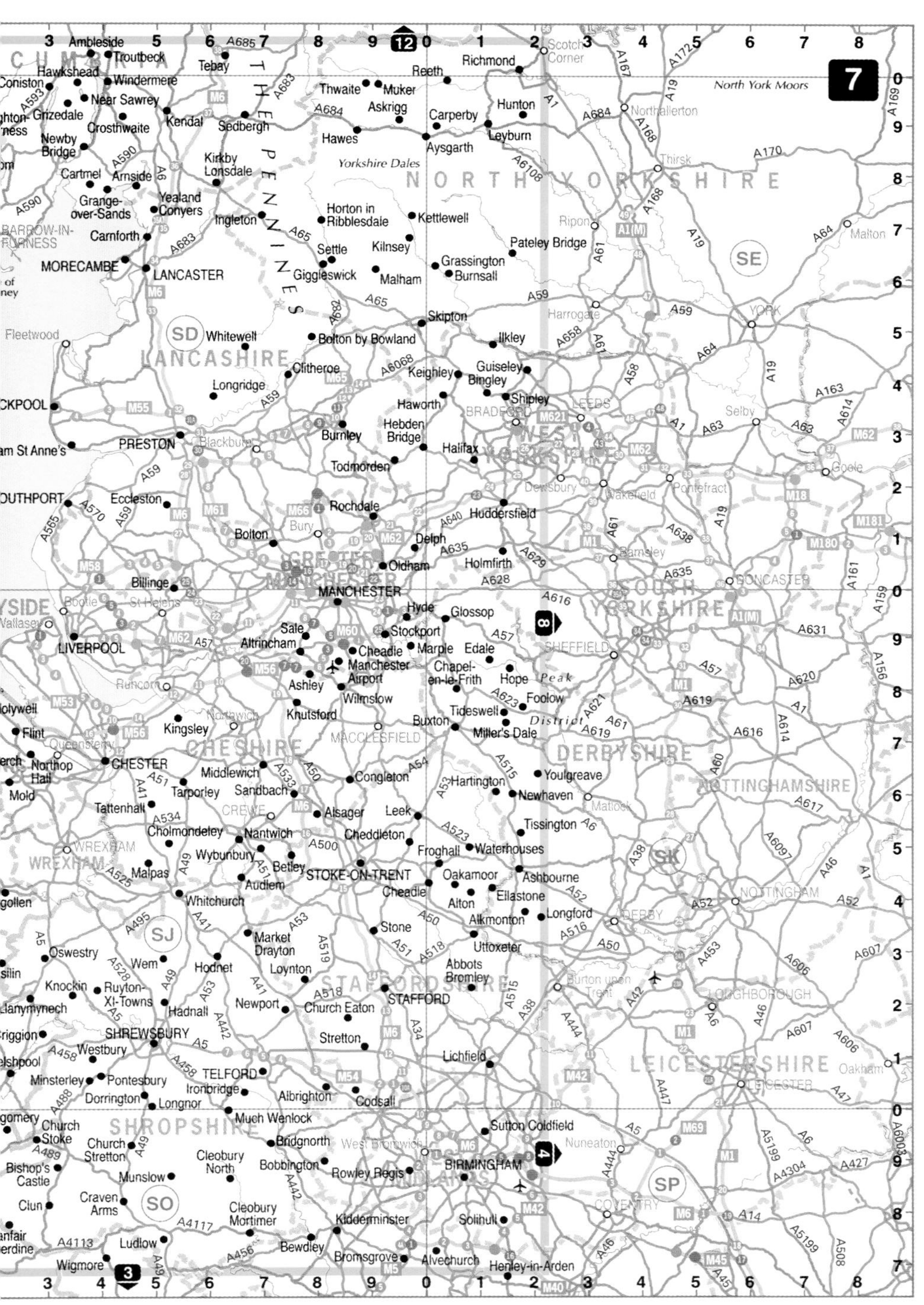7
12
8
4
3
CUMBRIA
Ambleside
Troutbeck
Hawkshead
Windermere
Coniston
Near Sawrey
Grizedale
Crosthwaite
Kendal
Newby Bridge
Cartmel
Arnside
Grange-over-Sands
Yealand Conyers
Carnforth
BARROW-IN-FURNESS
MORECAMBE
LANCASTER
Tebay
Sedbergh
Kirkby Lonsdale
Ingleton
THE PENNINES
Thwaite
Muker
Reeth
Richmond
Scotch Corner
Askrigg
Hawes
Carperby
Aysgarth
Hunton
Leyburn
Yorkshire Dales
NORTH YORKSHIRE
North York Moors
Northallerton
Thirsk
Ripon
Malton
Horton in Ribblesdale
Kettlewell
Settle
Kilnsey
Giggleswick
Malham
Grassington
Burnsall
Pateley Bridge
SE
SD
Fleetwood
Whitewell
Bolton by Bowland
Skipton
Harrogate
YORK
Ilkley
LANCASHIRE
Clitheroe
Keighley
Guiseley
Bingley
Shipley
Longridge
Haworth
BRADFORD
LEEDS
Selby
BLACKPOOL
PRESTON
Blackburn
Burnley
Hebden Bridge
Halifax
WEST YORKSHIRE
Lytham St Anne's
Todmorden
Dewsbury
Wakefield
Pontefract
Goole
SOUTHPORT
Eccleston
Rochdale
Huddersfield
Bury
Bolton
Delph
GREATER MANCHESTER
Oldham
Holmfirth
Barnsley
Billinge
MANCHESTER
DONCASTER
SOUTH YORKSHIRE
MERSEYSIDE
Bootle
St Helens
Wallasey
LIVERPOOL
Hyde
Glossop
Sale
Stockport
Altrincham
Cheadle
Marple
Edale
SHEFFIELD
Manchester Airport
Chapel-en-le-Frith
Hope
Peak District
Runcorn
Ashley
Wilmslow
Foolow
Holywell
Northwich
Knutsford
Tideswell
Flint
Kingsley
Buxton
Miller's Dale
Queensferry
MACCLESFIELD
CHESHIRE
DERBYSHIRE
Northop Hall
CHESTER
Mold
Middlewich
Congleton
Youlgreave
Tarporley
Sandbach
Hartington
Newhaven
Matlock
NOTTINGHAMSHIRE
Tattenhall
CREWE
Alsager
Leek
Cholmondeley
Nantwich
Cheddleton
Tissington
WREXHAM
Wybunbury
Betley
Froghall
Waterhouses
SK
Malpas
Audlem
STOKE-ON-TRENT
Oakamoor
Ashbourne
Cheadle
Alton
Ellastone
Whitchurch
NOTTINGHAM
Llangollen
Alkmonton
Longford
DERBY
SJ
Market Drayton
Stone
Oswestry
Wem
Hodnet
Loynton
Uttoxeter
Abbots Bromley
Burton upon Trent
Knockin
Ruyton-XI-Towns
STAFFORDSHIRE
STAFFORD
Llanymynech
Hadnall
Newport
Church Eaton
LOUGHBOROUGH
SHREWSBURY
Stretton
Westbury
Lichfield
LEICESTERSHIRE
Welshpool
TELFORD
Oakham
Minsterley
Pontesbury
Ironbridge
Albrighton
Codsall
LEICESTER
Dorrington
Longnor
Montgomery
Church Stoke
SHROPSHIRE
Much Wenlock
Sutton Coldfield
Church Stretton
Bridgnorth
West Bromwich
Nuneaton
Bishop's Castle
Cleobury North
Bobbington
Rowley Regis
BIRMINGHAM
WEST MIDLANDS
SP
Munslow
Clun
Craven Arms
SO
Cleobury Mortimer
COVENTRY
Kidderminster
Solihull
Llanfair Waterdine
Ludlow
Bewdley
Bromsgrove
Alvechurch
Henley-in-Arden
Wigmore
A685
A683
A684
A6108
A1
A167
A172
A19
A168
A170
A169
A593
A590
A6
A65
A682
A59
A61
A658
A64
A6068
A58
A163
A614
A63
M621
M62
M55
M65
M6
M61
M66
A640
A635
A629
A628
A570
A565
M58
M18
M181
M180
A161
A159
A616
A631
A57
A156
A620
M60
M62
M56
M53
A623
A621
A619
A6
A614
A616
A60
A617
A51
A41
A534
A533
A50
A54
A53
A515
A6097
A523
A500
A49
A525
A52
A38
A46
A495
A5
A528
A441
A53
A519
A518
A516
A453
A42
A607
A606
A442
A34
A444
A447
M1
M42
A458
A488
A489
M54
M6
A5199
A4304
A427
A6003
A4117
A4113
A456
M5
M40
M42
A14
M45
A45
A508
A5

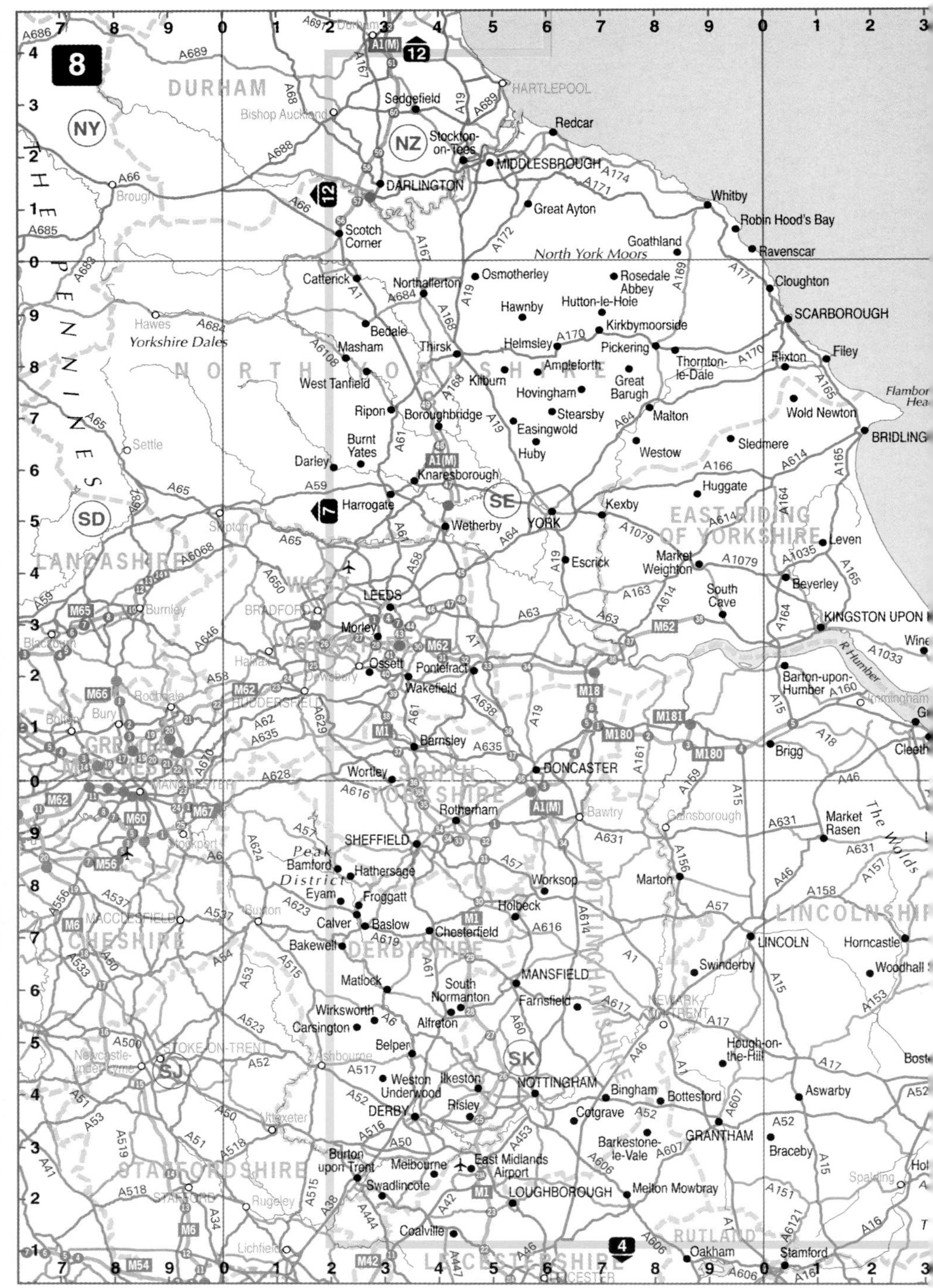

For continuation pages refer to numbered arrows

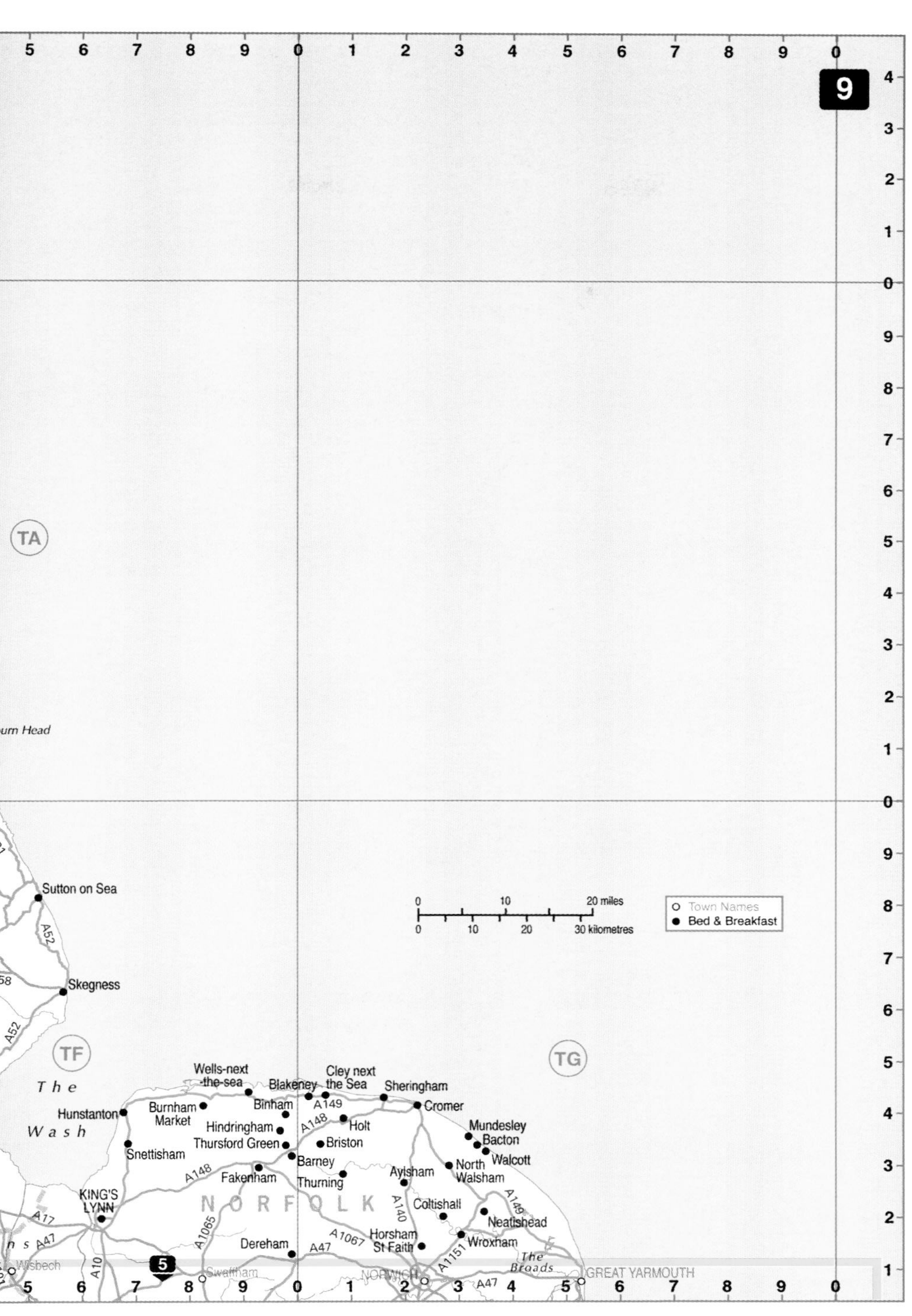
9
TA
TF
TG
Sutton on Sea
A52
Skegness
The Wash
Wells-next-the-sea
Blakeney
Cley next the Sea
Sheringham
Cromer
Hunstanton
Burnham Market
Binham
A149
A148
Holt
Hindringham
Thursford Green
Briston
Mundesley
Bacton
Walcott
Snettisham
Barney
North Walsham
Fakenham
Thurning
Aylsham
KING'S LYNN
NORFOLK
A140
Coltishall
A17
A47
A1065
A1067
Neatishead
Dereham
Horsham St Faith
Wroxham
A1151
The Broads
A10
Wisbech
Swaffham
NORWICH
GREAT YARMOUTH
0 10 20 miles
0 10 20 30 kilometres
Town Names
Bed & Breakfast

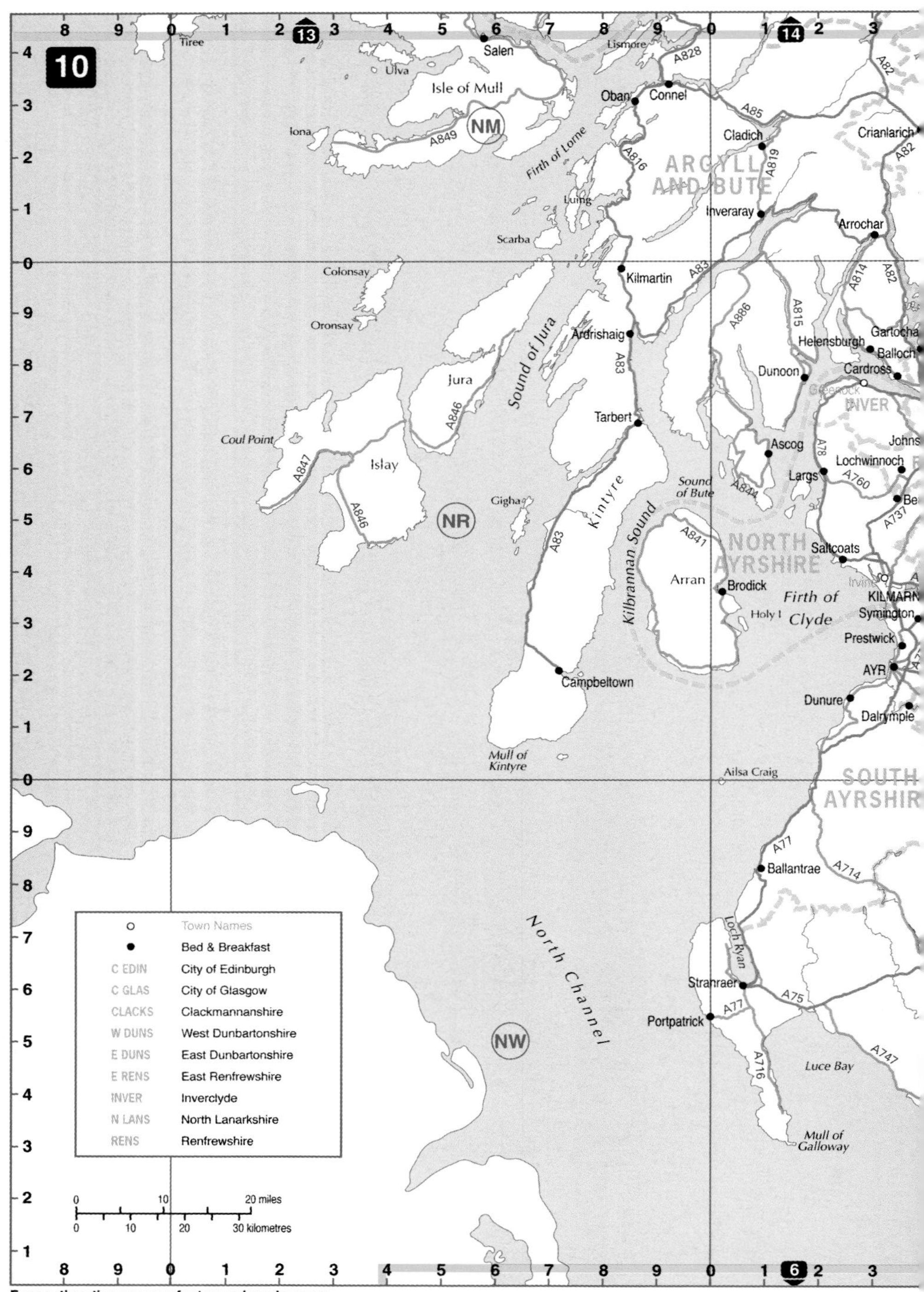

○	Town Names
●	Bed & Breakfast
C EDIN	City of Edinburgh
C GLAS	City of Glasgow
CLACKS	Clackmannanshire
W DUNS	West Dunbartonshire
E DUNS	East Dunbartonshire
E RENS	East Renfrewshire
INVER	Inverclyde
N LANS	North Lanarkshire
RENS	Renfrewshire

0 10 20 miles
0 10 20 30 kilometres

For continuation pages refer to numbered arrows

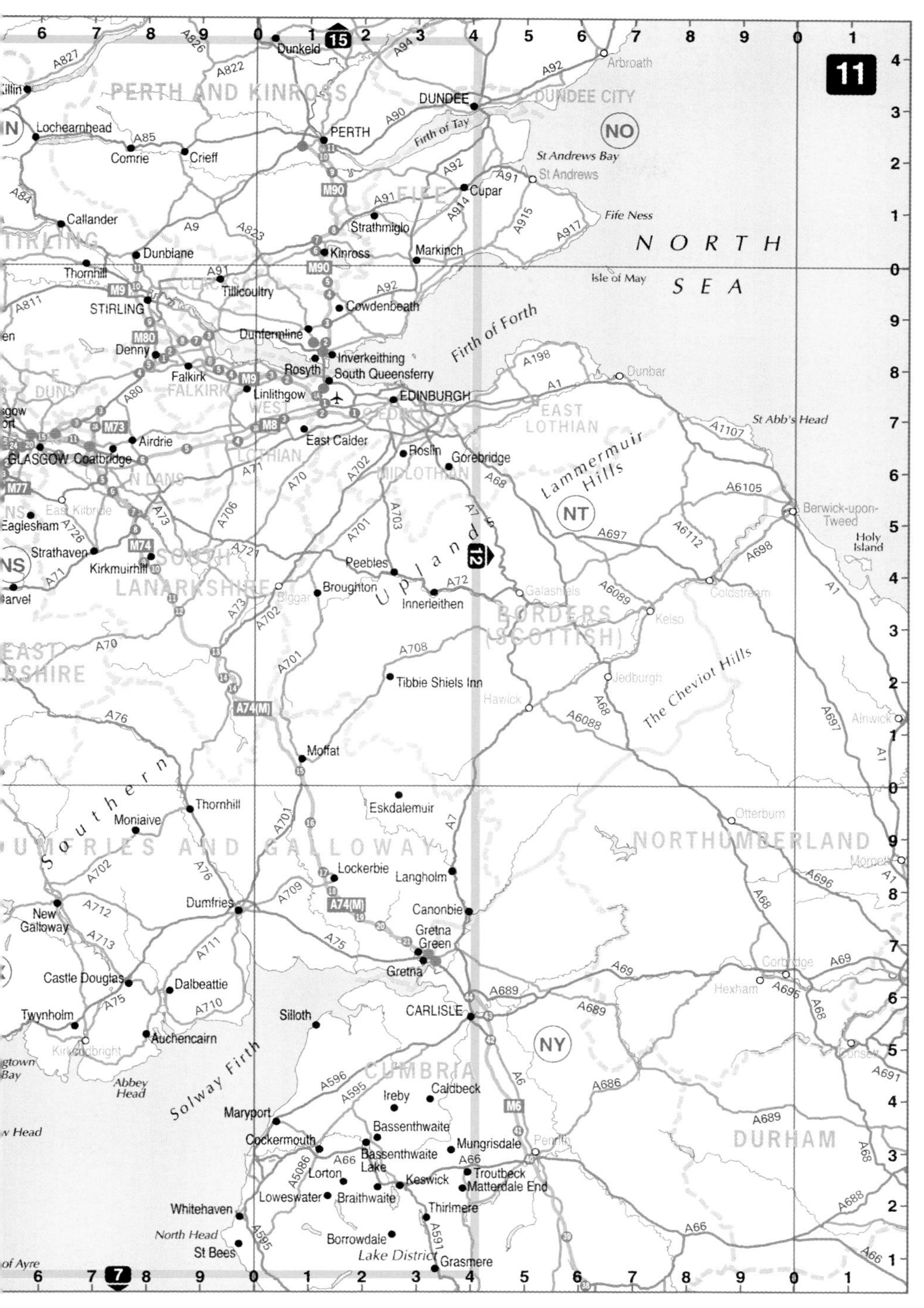

11
PERTH AND KINROSS
Dunkeld
Killin
Lochearnhead
Comrie
Crieff
PERTH
DUNDEE
DUNDEE CITY
Arbroath
Firth of Tay
St Andrews Bay
St Andrews
FIFE
Cupar
Strathmiglo
Fife Ness
Callander
Dunblane
Kinross
Markinch
NORTH
SEA
Isle of May
STIRLING
Thornhill
Tillicoultry
CLACKMANNAN
Cowdenbeath
Dunfermline
Firth of Forth
Denny
Inverkeithing
Rosyth
South Queensferry
Falkirk
FALKIRK
Linlithgow
EDINBURGH
Dunbar
WEST LOTHIAN
EAST LOTHIAN
St Abb's Head
Airdrie
East Calder
GLASGOW
Coatbridge
Roslin
Gorebridge
MIDLOTHIAN
Lammermuir Hills
East Kilbride
Eaglesham
Berwick-upon-Tweed
Holy Island
Strathaven
Kirkmuirhill
SOUTH LANARKSHIRE
Peebles
Upland
Biggar
Broughton
Innerleithen
Galashiels
Coldstream
Kelso
BORDERS (SCOTTISH)
EAST AYRSHIRE
Tibbie Shiels Inn
Jedburgh
Hawick
The Cheviot Hills
Alnwick
Moffat
Southern
Thornhill
Eskdalemuir
Otterburn
Moniaive
DUMFRIES AND GALLOWAY
NORTHUMBERLAND
Morpeth
Lockerbie
Langholm
Dumfries
New Galloway
Canonbie
Gretna Green
Gretna
Castle Douglas
Dalbeattie
Corbridge
Hexham
Twynholm
Silloth
CARLISLE
Kirkcudbright
Auchencairn
Solway Firth
Consett
Abbey Head
CUMBRIA
Caldbeck
Ireby
Maryport
Bassenthwaite
Cockermouth
Mungrisdale
Penrith
DURHAM
Bassenthwaite Lake
Lorton
Keswick
Troutbeck
Matterdale End
Loweswater
Braithwaite
Whitehaven
Thirlmere
North Head
Borrowdale
St Bees
Lake District
Grasmere
NO
NT
NY
NS

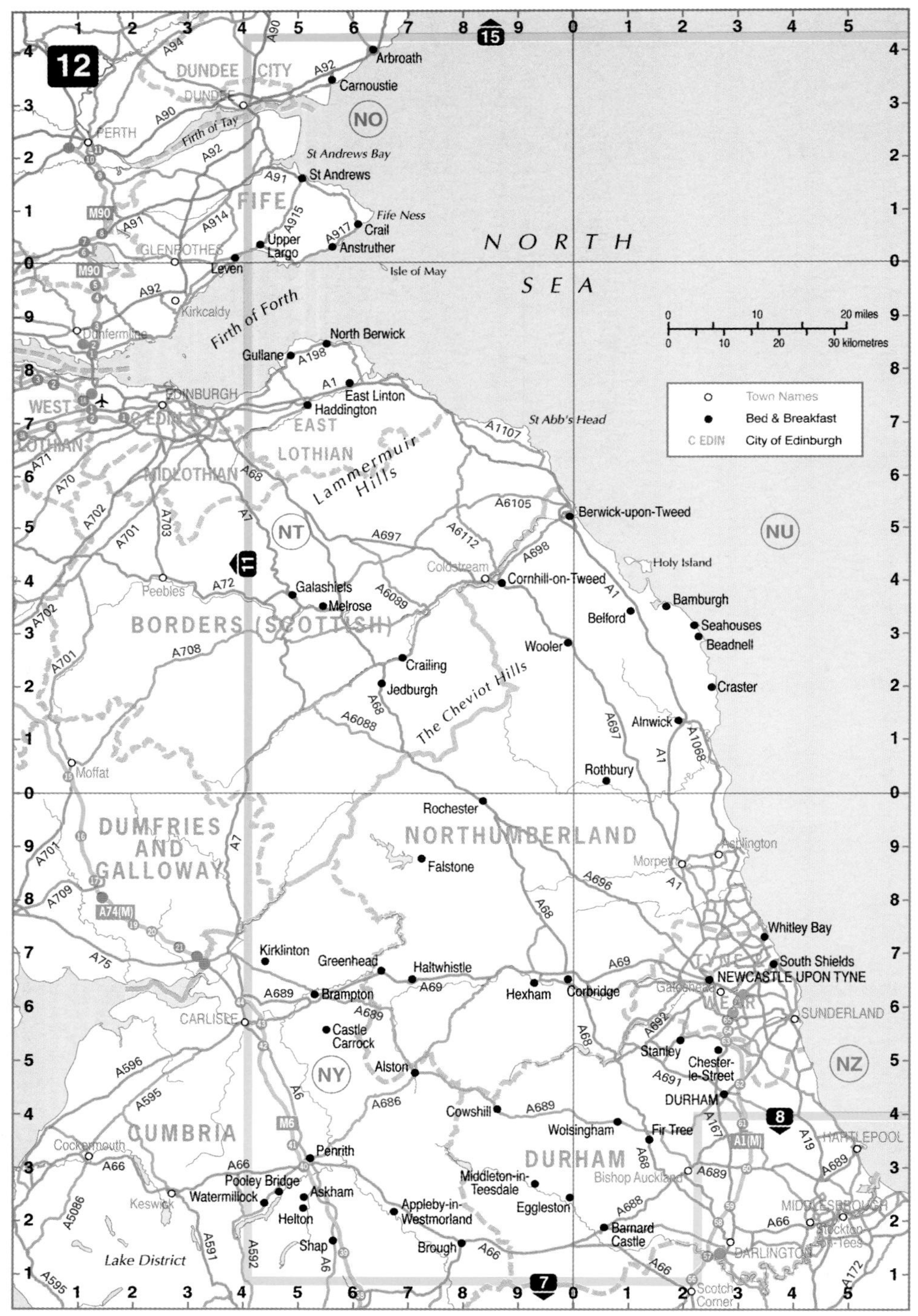

For continuation pages refer to numbered arrows

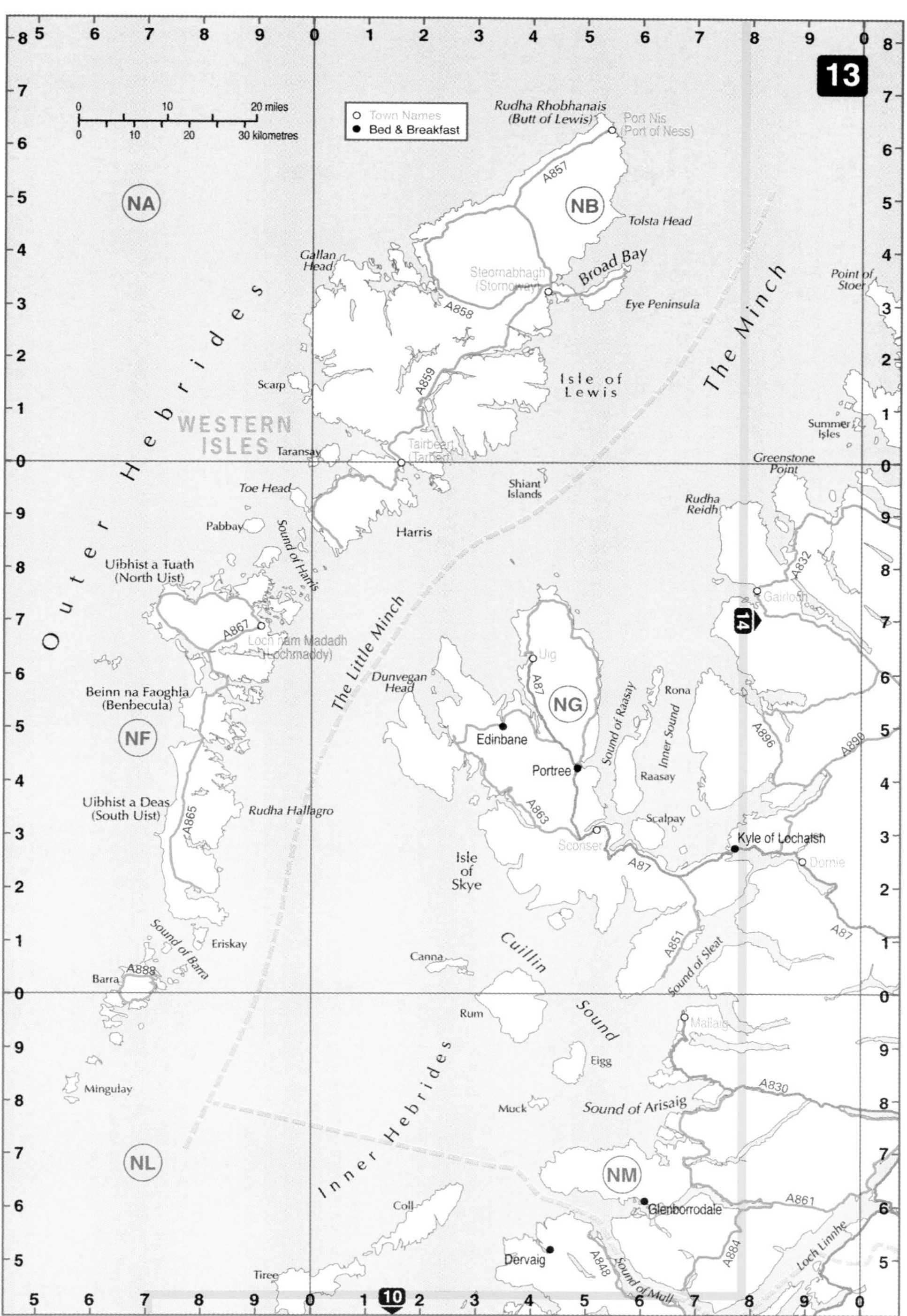

13
Town Names
Bed & Breakfast
0 10 20 miles
0 10 20 30 kilometres
Rudha Rhobhanais (Butt of Lewis)
Port Nis (Port of Ness)
NA
NB
NF
NG
NL
NM
Tolsta Head
Gallan Head
Steornabhagh (Stornoway)
Broad Bay
Eye Peninsula
The Minch
Point of Stoer
Scarp
Isle of Lewis
WESTERN ISLES
Outer Hebrides
Taransay
Tairbeart (Tarbert)
Summer Isles
Greenstone Point
Toe Head
Shiant Islands
Rudha Reidh
Pabbay
Sound of Harris
Harris
Uibhist a Tuath (North Uist)
Gairloch
Loch nam Madadh (Lochmaddy)
The Little Minch
Uig
Dunvegan Head
Beinn na Faoghla (Benbecula)
Rona
Edinbane
Sound of Raasay
Inner Sound
Portree
Raasay
Uibhist a Deas (South Uist)
Rudha Hallagro
Scalpay
Sconser
Kyle of Lochalsh
Dornie
Isle of Skye
Cuillin Sound
Eriskay
Sound of Barra
Canna
Barra
Rum
Mallaig
Sound of Sleat
Eigg
Mingulay
Inner Hebrides
Muck
Sound of Arisaig
Coll
Glenborrodale
Dervaig
Tiree
Sound of Mull
Loch Linnhe
A857
A858
A859
A867
A865
A888
A87
A863
A851
A832
A896
A890
A830
A861
A884
A848
14
10

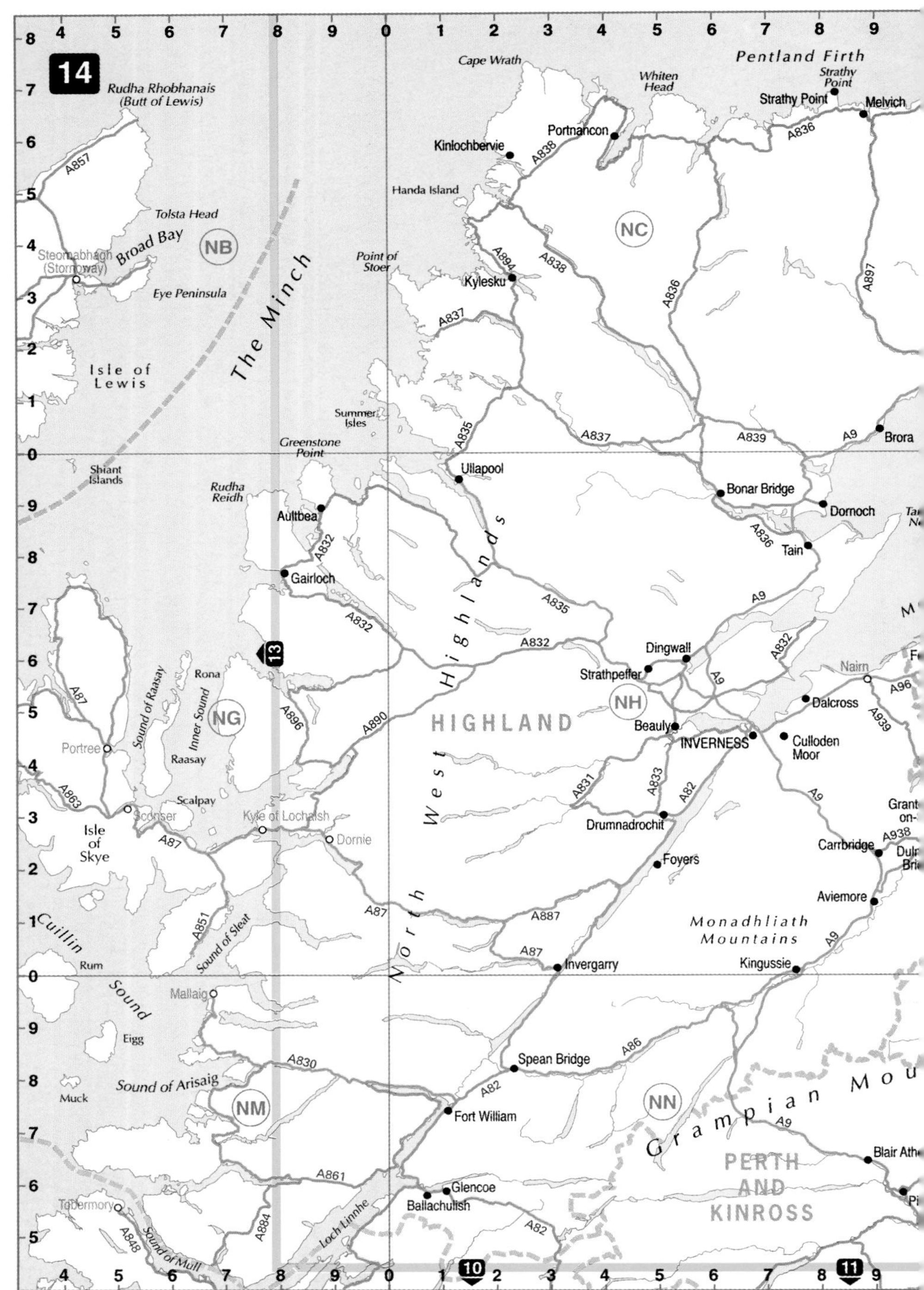

For continuation pages refer to numbered arrows

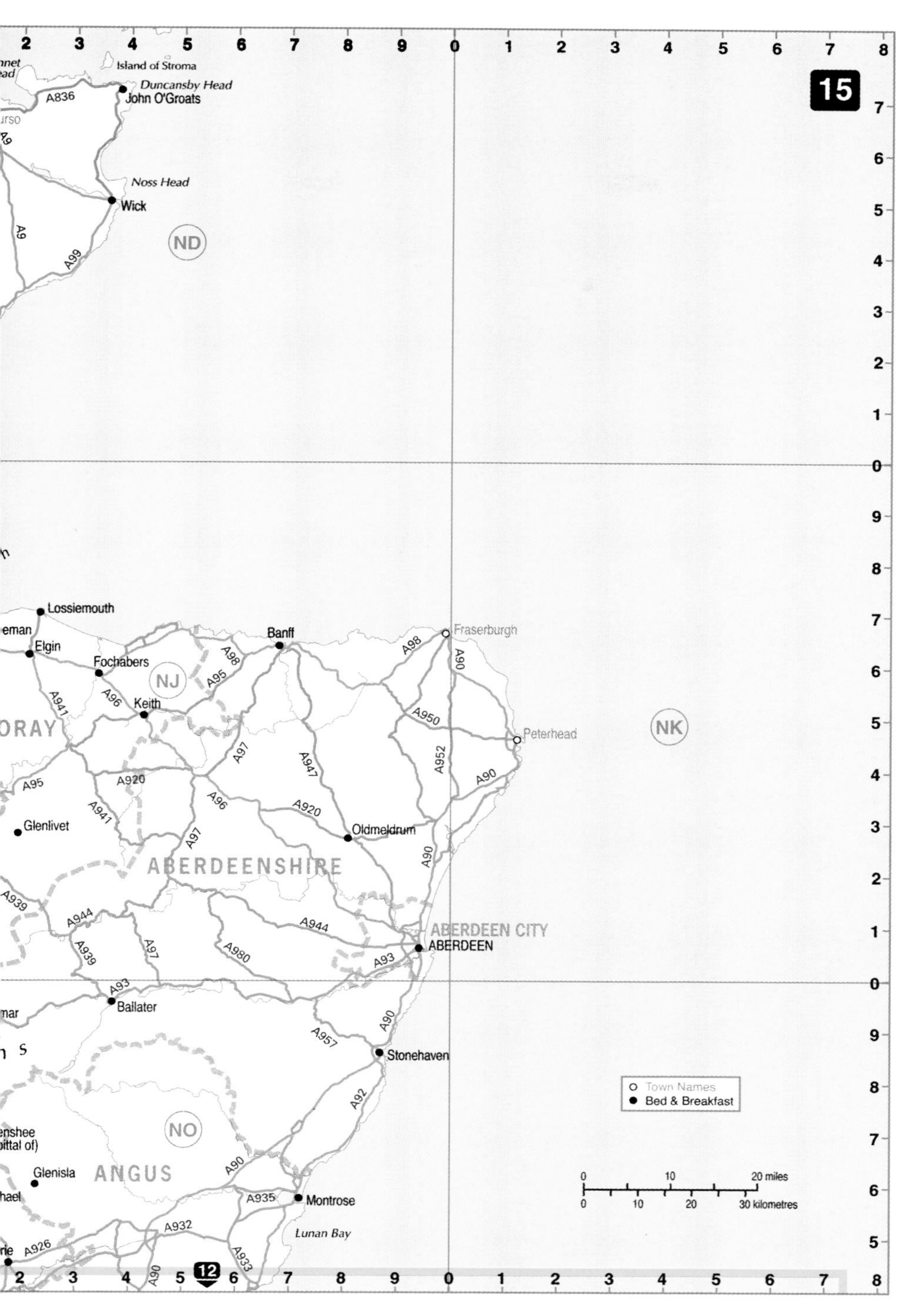
15
Island of Stroma
Duncansby Head
John O'Groats
Noss Head
Wick
ND
Lossiemouth
Elgin
Fochabers
Keith
Banff
Fraserburgh
Peterhead
NJ
NK
MORAY
Glenlivet
Oldmeldrum
ABERDEENSHIRE
ABERDEEN CITY
ABERDEEN
Ballater
Stonehaven
NO
Glenisla
ANGUS
Montrose
Lunan Bay
A836
A9
A99
A941
A96
A98
A95
A97
A947
A950
A952
A90
A920
A939
A944
A980
A93
A957
A92
A935
A932
A926
A933
12
Town Names
Bed & Breakfast
0
10
20 miles
0
10
20
30 kilometres

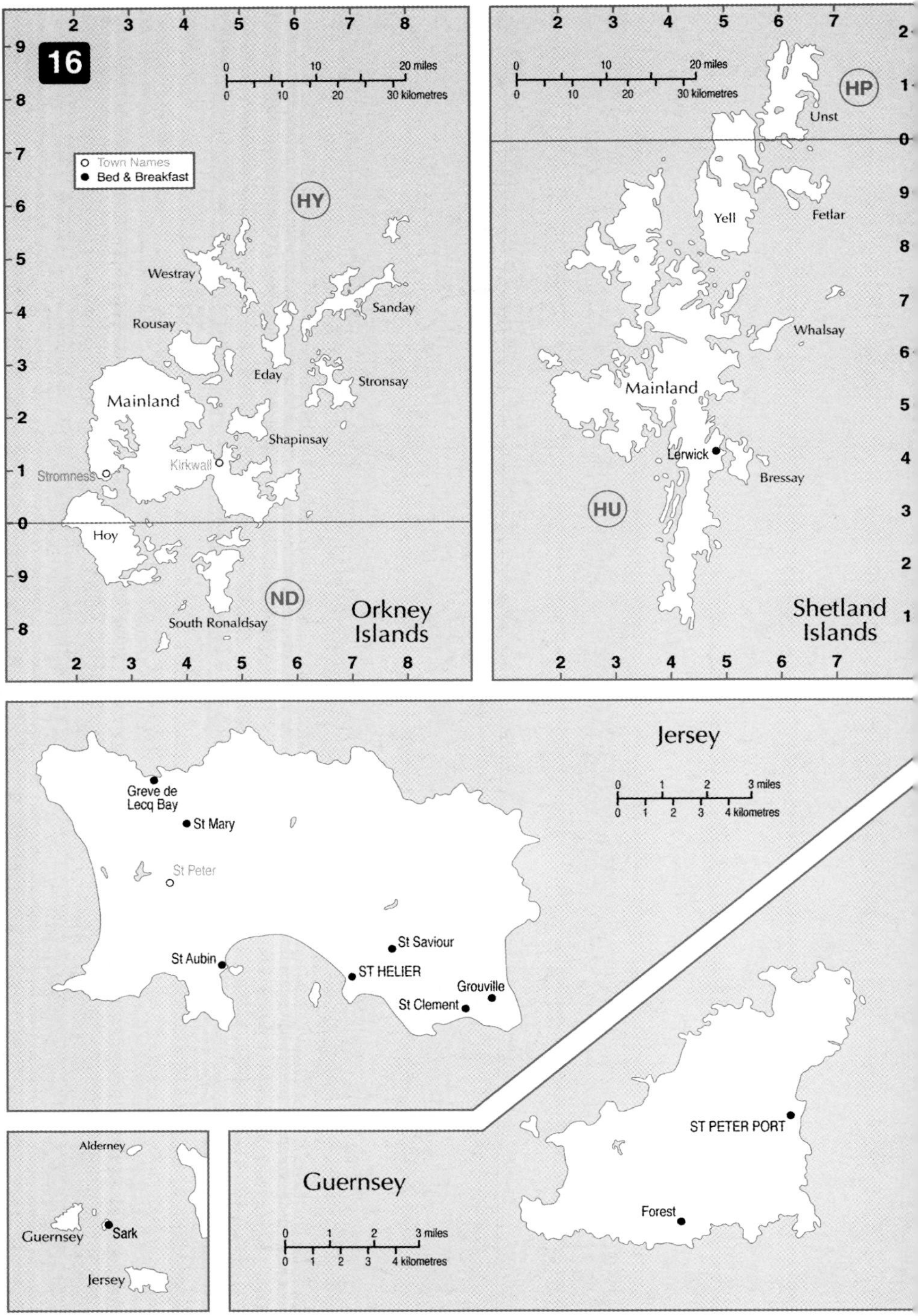
16
Town Names
Bed & Breakfast
Orkney Islands
HY
ND
0 10 20 miles
0 10 20 30 kilometres
Westray
Sanday
Rousay
Eday
Stronsay
Mainland
Shapinsay
Kirkwall
Stromness
Hoy
South Ronaldsay
Shetland Islands
HP
HU
Unst
Yell
Fetlar
Whalsay
Mainland
Lerwick
Bressay
Jersey
0 1 2 3 miles
0 1 2 3 4 kilometres
Greve de Lecq Bay
St Mary
St Peter
St Saviour
St Aubin
ST HELIER
Grouville
St Clement
Guernsey
0 1 2 3 miles
0 1 2 3 4 kilometres
ST PETER PORT
Forest
Alderney
Guernsey
Sark
Jersey

Central London

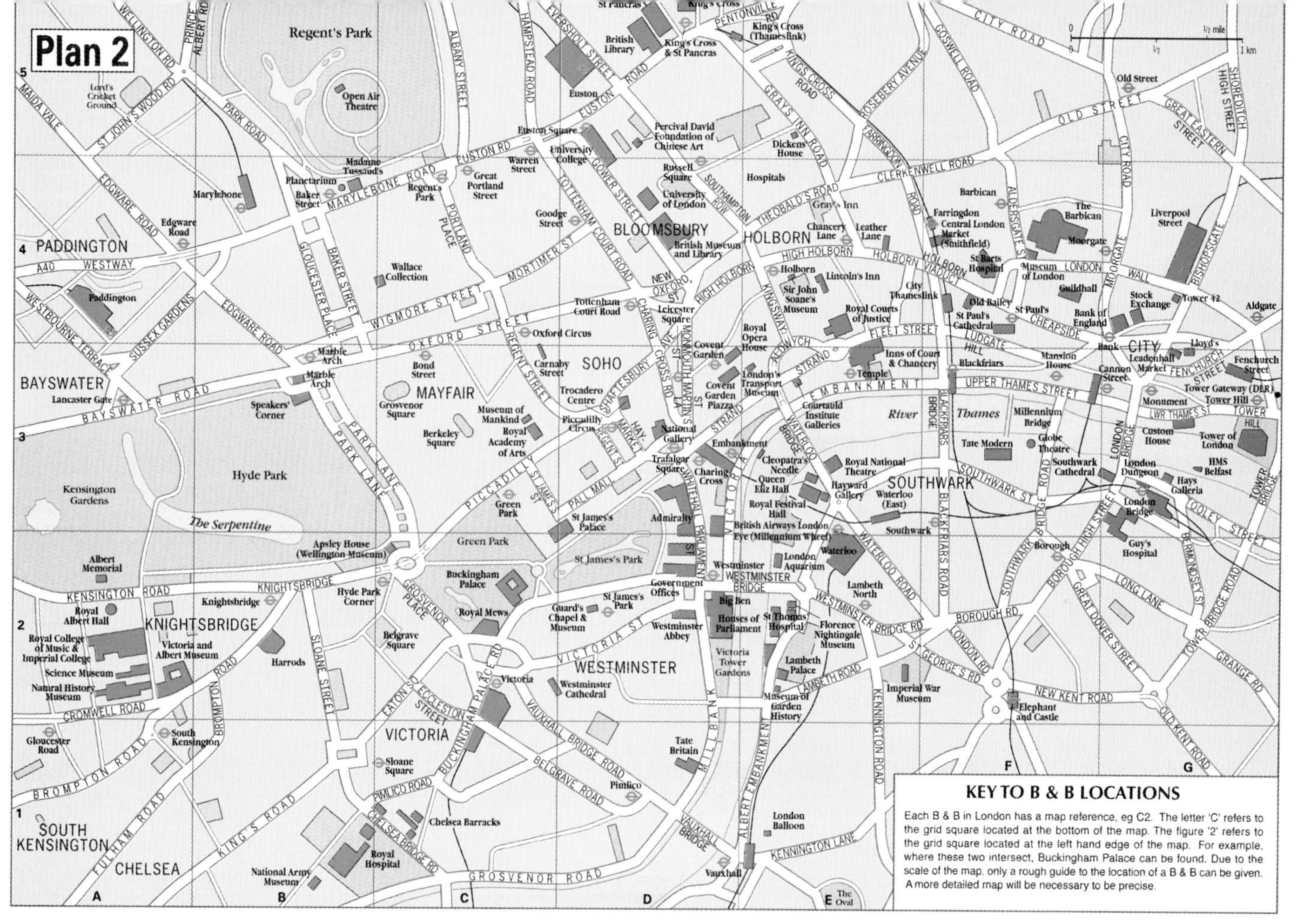

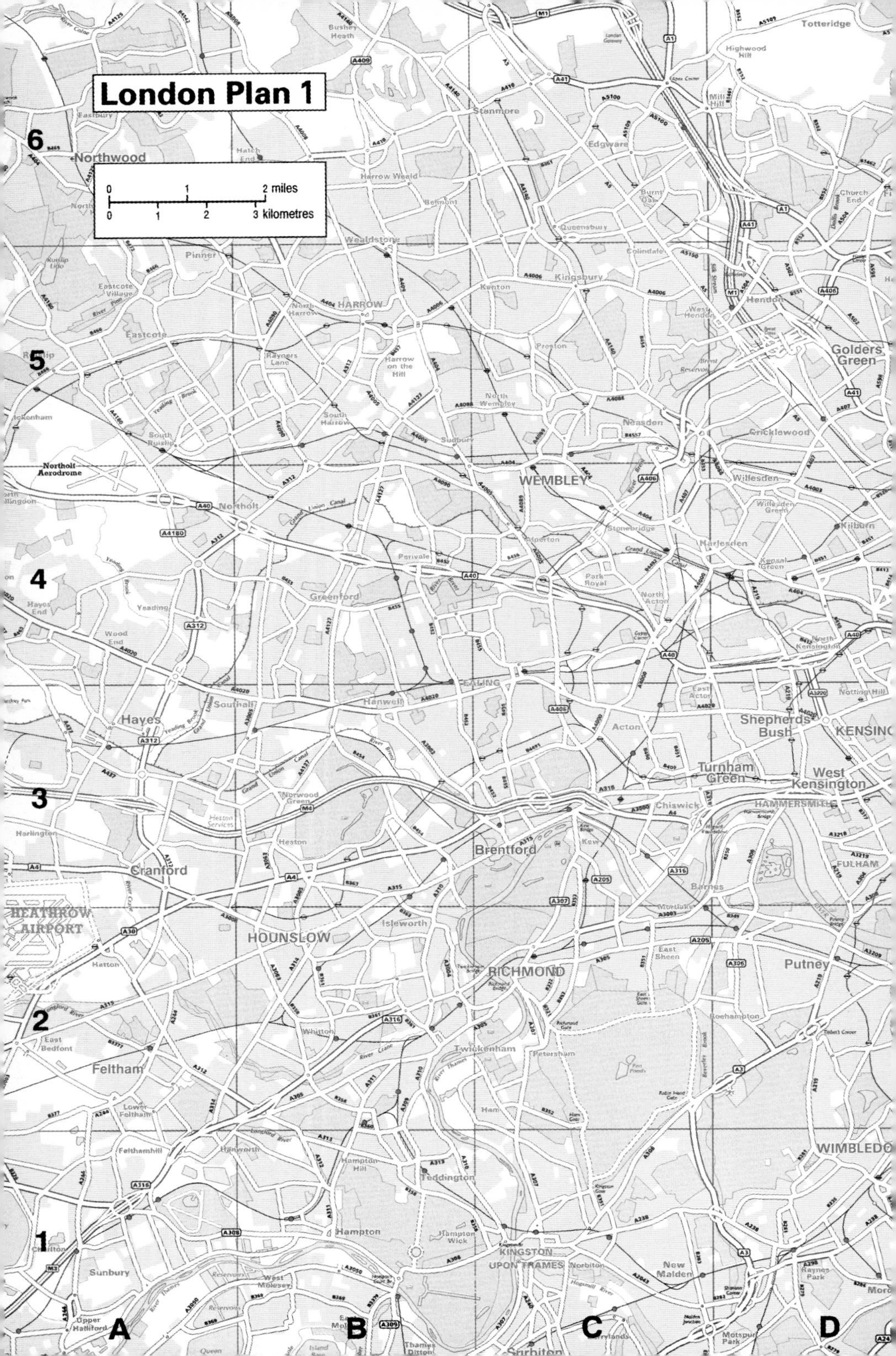

London Plan 1
0 1 2 miles
0 1 2 3 kilometres
6
5
4
3
2
1
A
B
C
D
Northwood
Eastbury
Bushey Heath
Hatch End
Stanmore
Edgware
Mill Hill
Highwood Hill
Totteridge
Harrow Weald
Belmont
Burnt Oak
Church End
Pinner
Wealdstone
Queensbury
Colindale
Eastcote Village
Kingsbury
Kenton
HARROW
North Harrow
Hendon
West Hendon
Eastcote
Rayners Lane
Harrow on the Hill
Preston
Golders Green
South Harrow
North Wembley
Neasden
Cricklewood
South Ruislip
Sudbury
Northolt Aerodrome
WEMBLEY
Willesden
Northolt
Willesden Green
Kilburn
Alperton
Stonebridge
Harlesden
Perivale
Kensal Green
Park Royal
Hayes End
Yeading
Greenford
North Acton
Wood End
North Kensington
EALING
Notting Hill
Hayes
Southall
Hanwell
East Acton
Shepherds Bush
KENSIN
Acton
Turnham Green
West Kensington
Norwood Green
Chiswick
HAMMERSMITH
Heston
Harlington
Kew
Cranford
Brentford
FULHAM
HEATHROW AIRPORT
Barnes
Mortlake
Isleworth
HOUNSLOW
East Sheen
Hatton
RICHMOND
Putney
Roehampton
East Bedfont
Whitton
Twickenham
Feltham
Petersham
Ham
Lower Feltham
WIMBLEDO
Hanworth
Felthamhill
Hampton Hill
Teddington
Hampton
Hampton Wick
KINGSTON UPON THAMES
Norbiton
New Malden
Raynes Park
Sunbury
West Molesey
Upper Halliford
Motspur Park
Surbiton
Thames Ditton
M1
M4
M3
A1
A40
A4
A3
A406
A312
A316
A205
A30
A4020
A4180
A409
A41
A306
A307
A308
A309
A3220

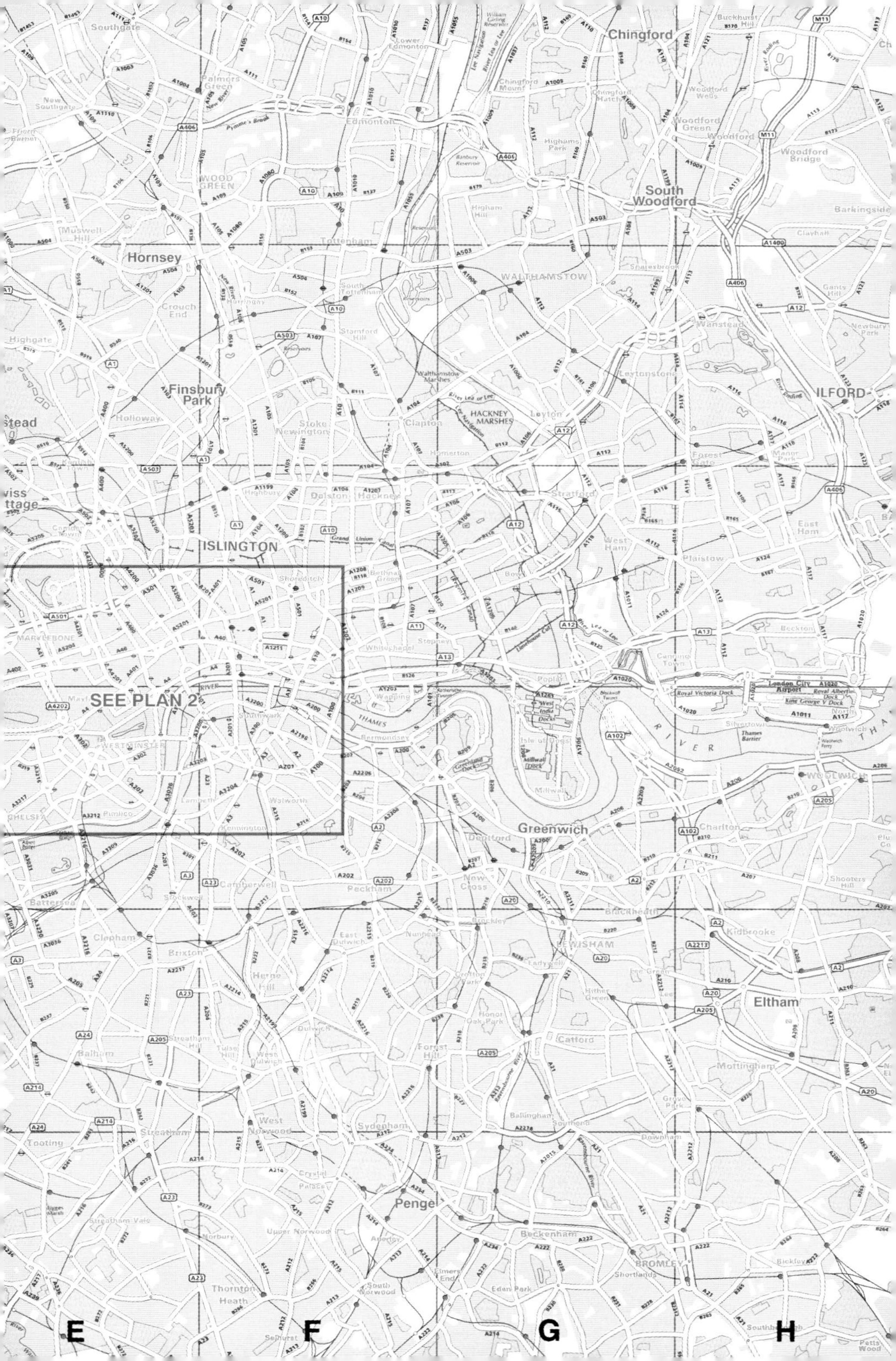
Southgate
Lower Edmonton
Chingford
Buckhurst Hill
Palmers Green
New Southgate
Edmonton
Chingford Mount
Chingford Hatch
Woodford Wells
Woodford Green
Woodford
Woodford Bridge
Highams Park
WOOD GREEN
South Woodford
Barkingside
Muswell Hill
Tottenham
Higham Hill
Clayhall
Hornsey
WALTHAMSTOW
Snaresbrook
Crouch End
South Tottenham
Gants Hill
Wanstead
Highgate
Stamford Hill
Newbury Park
Walthamstow Marshes
Leytonstone
Finsbury Park
HACKNEY MARSHES
ILFORD
Holloway
Stoke Newington
Clapton
Leyton
Homerton
Forest Gate
Manor Park
Dalston
Hackney
Stratford
East Ham
ISLINGTON
West Ham
Plaistow
Shoreditch
Bethnal Green
Bow
MARYLEBONE
Whitechapel
Stepney
Canning Town
Beckton
Poplar
London City Airport
Royal Victoria Dock
Royal Albert Dock
King George V Dock
SEE PLAN 2
Wapping
West India Docks
North Woolwich
Southwark
THAMES
RIVER
Silvertown
Thames Barrier
Woolwich Ferry
WESTMINSTER
Bermondsey
Isle of Dogs
Millwall Dock
Greenland Dock
WOOLWICH
Millwall
Lambeth
Walworth
Greenwich
Charlton
CHELSEA
Pimlico
Kennington
Deptford
Camberwell
Peckham
New Cross
Shooters Hill
Battersea
Stockwell
Brockley
Blackheath
Kidbrooke
Clapham
Brixton
East Dulwich
Nunhead
LEWISHAM
Ladywell
Lee Green
Herne Hill
Crofton Park
Hither Green
Lee
Eltham
Honor Oak Park
Dulwich
Balham
Streatham Hill
Tulse Hill
West Dulwich
Forest Hill
Catford
Mottingham
Streatham
West Norwood
Sydenham
Bellingham
Southend
Grove Park
Tooting
Downham
Crystal Palace
Penge
Streatham Vale
Upper Norwood
Anerley
Beckenham
Norbury
BROMLEY
Bickley
Elmers End
Shortlands
Thornton Heath
South Norwood
Eden Park
Selhurst
Southborough
Petts Wood
E
F
G
H

Index

A

ABBERLEY
Manor Arms Country Inn & Hotel 446
Whoppets Wood 446
ABBEY DORE
The Nevill Arms 233
Tan House Farm 233
ABBOTS BROMLEY
Marsh Farm 368
ABBOTSBURY
East Farm House 172
ABERAERON
Arosfa Guesthouse 560
ABERDEEN
Arkaig Guest House 494
Bimini Guest House 494
Corner House Hotel 494
Crown Private Hotel 494
The Jays Guest House 494
Kildonan Guest House 494
Manorville 494
Strathisla Guest House 494
ABERDYFI
Cartref Guest House 572
ABERGAVENNY
Hardwick Farm 579
Llanwenarth House 579
Oak Meadows 578
Penyclawdd Farm 579
ABERPORTH
Ffynonwen Country Guest House 560
ABERSOCH
Riverside Hotel 572
ABERYSTWYTH
Glyn-Garth 560
Llety Ceiro Country House 560
Llety Gwyn Hotel 561
Mount Pleasant Guest House 561
Queensbridge Hotel 561
Yr Hafod 561
ABINGDON
Dinckley Court 310
Rafters 310-1
ACHILL ISLAND
Finncorry House 634
Gray's Guest House 634
Lavelles Seaside House 635
West Coast House 635
ADARE
Adare Lodge 632
Avona House 632
Berkeley Lodge 632
Coatesland House 632
AIRDRIE
Calder Guest House 538
Easter Glentore Farm 537
Rosslee 538
Shawlee Cottage 538
ALBRIGHTON
Parkside Farm 320
ALBURY
Drummond Arms 384
ALDERMINSTER
The Bell 412
ALFRETON
Oaktree Farm 115
ALKMONTON
The Courtyard 115
Dairy House Farm 115
ALMONDSBURY
Abbotts Way Guesthouse 198
Hart's House 198
ALNWICK
Bondgate House Hotel 303
ALSAGER
Sappho Cottage 49
ALSTON
Greycroft 84
Ivy House 84
ALTON (Hants)
White Hart 219
ALTON (Staffs)
Bull's Head Inn 368
Farriers Cottage & Mews at Woodhouse Farm 368
ALTRINCHAM
Ash Farm Country Guest House 216
The Old Packet House 216
ALVECHURCH
Alcott Farm 446
AMBERLEY
Woody Banks 403
AMBLESIDE
Brathay Lodge 85
Chapel House Hotel 87
Compston House 86
Drunken Duck Inn 85
Easedale Lodge 86
Elterwater Park 86
Freshfields 86
Grey Friar Lodge Country House Hotel 84
Haven Cottage Guest House 87
Kent House 86
Meadowbank 87
Melrose 87
Rowanfield Country House 85
Rysdale Hotel 87
Stepping Stones 86
2 Cambridge Villas 87
Wateredge Inn 86
White Lion Hotel 86-7
AMESBURY
Catkin Lodge 431
Mandalay 431
Park House Motel 431
AMLWCH
Penycefn House 556
AMPLEFORTH
Shallowdale House 454
ANDOVER
Broadwater 219
Gunville House 219
Nether Cottage 219
New House Bed & Breakfast 219
Tilehurst 219
ANNESTOWN
Annestown House 639
ANSTRUTHER
Beaumont Lodge Guest House 517
The Grange 518
The Spindrift 518
APPLEBY-IN-WESTMORLAND
Bongate House 87
Clifton Cottage 87
Eden Grove Farmhouse 87
APPLEDORE
The Railway Hotel 241
ARBROATH
Kingsley Guest House 496
ARDARA
Bay View Country House 608
ARDINGLY
The Avins Bridge Restaurant & Rooms 403
ARDMORE
Newtown Farm Guesthouse 639
ARDRISHAIG
Fascadale House 496
ARLINGHAM
The Old Passage Inn 198
ARLINGTON
Bates Green 387
ARMSCOTE
Willow Corner 412
ARNSIDE
Willowfield Hotel 88
ARROCHAR
Bemersyde 497
ARTHURSTOWN
Glendine Country House 645
ARUNDEL
Arden Guest House 404
Blakehurst Farm 403
Bonham's Country House 403

Pindars 403
ASCOG
Balmory Hall 553
ASCOT
Ascot Corner 35
ASHBOURNE
Air Cottage Farm 117
Bramhall's 116
Common End Farm
Bed & Breakfast 116
Compton House 117
Green Man Inn 116
Homesclose House 117
Mercaston Hall 117
Millfields B & B 117
Omnia Somnia 115
Stone Cottage 117
Turlow Bank 116
ASHBURTON
Gages Mill 131
Greencott 131
The Rising Sun 131
ASHFORD (Kent)
Bethersden Old Barn 241
Croft Hotel 241
Vicky's Guest House 241
ASHFORD (Wicklow)
Ballyknocken House 649
ASHLEY
Birtles Farm B&B 49
ASKHAM
Queen's Head Inn 88
ASKRIGG
Whitfield 454
ASTHALL
Maytime Inn 311
ASTWICK
Tudor Oaks Lodge 34
ASWARBY
Tally Ho Inn 265
ATHERINGTON
Springfield Garden 131
ATHERSTONE
Mythe Farm
Bed & Breakfast 412
ATHLONE
Riverview House 644
Shelmalier House 644
ATHY
Coursetown
Country House 630
ATTLEBOROUGH
Conifers 288
AUCHENCAIRN
Balcary Mews 512
AUDLEM
Little Heath Farm 49
AULTBEA
Mellondale 522
AVIEMORE
Cairngorm Guest House 522
The Old Minister's
House 522
Ravenscraig
Guest House 522-3
AVOCA
Ashdene 649
Cherrybrook
Country Home 649
Old Coach House 649
Sheepwalk House
& Cottages 649
AXMINSTER
Goodmans House 132
Kerrington House 132
Lea Hill 132
Pump Farm 132
Sellers Wood Farmhouse 132
Shamwari 132
AYLESBURY
The Hamlet 40
AYLESFORD
Wickham Lodge 241
AYR
Belmont Guest House 546
Coila Guest House 546
Craggallan 546
Dargil 546
Daviot House 546
Glenmore Guesthouse 546
Greenan Lodge 546
Windsor Hotel 546
AYSGARTH
Stow House Hotel 454-5

B

BACTON
Keswick Hotel
& Restaurant 288
BADINGHAM
Colston Hall 374
BAGENALSTOWN
Orchard Grove 599
BAKEWELL
Avenue House 117
Barleycorn Croft 118
Bene-Dorme 117
Bourne House 118
Burre Close Cottage 118
Castle Cliffe Guest House 118
Croft Cottages 118
George Hotel 118-9
Holly House 118
White Lion 118
Wyeclose 118
Wyedale Bed & Breakfast 118
BALA
Erw Feurig Guest House 572
Pen-Y-Bryn Farmhouse 572
BALLACHULISH
Ballachulish House 523
Fern Villa 523
Lyn-Leven Guest House 523
BALLANTRAE
Cosses Country House 547
BALLATER
The Belvedere
Guest House 495
Glen Lui Hotel 494-5
Inverdeen House 495
Moorside Guest House 495
BALLINHASSIG
Blanchfield House 602
BALLOCH
Sunnyside 551
Willowdale B & B 551
BALLYHACK
Marsh Mere Lodge 645
BALLYLIFFIN
Rossaor House 609
BALLYMACARBRY
Glasha Farmhouse 640
Hanoras Cottage 640
BALLYSADARE
Seashore House 636
BALLYSHANNON
Dún Na Sí 609
BALLYVAUGHAN
Drumcreehy Guesthouse 600
Rusheen Lodge 600
BAMBURGH
Hillside Bed & Breakfast 303
BAMFORD
The Outpost 119
The White House 119
BAMPTON (Devon)
The Bark House 133
Newhouse Farm 133
The Old Rectory 133
BAMPTON (Oxon)
The Romany Inn 311
BANBURY
The Blinking Owl 311
Calthorpe Lodge
Guest House 312
Fairlawns Guest House 312
La Madonette
Country Guest House 311
The Lampet Arms 311
Roebuck Inn 312
BANDON
Glebe Country House 602
BANFF
Morayhill 495
BANGOR (Co Down)
Hebron House 595
Tara Guest House 596

BANGOR (Gwynedd)
Goetre Isaf Farmhouse 573
Gors-yr-Eira
Country Guest House 572
Nant y Fedw 572-3
BANSHA
Bansha House 637
BANTHAM
Sloop Inn 133
BANTRY
The Mill Bed
& Breakfast 602
BARKESTONE-LE-VALE
Woodside Farm 261
BARMOUTH
Llwyndu Farmhouse 573
BARNARD CASTLE
Greta House 191
The Homelands 191
Wilson House 191
BARNEY
The Old Brick Kilns 288
BARNINGHAM
College House Farm 374
BARNSLEY
Churchills Hotel 484
BARNSTAPLE
Cresta Guest House 133
Home Park Farm 133
Rowden Barton 134
The Spinney Country
Guest House 133
Twitchen Farm 134
Yeo Dale Hotel 133
BARTON-ON-SEA
Cleeve House 220
Tower House 219
BARTON-UPON-HUMBER
Tobias House 265
BASINGSTOKE
Fernbank Hotel 220
The Hatchings 220
BASLOW
Holly Cottage 119
BASSENTHWAITE LAKE
Link House 88
BATH
Ainsborough Hotel 336-7
Anchor Farm 337
Apsley House Hotel 331
Aquae Sulis Hotel 337
Aran House Number
Ninety Three 341
Armstrong House 337
Arney Guest House 341
Ashgrove Guest House 342
Ashley Villa Hotel 338
Athole Guest House 332
The Ayrlington 331
Badminton Villa 335
Bailbrook Lodge Hotel 341
Bath Lodge 332
Beckfords B + B 338
Brocks Guest House 336
Brompton House 338
Cairngorm 342
Cheriton House 332
The County Hotel 335
Cranleigh 338
Devonshire House 338-9
Dolphin House 342
Dorian House 332
Eagle House 339
Edgar Hotel 342
Grove Lodge 340
Haydon House 332
Henrietta Hotel 342
The Hermitage 342
Highfields 344
Highways House 340
Holly Lodge 334
Hotel St Clair 342-3
Kennard Hotel 334
Ko Ryu Guest House 343
Lamp Post Villa 343
Laura Place Hotel 340
Leighton House 334
Lynwood Guest House 343
Marlborough House 340
Mendip View
Guest House 343
Monkshill Guest House 334
Monmouth Lodge 334
North Lodge
Guest House 340-1
Oakleigh House 341
The Old Red House 343
Orchard Lodge 343
Owl House 341
The Parade Park and
Lambrettas Bar 341
Paradise House Hotel 334
The Plaine 336
Roman City Guest House 344
St Leonards 336
Tasburgh House Hotel 336
Victoria House 341
Villa Magdala Hotel 336
Waltons Guest House 343
Wheatsheaf Inn 341
The White Guest House 343
Widbrook Grange 335
BATTLE
Farthings Farm 387
Fox Hole Farm 387
BEACONSFIELD
The George Hotel 40
BEADNELL
Low Dover 304
BEAMINSTER
Watermeadow House 172
BEAULY
Heathmount Guest
House 523
BECKINGTON
Pickford House 344
BEDALE
The Castle Arms Inn 455
Elmfield Country House 455
Southfield 455
Upsland Farm 455
BEDDGELERT
Sygun Fawr
Country House 573
BEDFORD
Birch House 34
Hertford House Hotel 34
Knife & Cleaver Inn 34
BEER
Bay View Guest House 134
BEERCROCOMBE
Whittles Farm 344
BEITH
Shotts Farm 537
BELFAST
Malone Guest House 595
BELFORD
Market Cross
Guest House 304
BELPER
Chevin Green Farm 119
Dannah Farm
Country House 119
The Hollins 120
Shottle Hall Guest House 120
BERKHAMSTED
Laurel Cottage 238
BERWICK-UPON-TWEED
Dervaig Guest House 304
High Steads 304
The Old Vicarage 304
BETLEY
Betley Court Farm 369
BETTYSTOWN
Lis-Maura 636
BETWS GARMON
Betws Inn 573
BETWS-Y-COED
Aberconwy House 562
Afon View Non Smokers
Guest House 562
Bryn Llewelyn Non Smokers
Guest House 564
Church Hill House 564
Coed-y-Fron 562-3
The Ferns Non Smokers
Guest House 563

Fron Heulog
Country House 563
Henllys 564
Summer Hill Non Smokers
Guest House 564
Ty Gwyn 564
The White Horse Inn 564
BEVERLEY
Burton Mount
Country House 451
The Eastgate
Guest House 451
BEWDLEY
Bank House 446
BEXHILL
The Arosa Hotel 387
Park Lodge 387
BEYTON
Manorhouse 374-5
BIBURY
Cotteswold House 198
BICKINGTON
Chipley Farm 134
Dartmoor Halfway Inn 134
East Burne Farm 134
BIDDENDEN
Bishopsdale Oast 241
BIDEFORD
The Mount 134
The Pines at Eastleigh 134-5
Sunset Hotel 135
BIGGLESWADE
Crown Hotel 34
BILLERICAY
31 Mercer Road 194
BILLINGE
Woodside 287
BINGHAM
Yeung Sing Hotel
& Restaurant 308
BINGLEY
Five Rise Locks 486
BINHAM
Chequers Inn 288-9
BIRDWOOD
The Kings Head 198
BIRMINGHAM
Ashdale House Hotel 422
Awentsbury Hotel 423
Black Firs 421
Bridge House Hotel 421
Cape Race Hotel 422
Central Guest House 422
Charde Guest House 422
Comfort Inn 422
La Caverna Restaurant
& Hotel 422
Elston Guest House 423
Lyndhurst Hotel 422-3
The Old Barn
Guest House 423
Olton Cottage
Guest House 422
Robin Hood Lodge Hotel 423
Rollason Wood Hotel 423
Tri-Star Hotel 423
Westbourne Lodge 421
BISHOP'S CASTLE
The Boar's Head 320
The Old Brick
Guesthouse 320-1
BISHOP'S STORTFORD
Anglesey Guest House 238
Broadleaf Guest House 239
Harewood 238
Little Bullocks Farm 239
Pearse House 239
BISHOP'S WALTHAM
Brent Villa 220
BLACKPOOL
Ashcroft Private
Licensed Hotel 258
Briar Dene Hotel 256
Burlees Hotel 256
Castlemere Hotel 256
The Colby Hotel 256
Craigmore Hotel 257
Denely Private Hotel 257
Fern Royd Hotel 257
Hartshead Hotel 257
Mains Hall Hotel &
Restaurant 257
The New Central Hotel 258
The Old Coach House 256
Sunny Cliff Guest House 256
Sunray 256
Westdean Hotel 257
Wilmar 257
Windsor Hotel 258
Windsor Park Hotel 258
BLAIR ATHOLL
Dalgreine Guest House 538
BLAIRGOWRIE
Duncraggan 538
Gilmore House 538-9
BLAKENEY
Viney Hill Country
Guesthouse 198-9
BLANDFORD FORUM
Ramblers Cottage 172
BLARNEY
Ashlee Lodge 603
Blarney Vale House 603
Killarney House 603
The White House 603
BLEDLOW
Cross Lanes 40
BLOCKLEY
Arreton House 199
The Old Bakery 199
BLUE ANCHOR
The Langbury 344
BOBBINGTON
Blakelands Country
House 369
BODMIN
Mount Pleasant 54
Tremeere Manor 54
BOGNOR REGIS
Jubilee Guest House 404
The Old Priory 404
The Regis Lodge 404
BOLTON
Broomfield Hotel 216
Heron Lodge 216
BOLTON-BY-BOWLAND
Middle Flass Lodge 258
BONAR BRIDGE
Kyle House 524
BONCHURCH
Winterbourne 425
BOROUGHBRIDGE
The Crown Inn 455
BORROWDALE
Greenbank
Countryhouse Hotel 88
Hazel Bank
Country House 88
BOSCASTLE
Old Coach House 54
Tolcarne House
Hotel & Restaurant 54
BOSHAM
Kenwood 404
White Barn
Guest House 404-5
BOSTON
Boston Lodge 265
BOTTESFORD
The Old Whitehouse 262
The Thatch Hotel
& Restaurant 262
BOURNEMOUTH
Alexander Lodge Hotel 172-3
Alum Grange Hotel 176
Amitie Guest House 173
The Balincourt Hotel 173
The Boltons Hotel 173
Carisbrooke Hotel 173
Cherry View Hotel 176
Cransley Hotel 173
Denewood Hotel 176
Dorset House 176
East Cliff Cottage Hotel 176
Fenn Lodge 176
Fielden Court
Private Hotel 174

Linwood House Hotel 176
The Lodge at Meyrick Park 174
Newlands Hotel 176
Thanet Hotel 174
Tiffanys Hotel 174
Tudor Grange Hotel 174
The Ventura Hotel 176
Westcotes House Hotel 174-5
Whateley Hall Hotel 175
Willowdene Hotel 175
Wood Lodge Hotel 175
Wychcote Hotel 175
BOURTON-ON-THE-WATER
Chestnuts (formerly Polly Perkins) 200
Coombe House 199
The Cotswold House 199
Lansdowne Villa 199
Stepping Stone 200
BOVEY TRACEY
Brookfield House 135
Cleavelands 135
Cromwell Arms Hotel 135
Front House Lodge 135
BOX
The Hermitage 432
Lorne House 432
Owl House 432
Spinney Cross 431
White Smocks 431
BOXFORD
Cox Hill House 375
Hurrells Farmhouse 375
BRACEBY
Saddleback Cottage 265
BRADFORD-ON-AVON
Bradford Old Windmill 432
Home Farm 433
Midway Cottage 433
Serendipity 433
Widbrook Grange 432-3
BRAEMAR
Callater Lodge Hotel 495
BRAINTREE
Park Farmhouse 194
Spicers Farm 194
BRAITHWAITE
The Royal Oak 88-9
BRAMPTON
The Blacksmiths Arms 90
Bush Nook 89
Cracrop Farm 89
Hullerbank 89
BRANDON
Riverside Lodge 375
BRANSGORE
Tothill House 220
BRAUNTON
Denham House 135
BRAY
Woodville 650
BRECHFA
Glasfryn Guest House & Restaurant 558
BRECON
The Beacons 586
Borderers Guesthouse 586
Cherrypicker House 586
The Flag and Castle 586
Llanddetty Hall Farm 585
The Old Ford Inn 586
Ty Newydd 586
The Usk Inn 586
BRENTFORD
Primrose House 211
BRIDESTOWE
Week Farm 136
BRIDGNORTH
Oldfield Cottage 321
Wyndene Guest House 321
BRIDGWATER
The Boat & Anchor Inn 344-5
Chinar 345
Model Farm 344
Phoenicia 345
Rockfield House 345
BRIDLINGTON
Bay Ridge Hotel 452
Langdon Hotel 452
Lansdowne House 452
Marton Grange 451
The Mount Hotel 451
Pembroke 452
Royal Hotel 451
Ryburn Hotel 452
Sandra's Guest House 452
Southdowne Hotel 452
Thiswilldo 452
BRIDPORT
Britmead House 177
New House Farm 177
The Travellers Rest 177
BRIGG
Hamsden Garth 265
BRIGHTON
Adastral Hotel 391
Adelaide Hotel 387
Ainsley House Hotel 388
Allendale Hotel 391
Alvia Hotel 392
Ambassador Hotel 388
Amblecliff Hotel 388
Arlanda Hotel 388
Ascott House Hotel 388-9
The Brighton Beach Hotel 392
Brighton House Hotel 389
Brighton Marina House Hotel 392
Brighton Pavilions 389
Cavalaire Hotel 392
Chatsworth Hotel 392
Gullivers Guest House 392
Hotel Pelirocco 389
Hotel Seafield 392
Hotel Twenty One 389
Kempton House Hotel 392
New Steine Hotel 390
Nineteen 390
Paskins Town House 390
Penny Lanes 390
Prince Regent Hotel 391
Regency Hotel 390
Sandpiper Guest House 392
The Shalimar Hotel 392
Topps Hotel 391
Trouville Hotel 391
Westbourne Hotel 392
BRILL
Poletrees Farm 41
BRISTOL
Arches Hotel 40
Basca House 40
Downlands House 38
Downs Edge 38
Greenlands 39
Mayfair Lodge 39
Oakfield Hotel 39
Rowan Lodge 39
Shirehampton Lodge Hotel 39
Valley Farm 39
Washington Hotel 40
Westbury Park Hotel 39
BRISTON
The John H Stracey 289
BRIXHAM
Harbour View Hotel 136
Richmond House Private Hotel 136
BROAD CHALKE
Ebblesway Courtyard 433
BROADSTAIRS
Bay Tree Hotel 242
Devonhurst Hotel 242
Oakfield Private Hotel 242
BROADWAY
Barn House 448
Bowers Hill Farm 446-7
Cowley House 447
Leasow House 447
Lower Field Farm 447
Milestone House 447
Mill Hay House 446
Mount Pleasant Farm 447

Olive Branch
Guest House 447
Pathlow Guest House 448
Southwold House 448
Whiteacres 448
Windrush House 448
BROCKENHURST
Bridge House 220
Careys Cottages 221
The Cottage Hotel 220
Crossings 221
Seraya 221
BROCKHAMPTON
Ladyridge Farm 233
BRODICK
Allandale Guest House 553
Dunvegan House 553
BROMPTON REGIS
Bruneton House 346
Holworthy Farm 345
BROMSGROVE
Lower Bentley Farm 448
Rosa Lodge 448
BROMYARD
Linton Brook Farm 234
Little Hegdon 233
BROOKE
The Old Vicarage 289
BROOKTHORPE
Brookthorpe Lodge 200
BRORA
Glenaveron 524
Lynwood 524
BROUGH
Augill Castle 90
BROUGHTON
The Glenholm Centre 543
Over Tweed 543
BROUGHTON IN FURNESS
The Workshop Studios 90
BRUNTINGTHORPE
Knaptoft House Farm
& The Greenway 262
BRUREE
Ballyteigue House 632-3
BRUTON
Gants Mill 346
BUCKFAST
Furzeleigh Mill
Country Hotel 136
BUCKFASTLEIGH
Kilbury Manor 136
BUCKLAND ST MARY
Hillside Guest
Accommodation 346
BUDE
Bude Haven Hotel
& Annabel's Restaurant
54-5
Cliff Hotel 55
Fairway House 55
Pencarrol Guest House 55
Seagulls Guest House 55
BUDLEIGH SALTERTON
Long Range Hotel 136
Lufflands 136
BUILTH WELLS
Woodlands 586
BUNGAY
Earsham Park Farm 375
BUNRATTY
Park House 600
BUNTINGFORD
Buckland Bury Farm 239
BURFORD
Burford House 312
Jonathan's at the Angel 312
BURGESS HILL
The Homestead 405
BURNHAM MARKET
North Farmhouse 289
Staffordshire House 289
Whitehall Farm 289
BURNHAM-ON-SEA
Somewhere House 346
BURNLEY
Eaves Barn Farm 258
Ormerod Hotel 259
BURNSALL
Burnsall Manor
House Hotel 455
BURNT YATES
The New Inn 456
BURROWBRIDGE
Saltmoor House 346
BURRY PORT
The George Hotel 558
BURTON UPON TRENT
Delter Hotel 369
Edgecote Hotel 369
BURWASH
Judins 393
BURY ST EDMUNDS
The Abbey Hotel 376
Ash Cottage 376
Avery House 377
Brambles Lodge 377
The Chantry Hotel 376
Dunston Guest
House Hotel 377
83 Whiting Street 376
Hamilton House 377
Maypole Green Barns 376
The Old
Cannon Brewery 376
Orchard Crescent B & B 375
St Andrews Lodge 377
St Vincent Guest House 377
The Six Bells
Country Inn 376
South Hill House 376
The Three Kings 376
BUTLEIGH
Court Lodge 346
BUXTON
Buxton Wheel
House Hotel 120
Grendon Guest House 120
Grosvenor House 120
Hawthorn Farm
Guest House 121
Lakenham Guesthouse 120
The Old Manse 121
The Queen Anne 121
Roseleigh Hotel 120-1
Wellhead Farm 121

C

CADNAM
Budds Farm 221
Kents Farm 221
Walnut Cottage 221
CAERNARFON
Bryn Eisteddfod
Country House Hotel 574
Caer Menai 574
Hafoty 574
Menai View Guest
House & Restaurant 574
Pengwern Farm 574
CAERPHILLY
The Cottage Guest House 557
CAERSWS
Lower Ffrydd 587
The Talkhouse 587
CAHERDANIEL
Derrynane Bay House 622
CALDBECK
Swaledale Watch
Farm House 90
CALDICOT
Penylan 579
CALLANDER
Abbotsford
Lodge Guest House 549
Annfield Guest House 549
Arden House 548-9
Brook Linn
Country House 549
Easter Tarr Farmhouse 49
Leny House 548
Lubnaig House 549
CALLINGTON
Dozmary 55
Green Pastures
Bed & Breakfast 55
Penpill Farmhouse 55
CALNE
Chilvester Hill House 433

Maundrell House 434
The White Horse 434
CALVER
Valley View 121
CAMBRIDGE
Acorn Guest House 42
The Alpha Milton
Guest House 43
Apple Tree House 42
Arbury Lodge Guest House 44
Assisi Guest House 44
Aylesbray Lodge
Guest House 42
Benson House 44
Brooklands Guesthouse 44
Cristina's Guest House 44
De Freville House 42-3
Dykelands Guest House 44
Fairways Guest House 44
Hamden Guest House 43
Hamilton Hotel 44-5
Helen Hotel 43
Holmefields Barn 42
Lensfield Hotel 43
Southampton
Guest House 45
CAMELFORD
Pendragon House 56
Silvermoon 56
CAMP
Barnagh Bridge
Country House 622
Suan Na Mara 622
CAMPBELTOWN
Westbank Guest House 497
CAMPILE
Kilmokea Country
Manor & Gradens 645
CANONBIE
Four Oaks 512
CANTERBURY
Abberley House 244
Beech Bank 242-3
Canterbury Pilgrims
Hotel 244
Cathedral Gate Hotel 244
Chislet Court Farm 243
Clare Ellen Guest House 243
Ensigne Cottage 243
Ersham Lodge Hotel 244
Magnolia House 242
Thanington Hotel 242
Upper Ansdore 244
Waltham Court Hotel 243
The White House 244
Yorke Lodge 242
CAPPOQUIN
Richmond House 640
CARDIFF
Annedd Lon
Guest House 557
The Big Sleep Hotel 558
Courtfield Hotel 558
Marlborough
Guest House 558
Tanglewood 558
CARDIGAN
Brynhyfryd Guest House 561
The Webley
Waterfront Hotel 561
CARDROSS
Kirkton House 497
CARLINGFORD
Beaufort House 634
CARLISLE
Angus Hotel
& Almonds Bistro 91
Bessiestown Farm Country
Guest House 90-1
Blackwell Farm 92
Cambro House 91
Cherry Grove 92
Cornerways Guest House 91
Craighead 92
Dalroc 92
East View Guest House 92
Fern Lee Guest House 91
Howard House 91
Howard Lodge
Guest House 92
Kingstown Hotel 91
Lynebank House 91
New Pallyards 91
CARLOW
Barrowville Town House 600
Carlow Guest House 600
CARMARTHEN
Capel Dewi Uchaf
Country House 559
Glôg Farm 559
Sarnau Mansion 559
CARNA
Hillside House B&B 617
CARNFORTH
New Capernwray Farm 259
The Redwell Inn 259
The Silverdale Hotel 259
CARNOUSTIE
Park House 496
CARPERBY
Wheatsheaf Hotel 456
CARRBRIDGE
Carrmoor Guest House 524
The Pines
Country House 524
CARRIGANS
Mount Royd
Country Home 609
CARRIGBYRNE
Woodlands House 645
CARSINGTON
Henmore Grange 121
CARTMEL
Hill Farm 92
Uplands Hotel 92-3
CASHEL
Ashmore House 638
Aulber House 637
Baileys of Cashel 637
Dualla House 638
Knock-Saint-Lour House 638
Legend's Townhouse
and Restaurant 638
Thornbrook House 638
CASHMOOR
Cashmoor House 177
CASTLE CARROCK
Gelt Hall Farm 93
CASTLE CARY
Clanville Manor 346
The Horse Pond
Inn & Motel 346-7
CASTLE COMBE
Fairfield Farm 434
CASTLE DOUGLAS
Craigadam 512-3
Longacre Manor 513
CASTLEGREGORY
Griffin's Tip Top
Country Farmhouse 623
Sea-Mount House
Bed & Breakfast 623
The Shores
Country House 622
Strand View House 623
CATCOTT
Honeysuckle 347
CATTERICK
Rose Cottage
Guest House 456
CEMAES BAY
Hafod Country House 556
CHAGFORD
Parford Well 136-7
CHALE
Chale Bay Farm 425
The Old House 425
CHALLOCK
Hegdale Farmhouse 245
Heycroft 245
CHAPEL-EN-LE-FRITH
Craigside 122
CHARD
Bere Farm 347
Bellplot House Hotel 347

Higher Beetham Farm 347
Watermead Guest House 347
CHARLTON
Woodstock House Hotel 405
CHATTERIS
North Bank House 45
CHAWLEIGH
The Barn Rodgemonts 137
CHEADLE (Gt Man)
Spring Cottage Guest House 216
CHEADLE (Staffs)
The Grange 369
CHEDDAR
Market Cross Hotel 348
Tor Farm 348
CHEDDLETON
Choir Cottage and Choir House 369
CHEEKPOINT
Three Rivers Guest House 640
CHELMSFORD
Beechcroft Hotel 194
Boswell House Hotel 194
Tanunda Hotel 194
Yew Tree Farm 194
CHELTENHAM
The Battledown 201
Beaumont House Hotel 200
Beechworth Lawn Hotel 200-1
Cleeve Hill Hotel 200
Georgian House 200
Ivydene Guest House 202
Lonsdale House 201
Montpellier Hotel 201
Moorend Park Hotel 201
Pardon Hill Farm 201
Stray Leaves Guest House 202
Stretton Lodge Hotel 201
Wishmoor House 201
CHERITON BISHOP
Holly Farm 137
CHESTER
Alton Lodge Hotel 49
Cheltenham Lodge 50
Craigleith Lodge 50
Derry Raghan Guest House 51
The Glann Hotel 51
Gloster Lodge Hotel 51
Golborne Manor 50
Green Gables 50
Grove House 49
Lavender Lodge 50
The Mount 50
Redland Private Hotel 49
Rowton Poplars Hotel 50
Strathearn Guest House 51
CHESTERFIELD
Anis Louise Guest House 122
The Beeches 122
CHESTER-LE-STREET
Waldridge Fell Guest House 191
CHICHESTER
Cedar House 405
Chichester Lodge 405
Downfields 405
Old Chapel Forge 406
Wilbury House Bed & Breakfast 406
CHICKLADE
The Old Rectory 434
CHIDEOCK
Betchworth House 177
Rose Cottage 177
CHILGROVE
Forge Hotel 406
CHILLATON
Tor Cottage 137
CHIPPENHAM (Cambs)
The Old Bakery 46
CHIPPENHAM (Wilts)
Home Farm 434
Home From Home 434
Pickwick Lodge Farm 434
CHIPPING CAMPDEN
Catbrook House 202
Holly House 202
The Malt House 202
Manor Farm 202
Marnic House 202
Primrose Cottage 202
Wyldlands 203
CHIPPING NORTON
The Forge House 312-3
CHIPPING ONGAR
Diggins Farm 194
CHISLEHAMPTON
Coach & Horses Inn 313
CHOLMONDELEY
The Cholmondeley Arms 51
CHOLSEY
The Well Cottage 313
CHRISTCHURCH
Ashbourne Guest House 178
The Beech Tree 178
Brantwood Guest House 178
Bure Farmhouse 178
Druid House 177
Grosvenor Lodge 179
The Lord Bute Hotel & Restaurant 178
Lyndhurst Lodge Guest House 178-9
Number 19 179
The Pines Hotel 179
Sea Corner Guest House 178
Stour Villa 179
Three Gables 178
The White House 178
CHUDLEIGH
Farmborough House 138
CHULMLEIGH
The Old Bakehouse 138
CHURCH EATON
Slab Bridge Cottage 369
CHURCH STOKE
The Drewin Farm 587
CHURCH STRETTON
Belvedere Guest House 321
Brookfields Guesthouse 322
Gilberries Hall Farm 322
Jinlye Guest House 321
Malt House Farm 322
Rectory Farm 322
Willowfield Guest House 321
CHURCHINFORD
The York Inn 348
CIRENCESTER
The Bungalow 203
The Masons Arms 203
Smerrill Barns 203
Wimborne House 203
CLACTON-ON-SEA
Sandrock Hotel 195
CLADICH
Rockhill Farm 497
CLANE
Ashley 630
Silverspring House 630
CLARE
Ship Stores 377
CLEETHORPES
Adelaide Hotel 265
Burlington Guest House 266
Clee House 265
Comat Hotel 265
Dovedale Hotel 266
Ginnies Guest House 266
Holmhirst Hotel 266
Shellys 266
Tudor Terrace Guest House 266
CLEOBURY MORTIMER
The Crown Inn 322
The Old Bake House 322
CLEOBURY NORTH
Cleobury Court 323
CLEY NEXT THE SEA
Old Town Hall House 289
CLIFDEN
Ardmore House 617
Ben View House 618
Buttermilk Lodge 617
Byrne's Mal Dua House 617

Dan O'Hara's Farmhouse 618
Dun Ri Guest House 617
Failte 618
Faul House 618
Kingstown House 618
Mallmore House 618
O'Grady's Sunnybank House 617

CLITHEROE
Brooklyn Guest House 259

CLONAKILTY
An Garran Coir 603
Desert House 604
Duvane Farm 603
Springfield House 604

CLONMEL
Farrenwick Country House 638

CLOUGHTON
Blacksmiths Arms 456

CLOVELLY
Fuchsia Cottage 138

CLUN
Birches Mill 323
Hurst Mill Farm 323

CLUTTON
The Hunters Rest 348

COALVILLE
Church Lane Farm House 262

COATBRIDGE
Auchenlea 538

COCKERMOUTH
Highside Farmhouse 93
Rose Cottage 93
Sundawn 93

CODSALL
Moors Farm & Country Hotel 369

COLCHESTER
Fridaywood Farm 195
Globe Hotel 195
The Old Manse 195
Salisbury Hotel 195

COLEFORD
The New Inn 138

COLERAINE
Camus Country Guest House 598
Greenhill House 598

COLESHILL
The Old Vicarage 412
Ye Olde Station Guest House 412

COLTISHALL
The Hedges 290
Kings Head 290

COLWYN BAY
Cabin Hill Private Hotel 565
Crossroads 565
Northwood Hotel 565
Plas Rhos Hotel 564
Whitehall Hotel 565

COLYFORD
Lower Orchard 138

COLYTON
The White Cottage 138

COMBE HAY
Anchor Farm 348
Wheatsheaf Inn 348

COMBER
The Old Schoolhouse Inn 596

COMPTON MARTIN
Haydon Grange Farm 348-9

COMRIE
Mossgiel Guest House 539

CONG
Ballywarren House 635

CONGLETON
Egerton Arms Hotel 51
Sandhole Farm 51
Waggon and Horses 51

CONISTON
Arrowfield Country Guest House 94
Browside Guest House 94
Coniston Lodge Hotel 93
Wheelgate Country Guest House 93
Wilson Arms 94

CONNEL
Ards House 497
Kilchurn 497
Loch Etive House 497
Ronebhal Guest House 498

CONWY
Bryn Derwen 566
Glan Heulog Guest House 566
Gwern Borter Country Manor 566
Sychnant Pass House 565

CORBRIDGE
The Hayes 304
Priorfield 304
Riverside Guest House 304

CORBY
Raven Hotel 302
Thatches on the Green 302

CORK
Antoine House 604-5
Brazier's Westpoint House 605
Crawford House 604
Fairylawn Guest House 604
Garnish House 604
Lancaster Lodge 604
Lough Mahon House 605
Killarney Guest House 605
Roserie Villa 605

CORNHILL-ON-TWEED
Ivy Cottage 305

COROFIN
Fergus View 600

CORSCOMBE
The Fox Inn 179

CORSHAM
Church Farm 435
Pickwick Lodge Farm 434

CORWEN
Powys Country House 569

COTGRAVE
Jerico Farm 308

COVENTRY
Acacia Guest House 424
Ashdowns Guest House 424
Ashleigh House 424
Croft On The Green 424

COWBRIDGE
Crossways House 593

COWDENBEATH
Struan Bank Hotel 518

COWES
Windward House 425

COWSHILL
Low Cornriggs Farm 191

CRACKINGTON HAVEN
Coombe Barton Inn 56

CRAIL
Selcraig House 518

CRAILING
Crailing Old School B&B 544

CRANBROOK
Hallwood Farm Oast 245
Tolehurst Barn 245

CRANTOCK
Carrek Woth 56

CRASTER
Cottage Inn 305

CRAUGHWELL
St Clerans 618

CRAVEN ARMS
The Firs 323
Stokesay Castle Inn 323
Strefford Hall Farm 323

CREDITON
Fircroft 139

CRETINGHAM
Shrubbery Farmhouse 378

CREWKERNE
The Manor Arms 349
Manor Farm 349
Shores Farm 349

CRIANLARICH
Ben More Lodge Hotel 549
The Lodge House 549

CRICCIETH
Abereistedd Hotel 574
Bron Rhiw Hotel 575
Glyn-Y-Coed Hotel 575

Min y Gaer Hotel 575
CRICKHOWELL
Glangrwyney Court 587
CRICKLADE
Upper Chelworth Farm 435
CRIEFF
Comely Bank 539
Gwydyr House Hotel 539
Merlindale 539
Number Five B&B 539
CRIGGION
Brimford House 588
CROMER
Beachcomber Guest House 290
Birch House 291
Bon Vista 290
Brightside Guest House 290
Chellow Dene Guest House 291
Glendale Guest House 291
Morden House 290
Sandcliff Private Hotel 291
Shrublands Farm 290
Westgate Lodge Private Hotel 291
The White Cottage 291
CROSCOMBE
The Bull Terrier 349
CROSTHWAITE
Crosthwaite House 94
CROWBOROUGH
Plough & Horses Inn 393
CROWCOMBE
Home Leigh House 349
CROYDE
West Winds Guest House 139
The Whiteleaf 139
CROYDON
Kirkdale Hotel 211
CULLOMPTON
Weir Mill Farm 139
CUPAR
Rathcluan Country House 519
Todhall House 518
Westfield House 518-9
CUSHENDUN
Drumkeerin 595
The Villa Farm House 595
CWMDUAD
Neuadd-Wen Guest House 559

D

DALBEATTIE
Auchenskeoch Lodge 513
Pheasant Hotel 513
DALCROSS
Easter Dalziel Farmhouse 524
DALRYMPLE
The Kirkton Inn Hotel 516
DAMERHAM
The Compasses Inn 221
DARLEY
Elsinglea Guest House 456
DARLINGTON
Balmoral Guest House 192
Clow Beck House 192
DARTFORD
The Rising Sun Inn 245
DARTMEET
Brimpts Barn 139
DARTMOUTH
Broome Court 140
The Captain's House 140
Cherub's Nest 141-1
Courtyard House 141
Hill View House 141
Nonsuch House 140
The Seale Arms 141
Slide House 140
Warfleet Lodge 140
DEAL
The Hole in The Roof Hotel 246
Sondes Lodge 245
Sutherland House Hotel 245
DELPH
Globe Farm Guest House 217
DENBIGH
Bach-Y-Graig 569
Cayo Guest House 569
DERBY
Georgian House Hotel 122
The Longlands 122
Rangemoor Park Hotel 122
DEREHAM
Yaxham Mill 291
DERVAIG
Bellachroy Hotel 553
DEVIZES
Blounts Court Farm 435
Craven House 436
Eastcott Manor 435
Greenfields 435
Littleton Lodge 435
DIDMARTON
The Kings Arms Inn 203
DINDER
Crapnell Farm 350
DINGLE
Alpine Guesthouse 624
Ballyegan House 625
Bambury's Guest House 624
Cleevaun 624
Dingle Heights 624-5
Doyles Town House 624
Emlagh House 623
Gormans Clifftop House & Restaurant 623
Greenmount House 623
Heatons Guest House 624
Hurleys Farm 625
Milltown House 623
Mount Eagle Lodge 624
Pax House 624
DINGWALL
Braelangwell House 524
DINTON
Wallace Farm 41
DISS
Jasmine House 291
DITCHEAT
The Manor House Inn 350
DOLGELLAU
Clifton House Hotel 575
Ivy House 576
Tyddynmawr Farmhouse 575
DOLTON
The Union Inn 141
DONCASTER
Balmoral Hotel 484
Canda Lodge 484
DONEGAL
Ardeevin 609
DOOLIN
Cullinan's Guest House & Restaurant 601
DORCHESTER
The Casterbridge Hotel 179
Churchview Guest House 180
Lamperts Cottage 180
Long Barn House 181
Maiden Castle Farm 180
Westwood House Hotel 180
Yalbury Cottage Hotel & Restaurant 180
Yellowham Farmhouse 180
DORNOCH
Achandean B & B 525
Inistore House 525
DORRINGTON
Ashton Lees 323
DOUGLAS
All Seasons 491
Chesterfield Hotel 491
Dreem Ard 491
Engelwood Lodge 491
Rosslyn Guest House 492
DOVER
Ardmore Private Hotel 246
Beulah House 246
Castle House 246
Dovers Restover Bed & Breakfast 246
Gateway Hovertel 246
Hubert House 247
Kernow Guest House 247

Longfield Guest House 247
Number One
Guest House 246
The Old Vicarage 246
Penny Farthing
Guest House 247
Peverell House 247
St Albans Non-Smoking
Bed & Breakfast 248
St Martins Guest House 248
Swingate Inn & Hotel 248
DOWNHAM MARKET
The Dial House 292
DOWNPATRICK
Pheasants' Hill
Country House 596
DRAYCOTT
Oakland House 350
DROGHEDA
Boynehaven House 634
Tullyesker
Country House 634
DRUMLISH
Longford Country House 633
DRUMNADROCHIT
Beechwood 525
Glen Rowan House 525
Riverbank 525
DRYMEN
Croftburn Cottage 550
DUBLIN
Aaron House 612
Aaronmor Guest House 613
Aberdeen Lodge 610
Abrae Court 613
Antrim Arms
Guest House 616
Aran House 616
Ardagh House 615
Ariel House 611
Askill 615
Belgrave Guest House 615
Blakes Townhouse 611
Brownes Townhouse &
Brasserie 611
Butlers Town House 611
Cedar Lodge 611
Charleston Manor 615
Charleville Lodge
Guest House 613
Clifden Guest House 615
Eglinton Manor 611
Eliza Lodge 613
Ferryview House 613
The Fitzwilliam 615
Glenogra Guest House 612
Glenshandan Lodge 614
Harrington Hall 614
Hazelhurst B & B 614
Kilronan House 614
Kingswood
Country House 614
Lyndon Guest House 616
Merrion Hall 612
Merrion Square Manor 614
No 66 Townhouse 614
Pairc na Bhfuiseog 615
Pembroke Town House 612
Raglan Lodge 612
St Aiden's Guesthouse 616
Trinity Lodge 614
Waterloo House 612
DULNAIN BRIDGE
Bydand 525
DULVERTON
Higher Langridge Farm 350
Highercombe 350
Threadneedle 350-1
Town Mills 351
DUMFRIES
Southpark
Country House 513
DUN LAOGHAIRE
Cumberland Lodge 616
DUNBLANE
Rokeby House 550
DUNCHURCH
Toft Hill 413
DUNDALK
Rosemount 634
DUNDEE
Anlast Three Chimneys 516
Beach House Hotel 516
Homebank Guest House 516
Invermark House 516
DUNFERMLINE
Clarke Cottage 519
Hillview House 519
Hopetoun Lodge 519
Pitreavie Guest House 519
DUNGANNON
Grange Lodge 599
DUNGARVAN
An Bohreen 641
The Castle
Country House 640
Gortnadiha House 641
Powersfield House 641
Sliabh gCua Farmhouse 641
DUNKELD
Waterbury Guest House 539
DUNLAVIN
Tynte House 650
DUNOON
The Anchorage Hotel 498
Lyall Cliff Hotel 498
DUNSTER
Buttercross 351
Conygar House 351
Dollons House 351
DUNURE
Dunduff Farm 547
DURHAM
Cathedral View
Guest House 192
The Gables 192
Hillrise Guest House 192
DYLIFE
Star Inn 588
DYMCHURCH
Waterside Guest House 248

E

EAGLESHAM
New Borland 517
EASINGWOLD
Stillington Mill 456
EAST CALDER
Ashcroft Farmhouse 551
Overshiel Farm 552
Whitecroft
Bed & Breakfast 551
EAST LINTON
Kippielaw Farmhouse 517
EAST MIDLANDS AIRPORT
Donington Park
Farmhouse Hotel 263
Kegworth House 263
EAST TYTHERLEY
Star Inn 221
EASTBOURNE
Arden Hotel 394
Bay Lodge Hotel 394
Beachy Rise Guest House 393
Bella Vista 393
Birling Gap Hotel 394-5
Brayscroft Hotel 394
Camelot Lodge 395
Chalk Farm Hotel &
Restaurant 394
Cromwell Private Hotel 394
Far End Hotel 395
The Halcyon Hotel 395
Mowbray Hotel 395
Pinnacle Point 393
St Omer Hotel 394
Sheldon Hotel 395
Southcroft Hotel 394
Westways Guest House 395
EASTCHURCH
The Shurland 248
EASTLING
Carpenters Arms 248
EASTON-IN-GORDANO
The Tynings B & B 40
ECCLESTON
Parr Hall Farm 259
EDALE
Edale House 122

EDENBRIDGE
Ye Old Crown 248-9
EDINBANE
Shorefield House 554
EDINBURGH
Abbotsford Guest House 506
Acorn Lodge
Guest House 502-3
Adam Drysdale House 510
Adam Hotel 503
Adria Hotel 507
Ailsa Craig Hotel 507
Airport Bed & Breakfast 507
Arden Guest House 503
Ashgrove House 503
Averon City Centre
Guest House 510
Ben Doran Guest House 503
Boisdale Hotel 507
Bonnington Guest House 501
Brae Lodge Guest House 510
Classic House 507
Corstorphine
Guest House 507
Dorstan Private Hotel 504
Dukes of Windsor Street 510
Dunstane House Hotel 501
Ecosse International 507
The Eglinton Hotel 506
Elder York Guest House 507
Ellesmere House 504
Elmview 500
Galloway Guest House 507
Gildun Guest House 510
Greenside Hotel 504
Grosvenor Gardens Hotel 504
Heriott Park Guest House 508
Hermitage Guest House 508
The International
Guest House 504
Ivy House 506
Kariba Guest House 510
Kew House 502
Kildonan Lodge Hotel 502
The Lodge Hotel 502
MacKenzie Guest House 508
Mayville Guest House 508
Newington Cottage 500
The Newington
Guest House 506
Parklands Guest House 508
Priory Lodge 505
Quaich Guest House 508
Ravensdown
Guest House 505
Rowan Guest House 508
The St Valery 510
The Salisbury
Guest House 510
Sandaig Guest House 506
Sherwood Guest House 508-9
Six Mary's Place
Guesthouse 506
Southside Guest House 506
The Stuarts 502
Terrace Hotel 509
Thistle Court Hotel 509
The Walton Hotel 510
EGGLESTON
Pine Ridge B & B 192
ELGIN
The Croft 535
The Lodge Guest House 535
The Pines Guest House 535
ELLASTONE
Cross Farm 370
ELMSWELL
Kiln Farm 378
ELSTEAD
The White House 384
ELY
The Anchor Inn 46
Castle Lodge Hotel 47
Hill House Farm 46
The Nyton Hotel 47
Rosendale Lodge 46
Springfields 46
Red Lion 47
EMYVALE
Fortsingleton 636
ENNIS
Cill Eoin House 601
Fountain Court 601
ENNISCORTHY
Ballinkeele House 646
Lemongrove House 646
ENNISKILLEN
Aghnacarra House 598
Arch Tullyhona
Farm Guest House 598
Dromard House 598
ENNISTYMON
Grovemount House 601
EPSOM
Epsom Downs Hotel 384
The White House 384
ESCRICK
Black Bull Inn 457
Church Cottage 456-7
ESKDALEMUIR
Hart Manor 514
ETTINGTON
The Houndsmill 413
EVERSHOT
The Acorn Inn 181
EVESHAM
Buttercup House 448-9
EWELL
Nonsuch Park Hotel 385
EXETER
The Devon Arms 142-3
Dunmore Hotel 143
The Edwardian 141
Fairwinds Village House
Hotel 142
The Gissons Arms 142
Holbrook Farm 142
Hotel Gledhills 143
Kerswell Grange
Country House 141
Mill Farm 142
Park View Hotel 143
Rydon Farm 142
St Andrews Hotel 142
The Sunnymede
Guest House 143
Telstar Hotel 143
EYAM
Miners Arms 122
EYE
Gislingham
Westview House 378
The White Horse Inn 378

F

FAHAN
St John's Country
House & Restaurant 609
FAKENHAM
Abbott Farm 292
Holly Tree 292
The White Horse Inn 292
FALKIRK
Ashbank Guest House 517
FALMOUTH
The Clearwater 58
Cotswold House Hotel 57
Dolvean Hotel 56-7
Gayhurst 57
Ivanhoe Guest House 57
Melvill House Hotel 57
Penwarren Guest House 58
Prospect House 57
Rosemary Private Hotel 57
Rosemullion Private Hotel 58
Springfield 58
Tregenna Guest House 58
Westcott Hotel 58
FALSTONE
The Blackcock Inn 305
Pheasant Inn 305
FAREHAM
Avenue House Hotel 222
Catisfield Cottage
Guest House 222
Springfield Hotel 222

FARNBOROUGH
The White Residence 222
FARNHAM
The Museum Inn 181
Sandiway 385
FARNINGHAM
Beesfield Farm 249
FARNSFIELD
Grange Cottage 308-9
FAVERSHAM
Preston Lea 249
FELINDRE
Coynant Farm 591
FELIXSTOWE
Dorincourt Guest House 378
FELSTED
Potash Farmhouse 195
FERMOY
Ballyvolane House 605
Glanworth Mill
Country Inn 605
FERNS
Clone House 646
FFESTINIOG
Morannedd 576
Ty Clwb 576
FILEY
Abbots Leigh
Guest House 457
Gables Guest House 457
Seafield Hotel 457
FILLONGLEY
Bourne Brook Lodge 413
FINDON
Village House Hotel 406
FIR TREE
Duke of York Inn 193
Greenhead Country
House Hotel 192-3
FISHGUARD
Erw-Lon Farm 581
Stanley House 581
FITZHEAD
Fitzhead Inn 351
FLINT
Oakenholt Farm Country
Guest House 571
FLIXTON
Orchard Lodge 457
FLYFORD FLAVELL
The Boot Inn 449
FOCHABERS
Castlehill Farm 536
FOLKESTONE
Chilton House Hotel 249
The Cross Channel 249
Harbourside Hotel 249
The Rob Roy 249
FOOLOW
The Bulls Head Inn 123
FORDINGBRIDGE
Ad Astra 222-3
Alderholt Mill 223
Cottage Crest 222
The Three Lions 222
FOREST
Maison Bel Air
Guest House 489
FORRES
Knockomie Lodge 536
FORT WILLIAM
Ashburn House 526
Benview Guest House 527
Berkeley House 527
Distillery House 526
Glenlochy Guest House 527
The Grange 526
Lochan Cottage
Guest House 527
Lochview Guest House 527
Mansefield House 526
Seangan Croft 526
FOWEY
Carnethic House 58
King of Prussia 58-9
Trevanion Guest House 59
FOWNHOPE
The Bowens
Country House 234
FOYERS
Foyers Bay House 527
FRAMLINGHAM
Bridge House 378
Church Farm 378-9
Fieldway 378
Woodlands Farm 378
FRAMPTON ON SEVERN
The Old School House 204
FRESSINGFIELD
Chippenhall Hall 379
FRINTON-ON-SEA
Uplands Guest House 195
FRITHAM
Fritham Farm 223
FROGGATT
The Chequers Inn 123
FROGHALL
Hermitage Working Farm 370
FROME
Brookover Farm 352
The Fox & Hounds Inn 352
Garden House 351
Highview 352
The Olde Bath Arms
Hotel & Restaurant 352
The Talbot 15th-Century
Coaching Inn 352

G

GAIRLOCH
The Old Inn 527
GALASHIELS
Ashlyn Guest House 544
Island House 544
GALWAY
Almara House 619
Ardawn House 619
Atlantic Heights 619
Corrib Haven
Guest House 619
Four Seasons 620
Four Winds Lodge 619
Killeen House 619
Marian Lodge
Guest House 620
Rhondda 620
Sunrise Lodge 620
The Swallow 620
Woodhaven Lodge 620
GATWICK AIRPORT
April Cottage 408
The Beeches 408
Corner House Hotel 406-7
Cumberland House 407
Gainsborough Lodge 408
Gatwick Belmont
Guest House 408
Gatwick White
House Hotel 408
The Lawn Guest House 407
Prinsted 408
Rosemead Guest House 407
Springwood Guest House 408
Trumbles 407
Vulcan Lodge
Guest House 407
Wayside Manor Farm 407
GAYHURST
Mill Farm 41
GIGGLESWICK
Black Horse Hotel 457
Woodlands 457
GLASBURY
Fforddfawr Farmhouse 588
GLASGOW
The Belgrave
Guest House 511
Craigielea House B&B 512
Georgian House Hotel 512
Hotel Enterprise 511
Kelvin Private Hotel 511
Kelvingrove Hotel 511
Lomond Hotel 511
McLays Guest House 512
Victorian House 511
GLASGOW AIRPORT
East Lochhead 542

Myfarrclan Guest House 542
GLASTONBURY
Barrow Farm 353
Cradlebridge Farm 352
Greenacres 352
Melrose 353
100 Boundary Way 352
Wearyall Hill House 352-3
Wood Lane House 353
GLENBEIGH
Ocean Wave 625
GLENBORRODALE
Feorag House 527
GLENCOE
Fern Villa 527
Lyn-Leven Guest House 528
Scorrybreac Guest House 528
GLENDALOUGH
Pinewood Lodge 650
GLENISLA
The Glenisla Hotel 496
GLENLIVET
Roadside Cottage 536
GLENSHEE, SPITTAL OF
Dalhenzean Lodge 539
GLOSSOP
Brentwood 123
The Gables Hotel 124
Hollincross House 124
Peakdale Lodge 124
Rock Farm 124
White House Farm 124
GOATHLAND
Fairhaven Country Hotel 458
GOLEEN
Carraig-Mor House 606
The Heron's Cove 606
GOREBRIDGE
Ivory House 535
GOREY
Hillside House 646
Woodlands
Country House 646
GORRAN
Tregerrick Farm B & B 59
GRAMPOUND
Perran House 59
GRANARD
Toberphelim House 633
GRANGE
Rowanville Lodge 636
GRANGE-OVER-SANDS
Elton Hotel 94
Mayfields 94
GRANTHAM
The Roost 266
GRANTOWN-ON-SPEY
Ardconnel House 528
Garden Park 528
The Pines 528
Ravenscourt House Hotel 528
Rossmor Guest House 528-9
GRASMERE
Howbeck Vegetarian
Guest House 94
Raise View Guest House 95
Riversdale 94
Silverlea Guest House 94-5
Woodland Crag
Guest House 95
GRASSINGTON
Ashfield House Hotel 458
Grassington Lodge 458
GREAT AYTON
Royal Oak Hotel 458
GREAT BARUGH
Barugh House 458
GREAT DUNMOW
Homelye Farm 195
GREAT ELLINGHAM
Aldercarr Hall 292
GREAT YARMOUTH
Andover Hotel 293
Avalon Private Hotel 293
Barnard House 292
Church Farm 293
Harbour Hotel 293
Jennis Lodge 293
The Ryecroft 293
The Ship Hotel 292-3
Winchester Private Hotel 293
GREENHEAD
Holmhead Guest House 305
GRETNA
Surrone House 514
GRETNA GREEN
The Mill 514
GREVE DE LECQ BAY
Hotel Des Pierres 489
GRIMSBY
Peaks Top Farm 266
GRIZEDALE
Grizedale Lodge The
Hotel in the Forest 95
GROUVILLE
Lavender Villa Hotel 490
GUILDFORD
Blanes Court Hotel 386
GUISELEY
Moor Valley Park Motel 486
GUITING POWER
Guiting Guest House 204
The Hollow Bottom 204
GULLANE
Faussetthill House 517

H

HADDINGTON
Eaglescairnie Mains 517
HADLEIGH
Edgehall Hotel 379
HADLOW
Leavers Oast 250
HADNALL
Hall Farm House 323
HALIFAX
Pinfold Guest House 486
Shibden Mill Inn 486
HALTWHISTLE
Vallum Lodge 306
HAMPTON IN ARDEN
The Cottage 424
The Hollies Guest House 424
HANNINGTON
The Jolly Tar 436
HARLECH
Castle Cottage Restaurant
with Rooms 576
Gwrach Ynys Country
Guest House 576
Morlyn 576
Noddfa Guest House 576
HARLESTON
Heath Farmhouse 294
HARLYN BAY
Polmark Hotel 59
HARPENDEN
The Laurels Guest House 239
HARROGATE
Acacia Lodge 459
The Albany Hotel 461
Alexa House &
Stable Cottages 459
April House 459
Ashley House Hotel 459
Ashwood House
Guest House 460
Aston Hotel 461
Azalea Court Hotel 462
Britannia Lodge 460
The Camberley Hotel 460
The Cavendish Hotel 460
The Dales 460
Delaine Hotel 460
Fountains Hotel 460
Gillmore Hotel 461
Glenayr 462
Grafton Hotel 461
Kimberley Hotel 459
Pigeon Olde Farm 462
Princes Hotel 462
Roxanne Guest House 462
Ruskin Hotel 459
Shelbourne Guest House 462
Valley Hotel 461
Wharfedale House 462
Wynnstay House 461

HARTEST
The Hatch 379
HARTFIELD
Bolebroke Watermill 395
HARTINGTON
Bank House Guest House 124
HARTLAND
Fosfelle Guest House 144
HARWICH
New Farm House 195
HASLEMERE
The Wheatsheaf Inn 386
HASTINGS & ST LEONARDS
Beechwood 397
Eagle House 396
Filsham Farmhouse 396
Lionsdown House 396
Parkside House 396
Seaspray Guest House 397
Summerfields House 397
Tower House Hotel 396
White Cottage 396-7
HATHERSAGE
Highlow Hall 124
Hillfoot Farm 125
The Millstone Inn 125
Moorgate 125
The Mount 125
The Plough Inn 124-5
Polly's B + B 125
The Scotsman's Pack Inn 125
Sladen Cottage 125
HAVERFORDWEST
College Guest House 582
Lower Haythog Farm 582
HAWES
Board Hotel 463
Steppe Haugh 462
HAWKHURST
Southgate-Little Fowlers 250
The Wren's Nest 250
HAWKSHEAD
Ees Wyke Country House 95
Kings Arms Hotel 96
Sawrey Ground 95
The Sun Inn 96
West Vale Country House 96
HAWNBY
Laskill Grange 463
HAWORTH
Aitches Guest House 486
Old Registry 486
HAYLE
Beckside Cottage 59
Calize Country House 59
HAY-ON-WYE
Tinto House 588
York House Guest House 588
HAYTOR
Bel Alp House 144
HAYWARDS HEATH
Sliders Farm 408
HEADCORN
Curtis Farm 250
HEATHFIELD
Iwood Bed & Breakfast 397
Old Corner Cottage 397
HEATHROW AIRPORT
Civic Guest House 213
The Cottage 211
Harmondsworth Hall 212
Lampton Guest House 212
Longford Guest House 212
Shalimar Hotel 212
Shepiston Lodge 212
Skylark Bed & Breakfast
Guest House 212-3
HEBDEN BRIDGE
Redacre Mill 486-7
HELENSBURGH
Lethamhill 498
HELMSLEY
The Carlton Lodge 463
Plumpton Court 463
Shallowdale House 463
HELSTON
Colvennor Farmhouse 59
HELTON
Beckfoot Country House 96
HEMEL HEMPSTEAD
Alexandra Guest House 239
HENLEY-IN-ARDEN
Ashleigh House 413
HENLEY-ON-THAMES
The Knoll 313
Lenwade 313
Slater's Farm 313
Thamesmead
House Hotel 313
HEREFORD
Felton House 234
Grafton Villa Farm 234
Hedley Lodge 234
Sink Green Farm 234
HERNE BAY
Foxden 250
HERSTMONCEUX
Wartling Place 397
HESSENFORD
Copley Arms 60
HEXHAM
Dene House 306
Loughbrow House 307
Montcoffer Bed
& Breakfast 306
Peth Head Cottage 306
The Rose & Crown Inn 307
Rye Hill Farm 306-7
The Sun Inn 307
HIGH HALDEN
Draylands 250
HIGH WYCOMBE
Clifton Lodge Hotel 41
HILTON
The Prince of Wales 47
HINCKLEY
Ambion Court Hotel 263
Badgers Mount 263
HINDRINGHAM
Field House 294
HINTON ST GEORGE
The Lord Poulett Arms 353
HITCHIN
The Greyhound 240
The Lord Lister Hotel 240
Redcoats
Farmhouse Hotel 240
HOARWITHY
Aspen House 234
HODNET
The Grange 324
HOLBEACH
Elloe Lodge 266
Pipwell Manor 267
HOLBECK
Browns 309
HOLMFIRTH
Holme Castle
Country Hotel 487
HOLSWORTHY
Clawford Vineyard 144
The Hollies Farm
Guest House 144
Leworthy Farm House 144
HOLT (Norfolk)
The Old Telephone Exchange
Bed & Breakfast 294
HOLT (Wilts)
The Coppers
Bed & Breakfast 436
HOLYHEAD
Wavecrest 556
Yr Hendre 556
HOLYWELL
Greenhill Farm 571
HOLYWOOD
Beech Hill
Country House 596
Braeside Country House 596
HONITON
Atwell's at
Wellington Farm 145
Courtmoor Farm 145
The Crest 145
The Old Forge 145
Threshays 145
West Colwell Farm 144

HOOK
Cedar Court Country Guest House 223
Cherry Lodge Guest House 223
Oaklea Guest House 223
HOPE
Round Meadow Barn 126
Stoney Ridge 126
Underleigh House 126
HOPEMAN
Ardent House 536
HORNCASTLE
Greenfield Farm 267
HORNCHURCH
Dorothea Bed & Breakfast 213
HORN'S CROSS
Lower Waytown 145
HORSELEAP
Woodlands Farmhouse 644
HORSHAM
Random Hall 408-9
The Willows 409
HORSHAM ST FAITH
Elm Farm Country House 294
HORSTED KEYNES
The Croft 409
HOUGH-ON-THE-HILL
The Brownlow Arms Country House Hotel 267
HOVINGHAM
Sedgwick Country Guest House 463
HOW CAPLE
The Falcon Guest House 234
HOWTH
Inisradharc 616
HUBY
The New Inn Motel 464
HUDDERSFIELD
The Weavers Shed Restaurant with Rooms 487
HUGGATE
The Wolds Inn 452
HULL
Earlsmere Hotel 452-3
HUNGERFORD
Beacon House 36
Crown & Garter 35
Marshgate Cottage Hotel 36
The Queen's Arms Hotel 36
The Swan Inn 35
HUNSTANTON
Claremont Guest House 294
The Gables 294
Green Shutters Guest House 295
Narara House 295
The Priory Bed & Breakfast 295
Richmond House Hotel 295
Rosamaly Guest House 295
Sutton House Hotel 295
The White Cottage 295
HUNTINGDON
Holmefields Barn 47
HUNTON
The Countryman's Inn 464
HUTTON-LE-HOLE
Moorlands of Hutton-le-Hole 464
HYDE
Needhams Farm 217

I

IDBURY
Bould Farm 314
ILFORD
Cranbrook Hotel 214
Park Hotel 214
Woodville Guest House 214
ILFRACOMBE
Collingdale Hotel 146
Dedes Hotel 146
Devonshire Moonta Hotel 147
Langleigh Park House 146
Norbury House Hotel 147
Southcliffe Hotel 145
Strathmore Hotel 146
The Towers Hotel 147
Varley House 146
Waterloo House Hotel 146
ILKESTON
The Redhouse 126
ILKLEY
Grove Hotel 487
ILMINSTER
The Old Rectory 353
INGLETON
Ferncliffe Country Guest House 464
Inglenook Guest House 464
Seed Hill Guest House 465
INNERLEITHEN
Caddon View 544
Traquair Arms Hotel 544
INVERARAY
Claonairigh House 498
INVERGARRY
Craigard Guest House 529
Forest Lodge 529
INVERKEITHING
Forth Craig Private Hotel 520
The Roods 520
INVERNESS
Acorn House 530
Ardmuir House 531
Ballifeary House Hotel 529
Brae Ness Hotel 531
Cedar Villa 531
Craigside Lodge 530-1
Culduthel Lodge 530
Hawthorn Lodge 531
Melrose Villa 532
Moyness House 529
Park Guest House 531
St Ann's House 531
Sunnyholm 531
Taransay 530
Trafford Bank 530
Westbourne Guest House 530
IREBY
Daleside Farm 96
IRONBRIDGE
Broseley Guest House 324
The Grove Inn & Fat Frog Restaurant 324
The Library House 324
Woodlands Farm Guest House 324
IWERNE COURTNEY OR SHROTON
The Cricketers 181

J

JACOBSTOWE
Higher Cadham Farm 147
JEDBURGH
Bridge House 544-5
Ferniehirst Mill Lodge 545
Glenfriars House 544
Kenmore Bank Hotel 545
The Spinney 544
JOHN O'GROATS
Bencorragh House 532
JOHNSTONE
Nether Johnstone House 542-3

K

KANTURK
Assolas Country House 606
KEDINGTON
The White House 380
KEIGHLEY
Bankfield Guesthouse 487
KEITH
The Haughs Farm 536
KEMPSEY
Walter de Cantelupe Inn 449
KENDAL
Barrowfield Farm 96
Blaven Homestay 96
Burrow Hall Country Guest House 97
Garnett House Farm 97
Gilpin Bridge Inn 97

The Glen 98
Higher House Farm 97
Low Jock Scar 97
Martindales Licensed Guest House 97
Millers Beck Country Guest House 98
Sonata Guest House 98
KENILWORTH
Hollyhurst Guest House 413
Victoria Lodge Hotel 413
KENMARE
Ashberry Lodge 625
Davitts 625
Harbour View 626
Sallyport House 625
Sea Shore Farm 625
KESWICK
Abacourt House 101
Allerdale House 98
Amble House 99
Avondale 99
Badgers Wood 99
Brierholme 101
Charnwood Guest House 99
Claremont House 99
Clarence House 101
Craglands 99
Cragside 101
Dalegarth House Country Hotel 99
Derwent Cottage 98
Dorchester House 102
Goodwin House 100
The Grange Country House 98
Greystones Hotel 100
Hall Garth 100
Hazeldene Hotel 100
Heatherlea 102
Howe Keld Lakeland Hotel 100
The Mill Inn 102
Paddock Guest House 101
Parkfield Guest House 100
Richmond House 102
Rickerby Grange Country House Hotel 100-1
Skiddaw Grove Country House 101
Stonegarth 101
Sunnyside Guest House 101
Swinside Inn 102
Tarn Hows 101
Watendlath Guest House 102
KETTERING
Pennels Guest House 302
Wold Farm 302
KETTLEWELL
Littlebeck 465
KEXBY
Ivy House Farm 465
KEYNSHAM
Grasmere Court Hotel 354
KIDDERMINSTER
Victoria Hotel 449
KIDLINGTON
Bowood House Hotel 314
KILBURN
Forresters Arms Hotel 465
KILCULLEN
Chapel View Country Home 630
KILGARVAN
Birchwood 626
KILKENNY
Alcantra 631
Auburn Lodge 631
Butler House 631
Shillogher House 631
KILLARNEY
Applecroft House 627
Ashville 628
Coffey's Loch Lein Guesthouse 628
Crystal Springs 627
Earls Court House 626
Foleys Town House 626
Glena House 627
Gorman's 628
Green Acres 628
Hussey's Bar & Townhouse 628
Kathleen's Country House 626-7
Killarney Villa 627
McCarthy's Town House 628
Nashville 628
O'Donovans Farm & Muckross Riding Stables 628
Old Weir Lodge 627
Shraheen House 627
Sliabh Luachra House 628
KILLEAGH
Tattans 606
KILLIN
Fairview House 550
KILLORGLIN
Carrig House Country House & Restaurant 629
Dromin Farmhouse 629
The Grove Lodge 629
O'Regan's Country Home & Gardens 629
KILMALLOCK
Flemingstown House 633
KILMARNOCK
Aulton Farm 516
Burnside Hotel 516
Laigh Langmuir Farmhouse 516
KILMARTIN
Dunchraigaig House 498
KILMORE QUAY
Quay House Guest House & Restaurant 647
KILNSEY
Kilnsey Old Hall 465
KILRUSH
Bruach-na-Coille 601
Hillcrest View 601
KILTEGAN
Barraderry House 650
KILVE
Hood Arms Hotel 354
KIMBOLTON
Apothecary Guest House 47
KING'S LYNN
Fairlight Lodge 296
Guanock Hotel 296
Maranatha Guest House 296
Wallington Hall 295
KINGSBRIDGE
Ashleigh House 147
Highwell House 147
Staunton Lodge 147
KINGSLEY
Charnwood 51
KINGSTON BLOUNT
Lakeside Town Farm 314
KINGUSSIE
Arden House 532
Avondale House 532
Columba House Hotel & Restaurant 532
Osprey Hotel 532
KINLOCHBERVIE
Old School Hotel 532
KINROSS
Burnbank 540
The Muirs Inn Kinross 539
KINSALE
Chart House Luxury Accommodation 606
Desmond House 607
Kilcaw House 608
Long Quay House 607
The Old Bank House 606
The Old Presbytery 607
Rivermount House 607
Toddies 607
Waterlands 607
KIRKBY LONSDALE
The Copper Kettle 102
KIRKBY STEPHEN
Augill Castle 102

KIRKBYMOORSIDE
Appletree Court 465
Brickfields Farm 465
KIRKLINTON
Clift House Farm 102
KIRKMICHAEL
Cruachan Country Cottage 540
KIRKMUIRHILL
Dykecroft Farm 548
KIRTLING
Hill Farm 48
KNARESBOROUGH
Newton House Hotel 466
The Villa 466
KNOCKIN
Top Farm House 324
KNUTSFORD
The Dog Inn 52
The Hinton Guest House 52
Laburnum Cottage Guest House 52
The Old Vicarage 52
KYLE OF LOCHALSH
The Old Schoolhouse 533
KYLEMORE
Kylemore House 620
KYLESKU
Newton Lodge Hotel 533

L

LACOCK
At the Sign of the Angel 436
LAHINCH
Moy House 602
LAMPETER
Dremddu Fawr Farm 561
Haulfan 561
LANCASTER
Lancaster Town House 260
New Capernwray Farm 260
LANDFORD
Springfields 436
LANGHOLM
The Reivers Rest 514
LANGPORT
The Old Pound Inn 354
LARGS
Lea-Mar 537
South Whittlieburn Farm 537
Whin Park 537
LARNE
Derrin Guesthouse 595
Manor Guest House 595
LATCHINGDON
Neptune Cafe Motel 196
LAUNCESTON
Hurdon Farm 60
Stenhill Farm 60
Tyne Wells House 60
Withnoe Farm 60
LAVENHAM
Anchor House 380
Lavenham Priory 380
Wood Hall 380
LAVERTON
Leasow House 204
LEAMINGTON SPA (ROYAL)
Bubbenhall House 413
Hill Farm 413
Lansdowne Hotel 414
Milverton House Hotel 414
LECHLADE
Cambrai Lodge 205
The Five Bells Broadwell 205
LEDBURY
Bodenham Farm 235
LEEDS
Ash Mount Hotel 487
Highbank Hotel 488
Merevale Hotel 488
Trafford House & Budapest Hotel 488
LEEK
Abbey Inn 370
LEENANE
Killary Lodge 620-1
LEICESTER
Stoneycroft Hotel 264
LEISTON
Field End Guest House 380
LELANT
The Badger Inn 60
LEOMINSTER
Hills Farm 235
Lawton Bury Farm Bed & Breakfast 235
Woonton Court Farm 235
LERWICK
Glen Orchy House 554
LETTERKENNY
Ballyraine Guest House 610
Pennsylvania House 610
LEVEN (Fife)
Sandilands 520
LEVEN (Yorks, East Riding)
The New Inn 453
LEWDOWN
Stowford House 148
LEWES
Holly Cottage 398
Nightingales 397
No. 6 398
LEYBURN
The Old Horn Inn 466
LICHFIELD
Coppers End 370
Little Pipe Farm 370
Main View 370
Moat Cottage 370
Park View 370
Stone House Farm 370
LIGHTHORNE
Redlands Farm 414
LIGHTWATER
Carlton Guest House 386
LIMERICK
Clifton House 633
White House B & B 633
LINCOLN
Abbottsford House 268
Ashlin House Hotel 269
Carholme Guest House 268
Carline Guesthouse 268
D'Isney Place Hotel 268
Eagles Guest House 268
Edward King House 270
Elma Guest House 269
The Gables 269
The Hollies Hotel 269
Jaymar 270
Minster Lodge Hotel 267
New Farm 269
Newport Guest House 269
Orchard House 268
St Clements Lodge 267
Savill Guest House 269
Tennyson Hotel 268-9
30 Bailgate 269
Westlyn Guest House 269
LINDFIELD
The Pilstyes 409
LINLITHGOW
Belsyde House 552
Bomains Farm Guest House 552
Thornton 552
LISDOONVARNA
Kincora House Country Inn & Restaurant 602
LISKEARD
Elnor Guest House 61
Trecarne House 61
Tregondale Farm 61
LITTLE DEWCHURCH
Cwm Craig Farm 235
LIVERPOOL
Aachen Hotel 287
The Blenheim Lodge 287
LIVINGSTON
Whitecroft Bed & Breakfast 553
LIZARD
Penmenner House Hotel 62
LLANBEDR
Bryn Artro Country House 577
Pensarn Hall Country Guest House 576

Victoria Inn 576-7
LLANBERIS
Plas Coch Guest House 577
LLANDDAROG
Coedhirion Farm 559
LLANDOGO
The Sloop Inn 579
LLANDRINDOD WELLS
Brynllys Guest House 589
The Drovers Arms 589
Guidfa House 588-9
Holly Farm 589
Kincoed Hotel 589
LLANDUDNO
Abbey Lodge 566
Beach Cove 568
Bodnant Guest House 568
Brigstock Hotel 566
Britannia Hotel 568
Bryn Arthur 569
Bryn Derwen Hotel 566
Carmel Private Hotel 566
The Concord 567
Cornerways Hotel 567
Cranberry House Guest House 567
Lynton House Hotel 567
Minion Private Hotel 568
Quinton Hotel 568
Sefton Court Hotel 567
Sunnyside Private Hotel 568
Tudno Lodge Guest House 568
The Victoria Town House 568
Vine House 568
Wedgwood Hotel 569
White Lodge Hotel 567
LLANDYSUL
Plas Cerdin 562
LLANELLI
Awel Y Mor 560
Ffynnon Rhosfa 560
LLANERCHYMEDD
Llwydiarth Fawr 556
Tre-Wyn 556
LLANFACHRAETH
Holland Hotel 556
LLANFACHRETH
Cors-y-Garnedd 577
Ty Isaf Farmhouse 577
LLANFAIR WATERDINE
The Waterdine 325
LLANGEFNI
Doldir Bed & Breakfast 556
LLANGOLLEN
Oakmere 569
Tyn Celyn Farmhouse 570
Whitegate 570
LLANGURIG
Old Vicarage 589
LLANIDLOES
Mount Inn 589
LLANSILIN
The Old Vicarage 589
LLANYMYNECH
The Manse 590
LLOWES
Ty-Bach 590
LLYSWEN
Oakfield 590
LOCHEARNHEAD
Mansewood Country House 550
LOCHWINNOCH
Belltrees Beild 543
East Lochhead 543
LOCKERBIE
Rosehill Guest House 514
LONDON E4
Ridgeway Hotel 272
LONDON E18
Grove Hill Hotel 272
LONDON N1
Kandara Guest House 272
LONDON N4
Majestic Hotel 272
Mount View 272
Ossian House 273
LONDON N8
White Lodge Hotel 273
LONDON NW1
Euston Square Hotel 274
Four Seasons Hotel 274
LONDON NW3
La Gaffe 274
Langorf Hotel 274
Quality Hampstead 274
Swiss Cottage Hotel 274
LONDON NW6
Dawson House Hotel 275
LONDON NW11
Anchor Hotel 275
Central Hotel 275
LONDON SE9
Yardley Court Private Hotel 275
LONDON SE10
The Pilot Inn 275
LONDON SE20
Melrose House 276
LONDON SW1
Blades Hotel 276
Carlton Hotel 278
Central House Hotel 277
Colliers Hotel 278
Dover Hotel 278
Melbourne House Hotel 276
Sidney Hotel 276-7
Stanley House Hotel 278
The Victoria Inn 277
The Willett 276
Windermere Hotel 276
Winchester Hotel 277
LONDON SW3
Claverley Hotel 278
LONDON SW5
Henley House Hotel 278-9
The Maranton House Hotel 278
My Place Hotel 278
Rushmore Hotel 279
Swiss House Hotel 279
LONDON SW7
Five Sumner Place Hotel 279
The Gainsborough 280
The Gallery 279
LONDON SW15
The Lodge Hotel 280
LONDON SW19
Trochee Hotel 280
Wimbledon Hotel 280
Worcester House Hotel 280
LONDON W1
Bentinck House Hotel 283
Bryanston Court Guest House 282
Georgian House Hotel 282
Hart House Hotel 282
Lincoln House Hotel 282-3
Marble Arch Inn 283
Mermaid Suite Hotel 280
The Regency Hotel 282
St George Hotel 280-1
22 281
Wigmore Court Hotel 282
LONDON W2
Averard Hotel 284
Barry House Hotel 284-5
The Blakemore Hotel 283
Byron Hotel 284
Camelot House Hotel 284
Comfort Inn 284
Kingsway Hotel 285
Kingsway Park Hotel 284
Mitre House Hotel 284
Mornington Hotel 283
Norfolk Plaza Hotel 283
Norfolk Towers Hotel 283
Park Lodge Hotel 284
LONDON W4
Chiswick Lodge 285
LONDON W6
Hotel Orlando 286
LONDON W8
Atlas-Apollo Hotel 286
LONDON W14
Aston Court Hotel 286
Avonmore Hotel 286

LONDON WC1
Euro Hotel 286
Guildford House Hotel 287
Mentone Hotel 286-7
LONDONDERRY
Arkle House 599
Clarence House 599
LONG COMPTON
Ashby House 414
Tallett Barn B & B 414
LONGFORD
Russets 126-7
LONGLEAT
Sturford Mead Farm 436-7
LONGNOR
Cobblers Cottage 325
LONGRIDGE
Jenkinsons Farmhouse 260
LOOE
The Beach House 62
Bucklawren Farm 62
Coombe Farm Hotel 62
Gulls Hotel 63
Panorama Hotel 62
St Aubyn's Guest House 62
Trehaven Manor 63
Woodlands 63
LORTON
New House Farm 102
The Old Vicarage 103
Winder Hall
Country House 103
LOSSIEMOUTH
Carmania 536
Lossiemouth House 536
LOSTWITHIEL
Ship Inn 63
LOUGHBOROUGH
Croft Guest House 264
De Montfort Hotel 264
Garendon Park Hotel 264
LOUTH
Masons Arms 270
LOWESTOFT
Abbe House Hotel 381
The Albany Hotel 381
Coventry House 381
Edingworth Guest House 381
Fairways Guest House 382
Hotel Katherine 381
Kingsleigh Guest House 381
Longshore Guest House 381
Seavilla Hotel 382
Somerton House
Private Hotel 382
Wavecrest Guest House 382
LOWESWATER
Kirkstile Inn 103
LOYNTON
The Lodge 371
LUDLOW
The Charlton Arms 326
The Church Inn 326
Haynall Villa 326
Line Farm 325
The Marcle 326
Moor Hall 326
Number Twenty Eight 325
Ravenscourt Manor 326
Red Roofs 326
The Roebuck Inn 326
LUDWELL
The Grove Arms 437
LUSK
Brookfield Lodge 616
LUSTLEIGH
Woodley House 148
LUTON
Arlington Hotel 34
Leaside Hotel 34
LUTTERWORTH
The Old Rectory B & B 264
LYDFORD
Moor View House 148
LYME REGIS
Albany Guest House 181
Coverdale Guest House 181
Kent House Hotel 181
Lucerne 181
Old Lyme Guest House 181
Old Monmouth Hotel 181
The Orchard
Country Hotel 181
St Michael's 182
The White House 181
LYMINGTON
Auplands 224
Efford Cottage 223
Harts Lodge 224
Jevington 224
The Kings Arms 224
The Nurse's Cottage 223
The Olde Barn 224
Passford Farm 224
The Victoriana
Bed & Breakfast 224
LYNDHURST
Bartley Farmhouse 224
Clarendon Villa 225
Heather House Hotel 225
Ormonde House 225
Rufus House Hotel 225
Stable End 225
The Penny
Farthing Hotel 225
Whitemoor House Hotel 225
LYNMOUTH
Bonnicott House 148
Countisbury
Lodge Hotel 148-9
Glenville House 149
The Heatherville 149
Orchard House Hotel 149
Rock House 149
LYNTON
Alford House Hotel 150
The Denes 151
Highcliffe House 150
Longmead House 150
Lynhurst Hotel 150
Pine Lodge 150-1
St Vincent House 151
Victoria Lodge 150
Waterloo House Hotel 151
LYTHAM ST ANNES
Endsleigh Private Hotel 260
Monarch Hotel 260
Strathmore Hotel 260

M

MACHYNLLETH
Maenllwyd 590
Yr Hen Felin
(The Old Mill) 590
MAIDENHEAD
Beehive Manor 36
Moor Farm 36
MAIDSTONE
Aylesbury Hotel 252
Conway House 251
Grove House 251
The Howard Hotel 252
King Street Hotel 251
Langley Oast 251
Ringlestone Inn &
Farmhouse Hotel 251
Rock House Hotel 252
Scuffits 251
MALHAM
River House Hotel 466
MALLOW
Greenfield House 608
Oaklands House 608
MALMESBURY
Horse & Groom Inn 437
Lovett Farm 437
Manby's Farm 437
MALPAS
Millmoor Farm 52
Tilston Lodge 52
MALTON
The Brow 466
The Wentworth Arms 466
MALVERN
Bredon House Hotel 449
Chestnut Hill 450
The Dell House 449

Hills Reach 449
Hillside 450
Link Lodge 449
Pembridge Hotel 450
St Just 449
Sidney House Hotel 450
Woodpeckers 450
MANCHESTER
Crescent Gate Hotel 217
Thistlewood Hotel 217
Victoria Park Hotel 217
MANCHESTER AIRPORT
Rylands Farm
Guest House 218
MANNINGTREE
Dairy House Farm 196
MANSFIELD
Appleby Guest House 309
Parkhurst Guest House 309
MARAZION
Glenleigh Hotel 63
MARDEN
Merzie Meadows 252
MARGARET RODING
Greys 196
MARGATE
Elonville Hotel 252
The Greswolde Hotel 252
Westbrook Bay House 252
MARKET DRAYTON
The Four Alls Inn 326
Mickley House 326
MARKET HARBOROUGH
Hunters Lodge 264
MARKET RASEN
Blaven 270
Chuck Hatch 270
MARKET WEIGHTON
Robeanne House 453
MARKINCH
Town House Hotel 520
MARLBOROUGH
Merlin Hotel 437
The Vines 437
MARLOW
The Country House 41
Holly Tree House 41
MARPLE
Matteo's Bar &
Country Hotel 218
MARTINSTOWN
Caireal Manor
Guest House 595
MARTLEY
Admiral Rodney Inn 450
MARTOCK
Higher Farm 354
White Hart Hotel 354
Wychwood 354
MARTON
Black Swan
Guest House 270-1
MARYPORT
The Retreat Hotel 103
MASHAM
Bank Villa Guest House 466
MATLOCK
Bradvilla 128
Farley Farm 128
Glendon 127
Hearthstone Farm 127
Hodgkinsons Hotel 127
Kensington Villa 128
The Laurels 129
Littlemoor Wood Farm 127
Manor House 127
The Old Sunday School 127
Red House
Carriage Museum 128
The Red Lion 128
Victoria House 128-9
Wayside Farm 128
Woodside 128
MATTERDALE END
Bank House Farm 103
MAWNAN SMITH
Trevean Bed
and Breakfast 63
MAXEY
Abbey House 48
MELBOURNE
The Coach House 129
The Melbourne Arms 129
MELROSE
Dunfermline House 545
Fauhope House 545
Kilkerran House 545
MELTON MOWBRAY
Amberley Gardens 264
Bryn Barn 264
MELVICH
The Sheiling
Guest House 533
MENAI BRIDGE
Wern Farm 556-7
MENDHAM
Weston House Farm 382
MERE
Chetcombe House 438
The Talbot Hotel 438
MERIDEN
Meriden Hotel 424
MERTHYR TYDFIL
Llwyn Onn Guest House 578
Penrhadw Farm 578
Tredegar Arms Hotel 578
MEVAGISSEY
Headlands Hotel 64
Kerryanna Country House 64
The Ship Inn 64
Treleaven Farm House 64
MIDDLE WINTERSLOW
The Beadles 438
MIDDLESBROUGH
The Grey House Hotel 466
MIDDLETON-IN-TEESDALE
Brunswick House 193
MIDDLEWICH
Forge Mill Farm 52
MIDHURST
Amberfold
Bed & Breakfast 409
Whincote 409
MIDLETON
Old Parochial House 608
MILFORD ON SEA
Alma Mater 226
Cherry Trees 226
Ha' Penny House 226
MILLER'S DALE
Dale Cottage 129
MILLOM
The Duddon Pilot Hotel 104
Pavilion Hotel 104
MILTON
Milton Manor 582
MILTON KEYNES
Apple Tree House 41
MINCHINHAMPTON
Hyde Wood House 205
MINEHEAD
Gascony Hotel 354-5
Glendower Hotel 354
The Old Ship Aground 355
The Red House 355
MINSTERLEY
Woodhouse Farm 327
MOATE
Temple Country
House & Spa 644
MOFFAT
Barnhill Springs Country
Guest House 514-5
Hartfell House 514
Limetree House 514
Queensberry House 514
MOLD
Heulwen 571
MONIAIVE
Auchencheyne 515
MONMOUTH
Church Farm
Guest House 579
MONTGOMERY
Little Brompton Farm 590
MONTROSE
Oaklands Guest House 496
MORECAMBE
Hotel Prospect 260

Wimslow Private Hotel 261
MORETONHAMPSTEAD
Blackaller Hotel & Restaurant 151
Cookshayes Country Guest House 152
Gate House 152
Great Sloncombe Farm 152
Great Wooston Farm 152
Midfields 152
Moorcote Country Guest House 152
MORETON-IN-MARSH
Rigside 205
MORETON-ON-LUGG
Upper House Farm 235
MOULSFORD
White House 314
MOUSEHOLE
Ship Inn 64
MUCH WENLOCK
Gaskell Arms 327
MUKER
Oxnop Hall 467
MULLINGAR
Crookedwood House 644
Hilltop Country House 645
MULLION
Alma House 64
MUNDESLEY
Manor Hotel 296
MUNGRISDALE
The Mill Inn 104
MUNSLOW
Crown Country Inn 327

N

NAILSWORTH
Aaron Farm 205
Highlands 205
NANNERCH
The Old Mill 571
NANTGAREDIG
Dolau Guest House 560
NANTWICH
The Limes 53
Oakland House 53
NARBERTH
Highland Grange 582
NARBOROUGH
Fossebrook 264
NAVAN
Killyon 636
NAYLAND
Gladwins Farm 382
Hill House 382
The White Hart Inn 382
NEAR SAWREY
Beechmount Country House 105
Buckle Yeat Guest House 104-5
Ees Wyke Country House 104
High Green Gate 105
Sawrey House Country Hotel & Restaurant 104
NEATH
Cwmbach Cottages Guest House 580
Green Lanterns Guest House 580
NEATISHEAD
Regency Guest House 296
NEEDHAM MARKET
Pipps Ford Farm 383
NENAGH
Ashley Park House 638
Williamsferry House 638
NETHER STOWEY
Castle of Comfort 355
NETTLECOMBE
The Marquis of Lorne 182
NETTLETON
Fosse Farmhouse Country Hotel 438
NEW GALLOWAY
Kalmar 515
NEW MILTON
Cottage Bed & Breakfast 226
NEW QUAY
Brynarfor Hotel 562
NEW ROSS
Oakwood House 647
NEWBRIDGE
Gables Guest House & Leisure Centre 630-1
NEWBURY
Rookwood Farm House 36-7
NEWBY BRIDGE
The Coach House 105
Hill Crest 105
The Knoll Country House 105
Lakes End Guest House 105
Old Barn Farm 105
NEWCASTLE UPON TYNE
Chirton House Hotel 411
Imperial Guest House 411
NEWENT
George Hotel 206
NEWHAVEN
The Smithy 129
NEWMARKET
Birdcage Walk 383
NEWNHAM
Swan House Country Guest House 206
NEWPORT (Newport)
Chapel Guest House 581
Crescent Guest House 581
The Inn at the Elm Tree 580
Kepe Lodge Guest House 581
The Rising Sun Hotel 581
NEWPORT (Shropshire)
Adams House Hotel & Restaurant 327
Norwood House Hotel 327
NEWPORT (Isle Of Wight)
Elizabeth House 426
Redway Cottage 425
NEWPORT PAGNELL
The Limes 42
NEWQUAY
Colan Barton 65
Degembris Farmhouse 65
Hotel Trevalsa 66
Kallacliff Hotel 65
Kellsboro Hotel 65
Melancoose Mill 65
Pendeen Hotel 66
Priory Lodge Hotel 66
Rolling Waves 66
Tir Chonaill Lodge Hotel 66-7
Wenden Guest House 67
Windward Hotel & Restaurant 66
NEWTON ABBOT
Bulleigh Park Farm 152-3
Chipley Farm 153
Sampsons Hotel & Restaurant 153
Walmer Towers 153
NEWTOWN
Yesterdays 590
NEWTOWNARDS
Ballynester House 597
Edenvale House 597
NITON
Pine Ridge Country House 426
NOMANSLAND
Clovenway House 438
NORTH BERWICK
Glentruim 517
NORTH CURRY
Banana Cottage 355
NORTH PETHERTON
Lower Clavelshay Farm 355
NORTH WALSHAM
Green Ridges 296
White House Farm 296
NORTHALLERTON
Porch House 467
Windsor Guest House 467
NORTHAMPTON
Green Park Hotel 302
Poplars Hotel 302
NORTHLEACH
Northfield Bed & Breakfast 206

NORTHOP HALL
Brookside House 571
NORTHWOOD
Frithwood House 214
NORTON ST PHILIP
Bath Lodge 355
Monmouth Lodge 355
The Plaine 355
NORWICH
Arbor Linden Lodge 298
The Arrandale Lodge 298
Beaufort Lodge 297
Carr House 297
Catton Old Hall 296
Chesters Restaurant & Guesthouse 298
Church Farm 298
Earlham Guesthouse 297
The Gables Guest House 297
Harvey House Guest House 298
The Larches 298
Marlborough House Hotel 298
Marsham Arms Inn 298
Old Thorn Barn 297
Rosedale 298
NOTTINGHAM
Acorn Hotel 309
Andrews Private Hotel 310
Beech Lodge 309
Fairhaven Private Hotel 309
The Gallery Hotel 310
Grantham Hotel 310
Hall Farm House 310
Tudor Lodge Hotel 310
NUNEATON
Leathermill Grange 414

O

OAKAMOOR
Bank House 371
The Beehive Guest House 371
Crowtrees Farm 371
Ribden Farm 371
Tenement Farm Guest House 371
OAKHAM
Kirkee House 320
OBAN
Braeside Guest House 499
Corriemar House 500
Glenbervie House 499
Glenburnie Private Hotel 499
Greencourt Guest House 499
Rhumor 500
Roseneath Guest House 499
Thornloe Guest House 499
Wellpark House 500
OGONNELLOE
Lantern House 602
OKEHAMPTON
Heathfield House 154
Luxridge 154
Meadowlea 154
Pressland House 154
OLD SODBURY
The Sodbury House Hotel 206
OLDHAM
Boothstead Farm 218
Farrars Arms 218
OLDMELDRUM
Cromlet Hill Guest House 495
OLNEY
The Queen Hotel 42
OMAGH
Hawthorn House 599
OSMOTHERLEY
Queen Catherine Hotel 467
OSSETT
The Mews Hotel 488
OSWESTRY
Ashfield Farmhouse 328
The Bear Hotel 327
Bradford Arms Hotel 327
Elgar House 327
The Hawthorns 328
Old Vicarage 328
The Pentre 328
Top Farm House 328
OTTERY ST MARY
Bistro 154
Fairmile Inn 154
Fluxton Farm 155
Normandy House Hotel & Pitt Farm 155
OUGHTERARD
The Boat Inn 621
Lakeland Country House 621
River Run Lodge 621
Waterfall Lodge 621
OUNDLE
The Ship Inn 303
OXFORD
Acorn Guest House 318
All Seasons Guesthouse 316
Beaumont Guest House 316-7
Brown's Guest House 317
Burlington House 314
Casa Villa Guesthouse 318
Chestnuts Guest House 314
Conifer Guest House 317
Cotswold House 315
Gables Guest House 315
Galaxie Private Hotel 315
Green Gables 317
Heather House 317
Highfield Guest House 316
Kings Guest House 318
Marlborough House 315
Newton House 318
Pickwicks Guest House 316
Pine Castle Hotel 316
River Hotel 317
Sandfield House 316
Victoria House Hotel 316
OXHILL
Nolands Farm 414
OXWICH
Woodside Guest House 592

P

PADSTOW
Cross House Hotel 67
Newlands Hotel 68
The Old Cabbage Patch 67
Penjoly Cottage Guest House 67
Rick Stein's Cafe 68
Roselyn 68
St Petroc's Hotel and Bistro 67
Trevone Bay Hotel 68
PAIGNTON
Aquamarine Hotel 156
Bay Cottage Private Hotel 156
Bay Sands Hotel 156
Beresford Private Hotel 155
Birchwood House Hotel 156
Channel View Hotel 156
Cherra Hotel 156
The Clydesdale 155
The Haldon 156
Kingswinford Hotel 155
Rosslyn Hotel 155
St Weonard's Private Hotel 156
The Sealawn Hotel 156-7
Torland Hotel 156
Torbay Sands Hotel 157
Wentworth Hotel 157
PARKMILL
Parc-le-Breos House 592
PATELEY BRIDGE
Central House 467
PEEBLES
Venlaw Farm 545
PEMBROKE
Poyerston Farm 582
PENARTH
The Westbourne Guest House 593
PENRITH
Beckfoot Country House 106
Brandelhow Guest House 106

Brooklands Guest House 106
Glendale Guest House 106
Limes Country Hotel 106
Roundthorn
Country House 106
PENTRAETH
Parc-yr-Odyn 557
PENYGROES
Llwyndu Mawr
Farmhouse 577
PENZANCE
Blue Seas Hotel 69
Camilla House Hotel 69
Carlton Hotel 70
Chy-an-Mor 68
Coth'a Noweth 71
Dunedin 69
Ennys 68
Estoril Hotel 71
Georgian House 69
Hotel Minalto 70
Mount Royal Hotel 70
Penalva 70
Pendennis 71
Penmorvah Hotel 71
Rose Farm 70
Southern Comfort
Guest House 71
The Summerhouse 68-9
Tremont 70
PERRANUTHNOE
Ednovean Farm 71
Ednovean House 71
Quilkyns 72
The Victoria Inn 72
PERTH
Adam Guest House 540
Anglers Inn 541
Castleview 541
Clunie Guest House 541
Kinnaird 540
Over Kinfauns 540
Park Lane Guest House 540-1
Westview Guest House 541
PETERBOROUGH
Aaron Park Hotel 48
Charlotte House 48
Hawthorn House 48
The Lodge Hotel 48
PETERSFIELD
The Good Intent 226
PETT
Pendragon Lodge 398
PEVENSEY
Priory Court Hotel &
Restaurant 398
The Sandcastle 398
PEWSEY
Three Horseshoes
Cottage 438
PICKERING
Fox & Hounds
Country Inn 468
The Moorlands Country
House Hotel 467
The Old Manse 468
Warrington Guest House 468
PIDDLETRENTHIDE
The Poachers Inn 182
PITLOCHRY
Arrandale House 541
Craigroyston House 541
Dundarave House 542
Dunfallandy House 541
Torrdarach Hotel 542
The Well House 542
Wellwood House 542
PLESHEY
Yew Tree Farm 196
PLYMOUTH
Berkeley's of St James 157
Caraneal 158
Citadel House 158
Cranbourne Hotel 158
Devonshire Guest House 158
The Dudley Hotel 157
Four Seasons
Guest House 158
Georgian House Hotel 158
Hotel Royal 158
Jewell's 157
The Lamplighter Hotel 158
Squires Guest House 157
POLPERRO
Penryn House Hotel 72
Trenderway Farm 72
PONTEFRACT
Southmoor Hotel 488
Wentvale 488
PONTESBURY
Gatten Lodge 328
PONTYPOOL
Mill Farm 593
Ty-Cooke Farm 593
POOLE
Acorns 182
Blue Shutters Hotel 182
Burleigh Private Hotel 182
Centraltown Guest House 183
Harbour View
Guest House 183
Holly House 183
Lewina Lodge
Guest House 183
Sarnia Cherie 182
Seacourt Guesthouse 183
Towngate Guest House 183
POOLEY BRIDGE
Elm House 106
PORLOCK
Dunster Steep House 356
PORT ERIN
Rowany Cottier 492
PORT ISAAC
The Corn Mill 73
The Courtyard at
Pendragon House 73
PORT ST MARY
Aaron House 492
PORTAFERRY
The Narrows 597
PORTHALLOW
Gallen Treath Guest House 72
PORTHCAWL
Glenaub Hotel 557
Minerva Hotel 557
Penoyre Guest House 557
PORTHCURNO
The Porthcurno Hotel 72
PORTHLEVEN
Harbour Inn 72-3
PORTHMADOG
Owen's Hotel 578
Tyddyn Du
Farm Holidays 578
PORTLAND
Alessandria Hotel 184
Portland Lodge 184
Queen Anne House 184
PORTLAOISE
Ivyleigh House 632
O'Sullivan Guesthouse 632
PORTNANCON
Port-Na-Con House 533
PORTPATRICK
Blinkbonnie Guest House 515
PORTREATH
Benson's 73
PORTREE
Craiglockhart
Guest House 554
Quiraing House 554
PORTSMOUTH
Abbey Lodge 228
Amberley Court 227
Bembell Court Hotel 227
Collingham Guest House 228
The Elms Guest House 228
Fairlea 228
The Festing Grove
Guest House 228
Glencoe Guest House 228
Hamilton House 227
Norfolk Hotel 228
St Margarets 227
Sherwood Guest House 228

Upper Mount
House Hotel 227
POSTBRIDGE
Lydgate House 159
PRAA SANDS
Gwynoon Guest House 73
PRESTATYN
Roughsedge House 570
PRESTEIGNE
Gumma Farm 590
PRESTON
Tulketh Hotel 261
Whitestake Farm 261
Withy Trees Guest House 261
PRESTWICK
Fernbank Guest House 547
Golf View Hotel 547
Kincraig Private Hotel 547
PULBOROUGH
Harkaway 409
PURLEY
Arran Court 214

R

RAMSEY
The River House 492
RAMSGATE
Belvidere Guest House 253
Eastwood Guest House 253
RATHDRUM
Avonbrae Guesthouse 650
RATHVILLY
Baile Ricead 600
RAVENSCAR
Smugglers Rock
Country Guest House 468
REDCAR
Claxton Hotel 468
REDHILL
Ashleigh House Hotel 386
Hillside Cottage 386
Lynwood Guest House 386
REDRUTH
Aviary Court Hotel 73
REDWICK
Brickhouse Country
Guest House 581
REETH
Arkleside Hotel 468
Charles Bathurst Inn 468-9
RHANDIRMWYN
The Royal Oak Inn 560
RHYL
Barratts Restaurant 570
Pier Hotel 570
Tremorfa Hotel 570
RICHMOND
The Old Brewery
Guest House 469
Pottergate Guest House 469
Whashton Springs Farm 469
RICHMOND UPON THAMES
Hobart Hall Hotel 386
RINGWOOD
Amberwood 229
Fraser House 230
Little Forest Lodge 229
The Old Cottage 229
Old Stacks 229
Picket Hill House 230
RIPON
Bay Tree Farm 469
Moor End Farm 470
Ravencroft B & B 470
St George Court 469
RISLEY
Braeside Guest House 129
ROADWATER
Wood Advent Farm 356
ROBERTSBRIDGE
Swallowfield Farm 398
ROBIN HOOD'S BAY
The Flask Inn 470
ROCHDALE
Hindle Pastures 218
ROCHESTER
Redesdale Arms Hotel 307
ROCK
Roskarnon House Hotel 73
ROGATE
Mizzards Farm 410
ROMFORD
Havering Road
Guest House 214-5
The Orchard
Guest House 216
ROMSEY
Country Accommodation
Guest House 230
The Mill Arms 230
Springfields 230
ROSCREA
The Tower Guest House &
Restaurant/Bar 639
ROSEDALE ABBEY
Sevenford House 470
ROSLIN
Olde Original Rosslyn
Inn 535
ROSSLARE HARBOUR
Churchtown House 647
Euro Lodge 647
Kilrane House 647
The Light House 647
Oldcourt House 647
ROSSNOWLAGH
Smugglers Creek Inn 610
ROSS-ON-WYE
The Arches 237
Brookfield House 237
Brynheulog 236
Lea House 236
Lumleys 236
Raglan House 237
Sunnymount Hotel 236
Trecilla Farm 236
The Whitehouse 236
ROSYTH
Backmarch House B & B 520
ROTHBURY
Katerina's Guest House 308
Newcastle Hotel 308
Orchard Guest House 307
Whitton Farm Hotel 308
ROTHERHAM
Stonecroft Hotel 485
ROUNDSTONE
Ivy Rock House 621
ROWLANDS CASTLE
The Fountain Inn 230
ROWLEY REGIS
Highfield House Hotel 424-5
ROYAL TUNBRIDGE WELLS
Bentham Hill Stables 255
Danehurst House 254
Hadleigh 255
The Old Parsonage 254-5
RUGBY
The White Lion Inn 415
RUSTINGTON
Kenmore Guest House 410
RUTHIN
Eyarth Station 571
Tyddyn Chambers 571
RUYTON-XI-TOWNS
Brownhill House 328
Top House Inn 328
RYDE
Abingdon Lodge Hotel 426
Eleanor Cottage 426
Grange Farm B&B 426
Little Upton Farm 426
Newnham Farm 426
RYE
The Benson 398-9
Cliff Farm 401
Durrant House Hotel 399
Jeake's House 399
King Charles II
Guest House 399
Layces Bed & Breakfast 401
Little Orchard House 400
Little Saltcote 402
Manor Farm Oast 400
Old Borough Arms Hotel 401
The Old Vicarage 402
The Old Vicarage
Guest House 400

Playden Cottage
Guesthouse 400
The Strand House 401
White Vine House 401

S

SAFFRON WALDEN
The Bonnet 196
The Cricketer's Arms 196
Rowley Hill Lodge 196
Yardleys 196
ST AGNES
Driftwood Spars Hotel 74
Penkerris 74
ST ALBANS
Ardmore House 240
ST ANDREWS
Annandale Guest House 521
Craigmore Guest House 521
Edenside House 522
Fossil House
Bed & Breakfast 520
Hazelbank Private Hotel 521
The Larches 521
Lorimer House 521
Riverview Guest House 521
Spinkstown Farmhouse 521
West Park House 521
Yorkston House 522
ST AUBIN
The Panorama 490
Peterborough House 490
ST AUSTELL
Anchorage House
Guest Lodge 74
The Lodge at Carlyon Bay 75
Lower Barn 74-5
Poltarrow Farm 75
The Rashleigh Arms 75
T'Gallants 75
ST BEES
Queens Hotel 106
ST BLAZEY
Nanscawen Manor House 75
ST CLEMENT
Bon Air Hotel 490
ST DAVID'S
The Coach House 583
Ramsey House 582
Y Glennydd Hotel 583
Y-Gorlan Guest House 582
ST HELIER
Cliff Court Hotel 490
Millbrook House 490
ST HILARY
Ennys 76
ST IVES
Bay View Guest House 78
Beckside Cottage 76
Channings Hotel 78
Chy-an-Creet
Private Hotel 76
Chy-Garth 76
Chy-Roma Guest House 78
The Hollies Hotel 78
Island View Guest House 78
Kynance Guest House 76
Lyonesse Hotel 76
The Old Vicarage Hotel 76-7
The Pondarosa 77
Portarlington 78
Porthminster View 78-9
Primrose Valley Hotel 79
Queens Tavern 79
Regent Hotel 77
The Sloop Inn 77
Thurlestone Private Hotel 79
Tregony Guest House 77
Tregorran Hotel 77
Treliska 78
Trewinnard 78
The Willows 79
ST JUST [NEAR LAND'S END]
Wellington Hotel 79
ST KEVERNE
The White Hart Hotel 79
ST MARY'S
Carnwethers
Country House 81
Crebinick House 81
The Wheelhouse 81
ST MAWGAN
The Falcon Inn 80
ST MERRYN
Farmers Arms 80
ST NEOT
The London Inn 80
ST PETER PORT
Marine Hotel 489
ST SAVIOUR
Champ Colin 490-1
ST TEATH
Tregarthen
Bed & Breakfast 80
SALCOMBE
The Lodge 159
SALE
Brooklands Luxury Lodge 218
SALEN
Gruline Home Farm 554
SALISBURY
The Beadles 438
Briden House 440
The Butt of Ale 441
Byways House 441
Cathedral Hotel 440
Clovelly Hotel 439
Ebblesway Courtyard 439
The Edwardian Lodge 440
Glen Lyn House 440
Hayburn Wyke
Guest House 441
Holmhurst 442
Malvern Guest House 440
Newton Farmhouse 439
The Old House 439
Richburn Guest House 441
Salisbury Old Mill House 441
Stratford Lodge 441
Websters 440
Wyndham Park Lodge 441
SALTASH
Crooked Inn 80
Holland Inn Motel 80-1
The Weary Friar Inn 80
SALTCOATS
Lochwood Farm Steading 537
SANDBACH
Poplar Mount Guesthouse 53
SANDHURST
Hoads Farm 253
SANDOWN
Carisbrooke
House Hotel 426-7
Chester Lodge Hotel 427
Culver Lodge Hotel 427
Lawns Hotel 427
Lyndhurst Hotel 427
The Philomel Hotel 427
SANDY
Highfield Farm 35
SARK
Hotel Petit Champ 492
SAUNDERSFOOT
Vine Cottage 583
Woodlands Hotel 583
SAXLINGHAM THORPE
Foxhole Farm 298
SAXMUNDHAM
Church Farm 383
SCARBOROUGH
Argo Hotel 471
Brincliffe Edge Hotel 472
Croft Hotel 470
Hotel Columbus 470
Hotel Danielle 471
Interludes 470
Jalna House Hotel 472
Kenways Guest House 472
Kerry Lee (Non Smoking)
Private Hotel 472
Lonsdale Villa Hotel 471
Lyness 472
Lysander Hotel 471
Mount House Hotel 471
North End Farm Country
Guesthouse 471

Paragon Hotel 470-1
Parmelia Hotel 472
Plane Tree Cottage Farm 472
Premier Hotel 472
The Ramleh 471
Sefton Hotel 472
Stewart Hotel 472
The Whiteley Hotel 471
SCOTCH CORNER
Vintage Hotel 473
SEAFORD
Avondale Hotel 402
The Silverdale 402
SEAHOUSES
Railston House 308
SEATON
Bay View 159
Beach End Guest House 159
Beaumont Guest House 159
Mariners Hotel 159
SEAVIEW
Northbank Hotel 427
SEDBERGH
Cross Keys
Temperance Inn 107
SEDGEFIELD
Dun Cow Inn 193
SELSEY
St Andrews Lodge Hotel 410
SENNEN
Mayon Farmhouse 81
SENNYBRIDGE
Maeswalter 590
SETTLE
Golden Lion 473
Liverpool House 473
The Oast Guest House 473
Whitefriars
Country Guesthouse 473
SEVENOAKS
Barn Cottage 253
SHAFTESBURY
The Grove Arms 184
The Old Forge 185
SHANAGARRY
Ballymaloe House 608
SHANKLIN
Bedford Lodge Hotel 428
The Clarendon Hotel
Shanklin Ltd 429
Clifton Hotel 429
Hayes Barton Hotel 428
The Hazelwood 429
Holly Lodge 428
Jasmine Lodge Hotel 429
Mount House Hotel 428
Norfolk House Hotel 428
The Richmond Hotel 428
Rowborough Hotel 428
St Brelades Hotel 429
St Georges House Hotel 428
Shoreside Hotel 429
The Triton Hotel 428
The White House Hotel 429
SHAP
Brookfield Guest House 107
SHEERNESS
Sheppey Guest House 253
SHEFFIELD
Critchleys 485
Hunter House Hotel 485
Lindrick Hotel 485
Quarry House 485
Westbourne House Hotel 485
SHERBORNE
The Alders 186
Almshouse Farm 186
Cromwell House 186
The Grange Hotel &
Restaurant 185
Munden House 185
The Old Vicarage 185
Venn Farm 186
SHERINGHAM
Bayleaf Guest House 300
The Birches 299
Camberley House 300
Fairlawns 299
Highfield Guest House 299
Homefield Guest House &
Restaurant 299
Knollside Lodge 299
Providence Place 299
Willow Lodge 299
SHIMPLING
Gannocks House 383
SHIPLEY
Beeties 488
SHIPSTON ON STOUR
Crab Mill 415
The Red Lion Hotel 415
SHREWSBURY
Abbey Court
Guest House 329
The Day House 329
Fieldside Guest House 328-9
Glyndene 330
Lythwood Hall
Bed and Breakfast 329
Meole Brace Hall 328
Sandford House Hotel 329
The Stiperstones
Guest House 330
Sydney House Hotel 330
Tudor House 329
SIDMOUTH
Glendevon Hotel 160
Jubilee Cottage 160
The Old Farmhouse 160
The Salty Monk 160
SILLOTH
Nith View Guest House 107
SILSOE
The Old George Hotel 35
SIMONSBATH
Barkham 356
SITTINGBOURNE
Hempstead House
Country Hotel 253
Sandhurst Farm Forge 253
SIXPENNY HANDLEY
Town Farm Bungalow 186
SKEGNESS
Crawford Hotel 271
SKERRIES
Redbank House
& Restaurant 616-7
SKIBBEREEN
Ilenroy House 608
SKIPTON
Brylie House Bed
& Breakfast 473
Craven House 474
Cravendale Guest House 474
Herriots Hotel,
Bar & Dining Rooms 474
Low Skibeden
Farmhouse 473
Rockwood House 474
Westfield House 474
SLEDMERE
Triton Inn 453
SLIGO
Aisling 636
Chestnut Lawn 637
SLOUGH
Colnbrook Lodge 37
SMARDEN
The Chequers Inn 254
SNETTISHAM
Rose & Crown 300
SOLIHULL
The Gate House 425
Ivy House 425
SOLVA
Lochmeyler Farmhouse 584
SOMERTON
Church Farm
Guest House 357
Home Farm 356-7
Lower Farm 356
Lydford House 356
Somerton Court
Country House 356
SOUTH BRENT
Coombe House 160-1
The Pack Horse 161
SOUTH CAVE
The Fox and Coney Inn 453

Rudstone Walk Country Accommodation 453
SOUTH MOLTON
Kerscott Farm 161
Old Coaching Inn 161
West Down Guest House 161
SOUTH NORMANTON
The Boundary Lodge 129
SOUTH QUEENSFERRY
Priory Lodge 510
SOUTH SHIELDS
Beach Haven Guest House 411
SOUTHAMPTON
Alcantara Guest House 231
Ashelee Lodge 231
The Fenland Guest House 231
Hunters Lodge Hotel 231
Landguard Lodge 231
Lodge Guest House 231
SOUTHEND-ON-SEA
Ilfracombe House Hotel 197
Mayflower Hotel 197
Terrace Hotel 197
Tower Hotel & Restaurant 197
SOUTHPORT
Ambassador Private Hotel 287
Cambridge Town House Hotel 287
Edendale Hotel 288
Lyndhurst Guest House 288
Rosedale Hotel 287
Sidbrook Hotel 288
The White Lodge Private Hotel 288
Whitworth Falls Hotel 287
SPEAN BRIDGE
Corriechoille Lodge 533
Distant Hills 533
The Smiddy House 533
SPIDDAL
Ard Aoibhinn 622
Ardmor Country House 621
Suan Na Mara 622
Tigh Chualain 622
Tuar Beag 622
STADHAMPTON
The Crazy Bear Hotel 318
STAFFORD
Bailey Hotel 372
Leonards Croft Hotel 372
The Old School 372
Windsor Hotel 372
The Yew Tree Inn & Restaurant 371
STAMFORD
Rock Lodge 271
STANDON
Nags Head 240
STANLEY
Bush Blades Farm 193
STANTON DREW
Greenlands 357
Valley Farm 357
STANTON PRIOR
Poplar Farm 357
STAPLE FITZPAINE
Greyhound Inn 357
STEARSBY
The Granary 474
STEEPLE ASTON
Westfield Farm Motel 318
STEYNING
Springwells Hotel 410
STIRLING
Castlecroft 550
XI Victoria Square 550
STOCKBRIDGE
Carbery Guest House 231
York Lodge 231
STOCKLAND
The Kings Arms Inn 161
STOCKPORT
Henry's Hotel 218
The Red Lion Inn 218
STOCKTON-ON-TEES
Grange Guest House 193
STOFORD
The Swan Inn 442
STOGUMBER
Northam Mill 358
STOKE HOLY CROSS
Salamanca Farm Guest House 300
STOKE ST GREGORY
Meare Green Farm 358
STOKE-BY-NAYLAND
The Angel Inn 383
STOKE-ON-TRENT
The Limes 372
The Victoria Hotel 372
STONE
Field House 372
STONEHAVEN
Alexander Guest House 496
Arduthie House 496
Woodside Of Glasslaw 496
STONEHOUSE
The Grey Cottage 206-7
Oaktree Farm 207
Rose & Crown Inn 207
STOW-ON-THE-WOLD
Aston House 208
Corsham Field Farmhouse 208
Crestow House 207
Kings Head Inn & Restaurant 207
Limes Guest House 208
Rectory Farmhouse 207
Woodlands Guest House 208
STRADBALLY
Tullamoy House 632
STRAFFAN
Woodside Lodge 631
STRANRAER
Balyett Bed & Breakfast 515
Fernlea Guest House 515
Glenotter 515
STRATFORD-UPON-AVON
Aidan Guest House 416
Ambleside Guest House 416
Avon Lodge 418
Brook Lodge 416
Clomendy B & B 419
Compton House 419
Craig Cleeve House 416
The Croft 419
Curtain Call Guest House 419
The Dylan Guest House 418
Eastnor House Hotel 416
Eversley Bears Guest House 416
The Fox & Goose Inn 416
Glebe Farm House 415
Gravelside 416
Hardwick House 417
Highcroft 418
Hollies Guest House 419
Hunters Moon 419
Loxley Farm 415
Marlyn Guest House 420
Melita Private Hotel 417
Monk's Barn Farm 417
Moonraker House 417
Parkfield Guest House 420
Sequoia House Private Hotel 418
Stretton House Hotel 420
Twelfth Night 418
Travellers Rest 420
Victoria Spa Lodge 418
Whitchurch Farm 420
STRATHAVEN
Avonlea 548
Springvale Hotel 548
STRATHPEFFER
Craigvar 534
Dunraven Lodge 534
Inver Lodge 534
STRATHY POINT
Catalina 534
STREET
Kasuli Bed & Breakfast 358

STRETTON
Woodlands House 372
STROUD
The Downfield Hotel 209
George Inn 209
Hunters Lodge 208
Hyde Crest 208-9
The Priory 208
STURMINSTER NEWTON
Stourcastle Lodge 186
SUDBURY
The Old Bull Hotel & Restaurant 383
The Plough 383
SULHAMSTEAD
The Old Manor 37
SURBITON
Warwick Lodge 216
SUTTON
Ashling Tara Hotel 216
SUTTON COLDFIELD
Standbridge Hotel 425
Windrush 425
SUTTON-ON-SEA
Athelstone Lodge Hotel 271
SWADLINCOTE
Overseale House 130
SWAFFHAM
Corfield House 300
The Red Lion Motel 300
SWANAGE
Eversden Private Hotel 187
The Gillan Hotel 186-7
Sandringham Hotel 187
White Lodge Hotel 187
SWANSEA
Alexander Hotel 592
Cefn Bryn 592
Crescent Guest House 592
The Grosvenor House 592
SWAY
The Forest Heath Hotel 232
The Nurse's Cottage 232
SWINDERBY
Halfway Farm Motel 271
SWINDON
Grove Lodge 442
Parklands Hotel 442
Portquin Guest House 442
SYDLING ST NICHOLAS
Lamperts Cottage 187
SYMINGTON
Nether Underwood Country House 548
SYMONDS YAT [EAST]
Garth Cottage 237
SYMONDS YAT [WEST]
Norton House 237

T

TAHILLA
Tahilla Cove Guesthouse 629
TAIN
Aldie House 534-5
Golf View House 534
TALGARTH
Castle Inn 591
TAMWORTH
Harlaston Post Office 373
Middleton House Farm 373
Oak Tree Farm 373
The Old Rectory 373
The Sleepy Owl 373
TARBERT
The Victoria Hotel 500
TARPORLEY
Alvanley Arms Hotel 53
Hill House Farm 53
TARRANT LAUNCESTON
Ramblers Cottage 187
TARRANT MONKTON
The Langton Arms 187
TATTENHALL
Ivy Farm B & B 53
TAUNTON
Blorenge House 358
Brookfield House 358-9
Creechbarn Bed & Breakfast 359
Cutsey House 358
Gatchells 359
Heathfield Lodge 358
Higher Dipford Farm 359
Lower Farm 359
Lower Manor Farm 360
Lower Marsh Farm 360
Meryan House Hotel 360
Pare Mill 360
The Spinney 360
West View 360
Yallands Farmhouse 360
TAVISTOCK
April Cottage 162
The Coach House 162
Tor Cottage 161
TEBAY
The Cross Keys Inn 107
Primrose Cottage Guest House 107
TEIGNMOUTH
Potters Mooring 162
Thomas Luny House 162
TELFORD
Avenue Farm Bed & Breakfast 330
Bridge House 330
Church Farm 330
Shray Hill Guest House 330

TEMPLE GRAFTON
The Blue Boar Inn 420
TEMPLEMORE
Saratoga Lodge 639
TENBY
Castle View Private Hotel 585
Clarence House Hotel 585
Giltar Grove Country House 584
Gumfreston Private Hotel 585
Gwynne House Guest House 584
Rosendale Park 584
St Teresa's Old Convent 585
Weybourne Guest House 584
TENTERDEN
Collina House Hotel 254
The White Lion 254
TETSWORTH
Little Acre Bed & Breakfast 318
TEWKESBURY
Willow Cottages 210
THAME
The Dairy 318-9
THAXTED
Crossways Guest House 197
THETFORD
The Chequers Inn 300
THIRLMERE
Stybeck Farm Experience 107
THIRSK
The Old Manor House 474
Spital Hill 475
THOMASTOWN
Abbey House 631
Carrickmourne House 631
THORNCOMBE
Upperfold House 188
THORNHILL (D&G)
Gillbank House 515
THORNHILL (Stirling)
Easter Tarr Farmhouse 550-1
THORNTON LE DALE
Allerston Manor House 475
THRUXTON
May Cottage 232
THURLES
The Castle B & B 639
Inch House Country House & Restaurant 639
THURNING
Rookery Farm 300
THURSFORD GREEN
Holly Lodge 300-1
THWAITE
Kearton Country Hotel 475

TIBBIE SHIELS INN
Tibbie Shiels Inn 545
TIDESWELL
Greystones 130
Jaret House 130
Poppies 130
TILLICOULTRY
Westbourne House 512
TINTAGEL
The Cottage Teashop 82
The Old Borough House 82
Pendrin House 82
Port William Inn 82
Tintagel Arms Hotel 82
TINTERN
Fountain Inn 580
TIPPERARY
Ach-na-Sheen Guesthouse 639
TIRLEY
Town Street Farm 210
TISBURY
The Beckford Arms 442
TISSINGTON
Bent Farm 130
TITCHMARSH
The Wheatsheaf Inn & Hotel 303
TIVERTON
Angel Guest House 163
Hornhill Farmhouse 162
Lodge Hill Farm 162
Lower Collipriest Farm 162
Quoit-At-Cross 163
TOBERCURRY
Cruckawn House 637
TODMORDEN
Staff of Life 488-9
TOPPESFIELD
Ollivers Farm 197
TORPOINT
Edgcumbe Arms 82
TORQUAY
Abberley Hotel 167
Arran Lodge 167
Athina 169
Atlantis Hotel 163
Aveland Hotel 163
Avenue Park Guest House 169
Babbacombe Hall Hotel 164
Barclay Court Hotel 164
Belmont Hotel 164
The Birdcage Hotel 167
Blue Haze Hotel 164
Burleigh House 167
Cedar Court Hotel 164
Colindale Hotel 163
Coombe Court Hotel 164
Court Prior 165
The Cranmore 165
Crown Lodge 165
Devon Court Hotel 168
Elmdene Hotel 165
Everglades Hotel 165
Fircroft Guest House 168
Gainsboro Hotel 165
The Garlieston Hotel 168
Glenorleigh Hotel 165
Green Park Hotel 168
Grosvenor House Hotel 168
Harmony Hotel 166
Headland View 166
Hotel Blue Conifer 166
Ingoldsby Hotel 166
Knowle Court Hotel 166
Lindum Hotel 167
Manor Court Hotel 166
Mulberry House 163
Newton House 166
Norwood Hotel 166
Oscars Hotel 167
The Palms Hotel 168
Redlands 168
Riviera Lodge Hotel 168
Robin Hill International Hotel 167
Stover Lodge Hotel 169
Tyndale Guest House 169
Wayfarer Guest House 169
Westgate Hotel 167
TOTLAND BAY
Frenchman's Cove 429
Sandford Lodge 429
TOTNES
The Durant Arms 169
Four Seasons Guest House 170
The Old Forge at Totnes 170
The Red Slipper 170
Steam Packet Inn 170
TRALEE
Brianville Guest House 629
Heatherville Farm 629
Tralee Townhouse 630
TRAMORE
Glenorney 641
Cliff House 642
Sea View Lodge 642
TREARDDUR BAY
Moranedd Guest House 557
TREFIN
Awel-Mor Guest House 585
TROUTBECK
Lane Head Farm 108
Queens Head Hotel 108
TROWBRIDGE
Watergardens 442-3
TRURO
Bissick Old Mill 83
Manor Cottage 83
Marcorrie Hotel 83
Rock Cottage 83
Trevispian Vean Farm 83
TWO BRIDGES
Cherrybrook Hotel 170
TWYNHOLM
Fresh Fields Guest House 515
TYWARDREATH
Elmswood House Hotel 83
TYWYN
Eisteddfa 578

U

UCKFIELD
Hooke Hall 402
ULEY
Hodgecombe Farm 210
ULLAPOOL
Dromnan Guest House 535
UPPER LARGO
Monturpie Guest House 522
USK
Ty-Gwyn Farm 580
UTTOXETER
Hillcrest Guest House 373
Oldroyd Guest House & Motel 374
Parkbrook Lodge 374

V

VENTNOR
Cornerways 430
Lake Hotel 430
Little Span Farm 430
Llynfi Hotel 430
The Old Rectory 429
Picardie Hotel 430
St Andrews Hotel 430
Troubadour Hotel 430
VERYAN
Elerkey Guest House 84
The New Inn 84

W

WADEBRIDGE
Swan Hotel 84
WADHURST
Four Keys 402
Spring Cottage 402
WAKEFIELD
Kirklands Hotel 489
Stanley View Guest House 489
WALCOTT
Holly Tree Cottage 301
WANTAGE
Stanford Park House 319

The Star Inn 319
WAREHAM
Redcliffe Farm 188
WARMINSTER
The Angel Coaching Inn 443
The Angel Inn 443
The Barn 443
Deverill End 444
The Dove Inn 443
The George Inn 444
The Granary
Bed & Breakfast 443
White Lodge 444
WARREN STREET
The Harrow Hill Hotel 255
WARSASH
Dormy House Hotel 232
Solent View Hotel 232
WARWICK
Agincourt Lodge Hotel 420
Austin House 421
Croft Guesthouse 420-1
Dockers Barn Farm 421
The Hare On The Park 420
WASHFORD
The Washford Inn 361
WATCHET
The Georgian House 361
WATERBEACH
Inspiration 48
WATERFORD
Arlington Lodge 643
Ashbourne House 643
Belmont House 643
Brown's Town House 643
The Coach House 643
Diamond Hill
Guest House 643
Foxmount
Country House 642
O'Gradys 643
Sion Hill House
& Gardens 642
WATERHOUSES
Ye Olde Crown 374
WATERMILLOCK
Brackenrigg Inn 108
Knotts Mill
Country Lodge 108
WATERROW
The Rock Inn 361
WATERVILLE
Brookhaven House 630
Klondyke House 630
WATFORD
Upton Lodge 240
WELLINGBOROUGH
Oak House Private Hotel 303
WELLS
Amber House 365
Beaconsfield Farm 361
Bekynton House 362
Beryl 362
Birdwood House 365
Canon Grange 362-3
Double-Gate Farm 363
Furlong House 363
Garden Cottage 363
Highcroft 363
Highfield 363
Hollow Tree Farm 363
Infield House 364
Littlewell Farm 364
Manor Farm
Bed & Breakfast 364
19 St Cuthbert Street 365
Number One Portway 364
The Old Farmhouse 362
The Old Stores 364
Riverside Grange 362
Sedgemoor House 365
Tynings House 364
WELLS-NEXT-THE-SEA
Branthill Farm 301
WELSHPOOL
Heath Cottage 591
Lower Trelydan
Farmhouse 591
Moat Farm 591
Orchard House 591
WELWYN GARDEN CITY
Brocket Arms 241
WEM
Lowe Hall Farm 330
Soulton Hall 330-1
WEMBLEY
Adelphi Hotel 216
Arena Hotel 216
WEOBLEY
Hill Top Farm 238
The Salutation Inn 237
WEST BAGBOROUGH
Bashfords Farmhouse 365
Tilbury Farm 365
WEST MALLING
Eden Farm
Accommodation 255
WEST PENNARD
Ashcombe Farm 367
WEST TANFIELD
The Bruce Arms 475
The Bull Inn 475
WESTBURY
Barley Mow House 331
WESTBURY
Birchanger Farm 444
The Duke at Bratton 444
Glenmore Farm 444
WESTGATE ON SEA
Bridge Hotel 255
WESTON UNDERWOOD
Park View Farm 130
WESTON-SUPER-MARE
Ashcombe Court 366
Baymead Hotel 366
Bella Vista Hotel 366
Beverley Guest House 366
Braeside Hotel 366
Church House 365
Clifton Lodge 366
Corbiere Hotel 366-7
Goodrington
Guest House 367
Milton Lodge Hotel 366
Oakover Guest House 367
Sarnia Hotel 367
The Seafarers 366
The Weston Bay Hotel 367
WESTOW
The Blacksmith Arms 475
Woodhouse Farm 475
WESTPORT
Bertra House 635
Carrabaun House 635
Knockranny Lodge 635
Riverbank House 635
Seabreeze 636
Seapoint House 636
WESTWARD HO!
Culloden House Hotel 170
WETHERBY
Broadleys 489
Prospect House 489
WEXFORD
Clonard House 648
Darral House 648
Killiane Castle 648
Maple Lodge 648
McMenamin's
Town House 648
Mount Auburn 648
O'Briens Auburn House 648
Rathaspeck Manor 649
Slaney Manor 649
WEYMOUTH
A Room with a View 190
The Alendale
Guest House 189
The Bay Guest House 188
Bay Lodge 188
Bayview Hotel 188
Beachcomber
Guest House 189
Bedford House Hotel 189
Cavendish House 190
The Chandlers Hotel 190

Channel View
Guest House 188
Cumberland Hotel 188-9
Esplanade Hotel 188
Ferndown Guest House 190
Hotel Kinley 190
Kingswood Hotel 189
Letchworth Guest House 189
The Seaham 189
Sou'west Lodge Hotel 190
Suncroft Hotel 189
Tamarisk Hotel 189
Tara Guest House 190
Trelawney Hotel 190
Wadham Guesthouse 190
Warwick Court Hotel 190
Westwey Hotel 190
WHEATLEY
The Bat & Ball Inn 319
WHEDDON CROSS
Rest and be
Thankful Inn 367
WHEPSTEAD
Folly House
Bed & Breakfast 384
WHIMPLE
Woodhayes Country
House and Cottage 170
WHITBY
Chiltern Guest House 476
Corra Lynn 476
Crescent House 476
Kimberley House Hotel 476
Rosslyn 477
The Sandbeck Hotel 476
Seacliffe Hotel 476
The Waverley 476
Ye Olde Beehive Inn 477
WHITCHURCH
Dearnford Hall 331
WHITEHAVEN
Corkickle Guest House 108
WHITEPARISH
Newton Farmhouse 444-5
WHITEWELL
The Inn at Whitewell 261
WHITLEY BAY
Cherrytree House 411
Marlborough Hotel 411
York House
Hotel and Studios 411
WHITSTABLE
Belmont House 256
Windy Ridge
Guest House 256
WICK
The Clachan 535
WIDECOMBE IN THE MOOR
Manor Cottage 171
WIGGINTON
Rangers Cottage 241
WIGMORE
Compasses Hotel 238
WILMINGTON
Crossways Hotel 402-3
WILMSLOW
Pear Tree Cottage Country
Guest House 54
WIMBORNE MINSTER
Ashton Lodge 191
WINCHCOMBE
Isbourne Manor House 210
Postlip Hall Farm 210
Sudeley Hill Farm 210
2 Dryfield Cottage 211
Wesley House 211
WINCHESTER
Acacia 232-3
Shawlands 233
24 Clifton Road 233
The Wykeham Arms 233
WINDERMERE
Alice Howe 110
The Beaumont 109
Belsfield House 110
Blenheim Lodge Hotel 110
Broadlands
Guest House 112-3
Coach House 110
Dene House 110
Denehurst Guest House 111
Eagle & Child Inn 113
Elim House 114
Fair Rigg 111
The Fairfield 111
Fir Trees 112
Firgarth 114
Glencree Private Hotel 111
Green Gables 114
The Haven 114
Hawksmoor Guest House 111
Hazel Bank 111
Holly Lodge Guest House 114
Howbeck 109
Lakeshore House 108-9
Laurel Cottage 112
Montfort Guest House 114
Newstead 110
The Old Court House 112
Rosemount Guest House 114
St Johns Lodge 115
Storrs Gate House 112
White Lodge Hotel 112
Woodlands Hotel 112
WINDSOR
Clarence Hotel 38
Netherton Hotel 38
Oscar Hotel 38
WINESTEAD
Farm House B & B 454
WINFORTON
Well Farm B & B 238
WING
Kings Arms Inn
& Restaurant 320
WINKLEIGH
The Old Parsonage 171
WINSFORD
Karslake House 367
WINTERBOURNE STOKE
Scotland Lodge 445
Scotland Lodge Farm 445
WIRKSWORTH
The Old Lock-Up 130-1
WIX
Dairy House Farm 198
New Farm House 198
WOLD NEWTON
The Wold Cottage 454
WOLSINGHAM
The Old Barn 193
WOODBRIDGE
Grove House 384
WOODFALLS
The Woodfalls Inn 445
WOODHALL SPA
Claremont Guest House 272
The Vale 272
Village Limits Motel 272
WOODSTOCK
The Crown Inn 320
Kings Head Inn
& Restaurant 319
The Laurels 319
Punchbowl Inn 320
The Townhouse 319
WOOLACOMBE
Baycliffe Hotel 172
The Castle Hotel 171
The Cleeve House Hotel 171
Holmesdale Hotel 172
Ossaborough House 171
WOOLER
The Old Manse 308
WOOLSTONE
The White Horse 320
WOOTTON
Island Charters 430
WOOTTON BASSETT
Little Cotmarsh Farm 445
WORCESTER
Burgage House 450
Croft Guest House 450
Park House Guest
Accommodation 451
Wyatt Guesthouse 451
WORKSOP
Acorn Lodge 310

The Dukeries Park 310
WORTHING
The Conifers 410
Moorings 410
WORTLEY
Wortley Cottage Guest House 485
WROXHAM
Beech Tree House 301
Bramble House 301
Park Lodge Guest House 301
WYBUNBURY
Lea Farm 54
WYLYE
The Bell Inn 445
WYMONDHAM
Witch Hazel 301

Y

YARKHILL
Garford Farm 238
YARMOUTH
Medlars 430
YARNTON
Eltham Villa Guest House 320
YATTON KEYNELL
The Crown Inn 445
YEALAND CONYERS
The Bower 261
YELVERTON
Harrabeer Country House Hotel 172
The Rosemont 172
YEOVIL
The Helyar Arms 368
Holywell House 368
YEOVILTON
Cary Fitzpaine Farm 368
YORK
Adams House Hotel 480
Alexander House 477
Arndale Hotel 478
Ascot House 478
Ashbourne House 478
Bedford Hotel 480
Beech House 480
Bishopgarth Guest House 483
Blue Bridge Hotel 481
Bootham Bar Hotel 484
Bronte Guest House 478-9
Cavalier Private Hotel 481
City Guest House 479
Crescent Guest House 484
Cumbria House 482
Curzon Lodge and Stable Cottages 479
Farthings Hotel 482
Fourposter Lodge Hotel 484
The Granary 479
Greenside 482
Hazelwood 478
The Heathers Guest House 479
Hillcrest Guesthouse 482
Hobbits Hotel 479
Holgate Bridge Hotel 482
Holly Lodge 480
Holmwood House Hotel 480
Linden Lodge Hotel 482
Moat Hotel 482
Nunmill House 480
Priory Hotel and Garth Restaurant 482-3
St Denys Hotel 483
St Georges Hotel 483
Wellgarth House 483
YOUGHAL
Ahernes 608
YOULGREAVE
The Old Bakery 131

Picture Credits

Permission for the use of photographs in the preliminary pages of this guide was kindly given by the following: Ennys, Penzance 3; The Old Bakery, Blockley 5, 29; Cross Keys Temperance Inn, Sedburgh 5; Abbey House, Maxey 6t; Marquis of Lorne, Nettlecombe 6bl; Southside Guest House, Edinburgh 7; The Old Rectory, Ilminster 8t; Omnia Somnia, Ashbourne 10b, 12b, 27br; The Old Farmhouse, Sidmouth 11t & 11bl; Shallowdale House, Ampleforth 11br; St Aubyn's Guest House, Looe 12t; R Saunders, John Wright Photography (Loxley Farm, Stratford upon Avon) 13; Nonsuch House, Dartmouth 15; Lavenham Priory, Lavenham 19, 20t, 21t; Yesterdays, Newtown 21b; The Big Sleep Hotel, Cardiff 20bl, 20br; R Bird, Robert Bird Designs (Little Orchard House, Rye) 25, 26t, 27t, 28t, 29t, 30t, 31t, 32t; Nova Development Corp 4, 6br, 9, 10t, 11bc, 14, 22t, 23r, 26bl, 26br, 27bl, 27bc, 28, 31bl, 31br.

The remaining picture, 8b, is from the AA PHOTO LIBRARY and was taken by D Forss.
(Abbreviations: t = top, b = bottom, l = left, r = right, c = centre)

Readers' Report form

Please send this form to:
Editor, The B&B Guide,
Lifestyle Guides,
The Automobile Association,
Fanum House,
Basingstoke RG21 4EA

or fax: 01256 491647
or e-mail: lifestyleguides@theAA.com

Please use this form to recommend any guest house, farmhouse or inn you have visited, whether it is in the guide or not currently listed. Feedback from readers helps us to keep our guide accurate and up to date. Please note, however, that if you have a complaint to make during a visit, we strongly recommend that you discuss the matter with the establishment management there and then so that they have a chance to put things right before your visit is spoilt. The AA does not undertake to arbitrate between you and the hotel management, or to obtain compensation or engage in correspondence.

Date:

Your name (block capitals)

Your address (block capitals)

....

....

....

.... e-mail address:

Comments (please include the name & address of the establishment)

....

....

....

....

....

....

....

....

(please attach a separate sheet if necessary)

Please tick here if you DO NOT wish to receive details of AA offers or products ☐

PTO

	YES	NO
Have you bought this guide before?	☐	☐

Have you bought any other accommodation, restaurant, pub, or food guides recently? If yes, which ones?

....

....

Why did you buy this guide? (circle all that apply)

holiday short break business travel special occasion

overnight stop find a venue for another event e.g. conference

other...

How often do you stay in B&Bs? (circle one choice)

more than once a month once a month once in 2-3 months

once in six months once a year less than once a year

Please answer these questions to help us make improvements to the guide:

Which of these factors are most important when choosing a B&B?

Price Location Awards/ratings Service

Decor/surroundings Previous experience Recommendation

Other (please state):..

Do you read the editorial features in the guide? ....

Do you use the location atlas?..

Which elements of the guide do you find the most useful when choosing somewhere to stay?

Description Photo Advertisement Diamond rating

Can you suggest any improvements to the guide?

....

....

....

....

Readers' Report form

Please send this form to:
Editor, The B&B Guide,
Lifestyle Guides,
The Automobile Association,
Fanum House,
Basingstoke RG21 4EA

or fax: 01256 491647
or e-mail: lifestyleguides@theAA.com

Please use this form to recommend any guest house, farmhouse or inn you have visited, whether it is in the guide or not currently listed. Feedback from readers helps us to keep our guide accurate and up to date. Please note, however, that if you have a complaint to make during a visit, we strongly recommend that you discuss the matter with the establishment management there and then so that they have a chance to put things right before your visit is spoilt. The AA does not undertake to arbitrate between you and the hotel management, or to obtain compensation or engage in correspondence.

Date:

Your name (block capitals)

Your address (block capitals)

....

....

....

.... e-mail address:

Comments (please include the name & address of the establishment)

....

....

....

....

....

....

....

....

(please attach a separate sheet if necessary)

Please tick here if you DO NOT wish to receive details of AA offers or products ☐

PTO

	YES	NO
Have you bought this guide before?	☐	☐

Have you bought any other accommodation, restaurant, pub, or food guides recently? If yes, which ones?

....

....

Why did you buy this guide? (circle all that apply)

holiday   short break   business travel   special occasion

overnight stop   find a venue for another event e.g. conference

other...

How often do you stay in B&Bs? (circle one choice)

more than once a month   once a month   once in 2-3 months

once in six months   once a year   less than once a year

Please answer these questions to help us make improvements to the guide:

Which of these factors are most important when choosing a B&B?

Price   Location   Awards/ratings   Service

Decor/surroundings   Previous experience   Recommendation

Other (please state):...

Do you read the editorial features in the guide? ....

Do you use the location atlas?...

Which elements of the guide do you find the most useful when choosing somewhere to stay?

Description   Photo   Advertisement   Diamond rating

Can you suggest any improvements to the guide?

....

....

....

....

Readers' Report form

Please send this form to:
Editor, The B&B Guide,
Lifestyle Guides,
The Automobile Association,
Fanum House,
Basingstoke RG21 4EA

or fax: 01256 491647
or e-mail: lifestyleguides@theAA.com

Please use this form to recommend any guest house, farmhouse or inn you have visited, whether it is in the guide or not currently listed. Feedback from readers helps us to keep our guide accurate and up to date. Please note, however, that if you have a complaint to make during a visit, we strongly recommend that you discuss the matter with the establishment management there and then so that they have a chance to put things right before your visit is spoilt. The AA does not undertake to arbitrate between you and the hotel management, or to obtain compensation or engage in correspondence.

Date:

Your name (block capitals)

Your address (block capitals)

....

....

....

.... e-mail address:

Comments (please include the name & address of the establishment)

....

....

....

....

....

....

....

....

(please attach a separate sheet if necessary)

Please tick here if you DO NOT wish to receive details of AA offers or products ☐

PTO

Have you bought this guide before? YES ☐ NO ☐

Have you bought any other accommodation, restaurant, pub, or food guides recently? If yes, which ones?

....

....

Why did you buy this guide? (circle all that apply)

holiday short break business travel special occasion

overnight stop find a venue for another event e.g. conference

other...

How often do you stay in B&Bs? (circle one choice)

more than once a month once a month once in 2-3 months

once in six months once a year less than once a year

Please answer these questions to help us make improvements to the guide:

Which of these factors are most important when choosing a B&B?

Price Location Awards/ratings Service

Decor/surroundings Previous experience Recommendation

Other (please state):..

Do you read the editorial features in the guide? ....

Do you use the location atlas?..

Which elements of the guide do you find the most useful when choosing somewhere to stay?

Description Photo Advertisement Diamond rating

Can you suggest any improvements to the guide?

....

....

....

....

Readers' Report form

Please send this form to:
Editor, The B&B Guide,
Lifestyle Guides,
The Automobile Association,
Fanum House,
Basingstoke RG21 4EA

or fax: 01256 491647
or e-mail: lifestyleguides@theAA.com

Please use this form to recommend any guest house, farmhouse or inn you have visited, whether it is in the guide or not currently listed. Feedback from readers helps us to keep our guide accurate and up to date. Please note, however, that if you have a complaint to make during a visit, we strongly recommend that you discuss the matter with the establishment management there and then so that they have a chance to put things right before your visit is spoilt. The AA does not undertake to arbitrate between you and the hotel management, or to obtain compensation or engage in correspondence.

Date:

Your name (block capitals)

Your address (block capitals)

....

....

....

.... e-mail address:

Comments (please include the name & address of the establishment)

....

....

....

....

....

....

....

....

(please attach a separate sheet if necessary)

Please tick here if you DO NOT wish to receive details of AA offers or products ☐

PTO

	YES	NO
Have you bought this guide before?	☐	☐

Have you bought any other accommodation, restaurant, pub, or food guides recently? If yes, which ones?

....

....

Why did you buy this guide? (circle all that apply)

holiday short break business travel special occasion

overnight stop find a venue for another event e.g. conference

other..

How often do you stay in B&Bs? (circle one choice)

more than once a month once a month once in 2-3 months

once in six months once a year less than once a year

Please answer these questions to help us make improvements to the guide:

Which of these factors are most important when choosing a B&B?

Price Location Awards/ratings Service

Decor/surroundings Previous experience Recommendation

Other (please state):..

Do you read the editorial features in the guide? ....

Do you use the location atlas?..

Which elements of the guide do you find the most useful when choosing somewhere to stay?

Description Photo Advertisement Diamond rating

Can you suggest any improvements to the guide?

....

....

....

....

Please send this form to:
Editor, The B&B Guide,
Lifestyle Guides,
The Automobile Association,
Fanum House,
Basingstoke RG21 4EA

or fax: 01256 491647
or e-mail: lifestyleguides@theAA.com

Please use this form to recommend any guest house, farmhouse or inn you have visited, whether it is in the guide or not currently listed. Feedback from readers helps us to keep our guide accurate and up to date. Please note, however, that if you have a complaint to make during a visit, we strongly recommend that you discuss the matter with the establishment management there and then so that they have a chance to put things right before your visit is spoilt. The AA does not undertake to arbitrate between you and the hotel management, or to obtain compensation or engage in correspondence.

Date:

Your name (block capitals)

Your address (block capitals)

....

....

....

.... e-mail address:

Comments (please include the name & address of the establishment)

....

....

....

....

....

....

....

....

(please attach a separate sheet if necessary)

Please tick here if you DO NOT wish to receive details of AA offers or products ☐

PTO

	YES	NO
Have you bought this guide before?	☐	☐

Have you bought any other accommodation, restaurant, pub, or food guides recently? If yes, which ones?

....

....

Why did you buy this guide? (circle all that apply)

holiday short break business travel special occasion

overnight stop find a venue for another event e.g. conference

other..

How often do you stay in B&Bs? (circle one choice)

more than once a month once a month once in 2-3 months

once in six months once a year less than once a year

Please answer these questions to help us make improvements to the guide:

Which of these factors are most important when choosing a B&B?

Price Location Awards/ratings Service

Decor/surroundings Previous experience Recommendation

Other (please state):..

Do you read the editorial features in the guide? ....

Do you use the location atlas?..

Which elements of the guide do you find the most useful when choosing somewhere to stay?

Description Photo Advertisement Diamond rating

Can you suggest any improvements to the guide?

....

....

....

....

Readers' Report form

Please send this form to:
Editor, The B&B Guide,
Lifestyle Guides,
The Automobile Association,
Fanum House,
Basingstoke RG21 4EA

or fax: 01256 491647
or e-mail: lifestyleguides@theAA.com

Please use this form to recommend any guest house, farmhouse or inn you have visited, whether it is in the guide or not currently listed. Feedback from readers helps us to keep our guide accurate and up to date. Please note, however, that if you have a complaint to make during a visit, we strongly recommend that you discuss the matter with the establishment management there and then so that they have a chance to put things right before your visit is spoilt. The AA does not undertake to arbitrate between you and the hotel management, or to obtain compensation or engage in correspondence.

Date:

Your name (block capitals)

Your address (block capitals)

....

....

....

.... e-mail address:

Comments (please include the name & address of the establishment)

....

....

....

....

....

....

....

....

(please attach a separate sheet if necessary)

Please tick here if you DO NOT wish to receive details of AA offers or products ☐

PTO

	YES	NO
Have you bought this guide before?	☐	☐

Have you bought any other accommodation, restaurant, pub, or food guides recently? If yes, which ones?

....

....

Why did you buy this guide? (circle all that apply)

holiday short break business travel special occasion

overnight stop find a venue for another event e.g. conference

other..

How often do you stay in B&Bs? (circle one choice)

more than once a month once a month once in 2-3 months

once in six months once a year less than once a year

Please answer these questions to help us make improvements to the guide:

Which of these factors are most important when choosing a B&B?

Price Location Awards/ratings Service

Decor/surroundings Previous experience Recommendation

Other (please state):..

Do you read the editorial features in the guide? ....

Do you use the location atlas?...

Which elements of the guide do you find the most useful when choosing somewhere to stay?

Description Photo Advertisement Diamond rating

Can you suggest any improvements to the guide?

....

....

....

....

Please send this form to:
Editor, The B&B Guide,
Lifestyle Guides,
The Automobile Association,
Fanum House,
Basingstoke RG21 4EA

or fax: 01256 491647
or e-mail: lifestyleguides@theAA.com

Please use this form to recommend any guest house, farmhouse or inn you have visited, whether it is in the guide or not currently listed. Feedback from readers helps us to keep our guide accurate and up to date. Please note, however, that if you have a complaint to make during a visit, we strongly recommend that you discuss the matter with the establishment management there and then so that they have a chance to put things right before your visit is spoilt. The AA does not undertake to arbitrate between you and the hotel management, or to obtain compensation or engage in correspondence.

Date:

Your name (block capitals)

Your address (block capitals)

....

....

....

.... e-mail address:

Comments (please include the name & address of the establishment)

....

....

....

....

....

....

....

....

(please attach a separate sheet if necessary)

Please tick here if you DO NOT wish to receive details of AA offers or products ☐

PTO

	YES	NO
Have you bought this guide before?	☐	☐

Have you bought any other accommodation, restaurant, pub, or food guides recently? If yes, which ones?

....

....

Why did you buy this guide? (circle all that apply)

holiday short break business travel special occasion

overnight stop find a venue for another event e.g. conference

other..

How often do you stay in B&Bs? (circle one choice)

more than once a month once a month once in 2-3 months

once in six months once a year less than once a year

Please answer these questions to help us make improvements to the guide:

Which of these factors are most important when choosing a B&B?

Price Location Awards/ratings Service

Decor/surroundings Previous experience Recommendation

Other (please state):...

Do you read the editorial features in the guide? ....

Do you use the location atlas?..

Which elements of the guide do you find the most useful when choosing somewhere to stay?

Description Photo Advertisement Diamond rating

Can you suggest any improvements to the guide?

....

....

....

....